Hoover's Handbook of American Business

2000

BUSINESS PRESS

Austin, Texas

BUSINESS PRESS

10 9 8 7 6 5 4 3 2 1

Publishers Cataloging-in-Publication Data

Hoover's Handbook of American Business 2000, vol. 1.

Includes indexes.

1. Business enterprises — Directories. 2. Corporations — Directories.

HF3010 338.7

Hoover's Company Information is also available on America Online, Baseline, Bloomberg Financial Network, Dialog, Dow Jones Interactive, EBSCO, LEXIS-NEXIS, Reuters NewMedia, and on the Internet at Hoover's Online (www.hoovers.com), Alta Vista (www.altavista.digital.com), CBS MarketWatch (cbs.marketwatch.com), Infoseek (www.go.com), MSN MoneyCentral (moneycentral.com), The New York Times, (www.nytimes.com), dowjones.com (www.dowjones.com), The Washington Post (www.washingtonpost.com), Yahoo! (www.yahoo.com), and others.

A catalog of Hoover's products is available on the World Wide Web at www.hoovers.com.

ISBN 1-57311-055-8

ISSN 1055-7202

This book was produced by Hoover's Business Press using Claris Corporation's FileMaker Pro 3.04; Quark, Inc.'s Quark XPress 4.04; EM Software, Inc.'s Xtags 4.01; and fonts from Adobe's Clearface, Futura, and Myriad families. Cover design is by Shawn Harrington. Electronic prepress and printing were done by Quebecor Printing (USA) Corp. in Fairfield, Pennsylvania. Text paper is 60# Postmark White.

US AND WORLD DIRECT SALES

Hoover's, Inc.
1033 La Posada Drive, Suite 250
Austin, TX 78752
Phone: 512-374-4500
Fax: 512-374-4501
e-mail: orders@hoovers.com

EUROPE

William Snyder Publishing Associates
5 Five Mile Drive
Oxford OX2 8HT
England
Phone & fax: +44-186-551-3186
e-mail: williamsnyder@compuserve.com

HOOVER'S, INC.

Founder: Gary Hoover
Chairman, President, and CEO: Patrick J. Spain
EVP & COO: Carl G. Shepherd

DATABASE EDITORIAL

Editor in Chief: Gordon T. Anderson
Executive Editor: Britton E. Jackson
Director, Editorial Systems: Holly Hans Jackson
Managing Editor, Hoover's Business Press: George Sutton
Senior Editor, Books & Editorial Projects: Ruth McClendon Linton
Senior Editors: Chris Barton, Travis Brown, Elaine Conces, Tom Dowe, Valerie Pearcy, Amy Silverman, Barbara M. Spain
Senior Contributing Editors: Alan Chai, Paul Mitchell
Information Resources Manager: Toni Loftin
Director, Financial Information and MasterList: Dennis Sutton
Associate Editors: Sally Alt, Jodi Berls, Gene Bisbee, Larry Bills, Rachel Brush, Bobby Duncan, Jennifer Furl, Carrie Geis, Allan Gill, Joe Grey, Melanie Hall, Mary Mickle, John Mitchell, Jim Moore, Vanita Trippe, David Woodruff
Writers: Joy Aiken, Linnea Anderson, Alexander Blunt, Angela Boeckman, Amanda Bowman, Joe Bramhall, James Bryant, Troy Bryant, Justin Burrows, Robert Carranza, Jason Cella, Jason Cother, David Crosby, Kevin Dodds, Stewart Eisenhart, Max Farr, Kevin Furr, Dan Gattuso, Paul Geary, David Hamerly, Stuart Hampton, Jeanette Herman, Jennifer Hinger, Guy Holland, Kristen Hughes, John Katzman, John MacAyeal, Nancy McBride, Nell Newton, Sheri Olander, Lynett Oliver, Rob Reynolds, Patrice Sarath, Joe Simonetta, Mike Sims, Kevin Smokler, Randy Williams
Financial Editors: Adi Anand, Shaun McDonald, Bill Ramsey
Quality Control Editor, MasterList: John Willis
Senior Editor, MasterList: Yvonne Cullinan
Associate Editor, MasterList: April Karli
Editorial Training Coordinator: Diane Lee
Copyeditors: Regan Brown, Theresa Hackley, Kristi Kingston, Kerry O'Brien, Christina Vallery, Emily Weida
Assistant Editors: Margaret Claughton, Jim Harris, Callie Henning, Kathleen Kelly, Matt Saucedo
Senior Production Specialist: Cecilia Martinez VanGundy
Production Specialists: JoAnn Estrada, Kristin Jackson-Isbell
Editorial Assistants: Danny Cummings, Jenny Foster, Delia Garza, Gil Harris, Alexi Holford, Daniel Johnson, Pei Lee, Josh Lower, David Porter, Tranea Prosser, David Ramirez, Kcevin Rob, Ashley Schrump, Sara Taylor, Shannon Timmerman, Jennifer Westrom, Bryan Zilar
Editorial Projects Coordinator: Rebecca Bycott
Documents Coordinator: Carla Baker
Information Resources Assistant: Vanh Phoummisane
Library Assistants: Litto Paul Bacas, Melissa Chinn, Lisa Putnam
Intern: Daniel Croll

WEB EDITORIAL

Senior Editor: David King
Business Travel Editor: Kate Ewing
Industry Editor: Sarah Hallman
IPO Central Editor: Wei San Hui
Money Editor: Kenan Pollack
Professions Editor: Clemon Goodin
News Editors: Damon Arhos, Jackie Doyle, Natasha Rosofsky, Amy Young
Directory Editors: Tara Fatemi, Kerrie Green, Karin Marie
Online Editorial Assistant: Christian Ethridge

HOOVER'S, INC. MISSION STATEMENT

1. To produce business information products and services of the highest quality, accuracy, and readability.
2. To make that information available whenever, wherever, and however our customers want it through mass distribution at affordable prices.
3. To continually expand our range of products and services and our markets for those products and services.
4. To reward our employees, suppliers, and shareholders based on their contributions to the success of our enterprise.
5. To hold to the highest ethical business standards, erring on the side of generosity when in doubt.

Abbreviations

AFL-CIO – American Federation of Labor and Congress of Industrial Organizations
AMA – American Medical Association
AMEX – American Stock Exchange
ARM – adjustable-rate mortgage
ATM – asynchronous transfer mode
ATM – automated teller machine
CAD/CAM – computer-aided design/computer-aided manufacturing
CASE – computer-aided software engineering
CD-ROM – compact disc – read-only memory
CEO – chief executive officer
CFO – chief financial officer
CISC – complex instruction set computer
CMOS – complementary metal-oxide semiconductor
COO – chief operating officer
DAT – digital audiotape
DOD – Department of Defense
DOE – Department of Energy
DOS – disc operating system
DOT – Department of Transportation
DRAM – dynamic random access memory
DVD – digital versatile disk/digital videodisk
EPA – Environmental Protection Agency
EPROM – erasable programmable read-only memory
EPS – earnings per share
ESOP – employee stock ownership plan
EU – European Union
EVP – executive vice president
FCC – Federal Communications Commission
FDA – Food and Drug Administration
FDIC – Federal Deposit Insurance Corporation
FTC – Federal Trade Commission
FTP – file transfer protocol
GATT – General Agreement on Tariffs and Trade
GDP – gross domestic product
GUI – graphical user interface
HMO – health maintenance organization
HR – human resources
HTML – hypertext markup language
ICC – Interstate Commerce Commission
IPO – initial public offering
IRS – Internal Revenue Service
ISDN – integrated services digital network
kWh – kilowatt-hour
LAN – local area network

LBO – leveraged buyout
LCD – liquid crystal display
LNG – liquefied natural gas
LP – limited partnership
Ltd. – limited
mips – millions of instructions per second
MW – megawatt
NAFTA – North American Free Trade Agreement
NASA – National Aeronautics and Space Administration
Nasdaq – National Association of Securities Dealers Automated Quotations
NATO – North Atlantic Treaty Organization
NYSE – New York Stock Exchange
OCR – optical character recognition
OECD – Organization for Economic Cooperation and Development
OEM – original equipment manufacturer
OPEC – Organization of Petroleum Exporting Countries
OS – operating system
OSHA – Occupational Safety and Health Administration
OTC – over-the-counter
PBX – private branch exchange
PCMCIA – Personal Computer Memory Card International Association
P/E – price-to-earnings ratio
RAM – random access memory
R&D – research and development
RBOC – regional Bell operating company
RISC – reduced instruction set computer
REIT – real estate investment trust
ROA – return on assets
ROE – return on equity
ROI – return on investment
ROM – read-only memory
S&L – savings and loan
SEC – Securities and Exchange Commission
SEVP – senior executive vice president
SIC – Standard Industrial Classification
SPARC – scalable processor architecture
SVP – senior vice president
VAR – value-added reseller
VAT – value-added tax
VC – vice chairman
VP – vice president
WAN – wide area network
WWW – World Wide Web

Contents

VOLUME 1

List of Lists viii

Companies Profiled ix

About *Hoover's Handbook of American Business 2000* xv

Using the Profiles xvi

A List-Lover's Compendium 1

The Company Profiles • A-K 63

VOLUME 2

Companies Profiled...viii

The Company Profiles • L-Z 847

Index of Profiles by Industry 1570

Index of Profiles by Headquarters Location 1577

Index of Brands, Companies, and People Named in the Profiles...................................1585

List of Lists

HOOVER'S RANKINGS

The 300 Largest Companies by Sales in *Hoover's Handbook of American Business 2000*..............2–4
The 300 Most Profitable Companies in *Hoover's Handbook of American Business 2000*..............5–7
The 300 Most Valuable Public Companies in *Hoover's Handbook of American Business 2000*.....................8–10
The 300 Largest Employers in *Hoover's Handbook of American Business 2000*..........11–13
The 100 Fastest-Growing Companies by Sales Growth in *Hoover's Handbook of American Business 2000*.....................14
The 100 Fastest-Growing Companies by Employment Growth in *Hoover's Handbook of American Business 2000*...................15
The 100 Shrinking Companies by Sales Growth in *Hoover's Handbook of American Business 2000* 16
The 100 Shrinking Companies by Employee Growth in *Hoover's Handbook of American Business 2000*.....................17

THE BIGGEST AND THE RICHEST

The Hoover's 500: America's Largest Business Enterprises.....................18–22
The *FORTUNE* 500 Largest US Corporations...23–27
The *Forbes* 500 Largest Private Corporations....28–32
Forbes 20 Greatest US Fortunes............................33
Top 20 in CEO Compensation.................................33
Forbes 40 Most Powerful Celebrities......................34
The 20 Most Powerful Women in Business............34

HEALTHCARE

Top 10 Healthcare Systems.....................................35
Top 10 Pharmaceutical Companies by Worldwide Sales.....................................35
Top 10 Branded Over-the-Counter Drugs...............35
Top 10 Prescription Drugs.....................................35

LEGAL, BUSINESS, AND FINANCIAL SERVICES

Top 25 US Banks by Total Assets...........................36
America's Top 25 Money Managers.........................36
The 25 Largest Management Consulting Firms.....37
Top 25 Law Firms...37
Top 25 Tax and Accounting Firms..........................37

MEDIA

Advertising Age's Top 50 Companies.......................38
Top 25 US Daily Newspapers by Circulation..........39
The 25 Largest Magazines in the US by Revenue....39
Top 25 Television Groups in the US........................40
Top 20 Cable Companies...40
Top 20 US Trade Book Publishers...........................40
Top 25 US Advertising Agencies by US Revenue....41
Top 25 Megabrands by 1998 Ad Spending..............41
Top 15 Advertisers in Daily Newspapers................42
Top 20 Films at US Box Office................................42

RETAIL

Chain Store Age's Top 25 Chain Stores..................43

Supermarket News' Top 25 Supermarket Companies..43
Top 25 Restaurant Brands by Sales........................44
Top 15 Convenience Store Companies by Number of Stores.....................................44
Top 25 Beverage Companies by Sales.....................45
Top 10 Soft Drinks...45

TECHNOLOGY

Software Magazine's Top 50 Software Companies by Revenue.....................46
Computer Retail Week's Top 50 Computer Retailers.....................46
Top 25 Internet Companies by Sales......................47
Top 10 Telecommunications Companies.................47
Top 20 Semiconductor Manufacturers...................48
Top 15 Government, Military & Aerospace Contractors.....................48
Top 10 Companies Granted Patents in 1998..........48

TRANSPORTATION

US Car and Light-Truck Sales.................................49
Top 15 Dealer Groups by New-Vehicle Sales Volume.....................50
Top 10 Auto Parts Retailers by Sales......................50
Top Vehicle Sellers...50
The World's Top 25 Airlines...................................51
The Top 25 Airline Fleets.......................................51
The 30 Largest US Trucking Companies.................51

STOCK MARKETS

The 30 Companies in the Dow Jones Industrial Average.....................52
The 20 Companies in the Dow Jones Transportation Average.....................52
The 15 Companies in the Dow Jones Utility Average.....................52
The Companies in the Standard & Poor's 500.....................53-55
The 400 Companies in the Standard & Poor's Midcap Index...................55-57

THE WORKPLACE

FORTUNE's 100 Best Companies to Work for in America.....................58
America's Top 10 Most Admired Companies..........59
The Top 20 Black-Owned Businesses......................59
The Top 20 Hispanic-Owned Businesses................59
The Top 20 Woman-Owned Businesses..................60
The 25 Best Companies for Asians, Blacks, and Hispanics.....................60

SPORTS

Professional Football Teams....................................61
Professional Basketball Teams................................61
The 10 Most Valuable Sports Franchises................61
The 10 Least Valuable Sports Franchises...............61
Professional Baseball Teams...................................62
Professional Hockey Teams....................................62

Companies Profiled

VOLUME 1

3Com Corporation 64
7-Eleven, Inc. 66
Abbott Laboratories 68
Ace Hardware Corporation 70
Adobe Systems Incorporated 72
Adolph Coors Company 74
Advance Publications, Inc. 76
Advanced Micro Devices, Inc. 78
Aetna Inc. 80
AFLAC Incorporated 82
A.G. Edwards, Inc. 84
AGCO Corporation 86
Air Products and Chemicals, Inc. 88
Airborne Freight Corporation 90
Alaska Air Group, Inc. 92
Alberto-Culver Company 94
Albertson's, Inc. 96
Alcoa Inc. 98
Allegheny Teledyne Incorporated 100
Allergan, Inc. 102
Alliant Techsystems Inc. 104
Allied Waste Industries, Inc. 106
AlliedSignal Inc. 108
Allmerica Financial Corporation 110
The Allstate Corporation 112
ALLTEL Corporation 114
Amazon.com, Inc. 116
Amerada Hess Corporation 118
AMERCO 120
America Online, Inc. 122
America West Holdings Corporation 124
American Electric Power Company, Inc. 126
American Express Company 128
American Financial Group, Inc. 130
American General Financial Group 132
American Greetings Corporation 134
American Home Products Corporation 136
American International Group, Inc. 138
American Standard Companies Inc. 140
AmeriSource Health Corporation 142
Ameritech Corporation 144
Ames Department Stores, Inc. 146
Amgen Inc. 148
AMR Corporation 150
Amway Corporation 152
Andersen Worldwide 154
Anheuser-Busch Companies, Inc. 156
Anixter International Inc. 158
Aon Corporation 160
Apple Computer, Inc. 162
Applied Materials, Inc. 164
ARAMARK Corporation 166
Archer Daniels Midland Company 168
Armstrong World Industries, Inc. 170
Arrow Electronics, Inc. 172
Arvin Industries, Inc. 174
ASARCO Incorporated 176
Ashland Inc. 178
Associates First Capital Corporation 180
AT&T Corp. 182
Atlantic Richfield Company 184
Automatic Data Processing, Inc. 186

AutoNation Inc. 188
AutoZone, Inc. 190
Avery Dennison Corporation 192
Avis Rent A Car, Inc. 194
Avnet, Inc. 196
Avon Products, Inc. 198
AXA Financial, Inc. 200
Baker & McKenzie 202
Baker Hughes Incorporated 204
Ball Corporation 206
Bank of America Corporation 208
The Bank of New York Company, Inc. 210
BANK ONE CORPORATION 212
Barnes & Noble, Inc. 214
Bausch & Lomb Incorporated 216
Baxter International Inc. 218
The Bear Stearns Companies Inc. 220
Bechtel Group, Inc. 222
Becton, Dickinson and Company 224
Bed Bath & Beyond Inc. 226
Bell & Howell Company 228
Bell Atlantic Corporation 230
BellSouth Corporation 232
Bemis Company, Inc. 234
Bergen Brunswig Corporation 236
Berkshire Hathaway Inc. 238
Best Buy Co., Inc. 240
Bestfoods 242
Bethlehem Steel Corporation 244
Beverly Enterprises, Inc. 246
The BFGoodrich Company 248
Bindley Western Industries, Inc. 250
BJ's Wholesale Club, Inc. 252
The Black & Decker Corporation 254
Blockbuster Inc. 256
Blue Cross and Blue Shield Association 258
The Boeing Company 260
Boise Cascade Corporation 262
Borden, Inc. 264
Borders Group, Inc. 266
Borg-Warner Automotive, Inc. 268
Boston Celtics Limited Partnership 270
Boston Scientific Corporation 272
Bowater Incorporated 274
Briggs & Stratton Corporation 276
Brinker International, Inc. 278
Bristol-Myers Squibb Company 280
Brown Shoe Company Inc. 282
Brown-Forman Corporation 284
Bruno's, Inc. 286
Brunswick Corporation 288
Budget Group, Inc. 290
Burger King Corporation 292
Burlington Coat Factory
  Warehouse Corporation 294
Burlington Industries, Inc. 296
Burlington Northern Santa Fe Corporation 298
Burns International Services Corporation 300
Cabletron Systems, Inc. 302
Cablevision Systems Corporation 304
California Public Employees'
  Retirement System 306
Caltex Corporation 308

Campbell Soup Company 310
Canandaigua Brands, Inc. 312
Capital One Financial Corporation 314
Cardinal Health, Inc. 316
Caremark Rx Inc. 318
Cargill, Incorporated 320
Carlson Wagonlit Travel 322
Carnival Corporation 324
Carolina Power & Light Company 326
Carter-Wallace, Inc. 328
Case Corporation 330
Caterpillar Inc. 332
CBS Corporation 334
Cendant Corporation 336
Centex Corporation 338
Central and South West Corporation 340
Ceridian Corporation 342
Champion Enterprises, Inc. 344
Champion International Corporation 346
The Charles Schwab Corporation 348
The Chase Manhattan Corporation 350
Chevron Corporation 352
Chicago Title Corporation 354
Chiquita Brands International, Inc. 356
CHS Electronics, Inc. 358
The Chubb Corporation 360
CIGNA Corporation 362
Cinergy Corp. 364
Cintas Corporation 366
Circuit City Stores, Inc. - Circuit City Group ...368
Cisco Systems, Inc. 370
Citigroup Inc. 372
Clear Channel Communications, Inc. 374
The Clorox Company 376
CMS Energy Corporation 378
CNA Financial Corporation 380
CNF Transportation Inc. 382
The Coastal Corporation 384
The Coca-Cola Company 386
Coca-Cola Enterprises Inc. 388
Colgate-Palmolive Company 390
Collins & Aikman Corporation 392
Columbia Energy Group 394
Columbia/HCA Healthcare Corporation 396
Comcast Corporation 398
Comdisco, Inc. 400
Comerica Incorporated 402
Commercial Metals Company 404
Compaq Computer Corporation 406
CompuCom Systems, Inc. 408
CompUSA Inc. 410
Computer Associates International, Inc. 412
Computer Sciences Corporation 414
ConAgra, Inc. 416
Conoco Inc. 418
Conseco, Inc. 420
Consolidated Edison, Inc. 422
Consolidated Freightways Corporation 424
Consolidated Natural Gas Company 426
Consolidated Stores Corporation 428
Constellation Energy Group, Inc. 430
ContiGroup Companies, Inc. 432
Continental Airlines, Inc. 434
Converse Inc. 436

Cooper Industries, Inc. 438
Cordant Technologies Inc. 440
Corning Incorporated 442
Corporate Express, Inc. 444
Costco Companies, Inc. 446
Countrywide Credit Industries, Inc. 448
Cox Enterprises, Inc. 450
C. R. Bard, Inc. 452
Crane Co. 454
Crown Cork & Seal Company, Inc. 456
CSX Corporation 458
Cummins Engine Company, Inc. 460
CVS Corporation 462
Cyprus Amax Minerals Company 464
Dana Corporation 466
Danaher Corporation 468
Darden Restaurants, Inc. 470
Data General Corporation 472
Dayton Hudson Corporation 474
Dean Foods Company 476
Deere & Company 478
Del Monte Foods Company 480
Dell Computer Corporation 482
Deloitte Touche Tohmatsu 484
Delphi Automotive Systems Corporation 486
Delta Air Lines, Inc. 488
Deluxe Corporation 490
Dexter Corporation 492
DHL Worldwide Express 494
The Dial Corporation 496
Diebold, Incorporated 498
Dillard's Inc. 500
Dime Bancorp, Inc. 502
Dole Food Company, Inc. 504
Dollar General Corporation 506
Dominion Resources, Inc. 508
Domino's Pizza, Inc. 510
Donaldson, Lufkin & Jenrette, Inc. 512
Dover Corporation 514
The Dow Chemical Company 516
Dow Jones & Company, Inc. 518
DTE Energy Company 520
Duke Energy Corporation 522
The Dun & Bradstreet Corporation 524
Dynegy Inc. 526
E. & J. Gallo Winery 528
The Earthgrains Company 530
Eastman Chemical Company 532
Eastman Kodak Company 534
Eaton Corporation 536
Edison International 538
EG&G, Inc. 540
E. I. du Pont de Nemours and Company 542
El Paso Energy Corporation 544
Electronic Data Systems Corporation 546
Eli Lilly and Company 548
EMC Corporation 550
EMCOR Group, Inc. 552
Emerson Electric Co. 554
Engelhard Corporation 556
Enron Corp. 558
Entergy Corporation 560
EOTT Energy Partners, L.P. 562
Equifax Inc. 564

Ernst & Young International 566
The Estée Lauder Companies Inc. 568
The E. W. Scripps Company 570
Exide Corporation...572
Exxon Corporation..574
Family Dollar Stores, Inc. 576
Fannie Mae...578
Farmland Industries, Inc. 580
FDX Corporation 582
Federal-Mogul Corporation 584
Federated Department Stores, Inc.....................586
The First American Financial Corporation 588
First Data Corporation 590
First Union Corporation 592
Firstar Corporation...594
FirstEnergy Corp...596
Fisher Scientific International Inc. 598
Fleet Financial Group, Inc. 600
Fleetwood Enterprises, Inc. 602
Fleming Companies, Inc. 604
Florida Progress Corporation............................606
Flowers Industries, Inc. 608
Fluor Corporation...610
FMC Corporation 612
FMR Corp..614
Food Lion, Inc. 616
Foodmaker, Inc. 618
Ford Motor Company 620
Fort James Corporation 622
Fortune Brands, Inc. 624
Foster Wheeler Corporation..............................626
Foundation Health Systems, Inc. 628
Fox Entertainment Group, Inc. 630
FPL Group, Inc. 632
Fred Meyer, Inc. 634
Freddie Mac..636
Freeport-McMoRan Copper & Gold Inc............638
Fruit of the Loom, Ltd. 640
Furniture Brands International, Inc....................642
Gannett Co., Inc. 644
The Gap, Inc. 646
Gateway, Inc...648
GATX Corporation 650
Genentech, Inc..652
General Dynamics Corporation.........................654
General Electric Company 656
General Instrument Corporation.......................658
General Mills, Inc. 660
General Motors Corporation 662
Genuine Parts Company....................................664
Georgia-Pacific Corporation.............................666
The Gillette Company..668
Golden West Financial Corporation..................670
The Goldman Sachs Group, Inc. 672
The Goodyear Tire & Rubber Company.............674
GPU, Inc. 676
The Great Atlantic & Pacific Tea
    Company, Inc. 678
The Green Bay Packers, Inc. 680
GTE Corporation 682
Halliburton Company..684
Hallmark Cards, Inc. 686
H&R Block, Inc. 688
Hannaford Bros. Co. 690

Harcourt General, Inc. 692
Harley-Davidson, Inc. 694
Harnischfeger Industries, Inc. 696
Harrah's Entertainment, Inc.............................698
Harris Corporation 700
The Hartford Financial Services Group, Inc. 702
Hartford Life, Inc..704
Hartmarx Corporation......................................706
Hasbro, Inc. 708
HEALTHSOUTH Corporation 710
The Hearst Corporation.....................................712
Heilig-Meyers Company 714
Hercules Incorporated......................................716
Herman Miller, Inc. 718
Hershey Foods Corporation 720
The Hertz Corporation 722
Hewlett-Packard Company 724
Hillenbrand Industries, Inc. 726
Hilton Hotels Corporation 728
H.J. Heinz Company 730
The Home Depot, Inc. 732
HON INDUSTRIES Inc. 734
Honeywell Inc. 736
Hormel Foods Corporation 738
Host Marriott Corporation 740
Household International, Inc. 742
Hughes Electronics Corporation 744
Humana Inc. 746
Hyatt Corporation...748
IBP, inc. 750
IGA, INC. 752
IKON Office Solutions, Inc................................754
Illinois Tool Works Inc. 756
Imation Corp...758
IMC Global Inc..760
InaCom Corp. 762
Ingersoll-Rand Company...................................764
Ingram Industries Inc. 766
Ingram Micro Inc...768
Intel Corporation 770
Intergraph Corporation 772
International Business Machines Corporation..774
International Flavors & Fragrances Inc. 776
International Multifoods Corporation 778
International Paper Company 780
The Interpublic Group of Companies, Inc.........782
Interstate Bakeries Corporation........................784
Intimate Brands, Inc. 786
Iomega Corporation..788
ITT Industries, Inc. 790
Jacobs Engineering Group Inc. 792
J.B. Hunt Transport Services, Inc. 794
J. C. Penney Company, Inc................................796
Jo-Ann Stores, Inc. 798
John Hancock Mutual Life
    Insurance Company.......................................800
Johns Manville Corporation 802
Johnson & Johnson 804
Johnson Controls, Inc. 806
Jones Apparel Group, Inc. 808
J.P. Morgan & Co. Incorporated.......................810
Kaiser Foundation Health Plan, Inc..................812
Kaufman and Broad Home Corporation............814
Keebler Foods Company....................................816

Kellogg Company..818
Kelly Services, Inc. 820
Kerr-McGee Corporation 822
KeyCorp..824
Kimberly-Clark Corporation 826
King Ranch, Inc. 828
King World Productions, Inc. 830
Kmart Corporation 832
Knight Ridder 834
Koch Industries, Inc..836
Kohl's Corporation 838
KPMG International 840
The Kroger Co. 842

VOLUME 2
Lands' End, Inc..848
La-Z-Boy Incorporated 850
Lear Corporation 852
Leggett & Platt, Incorporated 854
Lehman Brothers Holdings Inc. 856
Lennar Corporation 858
Lennox International Inc. 860
Levi Strauss & Co. 862
Lexmark International Group, Inc. 864
LG&E Energy Corp. 866
Liberty Media Group...868
LifeStyle Furnishings International Ltd...........870
The Limited, Inc. 872
Lincoln National Corporation 874
Litton Industries, Inc. 876
Liz Claiborne, Inc. 878
Lockheed Martin Corporation...........................880
Loews Corporation..882
Longs Drug Stores Corporation.........................884
Loral Space & Communications Ltd. 886
Louisiana-Pacific Corporation...........................888
Lowe's Companies, Inc. 890
The LTV Corporation 892
Lucent Technologies Inc. 894
Lyondell Chemical Company.............................896
MacAndrews & Forbes Holdings Inc.................898
Magellan Health Services, Inc...........................900
Mandalay Resort Group 902
Manpower Inc. 904
Mark IV Industries, Inc. 906
Marriott International, Inc. 908
Mars, Inc. 910
Marsh & McLennan Companies, Inc. 912
Masco Corporation...914
Massachusetts Mutual Life
  Insurance Company..916
Mattel, Inc...918
Maxtor Corporation 920
MAXXAM Inc. 922
The May Department Stores Company.............924
Maytag Corporation 926
MBNA Corporation...928
McCormick & Company, Incorporated.............930
McDermott International, Inc............................932
McDonald's Corporation...................................934
The McGraw-Hill Companies, Inc. 936
MCI WorldCom, Inc..938
McKesson HBOC, Inc. 940
McKinsey & Company 942

The Mead Corporation......................................944
MediaOne Group, Inc. 946
Medtronic, Inc. 948
Mellon Bank Corporation..................................950
Merck & Co., Inc. 952
Merisel, Inc. 954
Meritor Automotive, Inc....................................956
Merrill Lynch & Co., Inc. 958
Metro-Goldwyn-Mayer Inc. 960
Metropolitan Life Insurance Company..............962
Michaels Stores, Inc. 964
Micro Warehouse, Inc.......................................966
MicroAge, Inc. 968
Micron Electronics, Inc.....................................970
Micron Technology, Inc.....................................972
Microsoft Corporation 974
MidAmerican Energy Holdings Company 976
Millennium Chemicals Inc.................................978
Minnesota Mining and Manufacturing
  Company 980
Mirage Resorts, Incorporated...........................982
Mitchell Energy & Development Corp. 984
Mobil Corporation 986
Monsanto Company 988
Montgomery Ward Holding Corp......................990
Morgan Stanley Dean Witter & Co. 992
Morrison Knudsen Corporation........................994
Motorola, Inc. 996
Musicland Stores Corporation 998
Nabisco Holdings Corp....................................1000
Nash Finch Company 1002
National Association of Securities
  Dealers, Inc...1004
National City Corporation 1006
National Semiconductor Corporation 1008
National Steel Corporation 1010
Nationwide Insurance Enterprise 1012
Navistar International Corporation 1014
NCR Corporation 1016
The Neiman Marcus Group, Inc. 1018
New York Life Insurance Company..................1020
New York Stock Exchange, Inc. 1022
The New York Times Company 1024
Newell Rubbermaid Inc...................................1026
Newmont Mining Corporation........................1028
Niagara Mohawk Holdings Inc. 1030
NIKE, Inc. 1032
NiSource Inc..1034
Nordstrom, Inc. 1036
Norfolk Southern Corporation........................1038
Northeast Utilities...1040
Northern States Power Company 1042
Northern Trust Corporation............................1044
Northrop Grumman Corporation 1046
Northwest Airlines Corporation......................1048
The Northwestern Mutual
  Life Insurance Company 1050
Novell, Inc. 1052
Nucor Corporation..1054
Occidental Petroleum Corporation.................1056
Office Depot, Inc. 1058
OfficeMax, Inc. 1060
Ogden Corporation 1062
Olin Corporation...1064

Olsten Corporation 1066
Omnicom Group Inc. 1068
Oracle Corporation 1070
OshKosh B'Gosh, Inc. 1072
Owens & Minor, Inc. 1074
Owens Corning 1076
Owens-Illinois, Inc. 1078
Oxford Health Plans, Inc. 1080
PACCAR Inc...1082
PacifiCare Health Systems, Inc. 1084
PacifiCorp...1086
Packard Bell NEC, Inc. 1088
Paine Webber Group Inc. 1090
Park Place Entertainment Corporation 1092
Parker Hannifin Corporation 1094
Payless Cashways, Inc. 1096
Payless ShoeSource, Inc. 1098
PECO Energy Company..................................1100
The Penn Traffic Company 1102
Pennzoil-Quaker State Company 1104
Penske Corporation 1106
PeopleSoft, Inc. 1108
The Pep Boys - Manny, Moe & Jack 1110
The Pepsi Bottling Group, Inc. 1112
PepsiCo, Inc. 1114
Perot Systems Corporation 1116
Peter Kiewit Sons', Inc. 1118
PETsMART, Inc..1120
Pfizer Inc..1122
PG&E Corporation..1124
Pharmacia & Upjohn, Inc. 1126
Phelps Dodge Corporation 1128
Philip Morris Companies Inc. 1130
Phillips Petroleum Company 1132
Phillips-Van Heusen Corporation 1134
Pier 1 Imports, Inc. 1136
Pilgrim's Pride Corporation 1138
Pillowtex Corporation...................................1140
The Pillsbury Company 1142
Pinnacle West Capital Corporation................1144
Pitney Bowes Inc. 1146
Pittston Brink's Group 1148
PNC Bank Corp...1150
Polaroid Corporation 1152
Polo Ralph Lauren Corporation 1154
PP&L Resources, Inc. 1156
PPG Industries, Inc. 1158
Praxair, Inc. 1160
Premark International, Inc. 1162
PricewaterhouseCoopers 1164
PRIMEDIA, Inc..1166
The Principal Financial Group........................1168
The Procter & Gamble Company 1170
The Progressive Corporation..........................1172
Promus Hotel Corporation.............................1174
The Prudential Insurance
   Company of America 1176
Public Service Enterprise
   Group Incorporated...................................1178
Publix Super Markets, Inc. 1180
Pulte Corporation 1182
The Quaker Oats Company 1184
QUALCOMM Incorporated..............................1186
Quantum Corporation....................................1188

Qwest Communications International Inc. 1190
Ralston Purina Company.................................1192
Raytheon Company..1194
The Reader's Digest Association, Inc. 1196
Read-Rite Corporation...................................1198
Reebok International Ltd. 1200
Regis Corporation 1202
Reliance Group Holdings, Inc. 1204
Reliant Energy, Incorporated 1206
Republic New York Corporation 1208
Revlon, Inc. 1210
Reynolds Metals Company.............................1212
Rite Aid Corporation......................................1214
R.J. Reynolds Tobacco Holdings Inc. 1216
Roadway Express, Inc. 1218
Rockwell International Corporation 1220
Rohm and Haas Company 1222
Ross Stores, Inc. 1224
Royal Caribbean Cruises Ltd. 1226
R. R. Donnelley & Sons Company 1228
Russell Corporation.......................................1230
Ryder System, Inc. 1232
Ryerson Tull, Inc. 1234
Sabre Inc..1236
SAFECO Corporation.....................................1238
Safeguard Scientifics, Inc. 1240
Safeway Inc. 1242
The St. Paul Companies, Inc. 1244
Saks Incorporated 1246
Sara Lee Corporation.....................................1248
SBC Communications Inc. 1250
S.C. Johnson & Son, Inc. 1252
Schering-Plough Corporation.........................1254
Schlumberger Limited 1256
SCI Systems, Inc. 1258
Scientific-Atlanta, Inc. 1260
Seagate Technology, Inc. 1262
Sealed Air Corporation 1264
Sears, Roebuck and Co. 1266
Sempra Energy 1268
Service Corporation International 1270
Service Merchandise Company, Inc. 1272
The ServiceMaster Company..........................1274
Sharper Image Corporation 1276
Shaw Industries, Inc. 1278
Shell Oil Company...1280
The Sherwin-Williams Company 1282
Shoney's, Inc. 1284
ShopKo Stores, Inc. 1286
Silicon Graphics, Inc. 1288
Simon Property Group, Inc. 1290
Skadden, Arps, Slate, Meagher & Flom 1292
SLM Holding Corporation...............................1294
Smithfield Foods, Inc. 1296
Smurfit-Stone Container Corporation 1298
Snap-on Incorporated....................................1300
Sodexho Marriott Services, Inc. 1302
Solectron Corporation....................................1304
Sonat Inc..1306
Sonoco Products Company 1308
Sotheby's Holdings, Inc. 1310
Southern Company..1312
Southwest Airlines Co. 1314
Spiegel, Inc. 1316

Springs Industries, Inc. 1318
Sprint Corporation 1320
The Stanley Works 1322
Staples, Inc. 1324
Starbucks Corporation 1326
Starwood Hotels & Resorts Worldwide, Inc. ...1328
State Farm Mutual Automobile
   Insurance Company...................................1330
State Street Corporation 1332
Steelcase Inc. 1334
Storage Technology Corporation 1336
Suiza Foods Corporation..............................1338
Sun Healthcare Group, Inc. 1340
Sun Microsystems, Inc. 1342
Sunbeam Corporation 1344
Sunoco, Inc. 1346
SunTrust Banks, Inc. 1348
SUPERVALU Inc. 1350
SYSCO Corporation......................................1352
Tandy Corporation 1354
Teachers Insurance and Annuity Association-
   College Retirement Equities Fund 1356
Tech Data Corporation 1358
Tektronix, Inc..1360
Tellabs, Inc. 1362
Temple-Inland Inc. 1364
Tenet Healthcare Corporation......................1366
Tenneco Inc. 1368
Tennessee Valley Authority...........................1370
Teradyne, Inc. 1372
Texaco Inc. 1374
Texas Instruments Incorporated 1376
Texas Utilities Company 1378
Textron Inc..1380
Thermo Electron Corporation 1382
Tiffany & Co. 1384
Time Warner Inc...1386
The Times Mirror Company 1388
The Timken Company 1390
The TJX Companies, Inc. 1392
Torchmark Corporation.................................1394
The Toro Company 1396
Tosco Corporation..1398
Toys "R" Us, Inc. 1400
Trammell Crow Company..............................1402
Trans World Airlines, Inc. 1404
Travelers Property Casualty Corp. 1406
Triarc Companies, Inc. 1408
Tribune Company 1410
TRICON Global Restaurants, Inc. 1412
Trinity Industries, Inc. 1414
The Trump Organization 1416
TruServ Corporation......................................1418
TRW Inc. 1420
Tupperware Corporation...............................1422
The Turner Corporation 1424
Tyco International Ltd....................................1426
Tyson Foods, Inc...1428
UAL Corporation...1430
Ultramar Diamond Shamrock Corporation.....1432
Unicom Corporation......................................1434
Union Carbide Corporation 1436
Union Pacific Corporation.............................1438
Unisource Worldwide, Inc. 1440

Unisys Corporation 1442
United Parcel Service of America, Inc. 1444
United States Postal Service..........................1446
United Stationers Inc.....................................1448
United Technologies Corporation 1450
UnitedHealth Group 1452
Universal Corporation 1454
Universal Studios, Inc. 1456
Unocal Corporation 1458
UNUMProvident 1460
US Airways Group, Inc. 1462
U.S. Bancorp 1464
U.S. Foodservice..1466
U.S. Industries, Inc. 1468
U.S. Office Products Company 1470
U S WEST, Inc. 1472
USA Networks, Inc. 1474
USAA...1476
USG Corporation 1478
UST Inc. 1480
USX-Marathon Group....................................1482
USX-U.S. Steel Group....................................1484
UtiliCorp United Inc. 1486
Valero Energy Corporation............................1488
Venator Group Inc...1490
VF Corporation 1492
Viacom Inc. 1494
Viad Corp..1496
Visa International 1498
Vlasic Foods International Inc. 1500
Vulcan Materials Company............................1502
Wachovia Corporation 1504
The Wackenhut Corporation.........................1506
Walgreen Co..1508
Wal-Mart Stores, Inc. 1510
The Walt Disney Company 1512
The Warnaco Group, Inc. 1514
Warner-Lambert Company.............................1516
Washington Mutual, Inc. 1518
The Washington Post Company......................1520
Waste Management, Inc. 1522
WellPoint Health Networks Inc. 1524
Wells Fargo & Company................................1526
Wendy's International, Inc. 1528
Western Digital Corporation 1530
Westvaco Corporation...................................1532
Weyerhaeuser Company 1534
Whirlpool Corporation 1536
Whitman Corporation 1538
Whole Foods Market, Inc. 1540
Willamette Industries, Inc. 1542
Wm. Wrigley Jr. Company.............................1544
The Williams Companies, Inc. 1546
Winn-Dixie Stores, Inc. 1548
World Color Press, Inc. 1550
W. R. Grace & Co..1552
W.W. Grainger, Inc..1554
Xerox Corporation 1556
Yellow Corporation 1558
York International Corporation 1560
Zale Corporation 1562
Zenith Electronics Corporation 1564
Ziff-Davis Inc. 1566

ABOUT *HOOVER'S HANDBOOK*
OF AMERICAN BUSINESS 2000

Welcome to the year 2000! Whether you believe that it's the last year of the decade, the turn of the century, or the start of a new millennium, the times are definitely changing. In the world of business there are changes, too. As we begin a new decade, century, or millennium, business points of view are just as varied as what we call this era. The stock markets are at all-time-high levels, more people than ever are trading shares, and IPO is the business plan of the moment. Whatever you need to stay ahead in this rapidly changing world of business, Hoover's can provide it for you.

As we begin the new year, we present the latest edition of the two-volume *Hoover's Handbook of American Business*. We've added some new features and brought back the favorite parts of the most valuable research tool you can find. *Hoover's Handbook of American Business* is the first of our four-title series of handbooks that is available as an indexed set, which includes *Hoover's Handbook of Emerging Companies*, *Hoover's Handbook of World Business*, and *Hoover's Handbook of Private Companies*. This series covers the biggest, fastest-growing and most influential enterprises in the world.

In addition to the 2,350 companies featured in our handbooks, coverage of nearly 50,000 business enterprises is available in electronic format on our World Wide Web site, Hoover's Online: The Business Network. Hoover's Online (www.hoovers.com), has been updated for the new year, too. We've redesigned the site to make it a comprehensive business information portal for the business professional. We have added more categories of business information, increased the number of companies we cover, and now offer channels dedicated to companies and industries, financial and industry news, business travel, business products and services, career development, and personal finance.

Our goal is to provide one site that addresses all the needs of business professionals. Hoover's has partnered with other prestigious business information and service providers to bring you all the right business information, services, and links in one place. Also, it is now organized in an easy-to-access new design that incorporates our two former Web sites, IPO Central and StockScreener. Additionally, Hoover's Company Information is available on more than 25 other sites on the Internet, including The Wall Street Journal, The New York Times, and online services Reuters, Infoseek, and America Online.

We welcome the recognition we have received as the premier provider of high-quality company information — online, electronically, and in print — and continue to look for ways to make our products more available and more useful to you.

We believe that anyone who buys from, sells to, invests in, lends to, competes with, interviews with, or works for a company should know all there is to know about that enterprise. Taken together, this book and the other Hoover's products and resources represent the most complete source of basic corporate information readily available to the general public.

This latest version of *Hoover's Handbook of American Business* contains, as always, profiles of the largest and most influential companies in the United States. Each of the companies profiled here was chosen because of its important role in American business. For more details on how these companies were selected, see the section titled "Using the Profiles."

This book has four sections in two volumes:

1. "Using the Profiles" describes the contents of our profiles and explains the ways in which we gather and compile our data.
2. "A List-Lover's Compendium" contains lists of the largest, smallest, best, most, and other superlatives related to companies involved in American business.
3. The Profiles section makes up the largest and most important part of the book — 750 profiles of major US enterprises, arranged alphabetically, with A-K in Volume 1 and L-Z in Volume 2.
4. Three indexes complete the book: In addition to the main index, which contains the names of brands, companies, and people mentioned in the profiles, the companies are also indexed by industry group and headquarters location. The indexes are at the end of Volume 2.

Additionally, a list of all profiled companies is found near the front of each volume.

As always, we hope you find our books useful. We invite your comments via phone (512-374-4500), fax (512-374-4501), mail (1033 La Posada Drive, Suite 250, Austin, Texas 78752), or e-mail (comments@hoovers.com).

The Editors,
Austin, Texas,
October 1999

USING THE PROFILES

SELECTION OF THE COMPANIES PROFILED

The 750 enterprises profiled in this book include the largest and most influential companies in America. Among them are:

- almost 700 publicly held companies, from 3Com to Ziff-Davis
- more than 30 large private companies (such as Hallmark Cards, UPS, and Cargill)
- several mutual and cooperative organizations (such as USAA and Ace Hardware)
- a selection of other enterprises (such as Kaiser Foundation Health Plan, the United States Postal Service, and the Tennessee Valley Authority) that we believe are sufficiently large and influential enough to warrant inclusion.

In selecting these companies, our foremost question was "What companies will our readers be most interested in?" Our goal was to answer as many questions as we could in one book — in effect, trying to anticipate your curiosity. This approach resulted in four general selection criteria for including companies in the book:

1. Size. The 500 or so largest American companies, measured by sales and by number of employees, are included in the book. In general, these companies have sales in excess of $2 billion, and they are the ones you will have heard of and the ones you will want to know about. These are the companies at the top of the various *FORTUNE*, *Forbes*, and *Business Week* lists. We have made sure to include the top private companies in this number.

2. Growth. We believe that relatively few readers will be going to work for, or investing in, the savings and loan industry. Therefore, only a few S&Ls are in the book. On the other hand, we have included a number of computer and peripheral makers and numerous other electronics and software firms.

3. Visibility. Most readers will have heard of Hilton Hotels and Wm. Wrigley. Their consumer or service natures make them household names, even though they are not among the corporate giants in terms of sales and employment.

4. Breadth of coverage. To show the diversity of economic activity, we've included, among others, two professional sports teams, one ranch, the

Big Five accounting firms, two of the largest law firms in the US, and the three principal US stock exchanges. We feel that these businesses are important enough to enjoy at least "token" representation. While we might not emphasize certain industries, the industry leaders are present.

ORGANIZATION

The profiles are presented in alphabetical order. This alphabetization is generally word by word, which means that Advance Publications precedes Advanced Micro Devices. We have shown the full legal name of the enterprise at the top of the page, unless the name is too long, in which case you will find it above the address in the Locations section of the profile. If a company name is also a person's name, like Walt Disney, it will be alphabetized under the first name; if the company name starts with initials, like J. C. Penney or H.J. Heinz, look for it under the combined initials (in the above examples, JC and HJ, respectively). All company names (past and present) used in the profiles are indexed in the last index in the book. Basic financial data is listed under the heading Historical Financials & Employees: where the company's stock is traded if it is public, the ticker symbol used by the stock exchange, and the company's fiscal year-end.

The annual financial information contained in the profiles is current through fiscal year-ends occurring as late as June 1999. We have included certain nonfinancial developments, such as officer changes, through September 1999.

OVERVIEW

In the first section of the profile, we have tried to give a thumbnail description of the company and what it does. The description will usually include information on the company's strategy, reputation, and ownership. We recommend that you read this section first.

HISTORY

This extended section reflects our belief that every enterprise is the sum of its history and that you have to know where you came from in order to know where you are going. While some companies have limited historical awareness and were unable to help us much and other companies are just plain boring, we think the vast majority of the enterprises in this book have colorful backgrounds. We have tried to focus on the people who made the enterprises what they are today. We have found these histories to be full of twists and ironies; they make fascinating reading.

OFFICERS

Here we list the names of the people who run the company, insofar as space allows. In the case of public companies, we have shown the ages and pay of key officers. In some cases the published data is for the previous year although the company has announced promotions or retirements since year-end. The pay represents cash compensation, including bonuses, but excludes stock option programs.

Although companies are free to structure their management titles any way they please, most modern corporations follow standard practices. The ultimate power in any corporation lies with the shareholders, who elect a board of directors, usually including officers or "insiders" as well as individuals from outside the company. The chief officer, the person on whose desk the buck stops, is usually called the chief executive officer (CEO). Often, he or she is also the chairman of the board.

As corporate management has become more complex, it is common for the CEO to have a "right-hand person" who oversees the day-to-day operations of the company, allowing the CEO plenty of time to focus on strategy and long-term issues. This right-hand person is usually designated the chief operating officer (COO) and is often the president of the company. In other cases one person is both chairman and president.

A multitude of other titles exists, including chief financial officer (CFO), chief administrative officer, and vice chairman (VC). We have always tried to include the CFO, the chief legal officer, and the chief human resources or personnel officer. Our best advice is that officers' pay levels are clear indicators of who the board of directors thinks are most important on the management team. The Officers section also includes the name of the company's auditing (accounting) firm, where available.

The people named in the profiles are indexed at the back of the book.

LOCATIONS

Here we include the company's headquarters, street address, telephone and fax numbers, and Web site, as available. The back of the book includes an index of companies by headquarters locations.

In some cases we have also included information on the geographic distribution of the company's business, including sales and profit data. Note that these profit numbers, like those in the Products/Operations section below, are usually operating or pretax profits rather than net profits. Operating profits are generally those before financing costs (interest income and payments) and before taxes, which are considered costs attributable to the whole company rather than to one division or part of the world. For this reason the net income figures (in the Historical Financials & Employees section) are usually much lower, since they are after interest and taxes. Pretax profits are after interest but before taxes.

PRODUCTS/OPERATIONS

This section lists as many of the company's products, services, brand names, divisions, subsidiaries, and joint ventures as we could fit. We have tried to include all its major lines and all familiar brand names. The nature of this section varies by company and the amount of information available. If the company publishes sales and profit information by type of business, we have included it. The brand, division, and subsidiary names are listed in the last index in the book.

COMPETITORS

In this section we have listed companies that compete with the profiled company. This feature is included as a quick way to locate similar companies and compare them. The universe of competitors includes all public companies and all private companies with sales in excess of $500 million. In a few instances we have identified smaller private companies as key competitors.

HISTORICAL FINANCIALS & EMPLOYEES

Here we have tried to present as much data

about each enterprise's financial performance as we could compile in the allocated space. While the information varies somewhat from industry to industry and is less complete in the case of private companies that do not release data (although we have always tried to provide annual sales and employment), the following information is generally present.

A 10-year table, with relevant annualized compound growth rates, covers:

- **Sales** — fiscal year sales (year-end assets for most financial companies)
- **Net income** — fiscal year net income (before accounting changes)
- **Income as a percent of sales** — fiscal year net income as a percent of sales (as a percent of assets for most financial firms)
- **Earnings per share** — fiscal year earnings per share (EPS)
- **Stock price** — the fiscal year high, low, and close
- **P/E** — high and low price/earnings ratio
- **Dividends per share** — fiscal year dividends per share
- **Book Value per share** — fiscal year-end book value (common shareholders' equity per share)
- **Employees** — fiscal year-end or average number of employees

The information on the number of employees is intended to aid the reader interested in knowing whether a company has a long-term trend of increasing or decreasing employment. As far as we know, we are the only company that publishes this information in print format.

The year at the top of each column in the Historical Financials & Employees section is the year in which the company's fiscal year actually ends. Thus, a company with a February 28, 1999, year-end is shown as 1999.

In addition, we have provided in graph form a stock price history for each company that was public prior to June 1999. The graphs show the range of trading between the high and the low price as well as the closing price for each quarter from January 1, 1999 through June 30, 1999. Generally, for private companies, we have graphed net income, or, if that is unavailable, sales.

Key year-end statistics in this section generally show the financial strength of the enterprise, including:

- Debt ratio (long-term debt as a percent of long-term debt and shareholders' equity)
- Return on equity (net income divided by the average of beginning and ending common shareholders' equity)
- Cash and cash equivalents
- Current ratio (ratio of current assets to current liabilities)
- Total long-term debt (including capital lease obligations)
- Number of shares of common stock outstanding
- Dividend yield (fiscal year dividends per share divided by the fiscal year-end closing stock price)
- Dividend payout (fiscal year dividends divided by fiscal year EPS)
- Market value at fiscal year-end (fiscal year-end closing stock price multiplied by fiscal year-end number of shares outstanding)

Per share data has been adjusted for stock splits. The data for public companies has been provided to us by Media General Financial Services, Inc. Other public company information was compiled by Hoover's, which takes full responsibility for the content of this section.

In the case of private companies that do not publicly disclose financial information, we usually did not have access to such standardized data. We have gathered estimates of sales and other statistics from numerous sources.

Hoover's Handbook of American Business

A LIST LOVER'S COMPENDIUM

The 300 Largest Companies by Sales in
Hoover's Handbook of American Business 2000

Rank	Company	Sales ($ mil.)	Rank	Company	Sales ($ mil.)
1	General Motors Corporation	161,315	51	GTE Corporation	25,473
2	Ford Motor Company	144,416	52	Nationwide Insurance Enterprise	25,301
3	Wal-Mart Stores, Inc.	137,634	53	United Parcel Service of America, Inc.	24,788
4	Exxon Corporation	100,697	54	E. I. du Pont de Nemours and Company	24,767
5	General Electric Company	99,820	55	ConAgra, Inc.	24,594
6	Blue Cross and Blue Shield	94,700	56	Safeway Inc.	24,484
7	International Business Machines	81,667	57	Costco Companies, Inc.	24,270
8	Citigroup Inc.	76,431	58	Johnson & Johnson	23,657
9	Philip Morris Companies Inc.	74,391	59	BellSouth Corporation	23,123
10	United States Postal Service	60,072	60	The Walt Disney Company	22,976
11	The Boeing Company	56,154	61	Conoco Inc.	22,796
12	AT&T Corp.	53,223	62	The Goldman Sachs Group, Inc.	22,478
13	Bank of America Corporation	51,794	63	PepsiCo, Inc.	22,348
14	Hewlett-Packard Company	47,061	64	Ingram Micro Inc.	22,034
15	Mobil Corporation	46,287	65	USX-Marathon Group	21,726
16	Cargill, Incorporated	46,000	66	First Union Corporation	21,543
17	TIAA-CREF	45,899	67	CIGNA Corporation	21,437
18	Sears, Roebuck and Co.	41,322	68	Loews Corporation	21,208
19	The Procter & Gamble Company	37,154	69	Caterpillar Inc.	20,977
20	Merrill Lynch & Co., Inc.	35,853	70	Aetna Inc.	20,604
21	Koch Industries, Inc.	35,000	71	Wells Fargo & Company	20,482
22	Kmart Corporation	33,674	72	Sara Lee Corporation	20,011
23	The Chase Manhattan Corporation	32,590	73	PG&E Corporation	19,942
24	Bell Atlantic Corporation	31,566	74	Lehman Brothers Holdings Inc.	19,894
25	Fannie Mae	31,499	75	International Paper Company	19,541
26	Enron Corp.	31,260	76	Raytheon Company	19,530
27	Compaq Computer Corporation	31,169	77	Xerox Corporation	19,449
28	Morgan Stanley Dean Witter & Co.	31,131	78	AMR Corporation	19,205
29	Dayton Hudson Corporation	30,951	79	American Express Company	19,132
30	Texaco Inc.	30,910	80	The Coca-Cola Company	18,813
31	American International Group, Inc.	30,760	81	Columbia/HCA Healthcare Corporation	18,681
32	J. C. Penney Company, Inc.	30,678	82	The Dow Chemical Company	18,441
33	McKesson HBOC, Inc.	30,382	83	J.P. Morgan & Co. Incorporated	18,425
34	The Home Depot, Inc.	30,219	84	New York Life Insurance Company	18,350
35	Lucent Technologies Inc.	30,147	85	Bristol-Myers Squibb Company	18,284
36	Motorola, Inc.	29,398	86	Dell Computer Corporation	18,243
37	SBC Communications Inc.	28,777	87	Freddie Mac	18,048
38	Delphi Automotive Systems Corporation	28,479	88	IGA, INC.	18,000
39	The Kroger Co.	28,203	89	MCI WorldCom, Inc.	17,678
40	State Farm Mutual Automobile Insurance Company	27,706	90	Duke Energy Corporation	17,610
41	CalPERS	27,514	91	UAL Corporation	17,561
42	The Prudential Insurance Company of America	27,087	92	SUPERVALU INC.	17,421
43	Metropolitan Life Insurance Company	27,077	93	Halliburton Company	17,353
44	Merck & Co., Inc.	26,898	94	Caltex Corporation	17,174
45	Intel Corporation	26,273	95	Ameritech Corporation	17,154
46	Lockheed Martin Corporation	26,266	96	Bergen Brunswig Corporation	17,122
47	Chevron Corporation	26,187	97	UnitedHealth Group	17,106
48	The Allstate Corporation	25,976	98	CNA Financial Corporation	17,074
49	United Technologies Corporation	25,687	99	Electronic Data Systems Corporation	16,891
50	BANK ONE CORPORATION	25,595	100	FDX Corporation	16,773

Source: Hoover's, Inc., Database, September 1999

The 300 Largest Companies by Sales in
Hoover's Handbook of American Business 2000 (continued)

Rank	Company	Sales ($ mil.)	Rank	Company	Sales ($ mil.)
101	AutoNation Inc.	16,118	151	U S WEST, Inc.	12,378
102	Archer Daniels Midland Company	16,109	152	Tyco International Ltd.	12,311
103	Sprint Corporation	16,017	153	Kimberly-Clark Corporation	12,298
104	Albertson's, Inc.	16,005	154	Lowe's Companies, Inc.	12,245
105	Cardinal Health, Inc.	15,918	155	Viacom Inc.	12,096
106	Federated Department Stores, Inc.	15,833	156	Publix Super Markets, Inc.	12,067
107	Kaiser Foundation Health Plan, Inc.	15,500	157	Tosco Corporation	12,022
108	Shell Oil Company	15,451	158	TRW Inc.	11,886
109	Alcoa Inc.	15,340	159	Phillips Petroleum Company	11,845
110	SYSCO Corporation	15,328	160	Schlumberger Limited	11,816
111	Walgreen Co.	15,307	161	Massachusetts Mutual Life Insurance Company	11,728
112	CVS Corporation	15,274			
113	AlliedSignal Inc.	15,128	162	Tech Data Corporation	11,529
114	Fleming Companies, Inc.	15,069	163	Entergy Corporation	11,495
115	The Hartford Financial Services Group, Inc.	15,022	164	Reliant Energy, Incorporated	11,489
			165	Southern Company	11,403
116	Minnesota Mining and Manufacturing Company	15,021	166	Anheuser-Busch Companies, Inc.	11,246
			167	Toys "R" Us, Inc.	11,170
117	Mars, Inc.	15,000	168	Ultramar Diamond Shamrock Corporation	11,135
118	ContiGroup Companies, Inc.	15,000			
119	PricewaterhouseCoopers	15,000	169	Carlson Wagonlit Travel	11,000
120	Fred Meyer, Inc.	14,879	170	AXA Financial, Inc.	10,919
121	Texas Utilities Company	14,736	171	Ernst & Young International	10,900
122	Time Warner Inc.	14,582	172	Tenet Healthcare Corporation	10,880
123	Microsoft Corporation	14,484	173	Weyerhaeuser Company	10,766
124	Dynegy Inc.	14,258	174	KPMG International	10,600
125	Delta Air Lines, Inc.	14,138	175	Union Pacific Corporation	10,553
126	Winn-Dixie Stores, Inc.	14,137	176	Travelers Property Casualty Corp.	10,451
127	Andersen Worldwide	13,900	177	Whirlpool Corporation	10,323
128	Berkshire Hathaway Inc.	13,832	178	Atlantic Richfield Company	10,303
129	John Hancock Mutual Life Insurance Company	13,653	179	American General Financial Group	10,251
			180	Food Lion, Inc.	10,220
130	Deere & Company	13,626	181	Warner-Lambert Company	10,214
131	Pfizer Inc	13,544	182	Edison International	10,208
132	Fluor Corporation	13,505	183	The Great Atlantic & Pacific Tea Company, Inc.	10,179
133	The Northwestern Mutual Life Insurance Company	13,479			
			184	Best Buy Co., Inc.	10,078
134	American Home Products	13,463	185	The Gillette Company	10,056
135	Emerson Electric Co.	13,447	186	Fleet Financial Group, Inc.	10,002
136	Coca-Cola Enterprises Inc.	13,414	187	CSX Corporation	9,898
137	The May Department Stores Company	13,413	188	Sun Microsystems, Inc.	9,791
138	Eastman Kodak Company	13,406	189	Textron Inc.	9,683
139	Georgia-Pacific Corporation	13,336	190	Humana Inc.	9,597
140	IBP, inc.	12,849	191	PacifiCare Health Systems, Inc.	9,522
141	Washington Mutual, Inc.	12,746	192	Associates First Capital Corporation	9,377
142	Rite Aid Corporation	12,732	193	The Limited, Inc.	9,347
143	Waste Management, Inc.	12,704	194	Circuit City Stores, Inc. - Circuit City Group	9,338
144	Bechtel Group, Inc.	12,645			
145	Goodyear Tire & Rubber	12,626	195	H.J. Heinz Company	9,300
146	Johnson Controls, Inc.	12,587	196	Eli Lilly and Company	9,237
147	UtiliCorp United Inc.	12,563	197	The St. Paul Companies, Inc.	9,108
148	Abbott Laboratories	12,478	198	Lear Corporation	9,059
149	Dana Corporation	12,464	199	The Gap, Inc.	9,055
150	McDonald's Corporation	12,421	200	Northwest Airlines Corporation	9,045

The 300 Largest Companies by Sales in
Hoover's Handbook of American Business 2000 (continued)

Rank	Company	Sales ($ mil.)	Rank	Company	Sales ($ mil.)
201	The Pillsbury Company	9,030	251	7-Eleven, Inc.	7,258
202	Deloitte Touche Tohmatsu	9,000	252	Paine Webber Group Inc.	7,250
203	Office Depot, Inc.	8,998	253	Unisys Corporation	7,208
204	Colgate-Palmolive Company	8,972	254	Marsh & McLennan Companies, Inc.	7,190
205	Burlington Northern Santa Fe Corporation	8,941	255	Unicom Corporation	7,151
206	Northrop Grumman Corporation	8,902	256	Staples, Inc.	7,123
207	Oracle Corporation	8,827	257	AFLAC Incorporated	7,104
208	Manpower Inc.	8,814	258	KeyCorp	7,100
209	Foundation Health Systems, Inc.	8,797	259	Consolidated Edison, Inc.	7,093
210	NIKE, Inc.	8,777	260	The Pepsi Bottling Group, Inc.	7,041
211	Farmland Industries, Inc.	8,775	261	Fox Entertainment Group, Inc.	7,023
212	Household International, Inc.	8,708	262	The Trump Organization	6,900
213	US Airways Group, Inc.	8,688	263	Pharmacia & Upjohn, Inc.	6,893
214	AmeriSource Health Corporation	8,669	264	Sunoco, Inc.	6,854
215	Monsanto Company	8,648	265	SCI Systems, Inc.	6,806
216	CHS Electronics, Inc.	8,546	266	CBS Corporation	6,805
217	TRICON Global Restaurants, Inc.	8,468	267	Seagate Technology, Inc.	6,802
218	Texas Instruments Incorporated	8,460	268	FMR Corp.	6,770
219	Cisco Systems, Inc.	8,459	269	Kellogg Company	6,762
220	Honeywell Inc.	8,427	270	Rockwell International Corporation	6,752
221	Nabisco Holdings Corp.	8,400	271	Tennessee Valley Authority	6,729
222	Bestfoods	8,374	272	Campbell Soup Company	6,696
223	Arrow Electronics, Inc.	8,345	273	FPL Group, Inc.	6,661
224	Crown Cork & Seal Company, Inc.	8,300	274	American Standard Companies Inc.	6,654
225	Ingersoll-Rand Company	8,292	275	Eaton Corporation	6,625
226	Schering-Plough Corporation	8,077	276	Genuine Parts Company	6,614
227	National City Corporation	8,071	277	Baxter International Inc.	6,599
228	The Bear Stearns Companies Inc.	7,980	278	Occidental Petroleum Corporation	6,596
229	Marriott International, Inc.	7,968	279	Amerada Hess Corporation	6,590
230	Continental Airlines, Inc.	7,951	280	Columbia Energy Group	6,551
231	The TJX Companies, Inc.	7,949	281	Ashland Inc.	6,534
232	PNC Bank Corp.	7,936	282	NCR Corporation	6,505
233	PACCAR Inc	7,895	283	Aon Corporation	6,493
234	Navistar International Corporation	7,830	284	SAFECO Corporation	6,452
235	Dillard's Inc.	7,797	285	Universal Studios, Inc.	6,439
236	Conseco, Inc.	7,716	286	ARAMARK Corporation	6,377
237	The Principal Financial Group	7,697	287	WellPoint Health Networks Inc.	6,369
238	USAA	7,687	288	The Chubb Corporation	6,350
239	U.S. Bancorp	7,664	289	American Electric Power Company, Inc.	6,346
240	Computer Sciences Corporation	7,660	290	Baker Hughes Incorporated	6,312
241	The Williams Companies, Inc.	7,658	291	Cummins Engine Company, Inc.	6,266
242	Bindley Western Industries, Inc.	7,621	292	General Mills, Inc.	6,246
243	Tenneco Inc.	7,597	293	Saks Incorporated	6,220
244	PPG Industries, Inc.	7,510	294	USX-U.S. Steel Group	6,184
245	Gateway, Inc.	7,468	295	Boise Cascade Corporation	6,162
246	Unisource Worldwide, Inc.	7,417	296	Case Corporation	6,149
247	Tyson Foods, Inc.	7,414	297	Lincoln National Corporation	6,087
248	SunTrust Banks, Inc.	7,392	298	Dominion Resources, Inc.	6,086
249	The Coastal Corporation	7,368	299	Levi Strauss & Co.	6,000
250	Fort James Corporation	7,301	300	Penske Corporation	6,000

The 300 Most Profitable Companies in
Hoover's Handbook of American Business 2000

Rank	Company	Net Income ($ mil.)	Rank	Company	Net Income ($ mil.)
1	MediaOne Group, Inc.	26,305	51	McDonald's Corporation	1,550
2	CalPERS	22,594	52	Sprint Corporation	1,535
3	Ford Motor Company	22,071	53	ITT Industries, Inc.	1,533
4	General Electric Company	9,296	54	Fleet Financial Group, Inc.	1,532
5	Exxon Corporation	6,433	55	Caterpillar Inc.	1,513
6	AT&T Corp.	6,398	56	U S WEST, Inc.	1,508
7	International Business Machines	6,328	57	Washington Mutual, Inc.	1,487
8	Intel Corporation	6,068	58	Dell Computer Corporation	1,460
9	Citigroup Inc.	5,807	59	The Times Mirror Company	1,417
10	Philip Morris Companies Inc.	5,372	60	Eastman Kodak Company	1,390
11	Merck & Co., Inc.	5,248	61	Cisco Systems, Inc.	1,350
12	Bank of America Corporation	5,165	62	Metropolitan Life Insurance Company	1,343
13	Microsoft Corporation	4,490	63	Travelers Property Casualty Corp.	1,343
14	E. I. du Pont de Nemours and Company	4,480	64	Chevron Corporation	1,339
15	Wal-Mart Stores, Inc.	4,430	65	AlliedSignal Inc.	1,331
16	SBC Communications Inc.	4,023	66	U.S. Bancorp	1,327
17	The Chase Manhattan Corporation	3,782	67	AMR Corporation	1,314
18	The Procter & Gamble Company	3,780	68	The Dow Chemical Company	1,310
19	American International Group, Inc.	3,766	69	CIGNA Corporation	1,292
20	Ameritech Corporation	3,606	70	Oracle Corporation	1,290
21	The Coca-Cola Company	3,533	71	Merrill Lynch & Co., Inc.	1,259
22	BellSouth Corporation	3,527	72	United Technologies Corporation	1,255
23	Fannie Mae	3,418	73	Warner-Lambert Company	1,254
24	Pfizer Inc.	3,351	74	Duke Energy Corporation	1,252
25	The Allstate Corporation	3,294	75	Anheuser-Busch Companies, Inc.	1,233
26	Morgan Stanley Dean Witter & Co.	3,276	76	Emerson Electric Co.	1,229
27	BANK ONE CORPORATION	3,108	77	Associates First Capital Corporation	1,224
28	Johnson & Johnson	3,059	78	The Bank of New York Company, Inc.	1,192
29	Bell Atlantic Corporation	2,965	79	Seagate Technology, Inc.	1,176
30	General Motors Corporation	2,956	80	Minnesota Mining and Manufacturing Company	1,175
31	Hewlett-Packard Company	2,945	81	Tyco International Ltd.	1,175
32	First Union Corporation	2,891	82	Kimberly-Clark Corporation	1,166
33	Bristol-Myers Squibb Company	2,836	83	Burlington Northern Santa Fe	1,155
34	Berkshire Hathaway Inc.	2,830	84	The Boeing Company	1,120
35	American Home Products	2,474	85	PNC Bank Corp.	1,115
36	The Goldman Sachs Group, Inc.	2,428	86	The Prudential Insurance Company of America	1,106
37	Abbott Laboratories	2,333	87	Ralston Purina Company	1,106
38	GTE Corporation	2,172	88	The Gillette Company	1,081
39	Liberty Media Group	2,157	89	National City Corporation	1,071
40	American Express Company	2,141	90	Sears, Roebuck and Co.	1,048
41	Eli Lilly and Company	2,098	91	Deere & Company	1,021
42	The Limited, Inc.	2,054	92	The Hartford Financial Services Group, Inc.	1,015
43	PepsiCo, Inc.	1,993	93	Schlumberger Limited	1,014
44	Wells Fargo & Company	1,950	94	State Farm Mutual Automobile Insurance Company	1,013
45	The Walt Disney Company	1,850	95	Delta Air Lines, Inc.	1,001
46	Schering-Plough Corporation	1,756	96	Lockheed Martin Corporation	1,001
47	United Parcel Service of America, Inc.	1,741	97	Gannett Co., Inc.	1,000
48	Mobil Corporation	1,704	98	KeyCorp	996
49	Freddie Mac	1,700	99	USAA	980
50	The Home Depot, Inc.	1,614	100	Southern Company	977

Source: Hoover's, Inc., Database, September 1999

The 300 Most Profitable Companies in
Hoover's Handbook of American Business 2000 (continued)

Rank	Company	Net Income ($ mil.)	Rank	Company	Net Income ($ mil.)
101	Comcast Corporation	972	151	Computer Associates International	626
102	SunTrust Banks, Inc.	971	152	Bestfoods	624
103	Lucent Technologies Inc.	970	153	Textron Inc.	608
104	J.P. Morgan & Co. Incorporated	963	154	Comerica Incorporated	607
105	Nationwide Insurance Enterprise	963	155	Automatic Data Processing, Inc.	605
106	Dayton Hudson Corporation	935	156	Cargill, Incorporated	597
107	Wachovia Corporation	874	157	J. C. Penney Company, Inc.	594
108	Mellon Bank Corporation	870	158	Texaco Inc.	578
109	Raytheon Company	864	159	Pitney Bowes Inc.	576
110	Amgen Inc.	863	160	Honeywell Inc.	572
111	Starwood Hotels & Resorts	860	161	Albertson's, Inc.	567
112	Alcoa Inc.	853	162	Ryerson Tull, Inc.	551
113	The May Department Stores Company	849	163	United States Postal Service	550
114	Colgate-Palmolive Company	849	164	Air Products and Chemicals, Inc.	547
115	Aetna Inc.	848	165	Aon Corporation	541
116	Carnival Corporation	836	166	Cendant Corporation	540
117	AXA Financial, Inc.	833	167	US Airways Group, Inc.	538
118	UAL Corporation	827	168	CSX Corporation	537
119	The Gap, Inc.	825	169	American Electric Power Company	536
120	The Northwestern Mutual Life Insurance Company	809	170	Dominion Resources, Inc.	536
121	Safeway Inc.	807	171	General Mills, Inc.	535
122	PPG Industries, Inc.	801	172	Dana Corporation	534
123	Marsh & McLennan Companies, Inc.	796	173	ALLTEL Corporation	526
124	EMC Corporation	793	174	Household International, Inc.	524
125	Entergy Corporation	786	175	Kmart Corporation	518
126	MBNA Corporation	776	176	PECO Energy Company	513
127	American General Financial Group	764	177	Walgreen Co.	511
128	Sun Microsystems, Inc.	763	178	Unicom Corporation	510
129	America Online, Inc.	762	179	Lincoln National Corporation	510
130	New York Life Insurance Company	753	180	Ingersoll-Rand Company	509
131	Electronic Data Systems Corporation	743	181	Kellogg Company	503
132	Texas Utilities Company	740	182	SLM Holding Corporation	502
133	Lehman Brothers Holdings Inc.	736	183	AutoNation Inc.	500
134	Norfolk Southern Corporation	734	184	Fort James Corporation	498
135	Consolidated Edison, Inc.	730	185	AFLAC Incorporated	487
136	PG&E Corporation	719	186	Lowe's Companies, Inc.	482
137	The Chubb Corporation	707	187	TRW Inc.	477
138	Enron Corp.	703	188	Masco Corporation	476
139	The Principal Financial Group	693	189	H.J. Heinz Company	474
140	Pharmacia & Upjohn, Inc.	691	190	Medtronic, Inc.	468
141	Goodyear Tire & Rubber	682	191	Conseco, Inc.	467
142	Illinois Tool Works Inc.	673	192	First Data Corporation	466
143	Edison International	668	193	Loews Corporation	465
144	FPL Group, Inc.	664	194	Costco Companies, Inc.	460
145	Federated Department Stores, Inc.	662	195	The Progressive Corporation	457
146	The Bear Stearns Companies Inc.	660	196	UST Inc.	455
147	Campbell Soup Company	660	197	Atlantic Richfield Company	452
148	Public Service Enterprise Group	644	198	NIKE, Inc.	451
149	FDX Corporation	631	199	Conoco Inc.	450
150	John Hancock	627	200	FMR Corp.	446

The 300 Most Profitable Companies in
Hoover's Handbook of American Business 2000 (continued)

Rank	Company	Net Income ($ mil.)	Rank	Company	Net Income ($ mil.)
201	TRICON Global Restaurants, Inc.	445	251	Eaton Corporation	349
202	The Coastal Corporation	444	252	The Charles Schwab Corporation	349
203	DTE Energy Company	443	253	Gateway, Inc.	346
204	Central and South West Corporation	440	254	Service Corporation International	342
205	Rohm and Haas Company	440	255	Computer Sciences Corporation	341
206	State Street Corporation	436	256	Hershey Foods Corporation	341
207	Golden West Financial Corporation	435	257	Johnson Controls, Inc.	338
208	Paine Webber Group Inc.	434	258	Reliance Group Holdings, Inc.	334
209	Southwest Airlines Co.	433	259	The McGraw-Hill Companies, Inc.	333
210	Firstar Corporation	430	260	Mattel, Inc.	332
211	Praxair, Inc.	425	261	USG Corporation	332
212	The TJX Companies, Inc.	424	262	Royal Caribbean Cruises Ltd.	331
213	Cooper Industries, Inc.	423	263	Constellation Energy Group, Inc.	328
214	The Washington Post Company	417	264	Whirlpool Corporation	325
215	PACCAR Inc	417	265	Parker Hannifin Corporation	320
216	Tribune Company	414	266	Baxter International Inc.	315
217	FirstEnergy Corp.	411	267	USX-Marathon Group	310
218	The Kroger Co.	411	268	The Interpublic Group of Companies	310
219	Texas Instruments Incorporated	407	269	Apple Computer, Inc.	309
220	3Com Corporation	404	270	Wm. Wrigley Jr. Company	305
221	Archer Daniels Midland Company	404	271	Navistar International Corporation	299
222	Union Carbide Corporation	403	272	The Clorox Company	298
223	Intimate Brands, Inc.	400	273	Hilton Hotels Corporation	297
224	Carolina Power & Light Company	399	274	SYSCO Corporation	297
225	Tellabs, Inc.	398	275	R. R. Donnelley & Sons Company	295
226	CVS Corporation	396	276	Weyerhaeuser Company	294
227	Newell Rubbermaid Inc.	396	277	Sempra Energy	294
228	Xerox Corporation	395	278	A.G. Edwards, Inc.	292
229	Corning Incorporated	394	279	Peter Kiewit Sons', Inc.	288
230	Marriott International, Inc.	390	280	Omnicom Group Inc.	285
231	VF Corporation	388	281	CMS Energy Corporation	285
232	Unisys Corporation	387	282	The Quaker Oats Company	285
233	Hartford Life, Inc.	386	283	Northern States Power Company	282
234	Countrywide Credit Industries, Inc.	385	284	CNA Financial Corporation	282
235	Continental Airlines, Inc.	383	285	Florida Progress Corporation	282
236	Columbia/HCA Healthcare Corporation	379	286	Maytag Corporation	281
237	Dover Corporation	379	287	The Dun & Bradstreet Corporation	280
238	Publix Super Markets, Inc.	378	288	Sunoco, Inc.	280
239	Donaldson, Lufkin & Jenrette, Inc.	371	289	The New York Times Company	279
240	Knight Ridder	366	290	The Hertz Corporation	277
241	General Dynamics Corporation	364	291	Capital One Financial Corporation	275
242	USX-U.S. Steel Group	364	292	Georgia-Pacific Corporation	274
243	UNUMProvident	363	293	The Sherwin-Williams Company	273
244	Occidental Petroleum Corporation	363	294	Food Lion, Inc.	273
245	GPU, Inc.	360	295	Avon Products, Inc.	270
246	Massachusetts Mutual Life Insurance Company	359	296	Columbia Energy Group	269
247	ConAgra, Inc.	358	297	Nucor Corporation	264
248	Genuine Parts Company	356	298	Fortune Brands, Inc.	263
249	Northern Trust Corporation	354	299	Cinergy Corp.	261
250	SAFECO Corporation	352	300	Vulcan Materials Company	256

The 300 Most Valuable Public Companies in Hoover's Handbook of American Business 2000

Rank	Company	Market Value* ($mil.)	Rank	Company	Market Value* ($mil.)
1	General Electric Company	333,672	51	The Walt Disney Company	52,049
2	Microsoft Corporation	269,285	52	American Express Company	46,339
3	Intel Corporation	196,513	53	Freddie Mac	44,797
4	Wal-Mart Stores, Inc.	191,264	54	EMC Corporation	42,809
5	Exxon Corporation	177,560	55	Medtronic, Inc.	42,101
6	Merck & Co., Inc.	174,083	56	Morgan Stanley Dean Witter & Co.	39,388
7	International Business Machines	170,719	57	Xerox Corporation	38,775
8	The Coca-Cola Company	165,190	58	The Gap, Inc.	36,711
9	Pfizer Inc	161,770	59	Motorola, Inc.	36,703
10	Bristol-Myers Squibb Company	133,068	60	Oracle Corporation	35,713
11	AT&T Corp.	132,847	61	Texas Instruments Incorporated	33,450
12	MCI WorldCom, Inc.	132,040	62	The Boeing Company	33,017
13	Philip Morris Companies Inc.	130,034	63	U S WEST, Inc.	32,503
14	Dell Computer Corporation	127,150	64	Tyco International Ltd.	32,412
15	The Procter & Gamble Company	121,784	65	The Allstate Corporation	31,493
16	America Online, Inc.	121,098	66	Anheuser-Busch Companies, Inc.	31,279
17	Johnson & Johnson	112,739	67	The Bank of New York Company, Inc.	31,118
18	Citigroup Inc.	112,193			
19	Berkshire Hathaway Inc.	106,298	68	Associates First Capital Corporation	30,844
20	SBC Communications Inc.	105,078			
21	Bank of America Corporation	103,693	69	Monsanto Company	29,892
22	American International Group	101,430	70	Safeway Inc.	29,879
23	Cisco Systems, Inc.	99,786	71	Kimberly-Clark Corporation	29,335
24	Eli Lilly and Company	97,448	72	Sprint Corporation	28,971
25	BellSouth Corporation	97,266	73	Pharmacia & Upjohn, Inc.	28,807
26	Lucent Technologies Inc.	91,173	74	Minnesota Mining and Manufacturing Company	28,589
27	The Home Depot, Inc.	89,265			
28	Bell Atlantic Corporation	85,116	75	MediaOne Group, Inc.	28,363
29	Schering-Plough Corporation	81,328	76	Waste Management, Inc.	28,362
30	Fannie Mae	75,850	77	Texaco Inc.	28,335
31	Abbott Laboratories	74,287	78	Dayton Hudson Corporation	28,165
32	American Home Products Corporation	73,993	79	Emerson Electric Co.	27,279
			80	Colgate-Palmolive Company	27,187
33	Ford Motor Company	71,719	81	Amgen Inc.	26,621
34	Compaq Computer Corporation	70,854	82	Sara Lee Corporation	25,770
35	Ameritech Corporation	69,655	83	U.S. Bancorp	25,765
36	Time Warner Inc.	69,383	84	Viacom Inc.	25,715
37	Mobil Corporation	68,008	85	Fleet Financial Group, Inc.	25,454
38	Wells Fargo & Company	65,664	86	Schlumberger Limited	25,330
39	GTE Corporation	62,920	87	Electronic Data Systems	24,750
40	Warner-Lambert Company	61,772	88	AlliedSignal Inc.	24,746
41	Hewlett-Packard Company	61,178	89	SunTrust Banks, Inc.	24,566
42	The Chase Manhattan Corporation	60,207	90	United Technologies Corporation	24,477
43	PepsiCo, Inc.	60,134	91	Campbell Soup Company	24,192
44	BANK ONE CORPORATION	60,113	92	Merrill Lynch & Co., Inc.	23,782
45	E. I. du Pont de Nemours and Company	59,755	93	National City Corporation	23,659
			94	Duke Energy Corporation	23,254
46	First Union Corporation	59,715	95	Eastman Kodak Company	23,241
47	General Motors Corporation	54,469	96	Washington Mutual, Inc.	22,775
48	Chevron Corporation	54,162	97	CBS Corporation	22,650
49	The Gillette Company	52,850	98	The Charles Schwab Corporation	22,578
50	McDonald's Corporation	52,092	99	Automatic Data Processing, Inc.	22,017
			100	Comcast Corporation	21,698

* Market value at most recent fiscal year-end
Source: Hoover's, Inc., Database, September 1999

The 300 Most Valuable Public Companies in
Hoover's Handbook of American Business 2000 (continued)

Rank	Company	Market Value* ($mil.)	Rank	Company	Market Value* ($mil.)
101	CVS Corporation	21,462	151	The Williams Companies, Inc.	13,359
102	Atlantic Richfield Company	21,008	152	Tellabs, Inc.	13,332
103	Lowe's Companies, Inc.	20,563	153	Staples, Inc.	13,200
104	Carnival Corporation	20,543	154	Texas Utilities Company	13,182
105	Firstar Corporation	20,344	155	Halliburton Company	13,037
106	Southern Company	20,214	156	Conoco Inc.	13,032
107	The Dow Chemical Company	20,041	157	AXA Financial, Inc.	12,915
108	American General Financial Group	19,641	158	Applied Materials, Inc.	12,761
109	Household International, Inc.	19,147	159	ConAgra, Inc.	12,722
110	Walgreen Co.	19,123	160	The Hartford Financial Services Group, Inc.	12,479
111	Computer Associates International, Inc.	19,050	161	The Progressive Corporation	12,280
112	Enron Corp.	18,880	162	General Mills, Inc.	12,218
113	MBNA Corporation	18,652	163	Consolidated Edison, Inc.	12,172
114	McKesson HBOC, Inc.	18,554	164	Travelers Property Casualty Corp.	12,148
115	Baxter International Inc.	18,414	165	PG&E Corporation	12,052
116	J.P. Morgan & Co. Incorporated	18,386	166	Norfolk Southern Corporation	12,023
117	Mellon Bank Corporation	18,010	167	Textron Inc.	11,751
118	Gannett Co., Inc.	17,996	168	AFLAC Incorporated	11,658
119	Raytheon Company	17,934	169	Avon Products, Inc.	11,617
120	Pitney Bowes Inc.	17,861	170	Archer Daniels Midland Company	11,613
121	Wachovia Corporation	17,749	171	State Street Corporation	11,267
122	Qwest Communications	17,350	172	Union Pacific Corporation	11,150
123	NIKE, Inc.	17,142	173	FPL Group, Inc.	11,137
124	Amazon.com, Inc.	17,038	174	The Interpublic Group of Companies, Inc.	11,129
125	ALLTEL Corporation	16,818	175	Aetna Inc.	11,108
126	H.J. Heinz Company	16,768	176	Loews Corporation	11,061
127	Lockheed Martin Corporation	16,655	177	Nabisco Holdings Corp.	10,984
128	Caterpillar Inc.	16,431	178	Phillips Petroleum Company	10,743
129	PNC Bank Corp.	16,400	179	Kohl's Corporation	10,731
130	Sun Microsystems, Inc.	16,347	180	Rite Aid Corporation	10,712
131	FDX Corporation	16,303	181	Comerica Incorporated	10,630
132	Sears, Roebuck and Co.	16,299	182	Boston Scientific Corporation	10,520
133	Burlington Northern Santa Fe Corporation	16,114	183	The Chubb Corporation	10,507
134	Cendant Corporation	16,091	184	Corning Incorporated	10,418
135	Columbia/HCA Healthcare	15,904	185	Wm. Wrigley Jr. Company	10,409
136	CIGNA Corporation	15,899	186	Cardinal Health, Inc.	10,399
137	The Kroger Co.	15,546	187	Costco Companies, Inc.	10,240
138	Albertson's, Inc.	15,292	188	Becton, Dickinson and Company	10,194
139	Marsh & McLennan Companies, Inc.	15,014	189	PPG Industries, Inc.	10,191
140	Bestfoods	14,981	190	Weyerhaeuser Company	10,112
141	Liberty Media Group	14,568	191	The McGraw-Hill Companies, Inc.	10,040
142	Illinois Tool Works Inc.	14,507	192	3Com Corporation	9,990
143	KeyCorp	14,478	193	The Clorox Company	9,914
144	Clear Channel Communications, Inc.	14,366	194	Service Corporation International	9,865
145	Coca-Cola Enterprises Inc.	14,352	195	Intimate Brands, Inc.	9,806
146	First Data Corporation	13,884	196	Omnicom Group Inc.	9,778
147	Kellogg Company	13,823	197	Edison International	9,773
148	International Paper Company	13,763	198	Masco Corporation	9,756
149	Alcoa Inc.	13,675	199	J. C. Penney Company, Inc.	9,750
150	The May Department Stores Company	13,477	200	Fred Meyer, Inc.	9,736

Rank	Company	Market Value* ($mil.)	Rank	Company	Market Value* ($mil.)
201	Delta Air Lines, Inc.	9,724	251	Harley-Davidson, Inc.	7,246
202	Northern Trust Corporation	9,710	252	Marriott International, Inc.	7,230
203	Conseco, Inc.	9,633	253	Carolina Power & Light Company	7,122
204	AMR Corporation	9,581	254	Unocal Corporation	7,046
205	The TJX Companies, Inc.	9,522	255	Mattel, Inc.	7,026
206	Honeywell Inc.	9,514	256	Rockwell International Corporation	6,909
207	Reliant Energy, Incorporated	9,495	257	Air Products and Chemicals, Inc.	6,840
208	Best Buy Co., Inc.	9,444	258	AutoNation Inc.	6,817
209	Aon Corporation	9,419	259	Dana Corporation	6,774
210	PECO Energy Company	9,381	260	Circuit City Stores, Inc. - Circuit City Group	6,724
211	USX-Marathon Group	9,294			
212	Office Depot, Inc.	9,156	261	TRW Inc.	6,722
213	Ralston Purina Company	9,139	262	Cintas Corporation	6,715
214	Dominion Resources, Inc.	9,093	263	Newell Rubbermaid Inc.	6,711
215	Public Service Enterprise Group Incorporated	9,066	264	The Bear Stearns Companies Inc.	6,663
			265	Hartford Life, Inc.	6,631
216	American Electric Power Company	9,027	266	Lexmark International Group, Inc.	6,582
217	CSX Corporation	9,010	267	The ServiceMaster Company	6,575
218	Hershey Foods Corporation	8,902	268	HEALTHSOUTH Corporation	6,502
219	Unisys Corporation	8,837	269	UST Inc.	6,351
220	Fort James Corporation	8,820	270	The New York Times Company	6,300
221	Computer Sciences Corporation	8,783	271	The Times Mirror Company	6,277
222	Federated Department Stores, Inc.	8,717	272	PacifiCorp	6,262
223	Kmart Corporation	8,663	273	DTE Energy Company	6,247
224	SYSCO Corporation	8,586	274	Royal Caribbean Cruises Ltd.	6,238
225	Unicom Corporation	8,364	275	Genuine Parts Company	6,003
226	Lincoln National Corporation	8,284	276	Nordstrom, Inc.	5,916
227	Deere & Company	8,277	277	R. R. Donnelley & Sons Company	5,885
228	The Estee Lauder Companies Inc.	8,244	278	Occidental Petroleum Corporation	5,870
229	UNUMProvident	8,098	279	Seagate Technology, Inc.	5,862
230	Dover Corporation	8,074	280	SAFECO Corporation	5,851
231	The Quaker Oats Company	8,052	281	WellPoint Health Networks Inc.	5,839
232	Gateway, Inc.	8,015	282	Central and South West Corporation	5,834
233	The St. Paul Companies, Inc.	7,969	283	The Washington Post Company	5,833
234	UnitedHealth Group	7,920	284	Sabre Inc.	5,778
235	Tribune Company	7,881	285	Baker Hughes Incorporated	5,767
236	SLM Holding Corporation	7,878	286	General Instrument Corporation	5,728
237	Goodyear Tire & Rubber	7,866	287	Tenneco Inc.	5,685
238	Ingersoll-Rand Company	7,767	288	Lehman Brothers Holdings Inc.	5,683
239	The Limited, Inc.	7,733	289	GPU, Inc.	5,656
240	FirstEnergy Corp.	7,719	290	CMS Energy Corporation	5,646
241	Entergy Corporation	7,677	291	Union Carbide Corporation	5,639
242	TRICON Global Restaurants, Inc.	7,670	292	Paine Webber Group Inc.	5,621
243	Tenet Healthcare Corporation	7,608	293	VF Corporation	5,601
244	Cablevision Systems Corporation	7,594	294	Maytag Corporation	5,554
245	Capital One Financial Corporation	7,552	295	Praxair, Inc.	5,554
246	Southwest Airlines Co.	7,538	296	Winn-Dixie Stores, Inc.	5,488
247	General Dynamics Corporation	7,475	297	Cinergy Corp.	5,455
248	The Coastal Corporation	7,473	298	The Dun & Bradstreet Corporation	5,411
249	CNA Financial Corporation	7,402	299	Fortune Brands, Inc.	5,311
250	Danaher Corporation	7,338	300	USA Networks, Inc.	5,261

The 300 Largest Employers in
Hoover's Handbook of American Business 2000

Rank	Company	Employees	Rank	Company	Employees
1	Manpower Inc.	2,015,000	51	Darden Restaurants, Inc.	116,700
2	Wal-Mart Stores, Inc.	910,000	52	Emerson Electric Co.	111,800
3	United States Postal Service	792,041	53	Viacom Inc.	111,730
4	Kelly Services, Inc.	740,000	54	The Gap, Inc.	111,000
5	Olsten Corporation	700,850	55	The Procter & Gamble Company	110,000
6	General Motors Corporation	594,000	56	Raytheon Company	108,200
7	Ford Motor Company	345,175	57	Halliburton Company	107,800
8	United Parcel Service of America	328,000	58	AT&T Corp.	107,800
9	Sears, Roebuck and Co.	324,000	59	Alcoa Inc.	103,500
10	General Electric Company	293,000	60	E. I. du Pont de Nemours and Company	101,000
11	International Business Machines Corporation	291,067	61	Albertson's, Inc.	100,000
12	McDonald's Corporation	284,000	62	Kaiser Foundation Health Plan, Inc.	100,000
13	Kmart Corporation	278,525	63	Sodexho Marriott Services, Inc.	100,000
14	J. C. Penney Company, Inc.	262,000	64	CVS Corporation	97,000
15	Columbia/HCA Healthcare Corporation	260,000	65	The Goodyear Tire & Rubber Company	96,950
16	TRICON Global Restaurants, Inc.	260,000	66	UAL Corporation	95,035
17	Dayton Hudson Corporation	244,000	67	Johnson & Johnson	93,100
18	The Boeing Company	231,000	68	Xerox Corporation	92,700
19	The Kroger Co.	213,000	69	Wells Fargo & Company	92,178
20	Delphi Automotive Systems Corporation	197,568	70	Food Lion, Inc.	92,125
21	United Technologies Corporation	178,800	71	AMR Corporation	92,000
22	Citigroup Inc.	173,700	72	Fred Meyer, Inc.	92,000
23	Bank of America Corporation	170,975	73	IGA, INC.	92,000
24	Safeway Inc.	170,000	74	BANK ONE CORPORATION	91,310
25	Lockheed Martin Corporation	165,000	75	Walgreen Co.	90,000
26	The Home Depot, Inc.	157,000	76	Rite Aid Corporation	89,900
27	ARAMARK Corporation	150,000	77	Johnson Controls, Inc.	89,000
28	Blue Cross and Blue Shield Association	150,000	78	BellSouth Corporation	88,400
29	PepsiCo, Inc.	150,000	79	Tyco International Ltd.	87,000
30	Philip Morris Companies Inc.	144,000	80	H&R Block, Inc.	86,500
31	Lucent Technologies Inc.	141,600	81	Dana Corporation	86,400
32	FDX Corporation	141,000	82	Eastman Kodak Company	86,200
33	Bell Atlantic Corporation	140,000	83	KPMG International	85,300
34	PricewaterhouseCoopers	140,000	84	American Express Company	85,000
35	Sara Lee Corporation	139,000	85	Ernst & Young International	85,000
36	Marriott International, Inc.	133,000	86	The Great Atlantic & Pacific Tea Company, Inc.	83,400
37	Motorola, Inc.	133,000	87	Blockbuster Inc.	82,400
38	Winn-Dixie Stores, Inc.	132,000	88	Cargill, Incorporated	82,000
39	Starwood Hotels & Resorts Worldwide, Inc.	130,000	89	Deloitte Touche Tohmatsu	82,000
40	SBC Communications Inc.	129,850	90	Seagate Technology, Inc.	82,000
41	The May Department Stores Company	127,000	91	Sun Healthcare Group, Inc.	80,720
42	The Limited, Inc.	126,800	92	ConAgra, Inc.	80,000
43	Tenet Healthcare Corporation	125,950	93	Hyatt Corporation	80,000
44	Hewlett-Packard Company	124,600	94	International Paper Company	80,000
45	Andersen Worldwide	123,791	95	Exxon Corporation	79,000
46	Electronic Data Systems Corporation	120,000	96	TRW Inc.	78,000
47	GTE Corporation	120,000	97	MCI WorldCom, Inc.	77,000
48	Federated Department Stores, Inc.	118,800	98	State Farm Mutual Automobile Insurance Company	76,257
49	Publix Super Markets, Inc.	117,000	99	Venator Group Inc.	75,118
50	The Walt Disney Company	117,000	100	Minnesota Mining and Manufacturing Company	73,564

Source: Hoover's, Inc., Database, September 1999

The 300 Largest Employers in
Hoover's Handbook of American Business 2000 (continued)

Rank	Company	Employees	Rank	Company	Employees
101	Beverly Enterprises, Inc.	73,000	151	Northwest Airlines Corporation	50,600
102	Burns International Services Corporation	73,000	152	Computer Sciences Corporation	50,000
103	The Chase Manhattan Corporation	72,683	153	The Prudential Insurance Company of America	50,000
104	First Union Corporation	71,486	154	SUPERVALU INC.	50,000
105	Compaq Computer Corporation	71,000	155	CIGNA Corporation	49,900
106	Delta Air Lines, Inc.	70,846	156	Northrop Grumman Corporation	49,600
107	Ameritech Corporation	70,525	157	Eaton Corporation	49,500
108	Tyson Foods, Inc.	70,500	158	Circuit City Stores, Inc. - Circuit City Group	49,362
109	AlliedSignal Inc.	70,400	159	Montgomery Ward Holding Corp.	49,000
110	Toys "R" Us, Inc.	70,000	160	American International Group, Inc.	48,000
111	VF Corporation	70,000	161	Ingersoll-Rand Company	46,500
112	The Wackenhut Corporation	70,000	162	Pfizer Inc	46,400
113	Waste Management, Inc.	68,000	163	CBS Corporation	46,189
114	Time Warner Inc.	67,500	164	CSX Corporation	46,147
115	Coca-Cola Enterprises Inc.	66,000	165	Morgan Stanley Dean Witter & Co.	45,712
116	Lowe's Companies, Inc.	66,000	166	Ryder System, Inc.	45,373
117	Caterpillar Inc.	65,824	167	Berkshire Hathaway Inc.	45,000
118	Union Pacific Corporation	65,000	168	Best Buy Co., Inc.	45,000
119	Sprint Corporation	64,900	169	Georgia-Pacific Corporation	45,000
120	Intel Corporation	64,500	170	Metropolitan Life Insurance Company	45,000
121	Schlumberger Limited	64,000	171	Aon Corporation	44,000
122	Textron Inc.	64,000	172	Office Depot, Inc.	44,000
123	Merrill Lynch & Co., Inc.	63,800	173	Continental Airlines, Inc.	43,900
124	Costco Companies, Inc.	63,000	174	Oracle Corporation	43,800
125	The TJX Companies, Inc.	62,000	175	The Gillette Company	43,100
126	DHL Worldwide Express	60,486	176	Burlington Northern Santa Fe Corporation	42,900
127	Lear Corporation	60,000	177	US Airways Group, Inc.	42,625
128	Saks Incorporated	60,000	178	IKON Office Solutions, Inc.	42,600
129	Whirlpool Corporation	59,000	179	Baxter International Inc.	42,000
130	Consolidated Stores Corporation	58,254	180	Bestfoods	42,000
131	Merck & Co., Inc.	57,300	181	Nordstrom, Inc.	42,000
132	American Standard Companies Inc.	57,100	182	AutoNation Inc.	42,000
133	Honeywell Inc.	57,000	183	Park Place Entertainment Corporation	42,000
134	Fluor Corporation	56,886	184	Pittston Brink's Group	41,800
135	Abbott Laboratories	56,236	185	Mobil Corporation	41,500
136	Cox Enterprises, Inc.	55,500	186	National City Corporation	41,218
137	Intimate Brands, Inc.	55,000	187	Rockwell International Corporation	41,000
138	Dillard's Inc.	54,921	188	Warner-Lambert Company	41,000
139	Bristol-Myers Squibb Company	54,700	189	IBP, inc.	40,000
140	Kimberly-Clark Corporation	54,700	190	Promus Hotel Corporation	40,000
141	U S WEST, Inc.	54,483	191	Parker Hannifin Corporation	39,873
142	Federal-Mogul Corporation	54,350	192	Gannett Co., Inc.	39,400
143	Marsh & McLennan Companies, Inc.	54,300	193	Chevron Corporation	39,191
144	Dole Food Company, Inc.	53,500	194	The Dow Chemical Company	39,000
145	The Allstate Corporation	53,000	195	Wendy's International, Inc.	39,000
146	Brinker International, Inc.	53,000	196	OfficeMax, Inc.	38,980
147	American Home Products Corporation	52,984	197	Fleming Companies, Inc.	38,900
148	HEALTHSOUTH Corporation	51,901	198	Owens-Illinois, Inc.	38,800
149	The ServiceMaster Company	51,740	199	H.J. Heinz Company	38,600
150	Nabisco Holdings Corp.	51,000	200	AutoZone, Inc.	38,500

Rank	Company	Employees	Rank	Company	Employees
201	Crown Cork & Seal Company, Inc.	38,459	251	Pharmacia & Upjohn, Inc.	30,000
202	Colgate-Palmolive Company	38,300	252	Mirage Resorts, Incorporated	29,850
203	Tandy Corporation	38,200	253	Dollar General Corporation	29,820
204	Hilton Hotels Corporation	38,000	254	Eli Lilly and Company	29,800
205	Smurfit-Stone Container	38,000	255	Yellow Corporation	29,700
206	Harrah's Entertainment, Inc.	37,400	256	Illinois Tool Works Inc.	29,200
207	Chiquita Brands International, Inc.	37,000	257	UnitedHealth Group	29,200
208	Deere & Company	37,000	258	Barnes & Noble, Inc.	29,000
209	The Pepsi Bottling Group, Inc.	36,900	259	Mattel, Inc.	29,000
210	Ames Department Stores, Inc.	36,400	260	Associates First Capital Corporation	28,662
211	R. R. Donnelley & Sons Company	36,300	261	The Coca-Cola Company	28,600
212	Fleet Financial Group, Inc.	36,000	262	Harris Corporation	28,500
213	Texas Instruments Incorporated	35,948	263	Mellon Bank Corporation	28,500
214	Omnicom Group Inc.	35,600	264	Cummins Engine Company, Inc.	28,300
215	American Greetings Corporation	35,475	265	Cooper Industries, Inc.	28,100
216	Cendant Corporation	35,000	266	FMR Corp.	28,000
217	Weyerhaeuser Company	35,000	267	Penske Corporation	28,000
218	Litton Industries, Inc.	34,900	268	Regis Corporation	28,000
219	Loews Corporation	34,300	269	Service Corporation International	27,618
220	Automatic Data Processing, Inc.	34,000	270	Fort James Corporation	27,500
221	The Interpublic Group of Companies, Inc.	34,000	271	The Pep Boys - Manny, Moe & Jack	27,460
			272	Washington Mutual, Inc.	27,330
222	Interstate Bakeries Corporation	34,000	273	Borders Group, Inc.	27,200
223	Avon Products, Inc.	33,900	274	Microsoft Corporation	27,055
224	Kohl's Corporation	33,800	275	Leggett & Platt, Incorporated	27,000
225	CNF Transportation Inc.	33,700	276	Mandalay Resort Group	27,000
226	Aetna Inc.	33,500	277	Pitney Bowes Inc.	26,792
227	SYSCO Corporation	33,400	278	U.S. Bancorp	26,526
228	Unisys Corporation	33,200	279	Sun Microsystems, Inc.	26,300
229	NCR Corporation	33,100	280	Tosco Corporation	26,300
230	ITT Industries, Inc.	33,000	281	Family Dollar Stores, Inc.	26,100
231	Nationwide Insurance Enterprise	32,815	282	Fortune Brands, Inc.	26,040
232	Jack in the Box Inc.	32,600	283	Roadway Express, Inc.	26,000
233	PPG Industries, Inc.	32,500	284	Shoney's, Inc.	26,000
234	7-Eleven, Inc.	32,368	285	Starbucks Corporation	26,000
235	Baker Hughes Incorporated	32,300	286	Payless ShoeSource, Inc.	26,000
236	Genuine Parts Company	32,000	287	KeyCorp	25,862
237	First Data Corporation	32,000	288	Southwest Airlines Co.	25,844
238	Newell Rubbermaid Inc.	32,000	289	Corporate Express, Inc.	25,700
239	Southern Company	31,848	290	Brunswick Corporation	25,500
240	Monsanto Company	31,800	291	PNC Bank Corp.	25,500
241	Masco Corporation	31,700	292	Schering-Plough Corporation	25,100
242	Fruit of the Loom, Ltd.	31,000	293	The Hartford Financial Services Group, Inc.	25,000
243	General Dynamics Corporation	31,000			
244	Smithfield Foods, Inc.	30,800	294	Universal Corporation	25,000
245	SunTrust Banks, Inc.	30,452	295	Solectron Corporation	24,857
246	Shaw Industries, Inc.	30,300	296	Praxair, Inc.	24,834
247	Bechtel Group, Inc.	30,000	297	The Sherwin-Williams Company	24,822
248	Levi Strauss & Co.	30,000	298	The Hertz Corporation	24,800
249	LifeStyle Furnishings	30,000	299	Texaco Inc.	24,628
250	Mars, Inc.	30,000	300	McKesson HBOC, Inc.	24,600

The 100 Fastest-Growing Companies by Sales Growth in
Hoover's Handbook of American Business 2000

Rank	Company	Annual % Change	Rank	Company	Annual % Change
1	Flowers Industries, Inc.	429.7%	51	Burger King Corporation	54.6%
2	Starwood Hotels & Resorts Worldwide, Inc.	403.4%	52	Enron Corp.	54.2%
3	Waste Management, Inc.	386.0%	53	Sun Healthcare Group, Inc.	53.6%
4	Liberty Media Group	316.6%	54	Countrywide Credit Industries, Inc.	53.3%
5	Amazon.com, Inc.	312.7%	55	The First American Financial Corporation	52.4%
6	Firstar Corporation	247.0%	56	Dana Corporation	50.3%
7	U.S. Foodservice	225.5%	57	First Union Corporation	50.3%
8	Qwest Communications International Inc.	221.9%	58	Metro-Goldwyn-Mayer Inc.	49.2%
9	Host Marriott Corporation	200.1%	59	The Pillsbury Company	49.2%
10	Sealed Air Corporation	197.4%	60	Dell Computer Corporation	48.0%
11	Fred Meyer, Inc.	171.5%	61	UnitedHealth Group	47.9%
12	PricewaterhouseCoopers	166.4%	62	Bergen Brunswig Corporation	46.8%
13	Pillowtex Corporation	160.3%	63	The St. Paul Companies, Inc.	46.5%
14	Federal-Mogul Corporation	147.4%	64	Cintas Corporation	46.2%
15	MCI WorldCom, Inc.	140.5%	65	McKesson HBOC, Inc.	45.7%
16	Bank of America Corporation	138.3%	66	Capital One Financial Corporation	45.5%
17	Wells Fargo & Company	112.0%	67	Cardinal Health, Inc.	45.1%
18	USA Networks, Inc.	108.8%	68	U.S. Industries, Inc.	45.0%
19	FirstEnergy Corp.	107.7%	69	Solectron Corporation	43.1%
20	Citigroup Inc.	103.2%	70	Raytheon Company	42.8%
21	Budget Group, Inc.	100.7%	71	Danaher Corporation	41.9%
22	Halliburton Company	96.8%	72	UtiliCorp United Inc.	40.7%
23	Clear Channel Communications, Inc.	93.8%	73	The Gap, Inc.	39.1%
24	BANK ONE CORPORATION	93.6%	74	USX-Marathon Group	38.7%
25	Tyco International Ltd.	86.6%	75	Conseco, Inc.	38.6%
26	Lennar Corporation	85.5%	76	Tellabs, Inc.	37.9%
27	Texas Utilities Company	85.5%	77	Staples, Inc.	37.5%
28	Suiza Foods Corporation	85.0%	78	Dean Foods Company	37.3%
29	America Online, Inc.	83.7%	79	SAFECO Corporation	37.0%
30	Allied Waste Industries, Inc.	80.1%	80	Cordant Technologies Inc.	36.4%
31	CHS Electronics, Inc.	79.7%	81	Royal Caribbean Cruises Ltd.	36.0%
32	Saks Incorporated	75.5%	82	The Warnaco Group, Inc.	35.8%
33	The Williams Companies, Inc.	73.7%	83	Starbucks Corporation	35.4%
34	Baker Hughes Incorporated	71.3%	84	EMC Corporation	35.3%
35	Washington Mutual, Inc.	69.4%	85	Cinergy Corp.	35.0%
36	Maxtor Corporation	69.1%	86	Champion Enterprises, Inc.	34.6%
37	Cablevision Systems Corporation	67.5%	87	Bowater Incorporated	34.4%
38	Reliant Energy, Incorporated	67.1%	88	Office Depot, Inc.	33.9%
39	Tech Data Corporation	63.4%	89	Simon Property Group, Inc.	33.5%
40	SunTrust Banks, Inc.	61.2%	90	Ingram Micro Inc.	32.9%
41	PeopleSoft, Inc.	61.1%	91	HEALTHSOUTH Corporation	32.8%
42	QUALCOMM Incorporated	59.7%	92	Sotheby's Holdings, Inc.	32.8%
43	ALLTEL Corporation	59.1%	93	Berkshire Hathaway Inc.	32.6%
44	Medtronic, Inc.	58.7%	94	Pittston Brink's Group	31.8%
45	Household International, Inc.	58.2%	95	The Bear Stearns Companies Inc.	31.3%
46	Sunbeam Corporation	57.2%	96	Chicago Title Corporation	31.3%
47	Trammell Crow Company	56.9%	97	Cisco Systems, Inc.	31.3%
48	National City Corporation	56.7%	98	Bed Bath & Beyond Inc.	31.0%
49	AutoNation Inc.	56.4%	99	Omnicom Group Inc.	31.0%
50	The Wackenhut Corporation	55.8%	100	Kaufman and Broad Home Corporation	30.3%

Note: Growth rates (compounded and annualized) are based on the sales histories detailed in each profile's HISTORICAL FINANCIALS & EMPLOYEES section; most, but not all, growth rates are for 9-year periods. These rates reflect acquisitions and divestitures.
Source: Hoover's, Inc., Database, September 1999

The 100 Fastest-Growing Companies by Employment Growth in *Hoover's Handbook of American Business 2000*

Rank	Company	Annual % Change	Rank	Company	Annual % Change
1	Lyondell Chemical Company	2,500.0%	51	First Union Corporation	51.8%
2	Starwood Hotels & Resorts	766.4%	52	EMC Corporation	51.6%
3	Qwest Communications	443.8%	53	Marsh & McLennan Companies, Inc.	50.8%
4	Federal-Mogul Corporation	308.6%	54	Baker Hughes Incorporated	50.2%
5	Waste Management, Inc.	284.2%	55	Trammell Crow Company	50.0%
6	MCI WorldCom, Inc.	279.3%	56	Texas Utilities Company	49.5%
7	Amazon.com, Inc.	242.0%	57	The Dial Corporation	48.4%
8	Sealed Air Corporation	234.1%	58	Pennzoil-Quaker State Company	47.2%
9	Cordant Technologies Inc.	228.3%	59	The Williams Companies, Inc.	45.9%
10	U.S. Foodservice	197.3%	60	Monsanto Company	45.2%
11	InaCom Corp.	185.7%	61	Firstar Corporation	45.1%
12	Jones Apparel Group, Inc.	177.0%	62	Gateway, Inc.	45.1%
13	Citigroup Inc.	152.1%	63	SunTrust Banks, Inc.	43.5%
14	Smurfit-Stone Container Corporation	140.5%	64	Countrywide Credit Industries, Inc.	42.5%
15	Suiza Foods Corporation	137.1%	65	America Online, Inc.	42.4%
16	PricewaterhouseCoopers	133.3%	66	Equifax Inc.	40.0%
17	Magellan Health Services, Inc.	132.0%	67	The St. Paul Companies, Inc.	40.0%
18	Compaq Computer Corporation	117.4%	68	R. R. Donnelley & Sons Company	39.6%
19	Bank of America Corporation	112.8%	69	National City Corporation	38.1%
20	Conseco, Inc.	105.9%	70	Washington Mutual, Inc.	37.5%
21	Hercules Incorporated	98.6%	71	The Gap, Inc.	37.0%
22	Sunbeam Corporation	89.3%	72	Solectron Corporation	36.5%
23	Lennar Corporation	88.4%	73	Danaher Corporation	36.4%
24	Pittston Brink's Group	86.6%	74	Cisco Systems, Inc.	36.4%
25	Dana Corporation	80.4%	75	Mandalay Resort Group	35.0%
26	McKesson HBOC, Inc.	79.6%	76	Archer Daniels Midland Company	34.8%
27	Armstrong World Industries, Inc.	78.3%	77	Valero Energy Corporation	34.8%
28	Ames Department Stores, Inc.	77.6%	78	AutoZone, Inc.	34.1%
29	Capital One Financial Corporation	76.4%	79	Jo-Ann Stores, Inc.	34.1%
30	Allied Waste Industries, Inc.	75.9%	80	The Goldman Sachs Group, Inc.	33.4%
31	Medtronic, Inc.	74.8%	81	Aon Corporation	33.3%
32	Mirage Resorts, Incorporated	74.7%	82	U.S. Industries, Inc.	33.3%
33	Kaufman and Broad Home Corporation	71.6%	83	National Association of Securities Dealers, Inc.	31.8%
34	Canandaigua Brands, Inc.	69.2%	84	ALLTEL Corporation	31.2%
35	Hallmark Cards, Inc.	66.8%	85	Omnicom Group Inc.	30.9%
36	Bowater Incorporated	66.0%	86	Genuine Parts Company	30.6%
37	Tech Data Corporation	62.4%	87	CompUSA Inc.	30.5%
38	Wells Fargo & Company	61.6%	88	Chicago Title Corporation	30.2%
39	BANK ONE CORPORATION	61.3%	89	Newell Rubbermaid Inc.	30.1%
40	Harrah's Entertainment, Inc.	59.8%	90	Cintas Corporation	29.7%
41	CHS Electronics, Inc.	59.6%	91	Clear Channel Communications, Inc.	29.6%
42	LG&E Energy Corp.	59.0%	92	QUALCOMM Incorporated	28.9%
43	PeopleSoft, Inc.	58.0%	93	Computer Associates International, Inc.	28.5%
44	Saks Incorporated	57.9%	94	Keebler Foods Company	28.4%
45	Smithfield Foods, Inc.	57.9%	95	Centex Corporation	28.3%
46	Household International, Inc.	57.7%	96	CNF Transportation Inc.	28.1%
47	EOTT Energy Partners, L.P.	55.3%	97	Boston Celtics Limited Partnership	27.9%
48	Dell Computer Corporation	52.5%	98	Boston Scientific Corporation	27.3%
49	Halliburton Company	52.4%	99	Sprint Corporation	27.3%
50	The First American Financial Corporation	52.1%	100	Sabre Inc.	27.1%

Note: Growth rates (compounded and annualized) are based on the employment histories detailed in each profile's HISTORICAL FINANCIALS & EMPLOYEES section; most, but not all, growth rates are for 9-year periods. These rates reflect acquisitions and divestitures.
Source: Hoover's, Inc., Database, September 1999

The 100 Shrinking Companies by Sales Growth in
Hoover's Handbook of American Business 2000

Rank	Company	Annual % Change	Rank	Company	Annual % Change
1	Sodexho Marriott Services, Inc.	(76.5%)	51	Zenith Electronics Corporation	(16.1%)
2	Hilton Hotels Corporation	(66.7%)	52	Campbell Soup Company	(15.9%)
3	Borden, Inc.	(59.8%)	53	Quantum Corporation	(15.6%)
4	Caremark Rx Inc.	(58.4%)	54	Silicon Graphics, Inc.	(15.3%)
5	Packard Bell NEC, Inc.	(54.0%)	55	Western Digital Corporation	(15.2%)
6	LG&E Energy Corp.	(53.0%)	56	Reynolds Metals Company	(14.9%)
7	Consolidated Natural Gas Company	(51.7%)	57	Corning Incorporated	(14.8%)
8	Ashland Inc.	(50.5%)	58	Burns International Services Corporation	(14.5%)
9	Lyondell Chemical Company	(49.7%)	59	McDermott International, Inc.	(14.3%)
10	ITT Industries, Inc.	(48.8%)	60	Micron Technology, Inc.	(14.3%)
11	Shell Oil Company	(46.6%)	61	Polaroid Corporation	(14.0%)
12	Atlantic Richfield Company	(44.9%)	62	Service Merchandise Company, Inc.	(13.5%)
13	Ryerson Tull, Inc.	(44.9%)	63	Unocal Corporation	(13.5%)
14	MediaOne Group, Inc.	(42.9%)	64	Yellow Corporation	(13.4%)
15	Millennium Chemicals Inc.	(41.2%)	65	Texas Instruments Incorporated	(13.2%)
16	Olin Corporation	(40.8%)	66	Levi Strauss & Co.	(13.0%)
17	E. I. du Pont de Nemours and Company	(37.7%)	67	Rockwell International Corporation	(13.0%)
18	Harnischfeger Industries, Inc.	(33.9%)	68	Union Carbide Corporation	(13.0%)
19	Montgomery Ward Holding Corp.	(32.5%)	69	Beverly Enterprises, Inc.	(12.9%)
20	Texaco Inc.	(31.6%)	70	Dover Corporation	(12.5%)
21	Converse Inc.	(31.5%)	71	TRICON Global Restaurants, Inc.	(12.5%)
22	Venator Group Inc.	(31.2%)	72	Eaton Corporation	(12.4%)
23	Cooper Industries, Inc.	(31.0%)	73	Freeport-McMoRan Copper & Gold Inc.	(12.2%)
24	EOTT Energy Partners, L.P.	(30.8%)	74	International Multifoods Corporation	(12.1%)
25	Read-Rite Corporation	(30.4%)	75	Marriott International, Inc.	(11.9%)
26	The Prudential Insurance Company of America	(26.9%)	76	Tupperware Corporation	(11.9%)
27	Bruno's, Inc.	(26.4%)	77	Mark IV Industries, Inc.	(11.8%)
28	The Mead Corporation	(25.7%)	78	Northwest Airlines Corporation	(11.5%)
29	Chevron Corporation	(25.2%)	79	Reebok International Ltd.	(11.5%)
30	Advance Publications, Inc.	(25.0%)	80	Micron Electronics, Inc.	(11.4%)
31	The Coastal Corporation	(23.7%)	81	Mitchell Energy & Development Corp.	(11.3%)
32	Cyprus Amax Minerals Company	(23.3%)	82	The Principal Financial Group	(11.2%)
33	Phillips Petroleum Company	(23.2%)	83	PacifiCorp	(11.1%)
34	Sunoco, Inc.	(23.0%)	84	Sonat Inc.	(11.1%)
35	National Semiconductor Corporation	(22.9%)	85	Tandy Corporation	(10.9%)
36	Phelps Dodge Corporation	(21.7%)	86	Tektronix, Inc.	(10.7%)
37	Dominion Resources, Inc.	(20.7%)	87	Cargill, Incorporated	(10.5%)
38	Mobil Corporation	(20.7%)	88	Pennzoil-Quaker State Company	(10.5%)
39	Amerada Hess Corporation	(20.0%)	89	Park Place Entertainment Corporation	(10.4%)
40	MacAndrews & Forbes Holdings Inc.	(19.3%)	90	The Dun & Bradstreet Corporation	(10.2%)
41	SLM Holding Corporation	(19.0%)	91	Sonoco Products Company	(10.2%)
42	Kerr-McGee Corporation	(18.4%)	92	Vlasic Foods International Inc.	(10.0%)
43	ASARCO Incorporated	(17.9%)	93	IMC Global Inc.	(9.8%)
44	Occidental Petroleum Corporation	(17.7%)	94	Southern Company	(9.6%)
45	Payless Cashways, Inc.	(16.4%)	95	Tosco Corporation	(9.5%)
46	Anixter International Inc.	(16.3%)	96	Delphi Automotive Systems Corporation	(9.4%)
47	Exxon Corporation	(16.3%)	97	National Steel Corporation	(9.3%)
48	The Hearst Corporation	(16.2%)	98	The Times Mirror Company	(9.3%)
49	Apple Computer, Inc.	(16.1%)	99	USX-U.S. Steel Group	(9.2%)
50	Dow Jones & Company, Inc.	(16.1%)	100	AGCO Corporation	(8.8%)

Note: Growth rates (compounded and annualized) are based on the sales histories detailed in each profile's HISTORICAL FINANCIALS & EMPLOYEES section; most, but not all, growth rates are for 9-year periods. These rates reflect acquisitions and divestitures.
Source: Hoover's, Inc., Database, September 1999

The 100 Shrinking Companies by Employee Growth in
Hoover's Handbook of American Business 2000

Rank	Company	Annual % Change	Rank	Company	Annual % Change
1	Borden, Inc.	(72.0%)	51	Dover Corporation	(18.8%)
2	Host Marriott Corporation	(63.6%)	52	Revlon, Inc.	(18.8%)
3	Packard Bell NEC, Inc.	(60.5%)	53	Viad Corp	(18.7%)
4	FirstEnergy Corp.	(53.9%)	54	Texas Instruments Incorporated	(18.6%)
5	Tenneco Inc.	(52.2%)	55	McDermott International, Inc.	(17.6%)
6	Sodexho Marriott Services, Inc.	(48.7%)	56	The Dun & Bradstreet Corporation	(17.2%)
7	Micron Electronics, Inc.	(48.1%)	57	Wendy's International, Inc.	(17.0%)
8	ITT Industries, Inc.	(43.6%)	58	Aetna Inc.	(16.9%)
9	Ashland Inc.	(43.0%)	59	Advance Publications, Inc.	(16.7%)
10	Ryerson Tull, Inc.	(42.7%)	60	Hasbro, Inc.	(16.7%)
11	Burger King Corporation	(42.0%)	61	Louisiana-Pacific Corporation	(16.7%)
12	Zenith Electronics Corporation	(40.4%)	62	Humana Inc.	(16.4%)
13	Toys "R" Us, Inc.	(39.7%)	63	Montgomery Ward Holding Corp.	(16.1%)
14	Hilton Hotels Corporation	(37.7%)	64	The Quaker Oats Company	(16.0%)
15	The Prudential Insurance Company of America	(37.5%)	65	Texaco Inc.	(16.0%)
16	Harcourt General, Inc.	(35.1%)	66	AT&T Corp.	(15.8%)
17	Imation Corp.	(34.7%)	67	Newmont Mining Corporation	(15.7%)
18	MacAndrews & Forbes Holdings Inc.	(34.7%)	68	The Penn Traffic Company	(15.6%)
19	Campbell Soup Company	(34.5%)	69	Yellow Corporation	(15.0%)
20	USA Networks, Inc.	(34.4%)	70	Metro-Goldwyn-Mayer Inc.	(14.7%)
21	Staples, Inc.	(33.2%)	71	Torchmark Corporation	(14.6%)
22	Caremark Rx Inc.	(32.9%)	72	The Mead Corporation	(14.5%)
23	Dow Jones & Company, Inc.	(32.5%)	73	King World Productions, Inc.	(14.2%)
24	IGA, INC.	(31.9%)	74	Payless Cashways, Inc.	(14.1%)
25	Cooper Industries, Inc.	(31.8%)	75	MidAmerican Energy Holdings Company	(13.9%)
26	Cyprus Amax Minerals Company	(31.4%)	76	SLM Holding Corporation	(13.9%)
27	Oxford Health Plans, Inc.	(30.6%)	77	Owens & Minor, Inc.	(13.9%)
28	Bruno's, Inc.	(28.7%)	78	Flowers Industries, Inc.	(13.7%)
29	Dominion Resources, Inc.	(28.6%)	79	Cabletron Systems, Inc.	(13.6%)
30	Entergy Corporation	(25.9%)	80	NCR Corporation	(13.6%)
31	Occidental Petroleum Corporation	(25.8%)	81	Applied Materials, Inc.	(13.4%)
32	TRICON Global Restaurants, Inc.	(25.7%)	82	Sonoco Products Company	(13.2%)
33	Ralston Purina Company	(25.6%)	83	Tandy Corporation	(13.2%)
34	AutoNation Inc.	(25.0%)	84	Intergraph Corporation	(13.0%)
35	Corning Incorporated	(24.9%)	85	Micro Warehouse, Inc.	(13.0%)
36	Olin Corporation	(24.5%)	86	Service Merchandise Company, Inc.	(12.7%)
37	Anixter International Inc.	(23.8%)	87	Owens Corning	(12.5%)
38	The Black & Decker Corporation	(23.8%)	88	American Home Products Corporation	(12.5%)
39	Atlantic Richfield Company	(23.3%)	89	Phelps Dodge Corporation	(12.3%)
40	Harnischfeger Industries, Inc.	(22.6%)	90	Tektronix, Inc.	(12.3%)
41	Ogden Corporation	(22.6%)	91	Columbia/HCA Healthcare Corporation	(11.9%)
42	Mitchell Energy & Development Corp.	(22.1%)	92	Champion International Corporation	(11.8%)
43	Ziff-Davis Inc.	(21.9%)	93	Eastman Kodak Company	(11.6%)
44	Reynolds Metals Company	(21.6%)	94	Russell Corporation	(11.4%)
45	Shoney's, Inc.	(21.2%)	95	Motorola, Inc.	(11.3%)
46	Read-Rite Corporation	(21.0%)	96	First Data Corporation	(11.1%)
47	Deluxe Corporation	(20.1%)	97	PacifiCare Health Systems, Inc.	(11.0%)
48	U S WEST, Inc.	(19.5%)	98	AmeriSource Health Corporation	(10.9%)
49	C. R. Bard, Inc.	(19.4%)	99	National Semiconductor Corporation	(10.8%)
50	Levi Strauss & Co.	(18.9%)	100	Sonat Inc.	(10.4%)

Note: Growth rates (compounded and annualized) are based on the employment histories detailed in each profile's HISTORICAL FINANCIALS & EMPLOYEES section; most, but not all, growth rates are for 9-year periods. These rates reflect acquisitions and divestitures.
Source: Hoover's, Inc., Database, September 1999

The Hoover's 500:
America's Largest Business Enterprises

Rank	Company	Sales ($ mil.)	Rank	Company	Sales ($ mil.)
1	General Motors Corporation	161,315	51	BANK ONE CORPORATION	25,595
2	Ford Motor Company	144,416	52	GTE Corporation	25,473
3	Wal-Mart Stores, Inc.	137,634	53	Nationwide Insurance Enterprise	25,301
4	Exxon Corporation	100,697	54	Cardinal Health, Inc.	25,034
5	General Electric Company	99,820	55	United Parcel Service	24,788
6	Blue Cross and Blue Shield	94,700	56	E. I. du Pont de Nemours and Company	24,767
7	International Business Machines	81,667			
8	Citigroup Inc.	76,431	57	ConAgra, Inc.	24,594
9	Philip Morris Companies Inc.	74,391	58	Safeway Inc.	24,484
10	United States Postal Service	60,072	59	Costco Companies, Inc.	24,270
			60	Johnson & Johnson	23,657
11	The Boeing Company	56,154			
12	AT&T Corp.	53,223	61	BellSouth Corporation	23,123
13	Bank of America Corporation	51,794	62	The Walt Disney Company	22,976
14	Hewlett-Packard Company	47,061	63	Conoco Inc.	22,796
15	Mobil Corporation	46,287	64	The Goldman Sachs Group, Inc.	22,478
16	Cargill, Incorporated	46,000	65	PepsiCo, Inc.	22,348
17	TIAA-CREF	45,899	66	Equilon Enterprises LLC	22,246
18	Sears, Roebuck and Co.	41,322	67	Ingram Micro Inc.	22,034
19	The Procter & Gamble Company	38,125	68	First Union Corporation	21,543
20	Merrill Lynch & Co., Inc.	35,853	69	CIGNA Corporation	21,437
21	Koch Industries, Inc.	35,000	70	Loews Corporation	21,208
22	Kmart Corporation	33,674	71	Caterpillar Inc.	20,977
23	The Chase Manhattan Corporation	32,590	72	Aetna Inc.	20,604
24	Bell Atlantic Corporation	31,566	73	Wells Fargo & Company	20,482
25	Fannie Mae	31,499	74	Sara Lee Corporation	20,012
26	Enron Corp.	31,260	75	PG&E Corporation	19,942
27	Compaq Computer Corporation	31,169	76	Lehman Brothers Holdings Inc.	19,894
28	Morgan Stanley Dean Witter & Co.	31,131	77	Microsoft Corporation	19,747
29	Dayton Hudson Corporation	30,951	78	International Paper Company	19,541
30	Texaco Inc.	30,910	79	Raytheon Company	19,530
31	American International Group, Inc.	30,760	80	Xerox Corporation	19,449
32	J. C. Penney Company, Inc.	30,678	81	Marathon Ashland Petroleum LLC	19,339
33	McKesson HBOC, Inc.	30,382	82	AMR Corporation	19,205
34	The Home Depot, Inc.	30,219	83	American Express Company	19,132
35	Lucent Technologies Inc.	30,147	84	The Coca-Cola Company	18,813
36	Motorola, Inc.	29,398	85	Columbia/HCA Healthcare Corporation	18,681
37	SBC Communications Inc.	28,777			
38	Delphi Automotive Systems	28,479	86	The Dow Chemical Company	18,441
39	The Kroger Co.	28,203	87	J.P. Morgan & Co. Incorporated	18,425
40	USX Corporation	27,887	88	New York Life Insurance Company	18,350
41	State Farm Mutual Automobile Insurance Company	27,706	89	Bristol-Myers Squibb Company	18,284
			90	Dell Computer Corporation	18,243
42	CalPERS	27,514	91	Freddie Mac	18,048
43	Prudential Insurance Company	27,087	92	IGA, INC.	18,000
44	Metropolitan Life Insurance Company	27,077	93	MCI WorldCom, Inc.	17,678
			94	Duke Energy Corporation	17,610
45	Merck & Co., Inc.	26,898	95	UAL Corporation	17,561
46	Intel Corporation	26,273	96	SYSCO Corporation	17,423
47	Lockheed Martin Corporation	26,266	97	SUPERVALU INC.	17,421
48	Chevron Corporation	26,187	98	Halliburton Company	17,353
49	The Allstate Corporation	25,976	99	Caltex Corporation	17,174
50	United Technologies Corporation	25,687	100	Ameritech Corporation	17,154

Source: Hoover's, Inc., Database, September 1999

Rank	Company	Sales ($ mil.)	Rank	Company	Sales ($ mil.)
101	Bergen Brunswig Corporation	17,122	151	McDonald's Corporation	12,421
102	UnitedHealth Group	17,106	152	U S WEST, Inc.	12,378
103	CNA Financial Corporation	17,074	153	Tyco International Ltd.	12,311
104	Nabisco Group Holdings Corp.	17,037	154	Kimberly-Clark Corporation	12,298
105	Electronic Data Systems Corporation	16,891	155	Lowe's Companies, Inc.	12,245
106	FDX Corporation	16,774	156	Cisco Systems, Inc.	12,154
107	AutoNation Inc.	16,118	157	Viacom Inc.	12,096
108	Sprint Corporation	16,017	158	Publix Super Markets, Inc.	12,067
109	Albertson's, Inc.	16,005	159	Tosco Corporation	12,022
110	Federated Department Stores, Inc.	15,833	160	TRW Inc.	11,886
111	Kaiser Foundation Health Plan, Inc.	15,500	161	Phillips Petroleum Company	11,845
112	Alcoa Inc.	15,340	162	Schlumberger Limited	11,816
113	Walgreen Co.	15,307	163	Massachusetts Mutual Life Insurance Company	11,728
114	CVS Corporation	15,274			
115	AlliedSignal Inc.	15,128	164	Sun Microsystems, Inc.	11,726
116	Fleming Companies, Inc.	15,069	165	Tech Data Corporation	11,529
117	The Hartford Financial Services Group, Inc.	15,022	166	Entergy Corporation	11,495
			167	Reliant Energy, Incorporated	11,489
118	Minnesota Mining and Manufacturing Company	15,021	168	Southern Company	11,403
			169	Anheuser-Busch Companies, Inc.	11,246
119	Mars, Inc.	15,000	170	Toys R Us, Inc.	11,170
120	ContiGroup Companies, Inc.	15,000	171	Ultramar Diamond Shamrock Corporation	11,135
121	PricewaterhouseCoopers	15,000			
122	Texas Utilities Company	14,736	172	Carlson Wagonlit Travel	11,000
123	Delta Air Lines, Inc.	14,711	173	Liberty Mutual Insurance Companies	10,964
124	Time Warner Inc.	14,582			
125	Archer Daniels Midland Company	14,283	174	AXA Financial, Inc.	10,919
126	Dynegy Inc.	14,258	175	Ernst & Young International	10,900
127	Winn-Dixie Stores, Inc.	14,137	176	Tenet Healthcare Corporation	10,880
128	Andersen Worldwide	13,900	177	Circuit City Stores, Inc.	10,804
129	Berkshire Hathaway Inc.	13,832	178	Weyerhaeuser Company	10,766
130	John Hancock Mutual Life Insurance Company	13,653	179	KPMG International	10,600
			180	Union Pacific Corporation	10,553
131	Deere & Company	13,626	181	Federal Reserve Bank of New York	10,482
132	Pfizer Inc	13,544	182	Travelers Property Casualty Corp.	10,451
133	Fluor Corporation	13,505	183	Whirlpool Corporation	10,323
134	The Northwestern Mutual Life Insurance Company	13,479	184	Atlantic Richfield Company	10,303
			185	American General Financial Group	10,251
135	American Home Products	13,463	186	Warner-Lambert Company	10,214
136	Emerson Electric Co.	13,447	187	Edison International	10,208
137	Coca-Cola Enterprises Inc.	13,414	188	The Great Atlantic & Pacific Tea Company, Inc.	10,179
138	The May Department Stores Company	13,413			
139	Eastman Kodak Company	13,406	189	Best Buy Co., Inc.	10,078
140	Georgia-Pacific Corporation	13,336	190	The Gillette Company	10,056
141	IBP, inc.	12,849	191	Fleet Financial Group, Inc.	10,002
142	Washington Mutual, Inc.	12,746	192	CSX Corporation	9,898
143	Rite Aid Corporation	12,732	193	Textron Inc.	9,683
144	Waste Management, Inc.	12,704	194	Humana Inc.	9,597
145	Bechtel Group, Inc.	12,645	195	PacifiCare Health Systems, Inc.	9,522
146	The Goodyear Tire & Rubber Company	12,626	196	Associates First Capital Corporation	9,377
147	Johnson Controls, Inc.	12,587	197	University of California	9,375
148	UtiliCorp United Inc.	12,563	198	The Limited, Inc.	9,347
149	Abbott Laboratories	12,478	199	H.J. Heinz Company	9,300
150	Dana Corporation	12,464	200	Eli Lilly and Company	9,237

The Hoover's 500:
America's Largest Business Enterprises (continued)

Rank	Company	Sales ($ mil.)	Rank	Company	Sales ($ mil.)
201	The St. Paul Companies, Inc.	9,108	251	Tenneco Inc.	7,597
202	Lear Corporation	9,059	252	Highmark Inc.	7,544
203	The Gap, Inc.	9,055	253	PPG Industries, Inc.	7,510
204	Northwest Airlines Corporation	9,045	254	Meijer, Inc.	7,500
205	Deloitte Touche Tohmatsu	9,000	255	Gateway, Inc.	7,468
206	Office Depot, Inc.	8,998	256	Tyson Foods, Inc.	7,414
207	Colgate-Palmolive Company	8,972	257	SunTrust Banks, Inc.	7,392
208	Burlington Northern Santa Fe Corporation	8,941	258	The Coastal Corporation	7,368
209	Northrop Grumman Corporation	8,902	259	Fort James Corporation	7,301
210	Oracle Corporation	8,827	260	7-Eleven, Inc.	7,258
211	Manpower Inc.	8,814	261	Paine Webber Group Inc.	7,250
212	Foundation Health Systems, Inc.	8,797	262	Unisys Corporation	7,208
213	NIKE, Inc.	8,777	263	Marsh & McLennan Companies, Inc.	7,190
214	Farmland Industries, Inc.	8,775	264	The Guardian Life Insurance Company of America	7,180
215	Household International, Inc.	8,708	265	Unicom Corporation	7,151
216	US Airways Group, Inc.	8,688	266	Staples, Inc.	7,123
217	AmeriSource Health Corporation	8,669	267	AFLAC Incorporated	7,104
218	Monsanto Company	8,648	268	KeyCorp	7,100
219	CHS Electronics, Inc.	8,546	269	Consolidated Edison, Inc.	7,093
220	TRICON Global Restaurants, Inc.	8,468	270	The Pepsi Bottling Group, Inc.	7,041
221	Texas Instruments Incorporated	8,460	271	H. E. Butt Grocery Company	7,000
222	Honeywell Inc.	8,427	272	John Hancock Financial Services, Inc.	6,902
223	Nabisco Holdings Corp.	8,400	273	The Trump Organization	6,900
224	Solectron Corporation	8,391	274	Pharmacia & Upjohn, Inc.	6,893
225	Bestfoods	8,374	275	Sunoco, Inc.	6,854
226	Arrow Electronics, Inc.	8,345	276	CBS Corporation	6,805
227	Crown Cork & Seal Company, Inc.	8,300	277	Seagate Technology, Inc.	6,802
228	Ingersoll-Rand Company	8,292	278	Army & Air Force Exchange Service	6,783
229	Schering-Plough Corporation	8,077	279	FMR Corp.	6,770
230	National City Corporation	8,071	280	Kellogg Company	6,762
231	Fox Entertainment Group, Inc.	8,057	281	Rockwell International Corporation	6,752
232	Marriott International, Inc.	7,968	282	Tennessee Valley Authority	6,729
233	Continental Airlines, Inc.	7,951	283	SCI Systems, Inc.	6,710
234	The TJX Companies, Inc.	7,949	284	FPL Group, Inc.	6,661
235	PNC Bank Corp.	7,936	285	American Standard Companies Inc.	6,654
236	PACCAR Inc	7,895	286	Eaton Corporation	6,625
237	The Bear Stearns Companies Inc.	7,882	287	Genuine Parts Company	6,614
238	Navistar International Corporation	7,830	288	Baxter International Inc.	6,599
239	Carlson Companies, Inc.	7,800	289	Occidental Petroleum Corporation	6,596
240	Dillard's Inc.	7,797	290	Amerada Hess Corporation	6,590
241	Blue Cross Blue Shield of Michigan	7,731	291	Columbia Energy Group	6,551
242	Conseco, Inc.	7,716	292	Ashland Inc.	6,534
243	The Principal Financial Group	7,697	293	NCR Corporation	6,505
244	USAA	7,687	294	Aon Corporation	6,493
245	U.S. Bancorp	7,664	295	SAFECO Corporation	6,452
246	Computer Sciences Corporation	7,660	296	Campbell Soup Company	6,424
247	The Williams Companies, Inc.	7,658	297	ARAMARK Corporation	6,377
248	Bindley Western Industries, Inc.	7,621	298	WellPoint Health Networks Inc.	6,369
249	Holberg Industries, Inc.	7,617	299	Avnet, Inc.	6,350
250	BankBoston Corporation	7,609	300	The Chubb Corporation	6,350

The Hoover's 500:
America's Largest Business Enterprises (continued)

Rank	Company	Sales ($ mil.)	Rank	Company	Sales ($ mil.)
301	American Electric Power Company	6,346	351	Cendant Corporation	5,284
302	CompUSA Inc.	6,321	352	Computer Associates International, Inc.	5,253
303	Baker Hughes Incorporated	6,312	353	The University of Texas System	5,244
304	Cummins Engine Company, Inc.	6,266	354	Fortune Brands, Inc.	5,241
305	General Mills, Inc.	6,246	355	Avon Products, Inc.	5,213
306	Saks Incorporated	6,220	356	PECO Energy Company	5,211
307	JM Family Enterprises, Inc.	6,200	357	Huntsman Corporation	5,200
308	U.S. Foodservice	6,198	358	MBNA Corporation	5,195
309	Daughters of Charity National Health System	6,170	359	ALLTEL Corporation	5,194
310	Boise Cascade Corporation	6,162	360	Ryder System, Inc.	5,189
311	Case Corporation	6,149	361	Land O'Lakes, Inc.	5,174
312	Alliant Foodservice Inc.	6,100	362	Centex Corporation	5,155
313	Lincoln National Corporation	6,087	363	Comcast Corporation	5,145
314	Dominion Resources, Inc.	6,086	364	CMS Energy Corporation	5,141
315	The Marmon Group, Inc.	6,032	365	Gannett Co., Inc.	5,121
316	Levi Strauss & Co.	6,000	366	C&S Wholesale Grocers Inc.	5,120
317	Penske Corporation	6,000	367	First Data Corporation	5,118
318	Hughes Electronics Corporation	5,964	368	Health Care Service Corporation	5,107
319	Apple Computer, Inc.	5,941	369	Nordstrom, Inc.	5,028
320	Public Service Enterprise Group Incorporated	5,931	370	R. R. Donnelley & Sons Company	5,018
321	Wachovia Corporation	5,914	371	Owens Corning	5,009
322	Anthem Insurance Companies, Inc.	5,878	372	Unocal Corporation	5,003
323	Cinergy Corp.	5,876	373	DHL Worldwide Express	5,000
324	FirstEnergy Corp.	5,861	374	S.C. Johnson & Son, Inc.	5,000
325	Reynolds Metals Company	5,859	375	Wakefern Food Corporation	5,000
326	Mellon Bank Corporation	5,814	376	Catholic Health Initiatives	5,000
327	The Bank of New York Company, Inc.	5,793	377	General Dynamics Corporation	4,970
328	Hartford Life, Inc.	5,788	378	Parker Hannifin Corporation	4,959
329	El Paso Energy Corporation	5,782	379	CNF Transportation Inc.	4,942
330	3Com Corporation	5,772	380	The Sherwin-Williams Company	4,934
331	Metropolitan Transportation Authority	5,707	381	Air Products and Chemicals, Inc.	4,919
332	Amway Corporation	5,700	382	Quantum Corporation	4,902
333	Union Carbide Corporation	5,659	383	MacAndrews & Forbes Holdings Inc.	4,900
334	Champion International Corporation	5,653	384	The Quaker Oats Company	4,843
335	Illinois Tool Works Inc.	5,648	385	Praxair, Inc.	4,833
336	IKON Office Solutions, Inc.	5,629	386	Litton Industries, Inc.	4,828
337	Cenex Harvest States Cooperatives	5,607	387	Tandy Corporation	4,788
338	PacifiCorp	5,580	388	Mattel, Inc.	4,782
339	Automatic Data Processing, Inc.	5,540	389	America Online, Inc.	4,777
340	Valero Energy Corporation	5,539	390	Science Applications International Corporation	4,740
341	MicroAge, Inc.	5,520	391	The ServiceMaster Company	4,724
342	Central and South West Corporation	5,482	392	Oxford Health Plans, Inc.	4,719
343	Sempra Energy	5,481	393	Starwood Hotels & Resorts Worldwide, Inc.	4,700
344	VF Corporation	5,479	394	New United Motor Manufacturing, Inc.	4,699
345	Donaldson, Lufkin & Jenrette, Inc.	5,407	395	Ralston Purina Company	4,653
346	Motiva Enterprises LLC	5,371	396	Olsten Corporation	4,603
347	Cox Enterprises, Inc.	5,355	397	State University of New York	4,564
348	Owens-Illinois, Inc.	5,306	398	The Black & Decker Corporation	4,560
349	EOTT Energy Partners, L.P.	5,295	399	Venator Group Inc.	4,555
350	The Progressive Corporation	5,292	400	Merisel, Inc.	4,553

The Hoover's 500:
America's Largest Business Enterprises (continued)

Rank	Company	Sales ($ mil.)	Rank	Company	Sales ($ mil.)
401	Foster Wheeler Corporation	4,537	451	GenAmerica Corporation	3,914
402	ITT Industries, Inc.	4,493	452	Hallmark Cards, Inc.	3,900
403	Eastman Chemical Company	4,481	453	American Family Insurance Group	3,888
404	Bethlehem Steel Corporation	4,478	454	Intimate Brands, Inc.	3,886
405	Federal-Mogul Corporation	4,469	455	Thermo Electron Corporation	3,868
406	Hershey Foods Corporation	4,436	456	Advance Publications, Inc.	3,859
407	Dole Food Company, Inc.	4,424	457	The Interpublic Group	3,844
408	K N Energy, Inc.	4,388	458	Meritor Automotive, Inc.	3,836
409	FMC Corporation	4,378	459	New York City Health and Hospitals	3,835
410	Equistar Chemicals, LP	4,363	460	Niagara Mohawk Holdings Inc.	3,826
411	Masco Corporation	4,345	461	Dairy Farmers of America	3,818
412	W.W. Grainger, Inc.	4,341	462	Catholic Health East	3,800
413	OfficeMax, Inc.	4,338	463	PP&L Resources, Inc.	3,786
414	TruServ Corporation	4,328	464	Flowers Industries, Inc.	3,776
415	The LTV Corporation	4,273	465	Smithfield Foods, Inc.	3,775
416	InaCom Corp.	4,258	466	The Mead Corporation	3,772
417	GPU, Inc.	4,249	467	Northeast Utilities	3,768
418	Harcourt General, Inc.	4,235	468	Dean Foods Company	3,755
419	State Street Corporation	4,234	469	Corporate Express, Inc.	3,753
420	DTE Energy Company	4,221	470	The Pittston Company	3,747
421	Norfolk Southern Corporation	4,221	471	Graybar Electric Company, Inc.	3,744
422	Pitney Bowes Inc.	4,221	472	Temple-Inland Inc.	3,740
423	Consolidated Stores Corporation	4,194	473	The McGraw-Hill Companies, Inc.	3,729
424	Enterprise Rent-A-Car	4,180	474	Rohm and Haas Company	3,720
425	Engelhard Corporation	4,175	475	Newell Rubbermaid Inc.	3,720
426	Southwest Airlines Co.	4,164	476	Sonat Inc.	3,710
427	Nash Finch Company	4,160	477	Willamette Industries, Inc.	3,700
428	The Hertz Corporation	4,154	478	The Mutual of Omaha Companies	3,700
429	Nucor Corporation	4,151	479	Avista Corporation	3,684
430	Medtronic, Inc.	4,134	480	Kohl's Corporation	3,682
431	AutoZone, Inc.	4,116	481	Pathmark Stores, Inc.	3,655
432	Kelly Services, Inc.	4,092	482	Cooper Industries, Inc.	3,651
433	Omnicom Group Inc.	4,092	483	Montgomery Ward Holding Corp.	3,634
434	New York State Lottery	4,085	484	Florida Progress Corporation	3,620
435	Maytag Corporation	4,069	485	New Century Energies, Inc.	3,611
436	American Financial Group, Inc.	4,050	486	BJ's Wholesale Club, Inc.	3,552
437	Giant Eagle Inc.	4,050	487	Shaw Industries, Inc.	3,542
438	Clark USA, Inc.	4,043	488	United Way of America	3,540
439	Applied Materials, Inc.	4,042	499	Republic New York Corporation	3,523
440	HEALTHSOUTH Corporation	4,006	490	Firstar Corporation	3,502
441	Universal Corporation	4,005	491	Rosenbluth International	3,500
442	The Clorox Company	4,003	492	Fleetwood Enterprises, Inc.	3,490
443	Topco Associates, Inc.	4,000	493	Corning Incorporated	3,484
444	Menard, Inc.	4,000	494	Smurfit-Stone Container Corporation	3,469
445	Dover Corporation	3,978	495	Phoenix Home Life Mutual Insurance	3,464
446	EMC Corporation	3,974	496	Avery Dennison Corporation	3,460
447	The Estée Lauder Companies Inc.	3,961	497	Interstate Bakeries Corporation	3,459
448	The BFGoodrich Company	3,951	498	Darden Restaurants, Inc.	3,458
449	Brunswick Corporation	3,945	499	Hechinger Company	3,449
450	Allegheny Teledyne Incorporated	3,923	500	Host Marriott Corporation	3,442

The *FORTUNE* 500 Largest US Corporations

Rank	Company	Revenues ($ mil.)	Rank	Company	Revenues ($ mil.)
1	General Motors Corporation	161,315	51	Johnson & Johnson	23,657
2	Ford Motor Company	144,416	52	BellSouth Corporation	23,123
3	Wal-Mart Stores, Inc.	139,208	53	The Walt Disney Company	22,976
4	Exxon Corporation	100,697	54	PepsiCo, Inc.	22,348
5	General Electric	100,469	55	Ingram Micro, Inc.	22,034
6	International Business Machines Corporation	81,667	56	First Union Corporation	21,543
			57	CIGNA Corporation	21,437
7	CitiGroup	76,431	58	Caterpillar, Inc.	20,977
8	Philip Morris Companies Inc.	57,813	59	McKesson HBOC	20,857
9	The Boeing Company	56,154	60	Loews Corporation	20,713
10	AT&T Corp.	53,588	61	Aetna, Inc.	20,604
11	BankAmerica Corporation	50,777	62	Wells Fargo & Company	20,482
12	State Farm Insurance Companies	48,114	63	Xerox Corporation	20,019
13	Mobil Corporation	47,678	64	Sara Lee Corporation	20,011
14	Hewlett-Packard Company	47,061	65	PG&E Corporation	19,942
15	Sears, Roebuck & Company	41,322	66	Lehman Brothers Holdings, Inc.	19,894
16	E. I. du Pont de Nemours	39,130	67	American Stores Company	19,867
17	Procter & Gamble	37,154	68	New York Life Insurance Company	19,849
18	TIAA-CREF	35,889	69	Raytheon Company	19,530
19	Merrill Lynch & Co., Inc.	35,853	70	International Paper Company	19,500
20	Prudential Insurance Company	34,427	71	AMR Corporation	19,205
21	Kmart Corporation	33,674	72	American Express Company	19,132
22	American International Group	33,296	73	The Coca-Cola Company	18,813
23	Chase Manhattan Corp.	32,379	74	Columbia/HCA Healthcare Corporation	18,681
24	Texaco	31,707	75	The Dow Chemical Company	18,441
25	Bell Atlantic	31,566			
26	Fannie Mae	31,499	76	J.P. Morgan & Co. Incorporated	18,425
27	Enron	31,260	77	Bristol-Myers Squibb Company	18,284
28	Compaq Computer	31,169	78	Dell Computer Corporation	18,243
29	Morgan Stanley Dean Witter	31,131	79	Freddie Mac	18,048
30	Dayton Hudson	30,951	80	MCI WorldCom	17,678
31	J. C. Penney Company, Inc.	30,678	81	Duke Energy Corporation	17,610
32	Home Depot	30,219	82	UAL Corporation	17,561
33	Lucent Technologies	30,147	83	Republic Industries, Inc.	17,487
34	Motorola	29,398	84	United Healthcare Corporation	17,355
35	SBC Communications	28,777	85	Halliburton Company	17,353
36	Kroger	28,203	86	SUPERVALU INC.	17,201
37	Merck	26,898	87	Ameritech Corporation	17,154
38	Chevron	26,801	88	Sprint Corporation	17,134
39	Metropolitan Life Insurance	26,735	89	RJR Nabisco Holdings Corp.	17,037
40	Intel	26,273	90	Electronic Data Systems	16,891
41	Lockheed Martin	26,266	91	Archer Daniels Midland Company	16,109
42	The AllState Corporation	25,879	92	Albertson's, Inc.	16,005
43	United Technologies	25,715	93	Cardinal Health, Inc.	15,918
44	BANK ONE CORPORATION	25,595	94	FDX Corp.	15,873
45	GTE Corporation	25,473	95	Federated Department Stores, Inc.	15,833
46	United Parcel Service	24,788	96	Alcoa, Inc.	15,489
47	USX Corporation	24,754	97	SYSCO Corporation	15,328
48	Safeway	24,484	98	Walgreen Co.	15,307
49	Costco	24,270	99	CVS Corporation	15,274
50	ConAgra, Inc.	23,841	100	AlliedSignal Inc.	15,128

Source: *FORTUNE*; April 26, 1999

The *FORTUNE* 500 Largest US Corporations (continued)

Rank	Company	Revenues ($ mil.)	Rank	Company	Revenues ($ mil.)
101	Fleming	15,069	151	Toys "R" Us	11,200
102	Hartford Financial Services	15,022	152	Weyerhaeuser	10,766
103	Minnesota Mining & Manufacturing	15,021	153	Massachusetts Mutual Life Ins.	10,668
104	Fred Meyer	14,879	154	Union Pacific	10,553
105	Texas Utilities	14,736	155	Whirlpool	10,323
106	Pfizer	14,704	156	American General	10,251
107	Northwestern Mutual Life Ins.	14,645	157	Warner-Lambert	10,214
108	Time Warner	14,582	158	Edison International	10,208
109	Microsoft	14,484	159	Gillette	10,056
110	Dynegy	14,258	160	Eli Lilly	10,051
111	Delta Air Lines	14,138	161	Fleet Financial Group	10,002
112	Berkshire Hathaway	13,832	162	CSX	9,898
113	Deere	13,822	163	Tenet Healthcare	9,895
114	Bergen Brunswig	13,720	164	Sun Microsystems	9,791
115	Winn-Dixie Stores	13,618	165	Humana	9,781
116	Fluor	13,505	166	Nike	9,553
117	American Home Products	13,463	167	Pacificare Health Systems	9,522
118	Emerson Electric	13,447	168	PacifiCorp	9,443
119	Coca-Cola Enterprises	13,414	169	The Limited, Inc.	9,347
120	May Department Stores	13,413	170	H.J. Heinz	9,209
121	Eastman Kodak	13,406	171	St. Paul Companies	9,108
122	Georgia-Pacific	13,223	172	CBS	9,061
123	Atlantic Richfield	13,195	173	Lear	9,059
124	Liberty Mutual Insurance Group	13,166	174	The Gap	9,055
125	Nationwide Ins. Enterprise	13,105	175	Northwest Airlines	9,045
126	IBP	12,849	176	Office Depot	8,998
127	Dana	12,839	177	Colgate-Palmolive	8,972
128	Washington Mutual	12,746	178	Burlington Northern Santa Fe	8,941
129	Waste Management	12,704	179	John Hancock Mutual Life Insurance	8,912
130	Goodyear Tire & Rubber	12,649	180	Northrop Grumman	8,902
131	Johnson Controls	12,587	181	Foundation Health Systems	8,896
132	Utilicorp United	12,563	182	Circuit City Group	8,871
133	Abbott Laboratories	12,478	183	Manpower	8,814
134	McDonald's	12,421	184	Farmland Industries	8,775
135	U S WEST	12,378	185	Household International	8,708
136	Kimberly-Clark	12,298	186	US Airways Group	8,688
137	Lowe's	12,245	187	Monsanto	8,648
138	Viacom	12,096	188	Amerisource Health	8,575
139	Publix Super Markets	12,067	189	CHS Electronics	8,546
140	Bankers Trust Corp.	12,048	190	Tricon Global Restaurants	8,468
141	Tosco	12,022	191	Texas Instruments	8,460
142	TRW	11,886	192	Cisco Systems	8,459
143	Phillips Petroleum	11,845	193	Honeywell	8,427
144	Textron	11,549	194	Bestfoods	8,374
145	Tech Data	11,529	195	Best Buy	8,358
146	Entergy	11,495	196	Ultramar Diamond Shamrock	8,347
147	Houston Industries	11,489	197	Arrow Electronics	8,345
148	Southern Company	11,403	198	Crown Cork & Seal	8,300
149	Rite Aid	11,375	199	Ingersoll-Rand	8,292
150	Anheuser-Busch	11,246	200	Schering-Plough	8,077

The *FORTUNE* 500 Largest US Corporations (continued)

Rank	Company	Revenues ($ mil.)	Rank	Company	Revenues ($ mil.)
201	National City Corp.	8,071	251	Amerada Hess	6,618
202	Rockwell International	8,025	252	Genuine Parts	6,614
203	Dillard's	8,012	253	Computer Sciences	6,601
204	Bear Stearns	7,980	254	Baxter International	6,599
205	Guardian Life Ins. Co. of America	7,974	255	Occidental Petroleum	6,596
206	Marriott International	7,968	256	Wellpoint Health Networks	6,573
207	Continental Airlines	7,951	257	Columbia Energy Group	6,568
208	TJX	7,949	258	NCR	6,505
209	PNC Bank Corp.	7,936	259	Aon	6,493
210	PACCAR	7,895	260	Safeco	6,452
211	Navistar International	7,885	261	Transamerica	6,429
212	Conseco	7,716	262	Aramark	6,377
213	Principal Financial	7,697	263	Chubb	6,350
214	United Services Automobile Assn.	7,687	264	American Electric Power	6,346
215	U.S. Bancorp	7,664	265	Baker Hughes	6,312
216	Williams	7,658	266	Cummins Engine	6,266
217	Bindley Western	7,623	267	Saks	6,220
218	BankBoston Corp.	7,609	268	Boise Cascade	6,162
219	Tenneco	7,605	269	Case	6,149
220	ITT Industries	7,523	270	Lincoln National	6,087
221	PPG Industries	7,510	271	Dominion Resources	6,086
222	Campbell Soup	7,505	272	General Mills	6,033
223	Gateway	7,468	273	Apple Computer	5,941
224	Ameriserve	7,421	274	Public Service Enterprise Group	5,931
225	Unisource Worldwide	7,417	275	Avnet	5,916
226	Tyson Foods	7,414	276	Wachovia Corp.	5,914
227	SunTrust Banks	7,392	277	R.R. Donnelley & Sons	5,900
228	Tele-Communications, Inc.	7,351	278	Anthem Insurance	5,878
229	Fort James	7,301	279	Cinergy	5,876
230	Paine Webber Group	7,250	280	FirstEnergy	5,861
231	Unisys	7,208	281	Reynolds Metals	5,859
232	Marsh & McLennan	7,190	282	Cendant	5,832
233	Unicom	7,151	283	Mellon Bank Corp.	5,814
234	Oracle	7,144	284	Quantum	5,805
235	Coastal	7,125	285	Bank of New York Companies	5,793
236	Staples	7,123	286	El Paso Energy	5,782
237	AFLAC	7,104	287	Venator	5,698
238	Keycorp	7,100	288	Union Carbide	5,659
239	Consolidated Edison	7,093	289	Champion International	5,653
240	Sunoco	7,024	290	Illinois Tool Works	5,648
241	MedPartners	7,004	291	Ikon Office Solutions	5,629
242	Ashland	6,933	292	Comcast	5,591
243	Pharmacia & Upjohn	6,893	293	Ralston Purina	5,577
244	Seagate Technology	6,819	294	Valero Energy	5,539
245	SCI Systems	6,806	295	LG&E Energy	5,529
246	Kellogg	6,762	296	Sempra Energy	5,525
247	Sodexho Marriott Services	6,704	297	MicroAge	5,520
248	FPL Group	6,661	298	U.S. Foodservice	5,507
249	American Standard	6,654	299	AMP	5,482
250	Eaton	6,625	300	Central & South West	5,482

The *FORTUNE* 500 Largest US Corporations (continued)

Rank	Company	Revenues ($ mil.)	Rank	Company	Revenues ($ mil.)
301	VF	5,479	351	Norfolk Southern	4,428
302	Owens-Illinois	5,450	352	Dole Food	4,424
303	3Com	5,420	353	Litton Industries	4,400
304	Unocal	5,379	354	KN Energy	4,388
305	Progressive	5,292	355	FMC	4,378
306	Solectron	5,288	356	Masco	4,345
307	CompUSA	5,286	357	W.W. Grainger	4,341
308	Avon Products	5,213	358	OfficeMax	4,338
309	Peco Energy	5,211	359	Pitney Bowes	4,334
310	MBNA	5,195	360	TruServ	4,328
311	Alltel	5,194	361	Universal	4,287
312	Ryder System	5,189	362	LTV	4,273
313	Airtouch Communications	5,181	363	InaCom	4,258
314	CMS Energy	5,141	364	GPU	4,249
315	Gannett	5,121	365	Harcourt General	4,235
316	First Data	5,118	366	State Street Corp.	4,234
317	Cooper Industries	5,101	367	Giant Food	4,231
318	Nordstrom	5,028	368	DTE Energy	4,221
319	Owens Corning	5,009	369	Consolidated Stores	4,194
320	General Dynamics	4,970	370	Engelhard	4,175
321	CNF Transportation	4,942	371	Southwest Airlines	4,164
322	Sherwin-Williams	4,934	372	Nash Finch	4,160
323	Air Products & Chemicals	4,934	373	Pacific Life Insurance	4,153
324	Dover	4,877	374	Nucor	4,151
325	Quaker Oats	4,843	375	Turner Corp.	4,130
326	Praxair	4,833	376	Ryerson Tull	4,093
327	Starwood Hotels & Resorts	4,832	377	Kelly Services	4,092
328	Automatic Data Processing	4,798	378	Omnicom Group	4,092
329	Fortune Brands	4,797	379	Maytag	4,069
330	Tandy	4,788	380	Hilton Hotels	4,064
331	Mattel	4,782	381	American Financial Group	4,050
332	Browning-Ferris Industries	4,746	382	Applied Materials	4,042
333	ServiceMaster	4,724	383	HEALTHSOUTH	4,006
334	Oxford Health Plans	4,719	384	American Family Insurance Group	4,003
335	Computer Associates Intl.	4,719	385	Centex	3,976
336	Parker Hannifin	4,633	386	EMC	3,974
337	UNUM	4,631	387	Interpublic Group	3,969
338	Olsten	4,603	388	B.F. Goodrich	3,951
339	Foster Wheeler	4,597	389	Brunswick	3,945
340	Mead	4,579	390	Harris	3,939
341	Allegiance	4,574	391	Allegheny Teledyne	3,923
342	Black & Decker	4,560	392	GenAmerica	3,914
343	Merisel	4,553	393	Provident Companies	3,904
344	Union Camp	4,503	394	Thermo Electron	3,868
345	Eastman Chemical	4,481	395	Smithfield Foods	3,867
346	Bethlehem Steel	4,478	396	KeySpan	3,836
347	Science Applications International	4,477	397	Meritor Automotive	3,836
348	Corporate Express	4,475	398	Niagara Mohawk Power	3,826
349	Federal-Mogul	4,469	399	Mutual of Omaha Insurance	3,820
350	Hershey Foods	4,436	400	Smurfit-Stone Container	3,794

Rank	Company	Revenues ($ mil.)	Rank	Company	Revenues ($ mil.)
401	PP&L Resources	3,786	451	Interstate Bakeries	3,266
402	Northeast Utilities	3,768	452	Cablevision Systems	3,265
403	Pittston	3,747	453	Hormel Foods	3,261
404	Graybar Electric	3,744	454	Trans World Airlines	3,259
405	Temple-Inland	3,740	455	Comdisco	3,243
406	McGraw-Hill	3,729	456	AutoZone	3,243
407	Newell	3,720	457	United States Filter	3,235
408	Rohm & Haas	3,720	458	Reebok International	3,225
409	Sonat	3,710	459	Dollar General	3,221
410	Willamette Industries	3,700	460	Comerica	3,220
411	Corning	3,689	461	Aid Association for Lutherans	3,218
412	Avista Corp.	3,684	462	Richfood Holdings	3,204
413	Kohl's	3,682	463	Sun Healthcare Group	3,142
414	Clark USA	3,668	464	Vencor	3,132
415	Pathmark Stores	3,655	465	Carolina Power & Light	3,130
416	Florida Progress	3,620	466	USG	3,130
417	Estée Lauder	3,618	467	Ace Hardware	3,120
418	New Century Energies	3,611	468	Becton, Dickinson	3,117
419	U.S. Office Products	3,604	469	Yellow	3,112
420	Consolidated Natural Gas	3,553	470	Silicon Graphics	3,101
421	BJ's Wholesale Club	3,552	471	Golden West Financial Corp.	3,100
422	Shaw Industries	3,542	472	Knight Ridder	3,100
423	Western Digital	3,542	473	Anixter International	3,084
424	Republic New York Corp.	3,523	474	Owens & Minor	3,082
425	Host Marriott	3,519	475	Airborne Freight	3,075
426	Flowers Industries	3,505	476	Regions Financial	3,073
427	Firstar Corp.	3,502	477	Conectiv	3,072
428	Autoliv	3,489	478	SLM Holding	3,065
429	IMC Global	3,483	479	Phelps Dodge	3,063
430	Avery Dennison	3,460	480	United Stationers	3,059
431	Hechinger	3,449	481	Fleetwood Enterprises	3,051
432	Phoenix Home Life Mutual Insurance	3,435	482	United Auto Group	3,045
433	Allmerica Financial	3,433	483	Lutheran Brotherhood	3,027
434	Peter Kiewit Sons'	3,403	484	Golden State Bancorp	3,026
435	Charles Schwab	3,388	485	Wesco International	3,025
436	Leggett & Platt	3,370	486	Lexmark International	3,021
437	Reliance Group Holdings	3,369	487	Micron Technology	3,012
438	U.S. Industries	3,362	488	BB&T Corp.	3,009
439	Baltimore Gas & Electric	3,358	489	Barnes & Noble	3,006
440	QUALCOMM	3,348	490	ShopKo Stores	2,994
441	Service Merchandise	3,327	491	Tribune	2,981
442	Hannaford Bros.	3,324	492	Integrated Health Services	2,973
443	Suiza Foods	3,321	493	SouthTrust Corp.	2,943
444	Ameren	3,318	494	AGCO	2,941
445	Hasbro	3,305	495	New York Times	2,937
446	Times Mirror	3,292	496	Mercantile Bancorporation	2,934
447	York International	3,289	497	Nipsco Industries	2,933
448	Darden Restaurants	3,287	498	Danaher	2,910
449	Dean Foods	3,269	499	Westvaco	2,905
450	Longs Drug Stores	3,267	500	Ball	2,896

The *Forbes* 500 Largest Private Companies in the US

Rank	Company	Revenues ($ mil.)	Rank	Company	Revenues ($ mil.)
1	Cargill	51,400	51	Schneider National	2,512
2	Koch Industries	36,200	52	Gulf States Toyota	2,500
3	United Parcel Service	22,458	53	Perdue Farms	2,480
4	Goldman Sachs	20,433	54	MacAndrews & Forbes Holdings	2,467
5	Continental Grain	15,000	55	Entex Information Services	2,457
6	Pricewaterhouse Coopers	15,000	56	Southern Wine & Spirits	2,450
7	Mars	14,500	57	Hendrick Automotive Group	2,434
8	Andersen Worldwide	13,700	58	Randalls Food Markets	2,419
9	Bechtel Group	11,300	59	Core-Mark International	2,396
10	Publix Super Markets	11,224	60	Hearst Corporation	2,375
11	KPMG Peat Marwick	10,600	61	Wegmans Food Markets	2,340
12	Ernst & Young	10,500	62	Jitney Jungle Stores of America	2,315
13	Holberg Industries	10,100	63	Peabody Holding	2,246
14	Deloitte Touche Tohmatsu	9,000	64	Belk Stores Services	2,225
15	Meijer	7,600	65	Kohler	2,200
16	H. E. Butt Grocery	7,000	66	McKinsey & Co	2,200
17	Levi Strauss & Co.	6,900	67	Raley's	2,193
18	ARAMARK	6,350	68	Keystone Foods	2,184
19	Alliant Foodservice	6,100	69	American Axle & Manufacturing	2,148
20	Marmon Group	6,003	70	Red Apple Group	2,115
21	Fidelity Investments	5,878	71	Transammonia	2,104
22	JM Family Enterprises	5,500	72	Jordan Motors	2,062
23	Montgomery Ward & Co.	5,386	73	International Data Group	2,060
24	Huntsman	5,200	74	Guardian Industries	2,000
25	C&S Wholesale Grocers	5,120	75	MBM	2,000
26	S.C. Johnson & Son	5,000	76	LifeStyle Furnishings International	1,960
27	Enterprise Rent-A-Car	4,180	77	Neuman Distributors	1,953
28	Hechinger Investment	4,100	78	Consolidated Electrical Distributors	1,950
29	Giant Eagle	4,065	79	Goodman Manufacturing	1,925
30	Clark USA	3,925	80	Gilbane Building	1,923
31	Pathmark Stores	3,696	81	Global Petroleum	1,900
32	Hallmark Cards	3,660	82	Metromedia	1,900
33	Menard	3,500	83	Penske Truck Leasing	1,900
34	Borden	3,482	84	Holman Enterprises	1,870
35	Graybar Electric	3,338	85	Black & Veatch	1,863
36	Hy-Vee	3,200	86	Ed Morse Automotive Group	1,855
37	Milliken & Co	3,200	87	QuikTrip	1,830
38	Cox Enterprises	3,130	88	Gulf Oil	1,800
39	Asbury Automotive Group	3,100	89	Schnuck Markets	1,800
40	Science Applications International	3,089	90	Ingram Industries	1,796
41	Amway	2,900	91	Carlson Companies	1,770
42	J.R. Simplot	2,900	92	J.F. Shea Co.	1,750
43	Schwan's Sales Enterprises	2,850	93	UniGroup	1,749
44	Peter Kiewit Sons'	2,764	94	Stater Bros. Markets	1,746
45	Lefrak Organization	2,750	95	DeMoulas Super Markets	1,742
46	Advance Publications	2,700	96	84 Lumber	1,700
47	Mid-Atlantic Cars	2,640	97	Gordon Food Service	1,700
48	Wesco Distribution	2,595	98	Flying J	1,641
49	VT	2,587	99	H.T. Hackney	1,623
50	Renco Group	2,550	100	Scoular	1,606

Source: *Forbes;* November 30, 1998

The *Forbes* 500 Largest Private Companies in the US (continued)

Rank	Company	Revenues ($ mil.)	Rank	Company	Revenues ($ mil.)
101	Eby-Brown	1,600	151	Lincoln Property	1,200
102	Golub	1,600	152	Prospect Motors	1,200
103	Southwire	1,600	153	Quad/Graphics	1,200
104	Sammons Enterprises	1,565	154	A.G. Spanos Companies	1,200
105	Brookshire Grocery	1,535	155	Connell Limited Partnership	1,190
106	Holiday Companies	1,520	156	Dillingham Construction	1,175
107	Haworth	1,510	157	Berwind Group	1,156
108	Grant Thornton	1,506	158	Crowley Maritime	1,153
109	RaceTrac Petroleum	1,500	159	DynCorp	1,146
110	Alex Lee	1,500	160	Riverwood International	1,139
111	Central National Gottesman	1,500	161	Edward Jones	1,135
112	Golden State Foods	1,500	162	Beaulieu of America Group	1,133
113	Quality King Distributors	1,500	163	Enterprise Products	1,130
114	Andersen Corporation	1,450	164	North Pacific Group	1,126
115	BDO Seidman	1,450	165	Towers Perrin	1,120
116	Lennox International	1,440	166	Micro Electronics	1,120
117	Booz, Allen & Hamilton	1,400	167	Schreiber Foods	1,120
118	Jeld-Wen	1,400	168	Avondale	1,100
119	Potamkin Manhattan Corp.	1,400	169	Bill Heard Enterprises	1,100
120	Purity Wholesale Grocers	1,400	170	IMG	1,100
121	Pilot	1,388	171	Mary Kay	1,100
122	H Group Holding	1,378	172	Larry H. Miller Group	1,100
123	Services Group of America	1,350	173	ICC Industries	1,099
124	Clark Enterprises	1,335	174	GSC Enterprises	1,082
125	Bridge Information Systems	1,330	175	Day & Zimmermann	1,080
126	Stroh Brewery	1,330	176	Follett	1,073
127	Grocers Supply Co.	1,325	177	DiGiorgio	1,072
128	Maritz	1,325	178	General Parts	1,067
129	Del Monte Foods	1,313	179	Comark	1,066
130	Save Mart Supermarkets	1,312	180	BE&K	1,061
131	E. & J. Gallo Winery	1,300	181	McGladrey & Pullen	1,060
132	Rich Products	1,300	182	Packerland Packing	1,056
133	Simpson Investment	1,300	183	Earle M. Jorgensen	1,050
134	J. M. Huber	1,299	184	Lykes Bros	1,050
135	W. L. Gore & Associates	1,280	185	Domino's Pizza	1,045
136	Parsons Corp	1,263	186	Young's Market	1,045
137	Amsted Industries	1,252	187	McCarthy	1,039
138	Connell	1,250	188	Whiting-Turner Contracting	1,035
139	Sinclair Oil	1,250	189	Asplundh Tree Expert Co.	1,026
140	Leprino Foods	1,240	190	National Distributing	1,025
141	Fry's Electronics	1,235	191	Huber Hunt & Nichols	1,015
142	DHL Airways	1,226	192	Wawa	1,011
143	Delaware North Companies	1,224	193	MTS	1,008
144	Flint Ink	1,216	194	L.L. Bean	1,008
145	Swagelok	1,210	195	Bashas'	1,000
146	Dunavant Enterprises	1,209	196	Dart Container	1,000
147	Cumberland Farms	1,206	197	Ebsco Industries	1,000
148	Bloomberg LP	1,200	198	Frank Consolidated Enterprises	1,000
149	Duchossois Industries	1,200	199	Helmsley Enterprises	1,000
150	Knowledge Universe	1,200	200	Honickman Affiliates	1,000

The *Forbes* 500 Largest Private Companies in the US (continued)

Rank	Company	Revenues ($ mil.)	Rank	Company	Revenues ($ mil.)
201	Irvine	1,000	251	Crown Equipment	856
202	Minyard Food Stores	1,000	252	Grove Worldwide	855
203	Nesco	1,000	253	Bose	850
204	Sierra Pacific Industries	1,000	254	MediaNews Group	850
205	Shamrock Foods	995	255	Parkdale Mills	850
206	CC Industries	992	256	Spitzer Management	850
207	Foster Farms	990	257	Boscov's Department Stores	846
208	Lanoga	986	258	Parsons & Whittemore	845
209	UIS	986	259	R.B. Pamplin	843
210	The Pantry	985	260	MacManus Group	843
211	Dade Behring	981	261	Club Corporation International	840
212	Walsh Group	980	262	J. Crew	834
213	Outboard Marine	980	263	ViewSonic	832
214	Westfield Companies	961	264	Printpack	832
215	ABC Supply	959	265	McKee Foods	831
216	Sheetz	952	266	Waremart	830
217	Kelley Automotive Group	950	267	PMC Global	828
218	Mark III Industries	950	268	Roll International	827
219	Tang Industries	950	269	Skadden, Arps, Slate, Meagher & Flom	826
220	Taylor Corporation	950	270	Rosenthal Automotive Organization	823
221	Marty Franich Auto Center	946	271	WWF Paper	821
222	Battelle Memorial Institute	946	272	Gould Paper	815
223	GAF	945	273	Wirtz	810
224	Coca-Cola Bottling Co. of Chicago	940	274	GS Industries	810
225	Big Y Foods	938	275	Inductotherm Industries	808
226	Tishman Realty & Construction	937	276	Republic Engineered Steels	803
227	American Bottling	935	277	M. A. Mortenson	803
228	Hensel Phelps Construction	934	278	Hoffman	800
229	Menasha	934	279	Stevedoring Services of America	800
230	Specialty Foods	920	280	Sealy	800
231	Sverdrup	919	281	Discount Tire	799
232	CH2M Hill Companies	918	282	Watkins Associated Industries	796
233	Ingram Entertainment	918	283	Baker & McKenzie	795
234	Ormet	910	284	Russ Darrow Group	795
235	Don Massey Cadillac	909	285	Swinerton	792
236	Schottenstein Stores	905	286	Courtesy Auto Group	791
237	Kinray	900	287	Fairchild Semiconductor	789
238	Wilbur-Ellis	900	288	Perot Systems	782
239	DPR Construction	895	289	M. Fabrikant & Sons	780
240	ACF Industries	891	290	Serra Investments	770
241	Lane Industries	890	291	Rooney Brothers	769
242	LDI	890	292	Favorite Brands International	766
243	Sweetheart Holdings	885	293	Big V Supermarkets	763
244	Baker & Taylor	880	294	Parsons Brinckerhoff	760
245	Carpenter	879	295	Sunbelt Beverage	760
246	Leo Burnett	878	296	Barton Malow	756
247	Chemcentral	875	297	Faulkner Organization	756
248	Burt Automotive Network	866	298	Roseburg Forest Products	756
249	AECOM Technology	860	299	O'Neal Steel	755
250	Hewitt Associates	858	300	Island Lincoln-Mercury Group	753

The *Forbes* 500 Largest Private Companies in the US (continued)

Rank	Company	Revenues ($ mil.)	Rank	Company	Revenues ($ mil.)
301	Topa Equities	752	351	Forever Living Products International	650
302	Community Health Systems	750	352	Inland Group	645
303	Fiesta Mart	750	353	Goya Foods	640
304	Horsehead Industries	750	354	Hartz Group	640
305	ICON Health & Fitness	749	355	Murphy Family Farms	640
306	American Commercial Lines	748	356	Ritz Camera	635
307	Drummond	746	357	Feld Entertainment	630
308	Deseret Management	742	358	Walbridge, Aldinger	630
309	Southern Foods Group	741	359	Great Lakes Cheese	625
310	Sutherland Lumber	741	360	Hubbard Broadcasting	625
311	Glazer's Wholesale Distributors	740	361	Steiner	625
312	Klaussner Furniture Group	738	362	Pepper Companies	623
313	TAC Worldwide Companies	737	363	American Century Investments	620
314	Lewis Homes Group of Cos.	732	364	Les Schwab Tire Centers	620
315	Hale-Halsell	731	365	Warren Equities	620
316	Bartlett and Company	725	366	Austin Industries	619
317	Genuardi Family Markets	725	367	Tutor-Saliba	619
318	King Kullen Grocery	725	368	Ingersoll International	611
319	Sherwood Food Distributors	725	369	Longaberger	611
320	DeBruce Grain	722	370	Tuttle-Click Automotive Group	609
321	Conair	716	371	Herb Chambers Cos	607
322	Newark Group	715	372	Little Caesar Enterprises	605
323	K-Va-T Food Stores	712	373	Peerless Importers	605
324	Lupient Automotive Group	708	374	Rudolph & Sletten	605
325	Jordan Industries	707	375	Turner Industries	602
326	McJunkin	701	376	Goss Graphic Systems	600
327	Cambridge Industries	700	377	Marnell Corrao Association	600
328	Celotex	700	378	Pella	600
329	Hunt Consolidated/Hunt Oil	700	379	Progressive Tool & Industries	600
330	McCombs Enterprises	700	380	Rooms to Go	600
331	OmniSource	700	381	TTC Illinois	597
332	SAS Institute	700	382	Koppers Industries	593
333	Washington Companies	700	383	Builder Marts of America	593
334	Watson Wyatt Worldwide	698	384	Empire Beef	591
335	Simplex Time Recorder	695	385	Arthur D. Little	589
336	Dunn Industries	686	386	Jim Koons Management	585
337	Freedom Communications	685	387	Fletcher Jones Management Group	584
338	MTD Products	685	388	Genmar Holdings	580
339	Ben E. Keith Co.	682	389	Oxford Automotive	576
340	Georgia Crown Distributing	680	390	Blue Bird	576
341	El Camino Resources	678	391	Gilman Investment	575
342	Journal Communications	675	392	Landmark communications	575
343	Charmer Industries	670	393	CMI International	574
344	Tasha	667	394	All-Phase Electric Supply	573
345	Medline Industries	665	395	Mel Farr Automotive Group	573
346	Guide	665	396	Pacifico Group	572
347	Earnhardt's Motor Cos	660	397	McWane	570
348	H.B. Zachry	660	398	Opus Group of Companies	570
349	Boston Consulting Group	655	399	Baugh Enterprises	565
350	American Golf	650	400	Darby Group Companies	565

The *Forbes* 500 Largest Private Companies in the US (continued)

Rank	Company	Revenues ($ mil.)	Rank	Company	Revenues ($ mil.)
401	Phil Long Dealerships	565	451	Furman Lumber	519
402	Manufacturers' Services	562	452	Houchens Industries	515
403	Lifetouch	560	453	Ris Paper	515
404	Unicco Service	555	454	United Supermarkets	515
405	Shapell Industries	554	455	Texas Petrochemicals	515
406	Moyer Packing	553	456	Beck Group	513
407	ASI	550	457	Santa Monica Ford	510
408	Simmons	550	458	Russell Stover Candies	510
409	Boler	550	459	Albert Trostel & Sons	510
410	The Iams Company	550	460	Ukrop's Super Markets	510
411	Perry H. Koplik & Sons	550	461	Williamson-Dickie Manufacturing	510
412	Rocco	550	462	Bob Rohrman Auto Group	509
413	Rosen's Diversified	550	463	GFI America	505
414	TRT Holdings	550	464	Morris Communications	505
415	Tube City	550	465	David Weekley Homes	503
416	Darcars	545	466	Neuberger Berman	502
417	Ricart Automotive	544	467	American Cast Iron Pipe	500
418	Dick Corporation	540	468	Cook Group	500
419	Greenwood Mills	540	469	Fellowes Manufacturing	500
420	Inserra Supermarkets	540	470	Green Bay Packaging	500
421	Kraus-Anderson	540	471	Henkels & McCoy	500
422	Copps Corporation	539	472	H.P. Hood	500
423	API Group	537	473	National Steel & Shipbuilding	500
424	Braman Enterprises	536	474	State Industries	500
425	Fareway Stores	535	475	TitanSports	500
426	Ourisman Automotive Enterprises	535	476	Atlas World Group	490
427	RTM Restaurant Group	535	477	Chronicle Publishing	490
428	American Color Graphics	533	478	Jones, Day, Reavis & Pogue	490
429	Galpin Motors	533	479	Sauder Woodworking	490
430	Soave Enterprises	533	480	Clark Material Handling	489
431	J.S. Alberici Construction Co.	531	481	Siegel-Robert	485
432	FNC Holdings	530	482	Safelite Glass	484
433	Johnson Brothers Wholesale Liquor	530	483	Gilster-Mary Lee	483
434	Spalding Holdings	530	484	Montgomery Watson	482
435	Thomason Auto Group	530	485	Shorenstein	481
436	Townsends	530	486	Field Container	480
437	Transtar Holdings	526	487	HBE Corporation	480
438	Grede Foundries	525	488	Richardson & Partners	480
439	Jockey International	525	489	Marcus Cable	479
440	Pacific Holding	525	490	Regal Cinemas	479
441	PC Richard & Son	525	491	Copley Press	477
442	Wolf Camera	525	492	Brasfield & Gorrie	477
443	Pitman	524	493	Bradco Supply	475
444	RAB Holdings	523	494	GoodTimes Entertainment	475
445	National Wine & Spirits	521	495	Krasdale Foods	475
446	American Foods Group	520	496	Oxbow	475
447	Bugle Boy Industries	520	497	Toresco Enterprises	475
448	George Koch Sons	520	498	FirstAmerica Automotive	474
449	Marathon Cheese	520	499	Dynatech	473
450	Pacific Coast Building Products	520	500	Four M	469

Forbes 20 Greatest US Fortunes

Rank	Name	Net Worth ($ bil.)	Rank	Name	Net Worth ($ bil.)
1	William H. Gates III	85.0	11	Gordon Earl Moore	15.0
2	Paul Gardner Allen	40.0	12	Lawrence Joseph Ellison	13.0
3	Warren Edward Buffett	31.0	13	Philip F. Anschutz	11.0
4	Steven Anthony Ballmer	23.0	13	John Werner Kluge	11.0
5	Michael Dell	20.0	15	Barbara Cox Anthony	9.7
6	Jim C. Walton	17.3	15	Anne Cox Chambers	9.7
7	Helen R. Walton	17.0	17	Sumner M. Redstone	9.4
8	Alice L. Walton	16.9	18	Jeffrey P. Bezos	7.8
9	John T. Walton	16.8	19	Abigail Johnson	7.4
10	S. Robson Walton	16.6	20	Kirk Kerkorian	7.0

Source: *Forbes;* October 11, 1999

Top 20 in CEO Compensation

Rank	Name	Company	Total Pay* ($ thou.)
1	Michael Eisner	Walt Disney	575,592
2	Mel Karmazin	CBS	201,934
3	Sanford Weill	CitiGroup	167,093
4	Stephen Case	America Online	159,233
5	Craig Barrett	Intel	116,511
6	John Welch	General Electric	83,664
7	Henry Schacht	Lucent Technologies	67,037
8	L. Dennis Kozlowski	Tyco International	65,264
9	Henry Silverman	Cendant	63,882
10	M. Douglas Ivester	Coca-Cola	57,322
11	Charles Heimbold	Bristol-Myers Squibb	56,279
12	Philip Purcell	Morgan Stanley Dean Witter	53,374
13	Reuben Mark	Colgate-Palmolive	52,703
14	Scott McNealy	Sun Microsystems	48,014
15	Louis Gerstner	IBM	46,335
16	Duane Burnham	Abbott Laboratories	45,995
17	Margaret Whitman	eBay	43,002
18	Randall Tobias	Eli Lilly	41,687
19	John Gifford	Maxim Integrated Products	40,097
20	Gordon Binder	Amgen	39,186

*includes salary, bonus, and long-term compensation
Source: *Business Week;* April 19, 1999

Forbes 40 Most Powerful Celebrities

Rank*	Company	Earnings ($ mil.)	Rank	Company	Earnings ($ mil.)
1	Michael Jordan	69.0	21	Eddie Murphy	47.5
2	Oprah Winfrey	125.0	22	Jim Carrey	32.5
3	Leonardo DiCaprio	37.0	23	Mark McGwire	10.0
4	Jerry Seinfeld	267.0	24	Dennis Rodman	15.3
5	Steven Spielberg	175.0	25	Tim Allen	77.0
6	Spice Girls	49.0	26	Master P	56.5
7	Harrison Ford	58.0	27	Stephen King	40.0
8	Robin Williams	56.0	28	Nicolas Cage	38.5
9	Celine Dion	55.5	29	Drew Carey	45.5
10	Rolling Stones	57.0	30	Michael Crichton	65.0
11	James Cameron	115.0	31	Martha Stewart	18.0
12	Tom Hanks	44.0	32	Kevin Costner	41.0
13	Helen Hunt	31.0	33	Sammy Sosa	10.0
14	Garth Brooks	54.0	34	Chris Carter	52.0
15	John Travolta	47.0	35	Ken Griffey Jr.	12.7
16	Mel Gibson	55.0	36	Andre Agassi	15.8
17	Brad Pitt	40.0	37	Howard Stern	20.0
18	Tiger Woods	26.8	38	Dale Earnhardt	24.1
19	Sean (Puffy) Combs	53.5	39	Larry David	242.0
20	Will Smith	34.0	40	Michael Schumacher	38.0

*Forbes' rankings are based on income and media recognition (Web prominence, magazine covers, radio/TV and newspaper coverage)
Source: *Forbes;* March 22, 1999

The 20 Most Powerful Women in Business

Rank	Name	Title	Company
1	Carly Fiorina	CEO, President	Hewlett-Packard
2	Heidi Miller	CFO	Citigroup
3	Mary Meeker	Managing Director	Morgan Stanley Dean Witter
4	Shelly Lazarus	Chairman, CEO	Ogilvy & Mather
5	Meg Whitman	CEO, President	eBay
6	Debby Hopkins	SVP, CFO	Boeing
7	Marjorie Scardino	CEO	Pearson
8	Martha Stewart	Chairman, CEO	Martha Stewart Living Omnimedia
9	Nancy Peretsman	EVP, Managing Director	Allen & Co.
10	Pat Russo	EVP Strategy, Business Development & Corporate Operations	Lucent Technologies
11	Patricia Dunn	Chairman	Barclays Global Investors
12	Abby Joseph Cohen	Managing Director	Goldman Sachs
13	Ann Livermore	CEO, President Enterprise Computing	Hewlett-Packard
14	Andrea Jung	President, COO	Avon Products
15	Sherry Lansing	Chairman: Motion Picture Group	Paramount Pictures
16	Karen Katen	EVP Global, President US Pharmaceuticals Group	Pfizer
17	Marilyn Carlson Nelson	Chairman, CEO	Carlson Cos.
18	Judy McGrath	President	MTV & M2
19	Lois Juliber	EVP, COO Developed Markets	Colgate-Palmolive
20	Gerry Laybourne	Chairman, CEO	Oxygen Media

Source: *FORTUNE;* October 25, 1999

Top 10 Healthcare Systems by Net Patient Revenues

Rank	System	Revenues ($ mil.)
1	U. S. Department of Veterans Affairs	20,027.1
2	Columbia/HCA Healthcare Corp.	18,681.0
3	Tenet Healthcare Corp.	8,821.0
4	Catholic Health Initiatives	4,587.3
5	New York City Health and Hospitals Corp.	3,834.5
6	Daughters of Charity National Health System	3,767.4
7	Catholic Healthcare West	3,301.3
8	New York Presbyterian Healthcare Network	3,238.0
9	Sisters of Mercy Health System-St. Louis	2,169.2
10	North Shore-Long Island Jewish Health System	2,164.9

Source: *Modern Healthcare;* May 24, 1999

Top 10 Pharmaceutical Companies by Worldwide Sales

Rank	Company	1998 Sales ($ mil.)
1	Novartis	10.6
2	Merck	10.6
3	Glaxo Wellcome	10.5
4	Pfizer	9.9
5	Bristol-Myers Squibb	9.8
6	Johnson & Johnson	9.0
7	American Home Products	7.8
8	Roche	7.6
9	Eli Lilly	7.4
10	SmithKline Beecham	7.3

Source: *Standard & Poor's Industry Survey – Healthcare: Pharmaceuticals;* July 29, 1999

Top 10 Prescription Drugs

Rank	Drug	Manufacturer	Use	Sales ($ mil.)
1	Prilosec	AstraZeneca	Antiulcer	2,933
2	Prozac	Eli Lilly	Antidepressant	2,181
3	Lipitor	Pfizer/Warner-Lambert	Cholesterol reducer	1,544
4	Zocor	Merck	Cholesterol reducer	1,481
5	Epogen	Amgen	Red blood cell stimulant	1,455
6	Zoloft	Pfizer	Antidepressant	1,392
7	Prevacid	TAP	Antiulcer	1,245
8	Paxil	SmithKline Beecham	Antidepressant	1,190
9	Claritin	Schering-Plough	Antihistamine	1,150
10	Norvasc	Pfizer	Antihypertensive	1,086

Source: *Standard & Poor's Industry Survey – Healthcare: Pharmaceuticals;* July 29, 1999

Top 10 Branded Over-the-Counter Drugs

Rank	Brand	Company	Total Sales ($ mil.)
1	Tylenol (analgesic)	Johnson & Johnson	541.8
2	Advil	American Home Products	366.6
3	Tylenol (cold medication)	Johnson & Johnson	257.3
4	Pepcid AC	Johnson & Johnson/Merck	224.6
5	Robitussin	American Home Products	206.7
6	Tums	SmithKline Beecham	182.0
7	Zantac	Warner-Lambert	170.8
8	Benadryl	Warner-Lambert	165.2
9	Sudafed	Warner-Lambert	161.7
10	Aleve	Bayer	149.3

Source: *Brandweek;* June 21, 1999

Top 25 US Banks by Total Assets

Rank	Company	Headquarters	1998 Total Assets ($ mil.)
1	NationsBank, N.A.	Charlotte, NC	317,268.0
2	CitiBank, N.A.	New York	304,316.0
3	The Chase Manhattan Bank	New York	291,476.0
4	Bank of America National Trust and Savings Assoc.	San Francisco	250,700.0
5	First Union National Bank	Charlotte, NC	208,670.0
6	Morgan Guaranty Trust Company of New York	New York	184,314.4
7	Bankers Trust Company	New York	98,919.0
8	Wells Fargo Bank, National Assoc.	San Francisco	86,269.0
9	Fleet National Bank	Providence, RI	78,152.0
10	Keybank National Association	Cleveland	72,925.4
11	BankBoston, National Association	Boston	70,258.8
12	U.S. Bank National Association	Minneapolis	69,781.0
13	The First National Bank of Chicago	Chicago	68,940.4
14	PNC Bank, National Association	Pittsburgh	68,257.3
15	Wachovia Bank, National Association	Winston-Salem, NC	61,879.0
16	The Bank of New York	New York	61,688.6
17	Republic National Bank of New York	New York	46,697.2
18	State Street Bank and Trust Company	Boston	45,726.6
19	Mellon Bank, N.A.	Pittsburgh	41,036.7
20	SouthTrust Bank, N.A.	Birmingham, AL	38,933.2
21	Regions Bank	Birmingham, AL	37,433.2
22	HSBC Bank USA	Buffalo, NY	33,581.9
23	Washington Mutual Bank	Seattle	33,401.7
24	Chase Manhattan Bank USA, National Association	Wilmington, DE	33,297.1
25	Union Bank of California, National Association	San Francisco	31,994.2

Source: *Federal Reserve Board's National Information Center;* September 2, 1999

America's Top 25 Money Managers

Rank	Company	Headquarters	1998 Total Assets ($ mil.)
1	Fidelity Investments	Boston	773,124
2	Barclays Global Investors	San Francisco	615,500
3	Merrill Lynch & Co.	Plainsboro, NJ	501,229
4	State Street Global Advisors	Boston	492,797
5	Capital Group Cos.	Los Angeles	424,235
6	Mellon Bank Corp.	Pittsburgh	400,975
7	Bankers Trust Co.	New York	361,884
8	Equitable Companies	New York	359,169
9	Morgan Stanley Dean Witter & Co.	New York	345,731
10	SSB Citi Asset Mgmt. Group	New York	327,027
11	J.P. Morgan Inv. Mgmt.	New York	316,193
12	UBS Brinson Division	Chicago	303,703
13	Putnam Investments	Boston	294,056
14	Scudder Kemper Investments	New York	281,188
15	Vanguard Group	Valley Forge, PA	276,318
16	TIAA-CREF	New York	244,171
17	Pimco Advisors	Newport Beach, CA	244,166
18	Prudential Insurance Co.	Newark, NJ	242,838
19	Bank of America Corp.	Charlotte, NC	233,500
20	Northern Trust Global Investments	Chicago	225,781
21	Franklin Group of Funds	San Mateo, CA	220,200
22	Amvescap	Atlanta	216,917
23	Wellington Mgmt. Co.	Boston	211,318
24	American Express Co.	New York	196,051
25	Chase Manhattan Corp.	New York	189,603

Source: *Institutional Investor;* July 1999

The 25 Largest Management Consulting Firms

Rank	Firm	1998 Revenues ($ mil.)
1	Andersen Consulting	7,129
2	PricewaterhouseCoopers	6,000
3	Ernst & Young	3,870
4	Deloitte Consulting	3,240
5	CSC	3,000
6	KPMG	3,000
7	McKinsey & Company	2,500
8	Cap Gemini	2,261
9	Mercer Consulting Group	1,543
10	Arthur Andersen	1,368
11	A.T. Kearney	1,234
12	Towers Perrin	1,230
13	Booz-Allen & Hamilton	1,204
14	IBM Consulting	990
15	American Management Systems	913
16	Keane	872
17	Hewitt Associates	858
18	Sema Group	836
19	Logica	790
20	The Boston Consulting Group	730
21	Watson Wyatt Worldwide	720
22	DMR Consulting Group	666
23	CMG	636
24	Aon Consulting	615
25	Cambridge Technology Partners	612

Source: *Consultants News;* June 1999; Kennedy Information
www.kennedyinfo.com, 800-531-0007

Top 25 Law Firms

Rank	Law Firm	Gross Revenue ($ mil.)
1	Skadden, Arps, Slate, Meagher & Flom	890.0
2	Baker & McKenzie	784.5
3	Jones, Day, Reavis & Pogue	530.0
4	Latham & Watkins	502.0
5	Davis Polk & Wardwell	435.0
6	Sullivan & Cromwell	426.5
7	Shearman & Sterling	425.5
8	Sidley & Austin	421.0
9	Mayer, Brown & Platt	400.0
10	Weil, Gotshal & Manges	399.5
11	Morgan, Lewis & Bockius	397.0
12	McDermott, Will & Emery	389.5
13	Simpson Thacher & Bartlett	386.0
14	Gibson, Dunn & Crutcher	374.0
15	Cleary, Gottlieb, Steen & Hamilton	366.0
16	White & Case	351.5
17	Cravath, Swaine & Moore	334.0
18	O'Melveny & Myers	328.0
19	Kirkland & Ellis	310.0
20	Akin, Gump, Strauss, Hauer & Feld	301.0
21	Fulbright & Jaworski	282.5
22	Vinson & Elkins	281.5
23	LeBoeuf, Lamb, Greene & MacRae	280.0
24	Foley & Lardner	277.0
25	Morrison & Foerster	274.0

Source: *American Lawyer;* July 1999

Top 25 Tax & Accounting Firms

Rank	Firm	1998 Revenue ($ mil.)	Rank	Firm	1998 Revenue ($ mil.)
1	Andersen Worldwide	6,828.0	16	Constantin Associates	85.1
2	PricewaterhouseCoopers	5,862.0	17	Clifton Gunderson	82.1
3	Ernst & Young	5,545.0	18	Moss Adams	82.0
4	Deloitte & Touche	4,700.0	19	Eisner	69.0
5	KPMG	3,800.0	20	Larson, Allen, Weishair & Co.	59.1
6	H&R Block	1,051.9	21	Olive	58.0
7	Century Business Services	363.0	22	Reznick Fedder & Silverman	46.9
8	Grant Thornton	336.0	23	David Berdon & Co.	41.1
9	McGladrey & Pullen	296.1	24	Triple Check	35.0
10	BDO Seidman	250.0	25	Wipfli Ullrich Bertelson	34.9
11	Jackson Hewitt	188.8			
12	American Express	149.5			
13	Crowe, Chizek and Co.	118.2			
14	Plante & Moran	104.7			
15	Baird Kurtz & Dobson	98.0			

Source: *Accounting Today;* March 15-April 4, 1999

Advertising Age's Top 50 Companies by Media Revenue

Rank	Company	Headquarters	Total 1998 Media Revenue ($ mil.)
1	Time Warner	New York	14,288.3
2	AT&T Corp.	New York	9,872.0
3	CBS Corp.	New York	7,684.9
4	Walt Disney Co.	New York/Burbank, CA	7,540.6
5	NBC TV (General Electric Co.)	Fairfield, CT	5,269.0
6	News Corp.	Sydney, Australia	4,972.2
7	Gannett Co.	Arlington, VA	4,910.0
8	America Online	Dulles, VA	4,800.0
9	Cox Enterprises	Atlanta	3,883.7
10	Advance Publications	Newark, NJ	3,859.1
11	DirecTV (General Motors Corp.)	El Segundo, CA	3,654.7
12	Hearst Corp.	New York	3,291.5
13	Viacom	New York	3,034.9
14	Knight Ridder	San Jose, CA	2,950.3
15	New York Times Co.	New York	2,937.2
16	Cablevision Systems Corp.	Woodbury, NY	2,896.5
17	Comcast Corp.	Philadelphia	2,732.8
18	Times Mirror Co.	Los Angeles	2,570.9
19	Tribune Co.	Chicago	2,515.6
20	Clear Channel Communications	San Antonio	2,079.0
21	Washington Post Co.	Washington, DC	1,901.9
22	AMFM Inc. (formerly Chancellor)	Dallas	1,581.4
23	Charter Communications	St. Louis	1,539.1
24	Dow Jones & Co.	New York	1,479.0
25	Adelphia Communications Corp.	Coudersport, PA	1,419.8
26	A.H. Belo Corp.	Dallas	1,407.3
27	Thomson Corp.	Toronto, Ontario	1,367.5
28	E.W. Scripps	Cincinnati	1,265.4
29	United News & Media	London	1,141.2
30	Primedia	New York	1,128.5
31	McClatchy Co.	Sacramento, CA	1,051.3
32	Advo Inc.	Windsor, CT	1,046.5
33	MediaNews Group	Denver	1,020.0
34	Reed Elsevier	London	968.8
35	Meredith Corp.	Des Moines, IA	961.0
36	Bloomberg	New York	936.0
37	International Data Group	Boston	857.1
38	Media General	Richmond, VA	845.7
39	USA Networks	New York	834.5
40	Reader's Digest Association	Pleasantville, NY	809.3
41	Central Newspapers	Phoenix	752.7
42	Discovery Communications	Bethesda, MD	750.0
43	Valassis Communications	Livonia, MI	741.4
44	EchoStar Communications Corp.	Littleton, CO	726.5
45	TV Guide Inc.	Tulsa, OK	716.8
46	Fox Family Worldwide	Los Angeles	705.9
47	Freedom Communications	Irvine, CA	672.6
48	McGraw-Hill	New York	652.3
49	Landmark Communications	Norfolk, VA	650.0
50	Ziff-Davis Publishing (Softbank)	New York	641.7

Source: *Advertising Age;* August 16, 1999

Top 25 US Daily Newspapers by Circulation

Rank	Newspaper	Parent Company	Circulation*
1	*Wall Street Journal*	Dow Jones & Company	1,792,452
2	*USA Today*	Gannett Co., Inc.	1,739,294
3	*New York Times*	The New York Times Company	1,134,974
4	*Los Angeles Times*	The Times Mirror Company	1,098,347
5	*Washington Post*	The Washington Post	809,059
6	*New York Daily News*	The Daily News	729,449
7	*Chicago Tribune*	Tribune Company	673,171
8	*Newsday*	The Times Mirror Company	573,542
9	*Houston Chronicle*	The Hearst Corporation	541,782
10	*Phoenix Arizona Republic*	Central Newspapers, Inc.	482,159
11	*Dallas Morning News*	A.H. Belo Corporation	479,248
12	*Chicago Sun-Times*	Hollinger International Inc.	477,302
13	*San Francisco Chronicle*	The Chronicle Publishing Company	475,244
14	*Boston Globe*	The New York Times Company	469,311
15	*New York Post*	The News Corporation Limited	433,774
16	*Newark Star-Ledger*	Advance Publications, Inc.	405,546
17	*Philadelphia Inquirer*	Knight Ridder	401,968
18	*Minneapolis/St. Paul Star Tribune*	The McClatchy Company	400,027
19	*Cleveland Plain Dealer*	Advance Publications, Inc.	394,740
20	*San Diego Union-Tribune*	The Copley Press, Inc.	381,256
21	*Denver Post*	Media News Groups, Inc.	370,423
22	*Detroit Free Press*	Knight Ridder	368,972
23	*Orange County Register*	Freedom Communications, Inc.	367,003
24	*St. Petersburg Times*	Times Publishing Company	359,214
25	*Rocky Mountain News*	E. W. Scripps Company	359,068

* For six months ended March 31, 1999
Source: *Editor & Publisher;* May 8, 1999

The 25 Largest Magazines in the US by Revenue

Rank	Magazine	Revenue ($ thou.)	1998 Total Paid Circulation	Parent Company
1	TV Guide	1,170,810	12,579,912	TV Guide Inc.
2	People	1,078,027	3,676,706	Time Warner
3	Sports Illustrated	850,057	3,286,489	Time Warner
4	Time	814,300	4,060,074	Time Warner
5	Reader's Digest	563,105	13,767,575	Reader's Digest Association
6	Better Homes & Gardens	559,124	7,613,249	Meredith Corp.
7	Newsweek	547,164	3,153,281	Washington Post Co.
8	Parade	517,116	37,079,772	Advance Publications
9	Business Week	416,922	908,953	McGraw-Hill Cos.
10	PC Magazine	378,607	1,182,181	Ziff-Davis
11	Good Housekeeping	344,829	4,584,879	Hearst Corp.
12	U.S. News & World Report	329,431	2,181,402	Mortimer Zuckerman
13	Family Circle	320,316	5,004,902	Bertelsmann
14	Woman's Day	319,554	4,242,097	Hachette Filipacchi
15	Forbes	315,752	785,065	Forbes Inc.
16	Cosmopolitan	306,087	2,768,260	Hearst Corp.
17	Fortune	305,916	781,883	Time Warner
18	Ladies' Home Journal	298,225	4,575,996	Meredith Corp.
19	USA Weekend	274,551	21,857,811	Gannett Co.
20	Entertainment Weekly	253,544	1,452,973	Time Warner
21	National Geographic	225,397	7,414,056	National Geographic Society
22	Money	215,015	1,905,158	Time Warner
23	Southern Living	211,379	2,518,732	Time Warner
24	Glamour	205,612	2,163,640	Advance Publications
25	Martha Stewart Living	202,828	2,354,284	Martha Stewart Living Omnimedia

Source: *Advertising Age;* June 14, 1999

Top 25 Television Groups in the US by Market Coverage

Rank	Group	Headquarters	% Coverage of Nation's 95.3 mil. TV Homes	No. of Stations
1	Fox Television Stations Inc.	Los Angeles	34.50	23
2	CBS Television Station Group	New York	32.80	15
3	Paxson Communications Corp.	West Palm Beach, FL	29.00	49
4	Tribune Broadcasting Co.	Chicago	27.00	20
5	NBC Inc.	New York	26.60	13
6	ABC Inc.	New York	24.00	10
7	United Television Inc./ Chris-Craft Industries Inc.	Beverly Hills, CA	18.80	10
8	Gannett Broadcasting	Arlington, VA	17.20	21
9	Hearst-Argyle Television Inc.	New York	16.10	32
10	USA Broadcasting Inc.	New York	15.50	13
11	Sinclair Broadcast Group Inc.	Baltimore	14.20	56
12	Paramount Stations Group Inc.	Los Angeles	13.60	19
13	Univision Communications Inc.	Los Angeles	13.50	13
14	A.H. Belo Corp.	Dallas	13.40	22
15	Telemundo Group Inc.	Hialeah, FL	10.70	8
16	Cox Broadcasting Inc.	Atlanta	9.60	11
17	Young Broadcasting Inc.	New York	9.00	13
18	E.W. Scripps Co.	Cincinnati	8.05	10
19	Hicks, Muse, Tate & Furst Inc.	Dallas	8.01	29
20	Shop at Home Inc.	Nashville, TN	7.70	6
21	Post-Newsweek Stations Inc.	Hartford, CT	7.20	6
22	Raycom Media Inc.	Montgomery, AL	6.60	30
23	Meredith Broadcast Group	Des Moines, IA	6.30	11
24	Media General Broadcast Group	Tampa	4.40	13
25	Clear Channel Communications	San Antonio	4.20	18

Source: *Broadcasting & Cable;* April 19, 1999

Top 20 US Cable Companies

Rank	Multiple System Operator	Basic Subscriptions
1	AT&T Broadband & Internet Services	10,870,350
2	Time Warner Cable	6,509,900
3	Comcast	5,387,659
4	MediaOne	5,127,548
5	TWE-Advance/Newhouse	4,500,000
6	Cox Communications	3,855,582
7	Cablevision Systems	3,438,975
8	Charter Communications	2,615,119
9	Adelphia Communications	2,263,429
10	Century Communications	1,471,397
11	InterMedia Partners	1,312,246
12	Falcon Communications	1,120,444
13	TCI/Time Warner	1,080,000
14	Lenfest Group	1,014,197
15	TCA Group	883,232
16	Cable One	736,843
17	FrontierVision Partners	702,362
18	Bresnan Communications	644,200
19	Cablecomm	636,200
20	Multimedia Cablevision	508,849

Source: *Cablevision;* August 30, 1999

Top 20 US Trade Book Publishers

Rank	Publisher	1998 Revenue ($ mil.)
1	Random House	2,020.0
2	Time Inc.	1,574.0
3	Reader's Digest	1,032.5
4	HarperCollins	737.0
5	Scholastic Inc.	787.0
6	Penguin Putnam	613.0
7	Simon & Schuster	583.3
8	Encyclopædia Britannica	465.0
9	Grolier Inc.	450.0
10	Harlequin	354.8
11	Holtzbrinck	275.0
12	Rodale Press	225.0
13	Hearst Book Group	210.0
14	Disney Publishing	165.0
15	Thomas Nelson	163.8
16	Barnes & Noble	160.0
17	IDG Books Worldwide	141.5
18	Golden Books	131.6
19	Andrews McMeel	115.0
20	DK Publishing	103.0

Taken from the pages of *Book Publishing Report*
Simba Information Inc. © 1999

Top 25 US Advertising Agencies by US Revenue

Rank	Agency	1998 Revenue ($ thou.)	Rank	Agency	1998 Revenue ($ thou.)
1	Grey Advertising	422,304	16	Campbell-Ewald	146,124
2	McCann-Erickson	421,000	17	MVBMS/EURO RSCG	116,400
3	Young & Rubicam	416,953	18	Arnold Communications	109,942
4	J. Walter Thompson	411,600	19	Lowe & Partners SMS	107,000
5	Leo Burnett Co.	396,280	20	Hill, Holliday, Connors, Cosmopulos	106,000
6	Foote, Cone & Belding	338,000			
7	DDB Needham	316,616	21	Campbell Mithun Esty	90,700
8	BBDO	307,000	22	Deutsch	86,390
9	Ogilvy & Mather	282,000	23	Publicis & Hal Riney	85,200
10	Saatchi & Saatchi	250,000	24	Publicis	83,000
11	Bozell	249,000	25	N.W. Ayer & Partners	79,800
12	Bates USA	228,000			
13	D'Arcy Masius Benton & Bowles	225,493			
14	TBWA Chiat/Day	223,380			
15	Ammirati Puris Lintas	155,602			

Source: *Adweek;* April 19, 1999

Top 25 Megabrands by 1998 Ad Spending

Rank	Brand, Product, or Service	Company	Total ($ mil.)
1	Chevrolet cars & trucks	General Motors Corp.	645.5
2	MCI telephone services	MCI WorldCom	636.2
3	Ford cars & trucks	Ford Division	621.4
4	Dodge cars & trucks	DaimlerChrysler	602.8
5	McDonald's restaurants	McDonald's Corp.	571.7
6	Sears stores	Sears, Roebuck & Co.	571.4
7	AT&T telephone services	AT&T Corp.	550.8
8	Toyota cars & trucks	Toyota Motor Sales USA	500.0
9	Sprint telephones services	Sprint Corp.	462.4
10	Burger King restaurants	Diageo	407.5
11	Circuit City stores	Circuit City Stores	403.7
12	Honda cars & trucks	American Honda Motor Co.	353.9
13	Macy's stores	Federated Department Stores	343.7
14	Nissan cars & trucks	Nissan Division	340.6
15	Chrysler cars & trucks	DaimlerChrysler	334.8
16	JCPenney stores	J. C. Penney Co.	318.5
17	Kmart stores	Kmart Corp.	309.6
18	General Mills cereals	General Mills	296.7
19	American Express credit cards	American Express	279.6
20	Kellogg's breakfast foods	Kellogg USA	278.7
21	IBM computers	IBM	270.3
22	General Motors cars & trucks	General Motors Corp.	262.4
23	Budweiser beers	Anheuser-Busch	261.0
24	Jeep vehicles	DaimlerChrysler	246.9
25	Oldsmobile cars & trucks	General Motors Corp.	242.3

Source: *Advertising Age;* July 12, 1999

Top 15 Advertisers in Daily Newspapers

Rank	Company	1998 Advertising ($ mil.)
1	Ford Motor Co. (local dealers)	529.82
2	Federated Dept. Stores	437.23
3	General Motors Corp. (local dealers)	408.00
4	May Dept. Stores Co.	382.70
5	DaimlerChrysler (local dealers)	342.63
6	Circuit City Stores	314.32
7	Toyota Motor Sales USA (local dealers)	276.24
8	Sears, Roebuck & Co.	228.60
9	Dayton Hudson Corp.	207.24
10	Dillard	201.65
11	Nissan Motor Corp. USA (local dealers)	184.82
12	J.C. Penney Co.	173.87
13	General Motors Corp. (dealer association)	150.31
14	American Honda Motor Co. (local dealers)	149.68
15	General Motors Corp.	147.90

Source: *Advertising Age;* April 26, 1999

Top 20 Films at US Box Office

Rank	Film	Distributor	1998 Box Office ($ mil.)
1	*Titanic**	Paramount	488.2
2	*Armageddon*	Buena Vista	201.6
3	*Saving Private Ryan*	DreamWorks	190.8
4	*There's Something About Mary*	Fox	174.4
5	*The Waterboy*	Buena Vista	147.9
6	*Dr. Dolittle*	Fox	144.2
7	*Deep Impact*	Paramount	140.5
8	*Godzilla*	Sony	136.3
9	*Rush Hour*	New Line Cinema	136.1
10	*Good Will Hunting**	Miramax	134.1
11	*Lethal Weapon 4*	Warner Bros.	130.4
12	*A Bug's Life*	Buena Vista	127.6
13	*The Truman Show*	Paramount	125.6
14	*As Good As It Gets**	Sony	124.1
15	*Mulan*	Buena Vista	120.6
16	*The Mask of Zorro*	Sony	93.7
17	*Enemy of the State*	Buena Vista	92.0
18	*Antz*	DreamWorks	88.7
19	*The Rugrats Movie*	Paramount	86.4
20	*The X-Files*	Fox	83.9

*1997 release; 1998 gross only
Source: *Variety;* January 11, 1999

Chain Store Age's Top 25 Chain Stores

Rank	Company	Headquarters	1998 Revenues ($ mil.)
1	Wal-Mart	Bentonville, AR	137,634,000
2	Sears, Roebuck and Co.	Hoffman Estates, IL	41,322,000
3	Kmart	Troy, MI	33,674,000
4	Dayton Hudson Corp.	Minneapolis	30,951,000
5	J. C. Penney	Plano, TX	30,678,000
6	The Home Depot	Atlanta	30,219,000
7	Kroger	Cincinnati	28,203,304
8	Safeway	Pleasanton, CA	24,484,200
9	Costco	Issaquah, WA	24,269,877
10	American Stores Co.	Salt Lake City	19,866,725
11	Dell Computer	Round Rock, TX	18,243,000
12	Ahold USA	Chantilly, VA	16,182,000
13	Albertson's	Boise, ID	16,005,115
14	Federated Department Stores	Cincinnati	15,833,000
15	Walgreen Co.	Deerfield, IL	15,307,000
16	CVS	Woonsocket, RI	15,273,600
17	Fred Meyer	Portland, OR	14,878,771
18	Winn-Dixie Stores	Jacksonville, FL	13,617,485
19	May Department Stores Co.	St. Louis	13,072,000
20	Rite Aid	Camp Hill, PA	12,731,900
21	Lowe's	North Wilksboro, NC	12,244,882
22	Publix	Lakeland, FL	12,067,125
23	Toys "R" Us	Paramus, NJ	11,170,000
24	Food Lion	Salisbury, NC	10,219,474
25	A&P	Montvale, NJ	10,179,358

Source: *Chain Store Age;* August 1999

Supermarket News' Top 25 Supermarket Companies

Rank	Company	1998 Revenues ($ bil.)	Rank	Company	1998 Revenues ($ bil.)
1	Kroger Co.	43.1	16	Wakefern Food Corp.	5.2
2	Albertson's	35.7	17	C&S Wholesale Grocers	5.1
3	Wal-Mart Supercenters	32.0	18	Super Kmart	4.4
4	Safeway	25.0	19	Nash Finch Co.	4.3
5	Ahold USA	19.7	20	Shaw's Supermarkets	4.2
6	SUPERVALU	17.8	21	Richfood Holdings	4.2
7	Fleming Companies	15.1	22	Giant Eagle	4.0
8	Winn-Dixie Stores	13.9	23	Pathmark Stores	3.7
9	Publix Super Markets	12.1	24	Hannaford Bros.	3.4
10	Loblaw Companies	11.0	25	Hy-Vee	3.2
11	A&P	10.5			
12	Food Lion	10.2			
13	Meijer Inc.	8.6			
14	Sobeys Canada	7.0			
15	H.E. Butt Grocery Co.	6.9			

Source: *Supermarket News;* January 25, 1999

Top 25 Restaurant Brands by Sales

Rank	Brand	Headquarters	Systemwide Sales* ($ mil.)
1	McDonald's Corp.	Oak Brook, IL	35,979.0
2	Burger King	Miami	10,333.0
3	KFC	Louisville, KY	8,446.0†
4	Pizza Hut	Dallas	7,800.0†
5	Wendy's	Dublin, OH	5,555.0
6	Taco Bell	Irvine, CA	5,000.0
7	Subway Sandwiches & Salads	Milford, CT	3,454.0†
8	Domino's Pizza	Ann Arbor, MI	3,224.0
9	Dairy Queen	Minneapolis	2,698.0†
10	Hardee's	Rocky Mountain, NC	2,476.0
11	Dunkin' Donuts	Randolph, MA	2,258.0
12	7-Eleven	Dallas	2,221.0
13	Arby's	Atlanta	2,200.0
14	Little Caesars	Detroit	2,193.0†
15	Sheraton Hotels	Boston	2,100.0
16	Applebee's Neighborhood Grill & Bar	Overland Park, KS	2,066.3
17	Denny's	Spartanburg, SC	1,960.0
18	Red Lobster	Orlando, FL	1,810.0
19	Outback Steakhouse	Tampa	1,522.0
20	T.G.I. Friday's	Dallas	1,440.0
21	Holiday Inn Worldwide	Atlanta	1,414.0†
22	Sonic Drive-Ins	Oklahoma City	1,389.2
23	Chili's Grill & Bar	Dallas	1,384.2
24	The Olive Garden	Orlando, FL	1,380.0
25	Jack In The Box	San Diego	1,224.1

* For calendar year 1998 or fiscal years ending between July 1, 1998, and June 30, 1999
† Estimate
Source: *Restaurants and Institutions;* July 15, 1999

Top 15 Convenience Store Companies by Number of Stores

Rank	Company	Headquarters	No. of Stores
1	Equilon Enterprises LLC	Houston	6,530
2	7-Eleven Inc.	Dallas	6,307
3	Mobil Corp.	Fairfax, VA	3,630
4	Tosco Corp.	Stamford, CT	3,099
5	BP Amoco plc	London	3,000
6	Chevron Corp.	San Francisco	2,700
7	Ultramar Diamond Shamrock Corp.	San Antonio	2,634
8	Speedway SuperAmerica LLC	Enon, Ohio	2,283
9	Alimentation Couche-Tard Inc.	Laval, Quebec	1,329
10	The Pantry Inc.	Sanford, NC	1,202
11	Casey's General Stores Inc.	Ankeny, IA	1,185
12	FEMSA Comercio S.A. de C.V.	Monterrey, Mexico	1,026
13	Atlantic Richfield Co.	Los Angeles	1,004
14	Exxon Corp.	Houston	1,000
15	Dillon Companies Inc.	Hutchinson, KS	797

Source: *Convenience Store News;* August 2, 1999

Top 25 Beverage Companies by Sales

Rank	Company	Headquarters	1998 Sales ($ mil.)
1	The Coca-Cola Company	Atlanta	18,813.0
2	Coca-Cola Enterprises, Inc.	Atlanta	13,414.0
3	PepsiCo. Inc.	Purchase, NY	11,373.0*
4	Anheuser-Busch Companies	St. Louis	9,238.6*
5	The Seagram Company, Ltd.	Montreal	4,670.0*
6	Philip Morris	New York	4,105.0*
7	FEMSA	Mexico City	2,824.0*
8	Panamerican Beverages Inc.	Mexico City	2,773.2
9	Southern Wine & Spirits	Miami	2,620.0
10	Cadbury Schweppes	Stamford, CT	1,989.7*
11	Adolph Coors	Golden, CO	1,899.5
12	Quaker Oats Company	Chicago	1,709.0*
13	Whitman Corporation	Rolling Meadows, IL	1,635.0
14	Sunbelt Beverage Corporation/ Charmer Industries	Astoria, NY	1,525.0
15	Brown-Forman Corporation	Louisville, KY	1,385.0*
16	The Stroh Brewery Company	Detroit, MI	1,330.0
17	National Distributing Company	Atlanta	1,275.0
18	Perrier Group of America	Greenwich, CT	1,272.9
19	Fortune Brands	Old Greenwich, CT	1,265.9*
20	E. & J. Gallo	Modesto, CA	1,250.0
21	Canandaigua Brands	Canandaigua, NY	1,213.8
22	Ocean Spray Cranberries	Lakeville-Middleboro, MA	1,200.0*
23	Young's Market Company	Los Angeles	1,045.0
24	Honickman Affiliates	Pennsauken, NJ	1,000.0*
24	Magnolia Marketing Company	New Orleans	1,000.0

* Represents beverage operations only
Source: *Beverage World;* July 15, 1999

Top 10 Soft Drinks

Rank	Brand	Company	1998 Gallonage (mil.)
1	Coca-Cola classic	Coca-Cola	3,122.1
2	Pepsi-Cola	PepsiCo	2,199.2
3	diet Coke	Coca-Cola	1,303.4
4	Mountain Dew	PepsiCo	1,017.6
5	Sprite	Coca-Cola	992.8
6	Dr Pepper	Cadbury Schweppes	899.1
7	Diet Pepsi	PepsiCo	759.6
8	7 UP	Cadbury Schweppes	316.4
9	caffeine free diet Coke	Coca-Cola	272.8
10	Minute Maid Orange*	Coca-Cola	189.4

* Includes regular and diet flavors, but total is predominantly regular Orange
Source: *Beverage World;* March 15, 1999

Software Magazine's Top 50 Software Companies by Revenue

Rank	Company	Worldwide 1998 ($ mil.)	Rank	Company	Worldwide 1998 ($ mil.)
1	Microsoft Corp.	16,327.0	26	Informix Software Inc.	637.1
2	IBM Corp.	11,863.0	27	Autodesk Inc.	617.1
3	Oracle Corp.	5,317.9	28	Symantec Corp.	614.0
4	Computer Associates International, Inc.	4,854.0	29	Acxiom Corp.	569.0
5	Hitachi Ltd.	4,184.0	30	J. D. Edwards & Co.	561.4
6	SAP AG	3,154.0	31	NCR Corp.	549.0
7	Hewlett-Packard Company	1,412.0	32	Intergraph Corp.	534.2
8	Sun Microsystems Inc.	1,367.3	33	Bull Worldwide Information Systems	492.0
9	Compaq Computer Corp.	1,174.0	34	Sterling Software Inc.	476.7
10	PeopleSoft Inc.	1,042.0	35	The Baan Company N.V.	460.7
11	Parametric Technology Corp.	1,009.3	36	EMC Corp.	445.0
12	Network Associates Inc.	990.1	37	Mentor Graphics Corp.	441.4
13	BMC Software Inc.	975.6	38	Hyperion Solutions	424.7
14	Cadence Design Systems Inc.	960.3	39	System Software Associates	421.0
15	Compuware Corp.	928.8	40	Siebel Systems Inc.	392.0
16	Adobe Systems Inc.	894.8	41	Rational Software Corp.	374.0
17	Sybase Inc.	867.5	42	GEAC Computer Corp. Ltd.	371.5
18	SAS Institute Inc.	846.0	43	JBA International Inc.	347.3
19	The Learning Company Inc.	839.3	44	Seagate Software	324.8
20	Andersen Consulting LLP	830.0	45	Candle Corp.	319.1
21	SunGard Data Systems Inc.	804.9	46	Sterling Commerce Inc.	316.2
22	Unisys Corp.	720.8	47	Merant Plc.	303.2
23	Platinum Technology Inc.	714.4	48	Attachmate Corp.	300.0
24	Novell Inc.	685.0	49	Environmental Systems Research Institute Inc.	278.0
25	Synopsys Inc.	682.8	50	i2 Technologies Inc.	273.0

*Total software revenue includes license fees and revenue from product maintenance and support.
Source: *Software Magazine;* June 1999

Computer Retail Week's Top 50 Computer Retailers

Rank	Company	1998 US Sales* ($ mil.)	Rank	Company	1998 US Sales* ($ mil.)
1	CompUSA	5,750.0	26	Future Shop	222.6
2	Best Buy	3,935.3	27	Babbage's Etc.	200.0
3	Office Depot	2,900.0	28	Onsale	168.0
4	Micro Warehouse	2,324.0	29	Computer Renaissance	150.0
5	Circuit City Stores	2,081.5	30	Damark	148.7
6	Staples	1,910.0	31	The Good Guys	144.9
7	CDW Computer Centers	1,675.0	32	QVC	130.0
8	OfficeMax	1,244.5	33	Nationwide Computers & Electronics	125.0
9	Micro Center	1,100.0	34	Barnes & Noble	123.7
10	Global DirectMail	1,083.0	35	Buy.com	110.0
11	Sam's Club	946.4	36	ComputerWare	100.0
12	Sears	905.0	37	Egghead.com	100.0
13	Insight Enterprises	900.0	38	Fingerhut	100.0
14	Wal-Mart Stores	890.0	39	NECX	100.0
15	Fry's Electronics	875.4	40	RCS Computer Experience	90.0
16	Gateway Country Stores	745.0	41	Computown	85.0
17	PC Connection	715.8	42	SBI Computer Warehouse	85.0
18	Creative Computers	710.0	43	PC Club	80.0
19	Costco	562.3	44	Cyberian Outpost	75.0
20	Multiple Zones	463.5	45	BJ's Wholesale Club	74.0
21	PC Warehouse	389.0	46	Toys "R" Us	73.8
22	RadioShack	356.9	47	Computer Town	70.0
23	J&R Computer World	330.8	48	DataVision	70.0
24	Army Air Force Exchange	266.3	49	Target Stores	70.0
25	Electronics Boutique	245.0	50	Kmart	68.2

*Stores selling PC-related merchandise
Source: *Computer Retail Week;* January 4, 1999

Top 25 Internet Companies by Sales

Rank	Company	Category	Sales ($ mil.)
1	America Online	ISP, portal	4.8B
2	Amazon.com	Retail	1B
3	E*Trade Group	Financial service	435
4	Yahoo!	Portal	390
5	PSINet	ISP	390
6	USWeb/CKS	Consulting	292
7	AmeriTrade	Financial service	274
8	ONSALE	Retail	266
9	EarthLink Network	ISP	254
10	CheckFree	Financial service	250
11	MindSpring	ISP	215
12	priceline.com	Retail	189
13	Security Dynamics	Security	188
14	Verio	ISP	188
15	Check Point	Security	170
16	Excite@Home	ISP, portal	159
17	CMGI	Miscellaneous	151
18	Network Solutions	Domain registrar	142
19	Prodigy	ISP	142
20	eBay	Retail	125
21	uBid	Retail	119
22	barnesandnoble.com	Retail	113
23	Concentric Network	ISP	110
24	Lycos	Portal	109
25	Exodus	ISP	108

Source: *Internet World;* September 15, 1999

Top 10 Telecommunications Companies

Rank	Company	Headquarters	1998 Sales ($ bil.)
1	AT&T	New York	53.2
2	Bell Atlantic	New York	31.5
3	MCI WorldCom	Jackson, MS	30.4
4	SBC	San Antonio, TX	28.7
5	GTE	Irving, TX	25.4
6	BellSouth	Atlanta	23.1
7	Ameritech	Chicago	17.1
8	Sprint	Westwood	16.0
9	Alltel	Little Rock, AR	5.1
10	Frontier	Rochester, NY	2.5

Source: *Brandweek;* June 21, 1999

Top 20 Semiconductor Manufacturers

Rank	Company	Segment Revenue ($ mil.)	Rank	Company	Segment Revenue ($ mil.)
1	Intel	22,332.1	11	Amkor Technology	1,568.0
2	Motorola	6,761.5	12	TSMC	1,559.3
3	Texas Instruments	6,345.0	13	LSI Logic	1,490.7
4	STMicroelectronics	4,247.8	14	Micron Technology	1,311.4
5	Applied Materials	3,476.5	15	Analog Devices	1,200.3
6	Tokyo Electron	3,252.4	16	Conexant Systems	1,200.0
7	Lucent Technologies	3,062.7	17	Fujitsu	1,123.9
8	Advanced Micro Devices	2,542.1	18	Atmel	1,111.1
9	National Semiconductor	2,139.8	19	ATI Technologies	930.0
10	Siemens	1,622.7	20	Kyocera	923.5

Source: *Electronic Business;* July 1999

Top 15 Government, Military & Aerospace Contractors

Rank	Company	Segment Revenue ($ mil.)
1	Raytheon	14,822.0
2	Lockheed Martin	7,342.0
3	General Electric Co. (GEC)	6,115.6
4	General Motors	5,968.0
5	TRW	4,900.2
6	Northrop Grumman	4,006.0
7	Litton Industries	2,841.1
8	Honeywell	2,528.0
9	The Boeing Company	2,527.0
10	Rockwell International	2,318.3
11	AlliedSignal	2,154.3
12	ITT Industries	1,220.3
13	Harris	937.1
14	Motorola	881.9
15	Sagem	739.3

Source: *Electronic Business;* July 1999

Top 10 Companies Granted Patents in 1998

Rank	Organization	1998 Patents
1	IBM	2,657
2	Canon Kabushiki Kaisha	1,928
3	NEC Corporation	1,627
4	Motorola Inc.	1,406
5	Sony Corporation	1,316
6	Samsung Electronics Co., Ltd.	1,304
7	Fujitsu Limited	1,189
8	Toshiba Corporation	1,170
9	Eastman Kodak Company	1,124
10	Hitachi, Ltd.	1,094

Source: US Patent & Trademark Office
(www.uspto.gov); January 7, 1999

US Car and Light-Truck Sales

Make	Cars Sold (thou.)	Trucks Sold (thou.)	Total (thou.)	Market Share % 1998	1997
Chevrolet	876	1,542	2,418	15.5	16.3
Pontiac	477	59	536	3.4	4.0
GMC	-	451	451	2.9	3.0
Buick	398	-	398	2.6	2.9
Oldsmobile	262	68	330	2.1	2.0
Saturn	232	-	232	1.5	1.7
Cadillac	182	5	187	1.2	1.2
General Motors	**2,427**	**2,125**	**4,552**	**29.2**	**31.1**
Ford	1,069	2,219	3,288	21.1	21.2
Mercury	324	86	410	2.6	2.9
Lincoln	143	44	187	1.2	1.1
Ford	**1,536**	**2,349**	**3,885**	**24.9**	**25.2**
Dodge	360	1,083	1,443	9.3	8.1
Jeep	-	459	459	2.9	3.1
Chrysler	236	72	308	2.0	1.8
Plymouth	140	157	297	1.9	2.1
Mercedes	127	43	170	1.1	0.8
Eagle	3	-	3	0.1	0.1
DaimlerChrysler	**866**	**1,814**	**2,680**	**17.3**	**16.0**
Toyota	765	440	1,205	7.7	7.5
Lexus	103	53	156	1.0	0.6
Toyota/Lexus	**868**	**493**	**1,361**	**8.7**	**8.1**
Honda	752	147	899	5.8	5.5
Acura	109	2	111	0.7	0.7
Honda/Acura	**861**	**149**	**1,010**	**6.5**	**6.2**
Nissan	368	190	558	3.6	4.4
Infiniti	44	20	64	0.4	0.4
Nissan/Infiniti	**412**	**210**	**622**	**4.0**	**4.8**
Mazda	187	54	241	1.5	1.5
Mitsubishi	148	43	191	1.2	1.2
Subaru	148	-	148	0.9	0.9
Isuzu	-	102	102	0.7	0.6
Hyundai	90	-	90	0.6	0.7
Kia	54	29	83	0.5	0.4
Suzuki	16	21	37	0.2	0.2
Daewoo	2	-	2	0.1	0.0
Other	1	-	1	0.1	0.0
Other — Asia	**646**	**249**	**895**	**5.8**	**5.5**
VW	218	2	220	1.4	0.9
BMW	132	-	132	0.8	0.8
Volvo	101	-	101	0.6	0.6
Audi	48	-	48	0.3	0.2
Saab	31	-	31	0.2	0.2
Jaguar	23	-	23	0.1	0.1
Land Rover	-	21	21	0.1	0.2
Porsche	17	-	17	0.1	0.1
Other — Europe	**570**	**23**	**593**	**3.6**	**3.1**
Total	**8,186**	**7,412**	**15,598**	**100.0**	**100.0**

Source: *Automotive News;* January 11, 1999

Top 15 Dealer Groups by New-Vehicle Sales Volume

Rank	Dealer Group	New-Vehicle Sales Volume	Total Revenue ($ mil.)
1	AutoNation Inc.	286,179	13,494.4
2	United Auto Group Inc.	77,403	3,343.1
3	Asbury Automotive Group	68,000	3,000.0
4	V.T. Inc.	64,296	2,646.5
5	Hendrick Automotive Group	56,667	2,235.1
6	Group 1 Automotive Inc.	39,822	1,631.0
7	Sonic Automotive Inc.	37,674	1,484.4
8	Planet Automotive	37,000	920.1
9	Bill Heard Enterprises Inc.	27,895	1,131.4
10	Penske Automotive Group	24,514	920.1
11	Ed Morse Automotive Group	23,441	1,053.4
12	Courtesy Auto Group	22,563	872.9
13	Serra Investments Inc.	22,087	810.9
14	Larry H. Miller Group	22,058	1,131.3
15	Rosenthal Automotive Organization	20,081	748.3

Source: *Automotive News;* April 19, 1999

Top 10 Auto Parts Retailers

Rank	Chain	No. of Stores	Sales ($ mil.)
1	AutoZone	2,700	3,200.0
2	Advance Auto Parts	1,567	1,220.8
3	General Parts Inc. (CARQUEST Auto Parts)	1,070	1,400.0
4	CSK Auto, Inc. (Checker/Schucks/Kragen)	893	1,090.4
5	Genuine Parts	758	3,300.0
6	Pep Boys	638	2,398.7
7	Discount Auto Parts	551	515.0
8	O'Reilly Auto Parts	521	616.0
9	Fisher Auto Parts	260	200.0
10	Midwest Auto Parts Dist. (Bumper to Bumper)	260	110.0

Source: *Automotive Marketing;* July 1999

Top 10 Vehicle Sellers

Rank	Vehicle	1998 Number Sold
1	Ford F-Series pickup	836,629
2	Chevrolet C/K pickup	555,989
3	Ford Explorer	431,488
4	Toyota Camry	429,575
5	Dodge Ram pickup	410,130
6	Honda Accord	401,071
7	Ford Taurus	371,074
8	Honda Civic	334,562
9	Ford Ranger	328,136
10	Dodge Caravan	293,819

Source: *Automotive News;* January 11, 1999

The World's Top 25 Airlines

Rank	Airline	1998 No. of RPKs*
1	United	200,496
2	American	175,309
3	Delta	166,271
4	British Airways	112,029
5	Northwest	107,381
6	Continental	86,741
7	Japan Airlines	78,813
8	Air France	74,542
9	Lufthansa	71,897
10	US Airways	66,564
11	Qantas	58,619
12	Singapore	57,737
13	KLM	57,304
14	All Nippon	53,825
15	Southwest	50,553
16	Cathay Pacific	40,679
17	TWA	39,401
18	Air Canada	37,346
19	Alitalia	35,527
20	Thai International	34,448
21	Iberia	32,521
22	Korean	32,277
23	Swissair	30,283
24	Varig	27,056
25	Malaysia	27,022

* revenue passenger kilometers

Source: *Air Transport World;* July 1999

The Top 25 Airline Fleets

Rank	Airline	No. of Aircraft
1	American	648
2	FedEx	625
3	Delta	605
4	United	577
5	Northwest	409
6	US Airways	381
7	Continental	353
8	Southwest	280
9	British Airways	271
10	Air France	227
11	Lufthansa	224
12	UPS	217
13	TWA	206
14	SAS	185
15	Air Canada	152
15	Alitalia	152
17	All Nippon	143
17	Qantas	143
19	Japan Airlines	138
20	Continental Express	135
21	Iberia	129
22	Aeroflot Russian	120
23	Mesa Air Group	115
24	Korean	113
25	Saudi Arabian	110
25	America West	110

Source: *Air Transport World;* July 1999

The 30 Largest US Trucking Companies

Rank	Company	1998 Revenue ($ thou.)	Rank	Company	1998 Revenue ($ thou.)
1	United Parcel Service	24,788,000	16	Allied Holdings	1,026,799
2	FDX Corp.	15,872,810	17	American Freightways Corp.	986,286
3	CNF Transportation	4,941,490	18	North American Van Lines	966,500
4	Yellow Corp.	2,900,577	19	Penske Truck Leasing Corp.	911,000
5	Schneider National	2,710,000	20	Swift Transportation Co.	873,433
6	Roadway Express	2,654,094	21	Werner Enterprises	863,417
7	Consolidated Freightways Corp.	2,238,423	22	Watkins Associated Industries	806,051
8	J.B. Hunt Transport Services	1,841,628	23	U.S. Xpress Enterprises	581,401
9	USFreightways Corp.	1,834,893	24	M.S. Carriers	528,841
10	UniGroup Inc.	1,807,496	25	Estes Express Lines	518,730
11	Arkansas Best Corp.	1,651,453	26	Atlas World Group	513,000
12	Ryder Integrated Logistics	1,501,000	27	Crete Carrier Corp.	511,563
13	NFC Americas	1,485,495	28	Comcar Industries	462,528
14	Landstar System	1,283,607	29	Southeastern Freight Lines	435,044
15	Overnite Transportation Co.	1,033,900	30	Averitt Express	428,893

Source: *Transport Topics;* August 9, 1999

The 30 Companies in the Dow Jones Industrial Average

Company	Ticker	Company	Ticker
AlliedSignal Inc.	ALD	Hewlett-Packard Co.	HWP
Aluminum Co. of America	AA	International Business Machines Corp.	IBM
American Express Co.	AXP	International Paper Co.	IP
AT&T Corp.	T	J.P. Morgan & Co.	JPM
Boeing Co.	BA	Johnson & Johnson	JNJ
Caterpillar Inc.	CAT	McDonald's Corp.	MCD
Chevron Corp.	CHV	Merck & Co.	MRK
Citigroup Inc.	C	Minnesota Mining & Manufacturing Co.	MMM
Coca-Cola Co.	KO	Philip Morris Cos.	MO
DuPont Co.	DD	Procter & Gamble Co.	PG
Eastman Kodak Co.	EK	Sears, Roebuck & Co.	S
Exxon Corp.	XON	Union Carbide Corp.	UK
General Electric Co.	GE	United Technologies Corp.	UTX
General Motors Corp.	GM	Wal-Mart Stores Inc.	WMT
Goodyear Tire & Rubber Co.	GT	Walt Disney Co.	DIS

Source: Dow Jones & Company (averages.dowjones.com); September 13, 1999

The 20 Companies in the Dow Jones Transportation Average

Company	Ticker
Airborne Freight Corp.	ABF
Alexander & Baldwin, Inc.	ALEX
AMR Corp.	AMR
Burlington Northern Santa Fe Corp.	BNI
CNF Transportation, Inc.	CNF
CSX Corp.	CSX
Delta Air Lines, Inc.	DAL
FDX Corp.	FDX
GATX Corp.	GMT
J.B. Hunt Transportation Services	JBHT
Norfolk Southern Corp.	NSC
Northwest Airlines Corp.	NWAC
Roadway Express, Inc.	ROAD
Ryder System, Inc.	R
Southwest Airlines Co.	LUV
UAL Corp.	UAL
Union Pacific Corp.	UNP
US Airways Group, Inc.	U
USFreightways	USFC
Yellow Corp.	YELL

Source: Dow Jones & Company (averages.dowjones.com); September 13, 1999

The 15 Companies in the Dow Jones Utility Average

Company	Ticker
American Electric Power Co.	AEP
Columbia Energy Group	CG
Consolidated Edison Inc.	ED
Consolidated Natural Gas Co.	CNG
Duke Energy Corp.	DUK
Edison International	EIX
Enron Corp.	ENE
Reliant Energy	REI
PECO Energy Co.	PE
PG&E Corp.	PCG
Public Service Enterprise Group	PEG
Southern Co.	SO
Texas Utilities Co.	TXU
Unicom Corp.	UCM
Williams Cos.	WMB

Source: Dow Jones & Company (averages.dowjones.com); September 13, 1999

The Companies in the Standard & Poor's 500

3Com Corp.
Abbott Labs
ADC Telecommunications
Adobe Systems
Advanced Micro Devices
AES Corp.
Aetna Inc.
AFLAC Corporation
Air Products & Chemicals
Alberto-Culver
Albertson's
Alcan Aluminium Ltd.
Alcoa Inc.
Allegheny Teledyne Inc
Allergan, Inc.
Allied Waste Industries
AlliedSignal
Allstate Corp.
ALLTEL Corp.
ALZA Corp. Cl. A
Amerada Hess
Ameren Corp.
America Online
American Electric Power
American Express
American General
American Greetings Cl A
American Home Products
American Int'l. Group
Ameritech
Amgen
AMR Corp.
AmSouth Bancorporation
Anadarko Petroleum
Andrew Corp.
Anheuser-Busch
Aon Corp.
Apache Corp.
Apple Computer
Applied Materials
Archer Daniels Midland
Armstrong World
ASARCO Inc.
Ashland Inc.
Associates First Capital
AT&T Corp.
Atlantic Richfield
Autodesk, Inc.
Automatic Data Processing Inc.
AutoZone Inc.
Avery Dennison Corp.
Avon Products
Baker Hughes
Ball Corp.
Bank of America Corp.
Bank of New York
Bank One Corp.
Bankboston Corp.
Bard (C.R.) Inc.
Barrick Gold Corp.
Bausch & Lomb
Baxter International Inc.
BB&T Corporation
Bear Stearns Companies
Becton, Dickinson
Bell Atlantic
BellSouth
Bemis Company
Best Buy Co., Inc.

BestFoods Inc.
Bethlehem Steel
Biomet, Inc.
Black & Decker Corp.
Block (H&R)
BMC Software
Boeing Company
Boise Cascade
Boston Scientific
Briggs & Stratton
Bristol-Myers Squibb
Brown-Forman Corp.
Brunswick Corp.
Burlington Northern Santa Fe Corp.
Burlington Resources
Cabletron Systems
Campbell Soup
Capital One Financial
Cardinal Health, Inc.
Carnival Corp.
Carolina Power & Light
Case Corp.
Caterpillar Inc.
CBS Corp.
Cendant Corporation
Centex Corp.
Central & South West
CenturyTel, Inc.
Ceridian Corp.
Champion International
Charles Schwab
Chase Manhattan
Chevron Corp.
Chubb Corp.
CIGNA Corp.
Cincinnati Financial
CINergy Corp.
Circuit City Group
Cisco Systems
Citigroup Inc.
Clear Channel Communications
Clorox Co.
CMS Energy
Coastal Corp.
Coca Cola Co.
Coca-Cola Enterprises
Colgate-Palmolive
Columbia Energy Group
Columbia/HCA Healthcare Corp.
Comcast Class A Special
Comerica Inc.
COMPAQ Computer
Computer Associates Intl.
Computer Sciences Corp.
Compuware Corp.
ConAgra Inc.
Conoco Inc.
Conseco Inc.
Consolidated Edison Hldgs.
Consolidated Natural Gas
Consolidated Stores
Constellation Energy Group
Cooper Industries
Cooper Tire & Rubber
Coors (Adolph)
Corning Inc.
Costco Wholesale Corp.
Countrywide Credit Industries
Crane Company

Crown Cork & Seal
CSX Corp.
Cummins Engine Co., Inc.
CVS Corp.
Cyprus Amax Minerals Co.
Dana Corp.
Danaher Corp.
Darden Restaurants
Data General
Dayton Hudson
Deere & Co.
Dell Computer
Delphi Automotive Systems
Delta Air Lines
Deluxe Corp.
Dillard Inc.
Dollar General
Dominion Resources
Donnelley (R.R.) & Sons
Dover Corp.
Dow Chemical
Dow Jones & Co.
DTE Energy Co.
Du Pont (E.I.)
Duke Energy
Dun & Bradstreet Corp. (New)
E G & G Inc.
Eastern Enterprises
Eastman Chemical
Eastman Kodak
Eaton Corp.
Ecolab Inc.
Edison Int'l
Electronic Data Systems
EMC Corp.
Emerson Electric
Engelhard Corp.
Enron Corp.
Entergy Corp.
Equifax Inc.
Exxon Corp.
Fannie Mae
FDX Holding Corp.
Federal Home Loan Mtg.
Federated Dept. Stores
Fifth Third Bancorp
First Data
First Union Corp.
Firstar Corporation
FirstEnergy Corp.
Fleet Financial Group
Fleetwood Enterprises
Florida Progress
Fluor Corp.
FMC Corp.
Ford Motor
Fort James Corp.
Fortune Brands, Inc.
Foster Wheeler
FPL Group
Franklin Resources Inc.
Freeport-McMoran Copper & Gold
Frontier Corp.
Fruit of the Loom Ltd. Hldg. Co.
Gannett Co.
Gap (The)
Gateway, Inc.
General Dynamics
General Electric

Source: Standard & Poor's Advisor Insight (www.advisorinsight.com/pub/indexes/index.html); July 29, 1999

The Companies in the Standard & Poor's 500 (continued)

General Instrument Corp.
General Mills
General Motors
Genuine Parts
Georgia-Pacific Group
Gillette Co.
Golden West Financial
Goodrich (B.F.)
Goodyear Tire & Rubber
GPU Inc.
Grace (W.R.) & Co. (New)
Grainger (W.W.) Inc.
Great A & P Tea Company
Great Lakes Chemical
GTE Corp.
Guidant Corp.
Halliburton Co.
Harcourt General Inc.
Harrah's Entertainment
Harris Corp.
Hartford Financial Svc. Group
Hasbro Inc.
HCR Manor Care
HEALTHSOUTH Corp.
Heinz (H.J.)
Helmerich & Payne
Hercules, Inc.
Hershey Foods
Hewlett-Packard
Hilton Hotels
Home Depot
Homestake Mining
Honeywell
Household International
Humana Inc.
Huntington Bancshares
IKON Office Solutions
Illinois Tool Works
IMS Health Inc.
Inco, Ltd.
Ingersoll-Rand
Intel Corp.
IBM
Int'l Flavors and Fragrances
International Paper
Interpublic Group
ITT Industries, Inc.
Jefferson-Pilot
Johnson & Johnson
Johnson Controls
Jostens Inc.
Kmart
Kansas City Southern Ind.
Kaufman & Broad Home Corp.
Kellogg Co.
Kerr-McGee
KeyCorp
Kimberly-Clark
King World Productions
KLA-Tencor Corp.
Knight Ridder Inc.
Kohl's Corp.
Kroger Co.
Laidlaw Inc.
Lehman Bros. Hldgs.
Lexmark Int'l. Group A
Lilly (Eli) & Co.
Limited, Inc.
Lincoln National

Liz Claiborne, Inc.
Lockheed Martin Corp.
Loews Corp.
Longs Drug Stores
Louisiana Pacific
Lowe's Companies
LSI Logic
Lucent Technologies
Mallinckrodt Inc.
Marriott Int'l. (New)
Marsh & McLennan
Masco Corp.
Mattel, Inc.
May Dept. Stores
Maytag Corp.
MBIA Inc.
MBNA Corp.
McDermott International
McDonald's Corp.
McGraw-Hill
MCI WorldCom
McKesson HBOC Inc.
Mead Corp.
MediaOne Group Inc.
Medtronic Inc.
Mellon Bank Corp.
Mercantile Bancorp
Merck & Co.
Meredith Corp.
Merrill Lynch
MGIC Investment
Micron Technology
Microsoft Corp.
Milacron Inc.
Millipore Corp.
Minnesota Mining & Mfg.
Mirage Resorts
Mobil Corp.
Monsanto Company
Morgan (J.P.) & Co.
Morgan Stanley, Dean Witter & Co.
Motorola Inc.
Nabisco Group Hldgs.
NACCO Ind. Cl. A
National City Corp.
National Semiconductor
National Service Ind.
Navistar International Corp.
Network Appliance
New Century Energies
New York Times Cl. A
Newell Rubbermaid Inc.
Newmont Mining
NEXTEL Communications
Niagara Mohawk Hldgs Inc.
NICOR Inc.
NIKE Inc.
Nordstrom
Norfolk Southern Corp.
Nortel Networks Corp.
Northern States Power
Northern Trust Corp.
Northrop Grumman Corp.
Novell Inc.
Nucor Corp.
Occidental Petroleum
Office Depot
Omnicom Group
ONEOK Inc.

Oracle Corp.
Owens Corning
Owens-Illinois
PACCAR Inc.
PacifiCorp
PaineWebber Group
Pall Corp.
Parametric Technology
Parker-Hannifin
Paychex Inc.
PE Corp.-PE Biosystems Group
PECO Energy Co.
Penney (J.C.)
Peoples Energy
PeopleSoft Inc.
Pep Boys
PepsiCo Inc.
Pfizer, Inc.
PG&E Corp.
Pharmacia & Upjohn, Inc.
Phelps Dodge
Philip Morris
Phillips Petroleum
Pioneer Hi-Bred Int'l
Pitney-Bowes
Placer Dome Inc.
PNC Bank Corp.
Polaroid Corp.
Potlatch Corp.
PP & L Resources
PPG Industries
Praxair, Inc.
Procter & Gamble
Progressive Corp.
Providian Financial Corp.
Public Serv. Enterprise Inc.
Pulte Corp.
Quaker Oats
QUALCOMM Inc.
Ralston-Ralston Purina Group
Raytheon Co.
Reebok International
Regions Financial Corp.
Reliant Energy
Republic New York
Reynolds Metals
Rite Aid
Rockwell International
Rohm and Haas
Rowan Cos.
Royal Dutch Petroleum
Russell Corp.
Ryder System
SAFECO Corp.
Safeway Inc.
Sara Lee Corp.
SBC Communications Inc.
Schering-Plough
Schlumberger Ltd.
Scientific-Atlanta
Seagate Technology
Seagram Co. Ltd.
Sealed Air Corp. (New)
Sears, Roebuck & Co.
Sempra Energy
Service Corp. International
Shared Medical Systems
Sherwin-Williams
Sigma-Aldrich

The Companies in the Standard & Poor's 500 (continued)

Silicon Graphics
SLM Holding Corp.
Snap-On Inc.
Solectron Corp.
Sonat Inc.
Southern Co.
SouthTrust Corp.
Southwest Airlines
Springs Industries Inc.
Sprint Corp. FON Group
Sprint Corp. PCS Group
St Jude Medical
St. Paul Companies
Stanley Works
Staples Inc.
State Street Corp.
Summit Bancorp
Sun Microsystems
Sunoco Inc.
SunTrust Banks
SUPERVALU Inc.
Synovus Financial
Sysco Corp.
Tandy Corp.
Tektronix Inc.
Tellabs, Inc.
Temple-Inland
Tenet Healthcare Corp.
Tenneco Inc.

Texaco Inc.
Texas Instruments
Texas Utilities Hldg.Cos.
Textron Inc.
Thermo Electron
Thomas & Betts
Time Warner Inc.
Times Mirror
Timken Co.
TJX Companies Inc.
Torchmark Corp.
Toys "R" Us Hldg. Cos.
Tribune Co.
TRICON Global Restaurants
TRW Inc.
Tupperware Corp.
Tyco International
U.S. Bancorp
Unicom Corp.
Unilever N.V.
Union Carbide
Union Pacific
Union Pacific Resources Group
Union Planters
Unisys Corp.
United HealthCare Corp.
United Technologies
Unocal Corp.
UNUMProvident Corp.

U S West Inc.
USAirways Group Inc.
UST Inc.
USX-Marathon Group
USX-U.S. Steel Group
V.F. Corp.
Viacom Inc.
Vulcan Materials
Wachovia Corp.
Wal-Mart Stores
Walgreen Co.
Walt Disney Co.
Warner-Lambert
Washington Mutual, Inc.
Waste Management (New)
Watson Pharmaceuticals
WellPoint Health Networks
Wells Fargo & Co. (New)
Wendy's International
Westvaco Corp.
Weyerhaeuser Corp.
Whirlpool Corp.
Willamette Industries
Williams Companies
Winn-Dixie
Worthington Ind.
Wrigley (Wm.) Jr.
Xerox Corp.

The 400 Companies in the Standard & Poor's Midcap Index

Abercrombie & Fitch Co.
ACNielsen
Acuson Corp.
Adtran Inc.
Affiliated Computer Svcs.
AGCO Corp.
Airborne Freight
Airgas Inc.
AK Steel Hldg. Corp.
Alaska Air Group
Albany International
Albemarle Corp.
Alexander & Baldwin
Allegheny Energy Inc.
Alliant Energy
Allmerica Financial
Altera Corp.
Ambac Financial Group
American Financial Group Hldg.
American Power Conversion
American Standard Cos.
American Water Works
Ametek, Inc.
Analog Devices
Apollo Group
Apria Healthcare Group
Arnold Ind.
Arrow Electronics

Arvin Industries
Associated Banc-Corp
Astoria Financial
AGL Resources Ltd.
Atmel Corp.
Avnet, Inc
Bandag Inc.
Banta Corp.
Barnes & Noble
Beckman Coulter Inc.
Bed Bath & Beyond
Belo (A.H.) Corp.
Bergen Brunswig
Beverly Enterprises (New)
Biogen, Inc.
BJ Services
BJ's Wholesale Club
Black Hills
Blyth Industries
Bob Evans Farms
Borders Group
Borg-Warner Automotive
Bowater Inc.
Brinker International
Buffets Inc.
Burlington Industries
Cabot Corp.
Cadence Design Systems

Callaway Golf Co.
Calpine Corp.
Cambridge Technology Partners
Carlisle Companies
Carpenter Technology
Carter-Wallace
CBRL Group, Inc.
CCB Financial
Centocor Inc.
Charter One Financial
Chesapeake Corp.
Chiron Corp.
Chris-Craft Industries
Church & Dwight
Cincinnati Bell
Cintas Corporation
Cirrus Logic
Citrix Systems
City National Corp.
CK Witco Corporation
Claire's Stores
Clayton Homes
Cleco Corp. Hldg. Co.
Cleveland-Cliffs
CMP Group Inc. Hldg. Co.
CNF Transportation Inc.
Comair Holdings
Comdisco, Inc.

Source: Standard & Poor's Advisor Insight (www.advisorinsight.com/pub/indexes/index.html); July 29, 1999

Compass Bancshares
CompUSA Inc.
COMSAT Corp.
Comverse Technology
Concord EFS Inc.
Conectiv
Consolidated Papers
Convergys Corp.
Cordant Technologies
Covance Inc.
Cypress Semiconductor
Cytec Industries
Dean Foods
Dentsply Int'l
Devon Energy Corp. (New)
Dexter Corp.
Dial Corp.
Diebold, Inc.
Dime Bancorp Inc.
Dole Foods
Dollar Tree Stores
Donaldson Co.
DPL Incorporated
Dreyer's Grand Ice Cream
DST Systems Inc.
E*Trade Group
Edwards (A.G.), Inc.
El Paso Energy
Electronic Arts
Energy East
Enesco Group
ENSCO Int'l
Ethyl Corp.
Everest Reinsurance Hldgs.
Family Dollar Stores
Fastenal Company
Federal Signal
Federal-Mogul
Ferro Corp.
FINOVA Group Inc.
First Health Group Inc.
First Security Corp. (Utah)
First Tennessee National
First Virginia Banks
FIserv Inc.
Flowers Industries
Flowserve Corp.
Forest Laboratories
Foundation Health Sys Inc.
Fuller (H.B.) Co.
Furniture Brands Int'l.
Gartner Group
GATX Corp.

GenCorp
Genzyme Corp.
Georgia Gulf
Gilead Sciences
P.H. Glatfelter Co.
Global Marine
Granite Construction
Greenpoint Financial Corp.
GTECH Holdings Corp.
Hanna (M.A.)
Hannaford Bros.
Harley-Davidson
Harsco Corp.
Harte-Hanks, Inc.
Hawaiian Electric Industries
Health Management Assoc.
Hispanic Broadcasting 'A'
Heilig-Meyers Co.
Hibernia Corp.
Hillenbrand Industries
HON Industries
Horace Mann Educators
Hormel Foods Corp.
Houghton Mifflin
HSB Group Inc.
Hubbell Inc. (Class B)
Hunt (J.B.) Transport Serv Inc.
IBP, Inc.
ICN Pharmaceuticals
IDACORP Inc. Hldg. Co.
Illinova Corp.
Imation Corp.
IMC Global Inc.
Indiana Energy
Informix Corp.
Integrated Devices Tech
International Game Technology
International Multifoods
Interstate Bakeries
Intuit, Inc.
Investment Technology Group
  (New)
IPALCO Enterprises
IVAX Corp.
Jabil Circuit
Jacobs Engineering Group
Jones Apparel Group
K N Energy
Kansas City Power & Light
Kaydon Corp.
Keane Inc.
Kelly Services
Kennametal Inc.

KeySpan Corp.
Keystone Financial
Lancaster Colony
Lance, Inc.
Lands' End
Lear Corporation
Lee Enterprises
Legato Systems Inc.
Leggett & Platt
LG&E Energy
Lincare Holdings
Linear Technology Corp.
Litton Industries
Lone Star Steakhouse
Longview Fibre
Lubrizol Corp.
Lyondell Chemical Co.
MagneTek, Inc.
Mandalay Resort Group
Manpower Inc.
Mark IV Industries
Marshall & Ilsley Corp.
Martin Marietta Materials
Maxim Integrated Prod
MAXXAM Inc.
McCormick & Co.
MCN Energy Group Inc.
Media General
MedImmune Inc.
Mentor Graphics
Mercantile Bankshares
Meritor Automotive Inc.
Micro Warehouse, Inc.
Microchip Technology
MidAmerican Energy Hldgs.
  (New)
Millennium Pharmaceuticals
Miller (Herman)
Minerals Technologies
MiniMed Inc.
Minnesota Power Inc.
Modine Mfg.
Modis Professional Svc.
Mohawk Industries
Molex Inc.
Montana Power
Murphy Oil
Mylan Laboratories
Nabors Industries
National Fuel Gas
Navigant Consulting
NCH Corp.
NCR Corp.

Network Associates Inc.
New England Electric System
Newport News Shipbuilding
NiSource Inc.
Noble Affiliates
Noble Drilling Corp.
Nordson Corporation
North Fork Bancorp.
Northeast Utilities
NOVA Corp.
Ocean Energy Inc. (New)
OfficeMax Inc.
Ogden Corp.
OGE Energy Corp.
Old Kent Financial
Old Republic Int'l
Olin Corp.
Olsten Corp.
Omnicare, Inc.
Oregon Steel Mills
Outback Steakhouse
Overseas Shipholding Group
Oxford Health Plans
Pacific Century Financial Corp.
PacifiCare Health Sys
Papa John's Int'l.
Payless ShoeSource Inc. Hldg. Co.
Pennzoil-Quaker State (New)
Pentair Corp.
Perrigo Co.
Pinnacle West Capital
Pioneer Natural Resources
Pittston Brink's Group
PMI Group
Policy Management Systems
Potomac Electric Power Co.
Precision Castparts
Premark International
Premier Parks
Promus Hotel Hldg.
Protective Life Corp.
Provident Financial Group Inc.
PSS World Medical Inc.
Public Service of New Mexico
Puget Sound Energy, Inc.
QLogic Corp.
Quantum Corp.-DSSG Stock
Questar Corp.
Quintiles Transnat'l
Quorom Health Group
Rational Software
Rayonier Inc.
Readers Digest Association

ReliaStar Fin'l Corp.
Reynolds & Reynolds
RJ Reynolds Tobacco Hldgs.
Robert Half Int'l
Rollins, Inc.
Ross Stores
RPM Inc.
Ruddick Corp.
Ryerson Tull, Inc. (New)
Saks Incorporated
Sanmina Corp.
Santa Fe Snyder Corp.
SCANA Corp.
Scholastic Corp.
Schulman (A.), Inc.
SCI Systems Inc.
Sensormatic Electronics
Sepracor Inc.
Sequa Corp.
Sequent Computer Systems
Shaw Industries
Siebel Systems, Inc.
Sierra Pacific Resources (New)
Smith International
Smucker (J.M.)
Snyder Communications
Solutia Inc.
Sonoco Products
Sotheby's Holdings
Southdown
Sovereign Bancorp
SPX Corp.
Standard Register Co.
Starbucks Corp.
STERIS Corp.
Sterling Commerce Inc.
Sterling Software Inc.
Stewart & Stevenson Services
Stewart Enterprises, Inc.
Storage Technology
Structural Dynamics Research
Stryker Corp.
Suiza Foods Corp.
SunGard Data Systems
Superior Industries
Swift Transportation
Sybron Int'l.
Sylvan Learning Systems
Symantec Corp.
Symbol Technologies
Synopsys Inc.
T. Rowe Price Assoc.
TCF Financial

Tech Data Corp.
TECO Energy
Tecumseh Products Co.
Teleflex
Telephone & Data Systems
Teradyne, Inc.
The Timber Co.
Tidewater Inc.
Tiffany & Co.
Tosco Corp.
Total Renal Care Hldgs.
Transaction Systems Architects
Transocean Offshore Inc.
Trigon Healthcare Inc.
Trinity Industries
Tyson Foods
U.S. Foodservice
UCAR International
Ultramar Diamond Shamrock
Unifi, Inc.
Unitrin, Inc.
Universal Corp.
Universal Foods
Univision Communications
USG Corp.
UtiliCorp United
Valero Energy
Varco Int'l
Veritas Software
Viad Corp.
Vishay Intertechnology
VISX Inc.
Vitesse Semiconductor
Vlasic Foods Int'l
Wallace Computer Services
Warnaco Group
Washington Gas Light
Washington Post
Waters Corporation
Watts Industries
Wausau-Mosinee Paper
Weatherford Int'l. Inc
Webster Financial Corp.
Wellman, Inc.
Westamerica Bancorp
Westpoint Stevens
Whitman Corp.
Wilmington Trust Corp.
Wisconsin Central Trans.
Wisconsin Energy
Xilinx, Inc.
York International
Zions Bancorp

FORTUNE's 100 Best Companies to Work for in America

1998 Rank	Company	1998 Rank	Company
1	Synovus Financial	51	Compuware
2	TDIndustries	52	K2
3	SAS Institute	53	Amgen
4	Southwest Airlines	54	Bureau of National Affairs
5	SCITOR	55	Starbucks
6	PeopleSoft	56	Genentech
7	Goldman Sachs	57	Erie Insurance
8	Deloitte & Touche	58	Enterprise Rent-A-Car
9	MBNA	59	Computer Associates
10	Hewlett-Packard	60	BE&K
11	Edward Jones	61	LensCrafters
12	Finova Group	62	Lucent Technologies
13	AFLAC	63	Sun Microsystems
14	First Tennessee Bank	64	Johnson & Johnson
15	Frank Russell	65	USAA
16	WRQ	66	Wal-Mart Stores
17	Janus	67	Medtronic
18	A.G. Edwards	68	Ingram Micro
19	Acxiom	69	Baptist Health Systems
20	W.L. Gore & Associates	70	Four Seasons Hotels
21	Kingston Technology	71	Merrill Lynch
22	J.M. Smucker	72	Alagasco
23	JM Family Enterprises	73	Enron
24	Cisco Systems	74	Arrow Electronics
25	UNUM	75	Ernst & Young
26	Timberland	76	Lands' End
27	Microsoft	77	Harley-Davidson
28	Merck	78	Publix Super Markets
29	Plante & Moran	79	FedEx
30	Great Plains	80	AlliedSignal
31	Guidant	81	Acipco
32	Lucas Digital	82	Quantum
33	Granite Rock	83	W.W. Grainger
34	Odetics	84	S.C. Johnson
35	Autodesk	85	Cerner
36	CDW	86	Alcon Laboratories
37	Valassis Communications	87	Herman Miller
38	REI	88	Union Pacific Resources
39	Fenwick & West	89	Worthington Industries
40	Continental Airlines	90	Honda of America Mfg.
41	Capital One	91	Kinko's
42	Ohio National Financial Services	92	Applied Materials
43	Wegmans	93	Quad/Graphics
44	Marriott International	94	3M
45	J.D. Edwards	95	3Com
46	BMC Software	96	Interface
47	QUALCOMM	97	Baldor Electric
48	Whole Foods Market	98	Nordstrom
49	Intel	99	Corning
50	Patagonia	100	L.L. Bean

Source: *FORTUNE;* January 11, 1999

America's 10 Most Admired Companies

Rank	Company	CEO	1998 Revenues ($ bil.)
1	General Electric	Jack Welch	99.8
2	Coca-Cola	Douglas Ivester	18.8
3	Microsoft	Bill Gates	14.5
4	Dell Computer	Michael Dell	12.3
5	Berkshire Hathaway	Warren Buffett	13.8
6	Wal-Mart Stores	David Glass	118.0
7	Southwest Airlines	Herb Kelleher	· 4.1
8	Intel	Craig Barrett	26.3
9	Merck	Raymond Gilmartin	27.0
10	Walt Disney	Michael Eisner	23.0

Source: *FORTUNE;* March 1, 1999

The Top 20 Black-Owned Businesses

Rank	Company	1998 Sales ($ mil.)
1	Philadelphia Coca-Cola Bottling Co. Inc.	389.0
2	Johnson Publishing Co.	371.9
3	TLC Beatrice International Holdings Inc.	322.0
4	Active Transportation	250.0
5	The Bing Group	232.0
6	World Wide Technology Inc.	201.0
7	FUCI Metals USA Inc.	200.0
8	Granite Broadcasting Corporation	193.9
9	H. J. Russell & Co.	184.4
10	BET Holdings II Inc.	178.0
11	Siméus Foods International Inc.	150.0
12	Anderson-Dubose Co.	143.7
13	Barden Companies Inc.	143.5
14	Midwest Stamping Inc.	135.0
15	Exemplar Manufacturing Co.	132.4
16	Mays Chemical Co.	130.0
17	Hawkins Food Group	129.7
18	Digital Systems International Corp.	116.1
19	Sayers Computer Source	110.0
19	Thomas Madison Inc.	110.0

Source: *Black Enterprise;* June 1999

The Top 20 Hispanic-Owned Businesses

Rank	Company	1998 Sales ($ mil.)
1	MasTec Inc.	1,005.10
2	Burt Automotive Network	837.53
3	Goya Foods Inc.	653.00
4	Ancira Enterprises Inc.	449.00
5	International Bancshares Corp.	367.87
6	IFS Financial Corp.	305.00
7	Related Group of Florida	297.00
8	Sedano's Supermarkets	294.00
9	Troy Ford	291.65
10	Lloyd A. Wise Companies	216.70
11	Rosendin Electric Inc.	206.00
12	Supreme International Corp.	190.70
13	AJ Contracting Company Inc.	183.18
14	Mexican Industries in Michigan Inc.	162.12
15	Pan American Hospital	156.00
16	Precision Trading Corp.	155.00
17	HUSCO International Inc.	150.00
18	Avanti/Case-Hoyt	145.00
19	Hamilton Bancorp Inc.	142.62
20	McBride & Associates Inc.	140.00

Source: *Hispanic Business;* June 1999

The Top 20 Woman-Owned Businesses

Rank	Company	Owner	1998 Sales ($ mil.)
1	JM Family Enterprises	Pat Moran	6,200
2	Fidelity Investments	Abigail Johnson	5,195
3	Golden West Financial	Marion O. Sandler	3,100
4	Carlson Companies	Marilyn Carlson Nelson	2,700
5	Raley's	Joyce Raley Teel	2,193
6	Washington Post	Katharine Graham	2,110
7	Little Caesar Enterprises	Marian Ilitch	2,100
8	Ingram Industries	Martha R. Ingram	2,000
9	Warnaco Group	Linda J. Wachner	1,950
10	Alberto-Culver	Bernice Lavin/Carol Bernick	1,835
11	84 Lumber	Maggie Hardy Magerko	1,600
12	Roll International	Lynda R. Resnick	1,570
13	Cumberland Farms	Lily Bentas	1,500
14	Frank Consolidated Enterprises	Elaine S. Frank	1,200
15	Axel Johnson	Antonia Axson Johnson	1,150
16	Charming Shoppes	Dorrit J. Bern	1,035
17	Minyard Food Stores	Liz Minyard/Gretchen M. Williams	1,000
18	Printpack	Gay Love	899
19	Software Spectrum	Judy Sims	884
20	J. Crew	Emily Woods	825

Source: *Working Woman;* June 1999

The 25 Best Companies for Asians, Blacks, and Hispanics

Rank	Company	1998 Sales ($mil.)	Minorities as % of Management*	Work Force
1	Union Bank of California	2,619	35.9	53.7
2	Fannie Mae	31,499	27.3	39.1
3	Public Service Company of New Mexico	1,252	34.2	47.3
4	Sempra Energy	5,525	28.0	46.8
5	Toyota Motor Sales	32,000	19.3	32.5
6	Advantica	1,962	16.6	46.3
7	SBC Communications	28,777	28.7	36.4
8	Lucent Technologies	30,147	19.5	24.5
9	Darden Restaurants	3,287	17.7	33.8
10	Wal-Mart Stores	139,208	42.0	N/A
11	Allstate	25,879	21.3	26.3
12	Chase Manhattan	32,379	25.1	40.4
13	Marriott International	7,968	20.7	56.9
14	U S WEST	12,378	16.0	16.9
15	Federal Express	13,200	27.8	41.5
16	Southern California Edison	8,847	24.5	42.0
17	Bank of America	50,777	23.3	39.8
18	Hyatt	3,250	27.0	61.7
19	TIAA-CREF	35,889	16.3	48.3
20	Xerox	20,019	23.0	27.9
21	BellSouth	23,123	23.1	28.0
22	Knight Ridder	3,100	16.0	27.7
23	AMR	19,205	15.2	29.0
24	Texas Instruments	8,460	15.9	28.0
25	Ameritech	17,154	23.2	26.8

N/A=Not Available
* Management includes both company officials and managers.
Source: *FORTUNE;* July 19, 1999

Professional Football Teams

Rank	Team	1998 Revenues ($ mil.)
1	Dallas Cowboys	118.0
2	Washington Redskins	115.1
3	Miami Dolphins	103.1
4	St. Louis Rams	91.9
5	Kansas City Chiefs	85.6
6	San Francisco 49ers	84.7
7	New England Patriots	84.0
8	Carolina Panthers	83.0
9	Philadelphia Eagles	83.0
10	San Diego Chargers	82.5
11	New York Giants	82.3
12	New Orleans Saints	80.9
13	Chicago Bears	79.0
14	Green Bay Packers	78.8
15	Buffalo Bills	78.7
16	Oakland Raiders	78.3
17	Minnesota Vikings	77.7
18	Atlanta Falcons	77.6
19	Seattle Seahawks	77.1
20	Arizona Cardinals	76.9
21	Tampa Bay Buccaneers	76.8
22	Denver Broncos	76.3
23	New York Jets	76.2
24	Pittsburgh Steelers	75.1
25	Detroit Lions	74.2
26	Baltimore Ravens	73.2
27	Tennessee Oilers*	71.5
28	Indianapolis Colts	70.9
29	Cincinnati Bengals	69.2
30	Jacksonville Jaguars	66.8

* now Tennessee Titans
Source: *Forbes;* December 14, 1998

Professional Basketball Teams

Rank	Team	1998 Revenues ($ mil.)
1	Chicago Bulls	112.2
2	New York Knicks	109.7
3	Portland Trail Blazers	94.1
4	Los Angeles Lakers	92.4
5	Phoenix Suns	87.0
6	Detroit Pistons	85.9
7	Utah Jazz	80.1
8	Washington Wizards	76.5
9	Houston Rockets	72.1
10	Philadelphia 76ers	69.9
11	New Jersey Nets	65.5
12	Boston Celtics	65.0
13	Seattle SuperSonics	64.9
14	Orlando Magic	63.7
15	Cleveland Cavaliers	61.9
16	Charlotte Hornets	56.4
17	Indiana Pacers	56.4
18	San Antonio Spurs	55.3
19	Sacramento Kings	51.9
20	Minnesota Timberwolves	51.8
21	Vancouver Grizzlies	51.1
22	Miami Heat	50.0
23	Golden State Warriors	48.0
24	Atlanta Hawks	46.6
25	Toronto Raptors	44.9
26	Milwaukee Bucks	42.7
27	Dallas Mavericks	41.2
28	Los Angeles Clippers	39.3
29	Denver Nuggets	37.8

Source: *Forbes;* December 14, 1998

The 10 Most Valuable Sports Franchises

Rank	Team	League	Current value ($ mil.)
1	Dallas Cowboys	NFL	413
2	Washington Redskins	NFL	403
3	Carolina Panthers	NFL	365
4	New York Yankees	MLB	362
5	Tampa Bay Buccaneers	NFL	346
6	Miami Dolphins	NFL	340
7	Baltimore Ravens	NFL	329
8	Seattle Seahawks	NFL	324
9	Baltimore Orioles	MLB	323
10	Cleveland Indians	MLB	322

Source: *Forbes;* December 14, 1998

The 10 Least Valuable Sports Franchises

Rank	Team	League	Current value ($ mil.)
1	Edmonton Oilers	NHL	67
2	Calgary Flames	NHL	78
3	Carolina Hurricanes	NHL	80
4	Phoenix Coyotes	NHL	87
5	Montreal Expos	MLB	87
6	Pittsburgh Penguins	NHL	89
7	Buffalo Sabres	NHL	91
8	Minnesota Twins	MLB	94
9	Milwaukee Bucks	NBA	94
10	Ottawa Senators	NHL	94

Source: *Forbes;* December 14, 1998

Professional Baseball Teams

Rank	Team	1998 Revenues ($ mil.)
1	New York Yankees	144.7
2	Baltimore Orioles	134.5
3	Cleveland Indians	134.1
4	Atlanta Braves	119.6
5	Colorado Rockies	116.6
6	Texas Rangers	97.6
7	Los Angeles Dodgers	94.3
8	Boston Red Sox	92.1
9	Seattle Mariners	89.8
10	Florida Marlins	88.2
11	St. Louis Cardinals	82.9
12	Chicago White Sox	82.3
13	Chicago Cubs	81.5
14	New York Mets	80.5
15	San Francisco Giants	69.8
16	Houston Astros	68.0
17	Toronto Blue Jays	67.1
18	Anaheim Angels	62.6
19	San Diego Padres	57.6
20	Philadelphia Phillies	57.1
21	Oakland Athletics	56.4
22	Kansas City Royals	51.2
23	Detroit Tigers	50.6
24	Cincinnati Reds	50.2
25	Pittsburgh Pirates	49.3
26	Milwaukee Brewers	46.9
27	Minnesota Twins	46.8
28	Montreal Expos	43.6

Source: *Forbes;* December 14, 1998

Professional Hockey Teams

Rank	Team	1998 Revenues ($ mil.)
1	Detroit Red Wings	80.1
2	Philadelphia Flyers	74.6
3	Washington Capitals	74.2
4	St. Louis Blues	70.0
5	New York Rangers	69.6
6	Boston Bruins	66.1
7	Chicago Blackhawks	63.1
8	Montreal Canadiens	61.8
9	New Jersey Devils	54.4
10	Colorado Avalanche	53.2
11	Pittsburgh Penguins	52.6
12	Mighty Ducks of Anaheim	49.6
13	San Jose Sharks	49.2
14	Toronto Maple Leafs	47.5
15	New York Islanders	46.2
16	Dallas Stars	45.6
17	Ottawa Senators	42.8
18	Tampa Bay Lightning	41.9
19	Vancouver Canucks	41.8
20	Buffalo Sabres	41.5
21	Phoenix Coyotes	41.2
22	Calgary Flames	38.9
23	Los Angeles Kings	38.5
24	Edmonton Oilers	33.6
25	Florida Panthers	32.7
26	Carolina Hurricanes	25.1

Source: *Forbes;* December 14, 1998

Hoover's Handbook of American Business

THE COMPANY PROFILES A-K

3COM CORPORATION

Often bullied by the sheer size of its rivals in the networking game, 3Com is forming its own league. The Santa Clara, California-based company is the #2 maker (although well behind Cisco) of hardware that lets computers communicate with each other across networks. Its products are playing a key role in the convergence of computer data, telephone calls, and video. To help it better compete, 3Com has beefed up its technology roster through acquisitions — more than a dozen in the last five years — and through alliances with such market leaders as Alcatel, IBM, and Microsoft. Business outside of the US accounts for almost half of the company's sales.

3Com is organized into three disparate units. Personal Connectivity focuses on the cards and modems that link PCs to corporate networks and the Internet. Network Systems makes hubs (network control devices), switches, routers (network linking devices), and network management software. It also designs communications technologies for public carriers and Internet service providers.

But Handheld Computing is the MVP of 3Com's team. The unit makes the Palm electronic organizer, licenses Palm technology, and operates Palm.Net, an Internet service for handheld computers. Palm has a 70% share of the global handheld computer market, and its introduction of the Internet-ready Palm VII has helped boost 3Com into the wireless connectivity major leagues.

HISTORY

Engineer Robert Metcalfe led the Xerox research team that invented Ethernet (now a PC networking standard) in 1973. Six years later, Metcalfe and several colleagues founded 3Com (for "computer, communication, and compatibility"). The company began as a computer network consulting firm before there were many PCs to network. In 1980 Xerox agreed to share its Ethernet patent to make the technology an industry standard, and $1.1 million in venture capital helped get 3Com rolling. The upstart introduced an Ethernet transceiver and adapter the next year. William Krause was hired away from Hewlett-Packard in 1981 to be 3Com's president. Sales took off in 1982 after IBM introduced its 16-bit PC.

3Com went public in 1984. Initially it sold network adapter cards to large computer makers and resellers, but by 1986 its manufacturing customers were integrating their own networking hardware. Krause responded by broadening the company's focus, and 3Com started providing network hardware and software systems.

In 1987 3Com gained a direct sales force when it acquired router supplier Bridge Communications. When Bridge co-founder Eric Benhamou was named to head 3Com in 1990, Metcalfe departed. Benhamou shed noncore businesses and developed the company's prosperous line of LAN adapters, hubs, and routers. He also started acquiring complementary products by purchasing their makers, including British hub specialist BICC Data Networks (1992) and LAN switch company Synernetics (1993). The company went into the red in 1994 when it bought Centrum Communications (re-mote-access technology) and NiceCom (a bandwidth data allocation innovator).

In an effort to build name recognition, the company plunked down $3.9 million in 1995 so that San Francisco's venerable Candlestick Park would be called 3Com Park through the year 2000. Also in 1995 the company bought high-end competitor Chipcom.

3Com's $7.3 billion purchase of U.S. Robotics in 1997 added remote-access units and the PalmPilot personal digital assistant to the company's lineup. Problems digesting the modem giant, however, led to layoffs and inventory backups. The first of several shareholder lawsuits alleging securities violations was filed that year. The company in 1998 named former Digital Equipment (now part of Compaq) heir apparent Bruce Claflin as president and COO (Benhamou remains chairman and CEO).

To shore up its competitive position, 3Com in 1999 made acquisitions including French data communications software firm Smartcode. The company also formed alliances, including a $1 billion technology-sharing pact with IBM, and computing and telephony convergence pacts with Alcatel and Microsoft. That year the company's Palm Computing unit announced the Palm VII, a handheld computer that provides e-mail access and wireless connections to content providers. To support the handheld device and expand its own role in wireless networking, 3Com formed a joint venture, dubbed OpenSky, to provide Internet access to wireless devices.

Chairman and CEO: Eric A. Benhamou, age 43,
$750,000 pay
President and COO: Bruce L. Claflin, age 47,
$528,127 pay
SVP and Chief Information Officer: David H. Starr,
age 47
SVP and Chief Technical Officer: John H. Hart, age 53
SVP; General Manager, Carrier Systems: Irfin Ali, age 35
SVP; General Manager, Network Systems: Edgar Masri,
age 41
SVP; General Manager, Personal Connectivity:
Jef Graham, age 43
SVP Corporate Services (HR): Eileen Nelson, age 52
SVP e-Commerce: Ralph B. Godfrey, age 59,
$443,750 pay
SVP Finance and CFO: Christopher B. Paisley, age 47
**SVP Legal and Government Relations, Secretary, and
General Counsel:** Mark D. Michael, age 48
SVP Marketing and Business Development:
Janice M. Roberts, age 43, $400,000 pay
SVP Worldwide Sales: Richard W. Joyce, age 43,
$406,165 pay
President Palm Computing: Alan J. Kessler, age 41,
$400,000 pay
Auditors: Deloitte & Touche LLP

LOCATIONS

HQ: 5400 Bayfront Plaza, Santa Clara, CA 95052
Phone: 408-326-5000   **Fax:** 408-326-5001
Web site: http://www.3com.com

3Com has manufacturing plants in Ireland, Singapore,
and the US; it operates 190 offices in 48 countries.

1999 Sales

	$ mil.	% of total
US	3,084	53
UK	443	8
Other countries	2,245	39
Total	**5,772**	**100**

PRODUCTS/OPERATIONS

1999 Sales

	$ mil.	% of total
Network Systems	2,612	45
Personal Connectivity	2,590	45
Handheld Computing	570	10
Total	**5,772**	**100**

COMPETITORS

Alcatel	Lucent
Boca Research	Madge Networks
Cabletron	Microsoft
Casio Computer	Motorola
Cisco Systems	Nokia
Com21	Nortel Networks
Compaq	Olivetti
Conexant Systems	Philips Electronics
Diamond Multimedia	Psion
D-Link	Sharp
Ericsson	Siemens
FORE Systems	Sony
General Instrument	Standard Microsystems
Hewlett-Packard	Symbian
IBM	Xircom
Intel	

HISTORICAL FINANCIALS & EMPLOYEES

Nasdaq symbol: COMS FYE: May 31	Annual Growth	1990	1991	1992	1993	1994	1995	1996	1997	1998	1999
Sales ($ mil.)	33.8%	419	399	408	617	827	1,295	2,327	3,147	5,420	5,772
Net income ($ mil.)	39.3%	21	(28)	4	39	(29)	126	178	374	30	404
Income as % of sales	—	4.9%	—	1.0%	6.3%	—	9.7%	7.6%	11.9%	0.6%	7.0%
Earnings per share ($)	22.2%	0.18	(0.25)	0.04	0.30	(0.23)	0.66	1.02	1.42	0.08	1.09
Stock price - FY high ($)	—	6.97	4.75	3.75	10.00	15.94	34.63	53.63	81.38	59.69	51.13
Stock price - FY low ($)	—	2.50	1.34	1.69	2.41	4.91	10.06	30.44	24.00	25.25	20.00
Stock price - FY close ($)	25.9%	3.44	2.16	2.94	6.75	11.75	32.00	49.25	48.50	25.38	27.31
P/E - high	—	39	—	94	33	—	52	53	57	746	47
P/E - low	—	14	—	42	8	—	15	30	17	316	18
Dividends per share ($)	—	0.00	0.00	0.00	0.00	0.00	0.00	0.00	0.00	0.00	0.00
Book value per share ($)	17.8%	2.00	1.75	1.80	2.09	2.16	3.36	5.80	8.51	7.82	8.74
Employees	23.1%	2,008	1,731	1,963	1,971	2,306	3,072	5,190	7,109	12,920	13,027

STOCK PRICE HISTORY

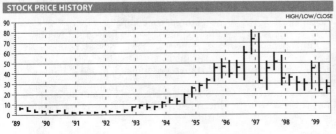

HIGH/LOW/CLOSE

1999 FISCAL YEAR-END

Debt ratio: 0.9%
Return on equity: 12.6%
Cash ($ mil.): 952
Current ratio: 2.85
Long-term debt ($ mil.): 30
No. of shares (mil.): 366
Dividends
  Yield: —
  Payout: —
Market value ($ mil.): 9,990

7-ELEVEN, INC.

OVERVIEW

"If convenience stores are open 24 hours, why are there locks on the doors?" If anyone knows, it's 7-Eleven. The Dallas-based company (formerly The Southland Corporation) operates about 5,600 7-Eleven convenience stores in more than 30 states and Canada (about half are franchised). Stores range from 2,400-3,000 sq. ft. and sell about 2,500 items. While most store locations offer Citgo gasoline, its merchandise (including Slurpees, beer, perishables, and tobacco items) accounts for more than 75% of sales.

7-Eleven also has an interest in about 240 stores in Mexico and licenses the 7-Eleven name worldwide. Seven-Eleven Japan, 51%-owned by Ito-Yokado (which also owns 65% of 7-Eleven, Inc.), runs more than 7,200 7-Eleven stores in Japan and Hawaii. Other licensees and affiliates in the US and 16 other countries operate about 5,700 stores.

The company is growing by building new stores and acquiring other chains, primarily in markets where it has a presence. 7-Eleven is boosting store sales by offering new products, including Café Cooler (a frozen cappuccino) and prepaid cellular phone cards.

HISTORY

Claude Dawley formed the Southland Ice Company in Dallas in 1927 when ice was a precious necessity during Texas summers for storing and transporting food. Dawley bought four other Texas ice plant operations with backing from Chicago utility magnate Martin Insull. The purchase included Consumers Ice, where Joe Thompson had increased profits by selling chilled watermelons off the truck docks. After the Dawley enterprise was underway, a dock manager in Dallas began stocking a few food items for customers. Ice docks were exempt from Texas' blue laws and could operate even on Sundays. He relayed the idea to Thompson, then running the ice operations, who adopted the idea at all company locations.

Thompson promoted the grocery operations by calling them Tote'm Stores and erecting totem poles by the docks. In 1928 he added gas stations to some store locations.

Insull bought out Dawley in 1930, and Thompson became president. He expanded Southland's operations even as the company operated briefly under the direction of bankruptcy court (1932-34). Having become the largest dairy retailer in the Dallas/Fort Worth area, in 1936 the company began its own dairy, Oak Farms, to supply some of its milk (it was sold in 1988). Ten years later the company changed its name to The Southland Corporation and adopted the name 7-Eleven, a reference to its stores' hours at the time.

After Thompson died in 1961, his eldest son, John, became president. John opened stores in Colorado, New Jersey, and Arizona in 1962 and in Utah, California, and Missouri in 1963. The company introduced the Slurpee, a fizzy slush drink, in 1965. Southland franchised the 7-Eleven format in the UK (1971) and in Japan (1973).

To supply its gas pumps, in 1983 the company purchased CITGO, a gasoline refining and marketing business with about 300 gas stations. It soon sold a 50% interest of the business to the Venezuelan government-owned oil company, Petróleos de Venezuela (PDVSA), in 1986.

In 1988 John and his two brothers borrowed heavily to buy 70% of Southland's stock in an LBO. Stymied by debt, the company sold its remaining 50% stake in Citgo to PDVSA in 1990. However, Southland defaulted on $1.8 billion in publicly traded debt later that year and filed for bankruptcy protection. The company then persuaded bondholders to restructure its debt and take 25% of its stock, clearing the way for the purchase of 70% of Southland in 1991 by its Japanese partner, Ito-Yokado. Company veteran Clark Matthews was named CEO that year.

From 1991 to 1993 sales declined as Southland closed underperforming stores, began renovating others, and upgraded its merchandise. Prepaid phone cards were added in 1995; in 1998 Southland introduced prepaid cellular phone services and began testing electronic banking kiosks, which allow users to cash checks, pay bills, and transfer funds.

Following the lead of its Japanese sibling, in 1998 Southland began implementing an electronic retail information system to connect stores to a company-wide network and allowing managers to fine-tune inventory on a store-by-store basis. New store openings and acquisitions (Christy's in New England, red D marts in Indiana) added 299 more units that year.

Southland changed its name to 7-Eleven, Inc., in April 1999 to better reflect the lone business of the company.

Chairman: Masatoshi Ito, age 74
VC: Toshifumi Suzuki, age 66
President, CEO, and Secretary: Clark J. Matthews II, age 62, $819,840 pay
EVP and CFO: James W. Keyes, $556,500 pay
SVP: Masaaki Asakura
SVP Distribution: Rodney A. Brehm, $321,510 pay
SVP Logistics: Joseph F. Gomes
SVP Merchandising: Gary R. Rose
SVP and General Counsel: Bryan F. Smith Jr., $367,490 pay
VP Development: Krista Fuller
VP Information Systems: Linda Svehlak
VP and Controller: Donald E. Thomas
VP, Canada Division: Terry Blocher
VP, Northeast Division: Frank Crivello
VP, Central Division: Cynthia Davis
VP, Southwest Division: Jeff Hamill
VP, Florida Division: John W. Harris
VP, Gasoline Supply: Gary Lockhart
VP, Great Lakes Division: Jeffrey A. Schenck
Auditors: PricewaterhouseCoopers LLP

LOCATIONS

HQ: 2711 N. Haskell Ave., Dallas, TX 75204-2906
Phone: 214-828-7011   **Fax:** 214-828-7848
Web site: http://www.7-eleven.com

7-Eleven owns and operates or franchises stores in more than 30 states in the US and in Canada.

PRODUCTS/OPERATIONS

1998 Sales

	% of total
Gasoline	23
Beverages	18
Tobacco products	18
Beer & wine	9
Candy & snacks	7
Food service	5
Nonfoods	5
Customer services	4
Dairy products	4
Baked goods	3
Other	4
Total	**100**

Selected Trademarks

7-Eleven	Deli Central
Big Bite	Quality Classic Selection
Big Gulp	Slurpee
Café Cooler	World Ovens
Café Select	

COMPETITORS

Casey's General Stores	Racetrac Petroleum
Chevron	Sheetz
Cumberland Farms	Shell
Dairy Mart	Texaco
Exxon	Tosco
FINA	Ultramar Diamond
Holiday Companies	Shamrock
Kroger	Uni-Marts
Mobil	Wawa
The Pantry	White Hen Pantry
QuikTrip	

HISTORICAL FINANCIALS & EMPLOYEES

Nasdaq symbol: SVEV FYE: December 31	Annual Growth	1989	1990	1991	1992	1993	1994	1995	1996	1997	1998
Sales ($ mil.)	(1.4%)	8,275	8,348	8,010	7,426	6,814	6,760	6,746	6,869	6,971	7,258
Net income ($ mil.)	—	(1,307)	(277)	83	(131)	71	92	271	90	70	74
Income as % of sales	—	—	—	1.0%	—	1.0%	1.4%	4.0%	1.3%	1.0%	1.0%
Earnings per share ($)	(4.8%)	—	—	0.24	(0.32)	0.17	0.22	0.65	0.20	0.16	0.17
Stock price - FY high ($)	—	—	—	3.03	4.25	7.69	6.75	4.72	4.94	3.69	3.03
Stock price - FY low ($)	—	—	—	0.94	1.19	2.97	3.81	2.88	2.44	1.72	1.56
Stock price - FY close ($)	0.2%	—	—	1.88	3.03	6.75	4.50	3.31	2.97	2.13	1.91
P/E - high	—	—	—	13	—	45	31	7	25	23	18
P/E - low	—	—	—	4	—	17	17	4	12	11	9
Dividends per share ($)	—	—	—	0.00	0.00	0.00	0.00	0.00	0.00	0.00	0.00
Book value per share ($)	—	—	—	(2.95)	(3.22)	(3.05)	(2.82)	(2.11)	(1.92)	(1.76)	(1.57)
Employees	(4.3%)	48,114	45,665	42,616	35,646	32,406	30,417	30,523	29,532	30,323	32,368

STOCK PRICE HISTORY

HIGH/LOW/CLOSE

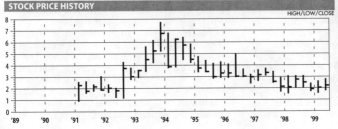

1998 FISCAL YEAR-END

Debt ratio: 100.0%
Return on equity: —
Cash ($ mil.): 27
Current ratio: 0.66
Long-term debt ($ mil.): 2,169
No. of shares (mil.): 410
Dividends
  Yield: —
  Payout: —
Market value ($ mil.): 783

ABBOTT LABORATORIES

OVERVIEW

Abbott Laboratories operates with Midwestern reserve: no overly hip marketing, no flamboyant CEO, no "dot-com" in its name.

But the times are a-changin' for the staid firm. While the Abbott Park, Illinois-based company's best-known brands are its nutritional products — such as Similac, a top infant formula, and Ensure, a leading nutrition supplement — far more of Abbott's sales come from medications and products used in hospitals.

Abbott's pharmaceuticals unit makes drugs ranging from antibiotics to protease inhibitors that treat HIV to stomach-ulcer medication. The hospital products division makes drug-delivery systems and products for anesthesia, critical care, and infection control. Its diagnostic products division makes medical diagnostic systems. Abbott also makes agricultural and chemical products.

The company's reputation as a formidable marketer results in much collaboration: Smaller firms invent new drugs and benefit from Abbott's size, expertise, and global market reach. Abbott, for its part, saves on development costs.

Abbott's conservative recent past is giving way to a more pugnacious and outward-looking style. The company has battled opponents ranging from the pharmaceutical lobby to the FDA and FTC to Ecuadoran environmentalists. Meanwhile, joint venture (with Takeda Chemical) TAP Holdings wants to enter the emerging erectile-dysfunction medication market with a new product, apomorphine, that may rival Pfizer's wildly profitable Viagra.

HISTORY

Dr. Wallace Abbott started making his dosimetric granule (a pill that supplied uniform quantities of drugs) at his home outside Chicago in 1888. By 1900 his Abbott Alkaloidal Company's sales hit $125,000, earning criticism from the American Medical Association for aggressive marketing, though much of the medical profession supported him.

During WWI Abbott scientists synthesized anesthetics previously available only from Germany. Abbott improved its research capacity in 1922 by buying Dermatological Research Laboratories; in 1928 it bought John T. Milliken and its well-trained sales force. Abbott went public in 1929.

Salesman DeWitt Clough became president in 1933 and company magazine *What's New* became a significant marketing tool. International operations began in the mid-1930s with branches in Argentina, Brazil, Cuba, Mexico, and the UK.

Abbott was integral to the WWII effort; the US made only 28 pounds of penicillin in 1943, prompting the company to ratchet up production. Abbott began marketing Erythrocin (erythromycin) in 1952. Consumer, infant and nutritional products (such as Selsun Blue shampoo, Murine eye drops, and Similac infant formula) joined the roster in the 1960s. The FDA banned the company's artificial sweetener Sucaryl in 1970 saying it might be carcinogenic, and in 1971 millions of intravenous solutions were recalled following contamination deaths.

Profits increased steadily after Robert Schoellhorn became CEO in 1979. He cut research and development and fired potential successors, which contributed to his ouster as chairman in 1990. In the 1980s Abbott began selling Japanese-developed pharmaceuticals in the US.

Duane Burnham became CEO in 1989; under his conservative management the company received FDA approvals to market ProSom (insomnia drug, 1990), Hytrin (hypertension drug for treatment of enlarged prostates, 1994), and Prevacid (ulcer treatment, 1995). In 1995 it got the OK to use its Depakote to treat manic depression and Lupron to treat anemia caused by fibroid tumors.

Abbott bought MediSense, a maker of blood sugar self-tests for diabetics in 1996, and also paid $32.5 million to settle claims of infant formula price-fixing from 17 states. In 1997 FTC action prompted Abbott to stop claiming that doctors recommended its Ensure nutritional supplement for healthy adults. That year the FDA allowed Abbott to use Norvir to treat HIV and AIDS in children after approving its use in adults in a record 72 days in 1996.

In 1999 Miles White became CEO. That year Abbott saw promising trial results for a new protease inhibitor to treat HIV and AIDS and a new post-stroke blood clot treatment; its Depacon did well in migraine testing. Outside the lab, Abbott agreed to buy California-based research pharmaceutical Alza Corp. for $7.3 billion; Alza makes products using "sustained release" technology, and urology and oncology products. On the downside, the FTC is probing Abbott, among others, for possible anti-competitive actions involving generic drugs.

Chairman and CEO: Miles D. White, age 43, $1,669,615 pay (prior to promotion)
President and COO: Robert L. Parkinson Jr., age 48, $1,298,461 pay
SVP Ross Products: Joy A. Amundson, age 44, $742,692 pay
SVP Finance and CFO: Gary P. Coughlan, age 55, $928,846 pay
SVP, Secretary, and General Counsel: Jose M. de Lasa
SVP Chemical and Agricultural Products: William G. Dempsey, age 47
SVP, Hospital Products: Richard A. Gonzalez, age 45
SVP Human Resources: Thomas M. Wascoe, age 52
SVP International Operations: Josef Wendler, age 49
Auditors: Arthur Andersen LLP

LOCATIONS

HQ: 100 Abbott Park Rd., Abbott Park, IL 60064-6400
Phone: 847-937-6100 **Fax:** 847-937-1511
Web site: http://www.abbott.com

Abbott Laboratories sells its products in 130 countries. It operates manufacturing facilities in Puerto Rico and the US, and in 12 other countries.

1998 Sales

	$ mil.	% of total
US	7,919	63
Japan	528	4
Germany	446	4
Canada	345	3
Italy	328	3
Other countries	2,912	23
Total	**12,478**	**100**

PRODUCTS/OPERATIONS

1998 Sales & Operating income

	Sales		Operating income	
	$ mil.	% of total	$ mil.	% of total
Diagnostics	2,790	22	448	13
Pharmaceutical	2,601	21	1,402	40
Hospital	1,890	15	369	11
Ross	1,820	15	540	16
Chemical & Agricultural	352	3	117	3
International	3,001	24	605	17
Other	24	—	—	—
Total	**12,478**	**100**	**3,481**	**100**

COMPETITORS

American Home Products
Amgen
AstraZeneca
Bausch & Lomb
Baxter
Bayer AG
Becton Dickinson
Bristol-Myers Squibb
Eli Lilly
Genentech
Glaxo Wellcome
Hoechst AG
Johnson & Johnson
Mallinckrodt
Merck
Novartis
Pfizer
Pharmacia & Upjohn
Rhône-Poulenc
Roche Holding
Schering-Plough
SmithKline Beecham
Solvay
Warner-Lambert

HISTORICAL FINANCIALS & EMPLOYEES

NYSE symbol: ABT FYE: December 31	Annual Growth	1989	1990	1991	1992	1993	1994	1995	1996	1997	1998
Sales ($ mil.)	9.8%	5,380	6,159	6,877	7,852	8,408	9,156	10,012	11,014	11,884	12,478
Net income ($ mil.)	11.7%	860	966	1,089	1,239	1,399	1,517	1,689	1,882	2,095	2,333
Income as % of sales	—	16.0%	15.7%	15.8%	15.8%	16.6%	16.6%	16.9%	17.1%	17.6%	18.7%
Earnings per share ($)	13.3%	0.49	0.56	0.64	0.74	0.85	0.94	1.05	1.19	1.34	1.51
Stock price - FY high ($)	—	8.80	11.59	17.44	17.09	15.44	17.00	22.38	28.69	34.88	50.06
Stock price - FY low ($)	—	5.78	7.81	9.81	13.06	11.31	12.69	15.31	19.06	24.88	32.53
Stock price - FY close ($)	21.5%	8.50	11.25	17.22	15.19	14.81	16.31	20.81	25.38	32.75	49.00
P/E - high	—	18	21	27	23	18	18	21	24	26	33
P/E - low	—	12	14	15	18	13	14	15	16	19	22
Dividends per share ($)	14.8%	0.17	0.20	0.24	0.29	0.33	0.37	0.41	0.47	0.53	0.59
Book value per share ($)	10.5%	1.54	1.65	1.88	2.00	2.24	2.52	2.79	3.07	3.27	3.77
Employees	3.8%	40,249	43,770	45,694	48,118	49,659	49,464	50,241	52,817	54,847	56,236

STOCK PRICE HISTORY

HIGH/LOW/CLOSE

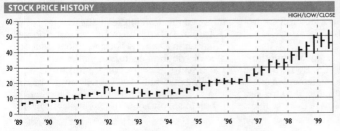

1998 FISCAL YEAR-END

Debt ratio: 19.0%
Return on equity: 40.8%
Cash ($ mil.): 308
Current ratio: 1.12
Long-term debt ($ mil.): 1,340
No. of shares (mil.): 1,516
Dividends
  Yield: 1.2%
  Payout: 39.1%
Market value ($ mil.): 74,287

ACE HARDWARE CORPORATION

OVERVIEW

Luckily, Ace has John Madden up its sleeve. Despite the growth of warehouse-style competitors, Ace Hardware has remained a household name, thanks to ads featuring the well-known football commentator (an appropriate choice considering the company primarily targets men). The Oak Brook, Illinois-based company is the US's #2 hardware cooperative, behind TruServ (operator of True Value and several other hardware chains). Ace dealer-owners operate about 5,100 Ace Hardware stores throughout the US and in more than 60 other countries. The company provides a number of member services, including advertising, insurance, purchasing incentives, and training.

Ace buys in bulk and distributes products, such as electrical and plumbing supplies, power tools, garden equipment, and housewares, to its members through about 20 warehouses nationwide. It also makes its own brand of paint and offers thousands of other Ace-brand products. Ace dealers own the company and receive dividends from Ace's profits.

HISTORY

A group of Chicago-area hardware dealers — Frank Burke, Richard Hesse, E. Gunnard Lindquist, and Oscar Fisher — decided in 1924 to pool their hardware buying and promotional costs. In 1928 the group incorporated as Ace Stores. Hesse became president the following year, retaining that position for the next 44 years. The company also opened its first warehouse in 1929, and by 1933 it had 38 dealers. That year Ace held its first convention so dealers could review and purchase merchandise.

The organization had 133 dealers in seven states by 1949. In 1953 Ace began to allow dealers to buy stock in the company through the Ace Perpetuation Plan. During the 1960s Ace expanded into the South and West, and by 1969 it had opened distribution centers in Georgia and California — its first such facilities outside Chicago.

By the early 1970s the do-it-yourself market began to surge as inflation pushed up plumber and electrician fees. As the market grew, large home center chains gobbled up market share from independent dealers such as those franchised through Ace. In response, Ace and its dealers became a part of a growing trend in the hardware industry — cooperatives.

Hesse sold the company to its dealers in 1973 for $6 million (less than half its book value), and the following year Ace began operating as a cooperative. Hesse stepped down in 1973 and Arthur Krausman became head of the co-op. In 1976 the dealers took full control when the company's first Board of Dealer-Directors was elected.

Two years later the co-op signed up a number of dealers in the eastern US. By 1979 it had dealers in all 50 states. Ace implemented an aggressive building program the following year to add more distribution centers to serve its growing network of dealers.

The co-op opened a paint plant in Matteson, Illinois, in 1984 and began making its own paint. By 1985 Ace had reached $1 billion in sales and had initiated its Store of the Future Program, allowing dealers to borrow up to $200,000 to upgrade their stores and conduct market analyses. Sports commentator and ex-professional football coach John Madden began representing the firm in 1988.

A year later the co-op began to test ACENET, a computer network that allowed Ace dealers to check inventory, send and receive e-mail, make special purchase requests, and keep up with prices on commodity items such as lumber. Also in 1989 it began an annual Lumber & Building Materials convention.

In 1990 Ace established an International Division to handle its overseas stores (it had been exporting products since 1975). EVP and COO David Hodnik was named president in 1995. That year the co-op added a net of 67 stores, including a three-store chain in Russia, and it added another 60 stores in 1996. (Since then growth has been stagnant.) Expanding further internationally, Ace signed a five-year joint-supply agreement in 1996 with Canadian lumber and hardware retailer Beaver Lumber. Hodnik added CEO to his title in 1996.

Ace fell further behind its old rival, True Value, in 1997 when SERVISTAR and True Value merged to form TruServ, a hardware giant that operated more than 10,000 outlets at the completion of the merger.

Late in 1997 Ace launched an expansion program in Canada. (The co-op already operated distribution centers in Ontario and Calgary.) In 1999 Ace merged its lumber and building materials division with Builder Marts of America to form a dealer-owned buying group to supply about 2,700 retailers.

OFFICERS

Chairman: Howard J. Jung, age 51
President and CEO: David F. Hodnik, age 51,
$600,000 pay
EVP Retail: William A. Loftus, age 60
SVP International and Technology: Paul M.
Ingevaldson, age 53
SVP Wholesale: Rita D. Kahle, age 42
VP Sales and Marketing: Michael C. Bodzewski, age 48
VP and Controller: Lori L. Bossmann, age 38
VP Merchandise: Ray A. Griffith, age 45
VP, General Counsel, and Secretary: David W. League,
age 59
VP Retail Support: David F. Myer, age 53
VP Human Resources: Fred J. Neer, age 59
VP Information Technology: Donald L. Schuman, age 60
Auditors: KPMG LLP

LOCATIONS

HQ: 2200 Kensington Ct., Oak Brook, IL 60523
Phone: 630-990-6600   **Fax:** 630-990-6838
Web site: http://www.acehardware.com

1998 Sales

	$ mil.	% of total
US	2,904	93
Other countries	216	7
Total	**3,120**	**100**

PRODUCTS/OPERATIONS

1998 Sales

	% of total
Paint, cleaning & related supplies	20
Plumbing & heating supplies	15
Hand & power tools	14
Electrical supplies	13
Garden, rural equipment & related supplies	13
General hardware	12
Sundries	7
Housewares & appliances	6
Total	**100**

Selected Services

Mail/office
Bridal registry
Care mail
Fax service
Film processing
Photocopies
Utility payments

Repair Work
Bikes
Chainsaws
Lamps
Power equipment and
tools
Screens and windows
Vacuums
VCRs

Specialty Services
Delivery
Hunting/fishing licenses
Key cutting and lock
servicing
Pipe cutting and
threading
Rentals
Trophies/engraving

Miscellaneous
Gift certificates
Live bait
Pool water and soil
testing

Subsidiaries
Ace Corporate Stores (operations of company-owned
stores)
Ace Hardware Canada (hardware wholesaler in Canada)
Ace Insurance Agency (dealer insurance program)
A.H.C. Store Development Corp. (operations of
company-owned stores)
Loss Prevention Services (security training and loss
prevention services for dealers)

COMPETITORS

84 Lumber	Lowe's
Akzo Nobel	McCoy
Benjamin Moore	Menard
Building Materials	Montgomery Ward
Holding	Payless Cashways
Carolina Holdings	Pergament Home
Costco Companies	Reno-Depot
D.I.Y. Home Warehouse	Rona
Do it Best	Sears
Grossman's	Sherwin-Williams
Hechinger	Sutherland Lumber
Home Depot	TruServ
HomeBase	United Hardware
ICI Americas	Distributing Co.
Kmart	Wal-Mart
Lanoga	Wickes

HISTORICAL FINANCIALS & EMPLOYEES

Cooperative FYE: December 31	Annual Growth	1989	1990	1991	1992	1993	1994	1995	1996	1997	1998
Sales ($ mil.)	8.1%	1,546	1,625	1,704	1,871	2,018	2,326	2,436	2,742	2,907	3,120
Net income ($ mil.)	6.2%	51	60	59	61	57	65	64	72	76	88
Income as % of sales	—	3.3%	3.7%	3.5%	3.2%	2.8%	2.8%	2.6%	2.6%	2.6%	2.8%
Employees	5.5%	2,875	2,931	3,110	3,256	3,405	3,664	3,917	4,352	4,685	4,672

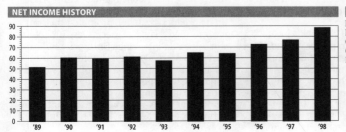

NET INCOME HISTORY

1998 FISCAL YEAR-END
Debt ratio: 30.6%
Return on equity: 33.6%
Cash ($ mil.): 54
Current ratio: 1.32
Long-term debt ($ mil.): 115

ADOBE SYSTEMS INCORPORATED

OVERVIEW

Adobe wants to be the foundation for the shape of things to come. At the forefront of the desktop publishing software industry, San Jose, California-based Adobe Systems offers the ubiquitous Acrobat Reader (distributed free of charge), a tool that enables users to display portable document format (PDF) files on the Internet. Adobe's top three products — Photoshop (photo enhancement), Illustrator (illustration and page design), and PageMaker (a page layout tool) — account for about 60% of its sales. The company's offerings also include print technology (page description language PostScript, printing architecture PrintGear) geared toward OEMs.

Adobe's activities aren't limited to developing its own software. In addition to investing directly in a handful of high-tech companies, Adobe has majority interests in two venture capital partnerships. Adobe's investments span nearly 20 companies whose products and services help buttress the use and acceptance of its own products. Among the partnerships' holdings are stakes in FileNet, PointCast, and Vignette.

Having survived a failed takeover bid from rival Quark, Adobe is taking action to rebound from slipping sales and to quell whispers about its less-than-speedy product growth track record. The company is banking on a restructuring effort and the impending debut of its InDesign publishing package (already branded a "Quark-killer" by industry observers) to propel it in the right direction.

HISTORY

When Charles Geschke hired John Warnock as chief scientist for Xerox's new graphics and imaging lab, he set the stage for one of the world's largest software makers. While at the Xerox lab, the pair developed the PostScript computer language, which tells a printer how to reproduce a digitized image on paper. When Xerox refused to market their product, the duo left the company and started Adobe (named after a creek near their homes in San Jose, California) in 1982.

Their original plan was to produce an electronic document processing system based on PostScript, but the company changed direction when Apple Computer whiz Steve Jobs hired it to co-design the software for his company's LaserWriter printer. A year later Adobe went public. Meanwhile, PostScript was pioneering the desktop publishing industry by enabling users to laser print nearly anything they created on a computer.

The company branched into the European market in 1987 with the establishment of its Adobe Systems Europe subsidiary. That year it entered the PC market by adapting PostScript for IBM's operating system. In 1989 the company began marketing its products in the Pacific Rim.

Adobe grew throughout the 1990s by acquiring other software companies, including OCR Systems and Nonlinear Technologies (1992) and AH Software and Science & Art (1993). Also in 1993 the company began licensing its PostScript software to printer manufacturers and marketing its Acrobat software. Adobe bought Aldus (1994), whose PageMaker software had been instrumental in establishing the desktop publishing market. (PageMaker's success depended on the font software that Adobe made and the two companies had a history of cooperation.) Next the company bought Frame Technology (FrameMaker publishing software, 1995), but the acquisition proved disastrous: Frame sales soon plummeted, partly the result of Adobe's move to eliminate Frame's technical support operations. The company's purchase of Web toolmaker Ceneca Communications that year was more successful.

In 1996 Adobe spun off its pre-press applications operations to Luminous Corporation. In 1997 the company issued stock dividends in technology startups in which it held stakes (such as Netscape). That year its licensing sales suffered a blow when one of its largest customers, Hewlett-Packard, introduced a clone version of PostScript. Also in 1997, for the first time, Adobe's revenues from Windows-based software exceeded those of its once-dominant Macintosh-based software.

In 1998 a hostile takeover bid by competitor Quark proved unsuccessful. Drooping sales that year, which Adobe blamed on the Asian economic flu (but which some analysts blamed on its product strategy), prompted the company to shed a layer of executives, 10% of its workforce, and its Adobe Enterprise Publishing Services and Image Club Graphics units. Adobe's 1999 acquisition of GoLive Systems expanded its Web-publishing product line, and the company planned to cut 250 jobs (9% of its workforce) to channel more money into marketing products and services on the Internet.

Co-Chairman and CEO: John E. Warnock, age 58
Co-Chairman and President: Charles M. Geschke, age 59
EVP Worldwide Products and Marketing:
Bruce R. Chizen, age 43
EVP and CFO: Harold Covert, age 52
SVP Worldwide Sales and Support: Graham Freeman
SVP; General Manager, Adobe Systems Europe:
Derek J. Gray, age 49
SVP Human Resources: Rebecca M. Guerra
SVP, General Counsel, and Secretary:
Colleen M. Pouliot, age 40
SVP Corporate Development: Jim Stephens
VP; General Manager, Adobe Systems North America:
Judi L. Webster
VP; General Manager, Enterprise Solutions Division:
George Cacciopo
VP; General Manager, Mass Market Division:
Kyle Mashima
**VP Product Marketing and Professional Publishing
Solutions:** Bryan Lamkin
President, Adobe Systems Japan: Jesse D. Young
Chief Internet Strategist: Andreas Poliza
Auditors: KPMG LLP

LOCATIONS

HQ: 345 Park Ave., San Jose, CA 95110-2704
Phone: 408-536-6000   **Fax:** 408-537-6000
Web site: http://www.adobe.com

1998 Sales

	$ mil.	% of total
North America	668	60
Europe	249	23
Other regions	192	17
Adjustments	(214)	—
Total	**895**	**100**

PRODUCTS/OPERATIONS

1998 Sales

	$ mil.	% of total
Products	731	82
Licensing fees	164	18
Total	**895**	**100**

1998 Sales

	% of total
Windows-based products	58
Other products	42
Total	**100**

COMPETITORS

Allaire	Linotype-Hell
America Online	Macromedia (CA)
Apple Computer	MetaCreations
Autodesk	MGI Software
Avid Technology	Micrografx
Corel	Microsoft
Electronics For Imaging	NetObjects
Harlequin Group	NewKidCo
Hewlett-Packard	Open Market
IBM	Quark
INSO	Vizacom
Interleaf	Xionics
Learning Company	

HISTORICAL FINANCIALS & EMPLOYEES

Nasdaq symbol: ADBE FYE: November 30	Annual Growth	1989	1990	1991	1992	1993	1994	1995	1996	1997	1998
Sales ($ mil.)	24.9%	121	169	230	266	314	598	762	787	912	895
Net income ($ mil.)	13.5%	34	40	52	44	57	6	94	153	187	105
Income as % of sales	—	27.8%	23.8%	22.5%	16.4%	18.2%	1.1%	12.3%	19.5%	20.5%	11.7%
Earnings per share ($)	7.9%	0.78	0.92	1.13	0.94	1.22	0.22	1.26	2.04	2.52	1.55
Stock price - FY high ($)	—	15.00	25.38	31.50	34.25	37.00	38.50	70.25	74.25	53.13	51.88
Stock price - FY low ($)	—	7.00	8.13	12.63	12.63	14.50	19.75	27.25	28.50	32.50	23.63
Stock price - FY close ($)	18.6%	9.63	12.63	24.00	17.00	23.13	33.00	67.63	39.50	42.00	44.75
P/E - high	—	19	28	28	36	30	175	56	36	21	33
P/E - low	—	9	9	11	13	12	90	22	14	13	15
Dividends per share ($)	8.0%	0.10	0.12	0.15	0.16	0.19	0.20	0.20	0.20	0.20	0.20
Book value per share ($)	21.6%	1.46	2.57	4.13	5.05	6.03	7.47	9.59	9.88	10.40	8.48
Employees	24.1%	383	508	701	887	1,000	1,584	2,319	2,266	2,702	2,680

STOCK PRICE HISTORY

High/Low/Close

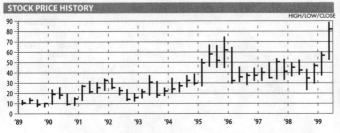

1998 FISCAL YEAR-END

Debt ratio: 0.0%
Return on equity: 20.4%
Cash ($ mil.): 111
Current ratio: 1.82
Long-term debt ($ mil.): —
No. of shares (mil.): 61
Dividends
 Yield: 0.4%
 Payout: 12.9%
Market value ($ mil.): 2,725

ADOLPH COORS COMPANY

OVERVIEW

If you've always thought of domestic beer as just a dull yellow beverage, look again. Golden, Colorado-based Adolph Coors, the parent of Coors Brewing, makes more than a dozen beers and other malt-based beverages available in amber, brown, gold, and red — and even in no color at all. Coors is the #3 US brewer, behind Anheuser-Busch and Philip Morris' Miller Brewing.

Nicknamed "The Silver Bullet," Coors Light is the company's premier product and the #4 US beer. Coors also makes Zima, a clear, lightly carbonated brew, and the Blue Moon line of specialty beers. Once known as a single-product, regional beer maker, the brewer has not been afraid to try new varieties, though it has discontinued several that have fallen short (Coors Dry, Keystone Dry, Blue Moon Raspberry Cream Ale).

Coors' Colorado plant is the world's largest single-site brewery. The company's beers are sold in more than 30 international markets, but almost all of its sales come from the US.

The heirs of founder Adolph Coors own all of the company's voting stock.

HISTORY

Adolph Coors landed in Baltimore in 1868, a 21-year-old stowaway fleeing Germany's military draft. He worked his way west to Denver, where he bought a bottling company in 1872 and became partners with Jacob Schueler, a local merchant, in 1873. The partners built a brewery in Golden, Colorado, a small town in the nearby Rocky Mountain foothills. Coors became sole owner of the Adolph Coors Company in 1880.

For most of its history, Coors confined its sales to western states. The cost of nationwide distribution was prohibitive because the company used a single brewery, natural brewing methods, and no preservatives; Coors beer was made, transported, and stored under refrigeration, with a shelf life of only one month.

The brewer survived Prohibition by making near beer and malted milk and by entering cement and porcelain chemical ware production. The Coors family built a vertically integrated company that did everything from growing brewing ingredients to pumping the oil that powered its breweries. By 1929, when Adolph died, son Adolph Jr. was running Coors. After repeal of the 18th Amendment, beer sales grew steadily in the company's 11-state market.

By the 1960s Coors beer had achieved cult status. Another result of the company's national reputation was that the Coors family had become notoriously private. In 1960 Adolph III was kidnapped and murdered, sending the clan into an even deeper state of secrecy.

Adolph Jr. died in 1970; his son Bill was named chairman and started the country's first aluminum-recycling program. Coors beer was the top seller in 10 of its 11 state markets by 1975, when the company went public. However, sales began to decline as Miller Brewing and Anheuser-Busch introduced new light and superpremium beers. Coors responded by introducing its own light and superpremium brands and expanding its market area to 16 states.

During the 1970s, Joe Coors, another grandson of the founder, supported many ultraconservative projects to express strong family opposition to student radicalism and liberal media. In the late 1970s and 1980s, Coors began rapid expansion while enduring boycotts and strikes due to alleged discriminatory labor practices. The brewer eventually developed progressive employment policies.

To meet increasing demand, Coors bought Stroh's Memphis brewery in 1990. The next year Coors committed more than $30 million to an effort to bring pro baseball to Denver. It spun off packaging and ceramics firm ACX Technologies in 1992. Also that year Coors introduced Zima, a high-priced, clear alcoholic beverage that briefly became a hit.

Leo Kiely became the first president of the company's brewing operations from outside the Coors family in 1993. The company cut its workforce by nearly 700; the severance program cost $70 million and resulted in Coors' first loss in over 10 years.

In 1994 the company opened a microbrewery (SandLot Brewery) at Coors Field, the new stadium for the Colorado Rockies baseball team. Coors' specialty Blue Moon products were piloted at the SandLot and went into production later in 1995.

Coors formed a partnership with Molson Breweries and Foster's in 1997 to manage the distribution of its brands in Canada (Foster's later sold its stake to Molson). In 1999 Coors joined the contentious bidding for ailing South Korean brewer Jinro Coors, which it had helped form in 1992 before selling its interest in 1997. It withdrew its bid in July 1999, citing an "unfair bidding process."

OFFICERS

Chairman and President; Chairman, Coors Brewing:
William K. Coors, age 82, $307,100 pay
VC: Joseph Coors, age 81
VP and Treasurer; VP, Finance and Treasurer, Coors Brewing: David G. Barnes
VP; VC and CEO, Coors Brewing: Peter H. Coors, age 52, $891,097 pay
VP; President and COO, Coors Brewing: W. Leo Kiely III, age 52, $739,500 pay
VP, Controller, and Assistant Treasurer; VP, Controller, and Assistant Treasurer, Coors Brewing:
Olivia M. Thompson, age 48
VP and Assistant Secretary; SVP, General Counsel, and Assistant Secretary, Coors Brewing:
M. Caroline Turner, age 49
VP and CFO; SVP and CFO, Coors Brewing:
Timothy V. Wolf, age 45
SVP of Sales, Coors Brewing: Carl L. Barnhill, age 50
Auditors: PricewaterhouseCoopers LLP

LOCATIONS

HQ: 17735 W. 32nd Ave., Golden, CO 80401
Phone: 303-279-6565 **Fax:** 303-277-6246
Web site: http://www.coors.com

Adolph Coors has production facilities in Colorado, Tennessee, Virginia, and Spain. It also has aluminum can and glass bottling plants in Colorado as well as distribution facilities in California, Colorado, Idaho, and Oklahoma. The company's products are sold in the US and more than 30 international markets in Asia, Australia, the Caribbean, Europe, Latin America, and North America.

1998 Sales

	$ mil.	% of total
US	1,873	99
Other countries	27	1
Total	**1,900**	**100**

PRODUCTS/OPERATIONS

Selected Brands

Blue Moon Abbey Ale	Keystone
Blue Moon Belgian White Ale	Keystone Ice
	Keystone Light
Blue Moon Harvest Pumpkin Ale	Original Coors
	Steinlager (licensed)
Coors Extra Gold	Winterfest
Coors Light	Zima Citrix
Coors Non-Alcoholic	Zima Clear
George Killian's Irish Red Lager (licensed)	

COMPETITORS

Anheuser-Busch	Grupo Modelo
Bass	Guinness Ltd.
Boston Beer	Heineken
Canandaigua Brands	Interbrew
Carlsberg	Miller Brewing
Foster's Brewing	Molson
Gambrinus	S&P
Genesee	

HISTORICAL FINANCIALS & EMPLOYEES

NYSE symbol: RKY FYE: December 31	Annual Growth	1989	1990	1991	1992	1993	1994	1995	1996	1997	1998
Sales ($ mil.)	0.8%	1,764	1,863	1,917	1,551	1,582	1,663	1,675	1,732	1,822	1,900
Net income ($ mil.)	20.0%	13	39	26	(2)	(42)	58	43	43	82	68
Income as % of sales	—	0.7%	2.1%	1.3%	—	(1.10)	3.5%	2.6%	2.5%	4.5%	3.6%
Earnings per share ($)	27.7%	0.20	0.87	0.50	(0.05)	(1.10)	1.51	1.13	1.14	2.16	1.81
Stock price - FY high ($)	—	24.38	27.38	24.25	22.88	22.63	20.88	23.25	24.25	41.25	56.75
Stock price - FY low ($)	—	17.38	17.13	17.38	15.50	15.00	14.75	15.13	16.75	17.50	29.25
Stock price - FY close ($)	12.4%	19.75	20.50	21.00	16.50	16.25	16.75	22.13	19.00	33.25	56.44
P/E - high	—	122	31	49	—	—	14	21	21	19	31
P/E - low	—	87	20	35	—	—	10	13	15	8	16
Dividends per share ($)	2.0%	0.50	0.50	0.50	0.50	0.50	0.50	0.50	0.50	0.55	0.60
Book value per share ($)	(3.4%)	28.75	29.20	29.33	18.17	16.54	17.59	18.29	18.87	19.98	21.14
Employees	(6.5%)	10,600	10,700	11,800	7,100	6,200	6,300	6,200	5,800	5,800	5,800

STOCK PRICE HISTORY

HIGH/LOW/CLOSE

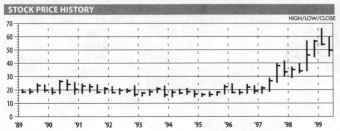

1998 FISCAL YEAR-END

Debt ratio: 11.9%
Return on equity: 8.8%
Cash ($ mil.): 160
Current ratio: 1.43
Long-term debt ($ mil.): 105
No. of shares (mil.): 37
Dividends
  Yield: 1.1%
  Payout: 33.1%
Market value ($ mil.): 2,069

ADVANCE PUBLICATIONS, INC.

OVERVIEW

Advance Publications is always moving forward. The Staten Island, New York-based publishing conglomerate is launching a major offensive to claim control of Internet real estate with specialized Web sites (The Yuckiest Site on the Internet) and online versions of its newspapers. It also owns AdOne Classified Network (online classified ad site) with four other media companies, and is a partner in Time Warner's Road Runner high-speed Internet access service.

But Advance has not retreated from words in print. Its high-profile Condé Nast Publications division is the source for lifestyle and fashion magazines *Glamour, Vogue,* and *GQ.* It also offers more thoughtful fare like *The New Yorker, Wired,* and *Vanity Fair.* Its acquisition of Disney's Fairchild Publications unit

(*W, Women's Wear Daily*) will give Condé Nast control of virtually the entire fashion publishing industry.

On the home front, the company owns small and midsized newspapers in 22 cities, including the *Times-Picayune* (New Orleans) and *The Plain Dealer* (Cleveland). It also publishes about 40 local business weeklies through its American City Business Journals unit, and it owns Parade Publications, purveyor of Sunday newspaper supplements *Parade* and the teen-focused *react.* Other interests include cable TV operations and a minority stake in Discovery Communications.

Advance Publications, secretive to the extreme, is controlled by CEO Samuel "Si" Newhouse Jr. and his brother, president Donald Newhouse.

HISTORY

Solomon Neuhaus (later Samuel I. Newhouse) got started in the newspaper business after dropping out of school at age 13. He went to work for a lawyer who had taken possession of the *Bayonne Times* in New Jersey as payment for a debt. The 16-year-old Newhouse was put in charge of the failing newspaper in 1911 and turned it around. In 1922 he bought his own newspaper, the *Staten Island Advance,* and used the profits to buy other papers in the New York area. By the 1950s he owned local papers in New York, New Jersey, and other middle markets and had expanded into Alabama.

In 1959 Newhouse bought magazine publisher Condé Nast as an anniversary gift for his wife. He joked that she had asked for a fashion magazine, so he bought her *Vogue.* Newhouse continued building his newspaper empire and expanded into cable television.

Newhouse died in 1979, leaving his sons Si and Donald as trustees of the company's voting stock. Although they reported inheritance taxes of $48.7 million, the IRS sought more. When the case — the largest until then — was decided in 1990, the IRS lost.

Meanwhile, the company continued to expand. The sons bought book publishing giant Random House from RCA in 1980. Si also built up the magazine business, resurrecting the Roaring Twenties standard *Vanity Fair* in 1983 and adding other titles under the Condé Nast banner, including *The New Yorker* in 1985.

During this period, Advance focused less on costs and more on creating prestigious products. Despite a recession and falling ad

revenues, editorial decisions became severed from financial considerations until the 1990s. As profits evaporated at some magazines, management shuffling became common. In 1993 Condé Nast added Knapp Publications (*Architectural Digest, Bon Appetit*) to its stable, but discontinued *House & Garden* (the magazine was revived in 1996). *New Yorker* president Steven Florio became president of Condé Nast in 1994 and helped most Condé Nast titles become profitable again in 1995.

Advance bought American City Business Journals in 1995. Two years later it began exploring links with the Discovery Channel, of which it owns about 25%. It also announced plans to debut new publications *Sports for Women* and *Businesses to Watch* (which profiles companies that advertise in *Vanity Fair*). The company sold the increasingly unprofitable Random House in 1998 for between $1.2 billion and $1.6 billion. That year also saw the purchase of Wired Ventures' trademark Internet magazine, *Wired.* Revered *New Yorker* editor Tina Brown, a former *Vanity Fair* editor credited with jazzing up the magazine's content and increasing its circulation by 200,000, left the company in 1998; staff writer and Pulitzer Prize winner David Remnick was named as Brown's replacement.

In 1999 Advance joined Donrey Media Group, E.W. Scripps, Hearst Corporation, and MediaNews Group to purchase the online classified advertising network AdOne and created strategic partnerships with Web sites such as Proteam.com and WeddingChannel.com.

**Chairman and CEO; Chairman, Condé Nast
Publications:** Samuel I. "Si" Newhouse Jr.
President: Donald E. Newhouse
Chairman, American City Business Journals: Ray Shaw
Chairman, Condé Nast International:
Jonathan Newhouse
President, Advance Internet: Steven Newhouse
President and CEO, Condé Nast Publications:
Steven T. Florio
**President, Condé Nast Asia-Pacific; Chairman,
Interculture Communications Ltd. (Taiwan):**
Didier Guerin
Publisher, Architectural Digest: Peter Hunsinger
Publisher, Condé Nast Traveler: Lisa Henriques Hughes,
age 39
Publisher, Details: Linda Mason
Publisher, Gourmet: Gina Sanders
Publisher, GQ: Thomas Florio, age 42
Publisher, Mademoiselle: Nina Lawrence
Publisher, The New Yorker: David Carey
Publisher, Staten Island Advance: Richard Diamond
EVP and CFO, Condé Nast Publications:
Eric C. Anderson
EVP, Condé Nast Publications: Catherine V. Johnston
SVP Human Resources, Condé Nast Publications:
Jill H. Bright
Comptroller, Staten Island Advance: Arthur Silverstein

LOCATIONS

HQ: 950 Fingerboard Rd., Staten Island, NY 10305
Phone: 718-981-1234   **Fax:** 718-981-1456
Web site: http://www.advance.net

Advance Publications has newspapers in 22 cities. Its
Condé Nast magazines are distributed throughout the US.

PRODUCTS/OPERATIONS

Selected Operations

American City Business
  Journals Inc. (39 weekly
  business newspapers)
Condé Nast Publications
  Allure
  Architectural Digest
  Bon Appetit
  Bride's
  Condé Nast Traveler
  Details
  Glamour
  Gourmet
  GQ
  House & Garden
  Mademoiselle
  The New Yorker
  Self

  Vanity Fair
  Vogue
  Wired
  *Women's Sports &
    Fitness*
Newhouse Broadcasting
  Cable television
  Discovery
    Communications
    (24%, cable TV
    channel)
Newhouse Newspapers
  (small to midsized
  papers in 22 cities)
Parade Publications
  Parade
  react

Selected Newspapers
The Birmingham News (Alabama)
The Plain Dealer (Cleveland)
The Times-Picayune (New Orleans)

COMPETITORS

American Express
Cablevision Systems
Comcast
Crain Communications
Dow Jones
E. W. Scripps
Gannett
Hachette Filipacchi
Hearst
Knight Ridder
McClatchy Company
McGraw-Hill
Meredith

New York Times
News Corp.
Pearson
PRIMEDIA
Reader's Digest
Salon
Time Warner
Times Mirror
Tribune
Viacom
Walt Disney
Washington Post

HISTORICAL FINANCIALS & EMPLOYEES

Private company FYE: December 31	Annual Growth	1989	1990	1991	1992	1993	1994	1995	1996	1997	1998
Sales ($ mil.)	(2.7%)	3,040	3,095	4,287	4,416	4,690	4,855	5,349	4,250	3,669	3,859
Employees	0.6%	19,000	19,500	19,000	19,000	19,000	19,000	24,000	24,000	24,000	20,000

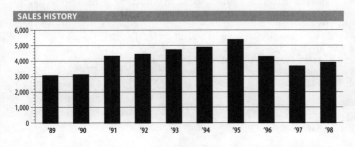

SALES HISTORY

ADVANCED MICRO DEVICES, INC.

OVERVIEW

In the microprocessor marketplace, Intel is the world's undisputed heavyweight champ and Advanced Micro Devices (AMD) is the stubborn challenger. Sunnyvale, California-based AMD is a major supplier of microprocessors and other integrated circuits (ICs). In addition to microprocessors, where it ranks #2 with more than 10% of the market, AMD makes nonvolatile memories and ICs for communications and networking.

Microprocessors, the brains of computers, continue to be AMD's focus. Many computer makers want an inexpensive alternative to Intel's chips, and AMD is taking a jab at Intel's 80% share of the PC market with its K6 (sixth-generation) chip and K6 with 3DNow!, which supports the multimedia capabilities built into most new PCs. Compaq (12% of sales), IBM,

and several second-tier PC makers, including Acer, have released K6-based systems. As a result, AMD has grabbed a big share of the consumer PC market and has a nearly 60% share in sub-$1,000 PC sales.

AMD's next-generation microprocessor expands AMD's reach into higher-end PCs. A strategic punch, the K7 (marketed as the Athlon) uses a different connection standard than the Pentium-system-compatible K6; this change will force some PC makers to choose between the Intel and AMD standards earlier in their design process.

In the battle with Intel, AMD has sometimes been its own worst enemy. Design flaws and other manufacturing problems have plagued the company, contributing to losses and testing the market's patience.

HISTORY

Management at Silicon Valley powerhouse Fairchild Camera & Instrument axed marketing whiz Jerry Sanders, reportedly for wearing a pink shirt on a sales call to IBM. So in 1969 Sanders started a semiconductor company, just as his former boss, Intel founder Robert Noyce, had done a year earlier.

At first Sanders used his marketing flair to sell products based on second-source agreements (chip designs licensed from other companies). Advanced Micro Devices (AMD) went public in 1972. Five years later it got an infusion of cash when Siemens, eager to get its foot in the door of the US semiconductor market, paid $30 million for nearly 20% of AMD (sold off by 1991). In 1982 AMD inked a deal with Intel that enabled AMD to make exact copies of Intel's iAPX86 microprocessors, used in IBM and compatible PCs.

By the mid-1980s AMD was developing its own chips. It suffered a setback in 1982 when a group of engineers left to start Cypress Semiconductor. In 1986, after prices for its old Intel microprocessor clones fell, AMD closed plants and announced its first layoffs. The next year AMD bought programmable logic chip maker Monolithic Memories and began legal action against Intel for breaking the 1982 agreement for AMD to second-source Intel's new 386 chips.

In 1990 Intel sued for copyright infringement when AMD introduced a version of Intel's 287 math coprocessor. Lawsuits also followed AMD's release of its 386 clone in 1991 and its 486 clone in 1993.

AMD signed a pact to develop microprocessors with Hewlett-Packard in 1993. It also formed a joint venture with Fujitsu to make

flash memory devices. A federal jury decided in AMD's favor in the 287 math coprocessor case in 1994. That year AMD began to sell its Am486 chip to Compaq (one of Intel's biggest customers).

After nearly a decade of legal wrangling, in 1995 AMD and Intel settled their differences. Each agreed to pay damages, and AMD won a perpetual license to the microcode in Intel's 386 and 486 chips. AMD's K5 microprocessor (a rival of Intel's Pentium chip) finally hit the market in 1996 — more than a year late.

In an effort to close the gap with Intel in processor performance, in 1996 AMD bought microprocessor developer NexGen and its technology for the K6 chip. That year AMD restructured its successful programmable logic devices unit as a subsidiary, Vantis. Product delays and declining sales led to a loss for the year.

AMD unveiled its K6 microprocessor in 1997, but had trouble increasing production to meet demand. In 1998 the prolonged slump in the chip market and pricing pressures depressed AMD's sales, which rose slightly thanks to the year-end holiday season. In 1999 it announced that another manufacturing snafu would lower output of K6 chips. AMD also sold Vantis to Lattice Semiconductor, raising $500 million to beef up its assault on Intel's market share.

Athlon, the company's ultrafast K7 chip, was unveiled in mid-1999 to positive reviews. Soon after, however, president and COO Atiq Raza — who had come to AMD with the NexGen purchase — resigned, signaling deepening problems for the company.

Chairman, CEO, Interim President, Interim COO, and Interim Chief Technical Officer: W. J. Sanders III, age 62, $1,012,167 pay
VC: Richard Previte, age 64, $778,479 pay (prior to title change)
EVP, Strategic Relations: Eugene D. Conner, $650,330 pay
SVP and CFO: Fran Barton
SVP and Co-Chief Marketing Executive: Robert R. Herb, $740,781 pay
SVP, General Counsel, and Secretary: Thomas M. McCoy
SVP, Technology Development and Wafer Fabrication Operations and Chief Scientist: William T. Siegle
SVP, Human Resources: Stanley Winvick
SVP and Co-Chief Marketing Executive: Stephen J. Zelencik
Group VP, Communications Group: Tom Eby
Group VP, Computation Products Group: Larry Hollatz
Group VP, Manufacturing Services Group: Donald M. Brettner
Group VP, Memory Group: Walid Maghribi
Group VP, Wafer Fabrication Group: Gary O. Heerssen
Group VP, Wafer Fabrication Technology Implementation: Daryl Ostrander
VP; General Manager, Communications Products Division: Gary Ashcraft
Auditors: Ernst & Young LLP

LOCATIONS

HQ: 1 AMD Place, Sunnyvale, CA 94086
Phone: 408-732-2400   **Fax:** 408-774-7023
Web site: http://www.amd.com

Advanced Micro Devices has manufacturing operations in California and Texas, and in China, Germany, Japan, Malaysia, Singapore, and Thailand.

1998 Sales

	$ mil.	% of total
US	1,149	45
Europe		
Germany	265	11
Other countries	465	18
Asia/Pacific	663	26
Total	**2,542**	**100**

PRODUCTS/OPERATIONS

1998 Sales

	$ mil.	% of total
Computation products	1,257	49
Memory	561	22
Communications	519	21
Vantis (programmable logic devices)	205	8
Total	**2,542**	**100**

COMPETITORS

3Com	Micron Technology
Alcatel	Motorola
Atmel	National Semiconductor
Cypress Semiconductor	NEC
Ericsson	Philips Electronics
Fujitsu	Samsung
Hitachi	Sharp
IBM	Siemens
Integrated Device Technology	STMicroelectronics
Intel	Texas Instruments
LSI Logic	Toshiba
Lucent	Zilog

HISTORICAL FINANCIALS & EMPLOYEES

NYSE symbol: AMD FYE: December 31	Annual Growth	1989	1990	1991	1992	1993	1994	1995	1996	1997	1998
Sales ($ mil.)	9.7%	1,105	1,059	1,227	1,515	1,648	2,135	2,430	1,953	2,356	2,542
Net income ($ mil.)	—	46	(54)	145	245	229	305	301	(69)	(21)	(104)
Income as % of sales	—	4.2%	—	11.8%	16.2%	13.9%	14.3%	12.4%	—	—	—
Earnings per share ($)	—	0.44	(0.78)	1.52	2.49	1.64	2.03	1.57	(0.51)	(0.15)	(0.72)
Stock price - FY high ($)	—	10.50	11.38	17.75	21.50	32.88	31.75	39.25	28.38	48.50	32.75
Stock price - FY low ($)	—	7.13	3.63	4.00	7.38	17.00	16.75	16.13	10.25	17.13	12.75
Stock price - FY close ($)	15.6%	7.88	4.88	17.50	18.13	17.75	24.88	16.50	25.75	17.75	29.00
P/E - high	—	24	—	12	9	20	16	25	—	—	—
P/E - low	—	16	—	3	3	10	8	10	—	—	—
Dividends per share ($)	—	0.00	0.00	0.00	0.75	0.00	0.00	0.01	0.00	0.00	0.00
Book value per share ($)	5.5%	8.51	7.73	9.32	11.86	14.63	18.19	20.09	14.70	14.28	13.78
Employees	0.6%	13,072	11,997	11,254	11,554	12,065	11,793	12,730	12,200	12,800	13,800

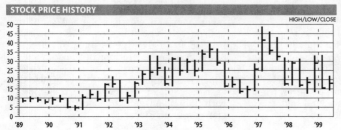

STOCK PRICE HISTORY HIGH/LOW/CLOSE

1998 FISCAL YEAR-END
Debt ratio: 40.6%
Return on equity: —
Cash ($ mil.): 362
Current ratio: 1.86
Long-term debt ($ mil.): 1,372
No. of shares (mil.): 145
Dividends
  Yield: —
  Payout: —
Market value ($ mil.): 4,219

AETNA INC.

OVERVIEW

Stop thinking Aetna is insurance, because now it's mostly managed health care.

Hartford, Connecticut-based Aetna's transformation included the sale of its property/casualty business to Travelers (now Citigroup) and a merger with U.S. Healthcare, a rapidly growing managed care firm. The merger turned Aetna into one of the nation's top managed health care firms. Its 1999 purchase of Prudential HealthCare shot it to the top of the heap and made it the health benefits provider for 10% of Americans.

Aetna provides group and individual health care, including indemnity insurance, PPOs, and HMOs. It also offers annuities, individual retirement advice, and asset management services, along with group pensions and pension plan management.

The company plans to slowly integrate Prudential's operations into its own to prevent the backlash it felt from doctors and patients after acquiring U.S. Healthcare. U.S. Healthcare founder Leonard Abramson owns about 9% of Aetna.

HISTORY

Hartford businessman and judge Eliphalet Bulkeley started Connecticut Mutual Life Insurance in 1846. Undeterred when he lost control of that company the next year, in 1853 Bulkeley and a group of Hartford businessmen founded Aetna Life Insurance as a spinoff of Aetna Fire Insurance.

Aetna's early growth is attributed to its nationwide agency network. It expanded in the 1860s by offering a participating life policy, which returned dividends to policyholders based on investment earnings, allowing Aetna to compete with mutual life insurers. In 1868 Aetna became the first firm to offer renewable term life policies.

Eliphalet's son, Morgan, became president in 1879. Aetna moved into accident (1891), health (1899), workers' compensation (1902), and automobile and other property insurance (1907) during his 43-year tenure. He increased Aetna's visibility by serving as mayor of Hartford, governor of Connecticut, and US senator, all the while leading Aetna.

By 1920 Aetna had added ocean and inland marine insurance, and by 1922 it was the US's largest multiline insurer. Aetna overexpanded its nonlife insurance lines (particularly automobiles) during the 1920s, threatening its solvency. It survived the Depression by restricting underwriting and rebuilding reserves.

After WWII the company expanded into group life, health, and accident insurance. In 1967 it reorganized under holding company Aetna Life and Casualty.

The 1960s, 1970s, and 1980s were go-go years for Aetna, which added lines and bought and sold everything from an oil-services firm to commercial real estate. But boom led to bust and a 1991 reorganization in which Aetna eliminated 8,000 jobs, withdrew from such lines as auto insurance, and sold its profitable American Reinsurance.

As part of Aetna's effort to take advantage of the boom in retirement savings, in 1995 it got permission to set up a bank, AE Trust Co., which allowed it to act as a pension trustee.

With its health care business accounting for almost 60% of sales by 1995, Aetna performed radical surgery in the late 1990s: It sold its property/casualty business to Travelers (now Citigroup); its behavioral managed care unit to Magellan Health Services (1997); and its individual life insurance business to Lincoln National (1998). The company also expanded overseas, merged with U.S. Healthcare, and bought the NYLCare managed health business from New York Life (1998).

A 1998 clash over contract terms — including a "gag" clause against discussing treatments not provided by Aetna — prompted 400 Texas doctors to leave its system; other defections followed in Kentucky and West Virginia. Consumers expressed discontent with the company, too, targeting Aetna with litigation over its refusal to provide treatment, particularly experimental procedures. One enterprising group even sued under the RICO statutes, claiming that Aetna's "commitment to quality" advertising was false and misleading. The company faced other troubles in 1998 as its decision to eliminate coverage of advanced fertility treatments from basic plans sparked controversy, prompting Aetna to reinstate it.

In an unprecedented move, the American Medical Association in 1998 asked the government to challenge Aetna's planned acquisition of Prudential's health care unit as anticompetitive. In 1999 the government required Aetna to sell off operations in Houston and Dallas to receive approval for the acquisition, which was completed later that year. Also that year the company agreed to a partnership with Columbia OneSource Health, a physicians group in Florida.

OFFICERS

Chairman, President, and CEO: Richard L. Huber,
age 62, $1,359,096 pay
VC Strategy and Finance: Alan J. Weber, age 49,
$302,885 pay
EVP; President, Aetna U.S. Healthcare:
Michael J. Cardillo, age 55, $1,181,092 pay
EVP; President, Aetna International:
Frederick C. Copeland Jr., age 57, $758,269 pay
EVP; President, Aetna Retirement Services:
Thomas J. McInerney, age 42, $761,538 pay
SVP Corporate Communications: Roger Bolton
SVP Aetna Investment Management Group:
Timothy A. Holt
SVP Federal Government Relations:
Vanda B. McMurtry
SVP Corporate Human Resources: Elease E. Wright
VP Acting General Counsel, and Secretary:
William J. Casazza
VP Diversity: Alfonso Martinez
VP Investor Relations: Robyn S. Walsh
Head of Telecommunications; Network And Distributed Services, Aetna Information Management:
Elizabeth A. Sage
General Counsel: L. Edward Shaw Jr.
Auditors: KPMG LLP

LOCATIONS

HQ: 151 Farmington Ave., Hartford, CT 06156
Phone: 860-273-0123 **Fax:** 860-273-3971
Web site: http://www.aetna.com

Aetna operates in Asia, Europe, Latin America, North
America, and the Pacific Rim.

1998 Sales

	$ mil.	% of total
The Americas		
US	18,428	89
Other countries	982	5
Asia/Pacific	1,192	6
Other regions	2	—
Total	**20,604**	**100**

PRODUCTS/OPERATIONS

1998 Sales

	$ mil.	% of total
Premiums	14,839	72
Investment income	3,191	16
Fees & other income	2,362	11
Realized capital gains	212	1
Total	**20,604**	**100**

1998 Premiums

	$ mil.	% of total
Healthcare	13,006	88
International	1,578	10
Retirement services	132	1
Large case pensions	123	1
Total	**14,839**	**100**

COMPETITORS

Blue Cross
CIGNA
Foundation Health
 Systems
Guardian Life
Humana
Kaiser Foundation
Mid Atlantic Medical

Oxford Health Plans
PacifiCare
UniHealth
UnitedHealth Group
USAA
WellPoint Health
 Networks

HISTORICAL FINANCIALS & EMPLOYEES

NYSE symbol: AET FYE: December 31	Annual Growth	1989	1990	1991	1992	1993	1994	1995	1996	1997	1998
Sales ($ mil.)	0.2%	20,290	19,743	19,196	17,497	17,118	17,525	12,978	15,163	18,540	20,604
Net income ($ mil.)	2.5%	676	614	505	230	(366)	468	252	651	901	848
Income as % of sales	—	3.3%	3.1%	2.6%	1.3%	—	2.7%	1.9%	4.3%	4.9%	4.1%
Earnings per share ($)	(1.2%)	6.02	5.52	4.59	0.51	(3.30)	4.14	2.20	4.72	5.60	5.41
Stock price - FY high ($)	—	62.50	58.38	49.13	48.88	66.25	65.75	76.75	82.50	118.13	89.38
Stock price - FY low ($)	—	46.63	29.00	31.88	38.00	43.38	42.25	46.75	55.38	66.31	60.19
Stock price - FY close ($)	3.7%	56.50	39.00	44.00	46.50	60.38	47.13	69.25	80.00	70.56	78.63
P/E - high	—	10	11	11	96	—	16	35	17	21	17
P/E - low	—	8	5	7	75	—	10	21	12	12	11
Dividends per share ($)	(12.9%)	2.76	2.76	2.76	2.76	2.76	2.76	2.76	2.47	0.80	0.80
Book value per share ($)	2.1%	61.94	64.23	67.09	65.64	62.77	48.85	63.39	66.79	70.85	74.51
Employees	(3.3%)	45,500	47,100	48,300	43,000	42,600	40,900	40,200	38,600	40,300	33,500

STOCK PRICE HISTORY

HIGH/LOW/CLOSE

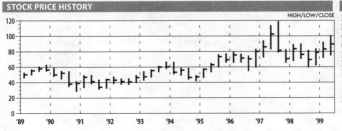

1998 FISCAL YEAR-END

Debt ratio: 19.7%
Return on equity: 8.1%
Cash ($ mil.): —
Current ratio: —
Long-term debt ($ mil.): 2,796
No. of shares (mil.): 141
Dividends
 Yield: 1.0%
 Payout: 14.8%
Market value ($ mil.): 11,108

AFLAC INCORPORATED

OVERVIEW

Too bad AFLAC's insurance didn't cover the Asian Economic Flu.

Despite its US roots, AFLAC makes most of its revenues selling "dread disease" cancer insurance in Japan. Along with being the largest foreign insurer in Japan — where it also sells supplemental medical and life insurance — AFLAC is also the US's largest seller of supplemental insurance. The Columbus, Georgia-based company sells policies that pay cash benefits for intensive care, long-term (nursing home) care, and in-home care.

Doing so much business in Japan (about 80% of sales) has its pitfalls. AFLAC is very vulnerable to yen/dollar currency fluctuations. It also will be vulnerable to increased competition in Japan beginning in 2001, when deregulation of its sector of the insurance industry begins.

AFLAC's primary sales tool in Japan is an agency system in which a corporation forms a subsidiary to sell AFLAC's insurance to its employees. Its US approach, known as cluster selling, is similar in that it sells to individuals through their workplaces. AFLAC is also working hard, through a growing agency staff, to garner clients who work at smaller enterprises in both countries.

HISTORY

American Family Life Assurance Co. (AFLAC) was founded in Columbus, Georgia, in 1955 by brothers John, Paul, and William Amos to sell life, health, and accident insurance. Competition was fierce, and the little company did poorly.

With AFLAC nearing bankruptcy, the brothers looked for a niche. Taking their cue from the polio scares of the 1940s and 1950s, which had spawned specialty insurance against that disease, the Amoses (whose father was a victim of cancer) decided to sell cancer insurance. In 1958 they introduced the world's first cancer-expense policy. It was a hit, and by 1959 the company had written nearly a million dollars in premiums and expanded across state lines.

The enterprise grew quickly during the 1960s, especially after developing its cluster-selling approach in the workplace, where employers were usually willing to make payroll deductions for premiums. By 1971 the company was operating in 42 states.

While visiting the World's Fair in Osaka in 1970, John Amos decided to market supplemental cancer coverage to the Japanese, whose national health care plan left them exposed to considerable expense from cancer treatment. After four years the company finally won approval to sell in Japan because the policies did not threaten existing markets and because the Amoses found notable backers in the insurance and medical industries. AFLAC became one of the first US insurance companies to enter the Japanese market, and it enjoyed an eight-year monopoly on the cancer market. In 1973 AFLAC organized a holding company and began buying television stations in the South and Midwest.

The 1980s were marked by US and state government inquiries into dread disease insurance. Many believed such policies were a poor value because they were relatively expensive and covered only one disease. However, the inquiries led nowhere and demand for such insurance increased, bringing new competition. As AFLAC's US sales growth slowed in the 1980s, business grew in Japan; soon Japan accounted for most of the company's sales. Attempts to sell the insurance in the UK and Australia failed.

In 1990 John Amos died of cancer and was replaced as CEO by his nephew Dan. Two years later the company officially renamed itself AFLAC (partly because Dan planned to increase the company's US profile and so many US companies already used the name "American").

AFLAC has sought to supplement its cancer insurance by introducing new products and improving old ones to encourage policyholders to add on or trade up. Its Japanese "living benefit" product, which includes lump sum payments for heart attacks and strokes, struck a chord with the aging population.

In 1997 Connecticut repealed its specified-disease insurance ban, while New York, New Jersey, and Massachusetts considered regulatory changes (New York has since allowed the insurance). Also in 1997 AFLAC sold its seven TV stations to Raycom Media to focus on insurance.

The company boosted its name recognition in the US from 2% in 1990 to more than 56%, primarily through advertising, including slots during the 1998 Olympic Winter Games and NASCAR races. In 1999 the company signed a three-year deal to cross-sell its supplemental insurance with human resources outsourcing firm NovaCare Employee Services.

Chairman, AFLAC Incorporated and AFLAC:
Paul S. Amos, age 72, $2,484,283 pay
President and CEO, AFLAC Incorporated and AFLAC:
Daniel P. Amos, age 47, $1,990,000 pay
EVP, CFO, and Treasurer, AFLAC Incorporated; EVP and CFO, AFLAC: Kriss Cloninger III, age 51, $900,000 pay
SVP Corporate Services, AFLAC Incorporated and AFLAC: Martin A. Durant III, age 50
SVP Human Resources: Angie Hart
SVP Investor Relations: Kenneth S. Janke Jr., age 40
SVP and Director Corporate and Market Development, AFLAC US: David A. Halmrast
Auditors: KPMG LLP

LOCATIONS

HQ: 1932 Wynnton Rd., Columbus, GA 31999
Phone: 706-323-3431 **Fax:** 706-324-6330
Web site: http://www.aflac.com

AFLAC conducts business throughout the US and several of its territories and in Japan.

1998 Sales & Operating Income

	Sales		Operating Income	
	$ mil.	% of total	$ mil.	% of total
Insurance				
Japan	5,657	79	502	69
US	1,418	20	230	31
Other operations	69	1	2	—
Adjustments	(40)	—	—	—
Total	**7,104**	**100**	**734**	**100**

PRODUCTS/OPERATIONS

1998 Assets

	$ mil.	% of total
Cash & equivalents	374	1
US Treasurys	3,003	10
Foreign government securities	14,657	47
Bonds	3,947	13
Stocks	177	1
Other securities	4,817	15
Mortgage loans	9	—
Other investments	10	—
Other assets	4,189	13
Total	**31,183**	**100**

1998 Sales

	$ mil.	% of total
Premiums		
Cancer-related	4,328	61
Other accident/health	1,099	15
Life	509	7
Net investment income	1,133	16
Other	35	1
Total	**7,104**	**100**

COMPETITORS

AIG	Provident Mutual
Chiyoda Mutual Life	Taiyo Mutual Life
Conseco	Toho Mutual Life
Daido Life Insurance	Insurance
Jefferson-Pilot	Torchmark
Lincoln National	UNUMProvident
Nippon Dantai Life	

HISTORICAL FINANCIALS & EMPLOYEES

NYSE symbol: AFL FYE: December 31	Annual Growth	1989	1990	1991	1992	1993	1994	1995	1996	1997	1998
Assets ($ mil.)	19.0%	6,515	8,035	10,145	11,901	15,443	20,287	25,338	25,023	29,454	31,183
Net income ($ mil.)	22.1%	81	117	149	183	255	293	349	394	585	487
Income as % of assets	—	1.2%	1.5%	1.5%	1.5%	1.7%	1.4%	1.4%	1.6%	2.0%	1.6%
Earnings per share ($)	23.2%	0.27	0.38	0.48	0.59	0.82	0.95	1.17	1.37	2.08	1.76
Stock price - FY high ($)	—	6.00	5.14	8.30	9.30	11.34	12.05	14.92	22.00	28.94	45.31
Stock price - FY low ($)	—	3.57	3.24	4.77	6.40	8.25	8.42	10.63	14.13	18.75	22.69
Stock price - FY close ($)	27.9%	4.80	5.10	7.97	9.20	9.50	10.67	14.51	21.38	25.56	43.88
P/E - high	—	22	14	17	16	14	13	13	16	14	26
P/E - low	—	13	9	10	11	10	9	9	10	9	13
Dividends per share ($)	13.5%	0.08	0.09	0.10	0.12	0.13	0.15	0.17	0.20	0.23	0.25
Book value per share ($)	22.4%	2.31	2.59	3.01	3.50	4.40	5.86	7.52	7.71	12.88	14.19
Employees	4.5%	3,005	3,150	3,318	3,618	3,902	4,321	4,070	4,421	4,032	4,450

STOCK PRICE HISTORY

HIGH/LOW/CLOSE

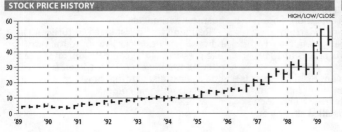

1998 FISCAL YEAR-END

Equity as % of assets: 12.1%
Return on assets: 1.6%
Return on equity: 12.9%
Long-term debt ($ mil.): 596
No. of shares (mil.): 266
Dividends
  Yield: 0.6%
  Payout: 14.2%
Market value ($ mil.): 11,658
Sales (mil.): $7,104

A.G. EDWARDS, INC.

OVERVIEW

With an attitude that's more Main Street than Wall Street, A.G. Edwards brings a midwestern sensibility to the investment business. The St. Louis-based firm owns investment firm A.G. Edwards & Sons, which operates one of the US's largest retail brokerage networks. The company has more than 630 offices nationwide. A.G. Edwards provides securities and commodities brokerage, asset management, mutual funds, insurance, trust services, and investment banking to individual, corporate, governmental, and institutional customers. The company also specializes in underwriting bonds for such public projects as schools and sports facilities.

Unlike most competitors, A.G. Edwards' brokers have no sales quotas. The company offers no proprietary mutual funds but does offer a no-load fund market, Fund Navigator, for a fee. Feeling pressure from discount brokers and from full-service firms that also have discount operations, A.G. Edwards has reluctantly begun to offer fee-based transactions on some types of accounts, rather than charging commissions. The company is family run: CEO Benjamin Edwards III is a fourth-generation descendant of the founder.

HISTORY

A. G. Edwards was born in 1812, six years before Illinois became a state. His father, Ninian Edwards (later the third governor of Illinois), named the child Albert Gallatin, after the secretary of the treasury during the presidencies of Jefferson and Madison. Albert's brother Ninian was Abraham Lincoln's brother-in-law; in 1836 both Ninian and Lincoln were elected to the Illinois legislature.

When the Civil War broke out in 1861, the Edwardses were fiercely loyal to Lincoln and the Union cause. Albert was a brigadier general in the Missouri state militia, then was appointed assistant secretary of the US Treasury in 1865, just six days before Lincoln's assassination. After serving five presidents, he retired in 1887 at age 75. Less than a year later he and his eldest son, Benjamin Franklin Edwards, formed brokerage firm A.G. Edwards & Son to handle trades on the NYSE for St. Louis banks. Albert died in 1892.

The brokerage survived the 1890s recession through conservative fiscal policies and in 1898 bought a seat on the NYSE. Two years later it opened a Wall Street office. After WWI the firm began targeting new middle-class investors. It handled its first IPO in 1925.

Although the firm weathered the Wall Street crash of 1929 better than many, the Depression and skepticism about investments made the 1930s a tough decade. But as a testament to A.G. Edwards' reputation, floor manager William McChesney Martin was elected the NYSE's first paid president in 1938. The company had six offices in 1940; four closed during WWII.

Third-generation president Presley Edwards (1929 to 1965) attended an IBM seminar in 1948 and, impressed by the new technology, had a computer system installed at company

headquarters in St. Louis. In the postwar boom, A.G. Edwards grew its branch network to 19 offices and 200 brokers by 1960.

Benjamin Edwards III, great-grandson of the founder, took over in 1965 and restructured the company, placing its emphasis squarely on retail business. To this end, the company, which went public in 1971, expanded its retail offices in small communities from 44 in the mid-1960s to 450 in the early 1990s.

In 1990 the firm installed a satellite-based communications system to link its headquarters with its branch offices. In 1994 it introduced a computerized bond-processing system and the Edwards Information Network, a regularly updated electronic information service for brokers. It put up its own Web site in 1996 to give investors access to investment information.

In 1997, in the face of the inevitable, A.G. Edwards began following the lead of the competition and introduced straight execution services as an alternative to its commissioned accounts. However, company brokers weren't happy about it, cautioning that clients rarely become wealthy when they trade on their own account. The company expanded its headquarters and added almost 500 more employees in 1998; it also received a thrift charter that would allow it to conduct its trust business nationwide.

Realizing that resistance was futile, A.G. Edwards the next year gave in to the Borg-like pressure of the competition, and began offering trading over the Internet. It held the line against discounting, however, offering only its traditional commission services.

Chairman, President, and CEO, A.G. Edwards and A.G. Edwards & Sons: Benjamin F. Edwards III, age 67, $1,826,278 pay

VC; VC, EVP, and Director Branch Division, A.G. Edwards & Sons: Robert L. Bagby, age 55, $1,208,766 pay

VC; VC, EVP, Director Sales and Marketing, and Director Investment Banking, A.G. Edwards & Sons: Benjamin F. Edwards IV, age 43, $1,065,620 pay (prior to promotion)

VP and Secretary; Corporate VP, Secretary, and Director Law and Compliance, A.G. Edwards & Sons: Douglas L. Kelly, age 50

VP and Treasurer; Corporate VP, Treasurer, Assistant Secretary, and Director Administration, A.G. Edwards & Sons: Robert L. Proost, age 61

VP and Director Personnel: Ron Hoenninger

Director Operations: Ron Kessler

SVP and Western Regional Officer, A.G. Edwards & Sons: Paul B. Coffee

SVP Securities Research, A.G. Edwards & Sons: Terry J. Dessent

Corporate VP and Director Information Technology, A.G. Edwards & Sons: Mary V. Atkin, age 44

Corporate VP and Director Market Analysis, A.G. Edwards & Sons: Alfred E. Goldman, age 65, $945,235 pay

Auditors: Deloitte & Touche LLP

LOCATIONS

HQ: 1 N. Jefferson Ave., St. Louis, MO 63103
Phone: 314-955-3000   **Fax:** 314-955-5402
Web site: http://www.agedwards.com

A.G. Edwards operates 630 offices in 49 states and the District of Columbia.

PRODUCTS/OPERATIONS

1999 Sales

	$ mil.	% of total
Commissions	1,202	54
Asset management & service fees	405	17
Investment banking	219	10
Interest	202	9
Principal transactions	202	9
Other	11	1
Total	**2,241**	**100**

Selected Subsidiaries

A.G. Edwards & Sons, Inc.
A.G. Edwards Capital, Inc.
A.G. Edwards Life Insurance Company
A.G. Edwards Trust Company
A.G.E. Properties, Inc.
AGE Commodity Clearing Corp.
GULL-AGE Capital Group, Inc. (real estate partnerships)

COMPETITORS

Ameritrade	National Discount Brokers
Charles Schwab	Group
CIBC World Markets	Paine Webber
DLJdirect	Principal Financial
E*TRADE	Quick & Reilly/Fleet
FMR	Raymond James Financial
Jones Financial	SEI
Companies	Siebert Financial
Hambrecht & Quist	Stephens
Lehman Brothers	TD Waterhouse Securities
Merrill Lynch	U. S. Bancorp Piper Jaffray
Morgan Keegan	
Morgan Stanley Dean	
Witter	

HISTORICAL FINANCIALS & EMPLOYEES

NYSE symbol: AGE FYE: February 28	Annual Growth	1990	1991	1992	1993	1994	1995	1996	1997	1998	1999
Sales ($ mil.)	15.6%	607	675	939	1,074	1,279	1,178	1,454	1,696	2,004	2,241
Net income ($ mil.)	19.5%	59	59	106	119	155	124	171	219	269	292
Income as % of sales	—	9.7%	8.8%	11.2%	11.1%	12.1%	10.5%	11.7%	12.9%	13.4%	13.0%
Earnings per share ($)	17.0%	0.73	0.73	1.25	1.37	1.71	1.33	1.77	2.24	2.75	3.00
Stock price - FY high ($)	—	8.08	8.29	17.18	14.81	16.94	15.01	18.01	27.51	43.00	48.81
Stock price - FY low ($)	—	5.14	4.34	7.94	9.20	12.01	11.01	13.59	15.01	20.51	22.63
Stock price - FY close ($)	20.6%	6.05	8.15	14.25	13.47	14.84	15.01	16.17	23.68	42.25	32.56
P/E - high	—	11	11	14	11	10	11	10	12	16	16
P/E - low	—	7	6	6	7	7	8	8	7	7	8
Dividends per share ($)	13.2%	0.18	0.19	0.23	0.28	0.33	0.37	0.39	0.43	0.50	0.55
Book value per share ($)	16.6%	4.31	4.80	6.06	7.11	8.72	9.84	11.70	13.13	15.21	17.16
Employees	8.5%	6,694	8,068	8,736	9,487	10,206	10,471	11,279	12,031	12,967	13,953

STOCK PRICE HISTORY

HIGH/LOW/CLOSE

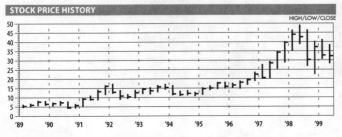

1999 FISCAL YEAR-END

Debt ratio: 0.0%
Return on equity: 17.9%
Cash ($ mil.): —
Current ratio: —
Long-term debt ($ mil.): —
No. of shares (mil.): 95
Dividends
  Yield: 1.7%
  Payout: 18.3%
Market value ($ mil.): 3,088

AGCO CORPORATION

OVERVIEW

AGCO has turned its dream of fields into reality. Based in Duluth, Georgia, the company is now the third-largest US farm equipment maker, behind Deere (#1) and Case (#2). AGCO sells tractors, rotary combines, harvesters, sprayers, related spare parts, and other farm equipment under more than a dozen brand names, including Massey Ferguson, GLEANER, Fendt, and Tye. Agricredit, a joint venture between AGCO and The Netherlands-based Rabobank, allows AGCO to offer financing services to customers and some of its 8,500 dealers. The company sells its products in more than 140 countries — Europe accounts for nearly half its revenues — and is expanding into South America.

AGCO has increased its product line rapidly by acquiring makers of other well-known brands of farm equipment. It outsources the manufacturing of most components and acts as an assembler of the equipment at its own plants. Despite its variety of brands, AGCO tries to keep costs low by employing common parts platforms. Its dealers are encouraged to carry multiple AGCO brands to capitalize on local product popularity.

HISTORY

In 1861, American Edward Allis purchased the bankrupt Reliance Works, a leading Milwaukee-based manufacturer of sawmills and flour-milling equipment. Under shrewd management, The Reliance Works of Edward P. Allis & Co. weathered financial troubles — bankruptcy in the Panic of 1873 — but managed to renegotiate its debt and recover. By the time Allis died in 1889, Reliance Works employed some 1,500 workers.

The company branched into different areas of manufacturing in the late 19th century, and by the 20th century the Edward P. Allis Co. (as it was then known) was the world leader in steam engines. In 1901 the company merged with another manufacturing giant, Fraser & Chalmers Company, to form the Allis-Chalmers Company. In the 1920s and 1930s, Allis-Chalmers threw its pitchfork into the farm equipment market.

Although overshadowed by John Deere and International Harvester (IH), Allis-Chalmers made key contributions to the industry — the first rubber-tired tractor (1932) and the All-Crop harvester. Allis-Chalmers spun off its farm equipment business in the 1950s, and phased out several unrelated products. The company, with its orange-colored tractors, expanded and prospered from the 1940s through the early 1970s. Then the chaffing farm economy of the late 1970s and early 1980s, coupled with a slew of bad management decisions, left Allis-Chalmers' sales out in the rain.

After layoffs and a plant shutdown in 1984, the capital-needy company was purchased in 1985 by German machinery maker Klockner-Humbolt-Deutz (KHD), who moved the company (renamed Deutz-Allis) to Georgia. In the mid-1980s low food prices hurt farmers and low demand hurt the equipment market. KHD was never able to bring profits up to a satisfactory level, and in 1990 the German firm sold the unit to the US management in a buyout led by Robert Ratliff. Ratliff believed the company could succeed by acquiring belly-up equipment makers, turning them around, and competing on price.

Renamed AGCO, the company launched a $186 million buying spree in 1991 that resulted in the acquisition of Fiat's Hesston (1991), White Tractor (1991), the North American distribution rights for Massey Ferguson (1993), and White-New Idea (1993). The bumper crop of product growth enabled AGCO to slice into competitors Deere and Case's market share. AGCO went public in 1992. Its 1994 purchase of the remainder of Massey Ferguson (with 20% of the world market) vaulted AGCO into the ranks of the world's leading farm equipment companies.

In 1996 AGCO launched a $1.5 billion, five-year plan for European growth. In 1997 the company acquired German farm equipment makers Fendt and Dronniberg. It also picked up Deutz Argentina, a supplier of agricultural equipment, engines, and vehicles, as part of an effort to expand into Latin and South America.

In 1998 AGCO entered the agricultural sprayer market by acquiring the Spra-Coupe line from Ingersoll-Rand and the Willmar line from Cargill. AGCO also announced it was cutting about 1,400 jobs, or about 13% of its workforce, because of a worldwide drop in farm equipment sales.

The company began 1999 with plans to acquire drill and sprayer company Great Plains Manufacturing, but soon withdrew the offer. That year New Holland's plan to acquire competitor Case sparked speculation that AGCO might also be on several shopping lists.

OFFICERS

Chairman: Robert J. Ratliff, age 67, $1,000,000 pay
President and CEO: John M. Shumejda, age 53, $484,115 pay
SVP Worldwide Sales: James M. Seaver, $394,418 pay
SVP Worldwide Marketing: Edward R. Swingle, $256,009 pay
VP Corporate Development: Norman L. Boyd
VP Corporate Relations: Judith A. Czelusniak
VP Parts, North America: Daniel H. Hazelton
VP Manufacturing Operations, Worldwide: Aaron D. Jones
VP Marketing, Europe, Africa, Middle East: Malcom P. Lines
VP and General Counsel: Stephen D. Lupton
VP Sales, North America: John G. Murdoch
VP and Treasurer: William A. Nix III
VP Worldwide Parts: Chris E. Perkins, $259,276 pay
VP Manufacturing: Bruce W. Plagman
VP Product Development, Worldwide: Dexter E. Schaible
VP and CFO: Patrick S. Shannon
VP and General Counsel: Michael F. Swick
VP Sales, Europe, Africa, Middle East: Adri Verhagen
VP Marketing, North America: Gerald A. Weaver
Auditors: Arthur Andersen LLP

LOCATIONS

HQ: 4205 River Green Pkwy., Duluth, GA 30096
Phone: 770-813-9200   **Fax:** 770-813-6118
Web site: http://www.agcocorp.com

AGCO has manufacturing plants in Argentina, Brazil, Denmark, France, the UK, and the US.

PRODUCTS/OPERATIONS

1998 Sales

	$ in mil.	% of total
Tractors	1,823	62
Replacement parts	500	17
Combines	294	10
Hay & forge	118	4
Implements & other	206	7
Total	**2,941**	**100**

Brand Names

AGCO Allis (tractors)
Black Machine (planters)
Deutz (tractors, combines, farm equipment)
Farmhand (loaders, grinders, mixers, rotary cutters)
Fendt (tractors, forklift trucks)
Fieldstar (precision farming systems)
Gleancoe (tillage equipment)
GLEANER (combines)
Hesston (hay tools and forage equipment)
IDEAL (combines)
Landini (tractors)
Massey Ferguson (tractors, rotary combines)
Spra-Coupe (sprayers)
Tye (grain drills, tillage equipment)
White (tractors)
White-New Idea (implements, planters)
Willmar (sprayers, spreaders, loaders)

COMPETITORS

Case	Renault
Caterpillar	Steyr-Daimler-Puch
Deere	Aktiengesellschaft
Ford	United Dominion
Kubota	Industries
New Holland	Volvo

HISTORICAL FINANCIALS & EMPLOYEES

NYSE symbol: AG FYE: December 31	Annual Growth	1989	1990	1991	1992	1993	1994	1995	1996	1997	1998
Sales ($ mil.)	29.8%	281	220	275	315	596	1,359	2,125	2,318	3,224	2,941
Net income ($ mil.)	36.8%	4	(12)	9	6	34	116	129	126	169	61
Income as % of sales	—	1.3%	—	3.2%	1.9%	5.7%	8.5%	6.1%	5.4%	5.2%	2.1%
Earnings per share ($)	24.2%	—	—	—	0.27	0.93	2.35	2.30	2.20	2.71	0.99
Stock price - FY high ($)	—	—	—	—	5.17	11.42	18.38	27.31	31.63	36.31	30.94
Stock price - FY low ($)	—	—	—	—	1.67	3.34	10.76	12.38	19.25	25.00	5.25
Stock price - FY close ($)	14.5%	—	—	—	3.50	11.38	15.19	25.50	28.63	29.25	7.88
P/E - high	—	—	—	—	19	12	8	12	14	13	31
P/E - low	—	—	—	—	6	4	5	5	9	9	5
Dividends per share ($)	26.0%	—	—	—	0.01	0.02	0.02	0.02	0.04	0.04	0.04
Book value per share ($)	29.5%	—	—	—	3.50	7.87	10.99	11.65	13.53	15.75	16.50
Employees	30.4%	960	991	1,145	1,201	2,417	5,789	5,548	7,800	11,000	10,500

STOCK PRICE HISTORY

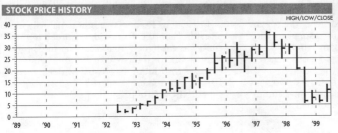

HIGH/LOW/CLOSE

1998 FISCAL YEAR-END

Debt ratio: 48.5%
Return on equity: 6.2%
Cash ($ mil.): 16
Current ratio: 2.35
Long-term debt ($ mil.): 924
No. of shares (mil.): 60
Dividends
  Yield: 0.5%
  Payout: 4.0%
Market value ($ mil.): 469

AIR PRODUCTS AND CHEMICALS

OVERVIEW

Change is in the air at Air Products and Chemicals. A leader in the US industrial gases market, the Allentown, Pennsylvania-based company produces argon, helium, hydrogen, nitrogen, oxygen, and other gases (which account for nearly 60% of sales) and chemicals and related equipment and services. It provides air pollution control systems, electric power services, and hydrogen purification and other equipment. Air Products' chemicals unit produces a range of industrial and specialty chemicals, including polyurethane, amines, emulsions, and surfactants.

The company supplies manufacturers in diverse markets with industrial gases by either building on-site plants or, for smaller needs, by truck delivery. Air Products has subsidiaries in 30 countries and exports to more than 100.

HISTORY

In the early 1900s, Leonard Pool, the son of a boilermaker, began selling oxygen to industrial users. By the time he was 30, he was district manager for Compressed Industrial Gases. In the late 1930s Pool hired engineer Frank Pavlis to help him design a cheaper and more efficient oxygen generator. In 1940 they had the design, and Pool established Air Products in Detroit (initially sharing space with the cadavers collected by his brother, who was starting a mortuary science college) on the basis of a simple, breakthrough concept: the provision of on-site gases. Instead of delivering oxygen in cylinders, Pool proposed to build oxygen-generating facilities near large-volume gas users and then lease them to the customers, reducing distribution costs.

Although industrialists encouraged Pool to pursue his ideas, few orders were forthcoming, and the company faced financial crisis. The outbreak of WWII got the company out of difficulty as the US military became a major customer. During the war the company moved to Chattanooga, Tennessee, for the available labor.

The end of the war brought with it another downturn as demand dried up. By waiting at the Weirton Steel plant until a contract was signed, Pool won a contract for three on-site generators. Weirton was practically the company's only customer. Pool relocated to Allentown, Pennsylvania, to be closer to the industrial markets of the Northeast and began securing more contracts with steel companies.

The Cold War and the launching of the Sputnik satellite in 1957 propelled the enterprise's growth. Convinced that Russian rockets were powered by liquid hydrogen, the US government asked Air Products to supply it with the volatile fuel. The company entered the overseas market for industrial gases that year through a joint venture with Butterley, a British firm to which it licensed its cryogenic (very low temperature) processes and equipment. In 1964 Air Products formed a subsidiary in Belgium.

The company diversified into chemicals in the 1960s. In 1962 it acquired Houdry Process, a firm specializing in chemicals and chemical-plant maintenance.

Business further expanded in the 1970s with the purchase of Airco's chemicals and plastics operations. Air Products began diversifying in the mid-1980s to use its skills in operating large-scale plants: it built an environmental- and energy-systems business, bought the industrial chemicals unit of Abbott Labs, and purchased Anchor Chemical. Air Products' Japanese affiliate merged with Hoxan KK in 1992. A 1994 restructuring merged its gases and equipment businesses.

Air Products has continued to invest globally. In 1995 and 1996 it won 20 contracts with semiconductor makers in China, among other countries. It acquired Carburos Metalicos, Spain's #1 industrial gas supplier, in 1996. The company shed most of its environmental- and energy-systems business.

Expanding in Europe, Air Products bought the methylamines and derivatives business of the UK's Imperial Chemical Industries PLC in 1997. Back at home the company sold its remaining interest in American Ref-Fuel (a waste-to-energy operation).

In 1998 the company bought Solkatronic Chemicals and opened a methylamines plant in Pensacola, Florida, to complement its purchase of Imperial Chemical Industries. It also formed two polymer ventures with Wacker-Chemie. The company formed Air Products Electronic Chemicals and formed an alliance with AlliedSignal Chemical.

In 1999 Air Products bought a majority interest in Hanyang Technology, Korea's top specialty gas equipment manufacturer for the semiconductor industry. Air Products and France's L'Air Liquide (#1 worldwide) agreed in 1999 to buy and break apart #2 industrial gas supplier BOC Group.

Chairman and CEO: Harold A. Wagner, age 63,
$1,814,561 pay
President and COO: John P. Jones III, age 48,
$764,262 pay
Corporate EVP: Joseph J. Kaminski, age 59,
$780,715 pay
EVP Chemicals, Asia, and Latin America:
Robert E. Gadomski, $764,262 pay
President, Air Products Asia: Wayne A. Hinman
President, Air Products Japan: Masataka Ono
President, Air Products Europe: Ronaldo Sullam
VP Finance and CFO: Leo J Daley
VP, Secretary and General Counsel: W. Douglas Brown
VP Engineering: Nirmal Chatterjee
VP Federal Relations: Jessica J. Holliday
VP and Corporate Controller: Paul E. Huck
VP Human Resources: Joseph P. McAndrew
VP Management Information Services:
Joseph H. McMakin
VP Technology: Stanley M. Morris
VP Taxes: Kenneth R. Petrini
VP Energy and Materials: Diane L. Sheridan
VP Corporate Planning: Scott A. Sherman
Corporate Treasurer: Marshall L. Sullivan
Auditors: Arthur Andersen LLP

LOCATIONS

HQ: 7201 Hamilton Blvd., Allentown, PA 18195-1501
Phone: 610-481-4911 **Fax:** 610-481-5900
Web site: http://www.airproducts.com

Air Products and Chemicals has operations in 30
countries.

PRODUCTS/OPERATIONS

1998 Sales & Operating Income

	Sales		Operating Income	
	$ mil.	% of total	$ mil.	% of total
Industrial gases	2,908	59	573	64
Chemicals	1,539	31	254	28
Equipment & services	472	10	73	8
Adjustments	—	—	(55)	—
Total	**4,919**	**100**	**845**	**100**

Principal Products and Services

Industrial Gases and	Nitrogen
Equipment	Oxygen
Air pollution control	Specialty, cutting, and
systems	welding gases
Air separation equipment	**Chemical**
Argon	Amines
Electric power services	Emulsions
Helium	Polyurethanes
Hydrogen	Polyvinyl alcohol
Hydrogen purification	Surfactants
equipment	
Natural gas liquefaction	
equipment	

COMPETITORS

AGA AB	Dow Chemical
Air Liquide	Hoechst AG
Airgas	Huntsman
BASF AG	ICI
BOC Group	Praxair
CHEMCENTRAL	Union Carbide

HISTORICAL FINANCIALS & EMPLOYEES

NYSE symbol: APD FYE: September 30	Annual Growth	1989	1990	1991	1992	1993	1994	1995	1996	1997	1998
Sales ($ mil.)	7.2%	2,642	2,895	2,931	3,217	3,328	3,485	3,865	4,008	4,638	4,919
Net income ($ mil.)	10.5%	222	230	249	271	201	248	368	416	429	547
Income as % of sales	—	8.4%	7.9%	8.5%	8.4%	6.0%	7.1%	9.5%	10.4%	9.3%	11.1%
Earnings per share ($)	10.7%	0.99	1.02	1.09	1.17	0.87	1.07	1.62	1.83	1.91	2.48
Stock price - FY high ($)	—	12.19	15.25	18.53	24.75	24.56	25.19	29.81	30.44	44.81	45.34
Stock price - FY low ($)	—	9.44	10.75	10.72	15.91	18.75	19.06	21.56	24.88	29.00	29.75
Stock price - FY close ($)	11.2%	11.44	11.22	16.78	22.19	19.38	23.38	26.06	29.13	41.47	29.75
P/E - high	—	12	15	17	21	28	24	18	17	23	18
P/E - low	—	10	11	10	14	22	18	13	14	15	12
Dividends per share ($)	4.2%	0.31	0.34	0.37	0.41	0.44	0.47	0.50	0.53	0.57	0.45
Book value per share ($)	6.5%	6.56	7.58	8.19	9.25	9.21	9.78	10.74	11.65	12.05	11.60
Employees	1.9%	14,100	14,000	14,600	14,500	14,100	13,300	14,800	15,200	16,400	16,700

STOCK PRICE HISTORY

HIGH/LOW/CLOSE

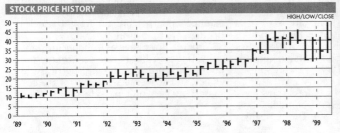

1998 FISCAL YEAR-END

Debt ratio: 46.0%
Return on equity: 20.5%
Cash ($ mil.): 62
Current ratio: 1.30
Long-term debt ($ mil.): 2,274
No. of shares (mil.): 230
Dividends
Yield: 1.5%
Payout: 18.1%
Market value ($ mil.): 6,840

AIRBORNE FREIGHT CORPORATION

OVERVIEW

Haulin', haulin', haulin' . . . though the rain is fallin' . . . you won't catch it crawlin' . . . Airborne! For more than a decade, Seattle-based Airborne Freight, popularly known as Airborne Express, has been the US's third-largest domestic airfreight express carrier, behind FDX and UPS. The company specializes in express service for high-volume corporate clients. Overnight delivery accounts for more than half of its domestic shipments, but it also offers next-afternoon and second-day services and ocean shipping. Airborne operates mainly through subsidiary ABX Air, which flies cargo throughout the US and Canada. ABX has more than 100 airplanes and runs the company's airport in Wilmington, Ohio — Airborne is the only US carrier with its own airport. ABX Air also owns or contracts almost 15,000 radio-dispatched delivery trucks and vans.

Airborne sells software and hardware that provides rate and tracking information and does metering and labeling for frequent shippers.

The company has strengthened its hand against global mail and package leaders DHL and FedEx. It has offices in Australia and New Zealand, the Far East, the Netherlands, and the UK and joint ventures in Japan, Malaysia, South Africa, and Thailand. Airborne is also going after e-commerce customers through an agreement with the US Postal Service: The nation's mail carriers will deliver its two-day shipments directly to residences.

HISTORY

Airborne Flower Traffic Association of California was founded in 1946 to ship fresh flowers from Hawaii to the mainland; it became Airborne Freight, an airfreight forwarder, in 1956. In 1968 it merged with Pacific Air Freight, which was founded in Seattle in 1947 by former US Army Air Corps officer Holt Webster to transport perishables to Alaska. Webster became the new company's first CEO.

Airborne introduced FOCUS, its proprietary package tracking system, in 1972 and began buying its own fleet of airplanes and trucks when the airline industry deregulated in 1977. Two years later it expanded into Europe and entered the young overnight delivery business. In 1980 Airborne bought Midwest Air Charter and its Wilmington, Ohio, airport, a former US Air Force base. Later called Airborne Air Park, the property became the company's principal hub and central sorting facility. In the early 1980s the company surpassed Emery Air Freight in shipments to become the third-largest express carrier in the US; it also entered the Australian and New Zealand markets. Webster retired in 1984.

In 1987 Australian transportation conglomerate TNT, which owned 15% of Airborne, tried to buy the rest, but after six months of negotiations, no agreement could be reached. That year, with a fleet of 37 planes, the company landed two major contracts: one to handle the US express air shipments of Purolator Courier of Canada; another to carry all of IBM's express shipments of 150 pounds or less (Airborne lost IBM's Pacific business in 1989). The company bought same-day shipper Sky Courier in 1989 and also created subsidiary ABX Air as its US airline.

In 1990 the company joined Japan's Mitsui and Panther Express International (owned by Mitsui and another Japanese firm, Tonami Transportation) to form Airborne Express Japan (40%-owned by Airborne). When FedEx challenged the company's high-volume corporate business the next year, Airborne cut prices, and in 1994 it began offering ocean shipping services as a less-expensive method of international transportation. In 1995 it added a runway to its small airport.

Airborne bought a small service partner in Scotland in 1996 and set up international ventures in Thailand and Malaysia. The next year, as the UPS strike was boosting Airborne's business — though severely taxing its resources — Airborne formed a joint venture in South Africa. It also increased its investment in Amarex International, an airfreight firm with a major presence in the Middle East, to about 9%, and in 1998 Airborne upped its stake in Pioneer Air Cargo of Thailand to 49%.

The next year the company teamed with the US Post Office to offer residential delivery services. The company also added two (of a planned 25) larger, quieter, freight-ready Boeing 767s to its fleet.

Airborne diversified as well, opening a facility, Optical Village (near its Wilmington hub), which provides storage, inventory, logistics, and delivery specifically for the designers, makers, and marketers of eyeglasses.

Chairman and CEO: Robert S. Cline, age 62,
$1,121,657 pay
President and COO: Robert G. Brazier, age 61,
$912,450 pay
EVP, International Division: John J. Cella, age 58
EVP, Marketing Division: Kent W. Freudenberger,
age 58, $517,640 pay
CFO and EVP, Finance Division: Roy C. Liljebeck,
age 61, $543,578 pay
EVP, Field Services Division:
Raymond T. Van Bruwaene, age 60, $508,069 pay
SVP, Information and Technology Systems:
David A. Billings
SVP, Human Resources: Richard G. Goodwin
SVP, Field Services, Area II: Thomas E. Nelson Jr.
SVP, Field Services, Area I: William R. Simpson
President and CEO, ABX Air: Carl D. Donaway, age 47,
$508,069 pay
COO, ABX Air: Joseph C. Hete
SVP, Aircraft Maintenance, ABX Air:
Dennis A. Manibusan
SVP, Flight Operations, ABX Air: Robert J. Morgenfeld
SVP, Ground Operations, ABX Air: Thomas W. Poynter
VP, Engineering and Cartage Administration:
William S. Ashby
Auditors: Deloitte & Touche LLP

LOCATIONS

HQ: 3101 Western Ave., Seattle, WA 98121
Phone: 206-285-4600   **Fax:** 206-281-1444
Web site: http://www.airborne.com

Airborne Freight provides delivery services in the US
(290 stations) and in more than 200 countries (45
stations).

1998 Sales

	$ mil.	% of total
US	2,713	88
Other countries	362	12
Total	**3,075**	**100**

PRODUCTS/OPERATIONS

Tracking and Shipping Services
EDI (Electronic Data Interchange, tracking and billing)
FOCUS (Freight Online Control and Update System)
LIBRA (customer-based metering, labeling, and
tracking system)
LIGHTSHIP TRACKER (rate, shipping, and tracking
information, plus labeling)
QUICKLINK (electronic invoicing and payment system)
WORLD DIRECTORY (worldwide shipping information)

Selected Subsidiaries
ABX Air, Inc.
Airborne Forwarding Corporation (doing business as
Sky Courier)
Airborne Freight Limited (New Zealand)

COMPETITORS

Air Express	FDX
American Freightways	Fritz
Arkansas Best	J. B. Hunt
Celadon	Pittston BAX
Circle International	Roadway Express
CNF Transportation	UAL
Consolidated Freightways	UPS
Continental Airlines	US Airways
Delta	U.S. Postal Service
DHL	Yellow Corporation

HISTORICAL FINANCIALS & EMPLOYEES

NYSE symbol: ABF FYE: December 31	Annual Growth	1989	1990	1991	1992	1993	1994	1995	1996	1997	1998
Sales ($ mil.)	13.9%	950	1,182	1,367	1,484	1,720	1,971	2,239	2,484	2,912	3,075
Net income ($ mil.)	24.5%	19	34	30	5	39	39	24	27	120	137
Income as % of sales	—	2.0%	2.8%	2.2%	0.4%	2.3%	2.0%	1.1%	1.1%	4.1%	4.5%
Earnings per share ($)	17.9%	0.62	0.88	0.70	0.06	0.92	0.87	0.55	0.64	2.44	2.72
Stock price - FY high ($)	—	9.91	13.50	15.00	14.88	17.63	19.94	14.75	14.19	37.22	42.88
Stock price - FY low ($)	—	5.22	6.75	8.31	6.25	9.00	9.00	9.19	9.75	11.38	14.25
Stock price - FY close ($)	16.9%	8.84	8.50	12.13	9.31	17.56	10.25	13.31	11.69	31.06	36.06
P/E - high	—	16	15	21	248	19	23	27	22	15	16
P/E - low	—	8	8	12	104	10	10	17	15	5	5
Dividends per share ($)	(2.4%)	0.15	0.15	0.15	0.15	0.15	0.15	0.15	0.19	0.15	0.12
Book value per share ($)	12.9%	5.32	7.00	7.55	7.44	8.23	9.24	9.64	9.99	13.44	15.92
Employees	9.8%	9,900	11,800	13,800	14,500	15,700	17,400	19,500	20,700	22,500	23,000

STOCK PRICE HISTORY

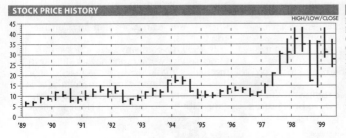

HIGH/LOW/CLOSE

1998 FISCAL YEAR-END
Debt ratio: 24.5%
Return on equity: 17.8%
Cash ($ mil.): 19
Current ratio: 1.31
Long-term debt ($ mil.): 249
No. of shares (mil.): 48
Dividends
  Yield: 0.3%
  Payout: 4.4%
Market value ($ mil.): 1,742

ALASKA AIR GROUP, INC.

OVERVIEW

Whether you want to capture a Kodiak moment or down a daiquiri by the Sea of Cortes, Alaska Air Group can fly you there. The Seattle-based company's Alaska Airlines subsidiary is a top 10 US airline. Alaska Air (which brings in more than 80% of group sales) serves 41 cities: 35 in Alaska and five other western US states, five in Mexico, and one in Canada. Alaska Air flies out of hubs in Anchorage, Alaska; Los Angeles; Portland, Oregon; and Seattle. The group also owns Horizon Air Industries, a Pacific Northwest regional carrier that serves 38 airports in five states and Canada.

On the chilling fields of competition the airlines are picking sides. Alaska Air's leadership in West Coast travel has made it an attractive code-sharing partner to American, British Airways, Canadian Airlines, Continental, KLM, Northwest, Qantas, and TWA. An additional code-sharing agreement with Reeve Aleutian Air puts customers on flights to Russia, a destination Alaska Air no longer serves directly.

The carrier competes profitably in the low-fare market against Southwest Airlines and UAL's United Shuttle. It maintains a young and efficient fleet (about 85 jets, 737s, and MD-80s, for Alaska Air), keeps costs low, and offers full-service passenger fare such as meals and first-class seating. About 5% of sales comes from delivering cargo, including halibut and other Alaskan seafood.

AXA Financial (formerly The Equitable Companies), which is majority-owned by European insurance firm AXA, owns 10% of Alaska Air Group.

HISTORY

Pilot Mac McGee started McGee Airways in 1932 to fly cargo between Anchorage and Bristol Bay, Alaska. He joined other local operators in 1937 to form Star Air Lines, which began airmail service between Fairbanks and Bethel in 1938. In 1944, a year after buying three small airlines, Star adopted the name Alaska Airlines.

The company bought two more local carriers and established freight service to Africa and Australia in 1950. This expansion, coupled with the seasonal nature of the airline's business, caused losses into the early 1970s. Developer Bruce Kennedy led a 1972 boardroom revolt, gaining control and turning the firm around by the end of 1973. But the Civil Aeronautics Board forced the carrier to drop service to cities in northwestern Alaska in 1975, and by 1978 it served only 10 Alaskan cities and Seattle.

Kennedy became CEO the next year. The 1978 Airline Deregulation Act allowed Alaska Air to move into new areas, such as California, and regain the routes it had lost. By 1982 it was the largest airline flying between Alaska and the lower 48 states.

In 1985 the airline reorganized, forming Alaska Air Group as its holding company. The next year Alaska Air Group bought Jet America Airlines (expanding its routes eastward to Chicago, St. Louis, and Dallas) and Seattle-based Horizon Air Industries (which served 30 Northwest cities). When competition in the East and Midwest cut profits in 1987, Kennedy shut down Jet America to focus on West Coast operations.

Hoping to counterbalance summer traffic to Alaska, the airline began service to two Mexican resorts in 1988. Fuel prices and sluggish traffic hurt 1990 earnings, but Alaska Air Group stayed in the black, unlike many other carriers. Kennedy retired as chairman in 1991.

That same year the airline began service to Canada and seasonal flights to two Russian cities. Neil Bergt's MarkAir airline (a former Alaska Air Group code-sharing partner) declared war, cutting fares and horning in on Alaska Air Group's territory. Nobody won. Alaska Air Group's profits were slashed, and MarkAir went into bankruptcy.

Alaska Air extended Russian flights to year-round in 1994.

In 1995 former Horizon boss John Kelly became CEO of the group, and George Bagley became Horizon's CEO.

The airline began service to Vancouver in 1996. That year it became the first major US carrier to use the GPS satellite navigation system. In 1997 it added service to more than a dozen new cities but took a step back the next year, halting service to Russia because of that country's economic woes.

Alaska Air Group and Dutch airline KLM agreed to a marketing alliance in 1998 that included reciprocal frequent-flier programs and code-sharing, and in 1999 it added code-sharing agreements with several major airlines — American, Canadian Air, Continental, and Qantas.

In 1999 the company faced a sick-out by customer service workers and a work slowdown by mechanics. Alaska Air Group got some labor relief when it hammered out a mechanics union contract for Alaska Air, but it continued haggling with the Teamsters and Horizon pilots.

Chairman, President, and CEO; Chairman and CEO, Alaska Airlines; Chairman, Horizon Air: John F. Kelly, age 55, $937,211 pay
President and CEO, Horizon Air: George D. Bagley, $401,069 pay
President, Alaska Airlines: William S. Ayer, $518,461 pay
EVP, Technical Operations and System Control, Alaska Airlines: John R. Fowler, $396,805 pay
SVP, Finance, Alaska Airlines: Harry G. Lehr, age 58, $405,711 pay
SVP, Operations, Horizon Air: Thomas M. Gerharter
VP, Legal and and Corporate Affairs and General Counsel, Alaska Air Group and Alaska Airlines: Keith Loveless, age 42
VP, Customer Services, Alaska Airlines: Edward W. White
VP, Employee Services, Alaska Airlines: Dennis J. Hamel
VP, Finance and Controller, Alaska Airlines: Bradley D. Tilden
VP, Finance and Treasurer, Alaska Airlines: Robin L. Krueger
VP, Flight Operations, Alaska Airlines: Michel A. Swanigan
VP, Flight Operations, Horizon Air: Daniel S. Scott
VP, Legal and Administration and Corporate Secretary, Horizon Air: Arthur E. Thomas
Auditors: Arthur Andersen LLP

HQ: 19300 Pacific Hwy. South, Seattle, WA 98188
Phone: 206-431-7040   **Fax:** 206-433-3379
Web site: http://www.alaska-air.com

1998 Sales

	$ mil.	% of total
Passenger service	1,728	91
Freight & mail	95	5
Other	75	4
Total	**1,898**	**100**

1998 Aircraft

	No. Owned	No. Leased
Alaska Airlines		
McDonnell Douglas MD-80	16	23
Boeing 737-200C	7	1
Boeing 737-400	4	33
Horizon		
Fokker F-28	7	13
de Havilland Dash 8	—	40
Total	**34**	**110**

America West	Lufthansa
AMR	Southwest Airlines
Air Canada	TWA
CINTRA	UAL
Continental Airlines	US Airways
Delta	

NYSE symbol: ALK FYE: December 31	Annual Growth	1989	1990	1991	1992	1993	1994	1995	1996	1997	1998
Sales ($ mil.)	8.4%	917	1,047	1,104	1,115	1,128	1,316	1,418	1,592	1,739	1,898
Net income ($ mil.)	12.6%	43	17	10	(85)	(31)	23	17	38	72	124
Income as % of sales	—	4.7%	1.6%	0.9%	—	—	1.7%	1.2%	2.4%	4.2%	6.6%
Earnings per share ($)	7.5%	2.51	0.82	0.27	(6.87)	(2.51)	1.62	1.26	2.05	3.53	4.81
Stock price - FY high ($)	—	30.50	26.00	25.38	23.88	18.13	18.88	21.38	30.75	40.13	62.56
Stock price - FY low ($)	—	19.88	13.88	17.50	14.75	12.25	13.13	13.50	15.88	20.75	26.00
Stock price - FY close ($)	8.8%	20.63	17.50	21.75	16.50	14.13	15.00	16.25	21.00	38.75	44.25
P/E - high	—	12	32	94	—	—	12	17	15	11	13
P/E - low	—	8	17	65	—	—	8	11	8	6	5
Dividends per share ($)	(100.0%)	0.20	0.20	0.20	0.20	0.00	0.00	0.00	0.00	0.00	0.00
Book value per share ($)	3.5%	22.08	21.23	21.49	14.76	12.50	14.30	15.67	18.83	26.00	30.11
Employees	3.7%	6,661	7,653	8,081	8,666	8,458	9,852	10,467	8,406	8,578	9,244

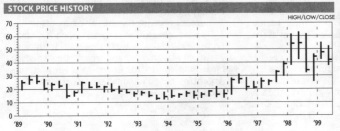

HIGH/LOW/CLOSE

Debt ratio: 17.8%
Return on equity: 15.8%
Cash ($ mil.): 29
Current ratio: 1.01
Long-term debt ($ mil.): 172
No. of shares (mil.): 26
Dividends
  Yield: —
  Payout: —
Market value ($ mil.): 1,160

ALBERTO-CULVER COMPANY

OVERVIEW

Sally promises beauty, Mrs. Dash seduces with spice, and Molly claims she's better than butter. Melrose Park, Illinois-based Alberto-Culver is the world's #1 distributor of professional beauty supplies through its Sally Beauty subsidiary. Alberto-Culver also makes consumer products, including Mrs. Dash seasonings, Molly McButter butter alternative, Alberto VO5 and St. Ives hair and skin care lines, FDS feminine deodorant spray, and Static Guard antistatic spray.

Sally operates more than 2,000 stores in Canada, Germany, Japan, the UK, and the US, selling hair and skin care goods, cosmetics, and styling appliances. Its Beauty Systems Group distributes products to beauty salons in the US and Canada.

Although dwarfed by consumer product and beauty care giants like Unilever and L'Oreal, Alberto-Culver has expanded its product lines through complementary acquisitions. Internationally, the firm plans to build its business in strong markets such as Scandinavia and the UK while expanding into Eastern Europe (with St. Ives) and Latin America (with Alberto VO5).

The Lavin and Bernick families run Alberto-Culver and own about 40% of the company.

HISTORY

Alberto VO5 Conditioning Hairdressing (featuring five vital oils in a water-free base) was developed in the early 1950s by a chemist named Alberto to rejuvenate the coiffures of Hollywood's movie stars from the damage of harsh studio lights. In 1955, 36-year-old entrepreneur Leonard Lavin and his wife, Bernice, borrowed $400,000, bought the Los Angeles-based firm that made VO5 from Blaine Culver, and relocated it to Chicago. That year Alberto-Culver implemented a key component of its corporate strategy — aggressive marketing — by running the first television commercial for VO5. Within three years Alberto VO5 led its category. In 1959 the company expanded its product line by buying TRESemme Hair Color.

Lavin built a new plant and headquarters in Melrose Park, Illinois, in 1960, took the company public in 1961, and formed an international marketing division. A series of product innovations included Alberto VO5 Hair Spray (1961), New Dawn Hair Color (the first shampoo-in, permanent hair color, 1963), Consort Hair Spray for Men (1965), and FDS (1966). Acquisitions in 1969 included low-calorie sugar substitute SugarTwin and 10-store beauty supply chain Sally Beauty.

Alberto-Culver restyled TV advertising in 1972 by putting two 30-second ads in a 60-second spot (it later pioneered the "split 30," back-to-back 15-second ads for two different products). It launched TCB (an ethnic hair care line) in 1975 and Static Guard antistatic spray in 1976.

The firm developed a series of food-substitute products in the 1980s, including Mrs. Dash (1983) and Molly McButter (1987). It also expanded the fast-growing Sally chain to the UK (1987). Lavin's son-in-law Howard Bernick succeeded him as president and COO in 1988.

By 1990 the Sally chain had about 800 stores, many added through the purchases of smaller chains. It bought the bankrupt Milo Beauty & Barber Supply chain (about 90 stores) in 1991. That year Alberto-Culver also bought Cederroth International, a Swedish maker of health and hygiene goods. Bernick became CEO in 1994, though Lavin stayed on as chairman.

In 1995 the firm acquired the toiletries division of Swedish beauty and cleaning product maker Molnlycke, combining it with Cederroth to form one of Scandinavia's largest consumer packaged goods marketers. Also that year Carol Bernick (Lavin's daughter) became head of Alberto-Culver USA and led the division to more than $300 million in sales.

The 1,500-store Sally chain opened its first 10 outlets in Japan through a joint venture in 1995 and acquired a small chain in Germany in 1996. In 1996 Alberto-Culver made its largest acquisition ever, paying $110 million for St. Ives Laboratories, maker of St. Ives Swiss Formula hair and skin care products.

In 1997 the consumer products division cut nearly 25% of its product line to focus on its best-sellers, and it introduced Cortexx, a gelatin-enhanced hair care line designed to reduce split ends. In 1998 Sally entered Canada by acquiring two beauty supply companies specializing in salon lines.

Cortexx had not reached the success in 1999 that Alberto-Culver had hoped for, and company-wide sales were sluggish. It announced plans to increase marketing spending by 16%. Also in 1999 Alberto-Culver bought Argentina-based La Farmaco, a personal care products company.

OFFICERS

Chairman: Leonard H. Lavin, age 79, $1,570,999 pay
VC, Secretary, and Treasurer: Bernice E. Lavin,
  $799,756 pay
**VC; President, Alberto-Culver North America and
  Secretary:** Carol L. Bernick, age 46, $786,422 pay
President and CEO: Howard B. Bernick, age 47,
  $1,674,002 pay
**SVP Finance and Controller (Principal
  Financial Officer):** William J. Cernugel
President, Sally Beauty Company: Michael H. Renzulli,
  $1,285,008 pay
President, Alberto-Culver International:
  Paul H. Stoneham
VP Human Resources, Alberto-Culver USA:
  Douglas E. Meneely
Auditors: KPMG LLP

LOCATIONS

HQ: 2525 Armitage Ave., Melrose Park, IL 60160
Phone: 708-450-3000   **Fax:** 708-450-3354
Web site: http://www.alberto.com

Alberto-Culver sells its products in more than 120
countries. It has manufacturing operations in Argentina,
Australia, Canada, Mexico, the Netherlands, Puerto Rico,
Spain, Sweden, the UK, and the US.

PRODUCTS/OPERATIONS

1998 Sales

	$ mil.	% of total
Sally Beauty	973	52
Alberto-Culver International	461	25
Alberto-Culver USA	418	23
Adjustments	(17)	—
Total	**1,835**	**100**

Selected Brands

Household and Food
Molly McButter (butter-flavored sprinkles)
Mrs. Dash (salt-free seasoning)
Static Guard (antistatic spray)
SugarTwin (sugar substitute)
Personal Use
Alberto VO5 (hair care products)
Consort (hair care products)
FDS (feminine deodorant spray)
St. Ives Swiss Formula (hair care
  and skin care products)
TCB (ethnic hair care products)
TRESemme (hair care products)

COMPETITORS

Allou	L'Oréal
Amway	Mary Kay
Avon	McCormick
Bristol-Myers Squibb	Monsanto
Burns, Philp	Perrigo
Church & Dwight	Procter & Gamble
Colgate-Palmolive	Regis
Cosmetic Center	Revlon
Cumberland Packing	Schwarzkopf & DEP
Del Labs	Shiseido
Gillette	Unilever
Helen of Troy	Wella
Johnson & Johnson	Windmere

HISTORICAL FINANCIALS & EMPLOYEES

NYSE symbol: ACV FYE: September 30	Annual Growth	1989	1990	1991	1992	1993	1994	1995	1996	1997	1998
Sales ($ mil.)	11.0%	717	796	874	1,091	1,148	1,216	1,358	1,590	1,775	1,835
Net income ($ mil.)	12.2%	29	35	30	39	41	44	53	63	85	83
Income as % of sales	—	4.1%	4.4%	3.4%	3.5%	3.6%	3.6%	3.9%	3.9%	4.8%	4.5%
Earnings per share ($)	10.2%	0.57	0.65	0.53	0.68	0.72	0.79	0.94	1.06	1.41	1.37
Stock price – FY high ($)	—	12.47	13.94	17.13	16.00	14.13	12.56	16.25	23.75	31.56	32.56
Stock price – FY low ($)	—	8.19	9.56	10.19	10.63	10.13	9.69	10.88	14.94	21.38	19.75
Stock price – FY close ($)	7.7%	12.00	10.38	11.75	11.94	11.31	11.69	15.25	21.69	30.44	23.38
P/E – high	—	22	21	32	24	20	16	17	22	22	24
P/E – low	—	14	15	19	16	14	12	12	14	15	14
Dividends per share ($)	11.0%	0.09	0.10	0.11	0.12	0.14	0.14	0.16	0.18	0.20	0.23
Book value per share ($)	13.2%	3.05	4.05	4.42	5.01	5.23	5.91	6.69	7.64	8.55	9.33
Employees	9.5%	5,600	5,900	7,300	7,600	8,600	9,300	9,900	10,700	11,000	12,700

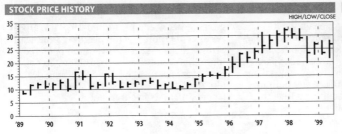

STOCK PRICE HISTORY

HIGH/LOW/CLOSE

1998 FISCAL YEAR-END

Debt ratio: 24.3%
Return on equity: 15.6%
Cash ($ mil.): 72
Current ratio: 1.89
Long-term debt ($ mil.): 172
No. of shares (mil.): 57
Dividends
  Yield: 1.0%
  Payout: 16.8%
Market value ($ mil.): 1,338

ALBERTSON'S, INC.

OVERVIEW

Albertson's grocery business has never been small potatoes, but now the Boise, Idaho-based company has really beefed up. The #2 supermarket chain in the US (after Kroger) operates more than 2,400 stores under several banners. Its namesake stores are located in 25 western, midwestern, and southern states; most are combination food and drugstores ranging from 35,000 to 82,000 sq. ft. The other outlets include more than 85 smaller grocery stores and about 30 no-frills warehouse stores (Max Food and Drug) emphasizing discounted meat and produce.

As a result of its purchase of American Stores, Albertson's also owns three regional supermarket chains: Acme Markets (in four states anchored by Philadelphia), Jewel (Chicago), and Lucky (California). The purchase also gave Albertson's the Osco Drug and Sav-on drugstore chains. To get approval for the acquisition, Albertson's agreed to sell 144 stores, mostly in California.

The new company intends to spend $11 billion to launch about 750 new food and drug combination stores, 500 stand-alone drugstores, 600 fuel centers, and remodel roughly 730 stores by the end of 2004. Blending the Albertson's and American Stores' cultures might take finesse: Unions represent about three-quarters of American Stores' employees, while only one-third of Albertson's stores are unionized. The acquisition places Albertson's in two tough union towns: Philadelphia and Chicago.

Theo Albrecht (his family owns supermarket chains ALDI and Trader Joe's) owns about 7% of Albertson's; the J.A. and Kathryn Albertson Foundation owns about 5% of the company.

HISTORY

J. A. "Joe" Albertson, Leonard Skaggs (whose family ran Safeway), and Tom Cuthbert founded Albertson's Food Center in Boise, Idaho, in 1939. Albertson, who left his position as district manager for Safeway to run the store, thought big from the start. The 10,000-sq.-ft. store was not only eight times the size of the average competitor, it offered an in-store butcher shop and bakery, one of the country's first magazine racks, and homemade "Big Joe" ice-cream cones. The men ended their partnership in 1945, the year Albertson's was incorporated, and by 1947 it operated six stores in Idaho.

The company opened its first combination food and drugstore, a 60,000-sq.-ft. superstore, in 1951 and began locating stores in growing suburban areas. Albertson's went public to raise expansion capital in 1959 and by 1960 had 62 stores in Idaho, Oregon, Utah, and Washington State. The food retailer acquired Greater All American Markets (1964), a grocery chain based in Downey, California, and Semrau & Sons (1965) of Oakland, which aided the company's thrust into the California market.

Albertson's and the Skaggs chain (by this time run by L. S. Skaggs Jr.) reunited temporarily in 1969, financing six Skaggs-Albertson's food-and-drug combination stores. (The partnership dissolved in 1977, with each side taking half of the units.) In 1973 Albertson's built its first full-line distribution facility. By 1986 the company had reached $5 billion in sales, a fivefold increase over 1975. Albertson's continued to add distribution facilities, including its first mechanized distribution center in 1988.

Gary Michael took over the reins as CEO in 1991. The next year the company purchased 74 Jewel Osco combination food and drugstores (mostly in Arkansas, Florida, Oklahoma, and Texas) from American Stores. The company's founder, Joe Albertson, died in 1993 at age 86.

In 1997 the United Food and Commercial Workers union, which represents supermarket employees, initiated a lawsuit against Albertson's, alleging the company forced employees to work overtime without pay. Also that year it began selling gasoline at a dozen stores. Albertson's widow, Kathryn, donated $660 million in Albertson's stock to the family's charitable foundation (benefiting Idaho's public schools) in 1997.

A year later Albertson's acquired Buttrey Food and Drug Stores in a $133 million deal that added about 30 stores in Montana, North Dakota, and Wyoming. Also in 1998 the company moved into Tennessee, Missouri, and Iowa by acquiring outlets from several regional grocery chains. In mid-1999 the grocer revisited its roots when it acquired American Stores (Skaggs' successor), which operated more than 1,550 stores in 26 states. To obtain regulatory approval for the $12 billion deal, Albertson's agreed to sell 144 stores in overlapping markets in three states.

Chairman and CEO: Gary G. Michael, age 58,
$1,656,223 pay
EVP, Marketing: Carl W. Pennington, age 61,
$556,342 pay
EVP, Development: Michael F. Reuling, age 52
EVP and General Counsel: Thomas R. Saldin, age 52
EVP, Operations: David G. Simonson, age 52
EVP, Information Systems and Technology:
Patrick S. Steele, age 49
EVP, Human Resources: Steven D. Young, age 50
SVP, Real Estate: Robert K. Banks, age 49
SVP, Distribution: Thomas E. Brother, age 57
SVP, Procurement: David G. Dean, age 48
SVP, Employee Development and Communications:
Peggy Jo Jones, age 46
SVP, Northwest Region: Dennis C. Lucas, age 51
SVP and Controller: Richard J. Navarro, age 46
SVP, Finance and CFO: A. Craig Olson, age 47
SVP, Labor Relations and Employment Law:
Bruce P. Paolini, age 41
President, Southern Region: William H. Emmons,
age 49
Auditors: Deloitte & Touche LLP

LOCATIONS

HQ: 250 E. Parkcenter Blvd., Boise, ID 83726
Phone: 208-395-6200   **Fax:** 208-395-6349
Web site: http://www.albertsons.com

PRODUCTS/OPERATIONS

Selected Operations
Acme Markets (supermarkets in Delaware, Maryland,
New Jersey, and Pennsylvania)
Albertson's (supermarkets in 25 southern
and western states)
Jewel Food Stores (supermarkets in Illinois, Indiana,
Iowa, and Wisconsin)
Lucky Stores (supermarkets in California,
Nevada, and New Mexico)
Max Food and Drug
(no-frills discount warehouse stores)
Osco (drugstores)
RxAmerica (pharmacy benefit management and mail-
order pharmacy joint venture with Longs Drug Stores)
Sav-on (drugstores)

Selected Specialty Departments
Bakery
Floral
Liquor
Pharmacy
Service delicatessen
Service meat and seafood
Video

COMPETITORS

A&P	Kash n' Karry	Randall's
Ahold USA	Food Stores	Rite Aid
Associated	Kroger	Safeway
Grocers	Longs	Stater Bros.
Costco	Minyard Food	Walgreen
Companies	Stores	Wal-Mart
Eckerd	Pathmark	Whole Foods
Food Lion	Publix	
H-E-B	Raley's	

HISTORICAL FINANCIALS & EMPLOYEES

NYSE symbol: ABS FYE: January 31	Annual Growth	1990	1991	1992	1993	1994	1995	1996	1997	1998	1999
Sales ($ mil.)	8.9%	7,423	8,219	8,681	10,174	11,284	11,895	12,585	13,777	14,690	16,005
Net income ($ mil.)	12.5%	197	234	258	269	340	400	465	494	517	567
Income as % of sales	—	2.6%	2.8%	3.0%	2.6%	3.0%	3.4%	3.7%	3.6%	3.5%	3.5%
Earnings per share ($)	13.4%	0.74	0.88	0.97	1.02	1.34	1.58	1.83	1.95	2.08	2.30
Stock price - FY high ($)	—	15.06	19.44	25.69	26.69	29.69	30.88	35.25	43.75	48.63	67.13
Stock price - FY low ($)	—	9.66	12.19	16.38	18.50	23.38	25.13	27.25	33.75	30.50	44.00
Stock price - FY close ($)	18.6%	13.09	19.38	20.00	24.44	26.75	29.88	33.88	35.00	47.75	61.00
P/E - high	—	20	22	26	26	22	20	19	22	23	29
P/E - low	—	13	14	17	18	17	16	15	17	15	19
Dividends per share ($)	15.0%	0.19	0.23	0.27	0.31	0.35	0.42	0.50	0.58	0.63	0.67
Book value per share ($)	13.9%	3.47	4.06	4.54	5.25	5.48	6.65	7.75	8.96	9.65	11.21
Employees	6.9%	55,000	58,000	60,000	71,000	75,000	76,000	80,000	88,000	94,000	100,000

STOCK PRICE HISTORY

HIGH/LOW/CLOSE

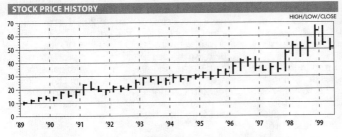

1999 FISCAL YEAR-END

Debt ratio: 37.5%
Return on equity: 20.2%
Cash ($ mil.): 81
Current ratio: 1.33
Long-term debt ($ mil.): 1,685
No. of shares (mil.): 251
Dividends
  Yield: 1.1%
  Payout: 29.1%
Market value ($ mil.): 15,292

ALCOA INC.

OVERVIEW

Alcoa is no lightweight, even though its products are. The Pittsburgh-based company (formerly Aluminum Company of America) is the world's top aluminum manufacturer. An integrated firm, Alcoa is also the largest producer of alumina (aluminum's principal ingredient, made from bauxite) and has operations in more than 30 countries. End products such as flat-rolled sheet aluminum are sold to makers of beverage cans and other packaging. The aerospace, automotive, railroad, and shipbuilding industries use sheet and plate products. Engineered products include extruded rods, tubes, and wire. Non-aluminum operations include packaging machinery, plastic bottles, vinyl siding, and car and truck electrical distribution systems.

Despite aluminum's drop in price, Alcoa continues to churn out healthy sales and profits through cost-cutting and the rapid assimilation of Alumax and Inespal, its major buys of 1998. Determined to remain at the top, Alcoa is buying Reynolds Metals (the #3 aluminum producer) in response to Canadian rival Alcan Aluminium's agreement to a three-way merger with Pechiney (France) and Alusuisse Lonza (Switzerland). Alcoa also has introduced new uses for aluminum, including its use in auto frames for the Audi A8 and the Plymouth Prowler.

HISTORY

In 1886 two chemists, one in France and one in the US, simultaneously discovered an inexpensive process for aluminum production. The American, Charles Hall, pursued commercial applications. Two years later, with an investor group led by Captain Alfred Hunt, Hall formed the Pittsburgh Reduction Company. Its first salesman, Arthur Davis, secured an initial order for 2,000 cooking pots.

In 1889 the Mellon Bank loaned the company $4,000. In 1891 the firm recapitalized as a million-dollar corporation, with the Mellon family holding 12% of the stock.

Davis led the business after Hunt died in 1899 and stayed on until 1957 (he died in 1962 at age 95). The company, the first industrial user of Niagara Falls (1893), introduced aluminum foil (1910) and found applications for aluminum in new products such as airplanes and cars. It became the Aluminum Company of America in 1907.

By the end of WWI, Alcoa had integrated backward into bauxite mining and forward into end-use production. By the 1920s the Mellons had raised their stake to 33%. The company transferred most foreign properties to Aluminum Ltd., a Canadian subsidiary, in 1928.

The government and Alcoa had debated antitrust issues in court for years since the smelting patent expired in 1912. Finally a 1946 federal ruling forced the company to sell many operations built during WWII as well as its Canadian subsidiary (today called Alcan, its largest competitor).

In the competitive aluminum industry of the 1960s, Alcoa's laboratories devised lower-cost production methods and seized market share, especially in beverage cans. In the 1970s Alcoa began offering engineered products such as aerospace components; in the 1980s it doubled spending on research and development and invested heavily in acquisitions and plant modernization.

CEO Paul O'Neill (former president of International Paper) arrived in 1987 and shifted the company's focus back to aluminum. Sales and earnings set records the next two years but plunged afterward, reflecting a weak global economy and record-low aluminum prices.

Alcoa sold some of its Latin American investments in 1992. O'Neill looked worldwide for new growth opportunities for aluminum, and the next year, as part of a joint venture with Kobe Steel, Alcoa opened a new beverage-can sheet mill. However, the fall of the Soviet Union in the early 1990s led to a worldwide glut as Russian exports soared.

In 1994 Alcoa cut its production as part of a two-year accord with Western and Russian producers. That year the company agreed to pool its alumina and chemical operations with Australia's Western Mining Corp.

Alcoa formed a joint venture with Shanghai Aluminum Fabrication Plant in China in 1995. The company expanded in Europe in 1996, acquiring Italy's state-run aluminum business, followed by the purchase of Inespal, Spain's state-run aluminum operations in 1998. Alcoa also bought #3 US aluminum producer Alumax for $3.8 billion in 1998. Known by the nickname Alcoa since the late 1920s, the company adopted that as its official name in 1999. O'Neill retired as CEO in 1999; COO Alain Belda succeeded him. Later that year, Alcoa bought the 50% of aluminum auto parts maker A-CMI it did not already own from Hayes Lemmerz International. Alcoa also agreed to buy Reynolds Metals for $4.4 billion after increasing its $4.1 billion hostile bid for the company.

Chairman: Paul H. O'Neill, age 63, $2,450,020 pay (prior to title change)
President and CEO: Alain J. P. Belda, age 55, $1,740,707 pay (prior to promotion)
EVP and CFO: Richard B. Kelson, age 52, $900,200 pay
EVP Allied Products: George E. Bergeron, age 57, $1,097,038 pay
EVP and Chairman's Counsel: Richard L. Fischer, age 62, $900,200 pay
EVP Environment, Health, Safety and General Counsel: Lawrence R. Purtell, age 51
EVP Human Resources and Communications: Robert F. Slagle, age 58
EVP Alcoa Business System: G. Keith Turnbull, age 63
VP and Controller: Timothy S. Mock
VP; President, Alcoa Forged Products: William F. Christopher
VP; President, Alcoa Rigid Packaging Division: Michael Coleman, age 48
VP; President, Alcoa Mill Products: John W. Collins
VP; President, Alcoa Closure Systems: Ronald A. Glah
VP; President, Alcoa Europe: L. Patrick Hassey, age 53, $938,931 pay
VP and Chief Information Officer: Patricia L. Higgins, age 49
Auditors: PricewaterhouseCoopers LLP

LOCATIONS

HQ: Alcoa Corporate Center, 201 Isabella St., Pittsburgh, PA 15212-5858
Phone: 412-553-4545   **Fax:** 412-553-4498
Web site: http://www.alcoa.com

Alcoa has 215 operating locations in 31 countries.

PRODUCTS/OPERATIONS

1998 Sales by Market

	$ mil.	% of total
Transportation	3,738	24
Packaging	3,304	22
Aluminum ingot	2,012	13
Alumina & chemicals	1,781	12
Building & construction	1,741	11
Distribution & other	2,764	18
Total	**15,340**	**100**

COMPETITORS

Alcan
Bethlehem Steel
BHP
British Steel
Budd Company
Commonwealth Industries
Crown Cork & Seal
Hayes Lemmerz
LTV
MAXXAM
Mitsubishi
Mitsui
Nippon Steel
Norsk Hydro
Nucor
Ormet
Preussag
Quanex
Reynolds Metals
Sumitomo
Superior Industries
Trans-World Metals
USX-U.S. Steel
VIAG

HISTORICAL FINANCIALS & EMPLOYEES

NYSE symbol: AA FYE: December 31	Annual Growth	1989	1990	1991	1992	1993	1994	1995	1996	1997	1998
Sales ($ mil.)	3.9%	10,910	10,710	9,884	9,492	9,056	9,904	12,500	13,061	13,319	15,340
Net income ($ mil.)	(1.1%)	945	295	63	(1,139)	5	375	791	515	805	853
Income as % of sales	—	8.7%	2.8%	0.6%	—	0.1%	3.8%	6.3%	3.9%	6.0%	5.6%
Earnings per share ($)	(1.1%)	2.67	0.85	0.18	(3.36)	0.01	1.05	2.22	1.47	2.31	2.42
Stock price - FY high ($)	—	19.91	19.31	18.28	20.16	19.59	22.56	30.13	33.13	44.81	40.63
Stock price - FY low ($)	—	13.81	12.41	13.44	15.25	14.75	16.06	18.44	24.56	32.13	29.00
Stock price - FY close ($)	7.9%	18.75	14.41	16.09	17.91	17.34	21.66	26.44	31.88	35.19	37.28
P/E - high	—	7	23	102	—	1,959	21	14	23	19	17
P/E - low	—	5	15	75	—	1,475	15	8	17	14	12
Dividends per share ($)	1.1%	0.68	0.77	0.45	0.40	0.40	0.40	0.45	0.67	0.49	0.75
Book value per share ($)	1.1%	14.85	15.05	14.34	10.35	9.98	11.03	12.45	12.77	12.97	16.36
Employees	6.1%	60,600	63,700	65,600	63,600	63,400	61,700	72,000	76,800	81,600	103,500

STOCK PRICE HISTORY

HIGH/LOW/CLOSE

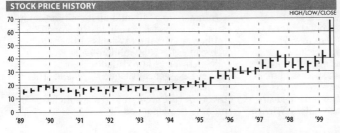

1998 FISCAL YEAR-END

Debt ratio: 32.2%
Return on equity: 14.2%
Cash ($ mil.): 342
Current ratio: 1.54
Long-term debt ($ mil.): 2,877
No. of shares (mil.): 367
Dividends
  Yield: 2.0%
  Payout: 31.0%
Market value ($ mil.): 13,675

ALLEGHENY TELEDYNE, INC.

OVERVIEW

Alloys are allies at Allegheny Teledyne. The Pittsburgh-based company, the result of a merger between diversified Teledyne and stainless-steel manufacturer Allegheny Ludlum, is a top maker of specialty alloys and steels (more than 50% of sales).

Its growing aerospace and electronics segment (about 25% of sales) offers such products as aircraft piston engines, and microwave components. Industrial products include forklifts. Allegheny Teledyne also makes air filters, equipment for dental labs, and Water Pik oral hygiene products.

Many of those businesses, picked up with

Allegheny Ludlum, have created confusion among investors. In response, the company is spinning off or selling the operations that don't fit with specialty alloys and metals. Aerospace, electronics, and high-tech software operations will be spun off into one publicly traded company, and consumer goods will be spun off into another to be renamed Allegheny Technologies. Allegheny Teledyne also plans to sell three industrial equipment divisions.

Chairman Richard Simmons (from Allegheny Ludlum) and his wife own about 8% of Allegheny Teledyne. Teledyne co-founder Henry Singleton owns about 7%.

HISTORY

Allegheny Ludlum Steel was established in 1938 through the merger of Allegheny Steel Company (founded in Pennsylvania in 1898) and Ludlum Steel Company (founded in New Jersey in 1854). Allegheny Steel veteran W. F. Detwiler became Allegheny Ludlum Steel's first chairman. During WWII the company developed heat-resisting alloys for aircraft turbine engines.

Following the war, the company focused on stainless steel and flat-rolled silicon electrical steel used to make electrical transformers. In 1956 it doubled its capacity for making specialty alloys and installed the industry's first semi-automated system for working hot steel. Allegheny Ludlum Steel established international operations in the 1960s with a plant in Belgium.

The company changed its name to Allegheny Ludlum Industries in 1970 and, after diversifying, sold its specialty steel division in a management-led buyout that formed Allegheny Ludlum Steel in 1980. In 1986 the company changed its name to Allegheny Ludlum Corp. It went public a year later. The company diversified the use of its metals in the 1990s, incorporating them into skis, cookware, razors, and PC diskettes.

Henry Singleton and George Kozmetsky, former Litton Industries executives, invested $225,000 each in 1960 to found Teledyne to make electronic aircraft components. Sales grew from $4.5 million the first year to nearly $90 million by 1964. Teledyne beat out IBM and Texas Instruments for a contract for a US Navy helicopter avionics system in 1965. Kozmetsky left the company a year later.

Under Singleton, Teledyne bought more than 100 companies, mostly small, successful manufacturing and technology firms in defense-related areas such as engines, unmanned aircraft, specialty metals, and computers. Teledyne

also moved into offshore oil-drilling equipment, insurance and finance, and the Water Pik line of oral care products.

In 1986 Teledyne spun off its Argonaut Insurance unit. It left the insurance business entirely with its 1990 spinoff of Unitrin. Its defense businesses were caught in a 1989 FBI fraud probe, and the company paid $4.4 million in restitution.

In 1991 Teledyne consolidated its operations from 130 units to 21 companies. Two years later it was indicted on charges of knowingly selling zirconium to a Chilean arms manufacturer for use in cluster bombs sold to Iraq. In 1995, protesting that the US government had approved of the deal, Teledyne pleaded guilty to the charges and paid a $13 million fine.

Despite Teledyne's rebuff of holding company WHX's 1994 takeover offer, in 1996 WHX came back with a new proposal that led to the $3.2 billion merger between Teledyne and Allegheny Ludlum in 1997. Also that year, CEO William Rutledge resigned with former Allegheny Ludlum CEO Richard Simmons succeeding him. The company also acquired the aerospace division of the UK's Sheffield Forgemaster's Group for $110 million and titanium producer Oregon Metallurgical for about $620 million.

In 1999 Allegheny announced its restructuring plan to focus on specialty metals; it sold Ryan Aeronautical (aerial drones) to Northrop Grumman for $140 million, its mining equipment business to Astec Industries for $18.5 million, and its fluid systems business to two companies for $350 million. Later that year, Allegheny picked up Canadian pool supply maker Les Agences Claude Marchand. The company also tapped Lockheed Martin executive Thomas Corcoran to replace Richard Simmons as president and CEO.

Chairman, President, and CEO: Richard P. Simmons, age 67, $1,715,312 pay
VC: Robert P. Bozzone, age 65
EVP; President and CEO, Aerospace and Electronics and Industrial: Robert Mehrabian, age 57, $871,953 pay
EVP Finance and Administration, and CFO: James L. Murdy, age 60, $671,888 pay
SVP Human Resources: Judd R. Cool, age 63
SVP, General Counsel, and Secretary: Jon D. Walton, age 56, $489,359 pay
Corporate VP Investor Relations and Corporate Communications: Richard J. Harshman, age 42
VP and Treasurer: Robert S. Park, age 54
VP, Controller, and Chief Accounting Officer: Dale G. Reid, age 43
President, Allegheny Ludlum: Jack W. Shilling
President, Allvac and High Performance Metals Group: John V. Andrews
President, ORMET-Wah Chang: Ralph A. Nauman
President, Titanium Industries: James S. Paddock
President, Rome Metals: John A. Dioguardi
President, Teledyne Electronic Technologies: Marvin H. Fink
President, Teledyne Brown Engineering: Richard A. Holloway
President, Teledyne Continental Motors: Bryan L. Lewis
President Metalworking Products, Industrial Segment: David M. Hogan
President, Teledyne Water Pik: Wayne S. Brothers
Auditors: Ernst & Young LLP

LOCATIONS

HQ: 1000 Six PPG Place, Pittsburgh, PA 15222-5479
Phone: 412-394-2800   **Fax:** 412-394-3034
Web site: http://www.alleghenyteledyne.com

PRODUCTS/OPERATIONS

1998 Sales

	$ mil.	% of total
Specialty metals	2,053	52
Aerospace & electronics	1,007	26
Industrial products	516	13
Consumer products	248	6
Adjustments	99	3
Total	**3,923**	**100**

COMPETITORS

Acerinox	Nippon Steel
Akzo Nobel	Northrop Grumman
Alcan	Nucor
AlliedSignal	Olympic Steel
Armco	Raytheon
Avesta Sheffield	Republic Technologies
Bausch & Lomb	Reynolds Metals
Bethlehem Lukens Plate	Rockwell International
Boeing	Rolls-Royce
British Steel	Siemens
Carpenter Technology	Texas Instruments
Emerson	Textron
FMC	Thomson SA
GE	Thyssen Krupp
General Dynamics	TRW
General Motors	United Technologies
J & L Specialty Steel	USX-U.S. Steel
Litton Industries	WCI Steel
Lockheed Martin	WHX
Masco	

HISTORICAL FINANCIALS & EMPLOYEES

NYSE symbol: ALT FYE: December 31	Annual Growth	1989	1990	1991	1992	1993	1994	1995	1996	1997	1998
Sales ($ mil.)	14.3%	1,180	1,085	1,005	1,036	1,100	1,077	1,494	3,816	3,745	3,923
Net income ($ mil.)	6.8%	134	69	41	47	71	18	112	213	298	241
Income as % of sales	—	11.3%	6.4%	4.1%	4.5%	6.4%	1.7%	7.5%	5.6%	7.9%	6.1%
Earnings per share ($)	1.7%	—	—	—	—	—	—	—	1.19	1.67	1.23
Stock price - FY high ($)	—	—	—	—	—	—	—	—	23.75	32.88	29.56
Stock price - FY low ($)	—	—	—	—	—	—	—	—	19.88	21.00	14.00
Stock price - FY close ($)	(5.7%)	—	—	—	—	—	—	—	23.00	25.88	20.44
P/E - high	—	—	—	—	—	—	—	—	20	20	24
P/E - low	—	—	—	—	—	—	—	—	17	13	11
Dividends per share ($)	100.0%	—	—	—	—	—	—	—	0.16	0.64	0.64
Book value per share ($)	17.3%	—	—	—	—	—	—	—	5.00	5.73	6.88
Employees	21.8%	—	—	5,400	5,400	6,100	6,000	6,000	24,000	22,000	21,500

1995 and prior information is for Allegheny Ludlum.

STOCK PRICE HISTORY

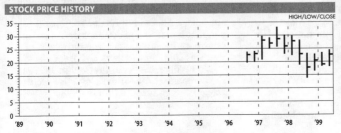

HIGH/LOW/CLOSE

1998 FISCAL YEAR-END

Debt ratio: 25.0%
Return on equity: 18.0%
Cash ($ mil.): 75
Current ratio: 2.19
Long-term debt ($ mil.): 447
No. of shares (mil.): 195
Dividends
  Yield: 3.1%
  Payout: 52.0%
Market value ($ mil.): 3,983

ALLERGAN, INC.

OVERVIEW

If your eyes are good and you have clear skin, you may not have heard of Allergan. But if you squint and scratch, its products are "killer apps."

Irvine, California-based Allergan's products include eye care medications, contact lens cleaners, surgical equipment, and intraocular lenses used in cataract surgery to replace the eye's natural lens. Allergan also makes Azelex acne treatment and Tazorac for acne and psoriasis. Its Botox — derived from the botulism toxin — is used to treat muscle spasms. Allergan is also seeking permission to extend the drug's uses to lower back pain and juvenile cerebral palsy. (A less orthodox use is to lessen wrinkles by relaxing facial muscles.)

Pressure from managed care companies and generic competition have led Allergan to trim its workforce and consolidate facilities. It is selling noncore operations, such as its over-the-counter eyedrops. Allergan is also looking for research and development partners and has formed pacts with drugmakers SUGEN and Cambridge NeuroScience to develop treatments for eye diseases such as glaucoma.

With US and European markets maturing, Allergan is looking to emerging markets to boost sales. It has made inroads in China, India, and Latin America. The firm is also developing new products to support its established offerings.

HISTORY

In 1950 Gavin Herbert set up a small ophthalmic business above one of his drugstores in Los Angeles. Chemist Stanley Bly invented the company's first product, antihistamine eyedrops called Allergan. The company adopted the name of the eyedrops and expanded the business and the product range. Herbert's son Gavin Jr., then a USC student, helped with the business (he's now chairman emeritus).

By 1960 Allergan was a $1 million company; it moved into the contact lens solution market with its liquifilm product that year. In 1964 it developed its first foreign distributorship, in Iraq, and the following year it started its first foreign subsidiary, in Canada. International expansion and limited competition for hard contact lens care products sustained sales growth at about 20% throughout the 1960s.

Allergan went public in 1971. During the 1970s the company became Bausch & Lomb's contractual supplier of Hydrocare lens solution and enzymatic cleaner for soft contact lenses. By 1975 Allergan had about a third of the hard contact lens care market. When Gavin Sr. died in 1978, Gavin Jr. succeeded him as president and CEO and also became chairman. By 1979 revenues topped $62 million.

SmithKline Beckman purchased Allergan for $236 million in 1980. The 1980s were a boom period for soft contact lens makers. In 1984 SmithKline acquired International Hydron, the #2 soft contact lens maker behind Bausch & Lomb; International Hydron became part of Allergan in 1987. In 1989 SmithKline merged with Beecham and spun off Allergan to its shareholders.

By the early 1990s the contact lens and lens care markets had begun to mature, leading to a company restructuring and a new focus on specialty pharmaceuticals. In 1992 Allergan sold its North and South American contact lens businesses; the rest of its contact lens businesses were sold in 1993.

The company boosted its presence in the intraocular lens market with the 1994 purchase of Ioptex Research. Also in 1994 Allergan and joint venture partner Ligand Pharmaceuticals made their enterprise an independently operating company, Allergan Ligand Retinoid Therapeutics (ALRT). The next year Allergan recalled about 400,000 bottles of contact lens solution because of potential eye irritation.

In 1995 Allergan acquired cataract surgery equipment maker Optical Micro Systems and the contact lens care business of Pilkington Barnes Hind. The company's 1995 income was hurt by a $50 million contribution to ALRT; its 1996 income is the result of a $70 million writeoff for restructuring. In 1996 Allergan inked development deals with SUGEN and Cambridge NeuroScience.

In 1997 Allergan received FDA approval for its multifocus eye lens for cataract patients and Tazorac for acne and psoriasis. In the UK Allergan received approval for its glaucoma treatment Alphagan. That year Allergan and Ligand acquired the assets of ALRT and formed a new subsidiary, Allergan Specialty Therapeutics, to conduct research and development of potential pharmaceutical products. The next year this unit was spun off to Allergan shareholders.

CEO William Shepherd retired in 1997, and the company chose former Novartis executive David Pyott to succeed him in 1998.

Chairman: Herbert W. Boyer, age 62
President and CEO: David E. I. Pyott, age 45,
$1,306,615 pay
SVP and Controller: Dwight J. Yoder, age 53
**Corporate VP, Science and Technology; President,
Research and Development and Global BOTOX:**
Lester J. Kaplan, age 48, $548,506 pay
**Corporate VP, Administration, Secretary, and General
Counsel:** Francis R. Tunney Jr., age 51, $521,949 pay
**Corporate VP; President, North America Region and
Global Eye Rx Business:** F. Michael Ball, age 43,
$515,145 pay
**Corporate VP; President, Europe, Africa, and Middle
East Region and Global Lens Care Products:**
James V. Mazzo, age 41, $404,420 pay
Corporate VP, Human Resources: Tom Burnham
Corporate VP; President, Asia/Pacific Region:
David A. Fellows, age 42
Corporate VP, Corporate Development:
George M. Lasezkay, age 47
Corporate VP; President, Latin America Region:
Nelson R. A. Marques, age 47
Corporate VP, Worldwide Operations:
Jacqueline J. Schiavo, age 50
Auditors: KPMG LLP

LOCATIONS

HQ: 2525 Dupont Dr., Irvine, CA 92612
Phone: 714-246-4500   **Fax:** 714-246-4971
Web site: http://www.allergan.com

Allergan has facilities in Argentina, Australia, Brazil,
Canada, China, France, Germany, Hong Kong, Ireland,
Italy, Japan, Spain, South Africa, the UK, and the US.

PRODUCTS/OPERATIONS

1998 Sales

	$ mil.	% of total
Pharmaceuticals	711	55
Medical devices	551	42
Research services	34	3
Total	**1,296**	**100**

Selected Products

Ophthalmic
Acular (solution for seasonal allergic conjunctivitis)
Betagan (ophthalmic solution)
Blephamide (ophthalmic anti-inflammatory
and anti-infective)
Ocuflox (solution for bacterial conjunctivitis
and corneal ulcers)
Phacoflex (natural lens replacement)
Polytrim (synthetic antimicrobial for ocular
bacterial infections)
Pred Forte (ocular corticosteroid
inflammation suspension)
Propine (ophthalmic solution)

Optical
Complete (contact lens solution)
UltraCare (contact lens neutralizer/disinfectant)

Other
Botox (neuromuscular disorder treatment)

COMPETITORS

Alcon	Merck
Bausch & Lomb	Novartis
Cooper Companies	Pharmacia & Upjohn
Hoffmann-La Roche	Schering-Plough
Johnson & Johnson	SmithKline Beecham

HISTORICAL FINANCIALS & EMPLOYEES

NYSE symbol: AGN FYE: December 31	Annual Growth	1989	1990	1991	1992	1993	1994	1995	1996	1997	1998
Sales ($ mil.)	5.4%	807	884	839	898	859	947	1,067	1,147	1,149	1,296
Net income ($ mil.)	—	57	81	(60)	104	109	111	73	77	128	(90)
Income as % of sales	—	7.1%	9.2%	—	11.5%	12.7%	11.7%	6.8%	6.7%	11.2%	—
Earnings per share ($)	—	0.86	1.21	(0.89)	1.53	1.65	1.73	1.12	1.17	1.95	(1.38)
Stock price - FY high ($)	—	25.50	19.38	25.50	27.25	26.38	30.88	33.75	42.00	37.19	66.50
Stock price - FY low ($)	—	15.63	12.25	16.75	20.38	20.75	20.00	25.75	30.00	25.88	31.75
Stock price - FY close ($)	15.7%	17.38	17.50	24.50	26.00	22.63	28.25	32.50	35.63	33.56	64.75
P/E - high	—	30	16	—	18	16	18	30	36	19	—
P/E - low	—	18	10	—	13	13	12	23	26	13	—
Dividends per share ($)	29.7%	0.05	0.28	0.33	0.38	0.40	0.42	0.47	0.62	0.52	0.52
Book value per share ($)	5.3%	6.63	7.82	6.61	7.48	8.04	9.48	10.37	11.45	12.89	10.53
Employees	(1.4%)	6,800	6,300	5,633	5,158	4,749	4,903	6,000	6,100	6,100	5,972

STOCK PRICE HISTORY

HIGH/LOW/CLOSE

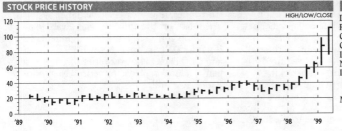

1998 FISCAL YEAR-END

Debt ratio: 22.4%
Return on equity: —
Cash ($ mil.): 182
Current ratio: 1.79
Long-term debt ($ mil.): 201
No. of shares (mil.): 66
Dividends
 Yield: 0.8%
 Payout: —
Market value ($ mil.): 4,281

ALLIANT TECHSYSTEMS INC.

OVERVIEW

If Rambo owned stock, he'd want a big chunk of Alliant Techsystems. The Hopkins, Minnesota-based company has three business groups: conventional munitions, aerospace systems, and defense systems.

Its conventional munitions group makes medium-caliber ammunition and tank ammunition, gunpowder, solid rocket propellant systems, munitions propellants, warheads, flares, and composite structures. The company's aerospace group makes solid propulsion systems for space vehicles, strategic missile systems, and reinforced composite structures for aircraft and spacecraft. Alliant's defense systems group turns out smart munitions, electronic systems, fuses, unmanned vehicles, and batteries. The US government (and its contractors) accounts for about 70% of sales.

The end of the Cold War forced Alliant to search for new markets, but regional conflicts have shown the importance of basic munitions. On the higher-tech side, the company has minimized direct competition with huge defense contractors such as Boeing and Raytheon by providing rocket motors to them.

Alliant hopes to increase international sales by expanding its offerings, seeking new customers, and continuing to forge alliances with defense and aerospace rivals.

HISTORY

Alliant Techsystems was formed in 1990 when Honeywell spun off its defense-related businesses to shareholders. Honeywell's roots in the defense business go back to 1941, when it was known as Honeywell-Minnesota. A maker of consumer electronics products such as switches, buttons, and appliances, Honeywell joined the war effort and began producing tank periscopes, turbo engine regulators, automatic ammunition firing control devices, and automatic bomb-release systems.

After WWII Honeywell-Minnesota found that the Cold War provided a reliable and profitable income stream for defense contractors. By 1964 the company had shortened its name to Honeywell and focused on electronics systems. The Vietnam War provided a boost in sales, but the fall of Saigon led to downsizing.

When the Iron Curtain fell in the late 1980s, Honeywell's defense businesses misfired and ran up huge losses. Honeywell sought to sell its defense businesses as an independent subsidiary, but was unable to obtain an acceptable bid. Honeywell spun off Alliant Techsystems to shareholders in 1990 under Toby Warson, the CEO of Honeywell's UK subsidiary.

A former naval commander, Warson began with about 8,300 employees and lots of bureaucratic layers; he quickly cut about 800 administrative jobs. Though the Soviet Union and its Eastern Bloc allies had collapsed, a new threat raised its head: Iraq. Saddam Hussein and his ilk presented a new enemy — the well-armed third world despot — that required meat-and-potatoes weapons. Cutbacks in the defense budget meant that advanced high-dollar systems were put on the back burner while cheaper alternatives, such as improved ammunition, were moved to the front.

During the Gulf War, Alliant's ordnance contributions included 120mm uranium-tipped anti-tank shells, 25mm shells for the Bradley Fighting Vehicle, and the 30mm bullets used by Apache helicopters and A-10 Warthog anti-tank planes.

Warson cut another 800 jobs after the Gulf War and reduced the number of management layers from 14 to seven. Alliant divested its only non-munitions unit, Metrum Information Storage (data recording and storage devices), in 1992. Metrum had incurred setbacks that caused the company to write-off millions of dollars. The next year Alliant acquired three companies: Accudyne Corporation (electronic and mechanical assemblies, fuses), Kilgore (infrared decoy devices, pyrotechnics, small detonators, 20mm ammunition), and Ferrulmatic (metal parts). Alliant expanded into additional aerospace markets and achieved vertical integration in propellant production in 1995 with the purchase of the aerospace division of Hercules Incorporated, a maker of space rocket motors, strategic and tactical weapons systems, and ordnance. In 1996 Alliant withdrew from demilitarization ventures in the former Soviet republics of Belarus and Ukraine.

Alliant refocused on its core operations in 1997 and jettisoned its marine systems group (torpedoes, underwater surveillance systems). The next year the company was awarded a $1 billion contract to make components for Boeing's Delta IV rockets. In 1999 chairman and CEO Dick Schwartz retired from the company and was replaced by retired Navy admiral Paul David Miller.

Chairman and CEO: Paul David Miller, age 57, $311,000 pay (prior to promotion)
President and COO: Peter A. Bukowick, age 55, $711,343 pay
Senior Group VP, Aerospace: Paul A. Ross, age 62, $413,292 pay
Group VP, Conventional Munitions: Nicholas G. Vlahakis, age 51, $303,170 pay
Group VP, Defense Systems: Don L. Sticinski, age 47
VP and Controller: Paula J. Patineau, age 45
VP and General Counsel: Daryl L. Zimmer, age 56, $290,778 pay
VP and Secretary: Charles H. Gauck, age 60
VP, Human Resources: Robert E. Gustafson, age 50
VP, Information Technology and Chief Information Officer: Geoffrey B. Courtright
VP, Investor Relations and Public Affairs and Assistant Treasurer: Richard N. Jowett, age 54
VP, Strategic Planning: Mark L. Mele, age 42
VP, Tax and Investments: John L. Lotzer, age 43
VP, Treasurer, and CFO: Scott S. Meyers, age 45, $451,538 pay
VP, Washington D.C. Operations: William R. Martin, age 58
Auditors: Deloitte & Touche LLP

LOCATIONS

HQ: 600 2nd St. NE, Hopkins, MN 55343
Phone: 612-931-6000   **Fax:** 612-931-5920
Web site: http://www.atk.com

Alliant Techsystems has facilities in California, Florida, Illinois, Kansas, Minnesota, Mississippi, New Jersey, New Mexico, Pennsylvania, Tennessee, Texas, Utah, Virginia, West Virginia, and Wisconsin.

1999 Sales

	% of total
US	94
Other countries	6
Total	**100**

PRODUCTS/OPERATIONS

1999 Sales

	$ mil.	% of total
Conventional munitions	480	44
Aerospace	395	36
Defense systems	224	20
Corporate	(9)	—
Total	**1,090**	**100**

1999 Sales

	% of total
US Government & contractors	
US Army	38
US Air Force	22
US Navy	10
Other	30
Total	**100**

COMPETITORS

Allied Research
Boeing
British Aerospace
Celsius
Cordant Technologies
GE
GenCorp
ITT Industries
K Systems
Litton Industries
Lockheed Martin
Northrop Grumman
Olin
Primex
Racal Electronics
Raytheon
Thomson SA

HISTORICAL FINANCIALS & EMPLOYEES

NYSE symbol: ATK FYE: March 31	Annual Growth	1990	1991	1992	1993	1994	1995	1996	1997	1998	1999
Sales ($ mil.)	(1.6%)	1,259	1,248	1,187	1,005	775	789	1,194	1,089	1,076	1,090
Net income ($ mil.)	2.1%	42	24	39	(114)	33	(74)	48	59	68	51
Income as % of sales	—	3.4%	2.0%	3.3%	—	4.2%	—	4.0%	5.4%	6.3%	4.7%
Earnings per share ($)	6.3%	—	2.55	3.88	(11.82)	3.21	(7.37)	3.56	4.41	5.10	4.15
Stock price - FY high ($)	—	—	15.25	29.25	31.00	30.00	40.63	53.00	57.38	69.00	88.00
Stock price - FY low ($)	—	—	8.63	19.88	19.13	22.00	21.75	35.63	42.00	40.50	57.88
Stock price - FY close ($)	24.7%	—	13.25	22.25	24.00	24.00	38.13	48.38	42.13	62.75	77.69
P/E - high	—	—	6	8	—	9	—	15	13	14	21
P/E - low	—	—	3	5	—	7	—	10	10	8	14
Dividends per share ($)	—	—	0.00	0.00	0.00	0.00	0.00	0.00	0.00	0.00	0.00
Book value per share ($)	(2.4%)	—	13.99	18.51	6.74	9.37	10.14	12.15	16.73	20.67	11.54
Employees	(2.8%)	7,900	7,600	6,700	4,500	4,900	8,200	7,700	6,800	6,550	6,110

STOCK PRICE HISTORY

HIGH/LOW/CLOSE

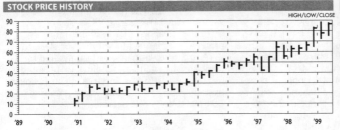

1999 FISCAL YEAR-END

Debt ratio: 72.1%
Return on equity: 42.8%
Cash ($ mil.): 21
Current ratio: 1.20
Long-term debt ($ mil.): 306
No. of shares (mil.): 10
Dividends
  Yield: —
  Payout: —
Market value ($ mil.): 799

ALLIED WASTE INDUSTRIES, INC.

OVERVIEW

Allied Waste Industries has collected enough garbage and garbage companies to make it the #2 trash company in the US, behind Waste Management. The Scottsdale, Arizona-based company believes that a bunch of little garbage piles is better than one big one — as long as it *owns* the little piles — and it is known for its decentralized management structure. The company's subsidiaries and affiliates serve some 9.9 million residential, commercial, and industrial customers in more than 60 markets in 46 states.

The vertically integrated firm operates about 360 collection companies, about 160 transfer stations, nearly 130 recycling facilities, and more than 160 landfills. Allied Waste handles only nonhazardous waste. The Blackstone Group of investors owns about 30% of the company.

Allied Waste has been piling up companies since it was created in 1987, but the $9.4 billion acquisition of Browning-Ferris Industries (which *had* been the #2 US waste company) in 1999 is a coup. Allied Waste is creating eight regional executive centers to handle the increased business, but it's leaving day-to-day management chores to local operators. BFI will operate as a subsidiary, at least in the short term.

Allied Waste is selling numerous assets to reduce its overlapping service areas, to unload noncore operations (such as medical waste handling and garbage-to-gas conversion facilities) and to meet requirements set up by the US Department of Justice as a result of the BFI deal. The firm continues to look for tuck-in acquisitions in both its new and old markets.

HISTORY

In 1987 entrepreneur Bruce Lessey looked around Houston at all the garbage trucks his Quick Wrench firm was servicing and saw an opportunity. He changed his company's name to Allied Waste, went public, and started buying waste companies. Two years later Allied Waste was in trouble. In stepped Roger Ramsey, co-founder of Browning-Ferris Industries (BFI), who left BFI in 1976. He was a partner in an investment company that owned part of Allied Waste. Ramsey joined the board (becoming CEO in 1989), and Lessey stepped down. Over the next seven years, the company acquired 30 waste haulers in seven states.

One of them (acquired in 1992) was R.18, an Illinois firm owned by Arizona native Thomas Van Weelden. Ramsey, the money man, and Van Weelden, a nonconformist whose entire family was in the garbage business, struck up a close partnership. Van Weelden became Allied Waste's president (and CEO in 1997), and the two moved the company to Scottsdale, Arizona, in 1993 to get away from Houston-based heavyweight (and future partner) BFI.

The two men implemented a rapid growth strategy through the loose consolidation of vertically integrated, locally managed operations. In 1996 Allied Waste bought a rich prize, Laidlaw Inc., for $1.6 billion, which tripled the company's revenues in 1997. It sold Laidlaw's Canadian operation to pay down debt.

Allied Waste acquired 54 other operators in 1998, including Seattle-based Rabanco Cos., which gave it a foothold in the Pacific Northwest. It also paid $1.1 billion for American Disposal Services. Late that year Van Weelden

succeeded Ramsey as chairman, and merger negotiations with big boy BFI got serious.

Between 1992 and the time Allied Waste made its biggest deal, it had collected more than 200 companies. In 1999 it bought its largest company yet, BFI, a $4.7 billion operation. The $9.4 billion acquisition sent Allied Waste's customer base soaring from 2.6 million to 9.9 million. At the time of its acquisition, BFI operated in 46 US states, Canada, and Puerto Rico.

Founded in 1967, BFI had been on the buyout trail for decades. During its first six years it acquired 157 waste-disposal companies and expanded overseas. In the 1980s it bought more than 500 firms and gained another 100 in the early 1990s.

All was not well at BFI, however. It had slipped in the late 1980s, when price-fixing charges and environmental violations cost it more than $5 million and a lot of bad press. By 1998 BFI was bloated and revenues were stagnant. It sold all operations outside of North America to Suez Lyonnaise in exchange for $1 billion and a 20% stake in SITA, Europe's #1 waste company. The rest of BFI's holdings went to Allied Waste in 1999.

To recoup about $1.7 billion from BFI's price, Allied planned to sell its 20% stake in SITA to Suez Lyonnaise, BFI's Canadian assets to Waste Management, medical waste services to Stericycle, BFI Gas Services to Gas Recovery Systems, and certain solid waste-handling operations to Republic Services.

Chairman, President and CEO: Thomas H. Van Weelden,
age 44, $1,273,000 pay (prior to promotion)
VP and Chief Accounting Officer: Peter S. Hathaway,
age 43
VP and CFO: Henry L. Hirvela, age 47, $675,000 pay
VP and COO: Larry D. Henk, age 39, $675,000 pay
VP, Compliance and Landfill Development:
Jim G. Van Weelden
VP, Legal and Corporate Secretary: Steven M. Helm,
age 51, $495,000 pay
VP, Mergers and Acquisitions: Michael G. Hannon, age 44
VP, Operations: Donald W. Slager, age 37, $405,000 pay
Regional VP, Great Lakes: Richard Van Hattem Jr.
Regional VP, Midwest: Joe Duncan
Regional VP, Northeast: Robert E. Deak
Regional VP, Southeast: Terry Armstrong
Regional VP, Southwest: Rick J. Krall
Regional VP, West: Donald A. Swierenga
Operations Integration: Roger Groen Jr.
Operations Integration: Pete Lindemulder
Treasurer: G. Thomas Rochford Jr.
Controller: James S. Eng
Director, Human Resources: Christine Caprice
Assistant Corporate Secretary and Corporate Counsel:
Jo Lynn White
Auditors: Arthur Andersen LLP

LOCATIONS

HQ: 15880 N. Greenway-Hayden Loop, Ste. 100,
Scottsdale, AZ 85260
Phone: 480-627-2700   **Fax:** 480-627-2701
Web site: http://www.alliedwaste.com

Allied Waste Industries operates in 46 US states in eight
regions: the Atlantic, Central, Great Lakes, Midwest,
Northeast, Northwest, Southeast, Southwest, and West.

PRODUCTS/OPERATIONS

1998 Sales

	% of total
Collection	56
Landfill	30
Transfer	7
Other	7
Total	**100**

COMPETITORS

Philip Services
Republic Services
Superior Services
Waste Connections
Waste Industries
Waste Management

HISTORICAL FINANCIALS & EMPLOYEES

NYSE symbol: AW FYE: December 31	Annual Growth	1989	1990	1991	1992	1993	1994	1995	1996	1997	1998
Sales ($ mil.)	88.3%	5	5	9	35	54	97	170	247	875	1,576
Net income ($ mil.)	—	(3)	(1)	0	1	1	(8)	9	(79)	0	(223)
Income as % of sales	—	—	—	4.3%	2.9%	2.4%	—	5.5%	—	0.0%	—
Earnings per share ($)	—	—	—	0.06	0.08	0.08	(0.24)	0.35	(0.84)	0.16	(1.22)
Stock price - FY high ($)	—	—	—	9.25	12.25	6.88	6.00	10.00	10.38	24.38	31.63
Stock price - FY low ($)	—	—	—	8.25	4.13	4.00	3.25	3.75	6.44	7.25	16.13
Stock price - FY close ($)	14.8%	—	—	9.00	4.75	5.25	4.00	7.13	9.25	23.31	23.63
P/E - high	—	—	—	154	153	86	—	29	—	152	—
P/E - low	—	—	—	138	52	50	—	11	—	45	—
Dividends per share ($)	—	—	—	0.00	0.00	0.00	0.00	0.00	0.00	0.00	0.00
Book value per share ($)	4.1%	—	—	3.82	4.00	5.98	6.02	2.66	3.64	5.76	5.04
Employees	61.1%	130	130	143	413	639	1,125	1,440	5,000	5,400	9,500

STOCK PRICE HISTORY

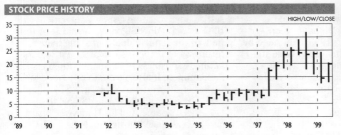

HIGH/LOW/CLOSE

1998 FISCAL YEAR-END

Debt ratio: 69.5%
Return on equity: —
Cash ($ mil.): 40
Current ratio: 1.10
Long-term debt ($ mil.): 2,119
No. of shares (mil.): 184
Dividends
  Yield: —
  Payout: —
Market value ($ mil.): 4,360

ALLIEDSIGNAL INC.

OVERVIEW

AlliedSignal comes in loud and clear, producing a broad band of products for the automotive, aerospace, pharmaceutical, plastics, fibers, and other markets. Based in Morristown, New Jersey, the company operates worldwide through its five industrial segments.

The aerospace operations of AlliedSignal include the manufacture of electronics and avionics such as flight safety systems and communication and navigation gear. Customers include Airbus and Boeing. The company also provides aircraft maintenance, overhaul, and training services.

The specialty chemicals & electronics segment is a leading producer of bulk pharmaceuticals and pharmaceutical intermediates. Its other chemical products include refrigerants, solvents, and agricultural materials. Performance polymers produced by the company range from nylon fibers to specialty films used to make everything from sports gear to body armor.

AlliedSignal's turbine technologies segment produces aircraft and marine engines and turbochargers for cars, trucks, off-road vehicles, and aircraft. The company is selling off its Bendix brake pads unit and its line of consumer automobile products.

CEO Larry Bossidy pumped up profitability by buying growth-oriented businesses. The company is buying controls maker Honeywell to become a leading aerospace parts-and-electronics manufacturer.

HISTORY

During WWI Germany controlled much of the world's chemical industry, causing dye and drug shortages. In response, *Washington Post* publisher Eugene Meyer and scientist William Nichols organized the Allied Chemical & Dye Corporation in 1920.

Allied opened a synthetic-ammonia plant in 1928 near Hopewell, Virginia, and became the world's leading producer of ammonia. After WWII Allied began making nylon, refrigerants, and other products. It became Allied Chemical Corporation in 1958.

Seeking a supplier of raw materials for its chemical products, in 1962 Allied bought Union Texas Natural Gas. In the early 1970s CEO John Connor sold many of the firm's unprofitable businesses and invested in oil and gas exploration. By 1979, when Edward Hennessy became CEO, Union Texas produced 80% of Allied's income.

Hennessy led the company into new fields, including electronics and health and scientific products. Under a new name, Allied Corporation (1981), it went on to buy the Bendix Corporation, an aerospace and automotive company, in 1983. By 1984 Bendix generated 50% of Allied's income.

In 1985 Allied merged with Signal Companies to form Allied-Signal (which changed to AlliedSignal in 1993). Founded by Sam Mosher in 1922 as the Signal Gasoline Company, the company merged with the Garrett Corporation, a Los Angeles-based aerospace firm, in 1964; acquired Mack Trucks in 1967 (spun off in 1983); and in 1968 became Signal Companies. Signal bought Ampex Corporation in 1981. The Allied merger added Signal's Garrett division to Bendix, making aerospace Allied's largest business sector. The company sold 50% of Union Texas in 1985 and spun off more than 40 unprofitable chemical and engineering businesses over the next two years.

Larry Bossidy, hired from GE in 1991 as the new CEO, streamlined the company. In 1994 AlliedSignal bought Ford Motor Company's UK spark plug operations and Textron's Lycoming Turbine Engine Division. In 1995 AlliedSignal bought a 96% stake in German specialty chemical maker Riedel-de Haen.

In 1996 the company sold much of its brakes business to Robert Bosch. In 1997 the company bought antifreeze maker Prestone Products and aircraft-lighting systems maker Grimes Aerospace. It sold its seatbelt- and airbag-producing business to BREED Technologies for $710 million. In 1998 the company made 13 acquisitions, including Banner Aerospace's aerospace fastener and chemical products distribution units for about $345 million and Pharmaceutical Fine Chemicals.

The company returned to the courts in 1999 in an attempt to block BFGoodrich's acquisition of Coltec Industries (a deal that would grab a majority of the market for landing gears), but settled after reaching a supply agreement with BFGoodrich. AlliedSignal then paid $655 million for the semiconductor-making materials business of UK's Johnson Matthey; it sold its laminates business to Germany's Ruetgers for $425 million. It also agreed to buy Honeywell, a maker of electronic controls, in a $14 billion deal. The plan called for AlliedSignal to take Honeywell's name, and for Honeywell chairman and CEO Michael Bonsignore to become CEO of the new company.

Chairman and CEO: Lawrence A. Bossidy, age 63, $6,000,000 pay
President and COO: Frederic M. Poses, age 56, $1,600,000 pay
SVP and Chief Information Officer: Larry E. Kittelberger, age 50
SVP, General Counsel, and Secretary: Peter M. Kreindler, age 53, $995,000 pay
SVP Human Resources and Communications: Donald J. Redlinger, age 54, $825,000 pay
SVP and CFO: Richard F. Wallman, age 47, $910,000 pay
President, Turbocharging Systems: William J. Amelio, age 41
President, Automotive Products Group: David E. Berges, age 49
President, Bendix/Jurid Products: Mark H. Breedlove Jr., age 42
President, Specialty Chemicals: Gary A. Cappeline, age 49
President, Federal Manufacturing & Technologies: Karen K. Clegg, age 50
President, Avionics & Lighting: Francis W. Daly
President, Aerospace Equipment Systems: Joseph DeSarla
President, AlliedSignal Aerospace: Robert D. Johnson, age 51
Auditors: PricewaterhouseCoopers LLP

LOCATIONS

HQ: 101 Columbia Rd., Morristown, NJ 07962
Phone: 973-455-2000 **Fax:** 973-455-4807
Web site: http://www.alliedsignal.com

AlliedSignal has facilities in about 40 countries worldwide.

PRODUCTS/OPERATIONS

1998 Sales & Operating Income

	Sales $ mil.	Sales % of total	Operating Income $ mil.	Operating Income % of total
Aerospace	4,871	32	920	43
Turbine technologies	3,638	24	458	22
Transportation products	2,441	16	106	5
Speciality chemicals & electronic solutions	2,241	15	327	15
Performance polymers	1,928	13	307	15
Other	9	—	—	—
Total	**15,128**	**100**	**2,118**	**100**

COMPETITORS

Akzo Nobel	Honeywell
Allegheny Teledyne	ITT Industries
American Standard	Litton Industries
BASF AG	Lockheed Martin
Beaulieu Of America	Northrop Grumman
BFGoodrich	Raytheon
Borg-Warner Automotive	Robert Bosch
Dana	Rockwell International
Dow Chemical	Rolls-Royce
DuPont	Siemens
Eaton	Tenneco
GE	Cordant Technologies
Hercules	Thomson SA
Hexcel	TRW
Hoechst AG	United Technologies

HISTORICAL FINANCIALS & EMPLOYEES

NYSE symbol: ALD FYE: December 31	Annual Growth	1989	1990	1991	1992	1993	1994	1995	1996	1997	1998
Sales ($ mil.)	2.7%	11,942	12,343	11,831	12,042	11,827	12,817	14,346	13,971	14,472	15,128
Net income ($ mil.)	10.8%	528	462	(273)	(712)	411	759	875	1,020	1,170	1,331
Income as % of sales	—	4.4%	3.7%	—	—	3.5%	5.9%	6.1%	7.3%	8.1%	8.8%
Earnings per share ($)	11.2%	0.89	0.84	(0.50)	(1.26)	0.73	1.34	1.52	1.76	2.02	2.32
Stock price - FY high ($)	—	10.09	9.47	11.25	15.50	20.03	20.34	24.94	37.19	47.13	47.56
Stock price - FY low ($)	—	7.94	6.22	6.47	10.22	14.38	15.19	16.69	23.56	31.63	32.63
Stock price - FY close ($)	19.8%	8.72	6.75	10.97	15.13	19.75	17.00	23.75	33.50	38.81	44.31
P/E - high	—	11	11	—	—	27	15	16	21	23	21
P/E - low	—	9	7	—	—	20	11	11	13	16	14
Dividends per share ($)	3.2%	0.45	0.45	0.40	0.25	0.29	0.34	0.39	0.45	0.52	0.60
Book value per share ($)	5.5%	5.88	6.27	5.40	3.97	4.21	5.27	6.35	7.39	7.86	9.48
Employees	(4.6%)	107,100	105,800	93,300	89,300	86,400	87,500	88,500	76,600	70,500	70,400

STOCK PRICE HISTORY

HIGH/LOW/CLOSE

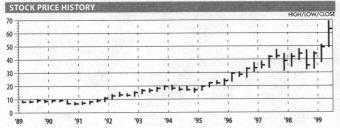

1998 FISCAL YEAR-END

Debt ratio: 21.8%
Return on equity: 25.1%
Cash ($ mil.): 712
Current ratio: 1.08
Long-term debt ($ mil.): 1,476
No. of shares (mil.): 558
Dividends
  Yield: 1.4%
  Payout: 25.9%
Market value ($ mil.): 24,746

ALLMERICA FINANCIAL CORP.

OVERVIEW

All secure? Allmerica Financial wants to help. The Worcester, Massachusetts-based company sells property/casualty insurance and asset management services. Primary subsidiaries Citizens Corporation and Hanover Insurance offer homeowners, personal and commercial auto, workers' compensation, and commercial multiperil insurance. The company's risk management group includes employee benefits management and third-party medical plan administration.

After bad weather damaged its property/casualty segment, Allmerica hitched its wagon to the wealth management star. As baby boomers near retirement, the company is emphasizing asset preservation products such as variable annuities, defined benefit plans, stable value products, investment management, and more.

HISTORY

In 1842 a group of Worcester, Massachusetts, businessmen tried to form a mutual life insurance company. They were denied a charter but tried again. The second time, with the assistance of a good lobbyist named Benjamin Balch, they succeeded. In 1844 the State Mutual Life Assurance Co. of Worcester set up business in the back room of secretary Clarendon Harris's bookstore. The first president was John Davis, a US senator. The company issued its first policy in 1845.

In the early years State Mutual reduced risk by issuing policies only for residents of "civilized" areas such as New England, New Jersey, New York, Ohio, and Pennsylvania. It also restricted movement, requiring policyholders to get permission for travel outside those areas. By the 1850s the company had begun issuing policies in the Midwest (with a 25% premium surcharge), the South (for 30% extra), and California (for a pricey extra $25 per $1,000), with a maximum coverage of $5,000. The Civil War was a problem for many insurers, who had to decide what to do about Southern policies and payment on war-related claims. State Mutual chose to pay out its Northern policyholders' benefits, despite the extra cost.

After the war, State Mutual shifted to a system in which only the general agent dealt directly with the company, instead of all agents contracting with the company.

In 1896 the firm began offering plans that paid out in installments, rather than a lump sum, for policyholders afraid that their beneficiaries would fritter away the whole payment.

The first 30 years of the 20th century were, for the company, a time of growth that was stopped short by the Depression. But despite a great increase in the number of policy loans and surrenders for cash value, State Mutual's financial footing remained sound.

After WWII the company entered group insurance and began offering individual sickness and accident coverage. In 1957 it was renamed State Mutual Life Assurance Co. of America. The firm added property/casualty insurance in the late 1950s through alliances with firms like Worcester Mutual Fire Insurance Co. During the 1960s State Mutual continued to develop property/casualty, buying interests in Hanover Insurance and Citizens Corporation.

The company followed the industrywide shift into financial services in the 1970s, adding mutual funds, a real estate investment trust, and an investment management firm. This trend accelerated in the 1980s and State Mutual began offering financial planning services, as well as administrative and other services for the insurance and mutual fund industries (the mutual fund administration operations were sold in 1995). Managing this growth was another story: The company's acquisitions left it bloated and disorganized. Technical systems were in disarray by the early 1990s and the agency force had grown to more than 1,400. In response, the company began a five-year effort to upgrade systems, cut fat, and reduce sales positions.

In view of its shifting focus, State Mutual changed its corporate name to Allmerica Financial Corporation in 1992. State regulators and the company's policyholders/owners allowed Allmerica to demutualize in 1995. In 1997 it bought the 40% of Allmerica Property & Casualty that it didn't already own. The next year heavy spring storms hammered Allmerica's bottom line, and the company incurred $15 million in catastrophe losses. That year it bought the portion of Citizens it didn't already own.

In 1999 Allmerica announced plans to sell its group life and health insurance operations to concentrate on its core businesses. It also said it would buy Advantage Insurance Network (AIN), a group of affiliated life insurance agencies.

OFFICERS

President and CEO: John F. O'Brien, age 55,
$1,550,553 pay
VP, Corporate Services: Bruce C. Anderson
VP and Chief Information Officer: Robert E. Bruce
VP and Chief Investment Officer: John P. Kavanaugh
VP, General Counsel, and Assistant Secretary:
John F. Kelly
VP, Human Resources: Renee Mikitarian-Bradley
VP, CFO, and Treasurer: Edward J. Parry III
President, The Hanover Insurance Company:
J. Barry May
President, Citizens Insurance: James R. McAuliffe
**President and CEO, Allmerica Financial Life Insurance
and Annuity:** Richard M. Reilly
President and CEO, Allmerica Property & Casualty:
Robert P. Restrepo Jr.
President, Allmerica Services: Eric A. Simonsen
VP, Allmerica Voluntary Benefits: Phillip E. Soule
Auditors: PricewaterhouseCoopers LLP

LOCATIONS

HQ: 440 Lincoln St., Worcester, MA 01653
Phone: 508-855-1000 **Fax:** 508-853-6332
Web site: http://www.allmerica.com

Allmerica Financial's business is focused in the
midwestern, northeastern and southern US.

PRODUCTS/OPERATIONS

1998 Assets

	$ mil.	% of total
Cash & equivalents	550	2
State & municipal bonds	2,487	9
Corporate bonds	4,991	18
Stocks	700	3
Mortgage loans	562	2
Policy loans	154	1
Separate account assets	13,698	48
Recoverables & receivables	511	2
Other assets	3,792	14
Other investments	163	1
Total	**27,608**	**100**

1998 Sales

	$ mil.	% of total
Premiums	2,305	67
Net investment income	624	18
Universal life & investment product policy fees	297	9
Other	207	4
Total	**3,433**	**100**

COMPETITORS

AIG	MassMutual
Allstate	MetLife
American Financial	Nationwide Insurance
AXA Financial	New York Life
Chubb	Northwestern Mutual
CIGNA	Progressive Corporation
CNA Financial	Prudential
GEICO	St. Paul Companies
The Hartford	State Farm
John Hancock	TIG Holdings
Liberty Mutual	Travelers
Lincoln National	USAA

HISTORICAL FINANCIALS & EMPLOYEES

NYSE symbol: AFC FYE: December 31	Annual Growth	1989	1990	1991	1992	1993	1994	1995	1996	1997	1998
Assets ($ mil.)	19.7%	—	—	—	9,367	10,291	10,503	17,758	18,998	22,549	27,608
Net income ($ mil.)	11.6%	—	—	—	104	115	40	134	182	209	201
Income as % of assets	—	—	—	—	1.1%	1.1%	0.4%	0.8%	1.0%	0.9%	0.7%
Earnings per share ($)	8.5%	—	—	—	—	—	—	2.61	3.63	3.82	3.33
Stock price - FY high ($)	—	—	—	—	—	—	—	28.63	34.38	51.00	75.25
Stock price - FY low ($)	—	—	—	—	—	—	—	23.38	24.75	32.63	38.38
Stock price - FY close ($)	28.9%	—	—	—	—	—	—	27.00	33.50	49.94	57.88
P/E - high	—	—	—	—	—	—	—	11	9	13	23
P/E - low	—	—	—	—	—	—	—	9	7	9	12
Dividends per share ($)	—	—	—	—	—	—	—	0.00	0.20	0.20	0.20
Book value per share ($)	10.1%	—	—	—	—	—	—	31.42	34.43	39.69	41.96
Employees	(2.5%)	—	—	—	—	—	—	6,800	6,800	6,300	6,300

STOCK PRICE HISTORY

HIGH/LOW/CLOSE

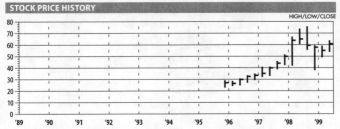

1998 FISCAL YEAR-END

Equity as % of assets: 8.9%
Return on assets: 0.8%
Return on equity: 8.2%
Long-term debt ($ mil.): 200
No. of shares (mil.): 59
Dividends
 Yield: 0.3%
 Payout: 6.0%
Market value ($ mil.): 3,392
Sales (mil.): $3,433

THE ALLSTATE CORPORATION

OVERVIEW

The "good hands" company has a stranglehold on the auto insurance business. Auto insurance accounts for some 75% of Northbrook, Illinois-based Allstate's property/casualty premiums. The company is the #2 personal lines insurer in the US (State Farm Mutual Automobile Insurance is #1).

Allstate's core insurance lines are home and auto; it is the #1 provider of nonstandard (high-risk) auto insurance. The company also offers life and annuity products and specialty lines. Allstate Federal Savings Bank provides financial services. The company is expanding its product lines in Europe and Asia.

For some folks, Allstate's good hands have been clutching a double-edged sword, as the company has been fighting several court battles. These include suits alleging it overcharged California customers and one brought by several states over its pamphlet, "Do I Need An Attorney?" sent to non-Allstate customers who had filed a claim against Allstate policyholders.

HISTORY

Allstate has its origins in a friendly game of bridge played in 1930 on a Chicago-area commuter train by Sears president Robert Wood and a friend, insurance broker Carl Odell. Odell suggested that Sears sell auto insurance through the mail. Wood liked the idea, financed the company, and in 1931 put Odell in charge (that hand of bridge must have shown Wood that Odell was no dummy). The company was named Allstate, after one of Sears' tire brands. Allstate was born just as Sears was beginning its push into retailing, and Allstate went with it, selling insurance out of all the new Sears stores.

Growth was slow during the Depression and WWII, but the postwar boom was a gold mine for both Sears and Allstate. Suburban development made cars a necessity, 1950s prudence necessitated car insurance, and Sears made it easy to buy the insurance at their stores and, increasingly, at freestanding agencies.

In the late 1950s Allstate added home and other property/casualty insurance lines. It also went into life insurance — in-force policies zoomed from zero to $1 billion in six years, the industry's fastest growth ever.

Sears formed Allstate Enterprises in 1960 as an umbrella for all its noninsurance operations. In 1970 that firm bought its first savings and loan (S&L). The insurer continued to acquire other S&Ls and to add subsidiaries throughout the 1970s and 1980s.

This strategy dovetailed with Sears' strategy, which was to become a diversified financial services company. In 1985 Sears introduced the Discover Card through Allstate's Greenwood Trust Company. However, by the late 1980s it was obvious Sears would never be a financial services giant. Moreover, it was losing so much in retailing that by 1987 Allstate was the major contributor to corporate net income. Sears began to dismantle its financial empire in the 1990s.

Allstate also suffered from a backlash against high insurance rates. When Massachusetts instituted no-fault insurance in 1989, Allstate stopped writing new auto insurance there. Later the company agreed to refund $110 million to customers to settle a suit with California over rate rollbacks required by 1988's Proposition 103.

Allstate went public in 1993, when Sears sold about 20% of its stake. That year it began reducing its operations in Florida to protect itself against high losses from hurricanes. Two years later the retailer spun off its remaining interest to its shareholders. Also in 1995 Allstate sold 70% of PMI, its mortgage insurance unit, to the public.

In 1996 Allstate worked to reduce its exposure to hurricane and earthquake losses. (Hurricane Andrew and the Northridge quake helped account for almost $4 billion in casualty losses alone.) It created a Florida-only subsidiary that would buy reinsurance to protect against losses that could arise from another major hurricane. Like many other insurers, the firm was required to help fund the California Earthquake Authority risk pool. That year Allstate sold its Northbrook (property/casualty) and Allstate Reinsurance operations to St. Paul and SCOR, respectively.

In 1998 Allstate sold its real estate portfolio for nearly $1 billion; chairman and CEO Jerry Choate retired and was succeeded by president and COO Edward Liddy; and Allstate opened a savings bank. In 1999 it set up a joint venture with Putnam Investments to sell variable annuities. That year agents filed a class-action suit claiming that Allstate treats them more like employees than independent contractors, without the requisite tax withholding and benefits.

Chairman, President, and CEO, Allstate Corporation and Allstate Insurance: Edward M. Liddy, age 53, $2,488,518 pay
President and CEO, Allstate Federal Savings Bank: Thomas W. Buckley
SVP and CFO: John L. Carl
VP, Secretary, and General Counsel; EVP, Secretary, and General Counsel, Allstate Insurance: Robert W. Pike, age 57
VP; SVP and Chief Investment Officer, Allstate Insurance: Casey J. Sylla, age 55
Chairman, Allstate Life Insurance: Louis G. Lower II, age 53, $989,763 pay
President, Allstate Property and Casualty Insurance: Richard I. Cohen, age 54
President, Allstate Life Insurance: Thomas J. Wilson, age 41
SVP Human Resources, Allstate Insurance: Joan M. Crockett, age 48
SVP Marketing and Brand Development, Allstate Insurance: Michael J. McCabe, age 53
SVP and Chief Information Officer, Allstate Insurance: Francis W. "Frank" Pollard, age 56
SVP Corporate Relations, Allstate Insurance; President, Allstate Indemnity and Deerbrook Insurance: Rita P. Wilson, age 52
Auditors: Deloitte & Touche LLP

LOCATIONS

HQ: Allstate Plaza, 2775 Sanders Rd., Northbrook, IL 60062-6127
Phone: 847-402-5000 **Fax:** 847-836-3998
Web site: http://www.allstate.com

Allstate sells life and property/casualty insurance in the US, Canada, and Germany, as well as in South Korea and other Asian countries.

PRODUCTS/OPERATIONS

1998 Assets

	$ mil.	% of total
Cash & equivalents	258	—
Treasury & agency securities	3,960	5
Asset-backed securities	4,251	5
Mortgage-backed securities	7,879	9
Municipal bonds	18,771	21
Corporate bonds	17,779	20
Stocks	6,421	7
Mortgage loans	3,458	4
Assets in separate account	10,098	11
Recoverables & receivables	5,014	6
Deferred policy acquisition costs	3,096	4
Other assets	6,706	8
Total	**87,691**	**100**

1998 Sales

	$ mil.	% of total
Personal property/ casualty insurance	19,307	74
Investment income	3,890	15
Life insurance	1,519	6
Other	1,260	5
Total	**25,976**	**100**

COMPETITORS

20th Century	Liberty Mutual
AIG	MetLife
American National Insurance	Nationwide Insurance
	Old Republic
Berkshire Hathaway	Progressive Corporation
Chubb	SAFECO
Cincinnati Financial	St. Paul Companies
CNA Financial	State Farm
The Hartford	Travelers
Kemper Insurance	USAA

HISTORICAL FINANCIALS & EMPLOYEES

NYSE symbol: ALL FYE: December 31	Annual Growth	1989	1990	1991	1992	1993	1994	1995	1996	1997	1998
Assets ($ mil.)	10.5%	35,583	41,478	43,378	52,098	59,358	61,369	70,029	74,508	80,918	87,691
Net income ($ mil.)	16.8%	815	701	723	(825)	1,302	484	1,904	2,075	3,105	3,294
Income as % of assets	—		2.3%	1.7%	1.7%	—	2.2%	0.8%	2.7%	2.8%	3.8%	3.8%
Earnings per share ($)	21.3%	—	—	—	—	1.50	0.54	2.12	2.32	3.56	3.94
Stock price - FY high ($)		—	—	—	—	17.13	14.94	21.19	30.44	47.19	52.38
Stock price - FY low ($)		—	—	—	—	13.56	11.31	11.75	18.69	28.13	36.06
Stock price - FY close ($)	21.2%	—	—	—	—	14.75	11.88	20.56	28.94	45.25	38.50
P/E - high		—	—	—	—	11	28	10	13	13	13
P/E - low		—	—	—	—	9	21	6	8	8	9
Dividends per share ($)	24.1%	—	—	—	—	0.18	0.36	0.39	0.43	0.36	0.53
Book value per share ($)	13.0%	—	—	—	—	11.44	9.38	14.17	15.22	18.36	21.08
Employees	(1.0%)	—	57,232	54,144	51,515	49,000	46,300	44,300	48,200	51,400	53,000

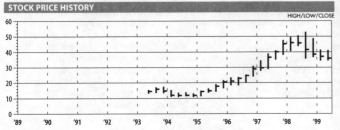

1998 FISCAL YEAR-END

Equity as % of assets: 19.7%
Return on assets: 3.9%
Return on equity: 19.1%
Long-term debt ($ mil.): 1,353
No. of shares (mil.): 818
Dividends
  Yield: 1.4%
  Payout: 13.5%
Market value ($ mil.): 31,493
Sales (mil.): $25,976

ALLTEL CORPORATION

OVERVIEW

ALLTEL wants to be all things to all of its communications customers. The Little Rock, Arkansas-based company offers wireless, local, and long-distance phone services and Internet access to about 6 million customers in 24 states, primarily in the southeastern and midwestern US. It has targeted acquisitions serving small and midsized cities.

ALLTEL provides local phone service to about 1.9 million customer lines in 15 US states through 574 rural exchanges. It is also approved to provide competitive local phone service in Arkansas, Florida, North Carolina, Texas, and Virginia, with plans to enter more. ALLTEL offers long-distance service to more than 500,000 customers; paging in Arkansas, Florida, and Nebraska; and Internet access in most ALLTEL service areas.

The 1998 acquisition of 360 Communications more than doubled ALLTEL's wireless customer base to about 4 million consumers in 22 US states. ALLTEL also offers PCS in Alabama and Florida and has PCS licenses in 73 markets in 12 US states. Putting it all together, the better to offer bundled services, the company is interconnecting its wireline and wireless properties with a massive, 12,000-mile fiber-optic cable network that it is building across 12 US states, crossing the southeast, the Eastern Seaboard, and the Great Lakes region.

Tying communications networks to a computer networking business? ALLTEL has it all. Its information services units provide processing software and services, such as mortgage loan data processing, in 48 countries. ALLTEL Publishing creates phone directories, and ALLTEL Supply distributes telecom equipment and materials.

HISTORY

ALLTEL traces its roots to the Western Reserve Telephone Company of Hudson, Ohio. In 1960 Weldon Case, grandson of Western Reserve's founder, merged it with four other Ohio phone companies to form the Mid-Continent Telephone Company. In 1983 Mid-Continent merged with the Allied Telephone Company (incorporated in 1954) to form ALLTEL Corporation, creating the US's fifth-largest telephone service. The merger, inspired by the competitive environment resulting from the AT&T breakup, included Mid-Continent's purchase of satellite-based carrier Argo Communications. Case became ALLTEL's chairman.

In 1984 ALLTEL Mobile launched its first wireless system in Charlotte, North Carolina. To concentrate on fast-growing Sun Belt markets, in 1987 ALLTEL sold cellular interests it had acquired in Ohio, Pennsylvania, and West Virginia.

As the 1990s began, ALLTEL combined its telecom business with information services. In 1990 the company bought Systematics, a provider of processing services and software to the financial industry. A year later ALLTEL bought C-TEC's cellular phone billing and information systems software, and in 1992 ALLTEL purchased Computer Power, Inc., which did data processing for the mortgage banking industry. These businesses would become part of ALLTEL Information Services.

When Case retired in 1991, Joe Ford became chairman and moved the company's headquarters to Little Rock. Building its southern presence, ALLTEL bought GTE's phone directory publishing business as well as GTE's Georgia phone properties in 1993. ALLTEL also acquired cellular properties in Arkansas, North Carolina, South Carolina, and Texas. In 1996 the company sold phone and cable TV lines in eight (mainly western) US states to Citizens Utilities.

Also in 1996 ALLTEL bought a 5% stake in Apex Global Information Services, a global Internet access provider, and the next year began offering Internet access in several of its US markets. The company began long-distance service that year and applied for permission to offer competitive local phone service in Arkansas and North Carolina.

ALLTEL won PCS licenses for 73 markets in 12 US states (including seven key southern states) in 1997. In a move to offer more bundled services, the company consolidated its wireline and wireless telephone operations that year into one unit, ALLTEL Communications.

In 1998 ALLTEL acquired Chicago-based 360 Communications (which had been struggling since its 1996 spin-off from Sprint) in a $6 billion deal; 360 brought 2.6 million cellular customers in 15 states, mostly in the Southeast and Mid-Atlantic. ALLTEL also bought about 2,400 miles of fiber-optic lines from Qwest, primarily in the South.

The next year the company bought Aliant Communications, a provider of both wireless and wireline services in Nebraska, for $1.8 billion, and agreed to acquire the smaller Liberty Cellular, based in Kansas, for $600 million.

Chairman and CEO: Joe T. Ford, age 61, $1,430,000 pay
VC: Dennis E. Foster, age 58, $1,958,379 pay
President and COO: Scott T. Ford, age 36, $956,250 pay
EVP External Affairs, General Counsel, and Secretary:
Francis X. Frantz, age 45
EVP: Tom T. Orsini
SVP Finance and Treasurer: Jeffery R. Gardner, age 39
SVP and Chief Technology Officer: John S. Haley, age 43
Chairman Information Services: William L. Cravens
Group President - Communications:
Kevin L. Beebe, age 39, $1,008,983 pay
Group President - Communications:
Michael T. Flynn, age 50
Group President - Information Services:
Jeffrey H. Fox, age 36, $760,000 pay
President Publishing: Kenneth W. Beach
President Supply: J. Scott Chesbro
President ALLTEL Telecommunications Services:
Roger Leitner
VP Human Resources: John L. Comparin, age 46
Controller: John M. Mueller, age 48
Assistant Treasurer: Jerry M. Green, age 51
Assistant Treasurer: Laura S. Hall, age 36
Auditors: Arthur Andersen LLP

LOCATIONS

HQ: 1 Allied Dr., Little Rock, AR 72202
Phone: 501-905-8000 **Fax:** 501-905-5444
Web site: http://www.alltel.com

ALLTEL provides telecommunications services in 24 US states. It also offers information processing software and services in 48 countries, including Canada, Germany, the UK, and the US.

PRODUCTS/OPERATIONS

1998 Sales

	$ mil.	% of total
Communications services		
Wireless	2,137	41
Wireline	1,309	25
Emerging businesses	100	2
Information services	1,162	22
Other	601	10
Adjustment	(115)	—
Total	**5,194**	**100**

Selected Operations
Cellular phone service
Directory publishing
Paging (paging networks)
PCS (personal communications services)
Telephone service (local and long-distance)

Selected Subsidiaries and Affiliates
360 Communications Company
ALLTEL Mobile Communications, Inc
ALLTEL Publishing Corporation
ALLTEL Supply, Inc.
ALLTEL Information Services, Inc.

COMPETITORS

AT&T
Bell Atlantic
BellSouth
EDS
Fiserv
Frontier Corporation
GTE
MCI WorldCom
Nextel
Powertel
Price Communications
PrimeCo
Qwest
R. R. Donnelley
SBC Communications
Sprint
Telephone & Data Systems
United States Cellular
Vodafone AirTouch

HISTORICAL FINANCIALS & EMPLOYEES

NYSE symbol: AT FYE: December 31	Annual Growth	1989	1990	1991	1992	1993	1994	1995	1996	1997	1998
Sales ($ mil.)	17.4%	1,226	1,574	1,748	2,092	2,342	2,962	3,110	3,192	3,264	5,194
Net income ($ mil.)	14.6%	154	193	189	229	262	272	355	292	508	526
Income as % of sales	—	12.6%	12.3%	10.8%	10.9%	11.2%	9.2%	11.4%	9.1%	15.6%	10.1%
Earnings per share ($)	5.9%	1.13	1.17	1.17	1.25	1.39	1.43	1.85	1.52	2.70	1.89
Stock price - FY high ($)	—	20.94	19.56	21.63	25.00	31.25	31.38	31.13	35.63	41.63	61.38
Stock price - FY low ($)	—	11.67	12.38	15.88	17.38	22.88	24.00	23.25	26.63	29.75	38.25
Stock price - FY close ($)	13.3%	19.44	17.00	19.50	23.88	29.50	30.13	29.50	31.38	41.06	59.81
P/E - high	—	19	17	18	20	22	22	17	23	15	32
P/E - low	—	10	11	14	14	16	17	13	18	11	20
Dividends per share ($)	8.0%	0.58	0.64	0.70	0.74	0.80	0.88	0.96	1.04	1.10	1.16
Book value per share ($)	6.3%	6.67	6.35	6.77	7.01	8.24	8.58	10.18	11.15	11.82	11.60
Employees	11.7%	7,919	11,359	12,660	12,876	14,864	16,333	15,865	16,307	16,393	21,504

STOCK PRICE HISTORY

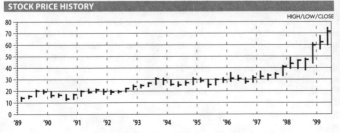

HIGH/LOW/CLOSE

1998 FISCAL YEAR-END

Debt ratio: 51.6%
Return on equity: 16.1%
Cash ($ mil.): 56
Current ratio: 0.81
Long-term debt ($ mil.): 3,492
No. of shares (mil.): 281
Dividends
 Yield: 1.9%
 Payout: 61.4%
Market value ($ mil.): 16,818

AMAZON.COM, INC.

OVERVIEW

A map of the Amazon River shows its tributaries spreading out like ever-grasping fingers, and a map showing namesake Amazon.com's reach within the online world would look pretty much the same. The Seattle-based company best known for selling books online has become the Internet's largest retailer—and much, much more.

While it still goes toe-to-toe with Barnes & Noble and others in the book business, Amazon.com now oversees a network of Internet sites. Its sites offer a host of other consumer goods, ranging from music to jewelry, prescription drugs, sporting goods, and groceries. Auctions conducted by Amazon.com offer an even longer list of items. The company's other services include a combo scheduler/address book, a Web-shopping comparison service, and one of the most comprehensive movie databases on the Internet.

In the half-decade since its formation, Amazon.com has gone from a venture-capital-funded startup in CEO Jeff Bezos' garage to a bellwether Internet stock and the standard by which other companies' online sales efforts are judged. It has defined the red-ink-drenched, spend-to-grow style of Internet companies whose jaw-dropping market values outpace those of much larger enterprises with much longer histories. Amazon.com has purchased outright or invested in so many different e-ventures that it's beginning to look like a venture capitalist firm itself.

Bezos and his family own about 42% of Amazon.com.

HISTORY

Jeff Bezos was researching the new Internet frontier in the early 1990s for hedge fund D.E. Shaw. He realized that book sales would be a perfect fit with electronic commerce because book distributors already kept meticulous electronic lists. Bezos, who as a teen had dreamed of entrepreneurship in outer space, took the idea to Shaw. The company passed on the idea, but Bezos ran with it, trekking cross country to Seattle (close to a facility owned by major book distributor Ingram) and typing up a business plan along the way.

Bezos founded Amazon.com in 1994. After months of preparation, he launched an efficient, easy-to-navigate Web site in July 1995. (Douglas Hofstadter's *Fluid Concepts and Creative Analogies* was Amazon.com's first sale.) By September the company had sales of $20,000 a week. Bezos and his team continued to work with the site, making it more seamless. They pioneered features that now seem mundane, like one-click shopping, customer reviews, and e-mail order verification.

Amazon.com went public in 1997. Moves to cement the Amazon.com brand included becoming the sole book retailer on America Online's public Web site and Netscape's commercial channel. Late that year it opened a distribution center in Delaware.

In 1998 the company launched its online music and video stores, and it began to sell toys and electronics. Amazon.com also expanded its European reach with the purchases of online booksellers Bookpages (UK) and Telebook (Germany), and it acquired the Internet Movie Database. Bezos also expanded the company's base of online services, buying Junglee, a comparison-shopping service, and PlanetAll, an address book, calendar, and reminder service.

By midyear Amazon.com had attracted so much attention that its market capitalization equaled the combined values of profitable bricks-and-mortar rivals Barnes & Noble and Borders, even though their combined sales were far greater than the upstart's.

Investors weren't the only ones paying attention to Amazon.com. Superseller Wal-Mart alleged in a 1998 lawsuit that the company lured away computer experts in order to steal distribution technology secrets (the suit was settled in 1999). In December 1998 Amazon.com formed a promotional link with Hoover's Online, publisher of this profile.

After rival Barnes & Noble's late-1998 agreement to buy the US's largest book distributor, Ingram Book Group (a deal later abandoned), Amazon.com expanded its own distribution system by acquiring large warehouses in Kansas and Nevada.

After raising $1.25 billion in a bond offering early in 1999, Amazon.com went on a spending spree with deals to buy all or part of drugstore.com, HomeGrocer.com, Pets.com, Gear.com, Web-use tracking firm Alexa Internet, auction site LiveBid.com, rare book and music marketplace Exchange.com, and e-commerce systems firm Accept.com. Amazon.com began conducting online auctions in early 1999 and soon partnered with 255-year-old auction house Sotheby's to offer live auctions for rare collectibles.

OFFICERS

Chairman, President, and CEO: Jeffrey P. Bezos, age 35, $81,840 pay
President and COO: Joseph Galli, age 41
CFO and VP Finance and Administration: Joy D. Covey, age 35
SVP Product Development: John D. Risher, age 33, $155,168 pay
VP Business Development: George T. Aposporos, $142,083 pay
VP and Executive Editor: Rick R. Ayre
VP and Chief Information Officer: Richard L. Dalzell, age 41, $201,512 pay
VP and Chief Technology Officer: Sheldon J. Kaphan, age 46
VP Strategic Growth: Ryan Sawyer
VP Business Development: Kavitark R. Shriram, age 42
VP and General Manager: Joel R. Spiegel, $116,352 pay
Auditors: Ernst & Young LLP

LOCATIONS

HQ: 1516 2nd Ave., Seattle, WA 98101
Phone: 206-622-2335   **Fax:** 206-622-2405
Web site: http://www.amazon.com

Amazon.com has customers in all 50 states and more than 160 countries.

PRODUCTS/OPERATIONS

Selected Merchandise

Books	Games
CDs	Jewelry
Computer Games	Toys
DVDs	Videos
Electronics	

Other Operations
Alexa Internet (Web tracking and recommendation site)
Amazon.com auctions
Drugstore.com (29%)
Gear.com (49%, close-out sporting goods)
HomeGrocer.com (35%)
IMDb (Internet Movie Database)
Junglee (online comparison shopping services)
Pets.com (50%, pet supply store)
PlanetAll (online address book, calendar, and reminder service)
sothebys.amazon.com (collectibles auctions)

COMPETITORS

Advanced Marketing	Hastings Entertainment
Barnes & Noble	Hollywood Entertainment
Bertelsmann	Infoseek
Best Buy	Lauriat's
Blockbuster	Microsoft
Book-of-the-Month Club	MTS
Books-A-Million	Musicland
Borders	mySimon
BUY.COM	Navarre
CDnow	ONSALE
Cendant	Peapod
Columbia House	PETsMART
Crown Books	PlanetRx.com
CVS	Shopping.com
eBay	toysmart.com
E-greetings	Toys "R" Us
eToys	Wal-Mart
Excite@Home	Webvan
Fogdog	WH Smith
Greg Manning Auctions	Yahoo!

HISTORICAL FINANCIALS & EMPLOYEES

Nasdaq symbol: AMZN FYE: December 31	Annual Growth	1989	1990	1991	1992	1993	1994	1995	1996	1997	1998
Sales ($ mil.)	—	—	—	—	—	—	0	1	16	148	610
Net income ($ mil.)	—	—	—	—	—	—	(0)	(0)	(6)	(28)	(125)
Income as % of sales	—	—	—	—	—	—	—	—	—	—	—
Earnings per share ($)	—	—	—	—	—	—	—	—	—	(0.21)	(0.84)
Stock price - FY high ($)	—	—	—	—	—	—	—	—	—	10.99	120.50
Stock price - FY low ($)	—	—	—	—	—	—	—	—	—	2.62	8.28
Stock price - FY close ($)	966.6%	—	—	—	—	—	—	—	—	10.03	106.98
P/E - high	—	—	—	—	—	—	—	—	—	—	—
P/E - low	—	—	—	—	—	—	—	—	—	—	—
Dividends per share ($)	—	—	—	—	—	—	—	—	—	0.00	0.00
Book value per share ($)	339.3%	—	—	—	—	—	—	—	—	0.20	0.87
Employees	299.2%	—	—	—	—	—	—	33	151	614	2,100

STOCK PRICE HISTORY

HIGH/LOW/CLOSE

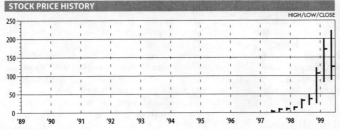

1998 FISCAL YEAR-END

Debt ratio: 71.5%
Return on equity: —
Cash ($ mil.): 26
Current ratio: 2.63
Long-term debt ($ mil.): 348
No. of shares (mil.): 159
Dividends
 Yield: —
 Payout: —
Market value ($ mil.): 17,038

AMERADA HESS CORPORATION

OVERVIEW

Amerada Hess has an armada of black gold assets. Based in New York City, the integrated oil and gas company conducts its exploration and production activities mainly in Gabon, Norway, the UK, and the US. Amerada Hess, which has its own fleet of tankers, has proved reserves of more than 1 billion barrels of oil equivalent. Its fields in the North Sea account for almost 60% of its oil reserves. The company also operates a refinery in St. Croix in the Virgin Islands in a venture with Venezuela's state oil company, PDVSA, and a refinery in New Jersey.

The company markets its petroleum products mainly in the eastern US. It has about 600 HESS gas stations; most are in Florida, New Jersey, New York, Pennsylvania, and South Carolina. About three-fourths of the stations are company-owned; more than half have Hess Express and Hess Mart convenience stores. Amerada Hess also sells natural gas in competitive UK and US markets and is beginning to sell electricity in the US's deregulating Northeast corridor.

Longtime CEO Leon Hess owned 13% of the firm when he died in 1999. His son, CEO John Hess, hopes to sail toward a profitable future for the company by exploiting attractive properties in Southeast Asia and offshore Brazil.

HISTORY

It was a logical match: Amerada Petroleum, which had been in the exploration and production business since the early 1900s, and Hess Oil and Chemical, involved in refining and marketing since the 1930s.

In 1919 British oil entrepreneur Lord Cowdray formed Amerada Corporation to explore for oil in North America. Cowdray soon hired geophysicist Everette DeGolyer, a pioneer in oil geology research. DeGolyer's systematic methods helped Amerada not only find oil deposits faster but also pick up fields missed by competitors. DeGolyer became president of Amerada in 1929 but left in 1932 to work independently.

After WWII Amerada began exploring overseas and during the 1950s entered pipelining and refining. It continued its overseas exploration through Oasis, a consortium formed in 1964 with Marathon, Shell, and Continental to explore in Libya.

Leon Hess began to buy stock in Amerada in 1966. The son of immigrants, he had entered the oil business during the Depression, selling "resid" — thick refining leftovers that refineries discarded — from a 1929 Dodge truck in New Jersey. He bought the resid cheap, kept it warm, and sold it as heating fuel to hotels. Hess also speculated, buying oil at low prices in the summer and selling it for a profit in the winter. He later bought more trucks, a transportation network, refineries, and gas stations, and went into oil exploration. Expansion pushed up debt, so in 1962 Leon's company went public as Hess Oil and Chemical after merging with Cletrac Corporation. In 1966 Hess began building a refinery in St. Croix, Virgin Islands.

Hess acquired Amerada in 1969, after an ownership battle with Phillips Petroleum.

During the 1970s Arab oil embargo, Amerada Hess began drilling on Alaska's North Slope. In 1978 it was one of five companies convicted of fixing retail gasoline prices.

The company took a roller-coaster ride in the 1980s, posting sales of $10 billion in 1981, which plunged, as oil prices fell, to only $4 billion in 1986. Oilman T. Boone Pickens bought up a chunk of the stock during the 1980s, spurring takeover rumors. They proved premature. In 1984 Leon Hess became the owner of the NFL's New York Jets football team, in which he had first invested in 1963.

Amerada Hess completed a pipeline in 1993 to carry natural gas from the North Sea to the UK. In 1995 Leon Hess stepped down as CEO (he died in 1999), and his son John took the position. Amerada Hess sold its 81% interest in the Northstar oil field in Alaska to British Petroleum (now BP Amoco), and the next year Petro-Canada bought the company's Canadian operations.

The company teamed with Dixons Stores Group in 1997 to market gas in the UK. It also purchased 66 Pick Wick convenience store/service stations.

In 1998 Amerada Hess sold half of its St. Croix refinery to Venezuela's state-owned PDVSA. The company also signed production-sharing contracts with a Malaysian oil firm as part of its strategy to move into Southeast Asia and began to sell natural gas to retail customers in the UK.

To offset losses brought on by depressed oil prices, Amerada Hess sold assets worth more than $300 million in 1999, including its southeastern pipeline network, gas stations in Georgia and South Carolina, and Gulf Coast terminals. It also moved into Latin America, announcing plans to explore fields offshore Brazil.

Chairman and CEO: John B. Hess, age 44,
$1,300,000 pay
President and COO: W. S. H. Laidlaw, age 43,
$1,150,000 pay
EVP and CFO: John Y. Schreyer, age 59, $725,000 pay
EVP and General Counsel: J. Barclay Collins II, age 54,
$725,000 pay
SVP: Alan A. Bernstein, age 54
SVP: Daniel F. McCarthy, age 54
SVP: F. Borden Walker, age 45
SVP: F. Lamar Clark, age 54
SVP Human Resources: Neal Gelfand, age 54
SVP: John A. Gartman, age 51
SVP: Lawrence H. Ornstein, age 47
SVP and Treasurer: Gerald A. Jamin, age 57
VP and Secretary: Carl T. Tursi
Managing Director, Amerada Hess Limited:
Francis R. Gugen, age 49, $560,000 pay
Auditors: Ernst & Young LLP

LOCATIONS

HQ: 1185 Avenue of the Americas, New York, NY 10036
Phone: 212-997-8500   **Fax:** 212-536-8390
Web site: http://www.hess.com

Amerada Hess conducts exploration and production
activities in Azerbaijan, Brazil, Denmark, Gabon,
Indonesia, Norway, Thailand, the UK, and in California,
Louisiana, New Mexico, North Dakota, Texas, and the
Gulf of Mexico in the US. It also sells natural gas in the
UK and the US and electricity in New Jersey, New York,
and Pennsylvania. It operates refineries in St. Croix on
the Virgin Islands and in New Jersey.

1998 Sales

	$ mil.	% of total
US	5,051	77
Europe	1,479	22
Other regions	60	1
Total	**6,590**	**100**

PRODUCTS/OPERATIONS

1998 Sales

	$ mil.	% of total
Refining & marketing	4,722	72
Exploration & production	1,867	28
Other	1	—
Total	**6,590**	**100**

1998 Sales

	$ mil.	% of total
Crude oil	894	14
Natural gas	1,711	26
Petroleum products	3,464	53
Other	521	7
Total	**6,590**	**100**

COMPETITORS

BHP	Marathon	Royal
BP Amoco	Ashland	Dutch/Shell
Chevron	Petroleum	Sinclair Oil
Coastal	Mobil	Sunoco
Devon Energy	Occidental	Texaco
Elf Aquitaine	Petrobras	Tosco
Exxon	Phillips	TOTAL FINA
Kerr-McGee	Petroleum	Unocal
Koch		USX-Marathon

HISTORICAL FINANCIALS & EMPLOYEES

NYSE symbol: AHC FYE: December 31	Annual Growth	1989	1990	1991	1992	1993	1994	1995	1996	1997	1998
Sales ($ mil.)	1.8%	5,589	6,948	6,267	5,875	5,852	6,602	7,302	8,272	8,234	6,590
Net income ($ mil.)	—	476	483	84	8	(268)	74	(394)	660	8	(459)
Income as % of sales	—	8.5%	6.9%	1.3%	0.1%	—	1.1%	—	8.0%	0.1%	—
Earnings per share ($)	—	5.87	5.96	1.04	0.09	(2.91)	0.79	(4.26)	7.09	0.08	(5.12)
Stock price - FY high ($)	—	51.88	56.00	59.13	51.25	56.38	52.63	53.63	60.50	64.50	61.06
Stock price - FY low ($)	—	31.00	42.88	42.50	36.63	42.38	43.75	43.25	47.50	47.38	46.00
Stock price - FY close ($)	0.2%	48.75	46.38	47.50	46.00	45.13	45.63	53.00	57.88	54.88	49.75
P/E - high	—	9	9	57	569	—	67	—	9	806	—
P/E - low	—	5	7	41	407	—	55	—	7	592	—
Dividends per share ($)	0.0%	0.60	0.75	0.45	0.45	0.45	0.60	0.60	0.60	0.60	0.60
Book value per share ($)	(0.9%)	31.69	38.34	38.63	36.59	32.71	33.33	28.60	36.35	35.16	29.26
Employees	(5.7%)	16,638	9,645	10,317	10,263	10,173	9,858	9,574	9,085	9,216	9,777

STOCK PRICE HISTORY

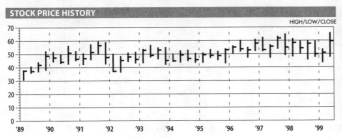

HIGH/LOW/CLOSE

1998 FISCAL YEAR-END

Debt ratio: 48.4%
Return on equity: —
Cash ($ mil.): 74
Current ratio: 1.05
Long-term debt ($ mil.): 2,476
No. of shares (mil.): 90
Dividends
 Yield: 1.2%
 Payout: —
Market value ($ mil.): 4,495

AMERCO

OVERVIEW

AMERCO is in business for the long haul. The Reno, Nevada-based company, best known for operating U-Haul International, has moved past the bitter legal battles within its founding Shoen family. With its house in order, AMERCO has refocused its attention on customers who need to get their stuff from here to there.

U-Haul has about 1,100 company-owned locations and nearly 15,000 independent dealers that rent about 190,000 trucks, trailers, and tow dollies to do-it-yourself movers across the US and Canada. It sells and rents moving supplies, and many sites rent floor- and carpet-cleaning equipment and install trailer hitches.

U-Haul is also a top provider of self-storage facilities, with more than 900 locations in the US and Canada. In addition, it manages units owned by others and has an interest in Private Mini Storage Realty of Texas.

Subsidiary Republic Western Insurance grew by providing short-term property/casualty insurance to U-Haul customers and is now expanding to offer coverage outside the company. AMERCO's other insurance unit, Oxford Life Insurance, offers life, health, and annuity insurance products and manages the company's self-insured group health and benefits programs.

The Shoen family, led by chairman and president Edward "Joe" Shoen, controls the company.

HISTORY

Leonard Samuel (L. S.) Shoen earned his nickname, "Slick," as a poor kid trying to make a buck during the Depression. In 1945, as a Navy veteran, he started U-Haul International in Ridgefield, Washington, to serve long-distance do-it-yourself movers who could not return a truck to its origin. Shoen bought used equipment and hit the road, convincing gas station owners to act as agents.

Shoen and his first wife, Anna Mary, who died in 1957, had six children. In 1958 Shoen remarried and with his second wife, Suzanne, had five children. Shoen bestowed stock on all his offspring but neglected to keep a controlling interest. In the 1960s Shoen brought his sons into the company.

U-Haul moved to Phoenix in 1967. Two years later it bought Oxford Life Insurance Co. Shoen formed AMERCO in 1971 as U-Haul's parent. The oil crunch of the 1970s caused U-Haul's network to shrink as gas stations closed, so the company opened its own agencies. New competitors entered the market, and the company's share of business dropped to below 50%. Shoen took AMERCO into debt to diversify into general consumer rentals. The company also established real estate and insurance subsidiaries.

Shoen's second wife divorced him after the out-of-wedlock birth of his 12th child in 1977. His brief marriage to the mother ended in a second divorce, and he remarried again (and, later, yet again). Meanwhile, Shoen tapped his eldest son Sam for help in pursuing the diversification strategy. In 1979 sons Edward "Joe" and Mark, disagreeing with this course, left the company. Sam became president.

In 1986 Joe and Mark gained the support of enough siblings to constitute a voting majority and ousted their father and brother. L. S. and Sam almost regained control two years later but were outmaneuvered by Joe, who as chairman issued enough stock to a few loyal employees to shift the balance. Then the outside faction sued the people who had been directors in 1988 over issuance of the stock.

Joe refocused on the self-moving business and began upgrading the fleet, reducing the average age of the equipment from 11 to 5 years. In 1993 AMERCO preferred stock began trading on the NYSE, and the next year its common stock was listed on Nasdaq.

Meanwhile, the lawsuit moved glacially through the courts. In 1994, the 1988 directors were found to have wrongfully excluded dissenting family members from the board. An initial award of $1.47 billion was later reduced to $462 million, due from the 1988 directors individually. However, they declared bankruptcy, and AMERCO indemnified them for the award. So in 1996 the company issued new stock and sold (and leased back) tens of thousands of vehicles and trailers to fulfill the judgment. In return, the dissenting family faction (including founder L. S.) gave up their 48% stake in AMERCO.

U-Haul went back to business, and in 1997 AMERCO held its first stockholders' meeting since 1993. The next year Joe lost an appeal to overturn a ruling that he had acted with malice in dealing with family members in the 1988 stock transaction; he was ordered to pay $7 million in punitive damages to relatives, exclusive of the $462 million previously awarded.

Chairman and President of AMERCO and U-Haul:
Edward J. "Joe" Shoen, age 50, $503,708 pay
VP of AMERCO: James P. Shoen, age 39,
$649,478 pay
Treasurer of AMERCO and Assistant Treasurer of U-Haul: Gary B. Horton, age 55
Secretary and General Counsel of AMERCO and U-Haul: Gary V. Klinefelter, age 52
Assistant Secretary of AMERCO and U-Haul:
John A. Lorentz, age 72
Assistant Secretary of AMERCO and U-Haul:
George R. Olds, age 57
President of U-Haul Phoenix Operations:
Mark V. Shoen, age 48
Assistant Treasurer of AMERCO and U-Haul:
Rocky D. Wardrip, age 41
VP Human Resources of U-Haul: Henry P. Kelly
Auditors: PricewaterhouseCoopers LLP

LOCATIONS

HQ: 1325 Airmotive Way, Ste. 100,
Reno, NV 89502-3239
Phone: 775-688-6300   **Fax:** 775-688-6338
Web site: http://www.uhaul.com

AMERCO's primary subsidiary, U-Haul International, rents consumer moving trucks and trailers throughout the US and Canada.

1999 Sales

	$ mil.	% of total
US	1,522	98
Canada	30	2
Total	**1,552**	**100**

PRODUCTS/OPERATIONS

1999 Sales

	$ mil.	% of total
Moving & storage	1,266	82
Property/casualty insurance	167	11
Life insurance	112	7
Real estate	7	—
Total	**1,552**	**100**

Operating Units
Amerco Real Estate Company (owner and manager of the company's real estate assets)
Oxford Life Insurance Company (life, health, and annuity direct writing and reinsurance)
Private Mini Storage (50%, storage)
Republic Western Insurance Company (property/casualty direct writing and reinsurance for U-Haul employees and customers)
U-Haul International, Inc. (do-it-yourself-moving truck rental and sales of packing supplies)

COMPETITORS

Budget Group
Penske Truck Leasing
Ryder
Shurgard Storage
Sovran
Storage USA

HISTORICAL FINANCIALS & EMPLOYEES

Nasdaq symbol: UHAL FYE: March 31	Annual Growth	1990	1991	1992	1993	1994	1995	1996	1997	1998	1999
Sales ($ mil.)	5.6%	951	987	972	1,041	1,135	1,241	1,294	1,425	1,425	1,552
Net income ($ mil.)	14.8%	18	(10)	21	32	40	60	60	52	35	63
Income as % of sales	—	1.9%	—	2.2%	3.1%	3.5%	4.8%	4.7%	3.6%	2.5%	4.0%
Earnings per share ($)	13.9%	—	—	—	—	—	1.23	1.33	0.66	0.66	2.07
Stock price - FY high ($)	—	—	—	—	—	—	22.50	25.50	49.25	37.00	33.88
Stock price - FY low ($)	—	—	—	—	—	—	15.75	14.75	19.50	22.63	19.63
Stock price - FY close ($)	0.1%	—	—	—	—	—	21.38	24.25	25.50	30.75	21.50
P/E - high	—	—	—	—	—	—	18	19	36	56	16
P/E - low	—	—	—	—	—	—	13	11	14	34	9
Dividends per share ($)	—	—	—	—	—	—	0.00	0.00	0.00	0.00	0.00
Book value per share ($)	11.2%	—	—	—	—	—	17.78	19.81	26.63	26.32	27.24
Employees	0.6%	13,600	10,000	9,300	10,900	13,500	12,000	13,000	14,400	14,000	14,400

STOCK PRICE HISTORY

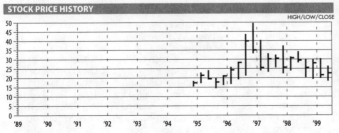

HIGH/LOW/CLOSE

1999 FISCAL YEAR-END

Debt ratio: 64.4%
Return on equity: 10.1%
Cash ($ mil.): —
Current ratio: —
Long-term debt ($ mil.): 1,115
No. of shares (mil.): 23
Dividends
  Yield: —
  Payout: —
Market value ($ mil.): 486

AMERICA ONLINE, INC.

OVERVIEW

The Ma Bell of the 21st century, America Online (AOL) is the world's #1 online service, with more than 18 million members. The Dulles, Virginia-based company's acquisition of #2 CompuServe (now subsidiary CompuServe Interactive Services) gave it 2 million more subscribers and dominant market share. AOL's acquisition of Internet browser software maker Netscape Communications solidified the company's pre-eminence and gave it control of Netscape's popular Navigator Web browser and its Netcenter Internet portal. As part of the deal, AOL also inked a three-year agreement with Sun Microsystems through which Sun will market and license Netscape's corporate

software. Sun and AOL also formed a joint venture (the Sun-Netscape Alliance) to develop enterprise software under the iPlanet name.

With flat-rate pricing and thousands of competitors offering Internet access, AOL is working to tap other revenue sources, particularly advertising and commerce. In an effort to expand its brand name beyond the PC, AOL plans to launch AOL TV, which will let users bookmark their favorite channels, access information and merchandise, and chat with other TV fans. The company also took a minority stake in TiVo, a maker of the new personal video recorder, which uses a hard-disk drive to store hours of video and television programming.

HISTORY

Stephen Case was in charge of developing new types of pizzas for Pizza Hut in the early 1980s when he began using an online service called the Source. He believed the user-unfriendly technology had possibilities but needed improvement. In 1983 he took a marketing job with Control Video, which ran an online service for users of Atari computer games. Control Video soon ran into trouble and Case helped the new CEO, entrepreneur Jim Kimsey, raise money to resurrect the company (venture capitalist Alan Patricof was among the investors). In 1985 Control Video was rechristened Quantum Computer Services, and it launched the Q-Link online service. Four years later the company unveiled a nationwide service called America Online, and in 1991 it changed its name to America Online.

AOL went public the next year, and Case became CEO (his lower-profile co-founder, Marc Seriff, was the company's first head of technology). AOL spent heavily on marketing in an effort to pass rivals Prodigy and CompuServe, and it also worked to expand its content lineup. In 1993 AOL began distributing a Windows-based version of its online software, which, with AOL's own easy-to-use interface, attracted even more subscribers.

Microsoft co-founder Paul Allen sold his 24.9% stake in AOL in 1994 when the company denied him a seat on its board. Also that year AOL bought multimedia developer Redgate Communications and Internet browser software maker Booklink Technologies (the latter from Internet investor CMGI). By the end of 1994, AOL had more than 1 million subscribers.

In 1995 AOL teamed with media conglomerate Bertelsmann to offer online services in Europe (French utility Vivendi bought an interest in 1998). The company also began offering

personal Web pages to its members. In 1996, facing growing competition, AOL started charging its members a flat rate, vastly increasing the amount of time they spent online. Seriff left in 1996.

In 1997, under the direction of new recruit (and MTV founder) Bob Pittman, the company scaled back marketing and focused on solving its network's traffic problems. Facing possible lawsuits, it agreed to pay refunds to customers who had experienced difficulty getting online. In 1998 it sold its ANS Communications transmission network to telecommunications provider WorldCom (now MCI WorldCom) in exchange for CompuServe's content operations, 2 million subscribers, and $175 million in cash. With a top competitor out of the way, AOL then announced a rate increase. AOL bought NetChannel that year in an effort to tap into the Interactive TV market.

In 1999 the company bought MovieFone, a provider of online movie times and tickets. AOL's 1999 acquisition of Internet browser software giant Netscape Communications (for about $10 billion) significantly expanded the company's profile. The acquisition also paved the way for AOL's joint venture with Sun Microsystems through which the two companies will develop enterprise software under the iPlanet name.

AOL teamed with Hughes Electronics to develop digital entertainment and Internet services. AOL TV, an interactive TV service, will be marketed in a package with DIRECTV, Hughes Electronics' direct broadcast satellite service. The companies will also collaborate on broadband satellite Internet service DirectPC. The agreement called for AOL to invest $1.5 billion in Hughes Electronics. In a departure from its subscription-based services, AOL plans to offer free Internet service in Europe.

Chairman and CEO: Stephen M. Case, age 40,
$1,176,667 pay
VC: Kenneth J. Novack, age 57, $999,053 pay
President and COO: Robert W. Pittman, age 44,
$1,291,665 pay (prior to title change)
SVP, CFO, Treasurer, and Assistant Secretary:
J. Michael Kelly, age 42
Chief Technology Officer: Marc Andreessen, age 27
SVP Global and Strategic Policy:
George Vradenburg III, age 55, $870,000 pay
SVP Communications: Ann Brackbill
SVP and Chief Communications Officer:
Kathryn A. Bushkin, age 49
SVP Brand Development: Marshall Cohen
SVP Business Affairs: David Colburn
SVP Corporate Development: Miles R. Gilburne, age 47
SVP Human Resources: Mark Stavish
SVP, AOL Products: John Paul
SVP and General Manager, Netcenter: Mike Homer
SVP, Netscape Enterprise Group: Barry Ariko
SVP, Netscape Enterprise Group: Steve Savignano
President, Interactive Services Group: Barry M. Schuler
President, Interactive Properties Group: Ted Leonsis
President, AOL International: Jack Davies
President and CEO, AOL Latin America:
Charles Herington
Auditors: Ernst & Young LLP

LOCATIONS

HQ: 22000 AOL Way, Dulles, VA 20166-9323
Phone: 703-448-8700   **Fax:** 703-918-1400
Web site: http://www.aol.com

America Online offers online services to subscribers
in more than 100 countries.

PRODUCTS/OPERATIONS

1999 Sales

	$ mil.	% of total
Subscription services	3,321	70
Enterprise solutions	456	9
Advertising, commerce & other	1,000	21
Total	**4,777**	**100**

Online Community
Buddy lists
Chat
E-mail
Instant messenger service
Internet address
  registration services
Online banking
Online radio and music

Selected Channels
Computing
Entertainment
Familes
Games
Health
International
Kids Only
Lifestyles
Local
Netscape Netcenter

News
Personal Finance
Radio
Research & Learn
Sports
Travel
WorkPlace

Selected Online Shopping
1-800-FLOWERS
Amazon.com
American Greetings
Eddie Bauer
FAO Schwarz
Godiva
Hickory Farms
JCPenney
Lands' End
N2K
NetGrocer
The Sharper Image

COMPETITORS

AT&T
CNET
Deutsche
  Telekom
Dow Jones
Excite@Home
Freeserve

Infoseek
Lycos
MCI WorldCom
Microsoft
Planet Direct
Prodigy
PSINet

Reuters
Thomson
  Corporation
Time Warner
Walt Disney
WebTV
Yahoo!

HISTORICAL FINANCIALS & EMPLOYEES

NYSE symbol: AOL FYE: June 30	Annual Growth	1990	1991	1992	1993	1994	1995	1996	1997	1998	1999
Sales ($ mil.)	84.3%	20	20	27	40	104	394	1,094	1,685	2,600	4,777
Net income ($ mil.)	150.0%	0	2	4	4	6	(34)	30	(499)	92	762
Income as % of sales	—	1.0%	7.7%	13.2%	10.5%	5.9%	—	2.7%	—	3.5%	16.0%
Earnings per share ($)	62.6%	—	—	0.02	0.02	0.01	(0.07)	0.04	(0.66)	0.09	0.60
Stock price - FY high ($)	—	—	—	0.28	0.61	1.44	3.01	8.88	7.77	27.44	175.25
Stock price - FY low ($)	—	—	—	0.17	0.19	0.57	0.86	2.67	2.80	7.06	17.25
Stock price - FY close ($)	144.6%	—	—	0.21	0.58	0.89	2.75	5.47	6.95	26.28	110.00
P/E - high	—	—	—	14	31	144	—	222	—	305	292
P/E - low	—	—	—	9	10	57	—	67	—	78	29
Dividends per share ($)	—	—	—	0.00	0.01	0.00	0.00	0.00	0.00	0.00	0.00
Book value per share ($)	75.4%	—	—	0.05	0.06	0.21	0.36	0.69	0.16	0.68	2.76
Employees	78.8%	—	116	124	236	527	2,481	5,828	7,371	8,500	12,100

STOCK PRICE HISTORY
HIGH/LOW/CLOSE

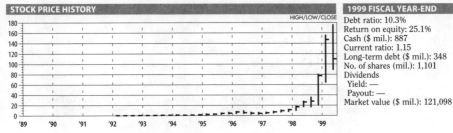

1999 FISCAL YEAR-END

Debt ratio: 10.3%
Return on equity: 25.1%
Cash ($ mil.): 887
Current ratio: 1.15
Long-term debt ($ mil.): 348
No. of shares (mil.): 1,101
Dividends
  Yield: —
  Payout: —
Market value ($ mil.): 121,098

AMERICA WEST HOLDINGS

OVERVIEW

For some, Western civilization means rattlesnakes, Vegas, and golfing in a desert oasis. America West Holdings specializes in delivering high-rollers, vacationers, and other travelers to the American West. The Tempe, Arizona-based holding company owns America West Airlines (AWA), a top 10 US carrier. AWA flies to about 50 US destinations as well as to six Mexican cities and Vancouver, British Columbia.

AWA, which flies about 600 flights per day, has a fleet of more than 110 aircraft (most of them Boeing 737s). Its primary hubs are in Phoenix and Las Vegas, and it has a mini-hub in Columbus, Ohio. It connects to additional destinations through code-sharing agreements with Continental Airlines, British Airways,

Northwest Airlines, Mesa Airlines, and Taiwan's EVA Airways.

Though it offers assigned seating and meals, on shorter flights AWA competes with low-fare carrier Southwest Airlines. Controlling costs allows it to undercut the fares of long-haul rivals as well. The airline has worked to raise its profile and promote local color through promotions with Arizona pro sports teams and with aircraft paint schemes with a Native American influence.

America West also owns a travel services subsidiary, The Leisure Company, which markets tour packages, such as golf vacations, under the America West Vacations brand. Investment firm TPG Partners controls 51% of America West; Continental Airlines controls about 9%.

HISTORY

For years airline consultant Edward Beauvais envisioned a Phoenix airline linking cities in the Southwest to California. He founded America West Airlines (AWA) in 1981 in the wake of airline deregulation. Beauvais' idea was simple: Offer low-fare flights with certain amenities (such as free newspapers) to woo business commuters and create a niche in a region overlooked by the major airlines. In 1983 AWA began flying from Phoenix to four cities. By 1986 AWA was serving 34 cities, turning a modest $2 million profit.

AWA added flights to Chicago, New York, and Baltimore in 1987. Beauvais established a second hub in Las Vegas, but expansion costs and competition from Southwest Airlines and USAir (now US Airways) in Phoenix led to a $46 million loss in 1987. AWA needed more capital to fuel its rapid expansion; to keep its stock in friendly hands, Beauvais and president Michael Conway (formerly of Continental) sold a 20% stake in AWA to its aircraft lessor, Australia's Ansett Airlines. AWA's employees already owned a 30% interest and were guaranteed up to 250% of their annual salaries in the event of a takeover.

Beauvais and Conway cut flights, sold planes, and furloughed 500 employees in 1988. But then AWA tried to expand by buying up bankrupt Eastern Airline's Washington, DC, route and, in 1991, by initiating service to Nagoya, Japan, via Hawaii. By the end of 1989, AWA had 286 daily flights to 56 cities, including Honolulu, New York, and Seattle.

Burdened with expansion-related debt and facing sluggish traffic and higher fuel prices, AWA succumbed to Chapter 11 in 1991. The

airline cut its fleet again and agreed to sell its Nagoya route to Northwest. But it still opened a third hub, in Columbus, Ohio, and began offering flights to Mexico City in 1992. That year Beauvais resigned as chairman and was replaced by turnaround specialist William Franke.

Conway and Franke never saw eye to eye. Their dispute gained force after an investment bid by the Pritzkers (owners of Hyatt Hotels) and favored by Conway was blocked by Franke, who enjoyed support from the board. In 1994 Conway was fired and replaced by Franke.

AWA emerged from bankruptcy in 1994. As part of restructuring, the carrier announced a 10% payroll reduction in 1995. An alliance with British Airways in 1996 expanded service, and to better manage its businesses, American West restructured as a holding company. In 1997 Richard Goodmanson became CEO of the airline, replacing Franke, who remained chairman.

In 1998 America West launched The Leisure Company (TLC), a tour package business. The company's profits were rising, but it wasn't out of turbulence. That year AWA was hit by the largest penalty yet levied against an airline by the FAA: $2.5 million for lapses in maintenance and structural inspections. Flight attendants threatened the company with a holiday strike and did not reach a contract agreement until 1999. That year America West rejected a takeover bid from United's holding company, UAL. Goodmanson resigned, and Franke succeeded him as CEO of AWA. On the sunnier side of the business, TLC agreed to buy National Leisure Group from Cendant.

Chairman and CEO; Chairman, President, and CEO, America West Airlines: William A. Franke, age 61, $458,333 pay
EVP and CFO, America West Holdings and America West Airlines: W. Douglas Parker, age 37, $421,375 pay (prior to promotion)
EVP and COO: Gilbert D. Mook, age 56
SVP and Chief Information Officer, America West Holdings and America West Airlines: Evon L. Jones
SVP Corporate Affairs, America West Holdings and America West Airlines: Stephen L. Johnson, age 42 pay (prior to promotion)
SVP Planning: Bernard L. Han, age 34
SVP Public Affairs, America West Holdings and America West Airlines: C. A. Howlett, age 55
President and CEO, The Leisure Company: John R. Garel, age 40, $376,738 pay
COO, The Leisure Company: Jack Richards
COO, The Leisure Company: Kevin P. Short, age 40
SVP Human Resources, America West Airlines: Bruce A. Johnson, age 42, $349,754 pay
SVP Marketing and Sales, America West Airlines: Michael A. Smith, age 45
SVP Operations, America West Airlines: Ronald A. Aramini, age 53
VP and Controller, America West Airlines: Michael R. Carreon, age 45
VP and General Counsel, America West Airlines: Kathleen Doyle, age 40
Auditors: KPMG LLP

PRODUCTS/OPERATIONS

1998 Sales

	$ mil.	% of total
Passenger	1,859	92
Leisure Co.	55	3
Cargo	45	2
Other	64	3
Total	**2,023**	**100**

1998 Aircraft Fleet

	No.
Boeing 737-100	1
Boeing 737-200	17
Boeing 737-300	46
Boeing 757-200	13
Airbus A319-100	3
Airbus A320-200	31
Total	**111**

COMPETITORS

AMR
Delta
Frontier Airlines
Hawaiian Airlines
Northwest Airlines
Southwest Airlines
TWA
UAL
US Airways

LOCATIONS

HQ: America West Holdings Corporation
111 W. Rio Salado Pkwy., Tempe, AZ 85281
Phone: 480-693-0800   **Fax:** 480-693-5546
Web site: http://www.americawest.com

HISTORICAL FINANCIALS & EMPLOYEES

NYSE symbol: AWA FYE: December 31	Annual Growth	1989	1990	1991	1992	1993	1994	1995	1996	1997	1998
Sales ($ mil.)	8.2%	993	1,316	1,414	1,294	1,325	1,409	1,551	1,740	1,875	2,023
Net income ($ mil.)	26.6%	13	(77)	(222)	(132)	37	62	54	9	75	109
Income as % of sales	—	1.3%	—	—	—	2.8%	4.4%	3.5%	0.5%	4.0%	5.4%
Earnings per share ($)	11.0%	—	—	—	—	—	1.58	1.16	0.16	1.63	2.40
Stock price - FY high ($)	—	—	—	—	—	—	16.38	19.00	23.75	18.94	31.31
Stock price - FY low ($)	—	—	—	—	—	—	6.38	6.38	10.88	12.00	9.56
Stock price - FY close ($)	20.7%	—	—	—	—	—	8.00	17.00	15.88	18.63	17.00
P/E - high	—	—	—	—	—	—	10	16	148	12	13
P/E - low	—	—	—	—	—	—	4	6	68	7	4
Dividends per share ($)	—	—	—	—	—	—	0.00	0.00	0.00	0.00	0.00
Book value per share ($)	6.8%	—	—	—	—	—	13.19	14.36	14.00	14.87	17.17
Employees	1.5%	10,700	13,700	12,142	10,929	10,544	10,715	8,712	9,652	11,639	12,204

STOCK PRICE HISTORY

HIGH/LOW/CLOSE

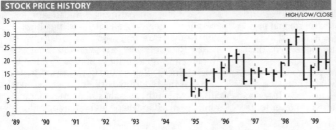

1998 FISCAL YEAR-END

Debt ratio: 23.7%
Return on equity: 16.2%
Cash ($ mil.): 108
Current ratio: 0.56
Long-term debt ($ mil.): 208
No. of shares (mil.): 39
Dividends
 Yield: —
 Payout: —
Market value ($ mil.): 663

AMERICAN ELECTRIC POWER

OVERVIEW

American Electric Power (AEP) takes its piece of the US power pie out of Middle America. Based in Columbus, Ohio, the utility holding company is one of the nation's largest electric providers, with seven utilities that serve more than 3 million customers in Indiana, Kentucky, Michigan, Ohio, Tennessee, Virginia, and West Virginia. Coal fuels almost all of the company's 21,650-MW capacity (its nuclear plant has been closed for safety problems since 1997). It also owns a 1,900-mile natural gas pipeline, storage and processing facilities in Louisiana.

In response to US utility deregulation, AEP intends to extend its reach from the Great Lakes to the Gulf Coast by acquiring Dallas-based Central and South West (CSW). After the merger AEP will serve the most electricity customers in the US, adding 1.7 million customers in Arkansas, Louisiana, Oklahoma, and Texas. To satisfy regulators' concerns about the CSW merger, AEP plans to relinquish control of about 22,000 miles of transmission lines to an independent operator.

Subsidiary AEP Resources handles the company's overseas operations, including Australian electric utility CitiPower and UK-based Yorkshire Electric. These will be bolstered by CSW's Mexico and UK holdings.

AEP is a major power marketer and trader. Other nonregulated subsidiaries provide energy construction and consulting services and offer communications services and fiber-optic products.

HISTORY

In 1906 Richard Breed, Sidney Mitchell, and Henry Doherty set up American Gas & Electric (AG&E) in New York to buy 23 utilities from Philadelphia's Electric Company of America. With properties in seven northeastern US states, AG&E began acquiring and merging small electric properties, creating the predecessors of Ohio Power (1911), Kentucky Power (1919), and Appalachian Power (1926). AG&E also bought the predecessor of Indiana Michigan Power (1925).

By 1926 the company was operating in Indiana, Kentucky, Michigan, Ohio, Virginia, and West Virginia. In 1935 AG&E engineer Philip Sporn, later known as the Henry Ford of power, introduced his high-voltage, high-velocity circuit breaker. AG&E picked up Kingsport Power in 1938.

Becoming president in 1947, Sporn began an ambitious building program that continued through the 1960s. Plants designed by AG&E (renamed American Electric Power in 1958) were among the world's most efficient, and electric rates stayed 25% to 38% below the national average.

AEP bought Michigan Power in 1967, six years after Donald Cook succeeded Sporn as president. Cook, who refused to attach scrubbers to the smokestacks of coal-fired plants, was criticized in the early 1970s by environmental protesters. AEP's first nuclear plant, named in Cook's honor, went on line in Michigan in 1975. He retired in 1976.

The firm moved from New York to Columbus, Ohio, in 1980 after buying what is now Columbus Southern Power (formed in 1883). It set up AEP Generating in 1982 to provide power to its electric utilities.

AEP began converting its second nuke, Zimmer, to coal in 1984. In 1992 AEP finally began installing scrubbers at its coal-fired Gavin plant in Ohio after being ordered to comply with the Clean Air Act. It also cleaned up its image by planting millions of trees in 1996.

The company formed AEP Communications after Congress passed the Telecommunications Act of 1996. The next year it created AEP Resources and jumped into the UK's deregulated electric market; AEP and New Century Energies bought Yorkshire Electricity for $2.8 billion. A $109 million UK windfall tax on the transaction — and increased wholesale competition — hurt AEP's bottom line. AEP also shut down its Cook nuke because of Nuclear Regulatory Commission safety concerns.

As the normally staid electric industry succumbed to merger mania, AEP agreed to buy Central and South West (CSW) of Texas in a $6.6 billion deal. AEP's sales would nearly double, and CSW was to bring its own UK utility, SEEBOARD, and other overseas holdings.

In 1998 AEP Resources bought a 20% stake in Pacific Hydro, an Australian power producer, and CitiPower, an Australian electric distribution company. AEP also bought Equitable Resources' Louisiana natural gas midstream operations, including an intrastate pipeline. In 1999 China's Pushan Power Plant (70%-owned by AEP Resources) began operations. That year AEP and four other utilities approached the Federal Energy Regulatory Commission to propose that they coordinate their transmission facilities (which they would still own) under a publicly traded independent system operator.

Chairman, President, and CEO, American Electric Power, AEP Service, and AEP Communications; Chairman and CEO, AEP Energy, AEP Resources, AEP Resources Service Company: E. Linn Draper Jr., age 57, $974,376 pay

President, AEP Energy Services; EVP, AEP Service: Paul D. Addis

President, AEP Communications, AEP Resources, and AEP Resources Service Company; EVP Corporate Development, AEP Service: Donald M. Clements Jr., $426,317 pay

EVP, AEP Service; VP, AEP Communications: William J. Lhota, age 59, $462,859 pay

EVP Power Generation, AEP Service: James J. Markowsky, age 54, $426,317 pay

VP and CFO; EVP Financial Services, AEP Services; VP, AEP Communications, AEP Energy Services, AEP Resources, and AEP Resources Service Company: Henry W. Fayne

EVP Corporate Services, AEP Service: Joseph H. Vipperman, $377,595 pay

SVP Fuel Supply, AEP Service: Charles A. Ebetino Jr.

SVP Corporate Communications, AEP Service: Luke M. Feck

SVP Generation Projects, AEP Service: John R. Jones

SVP Information Services and Chief Information Officer, AEP Services: Michael F. Moore

SVP Corporate Planning and Budgeting, AEP Service: Richard E. Munczinski

SVP Human Resources, AEP Service: Rodney B. Plimpton

SVP Nuclear Generation, AEP Service: Robert P. Powers

SVP Distribution, AEP Service: Peter Splawnyk

Auditors: Deloitte & Touche LLP

HQ: American Electric Power Company, Inc.,
1 Riverside Plaza, Columbus, OH 43215-2373
Phone: 614-223-1000   **Fax:** 614-223-1823
Web site: http://www.aep.com

Selected Subsidiaries
AEP Generating Co.
AEP Resources Inc.
  CitiPower (electricity distribution in Australia)
  Yorkshire Electricity Group (50%, electricity distributor in the UK)

Allegheny Energy
Cinergy
CMS Energy
Conectiv
Consolidated Natural Gas Group
Dominion Resources
Duke Energy
DTE
Dynegy
Enron
Entergy

FirstEnergy
Illinova
Indiana Energy
LG&E Energy
New Century Energies
Nicor
NiSource
Northern States Power
SIGCORP
Southern Company
TVA
Unicom
UtiliCorp

NYSE symbol: AEP FYE: December 31	Annual Growth	1989	1990	1991	1992	1993	1994	1995	1996	1997	1998
Sales ($ mil.)	2.4%	5,140	5,168	5,047	5,045	5,269	5,505	5,670	5,849	6,161	6,346
Net income ($ mil.)	(1.8%)	629	496	498	468	354	500	530	587	511	536
Income as % of sales	—	12.2%	9.6%	9.9%	9.3%	6.7%	9.1%	9.3%	10.0%	8.3%	8.4%
Earnings per share ($)	(1.6%)	3.25	2.65	2.70	2.54	1.92	2.71	2.85	3.14	2.70	2.81
Stock price – FY high ($)	—	33.38	33.13	34.25	35.25	40.38	37.38	40.63	44.75	52.00	53.31
Stock price – FY low ($)	—	25.75	26.00	26.63	30.38	32.00	27.25	31.25	38.63	39.13	42.06
Stock price – FY close ($)	4.0%	33.00	28.00	34.25	33.13	37.13	32.88	40.50	41.13	51.63	47.06
P/E – high	—	10	13	13	14	21	14	14	14	19	19
P/E – low	—	8	10	10	12	17	10	11	12	14	15
Dividends per share ($)	0.2%	2.36	2.40	2.40	2.40	2.40	2.40	2.40	2.40	2.40	2.40
Book value per share ($)	1.2%	22.71	22.58	22.88	23.01	22.50	22.83	23.25	24.15	24.62	25.24
Employees	(2.6%)	22,700	22,798	22,136	20,841	20,007	19,660	18,502	17,951	17,844	17,943

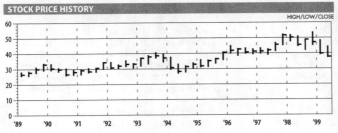

HIGH/LOW/CLOSE

Debt ratio: 57.6%
Return on equity: 11.1%
Cash ($ mil.): 173
Current ratio: 0.79
Long-term debt ($ mil.): 6,800
No. of shares (mil.): 192
Dividends
  Yield: 5.1%
  Payout: 85.4%
Market value ($ mil.): 9,027

AMERICAN EXPRESS COMPANY

OVERVIEW

American Express wants you to get out of town and take your charge card with you. The New York City-based company's Travel Related Services (TRS) is the world's largest travel agency (neck and neck with Japan Travel) and the largest issuer of charge cards. (Visa is the #1 credit card issuer, MasterCard is #2.)

TRS is the company's largest segment, with locations in 160 countries. TRS also publishes food- and travel-related magazines, and operates an online bank. American Express Financial Corporation and marketing subsidiary American Express Financial Advisors sell life insurance, annuities, investment funds, and financial advisory services. Subsidiary American Express Bank, the world's largest issuer of travelers' checks, serves 38 countries.

After snob-appeal tactics for its classic green charge card failed, American Express found success in the credit card business with Optima and other cards issued through various commercial partners. (Charge cards require full payment each month; credit cards can carry over a balance.) It has steadily built up the number of merchants who accept the cards and is pushing into overseas markets. American Express might also be able to boost its share of the credit card market with help from the Justice Department, which has sued Visa and MasterCard alleging that the companies' bylaws forbidding member banks from issuing cards of their competitors are monopolistic.

Warren Buffett's Berkshire Hathaway owns about 11% of American Express.

HISTORY

In 1850 Henry Wells and his two main competitors combined their delivery services to form American Express. When directors refused to expand to California in 1852, Wells and VP William Fargo formed Wells Fargo while remaining at American Express.

American Express merged with Merchants Union Express in 1868 and developed a money order to compete with the government's postal money order. Fargo's difficulty in cashing letters of credit in Europe led to the offering of Travelers Cheques in 1891.

In WWI the US government nationalized and consolidated all express delivery services, compensating the owners. After the war, American Express incorporated as an overseas freight and financial services and exchange provider (the freight operation was sold in 1970). In 1958 the company introduced the American Express charge card. It bought Fireman's Fund American Insurance (sold gradually between 1985 and 1989) and Equitable Securities in 1968.

James Robinson (CEO from 1977 to 1993) hoped to turn American Express into a financial services supermarket. The company bought brokerage Shearson Loeb Rhoades (1981) and investment banker Lehman Brothers (1984), among other banking, brokerage, and investment firms. In 1987 it introduced Optima, a revolving credit card, to compete with MasterCard and Visa; it had no experience in underwriting credit cards and was badly burned by losses.

Most of the financial units were combined as Shearson Lehman Brothers. But the financial services supermarket never came to

fruition, and losses in this area brought a steep drop in earnings in the early 1990s. Harvey Golub was brought in as CEO in 1993 to restore stability. He cut costs and restructured the company to increase efficiency.

The company sold its brokerage operations as Shearson (to Travelers, now Citigroup) and spun off investment banking as Lehman Brothers in 1994. In late 1996 the company announced an alliance with Advanta Corp. allowing Advanta Visa and MasterCard holders to earn points in the American Express Membership Rewards program. The move sparked a lawsuit from Visa and MasterCard, which prohibit their member banks from doing business with American Express. Efforts by Visa to set up similar restrictions in the European Union have been rebuffed, Advanta has countersued, and the US Justice Department has begun looking into possible antitrust violations by Visa and MasterCard.

In an effort to build its presence in the credit card market, American Express resuscitated the Optima card and introduced several co-branded cards with companies such as Credit Lyonnais and United Airlines. In 1997 Kenneth Chenault was named president and COO, a move that puts him in line to succeed Golub. (Golub announced in 1999 that he will retire from the CEO position in 2001 and the chairman position in 2002.) In 1998 the company bought Havas Voyages, France's largest travel agency.

That year American Express jumped on the Internet bandwagon by purchasing 14% of Barry Diller's Ticketmaster Online-CitySearch. American Express Membership B@nk, an online banking service, was also launched in 1999.

Chairman and CEO; Chairman, Travel Related Services:
Harvey Golub, age 60, $3,419,231 pay
**President and COO; President and CEO, Travel Related
Services:** Kenneth I. Chenault, age 47, $2,467,308 pay
VC and CFO: Richard K. Goeltz, age 56, $1,223,269 pay
VC: Jonathan S. Linen, age 55, $1,341,154 pay
**Chairman and CEO, American Express Bank;
President, Travelers Cheque Group:** John A. Ward III,
age 52
President and CEO, American Express Financial:
David R. Hubers, age 56, $1,100,000 pay
**President, American Express Relationship Services,
Travel Related Services:** Anne M. Busquet, age 49
President, Amex Canada: Alan Stark
**President, Consumer Card Services Group, Travel
Related Services:** Alfred F. Kelly Jr., age 40
President, Corporate Services, Travel Related Services:
Edward P. Gilligan, age 38
**President, Establishment Services Worldwide, Travel
Related Services:** David C. House, age 49
President, International, Travel Related Services:
James M. Cracchiolo
**President, Small Business Services, Travel Related
Services:** Steven W. Alesio, age 44
EVP and Chief Information Officer: Allan Z. Loren,
age 59
EVP Corporate Affairs and Communications:
Thomas Schick, age 51
EVP and General Counsel: Louise M. Parent, age 47
EVP Global Advertising: John D. Hayes, age 43
EVP Human Resources and Quality:
Ursula F. Fairbairn, age 56
**SVP, Global Supplier Relations, American Express
Corporate Services:** Pamela Arway
Auditors: Ernst & Young LLP

HQ: World Financial Center,
200 Vesey St., New York, NY 10285
Phone: 212-640-2000   **Fax:** 212-619-9802
Web site: http://www.americanexpress.com

1998 Sales

	$ mil.	% of total
US	14,535	73
Europe	2,476	13
Asia/Pacific	1,332	7
Other regions	1,444	7
Adjustments	(655)	—
Total	**19,132**	**100**

1998 Sales

	$ mil.	% of total
Travel Related Services	13,237	68
American Express Financial Advisors	5,095	26
American Express Bank	1,002	5
Other	112	1
Adjustments	(314)	—
Total	**19,132**	**100**

Accor	FMR	MasterCard
Allstate	GE	MBNA
BANK ONE	General Motors	Merrill Lynch
Barclays	Household	MetLife
Carlson Wagonlit	International	Morgan Stanley
Chase Manhattan	Japan Travel	Dean Witter
Citigroup	Bureau	Prudential
First USA Bank	John Hancock	Visa

NYSE symbol: AXP FYE: December 31	Annual Growth	1989	1990	1991	1992	1993	1994	1995	1996	1997	1998
Sales ($ mil.)	(2.9%)	25,047	24,332	25,763	26,961	14,173	14,282	15,841	16,237	17,760	19,132
Net income ($ mil.)	7.1%	1,157	181	789	462	1,478	1,413	1,564	1,901	1,991	2,141
Income as % of sales	—	4.6%	0.7%	3.1%	1.7%	10.4%	9.9%	9.9%	11.7%	11.2%	11.2%
Earnings per share ($)	6.2%	2.70	0.34	1.59	0.88	2.32	2.76	3.10	3.56	4.15	4.63
Stock price – FY high ($)	—	39.38	35.25	30.38	25.38	36.63	33.13	45.13	60.38	91.50	118.63
Stock price – FY low ($)	—	26.38	17.50	18.00	20.00	22.38	25.25	29.00	38.63	53.63	67.00
Stock price – FY close ($)	12.7%	34.88	20.63	20.50	24.88	30.88	29.50	41.38	56.50	89.25	102.50
P/E – high	—	15	104	19	29	16	12	15	17	22	26
P/E – low	—	10	51	11	23	10	9	9	11	13	14
Dividends per share ($)	0.8%	0.84	0.92	0.94	1.00	1.00	0.95	0.90	0.90	0.90	0.90
Book value per share ($)	5.8%	12.90	13.21	15.07	15.20	17.42	12.57	16.60	18.03	20.53	21.45
Employees	(2.6%)	107,542	106,836	110,728	114,352	64,654	72,412	70,347	72,300	73,620	85,000

HIGH/LOW/CLOSE

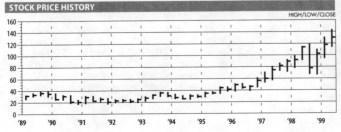

Debt ratio: 40.8%
Return on equity: 22.1%
Cash ($ mil.): —
Current ratio: —
Long-term debt ($ mil.): 7,019
No. of shares (mil.): 452
Dividends
  Yield: 0.9%
  Payout: 19.4%
Market value ($ mil.): 46,339

AMERICAN FINANCIAL GROUP, INC.

OVERVIEW

Carl Lindner is bananas for insurance.

Lindner is the chairman and CEO of Cincinnati-based American Financial Group (AFG), an insurance holding company that also owns 37% of Chiquita Brands International. But it's car insurance, especially high-risk motorist insurance, that drives the company's bottom line.

AFG insurance subsidiaries also sell standard risk auto insurance, as well as homeowners and multiperil insurance. It offers such specialty lines as workers' compensation, professional liability, ocean and inland marine, and multiperil crop insurance. The growing

retirement-savings market plays a big role in AFG's product mix, especially flexible and single-premium deferred annuities through its American Annuity Group subsidiary.

AFG's results in the 1990s have been uneven and it has typically not made an underwriting profit. The company has shed its commercial lines to concentrate on property/casualty and life and annuities businesses, though it continues to invest in noncore companies such as Chiquita and Provident Bank (49%).

The conservative Lindner is Cincinnati's wealthiest citizen; he and his family own about 44% of the company.

HISTORY

When his father became ill in the mid-1930s, Carl Lindner dropped out of high school to take over his family's dairy business. He built it into a large ice-cream store chain called United Dairy Farmers (now run by his brother Robert). Lindner branched out in 1955 with Henthy Realty, and in 1959 he bought three savings and loans. The next year Lindner changed the company's name to American Financial Corp. (AFC). He took it public in 1961, using the proceeds to buy United Liberty Life Insurance (1963) and Provident Bank (1966).

Lindner also diversified with the formation of American Financial Leasing & Services Company in 1968 to lease airplanes, computers, and other equipment. In 1969 the company acquired Phoenix developer Rubenstein Construction and renamed it American Continental. AFC bought several life, casualty, and mortgage insurance firms in the 1970s, including National General, parent of Great American Insurance Group, later the core of AFC's insurance segment. Also in the early 1970s the company moved into publishing by buying 95% of the *Cincinnati Enquirer,* paperback publisher Bantam Books, and hardback publisher Grosset & Dunlap.

But the publishing interests soon went back on the block, as Lindner concentrated on insurance, which was then suffering from an industrywide slowdown. In addition to selling the *Enquirer,* AFC spun off American Continental in 1976. American Continental's president was Charles Keating, who had joined AFC in 1972 and whose brother published the *Enquirer.* Keating (who was later jailed and released, then eventually pleaded guilty in connection with the failure of Lincoln Savings) underwent an SEC investigation during part of his time at AFC for alleged improprieties at Provident Bank. The bank was spun off in 1980.

Lindner took AFC private in 1981. That year, following a strategy of bottom-feeding, the company began building its interest in the nonrailroad assets of Penn Central, the former railroad that had emerged from bankruptcy as an industrial manufacturer. Later that decade AFC increased its ownership in United Brands (later renamed Chiquita Brands International) from 29% to 45%. Lindner installed himself as CEO and reversed that company's losses. In 1987 AFC acquired a TV company, Taft Communications (renamed Great American Communications), entailing a heavy debt load. To reduce its debt, AFC trimmed its holdings, including Circle K, Hunter S&L, Kings Island amusement park, and interest in Scripps Howard Broadcasting.

Great American Communications went bankrupt in 1992 and emerged the next year as Citicasters Inc. (sold 1996). In 1995 Lindner created American Financial Group to effect the merger of AFC and Premier Underwriters, of which he owned 42%. The result was American Financial Group (AFG).

In 1997 Lindner's bipartisan political donations gained publicity when it became known that he had been an overnight guest in the Clinton White House and that his gifts to Republicans had brought support in a dispute with the EU over the banana trade. That year AFG's holdings were reshuffled to streamline its corporate organization. It sold some noncore units, including Millennium Dynamics (its software consulting services) and its commercial insurance operations in 1998. The next year AFG bought direct response auto insurer Worldwide Insurance Company as part of its efforts to build depth in the highly commoditized auto insurance market.

Chairman and CEO: Carl H. Lindner, age 79,
$1,665,000 pay
Co-President: Carl H. Lindner III, age 45,
$1,665,000 pay
Co-President: Keith E. Lindner, age 39, $1,665,000 pay
Co-President: S. Craig Lindner, age 44, $1,665,000 pay
SVP and General Counsel: James E. Evans, age 53,
$1,638,000 pay
SVP Taxation: Thomas E. Mischell, age 51
SVP and Treasurer: Fred J. Runk, age 56
VP, Secretary and Deputy General Counsel:
James C. Kennedy
VP Human Resources: Lawrence Otto
VP Investor Relations: Anne N. Watson
Auditors: Ernst & Young LLP

LOCATIONS

HQ: 1 E. 4th St., Cincinnati, OH 45202
Phone: 513-579-2121   **Fax:** 513-579-2113
Web site: http://www.amfnl.com

PRODUCTS/OPERATIONS

1998 Assets

	$ mil.	% of total
Cash & equivalents	297	2
Treasury & agency securities	538	3
Utility bonds	718	5
Mortgage-backed securities	2,493	16
Corporate bonds	6,298	40
Reinsurance recoverables & prepaid premiums	1,974	12
Other assets	3,527	22
Total	**15,845**	**100**

1998 Sales

	$ mil.	% of total
Property & casualty premiums	2,699	66
Investment income	884	22
Life, accident & health premiums	170	4
Gains & other income	310	8
Adjustments	(13)	—
Total	**4,050**	**100**

COMPETITORS

20th Century
Allstate
AXA Financial
Chubb
CIGNA
Cincinnati Financial
Citigroup
Dole
Fresh Del Monte Produce
GEICO
Kemper Insurance
Liberty Mutual
MetLife
New York Life
Northwestern Mutual
Ohio Casualty
Progressive Corporation
Prudential
Reliance Group Holdings
St. Paul Companies
State Farm
Transamerica

HISTORICAL FINANCIALS & EMPLOYEES

NYSE symbol: AFG FYE: December 31	Annual Growth	1989	1990	1991	1992	1993	1994	1995	1996	1997	1998
Assets ($ mil.)	19.5%	3,178	3,547	3,383	3,531	4,050	4,194	14,954	15,051	15,755	15,845
Net income ($ mil.)	(3.7%)	174	98	3	305	232	—	191	233	192	124
Income as % of assets	—	5.5%	2.8%	0.1%	8.6%	5.7%	0.0%	1.3%	1.6%	1.2%	0.8%
Earnings per share ($)	(2.4%)	2.48	1.60	0.05	6.48	6.85	(0.83)	3.85	3.79	0.64	2.00
Stock price – FY high ($)	—	28.38	28.25	27.00	27.13	39.75	33.25	32.13	38.88	49.25	45.75
Stock price – FY low ($)	—	22.88	15.38	19.25	18.00	23.50	21.63	22.88	28.50	32.38	30.50
Stock price – FY close ($)	5.3%	27.50	19.88	26.13	24.88	32.38	25.88	30.63	37.75	40.31	43.88
P/E – high	—	11	18	540	4	6	—	8	10	77	23
P/E – low	—	9	10	385	3	3	—	6	8	51	15
Dividends per share ($)	10.7%	0.40	0.48	0.68	0.80	0.84	0.88	1.00	1.00	1.00	1.00
Book value per share ($)	0.1%	27.84	31.00	31.23	32.40	36.30	33.46	23.95	25.45	27.24	28.17
Employees	(8.1%)	—	19,700	12,100	11,100	5,400	4,300	9,800	9,500	10,500	10,000

1994 and prior information is for American Premier Underwriters, Inc.

STOCK PRICE HISTORY

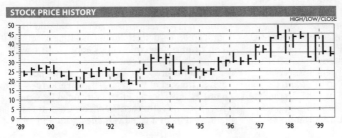

HIGH/LOW/CLOSE

1998 FISCAL YEAR-END

Equity as % of assets: 10.8%
Return on assets: 0.8%
Return on equity: 7.2%
Long-term debt ($ mil.): 592
No. of shares (mil.): 61
Dividends
  Yield: 2.3%
  Payout: 50.0%
Market value ($ mil.): 2,674
Sales (mil.): $4,050

AMERICAN GENERAL

OVERVIEW

American General Financial Group is no generalist when it comes to business.

The Houston-based company is focused on just three segments: retirement products, life insurance, and consumer finance. American General is the US's #3 life and health insurance company (behind Prudential and Met Life).

Subsidiaries American General Annuity (formerly Western National) and Variable Annuity Life Insurance Co. (VALIC) provide a variety of investment products, tax-deferred retirement plans, and planning services to individuals and businesses. VALIC targets health care, educational, and not-for-profit organizations. American General offers life insurance and annuities through its USLIFE and other subsidiaries.

The company offers consumer finance through American General Finance, which has some 1,300 offices in 41 states. This unit provides unsecured and home equity loans, home equity lines of credit, and retail financing. American General is merging its Standard Pacific Savings thrift into its finance operations to create American General Bank, which will also offer checking and savings accounts.

While American General continues to acquire competitors in its consolidating industry, the company is looking to grow by cross-selling its products and services.

HISTORY

In 1925 the Commission of Appeals of Texas ruled that insurers could underwrite more than one line of insurance. Gus Wortham formed American General Insurance Co. in 1926 to provide both fire and casualty insurance.

In 1939 the company established American General Investment to make acquisitions, buying Houston-based Seaboard Life Insurance in 1945. American General took off when Benjamin Woodson joined in 1953. The former managing director of the National Association of Life Underwriters used his contacts to find acquisitions to expand American General's life and health business. These included companies in Nebraska, Oklahoma, and Pennsylvania.

After concentrating on its life and health business through the 1950s, the company refocused on property/casualty insurance. In 1964 it doubled in size by acquiring Maryland Casualty Co., giving American General a presence across the US and in Canada.

In 1968 American General bought a third of California-Western States Life Insurance (Cal-West), increasing its stake to 100% by 1975. Cal-West's Harold Hook became president of American General in 1975 and succeeded Woodson as chairman in 1978. In 1976, senior vice president Charles Bauer and money managers Robert Graham and Gary Crum left the company to form mutual fund manager AIM Management Group (which merged with INVESCO in 1997 to form AMVESCAP).

The company became American General Corp. in the 1980s. It bought life insurer and Grand Ole Opry-owner NLT in 1982 and Gulf United's insurance business in 1984. In the late 1980s American General began shifting its emphasis, buying Manufacturers Hanover's consumer finance division in 1988 and selling its property/casualty business to Zurich Insurance Co. in 1989.

In 1990 Torchmark Corp. made a hostile takeover attempt. Hook won the ensuing proxy fight and then put American General up for sale. When no buyers appeared, he cut costs and boosted earnings by consolidating operations and laying off more than 500 employees in 1991.

After a six-year acquisition hiatus, the company bought insurer Conseco's 46% interest in Western National Corp. in 1994 and Franklin Life Insurance from American Brands in 1995. Through much of 1994 and into early 1995, American General pursued Chicago-based Unitrin, an insurer and consumer lender. Facing heavy resistance from Unitrin's management, American General instead bought Independent Insurance in 1996. James Tuerff resigned as president that year upon the announcement that Robert Devlin (VC at the time) would succeed Hook as CEO (he did so in 1997).

In 1997 American General bought USLIFE and Home Beneficial Life Insurance. The US-LIFE acquisition led the company to divide its life insurance business by sales channels, with independent-agency units including USLIFE in one division, and career agency operations in another. (That year American General sold its bank credit card portfolio to GE.) It also formed a Mexican retirement savings joint venture with Grupo Nacional Provincial.

The following year American General acquired the rest of Western National and renamed it American General Financial Group. To expand its retirement services, the company launched its first retail variable annuity in 1999.

OFFICERS

Chairman, President, and CEO: Robert M. Devlin, age 58, $3,201,346 pay
VC: Jon P. Newton, age 57, $1,679,808 pay
VC and Group Executive, Consumer Finance: Frederick W. Geissinger
VC and Group Executive, Life Insurance; Chairman, President and CEO, American General Life Companies: Rodney O. Martin Jr., age 46, $913,864 pay
VC and Group Executive, Retirement Services: John A. Graf
EVP and CFO: Nicholas R. Rasmussen, age 52
EVP and Chief Investment Officer; President and CEO, Investment Management: Richard W. Scott, age 45
EVP and General Counsel: Mark S. Berg, age 40
EVP Strategic Development: David W. Entrekin, age 37
SVP Corporate Relations: Robert D. Mrlik, age 40
Chairman, President and CEO, American General Life and Accident Insurance: Joe Kelley, age 51
President and CEO, American General Finance: Frederick W. Geissinger, age 53
EVP Investment Management: Peter V. Tuters, age 46
VP Corporate Human Resources: Laura Nichol
Auditors: Ernst & Young LLP

LOCATIONS

HQ: Amercian General Financial Group
2929 Allen Pkwy., Houston, TX 77019-2155
Phone: 713-522-1111   **Fax:** 713-523-8531
Web site: http://www.agc.com

American General provides insurance and other financial services in all 50 states, the District of Columbia, and Puerto Rico.

PRODUCTS/OPERATIONS

1998 Assets

	$ mil.	% of total
Cash & equivalents	341	—
Fixed maturity securities	62,731	60
Mortgage loans	3,368	3
Policy loans	2,329	2
Net finance receivables	9,275	9
Deferred policy acquisition costs	3,253	3
Separate account assets	16,158	15
Other	7,652	8
Total	**105,107**	**100**

1998 Sales

	$ mil.	% of total
Life Insurance	5,506	54
Retirement Services	3,095	30
Consumer Finance	1,609	16
Other	41	—
Total	**10,251**	**100**

COMPETITORS

AXA Financial	Lincoln National
CIGNA	MassMutual
Citigroup	MetLife
Conseco	New York Life
Guardian Life	Northwestern Mutual
The Hartford	Prudential
Household International	Sun Life
Jefferson-Pilot	Transamerica
John Hancock	USAA

HISTORICAL FINANCIALS & EMPLOYEES

NYSE symbol: AGC FYE: December 31	Annual Growth	1989	1990	1991	1992	1993	1994	1995	1996	1997	1998
Assets ($ mil.)	14.1%	32,062	33,808	36,105	39,742	43,982	46,295	61,153	66,254	80,620	105,107
Net income ($ mil.)	5.7%	464	562	480	533	204	513	564	577	542	764
Income as % of assets	—	1.4%	1.7%	1.3%	1.3%	0.5%	1.1%	0.9%	0.9%	0.7%	0.7%
Earnings per share ($)	5.2%	1.88	2.35	2.13	2.45	0.70	2.46	2.66	2.63	2.19	2.96
Stock price - FY high ($)	—	19.25	25.31	22.81	29.38	36.50	30.50	39.13	41.75	56.25	79.00
Stock price - FY low ($)	—	14.75	11.75	14.00	20.13	26.25	24.88	27.50	32.88	36.50	52.31
Stock price - FY close ($)	19.6%	15.63	15.38	22.25	28.50	28.63	28.25	34.88	40.88	54.06	78.00
P/E - high	—	10	11	11	12	52	12	15	16	26	27
P/E - low	—	8	5	7	8	38	10	10	13	17	18
Dividends per share ($)	8.0%	0.75	1.40	1.00	1.04	1.10	1.16	1.24	1.30	1.40	1.50
Book value per share ($)	6.3%	20.19	19.86	19.89	21.34	23.83	17.26	32.02	27.26	30.83	34.89
Employees	2.9%	12,500	12,000	11,000	11,600	11,500	12,900	15,300	15,300	16,200	16,100

STOCK PRICE HISTORY

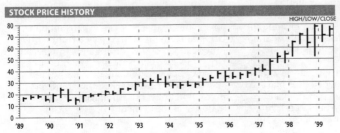

HIGH/LOW/CLOSE

1998 FISCAL YEAR-END

Equity as % of assets: 8.4%
Return on assets: 0.8%
Return on equity: 8.7%
Long-term debt ($ mil.): —
No. of shares (mil.): 252
Dividends
  Yield: 1.9%
  Payout: 50.7%
Market value ($ mil.): 19,641
Sales (mil.): $10,251

AMERICAN GREETINGS

OVERVIEW

American Greetings has been building its house of cards for nearly a century. The #2 US maker of greeting cards (behind Hallmark Cards), the Cleveland-based company markets its missives under the American Greetings, Carlton Cards, and Forget Me Not brand names. Written in more than 20 languages, American Greetings' cards are available in 110,000 stores across more than 80 countries. The company has 30 plants worldwide.

While greeting cards generate more than two-thirds of its revenue, American Greetings has branched into other products including DesignWare party goods, GuildHouse candles, Balloon Zone balloons, and Designers' Collection stationery. Subsidiary Learning Horizons offers supplemental educational products, and subsidiary Magnivision is one of the largest makers of nonprescription reading glasses.

The company's AG Industries subsidiary makes display fixtures for American Greetings and retailers such as Blockbuster. Its Plus Mark subsidiary makes gift wrap, boxed cards, and accessories.

American Greetings made the leap into cyberspace in 1995 when it began offering online greetings via the Internet. The company announced plans to spin off a minority interest in its online subsidiary, AmericanGreetings.com, in 1999. American Greetings has also initiated a productivity push to speed turnover of its cards at the retail level. Members of the founding Sapirstein family (including founder-chairman Irving Stone, chairman and CEO Morry Weiss, and senior VP Erwin Weiss) own about 5% of the company but control nearly 34% of the voting power.

HISTORY

In 1906 Polish immigrant Jacob Sapirstein founded Sapirstein Greeting Card Company and began selling postcards from a horse-drawn wagon. The outbreak of WWI and the resulting separation of numerous families helped spur demand for the company's products. The impact of the war also helped shape the company's future: After an embargo was imposed on cards produced in Germany, Sapirstein decided to begin manufacturing his own cards.

Sapirstein's sons eventually joined the burgeoning company and, in 1940, after adopting the American Greetings Publishers name, the company's sales topped $1 million. The company incorporated as American Greetings in 1944 and went public in 1952. It introduced Hi Brows, a line of funny studio cards, in 1956 and broke ground on a 1.5 million-sq.-ft. headquarters building the same year.

In 1960 Sapirstein's son, Irving Stone (all three Sapirstein sons changed their surname to Stone, a derivative of Sapirstein) was appointed president and Jacob Sapirstein became chairman. The ubiquitous Holly Hobbie made her first appearance on greeting cards in 1967 (within a decade, she had become the world's most popular licensed female character). In 1968 American Greetings' sales exceeded $100 million.

American Greetings introduced the Ziggy character in 1972 and launched Plus Mark, a maker of seasonal wrapping paper, boxed cards, and accessories six years later. Irving Stone succeeded his father as chairman and

CEO in 1978, and Morry Weiss, Irving Stone's son-in-law, was appointed president.

The success of Holly Hobbie licensing prompted American Greetings to create its own licensing division in 1980. In 1982 it introduced the Care Bears, licensed characters that appeared in animated films. Following the death of Jacob Sapirstein in 1987 (at the ripe old age of 102), Morry Weiss became chairman and CEO and Irving Stone became founder-chairman.

The company bought Magnivision (nonprescription reading glasses) in 1993. It ventured onto the Internet two years later, when it began offering online greeting cards. Its 1996 attempt to acquire #3 card maker Gibson Greetings proved unsuccessful. The company branched into supplemental educational products the following year when it unveiled its Learning Horizon product line.

Its acquisitions of greeting card companies Camden Graphics and Hanson White in 1998 helped American Greetings double its presence in the UK. As part of an international restructuring plan, in 1999 the company shuttered a Canadian plant, eliminating 650 jobs. Later that year, in an expansion of its existing agreement with America Online (AOL), American Greetings' online unit (American-Greetings.com) became AOL's exclusive provider of electronic greetings. The company subsequently filed to take AmericanGreetings.com public, but intended to retain a majority of the company.

OFFICERS

Founder-Chairman: Irving I. Stone, age 90, $318,626 pay
Chairman and CEO: Morry Weiss, age 59, $930,792 pay
President and COO: Edward Fruchtenbaum, age 51, $772,792 pay
SVP and CFO: William S. Meyer, age 52
SVP Consumer Products: Erwin Weiss, age 50, $351,784 pay
SVP Electronic Marketing; President and CEO Americangreetings.com: John M. Klipfell, age 49
SVP Human Resources and Communications: Patricia A. Papesh, age 51
SVP International: Mary Ann Corrigan-Davis, age 45
SVP Information Services: Thomas T. Zinn Sr., age 50
SVP Manufacturing: Michael B. Birkholm, age 47
SVP National Accounts: George A. Wenz, age 54
SVP Product Development: Jeffrey M. Weiss, age 35
SVP Sales: William R. Mason, age 54, $383,970 pay
SVP, Secretary, and General Counsel: Jon Groetzinger Jr., age 50, $366,267 pay
VP and Treasurer: Dale A. Cable, age 51
VP and Corporate Controller: Patricia L. Ripple, age 43
VP Creative: David R. Beittel
VP Communications: Jeffrey A. Petit
VP Human Resources: Brian T. McGrath
VP Manufacturing Everyday: Thomas O. Davis
Auditors: Ernst & Young LLP

LOCATIONS

HQ: American Greetings Corporation
1 American Rd., Cleveland, OH 44144-2398
Phone: 216-252-7300   **Fax:** 216-252-6777
Web site: http://www.americangreetings.com/corporate

American Greetings has operations in Australia, Canada, France, Ireland, Mexico, New Zealand, South Africa, the UK, and the US. Its products are marketed in more than 80 countries.

1999 Sales

	$ mil.	% of total
US	1,820	83
Other countries	386	17
Total	**2,206**	**100**

PRODUCTS/OPERATIONS

1999 Sales

	$ mil.	% of total
Everyday greeting cards	1,051	48
Seasonal greetings cards	451	20
Gift wrap & wrap accessories	302	14
Other	402	18
Total	**2,206**	**100**

Selected Products
AG Industries (retails display fixtures)
American Greetings (cards)
Balloon Zone (balloons)
Carlton Cards (cards)
Designers' Collection (stationery)
DesignWare (party goods)
Forget Me Not (cards)
GuildHouse (candles)
Learning Horizons (supplemental educational products)
Magnivision (nonprescription reading glasses)
Plus Mark (gift wrap, boxed cards, and accessories)

COMPETITORS

Blue Mountain Arts
Blyth Industries
CTI Industries
CSS Industries
Gibson Greetings
Hallmark
Marchon Eyewear
Successories
Vista Eyecare

HISTORICAL FINANCIALS & EMPLOYEES

NYSE symbol: AM FYE: February 28	Annual Growth	1990	1991	1992	1993	1994	1995	1996	1997	1998	1999
Sales ($ mil.)	6.2%	1,287	1,413	1,554	1,672	1,770	1,878	2,012	2,172	2,199	2,206
Net income ($ mil.)	10.7%	72	83	98	112	114	149	115	167	190	180
Income as % of sales	—	5.6%	5.8%	6.3%	6.7%	6.4%	7.9%	5.7%	7.7%	8.6%	8.2%
Earnings per share ($)	9.4%	1.13	1.31	1.40	1.55	1.54	1.98	1.53	2.22	2.55	2.53
Stock price - FY high ($)	—	18.56	20.31	21.56	26.19	34.25	31.38	33.00	31.38	45.88	53.75
Stock price - FY low ($)	—	10.63	13.31	15.63	18.88	23.88	25.75	25.50	23.50	29.25	22.00
Stock price - FY close ($)	4.7%	15.63	18.88	21.25	24.00	27.88	29.38	27.38	31.00	45.63	23.69
P/E - high	—	16	16	15	17	22	16	22	14	18	21
P/E - low	—	9	10	11	12	16	13	17	11	11	9
Dividends per share ($)	9.4%	0.33	0.35	0.37	0.41	0.47	0.53	0.60	0.66	0.70	0.74
Book value per share ($)	8.4%	9.44	10.39	12.05	13.07	14.21	15.61	16.53	18.16	18.90	19.49
Employees	1.6%	30,800	31,600	31,200	31,400	36,600	35,600	36,800	36,300	35,600	35,475

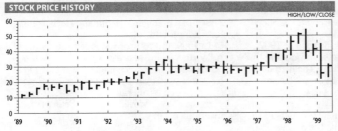

STOCK PRICE HISTORY
HIGH/LOW/CLOSE

1999 FISCAL YEAR-END

Debt ratio: 25.6%
Return on equity: 13.4%
Cash ($ mil.): 145
Current ratio: 2.74
Long-term debt ($ mil.): 463
No. of shares (mil.): 69
Dividends
  Yield: 3.1%
  Payout: 29.2%
Market value ($ mil.): 1,637

AMERICAN HOME PRODUCTS

OVERVIEW

Since this drugmaker also produces pest- and weed-control products, one might say that Madison, New Jersey-based American Home Products (AHP) kills the bugs in your body and your yard.

Subsidiary Wyeth-Ayerst Laboratories accounts for some 70% of sales; products include women's health care products (estrogen-replacement drug Premarin), nutritionals (Promil and Nursoy baby formulas), cardiovascular therapies (Cordarone), adult and children's vaccines, and mental health treatments (Effexor antidepressant). Consumer subsidiary Whitehall-Robins Healthcare makes profitable over-the-counter brands, such as Advil, Centrum, and Robitussin; subsidiary Fort

Dodge makes veterinary drugs. AHP's agricultural products subsidiary, Cyanamid (which may be on the block), makes insecticides and herbicides.

AHP's drug business lost some strength after the recall of diet drugs Redux and Pondimin (fen-phen) and the lawsuits that followed. The company has intensified a push to enhance its drug pipeline; it owns Genetics Institute, creator of drugs for anemia and other diseases, and a majority share of cancer drugmaker Immunex. The company is also looking to merge with another major pharmaceuticals player to remain competitive in a consolidating industry.

HISTORY

The history of American Home Products (AHP) is one of continuous acquisitions. Incorporated in 1926, it began by consolidating several small companies that made proprietary medicines. In the Depression the firm bought more than 30 food and drug companies. A sunburn oil bought in 1935 became the hemorrhoid treatment Preparation H; Anacin was also bought in the 1930s. AHP purchased Canada's Ayerst Laboratories in 1943 (cod-liver oil, vitamins, and Premarin) and acquired Chef Boyardee Quality Foods in 1946.

In alliance with the UK's Imperial Chemical Industries, Ayerst developed Inderal (1968), first of the beta-blocker class of antihypertensives. AHP bought Sherwood Medical Group (medical supplies) in 1982. Lawyer John Stafford became CEO in 1986. AHP bought Bristol-Myers' animal health division a year later, and in 1988 it took over A. H. Robins, which had been bankrupted by lawsuits over the Dalkon Shield contraceptive device. The following year AHP's Advil, introduced in 1984, outsold Bristol-Myers' Nuprin. In 1992 the company bought 60% of Genetics Institute (it bought the rest in 1996).

In 1994 AHP acquired American Cyanamid; the hostile takeover pumped up AHP's presence in biotechnology, generics, and agricultural products and increased research and development for its product pipeline.

American Cyanamid was founded in 1907 by Frank Washburn, who began producing the world's first synthetic fertilizer. The firm diversified into other chemicals in the 1920s and during WWII supplied US troops with typhus vaccine.

AHP introduced several new products in the US in 1996, including Redux, the first weight-

reduction drug to win FDA approval in more than two decades. It recalled Redux and Pondimin the next year after they were linked to heart valve problems. The recall led to a number of lawsuits. The firm also ran into problems with its painkiller Duract, which had to be pulled after a year for causing liver damage and death in some patients.

To cut debt and focus on high-margin pharmaceuticals, the company sold its food unit (Chef Boyardee, Jiffy Pop) to investment firm Hicks, Muse, Tate & Furst in two stages in 1996 and 1998.

In 1997 AHP bought the animal health operations of Belgian chemical and pharmaceuticals firm Solvay SA. The company sold off its remaining medical device units in 1998. Subsidiary American Cyanamid formed an alliance with Zeneca Seeds, a member company of seed giant Advanta, to breed canola varieties. The next year, however, agricultural sales fizzled, prompting AHP to put the operation up for sale.

In 1998 AHP saw merger plans with both SmithKline Beecham and Monsanto collapse. The next year it made plans to cut jobs and expenses as part of a restructuring effort. AHP also lost its multimillion-dollar battle to keep a potential Premarin rival off the market. As partial consolation, the company bought New Jersey-based Solgar Vitamin and Herb Company for $425 million.

In 1999, the company stopped shipments of a rotavirus vaccine because it was causing bowel obstructions in infants and recalled 600,000 allergy kits used by people at risk for anaphylactic shock caused by allergic reactions. That same year, the FDA approved Sonata, the firm's new insomnia drug.

Chairman, President, and CEO: John R. Stafford,
  age 61, $2,774,000 pay
SEVP (CFO): Robert G. Blount, age 60, $1,491,500 pay
EVP: Robert Essner, age 51, $1,282,500 pay
SVP Science and Technology: Robert I. Levy, age 61,
  $1,117,708 pay
SVP and General Counsel: Louis L. Hoynes Jr., age 63
Chairman and CEO, Immunex: Edward V. Fritzky
President, Cyanamid Agricultural Products:
  Marco A. Fonseca
President, Wyeth-Ayerst Research: L. Patrick Gage
President, Whitehall-Robins Healthcare:
  Kenneth J. Martin
President, Wyeth-Ayerst Global Pharmaceuticals:
  Bernard Poussot
President, Specialty Pharmaceuticals: David G. Strunce
Auditors: Arthur Andersen LLP

LOCATIONS

HQ: American Home Products Corporation,
  5 Giralda Farms, Madison, NJ 07940-0874
Phone: 973-660-5000   **Fax:** 973-660-7026
Web site: http://www.ahp.com

American Home Products has manufacturing plants in
Brazil, Canada, China, France, Germany, Ireland, Italy,
the Philippines, Puerto Rico, Taiwan, the UK, and the US.

1998 Sales

	$ mil.	% of total
US	7,725	57
Other countries	5,738	43
Total	**13,463**	**100**

PRODUCTS/OPERATIONS

1998 Sales

	$ mil.	% of total
Pharmaceuticals	8,902	66
Agricultural products	2,194	16
Consumer health care	2,175	16
Corporate & other	192	2
Total	**13,463**	**100**

Selected Subsidiaries
American Cyanamid Co.
Dimminaco AG
Genetics Institute, Inc.
Immunex Corp.
Wyeth Nutritionals, inc.
Wyeth-Ayerst Pharmaceuticals, Inc.
Wyeth-Lederle

COMPETITORS

Abbott Labs	Johnson & Johnson
Amgen	Merck
AstraZeneca	Monsanto
BASF AG	Novartis
Baxter	Novo Nordisk A/S
Bayer AG	Pfizer
Bristol-Myers Squibb	Pharmacia & Upjohn
Chiron	Procter & Gamble
DuPont	Rhône-Poulenc
Eli Lilly	Roche Holding
Genentech	Schering-Plough
Glaxo Wellcome	SmithKline Beecham
Hoechst AG	Warner-Lambert

HISTORICAL FINANCIALS & EMPLOYEES

NYSE symbol: AHP FYE: December 31	Annual Growth	1989	1990	1991	1992	1993	1994	1995	1996	1997	1998
Sales ($ mil.)	8.0%	6,747	6,775	7,079	7,874	8,305	8,966	13,376	14,088	14,196	13,463
Net income ($ mil.)	9.4%	1,102	1,231	1,375	1,461	1,469	1,528	1,680	1,883	2,043	2,474
Income as % of sales	—	16.3%	18.2%	19.4%	18.6%	17.7%	17.0%	12.6%	13.4%	14.4%	18.4%
Earnings per share ($)	8.6%	0.88	0.97	1.08	1.16	1.18	1.24	1.35	1.46	1.56	1.85
Stock price - FY high ($)	—	13.67	13.78	21.56	21.06	17.25	16.81	24.97	33.25	42.44	58.75
Stock price - FY low ($)	—	9.97	10.75	11.63	15.56	13.88	13.84	15.44	23.53	28.50	37.75
Stock price - FY close ($)	17.3%	13.44	13.16	21.16	16.88	16.19	15.69	24.25	29.31	38.25	56.38
P/E - high	—	16	14	20	18	15	14	18	23	27	32
P/E - low	—	11	11	11	13	12	11	11	16	18	20
Dividends per share ($)	3.4%	0.49	0.54	0.60	0.67	0.72	0.74	0.76	0.79	1.08	0.66
Book value per share ($)	18.6%	1.58	2.13	2.61	2.85	3.12	3.48	4.42	5.44	6.29	7.33
Employees	0.5%	50,816	48,700	47,938	50,653	51,399	74,009	64,712	59,747	60,523	52,984

STOCK PRICE HISTORY
HIGH/LOW/CLOSE

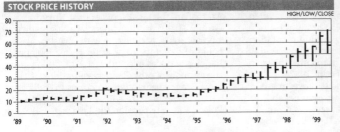

1998 FISCAL YEAR-END
Debt ratio: 28.6%
Return on equity: 25.7%
Cash ($ mil.): 1,182
Current ratio: 1.89
Long-term debt ($ mil.): 3,859
No. of shares (mil.): 1,312
Dividends
 Yield: 1.2%
 Payout: 35.7%
Market value ($ mil.): 73,993

AMERICAN INTERNATIONAL GROUP

OVERVIEW

American International Group (AIG) has the world covered. The New York City-based AIG is a global insurance presence, offering life insurance, property/casualty lines, and financial services in the US and internationally. The company used to separate its businesses along geographic lines (life operations outside the US, property/casualty within), but recent acquisitions have blurred those borders, especially the purchase of SunAmerica, a life and annuities company operating in the US. The move is also expected to jump-start AIG's property/casualty sales (SunAmerica's fastest-growing segment). AIG also leases aircraft and operates a ski resort in Vermont.

The company is one of the few insurers that makes an underwriting profit instead of depending on investments to stay in the black, largely due to legendary chairman and CEO Maurice Greenberg. Greenberg has taken steps to ensure that his legacy continues by naming his second son, Evan, as his successor (the eldest Greenberg son, Jeff, is president at Marsh & McClennan Companies).

Private companies owned by upper management own more than 24% of AIG.

HISTORY

Former ice cream parlor owner Cornelius Starr founded property/casualty insurer C. V. Starr & Co. in Shanghai, China in 1919. After underwriting business for other insurers, Starr began selling life insurance to the Chinese in 1921. In 1926 he opened a New York office specializing in risks incurred outside the US by American companies. As WWII approached, Starr moved his base to the US; when the war in Europe cut off business there, he concentrated on Latin America. After a brief postwar return to China, the company was kicked out by the communist government.

In the 1950s the company began providing disability, health, and life insurance and portable pension plans for employees who moved from country to country. Starr chose his successor, Maurice Greenberg, in 1967 and died the next year. Greenberg, who had come aboard in 1960 to help develop overseas accident and health insurance, took over the newly formed American International Group, a holding company for Starr's worldwide collection of insurance companies. Greenberg's policy of achieving underwriting profits forced the company to exercise exceptional discipline in accepting business and setting premiums. AIG went public in 1969.

By 1975 AIG was the largest foreign life insurer in Hong Kong, Japan, Malaysia, the Philippines, Singapore, and Taiwan and the only insurer with worldwide sales and support facilities. AIG's underwriting policies saved it when price wars from 1979 to 1984 brought heavy losses to most insurers. Its sterling reputation and hard work helped it become the second US-owned insurer (after Chubb) to enter the xenophobic South Korean market in 1987.

During the 1980s, AIG began investment operations in Asia, increased its presence in health care, and formed a financial services group. It bought International Lease Finance Corpora-tion, which leases and remarkets jets to airlines, in 1990. AIG soon moved into Poland, Hungary, and Estonia.

The company resumed its Chinese operations in 1993 after triumphing over stiff opposition from state-owned monopolies. It also resumed sending commissioned salespeople door-to-door to sell life policies.

With a strong presence in many developing markets, AIG began cross-selling a wide array of financial products. In 1995 the company formed the Asian Infrastructure Fund, a mutual fund for individual investors. The following year AIG acquired SPC Credit, a consumer and commercial finance company with offices in the Philippines, Taiwan, and Thailand.

In 1997 AIG teamed up with Brazil's Unibanco for an insurance joint venture. In hopes of expanding its sales to individuals, AIG agreed in late 1997 to acquire specialty insurer American Bankers Insurance, but diversified services company Cendant won the bidding war with its $3.1 billion offer (AIG walked away with a $100 million consolation prize). In 1998 AIG agreed to invest $1.35 billion in the Blackstone Group buyout firm. Later that year AIG bought SunAmerica for $18.3 billion, giving the company access to a sales-driven distribution network and greater flexibility in the consolidating financial services industry.

In 1999 the company expanded into Azerbaijan, forming an insurance joint venture with Azerbaijani financial services firm Nurgun Group. That year AIG's financial advisory division entered a partnership with investment banker Blackstone to provide acquisition and financing services in Southeast Asia. Following the example of other large corporations, it moved many back-office functions to India, where labor costs are quite low. It also entered Poland's private pension fund market.

Chairman and CEO; Chairman, Transatlantic Holdings and 20th Century Industries; President and CEO, C.V. Starr: Maurice R. "Hank" Greenberg, age 73, $6,000,000 pay
Senior VC, General Insurance: Thomas R. Tizzio, age 61, $1,136,623 pay
VC, Investments and Financial Services: Edward E. Matthews, age 67, $1,052,500 pay
VC, Life Insurance: Edmund S. W. Tse, age 61, $769,612 pay
VC, External Affairs: Frank G. Wisner, age 60
President and COO: Evan G. Greenberg, age 44, $822,692 pay
EVP, Life Insurance: R. Kendall Nottingham
EVP, CFO, and Comptroller: Howard I. Smith, age 54
SVP, Human Resources: Axel I. Freudmann, age 52
SVP and Chief Investment Officer: Win J. Neuge
SVP and General Counsel: Ernest T. Patrikis, age 55
Auditors: PricewaterhouseCoopers LLP

LOCATIONS

HQ: American International Group, Inc.,
70 Pine St., New York, NY 10270
Phone: 212-770-7000 **Fax:** 212-509-9705
Web site: http://www.aig.com

1998 Sales

	$ mil.	% of total
US & Canada	15,818	47
Far East	10,571	32
Other regions	6,907	21
Adjustments	(2,536)	—
Total	**30,760**	**100**

PRODUCTS/OPERATIONS

1998 Assets

	$ mil.	% of total
Cash & equivalents	5,141	3
Trading account	11,897	6
Foreign governments' securities	11,152	6
State & municipal bonds	19,524	10
Corporate bonds	27,969	14
Stocks	5,893	3
Other securities	24,292	13
Mortgage loans & real estate	8,247	4
Receivables & reinsurance	30,994	16
Flight equipent under lease	16,330	8
Other assets	32,959	17
Total	**194,398**	**100**

1998 Sales

	$ mil.	% of total
General insurance	16,495	52
Life insurance	13,444	42
Financial services	913	3
Adjustments	818	3
Total	**30,760**	**100**

COMPETITORS

AEGON	Jefferson-Pilot
Allianz	John Hancock
Allmerica Financial	Kemper Insurance
Allstate	MetLife
American Family Insurance	New York Life
AXA	Prudential
Berkshire Hathaway	Reliance Group Holdings
Chubb	SAFECO
CNA Financial	St. Paul Companies
The Hartford	Tokio Marine and Fire
	Travelers

HISTORICAL FINANCIALS & EMPLOYEES

NYSE symbol: AIG FYE: December 31	Annual Growth	1989	1990	1991	1992	1993	1994	1995	1996	1997	1998
Assets ($ mil.)	17.3%	46,143	58,143	69,390	79,835	101,015	114,346	134,136	148,431	163,971	194,398
Net income ($ mil.)	11.9%	1,368	1,442	1,553	1,657	1,939	2,176	2,510	2,897	3,332	3,766
Income as % of assets	—	3.0%	2.5%	2.2%	2.1%	1.9%	1.9%	1.9%	2.0%	2.0%	1.9%
Earnings per share ($)	11.8%	1.05	1.09	1.14	1.25	1.46	1.62	1.88	2.18	2.52	2.86
Stock price - FY high ($)	—	14.19	13.41	16.15	19.22	23.80	23.92	33.99	41.42	61.50	82.10
Stock price - FY low ($)	—	8.39	9.03	11.40	12.98	17.44	19.41	22.82	31.36	37.90	51.90
Stock price - FY close ($)	21.8%	13.11	12.17	15.58	18.37	20.83	23.26	32.92	38.53	58.03	77.30
P/E - high	—	14	12	14	15	16	15	18	19	24	29
P/E - low	—	8	8	10	10	12	12	12	14	15	18
Dividends per share ($)	9.0%	0.06	0.06	0.07	0.08	0.09	0.10	0.11	0.14	0.15	0.13
Book value per share ($)	13.7%	6.50	7.39	8.55	9.56	11.38	12.34	14.88	16.71	18.31	20.68
Employees	4.3%	33,000	33,600	32,000	33,000	33,000	32,000	34,500	36,600	40,000	48,000

STOCK PRICE HISTORY

HIGH/LOW/CLOSE

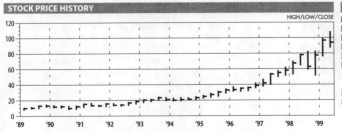

1998 FISCAL YEAR-END

Equity as % of assets: 14.0%
Return on assets: 2.1%
Return on equity: 13.9%
Long-term debt ($ mil.): 15,249
No. of shares (mil.): 1,312
Dividends
  Yield: 0.2%
  Payout: 4.5%
Market value ($ mil.): 101,430
Sales (mil.): $30,760

AMERICAN STANDARD COMPANIES

OVERVIEW

American Standard's "Trane" is on the right track, but it's hauling a heavy load of debt. The Piscataway, New Jersey-based company mainly sells residential and commercial air-conditioning and indoor environmental control systems under the American Standard and Trane names. Its other lines of business include American Standard, Ideal Standard, and Porcher plumbing fixtures and WABCO automotive braking systems, which are leaders in their markets. American Standard offers its customers financing through an alliance with Transamerica Corporation (now part of AEGON NV).

American Standard has suffered throughout the 1990s from slow sales growth and poor earnings. It has lost money in eight of the last 10 years, in part because of the maturity of its main environmental control and plumbing markets in the US. About 65% of US air-conditioning sales are for the replacement and repair market. These lines are also dependent on construction and weather cycles. In response, the company is expanding geographically, particularly European and warm-weather Asian markets such as India and Vietnam, to boost new-unit sales.

Increased use of automatic braking systems, which are required for new vehicles in many regions, has helped build American Standard's WABCO braking-systems operations. To decrease reliance on industrial businesses, the company has moved into a wholly unrelated area, diagnostic medical systems, by making sample-analysis equipment. This equipment is designed to provide multiple tests simultaneously on a single sample.

HISTORY

In 1881 American Radiator began making steam and water-heating equipment in Buffalo, New York. J. P. Morgan acquired the company, along with almost every other US heating-equipment firm, and consolidated them as American Radiator in 1899. That year Ahrens & Ott joined with Standard Manufacturing to create Standard Sanitary, which produced enameled cast-iron plumbing fixtures.

Both American Radiator and Standard Sanitary grew through acquisitions in the early 20th century. In 1929 the companies merged to form American Radiator & Standard Sanitary, expanding operations across North and South America and into Europe. By the 1960s the company was the world's #1 manufacturer of plumbing fixtures.

In 1967 the firm became American Standard and began diversifying through acquisitions. In 1968 it bought Westinghouse Air Brake (WABCO), which made railway brakes and, later, automotive products (WABCO traces its history to Union Switch and Signal, begun in 1882). During the 1970s and 1980s the firm consolidated operations and sold numerous businesses. It bought Trane (air conditioners) in 1984.

American Standard fought off a hostile takeover by Black & Decker in 1988 and then agreed to be purchased by ASI Holding (formed by LBO firm Kelso & Co.) and taken private. The transaction left the firm deeply in debt. To raise cash, it sold its Manhattan headquarters, its railway signal business, its Steelcraft division, and its pneumatic-controls business in 1988. American Standard sold its railway brake operations in 1990 and Tyler Refrigeration in 1991, losing $22 million in the deal.

In 1994 American Standard acquired 70% of Deutsche Perrot-Bremsen's automotive brake business in a joint venture. American Standard went public again in 1995 and bought the 67% of Etablissements Porcher Paris (bathroom fixtures) that it did not already own. The company introduced a commercial, non-CFC-based air conditioner and an electronic brake-by-wire system in 1996. Later that year American Standard fought off a takeover bid by Tyco. Continued poor results in the 1990s prompted the company to streamline operations, shake up management in several areas, and institute a just-in-time manufacturing system to help pare inventory. In late 1997 Horst Hinrichs (SVP at WABCO) was appointed VC of the corporation to provide management succession.

The company's medical systems group, which began operating in 1989, offers low-cost analyzers and diagnostic supplies for use in doctors' offices. In 1998 American Standard received European approval for its noninvasive test product, which uses breath samples to detect the H. pylori bacterium, now known to cause up to 80% of stomach ulcers. In 1999 the company bought the bathroom-fixtures business of the UK's Blue Circle for $417 million to boost sales in Europe.

Chairman, President, and CEO:
Emmanuel A. Kampouris, age 64, $2,700,000 pay
VC: Horst Hinrichs, age 66, $590,215 pay
SVP, Medical Systems: Fred A. Allardyce, age 57,
$515,000 pay
SVP, Automotive Products: W. Craig Kissel, age 48,
$550,000 pay
**VP Automotive Products, Order Obtainment,
Aftermarket:** Giancarlo Aimetti, age 62
**VP Plumbing Products, Product and Business
Development:** Alexander A. Apostolopoulos, age 56
VP and Treasurer: Thomas S. Battaglia, age 56
**VP and Group Executive, Plumbing Products, Asia
Pacific:** Gary A. Brogoch, age 48
VP Automotive Products, Leeds Operations:
Michael C. R. Broughton, age 58
VP Human Resources: Adrian B. Deshotel, age 54
VP, Secretary, and General Counsel: Richard A. Kalaher,
age 58
VP and CFO: George H. Kerckhove, age 61,
$650,000 pay
VP Investor Relations: Raymond D. Pipes, age 49
VP and Controller: G. Ronald Simon, age 57
Auditors: Ernst & Young LLP

LOCATIONS

HQ: American Standard Companies, Inc.
1 Centennial Ave., Piscataway, NJ 08855
Phone: 732-980-6000 **Fax:** 732-980-3340
Web site: http://www.americanstandard.com

American Standard Companies operates 120
manufacturing facilities in 35 countries.

PRODUCTS/OPERATIONS

1998 Sales & Operating Income

	Sales		Operating Income	
	$ mil.	% of total	$ mil.	% of total
Air conditioning	3,940	59	386	59
Plumbing	1,510	23	119	18
Automotive	1,106	17	153	23
Medical systems	98	1	(21)	—
Total	**6,654**	**100**	**637**	**100**

COMPETITORS

Black & Decker
Borg-Warner Automotive
Carrion Aircon
Dana
Eaton
Electrolux
Fortune Brands
Goodman Holding
Grohe
Knorr-Bremse
Kohler
Lennox
Masco
Meritor
Mueller Industries
Robert Bosch
Tecumseh Products
TOTO
United Technologies
U.S. Industries
Villeroy & Boch
Watsco
Whirlpool
York International

HISTORICAL FINANCIALS & EMPLOYEES

NYSE symbol: ASD FYE: December 31	Annual Growth	1989	1990	1991	1992	1993	1994	1995	1996	1997	1998
Sales ($ mil.)	8.0%	3,334	3,637	3,595	3,792	3,831	4,458	5,222	5,805	6,008	6,654
Net income ($ mil.)	—	(34)	(54)	(111)	(57)	(117)	(86)	112	(47)	96	(16)
Income as % of sales	—	—	—	—	—	—	—	2.1%	—	1.6%	—
Earnings per share ($)	—	—	—	—	—	—	—	1.47	(0.60)	1.26	(0.22)
Stock price - FY high ($)	—	—	—	—	—	—	—	32.00	39.75	51.63	49.25
Stock price - FY low ($)	—	—	—	—	—	—	—	19.63	25.50	34.63	21.63
Stock price - FY close ($)	8.7%	—	—	—	—	—	—	28.00	38.25	38.31	36.00
P/E - high	—	—	—	—	—	—	—	22	—	41	—
P/E - low	—	—	—	—	—	—	—	13	—	27	—
Dividends per share ($)	—	—	—	—	—	—	—	0.00	0.00	0.00	0.00
Book value per share ($)	—	—	—	—	—	—	—	(5.08)	(4.84)	(8.47)	(10.03)
Employees	6.2%	33,300	32,900	32,000	33,500	36,000	38,000	43,000	44,000	51,000	57,100

STOCK PRICE HISTORY

HIGH/LOW/CLOSE

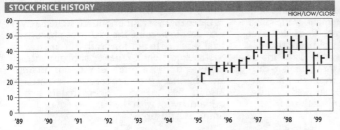

1998 FISCAL YEAR-END

Debt ratio: 100.0%
Return on equity: —
Cash ($ mil.): 65
Current ratio: 0.68
Long-term debt ($ mil.): 1,528
No. of shares (mil.): 70
Dividends
 Yield: —
 Payout: —
Market value ($ mil.): 2,517

AMERISOURCE HEALTH

OVERVIEW

AmeriSource Health offered the US government a deal that was too hard to swallow. The Malvern, Pennsylvania-based wholesale distributor of pharmaceuticals and health care products (#4 in the US) had agreed to be bought by market leader McKesson (now McKesson HBOC), but opposition from federal regulators killed the deal. AmeriSource supplies hospitals, managed care facilities, drugstores, nursing homes, clinics, supermarkets, and mass merchandisers from 23 facilities across the US.

The company has continued to expand the related services it provides customers. These include the Family Pharmacy program, which offers advertising and private-label product lines to 2,500 independent and small chain drugstores; Income Rx, which helps hospitals and pharmacies save money by finding generic pharmaceutical equivalents; MedAssess, a continuing education program for pharmacists; and American Health Packaging, which repackages bulk quantities of pharmaceuticals into smaller units, allowing customers to decrease their product, inventory, and dispensing costs.

The company has opened new distribution centers to increase its coverage across the US and has made acquisitions to bolster expansion in the Southeast.

HISTORY

In 1977 Tinkham Veale went into the drug wholesaling business. His company, Alco Standard, already owned chemical, electrical, metallurgical, and mining companies.

Alco's first drug wholesaler purchase was The Drug House (Delaware and Pennsylvania); the next was Duff Brothers (Tennessee). The company then bought other wholesalers in the South, East, and Midwest. Its *modus operandi* was to buy small, well-run companies for cash and Alco stock and leave the incumbent management in charge.

By the early 1980s Alco was the US's third-largest wholesale drug distributor and growing at a phenomenal rate (28% between 1983 and 1988). The company's growth coincided with a time of consolidation in the industry (the number of wholesalers dropped by half between 1980 and 1992), and in 1985 Alco Standard spun off its drug distribution operations as Alco Health Services Corporation, retaining 60% ownership.

Alco Health boosted its sales above $1 billion mostly via acquisitions and expanded product lines. The company also offered marketing and promotional help to its independent pharmacy customers (which were beleaguered by the growth of national discounters) and targeted hospitals, nursing homes, and clinics.

In 1988, when the US was in the midst of its LBO frenzy, an Alco management group failed in a leveraged buyout attempt. Rival McKesson then tried to acquire Alco Health, but that deal fell through for antitrust reasons. Later in 1988, management turned for backing to Citicorp Venture Capital Corp. in another buyout attempt. This time the move succeeded, and a new holding company, Alco Health Distribution, was formed.

In 1993 Alco Health was named as a defendant in suits by independent pharmacies charging discriminatory pricing policies; a ruling the next year limited its liability. To move away from a reliance on independent drugstores, Alco Health began targeting government entities, among others.

Alco Health went public as AmeriSource Health in 1995. AmeriSource made a series of acquisitions to move into related areas, including inventory management technology, drugstore pharmaceutical supplies in Florida and the Caribbean, and disease-management services for pharmacies.

In 1997 AmeriSource made its largest purchase yet when it acquired Alabama-based Walker Drug Company for $140 million, adding 1,500 independent and chain drugstores in the Southeast. That year the company agreed to assume control of food and drug chain Pathmark Stores' pharmaceutical inventory. Also in 1997 McKesson once again made an offer to buy AmeriSource, this time for $2.4 billion, and in similar agreements the #2 and #3 wholesale distributors, Cardinal Health and Bergen Brunswig, reached a similar pact. However, once again antitrust concerns reared up, and the deals were scrapped in 1998 when the Federal Trade Commission voted against both pacts and a federal judge supported that decision.

Later that year AmeriSource signed a five-year deal to become the exclusive pharmaceutical supplier to not-for-profit Sutter Health Systems; in 1999 it renewed similar contracts with the US Department of Veterans Affairs and Pharmacy Provider Services Corporation. Also in 1999 AmeriSource boosted its distribution network with the purchase of C.D. Smith Healthcare.

Chairman: Lawrence C. Karlson
President and CEO: R. David Yost
COO: Kurt J. Hilzinger
Corporate VP Sales & Marketing: Thomas P. Connolly
VP and Treasurer: John A. Aberant
VP Retail Sales & Marketing: Gerry Baker
VP Human Resources and Employment Practice:
  Eileen C. Clark
VP Institutional Sales: Ron Clerico
VP, Alternate Site Sales & Marketing: Alan Clock
VP and Controller: Michael D. DiCandilo
VP and CFO: George L. James III, age 52
VP and Chief Procurement Officer: Bonnie J. Keith
VP, Secretary, and General Counsel: William D. Sprague
VP and Chief Information Officer: Denny W. Steele
VP: Robert W. Meyer
Director, Investor Relations: Marybeth Alvin
Assistant Treasurer: M. Curtis Young
Auditors: Ernst & Young LLP

LOCATIONS

HQ: AmeriSource Health Corporation
  300 Chester Field Pkwy., Malvern, PA 19355
Phone: 610-296-4480   **Fax:** 610-647-0141
Web site: http://www.amerisource.com

AmeriSource Health has operations in Alabama, Arizona, California, Delaware, Florida, Idaho, Indiana, Kentucky, Maryland, Massachusetts, Minnesota, Missouri, New Jersey, North Carolina, Ohio, Oregon, Pennsylvania, Tennessee, Texas, Virginia, West Virginia, and Wisconsin.

PRODUCTS/OPERATIONS

1998 Sales

	% of total
Hospitals & managed care facilities	47
Independent pharmacies	34
Chain drug stores	19
Total	**100**

Selected Services
American Health Packaging (bulk purchasing and repackaging program)
The Diabetes Shoppe (care centers)
ECHO (ordering and inventory management assistance)
Family Pharmacy (merchandising and promotional campaigns)
Health Services Plus (oncology and specialty product distribution)
Income Rx (generic pharmaceutical sales)
MedAssess (continuing education program)

COMPETITORS

Bergen Brunswig
Bindley Western
Cardinal Health
D & K Healthcare Resources
McKesson HBOC
Neuman Distributors
Owens & Minor
PSS World Medical
Quality King

HISTORICAL FINANCIALS & EMPLOYEES

NYSE symbol: AAS FYE: September 30	Annual Growth	1989	1990	1991	1992	1993	1994	1995	1996	1997	1998
Sales ($ mil.)	14.5%	2,564	2,564	2,827	3,330	3,719	4,302	4,669	5,552	7,816	8,669
Net income ($ mil.)	—	(16)	(29)	(23)	(6)	(19)	(208)	10	36	45	51
Income as % of sales	—	—	—	—	—	—	—	0.2%	0.6%	0.6%	0.6%
Earnings per share ($)	54.9%	—	—	—	—	—	—	0.28	0.77	0.95	1.04
Stock price - FY high ($)	—	—	—	—	—	—	—	13.88	22.25	32.63	40.38
Stock price - FY low ($)	—	—	—	—	—	—	—	9.88	12.63	18.81	22.23
Stock price - FY close ($)	26.3%	—	—	—	—	—	—	13.50	22.25	29.22	27.22
P/E - high	—	—	—	—	—	—	—	50	29	34	39
P/E - low	—	—	—	—	—	—	—	35	16	20	21
Dividends per share ($)	—	—	—	—	—	—	—	0.00	0.00	0.00	0.00
Book value per share ($)	—	—	—	—	—	—	—	(2.66)	(0.68)	0.26	1.37
Employees	3.6%	2,400	2,323	2,560	2,269	2,403	2,370	2,600	3,000	3,700	3,298

STOCK PRICE HISTORY

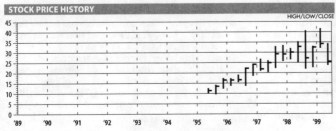

HIGH/LOW/CLOSE

1998 FISCAL YEAR-END

Debt ratio: 85.8%
Return on equity: 67.1%
Cash ($ mil.): 49
Current ratio: 1.40
Long-term debt ($ mil.): 454
No. of shares (mil.): 55
Dividends
  Yield: —
  Payout: —
Market value ($ mil.): 1,493

AMERITECH CORPORATION

OVERVIEW

The Baby Bell from the Great Lakes is joining the Baby Bell from the Lone Star State to become King of the Hill. Chicago-based Ameritech has agreed to be acquired by SBC Communications of San Antonio. Their merging will create the largest local phone company in the US, with control of about a third of the access lines.

Ameritech provides local phone service to more than 12 million customers in Illinois, Indiana, Michigan, Ohio, and Wisconsin, and it is seeking permission to offer long-distance in those states.

It also has more than 3.6 million US cellular customers, and two-thirds of those use its cellular long-distance service. It offers Internet access and provides paging service to more than 1.5 million units in its own territory, Minnesota, and Missouri. However, to gain approval for the SBC deal, it is selling nearly half of its wireless operations to a venture of GTE and investment firm Georgetown Partners.

Ameritech has diversified beyond phones into cable and security services. Its cable TV business has over 200,000 customers in some 80 Midwest communities, and its subsidiary SecurityLink, with more than 1.2 million customers, is the #2 US security firm (behind Tyco International's ADT) and the largest in Canada.

A Bell abroad, Ameritech owns a 20% stake in Bell Canada and has telecom holdings in Belgium, Denmark, Hungary, and Norway.

HISTORY

From 1878 to the 1920s the Bell System consolidated small phone companies into bigger companies that built long-distance lines to other Bell exchanges. These lines became AT&T Long Lines; local operations were retained by the Bell companies.

A century later, in 1983, Ma Bell was under attack. That year Ameritech (short for American Information Technologies) became the first US firm to offer commercial cellular service and the first Baby Bell to trade on the New York Stock Exchange. With the 1984 break-up of AT&T, Ameritech received five of AT&T's 22 phone companies and a share in Bellcore, the R&D arm shared by the Baby Bells.

Ameritech never looked back. In 1984 it became the first US firm to place fiber-optics into service, the first to lease its broadband network to a cable TV company, and the first (with sibling NYNEX) to use long-distance circuits from AT&T's competitors (including rival MCI, now MCI WorldCom) for its corporate customers.

Through the next decade, Ameritech ventured from the Midwest. It bought an interest in New Zealand's public phone system in 1990 (sold in 1998) and joined France Telecom and the Polish government in 1991 to build a cellular network in Poland (sold in 1996). Investments included 15% of MATAV, Hungary's phone company (1993), and stakes in Belgium's telecom company, Belgacom (1997), Denmark's Tele Danmark (1998), and Bell Canada, a unit of BCE (1999).

In 1992 retiring CEO William Weiss held a fateful meeting and asked top executives to profile the Ameritech they envisioned in 1995. Only four who shared Weiss' enthusiasm for radical corporate change (including Dick Notebaert, who succeeded Weiss as CEO in 1994) joined him in planning the company's future.

On a new path to diversification, Ameritech entered the home security business by buying small SecurityLink in 1994, then the bigger National Guardian in 1995. Although the Bells were banned from the security business for five years under the Telecommunications Act of 1996, a grandfather clause exempted Ameritech. Taking full advantage, it acquired the assets of nine companies by 1998, including Circuit City's alarm systems unit (1996) and Republic Industries' security division (1997).

In 1997 the Baby Bells, preparing to compete, sold Bellcore. Still, to shield their cash-cow Yellow Pages operations from online competition, Ameritech and three other Bells teamed up to offer a directory through Yahoo! Ameritech also sought clearance to enter the long-distance market and launched its Internet access service.

The Telecom Act prevented Bells from offering long-distance service in their own territory until they had strong local phone competitors. In 1998 Ameritech tried to outmaneuver the Act by marketing the long-distance services of Qwest for a per-customer finder's fee, but the FCC rejected the plan.

That year Texas Bell SBC agreed to buy the company in a $62 billion deal that would create the largest US local phone company. To allay regulators' concerns, Ameritech agreed in 1999 to sell its interests in 20 cellular properties — almost half of its wireless phone business — to a venture of GTE and minority-owned investment firm Georgetown Partners.

Chairman, President, and CEO: Richard C. Notebaert, age 51, $3,018,854 pay
EVP and CFO: Oren G. Shaffer, age 56, $1,123,528 pay
EVP Communications and Information Products: Thomas E. Richards, age 44, $832,983 pay
EVP Corporate Strategy and Business Development: W. Patrick Campbell, age 52, $956,389 pay
EVP and General Counsel: Kelly R. Welsh, age 46
EVP Regulatory and Wholesale Operations: Barry K. Allen, age 50, $947,246 pay
SVP Corporate Communications: Joan H. Walker, age 51
SVP Human Resources: Walter M. Oliver, age 53
VP and Comptroller: Barbara A. Klein, age 44
VP Federal Relations: Gary R. Lytle, age 54
VP Investor Relations: Sari L. Macrie, age 41
VP and Treasurer: Richard W. Pehlke, age 44
President, Ameritech Cellular Services: Walter S. Catlow
President, Ameritech International: Timothy J. Cawley
President, Ameritech Michigan: Robert N. Cooper
President, Consumer Services: John E. Rooney
President, General Business Services: Ronald L. Blake
President, Information Industry Services: Karen S. Vessely
President, SecurityLink from Ameritech: Neil E. Cox
Secretary: Deidra D. Gold, age 44
Auditors: Arthur Andersen LLP

LOCATIONS

HQ: 30 S. Wacker Dr., Chicago, IL 60606
Phone: 312-750-5000   **Fax:** 312-207-0016
Web site: http://www.ameritech.com

Ameritech provides local phone service in Illinois, Indiana, Michigan, Ohio, and Wisconsin; and cellular service in Hawaii, Illinois, Indiana, Kentucky, Michigan, Missouri, Ohio, and Wisconsin.

PRODUCTS/OPERATIONS

1998 Sales

	$ mil.	% of total
Local service	7,020	42
Cellular, directory & other	5,694	33
Interstate network access	2,481	14
Long-distance service	1,408	8
Intrastate network access	551	3
Total	**17,154**	**100**

Selected Affiliates
Belgacom SA (18%, Belgium)
MATAV (30%, long-distance and cellular services, Hungary)
NetCom (20%, cellular services, Norway)
SecurityLink (security services)
Tele Danmark (42%, Denmark)

COMPETITORS

American Cellular	PageNet
AT&T	Pittston Brink's
Bell Atlantic	Protection One
BellSouth	SBC Communications
BT	Sprint
Cable & Wireless	Telephone & Data Systems
Communications	Time Warner
CenturyTel	TSR Wireless
Frontier Corporation	Tyco International
GTE	United States Cellular
infoUSA	USA.NET
Intermedia	USN Communications
Communications	U S WEST
MCI WorldCom	Vodafone AirTouch
McLeodUSA	Voyager.net

HISTORICAL FINANCIALS & EMPLOYEES

NYSE symbol: AIT FYE: December 31	Annual Growth	1989	1990	1991	1992	1993	1994	1995	1996	1997	1998
Sales ($ mil.)	5.9%	10,211	10,663	10,818	11,153	11,710	12,570	13,428	14,917	15,998	17,154
Net income ($ mil.)	12.6%	1,238	1,254	1,166	(400)	1,513	(1,064)	2,008	2,134	2,296	3,606
Income as % of sales	—	12.1%	11.8%	10.8%	—	12.9%	—	15.0%	14.3%	14.4%	21.0%
Earnings per share ($)	12.2%	1.15	1.18	1.10	(0.37)	1.39	(0.97)	1.81	1.92	2.08	3.25
Stock price – FY high ($)	—	17.06	17.44	17.44	18.63	22.78	21.56	29.69	33.44	43.13	64.25
Stock price – FY low ($)	—	11.72	13.13	13.94	14.06	17.50	18.13	19.94	24.81	27.63	38.84
Stock price – FY close ($)	15.7%	17.00	16.69	15.88	17.81	19.19	20.19	29.44	30.31	40.25	63.38
P/E – high	—	15	15	16	—	16	—	16	17	21	20
P/E – low	—	10	11	13	—	13	—	11	13	13	12
Dividends per share ($)	5.7%	0.73	0.79	0.85	0.88	0.92	0.96	1.00	1.06	1.13	1.20
Book value per share ($)	3.7%	7.12	7.31	7.59	6.47	7.18	5.49	6.33	6.99	7.57	9.92
Employees	(1.0%)	77,326	75,780	73,967	71,300	67,192	63,594	65,345	66,128	74,359	70,525

STOCK PRICE HISTORY

HIGH/LOW/CLOSE

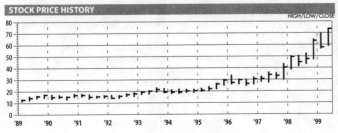

1998 FISCAL YEAR-END
Debt ratio: 33.8%
Return on equity: 33.1%
Cash ($ mil.): 139
Current ratio: 0.64
Long-term debt ($ mil.): 5,557
No. of shares (mil.): 1,099
Dividends
 Yield: 1.9%
 Payout: 36.9%
Market value ($ mil.): 69,655

AMES DEPARTMENT STORES, INC.

OVERVIEW

Like a heroine in an old movie, Ames Department Stores once tried to leave its humble roots behind, but it has found that true retail happiness lies with the simple folk. The Rocky Hill, Connecticut-based discount chain has more than 450 stores located mainly in small and midsized cities in 19 states in the Northeast, Midwest, and Mid-Atlantic.

Its stores offer apparel (larger sizes are a specialty), crafts, electronics, housewares, jewelry, sporting goods, and health and beauty items. Unlike discount retailers that stock a large mix of private-label products, Ames emphasizes national brands. Its stores are smaller than those of competitors like Wal-Mart and Kmart.

Ames aimed for more upscale customers with its purchase of Zayre in the late 1980s but wound up in bankruptcy. Since emerging in 1992, the company has returned to its traditional customer: lower- and middle-income women with families, as well as senior citizens. Ames has two programs to attract these shoppers. Its "Special Buy" promotion offers closeouts and canceled orders (apparel, mainly) at deep discounts. Its 55 Gold card provides shoppers 55 and over a 10% discount on Tuesdays.

The company bolstered its store count by 50% with its 1999 acquisition of the sickly, 155-store Hills Stores chain, whose key markets included Cleveland, Pittsburgh, and Buffalo, New York.

HISTORY

Poring through hundreds of possible names for their new discount department store, Milton and Irving Gilman decided to keep it short (because signs would be cheaper) and traditional (since the store would be located in the Ames Worsted Textile Company in Southbridge, Massachusetts). The brothers founded Ames Department Store in 1958 and were joined by brother Herbert the next year.

During the next few years, the Gilmans opened additional stores in abandoned factories in upstate New York and northern Vermont. The company went public in 1962 as Ames Department Stores, and by 1970 it had 23 Ames stores and $50 million in sales.

In the 1970s and 1980s, the company built new stores and bought other chains in the Northeast. As established retailers closed, Ames moved in. Acquisitions included Joseph Leavitt and K&R Warehouse (1972); Davis Wholesale (1978); Neisner Brothers' (1978); King's (1984); G.C. Murphy (1985); and the Zayre Discount Division of Zayre Corporation (now TJX Companies), with 392 stores, for $800 million (1988). Ames opened its Crafts & More stores in 1988.

After the Gilmans retired, nonfamily members took over. Peter Hollis, formerly of Zayre, became CEO in 1987. Ames closed 74 Zayre stores, and conversion of the remaining stores to Ames' format was costly and slow. Sales decreased at the former Zayre stores, which lost traditional customers when Ames eliminated periodic sales in favor of an everyday-low-price policy.

To raise capital, in 1989 Ames sold the Zayre shoe concession to J. Baker for $60 million. It also sold 130 G.C. Murphy stores and 25 Bargain World stores to Meshulam Riklis' McCrory Corporation for $77.6 million.

But a corporate restructuring was not enough. As the company's cash flow decreased, unpaid vendors refused to ship new merchandise in early 1990, pushing Ames into Chapter 11. Hollis resigned, and Stephen Pistner, formerly with Dayton Hudson's Target and Montgomery Ward, became CEO.

Ames sold its Mathews & Boucher (wholesale sporting goods) division in 1992. Later that year a management row resulted in the ouster of Pistner. Peter Thorner was promoted to president and COO. Also in 1992 Ames sued Wertheim Schroder & Co., the brokerage firm that had advised it to buy Zayre in 1988, saying it paid too much for the retail chain after receiving "inaccurate and misleading information and self-interested advice." (The suit was settled in 1994 for $19 million.)

The company emerged from bankruptcy at the end of 1992, 371 stores lighter than it was when it originally filed. The next year it closed the last three Crafts & More stores, along with other stores. When Thorner resigned in 1994, discount retail veteran Joseph Ettore was hired as president and CEO. Ames closed 17 stores in fiscal 1996.

In 1999 Ames bought Massachusetts-based Hills Stores for about $330 million and set out to spend $185 million to convert the Hills locations to the Ames banner. The deal moved it into Illinois, Indiana, Kentucky, North Carolina, and Tennessee. Also in 1999 Ames bought 10 Caldor stores in Massachusetts, Connecticut, and New Jersey.

Chairman: Paul M. Buxbaum, age 44
President and CEO: Joseph R. Ettore, age 59,
$1,689,423 pay
EVP, Chief Financial and Administrative Officer:
Rolando de Aguiar, age 50
EVP and COO: Denis T. Lemire, age 51, $547,500 pay
(prior to promotion)
SVP, Marketing: Eugene E. Bankers, age 59,
$345,014 pay
SVP, General Counsel, and Secretary: David H. Lissy,
age 55, $329,839 pay
Auditors: Arthur Andersen LLP

LOCATIONS

HQ: 2418 Main St., Rocky Hill, CT 06067
Phone: 860-257-2000   **Fax:** 860-257-2198
Web site: http://www.AmesStores.com

1999 Stores

	No.
Pennsylvania	99
New York	91
Ohio	53
Massachusetts	36
Maryland	24
Maine	23
Connecticut	22
New Hampshire	19
West Virginia	19
Virginia	14
New Jersey	12
Vermont	12
Other	28
Total	**452**

PRODUCTS/OPERATIONS

1999 Sales

	% of total
Home lines (housewares, appliances)	39
Softlines (apparel)	30
Hardlines (cosmetics, toys)	27
Shoes	4
Total	**100**

COMPETITORS

Ace Hardware
BJs Wholesale Club
Bradlees
Circuit City
Consolidated Stores
Costco Companies
Dollar General
Family Dollar Stores
Filene's Basement
Home Depot
J. C. Penney
Kmart
Kohl's
Lechters
McCrory
Meijer
Montgomery Ward
Sears
Service Merchandise
Target Stores
TJX
Toys "R00 Us
Value City
Wal-Mart

HISTORICAL FINANCIALS & EMPLOYEES

Nasdaq symbol: AMES FYE: January 31	Annual Growth	1990	1991	1992	1993	1994	1995	1996	1997	1998	1999
Sales ($ mil.)	(6.9%)	4,793	3,109	2,819	142	2,124	2,143	2,121	2,162	2,233	2,507
Net income ($ mil.)	—	(220)	(793)	(282)	(24)	11	17	(2)	17	35	34
Income as % of sales	—	—	—	—	—	0.5%	0.8%	—	0.8%	1.5%	1.3%
Earnings per share ($)	—	—	—	—	(1.19)	0.51	0.79	(0.08)	0.76	1.46	1.40
Stock price - FY high ($)	—	—	—	—	4.88	4.63	6.50	3.81	7.06	19.63	32.50
Stock price - FY low ($)	—	—	—	—	1.00	1.50	2.25	1.13	1.25	6.38	10.50
Stock price - FY close ($)	41.2%	—	—	—	3.88	2.88	2.75	1.56	6.31	14.38	30.75
P/E - high	—	—	—	—	—	9	8	—	9	13	23
P/E - low	—	—	—	—	—	3	3	—	2	4	8
Dividends per share ($)	—	—	—	—	0.00	0.00	0.00	0.00	0.00	0.00	0.00
Book value per share ($)	34.4%	—	—	—	2.31	3.00	4.22	4.07	5.28	7.70	13.59
Employees	(4.5%)	55,000	35,000	28,000	23,000	22,000	22,200	22,200	20,000	20,500	36,400

STOCK PRICE HISTORY

HIGH/LOW/CLOSE

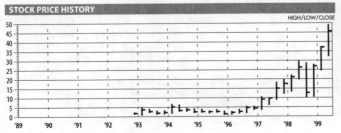

1999 FISCAL YEAR-END

Debt ratio: 47.0%
Return on equity: 10.4%
Cash ($ mil.): 36
Current ratio: 0.98
Long-term debt ($ mil.): 288
No. of shares (mil.): 24
Dividends
 Yield: —
 Payout: —
Market value ($ mil.): 733

AMGEN INC.

You need no microscope to see that Amgen is the world's largest biotechnology firm. The Thousand Oaks, California-based company has triple the sales of its nearest competitor, but has shown itself of late to be as susceptible as any biotech to the pitfalls of pairing business with science. Amgen develops therapeutic products in four areas: hematopoiesis (blood cell production), autoimmunity, neuroendocrinology, and soft-tissue repair. About one-fourth of the company's sales are funneled into research and development.

Amgen's primary products are anti-anemia drug Epogen (55% of sales) and immune system stimulator Neupogen (44%). Amgen also markets hepatitis C treatment Infergen. Besides finding new uses for existing drugs, Amgen also has about a dozen new products under development. These include treatments for blood and bone marrow disorders, AIDS, and rheumatoid arthritis.

Amgen has numerous licensing agreements with other companies, including Hoffmann-La Roche, Johnson & Johnson, and Kirin Brewery.

HISTORY

Amgen was formed as Applied Molecular Genetics in 1980 by a group of scientists and venture capitalists to develop health care products based on molecular biology. George Rathmann, a VP at Abbott Laboratories and researcher at UCLA, became the company's CEO and first employee. Rathmann decided to develop a few potentially profitable products rather than conduct research.

Amgen operated close to bankruptcy until 1983, when company scientist Fu-Kuen Lin cloned the human protein erythropoietin (EPO), which stimulates the body's red blood cell production. Amgen went public that year.

The company formed a joint venture with Japan's Kirin Brewery in 1984 to develop and market EPO. The two firms also collaborated on recombinant human granulocyte colony stimulating factor (G-CSF), a protein that stimulates the immune system.

Amgen joined Johnson & Johnson subsidiary Ortho Pharmaceutical in a marketing alliance in 1985 and created a tie with Roche Holding in 1988. Fortunes soared in 1989 when the FDA approved Epogen (the brand name of EPO) for the treatment of anemia. (It is most commonly used to counter side effects of kidney dialysis.) In 1991 Amgen received approval to market Neupogen, the brand name of G-CSF, to chemotherapy patients.

As the company grew, it needed to transform itself from startup to going concern; to do so, Amgen hired MCI veteran Kevin Sharer as president in 1992. Neupogen's usage was expanded in 1993 to include treatment of severe chronic neutropenia (low white blood cell count).

In 1993 Amgen became the first American biotech to gain a foothold in China, through an agreement with Kirin Pharmaceuticals to sell Neupogen (under the name Gran) and Epogen there. The acquisition of Synergen in 1994 added another research facility, accelerating the pace of and increasing the number of products in research and clinical trials.

Although Amgen now had two proven sellers in Epogen and Neupogen, its growth lay in its pipeline, which reported both good and bad news. In 1997 Amgen and its partner Regeneron reported the failure of human trials for a drug to help sufferers of Lou Gehrig's disease. On the other hand, a new drug, Stemgen, that stimulates the growth of white blood cells for breast cancer patients undergoing chemotherapy, was recommended for approval by an advisory committee to the FDA in 1998. That year its genome research program discovered a substance that allows the spread of cancer cells, a potential target for new drugs. Amgen also agreed to buy the rights to Guilford Pharmaceuticals' drug compounds for nervous system disorders.

Amgen had to swallow a couple of tough legal pills in 1998. A dispute with Johnson & Johnson over Amgen's 1985 licensing agreement with Ortho Pharmaceutical ended with Amgen paying about $200 million. The very next day Amgen's patent infringement lawsuit against Transkaryotic Therapies, which had developed its own EPO product, was rejected. Amgen did, however, win a legal battle with Johnson & Johnson over the rights to a promising anemia drug.

Problems plugged Amgen's product pipeline in 1999. Stemgen stalled in the FDA approval process; development of obesity and Parkinson's disease treatments ceased after discouraging trial results; and sales of Epogen, which help fund Amgen's research, began to stagnate. On the upside, that year the FDA announced that Amgen could skip Phase III trials for its rheumatoid arthritis drug because earlier tests were so successful.

Chairman Emeritus; Chairman, President, and CEO, ICOS Corporation: George B. Rathmann
Chairman and CEO: Gordon M. Binder, age 63, $1,766,135 pay
President and COO: Kevin W. Sharer, age 50, $1,447,309 pay
SVP, Sales and Marketing: Stanley M. Benson, age 47
SVP, Finance and CFO: Kathryn E. Falberg, age 38
SVP, General Counsel, and Secretary: George A. Vandeman, age 59, $876,591 pay
VP, Human Resources: Edward F. Garnett, age 51
VP, Product Development and Chief Medical Officer: George Morstyn, age 48, $824,192 pay
VP, U.S. Sales: William L. Ashton
VP, Controller, and Chief Accounting Officer: Marc M. P. de Garidel, age 40
Auditors: Ernst & Young LLP

LOCATIONS

HQ: 1 Amgen Center Dr., Thousand Oaks, CA 91320-1799
Phone: 805-447-1000   **Fax:** 805-447-1010
Web site: http://www.amgen.com

Amgen has research facilities in the US and Canada, manufacturing facilities in the US and Puerto Rico, and clinical development staff in Australia, Canada, Europe, Hong Kong, Japan, and the US.

1998 Sales

	$ mil.	% of total
US	2,441	90
Europe	277	10
Adjustments	(76)	—
Total	**2,642**	**100**

PRODUCTS/OPERATIONS

1998 Sales

	$ mil.	% of total
Epogen	1,382	51
Neupogen	1,116	41
Other products sales	16	1
Other revenue	204	7
Adjustments	(76)	—
Total	**2,642**	**100**

COMPETITORS

Abbott Labs	Interneuron
American Home Products	Pharmaceuticals
Baxter	Johnson & Johnson
Biogen	Merck
Bristol-Myers Squibb	Novartis
Cephalon	Novo Nordisk A/S
Chiron	Pfizer
Chugai	Pharmacia & Upjohn
Eli Lilly	Rhone-Poulenc
Genentech	Roche Holding
Glaxo Wellcome	Schering-Plough
Hoechst AG	Transkaryotic Therapies
Immunex	Warner-Lambert

HISTORICAL FINANCIALS & EMPLOYEES

Nasdaq symbol: AMGN FYE: December 31	Annual Growth	1989	1990	1991	1992	1993	1994	1995	1996	1997	1998
Sales ($ mil.)	33.9%	190	381	680	1,080	1,355	1,620	1,904	2,198	2,346	2,642
Net income ($ mil.)	52.7%	19	34	98	358	383	320	538	680	644	863
Income as % of sales	—	10.0%	9.0%	14.4%	33.1%	28.3%	19.7%	28.2%	30.9%	27.5%	32.7%
Earnings per share ($)	47.3%	0.05	0.06	0.17	0.61	0.69	0.57	0.96	1.21	1.18	1.63
Stock price - FY high ($)	—	2.63	11.09	19.00	19.56	17.94	15.06	29.88	33.25	34.69	54.00
Stock price - FY low ($)	—	1.49	2.45	4.70	12.31	7.75	8.69	14.03	25.69	22.44	23.31
Stock price - FY close ($)	39.8%	2.57	10.92	18.94	17.66	12.38	14.75	29.69	27.19	27.06	52.28
P/E - high	—	53	185	112	32	26	26	31	27	29	33
P/E - low	—	30	41	28	20	11	15	15	21	19	14
Dividends per share ($)	—	0.00	0.00	0.00	0.00	0.00	0.00	0.00	0.00	0.01	0.00
Book value per share ($)	30.8%	0.45	0.78	1.01	1.71	2.18	2.41	3.15	3.60	4.14	5.03
Employees	25.3%	721	1,179	1,723	2,335	3,100	3,546	4,046	4,646	5,308	5,500

STOCK PRICE HISTORY
HIGH/LOW/CLOSE

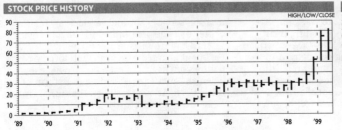

1998 FISCAL YEAR-END

Debt ratio: 8.0%
Return on equity: 33.7%
Cash ($ mil.): 201
Current ratio: 2.10
Long-term debt ($ mil.): 223
No. of shares (mil.): 509
Dividends
  Yield: —
  Payout: —
Market value ($ mil.): 26,621

AMR CORPORATION

OVERVIEW

AMR's American Airlines is taking on the world. The #2 US carrier (behind UAL's United Airlines), American serves about 180 destinations (some through code-sharing alliances) throughout the Caribbean, the Pacific, Europe, and the Americas. The airline has major hubs at Dallas/Fort Worth's DFW and Chicago's O'Hare, as well as in Miami and in San Juan, Puerto Rico. It plans to build a $1 billion terminal at New York City's JFK. Based in Fort Worth, Texas, AMR also owns commuter carrier American Eagle and 83% of Sabre, which has the #1 travel reservations system.

American's strategy for international expansion is based on making friends. The company leads Oneworld, an extensive marketing alliance with British Airways, Canadian Airlines, Cathay Pacific, and Qantas. It also has code-sharing agreements with carriers such as China Airlines, Iberia, and Japan Airlines and is expanding routes in Latin America, Asia, and Europe. In the US, American has formed marketing alliances with US Airways and Alaska Air; with the integration of Reno Air's operations the carrier has access to routes in the western US traditionally dominated by Southwest and United.

AMR CEO Donald Carty is working to build employee morale after the turbulent reign of his predecessor, Robert Crandall. The company is also selling noncore operations to concentrate on flying.

HISTORY

In 1929 Sherman Fairchild's Fairchild Aviation created a New York City holding company called the Aviation Corporation (AVCO). AVCO combined the routes of some 85 small airlines in 1930 to create American Airways. The company had its first dose of financial trouble in 1934 after the government suspended private airmail for months. Corporate raider E. L. Cord took over and named the company American Airlines.

Cord put former AVCO manager C. R. Smith in charge, and American became the leading US airline in the late 1930s. The Douglas DC-3, built to Smith's specifications, was introduced by American in 1936 and became the first commercial airliner to pay its way on passenger revenues alone.

After WWII American bought Amex Airlines, which flew to northern Europe, but another financial crisis prompted Amex's sale in 1950. The airline introduced Sabre, the first automated reservations system, in 1964. Smith left American four years later to serve President Lyndon Johnson as secretary of commerce.

In 1979, the year after the airline industry was deregulated, American moved from New York to Dallas/Fort Worth. Former CFO Bob Crandall became president in 1980 (he later became CEO). Using Sabre to track mileage, he introduced the industry's first frequent-flier program (AAdvantage). In 1982 American created AMR as its holding company. After acquiring Nashville Eagle, a commuter airline, in 1987, AMR established American Eagle, which continued to buy regional airlines.

Ducking an unsolicited takeover bid in 1989 by Donald Trump, AMR branched out internationally by purchasing routes to Japan, Latin America, and London from other carriers. A 1994 attempt by American to simplify its pricing led to a discounting war that bit into profits industrywide. Tragedy struck AMR's American Eagle subsidiary that year — two crashes resulted in 83 deaths. The next year American's 16-year fatality-free flying record ended when an airliner crashed into a mountain near Cali, Colombia, killing 160.

In 1996 AMR sold nearly 20% of Sabre to the public and struck a deal to convert its entire fleet to Boeing planes in exchange for preferred pricing. That year British Airways and American announced a code-sharing alliance (which still must clear regulatory hurdles). A wave of alliances followed, including the establishment of Oneworld in 1999.

Crandall retired in 1998 (after a major airline strike was averted only by President Bill Clinton's intervention) and was replaced by American's president, Donald Carty. American bought Reno Air in 1998, and concerns about integrating the smaller airline (completed in 1999) caused more labor strife, culminating in a slew of pilots calling in sick for more than a week in 1999. A federal judge ordered the pilots union to pay almost $46 million in compensation.

To focus on airlines, AMR sold its executive aviation services, ground services, and call-center management units in 1998 and 1999.

AMR had troubles in 1999: The Justice Department charged American with forcing competitors out of its hubs, and nine people died when an American jet landing in a storm in Little Rock, Arkansas, slid off the runway into a tower and caught fire.

Chairman, President, and CEO, AMR and American Airlines: Donald J. Carty, age 52, $1,773,198 pay
SVP and CFO, AMR and American Airlines: Gerard J. Arpey, age 40, $749,833 pay
SVP Human Resources: Thomas J. Kiernan
SVP and General Counsel, AMR and American Airlines: Anne H. McNamara, age 51
President, AAdvantage Marketing Programs: Bruce T. Chemel
President, AMR Global Services: Lauri L. Curtis
President AMR Training Group, AMR Global Services: David S. Levine
President, AMR Investment Services: William F. Quinn
EVP Operations, American Airlines: Robert W. Baker, $1,120,825 pay
SVP Marketing, American Airlines: Michael W. Gunn, $839,967 pay
SVP Miami, Caribbean, and Latin America, American Airlines: Peter J. Dolara
SVP Customer Services, American Airlines: Daniel A. Garton
SVP Maintenance and Engineering, American Airlines: David L. Kruse
VP Customer Services Planning: Bella G. Goren
Corporate Secretary: Charles D. MarLett
Auditors: Ernst & Young LLP

LOCATIONS

HQ: 4333 Amon Carter Blvd., Fort Worth, TX 76155
Phone: 817-963-1234   **Fax:** 817-967-9641
Web site: http://www.amrcorp.com

1998 Sales

	$ mil.	% of total
US	13,546	71
Latin America	2,968	15
Europe	2,247	12
Pacific	444	2
Total	**19,205**	**100**

PRODUCTS/OPERATIONS

1998 Sales

	$ mil.	% of total
Airline Group		
Passenger		
American Airlines	14,695	74
AMR Eagle Holding	1,121	6
Cargo	656	3
Other	977	5
Sabre Inc.	2,306	12
Other	119	—
Adjustments	(669)	—
Total	**19,205**	**100**

Selected Subsidiaries and Affiliates
American Airlines, Inc.
AMR Eagle Holding Corporation
Sabre Inc. (83%)

COMPETITORS

AirTran Holdings	Mesaba Holdings
Alaska Air	Northwest Airlines
America West	Southwest Airlines
Comair	SkyWest Airlines
Continental Airlines	TWA
Delta	UAL
Mesa Air	US Airways

HISTORICAL FINANCIALS & EMPLOYEES

NYSE symbol: AMR FYE: December 31	Annual Growth	1989	1990	1991	1992	1993	1994	1995	1996	1997	1998
Sales ($ mil.)	7.0%	10,480	11,720	12,887	14,396	15,816	16,137	16,910	17,753	18,570	19,205
Net income ($ mil.)	12.5%	455	(40)	(240)	(935)	(110)	228	167	1,016	985	1,314
Income as % of sales	—	4.3%	—	—	—	—	1.4%	1.0%	5.7%	5.3%	6.8%
Earnings per share ($)	8.6%	3.58	(0.32)	(1.77)	(6.25)	(1.13)	0.02	1.06	5.60	5.39	7.52
Stock price - FY high ($)	—	53.63	35.13	35.56	40.13	36.44	36.38	40.13	48.75	66.28	89.94
Stock price - FY low ($)	—	26.06	19.88	22.13	27.19	27.75	24.06	26.69	34.00	39.13	45.63
Stock price - FY close ($)	8.3%	29.00	24.19	35.25	33.75	33.50	26.63	37.13	44.06	64.25	59.38
P/E - high	—	15	—	—	—	—	1,819	38	9	12	12
P/E - low	—	7	—	—	—	—	1,203	25	6	7	6
Dividends per share ($)	—	0.00	0.00	0.00	0.00	0.00	0.00	0.00	0.00	0.00	0.00
Book value per share ($)	3.6%	30.25	29.91	27.75	22.21	21.08	21.75	23.84	31.14	35.89	41.51
Employees	0.4%	89,000	102,809	116,300	119,300	118,900	109,800	110,000	88,900	90,600	92,000

STOCK PRICE HISTORY

HIGH/LOW/CLOSE

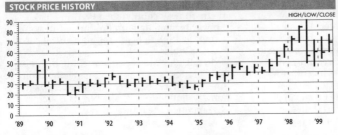

1998 FISCAL YEAR-END

Debt ratio: 38.5%
Return on equity: 19.6%
Cash ($ mil.): 95
Current ratio: 0.86
Long-term debt ($ mil.): 4,200
No. of shares (mil.): 161
Dividends
 Yield: —
 Payout: —
Market value ($ mil.): 9,581

AMWAY CORPORATION

OVERVIEW

They did it . . . Amway. The DeVos and Van Andel families' direct-sales firm has grown into a global enterprise, distributing home and personal care products in more than 80 countries and territories. The Ada, Michigan-based company includes about 50 affiliates and two majority-owned sister companies: Amway Japan (Japan is Amway's top market) and Amway Asia Pacific. About 70% of the firm's sales come from outside North America.

The world's largest direct-sales company, Amway sells what it calls "soap and hope." The "soap" is its line of more than 450 personal care, nutrition, home, and commercial products such as ARTISTRY cosmetics and NUTRILITE vitamins. Like rivals Herbalife and Mary Kay, Amway uses an army of distributors to sell products and bring in new sales recruits; to these 3 million (mostly part-time) distributors, it offers "hope," in part through giant rallies akin to fundamentalist Christian revivals.

Amway, a major Republican Party donor, is owned by billionaire founders Richard DeVos and Jay Van Andel and their families. A policy board composed of DeVos and Van Andel and four children from each family governs the firm.

HISTORY

After serving in the Army Air Corps in WWII, high school pals Richard DeVos and Jay Van Andel tried several moneymaking projects. In the late 1940s they became distributors for NUTRILITE, a California vitamin company that had pioneered network sales (in which distributors receive commissions on sales made by the people they recruit). In 1958, when NUTRILITE's leadership was failing, DeVos and Van Andel decided to develop their own product line. They founded the American Way Association (later shortened to Amway) in 1959. Van Andel oversaw Amway's nuts and bolts while DeVos provided the motivational spark.

Amway's first product was a multipurpose solution called L.O.C. (Liquid Organic Cleaner). The firm then began making laundry detergent, other household cleaners, and personal grooming products. In 1963 Amway established distributorships in Canada. By 1964 the company's sales had reached $10 million. Administration and sales support could barely keep up with the growth of the distributor network: 70 building projects, including factories and warehouses, were begun between 1960 and 1978. The "American Way" soon caught on in Australia and Europe.

In the early 1970s Amway bought NUTRILITE (1972) and expanded to Asia (Hong Kong, 1974). In 1977 the company bought the Mutual Broadcasting System (radio stations in Chicago and New York; sold 1985). Two years later an FTC ruling exonerated Amway of charges that it was a pyramid scheme, saying that because distributors receive commissions only on actual sales of their recruit network — and Amway buys back excess inventory — the business was legitimate. In 1982 Amway was charged with defrauding the Canadian government of $22 million in import duties. It pleaded guilty and paid $50 million.

Following several suits alleging abusive sales practices, in 1984 Amway brought in William Nicholson (a former assistant to President Gerald Ford) to help it reorganize; he beefed up training and added new products and services, including MCI long-distance service and a car discount program. In 1991 rival Procter & Gamble (P&G) won a $75,000 judgment against Amway distributors for spreading rumors linking P&G with Satanism. Nicholson stepped down as COO in 1992.

The company formed a $29 million joint venture in 1992 to build a plant in China. The next year, to finance its China strategy, it spun off 13.4% of Hong Kong-based subsidiary Amway Asia Pacific. Amway Japan also went public in 1993. That year DeVos retired as president and was replaced by his son Dick. In 1995 Van Andel retired, handing the chairmanship to his son Steve. P&G charged in 1996 that Amway distributors had used the company's AMVOX voice-mail system for continued rumor-mongering.

The next year Amway formed alliances with Rubbermaid (now Newell Rubbermaid) to sell its products overseas and with Waterford Crystal to sell vases in North America. After China banned direct selling in 1998, revised rules allowed Amway to sell its products there by having distributors act as sales representatives rather than buy the products and resell them. Amway countersued P&G in 1998. Amway teamed up with Columbia Energy Group in 1998 to begin selling natural gas to households.

In fall 1999 Amway began selling its household brands as well as brand-name items online. Internet subsidiary Quixtar operates like Amway, but neither its site nor its merchandise mention the Amway name.

OFFICERS

Chairman and Co-CEO; Chairman, Amway Asia Pacific:
Steve Van Andel, age 43
President and Co-CEO; Chairman, Amway Japan:
Richard M. DeVos Jr., age 43
SVP, CFO, and Treasurer: Lawrence Call
SVP New Business Ventures: David Brenner
SVP Operations: Al Koop
SVP Europe and Americas: Dave Van Andel
SVP Global Distributor Relations, Amway Asia Pacific:
Doug DeVos
**SVP and General Counsel, Amway and Amway Asia
Pacific:** Craig Meurlin
VP Human Resources: Pamela Linton
VP Catalog and Communications: Nan Van Andel

LOCATIONS

HQ: 7575 Fulton St. East, Ada, MI 49355-0001
Phone: 616-787-6000   **Fax:** 616-787-6177
Web site: http://www.amway.com

Amway has manufacturing facilities in the US, China,
and South Korea and farming operations in the US,
Mexico, and Brazil.

PRODUCTS/OPERATIONS

Selected Products

Cosmetics
ARTISTRY Cosmetics
ARTISTRY Skin Care

Home Care
Dish Drops dishwashing liquid
Household cleaners
L.O.C. multipurpose cleaner
SA8 laundry detergent

Home Tech (Living)
Queen cookware
Water treatment

Nutrition and Wellness
Active 8 Beverages
Modern Magic Meals foods
NUTRILITE multivitamins and dietary supplements
Positrim Weight Control System
Snack Sense snacks

Personal Care
Body washes and soaps
Children's care
Glister/Spreedent toothpaste
Hair care
Lotion

Other
Franklin Covey Day Planner
Oneida flatware
Rubbermaid food storage
Waterford Crystal stemware
Wedgwood Home dinnerware
WiltonArmetale serveware

Selected Services:

Auto leasing
Columbia Energy natural gas
Home mortgage
MCI WorldCom long distance

COMPETITORS

Avon
Brown-Forman
Clorox
Colgate-Palmolive
Daiei
Dial
Estée Lauder
Fingerhut
Gillette
GNC
Henkel
Herbalife
Johnson & Johnson
Kao
L'Oréal
MacAndrews & Forbes
Mary Kay
Newell Rubbermaid
Nu Skin USA
Procter & Gamble
S.C. Johnson
Shaklee
Tupperware
Unilever

HISTORICAL FINANCIALS & EMPLOYEES

Private company FYE: August 31	Annual Growth	1989	1990	1991	1992	1993	1994	1995	1996	1997	1998
Sales ($ mil.)	15.9%	1,513	1,842	2,550	3,069	3,465	4,309	4,958	5,352	6,000	5,700
Employees	8.0%	7,000	7,500	9,500	10,000	11,000	12,500	13,000	13,000	13,000	14,000

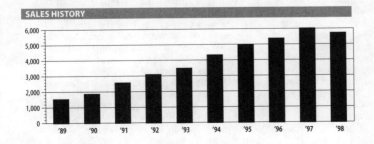

SALES HISTORY

ANDERSEN WORLDWIDE

OVERVIEW

The battle Andersen Worldwide faces with other accounting and consulting firms is nothing compared to what's going on within its own ranks.

The Chicago-based partnership — the #2 Big Five firm, behind PricewaterhouseCoopers — operates in 78 countries and has correspondent relationships with accounting firms in another 46 countries. In addition to its Arthur Andersen accounting unit — whose tradition of intensive training and discipline bordering on regimentation has earned its professionals the sobriquet "Arthur Androids" — the firm also operates Andersen Consulting, which accounts for 54% of sales.

The two halves of the firm are at war. Andersen's traditional auditing services business is increasingly subject to price competition and client mobility. In response, Andersen began offering internal audit and tax process oversight and outsourcing services, which provide steadier income. The unit also offers human resources, international trade, and risk consulting, as well as legal consulting. These services brought Arthur Andersen into direct competition with Andersen Consulting, increasing the tension created by the latter's growing financial dominance of the organization. The dispute dragged on through 1998, when it went into arbitration. The final battle is expected to take place in late 1999.

HISTORY

Arthur Andersen worked in Price Waterhouse's Chicago office in 1907. After becoming Illinois' youngest CPA, he began teaching accounting at Northwestern University in 1908, at age 23. He later became head of the accounting department at Northwestern. In 1913 Andersen formed a public accounting firm, Andersen, DeLany & Company, with Clarence DeLany.

The establishment of both the Federal Reserve System and the federal income tax that year increased the demand for accounting services. Early clients included ITT, Briggs & Stratton, and Parker Pen. In 1915 Andersen, DeLany opened a Milwaukee office. After DeLany's departure in 1918, the firm became Arthur Andersen & Co.

Andersen grew rapidly in the 1920s and began performing financial investigations, which formed the basis for its management consulting practice.

When Samuel Insull's utility empire collapsed in 1932, Andersen was appointed the bankers' representative and guarded the assets during the refinancing. Andersen opened additional offices in Boston and Houston (1937) and in Atlanta and Minneapolis (1940).

Andersen's presence dominated the firm until his death in 1947, when Leonard Spacek took the reins. During Spacek's tenure, the firm opened 18 new US offices and began its international expansion, first in Mexico and then continuing elsewhere. The firm entered the consulting business in 1954.

Andersen has been an innovator among the major accounting firms. The company opened Andersen University, its Center for Professional Education, in the early 1970s on a campus in St. Charles, Illinois, and provided the industry's first worldwide annual report in 1973.

During the 1970s Andersen increased its consulting business; by 1988 consulting fees made up 40% of revenues, making Andersen the world's largest consulting firm. Tension between consultants and auditors eventually forced a 1989 restructuring, which established Arthur Andersen and Andersen Consulting as distinct entities. The very next year, however, the accounting side set up its own consulting operation to serve companies with less than $175 million in annual sales.

In the 1990s Arthur Andersen was drawn into several lawsuits alleging that it should have detected the financial misdeeds that caused several S&Ls to fail. The firm negotiated a settlement in 1993 that disposed of all its potential liabilities. Arthur Andersen expanded its consulting business in 1994. In 1995 the firm restructured its career tracks to permit a longer learning curve and to provide a role for those uninterested in partnership. Andersen Consulting was chosen by the Frankfurt Stock Exchange in 1996 to create an off-floor trading system.

Managing partner and CEO Lawrence Weinbach announced his retirement in 1997, spurring a search for a successor. After two nominees were rejected by the company's partners, the board named accounting partner W. Robert Grafton as acting CEO. At year's end, Andersen Consulting's partners voted to seek their independence.

During 1998 a migration of workers between the units brought rumors that the split was at hand. In 1999, KPMG Canada planned to defect to join Arthur Andersen, but Andersen withdrew its acquisition offer.

Managing Partner and CEO: W. Robert Grafton
Worldwide Managing Partner, Arthur Andersen:
Jim Wadia
VP Finance and Administration and CFO:
James R. Kackley
Managing Partner and CFO, Arthur Andersen:
Clement W. Eibl
Managing Partner and General Counsel, Arthur Andersen: Daniel D. Beckel
Managing Partner Assurance and Business Advisory, Arthur Andersen: Michael L. Bennett
Managing Partner Strategy and Planning, Arthur Andersen: Richard E.S. Boulton
Managing Partner and Chief Information Officer: Eric C. Dean
Managing Partner Global 1000, Arthur Andersen: James D. Edwards
Area Managing Partner, Asia/Pacific, Arthur Andersen: Terry E. Hatchett
Managing Partner, Arthur Andersen Knowledge Enterprises: Thomas B. Kelly
Managing Partner Business Consulting, Arthur Andersen: Charles H. Ketteman
Managing Partner, Human Resources and Partner Matters, Arthur Andersen: Peter Pesce
Managing Partner, US; Arthur Andersen: Steve M. Samek
Managing Partner, Europe, Middle East, India, and Africa; Arthur Andersen: Xavier de Sarrau
Managing Partner, Andersen Consulting: George T. Shaheen
Managing Partner Global Corporate Finance, Arthur Andersen: John A. Talbot
Managing Partner Tax, Legal, and Business Advisory, Arthur Andersen: Alberto E. Terol
Managing Partner, Latin America; Arthur Andersen: Jose Luis Vazquez

LOCATIONS

HQ: 33 W. Monroe St., Chicago, IL 60603-5385
Phone: 312-580-0033   **Fax:** 312-507-6748
Web site: http://www.arthurandersen.com

Andersen Worldwide operates in 78 countries and has correspondent relationships with firms in 46 other countries.

PRODUCTS/OPERATIONS

1998 Sales

	$ mil.	% of total
Consulting	7,800	56
Accounting	6,100	44
Total	**13,900**	**100**

Operating Units

Andersen Consulting
Application management
Business process outsourcing
Design, Build, Run
Information technology outsourcing

Arthur Andersen
Assurance and Business Advisory Services
  Assurance and Process Assessment Services
  Business Ethics Services
  Business Risk Consulting Services and Assurance
  Contract Audit Services
  Contract Finance and Accounting Services
Business Consulting
Economic and Financial Consulting
  Actuarial and Insurance Services
  Corporate Finance
  Corporate Recovery
  Economic Consulting
  Emerging Markets
  Environmental Services
  Legal Consulting
  Privatization Services
  Real Estate Services
  Turnaround Group
  Valuation Services
Tax, Legal, and Business Advisory Services

COMPETITORS

American Management
Arthur D. Little
Bain & Company
BDO International
Booz, Allen
Boston Consulting
Computer Sciences
Deloitte Touche Tohmatsu
EDS
Ernst & Young
Grant Thornton
 International

IBM
KPMG
Marsh & McLennan
MCI WorldCom
McKinsey & Company
Perot Systems
Policy Management
 Systems
PricewaterhouseCoopers
Towers Perrin

HISTORICAL FINANCIALS & EMPLOYEES

Partnership FYE: August 31	Annual Growth	1989	1990	1991	1992	1993	1994	1995	1996	1997	1998
Sales ($ mil.)	17.0%	3,382	4,160	4,948	5,577	6,017	6,738	8,134	9,499	11,300	13,900
Employees	10.3%	51,414	56,801	59,797	62,134	66,478	72,722	82,121	91,572	104,933	123,791

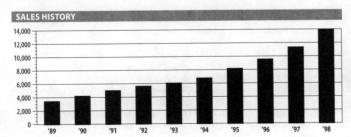

SALES HISTORY

14,000
12,000
10,000
8,000
6,000
4,000
2,000
0
  '89 '90 '91 '92 '93 '94 '95 '96 '97 '98

ANDERSEN WORLDWIDE

ANHEUSER-BUSCH COMPANIES, INC.

OVERVIEW

Anheuser-Busch Companies wants to be the life of the party, whether with its Bud-Weis-Er, as croaked by a trio of frogs in its TV commercials, or its theme parks. The St. Louis-based company is the world's largest brewer; it is also one of the nation's largest theme park operators, the #3 US manufacturer of aluminum cans, and the largest recycler of aluminum cans in the world.

Anheuser-Busch leads the US beer market with about a 48% share, and Budweiser is the nation's top-ranked beer. The company makes more than 30 different beers, including Bud Light, Michelob, and Busch. Its several malt and specialty brews, along with a joint venture with Japanese brewer Kirin Brewery and its

purchase of minority stakes in various small breweries, are an attempt by Anheuser-Busch to tap the premium and specialty beer sector. Internationally, the firm is seeking to better its sales through marketing — particularly the UK, China, and Japan — and investments in top brewers. Anheuser-Busch owns just over 50% of Mexico's Grupo Modelo (Corona).

The company's theme parks include Busch Gardens and Sea World. It also makes labels and cans for itself and soft-drink customers, has grain elevators and malt plants, and develops real estate.

Chairman and president August Busch III represents the fourth generation of the Busch family to lead the company.

HISTORY

George Schneider founded the Bavarian Brewery in St. Louis in 1852. Eight years later he sold the unprofitable brewery to Eberhard Anheuser. Anheuser's son-in-law, Adolphus Busch, joined the company in 1864 and in 1876 assisted restaurateur Carl Conrad in creating Budweiser, a light beer like those brewed in Bohemia. The brewery's rapid growth was based in part on the popularity of Budweiser over heavier, darker beers.

When Adolphus died in 1913, his son August took over the company, which was renamed Anheuser-Busch in 1919. During Prohibition (1920-33), August saved the company by selling yeast, refrigeration units, truck bodies, syrup, and soft drinks. When repeal came in 1933, August quickly resumed brewing; he delivered a case of Budweiser to Franklin Roosevelt in a carriage drawn by Clydesdale horses, which became Anheuser-Busch's symbol.

Anheuser-Busch acquired the St. Louis Cardinals baseball team in 1953. Four years later the brewer knocked Schlitz out of first place among US brewers. In 1959 the company established its Busch Entertainment theme park division.

In 1970 Miller Brewing held seventh place in the industry, but Philip Morris acquired Miller and challenged Budweiser's leadership. By 1978 Miller had passed Schlitz and Pabst to take second place, but Anheuser-Busch triumphed, becoming the first brewer to sell 40 million barrels a year.

The company bought Campbell Taggart (baked goods) and created its Eagle snack foods unit in 1982. Budweiser was introduced in England and Japan in 1984 through licensing. In 1989 Anheuser-Busch acquired Sea World from Harcourt Brace Jovanovich.

In 1993 the beer maker bought 18% of Corona maker, Grupo Modelo. Also that year the brewer became the first since Prohibition to list alcohol content on its beer, after a federal ban was overturned. Anheuser-Busch formed a joint venture with Kirin Brewery in 1993 to distribute Budweiser in Japan. A new beer, Ice Draft (now Bud Ice), was introduced the following year. The company also acquired a minority stake in Redhook Ale Brewery in 1994 and rights to distribute Redhook products.

Anheuser-Busch sold the Cardinals baseball team and stadium for $150 million and spun off its Campbell Taggart baking unit in 1996. The company then closed its Eagle Snacks unit, completing its exit from the food business.

To increase its presence in the specialty beer sector, the company began brewing and selling Kirin beers in the US in 1997. Anheuser-Busch's use of hardball tactics to discourage distributors from carrying competing brands — its "100% Share of Mind" program offers a combination of cash incentives and restrictions to keep distributors loyal — led to a Department of Justice investigation in 1997 (it ended in 1998 without legal action).

In 1998 the company and Teamsters union employees at its breweries struggled to agree on terms of a new contract. Also in 1998 it increased its holding in Grupo Modelo to over 50%. Anheuser-Busch started test-marketing plastic beer bottles in 1999 and was criticized for its advertising's appeal to youngsters, especially after it made a CD featuring lizards and frogs from its commercials. In September 1999 Anheuser-Busch recalled 5.8 million bottles of Budweiser brewed in Spain and distributed in Europe, due to defective glass bottles.

Chairman and President; Chairman and President of Anheuser-Busch, Inc.: August A. Busch III, age 61, $2,857,750 pay

VP and Group Executive; President of Anheuser-Busch, Inc.: Patrick T. Stokes, age 56, $1,450,000 pay

EVP and Group Executive; Chairman of Anheuser-Busch International: John H. Purnell, age 57, $704,000 pay

VP and CFO: W. Randolph Baker, age 52

Group VP and General Counsel: Stephen K. Lambright, age 56, $740,000 pay

VP - Corporate Engineering: Aloys H. Litteken, age 58

VP - Corporate Human Resource; Chairman and President of Busch Properties: William L. Rammes, age 57

Chairman and President of Busch Entertainment: John B. Roberts, age 54

VP and Group Executive; Chairman, President and CEO of Metal Container; Chairman, President, and CEO of Anheuser-Busch Recycling; Chairman, President and CEO of Precision Printing and Packaging; Chairman, President and CEO of Packaging Business Services: Joseph L. Goltzman, age 57

VP and Group Executive: Donald W. Kloth, age 57

EVP and Chief Communications Officer: John E. Jacob, age 64, $807,000 pay

Auditors: PricewaterhouseCoopers LLP

LOCATIONS

HQ: 1 Busch Place, St. Louis, MO 63118
Phone: 314-577-2000   **Fax:** 314-577-2900
Web site: http://www.anheuser-busch.com

Anheuser-Busch Companies brews beer in 11 countries and sells its beer in more than 80 countries.

PRODUCTS/OPERATIONS

1998 Sales

	$ mil.	% of total
Beer	9,239	82
Packaging	1,127	10
Entertainment	761	7
Other	119	1
Total	**11,246**	**100**

Selected Beverages
Azteca (imported)
Bud Light
Budweiser
Busch
Catalina Blonde
Hurricane Malt Liquor
King Cobra
Kirin Lager (joint venture)
Michelob
Natural Light
O'Doul's (nonalcoholic)
Pacific Ridge Ale
Red Wolf Lager
Redhook (distribution)
Safari Lager
Tequiza
ZiegenBock Amber

Theme Parks
Adventure Island (water park; Tampa)
Busch Gardens (theme parks; Tampa and Williamsburg, VA)
Port Adventura, SA (20%, Barcelona, Spain)
SeaWorld (marine adventure parks; Cleveland; Orlando, FL; SanAntonio; and San Diego)
Sesame Place (family play park; Langhorne, PA)
Water Country USA (water theme park; Williamsburg, VA)

COMPETITORS

Adolph Coors
Asahi Breweries
Bass
Carlsberg
Foster's Brewing
Guinness Ltd.
Heineken
Interbrew
Miller Brewing
Premier Parks
S&P
Universal Studios
Walt Disney

HISTORICAL FINANCIALS & EMPLOYEES

NYSE symbol: BUD FYE: December 31	Annual Growth	1989	1990	1991	1992	1993	1994	1995	1996	1997	1998
Sales ($ mil.)	1.9%	9,481	10,744	10,996	11,394	11,505	12,054	10,341	10,884	11,066	11,246
Net income ($ mil.)	5.4%	767	842	940	918	595	1,032	642	1,190	1,169	1,233
Income as % of sales	—	8.1%	7.8%	8.5%	8.1%	5.2%	8.6%	6.2%	10.9%	10.6%	11.0%
Earnings per share ($)	7.3%	1.34	1.47	1.62	1.60	1.09	1.94	1.24	2.34	2.34	2.53
Stock price - FY high ($)	—	23.00	22.63	31.00	30.38	30.13	27.69	34.00	45.00	48.25	68.25
Stock price - FY low ($)	—	15.31	17.00	19.63	25.88	21.50	23.56	25.38	32.38	38.50	42.94
Stock price - FY close ($)	14.6%	19.25	21.50	30.75	29.25	24.56	25.44	33.44	40.00	44.00	65.63
P/E - high	—	17	15	19	19	28	14	27	19	21	27
P/E - low	—	11	12	12	16	20	12	20	14	16	17
Dividends per share ($)	11.7%	0.40	0.47	0.53	0.60	0.68	0.76	0.84	0.92	1.00	1.08
Book value per share ($)	5.5%	5.48	6.52	7.78	8.30	7.97	8.58	8.73	8.10	8.30	8.85
Employees	(7.4%)	46,608	45,432	44,386	44,790	43,345	42,622	42,529	25,123	24,326	23,344

STOCK PRICE HISTORY

HIGH/LOW/CLOSE

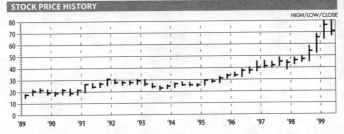

1998 FISCAL YEAR-END

Debt ratio: 52.8%
Return on equity: 29.3%
Cash ($ mil.): 225
Current ratio: 0.95
Long-term debt ($ mil.): 4,719
No. of shares (mil.): 477
Dividends
  Yield: 1.6%
  Payout: 42.7%
Market value ($ mil.): 31,279

ANIXTER INTERNATIONAL INC.

OVERVIEW

Anixter International's got connections. Based in the Chicago suburb of Skokie, Illinois, the company distributes more than 54,000 products that connect PCs, peripheral equipment, mainframe computers, and various networks to each other. As a leading global distributor of electrical wire and cable, Anixter operates about 80 warehouses with 110 connected sales offices in 40 countries.

Anixter sells copper and fiber-optic cable for data transmission and electrical wiring to transmit energy and monitor industrial processes. The company's more than 80,000 customers include governments, utilities, and manufacturers, as well as resellers such as contractors, architects, engineers, and wholesalers. More than 70% of Anixter's revenues come from sales in North America.

The company has shed its design, manufacturing, network integration, and consulting operations to focus on distribution.

Entities associated with Anixter's chairman, billionaire financier Samuel Zell, own 21% of the company.

HISTORY

Two San Francisco businessmen, Gary Friedman and Peter Redfield, founded SSI Computer in 1967 to lease computer systems. The company bought $90 million worth of IBM midsize computers and leased them at rates lower than IBM's.

In 1968 SSI entered the intermodal container and railcar leasing business when it purchased SSI Container Corp. In 1969 it bought Management Data Processing Corp., and the next year the company renamed itself Itel. Over the next decade it formed SSI Trailer (1970), SSI Navigation (1973), and SSI Rail Corp. (1975). During the 1970s the company diversified into aircraft leasing (Itel Air) and capital goods (Itel Capital).

By the mid-1970s Itel's computer-leasing business was starting to falter, but management continued an extravagant corporate culture of plush offices and shareholder cruises.

In 1979 Itel announced that it would leave the computer business and handed most of its sales and service over to one of its major suppliers, National Semiconductor. Afterward both Friedman and Redfield were dismissed. New CEO James Maloon focused Itel on its transportation services, but by 1981 the company was $1.3 billion in debt and had filed for Chapter 11 protection.

When reorganization failed to resurrect the debt-strapped company, Samuel Zell, a Chicago financier whose interests range from trailer parks to cruise ships, began accumulating Itel stock. In 1984 he earned a seat on the board and the following year became chairman.

Zell and VC Rod Dammeyer, former Household International CFO, acquired Great Lakes International (marine dredging, 1986), Anixter Bros. (wire and cable, 1986), Pullman (railcars, 1988), and a minority stake in Santa Fe Southern Pacific (railroad, 1988). Other acquisitions included Flexi-Van Leasing (1987), the assets of Evans Asset Holding (railcars, 1987), and B.C. Hydro (rail freight line, 1988). By 1988 Itel was North America's leading railcar leasing company.

In the 1990s Itel began to reposition itself: It sold its container-leasing business in 1990 and its Itel Distribution Systems and Great Lakes Dredge & Deck Co. in 1991. When the smoke cleared, Anixter was its core operation. Anixter's cable television products subsidiary ANTEC was spun off in a 1993 stock offering. Also that year Dammeyer replaced Zell as Itel's CEO.

Itel's focus became the development of new markets in the burgeoning global communications industry. The company sold its remaining rail-leasing interests in 1994. The next year Itel sold its stake in Santa Fe Energy Resources and changed its name to identify itself as an electrical equipment business.

When a wholly owned subsidiary of ANTEC merged with cable TV equipment firm TSX Corp. in 1997, Anixter's ownership in ANTEC was reduced to 19%. That year the company joined with security software maker Check Point Software Technologies to provide network-security products in Europe.

In 1998 Anixter sold its ANTEC holdings as part of a strategy to liquidate noncore assets in order to finance the repurchase of its common stock. That year it also bought Pacer Electronics, an electrical and data cabling distributor serving the Northeast US. Anixter sold its European network integration business to Persetel Q Data Holdings of South Africa and its data-network design and consulting unit to Ameritech for $200 million in cash in 1999.

Chairman: Samuel Zell, age 57
VC: Rod F. Dammeyer, age 58, $325,000 pay
President and CEO, Anixter International and Anixter Inc.: Robert W. Grubbs Jr., age 42, $773,970 pay
SVP Finance and CFO, Anixter International; EVP and CFO, Anixter Inc.: Dennis J. Letham, age 47, $455,800 pay
SVP, Law and Secretary: James E. Knox, age 61
SVP Network Services: Bill Collins
VP of Human Resources: Alan Drizd
VP and Controller: James M. Froisland, age 48, $254,820 pay
VP and Treasurer: Lisa K. Lanz, age 46, $236,220 pay
VP Taxes: Philip F. Meno, age 40
General Counsel and Assistant Secretary, Anixter International; General Counsel and Secretary, Anixter Inc.: John A. Dul, age 38
Auditors: Ernst & Young LLP

LOCATIONS

HQ: 4711 Golf Rd., Skokie, IL 60076
Phone: 847-677-2600   **Fax:** 847-677-8557
Web site: http://www.anixter.com

Anixter operates 79 warehouses and 110 sales offices based in 171 cities in 40 countries worldwide.

PRODUCTS/OPERATIONS

1998 Sales

	$ mil.	% of total
North America	1,683	72
Europe	518	22
Asia & Latin America	148	6
Total	**2,349**	**100**

1998 Sales

	% of total
Structural cable	80
Wire & cable	20
Total	**100**

Selected Products
Copper and fiber-optic cable
Electrical wiring systems
Mainframe peripheral equipment
PC peripheral equipment
Tubing and connectors

COMPETITORS

Cable Design Technologies	Okonite
Cabletron	Scientific-Atlanta
General Instrument	Southwire
Graybar Electric	Superior TeleCom
MicroAge	WESCO International

HISTORICAL FINANCIALS & EMPLOYEES

NYSE symbol: AXE FYE: December 31	Annual Growth	1989	1990	1991	1992	1993	1994	1995	1996	1997	1998
Sales ($ mil.)	1.1%	2,121	1,977	1,689	1,682	1,909	1,733	2,195	2,475	2,805	2,349
Net income ($ mil.)	9.1%	30	132	(114)	(104)	(1)	247	39	36	45	66
Income as % of sales	—	1.4%	6.7%	—	—	—	14.3%	1.8%	1.5%	1.6%	2.8%
Earnings per share ($)	22.1%	0.24	0.93	(1.75)	(1.90)	(0.07)	3.84	0.70	0.72	0.95	1.45
Stock price – FY high ($)	—	14.44	12.00	10.13	12.19	16.81	18.13	22.06	20.00	19.69	22.75
Stock price – FY low ($)	—	9.00	3.81	4.88	8.00	10.13	11.38	16.63	12.63	12.00	11.88
Stock price – FY close ($)	7.1%	11.00	4.81	9.44	11.44	14.00	17.31	18.63	16.13	16.50	20.31
P/E – high	—	60	13	—	—	—	5	32	28	21	16
P/E – low	—	38	4	—	—	—	3	24	18	13	8
Dividends per share ($)	—	0.00	0.00	0.00	0.00	0.00	0.00	0.00	0.00	0.00	0.00
Book value per share ($)	2.8%	7.65	8.34	6.70	5.05	6.14	9.24	8.55	9.07	10.09	9.83
Employees	(5.8%)	8,200	8,000	5,300	4,600	4,600	4,200	5,100	5,600	6,300	4,800

STOCK PRICE HISTORY

HIGH/LOW/CLOSE

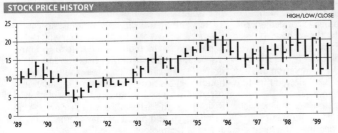

1998 FISCAL YEAR-END

Debt ratio: 56.9%
Return on equity: 15.9%
Cash ($ mil.): 21
Current ratio: 2.66
Long-term debt ($ mil.): 544
No. of shares (mil.): 42
Dividends
  Yield: —
  Payout: —
Market value ($ mil.): 851

AON CORPORATION

OVERVIEW

In the end, there can be only one. One top insurance brokerage and consulting firm, that is. Aon is a leader in the fast consolidating industry, but is currently #2 behind archnemesis, Marsh & McLennan. It is also a global purveyor of accident and health insurance, specialty and professional insurance, reinsurance, and risk management consulting services.

Aon operates in two business areas. Aon's youthful commercial insurance brokerage and consulting group is its largest segment. Anchored by the Aon Group, this segment includes subsidiaries that help groups and businesses choose industry-specific insurance and reinsurance coverage, as well as others that provide consulting on risk management for companies worldwide. The company's television advertising campaign is pushing this segment of its business and (hopefully) increasing name recognition.

The consumer insurance underwriting segment includes founder Clement Stone's original insurance underwriting business, Combined Insurance, which offers supplemental accident, life, and health insurance. The segment's Virginia Surety and London General Insurance offer extended consumer product warranties.

Chairman and CEO Patrick Ryan, who is largely responsible for Aon's growth in the brokerage and consulting field, owns about 12% of the company.

HISTORY

The story of Aon begins with Clement Stone's founding of Combined Insurance in 1947, but Stone's involvement with business started much earlier. At age six he started working as a paperboy in Chicago to supplement the earnings of his seamstress mother. The young Stone devoured the optimistic messages of the 19th-century Horatio Alger novels, which detailed the successes of plucky, enterprising heroes.

Mrs. Stone bought a small Detroit insurance agency and in 1918 brought her son into the business. Young Stone sold low-cost, low-benefit accident insurance, underwriting and issuing policies on-site. In 1922 Stone opened his own agency, the Combined Registry Co. While selling up to 122 policies per day, he recruited a nationwide force of agents.

As the Depression took hold, Stone reduced his workforce and improved training, offering agents the benefit of his experience and positive mental attitude. Forced by his son's respiratory illness to winter in the South, Stone followed the sun to Arkansas and Texas. In 1939 he bought American Casualty Insurance Co. of Dallas. It was consolidated with other acquisitions as the Combined Insurance Co. of America in 1947.

The company grew through the 1950s and 1960s, continuing to sell health and accident policies. In the 1970s Combined expanded overseas despite being hit hard by the recession.

In 1982, after 10 years of stagnant growth under Clement Stone Jr., the elder Stone (then 79) resumed control until the completion of a merger with Ryan Insurance Co. allowed him to transfer power to Patrick Ryan.

Ryan, the son of a Wisconsin Ford dealer, had started his company as an auto credit insurer in 1964. In 1976 the company acquired the insurance brokerage units of the Esmark conglomerate. Ryan's less-personal management style differed radically from Stone's rah-rah boosterism, but the men's shared interest in philanthropy helped seal the deal.

Ryan increased the company's emphasis on insurance brokering and added more upscale insurance products. He also trimmed staff and took other cost-cutting measures, and in 1987 he changed Combined's name to Aon. In 1995 the company sold its remaining direct life insurance holdings to General Electric Capital to focus on consulting. The following year Aon began offering hostile takeover insurance policies, which cover the expenses of successfully fighting off an unwanted suitor, to small and midsized companies.

Aon built a global presence through acquisitions. In 1997 it bought The Minet Group from The St. Paul Companies, as well as troubled insurance brokerage Alexander & Alexander Services in a deal that made Aon (temporarily) the largest insurance broker worldwide. The company made no US acquisitions in 1998, but doubled its employee base with purchases including Spain's largest retail insurance broker, Gil y Carvajal, and the formation of Aon Korea, the first non-Korean firm of its kind to be licensed there.

Responding to industry demands, Aon announced its new fee disclosure policy in 1999, and the company reorganized to focus on buying personal line insurance firms and to integrate its acquisitions. That year the company bought Nikols Sedgwick Group (an Italian insurance firm) and announced the formation of RiskAttack (in partnership with Zurich US), a risk analysis and financial management concern aimed at technology companies.

Chairman and CEO; Chairman, Aon Group Inc.: Patrick G. Ryan, age 61, $1,763,942 pay (prior to title change)
President and COO; Aon Group and Aon Corporation: Michael D. O'Halleran, age 48, $2,009,615 pay (prior to promotion)
Chairman, Aon Risk Services Worldwide: Dirk P. M. Verbeek
Chairman, Aon Risk Services, The Americas: Dick Riley
Chairman, Aon Services Group: Michael D. Rice
Chairman, Aon Group Limited: Dennis L. Mahoney
EVP; Chairman, Aon Consulting Worldwide: Daniel T. Cox, age 52, $1,064,980 pay
Chairman, Aon Credit Services: Gilbert N. Zitin
Chairman, Combined Insurance Company of America: Richard M. Ravin
EVP and CFO: Harvey N. Medvin, age 62, $1,298,076 pay
EVP and Chief Counsel: Raymond I. Skilling, age 59, $1,294,230 pay
VP Human Resources: Melody L. Jones
Auditors: Ernst & Young LLP

LOCATIONS

HQ: 123 N. Wacker Dr., Chicago, IL 60606
Phone: 312-701-3000 **Fax:** 312-701-3100
Web site: http://www.aon.com

1998 Sales

	$ mil.	% of total
US	3,736	58
Europe		
UK	1,244	19
Other countries	790	12
Other regions	723	11
Total	**6,493**	**100**

PRODUCTS/OPERATIONS

1998 Sales

	$ mil.	% of total
Brokerage commissions & fees	4,197	65
Premiums	1,706	26
Investments	590	9
Total	**6,493**	**100**

Selected Subsidiaries

Aon Consulting Worldwide
Aon Group
Aon Healthcare Alliance
Aon Re Worldwide
Aon Risk Services
Aon Services Group
Aon Warranty Group
Combined Insurance Company of America
London General Insurance Company
Virginia Surety Company

COMPETITORS

AFLAC
AIG
American General
Arthur Gallagher
Cerulean
Chubb
Citigroup
General Re
Health Care Service

Heath
Marsh & McLennan
StanCorp Financial Group
Torchmark
Transamerica
Trigon Healthcare
UNUMProvident
Willis Corroon

HISTORICAL FINANCIALS & EMPLOYEES

NYSE symbol: AOC FYE: December 31	Annual Growth	1989	1990	1991	1992	1993	1994	1995	1996	1997	1998
Assets ($ mil.)	8.9%	9,156	10,432	11,633	14,290	16,279	17,922	19,736	13,723	18,691	19,688
Net income ($ mil.)	9.8%	232	239	242	127	324	360	403	335	299	541
Income as % of assets	—	2.5%	2.3%	2.1%	0.9%	2.0%	2.0%	2.0%	2.4%	1.6%	2.7%
Earnings per share ($)	7.8%	1.05	1.07	1.10	0.52	1.27	1.39	1.53	1.26	39.27	2.07
Stock price - FY high ($)	—	12.83	12.65	12.39	16.02	17.36	15.90	22.63	28.81	39.27	50.40
Stock price - FY low ($)	—	8.01	7.94	8.83	11.61	13.72	13.01	13.96	21.13	26.80	32.18
Stock price - FY close ($)	12.8%	12.54	10.31	11.76	16.02	14.35	14.24	22.19	27.64	39.10	36.94
P/E - high	—	12	12	11	31	14	11	15	23	35	24
P/E - low	—	8	7	8	22	11	9	9	17	24	16
Dividends per share ($)	6.6%	0.41	0.44	0.47	0.49	0.53	0.56	0.59	0.63	0.68	0.73
Book value per share ($)	6.9%	6.48	6.64	8.05	9.67	9.97	9.53	10.86	11.34	11.21	11.83
Employees	19.3%	9,000	9,000	11,000	15,000	18,000	18,000	27,000	28,000	33,000	44,000

STOCK PRICE HISTORY

HIGH/LOW/CLOSE

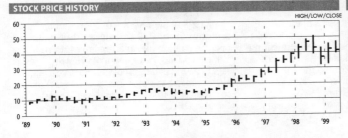

1998 FISCAL YEAR-END

Equity as % of assets: 15.3%
Return on assets: 2.8%
Return on equity: 17.9%
Long-term debt ($ mil.): 580
No. of shares (mil.): 255
Dividends
  Yield: 2.0%
  Payout: 35.3%
Market value ($ mil.): 9,419
Sales (mil.): $6,493

APPLE COMPUTER, INC.

OVERVIEW

Apple Computer may be writing its book of Jobs, but its devoted followers are the ones bearing the company's afflictions with faith and fortitude. The Cupertino, California-based pioneer is best known for the Macintosh computer (Mac), which brought consumers simplified computing with a graphically pleasing interface superimposed over complex instructions. Other products include the hot-selling, brightly colored iMac; the high-performance Power Mac G3 computer; the Mac OS (operating system); the Mac OS X server (Apple's first server); and FileMaker Pro database software. Once the world's top PC maker, Apple lost luster as it became a market also-ran behind the Microsoft/Intel-based PC juggernaut; but Mac maintained popularity in classrooms, Web-page design shops, and graphic arts studios, making Apple a major Web products provider.

Intense, inspirational Apple co-founder Steve Jobs has returned as semipermanent (and salary-less) interim CEO to counteract years of shrinking revenues, defecting executives, market-stealing clone sales, and such troubled products as the discontinued Newton handheld computers. And through it all, Apple owners remained among the industry's most loyal repurchasers.

Jobs has streamlined the company, squelched Mac cloning, bear-hugged old nemesis Microsoft, released the popular iMac low-end PC, and (taking a cue from Dell Computer) begun selling built-to-order systems online. The changes have resulted in some happy news: Apple's first profits since 1995 and a regained market toehold.

HISTORY

College dropouts Steve Jobs and Steve Wozniak founded Apple in 1976 in California's Santa Clara Valley. After Jobs' first sales call brought an order for 50 units, the duo built the Apple I in his garage and sold it without a monitor, keyboard, or casing. Demand convinced Jobs there was a distinct market for small computers; the company's name (a reference to Jobs' stint on an Oregon farm) and the computer's user-friendly look and feel set it apart from others.

By 1977 Wozniak added a keyboard, color monitor, and eight peripheral device slots (which gave the machine considerable versatility and inspired numerous third-party add-on devices and software). Sales jumped from $7.8 million in 1978 to $117 million in 1980, the year Apple went public. By 1983 Wozniak left the firm and Jobs hired PepsiCo's John Sculley as president. Apple then rebounded from failed 1983 product introductions by unveiling the Mac in 1984. After tumultuous struggles with Sculley, Jobs left in 1985 and founded NeXT Software, a designer of applications for developing software. That year Sculley ignored Microsoft founder Bill Gates' appeal for Apple to license its products and make its platform an industry standard.

In 1986 Apple blazed the desktop publishing trail with its Mac Plus and LaserWriter printers; the following year it formed the software firm that later became Claris. The late 1980s brought new competition from Microsoft, whose Windows operating system (OS) featured a graphical interface akin to Apple's.

Apple sued but lost its claim to copyright protection in 1992.

In 1993 Apple unveiled the Newton handheld computer, but sales were slow. Earnings fell drastically, so the company trimmed its workforce (Sculley was among the dearly departed). In 1994 Apple cried "uncle" and began licensing clones of its OS, hoping a flurry of Mac-alikes would boost the design of compatible software; but by 1996 struggling Apple realized Mac clones were stealing sales. That year it hired Gilbert Amelio, formerly of National Semiconductor, as CEO.

In 1997 Apple bought NeXT (intending to use its technology for future products), but sales kept dropping and it subsequently cut about 30% of its workforce, canceled projects, and trimmed research costs. Meanwhile Apple's board ousted Amelio and Jobs took charge. In typical Jobs fashion, the CEO forged a surprising alliance with Microsoft, including putting out a Mac version of Microsoft's popular office software. To protect market share, Jobs also stripped the cloning license from chief imitator Power Computing and put it out of business.

In 1998 Apple revamped its profitable Claris unit (by cutting 300 employees, shifting most operations to Apple, and renaming it FileMaker) and stopped making its Newton, MessagePad, and eMate products. That year Apple also jumped back into the race with its fruit-colored cocktail of iMacs and its first server, the Mac OS X.

OFFICERS

Interim CEO: Steven P. Jobs, age 43
EVP and CFO: Fred D. Anderson, age 54, $604,283 pay
SVP Worldwide Operations: Timothy D. Cook, age 38, $723,953 pay
SVP Worldwide Sales: Mitchell Mandich, age 50, $402,253 pay
SVP Hardware Engineering: Jonathan Rubinstein, age 42, $402,095 pay
SVP, Secretary, and General Counsel: Nancy R. Heinen
SVP Software Engineering: Avadis "Avie" Tevanian Jr.
SVP Service and Support: Sina Tamaddon, age 41
VP; General Manager, Apple Asia Pacific: J. Graham Long
VP Human Resources: Eileen Schloss
VP of Worldwide Marketing: Steve Wilhite, age 47
Managing Director, Apple Computer South Asia: Darke E. Sani
Auditors: KPMG LLP

LOCATIONS

HQ: 1 Infinite Loop, Cupertino, CA 95014
Phone: 408-996-1010   **Fax:** 408-974-2113
Web site: http://www.apple.com

1998 Sales & Operating Income

	Sales $ mil.	Sales % of total	Operating Income $ mil.	Operating Income % of total
North America	3,287	55	45	14
Europe, Middle East & Africa	1,345	23	117	36
Asia/Pacific	1,024	17	59	18
Other regions	285	5	8	2
Adjustments	—	—	100	30
Total	**5,941**	**100**	**329**	**100**

PRODUCTS/OPERATIONS

Selected Products

Color monitors
High-performance computers (Power Macintosh G3 and G4 families)
Internet tools
Multimedia software (QuickTime)
Networking and connectivity tools
Operating systems (Mac OS)

PCs (Power Macintosh, iMac)
Personal productivity software (FileMaker Pro)
Portable computers (Macintosh PowerBook, iBook)
Printers (ImageWriter)
Servers (Mac OS X)
Studio display monitors

COMPETITORS

Acer
Canon
Casio Computer
Compaq
Dell Computer
eMachines
Fujitsu
Gateway
Hewlett-Packard
IBM
Intel
Matsushita

Micron Technology
Microsoft
Novell
Oki Electric
Packard Bell
Philips Electronics
Samsung
Siemens
Sony
Sun Microsystems
Toshiba

HISTORICAL FINANCIALS & EMPLOYEES

Nasdaq symbol: AAPL FYE: September 30	Annual Growth	1989	1990	1991	1992	1993	1994	1995	1996	1997	1998
Sales ($ mil.)	1.3%	5,284	5,558	6,309	7,087	7,977	9,189	11,062	9,833	7,081	5,941
Net income ($ mil.)	(4.2%)	454	475	310	530	87	310	424	(816)	(1,045)	309
Income as % of sales	—	8.6%	8.5%	4.9%	7.5%	1.1%	3.4%	3.8%	—	—	5.2%
Earnings per share ($)	(5.6%)	3.53	3.77	2.58	4.33	0.73	2.61	3.45	(6.59)	(8.29)	2.10
Stock price - FY high ($)	—	50.25	50.38	73.25	70.00	65.25	38.50	50.13	42.50	29.75	43.75
Stock price - FY low ($)	—	33.50	27.25	24.25	41.50	23.00	22.00	32.50	16.00	12.75	12.75
Stock price - FY close ($)	(1.7%)	44.50	29.00	49.50	45.13	23.38	33.69	37.25	22.19	21.69	38.13
P/E - high	—	14	13	28	16	89	15	15	—	—	21
P/E - low	—	9	7	9	10	32	8	9	—	—	6
Dividends per share ($)	(100.0%)	0.40	0.44	0.48	0.48	0.48	0.48	0.48	0.12	0.00	0.00
Book value per share ($)	(0.7%)	11.77	12.54	14.92	18.46	17.45	19.94	23.60	16.53	8.21	11.04
Employees	(4.4%)	14,517	14,528	14,432	14,798	14,938	14,592	17,615	10,896	10,176	9,663

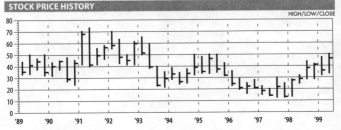

STOCK PRICE HISTORY
HIGH/LOW/CLOSE

1998 FISCAL YEAR-END

Debt ratio: 36.7%
Return on equity: 20.7%
Cash ($ mil.): 1,481
Current ratio: 2.43
Long-term debt ($ mil.): 954
No. of shares (mil.): 135
Dividends
 Yield: —
 Payout: —
Market value ($ mil.): 5,155

APPLIED MATERIALS, INC.

OVERVIEW

Thanks to the proliferation of semiconductors, we are spirits in an Applied Materials world. The Santa Clara, California-based company is the world's #1 maker of semiconductor wafer fabrication equipment. As microchips are incorporated into more and more products, the chip making process continues to create ever-smaller and increasingly complex products. Just as quickly, chip making machinery becomes obsolete — good news for Applied Materials' sales. The company's customers include top chip makers Advanced Micro Devices, Intel, Lucent, and Motorola.

Applied Materials' machines dominate most segments of the chip making industry, including deposition (layering film on wafers), etching (removing excess material from circuit patterns on the wafer), and ion implantation (altering electrical characteristics of certain areas in wafer coatings). The company also makes wafer and photomask inspection tools. It owns half of Applied Komatsu Technology, a Japanese maker of equipment for fabricating thin-film transistors for flat-panel displays.

The company relies on globalization, diversification, and anticipation of market cycles to help it weather recurrent downturns, like the 1997-98 slump. It also depends on heavy R&D efforts to maintain growth. The chip industry is moving to smaller line widths, larger wafers, and new technologies such as copper interconnects. Applied Materials introduced the industry's first systems that accommodate the larger 300mm wafers and facilitate copper interconnects. During the recent downturn it focused on helping chip makers migrate to the latest (0.18 micron) process technology.

HISTORY

Applied Materials was founded in 1967 in Mountain View, California, as a maker of chemical vapor deposition systems for fabricating semiconductor wafers. After growing more than 40% annually, the company went public in 1972. Two years later it purchased wafer maker Galamar Industries.

In 1975 Applied Materials suffered a 45% drop in sales as the semiconductor industry contracted along with the US economy. Financial and managerial problems plagued the company following the recession, so in 1976 James Morgan, a former division manager for conglomerate Textron, was chosen to replace founder Michael McNeilly as CEO. Two years later Morgan also became chairman.

After selling Galamar (1977) and other non-core units and persuading the company's main backer, the Bank of America, to extend Applied Materials' credit limit, Morgan announced a plan to move into Japan. The company's first joint venture, Applied Materials Japan, was set up in 1979.

Morgan's hunch that Japan would become a major producer of semiconductors paid off. His early arrival, plus his attention to Japanese ways of doing business, put Applied Materials way ahead of its American competitors. Morgan wrote *Cracking the Japanese Market* about his experiences doing business in Japan.

Another slump hit the computer chip industry in 1985; Morgan used the slowdown as an opportunity to rev up research and development. With two separate technologies competing for the next wave of wafer manufacturing machines, Morgan essentially bet on the fast but unproven one-at-a-time, multiple-chamber method (as opposed to the existing batch-process system). The resulting Precision 5000 series machines revolutionized the industry and catapulted Applied Materials to the top.

Applied Materials formed a joint venture with Japanese equipment maker Komatsu in 1993 to develop machinery for makers of flat-panel displays. That year Applied Materials' sales passed the $1 billion mark.

In 1995 Applied Materials added a yield increasing rapid thermal processing system to its line. The company skated through a 1996 industry slump caused by overcapacity. Late that year it acquired two Israeli companies, Opal (scanning electronic microscopes used in wafer inspection), and Orbot Instruments (wafer and photomask inspection systems) to grab 4% of the crowded chip inspection tools market. In 1997 Applied Materials received orders from Taiwan Semiconductor Manufacturing Co. worth $413 million (including the industry's largest-ever order, at $182 million).

Responding to an industry slowdown, in 1998 the company took charges totaling $285 million, some of which related to a restructuring plan, and initiated a series of job cuts to reduce its workforce by 25%. Late that year Applied Materials bought Consilium, a maker of factory-floor management software, for about $82 million.

Chairman and CEO: James C. Morgan, age 59, $1,012,104 pay
President: Dan Maydan, age 62, $773,135 pay
SVP, CFO, and Chief Administrative Officer:
Joseph R. Bronson, age 49, $498,977 pay
SVP: Sasson Somekh, age 51, $534,165 pay
SVP: David N. K. Wang, age 51, $534,165 pay
Group VP; President, Applied Materials Japan:
Yoichi Akasaka
Group VP; President, Applied Materials Europe:
Rodney Griffiths
Group VP; President, Applied Materials North America:
Steven A. Lindsay
Group VP, Corporate Affairs: Glen O. Toney
Group VP, Global Human Resources: Seitaro Ishii
VP and Chief Information Officer: Michael A. Graves
VP, Global Controller and Chief Accounting Officer:
Michael K. O'Farrell
VP, Global Finance and Treasurer: Nancy H. Handel
VP, Global Operations: Thomas M. Rohrs
VP, Worldwide Manufacturing Operations: Larry Ward
Auditors: PricewaterhouseCoopers LLP

LOCATIONS

HQ: 3050 Bowers Ave., Santa Clara, CA 95054-3298
Phone: 408-727-5555 **Fax:** 408-748-9943
Web site: http://www.appliedmaterials.com

Applied Materials has facilities in Israel, Japan, South Korea, Taiwan, the UK, and the US.

1998 Sales & Operating Income

	Sales		Operating Income	
	$ mil.	% of total	$ mil.	% of total
Asia/Pacific	1,848	46	386	47
North America	1,549	38	377	45
Europe	645	16	70	8
Adjustments	—	—	(445)	—
Total	**4,042**	**100**	**388**	**100**

PRODUCTS/OPERATIONS

Selected Products

Wafer Processing Systems
Chemical mechanical polishing
Deposition
Chemical vapor deposition
Epitaxial and polysilicon deposition
Physical vapor deposition
Etching
Ion implantation
Rapid thermal processing

Diagnostic Systems
Metrology
Wafer/reticle inspection

COMPETITORS

ASM International	Mattson Technology
Canon	Nikon Corporation
Eaton	Novellus Systems
Ebara	Silicon Valley Group
FSI International	SpeedFam-IPEC
GaSonics International	Steag
Hitachi	Teradyne
JDS Uniphase	Tokyo Electron
KLA-Tencor	Ulvac Japan
Lam Research	

HISTORICAL FINANCIALS & EMPLOYEES

Nasdaq symbol: AMAT FYE: October 31	Annual Growth	1989	1990	1991	1992	1993	1994	1995	1996	1997	1998
Sales ($ mil.)	26.1%	502	567	639	751	1,080	1,660	3,062	4,145	4,074	4,042
Net income ($ mil.)	18.1%	52	34	26	40	100	221	454	600	499	231
Income as % of sales	—	10.3%	6.0%	4.1%	5.3%	9.2%	13.3%	14.8%	14.5%	12.2%	5.7%
Earnings per share ($)	13.2%	0.20	0.13	0.10	0.14	0.31	0.66	1.28	1.63	1.32	0.61
Stock price - FY high ($)	—	2.05	2.53	2.38	3.81	10.00	13.63	29.94	27.75	54.19	40.13
Stock price - FY low ($)	—	1.05	1.08	1.03	1.41	3.66	7.31	9.25	10.88	12.94	21.56
Stock price - FY close ($)	40.8%	1.59	1.09	1.52	3.69	7.88	13.00	25.06	13.22	33.38	34.69
P/E - high	—	10	19	24	27	32	21	23	17	41	66
P/E - low	—	5	8	10	10	12	11	7	7	10	35
Dividends per share ($)	—	0.00	0.00	0.00	0.00	0.00	0.00	0.00	0.00	0.00	0.00
Book value per share ($)	27.1%	0.98	1.13	1.21	1.52	1.86	2.87	4.97	6.58	8.01	8.48
Employees	18.3%	2,651	3,281	3,543	3,909	4,739	6,497	10,537	11,403	13,924	12,060

STOCK PRICE HISTORY

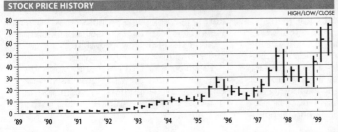

HIGH/LOW/CLOSE

1998 FISCAL YEAR-END

Debt ratio: 16.5%
Return on equity: 7.4%
Cash ($ mil.): 575
Current ratio: 3.15
Long-term debt ($ mil.): 617
No. of shares (mil.): 368
Dividends
Yield: —
Payout: —
Market value ($ mil.): 12,761

ARAMARK CORPORATION

OVERVIEW

"Take me out to the ball game, take me out to the crowd. Buy me some peanuts and ..." Sushi? It's a big seller at some ballparks where ARAMARK has the refreshment concession. The world's third-largest food service provider, the Philadelphia-based firm is a major concessionaire for sports and other recreational facilities and national parks. It also provides food, building maintenance, and housekeeping services for schools, businesses, hospitals, and prisons. Food and support operations make up more than 65% of sales.

In addition to its food business, ARAMARK is the US's second-largest uniform rental company (behind Cintas). It provides uniform services primarily to public employees and the public safety, hospitality, and health care industries. Through its Children's World Learning Centers, ARAMARK provides before- and after-school and employee on-site child care services. The company transferred its magazine distribution business to a joint venture project in which it retains a minority interest.

Chairman and CEO Joseph Neubauer owns about 25% of the privately held firm. Altogether, employees own more than 93% of the company. About 150 ARAMARK employees are "paper millionaires" thanks to the company's stock ownership program.

HISTORY

In 1959 Davidson Automatic Merchandising, owned by Davre Davidson of California, merged with a Chicago vending machine company owned by William Fishman. The two men had become friends through their individual roles as vending machine suppliers to local Douglas Aircraft factories during WWII. Davidson became chairman and CEO, and Fishman became president of the new enterprise, Automatic Retailers of America (ARA).

ARA serviced mainly candy, beverage, and cigarette machines and by 1961 was the US's leading vending machine company, with operations in 38 states. The firm moved into food vending in the early 1960s and served clients such as Southern Pacific Rail. Between 1959 and 1963 it acquired 150 food service businesses, including Slater Systems in 1961, making ARA a leader in the operation of cafeterias at colleges, hospitals, and work sites. ARA went into the food service business despite slimmer profit margins because food servicing was less capital-intensive and more responsive to price changes than vending machines. The company (which changed its name to ARA Services in 1966) grew so rapidly in this period that the FTC stepped in; ARA agreed to restrict future food-vending acquisitions.

ARA began providing food services to the Olympics at the 1968 Mexico City games and has been present at most subsequent Olympics. (Atlanta in 1996 was its tenth.) Also that year it began to diversify into other service businesses, such as publication distribution, and in 1970 it expanded into janitorial and maintenance services by buying Ground Services (airline cleaning and loading services; sold in 1990). A foray into residential care for the elderly — National Living Centers, now Living Centers of America — began in 1973 (and ended in fiscal 1993 with the sale of the last of its stock). This acquisition also led to ARA's entry into emergency room staffing services (sold in 1997). The company expanded into child care (National Child Care Centers) in 1980.

CFO Joseph Neubauer became CEO in 1983 and chairman a year later. Shortly after, to avoid a hostile takeover, he led a $1.2 billion LBO of ARA. Since then the company has been repurchasing shares from other investors (investment banks and employee-benefit plans).

After the buyout, the company began refining its core operations. It acquired Szabo (correctional food services) in 1986, Children's World Learning Centers in 1987, and Coordinated Health Services (medical billing services) in 1993. ARA sold its airport ground-handling service in 1990.

ARA became ARAMARK in 1994 as part of an effort to raise its profile with its ultimate clients, the public. But all has not been rosy — the company's concession operations suffered when baseball and hockey players went on strike in 1994 and 1995.

Acquisitions in 1996 included Gall's, North America's #1 supplier of public safety equipment. In 1997 ARAMARK cooked more than 3,000 pounds of barbecue for baseball fans during opening day of Atlanta's new Turner Field. That year it announced a plan, contingent on stockholder approval, to become 100% employee-owned.

In 1998 ARAMARK entered into a joint venture with privately held Anderson News Company, exchanging its magazine distribution operations for a minority stake in the new business.

OFFICERS

Chairman and CEO: Joseph Neubauer, age 57, $948,000 pay
VC: James E. Ksansnak, age 58, $399,000 pay
President and COO: William Leonard, age 50, $500,000 pay
EVP and CFO: L. Frederick Sutherland, age 46, $364,000 pay
EVP, Secretary, and General Counsel: Martin W. Spector, age 60, $359,500 pay
EVP: Charles E. Kiernan, age 53
EVP Human Resources: Brian G. Mulvaney, age 42
SVP and Treasurer: Barbara A. Austell, age 45
VP, Chief Accounting Officer, and Controller: Alan J. Griffith, age 44
VP: Dean E. Hill, age 47
VP: John P. Kallelis, age 60
Director Audit and Controls: Michael R. Murphy, age 41
Assistant Secretary and Associate General Counsel: Donald S. Morton, age 50
Assistant Treasurer: Richard M. Thon, age 43
Auditors: Arthur Andersen LLP

LOCATIONS

HQ: Aramark Tower, 1101 Market St., Philadelphia, PA 19107
Phone: 215-238-3000   **Fax:** 215-238-3333
Web site: http://www.aramark.com

ARAMARK has operations in Belgium, Canada, the Czech Republic, Germany, Hungary, Japan, Mexico, South Korea, Spain, the UK, and the US.

PRODUCTS/OPERATIONS

1998 Sales & Operating Income

	Sales		Operating Income	
	$ mil.	% of total	$ mil.	% of total
Food, leisure & support services	4,342	68	230	61
Uniform services	1,308	20	116	31
Health & education	361	6	31	28
Distribution services	366	6	(20)	—
Adjustments	—	—	(24)	—
Total	**6,377**	**100**	**333**	**100**

Major Operations

Food and Support Services Group
Business services (dining, meeting, janitorial)
Campus services (maintenance, grounds, custodial)
Correctional services (food, commissary, facility maintenance)
Facility services
Health care support services (patient transportation, groundskeeping, food & nutrition)
Refreshment services (snack and beverage vending)
School support services (facility & food management)
Sports and entertainment services (managed services for professional sports facilities, convention centers)

Educational Resources Group
Children's World Learning Centers (community child care centers)
Daybridge Child Development Centers (worksite child care facilities)
Medallion School Partnerships (before- & after-school programs)
Meritor Academy (private school system)

Uniform and Career Apparel Group
ARAMARK Uniform Services (general uniforms)
Crest Uniform Co. (hospitality and health care uniforms)
E.T. Wright (direct marketer of hard-to-find shoe sizes)
Gall's, Inc. (direct marketer of police, medical, fire/rescue equipment, public employee uniforms)
WearGuard (direct marketer of work clothes)

COMPETITORS

Alex Lee	KinderCare
Angelica	La Petite Academy
Cintas	Levy Restaurants
Compass Group	Ogden
Delaware North	Sara Lee
Fine Host	ServiceMaster
G&K Services	Sodexho Marriott Services
Host Marriott Services	UniFirst
International Multifoods	Viad
ISS	

HISTORICAL FINANCIALS & EMPLOYEES

Private company FYE: September 30	Annual Growth	1989	1990	1991	1992	1993	1994	1995	1996	1997	1998
Sales ($ mil.)	4.6%	4,244	4,596	4,774	4,865	4,891	5,162	5,601	6,122	6,310	6,377
Net income ($ mil.)	14.2%	39	52	64	67	77	86	94	110	146	129
Income as % of sales	—	0.9%	1.1%	1.3%	1.4%	1.6%	1.7%	1.7%	1.8%	2.3%	2.0%
Employees	2.0%	125,000	134,000	135,000	124,000	131,000	133,000	140,000	150,000	150,000	150,000

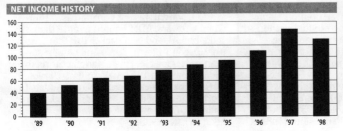

NET INCOME HISTORY

1998 FISCAL YEAR-END
Debt ratio: 100.0%
Return on equity: —
Cash ($ mil.): 21
Current ratio: 1.08
Long-term debt ($ mil.): 1,705

ARAMARK

ARCHER DANIELS MIDLAND

OVERVIEW

Inspect Archer Daniels Midland's (ADM) ingredients, and you're likely to see a lot of items you don't recognize but eat every day. Despite their scientific names, Decatur, Illinois-based ADM makes them primarily by processing the three largest crops in the US: corn, soybeans, and wheat. Once processed, the products are sold to food and beverage manufacturers, including Nabisco and PepsiCo.

ADM's corn by-products include syrups, sweeteners, citric and lactic acids, and ethanol. The company processes soybeans and other oilseeds into vegetable oils and by-products ranging from salad oils and margarine to industrial chemicals and pulp. ADM also produces wheat and durum flour for bakeries and pasta makers and makes its own pasta products. The company owns or leases more than 350 processing plants worldwide.

A price-fixing scheme that cost AMD $100 million not only blemished its image, but dented the bottom line in 1997 and 1998. In 1998 a trio of top executives were convicted in the scheme, including Michael Andreas — son of chairman emeritus Dwayne Andreas and cousin of chairman, president, and CEO Allen Andreas. The Andreas family owns about 5% of ADM.

The company has seen significant growth through the processing of cocoa beans and has expanded internationally, giving credence to its self-appointed title of "supermarket to the world." ADM has interests in food processors in Asia, Canada, Europe, and South America.

HISTORY

John Daniels started crushing flaxseed to make linseed oil in 1878, and in 1902 he formed Daniels Linseed Company in Minneapolis. George Archer, another flaxseed crusher, joined the company in 1903. In 1923 the company bought Midland Linseed Products and became Archer Daniels Midland (ADM). ADM continued to buy oil processing companies in the Midwest during the 1920s. It also started to conduct research (an uncommon practice at the time) on the chemical composition of linseed oil.

ADM entered the flour milling business in 1930 when it bought Commander-Larabee (then the #3 flour miller in the US). In the 1930s the company discovered a method for extracting lecithin (a food additive used in candy and other products) from soybean oil, significantly lowering its price.

The enterprise grew rapidly following WWII. By 1949 it was the leading processor of linseed oil and soybeans in the US and was fourth in flour milling. During the early 1950s ADM began foreign expansion in earnest.

In 1966 the company's leadership passed to Dwayne Andreas, a former Cargill executive who had purchased a block of Archer family stock. Andreas focused ADM on soybeans, including the production of textured vegetable protein, a cheap soybean by-product used in foodstuffs. Soybean oils later became the choice for cooking.

Andreas' restructuring paved the way for productivity and expansion. In 1971 the company acquired Corn Sweeteners (glutens, high-fructose syrups). Other acquisitions included Supreme Sugar in 1973 (sold 1995), Tabor (grain, 1975), and Colombian Peanut (1981).

ADM formed a grain-marketing joint venture with GROWMARK in 1985.

The company continued to expand its global presence in the early 1990s. In 1992 ADM bought Ogilvie Mills (four mills in Canada) from John Labatt. During the 1992 presidential race, the Andreas family made substantial donations to both parties in the hope that the winner would support the use of ethanol in gasoline. Two years later the EPA required that 10% of all gas sold in the US be blended with ethanol.

In 1995 the FBI — aided by company executive-turned-informer Mark Whitacre — joined a federal investigation of lysine and citric acid price-fixing by ADM. In 1996 ADM agreed to plead guilty to two criminal charges of price-fixing and paid $100 million in penalties, a record at that time for a US criminal antitrust case. Whitacre later lost his immunity when convicted of defrauding ADM out of $9 million. He and two other ADM executives, including onetime ADM heir apparent Michael Andreas, were tried and convicted in 1998 and sentenced to prison in 1999.

Meanwhile, ADM continued to grow. In 1997 it acquired W. R. Grace's cocoa business and, after naming Allen Andreas (Dwayne's nephew) as CEO, bought 42% of Canada-based United Grain Growers. ADM bought a more than 8% stake in pork and beef packer IBP that year (increased to 13% in 1998) and bought soybean processor Moorman Manufacturing for $296 million. In 1998 ADM sold its Harvest Burger line of meat replacement products to Worthington Foods for $9.3 million. Dwayne Andreas turned over the chairman post to Allen in early 1999.

OFFICERS

Chairman Emeritus: Dwayne O. Andreas
Chairman and CEO: G. Allen Andreas, age 55,
$2,128,495 pay (prior to promotion)
President: John D. McNamara,
age 50 pay (prior to promotion)
EVP: Charles T. Bayless, age 63, $628,728 pay
**SVP, Group VP, and VP; President ADM/Growmark,
Demeter, and Tabor Grain:** Burnell D. Kraft, age 67,
$861,502 pay
SVP and Assistant to Chairman: Martin L. Andreas,
age 59, $701,186 pay
SVP: Richard P. Reising, age 54, $554,454 pay
Director Corporate Personnel: Sheila Witts-Mannweiler
Auditors: Ernst & Young LLP

LOCATIONS

HQ: Archer Daniels Midland Company,
4666 Faries Pkwy., Decatur, IL 62526
Phone: 217-424-5200   **Fax:** 217-424-6196
Web site: http://www.admworld.com

Archer Daniels Midland operates nearly 250 plants in the
US and about 105 in foreign countries.

PRODUCTS/OPERATIONS

1998 Sales & Operating Income

	Sales		Operating Income	
	$ mil.	% of total	$ mil.	% of total
US	10,784	67	552	77
Europe	3,869	24	111	15
Other regions	1,456	9	57	8
Total	**16,109**	**100**	**720**	**100**

1998 Sales

	$ mil.	% of total
Oilseed products	10,152	63
Corn products	2,154	14
Wheat & other milled products	1,491	9
Other products & services	2,312	14
Total	**16,109**	**100**

COMPETITORS

Ag Processing	Eridania Beghin-Say
Agribrands International	Farmland Industries
Ajinomoto	GROWMARK
The Andersons	Pioneer Hi-Bred
Bartlett & Company	Riceland Foods
Cargill	Scoular
Cenex Harvest States	Southern States
ConAgra	Tate & Lyle
Continental Grain	Universal Corporation
Corn Products	
International	

HISTORICAL FINANCIALS & EMPLOYEES

NYSE symbol: ADM FYE: June 30	Annual Growth	1989	1990	1991	1992	1993	1994	1995	1996	1997	1998
Sales ($ mil.)	8.2%	7,929	7,751	8,468	9,232	9,811	11,374	12,672	13,314	13,853	16,109
Net income ($ mil.)	(0.6%)	425	484	467	504	568	484	796	696	377	404
Income as % of sales	—	5.4%	6.2%	5.5%	5.5%	5.8%	4.3%	6.3%	5.2%	2.7%	2.5%
Earnings per share ($)	0.0%	0.65	0.69	0.68	0.73	0.89	0.73	1.21	1.09	0.60	0.65
Stock price - FY high ($)	—	8.72	11.62	11.64	15.72	14.40	14.34	17.35	17.47	21.75	23.44
Stock price - FY low ($)	—	5.08	7.68	8.72	10.34	11.05	10.92	12.26	12.32	14.13	17.61
Stock price - FY close ($)	9.5%	8.14	10.98	10.63	11.17	11.73	12.19	15.30	16.50	21.30	18.45
P/E - high	—	13	17	17	22	16	20	14	16	36	36
P/E - low	—	8	11	13	14	12	15	10	11	24	27
Dividends per share ($)	18.9%	0.04	0.05	0.06	0.06	0.06	0.06	0.08	0.15	0.18	0.19
Book value per share ($)	8.7%	4.86	5.40	5.96	6.83	7.44	8.04	9.49	10.20	10.84	10.33
Employees	9.5%	10,214	11,861	13,049	13,524	14,168	16,013	14,833	14,811	17,160	23,132

STOCK PRICE HISTORY

HIGH/LOW/CLOSE

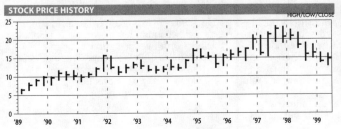

1998 FISCAL YEAR-END

Debt ratio: 30.4%
Return on equity: 6.2%
Cash ($ mil.): 346
Current ratio: 1.47
Long-term debt ($ mil.): 2,847
No. of shares (mil.): 629
Dividends
 Yield: 1.0%
 Payout: 29.2%
Market value ($ mil.): 11,613

ARMSTRONG WORLD INDUSTRIES

OVERVIEW

There is no ceiling too high, no floor too low for Armstrong World Industries. The Lancaster, Pennsylvania-based company makes a wide variety of floor coverings and ceiling systems for commercial and residential use. Armstrong's flooring products (48% of sales) include sheet and tile form, laminate and sports flooring, and linoleum. Its ceiling products are marketed to commercial, institutional, and residential customers, and include acoustical ceilings and suspended-ceiling systems. Armstrong's other products include pipe insulation, gasket materials, and supplies for the appliance, automotive, and textile industries.

Armstrong restructured its business to focus on its core products. It shed unsuccessful operations, including Thomasville Furniture and its stake in Dal-Tile, and entered the wood flooring industry through its Triangle Pacific acquisition, a provider of hardwood flooring and cabinets. Armstrong increased its presence in the global flooring market with the purchase of DLW Aktiengesellschaft, a German maker of flooring products and furniture.

Armstrong's restructuring in favor of core businesses, growth in international markets, and charges related to its workforce reduction affected the company's short-term earnings.

HISTORY

Thomas Armstrong and John Glass started the Armstrong Brothers cork-cutting shop in Pittsburgh in 1860. Armstrong carved the corks by hand, stamped his name on each one, and made his first deliveries in a wheelbarrow.

Concerned with fairness to his customers, Armstrong rejected the maxim "Let the buyer beware" and put a written guarantee in each burlap sack of corks before shipping. By the mid-1890s Armstrong Brothers was the largest cork company in the world. The enterprise changed its name to Armstrong Cork in 1895.

To make up for a dwindling cork market near the turn of the century, Armstrong found new uses for its cork in insulated corkboard and brick. In 1906 the business turned its attention to linoleum (which then was made with cork powder) and started building a new factory in Lancaster, Pennsylvania. Armstrong died in 1908, a year before the linoleum hit the market.

The company continued to make flooring and insulating materials through the 1950s while establishing foreign operations, primarily in Canada, Europe, and Australia. During the 1960s Armstrong expanded its line to include home furnishings by purchasing E & B Carpet Mills (1967) and Thomasville Furniture Industries (1968, sold 1995).

The firm changed its name to Armstrong World Industries in 1980. That decade it rapidly expanded through acquisitions, including Applied Color Systems (computerized color systems, 1981; sold 1989), Chemline Industries (chemicals, 1985), W. W. Henry (adhesives and powder products, 1986), and American Olean (ceramic tile, 1988). In 1989 the company sold its carpet operations.

Armstrong and Worthington Industries combined their suspended-ceiling businesses in 1992, and Armstrong sold its 50% interest in ArmStar (marble flooring tiles).

By the mid-1990s Armstrong had entered a period of cutbacks and other moves that would form a major restructuring. Even though the company's building-products division went on a two-year job-slashing spree (cutting its worldwide workforce by 25%), by the end of 1994 Armstrong's North American sheet flooring unit introduced 166 new products, representing nearly 30% of its sheet flooring line. In 1995 Armstrong sold its champagne cork operation to Spanish investors and exchanged its American Tile Olean subsidiary, plus $27 million, for a 37% stake in ceramic-tile maker Dal-Tile.

To expand international operations, Armstrong made a series of strategic maneuvers in 1996, including linking with Shanghai Advanced Building Materials to open a mineral fiber acoustical ceiling plant in China and forming a joint venture to make soft-fiber ceilings in Europe.

In 1998 Armstrong sold its 34% stake in ceramic tile maker Dal-Tile after failing to gain control of the underperforming company. Also that year the company bought Triangle Pacific, a maker of hardwood flooring and cabinets, for $1.15 billion. It also bought a 93% stake in Germany-based DLW, a flooring and furniture maker.

In 1999 Armstrong agreed to form a joint venture by combining its worldwide insulation business with two insulation companies — NMC/Nomaco of Belgium and Thermaflex of the Netherlands. Later that year, Armstrong agreed to sell its textile product operations to Day International Group, Inc.

Chairman, President, and CEO: George A. Lorch, age 57, $1,757,839 pay
SVP Human Resources: Douglas L. Boles, age 41
SVP, Secretary, and General Counsel: Deborah K. Owen, age 47
SVP Finance and CFO: Frank A. Riddick III, age 42, $718,448 pay
VP Corporate Strategy: Mark E. Adamczyk
VP: Alan L. Burnaford
VP and Controller: Edward R. Case, age 52
VP and Director Corporate Relations: Camilla L. Collova
VP and Treasurer: E. Follin Smith
VP: Stephen E. Stockwell, $557,614 pay
President, Worldwide Building Products Operations: Marc R. Olivie, age 45, $564,986 pay
President, Worldwide Floor Products Operations: Robert J. Shannon Jr., age 50
President, Wood Flooring and Cabinet Operations: Floyd F. Sherman, $671,432 pay
President, Armstrong Insulation Products: Ulrich J. Weimer, age 54, $531,760 pay
Director Taxes: Joseph R. DeSanto
Assistant Treasurer: Marko A. Alvarez
Assistant Treasurer: Joel R. Wittenberg
Auditors: KPMG LLP

LOCATIONS

HQ: Armstrong World Industries, Inc.,
2500 Columbia Ave., Lancaster, PA 17604-3001
Phone: 717-397-0611   **Fax:** 717-396-2787
Web site: http://www.armstrong.com

Armstrong World Industries operates 69 plants in 15 countries, including about 40 in the US. The company has additional plants in seven countries through various joint ventures.

1998 Sales

	$ mil.	% of total
The Americas	1,922	70
Europe	631	23
Other regions	193	7
Total	**2,746**	**100**

PRODUCTS/OPERATIONS

1998 Sales & Operating Income

	Sales		Operating Income	
	$ mil.	% of total	$ mil.	% of total
Floor coverings	1,317	48	176	46
Building products	757	28	117	30
Wood products	346	13	39	10
Industry products	230	8	46	12
Other	96	3	9	2
Total	**2,746**	**100**	**387**	**100**

Selected Products
Ceiling materials for residential and commercial structures
Floor coverings (sheet and tile) for residential and commercial structures
Gasket materials
Pipe insulation
Textile mill supplies
Wood flooring and cabinets

COMPETITORS

American Biltrite	Johns Manville
Celotex	3M
CertainTeed	Owens Corning
Congoleum	Sommer Allibert
Formica	USG
Interface	Wienerberger Group

HISTORICAL FINANCIALS & EMPLOYEES

NYSE symbol: ACK FYE: December 31	Annual Growth	1989	1990	1991	1992	1993	1994	1995	1996	1997	1998
Sales ($ mil.)	1.0%	2,513	2,531	2,439	2,550	2,525	2,753	2,085	2,156	2,199	2,746
Net income ($ mil.)	—	166	144	48	(234)	64	210	123	156	185	(9)
Income as % of sales	—	6.6%	5.7%	2.0%	—	2.5%	7.6%	5.9%	7.2%	8.4%	—
Earnings per share ($)	—	3.72	2.86	0.78	(6.51)	1.27	4.62	2.54	3.61	4.50	(0.23)
Stock price - FY high ($)	—	50.88	38.75	34.50	37.50	55.25	57.50	64.13	75.25	75.38	90.00
Stock price - FY low ($)	—	33.38	18.00	22.88	24.50	28.75	36.00	38.38	51.88	61.50	46.94
Stock price - FY close ($)	5.5%	37.25	25.00	29.25	31.88	53.25	38.50	62.00	69.50	74.75	60.31
P/E - high	—	14	14	44	—	44	12	25	21	17	—
P/E - low	—	9	6	29	—	23	8	15	14	14	—
Dividends per share ($)	6.7%	1.05	1.14	1.19	1.20	1.20	1.26	1.40	1.56	1.72	1.88
Book value per share ($)	0.7%	16.72	17.01	16.65	7.98	8.21	12.70	14.00	19.19	20.20	17.73
Employees	(3.3%)	25,607	25,200	24,066	23,500	21,682	20,583	13,433	10,580	10,600	18,900

STOCK PRICE HISTORY

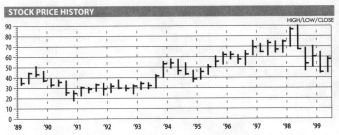

HIGH/LOW/CLOSE

1998 FISCAL YEAR-END

Debt ratio: 68.8%
Return on equity: —
Cash ($ mil.): 38
Current ratio: 1.49
Long-term debt ($ mil.): 1,563
No. of shares (mil.): 40
Dividends
  Yield: 3.1%
  Payout: —
Market value ($ mil.): 2,414

ARROW ELECTRONICS, INC.

OVERVIEW

Arrow Electronics is right on target, maintaining its position as the world's #1 distributor of electronic components and computer products. The Melville, New York-based company's inventory includes semiconductors (about 60% of sales) and computer peripherals. It also sells capacitors, power supplies, and other passive components and interconnect products. Arrow's customers are primarily manufacturers in industries such as aviation and aerospace, computers and office equipment, industrial equipment, medical and scientific devices, and telecommunications equipment, as well as resellers of computer systems. They include global manufacturers such as Alcatel, Cisco, Ericsson, Lucent, Motorola, and Siemens. The company has more than 600 suppliers, with semiconductor maker Intel accounting for 18% of products sold and Hewlett-Packard for 13%.

Acquisitions have helped Arrow best distribution rival Avnet. To help maintain its lead, the company has been consolidating units worldwide in a move toward global coordination. It has also realigned its North American operations — which account for more than two-thirds of sales — around customer segments.

HISTORY

Arrow Radio began in 1935 in New York City as an outlet for used radio equipment. In the mid-1960s the company was selling various home entertainment products and wholesaling electronic parts. In 1968 three Harvard Business School graduates got Arrow in their sights. Duke Glenn, Roger Green, and John Waddell led a group of investors that acquired the company for $1 million in borrowed money. The three also bought a company that reclaimed lead from used car batteries.

With the money they made in the lead reclamation business, the trio expanded Arrow's inventory in its wholesale electronics distribution business. By 1971 Arrow was the 10th-largest electronics parts distributor in the US. The company expanded rapidly during the 1970s, primarily through internal growth, and by 1977 had become the fourth-largest electronics distributor in the US. In 1979 Arrow bought the #2 US distributor, Cramer Electronics. Although the purchase of West Coast-based Cramer was financed with junk bonds and left Arrow deeply in debt, revenues doubled. Arrow went public in 1979.

One year later a hotel fire killed 13 members of Arrow's senior management, including Glenn and Green. Waddell, who had remained at company headquarters to answer questions about a stock split announced that day, was named acting CEO. Company stock fell 19% the first day it traded after the fire and another 14% before the end of the month. Adding to the company's woes, a slump hit the electronics industry in 1981. That year Arrow's board lured Alfred Stein to leave Motorola and lead the company's new management team as president and CEO; Waddell remained chairman. Stein did not mesh with Arrow, and in early 1982 the board fired him and put Waddell in charge again. By 1983 the industry slump was over, and Arrow was temporarily back in the black. However, another industry downturn led to significant losses between 1985 and 1987.

In the mid-1980s Arrow began a major global expansion, acquiring in 1985 a 40% interest in Germany's largest electronics distributor, Spoerle Electronic (it currently owns 90% of Spoerle). President Stephen Kaufman, a former McKinsey & Company consultant, was named CEO in 1986 (Waddell remains VC). Arrow bought Kierulff Electronics, the fourth-largest US distributor, in 1988, and Lex Electronics, the third-largest, three years later.

Arrow expanded into Asia in 1993 with the acquisition of Hong Kong-based Components Agents. Other acquisitions included Anthem Electronics (1994) and Components+Instrumentation (New Zealand, 1995). Italian subsidiary Silverstar (98% owned) in 1996 acquired Eurelettronica, one of Italy's biggest semiconductor distributors. In 1997 Arrow bought the electronic components distribution business of Premier Farnell (a UK-based electronics distributor with operations in 15 countries). The next year it purchased a majority stake in Scientific & Business Minicomputers, a distributor of Hewlett-Packard mid-range computers.

In 1999 Arrow acquired passive components distributor Richey Electronics and the Electronics Distribution Group of Bell Industries. The company also joined rival Avnet, CMP Media, and software firm Aspect Development in a joint venture called ChipCenter, which provides business-to-business, online electronics resources.

OFFICERS

Chairman and CEO; President and CEO, Arrow Electronics Europe: Stephen P. Kaufman, age 57, $1,025,000 pay
EVP and COO: Francis M. Scricco, age 49
EVP, Secretary, and General Counsel: Robert E. Klatell, age 53, $560,000 pay
SVP and CFO: Sam R. Leno, age 53
SVP: Betty Jane Scheihing, age 50, $475,000 pay
SVP; President, Arrow Electronics Asia: Steven W. Menefee, age 54
VP; President, Arrow Asia/Pacific: John Tam
VP; President, Arrow Semiconductor Group: Albert G. Streber
VP; President, North American Components: Jan M. Salsgiver, age 42
VP; President, North American Computer Products: Michael J. Long
VP; Managing Director, Central Europe: Jurgen Saalwachter
VP; Managing Director, Northern Europe: Harriet Green
VP; Managing Director, Southern Europe: Germano Fanelli
VP: John J. Powers III
VP: Paul J. Reiley
VP: Leon Shivamber
Chairman, Arrow Electronics Europe; Chairman and CEO, Spoerle Electronic: Carlo Giersch, age 61, $568,500 pay
President, Internet Business Group: Thomas F. Hallam
President, Arrow Alliance Group: James M. Rosenberg
President, Arrow Supplier Services Group: Wesley S. Sagawa
Auditors: Ernst & Young LLP

LOCATIONS

HQ: 25 Hub Dr., Melville, NY 11747
Phone: 516-391-1300   **Fax:** 516-391-1640
Web site: http://www.arrow.com

Arrow Electronics has 200 sales facilities and 27 distribution centers in 34 countries.

1998 Sales

	$ mil.	% of total
North America	5,351	64
Europe	2,397	29
Asia/Pacific	597	7
Total	**8,345**	**100**

PRODUCTS/OPERATIONS

1998 Sales

	$ mil.	% of total
Electronic components	6,344	76
Computer products	2,001	24
Total	**8,345**	**100**

COMPETITORS

All American Semiconductor
Avnet
Bell Microproducts
Electrocomponents
Future Electronics
Jaco Electronics
Kent Electronics
Marshall Industries
Nu Horizons Electronics
Pioneer-Standard Electronics
Premier Farnell
Rexel
Richardson Electronics
TTI
Wyle Electronics

HISTORICAL FINANCIALS & EMPLOYEES

NYSE symbol: ARW FYE: December 31	Annual Growth	1989	1990	1991	1992	1993	1994	1995	1996	1997	1998
Sales ($ mil.)	27.7%	925	971	1,044	1,622	2,536	4,649	5,919	6,535	7,764	8,345
Net income ($ mil.)	52.9%	3	10	9	45	82	112	203	203	164	146
Income as % of sales	—	0.3%	1.0%	0.8%	2.8%	3.2%	2.4%	3.4%	3.1%	2.1%	1.7%
Earnings per share ($)	—	(0.10)	0.22	0.14	0.77	1.22	1.16	2.03	1.98	1.64	1.50
Stock price - FY high ($)	—	3.38	3.50	8.25	15.25	21.56	22.56	29.88	27.69	36.00	36.25
Stock price - FY low ($)	—	1.56	1.81	1.81	7.19	13.25	16.81	17.56	17.63	25.13	11.75
Stock price - FY close ($)	33.8%	1.94	2.19	7.88	14.31	20.88	17.94	21.50	26.75	32.44	26.69
P/E - high	—		16	59	20	18	19	15	14	22	24
P/E - low	—		8	13	9	11	14	9	9	15	8
Dividends per share ($)	—	0.00	0.00	0.00	0.00	0.00	0.00	0.00	0.00	0.00	0.00
Book value per share ($)	10.7%	6.24	6.32	5.66	6.00	7.30	9.07	11.81	13.27	13.22	15.55
Employees	16.4%	2,475	2,280	4,200	4,100	4,600	6,500	7,000	7,900	9,800	9,700

STOCK PRICE HISTORY

HIGH/LOW/CLOSE

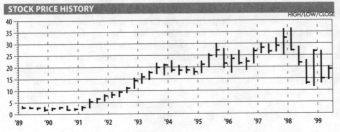

1998 FISCAL YEAR-END

Debt ratio: 41.2%
Return on equity: 9.8%
Cash ($ mil.): 159
Current ratio: 2.46
Long-term debt ($ mil.): 1,040
No. of shares (mil.): 96
Dividends
  Yield: —
  Payout: —
Market value ($ mil.): 2,552

ARVIN INDUSTRIES, INC.

OVERVIEW

Chances are, the next time you enjoy a smooth, quiet ride, you'll have Arvin Industries to thank. The Columbus, Indiana-based company is a manufacturer of automotive exhaust (mufflers, tailpipes) and ride-control systems (shock absorbers and struts). Arvin's other products include automotive filters (Purolator), power-steering pumps, and engine dampers. In addition to the OEM market (68% of sales), the company sells replacement parts under such brands as Arvin, Purolator, and private labels. Replacement customers include Pep Boys, Sears, and Meineke. On the OEM side, Ford and General Motors account for nearly a third of the company's sales; other customers include DaimlerChrysler, Toyota, and Volkswagen.

Arvin operates more than 70 facilities in 19 countries (about 45% of sales come from outside the US). Following the growth strategies of its customers, Arvin has focused on establishing global operations, primarily in Europe. The company is also steering toward developing markets such as Brazil, China, India, and Thailand.

HISTORY

Arvin Industries' origins go back to a 1919 partnership formed by Quintin Noblitt and Frank Sparks in Indiana. Mechanical engineer Noblitt and salesman Sparks formed the Indianapolis Air Pump Company, whose primary product was tire pumps.

In 1920 Air Pump agreed to make heaters designed by Richard Arvin for Ford cars. Air Pump (renamed Indianapolis Pump and Tube) bought out Arvin's stake in Arvin Heater in 1922. It grew in the 1920s, aided by contracts with Chevrolet and Ford. Indianapolis Pump and Tube changed its name to Noblitt-Sparks Industries in 1927. The company made a line of auto parts (including brake levers and hubcaps) and Arvin-brand heaters for every make of car on the market by the time it went public in 1928.

Noblitt-Sparks moved into the car radio market in 1933 and built its first home radio in 1935. By the mid-1930s its mufflers emerged as the company's top-selling product. Sparks left the company in 1937.

During WWII production shifted to the war effort; afterwards, the company began making consumer products such as laundry tubs, irons, and TVs. In 1950 the company changed its name to Arvin Industries, after its popular brand name. It left the TV business in 1955 because of low profits. The next year it launched Arvinyl, a vinyl-to-metal sheet laminate. By 1960 the company was the largest laminator in the US.

In 1962 Arvin Industries bought Westgate Laboratory, its first venture in advanced electronics. The company grew geographically during the 1960s, establishing plants across the US and in Canada, Hong Kong (sold 1973), and Taiwan. In 1974 it produced its first catalytic converter, and in 1978 it acquired Calspan Corporation (Buffalo, New York), a leading R&D company specializing in avionics and energy systems.

With company veteran James Baker at the helm (appointed CEO in 1981), Arvin Industries received several government contracts and expanded globally through joint ventures and acquisitions. In 1988 it bought Amortext, a French maker of shock absorbers, and two years later it began an Australian joint venture, Arvin-Tubemakers, to make exhaust systems. In 1993 it bought a major stake in Italian shock absorber maker Way Assauto, followed by the 1994 acquisition of MTA in Mosciano St. Angelo, Italy (to serve the nearby Fiat factories).

To focus on exhaust systems and ride control products, the company sold its Schrader Automotive unit (tire valves and related products) for $41 million in 1995. That year the company sold Space Industries International (the successor to Calspan) to a management-led group.

Arvin Industries inked a deal in 1996 with Bangkok-based supplier Able (stampings, fuel tanks, brake and fuel lines) to make exhaust systems and catalytic converters in Southeast Asia. The next year it bought out partner Sogefi's half of its Tesh exhaust-components joint venture in Europe and formed a joint venture with Argentina's Profile to make exhaust system parts for Renault and Chrysler. In 1998 William Hunt became CEO; he vowed to boost sales to $5 billion by 2002 through internal growth and acquisitions in core product areas. Arvin launched a joint venture with Japan-based Kayaba Industries in 1998 to make ride-control products. In 1999 Arvin bought a 49% stake in Germany-based Zeuna Starker (exhaust systems), Mark IV Industries' Purolator line of automotive filter products for $282 million, and Kentucky coil coating supplier WorldSource.

Chairman, President, and CEO: V. William Hunt,
age 54, $1,578,615 pay (prior to promotion)
VP Total Quality, Arvin Ride & Motion Control:
Kathaleen Banks
VP; Managing Director, Arvin Ride Control Europe:
Jose L. Berraondo
VP, Strategic Initiatives: Larry D. Blair, age 55
VP Public Affairs and Corporate Communications:
John W. Brown
**VP; Managing Director, Arvin Replacement Products,
Europe:** William K. Daniel
VP; President, Roll Coater: Donald E. Ebert
VP; President, Arvin Ride & Motion Control:
David S. Hoyte, age 52,
$622,832 pay (prior to title change)
VP Worldwide Purchasing: Karl A. Hurston
VP, Financial Operations and Chief Accounting Officer:
William M. Lowe
VP Human Resources: Raymond P. Mack, age 58
VP Finance and CFO: Richard A. Smith, age 53,
$647,554 pay
VP, General Counsel, and Secretary: Ronald R. Snyder,
age 54
VP: E. Leon Viars, age 59, $572,755 pay
Auditors: PricewaterhouseCoopers LLP

HQ: 1 Noblitt Plaza, Columbus, IN 47202-3000
Phone: 812-379-3000   **Fax:** 812-379-3688
Web site: http://www.arvin.com

Arvin Industries has major US manufacturing plants in
Alabama, Indiana, Missouri, South Carolina, and
Tennessee. Outside the US its principal plants are in
Brazil, Canada, France, Italy, Mexico, the Netherlands,
South Africa, Spain, and the UK.

1998 Sales & Operating Income

	Sales		Operating Income	
	$ mil.	% of total	$ mil.	% of total
Automotive original equipment	1,693	68	94	55
Automotive replacement equipment	686	27	72	42
Other	120	5	5	3
Total	**2,499**	**100**	**171**	**100**

Selected Products

Automotive Original Equipment
Catalytic converters
Exhaust pipes
Gas springs
Mufflers
Power-steering pumps
Shock absorbers
Struts
Vacuum actuators

Automotive Replacement Equipment
Catalytic converters
Exhaust pipes
Mufflers
Shock absorbers
Struts

A. O. Smith
Borg-Warner Automotive
Dana
Donnelly
Eaton
MascoTech

Simpson Industries
SPX
Tenneco
TRW
Williams Controls

NYSE symbol: ARV FYE: December 31	Annual Growth	1989	1990	1991	1992	1993	1994	1995	1996	1997	1998
Sales ($ mil.)	5.5%	1,541	1,687	1,676	1,890	1,939	2,040	1,966	2,213	2,349	2,499
Net income ($ mil.)	17.5%	18	34	23	6	40	(16)	19	47	67	78
Income as % of sales	—	1.2%	2.0%	1.4%	0.3%	2.1%	—	1.0%	2.1%	2.8%	3.1%
Earnings per share ($)	19.9%	0.63	1.41	0.81	0.03	1.67	1.15	0.85	2.03	2.85	3.23
Stock price - FY high ($)	—	26.75	19.00	26.38	32.25	37.75	33.75	24.88	25.25	41.63	44.13
Stock price - FY low ($)	—	14.50	13.38	16.25	20.38	25.25	22.81	16.13	16.75	21.00	31.00
Stock price - FY close ($)	11.4%	15.75	17.13	21.75	30.75	32.00	23.25	16.50	24.75	33.31	41.69
P/E - high	—	42	13	33	1,075	23	29	29	12	15	14
P/E - low	—	23	9	20	679	15	20	19	8	7	10
Dividends per share ($)	2.0%	0.68	0.68	0.68	0.70	0.76	0.76	0.76	0.76	0.77	0.81
Book value per share ($)	1.5%	19.07	20.72	20.58	18.45	19.04	17.81	17.76	17.95	19.76	21.83
Employees	(1.3%)	16,900	16,700	16,200	16,000	14,334	13,298	12,071	12,982	14,324	14,963

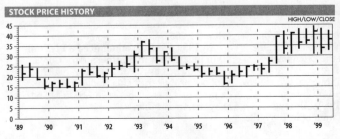

HIGH/LOW/CLOSE

Debt ratio: 35.3%
Return on equity: 13.9%
Cash ($ mil.): 107
Current ratio: 1.32
Long-term debt ($ mil.): 308
No. of shares (mil.): 26
Dividends
  Yield: 1.9%
  Payout: 25.1%
Market value ($ mil.): 1,077

ASARCO INCORPORATED

OVERVIEW

The malleable-metals marketplace is testing ASARCO's mettle. The New York City-based firm is a leading miner, refiner, and smelter of copper (70% of sales). The company also mines zinc and silver, smelts lead, and owns a specialty metals business. Its holdings include a 50% stake in a copper-molybdenum mine in Montana, 54% of Southern Peru Copper (mining and smelting operations), and 50% of Silver Valley Resources (silver mining). Other ASARCO businesses include aggregates (American Limestone Company) and specialty chemicals (Enthone-OMI).

Falling copper prices and the costs of environmental violations have left ASARCO's profits in the hole. A failed merger attempt with rival Cyprus Amax Minerals — the deal would have created the largest publicly held copper company in the world — has left ASARCO shopping for a buyer or partner. The company also is swapping its silver interests in Idaho, Peru, and Bolivia to partner Coeur d'Alene in return for a 20% stake in that silver-mining company. It also is selling its specialty chemicals business.

HISTORY

Henry Rogers, who helped create the Standard Oil Trust, tried to duplicate that effort in the US nonferrous metals industry by founding the American Smelting and Refining Company in 1899 (officially renamed ASARCO in 1975). Rogers began with 23 companies, 16 smelters, 18 refineries, and some mines. Competition from rival M. Guggenheims' Sons and labor strikes forced ASARCO to merge with Guggenheim in 1901. ASARCO became a public company when the Guggenheims sold all but 10% of their stock following the 1907 panic.

ASARCO expanded by acquiring five Mexican mines (1901), Federal Mining and Smelting in Idaho (1903), and a controlling interest in US Zinc (1903). In 1910 ASARCO bought copper mines in Arizona. (It began its first open-pit copper mine there in 1954.) In the 1920s the company started making products using its metals; it later bought a stake in Michigan Copper and Brass (1928; later Revere Copper and Brass, makers of Revere Ware; sold 1982). ASARCO expanded to Peru in 1921. In 1930 it invested in Mount Isa Mines (later M.I.M. Holdings), an Australian miner of silver, lead, zinc, and copper; 20 years later it made a huge copper strike. After WWII ASARCO diversified by producing secondary metals from its ores, and in the 1950s it expanded into asbestos and increased the size of its copper-mining operations in Peru (Southern Peru Copper).

ASARCO increased its copper holdings during the 1980s by buying properties in Arizona from Amoco (1985), British Petroleum's mine in Ray, Arizona (1986), and the Eisenhower Mine from a joint venture of Anaconda and AMAX (1987). ASARCO continued to diversify by buying chemical companies OMI International (1988) and IMASA Group (1989). Although ASARCO ended its asbestos mining in 1989, the company and two subsidiaries were defendants in hundreds of asbestos-related lawsuits, most of which were dismissed or settled by late 1994.

A price drop in 1992 forced ASARCO to suspend operations at its silver mine in Galena, Idaho (1992) and its silver and copper mine in Troy, Montana (1993). In 1993 ASARCO converted its stake in poorly performing Mexico Desarrollo Industrial Minero (copper, lead, and zinc) to a 23.6% stake in Mexico's largest nonferrous metals mining company, Grupo Mexico. That year it completed a $1 billion modernization and expansion program. In 1994 ASARCO sold its principal gold-mining operations, ASARCO Australia.

Despite rising demand, anticipation of a market glut due to higher production caused copper prices to drop in 1996. The price drop, coupled with the Sumitomo-related copper-trading scandal, pushed ASARCO's revenues lower for the year. ASARCO sold its remaining interest in M.I.M. Holdings in 1996 and its stake in Grupo Mexico in 1997. Also in 1996, the US government sued ASARCO and three other mining companies for damage caused to the Coeur d'Alene River by mining activities. The suit is still being contested. Environmental problems proved costly in 1998 as the company agreed to pay over $6 million in fines and spend about $62 million to clean up pollution from operations in Arizona and Montana. ASARCO also sold its Missouri lead business (two mines, a refinery, and a smelter) to Doe Run for $55 million.

In 1999 ASARCO announced a $1.2 million investment in Southern Peru Copper (54%- owned by ASARCO). Also in 1999 copper producer Phelps Dodge broke up a proposed merger between ASARCO and Cyprus Amax Minerals.

Chairman and CEO: Francis R. McAllister, age 56,
$518,750 pay (prior to promotion)
President and COO: Kevin R. Morano, age 45,
$382,258 pay (prior to promotion)
VP Finance and CFO: William Dowd, age 49
VP and General Counsel: Augustus B. Kinsolving,
age 59, $299,004 pay
VP, Government and Public Affairs:
Douglas E. McAllister
VP Commercial: William L. "Gus" Paul, age 48
VP Exploration: Gerald D. Van Voorhis, age 60
VP Environmental Operations: Michael O. Varner,
age 57
VP Human Resources: David B. Woodbury, age 58
Secretary: Robert Ferri, age 51
Treasurer: Christopher F. Schultz, age 47
Controller: Edward J. Melando, age 43
General Auditor: James L. Wiers, age 54
Auditors: PricewaterhouseCoopers LLP

LOCATIONS

HQ: 180 Maiden Ln., New York, NY 10038
Phone: 212-510-2000   **Fax:** 212-510-1855
Web site: http://www.asarco.com

ASARCO's principal mines are in the US (Arizona, Idaho, Montana, Tennessee), Canada, and Peru. Subsidiary Enthone-OMI has operations in Asia, Australia, Europe, and North America; American Limestone has operations in Tennessee and Virginia.

PRODUCTS/OPERATIONS

1998 Sales

	$ mil.	% of total
Copper	1,576	71
Specialty chemicals	351	16
Lead, zinc & precious metals	238	11
Aggregates	57	2
Other	11	—
Total	**2,233**	**100**

Principal Products
Aggregates
Copper
Lead
Molybdenum
Silver
Specialty chemicals
Zinc

COMPETITORS

Anglo American	Inco Limited
BHP	Koch
Carso	Grupo Mexico
Codelco	Mueller Industries
Cyprus Amax	Newmont Mining
Dow Chemical	Phelps Dodge
DuPont	Placer Dome
Echo Bay Mines	Rio Algom
FMC	Rio Tinto plc
Freeport-McMoRan	Union Carbide
Copper & Gold	Vulcan Materials
Homestake Mining	Zambia Copper

HISTORICAL FINANCIALS & EMPLOYEES

NYSE symbol: AR FYE: December 31	Annual Growth	1989	1990	1991	1992	1993	1994	1995	1996	1997	1998
Sales ($ mil.)	0.1%	2,211	2,209	1,910	1,909	1,736	2,032	3,198	2,697	2,721	2,233
Net income ($ mil.)	—	231	149	46	(83)	16	64	169	138	143	(131)
Income as % of sales	—	10.5%	6.8%	2.4%	—	0.9%	3.1%	5.3%	5.1%	5.3%	—
Earnings per share ($)	—	5.50	3.60	1.12	(2.01)	0.38	1.53	3.98	3.42	3.42	(3.29)
Stock price - FY high ($)	—	35.88	34.13	30.50	31.75	28.63	34.88	36.63	36.25	34.25	27.81
Stock price - FY low ($)	—	26.13	22.25	18.25	19.75	16.25	21.38	23.69	23.13	21.75	14.88
Stock price - FY close ($)	(7.3%)	29.88	27.13	21.38	25.00	22.88	28.50	32.00	24.88	22.44	15.13
P/E - high		7	9	27	—	75	23	9	11	10	—
P/E - low		5	6	16	—	43	14	6	7	6	—
Dividends per share ($)	(8.1%)	1.50	1.60	1.60	0.80	0.40	0.40	0.70	1.00	0.80	0.70
Book value per share ($)	1.2%	34.56	36.78	36.24	32.74	35.27	36.04	40.11	40.56	42.71	38.45
Employees	2.4%	9,000	9,300	9,055	8,900	8,500	8,000	12,200	11,800	11,800	11,100

STOCK PRICE HISTORY

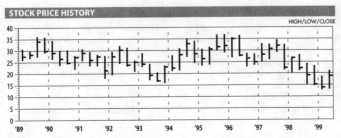

HIGH/LOW/CLOSE

1998 FISCAL YEAR-END

Debt ratio: 40.0%
Return on equity: —
Cash ($ mil.): 193
Current ratio: 1.86
Long-term debt ($ mil.): 1,015
No. of shares (mil.): 40
Dividends
 Yield: 4.6%
 Payout: —
Market value ($ mil.): 600

ASHLAND INC.

OVERVIEW

Ashland has changed its oil and shifted gears. The Covington, Kentucky-based company has spun off its petroleum refining and marketing business into a joint venture, Marathon Ashland Petroleum (MAP), to focus on growth markets in chemicals, highway construction, and automotive products. Acquisitions are paving Ashland's way: In 1998 it bought 20 companies, including specialty chemical makers and paving and construction businesses.

Ashland Chemical, its largest unit, distributes industrial chemicals, thermoplastics, resins, solvents, and fiberglass materials; it also makes specialty chemicals and petro chemicals. Highway construction firm APAC, with divisions in 14 states, is one of the US's top suppliers of asphalt and highway materials. The Valvoline unit, whose namesake motor oil is #2 in the US behind Pennzoil-Quaker State, operates a chain of oil-change centers and markets auto and industrial oils (such as Durablend), auto chemicals (such as Zerex antifreeze), and environmental services. Ashland also owns 58% of Arch Coal, the #2 US coal producer after Peabody Coal, but has announced plans to sell the investment.

The company exited oil exploration and production with the sale of its US operations to Norway's Statoil and its Nigerian upstream operations to Swiss firm Addax Oryx. Ashland owns 38% of the MAP venture; USX-Marathon owns the rest.

HISTORY

Fred Miles sold his Oklahoma oil drilling company in 1917 to wheel and deal in Kentucky. Finding financial backing, he established Swiss Oil Company. In 1924 Swiss bought a refinery in Catlettsburg, a rough town near sedate Ashland, and created the Ashland Refining unit. Miles battled Swiss directors for control, lost, and resigned in 1927.

Swiss bought Tri-State Refining in 1930 and Cumberland Pipeline's eastern Kentucky network in 1931. The company changed its name to Ashland Oil and Refining in 1936. Following WWII it acquired small independent oil firms, winning the venerable Valvoline name in 1950 by buying Freedom-Valvoline.

The firm formed Ashland Chemical in 1967 after buying Anderson-Prichard Oil (1958), United Carbon (1963), and ADM Chemical (1967). Changing its name to Ashland Oil, it added the SuperAmerica convenience store chain in 1970 and by 1973 had begun exploring in Nigeria for oil after OPEC nations raised oil prices.

Scandal hit in 1975, the year Ashland Coal was formed. CEO Orin Atkins admitted to ordering Ashland executives to make illegal contributions to the 1972 Nixon presidential campaign. He was deposed in 1981 after the company made questionable payments to highly placed "consultants" with connections to oil-rich Middle Eastern governments. Atkins was arrested in 1988 for trying to fence purloined documents regarding litigation between Ashland and the National Iranian Oil Company (NIOC). Ashland, which launched the federal investigation that led to Atkins' arrest, settled with NIOC in 1989. Atkins pleaded guilty and received probation.

It was business as usual in the 1990s. Ashland bought Permian (crude oil gathering and marketing) in 1991 and merged it into Scurlock Oil. In 1992 Ashland Chemical bought most of Unocal's chemical distribution business, and two years later it bought two companies that produce chemicals for the semiconductor industry. Also in 1994 Ashland made a promising oil discovery in Nigeria.

The company, now named Ashland Inc., spent $368 million on 14 acquisitions to expand its energy and chemical divisions in 1995. It also received $75 million from its settlement with Columbia Gas System (now Columbia Energy Group) for abrogated natural gas contracts resulting from Columbia's bankruptcy.

In 1996 Paul Chellgren came onboard as CEO, and under shareholder fire Ashland began a major reorganization. The next year Arch Mineral and Ashland Coal combined to form Arch Coal (Ashland is 58% owner), and Ashland made more than a dozen acquisitions to bolster its chemical and construction businesses. Its exploration unit, renamed Blazer Energy, was sold to Norway's Statoil for $566 million. Ashland also pulled ads for Valvoline's TM8 engine treatment: The ads' claims were inflated, said the Federal Trade Commission.

In 1998 Ashland joined with USX-Marathon to create Marathon Ashland Petroleum, thereby leaving the petroleum refining and marketing business. It also bought 20 companies, including Eagle One Industries, a maker of car care products, and Masters-Jackson, a group of highway construction companies. In 1999 Ashland offered to buy Denmark's Superfos, which has substantial highway construction holdings in the US.

Chairman and CEO: Paul W. Chellgren, age 55,
$1,919,135 pay
EVP: John A. "Fred" Brothers, age 58, $980,151 pay
**SVP and Group Operating Officer, APAC and Arch
Coal:** James R. Boyd, age 52, $837,704 pay
SVP and CFO: J. Marvin Quin, age 51, $751,594 pay
SVP; President, Ashland Chemical: David J. D'Antoni,
age 53, $711,079 pay
SVP, Secretary, and General Counsel:
Thomas L. Feazell, age 61
SVP; President, Valvoline: James J. O'Brien, age 44
SVP; President, APAC: Charles F. Potts, age 54
President, Ashland International: John D. Van Meter
Administrative VP and Controller: Kenneth L. Aulen,
age 49
Administrative VP Human Resources: Philip W. Block,
age 51
VP and Chief Information Officer: Roger B. Claycraft
VP: David L. Hausrath
VP Corporate Affairs: J. Dan Lacy
VP, Environmental, Health, Safety, and Medical Affairs:
Andrew C. Meko
VP Planning: Carl A. Peko
VP: Richard P. Thomas
Group VP Distribution, Ashland Chemical:
Peter M. Bokach
Treasurer: Daniel B. Huffman, age 53
Auditor: Lamar M. Chambers, age 44
Auditors: Ernst & Young LLP

LOCATIONS

HQ: 50 E. RiverCenter Blvd., Covington, KY 41012-0391
Phone: 606-815-3333 **Fax:** 606-815-5053
Web site: http://www.ashland.com

PRODUCTS/OPERATIONS

1998 Sales & Operating Income

	Sales		Operating Income	
	$ mil.	% of total	$ mil.	% of total
Chemicals	4,087	62	158	28
APAC	1,444	22	90	16
Valvoline	1,023	16	53	10
Refining & marketing	—	—	239	42
Coal	—	—	25	4
Adjustments	(20)	—	(118)	—
Total	**6,534**	**100**	**447**	**100**

Selected Subsidiaries

Ashland Chemical (chemicals, plastics,
and thermoplastics)
APAC, Inc. (construction)
The Valvoline Co. (auto products and services)
Marathon Ashland Petroleum LLC (38%, refining
and marketing)
Arch Coal, Inc. (58%, coal)

COMPETITORS

AlliedSignal	Old World Industries
BASF AG	PDVSA
Bayer AG	Peabody Group
BP Amoco	Pennzoil-Quaker State
Burmah Castrol	Phillips Petroleum
Chevron	Royal Dutch/Shell
Clark	Sunoco
DuPont	Texaco
ENI	Tosco
Exxon	TOTAL FINA
FINA	Ultramar Diamond
Granite Construction	Shamrock
Hoechst AG	Valero Energy
Lyondell Chemical	Vulcan Materials
Meadow Valley	Williams Companies
Mobil	

HISTORICAL FINANCIALS & EMPLOYEES

NYSE symbol: ASH FYE: September 30	Annual Growth	1989	1990	1991	1992	1993	1994	1995	1996	1997	1998
Sales ($ mil.)	(2.3%)	8,062	8,498	9,246	9,552	9,554	9,457	11,179	12,145	13,208	6,534
Net income ($ mil.)	10.0%	86	182	145	(336)	142	197	24	211	279	203
Income as % of sales	—	1.1%	2.1%	1.6%	—	1.5%	2.1%	0.2%	1.7%	2.1%	3.1%
Earnings per share ($)	6.1%	1.55	3.20	2.54	(5.75)	2.20	2.79	0.08	2.96	3.64	2.63
Stock price - FY high ($)	—	43.00	41.25	35.25	34.00	34.38	44.50	39.88	44.13	54.94	57.94
Stock price - FY low ($)	—	31.63	29.63	26.13	22.50	23.63	31.00	31.25	30.38	39.25	44.13
Stock price - FY close ($)	1.5%	40.38	30.75	30.38	24.88	33.88	35.38	33.38	39.75	54.38	46.25
P/E - high	—	28	13	14	—	16	16	499	15	15	22
P/E - low	—	20	9	10	—	11	11	391	10	11	17
Dividends per share ($)	1.1%	1.00	1.00	1.00	1.00	1.00	1.00	1.00	1.10	1.10	1.10
Book value per share ($)	4.1%	19.62	22.14	24.11	18.12	19.35	21.34	21.28	23.77	26.99	28.12
Employees	(6.2%)	37,800	33,400	33,000	33,700	31,800	31,600	32,800	36,100	37,200	21,200

STOCK PRICE HISTORY

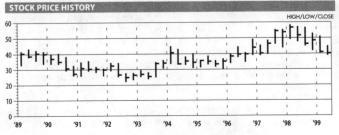

HIGH/LOW/CLOSE

1998 FISCAL YEAR-END

Debt ratio: 41.4%
Return on equity: 9.5%
Cash ($ mil.): 34
Current ratio: 1.34
Long-term debt ($ mil.): 1,507
No. of shares (mil.): 76
Dividends
 Yield: 2.4%
 Payout: 41.8%
Market value ($ mil.): 3,515

ASSOCIATES FIRST CAPITAL

OVERVIEW

Associates First Capital is taking the fast lane now that it has left Ford behind. The Irving, Texas-based company is the #1 consumer finance company in the US (ahead of Household International). It is a major provider of personal and commercial financing, with approximately 4,000 offices throughout the US and 16 countries. Formerly owned by Ford Motor, the company became completely independent in 1998.

Consumer offerings at Associates First Capital include home equity loans (the company's largest segment), manufactured-housing leasing and lease financing, unsecured personal loans, and credit-related and other insurance. Its commercial offerings include truck, tool, industrial, and communications equipment financing; automotive fleet management; employee relocation services; and corporate purchasing and credit card programs. The company has also been aggressive in making inroads into the private-label credit card business; Associates First Capital manages programs for such oil companies as Texaco and Shell Oil and for such retailers as OfficeMax and Tandy's RadioShack.

Independence from Ford has given Associates the opportunity to expand internally and through acquisitions. The company has been building up its credit card operations, with an eye toward cross-selling potential as a countermeasure to industry consolidation and increased competition.

HISTORY

E. M. Morris founded Associates in a South Bend, Indiana, garage in 1918 to lend people money for automobiles. After nearly 20 years of steady growth, the company went public in 1937.

In 1968 Associates was bought by Gulf + Western (the diverse acquirer was a player in the commodities market, as well as the parent of moviemaker Paramount Pictures and parts seller Western Auto). The business thrived in the consumer financing industry as a Gulf + Western subsidiary.

It formed Associates Commercial Corp. in 1975 to finance truck makers, sellers, and operators as well as purchasers of communications gear and heavy equipment. The next year it moved from South Bend to Irving, Texas, along with its parent company. In 1979 Associates expanded into Japan and the UK. Gulf + Western (renamed Paramount Communications) sold Associates in 1989 to concentrate on its entertainment and publishing operations. Ford Motor Company snapped Associates up for $3.3 billion to protect itself from the cyclical nature of the auto industry. The purchase made the automaker the US's second-largest provider of diversified financial services (after Citicorp, now part of Citigroup).

Seeking to protect itself from the ups and downs of operating in a single market, Associates did some buying of its own, including Chase Manhattan's equipment-financing unit (1992) and truck-leasing receivables from the financial unit of Mack Trucks (1993).

In 1995 the company expanded into Mexico, offering consumer finance loans, as well as financing for construction projects, trucking operations, and the communications industry. The firm also formed Associates Rental Systems, leasing over-the-road semitrailers in the Northeast and Midwest.

In 1996 Associates bought the recreational vehicle financing unit of mobile home maker Fleetwood (sold in 1999). Also in 1996 Ford sold to the public 19% of Associates, which lost no time in expanding. Afterwards, Ford melded the fleet service unit of subsidiary USL Capital into Associates, adding more than 100,000 cars, trucks, and vans under lease to more than 1,800 customers and making Associates one of the top vehicle lessors.

The next year Associates bought the credit operations of J. C. Penney, The Bank of New York Company, and Texaco. The company expanded its branch network into Costa Rica and Taiwan and broadened its presence in Canada by buying the consumer loan business of The Great Universal Stores P.L.C. and the commercial vehicle-leasing operations of AT&T Capital (now part of Newcourt Credit Group).

Associates continued to expand in 1998. It acquired SPS Transaction Services, boosting its private-label card processing operation. It also bought 90% of Japan's consumer-targeted DIC Finance, increasing its presence in that growing market. That year Ford spun off its remaining 81% stake in Associates to Ford shareholders, and the FTC included Associates in its probe of subprime lending practices. In 1999 Associates broadened its US and world presence, buying Textron subsidiary Avco Financial Services. Also in 1999 Associates sold one of its credit card payment processing units to Alliance Data Systems to focus on its core activities.

Chairman and CEO: Keith W. Hughes, age 52,
$1,712,500 pay
SEVP Insurance and Business Development:
David A. Brooks, age 59
SEVP and CFO: Roy A. Guthrie, age 45, $662,250 pay
SEVP International: Wilfred Y. Horie, age 53,
$662,500 pay
SEVP Commercial Operations: Lawrence J. Pelka
**SEVP Credit Card; President, Associates Credit Card
Services:** Joseph N. Scarpinato, age 54, $624,750 pay
**EVP Information Services; President, Associates
Information Services:** Walter B. Copeland, age 45
EVP and Chief Credit Officer: A. William Crowley Jr.
EVP, Secretary, and General Counsel:
Chester D. Longenecker, age 52
EVP Human Resources: Michael E. McGill, age 54
SVP Corporate Communications: Sandra J. Allen
SVP Investor Relations: Christopher T. Porter
President, Associates Diversified Services Group:
John D. Kines
Auditors: PricewaterhouseCoopers LLP

LOCATIONS

HQ: Associates First Capital Corporation,
250 E. Carpenter Fwy., Irving, TX 75062-2729
Phone: 972-652-4000   **Fax:** 972-652-7420
Web site: http://www.theassociates.com

1998 Sales

	$ mil.	% of total
US	8,158	87
Japan	750	8
Other countries	469	5
Total	**9,377**	**100**

PRODUCTS/OPERATIONS

1998 Sales

	$ mil.	% of total
Finance charges	7,910	84
Insurance premiums	472	5
Other income	995	11
Total	**9,377**	**100**

1998 Sales

	$ mil.	% of total
Consumer finance	5,878	59
Commercial finance	2,527	25
International finance	1,625	16
Adjustments	(653)	—
Total	**9,377**	**100**

COMPETITORS

AAA	FIRSTPLUS Financial
Advanta	Group
AMERCO	GE Capital
American Express	General Motors
Bank of America	Green Tree Financial
BANK ONE	Household International
Chase Manhattan	Money Store
Citigroup	Newcourt Credit
ContiFinancial	Ryder
Countrywide Credit	Transamerica
First Union	XTRA
First USA Bank	

HISTORICAL FINANCIALS & EMPLOYEES

NYSE symbol: AFS FYE: December 31	Annual Growth	1989	1990	1991	1992	1993	1994	1995	1996	1997	1998
Sales ($ mil.)	15.1%	—	—	3,496	3,696	4,115	4,926	6,107	7,098	8,279	9,377
Net income ($ mil.)	21.6%	—	—	312	410	494	603	723	857	1,032	1,224
Income as % of sales	—	—	—	8.9%	11.1%	12.0%	12.2%	11.8%	12.1%	12.5%	13.0%
Earnings per share ($)	19.3%	—	—	—	—	—	—	—	1.23	1.48	1.75
Stock price - FY high ($)	—	—	—	—	—	—	—	—	24.25	36.28	43.69
Stock price - FY low ($)	—	—	—	—	—	—	—	—	16.56	21.06	22.66
Stock price - FY close ($)	38.6%	—	—	—	—	—	—	—	22.06	35.59	42.38
P/E - high	—	—	—	—	—	—	—	—	20	25	25
P/E - low	—	—	—	—	—	—	—	—	13	14	13
Dividends per share ($)	44.9%	—	—	—	—	—	—	—	0.10	0.20	0.21
Book value per share ($)	22.2%	—	—	—	—	—	—	—	7.84	9.05	11.72
Employees	14.5%	—	—	11,142	12,430	13,933	15,318	16,647	18,980	22,600	28,662

STOCK PRICE HISTORY

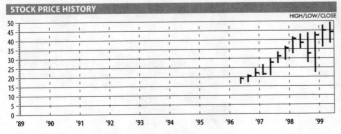

HIGH/LOW/CLOSE

1998 FISCAL YEAR-END

Debt ratio: 81.5%
Return on equity: 14.3%
Cash ($ mil.): —
Current ratio: —
Long-term debt ($ mil.): 37,597
No. of shares (mil.): 728
Dividends
  Yield: 0.5%
  Payout: 12.0%
Market value ($ mil.): 30,844

AT&T CORP.

OVERVIEW

Throw out the walker — old Ma Bell has a new spring in her step. The largest telecom company in the US (90 million customers), AT&T is ready for the race into new markets. The New York City-based company leads MCI WorldCom in US long-distance service and ranks among the frontrunners in other business areas: AT&T Wireless is the #1 wireless provider, with 10 million subscribers, and AT&T WorldNet is #3 among ISPs (behind America Online and Microsoft Network), with 1.5 million customers. AT&T also provides businesses with local and international phone services; data services; and communications outsourcing, consulting, and network integration.

Never satisfied, AT&T has rushed to pick up cable companies so that it can offer more services, including local phone service, over broadband networks. AT&T has acquired Tele-Communications, Inc. (TCI), the #2 US cable player (renamed AT&T Broadband & Internet Services), and has agreed to buy #4 cable firm MediaOne. With these two under its belt, AT&T will pass Time Warner as the US's #1 cable operator. It is negotiating with Time Warner and fellow cable operator Comcast to offer phone service over the companies' cable networks.

AT&T has left Unisource, the shaky European telecom consortium, for a global network services venture with British Telecommunications. With the purchase of IBM Global Network (now AT&T Global Network Services), which provides multinationals with data links, AT&T reaches the ends of the earth.

HISTORY

"Mr. Watson, come here. I want you."

Alexander Graham Bell spoke the telephone's first words in 1876. Bell's backers — fathers of deaf students he was tutoring — founded Bell Telephone (1877) and New England Telephone (1878), combined into National Bell Telephone in 1879.

After much litigation, National Bell barred rival Western Union, which had filed a patent hours after Bell, from the phone business in 1879. National Bell also wrested control of Western Electric, the US's #1 electrical equipment manufacturer, from Western Union in 1882. Bell was incorporated in 1885 as a subsidiary of American Bell Telephone.

Patents expired in the 1890s, and carriers raced into the market. Bell changed its name to American Telephone and Telegraph (AT&T) and became the parent of the Bell System in 1899.

J. P. Morgan gained control in 1907, and AT&T won Western Union in 1909. Facing antitrust action, AT&T sold it in 1913 and agreed not to buy phone companies without approval, beginning a 70-year run as a monopoly. Bell Labs, the heralded research division, was formed in 1925.

In 1949 the government tried to force AT&T to sell Western Electric: A 1956 settlement allowed AT&T to keep its prize but restricted it to phones. The FCC stripped AT&T of its phone equipment monopoly (1968) and allowed rivals, led by MCI (now MCI WorldCom), to use its network (1969). Finally a 1974 antitrust suit led to AT&T's 1984 breakup. Seven Baby Bells took over local service, and AT&T was left with long distance and Western Electric.

AT&T made the ill-advised buy of computer maker NCR in 1991. In 1994 the carrier formally became AT&T Corp. and made a better purchase, McCaw Cellular, then the US's #1 cell phone operator. After the Telecom Act passed in 1996, AT&T sharpened its focus on communications, spinning off NCR and Lucent (network products and Bell Labs) and offering personal communications services (PCS) and Internet access.

In 1997 Michael Armstrong, former Hughes Electronics CEO, became the first outsider to head AT&T. He envisioned the new AT&T as a one-stop telecom provider. The next year AT&T snagged local carrier Teleport Communications, and agreed to form an international venture with British Telecommunications (BT). In 1999 AT&T and BT bought a 30% stake in Japan Telecom. AT&T bought the Japanese and US portions of the IBM Global Network (now AT&T Global Network Services) as part of a step-by-step acquisition.

Also in 1999 AT&T bought cable giant TCI and gained Liberty Media (TV Guide, cable channels) and cable-based Internet company At Home (now Excite@Home). It agreed to pay $58 billion for cable firm MediaOne after persuading Comcast to drop its bid in return for two million cable subscribers. The proposed MediaOne purchase stalled AT&T's negotiations with Time Warner to offer local service over cable lines.

Microsoft agreed to invest $5 billion in AT&T in return for increased (though nonexclusive) use of its software in AT&T cable set-top boxes. AT&T also snapped up some 700,000 wireless customers by buying Vanguard Cellular.

OFFICERS

Chairman and CEO: C. Michael Armstrong, age 60, $3,300,150 pay
President; Chairman and CEO, AT&T Consumer Services: John D. Zeglis, age 51, $1,650,000 pay
SEVP and CFO: Daniel E. Somers, age 51, $1,042,900 pay
EVP, Merger and Joint Venture Integration: Harold W. Burlingame, age 58
EVP, Law and Governmental Affairs, and General Counsel: James W. Cicconi, age 46
EVP, Human Resources: Mirian M. Graddick, age 44
EVP; President and CEO, AT&T Wireless Services: Daniel R. Hesse, age 45
EVP; President, AT&T Network Services: Frank Ianna, age 49, $954,000 pay
EVP; President, Business Services: Michael G. Keith, age 50
EVP, Public Relations and Employee Communication: Richard J. Martin, age 52
EVP, Corporate Strategy and Business Development: John C. Petrillo, age 49, $954,000 pay
EVP; President and CEO, AT&T Solutions: Richard R. Roscitt, age 47
Chairman, Liberty Media Corporation: John C. Malone, age 58
President and CEO, AT&T Broadband and Internet Services: Leo J. Hindery Jr., age 51
President, AT&T Labs and Chief Technology Officer: David C. Nagel, age 54
Auditors: PricewaterhouseCoopers LLP

LOCATIONS

HQ: 32 Avenue of the Americas, New York, NY 10013-2412
Phone: 212-387-5400　　**Fax:** 212-387-5695
Web site: http://www.att.com

PRODUCTS/OPERATIONS

1998 Sales

	$ mil.	% of total
Business services	23,611	44
Consumer services	22,885	43
Wireless services	5,406	10
Local & other	1,321	3
Total	**53,223**	**100**

Selected Subsidiaries and Services

AT&T Broadband & Internet Services
AT&T Canada (22%)
AT&T Labs
AT&T Local Services Division
AT&T Solutions, Inc. (global network and computer management consulting)
AT&T Wireless Services
AT&T WorldNet Service (dial-up Internet access)

COMPETITORS

America Online
Ameritech
BCE
BCT.TELUS Communications
Bell Atlantic
BellSouth
BT
Cable & Wireless
Comcast
CompuServe
Deutsche Telekom
EarthLink
EXCEL Communications
France Telecom
Frontier Corporation
GTE
IXC Communications
Level 3 Communications

MCI WorldCom
Microsoft
MindSpring
Nextel
NTT
Prodigy
SBC Communications
SkyTel Communications
SNET
Sprint
Telco Communications
Time Warner
Qwest
United States Cellular
U S WEST
Vodafone AirTouch

HISTORICAL FINANCIALS & EMPLOYEES

NYSE symbol: T FYE: December 31	Annual Growth	1989	1990	1991	1992	1993	1994	1995	1996	1997	1998
Sales ($ mil.)	4.4%	36,112	37,285	63,089	64,904	67,156	75,094	79,609	52,184	51,319	53,223
Net income ($ mil.)	10.1%	2,697	2,735	522	3,807	(3,794)	4,710	139	5,908	4,638	6,398
Income as % of sales	—	7.5%	7.3%	0.8%	5.9%	—	6.3%	0.2%	11.3%	9.0%	12.0%
Earnings per share ($)	4.0%	1.67	1.67	0.27	1.91	(1.87)	2.01	0.06	2.40	1.90	2.38
Stock price – FY high ($)	—	24.01	22.39	19.81	25.51	31.22	27.44	32.90	33.08	42.69	52.69
Stock price – FY low ($)	—	13.51	13.93	13.93	17.59	24.13	22.69	22.87	22.18	20.51	32.27
Stock price – FY close ($)	9.8%	21.85	14.47	18.79	24.49	25.21	24.13	31.10	28.93	40.90	50.53
P/E – high	—	14	13	73	13	—	14	548	14	22	22
P/E – low	—	8	8	52	9	—	11	381	9	11	14
Dividends per share ($)	1.1%	0.80	0.86	0.88	0.88	0.88	0.88	0.88	0.88	0.88	0.88
Book value per share ($)	2.3%	7.90	8.61	8.27	9.42	6.83	7.62	7.22	8.34	9.30	9.71
Employees	(12.0%)	339,500	328,900	317,100	312,700	308,700	304,500	300,000	130,000	128,000	107,800

STOCK PRICE HISTORY

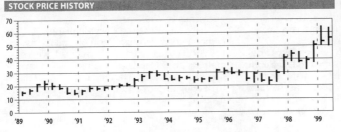

1998 FISCAL YEAR-END

Debt ratio: 17.9%
Return on equity: 25.1%
Cash ($ mil.): 3,160
Current ratio: 0.91
Long-term debt ($ mil.): 5,556
No. of shares (mil.): 2,629
Dividends
　Yield: 1.7%
　Payout: 37.0%
Market value ($ mil.): 132,847

ATLANTIC RICHFIELD COMPANY

OVERVIEW

No, the Atlantic is not the focus of exploration for integrated oil company Atlantic Richfield Company (ARCO). More than two-thirds of Los Angeles-based ARCO's proved reserves (2.8 billion barrels of oil equivalent) are located in the US, mainly in Alaska.

But ARCO engages in oil, natural gas, and natural gas liquids exploration, production, refining, and marketing around the world. Outside the US, ARCO's main production areas include Algeria, China, Indonesia, the North Sea, Pakistan, Russia, and Venezuela. It operates refineries in California and Washington State and has more than 1,700 ARCO-branded gas stations in Arizona, California, Nevada, Oregon, Washington State, and British Columbia. ARCO has an 82% stake in natural gas firm Vastar Resources.

ARCO has sold its US and Australian coal mining operations, as well as its 82% stake in ARCO Chemical, to focus on oil production. Low crude prices, however, have forced the company to cut jobs. Faced with a prolonged price slump and increasing industry consolidation, ARCO has agreed to be bought by UK-based BP Amoco, the world's third-largest integrated oil company.

HISTORY

In 1866 Charles Lockhart and other pioneers in the Pennsylvania oil industry formed Atlantic Petroleum Storage, changing its name to Atlantic Refining in 1870 after buying a small refinery. It became a secret affiliate of Standard Oil in 1874 and was spun off by order of the US Supreme Court in 1911.

In the 1920s Atlantic Refining explored for oil in Iraq, and in the 1930s it designed the first all-welded ship. Through the 1950s and 1960s, the company bought oil and plastics businesses, including Hondo Oil & Gas (1963) from larger-than-life oilman Robert Anderson, who became the company's top shareholder and was elected chairman in 1965.

Under Anderson, Atlantic Refining grew from a small East Coast oil refiner to a large West Coast integrated oil leader. In 1966 it purchased Richfield Oil and adopted Atlantic Richfield Company, or ARCO, as its name. Richfield brought an exploration site on Alaska's North Slope at Prudhoe Bay.

In 1968 ARCO, exploring on the North Slope with Humble Oil (later Exxon), drilled into North America's largest oil deposit. To transport the oil to the lower 48 states, eight oil companies formed the Trans-Alaska Pipeline System. The field began production in 1977, and oil flowed from Prudhoe Bay to the ice-free coastal waters of Valdez, 800 miles away.

ARCO bought Sinclair Oil in 1969, and in 1972 it relocated to Los Angeles. To diversify, it bought Anaconda (1977), a Montana copper and uranium mining enterprise.

ARCO foresaw that OPEC was a leaky cartel and that oil prices were destined to fall. So, in 1982, ARCO became the first oil major to introduce cut-rate, self-service stations. In 1985 it repurchased about $4 billion worth of stock to become a less appealing takeover target, dumped its noncore businesses, including Anaconda, and buttressed its energy and chemical concerns. It spun off part of a chemical unit to create wholly owned Lyondell Petrochemical (now Lyondell Chemical). In 1986 Anderson retired, and Lodwrick Cook, who had started out pumping gas at a family store, took the helm. The firm sold a stake in ARCO Chemical to the public in 1987. Two years later ARCO spun off 50.1% of Lyondell.

On Cook's watch, ARCO slowed oil and gas investments, and production declined. ARCO finally added to its Alaskan properties in 1993 when it acquired 130,000 acres of leases in partnership with Phillips Petroleum. It took a 10% stake in China's Zhenhai Refining & Chemical in 1994, as Cook made way for Texan Mike Bowlin.

ARCO was expanding internationally, including in some trouble spots. In 1995 ARCO bought about 8% of Russia's LUKOIL and in 1997 forged an oil and gas joint venture, LUKARCO. It also purchased Elf Aquitaine's Tunisian oil assets. Meanwhile, ARCO began selling noncore businesses, including the rest of Lyondell, to focus on oil again.

In 1998 ARCO bought Union Texas Petroleum for $3.3 billion. As oil prices plunged, it sold its 82% stake in ARCO Chemical to Lyondell and began unloading its coal businesses. In 1999 it agreed to sell Union Texas Petrochemicals to Williams.

That year ARCO and Chevron planned to combine their Permian Basin oil and gas assets. But ARCO had become overstretched, with operations in 29 countries, and its Russian investment was a disaster. Needing time and capital to develop its properties, it agreed to be bought by giant BP Amoco in a $27 billion deal.

Chairman and CEO: Mike R. Bowlin, age 56, $1,720,000 pay
President and COO: Michael E. Wiley, age 48, $858,269 pay
EVP and CFO: Marie L. Knowles, age 52, $810,000 pay
EVP: J. Kenneth Thompson, age 47, $714,231 pay
EVP: Donald R. Voelte Jr., age 46, $644,173 pay
SVP and Treasurer: Terry G. Dallas, age 48
SVP, Human Resources: John H. Kelly, age 44
SVP; President, ARCO Alaska: Kevin O. Meyers, age 44
SVP; President, ARCO Products: Roger E. Truitt, age 53
SVP, General Counsel, and Corporate Secretary: Bruce G. Whitmore, age 54
VP and Controller: Allan L. Comstock, age 55
VP, Exploration: Dodd W. DeCamp
VP and General Tax Officer: Patrick J. Ellingsworth
VP and Investment Officer; President, ARCO Investment Management: Beverly L. Hamilton
VP, Federal Government Relations: Robert L. Healy
VP, Corporate Planning: Dennis D. Schiffel, age 55
VP, Technology and Operations Services: Stephen G. Suellentrop
VP, Communications, Public Affairs, and Investor Relations: Beverly L. Thelander, age 43
Auditors: PricewaterhouseCoopers LLP

LOCATIONS

HQ: 515 S. Flower St., Los Angeles, CA 90071
Phone: 213-486-3511 **Fax:** 213-486-2063
Web site: http://www.arco.com

Atlantic Richfield has interests in Algeria, China, Indonesia, Pakistan, Russia, Tunisia, the UK, the United Arab Emirates, the US, and Venezuela, as well as in the Caspian Sea, Gulf of Mexico, and the UK sector of the North Sea. It owns service stations in Arizona, California, Nevada, Oregon, Washington State, and British Columbia and refineries in California and Washington State.

PRODUCTS/OPERATIONS

1998 Sales

	$ mil.	% of total
Exploration & production	5,934	51
Refining & marketing	5,484	47
Chemicals	172	2
Adjustments	(1,287)	—
Total	**10,303**	**100**

Selected Subsidiaries and Joint Ventures
ARCO Alaska, Inc.
ARCO Pipeline
ARCO Products
LUKARCO (46%, Russia)
Vastar Resources, Inc. (82%)

COMPETITORS

Amerada Hess	Occidental
Ashland	PDVSA
BHP	PEMEX
BP Amoco	Petrobras
Chevron	Phillips Petroleum
Coastal	Repsol-YPF
Conoco	Royal Dutch/Shell
Elf Aquitaine	Sunoco
Exxon	Texaco
Imperial Oil	Tosco
Kerr-McGee	TOTAL FINA
Koch	USX-Marathon
Mobil	

HISTORICAL FINANCIALS & EMPLOYEES

NYSE symbol: ARC FYE: December 31	Annual Growth	1989	1990	1991	1992	1993	1994	1995	1996	1997	1998
Sales ($ mil.)	(4.3%)	15,351	18,008	17,037	17,503	17,189	15,035	15,819	18,592	18,684	10,303
Net income ($ mil.)	(15.0%)	1,953	2,011	709	801	269	919	1,376	1,663	1,771	452
Income as % of sales	—	12.7%	11.2%	4.2%	4.6%	1.6%	6.1%	8.7%	8.9%	9.5%	4.4%
Earnings per share ($)	(14.3%)	5.63	6.08	2.20	2.48	0.83	2.82	4.22	3.86	3.71	1.40
Stock price – FY high ($)	—	57.19	71.13	67.88	60.88	63.88	56.19	58.94	71.25	87.25	84.69
Stock price – FY low ($)	—	40.19	52.75	49.56	49.06	50.25	46.25	50.25	53.75	62.19	56.25
Stock price – FY close ($)	1.8%	55.69	61.81	53.38	57.38	52.63	50.88	55.38	66.25	80.13	65.38
P/E – high	—	10	12	31	25	77	20	14	18	24	60
P/E – low	—	7	9	23	20	61	16	12	14	17	40
Dividends per share ($)	2.7%	2.25	2.50	2.75	2.75	2.75	2.75	2.80	2.75	2.83	2.85
Book value per share ($)	1.9%	19.98	22.49	21.67	21.14	19.15	19.52	21.01	24.21	26.89	23.59
Employees	(4.0%)	26,600	27,300	27,700	26,800	25,100	23,200	22,000	22,800	24,000	18,400

STOCK PRICE HISTORY

HIGH/LOW/CLOSE

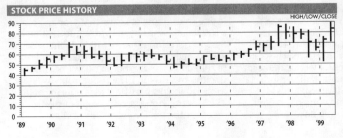

1998 FISCAL YEAR-END
Debt ratio: 36.4%
Return on equity: 6.0%
Cash ($ mil.): 657
Current ratio: 0.48
Long-term debt ($ mil.): 4,332
No. of shares (mil.): 321
Dividends
  Yield: 4.4%
  Payout: 203.6%
Market value ($ mil.): 21,008

AUTOMATIC DATA PROCESSING, INC.

OVERVIEW

ADP has withstood the process of time. With more than 425,000 accounts, Automatic Data Processing (ADP) is the #1 payroll services provider in the world. The Roseland, New Jersey-based company's payroll and tax processing services make up more than half of its revenues. ADP's Brokerage Services unit provides support and securities transaction processing for firms worldwide, while its Dealer Services unit provides inventory and other computing and data services to more than 18,000 auto and truck dealers. Other services include accounting and auto collision estimates for insurers.

Effective management and a focused strategy have steered ADP to double-digit per-share earnings growth for more than 35 years running, resulting in strong cash flow. The data processing giant has also been buoyed by the growing US economy and the trend toward outsourcing payroll by American corporations.

ADP is expanding internationally and extending its existing services through acquisitions (it bought 11 established providers from around the world in fiscal 1998 alone). It also continues to establish its contract-worker business, which has doubled since ADP entered the field in 1996.

HISTORY

In 1949, 22-year-old Henry Taub started Automatic Payrolls, a manual payroll preparation service in Paterson, New Jersey. Taub's eight accounts created gross revenues of around $2,000 that year. In 1952 his brother Joe joined the company, and a childhood friend, Frank Lautenberg, took a pay cut to become the firm's first salesman.

The company grew steadily during the 1950s. In 1961 it went public and changed its name to Automatic Data Processing. The next year it offered back-office services to brokerage houses and bought its first computer. ADP's revenues reached $1 million in 1962.

During the 1970s, ADP bought more than 30 companies in the US, Brazil, and the UK, all involved in data and payroll processing, shareholder services, computer networks, inventory control, or automated banking. Its stock began trading on the NYSE in 1970, revenues reached $50 million in 1971, and the company started data centers in Florida in 1972 and Connecticut in 1973. Lautenberg became CEO in 1975.

ADP bought more than 25 businesses during the 1980s in the US, Canada, and Germany, mainly in data and information services. Its purchases of stock information provider GTE Telenet (1983) and Bunker Ramo's information system business (1986) brought the company 45,000 stock quote terminals. When Lautenberg resigned as CEO to become one of New Jersey's US senators in 1983, Josh Weston, who had joined the company in 1970, replaced him.

By 1985 ADP revenues had climbed to $1 billion. Soon after, founder Taub retired. The company installed 15,000 computer workstations at brokerages in 1986; it began installing more than 38,000 new integrated workstations at Merrill Lynch and Shearson Lehman three years later. ADP shed units, including its

Canadian stock quote and Brazilian businesses, in 1989 and 1990.

After being deterred from major acquisitions by the inflated prices of the late 1980s, ADP purchased BankAmerica Corp.'s 17,000-client Business Services division (1992) and Industry Software Corp.'s back-office and international equities business (1993).

In 1994 the company purchased Peachtree Software (accounting and payroll software for small companies), National Bio Systems (medical bill auditing), and V-Crest (auto dealership management systems). ADP acquired chief rival AutoInfo and its network of 3,000 salvage yards in 1995, and further expanded into Western Europe with its purchase of Paris-based computing services firm GSI.

The buying binge continued in 1996 with such purchases as Global Proxy Services Corp. (proxy processing services), Health Benefits America (benefits management), and Merrin Financial (automated securities trade order management). Arthur Weinbach, a former Deloitte & Touche partner and ADP executive since 1980, was named CEO in 1996. ADP was ordered in an antitrust settlement the next year to help recreate AutoInfo as a viable competitor to ADP's salvage yard business.

Among its 11 acquisitions in 1998 was Swiss Reinsurance's European collision estimates business. The company also sold its money-losing stock quote business that year and took a 5% stake in the buyer, Bridge Information Systems. Weston retired in 1998; Weinbach was named chairman. The company also filed to spin off Peachtree, but in early 1999 it sold the unit to UK-based The Sage Group in a $145 million deal. In 1999 the company bought The Vincam Group, an employment management contractor, for about $295 million.

Chairman and CEO: Arthur F. Weinbach, age 55, $1,037,500 pay
President and COO: Gary C. Butler, age 51, $931,151 pay
SVP: Eugene A. Hall, age 42
Group President, Employer Services: Russell P. Fradin, age 43, $645,595 pay
Group President, Brokerage Services: Richard J. Daly, age 45, $513,269 pay
Group President, Brokerage Services: John P. Hogan, age 50, $508,270 pay
Group President, Dealer Services: S. Michael Martone, age 50
VP Finance and CFO: Richard J. Haviland, age 52
VP, Secretary, and General Counsel: James B. Benson, age 53
VP Human Resources: Richard C. Berke, age 53
VP and Treasurer: Raymond L. Colotti
VP Worldwide Business Development: G. Harry Durity, age 51
Auditors: Deloitte & Touche LLP

LOCATIONS

HQ: 1 ADP Blvd., Roseland, NJ 07068
Phone: 973-994-5000   **Fax:** 973-994-5387
Web site: http://www.adp.com

Automatic Data Processing has more than 55 processing centers in Asia, Australia, Canada, Europe, South Africa, South America, and the US.

1998 Sales

	$ mil.	% of total
US	4,013	84
Europe	493	10
Other regions	261	5
Adjustments	31	1
Total	**4,798**	**100**

PRODUCTS/OPERATIONS

1998 Sales

	$ mil.	% of total
Employer services	2,747	57
Brokerage services	1,100	23
Dealer services	698	15
Other	253	5
Total	**4,798**	**100**

Employer Services
Benefits outsourcing
Human resource record keeping and reporting
Payroll processing and tax filing

Brokerage Services
Desktop applications support
Investor support tools
Securities transaction processing

Dealer Services
Asset management
Computer systems sales/support
Employee productivity training
Manufacturer/dealer data communications networks
Vehicle registration services

Claims Services
Collision repair estimating
Parts identification, location, and pricing
Vehicle replacement valuation

COMPETITORS

BISYS	First Data	Paychex
Ceridian	Fiserv	Payroll 1
Computer	GSI SA	ProBusiness
Language	H&R Block	Services
Research	Intuit	SEI
Concentrex	Kronos	TEAM America
Concord EFS	Paradyme	TriNet

HISTORICAL FINANCIALS & EMPLOYEES

NYSE symbol: AUD FYE: June 30	Annual Growth	1989	1990	1991	1992	1993	1994	1995	1996	1997	1998
Sales ($ mil.)	12.4%	1,678	1,714	1,772	1,941	2,223	2,469	2,894	3,567	4,112	4,798
Net income ($ mil.)	13.9%	188	212	228	256	294	329	395	455	514	605
Income as % of sales	—	11.2%	12.4%	12.9%	13.2%	13.2%	13.3%	13.6%	12.7%	12.5%	12.6%
Earnings per share ($)	13.8%	0.31	0.36	0.41	0.46	0.52	0.57	0.68	0.77	0.86	0.99
Stock price - FY high ($)	—	5.19	7.34	9.25	12.25	14.03	14.22	16.50	21.69	25.06	36.44
Stock price - FY low ($)	—	4.33	4.94	5.66	7.56	9.69	11.75	12.69	15.47	17.81	22.19
Stock price - FY close ($)	24.6%	5.02	6.91	8.13	10.69	12.00	13.28	15.72	19.31	23.50	36.44
P/E - high	—	17	20	23	27	27	25	24	28	29	37
P/E - low	—	14	14	14	16	19	21	19	20	21	22
Dividends per share ($)	15.2%	0.07	0.08	0.09	0.10	0.12	0.13	0.15	0.19	0.22	0.25
Book value per share ($)	14.8%	1.63	1.91	1.90	2.31	2.65	3.01	3.64	4.02	4.54	5.64
Employees	5.5%	21,000	19,000	19,000	20,500	21,000	22,000	25,000	29,000	30,000	34,000

STOCK PRICE HISTORY

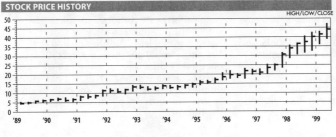

HIGH/LOW/CLOSE

1998 FISCAL YEAR-END

Debt ratio: 5.3%
Return on equity: 17.8%
Cash ($ mil.): 752
Current ratio: 1.50
Long-term debt ($ mil.): 192
No. of shares (mil.): 604
Dividends
  Yield: 0.7%
  Payout: 25.3%
Market value ($ mil.): 22,017

AUTONATION INC.

OVERVIEW

Never one to let a blockbuster idea go to waste, Wayne Huizenga has used rapid-fire acquisitions to build Fort Lauderdale, Florida-based AutoNation into the nation's #1 car dealer (United Auto Group is a distant second). The company is also #1 in the US rental car business, but has announced plans to divest its rental unit in order to focus on its auto retailing.

Formerly known as Republic Industries, the company has been a driving force in the consolidation of the US car-sales business. It owns or has agreed to buy about 400 new-car dealerships and 45 or so AutoNation USA used-vehicle megastores, often clustering its dealerships within markets so that they can share inventory, cross-sell to customers, and reduce marketing costs. AutoNation is still tinkering with dealership formats, most notably by combining national and local identities — as well as a no-haggling policy — at its John Elway AutoNation stores in Colorado. It also sells cars online.

The firm's car rental operations include Alamo Rent A Car, which caters to leisure travelers; National Car Rental System, which primarily serves business travelers; and insurance-replacement renter CarTemps USA. AutoNation operates, licenses, or franchises about 4,000 rental locations worldwide.

Huizenga owns about 5% of AutoNation.

HISTORY

AutoNation started in 1980 as Republic Resources, which brokered petroleum leases, did exploration and production, and blended lubricants. In 1989, after oil prices crashed and a stockholder group tried to force Republic into liquidation, Browning-Ferris Industries (BFI) founder Thomas Fatjo gained control of the company and refocused it on a field he knew well — solid waste. He renamed the firm Republic Waste.

Michael DeGroote, founder of BFI rival Laidlaw, bought into Republic in 1990. (Fatjo left the next year.) DeGroote's investment funded more acquisitions. Republic moved into hazardous waste in 1992, just before the industry nosedived due to stringent new environmental rules. In 1994 Republic spun off its hazardous-waste operations as Republic Environmental Systems, and Republic's stock began rising immediately.

That attracted the attention of Wayne Huizenga, who had founded Waste Management and Blockbuster Video. To him, Republic was not merely a midsized solid-waste firm. No, Huizenga saw Republic as a publicly traded vehicle that could allow him to tap into the stock market to fund his latest project: an integrated, nationwide auto dealer — a first for the highly fragmented and localized industry.

In 1995 Republic bought Hudson Management, a trash business owned by Huizenga's brother-in-law, and Huizenga bought a large interest in Republic. As a result, Huizenga took control of Republic's board. The firm became Republic Industries, and DeGroote stepped back from active management.

Huizenga's investment helped Republic acquire more waste businesses, and his name brought a flood of new investors. The company diversified with electronic security acquisitions, but growth in this field faltered with a failed bid to buy market leader ADT in 1996. (Republic sold its security division to Ameritech in 1997.)

By 1996 Huizenga's still-separate auto concept, AutoNation, was operational, with 55 automobile franchises and seven used-car stores. Republic bought Alamo Rent A Car and National Car Rental System, and in 1997 AutoNation (headed by Steven Berrard) was bought by Republic. The combined company continued buying dealerships and car rental firms at a sizzling rate. To gain a foothold in Europe, the company acquired EuroDollar Holdings, the UK's #2 rental car company, and folded its operations into National.

Republic spun off its solid-waste operations to the public in 1998 as Republic Services. That year Republic bought or agreed to buy 181 new-car franchises, opened nine AutoNation USA dealerships, and opened 62 CarTemps USA insurance-replacement locations.

Stepping up its marketing efforts, Republic hired John Costello (creator of the "Softer Side of Sears" campaign), who took over as president in 1999, but he quickly resigned. Republic trashed the most visible connection to its waste-hauling past in 1999 by adopting AutoNation as its corporate moniker. The company announced in midyear that co-CEO Berrard would leave AutoNation and that Huizenga would give up his own co-CEO title once a new chief was found.

The company joined forces in 1999 with online bidding service priceline.com to offer "name your own price" car sales through the Internet.

Chairman and Co-CEO: H. Wayne Huizenga, age 60, $1,000,000 pay
VC: Harris W. Hudson, age 56
Co-CEO: Steven R. Berrard, age 44, $1,400,000 pay (prior to title change)
President and COO: Michael E. Maroone
SVP Information Technology: H. Scott Barrett
SVP, General Counsel, and Secretary: James O. Cole, age 58, $402,876 pay
SVP Human Resources: Robert E. Dees Jr.
SVP Corporate Communications: James J. Donahue Jr., age 42
SVP Corporate Real Estate Services: Robert F. Dwors
SVP Corporate Development: Thomas W. Hawkins, age 37, $398,536 pay
SVP and CFO; President of AutoNation Rental Group: Michael S. Karsner, age 40, $458,975 pay
VP AutoRewards (SM): Maria Bailey, age 34
VP Operations Planning: Jeffrey G. Davis
VP Finance: Kathleen Hyle
VP Internal Communications: Leslye Mundy
VP and Corporate Controller: Mary E. Wood, age 43
President North American Rental Group: Jeffrey J. Parell
Auditors: Arthur Andersen LLP

LOCATIONS

HQ: 110 SE 6th St., Fort Lauderdale, FL 33301
Phone: 954-769-6000   **Fax:** 954-769-6408
Web site: http://www.autonation.com

AutoNation has new-car dealerships in 20 states and used-car dealerships in 13 states. Its Alamo Rent A Car, National Car Rental System, and CarTemps USA units have locations in more than 65 countries.

PRODUCTS/OPERATIONS

1998 Sales

	$ mil.	% of total
Auto sales	12,664	79
Auto rental	3,454	21
Total	**16,118**	**100**

Primary Operations
  Auto Retail Group
    AutoNation Financial Services (financing and insurance)
    AutoNation USA (used-vehicle megastores)
    AutoNationDirect.com (internet sales)
    Franchised vehicle dealerships
  Auto Rental Group
    Alamo Rent A Car (leisure travelers' car rental)
    CarTemps USA (insurance-replacement market car rental)
    National Car Rental System (business travelers' car rental)

COMPETITORS

ARRIVA	Hertz
Asbury Automotive	Holman Enterprises
Avis Europe	JM Family Enterprises
Bill Heard	Mid-Atlantic Cars
Budget Group	Morse Operations
CarMax	Penske Automotive
Cendant	Potamkin
Dollar Thrifty Automotive Group	Sixt
Enterprise Rent-A-Car	Sonic Automotive
Group 1 Automotive	United Auto Group
Hendrick Automotive	VT

HISTORICAL FINANCIALS & EMPLOYEES

NYSE symbol: AN FYE: December 31	Annual Growth	1989	1990	1991	1992	1993	1994	1995	1996	1997	1998
Sales ($ mil.)	210.5%	1	32	52	110	103	49	260	2,366	10,306	16,118
Net income ($ mil.)	—	(0)	2	2	(14)	(19)	11	23	(60)	440	500
Income as % of sales	—	—	6.0%	4.1%	—	—	23.4%	8.8%	—	4.3%	3.1%
Earnings per share ($)	26.7%	—	0.16	0.07	(0.27)	0.07	0.26	0.07	(0.05)	1.02	1.06
Stock price - FY high ($)	—	—	12.63	7.88	6.81	2.75	2.06	18.06	34.63	44.38	30.00
Stock price - FY low ($)	—	—	2.94	2.31	2.25	1.38	1.25	1.50	13.19	19.00	10.00
Stock price - FY close ($)	20.4%	—	3.38	6.06	2.63	1.69	2.00	18.06	31.19	23.31	14.88
P/E - high	—	—	79	113	—	39	8	258	—	44	28
P/E - low	—	—	18	33	—	20	5	21	—	19	9
Dividends per share ($)	—	—	0.00	0.00	0.00	0.00	0.00	0.00	0.00	0.00	0.00
Book value per share ($)	27.2%	—	1.73	4.52	1.78	1.42	1.62	2.87	4.93	8.05	11.84
Employees	95.3%	—	—	—	756	683	398	4,090	30,300	56,000	42,000

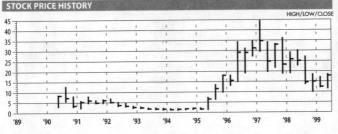

STOCK PRICE HISTORY
HIGH/LOW/CLOSE

1998 FISCAL YEAR-END
Debt ratio: 29.9%
Return on equity: 9.2%
Cash ($ mil.): 774
Current ratio: 1.52
Long-term debt ($ mil.): 2,316
No. of shares (mil.): 458
Dividends
  Yield: —
  Payout: —
Market value ($ mil.): 6,817

AUTOZONE, INC.

OVERVIEW

Imagine that you are in your garage making some weekend car repairs. The wheel cylinders are leaking . . .the brake shoe adjuster nut is rusted solid . . . you're about to enter . . . the AutoZone. The Memphis-based company is the largest retail auto parts chain in the US, operating more than 2,700 stores in about 40 states. Most of its stores cater to both do-it-yourself consumers and professional auto repair shops.

AutoZone stores sell hard parts (alternators, engines, batteries), maintenance items (oil, antifreeze), accessories (car stereos, floor mats), and other merchandise. The stores offer items under brand names as well as under AutoZone private labels such as Duralast and Deutsch.

The stores also offer diagnostic testing for starters, alternators, and batteries but do not sell tires or perform general auto repairs. AutoZone's TruckPro subsidiary sells heavy-duty truck parts at over 40 stores in 14 southern and midwestern states. Its ALLDATA unit sells automotive diagnostic and repair software.

The company has been expanding both through acquisitions and by opening an average of about 250 outlets per year. It recently began expanding outside the US. AutoZone also introduced a 3,800-sq.-ft. store format for markets too small to support its typical 7,700-sq.-ft. stores.

HISTORY

Joseph "Pitt" Hyde took over the family grocery wholesale business, Malone & Hyde (est. 1907) in 1968. He expanded into specialty retailing, opening drugstores, sporting goods stores, and supermarkets, but his fortunes began to race on Independence Day, 1979, when he opened his first Auto Shack auto parts store in Forrest City, Arkansas.

Using retailing behemoth Wal-Mart as a model, Hyde concentrated on smaller markets in the South and Southeast, emphasizing everyday low prices and centralized distribution operations. He stressed customer service to provide his do-it-yourself customers with expert advice on choosing parts. While a number of retailers have tried to copy Wal-Mart's successful model, Hyde had an inside track: Before starting Auto Shack he had served on Wal-Mart's board for seven years.

Auto Shack had expanded into seven states by 1980, and by 1983 it had 129 stores in 10 states. The next year Malone & Hyde's senior management, with investment firm Kohlberg Kravis Roberts (KKR), took the company private in an LBO. Auto Shack continued to expand, reaching 192 stores in 1984.

A year later Auto Shack introduced its Express Parts Service, the first service in the industry to offer a toll-free number and overnight delivery of parts. The following year it introduced another first: a limited lifetime warranty on its merchandise. Also in 1986 Auto Shack introduced its own Duralast line of auto products.

The company was spun off to Malone & Hyde's shareholders in 1987, and then Malone & Hyde's other operations were sold. Auto Shack brought its electronic parts catalog online that year. The company changed its name to AutoZone in 1987, in part to settle a lawsuit with Radio Shack. By this time it had 390 stores in 15 states.

In 1989 it opened its 500th store, 10 years to the day after the first store opened. AutoZone went public in 1991. By the end of that year, it had nearly 600 stores and five distribution centers. The company topped $1 billion in sales in 1992. The next year it opened new distribution centers in Illinois and Tennessee and closed its Memphis operation.

AutoZone introduced its Flexogram communication system, which allows stores to customize inventory according to local needs, in 1994. It opened 280 stores in 1996, mostly in existing markets, and began selling to commercial customers such as service stations and repair shops. It also acquired auto diagnostic software company ALLDATA. Hyde stepped down as CEO that year and as chairman in 1997 and was replaced by COO Johnston Adams.

The company made several key purchases in 1998. It acquired Chief Auto Parts for $280 million, adding 560 stores (most in California) that were converted to AutoZones in 1999. It also purchased Adap and its 112 Auto Palace stores in the Northeast; heavy-duty truck parts distributor TruckPro; and, from Pep Boys, 100 Express stores. Also in 1998 AutoZone opened its first Mexico store, in Nuevo Laredo.

Key shareholder KKR divested its 13% share in AutoZone that year, and Hyde sold much of his stake by early 1999. AutoZone plans to open 225 new stores in 1999, including two more in Mexico.

Chairman and CEO: Johnston C. Adams Jr., age 49,
$773,500 pay
President and COO: Timothy D. Vargo, age 47,
$618,800 pay
EVP and CFO: Robert J. Hunt, age 49, $417,000 pay
EVP Store Development and Assistant Secretary:
Lawrence E. Evans, age 54, $300,588 pay
SVP, Store Development: Gene Auerbach, age 54
SVP Stores: Gerald E. Colley, age 46, $304,750 pay
**SVP Systems Technology and Support and Chief
Information Officer:** Bruce Clark, age 52
SVP, Secretary, and General Counsel:
Harry L. Goldsmith, age 47
SVP Distribution: Michael E. Longo, age 37
SVP Advertising: Anthony D. Rose Jr., age 38
SVP International: Stephen W. Valentine, age 36
SVP Merchandising: David J. Wilhite, age 36
Chairman and CEO, TruckPro: Dale Dawson
VP Merchandising Analysis & Support:
Richard F. Adams Jr.
VP Real Estate: David W. Barczak
VP and Controller: Michael E. Butterick, age 47
VP Stores: Clete Faddis, age 36
VP Merchandising: Clifford E. Green
VP Distribution: Phillip J. Jackson
Auditors: Ernst & Young LLP

LOCATIONS

HQ: 123 S. Front St., Memphis, TN 38103
Phone: 901-495-6500   **Fax:** 901-495-8300
Web site: http://www.autozone.com

PRODUCTS/OPERATIONS

Selected Merchandise

Accessories	Engine additives
Car stereos	Oil
Floor mats	Power steering fluid
	Protectants
Hard Parts	Transmission fluid
Alternators	Waxes
Batteries	
Brake shoes and pads	**Selected Brands**
Carburetors	Albany
Clutches	ALLDATA
Engines	AutoZone
Starters	Deutsch
Water pumps	Duralast
	TruckPro
Maintenance Items	Ultra Spark
Antifreeze	Valucraft
Brake fluid	

COMPETITORS

Advance Auto Parts	Montgomery Ward
CARQUEST	NAPA
Costco Companies	O'Reilly Automotive
CSK Auto	PACCAR
Discount Auto Parts	Pep Boys
Genuine Parts	Sears
Goodyear	Target Stores
Kmart	Wal-Mart

HISTORICAL FINANCIALS & EMPLOYEES

NYSE symbol: AZO FYE: August 31	Annual Growth	1989	1990	1991	1992	1993	1994	1995	1996	1997	1998
Sales ($ mil.)	22.1%	536	672	818	1,002	1,217	1,508	1,808	2,243	2,691	3,243
Net income ($ mil.)	43.2%	9	23	44	63	87	116	139	167	195	228
Income as % of sales	—	1.7%	3.5%	5.4%	6.3%	7.1%	7.7%	7.7%	7.5%	7.2%	7.0%
Earnings per share ($)	23.9%	—	—	0.33	0.43	0.59	0.78	0.93	1.11	1.28	1.48
Stock price - FY high ($)		—	—	10.38	21.00	27.56	30.75	27.63	37.63	30.75	38.00
Stock price - FY low ($)		—	—	6.56	9.59	14.13	22.13	21.63	23.38	19.50	23.75
Stock price - FY close ($)	14.3%	—	—	10.19	14.50	26.88	24.88	26.88	27.25	28.25	25.94
P/E - high		—	—	31	49	47	39	30	34	24	26
P/E - low		—	—	20	22	24	28	23	21	15	16
Dividends per share ($)		—	—	0.00	0.00	0.00	0.00	0.00	0.00	0.00	0.00
Book value per share ($)	27.9%	—	—	1.53	2.02	2.75	3.63	4.66	5.77	7.11	8.56
Employees	19.2%	7,900	9,300	11,700	13,200	15,700	17,400	20,200	26,800	28,700	38,500

STOCK PRICE HISTORY

HIGH/LOW/CLOSE

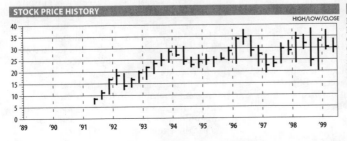

1998 FISCAL YEAR-END

Debt ratio: 29.5%
Return on equity: 17.5%
Cash ($ mil.): 7
Current ratio: 1.30
Long-term debt ($ mil.): 545
No. of shares (mil.): 152
Dividends
  Yield: —
  Payout: —
Market value ($ mil.): 3,945

AVERY DENNISON CORPORATION

OVERVIEW

Some people eschew labels, but Avery Dennison insists on them. The Pasadena, California-based company is, after all, a leading producer of adhesive labels used on everything from wine and shampoo bottles to cassette tapes and overnight mailers. Under its Avery Dennison and Fasson brands, the company makes papers, films, and foils coated with adhesive and sold in rolls to printers. It also makes school and office products (Avery, Marks-A-Lot, HI-LITER), such as notebooks, three-ring binders, and markers, as well as

Duracell battery-testing labels and the United States Postal Service's self-adhesive stamps.

Now Avery Dennison is out to label the world. Thanks to an increase in consumer spending in developing countries and the increasing use of PCs and bar codes, the business is growing internationally. The company has opened sales offices and distribution centers in the Asia/Pacific region, Latin America, and Eastern Europe. Employees, through a stock benefit trust, own approximately 13% of Avery Dennison.

HISTORY

Avery Dennison was created in 1990 by the merger of Avery International Corporation and Dennison Manufacturing Company. In 1935 Stanton Avery founded Kum-Kleen Products, which would become Avery International. The company made self-adhesive labels using machinery Avery had developed at the Adhere Paper Company. After a fire destroyed the plant's equipment in 1938, Avery, who had renamed the company Avery Adhesives, improved the machinery used in manufacturing the labels.

During and after WWII, Avery Adhesives shifted toward the industrial market for self-adhesives. The company incorporated in 1946. At that time Avery Adhesives sold 80% of its production, consisting of industrial labels, to manufacturers that labeled their own products.

The company lost its patent rights for self-adhesive labels in 1952, transforming the firm and the entire industry. As a result, a new division was created — the Avery Paper Company (later renamed Fasson) — to produce and market self-adhesive base materials.

Avery Adhesives began selling its stock on the over-the-counter market in 1961. Three years later it had four divisions: label products, base materials, Rotex (hand-operated embossing machines), and Metal-Cal (anodized and etched aluminum foil for nameplates). Renamed Avery International in 1976, the company closed some manufacturing facilities and initiated an 8% cut in its workforce in the late 1980s.

In 1990 Avery International merged with Dennison Manufacturing. Dennison was started in 1844 by the father-and-son team of Andrew and Aaron Dennison to produce jewelry boxes. By 1849 Aaron's younger brother, Eliphalet Whorf (E. W.), was running the business and expanding it into tags, labels, and tissue paper. Dennison was incorporated in 1878 with $150,000 in capital.

By 1911 Dennison sold tags, gummed labels, paper boxes, greeting cards, sealing wax, and tissue paper, and it had stores in Boston, Chicago, New York City, Philadelphia, St. Louis, and London. Henry Dennison, E. W.'s grandson, became president in 1917 and served in this capacity until 1952.

From the 1960s to the 1980s, Dennison spent heavily on research and development and helped to develop such products as electronic printers and pregnancy test supplies. In the mid-1980s the firm reorganized its operations, selling seven businesses, closing four others, and focusing on stationery, systems, and packaging.

In addition to office products and product identification and control systems, the 1990 merger combined Dennison's office products operations in France (Doret and Cheval Ordex) with Avery International's sizable self-adhesive base materials business. However, it was soon discovered that Avery Dennison was in worse shape than expected, and much of the early 1990s was spent improving its operating performance.

Avery Dennison sold its 50% interest in Japan's Toppan Ltd., in 1996, clearing the way to develop its own businesses in Asia. The next year Avery died at age 90. Also in 1997, an alliance with rival Four Pillars turned sour when Avery Dennison accused the Taiwanese firm of stealing trade secrets. (Two executives at Four Pillars were convicted of espionage in 1999.)

President Philip Neal was promoted to CEO in 1998. Adhering to its goal of global expansion, the label maker in early 1999 formed a joint venture with Germany's Zweckform Buro-Produkte.

With growth slowing, in 1999 Avery Dennison announced that it would close eight plants. In July 1999 the company bought Stimsonite, a maker of reflective safety products for the transportation industry.

OFFICERS

Chairman: Charles D. Miller, age 71, $880,000 pay
President and CEO: Philip M. Neal, age 58, $1,458,333 pay
EVP, Global Technology and New Business Development: Kim A. Caldwell, age 51, $658,333 pay
SVP Finance and CFO: Robert M. Calderoni, age 39, $620,000 pay
SVP, General Counsel, and Secretary: Robert G. van Schoonenberg, age 52, $642,667 pay
SVP, US Office Products: Jesse Beim
Senior Group VP, Worldwide Converting, Graphic Systems and Specialty Tapes: Geoffrey T. Martin, age 44, $606,667 pay
VP, Human Resources: J. Terry Schuler
Auditors: PricewaterhouseCoopers LLP

LOCATIONS

HQ: 150 N. Orange Grove Blvd., Pasadena, CA 91103
Phone: 626-304-2000   **Fax:** 626-792-7312
Web site: http://www.averydennison.com

Avery Dennison operates about 200 manufacturing and sales facilities in 89 countries.

1998 Sales

	$ mil.	% of total
US	2,207	63
Other countries	1,288	37
Adjustments	(35)	—
Total	**3,460**	**100**

PRODUCTS/OPERATIONS

Pressure-Sensitive Adhesives and Materials
Base materials
  Film
  Paper
Chemical products
  Binders
  Emulsion-based and solvent acrylic polymer adhesives
  Protective coatings
Graphic products
  Durable cast and reflective films
  Metallic dispersion products
  Proprietary woodgrain film laminates
  Specialty print-receptive films
Specialty tape products
  Single- and double-coated tapes and transfer adhesives
Transportation safety products
  Highway delineators
  Reflective pavement markers
  Work zone markers

Consumer and Converted Products Sector
Bar-coded tags
Battery-testing labels
Data processing labels
Laser print card and index products
Markers
Notebooks
Presentation and organizing systems
Printer labels
Sheet protectors
Three-ring binders

COMPETITORS

Bemis
Esselte
Fortune Brands
H.B. Fuller
Mead
3M
Moore Corporation
Newell Rubbermaid
Paxar
Standard Register
Wallace Computer

HISTORICAL FINANCIALS & EMPLOYEES

NYSE symbol: AVY FYE: December 31	Annual Growth	1989	1990	1991	1992	1993	1994	1995	1996	1997	1998
Sales ($ mil.)	8.0%	1,732	2,590	2,545	2,623	2,609	2,857	3,114	3,223	3,346	3,460
Net income ($ mil.)	11.1%	87	6	63	80	84	109	144	176	205	223
Income as % of sales	—	5.0%	0.2%	2.5%	3.1%	3.2%	3.8%	4.6%	5.5%	6.1%	6.5%
Earnings per share ($)	9.1%	0.98	0.06	0.52	0.68	0.74	1.00	1.32	1.63	1.93	2.15
Stock price - FY high ($)	—	15.94	16.50	12.88	14.56	15.75	18.00	25.06	36.50	45.75	62.06
Stock price - FY low ($)	—	10.50	7.75	9.50	11.63	12.56	13.19	16.56	23.75	33.38	39.44
Stock price - FY close ($)	12.2%	15.94	10.75	12.69	14.38	14.69	17.75	25.06	35.38	44.75	45.06
P/E - high	—	16	275	25	21	21	18	19	22	24	29
P/E - low	—	11	129	18	17	17	13	13	15	17	18
Dividends per share ($)	14.4%	0.26	0.40	0.38	0.42	0.46	0.50	0.56	0.62	0.72	0.87
Book value per share ($)	1.9%	6.09	6.83	6.65	6.82	6.40	6.81	7.69	6.84	7.03	7.24
Employees	3.6%	11,715	18,816	17,095	16,550	15,750	15,400	15,500	15,800	16,200	16,100

STOCK PRICE HISTORY

HIGH/LOW/CLOSE

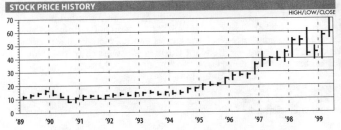

1998 FISCAL YEAR-END

Debt ratio: 35.9%
Return on equity: 26.8%
Cash ($ mil.): 19
Current ratio: 1.21
Long-term debt ($ mil.): 466
No. of shares (mil.): 115
Dividends
  Yield: 1.9%
  Payout: 40.5%
Market value ($ mil.): 5,185

AVIS RENT A CAR, INC.

OVERVIEW

Avis Rent A Car has spun out solo in a race to overtake Hertz. The Garden City, New York-based company is the largest franchisee of the Avis car rental system, owned by Cendant. The company maintains more than 205,000 vehicles at over 625 locations, mainly in North America (out of about 4,200 Avis locations worldwide). Cendant, which also owns real estate and hotel franchises, once owned the company in whole (through predecessor HFS) and still has about a 20% stake.

The company's link to Cendant affords cross-marketing opportunities (travelers using Cendant's hotels often need car rentals), but Avis Rent A Car must pay Cendant a steep 4% royalty on revenues each year to use the Avis name. Avis Rent A Car also has ties to another former owner, General Motors (GM); through a purchasing agreement, most of its cars are GM vehicles.

In step with its rivals, the Avis system uses a pricing model (patterned after the airline industry's) that charges higher prices during peak demand. The company is working on expanding its share of the leisure travel market (64% of sales come from business travelers); to that end, it is acquiring other Avis franchises with airport locations and intensifying marketing. In addition, Avis Rent A Car is moving into the corporate and government vehicle fleet business.

HISTORY

Young Detroit car dealer Warren Avis noticed in the 1940s that no car rental agencies, including Hertz, had airport operations. A former US Army pilot, Avis believed air travel was the wave of the future. In 1946 he invested his savings and borrowed funds to open Avis Airlines Rent-A-Car System outlets at Detroit's Willow Run Airport and Miami International Airport. Avis' idea was a success, and in 1948 his company opened inner-city locations to serve hotels and office buildings.

By 1954 Avis had expanded into Mexico, Canada, and Europe. That year he sold the company to Richard Robie, a Boston-based car rental agent, for $8 million. Robie then went broke and two years later sold Avis to Boston investors. After forming a holding company (Avis, Inc.), with Avis Rent-A-Car System as its main subsidiary, the new owners instituted car leasing. In 1962 they sold Avis to investment bankers Lazard Freres, who named Robert Townsend president and moved Avis' headquarters to Garden City, New York.

ITT bought Avis in 1965. Winston Morrow replaced Townsend and focused on overseas expansion. A headquarters serving Africa, Europe, and the Middle East (now Avis Europe) was established in the UK. In 1972 Avis pioneered the use of the Wizard System, now the industry's oldest computer reservation system. That year, as part of an antitrust settlement, ITT sold 48% of the company to the public; a court-appointed trustee held the rest. Avis returned to private ownership in 1977 when Norton Simon bought it for $174 million.

Former Hertz executive Joseph Vittoria became president in 1982. During the mid-1980s Avis was passed from owner to owner: Esmark bought Norton Simon (1983) and in turn was bought by Beatrice (1984). Kohlberg Kravis Roberts took Beatrice private in an LBO (1985) and sold Avis to William Simon's investment partnership, Wesray Capital Corporation (1986). Also in 1986 Avis sold its leasing operations to PHH Group and most of Avis Europe to the public on the London Exchange.

Led by Vittoria and aided by General Motors (GM), in 1987 Avis employees established an Employee Stock Ownership Plan (ESOP) and bought the company for $1.79 billion (the debt was retired in 1995). Avis then joined GM and Lease International to form Cilva Holdings, which bought Avis Europe in 1989.

In 1996 Avis employees (who owned 71% of Avis) and GM (which owned 29%) sold the company to HFS for $800 million; Craig Hoenshell succeeded Vittoria the next year. Also in 1997 HFS spun off Avis' #1 franchisee as Avis Rent A Car. In an effort to add more airport locations, that year Avis Rent A Car bought First Gray Line, the #2 Avis franchisee. In 1998 it acquired another key Avis franchisee, Hayes Leasing. Hoenshell left abruptly in late 1998, saying he'd accomplished his goals during his short tenure; board member Martin Edelman took over as the company sought a new chairman and CEO.

In July 1999 Avis Rent A Car bought Cendant's 700,000-vehicle fleet business — including PHH Vehicle Management Services, Cendant Business Answers (Europe), The Harpur Group, and Wright Express — for $5 billion.

Chairman: Martin Edelman, age 57
President and COO - Vehicle Management Services Group: Mark E. Miller
President and COO - Rental Car Group:
F. Robert Salerno, age 47,
$776,730 pay (prior to title change)
President - Corporate and Business Affairs:
Kevin M. Sheehan, age 45,
$582,451 pay (prior to title change)
SVP Sales: Thomas J. Byrnes, age 54, $366,945 pay
SVP Marketing: Maria M. Miller, age 42
VP International: Michael P. Collins, age 51
VP Tax: Richard S. Jacobson, age 55
VP and Treasurer: Gerard J. Kennell, age 54
VP Human Resources, Staffing and Diversity:
James A. Keyes, age 53
VP, General Counsel, and Secretary: Karen C. Sclafani, age 47
VP and Controller: Timothy M. Shanley, age 50
VP Operations, US Rent A Car: John Forsythe
VP, Western Area: Kerry L. Morris
VP, Southeast Area: George Proos
VP, Northeast Area: Thomas J. Tobias
VP, Central Area: James R. Weber
General Manager, AIM Network: Wade Cook
Director Group Sales: James R. Hommen
Auditors: Deloitte & Touche LLP

LOCATIONS

HQ: 900 Old Country Rd., Garden City, NY 11530
Phone: 516-222-3000   **Fax:** 516-222-6677
Web site: http://www.avis.com

Avis Rent A Car has vehicle rental operations at more than 625 locations in Argentina, Australia, Canada, New Zealand, Puerto Rico, the US, and the US Virgin Islands.

1998 Sales

	$ mil.	% of total
US	2,062	90
Other countries	236	10
Total	**2,298**	**100**

PRODUCTS/OPERATIONS

Selected Services
Additional liability insurance
Cellular phones
Child seats
Concession fee recovery
Loss damage waivers
Optional refueling services
Personal accident insurance
Personal effects protection
Ski racks

COMPETITORS

AutoNation
Budget Group
Dollar Thrifty Automotive Group
Enterprise Rent-A-Car
Hertz
Premier Car Rental

HISTORICAL FINANCIALS & EMPLOYEES

NYSE symbol: AVI FYE: December 31	Annual Growth	1989	1990	1991	1992	1993	1994	1995	1996	1997	1998
Sales ($ mil.)	11.0%	—	—	—	1,229	1,333	1,412	1,616	363	2,046	2,298
Net income ($ mil.)	(1.4%)	—	—	—	69	53	22	26	1	28	64
Income as % of sales	—	—	—	—	5.6%	4.0%	1.6%	1.6%	0.3%	1.3%	2.8%
Earnings per share ($)	106.8%	—	—	—	—	—	—	—	—	0.88	1.82
Stock price - FY high ($)	—	—	—	—	—	—	—	—	—	36.56	38.25
Stock price - FY low ($)	—	—	—	—	—	—	—	—	—	21.50	11.38
Stock price - FY close ($)	(24.3%)	—	—	—	—	—	—	—	—	31.94	24.19
P/E - high	—	—	—	—	—	—	—	—	—	42	21
P/E - low	—	—	—	—	—	—	—	—	—	24	6
Dividends per share ($)	—	—	—	—	—	—	—	—	—	0.00	0.00
Book value per share ($)	28.7%	—	—	—	—	—	—	—	—	14.55	18.72
Employees	6.5%	—	—	—	13,000	13,500	14,000	15,000	16,000	18,000	19,000

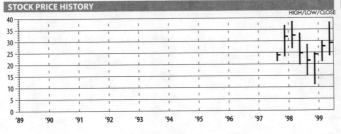

STOCK PRICE HISTORY HIGH/LOW/CLOSE

1998 FISCAL YEAR-END
Debt ratio: 82.9%
Return on equity: 10.2%
Cash ($ mil.): 30
Current ratio: 0.99
Long-term debt ($ mil.): 3,015
No. of shares (mil.): 33
Dividends
  Yield: —
  Payout: —
Market value ($ mil.): 804

AVNET, INC.

OVERVIEW

The Arrow in Avnet's gut has only made it more determined. Phoenix-based Avnet is the #2 US distributor of electronic components and computer products, behind Arrow Electronics. Avnet distributes parts from 250 manufacturers, buying in bulk and selling to Eastman Kodak, AT&T, Hewlett-Packard, and more than 100,000 other equipment makers. About half of the company's sales come from its Hamilton Hallmark unit, which distributes semiconductors for top chip makers such as Advanced Micro Devices, Intel, and Motorola. Avnet was the industry leader until Arrow bought the companies that put it on top (the rivals are known on Wall Street for trying to outdo each other through rousing games of dueling acquisitions). Avnet has purchased 20 firms in the past six years. Most of those have been outside the US, as it continues extending its worldwide presence in Africa, Asia, and Europe.

The company has restructured to consolidate subsidiaries, divesting itself of industrial operations, video communications, and other noncore businesses.

HISTORY

In 1921, before commercial battery-operated radios, Charles Avnet started a small ham radio replacement parts distributorship in lower Manhattan, selling parts to designers, inventors, and ship-to-shore radio users on docked ships. The stock market crash in 1929 left the business strapped, and it went bankrupt in 1931. Later that decade Avnet founded another company, making car radio kits and antennas. But competition got the best of him, and again his company went bankrupt.

During WWII Charles, with sons Lester and Robert, founded Avnet Electronic Supply to sell parts to government and defense contractors, since production of home radio sets was prohibited. After the war the company bought and sold surplus electrical and electronic parts. A contract from Bendix Aviation spurred company growth (it became the first franchised connector distributor), and Avnet opened a West Coast warehouse. In 1955 the company incorporated as Avnet Electronics Supply, with Robert as chairman and CEO and Lester as president. Sales reached $1 million that year, although the company lost $17,000. The company changed its name to Avnet Electronics in 1959.

One year later Avnet made its first acquisition, British Industries, and went public. The acquisitions continued throughout the 1960s with Hamilton Electro (1962), Fairmount Motor Products (1963), Carol Wire & Cable (1968), and Time Electronic Sales (1968). Semiconductor maker Hamilton remained autonomous but buoyed Avnet's connector component business.

To acknowledge its diversification into motors and other products, the company again changed its name, to Avnet, Inc., in 1964. Robert Avnet died the next year and Lester took over as chairman. When Lester died five years later, director Simon Sheib became chairman and CEO.

The company worked to absorb its purchases in the midst of a recession. In 1973 Intel, which had brought out the first microprocessor, signed Avnet as a distributor, and by 1979 sales had topped $1 billion. The next year Anthony Hamilton, founder of Hamilton Electro, became chairman and CEO when Sheib died, and Avnet took the top spot among US distributors of electronic components.

Avnet sold its wire and cable business in the wake of a 1982 economy that caused price declines. An earthquake in 1987 damaged the company's distribution facilities and left executives looking for a new home. Initial relocation in the Phoenix area began that year. When Hamilton died in 1989, Time Electronic founder Leon Machiz, an Avnet executive, was named chairman and CEO.

During 1991 and 1992 Avnet spent more than $100 million for acquisitions in the European market. The company outbid Wyle Laboratories for Hall-Mark Electronics, the US's third-largest distributor, in 1993, and it acquired Penstock, the top US distributor of microwave radio-frequency products, the next year.

The company continued to expand globally in 1995, acquiring Hong Kong distributor WKK Semiconductor, among others. Also that year Avnet began selling nonelectronics operations.

In 1998 the company reorganized around separate global computer and electronics businesses. President and COO Roy Vallee succeeded Machiz as chairman and CEO. Asia's economic crisis caused Avnet to suffer a drop in profits for fiscal 1998. The next year it sold its Allied Electronics subsidiary for $380 million and agreed to acquire smaller rival Marshall Industries in a deal valued at about $830 million.

Chairman and CEO: Roy Vallee, age 46, $1,248,000 pay
SVP, CFO, and Assistant Secretary: Raymond Sadowski, age 44
SVP; President, Time Electronics Division: Burton Katz, $564,604 pay
SVP; President, Computer Marketing Group: Richard Ward, age 58, $523,807 pay
SVP, Secretary, and Chief Legal Counsel: David R. Birk, age 50
SVP Global Operations and Chief Information Officer: Anthony T. DeLuca, age 48
SVP; Director, Product Business Group: Lori Hartman
SVP; Co-President, Avnet Electronics Marketing Group: Brian Hilton, age 56
SVP Supplier and Materials Management: Don Sweet
SVP: Keith Williams, age 50
SVP Human Resources: Robert Zierk
CEO, Penstock: Bruce White
Co-President, Avnet Electronics Marketing Group: Steven C. Church, age 49, $691,129 pay
VP; Chief Information Officer, Information Services Division: Steven Bandrowczak
Auditors: Arthur Andersen LLP

LOCATIONS

HQ: 2211 S. 47th St., Phoenix, AZ 85034
Phone: 623-643-2000 **Fax:** 623-643-7240
Web site: http://www.avnet.com

Avnet has operations in the Asia/Pacific region, Canada, Europe, South Africa, and the US.

1998 Sales

	$ mil.	% of total
US	4,450	75
Other countries	1,466	25
Total	**5,916**	**100**

PRODUCTS/OPERATIONS

1998 Sales

	$ mil.	% of total
Semiconductors	3,223	54
Computer products	1,589	27
Connectors	506	9
Other	560	10
Adjustments	38	—
Total	**5,916**	**100**

Selected Operations
Avnet Computer (computer systems and peripherals for users)
Avnet Direct (electronic commerce)
Avnet Integrated Material Services (materials management and logistics services)
Hall-Mark Computer Products (computer systems and peripherals for resellers)
Hamilton Hallmark (semiconductors)
Penstock (radio-frequency/microwave products and services distribution)
Time Electronics (connectors, cable assemblies, and other components)

COMPETITORS

Arrow Electronics
Bell Microproducts
Graybar Electric
Jaco Electronics
Marshall Industries
Nu Horizons Electronics
Pioneer-Standard Electronics
Richardson Electronics
TTI
Wyle Electronics

HISTORICAL FINANCIALS & EMPLOYEES

NYSE symbol: AVT FYE: June 30	Annual Growth	1989	1990	1991	1992	1993	1994	1995	1996	1997	1998
Sales ($ mil.)	13.3%	1,919	1,751	1,741	1,759	2,238	3,548	4,300	5,208	5,391	5,916
Net income ($ mil.)	12.1%	54	57	62	51	69	85	140	188	183	151
Income as % of sales	—	2.8%	3.2%	3.5%	2.9%	3.1%	2.4%	3.3%	3.6%	3.4%	2.6%
Earnings per share ($)	10.8%	1.51	1.57	1.72	1.42	1.91	2.09	3.32	4.31	4.25	3.80
Stock price - FY high ($)	—	25.75	33.50	30.00	30.00	37.00	45.00	49.75	55.63	64.88	74.50
Stock price - FY low ($)	—	19.00	23.38	21.50	23.25	26.75	30.75	31.50	38.00	39.13	53.69
Stock price - FY close ($)	9.9%	23.38	28.75	27.75	27.63	34.00	31.50	48.25	42.13	57.50	54.69
P/E - high	—	17	21	17	21	19	22	15	13	15	20
P/E - low	—	13	15	13	16	14	15	9	9	9	14
Dividends per share ($)	2.0%	0.50	0.58	0.60	0.60	0.60	0.60	0.60	0.60	0.60	0.60
Book value per share ($)	6.4%	20.60	21.46	22.60	23.56	24.35	27.26	30.38	34.67	36.55	36.09
Employees	0.3%	8,500	7,500	7,250	6,650	6,500	8,000	9,000	9,500	9,400	8,700

STOCK PRICE HISTORY

HIGH/LOW/CLOSE

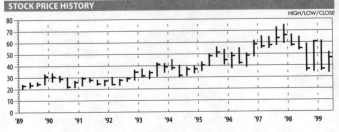

1998 FISCAL YEAR-END

Debt ratio: 38.1%
Return on equity: 11.5%
Cash ($ mil.): 83
Current ratio: 3.41
Long-term debt ($ mil.): 811
No. of shares (mil.): 36
Dividends
  Yield: 1.1%
  Payout: 15.8%
Market value ($ mil.): 1,994

AVON PRODUCTS, INC.

OVERVIEW

Makeovers are a staple of the cosmetics business, and Avon Products, the world's #1 direct seller of beauty products, is in the midst of a corporate makeover. As part of its new image, the New York City-based company is in the process of cutting $400 million in annual costs; to that aim, it has shed 30% of its product lines in favor of more upscale global brands that will be backed by global advertising campaigns. (Avon itself wants to become the "Coca-Cola of the beauty industry.") The Avon Lady in charge of putting on the company's new face is, in fact, a man — Charles Perrin — who consolidated brands and used globally shared ad campaigns as the chief of Duracell.

Avon is also moving away from its frumpy door-to-door saleslady image by exploring new sales channels. Although 98% of revenues still come from its sales representatives, the company now sells products through mail-order catalogs aimed at upscale shoppers, a toll-free phone number, the Internet, mall kiosks, and a very fashionable day spa (The Avon Centre) housed in Manhattan's Trump Tower.

The company's image in the US may need polishing, but it's shining brightly overseas, where about two-thirds of its sales are made. Long established in the US, Canada, and parts of Europe and the Pacific, the firm is aggressively pursuing new customers in emerging economies such as Taiwan, Malaysia, and Russia. Avon is also promoting its image as "The Company for Women" by providing business opportunities for women in countries where women have few choices.

HISTORY

In the 1880s book salesman David McConnell gave small bottles of perfume to New York housewives who listened to his sales pitch. The perfume was more popular than the books, so in 1886 McConnell created the California Perfume Company and hired women to sell door-to-door (he renamed the company Avon Products in 1950 after being impressed by the beauty of Stratford-upon-Avon in England). Through the 1950s these women, mostly housewives seeking extra income, made Avon a major force in the cosmetics industry. The firm first advertised on TV in 1953, using the now-famous doorbell ring. It began selling internationally during the 1950s and 1960s.

From the 1960s until the mid-1980s, Avon was the world's largest cosmetics company, known for its appeal to middle-class homemakers. But the company hit hard times in 1974 — the recession made many of its products too pricey for blue-collar customers, and women were leaving home for the workforce. Discovering that Avon's traditional products had little appeal for younger women, president David Mitchell began an overhaul of the product line, introducing the Colorworks line for teenagers with the slogan, "It's not your mother's makeup," and ads picturing active young women.

Avon acquired prestigious jeweler Tiffany & Co. in 1979 (sold 1984) to help improve the company's image. To boost profits, it entered the retail prestige fragrance business by launching a joint venture with Liz Claiborne (1985) and buying Giorgio (1987; the Giorgio Beverly Hills retail operations were sold in

1994). But Liz Claiborne dissolved the joint venture when Avon bought competitor Parfums Stern in 1987 (sold 1990). It sold 40% of Avon Japan (started 1969) to the Japanese public that year.

Avon Color cosmetics were introduced in 1988, and sleepwear, preschool toys, and videos followed in 1989. The company introduced apparel in 1994 and the next year worked with designer Diane Von Furstenberg to launch a line of clothing. Also in 1995 Avon bought Justin (Pty) Ltd., South Africa's second-largest direct seller of cosmetics.

The company debuted Avon Lifedesigns, a business unit offering goal-setting seminars and other services for women, in 1996. Avon and Mattel joined forces that year to sell toys — Winter Velvet Barbie became Avon's most successful product introduction ever. In 1997 the company launched a new home furnishings catalog and bought direct seller Discovery Toys (sold in early 1999). Late in 1997 it began its $400 million restructuring program.

Also in 1997 Avon passed over several high-ranking female Avon executives (it felt they weren't ready) when it hired Charles Perrin, who took over as CEO in mid-1998. Andrea Jung, the brain behind the makeover, became president. In keeping with its strategy to make products more accessible, Avon also began selling makeup in 1998 at mall kiosks and through a catalog. Late that year The Avon Centre day spa opened in Manhattan.

Chairman and CEO: Charles R. Perrin, age 53,
$1,798,163 pay (prior to promotion)
President and COO: Andrea Jung, age 40, $1,179,899 pay
EVP and President, Europe, Asia, and Africa:
Jose Ferreira Jr., age 42
EVP; President, North America: Susan J. Kropf, age 50,
$963,447 pay
EVP; President, Latin America: Fernando Lezama,
age 59, $806,742 pay
SVP and CFO: Robert J. Corti, age 49
SVP Global Operations: Harriet Edelman, age 42
SVP Global Marketing: Lynn Emmolo
SVP Human Resources: Jill Kanin-Lovers, age 47
SVP and Chief Information Officer: Sateesh B. Lele,
age 56
SVP, General Counsel, and Secretary:
Ward M. Miller Jr., age 66
Group VP Research and Development: Janice Teal, age 46
VP Global Advertising: Robert S. Gilbralter
VP and Controller: Janice Marolda, age 38
Auditors: PricewaterhouseCoopers LLP

LOCATIONS

HQ: 1345 Avenue of the Americas,
New York, NY 10105-0196
Phone: 212-282-5000 **Fax:** 212-282-6049
Web site: http://www.avon.com

1998 Sales

	$ mil.	% of total
The Americas		
US	1,774	34
Other countries	1,953	37
Europe	863	17
Pacific	623	12
Total	**5,213**	**100**

PRODUCTS/OPERATIONS

1998 Sales

	$ mil.	% of total
Cosmetics, fragrances & toiletries	3,182	61
Gift & decorative	1,051	20
Apparel	572	11
Fashion jewelry & accessories	408	8
Total	**5,213**	**100**

Selected Brands

Cosmetics
Beyond Color
Color Last
Color Rich
Face Lifting
Glimmersticks
Hydro Liner
Incredible Lengths
Natural Radiance
Perfect Wear
Satin Moisture
True Color
Voluptuous

Fragrances
Forest Lily
Josie

Millennia
Natori
Starring
Women of Earth

Skin Care, Bath, and Body
Anew
Milk Made
Moisture Therapy
Naturals
Skin-So-Soft

Other
Apparel
Barbie dolls
Giftware
Jewelry and accessories

COMPETITORS

Alberto-Culver
Amway
Beiersdorf
Body Shop
Colgate-
 Palmolive
Coty
Estee Lauder

Forever Living
Herbalife
Intimate Brands
Johnson &
 Johnson
L'Oréal
LVMH
Mary Kay

Perrigo
Procter &
 Gamble
Revlon
Shaklee
Shiseido
Unilever
Wella

HISTORICAL FINANCIALS & EMPLOYEES

NYSE symbol: AVP FYE: December 31	Annual Growth	1989	1990	1991	1992	1993	1994	1995	1996	1997	1998
Sales ($ mil.)	5.2%	3,300	3,454	3,593	3,810	4,008	4,267	4,492	4,814	5,079	5,213
Net income ($ mil.)	19.4%	55	195	136	175	132	196	257	318	339	270
Income as % of sales	—	1.7%	5.7%	3.8%	4.6%	3.3%	4.6%	5.7%	6.6%	6.7%	5.2%
Earnings per share ($)	32.7%	0.08	0.65	0.47	0.61	0.46	0.69	0.94	1.18	1.27	1.02
Stock price - FY high ($)	—	10.31	9.53	12.25	15.06	16.09	15.91	19.59	29.75	39.00	46.25
Stock price - FY low ($)	—	4.88	5.69	6.53	11.00	11.91	12.09	13.50	18.16	25.31	25.00
Stock price - FY close ($)	19.0%	9.22	7.34	11.50	13.84	12.16	14.94	18.84	28.56	30.69	44.25
P/E - high	—	129	15	26	25	35	23	21	25	31	45
P/E - low	—	61	9	14	18	26	18	14	15	20	25
Dividends per share ($)	11.8%	0.25	0.25	1.10	0.38	0.43	0.48	0.53	0.58	0.63	0.68
Book value per share ($)	1.7%	0.93	1.65	0.88	1.08	1.09	0.67	0.71	0.91	1.08	1.09
Employees	1.3%	30,100	30,300	30,500	29,700	29,800	30,400	31,800	33,700	34,995	33,900

STOCK PRICE HISTORY

HIGH/LOW/CLOSE

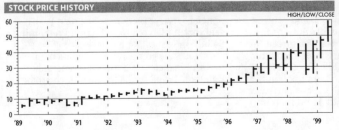

1998 FISCAL YEAR-END

Debt ratio: 41.3%
Return on equity: 94.7%
Cash ($ mil.): 106
Current ratio: 1.01
Long-term debt ($ mil.): 201
No. of shares (mil.): 263
Dividends
 Yield: 1.5%
 Payout: 66.7%
Market value ($ mil.): 11,617

AXA FINANCIAL, INC.

OVERVIEW

New York City-based AXA Financial (formerly The Equitable Companies) is taking an AXA down its middle. The company, 58%-owned by French insurance giant AXA, is separating its traditional life insurance offerings from its financial advisory services, for which a new brand identity (AXA Advisors) is being created. The company will continue to operate its life insurance business under the Equitable name.

The change may be a good fit for AXA Financial's 7,400 career insurance agents, because they are also licensed stockbrokers who can sell the company's myriad products. AXA Financial's subsidiaries Alliance Capital Management (57%; mutual funds, cash management, institutional services) and Donaldson, Lufkin & Jenrette (72%; brokerage, investment banking, venture capital services) should also benefit from the change. Equitable Life sells traditional life insurance products and acts as a retrocessionaire, assuming life and annuity reinsurance from reinsurers.

HISTORY

As a student in Catskill, New York, Henry Hyde (no relation to the adulterous Illinois representative) was advised by his teacher, General John Johnston (founder of Northwestern Mutual Life Insurance Co. in 1857), to go into life insurance. After a brief stint with Mutual Life of New York, Hyde left in 1859 at age 25 to found the Equitable Life Assurance Society in New York, a joint stock company named after the Equitable Life Assurance Society of London.

Business boomed during the Civil War, and Equitable expanded to Asia, Europe, the Middle East, and South America. It grew faster than the insurance industry overall and by 1899 was the world's first company to have $1 billion of life insurance in force.

Revelations in 1905 about the company's financial condition led to the resignation of management and, in 1917, its conversion to mutual status. It pioneered group insurance (for Montgomery Ward in 1911) and developed a way to apportion dividends within a particular group (eventually adopted by most of the industry).

After the boom of the 1920s, Equitable weathered the Depression and WWII. It continued to grow during the postwar boom. In the 1970s it diversified into computers, mining, and real estate. The next decade the company bought Donaldson, Lufkin & Jenrette (DLJ) and an HMO (EQUICOR, formed with Hospital Corporation of America, 1986; sold 1990).

Equitable also pioneered guaranteed investment contracts (GICs) — retirement plans that guaranteed principal and returns of up to 18% and allowed contributions for the life of the contract. This move forced the company to pay inflationary rates even after interest rates fell in the 1980s. To cover the difference, the firm invested in junk bonds and real estate but when the 1980s party was over, Equitable was left with $15 billion in GIC obligations and a lot of distressed real estate. The company almost went under.

In 1990 Richard Jenrette became CEO. He cut costs, sought new capital, and invested in new areas. By 1991 the company's situation had eased, yet rumors of Equitable's demise brought a run of policy redemptions, further increasing the need for cash. AXA stepped in and injected more than $1 billion into the firm in return for an active management role (sparking rumors of disharmony). But a bigger fix was needed. As a mutual, Equitable could not raise capital, so Jenrette took it public in 1992.

More cost-cutting, real estate sales, and an economic upturn contributed to a turn of the tide. But a little asset shuffling also helped. In 1993 the parent company capitalized the Life Assurance unit by buying 61% of DLJ from it, and the next year the corporation improved its asset quality by selling (through Alliance Capital Management) $700 million of collateralized, noninvestment-grade bonds, some of which the company then repurchased. It also sold 20% of DLJ in a 1995 IPO, after which Jenrette retired from active management.

Despite the gain from the stock sale, increased reserves (some still relating to the GICs) reduced 1996 earnings. Equitable began charting a course toward higher growth and closer relations with AXA.

In 1997 Equitable sold its Equitable Real Estate Investment Management unit to Lend Lease, an Australian public property and financial services company. The next year it said that it planned to sell half its remaining $4 billion real estate portfolio.

In 1999 the company changed its name to AXA Financial, retaining the venerable Equitable brand for its life insurance products.

OFFICERS

Chairman: Henri de Castries, age 44
VC and COO; President and COO, Equitable Life:
Michael Hegarty, age 54
President and CEO; Chairman and CEO, Equitable Life: Edward D. Miller, age 58, $5,747,019 pay
EVP and General Counsel, AXA Financial and Equitable Life: Robert E. Garber
EVP, AXA Financial and Equitable Life:
Jerome S. Golden, $1,291,450 pay
EVP and CFO; VC and CFO, Equitable Life:
Stanley B. Tulin
EVP and Chief Investment Officer, AXA Financial and Equitable Life: Peter D. Noris
EVP; SEVP and Chief Distribution Officer, Equitable Life: Jose S. Suquet
EVP and Chief Information Officer, Equitable Life: Leon B. Billis
Director of Human Resources: Carolyn Greene
Auditors: PricewaterhouseCoopers LLP

LOCATIONS

HQ: AXA Financial, Inc.,
1290 Avenue of the Americas, New York, NY 10104
Phone: 212-554-1234   **Fax:** 212-707-1755
Web site: http://www.equitable.com

PRODUCTS/OPERATIONS

1998 Assets

	$ mil.	% of total
Cash & equivalents	2,335	2
Trading account	13,195	8
Bonds	15,477	10
Other securities	24,287	15
Separate accounts	43,302	27
Receivables	34,590	22
Other assets	26,315	16
Total	**159,501**	**100**

1998 Sales

	$ mil.	% of total
Commissions, fees & other income	4,533	42
Investment income	4,499	41
Policy charges & fees	1,056	10
Premiums	588	5
Other	243	2
Total	**10,919**	**100**

1998 Sales

	% of total
Investment banking	50
Insurance	38
Asset management	12
Total	**100**

COMPETITORS

Chubb
CIGNA
Citigroup
John Hancock
Liberty Financial
Merrill Lynch
MetLife
MONY
New York Life
Northwestern Mutual
Prudential
State Farm
T. Rowe Price
Torchmark
USAA
Vanguard Group

HISTORICAL FINANCIALS & EMPLOYEES

NYSE symbol: AXF FYE: December 31	Annual Growth	1989	1990	1991	1992	1993	1994	1995	1996	1997	1998
Assets ($ mil.)	9.8%	68,574	69,789	74,918	78,869	98,991	94,640	113,749	128,811	151,438	159,501
Net income ($ mil.)	22.7%	132	(454)	(898)	(129)	235	297	350	99	561	833
Income as % of assets	—	0.2%	—	—	—	0.2%	0.3%	0.3%	0.1%	0.4%	0.5%
Earnings per share ($)	—	—	—	—	(0.08)	1.08	1.37	1.75	0.37	2.47	3.62
Stock price - FY high ($)	—	—	—	—	14.38	31.50	30.00	26.50	26.88	53.00	84.19
Stock price - FY low ($)	—	—	—	—	7.13	13.38	16.75	17.00	21.88	23.63	28.25
Stock price - FY close ($)	26.7%	—	—	—	14.00	27.00	18.13	24.00	24.63	49.75	57.88
P/E - high	—	—	—	—	—	29	22	15	73	21	23
P/E - low	—	—	—	—	—	12	12	10	59	10	8
Dividends per share ($)	12.2%	—	—	—	0.10	0.20	0.20	0.20	0.20	0.20	0.20
Book value per share ($)	9.9%	—	—	—	14.51	13.51	16.15	17.08	19.21	23.71	25.52
Employees	3.0%	—	—	—	12,300	13,100	13,600	13,300	14,700	12,700	14,700

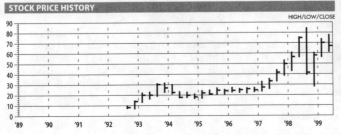

HIGH/LOW/CLOSE

1998 FISCAL YEAR-END

Equity as % of assets: 3.6%
Return on assets: 0.5%
Return on equity: 14.6%
Long-term debt ($ mil.): 6,300
No. of shares (mil.): 223
Dividends
 Yield: 0.3%
 Payout: 5.5%
Market value ($ mil.): 12,915
Sales (mil.): $10,919

BAKER & MCKENZIE

OVERVIEW

What do you call thousands of lawyers scattered across the globe? Whatever you call them, it's likely they're associated with Baker & McKenzie, the Chicago-based law firm that employs more lawyers and boasts more international offices than any other US law firm. With more than 2,300 lawyers in 59 offices across 35 countries, the firm offers legal services in areas such as banking, securities, labor, international trade, tax, and technology. It has handled the legal affairs of such heavy-duty clients as Chase Manhattan, Honeywell, and Ingersoll-Rand.

Its prolific global expansion has earned Baker & McKenzie the nickname McFirm (attorneys in rival firms joke that, like McDonald's, Baker & McKenzie has a franchise in every country). But Baker & McKenzie's knack for diving into developing regions (sometimes before the rule of law is even fully developed) has helped the firm establish market share before its competitors arrive to set up shop. Baker & McKenzie has established offices in such diverse areas as China, Hong Kong (the firm's largest office), Kazakhstan, Poland, Ukraine, and Vietnam. More than a third of its fees come from the Asia/Pacific region and more than 80% of its lawyers work in offices outside the US.

In spite of its girth, Baker & McKenzie is beginning to face new competition. Multinational accounting firms such as Andersen Worldwide are becoming more active in offering legal advice, charging lower fees than traditional law firms, while hiring away several tax partners from Baker & McKenzie.

HISTORY

Russell Baker traveled from his native New Mexico to Chicago on a railroad freight car to attend law school. Upon graduation in 1925 he started practicing law with his classmate Dana Simpson under the name Simpson & Baker. Inspired by Chicago's role as a manufacturing and agricultural center for the world and influenced by the international focus of his alma mater, the University of Chicago, Baker dreamed of developing an international law practice based in the Windy City. He began developing an expertise in international law. In 1934 Abbott Laboratories retained him to handle its worldwide legal affairs, and Baker was on his way to fulfilling his dream.

Baker joined forces in 1949 with Chicago litigator John McKenzie, forming Baker & McKenzie. The firm opened its first foreign office in 1955, in Caracas, Venezuela, to meet the needs of its expanding US client base. Over the next 10 years it opened outposts in Amsterdam, Brussels, Frankfurt, London, Madrid, Manila, Mexico City, Paris, Sao Paulo, Sydney, Tokyo, Toronto, and Zurich. Another 23 offices were added in the Americas, Asia, and Europe between 1965 and 1990.

Baker's death in 1979 neither slowed the firm's growth nor changed its international character. To manage the sprawling law firm, Baker & McKenzie created the position of chairman of the executive committee in 1984.

In late 1991 the firm dropped the Church of Scientology as a client, losing an estimated $2 million in business. It was speculated that pressure from client Eli Lilly (maker of the drug Prozac, which Scientologists actively oppose) influenced the decision. In 1992 Baker & McKenzie was ordered to pay $1 million for wrongfully firing an employee who later died of AIDS. The firm fought the verdict but eventually settled for an undisclosed amount in 1995.

In 1994 Baker & McKenzie closed its Los Angeles office (the former MacDonald, Halsted & Laybourne; acquired 1988) amid considerable rancor. Also that year a former secretary at the firm received a $7.1 million judgment for sexual harassment by a partner. (The award was later reduced by a San Francisco Superior Court judge to $3.5 million, and, after losing an appeal to further reduce the award, the firm paid the employee $3.5 million in 1998.)

John Klotsche, a senior partner from the firm's Palo Alto, California, office was appointed chairman in 1995. The following year the firm began a major expansion into California's Silicon Valley — the first step in an initiative to design services for technology companies around the world. It also expanded its Warsaw, Poland, office through a merger with the Warsaw office of Dickinson, Wright, Moon, Van Dusen & Freman.

In 1998 Baker & McKenzie formed a special unit in Singapore to deal with business generated from the financial troubles in Asia. The opening of offices in Taiwan and Azerbaijan in 1998 brought the firm's total number of offices to 59.

Chairman: John C. Klotsche
CFO: Suzanne M. Meyers
Executive Director: Lindy Reggiero
Director International Systems: Martin M. Moderi
Director International Administration:
Teresa A. Townsend
Manager Marketing and Public Relations: Joe Silverman
Supervisor Human Resources: Jennifer Pingolt
Auditors: Arthur Andersen LLP

LOCATIONS

HQ: 1 Prudential Plaza,
130 E. Randolph Dr., Ste. 2500, Chicago, IL 60601
Phone: 312-861-8800   **Fax:** 312-861-2899
Web site: http://www.bakerinfo.com

Baker & McKenzie has offices in 35 countries.

Office Locations

Argentina	The Netherlands
Australia	Philippines
Azerbaijan	Poland
Belgium	Russia
Brazil	Saudi Arabia
Canada	Singapore
Chile	Spain
China	Sweden
Colombia	Switzerland
Czech Republic	Taiwan
Egypt	Thailand
France	Ukraine
Germany	UK
Hungary	US
Indonesia	Venezuela
Italy	Vietnam
Japan	
Kazakhstan	
Mexico	

PRODUCTS/OPERATIONS

Selected Practice Areas
Banking and finance
  Aircraft and other asset-based finance
  Capital markets
  Derivatives
  Export credits
Corporate and securities
  Bond and note issues
  Domestic IPOs
  International equity offerings
International trade
  Antitrust and competition laws
  Customs duties
  Environmental and product safety regulations
  Import and export control regulations
IP, IT, and Communications
  Antipiracy
  Biotechnology and high technology
  Patent prosecution and counseling
Tax
  Customs duty
  Lobbying on tax matters
  Personal tax, trust, and estate planning
  Transfer pricing planning and defense
US Litigation
  Antitrust and unfair trade practices
  Construction
  Creditor's rights and bankruptcy
  Employment, labor, and civil rights
  Intellectual property
  Product liability & mass tort

COMPETITORS

Andersen Worldwide	McDermott, Will
Cleary, Gottlieb	Morgan, Lewis
Cravath, Swaine	Pillsbury Madison
Davis Polk	PricewaterhouseCoopers
Ernst & Young	Shearman & Sterling
Fulbright & Jaworski	Sidley & Austin
Gibson, Dunn & Crutcher	Simpson Thacher
Jones, Day	Skadden, Arps
Kirkland & Ellis	Sullivan & Cromwell
Latham & Watkins	Weil, Gotshal
Mayer, Brown & Platt	White & Case

HISTORICAL FINANCIALS & EMPLOYEES

Partnership FYE: June 30	Annual Growth	1989	1990	1991	1992	1993	1994	1995	1996	1997	1998
Sales ($ mil.)	9.7%	341	404	478	504	512	546	594	646	697	785
Employees	4.4%	—	4,736	4,887	4,919	5,054	5,114	5,248	5,680	6,100	6,700

SALES HISTORY

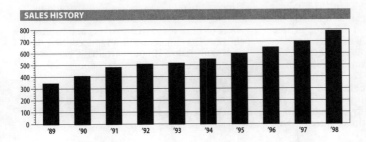

BAKER & MᶜKENZIE

BAKER HUGHES INCORPORATED

OVERVIEW

Baker Hughes has the drill down pat. The Houston-based company provides products and services to the worldwide oil field and process equipment industries. The firm helps energy companies locate oil and gas reserves and provides drill bits, drilling fluids, and other equipment used in the drilling process, as well as equipment and services used to complete and repair oil and gas wells. The company also provides waste-material separation and removal systems for industrial, mining, municipal, and papermaking operations. Baker Petrolite makes oil field specialty chemicals.

With the purchase of rival Western Atlas, Baker Hughes has reorganized its oil field operations to provide integrated services such as planning, engineering, and coordination of well drilling and completion. However, with oil prices hitting the bottom of the barrel, the company is tightening its belt — and trimming 18% of its workforce in the process.

HISTORY

Howard Hughes Sr. developed the first oil well drill bit for rock in 1909. Hughes and partner Walter Sharp opened a plant in Houston, and their company, Sharp & Hughes, soon had a near monopoly on rock bits. When Sharp died in 1912, Hughes bought his partner's half of the company, incorporating as Hughes Tool. Hughes held 73 patents when he died in 1924; the company passed to Howard Hughes Jr.

It is estimated that between 1924 and 1972 Hughes Tool provided Hughes Jr. with $745 million in pretax profits, which he used to diversify into movies (RKO), airlines (TWA), and Las Vegas casinos. In 1972 he sold the company to the public for $150 million. After 1972 the company expanded into tools for aboveground oil production. In 1974, under the new leadership of chairman James Leach, Hughes bought the oil field equipment business of Borg-Warner.

In 1913 drilling contractor Carl Baker organized the Baker Casing Shoe Company in California to collect royalties on his three oil tool inventions. The firm began to make its own products in 1918, and during the 1920s it expanded nationally, opened global trade, and formed Baker Oil Tools (1928). The company grew in the late 1940s and the 1950s as oil drilling boomed.

During the 1960s Baker prospered, despite fewer US well completions. International sales increased. From 1963 to 1975 Baker bought oil-related companies Kobe, Galigher, Ramsey Engineering, and Reed Tool. Sales topped $1 billion in 1979 for the first time.

US expenditures for oil services fell between 1982 and 1986 from $40 billion to $9 billion. In 1987 both Baker and Hughes faced falling revenues, and Hughes had large debts from expansion. The two companies merged to form Baker Hughes. By closing plants and combining operations, the venture became profitable by the end of 1988. The company bought Eastman Christensen (the world leader in directional and horizontal drilling equipment) and acquired the instrumentation unit of Tracor Holdings in 1990.

Baker Hughes spun off BJ Services (pumping services) to the public in 1991 and sold the Eastern Hemisphere operations of Baker Hughes Tubular Services (BHTS) to Tuboscope. It sold the Western Hemisphere operations of BHTS to ICO the following year.

Also in 1992 Baker Hughes bought Teleco Oilfield Services, a pioneer in directional drilling techniques, from Sonat. The next year the company consolidated its drilling-technology businesses into a single unit, named Baker Hughes INTEQ, to package services more efficiently.

The company continued expanding internationally in 1994, and in 1995 Baker Hughes sold EnviroTech Pumpsystems to the Weir Group of Glasgow, Scotland. In 1996 company veteran Max Lukens was promoted to CEO. He replaced James Woods as chairman the next year.

Baker Hughes formed an alliance with Schlumberger's oil field service operations in 1996. In a move to boost its oil field chemicals operations, in 1997 the company acquired Petrolite for about $693 million. Baker Hughes acquired rival Western Atlas for $3.3 billion in 1998 to keep up with the consolidation of the oil field services industry and to strengthen its land-based seismic data business (ranked #1 in that market) and testing business. As oil companies reduced their demand for Baker Hughes' products, because of the downturn in the Asian economy, disruptions from tropical storms, and slumping oil prices, the company announced job cuts in 1998 and again in 1999 that reduced their workforce more than 18%.

Chairman, President and CEO: Max L. Lukens, age 50, $800,000 pay
SVP: Thomas R. Bates, age 49, $270,351 pay
SVP Finance & Administration and CFO:
Ray A. Ballantyne
George S. Finley, age 47, $335,540 pay
SVP: Andrew J. Szescila, age 51, $425,577 pay
VP Marketing, Technology and Business Development:
Ray A. Ballantyne
VP and Treasurer: Douglas C. Doty
VP Government Affairs: Arthur T. Downey
VP and General Counsel: Lawrence O'Donnell III,
age 41, $284,620 pay
VP; President, Baker Petrolite: M. Glen Bassett
VP; President, Centrilift: Joseph F. Brady
VP; President, Baker Process: Matthew G. Dick
VP; President, E&P Solutions: Gerald M. Gilbert
VP; President, Baker Oil Tools: Edwin C. Howell,
$305,615 pay
VP; President, Baker Atlas: Gary E. Jones
VP; President, Baker Hughes INTEQ:
Timothy J. Probert
VP; President, Hughes Christensen: Douglas J. Wall
VP; President, Western Geophysical: Richard C. White
Manager of Human Resources: Nicole Boisburn
Auditors: Deloitte & Touche LLP

LOCATIONS

HQ: 3900 Essex Ln., Houston, TX 77027
Phone: 713-439-8600   **Fax:** 713-439-8699
Web site: http://www.bakerhughes.com

Baker Hughes operates 80 manufacturing plants around
the world, 67% of which are in the US.

PRODUCTS/OPERATIONS

1998 Sales

	$ mil.	% of total
Oil field equipment	5,802	92
Process equipment	490	8
Other	20	—
Total	**6,312**	**100**

Selected Subsidiaries
Baker Atlas
Baker Hughes INTEQ
Baker Oil Tools
Baker Petrolite
Centrilift
E&P Solutions
Hughes Christensen
Western Geophysical

COMPETITORS

BJ Services
Compagnie Generale de Geophysique
Fluor
FMC
Halliburton
Ingersoll-Rand
Nabors Industries
Petroleum Geo-Services
Schlumberger
Smith International
US Filter
Weatherford International

HISTORICAL FINANCIALS & EMPLOYEES

NYSE symbol: BHI FYE: December 31	Annual Growth	1989	1990	1991	1992	1993	1994	1995	1996	1997	1998
Sales ($ mil.)	11.7%	2,328	2,614	2,828	2,539	2,702	2,505	2,638	3,028	3,685	6,312
Net income ($ mil.)	—	85	142	174	5	59	43	105	176	97	(297)
Income as % of sales	—	3.7%	5.4%	6.1%	0.2%	2.2%	1.7%	4.0%	5.8%	2.6%	—
Earnings per share ($)	—	0.66	1.06	1.26	0.00	0.34	0.22	0.57	1.23	0.63	(0.92)
Stock price - FY high ($)	—	23.00	34.75	31.00	26.00	29.63	24.88	23.75	35.63	47.25	44.13
Stock price - FY low ($)	—	12.13	19.88	20.75	15.88	17.75	17.00	16.75	18.38	29.50	15.00
Stock price - FY close ($)	(1.9%)	21.00	29.00	24.50	23.38	23.50	18.63	20.38	30.38	43.81	17.63
P/E - high	—	35	33	25	—	87	113	42	29	75	—
P/E - low	—	18	19	16	—	52	77	29	15	47	—
Dividends per share ($)	2.6%	0.46	0.46	0.46	0.46	0.46	0.46	0.46	0.46	0.46	0.58
Book value per share ($)	1.8%	8.31	10.36	11.17	11.84	11.44	11.60	10.64	11.69	15.38	9.78
Employees	5.2%	20,400	20,900	21,300	19,600	18,400	14,700	15,200	16,800	21,500	32,300

STOCK PRICE HISTORY

HIGH/LOW/CLOSE

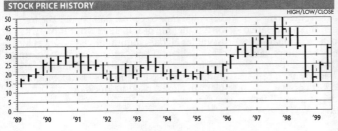

1998 FISCAL YEAR-END

Debt ratio: 46.0%
Return on equity: —
Cash ($ mil.): 17
Current ratio: 2.08
Long-term debt ($ mil.): 2,726
No. of shares (mil.): 327
Dividends
  Yield: 3.3%
  Payout: —
Market value ($ mil.): 5,767

BALL CORPORATION

OVERVIEW

Ball is trying to build up momentum as it leaves behind its century-old foundation as a glassmaker and rolls toward a future based on aluminum beverage cans and polyethylene terephthalate (PET) plastic packaging for food and beverages. Muncie, Indiana-based Ball also produces aerospace and communications items, including satellite ground station control software and spacecraft guidance and control instruments.

The company's packaging segment produces bottles, cans, and jars for the food and beverage industry. Customers include packagers of food, juices, soft drinks, beer, wine,

and spirits. PepsiCo and Coca-Cola bottlers account for about a fourth of sales. NASA, the US Department of Defense, and foreign governments all do business with the aerospace and technologies segment.

Ball's strategy is to build on its strength in cans (especially outside of the US, where can markets are growing rapidly) and to increase its output of plastic containers. The company is one of the leading makers of metal cans in North America and China, and it has can-manufacturing alliances in Brazil, the Philippines, and Thailand.

HISTORY

The Ball Corporation's history began in 1880 when Frank Ball and his four brothers started making wood-jacket tin cans to store and transport kerosene and other materials. In 1884 the company switched to tin-jacketed glass containers for kerosene lamps. The lamps, however, were soon displaced by Thomas Edison's electric lightbulb.

The Ball brothers then learned that the patent to the original sealed-glass storage container (the Mason jar) had expired. By 1886 the brothers had entered the sealed-jar business and imprinted their jars with the Ball name. In their first year, they made 12,500 jars and sparked a patent war with the two reigning jar producers, who asserted that they controlled the correct patents and threatened to sue. The Ball lawyers proved that the patents had expired, and the jar remained Ball's mainstay for many years.

By the late 1940s Ball's production facilities had become obsolete. The company began diversifying, but a 1947 antitrust ruling prohibited it from buying additional glass subsidiaries.

Ball decided to take advantage of the space race by buying Control Cells (aerospace science research) in 1957. The Soviets launched Sputnik that year, igniting a massive US scientific effort in 1958, and Ball's efforts led to federal contracts to make equipment for the US space program.

Ball established its metal beverage container business in 1969 when it bought Jeffco Manufacturing of Colorado. The company then won contracts to supply two-piece cans to Budweiser, Coca-Cola, Dr Pepper, Pepsi, and Stroh's Beer. John Fisher became president and CEO in 1971. The last company president who was a member of the Ball family, Fisher wanted Ball to diversify. He took

the company public in 1972 to fund his efforts. That year he acquired a Singapore-based petroleum equipment company. Next he led Ball into agricultural irrigation systems and prefabricated housing. In 1974 Ball acquired a small California computer firm, which formed the basis of its telecommunications division.

Fisher retired in 1981. Ball's metal-container business suffered in the late 1980s from overcapacity and price wars in its industry. In 1989 the aerospace division was hit hard by $10 million in losses on an Air Force contract and by reductions in defense spending.

Ball spun off its Alltrista subsidiary (a collection of seven diversified operations, including home canning jars) to shareholders in 1993 and purchased Heekin Can, a manufacturer for the food, pet food, and aerosol markets. That year Ball's $50 million mirror system corrected the Hubble Space Telescope's blurred vision. The company entered the polyethylene terephthalate (PET) container business in 1995 and placed its glass-container business into a newly formed company, Ball-Foster Glass Container. The next year Ball sold its 42% of the company to its partner, French materials company Saint-Gobain Group.

In 1996 Ball sold its aerosol-can business to BWAY Corp. In 1997 it acquired M.C. Packaging of Hong Kong to become a leading supplier of beverage cans to China. Ball popped the top on another big deal in 1998 when it bought Reynolds Metals' aluminum-can business for $746 million. It later announced it was closing two former Reynolds' plants in California and eliminating 300 jobs. In 1999 Ball announced plans to close a plant in Florida.

Chairman of the Executive Committee Emeritus:
Edmund F. Ball
Chairman Emeritus: John W. Fisher
Chairman and CEO: George A. Sissel, age 62,
$1,758,444 pay
VC and CFO: R. David Hoover, age 53, $876,378 pay
President; COO, Packaging Operations:
George A. Matsik, age 59, $872,223 pay
SVP Finance: Raymond J. Seabrook, age 47,
$475,416 pay
SVP Administration: David A. Westerlund, age 48,
$450,411 pay
VP and General Counsel: Donald C. Lewis, age 56
VP and Controller: Albert R. Schlesinger, age 57
VP Corporate Relations: Harold L. Sohn, age 52
Corporate Secretary: Elizabeth A. Overmyer
Treasurer: Douglas E. Poling
Assistant Corporate Secretary: Barbara J. Miller
Auditors: PricewaterhouseCoopers LLP

LOCATIONS

HQ: 10 Longs Peak Dr., Broomfield, CO 80021-2510
Phone: 303-469-3131
Web site: http://www.ball.com

Ball Corporation has more than 30 metal-packaging and
manufacturing facilities in the US, Canada, and Puerto
Rico. The company's aerospace and technologies group
has offices in California, Colorado, Georgia, New Mexico,
and Ohio. Ball also owns or has stakes in packaging
plants in Brazil, China, Hong Kong, the Philippines,
Russia, Taiwan, and Thailand.

PRODUCTS/OPERATIONS

1998 Sales

	$ mil.	% of total
Packaging	2,534	87
Aerospace & technologies	362	13
Total	**2,896**	**100**

Selected Products

Packaging
Metal
  Two- and three-piece metal food containers
  Two-piece metal beverage containers
Plastic
  PET plastic food and beverage containers

Aerospace and Technologies
Aerospace Systems
  Satellite ground station control hardware and software
  Spacecraft guidance, control instruments, and sensors
  Subsystems for surveillance, warning, target
    identification, and altitude control
Telecommunications Products
  Advanced antenna systems
  Video systems and products

COMPETITORS

Alcoa
Boeing
BWAY
CLARCOR
Continental Can
Crown Cork & Seal
PLM
Schmalbach-Lubeca
Sequa
SPX
Tetra Laval
Tyco International
U.S. Can

HISTORICAL FINANCIALS & EMPLOYEES

NYSE symbol: BLL FYE: December 31	Annual Growth	1989	1990	1991	1992	1993	1994	1995	1996	1997	1998
Sales ($ mil.)	10.1%	1,222	1,357	2,267	2,178	2,441	2,595	2,592	2,184	2,389	2,896
Net income ($ mil.)	(8.2%)	36	50	66	69	(65)	73	(19)	24	58	17
Income as % of sales	—	2.9%	3.7%	2.9%	3.2%	—	2.8%	—	1.1%	2.4%	0.6%
Earnings per share ($)	(12.3%)	1.44	1.95	2.29	2.34	2.35	2.35	(0.64)	0.68	1.74	0.44
Stock price - FY high ($)	—	34.38	34.50	38.25	39.50	37.25	32.13	38.75	32.25	39.00	47.94
Stock price - FY low ($)	—	25.25	26.00	25.63	28.00	25.13	24.38	25.75	23.13	23.75	28.63
Stock price - FY close ($)	3.5%	33.63	26.88	38.00	35.38	30.25	31.50	27.75	26.25	35.38	45.75
P/E - high	—	24	18	17	17	—	14	—	47	22	109
P/E - low	—	18	13	11	12	—	10	—	34	14	65
Dividends per share ($)	(6.5%)	1.10	1.14	1.18	1.22	1.24	0.60	0.60	0.60	0.60	0.60
Book value per share ($)	1.3%	17.39	18.28	21.39	22.55	19.11	20.25	18.84	19.22	20.23	19.52
Employees	6.2%	7,051	12,514	11,851	12,589	13,954	12,783	7,500	7,900	10,300	12,100

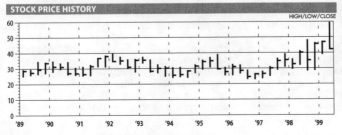

STOCK PRICE HISTORY
HIGH/LOW/CLOSE

1998 FISCAL YEAR-END
Debt ratio: 66.4%
Return on equity: 2.8%
Cash ($ mil.): 34
Current ratio: 1.29
Long-term debt ($ mil.): 1,230
No. of shares (mil.): 30
Dividends
  Yield: 1.3%
  Payout: 136.4%
Market value ($ mil.): 1,393

BANK OF AMERICA CORPORATION

OVERVIEW

Welcome to the machine.

Bank of America Corporation (formerly BankAmerica Corporation), the holding company formed by NationsBank's 1998 union with BankAmerica Corporation, is now the nation's largest bank. Headquartered in Charlotte, North Carolina, with wholesale operations in San Francisco, the bank has nearly 5,000 branches in 22 states and about 40 foreign countries. The new Bank of America and its subsidiaries offer a wide range of financial services, including consumer, commercial, and international banking; commercial real estate; investment and brokerage services; mortgage lending; insurance; mutual funds; and more.

Bank of America's predecessor banks (NationsBank, which is the surviving entity, and BankAmerica) had both been big dogs in the hunt for merger and acquisition targets. NationsBank, in particular, was known for its aggressiveness in expanding through acquisitions.

HISTORY

Bank of America predecessor NationsBank got started in 1874, when citizens of Charlotte organized Commercial National Bank. Commercial National merged with American Trust Company (founded 1901) in 1957 to become American Commercial Bank. American Commercial merged with Security National (founded 1933) in 1960 to form North Carolina National Bank, which operated 40 offices in 20 North Carolina cities.

The bank formed a holding company, NCNB Corp., in 1968. By 1980 NCNB was the largest bank in North Carolina. It became the first bank to expand into Florida by buying First National Bank of Lake City in 1982.

Under the leadership of Hugh McColl, who became chairman in 1983, NCNB became the first southern banking operation to span six states: Florida, Georgia, Maryland, North Carolina, South Carolina, and Virginia.

NCNB profited hugely from the savings and loan crisis of the late 1980s and early 1990s by managing assets and branches and by buying defunct thrifts at fire-sale prices. The company nearly doubled its assets in 1988 when the FDIC chose it to manage the shuttered First Republicbank Corp., formerly Texas' largest bank. The company took over C&S/Sovran in 1991. NCNB was then renamed NationsBank.

In 1993 the company diversified by buying Chicago Research & Trading, a government securities, derivatives, and options dealer and provider of oil and gas financing. It moved into Mexico in 1994 with the acquisition of 10% of Grupo Financiero Bancomer's factoring business.

A 1993 joint venture with Dean Witter, Discover to open securities brokerages in banks led to complaints; citing differences over sales practices, Dean Witter withdrew from the arrangement in 1994. SEC investigations and a class-action lawsuit ensued, with NationsBank settling the lawsuit for about $30 million. (The company agreed to settle similar charges in 1998.)

NationsBank acquired St. Louis-based Boatmen's Bancshares in 1997 and entered the formerly out-of-bounds investment banking field by purchasing Montgomery Securities (now Banc of America Securities). The next year it acquired Barnett Banks, Florida's leading bank.

Enter BankAmerica. Founded in 1904 as Bank of Italy, BankAmerica had at one time been the US's largest bank but fell behind as competitors consolidated. As the ink was drying on the Barnett Banks purchase, BankAmerica's board of directors was discussing whether the bank could become more competitive by acquiring or being acquired.

BankAmerica opted for the latter, and initiated talks with NationsBank. NationsBank caught its breath, then agreed to merge. Just after the merger, the bank announced it would write down a $1.4 billion bad loan to investment firm D.E. Shaw & Co., which followed the same Russian-investment-paved path of descent as Long-Term Capital Management. David Coulter (head of the old BankAmerica, which made the loan) took the fall for the loss, resigning as president; the balance of executive power shifted noticeably to the NationsBank side when in 1999 Kenneth Lewis took the post.

The Russian debacle and the difficulties of trying to mesh the two banks led the firm in early 1999 to reorganize and reduce overseas operations, including selling its private banking operations in Europe and Asia to UBS AG. Also that year it bought 50% of Denver-based mutual fund firm Marsico Capital Management. The bank changed its name from BankAmerica Corporation to Bank of America Corporation and linked up with America Online to offer online banking services through AOL's Banking Center.

OFFICERS

Chairman and CEO: Hugh L. McColl Jr., age 63, $3,500,000 pay
VC and CFO: James H. Hance Jr., age 54, $2,387,500 pay
President: Kenneth D. Lewis, age 51, $2,387,500 pay
President, Global Corporate and Investment Banking: Michael J. Murray, age 54, $2,387,500 pay
President, Principal Investing and Wealth Management: Michael E. O'Neill
Corporate Risk Mnagement Executive: F. William Vandiver Jr., age 56, $2,225,000 pay
EVP and Senior Personnel Executive: Charles Cooley
EVP and Principal Financial Executive: Marc D. Oken, age 52
COO, Bank in Europe, Middle East and Africa: John Weguelin
International Treasurer, Global Markets Group: Gordon Sangster
Director Europe, Middle East & Africa Corporate Banking Group: Alexandra McLeod
Director International Corporate Banking Group: Robert P. Morrow III, age 49

LOCATIONS

HQ: 100 N. Tryon St., 18th Fl., Charlotte, NC 28255
Phone: 704-386-5000   **Fax:** 704-386-6699
Web site: http://www.bankofamerica.com

Bank of America has more than 4,800 branches in 22 US states and the District of Columbia and maintains offices in 37 other countries.

PRODUCTS/OPERATIONS

1998 Assets

	$ mil.	% of total
Cash & equivalents	62,173	10
Trading account	39,602	6
US treasury securities	17,728	3
Foreign securities	6,494	1
Mortgage-backed securities	51,993	8
Derivative-dealer assets	16,400	3
Other securities	4,372	1
Net loans	350,206	57
Receivable	3,734	1
Other assets	64,977	10
Total	**617,679**	**100**

COMPETITORS

American Express	First Virginia
AmSouth	Fleet
Bank of Montreal	GE
Bank of New York	Golden West Financial
BANK ONE	Household International
BankBoston	J.P. Morgan
BB&T	KeyCorp
Canadian Imperial	MBNA
Chase Manhattan	Mellon Bank
Citigroup	SunTrust
Countrywide Credit	U. S. Bancorp
Credit Lyonnais	UnionBanCal
Credit Suisse First Boston	Wachovia
Dai-Ichi Kangyo	Washington Mutual
First Union	Wells Fargo

HISTORICAL FINANCIALS & EMPLOYEES

NYSE symbol: BAC FYE: December 31	Annual Growth	1989	1990	1991	1992	1993	1994	1995	1996	1997	1998
Assets ($ mil.)	28.2%	66,191	65,285	110,319	118,059	157,686	169,604	187,298	185,794	264,562	617,679
Net income ($ mil.)	27.9%	563	366	202	1,145	1,501	1,690	1,950	2,375	3,077	5,165
Income as % of assets	—	0.9%	0.6%	0.2%	1.0%	1.0%	1.0%	1.0%	1.3%	1.2%	0.8%
Earnings per share ($)	4.2%	—	—	—	2.26	2.86	3.03	3.52	3.92	4.17	2.90
Stock price - FY high ($)	—	—	—	—	26.69	29.00	28.69	37.38	52.63	71.69	88.44
Stock price - FY low ($)	—	—	—	—	19.81	22.25	21.69	22.31	32.19	48.00	44.00
Stock price - FY close ($)	15.2%	—	—	—	25.69	24.50	22.56	34.81	48.88	60.81	60.13
P/E - high	—	—	—	—	12	10	9	11	13	17	30
P/E - low	—	—	—	—	9	8	7	6	8	12	15
Dividends per share ($)	13.1%	—	—	—	0.76	0.82	0.94	1.04	1.20	1.37	1.59
Book value per share ($)	9.8%	—	—	—	15.21	18.03	19.71	23.15	23.61	29.83	26.59
Employees	13.0%	57,069	58,449	58,449	50,828	57,463	61,484	58,322	62,971	80,360	170,975

1997 and prior information is for NationsBank Corporation only.

STOCK PRICE HISTORY

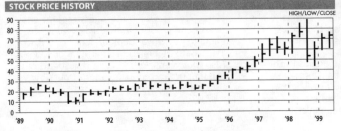

HIGH/LOW/CLOSE

1998 FISCAL YEAR-END

Equity as % of assets: 7.4%
Return on assets: 1.2%
Return on equity: 11.3%
Long-term debt ($ mil.): 45,888
No. of shares (mil.): 1,724
Dividends
  Yield: 2.6%
  Payout: 54.8%
Market value ($ mil.): 103,693
Sales (mil.): $51,794

THE BANK OF NEW YORK COMPANY

OVERVIEW

Big Apple-based The Bank of New York Company (BNY) is biting deeper into the custody and trust markets. The top retail bank in the suburban New York area, The company's operations include some 360 branches, mostly in tony suburbs in New York, New Jersey, and Connecticut. BNY offers real estate and consumer loans, as well as banking services for small and midsized businesses. BNY Capital Markets offers such investment banking services as structuring and syndication of credit facilities, debt and equity private placements, and advice on mergers and acquisitions.

The company also provides government and corporate clearing, transfer, and transaction services and corporate finance options such as mortgage-backed lending. BNY has especially cashed in on securities processing, including American depositary receipts (dollar-denominated foreign securities) services.

BNY has been building its fee-based operations through acquisitions, particularly securities processing and trust services. It will surpass Chase Manhattan as the #1 provider of custodial services after its planned acquisition of Royal Bank of Scotland's trust services.

HISTORY

In 1784 Alexander Hamilton (at 27, already a Revolutionary War hero and economic theorist) and a group of New York merchants and lawyers founded New York City's first bank, The Bank of New York Company (BNY). Hamilton saw a need for a credit system to finance the nation's growth and to establish credibility for the new nation's chaotic monetary system.

Hamilton became US secretary of the treasury in 1789 and soon negotiated the new US government's first loan — for $200,000 — from BNY. The bank also helped finance the War of 1812 by offering $16 million in subscription books, and the Civil War by loaning the government $150 million. In 1878 BNY became a US Treasury depository for the sale of government bonds.

The bank's conservative fiscal policies and emphasis on commercial banking enabled it to weather economic turbulence in the 19th century. In 1922 it merged with New York Life Insurance and Trust Co. (formed in 1830 by many of BNY's directors) to form Bank of New York and Trust Co. The bank survived the crash of 1929 and remained profitable, paying dividends throughout the Depression. In 1938 it reclaimed its Bank of New York name.

During the mid-20th century, BNY expanded its operations and its reach through acquisitions, including Fifth Avenue Bank (trust services, 1948) and Empire Trust Co. (serving developing industries, 1966). In 1968 the bank created holding company The Bank of New York Company, Inc., to expand statewide with purchases such as Empire National Bank (1980).

BNY relaxed its lending policies in the 1980s and began to build its fee-for-service side, boosting its American depositary receipts business by directly soliciting European companies and seeking government securities business. The bank bought New York competitor Irving Trust in a 1989 hostile takeover and in 1990 began buying other banks' credit card portfolios.

As the economy cooled in the early 1990s, BNY's book of highly leveraged transactions and nonperforming loans suffered, so the company sold many of those loans.

In the mid-1990s BNY bought processing and trust businesses and continued to build its retail business in the suburbs. It pared noncore operations, selling its mortgage banking unit (and in 1998 moved its remaining mortgage operations into a joint venture with Alliance Mortgage Company). However, BNY continues to originate mortgages.

The move into trust services accelerated in 1997 when BNY bought operations from Wells Fargo, Signet Bank (now part of First Union), and NationsBank (now Bank of America). By 1998 BNY had bought close to two dozen corporate trust businesses. The company also sold its credit card business to Chase Manhattan and announced plans in 1999 to sell its factoring and asset-based lending operations to General Motors Acceptance Corporation. In late 1997 and again in 1998, the bank tried to woo Mellon Bank into a merger but was rejected each time.

Also in 1998 BNY bought the Bank of Montreal's UK-based fiscal agency business. In 1999 the bank bought Estabrook Capital Management, which manages asset for businesses and wealthy individuals, and made plans to buy Royal Bank of Scotland's RBS Trust Bank to boost international business. Also that year, the US began investigating Russian organized-crime money possibly flowing through the bank.

Chairman and CEO: Thomas A. Renyi, age 53, $7,380,385 pay
VC: Alan R. Griffith, age 57, $3,617,308 pay
President: Gerald L. Hassell, age 47, $3,138,048 pay
SEVP and CFO: Bruce W. Van Saun, age 41, $925,385 pay
SEVP Asset Based Lending Sector, The Bank of New York: Robert J. Mueller
SEVP Financial Companies Services Sector, The Bank of New York: Thomas J. Perna
SEVP Worldwide Securities Processing Sector, The Bank of New York: Joseph M. Velli
EVP and Chief Credit Policy Officer, The Bank of New York: Harold F. Dietz
EVP Corporate Banking, The Bank of New York: Leslie V. Godridge
Director Personnel: Thomas Angers
Auditors: Ernst & Young LLP

LOCATIONS

HQ: The Bank of New York Company, Inc.,
1 Wall St., New York, NY 10286
Phone: 212-495-1784   **Fax:** 212-495-2546
Web site: http://www.bankofny.com

1998 Sales & Pretax Income

	Sales		Pretax Income	
	$ mil.	% of total	$ mil.	% of total
US	4,620	80	1,076	90
Europe	662	11	65	6
Asia	239	4	14	1
Other regions	272	5	37	3
Total	**5,793**	**100**	**1,192**	**100**

PRODUCTS/OPERATIONS

1998 Assets

	$ mil.	% of total
Net loans	37,750	59
Cash & equivalents	8,503	13
US Treasuries	3,444	5
Trading account	1,637	3
State & municipal bonds	662	1
Other securities	2,268	4
Other	9,239	15
Total	**63,503**	**100**

1998 Sales

	$ mil.	% of total
Loan interest	2,770	48
Processing fees	1,256	22
Trust & service charges	709	12
Other interest	740	13
Other	318	5
Total	**5,793**	**100**

COMPETITORS

Bank of America	Fleet
BANK ONE	HSBC Holdings
BankBoston	J.P. Morgan
Brown Brothers Harriman	KeyCorp
Canadian Imperial	Mellon Bank
Chase Manhattan	Northern Trust
Citigroup	Republic New York
Deutsche Bank	Royal Bank of Canada
First Union	UBS

HISTORICAL FINANCIALS & EMPLOYEES

NYSE symbol: BK FYE: December 31	Annual Growth	1989	1990	1991	1992	1993	1994	1995	1996	1997	1998
Assets ($ mil.)	3.0%	48,857	45,390	39,426	40,909	45,546	48,879	53,720	55,765	59,961	63,503
Net income ($ mil.)	42.0%	51	308	122	369	559	749	914	1,020	1,104	1,192
Income as % of assets	—	0.1%	0.7%	0.3%	0.9%	1.2%	1.5%	1.7%	1.8%	1.8%	1.9%
Earnings per share ($)	49.9%	0.04	0.50	0.16	0.53	0.68	0.93	1.09	1.20	1.36	1.53
Stock price - FY high ($)	—	6.88	5.22	4.52	6.83	7.81	8.31	12.25	18.06	29.28	40.56
Stock price - FY low ($)	—	4.59	1.66	2.06	3.75	6.33	6.23	7.13	10.88	16.38	24.00
Stock price - FY close ($)	26.0%	5.03	2.22	3.86	6.73	7.13	7.44	12.19	16.88	28.91	40.25
P/E - high	—	172	10	28	13	11	9	11	15	22	27
P/E - low	—	115	3	13	7	9	7	7	9	12	16
Dividends per share ($)	8.9%	0.25	0.27	0.21	0.19	0.22	0.28	0.34	0.42	0.49	0.54
Book value per share ($)	5.5%	4.36	4.49	4.48	4.82	5.04	5.56	6.46	6.49	6.67	7.05
Employees	0.0%	17,083	15,847	15,139	16,167	15,621	15,477	15,810	16,158	16,494	17,157

STOCK PRICE HISTORY

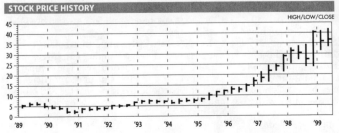

HIGH/LOW/CLOSE

1998 FISCAL YEAR-END

Equity as % of assets: 8.6%
Return on assets: 1.9%
Return on equity: 21.9%
Long-term debt ($ mil.): 2,086
No. of shares (mil.): 773
Dividends
  Yield: 1.3%
  Payout: 35.3%
Market value ($ mil.): 31,118
Sales (mil.): $5,793

BANK ONE CORPORATION

OVERVIEW

"Bigger is better" is the current banking industry mantra, and BANK ONE CORPORATION fits the mold right down to its all-caps name.

The Chicago-based company's acquisition of First Chicago NBD has made it one of the top five US banks by assets; its First USA unit is the top credit card issuer in the US (ahead of Citigroup and MBNA). BANK ONE has more than 2,000 branches in 14 states and has electronic banking facilities that allow customers to bank anywhere in the US.

The new BANK ONE is the product of consolidation and regulatory changes that allow banks to operate as unified national corporations. In BANK ONE's case, its one-stop shop is organized around credit card services, retail and commercial banking (including leasing and lease financing), investment management, and consumer finance (including mortgage lending and other consumer credit services). First Chicago has brought to the new entity its strengths in regional banking, corporate banking, corporate investments, and credit cards.

HISTORY

The 130-year journey from Columbus, Ohio, to Chicago started with BANK ONE's predecessor, BANC ONE, which traced its origins to 1868, when F. C. Session opened a bank in Columbus. By 1929 Session's bank combined with another local bank to form City National Bank and Trust. John H. McCoy became the bank's president in 1935, spawning a family dynasty.

John G. succeeded his father in 1958, and City National soon began to break with tradition. In the 1960s the bank helped launch comedienne Phyllis Diller by hiring her for radio and TV commercials.

In 1966 the bank introduced the first Visa (then BankAmericard) card service outside California. McCoy formed a holding company for City National, First Banc Group of Ohio, in 1967 (using a "c" because of legal restrictions on using "bank"). The firm then moved beyond Columbus, buying Farmers Savings and Trust of Mansfield, Ohio, in 1968. First Banc scored a coup in 1977 when Merrill Lynch hired it to handle the Cash Management Account, the first product to combine a brokerage account with checking and a debit card.

First Banc Group changed its name to BANC ONE in 1979; all affiliated banks took the name Bank One. Another McCoy, John B., succeeded his father as CEO in 1984 as barriers to interstate banking were loosened. BANC ONE expanded into Indiana, Kentucky, Michigan, and Wisconsin. It broke into the lucrative but troubled Texas market in 1989 by acquiring 20 failed MCorp bank branches, helped by a hefty dose of federal aid.

In 1991 the firm entered Illinois, and the next year it moved on to Arizona and Utah, all with stock swap acquisitions (continuing its policy of not diluting its investors' stock holdings). It formed a development alliance with Banco Nacional de Mexico in 1992.

The company was developing branded services and products, but affiliates could choose among offerings and maintain their own information systems. This setup made it difficult to track regional operations, and many positions were duplicated. Such excess could be tolerated when acquisitions were a cheap way of increasing sales, but when earnings took a dip after the bond market collapse of 1994, the effect on the bottom line became apparent.

In response, BANC ONE began a major consolidation effort. The company also continued to make acquisitions, and in 1996 it bought Premier Bancorp. Premier had been built up during the 1980s by C. W. "Chuck" McCoy — John B. McCoy's uncle. In 1997 BANC ONE bought Oklahoma City-based Liberty Bancorp. That year its acquisition of First USA, the fourth-largest credit card issuer in the US, made BANC ONE the #3 credit card issuer (behind Citicorp and MBNA); by 1999, BANC ONE had eclipsed its competitors as the world's largest issuer of Visa credit cards.

Founded in 1863, First Chicago NBD emerged from the Chicago Fire of 1871, weathered the bank runs of the Great Depression, but succumbed to the siren call of industry consolidation in early 1998. Needing a national partner to transcend its super-regional status, First Chicago agreed to be acquired by BANC ONE in a $30 billion stock swap in early 1998. The combined banks became BANK ONE, which was based in Chicago and 40%-owned by First Chicago stockholders and 60%-owned by BANC ONE holders.

In 1999 BANK ONE announced plans to cut 20% of its foreign banking employees and about 5% of its total workforce. The company also agreed to sell First Chicago's mortgage servicing portfolio to HomeSide for $18 billion and sold its transaction processing services to First Data.

Chairman: Verne G. Istock, age 58, $2,568,270 pay
VC: Richard Lehmann, age 54, $1,749,700 pay
VC: David Vitale, age 52, $1,519,616 pay
President and CEO: John B. McCoy, age 55,
$3,195,000 pay
SEVP and Head of Acquisitions: William P. Boardman,
age 57
EVP and CFO: Robert Rosholt, age 49
EVP and Chief Information Officer: Marvin Adams
EVP, General Counsel, and Secretary:
Sherman I. Goldberg, age 56
EVP and Head of Commercial Bank Products:
W.G. Jurgensen, age 47
EVP and Head of Investment Management:
David J. Kundert, age 56
EVP and Head of Human Resources: Timothy P. Moen,
age 46
EVP and Head of Commercial Bank Relationships:
Susan S. Moody, age 45
EVP and General Auditor: Robert A. O'Neil Jr., age 45
**EVP and Head of Commercial Bank - Real Estate and
Private Banking:** Ronald G. Steinhart, age 58
EVP and Head of Credit Card: Richard W. Vague, age 43,
$1,559,575 pay
EVP and Head of Finance One: Donald A. Winkler
Chairman, First Chicago Capital Markets:
F. Gerald Byrne
CEO, European Operations: James Corcoran
CEO, Canadian Division: Gary Heatherington
Auditors: Arthur Andersen LLP

LOCATIONS

HQ: 1 First National Plaza, Chicago, IL 60670
Phone: 312-732-4000   **Fax:** 312-732-3366
Web site: http://www.bankone.com

PRODUCTS/OPERATIONS

1998 Assets

	$ mil.	% of total
Cash & equivalents	34,382	13
Trading account	5,345	2
Securities	44,852	17
Net loans	153,127	59
Other	23,790	9
Total	**261,496**	**100**

1998 Sales

	$ mil.	% of total
Interest		
Loans	14,106	55
Securities	2,297	9
Other interest	1,121	4
Credit card income	3,276	13
Charge & fees	2,645	11
Other	2,150	8
Total	**25,595**	**100**

COMPETITORS

ABN Amro	Comerica	Huntington
Advanta	Cullen/Frost	Bancshares
American	Bankers	KeyCorp
Express	Fifth Third	Marshall & Ilsley
The Associates	Bancorp	Mellon Bank
Bank of America	First Security	Merrill Lynch
Bank of Montreal	Firstar Corp.	MBNA
Bank of New	Fleet	MNB Bancshares
York	Ford	Morgan Stanley
Capital One	GE	Dean Witter
Financial	General Motors	Northern Trust
Charles Schwab	Harris Bankcorp	PNC Bank
Chase Manhattan	Household	Washington
Citigroup	International	Mutual
CNB Bancshares		Wells Fargo

HISTORICAL FINANCIALS & EMPLOYEES

NYSE symbol: ONE FYE: December 31	Annual Growth	1989	1990	1991	1992	1993	1994	1995	1996	1997	1998
Assets ($ mil.)	28.9%	26,552	30,336	46,293	61,417	79,919	88,923	90,454	101,848	115,901	261,496
Net income ($ mil.)	26.9%	363	423	530	781	1,140	1,005	1,278	1,427	1,306	3,108
Income as % of assets	—	1.4%	1.4%	1.1%	1.3%	1.4%	1.1%	1.4%	1.4%	1.1%	1.2%
Earnings per share ($)	7.4%	1.37	1.51	1.75	1.96	2.09	1.80	2.20	2.52	1.99	2.61
Stock price - FY high ($)	—	18.37	18.09	28.81	32.15	36.95	31.40	33.15	43.52	54.43	65.63
Stock price - FY low ($)	—	11.04	10.38	13.59	25.31	26.66	19.93	20.76	28.41	35.68	36.13
Stock price - FY close ($)	13.7%	16.08	15.16	28.74	31.92	29.39	20.97	31.09	39.09	49.37	51.06
P/E - high	—	13	12	16	16	18	17	15	17	27	25
P/E - low	—	8	7	8	13	13	11	9	11	18	14
Dividends per share ($)	12.9%	0.50	0.55	0.62	0.70	0.85	1.00	1.38	0.93	1.35	1.49
Book value per share ($)	8.1%	8.55	9.89	11.54	12.83	14.72	15.23	16.89	17.96	15.89	17.30
Employees	19.9%	17,800	19,300	27,500	32,700	45,300	48,800	46,900	51,100	56,600	91,310

STOCK PRICE HISTORY

HIGH/LOW/CLOSE

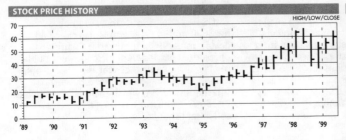

1998 FISCAL YEAR-END

Equity as % of assets: 7.8%
Return on assets: 1.6%
Return on equity: 15.3%
Long-term debt ($ mil.): 21,295
No. of shares (mil.): 1,177
Dividends
  Yield: 2.9%
  Payout: 57.1%
Market value ($ mil.): 60,113
Sales (mil.): $25,595

BARNES & NOBLE, INC.

OVERVIEW

Barnes & Noble books a lot of sales, and it sells a lot of books — one in every eight books sold in the US, as a matter of fact. The New York City-based retailer is the #1 US bookstore chain, with about 1,000 stores in every state and the District of Columbia. More than half of its stores are freestanding superstores operating under the Barnes & Noble, Bookstop, and Bookstar banners; the rest are mall-based stores under the names B. Dalton, Doubleday, and Scribner's. Barnes & Noble also owns a direct-mail bookselling business and several publishing companies. Chairman and CEO Lenny Riggio — who confesses he's not much of a reader these days — owns about 23% of the company. Riggio also owns 80% of sister company Barnes & Noble College Bookstores, a private textbook seller.

Riggio revolutionized bookselling by introducing huge stores (up to 60,000 sq. ft.) that stocked an extensive range of titles at deep discounts. He made them browser-friendly environments by adding children's areas and cafes. Although Riggio has made bookstores into popular hangouts, not everyone is pleased. Barnes & Noble (along with rival Borders Group) has been sued by independent retailers who claim they are being forced out of business.

The company's online book selling unit, barnesandnoble.com (a publicly traded joint venture with Bertelsmann), continues to play catch-up with leader Amazon.com. Although Barnes & Noble continues to close mall-based stores in favor of freestanding superstores, it is testing a new mall format: newsstands called ink.

HISTORY

Barnes & Noble dates back to 1873 when Charles Barnes went into the used-book business in Wheaton, Illinois. By the turn of the century, he was operating a thriving bookselling operation in Chicago. His son William took over as president in 1902. William sold his share in the firm in 1917 (to C. W. Follett, who built Follett Corp. into a major Barnes & Noble competitor) and moved to New York City, where he bought an interest in established textbook wholesalers Noble & Noble. The company was soon renamed Barnes & Noble. It first sold mainly to colleges and libraries, providing textbooks and opening a large Fifth Avenue shop. Over the next three decades, Barnes & Noble became one of the leading booksellers in the New York region.

Enter Lenny Riggio, who worked at a New York University bookstore to help pay for night school. He studied engineering but got the itch for bookselling. In 1965, at age 24, he borrowed $5,000 and opened Student Book Exchange NYC, a college bookstore. Beginning in the late 1960s, he expanded by buying other college bookstores.

In 1971 Riggio paid $1.2 million for the Barnes & Noble store on Fifth Avenue. He soon expanded the store, and in 1974 he began offering jaw-dropping, competitor-maddening discounts of up to 40% for best-sellers. Acquiring Marboro Books five years later, the company entered the mail-order and publishing business.

By 1986 Barnes & Noble had grown to about 180 outlets (including 142 college bookstores). Along with Dutch retailer Vendex, that year it bought Dayton Hudson's B. Dalton mall

bookstore chain (about 800 stores), forming BDB Holding Corp. (Vendex had sold its shares by 1997.) In 1989 the company acquired the Scribner's Bookstores trade name and the Bookstop/Bookstar superstore chain. BDB began its shift to superstore format and streamlined its operations to integrate Bookstop and Doubleday (acquired in 1990) into its business.

BDB changed its name to Barnes & Noble in 1991. With superstore sales booming, the retailer went public in 1993 (the college stores remained private). Despite Barnes & Noble's record sales, charges from its mall store closings led to a $53 million loss in fiscal 1996. It also bought 20% of Canadian bookseller Chapters that year (sold in 1999).

The bookseller went online in 1997 and in 1998 sold a 50% stake in its Web operation subsidiary to German media giant Bertelsmann. The $200 million deal was meant to strengthen both companies in the battle against online rival Amazon.com. A group of independent retailers (backed by the American Booksellers Association) sued Barnes & Noble in 1998 for allegedly pressuring publishers into granting unfair discounts and promotions.

Also in 1998 Barnes & Noble agreed to buy #1 US book distributor Ingram Book Group for $600 million; the companies called off the deal in mid-1999 after it ran into antitrust opposition. barnesandnoble.com went public in May 1999. Later that year Barnes & Noble bought small book publisher J.B. Fairfax International USA, which includes the Michael Friedman Publishing Group, a publisher of coffee-table books.

Chairman and CEO; Chairman, barnesandnoble.com:
Leonard Riggio, age 58, $1,223,077 pay
VC: Stephen Riggio, age 44, $793,846 pay
COO: J. Alan Kahn, age 52, $800,000 pay
EVP; President, Barnes & Noble Development:
Mitchell S. Klipper, age 41, $793,846 pay
EVP and CFO: Marie J. Toulantis, age 45, $480,000 pay
SVP Corporate Communications and Public Affairs:
Mary E. Keating, age 42
VP and Controller: Michael Archbold
VP; President, Barnes & Noble Distribution:
David K. Cully, age 46
VP Real Estate: David S. Deason, age 40
VP and Chief Information Officer: Joseph Giamelli,
age 49
VP Marketing and Advertising: Maureen H. Golden,
age 48
VP; President, B. Dalton Bookseller: Frank O'Neill,
age 49
VP Human Resources: Michelle Smith
VP; President, Barnes & Noble Booksellers:
Thomas A. Tolworthy, age 44
CEO, barnesandnoble.com: Jonathan Bulkeley
COO, barnesandnoble.com: Jeffery M. Killeen, age 44
Secretary: Michael N. Rosen, age 58
Auditors: BDO Seidman, LLP

LOCATIONS

HQ: 122 5th Ave., New York, NY 10011
Phone: 212-633-3300   **Fax:** 212-675-0413
Web site: http://www.shareholder.com/bks

Barnes & Noble has stores in all 50 states and
Washington, DC.

PRODUCTS/OPERATIONS

Selected Businesses
Mail-order business
  Marboro Books Corp.
Mall stores
  B. Dalton Bookseller
  Doubleday Book Shops
  Scribner's Bookstores
Online sales
  barnesandnoble.com (40%)
Publishing
  Barnes & Noble Books
  J.B. Fairfax International USA
  Michael Friedman Publishing
Superstores
  Barnes & Noble
  Bookstar
  Bookstop

COMPETITORS

Amazon.com
Book-of-the-Month Club
Books-A-Million
Borders
Cendant
Crown Books
Follett
Hastings Entertainment
Lauriat's
MTS
Musicland
Toys "R" Us
Viacom
Wal-Mart
WH Smith

HISTORICAL FINANCIALS & EMPLOYEES

NYSE symbol: BKS FYE: January 31	Annual Growth	1990	1991	1992	1993	1994	1995	1996	1997	1998	1999
Sales ($ mil.)	16.7%	749	880	921	1,087	1,337	1,623	1,977	2,448	2,797	3,006
Net income ($ mil.)	26.7%	11	7	(5)	(9)	8	26	(53)	51	53	92
Income as % of sales	—	1.5%	0.8%	—	—	0.6%	1.6%	—	2.1%	1.9%	3.1%
Earnings per share ($)	53.8%	—	—	—	—	0.15	0.41	(0.85)	0.75	1.10	1.29
Stock price - FY high ($)	—	—	—	—	—	17.00	15.69	21.13	18.88	34.25	48.00
Stock price - FY low ($)	—	—	—	—	—	10.31	10.00	10.81	11.88	15.19	22.19
Stock price - FY close ($)	28.3%	—	—	—	—	10.75	14.88	13.44	15.56	31.75	37.44
P/E - high	—	—	—	—	—	113	38	—	25	31	37
P/E - low	—	—	—	—	—	69	24	—	16	14	17
Dividends per share ($)	—	—	—	—	—	0.00	0.00	0.00	0.00	0.00	0.00
Book value per share ($)	12.4%	—	—	—	—	5.50	5.95	6.07	6.87	7.83	9.87
Employees	12.6%	—	—	12,600	13,500	14,700	20,000	21,400	23,900	29,500	29,000

STOCK PRICE HISTORY

HIGH/LOW/CLOSE

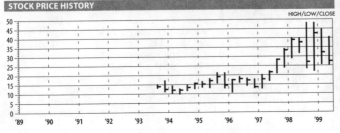

1999 FISCAL YEAR-END

Debt ratio: 26.8%
Return on equity: 13.6%
Cash ($ mil.): 31
Current ratio: 1.41
Long-term debt ($ mil.): 249
No. of shares (mil.): 69
Dividends
  Yield: —
  Payout: —
Market value ($ mil.): 2,574

BAUSCH & LOMB INCORPORATED

OVERVIEW

Eyes are the windows to profit for Bausch & Lomb. The Rochester, New York-based company is known for its contact lenses, ReNu and Sensitive Eyes lens care solutions, and eyedrops. A pharmaceutical division makes prescription and over-the-counter ophthalmic drugs; its Charles River Laboratories breeds genetically unique strains of laboratory animals and provides biomedical products and services. Its surgical division makes equipment for cataract and other ophthalmic surgery.

Bausch & Lomb prescribed a reorganization after years of strained eyewear sales and legal battles. Its Ray-Ban, Killer Loop, and other shades have been sold to rival Luxottica; Miracle Ear and Charles River Laboratories are being sold, too. The company has moved into the surgery business to cash in on the boom in cataract and corrective eye surgeries.

HISTORY

In 1853 German immigrant Jacob Bausch opened a small store in Rochester, New York, to sell European optical imports. Henry Lomb soon became a partner by loaning Bausch $60.

Bausch & Lomb's first major breakthrough came with Bausch's invention of Vulcanite (a hard rubber) eyeglass frames. The company fitted the frames with European lenses and by 1880 had a New York City sales office. Bausch & Lomb later began making microscopes, binoculars, and telescopes.

The company incorporated in 1908 as Bausch & Lomb Optical Co. In 1912 William Bausch, Jacob's son, became one of the few to make optical-quality glass in the US. During WWI, Bausch & Lomb supplied the military with lenses for binoculars, searchlights, rifle scopes, and telescopes.

The Army Air Corps commissioned the company in 1929 to create lenses to reduce sun glare for pilots. Bausch & Lomb responded with Ray-Ban sunglasses; they were made available to the public in 1936 and went on to become a company mainstay. Bausch & Lomb went public in 1938.

The company won an Oscar in the 1950s for its Cinemascope lens; it won government contracts for lenses used in satellite and missile systems in the 1960s. Bausch & Lomb also bought such firms as Ferson Optics (1968) and Reese Optical (1969). It began concentrating on contact lenses after the FDA approved its soft lenses in 1971.

In 1981 Daniel Gill, who had helped build the soft contact lens business, became CEO. He sold the company's prescription eyeglass services and industrial instruments units and diversified into medical products and research.

Earnings soared in the 1990s with overseas expansion and acquisitions: Dahlberg (Miracle-Ear hearing aids); Steri-Oss (dental implants); the Curel and Soft Sense skin care lines from S.C. Johnson; Award plc, a Scottish manufac-turer of disposable contacts (1996); and Arnette Optic Illusions sport sunglasses (1996).

However, Gill's insistence on double-digit growth contributed to a dubious ethical climate in which some executives used questionable tactics to put more sales on the books. This led to an SEC probe (closed in 1997 with no fines or penalties assessed) and a shareholder lawsuit (settled in 1997 for $42 million). That year, the company also paid $1.7 million to settle a customer class-action lawsuit alleging Bausch & Lomb was marketing a single type of contact lens under several different product names with varying prices. Gill resigned under fire in 1995 and was replaced by outside director William Waltrip; he turned the reins over to William Carpenter in 1997.

A $100 million restructuring program began that year. Noncore divisions were sold (oral care and dental implant businesses in 1996; skin care line to Kao subsidiary Andrew Jergens Co. in 1998) and 1,900 jobs were cut. The company entered the cataract and refractive surgery market, buying Chiron's vision unit and American Home Products' Storz Instrument unit in 1998, and ophthalmic diagnostic technology company Orbtek in 1999.

In 1998 a French appeals court ruled in favor of Bausch & Lomb in a patent lawsuit filed by Oakley over sunglass styles (a US suit is pending). The company decided to sell its sunglasses unit to Luxottica for $640 million in 1999.

Facing off with rivals Johnson & Johnson and Novartis' Ciba Vision over its new PureVision extended-wear lenses, the company withdrew disputed PureVision ads after receiving an FDA warning in 1999. That year the company made plans to develop eye disease treatment products through a pact with Control Delivery Systems; it also agreed to sell Miracle Ear (to Italy's Amplifon S.p.A.) and its Charles River Laboratories (to an affiliate of Donaldson, Lufkin & Jenrette).

Chairman and CEO: William M. Carpenter, age 46,
$1,499,400 pay
President and COO: Carl E. Sassano, age 49,
$690,802 pay
EVP; President, Eyewear: Dwain L. Hahs, age 46,
$591,675 pay
SVP Human Resources: Daryl M. Dickson, age 47
SVP; President, Surgical and Pharmaceuticals:
Hakan S. Edstrom, age 48
SVP; President and CEO, Charles River Laboratories:
James C. Foster, age 48, $526,874 pay
SVP and CFO: Stephen C. McCluski, age 46,
$383,443 pay
SVP and CTO: Thomas M. Riedhammer, age 50
SVP and General Counsel: Robert B. Stiles, age 49
VP and Chief Information Officer: Robert D. Colangelo,
age 39
VP Global Product Supply, Eyewear: James T. Horn
VP Corporate Communications: Barbara M. Kelley
VP and Controller: Jurij Z. Kushner, age 48
VP Global Operations, Vision Care: Thomas W. Lance
VP, Japan: James F. Milton
VP and Treasurer: Alan H. Resnick
Auditors: PricewaterhouseCoopers LLP

LOCATIONS

HQ: 1 Bausch & Lomb Place, Rochester, NY 14604-2701
Phone: 716-338-6000   **Fax:** 716-338-6007
Web site: http://www.bausch.com

Bausch & Lomb has divisions and subsidiaries in about
35 countries.

1998 Sales

	$ mil.	% of total
US	1,237	52
Other countries	1,126	48
Total	**2,363**	**100**

PRODUCTS/OPERATIONS

1998 Sales & Operating Income

	Sales		Operating Income	
	$ mil.	% of total	$ mil.	% of total
Vision care	961	41	207	60
Pharmaceuticals	626	26	92	26
Eyewear	456	19	6	2
Health care	320	14	41	12
Total	**2,363**	**100**	**346**	**100**

COMPETITORS

Akorn
Alcon
Allergan
Bacou USA
Cooper Companies
De Rigo
Escalon Medical
Essilor International
Eastman Chemical
GN ReSound
Johnson & Johnson
Lantis

LaserSight
Nestle
Novartis
Oakley
Ocular Sciences
Paradigm Medical
STAAR Surgical
Summit Technology
Vista Eyecare
VISX
Wesley Jessen

HISTORICAL FINANCIALS & EMPLOYEES

NYSE symbol: BOL FYE: December 31	Annual Growth	1989	1990	1991	1992	1993	1994	1995	1996	1997	1998
Sales ($ mil.)	7.6%	1,220	1,369	1,520	1,709	1,872	1,851	1,933	1,927	1,916	2,363
Net income ($ mil.)	(15.5%)	114	131	28	171	157	14	112	83	49	25
Income as % of sales	—	9.4%	9.6%	1.8%	10.0%	8.4%	0.7%	5.8%	4.3%	2.6%	1.1%
Earnings per share ($)	(14.7%)	1.89	2.19	0.46	2.84	2.31	0.52	1.93	1.47	0.89	0.45
Stock price - FY high ($)	—	32.94	36.50	60.00	60.50	57.50	53.88	44.50	44.50	47.88	60.00
Stock price - FY low ($)	—	20.38	26.38	31.75	44.50	43.00	30.63	30.88	32.50	32.50	37.75
Stock price - FY close ($)	7.0%	32.50	35.50	58.00	54.50	51.25	33.88	39.63	35.00	39.63	60.00
P/E - high	—	17	17	130	21	25	104	23	30	54	133
P/E - low	—	11	12	69	16	19	59	16	22	37	84
Dividends per share ($)	7.1%	0.56	0.64	0.71	0.78	0.86	0.93	1.00	1.04	1.04	1.04
Book value per share ($)	2.3%	12.16	14.44	13.77	15.11	15.68	15.50	16.32	15.92	14.82	14.95
Employees	2.0%	12,500	13,000	13,700	14,500	15,900	14,400	14,000	13,000	13,000	15,000

STOCK PRICE HISTORY

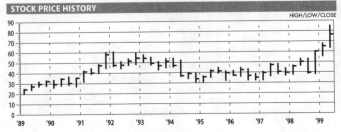

HIGH/LOW/CLOSE

1998 FISCAL YEAR-END

Debt ratio: 60.3%
Return on equity: 3.0%
Cash ($ mil.): 129
Current ratio: 1.95
Long-term debt ($ mil.): 1,281
No. of shares (mil.): 57
Dividends
  Yield: 1.7%
  Payout: 231.1%
Market value ($ mil.): 3,392

BAXTER INTERNATIONAL INC.

OVERVIEW

At Baxter International, blood is just the beginning. The Deerfield, Illinois-based medical products maker is a global leader in blood and circulatory products, including heart monitor catheters and automated blood-component collection and separation systems.

Products include tissue heart valves, blood transfusion systems, hemophilia treatments, home dialysis systems, heart surgery equipment, and intravenous products. Product development has focused on devices for

minimally invasive heart surgeries, as well as products to manage wounds and deactivate viruses in donated blood. Baxter is also researching ways to transplant animal organs into humans.

With more than half of the company's sales outside the US, Baxter is eyeing global expansion. Its plans include building more overseas plants, buying foreign-based companies, and focusing on such emerging markets as Latin America.

HISTORY

Idaho surgeon Ralph Falk, his brother Harry, and California physician Donald Baxter formed the Don Baxter Intravenous Products Corporation in 1931 to distribute intravenous (IV) solutions Baxter made in Los Angeles. Two years later the company opened its first plant, outside Chicago. Ralph Falk bought Baxter's interest in 1935 and began research and development efforts leading to the first sterilized vacuum-type blood collection device (1939), which could store blood for weeks instead of hours. Product demand during WWII spurred sales above $1.5 million by 1945.

In 1949 the company created Travenol Laboratories to make and sell drugs. Baxter went public in 1951 and began an acquisition program the following year. In 1953 failing health caused both Falks to give company control to William Graham, a manager since 1945. Under Graham's leadership, Baxter absorbed Wallerstein Company (1957); Fenwal Labs (1959); Flint, Eaton (1959); and Dayton Flexible Products (1967).

In 1975 Baxter's headquarters moved to Deerfield, Illinois. In 1978 the company debuted the first portable dialysis machine and had $1 billion in sales. Vernon Loucks Jr. became CEO two years later. Baxter claimed the title of the world's leading hospital supplier in 1985 when it bought American Hospital Supply (a Baxter distributor from 1932 until 1962).

Offering more than 120,000 products and an electronic order-entry system that connected customers with some 1,500 vendors, Baxter captured nearly 25% of the US hospital supply market in 1988. That year it became Baxter International.

In 1992 Baxter spun off Caremark (home infusion therapy and mail-order drugs) but kept a division that controlled 75% of the world's dialysis machine market.

In 1993 Baxter pleaded guilty (and was temporarily suspended from selling to the Veterans

Administration) to bribing Syria to remove Baxter from a blacklist for trading in Israel. The following year Baxter signed an eight-year agreement to supply IV products to Columbia/HCA's US hospitals and surgical centers.

The company entered the US market for cardiovascular perfusion services in 1995 with the purchases of PSICOR and SETA. Baxter, along with two other silicone breast-implant makers, also agreed to settle thousands of claims (at an average of $26,000 each) from women suffering side-effects from the implants. The next year Baxter spun off its multibillion-dollar cost management and hospital supply business, naming the firm Allegiance (sold to Cardinal Health, 1999).

Acquisitions in 1997 boosted Baxter's presence in Europe (Swiss blood plasma maker Immuno International), as well as its share of the market for open heart surgery devices (Research Medical). That year it agreed to pay about 20% of a $670 million legal settlement in a suit relating to hemophiliacs becoming HIV-infected through blood products. Baxter bought biotech firm Somatogen in 1998 as part of its push for a blood substitute. It also bought the anesthesia drug business of The BOC Group and the blood therapy operations of Bieffe Medital. At the end of 1998, the company chose president Harry Kraemer to succeed Loucks, who remains as chairman.

That year Baxter stopped testing its HemAssist artificial blood product after disappointing results. It had better luck when the FDA approved a heart-assist device for patients awaiting heart transplants. In 1999 Baxter said it would phase out the use of PVC (polyvinyl chloride) in intravenous systems after consumer and labor groups criticized the substance. It also said it would spin off its cardiovascular operations. Also that year, Baxter sued Spectranetics alleging patent infringement on its medical laser system.

Chairman Emeritus: William B. Graham
Chairman: Vernon R. Loucks Jr., age 64, $2,360,600 pay
President and CEO: Harry M. Jansen Kraemer Jr.,
  age 44, $1,303,770 pay
SVP and CFO: Brian P. Anderson, age 48
SVP Human Resources: Michael J. Tucker, age 46
Corporate VP Regulatory and Clinical Affairs:
  Fabrizio Bonanni, age 52
Corporate VP Research and Technical Services:
  Kshitij Mohan, age 54
Corporate VP Quality Management: John L. Quick, age 54
Corporate VP and General Counsel:
  Thomas J. Sabatino Jr., age 40
Treasurer: Steven J. Meyer, age 42
**Group VP Corporate Development and Strategy, Baxter
  World Trade Corporation:** Timothy B. Anderson
Group VP Renal, Baxter World Trade Corporation:
  Donald W. Joseph, age 61, $826,750 pay
**SVP Intercontinental and Asia, Baxter World Trade
  Corporation:** Carlos del Salto, age 56
Corporate VP; President, Fenwal: Roberto E. Perez
**Group VP I.V. Systems/Medical Products and Fenwal,
  Baxter Healthcare Corporation:** Jack L. McGinley,
  age 52, $826,750 pay
**Group VP Cardiovascular and Biopharmaceuticals,
  Baxter Healthcare Corporation:** Michael A. Mussallem,
  age 46, $761,750 pay
**Corporate VP; President I.V. Systems, Baxter
  Healthcare Corporation:** David F. Drohan, age 60
Auditors: PricewaterhouseCoopers LLP

LOCATIONS

HQ: 1 Baxter Pkwy., Deerfield, IL 60015
Phone: 847-948-2000   **Fax:** 847-948-3948
Web site: http://www.baxter.com

1998 Sales

	$ mil.	% of total
US	3,145	48
Japan	543	8
Other countries	2,911	44
Total	**6,599**	**100**

PRODUCTS/OPERATIONS

1998 Sales

	$ mil.	% of total
IV systems/international hospital	2,314	35
Blood therapies	1,861	28
Renal products	1,530	23
Cardiovascular products	894	14
Total	**6,599**	**100**

COMPETITORS

Abbott Labs	Johnson & Johnson
American Home Products	LifeStream International
Amgen	Medtronic
Bayer AG	Merck
Becton Dickinson	Novartis
C. R. Bard	Novo Nordisk A/S
Dow Corning	Pfizer
DuPont	Roche Holding
Eli Lilly	St. Jude Medical
Fresenius Medical	Teleflex
Genentech	Tutogen Medical
Guidant	United States Surgical
Hoechst AG	

HISTORICAL FINANCIALS & EMPLOYEES

NYSE symbol: BAX FYE: December 31	Annual Growth	1989	1990	1991	1992	1993	1994	1995	1996	1997	1998
Sales ($ mil.)	(1.3%)	7,399	8,100	8,921	8,471	8,879	9,324	5,048	5,438	6,138	6,599
Net income ($ mil.)	(3.8%)	446	40	591	441	(198)	596	649	669	300	315
Income as % of sales	—	6.0%	0.5%	6.6%	5.2%	—	6.4%	12.9%	12.3%	4.9%	4.8%
Earnings per share ($)	(3.4%)	1.49	(0.05)	2.00	1.54	(0.70)	1.44	2.31	2.41	1.06	1.09
Stock price - FY high ($)	—	25.88	29.50	40.88	40.50	32.75	28.88	44.75	48.13	60.25	66.00
Stock price - FY low ($)	—	17.50	20.50	25.63	30.50	20.00	21.63	26.75	39.75	39.88	48.50
Stock price - FY close ($)	11.1%	25.00	27.88	40.00	32.38	24.38	28.25	41.88	41.00	50.44	64.31
P/E - high	—	17	—	20	26	—	20	19	20	57	61
P/E - low	—	12	—	13	20	—	15	12	16	38	44
Dividends per share ($)	8.6%	0.55	0.62	0.72	0.83	0.97	1.01	1.09	1.17	1.13	1.16
Book value per share ($)	(3.4%)	13.49	13.45	14.45	13.59	11.52	13.18	13.62	9.19	9.35	9.92
Employees	(3.9%)	60,000	60,600	60,400	61,300	60,400	53,500	35,500	37,000	41,000	42,000

STOCK PRICE HISTORY

HIGH/LOW/CLOSE

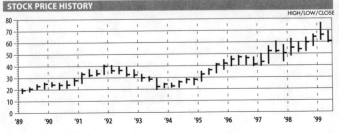

1998 FISCAL YEAR-END

Debt ratio: 52.2%
Return on equity: 11.1%
Cash ($ mil.): 709
Current ratio: 1.56
Long-term debt ($ mil.): 3,096
No. of shares (mil.): 286
Dividends
  Yield: 1.8%
  Payout: 106.4%
Market value ($ mil.): 18,414

THE BEAR STEARNS COMPANIES INC.

OVERVIEW

These days there are many bears on Wall Street but only one Bear Stearns. One of the US's top securities trading, investment banking, and brokerage firms, New York City-based Bear Stearns Companies serves a worldwide clientele of corporations, financial institutions, governments, and individuals. Bear Stearns diversifies its income by performing trade clearing services. In the 1990s it has added significant mergers and acquisitions capacities.

The company has a large presence in Latin America, where it is a market leader in underwriting equity offerings, and it has operated in Europe for 40 years and continues to add offices. Bear Stearns has made great strides in Asia, especially in China (where it has offices in Beijing and Shanghai) and Japan.

Much of Bear Stearns's success has been attributed to longtime chairman Alan "Ace" Greenberg, whose unusual cost-cutting tactics (such as reusing broken rubber bands) and philanthropy (he donated $1 million to pay for Viagra prescriptions for needy patients) often make the news.

HISTORY

Joseph Bear, Robert Stearns, and Harold Mayer founded Bear, Stearns & Co. in 1923 with $500,000 in capital. The firm grew rapidly and weathered the 1929 stock market crash with no layoffs. During the Depression, Bear Stearns aggressively promoted government bonds.

The firm opened its first branch office in Chicago in 1940; it created its international department in 1948 and in 1955 opened an office in Amsterdam. Other branches followed in Geneva (1963), San Francisco (1965), Paris (1967), and Los Angeles (1968).

Bear Stearns was guided in the 1950s and 1960s by trader Salim "Cy" Lewis, who began his career as a runner for Salomon Brothers. At Bear Stearns he worked his way up to chairman, becoming a Wall Street legend as the hard-charging, Scotch-drinking taskmaster of "The Bear," as the firm came to be known (driving Jerome Kohlberg out on his own with two young colleagues, Henry Kravis and George Roberts).

In 1973 Bear Stearns pulled profit out of some of its unused space by giving independent brokers free rent in return for their using the company for clearing — processing stock trades. This practice became a major contributor to the company's bottom line.

When Lewis died in 1978, Alan Greenberg became CEO and not only maintained his predecessor's reputation for aggressive trading but surpassed it. Greenberg, Kansas-born and Oklahoma-reared, had worked his way up from the risk arbitrage desk, to which he was assigned at the age of 25 (he had started as a clerk several years earlier).

Under Greenberg the firm formed the government securities department (1979), the mortgage-backed securities department (1981), and Bear Stearns Asset Management and Custodial Trust, a New Jersey bank and trust company (1984).

Bear Stearns went public in 1985 as The Bear Stearns Companies Inc. It moved into investment banking in the late 1980s and became the leading underwriter in the less-competitive Latin American market in 1991. The firm also created Bear Stearns Securities Corporation to handle its clearing business.

But along with success and a high profile came difficulties. The company's volume of underwritings prompted a deluge of lawsuits relating to junk bonds and hot IPOs that fizzled, including suits relating to point-of-sale and in-store advertising, and diet planner Jenny Craig.

The 1994 bond market crash mauled Bear Stearns, and its non-calendar fiscal year meant that decreased earnings arising from those events were not posted until mid-1995, when most of its competitors had recovered. Lower earnings brought reduced bonuses, which prompted several high-level bond executives to leave.

In 1997 Bear Stearns joined forces with the National Mortgage Bank of Greece to introduce mortgage/asset securitization to that country and opened an office in Ireland to provide access to the unifying European market.

Legal woes resurfaced in 1998 when the firm suffered adverse judgments over actions in the late 1980s. One jury award ($108 million) related to the acquisition of Cadnetix by now-defunct Daisy Systems; another related to bond underwriting for Weintraub Entertainment Group and may eventually cost more than $120 million. In 1999, Bear Stearns agreed to pay $38 million to settle SEC charges relating to the firm's relationship with a brokerage accused of defrauding customers. That year, Bear Stearns moved into the syndicated lending market.

Chairman, Bear Stearns Companies and Bear, Stearns and Co.: Alan C. Greenberg, age 71, $13,898,880 pay
President and CEO, Bear Stearns Companies and Bear, Stearns & Co.: James E. Cayne, age 64, $10,271,830 pay
COO, Bear Stearns Companies and Bear, Stearns and Co.: William J. Montgoris, age 51
EVP, Bear Stearns Companies and Bear, Stearns Co.: Alan D. Schwartz, age 48, $8,209,714 pay
EVP: Warren J. Spector, age 40, $4,375,000 pay
EVP and General Counsel; General Counsel, Bear, Stearns and Co.: Mark E. Lehman, age 47, $2,377,275 pay
SVP Finance and CFO: Samuel L. Molinaro Jr., age 40
VC, Bear, Stearns and Co.: E. John Rosenwald Jr.
VC, Bear, Stearns and Co.: Michael L. Tarnopol
Secretary, Bear, Stearns and Co.: Kenneth L. Edlow
Treasurer, Bear, Stearns and Co.: Michael Minikes
Controller and Assistant Secretary, Bear, Stearns and Co.: Michael J. Abatemarco
Senior Managing Director, Investment Banking Division, Bear, Stearns and Co.: Stephen Davidson
Managing Director Private Client Marketing, Bear Stearns Asset Management: Kenneth L. Henry
Managing Director, Latin American Equity Research Department, Bear, Stearns & Co.: Rowe Michels
Managing Director, Financial Analytics and Structured Transactions Department: Anant Patel
Personnel Director: Stephen A. Lacoff
Auditors: Deloitte & Touche LLP

HQ: 245 Park Ave., New York, NY 10167
Phone: 212-272-2000   **Fax:** 212-272-8239
Web site: http://www.bearstearns.com

1998 Sales

	$ mil.	% of total
Interest & dividends	4,286	54
Principal transactions	1,727	22
Investment banking	1,001	12
Commissions	903	11
Other	63	1
Total	**7,980**	**100**

Selected Services
Assisting in mergers, acquisitions, and restructurings
Brokerage
Fiduciary services
Financing customer activities
Investment management and advisory services
Securities clearance services
Securities lending
Securities trading
Trust services

AIG
American Express
Banc of America Securities
Brown Brothers Harriman
Charles Schwab
Credit Suisse First Boston
Deutsche Bank
Goldman Sachs
Lehman Brothers
Merrill Lynch
Morgan Stanley Dean Witter
Paine Webber
Prudential
Royal Bank of Canada
Salomon Smith Barney Holdings
UBS

NYSE symbol: BSC FYE: June 30	Annual Growth	1989	1990	1991	1992	1993	1994	1995	1996	1997	1998
Sales ($ mil.)	14.5%	2,365	2,386	2,380	2,677	2,857	3,441	3,754	4,964	6,077	7,980
Net income ($ mil.)	16.1%	172	119	143	295	362	387	241	491	613	660
Income as % of sales	—	7.3%	5.0%	6.0%	11.0%	12.7%	11.2%	6.4%	9.9%	10.1%	8.3%
Earnings per share ($)	18.6%	0.94	0.64	0.88	1.91	2.24	2.38	1.47	3.11	4.00	4.38
Stock price - FY high ($)	—	7.91	9.22	10.17	14.44	17.59	20.33	19.84	22.54	34.15	60.93
Stock price - FY low ($)	—	5.44	6.39	4.59	8.43	10.01	13.86	12.12	16.50	18.69	32.37
Stock price - FY close ($)	24.4%	7.60	7.86	8.75	11.69	17.49	13.96	18.44	21.41	32.55	54.15
P/E - high	—	8	14	12	8	8	9	13	7	9	14
P/E - low	—	6	10	5	4	4	6	8	5	5	7
Dividends per share ($)	7.4%	0.30	0.29	0.35	0.44	0.44	0.46	0.49	0.52	0.56	0.57
Book value per share ($)	19.9%	5.54	5.80	6.31	7.85	9.80	12.52	14.08	17.71	22.98	28.37
Employees	4.9%	5,994	5,732	5,612	5,873	6,036	7,321	7,481	7,749	8,309	9,200

HIGH/LOW/CLOSE

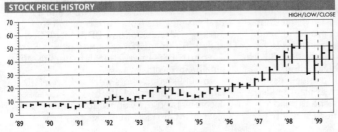

Debt ratio: 75.9%
Return on equity: 18.9%
Cash ($ mil.): —
Current ratio: —
Long-term debt ($ mil.): 13,496
No. of shares (mil.): 123
Dividends
 Yield: 1.1%
 Payout: 13.0%
Market value ($ mil.): 6,663

BECHTEL GROUP, INC.

OVERVIEW

Whether it's raising an entire city or razing a nuclear power plant, you can bet the Bechtel Group will be there to bid on the business. The engineering, construction, and project management firm, based in San Francisco, is #2 in the US heavy construction industry (behind Fluor).

Bechtel builds facilities for industries such as aerospace, chemical manufacturing, energy generation and transmission, mining and metals, surface transportation, telecommunications, and water and waste management. Bechtel has made a name for itself on huge projects, such as the building of the entire industrial city of Jubail in Saudi Arabia, and on difficult ones, such as the cleanup of

Chernobyl. It has worked in 140 countries on more than 19,000 projects, including the Hoover Dam. Some two-thirds of its business is outside the US.

In recent years Bechtel has cut costs by standardizing its designs while improving its communications with a worldwide computer network. Bechtel increasingly acts as a private investor in large public-sector projects, and it develops relationships with local suppliers and contractors.

The billionaire Bechtel family controls the company, which is headed by fourth-generation member Riley Bechtel.

HISTORY

In 1898 25-year-old Warren Bechtel left his Kansas farm to grade railroads in the Oklahoma Indian territories, then followed the rails west. Settling in Oakland, California, he founded his own contracting firm. Foreseeing the importance of roads, oil, and power, he won big projects such as the Northern California Highway and the Bowman Dam. By 1925 W.A. Bechtel was the West's largest construction company.

Steve Bechtel (president after his father's death in 1933) won the company projects such as the Hoover Dam and the San Francisco Bay Bridge and WWII defense contracts. Noted for his friendships with influential people, including Dwight Eisenhower, Adlai Stevenson, and Saudi Arabia's King Faisal, Steve developed projects that spanned nations and industries, such as pipelines in Saudi Arabia, Canada, and Australia and numerous power projects. By 1960, when Steve Bechtel Jr., took over, the company operated on six continents.

In the next two decades, Bechtel worked on transportation projects — such as San Francisco's Bay Area Rapid Transit (BART) system and the Washington, DC, subway system — and power projects, including nuclear plants. After the 1979 Three Mile Island accident, Bechtel tried its hand at nuclear cleanup. With nuclear power no longer in vogue, it focused on other markets, such as mining in New Guinea (gold and copper, 1981-84) and China (coal, 1984). Bechtel's Jubail project in Saudi Arabia, begun in 1976, raised an entire city.

The US recession and rising third-world debt of the early 1980s sent Bechtel reeling. It cut its workforce by 22,000 and stemmed losses by piling up small projects such as plant modernizations. One disaster was Bechtel's good fortune. When the Chernobyl nuclear plant

exploded in 1986, Bechtel became part of the cleanup team.

Riley Bechtel, great-grandson of Warren, became CEO in 1990. He soon profited from another disaster: After the 1991 Gulf War, Bechtel extinguished Kuwait's flaming oil wells and worked on the oil-spill cleanup. During the decade it also worked on such projects as the Channel Tunnel (Chunnel) between England and France, the new airport in Hong Kong, and pipelines in the former Soviet Union.

Bechtel was part of the consortium contracted in 1996 to build a high-speed passenger rail line between London and the Chunnel. International Generating (InterGen), Bechtel's joint venture with Pacific Gas & Electric (PG&E), was chosen to help build Mexico's first private power plant. In 1996 Bechtel bought PG&E's share of InterGen, then sold a 50% stake in InterGen to a unit of Royal Dutch/Shell in early 1997.

That year Bechtel began a venture, Netcon (Thailand), with Lucent to build telecom systems abroad. Bechtel also joined with Dresser (now part of Halliburton), Pacific Enterprises (now Sempra Energy), and Energy Asset Management to buy interests in energy projects in developing regions. In 1998 Bechtel won major contracts to construct a gas production plant in Abu Dhabi, with Technip, and a natural gas pipeline from Turkmenistan to Turkey, with Amoco (now BP Amoco). Bechtel and its Turkmenistan pipeline partners formed a venture, PSG International, to pursue other pipeline projects.

In 1999, based on its work at Three Mile Island and Chernobyl, Bechtel was hired to decommission the Connecticut Yankee nuclear plant at Haddam Neck.

OFFICERS

Chairman and CEO: Riley P. Bechtel
VC: Don Gunther
President and COO: Adrian Zaccaria
SVP and CFO: Georganne Proctor
SVP, Human Resources: Bob Baxter
SVP, Information Systems & Technology:
Hank Leingang
SVP, External Affairs: Chuck Redman
SVP, Legal and Risk Management: Foster Wollen
**President, Europe, Africa, Middle East, Southwest
Asia:** John Carter
President, Latin America: Ric Cesped
President, North America: Darrell Donly
President, Asia Pacific: Ted Kyzer
President, Bechtel Petroleum & Chemical:
Gary Hammond
President, Bechtel Telecommunications:
George Conniff
President, Bechtel Technology and Consulting:
Larry Papay
**President, Bechtel National, Inc.; Bechtel Systems &
Infrastructure, Inc.:** Lee McIntire
President, Bechtel Enterprises, Inc.: Paul Unruh
Acting President, Bechtel Civil: Bob Baxter
President, Bechtel Nuclear Power: Ken Hess
President, Bechtel Mining and Metals: Dick Harding
Auditors: PricewaterhouseCoopers LLP

LOCATIONS

HQ: 50 Beale St., San Francisco, CA 94105
Phone: 415-768-1234   **Fax:** 415-768-9038
Web site: http://www.bechtel.com

Bechtel Group provides heavy construction design and construction services in Africa, the Asia/Pacific region, Europe, Latin America, the Middle East, North America, and Southwest Asia.

1998 Sales

	% of total
North America	38
Europe, Africa, Middle East & Southwest Asia	31
Latin America	19
Asia/Pacific	12
Total	**100**

PRODUCTS/OPERATIONS

**Selected Industries
Served**
Aviation services
Chemicals
Commercial buildings
Environmental and
pollution control
Hazardous waste cleanup
Hotels, resorts, and theme
parks
Manufacturing
Mining and metals
Petroleum
Pipelines
Ports and harbors
Power
Space and defense

Surface transportation
Telecommunications
Water supply and
treatment

Selected Services
Automation technology
Community relations
Environmental health and
safety
Equipment operations
International consulting
Labor relations
Project management,
engineering, and
financing
Worldwide procurement

COMPETITORS

ABB Asea Brown Boveri
Black and Veatch
Bouygues
CH2M Hill
Chiyoda Corp.
EIFFAGE
EMCON
Enron
Fluor
Foster Wheeler
Halliburton
HOCHTIEF
Hyundai Engineering and
Construction
IT Group
ITOCHU
Jacobs Engineering
Kvaerner
Marubeni

Morrison Knudsen
NKK
Parsons
Perini
Peter Kiewit Sons'
Philipp Holzmann
PowerGen
Roy F. Weston
RWE
Safety-Kleen
Samsung
Schneider
Siemens
Societe Generale
d'Entreprises
Technip
URS
Waste Management

HISTORICAL FINANCIALS & EMPLOYEES

Private company FYE: December 31	Annual Growth	1989	1990	1991	1992	1993	1994	1995	1996	1997	1998
Sales ($ mil.)	10.6%	5,096	5,631	7,526	7,774	7,337	7,885	8,504	8,157	11,329	12,645
Employees	0.8%	27,800	32,500	30,900	30,900	29,400	29,200	29,400	30,000	30,000	30,000

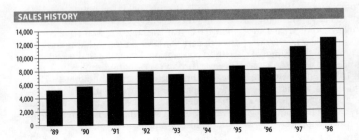

SALES HISTORY

Bechtel Group, Inc.

BECTON, DICKINSON AND COMPANY

OVERVIEW

Becton, Dickinson's products give people all over the world a shot in the arm. The Franklin Lakes, New Jersey-based company is the leading US maker of hypodermic needles and syringes (its diabetic syringes have an almost 90% share) and one of the leading makers in the world. Becton Dickinson's best-sellers include FACSCalibur flow cytometry (cell analysis) systems, Hypak prefillable syringes, and Vacutainer blood-collection products. The company also makes ACE bandages and other consumer health care products.

Becton Dickinson is eschewing its former frumpy, slow-growth strategy in favor of a market-pleasing regimen of new products, new acquisitions, and new technology. As part of the strategy, the company is accentuating R&D and targeting overseas markets, establishing manufacturing plants in China and India and investing in ailing Asian medical product companies. The company is also introducing its products, such as the Uniject prefilled syringe, to less-developed countries.

HISTORY

Maxwell Becton and Fairleigh Dickinson established a medical supply firm in New York in 1897. In 1907 the company moved to New Jersey and became one of the first US firms to make hypodermic needles.

During WWI, Becton Dickinson made all-glass syringes and introduced the cotton-elastic bandage. After the war, its researchers designed an improved stethoscope and created specialized hypodermic needles. The company supplied medical equipment to the armed forces during WWII. Along the way, Becton and Dickinson helped establish Fairleigh Dickinson Junior College (now Fairleigh Dickinson University) in 1942. Meanwhile, the company continued to develop products such as the VACUTAINER blood-collection apparatus, its first medical laboratory aid.

After the deaths of Dickinson (1948) and Becton (1951), their respective sons, Fairleigh Jr. and Henry, took over. The company introduced disposable hypodermic syringes in 1961 and went public in 1963.

During the 1960s the company opened plants in Brazil, Canada, France, and Ireland and climbed aboard the conglomeration bandwagon by diversifying into such businesses as industrial gloves (Edmont, 1966) and computer systems (Spear, 1968). It also went on a major acquisition spree in its core fields during the 1960s and 1970s, buying more than 25 medical supply, testing, and lab companies by 1980.

Wesley Howe, successor to Fairleigh Dickinson Jr., expanded the company's foreign sales in the 1970s. Howe thwarted a takeover by the diversifying oil giant Sun Company (now Sunoco) in 1978 and began to sell Becton Dickinson's nonmedical businesses in 1983, ending with the 1989 sale of Edmont. Acquisitions, including Deseret Medical (IV catheters, surgical gloves and masks; 1986), helped sharpen the company's focus on medical/surgical supplies.

In the 1990s Becton Dickinson formed a number of alliances and ventures with other companies, including a 1991 agreement to make and market Baxter's InterLink injection system and a 1993 joint venture with NeXagen to make and market in vitro diagnostics. With tuberculosis re-emerging in the US as a serious health threat, the company improved its TB detection and drug-resistance test systems. The US Centers for Disease Control recommended its TB testing methodology as the method of choice for detection.

In 1996 Becton Dickinson began marketing GlucoWatch (a painless, continuous glucose monitoring device developed by Cygnus), and acquired MicroProbe's diagnostic business and brand name. Later that year it formed a partnership to supply medical products to the Premier medical products purchasing networks.

Previously known on Wall Street as a homely company that concentrated primarily on cutting costs and slow and steady growth, Becton Dickinson effected an image change with a string of acquisitions beginning in 1997. The company acquired PharMingen, a maker of biomedical research reagents, and Difco Laboratories, a maker of microbiology media, which broadened its product lines. The company also signed a pact with Nanogen to collaborate on diagnosis products for infectious diseases.

In 1998 Becton Dickinson bought The BOC Group's medical devices business for $452 million. That year the company was sued by health care workers claiming that it continued selling conventional syringes that could spread disease through accidental needle sticks instead of promoting safer technology. In 1999, the company joined forces with Millennium Pharmaceuticals to develop cancer tests and treatments; it also bought genetic test-maker Clontech Laboratories.

Chairman, President, and CEO: Clateo Castellini,
age 63, $1,746,875 pay
VC and General Counsel: John W. Galiardo, age 64,
$765,833 pay
EVP: Edward J. Ludwig, age 47,
$551,667 pay (prior to promotion)
SVP Finance and CFO: Kenneth R. Weisshaar, age 48,
$516,667 pay (prior to promotion)
SVP Strategy and Development: Walter M. Miller,
age 55, $553,000 pay
SVP and Chief Technology Officer:
Vincent L. De Caprio, age 48
**President, Worldwide Infusion Therapy and Injection
Systems:** Robert F. Adrion, age 57
President, Worldwide Consumer Health Care:
Jean-Luc Butel, age 42
VP Finance Operations and Treasurer:
Geoffrey D. Cheatham
VP and Secretary: Bridget M. Healy
VP Human Resources: James V. Jerbasi
Auditors: Ernst & Young LLP

LOCATIONS

HQ: 1 Becton Dr., Franklin Lakes, NJ 07417-1880
Phone: 201-847-6800   **Fax:** 201-847-6475
Web site: http://www.bd.com

Becton, Dickinson has offices in more than 40 countries.

1998 Sales & Operating Income

	Sales		Operating Income	
	$ mil.	% of total	$ mil.	% of total
US	1,691	54	396	77
Europe	873	28	105	21
Other regions	553	18	12	2
Adjustments	—	—	(172)	—
Total	**3,117**	**100**	**341**	**100**

PRODUCTS/OPERATIONS

1998 Sales & Operating Income

	Sales		Operating Income	
	$ mil.	% of total	$ mil.	% of total
Medical supplies & devices	1,716	55	320	62
Diagnostic systems	1,401	45	193	38
Adjustments	—	—	(172)	—
Total	**3,117**	**100**	**341**	**100**

COMPETITORS

Abbott Labs
ALZA
American Home Products
Ballard Medical
Baxter
Boston Scientific
Bristol-Myers Squibb
C. R. Bard
Diagnostic Products
Isolyser
Johnson & Johnson
Mallinckrodt
Maxxim Medical
McKesson General Medical
Medex
Medical Action Industries
Medline Industries
Novo Nordisk A/S
Pfizer
Teleflex
Trinity Biotech
United States Surgical
Vital Signs

HISTORICAL FINANCIALS & EMPLOYEES

NYSE symbol: BDX FYE: September 30	Annual Growth	1989	1990	1991	1992	1993	1994	1995	1996	1997	1998
Sales ($ mil.)	6.2%	1,812	2,013	2,172	2,365	2,465	2,560	2,713	2,770	2,811	3,117
Net income ($ mil.)	1.1%	214	182	190	201	72	227	252	284	300	237
Income as % of sales	—	11.8%	9.1%	8.7%	8.5%	2.9%	8.9%	9.3%	10.2%	10.7%	7.6%
Earnings per share ($)	3.2%	0.68	0.59	0.61	0.65	0.22	0.76	0.89	1.05	1.15	0.90
Stock price - FY high ($)	—	7.36	9.25	10.19	9.86	10.52	12.06	15.88	22.44	27.81	43.81
Stock price - FY low ($)	—	6.05	6.88	7.88	7.25	8.16	8.50	11.28	15.53	18.50	20.94
Stock price - FY close ($)	21.4%	7.16	8.22	8.50	9.39	9.41	12.06	15.72	22.13	23.94	41.13
P/E - high	—	11	16	17	15	48	16	18	21	24	49
P/E - low	—	9	12	13	11	37	11	13	15	16	23
Dividends per share ($)	9.3%	0.13	0.14	0.15	0.15	0.15	0.17	0.19	0.21	0.23	0.26	0.29
Book value per share ($)	7.2%	3.38	3.92	4.33	5.05	4.68	5.07	5.16	5.15	5.46	6.31
Employees	1.6%	18,800	18,500	18,600	19,100	19,000	18,600	18,100	17,900	18,900	21,700

STOCK PRICE HISTORY

HIGH/LOW/CLOSE

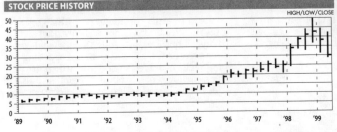

1998 FISCAL YEAR-END

Debt ratio: 40.4%
Return on equity: 15.1%
Cash ($ mil.): 83
Current ratio: 1.41
Long-term debt ($ mil.): 1,092
No. of shares (mil.): 248
Dividends
  Yield: 0.7%
  Payout: 32.2%
Market value ($ mil.): 10,194

BED BATH & BEYOND INC.

OVERVIEW

"Beyond" is really not much farther than your kitchen and living room, but it means more alliterative fun for Bed Bath & Beyond. The Union, New Jersey-based company is on top of the towel heap among superstore domestics retailers, a few folds ahead of #2 Linens 'n Things. The company operates about 200 outlets in 35 states, and it has stepped up its store-opening plans to 50 per year. Bed Bath & Beyond enters several states each year; about 40% of its stores are located in California, Florida, New York, and Texas.

Bed Bath & Beyond's shelves are stuffed with big-brand merchandise in two main categories: domestics (bed linens, bathroom items, and kitchen textiles) and home furnishings (a potpourri of goods ranging from cookware and cutlery to ironing boards and coffeemakers to picture frames and fancy soaps). In addition to offering brand-name items, the company has been slowly expanding its A Step Beyond private-label housewares line.

Targeting educated women with mid-to-upscale incomes, Bed Bath & Beyond's "big box" airy warehouse-type stores offer large selections of department-store-quality items discounted up to 40%. The chain eschews sales events, preferring instead to keep its prices routinely low. Vendors ship merchandise directly to the stores, eliminating the expense of a central distribution center and reducing warehousing costs. Most merchandise goes straight out to the sales floor, with minimal back-room warehousing.

The retailer's decentralized structure allows store managers to have more authority and control than their peers at other retailers. The debt-free company further cuts costs by locating its stores in strip shopping centers, freestanding buildings, and off-price malls — rather than in pricier regional malls — and by depending on word-of-mouth and inexpensive direct-delivery circulars for advertising. Its efforts show in its consistently high profit margins.

Low-profile founders Warren Eisenberg and Leonard Feinstein have slowly reduced their holdings in Bed Bath & Beyond; each now owns about 5% of the company

HISTORY

Warren Eisenberg and Leonard Feinstein, both employed by a discounter called Arlan's, brainstormed an idea in 1971 for a chain of stores offering only home goods. They were betting that customers were, in Feinstein's words, interested in a "designer approach to linens and housewares." The two men started two small linens stores (about 2,000 sq. ft.) named bed n bath, one in New York and one in New Jersey.

Expansion came at a fairly slow pace as the company moved only into California and Connecticut by 1985. By then the time was right for such a specialty retailer: Department stores were cutting back on their houseware lines to focus on the more profitable apparel segment, and baby boomers were spending more leisure time at their homes (and more money on spiffing them up). Eisenberg and Feinstein opened a 20,000-sq.-ft. superstore in 1985 that offered a full line of home furnishings. The firm changed its name to Bed Bath & Beyond two years later in order to reflect its new offerings.

With the successful superstore format, the company built all new stores in the larger design. Bed Bath & Beyond grew rapidly; square footage quadrupled between 1992 and 1996. The company went public in 1992. That year it eclipsed the size of its previous stores when it opened a 50,000-sq.-ft. store in Manhattan. (It later enlarged this store to 80,000 sq. ft.; the company's stores now average 42,000 sq. ft.)

Bed Bath & Beyond's management has attributed its success, in part, to the leeway it gives its store managers, who monitor inventory and have the freedom to try new products and layouts. One example often cited by the company is the case of a manager who decided to sell glasses by the piece instead of in sets. Sales increased 30%, and the whole chain incorporated the practice.

The retailer opened 28 new stores in fiscal 1997, 33 in fiscal 1998, and 45 in fiscal 1999, its first-ever billion dollar sales year. Bed Bath & Beyond said in 1999 that it would open about 50 new stores during fiscal 2000.

In 1999 the company dipped a toe into the waters of e-commerce by agreeing to buy a stake in Internet Gift Registries, which operates the WeddingNetwork Web site. By midyear, however, as Bed Bath & Beyond considered other possible approaches to selling online, its own Web site offered little more than the logos of a handful of suppliers and a toll-free number for finding store locations.

Co-Chairman and Co-CEO: Warren Eisenberg, age 68, $750,000 pay
Co-Chairman and Co-CEO: Leonard Feinstein, age 62, $750,000 pay
President and COO: Steven H. Temares, age 40, $383,000 pay (prior to promotion)
CFO and Treasurer: Ronald Curwin, age 69
SVP Stores: Matthew Fiorilli, age 42, $294,000 pay
SVP Merchandising: Arthur Stark, age 44, $304,000 pay
VP Administration and Corporate Operations: Michael Honeyman, age 40
VP Visual Merchandising: Phillip Kornbluh
VP Legal and General Counsel: Allan Rauch, age 39
VP Product Development and Marketing: Jonathan Rothstein, age 40
VP Finance: G. William Waltzinger, age 34
VP Stores, NYC and Long Island Region: P. Timothy Brewster, age 42
VP Stores, Northeast Region: Martin Eisenberg, age 44
VP Stores, Southern Region: Edward Kopil, age 38
VP Stores, Midwest and Western Region: Martin Lynch, age 37
VP Stores, Mid-Atlantic Region: William Onksen, age 41
Senior Regional Manager, Western Region: Alan Jacobson, age 35
General Merchandise Manager, Domestics Merchandise: Harold Kislik
Controller: Eugene Castagna, age 33
Director Human Resources: Connie Van Dyke
Auditors: KPMG LLP

HQ: 650 Liberty Ave., Union, NJ 07083
Phone: 908-688-0888   **Fax:** 908-688-6483
Web site: http://www.bedbath.com

Selected Merchandise

Domestics
Bath accessories
Bed linens
Kitchen textiles
Window treatments

Home Furnishings
Basic housewares
General home furnishings
Kitchen and tabletop items

Bombay Company
Container Store
Cost Plus
Dayton Hudson
Dillard's
Euromarket Designs
Federated
HomePlace
IKEA
J. C. Penney
Kmart
Lechters
Lillian Vernon
Linens 'n Things
May
Pier 1 Imports
Ross Stores
Saks Inc.
Sears
Strouds
Wal-Mart
Williams-Sonoma

Nasdaq symbol: BBBY FYE: February 28	Annual Growth	1990	1991	1992	1993	1994	1995	1996	1997	1998	1999
Sales ($ mil.)	34.0%	—	134	168	217	306	440	601	823	1,067	1,397
Net income ($ mil.)	32.2%	—	10	12	16	22	30	40	55	73	97
Income as % of sales	—	—	7.7%	7.2%	7.4%	7.2%	6.8%	6.6%	6.7%	6.9%	7.0%
Earnings per share ($)	33.5%	—	—	—	0.12	0.16	0.22	0.29	0.39	0.52	0.68
Stock price - FY high ($)	—	—	—	—	4.75	8.88	8.25	11.31	15.88	22.44	35.19
Stock price - FY low ($)	—	—	—	—	1.75	3.69	5.69	4.50	9.13	11.44	17.13
Stock price - FY close ($)	40.8%	—	—	—	3.78	6.81	6.06	11.16	13.00	21.59	29.44
P/E - high	—	—	—	—	40	56	38	39	41	43	52
P/E - low	—	—	—	—	15	23	26	16	23	22	25
Dividends per share ($)	—	—	—	—	0.00	0.00	0.00	0.00	0.00	0.00	0.00
Book value per share ($)	39.2%	—	—	—	0.40	0.57	0.80	1.11	1.56	2.14	2.95
Employees	28.8%	—	—	1,600	2,400	3,200	4,100	5,400	7,000	8,200	9,400

HIGH/LOW/CLOSE

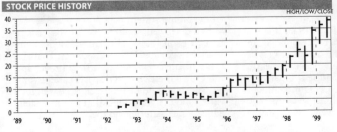

Debt ratio: 0.0%
Return on equity: 23.7%
Cash ($ mil.): 90
Current ratio: 2.21
Long-term debt ($ mil.): —
No. of shares (mil.): 139
Dividends
  Yield: —
  Payout: —
Market value ($ mil.): 4,104

BELL & HOWELL COMPANY

OVERVIEW

Bell & Howell has gone from helping your dad make home movies to helping your company manage information. The Skokie, Illinois-based company's information access unit offers scholarly papers, periodicals, and other publications online as research materials for libraries and schools. It also sells electronic and microfilm equipment for the storage and processing of technical reference documents, primarily for the automotive industry. The company's imaging business provides document management products for paper-intensive industries such as banking and insurance. Its mail processing systems subsidiary makes machines for high-volume commercial mail processing and helps businesses better target mass-mailing projects.

Long known for its low-end movie cameras (Dallas dressmaker Abraham Zapruder used an 8mm Bell & Howell camera to film President Kennedy's assassination), the company continues to reshape its image. It is expanding by targeting market niches such as law firms and automakers that have specific document management requirements, and has embraced the Internet as a natural tool for its information access business.

Texas billionaire Robert Bass' Keystone Inc. investment firm owns 19% of the company, French banking house Lazard Freres & Co. owns almost 8%, and investor Jeffrey Tannenbaum's Fir Tree Partners owns about 5%.

HISTORY

At the turn of the century, when Chicago was the US motion picture capital, Donald Bell worked as a projectionist in theaters around northern Illinois. He met Albert Howell, a mechanical expert who had patented an improvement to film projectors, and in 1907 they formed the Bell & Howell Company. Starting out mainly as a repair shop, the company rose to prominence in the movie industry by establishing 35mm as the standard film width. It made machines that used 35mm film and refused to repair machines that used any other width.

In 1912 Bell & Howell developed the 2079, its first all-metal camera, after one of its wood-and-leather models was eaten by termites.

Bell fired Howell and bookkeeper Joseph McNabb in 1916 for changing the company's operations while he was away on a sales trip. The next day Howell and McNabb, with financial backing from Rufus Kittredge and Charles Ziebarth, bought out Bell's interest for $183,895. By 1919 nearly all of the movie equipment used in rapidly growing Hollywood was made by Bell & Howell.

In the 1920s the company achieved widespread success with a 16mm camera for consumers. In 1932 it unveiled the 16mm sound-on-film projector.

Bell & Howell went public in 1945. It appointed 29-year-old Charles Percy CEO (at the time the youngest-ever chief executive of a large company) in 1949 after McNabb's death. Howell died in 1951. In 1954 the company was awarded its first Oscar (of three) for technical contributions to the film industry; it was the first Academy Award ever given to a company.

After WWII Bell & Howell used acquisitions to diversify into new fields, including microfilm equipment (Pathe Manufacturing, 1946), mail-order form equipment (the Inserting and Mailing Machine Co., 1958), a training school for electronics and media (DeVry Technical Institute, 1966), and publishing (Merrill Publishing, 1967).

In the 1970s Bell & Howell sold its camera business to focus on mail sorting and other operations. Restructuring, including the 1987 sale of DeVry, continued unabated until 1988, when Robert Bass took the company private in an LBO. The Bass-led management team focused on the information management technologies and sold noncore assets. In 1989 it sold Merrill Publishing.

The company restructured its massive debt load in 1993. By 1994 its database and mail processing businesses were thriving, and in 1995 it again went public.

In 1997 Bell & Howell renewed a contract to provide GM's European operations with an electronic parts catalog in 17 languages. The next year Bell & Howell became Canadian document management company UniRom's exclusive provider in the US. The company also teamed up with CheckFree to develop an electronic billing system.

Bell & Howell acquired two UK-based database firms in 1999: Information Publications International and Alison Associates. That year the company and Automatic Data Processing integrated their electronic parts catalog for auto dealers. Also in 1999 Bell & Howell joined with Follett Higher Education Group to deliver educational materials online.

Chairman, President, and CEO: James P. Roemer, age 51, $1,071,639 pay
EVP and CFO: Nils A. Johansson, age 50, $706,239 pay
VP, Finance and Chief Accounting Officer: Stuart T. Lieberman, age 47
VP, Investor Relations and Business Development: Dwight A. Mater, age 41
VP, Human Resources: Maria T. Rubly, age 44
President and CEO, Bell & Howell Information and Learning: Joseph P. Reynolds, age 49, $333,595 pay
President and CEO, Bell & Howell Mail and Messaging Technologies: Michael A. Dering, age 47, $481,916 pay
President and CEO, Bell & Howell Publishing Services: Wayne Mickiewicz, age 47, $284,616 pay
President, Document Management Products: Brian Longe
VP, Finance and Business Development, Bell & Howell Document Management Products and Bell & Howell Protocorp: Donald J. Deegan
VP, Human Resources, Bell & Howell Document Management Products and Bell & Howell Protocorp: Patricia A. Nolan
Secretary and General Counsel: Todd W. Buchardt, age 39
Auditors: KPMG LLP

LOCATIONS

HQ: 5215 Old Orchard Rd., Skokie, IL 60077-1076
Phone: 847-470-7100   **Fax:** 847-470-9825
Web site: http://www.bellhowell.com

Bell & Howell markets its products worldwide from facilities in Austria, Canada, France, Germany, Japan, the Netherlands, Singapore, Switzerland, the UK, and the US.

1998 Sales

	$ mil.	% of total
US	670	74
Europe	169	19
Other regions	61	7
Total	**900**	**100**

PRODUCTS/OPERATIONS

1998 Sales

	$ mil.	% of total
Products	664	74
Services	236	26
Total	**900**	**100**

1998 Sales

	$ mil.	% of total
Mail & messaging	404	45
Information access	321	36
Imaging	175	19
Total	**900**	**100**

COMPETITORS

ADP	National Computer
Anacomp	Systems
BRC Holdings	Pitney Bowes
CACI International	Reed Elsevier
Fujitsu	Ricoh
FYI	R. R. Donnelley
Hewlett-Packard	Siemens
IBM	SunGard Data Systems
Minolta	Thomson Corporation
Moore Corporation	Xerox

HISTORICAL FINANCIALS & EMPLOYEES

NYSE symbol: BHW FYE: December 31	Annual Growth	1989	1990	1991	1992	1993	1994	1995	1996	1997	1998
Sales ($ mil.)	4.0%	630	612	625	670	676	720	820	903	857	900
Net income ($ mil.)	4.0%	26	(31)	(24)	(22)	(183)	(9)	16	23	(32)	37
Income as % of sales	—	4.1%	—	—	—	—	—	2.0%	2.6%	—	4.1%
Earnings per share ($)	18.1%	—	—	—	—	—	—	0.96	1.24	(1.63)	1.58
Stock price - FY high ($)	—	—	—	—	—	—	—	29.38	35.38	33.25	37.81
Stock price - FY low ($)	—	—	—	—	—	—	—	15.50	22.00	19.13	21.50
Stock price - FY close ($)	10.5%	—	—	—	—	—	—	28.00	23.75	24.19	37.81
P/E - high	—	—	—	—	—	—	—	31	29	—	24
P/E - low	—	—	—	—	—	—	—	16	18	—	14
Dividends per share ($)	—	—	—	—	—	—	—	0.00	0.00	0.00	0.00
Book value per share ($)	—	—	—	—	—	—	—	(10.34)	(9.12)	(2.75)	(1.25)
Employees	(1.4%)	6,733	5,966	6,000	5,770	5,771	5,791	5,966	6,110	5,704	5,926

STOCK PRICE HISTORY

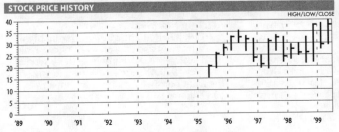

HIGH/LOW/CLOSE

1998 FISCAL YEAR-END

Debt ratio: 100.0%
Return on equity: —
Cash ($ mil.): 18
Current ratio: 1.01
Long-term debt ($ mil.): 445
No. of shares (mil.): 23
Dividends
  Yield: —
  Payout: —
Market value ($ mil.): 880

BELL ATLANTIC CORPORATION

OVERVIEW

This bouncing Baby Bell just won't stop growing. Still relishing its 1997 acquisition of sibling Bell NYNEX, Bell Atlantic is looking ahead to acquiring GTE and becoming a global communications leader.

The New York City-based local phone company is the largest Baby Bell and second-largest US telecommunications company (behind AT&T). Bell Atlantic has over 42 million access lines in 13 states from Maine to Virginia, plus Washington, DC, and telecommunications investments in 23 countries. It will nearly double in size when it acquires GTE. GTE serves more than 21 million local phone customers in 28 US states and offers long-distance service in all 50.

The Telecommunications Act of 1996 opened up competition, providing an impetus for the NYNEX and GTE deals, and gave Bell Atlantic a path into the long-distance market.

Hoping to become the first Bell to provide long-distance services, it has filed applications to do so in New York and Massachusetts. The requests face stiff opposition, however, and Bell Atlantic must convince the FCC that its local markets are open to competition.

The company offers wireless service in 24 states through its Bell Atlantic Mobile subsidiary and its PrimeCo affiliate (a partnership with Vodafone AirTouch). Bell Atlantic and Vodafone AirTouch are dividing PrimeCo's operations; the companies are also discussing an alliance that would create a nationwide wireless network in the US.

Bell Atlantic is expanding its Internet offerings as well. America Online is promoting the Bell's high-speed DSL (digital subscriber line) service, which allows subscribers to surf the Web without interfering with phone service.

HISTORY

Bell Atlantic is as old as the telephone: It is one of the 1870s-era phone companies that evolved into AT&T and its Bell System of regional telephone operations. AT&T lived happily as a regulated monopoly until a US government antitrust suit led to its breakup in 1984.

Seven regional Bell operating companies (RBOCs, or Baby Bells) emerged in 1984, including Bell Atlantic. The new company, based in Philadelphia, received local phone service rights in six states and Washington, DC; cellular company Bell Atlantic Mobile Systems; and one-seventh of Bellcore, the R&D subsidiary.

Bell Atlantic pursued unregulated businesses such as wireless, Internet, directory publishing, and catalog sales of computer parts and office supplies. It invested heavily in data-transport markets to supplement existing voice services, offering the first CO-LAN (central-office local area network) system in 1985. A year later it introduced a switched public data network and began testing integrated voice/data network (ISDN) services.

Bell Atlantic expanded internationally in the early 1990s: It was selected, with Ameritech, to buy New Zealand's public phone system (1990); it partnered with U S WEST to offer cellular services in the former Czechoslovakia (1991); and it bought 23% of Mexico's Grupo Iusacell, later raised to 47% (1993). Its 1992 acquisition of Metro Mobile gave it extensive East Coast cellular phone coverage.

In 1994 Bell Atlantic tried and failed to buy cable giant TCI (now part of AT&T), but succeeded in forming the PrimeCo partnership with NYNEX, U S WEST, and AirTouch, which began offering PCS. Enjoying freedom from wires, Bell Atlantic and NYNEX combined their cellular and paging operations in 1995. In 1996 Bell Atlantic and the six other RBOCs sold Bellcore to Science Applications International.

Bell Atlantic doubled in size with the $25.6 billion purchase of New York City-based NYNEX in 1997, moving from the Cradle of Liberty to the Big Apple. The deal created the second-largest US telecom services firm (after AT&T) but brought with it NYNEX's reputation for poor service. Raymond Smith, Bell Atlantic head since 1989, served as head of the combined company until NYNEX CEO Ivan Seidenberg took over at the end of 1998.

Bell Atlantic filed the first of several applications to sell long-distance service in New York (1998) and Massachusetts (1999), but the requests faced stiff opposition from rivals and scrutiny by the FCC. To prove its local phone market is open to rivals, Bell Atlantic began leasing its lines to telecom reseller UniDial and AT&T (in New York).

In 1999 Bell Atlantic began offering high-speed Internet and data access services, making a deal with AOL to promote these services. That year Bell Atlantic also agreed to buy GTE, the giant non-Bell local phone company, in a $53 billion deal.

OFFICERS

Chairman and CEO: Ivan G. Seidenberg, age 52,
$2,060,400 pay (prior to title change)
President and COO: Lawrence T. Babbio Jr., age 54,
$1,681,200 pay (prior to title change)
President and COO: James G. Cullen, age 56,
$1,681,200 pay (prior to title change)
SEVP and CFO/Strategy and Business Development:
Frederic V. Salerno, age 55, $1,681,200 pay
EVP Strategy and Corporate Development:
Alexander H. Good, age 49
EVP Human Resources: Donald J. Sacco, age 57
EVP External Affairs and Corporate Communications:
Morrison DeS. Webb, age 51
EVP General Counsel: James R. Young, age 47,
$909,300 pay
SVP Government Relations: Thomas J. Tauke, age 48
Group President Consumer: Frederick D. D'Alessio
Group President Enterprise Business: Bruce S. Gordon
Group President Network Services: Paul A. Lacouture
Group President General Business: Regina H. Novotny
Group President Directory: Matthew J. Stover
Group President Wireless: Dennis F. Strigl
VP Ethics and Corporate Compliance:
Jacquelyn B. Gates, age 47
VP Corporate Communications: Patrick F. X. Mulhearn,
age 47
VP and Controller: Doreen A. Toben, age 49
VP Internal Auditing: Chester N. Watson, age 48
VP Treasurer: Ellen C. Wolf, age 45
Auditors: PricewaterhouseCoopers LLP

LOCATIONS

HQ: 1095 Avenue of the Americas, New York, NY 10036
Phone: 212-395-2121   **Fax:** 212-869-3265
Web site: http://www.bellatlantic.com

PRODUCTS/OPERATIONS

1998 Sales

	$ mil.	% of total
Domestic telecom		
Local services	13,882	44
Network access services	7,656	24
Ancillary services	2,090	7
Long-distance services	1,929	6
Global wireless	3,798	12
Directory services	2,264	7
Other businesses	124	—
Adjustments	(177)	—
Total	**31,566**	**100**

COMPETITORS

ALLTEL
Ameritech
AT&T
BellSouth
BT
Comcast
Cox Enterprises
GTE
MCI WorldCom
Nextel
SBC Communications
SNET
Sprint
Telephone & Data Systems
Time Warner
U S WEST
Vodafone AirTouch

HISTORICAL FINANCIALS & EMPLOYEES

NYSE symbol: BEL FYE: December 31	Annual Growth	1989	1990	1991	1992	1993	1994	1995	1996	1997	1998
Sales ($ mil.)	11.9%	11,449	12,298	12,280	12,647	12,990	13,791	13,430	13,081	30,194	31,566
Net income ($ mil.)	11.9%	1,075	1,313	(223)	1,341	1,403	(755)	1,858	1,739	2,455	2,965
Income as % of sales	—	9.4%	10.7%	—	10.6%	10.8%	—	13.8%	13.3%	8.1%	9.4%
Earnings per share ($)	3.5%	1.36	1.69	(0.26)	1.57	(0.41)	0.04	(0.07)	2.19	1.57	1.86
Stock price - FY high ($)	—	28.06	28.56	27.06	26.94	34.56	29.81	34.44	37.44	45.88	61.19
Stock price - FY low ($)	—	17.34	19.75	21.50	20.13	24.81	24.19	24.19	27.56	28.38	40.44
Stock price - FY close ($)	7.7%	27.81	26.81	24.13	25.63	29.63	24.88	33.44	32.38	45.50	54.00
P/E - high	—	21	17	—	17	—	745	—	17	29	33
P/E - low	—	13	12	—	13	—	605	—	13	18	22
Dividends per share ($)	4.0%	1.08	1.16	1.24	1.29	1.33	1.37	1.40	1.43	1.49	1.54
Book value per share ($)	(3.0%)	10.89	11.36	9.89	9.01	9.43	6.97	7.66	8.48	8.23	8.26
Employees	6.5%	79,100	81,600	75,700	71,400	73,600	72,300	61,800	62,600	141,000	140,000

1996 and prior information is for Bell Atlantic Corporation only.

STOCK PRICE HISTORY

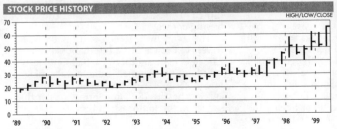

HIGH/LOW/CLOSE

1998 FISCAL YEAR-END

Debt ratio: 57.2%
Return on equity: 22.8%
Cash ($ mil.): 237
Current ratio: 0.86
Long-term debt ($ mil.): 17,646
No. of shares (mil.): 1,576
Dividends
  Yield: 2.9%
  Payout: 82.8%
Market value ($ mil.): 85,116

BELLSOUTH CORPORATION

OVERVIEW

In the telecommunications world, BellSouth is the belle of the South. And competition? Frankly, my dear, BellSouth doesn't give a damn . . . yet. The Atlanta-based phone company (the third-largest local phone company in the US, behind Bell Atlantic and SBC) still gets more than 40% of its sales from 23 million local phone customers in the Southeast. It also serves about 4.8 million wireless customers in 14 US states, through BellSouth Cellular and BellSouth Mobility (PCS) customers. BellSouth also publishes phone directories and provides digital TV.

This Baby Bell is making sure that Atlanta burns in the high-tech world. About 400 Atlanta homes will be the first in the US connected to passive optical network (PON), using fiber-optic networks and asynchronous transfer mode (ATM) protocol for high-speed communications transmission — without active electronics that require an external power source. BellSouth is also introducing high-speed Internet access through its BellSouth.net Fast Access ADSL (asymmetric digital subscriber line) service to certain US markets. The company has more than 500,000 dial-up Internet access customers across the southeastern US.

BellSouth is also a hot enchilada south of the border. When its 1998 sales from Latin America nearly doubled, the phone company warmed to more opportunities in that region, which is deregulating. BellSouth provides wireless phone service through telecom holdings to 2.3 million customers in nine Central and South American countries. BellSouth also serves wireless customers in Europe, India, and Israel.

HISTORY

As Boston-based National Bell struggled to market Alexander Graham Bell's telephone, general manager Theodore Vail recruited James Merrill Ormes to target the southern US in 1878. Ormes created several Bell exchanges, but competitor Western Union hampered growth. The next year the two rivals formed Southern Bell Telephone and Telegraph; Western Union took a controlling interest. In the 1890s Southern Bell's original patents expired, igniting competition, but the Bell responded by upgrading networks, cutting prices, and buying out its rivals.

The company relinquished its Virginia and West Virginia territory in 1912, and AT&T arranged Southern Bell's merger with Cumberland Telephone and Telegraph (Kentucky, Louisiana, Mississippi, and Tennessee). In the post-WWII boom the company grew rapidly.

Southern Bell was structured into two divisions in 1957, a prelude to its split in 1968 into Birmingham-based South Central Bell (Alabama, Kentucky, Louisiana, Mississippi, and Tennessee) and Atlanta-based Southern Bell (Florida, Georgia, North Carolina, and South Carolina). But the division was short-lived. The 1983 settlement of the antitrust case against AT&T broke up local phone service among seven Baby Bells, and the largest, BellSouth, reunited Southern Bell and South Central Bell.

BellSouth reached beyond local service in the 1980s and 1990s, acquiring a directory publisher (1986), paging and cellular company MCCA (1988), and a cellular license in Argentina (1988). In 1990 it created wireless provider BellSouth New Zealand (it sold out to Vodafone, now Vodafone AirTouch, in 1998). BellSouth also snapped up Graphic Scanning Corp. (1991, cellular and paging) and bought 18 Midwest cellular systems from McCaw Cellular (1992). Following the 1995 FCC auction, BellSouth teamed with Northern Telecom (now Nortel Networks) to build one of the first PCS systems in the US. BellSouth sold its paging division to MobileMedia in 1996.

In 1997 BellSouth made major investments in Latin America, including 49% of NICACEL, Nicaragua's only wireless company, and majority stakes in telecoms in Ecuador and Peru. It increased its stake in TelCel Cellular, Venezuela's biggest wireless operator, to more than 75% in 1998.

BellSouth tried to enter long-distance markets in South Carolina and Louisiana in 1998, but the FCC turned it down, saying that BellSouth had not opened its local markets to competition. Undaunted, the company tried to get a foot in the door again in 1999 when it bought a 10% stake in long-distance provider Qwest for about $3.5 billion. BellSouth also hinted in an SEC filing that it has considered buying control of Qwest.

The company in 1999 leased 1,850 wireless towers to Crown Castle International and agreed to lease another 773. BellSouth also rolled out its asymmetric digital subscriber line (ADSL) Internet access and formed an agreement with ISP MindSpring to offer the service in the southeastern US.

Chairman Emeritus: John L. Clendenin, age 64
Chairman, President, and CEO: F. Duane Ackerman, age 56, $2,990,000 pay
EVP and CFO: Ronald M. Dykes, age 51, $981,000 pay
EVP and Chief Information Officer: Francis A. Dramis Jr., age 50
EVP and General Counsel: Charles R. Morgan, age 52
Executive Staff Officer: C. Sidney Boren, age 55
SVP Advanced Data Networks: Robert L. Capell III, age 50
SVP Managed Network Solutions: Donna A. Lee, age 44
SVP Corporate Compliance and Corporate Secretary: Carl Swearingen, age 52
VP Corporate Development: Keith O. Cowen, age 42
VP Financial Management and Treasurer: Mark E. Droege Jr., age 45
VP Governmental Affairs: David J. Markey, age 58
VP Advertising and Public Relations: William C. Pate, age 38
VP Human Resources: Richard D. Sibbernsen, age 51
Group President, BellSouth Business: Richard A. Anderson, age 40
Group President, Value Added Networks: William F. Reddersen, age 51
President and CEO, BellSouth Communications Group: Jere A. Drummond, age 59, $1,480,000 pay
President, BellSouth Telecommunications: Charles B. Coe, age 51, $934,300 pay
President and CEO, BellSouth Enterprises: Earle Mauldin, age 58, $1,310,500 pay
Auditors: PricewaterhouseCoopers LLP

LOCATIONS

HQ: 1155 Peachtree St. NE, Atlanta, GA 30309-3610
Phone: 404-249-2000   **Fax:** 404-249-5599
Web site: http://www.bellsouthcorp.com

PRODUCTS/OPERATIONS

1998 Sales

	$ mil.	% of total
Local service	9,399	41
Network access	4,632	20
Domestic wireless	2,723	12
International operations	1,995	9
Directory advertising & publishing	1,891	8
Other wireline	1,657	7
Toll	713	3
Other services	113	—
Total	**23,123**	**100**

COMPETITORS

ALLTEL	Sprint
Ameritech	Telecom Italia
AT&T	Telecomunicaciones de
Bell Atlantic	Chile
CenturyTel	Telefonica
Comcast	Telefonica de Argentina
Cox Enterprises	Telefonica del Peru
GTE	Teleglobe
infoUSA	Telephone & Data Systems
MCI WorldCom	Time Warner
Millicom International	U S WEST
Nextel	Viacom
R. R. Donnelley	Vodafone AirTouch
SBC Communications	

HISTORICAL FINANCIALS & EMPLOYEES

NYSE symbol: BLS FYE: December 31	Annual Growth	1989	1990	1991	1992	1993	1994	1995	1996	1997	1998
Sales ($ mil.)	5.7%	13,996	14,345	14,446	15,202	15,880	16,845	17,886	19,040	20,561	23,123
Net income ($ mil.)	8.2%	1,741	1,632	1,472	1,618	880	2,160	(1,232)	2,863	3,261	3,527
Income as % of sales	—	12.4%	11.4%	10.2%	10.6%	5.5%	12.8%	—	15.0%	15.9%	15.3%
Earnings per share ($)	7.7%	0.91	0.85	0.76	0.83	0.43	1.09	(0.62)	1.44	1.64	1.78
Stock price - FY high ($)	—	14.53	14.81	13.75	13.88	15.97	15.88	21.94	22.94	29.06	50.00
Stock price - FY low ($)	—	9.75	12.25	11.34	10.84	12.59	12.63	13.41	17.63	19.06	27.06
Stock price - FY close ($)	14.7%	14.47	13.69	12.94	12.84	14.50	13.53	21.75	20.25	28.16	49.88
P/E - high	—	16	17	18	17	37	15	—	16	18	28
P/E - low	—	11	14	15	13	29	12	—	12	12	15
Dividends per share ($)	1.7%	0.62	0.66	0.69	0.69	0.69	0.69	0.70	0.72	0.72	0.72
Book value per share ($)	2.2%	6.80	6.57	6.75	7.01	6.80	7.24	5.95	6.68	7.64	8.26
Employees	(1.5%)	101,230	101,945	96,084	97,112	95,084	92,100	87,600	81,200	81,000	88,400

STOCK PRICE HISTORY

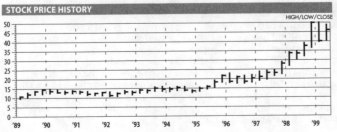

HIGH/LOW/CLOSE

1998 FISCAL YEAR-END

Debt ratio: 35.1%
Return on equity: 21.9%
Cash ($ mil.): 3,003
Current ratio: 0.95
Long-term debt ($ mil.): 8,715
No. of shares (mil.): 1,950
Dividends
 Yield: 1.4%
 Payout: 40.4%
Market value ($ mil.): 97,266

BEMIS COMPANY, INC.

OVERVIEW

The folks at Bemis Company can really pack a wallop . . . or a snack . . . or fertilizer, for that matter. The Minneapolis-based company is a leading US maker of flexible packaging and pressure-sensitive materials (used primarily for labeling). Flexible packaging accounts for 74% of sales and pressure-sensitive materials for the rest. The company's products protect and promote items from meat and bread to pet food and fertilizer. Customers such as General Mills, Green Giant, Mars, Nabisco, and Pillsbury make up the base of Bemis' largest segment, the food industry. Other markets include the agribusiness, chemical, graphic arts and printing, medical, and pharmaceutical industries. Bemis' pressure-sensitive graphics are also used for extra-large "packaging," including signage and advertisements on buses and trains.

New products, such as a lightweight flexible film with spoilage retardants have been important to Bemis' success. The company has also increased its presence in high-growth markets through acquisitions and expansion outside of the US.

HISTORY

Judson Moss Bemis founded J. M. Bemis and Company, Bag Manufacturers, in St. Louis in 1858. The 25-year-old received advice and equipment from cousin Simeon Farwell, who owned an established bag-making factory. St. Louis' role as a trading center supported by major railroads and the Mississippi River helped Bemis' business. The company introduced preprinted and machine-sewn flour sacks to the city's millers and by the end of its first year was making about 4,000 sacks a day. In the company's second year, Edward Brown, a relative of Farwell's, became Bemis' partner and the company was renamed Bemis and Brown.

During the Civil War Brown opened an office in Boston to make the most of fluctuating exchange rates. Bemis also began trading in raw cotton (priced sky-high because of the war) and recycling burlap shipping bags into gunnysacks. The company soon began producing its own burlap sacks from imported jute.

Stephen Bemis, Judson's brother, became a partner in the firm in 1870 and took over its St. Louis operations. Judson joined Brown in Boston, where he could be involved in commodity purchases and financial operations. Soon after, he bought out Brown's share of the firm for an amount that was extravagant at that time — $300,000.

By the early 1880s Bemis Bros. and Co. was the US's #2 bag maker. It opened a second factory in 1881 in Minneapolis, which had become the center of the nation's milling industry and home of such companies as General Mills and Pillsbury. During the late 1800s and the early 1900s, Bemis opened plants in Houston; Memphis; New Orleans; Omaha, Nebraska; San Francisco; and Seattle.

Judson retired in 1909, but the company continued to be run by successive generations of Bemises. In 1914 the company entered the emerging industry of paper milling and paper-bag making, but it continued to focus on textile packaging until WWII, when shortages of cotton and jute expanded the role of paper packaging and led to the development of polyethylene packaging. By the 1950s Bemis' core products had become paper and plastic packaging. In 1959 the company opened its own R&D facility. During the late 1950s and 1960s Bemis made several important acquisitions, including Curwood (packaging for medical products) and MACtac (pressure-sensitive materials). The company was renamed Bemis Company in 1965.

More than $100 million of noncore businesses were sold during the 1970s and 1980s and Bemis began a major capital expansion program aimed at making the company an industry leader. Bemis' sales topped $1 billion in 1988.

Bemis bought candy-packaging producer Milprint, Inc., in 1990; Princeton Packaging's bakery-packaging business in 1993; and Banner Packaging in 1995. In 1996 Bemis introduced the on-battery tester, developed with Eveready. Bemis' medical packaging segment was rejuvenated that year with the purchase of Malaysia-based Perfecseal. The company sold its packaging-equipment business in 1997 and began closing plants and consolidating operations.

In 1998 Bemis purchased a one-third interest in Brazil-based Dixie Toga's flexible-packaging operations and acquired Belgium's Techy International. To coincide with the general acceptance of the euro and the company's expansion in European markets, as well as to avoid any accounting problems, Bemis is installing "euro friendly" computer software.

OFFICERS

Chairman and CEO: John H. Roe, age 59, $879,000 pay
President and COO: Jeffrey H. Curler, age 48, $624,140 pay
VC; President and CEO, Morgan Adhesives (MACtac): Robert F. Mlnarik, age 57, $568,875 pay
SVP, General Counsel, and Secretary: Scott W. Johnson, age 58, $436,594 pay
SVP, CFO, and Treasurer: Benjamin R. Field III, age 60, $420,203 pay
VP Operations; President, Bemis Flexible Plastic Packaging: Thomas L. Sall, age 54, $450,253 pay
VP and Controller: Gene C. Wulf, age 48
VP, Human Resources: Lawrence E. Schwanke, age 59
VP, Tax and Assistant Controller: Stanley A. Jaffy, age 50
President, Curwood North America: Henry J. Theisen
President, Milprint and Polyethylene Packaging Division: Gary V. Stone
President, Perfecseal: Alan McClure
President, MacKay: James A. Elliott
President, Polyethylene Packaging Division: Neal J. Ganly
President, Banner Packaging: James A. Russler
President, Paper Products: Richard W. Lange
Auditors: PricewaterhouseCoopers LLP

LOCATIONS

HQ: 222 S. 9th St., Ste. 2300, Minneapolis, MN 55402-4099
Phone: 612-376-3000   **Fax:** 612-376-3180
Web site: http://www.bemis.com

Bemis Company has operations in Belgium, Brazil, Canada, France, Germany, Italy, Jamaica, Malaysia, Mexico, the Netherlands, Puerto Rico, Singapore, Spain, Sweden, Switzerland, the UK, and the US.

PRODUCTS/OPERATIONS

1998 Sales

	$ mil.	% of total
Flexible packaging	1,368	74
Pressure-sensitive materials	480	26
Total	**1,848**	**100**

Selected Products

Flexible Packaging
Coated and laminated film
Industrial and consumer paper-bag packaging
Machinery for flexible and industrial packaging
Polyethylene packaging

Pressure-Sensitive Materials
Graphic films
Label-application equipment
Narrow web roll label products
Printing products
Technical products

COMPETITORS

AEP Industries	Koc
Avery Dennison	Mead
Crown Cork & Seal	3M
Dow Chemical	Owens-Illinois
DuPont	Printpack
Flexcon Company	Smurfit-Stone Container
Fort James	Sonoco Products
Huntsman	Tenneco
International Paper	VIAG

HISTORICAL FINANCIALS & EMPLOYEES

NYSE symbol: BMS FYE: December 31	Annual Growth	1989	1990	1991	1992	1993	1994	1995	1996	1997	1998
Sales ($ mil.)	6.2%	1,077	1,128	1,142	1,181	1,204	1,391	1,523	1,655	1,877	1,848
Net income ($ mil.)	10.1%	47	51	53	57	44	73	85	101	108	111
Income as % of sales	—	4.4%	4.5%	4.6%	4.8%	3.7%	5.2%	5.6%	6.1%	5.7%	6.0%
Earnings per share ($)	9.8%	0.90	0.99	1.03	1.10	0.86	1.40	1.63	1.90	2.00	2.09
Stock price – FY high ($)	—	18.75	18.75	20.69	29.63	27.38	25.75	30.00	37.63	47.94	46.94
Stock price – FY low ($)	—	11.25	12.81	13.44	19.75	19.88	20.50	23.00	25.63	33.63	33.50
Stock price – FY close ($)	9.2%	17.19	14.81	20.50	25.13	23.63	24.00	25.63	36.88	44.06	37.94
P/E – high	—	21	19	20	27	32	18	18	20	24	22
P/E – low	—	13	13	13	18	23	15	14	13	17	16
Dividends per share ($)	12.7%	0.30	0.36	0.42	0.46	0.50	0.54	0.64	0.72	0.80	0.88
Book value per share ($)	10.5%	5.23	5.81	6.46	7.06	7.24	8.16	9.76	9.79	12.08	12.83
Employees	2.5%	7,500	7,950	7,796	7,733	7,565	8,120	8,515	8,900	9,300	9,400

STOCK PRICE HISTORY

HIGH/LOW/CLOSE

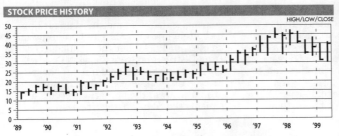

1998 FISCAL YEAR-END

Debt ratio: 35.6%
Return on equity: 16.6%
Cash ($ mil.): 24
Current ratio: 2.13
Long-term debt ($ mil.): 371
No. of shares (mil.): 52
Dividends
  Yield: 2.3%
  Payout: 42.1%
Market value ($ mil.): 1,983

BERGEN BRUNSWIG CORPORATION

OVERVIEW

This company is a drug kingpin.

Orange, California-based Bergen Brunswig is the #3 US wholesale drug distributor. It sells drugs and medical supplies to hospitals and managed care facilities. Through its approximately 65 locations in nearly 30 states, it also provides medical equipment, over-the-counter medications, beauty products, and sundries to independent drugstores and large pharmacy chains throughout the US. The acquisition of institutional pharmacy giant PharMerica added another half-million long-term-care and workers' compensation clients.

Pressed by a general resistance to the high cost of drugs and fallout from Medicare reimbursement cuts, the company has been working to slash costs. Bergen Brunswig is consolidating its distribution facilities and automating its order and inventory systems, offering computer links between suppliers and retailers. The company is also reducing the costs of inventory for its pharmacy customers by retaining ownership of drugs until they're dispensed.

Bergen Brunswig combines the buying power of its customers to negotiate the best prices on generic drugs from its affiliated suppliers. In addition, the company offers a variety of promotional assistance programs for small retailers under the Good Neighbor Pharmacy program.

Chairman Robert Martini owns nearly 6% of the company.

HISTORY

Lucien Napoleon Brunswig, the son of a French doctor, immigrated to America in 1871 to seek his fortune. He opened drugstores in Atchison, Kansas, and Fort Worth, Texas, which were so successful that he was offered a job at a New Orleans-based wholesale drug company in 1882. Brunswig took over in 1885 after his boss's death. He expanded the company westward to Los Angeles, moving there in 1903. In 1907 he the business Brunswig Drug Company. Brunswig died in 1943.

Brunswig Drug merged with Bergen Drug in 1969 to form Bergen Brunswig. Bergen had been founded in Hackensack in 1947 by Emil Martini and named after the New Jersey county in which it was headquartered. Emil Jr. took the helm after his father's death in 1956.

In the 1970s Bergen Brunswig acquired several businesses and pioneered the use of automated order-entry systems. Between 1975 and 1990 sales per employee skyrocketed from $200,000 to $1.6 million; these advances and an aging population spurred tremendous growth.

A stock recapitalization plan, which eventually left control of the company in the public's hands, was implemented in 1989, and the Martinis' voting stake fell to about 13%. That year Bergen Brunswig unveiled an ad campaign for pharmacies associated with its Good Neighbor Pharmacy program, giving independent pharmacists the buying power of a chain.

After running the company for 36 years, Emil Jr. died in 1992 and his brother Robert took over. That year the company agreed to buy Healthcare Distributors of Indiana. A bidding war with Cardinal Distribution (now Cardinal Health) for Durr-Fillauer Medical ended in Bergen Brunswig's favor.

The company signed supplier contracts in 1994 with Columbia/HCA, Safeway, and ShopKo and received six drug contracts from the Pentagon. These and other contracts will be worth $5 billion in business by 2000.

In 1995 Bergen Brunswig made acquisitions in the medical-surgical supply distribution sector, including Seattle-based distributor Biddle & Crowther (which also serves Alaska) and Lake Zurich, Illinois-based Colonial Healthcare Supply. The company then bought Alabama-based Oncology Supply Company in 1996 to augment its specialty product distribution subsidiary Alternate Site Distribution.

A $1.6 billion deal to acquire generic drugmaker IVAX was dropped in 1997 after Bergen Brunswig alleged IVAX breached the merger agreement. That year the firm signed distribution contracts with BJC Health System and Northwestern Healthcare, the Chicago-based parent of Northwestern Memorial Hospital. President Donald Roden succeeded Robert Martini as CEO in 1997.

Cardinal Health agreed to buy Bergen Brunswig for $2.6 billion in 1997, but in 1998 the FTC blocked the move. Bergen Brunswig went on to acquire a slew of companies that year and ended up nicking its bottom line with $110 million in special charges. In 1999 it bought Stadtlanders Drug Distribution from Canada's Counsel Corporation and acquired institutional pharmacy giant PharMerica. That acquisition proved costly as the number of Medicare patients served by PharMerica decreased.

OFFICERS

Chairman: Robert E. Martini, age 66
President and CEO: Donald R. Roden, age 52,
$1,287,150 pay
EVP and Chief Information Officer, Bergen Brunswig:
Linda M. Burkett, age 48
EVP and Chief Procurement Officer:
Charles J. Carpenter, age 49, $569,283 pay
EVP and CFO; President, Bergen Brunswig Specialty:
Neil F. Dimick, age 49, $829,150 pay
EVP; President, Bergen Brunswig Medical
and IntePlex: William J. "Bill" Elliott, age 49
EVP; President, Bergen Brunswig Drug:
Brent R. Martini, age 39, $597,933 pay
EVP, Chief Legal Officer, and Secretary:
Milan A. "Mike" Sawdei, age 52
EVP Human Resources, Bergen Brunswig and
Bergen Brunswig Drug: Carol E. Scherman, age 43
EVP East Region, Bergen Brunswig Drug: Bill Allen
EVP Central Region, Bergen Brunswig Drug:
Larry Burch
EVP West Region, Bergen Brunswig Drug:
Ralph Williamson
VP Operations (Central Region), Bergen Brunswig
Medical: Al Anderson
VP Operations (West Region), Bergen Brunswig
Medical: Jim Ross
VP Operations (East Region), Bergen Brunswig
Medical: Phillip Young
Auditors: Deloitte & Touche LLP

LOCATIONS

HQ: 4000 Metropolitan Dr., Orange, CA 92868-3598
Phone: 714-385-4000   **Fax:** 714-385-1442
Web site: http://www.bergenbrunswig.com

Bergen Brunswig Corporation operates 64 distribution
facilities in 29 states.

PRODUCTS/OPERATIONS

1998 Sales

	$ mil.	% of total
Sales	13,720	80
Bulk shipments to customers' warehouses	3,402	20
Total	**17,122**	**100**

Services
Advertising
Electronic ordering system
In-store merchandising programs
Inventory management
Just-in-time delivery
Logistics management
Marketing assistance
Pharmacy computers
Point-of-sale systems
Private-label products

Selected Subsidiaries
Bergen Brunswig Drug Company (pharmaceuticals and
other medical products)
Bergen Brunswig Medical Corporation (medical and
surgical products)
Bergen Brunswig Specialty Company (oncology and
pharmaceutical products)
IntePlex Inc. (managed care services)
Stadtlanders Drug Distribution (mail-order pharmacy)

COMPETITORS

AmeriSource
Bindley Western
Cardinal Health
D & K Healthcare
  Resources
Kinray

McKesson HBOC
Neuman Distributors
Owens & Minor
PSS World Medical
Quality King

HISTORICAL FINANCIALS & EMPLOYEES

NYSE symbol: BBC FYE: September 30	Annual Growth	1989	1990	1991	1992	1993	1994	1995	1996	1997	1998
Sales ($ mil.)	17.8%	3,923	4,442	4,838	5,048	6,824	7,484	8,448	9,943	11,661	17,122
Net income ($ mil.)	(26.2%)	48	66	64	61	26	56	64	74	82	3
Income as % of sales	—	1.2%	1.5%	1.3%	1.2%	0.4%	0.7%	0.8%	0.7%	0.7%	0.0%
Earnings per share ($)	(27.3%)	0.53	0.59	0.58	0.62	0.29	0.58	0.64	0.73	0.81	0.03
Stock price – FY high ($)	—	8.64	9.48	10.48	9.25	9.75	7.95	11.65	13.00	22.88	31.13
Stock price – FY low ($)	—	4.86	6.56	6.84	6.40	5.75	5.50	5.70	8.20	10.35	16.81
Stock price – FY close ($)	12.8%	8.58	7.40	8.72	7.70	7.00	6.55	8.55	12.70	20.19	25.28
P/E – high	—	16	16	18	15	34	14	18	18	28	1,038
P/E – low	—	9	11	12	10	20	9	9	11	13	560
Dividends per share ($)	11.5%	0.09	0.11	0.13	0.16	0.16	0.23	0.19	0.19	0.22	0.24
Book value per share ($)	5.5%	3.77	4.29	4.31	4.53	4.70	4.96	5.22	5.78	6.40	6.11
Employees	4.6%	3,600	3,800	3,700	3,500	4,250	4,243	4,770	4,900	5,100	5,400

1994 is a 13-month fiscal year.

STOCK PRICE HISTORY
HIGH/LOW/CLOSE

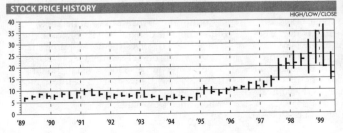

1998 FISCAL YEAR-END
Debt ratio: 41.6%
Return on equity: 0.5%
Cash ($ mil.): 79
Current ratio: 1.31
Long-term debt ($ mil.): 448
No. of shares (mil.): 103
Dividends
  Yield: 0.9%
  Payout: 800.0%
Market value ($ mil.): 2,601

BERKSHIRE HATHAWAY INC.

OVERVIEW

Is the Oracle of Omaha's crystal ball dimming?

Although Warren Buffett's Omaha, Nebraska-based Berkshire Hathaway is thriving, the master himself has made some very poor decisions lately (like selling most of his company's McDonald's holdings just before a stock rebound). The avatar of value investing, Buffett buys and holds, choosing undervalued companies with strong managements to whom he gives considerable autonomy.

Buffett and his partner Charles Munger invest in what they know, low-tech companies like Borsheim's Jewelry Company, See's Candy, a variety of shoe and furniture companies, and publishing (encyclopedias and newspapers).

And, increasingly, insurance. Buffett uses the float — the assets tied up in insurance company claim reserves — to increase his investment clout and to bolster Berkshire Hathaway's bottom line. Major holdings include GEICO and General Re. Other investments include holdings of Coca-Cola, American Express, Disney, Gillette, and Wells Fargo.

It's what the two don't know, however — namely high tech — that has driven the bull market. Berkshire Hathaway is now so large that it is hard-put to post sterling growth rates from its low-tech stable.

Buffett and wife Susan own 38% of Berkshire Hathaway.

HISTORY

Warren Buffett bought his first stock — three shares of Cities Service — at age 11. In the 1950s he studied at Columbia University under famed investor Benjamin Graham. Graham's axioms: Use quantitative analysis to discover companies whose intrinsic worth exceeds their stock prices; popularity is irrelevant; and the market will vindicate the patient investor.

In 1956 Buffett, then 25, founded Buffett Partnership, Ltd. The $105,000 in initial assets multiplied as the company bought Berkshire Hathaway (textiles, 1965; closed 1985) and National Indemnity (insurance, 1967). When Buffett dissolved the partnership in 1996 because he believed stocks were were overvalued, value per share had risen thirtyfold.

Buffett continued investing under the Berkshire Hathaway name, looking for solid businesses with strong management, like See's Candies (1972). Buffett liked the media companies that provided mass advertising outlets, so beginning with the stock market slump of 1973-74 he bought stakes in advertising agencies (Interpublic, Ogilvy & Mather), newspapers (*Washington Post, Boston Globe*, and *Buffalo News*), and television (Capital Cities/ABC, 1985). He also increased his insurance holdings: between 1976 and 1981 Buffett invested $45 million in auto insurer GEICO.

Continuing to invest in simple, branded businesses, regardless of current performance, Buffett bought Nebraska Furniture Mart (1983), uniform makers Fechheimer Brothers (1986), and Scott Fetzer (*World Book* encyclopedias and Kirby vacuum cleaners, 1986). The scale of investments increased as the company bought stakes in American Express (1991), Champion International (1990), Coca-Cola (1988-89), Gillette (1989), Salomon Brothers (investment banking, 1987), US Airways (1989), and Wells Fargo (1989-91).

In the 1990s, Buffet continued to buy strong brands and services, including shoes (H. H. Brown Shoe Co., 1991), furniture, jewelry retailing, and pilot-training company FlightSafety International (1996).

Salomon Brothers attracted attention when it became known that it had illegally bought up most of two successive issues of US government securities in 1991. Buffett appointed new management and revised compensation practices. The resulting exodus of talent took Salomon into a tailspin that ended when Travelers bought it and formed Salomon Smith Barney.

With undervalued companies rare in the long bull market, Buffett was increasingly attracted to maximizing his market power by directing the investments of insurance companies. He increased Berkshire Hathaway's insurance holdings, including an 82% stake in Central States Indemnity (credit insurance, 1992) and a total buyout of GEICO (1996).

In 1996, as the company's share price soared toward $35,000 and outsiders threatened to start a mutual fund to invest in Berkshire Hathaway stock, Buffett created a cheaper class B stock.

Continuing to invest in what he knew, Buffett bought General Re (1998), forcing it to reposition its investments, and time share private jets through Executive Jet's NetJets (1988). Berkshire also increased its holdings in fast foods with investments in International Dairy Queen (1998) and Dunkin' Donuts owner Allied Domecq (1999).

Chairman and CEO; Chairman of See's Candies:
Warren E. Buffett, age 68, $100,000 pay
VC; VC of See's Candies: Charles T. Munger, age 75,
$100,000 pay
VP and CFO: Marc D. Hamburg, age 49, $306,250 pay
Secretary: Forrest N. Krutter
Controller: Daniel J. Jaksich
Auditors: Deloitte & Touche LLP

LOCATIONS

HQ: 1440 Kiewit Plaza, Omaha, NE 68131
Phone: 402-346-1400   **Fax:** 402-346-3375
Web site: http://www.berkshirehathaway.com

Through its holdings, Berkshire Hathaway operates
primarily in the US.

PRODUCTS/OPERATIONS

1998 Sales

	$ mil.	% of total
Insurance	5,481	40
Sales and service	4,675	34
Interest, dividend and other	1,049	8
Financial products businesses	212	2
Realized investment gain	2,415	16
Total	**13,832**	**100**

Major Equity Investments
Allied Domecq (2%)
American Express (11%)
Coca-Cola (8%)
Gillette (14%)
Walt Disney (3%)
Washington Post Co. (17%)
Wells Fargo & Co. (4%)

Subsidiaries

Blue Chip Stamps
Borsheim's Jewelry Company, Inc.
The Cologne Reinsurance Company
Dexter Shoe Company
Europa Ruckversicherung AG
Fairfield Insurance Company
The Fechheimer Brothers Company
FlightSafety International Inc.
GEICO Corporation
General Re Corporation
Genesis Insurance Company
Helzberg's Diamond Shops, Inc.
Herbert Clough, Inc.
H. H. Brown Shoe Company, Inc.
Lowell Shoe, Inc.
National Re Corporation
The Scott Fetzer Company
See's Candies, Inc.
Star Furniture Company
Wesco Financial Corporation

COMPETITORS

AEA Investors	The Hartford
AIG	KKR
Allstate	Lincoln National
Andersen Group	Loews
AXA Financial	MacAndrews & Forbes
Blackstone Group	Munich Re
Chubb	Prudential
CIGNA	State Farm
Citigroup	Swiss Re
CNA Financial	Washington Mutual

HISTORICAL FINANCIALS & EMPLOYEES

NYSE symbol: BRK.A FYE: December 31	Annual Growth	1989	1990	1991	1992	1993	1994	1995	1996	1997	1998
Sales ($ mil.)	21.0%	2,484	1,580	3,106	3,029	3,654	3,848	4,488	10,500	10,430	13,832
Net income ($ mil.)	22.7%	448	394	440	407	759	495	725	2,489	1,902	2,830
Income as % of sales	—	18.0%	24.9%	14.2%	13.4%	20.8%	12.9%	16.2%	23.7%	18.2%	20.5%
Earnings per share ($)	21.6%	390.01	344	384	355.24	656	420	611	2,065	1,542	2,262
Stock price - FY high ($)	—	8,875	7,425	9,125	11,750	17,800	20,800	33,400	38,000	48,600	84,000
Stock price - FY low ($)	—	4,625	5,500	6,550	8,575	11,350	15,150	20,250	29,800	33,000	45,700
Stock price - FY close ($)	26.1%	8,675	6,675	9,050	11,750	16,325	20,400	32,100	34,100	46,000	70,000
P/E - high	—	23	22	24	33	27	50	55	18	32	37
P/E - low	—	12	16	17	24	17	36	33	14	21	20
Dividends per share ($)	—	0.00	0.00	0.00	0.00	0.00	0.00	0.00	0.00	0.00	0.00
Book value per share ($)	27.4%	4,283.00	4,612	6,440	7,743	8,853	10,083	14,030	19,011	24,646	7,801
Employees	9.4%	20,000	20,000	22,000	22,000	22,000	22,000	24,000	34,500	38,000	45,000

STOCK PRICE HISTORY

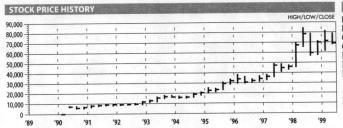

HIGH/LOW/CLOSE

1998 FISCAL YEAR-END

Debt ratio: 4.0%
Return on equity: 4.9%
Cash ($ mil.): 13,582
Current ratio: —
Long-term debt ($ mil.): 2,385
No. of shares (mil.): 2
Dividends
 Yield: —
 Payout: —
Market value ($ mil.): 106,298

BEST BUY CO., INC.

OVERVIEW

Richard Schulze has been busy building a better Best Buy. His Eden Prairie, Minnesota-based company is the #1 consumer electronics specialty retailer in the US, even though rival Circuit City has far more stores. Best Buy's more than 310 stores in about 40 states offer home office equipment, audio and video equipment, entertainment software (such as CDs, DVDs, videos, and video games), appliances, and other products such as cameras.

CEO Schulze, who founded Best Buy and owns about 18% of its stock, has been restructuring the chain following a period of ungainly growth. Though the company introduced itself to many consumers by offering a wide selection of cheap CDs — a tactic that brought traffic into the stores but didn't do much for profits — it is now emphasizing higher-margin items such as digital goods. After a hiatus from expansion, Best Buy is opening about 40 stores per year and is planning a major online sales effort.

HISTORY

Tired of working for a father who ignored his ideas to improve the business (electronics distribution), Richard Schulze quit. In 1966, with a partner, he founded Sound of Music, a Minnesota home/car stereo store. Schulze bought out his partner in 1971 and began to expand the chain.

While chairing a school board, Schulze saw declining enrollment and realized his target customer group, 15- to 18-year-old males, was shrinking. In the early 1980s he broadened his product line and targeted older, more affluent customers by offering appliances and VCRs.

After a 1981 tornado destroyed his best store (but not its inventory), Schulze spent his entire marketing budget to advertise a huge parking-lot sale. The successful sale taught him the benefits of strong advertising and wide selection combined with low prices. In 1983 Schulze changed the company's name to Best Buy and began to open larger superstores. The firm went public two years later.

Buoyed by the format change and the fast-rising popularity of the VCR, Best Buy grew rapidly. Between 1984 and 1987 it expanded from eight stores to 24, and sales jumped from $29 million to $240 million. The next year another 16 stores opened and sales jumped by 84%. However, by that time Best Buy had begun to butt heads with many expanding consumer electronics retailers, and its profits took a beating.

To set Best Buy apart from its competitors, in 1989 Schulze introduced the Concept II warehouse-like store format. Thinking that customers could buy products without much help, Schulze cut payroll by taking sales staff off commission and reducing the number of employees per store by about a third.

The concept proved to be such a hit in the company's home base, Minneapolis/St. Paul, that it drove major competitor Highland Appliance to bankruptcy. Customers were happy, but many of Best Buy's suppliers, believing sales help was needed to sell products, pulled their products from Best Buy stores. The losses didn't seem to hurt Best Buy; it took on Sears and Montgomery Wards in the Chicago market in 1989 and continued expanding over the next few years.

In 1994 the company debuted Concept III, an even larger store format with more hands-on features such as CD listening stations. Best Buy opened 47 new stores in 1995 but found itself swimming in debt. Earnings plummeted in fiscal 1997, partly due to a huge PC inventory made obsolete by Intel's newer product, which led to a $15 million writeoff.

Best Buy started selling CDs on its Web site in 1997. That year it realized it had overextended itself with its expansion, super-sized stores, and financing promotions. Best Buy underwent a speedy, massive, makeover by scaling back expansion, doing away with its policy of "no money down, no monthly payments, no interest" (and next-to-no profits), and narrowing and shifting inventory.

Thanks in part to increased sales of extended-service plans, higher-priced digital gadgets, and high-margin accessories, Best Buy posted record profits in fiscal 1998 and 1999. It began to enter new markets (including New England) and introduced its Concept IV stores, which highlight digital products and feature stations for computer software and DVD demonstrations.

In 1999 the company announced it would open smaller stores (30,000 sq. ft.) in smaller markets. To better compete with the prices offered by online computer retailers, it began a program in which Internet service provider Prodigy offers rebates to customers who purchase PCs at Best Buy and go online through Prodigy.

Founder, Chairman and CEO: Richard M. Schulze,
age 58, $2,460,500 pay
President and COO: Bradbury H. Anderson, age 49,
$1,730,550 pay
EVP Marketing: Wade R. Fenn, age 40, $1,159,150 pay
EVP and CFO: Allen U. Lenzmeier, age 55,
$1,183,050 pay
SVP Merchandising: Gary L. Arnold, age 47
SVP People & Learning: Nancy C. Bologna, age 46
SVP Advertising: Julie M. Engel, age 38
SVP Finance and Treasurer: Robert C. Fox, age 48
SVP Inventory Management: Kevin P. Freeland, age 41
**SVP Information Systems and Chief Information
Officer:** Marc D. Gordon, age 38
SVP Merchandising: Wayne R. Inouye, age 46
SVP Sales: Michael P. Keskey, age 44, $728,220 pay
SVP Strategic Marketing: Michael Linton, age 43
SVP Corporate Strategic Planning: George Z. Lopuch,
age 49
SVP Operations: Joseph T. Pelano Jr., age 51
SVP Services: Lowell Peters, age 58
SVP Merchandising: Philip J. Schoonover, age 39
SVP Sales: Kenneth R. Weller, age 50, $728,220 pay
President, E-Commerce Division: John Walden, age 39
Auditors: Ernst & Young LLP

HQ: 7075 Flying Cloud Dr., Eden Prairie, MN 55344
Phone: 612-947-2000 **Fax:** 612-947-2422
Web site: http://www.bestbuy.com

1999 Sales

	% of total
Home office	36
Consumer electronics	
Video	16
Audio	11
Entertainment software	20
Appliances	8
Other	9
Total	**100**

Amazon.com	Kmart
Blockbuster	Micro Warehouse
Borders	Montgomery Ward
BUY.COM	MTS
CDW Computer Centers	Musicland
Circuit City	Office Depot
CompUSA	OfficeMax
Costco Companies	PC Connection
Dell Computer	Sears
Fry's Electronics	Staples
Gateway	Tandy
Good Guys	Target Stores
Heilig-Meyers	Toys "R" Us
HMV Media Group	Ultimate Electronics
J. C. Penney	Wal-Mart

NYSE symbol: BBY FYE: February 28	Annual Growth	1990	1991	1992	1993	1994	1995	1996	1997	1998	1999
Sales ($ mil.)	39.2%	513	665	930	1,620	3,007	5,080	7,217	7,771	8,358	10,078
Net income ($ mil.)	50.4%	6	(10)	10	20	41	58	48	2	95	224
Income as % of sales	—	1.1%	—	1.0%	1.2%	1.4%	1.1%	0.7%	0.0%	1.1%	2.2%
Earnings per share ($)	37.7%	0.06	(0.10)	0.09	0.15	0.25	0.32	0.28	0.01	0.52	1.07
Stock price – FY high ($)	—	0.84	1.05	2.95	3.93	7.86	11.31	7.56	6.56	15.30	49.00
Stock price – FY low ($)	—	0.47	0.38	0.67	1.18	2.71	5.16	3.00	1.97	2.16	14.73
Stock price – FY close ($)	60.7%	0.65	0.70	1.82	3.43	6.91	5.44	4.19	2.31	14.89	46.38
P/E – high	—	14	—	33	26	31	35	27	656	29	46
P/E – low	—	8	—	7	8	11	16	11	197	4	14
Dividends per share ($)	—	0.00	0.00	0.00	0.00	0.00	0.00	0.00	0.00	0.00	0.00
Book value per share ($)	25.7%	0.67	0.57	1.17	1.36	1.87	2.23	2.52	2.53	3.12	5.23
Employees	31.2%	3,900	4,300	5,500	9,600	15,200	25,300	33,500	36,300	39,000	45,000

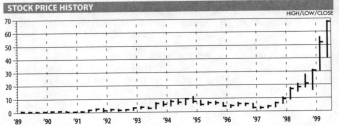

HIGH/LOW/CLOSE

Debt ratio: 2.8%
Return on equity: 21.1%
Cash ($ mil.): 786
Current ratio: 1.49
Long-term debt ($ mil.): 31
No. of shares (mil.): 204
Dividends
  Yield: —
  Payout: —
Market value ($ mil.): 9,444

BESTFOODS

OVERVIEW

Bestfoods doesn't just hold the mayo, it holds North America's #1 mayonnaise brand (Hellmann's). The Englewood Cliffs, New Jersey-based company also sells other market leaders, including Mazola corn oil, Thomas' English muffins and bagels, and Mueller's pasta. Formerly named CPC International, the company makes Boboli Italian breads; Entenmann's baked goods; Oroweat breads; Maizena corn starch; Skippy peanut butter; Karo syrup; and Knorr soups, sauces, and bouillons, among other products. However,

approximately 13% of Bestfoods' sales come from mayonnaise.

About 60% of Bestfoods' sales come from countries outside North America; its products are distributed in about 110 countries. The company has grown through acquisitions, by adding new products under existing brands (such as new flavors of Hellmann's pourable salad dressings), and by expanding brands across borders. Bestfoods has a food service business, called Caterplan outside the US, that serves nearly 60 countries.

HISTORY

American Linseed, a seed and flour miller incorporated in New Jersey in 1898, moved into consumer products in 1917 with its purchase of Nucoa Butter Company. Nucoa Butter's largest subsidiary, The Best Foods, made margarine, edible oil products, and the Best Foods brand of mayonnaise.

The businesses of Best Foods' parent changed during the 1920s and 1930s, although consumer products and milling remained its focus. In 1932 the Best Foods subsidiary acquired the Hellmann's mayonnaise brand from General Foods, which took a 29% stake in the subsidiary. Best Foods mayonnaise was marketed west of the Mississippi, while Hellmann's was marketed in the east. General Foods sold back its interest in 1942.

Several changes in 1955 moved the parent company away from milling and focused it more on consumer products: It changed its name to The Best Foods, acquired Rosefield Packaging (maker of Skippy peanut butter), and sold a major milling operation.

Best Foods merged with the Corn Products Refining Company, a corn refinery with brands such as Mazola, Karo, Argo, and Kingsford's, in 1958. The next year the new company, named Corn Products Company, acquired C.H. Knorr, a packaged soup maker founded in Germany in 1838. By the early 1960s the firm had expanded into Latin America, the Philippines, and other European countries. To reflect this expansion and the diminishing role of its corn refining operations, the company was renamed CPC International in 1969.

CPC continued to add consumer brands, including S. B. Thomas (English muffins, 1969), C. F. Mueller (pasta, 1983), and Arnold Foods (baked goods, 1986). In 1986 CPC thwarted a takeover attempt by financier Ronald Perelman by repurchasing more than 20% of its stock.

Charles Shoemate, with the company since 1962, was named CEO in 1990.

Between the late 1980s and mid-1990s, CPC spent nearly $1 billion to acquire more than 50 companies, including Ambrosia (desserts, UK), Conimex (Asian foods, the Netherlands), Milwaukee Seasonings, and Fearn International (soups and sauces, US). In 1993 it acquired Pfanni potato products, the largest such brand in Europe, and businesses in Costa Rica, the Czech Republic, Denmark, and Turkey.

In 1995 CPC bought Lesieur, a top French salad dressing maker, and it bought Kraft's baking unit, which included Entenmann's baked goods. Also that year the company acquired Brain's Frozen Foods, maker of Mr. Brain's Faggots (cakes), and UK's Pot Noodle. In 1996 CPC settled a lawsuit accusing it of fixing prices of high-fructose corn syrup (paying $7 million) and introduced pourable dressings in the US and Latin America.

The company closed its Muellers' pasta plant the following year and began contracting out pasta production to American Italian Pasta. Its 1997 purchase of Starlux (bouillons, Nocilla chocolate hazelnut spread) tripled its presence in Spain.

To protect earnings from volatility in the corn market, CPC spun off its corn refining business at year-end 1997 as Corn Products International. The company changed its name to Bestfoods in 1998; to mark the change, the company staged a "Bull Run" in front of the NYSE in which actors dressed as Hellmann's, Skippy, Mazola, and other branded products symbolically stayed ahead of the bulls.

Also in 1998 Bestfoods sold its Entenmann's baked-goods business in the UK and Ireland, as well as the Mr. Brain's meatballs business in the UK, to Hibernia Foods.

Chairman, President, and CEO: Charles R. Shoemate,
age 59, $2,526,667 pay
CFO: Bernard H. Kastory, age 53, $965,000 pay
EVP and President, Bestfoods Europe: Alain Labergere,
age 64, $1,335,000 pay
EVP Strategic Planning and Business Development:
Robert J. Gillespie, age 56, $1,325,000 pay
SVP Human Resources: Richard P. Bergeman, age 60
President, Bestfoods North America Division:
Axel C. A. Krauss, age 54
VP; President and CEO, Bestfoods Baking Company:
John J. Langdon, age 58, $830,000 pay
Auditors: KPMG LLP

LOCATIONS

HQ: 700 Sylvan Ave., International Plaza,
Englewood Cliffs, NJ 07632-9976
Phone: 201-894-4000   **Fax:** 201-894-2186
Web site: http://www.bestfoods.com

Bestfoods has 37 plants in Europe, 30 in the US, 20 in
Africa and the Middle East, 20 in Latin America, 18 in
Asia, and two in Canada.

1998 Sales

	$ mil.	% of total
Europe	3,490	42
North America	3,413	41
Latin America	1,149	13
Asia	322	4
Total	**8,374**	**100**

PRODUCTS/OPERATIONS

Selected Products and Brand Names

Baked Goods	**Dressings**
Arnold	Best Foods
Boboli	Hellmann's
Brownberry	
Entenmann's	**Pasta**
Freihofer's	Mueller's
Master's Best	
Oroweat	**Soups, Sauces, and**
Sahara	**Bouillons**
Thomas'	Fruco
	Knorr
Corn Oil	Pot Noodle
Mazola	Tastebreaks
Corn Syrup	**Spreads**
Karo	Marmite
	Nocilla
Cornstarch	Santa Rosa
Maizena	Skippy
Desserts	
Alsa	
Ambrosia	

COMPETITORS

Associated British Foods	Kraft Foods International
Barilla	Lancaster Colony
Borden	McCormick
Campbell Soup	Nabisco Holdings
ConAgra	Nestle
Diageo	New World Pasta
Earthgrains	Procter & Gamble
Flowers Industries	Quaker Oats
General Mills	Sara Lee
Heinz	Specialty Foods
Interstate Bakeries	Unilever

HISTORICAL FINANCIALS & EMPLOYEES

NYSE symbol: BFO FYE: December 31	Annual Growth	1989	1990	1991	1992	1993	1994	1995	1996	1997	1998
Sales ($ mil.)	5.7%	5,103	5,781	6,189	6,599	6,738	7,425	8,432	9,844	8,400	8,374
Net income ($ mil.)	7.4%	328	374	373	224	455	345	512	580	344	624
Income as % of sales	—	6.4%	6.5%	6.0%	3.4%	6.7%	4.6%	6.1%	5.9%	4.1%	7.5%
Earnings per share ($)	11.4%	0.79	0.88	0.93	0.41	1.14	0.79	1.69	1.85	1.15	2.09
Stock price - FY high ($)	—	18.44	21.19	23.38	25.81	25.56	27.81	37.25	42.13	54.38	60.88
Stock price - FY low ($)	—	12.34	15.50	18.00	19.88	19.94	22.13	25.81	32.44	37.69	43.25
Stock price - FY close ($)	12.5%	18.44	20.81	22.63	25.31	23.81	26.63	34.31	38.75	54.00	53.25
P/E - high	—	23	24	25	63	22	35	22	23	47	29
P/E - low	—	16	18	19	48	17	28	15	18	33	21
Dividends per share ($)	8.8%	0.43	0.49	0.54	0.59	0.63	0.67	0.73	0.78	0.84	0.92
Book value per share ($)	(1.5%)	3.36	4.15	4.73	4.86	5.22	5.30	6.17	6.60	2.93	2.93
Employees	2.5%	33,500	35,542	35,000	38,000	39,000	41,900	52,500	55,300	44,200	42,000

STOCK PRICE HISTORY

HIGH/LOW/CLOSE

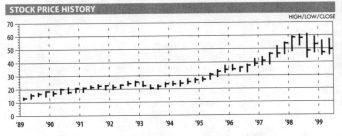

1998 FISCAL YEAR-END

Debt ratio: 67.7%
Return on equity: 75.7%
Cash ($ mil.): 142
Current ratio: 1.04
Long-term debt ($ mil.): 2,053
No. of shares (mil.): 281
Dividends
  Yield: 1.7%
  Payout: 44.0%
Market value ($ mil.): 14,981

BETHLEHEM STEEL CORPORATION

OVERVIEW

It's hard to get ahead when people are dumping steel on your figurative head. Just ask Bethlehem Steel, the US's #2 steel company (USX-U.S. Steel is #1). Widespread dumping of imported steel has hurt US steelmakers, and the Bethlehem, Pennsylvania-based company is running to stand still, although its 1998 purchase of Lukens expanded its steel-plate offerings.

Bethlehem owns two integrated steel mills that use blast furnaces and basic oxygen furnaces to convert iron ore into steel: The Burns Harbor and Sparrows Point divisions make steel plates and sheets for the appliance, automotive, construction, container, and service-center markets. In contrast, Bethlehem's

Pennsylvania Steel and Bethlehem Lukens Plate divisions use electric minimills to melt scrap metal in the production of such products as railroad rails, flat bars, pipe, and plate products. The company also owns seven short-line railroads and stakes in two iron mines (Minnesota and Brazil).

To stay competitive during the 1990s, Bethlehem cut steel production capacity from 16 million to 10 million tons and laid off about 40% of its workforce. While taking legal action over the dumping of foreign steel in the US, Bethlehem continues to focus its efforts on quality improvements and cost reductions through the construction of modern facilities.

HISTORY

Bethlehem Steel began as Saucona Iron in South Bethlehem, Pennsylvania, in 1857, rolling iron railroad rails. It changed its name to Bethlehem Rolling Mills & Iron in 1859 and to Bethlehem Iron in 1861, when it began forging armor plate for US Navy ships. In 1899 it became Bethlehem Steel.

Charles Schwab (president of United States Steel) bought, sold, and again bought Bethlehem Steel in 1901 and 1902. He then transferred Bethlehem to United States Shipbuilding, which soon failed. Bethlehem Steel, which then included a steel plant, shipbuilding yards on both US coasts, and Cuban iron-ore mines, was spun off in 1904 with Schwab as president. Schwab saw the potential in Henry Grey's one-piece, wide-flange steel I-beams for large buildings and built a structural mill at Saucon, Pennsylvania. He bought Grey's patents and found a market in the construction industry.

In 1912 Schwab bought the Tofo Iron Mines in Chile, a cheap source of superior-grade iron ore. Bethlehem purchased Pennsylvania Steel and Maryland Steel in 1916. With its myriad assets, Bethlehem was well prepared for the steel and shipbuilding needs of WWI.

Bethlehem bought Pacific Coast Steel and Southern California Iron & Steel in 1930. In 1931 it bought the fabricating business of McClintic-Marshall Construction. Bethlehem made the steelwork for structures such as the Golden Gate Bridge and the US Supreme Court building. During WWII the company built 1,121 ships.

In the face of growing US imports in the 1970s and 1980s, Bethlehem reduced production and sold some nonsteel operations. The

company undertook a major facilities modernization in 1981 and began building new facilities in 1986. In 1989 Bethlehem bought an interest in Walbridge Coatings (galvanized steel sheets).

A slimmer Bethlehem faced an industrywide slump in demand and the recession of the early 1990s. The company sold its Freight Car Division in 1991. The next year it sold a coal mine and closed its bar, rod, and wire unit (sold 1994).

In 1993 Bethlehem and Lafayette Steel formed a joint venture (Precision Blank Welding) to produce steel blanks for custom auto parts. Two years later General Motors subsidiary Saturn agreed to use Bethlehem as its principal steel source. In 1997 Bethlehem sold its BethShip shipbuilding facility and West Virginia coal-mining operations, as well as its money-losing BethForge and CENTEC subsidiaries. Bethlehem also agreed to acquire steelmaker Lukens to strengthen its share of the US steel-plate market. After a rival bid by Allegheny Teledyne pushed up the price to $740 million, the two suitors inked a deal in 1998 that gave each company what it wanted: Bethlehem got Lukens but sold most of its stainless-steel operations to Allegheny for $175 million.

Also that year Bethlehem joined other US steelmakers in filing trade complaints against competitors in Brazil, Japan, and Russia for dumping low-priced steel in the US. In 1999 Bethlehem closed two stainless-steel mills (acquired from Lukens) in Ohio and Pennsylvania, cutting 540 jobs. Bethlehem also sold its Washington Specialty Metals service center to Ryerson Tull for $70 million.

Chairman and CEO: Curtis H. Barnette, age 64, $1,178,800 pay
President and COO: Roger P. Penny, age 62, $832,050 pay
EVP Finance, Treasurer, and CFO: Gary L. Millenbruch, age 61, $683,050 pay
EVP Commercial and Business Development and Chief Commercial Officer: Duane R. Dunham, age 57, $438,900 pay
SVP Administration and Chief Administrative Officer: Augustine E. Moffitt Jr., age 53
VP Accounting and Controller: Lonnie A. Arnett, age 53
VP Public Affairs: Stephen G. Donches, age 53
VP Law, General Counsel, and Secretary: William H. Graham, age 53
VP Union Relations: John L. Kluttz, age 56
VP Planning: Carl F. Meitzner, age 59
VP Technology and Chief Technology Officer: Malcolm J. Roberts, age 56
VP Purchasing and Transportation and Chief Procurement Officer: Robert A. Rudzki, age 45
VP Human Resources: Dorothy L. Stephenson, age 49
President, Burns Harbor Division: Walter N. Bargeron, age 56
Auditors: PricewaterhouseCoopers LLP

LOCATIONS

HQ: 1170 8th Ave., Bethlehem, PA 18016-7699
Phone: 610-694-2424   **Fax:** 610-694-6920
Web site: http://www.bethsteel.com

Bethlehem Steel owns steel mills in Indiana, Maryland, and Pennsylvania. It also operates coke-making facilities in Indiana and New York. In addition, the company owns stakes in iron mines in Minnesota and Brazil.

PRODUCTS/OPERATIONS

1998 Sales

	% of total
Steel mill products	
Coated sheets	29
Plates	22
Cold-rolled sheets	17
Hot-rolled sheets	13
Tin mill products	7
Rail products	4
Other steel mill products	5
Other products & services	3
Total	**100**

1998 Steel Mill Sales

	% of total
Service centers, processors & convertors	47
Transportation (including automotive)	23
Construction	12
Containers	5
Machinery	5
Other	8
Total	**100**

COMPETITORS

AK Steel Holding Corporation
Anglo American
Armco
BHP
Chaparral Steel
Hyundai
IPSCO
Ispat International
Lone Star Technologies
LTV
Mitsubishi
National Steel
Nippon Steel
Northwestern Steel & Wire
Nucor
Roanoke Electric Steel
Rowan
Thyssen Krupp
USX-U.S. Steel
Weirton Steel

HISTORICAL FINANCIALS & EMPLOYEES

NYSE symbol: BS FYE: December 31	Annual Growth	1989	1990	1991	1992	1993	1994	1995	1996	1997	1998
Sales ($ mil.)	(1.8%)	5,251	4,899	4,318	4,008	4,323	4,819	4,868	4,679	4,631	4,478
Net income ($ mil.)	(7.6%)	246	(464)	(767)	(449)	(266)	81	180	(309)	281	120
Income as % of sales	—	4.7%	—	—	—	—	1.7%	3.7%	—	6.1%	2.7%
Earnings per share ($)	(15.3%)	2.86	(6.45)	(10.41)	(5.78)	(3.37)	0.35	1.23	(3.15)	2.03	0.64
Stock price - FY high ($)	—	28.50	21.13	18.50	17.25	21.00	24.25	19.13	15.88	12.88	17.13
Stock price - FY low ($)	—	15.25	10.63	10.75	10.00	12.88	16.25	12.63	7.63	7.63	7.00
Stock price - FY close ($)	(8.4%)	18.50	14.75	14.00	16.00	20.38	18.00	13.88	8.88	8.69	8.38
P/E - high	—	10	—	—	—	—	69	16	—	6	27
P/E - low	—	5	—	—	—	—	46	10	—	4	11
Dividends per share ($)	(100.0%)	0.20	0.40	0.40	0.00	0.00	0.00	0.00	0.00	0.00	0.00
Book value per share ($)	(7.3%)	22.37	15.56	8.71	4.08	7.46	10.39	11.06	8.51	10.63	11.34
Employees	(6.3%)	30,500	29,600	27,500	24,900	20,700	19,900	18,300	17,500	15,600	17,000

STOCK PRICE HISTORY
HIGH/LOW/CLOSE

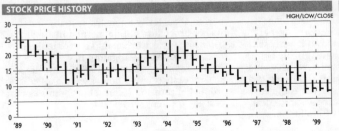

1998 FISCAL YEAR-END

Debt ratio: 29.6%
Return on equity: 8.1%
Cash ($ mil.): 138
Current ratio: 1.52
Long-term debt ($ mil.): 628
No. of shares (mil.): 130
Dividends
  Yield: —
  Payout: —
Market value ($ mil.): 1,091

BEVERLY ENTERPRISES, INC.

OVERVIEW

Beverly Enterprises has fallen — and it might not be able to get up. Fort Smith, Arkansas-based Beverly Enterprises has dropped to become the #2 US nursing home operator (behind Sun Healthcare Group). Beverly also runs assisted living centers and offers outpatient and rehabilitation services.

Like the rest of the nursing home industry, Beverly grappled with PPS, the prospective payment system adopted by Medicare, in 1999. (PPS pays operators per procedure, not actual costs.) Beverly says it was prepared for PPS, which has forced operators to wean themselves from inefficiency-breeding cost-plus pricing; some competitors, including Sun Healthcare, have apparently been harder hit. Beverly responded to PPS by trying to slim down or sell off underperforming operations.

Beverly's other woes include ongoing battles with unions and the National Labor Relations Board (the industry is notorious for paying low wages), run-ins with regulators for rules infractions, and accusations of patient maltreatment (resulting in record-setting punitive judgments).

HISTORY

In 1963 Utah accountant Roy Christensen founded Beverly as three convalescent hospitals near Beverly Hills, California. The emergence of the Great Society, Medicare, and Medicaid in the 1960s fueled the firm's growth. Beverly also dabbled in mirrors, plastics, real estate, and printing before going public in 1966.

Beverly sobered up to losses and industry-wide overexpansion by the early 1970s. The company turned to investment firm Stephens, Inc., to ward off a takeover. Beverly doubled in size in 1977, buying Leisure Lodges nursing homes from Stephens in exchange for 23% of Beverly. Acquisitions pushed Beverly into the #1 nursing home spot by 1983 (by then, Stephens had sold out for a tidy profit). Beverly also diversified, starting its Pharmacy Corporation of America unit.

Management later wrestled with labor unrest and problems with Medicaid. Beverly again turned to Stephens in the late 1980s to avoid another takeover and shake up management.

High turnover, low pay, and mismanagement in an already struggling industry led to allegations of unfair labor practices and patient neglect, including the company's implication in patients' deaths in California and Minnesota.

An inventive late 1980s plan to restructure debt by selling nursing homes cast a cloud over some of those involved in it, including lawyers from Little Rock's Rose Law Firm (William Kennedy and Vince Foster, who would become White House counsels, and Webster Hubbell, who would become associate attorney general and a felon). A loophole would let Beverly sell unprofitable Arkansas and Iowa nursing homes to not-for-profit shell companies, which would make the buys using funds raised through tax-free bonds. An $86 million sale was completed in Iowa; after public outcry, the Arkansas deal was killed by then-Governor Bill Clinton.

In 1990 Beverly's headquarters moved to Arkansas, near Stephen's Little Rock home. Beverly decentralized management of its 883 nursing homes (a move it would later try to use to shield it from liability in labor violations) and began selling some assets. In the mid-1990s Beverly sought relief in higher-margin businesses (post-acute care hospitals, pharmacy services, rehab and respiratory therapy). In 1996 Beverly backed out of managed care; divestitures included Pharmacy Corporation of America, sold to what is now Bergen Brunswig unit PharMerica. Beverly also exited Texas' punitive regulatory environment, selling 49 nursing homes in the state.

In 1993 the National Labor Relations Board (NLRB) concluded the company had illegally stifled workers' attempts to organize; a similar complaint was filed in 1996. (The company dismisses the NLRB's decisions as "fundamentally flawed".) In 1998 the company filed, then withdrew, a slander suit against a Cornell professor who characterized Beverly as "one of the nation's most notorious labor-law violators."

Beverly set records for punitive damages in 1997 and 1998, suffering $70 million and $95 million judgments (later reduced to $54 million and $3 million, respectively) relating to patient neglect.

Having whittled its nursing homes down to about 560 in 1999 and losing the top spot to Sun Healthcare, Beverly braced itself for a period of austerity as Medicare inaugurated its per-procedure billing method in 1999. That same year the federal government announced it was investigating Beverly's Medicare billings back to 1990; as a result, several of its nursing homes were banned from Medicare and Medicaid programs as part of a government settlement.

Chairman and CEO: David R. Banks, age 62,
$761,492 pay
President and COO: Boyd W. Hendrickson, age 54,
$543,923 pay
EVP; President, Beverly Healthcare: William A. Mathies,
age 39, $386,885 pay
EVP: T. Jerald Moore, age 58
EVP, Secretary, and General Counsel:
Robert W. Pommerville, age 58
EVP Asset Management: Bobby W. Stephens, age 54,
$321,415 pay
EVP and CFO: Scott M. Tabakin, age 40, $341,169 pay
EVP; President, Beverly Care Alliance: Mark D. Wortley,
age 43
EVP Strategic Planning and Operations Support:
Phillip W. Small, age 42
SVP and Treasurer: Schuyler Hollingsworth Jr., age 52
VP, Chief Accounting Officer, and Controller:
Pamela H. Daniels, age 35
SVP Quality Management: Eugene B. Clarke
SVP Labor and Employment: Donald L. Dotson
SVP and Chief Information Officer: Barry S. Ganley
**SVP Investor Relations and Corporate
  Communications:** James M. Griffith
SVP Sales and Marketing: Mark R. Mostow
SVP Human Resources: Carol C. Johansen
Auditors: Ernst & Young LLP

LOCATIONS

HQ: 5111 Rogers Ave., Ste. 40-A,
  Fort Smith, AR 72919-0155
Phone: 501-452-6712   **Fax:** 501-452-5131
Web site: http://www.beverlynet.com

Beverly Enterprises has operations in 32 states.

PRODUCTS/OPERATIONS

1998 Sales

	% of total
Medicaid	46
Medicare	28
Private & other	26
Total	**100**

Selected Operations
Assisted living centers
Home health centers
Hospice care
Nursing homes
Rehabilitation centers

COMPETITORS

American Healthcorp
Centennial HealthCare
Columbia/HCA
Genesis Health Ventures
HCR Manor Care
Integrated Health Services
Life Care Centers
Mariner Post-Acute Network
National HealthCare
NovaCare
Sun Healthcare
Tenet Healthcare
Vencor

HISTORICAL FINANCIALS & EMPLOYEES

NYSE symbol: BEV FYE: December 31	Annual Growth	1989	1990	1991	1992	1993	1994	1995	1996	1997	1998
Sales ($ mil.)	3.3%	2,104	2,113	2,301	2,597	2,871	2,969	3,229	3,267	3,230	2,812
Net income ($ mil.)	—	(104)	13	29	(10)	58	75	(8)	50	59	(31)
Income as % of sales	—	—	0.6%	1.3%	—	2.0%	2.5%	—	1.5%	1.8%	—
Earnings per share ($)	—	(1.87)	0.18	0.35	(0.14)	0.42	0.76	(0.16)	0.49	0.57	(0.24)
Stock price - FY high ($)	—	6.71	5.96	8.31	8.81	9.90	11.19	11.37	9.69	13.31	16.25
Stock price - FY low ($)	—	3.36	2.52	4.61	4.78	6.21	8.28	6.35	6.52	8.64	5.25
Stock price - FY close ($)	5.9%	4.03	5.79	5.96	8.73	8.89	10.13	7.49	8.99	13.00	6.75
P/E - high	—	—	33	24	—	24	15	—	20	23	—
P/E - low	—	—	14	13	—	15	11	—	13	15	—
Dividends per share ($)	—	0.00	0.00	0.00	0.00	0.00	0.00	0.00	0.00	0.00	0.00
Book value per share ($)	2.0%	6.34	6.03	6.71	6.58	7.19	7.91	8.32	8.70	8.15	7.58
Employees	(3.0%)	96,000	92,000	93,000	93,000	89,000	82,000	83,000	81,000	74,000	73,000

STOCK PRICE HISTORY

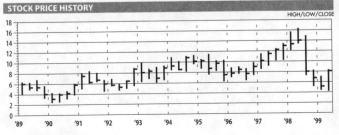

HIGH/LOW/CLOSE

1998 FISCAL YEAR-END

Debt ratio: 53.1%
Return on equity: —
Cash ($ mil.): 17
Current ratio: 1.95
Long-term debt ($ mil.): 878
No. of shares (mil.): 102
Dividends
  Yield: —
  Payout: —
Market value ($ mil.): 691

THE BFGOODRICH COMPANY

OVERVIEW

Literally tireless in its striving to be good and rich, BFGoodrich (BFG) is a global leader in aerospace systems and services and specialty chemicals. But the Charlotte, North Carolina-based company no longer makes tires. It licensed the BFGoodrich name to Michelin almost a decade ago. BFG's aerospace products include aircraft landing systems and sensing systems used for fuel management, navigation and power, and collision avoidance. The company also provides aircraft maintenance, repair, and overhaul services.

BFG's specialty chemicals include textile and industrial coatings; polymers for house-hold, personal care, and pharmaceutical products; and polymer additives and specialty plastics such as polyerethanes, heat-resistant plastics, antioxidants (for rubber, plastics, and lubricants), and molding resins.

The company continues to grow through acquisitions. Its 1997 $1.2 billion purchase of Rohr, the world's #1 maker of commercial aircraft nacelle systems, nearly doubled BFG's size. Its purchase of Coltec Industries, another aerospace component maker, will expand its product line to include seals, gaskets, and other engineered industrial products and make it #1 in landing gear for commercial and defense aircraft.

HISTORY

Orphan, doctor, Civil War veteran, and entrepreneur Benjamin Franklin Goodrich bought stock in the Hudson River Rubber Co. in 1869. He moved the firm to Akron, Ohio, in 1870. Its rubber products included fire hoses, bottle stoppers, rubber rings for canning jars, and billiard cushions. After the depression of the mid-1870s, the company reorganized as B.F. Goodrich & Co (BFG).

BFG's development of new uses for rubber galvanized the industry, but it was the advent of rubber tires that secured the company's future. In 1896 bicycle maker Alexander Winton asked BFG to make tires for his "horseless carriage." (A British company named Silvertown had invented the pneumatic tire, and BFG acquired the patent.) As the automobile's popularity grew, BFG continued to improve its tires. It added fabric cords and carbon black to make tires tougher and give them their black coloring.

BFG introduced the first rubber sponge in 1902. It began making aircraft tires in 1909, and its tires were standard on WWI airplanes. In the 1920s the company added sliding fasteners made by Universal Fastener to its rubber galoshes and began calling the boots "zippers." In 1926 BFG scientists formulated polyvinyl chloride (PVC). The following year the company supplied the tires for Charles Lindbergh's *Spirit of St. Louis,* and in the 1930s BFG introduced the first commercial aircraft de-icer.

BFG was at the forefront of the effort to make synthetic rubber, especially after Japan cut off the US's supply of natural rubber during WWII. The company's chemicals division was organized in 1943. During the war BFG introduced continuous rubber tracks for tanks, as well as the technology used in pilots' "Mae West" life vests.

The company began selling tubeless tires in 1947, and by the mid-1950s new cars came equipped with the safer tires. In 1956 it formed its aerospace division. A few years later the company provided the space suit worn by Alan Shepard, the first American in space. BFG also made P-F Flyers, sneakers popular with children in the 1960s.

John Ong became chairman in 1979 and reduced the company's dependence on tires. In 1986 BFG and Uniroyal formed the Uniroyal Goodrich Tire Co. When Michelin bought the unit in 1990, BFG was out of the tire business.

In 1993 BFG sold Geon, its vinyl division and Ong poured the proceeds back into chemical and aerospace businesses. Acquisitions since 1990 include Hercules Aircraft and Electronics Group (aircraft engine electrical systems, 1990), Eastern Airlines Avionics (test equipment, 1991), GE Specialty Heating and Avionics Power (heated and electrical components, 1994), Rhône-Poulenc's textile coating business (1994), Algan (graphic arts coatings and additives, 1996), Zimchem (acrylic polymers, 1996), a textile chemical and dye unit from Triarc (1997), and Rohr (commercial airline engine nacelles, 1997).

In 1998 BFG acquired specialty chemicals maker Freedom Chemical. BFG acquired Coltec Industries (aerospace components and engineeered industrial products) for about $2 billion in 1999 after settling a prolonged court battle over the acquisition with rivals Crane and AlliedSignal. BFG moved its headquarters from Richfield, Ohio, to Charlotte, North Carolina.

Chairman, President, and CEO: David L. Burner, age 59, $1,284,110 pay
EVP; President and COO, Industrial Segment: John W. Guffey
EVP; President and COO, Aerospace Segment: Marshall O. Larsen, age 50, $786,394 pay
EVP; President and COO, Performance Materials Segment: David B. Price Jr., age 53, $510,807 pay
SVP Finance and CFO: Laurence A. Chapman, age 49
SVP and General Counsel: Terrence G. Linnert, age 52
VP; Group VP, Maintenance, Repair, and Overhaul: Robert L. Avery
VP, Associate General Counsel, and Secretary: Nicholas J. Calise
VP; Group VP, Polymer Additives and Specialty Plastics: Sarah Coffin
VP; Group VP, Sensors and Integrated Systems: John J. Grisik
VP; VP Operations, Performance Materials: Steven R. Guidry
VP Human Resources and Administration: Gary L. Habegger
VP Research and Development: Victoria F. Haynes
VP Strategic Planning and Chief Knowledge Officer: Stephen R. Huggins
VP and Controller: Robert D. Koney Jr., age 42
VP; Group VP, Landing Systems: Ernest F. Schaub
VP; Group VP, Consumer Specialties: William B. Sedlacek
Auditors: Ernst & Young LLP

HQ: 3 Coliseum Centre, 2550 W. Tyvola Rd., Charlotte, NC 28217-3597
Phone: 704-423-7000   **Fax:** 704-423-7100
Web site: http://www.bfgoodrich.com

1998 Sales & Operating Income

	Sales		Operating Income	
	$ mil.	% of total	$ mil.	% of total
Aerospace	2,755	70	386	73
Specialty chemicals	1,196	30	146	27
Total	**3,951**	**100**	**532**	**100**

1998 Aerospace Sales

	$ mil.	% of total
Aerostructures	1,144	41
Landing systems	598	22
Sensors & integrated systems	575	21
Maintenance & repair	438	16
Total	**2,755**	**100**

1998 Specialty Chemicals Sales

	$ mil.	% of total
Textile & industrial coatings	606	51
Polymer additives & plastics	432	36
Consumer specialties	158	13
Total	**1,196**	**100**

AlliedSignal
Ashland
Banner Aerospace
Degussa-Huls
Dow Chemical
DuPont
Eastman Chemical
Great Lakes Chemical
Gulfstream Aerospace
H.B. Fuller
Hercules
Honeywell
Huntsman
M. A. Hanna
Moog
Northrop Grumman
Rhône-Poulenc
Union Carbide
Whittaker

NYSE symbol: GR FYE: December 31	Annual Growth	1989	1990	1991	1992	1993	1994	1995	1996	1997	1998
Sales ($ mil.)	5.6%	2,420	2,433	2,472	2,526	1,818	2,199	2,409	2,239	3,373	3,951
Net income ($ mil.)	3.1%	172	136	(81)	(296)	128	76	118	152	178	227
Income as % of sales	—	7.1%	5.6%	—	—	7.1%	3.4%	4.9%	6.8%	5.3%	5.7%
Earnings per share ($)	(0.4%)	3.14	2.48	(1.75)	(5.96)	(0.37)	0.91	1.34	1.65	2.41	3.02
Stock price - FY high ($)	—	34.50	23.69	23.81	29.06	27.13	24.19	36.31	45.88	48.25	56.00
Stock price - FY low ($)	—	19.25	14.75	18.00	19.44	19.75	19.50	20.81	33.38	35.13	26.50
Stock price - FY close ($)	6.3%	20.75	18.88	21.00	24.44	20.13	21.69	34.00	40.50	41.44	35.88
P/E - high	—	11	10	—	—	—	27	27	28	20	19
P/E - low	—	6	6	—	—	—	21	16	20	15	9
Dividends per share ($)	1.1%	1.00	1.06	1.10	1.10	1.10	1.10	1.10	1.35	1.10	1.10
Book value per share ($)	(0.8%)	23.04	24.64	21.73	14.03	15.31	15.75	16.73	19.53	19.56	21.51
Employees	3.8%	12,302	14,701	14,415	13,375	13,416	13,392	12,287	14,160	16,838	17,175

HIGH/LOW/CLOSE

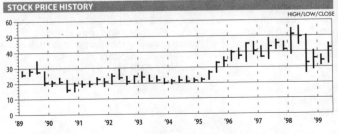

Debt ratio: 38.4%
Return on equity: 14.2%
Cash ($ mil.): 32
Current ratio: 1.63
Long-term debt ($ mil.): 995
No. of shares (mil.): 74
Dividends
  Yield: 3.1%
  Payout: 36.4%
Market value ($ mil.): 2,668

BINDLEY WESTERN INDUSTRIES

OVERVIEW

Bindley Western Industries keeps the drugs coming.

The fifth-largest wholesale drug distributor in the US (McKesson HBOC is #1), Indianapolis-based Bindley Western supplies prescription drugs, health care products, and beauty supplies to drugstore chains, independent drugstores, and health care providers nationwide.

The company traditionally focused on stocking the warehouses of such retail drugstore chains as Eckerd and CVS, which together account for about 35% of Bindley Western's total sales. In recent years, however, Bindley Western has also increased direct sales of supplies to the growing independent pharmacy and nonwarehouse chain market (about 35% of revenues).

Until Priority Healthcare Corporation was completely spun off to shareholders in 1999, Bindley Western's subsidiary targeted specialty care providers; the company sold its stake in Priority Healthcare in order to focus on its wholesale distribution business.

Founder and chairman William Bindley owns about 20% of Bindley Western.

HISTORY

William Bindley was born into the pharmaceutical distribution business. In 1865 his great-grandfather founded E. H. Bindley & Co., which distributed to independent local drugstores in Terre Haute, Indiana.

One hundred years later William joined the family business. When his father thwarted his idea for bringing the company into the modern era by serving drugstore chains, the younger Bindley started his own company, Bindley Western.

Bindley Western supplied pharmaceuticals to chain stores while the older company continued to supply independent local drugstores. Bindley carved out his company's market niche by combining volume purchasing with an efficient warehousing and distribution operation.

In 1973 Bindley Western moved to its own offices in Indianapolis. The company ranked among the country's top 10 drug wholesalers by 1977. When the family sold E. H. Bindley & Co. in 1979, the way was opened for Bindley Western to expand into new markets. It soon began distributing beauty supplies, food, and nonpharmaceutical health products.

The company went public in 1983. Two years later the FBI launched an investigation into allegations that three company employees had diverted drugs illegally and had accepted kickbacks from vendors. Although the firm was held blameless and the drug-diversion charges were proved false, the three employees were found guilty of receiving kickbacks.

In 1987 the company acquired the Osmon Drug Group, marking Bindley Western's entry into the growing market for direct supplies to independent stores. The company also began computerizing to make distribution more cost-effective.

In the early 1990s Bindley Western began developing new markets, including alternative care delivery (shipping directly to patients, physicians' offices, hospitals, nursing homes, and surgical centers). In 1993 the company acquired two Florida-based distributors of specialty medical products: Charise Charles (dialysis and oncology products) and PRN Medical (dialysis and renal supplies and equipment). The next year Bindley Western rolled these two into a new company, Priority Healthcare Corporation, to focus on the alternative care market. In 1995 Priority picked up 3C Medical, a California-based distributor of hemodialysis products. Also in 1994 Bindley Western bought Kendall Drug Co., a North Carolina-based wholesale drug distributor.

The firm augmented its alternative care holdings with the 1995 acquisition of IV One Companies, which included a clinical and infusion pharmacy, a nursing service, and a specialty wholesaler.

Bindley Western started National Infusion Services (NIS) in 1996 to purchase the infusion services division of Infectious Disease of Indiana. Wanting NIS to do more than supply infusion services (such as become a managed care provider), in 1997 the company renamed the unit Priority Healthcare Services. Bindley Western also bought Tennessee Wholesale Drug and spun off 20% of Priority Healthcare Corporation in an IPO.

In 1998 Bindley Western signed a deal that nearly doubled the number of CVS stores supplied by the company. In 1999 it signed multi-year supply contracts with drug-purchasing organization Minnesota Multistate Contracting Alliance for Pharmacy and with a group-purchasing organization representing half of the US's Catholic hospitals. That year Bindley Western spun off the rest of Priority Healthcare Corporation to its shareholders.

Chairman, President, and CEO: William E. Bindley, age 58, $1,293,750 pay
EVP; President, Bindley Western Drug: Keith W. Burks, age 41, $635,418 pay
EVP, Secretary, and General Counsel: Michael D. McCormick, age 51, $635,418 pay
EVP and CFO: Thomas J. Salentine, age 59, $638,333 pay
VP and Controller: Gregory S. Beyerl, age 41
Treasurer: Michael L. Shinn, age 44, $166,542 pay
Director Compensation and Benefits: Marion A. McDermott, age 52
Associate General Counsel: Scott D. Teets, age 41
Director Human Resources: Thomas J. Weakley, age 56
Director Investor Relations: Paul G. Blair, age 36
Director Corporate Communications and Community Affairs: Sally A. Bindley, age 29
SVP Purchasing and Marketing, Bindley Western Drug: David D. Dunlop, age 53
SVP Sales, Bindley Western Drug: J. Michael Gattis, age 52
SVP Operations, Bindley Western Drug: Michael J. McMahon, age 44
SVP Hospital and Managed Care Sales, Bindley Western Drug: Daniel F. Skalecki, age 50
SVP Information Services, Bindley Western Drug: Jon Mark Wiley, age 48
VP Chain Account Procurement, Bindley Western Drug: Kathleen Byrne, age 45
President and CEO, Priority Healthcare: Robert L. Myers
Auditors: PricewaterhouseCoopers LLP

HQ: 8909 Purdue Rd., Indianapolis, IN 46268
Phone: 317-704-4000   **Fax:** 317-704-4601
Web site: http://www.bindley.com

1998 Sales

	$ mil.	% of total
Direct store delivery	3,878	51
Chain drug warehouse	3,743	49
Total	**7,621**	**100**

Selected Subsidiaries
BW Food Distributors, Inc.
BW Transportation Services, Inc.
College Park Plaza Associates, Inc.
Special Services Company

Major Customers
CVS Corporation (17% of sales)
Consorta, Catholic Resource Partners
Eckerd Corporation (18% of sales)
Rite Aid Corporation

AmeriSource
Avon
Bergen Brunswig
Cardinal Health
Grocers Supply
McKesson HBOC
Neuman Distributors
Owens & Minor
PSS World Medical
Quality King

NYSE symbol: BDY FYE: December 31	Annual Growth	1989	1990	1991	1992	1993	1994	1995	1996	1997	1998
Sales ($ mil.)	19.3%	1,561	2,042	2,393	2,912	3,426	4,034	4,670	5,318	7,310	7,621
Net income ($ mil.)	24.8%	3	7	11	13	10	15	16	18	24	19
Income as % of sales	—	0.2%	0.3%	0.5%	0.4%	0.3%	0.4%	0.4%	0.3%	0.3%	0.3%
Earnings per share ($)	11.8%	0.23	0.53	0.75	0.68	0.49	0.68	0.72	0.77	0.89	0.63
Stock price - FY high ($)	—	6.05	8.02	10.27	11.67	8.16	8.79	10.97	11.81	18.25	36.94
Stock price - FY low ($)	—	3.94	4.85	6.40	6.54	5.34	6.26	7.70	8.44	9.77	15.19
Stock price - FY close ($)	22.6%	5.91	6.96	9.63	7.10	6.68	8.72	9.56	10.90	17.37	36.94
P/E - high	—	26	15	14	17	17	13	15	15	21	59
P/E - low	—	17	9	9	10	11	9	11	11	11	24
Dividends per share ($)	—	0.00	0.02	0.04	0.04	0.04	0.05	0.05	0.05	0.05	0.06
Book value per share ($)	10.7%	4.41	4.85	7.06	8.21	8.65	9.36	9.77	10.84	12.34	10.99
Employees	13.3%	406	429	464	628	657	801	912	909	1,283	1,254

HIGH/LOW/CLOSE

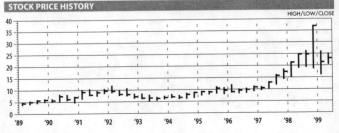

Debt ratio: 0.2%
Return on equity: 5.7%
Cash ($ mil.): 43
Current ratio: 1.24
Long-term debt ($ mil.): 1
No. of shares (mil.): 30
Dividends
  Yield: 0.2%
  Payout: 9.5%
Market value ($ mil.): 1,120

BJ'S WHOLESALE CLUB, INC.

OVERVIEW

Long indistinguishable from the nation's leading warehouse retailers (Costco and Sam's Club), BJ's Wholesale Club wants to find its own identity, as well as new space to grow in. The Natick, Massachusetts-based company is the US's #3 discount warehouse chain, with more than 5 million members and more than 100 stores in 13 states, mostly in the Northeast, but also in Florida, Virginia, and Ohio.

Like Costco, BJ's gets more than 60% of its sales from typical supermarket items; it sells frozen food, meat and dairy products, fresh produce, canned goods, dry food items, and household products at prices about 25% cheaper than supermarkets. The rest of its sales come from merchandise common to warehouse stores: apparel, tires, electronics, and office equipment, among other items. Like both its rivals, BJ's requires membership

and offers a limited selection of items in warehouses that span 2 1/2 acres (although it does operate some smaller warehouses in small cities).

So where does BJ's detect a niche? Unlike Costco, it has liberal membership policies, offers a slightly larger product line, and accepts coupons and most major credit cards, including BJ's co-branded MasterCard. BJ's has added other consumer-minded accoutrements, such as one-hour photo service, optical stores, and food courts with Pizza Huts and Ben and Jerry's ice cream.

In addition to opening new stores in existing markets, the company has been expanding into the Midwest and in Florida. BJ's also is adding gas stations to several of its stores, offering discounted gas to members.

HISTORY

In 1984, with Price Club (now part of Costco) thriving and Wal-Mart's Sam's Club beginning to dot the horizon, Zayre Corp. opened BJ's Wholesale Club, New England's first warehouse club. Zayre, a Massachusetts-based chain of discount department stores, placed the first store in Medford, Massachusetts, and named the operation after top executive Mervyn Weich's wife, Barbara Jane. In return for an annual membership fee, customers could buy a mix of goods priced at around 8%-10% above what they cost BJ's.

Zayre's bought the California-based Home-Club chain of home improvement warehouses in 1986 and combined HomeClub with BJ's to form Zayre's warehouse division. Weich was replaced by John Levy the next year.

By mid-1987 BJ's had 15 stores and more than half a billion dollars in annual sales. Over the next few years, the chain expanded into 11 states in the Northeast and Midwest, including stores in the Chicago area. Despite the chain's rapid growth — or because of it — BJ's failed to post profits.

A debt-burdened Zayre began shifting its focus to its moderate-priced chains (including T.J. Maxx and Hit or Miss) during the late 1980s. In 1989 it spun off its warehouse division to shareholders and renamed it Waban (after a nearby Massachusetts town). Zayre was renamed TJX Companies.

Waban cracked the $1 billion sales mark in 1990. During the early 1990s the company moved into the midwestern US, but its stores failed to thrive. In 1991 it closed one of its

four Chicago stores, and in 1992 it turned the other three into HomeBase stores.

Also during those years, BJ's added fresh meats, bakery items, optical departments, and travel agents to its stores. In 1993 Herbert Zarkin, BJ's president, replaced Levy as CEO. That year BJ's had 52 stores and 2.6 million members; its sales reached $2 billion. A new inventory scanning system implemented by the company helped cut costs.

Once again, however, strong sales didn't add up to big profits. In 1993 BJ's per-store profits were far below those of its competitors, primarily due to intense competition and a regional recession.

Two years later BJ's became the first warehouse club to accept MasterCard and issued its own store-brand version of that card. BJ's added nine stores in 1995, 10 the next year, and four in 1997.

Meanwhile, Waban was struggling with HomeBase, which was still failing to show a profit due to restructuring charges. In 1997 Waban spun off BJ's Wholesale Club — its star performer — to keep it from being undervalued; Waban then changed its name to HomeBase. Also in 1997 John Nugent was named BJ's CEO.

BJ's added gas stations in several of its northeastern stores in 1998. Also that year it introduced its private-label products under the Executive Choice and Berkley & Jensen names.

In 1999 BJ's announced it planned to open its first store in North Carolina.

OFFICERS

Chairman: Herbert J. Zarkin, age 60, $570,000 pay
President and CEO: John J. Nugent, age 52, $932,404 pay
EVP and CFO: Frank D. Forward, age 44, $316,830 pay
EVP, Merchandising: Laura J. Sen, age 42, $358,155 pay
EVP, Club Operations: Michael T. Wedge, age 45, $358,155 pay
SVP, Food Merchandise: Paul M. Bass
SVP, General Merchandise: Edward A. Beevers
SVP, Human Resources: Thomas Davis III
SVP, Real Estate and Property Development: George L. Drummey
SVP, Marketing: Edward F. Gillooly
SVP, Information Systems: Ronald A. Laferriere
Auditors: PricewaterhouseCoopers LLP

LOCATIONS

HQ: 1 Mercer Rd., Natick, MA 01760
Phone: 508-651-7400   **Fax:** 508-651-6114
Web site: http://www.bjswholesale.com

1999 Stores

	No.
New York	23
Massachusetts	13
New Jersey	12
Pennsylvania	10
Connecticut	7
Florida	6
Maryland	6
Virginia	6
Ohio	4
New Hampshire	4
Maine	2
Rhode Island	2
Delaware	1
Total	**96**

PRODUCTS/OPERATIONS

1998 Sales

	$ mil.	% of total
Merchandise & services	3,477	98
Membership fees	75	2
Total	**3,552**	**100**

Selected Merchandise

Food
Baked goods
Canned goods
Dairy products
Dry grocery items
Fresh produce
Frozen foods
Meat and fish

General Merchandise
Apparel
Auto accessories
Books
Computer software

Consumer electronics
Greeting cards
Hardware
Health and beauty aids
Household paper products and cleaning supplies
Housewares
Jewelry
Office supplies
Small appliances
Tires
Toys

COMPETITORS

Ahold USA
Ames
Best Buy
Bradlees
Circuit City
Costco Companies
Dayton Hudson
Family Dollar Stores
Grand Union
Hannaford Bros.

J. C. Penney
Kmart
Office Depot
Pathmark
Penn Traffic
Sears
Service Merchandise
Staples
Wal-Mart
Weis Markets

HISTORICAL FINANCIALS & EMPLOYEES

NYSE symbol: BJ FYE: January 31	Annual Growth	1990	1991	1992	1993	1994	1995	1996	1997	1998	1999
Sales ($ mil.)	12.1%	—	—	—	1,787	2,003	2,293	2,530	2,923	3,227	3,552
Net income ($ mil.)	19.8%	—	—	—	21	20	31	42	54	68	63
Income as % of sales	—	—	—	—	1.2%	1.0%	1.3%	1.6%	1.8%	2.1%	1.8%
Earnings per share ($)	(9.9%)	—	—	—	—	—	—	—	—	0.91	0.82
Stock price - FY high ($)	—	—	—	—	—	—	—	—	—	16.16	23.16
Stock price - FY low ($)	—	—	—	—	—	—	—	—	—	13.00	14.94
Stock price - FY close ($)	45.9%	—	—	—	—	—	—	—	—	15.00	21.88
P/E - high	—	—	—	—	—	—	—	—	—	18	28
P/E - low	—	—	—	—	—	—	—	—	—	14	18
Dividends per share ($)	—	—	—	—	—	—	—	—	—	0.00	0.00
Book value per share ($)	10.4%	—	—	—	—	—	—	—	—	5.95	6.57
Employees	6.6%	—	—	—	—	—	—	—	11,000	11,600	12,500

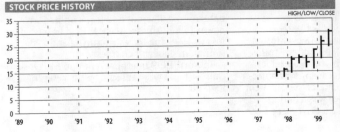

STOCK PRICE HISTORY
HIGH/LOW/CLOSE

1999 FISCAL YEAR-END

Debt ratio: 6.2%
Return on equity: 12.9%
Cash ($ mil.): 12
Current ratio: 1.31
Long-term debt ($ mil.): 32
No. of shares (mil.): 74
Dividends
  Yield: —
  Payout: —
Market value ($ mil.): 1,615

BLACK & DECKER

OVERVIEW

For The Black & Decker Corporation, the wave of the future is cordless. Maybe that's why it pulled the plug on its household appliances business. The Towson, Maryland-based company is the world's leading maker of power tools and accessories. It also makes electric lawn and garden tools, building products, plumbing products, and industrial fastening systems. The Home Depot accounts for 14% of sales.

Black & Decker has assembled a bevy of famous brands, including Black & Decker and DeWALT (power tools and accessories), Kwik-

set (security hardware), and Price Pfister (faucets, #3 in North America).

Despite its brands' high profiles, Black & Decker is retooling. The company sold its household appliances operations (toasters, irons, coffeemakers) in North America, Latin America, and Australia — in part because of their low profit margins and in part because the light-duty appliances had hurt its power tools' image. Black & Decker has kept its lighting and cleaning appliances, including its popular Dustbuster handheld vacuum line.

HISTORY

When Duncan Black and Alonzo Decker opened The Black & Decker Manufacturing Company in Baltimore in 1910 with a $1,200 investment, they began a partnership that would last over 40 years. Starting with milk-bottle-cap machines and candy dippers, the partners introduced their first major tool in 1916 — a portable half-inch electric drill with patented pistol grip and trigger switch, now on display at the Smithsonian.

In 1917 the company built its first manufacturing plant, which would become its headquarters, in rural Towson, Maryland. Sales passed $1 million in 1919, and the company added a 20,000-sq.-ft. factory. Black & Decker quickly established itself in international markets with sales representatives in Australia, Japan, and Russia that year, and it built a manufacturing plant in England in 1939.

Black & Decker produced tools that defined the power tool industry — the first portable screwdriver (1922), the half-inch BB special drill (1923), the first electric hammer (1936), portable electric drills for do-it-yourself home repair (1946), finishing sanders and jigsaws (1953), and the Dustbuster handheld vacuum (1978). The founders led Black & Decker until they died — Black in 1951 (a year before the company went public) and Decker in 1956 — then family members took control of its operations until the 1970s.

The company acquired the General Electric (GE) housewares operations in 1984, replacing GE's trademark with the Black & Decker hexagonal trademark on items such as toaster ovens, can openers, and irons. Black & Decker lost market share in the mid-1980s. Administrative and production costs were high, and product quality was suffering. The company's manufacturing network was inefficient, its management was fat, and customer service was faltering. Nolan Archibald became Black & Decker's CEO

in 1986 and began a major restructuring. Renamed The Black & Decker Corporation, it closed five plants, streamlined distribution systems, consolidated overseas facilities, and cut payroll 10%. Earnings doubled in 1987.

Two years later Black & Decker acquired megaconglomerate Emhart (formerly American Hardware), but the purchase caused earnings to fall. To service its debt, the firm sold off pieces of its acquisition, including Emhart's Bostik adhesives, True Temper Hardware, and North American Mallory Controls. The divestitures resumed in 1993 when Black & Decker sold the architectural hardware business of Corbin Russwin and the through-hole machinery business of Dynapert (a maker of printed circuit board assembly equipment).

Black & Decker expanded its international presence in 1995, beginning joint operations in India and China and introducing DeWALT power tools to Europe and Latin America. In 1997 it teamed up with British industrial giant Imperial Chemical to introduce an automated paint application device, the Paintmate.

The next year Black & Decker sold its sluggish household products operations in the US and Latin America (except Brazil) to small-appliance maker Windmere-Durable (it kept the more profitable lighting and cleaning lines). It also sold True Temper Sports to Cornerstone Equity Investors and sold Emhart Glass to Bucher Holdings of Switzerland. The sales are part of the company's plan to eliminate up to 3,000 jobs and focus on its DeWALT power tool business. Black & Decker posted a loss in 1998 due to restructuring and $900 million in goodwill charges.

In April 1999 heir apparent and EVP Joseph Galli left and was replaced by GE veteran Paul McBride.

OFFICERS

Chairman, President, and CEO: Nolan D. Archibald,
age 55, $2,966,667 pay
**EVP; President, Fastening and Assembly Systems
Group:** Paul A. Gustafson, age 56
EVP; President, Security Hardware Group:
Dennis G. Heiner, age 55
EVP; President, Power Tools and Accessories Group:
Paul McBride
SVP and CFO: Thomas M. Schoewe, age 46, $700,000 pay
SVP and General Counsel: Charles E. Fenton, age 50,
$848,333 pay
SVP Public Affairs and Corporate Secretary:
Barbara B. Lucas, age 53
SVP Human Resources: Leonard A. Strom, age 53
**VP; President, Europe, Power Tools and Accessories
Group:** Frederik B. van den Bergh, age 53, $632,375 pay
Auditors: Ernst & Young LLP

LOCATIONS

HQ: The Black and Decker Corporation,
701 E. Joppa Rd., Towson, MD 21286
Phone: 410-716-3900 **Fax:** 410-716-2933
Web site: http://www.blackanddecker.com

The Black & Decker Corporation's products are
marketed in more than 100 countries.

1998 Sales

	$ mil.	% of total
US	2,704	59
Europe	1,365	30
Other regions	491	11
Total	**4,560**	**100**

PRODUCTS/OPERATIONS

1998 Sales

	$ mil.	% of total
Power tools & accessories	2,946	64
Building products	851	19
Fastening & assembly systems	463	10
Other	334	7
Adjustments	(34)	—
Total	**4,560**	**100**

COMPETITORS

American Standard	Makita
Assa Abloy	Masco
Atlas Copco	Matsushita
Cooper Industries	Pentair
Danaher Corporation	Robert Bosch
Eaton	Royal Appliance
Electrolux	SANYO
Emerson	Snap-on
Fortune Brands	Stanley Works
Greenfield Industries	Textron
Hitachi	Toro
Illinois Tool Works	TRW
Ingersoll-Rand	U.S. Industries
Kohler	

HISTORICAL FINANCIALS & EMPLOYEES

NYSE symbol: BDK FYE: December 31	Annual Growth	1989	1990	1991	1992	1993	1994	1995	1996	1997	1998
Sales ($ mil.)	4.0%	3,190	4,832	4,637	4,780	4,882	5,248	4,766	4,914	4,941	4,560
Net income ($ mil.)	—	30	51	53	(334)	66	127	224	230	227	(755)
Income as % of sales	—	0.9%	1.1%	1.1%	—	1.4%	2.4%	4.7%	4.7%	4.6%	—
Earnings per share ($)	—	0.51	0.84	0.81	(4.52)	0.64	1.36	2.37	2.39	2.35	(8.22)
Stock price - FY high ($)	—	25.25	20.13	19.63	26.88	22.25	25.75	38.13	44.25	43.44	65.50
Stock price - FY low ($)	—	18.13	8.00	8.50	14.63	16.63	17.00	22.88	29.00	29.63	37.94
Stock price - FY close ($)	10.4%	23.00	9.38	17.00	18.13	19.75	23.75	35.25	30.13	39.06	56.06
P/E - high	—	50	24	24	—	35	19	16	19	18	—
P/E - low	—	36	10	10	—	26	13	10	12	13	—
Dividends per share ($)	2.0%	0.40	0.40	0.40	0.40	0.40	0.40	0.40	0.48	0.48	0.48
Book value per share ($)	(6.7%)	12.23	14.94	14.18	11.08	10.72	12.04	14.72	17.32	18.89	6.56
Employees	(6.2%)	38,600	43,400	38,600	38,800	37,300	35,800	29,300	29,200	28,600	21,800

STOCK PRICE HISTORY

HIGH/LOW/CLOSE

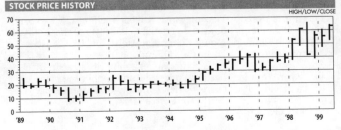

1998 FISCAL YEAR-END

Debt ratio: 66.7%
Return on equity: —
Cash ($ mil.): 88
Current ratio: 1.27
Long-term debt ($ mil.): 1,149
No. of shares (mil.): 87
Dividends
  Yield: 0.9%
  Payout: —
Market value ($ mil.): 4,905

BLOCKBUSTER INC.

OVERVIEW

Anxious parent Viacom is pushing Blockbuster out of the nest. The world's #1 home video products retailer, Dallas-based Blockbuster operates about 6,500 video stores in 26 countries (more than 1,000 of the stores are franchised). In addition to video and DVD sales and rentals, Blockbuster stores offer rentals of VCRs, DVD players, video games, and video game consoles.

Viacom never achieved the synergy it anticipated with the 1994 purchase of Blockbuster; it had hoped for cross-marketing between its video stores and movie studios and between its music stores (which it has sold) and the MTV cable networks. Blockbuster has had a hard time sustaining growth, in part because more viewers are building their own video libraries, accessing pay-per-view channels, or buying satellite dishes. Blockbuster has also been weak internally, with three CEOs in three years and a headquarters move from Florida to Texas that many employees refused to make. However, Blockbuster has been on the mend, thanks in large part to a revenue-sharing agreement with film studios such as Warner Brothers that allows Blockbuster to stock more copies of films by paying studios less for each copy. (The revenue-sharing agreements have brought trouble in the form of an antitrust lawsuit against the company filed by two small video store operators in Texas.)

Viacom sold about 20% of Blockbuster to the public in 1999 and plans to sell the rest before the end of the year (Viacom controls about 95% of Blockbuster's voting shares). Viacom chairman Sumner Redstone controls Viacom through his privately held company, National Amusements.

HISTORY

In 1982 David Cook founded Cook Data Services in Dallas to sell software and computing services to the oil and gas industries. The company went public that year. When the energy industry slowed in the mid-1980s, Cook sold these businesses and shifted direction in favor of flashy, computerized video rental stores. The company opened its first store in 1985 and changed its name to Blockbuster Entertainment in 1986.

Then Midas-like entrepreneur Wayne Huizenga took over, injecting $18 million in Blockbuster in 1987 and buying the company by the end of the year. Huizenga embarked on an acquisition program, increasing the number of Blockbuster stores to 130 by year's end. (Stock appreciation was so rapid in 1988 that the company declared two two-for-one stock splits in the space of 20 weeks.) Other acquisitions (including Major Video, a 175-store chain based in Las Vegas, and Virginia-based Erol's, the US's third-largest video chain) increased the number of stores to 1,500 by 1990.

Blockbuster became the largest video renter in the UK in 1992 through the purchase of the 875-unit Cityvision chain. It also bought the Sound Warehouse and Music Plus music store chains from Shamrock Holdings. In 1993 the company acquired a majority stake in Spelling Entertainment and an interest in movie producer Republic Pictures.

The firm acquired software developer Virgin Interactive Entertainment in 1994 and folded it into Spelling. That year Viacom paid $8.4 billion for Blockbuster and formed a new division called Blockbuster Entertainment Group. Following the acquisition, Huizenga left the company. (He's now CEO of AutoNation.)

Steven Berrard, who became Blockbuster CEO after the 1994 takeover, resigned in 1996 to head Huizenga's used-car operations. Wal-Mart veteran Bill Fields, who replaced him, wanted to promote the retailer as a "neighborhood entertainment center," selling videotapes (instead of renting them), books, CDs, gift items, and music. In 1996 Viacom closed 50 music outlets and moved Blockbuster's headquarters.

In 1997 Viacom scaled back Blockbuster's expansion plans, and after Fields resigned as CEO, Viacom began unraveling many of his efforts, especially his focus on non-rental operations. Viacom hired Taco Bell *jefe* John Antioco in hopes that he would lead Blockbuster to a replay of its earlier success. Antioco's reign began with Viacom taking a $300 million charge related to the turmoil at Blockbuster. Antioco's efforts to stock more copies of hit movies by sharing rental revenues with studios but paying less for each video copy caused rental revenues to jump by 1998. Also that year Viacom, which had been selling assets to pare down debt related to its 1994 purchase of Paramount Communications, sold Blockbuster Music for $115 million.

Viacom spun off a minority stake in Blockbuster in mid-1999 and announced plans to open 900 new company-owned stores per year for the next three years.

Chairman, President, and CEO: John F. Antioco, age 49
EVP, Real Estate, Franchising, and New Business Development: Mark T. Gilman, age 35
EVP and Chief Marketing Officer: James Notarnicola, age 47
EVP and COO: Gary J. Peterson, age 48
EVP and Chief Information Officer: Alva J. Phillips, age 54
EVP, Domestic Video Operations: Michael K. Roemer, age 50
EVP, General Counsel, and Secretary: Edward B. Stead, age 52
EVP; President, Worldwide Retail Operations: Nigel Travis, age 49
EVP, Merchandising: Dean M. Wilson, age 41
EVP and CFO: Larry J. Zine, age 44
SVP Worldwide Human Resources: Steve Becker
Auditors: PricewaterhouseCoopers LLP

LOCATIONS

HQ: 1201 Elm St., Dallas, TX 75270
Phone: 214-854-3000   **Fax:** 214-854-4848
Web site: http://www.blockbuster.com

Blockbuster operates about 6,500 home video stores in 26 countries including Argentina, Australia, Brazil, Canada, Chile, China, Colombia, Denmark, Ecuador, El Salvador, Israel, Italy, Mexico, New Zealand, Panama, Peru, Poland, Portugal, Spain, Taiwan, Thailand, the UK, Uruguay, the US, and Venezuela.

1998 Stores

	No.	% of total
US	4,258	66
Other countries	2,241	34
Total	**6,499**	**100**

PRODUCTS/OPERATIONS

Selected Merchandise
Equipment (rentals)
    DVD players
    Video game consoles
    Video players
Movies
    DVD
    Video
Video games
    N64
    PlayStation

COMPETITORS

Best Buy
Borders
Circuit City
Hastings Entertainment
Hollywood Entertainment
Movie Gallery
Musicland
MTS
Trans World Entertainment
Video Update
Walt Disney
West Coast Entertainment

HISTORICAL FINANCIALS & EMPLOYEES

NYSE symbol: BBI FYE: December 31	Annual Growth	1989	1990	1991	1992	1993	1994	1995	1996	1997	1998
Sales ($ mil.)	15.0%	—	—	—	—	—	—	—	2,942	3,314	3,893
Net income ($ mil.)		—	—	—	—	—	—	—	78	(318)	(337)
Income as % of sales		—	—	—	—	—	—	—	2.6%	—	—
Employees		—	—	—	—	—	—	—	—	—	82,400

NET INCOME HISTORY

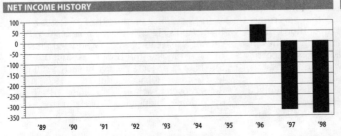

1998 FISCAL YEAR-END

Debt ratio: 23.3%
Return on equity: —
Cash ($ mil.): 99
Current ratio: 0.75
Long-term debt ($ mil.): 1,715

BLUE CROSS AND BLUE SHIELD

OVERVIEW

The rise of managed health care has had some of its members singing the blues, but Blue Cross and Blue Shield Association still has major market power. The Chicago-based association governs 51 chapters that offer health care coverage to nearly 73 million Americans via indemnity insurance, HMOs, PPOs, point-of-service (POS) plans, and Medicare plans.

While some Blues always faced competition head-on, most received tax benefits for taking all comers. But as lower-cost plans attracted the hale and hearty, the Blues' customers became older, sicker, and more expensive. With their quasi-charitable status and outdated rate structures, many Blues lost market share.

They have fought back by merging among themselves, creating for-profit subsidiaries, forming alliances with for-profit enterprises, or dropping their not-for-profit status and going public — while still using the Blue Cross Blue Shield name. A history of tax breaks complicates some of these efforts and usually requires the creation of charitable foundations. As a result, the umbrella association is becoming a licensing and brand-marketing entity. As industry consolidation threatens their market advantage, many Blues are competing among themselves as they push beyond the boundaries of their home states.

HISTORY

Blue Cross was born in 1929, when Baylor University official Justin Kimball offered schoolteachers 21 days of hospital care for $6 a year. A major plan feature was a community rating system that based premiums on the community claims experience rather than members' conditions.

The Blue Cross symbol was devised in 1933 by Minnesota plan executive E. A. van Steenwyck. By 1935 many of the 15 plans in 11 states used the symbol. Many states gave the plans nonprofit status, and in 1936 the American Hospital Association formed the Committee on Hospital Service (renamed the Blue Cross Association in 1948) to coordinate them.

As Blue Cross grew, state medical societies began sponsoring prepaid plans to cover doctors' fees. In 1946 they united under the aegis of the American Medical Association (AMA) as the Associated Medical Care Plans (later the Association of Blue Shield Plans).

In 1948 AMA thwarted a Blue Cross attempt to merge with Blue Shield. But the Blues increasingly cooperated on public policy matters while competing for members, and each Blue formed a not-for-profit corporation to coordinate its plan's activities.

By 1960 Blue Cross insured about a third of the US. Over the next decade the Blues started administering Medicare and other government health plans, and by 1970 half of Blue Cross' premiums came from government entities.

In the 1970s the Blues adopted such cost-control measures as review of hospital admissions; many plans even abandoned the community rating system. Most began emphasizing preventive care in HMOs or PPOs.

The two Blues finally merged in 1982, but this had little effect on the associations' bottom lines as losses grew.

By the 1990s the Blues were big business; some of the state associations offered officers high salaries and perks but still insisted on special regulatory treatment.

Blue Cross of California became the first chapter to give up its tax-free status when it was bought by WellPoint Health Networks, a managed care subsidiary it had founded in 1992. In a 1996 deal, WellPoint became the chapter's parent and converted it to for-profit status, assigning all of the stock to a public charitable foundation, which received the proceeds of its subsequent IPO. WellPoint also bought the group life and health division of Massachusetts Mutual Life Insurance (better known as MassMutual).

The for-profit switches picked up in 1997. Blue Cross of Connecticut merged with insurance provider Anthem, and other mergers followed. Half the nation's Blues formed an alliance called BluesConnect, competing with national health plans by offering employers one nationwide benefits organization. The association also pursued overseas licensing agreements in Europe, South America, and Asia, assembling a network of Blue Cross-friendly caregivers aiming for worldwide coverage.

In 1998 Blues in more than 35 states sued the nation's big cigarette companies to recoup the costs of treating smoking-related illnesses. In a separate lawsuit, Blue Cross and Blue Shield of Minnesota received nearly $300 million from the tobacco industry. In 1999, Anthem moved to acquire or affiliate with Blues in Colorado, Maine, and New Hampshire.

President and CEO: Patrick G. Hays
EVP Business Alliances: Harry P. Cain II
EVP Systems Development and COO: Scott P. Serota
SVP, Corporate Secretary, and General Counsel:
  Roger G. Wilson
SVP Policy, Representation, and Membership Services:
  Mary Nell Lehnhard
VP and Chief Administration Officer: Steve Heath
VP Finance and Administration: Ralph Rambach
Human Resources: Bill Colbourne
Auditors: PricewaterhouseCoopers LLP

LOCATIONS

HQ: Blue Cross and Blue Shield Association,
  225 N. Michigan Ave., Chicago, IL 60601-7680
Phone: 312-297-6000   **Fax:** 312-297-6609
Web site: http://www.blueshield.com

The Blue Cross and Blue Shield Association has offices
in Chicago and Washington, DC, with licensees
operating throughout the US as well as in Jamaica,
Japan, Mexico, Uruguay, and Western Europe.

PRODUCTS/OPERATIONS

1998 Members

	No. (mil.)	% of total
PPO plans	25.7	35
HMO plans	14.2	20
POS plans	6.4	9
Federal health benefits program	3.9	5
Other	22.5	31
Total	**72.7**	**100**

Selected Operations
BlueCard Worldwide (care of US members in foreign
  countries)
BluesConnect (nationwide alliance)
Federal Employee Program (federal employees and
  retirees)
Health maintenance organizations
Medicare management
Point-of-service programs
Preferred provider organizations

COMPETITORS

Aetna
CIGNA
Foundation Health Systems
Humana
Oxford Health Plans
Prudential
UniHealth
UnitedHealth Group

HISTORICAL FINANCIALS & EMPLOYEES

Association FYE: December 31	Annual Growth	1989	1990	1991	1992	1993	1994	1995	1996	1997	1998
Sales ($ mil.)	6.0%	56,040	62,566	67,068	70,913	71,161	71,414	74,400	75,200	76,500	94,700
Employees	1.7%	129,000	133,000	138,000	143,000	135,883	146,352	146,000	150,000	150,000	150,000

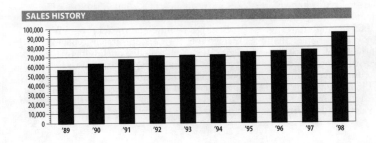

SALES HISTORY

Blue Cross
Blue Shield

THE BOEING COMPANY

From Delta rockets and the Space Shuttle to the Apache helicopter and the 747 jumbo jet, Boeing is the 400-pound gorilla of US aerospace. The only maker of big commercial jets in the US, the Seattle-based firm is the world's largest aerospace company. It has divisions devoted to commercial airplanes, military aircraft and missiles, and space and communications systems.

The company's commercial planes (63% of sales) include the Boeing 737 (the world's most popular commercial aircraft), 747, 757, 767, and 777 jets, which represent a variety of passenger and cargo configurations and range capabilities. The dominant producer of large commercial aircraft, its only competition comes from the French consortium, Airbus.

Boeing's military aircraft include the F/A-18 Hornet strike fighter, the venerable F-15E Eagle fighter-bomber, the AH-64D Apache Longbow helicopter, and the C-17 Globemaster III transport. Missiles include the Standoff Land Attack Missile (SLAM ER) and the Joint Direct Attack Munition (JDAM).

Major Boeing space systems include the Space Shuttle (with Lockheed Martin), the Delta family of rockets, global positioning systems (GPS), and communications satellites. Through partnerships with other companies, Boeing is planning to offer satellite communication services. Boeing is also the prime contractor for the International Space Station.

After severe production problems in 1997 Boeing has regained its footing. Now it is bracing itself for the downturn in commercial plane orders that is widely expected to occur over the next several years.

Bill Boeing built his first airplane in 1916 with naval officer Conrad Westervelt. His Seattle company, Pacific Aero Products, changed its name to Boeing Airplane Company the next year.

During WWI Boeing built training planes for the US Navy. After the war it began the first international airmail service (between Seattle and Victoria, British Columbia). The company added a Chicago-San Francisco route in 1927 and established an airline subsidiary, Boeing Air Transport. The airline's success was aided by Boeing's Model 40A, the first plane using Frederick Rentschler's new air-cooled engine, the Wasp.

Rentschler and Boeing combined their companies as United Aircraft and Transport in 1929. United soon owned a number of aviation businesses, including Sikorsky Aviation, Stout Air Services, and Clement Keys' National Air Transport.

The company introduced the all-metal airliner in 1933. The next year new airmail rules forced United to sell its airline operations. This left Boeing Airplane (as it was known until 1961) with the manufacturing concerns.

Between 1935 and 1965 Boeing's new planes included the Model 314 Clipper (flying boat) used by Pan Am, the Model 307 Stratoliner (the first aircraft with a pressurized cabin), and the 707 (the first successful jetliner) and 727. In the 1960s it built the first stage of the rockets used in the Apollo space program. The company delivered the first 737 in 1967. The 747 (the first jumbo jet) also went into production in the late 1960s.

Boeing expanded its information services and aerospace capabilities by establishing Boeing Computer Services in 1970. World fuel shortages and concern over aircraft noise prompted Boeing to design the efficient and quiet 757 and 767 models in the late 1970s.

The company's wide-body 777, its first new commercial aircraft in 11 years, made its maiden flight in 1995. In 1996 Boeing bought Rockwell's aerospace and defense operations. The next year Boeing agreed to build a $9 billion network of communications satellites for affiliate Teledesic.

In 1997 Boeing bought rival and leading military aircraft maker McDonnell Douglas for $16 billion. That year production problems idled much of its workforce, causing huge losses. In 1998 Boeing announced several production changes, including halting manufacture of the MD-11, -80, and -90 lines by early 2000, and the consolidation of facilities. The cost cutting moves are expected to result in the loss of 48,000 jobs (20% of its workforce) through 2000.

Boeing's commercial rocket program was thrown into turmoil after its large-payload Delta III rocket exploded during its maiden launch. The Air Force, however, awarded the bulk of a satellite-launching contract to Boeing over rival Lockheed Martin. Boeing's Delta III blues continued in 1999 when the rocket failed to lift a satellite to the proper orbit.

Chairman and CEO: Philip M. Condit, age 57,
$998,896 pay
President and COO: Harry C. Stonecipher, age 62,
$899,007 pay
SVP; President, Space and Communications Group:
James F. Albaugh, age 48, $499,582 pay
SVP and General Counsel: Theodore J. Collins, age 62
SVP, People: James B. Dagnon, age 59
SVP and CFO: Deborah C. Hopkins, age 44
SVP; President, Boeing Commercial Airplane Group:
Alan R. Mulally, age 53, $778,601 pay
SVP; President, Boeing Shared Services Group:
James F. Palmer, age 49, $525,046 pay
**SVP; President, Military Aircraft and Missile Systems
Group:** Michael M. Sears, age 51, $664,169 pay
SVP and Chief Administrative Officer: John D. Warner,
age 59
VP and Controller: Gary W. Beil
**VP, Corporate Secretary, and Assistant General
Counsel:** James C. Johnson
VP of Communications: Judith A. Muhlberg, age 46
VP of Finance and Treasurer: Walter E. Skowronski,
age 50
**EVP, Single-Aisle Airplane Programs, Boeing
Commercial Airplanes Group:** James M. Jamieson,
age 50
Auditors: Deloitte & Touche LLP

LOCATIONS

HQ: 7755 E. Marginal Way South, Seattle, WA 98108
Phone: 206-655-2121   **Fax:** 206-544-1581
Web site: http://www.boeing.com

Boeing has customers in 145 countries, including
Australia and Canada, but the bulk of its operations take
place in the US.

PRODUCTS/OPERATIONS

1998 Sales

	$ mil.	% of total
Commercial airplanes	35,545	63
Military aircraft & missiles	12,990	23
Space & Communications	6,889	12
Financing & other	730	2
Total	**56,154**	**100**

COMPETITORS

Aerospatiale
Airbus
BFGoodrich
Bombardier
British Aerospace
Cordant Technologies
DaimlerChrysler
Dassault Aviation
Kaman
Lockheed Martin
Northrop Grumman
Raytheon
Sextant Avionique
Textron
Thomson SA
United Technologies

HISTORICAL FINANCIALS & EMPLOYEES

NYSE symbol: BA FYE: December 31	Annual Growth	1989	1990	1991	1992	1993	1994	1995	1996	1997	1998
Sales ($ mil.)	12.0%	20,276	27,595	29,314	30,184	25,438	21,924	19,515	22,681	45,800	56,154
Net income ($ mil.)	1.6%	973	1,385	1,567	552	1,244	856	393	1,095	(178)	1,120
Income as % of sales	—	4.8%	5.0%	5.3%	1.8%	4.9%	3.9%	2.0%	4.8%	—	2.0%
Earnings per share ($)	(2.2%)	1.41	2.01	2.28	0.81	1.64	1.48	(0.04)	1.85	(0.18)	1.15
Stock price - FY high ($)	—	20.64	30.94	26.50	27.31	22.38	25.06	40.00	53.75	60.50	56.25
Stock price - FY low ($)	—	12.87	18.88	20.63	16.06	16.69	21.06	22.19	37.06	43.00	29.00
Stock price - FY close ($)	5.7%	19.80	22.69	23.88	20.06	21.63	23.50	39.19	53.25	48.94	32.63
P/E - high	—	15	15	12	34	14	17	—	29	—	49
P/E - low	—	9	9	9	20	10	14	—	20	—	25
Dividends per share ($)	4.1%	0.39	0.48	0.50	0.50	0.50	0.50	0.50	0.42	0.56	0.56
Book value per share ($)	3.6%	8.87	10.15	11.86	11.87	13.20	14.23	14.39	15.75	13.31	12.17
Employees	3.9%	163,900	160,500	155,700	142,000	123,000	117,000	105,000	143,000	238,000	231,000

STOCK PRICE HISTORY

HIGH/LOW/CLOSE

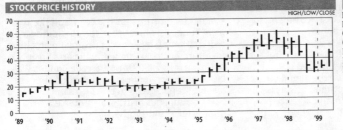

1998 FISCAL YEAR-END

Debt ratio: 33.1%
Return on equity: 9.1%
Cash ($ mil.): 2,183
Current ratio: 1.22
Long-term debt ($ mil.): 6,103
No. of shares (mil.): 1,012
Dividends
  Yield: 1.7%
  Payout: 48.7%
Market value ($ mil.): 33,017

BOISE CASCADE CORPORATION

OVERVIEW

Although Boise Cascade doesn't make paper money, it does make money from paper. The Boise, Idaho-based company manages more than 2 million acres of forests to support its manufacturing of paper, building products, and office products. Through its publicly traded Boise Cascade Office Products subsidiary, Boise Cascade also distributes office paper and furniture, along with computer supplies. The company operates about 70 distribution centers in Australia, Canada, France, Spain, the UK, and the US. Its building products range from laminated veneer lumber to I-joists and plywood.

Paper products made by Boise Cascade include uncoated printing papers, newsprint, market pulp, containerboard, business paper, and forms.

The Asian economic crisis eroded demand for paper there and also resulted in increased paper imports to the US, which decreased prices. As a result, Boise Cascade restructured by closing four wood products plants and its Portland, Oregon-based paper research and development facility. Finding American trees increasingly difficult to harvest due to environmental concerns, the firm is buying timberland in countries such as Chile.

HISTORY

Boise Cascade got its start in 1957 with the merger of two small lumber companies — Boise Payette Lumber Company (based in Boise, Idaho) and Cascade Lumber Company (Yakima, Washington). The business diversified in the 1960s under the leadership of Robert Hansberger, moving into office products distribution in 1964. A number of acquisitions followed, including Ebasco Industries (1969), a consulting, engineering, and construction firm. By 1970 Boise Cascade had made more than 30 buys to diversify into building materials, paper products, real estate, recreational vehicles (RVs), and publishing.

In the early 1970s the company suffered a timber shortage as its access to public timberlands dwindled. Its plans to develop recreational communities in Hawaii, Washington, and California met opposition from residents, causing Boise Cascade to scrap all but six of the 29 projects. In 1972 high costs related to the remaining projects left the company in debt.

John Fery replaced Hansberger as president that year and sold companies not directly related to the company's core forest product operations.

In the late 1980s and early 1990s, Boise Cascade sold more nonstrategic operations, including its Specialty Paperboard Division in 1989. It sold more than half of its corrugated container plants in 1992 to focus on manufacturing forest products and distributing building materials and office supplies.

Boise Cascade also sold its wholesale office product business in 1992 to focus on direct sales to big buyers such as IBM and Boeing. Two years later it entered direct-mail distribution by acquiring the direct-mail business of Reliable, a Chicago-based national office products supplier. Boise Cascade then bought a 10% stake in Reliable's 18 retail stores, located mostly in the Midwest. The company sold off its Canadian subsidiary, Rainy River Forest Products, in 1994 and 1995. Resurgent paper prices resulted in a profit in 1995, Boise Cascade's first since 1990.

Also in 1995, in a move into the international paper market, Boise Cascade signed a joint venture agreement with Shenzhen Leasing to form Zhuhai Hiwin Boise Cascade, a Chinese manufacturer of carbonless paper. That year it sold a minority stake in Boise Cascade Office Products (BCOP) to the public.

The company sold its coated papers business to paper and packaging heavyweight Mead in 1996 for $639 million. The following year Boise Cascade began harvesting its first quick-growth cottonwood trees (specially grown to cut the cost of harvesting from traditional slow-growth hardwood plantations). Also in 1997 BCOP bought Jean-Paul Guisset, the #3 office products direct marketer in France. Although this acquisition boosted sales and increased the company's European presence, company profits suffered that year because of weak paper prices.

The low price of paper in 1998 prompted the company to close four sawmills and a research and development center. Restructuring costs associated with the closures and a fire at the company's Medford, Oregon, plywood plant led to a net income loss for the year. Still the company bought six firms that year, including a direct marketing business in Spain and an office furniture business and a graphic arts business in Canada. In 1999 Boise Cascade bought Wallace Computer Services, a contract stationer business, and agreed to buy Furman Lumber, a building supplies distributor in the eastern, midwestern, and southern US.

OFFICERS

Chairman and CEO: George J. Harad, age 54,
$1,542,912 pay
SVP Building Products: John C. Bender
SVP and CFO: Theodore Crumley, age 53, $528,934 pay
SVP Manufacturing Paper: A. Ben Groce, age 57
SVP and General Counsel: John W. Holleran, age 44
SVP International: Terry R. Lock, age 57
SVP; CEO, Boise Cascade Office Products:
Christopher C. Milliken, age 53, $573,972 pay
SVP and General Manager, Paper: N. David Spence,
age 63, $544,967 pay
VP; SVP, CFO, and Treasurer, Boise Cascade Office
Products: A. James Balkins III, age 46
VP Building Materials Distribution and Engineered
Wood Products Sales and Marketing: Stanley R. Bell,
age 52
VP and Controller: Tom E. Carlile, age 47
VP Marketing and Sales: Graham L. Covington, age 56
VP and Corporate Secretary: Karen E. Gowland, age 40
VP Human Resources: J. Michael Gwartney, age 57
VP Corporate Communications and Investor Relations:
Vincent T. Hannity, age 54
VP and Treasurer: Irving Littman, age 58
Auditors: Arthur Andersen LLP

LOCATIONS

HQ: 1111 W. Jefferson St., Boise, ID 83728-0001
Phone: 208-384-6161 **Fax:** 208-384-7189
Web site: http://www.bc.com

Boise Cascade operates 23 wood products mills, 14 pulp
and paper mills, seven corrugated container plants, 16
wholesale building products distribution centers, and 68
office products distribution centers.

PRODUCTS/OPERATIONS

1998 Sales

	$ mil.	% of total
Office products	3,067	46
Paper	1,752	27
Building products	1,722	26
Other	80	1
Adjustments	(459)	—
Total	**6,162**	**100**

Office Products
Distribution
Office and computer
supplies
Office furniture
Paper products
Promotional products

Selected Building
Products
Engineered wood products
I-joists
Laminated beams
Laminated veneer
lumber
Oriented strand board

Lumber
Particleboard
Plywood

Selected Paper Products
Business papers
Colored papers
Containerboard
Corrugated containers
Market pulp
Newsprint
Security papers

COMPETITORS

Abitibi-Consolidated
Blandin Paper
Champion International
Corporate Express
Georgia-Pacific

International Paper
Mead
Smurfit-Stone Container
Weyerhaeuser
Willamette

HISTORICAL FINANCIALS & EMPLOYEES

NYSE symbol: BCC FYE: December 31	Annual Growth	1989	1990	1991	1992	1993	1994	1995	1996	1997	1998
Sales ($ mil.)	4.0%	4,338	4,186	3,951	3,716	3,958	4,140	5,074	5,108	5,494	6,162
Net income ($ mil.)	—	268	75	(80)	(228)	(77)	(63)	352	9	(30)	(37)
Income as % of sales	—	6.2%	1.8%	—	—	—	—	6.9%	0.2%	—	—
Earnings per share ($)	—	5.70	1.62	(2.46)	(6.73)	(3.17)	(3.08)	5.39	(0.63)	(1.19)	(1.00)
Stock price - FY high ($)	—	48.00	46.25	29.25	25.38	27.50	30.50	47.50	47.25	45.56	40.38
Stock price - FY low ($)	—	39.75	19.75	18.38	16.38	19.50	19.00	26.25	27.38	27.75	22.25
Stock price - FY close ($)	(3.9%)	44.38	26.00	22.25	21.13	23.50	26.75	34.50	31.75	30.25	31.00
P/E - high	—	8	29	—	—	—	—	9	—	—	—
P/E - low	—	7	12	—	—	—	—	5	—	—	—
Dividends per share ($)	(9.7%)	1.50	1.52	1.52	0.60	0.60	0.60	0.60	0.45	0.60	0.60
Book value per share ($)	(5.9%)	41.23	41.07	37.49	29.95	25.92	21.77	28.17	27.30	25.39	23.84
Employees	1.8%	19,539	9,810	19,619	17,222	17,362	16,618	17,820	19,976	22,514	23,039

STOCK PRICE HISTORY

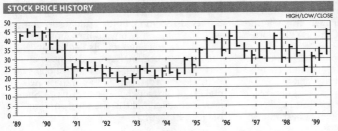

HIGH/LOW/CLOSE

1998 FISCAL YEAR-END

Debt ratio: 54.8%
Return on equity: —
Cash ($ mil.): 74
Current ratio: 1.21
Long-term debt ($ mil.): 1,734
No. of shares (mil.): 56
Dividends
Yield: 1.9%
Payout: —
Market value ($ mil.): 1,746

BORDEN, INC.

OVERVIEW

After giving Elsie the cow and the Cracker Jack boy their pink slips, Borden has reinvented itself as a specialty chemicals company. The Columbus, Ohio-based company, controlled by Kohlberg Kravis Roberts (KKR), has sold its dairy division and its decorative-products unit, as well as its Cracker Jack snack food and Eagle Brand condensed-milk units. Borden is sticking with its pasta brands (including Creamette and Prince), along with its Classico pasta sauces and Wyler's bouillon and dry soups.

Borden operates the affiliated salty-snack company Wise Foods, Elmer's Products unit (consumer adhesives), and chemicals divisions (resins, coatings, adhesives, melamine crystal, and specialty inks). It is North America's #1 producer of formaldehyde (followed by Georgia-Pacific and Neste Resins), the bulk of which is used to produce thermosetting resins.

The company is growing its chemicals business through acquisitions. Borden has agreed to buy Spurlock Industries and the chemicals unit of Blagden PLC. Both companies make formaldehyde and resins.

HISTORY

Galveston, Texas, resident Gail Borden Jr. was the founder of one of Texas' first newspapers, the *Telegraph and Texas Register,* in which he headlined the phrase, "Remember the Alamo." He was also an inventor whose creations included a portable bathhouse and a nonperishable meat biscuit. By 1853 he had developed a process to preserve milk by condensing it in a vacuum.

Borden located his business in Burrville, Connecticut, in 1857 and called it Gail Borden, Jr., and Company; he formed New York Condensed Milk with grocer Jeremiah Milbank the next year. A big break came with the Civil War, when the US Army ordered 500 pounds of condensed milk. Condensed milk was later carried on Robert Peary's North Pole and Annapurna expeditions. When Borden died in 1874, the company was the leading US milk condenser.

The company incorporated in 1899 and took the name Borden Company in 1919. Between 1928 and 1929 Borden doubled in size and gained operations in ice cream, cheese, and powdered milk. By 1929 it had diversified by buying glue maker Casein.

The company was well-positioned internationally and in the chemicals market by the end of WWII. To reduce dependence on dairy revenues, Borden expanded its chemicals business by buying Columbus Coated Fabrics (1961) and Smith-Douglass (1964). Expansion into snacks began in 1964 with the purchase of Wise Foods and Cracker Jack. In 1979 Borden bought Buckeye and Guy's Food potato chip makers.

In the 1980s Borden spent $1.9 billion on 91 acquisitions, mainly regional makers of snack foods and pasta, but the lack of a centralized manufacturing and selling network slowed growth and resulted in lost market share for many of the company's best-known products. At that time, Borden was the world's largest pasta maker.

By late 1993 Borden had axed CEO Anthony D'Amato, under whose leadership the company's market value had dropped 50% in two years to $2.4 billion. In 1994 Borden sold its food service unit (to Heinz) and several other small food divisions. Later that year Kohlberg Kravis Roberts & Co. (KKR) bought 64% of Borden, paying for it with $2 billion in RJR Nabisco stock, which had been a disappointment to KKR. Eventually, affiliates of KKR owned virtually all of Borden.

Still saddled with debt, in 1996 Borden sold its Global Packaging business to AEP Industries. Borden sold its Borden Foods Corporation and Wise salty-snacks business to other branches of KKR, which kept them affiliated with Borden.

In 1997 Borden sold Cracker Jack to PepsiCo's Frito-Lay. The Borden/Meadow Gold Dairies division was sold to a group led by giant dairy co-op Mid-America Dairymen (now part of Dairy Farmers of America). Also that year the company's Borden Chemical subsidiary acquired Melamine Chemicals, which makes melamine crystals used in adhesives and coatings.

In 1998 it bought the chemicals unit of Sun Coast Industries, which makes specialty resins and compounds. Also in 1998 KKR affiliate BW Holdings, Borden's parent, acquired 92% of Corning Consumer Products, to be managed by Borden. In addition, Borden sold its decorative-products business to buyout firm American Capital Strategies and sold its Eagle Brand, Cremora, ReaLemon, Kava, and None Such grocery brands to startup Eagle Family Foods.

In 1999 Borden agreed to purchase two makers of formaldehyde and resins — Spurlock Industries and the chemicals unit of Blagden PLC (UK).

Chairman, President, and CEO; Chairman, Corning Consumer Products; Chairman, Borden Foods: C. Robert Kidder, age 54, $1,647,470 pay
EVP and CFO: William H. Carter, age 45, $565,000 pay
EVP, Corporate Strategy and Development: Kevin M. Kelley
EVP; Chairman and CEO, Elmer's Products: Ronald C. Kesselman
EVP; Chairman and CEO, Borden Chemical: Joseph M. Saggese, age 67, $736,671 pay
SVP Human Resources and Corporate Affairs: Nancy A. Reardon, age 46, $453,223 pay
SVP and Treasurer: Ronald P. Starkman, age 44
SVP and General Counsel: William F. Stoll Jr., age 50, $441,953 pay
President and CEO, Corning Consumer Products: Peter Campanella
Chairman and COO, Borden Foods: Peter M. Dunn
Auditors: Deloitte & Touche LLP

LOCATIONS

HQ: 180 E. Broad St., Columbus, OH 43215
Phone: 614-225-4000

1998 Sales

	$ mil.	% of total
US	942	67
Canada	142	10
Other countries	316	23
Total	**1,400**	**100**

PRODUCTS/OPERATIONS

1998 Sales

	$ mil.	% of total
Chemicals	1,260	90
Businesses held for sale	37	3
Other	103	7
Total	**1,400**	**100**

Selected Subsidiaries and Affiliates

BCP Finance Corporation
BCP Management, Inc.
Borden Chemical, Inc.
Borden Chemical International, Inc.
Borden Foods Corporation
Borden International Philippines (98%)
Corning Consumer Products Company
Elmer's Products Canada, Inc.
Elmer's Products, Inc.
Melamine Chemicals, Inc.
Quimica Borden Espana SA (96%, Spain)
Wise Foods, Inc.

COMPETITORS

Akzo Nobel	Hormel
American Italian Pasta	Huntsman
Ashland	ICI
BASF AG	Kraft Foods
Bestfoods	Lancaster Colony
Borden Chemicals	Lawter International
Campbell Soup	M. A. Hanna
Celanese	McWhorter Technologies
ConAgra	New World Pasta
Dainippon Ink &	Newell Rubbermaid
Chemicals	Procter & Gamble
DuPont	R.J. Reynolds Tobacco
Frito-Lay	Rohm and Haas
General Mills	Sara Lee
Georgia Gulf	Unilever PLC
Georgia-Pacific	Valspar

HISTORICAL FINANCIALS & EMPLOYEES

Private company FYE: December 31	Annual Growth	1989	1990	1991	1992	1993	1994	1995	1996	1997	1998
Sales ($ mil.)	(17.1%)	7,593	7,633	6,756	5,872	5,506	5,626	5,944	5,765	3,482	1,400
Net income ($ mil.)	—	(61)	364	295	(364)	(631)	(598)	(366)	82	278	63
Income as % of sales	—	—	4.8%	4.4%	—	—	—	—	1.4%	8.0%	4.5%
Employees	(23.4%)	46,500	46,300	44,400	41,900	41,900	32,300	27,500	20,000	15,000	4,200

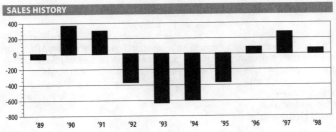

SALES HISTORY

Debit ratio: 86.1%
Return on equity: 70.1%
Cash ($ mil.): 672
Current ratio: 1.05
Long-term debt ($ mil.): 552

BORDERS GROUP, INC.

OVERVIEW

Although a great writer's imagination has no borders, inside Borders you can find the works of many great writers. Ann Arbor, Michigan-based Borders Group, the nation's #2 bookstore retailer, operates more than 1,150 US stores (in all 50 states) under two names: Borders (about 260 superstores) and Waldenbooks (the #1 US mall bookstore chain). The company also owns about 25 Books etc. stores in the UK and has opened Borders stores in the UK, Australia, and Singapore.

In addition to international expansion, the firm continues to open US superstores in its bid to take sales from best-seller Barnes &

Noble. Most superstores sell music in addition to books and have cafes. Since many book-worms now shop online, Borders sells books, music, and videos on its Web site, which also offers live chats with authors and musicians. Slow to join the e-commerce revolution, the company trails Amazon.com and Barnes & Noble significantly in that arena.

With book sales moving online, Borders strives to reflect local tastes and interests in its superstores, even employing community relations representatives. The stores also host literary and community events, including author signings and lectures.

HISTORY

Brothers Louis and Tom Borders founded their first bookstore in 1971 in Ann Arbor, Michigan. The store originally sold used books but soon added new books. As titles were added, Louis developed tracking systems for the growing inventory. It's been said that the former MIT student stumbled upon the system while trying to create a software program to predict horse race winners. In the mid-1970s the brothers formed Book Inventory Systems to market the system to other independent bookstores.

Through the late 1970s and early 1980s, the brothers focused on building the service part of their business, but by the mid-1980s they were having trouble finding enough large, independent bookstore customers. Refocusing on retail, they opened their second store (Birmingham, Michigan) in 1985.

They had five stores by 1988 and hired Robert DiRomualdo (president of cheeselog chain Hickory Farms) to run Borders and mount a national expansion. Discount retailer Kmart bought Book Inventory Systems (including 19 Borders bookstores) in 1992.

Kmart already owned Waldenbooks, which had been founded in 1933 and named for the Massachusetts pond that inspired Thoreau. Started by Larry Hoyt as a book rental library, Waldenbooks had 250 outlets by 1948. In 1968 the bookseller opened its first all-retail bookstore in Pittsburgh.

By placing stores in the growing number of US shopping malls, Waldenbooks expanded rapidly during the 1970s. In 1979 the company hired former Procter & Gamble executive Harry Hoffman to run the company. Hoffman drew the ire of traditionalists in the book retailing industry because he focused on bestsellers instead of literary works. Hoffman also added nonbook items such as greeting cards to the stores' merchandise mix.

In 1981 Waldenbooks became the first bookseller to operate in all 50 states. Kmart acquired the chain three years later. As part of a plan to revive its discount business, Kmart spun off Borders Group (which by this time included Waldenbooks, Borders, and part of Planet Music, formerly CD Superstore) to the public in 1995. Borders consolidated its three divisions under one roof and bought the rest of Planet Music (closed in 1997). With mall traffic slowing nationally, Borders CEO DiRomualdo steered the company away from Waldenbooks and toward superstores.

Moving beyond its existing borders, the company acquired the UK chain Books etc., opened a store in Singapore in 1997, and entered Australia the next year. Borders finally began offering books, music, and videos through its borders.com Web site in 1998, three years after Amazon.com began selling online.

Also in 1998 a group of independent retailers sued Borders (and rival Barnes & Noble) for allegedly pressuring publishers into granting unfair discounts and promotions. Philip Pfeffer, a former top executive with publisher Random House and book distributor Ingram who succeeded DiRomualdo as CEO in late 1998, was forced out five months later, in part for being slow to address the company's lagging efforts online.

In 1999 Borders acquired 20% of UK stationery retailer Paperchase Products; All Wound Up, a kiosk-based seller of interactive toys and novelties; and 20% of Sprout, Inc., which offers on-demand book printing.

Chairman, CEO, and President: Robert F. DiRomualdo, age 54
VC: George R. Mrkonic, age 46
VC: Bruce A. Quinnell, age 50
SVP Finance, CFO, and Treasurer: Kenneth E. Scheve, age 52
VP, General Counsel, and Secretary: Thomas D. Carney, age 52
VP, Internet Services: Karen Tyree
Chairman and CEO, Borders (UK) Ltd.:
Richard D. Joseph, age 42
President, International: Vincent E. Altruda, age 49
President, Borders Stores: Richard L. Flanagan, age 46
President, Merchandising and Distribution:
Timothy J. Hopkins, age 45
President, Waldenbooks Stores: Ronald S. Staffieri, age 49
President, Borders Group Stores:
Kathryn L. Winkelhaus, age 43
Online Staff Editor: Rich Fahle
Associate Director of Online Services: Carol Mjoseth
Auditors: PricewaterhouseCoopers LLP

LOCATIONS

HQ: 100 Phoenix Dr., Ann Arbor, MI 48108
Phone: 734-477-1100   **Fax:** 734-477-1965
Web site: http://www.bordersgroupinc.com

Borders Group has stores in Australia, Singapore, the UK, and the US.

PRODUCTS/OPERATIONS

1999 Sales

	$ mil.	% of total
Borders	1,563	60
Waldenbooks	942	37
Borders.com	5	—
Other	85	3
Total	**2,595**	**100**

Selected Operations
All Wound Up (interactive toy and novelty kiosks)
Books etc. (UK bookstores)
Borders (superstores with books, videos, and multimedia products)
Borders.com (Web site with online book, music, and video sales)
Paperchase (20%; gift wrap, greeting cards, stationery)
Sprout (20%, on-demand book printing)
Waldenbooks (mall bookstores)

COMPETITORS

Amazon.com	HMV Media Group
Barnes & Noble	Lauriat's
Best Buy	MTS
Blockbuster	Musicland
Book-of-the-Month Club	Toys "R" Us
Books-A-Million	Trans World
CDnow	Entertainment
Columbia House	Wal-Mart
Crown Books	WH Smith
Follett	Wherehouse
Hastings Entertainment	Entertainment

HISTORICAL FINANCIALS & EMPLOYEES

NYSE symbol: BGP FYE: January 31	Annual Growth	1990	1991	1992	1993	1994	1995	1996	1997	1998	1999
Sales ($ mil.)	11.8%	—	1,064	1,140	1,183	1,370	1,511	1,749	1,959	2,266	2,595
Net income ($ mil.)	61.4%	—	2	17	23	(38)	21	(211)	58	80	92
Income as % of sales	—	—	0.2%	1.5%	1.9%	—	1.4%	—	3.0%	3.5%	3.5%
Earnings per share ($)	—	—	—	—	—	—	—	(2.94)	0.70	0.98	1.12
Stock price - FY high ($)	—	—	—	—	—	—	—	10.94	22.44	33.44	41.75
Stock price - FY low ($)	—	—	—	—	—	—	—	6.94	9.69	18.50	16.31
Stock price - FY close ($)	17.5%	—	—	—	—	—	—	10.56	22.31	32.25	17.13
P/E - high	—	—	—	—	—	—	—	—	32	34	37
P/E - low	—	—	—	—	—	—	—	—	14	19	15
Dividends per share ($)	—	—	—	—	—	—	—	0.00	0.00	0.00	0.00
Book value per share ($)	13.7%	—	—	—	—	—	—	6.27	6.74	7.93	9.20
Employees	14.8%	—	—	—	—	13,650	16,700	20,000	22,800	24,300	27,200

STOCK PRICE HISTORY

HIGH/LOW/CLOSE

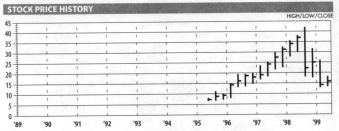

1999 FISCAL YEAR-END

Debt ratio: 0.9%
Return on equity: 12.9%
Cash ($ mil.): 43
Current ratio: 1.15
Long-term debt ($ mil.): 6
No. of shares (mil.): 78
Dividends
  Yield: —
  Payout: —
Market value ($ mil.): 1,331

BORG-WARNER AUTOMOTIVE, INC.

OVERVIEW

Borg-Warner Automotive couldn't be happier that millions of American surburbanites are buying four-wheel drive sport utility vehicles to navigate treacherous cul-de-sacs and quicksand-ridden mall parking lots. Based in Chicago, Borg-Warner is one of the world's leading makers of four-wheel-drive transfer cases, which account for 27% of its sales. In addition to making powertrain components for cars, light trucks, and RVs, Borg-Warner supplies auto parts to every major automaker. Its products include automatic transmissions, transfer cases, turbochargers, emission-control systems, clutches, friction plates, and timing-chain systems. A buoyant US auto market has helped the company earn most of its growing revenues from long-term clients Ford (32% of sales), DaimlerChrysler (17%), and General Motors (14%).

Borg-Warner plans to hit $4 billion in sales by the year 2005 by creating new products and acquiring companies. The company operates more than 50 plants in 12 countries and has manufacturing joint ventures in China, Japan, and Korea.

HISTORY

Borg-Warner Automotive traces its roots to the 1928 merger of four major Chicago auto parts companies (Borg & Beck, clutches; Warner Gear, transmissions; Mechanics Universal Joint; and Marvel Carburetor). The newly named Borg-Warner Corporation quickly began diversifying by buying other companies, including Ingersoll Steel & Disc (agricultural blades and discs) and Norge (refrigerators).

The company survived the Depression largely through the contributions of its Norge and Ingersoll divisions. In the last half of the 1930s the manufacturer purchased several companies, including Calumet Steel (1935) and US Pressed Steel (1937).

During the early 1940s Borg-Warner made parts for planes, trucks, and tanks. Between 1942 and 1945 the company made more than 1.6 million automotive transmissions and gained the experience and manufacturing capacity to handle the post-war car boom. Its 1948 contract with Ford to build half of its transmissions resulted in massive growth.

Roy Ingersoll, president of the Ingersoll Steel & Disc division, assumed leadership of Borg-Warner in 1950 and embarked on a major diversification program. In 1956 Borg-Warner purchased several companies, including York, Humphreys Manufacturing, Industrial Crane & Hoist, Dittmer Gear, and the Chemical Process Company.

James Bert became president in 1968 and continued to broaden the company.

Borg-Warner entered the security business in 1978 when it bought Baker Industries (which provided armored transport under the Wells Fargo name). In 1980 Borg-Warner sold its Ingersoll Products division to a group of investors led by Jack Maxwell. It acquired Burns International Security Services in 1982. Borg-Warner spun off York to its shareholders in 1986.

In the face of a takeover attempt in 1987, Merrill Lynch Capital Partners organized an LBO and took the company private, assuming $4.5 billion in debt. Borg-Warner then sold off everything but its automotive and security units, including its chemical group to General Electric for $2.3 billion (1988) and its credit unit, Chilton, to TRW for $330 million (1989).

The company went public again in 1993 as Borg-Warner Security; it spun off Borg-Warner Automotive to its shareholders. (Borg-Warner Security changed its name to Burns International Services in 1999). In 1995 Borg-Warner Automotive formed a joint venture in India (Divgi-Warner) to make transmissions and purchased the precision-forged products division of US-based Federal-Mogul for $28 million.

To expand Borg-Warner Automotive's air- and fluid-control business, the company acquired three businesses (Holley Automotive, Coltec Automotive, and Performance Friction Products) from auto component maker Coltec Industries in 1996. The next year the company acquired a majority stake in Kuhnle, Kopp & Kausch, a Germany-based turbocharger subsidiary of Penske. That same year Borg-Warner Automotive divested its money-losing manual transmission business.

Reduced production of Ford trucks, the weak Asian economy, and the GM strike hurt Borg-Warner Automotive's 1998 sales. The following year the company bought diesel engine component maker Kuhlman for $680 million, then agreed to sell Kuhlman's electrical transformer business to The Carlyle Group for $120 million. Borg-Warner also sold its interests in joint ventures Warner-Ishi and Warner-Ishi Europe to its partner, Ishikawajima-Harima Heavy Industries. Later that year, the company agreed to acquire the Fluid Power Division of Eaton Corporation.

Chairman and CEO: John F. Fiedler, age 60,
$745,549 pay
**EVP; Group President and General Manager, Air/Fluid
Systems:** Gary P. Fukayama, age 51, $564,961 pay
**EVP; Group President and General Manager, Morse
TEC:** Ronald M. Ruzic, age 60, $555,592 pay
Acting Treasurer: Jeffrey L. Obermayer, age 44
VP and Controller: William C. Cline, age 49
VP Business Development: Christopher A. Gebelein,
age 52
VP, Secretary, and General Counsel:
Laurene H. Horiszny, age 43
VP and Chief Information Officer: John A. Kalina,
age 53
VP Human Resources: Geraldine Kinsella, age 51
**VP; President and General Manager, Powertrain
Systems:** Timothy M. Manganello, age 49
VP Engineering, Powertrain Systems: Mark Perlick
**VP; President and General Manager, Automatic
Transmission Systems:** Robert D. Welding, age 50,
$353,109 pay
President and General Manager, BWA Turbo Systems:
Tim Campbell
Auditors: Deloitte & Touche LLP

LOCATIONS

HQ: 200 S. Michigan Ave., Chicago, IL 60604
Phone: 312-322-8500   **Fax:** 312-461-0507
Web site: http://www.bwauto.com

Borg-Warner Automotive operates more than 50
manufacturing facilities in 12 countries.

PRODUCTS/OPERATIONS

1998 Sales

	$ mil.	% of total
Morse TEC	536	28
Powertrain systems	519	27
Automatic transmission systems	403	22
Air/fluid systems	351	19
Divested operations	74	4
Adjustments	(46)	—
Total	**1,837**	**100**

Selected Products

Morse TEC
Chain tensioners and snubbers
Crankshaft and camshaft sprockets
Front-wheel and four-wheel drive chain and
timing chain systems

Powertrain Systems
Four-wheel drive and all-wheel drive transfer cases

Automatic Transmission Systems
Friction plates
One-way clutches
Torque converters
Transmission bands

Air/Fluid Systems
Engine and emission-control components and systems
Fuel- and vapor-management components and systems
Transmissions and steering suspension systems

COMPETITORS

A. O. Smith	Renold
Arvin Industries	Siemens
Dana	Simpson Industries
Eaton	SPX
Intermet	TRW
PACCAR	Valeo

HISTORICAL FINANCIALS & EMPLOYEES

NYSE symbol: BWA FYE: December 31	Annual Growth	1989	1990	1991	1992	1993	1994	1995	1996	1997	1998
Sales ($ mil.)	7.4%	965	926	820	926	985	1,223	1,329	1,540	1,767	1,837
Net income ($ mil.)	18.9%	20	(13)	(36)	(12)	(98)	64	74	42	103	95
Income as % of sales	—	2.1%	—	—	—	—	5.3%	5.6%	2.7%	5.8%	5.2%
Earnings per share ($)	—	—	—	—	—	(4.23)	2.75	3.15	1.75	4.31	4.00
Stock price – FY high ($)	—	—	—	—	—	28.00	34.00	33.88	43.00	61.50	68.38
Stock price – FY low ($)	—	—	—	—	—	20.50	21.63	22.38	28.38	38.38	33.06
Stock price – FY close ($)	14.8%	—	—	—	—	28.00	25.13	32.00	38.50	52.00	55.81
P/E – high	—	—	—	—	—	—	12	11	25	14	17
P/E – low	—	—	—	—	—	—	8	7	16	9	8
Dividends per share ($)	—	—	—	—	—	0.00	0.58	0.60	0.60	0.60	0.60
Book value per share ($)	10.5%	—	—	—	—	20.19	23.13	25.57	26.59	29.46	33.24
Employees	8.8%	—	—	—	—	6,610	7,330	8,600	9,800	10,400	10,100

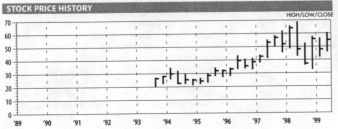

STOCK PRICE HISTORY
HIGH/LOW/CLOSE

1998 FISCAL YEAR-END
Debt ratio: 24.2%
Return on equity: 12.2%
Cash ($ mil.): 44
Current ratio: 0.83
Long-term debt ($ mil.): 249
No. of shares (mil.): 23
Dividends
  Yield: 1.1%
  Payout: 15.0%
Market value ($ mil.): 1,305

BOSTON CELTICS LIMITED

OVERVIEW

The tradition-rich Boston Celtics sports franchise, owned by the Boston Celtics Limited Partnership, has seen better days. Although no other professional basketball franchise can match its record of success, it has been more than a decade since the team won its last championship. The once-dominant team was a charter member of the Basketball Association of America (which evolved into the NBA) and boasts 16 NBA titles and 25 Hall-of-Famers (including newly inducted Larry Bird and Kevin McHale).

The partnership's revenues come from Celtics home-game ticket sales and the licensing of Celtics games for TV, cable, and radio.

The team has moved from its original home venue, Boston Garden, to the larger FleetCenter, which boasts a seating capacity of about 19,300. (The team still plays on a parquet floor moved from Boston Garden.)

A complex reorganization in 1998 split the partnership into two parts, a private partnership and a public one. Don Gaston, his son Paul (chairman), and the Gaston family control the team through the private partnership. More than 80,000 investors (many of whom hold less than 10 shares as souvenirs) own about 48% of the team through the public partnership.

HISTORY

Walter Brown founded the Boston Celtics basketball team (so named partially because of Brown's Irish background) in 1946. Brown hired Arnold "Red" Auerbach as head coach in 1950.

Auerbach turned the Celtics into a competitive organization by acquiring such players as Bob Cousy, Chuck Cooper (the first black player in the NBA), Bill Sharman, and Frank Ramsey. Although the Celtics greatly improved during Auerbach's first six years as coach, they were unable to win an NBA title.

The turning point came in 1956, when Auerbach traded two players to the St. Louis Hawks for a first-round draft pick, who turned out to be center Bill Russell. Auerbach created the greatest dynasty in basketball history around Russell's gifted play, winning nine NBA championships from 1957 through 1966. Auerbach left coaching to become the team's general manager in 1966. Russell took over and, as the first black NBA coach, led the team to two more titles in 1968 and 1969.

During the early 1970s, under coach Tom Heinsohn, the team was restructured and, with the talents of players like John Havlicek, Don Nelson, Jo Jo White, and Dave Cowens, won NBA titles in 1974 and 1976. By the late 1970s, however, they had slipped into last place, and Brown sold his interest to Harry Mangurian. During the 1979-80 season the Celtics registered another major turnaround, largely due to the efforts of 1978 draft choice Larry Bird. With the help of Kevin McHale and Robert Parish, the Celtics won their 14th title in 1981.

Mangurian sold control of the team in 1983 to Don Gaston, Paul Dupee, and Alan Cohen for $19 million. K. C. Jones became head coach in 1983 and led the team to titles in

1984 and 1986. Following their 1986 championship, the Celtics selected University of Maryland forward Len Bias as the second overall draft pick. However, Bias died two days later of a cocaine-induced cardiac arrest.

Also that year the three owners established a publicly traded master limited partnership and offered "units" to investors (a first for a pro franchise). The offering yielded gains of more than $44 million for the three principal shareholders.

In 1992 Paul Gaston (Don's son) became company chairman and Stephen Schram president. Auerbach, now VC, continued as basketball president.

The legendary Bird and seven-time All Star McHale retired before and after the 1992-93 season, respectively. Tragedy struck again that summer when 27-year-old All Star Reggie Lewis collapsed and died from cardiac arrest.

Gaston bought out Cohen's 11% stake in the company for $16.3 million in 1995. That same year the Celtics played their final game at the historic Boston Garden. To allow room for bigger crowds, the team moved to the FleetCenter for the 1995-96 season.

In 1997 the Celtics signed successful University of Kentucky coach Rick Pitino to a 10-year, $70 million contract. The same year the Celtics announced an exclusive five-year partnership with Citizens Bank after Fleet, the largest bank in New England, refused to spend $6 million over five years for marketing and promotion (Fleet is paying $30 million over 15 years for the sports arena's naming rights).

Like other NBA teams, the Celtics in 1998 began recording losses in the millions as a player-owner standoff forced the cancellation of the first three months of the season.

OFFICERS

Chairman and CEO: Paul E. Gaston, age 41,
$1,324,596 pay
EVP, COO, CFO, Secretary, and Treasurer:
Richard G. Pond, age 38, $650,000 pay
VC, Boston Celtics: Arnold "Red" Auerbach,
$750,000 pay
**President, Director Basketball Operations, and Head
Coach, Boston Celtics:** Rick Pitino, age 46,
$6,750,000 pay
EVP Corporate Development, Boston Celtics:
Michael L. Carr
EVP Marketing and Sales, Boston Celtics: Stuart Layne
General Manager, Boston Celtics: Chris Wallace
VP Administration, Boston Celtics: Joseph DiLorenzo
Director Human Resources and Shareholder Services:
Barbara Reed
Auditors: Ernst & Young LLP

LOCATIONS

HQ: 151 Merrimac St., Boston, MA 02114
Phone: 617-523-6050   **Fax:** 617-523-5949
Web site: http://www.nba.com/celtics

The Boston Celtics is a member of the Atlantic Division
of the Eastern Conference of the National Basketball
Association.

PRODUCTS/OPERATIONS

1998 Sales

	$ mil.	% of total
Ticket sales	39	51
TV, cable & radio broadcast rights fees	28	37
Other (promotional, novelty & royalties)	9	12
Total	**76**	**100**

NBA Championship Titles

1957	1964	1976
1959	1965	1981
1960	1966	1984
1961	1968	1986
1962	1969	
1963	1974	

Former Celtics
Arnold "Red" Auerbach
Larry Bird
Walter Brown
Bob Cousy
Dave Cowens
John Havlicek
Tom Heinsohn
Dennis Johnson
K.C. Jones
Sam Jones
Reggie Lewis
Jim Loscutoff
"Easy Ed" Macauley
Kevin McHale
Don Nelson
Robert Parish
Frank Ramsey
Bill Russell
Tom "Satch" Sanders
Bill Sharman
Jo Jo White

COMPETITORS

Miami Heat
New Jersey Nets
New York Knicks
Orlando Magic
Philadelphia 76ers
Washington Wizards

HISTORICAL FINANCIALS & EMPLOYEES

NYSE symbol: BOS FYE: June 30	Annual Growth	1989	1990	1991	1992	1993	1994	1995	1996	1997	1998
Sales ($ mil.)	12.0%	27	30	41	46	81	83	52	65	63	76
Net income ($ mil.)	0.1%	12	8	11	8	5	24	16	54	0	12
Income as % of sales	—	44.5%	26.8%	27.0%	16.8%	6.4%	28.7%	30.8%	83.6%	0.6%	16.2%
Employees	3.9%	39	43	43	42	173	125	66	47	43	55

STOCK PRICE HISTORY

HIGH/LOW/CLOSE

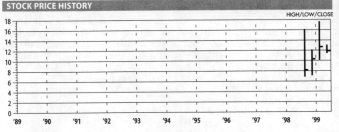

1998 FISCAL YEAR-END
Debt ratio: 211.4%
Return on equity: —
Cash ($ mil.): 8
Current ratio: 4.04
Long-term debt ($ mil.): 63

BOSTON SCIENTIFIC CORPORATION

OVERVIEW

Attention, surgeon generals: If you need a minimal invasion, Boston Scientific can supply the troops. Based in Natick, Massachusetts, the company makes medical devices for use in minimally invasive surgeries. These devices, which are inserted into the body either through natural openings or incisions, can be moved throughout the body to detect and treat a host of ailments. Boston Scientific's products — steerable catheters, micro-guidewires, and polypectomy snares — are used in such fields as cardiology, gastroenterology, radiology, urology, and vascular medicine.

Boston Scientific, with a recent history of growth through acquisitions, expects to continue benefiting from the trend toward consolidation (spurred by the dwindling number of distributors favored by HMOs) surging through the medical equipment industry. The company has also focused on its overseas growth, doubling its investment in the Pacific Rim.

Together with their families, co-founders John Abele and Peter Nicholas each control about 17% of the company.

HISTORY

Although many medical companies start in or around a hospital, Boston Scientific can trace its origins to a children's soccer game. It was there that two dads, John Abele and Peter Nicholas, found common ground. Both had fathers who had been WWII submarine commanders. The two also had complementary talents and interests. Nicholas, a Wharton MBA, wanted to run his own company; Abele, a philosophy and physics graduate, wanted a job that would help people.

In 1979 the two soccer dads founded Boston Scientific to buy medical device maker Medi-Tech. To make the buy, Abele and Nichols had to borrow half a million dollars from a bank and raise an additional $300,000. Medi-Tech's primary product was a steerable catheter, a soft-tipped device that could be maneuvered within the body. After the purchase, Boston Scientific expanded on the success of the catheter, which had revolutionized gallstone operations in the early 1970s. The company adapted it for a slew of new procedures for the heart, lungs, intestines, and other organs.

Boston Scientific's sales were healthy in 1983, but the company still lacked funds, so it eagerly accepted $21 million from Abbott Laboratories in exchange for a 20% stake. New FDA regulations slowed product introduction and put a crimp in the company's growth. By the late 1980s, however, Boston Scientific had found a legal loophole to avoid lengthy delays: The company began to describe its products in the vaguest terms possible, so that upgraded devices could be considered similar enough to their predecessors to escape the in-depth scrutiny of a new approval process. Still, before this linguistic legerdemain cleared away government red tape, Abele and Nicholas had to mortgage their personal properties to stay afloat. After Boston Scientific returned to profitability in 1991, it went public the next year and bought back Abbott Laboratories' interest in the company.

In 1995 Boston Scientific acquired a bevy of medical device companies. Among the most important acquisitions were SCIMED Life Systems, which specialized in cardiology products; Heart Technology, Inc., a maker of systems to treat coronary atherosclerosis; and Meadox Medicals, which made arterial grafts. As a result of these acquisitions, Boston Scientific's sales more than doubled in 1995.

The company continued its buying spree, adding EP Technologies and Symbiosis Corp. in 1996 and Target Therapeutics in 1997. The company's many acquisitions brought operational problems that year, causing inventories to soar while Boston Scientific worked to integrate its new operations. Purchases continued in 1998, however, as Boston Scientific bought Pfizer's catheter, stent, and angioplasty equipment business. The Justice Department kicked off an investigation of the Nir-Sox stent, which had been launched and subsequently recalled earlier in the year.

Late that year news came out that Boston Scientific's Japanese subsidiary had inflated sales over several years by as much as $90 million. Restated earnings subsequently revealed a loss, compounded by the company's problems with assimilating acquisitions and product recall. Takeover rumors started to fly, as well. The 1998 acquisition of stent maker Schneider Worldwide fattened Boston Scientific's pipeline and payroll; the company in 1999 said it would cut 14% of workers. That year a federal judge ruled that the company's Bandit PTCA catheter infringed on a Guidant patent.

Chairman: Peter M. Nicholas, age 57, $725,400 pay
President and CEO: James R. Tobin, age 54
SVP Finance and Administration and CFO:
Lawrence C. Best, age 47, $365,000 pay
SVP; President, Boston Scientific International:
Paul A. LaViolette, age 40
SVP; Group President Vascular Businesses:
Philip Le Goff, age 47, $350,000 pay
SVP Operations: C. Michael Mabrey, age 56
SVP Human Resources: Robert G. MacLean, age 54
SVP and Chief Development Officer:
Arthur L. Rosenthal, age 51
SVP, Secretary, and General Counsel: Paul W. Sandman, age 50, $297,000 pay
SVP; President Scimed Life Systems; Group President Cardiology Businesses: Michael Berman, age 40, $290,000 pay
President, Boston Scientific Europe: Michel Darnaud
Auditors: Ernst & Young LLP

LOCATIONS

HQ: 1 Boston Scientific Place, Natick, MA 01760-1537
Phone: 508-650-8000   **Fax:** 508-647-2200
Web site: http://www.bsci.com

1998 Sales

	$ mil.	% of total
US	1,394	63
Europe	381	17
Japan	333	15
Emerging markets	119	5
Other regions	7	—
Total	**2,234**	**100**

PRODUCTS/OPERATIONS

1998 Sales

	$ mil.	% of total
Vascular	1,777	80
Nonvascular	426	19
Other	31	1
Total	**2,234**	**100**

Selected Products

Vascular Devices
Catheters
Electrophysiology products
Intraluminal ultrasound imaging systems
Micro-guidewires
Stents
Surgical and endovascular grafts
Vena cava filter systems

Nonvascular Devices
Automatic disposable needle biopsy systems
Balloon dilatation catheters
Enteral feeding devices
Hemostatic catheters
Incorporeal shock wave lithotripsy devices
Multiple banding devices
Polypectomy snares
Sphincterotomes
Ureteral stents

COMPETITORS

Arrow International	EndoSonics
Arterial Vascular	Guidant
Baxter	Johnson & Johnson
Becton Dickinson	Maxxim Medical
Cook Group	Medtronic
C. R. Bard	Spectranetics
Datascope	St. Jude Medical
Electro-Catheter	United States Surgical

HISTORICAL FINANCIALS & EMPLOYEES

NYSE symbol: BSX FYE: December 31	Annual Growth	1989	1990	1991	1992	1993	1994	1995	1996	1997	1998
Sales ($ mil.)	38.4%	—	—	230	315	380	449	1,107	1,462	1,872	2,234
Net income ($ mil.)	—	—	—	42	57	70	80	8	167	139	(264)
Income as % of sales	—	—	—	18.2%	18.0%	18.3%	17.8%	0.8%	11.4%	7.4%	—
Earnings per share ($)	—	—	—	—	0.29	0.20	0.38	(0.05)	0.42	0.35	(0.68)
Stock price - FY high ($)	—	—	—	—	10.44	11.81	8.94	24.69	30.75	39.22	40.84
Stock price - FY low ($)	—	—	—	—	7.00	4.69	5.94	8.31	18.88	20.50	20.13
Stock price - FY close ($)	17.0%	—	—	—	10.44	6.25	8.69	24.63	30.00	22.94	26.81
P/E - high	—	—	—	—	36	59	24	—	73	112	—
P/E - low	—	—	—	—	24	23	16	—	45	59	—
Dividends per share ($)	—	—	—	—	0.00	0.00	0.00	0.00	0.00	0.00	0.00
Book value per share ($)	9.4%	—	—	—	1.22	1.27	1.75	2.17	2.57	2.54	2.09
Employees	34.7%	—	—	1,738	2,051	2,051	2,838	8,000	9,580	11,000	14,000

STOCK PRICE HISTORY

HIGH/LOW/CLOSE

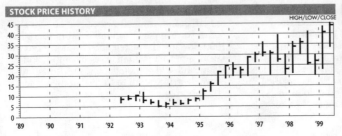

1998 FISCAL YEAR-END

Debt ratio: 62.4%
Return on equity: —
Cash ($ mil.): 70
Current ratio: 0.78
Long-term debt ($ mil.): 1,364
No. of shares (mil.): 392
Dividends
  Yield: —
  Payout: —
Market value ($ mil.): 10,520

BOWATER INCORPORATED

OVERVIEW

Extra! Extra! Read all about it! Bowater, the largest newsprint producer in the US, became the second-largest newsprint producer in the world (behind Canada's Abitibi-Consolidated) after buying Montreal's Avenor. The Greenville, South Carolina-based Bowater can churn out about 3 billion tons of newsprint annually from its 11 paper/saw mills in Canada, South Korea, and the US. Other products include coated papers, directory and specialty-grade papers, and lumber.

In addition to the company's 2 million acres of owned and leased timber holdings in the US and Canada, Bowater has about 14 million acres of timber-cutting rights in Canada. In a move to maximize its timberland assets, Bowater has created a separate forest-products division for considered sale or spinoff. Low prices in recent years have unleashed a chain of consolidation moves in the industry, which has had trouble balancing production and demand. Paper companies are cautiously optimistic that prices and earnings will improve, barring further global economic shocks.

HISTORY

The roots of Bowater can be traced to the founders of its British parent, Bowater PLC (renamed Rexam plc in 1995). In 1881 William Bowater, after several years with a Manchester papermaking firm, set up his own business in London at the age of 43. Cashing in on the boom in newspaper readership in the UK at the turn of the century, W. V. Bowater & Sons secured contracts as a paper wholesaler with two leading newspaper publishers — Alfred Harmsworth (the *Daily Mail* and the *Daily Mirror*) and Edward Lloyd (the *Daily Chronicle*).

Bowater set up a US marketing subsidiary, Hudson Packaging & Paper Co., in 1914 and an office in Sydney, Australia, in 1919. Eric Bowater, the founder's grandson, took over as chairman in 1927 at the age of 32 and led the company in a major expansion. By 1936 Bowater accounted for 60% of British newsprint output, up from just 22% only six years before. Bowater began its North American manufacturing operations in 1938, when it purchased a pulp and newsprint mill in Corner Brook, Newfoundland.

WWII had a devastating impact on the company's UK newsprint business, and output fell by 80%. Bowater PLC diversified into paper packaging in 1944, buying Acme Corrugated Cases.

Bowater PLC expanded its presence in the US in 1954 with the opening of Bowater Southern, a newsprint mill in Calhoun, Tennessee. That year Eric Bowater died. Christopher Chancellor, formerly with Reuters, became CEO.

In 1964 Bowater formed Bowater United States Corp. to manage its US operations. Bowater moved away from paper production in the 1970s, diversifying into such areas as packaging, tissue products, building products, commodity trading, and foodstuffs. In 1984 Bowater exited the paper and pulp business, spinning off its US operations as Bowater Incorporated.

After the spinoff, Bowater expanded its range of products. In 1991 the company acquired an 80% interest in Great Northern Paper from Georgia-Pacific for $300 million. It acquired the remaining 20% in 1992.

The next year Bowater started up the Great Northern Paper recycling facilities, completed the consolidation of its corporate headquarters in Greenville, South Carolina, and sold 70,000 acres of nonstrategic timberlands.

Arnold Nemirow, former CEO of Wausau Paper Mills in Wisconsin, became Bowater's COO in 1994; subsequently, he became CEO and chairman. After three years of losses (largely fueled by a slump in paper prices), the company turned around in 1995, due in part to cost-reduction programs, the sale of timberlands, and higher paper prices.

In 1996 Bowater sold its Star Forms subsidiary to CST Office Products. In 1997 the company committed $180 million to upgrade its Calhoun newsprint plant. It created a forest-products division, a reorganization of its US and Canadian forest and woods products operations, that was expected to lead to restructuring the business as a separate entity.

In 1998 Bowater paid $2.37 billion for Montreal-based Avenor, 25% more than tendered in a hostile takeover bid from Abitibi-Consolidated, contributing to a loss in earnings. Bowater then sold three former Avenor mills in Ontario to Weyerhaeuser for $520 million and closed a former Avenor mill in British Columbia. Bowater also bought a South Korean paper mill for $201 million. In 1999 Bowater harvested $216 million from the sale of almost a million acres of timberland in Maine and sold 400,000 acres, two mills, and a hydroelectric system to Canadian investment group Inexcon Maine.

Chairman, President, and CEO: Arnold M. Nemirow,
age 54, $1,161,160 pay
EVP; President, Newsprint and Directory Division:
Arthur D. Fuller, age 54, $613,169 pay
SVP and CFO: David G. Maffucci, age 48, $473,633 pay
SVP Corporate Affairs and General Counsel:
Anthony H. Barash, age 56, $439,564 pay
SVP; President, Coated Paper Division:
E. Patrick Duffy, age 57, $527,112 pay
VP Corporate Development and Strategy:
James H. Dorton, age 42
VP, North American Newsprint and Directory Sales:
C. Randy Ellington
VP, US and Korea Newsprint Operations:
Jerry R. Gilmore, age 50
VP, Purchasing and Transportation: Larry G. Green
VP; President, Forest Products Division:
Richard K. Hamilton, age 50
VP Information Technology: Steven G. Lanzl, age 50
VP Manufacturing Services: Robert A. Moran, age 54
VP and Controller: Michael F. Nocito, age 43
VP, Secretary, and Assistant General Counsel:
Wendy C. Shiba, age 48
VP Human Resources: James T. Wright, age 52
Auditors: KPMG Peat Marwick LLP

LOCATIONS

HQ: 55 E. Camperdown Way, Greenville, SC 29602
Phone: 864-271-7733   **Fax:** 864-282-9482
Web site: http://www.bowater.com

Bowater has pulp and paper mills in South Carolina,
Tennessee, and Washington State in the US; in New
Brunswick, Ontario, and Quebec in Canada; and in
South Korea. It also operates sawmills in Alabama, Nova
Scotia, and Quebec.

PRODUCTS/OPERATIONS

1998 Sales

	$ mil.	% of total
Newsprint	1,357	57
Coated groundwood	474	20
Forest products division	517	22
Corporate/other	17	1
Adjustments	(370)	—
Total	**1,995**	**100**

1998 Sales

	$ mil.	% of total
Newsprint	1,109	52
Coated groundwood	391	18
Directory paper	174	8
Market pulp	272	13
Undercoated groundwood specialties	49	2
Lumber & other products	148	7
Adjustments	(148)	—
Total	**1,995**	**100**

COMPETITORS

Abitibi-Consolidated	Norske Skog
Boise Cascade	Potlatch
Champion International	Rayonier
Consolidated Papers	Smurfit-Stone Container
Donohue	Sonoco Products
Fort James	UPM-Kymmene
Georgia-Pacific	Westvaco
International Paper	Weyerhaeuser
Louisiana-Pacific	Willamette
Mead	

HISTORICAL FINANCIALS & EMPLOYEES

NYSE symbol: BOW FYE: December 31	Annual Growth	1989	1990	1991	1992	1993	1994	1995	1996	1997	1998
Sales ($ mil.)	3.6%	1,450	1,380	1,289	1,494	1,354	1,359	2,001	1,718	1,485	1,995
Net income ($ mil.)	—	145	78	46	(82)	(65)	(5)	247	200	54	(19)
Income as % of sales	—	10.0%	5.7%	3.5%	—	—	—	12.3%	11.7%	3.6%	—
Earnings per share ($)	—	3.86	2.05	1.15	(2.34)	(1.84)	(0.59)	5.22	4.55	1.25	(0.44)
Stock price – FY high ($)	—	34.13	28.50	30.38	27.25	24.63	29.63	54.38	41.63	57.00	60.50
Stock price – FY low ($)	—	25.75	16.13	18.63	17.63	18.00	20.38	26.38	31.50	36.88	31.19
Stock price – FY close ($)	4.6%	27.63	21.25	22.13	24.13	23.00	26.63	35.50	37.63	44.44	41.44
P/E – high	—	9	14	26	—	—	—	10	9	46	—
P/E – low	—	7	8	16	—	—	—	5	7	30	—
Dividends per share ($)	(3.7%)	1.12	1.20	1.20	1.20	0.75	0.60	0.60	0.75	0.80	0.80
Book value per share ($)	3.2%	25.37	26.24	26.21	22.55	20.10	19.07	24.52	27.94	27.99	33.72
Employees	5.6%	5,100	5,100	7,200	6,900	6,600	6,000	5,500	5,025	5,000	8,300

STOCK PRICE HISTORY

HIGH/LOW/CLOSE

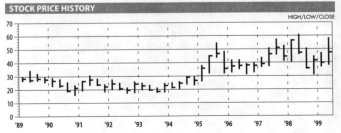

1998 FISCAL YEAR-END

Debt ratio: 46.3%
Return on equity: —
Cash ($ mil.): 58
Current ratio: 0.90
Long-term debt ($ mil.): 1,535
No. of shares (mil.): 52
Dividends
  Yield: 1.9%
  Payout: —
Market value ($ mil.): 2,152

BRIGGS & STRATTON CORPORATION

OVERVIEW

Briggs & Stratton, the world's #1 maker of air-cooled gasoline engines, doesn't mind getting yanked around; one good pull is usually enough to start one of the Wauwatosa, Wisconsin-based company's ubiquitous three- to 22-horsepower engines. About 80% of its engines are used in lawn and garden equipment such as lawn mowers, edgers, and garden tillers. Customers include US lawn mower maker MTD Products (18% of sales), AB Electrolux (15%), and Tomkins PLC (13%).

As part of a move to reduce costs, the company has opened three manufacturing plants in the South, where wages are lower. The plants have not produced the expected efficiencies, however, and the expense of setting up the plants has hurt results. Briggs & Stratton has been selling off noncore businesses to concentrate on its engines. It has also begun using joint ventures for greater international penetration.

HISTORY

In 1909 inventor Stephen Foster Briggs and grain merchant Harold Stratton gathered $25,000 and founded Briggs & Stratton to produce a six-cylinder, two-cycle engine that Briggs had developed while in college. However, the engine proved too expensive for mass production. A brief foray into the automobile assembly business also failed, as the company skirted bankruptcy. But in 1910 Briggs received a patent for a single-spark gas engine igniter. It wasn't a run-away success, but the company had found its niche making automotive electrical components. By 1920 Briggs & Stratton was the largest US producer of specialty lights, ignitions, regulators, and starting switches. These specialties accounted for two-thirds of the firm's total business through the mid-1930s.

The company acquired the A. O. Smith Motor Wheel (a gasoline-driven wheel designed to be attached to bicycles) and the Flyer (a two-passenger vehicle similar to a buckboard) in 1919. Neither product was successful and both were soon sold, but the company gained crucial knowledge and experience. In 1923 Briggs & Stratton introduced a stationary version of the Motor Wheel designed to power washing machines, garden tractors, and lawn mowers. The company continued to diversify, moving into the automotive lock business in 1924. Its die-cast cylinder lock outsold competitors' brass models, and by the end of the decade, Briggs & Stratton had the lion's share of the market. The company formed a new unit, BASCO, to make autobody hardware such as door handles, hinges, knobs, locks, levers, and keys. Briggs & Stratton bought Evinrude Outboard Motor Company in 1928, but sold the business within a year.

As with many other industrial manufacturers, WWII provided a nearly insatiable market for the company. Its wartime contributions included airplane ignition switches, artillery

ammunition, and engines for generators, pumps, compressors, fans, repair shops, emergency hospitals, and mobile kitchens.

After the war, Briggs & Stratton focused on small engines for lawn and garden equipment and soon dominated the market. In 1953 the company introduced an aluminum die cast engine that was lighter than competing models and could withstand greater operating temperatures and pressures. Baby boomer's parents fueled sales and the small market attracted little competition; Briggs & Stratton thrived making air-cooled engines and automobile components such as locks and switches.

By the end of the 1970s, sales had risen to about $590 million and as the low-cost producer in the industry, the company was without a rival. But during the early 1980s, Japanese companies, including Honda, Kawasaki, Mitsubishi, and Suzuki, entered the market after motorcycle sales crested. As a result of the strong dollar, these new competitors were able to provide engines to equipment makers more cheaply than could Briggs & Stratton; the company suffered a decline in the late 1980s.

During the early 1990s the company experienced a resurgence: Frederick Stratton Jr., grandson of the co-founder, took over as president in 1992, and Briggs & Stratton benefited from a dollar that was weak relative to the yen. It spun off its car-and-truck lock business as STRATTEC in 1995.

In fiscal 1996 the company started up three new engine plants in Missouri, Alabama, and Georgia. The next year it began selling noncore operations, including a foundry business. In 1998 it sold another foundry and decided to sell its long-life engine (for residential heat pumps) and computer software operations. Also in 1998 the company agreed to form two joint ventures in India.

OFFICERS

Chairman and CEO: Frederick P. Stratton Jr., age 59, $813,225 pay
President and COO: John S. Shiely, age 46, $502,087 pay
EVP Sales and Service: Michael D. Hamilton, age 56, $367,164 pay
EVP, Secretary, and Treasurer: Robert H. Eldridge, age 59, $315,580 pay (prior to title change)
SVP and CFO: James E. Brenn, age 50
SVP, Engine Group: Richard J. Fotsch, age 43
SVP Administration: Thomas R. Savage, age 50
VP International: Hugo A. Keltz, age 50
VP Distribution Sales and Service: Curtis E. Larson Jr., age 50
VP; General Manager, Spectrum Division: Paul M. Neylon, age 51
VP Marketing: William H. Reitman, age 42
VP Sales: Stephen H. Rugg, age 51
VP; General Manager, Castings Division: Gregory D. Socks, age 49
VP Human Resources: Gerald E. Zitzer, age 51
Controller: Todd J. Teske
Auditors: Arthur Andersen LLP

LOCATIONS

HQ: 12301 W. Wirth St., Wauwatosa, WI 53222
Phone: 414-259-5333   **Fax:** 414-259-5773
Web site: http://www.briggsandstratton.com

Briggs & Stratton has manufacturing facilities in Auburn, Alabama; Milwaukee, Wisconsin; Murray, Kentucky; Poplar Bluff and Rolla, Missouri; Ravenna, Michigan; and Statesboro, Georgia.

PRODUCTS/OPERATIONS

1998 Sales

	% of total
Lawn & garden	79
Industrial, construction, agricultural, consumer	21
Total	**100**

Selected Applications
Garden tillers and tractors
Generators
Pressure washers
Pumps
Riding and walking lawn mowers
Snow blowers
Tillers

Selected Brand Names
Classic
Diamond I/C
I/C
Industrial Plus
Quantum
Quattro
Sprint
Vanguard

COMPETITORS

Honda
Kawasaki Heavy Industries
Kohler
Mitsubishi
Suzuki
Tecumseh Products
Toro

HISTORICAL FINANCIALS & EMPLOYEES

NYSE symbol: BGG FYE: June 30	Annual Growth	1989	1990	1991	1992	1993	1994	1995	1996	1997	1998
Sales ($ mil.)	4.7%	876	1,003	951	1,042	1,140	1,286	1,340	1,287	1,316	1,328
Net income ($ mil.)	—	(20)	35	37	52	70	70	105	92	62	71
Income as % of sales	—	—	3.5%	3.8%	4.9%	6.2%	5.4%	7.8%	7.2%	4.7%	5.3%
Earnings per share ($)	—	(0.70)	1.23	1.26	1.78	2.43	2.40	3.61	3.18	2.15	2.85
Stock price - FY high ($)	—	17.44	17.00	16.88	27.38	34.31	45.13	39.25	46.88	53.63	53.38
Stock price - FY low ($)	—	12.38	12.06	10.25	16.44	21.06	32.44	30.50	32.75	36.50	36.88
Stock price - FY close ($)	12.3%	13.19	16.44	16.44	22.44	33.06	33.44	34.50	41.13	50.00	37.44
P/E - high	—	—	14	13	15	14	19	11	15	25	19
P/E - low	—	—	10	8	9	9	14	8	10	17	13
Dividends per share ($)	3.8%	0.80	0.80	0.80	0.80	0.64	0.90	0.98	1.05	1.09	1.12
Book value per share ($)	4.5%	8.96	9.38	9.84	10.80	12.44	13.96	15.19	17.30	13.82	13.28
Employees	(0.1%)	7,316	7,994	7,242	7,799	7,950	8,628	6,958	7,507	7,661	7,265

STOCK PRICE HISTORY

HIGH/LOW/CLOSE

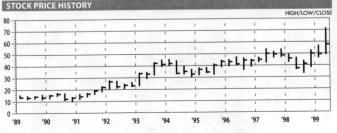

1998 FISCAL YEAR-END

Debt ratio: 28.8%
Return on equity: 22.3%
Cash ($ mil.): 85
Current ratio: 1.71
Long-term debt ($ mil.): 128
No. of shares (mil.): 24
Dividends
  Yield: 3.0%
  Payout: 39.3%
Market value ($ mil.): 892

BRINKER INTERNATIONAL, INC.

OVERVIEW

Brinker International can satisfy most of your culinary cravings. With nine chains of nearly 850 restaurants, Dallas-based Brinker is one of the largest casual-dining companies in the US. Its largest restaurant chain is the full-service, southwestern-themed Chili's Grill & Bar, which accounts for about 70% of sales.

The company also operates Romano's Macaroni Grill Italian restaurants, which feature family-style recipes and exhibition cooking, and On the Border Cafes, which offer southwestern and northern Mexican entrees. Other concepts include Cozymel's Coastal Mexican Grill, Maggiano's Little Italy (southern Italian dining), and Corner Bakery (baked goods). In addition, the company is developing

and testing three emerging chains: eatZi's Market & Bakery (upscale, chef-prepared, takeout entrees), Big Bowl (Asian food), and Wildfire (1940s-style steak houses). Brinker operates restaurants throughout Asia, Australia, Europe, North America, and South America.

In an effort to revitalize stagnant chains, the company has reorganized its management structure, giving each chain its own team of executives, chefs, and marketers. It has also increased its focus on its product, overhauling the Chili's menu and emphasizing food consistency and quality at On the Border. Brinker plans to accelerate the expansion of its chains, particularly the Corner Bakery concept.

HISTORY

Brinker International was founded as Chili's Bar & Grill in Dallas in 1975 by Larry Lavine and became Chili's Inc. the following year. By the early 1980s its first restaurant chain, Chili's, had become one of the Southwest's most popular. Norman Brinker, who pioneered the so-called "casual-dining" segment with Steak and Ale (including an innovation known as the salad bar) in the 1960s, left restaurant chain owner Pillsbury (Burger King, Pillsbury's Poppin' Fresh Restaurants) to strike out on his own and bought control of Chili's Inc. in 1983. With plans to develop the small company into a major chain, Brinker took Chili's public in 1984.

The company began aggressively recruiting joint venture and franchise partners. It also expanded the Chili's menu to include items such as fajitas, staking the company's growth on aging baby boomers who were looking for something more than fast food. After attempts to regain control of Brinker's former S&A Restaurant and to acquire fast-food chains like Taco Cabana and Flyer's Island Express were stymied, Brinker decided to focus on the casual, low-priced restaurant market.

In 1989 Chili's Inc. acquired Grady's Goodtimes (a Knoxville, Tennessee-based restaurant chain owned by the Regas family, who had been in the restaurant business in Tennessee since 1919). That year Chili's also bought Romano's Macaroni Grill (a small Italian chain founded by Texas restaurateur Phil Romano in 1988). Reflecting the expansion of its restaurant offerings, the company changed its name to Brinker International in 1990.

Brinker introduced Spageddies (a casual,

lower-priced pasta restaurant) in 1992. With two Italian-cuisine chains in his network, the entrepreneur began to take on rival Olive Garden. Brinker suffered a major head injury in 1993 while playing polo, leaving him comatose for two weeks. Despite the traumatic event and poor early prognosis, he made a rapid recovery and returned to running the company.

In 1994 Brinker International expanded to cash in on the popularity of Mexican food. It acquired Cozymel's Coastal Mexican Grill that year and bought the $50 million, 21-unit On the Border Mexican-food chain the following year.

In 1995 Brinker retired as CEO (he remains chairman). That year, led by new CEO Ronald McDougall, the company sold Grady's and Spageddies to Quality Dining, as they no longer fit the company's overall strategy, and acquired two restaurant concepts from Rich Melman's Lettuce Entertain You Enterprises for $67 million.

In 1996 it opened a test location in Dallas of its eatZi's Market & Bakery (a joint venture with Romano), a gourmet grocery takeout concept, to capitalize on the public's increasing desire to dine at home.

The company began a major overhaul of Chili's menu in 1997, led by 34-year old Brian Kolodziej, a former chef at Dallas' ritzy Mansion on Turtle Creek hotel. In 1998 Brinker announced plans to open as many as 1,500 Corner Bakery shops (a newly introduced eatery featuring sandwiches and "trendy" baked goods) over a 10-year period.

Chairman: Norman E. Brinker, age 67
VC and CEO: Ronald A. McDougall, age 56,
$1,895,173 pay (prior to promotion)
President and COO: Douglas H. Brooks, age 46,
$642,931 pay (prior to promotion)
EVP, CFO, and Chief Strategic Officer:
Russell G. Owens, age 39, $515,839 pay
**EVP, Chief Administrative Officer, Secretary, and
General Counsel:** Roger F. Thomson, age 49,
$602,446 pay
EVP Human Resources: Carol Kirkman, age 41
SVP Finance and Treasurer: R. Chris Busbee
SVP Purchasing: W. Thomas Campbell
SVP; President, On The Border: Leslie J. Christon,
age 44
SVP; President, Cozymel's: Kenneth D. Dennis, age 45
SVP; President, Chili's Grill & Bar Concepts:
Todd E. Diener, age 41
SVP and Controller: Thomas J. Gispanski
SVP; President, Romano's Macaroni Grill:
John C. Miller, age 43
SVP and Chief Information Officer: Jodie N. Ray
SVP Investor Relations: Charles M. Sonsteby
SVP Corporate Development: Roy E. Study
VP Food and Beverage Purchasing: Robert P. Hall
VP Design and Architecture: Richard A. McCaffrey
VP Franchise Business Development: David N. Tyner
Auditors: KPMG LLP

LOCATIONS

HQ: 6820 LBJ Fwy., Dallas, TX 75240
Phone: 972-980-9917   **Fax:** 972-770-4139
Web site: http://www.brinker.com

Brinker International operates nearly 850 restaurants
worldwide.

PRODUCTS/OPERATIONS

1998 Restaurants

	No.
Chili's Grill & Bar	
Company-owned	414
Franchised & joint ventures	159
Romano's Macaroni Grill	
Company-owned	111
Franchised	2
On the Border	
Company operated	50
Franchised	15
Corner Bakery	30
Cozymel's Coastal Mexican Grill	12
Maggiano's Little Italy	7
eatZi's	3
Big Bowl	2
Wildfire	1
Total	**806**

COMPETITORS

Advantica Restaurant
 Group
American Restaurant
 Group
Applebee's
Avado Brands
Bertucci's
California Pizza Kitchen
Carlson Restaurants
 Worldwide
CBRL Group
Champps Entertainment
Chart House
CKE Restaurants

Darden Restaurants
Eateries
El Chico Restaurants
Landry's Seafood
Lone Star Steakhouse
Metromedia
NPC International
Outback Steakhouse
Prandium
Quality Dining
Ruby Tuesday
Taco Cabana
Tanner's Restaurant Group
VICORP Restaurants

HISTORICAL FINANCIALS & EMPLOYEES

NYSE symbol: EAT FYE: June 30	Annual Growth	1989	1990	1991	1992	1993	1994	1995	1996	1997	1998
Sales ($ mil.)	20.9%	285	347	427	519	653	879	1,042	1,163	1,335	1,574
Net income ($ mil.)	19.4%	14	18	26	36	49	62	73	34	61	69
Income as % of sales	—	4.9%	5.2%	6.1%	6.9%	7.5%	7.0%	7.0%	3.0%	4.5%	4.4%
Earnings per share ($)	16.4%	0.26	0.33	0.40	0.51	0.69	0.83	0.98	0.44	0.81	1.02
Stock price - FY high ($)	—	5.89	7.62	12.31	18.35	24.68	33.68	26.00	19.00	19.00	24.63
Stock price - FY low ($)	—	3.04	5.47	5.05	11.20	13.79	20.00	14.75	11.88	10.63	13.63
Stock price - FY close ($)	14.3%	5.79	7.17	11.35	14.68	22.84	21.00	17.25	15.00	14.25	19.25
P/E - high	—	23	23	31	36	36	41	27	43	23	24
P/E - low	—	12	17	13	22	20	24	15	27	13	13
Dividends per share ($)	—	0.00	0.00	0.00	0.00	0.00	0.00	0.00	0.00	0.00	0.00
Book value per share ($)	21.4%	1.58	2.30	3.25	3.91	4.88	5.87	6.89	7.87	8.03	9.01
Employees	15.9%	14,000	15,000	20,000	28,000	29,000	38,000	37,500	39,900	47,000	53,000

STOCK PRICE HISTORY

HIGH/LOW/CLOSE

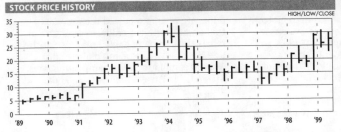

1998 FISCAL YEAR-END

Debt ratio: 19.9%
Return on equity: 11.6%
Cash ($ mil.): 31
Current ratio: 0.53
Long-term debt ($ mil.): 147
No. of shares (mil.): 66
Dividends
 Yield: —
 Payout: —
Market value ($ mil.): 1,269

BRISTOL-MYERS SQUIBB COMPANY

OVERVIEW

No pain, no gain for Bristol-Myers Squibb. The New York City-based company's best-known brands include Excedrin and Bufferin analgesics and personal care products Clairol and Sea Breeze, but nearly 70% of sales come from pharmaceuticals, particularly anticancer, cardiovascular, and anti-infective treatments. The company also makes infant formula, nutritional supplements, and orthopedic products.

Bristol-Myers Squibb's strategy is to produce several leading products within each market. For example, its TAXOL, Paraplatin,

Platinol, and VePesid make it a top producer of anticancer drugs. Another best-seller is its anticholesterol drug Pravachol.

But none of these can compare with competitors' sexier products, so despite progress made under chairman and CEO Charles Heimbold, the company lags in investors' esteem. In response, it has cut costs, refined its product line, and expanded R&D operations. Bristol-Myers Squibb now has more than 40 drugs in its pipeline and has tripled its licensing and research partnerships since 1994.

HISTORY

Bristol-Myers Squibb is the product of a merger of rivals.

Squibb was founded by Dr. Edward Squibb in New York City in 1858. He developed techniques for making pure ether and chloroform; he turned the business over to his sons in 1891. Sales of $414,000 in 1904 grew to $13 million by 1928. The company supplied penicillin and morphine during WWII. In 1952 it was bought by Mathieson Chemical, which in turn was bought by Olin Industries in 1953, forming Olin Mathieson Chemical. Squibb maintained its separate identity.

From 1968 to 1971 the company went through repeated reorganizations and changed its name to Squibb Corporation. Capoten and Corgard, two major cardiovascular drugs, were introduced in the late 1970s. Capoten was the first drug engineered to attack a specific disease-causing mechanism. Squibb formed a joint venture with Denmark's Novo in 1982 to sell insulin.

William Bristol and John Myers founded Clinton Pharmaceutical in Clinton, New York, in 1887 (renamed Bristol-Myers in 1900) to sell bulk pharmaceuticals. Bristol-Myers made antibiotics after the 1943 purchase of Cheplin Biological Labs. The company began overseas expansion in the 1950s. It bought Clairol (1959), Mead Johnson (drugs, infant and nutritional formula; 1967), and Zimmer (orthopedic implants, 1972). It introduced new drugs for treating cancer (Platinol, 1978) and anxiety (BuSpar, 1986). That year it acquired biotech companies Oncogen and Genetic Systems.

Bristol-Myers bought Squibb in 1989. In 1990 the new company bought Concept (arthroscopy products, US) and Orthoplant (implants, Germany). In 1993 it joined Eastman Kodak and Elf Aquitaine in developing new heart drugs. Despite these initiatives, earnings slipped. In 1994 company veteran

Charles Heimbold became CEO and moved to turn profits upward. Bristol-Myers Squibb in 1995 acquired wound- and skin-care products company Calgon Vestal Laboratories and Scandinavian generic pharmaceuticals producer A/S GEA Farmaceutisk Fabrik. Also that year the company, along with fellow silicone breast-implant makers 3M and Baxter International, agreed to settle thousands of personal-injury claims at an average of $26,000 per claim.

In response to an antitrust suit filed by independent drugstores, Bristol-Myers Squibb and other major drugmakers agreed in 1996 to charge pharmacies the same prices as managed care groups for medications. That year the company formed a unit to produce generic drugs. Also in 1996 Bristol-Myers Squibb began marketing Pravachol.

Over the next two years the company tweaked its product line, acquiring drug, cosmetics, and consumer products companies and brands. It sold its Linvatec unit (arthroscopic products and powered surgical instruments) to CONED in 1997 and the next year sold its Ban antiperspirant brand to personal care products maker Chattem. Having refined its product line, the company began a series of officer reassignments that were widely interpreted as the beginning of the process of finding a successor for Charles Heimbold, who announced he would retire in 2001.

In 1999 Bristol-Myers Squibb pulled its backing for EntreMed after being unable to duplicate results reported the previous year that angiostatin had eradicated tumors in mice. The company helped market SmithKline Beecham's promising diabetes drug, Avandia, and launched a campaign against AIDS/HIV in Africa, hoping to safeguard its drug patents there.

Chairman and CEO: Charles A. Heimbold Jr., age 65, $3,194,375 pay
President Technical Operations, Worldwide Medicines Group: Hamed M. Abdou, age 58
VP, Head of the Office of Corporate Conduct, and Secretary: Alice C. Brennan, age 46
SVP Corporate Development: George P. Kooluris, age 54
President, U.S. Medicines and Global Marketing: Richard J. Lane, age 48
SVP and General Counsel; President, Medical Devices Group: John L. McGoldrick, age 58, $884,448 pay
SVP and CFO: Michael F. Mee, age 56, $974,157 pay
President, International Medicines: Christine A. Poon, age 46
President, Bristol-Myers Squibb Pharmaceutical Research Institute: Peter S. Ringrose, age 53, $907,411 pay
SVP; President, Worldwide Beauty Care and Nutritionals: Stephen I. Sadove, age 47
VP Financial Operations and Controller: Frederick S. Schiff, age 51
SVP Corporate and Environmental Affairs: John L. Skule, age 55
SVP Human Resources: Charles G. Tharp, age 47
EVP: Kenneth E. Weg, age 60, $1,414,520 pay
Auditors: PricewaterhouseCoopers LLP

LOCATIONS

HQ: 345 Park Ave., New York, NY 10154-0037
Phone: 212-546-4000   **Fax:** 212-546-4020
Web site: http://www.bms.com

Bristol-Myers Squibb has 43 manufacturing plants worldwide.

1998 Sales

	$ mil.	% of total
Western Hemisphere		
US	12,527	61
Other countries	1,749	8
Europe, Middle East & Africa	4,873	24
Pacific	1,457	7
Adjustments	(2,322)	—
Total	**18,284**	**100**

PRODUCTS/OPERATIONS

1998 Sales

	$ mil.	% of total
Medicines	12,573	69
Beauty care	2,305	12
Nutritionals	1,759	10
Medical devices	1,647	9
Total	**18,284**	**100**

COMPETITORS

Abbott Labs	Hoechst AG
American Home Products	Johnson & Johnson
Amgen	Merck
Bayer AG	Novartis
Biomet	Pfizer
Boehringer Ingelheim	Pharmacia & Upjohn
Dial	Procter & Gamble
Eli Lilly	Rhône-Poulenc
G.D. Searle	Roche Holding
Gillette	Solvay
Glaxo Wellcome	Warner-Lambert

HISTORICAL FINANCIALS & EMPLOYEES

NYSE symbol: BMY FYE: December 31	Annual Growth	1989	1990	1991	1992	1993	1994	1995	1996	1997	1998
Sales ($ mil.)	7.9%	9,189	10,300	11,159	11,156	11,413	11,984	13,767	15,065	16,701	18,284
Net income ($ mil.)	16.0%	747	1,748	2,056	1,962	1,959	1,842	1,812	2,850	3,205	2,836
Income as % of sales	—	8.1%	17.0%	18.4%	17.6%	17.2%	15.4%	13.2%	18.9%	19.2%	15.5%
Earnings per share ($)	21.2%	0.36	0.84	0.99	0.96	0.95	0.91	0.89	1.40	1.57	2.03
Stock price - FY high ($)	—	14.50	17.00	22.34	22.53	16.81	15.25	21.78	29.09	49.09	67.63
Stock price - FY low ($)	—	11.00	12.63	15.28	15.00	12.72	12.50	14.44	19.50	26.63	44.16
Stock price - FY close ($)	19.0%	14.00	16.75	22.06	16.84	14.56	14.47	21.47	27.25	47.31	66.91
P/E - high	—	40	20	23	23	18	17	24	21	31	33
P/E - low	—	31	15	15	16	13	14	16	14	17	22
Dividends per share ($)	5.1%	0.50	0.53	0.60	0.69	0.72	0.73	0.74	0.75	0.76	0.78
Book value per share ($)	5.2%	2.42	2.59	2.79	2.91	2.90	2.81	2.88	3.28	3.63	3.81
Employees	0.1%	54,100	52,900	53,500	52,600	49,500	47,700	49,140	51,200	53,600	54,700

STOCK PRICE HISTORY

HIGH/LOW/CLOSE

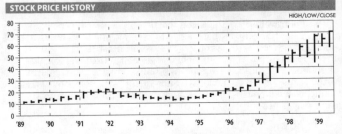

1998 FISCAL YEAR-END

Debt ratio: 15.3%
Return on equity: 37.4%
Cash ($ mil.): 2,244
Current ratio: 1.52
Long-term debt ($ mil.): 1,364
No. of shares (mil.): 1,989
Dividends
  Yield: 1.2%
  Payout: 38.4%
Market value ($ mil.): 133,068

BROWN SHOE COMPANY INC.

OVERVIEW

There's no business like shoe business for Brown Shoe Company (formerly Brown Group). A footwear wholesaler and retailer, the St. Louis-based company is a leader in both men's and women's nonathletic shoes. Brown Shoe operates three retail chains: Famous Footwear, one of the nation's largest family shoe chains, with about 850 stores in the US (it accounts for more than half of the company's sales); more than 450 Naturalizer stores in the US and Canada; and 16 F. X. LaSalle stores in Canada.

Through its Pagoda, Brown Branded Marketing, and Canadian wholesale divisions, the company sells shoes to 2,800 department stores, mass merchandisers, and independent retailers, primarily in the US and Canada. In addition to its own brands (Buster Brown, Connie, Naturalizer), Brown Shoe sells private-label products and licensed brands such as Barbie, Dr. Scholl's, and several Mickey brands (Walt Disney). More than three-fourths of the company's products are made in China.

Brown Shoe is expanding its Famous Footwear chain and introducing new styles to appeal to younger customers.

HISTORY

Salesman George Brown began mass-producing women's shoes in St. Louis in 1878, unusual at a time when the shoe industry was firmly entrenched in New England. With the financial backing of partners Alvin Bryan and Jerome Desnoyers, Brown hired five shoemakers and opened Bryan, Brown and Company. The firm's fashionable first shoes were a pleasant contrast to the staid, black shoes typical of New England and were an instant success. The enterprise grew rapidly, and in 1893, Brown, by then the sole remaining partner, renamed the operation Brown Shoe Company. By 1900 sales had reached $4 million.

Company executive John Bush introduced cartoonist Richard Outcault's Buster Brown comic strip character in 1902 at the St. Louis World's Fair as a trademark for Brown's children's shoes. Bush failed to purchase the exclusive rights, and Buster Brown became the trademark for scores of products, even cigars and whiskey. Nevertheless, Buster Brown became a famous trademark for the company. Bush eventually hired midgets to dress as Buster Brown and crisscross the country selling Brown shoes, always with the catchy jingle, "I'm Buster Brown; I live in a shoe. (WOOF! WOOF!) That's my dog Tige; he lives there too."

During the Great Depression, company VP Clark Gamble developed the concept, later commonplace, of having salesmen sell only specific branded shoe lines instead of traveling with samples of all the company's shoes. Brown Shoe modernized its operations and entered the retailing business during the 1950s by purchasing Wohl Shoe, Regal Shoe, and G. R. Kinney (sold in 1963 to Woolworth because of antitrust litigation). It also launched a national advertising push through major magazines and children's TV shows.

Diversifying, Brown Shoe bought Cloth World stores (1970), Eagle Rubber (toys and sporting goods, 1971), Hedstrom (bicycles and equipment, 1971), Meis Brothers (department stores, 1972), and Outdoor Sports Industries (1979), among others. It became the Brown Group in 1972.

The company acquired the 32-store Famous Footwear chain in 1981 and expanded it rapidly (especially from 1990 to 1995, when it added more than 500 stores, reaching a total of about 815). B. A. Bridgewater became Brown Group's CEO in 1982. In 1985 the company sold its recreational products segment and in 1989 shed all of its specialty retailers except Cloth World.

As the US shoe manufacturing industry fell prey to cheaper foreign imports, Brown Group began closing its US shoemaking plants. In 1991 and 1992 it closed nine US shoe factories, cutting capacity in half. It discontinued its Wohl Leased Shoe Department business in 1994 and, still facing declining sales and profits, closed five shoe factories and discontinued its Connie and Regal footwear chains. Brown Group also sold its Cloth World chain and discontinued its Maryland Square catalog business.

Brown Group continued its restructuring in 1995, closing its last five plants in the US (it still has two in Canada). Also that year it bought the upscale Larry Stuart Collection and the le coq sportif athletic shoe business. Charges tied to overstocking in its overseas division led to a loss for fiscal 1998.

In 1999 Bridgewater retired and Ronald Fromm was promoted to president, chairman, and CEO. Subsequently, the company changed its name back to Brown Shoe Company.

OFFICERS

Chairman, President, and CEO: Ronald A. Fromm Jr., age 47, $697,471 pay
EVP; President, Famous Footwear: Brian C. Cook, age 59, $855,000 pay (prior to promotion)
EVP and CFO: Harry E. Rich, age 59, $667,000 pay
President, Naturalizer Retail Division: Byron D. Norfleet, age 37
President, Pagoda: Gary M. Rich, age 48
President, Brown Shoe Sourcing: David H. Schwartz, age 53, $607,000 pay
President, Brown Branded: Gregory J. Van Gasse, age 48
Director Human Resources: James Preuss
Auditors: Ernst & Young LLP

LOCATIONS

HQ: 8300 Maryland Ave., St. Louis, MO 63105
Phone: 314-854-4000   **Fax:** 314-854-4274
Web site: http://www.brownshoecompany.com

Brown Shoe Company has about 1,300 retail stores in the US and Canada. It also sells shoes wholesale to about 2,800 retailers in Canada, Europe, the Far East, South America, and the US.

1999 Sales

	$ mil.	% of total
US	1,222	79
Far East	224	14
Canada	75	5
Other regions	26	2
Adjustments	(8)	—
Total	**1,539**	**100**

PRODUCTS/OPERATIONS

Children's Shoes
Barbie (licensed)
Buster Brown
Disney Babies (licensed)
Flash Tech
Hello Kitty
le coq sportif
Live Wires
Mickey & Co. (licensed)
Mickey for Kids (licensed)
Mulan (licensed)
Simba's Pride (licensed)
Star Wars (licensed)
Tarzan (licensed)
The Land Before Time
The Lion King (licensed)
Wildcats

Men's Shoes
Big Country
Cedar Trail
Dr. Scholl's (licensed)

Jean Pier Clemente
le coq sportif
Penn (licensed)
Regal
Russell Athletic (licensed)

Women's Shoes
Air Step
Connie
Dr. Scholl's (licensed)
Fanfares
Larry Stuart Collection
le coq sportif
Life Stride
LS Studio
Mickey Unlimited (licensed)
Naturalizer
Night Life
Penn (licensed)
Russell Athletic (licensed)
Unionbay (licensed)

COMPETITORS

Berkshire Hathaway
Dayton Hudson
Dillard's
Federated
Florsheim
Footstar
Genesco
J. Baker
J. C. Penney
Kenneth Cole
Kmart
May

Nine West
Nordstrom
Payless ShoeSource
Phillips-Van Heusen
Reebok
Ross Stores
Saks Inc.
Sears
Shoe Carnival
Stride Rite
TJX
Wal-Mart

HISTORICAL FINANCIALS & EMPLOYEES

NYSE symbol: BWS FYE: January 31	Annual Growth	1990	1991	1992	1993	1994	1995	1996	1997	1998	1999
Sales ($ mil.)	(1.9%)	1,821	1,764	1,728	1,791	1,598	1,462	1,456	1,525	1,567	1,539
Net income ($ mil.)	(3.9%)	34	32	4	5	(32)	39	3	20	(21)	24
Income as % of sales	—	1.9%	1.8%	0.2%	0.3%	—	2.7%	0.2%	1.3%	—	1.5%
Earnings per share ($)	(4.2%)	1.95	1.85	0.22	0.27	(1.83)	2.23	0.19	1.15	(1.19)	1.32
Stock price - FY high ($)	—	35.50	30.00	28.75	29.88	36.00	38.88	33.38	23.38	20.13	20.00
Stock price - FY low ($)	—	22.38	19.75	21.63	21.00	28.75	29.75	12.50	11.88	12.44	12.50
Stock price - FY close ($)	(3.9%)	23.00	24.50	26.13	29.25	35.13	31.88	13.75	16.50	14.50	16.06
P/E - high	—	18	16	131	111	—	17	176	20	—	15
P/E - low	—	11	11	98	78	—	13	66	10	—	9
Dividends per share ($)	(14.3%)	1.60	1.60	1.60	1.60	1.60	1.60	1.30	0.75	0.85	0.40
Book value per share ($)	(5.2%)	19.39	19.47	18.10	16.69	13.27	13.90	12.92	13.19	11.04	11.96
Employees	(9.9%)	28,000	27,500	25,500	23,000	22,000	14,500	11,000	11,500	11,500	11,000

STOCK PRICE HISTORY

HIGH/LOW/CLOSE

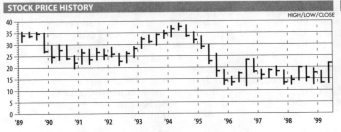

1999 FISCAL YEAR-END

Debt ratio: 44.2%
Return on equity: 10.9%
Cash ($ mil.): 46
Current ratio: 2.02
Long-term debt ($ mil.): 172
No. of shares (mil.): 18
Dividends
  Yield: 2.5%
  Payout: 30.3%
Market value ($ mil.): 292

BROWN-FORMAN CORPORATION

OVERVIEW

Straight-up or mixed, whiskey or wine — Brown-Forman's got a drink for you, and a glass to serve it in. The Louisville, Kentucky-based company is best known for producing some of the top-selling wines and spirits in their respective categories, including Jack Daniel's (whiskey), Canadian Mist (Canadian whiskey), Korbel (premium champagne), and Bolla (premium wine). Other drinks include Southern Comfort liqueurs, Old Forester (bourbon), Early Times (whiskey), and Pepe Lopez tequila. The company also licenses its beverage brand names; makes Hartmann luggage and leather goods; and makes tableware, crystal, silver, and collectibles under the Lenox, Dansk, and Gorham names (it is the #1 US maker of fine china).

Brown-Forman has found global success by introducing Jack Daniel's into new markets overseas (it has become the leading US whiskey sold worldwide). Its Wines International unit markets Fetzer and 25 other brands in 75 countries and is expanding rapidly.

Descendants of the co-founding Brown family, including CEO Owsley Brown II, control Brown-Forman.

HISTORY

George Brown and John Forman opened the Brown-Forman Distillery in Louisville, Kentucky, in 1870 to produce Old Forester-brand bourbon. Old Forester sold well through the end of the century, in part because of the company's innovative packaging (safety seals and quality guarantees on the bottles). When Forman died in 1901, Brown bought his interest in the company.

Old Forester continued to be successful under the Brown family. Brown-Forman obtained government approval to produce alcohol for medicinal purposes during Prohibition. In 1923 it made its first acquisition, Early Times, but stored its whiskey in a government warehouse (removed only by permit). The firm went public in 1933 and re-established the Old Forester image as an alcoholic beverage after the repeal of Prohibition.

During WWII the government greatly curtailed alcoholic beverage production (alcohol was needed for the war effort). The company compensated by providing alcohol for wartime rubber and gunpowder production. In 1941 Brown-Forman correctly predicted that the war would be over by the end of 1945 and started the four-year aging process for its bourbon. As a result, Early Times dominated the whiskey market after the war.

In 1956 Brown-Forman expanded beyond Old Forester by purchasing Lynchburg, Tennessee-based Jack Daniel's (sour mash whiskey). The company retained the simple, black Jack Daniel's label and promoted the image of a small Tennessee distillery for the brand.

Brown-Forman continued to expand its alcohol line during the 1960s and 1970s, acquiring Korbel (champagne and brandy, 1965), Quality Importers (Ambassador Scotch, Ambassador Gin, and Old Bushmills Irish Whiskey; 1967), Bolla and Cella (wines, 1968), and Canadian Mist (blended whiskey, 1971). In 1979 it purchased Southern Comfort (a top-selling liqueur).

Non-beverage acquisitions included Lenox (a leading US maker of fine china, crystal, gifts, and Hartmann luggage; 1983), Kirk Stieff (silver and pewter, 1990), and Dansk International Designs (china, crystal, silver, and the high-quality Gorham line; 1991). Brown-Forman launched Gentleman Jack Rare Tennessee Whiskey in 1988, its first new whiskey from its Jack Daniel's distillery in more than 100 years.

The company acquired wine maker Jekel Vineyards in 1991 and the next year bought the family-owned Fetzer Vineyards in Mendocino County, California. In 1993 Owsley Brown II succeeded his brother Lee as CEO. Faced with flat sales in the US, Brown-Forman reorganized its beverage operations in 1994 to facilitate international sales. A year later Moore County, Tennessee, voters approved a referendum that allowed whiskey sales in Lynchburg (home of Jack Daniel's) for the first time since Prohibition. Also in 1995 Brown-Forman formed a 50-50 joint venture with Jagatjit Industries, India's third-largest spirits producer and, in 1996, introduced Southern Comfort to that market.

A 1997 licensing agreement with Carlson, whose T.G.I. Friday's restaurants came out with a Jack Daniel's line of meat dishes, stealthily slipped the brand into national television advertising. Brown-Forman said in 1998 that it would spend $60 million over five years to promote Finlandia Vodka (it obtained exclusive US distribution in 1996).

Brown-Forman bought an 80% stake in premium wine maker Sonoma-Cutrer Vineyards in 1999. It also began advertising Korbel as the "Official Champagne of the Millennium."

OFFICERS

Chairman and CEO: Owsley Brown II, age 56, $1,373,995 pay
VC: Owsley B. Frazier, age 63, $640,436 pay
VC; President and CEO, Brown-Forman Beverages Worldwide: William M. Street, age 60, $984,268 pay
EVP and CFO: Steven B. Ratoff, age 56, $555,158 pay
SVP and Director Corporate Development: John P. Bridendall, age 49
SVP and Executive Director Human Resources and Information Services: Russell C. Buzby
SVP, General Counsel, and Secretary: Michael B. Crutcher, age 55
SVP Corporate Communications and Corporate Services: Lois A. Mateus, age 52
SVP Human Resources: James D. Wilson
President, Lenox: Stanley E. Krangel, age 48, $576,101 pay
Auditors: PricewaterhouseCoopers LLP

LOCATIONS

HQ: 850 Dixie Hwy., Louisville, KY 40210
Phone: 502-585-1100   **Fax:** 502-774-7876
Web site: http://www.brown-forman.com

Brown-Forman's Wines and Spirits segment owns seven plants in the US, two in Italy, and one each in the US Virgin Islands and Canada. Its Consumer Durables segment owns plants in New Jersey, North Carolina, Pennsylvania, Rhode Island, and Tennessee.

1999 Sales

	$ mil.	% of total
US	1,649	72
Other countries	381	28
Adjustment	(254)	—
Total	**1,776**	**100**

PRODUCTS/OPERATIONS

1999 Sales & Operating Income

	Sales		Operating Income	
	$ mil.	% of total	$ mil.	% of total
Wines & Spirits	1,468	72	284	88
Consumer Durables	562	28	38	12
Adjustment	(254)	—	—	—
Total	**1,776**	**100**	**322**	**100**

Selected Brands

Wines
Armstrong Ridge
Bel Arbor
Bolla
Bonterra Vineyards
Fetzer Vineyards
Jekel Vineyards
Korbel champagne and wines
Sonoma-Cutrer Vineyards

Spirits
Black Bush (whiskey)
Canadian Mist (whiskey)
Early Times (whiskey)
Gentleman Jack (whiskey)
Jack Daniel's (whiskey)
Old Forester (bourbon)

Pepe Lopez (tequila)
Southern Comfort (liqueur)
Tropical Freezes (low-alcohol freezer cocktails)
Woodford Reserve (whiskey)

Consumer Durables
Dansk (crystal, dinnerware, glassware, flatware, giftware)
Gorham (crystal, flatware, giftware, silver)
Hartmann (luggage, leather goods)
Lenox (china, collectibles, crystal, dinnerware, giftware)

COMPETITORS

Allied Domecq
Anheuser-Busch
Bacardi-Martini
Beringer
Canandaigua Brands
Diageo
Fortune Brands
Gallo
Gucci
Heaven Hill
Jose Cuervo
Kendall-Jackson
Libbey
LVMH
Mikasa
Oneida
Robert Mondavi
Samsonite
Seagram
Taittinger
Waterford
Wedgwood

HISTORICAL FINANCIALS & EMPLOYEES

NYSE symbol: BF.B FYE: April 30	Annual Growth	1990	1991	1992	1993	1994	1995	1996	1997	1998	1999
Sales ($ mil.)	6.4%	1,017	1,119	1,260	1,415	1,401	1,420	1,544	1,584	1,669	1,776
Net income ($ mil.)	9.1%	93	145	146	156	129	149	160	169	185	202
Income as % of sales	—	9.1%	13.0%	11.6%	11.0%	9.2%	10.5%	10.4%	10.7%	11.1%	11.4%
Earnings per share ($)	11.5%	1.10	1.73	1.76	1.88	1.63	2.15	2.31	2.45	2.67	2.93
Stock price - FY high ($)	—	30.55	26.64	29.97	29.47	30.47	33.88	42.50	51.88	59.00	77.25
Stock price - FY low ($)	—	19.44	18.65	22.98	24.23	24.31	26.13	31.50	35.25	45.00	54.94
Stock price - FY close ($)	15.4%	20.35	25.97	25.31	26.89	29.89	33.00	39.50	50.50	56.63	73.69
P/E - high	—	28	15	17	16	19	16	18	21	22	26
P/E - low	—	18	11	13	13	15	12	14	14	17	19
Dividends per share ($)	6.9%	0.63	0.72	0.78	0.86	0.93	0.97	1.02	1.06	1.10	1.15
Book value per share ($)	7.6%	6.95	7.82	8.74	9.74	6.55	7.74	9.02	10.41	11.72	13.39
Employees	3.9%	5,400	5,600	6,900	6,700	7,100	7,300	7,400	7,500	7,600	7,600

STOCK PRICE HISTORY

HIGH/LOW/CLOSE

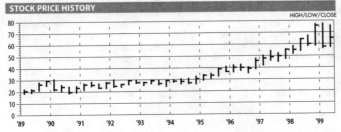

1999 FISCAL YEAR-END

Debt ratio: 5.5%
Return on equity: 22.0%
Cash ($ mil.): 171
Current ratio: 1.93
Long-term debt ($ mil.): 53
No. of shares (mil.): 69
Dividends
  Yield: 1.6%
  Payout: 39.2%
Market value ($ mil.): 5,048

BRUNO'S, INC.

OVERVIEW

Bruno's is hoping it has finally thawed out from its deep financial freeze. Once Dixie's hottest grocery chain, with nearly 250 stores in the early 1990s, Birmingham, Alabama-based Bruno's lost five key executives to a plane crash in 1991, encountered an onslaught of competition, and now operates under Chapter 11 bankruptcy protection. Downsized to a more manageable size, today Bruno's has about 150 stores, primarily in Alabama, but also in Florida, Georgia, and Mississippi. Value-priced Food World and FoodMax account for most of its stores; upscale Bruno's and the rural Food Fair chain make up the rest. It also runs eight liquor stores next to Food World stores in Florida. Investment firm Kohlberg Kravis Roberts (KKR) acquired 82% of Bruno's in 1995.

The company has floundered under KKR. An effort to convert the chain from its low-priced format to a frequent-shopper format alienated customers, who left for the cheaper prices offered by Wal-Mart and Winn-Dixie. In 1997 KKR named James Demme, who had turned around Oklahoma City-based Homeland Stores, as chairman, president, and CEO, but it was too late to stave off a bankruptcy filing.

HISTORY

Brothers Joseph and Sam Bruno — sons of Italian immigrants — founded Bruno's in 1932 in Birmingham, Alabama, with $600 of their mother's savings. Their father, Vincent, a former steelworker, and their mother, Theresa, ran the 800-sq.-ft. food store, with other Bruno siblings helping after school. A second store opened three years later.

Sam and Joe, along with their brothers, Lee and Angelo, incorporated in 1959 with 10 stores. Bruno's opened Big B Discount Drug Stores in 1968. By 1970 there were 29 Bruno's Food Stores in Alabama. The company went public in 1971 and began the Food World chain in 1972, opening large (40,000 to 48,000 sq. ft.) discount supermarkets. It spun off its 70-store Big B subsidiary in 1981.

Bruno's Food Stores were remodeled as Bruno's Food and Pharmacy stores in 1983. Located in suburban markets, the combination grocery and drug stores (52,000 to 60,000 sq. ft.) featured more extensive meat, seafood, produce, bakery, and deli departments than conventional supermarkets. The company also opened Bruno's Finer Foods (1983) and Food Fair (1985) stores.

The grocer acquired the Megamarket stores in Birmingham (1985) and converted them to FoodMax stores, large warehouse supermarkets (48,000 to 65,000 sq. ft.). In the 1970s and 1980s, Bruno's also expanded into adjacent states. Acquisitions included Steven's Supermarket (Nashville, Tennessee; 1987), Piggly Wiggly (central and southern Georgia, 1988), and seven BiLo supermarkets (Macon, Georgia; 1988).

Joe had studied European hypermarkets in the 1970s, and he believed they were the future of food retailing. In 1990, as a joint venture, Bruno's and Kmart opened American Fare, a 240,000-sq.-ft hypermarket with food and general merchandise, in Atlanta. Citing annual losses of more than $3.5 million, Bruno's withdrew from the partnership in 1992, taking a $12.9 million charge.

The company was added to the Standard & Poor's 500 index in 1991. Late that year Angelo and Lee Bruno, son and grandson of one of the company founders, were killed in a plane crash along with three other top managers.

Bruno's folded its Piggly Wiggly southern division into its Birmingham corporate office operations in 1992. The company's chairman, Ronald Bruno, stepped down in 1995 after the $1.15 billion takeover by Kohlberg Kravis Roberts (KKR), a firm known for buying undervalued food retailers (most notably Safeway and Fred Meyer) and selling them for a profit to companies active in consolidating the industry. Former American Stores executive William Bolton briefly took the helm. A year later Bruno's shut down one of its two distribution centers and sold or closed 47 stores.

Late in 1997 KKR brought in James Demme, who turned around Oklahoma City-based Homeland Stores, to revitalize the troubled company. To cut costs, Bruno's sold its 10 Seessel's supermarkets to Albertson's for $88 million in January 1998 (it had acquired the chain late in 1996 for $62 million). The company also sold 13 stores in Georgia to Ingles Markets. The next month, only four months after Demme arrived, Bruno's entered Chapter 11 bankruptcy protection. Later that year the company ended up selling 15 more stores in Tennessee to Albertson's and closed 20 underperforming stores.

In 1999 Bruno's closed 14 more stores in Alabama, Florida, and Georgia.

Chairman, CEO, and President: James A. Demme, age 58, $900,010 pay
EVP Marketing: Steve Slade, age 48
SVP Merchandising: Bruce A. Efird, age 40
SVP, General Counsel, and Secretary: Walter M. Grant, age 54, $396,010 pay
SVP Human Resources: Laura Hayden, age 41, $285,012 pay
SVP and CFO: Arthur B. McCarter, age 48
SVP Operations: William D. Shoemaker, age 46
Auditors: Deloitte & Touche LLP

LOCATIONS

HQ: 800 Lakeshore Pkwy., Birmingham, AL 35211
Phone: 205-940-9400   **Fax:** 205-912-4534
Web site: http://www.brunos.com

Bruno's operates supermarkets under several banners in Alabama, Florida, Georgia, and Mississippi. It also runs liquor stores in Florida.

1999 Stores

	No.
Alabama	108
Georgia	27
Florida	10
Mississippi	4
Total	**149**

PRODUCTS/OPERATIONS

1999 Stores

	No.
Food World	72
FoodMax	31
Bruno's	25
Food Fair	19
Other	2
Total	**149**

COMPETITORS

Albertson's
CVS
Fleming Companies
Jitney-Jungle
Kroger
Rite Aid
Walgreen
Wal-Mart
Winn-Dixie

HISTORICAL FINANCIALS & EMPLOYEES

OTC symbol: BRNOQ FYE: January 31	Annual Growth	1990	1991	1992	1993	1994	1995	1996	1997	1998	1999
Sales ($ mil.)	(3.9%)	—	2,586	2,658	2,872	2,835	2,870	2,891	2,899	2,560	1,883
Net income ($ mil.)	—	—	67	43	47	41	33	(71)	(50)	(156)	(52)
Income as % of sales	—	—	2.6%	1.6%	1.6%	1.4%	1.2%	—	—	—	—
Earnings per share ($)	—	—	—	—	—	—	—	(1.31)	(1.97)	(6.07)	(2.06)
Stock price - FY high ($)	—	—	—	—	—	—	—	11.75	17.25	16.13	2.17
Stock price - FY low ($)	—	—	—	—	—	—	—	10.00	9.88	1.25	0.20
Stock price - FY close ($)	(51.7%)	—	—	—	—	—	—	10.00	15.63	2.63	1.08
P/E - high	—	—	—	—	—	—	—	—	—	—	—
P/E - low	—	—	—	—	—	—	—	—	—	—	—
Dividends per share ($)	—	—	—	—	—	—	—	0.00	0.00	0.00	0.00
Book value per share ($)	—	—	—	—	—	—	—	(11.25)	(13.03)	(19.01)	(21.07)
Employees	(6.4%)	—	21,600	23,454	26,486	27,220	25,600	26,000	25,000	17,800	12,700

STOCK PRICE HISTORY

HIGH/LOW/CLOSE

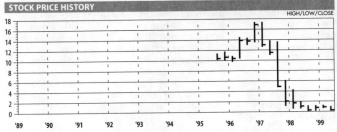

1999 FISCAL YEAR-END

Debt ratio: 100.0%
Return on equity: —
Cash ($ mil.): 66
Current ratio: 2.55
Long-term debt ($ mil.): —
No. of shares (mil.): 26
Dividends
  Yield: —
  Payout: —
Market value ($ mil.): 28

BRUNSWICK CORPORATION

OVERVIEW

Brunswick takes the business of leisure quite seriously. The Lake Forest, Illinois-based company once scored most of its sales from making billiards and bowling equipment. Today about two-thirds of the company's sales come from making marine equipment, including outboard motors (Mercury, Mariner) and boats designed for sport fishing (Robalo), pleasure (Bayliner), performance (Baja), and yachting (Sea Ray). Brunswick also makes camping and fishing goods (Igloo coolers, Zebco rods),

fitness equipment (Life Fitness), bicycles (Mongoose), gun accessories (Hoppe's), and sleds (Flexible Flyer).

The diversified company hasn't forgotten its roots. The world's leading producer of bowling and billiards equipment, Brunswick also operates about 125 bowling alleys (Brunswick Recreation Centers) worldwide. Working hard to freshen the game, most Brunswick alleys offer "Cosmic Bowling," where pins and lanes glow amidst fog and loud music.

HISTORY

Swiss immigrant woodworker John Brunswick built his first billiard table in 1845 in Cincinnati. In 1874 he formed a partnership with Julius Balke, and a decade later they teamed with H. W. Collender, forming the Brunswick-Balke-Collender Company.

Following Brunswick's death, son-in-law Moses Bensinger became president and diversified into bowling equipment in the 1880s. Bensinger's son B. E. followed as president (1904) and led the company into wood and rubber products, phonographs, and records. (Al Jolson recorded *Sonny Boy* on the Brunswick label.) Brunswick went public after WWI.

By 1930 Brunswick focused on bowling and billiards, sports that had seedy reputations during the 1920s and 1930s. When B. E. died in 1935, his son Bob became CEO and launched a massive promotional campaign to make his meal tickets respectable.

Bob's brother Ted succeeded him as CEO in 1954. Bowling equipment rival A.M.F. introduced the first automatic pinsetter in 1952, and Brunswick followed in 1956, capturing the lead by 1958. Brunswick diversified, adding Owens Yacht, MacGregor (sporting goods, 1958), Aloe (medical supplies, 1959), Mercury (marine products, 1961), and Zebco (fishing equipment, 1961). The company adopted its present name in 1960.

Bowling sales plummeted in the 1960s, and the company cut costs by selling unprofitable enterprises and focusing on new products such as an automatic scorer. In the 1970s acquisitions brought Brunswick into the medical diagnostics and energy and transportation products markets. CEO Jack Reichert, a former pin boy who became chairman in 1983, cut corporate staff in half and promoted the marine business.

The company sparked an industrywide consolidation trend in 1986 by buying boat builders Bayliner and Ray Industries. It

followed with purchases of Kiekhaefer Aeromarine (marine propulsion engines, 1990) and Martin Reel Company (fly reels, 1991). In 1992 Brunswick and Tracker Marine (a Missouri-based boat manufacturer) agreed to form a partnership to manufacture boats and marine equipment. That year it also acquired the Browning line of rods and reels.

In 1993 Brunswick began selling its businesses unrelated to recreation in the automotive, electronics, and defense industries. The company sold its Circus World Pizza business and closed its golf club shaft business two years later. Also in 1995 the Brunswick Indoor Recreation division opened new family entertainment centers that offered bowling and billiards in Brazil, China, Japan, South Korea, and Thailand.

Brunswick expanded its outdoor recreation business in 1996, purchasing camping business Nelson/Weather Rite from recreational giant Roadmaster Industries (now called RDM Sports Group) along with Roadmaster's bicycle business. Brunswick also sold several of its freshwater boat manufacturing operations to Tracker Marine and acquired the Boston Whaler line of saltwater boats from Meridian Sports that year.

In 1997 the company acquired ice chest and cooler manufacturer Igloo Holdings, Bell Sports' Mongoose bicycle unit, Mancuso's Life Fitness (a maker of exercise equipment), Hoppe's gun cleaning and hunting accessory business, Hammer Strength (plate-loaded strength training equipment), and DBA products, a manufacturer of bowling lane machines and equipment. In 1998 Brunswick bought ParaBody, a manufacturer of multi-station gyms, benches, and racks.

That year 22 boat builders won a $133 million antitrust suit against Brunswick. Several suits related to the decision followed in 1999.

Chairman and CEO: Peter N. Larson, age 59, $3,206,293 pay
EVP and CFO; Chairman, Indoor Recreation: Peter B. Hamilton, age 52, $794,597 pay
SVP; President, Mercury Marine Group: George W. Buckley, age 53, $1,032,197 pay
SVP Strategic Planning and Business Development; Chairman, US Marine: Dudley E. Lyons, age 58, $616,997 pay
VP, General Counsel, and Secretary: Mary D. Allen, age 53
VP; President, Sea Ray: William J. Barrington, age 48, $819,173 pay
VP and Chief Human Resources Officer: B. Russell Lockridge
Auditors: Arthur Andersen LLP

LOCATIONS

HQ: 1 N. Field Ct., Lake Forest, IL 60045-4811
Phone: 847-735-4700   **Fax:** 847-735-4765
Web site: http://www.brunswickcorp.com

Brunswick operates approximately 50 plants, primarily in the US. It also operates about 125 bowling centers worldwide and an additional 30 centers through international joint ventures.

1998 Sales

	$ mil.	% of total
US	3,138	80
Other countries	807	20
Total	**3,945**	**100**

PRODUCTS/OPERATIONS

Selected Brand Names and Products

Boat Motors
Mariner
MerCruiser
Mercury Marine
Motorguide

Boats
Baja
Bayliner
Boston Whaler
Maxum
Robalo
Sea Ray
Trophy

Recreation Centers
Brunswick Recreation
  Centers

Sporting Goods
Bicycles
  Mongoose
  Roadmaster
Billiards
  Brunswick

Bowling
  Brunswick
  DBA
Camping
  American Camper
  Igloo
  Remington
Fishing
  Browning
  Lew's
  Martin
  Quantum
  Swivl-Eze
  Zebco
Fitness Equipment
  Hammer Strength
  Life Fitness
  Parabody
Gun Care and Accessories
  Hoppe's
Sleds and Wagons
  Flexible Flyer

COMPETITORS

AMF Bowling
Coleman
Cybex International
Dave & Buster's
First Leisure
Genmar Holdings
Honda
Huffy

Johnson Worldwide
K2
MacAndrews & Forbes
Outboard Marine
Schwinn/GT
Suzuki
Tomkins
Yamaha

HISTORICAL FINANCIALS & EMPLOYEES

NYSE symbol: BC FYE: December 31	Annual Growth	1989	1990	1991	1992	1993	1994	1995	1996	1997	1998
Sales ($ mil.)	3.8%	2,826	2,478	2,088	2,059	2,207	2,700	3,041	3,160	3,657	3,945
Net income ($ mil.)	—	(71)	71	(24)	(26)	23	129	127	186	151	186
Income as % of sales	—	—	2.9%	—	—	1.0%	4.8%	4.2%	5.9%	4.1%	4.7%
Earnings per share ($)	—	(0.81)	0.80	(0.27)	(0.28)	0.24	1.35	1.32	1.88	1.50	1.88
Stock price – FY high ($)	—	21.50	16.13	16.38	17.75	18.50	25.38	24.00	25.88	37.00	35.69
Stock price – FY low ($)	—	13.00	6.38	8.00	12.13	12.50	17.00	16.25	17.25	23.13	12.00
Stock price – FY close ($)	6.4%	14.13	9.00	13.88	16.25	18.00	18.88	24.00	24.00	30.31	24.75
P/E – high	—	—	20	—	—	77	19	18	14	25	19
P/E – low	—	—	8	—	—	52	13	12	9	15	6
Dividends per share ($)	1.4%	0.44	0.44	0.44	0.44	0.44	0.44	0.50	0.50	0.50	0.50
Book value per share ($)	5.5%	8.82	9.33	8.79	8.65	8.44	8.44	9.54	10.65	12.16	13.22	14.27
Employees	(0.1%)	25,700	20,500	19,500	17,000	18,000	20,800	20,900	22,800	25,300	25,500

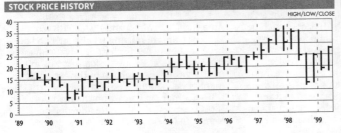

STOCK PRICE HISTORY
HIGH/LOW/CLOSE

1998 FISCAL YEAR-END

Debt ratio: 32.6%
Return on equity: 14.2%
Cash ($ mil.): 126
Current ratio: 1.40
Long-term debt ($ mil.): 635
No. of shares (mil.): 92
Dividends
  Yield: 2.0%
  Payout: 26.6%
Market value ($ mil.): 2,274

BUDGET GROUP, INC.

OVERVIEW

Budget Group has gone from franchise player to franchise owner — and then some. The Daytona Beach, Florida-based company used to be Team Rental Group, the largest franchisee of Budget Rent a Car Corporation (BRACC). The renamed company now owns BRACC, operator of one of the world's largest car rental systems. It is also the US's #2 renter of moving trucks (behind AMERCO's U-Haul), including Budget trucks as well as yellow Ryder trucks. Worldwide, Budget Group oversees a system of about 6,400 car and truck rental locations, most of them operated by franchisees.

The company also leases vehicles for vanpools in 60 US markets, sells cars (mostly used), and sells and rents RVs (Cruise America).

In addition, Budget Group operates parking lots at 13 US airports.

After growing quickly through acquisitions, the company is cutting costs by consolidating franchises and streamlining operations. It's also hiking rental prices and expanding its European operations. Budget Group has increased its marketing efforts through alliances with Storage USA and airline frequent-flier programs. BRACC's Perfect Drive program rewards frequent renters with such prizes as vacation packages, K2 skis, Callaway golf equipment, and free car rentals.

Chairman and CEO Sandy Miller controls 19% of Budget Group's voting stock; VC Jeffrey Congdon and director John Kennedy each control over 10%.

HISTORY

Car-rental industry veteran Sandy Miller had logged miles on his odometer with the Avis, Budget, and Dollar systems by 1987. That year he joined Jeffrey Congdon and John Kennedy in forming Team Rental Group to operate the Budget Rent a Car Corporation (BRACC) franchise in San Diego. In 1991 Team Rental began methodically expanding its BRACC franchise operations with acquisitions in New York and Virginia.

Three years later the company bought franchises in Pennsylvania and Ohio, went public, and began selling used rental cars. Next came acquisitions of franchises in California and Arizona (more than 90 locations combined), as well as in Indiana, North Carolina, and Connecticut.

By 1996 Team Rental's 160 or so locations made it BRACC's largest franchisee. That year it bought Chrysler's Van Pool Services (van rentals for commuter groups), further increasing its vehicle purchasing power.

Amid an industrywide shift in the ownership of major car rental firms, BRACC became available, and in 1997 Team Rental acquired the franchisor — a much larger company — for $350 million.

Morris Mirkin had begun Budget Rent a Car in Los Angeles in 1958 with 10 cars, which he rented for four dollars a day and four cents a mile. Distant relative Jules Lederer, then-husband of advice columnist Ann Landers, began leasing cars to Mirkin the next year and in 1960 formed Budget Rent a Car Corp. of America. Lederer's firm grew through franchising and focusing on the leisure travel market. In 1968 Transamerica bought Lederer's

company. (Mirkin's company continued to operate in California and Nevada.)

In 1986 BRACC management and LBO firm Gibbons, Green, van Amerongen bought the company for $205 million. It went public in 1987, only to be taken private again two years later in a buyout worth $333 million, with $300 million plunked down by Ford Motor and the rest by BRACC management and Gibbons' general partner.

BRACC began opening corporate-owned units in Europe in 1989 and purchased Diversified Services, its biggest franchisee, in 1990. That buyout gave BRACC direct access to Florida and Los Angeles, the two largest US car rental markets. BRACC lost $125 million in 1995 but broke even the next year after a round of cost-cutting under new management.

Ford owned rental car leader Hertz by 1996 and decided to buy all of BRACC as well. When that deal ran into antitrust concerns the next year, Team Rental moved in, bought BRACC for $350 million, and changed its own name to Budget Group. Budget Group agreed to buy about 80,000 vehicles per year from Ford for 10 years. Also in 1997 Budget Group bought Premier Car Rental (insurance replacement).

In 1998 the company acquired Cruise America (RV rentals) and Ryder TRS (consumer rentals of moving trucks), which had been sold by Ryder System to private investors in 1996. Budget Group took about $71 million in charges in 1998 related to the extinguishment of debt and its restructuring efforts.

To get more of its cars on the road, in 1999 BRACC launched a Web site allowing customers to bid on cars — an industry first.

Chairman and CEO: Sanford Miller, age 46, $795,807 pay
VC: Jeffrey D. Congdon, age 55, $693,374 pay
EVP, General Counsel, and Secretary: Robert L. Aprati, age 54, $370,444 pay
President, Budget Rent a Car, North America: Mark Sotir, age 35
President and COO, Budget International: Jean-Claude Ghiotti
EVP and CFO: Michael B. Clauer, age 42, $258,563 pay
President, Budget Truck Group: Thomas B. Zorn
President, Diversified Business Group: Randall S. Smalley
President, Budget Car Sales: Michael F. Katzin
President, Cruise America: Robert A. Smalley Jr.
President, Premier Car Rental: James R. Dreesen
President and CEO, VPSI: R. J. Henning
SVP, BGI Corporate Integration: Sandra Hughes
SVP Human Resources: Vickie Pyne
VP Corporate Communications: Kimberly Mulcahy
Auditors: Arthur Andersen LLP

LOCATIONS

HQ: 125 Basin St., Ste. 210, Daytona Beach, FL 32114
Phone: 904-238-7035 **Fax:** 904-238-7461
Web site: http://www.bgi.com

Budget Group and its franchisees have operations in more than 120 countries and territories.

PRODUCTS/OPERATIONS

1998 Sales

	% of total
Vehicle rentals	74
Retail car sales	22
Royalty fees & other	4
Total	**100**

Major Business Units

Car Rental
Budget Rent a Car (car and truck rental system)
Premier Car Rental (insurance replacement rentals)
Van Pool Services (commuter van leasing)

Car Sales
Budget Car Sales (used- and new-car sales)

Truck Rental
Budget Truck Rental (truck rental system)
Cruise America (camper, RV, and motorcycle sales and rentals)
Ryder TRS (truck rental system)

COMPETITORS

AMERCO
AutoNation
Avis Europe
Cendant
Dollar Thrifty Automotive Group
Enterprise Rent-A-Car
Hertz
Penske
Rent-A-Wreck
Sixt

HISTORICAL FINANCIALS & EMPLOYEES

NYSE symbol: BD FYE: December 31	Annual Growth	1989	1990	1991	1992	1993	1994	1995	1996	1997	1998
Sales ($ mil.)	159.3%	—	—	—	—	22	39	150	357	1,304	2,616
Net income ($ mil.)	—	—	—	—	—	0	0	0	5	37	(49)
Income as % of sales	—	—	—	—	—	1.8%	1.0%	0.2%	1.3%	2.8%	—
Earnings per share ($)	—	—	—	—	—	—	0.07	0.05	0.47	1.60	(1.53)
Stock price - FY high ($)	—	—	—	—	—	—	12.00	11.75	20.25	37.75	39.50
Stock price - FY low ($)	—	—	—	—	—	—	9.00	6.19	8.25	16.00	11.00
Stock price - FY close ($)	13.7%	—	—	—	—	—	9.50	8.50	16.13	34.56	15.88
P/E - high	—	—	—	—	—	—	171	235	43	24	—
P/E - low	—	—	—	—	—	—	129	124	18	10	—
Dividends per share ($)	—	—	—	—	—	—	0.00	0.00	0.00	0.00	0.00
Book value per share ($)	41.7%	—	—	—	—	—	4.50	5.81	8.35	16.97	18.16
Employees	129.2%	—	—	—	—	—	525	1,709	2,000	12,000	14,500

1993-96 information is for Team Rental Group.

STOCK PRICE HISTORY

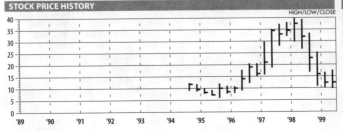

HIGH/LOW/CLOSE

1998 FISCAL YEAR-END

Debt ratio: 84.8%
Return on equity: —
Cash ($ mil.): 136
Current ratio: 2.06
Long-term debt ($ mil.): 3,635
No. of shares (mil.): 36
Dividends
 Yield: —
 Payout: —
Market value ($ mil.): 569

BURGER KING CORPORATION

OVERVIEW

Burger King's not the world's burger king yet, but it's pretty close. The Miami-based company is the world's #2 hamburger chain, ahead of Wendy's but still trailing McDonald's. Burger King feeds about 14 million hungry customers each day, about half of them from its drive-through windows. A whopping 1.5 billion Whoppers, Burger King's flame-broiled signature hamburger, are sold each year at the roughly 10,000 Burger King restaurants worldwide (nearly 80% are in the US). The company also offers other fast-food fare such as the BK Broiler (grilled chicken sandwich), fries, soft drinks, and breakfast items such as the Croissan'wich.

With about 20% of the US market, Burger King still has quite a bit to go before reaching McDonald's 44% share. To breach this gap, Burger King has introduced the Big King, a double-decker hamburger concocted to compete with the better-known Big Mac. Burger King also upgraded its french fries, heralding the change with an ad campaign inviting customers to "Taste the french fry that beat McDonald's." A heavy proponent of advertising, Burger King hopes this campaign and its "It just tastes better" promotion will help lure customers away from the land of the Happy Meal.

Burger King is a subsidiary of British food and spirits giant Diageo.

HISTORY

In 1954 restaurant veterans James McLamore and David Edgerton founded the first Burger King in Miami. Three years later the company added an item to its menu of hamburgers, milk shakes, and sodas: the Whopper sandwich, which then sold for 37 cents. Burger King used television to help advertise the Whopper (its first TV commercial appeared in 1958). During its infancy Burger King broke the mold of the fast food business by being the first chain to offer dining rooms.

Looking to expand nationwide, Burger King turned to franchising in 1959. McLamore and Edgerton took a very hands-off approach to their franchisees, allowing them to buy large territories and to operate with a high degree of autonomy. Although their technique did spur growth, it also created large service inconsistencies among Burger Kings across the US; this bugaboo would haunt the company for years to come. Having grown from a single store to a chain of 274 stores located in both the US and abroad, Burger King was sold to Pillsbury for $18 million in 1967.

During the early 1970s Burger King continued to add locations while parent Pillsbury fought to rein in large franchisees, some of whom argued they could run their Burger Kings better than a packaged-goods company. In 1977 Pillsbury handed control of Burger King to Donald Smith, a McDonald's veteran, who soon silenced the insurrection. Smith tightened franchising regulations, created 10 regional management offices, and instituted annual visits; in many ways, he "McDonaldized" the company's structure. Burger King did well during this time, launching its successful "Have It Your Way"

campaign in 1974 and introducing drive-through service a year later.

Smith left for Pizza Hut in 1980, and by 1982 Burger King had reached the #2 fast-food plateau, trailing McDonald's. The company struggled through the rest of the 1980s, though, hurt by high management turnover and a string of unsuccessful ad campaigns. (Remember "Herb the Nerd"? Few do.) Pillsbury became the target of a hostile takeover by UK-based Grand Metropolitan, and in 1988 Grand Met acquired Pillsbury along with its 5,500 Burger King restaurants.

After acquiring more than 520 Wimpey Hamburger restaurants from United Biscuits, Grand Met bolstered Burger King's international operations by converting about 200 UK-based Wimpey hamburger stores into Burger Kings in 1990. Also that year the company introduced the BK Broiler, a chicken sandwich that quickly became the rage among health-conscious fast-food customers. International expansion increased that decade, with new restaurants in Mexico (1991), Saudi Arabia (1993), and Paraguay (1995).

Starting in 1992, promotional tie-ins with Walt Disney and its widely popular *Beauty and the Beast* and *The Lion King* movies helped boost Burger King's sales (McDonald's garnered the Walt Disney contract in 1996). In 1997 Grand Metropolitan and Guinness combined their operations to form Diageo, making Burger King a subsidiary of the newly-formed company. Burger King tested a smart card loyalty program in 1998, which allowed customers to earn points by using Burger King smart cards to purchase food.

OFFICERS

CEO: Dennis Malamatinas, age 43
SVP and CFO: Colin Heggie
SVP Operations and Support: Vince Berkeley
SVP Management Information Systems and Chief Information Officer: Tom Giordano
SVP Human Resources: Yvonne Jackson
SVP Research and Development and Chief Technology Officer: Tulin Tuzel
President, Asia Pacific Region: David Chapman
President, Burger King North America: Paul E. Clayton, age 40
President, Canada: George Michel
President, Latin America, Caribbean, Mexico Region: Julio Ramirez
President, Europe, Middle East, Africa Region: David G. Williams
SVP Company Restaurants, U.S.: Roy Blauer
SVP Franchise Operations and Development, U.S.: Mark Giresi
VP Marketing Services: Richard Taylor
VP Marketing, USA: Rob Calderin
VP, Central Region: Jim Joy
VP, Western Region: Ray Miolla
VP, Southwestern Region: Susan Stanley
VP, Southeast Region: Melanie Wisniewski
Auditors: KPMG Audit Plc

LOCATIONS

HQ: 17777 Old Cutler Rd., Miami, FL 33157
Phone: 305-378-7011   **Fax:** 305-378-7262
Web site: http://www.burgerking.com

Burger King has restaurants in all 50 states and in about 55 other countries.

1998 Restaurants

	No.	% of total
US	7,801	78
Other countries	2,191	22
Total	**9,992**	**100**

PRODUCTS/OPERATIONS

1998 Sales

	% of total
Drive-through	50
Dine-in	35
Take-out	15
Total	**100**

1998 Restaurants

	No.	% of total
Franchised	9,189	92
Company-owned	803	8
Total	**9,992**	**100**

Selected Products

Big King sandwich	Dutch apple pie
Biscuits	French fries
BK Big Fish	French toast sticks
BK Broiler	Hamburger
Broiled chicken salad	Hash browns
Cheeseburger	Onion rings
Chicken sandwich	Salads
Chicken tenders	Shakes
Croissan'wich	Soft drinks
Double cheeseburger	Whopper
Double Whopper	Whopper, Jr.

COMPETITORS

Advantica Restaurant Group	Long John Silver's
AFC Enterprises	McDonald's
Checkers Drive-In	Shoney's
Chick-fil-A	Sonic
CKE Restaurants	Subway
Dairy Queen	Taco Cabana
Davco Restaurants	TRICON
Domino's Pizza	Wendy's
Foodmaker	Whataburger
Little Caesar	White Castle

HISTORICAL FINANCIALS & EMPLOYEES

Subsidiary FYE: June 30	Annual Growth	1989	1990	1991	1992	1993	1994	1995	1996	1997	1998
Sales ($ mil.)	26.8%	—	—	—	—	—	—	—	1,342	1,396	2,158
Employees	(42.0%)	—	—	—	—	—	—	—	—	29,590	17,149

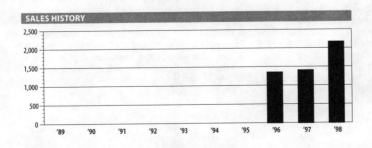

SALES HISTORY

BURLINGTON COAT FACTORY

OVERVIEW

When the weather outside is frightful, sales at Burlington Coat Factory Warehouse heat up. The Burlington, New Jersey-based company sells off-price, brand-name men's, women's, and children's clothing and outerwear at its 260-plus stores in 42 states. Many of its stores also carry linens, housewares, and gifts.

The firm is best known for its year-round selection of about 10,000 to 20,000 discounted coats (compared to about 1,500 to 2,000 coats at the typical department store). Burlington Coat Factory also runs stores under the names Cohoes Fashions (upscale apparel and accessories), Decelle (moderately priced family apparel), Luxury Linens (bed and bath items), Totally 4 Kids (children's clothing, books, toys), and Baby Depot (infant and toddler clothes and furniture). Some stores, such as Baby Depot, are also found as departments within its stores.

Burlington Coat Factory takes less of a markup than its department store competition and has lower profit margins than other clothing retailers, but chairman, president, and CEO Monroe Milstein has kept the company competitive by running a tight ship. It buys the coats early in the season (up to five months before department store rivals) to lock in lower prices. Burlington Coat Factory prefers to lease existing buildings and refurbish rather than build new stores, keeping overhead low. Unlike other off-price retailers, it buys directly from manufacturers and does not rely on leftovers or closeouts.

The Milstein clan owns 62% of Burlington Coat Factory. Monroe's wife, Henrietta, and their sons Andrew and Stephen are company executives and directors.

HISTORY

Russian-Jewish immigrant Abe Milstein and a partner started coat wholesaler and manufacturer Milstein and Feigelson in 1924. Abe's son, Monroe, was a quick study. He graduated from New York University with a business degree in 1946 at age 19 and started his own coat and suit wholesaling business called Monroe G. Milstein, Inc. His mother provided free labor at her son's company six days a week to keep the business alive. Abe ended his partnership in 1953 and joined his son's business.

Family relations were strained temporarily in 1972, when Monroe disregarded his father's advice not to buy a faltering coat factory outlet store in Burlington, New Jersey. (Abe believed that his son did not have enough retailing experience.) Monroe, however, thought owning a retail store would provide a guaranteed sales outlet for their merchandise, and he bought Burlington Coat Factory for $675,000 (using $60,000 of his wife Henrietta's savings). His company also adopted the Burlington Coat Factory Warehouse moniker as its own.

To become less dependent on the season-specific coat business, the company soon expanded its merchandise mix by adding a children's division (started by Henrietta) and subleased departments. It opened a second store in Long Island, New York, in 1975.

Settling a trademark dispute with fabric maker Burlington Industries in 1981, Burlington Coat Factory agreed to say in advertising — as it does to this day — that the two companies are not affiliated. The 31-store company went public two years later, using the money it raised to open almost 30 stores that year. As part of its expansion in the 1980s, Burlington Coat Factory opened stores in warmer climates such as Texas and Florida.

The firm tried to grow through acquisitions that decade but failed in its attempts to buy department store retailers (Woodward & Lathrop, Wanamakers), an off-price retailer (Dry Goods), and coat manufacturer Londontown (London Fog). It made a successful bid in 1989 for New York discount retailer Cohoes.

Burlington Coat Factory's sales topped the $1 billion mark for the first time in fiscal 1993. The company bought Boston-based off-price family apparel chain Decelle in 1993. It then opened its first store outside the US (in Mexico) and tried new stand-alone store concepts based on successful in-store departments such as Luxury Linens and Baby Depot. A warm winter in 1994 hurt the company: Profits fell by two-thirds, and it sold off inventory for two years afterward.

In fiscal 1999 the company moved its fiscal year-end from June to May. The company pulled a line of men's parkas in late 1998 after a Humane Society investigation revealed that the coats were trimmed with hair from dogs killed inhumanely in China. Burlington Coat Factory said its vendor told them the coats — labeled "Mongolian dog fur" — were made with coyote hair.

Chairman, President, and CEO: Monroe G. Milstein, age 72
EVP, Executive Merchandise Manager, and Assistant Secretary: Andrew R. Milstein, age 46
EVP and Secretary: Henrietta Milstein, age 70
EVP and General Merchandise Manager: Stephen E. Milstein, age 43
EVP and COO: Mark A. Nesci, age 43
EVP, General Counsel, and Assistant Secretary: Paul C. Tang, age 46
VP and Treasurer: Bernard Brodsky, age 59
VP, Corporate Controller, and Chief Accouting Officer: Robert L. LaPenta Jr., age 45
Manager Human Resources: Chris Pilla
Auditors: Deloitte & Touche LLP

LOCATIONS

HQ: Burlington Coat Factory Warehouse,
1830 Rte. 130, Burlington, NJ 08016
Phone: 609-387-7800   **Fax:** 609-387-7071
Web site: http://www.coat.com

Burlington Coat Factory Warehouse has locations in Alabama, Alaska, Arizona, Arkansas, California, Colorado, Connecticut, Delaware, Florida, Georgia, Idaho, Illinois, Indiana, Iowa, Kansas, Kentucky, Louisiana, Maine, Maryland, Massachusetts, Michigan, Minnesota, Missouri, Nebraska, Nevada, New Hampshire, New Jersey, New Mexico, New York, North Carolina, Ohio, Oklahoma, Oregon, Pennsylvania, Rhode Island, South Carolina, Tennessee, Texas, Utah, Virginia, Washington, and Wisconsin.

PRODUCTS/OPERATIONS

1999 Sales

	$ mil.	% of total
Apparel	1,564	78
Non-apparel	424	21
Other	18	1
Total	**2,006**	**100**

1999 Stores

	No.
Burlington Coat Factory	242
Decelle	8
Luxury Linens	6
Cohoes Fashions	4
Baby Depot	1
Totally 4 Kids	1
Total	**262**

Stores

Baby Depot (accessories, clothes, furniture for babies and toddlers)
Burlington Coat Factory (off-price clothing, accessories, linens, bath items, gifts)
Cohoes Fashions (upscale apparel and accessories)
Decelle (family apparel with an emphasis on youth clothing)
Luxury Linens (linens, bath items, gifts)
Totally 4 Kids (children's clothing, furniture, books, toys)

COMPETITORS

Bed Bath & Beyond	J. C. Penney	Saks Inc.
Belk	Linens 'n Things	Sears
Dayton Hudson	May	Stein Mart
Dillard's	Montgomery	Toys "R" Us
Federated	Ward	TJX
	Ross Stores	Value City

HISTORICAL FINANCIALS & EMPLOYEES

NYSE symbol: BCF FYE: May 31	Annual Growth	1990	1991	1992	1993	1994	1995	1996	1997	1998	1999
Sales ($ mil.)	10.9%	790	887	998	1,198	1,468	1,585	1,592	1,758	1,796	2,006
Net income ($ mil.)	8.0%	24	25	31	43	45	15	29	57	64	48
Income as % of sales	—	3.0%	2.8%	3.1%	3.6%	3.1%	0.9%	1.8%	3.2%	3.5%	2.4%
Earnings per share ($)	8.2%	0.50	0.52	0.65	0.88	0.93	0.30	0.59	1.17	1.34	1.02
Stock price - FY high ($)	—	6.21	5.61	9.59	15.56	23.64	20.62	11.97	16.66	20.50	28.06
Stock price - FY low ($)	—	4.45	3.15	4.82	6.62	10.97	7.08	7.81	8.33	12.39	10.75
Stock price - FY close ($)	14.9%	4.82	5.19	6.76	12.99	14.37	8.64	8.75	16.24	20.06	16.88
P/E - high	—	12	11	15	18	25	69	20	14	15	28
P/E - low	—	9	6	7	8	12	24	13	7	9	11
Dividends per share ($)	—	0.00	0.00	0.00	0.00	0.00	0.00	0.00	0.00	0.02	0.02
Book value per share ($)	11.1%	4.56	5.09	5.68	6.63	7.49	7.88	8.37	9.29	10.97	11.80
Employees	7.8%	10,200	10,300	10,300	12,800	17,000	15,000	17,000	17,600	20,000	20,000

STOCK PRICE HISTORY

HIGH/LOW/CLOSE

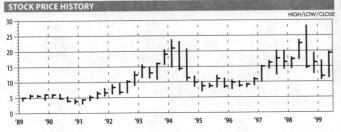

1999 FISCAL YEAR-END

Debt ratio: 8.8%
Return on equity: 8.7%
Cash ($ mil.): 107
Current ratio: 2.04
Long-term debt ($ mil.): 53
No. of shares (mil.): 46
Dividends
  Yield: 0.1%
  Payout: 2.0%
Market value ($ mil.): 784

BURLINGTON INDUSTRIES, INC.

OVERVIEW

In an industry where speedy production is a key to profits, "A stitch in time saves nine" could be Burlington's motto. The Greensboro, North Carolina-based company is one of the top US fabric makers, along with Milliken and Springs Industries. Its apparel fabrics include worsted and worsted wool blends, woven synthetic fabrics, polyesters and polyester blends, synthetic outerwear fabrics, and denims.

Burlington's fabrics for interior furnishing include woven jacquard mattress ticking and woven jacquard and textured fabrics used to make furniture, comforters, and window treatments. Finished interior furnishing products include window coverings, table linens, area and accent rugs, and commercial carpets. The carpet division's tufted synthetic carpet and carpet tiles are sold under the Duracolor and Lees brand names.

By combining new products with quick production, Burlington hopes to stay ahead in the fast-changing fabrics industry, where profits are tied to nimble product development, short production cycles, and the ability to replenish stock quickly. The company has accelerated its expansion in Mexico and plans to spend almost $300 million on facilities there, including a denim plant, a worsted wool plant, and five garment-manufacturing plants. Meanwhile, low-priced imported goods from Asia have forced Burlington to close mills and slash employment in the US.

HISTORY

Spencer Love, who had entered the milling business after WWI, moved his North Carolina cotton mill from Gastonia to Burlington in 1923. To finance the new mill, he convinced the citizens of Burlington to help him sell stock in a new company, Burlington Mills. In 1924, when the mill was struggling with waning demand for its cotton products, Love switched from cotton milling to rayon.

When textile prices dropped during the Depression, many mills went out of business, especially in the North, where labor was more expensive. Burlington bought several of these failed businesses. Corporate headquarters moved to Greensboro in 1935, and Burlington started producing hosiery in 1940. The company continued to expand in the 1950s, buying Pacific Mills and Klopman Mills, and it changed its name to Burlington Industries in 1955.

The company diversified further into consumer products with the acquisitions of Charm Tred Mills, a manufacturer of scatter rugs (1959), and Philadelphia carpet producer James Lees & Company (1960). Burlington bought Globe Furniture in 1966 and made several other acquisitions in the furniture business throughout the 1970s (it subsequently exited that line). William Klopman, son of Klopman Mills' founder, became CEO in 1976. He focused the company on consumer products and clothing fabrics in response to increasing international competition in its traditional textile markets.

By 1980 Burlington was by far the world's largest textile producer. Most of its profits came from consumer products sold under private labels and its own brand names. The company's inability to move beyond the commodity textiles business led to several years of poor profits and a takeover attempt by Montreal-based Dominion Textile. Chairman Frank Greenberg led an LBO, taking the company private in 1987.

The company continued to sell noncore businesses, including its automotive interior carpet and trim-manufacturing subsidiary (C. H. Masland & Sons) in 1991. Burlington went public in 1992.

That year two company employees representing the 20,000-member Employee Stock Ownership Plan (ESOP) sued Burlington management and investment banker Morgan Stanley, alleging breach of fiduciary duty and other violations of the ESOP. (Employees settled the suit in 1996 for $26.5 million — one of the largest settlements in a US retirement-plan suit.)

In 1994 the company sold its decorative prints business, and in 1995 it acquired Bacova Guild, a maker of rugs, welcome mats, and kitchen and bath accessories. It entered a joint venture with Mafatlal Industries, India's #1 textile producer, to make and market denim in India, beginning in 1997.

Burlington closed its struggling knit fabrics division in 1996. In 1997 the firm sold Sedgefield Specialties, its textile chemicals unit, to Sequa. The next year the company kicked its Mexican expansion plans into high gear after shedding its synthetic yarn business. In 1999 Burlington announced it would eliminate 2,900 jobs and close seven plants to slash production of apparel fabrics in the US by 25%. Burlington then agreed to buy a jean-sewing plant in Mexico as it constructed other garment plants there.

Chairman and CEO: George W. Henderson III, age 50, $1,092,100 pay
VC: Abraham B. Stenberg, age 63, $784,617 pay
EVP: Gary P. Welchman, age 55, $408,883 pay
SVP and CFO: Charles E. Peters Jr., age 46, $395,500 pay
SVP Corporate Development and Law: John D. Englar, age 51, $423,667 pay
President, Burlington House Group: John P. Ganley
President, Burlington House Floor Accents: Ralph Grogan
President, Burlington Denim: Bernard J. Leonard
President, Burlington Tailored Fashions: Lawrence F. Himes
President, Textiles Morelos: Michael G. Taylor
EVP, Burlington Sportswear: Kenneth Kunberger
Group VP: George C. Waldrep Jr., age 59
VP and Chief Information Officer: Judith J. Altman, age 40
VP Human Resources and Public Relations: James M. Guin, age 55
VP Investor Relations and Treasurer: Lynn L. Lane, age 47
VP and General Counsel: Robert A. Wicker, age 54
Corporate Secretary and Associate General Counsel: Alice Washington Grogan, age 42
Auditors: Ernst & Young LLP

LOCATIONS

HQ: 3330 W. Friendly Ave., Greensboro, NC 27410
Phone: 336-379-2000   **Fax:** 336-379-4504
Web site: http://www.burlington-ind.com

Burlington Industries operates manufacturing plants in the US and Mexico.

PRODUCTS/OPERATIONS

1998 Sales & Operating Income

	Sales		Operating Income	
	$ mil.	% of total	$ mil.	% of total
Apparel fabric	1,163	58	102	56
Interior furnishings	847	42	81	44
Total	**2,010**	**100**	**183**	**100**

COMPETITORS

Avondale Incorporated
Cone Mills
Culp
Delta Woodside
Dixie Group
DuPont
Dyersburg
Fab Industries
Galey & Lord
Greenwood Mills
Guilford Mills
JPS Industries
Milliken
Mohawk Industries
R. B. Pamplin
Shaw Industries
Springs Industries
Texfi Industries
Thomaston Mills
Unifi
WestPoint Stevens

HISTORICAL FINANCIALS & EMPLOYEES

NYSE symbol: BUR FYE: September 30	Annual Growth	1989	1990	1991	1992	1993	1994	1995	1996	1997	1998
Sales ($ mil.)	(0.9%)	2,181	2,043	1,926	2,066	2,058	2,127	2,209	2,182	2,091	2,010
Net income ($ mil.)	—	(36)	(117)	(39)	(183)	85	95	68	41	59	81
Income as % of sales	—	—	—	—	—	4.1%	4.5%	3.1%	1.9%	2.8%	4.0%
Earnings per share ($)	—	—	—	—	(4.83)	1.25	1.38	1.04	0.64	0.95	1.32
Stock price - FY high ($)	—	—	—	—	15.00	16.88	17.13	13.63	14.88	14.69	18.88
Stock price - FY low ($)	—	—	—	—	10.88	11.00	10.25	9.25	9.88	9.75	8.19
Stock price - FY close ($)	(5.0%)	—	—	—	13.13	14.25	10.50	12.63	9.88	14.00	9.63
P/E - high	—	—	—	—	—	14	12	13	23	15	14
P/E - low	—	—	—	—	—	9	7	9	15	10	6
Dividends per share ($)	—	—	—	—	0.00	0.00	0.00	0.00	0.00	0.00	0.00
Book value per share ($)	9.7%	—	—	—	6.96	8.22	8.51	9.45	9.46	10.57	12.15
Employees	(4.1%)	27,500	28,000	24,000	23,400	23,600	23,800	22,500	21,000	20,100	18,900

STOCK PRICE HISTORY

HIGH/LOW/CLOSE

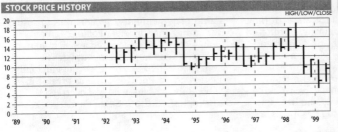

1998 FISCAL YEAR-END

Debt ratio: 53.4%
Return on equity: 11.5%
Cash ($ mil.): 18
Current ratio: 2.97
Long-term debt ($ mil.): 802
No. of shares (mil.): 58
Dividends
  Yield: —
  Payout: —
Market value ($ mil.): 555

BURLINGTON NORTHERN SANTA FE

OVERVIEW

It's true that Santa leaves trains as gifts for little boys, but Burlington Northern Santa Fe (BNSF) is a big boy now, and has to buy them. Based in Fort Worth, Texas, BNSF is purchasing billions of dollars of locomotives and upgrading track and yard facilities.

The second-largest US railroad behind Union Pacific, BNSF makes tracks through 28 states in the West, Midwest, and Sunbelt regions of the US and in two Canadian provinces. Trackage rights (which allow BNSF to operate its trains on another railroad's tracks) account for almost 8,000 miles of BNSF's 34,000-mile system. BNSF also partners with rival Union

Pacific to operate joint dispatching centers covering the Gulf Coast, Southern California, and Wyoming's Powder River Basin areas. The two are opening another joint center in Kansas City, Missouri.

BNSF transports a variety of manufacturing, agricultural, and natural resource commodities (forest products, metals, and minerals), chemicals, consumer and food products, and motor vehicles and automotive parts. Coal shipping accounts for 25% of the company's sales, and intermodal services (shipping by a combination of ship, train, or truck) contribute 28%.

HISTORY

Burlington Northern (BN) was largely created by James Hill, who bought the St. Paul & Pacific Railroad in Minnesota in 1878. By 1893 Hill had completed the Great Northern Railway, extending from St. Paul to Seattle. The next year he gained control of Northern Pacific (chartered in 1864), which had been built between Minnesota and Washington State. In 1901, with J.P. Morgan's help, Hill acquired the Chicago, Burlington & Quincy (Burlington), whose routes included Chicago-St. Paul and Billings, Montana-Denver-Fort Worth, Texas-Houston. The Spokane, Portland & Seattle Railway (SP&S), completed in 1908, gave Great Northern an entrance to Oregon.

Hill intended to merge Great Northern, Northern Pacific, SP&S, and Burlington under his Morgan-backed Northern Securities Company, but in 1904 the Supreme Court found that Northern Securities had violated the Sherman Antitrust Act. The holding company was dissolved, but Hill controlled the individual railroads until he died in 1916. Hill's railroads produced well-known passenger trains: Great Northern's Empire Builder (now operated by Amtrak) began service in 1929, and in 1934 Burlington Zephyr was the nation's first streamlined passenger diesel.

After years of deliberation, the Interstate Commerce Commission allowed Great Northern and Northern Pacific to merge in 1970, along with jointly owned subsidiaries Burlington and SP&S. The new company, Burlington Northern (BN), acquired the St. Louis-San Francisco Railway in 1980, adding more than 4,650 miles to its rail network.

The company formed Burlington Motor Carriers (BMC) in 1985 to manage five trucking companies it had acquired. It sold BMC in 1988 and spun off Burlington Resources, a

holding company for its nonrailroad businesses (including oil, minerals, and property). In 1991 BN formed a rail-barge joint venture with Mexican industrial firm Grupo Protexa.

A fiery collision between a BN freight train and a Union Pacific (UP) freight in 1995 propelled the rivals to begin joint testing of global positioning satellites for guiding trains. Besides improving safety, the two hoped to end rail bottlenecks.

That year BN and Santa Fe Pacific (SFP), founded in 1859, formed Burlington Northern Santa Fe in a $4 billion merger. BN's strength lay in transporting manufacturing, agricultural, and natural resource commodities, and SFP specialized in intermodal shipping (combining train, truck, and ship). SFP (originally the Atchison, Topeka & Santa Fe) had taken the name Santa Fe Pacific in 1989 after its forced sale of Southern Pacific.

The new BNSF acquired Washington Central Railroad in 1996, adding a third connection between central Washington State and the Pacific Coast. In 1997 customers protested when BNSF couldn't come up with enough cars and locomotives for grain shipping. A year later UP was in trouble with clogged rail lines: BNSF opened a joint dispatching center in Houston with UP to help unsnarl traffic. The effort proved successful, and in 1999 BNSF and UP began to combine dispatching in Southern California; the Kansas City, Missouri area; and Wyoming's Powder River Basin.

In 1999 BNSF announced a $2.5 billion capital improvement program, but later decided to trim spending to $2.28 billion and cut 1,400 jobs. Matthew Rose took over as president, while Robert Krebs, who had overseen the Burlington Northern-Santa Fe merger, remained as chairman and CEO.

Chairman and CEO: Robert D. Krebs, age 56,
$565,961 pay (prior to title change)
President and COO: Matthew K. Rose, age 39,
$434,579 pay (prior to promotion)
EVP and Chief Marketing Officer: Charles L. Schultz,
age 51, $418,926 pay (prior to promotion)
SVP and CFO: Denis E. Springer, age 53, $637,550 pay
SVP Operations: Carl Ice
SVP Law and Chief of Staff: Jeffrey R. Moreland, age 54
VP Litigation: Gary L. Crosby
VP Government Relations: A. R. "Skip" Endres Jr.
VP and Chief Information Officer: Bruce E. Freeman
VP Human Resources: Ricki Gardner
VP and Controller: Thomas N. Hund, age 45
VP Investor Relations and Corporate Secretary:
Marsha K. Morgan
VP Finance and Treasurer: Patrick J. Ottensmeyer
VP Corporate Relations: Richard A. Russack
VP and General Counsel: Richard E. Weicher
VP and General Tax Counsel: Daniel J. Westerbeck
Auditors: PricewaterhouseCoopers LLP

LOCATIONS

HQ: Burlington Northern Santa Fe Corporation,
2650 Lou Menk Dr., 2nd Fl.,
Fort Worth, TX 76131-2830
Phone: 817-333-2000   **Fax:** 817-352-7171
Web site: http://www.bnsf.com

Burlington Northern Santa Fe operates in 28 US states
and in two Canadian provinces.

PRODUCTS/OPERATIONS

1998 Sales

	$ mil.	% of total
Intermodal	2,469	28
Coal	2,239	25
Agricultural commodities	1,077	12
Chemicals	841	10
Metals & minerals	757	8
Forest products	598	7
Consumer goods	553	6
Automotive	388	4
Other	19	—
Total	**8,941**	**100**

COMPETITORS

APL
Canadian National Railway
Canadian Pacific
CNF Transportation
CSX
J. B. Hunt
Landstar System
Norfolk Southern
Schneider National
Union Pacific
U.S. Xpress
Werner

HISTORICAL FINANCIALS & EMPLOYEES

NYSE symbol: BNI FYE: December 31	Annual Growth	1989	1990	1991	1992	1993	1994	1995	1996	1997	1998
Sales ($ mil.)	7.6%	4,606	4,674	4,559	4,630	4,699	4,995	6,183	8,187	8,413	8,941
Net income ($ mil.)	18.9%	243	222	(306)	299	296	426	92	889	885	1,155
Income as % of sales	—	5.3%	4.7%	—	6.5%	6.3%	8.5%	1.5%	10.9%	10.5%	12.9%
Earnings per share ($)	122.7%	—	—	—	—	—	—	0.22	1.91	1.88	2.43
Stock price - FY high ($)	—	—	—	—	—	—	—	28.22	30.01	33.61	35.67
Stock price - FY low ($)	—	—	—	—	—	—	—	23.48	24.48	23.39	26.88
Stock price - FY close ($)	9.7%	—	—	—	—	—	—	25.97	28.76	30.95	34.25
P/E - high	—	—	—	—	—	—	—	128	16	18	15
P/E - low	—	—	—	—	—	—	—	107	13	12	11
Dividends per share ($)	—	—	—	—	—	—	—	0.00	0.40	0.40	0.42
Book value per share ($)	13.8%	—	—	—	—	—	—	11.21	12.93	14.51	16.52
Employees	3.0%	32,900	32,905	31,760	31,204	30,502	30,711	45,500	43,000	44,500	42,900

STOCK PRICE HISTORY

HIGH/LOW/CLOSE

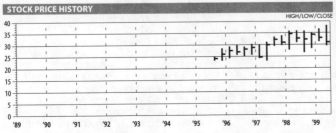

1998 FISCAL YEAR-END

Debt ratio: 40.0%
Return on equity: 14.9%
Cash ($ mil.): 25
Current ratio: 0.55
Long-term debt ($ mil.): 5,188
No. of shares (mil.): 470
Dividends
  Yield: 1.2%
  Payout: 17.3%
Market value ($ mil.): 16,114

BURNS INTERNATIONAL SERVICES

OVERVIEW

They're packin' heat, patrolling halls, and riding shotgun while on the alert for desperadoes — Burns International Services provides that warm sense of security. Chicago-based Burns International, formerly Borg-Warner Security, provides security guards (more than 65,000 on staff), background screening, investigative services, nuclear utility security, and other security services to about 14,000 clients in Canada, Colombia, Mexico, the UK, and the US. The firm's brand names include Burns and Globe. Its 49%-owned Loomis, Fargo unit also provides armored transport services.

A strong brand name is a company's best security. In recognition of this, Burns has become quite the name-dropper: Besides changing its corporate name, Burns International has agreed to cede the Wells Fargo trade name to the bank and is consolidating services under the Burns name. These actions follow recent efforts by the firm to focus on physical security; it has shed Pony Express (courier service) and Wells Fargo Alarm (electronic security). Meanwhile, Burns has formed a strategic alliance with Wells Fargo Alarm's buyer, Tyco International, to provide electronic security services.

Burns International applied the proceeds of its sales to reducing debt, the legacy of a 1987 leveraged buyout. Merrill Lynch-affiliated partnerships that executed the LBO still own part of the company but plan to sell their remaining shares.

HISTORY

Burns International Services began as Borg-Warner, the product of a 1928 merger of four Chicago auto parts companies. The firm diversified over the next 50 years, buying agricultural equipment, steel, air-conditioning and refrigeration, and furniture interests. It entered the security business in 1977 when it acquired Baker Industries, a provider of armored car and security services under the Wells Fargo and Pony Express names.

Wells Fargo had been founded in 1852 by American Express executives Henry Wells and William Fargo as a stagecoach delivery company serving the wild West. In 1905 it separated its banking and delivery operations (creating San Francisco's Wells Fargo Bank).

Pony Express jumped out of the gate in 1858, when William Russell and other horseback riders launched the short-lived mail route between Missouri and California. Wells Fargo operated the Salt Lake City-to-San Francisco leg of the route. Transcontinental telegraph lines put the Pony to pasture in 1861, and both the Pony Express and Wells Fargo trademarks reverted to American Express until Baker Industries bought them in 1967.

Between 1977 and 1991 Borg-Warner acquired 72 protective-services companies while maintaining its automotive lines and adding chemical and credit services. In 1982 it bought security guard firm Burns International Security Services. Burns International had been founded in 1910 by William Burns, a famous Chicago investigator and the first head of the FBI's predecessor agency.

In 1987 Borg-Warner was threatened with a takeover by Irwin Jacobs and Samuel Heyman until Merrill Lynch Capital Partners organized an LBO and took the company private, assuming $4.5 billion in debt. Saddled by the huge debt, Borg-Warner sold virtually all its businesses to GE in 1988 and its Chilton credit unit to TRW in 1989. It kept its automotive and security operations and continued making acquisitions, including guard firm Security Bureau in 1992.

The company went public again as Borg-Warner Security in 1993 and spun off Borg-Warner Automotive. The firm won a high-profile assignment to provide security services at the 1996 Summer Olympics in Atlanta, but its image took a hit when a bomb exploded at an outdoor concert there. In 1997 the company merged its Wells Fargo armored transport unit with Loomis Armored (owned by buyout firm Wingate Partners). Borg-Warner Security received 49% of the resulting Loomis, Fargo & Co.

Borg-Warner Security moved forward with a plan to focus on physical security and improve its balance sheet. It sold the struggling Pony Express courier to Mustang Holdings in 1998 and its Wells Fargo Alarm electronic security company to ADT's owner, Tyco International.

In 1999 former United Air Lines president John Edwardson became CEO. Also that year, the bank Wells Fargo had grown increasingly protective of its brand name, so Borg-Warner agreed to drop the Wells Fargo brand by 2001. It changed its name to Burns International Services and announced plans to consolidate its offerings under the Burns brand name. The firm also bought back nearly half of the shares owned by the Merrill Lynch LBO partnerships.

Chairman, President and CEO: John A. Edwardson, age 49
EVP, Sales and Marketing: James F. McNulty, age 48
SVP: John D. O'Brien, age 56, $604,000 pay
VP, Finance and CFO: Timothy M. Wood, age 51, $542,000 pay
VP, General Counsel, and Secretary: Robert E. T. Lackey, age 50, $314,200 pay
VP, Human Resources: Nancy E. Kittle
VP, Risk Management: Craig J. Bollinger
Treasurer: Brian S. Cooper
Director, Corporate Affairs: Anne B. Ireland
Director, Investor Relations: Jeff Cartwright
Manager, Corporate Communications: Lynne Glovka
Auditors: Deloitte & Touche LLP

LOCATIONS

HQ: 200 S. Michigan Ave., Chicago, IL 60604
Phone: 312-322-8500   **Fax:** 312-322-8704
Web site: http://www.bwsc.com

Burns International Services operates in Canada, Colombia, Mexico, the UK, and the US.

1998 Sales

	$ mil.	% of total
US	1,202	91
Other countries	121	9
Total	**1,323**	**100**

PRODUCTS/OPERATIONS

Selected Services
Armored transport services
Aviation security services
Background screening
Contract staffing services
Investigative services
Nuclear utility security
Physical security personnel and patrol services
Safety and security compliance audits
Telecommunications/MIS security

Selected Subsidiaries
Borg-Warner Protective Services Corporation
  Borg-Warner Information Services, Inc.
  Burns International Security Services, Inc.
  Wells Fargo Guard Services, Inc.
BW-Canadian Guard Corporation
BW-Colombia Guard Corporation
BW-U.K. Guard Corporation
Globe Aviation Services Corporation
Loomis, Fargo & Co. (49%)

COMPETITORS

American Protective
American Security
Armored Transport
Command Security
International Total Services
Pinkerton's
Pittston Brink's
Securicor
Wackenhut

HISTORICAL FINANCIALS & EMPLOYEES

NYSE symbol: BOR FYE: December 31	Annual Growth	1989	1990	1991	1992	1993	1994	1995	1996	1997	1998
Sales ($ mil.)	(5.6%)	2,216	2,340	1,555	1,621	1,765	1,793	1,863	1,711	1,548	1,323
Net income ($ mil.)	(2.3%)	36	12	11	39	(243)	13	1	(15)	19	29
Income as % of sales	—	1.6%	0.5%	0.7%	2.4%	—	0.7%	0.1%	—	1.2%	2.2%
Earnings per share ($)	—	—	—	—	—	(10.65)	0.59	0.05	(0.62)	0.79	1.21
Stock price – FY high ($)	—	—	—	—	—	22.88	22.00	13.00	13.13	19.75	24.75
Stock price – FY low ($)	—	—	—	—	—	18.00	8.25	5.50	8.25	10.13	13.06
Stock price – FY close ($)	(1.8%)	—	—	—	—	20.50	9.75	12.50	10.75	17.63	18.75
P/E – high	—	—	—	—	—	—	37	260	—	25	20
P/E – low	—	—	—	—	—	—	14	110	—	13	11
Dividends per share ($)	—	—	—	—	—	0.00	0.00	0.00	0.00	0.00	0.00
Book value per share ($)	30.6%	—	—	—	—	1.21	2.17	2.42	2.00	3.05	4.59
Employees	(0.3%)	75,300	76,800	74,500	78,350	87,000	91,698	96,974	73,000	68,000	73,000

STOCK PRICE HISTORY

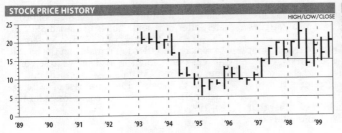

HIGH/LOW/CLOSE

1998 FISCAL YEAR-END

Debt ratio: 56.2%
Return on equity: 30.0%
Cash ($ mil.): 106
Current ratio: 1.74
Long-term debt ($ mil.): 124
No. of shares (mil.): 21
Dividends
  Yield: —
  Payout: —
Market value ($ mil.): 396

CABLETRON SYSTEMS, INC.

OVERVIEW

Cabletron Systems will have to switch *and* fight if it wants to recapture its share of the networking hardware market. The Rochester, New Hampshire-based company makes switches and other devices that transfer data between computers and networks. A portion of its sales also comes from software, such as its SPECTRUM Enterprise Manager for network administration, as well as consulting, project management, and other ancillary services. Customers include government agencies (15% of sales), manufacturers, banks, and universities.

Cabletron climbed the network equipment ladder by combining product innovation (it produced one of the first network hubs), aggressive sales, and a no-frills, zero-tolerance corporate culture. But the high-growth market has attracted big players — traditional industry leaders Cisco and 3Com have been joined by such behemoths as Lucent, Alcatel, Intel, and Nortel Networks. To hold on to its business, Cabletron is using acquisitions to expand, especially into newer networking technologies. Its purchases include the networking unit of Digital Equipment (now Compaq) and switch maker NetVantage. Meanwhile, Cabletron itself remains the subject of takeover rumors.

Director Craig Benson, Cabletron's cofounder and former CEO, owns 11% of the company.

HISTORY

Cabletron got its start in 1983 when Robert Levine, a salesman for his father's cable company, needed 1,000 feet of cable for a customer's computer network. He could only find rolls of 10,000 feet. Levine's friend Craig Benson suggested they cut the cable and sell short segments to business associates. By guaranteeing delivery within 48 hours (the industry norm was 90 days), they created a niche. A year later the company had 10 part-time employees and $100,000 in sales.

The two-man garage startup soon began installing networks, then designing networking equipment. The company was known for parsimony; its office furniture was secondhand and its boardrooms had no chairs (which undoubtedly discouraged long meetings).

Rapid growth began in 1988 with the release of an intelligent wiring hub used to simplify network installation and aid in troubleshooting and modification. Cabletron went public in 1989. It introduced network management software in 1990 and an adapter that let Macintosh users connect to networks in 1992. It also introduced the industry's first bridge that linked remote networks.

Levine's macho bluster (he sometimes drove a tank around Rochester's streets) created a company culture steeped in conflict. To rally employees, Levine dressed in combat fatigues or leather biker duds.

To counter the 1994 merger of rivals Synoptics and Wellfleet (later Bay Networks), Cabletron signed an aggressive marketing deal with Cisco. A licensing disagreement turned the partners into archrivals.

Cabletron's release in 1995 of switches that connected four times as many computers on a network increased the speed of its products more than fivefold. That year the company also began buying complementary technologies, such as the high-speed network switch operations of Standard Microsystems (1995), and networking connector maker ZeitNet and net access developer Netlink (1996). Also in 1996 the company unveiled software for managing virtual networks, and letting users oversee switches via the Web.

In 1997 Levine resigned as CEO and was replaced by former NYNEX executive Don Reed. To boost its product offerings and international sales, in 1998 the company bought Digital Equipment's (now part of Compaq) computer network equipment business, and the 75% of switch router maker Yago Systems that it didn't already own. Benson took over as president and CEO that year when Reed resigned after just eight months on the job. Acquisition-related charges led to a loss for fiscal 1998.

To recover, Cabletron in 1999 began trimming its workforce and selling certain manufacturing assets to contract manufacturer Celestica. That year Cabletron restated its earnings back to fiscal 1997 following a review by the SEC of the company's acquisition-related accounting. Benson resigned immediately afterward, and Cabletron named SVP Piyush Patel, formerly CEO of Yago Systems, to replace him (Benson remains on the board). Also in 1999 Cabletron made plans to sell or spin off its software business. Acquisitions, such as Cabletron's 1998 purchase of switch maker NetVantage, helped cause losses for fiscal 1999.

Chairman, President, and CEO: Piyush Patel, age 43
COO: Romulus Pereira
EVP, Finance and CFO: David J. Kirkpatrick, age 47, $366,837 pay
EVP, Global Services and Support: Earle Humphreys, age 52, $316,212 pay
EVP, North and South American Sales: Carl Boisvert, age 41, $337,654 pay
EVP, Software: Michael Skubisz, age 32
SVP and Legal Counsel: Eric Jaeger, age 36
SVP, Human Resources: Linda Pepin, age 46
President, Asia/Pacific: Gary Workman
President, European Relations: Joe Solari
Chief Information Officer: Henry Fiallo, age 46
Auditors: KPMG LLP

LOCATIONS

HQ: 35 Industrial Way, Rochester, NH 03867
Phone: 603-332-9400   **Fax:** 603-332-8007
Web site: http://www.cabletron.com

Cabletron Systems has operations in Argentina, Australia, Brazil, Canada, Chile, China, Colombia, the Czech Republic, France, Germany, Hong Kong, India, Ireland, Italy, Japan, Malaysia, Mexico, the Netherlands, Singapore, South Korea, Spain, Sweden, Switzerland, the UK, the US, and Venezuela.

1999 Sales

	$ mil.	% of total
US	829	59
Europe	430	30
Pacific Rim	114	8
Other regions	38	3
Total	**1,411**	**100**

PRODUCTS/OPERATIONS

1999 Sales

	$ mil.	% of total
Switched products	777	55
Shared media products	170	12
Software, services & other	464	33
Total	**1,411**	**100**

Products

Bandwidth-heavy devices (ATM SmartSwitch)
Internet Security firewalls (with Nokia)
Network management tools
  (SPECTRUM Enterprise Manager)
Office/home network switches
  (LAN SmartSwitch, SmartSTACK)
Remote access switches
Routers (SmartSwitch)

Services

Certification and documentation
Consulting & Training
Maintenance
Project planning, design, and management
Testing and performance analysis

COMPETITORS

3Com	Lucent
Alcatel	Madge Networks
Cisco Systems	Motorola
Computer Associates	MRV Communications
Datapoint	Network Associates
Digi International	Newbridge Networks
D-Link	Nokia
Ericsson	Nortel Networks
FORE Systems	Novell
GVC	Siemens
Intel	

HISTORICAL FINANCIALS & EMPLOYEES

NYSE symbol: CS FYE: February 28	Annual Growth	1990	1991	1992	1993	1994	1995	1996	1997	1998	1999
Sales ($ mil.)	33.5%	105	181	291	418	598	811	1,070	1,407	1,377	1,411
Net income ($ mil.)	—	23	36	58	84	119	162	164	222	(127)	(245)
Income as % of sales	—	21.5%	19.9%	20.0%	20.0%	19.9%	20.0%	15.4%	15.8%	—	—
Earnings per share ($)	—	0.18	0.27	0.42	0.60	0.81	1.07	0.93	1.40	(0.81)	(1.47)
Stock price - FY high ($)	—	3.35	7.90	13.18	18.45	25.25	26.50	43.88	43.56	46.50	17.13
Stock price - FY low ($)	—	1.38	2.13	6.05	8.43	15.30	16.53	19.44	26.50	12.63	6.63
Stock price - FY close ($)	15.7%	2.18	7.38	12.15	15.63	25.00	19.81	37.56	30.13	15.50	8.13
P/E - high	—	19	29	31	31	31	25	47	31	—	—
P/E - low	—	8	8	14	14	19	15	21	19	—	—
Dividends per share ($)	—	0.00	0.00	0.00	0.00	0.00	0.00	0.00	0.00	0.00	0.00
Book value per share ($)	32.2%	0.51	1.01	1.45	2.04	2.97	4.11	5.38	6.92	6.25	6.32
Employees	19.2%	1,223	1,825	2,032	2,625	3,663	4,970	5,377	6,607	6,887	5,951

STOCK PRICE HISTORY

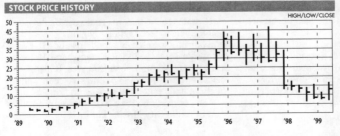
HIGH/LOW/CLOSE

1999 FISCAL YEAR-END

Debt ratio: 0.0%
Return on equity: —
Cash ($ mil.): 159
Current ratio: 1.79
Long-term debt ($ mil.): —
No. of shares (mil.): 172
Dividends
  Yield: —
  Payout: —
Market value ($ mil.): 1,402

CABLEVISION SYSTEMS

OVERVIEW

What's the best thing to do when you're in the city that never sleeps? Stay up and watch TV! Bethpage, New York-based Cablevision Systems provides cable TV to about 3.4 million subscribers in New York City (about 80% of subscribers), Boston, and Cleveland.

Prop your eyes open because Cablevision has a remote control-ful of entertainment options. Rainbow Media Holdings (25%-owned by NBC) owns several cable channels, including American Movie Classics and Bravo. Rainbow's sports business (40%-owned by Fox Sports Networks) comprises regional sports networks and the Madison Square Garden company, which holds the famous NYC arena, the New York Knicks, the New York Rangers, and Radio City Music Hall. Cablevision's Clearview Cinema Group operates about 65 theaters in Connecticut, New Jersey, New York, and Pennsylvania.

Besides the convergence of cable, entertainment, and sports, Cablevision has been pursuing another kind of convergence — bringing together cable TV, phone, and PCs. It owns electronics retailer Nobody Beats The Wiz and competitive local-exchange carrier Lightpath; it also operates a residential phone service over its Long Island cable network.

AT&T Broadband & Internet Services owns 33% of Cablevision's stock. However, chairman and founder Charles Dolan and his family (including son James Dolan, the CEO) control 80% of the votes.

HISTORY

In 1954 Charles Dolan helped form Sterling Manhattan Cable, which won the cable TV franchise for Lower Manhattan in 1965. It began broadcasting pro basketball and hockey, courtesy of Madison Square Garden (MSG), in 1967. In 1970 Dolan started Home Box Office (HBO), the first nationwide pay-TV channel, and hired Gerald Levin (now Time Warner CEO) to run it.

Dolan took the company public as Sterling Communications; its partner, media giant Time (now part of Time Warner), came to own 80% of Sterling. Costs mounted, however, and in 1973 Time liquidated Sterling (but kept HBO).

Dolan bought back the New York franchises and formed Long Island Cable Communications Development. He changed its name to Cablevision and expanded around New York and Chicago. In 1980 Cablevision formed Rainbow Programming, which soon included the American Movie Classics and Bravo channels; in 1983 it launched the popular SportsChannel (now Fox Sports New York). Cablevision went public in 1986. It bought two Connecticut cable systems that year and one in Massachusetts the next.

In 1989 Cablevision helped NBC launch the CNBC cable network but sold its interest to NBC in 1991. Cablevision started The Independent Film Channel in 1994 and also began offering cable phone service to businesses on Long Island — two years before the Telecommunications Act was passed. Subsidiary Cablevision Lightpath, a competitive local-exchange carrier, signed a groundbreaking co-carrier agreement with Baby Bell NYNEX (now part of Bell Atlantic) in 1995, allowing it to connect to the NYNEX network.

To get a grip on NYC entertainment, Cablevision partnered with ITT in 1995 to buy MSG, which included the arena, the New York Knicks, the New York Rangers, and the MSG Network (with about 5 million subscribers). Three years later ITT had been bought out and was no more (acquired by Starwood).

Meanwhile, on-again, off-again merger talks with U S WEST Media stalled over Dolan's high asking price. In late 1996 Charles' son, James Dolan, became CEO.

In 1997 Cablevision began dumping cable holdings, which were spread over 19 states, to focus on its New York, New Jersey, and Connecticut operations and the upgrading of its cable infrastructure for Internet and phone services. It began a series of swaps with TCI in order to cluster its cable systems. (As a result, TCI, which had been bought by AT&T, held 33% of Cablevision stock by 1999.)

Cablevision sold 40% of Rainbow Media's regional sports business to Fox/Liberty (now Fox Sports Networks, owned by News Corp.) to create a rival to Disney's ESPN. Fox/Liberty got 40% of MSG, and Cablevision got Fox Sports Net, a chain of 22 regional sports networks. MSG also bought Radio City Entertainment (and the famed Rockettes) in 1997.

In early 1998 the company sold cable systems in 10 states to Mediacom. That year Cablevision bought beleaguered retailer Nobody Beats The Wiz (aiming to sell cable modems and HDTV alongside TVs), Clearview Cinema, and 16 New York theaters from Loews Cineplex. It also began offering business phone service in Connecticut and residential service on Long Island.

The company began a $70 million renovation of Radio City Music Hall in 1999.

OFFICERS

Chairman: Charles F. Dolan, age 72, $2,060,000 pay
VC: William J. Bell, $2,600,000 pay
President and CEO: James L. Dolan, age 43, $3,150,000 pay
EVP, Communications, Government, and Public Affairs: Sheila A. Mahony, age 57
EVP, Finance and Controller: Andrew B. Rosengard, age 41
EVP, General Counsel, and Secretary: Robert S. Lemle, age 46, $1,525,000 pay
EVP, Planning and Operations: Margaret A. Albergo, age 45
SVP and Chief Information Officer: Thomas C. Dolan, age 46
SVP, Regional News: Patrick F. Dolan, age 48
President and CEO, Madison Square Garden: David W. Checketts
President and CEO, Rainbow Media Holdings: Joshua W. Sapan
President and CEO, The Wiz: Bill Marginson
President, Product Management and Marketing: Michael Bair
Director, Human Resources: Harvey Benenson
President, Telecommunications Services: Joseph Azznara
Auditors: KPMG LLP

LOCATIONS

HQ: 1111 Stewart Ave., Bethpage, NY 11714
Phone: 516-803-2300   **Fax:** 516-803-2273
Web site: http://www.cablevision.com

Cablevision Systems provides cable TV service in and around Boston, Cleveland, and New York City. It operates movie theaters in Connecticut, New Jersey, New York, and Pennsylvania.

PRODUCTS/OPERATIONS

1998 Sales

	$ mil.	% of total
Telecommunications services	1,889	56
Rainbow Media	1,008	30
Retail electronics	464	13
Other	7	1
Adjustments	(103)	—
Total	**3,265**	**100**

Selected Operations

Cable Holdings
Rainbow Media Holdings Inc.

Consumer Electronics
Nobody Beats The Wiz (consumer electronics retailer)

Telephone Holdings
Cablevision Lightpath Inc. (local telephone service)

Rainbow Media Entertainment and Sports Operations: Madison Square Garden Properties
Fox Sports New York (NYC regional sports programming)
Madison Square Garden, L.P. (96.3%)
  New York Knickerbockers (men's basketball)
  New York Rangers (men's hockey)
  Radio City Music Entertainment

COMPETITORS

Adelphia Communications	Cox Communications
America Online	DIRECTV
AT&T Broadband &	MediaOne Group
Internet Services	NBC
Bell Atlantic	RCN
CBS	Tandy
Circuit City	Time Warner
Comcast	Viacom
CompUSA	Walt Disney

HISTORICAL FINANCIALS & EMPLOYEES

AMEX symbol: CVC FYE: December 31	Annual Growth	1989	1990	1991	1992	1993	1994	1995	1996	1997	1998
Sales ($ mil.)	23.4%	493	563	603	573	667	837	1,078	1,315	1,949	3,265
Net income ($ mil.)	—	(154)	(271)	(227)	(251)	(247)	(315)	(318)	(332)	137	(449)
Income as % of sales	—	—	—	—	—	—	—	—	—	7.0%	—
Earnings per share ($)	—	(1.78)	(3.09)	(2.58)	(2.80)	(2.71)	(3.43)	(3.55)	(4.63)	(0.12)	(3.16)
Stock price - FY high ($)	—	11.81	9.59	8.88	9.13	18.00	16.97	17.44	15.09	24.56	50.25
Stock price - FY low ($)	—	7.44	2.47	3.09	6.22	7.34	9.75	12.19	6.25	6.78	21.78
Stock price - FY close ($)	20.6%	9.28	3.88	8.75	8.75	16.97	12.63	13.56	7.66	23.94	50.13
P/E - high	—	—	—	—	—	—	—	—	—	—	—
P/E - low	—	—	—	—	—	—	—	—	—	—	—
Dividends per share ($)	—	0.00	0.00	0.00	0.00	0.00	0.00	0.00	0.00	0.00	0.00
Book value per share ($)	—	(4.83)	(7.84)	(10.37)	(13.82)	(16.19)	(19.27)	(19.15)	(23.90)	(23.72)	(17.24)
Employees	18.6%	3,400	2,960	3,392	3,444	3,636	4,698	5,801	7,118	15,020	15,824

STOCK PRICE HISTORY

HIGH/LOW/CLOSE

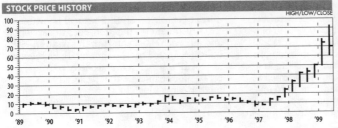

1998 FISCAL YEAR-END

Debt ratio: 100.0%
Return on equity: —
Cash ($ mil.): 174
Current ratio: 0.59
Long-term debt ($ mil.): 5,358
No. of shares (mil.): 151
Dividends
  Yield: —
  Payout: —
Market value ($ mil.): 7,594

CALPERS

California's public sector retirees already have a place in the sun; CalPERS gives them the money to enjoy it.

The California Public Employees' Retirement System (CalPERS), based in Sacramento, is the largest public pension system in the US, with about $150 billion in assets. It manages retirement and health plans for 2,500 government agencies representing more than a million California employees and retirees and their beneficiaries. CalPERS has established itself as a powerful negotiator for services such as insurance; rates established by CalPERS serve as a benchmark for other employers.

Less than 20% of revenues come from employee contributions; most come from the funds' investments. Because of its size, CalPERS has immense power in the investment world and is one of the most active institutional investors in the US on issues such as corporate performance and executive compensation; it even puts out a high-profile list each year of the worst-performing US companies.

CalPERS is governed by a 13-member board (six elected, three appointed, and four designated). Designated members include the director of the state's Department of Personnel Administration, the state controller, the state treasurer, and a member of the State Personnel Board.

HISTORY

Legislation established CalPERS in 1931 to administer a pension fund for state employees. By the 1940s the system allowed other public agencies and some school employees to contract for retirement benefits.

When the Public Employees' Medical & Hospital Care Act was passed in 1962, CalPERS began providing health insurance for members. The fund was managed internally and very conservatively with little exposure to stocks. Despite its slow asset growth, the state saw it as a source of funds to meet its own cash shortfalls.

CalPERS began its aggressive involvement in corporate governance issues in the mid-1980s, when California treasurer Jesse Unruh became outraged by various corporate greenmail schemes. Unruh hired Dale Hanson (formerly with the Wisconsin pension board) as CEO in 1987; under Hanson, CalPERS led the movement to force corporations to be accountable to institutional investors.

In the late 1980s CalPERS moved into real estate and the Japanese stock market. When both crashed around 1990, Hanson came under pressure. CalPERS was twice forced to take major write-downs for its real estate holdings. CalPERS turned to expensive outside fund managers, but its investment performance deteriorated and member services suffered.

Legislation passed in 1990 allowed CalPERS to offer long-term health insurance. In 1991 Governor Pete Wilson tried to take $1.6 billion from CalPERS to help the state meet its budget shortfall. This resulted in legislation preventing future raids. CalPERS made its first direct investment in 1993 when it formed a partnership with energy giant Enron to invest in gas pipelines and similar projects.

With interest rates rising and the bond market crashing, in 1994 CalPERS suffered its worst performance in a decade. That year Hanson resigned amid criticism that his focus on corporate governance had interfered with his running CalPERS. The system moved to an indexing management strategy.

After Hanson left, CalPERS tried being less confrontational with the corporations in which it invested; the pension plan had gained little in terms of better performance. CalPERS created a separate office to handle investor issues and launched an International Corporate Governance Program. The next year, because of its activism, CalPERS was disinvited from joining the newest investment pool formed by Kohlberg Kravis Roberts & Co.

In 1996 the system partnered with the Asian Development Bank to invest in the Asia/Pacific region. The next year the organization took a major hit in the Asian financial crisis but used the downturn as an opportunity to expand its position there in undervalued stocks. In 1998 CalPERS pressured international companies to adopt more transparent financial reporting methods. That year board member and State Controller Kathleen Connell, up for re-election, sued CalPERS because it forbid current and would-be trustees from donating to political campaigns; the rule was rescinded because CalPERS had not followed the proper procedures to enact it. CalPERS teamed up with REIT Burnham Pacific Properties to develop and manage retail centers in the West. In 1999 CalPERS agreed to a premium rate increase of almost 10% which portends hefty rate increases for businesses that lack CalPERS mighty bargaining clout.

OFFICERS

President of the Board: William Dale Crist
Vice President of the Board: Charles P. Valdez
CEO: James E. Burton
Deputy Executive Officer: James H. Gomez
Assistant Executive Officer, Investment Operations: Robert Aguallo
Assistant Executive Officer, Financial and Administration Services: Vincent P. Brown
Assistant Executive Officer, Member and Benefit Services: Barbara D. Hegdal
Assistant Executive Officer, Governmental Affairs, Planning, and Research: Robert D. Walton
Chief, Information Technology Services Division: Jack Corrie
Chief, Office of Public Affairs: Patricia K. Macht
Chief Human Resources: Tom Pettey
Chief Investment Officer: Sheryl Pressler
Chief Actuary: Ronald L. Seeling
General Counsel: Kayla J. Gillan
Deputy General Counsel: Linda K. McAtee
Principal Investment Officer, Alternative Investments and Private Equity: Richard J. Hayes
Health Benefits Services: Margaret T. Stanley
Auditors: PricewaterhouseCoopers LLP

LOCATIONS

HQ: California Public Employees' Retirement System, Lincoln Plaza, 400 P St., Sacramento, CA 95814
Phone: 916-326-3829 **Fax:** 916-326-3410
Web site: http://www.calpers.ca.gov

PRODUCTS/OPERATIONS

1998 Assets

	$ mil.	% of total
Cash & equivalents	14,266	9
Treasury & agency securities	5,190	3
Corporate bonds	11,696	8
International bonds	4,786	3
Stocks	92,502	59
Mortgage loans	15,830	10
Real estate equities	6,020	4
Other investments	4,382	3
Receivables	1,899	1
Other assets	72	—
Total	**156,643**	**100**

Funds
Judges' Retirement Fund
Judges' Retirement Fund II
Legislators' Retirement Fund
Public Employees' Contingency Reserve Fund
Public Employees' Deferred Compensation Fund
Public Employees' Health Care Fund
Public Employees' Long-Term Care Fund
Public Employees' Retirement Fund

1999 Underperformers List
Cummins Engine Company, Inc.
Mallinckrodt Inc.
Mandalay Resort Group
National Semiconductor Corporation
Pacific Century Financial Corporation
Pioneer Natural Resources Company
St. Jude Medical, Inc.
Sierra Health Services, Inc.
Tyson Foods, Inc.

HISTORICAL FINANCIALS & EMPLOYEES

Government-owned FYE: June 30	Annual Growth	1989	1990	1991	1992	1993	1994	1995	1996	1997	1998
Assets ($ mil.)	17.7%	—	—	—	—	69,484	76,935	90,417	102,797	128,880	156,643
Net income ($ mil.)	19.9%	—	—	—	—	9,111	738	11,622	12,274	19,477	22,594
Income as % of assets	—	—	—	—	—	13.1%	1.0%	12.9%	11.9%	15.1%	14.4%
Employees	8.5%	—	—	—	—	—	900	1,000	1,037	1,089	1,247

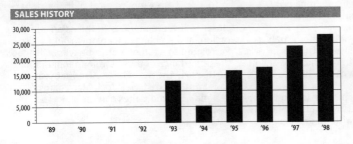

SALES HISTORY

CALTEX CORPORATION

OVERVIEW

Go east, young person, and you'll find Caltex and its petroleum refining and marketing operations. One of the oldest and most successful joint ventures in the history of business, Singapore-based Caltex (formerly Caltex Petroleum) is owned 50-50 by US energy titans Texaco and Chevron.

With operations in more than 60 countries, primarily in Africa, the Asia/Pacific region, and the Middle East, Caltex sells 1.5 million barrels of crude oil and petroleum products per day.

The company has stakes in 13 fuel refineries, two lubricant refineries, 17 lubricant-blending plants, six asphalt plants, and more than 500 ocean terminals and depots. It markets products through 8,000 retail outlets, including 425 Star Mart convenience stores.

Despite the Asian economic downturn, the company is bullish on the Asia/Pacific region. In 1999 Caltex moved its headquarters to Singapore, where it is the country's largest private company.

HISTORY

In the 1930s Standard Oil of California (Socal, now Chevron) had a problem most oil companies would wish for: It had oil reserves in Bahrain with a potential 30,000-barrel-a-day production capacity, but didn't have the refining or marketing network to sell the oil profitably.

While Socal's oil sat idly in the Bahraini soil, Texaco had its own problems. It had a large marketing network in Asia and Africa but lacked a crude supply in the Eastern Hemisphere; it was shipping its products from the US. Enter James Forrestal, head of the American investment bank Dillon Read, with plans for a little matchmaking. Forrestal brought the two companies together, and in 1936 they formed the California-Texas Oil Company (Caltex).

Although disrupted by WWII, Caltex still expanded quickly, organizing itself geographically. It formed companies in Malaysia, Thailand, and Yemen, and it increased its refining capacity in Bahrain (1945), began building and expanding refineries in other areas (1946), and bought Texaco's European and North African marketing operations (1947). In 1951 Caltex formed a joint venture with Nippon Oil (now called Nippon Mitsubishi Oil) to refine crude oil supplied by Caltex in Japan and bought 50% of Japan's Koa Oil Company.

Caltex sold its European operations to Socal and Texaco in 1967 to concentrate on building its presence in Africa, Asia, and Australasia. A year later Caltex entered South Korea and formed the Honam Oil Refinery (renamed LG-Caltex Oil in 1996) in a partnership with Lucky Chemical (now LG Chemical).

During the 1970s several of Caltex's Arab holdings were nationalized as an OPEC-spawned upheaval shook the oil industry, and in 1978 the Indian government nationalized Caltex Oil Refining (India) Ltd.

In 1980 Caltex tried its hand in the convenience store business, setting up Majik Markets in an Australian venture with US grocer Munford. (Though Caltex had turned the MM stores over to the 7-Eleven franchise by 1990, it later began adding Star Marts to its gas stations.) In 1982 Caltex moved from New York to Irving, Texas, in the Dallas area.

Four years later it began modernizing its refineries in Australia, the Philippines, and Singapore. In 1988 it created Caltex Services Corporation to provide tech support to Caltex companies.

Caltex formed a joint venture for blending and marketing lubricants with Indian oil company IBP in 1993. The next year the company opened offices in Vietnam and Indonesia.

In 1995 company veteran David Law-Smith became CEO. The Japanese government announced plans to lift import restrictions on refined oil in 1996, allowing Caltex to sell to Japanese customers from elsewhere in Asia; Caltex, which had completed a refinery in Thailand, sold its 50% stake in Nippon Oil. That year the company and Shantou Ocean Enterprises announced plans to build China's largest liquid propane gas storage facility.

In 1997 Caltex sold its 40% share of the Bahrain Refining Co. The company also merged its Australian refining and marketing unit with Pioneer International's Ampol unit.

Caltex restructured in 1998, organizing around functions — such as marketing, refining, and trading — rather than geography. It hoped to save about $250 million annually.

In 1999 Caltex moved most of its headquarters operations from Texas to Singapore to be closer to its core markets in the Asia/Pacific region, and it changed its name from Caltex Petroleum to plain ol' Caltex to acknowledge the importance of non-petroleum operations, particularly the Star Marts. Also that year, Law-Smith retired, SVP Jock McKenzie became CEO and Caltex sold its stake in Koa Oil.

Chairman and CEO: Jock McKenzie
EVP: Guy J. Camarata
CFO: Malcolm J. McAuley
VP, Secretary, and General Counsel: Frank W. Blue
VP; Head of Worldwide Trading, Singapore:
Leo G. Lonergan
VP Human Resources: Stephen H. Nichols
VP: Shariq Yosufzai
Auditors: KPMG LLP

LOCATIONS

HQ: 125 E. John Carpenter Fwy., Irving, TX 75062-2794
Phone: 533-3000   **Fax:** 972-830-1081
Web site: http://www.caltex.com

Caltex Petroleum has operations in more than 60 countries, primarily in Africa, the Asia/Pacific region, Australia, the Middle East, and New Zealand.

PRODUCTS/OPERATIONS

Selected Products
Asphalt/Bitumen
Automotive fuel
Automotive lubes
Aviation fuel
Commercial lubes
Industrial oils
LPG
Marine and railroad fuel
Motorcycle oils
Specialty products

Selected Subsidiaries and Affiliates
American Overseas Petroleum Ltd. (coordinates
activities of P. T. Caltex Pacific Indonesia)
LG-Caltex Oil Corp. (50%, refining, South Korea)
P. T. Caltex Pacific Indonesia (oil and gas exploration)
Star Petroleum Refining Co. Ltd. (64%, Thailand)

COMPETITORS

7-Eleven	Mitsubishi
Amerada Hess	Mobil
BHP	Occidental
BP Amoco	Petronas
Coastal	Royal Dutch/Shell
Devon Energy	SK Corporation
Elf Aquitaine	TOTAL FINA
ENI	Unocal
Exxon	USX-Marathon
Kerr-McGee	Woolworths

HISTORICAL FINANCIALS & EMPLOYEES

Joint venture FYE: December 31	Annual Growth	1989	1990	1991	1992	1993	1994	1995	1996	1997	1998
Sales ($ mil.)	4.5%	11,507	15,147	15,445	17,281	15,409	14,751	15,067	18,166	18,357	17,174
Net income ($ mil.)	(14.9%)	609	601	839	720	720	689	899	1,193	846	143
Income as % of sales	—	5.3%	4.0%	5.4%	4.2%	4.7%	4.7%	6.0%	6.6%	4.6%	0.8%
Employees	0.3%	—	7,700	7,700	7,600	7,800	8,000	7,000	7,300	7,600	7,900

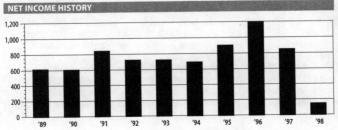

NET INCOME HISTORY

1998 FISCAL YEAR-END
Debt ratio: 17.5%
Return on equity: 3.3%
Cash ($ mil.): 178
Current ratio: 0.70
Long-term debt ($ mil.): 930

CAMPBELL SOUP COMPANY

OVERVIEW

Campbell Soup is souping up its line to go beyond the basics. Although Camden, New Jersey-based Campbell accounts for about 75% of all soup sold in the US, sales of condensed soups (led by tomato, chicken noodle, and cream of mushroom) have slowed as consumers use them less often in casseroles and other dishes.

To keep up with today's on-the-go population, the firm has launched ready-to-serve soups in resealable plastic containers and microwaveable single-serving bowls (US) and long-life cartons (UK). Building its food service business, Campbell created the Away From Home unit to target cafeterias and fast-food outlets. Campbell also makes Pepperidge Farm cookies and crackers and Godiva chocolates (#1 in US specialty chocolate).

The company holds about 7% of the European soup market and is trying to expand its share, partly through acquisitions. To reduce costs and focus on core segments (soups and sauces, biscuits and confectionery, and food service), in 1998 the firm spun off its Swanson frozen foods and Vlasic pickles lines, along with several smaller businesses, as Vlasic Foods International.

Descendants of condensed soup inventor John Dorrance own more than 50% of Campbell.

HISTORY

Campbell Soup began in Camden, New Jersey, in 1869 as a canning and preserving business founded by icebox maker Abram Anderson and fruit merchant Joseph Campbell. Anderson left in 1876 and Arthur Dorrance took his place. The Dorrance family assumed control after Campbell retired in 1894.

Arthur's nephew, John Dorrance, joined Campbell in 1897. The young chemist soon found a way to condense soup by eliminating most of its water. Without the heavy bulk of water-filled cans, distribution was cheaper, and Campbell products quickly spread.

In 1904 the firm introduced the Campbell Kids characters. Entering the California market in 1911, Campbell became one of the first US companies to achieve national distribution of a food brand. It bought Franco-American, the first American soup maker, in 1915.

Campbell's ubiquity in American kitchens made its soup can an American pop-culture icon (it was even illustrated by Andy Warhol in his celebrated 1960s print) and brought great wealth to the Dorrance family.

With a reputation for conservative management, Campbell began to diversify, acquiring V8 juice (1948), Swanson (1955), Godiva Chocolatier (33% in 1966; full ownership in 1974), Vlasic pickles (1978), and Mrs. Paul's seafood (1982; sold 1996). It introduced Prego spaghetti sauce and LeMenu frozen dinners in the early 1980s.

Much of Campbell's sales growth in the 1990s came not from unit sales but from increasing its prices. In 1993 it took a $300 million restructuring charge, and over the next two years it sold poor performers at home and abroad. John Sr.'s grandson Bennett Dorrance took up the role of VC in 1993, becoming the first family member to take a senior executive position in 10 years.

In 1995 Campbell paid $1.1 billion for picante sauce maker Pace Foods and acquired Fresh Start Bakeries (buns and muffins for McDonald's) and Homepride (#1 cooking sauce in the UK).

As part of its international expansion, in 1996 the firm acquired Grand Metropolitan's #1 German soup maker, Erasco, and Cheong Chan, a food manufacturer in Malaysia. That year it sold Mrs. Paul's and reorganized into two operating divisions: U.S. Grocery, and Campbell International and Specialty Foods. In 1997 Campbell sold its Marie's salad dressing operations and bought Danone's Liebig (France's leading wet-soup brand). Also that year Dale Morrison, a relative newcomer to the firm, succeeded David Johnson as president and CEO.

The company spun off lower-margin businesses with combined sales of $1.4 billion in 1998 as Vlasic Foods International. After disappointing test-market sales that year, Campbell canceled its Intelligent Quisine mail-order line of "functional" foods. It then bought Fortun Foods, maker of refrigerated soups sold in the US and more than 20 countries, and launched Away From Home, a new unit to focus on school and office cafeterias and fast-food outlets in addition to its existing restaurant service.

In 1999 Campbell's Pepperidge Farm unit, maker of goldfish crackers, emerged victorious after rival Nabisco sued for the right to sell fish-shaped cheese crackers. Also in 1999 Campbell's agreed to sell its Fresh Start business, primarily to the unit's management and Berkshire Partners. In August the company unveiled its redesigned soup can labels, changing an American icon.

OFFICERS

President and CEO: Dale F. Morrison, age 49,
$1,893,500 pay
EVP and CFO: Basil L. Anderson, age 53, $818,520 pay
SVP; President, North American Soup and Sauce:
F. Martin Thrasher, age 48, $776,507 pay
SVP Global Sourcing and Engineering: Robert Subin,
age 60, $661,555 pay
SVP Law and Government Affairs: Ellen Oran Kaden,
age 47
VP; President, Pepperidge Farm: David L. Albright,
age 51
VP and Chief Information Officer: Roger D. Berry
VP Public Affairs: Jerry S. Buckley, age 43
VP Global Business Development: Timothy M. Callahan
VP Supply Chain: T. Ron Gable, age 50
VP Corporate Development: Ralph A. Harris
VP and Controller: Gerald S. Lord, age 52
VP Global Research and Development:
R. David C. Macnair, age 44
VP Human Resources: Edward F. Walsh, age 57
Auditors: PricewaterhouseCoopers LLP

LOCATIONS

HQ: Campbell Place, Camden, NJ 08103-1799
Phone: 856-342-4800 **Fax:** 856-342-3878
Web site: http://www.campbellsoups.com

1998 Sales & Operating Income

	Sales		Operating Income	
	$ mil.	% of total	$ mil.	% of total
US	4,850	72	1,124	88
Europe	859	13	36	3
Australia	627	9	50	4
Other regions	417	6	73	5
Adjustments	(57)	—	(35)	—
Total	**6,696**	**100**	**1,248**	**100**

PRODUCTS/OPERATIONS

1998 Sales

	$ mil.	% of total
Soup & sauces	4,434	66
Biscuits & confectionery	1,522	22
Food service	455	7
Other	334	5
Adjustments	(49)	—
Total	**6,696**	**100**

Selected Brand Names
Arnott's (biscuits)
Campbell's (soups)
Erasco (soups)
Franco-American (canned pasta)
Godiva (chocolate)
Homepride (sauces)
Liebig (soups)
Pace (Mexican sauces)
Pepperidge Farm (biscuits and crackers)
Prego (pasta sauces)
Stockpot (soups)
Swanson (broths)
V8 & V8 Splash (vegetable and fruit juices)

COMPETITORS

Bestfoods
Borden
Cadbury
 Schweppes
ConAgra
Danone
Diageo
General Mills
Heinz
Hershey
Hormel
Keebler
Kraft Foods
Lindt & Sprungli
Mars
Nabisco Holdings
Nestle
Philip Morris
Quaker Oats
Sara Lee
Specialty Foods
Unilever

HISTORICAL FINANCIALS & EMPLOYEES

NYSE symbol: CPB FYE: July 31	Annual Growth	1989	1990	1991	1992	1993	1994	1995	1996	1997	1998
Sales ($ mil.)	1.9%	5,672	6,206	6,204	6,263	6,586	6,690	7,278	7,678	7,964	6,696
Net income ($ mil.)	54.6%	13	4	402	491	8	630	698	802	713	660
Income as % of sales	—	0.2%	0.1%	6.5%	7.8%	0.1%	9.4%	9.6%	10.4%	9.0%	9.9%
Earnings per share ($)	53.7%	0.03	0.01	0.79	0.98	0.01	1.26	1.40	1.59	1.49	1.44
Stock price - FY high ($)	—	15.16	15.50	21.78	21.94	22.69	21.63	25.63	35.38	52.81	62.88
Stock price - FY low ($)	—	6.44	10.53	10.94	15.75	17.63	17.13	18.50	22.13	32.00	46.00
Stock price - FY close ($)	15.6%	14.63	13.34	19.94	18.94	17.94	18.50	23.38	33.94	51.88	54.00
P/E - high	—	505	1,550	28	22	2,269	17	18	22	35	44
P/E - low	—	215	1,053	14	16	1,763	14	13	14	21	32
Dividends per share ($)	15.0%	0.23	0.25	0.28	0.26	0.43	0.53	0.75	0.68	0.56	0.81
Book value per share ($)	(6.1%)	3.43	3.27	3.53	4.04	3.38	4.01	4.78	5.55	2.98	1.95
Employees	(8.8%)	55,412	49,941	44,934	43,256	46,920	44,378	43,781	40,650	37,000	24,250

STOCK PRICE HISTORY

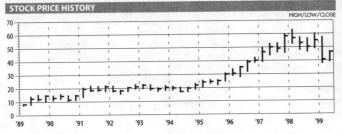

HIGH/LOW/CLOSE

1998 FISCAL YEAR-END

Debt ratio: 57.2%
Return on equity: 75.5%
Cash ($ mil.): 16
Current ratio: 0.51
Long-term debt ($ mil.): 1,169
No. of shares (mil.): 448
Dividends
 Yield: 1.5%
 Payout: 56.3%
Market value ($ mil.): 24,192

CANANDAIGUA BRANDS, INC.

OVERVIEW

Canandaigua Brands has welcomed some fancier labels to its table, but it still dances with the Wild Irish Rose who brought it to the party. The Fairport, New York-based beverage maker sells more than 170 brands of wine, beer, cider, distilled spirits, and bottled water in the US and the UK.

The company is the second-largest wine producer in the US, after E. & J. Gallo Winery. Its wines range from the inexpensive Almaden and Inglenook brands up to the classier Franciscan Oakville Estate and Simi labels, and Canandaigua continues to make the domestic dessert wine, Richards Wild Irish Rose, that brought it early success. The company's Canandaigua Wine unit also produces grape juice concentrate, used to make juice-based foods and beverages.

Through its Barton division, Canandaigua sells a number of regional beers and imports, such as Corona and Tsingtao, as well as several Canadian whiskey labels, including Black Velvet. Its Matthew Clark unit is a leading producer and distributor of wine, cider, and bottled water in the UK, as well as a wholesaler of beverages to the food service industry in the UK.

Canandaigua has built up a diverse product range in recent years through acquisitions, which, coupled with internal growth, have more than doubled its sales. The founding Sands family controls about 61% of the company's voting power.

HISTORY

Marvin Sands, the son of wine maker Mordecai (Mack) Sands, exited the Navy in 1945 and entered distilling by purchasing a Canandaigua, New York, winery. His business, which he named Canandaigua Industries, struggled while making fruit wines in bulk for local bottlers in the East. Aiming at regional markets, the company began producing its own brands two years later. Marvin opened the Richards Wine Cellar in Petersburg, Virginia, in 1951 and put his father in charge of the unit. In 1954 Marvin developed his own brand of "fortified" (20% alcohol content) sweet dessert wine, naming it Richards Wild Irish Rose after one of his sons.

On the strength of its sales, the company slowly expanded, buying a number of small wineries in the 1960s and 1970s, including Tenner Brothers Winery (1965) and Hammondsport Wine Company (1969). It went public in 1973, changing its name to Canandaigua Wine. A year later, expanding to the West Coast, it acquired the Bisceglia Brothers Winery in Madera, California, thus gaining access to the growing varietal market.

Canandaigua continued to grow through acquisitions and new product introductions in the early 1980s. In 1984, when wine coolers became popular, the company introduced Sun Country Coolers, doubling sales to $173 million by 1986. Marvin's son Richard took over as president that year. He headed the enterprise during the sudden cooling of the wine cooler market, and the business lost a total of $20 million in 1987 and 1988.

The short-lived wine cooler fad made Canandaigua realize that its distribution network could handle more volume, so it began looking for additional brands. The company picked up Kosher wine maker Manischewitz and East Coast wine maker Widmer's Wine Cellars, both in 1987. The following year Canandaigua acquired Cal-Products, a maker of grape products. The company made a major purchase in 1991 when it bought Guild Wineries & Distillers (Cook's champagne) for $60 million.

Subsequent acquisitions included Barton (beer importing, branded spirits; 1993), Vintners International (Paul Masson and Taylor, 1993), Heublein's Almaden and Inglenook (1994), and 12 distilled spirits brands from United Distillers Glenmore (1995). The moves doubled Canandaigua's share of the spirits market, making it the #4 US spirits supplier. After the flurry of acquisitions, the company changed its name in 1997 to Canandaigua Brands.

In 1998 Canandaigua scored high sales with its new Arbor Mist, a fruitier, low-alcohol "wine product" aimed at female consumers. That year it also bought Matthew Clark, a UK-based maker of cider, wine, and bottled water, for $359 million.

Further stocking its cabinet, in 1999 Canandaigua bought several whiskey brands (including Black Velvet) and two Canadian production facilities from Diageo, and it agreed to provide packaging and distilling services for some Diageo brands. Also in 1999 Canandaigua entered the premium wine business with the purchases of vintners Simi Winery and Franciscan Estates.

Founder Marvin Sands died in August 1999. Richard, who had been CEO since 1993, succeeded his father as chairman.

OFFICERS

Chairman, President, and CEO: Richard Sands, age 48, $926,138 pay (prior to promotion)
EVP and General Counsel; CEO, International; Interim President and Interim CEO, Canandaigua Wine Company: Robert Sands, age 40, $899,595 pay
SVP and Chief Human Resources Officer: George Murray, age 52
SVP and CFO: Thomas S. Summer, age 45
President and CEO, Matthew Clark: Peter Aikens, age 60
President and CEO, Barton: Alexander L. Berk, age 49, $711,288 pay
Auditors: Arthur Andersen LLP

LOCATIONS

HQ: 300 Willowbrook Office Park, Fairport, NY 14450
Phone: 716-218-2169   **Fax:** 716-394-6017

PRODUCTS/OPERATIONS

Selected Brands

Canandaigua Wine

Almaden	Manischewitz
Arbor Mist	Marcus James
Cook's	Mt. Veeder Winery
Deer Valley	Mystic Cliffs
Dunnewood	Paul Masson
Estancia Estates	Richards Wild Irish Rose
Estate Cellars	Riverland Vineyards
Franciscan Oakville Estate	Simi
Inglenook	Taylor California Cellars
J. Roget	Vina Santa Carolina

Barton

Distilled Spirits

Barton	Domestic Beer
Black Velvet	Point Special
Canadian LTD	
Chi Chi's	Imported Beer
di Amore	(Distribution)
Fleischmann's	Corona Extra
Glenmore	Corona Light
Golden Wedding	Double Diamond Ale
Inver House	Modelo Especial
Kentucky Tavern	Negra Modelo
MacNaughton	Pacifico
McMaster's	Peroni
Monte Alban	St. Pauli Girl
Montezuma	Tsingtao
Mr. Boston	
OFC	**Matthew Clark**
Old Thompson	Blackthorn (cider)
Schenley	Gaymer's Olde
Skol	English (cider)
Ten High	QC (fortified wine)
Triple Crown	Stone's (fortified wine)
	Strathmore (bottled water)

COMPETITORS

Adolph Coors	Heaven Hill
Allied Domecq	Heineken
Anheuser-Busch	Kendall-Jackson
Bacardi-Martini	Miller Brewing
Beringer	National Grape Co-op
Brown-Forman	Robert Mondavi
Diageo	Seagram
Fortune Brands	Wine Group
Gallo	

HISTORICAL FINANCIALS & EMPLOYEES

Nasdaq symbol: CBRNA FYE: February 28	Annual Growth	1990	1991	1992	1993	1994	1995	1996	1997	1998	1999
Sales ($ mil.)	26.6%	180	177	245	306	630	907	535	1,135	1,213	1,497
Net income ($ mil.)	31.1%	4	8	11	16	12	41	3	28	50	51
Income as % of sales	—	2.4%	4.4%	4.6%	5.1%	1.9%	4.5%	0.6%	2.4%	4.1%	3.4%
Earnings per share ($)	21.7%	0.46	0.84	1.01	1.20	0.74	2.16	0.17	1.42	2.62	2.69
Stock price - FY high ($)	—	6.34	11.18	17.01	23.75	32.00	48.00	53.00	39.50	58.50	61.50
Stock price - FY low ($)	—	4.34	4.12	10.09	10.75	20.25	29.75	29.75	15.75	21.88	35.25
Stock price - FY close ($)	30.1%	5.01	11.12	13.50	22.25	30.50	47.25	38.00	30.75	55.75	53.38
P/E - high	—	14	13	17	20	43	22	312	28	22	23
P/E - low	—	9	5	10	9	27	14	175	11	8	13
Dividends per share ($)	—	0.00	0.00	0.00	0.00	0.00	0.00	0.00	0.00	0.00	0.00
Book value per share ($)	19.4%	4.90	5.77	8.21	9.92	12.80	17.99	18.17	19.32	22.16	24.22
Employees	23.1%	650	900	900	1,950	2,650	2,150	2,500	2,500	2,500	4,230

1996 is a 6-month fiscal year.

STOCK PRICE HISTORY

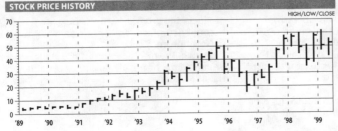

1999 FISCAL YEAR-END

Debt ratio: 65.6%
Return on equity: 11.6%
Cash ($ mil.): 28
Current ratio: 2.06
Long-term debt ($ mil.): 832
No. of shares (mil.): 18
Dividends
  Yield: —
  Payout: —
Market value ($ mil.): 959

CAPITAL ONE FINANCIAL

OVERVIEW

Maybe the company should be called Capital Four-One-One.

Capital One Financial's database has information on one in seven US households, and uses it to match customers with more than 6,000 different Visa and MasterCard credit card products. The Falls Church, Virginia company offers the cards through its Capital One Bank and Capital One F.S.B. banking subsidiaries (the company has no retail banking operations). All told, the company manages more than $17 billion in consumer debt derived from some 18 million accounts.

Capital One works hard to keep the *custom* in customer. Its cards sport graphic themes ranging from kittens to pro wrestlers; card terms run the gamut from a $200 limit and $50 annual fee (for those with spotty credit) to a 9.9% annual interest rate and no fee (for affluent and responsible "superprime" customers. No word yet on any "superduperprime" offerings). Capital One has extended its superprime credit offerings to Canada and the UK. The company also markets to college students, which it refers to as "tomorrow's superprime customers."

Capital One Financial hopes to pursue mammon through its mammoth database. When customers call Capital One to check balances or make payments, chances are they'll be offered goods or services that match their profiles. Under its Information-Based Strategy, Capital One pitches such customized products as home mortgages, car insurance, and shopping catalogs to incoming callers. (This plan lets the company avoid making those annoying unsolicited sales calls.) As part of the strategy, Capital One has moved into wireless phone service and auto finance (America One Communications and Summit Acceptance, respectively).

HISTORY

Capital One is a descendant of the Bank of Virginia, which was formed in 1945. Acquisitions and mergers brought some 30 banks and several finance and mortgage companies under the bank's umbrella between 1962 and 1986, when the Bank of Virginia became Signet Banking. The company began issuing products similar to credit cards in the 1950s and was MasterCard issuer #001.

Signet's credit card operations had reached 1 million customers in 1988, when the bank hired consultants Richard Fairbank and Nigel Morris (now the top two officers at Capital One) to implement their Promethean "Information-Based Strategy." Under the duo's leadership, the bank began using sophisticated data-collection methods to gather massive amounts of information on existing or prospective customers; it then used the information to design and mass-market customized products to the customer.

In 1991 — after creating the largest Oracle database in the world and developing sophisticated screening processes and direct-mail marketing tactics — Signet escalated the credit card wars, snagging away many lucrative customers from its rivals with its innovative balance-transfer credit card. The card let customers of other companies transfer what they owed on higher-interest cards to a Signet card with a lower introductory rate.

The new card immediately drew imitators (by 1997 balance-transfer cards accounted for 85% of credit card solicitations). After skimming off the least risky customers, Fairbank and Morris began going after less-desirable credit customers who could be charged higher rates. The result was what they call second-generation products — secured and unsecured cards with lower credit lines and higher annual percentage rates and fees for higher-risk customers.

The credit card business had grown to 5 million customers by 1994, but at a high cost to Signet, which had devoted most of its resources to finding and servicing credit card holders. That year Signet spun off its credit card business as Capital One to focus on banking (Signet was later acquired by First Union).

The company expanded into Florida and Texas in 1995 and into Canada and the UK in 1996; that year it established its savings bank, mainly to offer other products and services to cardholders. In 1997 the company used this unit to move into deposit accounts, buying a deposit portfolio from J. C. Penney. In 1998 the company began marketing its products to such clients as immigrants and high school students (whose parents must co-sign for the card). The company also expanded in terms of products and geography, acquiring auto lender Summit Acceptance and opening a new office in Nottingham, England.

In 1999 the firm's continued growth spurt prompted the hiring of 800 employees at its Dallas location.

Chairman and CEO: Richard D. Fairbank, age 48
President and COO: Nigel W. Morris, age 40
SVP Credit Card Operations: Marjorie M. Connelly, age 37
SVP: Matthew J. Cooper, age 32, $365,878 pay
SVP and Chief Information Officer: James P. Donehey, age 50, $323,564 pay
SVP, Corporate Secretary, and General Counsel: John G. Finneran Jr., age 49, $353,250 pay
SVP Human Resources: Dennis H. Liberson, age 43
SVP Brand Management: William J. McDonald, age 43
SVP Marketing and Analysis: Peter Schnall, age 35
SVP Finance and Accounting, Treasurer and Assistant Secretary: David M. Willey, age 38
Auditors: Ernst & Young LLP

LOCATIONS

HQ: 2980 Fairview Park Dr., Ste. 1300,
Falls Church, VA 22042-4525
Phone: 703-205-1000 **Fax:** 703-205-1755
Web site: http://www.capitalone.com

Capital One Financial has operations centers in Florida, Massachusetts, Texas, Virginia, Washington, and the UK.

PRODUCTS/OPERATIONS

1998 Sales

	$ mil.	% of total
Consumer loan interest	1,003	39
Other interest	108	4
Servicing & securitization	790	30
Service charges	612	24
Other income	87	3
Total	**2,600**	**100**

Subsidiaries
America One Communications, Inc. (wireless phone services)
Capital One Bank (credit card products)
Capital One, F.S.B. (consumer lending and deposit services)
Capital One Services, Inc. (operating, administrative, and other services to the corporation and its subsidiaries)
Summit Acceptance Corporation (automobile loans)

COMPETITORS

American Express	Household International
The Associates	MBNA
BANK ONE	Morgan Stanley Dean
Bank of America	Witter
CellStar	Providian Financial
Chase Manhattan	Toronto-Dominion Bank
Citigroup	Wells Fargo

HISTORICAL FINANCIALS & EMPLOYEES

NYSE symbol: COF FYE: December 31	Annual Growth	1989	1990	1991	1992	1993	1994	1995	1996	1997	1998
Sales ($ mil.)	48.5%	—	—	—	242	455	656	1,010	1,424	1,787	2,600
Net income ($ mil.)	42.9%	—	—	—	32	111	95	127	155	189	275
Income as % of sales	—	—	—	—	13.3%	24.3%	14.5%	12.5%	10.9%	10.6%	10.6%
Earnings per share ($)	28.8%	—	—	—	—	—	0.48	0.64	0.77	0.93	1.32
Stock price - FY high ($)	—	—	—	—	—	—	5.54	9.87	12.28	18.09	43.27
Stock price - FY low ($)	—	—	—	—	—	—	4.62	5.12	7.24	10.16	16.84
Stock price - FY close ($)	63.7%	—	—	—	—	—	5.33	7.95	11.99	18.04	38.30
P/E - high	—	—	—	—	—	—	12	15	16	19	33
P/E - low	—	—	—	—	—	—	10	8	9	11	13
Dividends per share ($)	—	—	—	—	—	—	0.00	0.08	0.11	0.11	0.11
Book value per share ($)	28.1%	—	—	—	—	—	2.39	3.02	3.72	4.55	6.44
Employees	33.6%	—	—	—	2,451	2,629	3,500	5,552	5,913	10,432

STOCK PRICE HISTORY

HIGH/LOW/CLOSE

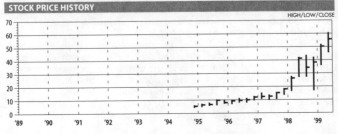

1998 FISCAL YEAR-END

Debt ratio: 75.1%
Return on equity: 21.7%
Cash ($ mil.): —
Current ratio: —
Long-term debt ($ mil.): 3,837
No. of shares (mil.): 197
Dividends
  Yield: 0.3%
  Payout: 8.3%
Market value ($ mil.): 7,552

CARDINAL HEALTH, INC.

OVERVIEW

Cardinal Health is in the pink.

The Dublin, Ohio-based company is the #2 US wholesale drug distributor (McKesson HBOC is #1). Cardinal distributes pharmaceutical products, health and beauty care products, and surgical and hospital supplies through a network of more than 30 distribution centers in 26 states. It also sells therapeutic plasma and other specialty pharmaceutical products using direct marketing and telemarketing.

Cardinal Health's aggressive acquisition program has absorbed more than a dozen companies since 1984. The firm is the largest franchisor of independent retail pharmacies through its Medicine Shoppe subsidiary. Other units include Owen Healthcare (pharmacy management), Pyxis (automated drug dispensing and medication management systems used by health care facilities), Allegiance (medical products distribution), and R.P. Scherer (softgels — gelatin capsules used to encase drugs and vitamins). Kmart, Cardinal's largest customer, accounts for about 12% of revenues.

Cardinal was stymied by federal opposition to its 1998 bid to buy #3 wholesaler Bergen Brunswig; it bought Allegiance in an even bigger deal the next year.

HISTORY

Cardinal Health harks back to Cardinal Foods, a food wholesaler named for Ohio's state bird. In 1971 Robert Walter, then only 26 and with the ink still fresh on his Harvard MBA, acquired Cardinal in a leveraged buyout. Walter hoped to grow Cardinal by acquisitions but was frustrated when he found that the food distribution industry was already highly consolidated.

In 1980 Cardinal acquired Zanesville, a small pharmaceutical distributor, and the company was on its way as a drug distributor. It went public in 1983 as Cardinal Distribution. Walter promptly started looking for new acquisitions, and the company subsequently expanded from coast to coast by swallowing other distributors. During the 1980s these purchases included Ellicott Drug Co. (1984, pharmaceuticals, New York), James W. Daly, Inc. (1985, pharmaceuticals and food, Massachusetts), and John L. Thompson Sons & Co. (1986, pharmaceuticals, New York).

In 1988 Cardinal sold its food group, including Midland Grocery Co. and Mr. Moneysworth Inc., to Roundy's and narrowed its focus to pharmaceuticals.

Drug distributors joined the rest of the pharmaceutical industry in its rush toward consolidation during the 1990s. Cardinal's acquisitions in those years included Ohio Valley-Clarksburg (1990, the Mid-Atlantic), Chapman Drug Co. (1991, Tennessee), PRN Services (1993, Michigan), Solomons Co. (1993, Georgia), Humiston-Keeling (1994, Illinois), and Behrens (1994, Texas).

One of Cardinal's most important acquisitions during this period was its cash purchase of Whitmire Distribution in 1994. Formerly Amfac Health Care, Whitmire had been a subsidiary of Amfac, one of Hawaii's "Big Five" landholders. When Amfac Health Care was spun off in 1988, its president, Melburn Whitmire, led a management group that acquired a majority interest. When Cardinal bought it, Whitmire was the US's #6 drug wholesaler; the purchase bumped Cardinal up to #3. At that time the company changed its name to Cardinal Health and Melburn Whitmire became Cardinal's VC.

In 1995 Cardinal made its biggest acquisition yet when it purchased St. Louis-based Medicine Shoppe International, the US's largest franchiser of independent retail pharmacies. The Medicine Shoppe enterprise had been started by two St. Louis obstetricians in 1970. When purchased by Cardinal for $348 million in stock, the chain had 987 outlets in the US and 109 abroad.

The company acquired Pyxis Corp. in 1996 in a stock swap worth $870 million. San Diego-based Pyxis provides hospitals with machines that automatically distribute pills to patients and provides pharmacy management services to hospital pharmacies. Later that year Cardinal bought PCI Services Inc., a pharmaceutical packaging company.

In 1997 Cardinal acquired Owen Healthcare, a provider of pharmacy management services, and also agreed to buy Bergen Brunswig; market leader McKesson countered Cardinal's latter move with a bid to acquire AmeriSource Health. In 1998 the Federal Trade Commission voted to block both deals; a federal judge supported that decision, and the agreements were scrapped.

That year Cardinal further expanded beyond marketing and distribution when it acquired R.P. Scherer, the world's largest maker of softgels. In 1999, Cardinal bought Allegiance, the largest medical products distributor in the US and made plans to buy Automatic Liquid Packaging, a liquid drug packager.

Chairman and CEO: Robert D. Walter, age 53, $1,524,231 pay
VC: Lester B. Knight
President and COO: John C. Kane, age 58, $978,407 pay
EVP; Group President, Pharmacy Automation and Management: Robert J. Zollars, age 41, $555,937 pay
EVP; Group President, Cardinal Distribution: James F. Millar, age 50, $532,311 pay
EVP; President, PCI Services: Daniel F. Gerner, $526,182 pay
EVP; President, Medicine Shoppe International: David A. Abrahamson, age 58
EVP; Group President, Allegiance: Joseph F. Damico
EVP, Secretary and General Counsel: Steven A. Bennett
EVP; President R.P. Scherer Corporation: George L. Fotiades, age 44
EVP and Chief Information Officer: Kathy Brittain White
SVP Human Resources: Carole W. Tomko
Corporate VP and Treasurer: Leonard G. Kuhr, age 40
Corporate VP: John L. Hatcher, age 52
VP and CFO: Richard J. Miller, age 42
President, Pyxis Corporation: Stephen S. Thomas
President, Cardinal Health Corporation: Stephanie A. Wagoner
President, Owen Healthcare, Inc.: Dwight Winstead
Auditors: Deloitte & Touche LLP

LOCATIONS

HQ: 5555 Glendon Ct., Dublin, OH 43016
Phone: 614-717-5000   **Fax:** 614-717-8871
Web site: http://www.cardinal-health.com

Cardinal Health distributes products from more than 30 facilities located Germany, Puerto Rico, the UK, and the US.

States with Cardinal Distribution Centers

Arizona	Missouri
California	Nevada
Colorado	New Mexico
Connecticut	New York
Delaware	North Carolina
Florida	Ohio
Georgia	Pennsylvania
Illinois	Tennessee
Kentucky	Texas
Louisiana	Utah
Massachusetts	Washington
Minnesota	West Virginia
Mississippi	Wisconsin

PRODUCTS/OPERATIONS

Selected Subsidiaries
Allegiance Corporation
Medicine Shoppe International, Inc.
Owen Healthcare, Inc.
PCI Services, Inc.
Pyxis Corporation
R.P. Scherer Corporation

COMPETITORS

AmeriSource
Bergen Brunswig
Bindley Western
Core-Mark
D & K Healthcare Resources
McKesson HBOC
Moore Medical
Owens & Minor
PSS World Medical
Quality King

HISTORICAL FINANCIALS & EMPLOYEES

NYSE symbol: CAH FYE: June 30	Annual Growth	1989	1990	1991	1992	1993	1994	1995	1996	1997	1998
Sales ($ mil.)	41.5%	700	874	1,184	1,648	1,967	5,790	7,806	8,862	10,968	15,918
Net income ($ mil.)	44.9%	9	13	17	25	34	35	85	112	181	247
Income as % of sales	—	1.3%	1.5%	1.5%	1.5%	1.7%	0.6%	1.1%	1.3%	1.7%	1.6%
Earnings per share ($)	22.4%	0.24	0.28	0.36	0.45	0.58	0.59	0.93	0.79	1.13	1.48
Stock price - FY high ($)	—	3.64	5.69	10.54	13.79	11.66	18.42	22.63	34.03	43.61	64.95
Stock price - FY low ($)	—	2.24	3.46	4.95	8.01	8.45	9.43	16.24	19.35	29.42	36.35
Stock price - FY close ($)	37.7%	3.51	4.90	10.11	10.94	10.59	17.44	21.02	32.09	38.19	62.53
P/E - high	—	15	20	29	31	20	31	24	43	39	44
P/E - low	—	9	12	14	18	15	16	17	24	26	25
Dividends per share ($)	24.1%	0.01	0.01	0.02	0.03	0.03	0.05	0.05	0.05	0.08	0.07
Book value per share ($)	18.0%	2.20	2.68	3.69	4.15	4.76	4.33	5.81	6.47	8.16	9.77
Employees	33.4%	840	830	1,100	1,400	1,600	3,500	4,000	4,800	11,000	11,200

STOCK PRICE HISTORY

HIGH/LOW/CLOSE

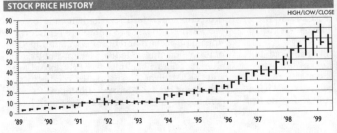

1998 FISCAL YEAR-END

Debt ratio: 14.4%
Return on equity: 15.2%
Cash ($ mil.): 305
Current ratio: 1.75
Long-term debt ($ mil.): 273
No. of shares (mil.): 166
Dividends
  Yield: 0.1%
  Payout: 4.7%
Market value ($ mil.): 10,399

CAREMARK RX INC.

OVERVIEW

Practice and practice and never get it right. And Birmingham, Alabama-based Caremark Rx (formerly MedPartners) did no better. Once the US's #1 practice management company (ahead of PhyCor), Caremark Rx has had enough of rising health care costs and fractious physicians. It's getting rid of its clinics to build its prescription benefits program, Caremark.

Caremark Rx became a giant in the physician practice management (PPM) industry by acquiring and managing practices and negotiating contracts with HMOs and other payers for nearly 13,500 physicians in about 240 clinics in some 40 states. Watching profits plunge as the costs of medical care and integrating

new clinics soared, and facing lawsuits from shareholders and physicians, the company decided to pull out of PPM.

The company focuses now on Caremark, which buys drugs directly from manufacturers to distribute to members through some 50,000 pharmacies and three mail-order services. The unit also offers disease management programs to members suffering from cystic fibrosis, multiple sclerosis, hemophilia, and other diseases. Unlike its rivals (Express Scripts is #1), Caremark is not owned by a pharmaceutical manufacturer and will exploit that status to gain market share.

HISTORY

MedPartners was formed by Richard Scrushy, the entrepreneurial chairman and president of HEALTHSOUTH Corp., the #1 US rehabilitation services company. HEALTHSOUTH grew by consolidating rehabilitation practices, many of which had a financial interest in the rehabilitation facilities to which they referred patients. In the 1990s, as HEALTHSOUTH restructured its agreements after self-referrals were restricted, Scrushy became interested in physician practice management (PPM).

Scrushy formed MedPartners in January 1993 and the next month bought a medical billing service. In June MedPartners landed its first contract, managing one of HEALTHSOUTH's practices. Larry House, HEALTHSOUTH's COO, became the company's chairman, president, and CEO. Funded by venture capitalists, House began acquiring other PPM companies. In 1993 MedPartners managed four practices; by the end of 1994, it managed 25.

MedPartners went public in 1995 and used the proceeds to buy more practices in the Southeast. Later that year it expanded to the West Coast, merging with Mullikin Medical Enterprises, then the US's largest private PPM (with about 3,000 doctors).

MedPartners/Mullikin, as it was known, had the size (4,900 doctors in 23 states) to go after market share. It targeted practices in markets where it could represent at least 20% of the physicians and where it could negotiate with the big HMOs.

In 1996 MedPartners/Mullikin secured its position as the leader in its field by buying Caremark, which managed the practices of about 1,000 doctors, provided pharmacy benefits management services nationwide, and had international operations.

After the Caremark deal, the company (renamed MedPartners) had some 7,400 doctors in its network. In 1997 it bought Florida-based InPhyNet Medical Management and formed a Southern California hospital-doctor network with Tenet Healthcare (the #2 US hospital chain) that gave both companies negotiating heft with HMOs.

MedPartners moved into several more southwestern markets before agreeing to merge with PhyCor (serving 19,000 doctors, mainly in rural areas). However, the company was badly bloated, and the PhyCor deal quickly fell apart when its fiscal shape came to light. To recover, the company cut operations and sold low-performance practices, racking up nearly $700 million in restructuring charges and recording another in a string of annual losses.

In the aftermath, House resigned as chairman and CEO. Mac Crawford, who had turned around managed behavioral care provider Magellan Health Services, replaced him. With cutbacks continuing in Southern California, the firm sold its contract emergency physicians management operations to investors in 1999 and planned to divest its government services business. Later that year the company announced plans to leave physician management entirely. Also in 1999 its California operations went into involuntary Chapter 11 bankruptcy protection; an interim settlement calls for MedPartners to pay $18 million to reimburse unpaid physicians and hospitals, claiming 92% of future earnings. MedPartners promptly sold all of its California clinics to KPC Global Care and KPC Medical Management. To reflect its refocusing on its Caremark subsidiary, the company changed its name to Caremark Rx.

Chairman, President, and CEO: Edwin M. Crawford,
age 50, $3,788,466 pay
EVP and CFO: James H. Dickerson Jr., age 52,
$750,000 pay
Chief Medical Officer: Rosalio J. Lopez, age 46
President, Pharmaceutical Services: John J. Arlotta,
age 49, $802,370 pay
EVP Corporate Strategies: Charles C. Clark, age 49
EVP and Chief Information Officer: John M. Deane,
age 44
EVP and General Counsel: Edward L. Hardin Jr., age 58,
$643,750 pay
EVP Managed Care: Edward J. Novinski, age 39
EVP and Chief Administrative Officer:
C. Clark Wingfield Jr., age 48
SVP Finance and Treasurer: Peter J. Clemens IV, age 34
SVP, Assistant General Counsel, and Corporate
Secretary: Sara J. Finley
SVP and Chief Accounting Officer: Howard A. McLure,
age 42
VP Finance and Controller: Mark S. Weeks, age 36
SVP Human Resources: Kirk McConnell
Auditors: Ernst & Young LLP

HQ: 3000 Galleria Tower, Ste. 1000,
Birmingham, AL 35244
Phone: 205-733-8996   **Fax:** 205-733-0704
Web site: http://www.caremark.com

Caremark operates across the US, as well as in Australia,
Bermuda, the British Virgin Islands, the Netherlands,
and New Zealand.

Subsidiaries
5000 Airport Plaza, L.P.
Acute Care Medical Management, Inc.
ADS Health Management, Inc.
Bay Area Practice Management Group, Inc.
BGS Healthcare, Inc.
Caremark Inc.
Caremark International Inc.
Cerritos Investment Group (I and II)
CHS Management, Inc.
Family Medical Center
Friendly Hills Healthcare Network Inc.
HealthWays, Inc.
Home Health Agency of Greater Miami, Inc.
LFMG, Inc.
MedGP, Inc.
MedPartners Aviation, Inc.
MPI/Memorial IPA, LLC
Pacific Medical Group, Inc.
Physicians' Hospital Management Corporation
PPS Indemnity, Inc.
PPS Valley Management, Inc.
Prescription Health Services, Inc.
Reliant Healthcare Systems, Inc.
Sachs, Morris & Sklaver, Inc.
Sierra Meadows Associates, Ltd.
Strategic Healthcare Management, Inc.
Talbert Health Services Corporation

Advance Paradigm
Columbia/HCA
CompScript
Express Scripts
Merck

ProVantage Health
 Services
Rite Aid
SmithKline Beecham

NYSE symbol: CMX FYE: December 31	Annual Growth	1989	1990	1991	1992	1993	1994	1995	1996	1997	1998
Sales ($ mil.)	362.8%	—	—	—	—	1	75	726	4,814	6,331	2,634
Net income ($ mil.)	—	—	—	—	—	(1)	(2)	(10)	(159)	(821)	(1,260)
Income as % of sales	—	—	—	—	—	—	—	—	—	—	—
Earnings per share ($)	—	—	—	—	—	—	—	(0.66)	(0.85)	(4.42)	(6.66)
Stock price – FY high ($)	—	—	—	—	—	—	—	34.50	36.00	28.38	22.38
Stock price – FY low ($)	—	—	—	—	—	—	—	14.75	16.38	17.88	1.63
Stock price – FY close ($)	(45.8%)	—	—	—	—	—	—	33.00	20.75	22.38	5.25
P/E – high		—	—	—	—	—	—	—	—	—	—
P/E – low		—	—	—	—	—	—	—	—	—	—
Dividends per share ($)	—	—	—	—	—	—	—	0.00	0.00	0.00	0.00
Book value per share ($)	—	—	—	—	—	—	—	3.24	4.47	0.46	(5.75)
Employees	102.2%	—	—	—	—	—	1,175	20,000	20,400	29,256	19,636

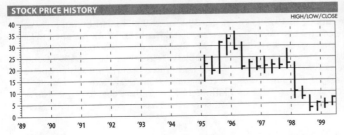

HIGH/LOW/CLOSE

Debt ratio: 293.6%
Return on equity: —
Cash ($ mil.): 23
Current ratio: 1.08
Long-term debt ($ mil.): 1,735
No. of shares (mil.): 199
Dividends
 Yield: —
 Payout: —
Market value ($ mil.): 1,045

CARGILL, INCORPORATED

OVERVIEW

On the global corporate battlefield, Cargill is the US's highest-ranking private. The largest private corporation in the US, Wayzata, Minnesota-based Cargill has diversified operations including commodities trading (grain, coffee, and petroleum); food processing; financial trading; futures brokering; seed, feed, and fertilizer producing; shipping; and steelmaking. In addition to making ingredients used in many food products, Cargill has its own food brands, including Honeysuckle White and

Riverside (poultry), Sunny Fresh (processed eggs), and Gerkens (cocoa).

Cargill has 29 subsidiaries with operations in more than 1,000 locations in about 60 countries; it trades in about 130 others. The company is the US's #1 grain exporter and one of the world's largest food processors. Its Excel unit slaughters about one-fifth of US cattle.

Nearly 100 descendants of the founders own about 85% of Cargill.

HISTORY

William W. Cargill founded Cargill in 1865 when he bought his first grain elevator, in Conover, Iowa. He and his brother Sam bought grain elevators all along the Southern Minnesota Railroad in 1870, just as Minnesota was becoming an important shipping route. Sam and a third brother, James, expanded the elevator operations while William worked with the railroads to monopolize transport of grain to markets and coal to farmers.

Around the turn of the century, William's son William S. invested in a number of ill-fated projects. William W. found that his name had been used to finance the projects; shortly afterward, he died of pneumonia. Cargill's creditors pressed for repayment, which threatened to bankrupt the company. John MacMillan, William W.'s son-in-law, took control and rebuilt Cargill. It had recovered by 1916 but lost its holdings in Mexico and Canada. MacMillan opened offices in New York (1922) and Argentina (1929), expanding grain trading and transport operations.

In 1945 Cargill bought Nutrena Mills (animal feed) and entered soybean processing; corn processing began soon after and grew with the demand for corn sweeteners. In 1954 Cargill benefited when the US began making loans to help developing countries buy American grain. Subsidiary Tradax, established in 1955, became one of the largest grain traders in Europe. A decade later Cargill began trading sugar by purchasing sugar and molasses in the Philippines and selling them abroad.

Cargill made its finances public in 1973 (as a requirement for its unsuccessful takeover bid of Missouri Portland Cement), revealing it to be one of the US's largest companies, with $5.2 billion in sales. In the 1970s it expanded into coal, steel, and waste disposal and became a major force in metals processing, beef, and salt production.

In the early 1990s Cargill began selling branded meats and packaged foods directly to supermarkets. To placate family heirs who wanted to take Cargill public, CEO Whitney MacMillan, grandson of John, created an employee stock plan in 1991 that allowed shareholders to cash in their shares. He also boosted dividends and reorganized the board, reducing the family's control. MacMillan retired in 1995 and nonfamily member Ernest Micek became CEO and chairman.

The firm bought Akzo Nobel's North American salt operations in 1997, becoming the #2 US salt company, behind Morton (acquired by Rohm and Haas in 1999).

Taking advantage of the high prices being paid for seed companies, in 1998 Cargill sold its foreign seed operations to Monsanto for $1.4 billion. Adding to its poultry operations, Cargill purchased turkey processor Plantation Foods that year. Internationally, the company became the manager of Toshoku, a bankrupt Japanese food trader (which it plans to buy). It also bought 60% of the Venezuelan grain and cereals business of commodities giant Bunge International.

In 1999 Cargill bought the #2 US grain export operation from Continental Grain in a deal estimated between $300 to $450 million (the firms agreed to sell some facilities to assuage antitrust interest). Both companies handle about 35% of US total grain sales and over 40% of US corn sales.

Cargill reported depressed earnings during fiscal 1998 and 1999, in part because of weaker international markets. Micek resigned as CEO in 1999 (but remained chairman) and was replaced by Warren Staley. Also in 1999 Cargill fessed up to misappropriating some genetic seed material from rival Pioneer Hi-Bred, killing its $650 million deal to sell its North American seed assets to Germany's AgrEvo.

OFFICERS

Chairman: Ernest S. Micek
VC: F. Guillaume Bastiaens
VC and CFO: Robert L. Lumpkins
President and CEO: Warren R. Staley, age 57
EVP: David W. Raisbeck
Corporate VP and Chief Technology Officer:
Ronald L. Christenson
Corporate VP and Controller: Galen G. Johnson
Corporate VP, General Counsel and Secretary:
James D. Moe
Corporate VP, Human Resources: Nancy Siska
Corporate VP, Information Technology: Lloyd B. Taylor
Corporate VP, Public Affairs: Robbin S. Johnson
Corporate VP, Research and Development:
Austen S. Cargill II
Corporate VP and Sector President: Gregory R. Page
Corporate VP and Treasurer: William W. Veazey
**Corporate VP, Worldwide Cargill Foods and
Procurement:** Tyrone K. Thayer
President, Agriculture-Biosciences Group:
Frederic W. Corrigan
President, Cargill Juice: Martin G. Dudley
President, Animal Nutrition: Richard D. Frasch
President, Dry Milling: John E. Geisler
President, Asia/Pacific Sector: Daniel R. Huber

LOCATIONS

HQ: 15407 McGinty Rd. West, Wayzata, MN 55391
Phone: 612-742-7575   **Fax:** 612-742-7393
Web site: http://www.cargill.com

Cargill and its subsidiaries and affiliates have more than
1,000 locations in 65 countries, and operate in about
130 others.

Regional US Sales Offices
Central Atlantic Region (Baltimore)
Mideast Region (Cincinnati)
Midwest Region (Hutchinson, KS)
North Atlantic Region (Watkins Glen, NY)
Northern and Central Region (Minneapolis)
Northern California (Newark, CA)
Northwest Region (Portland, OR)
Southern Region (Breaux Bridge, LA)

PRODUCTS/OPERATIONS

Selected Businesses

Financial
Financial instrument
trading
Futures brokerage and risk
management
Investment in real estate
and other financial
assets
Leasing
Trade and structured
finance

Industrial
Global steel
merchandising
Steel processing,
manufacturing, and
recycling

Processing
Animal nutrition
Cattle feedlots and
contract hog production

Cocoa
Corn, flour, and rice
milling
Fertilizer production and
distribution
Fruit juices
Malt
Meat (beef, pork, poultry,
eggs)
Oilseeds processing
Salt
Seed

Trading
Coffee
Cotton
Energy
Fats and oils
Freight operations and
vessel chartering
Grain
Rubber
Sugar

COMPETITORS

ADM
Ag Processing
Ajinomoto
BASF AG
Bethlehem Steel
Cenex Harvest States
ConAgra
Continental Grain
Corn Products
International
Dole
Dow Chemical
DuPont
Eridania Beghin-Say
Farmland Industries
General Mills

Heinz
Hormel
IBP
Ingram Industries
Koch
Mitsubishi
Monsanto
Nippon Steel
Novartis
Nucor
Rohm and Haas
Sara Lee
Smithfield Foods
Tate & Lyle
USX-U.S. Steel

HISTORICAL FINANCIALS & EMPLOYEES

Private company FYE: May 31	Annual Growth	1990	1991	1992	1993	1994	1995	1996	1997	1998	1999
Sales ($ mil.)	0.5%	44,000	49,100	46,800	47,100	47,135	51,000	56,000	56,000	51,400	46,000
Net income ($ mil.)	5.4%	372	382	450	358	571	671	902	814	468	597
Income as % of sales	—	0.8%	0.8%	1.0%	0.8%	1.2%	1.3%	1.6%	1.5%	0.9%	1.3%
Employees	4.5%	55,200	60,000	63,500	70,000	70,700	73,300	76,000	79,000	80,600	82,000

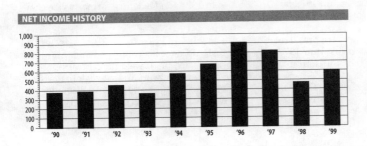

NET INCOME HISTORY

CARLSON WAGONLIT TRAVEL

OVERVIEW

History was bunk for Henry Ford, but for Carlson Wagonlit Travel it was a bunk bed. Minnetonka, Minnesota-based Carlson Wagonlit (pronounced Vah-gon-LEE) Travel descends from Europe's Wagons-Lits (literally, sleeping cars) company, which was founded by the creator of the Orient Express, and from the US's oldest travel agency chain (Ask Mr. Foster).

Carlson Wagonlit Travel is the third-largest travel company in the world behind American Express and Japan Travel Bureau (which are virtually tied for the #1 position). The company manages business travel from about 3,000 locations in more than 140 countries.

Carlson Wagonlit Travel is co-owned by France's Accor Group (motel and hotel franchises, travel and tourism services) and the US's Carlson Companies.

Carlson Companies is a service conglomerate whose nonbusiness travel operations include hospitality (it franchises Radisson Hotels, T.G.I. Friday's and Italianni's restaurants, and luxury cruise lines) and marketing services (motivational and incentive programs for businesses).

HISTORY

Belgian inventor Georges Nagelmackers' first enterprise was adding sleeping compartments to European trains in 1872. Nagelmackers later created the Orient Express. Over the years his Wagons-Lits company expanded its mission and eventually became Wagonlit Travel.

While Nagelmackers was establishing his business in Europe, Ward G. Foster was giving out steamship and train schedules from his gift shop facing the stately Ponce de Leon Hotel in St. Augustine, Florida.

As legend has it, locals directed hotel patrons with travel questions to Foster's shop with the oft-repeated phrase: "Ask Mr. Foster. He'll know."

In 1888 he founded Ask Mr. Foster Travel (it became the oldest travel agency in the US). By 1913 the company had offices located in pricey department stores and in the lobbies of upscale hotels and resorts throughout the country. After 50 years at the helm, Foster sold his business in 1937, three years before his death.

After suffering hard times during WWII and into the 1950s, the company changed hands again in 1957 when Donald Fisher and Thomas Orr, two Ask Mr. Foster shareholders, bought controlling interests for $157,000.

In 1972 Peter Ueberroth (Major League Baseball commissioner and Los Angeles Olympic Organizing Committee president) bought the company, then sold it in 1979 to Carlson Companies, Inc., Carlson Wagonlit's parent.

In 1990 Ask Mr. Foster became Carlson Travel Network. Also that year Carlson Companies acquired the UK's A.T. Mays, the Travel Agents — a leading UK seller of vacation and tour packages. By 1992 Carlson Companies, besides adding a travel agency a day to the 2,000-plus it already owned, was adding a new hotel every 10 days.

Europe's Wagonlit Travel and the US's Carlson Travel Network joined forces in 1994 to pursue expansion efforts. Under a dual-president ownership, the parent companies owned operations in specific world regions. The two companies began developing new business technology and expanded into new global business markets.

In 1994 the venture acquired Germany's Brune Reiseburo travel agency and opened a branch office in Moscow. Through 1995 and 1996 acquisitions targeted the Asia/Pacific region, including Hong Kong's and Japan's Dodwell Travel and the corporate travel business of Singapore's Jetset Travel. It also formed a partnership with Traveland, an Australian travel agency.

In 1997 Wagonlit Travel and Carlson Travel Network finalized the merger of their business activities operations, renamed Carlson Wagonlit Travel. The following year the new company acquired Florida's Travel Agents International, with more than 300 franchised operations and $600 million in annual sales. Also in 1998 Jon Madonna, formerly vice chairman of The Travelers Group, replaced Travis Tanner as CEO.

The following year three travel agencies in eastern Canada consolidated under the Carlson Wagonlit Travel brand, creating the largest travel network in that region. Carlson Companies founder and Carlson Wagonlit Travel chairman Curtis Carlson died.

OFFICERS

President and CEO: Jon Madonna
EVP Global Sales and Account Management:
Liliana Frigerio
EVP Products and Services: Jim Giancola
EVP North America Operations: Dean Hatton
EVP and CFO: Clive Hole
EVP EMEA Operations and Regions: Richard Lovell
EVP North America Sales and Account Management:
Ron Merriman
EVP Latin America: Ross Mersinger
VP Industry Relations - Worldwide: Gary Alexander
VP Finance, Americas: Tim Hennessy
Chief Information Officer: Loren Brown
President, Europe, Middle East, and Africa:
Herve Gourio
President, Asia Pacific: Geoffrey Marshall

LOCATIONS

HQ: 701 Carlson Pkwy., Minnetonka, MN 55459
Phone: 612-212-5000   **Fax:** 612-212-1288
Web site: http://www.carlsonwagonlit.com

Carlson Wagonlit Travel has offices in more than 3,000 locations worldwide.

PRODUCTS/OPERATIONS

Selected Services
Carlson Wagonlit Travel Services (advice, information, reservations)

COMPETITORS

American Express
Japan Travel Bureau
Maritz
Rosenbluth International
WorldTravel

HISTORICAL FINANCIALS & EMPLOYEES

Joint venture FYE: December 31	Annual Growth	1989	1990	1991	1992	1993	1994	1995	1996	1997	1998
Sales ($ mil.)	7.6%	—	—	—	—	—	—	—	9,500	10,600	11,000
Employees	0.2%	—	—	—	—	—	—	—	20,000	20,000	20,100

SALES HISTORY

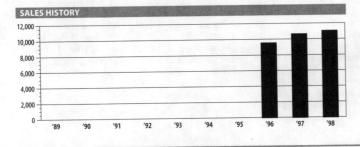

CARNIVAL CORPORATION

Carnival invites tourists to party hearty on the high seas. The Miami-based company is the world's #1 cruise operator, with about a third of the global market. The company operates three cruise lines, tour operations, and hotels in Alaska, Washington, and Canada, and it has stakes in four other cruise lines. Altogether, its holdings include more than 30 ships.

The company's Carnival Cruise Lines is its best-known line. Its 13 ships (with such names as *Ecstasy* and *Carnival Destiny*) cater to budget-minded vacationers traveling to the Caribbean and the Mexican Riviera. Its premium Holland America Line (HAL, eight ships) primarily serves Alaska and the Caribbean, while its Windstar Cruises operates four luxury sailing ships in the Caribbean, Mediterranean, and South Pacific. Carnival

also owns 68% of luxury cruise line Cunard as well as a stake in one of Europe's top cruise lines, Italy-based Costa Crociere.

Carnival's cruise and tour business (Holland America Westours) conducts bus, train, and cruise tours of Washington, Alaska, and Canada (it owns or operates 14 hotels in the latter two regions). It also has a 26% interest in Airtours, one of the UK's largest tour operators (airplanes, cruise ships, hotels, and travel agencies).

Carnival is riding the wave of maritime tourism. It is building eight new Carnival and HAL ships, which it plans to launch through the year 2003.

CEO Micky Arison and his family control the company through a 45% voting and 19% equity interest. The Arison family also owns the NBA's Miami Heat.

In 1972 Ted Arison (formerly with Norwegian Caribbean Lines) persuaded old friend Meshulam Riklis to bankroll his $6.5 million purchase of the *Empress of Canada*. Riklis owned (among other things) the Boston-based American International Travel Service (AITS). Setting up Carnival Cruise Lines as an AITS subsidiary, Arison renamed his ship the *Mardi Gras*. Unfortunately, she ran aground on her maiden voyage, sending Carnival into red ink for three years.

Arison bought out Riklis in 1974 for $1 and assumed Carnival's $5 million debt. He envisioned a cruise line that would offer affordable vacation packages to young, middle-class consumers, and invented a new type of cruise ship featuring live music, gambling, and other entertainment on board. Within a month Carnival was profitable. By the end of the following year, Arison had paid off Carnival's debt and bought its second ship.

He added a third ship in 1977, and the next year, when shipbuilding costs and fuel prices were very high, Arison stunned the cruise industry by announcing that Carnival would build a new ship; it set sail in 1982, and its overwhelming success led Micky Arison (who had succeeded his father as CEO in 1979) to build three more. Carnival became the world's #1 cruise operator. It went public in 1987.

In the meantime, the company had added three- and four-day short cruises to the Bahamas, and in 1988 it opened Carnival's Crystal Palace Resort (hotel/casino) there. Carnival started offering luxury cruises in 1989 after buying Holland America Line, which operated

cruises to Alaska and the Caribbean through Holland America Cruises and to the Caribbean and the South Pacific through Windstar Cruises. It also ran Westours and the Westmark hotel chain.

Carnival's partnership with Seabourn Cruise Lines came about through a 1992 joint venture, and in 1994 the company changed its name to Carnival Corporation. Subsequently it announced that it would merge its land-based gaming interests with the Continental Companies to form Carnival Hotels and Casinos.

In 1996 the company stepped up its European expansion and bought 28% of UK-based Airtours. The next year Carnival and Airtours jointly acquired European cruise giant Costa Crociere for about $275 million. In early 1998 Carnival closed a deal with Finnish shipbuilder Kvaerner Masa-Yards (which will build up to three ships for Carnival for about $375 million each) and led a group of investors in a $500 million deal to purchase the prestigious Cunard Line, which numbers the *Queen Elizabeth 2* among its five ships. Carnival merged its 50%-owned Seabourn line with Cunard. Also that year Carnival took a $7 million charge due to a fire on its *Ecstasy* cruise ship. After a woman who claims to have been sexually assaulted while on a Carnival ship filed a lawsuit against the company in 1999, Carnival acknowledged that it had received more than 100 other similar complaints against its cruise employees since 1995.

OFFICERS

Chairman and CEO: Micky Arison, age 49,
$2,001,000 pay
VC and COO: Howard S. Frank, age 57, $1,708,000 pay
SVP Finance and CFO: Gerald R. Cahill, age 47
Chairman and CEO, Holland America Line-Westours:
A. Kirk Lanterman, age 67, $1,087,000 pay
President and COO, Carnival Cruise Lines:
Robert H. Dickinson, age 56, $1,415,000 pay
President and CEO, Cunard Line Ltd.: Larry Pimentel
President and COO, Holland America Line-Westours:
Peter T. McHugh, age 51
SVP Operations, Carnival Cruise Lines:
Meshulam Zonis, age 65, $828,000 pay
VP Marketing: Jack Anderson, age 46
VP Strategic Planning: Pamela C. Conover
VP and Treasurer: Lowell Zemnick, age 55
Director of Human Resources: Susan Herrmann
Auditors: PricewaterhouseCoopers LLP

LOCATIONS

HQ: 3655 NW 87th Ave., Miami, FL 33178-2428
Phone: 305-599-2600 **Fax:** 305-406-4700
Web site: http://www.carnivalcorp.com

PRODUCTS/OPERATIONS

1998 Sales

	$ mil.	% of total
Cruise	2,798	91
Tour	274	9
Adjustments	(63)	—
Total	**3,009**	**100**

Selected Cruise Ships

Carnival Cruise Lines
Carnival Destiny (Caribbean, 2,642 passengers)
Celebration (Caribbean, 1,486)
Ecstasy (Caribbean, 2,040)
Elation (Mexico, 2,040)
Fantasy (Bahamas, 2,044)
Fascination (Caribbean, 2,040)
Holiday (Mexico, 1,448)
Imagination (Caribbean, 2,040)
Inspiration (Caribbean, 2,040)
Jubilee (Alaska, Hawaii, and Mexico; 1,486)
Paradise (Caribbean, 2,040)
Sensation (Caribbean, 2,044)
Tropicale (Alaska and Caribbean, 1,014)

Holland American Line
Maasdam (Alaska and Panama Canal, 1,266)
Nieuw Amsterdam (Alaska and Caribbean, 1,214)
Noordam (Alaska and Asia/Pacific, 1,214)
Rotterdam (worldwide, 1,316)
Ryndam (Alaska and Caribbean, 1,266)
Statendam (Alaska and Hawaii, 1,266)
Veendam (Canada and Caribbean, 1,266)
Westerdam (Alaska and Caribbean, 1,494)

Windstar Cruises
Wind Song (Costa Rica and Europe, 148)
Wind Spirit (Caribbean and Europe, 148)
Wind Star (Caribbean and Europe, 148)
Wind Surf (Caribbean and Europe, 312)

COMPETITORS

Canadian Pacific	Royal Caribbean Cruises
Carlson	Royal Olympic Cruises
Club Med	Siem Industries
Peninsular and Oriental	Vard
Princess Cruises	Walt Disney

HISTORICAL FINANCIALS & EMPLOYEES

NYSE symbol: CCL FYE: November 30	Annual Growth	1989	1990	1991	1992	1993	1994	1995	1996	1997	1998
Sales ($ mil.)	11.3%	1,148	1,391	1,405	1,474	1,557	1,806	1,998	2,213	2,448	3,009
Net income ($ mil.)	17.6%	194	206	85	277	318	382	451	566	666	836
Income as % of sales	—	16.9%	14.8%	6.1%	18.8%	20.4%	21.1%	22.6%	25.6%	27.2%	27.8%
Earnings per share ($)	16.3%	0.36	0.39	0.16	0.49	0.57	0.67	0.79	0.96	1.12	1.40
Stock price - FY high ($)	—	6.59	6.22	7.31	8.50	12.09	13.06	13.56	15.94	27.13	42.63
Stock price - FY low ($)	—	3.47	2.69	3.03	5.63	7.56	10.28	9.56	11.38	14.88	19.00
Stock price - FY close ($)	24.2%	4.91	3.31	5.78	8.06	12.03	10.81	13.00	15.81	27.03	34.50
P/E - high	—	18	16	46	17	21	19	17	17	24	30
P/E - low	—	10	7	19	11	13	15	12	12	13	14
Dividends per share ($)	5.2%	0.19	0.12	0.12	0.14	0.14	0.14	0.15	0.18	0.22	0.30
Book value per share ($)	17.9%	1.64	1.90	2.08	2.45	2.88	3.41	4.12	5.14	6.07	7.20
Employees	4.8%	14,450	15,500	16,000	14,870	15,650	17,250	15,280	18,110	18,100	22,000

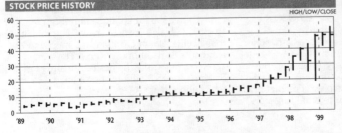

STOCK PRICE HISTORY HIGH/LOW/CLOSE

1998 FISCAL YEAR-END
Debt ratio: 26.7%
Return on equity: 19.5%
Cash ($ mil.): 137
Current ratio: 0.33
Long-term debt ($ mil.): 1,563
No. of shares (mil.): 595
Dividends
  Yield: 0.9%
  Payout: 21.4%
Market value ($ mil.): 20,543

CAROLINA POWER & LIGHT

OVERVIEW

Carolina Power & Light (CP&L) is an old utility learning new tricks. Traditionally the Raleigh, North Carolina-based company has generated, transmitted, and distributed electricity in the Carolinas, but it is adding some new moves in order to chase deregulating markets. In its home states CP&L serves 1.2 million customers, and its 10 power plants generate almost 10,000 MW, most of which is powered by coal and nuclear sources.

Even though North and South Carolina have no deregulation plans on the books, CP&L is keeping up with the changing utility industry. It has jumped into wholesale power marketing and trading, and it's adding another 2,300 MW to its portfolio by 2002 to sell on the wholesale market and to retail customers. Its purchase of North Carolina Natural Gas has added 178,000 gas customers. CP&L is also hedging its bets by forming nonutility companies such as Interpath Communications, an Internet and telecommunications operation, and Strategic Resource Solutions, an energy services provider.

Still hungry for growth, CP&L has agreed to buy utility holding company Florida Progress, which provides electricity to 1.3 million customers in Florida's west and central regions and along the Gulf Coast.

HISTORY

Central Carolina Power was incorporated in 1908. Later that year, under the aegis of the Electric Bond and Share Co. (EBS, a subsidiary of General Electric), Central Carolina Power crossed lines with Raleigh Electric and Consumers Light & Power to form Carolina Power & Light (CP&L).

EBS president S. Z. Mitchell was a leader in the young industry, espousing economies of scale through mergers and promoting lower rates to encourage higher-volume sales. CP&L had three hydroelectric plants by 1911, and by 1912 it had acquired three neighboring utilities, including Asheville Power & Light. In addition to retail sales, it began selling power wholesale to municipal utilities.

Demand soared after WWI as textile mills switched from steam engines to electricity and residential customers became enamored of modern appliances sold by CP&L. The company merged with four other utilities and reincorporated in 1926. The next year it became part of National Power & Light, a huge utility holding company created by EBS.

CP&L struggled during the Depression as demand slackened. To add legislative insult to financial injury, Congress passed the Public Utility Holding Company Act of 1935 to break up vast utility trusts. The act inaugurated 60 years of regional monopolies regulated by state and federal authorities. In 1948 CP&L was divested from EBS and went public.

The postwar boom increased the demand for power, and to keep up CP&L built several large coal-fired plants. By the early 1960s the company had begun building its first nuclear facility, its Robinson plant, which was completed in 1971. CP&L also continued to build huge, coal-fired plants.

The company completed its second nuke (Brunswick) in 1977. But two years later the accident at Pennsylvania's Three Mile Island cast a pall on the industry. After numerous delays CP&L decided to complete just one more nuke (Harris). The plant went on line in 1987, and CP&L requested a 13% rate increase to help cover its $3.8 billion cost. In contrast to its brothers, Harris ran quite well. But problems continued to plague CP&L's nuclear program into the early 1990s.

The Federal Energy Policy Act of 1992 dramatically changed the utility industry by allowing wholesale power competition. The following year CP&L hired new nuke management to turn around its troubled Brunswick plant. In 1994 CP&L formed CaroNet, an Internet and telecommunications services provider that later became Interpath Communications.

Damages to the utility's infrastructure — incurred in 1996 when Hurricane Fran struck the Carolinas — cost about $100 million. The following year the company unveiled Strategic Resource Solutions, an unregulated energy services company created out of the former Knowledge Builders. In 1998 Interpath Communications acquired Internet services provider TriNet Services.

To expand into natural gas distribution, CP&L bought North Carolina Natural Gas (NCNG) in 1999 for about $354 million in stock. CP&L also opened a new electric plant in Asheville, North Carolina, and moved to expand outside its home territory: The company agreed to buy utility holding company Florida Progress for $5.3 billion in cash and stock and $2.7 billion in assumed debt.

OFFICERS

Chairman, President, and CEO: William Cavanaugh III, age 60, $1,100,027 pay (prior to promotion)
EVP and CFO, Financial Services: Glenn E. Harder, age 48, $390,306 pay
EVP, Energy Supply: William S. Orser, age 54, $557,345 pay
SVP and Chief Nuclear Officer, Nuclear Generation: C. S. Hinnant, age 54
SVP, Energy Delivery: Fred N. Day IV, age 55
SVP and General Counsel, Administrative Services and Corporate Relations: Roger B. McGehee, age 56
SVP, Power Operations: Tom D. Kilgore, age 51
SVP, Retail Sales and Services: Cecil L. Goodnight, age 55, $305,009 pay
VP, Human Resources: Brenda Castonguay
Auditors: Deloitte & Touche LLP

LOCATIONS

HQ: 411 Fayetteville St., Raleigh, NC 27601
Phone: 919-546-6111 **Fax:** 919-546-2920
Web site: http://www.cplc.com

Carolina Power & Light distributes electricity in more than 200 communities in North and South Carolina. Its service territory includes the Atlantic coast, the lower Piedmont section, and the greater Asheville area in North Carolina, and northeastern South Carolina.

1998 Sales

	$ mil.	% of total
North Carolina retail	2,097	67
North Carolina wholesale	407	13
South Carolina retail	407	13
South Carolina wholesale	31	1
Other	188	6
Total	**3,130**	**100**

PRODUCTS/OPERATIONS

1998 Sales

	$ mil.	% of total
Residential	1,033	33
Industrial	720	23
Commercial	688	22
Wholesale	407	13
Other	282	9
Total	**3,130**	**100**

1998 Fuel Sources

	% of total
Coal	53
Nuclear	32
Oil and gas	13
Hydro	2
Total	**100**

Subsidiaries

Interpath Communications, Inc. (Internet and telecommunications)
North Carolina Natural Gas (natural gas sales and distribution)
Strategic Resource Solutions (energy management services)

COMPETITORS

AEP
Cinergy
Dominion Resources
Duke Energy
Enron
Entergy
SCANA
Southern Company
TVA

HISTORICAL FINANCIALS & EMPLOYEES

NYSE symbol: CPL FYE: December 31	Annual Growth	1989	1990	1991	1992	1993	1994	1995	1996	1997	1998
Sales ($ mil.)	2.6%	2,481	2,617	2,686	2,767	2,895	2,877	3,007	2,996	3,024	3,130
Net income ($ mil.)	0.7%	376	280	377	380	347	313	373	391	388	399
Income as % of sales	—	15.2%	10.7%	14.0%	13.7%	12.0%	10.9%	12.4%	13.1%	12.8%	12.8%
Earnings per share ($)	3.0%	2.10	1.58	2.27	2.36	2.10	2.03	2.48	2.66	2.66	2.75
Stock price - FY high ($)	—	24.00	23.81	27.13	28.19	34.63	30.00	34.63	38.75	42.69	49.63
Stock price - FY low ($)	—	17.50	19.00	21.63	24.44	27.00	22.50	26.13	33.75	32.75	39.19
Stock price - FY close ($)	8.2%	23.19	23.31	27.06	27.75	30.13	26.63	34.50	36.50	42.38	47.06
P/E - high	—	11	15	12	12	16	15	14	15	16	18
P/E - low	—	8	12	10	10	13	11	11	13	12	14
Dividends per share ($)	3.4%	1.43	1.46	1.52	1.58	1.64	1.70	1.76	1.37	1.88	1.94
Book value per share ($)	3.8%	13.88	14.02	14.87	15.76	16.38	16.54	16.93	17.77	18.63	19.49
Employees	(2.3%)	—	—	8,500	8,120	8,101	7,900	7,812	6,701	6,900	7,200

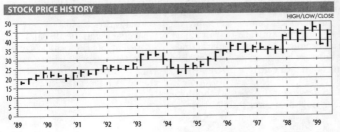

STOCK PRICE HISTORY
HIGH/LOW/CLOSE

1998 FISCAL YEAR-END

Debt ratio: 46.5%
Return on equity: 13.5%
Cash ($ mil.): 29
Current ratio: 1.48
Long-term debt ($ mil.): 2,614
No. of shares (mil.): 151
Dividends
  Yield: 4.1%
  Payout: 70.5%
Market value ($ mil.): 7,122

CARTER-WALLACE, INC.

OVERVIEW

If the body is a temple, Carter-Wallace sells the janitorial supplies that keep it tidy. The New York City-based company makes personal care products and prescription drugs. Its Consumer Products segment (about 40% of sales) makes Nair (the #1 line of depilatories), Arrid deodorant, and Pearl Drops tooth polish. It is also a leading maker of pregnancy tests (First Response) and condoms (the US leader with its Trojan and Class brands). The Health Care division includes Wallace Laboratories (pharmaceuticals) and Wampole Laboratories (medical diagnostic and testing products). Subsidiary Lambert Kay makes pet supplies.

Through holding company CPI Development, chairman and CEO Henry Hoyt Jr. and the founding Hoyt family own about 36% of the firm; investor "Super" Mario Gabelli owns another 19%.

HISTORY

In the late 1920s Henry Hoyt observed from the sidelines his father-in-law's company, which made Carter's Little Liver Pills. Hoyt was frustrated; he believed the company should spend more on new product development. In 1929 he took matters into his own hands and secretly purchased a controlling interest in the firm.

Hoyt sacrificed dividend payouts to invest in intensive research and development. His strategy paid off over the next couple of decades as the company (renamed Carter Products in 1937) introduced several successful products, including Arrid (1935), Nair (1940), and Rise (shaving cream, 1949; sold to Faberge 1988). Arrid was formulated by Princeton research chemist John Wallace.

Carter Products broke into the drug industry in the 1950s with the purchase of Miltown, a prescription tranquilizer. In 1959 the US government claimed the name "Carter's Little Liver Pills" was misleading (the pills had nothing to do with treating the liver) and ordered a change. Carter-Wallace still sells the renamed Carter's Little Pills as a laxative.

The company launched an aggressive acquisition program in the 1960s, including Lambert Kay (1968) and Zavala Hermanos (toiletries, 1969). In 1965, in light of the hefty boost its Wallace Laboratory division gave to its bottom line, Carter Products changed its name to Carter-Wallace.

Expansion continued in the 1970s and 1980s with acquisitions that included Winsted Company (pet products, 1971), Maltsupex and Syllamalt laxative products (from Abbott Laboratories, 1974), Mallinckrodt's pharmaceuticals division (1979), Youngs Drug Products (maker of Trojans, 1985), Mentor's condom business (1989), and the Poupina line of infant health care products (from Groupe Monot, 1989).

Henry Hoyt retired in 1986, leaving son Henry Jr. in charge. The elder Hoyt died three years later.

Carter-Wallace went on broadening its consumer and health products line by acquiring Tambrands' First Response pregnancy tests (1990), American Cyanamid's Lady's Choice antiperspirants and deodorants (1990), DuPont's Isostat Microbial System (1991), and the Cossack line of men's grooming products from the UK's Reckitt & Colman (1991). The company bought Spain's Icart (hand creams and foot care products) in 1993. Carter-Wallace's Italian subsidiary, Bouty SpA, continued the firm's European expansion the next year with the acquisition of Technogenetics, the diagnostic arm of Recordati Italy.

In the mid-1990s the company suffered from adverse reactions to some of its newer drugs; antiepileptic Felbatol was found to cause liver damage and expectorant Organidin was carcinogenic to lab animals. Charges relating to discontinuing or restricting the use of these drugs brought a steep loss in 1995, following a smaller one in 1994.

In 1996 Carter-Wallace entered the burgeoning diagnostics business, buying Cambridge Biotech, which made tests to detect intestinal pathogens and Lyme disease; the firm also added a line of autoimmune diagnostic kits from BioWhittaker. That year the company turned down investor Marvin Davis's near-billion-dollar buyout offer. The rejection — on top of losses and followed by lackluster earnings — stirred shareholder discontent; outside stockholders, including Roy Disney's Shamrock Holdings, demanded that the company be put up for sale the next year. Predictably, the proposal was rejected.

In 1999 Carter-Wallace won the US sales and marketing rights for Calypte Biomedical's professional-use HIV test products; it will also distribute Uriscreen, a home test for urinary tract infections, developed by Israel's Healthcare Technologies.

Chairman and CEO: Henry H. Hoyt Jr., age 71, $2,075,900 pay
President and COO: Ralph Levine, age 63, $1,432,100 pay
EVP and CFO: Paul A. Veteri, age 57, $1,263,600 pay
VP and Controller: Peter J. Griffin, age 56
VP, Secretary, and General Counsel: Stephen R. Lang, age 64, $672,092 pay
VP and Treasurer: James L. Wagar, age 64
VP, Consumer Products, U.S.: T. Rosie Albright, age 52, $722,900 pay
VP, Corporate Development: C. Richard Stafford, age 63
VP, Diagnostics, U.S.: John Bridgen, age 52
VP, Human Resources: Thomas B. Moorhead, age 65
VP, International: Adrian J. L. Huns, age 51
VP, Manufacturing: Michael J. Kopec, age 59
VP, Medical and Scientific Affairs: James C. Costin, age 55
VP, Pharmaceuticals, U.S.; President, Wallace Laboratories: Thomas G. Gerstmyer, age 56
VP, Quality Control: Donald R. Daoust, age 63
VP, Taxes: Mark Wertlieb, age 43
Auditors: KPMG LLP

LOCATIONS

HQ: 1345 Avenue of the Americas, New York, NY 10105
Phone: 212-339-5000   **Fax:** 212-339-5100
Web site: http://www.carterwallace.com

Carter-Wallace operates manufacturing plants in Canada, Italy, Mexico, New Zealand, Spain, the UK, and the US. It has warehouses and offices in Australia, Canada, France, the UK, and the US.

PRODUCTS/OPERATIONS

1999 Sales

	$ mil.	% of total
Domestic		
Consumer products	283	42
Health care	181	27
International	205	31
Total	**669**	**100**

COMPETITORS

Abbott Labs	Merck
American Home Products	Meridian Diagnostics
Amway	Nature's Sunshine
Bristol-Myers Squibb	Novartis
Chiron	Pacific Dunlop
Colgate-Palmolive	Perrigo
Dade Behring	Pharmacia & Upjohn
Del Labs	Procter & Gamble
Diagnostic Products	Reckitt & Colman
Eli Lilly	Rhône-Poulenc
Gillette	Roche Holding
Glaxo Wellcome	Schering-Plough
Hartz	SSL International
IVAX	Unilever
Johnson & Johnson	Warner-Lambert
Lee Pharmaceuticals	

HISTORICAL FINANCIALS & EMPLOYEES

NYSE symbol: CAR FYE: March 31	Annual Growth	1990	1991	1992	1993	1994	1995	1996	1997	1998	1999
Sales ($ mil.)	2.1%	555	635	673	654	665	664	659	649	662	669
Net income ($ mil.)	(6.2%)	50	52	46	47	(20)	(56)	8	27	27	28
Income as % of sales	—	9.1%	8.2%	6.8%	7.2%	—	—	1.2%	4.1%	4.1%	4.2%
Earnings per share ($)	(6.2%)	1.10	1.12	1.00	1.03	(0.44)	(1.22)	0.16	0.58	0.59	0.62
Stock price - FY high ($)	—	20.15	21.10	45.79	40.50	33.88	25.63	16.75	18.00	19.75	19.69
Stock price - FY low ($)	—	13.32	14.94	20.02	22.63	19.88	9.88	10.13	10.38	12.75	14.38
Stock price - FY close ($)	0.5%	17.15	20.10	31.05	28.00	21.00	12.00	16.50	13.75	18.31	18.00
P/E - high	—	18	19	46	39	—	—	105	31	33	32
P/E - low	—	12	13	20	22	—	—	63	18	22	23
Dividends per share ($)	(1.8%)	0.26	0.30	0.33	0.33	0.33	0.29	0.16	0.16	0.16	0.22
Book value per share ($)	0.7%	7.51	8.35	8.94	9.42	8.54	7.08	7.18	7.54	7.71	7.99
Employees	(2.4%)	4,110	4,270	4,170	4,020	4,060	3,670	3,610	3,460	3,360	3,310

STOCK PRICE HISTORY

HIGH/LOW/CLOSE

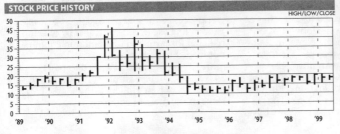

1999 FISCAL YEAR-END

Debt ratio: 15.3%
Return on equity: 7.9%
Cash ($ mil.): 49
Current ratio: 1.94
Long-term debt ($ mil.): 65
No. of shares (mil.): 45
Dividends
  Yield: 1.2%
  Payout: 35.5%
Market value ($ mil.): 810

CASE CORPORATION

OVERVIEW

Case is chasing Deere. The Racine, Wisconsin-based company is North America's #2 maker of farm machinery (after Deere & Company) and the world's largest maker of light to medium-size construction equipment. It makes combines, cotton pickers, sprayers, and tractors for use on the farm, and backhoes, crawler dozers, and trenchers for use in the city. Case sells through a network of 4,900 outlets in more than 150 countries. Subsidiary Case Capital provides customer loans and leasing contracts.

New Holland, which makes farm machinery, is buying Case, bringing both closer to their goal of catching Deere. But all three players are hurting from the global decline in demand for farm machinery. To ease the pain, Case has reduced production, cut 3,400 jobs, and focused on financial services and contruction equipment. Case is also sowing seeds in emerging markets such as Argentina, Brazil, China, and Russia, but it may be a while before Case reaps the benefits.

HISTORY

In 1842 Jerome I. Case moved to Rochester, Wisconsin, with a crude mechanized thresher that he modified to separate straw from grain. He moved to Racine in 1844 and three years later began building his separator-threshers as the Jerome Increase Case Machinery Co. The company's name changed to Racine Threshing Machine Works in 1848.

During the Civil War, Case and three partners founded J.I. Case & Co. The company debuted its first self-propelled steam traction engine in 1876 and began to make road machinery. In 1880 the company changed its name again, to J.I. Case Threshing Machine Co.

Case died in 1891. Partner Stephen Bull took over and, with three others, bought all the stock from the Case family. By WWI the company was listed on the New York Stock Exchange.

Between 1893 and 1924 the company diversified and expanded overseas. A former John Deere executive, Leon Clausen, became president in 1924 when Case was losing sales to competitors.

Clausen (president until 1948) improved designs, expanded the line, modernized Case's factories, and built the company's dealership network. Following a reorganization in 1928, the company's name became J.I. Case Co.

In the 1920s and 1930s the company acquired agricultural manufacturers Emerson-Brantingham and the Rock Island Plow Co. By 1937 it was the #3 maker of farm equipment.

During WWII Case made tractors and other equipment for the military. A 440-day strike at Case from 1945 to 1947 — the longest in US history at the time — hurt the company and forced Clausen to step down as president, although he remained chairman until 1958.

The company's merger with American Tractor in 1957 expanded its product line, but Case was unable to meet its debts by 1962. The company reorganized, finding a majority buyer

(Kern County Land) in 1964. Tenneco, a Houston-based holding company, bought Kern in 1967 and acquired the rest of Case in 1970.

Case prospered in the 1970s as it focused on overseas markets and construction equipment. A recession in farming in the early 1980s hurt US sales and led to consolidation in the industry. Case bought International Harvester's farm-equipment operations in 1985 to become the #2 maker of farm equipment.

After losses forced plant closings, Tenneco restructured Case in 1991. Three years later Tenneco began divesting Case via a public offering. It reduced its stake to 45% and spun off the rest in 1996, two years after Jean-Pierre Rosso became Case's CEO.

Case made a series of buys in 1996: Concord Inc., a leading supplier of air drills in the US; Austoft Holdings Ltd. of Australia, the world's largest maker of sugarcane-harvesting equipment; Fermec, a UK-based construction equipment firm; and a 75% stake in Steyr Landmaschinentechnik AG, an Austrian tractor maker.

In 1997 Case bought agricultural software developer Agri-Logic from Fluid Power Industries and also purchased bor-mor Inc., a maker of drilling equipment. Case bought Tyler Industries (spraying equipment) and DMI (tillage and fertilizer equipment) the next year. Case reduced production of its farm equipment in 1998 because of poor demand and announced plans to cut about 3,400 jobs, nearly 19% of its workforce, by the end of 1999. Case also expanded its Case Capital business by offering financing for farm and construction equipment not made by the company.

In 1999 New Holland agreed to buy Case for $4.3 billion. Italian automaker Fiat, which owns 69% of New Holland, would take a 71% stake in the merged company.

OFFICERS

Chairman and CEO: Jean-Pierre Rosso, age 58, $850,008 pay
President and COO: Steven G. Lamb, age 42, $560,004 pay
CFO; President, Financial Services: Theodore R. French, age 44, $440,004 pay
SVP, Strategy and Corporate Development: Richard M. Christman, age 48, $285,000 pay
VP, Supply Chain Management: Daniel E. Bridleman
VP Corporate Development: Frank A. Brooke
VP Human Resources: Marc J. Castor
VP and Chief Information Officer: Richard B. Davidson
VP Tax: John E. Evard Jr.
VP and Treasurer: Peter Hong
VP and Controller: Robert J. Naglieri
VP Communications and Government Affairs: Ellen Robinson
VP, Functional Engineering: Duane D. Tiede
Secretary and General Counsel: Richard S. Brennan, age 60, $335,000 pay
President, Case Capital: Andrew E. Graves
President, Case Europe: Leopold Plattner
President, Case Credit Corporation: Kenneth R. Gangl
SVP and General Manager, North American Region: Harold D. Boyanovsky
Auditors: Arthur Andersen LLP

LOCATIONS

HQ: 700 State St., Racine, WI 53404
Phone: 414-636-6011 **Fax:** 414-636-5043
Web site: http://www.casecorp.com

Case has 12 manufacturing facilities in North America and 13 in Australia, Austria, Brazil, France, Germany, and the UK.

1998 Sales

	$ mil.	% of total
US	3,931	49
France	1,070	13
UK	831	10
Canada	471	6
Other countries	1,778	22
Adjustments	(1,932)	—
Total	**6,149**	**100**

PRODUCTS/OPERATIONS

1998 Sales

	$ mil.	% of total
Farm equipment	3,533	57
Construction equipment	2,205	36
Parts	411	7
Total	**6,149**	**100**

COMPETITORS

AGCO
Blount
Caterpillar
Daewoo
Deere
Hitachi
Hyundai
Ingersoll-Rand
Isuzu
Komatsu
Kubota
New Holland
Samsung
Volvo

HISTORICAL FINANCIALS & EMPLOYEES

NYSE symbol: CSE FYE: December 31	Annual Growth	1989	1990	1991	1992	1993	1994	1995	1996	1997	1998
Sales ($ mil.)	1.6%	5,343	5,715	4,763	4,150	3,995	4,262	4,937	5,176	5,796	6,149
Net income ($ mil.)	(3.7%)	90	41	(985)	(1,107)	(22)	131	337	316	403	64
Income as % of sales	—	1.7%	0.7%	—	—	—	3.1%	6.8%	6.1%	7.0%	1.0%
Earnings per share ($)	(19.5%)	—	—	—	—	—	1.81	4.48	4.07	5.11	0.76
Stock price - FY high ($)	—	—	—	—	—	—	21.50	45.88	56.50	72.94	71.44
Stock price - FY low ($)	—	—	—	—	—	—	18.25	20.50	40.00	48.38	17.31
Stock price - FY close ($)	0.4%	—	—	—	—	—	21.50	45.75	54.50	60.44	21.81
P/E - high	—	—	—	—	—	—	12	10	14	14	94
P/E - low	—	—	—	—	—	—	10	5	10	9	23
Dividends per share ($)	41.4%	—	—	—	—	—	0.05	0.20	0.20	0.20	0.20
Book value per share ($)	14.3%	—	—	—	—	—	16.74	21.28	25.83	29.53	28.55
Employees	(5.4%)	29,100	28,500	24,200	18,500	17,100	16,900	15,700	17,500	18,300	17,700

STOCK PRICE HISTORY

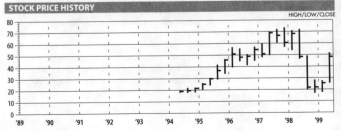

HIGH/LOW/CLOSE

1998 FISCAL YEAR-END

Debt ratio: 58.5%
Return on equity: 3.0%
Cash ($ mil.): 142
Current ratio: 1.51
Long-term debt ($ mil.): 3,080
No. of shares (mil.): 74
Dividends
  Yield: 0.9%
  Payout: 26.3%
Market value ($ mil.): 1,612

CATERPILLAR INC.

OVERVIEW

Like its namesake, Peoria, Illinois-based Caterpillar is trying to metamorphose and fly away from cyclical downturns in the construction industry. Caterpillar (or Cat) is the world's #1 manufacturer of earthmoving machinery and a leading supplier of agricultural equipment. In an attempt to combat downturns in these industries, the company has expanded into engine manufacturing and financing. It also provides insurance to Cat customers and dealers. The company also makes mining, logging, and oil industry equipment. Cat has manufacturing operations in 22 countries and a global network of 195 dealers serving 166

countries. Cat distributes its own line of Cat boots, caps, and jeans, as well as other manufacturer's auto parts (DaimlerChrysler) and sneakers (Puma).

Already a global organization — non-US sales account for 49% of the company's sales — Caterpillar is investing in new markets such as China, the former Soviet republics, Central Europe, and a number of other developing nations. Still, earnings have declined because economy downturns in Asia and South America have offset the booming US construction industry, and the mining, logging, and agricultural industries remain in a deep slump.

HISTORY

In 1904 in Stockton, California, combine maker Benjamin Holt modified the farming tractor by substituting a gas engine for steam and replacing iron wheels with crawler tracks. This improved the tractor's mobility over dirt.

The British adapted the "caterpillar" (Holt's nickname for the tractor) design to the armored tank in 1915. Following WWI, the US Army donated tanks to local governments for construction work. The caterpillar's efficiency spurred the development of earthmoving and construction equipment.

Holt merged with Best Tractor in 1925. The new company, named Caterpillar, moved to Peoria, Illinois, three years later. In the 1930s Cat expanded into international markets and phased out combine production to concentrate on construction and road-building equipment.

Sales volume more than tripled during WWII when Cat supplied the military with earthmoving equipment. Returning servicemen touted its durability and quality, and high demand continued during the postwar years. Cat emerged solidly in first place in the industry, far ahead of #2 International Harvester.

Expanding beyond US borders, the company established its first plant overseas in the UK (1951). It entered a joint venture with Japanese industrial titan Mitsubishi in 1963. Cat bought Solar Turbines (gas turbine engines, 1981). Fifty consecutive years of profits ended, however, when Cat ran up $953 million in losses between 1982 and 1984 as equipment demand fell and competition from international firms intensified. Cat doubled its product line between 1984 and 1989 and shifted production toward smaller equipment.

In 1990 CEO Donald Fites reorganized Cat along product lines. The next year the company clashed with the United Auto Workers (UAW)

over wage and health benefits. A strike resulted, and Cat reported its first annual loss since 1984. Most of the striking workers returned to work without a contract by mid-1992.

The firm completed a six-year, $1.8 billion modernization program in 1993 that automated many of its factories. That investment benefited the company when almost two-thirds of Cat's UAW employees at eight plants in Colorado, Illinois, and Pennsylvania went on strike in 1994.

Company management hired replacement workers and used its foreign factories to help fill orders. In 1995, after two years of record earnings at Cat, the UAW called off the strike. Cat set up a holding company, Caterpillar China Investment Co. Ltd., in 1996 for joint ventures there.

In 1998 Cat and the UAW (with federal mediation) hammered out their first contract agreement in more than six years. That year Cat paid $1.33 billion for LucasVarity's UK-based Perkins Engines, expanding its capacity to produce small and midsized diesel engines. Other 1998 purchases included Veratech Holdings (bucket and work tools), Material Handling Crane Systems (hydraulic excavators), and Wrightech (dragline buckets).

Chairman and CEO Fites retired in 1999, and was succeeded by VC Glen Barton. Caterpillar sold its Kato Engineering electric generator subsidiary to Emerson Electric in exchange for Emerson's stake in their diesel generator set joint venture, F.G. Wilson. Cat then prepared for layoffs and production cutbacks after slowdowns in agriculture, mining, and oil exploration reduced machinery orders.

Chairman and CEO: Glen A. Barton, age 59,
$972,003 pay (prior to title change)
Group President: Gerald S. Flaherty, age 60,
$839,304 pay
Group President: James W. Owens, age 52, $746,904 pay
Group President: Gerald L. Shaheen, age 54
Group President: Richard L. Thompson, age 59,
$746,904 pay
VP, Secretary, and General Counsel:
R. Rennie Atterbury III, age 61
VP: James W. Baldwin, age 61
VP: Sidney C. Banwart, age 53
VP; Chairman, Caterpillar Overseas:
Vito H. Baumgartner, age 58
VP: Michael J. Baunton, age 47
VP; President, Caterpillar Financial Services:
James S. Beard, age 57
VP; President, Caterpillar Industrial:
Richard A. Benson, age 55
VP: Ronald P. Bonati, age 59
VP: James E. Despain, age 61
VP: Michael A. Flexsenhar, age 59
VP: Donald M. Ings, age 50
VP: Duane H. Livingston, age 57
VP: Robert R. Macier, age 50
VP and CFO: F. Lynn McPheeters, age 56
VP Human Resources: Alan J. Rassi
Auditors: PricewaterhouseCoopers LLP

LOCATIONS

HQ: 100 NE Adams St., Peoria, IL 61629-7310
Phone: 309-675-1000   **Fax:** 309-675-1182
Web site: http://www.caterpillar.com

Caterpillar has manufacturing plants in 22 countries
and 195 dealerships worldwide.

PRODUCTS/OPERATIONS

1998 Sales & Operating Income

	Sales		Operating Income	
	$ mil.	% of total	$ mil.	% of total
Machinery	13,448	71	1,584	68
Engines	6,524	25	504	22
Financial services	1,005	4	239	10
Total	**20,977**	**100**	**2,540**	**100**

Selected Brands
Barber-Greene
Cat
Caterpillar
MaK
Perkins
Solar

COMPETITORS

AGCO
Allied Products
Case
Cummins Engine
DaimlerChrysler
Deere
FMC
Ford
Halliburton
Harnischfeger
Hitachi
Hyundai
Ingersoll-Rand
Isuzu
Komatsu

Kubota
Marubeni
Navistar
New Holland
Penske
Peterson Tractor
Peugeot
Rolls-Royce
Stewart & Stevenson
Terex
Thyssen Krupp
United Dominion
Industries
Volvo

HISTORICAL FINANCIALS & EMPLOYEES

NYSE symbol: CAT FYE: December 31	Annual Growth	1989	1990	1991	1992	1993	1994	1995	1996	1997	1998
Sales ($ mil.)	7.3%	11,126	11,436	10,182	10,194	11,615	14,328	16,072	16,522	18,925	20,977
Net income ($ mil.)	13.2%	497	210	(404)	(2,435)	652	955	1,136	1,361	1,665	1,513
Income as % of sales	—	4.5%	1.8%	—	—	5.6%	6.7%	7.1%	8.2%	8.8%	7.2%
Earnings per share ($)	14.3%	1.23	0.52	(1.00)	(6.03)	1.52	2.33	2.84	3.50	4.37	4.11
Stock price - FY high ($)	—	17.25	17.13	14.41	15.53	23.28	30.38	37.63	40.50	61.63	60.75
Stock price - FY low ($)	—	13.22	9.53	9.41	10.31	13.47	22.19	24.13	27.00	36.25	39.06
Stock price - FY close ($)	13.7%	14.47	11.75	10.97	13.41	22.25	27.56	29.38	37.63	48.50	46.00
P/E - high	—	14	33	—	—	15	13	13	12	14	15
P/E - low	—	11	18	—	—	9	10	8	8	8	10
Dividends per share ($)	15.5%	0.30	0.30	0.30	0.15	0.15	0.23	0.60	0.75	0.90	1.10
Book value per share ($)	3.0%	11.03	11.25	10.02	3.90	5.40	7.26	8.73	10.81	12.71	14.36
Employees	0.9%	60,784	59,662	55,950	52,340	50,443	53,986	54,352	57,026	59,863	65,824

STOCK PRICE HISTORY

HIGH/LOW/CLOSE

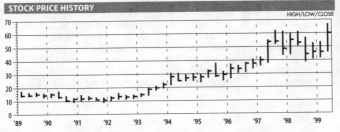

1998 FISCAL YEAR-END

Debt ratio: 64.7%
Return on equity: 29.5%
Cash ($ mil.): 360
Current ratio: 1.44
Long-term debt ($ mil.): 9,404
No. of shares (mil.): 357
Dividends
  Yield: 2.4%
  Payout: 26.8%
Market value ($ mil.): 16,431

CBS CORPORATION

OVERVIEW

Reinforcing the nickname it has carried for half a century, the "Tiffany Network" has shed the industrial vestiges of its former self (Westinghouse Electric) and is polishing its media empire. Best known for its television network, New York City-based CBS also has substantial radio holdings and interests in cable and Internet companies.

CBS ascended to the top of the TV network ratings heap during the 1998-99 season. But its audience skews older than those of its rivals, a thorny issue resulting in some of its top-rated programs generating lower ad revenues than other networks' less popular but "younger" shows. The CBS Television Network has more than 200 affiliates, and CBS itself owns 15 TV stations. It has also entered the cable arena with purchases of The Nashville Network (TNN) and Country Music Television (CMT). Through its 82% interest in Infinity Broadcasting, CBS boasts an extensive reach into radio. Spun off from CBS in 1998, Infinity owns 160 radio stations in 34 US markets. CBS also owns 37% of MarketWatch.com and 21% of SportsLine USA, and has inked a deal to provide broadcast news to America Online.

Under the leadership of president and CEO Mel Karmazin, CBS has been tightening its financial belt in the face of escalating programming costs and sluggish ad revenues. Its agreement to acquire mega-syndicator King World Productions (whose stable of programs includes powerhouses such as *The Oprah Winfrey Show* and *Wheel of Fortune*) will add a syndication dimension to its profile. Entertainment conglomerate Viacom agreed to purchase CBS in 1999. Viacom CEO Sumner Redstone will continue to lead the combined firm, with Karmazin taking over as president and COO.

HISTORY

Arthur Judson founded United Independent Broadcasters (UIB), a radio broadcasting company, in 1927. When Columbia Phonograph bought UIB's broadcasting rights later that year, the company was re-christened as the Columbia Phonograph Broadcasting System, a moniker later shortened to the Columbia Broadcasting System. When cigar maker Sam Paley took a controlling interest in the company in 1928, he installed his son William as president, and the younger Paley set about changing the face of broadcasting. He promoted daytime dramas, raided stars from NBC, and built a strong news organization.

CBS branched into TV broadcasting during the 1940s, picking up the Tiffany Network nickname as it became known for programming considered classier than the norm. During the 1950s CBS News exposed McCarthyism, but the network found itself red-faced when its *$64,000 Question* was front and center in a 1958 quiz show scandal. Thanks to shows such as *Mr. Ed* and *The Beverly Hillbillies,* CBS was #1 in entertainment ratings during much of the 1950s and 1960s. It also began to diversify, taking stakes in ventures ranging from publishing to the New York Yankees (CBS later sold its 80% ownership in the baseball team).

In spite of a flurry of turnover among top management during the 1970s, programming such as *The Mary Tyler Moore Show* and *All in the Family* helped CBS lead the ratings race. Laurence Tisch became CEO in 1987; he led the sale of CBS's publishing and record operations. When William Paley died in 1990, Tisch became chairman.

In 1994 a stunned CBS lost broadcasting rights to NFL football games and several affiliates to the Fox network. The next year, after a no confidence vote from one of its top institutional investors, Westinghouse Electric acquired CBS for $5.4 billion. Committing itself to broadcasting, Westinghouse began selling its non-broadcasting holdings and acquired Infinity Broadcasting in 1996. It expanded into cable with acquisitions of The Nashville Network and Country Music Television. The company changed its name from Westinghouse to CBS Corporation in 1997.

CBS's 1998 acquisition of American Radio Systems brought 90 additional radio stations to its fold. Its sale of nearly 20% of Infinity Broadcasting later that year was one of the most successful IPOs of all time. Also in 1998 the company outbid NBC for a key contract with the NFL ($4 billion over eight years).

President and COO Mel Karmazin (former CEO of Infinity Broadcasting) was appointed CEO in 1999 and David McLaughlin was appointed chairman. CBS also bought 50% of StoreRunner.com, 35% of Internet directory firm Switchboard, 35% of medical Web site Medscape, and agreed to buy 20% of Rx.com. Other deals include the $2.5 billion agreement to buy syndication giant King World Productions and the pending acquisition of a 30% stake in online entertainment firm Big Entertainment. Entertainment conglomerate Viacom has agreed to buy the company for a whopping $35 million.

Chairman: David McLaughlin, age 66
President and CEO: Mel Karmazin, age 55,
$4,000,000 pay (prior to promotion)
EVP and CFO: Fredric G. Reynolds, age 48,
$1,147,000 pay
EVP and General Counsel: Louis J. Briskman, age 50,
$895,000 pay
EVP Human Resources: David Zemelman
SVP Communications: Gil Schwartz
VP and Controller: Robert G. Freedline, age 41
President and CEO, CBS Television: Leslie Moonves,
age 49, $4,000,000 pay
President, CBS Entertainment: Nancy Tellem
President Sales, CBS Television: Joseph Abruzzese
SVP Comedy Development, CBS Entertainment:
Gene Stein
SVP Communications, CBS Entertainment:
Chris Ender
**SVP Current Programming and Specials, CBS
Entertainment:** Terry Botwick
SVP Drama Development, CBS Entertainment:
Nina Tassler
**SVP Movies for Television and Mini-Series, CBS
Entertainment:** Sunta Izzicupo
**SVP Program Planning and Scheduling, CBS
Entertainment:** Kelly Kahl
SVP Programming, East Coast, CBS Entertainment:
Mitch Semel
SVP Talent and Casting, CBS Entertainment:
Peter Golden
Secretary: Angeline C. Straka
Director of Recruitment and Placement:
Linda Kalarchian
Auditors: KPMG LLP

LOCATIONS

HQ: 51 W. 52nd St., New York, NY 10019
Phone: 212-975-4321   **Fax:** 212-975-4516
Web site: http://www.cbs.com

CBS has operations in Belgium, Canada, Ireland, New
Zealand, Singapore, Spain, Switzerland, Ukraine, the
UK, and the US.

PRODUCTS/OPERATIONS

1998 Sales

	$ mil.	% of total
Television	4,919	72
Radio	1,893	28
Adjustments	(7)	—
Total	**6,805**	**100**

COMPETITORS

A&E Networks
ABC
AMFM
AT&T Broadband & Internet Services
BHC Communications
Clear Channel
Cox Enterprises
Discovery Communications
Fox Entertainment
Liberty Media
NBC
Time Warner
Tribune
Univision Communications
USA Networks
Viacom

HISTORICAL FINANCIALS & EMPLOYEES

NYSE symbol: CBS FYE: December 31	Annual Growth	1989	1990	1991	1992	1993	1994	1995	1996	1997	1998
Sales ($ mil.)	(6.8%)	12,844	12,915	12,794	8,447	8,875	8,848	6,296	8,449	5,363	6,805
Net income ($ mil.)	—	922	268	(1,086)	(1,291)	(270)	77	15	30	549	(21)
Income as % of sales	—	7.2%	2.1%	—	—	—	0.9%	0.2%	0.4%	10.2%	—
Earnings per share ($)	—	3.15	0.91	(3.46)	(3.81)	(1.07)	(0.11)	(0.25)	0.12	0.84	(0.03)
Stock price – FY high ($)	—	42.31	39.38	31.00	21.13	17.13	15.25	17.88	21.13	32.06	36.63
Stock price – FY low ($)	—	25.63	24.25	13.75	9.38	12.75	10.88	12.13	15.38	16.00	18.00
Stock price – FY close ($)	(1.3%)	37.00	28.50	18.00	13.38	14.13	12.25	16.38	19.88	29.44	32.81
P/E – high		13	43	—	—	—	—	—	176	38	—
P/E – low		8	27	—	—	—	—	—	128	19	—
Dividends per share ($)	(29.4%)	1.15	1.35	1.40	0.72	0.40	0.20	0.20	0.20	0.20	0.05
Book value per share ($)	(1.6%)	15.10	13.43	11.04	6.77	2.97	4.56	3.81	9.79	11.61	13.12
Employees	(10.2%)	121,963	115,774	113,664	109,050	101,654	84,400	77,813	59,275	51,444	46,189

STOCK PRICE HISTORY

HIGH/LOW/CLOSE

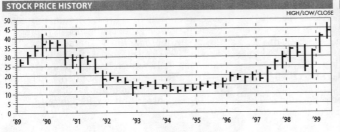

1998 FISCAL YEAR-END

Debt ratio: 21.7%
Return on equity: —
Cash ($ mil.): 798
Current ratio: 1.74
Long-term debt ($ mil.): 2,506
No. of shares (mil.): 690
Dividends
 Yield: 0.2%
 Payout: —
Market value ($ mil.): 22,650

CENDANT CORPORATION

OVERVIEW

If Cendant's history were set to music, it would be a country song about a marriage gone wrong and the road to recovery. Cendant, based in New York City, resulted from the 1997 merger of direct marketer CUC International and hospitality franchisor HFS. Immediately following the merger, hundreds of millions of dollars in "fictitious revenues" at CUC was discovered. To recover from the CUC scandal, Cendant has sold many of that predecessor's operations, and more sales are in the works.

Cendant offers travel, real estate, direct marketing, and other consumer and business services. It is the world's largest hotel franchisor, with more than 6,000 middle- and economy-priced properties, although it doesn't own any hotels itself. Cendant owns the world's #1 time-share exchange service (Resort Condominiums International) and the Avis rental-car franchise system. It also owns the nation's #1 and #3 real estate brokerage franchises (Century 21, Coldwell Banker). Cendant offers discounted products and services through direct marketing to more than 63 million members. Other services include tax preparation (Jackson Hewitt).

Cendant has operations in more than 100 countries.

HISTORY

Acting on what seemed like a good idea at the time, CUC International and HFS merged in 1997 to form Cendant. CUC got its start in 1973 when a group led by Walter Forbes, envisioning a computer-based home shopping network, founded Comp-U-Card America, later known as CUC. In the 1980s CUC became a discount direct marketer and catalog-based shopping club. It went public in 1983 with 100,000 members. CUC offered wholesale memberships to banks and other credit institutions, whose customers enjoyed discounts and other services. It acquired Financial Institution Services in 1985 and American Direct Response in 1986.

With no inventory and low overhead, CUC sold merchandise at 6%-8% over wholesale prices. Between 1989 and 1993 it signed up 7.6 million members. In 1996 CUC acquired Advance Ross Corporation, a processor of value-added tax refunds to travelers in Europe; Rent Net, an online apartment rental service; the Ideon Group, a credit card enhancement service; and entertainment software publishers Davidson & Associates and Sierra On-Line. In 1997 CUC bought software maker Knowledge Adventure and launched a new online shopping site, NetMarket.

HFS's growth was similarly explosive. In the 1980s Henry Silverman helped transform roadside chain Days Inn into the world's #3 hotel franchisor. In 1990 he joined LBO specialist Blackstone Group and led its purchases of the Howard Johnson and Ramada brands. In 1992 Blackstone bought Days Inn, taking it and the other two operations public as Hospitality Franchise Systems (later HFS). In 1996 it bought the Super 8 Motels brand.

In 1995 HFS entered the residential real estate market with the purchase of Century 21.

In 1996 it bought Electronic Realty Associates (ERA), real estate firm Coldwell Banker, time-share operator Resort Condominiums International, and car-rental firm Avis. In 1997 HFS sold 75% of Avis's #1 franchisee to the public. Also that year HFS bought relocation service firm PHH.

CUC and HFS completed their $14.1 billion merger in December 1997. The name Cendant was derived from "ascendant," but the marriage quickly headed the opposite direction. The honeymoon ended in 1998 amid revelations of accounting irregularities (about $500 million in fake revenue and pretax profit) at CUC prior to the merger. The resulting fall in Cendant's stock price cost CEO Silverman almost $1 billion in the value of his stock options between April and July. Chairman Forbes resigned at the end of July 1998.

Cendant's 1998 acquisitions included Jackson Hewitt, the US's #2 tax-preparation firm, and UK-based National Parking. After Forbes resigned, Silverman began to reshape the firm largely in the image of the former HFS. Cendant sold Cendant Software, Hebdo Mag, Essex, National Leisure Group, National Library of Poetry, and Match.Com for a total of about $1.4 billion.

The company agreed in 1999 to take a $220 million charge to settle a class-action lawsuit filed by disgruntled shareholders. Cendant sued accounting firm Ernst & Young in 1999, charging it with gross negligence in failing to detect the improper financial practices at CUC. Also in 1999 Cendant sold its fleet business — including PHH Vehicle Management Services — to Avis Rent A Car for $5 billion, and it put its Entertainment Publications, Green Flag, and other noncore units up for sale.

OFFICERS

Chairman, President, and CEO: Henry R. Silverman,
age 58, $2,818,142 pay
VC and General Counsel: James E. Buckman,
$769,056 pay
VC; Chairman and CEO, Travel Division:
Stephen P. Holmes, age 42, $1,035,384 pay
VC; Chairman and CEO, Alliance Marketing Division:
Michael P. Monaco, age 51, $1,035,384 pay
SEVP Finance and CFO: David M. Johnson, age 38
EVP Human Resources: Thomas D. Christopoul
EVP Finance and Chief Accounting Officer:
Jon F. Danski
EVP Strategic Development: Samuel L. Katz, age 33
EVP; President and CEO, Lifestyle Unit:
Michael H. Wargotz, age 39
Auditors: Deloitte & Touche LLP

LOCATIONS

HQ: 9 W. 57th St., New York, NY 10019
Phone: 212-413-1800   **Fax:** 212-413-1918
Web site: http://www.cendant.com

PRODUCTS/OPERATIONS

1998 Sales

	$ mil.	% of total
Travel	1,063	20
Individual Membership	929	18
Insurance/Wholesale	544	10
Real Estate Franchise	456	9
Relocation	444	8
Fleet	388	7
Mortgage	353	7
Other	1,107	21
Total	**5,284**	**100**

Services

Alliance Marketing
Entertainment publications
Individual memberships
Insurance/wholesale

Real Estate Franchises
Brokerage
Century 21 Corp.
Coldwell Banker Corp.
ERA
Mortgage
Relocation

Travel
Car rental
Avis (car-rental
franchise)
Hotel franchises
Days Inn
Howard Johnson
Knights Inn

Ramada (in the US)
Super 8
Travelodge (in North
America)
Villager Lodge
Wingate Inn
Time-share exchange
Resort Condominiums
International (RCI)

Other Services
Green Flag (motorist
assistant in the UK)
Jackson Hewitt, Inc. (tax
preparation)
National Car Parks (car
park operators in the UK)
Welcome Wagon
Wizcom (hotel and car
rental reservations
processor)

COMPETITORS

AAA
AARP
Accor
AutoNation
Bass Hotels & Resorts
Budget Group
Choice Hotels
Enterprise Rent-A-Car
Experian
GE Capital
Hertz
Hilton

Interval International
J. C. Penney
Marriott International
Promus Hotel
Reader's Digest
RE/MAX
Sears
Starwood Hotels & Resorts
Worldwide
USAA
Wal-Mart

HISTORICAL FINANCIALS & EMPLOYEES

NYSE symbol: CD FYE: December 31	Annual Growth	1989	1990	1991	1992	1993	1994	1995	1996	1997	1998
Sales ($ mil.)	34.6%	365	451	641	739	875	1,045	1,415	2,348	5,315	5,284
Net income ($ mil.)	59.4%	8	18	25	59	87	118	163	164	55	540
Income as % of sales	—	2.2%	3.9%	3.9%	8.0%	10.0%	11.3%	11.5%	7.0%	1.0%	10.2%
Earnings per share ($)	32.0%	0.05	0.10	0.11	0.25	0.34	0.45	0.56	0.41	0.06	0.61
Stock price - FY high ($)	—	2.74	3.35	6.53	8.61	17.68	16.13	26.18	27.50	34.38	41.69
Stock price - FY low ($)	—	1.39	1.65	3.25	5.12	7.38	11.12	15.29	18.34	19.25	6.50
Stock price - FY close ($)	31.7%	1.62	3.32	6.21	8.09	14.24	15.40	24.60	24.88	34.38	19.31
P/E - high	—	55	34	59	34	52	36	47	67	573	68
P/E - low	—	28	17	30	20	22	25	27	45	321	11
Dividends per share ($)	(100.0%)	0.66	0.00	0.00	0.00	0.00	0.00	0.00	0.00	0.00	0.00
Book value per share ($)	—	(0.25)	(0.13)	(0.00)	0.62	1.13	1.72	2.57	3.12	5.38	5.80
Employees	34.1%	2,500	3,000	3,200	5,000	6,000	6,500	8,000	11,000	34,000	35,000

1998 and prior information is for CUC International only.

STOCK PRICE HISTORY

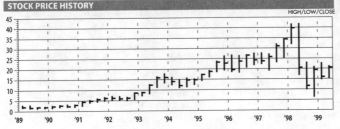

1998 FISCAL YEAR-END

Debt ratio: 68.0%
Return on equity: 11.2%
Cash ($ mil.): 1,009
Current ratio: 1.58
Long-term debt ($ mil.): 10,260
No. of shares (mil.): 833
Dividends
  Yield: —
  Payout: —
Market value ($ mil.): 16,091

CENTEX CORPORATION

OVERVIEW

Centex Corporation has built its way to the top of its profession: The Dallas-based company, which constructs houses for first-time buyers (starter homes begin at $54,000) and move-up buyers (up to $869,000), is the leading US homebuilder. Centex also buys and develops land, provides mortgage loans and insurance to home purchasers, and offers commercial contracting and construction services.

Its main subsidiary, Centex Homes, builds more than 14,000 homes each year in 19 states and Washington, DC. More than 90% of its homes are single-family detached houses; townhomes and condominiums make up the balance. Centex also has holdings in Latin America and the UK, including British builder Fairclough Homes, and owns 80% of Cavco

Industries, a leading builder of the manufactured homes used in mobile home parks.

Centex Construction Group is made up of six independent regional construction firms, with projects in both the private sector (such as office and apartment buildings) and public sector (such as education, government, and health care facilities).

Centex has cemented its leadership position by offering home-related products and services. Its majority-owned subsidiary, Centex Construction Products, makes and sells gypsum wallboard, aggregates, and ready-mix concrete. CTX Mortgage makes loans to more than 70% of its parent's homebuyers. The firm's Centex HomeTeam subsidiary provides pest control, security, and lawn services.

HISTORY

Tom Lively and Ira Rupley, who built their first large subdivision near Dallas in 1949, founded a homebuilding company, Centex, the next year. Centex's first out-of-Texas project was a development of 7,000 houses near Chicago.

By 1960 it had built 25,000 houses. Branching out from homebuilding, Centex built its first cement plant in 1963 and established four more plants over the next 25 years. Centex expanded into commercial construction with the purchase in 1966 of Dallas contractor J. W. Bateson (founded 1936), later buying other general contractors in Florida, California, and Washington, DC, in the 1970s. To combine homebuilding with home financing, Centex began mortgage banking in 1973, and when oil prices soared during the 1970s, the enterprising company formed subsidiary Cenergy to go digging for petroleum (spun off in 1984).

Centex increasingly built outside its Southwest territory — from 28% of all new homes in 1979 to 45% in 1984. Larry Hirsch, a New York-reared lawyer who had headed a Houston cement and energy company, became COO in 1984 (and CEO in 1988). The early 1980s were a boom time for Texas real estate as deregulation spurred S&Ls to make loans — any loans. The market became overbuilt, and when oil prices collapsed in 1986-87, credit dried up. With the spectacular failure of several Texas S&Ls, the Texas real estate market crashed. Centex was pinched, but it survived on sales from less-depressed areas of the US.

Centex Development Company was established in 1987 as a custodian for land the company could not develop during the bust. Centex created Centex-Rodgers Construction that year

to focus on medical facility construction. In 1994 the company took its construction products division public and sold off its S&Ls.

In 1995 Centex entered into ventures to build luxury houses in the UK and living centers for people suffering from Alzheimer's disease and memory disorders. The next year Centex purchased parts of security systems firm Advanced Protection Systems and pest-control company Environmental Safety Systems — both are now part of Centex HomeTeam.

The company was selected by *Builder* and *Home* magazines in 1997 to build the Home of the Future, showcasing cutting-edge products and design. On the other end of the housing spectrum, Centex acquired 80% of manufactured-home maker Cavco Industries; the next year Cavco bought AAA Homes, which had about 260 manufactured-home retail outlets in 12 states, Canada, and Japan. In 1998 Centex entered Ohio and New Jersey by acquiring Wayne Homes and Calton Homes, respectively.

Along with other Houston builders, Centex contracted ClearWorks Technologies in 1999 to pre-wire Houston homes for Internet, networking, and other "smart home" capabilities. The US company also went further abroad: It bought UK builder Fairclough Homes (operating in the North West, Midlands, and South East) from AMEC for $175 million.

Meanwhile, CTX Mortgage was sued by a Washington-based ISP, Connect Northwest, for breaking that state's spam laws, allegedly sending out thousands of e-mail advertisements with false return addresses.

Chairman and CEO: Laurence E. Hirsch, $2,450,000 pay
VC and CFO: David W. Quinn, $2,050,000 pay
EVP; Chairman and CEO, Centex Homes:
Timothy R. Eller, $1,764,400 pay
**EVP, Chief Legal Officer, General Counsel, and
Secretary:** Raymond G. Smerge, $890,000 pay
SVP, Strategic Planning and Mergers and Acquisitions:
Robert M. Swartz
VP: Peter M. McParlin
VP Corporate Communications: Sheila E. Gallagher
VP Taxes: Richard C. Harvey
President and CEO, Centex Development:
Richard C. Decker
President and CEO, Centex Home Equity:
Anthony H. Barone
EVP and COO, Centex Home Equity:
Stephen D. Janawsky
President and COO, Centex Homes:
Andrew J. Hannigan
EVP and CFO, Centex Homes: William D. Albers
EVP, Centex Homes: Thomas M. Boyce
EVP, Centex Homes: Robert D. Hillmann
EVP, Centex Homes: Steven R. Muller
President, Centex Multi-Family: Michael M. Vick
President and CEO, CTX Mortgage: Judson H. Croom
Controller: Barry G. Wilson
Auditors: Arthur Andersen LLP

HQ: 2728 N. Harwood, Dallas, TX 75201-1516
Phone: 214-981-5000   **Fax:** 214-981-6859
Web site: http://www.centex.com

Centex builds houses in more than 60 markets in 19
US states and the District of Columbia. It also invests in
homebuilding activities in Latin America and the UK.

1999 Sales

	$ mil.	% of total
Homebuilding	2,998	58
Contracting & construction services	1,351	26
Financial services	436	8
Construction products	336	7
Investment real estate	34	1
Total	**5,155**	**100**

Selected Subsidiaries
Cavco Industries (80%, manufactured housing)
Centex Homes (home building)
Centex HomeTeam Services (security monitoring, pest
control, lawn care, and home systems)
CTX Mortgage Company (home mortgage lender)
Fairclough Homes Group Ltd. (homebuilding in the UK)

Ameritech	M.D.C. Holdings
Barratt Developments	MGIC Investment
Beazer Homes	M I Schottenstein Homes
Countrywide Credit	NVR
Del Webb	Peter Kiewit Sons'
D.R. Horton	Pittston Brink's
Fleet	PMI Group
Fluor	Pulte
Foster Wheeler	Rollins
George Wimpey	Ryland
GE Capital	Toll Brothers
Hovnanian Enterprises	Turner Corporation
Kaufman & Broad	Tyco International
Lennar	U.S. Home

NYSE symbol: CTX FYE: March 31	Annual Growth	1990	1991	1992	1993	1994	1995	1996	1997	1998	1999
Sales ($ mil.)	10.7%	2,073	2,244	2,166	2,503	3,215	3,278	3,103	3,785	3,976	5,155
Net income ($ mil.)	15.8%	62	44	35	61	85	92	53	107	145	232
Income as % of sales	—	3.0%	1.9%	1.6%	2.4%	2.7%	2.8%	1.7%	2.8%	3.6%	4.5%
Earnings per share ($)	15.7%	1.01	0.71	0.56	0.96	1.51	1.51	0.91	1.80	2.36	3.75
Stock price - FY high ($)	—	10.47	11.06	13.75	17.31	22.88	16.19	18.00	21.00	41.63	45.75
Stock price - FY low ($)	—	7.00	4.81	8.47	9.94	13.38	10.06	11.75	12.63	16.75	26.38
Stock price - FY close ($)	14.7%	9.72	8.56	12.09	15.81	15.44	12.13	15.50	17.63	38.13	33.38
P/E - high	—	10	16	25	18	18	11	20	12	18	12
P/E - low	—	7	7	15	10	10	7	13	7	7	7
Dividends per share ($)	5.4%	0.10	0.10	0.10	0.10	0.10	0.10	0.10	0.10	0.12	0.16
Book value per share ($)	11.7%	7.44	7.92	8.49	9.29	10.56	11.90	12.71	14.40	16.65	20.17
Employees	11.1%	5,100	5,300	5,500	6,500	8,430	6,395	6,186	8,926	10,259	13,161

HIGH/LOW/CLOSE

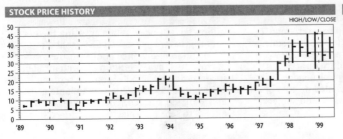

Debt ratio: 19.2%
Return on equity: 19.4%
Cash ($ mil.): 111
Current ratio: 1.37
Long-term debt ($ mil.): 284
No. of shares (mil.): 59
Dividends
  Yield: 0.5%
  Payout: 4.3%
Market value ($ mil.): 1,982

CENTRAL AND SOUTH WEST

OVERVIEW

Electricity provider Central and South West (CSW) is pulling a power play that will turn into a disappearing act if it comes off. The proposed acquisition of Dallas-based CSW by American Electric Power (AEP) — one of the biggest mergers of investor-owned electric utilities in US history — will bring 9 million customers under one roof. Then CSW will be dissolved.

The merger's critics, who *haven't* disappeared yet, complain that CSW is just too big. CSW currently operates four regulated US utilities (with a combined generating capacity of 14,000 MW) that serve about 1.7 million customers. Central Power and Light (CPL) and West Texas Utilities (WTU) operate in Texas, Public Service Company of Oklahoma (PSC)

provides power for Oklahoma, and Southwestern Electric Power Company (SWEPCO) serves Arkansas and Louisiana. CSW is active overseas as well. It owns a UK regional electric company, SEEBOARD, that provides power for 2 million customers, and its Brazilian utility, VALE, serves 1.9 million more. CSW is also involved in power trading.

CSW has long believed in the power of non-regulated activities. CSW Energy and CSW International have independent power projects in the US and abroad. Subsidiary EnerShop helps large-volume users manage their energy use more efficiently, while C3 Communications offers automated meter reading systems to other utilities and is building a fiber-optic network in Texas and Louisiana.

HISTORY

Utility magnate Samuel Insull and his brother Martin formed Central and South West Utilities (CSU) as a subsidiary of their huge Middle West Utilities in 1925. CSU, in turn, united five firms that provided power, water, and gas in Kansas, Louisiana, Mississippi, Oklahoma, and Texas.

The 1935 Public Utility Holding Company Act restricted the gigantic utility holding companies. CSU was divested from Middle West in 1947 and merged with a subsidiary, American Public Service, to become Central and South West (CSW).

The growth of the oil industry in Oklahoma and Texas helped CSW reach over $200 million in sales by the early 1960s. In 1961 it bought Transok Pipe Line to supply natural gas to its Oklahoma power stations, and within a decade its revenues had more than doubled, to $425 million. Natural gas fueled all its plants, most of which were in rural areas.

Led by chairman Silas Bent Phillips, CSW embarked on a major construction and fuel diversification program in 1972. By 1978 the company was still 96% dependent on natural gas and its fuel costs were 50% above that of Texas rivals Houston Lighting & Power (HP&L, now Reliant Energy) and Texas Utilities (TXU). Phillips decided to interconnect CSW's utilities throughout their four-state service area to make cheaper wholesale power available systemwide. Until then the Texas power grid was completely independent of the US grid. HP&L and TXU wanted no part of this interstate commerce (which would subject them to federal regulation) and held up the plan in court for years. Finally, a compromise

allowed CSW to convert its AC power to DC, transmit it across state lines, then reconvert it to AC while the feds looked the other way.

CSW's 25% ownership of the South Texas Nuclear Project mired the firm in spiraling construction costs during the 1980s. Generating Unit 1 went on line in 1988, eight years behind schedule. Unit 2 powered up in 1989.

In 1990, with competition fast approaching, CSW adopted a policy of diversification under president E. R. Brooks (who became CEO in 1991). In 1992 the Energy Policy Act opened utilities' once-exclusive service areas to wholesale competition. CSW restructured in 1994 and formed two nonregulated subsidiaries: CSW Communications (later C3 Communications) and CSW International.

Things took a turn for the worse in the mid-1990s. First CSW attempted to buy two bankrupt utilities, El Paso Electric and Cajun Electric, but failed. In 1996, eyeing the UK's deregulated market, CSW paid $2.1 billion to buy SEEBOARD and sold off Transok to pay down the debt. But it got hit by a windfall tax levied by the UK the next year.

After a 1997 rate cut by Texas' public utility commission hit Central Power & Light hard, CSW agreed to American Electric Power's $6.6 billion buyout offer. While awaiting the necessary regulatory approvals, CSW sold off the C3 local and long-distance phone business to partner ICG, began building merchant plants in Texas and England's West Sussex, and in 1998 opened two cogeneration plants in Texas and Tampico, Mexico. The next year CSW agreed to set up an electricity interexchange system with Mexico.

Chairman and CEO: E. R. Brooks, age 61,
$1,191,345 pay
President and COO: Thomas V. Shockley III, age 53,
$818,462 pay
EVP and CFO: Glenn D. Rosilier, age 51, $422,636 pay
EVP and General Counsel: Ferdinand C. Meyer Jr.,
age 59, $544,272 pay
**SVP Customer Relations & Corporate Development and
Assistant Corporate Secretary:** Venita McCellon-Allen,
age 39
SVP Electric Operations: Glenn Flies, age 51,
$517,307 pay
SVP External Affairs: Thomas M. Hagan, age 54
VP, AEP Merger: Stephen J. McDonnell
VP, Opportunities: Michael D. Smith
**VP, Corporate Secretary, and Associate General
Counsel:** Kenneth C. Raney Jr., age 47
**President, Energy Delivery, Central and South West
Services:** Robert L. Zemanek, $372,529 pay
**President, Energy Services, Central and South West
Services:** Richard H. Bremer
**President, Production, Central and South West
Services:** Richard P. Verret
**VP, Customer Relations, Central and South West
Services:** M. Bruce Evans
**VP, Human Resources, Central and South West
Services:** Lana L. Hillebrand
Treasurer: Wendy G. Hargus, age 41
Controller: Lawrence B. Connors, age 47
Auditors: Arthur Andersen LLP

LOCATIONS

HQ: Central and South West Corporation,
1616 Woodall Rodgers Fwy., Dallas, TX 75202-1234
Phone: 214-777-1000   **Fax:** 214-777-1033
Web site: http://www.csw.com

PRODUCTS/OPERATIONS

1998 Energy Marketed

	kWh (mil.)	% of total
Industrial	21,481	32
Residential	19,757	30
Commercial	15,554	23
Wholesale	8,296	12
Other	1,906	3
Total	**66,994**	**100**

Utility Subsidiaries
Central Power and Light Company (South Texas)
Public Service Company of Oklahoma (eastern and
southwestern Oklahoma)
SEEBOARD plc (provides electricity in the UK)
Southwestern Electric Power Company (northern
Louisiana, northern Texas, and Arkansas)
West Texas Utilities Company

Nonutility Subsidiaries
C3 Communications, Inc. (designs, builds, and
maintains telecommunications networks)
CSW Energy, Inc. (develops and operates independent
power and cogeneration projects)
CSW International, Inc. (develops and operates foreign
independent power projects)
EnerShop Inc. (energy-efficiency services)

COMPETITORS

Cleco	Pedernales Electric
Dynegy	Reliant Energy
El Paso Electric	Southwestern Public
Empire District Electric	Service
Entergy	TNP Enterprises
LCRA	Texas Utilities
OGE	

HISTORICAL FINANCIALS & EMPLOYEES

NYSE symbol: CSR FYE: December 31	Annual Growth	1989	1990	1991	1992	1993	1994	1995	1996	1997	1998
Sales ($ mil.)	8.9%	2,549	2,744	3,047	3,289	3,687	3,623	3,735	5,155	5,268	5,482
Net income ($ mil.)	3.0%	337	386	401	404	327	412	421	447	163	440
Income as % of sales	—	13.2%	14.1%	13.2%	12.3%	8.9%	11.4%	11.3%	8.7%	3.1%	8.0%
Earnings per share ($)	2.7%	1.63	1.90	1.99	2.03	0.72	2.07	2.10	2.07	0.72	2.07
Stock price - FY high ($)	—	20.13	23.00	27.19	30.00	34.25	30.88	28.50	29.50	27.50	30.75
Stock price - FY low ($)	—	14.88	18.31	20.75	24.25	28.25	20.13	22.38	25.38	18.00	24.88
Stock price - FY close ($)	3.5%	20.06	22.00	27.00	29.13	30.25	22.63	27.88	25.63	27.06	27.44
P/E - high	—	12	12	14	15	48	15	14	14	38	15
P/E - low	—	9	10	10	12	39	10	11	12	25	12
Dividends per share ($)	3.3%	1.30	1.38	1.46	1.54	1.62	1.70	1.72	1.74	1.74	1.74
Book value per share ($)	2.2%	14.07	14.57	15.05	15.54	15.55	16.01	16.47	17.98	16.76	17.05
Employees	3.0%	8,423	8,377	8,581	8,595	8,707	8,055	12,064	11,437	11,415	10,956

STOCK PRICE HISTORY

HIGH/LOW/CLOSE

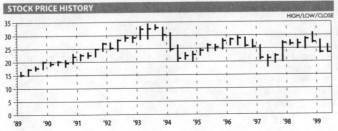

1998 FISCAL YEAR-END

Debt ratio: 49.9%
Return on equity: 12.1%
Cash ($ mil.): 157
Current ratio: 0.61
Long-term debt ($ mil.): 3,785
No. of shares (mil.): 213
Dividends
Yield: 6.3%
Payout: 84.1%
Market value ($ mil.): 5,834

CERIDIAN CORPORATION

OVERVIEW

Ceridian loves to crunch numbers. The Minneapolis-based information services company's Human Resource Services unit (HRS, 60% of Ceridian's sales) is a leading provider of human resources information systems, payroll and tax services, employee training, and related services and software, serving more than 100,000 customers in the US, Canada, and the UK. Ceridian's Comdata unit provides services to the transportation industry, including fuel cards, licensing, and fuel tax reporting. The

company's Arbitron subsidiary measures broadcast audiences, providing data that helps advertisers decide where to spend their money most effectively.

Having divested its defense electronics business, Ceridian is firmly focused on information services. The company is using acquisitions and new products and services to help meet its ambitious goal of growing revenues by 15%-20% a year.

HISTORY

Ceridian has its roots in Control Data Corporation (CDC), which William Norris founded in 1957 to challenge IBM in mainframe computers for scientific applications. Norris, a WWII cryptologist, after the war helped found Engineering Research Associates (ERA), which was sold to Remington Rand and formed the nucleus of Sperry Rand. Norris managed Sperry Rand's UNIVAC division, where Seymour Cray (who later founded Cray Computers and Cray Research) created a line of pioneering computers.

During the 1960s and 1970s CDC was a powerhouse. It bought more than 80 companies, primarily in peripherals and data services. The company's service segment grew substantially in 1973 when, in the settlement of an antitrust suit, CDC was allowed to buy IBM's service bureau for less than market value. (This business later evolved into Human Resource Services.) CDC also began providing lease financing services for its customers through the 1968 purchase of Commercial Credit Company. (During this period Norris directed the company into social remediation projects, building facilities in low-income areas and offering benefits such as day care and counseling.)

In the early 1980s CDC plunged into supercomputers and encountered heated competition from Japanese companies. It also entered the fiercely competitive semiconductor business. These operations sucked cash out of the organization and never became profitable.

Norris retired following huge losses in 1985. His successor, Robert Price, divested such operations as Commercial Credit. Sales rose modestly and then fell again. Price resigned and Lawrence Perlman was brought in as CEO in 1990. He turned the company away from proprietary systems and made alliances with other manufacturers, including Silicon Graphics and Volkswagen (to develop computer-assisted engineering and manufacturing

software). But new cost controls could not overcome the effects of recession in the early 1990s and sales remained weak. In 1992 CDC spun off its computer products and services subsidiary, Control Data Systems, and changed its name to Ceridian (a made-up word).

The remaining company consisted of the human resources management and benefits administration operations, Arbitron, and Defense Electronics. Reaching for a common thread, Ceridian redefined itself as a diversified information services company. Bankrolled by higher earnings at last, plus about $1 billion in tax credits from its past losses, the company shopped for acquisitions. In 1995 it bought Comdata, a provider of information services to the trucking industry and casino cash advances. In 1996 the company acquired nine additional human resources and transportation services companies.

In 1997 Ceridian expanded its information business to the UK through the purchase of Continental Research. Later that year it exited the defense electronics business by selling Computing Devices International to General Dynamics for $600 million. In 1998 the company swapped Comdata's casino services unit for First Data's trucking services business and purchased the payroll divisions of Canadian Imperial Bank of Commerce and Toronto-Dominion Bank (now Ceridian Canada Ltd.).

Ceridian in 1999 bought competitor ABR Information Services (benefits and payroll services, now Ceridian Benefits Services) for $750 million. It also purchased the LifeWorks line of workplace effectiveness training products and jumped on the WWW wagon with PowerPay, software that lets businesses transmit human resources data over the Internet. The company also announced that COO Ronald Turner will succeed Perlman as CEO in the new year.

Chairman and CEO: Lawrence Perlman, age 60,
$1,522,350 pay
President and COO: Ronald L. Turner, age 52,
$746,979 pay
EVP and CFO: John R. Eickhoff, age 58, $589,370 pay
EVP; President, Arbitron: Stephen B. Morris, age 55,
$235,770 pay
SVP Human Resources: Shirley Hughes, age 53
VP and Corporate Controller: Loren D. Gross, age 53
VP, Secretary, and General Counsel: Gary M. Nelson,
age 47
VP Diversity Resources and Public Affairs:
Norma Anderson
VP Government Relations: James O'Connell
VP; President, Ceridian Employer Services:
Carl O. Keil, age 57, $580,930 pay
VP; President, Ceridian Performance Partners:
Linda Hall Whitman, age 50
VP; President, Comdata: Tony G. Holcombe, age 43,
$486,903 pay
President, Ceridian Canada: Jim Jarvis
Auditors: KPMG LLP

LOCATIONS

HQ: 8100 34th Ave. South, Minneapolis, MN 55425-1640
Phone: 612-853-8100   **Fax:** 612-853-4068
Web site: http://www.ceridian.com

Ceridian serves customers in Canada, the UK, and the US.

1998 Sales

	$ mil.	% of total
US	1,034	89
Canada & UK	128	11
Total	**1,162**	**100**

PRODUCTS/OPERATIONS

1998 Sales

	$ mil.	% of total
Human Resource Services	700	60
Comdata	267	23
Arbitron	195	17
Total	**1,162**	**100**

Operations
Human Resource Services
Centrefile (payroll processing and human resource
information system services in the UK)
Ceridian Benefits Services (benefits and payroll)
Ceridian Employer Services (payroll processing, tax
filing, time and attendance software, benefits
administration)
Ceridian Performance Partners (workplace
effectiveness, including employee recruitment,
retention, and productivity)
Usertech (end user training and support programs)
Comdata (trucking and truck stop information services:
cash advances, fuel purchasing cards, vehicle escort)
Arbitron (radio and other media ratings services,
marketing databases)
Scarborough Research Partnership (joint venture,
product and service usage reporting)
Tapscan, Inc. (software for broadcasters and advertisers)

COMPETITORS

ACNielsen	Kelly Services
Administaff	Kronos
ADP	Paradyme
Computer Language	Paychex
Research	PeopleSoft
Concord EFS	ProBusiness Services
Interim Services	TeamStaff

HISTORICAL FINANCIALS & EMPLOYEES

NYSE symbol: CEN FYE: December 31	Annual Growth	1989	1990	1991	1992	1993	1994	1995	1996	1997	1998
Sales ($ mil.)	(9.8%)	2,935	1,691	1,525	830	886	916	1,333	1,496	1,075	1,162
Net income ($ mil.)	—	(680)	3	(10)	(393)	(30)	79	59	182	472	190
Income as % of sales	—	—	0.2%	—	—	—	8.6%	4.4%	12.2%	44.0%	16.3%
Earnings per share ($)	—	(8.06)	0.03	(0.13)	(4.62)	(1.96)	0.63	0.33	1.13	2.97	1.29
Stock price - FY high ($)	—	12.00	10.81	6.88	8.63	9.94	13.75	23.75	27.44	23.88	36.00
Stock price - FY low ($)	—	8.13	3.81	3.38	4.56	6.50	9.25	13.06	18.50	14.75	21.75
Stock price - FY close ($)	16.2%	9.06	4.44	5.44	7.63	9.50	13.44	20.63	20.25	22.91	34.91
P/E - high	—	—	360	—	—	—	22	72	24	8	28
P/E - low	—	—	127	—	—	—	15	40	16	5	17
Dividends per share ($)	—	0.00	0.00	0.00	0.00	0.00	0.00	0.00	0.00	0.00	0.00
Book value per share ($)	(0.4%)	4.69	5.24	5.12	(1.18)	1.20	2.00	1.08	2.17	3.98	4.53
Employees	(6.7%)	18,000	14,500	13,000	8,800	7,600	7,500	10,200	10,800	8,000	9,600

STOCK PRICE HISTORY

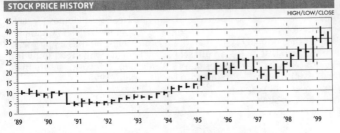

HIGH/LOW/CLOSE

1998 FISCAL YEAR-END

Debt ratio: 7.7%
Return on equity: 29.2%
Cash ($ mil.): 102
Current ratio: 1.45
Long-term debt ($ mil.): 54
No. of shares (mil.): 144
Dividends
  Yield: —
  Payout: —
Market value ($ mil.): 5,010

CHAMPION ENTERPRISES, INC.

OVERVIEW

Its homes may not be so mobile, but Champion Enterprises is still leading the race. Based in Auburn Hills, Michigan, Champion is barely ahead of Fleetwood Enterprises in the chase for #1 among US makers of manufactured housing. Champion's 65 factories make single- and multi-section (63% of sales) manufactured homes that sell for $15,000 to $150,000 and range from 400 sq. ft. to 6,100 sq. ft. The company sells homes in the US and western Canada through about 3,500 independent retailers and more than 280 company-owned locations in 28 states and Canada.

Under CEO Walter Young, Champion has started living up to its name. During the 1990s the company grew both internally and through acquisitions of about two companies annually. Young keeps Champion flexible with a small central staff that offers financial, legal, and purchasing help to its plants. Champion plants aren't obliged to use the services, but they are available for free.

In a rapidly consolidating manufactured-housing market, Champion is trying to become even more vertically integrated. Because its houses must be shipped, Champion bought a freight-hauling company in 1996 to bring that service in-house. To ensure venues for its homes, it is buying independent retailers. Deutsche Bank subsidiary Bankers Trust owns about 15% of Champion.

HISTORY

Champion Home Builders started in 1953, just in time to take advantage of the burgeoning postwar American economy and the passage of a 1956 law allowing mobile homes to be up to 10 feet wide. The 2-foot increase made mobile homes increasingly popular — by 1960 a majority were "10-wides." The change shifted the main benefit of mobile homes from mobility to affordability. Champion prospered and the growing company went public in 1962. By the mid-1960s it was one of the leaders in its market.

Part of Champion's success could be attributed to its vertically integrated manufacturing process. Champion made and installed all the components in a home, from plumbing to drapes. This policy increased efficiency, and productivity was exemplary — twice that of most of its rivals. Despite these advantages, the mid-1970s recession hit the company hard. Industry sales fell about a third from their 1972 peak. Champion felt the recession's brunt in its mobile-home sales, but sales of recreational vehicles (RVs) and low-priced motor homes helped temper the losses. The rapid increase of prices for site-built housing helped Champion and other mobile-home makers out of the slump. Mobile homes then experienced a resurgence in popularity, their relative affordability greater than ever before.

At the start of the 1980s, Champion recovered briefly, but by the mid-1980s the company was again struggling. By 1990 the firm had lost $30 million over the previous five years and was considering Chapter 11 bankruptcy proceedings. Walter Young took over that year and quickly revamped the company. To stave off bankruptcy, Young sold some businesses (RV making and component manufacturing) for much-needed cash. Young also gutted the central office and eliminated 248 of 260 jobs. This move took the decision-making process out of corporate hands — which Young saw as needlessly bureaucratic — and gave it to customers and local designers.

In 1993 Champion settled on a growth strategy involving both internal sales and acquisitions. The company soon acted on its plan by purchasing Dutch Housing in 1994 and Chandeleur Homes and Crest Ridge Homes a year later. In 1996 Champion acquired Redman Industries, the #3 US manufactured-housing builder at that time (Champion was #2). The acquisition vaulted Champion to the top spot in terms of sales during 1996. In addition to its acquisition of Redman, Champion opened five new plants. Combined with the Redman purchase, Champion more than doubled the number of plants it operated from 23 to about 50.

In 1998 Champion sold its midsize-bus business to narrow its focus on housing. That year the company bought manufactured-housing seller The ICA Group, operator of 23 retail outlets under the A-1 Homes, USA Homes, and Homes of America names. In 1999 Champion bought Care Free Homes (Utah), Central Mississippi Manufactured Housing, Homes of Merit (Florida), and Heartland Homes (Texas). In an example of corporate largesse, Champion kept all of its Titan Mobile Homes employees on full salary and benefits while rebuilding the subsidiary's Waterville, New York, factory that burned to the ground in 1999.

OFFICERS

Chairman, President, and CEO: Walter R. Young Jr.,
age 54, $1,437,333 pay
EVP, Chief Strategic and Finance Officer:
Joseph H. Stegmayer, age 48, $761,129 pay
COO: Philip C. Surles, age 57, $889,781 pay
President, Retail Operations: M. Mark Cole, age 37,
$1,010,533 pay
VP, General Counsel, and Secretary: John J. Collins Jr.,
age 47, $380,333 pay
VP and Controller: Richard P. Hevelhorst, age 51
Treasurer: Carmel E. Thomas
VP of Human Resources: Hugh Beswick
VP, Marketing: Byron E. Stroud
President, Western Region: Michael L. Barker
President, Southern Region: Richard A. Brugge
President, Midwestern Region: Brian J. Lapelle
President, Eastern Region: Bobby J. Williams
Chief Marketing Officer: Donald D. Williams
Auditors: PricewaterhouseCoopers LLP

LOCATIONS

HQ: 2701 University Dr., Ste. 300,
Auburn Hills, MI 48326
Phone: 248-340-9090   **Fax:** 248-340-9345
Web site: http://www.champent.com

Champion Enterprises sells its manufactured homes
throughout the US and western Canada. The company
has manufacturing and retail facilities in 32 US states
and two Canadian provinces.

PRODUCTS/OPERATIONS

Selected Subsidiaries
Champion Home Builders Co.
Champion Home Centers, Inc.
Chandeleur Homes, Inc.
Crest Ridge Homes, Inc.
Dutch Housing, Inc.
Grand Manor, Inc.
Homes of Legend, Inc.
Homes of Merit, Inc.
Moduline International, Inc.
    Lamplighter Homes, Inc.
    Lamplighter Homes (Oregon), Inc.
    Moduline Industries (Canada) Ltd.
Redman Industries, Inc.
    Redman Homes, Inc.
    Western Homes Corporation

COMPETITORS

American Homestar
Cavalier Homes
Cavco
Clayton Homes
Coachmen Industries
Fairmont Homes
Fleetwood Enterprises
General Housing
Horton Homes
Liberty Homes
KIT Manufacturing
Nobility Homes
Oakwood Homes
Palm Harbor Homes
Skyline
Southern Energy Homes

HISTORICAL FINANCIALS & EMPLOYEES

NYSE symbol: CHB FYE: December 31	Annual Growth	1989	1990	1991	1992	1993	1994	1995	1996	1997	1998
Sales ($ mil.)	24.5%	314	288	270	235	342	616	798	1,644	1,675	2,254
Net income ($ mil.)	—	(14)	—	(1)	3	11	27	32	54	75	94
Income as % of sales	—	—	0.1%	—	1.2%	3.3%	4.4%	4.0%	3.3%	4.5%	4.2%
Earnings per share ($)	—	(0.50)	0.02	(0.03)	0.09	0.30	0.96	1.14	1.09	1.54	1.91
Stock price - FY high ($)	—	1.22	1.19	1.47	2.72	4.94	10.16	15.50	26.13	21.25	30.00
Stock price - FY low ($)	—	0.47	0.47	0.59	0.72	2.28	4.38	6.78	11.88	13.75	17.50
Stock price - FY close ($)	57.1%	0.47	1.03	1.09	2.63	4.41	7.63	15.44	19.50	20.56	27.38
P/E - high	—	—	60	—	30	16	11	14	24	14	16
P/E - low	—	—	24	—	8	8	5	6	11	9	9
Dividends per share ($)	—	0.00	0.00	0.00	0.00	0.00	0.00	0.00	0.00	0.00	0.00
Book value per share ($)	29.0%	0.85	0.89	1.16	1.22	1.59	2.62	3.70	4.75	6.02	8.39
Employees	20.1%	2,700	2,700	2,200	2,100	2,800	4,500	2,300	11,000	11,300	14,000

STOCK PRICE HISTORY

HIGH/LOW/CLOSE

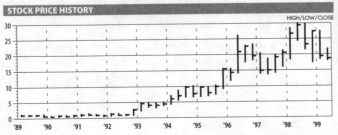

1998 FISCAL YEAR-END

Debt ratio: 22.6%
Return on equity: 23.2%
Cash ($ mil.): 24
Current ratio: 0.98
Long-term debt ($ mil.): 118
No. of shares (mil.): 48
Dividends
  Yield: —
  Payout: —
Market value ($ mil.): 1,322

CHAMPION INTERNATIONAL

OVERVIEW

Champion is almost down to fighting weight. Stamford, Connecticut-based Champion International produces coated and uncoated paper, kraft papers (used in such products as paper grocery bags), pulp, lumber, and plywood and distributes paper products through 27 distribution centers in 27 states. Champion also owns mineral, oil, and gas rights to about half of its timberland holdings in the US and Canada.

In the face of intense competition and low paper prices, Champion is selling off its less-profitable business segments. It's already axed its newsprint and paperboard foodservice packaging businesses. The company has amassed a substantial amount of timberland (controlling a total of about 5 million acres), to ensure a steady supply of lumber, and has increased its presence in Brazil. Champion also plans to pursue alliances and joint ventures to improve its competitive position, without large cash outlays.

HISTORY

Champion International was formed by the 1967 merger of US Plywood and Champion Paper & Fibre. US Plywood, founded in New York by Lawrence Ottinger in 1919, began by selling glue and WWI surplus plywood. By 1932 the company made its own products, and in 1937 it consolidated operations with Aircraft Plywood. Champion Paper & Fibre was formed when Reuben Robertson, who founded Champion Fibre in Ohio in 1906, married the daughter of the founder of similarly named Champion Coated Paper, incorporated in Ohio in 1893.

The first years for US Plywood-Champion Paper (the resulting company) were marked by internal strife between the paper and plywood units over such issues as timber resource allocation. During that period the business diversified, buying Drexel Enterprises (furniture, 1968; sold 1977), Trend Industries (carpet, 1969; sold 1978), Path Fork Harlan Coal (to power the company's pulp and paper mills, 1970), and AW Securities (carpets, 1974; sold 1980). It adopted the present name in 1972.

Director Karl Bendetson, who disapproved of plans to diversify Champion into chemicals, persuaded the board in 1974 to fire CEO Thomas Willers. Andrew Sigler replaced Willers and quickly sold more than a dozen non-forest businesses.

In 1977 Champion bought Hoerner Waldorf, the fourth-largest American producer of paper packaging products such as grocery bags and cardboard boxes. With its $1.8 billion acquisition of St. Regis in 1984, Champion tightened its focus on pulp and paper production. It sold the office products businesses (1984); 55 corrugated container plants, packaging plants, and paperboard mills (1986); two Texas mills (1987); and its Columbus, Ohio, specialty paper plant (1988). In 1991 and 1992 Champion sold large tracts of difficult-to-access western timberlands.

Champion also fought a $5 billion class-action lawsuit alleging that its Canton, North Carolina, mill had dumped pollutants into the Pigeon River: A $6.5 million settlement was approved in 1993. That year Champion sold 870,000 acres of Montana woods to Plum Creek Timber and two wood-products mills to Stimson Lumber. It also announced a breakthrough in bleach filtrate recycling (BFR) technology that reduces the waste of bleached-pulp mills.

Two years later Champion expanded its newsprint subsidiary's paper-collection efforts beyond Texas to major cities in Alabama, Georgia, and Tennessee. Wheelabrator Technologies acquired exclusive licensing rights to the BFR process that year. Also in 1995 Champion's Brazilian subsidiary earned about $110 million on sales of $404 million.

Richard Olson took over as CEO in 1996. The next year Champion announced plans to unload its newsprint and paper-recycling operations along with other peripheral businesses. It inked a deal with Asia Pacific Resources International, whereby Champion gained exclusive rights to the US distribution of Asia Pacific's uncoated free sheet paper. In 1998 the company bought Brazilian papermaker Industria de Papel Arapoti and sold three recycling centers and two newsprint plants to Donohue, the newsprint unit of Quebecor.

In 1999 Champion sold a paper mill and its liquid packaging business to Blue Ridge Paper Products (55% owned by KPS Special Situations Fund LP) and sold its groundwood specialty mill to Crabar Paper & Allied Products. It also sold 143,000 acres of forestland in New York to a preservation group, Conservation Fund, for $46 million. It also has put up another 54,000 acres of timberland in North Carolina for sale.

Chairman and CEO: Richard E. Olson, age 61,
$1,275,000 pay
VC and Executive Officer: Kenwood C. Nichols, age 59,
$985,000 pay
EVP Distribution, Pulp Sales, and International Sales:
L. Scott Barnard, age 56, $621,000 pay
EVP Forest Products: Mark V. Childers, age 46
EVP Coated Papers and Kraft Papers:
Thomas L. Griffin, age 56, $456,580 pay
EVP Uncoated Papers: Richard L. Porterfield, age 52,
$546,000 pay
SVP and General Counsel: Stephen B. Brown, age 59
**SVP Marketing, Strategic Planning, Mineral Resources,
and Real Estate:** Michael P. Corey, age 55
SVP Environmental, Health, and Safety Affairs:
Richard J. Diforio Jr., age 63
VP and Secretary: Lawrence A. Fox
VP Finance and Treasurer: Thomas L. Hart
VP and Controller: John M. Nimons
**President and Managing Director, Champion Papel e
Celulose:** Odair A. Garcia
Chairman, President, and CEO, Weldwood of Canada:
George R. Richards
Auditors: Arthur Andersen LLP

LOCATIONS

HQ: Champion International Corporation,
1 Champion Plaza, Stamford, CT 06921
Phone: 203-358-7000   **Fax:** 203-358-6444
Web site: http://www.championpaper.com

Champion International has manufacturing facilities in
Brazil, Canada, and the US.

PRODUCTS/OPERATIONS

1998 Sales

	$ mil.	% of total
Pulp & paper	4,640	82
Wood products	1,013	18
Total	**5,653**	**100**

Selected Products and Operations
Coated papers
Northern softwood and hardwood pulps
Paper distribution
Softwood lumber
Softwood timberlands
Unbleached packaging
Uncoated free sheet papers

COMPETITORS

Boise Cascade
Bowater
Chesapeake Corporation
Consolidated Papers
Fort James
Georgia-Pacific
International Paper
Kimberly-Clark
Louisiana-Pacific
MacMillan Bloedel
Mead
Plum Creek Timber
Potlatch
Rayonier
Smurfit-Stone Container
Temple-Inland
Westvaco
Weyerhaeuser
Willamette

HISTORICAL FINANCIALS & EMPLOYEES

NYSE symbol: CHA FYE: December 31	Annual Growth	1989	1990	1991	1992	1993	1994	1995	1996	1997	1998
Sales ($ mil.)	1.0%	5,163	5,090	4,786	4,927	5,069	5,318	6,972	5,880	5,736	5,653
Net income ($ mil.)	(17.7%)	432	223	40	(440)	(156)	63	772	141	(549)	75
Income as % of sales	—	8.4%	4.4%	0.8%	—	—	1.2%	11.1%	2.4%	—	1.3%
Earnings per share ($)	(17.6%)	4.43	2.08	0.14	(5.05)	(1.98)	0.38	7.67	1.48	(5.72)	0.78
Stock price - FY high ($)	—	37.75	33.75	30.63	30.25	34.63	40.00	60.25	51.13	66.50	58.44
Stock price - FY low ($)	—	28.88	23.13	22.25	23.50	27.13	28.00	36.13	39.00	41.38	40.50
Stock price - FY close ($)	2.7%	32.00	25.63	24.00	28.75	33.38	36.50	42.00	43.25	45.31	40.50
P/E - high	—	9	16	219	—	—	105	8	35	—	75
P/E - low	—	7	11	159	—	—	74	5	26	—	33
Dividends per share ($)	(17.1%)	1.08	1.10	0.48	0.20	0.20	0.20	0.20	0.20	0.20	0.20
Book value per share ($)	(1.9%)	38.60	39.58	39.51	32.85	30.61	31.74	38.12	39.30	33.39	32.39
Employees	(3.6%)	29,500	28,500	27,500	27,300	25,250	24,615	24,129	24,379	23,969	21,137

STOCK PRICE HISTORY   HIGH/LOW/CLOSE

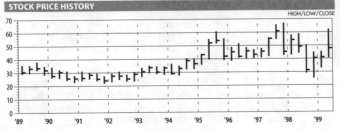

1998 FISCAL YEAR-END
Debt ratio: 48.8%
Return on equity: 2.4%
Cash ($ mil.): 300
Current ratio: 1.37
Long-term debt ($ mil.): 2,948
No. of shares (mil.): 96
Dividends
  Yield: 0.5%
  Payout: 25.6%
Market value ($ mil.): 3,871

CHARLES SCHWAB CORPORATION

OVERVIEW

Like it or not, pioneering discount brokerage Charles Schwab is beginning to resemble the old fogies.

San Francisco-based Schwab now offers services typical of the traditional brokerage houses it rebelled against more than 20 years ago. To compete with rivals' cheaper fees, Schwab offers research and asset allocation advice in-house; its AdvisorSource refers customers who need more help to independent money managers that execute trades with Schwab.

Schwab's main business is still discount brokerage — making trades for investors who make their own decisions. The company's other services include Touch-Tone phone and online trading, futures and commodities trading, access to IPOs, and investment educational material. Its eSchwab unit dominates the online trading market and accounts for more than half of the firm's trading volume. Schwab is also one of the top three mutual fund distributors (with Vanguard and FMR's Fidelity Investments). Schwab's OneSource mutual fund marketplace offers more than 1,600 no-load mutual funds from 260 families (including its proprietary funds).

Schwab has some 290 offices, and has exported its no-frills concept to the UK and Canada. In an example of financial services convergence, Schwab is also moving into online banking.

Founder Charles Schwab owns about 20% of the company.

HISTORY

During the 1960s Stanford graduate Charles Schwab founded First Commander Corp. to manage investments and publish a newsletter. But he failed to properly register with the SEC, and after a hiatus he returned to the business in 1971 under the name Charles Schwab & Company. Initially a full-service broker, Schwab moved into discount brokerage after the SEC outlawed fixed commissions in 1975. While most brokers defiantly raised commissions, Schwab cut its rates steeply.

From 1977 to 1983 Schwab's client list increased thirtyfold and revenues grew, enabling the firm to automate its operations and develop cash-management account systems. To gain capital, Charles sold the company to BankAmerica (now Bank of America) in 1983. Schwab grew, but expansion into mutual funds and services like telephone trading was prevented by federal regulations against banks acting as brokerages. Charles bought his company back in 1987 and took it public.

When the stock market crashed later that year, trading volume fell by nearly half. Stung, Schwab diversified further, offering new fee-based services. Commission revenues fell from 64% of sales in 1987 to 39% in 1990, but by 1995 the long bull market had pushed commissions to more than 50% (where they still hover).

In 1989 Schwab introduced TeleBroker, a 24-hour Touch-Tone telephone trading service available in English, Spanish, Mandarin, or Cantonese.

Among Schwab's acquisitions was the 1991 purchase of Mayer & Schweitzer, an OTC market maker that accounted for about 7% of all Nasdaq trades.

Schwab continued to diversify, courting the business of independent financial advisors. In 1993 the company opened its first overseas office in London, but was relegated to trading only in dollar-denominated stocks until its 1995 acquisition of Share-Link (now Charles Schwab Europe), the UK's largest discount brokerage.

During the next year Schwab made a concerted effort to build its retirement services by creating a new unit to provide 401(k) administration and investment services. In 1997 Schwab formed alliances with securities underwriters J.P. Morgan & Co., Hambrecht & Quist, and Credit Suisse First Boston (CSFB) to give its customers access to IPOs; the next year the relationship with CSFB deepened with an agreement to give Schwab access to debt offerings. In late 1997 and early 1998, Schwab reorganized to reflect its new business lines. The company also began recruiting talent rather than promoting from within.

In 1999 Schwab formed Charles Schwab Canada (from acquisitions Priority Brokerage and Porthmeor Securities) and started a joint venture in Japan with companies led by Tokyo Marine & Fire Insurance. It also said it would upgrade computer systems after excess demand caused several online trading outages and later in the year announced that IBM would help to solve Schwab's technology woes. That year Schwab joined those online brokers using advertising to urge traders to invest more cautiously; meanwhile the company is linking up with FMR and stock dealer Spear, Leeds, & Kellogg to eventually offer after-hours trading. Also in 1999, Schwab introduced Velocity, a desktop trading system designed to make trading easier for fiscally endowed investors.

Chairman and Co-CEO: Charles R. Schwab, age 61,
$6,945,229 pay
President and Co-CEO: David S. Pottruck, age 50,
$6,945,229 pay
**VC and Enterprise President, Retirement Plan
Services:** John P. Coghlan, age 47, $1,177,225 pay
VC; President, Retail Group: Linnet F. Deily, age 53,
$1,169,392 pay
**VC and Enterprise President, Capital Markets and
Trading:** Lon Gorman, age 50
VC and Chief Information Officer: Dawn G. Lepore
EVP Corporate Oversight and General Counsel:
Carrie E. Dwyer
EVP Brokerage Operations: Wayne W. Fieldsa
EVP Retail Branch Network: James M. Hackley
EVP and Chief Strategy Officer: Daniel O. Leemon
EVP Technology Services: Frederick E. Matteson
EVP Human Resources: George A. Rich
EVP and Enterprise President, Electronic Brokerage:
Gideon Sasson, age 43
CFO: Christopher V. Dodds
Enterprise President, General Investor Segment:
Karen W. Chang, age 50
Enterprise President, Retail Client Services:
Susanne D. Lyons, age 41
Auditors: Deloitte & Touche LLP

LOCATIONS

HQ: The Charles Schwab Corporation,
101 Montgomery St., San Francisco, CA 94104
Phone: 415-627-7000 **Fax:** 415-627-8840
Web site: http://www.schwab.com

Charles Schwab has about 290 branch offices in Canada,
the Cayman Islands, Hong Kong, Puerto Rico, the UK,
the US, and the Virgin Islands.

PRODUCTS/OPERATIONS

1998 Sales

	$ mil.	% of total
Commissions	1,309	39
Interest	1,128	33
Mutual fund service fees	559	17
Principal transactions	287	8
Other	105	3
Total	**3,388**	**100**

Subsidiaries

Charles Schwab & Co., Inc. (securities broker-dealer)
Charles Schwab Europe (retail securities brokerage)
Charles Schwab Investment Management, Inc. (mutual
fund investment adviser)
The Charles Schwab Trust Company
Mayer & Schweitzer, Inc. (market maker and
trade services)
Schwab Holdings, Inc.

COMPETITORS

American Express
Ameritrade
Citigroup
Datek Online
DLJdirect
Jones Financial
Companies
E*TRADE
FMR
John Hancock
Merrill Lynch

Morgan Stanley Dean
Witter
Paine Webber
Prudential
Quick & Reilly/Fleet
Raymond James Financial
TD Waterhouse Securities
Transamerica
Transterra
U. S. Bancorp Piper Jaffray
Wachovia

HISTORICAL FINANCIALS & EMPLOYEES

NYSE symbol: SCH FYE: December 31	Annual Growth	1989	1990	1991	1992	1993	1994	1995	1996	1997	1998
Sales ($ mil.)	22.3%	553	626	795	909	1,097	1,263	1,777	2,277	2,845	3,388
Net income ($ mil.)	38.2%	19	17	50	81	118	135	173	234	270	349
Income as % of sales	—	3.4%	2.7%	6.2%	8.9%	10.7%	10.7%	9.7%	10.3%	9.5%	10.3%
Earnings per share ($)	34.4%	0.03	0.02	0.07	0.11	0.14	0.17	0.22	0.29	0.33	0.43
Stock price - FY high ($)	—	0.56	0.59	1.58	1.87	2.85	2.74	6.45	7.31	14.76	34.25
Stock price - FY low ($)	—	0.22	0.35	0.38	0.82	1.23	1.76	2.46	4.00	6.76	9.25
Stock price - FY close ($)	57.9%	0.46	0.38	1.50	1.29	2.40	2.59	4.48	7.12	13.99	28.09
P/E - high	—	19	30	23	17	20	16	29	25	45	80
P/E - low	—	7	18	5	7	9	10	11	14	20	22
Dividends per share ($)	22.0%	0.01	0.01	0.01	0.01	0.02	0.03	0.03	0.04	0.05	0.06
Book value per share ($)	25.9%	0.22	0.21	0.26	0.34	0.49	0.61	0.81	1.09	1.44	1.78
Employees	19.4%	2,700	2,900	3,800	4,500	6,500	6,500	9,200	10,400	12,700	13,300

STOCK PRICE HISTORY

HIGH/LOW/CLOSE

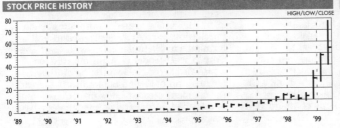

1998 FISCAL YEAR-END

Debt ratio: 19.7%
Return on equity: 24.4%
Cash ($ mil.): —
Current ratio: —
Long-term debt ($ mil.): 351
No. of shares (mil.): 804
Dividends
Yield: 0.2%
Payout: 14.0%
Market value ($ mil.): 22,578

CHASE MANHATTAN CORPORATION

OVERVIEW

Once the biggest in the land, this bank is now giving chase. New York City's Chase Manhattan is now the #2 bank in the US (behind Bank of America). The bank offers commercial and consumer loans and, increasingly, investment banking services.

Chase's customers include large corporate and government institutions and individual consumers, which it serves through some 600 branches in the New York State-area and another 125 in Texas. The bank also has branches in Brazil, the Caribbean, Hong Kong, and Panama. In the US, Chase is the fourth-largest issuer of credit cards (BANK ONE's First USA is #1), the largest financier of auto loans, and the third-largest originator of residential mortgage loans. The company's Chase Technology Solutions group offers labor- and technology-intensive transaction processing services, including cash management, transaction processing, and fiduciary services.

Expansion is the touchstone of Chase's strategy: The bank longs to become a national presence but remains regionalized in New York and Texas. It is pursuing acquisition-powered expansion into investment banking — eyeing the likes of Merrill Lynch and Paine Webber. And even though it has historically specialized in underwriting debt and not stocks, Chase now seeks to enter such diverse markets as money management, mergers and acquisitions consulting, and investment research.

HISTORY

Chase Manhattan started as a water utility. In 1799 The Manhattan Company was created to bring pure water to New York City. Buried in the company's incorporation documents was a provision that also allowed the company to provide banking services. The move into banking services was the brainchild of investor and future Vice President Aaron Burr. Burr brought The Manhattan Company into banking competition with The Bank of New York, which was founded by rival Alexander Hamilton, whom Burr would eventually slay in a notorious 1804 duel. Chase Manhattan still owns the dueling pistols.

In 1877 John Thompson formed Chase National, naming it for Salmon Chase, Abraham Lincoln's secretary of the treasury and the architect of the national bank system. Chase National merged with John D. Rockefeller's Equitable Trust in 1930, becoming the world's largest bank and beginning a long relationship with the Rockefellers. Chase National continued growing after WWII, and in 1955 it merged with the Bank of Manhattan. Chase Manhattan remained the US's largest bank into the 1960s.

When soaring oil prices in the 1970s made energy loans attractive, Chase invested in Penn Square, an obscure oil-patch bank in Oklahoma and the first notable bank failure of the 1980s. Chase struggled as the legal aftereffects of Penn Square's 1982 failure dragged on until 1993. The company was also hit with losses following the 1987 foreign loan crisis and then by the real estate crash. In 1995 the bank went looking for a partner. After talks with BankAmerica (now part of Bank of America), it settled on Chemical Bank.

Chemical Bank opened in 1824 and became one of the US's largest banks by 1900. Like The Manhattan Company, Chemical Bank started in an unrelated business as the New York Chemical Manufacturing Company in 1823, largely in order to be able to open a bank (it dropped its chemical operations in 1844). Chemical would merge with Manufacturer's Hanover in 1991.

After its merger with Chase in 1996, Chemical Bank was the surviving entity but assumed Chase's more prestigious name. Initial cost savings from the merger were substantial, as 8,000 jobs and 400 New York City-area branch offices were eliminated. In 1997 Chase acquired the credit business of The Bank of New York and the corporate trustee business of Mellon Bank.

The company underwent another round of belt-tightening in 1998 when it announced that it would take a $320 million charge and cut 4,500 jobs to save $460 million a year in redundancies. Chase also consolidated its global custody business that year and bought Morgan Stanley Dean Witter's global custody operations. The bank also suffered losses that year related to its involvement with the ill-starred Long-Term Capital Management hedge fund.

In 1999 Chase leaned toward more lending, purchasing two mortgage originators and forming a marketing alliance with AmeriCredit Corp., the #1 lender of subprime auto loans; Chase also agreed to acquire the mortgage-lending unit of Mellon Bank Corp. That year the company created a new unit, Chase.com, to manage Internet and new technology-based operations.

Chairman, Chase Manhattan and Chase Bank:
Walter V. Shipley, age 63,
$6,228,686 pay (prior to title change)
VC, President, and CEO, Chase Manhattan and Chase Bank: William B. Harrison Jr., age 55,
$5,842,148 pay (prior to promotion)
VC National Consumer Services, Chase Manhattan and Chase Bank: Donald L. Boudreau, age 58,
$2,311,058 pay
VC Finance and Risk Management, Chase Manhattan and Chase Bank: Marc J. Shapiro, age 51,
$1,797,596 pay
VC Global Markets and International: Donald H. Layton
VC Global Investment Banking: James B. Lee Jr.
VC Chase Technology Solutions, Chase Manhattan and Chase Bank: Joseph G. Sponholz, age 54
EVP, CFO, and Treasurer: Dina Dublon
EVP and National Consumer Services: Denis O'Leary
COO, Chase Home Finance: Stephan J. Rotella
VP, Global Securitization Unit: Peter Rubinstein
Managing Director: John Collett
Director Human Resources, Chase Manhattan and Chase Bank: John J. Farrell, age 46
Director Corporate Marketing and Communications: Frederick W. Hill, age 48
General Counsel, Chase Manhattan and Chase Bank: William H. McDavid, age 52
Auditors: PricewaterhouseCoopers LLP

LOCATIONS

HQ: The Chase Manhattan Corporation,
270 Park Ave., New York, NY 10017
Phone: 212-270-6000   **Fax:** 212-270-2613
Web site: http://www.chase.com

PRODUCTS/OPERATIONS

1998 Assets

	$ mil.	% of total
Cash & equivalents	42,767	12
Securities	89,334	24
Derivative contracts	32,848	9
Net loans	169,202	46
Other	31,724	9
Total	**365,875**	**100**

1998 Sales

	$ mil.	% of total
Interest		
Loans	13,389	41
Securities	3,616	11
Other	5,284	16
Noninterest		
Service & management fees	5,138	16
Credit card revenue	1,474	5
Trading revenue & other	3,689	11
Total	**32,590**	**100**

COMPETITORS

American Express	Dime Bancorp
The Associates	DLJ
Bank of America	Fleet
Bank of New York	GE
BANK ONE	HSBC Holdings
Barclays	KeyCorp
Capital One Financial	Lehman Brothers
Citigroup	MBNA
Countrywide Credit	Merrill Lynch
Credit Suisse First Boston	Morgan Stanley Dean
Deutsche Bank	Witter

HISTORICAL FINANCIALS & EMPLOYEES

NYSE symbol: CMB FYE: December 31	Annual Growth	1989	1990	1991	1992	1993	1994	1995	1996	1997	1998
Assets ($ mil.)	19.9%	71,513	73,019	138,930	139,655	149,888	171,423	182,926	336,099	365,521	365,875
Net income ($ mil.)	—	(482)	291	154	1,086	1,604	1,294	1,805	2,461	3,708	3,782
Income as % of assets	—	—	0.4%	0.1%	0.8%	1.1%	0.8%	1.0%	0.7%	1.0%	1.0%
Earnings per share ($)	—	(4.15)	1.19	0.06	1.95	2.40	2.49	3.02	2.47	4.02	4.24
Stock price - FY high ($)	—	20.56	15.69	15.06	19.75	23.19	21.06	22.38	47.94	63.28	77.56
Stock price - FY low ($)	—	14.25	4.81	5.25	10.94	17.50	16.81	17.88	26.06	42.31	35.56
Stock price - FY close ($)	18.9%	14.94	5.38	10.63	19.31	20.06	17.94	29.38	44.69	54.75	71.00
P/E - high	—	—	13	251	10	10	8	11	19	16	18
P/E - low	—	—	4	88	6	7	7	6	11	11	8
Dividends per share ($)	0.2%	1.36	1.36	0.50	0.60	0.65	0.79	0.94	1.09	1.21	1.39
Book value per share ($)	9.2%	12.16	12.12	13.14	16.21	18.80	18.94	21.28	21.29	23.76	26.90
Employees	4.4%	49,173	45,636	43,169	39,687	41,567	42,130	72,696	67,785	69,033	72,683

STOCK PRICE HISTORY

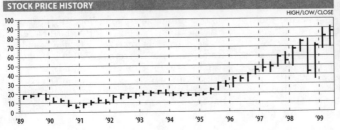

HIGH/LOW/CLOSE

1998 FISCAL YEAR-END

Equity as % of assets: 6.2
Return on assets: 1.0
Return on equity: 16.6%
Long-term debt ($ mil.): 18,375
No. of shares (mil.): 848
Dividends
  Yield: 2.0%
  Payout: 32.8%
Market value ($ mil.): 60,207
Sales (mil.): $32,590

CHEVRON CORPORATION

Chevron has earned its stripes as one of the world's top oil companies. The San Francisco-based enterprise, operating in more than 90 countries, is the US's fourth-largest oil and gas company (behind Exxon, Mobil, and Texaco).

One of the biggest US oil refiners and a leading marketer of gasoline and lubricants, Chevron operates some 7,900 service stations in the US and 200 in Canada: It is the leader in the West Coast retail market and a major player on the Gulf Coast. Overseas, Chevron and Texaco jointly own Caltex, which markets refined products in Africa, the Asia/Pacific region, and the Middle East. It also makes chemicals (including ethylene, benzene, and styrene), mines coal, and holds a 28% stake in gas marketer Dynegy.

The company, which has a commanding presence in West Africa, the Caspian Sea region, and Australia, is marching further into non-US territories to boost its proved reserves of oil (4.7 billion barrels of crude, condensate, and natural gas liquids) and natural gas (9.3 trillion cu. ft.). It has a stake in the giant Tengiz oil field in Kazakhstan, as well as oil fields off the Angolan coast and in the Gulf of Mexico.

With oil prices falling, Chevron is tightening its belt a few more notches. Although it has already slashed its operating costs by $2.4 billion (about 25%) since 1991, it plans to cut $500 million more in 1999. Employees own 11% of Chevron.

HISTORY

Thirty years after the California gold rush, a small company began digging for a new product — oil. The crude came from wildcatter Frederick Taylor's well north of Los Angeles. In 1879 Taylor and other oilmen formed Pacific Coast Oil, attracting the attention of John D. Rockefeller's Standard Oil. The two firms competed fiercely until Standard took over Pacific Coast in 1900.

When Standard Oil was broken up in 1911, its West Coast operations became the stand-alone Standard Oil Company (California), which was nicknamed Socal, and sold Chevron-brand products. After winning drilling concessions in Bahrain and Saudi Arabia in the 1930s, Socal summoned Texaco to help market the desert crude, and they formed Caltex (California Texas Oil Company) as equal partners. In 1948 Socony (later Mobil) and Jersey Standard (later Exxon) bought 40% of Caltex's Saudi operations, and the Saudi arm became Aramco (Arabian American Oil Company).

Socal exploration pushed into Louisiana and the Gulf of Mexico in the 1940s. In 1961 Socal bought Standard Oil Company of Kentucky (Kyso). The 1970s brought setbacks: Caltex holdings were nationalized during the OPEC-spawned upheaval, and in 1980 Aramco was claimed by the Saudi Arabian government.

In 1984 Socal was renamed Chevron and doubled its reserves with its record $13.3 billion purchase of Gulf Corp. Gulf's origins went back to the 1901 Spindletop gusher in Texas as J. M. Guffey Petroleum, bankrolled by the Mellon family. Founder Guffey was unseated by William Larimer Mellon (1902), and the company's name was changed to Gulf (1907). Gulf became an oil power by developing Kuwaiti

concessions after WWII but was hobbled by that country's oil cutbacks in the 1970s.

Chevron bought Tenneco's Gulf of Mexico oil and gas properties in 1988 and in 1992 swapped fields valued at $1.1 billion for 15.7 million shares of Chevron stock owned by Pennzoil. Chevron and rival Conoco won permission from UK authorities in 1994 to develop the North Sea's Britannia Field.

In the 1990s Chevron gave its retailing units a tune-up. It allied with McDonald's (1995) to combine burger stands and gas stations in 12 western states and launched Foodini's (1998), a chain of pre-made-meal markets. The company also shed 450 UK gas stations and a refinery in a sale to Shell (1997).

Chevron sold its natural gas operation in 1996 for a stake in Houston-based NGC (now Dynegy). In 1997 Chevron signed its first on-shore exploration contract in China and began construction on a Saudi Arabian petrochemical complex. The next year it bought Amoco's (now BP Amoco) North American lubricants business.

Poor economic conditions in Asia and slumping oil prices in 1998 forced Chevron to shed some US holdings — including Gulf of Mexico and California properties — and in 1999 it agreed to sell its Pittsburg & Midway US coal mining operations. Focusing on overseas operations, it bought Rutherford-Moran Oil to increase its interests in Thailand, and teamed up with Nigeria's SASOL in a joint venture to convert natural gas to liquids. Chevron also discussed merging with its Caltex partner, Texaco, but talks collapsed after the two could not agree on terms.

Chairman and CEO: Kenneth T. Derr, age 62, $2,460,000 pay
VC Worldwide Refining, Marketing, Chemicals, and Coal Mining: James N. Sullivan, age 61, $1,280,000 pay
VC Worldwide Oil and Gas Exploration and Production and Corporate Human Resources: David J. O'Reilly, age 52, $889,167 pay
VP; President, Chevron Chemical Company: Darry W. Callahan, age 56
VP; President, Chevron Services Company: Lloyd E. Elkins, age 55
VP; President, Chevron U.S.A. Production Company: Peter J. Robertson, age 52
VP; President, Chevron Products Company: Patricia Woertz, age 46
VP Public Affairs: Aldo M. Caccamo, age 61
VP and Treasurer: George K. Carter, age 63
VP and General Counsel: Harvey D. Hinman, age 58
VP and CFO: Martin R. Klitten, age 54, $788,750 pay
VP Human Resources and Quality: Gregory Matiuk, age 53
VP Technology and Environmental Affairs: Donald L. Paul, age 52
VP Strategic Planning: John S. Watson, age 42
Secretary: Lydia I. Beebe, age 46
Comptroller: Stephen J. Crowe, age 51
General Tax Counsel: R. Bruce Marsh, age 56
Auditors: KPMG LLP

LOCATIONS

HQ: 575 Market St., San Francisco, CA 94105
Phone: 415-894-7700   **Fax:** 415-894-0583
Web site: http://www.chevron.com

PRODUCTS/OPERATIONS

1998 Sales & Operating Income

	Sales		Operating Income	
	$ mil.	% of total	$ mil.	% of total
Petroleum	28,732	90	1,672	93
Chemicals	3,216	9	122	7
Other	456	1	—	—
Adjustments	(6,217)	—	—	—
Total	**26,187**	**100**	**1,794**	**100**

Selected Subsidiaries and Affiliates
Caltex Corporation (50%, refining and marketing)
Chevron Chemical Company (chemicals)
Dynegy (28%, natural gas)
Tengizchevroil (45%, oil exploration, Kazakhstan)

COMPETITORS

7-Eleven	Norsk Hydro
Amerada Hess	Occidental
Ashland	PDVSA
BHP	PEMEX
BP Amoco	Petrobras
Coastal	Phillips Petroleum
Conoco	Racetrac Petroleum
Costco Companies	Royal Dutch/Shell
Devon Energy	Sinclair Oil
Dow Chemical	Sunoco
DuPont	Texaco
Eastman Chemical	Tosco
Elf Aquitaine	TOTAL FINA
Exxon	Ultramar Diamond
Huntsman	Shamrock
ICI	Union Carbide
Kerr-McGee	Unocal
Koch	USX-Marathon
Lyondell Chemical	Valero Energy
Mobil	

HISTORICAL FINANCIALS & EMPLOYEES

NYSE symbol: CHV FYE: December 31	Annual Growth	1989	1990	1991	1992	1993	1994	1995	1996	1997	1998
Sales ($ mil.)	(1.3%)	29,443	38,607	36,461	37,464	32,123	30,340	31,322	37,580	35,009	26,187
Net income ($ mil.)	20.4%	251	2,157	1,293	1,569	1,265	1,693	930	2,607	3,256	1,339
Income as % of sales	—	0.9%	5.6%	3.5%	4.2%	3.9%	5.6%	3.0%	6.9%	9.3%	5.1%
Earnings per share ($)	20.9%	0.37	3.05	1.85	2.31	1.94	2.59	1.43	3.98	4.95	2.04
Stock price - FY high ($)	—	36.75	40.81	40.06	37.69	49.38	49.19	53.63	68.38	89.19	90.19
Stock price - FY low ($)	—	22.69	31.56	31.75	30.06	33.69	39.88	43.38	51.00	61.75	67.75
Stock price - FY close ($)	10.5%	33.88	36.31	34.50	34.75	43.56	44.63	52.38	65.00	77.00	82.94
P/E - high	—	99	13	22	16	25	19	38	17	18	44
P/E - low	—	61	10	17	13	17	15	30	13	12	33
Dividends per share ($)	6.4%	1.40	1.48	1.63	1.65	1.75	1.85	1.93	2.08	2.28	2.44
Book value per share ($)	3.2%	19.69	21.15	21.25	21.11	21.48	22.40	22.01	23.92	26.64	26.08
Employees	(3.7%)	54,826	54,208	55,123	49,245	47,576	45,758	43,019	40,820	39,362	39,191

STOCK PRICE HISTORY

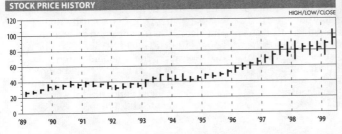

HIGH/LOW/CLOSE

1998 FISCAL YEAR-END
Debt ratio: 20.5%
Return on equity: 7.9%
Cash ($ mil.): 569
Current ratio: 0.88
Long-term debt ($ mil.): 4,393
No. of shares (mil.): 653
Dividends
  Yield: 2.9%
  Payout: 119.6%
Market value ($ mil.): 54,162

CHICAGO TITLE CORPORATION

Chicago Title will insure that you own what you say you own. Through such subsidiaries as Chicago Title and Trust, Chicago Title Insurance, Security Union Title Insurance, and Ticor Title Insurance, the company provides title insurance and other real estate-related services, including title search and examination, flood certification, credit reporting, escrow account management, document recording, and disbursement of funds.

Alleghany Corporation spun off the company in 1998 to capitalize on a booming real estate market and consolidating industry. Chicago Title focuses on three customer

segments: financial institutions heavily involved in residential lending, local firms involved with real estate and title transactions, and corporate clients involved in large commercial property transactions. Alleghany chairman Fred Kirby, his siblings, and their estates together own more than a third of Chicago Title.

The company once duked it out with rivals LandAmerica and First American to be the US's #1 title insurance writer; each now claims about one-fifth of the pie. However, Fidelity National Financial's plan to create a truly national company by purchasing Chicago Title will make the new title firm the largest in the US.

HISTORY

Chicago Title is an amalgam of several title companies whose histories date back to 1847. The title ledgers of three of these companies (Shortall and Hoard, Jones and Sellers, and Chase Brothers) were literally snatched from the flames in the Chicago Fire of 1871, when the city's official property records were lost. The private records, which included copies of the city's real estate plats, were adopted in 1872 as the basis of new property records and facilitated the city's rebuilding. The title business in Chicago underwent a period of change and consolidation, and after the adoption of the General Trust Company Act by Illinois in 1887, one of the surviving firms (Handy, Simmons, Smith and Stocker) added a trust business, changing its name to Title Guarantee and Trust. Title Guarantee began issuing insurance in 1888 to protect buyers from claims against property titles. In 1891 the company became Chicago Title and Trust Co. (CT&T) and incorporated in 1912.

CT&T expanded within Illinois and by the 1950s had also moved into other states. In 1961 the company formed Chicago Title Insurance Co. (CTI) for its growing national title insurance business. Lincoln National of Fort Wayne, Indiana, bought CT&T in 1969.

Looking for another investment after selling its cash cow, IDS (the US's largest mutual fund administrator), Alleghany bought CT&T in 1985, then merged several other title operations into it. The company expanded west, acquiring SAFECO Title Insurance (1987, renamed Security Union Title Insurance in 1988) and Ticor Title Insurance and Ticor Title Guarantee (1991). These acquisitions made Alleghany the largest US title insurance company.

The boom of 1992-93 was followed by rising interest rates and dropping real estate activity; CT&T took a hit. The firm took cost-control measures and responded to the trend of mortgage companies providing title and closing services in addition to title insurance. It bought mortgage credit (Credit Data Reporting Services, renamed Chicago Title Credit Services) and flood information service (National Flood Information Services, renamed Chicago Title Flood Services) providers in 1995. It added debt collection, property appraisal and field inspection (Market Intelligence Inc., renamed Chicago Title Market Intelligence), foreclosure, and reconveyance companies in 1996; the company also began operating in Mexico that year.

A strong commercial market lifted CT&T's sales in 1997. The former dean of Indiana University's business school, John Rau, stepped into its leadership position that year. As the title insurance industry consolidated, the country's largest lenders provided more and more mortgages. CT&T introduced Castlelink to provide customers with one source to order and receive its products and documents electronically at any location.

In 1998 Alleghany spun off to stockholders Chicago Title Corp., created as the holding company for CT&T, CTI, Security Union, and Ticor Title. The new company then bought United Title of Nevada, Consolidated Reconveyance, The Escondido Escrow Co., and Ranch & Coast Escrow to add more services to its portfolio. In 1999 Fidelity National Financial announced it would buy Chicago Title for $1.2 billion.

Chairman: Richard P. Toft, age 62
President and CEO: John Rau, age 50, $1,185,384 pay
EVP and CFO: Peter G. Leemputte, age 41, $437,669 pay
EVP and Chief Technology and Information Officer: Louis A. Iannaccone, age 50
SVP Corporate Planning and Development and Manager, Western Division: William T. Halvorsen Jr., age 52
EVP, Secretary, and General Counsel: Paul T. Sands Jr., age 55, $278,695 pay
VP and Internal Audit Director: William E. August
SVP and Manager, Eastern Division: Christopher Abbinante, age 48, $564,077 pay
SVP and Chief Underwriting Counsel, Chicago Title Insurance Company: Joseph C. Bonita
VP Investor Relations, Chicago Title and Trust Company: Toshie Y. Davis
SVP Commercial Sales, Chicago Title Insurance Company and Ticor Title Insurance Company: Jack A. Marino
SVP Human Resources, Chicago Title and Trust Company: LaNette Zimmerman
VP and Treasurer, Chicago Title and Trust Company and Chicago Title Insurance Company: A. Larry Sisk
EVP Commercial Business/Best Practices: Thomas C. Hodges, age 53, $504,615 pay
EVP Institutional Sector: Jeffery A. Wilson
Auditors: KPMG LLP

LOCATIONS

HQ: 171 N. Clark St., Chicago, IL 60601
Phone: 312-630-2000 **Fax:** 312-223-5955
Web site: http://www.ctt.com

PRODUCTS/OPERATIONS

1998 Sales

	$ mil.	% of total
Title premiums, escrow & trust fees	1,862	97
Investment income	64	3
Net realized investment gain on sales to Alleghany	1	—
Total	**1,927**	**100**

Selected Subsidiaries
Chicago Title and Trust Company
Chicago Title Credit Services, Inc.
Chicago Title Insurance Company
Decator Title Company
Heritage American Insurance Services
Iowa Land Services Corporation
LC Investment Corporation
McNamara, Inc.
Real Info, LLC
Security Title Agency, Inc.
Security Union Title Insurance Company
Ticor Financial Company
Ticor Title Insurance Company
Title Accounting Services Corporation
United Financial Management Company
United Title of Nevada, Inc.
Washington Title Company

COMPETITORS

American National Financial
Capital Title Group
Fidelity National
First American Financial
Investors Title
LandAmerica Financial Group
Old Republic
PMI Group
Stewart Information

HISTORICAL FINANCIALS & EMPLOYEES

NYSE symbol: CTZ FYE: December 31	Annual Growth	1989	1990	1991	1992	1993	1994	1995	1996	1997	1998
Sales ($ mil.)	19.4%	—	—	—	—	—	—	1,132	1,328	1,467	1,927
Net income ($ mil.)	47.3%	—	—	—	—	—	—	30	52	68	97
Income as % of sales	—	—	—	—	—	—	—	2.7%	3.9%	4.6%	5.0%
Earnings per share ($)	—	—	—	—	—	—	—	—	—	—	4.44
Stock price - FY high ($)	—	—	—	—	—	—	—	—	—	—	51.44
Stock price - FY low ($)	—	—	—	—	—	—	—	—	—	—	35.00
Stock price - FY close ($)	—	—	—	—	—	—	—	—	—	—	46.94
P/E - high	—	—	—	—	—	—	—	—	—	—	12
P/E - low	—	—	—	—	—	—	—	—	—	—	8
Dividends per share ($)	—	—	—	—	—	—	—	—	—	—	0.68
Book value per share ($)	—	—	—	—	—	—	—	—	—	—	21.05
Employees	30.2%	—	—	—	—	—	—	—	—	8,100	10,550

STOCK PRICE HISTORY

HIGH/LOW/CLOSE

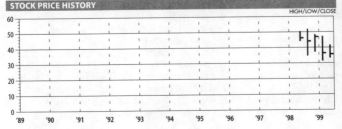

1998 FISCAL YEAR-END

Debt ratio: 0.0%
Return on equity: 21.1%
Cash ($ mil.): —
Current ratio: —
Long-term debt ($ mil.): —
No. of shares (mil.): 22
Dividends
  Yield: 1.4%
  Payout: 15.3%
Market value ($ mil.): 1,029

CHIQUITA BRANDS INTERNATIONAL

OVERVIEW

That's not just a banana in Chiquita's pocket — it's a banana empire. Chiquita Brands International is the world's #1 producer, marketer, and distributor of bananas, which account for nearly 60% of the Cincinnati-based company's total sales. Chiquita also offers other fresh fruits and vegetables. Subsidiary Chiquita Processed Foods sells juices and processed bananas and is the nation's largest private-label vegetable canner; its branded lines include the Stokely's label.

Chiquita has howled loudly about trade restrictions in the European market and was a strong force behind the US levying of retaliatory tariffs on European Union luxury imports. Meanwhile, along with growing its private-label canned vegetable business, Chiquita aims to take advantage of its distribution networks and sell more fresh produce to existing customers.

Financier Carl Lindner and his family own nearly 40% of Chiquita, largely through American Financial Group.

HISTORY

Lorenzo Baker sailed into Jersey City, New Jersey, in 1870 with 160 bunches of Jamaican bananas. Finding the fruit profitable, Baker arranged to sell bananas through Boston produce agent Andrew Preston. With the support of Preston's partners, the two formed the Boston Fruit Company in 1885. In 1899 Boston Fruit merged with three other banana importers and incorporated as United Fruit Company. Soon the company was importing bananas from numerous Central American plantations for expanded distribution in the US.

United Fruit entered the Cuban sugar trade with the purchase of Nipe Bay (1907) and Saetia Sugar (1912). It bought Samuel Zemurray's Cuyamel Fruit Company in 1930, leaving Zemurray as the largest shareholder. Zemurray, who had masterminded the overthrow of the Honduran regime in 1905 to establish one favorable to his business, forcibly established himself as United Fruit's president in 1933.

In 1944 the company introduced its catchy calypso-style Chiquita Banana jingle. (It was designed to teach consumers how to store and eat bananas.)

The term "banana republic" originates from United Fruit's involvement in establishing Central American regimes friendly to its operations. In 1954, when leftist Guatemalan leader Jacobo Arbenz threatened to seize United Fruit's holdings, the company claimed he was a communist threat and provided ships to transport CIA-backed troops and ammunition for his ultimate overthrow. United Fruit also provided two ships for the ill-fated Bay of Pigs invasion of Cuba in 1961.

Diversifying in the 1960s, United Fruit purchased A&W (restaurants and root beer, 1966) and Baskin-Robbins (ice cream, 1967). Eli Black, founder of AMK (which included the Morrell meat company), bought United Fruit in 1970 and changed its name to United Brands. Through American Financial Group, Carl Lindner began acquiring large amounts of United Brands' stock in 1973; he became chairman of the company in 1984. During the 1970s and 1980s, United Brands sold many of its holdings, including Baskin-Robbins (1973) and A&W (restaurants, 1982; soft drinks, 1987).

The firm became Chiquita Brands International in 1990. Chiquita acquired Friday Canning two years later. It then began divesting its meat operations, and all were sold by 1995.

In 1993 the European Union (EU) set up trade barriers against banana imports from Latin America, favoring banana-producing former European colonies in the Caribbean. The preference system annoyed Chiquita, whose bananas come from non-favored countries but still retained more than 20% of the European market. In 1997 the EU's trade policy was ruled illegal; the battle continued, however, over just how open the market should be.

Chiquita bought vegetable canners Owatonna Canning (1997), American Fine Foods (1997), and Stokely USA (1998) and merged them with Friday Canning in 1998 to create Chiquita Processed Foods. That year *The Cincinnati Enquirer* (once owned by Lindner) retracted a series of scathingly critical articles on Chiquita based in part on illegally obtained company voice-mail messages. Media coverage of the newspaper's actions spread the original articles' allegations — of bribery, illegal land ownership, and care less use of pesticides — to an audience far beyond Cincinnati.

In 1998 Hurricane Mitch destroyed Chiquita plantations in Honduras and Guatemala, costing the company $74 million (flooding in 1996 had cost $70 million). Sales were not affected though, as Chiquita was able to turn to growers in Ecuador and Panama.

OFFICERS

Chairman and CEO: Carl H. Lindner, age 79,
$115,000 pay
VC: Keith E. Lindner, age 39, $100,000 pay
President and COO: Steven G. Warshaw, age 45,
$1,325,000 pay
SVP and CFO: Warren J. Ligan, age 45
SVP, General Counsel, and Secretary: Robert W. Olson,
age 53, $510,000 pay
VP, Corporate Planning: Carla A. Byron
VP, Corporate Affairs: Joseph W. Hagin II
VP, Information Systems: Jeffrey T. Klare
VP and Treasurer: Gerald R. Kondritzer
VP, Human Resources: Jean B. Lapointe
VP, Investor Relations: Michael B. Sims
VP and Controller: William A. Tsacalis, age 55
VP, Internal Audit: Steven A. Tucker
President, Diversified Foods Group:
Anthony D. Battaglia, age 54, $575,000 pay
President and COO, Chiquita Banana Group:
Robert F. Kistinger, age 46, $875,000 pay
Auditors: Ernst & Young LLP

LOCATIONS

HQ: Chiquita Brands International, Inc.,
250 E. 5th St., Cincinnati, OH 45202
Phone: 513-784-8000   **Fax:** 513-784-8030
Web site: http://www.chiquita.com

Chiquita Brands International distributes its fruit and
vegetable products in more than 60 countries.

1998 Sales

	$ mil.	% of total
North America	1,603	59
Central & South America	47	2
Europe & other regions	1,070	39
Total	**2,720**	**100**

PRODUCTS/OPERATIONS

1998 Sales

	$ mil.	% of total
Fresh produce	2,243	82
Processed foods	477	18
Total	**2,720**	**100**

Major Brands
Amigo (bananas)
Chiquita (fresh bananas, other fresh fruit, juices,
processed bananas)
Chiquita Jr. (bananas)
Consul (bananas)
Ferraro's Earth Juice (fresh fruit and vegetable juices)
Naked Juice (fresh fruit and vegetable juices)
Premium (fresh vegetables)
Read (canned vegetables)
Stokely's (canned vegetables)

COMPETITORS

CHR	Lykes Bros.
Coca-Cola	Ocean Spray
Del Monte	Pillsbury
Dole	Pro-Fac
Fresh Del Monte Produce	Seneca Foods
Fyffes	Tri Valley Growers
Goya	Tropicana Products
J. M. Smucker	United Foods

HISTORICAL FINANCIALS & EMPLOYEES

NYSE symbol: CQB FYE: December 31	Annual Growth	1989	1990	1991	1992	1993	1994	1995	1996	1997	1998
Sales ($ mil.)	(3.7%)	3,823	4,273	4,627	2,723	2,533	3,962	2,566	2,435	2,434	2,720
Net income ($ mil.)	—	68	94	129	(284)	(51)	(72)	9	(51)	—	(18)
Income as % of sales	—	1.8%	2.2%	2.8%	—	—	—	0.4%	—	0.0%	—
Earnings per share ($)	—	1.67	2.20	2.52	(5.48)	(0.99)	(1.51)	0.02	(1.13)	(0.29)	(0.55)
Stock price - FY high ($)	—	17.63	32.13	50.75	40.13	17.75	19.38	18.13	16.50	18.13	16.25
Stock price - FY low ($)	—	12.88	16.00	29.38	15.25	10.00	11.25	12.13	11.13	12.63	9.31
Stock price - FY close ($)	(6.4%)	17.38	32.00	40.00	17.25	11.50	13.63	13.75	12.75	16.31	9.56
P/E - high	—	11	15	20	—	—	—	907	—	—	—
P/E - low	—	8	7	12	—	—	—	607	—	—	—
Dividends per share ($)	0.0%	0.20	0.35	0.55	0.66	0.44	0.20	0.20	0.20	0.20	0.20
Book value per share ($)	(4.0%)	11.94	15.21	19.39	12.93	11.33	9.21	9.75	8.51	8.61	8.26
Employees	(1.9%)	44,000	46,000	50,000	45,000	45,000	40,000	36,000	36,000	40,000	37,000

STOCK PRICE HISTORY

HIGH/LOW/CLOSE

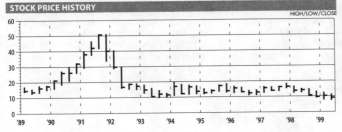

1998 FISCAL YEAR-END

Debt ratio: 55.8%
Return on equity: —
Cash ($ mil.): 89
Current ratio: 1.58
Long-term debt ($ mil.): 1,003
No. of shares (mil.): 65
Dividends
  Yield: 2.1%
  Payout: —
Market value ($ mil.): 626

CHS ELECTRONICS, INC.

OVERVIEW

CHS Electronics keeps its passport handy and its pocketbook open. The Miami-based company is the #3 distributor of computers, networking products, peripherals, and software in the world (behind Ingram Micro and Tech Data). CHS serves more than 150,000 resellers in some 45 countries outside the US. The company focuses on products from high-profile vendors such as Hewlett-Packard, Microsoft, IBM, and Intel.

Founder, chairman, and CEO Claudio Osorio has led dozens of acquisitions in fragmented markets to build CHS's heft. Already a leader in Europe (about 75% of sales) and Latin America, the company continues to expand its Asian and Middle Eastern presence. Instead of absorbing the distributors it purchases, CHS favors keeping the existing management to benefit from their local experience.

To better compete with its larger rivals, CHS is using its European facilities to enter the higher-margin market of channel assembly, a process in which distributors piece together branded and private-label components to suit the needs of specific customers. CHS is also working to establish an e-commerce presence and expand its enterprise systems business.

Venezuela-born Osorio owns almost 13% of the company; EVP Carsten Frank, 8%; and Mellon Bank, 7%.

HISTORY

As a teenager in Venezuela, Claudio Osorio built a bicycle parts trading venture into a full-time sporting goods store. At age 18, more enamored with distribution than retail, Osorio flew to California, rented a business suit, and won his first six-figure deal, to resell scuba gear in his home country.

The sporting goods business was sold in the early 1980s for $4 million to a man who didn't want the company's PC systems. CHS began in 1985 as Comtrad after Osorio stuck an ad in a local paper to sell the computers; the considerable response convinced him there was a demand.

To avoid the tapped US distribution market, the company set its sights on Europe and sold $10 million worth of products in its first year. Comtrad tried to distinguish itself from other distributors early on through aggressive marketing (Osorio's full-page print ads took IBM to task for selling older PCs) and quick turnaround. Instead of shipping the computers by boat to Venezuela, Osorio convinced air shippers to pack computer parts in canvas bags they used for letters, and had the parts assembled in Caracas.

In 1993 the company bought a German distributor of Hewlett-Packard (HP) products, a deal that would define its future — HP remains CHS's main supplier. The next year the company entered the South American market with the purchase of Florida-based CHS Promark. The acquisition led the company to change its name to CHS and relocate its headquarters to Miami.

In 1995 CHS bought nine firms in as many countries, intensifying its practice of buying companies seasoned in local markets in lieu of opening its own distribution centers. When rival Merisel tired of trying to squeeze profits out of its European and Latin American operations, CHS bought those operations (1996). The purchase boosted sales from $862 million in 1995 to $1.86 billion in 1996, the year CHS went public. To finance continued acquisitions Osorio sold 40% of CHS the following year in a secondary offering.

CHS made 15 acquisitions in 1997, including Scandinavia's largest computer products distributor, Santech Micro Group; Switzerland-based Karma International, with operations in Europe, the Middle East, and Asia; and German firm Frank & Walter Computer. Purchases in 1998 included a majority stake of French distributor Metrologie International and three distribution firms in Miami and Argentina, as part of a total of 16 acquisitions that year. CHS also agreed to buy four European PC subsidiaries of German retailer Metro AG, but the deal fell through.

Errors reporting vendor rebates prompted CHS in 1999 to restate earnings for the last three quarters of 1998; Osorio blamed the problems on a top-ranking European officer, who resigned. (A class-action shareholder suit followed soon thereafter.)

In a move to cut costs amid slumping margins, CHS announced in 1999 that it would lay off about 600 employees and close as many as 30 warehouses worldwide. Later that year CHS received a shot in the arm (estimated at as high as $50 million) from software giant Computer Associates as part of a distribution alliance. CHS also agreed to sell its Sun Microsystems distribution operations in Austria, Denmark, Germany, and Sweden for $50 million.

OFFICERS

Chairman, President, and CEO: Claudio E. Osorio, age 40, $750,000 pay
COO: Mark E. Keough, age 44
EVP, Worldwide Logistics: Carsten Frank, age 35, $500,000 pay
VP, Finance, CFO, and Treasurer: Craig S. Toll, age 50, $346,925 pay
Chief Technology Officer: Clifford Dyer
Chief Information Officer: Surinder Khurana
Chief Officer, Mergers and Acquisitions and Secretary: Antonio Boccalandro, age 31
COO, Asian Region: K. H. Lim
COO, Central European Region: Helmut Schmitt
COO, European Region: Jean-Pierre Robinot
COO, Karma Operations: Ofer Magen
COO, Latin American Region: Anthony Shalom
COO, Southern and Eastern European Regions: Salvatore Cacioppo
Managing Director, CHS Finance SA: Marc J. P. Schurtz
Regional Director, Nordic and British Isles Region: Lars Krull
Director, Human Resources: Isabel Viteri
Director, Investor Relations: Richard Kaminsky
Auditors: Grant Thornton LLP

LOCATIONS

HQ: 2000 NW 84th Ave., Miami, FL 33122
Phone: 305-908-7200   **Fax:** 305-908-7040
Web site: http://www.chse.com

CHS Electronics operates in more than 45 countries in Asia, Europe, and Latin America.

1998 Sales

	$ mil.	% of total
Western Europe	5,535	65
Latin America	1,517	18
Eastern Europe	984	11
Asia & Middle East	510	6
Total	**8,546**	**100**

PRODUCTS/OPERATIONS

1998 Sales

	% of total
Mass storage	25
PCs	20
Printers	12
Software	11
Components	8
Networking & multimedia	8
Peripherals	7
Other	9
Total	**100**

COMPETITORS

Arrow Electronics
Avnet
Comark
Computer 2000
InaCom
Ingram Micro
Merisel
MicroAge
SED International
Tech Data

HISTORICAL FINANCIALS & EMPLOYEES

NYSE symbol: HS FYE: December 31	Annual Growth	1989	1990	1991	1992	1993	1994	1995	1996	1997	1998
Sales ($ mil.)	114.0%	—	—	42	80	147	244	862	1,856	4,756	8,546
Net income ($ mil.)	115.0%	—	—	0	1	(1)	(0)	5	12	48	46
Income as % of sales	—	—	—	0.5%	1.4%	—	—	0.5%	0.7%	1.0%	0.5%
Earnings per share ($)	30.4%	—	—	—	—	—	—	0.37	0.78	1.32	0.82
Stock price – FY high ($)	—	—	—	—	—	—	—	7.67	13.01	30.75	24.81
Stock price – FY low ($)	—	—	—	—	—	—	—	4.67	5.34	10.34	4.50
Stock price – FY close ($)	41.3%	—	—	—	—	—	—	6.00	11.42	17.13	16.94
P/E – high	—	—	—	—	—	—	—	21	17	23	30
P/E – low	—	—	—	—	—	—	—	13	7	8	5
Dividends per share ($)	—	—	—	—	—	—	—	0.00	0.00	0.00	0.00
Book value per share ($)	32.2%	—	—	—	—	—	—	6.53	5.62	13.65	15.07
Employees	138.3%	—	—	—	—	—	211	968	2,296	4,260	6,800

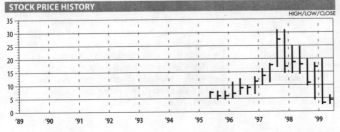

STOCK PRICE HISTORY
HIGH/LOW/CLOSE

1998 FISCAL YEAR-END

Debt ratio: 31.0%
Return on equity: 5.5%
Cash ($ mil.): 177
Current ratio: 1.14
Long-term debt ($ mil.): 376
No. of shares (mil.): 56
Dividends
  Yield: —
  Payout: —
Market value ($ mil.): 942

THE CHUBB CORPORATION

OVERVIEW

Chubb Corporation is getting back into shape. The Warren, New Jersey-based property/casualty insurer is cutting the fat (read: unprofitable lines) and making the commitment to become a leaner and meaner operation. No more Mr. Nice Guy: Chubb is serious about raising premium rates and making the increases stick.

Chubb divested its life, health, and real estate operations to concentrate on property/casualty insurance for midsized businesses and on personal lines for wealthy individuals. It of-fers traditional and niche coverage, including such specialty lines as executive protection. Its acquisition of what is now Chubb Executive Risk is expected to give it heft in the specialty commercial coverage market.

Another element in Chubb's growth strategy is focusing on developing international markets, particularly Latin America. The company already does business in more than 30 countries.

British insurer Royal & Sun Alliance Insurance Group owns nearly 6% of Chubb.

HISTORY

Thomas Caldecot Chubb and his son Percy formed Chubb & Son in New York in 1882 to underwrite cargo and ship insurance. The company soon became the US manager for Sea Insurance Co. of England and co-founded New York Marine Underwriters (NYMU). In 1901 NYMU became Chubb's chief property/casualty affiliate, Federal Insurance Co.

Chubb expanded in the 1920s, opening a Chicago office (1923) and, just before the 1929 crash, organizing Associated Aviation Underwriters. Growth slowed during the Depression, but Chubb recovered enough by 1939 to buy Vigilant Insurance Co.

The company bought Colonial Life in 1959 and Pacific Indemnity in 1967. That year Chubb Corporation was formed as a holding company, with Chubb & Son designated as the manager of the property/casualty insurance businesses. A 1969 takeover attempt by First National City Corp. (predecessor of Citigroup) was foiled by federal regulators.

Chubb acquired Bellemead Development in 1970 to expand its real estate portfolio. Following a strategy of offering specialized insurance, Chubb in the 1970s launched insurance packages for the entertainment industry, including films and Broadway shows. After the Tylenol poisonings of 1982, Chubb developed insurance against product tampering (which it no longer offers). During the 1980s Chubb focused on specialized property/casualty insurance lines; in 1985 it retreated from medical malpractice insurance.

The company combined three subsidiaries into Chubb Life Insurance Co. of America in 1991. The next year Chubb subsidiary Pacific Indemnity settled a suit over Fibreboard Corporation's asbestos liability (Fibreboard was later bought by Owens Corning); the company ultimately paid some $675 million in asbestos-related settlements.

Financial difficulties at Lloyd's of London caused that company to rethink and subsequently relax its rules about doing business with corporate insurance companies. Chubb took advantage of the opportunity and, in 1993, opened an office at Lloyd's. The next year Chubb's acquisitions included the personal lines business of Alexander & Alexander (now part of Aon Corporation).

Since the 1880s, Chubb had maintained an alliance with UK-based Royal & Sun Alliance Insurance Group and its predecessors. Royal & Sun Alliance owned about 5% of Chubb, and Chubb held about 3% of Royal & Sun Alliance. In 1993 the US insurer formed a new joint venture with the British company, with the purpose of extending to the UK Chubb's insurance products targeting the affluent. But in 1996, a major client of Royal & Sun Alliance Insurance Group defected and Chubb ended the agreement.

To focus on the property/casualty market, in 1997 Chubb sold its life and health insurance operations to Jefferson Pilot and its Bellemead real estate business to Paine Webber and Morgan Stanley Dean Witter. (Chubb had attributed its lower 1996 earnings to real estate.) The next year the commercial lines market tanked and with it went Chubb's earnings. With losses dragging down its otherwise profitable property/casualty segment, Chubb vowed to get tough — raising rates and getting out of unprofitable businesses — no matter how much it hurt. It also forged ahead with its overseas plans, buying Venezuelan insurer Italseguros Internacional and creating Chubb Re to offer international reinsurance. In 1999 Chubb bought corporate officer insurer Executive Risk (renamed Chubb Executive Risk) to beef up its executive protection and financial services lines.

Chairman and CEO: Dean R. O'Hare, age 56,
$1,775,424 pay
President: John J. Degnan, age 54, $750,193 pay
EVP and CFO: David B. Kelso, age 46, $712,116 pay
EVP: Thomas F. Motamed, age 50, $721,154 pay
EVP: Donn H. Norton, age 57
EVP: Michael O'Reilly, age 55, $676,250 pay
SVP: Daniel J. Conway
SVP: Gail E. Devlin, age 60
SVP: David S. Fowler, age 53
SVP: Frederick W. Gaertner
SVP: Ned I. Gerstman
SVP: Andrew A. McElwee Jr., age 44
SVP: Glenn A. Montgomery, age 46
SVP: Marjorie D. Raines
SVP: Henry B. Schram, age 52
SVP and General Counsel: Joanne L. Bober
VP and General Counsel: Michael J. O'Neill Jr., age 50
VP and Secretary: Henry G. Gulick, age 55
EVP, Chubb & Son: George R. Fay, age 50
EVP, Chubb & Son: Charles M. Luchs, age 59
Auditors: Ernst & Young LLP

LOCATIONS

HQ: 15 Mountain View Rd., Warren, NJ 07061-1615
Phone: 908-903-2000   **Fax:** 908-903-3402
Web site: http://www.chubb.com

Chubb has more than 120 offices throughout the
Americas, Europe, and the Pacific Rim.

PRODUCTS/OPERATIONS

1998 Assets

	$ mil.	% of total
Cash & equivalents	8	—
Treasury & agency securities	353	2
Tax-exempt securities	9,075	44
Mortgage-backed securities	1,778	9
Foreign bonds	1,202	6
Corporate bonds	1,076	5
Real estate assets	746	4
Receivables & recoverables	2,506	11
Other	4,002	19
Total	**20,746**	**100**

1998 Sales

	$ mil.	% of total
Property/casualty insurance premiums	5,304	84
Investment income	760	12
Other	286	4
Total	**6,350**	**100**

COMPETITORS

AIG	GEICO
Allianz	General Re
Allstate	The Hartford
AXA	Liberty Mutual
CGU plc	St. Paul Companies
CIGNA	State Farm
Citigroup	Tokio Marine and Fire
CNA Financial	

HISTORICAL FINANCIALS & EMPLOYEES

NYSE symbol: CB FYE: December 31	Annual Growth	1989	1990	1991	1992	1993	1994	1995	1996	1997	1998
Assets ($ mil.)	7.1%	11,179	12,268	13,775	15,019	19,437	20,723	22,997	19,939	19,616	20,746
Net income ($ mil.)	5.9%	421	522	552	617	324	529	697	513	770	707
Income as % of assets	—	3.8%	4.3%	4.0%	4.1%	1.7%	2.6%	3.0%	2.6%	3.9%	3.4%
Earnings per share ($)	6.1%	2.46	3.04	3.16	3.48	1.83	2.96	3.90	2.88	4.39	4.19
Stock price - FY high ($)	—	24.88	27.38	39.00	45.50	48.19	41.56	50.31	56.25	78.50	88.81
Stock price - FY low ($)	—	14.41	17.31	25.00	31.19	38.00	34.31	38.06	40.88	51.13	55.38
Stock price - FY close ($)	11.8%	23.81	27.13	38.50	44.44	38.94	38.69	48.38	53.75	75.63	64.75
P/E - high	—	10	9	12	13	26	14	13	20	18	21
P/E - low	—	6	6	8	9	21	12	10	14	12	13
Dividends per share ($)	11.6%	0.57	0.64	0.72	0.79	0.85	0.91	0.97	1.06	1.14	1.53
Book value per share ($)	9.5%	15.42	17.60	20.37	22.59	23.92	24.46	30.14	31.24	33.53	34.78
Employees	0.6%	10,100	10,100	10,100	10,000	10,500	11,200	10,900	11,600	11,000	10,700

STOCK PRICE HISTORY

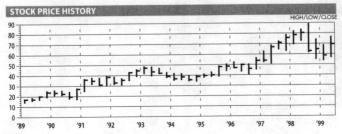
HIGH/LOW/CLOSE

1998 FISCAL YEAR-END

Equity as % of assets: 27.2%
Return on assets: 3.5%
Return on equity: 12.5%
Long-term debt ($ mil.): 608
No. of shares (mil.): 162
Dividends
  Yield: 2.4%
  Payout: 36.5%
Market value ($ mil.): 10,507
Sales (mil.): $6,350

CIGNA CORPORATION

OVERVIEW

A casualty of CIGNA's growing health care segment: property/casualty insurance.

The Philadelphia-based company's property/casualty insurance is making way for its growing health care segment. CIGNA offers group life and disability insurance and retirement and investment services and management. It also operates one of the nation's largest HMOs, with more than 6 million members. Related businesses, such as dental plans, specialty medical management programs, and pharmacy benefits management, cover about 15 million people.

Outside the US, CIGNA offers insurance to individuals (life, accident, and health) and large commercial customers (group insurance and benefits). CIGNA also provides reinsurance (group and individual life, personal accident, and health care coverage). The company operates in over 30 countries throughout North and South America, Europe, and the Pacific Rim. Property/casualty insurance, once the company's main business, had declined to about 15% of sales before CIGNA sold the operations to ACE Limited, based in Bermuda.

HISTORY

The Insurance Company of North America (INA) was founded in 1792 by Philadelphia businessmen. INA was the US's first stock insurance company and its first marine insurer. It later issued life insurance, fire insurance, and coverage for the contents of buildings. In 1808 it began using agents outside Pennsylvania. INA grew internationally in the late 1800s, appointing agents in Canada, as well as in London and Vienna, Austria. It was the first US company to write insurance in China, beginning in Shanghai in 1897.

In 1942 INA provided both accident and health insurance for men working on the Manhattan Project, which developed the atomic bomb. It introduced the first widely available homeowner coverage in 1950. INA bought HMO International, then the largest publicly owned health maintenance organization in the US, in 1978 and merged with Connecticut General in 1982 to form CIGNA.

Connecticut General began selling life insurance in 1865 and health insurance in 1912. It wrote its first group insurance (for the *Hartford Courant* newspaper) in 1913, and the first individual accident coverage for airline passengers in 1926. In the late 1930s Connecticut General was a leader in developing group medical coverage. The company offered the first group medical coverage for general use in 1952 and in 1964 added group dental insurance.

After the merger, CIGNA bought Crusader Insurance (UK, 1983; sold 1991) and AFIA (1984). It sold its individual insurance products division to InterContinental Life in 1988 and its Horace Mann Cos. (individual financial services) to an investor group in 1989 to begin positioning itself as a provider of managed health care. To this end, in 1990 CIGNA bought EQUICOR, an HMO started by Hospital Corporation of America (now part of Columbia/HCA)

and Equitable Life Assurance. It began to withdraw from the personal property/casualty business to focus on small and midsized commercial clients in the US. In the early 1990s CIGNA reduced its property/casualty business, cutting sales overseas and combining them with life and health operations. It also exited areas such as airline insurance and surety bonds. The company sold its individual life insurance and annuity business to Lincoln National in 1998.

CIGNA has expanded internationally, opening a Beijing office in 1993, 43 years after its departure from China. The next year the company bought 60% of an Indonesian insurance company. CIGNA started offering investment and pension products in Japan in 1999. It also acquired 45% of Mediplan, a managed health care organization in Mexico.

The company continued to cultivate its health care segment, acquiring managed care provider Healthsource in 1997. The company expanded its group benefits operations to India, Brazil, and Poland; at home, it cut its payroll by 1,300 in the US to counter rising costs.

Reeling from unforeseen environmental liabilities from pollution (chiefly related to asbestos), in 1995 CIGNA split property/casualty between a healthy segment that continued to write new policies and one for run-off business. (Policyholder objections and court rulings have kept CIGNA from finalizing the restructuring.) Having limited new property/casualty business to niche segments in the late 1990s, the company sold these operations (including Cigna Insurance Co. of Europe) to ACE Limited in 1999 to fund internal growth and acquisitions.

Chairman and CEO: Wilson H. Taylor, age 55,
$4,869,000 pay
President and COO: H. Edward Hanway, age 47,
$1,436,500 pay
EVP, Human Resources and Services:
Donald M. Levinson, age 53, $1,155,800 pay
EVP and CFO: James G. Stewart, age 56, $1,465,600 pay
EVP and General Counsel: Thomas J. Wagner, age 59
SVP and Chief Information Officer: Andrea Anania
SVP and Treasurer: David B. Gerges
SVP, Strategic Planning: Paul H. Rohrkemper
SVP and Associate General Counsel: Judith E. Soltz
Chief Accounting Officer: James A. Sears
President, CIGNA Domestic Property and Casualty:
Gerald A. Isom, age 60, $1,268,300 pay
President, CIGNA Investment Management:
Thomas C. Jones III, age 52
**President, CIGNA International Employee Benefits and
Life Insurance:** Terry L. Kendall, age 52
President, CIGNA Group Insurance: John K. Leonard
President, CIGNA Reinsurance: Francine M. Newman
President, CIGNA Retirement and Investment Services:
Byron D. Oliver, age 56
President, CIGNA HealthCare: William M. Pastore
Auditors: PricewaterhouseCoopers LLP

LOCATIONS

HQ: 1 Liberty Place, Philadelphia, PA 19192-1550
Phone: 215-761-1000   **Fax:** 215-761-5515
Web site: http://www.cigna.com

1998 Premiums and Fees

	% of total
US	84
Other countries	16
Total	**100**

PRODUCTS/OPERATIONS

1998 Assets

	$ mil.	% of total
Cash & equivalents	3,797	3
Government securities	6,691	6
Asset-backed securities	8,068	7
Corporate bonds	17,852	16
Mortgage loans	9,599	8
Policy loans	6,185	6
Assets in separate account	34,808	30
Recoverables & receivables	17,394	15
Other assets	10,218	9
Total	**114,612**	**100**

1998 Sales

	$ mil.	% of total
Employee life & health	12,552	59
Retirement & investment	1,870	9
International life & health	1,346	6
Property/casualty	3,254	15
Other	2,415	11
Total	**21,437**	**100**

COMPETITORS

Aetna	Kemper Insurance
Allianz	MassMutual
Allstate	MetLife
American Express	New York Life
Aon	Northwestern Mutual
AXA Financial	Oxford Health Plans
Blue Cross	Principal Financial
Chubb	Prudential
CNA Financial	State Farm
The Hartford	TIAA-CREF
John Hancock	Travelers
Kaiser Foundation	UnitedHealth Group

HISTORICAL FINANCIALS & EMPLOYEES

NYSE symbol: CI FYE: December 31	Annual Growth	1989	1990	1991	1992	1993	1994	1995	1996	1997	1998
Assets ($ mil.)	7.9%	57,779	63,691	66,737	69,827	84,975	86,102	95,903	98,932	108,199	114,612
Net income ($ mil.)	9.7%	562	330	449	311	234	554	211	1,056	1,086	1,292
Income as % of assets	—	1.0%	0.5%	0.7%	0.4%	0.3%	0.6%	0.2%	1.1%	1.0%	1.1%
Earnings per share ($)	11.2%	2.33	1.45	2.09	1.45	1.09	2.50	0.96	4.63	4.88	6.05
Stock price – FY high ($)	—	22.23	20.19	20.56	20.27	22.77	24.64	38.30	47.74	66.85	82.38
Stock price – FY low ($)	—	15.28	11.07	11.99	15.69	18.81	18.98	20.73	33.55	44.66	55.94
Stock price – FY close ($)	16.3%	19.81	13.61	20.35	19.52	20.90	21.19	34.38	45.50	57.40	77.31
P/E – high	—	10	14	10	14	21	10	40	10	14	14
P/E – low	—	7	8	6	11	17	8	22	7	9	9
Dividends per share ($)	(1.7%)	0.99	1.01	1.01	1.01	1.01	1.01	1.01	1.05	1.10	0.85
Book value per share ($)	6.2%	23.50	24.48	27.28	26.67	30.41	26.87	31.22	32.35	36.56	40.25
Employees	0.5%	47,677	56,973	55,961	52,255	50,600	48,300	44,707	42,800	47,700	49,900

STOCK PRICE HISTORY

HIGH/LOW/CLOSE

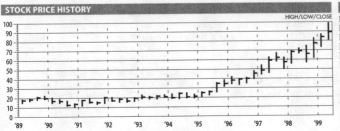

1998 FISCAL YEAR-END

Equity as % of assets: 7.2%
Return on assets: 1.2%
Return on equity: 15.6%
Long-term debt ($ mil.): 1,431
No. of shares (mil.): 206
Dividends
 Yield: 1.1%
 Payout: 14.0%
Market value ($ mil.): 15,899
Sales (mil.): $21,437

CINERGY CORP.

OVERVIEW

A multibillion-dollar underdog? That's how Cinergy wants to be perceived. The Cincinnati-based utility holding company wants to avoid the fate of large, lumbering companies by staying nimble in the dog-eat-dog world of competition. Its regulated subsidiaries, Cincinnati Gas & Electric and PSI Energy, have a generating capacity of 11,000 MW and provide power to about 1.4 million electricity customers and 470,000 gas customers in Ohio, Indiana, and Kentucky. However, Cinergy is busting out of its regional utility role and taking on deregulated

markets. The company is in the risky business of wholesale power trading and trying a customer-choice pilot program for its Ohio natural gas customers.

Cinergy is also chasing global ambitions. It has formed Cinergy Global Resources to handle its international business and plans on participating in deregulating markets worldwide. The company holds interests in power generation, transmission, and distribution facilities in Bangladesh, the Czech Republic, Estonia, Spain, the UK, and Zambia.

HISTORY

Cinergy is the product of the 1994 merger between Cincinnati Gas & Electric (CG&E) and PSI Resources. CG&E began in 1837 when James Conover was granted a charter for the Cincinnati Gas Light & Coke Company. Conover began supplying manufactured gas to Cincinnati residents in 1843. The utility industry was still in its early days: For example, whiskey was used as an antifreeze in early liquid-filled gas meters.

Then the incandescent bulb sprang to light. Hedging its bets, Conover's company began buying the stock of Cincinnati Electric Light in 1887 and renamed itself Cincinnati Gas & Electric Company in 1901. CG&E became a subsidiary of Columbia Gas & Electric in 1911.

After WWII, Columbia had to divest CG&E under the 1935 Public Utility Holding Company Act, which broke up the powerful utility trusts and ushered in the era of regulated regional monopolies.

During the 1950s and 1960s, CG&E expanded and built new plants fired with cheap, plentiful coal. However, the lure of cheaper nuclear power led CG&E to begin building Zimmer Station in the early 1970s. Over the next decade, however, costs and controversy forced CG&E to convert the nearly completed nuke to coal. Competition was on the horizon in the early 1990s, and CG&E began looking for a merger partner.

Enter PSI. PSI dates back to the early 1900s, when utility magnate Samuel Insull created a huge holding company, Middle West Utilities. In 1902 subsidiary United Gas & Electric Company of New Albany was created to invest in Indiana power plants and electric railways. Renamed Public Service Company of Indiana, or PSI, in 1931, the company was divested by Midland United (successor to Middle West) in 1948.

PSI's postwar growth focused on new coal-fired plants, but in 1978 it began building the

Marble Hill nuke. Mounting costs nearly bankrupted PSI, but in 1986 it was allowed a rate hike to cover the subsequent $1.34 billion write-off of Marble Hill.

In 1988 PSI hired former Federal Energy Regulatory Commission official James Rogers as chairman. Rogers realized he needed a partner to help absorb rising industry costs, such as smokestack scrubbers required by the 1990 Clean Air Act. The company became PSI Resources in 1990, and PSI and neighboring CG&E agreed to merge in 1992.

Cinergy was born in 1994; its name was derived from CG&E's stock symbol (CIN) and the word synergy. In 1996 GPU and Cinergy formed Avon Energy Partners to buy UK-based Midlands Electricity. It also formed a venture with Trigen Energy, a pioneer in cogeneration technology, to build on-site cogeneration facilities for big energy users such as hospitals and shopping malls. That year Cinergy paid $6 million to have Cincinnati's Riverfront Stadium renamed Cinergy Field for five years.

In 1997 Cinergy and fellow utilities Florida Progress and New Century Energies teamed up to form Cadence Network to market energy and related services to national chains of restaurants, hotels, and stores. Building up its energy trading operations, Cinergy also became a member of NYMEX that year. To get into gas commodity trading, it bought Greenwich Energy Partners (1997) and ProEnergy (1998). After dumping Midlands' power generation business in 1998, Cinergy sold its stake in Midlands' distribution unit to GPU in 1999; Cinergy retained its gas trading operation. But trading wholesale power proved to be perilous during the 1999 heatwave in the Midwest when Cinergy failed to relay power to marketers with which the firm held contracts.

Chairman: Jackson H. Randolph, $906,750 pay
VC, President, and CEO: James E. Rogers,
  $1,429,200 pay
VP; Managing Director, Cinergy Global Power Services:
  John Bryant
VP; COO, Energy Commodities Business Unit:
  Michael J. Cyrus
VP, Secretary, and General Counsel; President,
  International Business Unit: Cheryl M. Foley
VP Corporate Services and Chief Strategic Officer;
  President, Cinergy Investments: William J. Grealis,
  $577,490 pay
VP Corporate Communications; Interim VP President
  Energy: J. Joseph Hale Jr.
VP; EVP and COO, Trigen-Cinergy Solutions:
  M. Stephen Harkness
VP; President, Energy Services Business Unit:
  Donald B. Ingle Jr.
VP Human Resources Strategy: Jerry W. Liggett
VP; President, Energy Services Business Unit:
  Madeleine W. Ludlow
VP and Treasurer: William L. Sheafer
VP and Controller: John P. Steffen
VP; President, Energy Delivery Business Unit:
  Larry E. Thomas, $522,215 pay
VP and CFO: Charles J. Winger, age 52
President, Cincinnati Gas & Electric: James L. Turner
Auditors: Arthur Andersen LLP

LOCATIONS

HQ: 139 E. 4th St., Cincinnati, OH 45202
Phone: 513-421-9500   **Fax:** 513-287-3171
Web site: http://www.cinergy.com

PRODUCTS/OPERATIONS

1998 Sales

	$ mil.	% of total
Electricity		
Utilities	2,553	44
Wholesale	2,140	36
Other	54	1
Gas		
Wholesale	659	11
Utilities	357	6
Transportation	41	1
Other	4	—
Other	68	1
Total	**5,876**	**100**

Selected Subsidiaries
The Cincinnati Gas & Electric Company (CG&E, electric
  and gas utility)
Cinergy Global Resources, Inc. (international projects)
Cinergy Investments, Inc. (nonutility operations)
PSI Energy, Inc. (electric utility)

COMPETITORS

AEP	IPALCO Enterprises
Allegheny Energy	Koch
Avista	LG&E Energy
Columbia Energy	NiSource
Consolidated Natural Gas	Peabody Group
DPL	PG&E
Duke Energy	Reliant Energy
Dynegy	Sempra Energy
El Paso Energy	SIGCORP
Enron	Southern Company
Entergy	TVA
Equitable Resources	UtiliCorp
FirstEnergy	Williams Companies
Indiana Energy	

HISTORICAL FINANCIALS & EMPLOYEES

NYSE symbol: CIN FYE: December 31	Annual Growth	1989	1990	1991	1992	1993	1994	1995	1996	1997	1998
Sales ($ mil.)	16.9%	1,438	1,439	1,518	1,553	1,752	2,924	3,031	3,243	4,353	5,876
Net income ($ mil.)	1.0%	240	235	207	202	(9)	191	347	316	253	261
Income as % of sales	—	16.7%	16.3%	13.6%	13.0%	—	6.5%	11.5%	9.8%	5.8%	4.4%
Earnings per share ($)	(6.0%)	2.89	2.75	2.21	2.04	0.43	1.29	2.20	1.99	1.59	1.65
Stock price - FY high ($)	—	21.59	21.18	26.76	26.60	29.63	27.75	31.13	34.25	39.13	39.88
Stock price - FY low ($)	—	16.26	18.68	18.59	22.26	23.88	20.75	23.38	27.50	32.00	30.81
Stock price - FY close ($)	5.6%	21.01	19.93	26.76	24.88	27.50	23.50	30.63	33.38	38.31	34.38
P/E - high	—	7	8	12	13	69	22	14	17	25	24
P/E - low	—	6	7	8	11	56	16	11	14	20	19
Dividends per share ($)	1.8%	1.53	1.60	1.65	1.65	1.68	1.39	1.72	1.74	1.80	1.80
Book value per share ($)	1.5%	13.96	17.92	18.71	19.16	17.25	15.56	16.17	16.39	16.10	16.02
Employees	6.5%	5,000	5,300	5,400	4,900	5,000	8,868	8,602	7,973	7,609	8,794

STOCK PRICE HISTORY

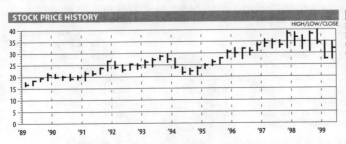

HIGH/LOW/CLOSE

1998 FISCAL YEAR-END

Debt ratio: 50.6%
Return on equity: 10.3%
Cash ($ mil.): 100
Current ratio: 0.60
Long-term debt ($ mil.): 2,605
No. of shares (mil.): 159
Dividends
  Yield: 5.2%
  Payout: 109.1%
Market value ($ mil.): 5,455

CINTAS CORPORATION

OVERVIEW

Where do you wear Cintas' wares? Why, at work, of course. Based in Cincinnati, Cintas is the nation's largest supplier of uniforms, with more than 300,000 client firms, including Merck & Co., Delta Air Lines, and Hilton Hotels. In all, it rents and leases work-wear to about 4 million workers. Cintas also offers uniform services — from custom design and embroidering to laundry, maintenance, and weekly pickup and delivery. In addition to regular work clothes, the company offers flame-resistant clothing and cleanroom suits. Cintas has some 260 facilities in the US, Canada, and Mexico, including more than 20 manufacturing and distribution centers.

Cintas has achieved substantial growth primarily through consolidation in its fragmented industry, gobbling up some 30 to 40 small firms in 1998. Its 1999 acquisition of Kansas City-based Unitog, however, launched Cintas past rival ARAMARK and into the top spot in the uniform rental business. The company is trying to leverage its position to offer more services like maintaining floor mats and providing janitorial supplies (now about 25% of sales) to its regular customers.

Along with acquisitions, the company hopes to grow by persuading potential clients that uniforms foster team spirit among employees.

Chairman Richard Farmer owns about 23% of the company; director James Gardner and his wife own about 7%.

HISTORY

In 1929 onetime animal trainer, boxer, and blacksmith Richard "Doc" Farmer started a business of salvaging old rags, cleaning them, and then selling them to factories. Farmer later began renting the rags to his customers. He would pick up the dirty rags, clean them, and return them to the factory. By 1936 the Acme Overall & Rag Laundry had established itself in Cincinnati with plans to convert an old bathhouse into a laundry. Farmer, along with his adopted son Herschell, suffered a setback from flood damage in 1937, but the family rebuilt and continued to grow the business.

In 1952 Doc Farmer died, and Herschell assumed command of the company. Five years later Herschell turned the reins over to his 23-year-old son, Richard, a former marine. Richard Farmer immediately moved Acme into the uniform rental market, and the company blossomed. Throughout the 1960s the company grew enormously, aided by Richard's innovative leadership. (The company was the first to use a polyester-cotton blend that lasted twice as long as normal cotton work uniforms.) Through a holding company, Richard established a string of uniform plants in the Midwest, starting with a factory in Cleveland in 1968. Four years later the company changed its name to Cintas.

At this time the company began tapping into the new corporate identity market, pushing the idea that uniforms convey a sense of professionalism and present a cleaner, safer image. The company began to custom design the uniforms, adding logos and distinctive colors to create "uniform" company uniforms. This aspect of the business compelled Cintas to expand to help accommodate its national clients; by 1972 the company had offices throughout Ohio and in Chicago, Detroit, and Washington, DC. By 1975 Cintas was operating in 13 states.

The company went public in 1983. For the rest of the 1980s Cintas rode the wave of consolidation in the uniform rental industry, making a slew of acquisitions to expand its geographic reach. The company also expanded from its blue-collar base into the service industry and began to supply uniforms to hotels, restaurants, and banks. By the early 1990s Cintas was a presence in most major US cities, and its share of the US market had climbed to about 10%. Farmer turned over the title of CEO to president Robert Kohlhepp in 1995. That same year the company acquired Cadet Uniform Services, a Toronto uniform rental business, for $41 million.

Scott Farmer, Richard's 38-year-old son, was named president and COO in 1997. That year Cintas made a number of acquisitions, including Micron-Clean Uniform Service and Canadian firms Act One Uniform Rentals and DW King Services. The company also moved into the first aid supplies industry with its purchase of American First Aid, and added cleanroom garments to its expanding list of uniform rentals. In 1998 Cintas acquired uniform rental company Apparelmaster, as well as Chicago-based Uniforms To You, a $150 million design and manufacturing company. In an effort to expand its corporate uniform business, the company acquired rival Unitog in 1999 for about $460 million.

OFFICERS

Chairman: Richard T. Farmer, age 64, $517,500 pay
CEO: Robert J. Kohlhepp, age 55, $687,800 pay
President and COO: Scott D. Farmer, age 40, $576,800 pay
SVP; President, Uniform Rental Division: Robert R. Buck, age 51, $495,207 pay
SVP and Secretary: David T. Jeanmougin, age 58, $350,000 pay
SVP, Southcentral Rental Group: John S. Kean III
VP and CFO: William C. Gale
VP: Bruce L. Burgess
VP and Treasurer: Karen L. Carnahan
VP Marketing and Merchandising: William W. Goetz
VP Research and Development: J. Phillip Holloman
VP, Midwest Rental Group: James A. Cain
VP, Southwest Rental Group: James J. Case
VP, Northcentral Rental Group: James V. Critchfield
VP, Northeast Rental Group: William L. Cronin
VP, Cleanroom Division: Michael P. Gaburo
VP, Canadian Rental Group: Arnold Gedmintas
VP, Western Rental Group: James J. Krupansky
VP, Great Lakes Rental Group: John W. Milligan
Director of Human Resources: Rick Sorrels
Auditors: Ernst & Young LLP

LOCATIONS

HQ: 6800 Cintas Blvd., Cincinnati, OH 45262-5737
Phone: 513-459-1200   **Fax:** 513-573-4130
Web site: http://www.cintas-corp.com

Cintas has about 260 facilities in Canada, Central America, Mexico, and the US.

Selected Manufacturing Locations

Cincinnati	Mexico City
Chicago	Mt. Vernon, Kentucky
Clay City, Kentucky	Owingsville, Kentucky
Fort Smith, Arkansas	Portal, Georgia
Hazard, Kentucky	San Buenaventura, Mexico
Irapuato, Mexico	San Jose, Costa Rica
La Cieba, Honduras	

PRODUCTS/OPERATIONS

1999 Sales

	$ mil.	% of total
Rentals	1,298	74
Other	454	26
Total	**1,752**	**100**

Selected Subsidiaries

Affirmed Medical
American First Aid
Benjamin's Uniform
Custom Uniform Service
Mechanics Uniform Holding
Mechanic Uniform Rental
Petragon
Respond Industries
SanDVans
Standard Uniform Service
Uniforms to You and Company
Unitog

COMPETITORS

Angelica
ARAMARK
G&K Services
Superior Uniform Group
UniFirst

HISTORICAL FINANCIALS & EMPLOYEES

Nasdaq symbol: CTAS FYE: May 31	Annual Growth	1990	1991	1992	1993	1994	1995	1996	1997	1998	1999
Sales ($ mil.)	22.4%	285	323	402	453	523	615	730	840	1,198	1,752
Net income ($ mil.)	20.2%	27	31	39	45	52	63	75	91	123	139
Income as % of sales	—	9.3%	9.7%	9.8%	9.9%	10.0%	10.2%	10.3%	10.8%	10.3%	7.9%
Earnings per share ($)	16.1%	0.32	0.36	0.42	0.50	0.60	0.75	0.88	1.05	1.19	1.23
Stock price - FY high ($)	—	7.84	12.25	16.06	15.50	17.25	20.13	28.00	32.19	52.88	78.38
Stock price - FY low ($)	—	5.92	6.42	10.44	11.88	12.38	14.88	16.75	24.63	30.75	39.88
Stock price - FY close ($)	26.5%	7.67	11.88	14.25	13.75	15.59	17.25	26.75	31.00	45.69	63.50
P/E - high	—	25	34	38	31	29	27	32	31	44	64
P/E - low	—	19	18	25	24	21	20	19	23	26	32
Dividends per share ($)	20.9%	0.04	0.05	0.06	0.07	0.09	0.10	0.13	0.15	0.18	0.22
Book value per share ($)	18.0%	1.85	2.14	2.45	2.84	3.31	3.88	4.55	5.31	6.26	8.24
Employees	17.2%	5,270	5,270	6,386	7,797	8,581	9,724	10,803	11,996	16,957	22,000

STOCK PRICE HISTORY

HIGH/LOW/CLOSE

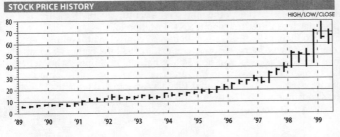

1999 FISCAL YEAR-END

Debt ratio: 24.6%
Return on equity: 15.9%
Cash ($ mil.): 16
Current ratio: 2.99
Long-term debt ($ mil.): 284
No. of shares (mil.): 106
Dividends
  Yield: 0.3%
  Payout: 17.9%
Market value ($ mil.): 6,715

CIRCUIT CITY

OVERVIEW

Circuit City is plugged in to almost every state in the US. Circuit City Stores' Circuit City Group is the #2 US appliance and electronics retailer, even though it has more stores than archrival Best Buy. Most of Richmond, Virginia-based Circuit City Group's about 600 US locations are Circuit City Superstores, which average from 9,500 to 43,000 sq. ft. and offer a broad selection of merchandise such as home office products (computers, software), audio and video equipment (home stereos, TVs), and major appliances.

To make up for the shrinking profit levels among PC sales, the company has turned to hot-ticket items such as satellite television systems and cellular phones. To tap in to new markets, Circuit City has been adding smaller stores in suburbs and less-populated cities. The company also sells small gift items through about 50 mall-based Circuit City Express stores (2,000 to 3,000 sq. ft.) and has two electronics-only stores. It has been growing at a rate of about 30 to 50 stores yearly.

Circuit City Stores is a holding company for Circuit City Group and used-car seller CarMax Group, which owns more than 30 used-car superstores and more than 20 new-car franchises.

HISTORY

While on vacation in Richmond, Virginia, in 1949, Samuel Wurtzel learned from a local barber that the first TV station in the South was about to go on the air. Wurtzel decided to launch a southern TV-retailing operation and founded Wards Company (an acronym for family names Wurtzel, Alan, Ruth, David, and Samuel) in Richmond that year, gradually diversifying into small appliances. Wards went public in 1961.

Throughout the 1960s and early 1970s, Wards expanded by acquiring several appliance retailers. Samuel's son Alan joined the business in 1966, when the company was focused on selling stereos. Predicting the end of the stereo boom, Alan converted the stores into full-line electronics specialty retailers.

Wards took a bold step in 1975, when it spent half of its net worth to open an electronics superstore in Richmond. It was an immediate success, and in 1981 it branched into the New York City market with the purchase of Lafayette Radio Electronics. The company found itself unable to compete with exuberant competitors in New York, such as Crazy Eddie (which eventually went out of business), and abandoned the market. From its New York experience, Wards developed a strategy of blitzing single markets in the South and the West with a high number of stores. In 1984 the company changed its name to Circuit City Stores.

Two years later Alan stepped down as CEO, and company leadership passed to Richard Sharp, a former computer consultant who had designed Circuit City's computerized sales system. Sharp made it a priority to maintain an efficient distribution and records system.

Earnings slipped in 1990 as consumer spending dropped and the industry was slow to introduce new products. During this time, Circuit City started opening mall stores named Impulse and introduced the Circuit City credit card.

Circuit City began selling recorded music in its superstores in 1992. The next year it entered Chicago with 18 stores and renamed its Impulse stores Circuit City Express. Also in 1993 Circuit City opened its first used-car-retailing venture, a CarMax dealership in Richmond. (The company offered a CarMax tracking stock in 1997.)

Partly due to Best Buy's aggressive expansion, this rival surpassed Circuit City's sales in fiscal year 1996. That year Circuit City and Mexico City-based electronics retailer Grupo Elektra launched a service whereby products bought at Circuit City stores in the US could be picked up at Elektra stores in Mexico. The next year the firm opened superstores in the New York City metropolitan area, part of its ongoing expansion.

The company formed Digital Video Express (DIVX), a joint venture with entertainment law firm Ziffren, Brittenham, Branca & Fischer, in 1998. DIVX offered DVD players and movies on limited-use, disposable discs available in Circuit City outlets and licensed to other stores. Frustrated by a lack of support from movie studios and other retailers, Circuit City pulled the plug on the venture in 1999, incurring about a $375 million loss.

In an effort to compete with online computer retailers, in 1999 the company began offering $400 rebates to customers who signed up with Internet service provider CompuServe. Circuit City also announced it planned to offer online shopping in 1999.

OFFICERS

Chairman and CEO: Richard L. Sharp, age 52, $2,179,911 pay
President and COO: W. Alan McCollough, age 49, $1,278,661 pay
EVP Operations: Richard S. Birnbaum, age 46, $1,030,488 pay
SVP, CFO, and Corporate Secretary: Michael T. Chalifoux, age 52, $993,469 pay
SVP and Chief Information Officer: Dennis J. Bowman
SVP and General Counsel: W. Stephen Cannon, age 47
SVP Administration: John A. Fitzsimmons, age 56, $921,354 pay
SVP Merchandising: John Froman, age 45
SVP Human Resources: Jeffrey S. Wells, age 53
Auditors: KPMG LLP

LOCATIONS

HQ: Circuit City Stores, Inc.–Circuit City Group, 9950 Mayland Dr., Richmond, VA 23233
Phone: 804-527-4000   **Fax:** 804-527-4194
Web site: http://www.circuitcity.com

1999 Stores

	No.
California	85
Texas	47
Florida	38
Illinois	33
Virginia	28
New York	27
Ohio	27
Michigan	23
Pennsylvania	21
Georgia	19
Other	242
Total	**590**

PRODUCTS/OPERATIONS

1999 Stores

	No.
Circuit City Superstores	540
Circuit City Express (mall stores)	48
Circuit City (electronics only)	2
Total	**590**

1999 Sales

	% of total
Home office	27
Televisions	18
Audio	16
Appliances	15
VCRs & camcorders	13
Other	11
Total	**100**

COMPETITORS

Amazon.com	Montgomery Ward
Best Buy	MTS
Blockbuster	Musicland
BUY.COM	Office Depot
CDW Computer Centers	OfficeMax
CompUSA	PC Connection
Costco Companies	REX Stores
Dell Computer	Sears
Fry's Electronics	Service Merchandise
Gateway	Staples
Good Guys	Tandy
HMV Media Group	Tops Appliance City
J&R Music	Wal-Mart
Kmart	The Wiz
Micro Warehouse	

HISTORICAL FINANCIALS & EMPLOYEES

NYSE symbol: CC FYE: February 28	Annual Growth	1990	1991	1992	1993	1994	1995	1996	1997	1998	1999
Sales ($ mil.)	18.1%	2,097	2,367	2,790	3,270	4,130	5,583	7,029	7,664	7,997	9,338
Net income ($ mil.)	7.4%	78	3	78	110	132	168	179	136	112	148
Income as % of sales	—	3.7%	0.1%	2.8%	3.4%	3.2%	3.0%	2.6%	1.8%	1.4%	1.6%
Earnings per share ($)	7.7%	0.38	0.02	0.42	0.58	0.69	0.87	0.92	0.70	0.57	0.74
Stock price - FY high ($)	—	6.75	7.25	8.32	14.10	16.94	13.75	19.00	19.38	22.75	32.07
Stock price - FY low ($)	—	4.66	2.25	3.82	6.91	8.25	8.63	10.75	14.32	15.44	14.41
Stock price - FY close ($)	19.7%	5.38	3.91	7.82	11.88	9.50	10.82	14.82	15.63	19.32	27.13
P/E - high	—	18	483	20	24	25	16	21	28	40	43
P/E - low	—	12	150	9	12	12	10	12	21	27	19
Dividends per share ($)	14.9%	0.02	0.03	0.03	0.03	0.04	0.05	0.06	0.07	0.07	0.07
Book value per share ($)	15.9%	1.96	1.98	2.39	3.01	3.70	4.55	5.47	8.23	8.30	7.37
Employees	15.9%	13,092	14,982	16,635	20,107	23,625	31,413	36,430	40,071	42,246	49,362

STOCK PRICE HISTORY

HIGH/LOW/CLOSE

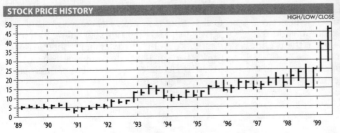

1999 FISCAL YEAR-END

Debt ratio: 18.3%
Return on equity: 8.1%
Cash ($ mil.): 248
Current ratio: 2.33
Long-term debt ($ mil.): 287
No. of shares (mil.): 124
Dividends
 Yield: 0.3%
 Payout: 9.5%
Market value ($ mil.): 6,724

CISCO SYSTEMS, INC.

OVERVIEW

When it comes to networks, Cisco isn't kidding. The San Jose, California-based company is the #1 supplier of computer networking products and a top gun in the telecommunications networking segment. Cisco controls 85% of the global market for routers and switches. Its other products include dial-up access servers and network management software. The company targets the high-end market, including service providers and large corporations, but it also sells to midsize and small businesses and consumers. Cisco's expansion beyond its traditional data networking role includes devices that accommodate voice and video traffic, with a focus on fiber-optic networking. The company gets a third of sales from phone companies.

Cisco products are at the heart of nearly every big computer network, and CEO John Chambers intends to keep it that way. He's using acquisitions (nearly 40 since 1993) to broaden its product line so it can offer one-stop shopping for networking gear. He is also making sure Cisco absorbs each acquisition without skipping a beat. Chambers has formed strategic relationships with the industry's major players, including software champ Microsoft and telecom equipment heavyweight Motorola. He is also using licensing to widen the influence of the company's Cisco Internetwork Operating System software (Cisco IOS) in hopes of making it a networking industry standard.

HISTORY

Cisco Systems was founded by Stanford University husband-and-wife team Leonard Bosack and Sandra Lerner and three colleagues in 1984. Bosack developed technology to link his computer lab's network with his wife's network in the graduate school of business. Deciding there could be a market for networking devices, the couple mortgaged their house, bought a used mainframe and got friends and relatives to work for deferred pay. They sold their first network router in 1986.

At first Cisco targeted universities, the aerospace industry, and government facilities. In 1988 the company expanded its marketing to include large corporations. Short of cash, Cisco turned to Donald Valentine of Sequoia Capital. Valentine bought a controlling stake in the company and became chairman. He hired John Morgridge, from GRiD Systems as president and CEO.

Cisco had a head start as the market for network routers opened up in the late 1980s. Sales leapt from $1.5 million in 1987 to $28 million in 1989. The company went public in 1990. That year Morgridge fired Lerner, with whom he had constantly battled, and Bosack quit.

By 1991 Cisco's sales had reached $183 million, but it was facing increased competition. Cisco began using acquisitions for expansion with its 1993 purchase of networking company Crescendo Communications. The next year it bought Kalpana, the leading maker of Ethernet switches.

In 1995 Cisco pumped up its position in the ATM (asynchronous transfer mode) switching market, buying LightStream. That year EVP John Chambers succeeded Morgridge as president and CEO; Morgridge became chairman.

In 1997 Cisco formed an alliance with Alcatel to provide networking to telecommunications and Internet access providers. The company's purchases that year included Ardent Communications (networking equipment) and Global Internet Software Group (network security products).

In 1998 Cisco acquired Precept Software (video transmission software) and American Internet Corporation (software for networking set-top boxes and cable modems). That year the company formed a pact with Dell and U S WEST to offer U S WEST customers Internet access using Cisco modems. Cisco's market capitalization passed the $100 billion milestone, a landmark accomplishment for a company its age.

The company in 1999 said it would build a $1 billion factory in San Jose, California, and invest more than $1 billion for 20% of KPMG's consulting business. That year Cisco joined with Motorola to acquire the fixed wireless assets of Bosch Telecom and form a joint venture, SpectraPoint Wireless, to provide data, voice, and video service. Cisco and Qwest Communications agreed to collaborate on what will be the biggest Internet-based network in the US.

In 1999 Cisco snapped up Sentient Networks (ATM products) and GeoTel Communications (call routing software). The company also agreed to buy Cerent (for $6.9 billion, Cisco's largest acquisition to date) and Monterey Networks, two small private companies whose products facilitate the movement of information over fiber-optic networks.

Chairman: John P. Morgridge, age 65
VC: Donald T. Valentine, age 66
President and CEO: John T. Chambers, age 49, $890,517 pay
EVP Service Provider and Consumer Lines: Donald J. Listwin, age 39, $930,668 pay (prior to promotion)
EVP Worldwide Operations: Gary J. Daichendt, age 48, $869,829 pay (prior to promotion)
SVP Finance and Administration, CFO, and Secretary: Larry R. Carter, age 55, $881,591 pay
SVP Strategic Technology Planning and Business Development and Chief Technology Officer: Judith Estrin, age 43
SVP Enterprise Line: Mario Mazzola, age 51, $884,192 pay
SVP Customer Advocacy: Douglas C. Allred
SVP Human Resources: Barbara Beck
SVP: Howard S. Charney
SVP, Global Alliances and Small-to-Medium Business: Charles H. Giancarlo, age 41
SVP Service Provider Line: Kevin J. Kennedy
SVP Corporate Development: Edward R. Kozel, age 43
SVP; General Manager, IOS Technology and Engineering Operations: Clifford B. Meltzer
SVP Manufacturing and Logistics: Carl Redfield, age 51
Auditors: PricewaterhouseCoopers LLP

LOCATIONS

HQ: 170 W. Tasman Dr., San Jose, CA 95134
Phone: 408-526-4000   **Fax:** 408-526-4100
Web site: http://www.cisco.com

Cisco Systems has more than 200 offices in 55 countries. The company's regional headquarters are in San Jose, California; Paris; and Tokyo.

PRODUCTS/OPERATIONS

Products and Services
Access
  Dial-up access servers
  Digital subscriber line (DSL) products
  Network security and management software
  Remote access routers
Cisco IOS (Internetwork Operating System)
Internet
  Cisco Cache Engine, Cisco DistributedDirector, and Cisco LocalDirector (balance the load among servers)
  Internet Commerce Solution
  NetRanger, NetSonar, and PIX Firewall (network security products)
LAN and WAN switches
Network management
  Assured Network Services (ANS, enterprise network management)
  Cisco Service Management (CSM, network service and delivery management system)
Routers (move data between networks)
SNA-to-LAN products (products that connect IBM mainframes to LANs)

COMPETITORS

3Com	Intel
Alcatel	Kingston Technology
Cabletron	Lucent
Compaq	Madge Networks
Digi International	Microsoft
Ericsson	MRV Communications
FORE Systems	Newbridge Networks
Fujitsu	Nortel Networks
IBM	Novell

HISTORICAL FINANCIALS & EMPLOYEES

Nasdaq symbol: CSCO FYE: July 31	Annual Growth	1989	1990	1991	1992	1993	1994	1995	1996	1997	1998
Sales ($ mil.)	88.8%	28	70	183	340	649	1,243	1,979	4,096	6,440	8,459
Net income ($ mil.)	89.9%	4	14	43	84	172	315	421	913	1,049	1,350
Income as % of sales	—	15.2%	19.9%	23.6%	24.9%	26.5%	25.3%	21.3%	22.3%	16.3%	16.0%
Earnings per share ($)	59.6%	—	0.01	0.02	0.04	0.08	0.12	0.16	0.31	0.34	0.42
Stock price - FY high ($)	—	—	0.21	0.55	1.49	3.18	4.53	6.53	13.15	18.00	34.85
Stock price - FY low ($)	—	—	0.07	0.14	0.52	1.23	2.09	2.27	5.70	10.07	15.15
Stock price - FY close ($)	91.0%	—	0.18	0.55	1.48	2.88	2.34	6.20	11.51	17.70	31.93
P/E - high	—	—	21	28	37	40	38	41	42	53	83
P/E - low	—	—	7	7	13	15	17	14	18	30	36
Dividends per share ($)	—	—	0.00	0.00	0.00	0.00	0.00	0.00	0.00	0.00	0.00
Book value per share ($)	67.9%	—	0.04	0.06	0.11	0.21	0.37	0.56	0.97	1.42	2.27
Employees	75.7%	94	254	505	882	1,451	2,443	4,086	8,782	11,000	15,000

STOCK PRICE HISTORY

HIGH/LOW/CLOSE

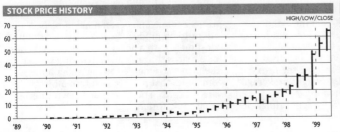

1998 FISCAL YEAR-END

Debt ratio: 0.0%
Return on equity: 19.0%
Cash ($ mil.): 535
Current ratio: 2.13
Long-term debt ($ mil.): 0
No. of shares (mil.): 3,125
Dividends
  Yield: —
  Payout: —
Market value ($ mil.): 99,786

CITIGROUP INC.

OVERVIEW

Can it all fit under one umbrella? Formed by the merger of banking company Citicorp and insurer Travelers Group, New York City-based Citigroup is the world's #1 financial services firm and one of the top US credit card issuers (neck-and-neck for first, with BANK ONE's First USA unit), as well as a full-service bank for consumers and commercial customers in 100 countries.

Travelers brings to the table its top US brokerage Salomon Smith Barney. Other subsidiaries include Primerica Financial Services (life insurance, mutual funds, and consumer loans), Commercial Credit (secured and unsecured personal and home equity loans), Travelers Bank (credit cards), and Travelers Life & Annuity (life and long-term-care insurance, annuities, and other retirement products). The company owns 84% of Travelers Property Casualty.

Citigroup may have to shed some operations if Congress fails to drop long-standing restrictions against banking and insurance combinations.

HISTORY

Citigroup travels under a fairly ancient umbrella. Predecessor Travelers Group (the first US accident insurer) was founded in 1864 by a group of businessmen in Hartford, Connecticut, and began using the red umbrella logo by 1870. Travelers soon added life insurance, annuities, and liability insurance; in 1897 it issued the first auto policy. It later added group life, and sold President Woodrow Wilson the first air travel policy.

A decision on the eve of the 1929 crash to buy federal bonds helped the firm survive the Depression. Travelers thrived after WWII and issued space travel insurance to *Apollo 11* astronauts for the first moon landing.

In the late 1970s and early 1980s Travelers got into financial services, briefly owning Keystone (mutual funds) and Dillon, Read (investment banking). When real estate soured in the late 1980s, it sold its home mortgage and relocation units. The firm entered the 1990s enfeebled, and thus caught the eye of empire builder Sanford "Sandy" Weill.

Weill had built brokerage firm Shearson Loeb Rhoades and sold it to American Express (AmEx) in 1981. Forced out of AmEx in 1985, Weill bounced back in 1986, buying Control Data's Commercial Credit unit (founded in 1912 to deal in commercial paper).

Primerica caught Weill's eye next. Its earliest antecedent, American Can, was founded in 1901 as a New Jersey canning company. During the 1960s it diversified into paper and forest products and in the 1970s it moved into retailing. In 1981 American Can bought life insurer Associated Madison; five years later it sold its container operations and became a financial services company. In 1987 the firm was renamed Primerica and also bought brokerage Smith Barney, Harris Upham & Co.

Weill's Commercial Credit bought Primerica in 1988 and in 1993 Primerica bought Shearson from AmEx. It also bought Travelers and took its name and logo.

Weill set about trimming Travelers. He sold several life subsidiaries and MetraHealth (a joint venture between Travelers and MetLife) in 1995 and bought Aetna's property/casualty business. In 1996 he combined Travelers' and Aetna's property/casualty operations to form Travelers Property Casualty and took it public. In 1997 Travelers bought Salomon Brothers and formed Salomon Smith Barney Holdings.

Weill won over Citicorp chairman and CEO John Reed in 1998. By the time of the fall merger, a slowed US economy and foreign-market turmoil brought significant losses to both sides. (Even as the deal closed, Citigroup was asked to help bail out hedge fund Long-Term Capital Management, brought to its knees by Russia's economic woes.)

The company consolidated in 1998 and 1999, laying off some 10,400 employees and shuffling management. So many executives (including co-chairmen and co-CEOs Weill and Reed) were paired through "co" titling that the company was dubbed "the ark." (It later rejiggered executive responsibilities in many areas.) In the turmoil at least two highly placed executives departed, including the erstwhile heir apparent to Reed and Weill; succession continued to be a critical and unresolved issue for the disparate co-leaders.

In 1999 Citigroup began dabbling more heavily in a traditionally Travelers' area, subprime lending, and began making niche acquisitions to fill product gaps. It targeted online consumers with a deal to offer Internet banking services through AOL's Banking Center. The firm also emerged as the leader among companies that provide government benefits via ATM cards, and it started its own Internet-based bank, Citi f/i.

Co-Chairman and Co-CEO: Sanford I. Weill, age 65, $7,192,816 pay
Co-Chairman and Co-CEO: John S. Reed, age 60, $9,525,000 pay
VC: Paul J. Collins, age 62
VC: Deryck C. Maughan, age 51, $3,922,792 pay
CFO: Heidi G. Miller, age 45
SVP Strategy and Business Development: Todd S. Thomson, age 38
Senior Human Resources Officer: Lawrence R. Phillips
VC and Senior International Officer, Citibank: William R. Rhodes, age 63
VP Investor Relations, Citigroup and Travelers Property Casualty: William F. Pike
Co-Chairman and CEO, SSB Citi Asset Management Planning Group: Thomas W. Jones, age 49
Co-Chairman and Global Chief Investment Officer, SSB Citi Asset Management Planning Group: Peter Carman
COO Affiliates, SSB Citi Asset Management Planning Group: Virgil H. Cumming
Co-CEO, Global Corporate and Investment Bank Planning Group: Michael A. Carpenter, age 51, $2,160,027 pay
Co-CEO, Global Corporate and Investment Bank Planning Group: Victor J. Menezes, age 49
CEO, Global Consumer Planning Group: Robert I. Lipp, age 60, $3,585,034 pay
President and CEO, Travelers Life and Annuity: J. Eric Daniels
Auditors: KPMG LLP

LOCATIONS

HQ: 399 Park Ave., New York, NY 10043
Phone: 212-559-1000   **Fax:** 212-793-3946
Web site: http://www.citi.com

PRODUCTS/OPERATIONS

1998 Assets

	$ mil.	% of total
Cash & equivalents	120,311	18
Trading account	119,845	18
Policy loans	215,341	32
Other investments	103,672	16
Recoverables & receivables	30,905	4
Other assets	78,567	12
Total	**668,641**	**100**

1998 Sales

	$ mil.	% of total
Loan interest & fees	22,543	30
Other interest & dividends	23,696	31
Commissions & fees	11,589	15
Insurance premiums	9,850	13
Asset management & fees	2,292	3
Principle transactions	1,780	2
Gains from sales of investments	840	1
Other	3,841	5
Total	**76,431**	**100**

COMPETITORS

Allstate	Chubb	Merrill Lynch
AXA Financial	CNA Financial	Morgan Stanley
Bank of America	Credit Suisse	Dean Witter
Bank of New York	First Boston	New York Life
	Deutsche Bank	Paine Webber
BANK ONE	FMR	Prudential
Bear Stearns	Goldman Sachs	State Farm
Capital One Financial	J.P. Morgan	Transamerica
Chase Manhattan	Lehman Brothers	
	MBNA	

HISTORICAL FINANCIALS & EMPLOYEES

NYSE symbol: C FYE: December 31	Annual Growth	1989	1990	1991	1992	1993	1994	1995	1996	1997	1998
Assets ($ mil.)	49.5%	17,955	19,689	21,561	23,397	101,360	115,297	114,475	151,067	386,555	668,641
Net income ($ mil.)	39.6%	289	373	479	728	916	1,326	1,834	2,331	3,104	5,807
Income as % of assets	—	1.6%	1.9%	2.2%	3.1%	0.9%	1.2%	1.6%	1.5%	0.8%	0.9%
Earnings per share ($)	20.2%	0.31	0.37	0.47	0.71	1.21	0.45	1.24	1.60	1.69	1.62
Stock price - FY high ($)	—	3.34	4.20	4.47	5.55	11.02	9.60	14.22	21.13	38.27	49.02
Stock price - FY low ($)	—	2.25	1.88	2.44	3.98	5.36	6.76	7.21	12.57	19.46	19.01
Stock price - FY close ($)	29.8%	3.17	2.55	4.38	5.39	8.65	7.21	13.94	20.19	35.93	33.14
P/E - high	—	11	11	10	8	9	21	11	13	23	30
P/E - low	—	7	5	5	6	4	15	6	8	12	12
Dividends per share ($)	32.2%	0.03	0.04	0.05	0.08	0.11	0.13	0.21	0.20	0.27	0.37
Book value per share ($)	18.3%	2.62	2.94	3.36	3.94	5.72	5.44	7.63	8.58	11.33	11.93
Employees	19.5%	35,000	34,000	32,000	30,000	65,000	52,000	47,600	58,900	68,900	173,700

1997 and prior financial information is for Travelers Group Inc. only.

STOCK PRICE HISTORY

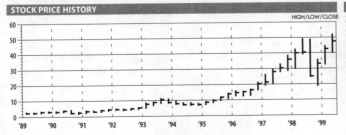

HIGH/LOW/CLOSE

1998 FISCAL YEAR-END

Equity as % of assets: 59.4%
Return on assets: 1.1%
Return on equity: 14.4%
Long-term debt ($ mil.): 62,711
No. of shares (mil.): 3,385
Dividends
  Yield: 1.1%
  Payout: 22.8%
Market value ($ mil.): 112,188
Sales (mil.): $76,431

CLEAR CHANNEL

OVERVIEW

In a media landscape dominated by flashy Internet companies, it's tempting to dismiss radio and billboards as yesterday's news. But don't write off these media pioneers just yet — Clear Channel Communications is here to remind us that the health of radio and billboards is still vigorous. The San Antonio-based company's 1999 acquisition of Jacor Communications elevated it to the #2 spot in US radio station ownership (behind AMFM). Clear Channel is also one of the world's largest outdoor advertising companies.

Nationwide, the company owns, programs, or sells airtime for more than 435 radio stations in about 100 markets. Clear Channel also has stakes in four international radio companies and a 29% interest in Heftel Broadcasting (the #1 Spanish-language radio broadcaster in the US). Its acquisition of Jacor brought more than 50 syndicated programs (*Rush Limbaugh, The Dr. Laura Schlessinger Show*) into its fold. Clear Channel also owns 18 US TV stations. Generating more than half of Clear Channel's 1998 revenue, the company's outdoor advertising activities encompass more than 300,000 outdoor advertising displays (billboards, kiosks, transit displays) across the US and 14 international markets. Clear Channel also boasts investments in half a dozen international outdoor advertising companies.

Clear Channel's purchase of Jacor was the largest in a long line of acquisitions made by the company to tighten its grip on the consolidating radio industry. Its acquisitive streak also extends to its outdoor advertising endeavors, which the company continues to expand. Co-founder, chairman, and CEO L. Lowry Mays and his family own 12% of Clear Channel. Co-founder and director B. J. "Red" McCombs and his family own 8% of the company.

HISTORY

In 1972 investment banker L. Lowry Mays found himself in a predicament. Investors looking to buy a San Antonio radio station had reneged on the financing that he had arranged for them, leaving Mays in a tight spot. He turned to local car dealer B. J. "Red" McCombs, and the two decided to buy the station themselves. The pair bought three more radio stations in 1973 and another station two years later. In 1975, after leaving investment banking to devote his time to radio stations, Mays changed the company's name from San Antonio Broadcasting to Clear Channel Communications (a moniker borrowed from the industry expression for a high-powered station that has exclusive use of its frequency).

The company went public in 1984, and its acquisition of Broad Street Communications later that year brought five new radio stations under its umbrella. Clear Channel soon earned a reputation for buying unsuccessful stations and turning them around. By the mid-1980s, its collection of radio stations numbered 16. Reluctant to pay the high prices asked for radio stations in the late 1980s, Clear Channel temporarily bowed out of radio acquisitions and tried its luck in the TV market. It created subsidiary Clear Channel Television in 1988, and, by 1992, had purchased seven TV stations (most were affiliates of the fledgling Fox network).

After the Federal Communications Commission loosened restrictions on radio station ownership in 1992, Clear Channel resumed the expansion of its radio empire. By 1994 its portfolio included 35 radio stations and nine TV stations. The company expanded internationally in 1995 through its purchase of a half interest in the Australian Radio Network. It also dipped a toe in the US Spanish-language radio market, buying 20% of Heftel Broadcasting (its stake in Heftel now stands at 29%).

When regulations on nationwide radio station ownership were lifted in 1996, Clear Channel wasted no time in extending its reach into radio. By the end of 1997, it owned or programmed 175 radio stations and 18 TV stations. It also crossed the threshold of the outdoor advertising industry with acquisitions of Eller Media in 1997 and Universal Outdoor Holdings and UK-based More Group in 1998. Clear Channel's foray into outdoor advertising was largely responsible for the company's 93% increase in sales in 1998. Its $4 billion purchase of Jacor Communications in 1999 marked the company's largest acquisition to date and positioned Clear Channel as the second-largest radio station owner in the country.

Chairman and CEO: L. Lowry Mays, age 63, $3,253,425 pay
President and COO: Mark P. Mays, age 35, $916,250 pay
EVP and CFO: Randall T. Mays, age 33, $891,667 pay
SVP and Chief Administrative Officer: Herbert W. Hill Jr.
SVP Corporate Development: Mark Hubbard, age 49
SVP Legal Affairs: Kenneth E. Wyker, age 37
Chairman and CEO, Eller Media: Karl Eller, age 70, $805,815 pay
CEO, Clear Channel International: Roger Parry
President, Eller Media: Scott Eller, age 42, $429,123 pay
COO, Clear Channel International: Coline McConville
EVP Television, Clear Channel Broadcasting: Rip Riordan
SVP Operations, Clear Channel Broadcasting: Peter Ferrara
SVP Operations, Clear Channel Broadcasting: James D. Smith
SVP Operations, Clear Channel Broadcasting: George L. Sosson
SVP Operations, Clear Channel Broadcasting: Stan Webb
VP and Chief Accounting and Information Officer: David Wilson
VP Communications: Kathryn Johnson
VP Finance: S. Houston Lane IV, age 26
VP Human Resources and Corporate Counsel: Demetra Koelling
VP Real Estate: Chad Dan
Auditors: Ernst & Young LLP

1998 Sales

	$ mil.	% of total
Outdoor advertising	702	52
Broadcasting	649	48
Total	**1,351**	**100**

Selected Investments
Adshel Street Furniture Pty. (50% ownership, street furniture displays in Australia and New Zealand)
Capital City Posters Pty., Ltd, (30% ownership, street furniture and billboard displays in Singapore)
Dauphin OTA (50% ownership, operations in Belgium, France, Italy, and Spain)
Expoplakat AS (40%, billboard displays in Estonia)
Grupo Acir Communicaciones, S.A. de C.V. (40% ownership, radio broadcasting in Mexico)
Hainan White Horse Advertising Media Investment Co. Ltd. (50% ownership, street furniture displays in China)
Heftel Broadcasting Corporation (29%)
Master & More Co., Ltd, (32% ownership, billboard displays in Thailand)
Plakanda Holdings (82% ownership, Switzerland and Poland)
Radio Bonton, a.s. (50% ownership, FM radio station in the Czech Republic)
Sirocco International SA, (50% ownership, outdoor advertising in France)

HQ: Clear Channel Communications, Inc., 200 Concord Plaza, Ste. 600, San Antonio, TX 78216-6940
Phone: 210-822-2828 **Fax:** 210-822-2299
Web site: http://www.clearchannel.com

ABC	Hearst-Argyle Television
AMFM	Infinity Broadcasting
Belo	Lamar Advertising
Cox Enterprises	Outdoor Systems
Donrey	Sinclair Broadcast Group
Gannett	Spanish Broadcasting

NYSE symbol: CCU FYE: December 31	Annual Growth	1989	1990	1991	1992	1993	1994	1995	1996	1997	1998
Sales ($ mil.)	45.7%	46	70	64	82	118	173	244	352	697	1,351
Net income ($ mil.)	—	(0)	(0)	1	4	9	22	32	38	64	54
Income as % of sales	—	—	—	1.7%	5.2%	7.7%	12.7%	13.1%	10.7%	9.1%	4.0%
Earnings per share ($)	—	(0.01)	(0.01)	0.02	0.04	0.08	0.16	0.23	0.26	0.34	0.22
Stock price - FY high ($)	—	0.70	0.77	0.99	1.81	4.61	6.50	11.06	22.63	39.94	62.31
Stock price - FY low ($)	—	0.43	0.49	0.67	0.86	1.62	3.93	6.27	10.19	16.81	31.00
Stock price - FY close ($)	64.4%	0.62	0.68	0.90	1.63	4.60	6.34	11.03	18.06	39.72	54.50
P/E - high	—	—	—	50	45	58	41	48	87	117	283
P/E - low	—	—	—	34	22	20	25	27	39	49	141
Dividends per share ($)	(100.0%)	0.13	0.00	0.00	0.00	0.00	0.00	0.00	0.00	0.00	0.00
Book value per share ($)	105.8%	0.03	0.03	0.22	0.72	0.26	0.95	1.18	3.34	8.89	17.01
Employees	29.2%	700	764	800	1,150	1,354	1,549	1,779	3,219	5,400	7,000

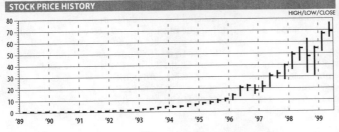

HIGH/LOW/CLOSE

Debt ratio: 34.1%
Return on equity: 1.2%
Cash ($ mil.): 37
Current ratio: 1.59
Long-term debt ($ mil.): 2,324
No. of shares (mil.): 264
Dividends
  Yield: —
  Payout: —
Market value ($ mil.): 14,366

THE CLOROX COMPANY

OVERVIEW

The Clorox Company makes consumer products for cleaning, cooking, and killing. The Oakland, California-based company is best known for its namesake bleach (the top bleach in the world), but its bevy of brand names also includes Formula 409, Soft Scrub, and S.O.S. cleaning products; Brita water filtration systems; Kingsford charcoal briquettes; Combat and Black Flag insecticides; and Fresh Step cat litter.

International markets (in more than 80 countries) make up about 20% of the firm's total sales; much of Clorox's foreign growth comes from its Latin American operations. The company has been building on existing lines through acquisitions, such as its 1999 purchase of First Brands, maker of top brands of cat litter, car-care products, and plastic wraps (its Glad brand is #1 in its market). Clorox has also cleaned up with new versions of old products and through the introduction of new products (more than 40 in 1998, including household items such as bleach-free laundry booster).

German chemical giant Henkel owns 30% of Clorox.

HISTORY

Known in its first few years as the Electro-Alkaline Company, The Clorox Company was founded in 1913 by five Oakland, California, investors to make bleach using water from salt ponds around San Francisco Bay. The next year the company registered the brand name Clorox (the name combines the bleach's two main ingredients, chlorine and sodium hydroxide). At first the company sold only industrial-strength bleach, but in 1916 it formulated a less-concentrated household solution.

With the establishment of a Philadelphia distributor in 1921, Clorox began a national expansion. The company went public in 1928 and built two more plants (in Illinois and New Jersey) in the late 1930s; it opened nine more US plants throughout the late 1940s and early 1950s. In 1957 Procter & Gamble (P&G) bought Clorox. The FTC raised antitrust questions, and litigation ensued over the next decade. P&G was ordered to divest Clorox, and in 1969 Clorox again became an independent company.

Following its split with P&G, the firm added new products, mostly household consumer goods and foods, acquiring the brands Liquid-Plumr (drain opener, 1969), Formula 409 (spray cleaner, 1970), Litter Green (cat litter, 1971), and Hidden Valley (salad dressings, 1972). In 1970 the company introduced Clorox 2, a non-chlorine bleach to compete with the new enzymatic cleaners. Clorox entered the specialty food products business by buying Grocery Store Products (Kitchen Bouquet, 1971) and Kingsford (charcoal briquettes, 1973).

In 1974 Henkel, a large West German maker of cleansers and detergents, purchased 15% of Clorox's stock as part of an agreement to share research. The agreement was later expanded to include joint manufacturing and marketing.

Beginning in 1977, Clorox sold off subsidiaries and brands, such as Country Kitchen Foods (1979), to focus on household goods, particularly those sold through grocery stores. Also in 1977 it introduced Soft Scrub, the first liquid cleanser in the US.

During the 1980s Clorox launched a variety of new products, including Match Light (instant-lighting charcoal, 1980), Tilex (mildew remover, 1981), and Fresh Step (cat litter, 1984). In 1990 it paid $465 million for American Cyanamid's household products group (including Pine-Sol cleaner and Combat insecticide).

Clorox pulled out of the laundry detergent business (entered in 1988) in 1991 after it was battered by heavyweights P&G and Unilever. Household products VP G. Craig Sullivan became CEO the next year and began a flurry of market research studies to determine how the company could improve its existing brands (one result: The chlorine smell of its flagship bleach was toned down). In 1993 Clorox divested its frozen food and bottled water operations. It began marketing its liquid bleach in Hungary through a Henkel subsidiary in 1994 and also bought S.O.S. soap pads from Miles Inc.

A string of acquisitions brought the company into new markets as it built on existing brands. Clorox bought Brita International Holdings, an Ontario-based water filtration systems manufacturer, in 1995 (Clorox had marketed Brita products in the US since 1988). It bought Black Flag and Lestoil in 1996 and car-care products manufacturer Armor All in 1997. With its 1999 purchase of First Brands — for about $2 billion in stock and debt — Clorox added complementary items (such as four more brands of cat litter) and diversified into plastic products (Glad).

OFFICERS

Chairman and CEO: G. Craig Sullivan, age 58, $1,898,250 pay
President and COO: Gerald E. Johnston, age 51, $654,150 pay (prior to promotion)
SVP, Secretary, and General Counsel: Peter D. Bewley, age 52
Group VP and CFO: Karen M. Rose, age 50
Group VP: Peter N. Louras Jr., age 48, $660,400 pay
Group VP: Lawrence S. Peiros, age 43, $489,750 pay
VP Product Supply: Anthony W. Biebl, age 49
VP Corporate Marketing Services: Robert H. Bolte, age 58
VP Human Resources: Janet M. Brady, age 44
VP and General Manager, Armor All and STP Business: Richard T. Conti, age 43
VP and General Manager, Brita Products: Charles M. Couric, age 52
VP Latin America: Scott D. House, age 37
VP Corporate Administration: Robert C. Klaus, age 53
VP and Controller: Henry J. Salvo Jr., age 50
VP and General Manager, Food and Professional Products: Glenn R. Savage, age 42
VP Corporate Communications and Public Affairs: Steven S. Silberblatt
VP Strategy and Planning: Daniel G. Simpson, age 44
VP Information Services: Keith R. Tandowsky, age 41
VP Sales: Frank A. Tataseo, age 44
Auditors: Deloitte & Touche LLP

LOCATIONS

HQ: 1221 Broadway, Oakland, CA 94612-1888
Phone: 510-271-7000   **Fax:** 510-832-1463
Web site: http://www.clorox.com

The Clorox Company sells its products in more than 80 countries.

PRODUCTS/OPERATIONS

Selected Brands
Armor All (automotive cleaning products)
Black Flag (insecticides)
Brita (water filter systems)
Clorox (liquid bleach; toilet bowl cleaner)
Combat (insecticides)
EverFresh (cat litter)
Formula 409 (spray cleaner)
Fresh Step (cat litter)
Glad (plastic wrap)
Handi Wipes (cloths and towelettes)
Hidden Valley (salad dressings)
Jonny Cat (cat litter)
K.C. Masterpiece (barbecue sauce)
Kingsford (charcoal briquettes and lighter)
Lestoil (heavy-duty household and bathroom cleaner)
Liquid-Plumr (drain opener)
Match Light (instant-lighting charcoal briquettes)
Maxforce (professional insecticide)
Pine-Sol (cleaner)
Scoop Away (cat litter)
Soft Scrub (liquid cleanser)
S.O.S. (steel wool soap pads and cleaning products)
StarterLogg (fire logs)
STP (automotive products)
Tilex (mildew remover, shower cleaner)
Wash 'n Dri (cloths and towelettes)

COMPETITORS

Amway
Church & Dwight
Colgate-Palmolive
Dial
Duraflame
Oil-Dri
Procter & Gamble
Ralston Purina
Reckitt & Colman
Reynolds Metals
S.C. Johnson
Tenneco
Turtle Wax
Unilever
USA Detergents

HISTORICAL FINANCIALS & EMPLOYEES

NYSE symbol: CLX FYE: June 30	Annual Growth	1989	1990	1991	1992	1993	1994	1995	1996	1997	1998
Sales ($ mil.)	8.1%	1,356	1,484	1,647	1,717	1,634	1,837	1,984	2,218	2,533	2,741
Net income ($ mil.)	10.2%	124	154	53	99	167	212	201	222	249	298
Income as % of sales	—	9.2%	10.4%	3.2%	5.7%	10.2%	11.5%	10.1%	10.0%	9.8%	10.9%
Earnings per share ($)	2.6%	1.12	0.70	0.25	0.46	0.76	0.99	0.95	1.06	1.19	1.41
Stock price - FY high ($)	—	20.13	11.13	11.34	13.00	13.34	13.94	16.44	22.34	33.55	48.31
Stock price - FY low ($)	—	13.75	9.03	8.03	9.13	10.19	11.75	11.94	15.22	21.72	30.94
Stock price - FY close ($)	10.9%	18.88	10.53	9.81	11.34	13.03	12.22	16.31	22.16	33.05	47.81
P/E - high	—	18	16	45	28	18	14	17	21	28	34
P/E - low	—	12	13	32	20	13	12	13	14	18	22
Dividends per share ($)	1.7%	0.55	0.33	0.37	0.40	0.43	0.45	0.48	0.53	0.58	0.64
Book value per share ($)	(3.3%)	7.10	3.75	3.62	3.73	4.01	4.26	4.50	4.53	5.02	5.23
Employees	2.5%	5,300	5,500	6,100	5,800	4,700	4,850	4,700	5,300	5,500	6,600

STOCK PRICE HISTORY

HIGH/LOW/CLOSE

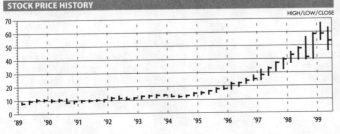

1998 FISCAL YEAR-END

Debt ratio: 22.6%
Return on equity: 27.5%
Cash ($ mil.): 90
Current ratio: 0.65
Long-term debt ($ mil.): 316
No. of shares (mil.): 207
Dividends
  Yield: 1.3%
  Payout: 45.4%
Market value ($ mil.): 9,914

CMS ENERGY CORPORATION

OVERVIEW

Though most of its revenue still comes from utility subsidiary Consumers Energy, Dearborn, Michigan-based holding company CMS Energy is hitching its power lines to a galloping horse: runaway demand for power in developing countries.

Consumers Energy generates (6,000 MW-capacity) and distributes electricity (principally from coal) to 1.6 million customers and natural gas to almost 1.6 million customers in Michigan's Lower Peninsula. While these utility mules are trudging consistently, another subsidiary, CMS Enterprises, is seeing its international energy-related businesses racing.

CMS Generation is the largest independent power developer in the world, with interests in about 40 plants powered by natural gas, coal,

and other fuels throughout 22 countries. It has won a bid to build a major power plant in energy-hungry India and is targeting power projects in Southeast Asia. The company's CMS Oil and Gas (formerly CMS NOMECO) unit engages in petroleum exploration and development, primarily overseas.

At home, management supports a restructuring plan by Michigan regulators in the electric utility industry's move from regional monopolies to retail competition. CMS has retired a nuclear plant and formed CMS MST to engage in energy marketing, services, and trading. CMS Panhandle Eastern Pipe Line, part of the company's CMS Gas Transmission unit, manages 10,400 miles of natural gas pipeline acquired from Duke Energy.

HISTORY

In the late 1880s W. A. Foote and partner Samuel Jarvis formed hydroelectric company Jackson Electrical Light Works in Jackson, Michigan. They established similar firms in other Michigan towns, ascribing their early success to Foote's ability to woo wealthy investors.

Foote's investments grew, and by 1910 he had formed Consumers Power as an electric utility holding company. That year the company merged with Michigan Light to create Commonwealth Power Railway and Light (CPR&L). Fresh capital helped build an integrated statewide transmission system.

Foote died in 1915, and after nine years of acquisitions, Bernard Cobb (Foote's successor) decided to sell the rail systems and split CPR&L into two companies: Commonwealth Power (CP) and Electric Railway Securities. In 1928 Cobb acquired Southeastern (US) Power & Light (SP&L). That year CP merged with Penn-Ohio Edison to form Allied Power & Light. A new company, Commonwealth and Southern (C&S), was then created as the parent of Allied and SP&L.

Cobb left in 1932 and future GOP presidential nominee Wendell Willkie became president of C&S. Willkie became a national political figure through his opposition to the Public Utility Holding Company Act, which ushered in a 60-year era of regulated regional monopolies.

After WWII Consumers Power was divested from C&S. In 1962 the company brought a small nuclear plant on line. The following year Consumers began diversifying with the purchase of oil and gas fields in Michigan, and in 1967 it formed NOMECO to guide its oil and gas exploration.

The completion of the Palisades nuclear plant in 1971 started a 13-year nightmare for Consumers as chronic problems caused lengthy shutdowns at the plant. The firm's third nuclear project (Midland) fared no better: Construction cost overruns and an environmental lawsuit delayed and ultimately killed the plant in 1984 — after $4.1 billion was spent.

In 1985 a temporary rate hike and the hiring of William McCormick as CEO set the firm on a new path. McCormick reincorporated the company as CMS (short for "Consumers") Energy in 1987 and created the Midland Cogeneration Venture (MCV) with six partners. MCV converted the former nuke to a natural gas-fueled, combined-cycle cogeneration plant. CMS Gas Transmission was formed in 1989.

In 1990 CMS Energy wrote off $657 million from its losses at Midland. But the firm regained profitability in 1993 and by 1994 was aggressively acquiring nonutility assets.

In the shadow of deregulation, McCormick in 1995 split the utilities into separate electric and gas divisions. That year the company issued a new class of stock to draw attention to its gas utility and transmission businesses, Consumers Gas Group.

In 1996 and 1997 CMS Energy led partners in power-plant acquisitions in Morocco and Australia. On the same track in 1998, the company acquired a half interest in Ghana's Takoradi power plant and bid successfully to build and manage a power plant and desalination project in Abu Dhabi, United Arab Emirates.

CMS Energy bought Panhandle Eastern Pipe Line, Trunkline Gas, and Trunkline LNG from Duke Energy for $2.2 billion in 1999.

Chairman and CEO; Chairman, Consumers Energy and CMS Enterprises: William T. McCormick Jr., age 54, $1,565,000 pay
President and COO; VC and President, Consumers Energy; President and CEO, CMS Enterprises: Victor J. Fryling, age 51, $1,007,440 pay
SVP and CFO, CMS Energy, Consumers Energy, and CMS Enterprises: Alan M. Wright, age 53, $524,220 pay
SVP, CMS Energy and Consumers Energy: John W. Clark, age 54
SVP, CMS Energy and CMS Enterprises: James W. Cook, age 58
SVP, Chief Accounting Officer, and Controller; SVP and Chief Accounting Officer, CMS Enterprises: Preston D. Hopper, age 48
SVP and General Counsel, CMS Energy and CMS Enterprises: Rodger A. Kershner, age 50
VP Human Resources: John F. Drake
VP Planning and Investor Relations: Laura L. Mountcastle
VP and Secretary: Thomas A. McNish
President and CEO, Electric Business Unit; EVP, Consumers Energy: David W. Joos, age 45, $693,520 pay
President and CEO, CMS Gas Transmission; SVP, CMS Enterprises: William J. Haener, age 57
President and CEO, CMS Generation; SVP, CMS Enterprises: Rodney E. Boulanger, age 58
President and CEO, CMS Oil and Gas: Bradley W. Fischer, age 49
President and CEO, Gas Business Unit; EVP, Consumers Energy: Paul A. Elbert, age 49, $531,740 pay
SVP, Consumers Energy: Robert A. Fenech, age 51
Auditors: Arthur Andersen LLP

HQ: Fairlane Plaza South, Ste. 1100, 330 Town Center Dr., Dearborn, MI 48126
Phone: 313-436-9200   **Fax:** 313-436-9225
Web site: http://www.cmsenergy.com

1998 Sales

	$ mil.	% of total
Electric utility	2,606	51
Gas utility	1,051	21
Marketing, services, and trading	939	18
Independent power production	277	5
Natural gas transmission, storage and processing	160	3
Oil and gas exploration and production	63	1
Other	45	1
Total	**5,141**	**100**

Selected Subsidiaries
CMS Enterprises
  CMS Gas Transmission (nonutility gas transmission and storage)
  CMS Panhandle Eastern Pipe Line
  CMS Generation (independent power projects)
  CMS MST (energy marketing, services and trading)
  CMS Oil and Gas (exploration and production)
  Consumers Gas Group
Consumers Energy

AEP	Edison	Reliant Energy
AES	International	Sempra Energy
DTE	Enron	UtiliCorp
Duke Energy	Illinova	

NYSE symbol: CMS FYE: December 31	Annual Growth	1989	1990	1991	1992	1993	1994	1995	1996	1997	1998
Sales ($ mil.)	6.3%	2,961	2,977	2,941	3,073	3,482	3,619	3,890	4,333	4,787	5,141
Net income ($ mil.)	(1.0%)	312	(494)	(276)	(297)	155	179	204	240	268	285
Income as % of sales	—	10.5%	—	—	—	4.5%	4.9%	5.2%	5.5%	5.6%	5.5%
Earnings per share ($)	(0.3%)	3.80	(6.07)	(3.44)	(3.72)	1.90	2.08	2.26	2.44	2.61	3.71
Stock price – FY high ($)	—	39.63	38.50	33.00	22.75	27.50	25.00	30.00	33.75	44.06	50.13
Stock price – FY low ($)	—	22.50	24.88	16.63	14.88	17.88	19.63	22.50	27.81	31.13	38.75
Stock price – FY close ($)	2.7%	38.00	27.88	18.38	18.38	25.13	22.88	29.88	33.63	44.06	48.44
P/E – high	—	10	—	—	—	14	12	13	14	17	14
P/E – low	—	6	—	—	—	9	9	10	11	12	10
Dividends per share ($)	35.7%	0.10	0.42	0.48	0.48	0.60	0.78	0.90	1.02	1.14	1.56
Book value per share ($)	(2.5%)	23.86	17.31	13.28	9.09	11.34	12.79	16.04	16.57	18.14	19.01
Employees	0.1%	9,646	9,484	9,212	9,971	10,013	9,972	10,072	9,663	9,659	9,710

HIGH/LOW/CLOSE

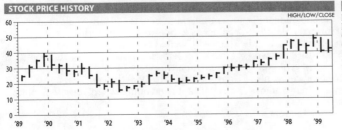

Debt ratio: 68.6%
Return on equity: 12.9%
Cash ($ mil.): 101
Current ratio: 0.78
Long-term debt ($ mil.): 4,831
No. of shares (mil.): 117
Dividends
  Yield: 3.2%
  Payout: 42.0%
Market value ($ mil.): 5,646

CNA FINANCIAL CORPORATION

OVERVIEW

It's no accident that CNA Financial writes so many commercial property/casualty insurance policies. The Chicago-based holding company's subsidiaries offer workers' compensation, general liability, multiple peril, reinsurance, marine, and other coverages for businesses, groups, and associations. CNA also provides special liability insurance for such professionals as doctors, lawyers, and architects.

CNA also offers life, accident, and health insurance (including annuity and pension products) for individuals and groups. Its personal insurance lines, which include auto and homeowners coverage, are being sold to Allstate. CNA is 85% owned by the Tisch family's Loews Corporation.

HISTORY

CNA Financial was founded in 1852 as the Continental Insurance Co. when merchant Henry Bowen could not find the type of fire insurance he wanted. Bowen assembled a group of investors and started out with about $500,000 in capital. In 1882 Continental Insurance added marine insurance and tornado insurance. Seven years later Francis Moore became president; he was developer of the Universal Mercantile Schedule, a system of assessing fire hazards in buildings.

About the time Continental Insurance was writing the book on fire insurance, several midwestern investors were having trouble assessing risk in their own insurance field — disability. In 1897 this group founded the Continental Casualty Co. in Hammond, Indiana. In the early years its primary clients were railroads. Continental Casualty eventually merged with other companies in the field, and by 1905 had branch offices in nine states and Hawaii and was writing business in 41 states and territories.

Both Continentals added new insurance lines in 1911: Continental Insurance went into personal auto, and Continental Casualty formed subsidiary Continental Assurance to sell life insurance. By 1915 Continental Insurance had four primary companies; spurred by growing prewar patriotism, they were called the America Fore Group. Both Continentals rose to the challenges presented by the world wars and the Depression; they entered the 1950s ready for new growth.

In the 1960s the companies began to diversify into other fields. Continental Insurance added interests in Diners Club and Capital Financial Services; in 1968 it formed holding company Continental Corp. Meanwhile, Continental Assurance (which had formed its own holding company, CNA Financial) went even farther afield, adding mutual fund companies, consumer finance companies, nursing homes, and residential construction.

By the early 1970s CNA was on the ropes

because of the recession and setbacks in the housing business. In 1974 Robert and Laurence Tisch bought most of the company and cut costs ruthlessly. Continental had its own problems in the 1970s, including an Iranian joint venture that got caught up in the revolution.

Both companies suffered losses arising from Hurricane Andrew in 1992, but CNA, which did its housecleaning in the 1970s, was better able to deal with the blow than was Continental, which entered the 1990s in need of restructuring.

Rising interest rates in 1994 hurt Continental, whose merger with CNA in 1995 made CNA one of the US's top 10 insurance companies. CNA consolidated the two operations to cut costs and eliminated about 5,000 jobs.

CNA bought Arizona-based Western National Warranty in 1995, followed by managed care provider CoreSource the next year. Also in 1996 CNA denied O. J. Simpson's claim on his business liability policy to fund his defense against the Brown/Goldman wrongful-death suit.

In 1997 the company spun off its surety business in a deal with Capsure Holdings and formed CNA Surety Corporation. Taking advantage of outsourcing trends, CNA created CNA UniSource, which provides payroll and human resources services. CNA UniSource bought its payroll servicer, Indiana-based Interlogic Systems, the next year.

CNA pursued a global strategy, buying majority interests in an Argentine workers' compensation carrier and a British marine insurer, but with 1998 sales flat and earnings down the tube, the company did more slashing than accumulating. It cut 2,400 jobs and exited such lines as agriculture and entertainment insurance, as well as certain types of employer health coverage. It also tightened its property/casualty underwriting as part of the turnaround plan. In 1999 the company agreed to sell its auto and homeowners lines to Allstate.

Chairman: Edward J. Noha, age 71
CEO: Laurence A. Tisch, age 76
Chairman and CEO, CNA Insurance Companies:
Bernard L. Hengesbaugh, age 52, $1,434,423 pay
President, CNA Insurance Companies: Philip L. Engel,
age 58, $800,000 pay
SVP Reinsurance, CNA Insurance Companies:
William J. Adamson Jr.
SVP Risk Management, CNA Insurance Companies:
Peter P. Conway Jr.
SVP Human Resources: Carol Dubnicki
SVP Claims, CNA Insurance Companies: James P. Flood
**SVP, CNA Consulting Group, CNA Insurance
Companies:** Michael C. Garner
SVP Life Operations, CNA Insurance Companies:
Peter E. Jokiel
**SVP, Secretary, and General Counsel, CNA Financial
Corporation:** Jonathan D. Kantor
CFO, Insurance Unit: Robert V. Deutsch, age 39
**SVP Commercial Operations, CNA Insurance
Companies:** Michael McGavick
SVP Specialty Operations: Thomas F. Taylor
SVP Global Operations: Robert T. Van Gieson
**SVP Information Technology, CNA Insurance
Companies:** David W. Wroe
SVP Marketing, CNA Insurance Companies:
William H. Sharkey Jr.
Auditors: Deloitte & Touche LLP

LOCATIONS

HQ: CNA Plaza, Chicago, IL 60685
Phone: 312-822-5000   **Fax:** 312-822-6419
Web site: http://www.cna.com

CNA Financial has offices throughout the US, Europe,
and South America.

PRODUCTS/OPERATIONS

1998 Assets

	$ mil.	% of total
Cash & equivalents	217	—
Corporate bonds	30,073	48
Stocks	1,970	3
Mortgage loans	62	—
Policy loans	177	—
Receivables	24,965	40
Other assets	4,895	8
Total	**62,359**	**100**

1998 Sales

	$ mil.	% of total
Premiums	13,375	78
Investment income	2,146	13
Investment gains	695	4
Other	858	5
Total	**17,074**	**100**

COMPETITORS

20th Century	MassMutual
AIG	MetLife
Allstate	Mutual of Omaha
American Financial	Nationwide Insurance
Chubb	New York Life
CIGNA	Pacific Mutual
GEICO	Prudential
General Re	Reliance Group Holdings
Guardian Life	St. Paul Companies
The Hartford	State Farm
John Hancock	Travelers
Liberty Mutual	USAA

HISTORICAL FINANCIALS & EMPLOYEES

NYSE symbol: CNA FYE: December 31	Annual Growth	1989	1990	1991	1992	1993	1994	1995	1996	1997	1998
Assets ($ mil.)	9.0%	28,682	31,089	35,673	36,681	41,912	44,320	59,902	60,735	61,269	62,359
Net income ($ mil.)	(8.3%)	614	367	613	(331)	268	37	757	965	966	282
Income as % of assets	—	2.1%	1.2%	1.7%	—	0.6%	0.1%	1.3%	1.6%	1.6%	0.5%
Earnings per share ($)	(8.3%)	3.24	1.92	3.26	(1.80)	1.42	0.17	4.04	5.16	5.17	1.49
Stock price - FY high ($)	—	36.21	33.30	33.05	34.80	33.63	27.39	41.04	39.13	44.04	53.26
Stock price - FY low ($)	—	19.19	16.48	20.90	26.14	24.73	19.98	21.56	31.88	32.09	34.50
Stock price - FY close ($)	2.4%	32.63	22.85	32.63	32.63	25.81	21.60	37.80	35.63	42.54	40.25
P/E - high	—	11	17	10	—	24	161	10	8	9	36
P/E - low	—	6	9	6	—	17	118	5	6	6	23
Dividends per share ($)	—	0.00	0.00	0.00	0.00	0.00	0.00	0.00	0.00	0.00	0.00
Book value per share ($)	9.3%	21.56	23.39	26.72	25.00	28.17	23.67	35.49	37.23	43.96	47.89
Employees	3.9%	16,700	17,200	17,800	17,200	16,800	15,600	25,000	24,300	24,700	23,600

STOCK PRICE HISTORY

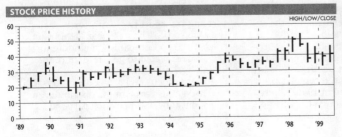

HIGH/LOW/CLOSE

1998 FISCAL YEAR-END

Equity as % of assets: 14.1%
Return on assets: 0.5%
Return on equity: 3.2%
Long-term debt ($ mil.): 3,160
No. of shares (mil.): 184
Dividends
  Yield: —
  Payout: —
Market value ($ mil.): 7,402
Sales (mil.): $17,074

CNF TRANSPORTATION INC.

OVERVIEW

CNF Transportation (CNF) has been traveling long enough to know what works. Based in Palo Alto, California, the global transportation company moves freight on the ground and in the air and operates through three primary business groups: Emery Worldwide, Con-Way Transportation Services, and Menlo Logistics. Its Road Systems unit also makes trailers and transportation equipment.

Emery, CNF's largest revenue generator, provides air cargo services and focuses mainly on heavy airfreight. In North America the firm relies on its fleet of 76 aircraft and 2,000 trucks, tractors, and trailers; internationally it acts as an airfreight forwarder in some 200 countries. Con-Way, a nonunion carrier, mainly provides less-than-truckload services in the US, Puerto Rico, and large cities in Canada and Mexico. It owns some 26,000 trucks, trailers, and tractors. Other Con-Way services include truckload and intermodal shipping. Menlo Logistics manages distribution networks and develops software for logistics optimization and order tracking.

CNF also works for the U.S. Postal Service: It provides air delivery for next-day express mail, sorts and transports second-day priority mail in the eastern US, and carries mail in peak times.

HISTORY

Leland James, co-owner of a bus company in Portland, Oregon, founded Consolidated Truck Lines in 1929 to provide transport services in the Pacific Northwest. Operations extended to San Francisco and Idaho by 1934 and to North Dakota by 1936. It adopted the name Consolidated Freightways (CF) in 1939.

James formed Freightways Manufacturing that year, making CF the only trucking company to design and build its own trucks (Freightliners). In the 1940s CF extended service to Chicago, Minneapolis, and Los Angeles.

CF went public in 1951 and moved to Menlo Park, California, in 1956. It continued to buy companies (52 between 1955 and 1960) and extended its reach throughout the US and Canada. When an attempt to coordinate intermodal services with railroads and shipping lines failed in 1960, William White became president and exited intermodal operations to focus on less-than-truckload shipping.

In 1966 CF formed CF AirFreight to offer air cargo services in the US. Three years later it bought Pacific Far East Lines, a San Francisco shipping line (now a part of Con-Way). White retired in 1971.

CF sold Freightways Manufacturing to Daimler-Benz (now DaimlerChrysler) in 1981 and started the Con-Way carriers, its regional trucking businesses, in 1983 after the US trucking industry was deregulated. In the 1980s Con-Way moved back into intermodal rail, truck, and ocean shipping.

The company bought Emery Air Freight in 1989 and combined it with CF AirFreight as a US and international air cargo company, Emery Worldwide. Founded in 1946, Emery Air Freight had expanded across the US and overseas, first by using extra cargo space on scheduled airline flights, then by chartering aircraft. It bought its first plane in 1979. Emery began having troubles in the 1980s, including difficulties in integrating its 1987 acquisition, Purolator Courier. A 1988 takeover attempt by former FedEx president Arthur Bass further plagued Emery; fending off the takeover resulted in losses of almost $100 million. Emery brought CF a 1989 deal with the U.S. Postal Service to handle its next-day express mail.

CF formed Menlo Logistics in 1990 to provide its customers with a range of third-party logistics services. In 1993 the company invested $201 million in integrating its technology improvements. A Teamsters' strike in 1994 that halted union carriers nationwide boosted demand for Con-Way's services as customers sought nonunion carriers to move their shipments. The next year Con-Way opened 40 service centers and bought another 3,300 tractors and trailers.

In 1996 CF spun off most of its long-haul transportation businesses (including CF MotorFreight, Canadian Freightways, and Milne & Craighead) and renamed the resulting entity Consolidated Freightways. CF then changed its own name to CNF Transportation (CNF).

CNF received a five-year, $1.7 billion contract from the U.S. Postal Service in 1997 to sort and transport two-day priority mail in the eastern US. The next year Menlo won contracts from six companies, including Intel and IBM, expected to generate more than $1 billion by 2003.

To better focus on its core operations, CNF sold its VantageParts unit (a distributor of heavy-duty aftermarket truck parts) to HDA Parts System in 1999.

Chairman: Donald E. Moffitt, $796,044 pay
President and CEO: Gregory L. Quesnel, age 50,
$942,295 pay (prior to promotion)
SVP and CFO: Chutta Ratnathicam, age 51,
$535,646 pay
SVP, General Counsel, and Secretary:
Eberhard G. H. Schmoller, age 55, $513,117 pay
**SVP; President and CEO, Con-Way Transportation
Services:** Gerald L. Detter, age 54, $1,251,135 pay
SVP; President and CEO, Emery Worldwide:
Roger Piazza, age 59
SVP; President and CEO, Menlo Logistics:
John H. Williford, age 42, $396,673 pay
President and CEO, Con-Way Central Express:
Richard V. Palazzo
President and CEO, Con-Way Southern Express:
John T. Hickerson
President and CEO, Con-Way Truckload Services:
J. Ronald Linkous
President and CEO, Con-Way Western Express:
Charles E. Boone
President and CEO, Emery Worldwide Airlines:
Kent T. Scott
**EVP Sales and Marketing, Con-Way Transportation
Services:** Bryan M. Millican
VP Human Resources and Deputy General Counsel:
David L. Slate
Auditors: Arthur Andersen LLP

LOCATIONS

HQ: 3240 Hillview Ave., Palo Alto, CA 94304
Phone: 650-494-2900   **Fax:** 650-813-5311
Web site: http://www.cnf.com

PRODUCTS/OPERATIONS

1998 Sales & Operating Income

	Sales		Operating Income	
	$ mil.	% of total	$ mil.	% of total
Emery Worldwide	2,204	45	64	22
Con-Way Transportation	1,684	34	207	71
Other	1,054	21	20	7
Total	**4,942**	**100**	**291**	**100**

Selected Subsidiaries and Operations
Emery Worldwide
Con-Way Transportation Services
Menlo Logistics
Road Systems

COMPETITORS

Air Express	GeoLogistics
Airborne Freight	J. B. Hunt
American Freightways	Norfolk Southern
Arkansas Best	Pittston BAX
Central Freight Lines	Roadway Express
CHR	Ryder
Circle International	Schneider National
CSX	TNT Post Group
DHL	Union Pacific
DSC Logistics	UPS
Eagle USA	U.S. Postal Service
Expeditors International	USFreightways
FDX	Werner
Fritz	Yellow Corporation

HISTORICAL FINANCIALS & EMPLOYEES

NYSE symbol: CNF FYE: December 31	Annual Growth	1989	1990	1991	1992	1993	1994	1995	1996	1997	1998
Sales ($ mil.)	3.1%	3,760	4,209	4,082	4,056	4,192	4,681	5,281	3,662	4,267	4,942
Net income ($ mil.)	24.1%	20	(28)	(40)	(81)	51	55	57	28	121	139
Income as % of sales	—	0.5%	—	—	—	1.2%	1.2%	1.1%	0.8%	2.8%	2.8%
Earnings per share ($)	25.0%	0.33	(1.16)	(1.52)	(2.78)	0.46	1.64	1.64	1.48	2.19	2.45
Stock price - FY high ($)	—	37.75	26.88	21.50	19.63	24.00	29.25	28.75	29.38	50.88	49.94
Stock price - FY low ($)	—	25.25	10.75	9.50	12.50	13.63	17.88	20.25	16.25	20.25	21.56
Stock price - FY close ($)	4.0%	26.50	11.75	15.38	17.63	23.63	22.38	26.50	22.25	38.75	37.56
P/E - high	—	114	—	—	—	52	18	18	20	23	20
P/E - low	—	77	—	—	—	30	11	12	11	9	9
Dividends per share ($)	(10.1%)	1.04	0.53	0.00	0.00	0.00	0.00	0.40	0.50	0.40	0.40
Book value per share ($)	(1.7%)	18.01	16.45	15.30	12.64	13.65	14.58	15.76	10.86	13.89	15.48
Employees	(2.1%)	40,800	41,300	37,700	37,900	39,100	40,500	41,600	25,100	26,300	33,700

STOCK PRICE HISTORY
HIGH/LOW/CLOSE

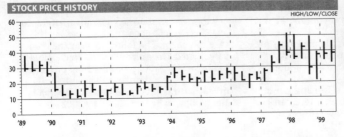

1998 FISCAL YEAR-END
Debt ratio: 43.3%
Return on equity: 18.8%
Cash ($ mil.): 74
Current ratio: 1.21
Long-term debt ($ mil.): 593
No. of shares (mil.): 48
Dividends
  Yield: 1.1%
  Payout: 16.3%
Market value ($ mil.): 1,798

THE COASTAL CORPORATION

OVERVIEW

Coastal's business is a gas. The Houston-based energy holding company's primary operations consist of natural gas marketing, transmission, and storage; petroleum refining and marketing; petrochemicals; oil and gas exploration; and coal mining.

A major portion of Coastal's earnings comes from the transmission and storage of natural gas. Its ANR Pipeline subsidiary operates 14 gas processing plants, 27 underground storage facilities, and about 18,000 miles of pipeline that links gas fields in the Gulf of Mexico, the Rockies, and the mid-continent region with its primary markets in Illinois, Michigan, and Wisconsin. Coastal's exploration and production unit has interests in more than 3,000 producing wells, mostly in South Texas and in the Gulf of Mexico; it also has agreements to exploit reserves in Australia, Indonesia, and Venezuela. Coastal owns four refineries and sells gasoline in 34 states through 1,550 Coastal-branded retail outlets.

The company is continuing a tradition started by controversial founder Oscar Wyatt of venturing into the troubled Mideast — where others fear to tread — striking a deal with Saddam Hussein to buy crude as part of Iraq's oil-for-food agreement with the UN.

HISTORY

After spending boyhood summers as an oil field worker, serving as a bomber pilot in WWII, and earning a mechanical engineering degree from Texas A&M, Oscar Wyatt started a small natural-gas gathering business in 1951 in Corpus Christi, Texas. The company became Coastal States Gas Producing Company in 1955. It collected and distributed natural gas from oil fields in South Texas.

In 1962 Coastal purchased Sinclair Oil's Corpus Christi refinery and pipeline network. Also in the early 1960s, Coastal subsidiary Lo-Vaca Gathering supplied natural gas to Texas cities and utilities. During the energy crisis of the early 1970s, Lo-Vaca hoarded its natural gas supplies and then raised prices. Unhappy customers sued Coastal, and in 1977 regulators ordered Lo-Vaca to refund $1.6 billion. To finance the settlement, Coastal spun off Lo-Vaca as Valero Energy.

Meanwhile, Wyatt had been expanding the company through a series of deals. Coastal won Rio Grande Valley Gas, a small South Texas pipeline (1968); in 1973 it mounted a successful $182 million hostile bid for Colorado Interstate Gas. That year it changed its name to Coastal States Gas Corporation. With aggressive acquisitions, the firm moved into low-sulfur Utah coal (Southern Utah Fuel, 1973), New England pipelines (Union Petroleum, 1973), California refining (Pacific Refining, 1976), and Florida petroleum marketing and transportation (Belcher Oil, 1977; renamed 1990). In 1980 Coastal adopted its present name. It bought American Natural Resources five years later in a $2.5 billion hostile takeover.

Wyatt struck a deal in 1987 giving Libyan dictator Muammar Qaddafi an interest in Coastal's Hamburg, Germany, refinery in exchange for discounts on Libyan oil. In 1991 the US government forbade American citizens from working for the venture.

Before the Persian Gulf War, Wyatt offered to sell Iraqi president Saddam Hussein a stake in Coastal's international refining and marketing operations. After hostilities broke out, Wyatt publicly accused President George Bush of trading US soldiers' lives for Saudi oil. Postwar US sanctions on Iraq left Coastal in the lurch. In 1992 Coastal closed its Kansas refinery after its Refining and Marketing Group posted a $192 million operating loss.

The next year Coastal completed construction on the Empire State Pipeline. The 156-mi. pipeline system, in which Coastal holds a 50% interest, runs from Niagara Falls to Syracuse, New York. In 1995 Wyatt stepped down as CEO, handing the job to president David Arledge. To finance more promising ventures, Coastal sold its Utah coal operations to Atlantic Richfield and Japan's ITOCHU for $610 million a year later.

In 1997 Wyatt retired as chairman, giving Arledge that position too. That year a New York City grand jury indicted a Coastal subsidiary and two of its former employees on charges of overbilling the city by about $1 million for heating oil.

Also in 1997 Coastal bought an 11% stake in the Alliance pipeline project, as part of a strategy to invest in natural gas transmission projects between Canada and US cities (in this case, Chicago). The following year the company joined Chevron and Mobil in contracting to buy nearly $200 million of Iraqi crude oil.

In 1999 Coastal unveiled a plan to build a major natural gas pipeline from Alabama to Tampa Bay, to be completed by 2002.

Chairman, President, and CEO: David A. Arledge, age 54, $1,122,527 pay
EVP Administration: Coby C. Hesse, age 51, $493,597 pay
EVP, Refining, Engineering, and Chemicals: James A. King, age 59, $477,030 pay
SVP, Coal: James L. Van Lanen, age 54
SVP and Corporate Secretary: Austin M. O'Toole, age 63
SVP, Crude Oil Supply and Marketing: Thomas M. Wade, age 46
SVP, Exploration and Production: Rodney D. Erskine, age 54
SVP, Finance: Donald H. Gullquist, age 55
SVP and General Counsel: Carl A. Corrallo, age 55, $409,901 pay
SVP, International Refining and Marketing: Jack C. Pester, age 64
SVP, Marketing: Dan J. Hill, age 58
SVP, Natural Gas: Jeffrey A. Connelly, age 52, $434,884 pay
SVP, Special Projects: Kenneth O. Johnson, age 78
VP, Administrative Services: M. Truman Arnold, age 70
VP, Controller, and General Auditor; VP, Coastal States Management: Jeffrey B. Levos, age 38
VP, Corporate Tax: Thomas E. Jackson, age 59
VP, Government and Corporate Affairs; SVP, Coastal States Management: M. Frank Powell, age 48
VP, Investor Relations: Stirling D. Pack Jr., age 51
Director, Human Resources: Lloyd Healy
Auditors: Deloitte & Touche LLP

LOCATIONS

HQ: Coastal Tower, 9 Greenway Plaza, Houston, TX 77046-0995
Phone: 713-877-1400   **Fax:** 713-877-6754
Web site: http://www.coastalcorp.com

PRODUCTS/OPERATIONS

1998 Sales

	$ mil.	% of total
Refining, marketing & chemicals	5,200	71
Natural gas	1,357	18
Exploration & production	437	6
Coal	242	3
Power	121	2
Other	11	—
Total	**7,368**	**100**

Selected Subsidiaries

Refining, Marketing, and Distribution
Coastal Refining & Marketing, Inc.

Natural Gas
ANR Pipeline Co.
Coastal Gas Services Co.

Exploration and Production
ANR Production Co.
Coastal Oil & Gas Corp.

COMPETITORS

ARCO	PDVSA
Ashland	PEMEX
BP Amoco	Phillips Petroleum
Chevron	Shell
Conoco	Sunoco
Duke Energy	Texaco
Dynegy	Tosco
Elf Aquitaine	TOTAL FINA
Enron	Ultramar Diamond
Exxon	Shamrock
Koch	Unocal
Mobil	Williams Companies

HISTORICAL FINANCIALS & EMPLOYEES

NYSE symbol: CGP FYE: December 31	Annual Growth	1989	1990	1991	1992	1993	1994	1995	1996	1997	1998
Sales ($ mil.)	(1.3%)	8,271	9,381	9,549	10,063	10,136	10,215	10,448	12,167	9,653	7,368
Net income ($ mil.)	11.3%	170	226	96	(127)	116	233	270	403	302	444
Income as % of sales	—	2.1%	2.4%	1.0%	—	1.1%	2.3%	2.6%	3.3%	3.1%	6.0%
Earnings per share ($)	9.5%	0.90	1.08	0.46	(0.62)	0.50	1.02	1.20	1.79	1.33	2.03
Stock price - FY high ($)	—	16.55	19.81	18.38	15.00	15.69	16.88	18.88	25.75	32.53	38.75
Stock price - FY low ($)	—	11.00	14.63	11.88	11.00	11.75	12.38	12.56	17.44	21.94	25.25
Stock price - FY close ($)	8.7%	16.55	16.13	12.31	11.94	14.13	12.88	18.50	24.44	30.97	35.13
P/E - high	—	18	18	40	—	31	17	16	14	24	19
P/E - low	—	12	14	26	—	24	12	10	10	16	12
Dividends per share ($)	5.7%	0.14	0.20	0.20	0.20	0.20	0.20	0.20	0.20	0.20	0.23
Book value per share ($)	7.3%	8.68	9.56	9.84	9.66	10.88	11.72	12.72	14.35	15.46	16.34
Employees	0.2%	13,100	13,900	16,500	16,600	16,000	16,300	15,500	14,700	13,200	13,300

STOCK PRICE HISTORY

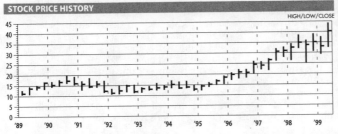

HIGH/LOW/CLOSE

1998 FISCAL YEAR-END

Debt ratio: 53.5%
Return on equity: 12.8%
Cash ($ mil.): 107
Current ratio: 0.98
Long-term debt ($ mil.): 3,999
No. of shares (mil.): 213
Dividends
  Yield: 0.7%
  Payout: 11.3%
Market value ($ mil.): 7,473

THE COCA-COLA COMPANY

OVERVIEW

According to The Coca-Cola Company, the two most famous expressions in the world are "OK" and "Coca-Cola." And if Coca-Cola had its way, you'd forget the other one. Atlanta-based Coca-Cola's flagship product is one of the planet's most valuable brands. The #1 soft-drink company (ahead of PepsiCo), it sells more than 160 beverages, such as carbonated and sports drinks, juices, teas, and coffees, in almost 200 countries.

Worldwide, Coca-Cola has two of the three top-selling soft drinks (#1 Coca-Cola classic and #3 diet Coke) and a 51% market share. The company's rivalry with PepsiCo has moved beyond Coke and Pepsi to juice products (Coca-Cola's Minute Maid vs. PepsiCo's Tropicana),

high-caffeine drinks (Surge vs. Mountain Dew), and bottled water (Dasani vs. Aquafina).

About two-thirds of Coca-Cola's sales come from outside North America, making the company sensitive to global economic turmoil. On the other hand, that turmoil has enabled the company to make international investments on the cheap. Coca-Cola's affiliates have been buying numerous bottlers in the US and around the world to reorganize its global bottling system into major anchors in prime markets.

SunTrust Banks, which helped underwrite Coca-Cola's first public stock sale, owns about 6% of the company, and Warren Buffett's Berkshire Hathaway owns 8%.

HISTORY

Atlanta pharmacist John Pemberton invented Coke in 1886. His bookkeeper, Frank Robinson, named the product after two ingredients, coca leaves (later cleaned of narcotics) and kola nuts. By 1891 druggist Asa Candler had bought The Coca-Cola Company, and within four years the soda-fountain drink was available in all states; it was in Canada and Mexico by 1898.

Candler sold most US bottling rights in 1899 to Benjamin Thomas and John Whitehead of Chattanooga, Tennessee, for $1. The men began a regional franchise bottling system, creating over 1,000 bottlers within 20 years. The famous contoured Coke bottle was designed in 1915 by the C. J. Root Glass Company.

In 1916 Candler retired to become Atlanta's mayor; his family sold the company to Atlanta banker Ernest Woodruff for $25 million in 1919. Coca-Cola went public that year. In 1923 Woodruff appointed his son Robert president.

Robert's contributions were in advertising and overseas expansion. He introduced the slogans "The Pause that Refreshes" (1929) and "It's the Real Thing" (1941). Woodruff decreed that every soldier would have access to a five-cent bottle of Coke during WWII; the government helped build 64 overseas bottling plants. Coca-Cola bought Minute Maid in 1960 and began launching new drinks — Fanta (1960), Sprite (1961), TAB (1963), and diet Coke (1982).

Woodruff headed the firm for six decades and was succeeded in 1981 by Roberto Goizueta, a Cuban-born chemical engineer who rejuvenated the business. Although Coca-Cola had dabbled in several industries over the years, Goizueta engineered the largest of these diversifications, the $700 million acquisition of

Columbia Pictures in 1982. (Coca-Cola made a profit of over $1 billion on Columbia when it — and other entertainment purchases that followed — was sold to Sony in 1989.)

In 1985, with Coke slipping in market share, the firm changed its formula. Consumers roundly rejected New Coke, so the company quickly brought back the original recipe as Coca-Cola classic. In 1986 it consolidated the US bottling operations it owned into Coca-Cola Enterprises and sold 51% of the new company to the public.

Coca-Cola introduced POWERaDE, its entry in the rapidly growing sports drink market, in 1990, and Fruitopia in 1994. In 1995 it bought root beer maker Barq's.

Goizueta died of lung cancer in 1997; while he was at the helm, the firm's value rose from $4 billion to $145 billion. Douglas Ivester, the architect of Coca-Cola's restructured bottling operations, succeeded him.

Ivester ran into a series of scrapes. The company's 1997 bid to buy Orangina from Pernod Ricard was blocked by the French government. An antitrust lawsuit from PepsiCo in 1998 challenged Coca-Cola's dominance in the US fountain-drink business. Global financial woes hurt the company's bottom line. International anti-trust scrutiny forced Coca-Cola to scale back an agreement to buy the rights (outside the US and France) to about 30 Cadbury Schweppes beverage brands, including Dr Pepper.

More bad news came in 1999 when Coca-Cola products were recalled in a handful of European countries and the European Commission ordered an investigation into alleged antitrust actions by the company.

OFFICERS

Chairman and CEO: M. Douglas Ivester, age 52,
$2,750,000 pay
SVP and CFO: James E. Chestnut, age 48, $365,000 pay
SVP and Chief Marketing Officer: Charles S. Frenette,
age 46
SVP and General Counsel: Joseph R. Gladden Jr., age 56
SVP of Corporate Affairs: Earl T. Leonard Jr., age 60
SVP; President and CEO of The Minute Maid Company:
Ralph H. Cooper, age 59, $599,583 pay
SVP; President of the Middle and Far East Group:
Douglas N. Daft, age 56, $690,250 pay
SVP; President of the North American Group:
Jack L. Stahl, age 46, $740,000 pay
SVP; President of the Africa Group: Carl Ware, age 55
VP; VP of Human Resources: Michael W. Walters, age 52
Auditors: Ernst & Young LLP

LOCATIONS

HQ: 1 Coca-Cola Plaza, Atlanta, GA 30313
Phone: 404-676-2121   **Fax:** 404-676-6792
Web site: http://www.cocacola.com

1998 Sales & Operating Income

	Sales $ mil.	Sales % of total	Operating Income $ mil.	Operating Income % of total
North America	6,915	37	1,460	27
Greater Europe	4,834	26	1,473	27
Middle & Far East	4,040	21	1,299	24
Latin America	2,244	12	999	18
Africa	603	3	216	4
Other regions	177	1	(480)	—
Total	**18,813**	**100**	**4,967**	**100**

PRODUCTS/OPERATIONS

Selected Brand Names

Soft Drinks
Aquarius
Barq's
Cherry Coke
Citra
Coca-Cola classic
diet Coke
Fanta
Fresca
Lift
Mello Yello
Mr. PiBB
Smart (soft drink for
Chinese market)
Sprite
Surge
TAB
Thums Up (cola beverage
sold in India)

Other Beverages
Bacardi (fruit mixers)
Bonaqua (bottled water)

Bright & Early (breakfast
beverages)
Ciel (bottled water for
Mexican market)
Dasani (bottled water)
Five Alive (fruit beverages)
Fruitopia (fruit juices and
teas)
Georgia (coffee drinks,
Japan)
Hi-C (fruit drinks)
Kuat (berry drink for
Brazilian market)
Minute Maid (juices and
juice drinks)
Nestea (tea-based drinks)
POWERaDE (sports drink)
Saryusaisai (tea drink,
Japan)
Tian Yu Di ("Heaven and
Earth" juice drinks,
China)

COMPETITORS

Bass
Cadbury Schweppes
Celestial Seasonings
Chiquita Brands
Cott
Dole
Ferolito, Vultaggio
Florida's Natural
Kirin
Lykes Bros.

National Beverage
National Grape Co-op
Ocean Spray
PepsiCo
Philip Morris
Procter & Gamble
Quaker Oats
Triarc
Unilever
Virgin Group

HISTORICAL FINANCIALS & EMPLOYEES

NYSE symbol: KO FYE: December 31	Annual Growth	1989	1990	1991	1992	1993	1994	1995	1996	1997	1998
Sales ($ mil.)	8.6%	8,966	10,236	11,572	13,074	13,957	16,172	18,018	18,546	18,868	18,813
Net income ($ mil.)	12.6%	1,214	1,382	1,618	1,664	2,176	2,554	2,986	3,492	4,129	3,533
Income as % of sales	—	13.5%	13.5%	14.0%	12.7%	15.6%	15.8%	16.6%	18.8%	21.9%	18.8%
Earnings per share ($)	11.3%	0.54	0.50	0.60	0.62	0.83	0.98	1.17	1.38	1.64	1.42
Stock price - FY high ($)	—	10.13	12.25	20.44	22.69	22.56	26.75	40.19	54.25	72.63	88.94
Stock price - FY low ($)	—	5.42	8.16	10.66	17.78	18.75	19.44	24.38	36.06	50.00	53.63
Stock price - FY close ($)	24.0%	9.66	11.63	20.06	20.94	22.31	25.75	37.13	52.63	66.69	67.00
P/E - high	—	19	25	34	37	27	27	34	39	44	63
P/E - low	—	10	16	18	29	23	20	21	26	30	38
Dividends per share ($)	15.0%	0.17	0.20	0.24	0.28	0.34	0.39	0.44	0.50	0.56	0.60
Book value per share ($)	12.5%	1.18	1.41	1.67	1.49	1.77	2.05	2.15	2.48	2.96	3.41
Employees	3.5%	20,960	24,000	28,900	31,300	34,000	33,000	32,000	26,000	29,500	28,600

STOCK PRICE HISTORY

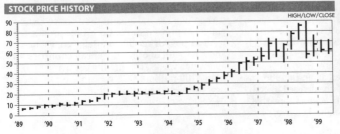

HIGH/LOW/CLOSE

1998 FISCAL YEAR-END

Debt ratio: 7.6%
Return on equity: 42.0%
Cash ($ mil.): 1,648
Current ratio: 0.74
Long-term debt ($ mil.): 687
No. of shares (mil.): 2,466
Dividends
  Yield: 0.9%
  Payout: 42.3%
Market value ($ mil.): 165,190

COCA-COLA ENTERPRISES INC.

OVERVIEW

Scientists and suits at The Coca-Cola Company concoct the secret recipes and market the brand, but Coca-Cola Enterprises (CCE) does much of the bottling and distribution of Coca-Cola products, including Coke, Sprite, Minute Maid, Fruitopia, and Barq's. Atlanta-based CCE is the world's #1 soft-drink bottler.

CCE blends Coca-Cola syrups and concentrates with carbonated water; pours them into Coke's trademark bottles, cans, and fountain containers; and distributes them in North America and Europe. Coca-Cola products account for almost 90% of its sales. CCE also bottles, markets, and/or distributes other beverage brands, including Canada Dry, Dr Pepper, Evian, NAYA, Nestea, Seven Up, and Schweppes.

One of many major "anchor" bottlers for The Coca-Cola Company, CCE distributes about 74% of that company's total volume in North America and about 20% worldwide. CCE has been increasing its share of the Coke market by acquiring other bottlers in the US, Canada, and Europe. It is trying to restore consumer confidence and sales volume in Europe after a contamination scare and product recall.

The Coca-Cola Company is CCE's principal shareholder, with a stake of about 40%. CCE chairman Summerfield Johnston Jr. owns about 8% of the company.

HISTORY

Coca-Cola Enterprises (CCE) was formed in 1986 when The Coca-Cola Company bought its two largest bottlers — JTL Corp. and BCI Holdings — and formed a single corporation. The company went public immediately, though Coca-Cola retained a significant interest in it.

CCE set about acquiring smaller bottling concerns across the US in its quest to consolidate and dominate the historically fragmented industry. By 1988 the company had become the #1 bottler in the world, but profits lagged. In an effort to boost performance, CCE reorganized, centralizing its operations.

Change came in 1991 when CCE merged with the Johnston Coca-Cola Bottling Group, the #2 US Coca-Cola bottler. The acquisition cost the ailing CCE $125 million, increased the company's already sizable debt, and led a number of disaffected investors to protest. Johnston executives took control when Summerfield Johnston Jr. (whose grandfather had co-founded the first Coke bottling franchisee) assumed the post of CEO, and Henry Schimberg, a former RC Cola route salesman, became president and COO.

In 1992 the bottler was reorganized into 10 US operating regions to allow for better control of individual market dynamics. A $1.5 billion public debt offering occurred that year, and the following year the company began looking outward for growth, acquiring Nederland B.V. (the Coca-Cola bottler of the Netherlands) as well as two Tennessee bottlers. In 1994 CCE recorded its first profitable year since 1990.

The company reorganized again in 1996, forming four operating groups defined by market and geographic lines. Its acquisitions that year included Montana-based Coke West, Louisiana's Ouachita Coca-Cola Bottling, and bottlers in Belgium and France.

CCE bought Cadbury Schweppes' 51% stake in the Coca-Cola & Schweppes Beverages UK joint venture for $2 billion in 1997, and it also purchased Coca-Cola's shares in Coca-Cola Beverages Ltd. (Canada's leading bottler) and The Coca-Cola Bottling Company of New York.

A half-dozen deals in 1998 included the $1.1 billion purchase of Coke Southwest and other bottling acquisitions in the US and Luxumbourg worth $355 million. Schimberg became CEO that year.

Also in 1998 CCE announced a major increase in spending on vehicles, equipment, and the like. The bottler expanded its vending-machine business, and many distributors and vending-machine owners (who use CCE as a supplier) complained that the firm was using its dominant position unfairly — for example, charging lower prices in its own machines than independent owners could for the same products.

CCE bought a half-dozen more US bottlers in January 1999 for $620 million. In April 1999 CEO Schimberg announced he would retire in April 2000.

Bad news came in June 1999 when products bottled by CCE in Antwerp, Belgium, and Dunkirk, France, were contaminated by bad carbon dioxide and a paint used on wooden pallets to prevent mold. Coca-Cola products were banned or recalled in Belgium, France, and a handful of other European countries for about two weeks, costing the company more than $100 million. CCE has since established new precautions at its bottling plants.

OFFICERS

Chairman: Summerfield K. Johnston Jr.
President and CEO: Henry A. Schimberg
Principal Operating Officer: John R. Alm
Principal Operating Officer: Norman P. Findley
CFO: Patrick J. Mannelly
SVP; President, Eastern North America Group:
Summerfield K. Johnston III
SVP; President, Western North America Group:
Gary P. Schroeder
SVP; President, Central North America Group:
G. David Van Houten Jr.
**VP, Director of Acquisitions, and Deputy General
Counsel:** E. Liston Bishop III
VP Investor Relations and Planning: Margaret F. Carton
VP Public Affairs: John H. Downs Jr.
VP Human Resources: Paul M. Gunderson
VP Operations: John C. Heinrich
VP Marketing: Daniel G. Marr
VP, Operations, Planning, and Development:
Michael W. McNally
VP and Treasurer: Vicki R. Palmer
Auditors: Ernst & Young LLP

LOCATIONS

HQ: 2500 Windy Ridge Pkwy., Atlanta, GA 30339
Phone: 770-989-3000   **Fax:** 770-989-3788
Web site: http://www.cokecce.com

Coca-Cola Enterprises has operations in 46 states and in
Belgium, Canada, France, Luxembourg, the Netherlands,
and the UK.

1998 Sales

	$ mil.	% of total
North America	10,056	75
Europe	3,358	25
Total	**13,414**	**100**

PRODUCTS/OPERATIONS

1998 Bottle & Can Brand Distribution

Company	North America % of total	Europe % of total	Total % of total
Coca-Cola Classic	40	51	42
diet Coke/Coca-Cola light	21	17	20
Sprite	14	3	11
Other Coca-Cola products	15	13	15
Other franchise products	10	16	12
Total	**100**	**100**	**100**

COMPETITORS

American Bottling
Buffalo Rock
Cadbury Schweppes
Coca-Cola Bottling Consolidated
Coca-Cola Bottling (IL)
Cott
Honickman
National Beverage
Ocean Spray
Pepsi Bottling
Philadelphia Coca-Cola
Quaker Oats
Triarc
Virgin Group
Whitman

HISTORICAL FINANCIALS & EMPLOYEES

NYSE symbol: CCE FYE: December 31	Annual Growth	1989	1990	1991	1992	1993	1994	1995	1996	1997	1998
Sales ($ mil.)	14.8%	3,882	4,034	4,051	5,127	5,465	6,011	6,773	7,921	11,278	13,414
Net income ($ mil.)	7.9%	72	93	(82)	(186)	(15)	69	82	114	171	142
Income as % of sales	—	1.8%	2.3%	—	—	—	1.1%	1.2%	1.4%	1.5%	1.1%
Earnings per share ($)	10.7%	0.14	0.22	(0.27)	(0.48)	(0.04)	0.17	0.20	0.28	0.43	0.35
Stock price - FY high ($)	—	6.24	5.62	6.78	5.41	5.29	6.49	9.95	16.36	36.00	41.56
Stock price - FY low ($)	—	4.91	4.08	3.91	3.75	3.91	4.66	5.91	7.99	15.69	22.88
Stock price - FY close ($)	23.5%	5.33	5.16	5.12	4.08	5.08	5.99	8.95	16.15	35.56	35.75
P/E - high	—	45	26	—	—	—	38	50	58	84	119
P/E - low	—	35	19	—	—	—	27	30	29	36	65
Dividends per share ($)	25.1%	0.02	0.02	0.02	0.02	0.02	0.02	0.02	0.03	0.08	0.15
Book value per share ($)	4.9%	3.87	3.99	3.74	3.23	3.25	3.38	3.64	3.76	4.61	5.95
Employees	13.0%	22,000	20,000	20,000	25,000	26,000	26,500	30,000	43,200	56,000	66,000

STOCK PRICE HISTORY — HIGH/LOW/CLOSE

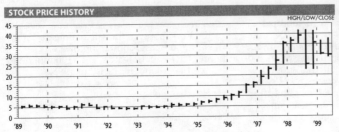

1998 FISCAL YEAR-END

Debt ratio: 79.8%
Return on equity: 5.9%
Cash ($ mil.): 68
Current ratio: 0.67
Long-term debt ($ mil.): 9,605
No. of shares (mil.): 401
Dividends
  Yield: 0.4%
  Payout: 42.9%
Market value ($ mil.): 14,352

COLGATE-PALMOLIVE COMPANY

OVERVIEW

Colgate-Palmolive wants you to get up close and personal. Headquartered in New York City, the company is the #1 maker of toothpaste in the US, ahead of Procter & Gamble. Colgate is also a major supplier of personal care products (baby care, deodorants, shampoos, and soaps), dishwashing soaps (Palmolive is a leading brand worldwide), and household cleaning products (Ajax, Axion). The company's pet food brand (Hill's Science Diet) is a best-seller globally. Colgate has operations in approximately 70 countries and markets its products in more than 200.

The company is aggressively going after market share, introducing a bevy of new products and supporting them with the highest level of advertising in more than a decade. Though foreign sales have always been critical to Colgate (nearly 70% of sales), the company has refocused on the US market. Efforts include a $100 million marketing blitz for Colgate Total toothpaste, the first toothpaste to get FDA approval to advertise its ability to heal gingivitis.

HISTORY

William Colgate founded The Colgate Company in Manhattan in 1806 to produce soap, candles, and starch. Colgate died in 1857, and the company passed to his son Samuel, who renamed it Colgate and Company. In 1873 the company introduced toothpaste in jars, and in 1896 it began selling Colgate Dental Cream in tubes. By 1906 Colgate was making 160 kinds of soap, 625 perfumes, and 2,000 other products. The company went public in 1908 and moved to Jersey City two years later.

In 1898 Milwaukee's B. J. Johnson Soap Company (founded 1864) introduced Palmolive, a soap made of palm and olive oils. It became so popular that the firm changed its name to The Palmolive Company in 1916. Ten years later Palmolive merged with Peet Brothers, a Kansas City-based soap maker founded in 1872. Palmolive-Peet merged with Colgate in 1928, forming Colgate-Palmolive-Peet (shortened to Colgate-Palmolive in 1953). The stock market crash of 1929 prevented a planned merger of the company with Hershey and Kraft.

During the 1930s the firm purchased French and German soap makers and opened branches in Europe. Colgate introduced Fab detergent and Ajax cleanser in 1947, and the brands soon became top sellers in Europe. The company expanded to the Far East in the 1950s, and by 1961 foreign sales were 52% of the total.

Colgate introduced a host of products in the 1960s and 1970s, including Palmolive dishwashing liquid (1966), Ultra Brite toothpaste (1968), and Irish Spring soap (1972). During the same time, the company diversified by buying approximately 70 other businesses, including Kendall hospital and industrial supplies (1972), Helena Rubinstein cosmetics (1973), Ram Golf (1974), and Riviana Foods and Hill's Pet Products (1976). The strategy had mixed results, and most of these acquisitions were sold in the 1980s.

Reuben Mark became CEO of Colgate in 1984. The company bought 50% of Southeast Asia's leading toothpaste, Darkie, in 1985; it changed its name to Darlie in 1989 following protests of its minstrel-in-blackface trademark.

Both Palmolive automatic dishwasher detergent and Colgate Tartar Control toothpaste were introduced in 1986. That year Colgate purchased the liquid soap lines of Minnetonka, the most popular of which is Softsoap. In 1992 the company bought Mennen, maker of Speed Stick (the leading US deodorant).

Increasing its share of the oral care market in Latin America to 79% in 1995, Colgate acquired Brazilian company Kolynos (from American Home Products for $1 billion) and 94% of Argentina's Odol Saic. The company also bought Ciba-Geigy's oral hygiene business in India, increasing its share of that toothpaste market. At home, however, sales and earnings in key segments were dismal, so in 1995 Colgate began a restructuring that included cutting more than 8% of its employees and closing or reconfiguring 24 factories over two years.

The company introduced a record 602 products in 1996 and continued to expand its operations in countries with emerging economies. The next year Brazilian antitrust regulators approved the Kolynos sale with the provision that Colgate stop selling Kolynos toothpaste for four years. Also in 1997 — as Colgate took the lead in the US toothpaste market for the first time in 35 years (displacing Procter & Gamble) — the FDA approved the sale of Colgate Total, the first toothpaste containing the germ-fighter triclosan. Colgate spent $100 million to launch the product in the US in 1998.

In 1999 the company sold the rights to Baby Magic (shampoos, lotions, oils) in the US, Canada, and Puerto Rico to Playtex Products for $90 million.

Chairman and CEO: Reuben Mark, age 60,
$3,456,334 pay
President and COO: William S. Shanahan, age 58,
$2,254,229 pay
CFO: Stephen C. Patrick, age 49, $916,342 pay
SVP, Secretary, and General Counsel:
Andrew D. Hendry, age 51
VP Global Human Resources: Robert J. Joy, age 52
EVP and COO, Developed Markets: Lois D. Juliber,
age 50, $1,176,454 pay
EVP and COO, High Growth Markets: David A. Metzler,
age 56, $1,132,229 pay
Auditors: Arthur Andersen LLP

LOCATIONS

HQ: 300 Park Ave., New York, NY 10022
Phone: 212-310-2000   **Fax:** 212-310-3405
Web site: http://www.colgate.com

Colgate-Palmolive has operations in more than 70
countries and sells its products in more than 200
countries.

1998 Sales & Operating Profit

	Sales		Operating Profit	
	$ mil.	% of total	$ mil.	% of total
Oral, personal & household care				
Latin America	2,408	27	502	32
Europe	2,068	23	318	21
North America	2,047	23	396	26
Asia & Africa	1,453	16	159	10
Pet nutrition & other	996	11	174	11
Total	**8,972**	**100**	**1,549**	**100**

PRODUCTS/OPERATIONS

Selected Brands

Household and Fabric Care	Kolynos
Ajax	Lady Speed Stick
Ajax Fiesta de Flores	Mennen
Fab	Orabase
Murphy Oil Soap	Palmolive
Palmolive	Softsoap
Protex	Speed Stick
Soupline/Suavitel	

Personal Care	**Pet Nutrition**
Baby Magic	Hill's Prescription Diet
Colgate	Prescription Diet n/d
Irish Spring	Science Diet

COMPETITORS

Alberto-Culver	Iams
Amway	Johnson & Johnson
Avon	Mars
Block Drug	Nestle
Carter-Wallace	Nu Skin
Chattem	Perrigo
Church & Dwight	Procter & Gamble
Clorox	Ralston Purina
Cosmair	Reckitt & Colman
Dial	S.C. Johnson
Gillette	SmithKline Beecham
Heinz	Warner-Lambert
Henkel	Unilever
Herbalife	USA Detergents

HISTORICAL FINANCIALS & EMPLOYEES

NYSE symbol: CL FYE: December 31	Annual Growth	1989	1990	1991	1992	1993	1994	1995	1996	1997	1998
Sales ($ mil.)	6.6%	5,039	5,691	6,060	7,007	7,141	7,588	8,358	8,749	9,057	8,972
Net income ($ mil.)	13.1%	280	321	125	477	190	580	172	635	740	849
Income as % of sales	—	5.6%	5.6%	2.1%	6.8%	2.7%	7.6%	2.1%	7.3%	8.2%	9.5%
Earnings per share ($)	11.8%	0.48	0.53	0.19	0.69	0.26	0.89	0.26	0.98	1.14	1.31
Stock price - FY high ($)	—	8.11	9.44	12.28	15.16	16.81	17.44	19.34	24.13	39.34	49.44
Stock price - FY low ($)	—	5.52	6.59	8.41	11.28	11.69	12.38	14.50	17.22	22.50	32.53
Stock price - FY close ($)	21.7%	7.94	9.22	12.22	13.94	15.59	15.84	17.56	23.06	36.75	46.44
P/E - high	—	17	18	65	22	65	20	74	25	35	38
P/E - low	—	12	12	44	16	45	14	56	18	20	25
Dividends per share ($)	11.9%	0.20	0.23	0.26	0.29	0.34	0.39	0.44	0.47	0.53	0.55
Book value per share ($)	9.2%	1.32	1.77	2.45	3.43	2.45	2.45	2.19	2.79	3.04	2.92
Employees	5.3%	24,100	24,800	24,900	28,800	28,000	32,800	38,400	37,900	37,800	38,300

STOCK PRICE HISTORY

HIGH/LOW/CLOSE

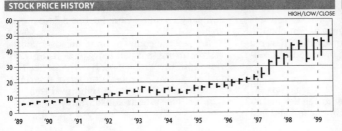

1998 FISCAL YEAR-END

Debt ratio: 52.5%
Return on equity: 49.6%
Cash ($ mil.): 182
Current ratio: 1.06
Long-term debt ($ mil.): 2,301
No. of shares (mil.): 585
Dividends
  Yield: 1.2%
  Payout: 42.0%
Market value ($ mil.): 27,187

COLLINS & AIKMAN CORPORATION

OVERVIEW

Collins & Aikman loves that new-car smell. The Charlotte, North Carolina-based company is a leading maker of automotive interior systems for carmakers around the world. Its products include floor mats, molded carpeting, plastic trim, convertible tops, acoustic materials, automotive fabrics, and luggage-compartment trim. Major customers include General Motors, Ford, DaimlerChrysler, Honda, and Toyota. Collins & Aikman also makes such nonautomotive products as casket liners and velvet furniture fabrics. The company has more than 60 facilities in 12 countries.

Collins & Aikman is undergoing a major restructuring that will create two divisions from the company's global automotive businesses: North America Automotive Interior Systems (Detroit) and Europe Automotive Systems (Germany). The company also is establishing a Specialty Automotive Products Division comprised of its Dura Convertible Systems and Automotive Fabrics businesses. The company intends to move from a mass of sprawling operating groups to three tightly knit units. Collins & Aikman has exited its businesses in wall coverings and upholstery fabric and floor coverings. Blackstone Partners and WP Partners collectively own about 80% of Collins & Aikman.

HISTORY

Collins & Aikman was founded as G. L. Kelty, a window shade shop, by Gibbons Kelty in 1843 in New York City. Following the death of Kelty, investor William Collins and nephew Charles Aikman bought Kelty's holding in a Philadelphia weave plant. They incorporated the company as Collins & Aikman in 1891 and specialized in heavy fabric for upholstery. During the 1920s the company began to make fabrics for auto seats. Collins & Aikman went public in 1926. When plastics supplanted textiles for many auto interior components after WWII, the company diversified into institutional carpets to boost its upholstery and apparel lines. Collins & Aikman was acquired by retail lumber firm Wickes in 1986.

The Wickes Corporation began as a foundry and machine shop in 1854 and developed a steam-powered mill saw that revolutionized the lumber industry. Wickes later diversified by building steam boilers. Exploiting the post-WWII building boom, the company's building-supply stores took off; they were renamed Wickes Lumber in 1962. Wickes's continued expansion and acquisitions through the 1970s and early 1980s led the company to bankruptcy, which it emerged from in 1985.

In 1988, two years after Wickes's acquisition of Collins & Aikman, the company sold Wickes Lumber. That year James Birle led a group of investors that took Wickes private, and Wickes Lumber's former parent changed its name to Collins & Aikman. Birle lowered the firm's debt by cutting overhead and selling assets.

Bruce Wasserstein joined Birle as co-CEO of Collins & Aikman in 1992. The company sold its engineering group to Teleflex in 1993 and also closed Builders Emporium and laid off 4,300 workers. Collins & Aikman reorganized in 1994 and raised $145 million when it went public — about half as much as it had hoped. The restructured company placed an emphasis on its automotive division, where contracts with the Big Three automakers helped lift the company to a leading position in the car interior market. The company also expanded globally with plants in Kapfenberg, Austria, and Toluca, Mexico.

Collins & Aikman got busy in 1996. Acquisitions that year included Manchester Plastics, which added a variety of plastic-based products such as door panels and headrests; BTR Fatati Limited, a European maker of floor carpet and trim; JPS Automotive, a maker of molded floor carpet and bodycloth; and Perstorp AB's auto supply operations in North America, Spain, and the UK (Perstorp is primarily a maker of acoustic products).

In 1997 Collins & Aikman sold its floor-coverings operations and its Mastercraft upholstery unit. That year the Manchester Plastics subsidiary entered a joint venture to make instrument panels for GM. The company also sold the airbag-fabric division of JPS to Safety Components International. In 1998 Collins & Aikman sold its Imperial Wallcoverings unit to a company sponsored by Blackstone Capital Partners. That year the company's earning were hurt by a 54-day strike at GM.

In 1999 the company announced a major restructuring that will reorganize its operations into three divisions: North America Interior Systems, Europe Automotive Interior Systems, and Specialty Automotive Products (convertible systems and fabrics).

Chairman and CEO; President, Collins & Aikman Products Co.: Thomas E. Evans, age 48
EVP, General Counsel, and Secretary: Elizabeth R. Philipp, age 42, $392,252 pay
EVP and CFO: Rajesh K. Shah
President, North America Automotive Interior Systems: Dennis E. Hiller, age 44, $401,750 pay
President, European Automotive Interior Systems: D. Michael Weston, age 53, $353,750 pay
President, Collins & Aikman Automotive Fabrics: Dean C. Gaskins
VP, General Counsel, and Secretary, Collins & Aikman Products: Ronald T. Lindsay
VP Human Resources, Collins & Aikman Products: Harold R. Sunday
Auditors: Arthur Andersen LLP

HQ: 701 McCullough Dr., Charlotte, NC 28262
Phone: 704-547-8500   **Fax:** 704-548-2081

Collins & Aikman operates more than 60 manufacturing facilities in Austria, Belgium, Canada, France, Germany, Japan, Mexico, the Netherlands, Spain, Sweden, the UK, and the US.

1998 Sales

	$ mil.	% of total
US	1,049	57
Canada	356	20
UK	144	8
Mexico	83	4
Other countries	194	11
Total	**1,826**	**100**

1998 Sales

	% of total
General Motors	31
Chrysler	18
Ford	20
Other	31
Total	**100**

1998 Sales

	$ mil.	% of total
Molded carpet	417	21
Plastic trim	295	20
Bodycloth	267	16
Acoustic systems	225	11
Floormats	139	8
Convertible systems	104	7
Luggage compartment trim	96	5
Other	283	12
Total	**1,826**	**100**

ASC
Eagle-Picher
Faurecia
Guilford Mills
Johnson Controls
Johnston Industries
Lancaster Colony
Lear
Magna International
Milliken
Textron

NYSE symbol: CKC FYE: December 31	Annual Growth	1989	1990	1991	1992	1993	1994	1995	1996	1997	1998
Sales ($ mil.)	(6.9%)	3,477	1,689	1,726	1,632	1,542	1,536	1,292	1,056	1,629	1,826
Net income ($ mil.)	—	84	(123)	234	(83)	(171)	(31)	206	41	155	(4)
Income as % of sales	—	2.4%	—	13.6%	—	—	16.0%	3.9%	9.5%	—
Earnings per share ($)	—	—	—	—	—	—	(2.40)	2.90	0.58	2.34	(0.06)
Stock price – FY high ($)	—	—	—	—	—	—	11.00	9.38	8.38	12.38	9.69
Stock price – FY low ($)	—	—	—	—	—	—	7.63	5.75	5.38	6.13	4.88
Stock price – FY close ($)	(10.9%)	—	—	—	—	—	8.13	6.88	6.25	8.63	5.13
P/E – high	—	—	—	—	—	—	—	3	14	5	—
P/E – low	—	—	—	—	—	—	—	2	9	3	—
Dividends per share ($)	—	—	—	—	—	—	0.00	0.00	0.00	0.00	0.00
Book value per share ($)	—	—	—	—	—	—	(5.85)	(3.23)	(2.87)	(1.02)	(1.28)
Employees	(6.4%)	—	—	25,200	25,200	22,300	16,000	12,000	12,800	15,100	15,900

1996 is an 11-month fiscal year.

HIGH/LOW/CLOSE

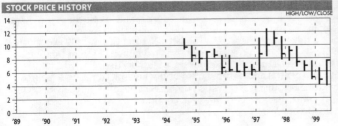

Debt ratio: 100.0%
Return on equity: —
Cash ($ mil.): 24
Current ratio: 1.48
Long-term debt ($ mil.): 846
No. of shares (mil.): 62
Dividends
  Yield: —
  Payout: —
Market value ($ mil.): 319

COLUMBIA ENERGY GROUP

OVERVIEW

Columbia Energy Group has energy not only for the District of Columbia but also for 35 states in the eastern US. Based in Reston, Virginia, the holding company operates one of the US's largest natural gas transmission and underground storage systems; its pipeline system connects the Gulf of Mexico to the northeastern US and spans 16,700 miles. Through five local distribution companies, Columbia Energy also supplies gas to more than 2 million customers in Kentucky, Maryland, Ohio, Pennsylvania, and Virginia.

The company doesn't just move gas: It explores for and produces oil and gas in eight Appalachian states and Canada and has proved reserves of 802 billion cu. ft. of natural gas equivalent. In addition, Columbia Energy is building up its retail gas business. Subsidiary Columbia Energy Services is exiting wholesale energy marketing and trading to focus on grabbing residential customers in newly competitive markets. Columbia Propane, which tripled its customer base with the purchase of National Propane Partners, serves more than 335,000 customers in 35 states.

Adding electricity to the mix, the company owns interests in three power plants and is developing four more. Columbia Energy is also dipping into telecommunications, building a fiber-optic network along its pipeline system.

HISTORY

Columbia Corporation was founded in 1906 in Huntington, West Virginia, to manage oil and gas fields in Kentucky and West Virginia. By 1909 it operated a 180-mile natural gas pipeline serving four cities in Kentucky and Ohio. It was renamed Columbia Gas & Electric when it merged with George Crawford's Ohio Fuel (natural gas distribution in Ohio, Pennsylvania, and West Virginia) in 1926. With Crawford as chairman, Columbia relocated to Delaware that year and went public.

Purchases over the next 40 years expanded Columbia's service area to New York, Maryland, and the District of Columbia. In 1931 Columbia completed a 460-mile pipeline linking Washington, DC, to gas fields in Kentucky. The company became Columbia Gas System in 1948.

In 1958 Columbia bought Gulf Interstate Gas, which operated an 845-mile pipeline linking Louisiana gas fields to eastern Kentucky. By 1972 Columbia supplied 10% of the US's gas customers.

With fuel shortages predicted for the 1970s, Columbia explored for gas in Canada (1971) and arranged for gas delivery from Alaska (1974). Still, supplies ran short, forcing schools and factories to close in company territory during the winter of 1976-77.

In 1978 Columbia and Consolidated System LNG built a liquefied natural gas plant, which was closed in 1980 because of price disputes with Algerian suppliers (the mothballed plant was not reopened until 1994).

Columbia bought Commonwealth Natural Resources in 1981 to expand into central and eastern Virginia. To secure future gas supplies, Columbia entered take-or-pay contracts between 1982 and 1984, agreeing to buy large amounts of gas at preset prices. But demand fell, and Columbia faced bankruptcy by 1985, mostly as a result of those contracts. To retain customers, it cut its rates to $1 billion below cost over two years. It also looked into another energy business, setting up Columbia Electric in 1987 to invest in power projects.

A mild winter in 1990 hurt earnings, and gas prices fell below the company's supply costs, ultimately causing Columbia to enter bankruptcy in 1991. The company divested Columbia Gas Development of Canada in 1992.

Oliver Richard (who had been a member of the Federal Energy Regulatory Commission at age 29) took over as CEO in 1995, and the company emerged from bankruptcy. The firm sold Columbia Gas Development to Hunt Petroleum in 1996 and moved its headquarters to the Virginia suburbs of Washington, DC.

In 1997 Columbia bought oil and gas producer Alamco, and in 1998 the company took the name Columbia Energy Group to reflect its move beyond gas transmission. That year it teamed with Amway to market natural gas and also began marketing wholesale power. Like other power marketers, it decided to exit the business in 1999 after disappointing results.

That year Columbia Propane expanded by buying National Propane Partners. Columbia also began building a fiber-optic telecommunications network beside its pipelines in the eastern US. Columbia's $9 billion offer for Consolidated Natural Gas in 1999 was spurned in favor of a $6.3 billion bid from Dominion Resources. Columbia itself fielded a takeover bid from utility holding company NiSource, which Columbia's board rejected. NiSource, however, continued to press its offer.

Chairman, President, and CEO, Columbia Energy Group and Columbia Energy Group Service Corporation: Oliver G. Richard III, age 46, $1,082,800 pay
SVP, Strategy and Communications: Patricia A. Hammick, age 52
SVP and CFO, Columbia Energy Group and Columbia Energy Group Service Corporation: Michael W. O'Donnell, age 54, $422,500 pay
SVP and Chief Legal Officer, Columbia Energy Group and Columbia Energy Group Service Corporation: Peter M. Schwolsky, age 52, $422,500 pay
VP and Controller: Jeffrey W. Grossman
President, Columbia Gulf Transmission: Terrance L. McGill
President, Columbia Insurance: Nicholas A. Parillo
President, Columbia LNG and Columbia Atlantic Trading: L. Michael Bridges
President, Columbia Network Services: Philip R. Aldridge
President and CEO, Columbia Electric: Michael J. Gluckman
President and CEO, Columbia Energy Resources: W. Henry Harmon
President and CEO, Columbia Energy Services: Paul J. Feldman
SVP, Human Resources, Columbia Energy Group Services Corporation: Louis E. Font
Auditors: Arthur Andersen LLP

LOCATIONS

HQ: 13880 Dulles Corner Ln., Herndon, VA 20171-4600
Phone: 703-561-6000   **Fax:** 703-561-7324
Web site: http://www.columbiaenergygroup.com

PRODUCTS/OPERATIONS

1998 Sales

	$ mil.	% of total
Marketing, propane & power generation	4,072	59
Distribution	1,870	27
Transmission & storage	839	12
Exploration & production	128	2
Adjustments	(358)	—
Total	**6,551**	**100**

Selected Operations and Subsidiaries

Marketing, Propane, and Power Generation
Columbia Electric Corporation
Columbia Energy Services Corporation
Columbia Propane Corporation

Transmission and Storage
Columbia Gas Transmission Corporation
Columbia Gulf Transmission Company

Exploration
Columbia Energy Resources, Inc.

COMPETITORS

AES	Enron
Cabot Oil & Gas	Equitable Resources
Coastal	FirstEnergy
Conectiv	Koch
Consolidated Natural Gas	Occidental
Dominion Resources	Range Resources
Duke Energy	Tejas Energy
Dynegy	Williams Companies

HISTORICAL FINANCIALS & EMPLOYEES

NYSE symbol: CG FYE: December 31	Annual Growth	1989	1990	1991	1992	1993	1994	1995	1996	1997	1998
Sales ($ mil.)	8.3%	3,204	2,358	2,577	2,922	3,391	2,833	2,635	3,354	5,054	6,551
Net income ($ mil.)	7.1%	146	105	(694)	51	152	241	(361)	222	273	269
Income as % of sales	—	4.5%	4.4%	—	1.8%	4.5%	8.5%	—	6.6%	5.4%	4.1%
Earnings per share ($)	4.7%	2.13	1.47	(9.17)	0.67	2.01	3.18	(4.77)	2.74	3.27	3.21
Stock price - FY high ($)	—	35.18	36.52	31.68	15.92	18.34	20.51	29.43	44.19	52.44	60.75
Stock price - FY low ($)	—	22.51	27.68	8.59	9.34	12.09	14.34	15.42	27.93	37.35	47.36
Stock price - FY close ($)	5.8%	34.68	31.27	11.51	12.76	14.92	15.67	29.26	42.44	52.40	57.75
P/E - high	—	17	25	—	24	9	6	—	16	16	19
P/E - low	—	11	19	—	14	6	5	—	10	11	15
Dividends per share ($)	(5.9%)	1.33	1.47	0.77	0.00	0.00	0.00	0.00	0.40	0.60	0.77
Book value per share ($)	0.2%	23.68	23.19	13.28	14.18	16.18	19.37	15.12	18.75	21.52	24.01
Employees	(2.5%)	10,800	10,829	10,367	10,172	10,114	10,600	9,981	9,274	8,529	8,564

STOCK PRICE HISTORY
HIGH/LOW/CLOSE

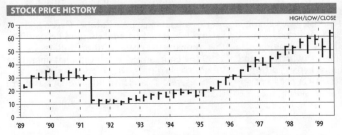

1998 FISCAL YEAR-END
Debt ratio: 50.0%
Return on equity: 13.4%
Cash ($ mil.): 26
Current ratio: 1.05
Long-term debt ($ mil.): 2,003
No. of shares (mil.): 84
Dividends
 Yield: 1.3%
 Payout: 24.0%
Market value ($ mil.): 4,823

COLUMBIA/HCA HEALTHCARE

OVERVIEW

It doesn't take a federal investigation to show that Columbia/HCA Healthcare is the US's #1 hospital operator. The Nashville, Tennessee-based company owns or operates some 220 facilities (down from some 345 in 1997) in the US, Switzerland, and the UK.

After an aggressive expansion that created an empire of hospitals and outpatient, diagnostic, and acute care clinics, Columbia/HCA wielded its power to drive hard bargains with its suppliers and undercut competitors, particularly small, not-for-profit hospitals. Federal and state

authorities cried foul and are suing the company for a host of civil and criminal violations.

The company draws about 40% of its sales from Medicare and Medicaid, and its profits have been hit not only by the soaring costs of medical care but also by government cutbacks in reimbursement rates. Columbia/HCA has attempted to remake itself into a leaner yet kinder company by spinning off some of its hospitals and selling its home care and prescription benefit management units and some of its surgery centers.

HISTORY

In 1987 Dallas lawyer Rick Scott and Fort Worth, Texas, financier Richard Rainwater founded Columbia Hospital Corp. to buy two hospitals in El Paso, Texas. The partners eventually sold 40% of the hospitals to local doctors, hoping that ownership would motivate physicians to increase productivity and efficiency.

The company entered the Miami market the next year and by 1990 had four hospitals. After merging with Smith Laboratories that year, Columbia went public and then acquired Sutter Laboratories (orthopedic products). By the end of 1990, it had 11 hospitals.

Columbia moved into Fort Myers, Florida, in 1992 with the purchase of eight hospitals. Other purchases that year included several facilities around Miami and a psychiatric hospital in El Paso. The next year it acquired Galen Health Care, which operated 73 hospitals and had been spun off from health plan operator Humana earlier in the year. The merger thrust the hospital chain into about 15 new markets.

Columbia bought Hospital Corporation of America (HCA) for $5.9 billion in 1994. (Scott's first bid for the hospital operator in 1987 failed.) Thomas Frist, his son Thomas Frist Jr., and Jack Massey (founder of Kentucky Fried Chicken, now part of TRICON) founded HCA in Nashville, Tennessee, in 1968. From a single hospital, the company had grown to 50 by 1973, and 10 years later it owned 376 hospitals in the US and seven other countries.

Meanwhile, the medical industry was changing as insurers, Medicare, and Medicaid began examining payment procedures more closely; in addition, the growth of HMOs (which aimed to restrict hospital admissions) began cutting into hospital occupancy rates. HCA began paring operations in the late 1980s, selling more than 100 hospitals. In 1989 Frist Jr. led a $5.1 billion LBO of the company. He sold more

assets and in 1992 took HCA public again, but losses and a tumbling stock price made it a takeover target.

Later in 1994 the newly christened Columbia/HCA acquired the US's largest operator of outpatient surgery centers, Dallas-based Medical Care America. A year later it completed the $3.6 billion takeover of 117-hospital HealthTrust, a 1987 offshoot of HCA.

Columbia/HCA was unstoppable in 1996. It made some 150 acquisitions, though it ultimately failed to buy 85% of insurer Blue Cross of Ohio.

In 1997 the government began investigating the company's business practices. After executive indictments, the company fired Scott and several other top officers. Frist Jr. — a doctor — became chairman and CEO, pledging to shrink the company and tone down its aggressive approach. Columbia/HCA sold its home care business, more than 100 of its less-desirable hospitals, and almost all the operations of Value Health (pharmacy benefits management and behavioral health care management), which it had just bought for about $1.1 billion.

The trimming continued in 1998 when it sold nearly three dozen outpatient surgery centers to HEALTHSOUTH and 14 hospitals to a consortium including Alliant Health System of Kentucky, Baptist Health of Alabama, and Johnson City Medical Center Hospital of Tennessee. That year Columbia/HCA sued former financial executive Samuel Greco and several vendors, accusing them of defrauding the company of several million dollars. In 1999 the company spun off regional operators LifePoint Hospitals, which operates about 23 facilities, and Triad Hospitals, which has more than 40.

Chairman and CEO: Thomas F. Frist Jr., age 60, $2,223 pay
President and COO: Jack Bovender Jr., age 53, $791,667 pay
VP Finance and Treasurer: David G. Anderson, age 51
President, Western Group: Richard M. Bracken, age 46, $478,958 pay
SVP and CFO, America's Group: Kenneth C. Donahey, age 48
President, Physician Services: W. Leon Drennan, age 43
VP Operations Finance: Rosalyn S. Elton, age 37
VP Contracts and Operations Support: James A. Fitzgerald Jr., age 44
President and CEO, America Group: James M. Fleetwood Jr., age 51
VP Development: V. Carl George, age 55
President, Eastern Group: Jay F. Grinney, age 48, $478,958 pay
SVP Administration and Human Resources, America's Group: Neil Hemphill, age 45
SVP Quality and Medical Director: Frank M. Houser
VP and Controller: R. Milton Johnson, age 42
CEO, America's Group: Scott L. Mercy, age 37
SVP Human Resources: Philip Patton, age 46
SVP and General Counsel: Robert A. Waterman, age 45, $494,792 pay
SVP and Chief Information Officer: Noel B. Williams
SVP Ethics, Compliance, and Corporate Responsibility: Alan Yuspeh, age 49
Auditors: Ernst & Young LLP

LOCATIONS

HQ: Columbia/HCA Healthcare Corporation, 1 Park Plaza, Nashville, TN 37203
Phone: 615-344-9551   **Fax:** 615-344-2266
Web site: http://www.columbia-hca.com

PRODUCTS/OPERATIONS

1998 Sales

	% of total
Managed care	32
Medicare	30
Medicaid	6
Other	32
Total	**100**

1998 Sales

	$ mil.	% of total
East Group	7,784	42
West Group	6,853	37
Atlantic Group	1,600	8
Pacific Group	1,589	8
America Group	498	3
Corporate & other	357	2
Total	**18,681**	**100**

COMPETITORS

Allina Health
American Medical Holdings
Catholic Health Initiatives
Catholic Healthcare West
Daughters of Charity
HEALTHSOUTH
Holy Cross
In Home Health
Integrated Health Services
Kaiser Foundation
Mercy Health Services
New York City Health and Hospitals
Sisters of Charity Health
SSM Health Care
Tenet Healthcare
Universal Health Services

HISTORICAL FINANCIALS & EMPLOYEES

NYSE symbol: COL FYE: December 31	Annual Growth	1989	1990	1991	1992	1993	1994	1995	1996	1997	1998
Sales ($ mil.)	70.6%	153	273	461	762	10,252	11,132	17,695	19,909	18,819	18,681
Net income ($ mil.)	58.5%	6	10	15	26	507	630	961	1,505	(305)	379
Income as % of sales	—	3.9%	3.6%	3.2%	3.3%	4.9%	5.7%	5.4%	7.6%	—	2.0%
Earnings per share ($)	0.9%	—	0.55	0.60	0.78	1.03	1.26	1.43	2.22	(0.46)	0.59
Stock price - FY high ($)	—	—	10.34	12.51	14.67	22.59	30.18	36.02	41.88	44.88	34.63
Stock price - FY low ($)	—	—	6.67	2.25	9.17	10.84	22.18	23.60	31.68	25.75	17.00
Stock price - FY close ($)	15.5%	—	7.84	11.34	14.17	22.09	24.35	33.85	40.75	29.63	24.75
P/E - high	—	—	19	21	19	22	24	25	19	—	59
P/E - low	—	—	12	4	12	11	18	17	14	—	29
Dividends per share ($)	—	—	0.00	0.00	0.00	0.02	0.08	0.08	0.09	0.08	0.08
Book value per share ($)	25.2%	—	1.95	4.27	6.84	6.88	9.63	10.67	12.82	11.30	11.80
Employees	60.5%	—	5,900	6,300	13,300	131,600	157,000	240,000	285,000	295,000	260,000

1989-92 information is for Columbia Hospital Corporation.

STOCK PRICE HISTORY

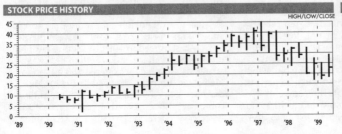

HIGH/LOW/CLOSE

1998 FISCAL YEAR-END

Debt ratio: 42.9%
Return on equity: 5.0%
Cash ($ mil.): 297
Current ratio: 1.09
Long-term debt ($ mil.): 5,685
No. of shares (mil.): 643
Dividends
  Yield: 0.3%
  Payout: 13.6%
Market value ($ mil.): 15,904

COMCAST CORPORATION

OVERVIEW

Comcast casts a wide net across communications industries. The Philadelphia-based cable operator has about 4.5 million subscribers in 21 US states. Comcast has been investing heavily in its cable networks, adding fiber-optics so that it can offer next-generation broadband services such as digital video and high-speed Internet services.

Comcast is getting 2 million more cable subscribers from AT&T after agreeing to drop its bid to buy rival MediaOne, which AT&T is acquiring. When the dust settles, Comcast will be the #3 US cable operator, behind AT&T Broadband & Internet Service (the former TCI) and Time Warner. As part of the deal, Comcast will carry AT&T phone service over its cable systems.

The company owns shares in QVC, the global electronic retailer (57%), and E! Entertainment Television, a joint venture with Disney (40%). It also has a two-thirds stake in Comcast-Spectacor, a venture that owns Philadelphia's Flyers hockey team and 76ers basketball team, as well as 46% of SportsNet, a regional sports programming network shared with the owners of Major League Baseball team Philadelphia Phillies.

President Brian Roberts, son of founder and chairman Ralph Roberts, owns about 24% of Comcast, and the Roberts family controls 80% of the voting rights. Software giant Microsoft owns an 11% stake.

HISTORY

In 1963 Ralph Roberts, Daniel Aaron, and Julian Brodsky bought American Cable Systems in Tupelo, Mississippi. The company soon expanded throughout the state. In 1969 the company got a new name: Comcast, combining "communications" and "broadcast." Two years later Comcast acquired franchises in western Pennsylvania, and when it went public in 1972, it moved to Philadelphia.

Comcast bought up local operations nationwide through the early 1980s and gained its first foreign cable franchise in 1983 in London (it sold its affiliate there to NTL in 1999). It took a 26% stake in the large Group W Cable in 1986. Roberts also lent financial support that year to a fledgling home-shopping channel called QVC — for "quality, value, and convenience."

A big step into telecommunications came in 1988 when Comcast bought American Cellular Network, with Delaware and New Jersey franchises. Two years later Roberts' son Brian — who had trained as a cable installer during a summer away from college — became Comcast's president.

In 1992 Comcast bought Metromedia's Philadelphia-area cellular operations and began investing in fiber-optic and wireless phone companies. By then the company was a major QVC shareholder. With an eye toward Comcast's programming needs, Brian persuaded Fox network head Barry Diller to become QVC's chairman. But when Diller tried to use QVC to take over CBS, Comcast bought control of QVC in 1994 to quash the bid, which went against cross-ownership bans. To pay for QVC, Comcast had to sell its 20% stake in cable firm Heritage Communications in 1995. Diller left the company (he now oversees USA

Networks, parent of QVC's archrival Home Shopping Network). Also in 1995 Comcast funded former Disney executive Richard Frank to launch the C3 (Comcast Content and Communication) programming company.

In 1996 the company formed Comcast-Spectacor, a regional sports venture that led to the regional all-sports channel SportsNet, and invested in cable-based Internet company @Home (now Excite@Home).

The next year Microsoft invested $1 billion in Comcast, crowning cable as the preferred pathway into the home for information delivery. Comcast's C3 also paired with Disney to buy out Time Warner's majority stake in E! Entertainment Television, but by 1998 C3 had folded and Comcast took control.

Comcast, TCI, and Cox sold Teleport, their local phone venture, to AT&T in 1998, but Comcast turned around and bought long-distance service provider GlobalCom (now Comcast Telecommunications). That year Sprint Spectrum — Comcast's PCS venture with Sprint, Cox, and the former TCI — was rolled into Sprint PCS, under Sprint's management.

In 1999 Comcast bought a controlling interest in Jones Intercable, with about 1.4 million subscribers, and agreed to swap some 400,000 subscribers in Los Angeles and Palm Beach, Florida, to rival Adelphia for more than 450,000 subscribers in eastern and midwestern markets.

Comcast agreed in 1999 to acquire rival MediaOne. Soon after the $54 billion deal was struck, however, AT&T offered $58 billion for MediaOne. Comcast dropped its bid for MediaOne when AT&T offered to sell it 2 million cable subscribers. Also that year Comcast sold its cellular operations to SBC for $1.7 billion.

Chairman: Ralph J. Roberts, age 79, $1,500,000 pay
VC: Julian A. Brodsky, age 65, $1,033,595 pay
President: Brian L. Roberts, age 39, $1,402,313 pay
EVP: Lawrence S. Smith, age 51, $1,102,863 pay
SVP and Treasurer: John R. Alchin, age 50,
$898,220 pay
SVP, General Counsel, and Secretary: Stanley L. Wang,
age 58
Chairman, Comcast-Spectator: Edward M. Snider
VC, Comcast-Spectator: Fred A. Shabel
President, Comcast Cable: Stephen B. Burke
President, QVC: Douglas S. Briggs
President and General Manager, Philadelphia Flyers:
Robert E. Clarke
President, Comcast Telecommunications:
Nathaniel Cohen
President, Philadelphia 76ers: Pat W. Croce
President, Hebenstreit Communications:
Barbara B. Gatison
President and CEO, First Union Complex:
Peter A. Luukko
President, E! Entertainment Television: Fran Shea
President, Comcast SportsNet: Jack L. Williams
EVP, Comcast Cable: Michael S. Tallent
EVP, Marketing and Customer Service, Comcast Cable:
David N. Watson
VP, Human Resources and Planning and Development:
Richard A. Petrino
Auditors: Deloitte & Touche LLP

LOCATIONS

HQ: 1500 Market St., Philadelphia, PA 19102-2148
Phone: 215-665-1700   **Fax:** 215-981-7790
Web site: http://www.comcast.com

PRODUCTS/OPERATIONS

1998 Sales

	$ mil.	% of total
Electronic retailing	2,403	47
Domestic cable communications	2,277	44
Corporate & other	465	9
Total	**5,145**	**100**

Selected Programming Investments

Comcast SportsNet (46%, regional sports programming
and events)
E! Entertainment (40%, entertainment-related news and
original programming)
The Golf Channel (43%, golf-related programming)
QVC (57%, electronic retailer)
Speedvision Network (15%, automotive, marine, and
aviation)
Sunshine Network (13%, regional sports, public affairs,
and general entertainment)
Viewer's Choice (11%, pay-per-view programming)

COMPETITORS

Adelphia Communications
American Telecasting
Ameritech
AT&T Broadband &
  Internet Services
BSkyB
Cablevision Systems
CAI Wireless
Charter Communications
Cox Communications
DIRECTV
EchoStar
  Communications
GTE
Insight Communications
  Company
Lenfest Communications
Liberty Media
MediaOne Group
Pegasus Communications
RCN
SBC Communications
Time Warner
USA Networks
ValueVision
Viacom

HISTORICAL FINANCIALS & EMPLOYEES

Nasdaq symbol: CMCSK FYE: December 31	Annual Growth	1989	1990	1991	1992	1993	1994	1995	1996	1997	1998
Sales ($ mil.)	27.9%	562	657	721	900	1,338	1,375	3,363	4,038	4,913	5,145
Net income ($ mil.)	—	(149)	(178)	(156)	(270)	(859)	(87)	(44)	(54)	(239)	972
Income as % of sales	—	—	—	—	—	—	—	—	—	—	18.9%
Earnings per share ($)	—	(0.47)	(0.53)	(0.44)	(0.67)	(2.01)	(0.19)	(0.09)	(0.11)	(0.38)	1.20
Stock price - FY high ($)	—	6.28	5.67	5.79	6.17	13.01	12.01	11.19	10.69	16.53	30.13
Stock price - FY low ($)	—	3.59	2.46	3.71	4.46	5.25	7.00	6.88	6.88	7.31	14.75
Stock price - FY close ($)	20.6%	5.42	4.29	5.54	6.04	12.01	7.84	9.09	8.91	15.78	29.34
P/E - high	—	—	—	—	—	—	—	—	—	—	25
P/E - low	—	—	—	—	—	—	—	—	—	—	12
Dividends per share ($)	2.5%	0.04	0.04	0.05	0.10	0.05	0.05	0.05	0.05	0.05	0.05
Book value per share ($)	29.6%	0.50	(0.06)	0.05	(0.45)	(1.96)	(1.52)	(1.62)	0.90	2.26	5.12
Employees	20.0%	3,292	3,478	3,722	5,327	5,391	6,700	12,200	16,400	17,600	17,000

STOCK PRICE HISTORY

HIGH/LOW/CLOSE

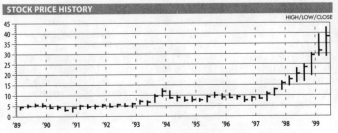

1998 FISCAL YEAR-END

Debt ratio: 58.9%
Return on equity: 25.7%
Cash ($ mil.): 871
Current ratio: 1.82
Long-term debt ($ mil.): 5,464
No. of shares (mil.): 740
Dividends
  Yield: 0.2%
  Payout: 4.2%
Market value ($ mil.): 21,698

COMDISCO, INC.

OVERVIEW

Many businesses choose to lease rather than buy their information-technology equipment, and that's the way, uh-huh uh-huh, Comdisco likes it. But the company from Rosemont, Illinois, is changing its footwork. For more than 20 years Comdisco has gone eyeball-to-eyeball with IBM in the mainframe leasing business. Comdisco is now shedding those mainframe operations — to IBM — to concentrate on leasing PCs and network servers and providing other information-technology services — asset management (procurement, administration, and disposal of a company's PCs and other high-tech equipment), network maintenance, and continuity services (backup computer systems).

The company, which operates from more than 100 offices and facilities in North America, Europe, and the Pacific Rim, also leases medical equipment (including MRI Systems and CT scanners) and semiconductor production and test equipment.

Though the dance is different, in many ways the tune is the same. To position itself as a tech services company rather than a simple equipment lessor, Comdisco has always touted its status as a third-party servicer, unaffiliated with specific computer hardware (unlike IBM). It also hasn't sought long-term relationships, as some consulting firms have done, preferring to solve problems on an as-needed basis.

CEO Nicholas Pontikes, son of the company's founder, and his family own 24% of Comdisco.

HISTORY

In 1969, at age 29, former IBM salesman Kenneth Pontikes borrowed $5,000 from his father to set up Computer Discount Corp. Gambling that companies would rather lease than pay outright for expensive and quickly obsolete computer equipment, Pontikes built Computer Discount by leasing IBM mainframes. It grew quickly, recording sales of $1 million in its first year.

In 1971 the company reincorporated as Comdisco and went public. It grew rapidly until 1974, when Intel put $250 million worth of used IBM System/360 computers up for sale just after Comdisco had agreed to purchase hundreds of 360s. The drop in prices for the model caused Comdisco to lose nearly $1 million that year.

Comdisco Financial Services was created in 1976 to help customers finance equipment leases and dispose of their old computers. Four years later Comdisco Disaster Recovery Services (now Comdisco Continuity Services) was formed to help businesses whose computer systems were down because of flood, fire, or other misfortune. The company also began expanding overseas in Germany and Switzerland (1979) and Japan (1986).

The staff had gained specialized knowledge of the computer industry, so in 1984 Pontikes formed Comdisco Equities. That subsidiary was shut down after the 1987 stock market crash caused a net loss of $80 million. Comdisco still participated in high-risk computer stocks through its Venture Lease Division (now Comdisco Ventures), which leased equipment to high-tech startups for a fee and the right to purchase a stake in the company.

As 1985 sales topped $1 billion, Comdisco began leasing more equipment: phone equipment in 1985, medical in 1988, and semiconductor manufacturing in 1992. By the end of the 1980s, Comdisco gained half of its revenue through non-IBM products. Still, the widespread switch from mainframes to PCs and the 1990-1991 recession cut its profits. Compounding those problems was a $70 million payment in 1994 to settle a lawsuit brought by IBM that accused Comdisco of using older IBM parts to produce computers to compete with newer IBM models (Comdisco denied any wrongdoing). That year Pontikes died of cancer. He was succeeded by Jack Slevin, the company's COO.

In 1995 Comdisco began serious expansion. It acquired firms to form Comdisco Network Services, a computer network consulting firm, and created a unit to provide equipment to the biotech, chemical, pharmaceutical, and other industries. In 1996 Comdisco added to its growing continuity service operations, buying CSC CompuSource (a unit of high-tech consultant Computer Sciences). Comdisco bought the used equipment division of Integrated Solutions Inc. in 1998 to beef up its refurbished semiconductor equipment unit. It also took a 25% stake in newly formed Transwire, which was building a high-speed data network in the Northeast.

In 1999 Slevin was succeeded as CEO by the founder's son, Nicholas Pontikes, and Comdisco agreed to sell its mainframe leasing operations to IBM, exiting the market it helped create. Switching its focus to leasing PCs and network servers and providing other information technology services, Comdisco completed its acquisition of Prism, a New York ISP.

OFFICERS

President and CEO: Nicholas K. Pontikes, age 34, $650,000 pay (prior to promotion)
EVP and CFO: John J. Vosicky, age 49, $455,000 pay
EVP and National Sales Manager: John C. Kenning, $534,000 pay
EVP: William N. Pontikes, age 57, $460,000 pay
SVP and Secretary: Philip A. Hewes, age 46
SVP and Corporate Controller: David J. Keenan
SVP: Gregory D. Sabatello
SVP Marketing and Business Development: David W. Sloboda, age 41
President, Europe: Thomas Flohr
President, Financial Management Division: Rosemary P. Geisler
President, Diversified Technology Group: Michael F. Herman
President, Electronics: Roger D. Innes, age 43
President, Technology Services Division: Jeffrey P. Keohane
President, Ventures Division: James P. Labe
VP Human Resources: Lucie A. Buford
VP Delivery Processes For Desktop Management: Dan Galardini, age 38
VP Corporate Communications: Mary Moster
VP Sales: Christopher M. Riley, age 34
Auditors: KPMG LLP

LOCATIONS

HQ: 6111 N. River Rd., Rosemont, IL 60018
Phone: 847-698-3000   **Fax:** 847-518-5440
Web site: http://www.comdisco.com

1998 Sales

	$ mil.	% of total
US	2,521	78
Europe	608	18
Pacific Rim	73	2
Canada	71	2
Adjustments	(30)	—
Total	**3,243**	**100**

PRODUCTS/OPERATIONS

1998 Sales

	$ mil.	% of total
Leasing	2,435	75
Business continuity & network services	433	14
Equipment sales	329	10
Other	46	1
Total	**3,243**	**100**

COMPETITORS

Amdahl	Hitachi
Andersen Worldwide	IBM
Cap Gemini	KeyCorp
CompuCom	MCI WorldCom
Computer Sciences	Newcourt Credit
EDS	Origin
El Camino Resources International	Siemens
ENTEX	SunGard Data Systems
GE	Sunrise International Leasing
Hewlett-Packard	

HISTORICAL FINANCIALS & EMPLOYEES

NYSE symbol: CDO FYE: September 30	Annual Growth	1989	1990	1991	1992	1993	1994	1995	1996	1997	1998
Sales ($ mil.)	7.6%	1,678	1,935	2,174	2,205	2,153	2,098	2,240	2,431	2,819	3,243
Net income ($ mil.)	3.9%	108	85	69	(9)	87	53	104	114	131	153
Income as % of sales	—	6.4%	4.4%	3.2%	—	4.0%	2.5%	4.6%	4.7%	4.6%	4.7%
Earnings per share ($)	6.0%	0.55	0.45	0.37	(0.05)	0.44	0.26	0.57	0.67	0.93	0.93
Stock price - FY high ($)	—	7.20	7.20	6.01	5.37	3.87	5.39	7.23	9.92	16.53	23.28
Stock price - FY low ($)	—	4.05	3.10	3.12	2.78	2.92	3.73	4.31	6.56	9.13	12.44
Stock price - FY close ($)	7.6%	7.07	3.23	4.13	3.59	3.78	4.62	6.62	9.63	16.34	13.63
P/E - high	—	13	16	16	—	9	21	13	15	21	25
P/E - low	—	7	7	8	—	7	14	8	10	12	13
Dividends per share ($)	8.0%	0.05	0.06	0.06	0.06	0.07	0.08	0.08	0.10	0.10	0.10
Book value per share ($)	9.7%	2.79	3.20	3.48	3.42	3.68	3.89	4.37	4.77	5.24	6.44
Employees	4.6%	1,875	1,960	2,179	2,087	2,000	2,000	2,100	2,100	2,400	2,800

STOCK PRICE HISTORY

HIGH/LOW/CLOSE

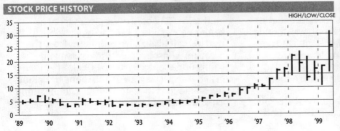

1998 FISCAL YEAR-END

Debt ratio: 81.9%
Return on equity: 15.6%
Cash ($ mil.): 63
Current ratio: 1.86
Long-term debt ($ mil.): 4,439
No. of shares (mil.): 152
Dividends
 Yield: 0.7%
 Payout: 10.8%
Market value ($ mil.): 2,073

COMERICA INCORPORATED

OVERVIEW

Comerica is a Loan Ranger. The Detroit-based bank holding company has long been strong in commercial lending, with an emphasis on small-business loans.

Comerica is organized into three operating units. The Business Bank focuses on business and asset-based lending, global finance, and institutional trusts; it offers commercial loans and lines of credit and international trade finance, among other services. The Individual Bank provides consumer lending and deposit gathering, mortgage loan servicing, small-business banking, private banking, and credit cards. The Investment Bank deals in mutual fund and annuity investment services, as well as life and disability insurance. Comerica

operates banks in California, Florida, Michigan, and Texas.

The company has been diversifying its fee-based business and investment services via strategic alliances. Links include National Data Corporation (to offer its business customers merchant processing services), Paine Webber (to gain new clients for its trust department), SPP Hambro & Co. (for greater access to capital markets), and Liberty Mutual Insurance (to offer discount auto and home insurance). Comerica has also expanded its insurance line to include property/casualty coverage for small-business and retail customers.

HISTORY

Comerica traces its history to 1849, when Michigan governor Epaphroditus Ransom tapped Elon Farnsworth to found the Detroit Savings Fund Institute. At that time Detroit was a major transit point for shipping between Lakes Huron and Erie, as well as between the US and Canada. The bank grew with the town and in 1871 became Detroit Savings Bank.

By 1899 Detroit was one of the top 10 US manufacturing centers and, thanks to a group of local tinkerers and mechanics that included Henry Ford, was on the brink of even greater growth. Detroit Savings grew also, fueled by the deposits of workers whom Ford paid up to $5 a day. Detroit Savings was not, however, the beneficiary of significant business with the auto companies; for corporate banking they turned first to eastern banks and then to large local banks in which they had an interest.

Detroit boomed during the 1920s as America went car-crazy, but after the 1929 crash Detroiters defaulted on mortgages by the thousands. By 1933 Michigan's banks were in such disarray that the governor shut them down three weeks prior to the federal bank holiday. Detroit Savings was one of only four Detroit banks to reopen. None of the major banks associated with auto companies survived.

A few months later Manufacturers National Bank, backed by a group of investors that included Edsel Ford (Henry's son), was founded. Although its start was rocky, Manufacturers National was on firm footing by 1936; around the same time Detroit Savings Bank renamed itself the Detroit Bank to appeal to a more commercial clientele.

WWII and the postwar boom put Detroit back in gear. In the 1950s and 1960s, both

banks thrived. In the 1970s statewide branching was permitted and both banks formed holding companies (DETROITBANK Corp. and Manufacturers National Corp.) and expanded throughout Michigan. As they grew, they added services; when Detroit's economy was hit by the the oil shocks of the 1970s these diversifications helped them through the lean years.

DETROITBANK opened a trust operation in Florida in 1982 to maintain its relationship with retired customers and renamed itself Comerica to be less area-specific. Manufacturers National also began operating in Florida (1983) and made acquisitions in the Chicago area (1987). Comerica went farther afield, buying banks in Texas (1988) and California (1991).

Following the national consolidation trend, in 1992 Comerica and Manufacturers National merged, retaining the Comerica name, but did not fully integrate until 1994, when the new entity began making more acquisitions. To increase sales and develop its consumer business, the company reorganized in 1996, selling its Illinois bank and its Michigan customs brokerage business. That year Comerica bought Fairlane Associates, expanding the company's property/casualty insurance line.

As part of its strategy to have operations in all the NAFTA countries Comerica opened a bank in Mexico in 1997 and one in Canada the next year; it also added online trading. The company consolidated its Michigan and Florida banks under one charter in 1999. That year it began prospecting for acquisitions in California and tapped its Paine Webber connection to expand its trust business.

OFFICERS

Chairman, President, and CEO, Comerica and Comerica Bank: Eugene A. Miller, age 61, $1,950,000 pay (prior to title change)
VC of the Business Bank: Joseph J. Buttigieg III, age 53, $693,000 pay
VC, Comerica and Comerica Bank: John D. Lewis, age 50, $984,000 pay
VC of Finance and Administration and CFO: Ralph W. Babb Jr., age 50, $748,000 pay
EVP and Chief Information Officer: John R. Beran, age 46
EVP, Corporate Staff: Richard A. Collister, age 54
EVP Investment Bank: George C. Eshelman, age 46
EVP Credit Administration: Dale E. Greene, age 52
EVP, Small Business and Individual Lending; Chairman and President, Comerica Acceptance Corporation; Chairman and President, Comerica Bank National Association: John R. Haggerty, age 55
EVP Credit Policy: Thomas R. Johnson, age 55
EVP, Corporate Secretary, and General Counsel: George W. Madison, age 45
EVP National Business Finance: Ronald P. Marcinelli, age 49
EVP Private Banking: David B. Stephens, age 53
SVP, Controller, and Chief Accounting Officer, Comerica and Comerica Bank: Marvin J. Elenbaas
SVP and General Auditor: James R. Tietjen, age 39
SVP Human Resources: Ted Bennett
Auditors: Ernst & Young LLP

LOCATIONS

HQ: Comerica Tower at Detroit Center, 500 Woodward Ave., Detroit, MI 48226
Phone: 313-222-4000   **Fax:** 313-965-4648
Web site: http://www.comerica.com

PRODUCTS/OPERATIONS

1998 Assets

	$ mil.	% of total
Cash & equivalents	1,773	5
Government & agency securities	2,206	6
Other securities	616	2
Commercial loans	19,086	52
Mortgage loans	5,217	14
Consumer loans	1,862	5
Other loans (net)	3,988	11
Other assets	1,853	5
Total	**36,601**	**100**

1998 Sales

	$ mil.	% of total
Loan interest & fees	2,382	74
Other interest	235	7
Investment management & fiduciary fees	184	6
Service charges	158	5
Commercial lending fees	43	1
Other	218	7
Total	**3,220**	**100**

KEY COMPETITORS

Bank of America
BANK ONE
Citigroup
Cullen/Frost Bankers
Huntington Bancshares
Michigan Heritage Bancorp
National City
Northern Trust
Silicon Valley Bancshares
SunTrust
U. S. Bancorp
Wells Fargo

HISTORICAL FINANCIALS & EMPLOYEES

NYSE symbol: CMA FYE: December 31	Annual Growth	1989	1990	1991	1992	1993	1994	1995	1996	1997	1998
Assets ($ mil.)	13.0%	12,150	13,300	14,451	26,587	30,295	33,430	35,470	34,206	36,292	36,601
Net income ($ mil.)	25.7%	78	129	153	226	341	387	413	417	531	607
Income as % of assets	—	0.6%	1.0%	1.1%	0.9%	1.1%	1.2%	1.2%	1.2%	1.5%	1.7%
Earnings per share ($)	15.6%	1.01	1.65	1.67	0.64	1.90	2.19	2.37	2.38	3.19	3.72
Stock price - FY high ($)	—	13.07	10.90	17.93	21.84	23.51	20.84	28.51	39.60	61.91	73.00
Stock price - FY low ($)	—	10.07	7.17	9.29	17.51	16.76	16.09	16.09	24.18	34.18	46.50
Stock price - FY close ($)	22.8%	10.73	9.37	17.93	21.34	17.76	16.26	26.68	34.93	60.20	68.19
P/E - high	—	13	7	11	34	12	10	12	17	19	20
P/E - low	—	10	4	6	27	9	7	7	10	11	13
Dividends per share ($)	11.0%	0.49	0.57	0.60	0.63	0.70	0.80	0.89	0.99	1.12	1.25
Book value per share ($)	7.9%	9.02	10.06	10.86	11.56	12.67	13.65	15.18	14.77	16.02	17.94
Employees	5.2%	6,783	6,960	7,180	13,322	12,670	13,498	13,572	11,969	10,877	10,739

STOCK PRICE HISTORY

HIGH/LOW/CLOSE

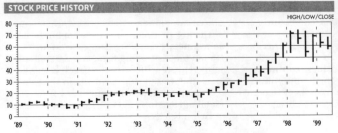

1998 FISCAL YEAR-END

Equity as % of assets: 7.6%
Return on assets: 1.7%
Return on equity: 21.7%
Long-term debt ($ mil.): 5,282
No. of shares (mil.): 156
Dividends
  Yield: 1.8%
  Payout: 33.6%
Market value ($ mil.): 10,630
Sales (mil.): $3,220

COMMERCIAL METALS COMPANY

OVERVIEW

There's no such thing as the end of the line at Commercial Metals Company (CMC), where old cars never die; they just get reincarnated into new metal products. The Dallas-based firm's CMC Steel Group operates four minimills in Alabama, Arkansas, South Carolina, and Texas. These mills process scrap metal from wrecked cars and other sources into structural steel for construction uses.

CMC owns 28 plants that produce goods such as steel fence posts, copper tubing, and signposts; a heat treating plant; 48 metal recycling plants; 12 warehouse stores that sell equipment and supplies to the concrete installation and construction trade; two industrial products supply centers; a rail salvage business; and a network of 16 international trading offices.

CMC's recycling segment processes scrap metal for sale to other steel mills and foundries. The company's marketing and trading segment brokers primary and secondary metals, steel, ores, concentrates, industrial minerals, ferroalloys, chemicals, and other materials used by a range of industries. This business unit also provides physical market pricing and trend information.

Facing uncertain economic conditions in Asia, CMC is relying on strong demand for steel from the US construction industry. It also expects to benefit from the 1997 six-year, $217 billion transportation law that provides funds for highway infrastructure rebuilding.

The Feldman family, descendants of CMC's founder, owns about 9% of the company.

HISTORY

In 1914 Russian immigrant Moses Feldman moved to Dallas, and the following year he founded a scrap metal company, American Iron & Metal.

In the 1920s Feldman suffered a heart attack. His son Jake attended Southern Methodist University in Dallas instead of Yale so he could help with the business. During the Depression the company was hurt by low metal prices. In 1932 Jake formed a two-man brokerage firm, which was combined as a partnership with his father's scrap metal operations; the new enterprise was named Commercial Metals Company (CMC). Moses Feldman died in 1937. The company was incorporated in 1946 and began buying related businesses in the 1950s.

In 1960 CMC was listed on the American Stock Exchange. It diversified and moved into other geographic markets in the 1960s. The company bought a stake in Texas steelmaker Structural Metals (1963). It formed Commercial Metals Europa (the Netherlands, 1965), its first overseas subsidiary, and expanded into New York by forming Commonwealth Metal. By 1966 the firm was one of the world's three largest scrap metal companies.

CMC bought Virginia-based copper tube manufacturer Howell Metals in 1968, the remainder of Structural Metals, and major stakes in seven affiliated businesses. Over a 10-year period CMC opened trading offices around the world.

During the 1970s the business continued to grow. The firm added a small minimill in Arkansas (1971) and certain assets of General Export Iron and Metal in Corpus Christi, Texas (1976).

CMC began trading on the New York Stock Exchange in 1982. The next year the company bought its third minimill, Birmingham, Alabama-based Connors Steel. In 1984 it formed a financial subsidiary, CMC Finanz, in Switzerland and by the end of the year was operating 20 metal recycling plants from Texas to Florida.

In the 1990s CMC modernized its minimills. In 1994 it acquired small scrap-metal operations and Shepler's, a concrete-related products business.

CEO Stanley Rabin completed the $50 million purchase of Owen Steel (a South Carolina minimill) in 1994, expanding CMC's reach into the Mid-Atlantic and Southeast. The company wrapped up a $30 million capital improvement program at its Alabama minimill in 1995 — just in time to ride a strong steel market to record profits.

Although a correction occurred in the steel and metals industry in 1996, which depressed prices, CMC achieved record earnings. The next year lower steel and scrap prices contributed to a decrease in the company's profits and revenues.

In 1997 CMC acquired Allegheny Heat Treating, a Pennsylvania-based provider of heat treatment services to steel mills. CMC also acquired two Florida-based auto salvage plants.

During 1998 CMC bought a Joplin, Missouri, metals recycling company, an Australian metals trading firm, and entered into a joint venture with Trinec, a Czech Republic steel mill, to sell steel products in the German market. CMC also bought A-1 Iron & Metal of Houston, and Construction Materials of Baton Rouge.

OFFICERS

President and CEO: Stanley A. Rabin, age 60,
$995,000 pay
SVP: Bert Romberg, age 68
Chairman and CEO, CMC Steel Group: Marvin Selig,
age 75, $955,000 pay
President, Commonwealth Metal: Charles J. Shrem
President, Cometals: Eliezer Skornicki
EVP, International Division: Michael Arwas
EVP, Dallas Trading Division: J. Matthew Kramer
EVP, Cometals: John Rothschild
SVP, International Division: Hanns Zoellner
VP, CFO, and Treasurer: Lawrence A. Engels, age 65
VP; President and COO, CMC Steel Group:
Clyde P. Selig, age 66, $705,030 pay
VP; President, Howell Metal: A. Leo Howell, age 77,
$685,000 pay
VP; President, Fabrication Plants, CMC Steel Group:
Hugh M. Ghormley, age 69, $666,097 pay
VP; President, Secondary Metals Processing Division:
Harry J. Heinkele, age 66
VP; President, International Division:
Murray R. McClean, age 50
VP, Secretary, and General Counsel: David M. Sudbury,
age 53
Controller: William B. Larson, age 45
Director Human Resources: Jesse Barnes
Assistant Controller: Milton L. Davis
Auditors: Deloitte & Touche LLP

LOCATIONS

HQ: 7800 Stemmons Fwy., Dallas, TX 75247
Phone: 214-689-4300   **Fax:** 214-689-5886
Web site: http://www.commercialmetals.com

CMC operates in more than 100 locations around
the world.

PRODUCTS/OPERATIONS

1998 Sales & Operating Income

	Sales		Operating Income	
	$ mil.	% of total	$ mil.	% of total
Manufacturing	1,234	51	75	78
Marketing & trading	789	32	20	22
Recycling	415	17	(1)	—
Adjustments	(70)	—	(8)	—
Total	**2,368**	**100**	**86**	**100**

COMPETITORS

AK Steel Holding
 Corporation
Armco
Bethlehem Steel
BHP
Birmingham Steel
Blue Tee
Chaparral Steel
Connell Limited
 Partnership
Keywell
LTV
Metal Management

Newell Recycling
Northwestern Steel & Wire
Nucor
OmniSource
Oregon Steel Mills
Quanex
Roanoke Electric Steel
Rouge Industries
Schnitzer Steel
Tube City
USX-U.S. Steel
Worthington Industries

HISTORICAL FINANCIALS & EMPLOYEES

NYSE symbol: CMC FYE: August 31	Annual Growth	1989	1990	1991	1992	1993	1994	1995	1996	1997	1998
Sales ($ mil.)	6.9%	1,303	1,137	1,161	1,166	1,569	1,666	2,117	2,322	2,258	2,368
Net income ($ mil.)	4.6%	29	26	12	13	22	26	38	46	39	43
Income as % of sales	—	2.2%	2.3%	1.0%	1.1%	1.4%	1.6%	1.8%	2.0%	1.7%	1.8%
Earnings per share ($)	4.8%	1.85	1.70	0.84	0.87	1.46	1.75	2.51	3.01	2.54	2.82
Stock price - FY high ($)	—	17.91	16.69	16.69	18.94	28.50	30.00	29.13	33.25	33.50	36.00
Stock price - FY low ($)	—	12.59	13.13	12.09	13.03	16.78	21.00	23.38	23.00	27.13	24.13
Stock price - FY close ($)	4.7%	16.13	14.25	14.72	17.25	28.31	26.75	28.25	30.13	30.75	24.38
P/E - high	—	10	10	20	22	20	17	12	11	13	13
P/E - low	—	7	8	14	15	11	12	9	8	11	9
Dividends per share ($)	5.9%	0.31	0.38	0.39	0.39	0.39	0.46	0.48	0.48	0.52	0.52
Book value per share ($)	8.4%	12.68	13.96	14.44	14.91	15.96	17.01	19.73	22.20	24.04	26.18
Employees	9.0%	3,386	3,838	3,709	3,834	3,904	4,353	6,272	6,700	7,150	7,350

STOCK PRICE HISTORY
HIGH/LOW/CLOSE

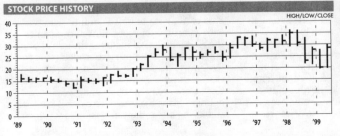

1998 FISCAL YEAR-END

Debt ratio: 31.3%
Return on equity: 11.2%
Cash ($ mil.): 31
Current ratio: 1.58
Long-term debt ($ mil.): 174
No. of shares (mil.): 15
Dividends
 Yield: 2.1%
 Payout: 18.4%
Market value ($ mil.): 355

COMPAQ COMPUTER CORPORATION

OVERVIEW

Compaq's aggressive expansion has built both success and aggravation. The Houston-based company has blossomed from leading PC maker — PCs account for over half of its sales — to the third-largest global computer firm, behind IBM and Hewlett-Packard. Other Compaq offerings include systems ranging from handheld portables to corporation-running servers to technology services. Compaq sells to businesses, consumers, government agencies, and education institutions.

The fast growth has taken its toll. Former CEO Eckhard Pfeiffer, the architect behind Compaq's rise, used the acquisitions of com-

modities like Tandem Computers and Digital Equipment (the biggest buy in the history of bits and bytes) to conquer the industry. But trouble integrating the purchases, competing with Dell Computer's direct sales strategy while appeasing wary resellers, and finding profit in an under-$500 PC world led Compaq to oust Pfeiffer in a bid to revitalize its fortunes.

A latecomer to the Web, Compaq is establishing its presence through its 16% ownership of powerhouse Internet investor CMGI, which acquired a majority stake in the Web destination operation formed by Compaq out of Digital's search engine, AltaVista Company.

HISTORY

Joseph "Rod" Canion and two other ex-Texas Instruments engineers started Compaq in Houston in 1982 to manufacture and sell portable IBM-compatible computers. Compaq's first portable was developed from a prototype the three sketched on a paper place mat when they first discussed the product idea.

Compaq shipped its first computer in 1982, and in 1983 (the year it went public) it recorded sales of $111 million — unprecedented growth for a computer startup. The success was due in part to emphasis on leading-edge technology. That year Benjamin Rosen was named chairman. Also in 1983 the company introduced a 28-pound portable computer — 18 months before IBM did — and in 1986 it was first out with a computer based on Intel's 386 chip. However, Compaq delayed introduction of its laptop until the prototype's display and battery technologies met engineering specifications. Although introduced late (1988), the laptop became an immediate success.

To sell its products, Compaq capitalized on the extensive base of dealers and suppliers built up around the IBM PC. Rather than establish a large sales force, the company gave exclusive rights to dealers for sales and service of its products. In 1988 Compaq became the first company to exceed the $2 billion sales mark within six years of its first product introduction.

Economic recession and stiff price competition slashed Compaq's revenues in 1991. Canion was forced to resign as CEO; he was replaced with German-born Eckhard Pfeiffer, the company's COO and a former marketing head at Texas Instruments. Pfeiffer took a no-nonsense approach to battle the glut of IBM cloners, cutting gross profit margins nearly in half. The move caused an intense price war;

when the dust settled in 1994, Compaq had passed Big Blue to lead the world in PC sales.

In 1996 Compaq reorganized divisions to reflect a more global emphasis. The next year it released a PC priced under $1,000 and sporting a Pentium-compatible chip made by Cyrix. To shore up its breadth of products, Compaq in 1997 also bought high-performance, low-failure specialist Tandem Computers for $3 billion.

In 1998 Compaq bought high-end hardware and Web search engine (AltaVista) specialist Digital Equipment for $9 billion in efforts to boost its oft-criticized service prowess. Digital was absorbed into Compaq, which eventually trimmed more than 15,000 jobs and recorded $1.7 billion in restructuring costs in 1998. To intensify a head-to-head battle with Dell's booming direct sales, Compaq began using the Internet to sell PCs to businesses, a strategy reversed later that year due to weak sales. In 1999 Compaq intensified its Internet focus by forming AltaVista Company and purchasing online retailer Shopping.com.

But bottom-line results came too slow for Compaq's board, which that year unceremoniously pressured Pfeiffer to resign in the wake of disappointing earnings and shareholder suits; Rosen assumed the interim CEO post. As shortfalls continued and a handful of Pfeiffer's executives left Compaq, the company was forced to restructure. As part of that plan, Compaq sold 83% of AltaVista to CMGI, an Internet investor with a portfolio of about 40 Web companies; the $2.3 billion deal included the sale of Shopping.com and other purchased electronic content providers. Also in 1999 Compaq chose COO Michael Capellas as its new president and CEO; Rosen remains chairman. Capellas announced plans that included closing facilities and laying off as many as 8,000 more workers.

Chairman: Benjamin M. Rosen, age 65
President and CEO: Michael D. Capellas, age 44,
$850,000 pay
Acting CFO and Treasurer: Ben Wells
SVP; Group General Manager, Consumer:
Michael J. Larson, age 45
SVP; Group General Manager, Personal Computers:
Michael J. Winkler, age 54
SVP, General Counsel, and Secretary:
Thomas C. Siekman, age 57
**SVP; Group General Manager, Enterprise Solutions and
Services:** Enrico Pesatori, age 58
SVP Europe, Middle East, and Africa: Andreas Barth,
age 54
**SVP Information Management and Chief Information
Officer:** Robert V. Napier
SVP Sales and Marketing: Peter Blackmore
SVP Supply Chain Management: Edward M. Straw, age 59
SVP Technology and Corporate Development and CTO:
William D. Strecker, age 54
VP; General Manager, Europe, Middle East and Africa:
Werner Koepf
VP eCommerce: Flint J. Brenton
VP Quality and Customer Satisfaction:
William B. "Bo" McBee III
Auditors: PricewaterhouseCoopers LLP

LOCATIONS

HQ: 20555 State Hwy. 249, Houston, TX 77070
Phone: 281-370-0670   **Fax:** 281-514-2656
Web site: http://www.compaq.com

Compaq Computer has operations worldwide and
manufacturing facilities in Brazil, China, Scotland,
Singapore, and the US.

1998 Sales

	$ mil.	% of total
US	13,981	45
Other countries	17,188	55
Total	**31,169**	**100**

PRODUCTS/OPERATIONS

1998 Sales

	$ mil.	% of total
Commercial PC	11,621	37
Enterprise	10,700	34
Consumer PC	4,945	16
Services	3,903	13
Total	**31,169**	**100**

COMPETITORS

Acer	Intel
Apple Computer	Matsushita
Bull	Micron Technology
Computer Sciences	NCR
Concurrent Computer	Oki Electric
Data General	Packard Bell
Dell Computer	Samsung
eMachines	Sequent
Fujitsu	SGI
Gateway	Siemens
Hewlett-Packard	Sun Microsystems
Hitachi	Toshiba
IBM	Unisys

HISTORICAL FINANCIALS & EMPLOYEES

NYSE symbol: CPQ FYE: December 31	Annual Growth	1989	1990	1991	1992	1993	1994	1995	1996	1997	1998
Sales ($ mil.)	30.3%	2,876	3,599	3,271	4,100	7,191	10,866	14,755	18,109	24,584	31,169
Net income ($ mil.)	—	333	455	131	213	462	867	789	1,313	1,855	(2,743)
Income as % of sales	—	11.6%	12.6%	4.0%	5.2%	6.4%	8.0%	5.3%	7.3%	7.5%	—
Earnings per share ($)	—	0.26	0.34	0.10	0.17	0.01	0.68	0.60	0.87	1.19	(1.71)
Stock price - FY high ($)	—	3.75	4.52	4.95	3.32	5.05	8.43	11.35	17.43	39.78	44.75
Stock price - FY low ($)	—	1.97	2.36	1.47	1.48	2.78	4.83	6.23	7.18	14.20	22.94
Stock price - FY close ($)	35.9%	2.65	3.75	1.76	3.25	4.92	7.90	9.60	14.88	28.25	42.00
P/E - high	—	14	13	50	20	505	12	19	20	33	—
P/E - low	—	8	7	15	9	278	7	10	8	12	—
Dividends per share ($)	—	0.00	0.00	0.00	0.00	0.00	0.00	0.00	0.00	0.00	0.05
Book value per share ($)	23.7%	0.99	1.44	1.53	1.67	2.10	2.82	3.45	4.49	6.21	6.73
Employees	25.0%	9,500	11,400	11,600	11,300	10,541	14,372	17,055	18,900	32,656	71,000

STOCK PRICE HISTORY HIGH/LOW/CLOSE

1998 FISCAL YEAR-END

Debt ratio: 0.0%
Return on equity: —
Cash ($ mil.): 4,091
Current ratio: 1.41
Long-term debt ($ mil.): 0
No. of shares (mil.): 1,687
Dividends
 Yield: 0.1%
 Payout: —
Market value ($ mil.): 70,854

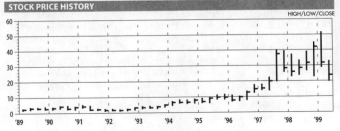

COMPUCOM SYSTEMS, INC.

OVERVIEW

CompuCom Systems helps *FORTUNE* 1000 customers piece together the computing puzzle. The Dallas-based company provides distributed network products (in a distributed network, data and application storage is spread across computers on the network) and network integration services to more than 6,000 business customers. CompuCom stocks goods from such leading computer makers as Compaq, IBM, and Hewlett-Packard; software publisher Microsoft; and peripherals manufacturers Toshiba and 3Com.

CompuCom's services business, which offers a variety of consulting, integration, help desk, asset management, and network management assistance, has hovered around 10% of sales each of the past three years, despite a strategic push into that market (it has tripled its service personnel since 1995). The company continues to expand its support operations, partially through acquisitions.

Facing sagging profits, CompuCom implemented a major restructuring to reduce costs. It created distribution centers close to supplier manufacturing sites and closed down all of its sales offices — more than 60 — in favor of virtual offices.

Investment and management firm Safeguard Scientifics owns about 56% of the company.

HISTORY

CompuCom Systems was founded by Stanley Sternberg in Michigan in 1981 to make factory automation products. Originally called CytoSystems, the company changed its name in 1983 to Machine Vision International (MVI) to reflect its focus on designing artificial vision systems for computers. Its main customers were Detroit automakers, which used MVI's automated inspection guidance systems to control industrial robots.

By the mid-1980s MVI was one of the largest machine vision companies in the US. In 1984 Safeguard Scientifics bought 31.5% of the company; Safeguard had been founded in 1953 by Warren Musser and Frank Diamond to raise funds for small, promising businesses. To raise more capital for MVI, Safeguard and MVI's management took the company public in 1985. However, MVI soon ran into trouble as the machine vision industry began to slow down. General Motors, the company's biggest customer, cut its orders, and MVI lost more than $13 million in 1986.

The following year MVI acquired New Jersey-based computer retailer TriStar Data Systems and Office Automation. The company moved its headquarters to New Jersey, changed its name to CompuCom Systems, and shifted its focus to selling and supporting microcomputers.

CompuCom exited the machine vision business in 1988 and acquired CompuShop, a Dallas-based computer retailer, from Bell Atlantic. CompuCom then relocated to Dallas. In 1989 the company named Avery More (EVP of an Apple Computer reseller) president, and co-CEO along with CompuShop CEO James Dixon.

In 1991 the company flirted briefly with retailing but abandoned the market and to focus on direct sales to corporate customers.

CompuCom expanded its networking business when it bought network integrator MicroSolutions in 1992 and International Micronet Systems two years later. When More left the company in 1993 to start his own venture capital firm, COO and reseller channel veteran Ed Anderson became CEO.

In 1995 the company bought network integrators in New Jersey and Texas. CompuCom and Unisys joined forces the next year to provide support services for multiple manufacturer desktop and network systems. The company also won a contract in 1996 to establish and operate two computer stores for the State of California (one in Los Angeles, the other in San Francisco). The next year the company added software management to its list of services.

In 1998 CompuCom bought Computer Integration, a computer reseller, and expanded its presence in the southeastern US with its purchase of Florida-based Dataflex. That year, when sales expenses grew faster than revenues, the company laid off close to 10% of its workforce. The reorganization was partly to blame for a drop in profits that year.

Boosting its sales in 1999, CompuCom bought the resale products business of rival ENTEX Information Services for $137 million. (The division had been credited for $1.8 billion of ENTEX's 1998 sales.) That year the company merged its ClientLink applications development subsidiary with Internet security services specialist E-Certify. Anderson left CompuCom to become president and CEO of E-Certify; chairman Harry Wallaesa (also president of Safeguard Scientifics) assumed the interim CEO post.

Chairman and Interim CEO: Harry Wallaesa, age 48
President and COO: Tom Lynch, age 56,
  $55,385 pay (prior to promotion)
SVP and CFO: M. Lazane Smith, age 44, $221,581 pay
SVP and Chief Information Officer: Jack D. Dowling
SVP, Distribution and Configuration: David W. Hall
SVP, Human Resources: David A. Loeser
VP, Architecture Development: David I. Robinson
VP, Business Development: Thomas Ducatelli
VP, Finance and Corporate Controller: Daniel L. Celoni
VP, Financial Operations: Mark J. Loder
VP, Help Desk Services: R. Ronald McIntire
VP, Managed Desktop Services: John F. McKenna
VP, Operations: Mark M. Warshauer
VP, Product Operations: John H. "Jay" Scott
VP, Professional Services: Robert J. D'Orazio
VP, Purchasing: Mark Killingsworth
VP, Sales International: Jonathan Edwards
VP, Telesales: Richard Rose
Auditors: KPMG LLP

LOCATIONS

HQ: 7171 Forest Ln., Dallas, TX 75230
Phone: 972-856-3600 **Fax:** 972-856-5395
Web site: http://www.compucom.com

CompuCom Systems has distribution centers in
California, New Jersey, North Carolina, and Texas.

PRODUCTS/OPERATIONS

1998 Sales

	$ mil.	% of total
Products	1,981	88
Services	258	11
Other	16	1
Total	**2,255**	**100**

Products	Network management
Computers	Networking support
Networking equipment	Product procurement
Peripherals	Software management
Software	
	Selected Suppliers
Services	3Com
Asset tracking	Compaq
Configuration	Hewlett-Packard
Consulting	IBM
Distribution	Intel
Field engineering	Microsoft
Help desk support	Toshiba

COMPETITORS

BT	Ingram Micro
CHS Electronics	Merisel
Comark	MicroAge
Compaq	Software Spectrum
ENTEX	Tech Data
Hewlett-Packard	Unisys
IBM	
InaCom	

HISTORICAL FINANCIALS & EMPLOYEES

Nasdaq symbol: CMPC FYE: December 31	Annual Growth	1989	1990	1991	1992	1993	1994	1995	1996	1997	1998
Sales ($ mil.)	26.6%	271	343	529	713	1,016	1,256	1,442	1,995	1,950	2,255
Net income ($ mil.)	(14.3%)	2	4	5	7	11	15	21	31	35	0
Income as % of sales	—	0.6%	1.0%	0.9%	1.0%	1.1%	1.2%	1.4%	1.5%	1.8%	0.0%
Earnings per share ($)	—	0.06	0.13	0.16	0.22	0.29	0.34	0.45	0.61	0.71	(0.01)
Stock price - FY high ($)	—	2.31	2.13	3.56	2.88	4.63	7.25	10.63	13.88	11.13	9.75
Stock price - FY low ($)	—	1.00	0.75	1.31	1.44	2.19	2.75	3.13	6.25	4.00	2.25
Stock price - FY close ($)	13.4%	1.13	1.31	2.25	2.19	4.06	3.13	9.50	10.75	8.25	3.50
P/E - high	—	39	16	22	13	16	21	24	23	16	—
P/E - low	—	17	6	8	7	8	8	7	10	6	—
Dividends per share ($)	—	0.00	0.00	0.00	0.00	0.00	0.00	0.00	0.00	0.00	0.00
Book value per share ($)	19.9%	0.81	0.93	1.14	1.39	1.78	2.21	2.80	3.30	4.23	4.12
Employees	26.2%	590	683	1,061	1,156	1,542	1,975	2,615	3,700	4,300	4,800

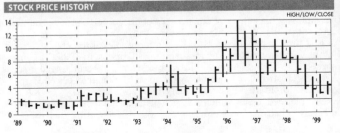

STOCK PRICE HISTORY
HIGH/LOW/CLOSE

1998 FISCAL YEAR-END
Debt ratio: 28.0%
Return on equity: 0.2%
Cash ($ mil.): 5
Current ratio: 1.65
Long-term debt ($ mil.): 82
No. of shares (mil.): 47
Dividends
 Yield: —
 Payout: —
Market value ($ mil.): 166

COMPUSA INC.

The nation's leading retailer of computers, Dallas-based CompUSA is determined to stay on top. Through more than 200 stores in 40 states, the company offers PCs and other hardware from leading OEMs, plus software and accessories such as CD-ROM drives and sound cards.

In addition to retail sales, CompUSA conducts mail order and direct sales to corporate, government, and education customers. Its CompUSA Net.com subsidiary concentrates on Internet sales. Growth in direct sales (which now brings in about 40% of sales) has enabled the company to fare better than some of its competitors, which are more dependent on sales to individual consumers. CompUSA's services include training programs (through some 500 classrooms located in or near its stores) and an array of technical support.

Its 1998 purchase of rival (but unprofitable) retail chain Computer City hurt profits, as have plunging PC prices, slumping sales at its retail stores, and the expense of promoting on-line sales. To boost profits and secure its lead, CompUSA is closing stores and laying off 7% of its workforce, with plans to hand management of its direct sales operations to Ingram Micro.

HISTORY

CompUSA was founded in 1984 when Mike Henochowicz (a native of South Africa and former Highland Appliance salesman) and Errol Jacobson invested $2,000 to open Soft Warehouse, a software store near Dallas.

Soft Warehouse prospered by offering a wide selection of titles. When the business opened, profit margins on computer programs were huge, and deep discounting, with little competition, still offered healthy profits. In 1985 Henochowicz and Jacobson opened their first superstore in Dallas.

Buyers in the early 1980s often did not know very much about computers and would go to one store to purchase hardware and another to buy software, relying on each store's technical expertise to guide their buying decisions. Soft Warehouse's one-stop-shopping concept coincided with the rise of savvy buyers who knew what they wanted.

In 1988 the partners opened a 24,000-sq.-ft. store in Atlanta. The next year Dubin Clark & Co., a private investment firm, bought a 50% interest in Soft Warehouse and brought in Nathan Morton, a former SVP of Home Depot, as the new COO. Morton immediately began an expansion program and was appointed CEO in 1990.

Decisions by Dell in 1990 and Apple in 1991 to sell their products through Soft Warehouse built the company's credibility. In 1991 the company adopted the name CompUSA to reflect its broader product lines and national expansion. That year CompUSA went public. (The two founders left about that time to pursue other interests.) By 1992 the company was operating 31 stores in 21 markets.

To manage its growth, CompUSA restructured in 1993 and announced plans for an international division to service its planned worldwide markets. Morton became chairman, and James Halpin (former president of Home-Base) was named president. Seven months later Morton resigned in the face of board dissatisfaction with CompUSA's poor earnings, which analysts blamed on inefficiencies stemming from rapid growth. Under Morton the company had become extremely decentralized, and in late 1994 the company had to auction off excess inventory.

Halpin became CEO and nixed plans for the international division. He also initiated staff cutbacks and instituted centralized buying. In 1995 CompUSA opened its first stand-alone customer training centers.

CompUSA in 1996 bought mail-order operation PCs Compleat (now CompUSA Net.com) and a minority stake in software developer InfoSource. The company continued to open new stores the following year, including locations in Richmond, Virginia; and Clearwater, Florida; and a handful of smaller stores in towns with populations under 150,000. Also in 1997 the company began selling build-to-order PCs.

In 1998 Apple set up its "store within a store" in CompUSA outlets and announced CompUSA would be its sole national retailer (although it later relented, permitting Best Buy to sell its products). Later that year CompUSA purchased Tandy's Computer City chain in a $211 million deal and launched a computer leasing program. It also increased its stake in InfoSource (to 50%), and teamed with IBM to offer a package of e-commerce products aimed at small businesses.

Hurt by slumping sales at its retail stores and by shrinking PC prices, in 1999 the company closed four stores, and announced it would lay off up to 1,500 employees and turn over management of its direct sales to Ingram Micro. It also plans to add more digital consumer products to its retail store shelves.

OFFICERS

Chairman: Giles H. Bateman, age 53
President and CEO: James F. Halpin, age 47, $959,615 pay
EVP and COO; President, CompUSA Stores: Harold F. Compton, age 51, $796,154 pay
EVP, CFO, Treasurer, and Assistant Secretary: James E. Skinner, age 45, $336,538 pay
EVP Merchandising: Lawrence N. Mondry, age 38, $385,192 pay
EVP Operations: J. Samuel Crowley, age 48, $332,500 pay
EVP Marketing: Ronald J. Gilmore, age 43
EVP Business Solutions: Anthony A. Weiss, age 31
SVP Merchandising: Paul F. Ewert, age 50
SVP of Technical Services: Rick L. Fountain, age 46
SVP Inventory Management: Harold D. Greenberg, age 51
SVP Human Resources: Melvin D. McCall, age 53
SVP; President, CompUSA Direct: Stuart M. Needleman, age 50
SVP Process Engineering and Chief Information Officer: Honorio J. Pardon, age 46
SVP Operations: Robert S. Seay, age 35
SVP, Secretary, and General Counsel: Mark R. Walker, age 41
Auditors: Ernst & Young LLP

LOCATIONS

HQ: 14951 N. Dallas Pkwy., Dallas, TX 75240
Phone: 972-982-4000   **Fax:** 972-982-4276
Web site: http://www.compusa.com

CompUSA has more than 200 retail stores in 40 states.

PRODUCTS/OPERATIONS

Selected Products

Hardware
  CD-ROM drives
  Cellular phones
  Connectivity products
  Data storage devices
  Desktop and laptop PCs
  Digital cameras
  Fax machines
  Handheld PCs
  Media storage products
  Modems
  Monitors
  Pagers
  Printers
  Sound cards
  Videoconferencing equipment

Virtual reality accessories
Software lines
  Business and personal productivity
  Education/ Entertainment
  Reference
  Utility

Selected Services
Computer training courses
Maintenance
Network design
Telephone help desk support
Upgrades

COMPETITORS

Babbage's Etc.
Best Buy
CDW Computer Centers
Circuit City
Comark
Compaq
CompuCom
Costco Companies
Creative Computers
DAMARK International
Dell Computer
Egghead.com
Fry's Electronics
Gateway

Good Guys
InaCom
Insight Enterprises
Micro Electronics
Micro Warehouse
MicroAge
OfficeMax
Sears
Software Spectrum
Staples
Supercom
Systemax
Tandy
Wal-Mart

HISTORICAL FINANCIALS & EMPLOYEES

NYSE symbol: CPU FYE: June 30	Annual Growth	1989	1990	1991	1992	1993	1994	1995	1996	1997	1998
Sales ($ mil.)	50.1%	137	300	544	827	1,342	2,146	2,813	3,830	4,611	5,286
Net income ($ mil.)	35.8%	2	2	(10)	10	12	(17)	23	60	94	32
Income as % of sales	—	1.5%	0.7%	—	1.2%	0.9%	—	0.8%	1.6%	2.0%	0.6%
Earnings per share ($)	11.7%	—	—	—	0.17	0.17	(0.23)	0.31	0.66	0.99	0.33
Stock price - FY high ($)	—	—	—	—	10.13	10.13	8.09	8.41	24.38	30.88	38.00
Stock price - FY low ($)	—	—	—	—	3.75	5.50	2.09	1.69	6.41	13.25	14.50
Stock price - FY close ($)	17.1%	—	—	—	7.03	7.38	2.22	8.31	17.06	21.50	18.13
P/E - high	—	—	—	—	60	60	—	27	37	31	115
P/E - low	—	—	—	—	22	32	—	5	10	13	44
Dividends per share ($)	—	—	—	—	0.00	0.00	0.00	0.00	0.00	0.00	0.00
Book value per share ($)	21.8%	—	—	—	1.40	2.20	1.98	2.26	3.63	4.68	4.56
Employees	48.1%	543	1,208	1,782	2,767	5,086	7,819	7,963	11,152	14,251	18,600

STOCK PRICE HISTORY

HIGH/LOW/CLOSE

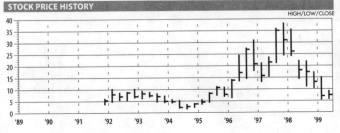

1998 FISCAL YEAR-END

Debt ratio: 21.3%
Return on equity: 7.6%
Cash ($ mil.): 152
Current ratio: 1.46
Long-term debt ($ mil.): 112
No. of shares (mil.): 91
Dividends
  Yield: —
  Payout: —
Market value ($ mil.): 1,647

COMPUTER ASSOCIATES

OVERVIEW

Computer Associates International (CA) is long on software products and short on hardball tactics. Or so it claims. Islandia, New York-based CA is the world's #3 independent software company (after Microsoft and Oracle; Microsoft and IBM are #1 and #2 overall). It sells more than 500 applications for all manner of computer systems. Although its name is not as recognizable as Microsoft's, CA makes the plumbing that keeps a company's technology humming, from connectivity and data access to network management. Its flagship product, Unicenter (25% of sales), gives corporations centralized control over complex computer networks.

Known as the scavenger of the software industry for its 20-year practice of swallowing rivals, CA has alienated customers and partners with its ruthlessness. Recent purchases, such as Computer Management Sciences, have a tender side — pumping up CA's support arm.

The man who took CA from a Swiss-owned fledgling US branch to a giant in its own right, billionaire CEO Charles Wang (pronounced "wong") runs a company that stresses the thrill of work. Although there is no art on its walls, Wang considers his programmers artists and rewards CA's talent with an indoor gym, day care facilities, and free breakfasts.

Wang owns 6% of the company; Swiss billionaire Walter Haefner owns 23%.

HISTORY

Born in Shanghai, Charles Wang fled Communist China with his family in 1952 and grew up in Queens, New York. After working in sales for software developer Standard Data, Wang started a joint venture in 1976 with Swiss-owned Computer Associates (CA) to sell software in the US. He started with four employees and one product, a file organizer for IBM storage systems. It was a great success, and in 1980 Wang bought out his Swiss partners. CA went public in 1981.

Wang realized that a far-flung distribution and service network, continuously fed by new products, was the key to success; acquiring existing software (and its customers) reduced risky in-house development and moved products to market sooner.

The company moved beyond mainframe utilities into computer software, buying the popular SuperCalc spreadsheet (1984) as well as accounting and data security software. The 1987 purchase of chief utilities rival UCCEL gave investor Walter Haefner a stake in CA.

CA's purchases of mostly struggling software firms made it in 1989 the first independent software company to reach $1 billion in sales. The $300 million acquisition of Cullinet that year added database and banking applications to CA's product line. But the new software was incompatible with some of CA's other products, which left customers with support concerns. This and other problems in assimilating Cullinet prompted CA to integrate its acquisitions and develop a way to have its software communicate regardless of hardware platform or operating system.

In the early 1990s CA acquired On-Line Software, a maker of debugging software, and Pansophic Systems, a maker of IBM software. Its acquisition methods by then were seen by some as relentless — swoop in, gobble up, cut costs, and get rid of employees. As a new owner, CA strongly defended its licensing contracts — often in court.

In 1994 CA promoted EVP of operations Sanjay Kumar to president (he is also COO). With his help, the company shifted away from its older systems to focus on network software; acquisitions (database software firm ASK Group, 1994; rival LEGENT, 1995; and network management expert Cheyenne Software, 1996) began to reflect this. CA continued its practice of buying in cash to avoid diluting stock.

Charges related to the LEGENT acquisition caused losses for fiscal 1996. Income rose again in 1997 and CA bought a stake in 3Name3D, a designer of 3-D models for entertainment companies. With its lack of a major service operation taking a bite out of potential business, CA made a $9.8 billion hostile takeover offer for consulting firm Computer Sciences Corp. (CSC) in 1998. CA soon dropped its bid in the face of CSC's fierce opposition and later acquired smaller computer service specialist Realogic.

The acquisitions helped cause a drop in profits for fiscal 1999. Later that year the company bought dominant support specialist Computer Management Sciences and database management software company PLATINUM technology (at about $3.5 billion, the industry's largest software deal to date). CA also formed a distribution alliance with CHS Electronics that included a $50 million investment in that company.

OFFICERS

Chairman and CEO: Charles B. Wang, age 54, $4,600,000 pay
President and COO: Sanjay Kumar, age 37, $3,300,000 pay
EVP; General Manager, Global Professional Services: Christopher Wagner
EVP, Global Information and Administrative Services: Gary Quinn
EVP, Research and Development: Russell M. Artzt, age 52, $1,470,000 pay
SVP; General Manager, Global Marketing: Mark Sokol
SVP; General Manager, Worldwide Channel Sales: Gayle Kemper
SVP, Advanced Technology: J. P. Corriveau
SVP, Business Development: Charles P. McWade, age 54, $650,000 pay
SVP, Finance and CFO: Ira Zar, age 37, $587,500 pay
SVP, Human Resources: Deborah J. Coughlin
SVP, Investor Relations: Doug Robinson
SVP, Product Strategy: Yogesh Gupta
SVP, Research and Development: Mark Combs
SVP, Worldwide Alliances: Ken Farber
Auditors: Ernst & Young LLP

PRODUCTS/OPERATIONS

Selected Software
Application life cycle
Assessment, remediation, and testing tools
Asset management
Data access and connectivity (Ingres II)
Data warehousing and business intelligence
Database management
Distributed network management (NetworkIT Pro)
Help desk
Information management
Internet commerce development tools (Jasmine TND)
Management software (Unicenter)
Security
Storage management (ARCserveIT)
Systems management
Text-to-multimedia interface (Opal)

Selected Services
Consulting
Custom development
Implementation
Maintenance
Outsourcing
Training

LOCATIONS

HQ: Computer Associates International, Inc., 1 Computer Associates Plaza, Islandia, NY 11749
Phone: 516-342-5224   **Fax:** 516-342-5329
Web site: http://www.cai.com

1999 Sales

	$ mil.	% of total
US	3,262	62
Europe	1,272	24
Other regions	719	14
Total	**5,253**	**100**

COMPETITORS

Amdahl
BMC Software
Candle Corporation
Compaq
Compuware
Forte Software
Hewlett-Packard
IBM
Informix
Landmark Systems
Microsoft
Network Associates
Oracle
Remedy
SAP
Sterling Software
Sun Microsystems
Sybase
Symantec
Unisys

HISTORICAL FINANCIALS & EMPLOYEES

NYSE symbol: CA FYE: March 31	Annual Growth	1990	1991	1992	1993	1994	1995	1996	1997	1998	1999
Sales ($ mil.)	16.8%	1,296	1,348	1,509	1,841	2,149	2,623	3,505	4,040	4,719	5,253
Net income ($ mil.)	16.5%	158	159	163	246	401	432	(56)	366	1,169	626
Income as % of sales	—	12.2%	11.8%	10.8%	13.3%	18.7%	16.5%	—	9.1%	24.8%	11.9%
Earnings per share ($)	18.0%	0.25	0.25	0.27	0.43	0.69	0.76	(0.10)	0.64	2.06	1.11
Stock price - FY high ($)	—	6.57	5.01	5.04	8.12	13.32	19.10	34.03	45.27	58.63	61.94
Stock price - FY low ($)	—	3.12	1.30	2.15	3.23	6.49	8.12	16.43	24.85	25.01	26.00
Stock price - FY close ($)	27.1%	4.12	2.63	4.60	7.08	9.16	17.62	31.87	25.93	57.75	35.56
P/E - high	—	26	20	19	19	19	25	—	71	28	56
P/E - low	—	12	5	8	8	9	11	—	39	12	23
Dividends per share ($)	—	0.00	0.03	0.03	0.03	0.04	0.06	0.06	0.07	0.09	0.08
Book value per share ($)	13.9%	1.58	1.78	1.65	1.86	2.26	2.79	2.72	2.77	4.54	5.09
Employees	8.7%	6,900	6,700	7,400	7,200	6,900	7,550	8,800	9,850	11,400	14,650

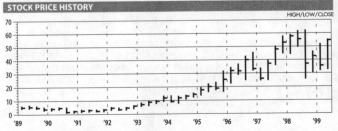

STOCK PRICE HISTORY
HIGH/LOW/CLOSE

1999 FISCAL YEAR-END
Debt ratio: 42.7%
Return on equity: 22.9%
Cash ($ mil.): 399
Current ratio: 1.41
Long-term debt ($ mil.): 2,032
No. of shares (mil.): 536
Dividends
  Yield: 0.2%
  Payout: 7.2%
Market value ($ mil.): 19,050

COMPUTER SCIENCES

OVERVIEW

Wherever there is a cluster of computers, an office of Computer Sciences Corporation (CSC) is probably nearby. El Segundo, California-based CSC is one of the world's largest information technology services companies. Its services include outsourcing (applications development, business process management, systems analysis), management consulting (business process re-engineering, change management), and systems integration. The company primarily targets global corporations and the US government (almost 25% of sales) as customers.

Chairman and CEO Van Honeycutt, known for his hands-on management style, oversees a corporate environment much like that of CSC's suburban Los Angeles location — laid-back and low-profile. The company ducks publicity and works closely with customers to establish long-lasting relationships. Long-term outsourcing contracts have helped CSC grow by about $1 billion a year since 1994.

But the company is also aggressively pushing into new markets. CSC continues to use acquisitions — more than 60 since 1986 — to boost its international presence, especially in Europe. The company is also beefing up its e-commerce capabilities with new services geared for the Internet such as electronic billing and online security.

Information processing specialist DST Systems owns about 5% of CSC.

HISTORY

Computer Sciences Corporation (CSC) was founded in Los Angeles in 1959 by Fletcher Jones and Roy Nutt to write software for computer manufacturers. Among its first customers were Honeywell and Univac. In 1963 CSC became the first software company to go public. Three years later it signed a $5.5 million contract to support NASA's computation laboratory. Annual sales had climbed to just over $53 million by 1968.

That year CSC agreed to merge with Western Union. The two companies had been working together for four years developing ways to transmit computerized information over telegraph wires, but the merger deal fell through. In 1969 William Hoover, who had joined the company from NASA's Jet Propulsion Laboratory in 1964, took over daily operations as president.

Jones turned his focus to strategy and started work on Infonet, a nationwide computer network, and Computicket, a computerized system for selling tickets. The excessive costs of developing these systems proved crippling to the company, and it was forced to write off millions of dollars in losses.

When Jones died in a plane crash in 1972, Hoover became chairman and CEO. CSC recovered from its losses with the help of a profitable government contract with the General Services Administration.

Under Hoover, CSC began transforming itself into a systems integrator. In 1986, when federal contracts still accounted for 70% of sales, the company started diversifying into the commercial sector. That year it bought Computer Partners, enhancing its presence in retail markets.

In 1991 CSC signed a 10-year, $3 billion contract with defense supplier General Dynamics. The following year the EPA canceled a $347 million contract with the company, citing problems with CSC's accounting practices. The Justice Department stepped in, and CSC agreed to pay $2.1 million to settle the charges.

The company secured an eight-year, $1.5 billion contract to handle data processing for Hughes Aircraft (now part of Raytheon) in 1995. That year Hoover, after more than two decades with CSC, stepped down as CEO (remaining chairman until 1997). He was succeeded by president and COO Van Honeycutt. Also in 1995 CSC bought Germany's largest independent computer services company, Ploenzke.

In 1996 CSC acquired insurance services provider Continuum Company for $1.5 billion. The next year it bought systems integrator Pinnacle Group and London-based information technology strategist Kalchas.

In 1998 CSC found itself on the other side of the bargaining table with a $9.8 billion hostile takeover bid from software giant Computer Associates (CA). After weeks of contentious battle, CA withdrew its bid. The IRS chose CSC to head a team including IBM, KPMG LLP, Lucent, and Unisys in a multibillion dollar project to update the agency's computer system.

That year CSC continued its acquisition spree, buying consulting firms in Europe including Informatica Group (Italy), KMPG Peat Marwick (France), Pergamon (Germany), and SYS-AID (the Netherlands). In 1999 CSC inked an 11-year, $1 billion deal to manage the back office functions of oil and gas giant Enron's energy services unit.

OFFICERS

Chairman, President, and CEO: Van B. Honeycutt, age 54, $980,793 pay
VP and Deputy General Counsel: Harvey N. Bernstein, age 52
VP; President, Financial Services Group: Edward P. Boykin, age 60
VP; President, Federal Sector: Milton E. Cooper, age 60, $721,831 pay
VP and Controller: Scott M. Delanty, age 44
VP, Secretary, and General Counsel: Hayward D. Fisk, age 56
VP and CFO: Leon J. Level, age 58, $732,359 pay
VP; President, European Group: Ronald W. Mackintosh, age 50, $892,586 pay
VP, Corporate and Marketing Communications: C. Bruce Plowman, age 61
VP, Corporate Development: Paul T. Tucker, age 51
VP, Human Resources: Frederick E. Vollrath
President, Consulting Group: Kirk E. Arnold, age 39
Auditors: Deloitte & Touche LLP

LOCATIONS

HQ: Computer Sciences Corporation,
2100 E. Grand Ave., El Segundo, CA 90245
Phone: 310-615-0311 **Fax:** 310-322-9768
Web site: http://www.csc.com

Computer Sciences Corporation has major operations in Australia, Belgium, Denmark, France, Germany, Italy, the Netherlands, Singapore, the UK, and the US.

1999 Sales

	$ mil.	% of total
US	4,894	64
Europe	2,250	29
Other regions	516	7
Total	**7,660**	**100**

PRODUCTS/OPERATIONS

1999 Sales

	% of total
Outsourcing	41
Management consulting	36
Systems integration	23
Total	**100**

Selected Services

Outsourcing	Management Consulting
Applications development	Business process
Claims processing	re-engineering
Credit checking	Information technology
Customer call centers	strategy
Data center management	
Desktop computing	**Systems Integration**
Network operations	Design
Systems analysis	Development
	Integration

COMPETITORS

American Management	Getronics
Andersen Consulting	IBM
Arthur D. Little	ICL
Cambridge Technology	KPMG
Cap Gemini	Lockheed Martin
Deloitte Touche Tohmatsu	McKinsey & Company
EDS	Origin
Ernst & Young	Perot Systems
Finsiel	PricewaterhouseCoopers
First Data	Unisys
Fiserv	

HISTORICAL FINANCIALS & EMPLOYEES

NYSE symbol: CSC FYE: March 31	Annual Growth	1990	1991	1992	1993	1994	1995	1996	1997	1998	1999
Sales ($ mil.)	19.9%	1,500	1,738	2,113	2,480	2,583	3,373	4,242	5,616	6,601	7,660
Net income ($ mil.)	20.1%	66	65	68	78	96	111	142	192	260	341
Income as % of sales	—	4.4%	3.7%	3.2%	3.1%	3.7%	3.3%	3.3%	3.4%	3.9%	4.5%
Earnings per share ($)	13.4%	0.68	0.67	0.69	0.78	0.53	1.00	0.71	1.23	1.64	2.11
Stock price - FY high ($)	—	9.74	11.16	14.13	13.40	20.88	26.31	40.38	43.25	56.75	74.88
Stock price - FY low ($)	—	7.28	6.12	8.70	9.49	11.66	17.63	23.25	30.81	28.94	46.25
Stock price - FY close ($)	24.7%	7.58	11.07	11.43	13.22	18.25	24.69	35.19	31.06	55.00	55.19
P/E - high	—	14	17	20	17	39	26	57	35	35	35
P/E - low	—	11	9	13	12	22	18	33	25	18	22
Dividends per share ($)	—	0.00	0.00	0.00	0.00	0.00	0.00	0.00	0.00	0.00	0.00
Book value per share ($)	13.6%	4.79	5.44	6.16	6.97	7.76	10.41	11.65	10.90	12.75	15.08
Employees	9.8%	21,600	22,900	26,500	26,000	29,000	32,900	33,850	42,200	45,000	50,000

STOCK PRICE HISTORY

HIGH/LOW/CLOSE

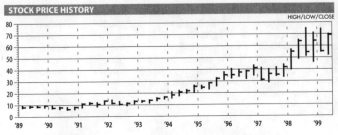

1999 FISCAL YEAR-END

Debt ratio: 14.2%
Return on equity: 14.2%
Cash ($ mil.): 603
Current ratio: 1.28
Long-term debt ($ mil.): 398
No. of shares (mil.): 159
Dividends
  Yield: —
  Payout: —
Market value ($ mil.): 8,783

CONAGRA, INC.

OVERVIEW

From fertilizer to french fries, ConAgra connects the links in the food chain. The Omaha, Nebraska-based diversified company is the #2 US food company, after Philip Morris' Kraft Foods. ConAgra's own name is nowhere near as famous as its 70-plus brands; it has 25 that account for more than $100 million each in annual sales, including Healthy Choice prepared foods and Butterball poultry.

The largest of ConAgra's three business segments is refrigerated foods, which brings in almost half of the company's sales. The US's top meat seller, it produces beef and pork products, cold cuts, and poultry under brands such as Armour, Cook's, and Country Pride. Its packaged foods segment, which wraps up about 30% of sales, makes shelf-stable and frozen foods (it's #2 in US frozen foods, after Nestle USA) under names including Banquet, Hunt's,

Marie Callender's, Orville Redenbacher's, Peter Pan, and Wesson. This segment also produces seafood and dairy products such as cheese, dessert toppings, and tablespreads (Parkay). ConAgra's agriculture segment is a leading US flour and dry corn miller and also trades and distributes crop protection chemicals, fertilizers, food ingredients, grain-based products, and seeds across the world. This segment reaps about 23% of sales.

The food industry has struggled to grow, resulting in depressed earnings. ConAgra launched a restructuring initiative, which, over the course of three years, will close at least 15 plants and 70 other facilities, exit 20 noncore businesses, and reduce the workforce by about 7,000 employees. Different units, which previously operated as independents, will pool resources to reduce overhead.

HISTORY

Alva Kinney founded Nebraska Consolidated Mills in 1919 by combining the operations of four Nebraska grain mills. It did not expand outside Nebraska until it opened a mill and feed processing plant in Alabama in 1942.

Consolidated Mills developed Duncan Hines cake mix in the 1950s. But Duncan Hines failed to raise a large enough market share, and the company sold it to Procter & Gamble in 1956. Consolidated Mills used the proceeds to expand, opening a flour and feed mill in Puerto Rico the next year. In the 1960s, while competitors were moving into prepared foods, the firm expanded into animal feeds and poultry processing. By 1970 it had poultry processing plants in Alabama, Georgia, and Louisiana. In 1971 the company changed its name to ConAgra (Latin for "in partnership with the land"). During the 1970s it expanded into the fertilizer, catfish, and pet accessory businesses.

Poorly performing subsidiaries and commodity speculation caused ConAgra severe financial problems until 1974, when Mike Harper, a former Pillsbury executive, took over. Harper trimmed properties to reduce debt and had the company back on its feet by 1976. ConAgra stayed focused on the commodities side of the business, but was thus tied to volatile price cycles. In 1978 it bought United Agri Products (agricultural chemicals).

ConAgra moved into food products in the 1980s with aggressive acquisitions. It bought Banquet (frozen food, 1980) and within six years had introduced almost 90 new products

under that label. Other purchases included Singleton Seafood (1981), Armour Food Company (meats, dairy products, frozen food; 1983), and RJR Nabisco's frozen food business (1986). ConAgra became a major player in the red meat market with the 1987 purchases of E. A. Miller (boxed beef), Monfort (beef and lamb), and Swift Independent Packing.

It bought Beatrice Foods (Orville Redenbacher's popcorn, Hunt's tomato products) in 1991. ConAgra reorganized in the late 1990s, closing more than 20 production plants.

In 1997 the company agreed to pay $8.3 million to settle federal charges that, among other things, it committed wire fraud and watered down grain before selling it. ConAgra also named VC and president Bruce Rohde as CEO; he became chairman in 1998.

The company introduced a vegetarian entree line in 1998, Advantage 10, developed with health guru Dean Ornish. It then bought GoodMark Foods, maker of Slim Jim and other meat snacks, and Nabisco's Egg Beaters and tablespreads units (Parkay, Blue Bonnet, Fleischmann's). Later that year ConAgra introduced a dietary supplement, Culturelle, which is a strain of "good" bacteria that can fight off "bad" bacteria. The firm acquired Holly Ridge Foods (pastries) in 1999. ConAgra then announced a three-year restructuring initiative in May 1999 designed to reduce expenses and boost earnings.

Chairman, President and CEO: Bruce C. Rohde,
$1,874,137 pay (prior to promotion)
EVP, CFO and Corporate Secretary: James P. O'Donnell,
$471,818 pay
SVP, Profit Improvement: Kenneth W. DiFonzo,
$406,300 pay
SVP and Chief Information Officer:
Kenneth W. Gerhardt
SVP, Mergers and Aquisitions: Dwight J. Goslee
SVP, Human Resources and Administration:
Owen C. Johnson
SVP, Sales and Marketing Development:
Timothy P. McMahon
**SVP, Commodity Procurement and Customer Risk
Management:** Kevin W. Tourangeau
SVP, Commodity Procurement and Risk Management:
Michael D. Walter
President and COO, ConAgra Frozen Foods:
James T. Smith, $414,368 pay
Auditors: Deloitte & Touche LLP

LOCATIONS

HQ: 1 ConAgra Dr., Omaha, NE 68102-5001
Phone: 402-595-4000   **Fax:** 402-595-4707
Web site: http://www.conagra.com

ConAgra has operations in 35 countries.

PRODUCTS/OPERATIONS

1999 Sales

	$ mil.	% of total
Refrigerated foods	11,549	47
Packaged foods	7,465	30
Agricultural products	5,580	23
Total	**24,594**	**100**

Selected Subsidiaries, Brands, and Products

Beatrice Cheese Co. (Healthy Choice and County Line
cheeses; Reddi-Wip dessert toppings; Blue Bonnet,
Chiffon, Fleischmann's, Move Over Butter, Parkay, and
Touch of Butter tablespreads; Egg Beaters)
Butterball Turkey Co.
ConAgra Frozen Foods (Banquet, Healthy Choice, Kid
Cuisine, Marie Callender's, Morton)
GoodMark Foods (Andy Capp's grain snacks, Slim Jim
meat snacks)
Hunt Foods Company (Chun King, Healthy Choice,
Hunt's, LaChoy, Rosarita/Gebhardt)
Lamb-Weston (frozen potato products)
Orville Redenbacher/Swiss Miss Foods Company
(popcorn, puddings, and cocoa mixes)
Swift & Company (fresh pork)
United Agri Products (crop protection chemicals)
Wesson/Peter Pan (Knott's Berry Farm products,
Peter Pan, Wesson)

COMPETITORS

ADM	Diageo	Nabisco Holdings
Agway	Dow Chemical	Nestle
Bestfoods	DuPont	Novartis
Borden	Farmland	Perdue
Bunge	Industries	Philip Morris
International	Frito-Lay	Procter &
Campbell Soup	General Mills	Gamble
Cargill	Gold Kist	Quaker Oats
Cenex Harvest	Heinz	Sara Lee
States	Hershey	Schwan's
Continental	Hormel	Smithfield Foods
Grain	IBP	Suiza Foods
Corn Products	Land O'Lakes	Tyson Foods
International	Mars	Unilever
Danone	McCain Foods	
Dean Foods	Monsanto	

HISTORICAL FINANCIALS & EMPLOYEES

NYSE symbol: CAG FYE: May 31	Annual Growth	1990	1991	1992	1993	1994	1995	1996	1997	1998	1999
Sales ($ mil.)	5.3%	15,501	19,505	21,219	21,519	23,512	24,109	24,822	24,002	23,841	24,594
Net income ($ mil.)	5.0%	232	311	372	270	437	496	189	615	613	358
Income as % of sales	—	1.5%	1.6%	1.8%	1.3%	1.9%	2.1%	0.8%	2.6%	2.6%	1.5%
Earnings per share ($)	2.0%	0.63	0.71	0.75	0.53	0.91	1.04	0.40	1.36	1.33	0.75
Stock price - FY high ($)	—	10.63	16.26	18.13	17.13	14.69	17.25	23.56	30.75	38.75	34.38
Stock price - FY low ($)	—	7.07	9.84	12.25	11.38	11.50	14.13	16.31	20.75	27.00	22.56
Stock price - FY close ($)	10.7%	10.42	15.26	12.94	12.56	14.38	16.69	21.31	30.19	29.25	26.06
P/E - high	—	17	23	24	32	16	17	59	23	29	46
P/E - low	—	11	14	16	21	13	14	41	15	20	30
Dividends per share ($)	15.0%	0.19	0.22	0.25	0.29	0.34	0.39	0.45	0.51	0.59	0.67
Book value per share ($)	8.0%	2.98	4.34	4.81	4.08	4.49	5.08	4.64	5.19	5.79	5.96
Employees	3.6%	58,369	74,718	80,787	83,000	87,000	90,871	80,000	80,000	82,169	80,000

STOCK PRICE HISTORY

HIGH/LOW/CLOSE

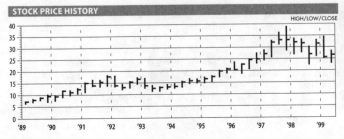

1999 FISCAL YEAR-END

Debt ratio: 42.5%
Return on equity: 12.3%
Cash ($ mil.): 63
Current ratio: 1.05
Long-term debt ($ mil.): 2,543
No. of shares (mil.): 488
Dividends
  Yield: 2.6%
  Payout: 89.3%
Market value ($ mil.): 12,722

CONOCO INC.

Emerging from its DuPont cocoon, Conoco (which was spun off from the chemical giant in 1998) has a mighty big wingspan: The Houston-based integrated energy company, which is engaged in oil and gas exploration, production, refining, marketing, and transportation, explores for petroleum in 15 countries. With proved reserves of 2.6 billion barrels of oil equivalent, Conoco has major holdings in the Gulf of Mexico, South Texas, the UK's North Sea, Venezuela, and Malaysia. It also operates about 10,000 miles of pipeline and four refineries in the US and one UK refinery.

Conoco sells gasoline, diesel fuel, and other petroleum products through 7,900 outlets in Europe, Thailand, and the US under the brands Conoco, Jet, Seca, and Turkpetrol. It is a major supplier of petroleum coke, industrial lubricants, and specialty products.

The company is also winging its way into power generation and wholesale marketing. Its Conoco Global Power unit markets and trades electricity and natural gas, and it develops and builds power plants, including a congeneration plant in Texas for former parent DuPont.

Conoco gained its full independence in 1999 when DuPont sold its 70% interest in Conoco to its stockholders.

HISTORY

Isaac Elder Blake, an Easterner who had lost everything on a bad investment, came to Ogden, Utah, and founded Continental Oil & Transportation (CO&T) in 1875. To transport petroleum from the East Coast to the West, Blake used railroad tank cars, an unusual concept at the time and just one of Blake's many innovations.

In 1885 CO&T merged with Standard Oil's operations in the Rockies and was reincorporated in Colorado as Continental Oil. Blake, always a speculator, was hit hard by the western financial panic of 1892 and left the company the next year. Continental tightened its grip on the Rocky Mountain area and by 1906 had taken over 98% of the western market. Its monopoly ended in 1911 when the US Supreme Court ordered Standard to divest several holdings: Continental was one of 34 independent oil companies created in 1913.

Seeing opportunity in autos, Continental built a gas station in 1914. Two years later it got into oil production when it bought United Oil, and by 1924 it had become fully integrated by merging with Mutual Oil, which owned production, refining, and distribution assets. Continental's biggest merger came in 1929 when it merged with Marland Oil of Oklahoma.

During the Depression, Continental envisioned a pipeline running from Oklahoma to Chicago and Minnesota to reduce transportation costs; it created a partnership to pursue the project. After WWII Continental helped pioneer the first offshore oil production boat, and in 1956 the company (with Union, Shell, and Superior oil companies) launched CUSS I, the first drill ship. Continental expanded in the 1950s and 1960s, acquiring oil fields in Africa, the Middle East, and South America. It also bought gas station chains (SOPI, Jet, Seca, and others) across Europe.

Continental then diversified, acquiring American Agricultural Chemicals in 1963 and Consolidation Coal (Consol) in 1966. Restructuring in the 1970s into Conoco Chemical, Consol, and two petroleum divisions, the firm ramped up oil exploration and entered ventures to develop uranium. In 1979 it changed its name to Conoco.

In the late 1970s, Conoco began joint ventures with chemical titan DuPont and was acquired by DuPont in 1981 to forestall hostile takeover attempts by Mobil and Seagram. In the midst of a worldwide oil crisis, DuPont saw Conoco as a reliable source of crude oil. DuPont sold off $1.5 billion of Conoco's assets and absorbed Conoco Chemicals.

During the 1980s Conoco made big oil finds in the Gulf of Mexico, the North Sea, Indonesia, and Ecuador, but by 1990 it was spread thin among 30 countries. It refocused on 15 countries, including high-risk areas: It had a 1991 venture with Lukoil to look for oil in the Russian Arctic and a 1996 deal to drill in disputed waters off Vietnam. (However, its plan to produce oil in Iran was vetoed by the US government in 1995.) Conoco also committed to Asia: Its largest overseas investment, a Malaysian refinery, was finished in 1998. Conoco began to pursue opportunities in electric power in 1995.

In 1998 DuPont spun off Conoco in the US's largest-ever IPO (DuPont had completely divested its 70% stake by the next year). Meanwhile, oil prices dropped, and the newly independent Conoco laid off workers and slashed capital spending by about 20%.

The company announced major oil finds in 1999 offshore Venezuela and in the Gulf of Mexico.

OFFICERS

Chairman, President and CEO: Archie W. Dunham, age 60, $2,201,261 pay (prior to promotion)
EVP, Exploration Production: Robert E. McKee III, age 52, $790,775 pay
EVP, Refining, Marketing, Supply, and Transportation: Gary W. Edwards, age 57, $858,460 pay
SVP Finance and CFO: Robert W. Goldman, age 56, $402,750 pay
SVP, Government Affairs, Corporate Strategy, and Communications: J. Michael Stinson
SVP, Human Resources: Mario Rocconi
SVP, Legal and General Counsel: Rick A. Harrington, age 54, $436,500 pay
President, Exploration and Production - Africa, Asia Pacific, and Middle East: T. E. Davis
President, Exploration and Production - Americas: J. R. Kemp III
President, Refining and Marketing - Asia Pacific: P. W. Lashbrooke
President, Exploration and Production - Europe: T. C. Knudson
President, Refining and Marketing - Europe: D. O. Kem
President, Refining and Marketing - North America: J. W. Nokes
Auditors: PricewaterhouseCoopers LLP

LOCATIONS

HQ: 600 N. Dairy Ashford, Houston, TX 77079
Phone: 281-293-1000   **Fax:** 281-293-1440
Web site: http://www.conoco.com

1998 Sales

	$ mil.	% of total
Downstream		
US	8,949	39
International	8,297	37
Upstream		
US	3,200	14
International	1,601	7
Corporate and other	749	3
Total	**22,796**	**100**

PRODUCTS/OPERATIONS

1998 Sales

	$ mil.	% of total
Refined products	13,729	60
Crude oil	3,737	16
Natural gas	3,139	14
Other	2,191	10
Total	**22,796**	**100**

COMPETITORS

ARCO	Occidental
Ashland	PDVSA
BP Amoco	PEMEX
Chevron	Petrobras
Coastal	Phillips Petroleum
Elf Aquitaine	Royal Dutch/Shell
ENI	Southern Company
Enron	Sunoco
Exxon	Texaco
Kerr-McGee	TOTAL FINA
Mobil	Unocal
Norsk Hydro	USX-Marathon

HISTORICAL FINANCIALS & EMPLOYEES

NYSE symbol: COC.B FYE: December 31	Annual Growth	1989	1990	1991	1992	1993	1994	1995	1996	1997	1998
Sales ($ mil.)	5.3%	—	—	15,851	16,065	15,035	13,956	14,695	18,779	20,447	22,796
Net income ($ mil.)	(7.8%)	—	—	795	316	755	422	575	863	1,097	450
Income as % of sales	—	—	—	5.0%	2.0%	5.0%	3.0%	3.9%	4.6%	5.4%	2.0%
Earnings per share ($)	—	—	—	—	—	—	—	—	—	—	0.71
Stock price - FY high ($)	—	—	—	—	—	—	—	—	—	—	25.75
Stock price - FY low ($)	—	—	—	—	—	—	—	—	—	—	19.38
Stock price - FY close ($)	—	—	—	—	—	—	—	—	—	—	20.75
P/E - high	—	—	—	—	—	—	—	—	—	—	36
P/E - low	—	—	—	—	—	—	—	—	—	—	27
Dividends per share ($)	—	—	—	—	—	—	—	—	—	—	0.00
Book value per share ($)	—	—	—	—	—	—	—	—	—	—	7.07
Employees	4.1%	—	—	—	—	—	—	—	—	16,000	16,650

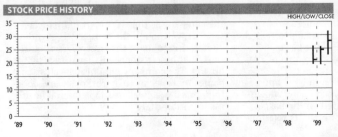

STOCK PRICE HISTORY
HIGH/LOW/CLOSE

1998 FISCAL YEAR-END

Debt ratio: 51.4%
Return on equity: 10.1%
Cash ($ mil.): 394
Current ratio: 1.02
Long-term debt ($ mil.): 4,689
No. of shares (mil.): 628
Dividends
 Yield: —
 Payout: —
Market value ($ mil.): 13,032

CONSECO, INC.

OVERVIEW

Conseco wrote the book on insurance industry consolidation; now we'll see what customers who live in trailers add to the mix. The Carmel, Indiana-based company has spent the 1990s doing business 1980s-style: buying insurance businesses rather than developing them. Conseco has gobbled up about 40 companies in a decade-and-a-half; the company's success has been its own worst enemy, as copycats are increasing the competition for bargain buys.

Conseco's stable of companies sells supplemental health, life, and group medical insurance; annuities; and other insurance products, primarily to working-class prospects. It has also introduced a series of mutual funds operated by its subsidiary Conseco Capital Management.

Conseco's conquests include Bankers Life and Casualty, Providential Life Insurance, and Wabash Life Insurance. Synergy being all the rage, it moved into finance by buying Green Tree Financial, the top lender to mobile home buyers. With Green Tree's focus on the lower-income customer, Conseco is hoping for cross-selling opportunities arising from its own customer demographics.

CEO Stephen Hilbert is among the highest paid executives in the US.

HISTORY

Conseco evolved from Security National, a small Indiana insurance company formed in 1979 by Stephen Hilbert. The former encyclopedia salesman and Aetna executive believed most insurers were bloated and that the industry was ripe for the picking by a smart, lean organization.

After raising capital, in 1982 the company implemented a growth-by-acquisition strategy with the purchase of Executive Income Life Insurance (renamed Security National Life Insurance). The next year it bought Consolidated National Life Insurance and renamed the expanded company Conseco.

In 1985 the firm went public, and bought Lincoln American Life Insurance. In 1986 it bought Lincoln Income Life (sold 1990) and Bankers National Life Insurance. Other acquisitions during that period included Western National Life Insurance (sold 1994) and National Fidelity Life Insurance.

In 1990 the company formed Conseco Capital Partners (with General Electric and Bankers Trust) to finance insurance acquisitions without burdening the parent company with debt. This device financed the purchase of Great American Reserve and the 1991 acquisition of Beneficial Standard Life. In 1992 Conseco bought Bankers Life Insurance, then sold 67% of it the next year. Also in 1993 the company formed the Private Capital Group to invest in noninsurance companies.

In 1994 the company pursued a protracted negotiation to acquire the much larger Kemper Corp., but decided the requisite $2.6 billion would cause too much debt. The aborted deal cost $36 million in bank and accounting fees. A Merrill Lynch analyst downgraded Conseco's stock based on the fiasco, prompting Conseco to terminate its relationship with Merrill, though it had underwritten Conseco's IPO.

Meanwhile, Private Capital's success led Conseco to form Conseco Global Investments. Other investments included stakes in race track and riverboat gambling operations in Indiana.

In 1996 and 1997 Conseco's acquisitiveness continued; it absorbed eight insurance companies, along with their expertise in life, health, property/casualty, and specialty insurance, including insurance for the elderly. It purchased the 62% of American Life Holdings it didn't already own.

In 1998, citing similar demographics, Conseco bought Green Tree Financial, the US's #1 mobile home financier. Green Tree has had its share of controversy, such as charges of fuzzy accounting practices and discrimination, which may hinder Conseco's quest for a federal thrift charter. And its segment has been hit by a new trend — the increasing sophistication of its customers, many of whom refinanced their double-wides at lower interest rates. Prepayments resulted in millions of dollars in charges for Green Tree that year, reducing Conseco's earnings.

Also in 1998, the company sought brand recognition: The Indiana Pacers will begin to play in the Conseco Fieldhouse in 1999. Conseco launched an ad campaign in 1999 targeting low-net-worth clients portraying the company as the "Wal-Mart of financial services." Although the company is spending 1999 trying to make the Green Tree acquisition fit, it hasn't stopped its favorite activity: buying. The company bought marketing companies that specialize in workplace and door-to-door sales, as well as supplemental health insurer Inter-State Service.

OFFICERS

Chairman, President, and CEO: Stephen C. Hilbert, age 53, $14,500,000 pay
EVP and CFO: Rollin M. Dick, age 67, $4,066,000 pay
EVP Corporate Development; President and CEO, Conseco Private Capital Group: Ngaire E. Cuneo, age 48
SVP, Chief Accounting Officer, and Treasurer: James S. Adams, age 39
SVP Investments; President and CEO, Conseco Capital Management: Maxwell E. Bublitz, age 43, $1,650,000 pay
President, Conseco Financial Group: Bruce A. Crittenden, age 47
EVP and COO; President and CEO, Conseco Services and President, Conseco Marketing: Thomas J. Kilian, age 48, $1,500,000 pay
EVP, Secretary, and General Counsel: John J. Sabl, age 47
SVP Finance: David J. Barra
SVP and Chief Accounting Officer: Gregory R. Barstead
SVP and Valuation Actuary: David L. Baxter
SVP Information Technology: Robert G. Clancy
SVP Marketing Services: Robert M. Dahl
SVP Human Resources: Dennis J. Dunlap
EVP Marketing: L. Gregory Gloeckner
President, Career Division: Dennis M. McComb
SVP Finance and Assistant Treasurer, Conseco Services: Daniel Murphy
SVP Corporate Communications: James W. Rosensteele
Auditors: PricewaterhouseCoopers LLP

LOCATIONS

HQ: 11825 N. Pennsylvania St., Carmel, IN 46032
Phone: 317-817-6100   **Fax:** 317-817-2847
Web site: http://www.conseco.com

PRODUCTS/OPERATIONS

1998 Assets

	$ mil.	% of total
US Treasuries	382	1
Foreign securities	127	—
Mortgage-backed securities	6,377	15
State & municipal bonds	105	—
Corporate bonds	12,837	29
Stocks	376	1
Mortgage loans	1,130	3
Policy loans	686	2
Assets in separate account	899	2
Receivables	4,034	9
Other securities & assets	16,647	38
Total	**43,600**	**100**

1998 Sales

	$ mil.	% of total
Insurance segment		
Premiums	3,949	51
Investments	2,082	27
Other	296	4
Finance segment		
Sale of receivables	745	10
Investments, fees & other	644	8
Total	**7,716**	**100**

COMPETITORS

Aetna	AXA Financial	MetLife
AFLAC	Fortis	New York Life
Allstate	GenAmerica	Northwestern
American General	Guardian Life	Mutual
American National Insurance	Household International	Principal Financial
	John Hancock	Prudential
	MassMutual	Torchmark

HISTORICAL FINANCIALS & EMPLOYEES

NYSE symbol: CNC FYE: December 31	Annual Growth	1989	1990	1991	1992	1993	1994	1995	1996	1997	1998
Assets ($ mil.)	26.7%	5,176	8,284	11,596	11,773	13,749	10,812	17,298	25,613	35,915	43,600
Net income ($ mil.)	29.0%	47	42	116	170	297	158	220	252	567	467
Income as % of assets	—	0.9%	0.5%	1.0%	1.4%	2.2%	1.5%	1.3%	1.0%	1.6%	1.1%
Earnings per share ($)	17.8%	0.32	0.34	1.01	1.35	2.20	1.82	2.12	1.82	2.64	1.40
Stock price - FY high ($)	—	1.75	1.88	8.42	11.84	18.94	16.56	15.78	33.13	50.06	58.13
Stock price - FY low ($)	—	0.70	1.06	1.49	5.16	11.16	8.97	8.13	14.91	30.75	21.94
Stock price - FY close ($)	38.0%	1.68	1.76	7.73	11.63	13.94	10.81	15.66	31.88	45.44	30.50
P/E - high	—	5	6	8	9	9	9	7	18	19	42
P/E - low	—	2	3	1	4	5	5	4	8	12	16
Dividends per share ($)	43.6%	0.02	0.02	0.02	0.02	0.05	0.13	0.08	0.06	0.22	0.52
Book value per share ($)	35.3%	1.08	1.46	3.87	5.46	8.45	5.22	7.93	16.86	20.22	16.36
Employees	44.5%	510	876	1,098	2,860	3,290	3,550	3,250	3,700	6,800	14,000

STOCK PRICE HISTORY

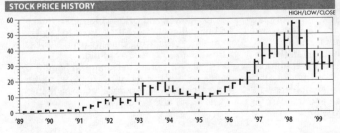

HIGH/LOW/CLOSE

1998 FISCAL YEAR-END

Equity as % of assets: 11.9%
Return on assets: 1.2%
Return on equity: 9.0%
Long-term debt ($ mil.): 5,322
No. of shares (mil.): 316
Dividends
  Yield: 1.7%
  Payout: 37.1%
Market value ($ mil.): 9,633
Sales (mil.): $7,716

CONSOLIDATED EDISON, INC.

Consolidated Edison, Inc. (CEI) makes the Big Apple shine. Based in New York City, the energy holding company supplies electricity through its largest subsidiary — Consolidated Edison Company of New York (better known as ConEd) — to more than 3 million customers in its hometown (except part of Queens) and most of Westchester County. It also distributes gas to more than a million customers in Manhattan, The Bronx, and parts of Queens and Westchester County, and provides steam service in Manhattan.

With the New York electricity market deregulating (to be completed in 2001), ConEd is selling most of its New York generation assets to focus on distribution and transmission. ConEd has also expanded its service area through the 1999 purchase of suburban supplier Orange and Rockland Utilities (operating in New York, Pennsylvania, and New Jersey).

CEI is moving toward competition rather cautiously, but it has established nonregulated subsidiaries to sell energy to New York retail customers and wholesale customers in the northeastern US. Another subsidiary invests in energy infrastructure and has interests in generating facilities in California, Michigan, Guatemala, and the Netherlands. CEI is also exploring a communications business based on its infrastructure experience.

A group of New York professionals, led by Timothy Dewey, founded the New York Gas Light Company in 1823 to provide utility service to part of Manhattan. Various companies served other areas of the city, and in 1884 five of these joined with New York Gas Light to form the Consolidated Gas Company of New York.

This unification occurred on the heels of the introduction of Thomas Edison's incandescent lamp (1879). The Edison Electric Illuminating Company of New York was formed in 1880 to build the world's first commercial electric power station, financed by a group led by J.P. Morgan. Edison supervised the project, known as the Pearl Street Station, and in 1882 New York became the first major city with electric lighting.

Realizing electricity would replace gas, Consolidated Gas began acquiring electric companies, including Anthony Brady's New York Gas and Electric Light, Heat and Power Company (1900), which consolidated with Edison's Illuminating Company in 1901 to form the New York Edison Company. More than 170 purchases followed, including that of the New York Steam Company (1930), a cheap source of steam for the company's electric turbines.

In 1935 Congress enacted the Public Utility Holding Company Act, which regulated regional monopolies. The next year New York Edison combined its holdings to form the Consolidated Edison Company of New York (ConEd).

ConEd opened its first nuclear station in 1962. By this time, ConEd had a reputation with its customers for being inefficient and offering poor service, and shareholders were angry about its slow growth and low earnings. Environmentalists joined the grousers in 1963 when ConEd began constructing a pumped-storage plant in Cornwall near the Hudson River. Charles Luce, a former undersecretary with the Department of Interior, was recruited to rescue ConEd in 1967. He began adding new power plants and beefing up customer service.

In the 1970s inflation and the OPEC oil embargo drove up oil prices (ConEd's main energy source), and in 1974 Luce withheld dividends for the first time since 1885. He persuaded the New York State Power Authority to buy two unfinished power plants, saving the company about $200 million. Luce ended the Cornwall controversy in 1980 by halting construction of the pumped-storage plant and donating the land for park use. Luce retired in 1982.

The utility started buying power from various suppliers and in 1984 agreed to a two-year price freeze, a boon to rate-hike-weary New Yorkers. It wasn't until 1992 that the New York State Public Service Commission approved a rate increase.

In 1997 ConEd, government officials, consumer groups, and other energy companies outlined how ConEd would make the transition to competition. The Consolidated Edison holding company was formed at the beginning of 1998, and the next year it sold New York City generating facilities to KeySpan, Northern States Power, and Orion Power for a total of $1.65 billion. ConEd also agreed to buy Massachusetts' generating capacity from Northeast Utilities in 1999 for $47 million.

That year Consolidated Edison bought Orange and Rockland Utilities for $790 million to increase its New York base and expand into New Jersey and Pennsylvania.

Chairman, President, and CEO; Chairman and CEO, Consolidated Edison Company of New York:
Eugene R. McGrath, age 57, $1,459,750 pay
President and COO, Consolidated Edison Company of New York: J. Michael Evans, age 53,
$616,333 pay (prior to promotion)
EVP and CFO, Consolidated Edison, Inc., and Consolidated Edison Company of New York:
Joan S. Freilich, age 57, $439,053 pay
SVP and Executive Assistant to the Chairman:
Horace S. Webb, age 58
SVP and General Counsel, Consolidated Edison, Inc., and Consolidated Edison Company of New York:
John D. McMahon, age 47
EVP Central Services, Consolidated Edison Company of New York: Charles F. Soutar, age 62, $541,333 pay
SVP Central Operations, Consolidated Edison Company of New York: Stephen B. Bram, age 56, $417,333 pay
SVP Gas, Consolidated Edison Company of New York:
Mary Jane McCartney, age 50
SVP Nuclear Operations, Consolidated Edison Company of New York: Neil S. Carns, age 59
VP Employee Relations, Consolidated Edison Company of New York: Richard P. Cowie, age 52
Auditors: PricewaterhouseCoopers LLP

LOCATIONS

HQ: Consolidated Edison, Inc.,
4 Irving Place, New York, NY 10003
Phone: 212-460-4600   **Fax:** 212-982-7816
Web site: http://www.conedison.com

PRODUCTS/OPERATIONS

1998 Sales

	$ mil.	% of total
Electric operations	5,674	80
Gas	960	14
Steam	322	4
Other	137	2
Total	**7,093**	**100**

Subsidiaries
Consolidated Edison Communications, Inc.
Consolidated Edison Company of New York, Inc.
Consolidated Edison Development, Inc.
Consolidated Edison Energy, Inc.
Consolidated Edison Solutions, Inc.
Orange and Rockland Utilities, Inc.

COMPETITORS

Amerada Hess
Central Hudson Gas & Electric Corporation
Cinergy
CMS Energy
Conectiv
Duke Energy
Energy East
Enron
KeySpan Energy
New Century Energies
New York Power Authority
Niagara Mohawk
NUI
PG&E
PSEG
Reliant Energy
RGS Energy Group
Texas Utilities
UtiliCorp

HISTORICAL FINANCIALS & EMPLOYEES

NYSE symbol: ED FYE: December 31	Annual Growth	1989	1990	1991	1992	1993	1994	1995	1996	1997	1998
Sales ($ mil.)	2.8%	5,551	5,739	5,873	5,933	6,265	6,373	6,537	6,960	7,121	7,093
Net income ($ mil.)	2.1%	606	572	567	604	659	734	724	708	713	730
Income as % of sales	—	10.9%	10.0%	9.7%	10.2%	10.5%	11.5%	11.1%	10.2%	10.0%	10.3%
Earnings per share ($)	2.2%	2.49	2.34	2.32	2.46	2.66	2.98	2.93	2.93	2.95	3.04
Stock price - FY high ($)	—	29.88	29.25	28.75	32.88	37.75	32.38	32.25	34.75	41.50	56.13
Stock price - FY low ($)	—	22.19	19.75	22.50	25.00	30.25	23.00	25.50	25.88	27.00	39.06
Stock price - FY close ($)	6.8%	29.13	23.63	28.63	32.63	32.13	25.75	31.75	29.13	41.00	52.88
P/E - high	—	12	13	12	13	14	11	11	12	14	18
P/E - low	—	9	8	10	10	11	8	9	9	9	13
Dividends per share ($)	2.4%	1.72	1.82	1.86	1.90	1.94	2.00	2.04	2.08	2.10	2.12
Book value per share ($)	3.5%	19.21	19.73	20.18	20.89	21.66	22.63	23.51	24.37	25.18	26.18
Employees	(3.5%)	19,798	19,483	19,087	18,718	17,586	17,097	16,582	15,801	15,029	14,322

STOCK PRICE HISTORY

HIGH/LOW/CLOSE

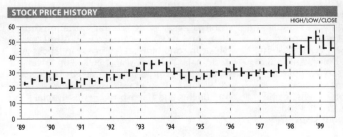

1998 FISCAL YEAR-END

Debt ratio: 39.4%
Return on equity: 12.1%
Cash ($ mil.): 102
Current ratio: 0.96
Long-term debt ($ mil.): 4,087
No. of shares (mil.): 230
Dividends
  Yield: 4.0%
  Payout: 69.7%
Market value ($ mil.): 12,172

CONSOLIDATED FREIGHTWAYS

OVERVIEW

Over the long haul, few trucking companies carry more less-than-truckload (LTL, shipments of less than 10,000 pounds) shipments than Consolidated Freightways. The company, based in Menlo Park, California, is the US's third-largest LTL trucking company, after Yellow Corp. and Roadway Express. It has more than 39,000 tractors, trailers, and other vehicles and more than 350 terminals in North America. Besides providing transport services throughout the US and to Canada and Mexico, the company offers freight services between the US and more than 80 other countries through agreements with ocean carriers and other partners.

Subsidiary Redwood Systems provides comprehensive logistics services, including warehousing, contract hauling, and inventory management; Leland James Service Corp. provides administrative services. Consolidated Freightway's Canadian trucking and warehousing subsidiaries include Canadian Freightways, Milne & Craighead, Canadian Sufferance Warehouses, and Epic Express.

Although it formerly operated on a hub-and-spoke system, Consolidated Freightways is increasingly routing its trucks directly between cities to improve productivity, and it is offering more time-definite air and ground services.

HISTORY

Leland James, co-owner of a Portland, Oregon, bus company, founded Consolidated Truck Lines in 1929. The company offered heavy hauling, moving, and other transportation services in the Pacific Northwest. Operations extended to San Francisco and Idaho by 1934 and to North Dakota by 1936. The company became Consolidated Freightways (CF) in 1939.

James formed Freightways Manufacturing that year, making CF the only trucking company to design and build its own trucks (Freightliners). Between 1940 and 1950, CF used acquisitions to extend service to Chicago, Minneapolis, and Los Angeles.

CF went public in 1951 and moved to Menlo Park, California, in 1956. More acquisitions (52 between 1955 and 1960) extended operations throughout the US and Canada. By 1959 CF was the largest common carrier in the US; it operated in 34 states and Canada and had $146 million in sales. When an attempt to coordinate intermodal services with railroads and shipping lines failed, CF ended the intermodal operations and focused on less-than-truckload (LTL) trucking.

In 1969 the company bought Pacific Far East Lines, a San Francisco shipping line. CF formed CF AirFreight in 1970 to ship air cargo in the US and Canada. It used the proceeds from the 1981 sale of Freightways Manufacturing to establish a regional trucking operation, Con-Way Transportation Services (1983). In 1989 the company bought Emery Air Freight, an international air cargo service, but Emery's losses dragged CF into the red.

CF invested $201 million in vehicle and technology improvements in 1993 and achieved its first profit in four years. CF

MotorFreight (CFMF), the long-haul division, cut expenses by closing 100 terminals during 1992-93.

In 1994 CFMF suffered the longest strike (18 working days) in its history; it had an operating loss of almost $47 million for the year, most of which was related to the Teamsters strike. CFMF continued to feel the effects of the labor stoppage in 1995 as it tried to woo back customers which had taken their business elsewhere during the strike. Hoping to get back on track, CF spent about $26 million to implement a new Business Accelerator System, which reorganized the way the unit handled shipments. In 1996 CFMF won a three-year, $25 million contract to serve as the primary LTL carrier for railroad company Burlington Northern Santa Fe.

That year CF spun off its long-haul businesses — including CFMF and the Canadian trucking and warehousing businesses, Canadian Freightways, Milne & Craighead, Canadian Sufferance Warehouses, and Epic Express — as Consolidated Freightways Corporation. CF (air freight and short-haul regional trucking lines) became CNF Transportation.

Consolidated Freightways established a logistics unit, Redwood Systems, in 1997. In 1998 the company launched two international alliances: one in Europe with Corneel Geerts International, a Swedish transportation company; and another in Mexico with Alfri Loder, a Mexican conglomerate, to invest in trucks and terminals. The next year it picked up drivers and delivery routes left stranded by bankrupt rival NationsWay, as well as NationsWay's hubs in Phoenix and Harrisburg, Pennsylvania.

OFFICERS

CEO: W. Roger Curry, age 60,
$711,121 pay (prior to title change)
President and COO: Patrick H. Blake, age 49,
$368,517 pay (prior to promotion)
EVP Sales and Marketing: Joseph R. Schillaci, age 56
SVP and CFO: Sunil Bhardwaj
SVP and Controller: Robert E. Wrightson, age 59,
$359,960 pay
SVP and General Counsel: Stephen D. Richards, age 55,
$313,784 pay
SVP Operations: Thomas A. Paulsen
VP and Chief Information Officer: Matt Saikkonen
VP Corporate Relations and Secretary: Maryla R. Fitch
VP Eastern Region: Patrick J. Brady
VP Maintenance and Purchasing: Tom C. Jarvi
VP National Sales: Thomas C. Gardner
VP National Sales: David A. Kramer
VP National Sales: William H. Mason
VP National Sales: Robert J. Morrey
VP Pricing Services: Robert H. Newell
VP Western Region: John Paiva
President, Canadian Freightways: Darshan S. Kailly
Director Human Resources: Wayne Bolio
Assistant Treasurer: Joy R. Arns
Auditors: Arthur Andersen LLP

LOCATIONS

HQ: Consolidated Freightways Corporation,
175 Linfield Dr., Menlo Park, CA 94025
Phone: 650-326-1700   **Fax:** 650-617-6700
Web site: http://www.cfwy.com

Consolidated Freightways provides less-than-truckload
service across North America and maintains air and
ocean container connections to more than 80 countries.

1998 Sales

	$ mil.	% of total
US	2,117	95
Canada	121	5
Total	**2,328**	**100**

PRODUCTS/OPERATIONS

Selected Services
Contract hauling
Inventory management
Less-than-truckload services
Logistics services
Warehousing

Selected Operations
Canadian Freightways
Canadian Sufferance Warehouses
Epic Express
Leland James Service Corp.
Milne & Craighead
Redwood Systems

COMPETITORS

American Freightways	Overnite Transportation
A-P-A Transport	Roadway Express
Arkansas Best	Ryder
FDX	Union Pacific
Hub Group	USFreightways
Motor Cargo Industries	Vitran
Nationsway Transport	Werner
Old Dominion Freight	Yellow Corporation
Line	

HISTORICAL FINANCIALS & EMPLOYEES

Nasdaq symbol: CFWY FYE: December 31	Annual Growth	1989	1990	1991	1992	1993	1994	1995	1996	1997	1998
Sales ($ mil.)	0.7%	—	—	2,132	2,155	2,074	1,936	2,107	2,146	2,299	2,238
Net income ($ mil.)	1.3%	—	—	24	(9)	20	(32)	(30)	(56)	20	26
Income as % of sales	—	—	—	1.1%	—	1.0%	—	—	—	0.9%	1.2%
Earnings per share ($)	—	—	—	—	—	—	—	—	(2.52)	0.89	1.12
Stock price - FY high ($)	—	—	—	—	—	—	—	—	9.13	18.50	19.75
Stock price - FY low ($)	—	—	—	—	—	—	—	—	6.00	7.00	7.50
Stock price - FY close ($)	33.7%	—	—	—	—	—	—	—	8.88	13.63	15.88
P/E - high	—	—	—	—	—	—	—	—	—	21	18
P/E - low	—	—	—	—	—	—	—	—	—	8	7
Dividends per share ($)	—	—	—	—	—	—	—	—	0.00	0.00	0.00
Book value per share ($)	11.1%	—	—	—	—	—	—	—	9.57	10.57	11.81
Employees	(1.4%)	—	—	23,200	23,200	22,100	22,000	20,200	20,300	21,600	21,000

STOCK PRICE HISTORY

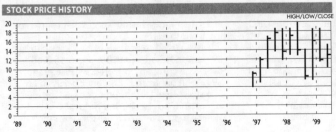

HIGH/LOW/CLOSE

1998 FISCAL YEAR-END

Debt ratio: 5.4%
Return on equity: 9.9%
Cash ($ mil.): 123
Current ratio: 1.33
Long-term debt ($ mil.): 15
No. of shares (mil.): 23
Dividends
  Yield: —
  Payout: —
Market value ($ mil.): 359

CONSOLIDATED NATURAL GAS

OVERVIEW

Consolidated Natural Gas (CNG) hopes that adding electricity to its energy mix will spark a business explosion. The Pittsburgh-based gas company has agreed to be acquired by electricity provider Dominion Resources to form integrated electricity and natural gas operations. The new company, which is taking Dominion's name, will tackle deregulated energy markets in the US.

CNG already serves 20,000 electric and 150,000 gas customers through its nonregulated arm, CNG Retail Services, but about half of the holding company's sales are generated by its four regulated gas utilities, which provide gas to 1.9 million customers in Ohio, Pennsylvania, Virginia, and West Virginia. The deal with Dominion is part of CEO

George Davidson's strategy to transform the company into a national one-stop energy services provider.

The company's gas roots reach beyond its distribution activities. CNG Transmission has 10,000 miles of pipeline in the northeastern, mid-Atlantic, and midwestern US; it also operates one of the largest underground natural gas storage systems in North America. CNG Producing explores for and produces gas and oil in the Gulf of Mexico and elsewhere in the US and Canada. It has proved reserves of 1.3 trillion cu. ft. of natural gas and 57.1 million barrels of oil. CNG International has holdings in electric and gas utilities in Argentina and owns part of a pipeline system in Australia.

HISTORY

Consolidated Natural Gas has its origins in John D. Rockefeller's Standard Oil Company and its US oil exploration efforts in the Northeast and Midwest. Standard subsidiary South Penn Oil accidentally discovered natural gas, and by the late 1890s Standard controlled natural gas fields in Ohio, Pennsylvania, and West Virginia (accounting for 80% of US production) and carried most of the nation's natural gas in its pipelines. With the idustrialization of America, natural gas use rose, and in 1898 Rockefeller organized the Hope Natural Gas Company to produce, gather, and transport gas from Standard's fields and the East Ohio Gas Company to distribute it.

The Sherman Antitrust Act broke up Standard's monopoly into 34 companies in 1911. One of these, Standard Oil Company (New Jersey), held Hope as well as East Ohio Gas, Peoples Natural Gas (Pittsburgh, founded 1885) and River Gas (Marietta, Ohio; 1894). In 1913 Hope designed the first commercial oil absorption plant to extract gasoline from natural gas, and in 1936 it constructed the first all-welded high-pressure gas pipeline. Hope and East Ohio Gas pioneered liquefied natural gas technology between 1937 and 1941.

In 1942 the gas companies and a New York pipeline (acquired in 1930) merged into CNG, a subsidiary of Standard Oil (New Jersey). After eight years of fighting the Public Utility Holding Company Act of 1935, which required diversified companies to shed their public utility subsidiaries, Standard spun off CNG to shareholders in 1943.

CNG added natural gas sources in the 1940s and 1950s, mainly in the Southwest,

and in 1957 it began drilling in the Gulf of Mexico. In 1975 it became the first gas utility to sell gas (and, later, storage) to neighboring utilities and pipelines.

In 1987 CNG veteran George Davidson became chairman and CEO; three years later CNG acquired Virginia Natural Gas. Deregulation in 1993 heated up competition in the natural gas industry, causing the firm to merge River Gas with East Ohio Gas in 1994.

CNG's first deepwater Gulf project produced gas in 1995. CNG allied with electric utility EnergyAustralia to develop cogeneration and gas projects in Asia and Australia, and in 1996 the firm formed CNG International to own 33% of Epic Energy, an Australian natural gas supplier, of which El Paso Energy also owned 33%.

In 1997 CNG signed a 10-year, $1 billion agreement (to begin in 2000) to supply electricity to Ormet Corporation's aluminum reduction plant and rolling mill in Ohio. It also received permission to sell electricity directly to residential and industrial customers in a pilot program in Pennsylvania.

In a competitive environment, wholesale margins in the natural gas business dried up. In 1998 the company sold CNG Energy Services, its money-losing wholesale gas marketing unit, to Sempra Energy.

CNG agreed to be bought by Virginia-based Dominion Resources in 1999 in a $6.3 billion deal. The company rejected a subsequent $9 billion bid from Columbia Energy in favor of a sweetened Dominion offer. CNG agreed to sell or spin off its Virginia Natural Gas subsidiary to gain approval for the Dominion deal.

OFFICERS

Chairman and CEO: George A. Davidson Jr., age 60, $689,700 pay
SVP and General Counsel: Stephen E. Williams, age 50, $275,967 pay
SVP, Nonregulated Business and CFO:
David M. Westfall, age 51, $331,867 pay
SVP, Organizational and Financial Performance:
Laura J. McKeown
SVP, Regulated Business: Ronald L. Adams, age 39, $422,600 pay
SVP, Technology and Implementation: William A. Fox
VP, Accounting and Financial Control:
Stephen R. McGreevy, age 48
VP, Human Resources: Anderson Haas
VP and Treasurer: Robert M. Sable Jr., age 47, $183,333 pay
President, Asset Operations: Jimmy D. Staton
President, CNG International: James S. Thomson
President, CNG Producing: H. Patrick Riley
President, Commercial Operations: Paul D. Koonce
Secretary: E. J. Marks III, age 35
Controller: Thomas F. Garbe, age 46
Auditors: PricewaterhouseCoopers LLP

LOCATIONS

HQ: CNG Tower, 625 Liberty Ave.,
Pittsburgh, PA 15222-3199
Phone: 412-690-1000 **Fax:** 412-690-1304
Web site: http://www.cng.com

Consolidated Natural Gas (CNG) distributes natural gas in Ohio, Pennsylvania, Virginia, and West Virginia. Subsidiary CNG Producing produces oil and gas in the US (mainly in the Appalachian Basin, the Gulf Coast region, and in the Gulf of Mexico) and Canada. CNG International has holdings in Argentina and Australia.

PRODUCTS/OPERATIONS

1998 Sales

	$ mil.	% of total
Regulated gas	1,374	50
Gas transportation & storage	546	20
Nonregulated gas	494	18
Other	346	12
Total	**2,760**	**100**

Selected Subsidiaries
Regulated Gas Utilities
The East Ohio Gas Company
Hope Gas, Inc.
The Peoples Natural Gas Company
Virginia Natural Gas, Inc.

Other Operations
CNG International Corporation
    Epic Energy Pipelines (33%, pipelines in Australia)
CNG Producing Company
CNG Research Company
CNG Retail Services Corporation
CNG Transmission Corporation

COMPETITORS

AEP	El Paso Energy
BP Amoco	Enron
Cabot Oil & Gas	Equitable Resources
Chevron	Exxon
Cinergy	Mobil
Coastal	Reliant Energy
Columbia Energy	Shell
Dominion Resources	Sonat
Duke Energy	Texaco
Dynegy	Williams Companies

HISTORICAL FINANCIALS & EMPLOYEES

NYSE symbol: CNG FYE: December 31	Annual Growth	1989	1990	1991	1992	1993	1994	1995	1996	1997	1998
Sales ($ mil.)	(0.2%)	2,802	2,715	2,607	2,521	3,184	3,036	3,307	3,794	5,710	2,760
Net income ($ mil.)	3.1%	182	164	169	195	206	183	21	298	304	239
Income as % of sales	—	6.5%	6.0%	6.5%	7.7%	6.5%	6.0%	0.6%	7.9%	5.3%	8.7%
Earnings per share ($)	1.4%	2.20	1.91	1.94	2.19	2.22	1.97	0.23	3.13	3.15	2.49
Stock price - FY high ($)	—	51.50	52.88	45.00	48.63	55.38	47.00	46.25	59.63	60.94	60.50
Stock price - FY low ($)	—	37.13	41.00	37.88	33.63	42.63	33.38	33.63	41.50	47.38	41.69
Stock price - FY close ($)	0.8%	50.38	44.00	43.00	45.50	47.00	35.50	45.38	55.25	60.50	54.00
P/E - high	—	23	28	23	22	25	24	201	19	19	24
P/E - low	—	17	21	20	15	19	17	146	13	15	17
Dividends per share ($)	1.1%	1.76	1.84	1.88	1.90	1.92	1.94	1.94	1.94	1.94	1.94
Book value per share ($)	2.4%	20.26	21.37	21.64	23.04	23.42	23.49	21.86	23.23	24.66	25.14
Employees	(1.8%)	7,357	7,753	7,726	7,615	7,625	7,566	6,600	6,426	6,412	6,224

STOCK PRICE HISTORY
HIGH/LOW/CLOSE

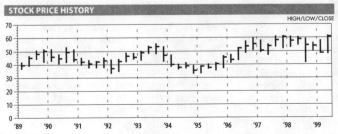

1998 FISCAL YEAR-END
Debt ratio: 36.5%
Return on equity: 10.0%
Cash ($ mil.): 138
Current ratio: 0.75
Long-term debt ($ mil.): 1,380
No. of shares (mil.): 95
Dividends
  Yield: 3.6%
  Payout: 77.9%
Market value ($ mil.): 5,154

CONSOLIDATED STORES

OVERVIEW

Consolidated Stores provides homes for the toys and other products that other retailers don't seem to want. The Columbus, Ohio-based holding company is the US's #1 closeout retailer, with about 1,200 closeout stores.

Consolidated runs four closeout retail chains — Big Lots, Odd Lots, Mac Frugal's, and Pic 'N' Save — in 40 southwestern, midwestern, southern, and mid-Atlantic states. Its merchandise includes name-brand and private-label housewares, electronics, foods, toiletries, tools, toys, and clothing. To stock the shelves of its stores, Consolidated buys truckloads of orphaned bric-a-brac (discontinued, overproduced, and outdated items) at steep discounts from stores and manufacturers.

The company is also the #2 toy store chain (after Toys "R" Us). It operates more than 1,330 toy stores under four toy store formats: K-B Toys in malls, K-B Toy Works in strip centers, K-B Toy Outlet in outlet malls, and K-B Toy Express in malls selling closeout toys during the Christmas season. Consolidated owns 80% of online toy retailer KBkids.com.

Another Consolidated closeout chain, Big Lots Furniture, is expanding quickly. Consolidated also operates a wholesale business, selling its discounted merchandise to a variety of retailers, manufacturers, distributors, and other wholesalers.

HISTORY

As a kid growing up in Columbus, Ohio, Russian-born Sol Shenk (pronounced "Shank") couldn't stand to pay full price for anything. His frugality blossomed into a knack for buying low and wholesaling. After a failed effort to make auto parts, Shenk began the precursor to Consolidated Stores in 1967, backed by brothers Alvin, Saul, and Jerome Schottenstein.

The company started by wholesaling closeout auto parts and buying retailers' closeout items to sell to other retailers. By 1971 Shenk had branched into retailing, selling closeout auto parts through a small chain of Corvair Auto Stores.

One of Shenk's sons suggested they devote space in the Corvair stores to closeout merchandise other than car parts. Sales surged, and Shenk decided to sell the Corvair outlets and focus on closeout stores. The first Odd Lots opened in 1982. (That year Shenk took a flier by buying 2,800 coupes from the bankrupt De Lorean car company at a price so low he was later sued by a court-appointed receiver, who sought to recover some of Shenk's profits.) Consolidated grew more than 100% annually for the next three years. By 1986, the year after it went public, the company was opening two stores a week in midsized markets around the Midwest.

Shenk found people would buy anything as long as the price was right. Two years after the mania for Rubik's Cubes had faded, Odd Lots bought 6 million of the puzzles (once retailed for $8) at eight cents apiece, marked them up 500%, and sold out the lot.

By 1987 the company had nearly 300 Odd Lots/Big Lots stores. But Consolidated's runaway growth had created massive inventory shortages and losses as disappointed customers stopped browsing the depleted outlets. The company was forced to stop relying on great deals in order to maintain stock at all times. Suppliers also complained that Consolidated was beginning to compete with retail outlets that sold the vendors' products at full price. The woes coincided with a falling-out with the Schottensteins. Shenk retired in 1989.

Apparel and electronics retail executive William Kelley was named chairman and CEO the next year. Kelley returned Consolidated to its closeout roots and concentrated on winning back the favor of suppliers. He used acquisitions through the early 1990s to boost sales and create new chains, such as All for One (discontinued in 1996), Toys Unlimited, and Toy Liquidators.

Consolidated doubled its size in 1996 with the $315 million purchase of struggling Kay-Bee Toys (renamed K-B Toys) and its more than 1,000 Kay-Bee toy stores from Melville Corp. Already operating about 100 closeout toy stores, Consolidated added more profitable closeout items to the K-B Toys selection.

The expansion continued with the 1998 purchase of top closeout competitor Mac Frugal's Bargains - Close-outs. (Mac Frugal's had nearly bought Consolidated in 1989 before Consolidated board members vetoed the deal.) The $1 billion acquisition of Mac Frugal's gave Consolidated another 326 western stores under the Pic 'N' Save and Mac Frugal's names.

In 1999 Consolidated combined its online toy sales operations with those of BrainPlay.com. to form KBkids.com.

Chairman, CEO, and President: William G. Kelley,
age 53, $935,000 pay
EVP, General Counsel, and Secretary: Albert J. Bell,
age 39, $375,000 pay
EVP and CFO: Michael J. Potter, age 37, $375,000 pay
EVP, Merchandising and Operations - Toy Division:
Salvatore Vasta
SVP, Store Operations: Patrick J. Barry
SVP, Human Resources: Brad A. Waite, age 41
VP, Market Research: Kevin A. Day
VP, Real Estate Administration: Kathleen R. Hupper
VP and Treasurer: James McGrady, age 48
VP and Controller: Mark Shapiro, age 39
VP, Strategic Planning and Investor Relations:
Michael J. Wagner
VP, Tax: L. Michael Watts
CEO and President, KB Toy Division:
Michael L. Glazer, age 51, $630,000 pay
**EVP, Merchandising and Sales Promotion - Closeout
Division:** Kent Larsson
EVP, Store Operations - Closeout Division:
Donald A. Mierzwa, age 48, $300,000 pay
Auditors: Deloitte & Touche LLP

LOCATIONS

HQ: Consolidated Stores Corporation
300 Phillipi Rd., Columbus, OH 43228-0512
Phone: 614-278-6800   **Fax:** 614-278-6676
Web site: http://www.cnstores.com

Consolidated Stores operates stores in all 50 states and
in Puerto Rico.

PRODUCTS/OPERATIONS

1999 Sales

	$ mil.	% of sales
Closeout stores	2,511	60
Toy stores	1,643	39
Other	40	1
Total	**4,194**	**100**

Stores
Big Lots
Big Lots Furniture
K-B Toys
K-B Toy Express
K-B Toy Outlet
K-B Toy Works
Mac Frugal's Bargains Close-outs
Odd Lots
Pic 'N' Save

COMPETITORS

99 CENTS Only	Kmart
Amazon.com	Liquidation World
Ames	Mazel Stores
Bill's Dollar Stores	One Price Clothing Stores
BJs Wholesale Club	Quality King
Bradlees	Ross Stores
Costco Companies	Salvation Army
Dayton Hudson	Sears
Dollar General	Service Merchandise
Dollar Tree	TJX
eToys	Toys "R" Us
Factory 2-U Stores	Tuesday Morning
Family Dollar Stores	Value City
Fred's	Variety Wholesalers
Goodwill	Wal-Mart
J. C. Penney	

HISTORICAL FINANCIALS & EMPLOYEES

NYSE symbol: CNS FYE: January 31	Annual Growth	1990	1991	1992	1993	1994	1995	1996	1997	1998	1999
Sales ($ mil.)	23.9%	609	679	772	929	1,055	1,279	1,512	2,648	4,055	4,194
Net income ($ mil.)	—	(7)	5	20	37	43	55	64	84	86	97
Income as % of sales	—	—	0.7%	2.6%	4.0%	4.1%	4.3%	4.3%	3.2%	2.1%	2.3%
Earnings per share ($)	—	(0.10)	0.06	0.28	0.50	0.73	0.92	0.78	1.17	0.77	0.86
Stock price - FY high ($)	—	5.36	3.68	8.88	12.00	14.24	12.80	16.40	28.32	50.00	46.13
Stock price - FY low ($)	—	1.36	1.20	2.24	6.40	9.04	7.36	10.08	12.80	25.80	15.50
Stock price - FY close ($)	32.1%	1.36	2.32	8.32	10.96	11.60	11.84	12.80	26.30	41.13	16.69
P/E - high	—	—	61	32	24	20	14	21	24	65	54
P/E - low	—	—	20	8	13	12	8	13	11	34	18
Dividends per share ($)	—	0.00	0.00	0.00	0.00	0.00	0.00	0.00	0.00	0.00	0.00
Book value per share ($)	20.3%	2.04	2.10	2.27	2.90	3.56	4.30	5.22	8.15	9.60	10.79
Employees	24.8%	7,926	7,926	16,518	16,000	16,399	19,699	21,633	38,000	50,324	58,254

STOCK PRICE HISTORY

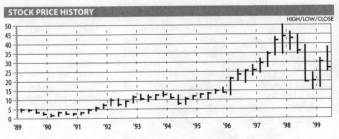

HIGH/LOW/CLOSE

1999 FISCAL YEAR-END

Debt ratio: 20.0%
Return on equity: 8.2%
Cash ($ mil.): 76
Current ratio: 2.90
Long-term debt ($ mil.): 296
No. of shares (mil.): 110
Dividends
  Yield: —
  Payout: —
Market value ($ mil.): 1,828

CONSTELLATION ENERGY GROUP

OVERVIEW

There's a new constellation in the wide open skies of the US power marketplace. Based in Baltimore, Maryland, Constellation Energy Group was created as a holding company in 1999 to separate its main subsidiary, regulated utility Baltimore Gas and Electric (BGE), from its nonutility businesses. BGE provides energy to more than 1.1 million electricity customers and almost 575,000 gas customers in Maryland; it accounts for about 80% of its parent's revenues. Coal and nuclear energy are the main fuels for BGE's 6,200 MW-generating capacity. To comply with Maryland's industry restructuring legislation (full-scale competition arrives in 2001), Constellation Energy is transferring BGE's power plants to an unregulated subsidiary; Constellation Power Source, a power marketer and trader, will sell the power wholesale.

As international power markets deregulate, the sky's the limit. Subsidiary Constellation Power is buying and developing independent power projects around the world. It has 29 projects in the US (including 15 plants in California) and 15 in Latin America. Constellation Energy has also teamed up with Goldman Sachs to form Orion Power, a venture that buys generation facilities in the US and Canada. Other nonutility operations include power plant management, real estate, and home products and services such as heating/cooling and plumbing installation.

HISTORY

In 1816, back when gas was manufactured out of tar, Rembrandt Peale (an artist and son of painter Charles Willson Peale), William Lorman, and three other partners formed the first gas utility in the US, Gas Light Company of Baltimore; Lorman was president until 1832. The firm soon ran out of money and successfully issued stock to raise capital.

Baltimore's growth outstripped the firm's gas-main capacity, and by 1860 it had a fierce rival in the People's Gas Light Co. In 1871 the two firms divided the city up and then fought a price war with yet another rival. Finally, the three merged as the Consolidated Gas Company of Baltimore City in 1880.

The next year the Brush Electric Light Company and the United States Electric Light and Power Company were established. In 1906 their descendants merged with Consolidated Gas to form the Consolidated Gas Electric Light and Power Co.

As demand for electricity grew, the company began to turn from hydroelectric power to steam generators in the 1920s. Its revenues increased despite the Depression, and it later set records producing gas and electricity during WWII. Despite a postwar boom in sales, earnings fell as Consolidated spent money on new plants, shifting to natural gas, and converting downtown Baltimore from DC to AC.

In 1955 Consolidated changed its name to Baltimore Gas and Electric Company (BGE). BGE announced plans in 1967 for Maryland's first nuclear power plant. Calvert Cliffs Unit 1 went on line in 1975; Unit 2 followed in 1997.

BGE began making additions to the Safe Harbor Hydroelectric Project in 1981. Over the next two years it sought to form a holding company in order to diversify, but state regulators rejected the request in 1983. Undaunted, the firm formed subsidiary Constellation Holdings in 1985 and began investing in nonutility businesses and pursuing independent power projects.

Both Calvert Cliffs nukes were shut down in 1989-90 for repairs, and BGE had to spend $458 million to replace power that the units would have produced.

The Energy Policy Act fundamentally changed the electric utility industry in 1992. Allowing wholesale power competition in monopoly territories, it set the stage for open power markets. In response BGE began aggressively expanding its gas division, and three years later it ventured into Latin America, taking a stake in a Bolivian power firm.

BGE also planned to get bigger in 1995 by merging with Potomac Electric Power Company (PEPCO). However, state and federal regulators insisted on rate caps and reductions, leading BGE and PEPCO to conclude in 1997 that the merger wasn't worth the trouble.

The company formed its power marketing arm that year with Goldman Sachs as its adviser. In 1998 BGE continued to work with Goldman Sachs, forming a joint venture, Orion Power Holdings, to buy electric plants in the US and Canada. In 1999 Orion bought hydro plants from Niagara Mohawk, three New York City power plants from ConEd, and a power plant from U.S. Generating.

That year Maryland passed legislation to introduce competition into its power markets, and Constellation Energy Group was formed in 1999 as the holding company for BGE and its nonregulated subsidiaries.

Chairman, President and CEO, Constellation Energy Group and Baltimore Gas and Electric:
Christian H. Poindexter, age 60,
$816,959 pay (prior to title change)
VC, Constellation Energy Group and Baltimore Gas and Electric; Chairman, President, and CEO, Constellation Enterprises: Edward A. Crooke, age 60,
$565,639 pay (prior to title change)
EVP, Generation, Baltimore Gas and Electric:
Robert E. Denton, age 56, $337,716 pay
EVP, Utility Operations, Baltimore Gas and Electric:
Frank O. Heintz, age 55, $313,955 pay
VP, Corporate Strategy and Development, Constellation Energy Group and Baltimore Gas and Electric:
Thomas F. Brady, age 49
VP, Corporate Affairs and General Counsel, Constellation Energy Group and Baltimore Gas and Electric: Robert S. Fleishman, age 45
VP, Finance and Accounting, CFO, and Secretary, Constellation Energy Group and Baltimore Gas and Electric: David A. Brune, age 57
VP, General Services, Baltimore Gas and Electric:
Gregory C. Martin, age 50
VP, Human Resources, Constellation Energy Group and Baltimore Gas and Electric: Linda D. Miller, age 48
Chairman, President, and CEO, Constellation Power Source: Charles W. Shivery, age 53, $607,007 pay
Treasurer and Assistant Secretary:
Thomas E. Ruszin Jr., age 43
Auditors: Mitchell & Titus LLP

HQ: Constellation Energy Group, Inc.,
39 W. Lexington St., Baltimore, MD 21201
Phone: 410-234-5678   **Fax:** 410-234-5220
Web site: http://www.constellationgroup.com

1998 Revenues

	$ mil.	% of total
Electric	2,219	66
Gas	449	13
Diversified businesses	690	21
Total	**3,358**	**100**

Selected Subsidiaries
Baltimore Gas and Electic Company (BGE, gas and electric utility)
BGE Home Products & Services, Inc. (HVAC and plumbing, appliances, home improvements)
Constellation Enterprises, Inc.
Constellation Power, Inc. (power generation projects in the US and Latin America)
Constellation Power Source, Inc. (wholesale power marketing and risk-management services)
Orion Power Holdings, Inc. (joint venture with Goldman Sachs, power generation acquisition in Canada and the US)

AEP	GPU
Allegheny Energy	Peabody Group
Avista	PEPCO
Chesapeake Utilities	PG&E
Columbia Energy	PP&L Resources
Conectiv	PSEG
Dominion Resources	Reliant Energy
Duke Energy	Sempra Energy
Dynegy	Southern Company
Enron	UtiliCorp
Entergy	Williams Companies

NYSE symbol: CEG FYE: December 31	Annual Growth	1989	1990	1991	1992	1993	1994	1995	1996	1997	1998
Sales ($ mil.)	5.9%	2,004	2,159	2,460	2,491	2,669	2,783	2,935	3,153	3,308	3,358
Net income ($ mil.)	1.9%	276	213	234	264	310	324	338	311	283	328
Income as % of sales	—	13.8%	9.9%	9.5%	10.6%	11.6%	11.6%	11.5%	9.9%	8.6%	9.8%
Earnings per share ($)	0.2%	2.03	1.55	1.52	1.63	1.85	1.93	2.02	1.85	1.72	2.06
Stock price - FY high ($)	—	23.26	23.09	22.84	24.38	27.50	25.50	29.00	29.50	34.31	35.25
Stock price - FY low ($)	—	19.01	16.26	17.18	19.76	22.38	20.50	22.00	25.00	24.75	29.25
Stock price - FY close ($)	3.3%	23.01	18.68	22.84	23.38	25.38	22.13	28.50	26.75	34.13	30.88
P/E - high	—	11	15	15	15	15	13	14	16	20	17
P/E - low	—	9	10	11	12	12	11	11	14	14	14
Dividends per share ($)	2.2%	1.37	1.40	1.40	1.42	1.46	1.50	1.54	1.58	1.62	1.66
Book value per share ($)	2.1%	16.61	16.59	17.01	17.63	17.94	18.42	19.07	19.35	19.44	19.98
Employees	0.4%	9,103	9,295	9,626	9,265	10,018	9,000	9,379	7,032	9,000	9,400

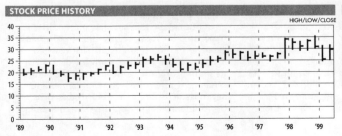

HIGH/LOW/CLOSE

Debt ratio: 49.7%
Return on equity: 11.0%
Cash ($ mil.): 174
Current ratio: 1.01
Long-term debt ($ mil.): 3,128
No. of shares (mil.): 149
Dividends
  Yield: 5.4%
  Payout: 80.6%
Market value ($ mil.): 4,609

CONTIGROUP COMPANIES, INC.

OVERVIEW

Talk about going against the grain. New York City-based ContiGroup Companies (CGC, formerly Continental Grain) has gotten out of the business in which it literally made its name. CGC was once the US's #2 grain exporter, but grain accounted for only one-fourth of the company's income before its commodities marketing business was bought in 1999 by Cargill.

CGC's largest business is ContiAgriIndustries, the world's #1 cattle feeder and one of the top pork and poultry producers in the US.

It also has interests in flour milling and animal feed and nutrition. CGC owns about 78% of publicly traded ContiFinancial, a consumer and commercial finance company specializing in home equity loans. CGC's investment arm, ContiInvestments, has interests in real estate, shipping, fund management, and natural resources.

Chairman emeritus Michel Fribourg (the great-great-grandson of ContiGroup's founder) and his family own the company.

HISTORY

Simon Fribourg founded a commodity trading business in Belgium in 1813. It operated there until 1848, when a drought in Belgium forced it to buy large stocks in Russian wheat.

As the Industrial Revolution swept across Europe and populations shifted to cities, people consumed more traded grain. In the midst of such rapid changes, the company prospered.

After WWI, Russia, which had been Europe's primary grain supplier, ceased to be a major player in the trading game, and Western countries picked up the slack. Sensing the shift, Jules and Rene Fribourg reorganized the business as Continental Grain and opened its first US office in Chicago in 1921.

Throughout the Depression the company bought US grain elevators wherever it could find them, often at low prices. Through its purchases, Continental Grain built a North American grain network that included major locations like Kansas City, Missouri; Nashville, Tennessee; and Toledo, Ohio.

In Europe, meanwhile, the Fribourgs were forced to endure constant political and economic upheaval, often profiting from it (they supplied food to Republican forces during the Spanish Civil War). When Nazis invaded Belgium in 1940, the Fribourgs were forced to flee, but after the war they reorganized the business in New York City.

After the war, Continental Grain pioneered US grain trade with the Soviets. The company went on a buying spree in the 1960s and 1970s, acquiring Allied Mills (feed milling, 1965) and absorbing many agricultural and transport businesses, including Texas feedlots and the Quaker Oats agricultural products unit.

During the 1980s Continental Grain sold its baking units (Oroweat and Arnold) and its commodities brokerage house and, amid an agricultural bust, formed ContiFinancial and other financial units.

Michel Fribourg stepped down as CEO in 1988 and was succeeded by Donald Staheli, the first non-family-member CEO. Soon after, Continental Grain realigned its international grain and oilseeds operations into the World Grain and Oilseeds Processing Group under the leadership of Michel's son Paul. The company entered a grain-handling and selling joint venture with Scoular in 1991. Three years later Staheli added the title of chairman, and Paul Fribourg became president. Continental Grain sold a stake in ContiFinancial (its most profitable business, including home equity loans and investment banking) to the public in 1996. Also in 1996 the firm formed ContiInvestments, an investment arm geared toward the parent company's areas of expertise.

That year Continental Grain and an overseas affiliate (Arab Finagrain) agreed to pay the US government $35 million, which included a $10 million fine against Arab Finagrain, to settle a fraud case involving commodity sales to Iraq.

Paul Fribourg succeeded Staheli as CEO in 1997. The company bought Campbell Soup's poultry processing units that year, and in 1998 it bought a 51% stake in pork producer/processor Premium Standard Farms, adding those operations (Texas and Missouri) to its own Missouri swine production business. Meanwhile, ContiFinancial diversified into retail home mortgage and home equity lending, among other areas.

Continental Grain sold its commodities marketing business in July 1999 to #1 grain exporter Cargill, though antitrust restrictions excluded seven facilities from the deal. With its grain operations gone, in 1999 the company renamed itself ContiGroup Companies and began to focus on its ContiAgriIndustries, ContiFinancial, and ContiInvestments units.

Chairman Emeritus: Michel Fribourg, age 82
Chairman and CEO: Paul J. Fribourg

LOCATIONS

HQ: ContiGroup Companies, Inc.,
277 Park Ave., New York, NY 10172-0002
Phone: 212-207-5100   **Fax:** 212-207-2910
Web site: http://www.contigroup.com

ContiGroup Companies operates in about 60 countries.

PRODUCTS/OPERATIONS

Selected Subsidiaries and Affiliates

Commodity Marketing Group
Astral International Shipping (shipping agents,
New Orleans)
ContiCarriers & Terminals (transport, Chicago)
ContiChem (liquefied petroleum gases; Norwalk, CT)
ContiCotton (cotton merchandising, Memphis)
ContiLatin (Latin American trading unit, New York)
Continental Grain Canada (Vancouver)
ContiQuincy Bunge Export (soybean merchandising
partnership with Quincy Soybean, New York)
ContiTec Engineering (grain processing consulting)
Finagrain (European trading unit, Geneva)
North American Grain Division (Chicago)
Rice Division (rice trading, New York)
Stellar Chartering and Brokerage
(ocean vessels, Chicago)
Wayne Farms (poultry, swine operations)

ContiFinancial Corporation (75%)
ContiFinancial Services (New York)
ContiLeasing (Voorhees, NJ)
ContiMortgage Corp. (Horsham, PA)
ContiTrade Services (New York)

Meat Group
Cattle Feeding Division (Boulder, CO)
Pork Division (Chicago)
Premium Standard Farms (51%; Princeton, MO)
Poultry Division (Gainesville, GA)
Dutch Quality House

Milling Group
Allied Mills/Wayne Feed (Chicago)
Asian Industries (Hong Kong)

COMPETITORS

ADM
Ag Processing
Agribrands International, Inc.
The Associates
Cactus Feeders
Cargill
Cenex Harvest States
ConAgra
Farmland Industries
Gold Kist
Household International
IBP
IMC Mortgage
Pilgrim's Pride
Purina Mills
Smithfield Foods
Tyson Foods

HISTORICAL FINANCIALS & EMPLOYEES

Private company FYE: March 31	Annual Growth	1990	1991	1992	1993	1994	1995	1996	1997	1998	1999
Estimated sales ($ mil.)	0.1%	14,850	15,000	15,000	15,000	15,000	14,000	15,000	16,000	15,000	15,000
Employees	2.1%	14,500	14,500	14,750	14,700	15,500	16,000	16,000	16,800	17,500	17,500

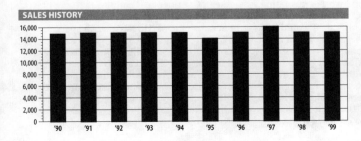

SALES HISTORY

ContiGroup
COMPANIES, INC.

CONTINENTAL AIRLINES, INC.

OVERVIEW

Not so long ago, a bankrupt Continental Airlines was singing for its supper. Now, a revitalized Continental is eating the breakfasts and lunches of its competitors. One of the top 10 US carriers, Houston-based Continental offers more than 2,200 flights to about 130 domestic and 80 international destinations. Continental's hubs are in Cleveland, Houston, Los Angeles, and Newark, New Jersey, and its Continental Micronesia division serves the western Pacific through a hub in Guam. Regional air carrier Continental Express offers more than 900 daily departures to about 80 US cities from Cleveland, Houston, and Newark. Continental also has an 8% stake in regional airline America West, and it owns part of Amadeus, one of the world's largest computerized reservation systems.

CEO Gordon Bethune has helped steer a turnaround at Continental. The carrier is courting business travelers, upgrading and expanding its fleet, reinforcing service at its US hubs, and expanding into markets such as Latin America and Asia through alliances. Continental shares codes with airlines such as Air France, Alitalia, Air China, and Virgin to overseas destinations.

Continental vastly expanded its reach via a code-sharing deal with #4 US carrier Northwest Airlines. As part of the deal, Northwest acquired a 13.5% stake in Continental and 46% of its voting stock. Northwest, Continental, and KLM Royal Dutch Airlines are members of the global Wings alliance.

HISTORY

Varney Speed Lines, the fourth airline begun by Walter Varney, was founded in 1934. It became Continental Airlines three years later when Robert Six, whose own airline had folded during the Depression, bought 40% of the carrier. Six convinced his father-in-law, chairman of drugmaker Charles Pfizer Co., to lend him $90,000 for the stake in Varney.

In 1951 Continental spent $7.6 million to update its fleet, a sum equal to its profit that year. It was a bold move for a small airline in an industry moving toward ever-larger aircraft. Two years later Continental merged with Pioneer Airlines, adding routes to 16 cities in Texas and New Mexico. It also added jets in the late 1950s to compete on cross-country routes. To maintain its small Boeing 707 fleet, Continental developed a maintenance system that enabled it to fly the planes 15 hours a day, seven days a week.

In 1962 the carrier suffered its first crash. The next year it moved its headquarters from Denver to Los Angeles. A transport service contract with the US military during the Vietnam War led to the formation of Air Micronesia in 1968.

Economic downturn, industry deregulation, and rising fuel costs left Continental with a string of losses in the late 1970s (it would lose more than $500 million between 1978 and 1983). Over the objections of Continental's unions, Frank Lorenzo's Texas Air bought the company in 1982. Texas Air had been founded in 1947 to provide service within Texas, and by 1970 it also flew to the West Coast and Mexico. Bankrupt two years later, the company was acquired by Lorenzo, who returned it to

profitability by 1976 — just in time for airline deregulation in 1978.

When Continental's union employees went on strike in 1983, Lorenzo maneuvered the airline into Chapter 11. Continental emerged from bankruptcy in 1986 as a low-fare carrier with the industry's lowest labor costs. That year Texas Air bought Eastern Airlines (founded as Pitcairn Aviation in 1927 and run for a time by WWI ace Eddie Rickenbacker), People Express Airlines, and Frontier Airlines.

In 1990 Lorenzo resigned as head of the company after selling most of his Continental investments. Texas Air changed its name to Continental Airlines Holdings. With fuel prices soaring because of the Mideast conflict, Continental again filed for bankruptcy. Gordon Bethune became CEO in 1994 and piloted Continental to a comeback with an investment by Air Partners/Air Canada and a reduction in routes and staff.

In 1997 Bethune's honeymoon with employees ended as the pilots union negotiated for an accelerated pay-raise schedule; a five-year contract was ratified in 1998. That year Northwest Airlines agreed to pay $519 million for a 14% stake in Continental, beating a takeover bid from Delta. Although Northwest became mired in labor problems, threatening the pact, it ended up paying $370 million for 13.5% of Continental. Meanwhile Continental bought 20 Boeing aircraft and acquired stakes in airlines in Colombia and Panama.

The next year Continental announced that it would launch service to Tel Aviv, its first route to the Middle East.

Chairman and CEO: Gordon M. Bethune, age 57, $2,146,500 pay
President and COO: Gregory D. Brenneman, age 37, $1,605,260 pay
EVP and CFO: Lawrence W. Kellner, age 40, $1,103,400 pay
EVP Operations: C. D. McLean, age 57, $1,001,852 pay
EVP, General Counsel, and Secretary: Jeffery A. Smisek, age 44, $944,496 pay
SVP Human Resources and Labor Relations: Michael H. Campbell, age 50
SVP Airport Services: Mark A. Erwin, age 43
SVP Corporate Development: J. David Grizzle, age 44
SVP Technical Operations: George L. Mason, age 52
SVP Asia: James B. Ream, age 43
SVP Sales and Distribution: Bonnie S. Reitz, age 46
SVP International: Barry P. Simon, age 56
SVP Purchasing and Materials Services: Kuniaki Tsuruta, age 63
SVP and Chief Information Officer: Janet P. Wejman, age 41
President Continental Express: David N. Seigel
Auditors: Ernst & Young LLP

LOCATIONS

HQ: 1600 Smith St., Dept. HQSEO, Houston, TX 77002
Phone: 713-324-5000   **Fax:** 713-324-6155
Web site: http://www.continental.com

Continental Airlines has hubs in Cleveland, Houston, Los Angeles, and Newark, New Jersey and in Guam.

1998 Sales

	$ mil.	% of total
US	5,620	71
Atlantic	995	12
Latin America	769	10
Pacific	567	7
Total	**7,951**	**100**

PRODUCTS/OPERATIONS

1998 Sales

	$ mil.	% of total
Passenger	7,366	93
Cargo	275	3
Mail & other	310	4
Total	**7,951**	**100**

Major Subsidiaries
Continental Express (regional airline)
Continental Micronesia, Inc. (air service in the Pacific)

COMPETITORS

Air Canada	Lufthansa
AirTran Holdings	Northwest Airlines
Alitalia	Qantas
All Nippon Airways	SAirGroup
AMR	SAS
British Airways	Singapore Airlines
Cathay Pacific	Southwest Airlines
Delta	TWA
JAL	UAL
KLM	US Airways

HISTORICAL FINANCIALS & EMPLOYEES

NYSE symbol: CAL FYE: December 31	Annual Growth	1989	1990	1991	1992	1993	1994	1995	1996	1997	1998
Sales ($ mil.)	2.0%	6,650	6,184	5,487	5,575	3,907	5,670	5,825	6,360	7,213	7,951
Net income ($ mil.)	—	(908)	(2,403)	(306)	(125)	(39)	(613)	215	319	385	383
Income as % of sales	—	—	—	—	—	—	—	3.7%	5.0%	5.3%	4.8%
Earnings per share ($)	—	—	—	—	—	(1.17)	(11.88)	3.37	4.17	4.99	5.02
Stock price - FY high ($)	—	—	—	—	—	15.25	13.63	23.75	31.44	50.19	65.13
Stock price - FY low ($)	—	—	—	—	—	6.50	3.75	3.25	19.44	27.00	28.88
Stock price - FY close ($)	26.7%	—	—	—	—	10.25	4.63	21.75	28.25	48.13	33.50
P/E - high	—	—	—	—	—	—	—	7	8	10	13
P/E - low	—	—	—	—	—	—	—	1	5	5	6
Dividends per share ($)	—	—	—	—	—	0.00	0.00	0.00	0.00	0.00	0.00
Book value per share ($)	30.1%	—	—	—	—	4.97	1.94	5.51	10.15	15.55	18.53
Employees	3.8%	31,400	34,800	36,300	38,300	43,100	37,800	32,300	35,400	39,300	43,900

STOCK PRICE HISTORY

HIGH/LOW/CLOSE

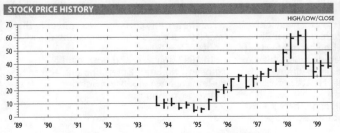

1998 FISCAL YEAR-END

Debt ratio: 65.5%
Return on equity: 32.1%
Cash ($ mil.): 1,399
Current ratio: 0.96
Long-term debt ($ mil.): 2,480
No. of shares (mil.): 64
Dividends
  Yield: —
  Payout: —
Market value ($ mil.): 2,157

CONVERSE INC.

OVERVIEW

As Converse has shown, even teams full of All Stars can find themselves in a slump. The North Reading, Massachusetts-based maker of athletic and leisure footwear — including the classic Chuck Taylor All Star canvas basketball sneaker — has been struggling with an industrywide downturn in demand for traditional athletic shoes.

Basketball shoes have taken the biggest hit. While Converse continues to make technological strides in the segment, it is increasingly interested in other categories: athletic originals (Chuck Taylors, casual shoes), children's shoes (including a line featuring Koosh characters licensed from OddzOn), and action sports (footwear for skateboarding, climbing, and mountain biking). It has introduced helium cushioning in its basketball and skating lines.

Converse's products are sold through about 9,000 athletic specialty, sporting goods, department, and shoe stores. The company itself operates about 30 retail outlets, and Converse also licenses its name to other companies for sports apparel and accessories.

Leon Black's Apollo Investment Fund owns 65% of the firm.

HISTORY

With a capital investment of $250,000, in 1908 Marquis Converse established the Converse Rubber Co. in Malden, Massachusetts, with 15 employees. The company got its big break shortly after its Converse canvas All Star shoe was launched in 1917. The shoe was chosen by young basketball star Chuck Taylor as his favorite basketball sneaker. Taylor joined the Converse sales team in 1921 and — in one of the first examples of sports endorsement — peddled the shoes at basketball clinics he hosted at schools and colleges. In 1923 Taylor's signature was added to the brand.

Converse fell into bankruptcy in 1929 and was acquired by Hodgman Rubber. The Depression and reduced profits led to another takeover in 1933, when the Stone family of Boston began its lucrative 39-year period of ownership. WWII provided a boost to the firm as it supplied the US military with protective footwear, parkas, and other equipment.

The company expanded after WWII, establishing plants in New Hampshire (1946) and a subsidiary in Puerto Rico (1953), then acquiring Tyler Rubber Co. (1961) and the Hodgman line of sporting goods (1964). Taylor retired from Converse in 1968. By the early 1970s the company had diversified into products ranging from hockey pucks to teethguards to industrial boots.

In 1972 Converse was acquired by Eltra, which made electrical and typesetting equipment. Within a year Converse expanded with the purchase of B.F. Goodrich's footwear division. The Goodrich acquisition brought with it the Jack Purcell brand of tennis shoe, which had been named for a Canadian badminton star and introduced in 1935. However, the high-performance leather athletic shoes introduced in the 1970s by NIKE and others proved immensely popular and put intense competitive pressure on Converse's canvas product. The company's sales sank.

Eltra was acquired by conglomerate Allied Corp. in 1979. Converse executives led a buyout of the division in 1982 before taking it public in 1983. The rise of the retro look in fashion starting in the mid-1980s made the old Chuck Taylor sneaker (and the Jack Purcell, to a lesser extent) hot with models, film stars, and the fashion-conscious.

Furniture, footwear, and apparel firm INTERCO added Converse to its list of assets in 1986. After being financially overstretched in fighting off a 1988 hostile takeover by the Rales brothers of Washington, DC, INTERCO filed for bankruptcy in 1991 — one of the largest bankruptcy cases in US history.

As part of INTERCO's reorganization, Converse emerged in 1994 as a public company controlled by financial adviser Leon Black. The next year it dumped its outdoor, running, walking, tennis, and football lines. Converse, hurt particularly by weak sales of basketball sneakers and restructuring charges, posted losses and saw its revenues fall in 1995 and 1996.

Sporting goods veteran Glenn Rupp was hired as chairman and CEO in 1996. Converse had record sales in 1997, but still finished in the red, due in part to a slowdown in retail demand in the last half of the year. The company laid off 5% of its workforce in 1998. It also entered the action sports footwear category that year ("for athletes who enjoy testing their limits of fear").

In 1999 Converse and rap mogul Master P's company, No Limit Entertainment, agreed to co-brand a line of footwear, starting with the Converse All Star Smooth.

Chairman and CEO: Glenn N. Rupp, age 54,
$500,000 pay
SVP and CFO: Donald J. Camacho, age 48
SVP, Research, Design, and Development:
Edward C. Frederick, age 52, $252,885 pay
SVP, Administration, General Counsel, and Secretary:
Jack A. Green, age 53, $197,227 pay
SVP, Production: Herbert R. Rothstein, age 57
SVP, Sales and Marketing: James E. Solomon, age 43,
$295,192 pay
SVP, International: Alistair Thorburn, age 41,
$235,000 pay
VP, Finance and Treasurer: James E. Lawlor
Auditors: PricewaterhouseCoopers LLP

LOCATIONS

HQ: 1 Fordham Rd., North Reading, MA 01864
Phone: 978-664-1100   **Fax:** 978-664-7472
Web site: http://www.converse.com

Converse distributes its products in 90 countries
through 9,000 athletic specialty, sporting goods,
department, and shoe stores and in about 30 company-
owned retail outlet stores.

1998 Sales

	$ mil.	% of total
US	166.6	54
Other countries	141.8	46
Total	**308.4**	**100**

PRODUCTS/OPERATIONS

Product Lines and Selected Brand Names
Action Sports (ECO system footwear for skateboarding,
adventure running, mountain biking, and climbing)
Athletic Originals (Chuck Taylor All Star and Jack
Purcell casual footwear)
Basketball (All Star high-performance footwear)
Children's (licensed Koosh footwear)
Cross-training (All Star high-performance footwear)

COMPETITORS

adidas-Salomon
Deckers Outdoor
Fila
K-Swiss
New Balance
NIKE
Puma
R. Griggs
Reebok
Skechers U.S.A.
Stride Rite
Timberland
Vans

HISTORICAL FINANCIALS & EMPLOYEES

NYSE symbol: CVE FYE: December 31	Annual Growth	1989	1990	1991	1992	1993	1994	1995	1996	1997	1998
Sales ($ mil.)	0.7%	—	292	289	316	380	437	408	349	450	308
Net income ($ mil.)	—	—	—	(30)	(11)	12	18	(72)	(18)	(5)	(23)
Income as % of sales	—	—	—	—	—	3.2%	4.0%	—	—	—	—
Earnings per share ($)	—	—	—	—	—	—	0.96	(4.30)	(1.10)	(0.29)	(1.32)
Stock price - FY high ($)	—	—	—	—	—	—	12.63	11.75	17.38	28.00	8.31
Stock price - FY low ($)	—	—	—	—	—	—	9.25	3.50	3.88	5.56	1.75
Stock price - FY close ($)	(33.1%)	—	—	—	—	—	11.88	4.13	17.00	6.00	2.38
P/E - high	—	—	—	—	—	—	13	—	—	—	—
P/E - low	—	—	—	—	—	—	10	—	—	—	—
Dividends per share ($)	—	—	—	—	—	—	0.00	0.00	0.00	0.00	0.00
Book value per share ($)	—	—	—	—	—	—	2.70	(1.36)	(2.33)	(2.77)	(4.00)
Employees	(2.7%)	—	—	—	—	3,042	3,053	2,459	2,249	2,956	2,658

STOCK PRICE HISTORY

HIGH/LOW/CLOSE

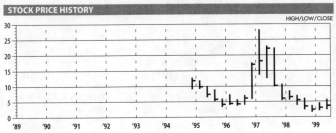

1998 FISCAL YEAR-END

Debt ratio: 100.0%
Return on equity: —
Cash ($ mil.): 3
Current ratio: 1.05
Long-term debt ($ mil.): 102
No. of shares (mil.): 17
Dividends
  Yield: —
  Payout: —
Market value ($ mil.): 41

COOPER INDUSTRIES, INC.

OVERVIEW

Cooper Industries can light up your life. The Houston-based company's electrical division (about 75% of sales) makes construction and lighting equipment for industrial and consumer use. Products include Arrow Hart wiring devices, Buss fuses, Crouse-Hinds electrical fixtures, and Metalux fluorescent lighting. The tools and hardware division's stock includes Apex sockets, Crescent wrenches, Plumb hammers, and Weller soldering equipment.

A global player, the company operates more than 90 plants in 19 countries. Cooper has shed its stalled automotive business to improve profitability and help pay for an acquisition spree in its tools and lighting divisions.

HISTORY

In 1833 Charles Cooper sold a horse for $50 and borrowed additional money to open a foundry with his brother Elias in Mount Vernon, Ohio. Known as C. & E. Cooper, the company made plows, hog troughs, maple syrup kettles, stoves, and wagon boxes.

C. & E. Cooper began making steam engines in the 1840s for use in mills and on farms; it later adapted the engines for wood-burning locomotives. In 1868 the company built its first Corliss steam engine and in 1875 it introduced the first steam-powered farm tractor. By 1900 its steam engines were sold in the US and overseas. The company debuted an internal combustion engine-compressor in 1909 for natural gas pipelines.

In the 1920s the company became the #1 seller of compression engines for oil and gas pipelines. A 1929 merger with Bessemer (small gas and diesel engines) created Cooper-Bessemer, whose diesel engines powered boats.

Diversification began in 1959 with the purchase of Rotor Tools. Cooper adopted its current name in 1965 and moved its headquarters to Houston in 1967. It went on to buy 20 other firms, including Lufkin Rule (measuring tapes, 1967), Crescent (wrenches, 1968), and Weller (soldering tools, 1970).

The 1979 purchase of Gardner-Denver gave Cooper a strong footing in oil-drilling and mining equipment, and the 1981 buy of Crouse-Hinds was a key diversification into electrical materials. The decline in oil prices in the early 1980s caused sales to drop more than 35% between 1981 and 1983, but Cooper stayed profitable because of its tools and electrical products.

Its electrical segment grew with the 1985 purchase of McGraw-Edison, maker of consumer products (Buss fuses) and heavy transmission gear for electrical utilities. Cooper grew further by buying RTE (electrical equipment, 1988), Cameron Iron Works (oil-drilling equipment, 1989), and Ferramentas Belzer do Brasil (hand-tool maker, 1992).

Expanding into automotive parts, Cooper bought Champion Spark Plug (1989) and Moog (auto replacement parts, 1992). From 1991 to 1993, the company divested 11 businesses and bought 13 complementary lines. Cooper sold Belden Inc. (electrical wires and cables) in 1993 and made five product-line acquisitions, including Hawker Fusegear of the UK (electrical fuses), Triangle Tool Group (hand tools), and Fail-Safe Lighting Systems (security lighting). In 1994 the company spun off Gardner-Denver Industrial Machinery, sold Cameron Forged Products, and added Abex Friction Products (brake materials) and Zanxx (lighting components) to its auto parts line.

In 1995 Cooper spun off Cooper Cameron (petroleum equipment) and the next year boosted its automotive segment with the purchase of Blazer International. Also in 1996 Cooper bought electrical fuse supplier Karp Electric, tool manufacturer Master Power, and electrical hub maker Myers Electric Products. Company veteran John Riley took over as chairman that year.

Some of its eight acquisitions in 1997 bolstered its electrical segment, including Menvier-Swain Group (UK), a maker of emergency lights and alarms. Cooper completed 11 acquisitions in 1998, including the tool business of Global Industrial Technologies (Quackenbush and Rotor Tool brands), two German firms, Apparatebau Hundsbach (electronic sensors) and Metronix Elektronik (power tool controls), and three makers of consumer tools and hardware in Mexico and Colombia. Cooper also traded its temperature-control business for Standard Motor's brake business. Also that year the company sold its automotive segment to Federal-Mogul, a maker of automotive and trucking parts. When the buying spree ended, the company announced it would cut 1,000 jobs and close 12 plants to cut costs. The company continued acquisitions in 1999, buying two electrical products operations — JSB Electrical (emergency lighting, UK) and Corelite (indirect lighting fixtures).

Chairman, President, and CEO: H. John Riley Jr.,
age 58, $1,172,666 pay
EVP Operations: Ralph E. Jackson Jr., age 57,
$571,167 pay
SVP and CFO: D. Bradley McWilliams, age 57,
$450,459 pay
SVP, General Counsel, and Secretary:
Diane K. Schumacher, age 45, $391,417 pay
SVP Human Resources: David R. Sheil Jr., age 42
SVP Strategic Planning: David A. White Jr., age 57
VP Investor Relations: Richard J. Bajenski, age 46
VP Public Affairs: Victoria Guennewig, age 48
VP and Treasurer: Alan J. Hill, age 54
VP and Controller: Terry A. Klebe, age 44
VP Taxes: E. Daniel Leightman, age 58
VP Information Systems: Terrance M. Smith, age 49
VP Environmental Affairs and Risk Management:
Robert W. Teets, age 48
President, Cooper Tools: J. David Cartwright
President, Cooper Power Tools: A. Peter Held
President, Cooper Power Systems: William D. Martino
President, Cooper Bussmann: Barry C. McHone
Managing Director, Cooper Menvier: J. Eric Scrimshaw
President, Crouse-Hinds: Sidney L. Sisney
President, Cooper Lighting: R. Fritz Zeck
Auditors: Ernst & Young LLP

LOCATIONS

HQ: 600 Travis, Ste. 5800, Houston, TX 77002-1001
Phone: 713-209-8400 **Fax:** 713-209-8995
Web site: http://www.cooperindustries.com

Cooper manufactures electrical products, hardware, and
tools in 19 countries and sells its products worldwide.

PRODUCTS/OPERATIONS

1998 Sales

	$ mil.	% of total
Electrical products	2,824	77
Tools & hardware	827	23
Total	**3,651**	**100**

COMPETITORS

ABB Asea Brown Boveri
Black & Decker
Danaher Corporation
Eaton
Emerson
GE
Illinois Tool Works
Ingersoll-Rand
Newell Rubbermaid
Philips Electronics
Siemens
SL Industries
Snap-on
Stanley Works
Waxman

HISTORICAL FINANCIALS & EMPLOYEES

NYSE symbol: CBE FYE: December 31	Annual Growth	1989	1990	1991	1992	1993	1994	1995	1996	1997	1998
Sales ($ mil.)	(3.7%)	5,129	6,222	6,163	6,159	6,274	4,588	4,886	5,284	5,289	3,651
Net income ($ mil.)	5.2%	268	361	393	(229)	367	(20)	94	315	395	423
Income as % of sales	—	5.2%	5.8%	6.4%	—	5.9%	—	1.9%	6.0%	7.5%	11.6%
Earnings per share ($)	7.5%	1.93	1.94	1.60	(3.55)	2.15	(0.64)	0.84	2.77	3.26	3.69
Stock price - FY high ($)	—	47.00	46.00	58.00	59.38	54.75	52.25	40.50	44.63	59.69	70.38
Stock price - FY low ($)	—	26.88	31.25	38.50	41.75	45.63	31.63	32.88	34.13	40.00	36.88
Stock price - FY close ($)	2.0%	40.00	41.13	57.25	47.38	49.25	34.00	36.75	42.13	49.00	47.69
P/E - high	—	24	24	36	—	25	—	48	16	18	19
P/E - low	—	14	16	24	—	21	—	39	12	12	10
Dividends per share ($)	3.4%	0.98	1.06	1.14	1.22	1.30	1.32	1.65	0.99	1.32	1.32
Book value per share ($)	(4.3%)	24.75	27.66	29.96	24.99	25.84	23.16	15.90	17.50	21.44	16.60
Employees	(7.8%)	58,100	57,500	53,900	52,900	49,500	40,800	40,400	42,000	41,200	28,100

STOCK PRICE HISTORY

HIGH/LOW/CLOSE

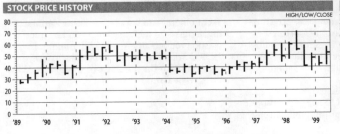

1998 FISCAL YEAR-END

Debt ratio: 33.1%
Return on equity: 27.1%
Cash ($ mil.): 20
Current ratio: 1.46
Long-term debt ($ mil.): 775
No. of shares (mil.): 94
Dividends
  Yield: 2.8%
  Payout: 35.8%
Market value ($ mil.): 4,492

CORDANT TECHNOLOGIES INC.

OVERVIEW

Since the Cold War's thaw, Cordant Technologies (formerly Thiokol) has warmed up to less-warlike ways of making money. Based in Salt Lake City, Cordant is a leader in producing solid rocket propulsion systems. Perhaps best known for its part in the *Challenger* space shuttle disaster, it is still the sole maker of the reusable solid rocket motors used on NASA space shuttles. Its propulsion business (Thiokol Propulsion group) also services the Trident submarine missile program and makes flare and decoy components and tactical propulsion systems.

Subsidiary Huck International, which accounts for about 55% of Cordant's sales, manufactures specialty fasteners, rivets, and lock bolts for the aerospace, automotive, and construction industries. Cordant also owns about 85% of Howmet International, a leading maker of precision castings for aircraft and industrial gas turbine engines. Huck and Howmet have helped Cordant reduce its reliance on government contracts and expand its customer base across other industry segments.

HISTORY

Joseph Patrick, a chemist conducting an experiment to develop cheap antifreeze, discovered synthetic rubber and founded Thiokol (Greek for "sulfur glue") Chemical Company in 1929. In 1943 the company developed a liquid polysulfide polymer, a nearly indestructible sealant for airplane fuel tanks and seams of aircraft carriers. Scientists at the California Institute of Technology's Jet Propulsion Laboratory discovered in the late 1940s that liquid polymer was the best solid propellant fuel binder. Thiokol immediately began rocket operations in Elkton, Maryland, with a US Army contract.

In 1958 Thiokol got a US Air Force contract to make the first stage of the Minuteman missile, the largest solid rocket motor built to that date. The company joined a US Air Force research program for giant solid rocket motors in 1963. At the same time, Thiokol and Hercules entered into a joint venture that developed propulsion systems for the Navy's *Poseidon* submarine-launched missile and the Trident I and Trident II programs.

Thiokol diversified into specialty chemicals by buying Dynachem (photopolymers and finishing compounds for printed circuits, 1974) and Ventron (sodium borohydride for pharmaceuticals and fine chemicals, 1976). In 1982 Thiokol merged with Morton International to become Morton Thiokol, a specialty chemicals, solid propulsion, and salt company. The company came under intense scrutiny after the 1986 explosion of the *Challenger* space shuttle, blamed on the failure of the Morton Thiokol-manufactured O-rings for the solid-fuel booster rockets. To mend its ties with NASA, the company redesigned the solid rocket motor.

Limited growth in the defense sector prompted Morton Thiokol to spin off its specialty chemicals, salt, and automobile airbag units into the newly formed Morton International in 1989. The remaining defense operations were renamed Thiokol Corporation, with retired Air Force general Robert Marsh as chairman and former astronaut Neil Armstrong on the board.

Marsh retired in 1991 and Edwin Garrison succeeded him. That year Thiokol signed a $2.6 billion contract to supply more than 140 solid rocket motors to the space shuttle program through 1997. The company entered the commercial market by buying Huck Manufacturing (now Huck International) in 1991. In 1993 James Wilson succeeded John Meyers as CEO of Thiokol. Wilson succeeded Garrison as chairman in 1995.

Also in 1995 Thiokol and Alliant Techsystems won a $123 million contract from Lockheed to make propulsion systems for the Trident II missile, and Thiokol and The Carlyle Group acquired jet- and turbine-engine component maker Howmet from Pechiney International SA. In 1996 Robert Crippen, former astronaut and director of the Kennedy Space Center, became president of the new Thiokol Propulsion group. The company entered into several international ventures in 1997, including agreements to supply solid rocket motors for Japan's H-IIA launch vehicle and Spain's Capricornio rocket. Thiokol increased its stake in Howmet from 49% to more than 60% later that year. In 1998 the company changed its name to Cordant Technologies and bought Jacobson Manufacturing, a maker of metal fasteners and engineered plastic products, for about $270 million. In 1999 Cordant again raised its stake in Howmet (to 85%) with the purchase of shares owned by the Carlyle Group.

OFFICERS

Chairman, President, and CEO: James R. Wilson, age 57, $840,000 pay (partial-year salary)
EVP and CFO: Richard L. Corbin, age 52, $315,000 pay (partial-year salary)
EVP Human Resources and Administration: James E. McNulty, age 54, $300,000 pay (partial-year salary)
VP; President, Thiokol Propulsion: Robert L. Crippen, age 61, $298,500 pay
VP; President, Huck International: Bruce M. Zorich, age 44, $275,000 pay (partial-year salary)
SVP and General Counsel: Daniel S. Hapke Jr., age 52
VP and Controller: Michael R. Ayers, age 48
VP and Treasurer: Nicholas J. Iuanow, age 39
VP and Corporate Secretary: Edwin M. North, age 53
VP Tax and Tax Counsel: Paul Cherecwich Jr.
VP and Chief Information Officer: Brad S. Stout
VP Compensation and Benefits: Richard T. Smith
President and CEO, Howmet International: David L. Squier
President, Industrial Fasteners, Huck International: Donald C. Busby
President, Aerospace Fasteners, Huck International: Gary Hourselt
SVP International Operations, Howmet International: Marklin Lasker
Auditors: Ernst & Young LLP

LOCATIONS

HQ: 15 W. South Temple, Ste. 1600, Salt Lake City, UT 84101-1532
Phone: 801-933-4000   **Fax:** 801-933-4014
Web site: http://www.cordanttech.com

PRODUCTS/OPERATIONS

1998 Sales

	$ mil.	% of total
Investment castings (Howmet)	1,351	56
Propulsion systems (Thiokol)	643	26
Fastening systems (Huck)	433	18
Total	**2,427**	**100**

Howmet Castings 1998 Sales

	% of total
Industrial gas turbine	35
Aero engine OEM	28
Aero engine aftermarket	23
Airframe structural	8
Other	6
Total	**100**

Thiokol Propulsion 1998 Sales

	% of total
Reusable solid rocket motor	60
Defense	30
Commercial space	10
Total	**100**

COMPETITORS

AAR	K Systems
Alliant Techsystems	Kellstrom
AlliedSignal	Labinal
Boeing	Lockheed Martin
British Aerospace	Precision Castparts
DASA	Rolls-Royce Allison
Fairchild	Sequa
Federal Screw Works	SPS Technologies
GE Aircraft Engines	TRW
GenCorp	United Technologies
Illinois Tool Works	

HISTORICAL FINANCIALS & EMPLOYEES

NYSE symbol: CDD FYE: December 31	Annual Growth	1989	1990	1991	1992	1993	1994	1995	1996	1997	1998
Sales ($ mil.)	8.3%	1,181	1,255	1,312	1,202	1,044	957	890	890	1,779	2,427
Net income ($ mil.)	14.7%	41	53	63	64	(4)	47	58	82	119	142
Income as % of sales	—	3.5%	4.3%	4.8%	5.3%	—	5.0%	6.6%	9.3%	6.7%	5.9%
Earnings per share ($)	15.0%	1.08	1.38	1.56	1.57	(0.09)	1.26	1.57	2.21	3.15	3.79
Stock price - FY high ($)	—	8.00	9.31	10.63	11.13	14.50	15.94	22.31	38.13	55.75	55.75
Stock price - FY low ($)	—	4.88	4.56	6.81	7.06	10.56	11.38	14.88	17.31	33.88	31.38
Stock price - FY close ($)	23.0%	5.81	7.56	8.00	10.94	12.06	15.13	19.75	35.00	46.13	37.50
P/E - high	—	7	7	7	7	—	13	14	17	18	15
P/E - low	—	5	3	4	4	—	9	9	8	11	8
Dividends per share ($)	3.2%	0.15	0.15	0.18	0.24	0.34	0.34	0.34	0.35	0.40	0.20
Book value per share ($)	11.1%	7.10	8.31	9.68	10.97	10.28	11.09	12.30	14.16	16.70	18.30
Employees	4.1%	12,100	11,500	11,500	11,200	9,300	8,000	7,200	5,900	5,300	17,400

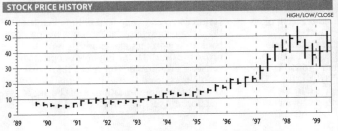

STOCK PRICE HISTORY
HIGH/LOW/CLOSE

1998 FISCAL YEAR-END

Debt ratio: 32.7%
Return on equity: 21.3%
Cash ($ mil.): 45
Current ratio: 1.08
Long-term debt ($ mil.): 325
No. of shares (mil.): 37
Dividends
  Yield: 0.5%
  Payout: 5.3%
Market value ($ mil.): 1,369

CORNING INCORPORATED

OVERVIEW

Like a beam of light racing along a fiber-optic strand, glassmaker Corning is narrowing its focus and moving forward. The Corning, New York-based materials company is a leading producer of fiber-optic cable, which it invented more than 20 years ago. Corning makes about 60,000 products, including nose cones for spacecraft and giant mirrors for high-powered telescopes.

Corning's Telecommunications unit (about half of sales) makes optical fiber and cable and photonic components, which use photons to transmit data. The company's Advanced Materials unit (about 30% of sales) produces a variety of industrial and scientific products, including environmental and semiconductor materials and optical and lighting products. Its Information Display segment makes glass products for TVs and VCRs, projection video lenses, and glass for flat-panel displays. The company also owns crystal maker Steuben Glass.

The Corning of the 21st century will be substantially different from its predecessor. During the mid-1990s losses at Dow Corning (the company's joint venture with Dow Chemical, which is embroiled in breast implant litigation) and a downturn in Corning's laboratory business prompted the company to sell most of its smallest but best-known unit, glassware and cookware maker Corning Consumer Products (Pyrex, Corning Ware, Revere Ware).

HISTORY

Amory Houghton started Houghton Glass in Massachusetts in 1851 and moved it to Corning, New York, in 1868. By 1876 the company, renamed Corning Glass Works, was making several types of technical and pharmaceutical glass. In 1880 it supplied the glass for Thomas Edison's first lightbulb. Other early developments included the red-yellow-green traffic light system (initially used for railroad signals) and borosilicate glass (which can withstand sudden temperature changes) for Pyrex oven and laboratory ware.

Joint ventures have been crucial to Corning's success. Early ones included Pittsburgh Corning (with Pittsburgh Plate Glass, 1937, glass construction blocks), Owens-Corning (with Owens-Illinois, 1938, fiber glass), and Dow Corning (with Dow Chemical, 1943, silicones).

By 1945 the company's laboratories (established in 1908) had made it the undisputed leader in the manufacture of specialty glass. Applications for its glass technology included the first mass-produced TV tubes, freezer-to-oven ceramic cookware (Pyroceram, Corning Ware), and car headlights.

After WWII Corning emphasized consumer product sales and expanded globally. In the 1970s the company pioneered the development of optical fiber and auto emission technology (now two of its principal products).

Seeing maturing markets for such established products as lightbulbs and TV tubes, Corning began buying higher-growth laboratory services companies (MetPath, 1982; Hazleton, 1987; Enseco, 1989; G.H. Besse-laar, 1989). It also established international joint ventures with Siemens, Mitsubishi, and Samsung. In 1988 Corning bought Revere Ware (cookware). The next year the company dropped Glass Works from its name.

In 1993 AT&T chose Corning to provide fiber-optic couplers for its undersea telecommunications system. Corning also developed an electrically heated catalytic converter (which beat tough California emissions standards set for 1997). In 1994 the company and Siecor (joint venture with Siemens) acquired several fiber and cable businesses from Northern Telecom (now Nortel Networks), expanding the firms' presence in Canada.

Joint venture Dow Corning, under assault from thousands of women seeking damages because of leaking silicone breast implants, entered Chapter 11 bankruptcy protection in 1995. The next year the company spun off its laboratory testing division to shareholders, creating Covance Inc. and Quest Diagnostics. Corning also formed Biccor to invest in fiber-optic ventures in Asia.

After deals to sell a stake in Corning Consumer Products to AEA Investors fell through in 1997, Corning sold the housewares unit to Kohlberg Kravis Roberts the next year. The company kept an 8% stake in the unit and held on to crystal maker Steuben Glass. Also in 1998 its Dow Corning joint venture agreed to pay $3.2 billion to settle breast implant claims and get out from under bankruptcy protection (plaintiffs must approve the deal). Declining product prices caused a drop in sales for fiscal 1998.

In 1999 Corning bought UK-based BICC Group's telecommunications cable business and Corning veteran Van Campbell retired.

Chairman and CEO: Roger G. Ackerman, age 60,
$1,147,107 pay
Co-COO; Sector President, Corning Communications:
John W. Loose, age 56, $739,297 pay
Co-COO; Sector President, Corning Technologies:
Norman E. Garrity, age 57, $739,297 pay
SVP, CFO, and Treasurer: James B. Flaws, age 50
SVP and General Counsel: William D. Eggers, age 54
SVP, International; President, Corning International:
Larry Aiello Jr.
**SVP, Manufacturing Effectiveness and Corporate
Quality:** Robert A. Gilchrist
SVP, Science and Technology: Charles W. Deneka,
age 54, $375,462 pay
VP and Controller: Katherine A. Asbeck, age 42
VP, Human Resources and Diversity Officer:
Pamela C. Schneider
Auditors: PricewaterhouseCoopers LLP

LOCATIONS

HQ: 1 Riverfront Plaza, Corning, NY 14831-0001
Phone: 607-974-9000   **Fax:** 607-974-8091
Web site: http://www.corning.com

Corning operates approximately 40 plants in Australia,
Belgium, China, France, Germany, India, Japan, Russia,
South Korea, the UK, and the US.

1998 Sales

	$ mil.	% of total
North America	2596	75
Asia/Pacific	443	12
Europe	374	11
Latin America & other regions	71	2
Total	**3,484**	**100**

PRODUCTS/OPERATIONS

1998 Sales

	$ mil.	% of total
Telecommunications	1,792	51
Advanced materials	1,020	29
Information display	645	19
Steuben Glass & other	27	1
Total	**3,484**	**100**

Selected Products

Telecommunications
Optical cable and fiber
Optical hardware and equipment
Photonic components

Advanced Materials
Environmental and science products
Optical and lighting products
Semiconductor products

Information Display Products
Glass panels and funnels for TVs and VCRs
LCD glass for flat-panel displays
Projection video lens assemblies

COMPETITORS

ACX Technologies	Pilkington
Alcatel	Pirelli S.p.A.
Apogee Enterprises	PPG
Asahi Glass	Saint-Gobain
BICC	Showa Electric Wire
Cookson Group	& Cable
Cristaleria Espanola	Taiheiyo Cement
Fisher Scientific	VIAG
Guardian Industries	Vitro
Nippon Sheet Glass	Waterford Wedgwood
Owens-Illinois	

HISTORICAL FINANCIALS & EMPLOYEES

NYSE symbol: GLW FYE: December 31	Annual Growth	1989	1990	1991	1992	1993	1994	1995	1996	1997	1998
Sales ($ mil.)	4.0%	2,439	2,941	3,259	3,709	4,005	4,771	5,313	3,652	4,090	3,484
Net income ($ mil.)	4.8%	259	292	317	(13)	(15)	281	(51)	176	440	394
Income as % of sales	—	10.6%	9.9%	9.7%	—	—	5.9%	—	4.8%	10.8%	11.3%
Earnings per share ($)	2.0%	1.40	1.56	1.69	(0.08)	(0.09)	1.30	(0.23)	0.78	1.85	1.67
Stock price - FY high ($)	—	21.69	25.88	43.13	40.31	39.00	35.06	37.38	46.25	65.13	45.69
Stock price - FY low ($)	—	16.00	17.38	21.06	28.75	24.00	27.63	24.13	27.88	33.75	22.88
Stock price - FY close ($)	8.6%	21.50	22.44	38.38	37.50	28.00	29.88	32.00	46.25	37.13	45.00
P/E - high	—	15	17	26	—	—	27	—	59	35	27
P/E - low	—	11	11	12	—	—	21	—	36	18	14
Dividends per share ($)	4.1%	0.50	0.69	0.68	0.62	0.68	0.69	0.72	0.72	0.72	0.72
Book value per share ($)	(3.6%)	9.08	10.07	10.43	9.30	8.40	11.51	9.15	4.20	5.38	6.50
Employees	(6.2%)	27,500	28,600	30,700	31,100	39,200	43,000	41,000	20,000	20,500	15,400

STOCK PRICE HISTORY

HIGH/LOW/CLOSE

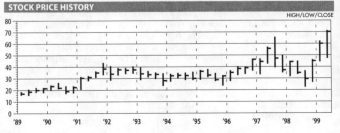

1998 FISCAL YEAR-END

Debt ratio: 39.6%
Return on equity: 26.2%
Cash ($ mil.): 45
Current ratio: 1.22
Long-term debt ($ mil.): 998
No. of shares (mil.): 232
Dividends
  Yield: 1.6%
  Payout: 43.1%
Market value ($ mil.): 10,418

CORPORATE EXPRESS, INC.

OVERVIEW

Corporate Express took the express route to success, making a lot of stops along the way to pick up hundreds of office supply firms. Now it finds itself being bought by Dutch office supply group Buhrmann. The Broomfield, Colorado-based company is one of the world's largest office products suppliers, offering everything from office and janitorial supplies to advertising specialties. Its customers, mostly large corporations, order from the company's catalog (featuring about 10,000 office and computer supply products) by phone, fax, e-mail, or through the Internet.

Founder Jirka Rysavy, a Czechoslovakian entrepreneur who once discussed the "sacred geometry" of the company's business strategy in its annual report, pursued a dizzying course of acquisitions during the 1990s, expanding Corporate Express throughout the US and overseas. However, disappointing results and a heavy debt load led the company to seek a buyer; it has also begun to distance itself from its unconventional founder.

Rysavy owns about 5% of the company. Director Martin Franklin owns about 8%.

HISTORY

Jirka Rysavy (YER-ka RIS-a-vee), recognized as a mathematical boy genius in his native Czechoslovakia, was a track star on his way to the Olympics until an injury sidelined him in 1974. He bummed around the world for several years, eventually landing in Boulder, Colorado, in 1984. Though he spoke little English, Rysavy got a job in a Boulder print shop, earning $3.35 an hour and working 16 hours a day.

Within six months the plain-living Rysavy (a strict vegetarian who still lives in a two-room cabin with no indoor plumbing) had saved $600, which he used to start his first business — Transecon (for Transformational Economy), a distribution company for recycled products that made a $100,000 profit in its first year. Rysavy took $30,000 from that venture and in 1985 began Crystal Market, a health foods store that he sold the next year for $300,000 (it became the first Wild Oats Market).

The following year he bought a small, unprofitable office supplies dealer for $100 cash. Rysavy realized that most of its revenues came from a few companies that were buying large quantities of office supplies. His new strategy of focusing on corporate sales instead of retail took Corporate Express from $300,000 to $2 million in the first year.

In 1988, leveraging the $300,000 he made from the health foods store's sale, Rysavy got the bank to finance the $7.8 million purchase of NBI's stationery division in Denver. More acquisitions followed, including the company's first venture capital purchase in 1991 and the beginning of national expansion with the 1992 acquisition of three Seattle-area office supply companies. In 1994 the company bought UK-based Hanson Office Products from Hanson PLC. Corporate Express

went public that year, having grown from 1990 sales of $71 million to $622 million.

Sales more than doubled the next year, jumping to $1.6 billion, as Corporate Express made acquisitions in Canada and Australia. The company added another 100 companies in 1996 and entered new markets such as software, computer supplies, and same-day local delivery service (through Houston-based U.S. Delivery Systems, the nation's #1 company of its kind). Corporate Express made more than 30 acquisitions in 1997, including several European stationers, and the company's most significant purchase, that of business forms maker Data Documents for $195 million (it later grouped the company with several others under a subsidiary renamed Corporate Express Document & Print Management).

With its stock price sagging, in 1998 Corporate Express began its plan to buy back 35 million (25%) of its outstanding shares and began cutting 1,700 jobs to eliminate overlap from recent acquisitions. Also in 1998 the company launched E-Way, its e-commerce-based ordering and fulfillment system, and promoted president Robert King to CEO.

Investment firms Brahman Management and Marlin Management (which had stakes in the firm) urged Corporate Express in early 1999 to oust Rysavy and consider a merger and other ways of "achieving shareholder value." In February 1999 Rysavy relinquished the chairman role, becoming chairman emeritus. The firm sold its same-day delivery business and Sofco paper product distributing business in 1999. (The delivery business and UK operations contributed to a loss in fiscal 1999.) In a $2.3 billion deal, Dutch distributor Buhrmann agreed in July 1999 to acquire Corporate Express.

OFFICERS

Chairman Emeritus: Jirka Rysavy, age 45, $465,192 pay
President and CEO: Robert L. King, age 48, $450,481 pay (prior to promotion)
EVP, CFO, and Secretary: Gary M. Jacobs, age 52, $344,781 pay
VP and Chief Information Officer: Monty Sooter
VP and Chief Technology Officer: David J. Leonard
VP, Corporate Communications: Van G. Hindes
VP, Distribution Operations: Timothy J. Beauchamp
VP, General Counsel and Corporate Development: Richard L. Millett Jr.
VP, Human Resources: John P. O'Loughlin
VP, Information Systems: Lisa L. Peters
VP, Merchandising: R. Todd Elmers
VP, Sales and Marketing: Sam Reese
VP, Strategic Planning and Investor Relations: Linda J. Dill
Auditors: PricewaterhouseCoopers LLP

LOCATIONS

HQ: 1 Environmental Way, Broomfield, CO 80021
Phone: 303-664-2000 **Fax:** 303-664-3324
Web site: http://www.corporate-express.com

Corporate Express has about 90 distribution centers and 570 sales and service centers, mostly in the US, but also in Australia, Canada, France, Germany, Ireland, Italy, the Netherlands, New Zealand, Switzerland, and the UK.

1998 Sales

	$ mil.	% of total
US	2,813	75
Other countries	940	25
Total	**3,753**	**100**

PRODUCTS/OPERATIONS

1998 Sales

	$ mil.	% of total
Office products	2,885	77
Desktop software distribution	582	15
Other	293	8
Adjustment	(7)	—
Total	**3,753**	**100**

Selected Products and Services

Advertising specialties	Forms management
Breakroom supplies	Fulfillment service
Business forms	Inbound telemarketing
Computer and imaging supplies	Janitorial and cleaning supplies
Computer software	Moving service
Computer training	Office equipment
Corporate call centers	Office equipment servicing
Courier service	Office furniture
Delivery service	Office supplies
Direct mail service	Presentation supplies
Distribution logistics management	Pressure-sensitive labels
Ergonomic products	Promotion service

COMPETITORS

Beyond.com	Office Depot
Boise Cascade Office Products	OfficeMax
Buhrmann	Staples
Costco Companies	United Stationers
Daisytek	U.S. Office Products
IKON	Wallace Computer
Moore Corporation	Wal-Mart

HISTORICAL FINANCIALS & EMPLOYEES

Nasdaq symbol: CEXP FYE: January 31	Annual Growth	1990	1991	1992	1993	1994	1995	1996	1997	1998	1999
Sales ($ mil.)	55.3%	71	79	78	103	165	622	1,590	3,196	3,573	3,753
Net income ($ mil.)	—	(0)	(4)	(1)	(5)	(9)	5	3	42	44	(73)
Income as % of sales	—	—	—	—	—	—	0.9%	0.2%	1.3%	1.2%	—
Earnings per share ($)	—	—	—	—	—	—	0.05	0.31	0.26	0.32	(0.64)
Stock price – FY high ($)	—	—	—	—	—	—	11.79	20.51	31.18	23.75	13.38
Stock price – FY low ($)	—	—	—	—	—	—	7.23	9.68	16.34	7.94	4.00
Stock price – FY close ($)	(11.8%)	—	—	—	—	—	10.62	19.84	18.75	8.84	6.44
P/E – high	—	—	—	—	—	—	236	66	120	74	—
P/E – low	—	—	—	—	—	—	145	31	63	25	—
Dividends per share ($)	—	—	—	—	—	—	0.00	0.00	0.00	0.00	0.00
Book value per share ($)	6.0%	—	—	—	—	—	3.38	4.79	5.50	6.55	4.27
Employees	81.2%	—	—	400	3,109	3,300	4,047	12,413	27,000	27,300	25,700

1998 is an 11-month fiscal year.

STOCK PRICE HISTORY

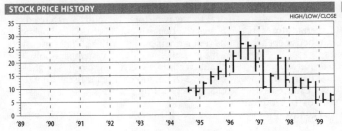

HIGH/LOW/CLOSE

1999 FISCAL YEAR-END

Debt ratio: 73.1%
Return on equity: —
Cash ($ mil.): 15
Current ratio: 1.67
Long-term debt ($ mil.): 1,207
No. of shares (mil.): 104
Dividends
  Yield: —
  Payout: —
Market value ($ mil.): 671

COSTCO COMPANIES, INC.

OVERVIEW

At Costco Companies, buying paper towels is a privilege, not a right. The Issaquah, Washington-based company (formerly Price/Costco) is the largest wholesale club operator in the US (ahead of Wal-Mart's Sam's Club). Costco operates or has stakes in about 300 warehouse stores, primarily under the Costco Wholesale name, serving 27 million members in Canada, Japan, Mexico, South Korea, Taiwan, the UK, and the US. The company's typical warehouse store, averaging 129,000 sq. ft., offers products ranging from alcoholic beverages to pharmaceuticals at sharply discounted prices. Costco carries a tenth of the variety offered by regular discount retailers, instead stocking 3,600 to 4,000 of the fastest-selling, highest-volume products.

In order to shop at Costco stores, customers must be members — a policy the company believes reinforces customer loyalty and provides a steady source of fee revenue. Three types of annual memberships are available: Business ($35 each and $25 for each additional card), Gold Star ($40 per individual), and Executive ($100; allows members to purchase products and services, including insurance, mortgage services, and check printing, at reduced rates). The company introduced the Executive membership in 1997 primarily to profit from the higher membership fees.

Facing competition from discounters that don't charge a membership fee, as well as from rival Sam's Club, Costco is expanding and retrofitting its warehouses to accommodate fresh food sections and other ancillary units, such as gas stations and optical departments.

HISTORY

From 1954 to 1974 retailer Sol Price built his Fed-Mart discount chain into a $300 million behemoth selling general merchandise to government employees. Price sold the company to Hugo Mann in 1975 and the next year, with son Robert, Rick Libenson, and Giles Bateman, opened the first Price Club warehouse, in San Diego, to sell in volume to small businesses at steep discounts. Several former Fed-Mart employees added $500,000 to Sol's $800,000 to help get the venture going.

Posting a large loss its first year prompted Price Club's decision to expand membership to include government, utility, and hospital employees, as well as credit union members. In 1978 it opened a second store, in Phoenix. Laurence, Sol's other son, who had declined to join the startup company, began a chain of tire-mounting stores with the help of his father. The stores, located adjacent to Price Club outlets on land leased from the company, used tires sold by the Price Clubs.

The company went public in 1980 with four stores in California and Arizona. Price Club moved into the eastern US with its 1984 opening of a store in Virginia and continued to expand, including a joint venture with Canadian retailer Steinberg in 1986 to operate stores in Canada; the first Canadian warehouse opened that year in Montreal.

Two years later Price Club acquired A. M. Lewis (grocery distributor, Southern California and Arizona), and the next year it started a delivery service to strengthen ties to its 1 million small-business customers. The company also opened two Price Club Furnishings, home and office furniture extensions of the company's discount format.

It bought out Steinberg's interest in the Canadian locations in 1990 and added stores on the East Coast and in California, Colorado, and British Columbia. However, competition in the East from ensconced rivals such as Sam's Club and PACE forced the closure of two stores two years later. A 50-50 joint venture with retailer Controladora Comercial Mexicana led to the opening of two Price Clubs in Mexico City in 1992 and 1993.

Price Club merged with Costco Wholesale in 1993. Founded in 1983 by Jeffrey Brotman and James Sinegal (a former EVP of Price Company), Costco Wholesale went public in 1985 and expanded into Canada.

In 1993 Price/Costco opened its first warehouse outside the Americas in a London suburb. Merger costs led to a loss the following year, and Price/Costco spun off its commercial real estate operations as Price Enterprises. In 1997 the company changed its corporate name to Costco Companies.

Costco began online sales in 1998, struck a deal to buy two stores in South Korea from Shinsegae Department Store Co., and opened its first store in Japan in 1999. Under industry-wide pressure over the way members-only chains record fees, Costco warned it might take a $118 million charge for fiscal 1999 to change accounting practices.

Chairman: Jeffrey H. Brotman, age 56, $532,692 pay
President and CEO: James D. Sinegal, age 62,
$532,692 pay
SEVP and COO, Merchandising, Distribution,
Construction, and Marketing: Richard D. DiCerchio,
age 55, $449,904 pay
EVP and CFO: Richard A. Galanti, age 42, $404,904 pay
EVP International Operations: Franz E. Lazarus, age 51,
$396,495 pay
EVP Manufacturing and Ancillary Businesses:
David B. Loge, age 56
SVP Human Resources and Risk Management:
John Matthews
Auditors: Arthur Andersen LLP

LOCATIONS

HQ: 999 Lake Dr., Issaquah, WA 98027
Phone: 425-313-8100   **Fax:** 425-313-8103
Web site: http://www.costco.com

Costco Companies operates stores primarily in the
Eastern and Western US and Canada. Through joint
ventures it operates stores in Japan, Mexico (50%-
owned, with Controladora Comercial Mexicana), South
Korea (94%), Taiwan (55%), and the UK (60%).

1998 Sales

	$ mil.	% of total
US	19,634	81
Other countries	4,636	19
Total	**24,270**	**100**

PRODUCTS/OPERATIONS

1998 Sales

	$ mil.	% of total
Sales	23,830	98
Membership fees	440	2
Total	**24,270**	**100**

1998 Sales

	% of total
Food (fresh & dry, institutionally packaged)	32
Sundries (snacks, beverages, health/beauty aids)	30
Hardlines (major appliances, electronics)	20
Softlines (apparel, cameras, jewelry)	12
Other (pharmacy, optical)	6
Total	**100**

Private Label
Kirkland Signature

COMPETITORS

Albertson's	Kroger
Ames	Loblaw
Army & Air Force	Office Depot
Exchange	OfficeMax
AutoZone	Petco
Barnes & Noble	PETsMART
Best Buy	Service Merchandise
BJs Wholesale Club	Smart & Final
Canadian Tire	Staples
Circuit City	Target Stores
CompUSA	Toys "R" Us
Home Depot	Walgreen
Hudson's Bay	Wal-Mart
Kmart	

HISTORICAL FINANCIALS & EMPLOYEES

Nasdaq symbol: COST FYE: August 31	Annual Growth	1989	1990	1991	1992	1993	1994	1995	1996	1997	1998
Sales ($ mil.)	19.5%	4,901	5,287	6,598	7,320	15,155	16,481	17,906	19,567	21,874	24,270
Net income ($ mil.)	16.4%	117	125	134	129	223	(112)	134	249	312	460
Income as % of sales	—	2.4%	2.4%	2.0%	1.8%	1.5%	—	0.7%	1.3%	1.4%	1.9%
Earnings per share ($)	12.4%	0.71	0.82	0.98	1.06	1.00	(0.51)	0.68	1.22	1.46	2.03
Stock price - FY high ($)	—	22.39	23.22	30.60	30.37	21.11	21.63	18.75	21.88	38.88	65.75
Stock price - FY low ($)	—	16.30	14.19	12.43	13.84	13.25	13.00	12.00	13.63	16.75	33.88
Stock price - FY close ($)	9.5%	20.87	15.59	29.78	14.42	17.82	15.69	16.88	19.88	36.06	47.06
P/E - high	—	32	28	31	29	21	—	28	18	27	32
P/E - low	—	23	17	13	13	13	—	18	11	11	17
Dividends per share ($)	(100.0%)	0.70	0.00	0.00	0.00	0.00	0.00	0.00	0.00	0.00	0.00
Book value per share ($)	11.7%	5.04	5.95	7.34	8.14	8.28	7.74	7.84	9.05	11.56	13.63
Employees	19.6%	12,545	13,336	19,142	20,777	43,000	47,000	52,000	53,000	57,000	63,000

STOCK PRICE HISTORY
HIGH/LOW/CLOSE

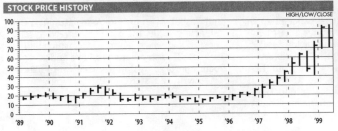

1998 FISCAL YEAR-END

Debt ratio: 23.9%
Return on equity: 15.5%
Cash ($ mil.): 362
Current ratio: 1.20
Long-term debt ($ mil.): 930
No. of shares (mil.): 218
Dividends
  Yield: —
  Payout: —
Market value ($ mil.): 10,240

COUNTRYWIDE CREDIT INDUSTRIES

OVERVIEW

Countrywide gives credit where credit is due. The company is the nation's largest independent residential mortgage lending and servicing firm. Pasadena, California-based Countrywide Credit Industries and its subsidiaries also offer insurance products, lines of credit, loan-closing products, subprime loans, home equity loans, mutual funds, and investment services through more than 400 US branch offices and the Internet. A new joint venture to service loans for the UK's Woolwich plc will give it exposure in the European market. The company specializes in prime quality first mortgages and is renowned for its highly automated system for managing the loans of more than 2 million customers.

Countrywide retains servicing on all loans it originates, buys, or sells. Its wholesale

operations produce prime mortgage and home equity loans through brokers; its retail division, through its Full Spectrum Lending subsidiary, offers subprime mortgage and home equity loans for the credit-impaired.

Countrywide also provides its own title insurance, credit reporting, home appraisal, and escrow services, which are linked through an electronic network to close loans quickly and reduce costs.

Having captured the US, Countrywide is eyeing the rest of the world. In addition to its UK joint venture, possibilities include France and Italy. Countrywide is also beefing up its insurance segment, which sells homeowners, auto, home warranty, disability, annuities, and term life products.

HISTORY

Countrywide was formed in 1969 by business associates David Loeb and Angelo Mozilo. Loeb had already founded mortgage banking business United Mortgage Servicing; Mozilo was his best salesman. Loeb was forced to give up his stake in the company to corporate raiders, and shortly thereafter the pair opened the first Countrywide office in Anaheim, California.

The company went public in the early 1970s, but the partners received only $800,000 in capital. Business picked up despite inflation and high interest rates. By 1974 Countrywide's eight branches were doing well, but the company could barely handle operating costs.

Loeb decided to reinvent the company. Mozilo grudgingly agreed; they closed all of the branches and fired all 95 employees except themselves and a secretary. They transformed Countrywide from a sales-driven to a product-driven enterprise, dropping its commissioned sales force in favor of direct solicitation of realtors. Guaranteed low interest rates eventually drummed up enough business to reopen a California branch that was soon seeing more business than it could handle. By 1978 the company was in the black.

By the mid-1980s Countrywide had 104 branches in 26 states. It also diversified during the decade, forming Countrywide Securities Corporation (1981) and Countrywide Asset Management (1985). Like other mortgage companies, Countrywide benefited from the savings and loan crisis of the late 1980s, moving in to fill a void in home loan production.

After the 1989-91 recession business picked up again as low interest rates prompted more

refinancing. Marginally rising interest rates in 1994 resulted in a flat housing market and a shrinking volume of mortgage refinancing industrywide. In response, Countrywide trimmed staff and took cost-cutting measures. By 1996 profits had rebounded.

But the company still faced the problem of mortgage refinancing, which provides one-time fees but has little effect on loan volume. In response, the company in 1997 began a nationwide advertising campaign to build brand awareness and to target new customer groups (a Spanish language ad campaign reached out to Hispanics). It also bought mutual funds broker and administrator Leshner Financial (now Countrywide Financial Services, being sold to Western and Southern Life Insurance) and signaled its intent to acquire more money managers.

Another tactic to increase loan volume was more risky. In 1998, as personal bankruptcies continued at record levels, the company moved into the subprime market through its Full Spectrum Lending subsidiary. The next year Countrywide said it would pump up its insurance business through the $425 million purchase of most of the operations of Balboa Life and Casualty Group from Associates First Capital. Also in 1999, the company agreed to sell most of its loans to Fannie Mae, which will promote Countrywide's products and accept loans approved by Countrywide's automated underwriting system.

Chairman and CEO: Angelo R. Mozilo, age 60, $5,335,821 pay
President: David S. Loeb, age 75, $5,235,821 pay
Senior Managing Director and COO; President and CEO, Countrywide Home Loans: Stanford L. Kurland, age 46, $1,939,927 pay
Managing Director Finance, CFO, and Chief Accounting Officer: Carlos M. Garcia, age 43, $699,471 pay
Managing Director and Chief Technology Officer: Jeremy V. Gross
Managing Director and Treasurer: Thomas K. McLaughlin
Managing Director Legal, Secretary, and General Counsel: Sandor E. Samuels, age 46
Managing Director Capital Markets: David Sambol, age 39, $1,085,200 pay
Managing Director Corporate Finance and Communications: Eric P. Sieracki
Managing Director Developing Markets: Marshall M. Gates, age 47
Managing Director Global Administration: Richard S. Lewis
Managing Director Human Resources: Anne D. McCallion
Managing Director Loan Administration: Richard DeLeo
Managing Director Marketing: Andrew S. Bielanski
Managing Director Risk Management and Strategic Planning: Jeffrey K. Speakes
Auditors: Grant Thornton LLP

HQ: Countrywide Credit Industries, Inc.,
4500 Park Granada, Calabasas, CA 91302-1613
Phone: 818-225-3000   **Fax:** 818-225-4051
Web site: http://www.countrywide.com

1999 Sales

	$ mil.	% of total
Loan production	1,323	45
Interest earned	1,029	35
Net loan servicing	423	14
Commissions, fees & other income	188	6
Total	**2,963**	**100**

Selected Subsidiaries
Countrywide Agency, Inc. (homeowners, property/casualty, annuities, and other insurance)
Countrywide Servicing Exchange (national servicing brokerage and consulting firm)
CTC Real Estate Services (trustee in connection with foreclosures)
Full Spectrum Lending, Inc. (subprime and home equity loans)
LandSafe, Inc. (title insurance agent and escrow services)
Second Charter Reinsurance Corp. (mortgage loan reinsurance)

Advanta
The Associates
Bank of America
Dime Bancorp
First American Financial
First Union
Freddie Mac
Golden West Financial
Green Tree Financial
HomeSide
Impac Mortgage Holdings
Insignia Financial Group
Irwin Financial
NVR
PN Holdings
Southern Pacific Funding
Washington Mutual
Wells Fargo

NYSE symbol: CCR FYE: February 28	Annual Growth	1990	1991	1992	1993	1994	1995	1996	1997	1998	1999
Assets ($ mil.)	38.4%	839	1,122	2,410	3,299	5,586	5,580	8,658	8,089	12,219	15,648
Net income ($ mil.)	45.6%	13	22	60	140	180	88	196	257	345	385
Income as % of assets	—	1.6%	2.0%	2.5%	4.2%	3.2%	1.6%	2.3%	3.2%	2.8%	2.5%
Earnings per share ($)	30.0%	0.31	0.43	0.81	1.52	1.97	0.96	1.95	2.44	3.09	3.29
Stock price - FY high ($)	—	4.25	5.40	19.64	22.07	23.35	18.88	26.75	31.13	48.50	56.25
Stock price - FY low ($)	—	2.59	2.28	5.08	10.85	15.26	12.38	15.50	19.75	24.38	28.63
Stock price - FY close ($)	32.0%	3.12	5.35	15.41	21.75	16.68	16.25	21.00	29.13	44.44	37.88
P/E - high	—	14	13	24	15	12	20	14	13	16	17
P/E - low	—	8	5	6	7	8	13	8	8	8	9
Dividends per share ($)	12.6%	0.11	0.12	0.16	0.23	0.28	0.32	0.32	0.32	0.32	0.32
Book value per share ($)	25.5%	2.90	3.33	7.03	8.30	9.66	10.32	12.91	15.19	19.12	22.37
Employees	31.1%	997	1,124	1,786	3,235	4,867	3,613	4,825	6,134	7,983	11,378

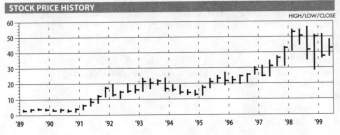

HIGH/LOW/CLOSE

Equity as % of assets: 16.1%
Return on assets: 2.8%
Return on equity: 15.3%
Long-term debt ($ mil.): 9,936
No. of shares (mil.): 113
Dividends
  Yield: 0.8%
  Payout: 9.7%
Market value ($ mil.): 4,266
Sales (mil.): $2,963

COX ENTERPRISES, INC.

OVERVIEW

Like an octopus at an all-you-can-eat buffet, Cox Enterprises has a lot on its plate. The Atlanta-based company is one of the US's largest media conglomerates, with interests in newspapers, radio, and broadcast and cable TV. Cox publishes 16 daily newspapers (including its flagship, *The Atlanta Journal-Constitution*) and 15 weeklies and shoppers. It owns 11 broadcast TV stations and owns or operates nearly 60 radio stations through its 70% stake in Cox Radio. In addition, the company owns about 80% of Cox Communications, one of the largest cable systems in the US with nearly 5 million subscribers, and provides telecommunications services (local and long-distance telephone, data transport network) to a variety of businesses. Cox's Manheim Auctions (more

than 80 traditional and Internet auctions) is the nation's largest used-car auction company.

With the growth of wireless communications and the Internet, Cox is sticking with its strategy of finding opportunity in emerging technologies. Its Cox Interactive Media operates a network of 28 online city sites, including Access Atlanta and InsideNewOrleans.com. The company is also a leader in digital television (its WSB-TV station in Atlanta was one of the first in the nation to offer digital programming) and provides Internet access to nearly 70,000 customers.

The company is owned by Barbara Cox Anthony (mother of CEO James Kennedy) and Anne Cox Chambers, daughters of founder James Cox.

HISTORY

James Middleton Cox dropped out of school in 1886 at age 16 and worked as a teacher, reporter, and congressional secretary before buying the *Dayton Daily News* in 1898. He acquired the nearby *Springfield Press-Republican* in 1905 and soon took up politics. Cox served two terms in the US Congress (1909-13) and three terms as Ohio governor (1913-15; 1917-21). In 1920 he was the Democratic candidate for president, with running mate Franklin D. Roosevelt, but he lost to rival Ohio publisher Warren Harding. In 1923 Cox bought the *Miami Daily News* and founded WHIO, Dayton, Ohio's first radio station. He bought Atlanta's WSB ("Welcome South, Brother"), the South's first radio station, in 1939, and in 1948 he added WSB-FM and WSB-TV, the South's first FM and TV stations. The next year Cox started WHIO-FM and WHIO-TV, Dayton's first FM and TV stations. *The Atlanta Constitution* joined his collection in 1950. When Cox died in 1957, his company owned seven newspapers, three TV stations, and several radio stations.

Cox Enterprises expanded its broadcast interests in the late 1950s and early 1960s. It was one of the first major broadcasting companies to enter cable TV when it purchased a system in Lewistown, Pennsylvania (1962). The Cox family's broadcast properties were placed in publicly held Cox Broadcasting in 1964. Two years later, its newspapers were placed into privately held Cox Enterprises, and the cable holdings became publicly held Cox Cable Communications. The broadcasting arm diversified, buying Manheim Services (auto auctions, 1968) and Kansas City Automobile Auction (1969).

Cox Broadcasting bought TeleRep, a TV advertising sales firm, in 1972. Cox Cable was in nine states and had 500,000 subscribers by 1977, when it rejoined Cox Broadcasting. The broadcasting company changed its name to Cox Communications in 1982; the Cox family took the company private again in 1985 and combined it with Cox Enterprises. James Kennedy, the founder's grandson, became chairman in 1987.

In 1991 Cox merged its Manheim unit with the auto auction business of Ford Motor Credit and GE Capital. It formed Sprint Spectrum LP, a partnership with long-distance operator Sprint and cable leviathans TCI (now part of AT&T) and Comcast in 1994 to bundle telephone service, cable TV, and other communication services. (Sprint bought Cox out in 1999.) The next year Cox bought Times Mirror's cable TV operations for $2.3 billion and folded those systems and its own into a new, publicly traded company, Cox Communications Inc. In 1996 the company formed Cox Interactive Media to expand its presence on the Internet.

Cox acquired two Seattle TV stations in 1997. In 1998 Manheim began an auction Web site for automobile wholesalers and Cox Interactive Media introduced interactive classified advertising Web sites.

The company entered into a joint venture with MP3.com in 1999 to develop and run a number of music-related Web sites.

Chairman and CEO: James C. Kennedy, age 51
President and COO: David E. Easterly, age 56
SVP and CFO: Robert C. O'Leary
SVP Administration: Timothy W. Hughes
President and CEO, Manheim Auctions:
Dennis G. Berry
President and CEO, Cox Communications, Inc.:
James O. Robbins
President, Cox Newspapers: Jay R. Smith
President, Cox Broadcasting: Nicholas D. Trigony
President, Cox Interactive Media: Peter M. Winter
SVP, Operations Cox Communications:
Margaret A. Bellville
VP Tax: Preston B. Barnett
VP Business Development and Planning:
Dean H. Eisner
VP and Chief Information Officer: Scott A. Hatfield
VP and Treasurer: Richard J. Jacobson
VP New Media: William L. Killen Jr.
VP Human Resources: Marybeth H. Leamer
VP Materials Management: Michael J. Mannheimer
VP Legal Affairs and Secretary: Andrew A. Merdek
VP Public Policy: Alexander V. Netchvolodoff
VP Marketing and Communication: John C. Williams

LOCATIONS

HQ: 1400 Lake Hearn Dr., Atlanta, GA 30319
Phone: 404-843-5000   **Fax:** 404-843-5109
Web site: http://www.CoxEnterprises.com

Cox Enterprises operates in Canada, France, Puerto
Rico, the UK, and the US.

Top Cable System Clusters
Hampton Roads, VA
Las Vegas
New England
New Orleans
Omaha, NE
Orange County, CA
Pensacola-Ft. Walton Beach, FL
Phoenix
San Diego
Tucson-Sierra Vista, AZ

PRODUCTS/OPERATIONS

Selected Daily Newspapers
The Atlanta Journal-Constitution
Austin American-Statesman (Texas)
The Daily Reflector (Greenville, NC)
The Daily Sentinel (Grand Junction, CO)
The Daily Sentinel (Nacogdoches, TX)
Dayton Daily News (Ohio)
Longview News-Journal (Texas)
The Lufkin Daily News (Texas)
Palm Beach Post (Florida)

Selected Radio Stations

KACE-FM, Los Angeles	WODL-FM;
KCYY-FM; San Antonio	Birmingham, AL
KOST-FM, Los Angeles	WRKA-FM; Louisville, KY
WCOF-FM, Tampa	WRVI-FM; Louisville, KY
WFLC-FM, Miami	WSB-AM, Atlanta
WHIO-AM; Dayton, OH	WSB-FM, Atlanta
WHKO-FM; Dayton, OH	WSUN-AM, Tampa
WHQT-FM, Miami	WWKA-FM, Orlando

Selected Television Stations

KIRO, Seattle	WHIO, Dayton, OH
KTVU, San Francisco-	WPXI, Pittsburgh
Oakland	WSB-TV, Atlanta
WFTV, Orlando, FL	WSOC, Charlotte, NC

Selected Cable and Television Operations
Cox Communications, Inc. (80%, cable television
operator)
Harrington, Righter & Parsons (sales representation)
MMT Sales (sales representation)
TeleRep, Inc. (sales representation)

Other Operation
Manheim Auctions (auto auctions at 83 locations in the
US, Canada, France, and the UK)

COMPETITORS

Advance	E. W. Scripps	SBC
Publications	Gannett	Communications
Belo	GTE	Time Warner
Ameritech	Hearst	Tribune
AT&T	Infinity	Viacom
Bell Atlantic	Broadcasting	Vodafone
Cablevision	Knight Ridder	AirTouch
Systems	MediaOne Group	Walt Disney
Comcast	New York Times	Washington Post
Dow Jones	News Corp.	

HISTORICAL FINANCIALS & EMPLOYEES

Private company FYE: December 31	Annual Growth	1989	1990	1991	1992	1993	1994	1995	1996	1997	1998
Sales ($ mil.)	11.7%	1,973	2,094	2,323	2,495	2,675	2,939	3,806	4,591	4,936	5,355
Employees	10.6%	22,487	24,864	29,943	30,865	31,000	37,000	38,000	43,000	50,000	55,500

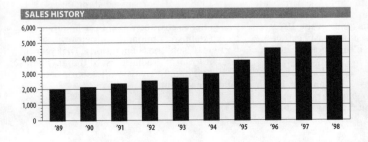

SALES HISTORY

C. R. BARD, INC.

OVERVIEW

If you laid all of C.R. Bard's catheters end to end — ouch! That would hurt.

The Murray Hill, New Jersey-based company is best known for its urological products; its Foley catheter is still one of the top bladder-drainage products, and the company proudly proclaims leadership in urine drainage and collection. Bard also makes vascular products, including stents, fabrics, and meshes for blood vessel repair. Bard also sells oncological diagnosis and treatment products, including

brachytherapy seeds (radioactive seeds placed at tumor sites) and specialty surgical products.

Bard once owned the cardiovascular products market, but for years the business languished in the face of some stiff competition. The company has finally decided to jettison those operations to focus on its urological, oncological, and other vascular products. Bard has reorganized around disease state management, delivering products along the continuum of care (prevention, treatment, and cure).

HISTORY

When visiting Europe at the turn of the century, silk importer Charles Russell Bard discovered that gomenol, a mixture of olive oil with a eucalyptus extract, offered him relief from urinary problems caused by tuberculosis. He brought gomenol to America and began distributing it.

In 1907 C. R. Bard began selling a ureteral catheter developed by J. Eynard, a French firm. The company incorporated in 1923 with its present name. When Charles Bard's health declined in 1926, he sold the business to John Willits and Edson Outwin (his sales manager and accountant, respectively).

In 1934 Bard became the sole agent for Davol Rubber's new Foley catheter, which helped the company achieve $1 million in sales by 1948. During the 1950s, sales increased more than 400% when the firm introduced its first presterilized packaged product and expanded its product line to include disposable drainage tubes and an intravenous feeding device.

Bard went public in 1963. During the 1960s the company began expanding operations both vertically, by boosting its manufacturing capabilities (it began making its own plastic tubing), and through acquisitions (it acquired United States Catheter and Instrument, 1966). It also established joint ventures with Davol to manufacture and distribute hospital and surgical supplies internationally.

The company diversified into the cardiovascular, respiratory therapy, home care products, and kidney-dialysis fields in the 1970s, and introduced the first angioplasty catheter, a nonsurgical device to clear blocked arteries, in 1979.

In 1984 Bard watched its urological business go limp. In response, the company began an acquisitions spree to gain market share in a consolidating hospital products industry. It swallowed up around a dozen companies,

including Davol, which made its best-selling Foley catheter, garnering such products as catheters and other products for angioplasty, diagnostics, and urinary incontinence. In 1988 it faced increasing competition in the coronary catheter market from such giants as Eli Lilly and Pfizer. Bard struck back with innovative products of its own, but it was too little too late — though the company struggled for the next 10 years, it finally had to pull out of the cardiovascular market.

Bard agreed in 1993 to pay a then-record $61 million for mislabeling and improperly testing angioplasty catheters blamed for the deaths of two people (and later taken off the market). However, a year later Bard's sales topped $1 billion for the first time, and it purchased catheter-related companies in Canada, France, and Germany.

Acquisitions in 1995 and 1996 included medical device manufacturers American Hydro-Surgical Instruments, MedChem Products, and the Cardiac Assist Division of St. Jude Medical. In 1996 Bard purchased a majority stake in Italy-based coronary stent producer X-Trode and acquired IMPRA, Inc., a leading supplier of vascular grafts (its largest deal ever, at $143 million). That year the ongoing catheter litigation snared three former Bard executives, who received 18-month prison sentences for conspiring to hide potentially fatal flaws in the products.

In 1998 Bard reorganized along disease state management lines. Determining that it was going to cost too much time and money to re-establish dominance in the cardiovascular field, it sold those operations. That year it bought ProSeed (radiation seed therapy) and in 1999 it bought Dymax (ultrasound catheter guidance systems).

Chairman and CEO: William H. Longfield, age 60, $1,297,700 pay
Group President: Guy J. Jordan, age 50, $466,083 pay
Group President: Timothy M. Ring, age 41, $542,927 pay
Group President: John H. Weiland, age 43, $509,921 pay
SVP and CFO: Charles P. Slacik, age 44
VP, Secretary, and General Counsel: Nadia C. Adler, age 54
VP Medical Affairs: James R. Adwers, age 55
VP Planning and Development: E. Robert Ernest, age 58
VP Quality Assurance: Christopher D. Ganser, age 46
VP Human Resources: Hope Greenfield, age 47
VP and Controller: Charles P. Grom, age 51
VP Information Technology: Vincent J. Gunari Jr.
VP Scientific Affairs: Richard D. Manthei, age 63
VP; President, Corporate Healthcare Services: James L. Natale
VP and Chief Investor Relations: Earle L. Parker, age 55
VP and Treasurer: Todd C. Schermerhorn, age 38
Assistant Secretary: Jean F. Miller
Auditors: Arthur Andersen LLP

LOCATIONS

HQ: 730 Central Ave., Murray Hill, NJ 07974
Phone: 908-277-8000   **Fax:** 908-277-8240
Web site: http://www.crbard.com

1998 Sales

	% of total
US	71
Europe	19
Japan	5
Other regions	5
Total	**100**

PRODUCTS/OPERATIONS

1998 Sales

	$ mil.	% of total
Urology	340	29
Oncology	213	18
Vascular	209	18
Divested products	196	17
Surgery	148	13
Other	59	5
Total	**1,165**	**100**

Major Business Groups and Products

Vascular Diagnosis and Intervention
Fabrics and meshes for blood vessel repair
Implantable blood vessel replacements

Urological Diagnosis and Intervention
Foley catheters, procedural kits and trays, and ureteral stents
Specialty devices for incontinence, endoscopic procedures, and stone removal

Oncological Diagnosis and Intervention
Biopsy and other cancer detection products
Gastroenterological products
Specialty access catheters and ports

Surgical Specialties
Irrigation devices for orthopedic and laparoscopic procedures
Topical hemostasis

COMPETITORS

Abbott Labs
Arrow International
Baxter
Becton Dickinson
Boston Scientific
Bristol-Myers Squibb
Johnson & Johnson
Maxxim Medical
Medline Industries
Pfizer
St. Jude Medical
Teleflex
United States Surgical

HISTORICAL FINANCIALS & EMPLOYEES

NYSE symbol: BCR FYE: December 31	Annual Growth	1989	1990	1991	1992	1993	1994	1995	1996	1997	1998
Sales ($ mil.)	4.6%	778	785	876	990	971	1,018	1,138	1,194	1,214	1,165
Net income ($ mil.)	16.2%	65	40	57	75	56	75	87	93	72	252
Income as % of sales	—	8.4%	5.1%	6.5%	7.6%	5.8%	7.4%	7.6%	7.7%	6.0%	21.7%
Earnings per share ($)	16.1%	1.18	0.76	1.08	1.42	0.89	1.33	1.52	1.61	1.26	4.51
Stock price - FY high ($)	—	26.50	22.50	31.75	35.88	35.25	30.50	32.25	37.38	39.00	50.25
Stock price - FY low ($)	—	18.75	12.88	14.88	22.50	20.50	22.25	25.50	25.88	26.38	28.50
Stock price - FY close ($)	9.4%	22.13	17.00	30.63	33.13	25.25	27.00	32.25	28.00	31.31	49.50
P/E - high	—	22	30	29	25	40	23	21	23	31	11
P/E - low	—	16	17	14	16	23	17	17	16	21	6
Dividends per share ($)	8.3%	0.36	0.42	0.46	0.50	0.54	0.58	0.62	0.66	0.70	0.74
Book value per share ($)	6.8%	6.12	6.45	6.90	7.43	7.35	8.45	9.89	10.56	10.09	11.02
Employees	(0.8%)	8,300	8,750	9,100	8,850	8,450	8,650	9,400	9,800	9,550	7,700

STOCK PRICE HISTORY

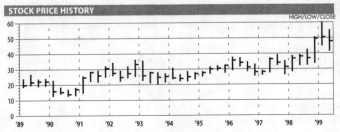

HIGH/LOW/CLOSE

1998 FISCAL YEAR-END

Debt ratio: 22.0%
Return on equity: 44.5%
Cash ($ mil.): 41
Current ratio: 1.61
Long-term debt ($ mil.): 160
No. of shares (mil.): 51
Dividends
 Yield: 1.5%
 Payout: 16.4%
Market value ($ mil.): 2,549

CRANE CO.

OVERVIEW

When it comes to acquisitions, Crane Co. is accustomed to heavy lifting — it has spent $725 million to purchase nearly 20 companies in the last seven years. The Stamford, Connecticut-based company is involved in everything from distribution (36% of sales) to fluid-handling components (20% of sales). It has seven business segments: wholesale distribution (millwork and plumbing fixtures), fluid handling (valves and wastewater treatment systems), aerospace (braking systems, fuel pumps), engineered material (liners for trucks and other vehicles), merchandising systems (vending machines), crane controls (switches

and control valves), and defense (elevators, winches, and cranes). Customers include the aerospace, truck and RV, construction, defense, and fluid-handling industries.

Crane works to build dominant positions in a number of niche markets through acquisitions. Examples of Crane's market dominance include Kemlite (fiberglass panels), National Vendors (vending machines), and its aerospace and controls businesses. Market segment domination often makes Crane a low-cost supplier, enabling it to attract more customers and outperform its rivals. The Crane Fund, a charitable trust, owns 11% of the company.

HISTORY

Crane was started in 1855 by Richard Teller Crane as a small foundry in a lumberyard owned by his uncle, Martin Ryerson. Crane grew with Chicago and its railroads, receiving its first big order supplying parts to a maker of railroad cars. In 1872 the company began making passenger elevators through the Crane Elevator Company, which was sold in 1895 to a joint venture that became the Otis Elevator Company. Although it had made plumbing materials since 1886, Crane developed a broader line in the 1920s and became a household name. The company remained under the leadership of the Crane family until Thomas Mellon Evans was elected chief executive in 1959. Evans diversified the company through acquisitions, including Huttig Sash & Door (1968) and CF&I Steel (1969). But Crane also added basic materials, buying Medusa (cement and aggregates) in 1979.

Mellon Evans' son Robert took over as Crane chairman in 1984 and began restructuring. That year Crane sold its U.S. Plumbing Division, and the next year it spun off CF&I Steel to its shareholders. The company then began buying manufacturing companies in the defense, aerospace, fluid controls, vending machines, fiberglass panels, and electronic components markets.

Crane expanded its Ferguson Machine business with the purchase of PickOmatic Systems of Detroit, a maker of mechanical parts handling equipment. The company boosted its wood building distribution segment with the 1988 acquisitions of Pozzi-Renati Millwork Products and Palmer G. Lewis.

In 1990 Crane acquired Lear Romec, a maker of pumps for the aerospace industry, and Crown Pumps' diaphragm pump business. Despite slumps in the defense, aerospace, and

other industries in the early 1990s, the company continued its successful strategy of selective acquisitions, including Jenkins Canada (bronze and iron valves, 1992), Rondel's millwork distributions and Burks Pumps (both in 1993), and Mark Controls (valves, instruments and controls, 1994). In 1995 the company signed a joint venture agreement with the Hebei Ningjin Valve Plant of China to produce industrial iron valves.

Crane slowed down acquisitions in 1996, picking up only two companies: Interpoint, a maker of DC-DC power converters, and UK-based Grenson Electronics, a producer of low-voltage power conversion components. In 1997 Crane acquired five businesses, the largest of which was Stockham Valves & Fittings, which is being integrated into the company's valve group.

The company's six 1998 acquisitions included Environmental Products USA (water purification systems), Number One Supply (buildings products distribution), Consolidated Lumber Company (wholesale distributor of lumber and millwork products), Sequentia Holdings (fiberglass reinforced plastic panels), Liberty Technologies (diagnostic equipment for the power and process industries), and the plastic-lined piping products division of Dow Chemical. Crane also sold two of its foundries in Tennessee and Alabama in 1998.

In 1999 the company lost an appeal to block BFGoodrich's purchase of Coltec Industries, an aerospace and industrial concern Crane wished to acquire. Crane filed a federal antitrust suit, but later settled out of court. Crane also began studying the possible spinoff of a subsidiary, Huttig Sash & Door.

Chairman and CEO: Robert S. Evans, age 54,
$1,777,159 pay
President and COO: Eric C. Fast
VP, Secretary, and General Counsel:
Augustus I. duPont, age 47, $433,442 pay
VP and Chief Information Officer: Bradley L. Ellis,
age 30
VP Environment, Health, and Safety:
Anthony D. Pantaleoni, age 44
VP Human Resources: John R. Packard, age 44
VP Finance and CFO: David S. Smith, age 41,
$650,974 pay
Controller: Michael L. Raithel, age 51, $455,410 pay
Treasurer: Gil A. Dickoff, age 37
Auditors: Deloitte & Touche LLP

LOCATIONS

HQ: 100 1st Stamford Place, Stamford, CT 06902
Phone: 203-363-7300   **Fax:** 203-363-7295
Web site: http://www.shareholder.com/crane

Crane Co. has more than 30 manufacturing facilities
in the US and five in Canada, as well as about 20
international sites.

PRODUCTS/OPERATIONS

1998 Sales & Operating Profit

	Sales		Operating Profit	
	$ mil.	% of total	$ mil.	% of total
Wholesale distribution	816	36	34	13
Fluid handling	445	20	28	11
Aerospace	395	17	118	45
Engineered materials	276	12	40	15
Merchandising systems	192	8	33	13
Crane controls	131	6	9	3
Other	14	1	(23)	—
Total	**2,269**	**100**	**239**	**100**

COMPETITORS

Azkoyen
BFGoodrich
Cameron Ashley
Dover
IMI
Kohler
PACCAR
Precision Castparts
PrimeSource Building
Swagelok
Tyco International

HISTORICAL FINANCIALS & EMPLOYEES

NYSE symbol: CR FYE: December 31	Annual Growth	1989	1990	1991	1992	1993	1994	1995	1996	1997	1998
Sales ($ mil.)	5.1%	1,456	1,438	1,303	1,307	1,310	1,654	1,782	1,848	2,037	2,269
Net income ($ mil.)	10.6%	56	63	22	24	49	56	76	92	113	138
Income as % of sales	—	3.8%	4.4%	1.7%	1.9%	3.7%	3.4%	4.3%	5.0%	5.5%	6.1%
Earnings per share ($)	11.2%	0.77	0.86	0.32	0.35	0.73	0.83	1.12	1.35	1.63	2.00
Stock price - FY high ($)	—	11.12	12.35	13.35	12.40	13.74	13.12	17.57	21.02	31.52	37.60
Stock price - FY low ($)	—	6.67	7.90	8.34	9.68	10.07	10.73	11.51	16.02	18.34	21.75
Stock price - FY close ($)	12.6%	10.34	8.90	10.51	10.51	11.01	11.96	16.41	19.34	28.93	30.19
P/E - high	—	14	14	42	35	19	16	16	16	19	19
P/E - low	—	9	9	26	28	14	13	10	12	11	11
Dividends per share ($)	2.0%	0.31	0.33	0.33	0.33	0.33	0.33	0.33	0.33	0.33	0.37
Book value per share ($)	10.0%	3.97	4.51	4.35	4.03	4.33	4.86	5.53	6.76	7.80	9.39
Employees	1.7%	10,737	10,000	9,000	8,500	8,700	10,700	8,500	10,700	11,000	12,500

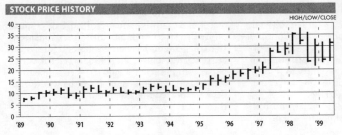

STOCK PRICE HISTORY HIGH/LOW/CLOSE

1998 FISCAL YEAR-END
Debt ratio: 35.8%
Return on equity: 21.5%
Cash ($ mil.): 16
Current ratio: 1.99
Long-term debt ($ mil.): 359
No. of shares (mil.): 68
Dividends
 Yield: 1.2%
 Payout: 18.5%
Market value ($ mil.): 2,068

CROWN CORK & SEAL COMPANY

OVERVIEW

Crown Cork & Seal Company (CC&S) has the packaging industry all wrapped up. The Philadelphia-based company is a leading producer of packaging containers. The company's metals packaging unit (which accounts for about 80% of sales) makes cans, closures, and ends for beer, pet food, soups, ready-made meals, and other products. CC&S also produces plastic containers for food, lipstick, nasal spray, and other goods. In addition, the company sells can-making equipment.

CC&S's strategy of growth through acquisition resulted in its purchasing about 20 companies, more than doubling its size and diversifying its product line and geographic base. The US now accounts for less than half of the company's sales and number of factories, and Europe is becoming CC&S's primary market. The company is also focused on capital improvements.

Chairman William Avery and CFO Alan Rutherford together own about 5% of CC&S.

HISTORY

Formed as Crown Cork & Seal Co. (CC&S) of Baltimore in 1892, the company was consolidated into its present form in 1927 when it merged with New Process Cork and New York Patents. The next year CC&S expanded overseas and formed Crown Cork International.

In 1936 CC&S acquired Acme Can and benefited from the movement at the time from home canning to processed canning. The company was the first to develop the aerosol can (1946).

By 1957 a heavy debt load had CC&S in trouble. Teetering on the brink of bankruptcy, the company hired Irishman John Connelly as president. Connelly immediately stopped can production (sending stockpiled inventory to customers), discontinued unprofitable product lines (ice cube trays), and reduced costs (25% of CC&S's employees were laid off over a 20-month period). He then directed CC&S to take advantage of new uses for aerosol cans (insecticides, hair spray, and bathroom cleaning supplies) and to expand overseas. CC&S obtained "pioneer rights" between 1955 and 1960 from foreign countries that granted it the first crack at new closure and can businesses.

The introduction of the pull tab pop-top in 1963 hit the can business like an exploding grenade. Connelly embraced pull tabs, but he rejected getting into the production of two-piece aluminum cans (first introduced in the mid-1970s), focusing instead on existing technology for three-piece cans. He also resisted the diversification trend then popular in the can-making industry, which later led to the declining performances of competitors Continental Can and American Can.

In 1970 CC&S moved into the printing end of the industry. It gained the ability to imprint color lithography on its bottle caps and cans through its acquisition of R. Hoe.

Connelly, known as the "Iron Man" for his tight-fisted control of fiscal matters, kept CC&S debt-free through most of the 1980s, using cash flow to buy back about half of CC&S's stock. In 1989 he picked Bill Avery to succeed him. With Connelly's blessing, Avery started a buying spree. CC&S bought the plants of Continental Can in three stages, paying $800 million. Connelly died in 1990. Two years later CC&S acquired CONSTAR International, the #1 maker of polyethylene terephthalate (PET) plastic containers.

In 1993 the company acquired another PET provider in Europe (Wellstar Holdings) and can maker Van Dorn. The following year CC&S acquired the can-manufacturing unit of Tri Valley Growers, one of the biggest in the country, for $61 million. Also in 1994 the Northridge earthquake ruined the company's plant in Van Nuys, California.

CC&S bought French packaging company CarnaudMetalbox in 1996. The purchase united CC&S's efficient operations and strong presence in North America with the French packaging concern's state-of-the-art manufacturing technology and international marketing experience. That year strikes over contract disputes halted production at eight of the company's plants. Also in 1996 CC&S agreed to sell its paint- and oblong-can business to Atlanta-based BWAY Corp. In addition, CC&S acquired Polish packaging company Fabryka Opakowan Blaszanyck.

In 1997 CC&S bought a 96% stake in Golden Aluminum from ACX Technologies, but returned the aluminum recycler in 1999 at a cost of $10 million. Also in 1997 CC&S spun off its Crown-Simplimatic machinery business to management. Dropping sales and foreign currency fluctuations in 1998 forced the company to announce it would close seven factories and cut 2,700 jobs, or 7% of its workforce. CC&S expected the restructuring to last through 1999.

Chairman and CEO: William J. Avery, age 58,
$1,575,950 pay
VC: Michael J. McKenna, age 64, $902,031 pay
President and COO; President, Americas Division:
John W. Conway, age 53, $642,531 pay
EVP; President, European Division:
Tommy H. Karlsson, age 52, $709,098 pay
EVP, Secretary, and General Counsel:
Richard L. Krzyzanowski, age 66
EVP and CFO: Alan W. Rutherford, age 55, $622,275 pay
EVP Corporate Technologies: Daniel A. Abramowicz
EVP Procurement and Traffic: Ronald R. Thoma, age 64
EVP; President, Asia-Pacific Division: William H. Voss,
age 53
SVP Taxes: Reda H. Amiry
SVP Finance and Treasurer: Craig R. L. Calle, age 39
SVP and Corporate Controller: Timothy J. Donahue,
age 36
SVP Corporate Operations: William R. Howard
VP Human Resources: Gary L. Burgess
VP Treasury Management: Michael B. Burns
VP Internal Audit: Gregory L. Cowan
VP Energy and Facilities: Daniel J. Donaghy
VP Business Development: Michael F. Dunleavy
VP Metal Purchasing: Charles E. Finnegan
VP Global Customer Business: Keith E. Lucas
Auditors: PricewaterhouseCoopers LLP

LOCATIONS

HQ: Crown Cork & Seal Company, Inc.,
1 Crown Way, Philadelphia, PA 19154-4599
Phone: 215-698-5100   **Fax:** 215-676-7245
Web site: http://www.crowncork.com

PRODUCTS/OPERATIONS

1998 Sales

	$ mil.	% of total
Metal food cans & ends	2,562	31
Metal beverage cans & ends	2,554	31
Plastic packaging	1,535	18
Other metal packaging	1,478	18
Other products	171	2
Total	**8,300**	**100**

Selected Products

Metal Packaging
Aerosol cans
Beverage cans
Closures
Food cans

Plastic Packaging
Bottles
Closures
Personal care product containers
PET (polyethylene terephthalate) bottles
Pharmaceutical packaging

COMPETITORS

Alcoa	Pechiney
Ball Corporation	Reynolds Metals
Berlin Packaging	Schmalbach-Lubeca
BWAY	Sealright
Century Aluminum	Silgan
Continental Can	Tetra Laval
Kerr Group	U.S. Can
Owens-Illinois	VIAG

HISTORICAL FINANCIALS & EMPLOYEES

NYSE symbol: CCK FYE: December 31	Annual Growth	1989	1990	1991	1992	1993	1994	1995	1996	1997	1998
Sales ($ mil.)	17.7%	1,910	3,072	3,807	3,781	4,163	4,452	5,054	8,332	8,495	8,300
Net income ($ mil.)	1.2%	94	107	128	155	99	131	75	284	294	105
Income as % of sales	—	4.9%	3.5%	3.4%	4.1%	2.4%	2.9%	1.5%	3.4%	3.5%	1.3%
Earnings per share ($)	(5.6%)	1.19	1.24	1.48	1.79	1.11	1.46	0.83	2.14	2.10	0.71
Stock price - FY high ($)	—	18.98	22.31	30.89	41.13	41.88	41.88	50.63	55.50	59.75	55.19
Stock price - FY low ($)	—	14.61	16.48	18.15	27.39	33.25	33.50	33.50	40.63	43.56	24.00
Stock price - FY close ($)	6.4%	17.69	18.90	29.89	39.88	41.88	37.75	41.75	54.38	50.13	30.81
P/E - high	—	16	18	21	23	38	29	61	26	28	78
P/E - low	—	12	13	12	15	30	23	40	19	21	34
Dividends per share ($)	—	0.00	0.00	0.00	0.00	0.00	0.00	0.00	1.00	1.00	1.00
Book value per share ($)	9.6%	9.39	10.97	12.44	13.24	14.09	15.28	16.12	23.69	23.43	21.45
Employees	11.2%	14,747	17,205	17,763	20,378	21,254	22,373	20,409	44,611	40,985	38,459

STOCK PRICE HISTORY

HIGH/LOW/CLOSE

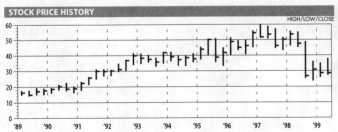

1998 FISCAL YEAR-END

Debt ratio: 51.7%
Return on equity: 4.0%
Cash ($ mil.): 284
Current ratio: 0.67
Long-term debt ($ mil.): 3,188
No. of shares (mil.): 122
Dividends
 Yield: 3.2%
 Payout: 140.8%
Market value ($ mil.): 3,769

CSX CORPORATION

CSX is banking on the railway and the seaway as the right ways to make money. The Richmond, Virginia-based company delivers freight by rail and ship, and it provides contract logistics services. CSX Transportation (CSXT), CSX's largest unit, is the third-largest railroad company in the US, after Union Pacific and Burlington Northern Santa Fe. A major coal carrier, CSXT has more than 23,000 route miles in 23 states in the eastern half of the US and two Canadian provinces.

With its purchase of 42% of Conrail (Norfolk Southern owns the rest), the firm has taken the fast track in the railroad industry's consolidation. The Conrail operations give CSX major rail links in the Northeast, such as Boston to Cleveland and New York to Chicago, and connect these cities with CSX's southern rail network. The company is focused on making the Conrail integration more successful than was Union Pacific's absorption of Southern Pacific, which resulted in massive railway congestion.

CSX's container shipping unit, Sea-Land Service, is one of the largest in the world; it operates a fleet of about 100 ships and reaches 120 ports worldwide. Sea-Land's international shipping business is being sold to A.P. Moller; CSX will retain its domestic shipping operations. Other units offer intermodal services (such as truck-to-train and train-to-ship) and logistical support. The company also owns The Greenbrier, a resort in West Virginia, and develops real estate.

CSX Corporation was formed in 1980, when Chessie System and Seaboard Coast Line (SCL) merged in an effort to improve the efficiency of their railroads.

Chessie's oldest railroad, the Baltimore & Ohio (B&O), was chartered in 1827 to help Baltimore compete against New York and Philadelphia for freight traffic. By the late 1800s the railroad served Chicago, Cincinnati, New York City, St. Louis, and Washington, DC. Chesapeake & Ohio (C&O) acquired it in 1962.

C&O originated in Virginia with the Louisa Railroad in 1836. It gained access to Chicago, Cincinnati, and Washington, DC, and by the mid-1900s was a major coal carrier. After B&O and C&O acquired joint control of Baltimore-based Western Maryland Railway (1967), the three railroads became subsidiaries of the newly formed Chessie System (1973).

One of SCL's two predecessors, Seaboard Air Line Railroad (SAL), grew out of Virginia's Portsmouth & Roanoke Rail Road of 1832. By 1875 the line was controlled by John Robinson, who gave the system its name. SAL acquired routes in Georgia, Florida, and Alabama.

SCL's other predecessor, Atlantic Coast Line Railroad (ACL), took shape between 1869 and 1893 as William Walters acquired several southern railroads. In 1902 ACL bought the Plant System (railroads in Georgia, Florida, and other southern states) and the Louisville & Nashville (a north-south line connecting New Orleans and Chicago), giving ACL the basic form it was to retain until 1967, when it merged with SAL to form SCL.

After CSX inherited the Chessie System and SCL, it bought Texas Gas Resources (gas pipeline, 1983), American Commercial Lines (Texas Gas' river barge subsidiary, 1984), and Sea-Land Corporation (ocean container shipping, 1986). To improve its market value, CSX sold most of its oil and gas properties, its communications holdings (LightNet), and most of its resort properties (Rockresorts) in 1988 and 1989.

Sea-Land formed joint ventures to operate in the former Soviet Union and in South America in the early 1990s. American Commercial Lines acquired Valley Line in 1992, boosting its barge capacity by more than one-third.

Sea-Land struck a deal with Danish shipping company Maersk Line in 1996 to share vessels and terminals. That year CSX made a friendly offer to buy rail company Conrail, which had prized access to the New York area, but the bid led to a takeover battle with rival Norfolk Southern. So, the next year Conrail decided to split its assets between the two; CSX paid $4.3 billion for 42%. The division took place in 1999.

CSX combined the American Commercial Lines barge business with the barge business of Vectura Group in 1998; CSX received $850 million from the sale and took a 32% stake in the new company, which retained the American Commercial Lines name.

In 1999 CSX sold Grand Teton Lodge to Vail Resorts for $50 million. Also that year CSX divided Sea-Land into three businesses: international terminal operations, domestic trade, and global container shipping, and announced plans to sell its international shipping business (including some terminals) to Denmark's A. P. Moller for $800 million.

Chairman, President, and CEO: John W. Snow, age 59,
$1,100,008 pay
EVP-Finance and CFO: Paul R. Goodwin, age 56,
$723,358 pay
EVP-Law and Public Affairs: Mark G. Aron, age 56,
$574,175 pay
SVP-Corporate Services: Andrew B. Fogarty, age 54
SVP-Executive Department: Thomas E. Hoppin
President and CEO-CSX Intermodal: Lester M. Passa,
age 44
President and CEO-CSX Transportation:
Alvin R. "Pete" Carpenter, age 57, $777,563 pay
President and CEO, Sea-Land Service: John P. Clancey,
age 54
**Group VP-Corporate Communications and Investor
Relations:** Jesse R. Mohorovic, age 56
VP-Administration: James A. Searle Jr.
VP-Audit and Advisory Services: William F. Miller
VP-Corporate Communications: Craig R. MacQueen
VP-Federal Affairs: Arnold I. Havens
VP-Financial Planning: Anita P. Beier
VP, General Counsel, and Corporate Secretary:
Alan A. Rudnick
VP-Law and General Counsel: Peter J. Shudtz
VP-State Relations: Michael J. Ruehling
VP and Treasurer: Gregory R. Weber, age 53
Director-Human Resources: Linda Amato
General Counsel-Corporate: Ellen M. Fitzsimmons
Auditors: Ernst & Young LLP

LOCATIONS

HQ: 1 James Center, 901 E. Cary St.,
Richmond, VA 23219-4031
Phone: 804-782-1400   **Fax:** 804-782-6747
Web site: http://www.csx.com

PRODUCTS/OPERATIONS

1998 Sales

	$ mil.	% of total
Rail commodities		
Coal	1,498	15
Chemicals	731	7
Automobiles	533	5
Forest products	493	5
Minerals	398	4
Agricultural products	360	4
Metals	318	3
Phosphates & fertilizer	302	3
Food & consumer	156	2
Other	167	2
Container shipping	3,916	40
Intermodal	618	6
Contract logistics	408	4
Total	**9,898**	**100**

Selected Subsidiaries and Affiliates
American Commercial Lines (32%, river barges and
tugboats)
CSX Transportation Inc. (rail transportation and
distribution services)
Sea-Land Service Inc. (container shipping worldwide)

COMPETITORS

APL
Atlantic Container
Burlington Northern
 Santa Fe
Canadian Pacific
CHR
CNF Transportation
Evergreen Marine

FDX
Hanjin Shipping
J. B. Hunt
Neptune Orient
Norfolk Southern
Peninsular and Oriental
Schneider National
Union Pacific

HISTORICAL FINANCIALS & EMPLOYEES

NYSE symbol: CSX FYE: December 31	Annual Growth	1989	1990	1991	1992	1993	1994	1995	1996	1997	1998
Sales ($ mil.)	2.8%	7,745	8,205	8,636	8,734	8,940	9,608	10,504	10,536	10,621	9,898
Net income ($ mil.)	2.5%	429	416	(272)	20	359	652	618	855	799	537
Income as % of sales	—	5.5%	5.1%	—	0.2%	4.0%	6.8%	5.9%	8.1%	7.5%	5.4%
Earnings per share ($)	2.2%	2.06	2.08	(1.36)	0.10	1.71	3.08	2.91	3.96	3.62	2.51
Stock price - FY high ($)	—	19.31	19.06	29.00	36.81	44.06	46.19	46.13	53.13	62.44	60.75
Stock price - FY low ($)	—	14.88	13.00	14.88	27.25	33.19	31.56	34.69	42.13	41.25	36.50
Stock price - FY close ($)	9.8%	17.94	15.88	28.94	34.38	40.94	34.81	45.63	42.25	54.00	41.50
P/E - high	—	9	9	—	368	26	15	16	13	17	24
P/E - low	—	7	6	—	273	19	10	12	11	11	15
Dividends per share ($)	7.2%	0.64	0.70	0.72	0.76	0.79	0.88	0.92	1.04	1.08	1.20
Book value per share ($)	5.6%	16.62	17.97	15.54	14.38	15.28	17.81	20.15	23.03	26.41	27.08
Employees	(1.4%)	52,582	50,931	49,883	47,597	48,308	47,703	47,965	47,314	46,911	46,147

STOCK PRICE HISTORY

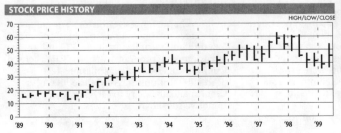

HIGH/LOW/CLOSE

1998 FISCAL YEAR-END

Debt ratio: 52.2%
Return on equity: 9.1%
Cash ($ mil.): 105
Current ratio: 0.76
Long-term debt ($ mil.): 6,432
No. of shares (mil.): 217
Dividends
 Yield: 2.9%
 Payout: 47.8%
Market value ($ mil.): 9,010

CUMMINS ENGINE COMPANY, INC.

OVERVIEW

Instead of livin' on reds, vitamin C, and cocaine to keep on truckin', many people just fire up a Cummins diesel. Headquartered in Columbus, Indiana, Cummins Engine is the world's #1 manufacturer of diesel engines larger than 200 horsepower (hp). Cummins' diesel and natural gas engines, which range from 60 to 6,000 hp, also power light commercial and midrange trucks, pickups, power generators, buses, construction equipment, farm tractors, recreational boats, and ships.

The company's power generation unit makes Onan and Petbow generator sets and Newage alternators. Cummins' Fleetguard and Nelson filtration units produce fuel and air filters and exhaust systems for heavy-duty engines.

Since 1994 the company has focused on upgrading or replacing its engines to incorporate advanced electronics, combustion, air-handling, and electronic controls. It also has entered several joint ventures to capitalize on its partners' geographic location and technical expertise. Cummins' strong performance in North America has been offset by weakness in Asian, South American, and agricultural markets.

HISTORY

Chauffeur Clessie Cummins believed that Rudolph Diesel's cumbersome and smoky engine could be improved for use in transportation. Borrowing money and work space from his employer — Columbus, Indiana, banker W. G. Irwin — Cummins founded Cummins Engine in 1919. Irwin invested more than $2.5 million and in the mid-1920s Cummins produced a mobile diesel engine. Truck manufacturers were reluctant to switch from gas to diesel, so Cummins used publicity stunts (such as racing in the Indianapolis 500) to advertise his engine.

The company earned its first profit in 1937, the year Irwin's grandnephew, J. Irwin Miller, took over. During WWII the Cummins engine was used in heavy cargo trucks. Sales jumped from $20 million in 1946 to more than $100 million by 1956. In the 1950s Cummins pioneered a line of four-stroke diesel engines, started its first overseas plant in Scotland (1956), and bought Atlas Crankshaft (1958). By 1967 it had 50% of the diesel engine market.

Cummins diversified in 1970 by acquiring the K2 Ski Company (fiberglass skis) and Coot Industries (all-terrain vehicles), but sold them by 1976. CEO Henry Schacht began modernizing company plants after touring Japanese factories.

In the early 1980s Cummins introduced a line of midrange engines developed in a joint venture with oil and gas concern J. I. Case, a subsidiary of Tenneco. To remain competitive, Cummins cut costs by 22%, doubled productivity in its US and UK plants, and spent $1.8 billion to retool its factories. The strategy yielded mixed results. Profits were erratic, and restructuring prevented the company from taking advantage of an industry boom in 1987 and 1988.

Having twice repelled unwelcome foreign suitors in 1989, Cummins sold 27% of its stock to Ford, Tenneco, and Japanese tractor maker Kubota for $250 million in 1990. The move raised cash and protected Cummins from future takeover bids. In 1992 Cummins agreed to develop a high-pressure fuel-injection system with Sweden's Saab-Scania.

The following year Cummins established engine-making joint ventures with Tata Engineering & Locomotive, India's largest heavy-vehicle maker, and Komatsu, a leading Japanese construction equipment maker.

In 1993 Cummins introduced a natural-gas engine for school buses and formed a joint venture to produce turbochargers in India. In 1995 the company entered a joint venture with Wartsila NSD, an engineering company, to develop high-speed diesel and natural gas engines in France and the UK. It also began a restructuring in 1995, selling plants and laying off workers.

Continuing its strategy of teaming with other manufacturers, Cummins agreed in 1996 to make small and midsize diesel engines with Fiat's Iveco and New Holland subsidiaries.

In 1997 subsidiary Cadec Systems signed a license to develop and sell Montreal-based Canadian Marconi's fleet tracking system, which uses satellites and computers. In early 1998 Cummins bought diesel exhaust and air filtration company Nelson Industries for $490 million. That year the Cummins took a $114 million charge for restructuring. The company also agreed, without admitting guilt, to pay a $25 million fine and contribute $35 million to environmental programs after the EPA accused Cummins of cheating on emissions tests.

In 1999 Cummins agreed to sell its Atlas Crankshaft subsidiary to Thyssen Krupp's automotive subsidiary.

OFFICERS

Chairman and CEO: James A. Henderson, age 64, $1,120,430 pay
President and COO: Theodore M. Solso, age 51, $770,983 pay
EVP and Chief Technical Officer; Group President, Industrial: F. Joseph Loughrey, age 49, $509,285 pay
EVP; Group President, Automotive: C. Roberto Cordaro, age 48, $428,451 pay
EVP; Group President, Power Generation and International: John K. Edwards, age 54
VP and CFO: Kiran M. Patel, age 50
VP Human Resources: Jean S. Blackwell, age 44
VP, Secretary, and General Counsel: Pamela F. Carter, age 49
VP Business Development: George Fauerbach
VP Quality: Frank J. McDonald
VP and Corporate Controller: Rick J. Mills, age 51
VP Corporate Responsibility and Diversity: Brenda S. Pitts
VP and Treasurer: Donald W. Trapp
President and Director General, Cummins Wartsila: Iain M. Barrowman
VP Worldwide Marketing, Medium-Duty and Heavy-Duty Trucks: Martha F. Brooks
Auditors: Arthur Andersen LLP

LOCATIONS

HQ: 500 Jackson St., Columbus, IN 47202-3005
Phone: 812-377-5000   **Fax:** 812-377-4937
Web site: http://www.cummins.com

Cummins has manufacturing operations in Australia, Brazil, China, France, India, Mexico, the UK, and the US. It also has joint ventures or licensing deals in China, France, India, Indonesia, Japan, Pakistan, South Korea, and Turkey.

PRODUCTS/OPERATIONS

1998 Sales

	$ mil.	% of total
Engine Business	3,982	63
Power generation	1,230	20
Filters & other	1,054	17
Total	**6,266**	**100**

Selected Products
Engines for trucks (pickups and heavy-duty), buses, and light commercial vehicles
Filtration products
   Fleetguard
   Nelson
Heavy- and medium-duty truck engines
   120 hp-300 hp diesel engines for midrange trucks
   260 hp-525 hp diesel engines for heavy-duty trucks
Industrial engines for construction, logging, mining, agricultural, and marine equipment
Power generation products
   Newage (alternators)
   Onan (gasoline engines and generator sets)
   Petbow (generator sets)

COMPETITORS

Caterpillar	Mitsubishi
DaimlerChrysler	Navistar
Detroit Diesel	Nissan
Emerson	Outboard Marine
Invensys	Scania
Isuzu	Thyssen Krupp
Kohler	Volvo
Mack Trucks	

HISTORICAL FINANCIALS & EMPLOYEES

NYSE symbol: CUM FYE: December 31	Annual Growth	1989	1990	1991	1992	1993	1994	1995	1996	1997	1998
Sales ($ mil.)	6.6%	3,511	3,462	3,406	3,749	4,248	4,737	5,245	5,257	5,625	6,266
Net income ($ mil.)	—	(6)	(138)	(14)	(190)	177	253	224	160	212	(21)
Income as % of sales	—	—	—	—	—	4.2%	5.3%	4.3%	3.0%	3.8%	—
Earnings per share ($)	—	(0.76)	(6.13)	(0.74)	(6.01)	4.63	6.11	5.52	4.01	5.48	(0.55)
Stock price - FY high ($)	—	36.13	27.75	27.25	40.44	54.38	57.63	48.63	47.75	83.00	62.75
Stock price - FY low ($)	—	24.00	15.56	16.25	26.63	37.38	35.88	34.00	34.50	44.25	28.31
Stock price - FY close ($)	3.8%	25.38	18.63	27.13	39.00	53.75	45.25	37.00	46.00	59.06	35.50
P/E - high	—	—	—	—	—	12	9	9	12	15	—
P/E - low	—	—	—	—	—	8	6	6	9	8	—
Dividends per share ($)	0.0%	1.10	1.10	0.35	0.10	0.20	0.63	1.00	1.00	1.08	1.10
Book value per share ($)	4.8%	19.89	18.68	17.14	11.21	18.41	25.78	29.43	33.30	33.78	30.29
Employees	1.3%	25,100	24,900	22,900	23,400	23,600	25,600	24,300	23,500	26,300	28,300

STOCK PRICE HISTORY

HIGH/LOW/CLOSE

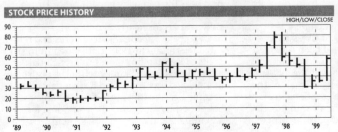

1998 FISCAL YEAR-END

Debt ratio: 47.2%
Return on equity: —
Cash ($ mil.): 38
Current ratio: 1.75
Long-term debt ($ mil.): 1,137
No. of shares (mil.): 42
Dividends
   Yield: 3.1%
   Payout: —
Market value ($ mil.): 1,491

CVS CORPORATION

OVERVIEW

Drugs are not merely recreational at CVS, which fills 10.5% of the nation's prescriptions. The Woonsocket, Rhode Island-based company is the #2 drugstore chain in the US (behind Walgreens) in total sales and #1 in store count and prescriptions filled. In addition to prescriptions, CVS's 4,200 or so drugstores — located east of the Mississippi — have "front-store" sections offering other medications, cosmetics, food, film processing, and general merchandise. Subsidiary PharmaCare Management Services provides prescription benefit management services.

Formerly known as Melville Corporation, in the mid-1990s the company shucked its apparel, home goods, and shoe retailing operations to concentrate on its star performer, the CVS chain. CVS then bulked up by acquiring Revco D.S. and Arbor Drugs.

CVS has since revved up its store-opening efforts, remodeled many existing stores, and moved others from strip malls to freestanding locations. In addition, the company has increased its private-label offerings to 1,400 items (accounting for about 11% of front-store sales) and has begun tapping the Internet market with an online pharmacy. CVS has played hardball with HMOs, refusing to fill prescriptions from certain health care plans that did not provide high enough reimbursement levels.

HISTORY

Brothers Stanley and Sid Goldstein, who ran health and beauty products distributor Mark Steven, branched out into retail in 1963 when they opened up their first Consumer Value Store in Lowell, Massachusetts, with partner Ralph Hoagland.

The chain grew rapidly, amassing 17 stores by the end of 1964 (the year the "CVS" name was first used) and 40 by 1969. That year the Goldsteins sold the chain to Melville Shoe to finance further expansion.

Melville had been founded in 1892 by shoe supplier Frank Melville. Melville's son, Ward, grew the company, creating the Thom McAn shoe store chain and later buying its supplier. By 1969 Melville had opened leased shoe shops in Kmart stores (through its Meldisco unit), launched one apparel chain (Chess King; sold in 1993), and purchased another (Foxwood Stores; renamed Foxmoor and sold in 1985).

In 1972 CVS bought the 84-store Clinton Drug and Discount, a Rochester, New York-based chain. Two years later, when sales hit $100 million, CVS had 232 stores — only 45 of which had pharmacies. The company bought New Jersey-based Mack Drug (36 stores) in 1977. By 1981 CVS had more than 400 stores.

CVS's sales hit $1 billion in 1985 as it continued to add pharmacies to many of its older stores. In 1987 Stanley's success was recognized companywide when he was named chairman and CEO of CVS's parent company, which by then had been renamed Melville Corporation.

Three years later CVS bought the 490-store Peoples Drug Stores chain from Imasco. The $330 million deal gave CVS locations in Maryland, Pennsylvania, Virginia, Washington, DC, and West Virginia. The next year the firm pulled out of California, where it had accumulated about 85 stores.

CVS created PharmaCare Management Services in 1994 to take advantage of the growing market for pharmacy services and managed-care drug programs. Pharmacist Tom Ryan took the helm of the CVS chain that year. The company opened its first New York City store in 1995, sparking an intense fight for territory there.

With CVS outperforming Melville's other operations, in 1995 Melville decided to concentrate on the drugstore chain. By that time Melville's holdings had grown to include discount department store chain Marshalls and furniture chain This End Up, both sold in 1995; athletic footwear chain Footaction, spun off as part of Footstar in 1996, along with Meldisco; the Linens 'n Things chain, spun off in 1996; the Kay-Bee Toys chain, sold in 1996; and Bob's Stores (apparel and footwear), sold in 1997.

Melville was renamed CVS in late 1996. Amid consolidation in the drugstore industry, in 1997 CVS — with about 1,425 stores — paid $3.7 billion for Revco D.S., which had nearly 2,600 stores in 17 states, including a strong presence in the Midwest and Southeast. The next year the company bought Arbor Drugs (200 stores in Michigan, later converted to the CVS banner) for nearly $1.5 billion.

CVS opened about 180 new stores and relocated nearly 200 in 1998 as it shifted from strip malls to freestanding stores (it also closed nearly 160 stores). Stanley retired as chairman in 1999 and was succeeded by Ryan, who had become CEO in 1998. In 1999 the company bought online drugstore pioneer Soma for $30 million and renamed it CVS.com.

OFFICERS

Chairman and CEO; President and CEO of CVS Pharmacy: Thomas M. Ryan, age 46, $2,003,250 pay (prior to promotion)
President and COO: Charles C. Conaway, age 38, $1,264,100 pay (prior to promotion)
EVP and CFO: David B. Rickard
EVP - Corporate Development: Lawrence Zigerelli, age 40
VP; EVP - Marketing of CVS Pharmacy: Daniel C. Nelson, $805,580 pay
VP; EVP - Stores of CVS Pharmacy: Larry J. Merlo, $771,200 pay
VP; SVP - Human Resources of CVS Pharmacy: Rosemary Mede
Auditors: KPMG LLP

LOCATIONS

HQ: 1 CVS Dr., Woonsocket, RI 02895
Phone: 401-765-1500 **Fax:** 401-766-2917
Web site: http://www.cvs.com

1998 Stores

	No.
Ohio	414
New York	363
Massachusetts	321
Pennsylvania	319
Georgia	304
North Carolina	296
Indiana	291
Virginia	253
Michigan	225
South Carolina	196
Other	1140
Total	**4,122**

PRODUCTS/OPERATIONS

1998 Sales

	% of total
Pharmacy	58
Front of store	42
Total	**100**

Store Operations
Pharmacy
Front of store (over-the-counter drugs, greeting cards, film and photofinishing services, beauty items, seasonal merchandise, and convenience foods)

COMPETITORS

Albertson's
Dayton Hudson
drugstore.com
Duane Reade
Eckerd
Kmart
Kroger
Rite Aid
Walgreen
Wal-Mart

HISTORICAL FINANCIALS & EMPLOYEES

NYSE symbol: CVS FYE: December 31	Annual Growth	1989	1990	1991	1992	1993	1994	1995	1996	1997	1998
Sales ($ mil.)	8.1%	7,554	8,687	9,886	10,433	10,435	11,286	9,689	5,528	12,738	15,274
Net income ($ mil.)	(0.0%)	398	385	347	133	332	308	(657)	75	38	396
Income as % of sales	—	5.3%	4.4%	3.5%	1.3%	3.2%	2.7%	—	1.4%	0.3%	2.6%
Earnings per share ($)	(6.4%)	1.78	1.80	1.60	0.56	1.19	1.10	(1.79)	0.49	0.07	0.98
Stock price - FY high ($)	—	26.81	28.88	27.63	27.50	27.38	20.81	19.94	23.00	35.00	56.00
Stock price - FY low ($)	—	18.44	16.38	19.13	21.25	19.44	14.75	14.31	13.63	19.50	30.44
Stock price - FY close ($)	10.5%	22.31	21.00	22.25	26.56	20.31	15.44	15.38	20.69	32.03	55.00
P/E - high	—	15	16	17	49	23	19	—	47	500	57
P/E - low	—	10	9	12	38	16	13	—	28	279	31
Dividends per share ($)	(13.8%)	0.65	0.71	0.72	0.74	0.76	0.76	0.57	0.22	0.22	0.17
Book value per share ($)	(0.9%)	7.84	8.95	9.97	9.83	10.58	11.21	7.36	4.44	6.02	7.25
Employees	(0.4%)	100,541	119,590	110,148	115,644	111,082	117,000	96,832	44,000	90,000	97,000

STOCK PRICE HISTORY

HIGH/LOW/CLOSE

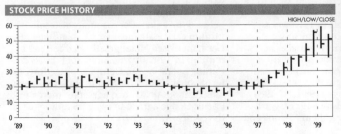

1998 FISCAL YEAR-END

Debt ratio: 8.1%
Return on equity: 14.0%
Cash ($ mil.): 181
Current ratio: 1.37
Long-term debt ($ mil.): 276
No. of shares (mil.): 390
Dividends
Yield: 0.3%
Payout: 17.3%
Market value ($ mil.): 21,462

CYPRUS AMAX MINERALS

OVERVIEW

Cyprus Amax Minerals won't be mining its own business much longer as rival Phelps Dodge is buying the company. The Englewood, Colorado-based mining company is the world's largest producer of molybdenum (used in steel-making) and a top producer of copper in the US and South America and coal in Australia. Through its 31% interest in Kinross Gold, Cyprus Amax holds a significant position in the international gold market. The company owns all its copper and molybdenum mines in the US and has shares in its operations in South America and Australia.

After getting shafted by low copper and molybdenum prices, Cyprus Amax has sold both its lithium business and US coal mines to concentrate on its core copper, gold, and molybdenum operations; it's seeking buyers for its stake in Kinross Gold and Australian coal operations. Low prices and high demand (particularly by wire and cable manufacturers) had prompted Cyprus Amax to merge with rival ASARCO until Phelps Dodge stepped in and broke up the deal. Cyprus Amax had been planning to increase its overall copper production by 50% over the next five to seven years, first through high-yield, large-reserve mines in Chile and Peru.

HISTORY

Cyprus Amax Minerals was created in 1993 when Cyprus Minerals, a coal and copper producer, merged with AMAX, a diversified metals and energy company.

Berthold Hochschild founded the American Metal Company (Amco) to trade in metals for a German banking firm. After severing ties with Germany during WWI, Amco formed an independent syndicate in 1916 to exploit Colorado deposits of molybdenum. In 1957 Amco merged with the syndicate, creating American Metal Climax, informally known as AMAX until the name became official in 1974.

The company ventured into other mining operations, including aluminum in 1962 when it purchased Kawneer of Michigan and Apex Smelting of Chicago. Combined under the name Alumax, the unit later became the US's third-largest aluminum company.

AMAX acquired Ayrshire Collieries in 1969 and coal mines in Wyoming in the 1970s. During the 1980s the company branched into gold. It made a foray into energy in 1990 with the purchase of Ladd Petroleum. A weak global economy, low metals prices, and excess imports of aluminum from the former Soviet Union hurt Alumax's earnings in the early 1990s.

Cyprus Minerals evolved from Amoco Minerals, a subsidiary of integrated oil company Amoco (now BP Amoco), created in 1969 to handle mineral rights. The subsidiary changed its name to Cyprus Minerals in 1979 when it acquired a diversified mining company. In 1985 Amoco spun off Cyprus Minerals.

The new publicly traded company went on a buying spree, purchasing coal mines in Utah (1985), Colorado (1985), and Wyoming (1987), and copper mines in Arizona (1986 and 1987) and New Mexico (1987). Also in 1987 Cyprus Minerals began mining for gold in Arizona and Australia. Sales topped $1 billion by 1988. Cyprus Minerals continued to expand, buying up lithium and copper producers between 1988 and 1990. It entered a coal mining joint venture with Carbones del Zulia (a subsidiary of Petroleos de Venezuela) in 1991.

The 1993 merger of Cyprus Minerals and AMAX consolidated certain operations of both companies and greatly reduced AMAX's debt. Spun off in the merger were Alumax and Amax Gold, in which the new company acquired a 42% stake. Job cuts, other cost cuts, and productivity boosts made Cyprus Amax a low-cost, high-volume worldwide producer. The company sold its AMAX Oil and Gas subsidiary in 1994 to finance mining projects in South America.

In early 1996 Cyprus Amax bought a 50% interest in the Springvale underground coal mine in Australia (South Korean conglomerate Samsung owns the other 50%) and purchased the Twentymile coal mine in Colorado. That year a copper price slump and a charge for environmental remediation depressed Cyprus Amax's results.

The company acquired 80% of the Kansanshi copper mine from Zambia Consolidated Copper Mines in 1997. In 1998 the company bought a stake in a copper and gold exploration project in Papua New Guinea and gained a 31% stake in Kinross Gold when it acquired Amax Gold (in which Cyprus Amax held a 59% stake). Cyprus Amax also sold its lithium carbonate business to an affiliate of Germany-based Metallgesellschaft for $305 million. In 1999 Cyprus Amax sold its US coal-mining operations to Germany-based RAG International Mining for $1.1 billion. Cyprus Amax and ASARCO then agreed to merge until Phelps Dodge agreed to pay $1.8 billion for the company.

Chairman, President, and CEO: Milton H. Ward, age 66,
$2,108,524 pay
EVP: Jeffrey G. Clevenger, age 49, $550,875 pay
EVP: Garold R. Spindler, age 51, $550,875 pay
SVP and CFO: Gerald J. Malys, age 54, $557,938 pay
SVP, General Counsel, and Secretary: Philip C. Wolf,
age 51, $423,750 pay
SVP Exploration: David H. Watkins, age 54
VP and Treasurer: Farokh S. Hakimi, age 50
VP Engineering and Development: Robin J. Hickson,
age 55
VP and Controller: John Taraba, age 50
Director Organizational Services (HR): Chris Crowl
Auditors: PricewaterhouseCoopers LLP

LOCATIONS

HQ: Cyprus Amax Minerals Company,
9100 E. Mineral Circle, Englewood, CO 80112
Phone: 303-643-5000   **Fax:** 303-643-5049
Web site: http://www.cyprusamax.com

Cyprus Amax Minerals has mining and related
operations in Australia, Chile, Japan, the Netherlands,
Panama, Papua New Guinea, Peru, Russia, Sweden, the
UK, the US, and Zambia.

1998 Sales

	$ mil.	% of total
US	2,203	86
Other countries	363	14
Total	**2,566**	**100**

PRODUCTS/OPERATIONS

1998 Sales

	$ mil.	% of total
Copper & molybdenum	1,284	50
Coal	934	36
Lithium	218	9
Other	130	5
Total	**2,566**	**100**

Principal Subsidiaries
Cyprus Climax Metals Co. (copper and molybdenum)
Cyprus Exploration & Development Corp.

COMPETITORS

Anglo American	Inco Limited
ASARCO	Mueller Industries
BHP	Newmont Mining
Carso	Phelps Dodge
Centromin	Placer Dome
Codelco	Rio Algom
Cominco	Rio Tinto plc
Fluor	Southern Peru Copper
Freeport-McMoRan	Trelleborg
Copper & Gold	TrizecHahn
Gencor	UM
Grupo Mexico	USX-U.S. Steel
Homestake Mining	

HISTORICAL FINANCIALS & EMPLOYEES

NYSE symbol: CYM FYE: December 31	Annual Growth	1989	1990	1991	1992	1993	1994	1995	1996	1997	1998
Sales ($ mil.)	4.1%	1,790	1,866	1,657	1,641	1,764	2,788	3,207	2,843	3,346	2,566
Net income ($ mil.)	—	250	111	43	(334)	100	175	124	77	69	(75)
Income as % of sales	—	14.0%	5.9%	2.6%	—	5.7%	6.3%	3.9%	2.7%	2.1%	—
Earnings per share ($)	—	3.50	2.29	0.72	(8.46)	1.85	1.69	1.13	0.62	0.54	(1.02)
Stock price - FY high ($)		33.00	28.50	25.38	32.00	36.38	33.38	32.13	29.13	26.81	17.88
Stock price - FY low ($)	—	21.34	13.88	17.50	18.50	21.25	23.13	24.25	19.88	14.44	9.00
Stock price - FY close ($)	(10.3%)	26.50	18.50	22.88	31.50	25.88	26.13	26.13	23.50	15.38	10.00
P/E - high	—	9	12	35	—	20	20	28	47	50	—
P/E - low	—	6	6	24	—	11	14	21	32	27	—
Dividends per share ($)	2.7%	0.63	0.80	0.80	0.85	0.80	0.80	0.80	0.60	0.80	0.80
Book value per share ($)	(2.8%)	30.92	27.94	28.02	19.52	24.16	25.11	25.39	25.33	24.87	23.85
Employees	(1.8%)	8,500	8,000	8,100	7,000	10,750	9,500	9,700	11,000	10,500	7,200

STOCK PRICE HISTORY

HIGH/LOW/CLOSE

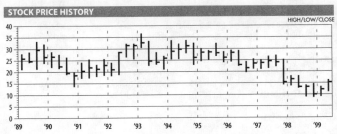

1998 FISCAL YEAR-END

Debt ratio: 44.3%
Return on equity: —
Cash ($ mil.): 353
Current ratio: 1.37
Long-term debt ($ mil.): 1,718
No. of shares (mil.): 90
Dividends
 Yield: 8.0%
 Payout: —
Market value ($ mil.): 902

DANA CORPORATION

Just call Dana Mr. Heavy-duty. The Toledo, Ohio-based manufacturer has built a global distribution empire by producing automotive components (axles, driveshafts, filters, valves, and piston rings). Its major customers include automakers Ford and DaimlerChrysler and truck maker Mack. The company is also a leading supplier of components to industrial markets and makers of construction and agricultural machinery. Dana's acquisition of Echlin made it a leader in the replacement parts aftermarket that sells to jobbers and do-it-yourselfers through parts distributorships. Its Dana Commercial Credit subsidiary provides leasing and financing services.

The company operates through seven business units: automotive systems group, automotive aftermarket group (created in 1998 to merge Echlin and Dana operations), engine systems group, heavy truck group, off-highway systems group, industrial group, and leasing services.

In a flurry of activity, Dana is selling non-core businesses and is replacing them with companies that fit into its heavy-duty parts profile, as it strives to reach its goal of 50% international sales by the year 2000. (Sales to countries other than the US now account for about 40% of Dana's revenues.)

HISTORY

Clarence Spicer began developing a universal joint and a driveshaft for automobiles while studying at Cornell University. Leaving Cornell in 1904, he patented his design, founded Spicer Manufacturing in Plainfield, New Jersey, and marketed the product himself.

The company ran into financial trouble in 1913, and the following year New York attorney Charles Dana joined the firm, advancing Spicer money to refinance.

Acquisitions after WWI strengthened Spicer's position in the growing truck industry. The business moved to Toledo, Ohio, in 1929 to be nearer to the emerging Detroit automotive center. In 1946 the company was renamed in honor of Dana, who became chairman two years later. In the 1950s sales topped $150 million.

In 1963 the company entered the replacement parts market by purchasing Perfect Circle and Aluminum Industries. Dana added Victor Manufacturing and Gasket in 1966. Charles Dana retired that year.

The firm bought the Weatherhead Company (hoses, fittings, and couplings; 1977) and Tyrone Hydraulics (pumps and motors, 1980), and later branched into financial services.

In 1989 the firm introduced a nine-speed, heavy-duty truck transmission (developed jointly with truck maker Navistar), the first all-new design of its type in over 25 years. Sluggish truck markets reduced 1990 and 1991 earnings.

Dana sold its mortgage banking business and some other financial services in 1992. Also that year it acquired Delta Automotive and Krizman, two leading makers and distributors of automotive aftermarket parts.

Dana acquired the Reinz Group, a German gasket maker with operations around the world, in 1993. The next year the company bought Sige, an Italian axle maker; Stieber Heidelberg, a German industrial components manufacturer; Tece, a Dutch auto parts distributor; and Tremec, a Mexican transmission maker.

In 1995 the firm bought the Plumley Companies (molded-rubber), US custom-molded plastics maker Mohawk Plastics, and the outstanding shares of its Canadian subsidiary Hayes-Dana. The next year Dana bought several Australian filter makers (J.B. Morgan and Co. and James N. Kirby), a German plastic components maker (Thermoplast), a Brazilian maker of oil seals and gaskets (Stevaux), and a 70% stake in Centrust SA, an Argentina-based holding company for auto parts maker Armetal.

In 1997 the company acquired Clark-Hurth Components (drivetrains) and the piston ring and cylinder liner operations of SPX Corporation; it also increased its shares in a Polish manufacturer of filtration products (Wix Filtron) and in an Argentine heavy-duty structural component maker (EASA).

Also in 1997, Dana sold its sheet-rubber and conveyor belt business to Coltec Industries, its European warehouse distribution operations to Partco Group, and its Spicer clutch business to Eaton. In 1998 the company bought Eaton's heavy axle and brake business, then paid $3.9 billion for auto parts maker Echlin. Dana then announced it was cutting 3,500 jobs, or 4.4% of its workforce, and closing 15 plants, mostly former Echlin facilities. It also paid $430 million in 1998 for the bearings, washers, and camshafts businesses of auto parts maker Federal-Mogul.

Chairman: Southwood J. "Woody" Morcott, age 60,
$2,395,000 pay (prior to title change)
President and CEO: Joseph M. Magliochetti, age 56,
$1,247,000 pay (prior to promotion)
EVP and CFO: John S. Simpson, age 57
VP, Secretary, and General Counsel: Martin J. Strobel,
age 58, $885,000 pay
Chairman and President, Dana Credit:
Edward J. Shultz, age 54, $910,400 pay
President, Automotive Systems Group:
William J. Carroll, age 54, $888,100 pay
President, Off-Highway Systems Group:
Bernard N. "Nick" Cole, age 56
President, Dana South America: Hugo Ferreira
President, Dana International:
Marvin A. "Gus" Franklin III, age 51
President, Engine Systems Group: Charles F. Heine,
age 46
President, Automotive Aftermarket Group:
Larry W. McCurdy, age 63
President, Dana Asia/Pacific: Kevin P. Moyer, age 41
President, Automotive Axle Products: W. L. Myers,
age 58
President, Dana Europe: Karl A. Nitsch
President, Industrial Group: Michael A. Plumley, age 48
VP, Heavy Truck Systems Group: Richard L. Clayton,
age 38
Auditors: PricewaterhouseCoopers LLP

LOCATIONS

HQ: 4500 Dorr St., Toledo, OH 43615
Phone: 419-535-4500   **Fax:** 419-535-4643
Web site: http://www.dana.com

Dana operates manufacturing and distribution facilities
in more than 30 countries worldwide.

PRODUCTS/OPERATIONS

1998 Sales & Operating Income

	Sales		Operating Income	
	$ mil.	% of total	$ mil.	% of total
Auto systems group	4,268	34	328	42
Auto aftermarket group	2,762	22	152	20
Engine systems group	2,013	16	91	12
Heavy truck group	1,629	13	89	11
Off-highway systems	898	7	47	6
Industrial group	712	6	40	5
Leasing services	—	—	34	4
Other	182	2	(190)	—
Total	**12,464**	**100**	**591**	**100**

COMPETITORS

AlliedSignal
American Axle &
 Manufacturing
Arvin Industries
Borg-Warner Automotive
Budd Company
Champion Parts
Deere
Eaton
Federal-Mogul
GE

Ingersoll-Rand
ITT Industries
Magna International
Mark IV
MascoTech
Meritor
Robert Bosch
SPX
TRW
Valeo

HISTORICAL FINANCIALS & EMPLOYEES

NYSE symbol: DCN FYE: December 31	Annual Growth	1989	1990	1991	1992	1993	1994	1995	1996	1997	1998
Sales ($ mil.)	11.0%	4,865	4,952	4,398	4,872	5,460	6,614	7,598	7,686	8,291	12,464
Net income ($ mil.)	16.8%	132	76	14	(382)	80	228	288	306	369	534
Income as % of sales	—	2.7%	1.5%	0.3%	—	1.5%	3.5%	3.8%	4.0%	4.5%	4.3%
Earnings per share ($)	8.4%	1.55	0.91	0.17	(4.35)	0.86	2.28	2.80	2.81	3.49	3.20
Stock price - FY high ($)	—	21.44	19.06	18.25	24.13	30.13	30.69	32.63	35.50	54.38	61.50
Stock price - FY low ($)	—	16.50	9.94	12.31	13.38	22.00	19.63	21.38	27.25	30.63	31.31
Stock price - FY close ($)	10.0%	17.31	14.94	13.88	23.50	29.94	23.50	29.25	32.63	47.50	40.88
P/E - high	—	14	21	107	—	35	13	12	13	16	19
P/E - low	—	11	11	72	—	26	9	8	10	9	10
Dividends per share ($)	4.0%	0.80	0.80	0.80	0.80	0.80	0.83	0.90	0.98	1.04	1.14
Book value per share ($)	4.0%	12.47	12.78	12.02	7.70	8.73	9.51	11.47	13.87	16.19	17.74
Employees	9.7%	37,500	33,300	35,000	35,000	36,000	39,500	42,200	45,500	47,900	86,400

STOCK PRICE HISTORY

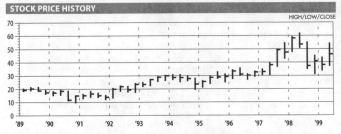

HIGH/LOW/CLOSE

1998 FISCAL YEAR-END

Debt ratio: 36.9%
Return on equity: 18.2%
Cash ($ mil.): 230
Current ratio: 1.09
Long-term debt ($ mil.): 1,718
No. of shares (mil.): 166
Dividends
 Yield: 2.8%
 Payout: 35.6%
Market value ($ mil.): 6,774

DANAHER CORPORATION

OVERVIEW

Danaher's namesake, a fishing stream off Montana's Flat Head River, took its name from a word meaning "swift flowing." The phrase is also apt for describing the acquisition-fueled growth of Danaher's process/environmental controls and tools businesses.

Danaher's controls group (56% of sales) produces a wide range of monitoring, sensing, controlling, and testing products. Notable brands include Veeder-Root (measuring and leak-detection systems for underground fuel-storage tanks), Fluke (devices for measuring electronic voltage, frequency, pressure, and temperature), and Pacific Scientific (electric motors, drives, and safety equipment).

The company is also a producer of mechanics' hand tools, automotive specialty tools, and accessories, which it makes under numerous brand names. For example, Danaher is the sole

maker of Sears' line of Craftsman tools (Sears accounts for about 10% of sales). Danaher is also the primary tool supplier for auto parts company NAPA.

Spotlight-averse brothers Steve and Mitch Rales — company chairman and chairman of the executive committee, respectively — own 33% of Danaher. The brothers have proven themselves fishers not only of trout but also of companies. Along with equally publicity-shy president and CEO George Sherman, they have grown Danaher by buying underperforming companies with strong market shares and recognizable brand names. Noted for cutting costs and improving productivity at purchased companies, Danaher plans further growth through new products, international expansion, and more acquisitions.

HISTORY

Once dubbed "raiders in short pants" by *Forbes,* Steven and Mitchell Rales began making acquisitions in their 20s. In 1981 they bought their father's 50% stake in Master Shield, a maker of vinyl building products. The brothers bought tire manufacturer Mohawk Rubber the next year. In 1983 they acquired control of publicly traded DMG, a distressed Florida real estate firm; the next year they sold DMG's real estate holdings and folded Mohawk and Master Shield into the company, which they renamed Danaher.

Danaher then began taking over low-profile industrial firms that weren't living up to their growth potential. Backed by junk bonds from Michael Milken, within two years it had purchased 12 more companies. Among these early acquisitions were makers of tools (Jacobs, Matco Tools), controls (Partlow, QualiTROL, Veeder-Root), precision components (Allen, maker of the namesake hexagonal wrench), and plastics (A.L. Hyde). With its purchases, Danaher proceeded to cut costs and pay down debt by unloading underperforming assets.

The Rales brothers' takeover efforts weren't always successful. They lost out to Warren Buffett when they tried to buy Scott & Fetzer (encyclopedias, vacuum cleaners) in 1985. They also missed in 1988 when they offered $2.8 billion for INTERCO (furniture, shoes, apparel), although they made off with $75 million for their troubles — and drove INTERCO into dismantlement and bankruptcy in the process.

In 1989 Danaher bought Easco Hand Tools, the main maker of tools for Sears, Roebuck's Craftsman line. (The Raleses already controlled Easco Hand Tools; a private partnership they controlled had bought the company from its parent in 1985 and taken it public in 1987.) The deal established the tool division as Danaher's largest, and two years later Sears selected Danaher as the sole manufacturer of Craftsman mechanics' hand tools.

The brothers hired Black & Decker power tools executive George Sherman as president and CEO in 1990. Between 1991 and 1995 Danaher grew through purchases such as Delta Consolidated Industries, Armstrong Brothers Tool, Joslyn, and four controls and instrument units of Mark IV Industries. The firm improved its international distribution channels with its purchases of the UK's West Instruments (1993) and Germany's Hengstler (1994).

Focusing on tools and controls, Danaher sold its automotive components business in 1995. After a lengthy battle, it bought test maker and controls firm Acme-Cleveland in 1996.

Danaher set its sights on Asia with its 1997 purchase of hand tool companies with plants in China and Taiwan. Other 1997 purchases included Current Technology and GEMS Sensors. Danaher made its two largest purchases to date in 1998 when it bought Pacific Scientific (motion controls and safety equipment) for $460 million and Fluke (electronic tools) for $625 million. In 1999 Danaher bought lab equipment maker Hach for $325 million.

Chairman: Steven M. Rales, age 47
Chairman of the Executive Committee:
Mitchell P. Rales, age 42
President and CEO: George M. Sherman, age 57,
$2,300,000 pay
SVP, CFO, and Secretary: Patrick W. Allender, age 52,
$697,000 pay
VP and Group Executive: Dennis D. Claramunt, age 53
VP and Group Executive: H. Lawrence Culp Jr.,
$496,000 pay
VP and Group Executive: Steven E. Simms, age 43,
$538,000 pay
VP and Group Executive: John P. Watson, age 54
VP Administration and Controller: C. Scott Brannan,
age 40
VP Corporate Development: Daniel L. Comas, age 34
VP Danaher Business System: Mark C. DeLuzio, age 41
VP Human Resources: Dennis Longo, age 42
Auditors: Arthur Andersen LLP

LOCATIONS

HQ: 1250 24th St. NW, Ste. 800, Washington, DC 20037
Phone: 202-828-0850　　**Fax:** 202-828-0860
Web site: http://www.danaher.com

Danaher has major facilities in Brazil, Canada, China,
Germany, the Netherlands, Slovakia, Switzerland,
Taiwan, the UK, and the US.

1998 Sales

	$ mil.	% of total
US	2,328	80
Europe	271	9
Other regions	311	11
Total	**2,910**	**100**

PRODUCTS/OPERATIONS

1998 Sales & Operating Income

	Sales		Operating Income	
	$ mil.	% of total	$ mil.	% of total
Environmental controls	1,615	56	223	58
Tools & components	1,295	44	159	42
Adjustments	—	—	(15)	—
Total	**2,910**	**100**	**367**	**100**

COMPETITORS

American Precision Industries
Black & Decker
Cooper Industries
Honeywell
Johnson Controls
Kollmorgen
Matrix Service
Snap-on
Stanley Works
Tektronix

HISTORICAL FINANCIALS & EMPLOYEES

NYSE symbol: DHR FYE: December 31	Annual Growth	1989	1990	1991	1992	1993	1994	1995	1996	1997	1998
Sales ($ mil.)	16.3%	749	840	832	949	1,067	1,289	1,487	1,812	2,051	2,910
Net income ($ mil.)	13.0%	61	36	13	32	18	82	108	208	155	183
Income as % of sales	—	8.2%	4.3%	1.6%	3.3%	1.7%	6.3%	7.3%	11.5%	7.5%	6.3%
Earnings per share ($)	8.2%	0.65	0.34	0.12	0.28	0.16	0.70	0.93	2.41	1.29	1.32
Stock price - FY high ($)	—	4.59	5.91	5.88	6.84	9.81	13.28	17.19	23.31	32.00	55.25
Stock price - FY low ($)	—	3.22	3.38	3.94	4.94	6.03	9.00	12.13	14.63	19.50	28.00
Stock price - FY close ($)	34.3%	3.81	4.00	5.06	6.50	9.53	13.06	15.88	23.31	31.56	54.31
P/E - high	—	7	17	49	24	61	19	18	10	25	42
P/E - low	—	5	10	33	18	38	13	13	6	15	21
Dividends per share ($)	—	0.00	0.00	0.00	0.00	0.03	0.03	0.04	0.05	0.05	0.04
Book value per share ($)	19.2%	2.07	2.71	2.83	3.07	3.20	4.08	5.01	6.79	7.84	10.01
Employees	11.8%	6,600	8,000	7,000	7,100	7,300	9,960	10,500	11,600	13,200	18,000

STOCK PRICE HISTORY

HIGH/LOW/CLOSE

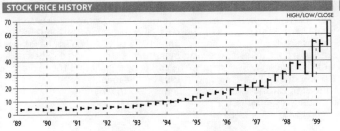

1998 FISCAL YEAR-END

Debt ratio: 23.4%
Return on equity: 13.5%
Cash ($ mil.): 42
Current ratio: 1.29
Long-term debt ($ mil.): 413
No. of shares (mil.): 135
Dividends
　Yield: 0.1%
　Payout: 3.0%
Market value ($ mil.): 7,338

DARDEN RESTAURANTS, INC.

OVERVIEW

Darden Restaurants has clawed its way to the top. The #1 casual-dining restaurateur in the land provides sustenance to nearly 5 million famished folks each week. The Orlando, Florida-based company's portfolio is bulging with the 668-unit Red Lobster chain of seafood restaurants, the 470-unit Olive Garden Italian restaurant chain, and the six-unit string of Bahama Breeze Caribbean restaurants. With the exception of 38 licensed Red Lobster units in Japan, Darden has built its eatery empire across the US and Canada without the benefit of franchises.

Red Lobster, Darden's oldest restaurant chain, has been credited with introducing fare

such as snow crab and calamari to landlocked clientele across the Midwest. The restaurants provide menus featuring fish, shrimp, crab, and lobster. Darden's Olive Garden chain offers fare including appetizers, soups, salads, pastas, seafood, and grilled entrees. Bahama Breeze, which serves only dinner, features Caribbean cuisine spotlighting an array of seafood, beef, pork, and chicken dishes.

Darden has revived its once-ailing Red Lobster chain and plans to continue expanding the number of its Bahama Breeze units. The company also is joining the barbecue brigade with Smokey Bones BBQ, a restaurant concept it has begun testing.

HISTORY

Nineteen-year-old Bill Darden entered the restaurant business in the late 1930s with a 25-seat luncheonette called the Green Frog in Waycross, Georgia. The restaurant, which featured the slogan "Service with a Hop," was a hit, and his career was born. During the 1950s he owned a variety of restaurants, including several Howard Johnson's, Bonanza, and Kentucky Fried Chicken outlets.

In 1963 Darden teamed with a group of investors to buy an Orlando restaurant, Gary's Duck Inn. The restaurant became the prototype for Darden's idea for a moderately priced, sit-down seafood chain. He decided to name the new chain Red Lobster, a takeoff on the old Green Frog.

The first Red Lobster opened in Lakeland, Florida, in 1968 with Joe Lee, who had worked in one of Darden's other restaurants, as its manager. It was such a success that within a month the restaurant had to be expanded. In 1970, when there were three Red Lobsters in operation and two under construction in central Florida, Betty Crocker's boss, General Mills, bought the chain — keeping Darden on to run it.

Red Lobster was not General Mills' first foray into the restaurant business. In 1968 the company opened Betty Crocker Tree House Restaurant and acquired a fish-and-chips chain and a barbecue chain. But Red Lobster would be its first success. Rather than franchise the Red Lobster name, it chose to develop the chain on its own. In 1975 Lee was named president of Red Lobster, and Darden became chairman of General Mills Restaurants.

While General Mills continued to expand Red Lobster, it also sought another restaurant idea to complement the seafood chain.

Among concepts tried and discarded were a steak house, as well as Mexican and health-food restaurants. In 1980 the company decided on Italian. After two years of marketing questionnaires and recipe tests, General Mills opened a prototype Olive Garden in Orlando featuring moderately priced Italian food. General Mills began to add outlets in the mid-1980s, and Olive Garden became another success story of the casual-dining industry.

After testing a new Chinese restaurant concept, General Mills opened its first China Coast in Orlando in 1990; the chain grew rapidly, with more than 45 units opening in a single year. The Olive Garden began to cool off in 1993: Same-store sales slid as competitors added Italian items to their menus. The next year Olive Garden increased its advertising budget, introduced new menu items, and began testing new formats, including smaller cafes for malls.

In 1995 General Mills decided to spin off the restaurant business as a public company and focus on consumer foods. The restaurants were renamed Darden Restaurants in honor of Bill Darden (who had died in 1994, the same year that Joe Lee was appointed CEO). Sagging performance prompted the company to abandon its China Coast chain in 1995. Darden tried again in 1997 with Bahama Breeze, opening a test restaurant in Orlando. Red Lobster's sales flagged in 1997, but the company initiated a turnaround in the following year, in part by revamping Red Lobster's menu. The company dipped into the barbecue sauce in 1999 and opened its inaugural Smokey Bones BBQ in Orlando.

Chairman and CEO: Joe R. Lee, age 58, $1,699,650 pay
EVP; President, New Business: Blaine Sweatt III, age 51, $733,026 pay
EVP; President, Olive Garden: Bradley D. Blum, age 45, $965,445 pay
EVP; President, Red Lobster: Richard E. Rivera, age 52, $963,826 pay
SVP; President, Bahama Breeze: Gary Heckel, age 46
SVP; EVP Operations, Olive Garden: Robert W. Mock, age 47, $533,996 pay
SVP and General Counsel: Paula J. Shives, age 48
SVP Business Information Systems and Corporate Controller: Linda J. Dimopoulos, age 48
SVP Corporate Relations: Richard J. Walsh, age 47
SVP Finance and Treasurer: Clarence Otis Jr., age 43
SVP Human Resources: Daniel M. Lyons, age 46
SVP Real Estate, Design, and Construction: James D. Smith, age 56
SVP Purchasing, Distribution, and Food Safety: Barry Moullet, age 41
SVP, Development, Bahama Breeze: Greg Buchanan
VP Communications: Rick Van Warner
VP Seafood Purchasing: Bill Herzig
EVP, Operations, Olive Garden: Bob Mock
EVP, Operations, Red Lobster: Edna Morris
Auditors: KPMG LLP

LOCATIONS

HQ: 5900 Lake Ellenor Dr., Orlando, FL 32809
Phone: 407-245-4000   **Fax:** 407-245-5114
Web site: http://www.darden.com

Darden Restaurants operates restaurants in the US and Canada. It also licenses restaurants in Japan.

PRODUCTS/OPERATIONS

1999 Sales

	$ mil.	% of total
Red Lobster	1,960	56
Olive Garden	1,480	43
Other (includes Bahama Breeze)	18	1
Total	**3,458**	**100**

1999 Sales

	% of total
Food	92
Alcoholic beverages	8
Total	**100**

Selected Menu Items

Bahama Breeze	Olive Garden	Red Lobster
Beef	Appetizers	Appetizers
Chicken	Chicken	Crab
Pasta	Desserts	Desserts
Pizza	Grilled meats	Fish
Pork	Pasta	Lobster
Seafood	Salads	Scallops
	Seafood	Shrimp
	Soup	
	Vegetables	
	Wine	

COMPETITORS

Advantica Restaurant Group	Landry's Seafood
Applebee's	Lone Star Steakhouse
Brinker	Metromedia
Carlson Restaurants Worldwide	Outback Steakhouse
Chart House	Prandium
Il Fornaio	Ruby Tuesday
	Shoney's

HISTORICAL FINANCIALS & EMPLOYEES

NYSE symbol: DRI FYE: May 31	Annual Growth	1990	1991	1992	1993	1994	1995	1996	1997	1998	1999
Sales ($ mil.)	6.7%	1,928	2,214	2,542	2,737	2,963	3,163	3,192	3,172	3,287	3,458
Net income ($ mil.)	3.3%	—	—	112	92	123	52	74	(91)	102	141
Income as % of sales	—	—	—	4.4%	3.4%	4.2%	1.7%	2.3%	—	3.1%	4.1%
Earnings per share ($)	33.7%	—	—	—	—	—	0.31	0.46	(0.59)	0.67	0.99
Stock price - FY high ($)	—	—	—	—	—	—	11.38	14.00	12.13	18.13	23.38
Stock price - FY low ($)	—	—	—	—	—	—	9.13	9.75	6.75	8.13	14.19
Stock price - FY close ($)	18.0%	—	—	—	—	—	11.00	11.88	8.38	15.44	21.31
P/E - high	—	—	—	—	—	—	37	30	—	27	24
P/E - low	—	—	—	—	—	—	29	21	—	12	14
Dividends per share ($)	—	—	—	—	—	—	0.00	0.04	0.08	0.08	0.08
Book value per share ($)	(0.5%)	—	—	—	—	—	7.43	7.66	7.07	7.23	7.30
Employees	4.8%	76,305	85,799	90,626	109,875	115,518	124,730	119,123	114,582	114,800	116,700

STOCK PRICE HISTORY
HIGH/LOW/CLOSE

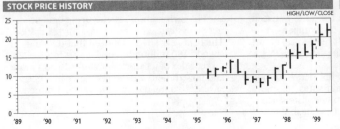

1999 FISCAL YEAR-END

Debt ratio: 24.6%
Return on equity: 14.6%
Cash ($ mil.): 41
Current ratio: 0.61
Long-term debt ($ mil.): 314
No. of shares (mil.): 132
Dividends
 Yield: 0.4%
 Payout: 8.1%
Market value ($ mil.): 2,815

DATA GENERAL CORPORATION

OVERVIEW

There's a new soul in the old machine. Westborough, Massachusetts-based Data General (DG), once a specialist in minicomputers for the reseller market and the hero of Tracy Kidder's 1981 best-seller about system development, *The Soul of a New Machine*, has agreed to be bought by high-level data storage specialist EMC.

DG has repositioned itself to offer servers and high-end storage products. More than half of its product sales come from AViiON, server systems geared to power transaction-heavy computer networks. Its CLARiiON mass-storage subsystems account for nearly 40% of product sales. DG also makes PCs, handhelds, network storage management software, and Internet appliances. Its customers include Columbia/HCA, Bloomberg, and Baan Company.

For a decade DG had revenues as flat as a silicon wafer (and consistently over $1 billion). After years of cutting costs, the company emerged from a close brush with bankruptcy in the mid-1990s. DG continues to let rivals market CLARiiON products under their own brands.

Because the Internet is driving technology in the direction of viewing information rather than processing it, DG established its THiiN line of Internet access computers with limited memory and processing power.

HISTORY

Edson de Castro and two other engineers left minicomputer maker Digital Equipment Corporation (DEC) in 1968 to form Data General (DG). Starting with $800,000 the company developed a minicomputer targeted at value-added resellers with specialized markets such as manufacturers and hospitals.

DG's first computer, the 16-bit NOVA minicomputer, quickly became a success by filling a gap in DEC's product line. The NOVA's simple design incorporated large printed circuit boards that reduced the computer's costs. With low overhead, an aggressive pricing strategy, and brash marketing, DG soon became a major contender in the minicomputer market. The firm later began making computers ranging from microcomputers to the $600,000 ECLIPSE, all based on the NOVA architecture. In 10 years (1969-79) DG sold over 70,000 computers.

By 1979, however, DG was slipping. Many of its rivals had already introduced 32-bit super minicomputers. In response, DG introduced the MV8000 in 1980. Between 1980 and 1984, DG's sales climbed because of the introduction of new machines and the highly rated CEO (comprehensive electronic office) software, an office automation product that included e-mail, word processing, and a filing system.

DG's growth slowed after 1985 because it failed to move into PCs and servers. Between 1985 and the end of 1989, the company reduced its workforce and closed several plants. Results continued to decline. The AViiON line was launched in 1989.

De Castro left DG in 1990. Price Waterhouse vet and former CFO Ronald Skates became CEO and continued to trim operations. He scuttled many R&D projects, choosing to focus on RISC servers (AViiON) and maintenance of the ECLIPSE MV customer base (which declined quickly anyway). He also began outsourcing and continued closing plants and cutting jobs, eventually paring away almost three-quarters of the workforce.

The company sold its Japanese distribution unit to Omron in 1991. The next year it introduced the CLARiiON family of mass-storage devices as a separate line rather than as part of the AViiON line.

In 1995 DG failed to stanch the flow of red ink, despite receiving $53 million from defense contractor Northrop Grumman to settle a lingering lawsuit for copyright and trade-secret infringement. On the positive side, Data General chose Intel-based architecture when its old Motorola chip had to be abandoned. DG in 1996 recorded its first profit since 1991.

In 1997 DG began delivering CLARiiON products based on Fibre Channel technology, which offers increased bandwidth and greater scalability. DG's first THiiN (Internet-specific) device, a Web server, hit the market that year. In 1998 DG consolidated several facilities and trimmed jobs. A lucrative agreement with Hewlett-Packard, which sold DG's hardware under the HP name, ended that year. DG formed a unit dedicated to product repair and logistics services for global firms. The end of the HP partnership, restructuring, and product delays caused a sizable loss for fiscal 1998. The next year DG announced that it would spend $100 million to build a staff to increase direct sales of its storage systems to corporate and government customers. Later in 1999, rival EMC agreed to buy DG for $1.1 billion.

President and CEO: Ronald L. Skates, age 57,
$750,000 pay
SVP Manufacturing, Information Management, and Customer Services: William J. Cunningham, $360,000 pay
SVP and General Manager, CLARiiON Advanced Storage Division: Joel Schwartz, $340,000 pay
SVP and General Manager, AViiON Enterprise Server Division: Ethan Allen Jr., $279,200 pay
VP Europe/Pacific: Stephen P. Baxter
VP and General Counsel: Jacob Frank
VP CFO, and Corporate Controller: John J. Gavin Jr.
VP Chief Administrative Officer, and Treasurer: Robert C. McBride
VP Human Resources: Erin Motameni
VP Sales Expansion: Anthony C. Nicoletti
VP Information Management Group: James J. Ryan
Secretary: Carl E. Kaplan
Auditors: PricewaterhouseCoopers LLP

LOCATIONS

HQ: 4400 Computer Dr., Westborough, MA 01580
Phone: 508-898-5000   **Fax:** 508-366-1319
Web site: http://www.dg.com

Data General has manufacturing operations in Massachusetts, North Carolina, and the Philippines.

1998 Sales & Operating Income

	Sales		Operating Income	
	$ mil.	% of total	$ mil.	% of total
US	1,179	73	(118)	—
Europe	286	18	(24)	—
Other regions	142	9	(5)	—
Adjustments	(145)	—	(1)	—
Total	**1,462**	**100**	**(148)**	**—**

PRODUCTS/OPERATIONS

1998 Sales

	$ mil.	% of total
Products	1,068	73
Services	394	27
Total	**1,462**	**100**

1998 Product Sales

	% of total
Servers	51
Storage	38
PCs & other equipment	8
Contract manufacturing	3
Total	**100**

Products
Compilers (EPC family)
Handheld computers (DataGenie family)
Internet appliances (THiiN)
Network server computers (AViiON)
Network storage management software (Navisphere)
Operating system software (DG/UX)
PCs (DG/ViiSION family)
Printers
Storage systems (CLARiiON)

COMPETITORS

Amdahl	MTI Technology
Compaq	NEC
Dell Computer	Sequent
EMC	Siemens
Fujitsu	Sun Microsystems
Hitachi	Toshiba
IBM	Unisys
Legato Systems	VERITAS Software

HISTORICAL FINANCIALS & EMPLOYEES

NYSE symbol: DGN FYE: September 30	Annual Growth	1989	1990	1991	1992	1993	1994	1995	1996	1997	1998
Sales ($ mil.)	1.2%	1,314	1,216	1,229	1,116	1,078	1,121	1,159	1,322	1,533	1,462
Net income ($ mil.)	—	(120)	(140)	86	(63)	(61)	(88)	(47)	28	56	(152)
Income as % of sales	—	—	—	7.0%	—	—	—	—	2.1%	3.6%	—
Earnings per share ($)	—	(4.10)	(4.65)	2.45	(1.91)	(1.73)	(2.45)	(1.23)	0.68	1.26	(3.11)
Stock price – FY high ($)	—	20.75	15.63	22.38	22.50	13.88	10.75	12.00	19.13	37.94	27.50
Stock price – FY low ($)	—	14.25	4.63	3.50	7.13	7.75	6.63	6.75	8.88	12.88	7.00
Stock price – FY close ($)	(3.8%)	15.25	5.25	19.50	11.00	10.25	10.00	10.38	14.00	26.63	10.81
P/E – high	—	—	—	9	—	—	—	—	28	30	—
P/E – low	—	—	—	1	—	—	—	—	13	10	—
Dividends per share ($)	—	0.00	0.00	0.00	0.00	0.00	0.00	0.00	0.00	0.00	0.00
Book value per share ($)	(8.8%)	17.68	13.21	15.50	13.41	10.69	8.46	7.37	8.31	10.68	7.75
Employees	(11.2%)	13,700	10,600	8,500	7,100	6,500	5,800	5,000	4,900	5,100	4,700

STOCK PRICE HISTORY

HIGH/LOW/CLOSE

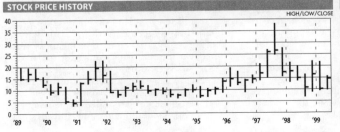

1998 FISCAL YEAR-END

Debt ratio: 35.6%
Return on equity: —
Cash ($ mil.): 158
Current ratio: 1.85
Long-term debt ($ mil.): 213
No. of shares (mil.): 50
Dividends
  Yield: —
  Payout: —
Market value ($ mil.): 537

DAYTON HUDSON CORPORATION

OVERVIEW

Keeping its aim on Target has made Dayton Hudson one of the largest retailers in the US. The Minneapolis-based company operates nearly 1,200 stores nationwide in three different retail niches: discount chain Target (nationwide); midrange department store Mervyn's California (mainly in the West and Southwest); and upscale department stores Dayton's, Hudson's, and Marshall Field's (Midwest).

The Target chain accounts for nearly three-fourths of Dayton Hudson's sales. The #3 US discounter, Target has positioned itself as an upscale alternative to larger rivals Wal-Mart and Kmart. It is expanding primarily in the Mid-Atlantic and Northeast. The chain, a relative latecomer to the booming supercenter category, is trying to make up for lost time: Its SuperTarget format, a 175,000-sq.-ft. grocery/discount store, is slated to grow from fewer than two dozen stores to over 200 in the next decade.

Dayton Hudson has repositioned its Marhsall Field's, Hudson's, and Dayton's chains by closing and selling off underperforming stores. Mervyn's California, meanwhile, is being squeezed by discounters and higher-end retailers alike as it attempts to trim costs, add new brands, and boost storewide promotions. Although its department store divisions haven't been as successful, Dayton Hudson continues to resist calls to split itself up, reminding skeptics that its department stores provide crucial funding for Target's growth.

HISTORY

The panic of 1873 left Joseph Hudson bankrupt. After he paid his debts at 60 cents on the dollar, he saved enough to open a men's clothing store in Detroit in 1881. Among his innovations were merchandise return privileges and price marking in place of bargaining. By 1891 Hudson's was the largest retailer of men's clothing in America. Hudson repaid his creditors from 1873 in full, with interest.

When Hudson died in 1912, four nephews expanded the business. In 1928 Hudson's built a new store in downtown Detroit that became the second-largest retail building in the US, growing to 25 stories with 49 acres of floor space.

Former banker George Dayton established a dry-goods store in 1902 in Minneapolis on a spot with a lot of foot traffic. Like Hudson, he offered return privileges and liberal credit. His store grew to a 12-story, full-line department store.

After WWII, both companies saw that the future lay in the suburbs. In 1954 Hudson's built Northland in Detroit, then the largest US shopping center. Dayton's built the world's first fully enclosed shopping mall in Edina, a Minneapolis suburb, in 1956; in 1962 it opened its first Target discount store.

Dayton's went public in 1966, the same year it began the B. Dalton bookstore chain. Three years later it merged with the family-owned Hudson's, forming Dayton Hudson. Dayton Hudson increased its ownership of malls and invested in such specialty areas as consumer electronics and hard goods.

Target became the company's top moneymaker in 1977. Dayton Hudson then bought California-based Mervyn's. In the late 1970s and 1980s, it sold nine regional malls and several other businesses, including the 800-store B. Dalton chain (to Barnes & Noble). In the late 1980s Dayton Hudson took Target to Los Angeles and the Northwest.

In 1990 Dayton Hudson bought the Marshall Field's chain of 24 department stores from B.A.T Industries. Marshall Field's began as a dry-goods business that Marshall Field bought in 1865 and subsequently built into Chicago's premier upscale retailer.

Dayton Hudson moved Mervyn's into Florida in 1991. To improve Mervyn's operations, in 1993 the company introduced a value pricing strategy, reintroduced women's dresses, and replaced about 70% of the chain's senior management.

The head of the Target division, Robert Ulrich, became Dayton Hudson's chairman and CEO in 1994. Target introduced its SuperTarget stores in 1995.

Target opened stores in the Mid-Atlantic and Northeast the next year, while the department store division began selling off its Marshall Field's locations in Texas and refocusing on the Midwest. In 1997 the company refined its operations by closing Mervyn's stores where it had low market share (such as Florida).

In 1998 Dayton Hudson bought direct-marketing company Rivertown Trading to bolster its Internet commerce business. Also that year the company acquired Associated Merchandising Corporation, which supplies apparel to department store chains. In 1999 Dayton Hudson announced it will unveil a number of e-commerce sites for its stores, including Marshall Field's and Hudson's.

Chairman and CEO, Dayton Hudson and Target:
Robert J. Ulrich, age 55, $3,342,524 pay
EVP and Chief Information Officer:
Vivian M. Stephenson, age 61
SVP and CFO: Douglas A. Scovanner, age 43
SVP, General Counsel, and Secretary: James T. Hale
VP E-Commerce, Technology, and Strategy:
Brigid Bonner
VP Year 2000: Dennis Breck
VP Communications, Dayton Hudson and Target:
Gail J. Dorn
VP and Treasurer: Stephen C. Kowalke
VP Guest, Distribution, and Advertising: Larry Wobig
President, Department Store Division: Linda L. Ahlers,
age 48, $1,219,199 pay
President, Rivertown Trading: Donna L. Avery
President, Mervyn's: Bart Butzer, age 43
President, Credit and New Businesses:
Gerald L. Storch, age 42
President, Target: Gregg Steinhafel, age 44,
$1,392,038 pay (prior to promotion)
EVP Stores, Mervyn's: Shannon M. Buscho
EVP Team, Guest, and Community Relations, Target:
Larry V. Gilpin, age 55, $1,068,223 pay
EVP Marketing, Target: John E. Pellegrene, age 62,
$980,906 pay
SVP Property Development, Target:
Robert G. McMahon, age 50
Chief Accounting Officer and Controller:
JoAnn Bogdan, age 46
Auditors: Ernst & Young LLP

LOCATIONS

HQ: 777 Nicollet Mall, Minneapolis, MN 55402-2055
Phone: 612-370-6948　　**Fax:** 612-370-5502
Web site: http://www.dhc.com

PRODUCTS/OPERATIONS

1999 Sales & Pretax Income

	Sales		Pretax Income	
	$ mil.	% of total	$ mil.	% of total
Target	23,056	75	1,578	75
Mervyn's	4,176	13	240	12
Department stores	3,285	11	279	13
Corporate & other	434	1	—	—
Total	**30,951**	**100**	**2,097**	**100**

Store Formats
Dayton's (upscale department stores)
Hudson's (upscale department stores)
Marshall Field's (upscale department stores)
Mervyn's California (midrange department stores)
Target, SuperTarget, Target Greatland (stores offering
groceries and general merchandise)

Other Operations
Associated Merchandising Corporation (apparel sourcing
for department stores)
Rivertown Trading
Circa: The Collectors Catalog (collectibles)
The Daily Planet (ethnic and global)
Seasons (traditional)
Signals (educational)
Well & Good (self-care and healthy living)
Wireless (home electronics)

COMPETITORS

Bed Bath &	J. C. Penney	Saks Inc.
Beyond	Kmart	Sears
Costco	The Limited	TJX
Companies	May	Toys "R" Us
Dillard's	Montgomery	Wal-Mart
Federated	Ward	
The Gap	Nordstrom	

HISTORICAL FINANCIALS & EMPLOYEES

NYSE symbol: DH FYE: January 31	Annual Growth	1990	1991	1992	1993	1994	1995	1996	1997	1998	1999
Sales ($ mil.)	9.5%	13,644	14,739	16,115	17,927	19,233	21,311	23,516	25,371	27,757	30,951
Net income ($ mil.)	9.6%	410	412	301	383	375	434	311	463	751	935
Income as % of sales	—	3.0%	2.8%	1.9%	2.1%	1.9%	2.0%	1.3%	1.8%	2.7%	3.0%
Earnings per share ($)	9.3%	0.89	0.87	0.62	0.80	0.80	0.92	0.65	0.97	1.59	1.98
Stock price - FY high ($)	—	11.16	13.24	13.36	13.24	14.15	14.46	13.40	20.31	37.25	64.50
Stock price - FY low ($)	—	7.20	7.70	9.28	9.80	10.43	10.80	10.53	12.09	18.81	31.44
Stock price - FY close ($)	22.9%	9.93	10.91	10.84	12.95	10.95	11.43	12.36	18.81	35.97	63.75
P/E - high	—	13	15	22	17	18	16	21	21	23	33
P/E - low	—	8	9	15	12	13	12	16	12	12	16
Dividends per share ($)	4.0%	0.19	0.22	0.24	0.26	0.27	0.28	0.29	0.31	0.33	0.27
Book value per share ($)	12.0%	4.12	4.80	5.21	5.80	6.35	7.07	7.31	8.10	9.55	11.41
Employees	6.0%	144,000	161,000	168,000	170,000	174,000	194,000	214,000	218,000	230,000	244,000

STOCK PRICE HISTORY

HIGH/LOW/CLOSE

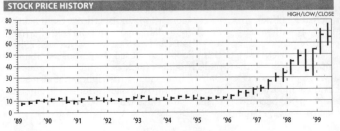

1999 FISCAL YEAR-END

Debt ratio: 45.5%
Return on equity: 18.5%
Cash ($ mil.): 255
Current ratio: 1.19
Long-term debt ($ mil.): 4,452
No. of shares (mil.): 442
Dividends
　Yield: 0.4%
　Payout: 13.6%
Market value ($ mil.): 28,165

DEAN FOODS COMPANY

OVERVIEW

Creating the cream of the crop, Dean Foods is the leading US fluid milk processor. The Franklin Park, Illinois-based company has nearly 35 dairy processing plants that produce branded and private-label milk, ice cream, and cultured dairy products for retail and institutional customers in the US and Mexico.

While dairy products bring in nearly 80% of sales, Dean Foods is also the largest pickle packer in the US, making pickles and relishes for sale under private and regional brands. The firm's specialty division is the largest producer of powdered nondairy coffee creamer (it invented the stuff), mostly sold to institutional customers; it also makes Marie's salad dressings and branded nondairy dips for retail sale, as well as shelf-stable sauces and puddings for food service use.

Once the largest US frozen vegetable processor, Dean Foods sold its vegetable division to the Pro-Fac Cooperative in order to focus on its core businesses. In addition, Dean Foods operates a trucking subsidiary, DFC Transportation, which hauls small refrigerated and frozen loads.

The company's growth has been tied to its steady acquisition of regional dairies and complementary food manufacturers. Its recent product introductions include single-serving Milk Chugs and the Picklevator, a plastic basket inside a jar that lifts pickles. Dean Foods is growing in the natural foods niche as a result of its purchases of Alta Dena Certified Dairy and Berkeley Farms (both dairies which reject the use of synthetic hormones) and its investment in White Wave (soy foods).

HISTORY

Pecatonica, Illinois-based Dean Evaporated Milk was founded in 1925 by Sam Dean, a Chicago evaporated-milk broker. By the mid-1930s it had moved into the fresh milk industry. Dean began making ice cream in 1947, about the time that geographic expansion became its priority. It bought a number of established regional dairies outside the Midwest throughout the late 1940s and the 1950s.

In 1952 Dean's research and development lab developed the first powdered nondairy coffee creamer, the bedrock of its specialty foods division. The company went public in 1961, the year it acquired Green Bay Food and entered the pickle business. It was renamed Dean Foods in 1963.

Howard Dean, grandson of the founder, joined Dean Foods in 1965. The company pursued acquisitions throughout that decade, though it ran into FTC trouble in the late 1960s. Howard became president in 1970. The firm acquired Gandy's Dairy of Texas in 1976 and further expanded its dairy operations into the Southwest with the 1978 purchases of Bell Dairy and Creamland Dairy.

Acquisitions in the 1980s moved Dean Foods into Florida, Kentucky, Ohio, and Pennsylvania. In 1985 it reached $1 billion in sales and acquired Ryan Milk of Kentucky, entering the ultrahigh-temperature processed product market.

Dean Foods diversified into vegetables with the 1986 acquisition of Larsen, a processor of branded and private-label canned and frozen vegetables. By 1987 the company had become the US's third-largest canned/frozen vegetable

purveyor. Howard became CEO that year. Other acquisitions in this growing market included Big Stone (canned vegetables, 1989), Birds Eye (second-largest US frozen vegetable brand, 1993), and Rio Grande Foods (frozen vegetables, 1995).

In 1996 Dean Foods closed a number of plants, including seven of its 20 vegetable facilities, due to overcapacity. Also in 1996 it was fined over $4 million — the largest Clean Water Act penalty ever imposed — for discharging pollutants into a public water treatment facility.

The firm bought Meadows Distributing (Chicago's top ice-cream/frozen dessert distributor) and Campbell Soup's Marie's salad dressing business in 1997. Dean Foods also created a new product: Milk Chugs, single-serving milk drinks in resealable plastic bottles. In 1998 it gave up on vegetables, selling its entire vegetable business to Agrilink Foods, a Pro-Fac Cooperative subsidiary, in exchange for $400 million and Agrilink's shelf-stable foods business (cheese sauces, pudding).

In fiscal 1998 Dean Foods purchased eight regional dairies, adding about $750 million in sales. Acquisitions in fiscal 1999 included the purchase of dairy operation Berkeley Farms and Alta Dena Certified Dairy. During 1999 Dean Foods purchased Oregon-based Steinfeld's Products (pickles, condiments) and Dairy Express (dairy distributor); it also acquired a minority stake in Boulder, Colorado-based White Wave (soy milk, tofu).

OFFICERS

Chairman and CEO: Howard M. Dean, age 62, $1,148,630 pay
President and COO: Richard Bailey, $978,438 pay
SVP: Thomas A. Ravencroft, age 62, $502,145 pay
Group VP; President, Dean Pickle and Specialty Products: James R. Greisinger, age 58, $402,720 pay
Group VP; President, Specialty Business Unit: Dennis J. Purcell, age 56
VP; President, Dairy Division: Eric A. Blanchard, age 43
VP Business Strategy: Luis P. Nieto, age 44
VP Dairy Sales and Marketing: Douglas A. Parr, age 57
VP Finance and CFO: William R. McManaman, age 52, $469,125 pay
VP Governmental and Dairy Industry Relations: Gary A. Corbett, age 51
VP Human Resources: Daniel M. Dressel, age 56
VP Manufacturing and Engineering: Gary D. Flickinger
VP Research and Development: George A. Muck, age 61
Auditors: PricewaterhouseCoopers LLP

LOCATIONS

HQ: 3600 N. River Rd., Franklin Park, IL 60131
Phone: 847-678-1680   **Fax:** 847-233-5505
Web site: http://www.deanfoods.com

Dean Foods operates dairies and processing facilities in 19 states and the UK.

PRODUCTS/OPERATIONS

1999 Sales

	$ mil.	% of total
Dairy	2,985	79
Specialty	407	11
Pickles	363	10
Total	**3,755**	**100**

Selected Brands

Dairy
Alta Dena
Barber's
Berkeley Farms
Bud's of San Fransisco
Coburg
Cream o' Weber
Creamland
Dairy Pure
Dean's
Fitzgerald
Gandy's
Maplehurst
Mayfield
McArthur
Meadow Brook
Price's
Purity
Reiter
T.G. Lee
Verifine
Wengert's

Specialty (dips, dressings, and sauces)
Bennett's
Dean's
Hoffman House
Imo
King
Marie's
Northwoods
Rod's

Pickles
Atkins
Aunt Jane's
Cates
Dailey
Heifetz
Paramount
Peter Piper
Rainbo
Roddenbery
Schwartz's
Steinfeld's

COMPETITORS

B&G Foods
California Dairies Inc.
ConAgra
Dairy Farmers of America
Danone
Darigold
Dreyer's
Foremost Farms
Heinz
Land O'Lakes

Nestle
Parmalat Finanziaria
Pillsbury
Prairie Farms Dairy
Pro-Fac
Shamrock Foods
Suiza Foods
Unilever
Vlasic Foods

HISTORICAL FINANCIALS & EMPLOYEES

NYSE symbol: DF FYE: May 31	Annual Growth	1990	1991	1992	1993	1994	1995	1996	1997	1998	1999
Sales ($ mil.)	7.3%	1,988	2,158	2,289	2,274	2,431	2,630	2,814	3,018	2,736	3,755
Net income ($ mil.)	10.6%	61	73	62	68	72	80	(50)	87	106	151
Income as % of sales	—	3.1%	3.4%	2.7%	3.0%	3.0%	3.0%	—	2.9%	3.9%	4.0%
Earnings per share ($)	10.4%	1.53	1.79	1.53	1.73	1.84	2.00	(1.24)	2.15	2.57	3.74
Stock price - FY high ($)	—	25.26	33.02	33.50	29.88	33.50	33.00	29.75	40.00	60.69	57.44
Stock price - FY low ($)	—	19.26	20.84	22.75	23.13	24.50	25.25	22.25	21.75	37.25	32.94
Stock price - FY close ($)	5.5%	23.18	31.10	24.63	26.50	27.25	28.00	24.38	38.00	49.25	37.50
P/E - high	—	17	18	22	17	18	17	—	19	24	15
P/E - low	—	13	12	15	13	13	13	—	10	14	9
Dividends per share ($)	7.6%	0.43	0.48	0.54	0.59	0.63	0.67	0.71	0.75	0.79	0.83
Book value per share ($)	8.2%	8.94	10.24	10.87	12.00	13.19	14.58	12.65	14.09	15.49	18.17
Employees	4.8%	8,900	9,600	10,100	10,500	12,100	11,800	11,500	11,800	14,500	13,600

STOCK PRICE HISTORY

HIGH/LOW/CLOSE

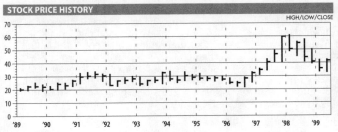

1999 FISCAL YEAR-END

Debt ratio: 46.8%
Return on equity: 21.1%
Cash ($ mil.): 16
Current ratio: 1.32
Long-term debt ($ mil.): 631
No. of shares (mil.): 39
Dividends
  Yield: 2.2%
  Payout: 22.2%
Market value ($ mil.): 1,478

DEERE & COMPANY

OVERVIEW

Old McDonald probably had a Deere, too. Based in Moline, Illinois, Deere & Company is the world's top maker of farm equipment (52% of sales) and a leading producer of construction and lawn care equipment. While farmers use Deere's tractors, harvesters, sprayers, and crop-handling equipment (most painted in its signature green), homeowners and grounds crews use its chain saws, snowblowers, and lawn trimmers. Construction workers use Deere's backhoes and excavators.

Deere offers financing and leasing services for its customers and dealers. Its health care operation, originally developed for employees only, now serves some 428,000 people.

Deere has bounded into making hay equipment and machines for commercial spraying and air-seeding. It had its eye on international markets, particularly Latin America and Eastern Europe, but the financial turmoil that began in Asia and spread to South America and even the US has hurt sales and led to layoffs and severe production cutbacks. Deere is selling its insurance business to Sentry Insurance.

HISTORY

Vermont-born John Deere moved to Grand Detour, Illinois, in 1836 and set up a blacksmith shop. Deere and other pioneers had trouble with the rich, black midwestern soil sticking to the iron plows designed for sandy eastern soils, so in 1837 Deere used a circular steel saw blade to create a self-scouring plow that moved so quickly it was nicknamed the whistling plow. He sold only three in 1838 but was making 25 a week by 1842.

Deere moved to Moline in 1847. His son Charles joined the firm in 1853, beginning a tradition of family management: All five presidents before 1982 were related by blood or marriage. Charles set up an independent dealership distribution system and expanded the product line to include wagons, buggies, and corn planters.

Under Charles Deere's son-in-law William Butterworth (president from 1907 to 1928), the company bought other agricultural equipment companies and developed harvesters and tractors with internal combustion engines. Butterworth's nephew Charles Wiman became president in 1928. He extended credit to farmers during the Depression; the policy won customer loyalty. In 1931 Deere opened its first international plant in Canada.

William Hewitt, Wiman's son-in-law, became CEO in 1955. Deere passed International Harvester in 1958 to become the #1 US maker of agricultural equipment, and by 1963 it was the world's largest. Deere expanded into Argentina, France, Mexico, and Spain; today Deere products are sold worldwide. Deere has used joint ventures abroad (Yanmar, small tractors, 1977; Hitachi, excavators, 1983) and internal research to diversify.

Despite an industrywide sales slump culminating in losses totaling $328 million in 1986 and 1987, Deere was the only major agricultural equipment maker to neither change ownership nor close factories during the 1980s. Instead, the company cut its workforce 44% and improved efficiency, lowering the manufacturing break-even point from 70% to 35% of capacity.

Robert Hanson became the first nonfamily CEO in 1982. He poured $2 billion into research and development during the 1980s, and in 1989 Deere introduced its largest new product offering up to then, including the 9000 series of combines (which had taken 15 years to develop). It acquired Funk Manufacturing, which makes powertrain components, for $87 million in 1989. That year Hans Becherer succeeded Hanson as CEO.

In recent years Deere has expanded its lawn care equipment business, especially in Europe. In 1991 it acquired a majority stake in Sabo-Maschinenfabrik, a German maker of commercial lawn mowers. Two years later Deere gained distribution rights to Zetor tractors and Brno diesel engines (from the Czech Republic), which the company marketed in Latin America and the Far East.

After spending most of the early 1990s in the doldrums because of recession and weak farm prices, Deere rebounded. By 1994 it had replaced its tractor line with all-new models. That year it bought Homelite, a maker of handheld outdoor power equipment, from industrial conglomerate Textron.

Deere signed a deal to sell more than 1,000 combines to Ukraine in 1996 and formed a joint venture the following year to make combines in China. With dwindling demand for agricultural equipment at home and failing economies in Asia, Brazil, and former Soviet states, Deere announced layoffs of about 2,400 workers in 1998 and production cutbacks in 1998 and 1999. It also agreed to sell its insurance business to Sentry Insurance.

Chairman and CEO: Hans W. Becherer, age 63,
$2,529,824 pay
SVP, General Counsel, and Corporate Secretary:
Frank S. Cottrell
SVP, Worldwide Parts and Corporate Administration:
Joseph W. England, age 58, $788,826 pay
SVP, Finance and Accounting and CFO: Nathan J. Jones
SVP Engineering, Technology, and Human Resources:
John K. Lawson
VP Industrial Relations: G. Bart Bontems
VP Government Affairs: Wade P. Clarke Jr.
VP Human Resources: Mertroe B. Hornbuckle
VP Quality: Will R. Hubbard
VP Corporate Communications: Curtis G. Linke
VP, Worldwide Supply Management: R. David Nelson
VP and Controller: James S. Robertson
VP Engineering: Robert J. Wismer
President, Worldwide Agricultural Equipment Division:
Bernard L. Hardiek, age 58, $927,006 pay
**President, Worldwide Construction Equipment
Division:** Pierre E. Leroy, age 50, $796,945 pay
**President, Worldwide Commercial and Consumer
Equipment Division and Deere Power Systems
Group:** Ferdinand F. Korndorf, age 49, $790,503 pay
President, Financial Services: Michael P. Orr
Auditors: Deloitte & Touche LLP

LOCATIONS

HQ: 1 John Deere Place, Moline, IL 61265-8098
Phone: 309-765-8000 **Fax:** 309-765-5772
Web site: http://www.deere.com

Deere & Company has manufacturing plants in
Argentina, Canada, France, Germany, Mexico, South
Africa, Spain, and the US.

PRODUCTS/OPERATIONS

1998 Sales & Operating Income

	Sales $ mil.	Sales % of total	Operating Income $ mil.	Operating Income % of total
Farm equipment	7,217	52	962	55
Construction equipment	2,585	19	300	17
Commercial & consumer equipment	2,124	15	214	12
Credit	971	7	256	15
Insurance & health care	766	6	15	1
Other	159	1	—	—
Adjustment	(196)	—	—	—
Total	**13,626**	**100**	**1,747**	**100**

COMPETITORS

AGCO
Black & Decker
Blue Cross
Case
Caterpillar
CIGNA
FMC
Ford
GE
Honda
Hyundai
Ingersoll-Rand
Kubota
Mitsubishi
Navistar
New Holland
Prudential
Toro
Volvo

HISTORICAL FINANCIALS & EMPLOYEES

NYSE symbol: DE FYE: October 31	Annual Growth	1989	1990	1991	1992	1993	1994	1995	1996	1997	1998
Sales ($ mil.)	9.1%	6,234	7,848	7,034	6,931	7,694	8,967	10,118	11,128	12,617	13,626
Net income ($ mil.)	11.6%	380	411	(20)	37	(921)	604	706	817	960	1,021
Income as % of sales	—	6.1%	5.2%	—	0.5%	(3.96)	6.7%	7.0%	7.3%	7.6%	7.5%
Earnings per share ($)	10.7%	1.67	1.79	(0.09)	0.16	(3.96)	2.32	2.69	3.11	3.74	4.16
Stock price - FY high ($)	—	21.40	26.10	19.11	18.94	26.10	30.26	31.72	45.00	60.50	64.13
Stock price - FY low ($)	—	14.65	12.53	12.82	12.28	12.24	21.48	20.40	28.31	39.13	28.38
Stock price - FY close ($)	7.7%	18.27	13.32	18.86	13.15	25.72	23.85	29.76	41.88	52.81	35.63
P/E - high	—	13	15	—	118	—	13	12	14	16	15
P/E - low	—	9	7	—	77	—	9	8	9	10	7
Dividends per share ($)	9.5%	0.38	0.62	0.67	0.67	0.67	0.67	0.73	0.80	0.80	0.86
Book value per share ($)	4.1%	12.24	13.14	12.39	11.56	8.12	9.86	11.78	13.83	16.57	17.56
Employees	(0.6%)	38,949	38,493	36,469	25,250	33,070	34,300	33,400	33,900	34,400	37,000

STOCK PRICE HISTORY

HIGH/LOW/CLOSE

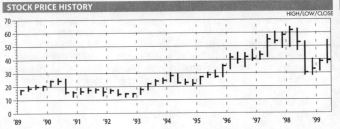

1998 FISCAL YEAR-END

Debt ratio: 40.6%
Return on equity: 25.0%
Cash ($ mil.): 310
Current ratio: 1.67
Long-term debt ($ mil.): 2,792
No. of shares (mil.): 232
Dividends
  Yield: 2.4%
  Payout: 20.7%
Market value ($ mil.): 8,277

DEL MONTE FOODS COMPANY

OVERVIEW

Del Monte Foods is one packer that roots for the 49ers. The San Francisco-based company is the largest produce canner and distributor in the US. It packages vegetables (corn, green beans, peas), fruit (peaches, pineapple, fruit cocktail), and tomatoes (sauce, ketchup, sloppy joe sauce) from produce supplied by more than 2,500 independent US growers. Del Monte sells nearly 80% of its products through US grocers and other retailers.

New CEO Richard Wolford (a former Dole executive installed by Texas Pacific Group, which owns about 47% of Del Monte) is trying to reheat the canned fruit and vegetable market. Del Monte is expanding through acquisitions, aggressive marketing (its first ad campaign in eight years is planned for 1999), and the introduction of new products, such as Orchard Select (fruit packed in glass jars sold in the produce section) and fruit smoothie concentrates.

HISTORY

Fred Tillman adopted the name Del Monte (originally the name of a coffee blend made for the fancy Hotel Del Monte in Monterey, California) in 1891 for use at his newly formed Oakland Preserving Company. Brand-name labeling was becoming a significant marketing tool, and Del Monte (Spanish for "of the mountain") became known for high value.

In 1899 Oakland Preserving merged into the California Fruit Canners Association (CFCA) with 17 other canneries (half of California's canning industry). The new company, adopted Del Monte as its main brand name. CFCA merged with other California canneries in 1916 to form Calpak and created national demand for Del Monte products through mass advertising. The company's first ad appeared in the *Saturday Evening Post* in 1917.

Calpak expanded into the Midwest in 1925 by acquiring Rochelle Canneries (Illinois). That year it established British Sales Limited and Philippine Packing Corporation. In later years the company expanded into the Philippines.

The Depression had a disastrous effect on Calpak. Share prices fell from $6.16 in 1930 to $0.09 in 1931, and the decade was marked by labor unrest. In 1932 the company took an $8.9 million loss. Profits recovered in 1934, but the Depression slowed growth. However WWII jump-started Calpak's operations — in 1942 about 40% of the company's products went to feed US troops — and the postwar boom kicked them into high gear.

The company bought control of Canadian Canners Limited, the world's second-largest canner, in 1956, gaining entry into the heavily protected British market. In the 1960s a venture into soft-drink products ended in failure. Calpak changed its name to Del Monte Foods in 1967.

RJR Industries bought Del Monte in 1979 as part of a diversification strategy. In 1989, after its buyout by Kohlberg Kravis Roberts, the newly named, debt-laden RJR Nabisco began selling assets, including Del Monte's Hawaiian Punch line in 1990 and its tropical fruit unit. Merrill Lynch and Del Monte executives bought Del Monte's domestic canning operations in 1990, but the transaction loaded the new company with debt.

To reduce debt, Del Monte sold its dried fruit operations to Yorkshire Food Group in 1993 and its pudding division to Kraft in 1995. A $1 billion deal in 1994 to sell the whole company to Mexico's Grupo Cabal, then-owner of Fresh Del Monte Produce, collapsed when Grupo Cabal's head, Carlos Cabal Peniche, was charged with illegal loan transactions and then disappeared. (He was captured in Australia in fall 1998.)

In 1995 Del Monte made a $4 million severance payment to Pacific Coast Producers after the FTC found that Del Monte's supply pact with Pacific Coast greatly reduced competition in the processed-fruit market.

Unloading international operations, Del Monte sold its Mexican subsidiary to private investment firm Hicks, Muse, Tate & Furst in 1996. The next year Del Monte was acquired by Texas Pacific Group, an investment partnership known for recruiting specialists to revive companies. It installed Richard Wolford, former president of Dole Packaged Foods, as CEO. Also in 1997 Del Monte bought Contadina's canned tomato products from Nestle.

Del Monte announced in 1998 that plant closings in California would cost 1,000 jobs. Interested again in expanding international markets, it bought back from Nabisco the rights to the Del Monte brand in South America, and it purchased Nabisco's canned fruits and vegetables business in Venezuela. Del Monte filed to go public in 1998 in order to raise money for debt reduction, but it postponed the offering because of a flat IPO market. In 1999, as market conditions improved, the company completed its IPO.

Chairman: Richard W. Boyce, age 44
CEO: Richard G. Wolford, age 53, $750,000 pay
COO: Wesley J. Smith, age 51, $600,000 pay
EVP Administration and CFO: David L. Meyers, age 52, $447,000 pay
EVP Sales: Glynn M. Phillips, age 61, $357,095 pay
EVP Marketing: Brent D. Bailey, age 46
SVP and Treasurer: Thomas E. Gibbons, age 50, $248,667 pay
SVP and Chief Accounting Officer: Richard L. French, age 41
SVP Technology: William J. Spain, age 56
VP Corporate Personnel: Mark J. Buxton
VP, Secretary, and General Counsel: William R. Sawyers, age 36
Auditors: KPMG LLP

LOCATIONS

HQ: 1 Market St., San Francisco, CA 94105
Phone: 415-247-3000 **Fax:** 415-247-3565
Web site: http://www.delmonte.com

1998 Production Facilities

	No.
California	6
Wisconsin	3
Washington	2
Illinois	1
Indiana	1
Minnesota	1
Texas	1
Total	**15**

1998 Distribution Facilities

	No.
Alabama	1
California	1
Illinois	1
New Jersey	1
Texas	1
Utah	1
Total	**6**

PRODUCTS/OPERATIONS

1998 Sales

	$ mil.	% of total
Canned vegetables	466	35
Canned fruits	456	35
Tomato products	313	24
Other	78	6
Total	**1,313**	**100**

Selected Brand Names

Apple Cup
Contadina
Del Monte
Del Monte Lite
Fruit Cup
Fruit Naturals
Fruit Pleasures
Fruit Rageous
Fruit Smoothie Blenders
Orchard Select

Selected Products

Fruit (peaches, pears, fruit cocktail, apricots, mandarin oranges, cherries, pineapple)
Tomatoes (stewed, crushed, diced, chunk, wedges, ketchup, tomato sauce, tomato paste, sloppy joe sauce)
Vegetables (corn, green beans, peas, mixed vegetables, spinach, beets, baby beets, carrots, potatoes, sauerkraut, asparagus, zucchini, flavored vegetables)

COMPETITORS

Campbell Soup
Chiquita Brands
ConAgra
Dole
Goya
Heinz
Lykes Bros.
Nestlé
Pillsbury
Pro-Fac
Seneca Foods
Tri Valley Growers
Unilever

HISTORICAL FINANCIALS & EMPLOYEES

NYSE symbol: DLM FYE: June 30	Annual Growth	1989	1990	1991	1992	1993	1994	1995	1996	1997	1998
Sales ($ mil.)	(2.9%)	1,717	1,317	1,435	1,431	1,555	1,499	1,527	1,305	1,217	1,313
Net income ($ mil.)	(23.5%)	56	(108)	(27)	(58)	(188)	3	5	88	(56)	5
Income as % of sales	—	3.3%	—	—	—	—	0.2%	0.3%	6.7%	—	0.4%
Employees	(1.9%)	—	—	15,340	14,500	14,000	12,500	12,500	12,000	14,100	13,450

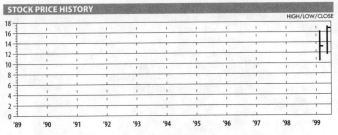

STOCK PRICE HISTORY
HIGH/LOW/CLOSE

1998 FISCAL YEAR-END

Debt ratio: 100.0%
Return on equity: —
Cash ($ mil.): 7
Current ratio: 1.72
Long-term debt ($ mil.): 677

DELL COMPUTER CORPORATION

OVERVIEW

The entire PC hardware industry is going to Dell in a handbasket. Round Rock, Texas-based Dell Computer makes desktop PCs, notebooks, and network servers, nearly 70% of which it sells to government entities and large corporations. It also markets peripherals and software from other manufacturers. Dell, which is challenging Compaq for the top spot among PC makers, continues to broaden its service offerings as it rises up the ranks of the world's largest computer companies.

With the industry-standard Wintel platform (Microsoft Windows operating system and Intel microprocessor) as its foundation, Dell has firmed its place as the world's #1 direct seller of computers and spawned a begrudging industry of copycats. Dell's built-to-order boxes mean lower inventories, which translate to lower costs and higher margins.

The proven formula has built Dell's status as the only *FORTUNE* 500 company with annual sales and earnings increases of more than 40% for the past four years. It's made Dell the best-performing stock in the past decade measured against other companies in the S&P 500 Index. Dell's Web site, which features some 50 country-specific pages, claims up to $18 million in computer sales daily and is expected to be processing half of Dell's transactions by the year 2000.

Founder and chairman Michael Dell, who (despite his youth) is the longest-tenured CEO at any major US computer firm, owns 14% of the company.

HISTORY

At age 13 Michael Dell was already a successful businessman. From his parents' home in Houston, Dell ran a mail-order stamp trading business that, within a few months, grossed over $2,000. At 16 he sold newspaper subscriptions and at 17 Dell bought his first BMW. When he enrolled at the University of Texas in 1983, he was thoroughly bitten by the business bug.

Dell started college as a pre-med student but found time to establish a business selling RAM (random-access memory) chips and disk drives for IBM PCs. Dell bought his products at cost from IBM dealers, who, at the time, were required to order from IBM large monthly quotas of PCs, which frequently exceeded demand. Dell resold his stock through newspapers (and later through computer magazines) at 10%-15% below retail.

By April 1984 Dell's dorm room computer components business was grossing about $80,000 a month — enough to persuade him to drop out of college. At about that time he started making and selling his own IBM clones under the brand name PC's Limited. Dell sold his machines directly to end users rather than through retail outlets, as most manufacturers did. By eliminating the retail markup, Dell could sell his PCs at about 40% of the price of an IBM.

The company was plagued by management changes during the mid-1980s. Renamed Dell Computer, it added international sales offices in 1987. In 1988 the company started selling to government agencies, added a sales force to serve larger customers, and went public.

The company tripped in 1990, reporting a 64% drop in profits. Sales were growing — but so were costs, mostly because of efforts to design a PC using proprietary components and RISC chips. Also, the company's warehouses were oversupplied. Within a year Dell turned itself around by cutting inventories and coming out with eight new products.

Dell entered the retail arena by letting Soft Warehouse Superstores (now CompUSA) in 1990 and office supply chain Staples in 1991 sell its PCs at mail-order prices. Also in 1991 Dell opened a plant in Limerick, Ireland.

In 1992 Xerox agreed to sell Dell machines in Latin America. Dell opened subsidiaries in Japan and Austria in 1993. The computer maker abandoned retail stores in 1994 to refocus on its mail-order origins. It also retooled its troubled notebook computer line and introduced a line of servers.

In 1995 the company started offering Pentium-based notebooks. The following year it ramped up operations in the Pacific Rim. In 1997 Dell entered the market for workstations and built up its consumer business by separating that operation from its small-business unit and launching a leasing program for individuals. Dell opened a plant in China in 1998 and made plans for a manufacturing and customer center in Brazil. It began selling a $999 PC in 1999 and agreed to buy ConvergeNet Technologies, a California-based maker of storage area network equipment, in a $340 million deal — the first acquisition in its history.

OFFICERS

Chairman and CEO: Michael S. Dell, age 34,
$3,459,236 pay
VC: Morton L. Topfer, age 62, $2,618,647 pay
VC: Kevin B. Rollins, age 46, $2,083,262 pay
SVP and CFO: Thomas J. Meredith, age 48,
$1,324,433 pay
SVP, Americas Home and Small Business Group:
Paul D. Bell, age 38
SVP, Americas Public and International Group:
Rosendo G. Parra, age 39
SVP, Americas Relationship Group: Joe Marengi, age 45
SVP, Enterprise Systems Group: Michael D. Lambert,
age 52
SVP, Finance: James M. Schneider, age 46
SVP, Law and Administration and Secretary:
Thomas B. Green, age 44
SVP, Personal Systems Group: G. Carl Everett Jr.,
age 48, $999,894 pay
SVP, Worldwide Operations Group: Keith Maxwell, age 50
VP and Chief Information Officer: Jerome N. Gregoire,
age 47
**VP; President, Europe, Middle East, and Africa, and
President, Asia/Pacific Group:** John L. Legere, age 41
VP; President, Dell Japan: Charles H. Saunders, age 55
VP of Worldwide Operations: David Allen, age 38
Auditors: PricewaterhouseCoopers LLP

LOCATIONS

HQ: 1 Dell Way, Round Rock, TX 78682-2244
Phone: 512-338-4400   **Fax:** 512-728-3653
Web site: http://www.dell.com

Dell Computer sells its products in more than 170
countries. The company has manufacturing facilities in
China, Ireland, Malaysia, and the US.

1999 Sales

	$ mil.	% of total
The Americas	12,420	68
Europe	4,674	26
Asia/Pacific	1,149	6
Total	**18,243**	**100**

PRODUCTS/OPERATIONS

1999 Sales

	$ mil.	% of total
Desktop computers	10,979	60
Notebooks	3,859	21
Enterprise systems	2,193	12
Other	1,212	7
Total	**18,243**	**100**

Products
Computer peripherals
Desktop computers (Dell Dimension, OptiPlex)
Network servers (PowerEdge)
Notebook computers (Inspiron, Latitude)
Software
Storage (PowerVault)
Workstations (Dell Precision)

COMPETITORS

Acer	Oki Electric
Apple Computer	Packard Bell
Bull	Sequent
Compaq	SGI
Data General	Sharp
Fujitsu	Sun Microsystems
Gateway	Tandy
Hewlett-Packard	Toshiba
IBM	Unisys
Micron Electronics	

HISTORICAL FINANCIALS & EMPLOYEES

Nasdaq symbol: DELL FYE: January 31	Annual Growth	1990	1991	1992	1993	1994	1995	1996	1997	1998	1999
Sales ($ mil.)	53.4%	389	546	890	2,014	2,873	3,475	5,296	7,759	12,327	18,243
Net income ($ mil.)	87.5%	5	27	51	102	(36)	149	272	518	944	1,460
Income as % of sales	—	1.3%	5.0%	5.7%	5.0%	—	4.3%	5.1%	6.7%	7.7%	8.0%
Earnings per share ($)	55.4%	0.01	0.02	0.03	0.05	(0.02)	0.05	0.09	0.17	0.32	0.53
Stock price - FY high ($)	—	0.10	0.24	0.38	0.78	0.77	0.75	1.54	4.52	12.98	50.19
Stock price - FY low ($)	—	0.05	0.05	0.21	0.23	0.22	0.30	0.62	0.84	3.74	12.61
Stock price - FY close ($)	115.4%	0.05	0.24	0.33	0.72	0.34	0.67	0.86	4.13	12.43	50.00
P/E - high	—	10	12	13	16	—	15	17	27	41	95
P/E - low	—	5	3	7	5	—	6	7	5	12	24
Dividends per share ($)	—	0.00	0.00	0.00	0.00	0.00	0.00	0.00	0.00	0.00	0.00
Book value per share ($)	40.0%	0.04	0.06	0.12	0.16	0.19	0.26	0.32	0.29	0.50	0.91
Employees	36.3%	1,500	2,050	2,970	4,650	5,980	6,400	8,400	10,350	16,000	24,400

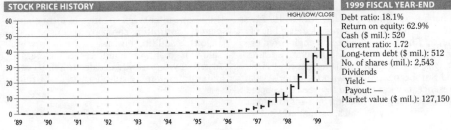

STOCK PRICE HISTORY   HIGH/LOW/CLOSE

1999 FISCAL YEAR-END

Debt ratio: 18.1%
Return on equity: 62.9%
Cash ($ mil.): 520
Current ratio: 1.72
Long-term debt ($ mil.): 512
No. of shares (mil.): 2,543
Dividends
  Yield: —
  Payout: —
Market value ($ mil.): 127,150

DELOITTE TOUCHE TOHMATSU

OVERVIEW

There's more than a touch of teamwork at Deloitte Touche Tohmatsu (DTT), known in the US as Deloitte & Touche. The New York City-based firm operates in more than 130 countries, using industry specialists to provide complete service. Its consulting specialties include strategic planning, information technology, financial management, and productivity. The commodification of the auditing side of the business (whose driving force has moved from relationships to pricing) has made the consulting side more important. In recognition of this, DTT has made its consulting group an autonomous unit (à la Andersen Worldwide).

The 1998 merger of Price Waterhouse and Coopers & Lybrand into PricewaterhouseCoopers (and the proposed but abandoned pairing of Ernst & Young and KPMG International) made size more important than ever. The PricewaterhouseCoopers combination dropped DTT to last place among the Big Five, prompting the company to begin an aggressive new advertising campaign.

HISTORY

In 1845 William Deloitte opened an accounting office in London. At first Deloitte, a former staff member of the Official Assignee in Bankruptcy of the City of London, solicited business from bankrupts. The development of joint stock companies in the mid-19th century fueled the rise of accounting because of the need for standardized financial reporting. Deloitte moved into the new field.

The firm added partners, among them John Griffiths (1869), who opened the company's first US office in New York City in 1890. Other branches followed in Cincinnati (1905), Chicago (1912), Montreal (1912), Boston (1930), and Los Angeles (1945). In 1952 the firm formed an alliance with Haskins & Sells.

Deloitte's aim was to be "the Cadillac, not the Ford" of accounting. The firm, which became Deloitte Haskins & Sells in 1978, began shedding its conservatism as competition heated up; it was the first of the Big Eight firms, for example, to advertise aggressively.

In 1984, in a taste of what was to come, Deloitte Haskins & Sells tried to merge with Price Waterhouse. The deal was dropped after Price Waterhouse's UK partners objected.

The Big Eight accounting firms became the Big Six in 1989 when Ernst & Whinney merged with Arthur Young to become Ernst & Young, and the staid Deloitte Haskins & Sells joined the flamboyant Touche Ross (whose Japanese affiliate's name, Ross Tohmatsu, rounds out the current name) to form Deloitte & Touche. Touche Ross, founded in New York in 1947, was the hard-charging, bare-knuckled, bad boy of the Big Eight. The merger was engineered by Deloitte's Michael Cook and Touche's Edward Kangas, in part to unite the former firm's US and European strengths with the latter's Asian presence. Cook continued to oversee US operations with Kangas presiding over international operations. Many affiliates, particularly in the UK, rejected the merger and defected to competing firms.

As auditors have increasingly been held accountable for the financial results of their clients, legal action has soared. In the 1990s Deloitte was sued because of activities relating to Drexel Burnham Lambert's Michael Milken, the failure of several savings and loans, and the bankruptcy of business clients.

But Deloitte's reputation remained strong enough that in 1995 the SEC chose Michael Sutton, the firm's national director of auditing and accounting practice, as its chief accountant. That year DTT formed Deloitte & Touche Consulting to consolidate its US and UK consulting operations; its Asian operations were later added to the group to facilitate regional expansion.

In 1996 the firm formed a corporate fraud unit (with special emphasis on the Internet) and bought PHH Fantus, the leading corporate relocation consulting company. The next year, amid a new round of mergers in the industry, rumors swirled that a merger of DTT and Ernst & Young had been scrapped because the firms could not agree on relative ownership of the two firms' partners. DTT disavowed plans to merge and launched an ad campaign directly targeted against its rivals.

In 1998 the firm's overseas expansion was hit by the Asian economic crisis, but the silver lining of the situation was a rise in restructuring and workout consulting. In 1999, about 1,000 consultants left the firm to form an independent consulting company unconstrained by Deloitte's auditing business; the new firm was sold to its managers and Evercore Partners. Also that year, Deloitte decided to sell its computer programming subsidiary to CGI Group.

Chairman: Edward A. Kangas
CEO: James E. Copeland Jr., age 54
COO: J. Thomas Presby
Chairman and CEO, Deloitte & Touche LLP:
Douglas M. McCracken, age 50
Chief Executive and Senior Partner, Deloitte & Touche (UK): John P. Connolly
CEO, Deloitte & Touche Consulting Group Global:
Pasquale "Pat" Loconto
National Director U. S. International Operations:
Rocco Laterzo
Director Human Resources: Martyn Fisher
Director Communications: David Read
Director Finance: Gerald W. Richards
National Director of Human Capital and Actuary Practice, Deloitte & Touche LLP: Ainar D. Aijala Jr., age 42
National Managing Director Finance, Deloitte & Touche LLP: William A. Fowler
National Director Marketing, Communications, and Public Relations, Deloitte & Touche LLP: Gary Gerard
National Director Operations, Deloitte & Touche LLP:
William H. Stanton
National Director Human Resources, Deloitte & Touche LLP: James H. Wall
Counsel: Joseph J. Lambert
General Counsel, Deloitte & Touche LLP:
Philip R. Rotner

LOCATIONS

HQ: 1633 Broadway, New York, NY 10019-6754
Phone: 212-492-4000   **Fax:** 212-492-4154
Web site: http://www.deloitte.com

Deloitte Touche Tohmatsu operates through about 700 offices in more than 130 countries.

1998 Sales

	$ mil.	% of total
North America	4,991	55
Europe	2,652	29
Asia/Pacific	883	10
Latin America/Caribbean	268	3
Africa	161	2
Middle East	45	1
Total	**9,000**	**100**

PRODUCTS/OPERATIONS

Selected Services
Accounting and auditing
Information technology consulting
Management consulting
Mergers and acquisitions consulting
Tax advice and planning

Selected Representative Clients
Allstate
DaimlerChrysler
General Motors
Merrill Lynch
MetLife
Microsoft
Mitsubishi
Nortel Networks
Procter & Gamble
Sears

Selected Affiliates
Akintola Williams & Co. (Cameroon)
Braxton Associates
C. C. Chokshi & Co. (India)
D&T Corporate Finance Europe Ltd. (UK)
Deloitte & Touche Central Europe (Czech Republic)
Deloitte & Touche Consulting Group/ICS
Hans Tuanakotta & Mustofa (Indonesia)
The IDOM Group
Nautilus Indemnity Holdings Ltd. (Bermuda)
Shawki & Co. (Egypt)
Tohmatsu & Co. (Japan)

COMPETITORS

Andersen Worldwide	Grant Thornton
Arthur D. Little	International
BDO International	H&R Block
Booz, Allen	KPMG
Boston Consulting	Marsh & McLennan
EDS	McKinsey & Company
Ernst & Young	PricewaterhouseCoopers
Gemini Consulting	Towers Perrin
	Watson Wyatt

HISTORICAL FINANCIALS & EMPLOYEES

Partnership FYE: August 31	Annual Growth	1989	1990	1991	1992	1993	1994	1995	1996	1997	1998
Sales ($ mil.)	9.7%	3,900	4,200	4,500	4,800	5,000	5,200	5,950	6,500	7,400	9,000
Employees	4.0%	—	59,700	56,000	56,000	56,000	56,600	59,000	63,440	65,000	82,000

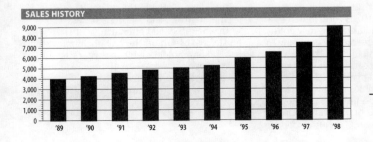

SALES HISTORY

Deloitte & Touche

DELPHI AUTOMOTIVE SYSTEMS

OVERVIEW

Exactly what goes on beneath the hood of a car might be Greek to most people, but it's no mystery to Delphi Automotive Systems, the world's #1 maker of auto parts. The Troy, Michigan-based auto parts manufacturer gets its name from ancient Greece, where people sought predictions and answers from the oracle at Delphi. Delphi Automotive doesn't claim to predict the future, but it can provide answers about almost everything mechanical or electrical that goes into a car.

Delphi's dynamics and propulsion division accounts for 45% of sales and produces brake, chassis, ignition, steering, and fuel management systems. Its safety, thermal, and electrical architecture unit, accounting for 39% of sales, makes climate-control, powertrain-cooling, air bag, and door module systems.

Delphi's electronics and mobile communications segment, including subsidiary Delco Electronics, manufactures audio, collision-warning, security, and fiber-optic data-transmission systems.

Delphi operates 168 manufacturing plants in 36 countries. It sells about 80% of its products to GM, but also supplies other automakers such as Ford, Toyota, and DaimlerChrysler.

Delphi went out on its own after a two-step spin by GM in 1999. About one-third of GM's 600,000 employees made the move with Delphi, which had been anticipating independence so it could expand its customer base and cut costs. Delphi plans to reduce labor costs by renegotiating United Auto Workers contracts. Meanwhile, Delphi has shed more than $3 billion in unprofitable operations to stay competitive.

HISTORY

Delphi Automotive Systems traces its roots back to the 1908 birth of General Motors (GM), originally formed as a consortium among Buick, Oldsmobile, and Cadillac. During WWI 90% of GM's trucks were targeted for the war effort. Chevrolet joined the group in 1918, and by 1920 GM had bought more than 30 companies.

GM expanded its product line in 1936 to include radios by buying Delco Electronics (transferred to Delphi in 1997). Delco was founded in 1912 by C. F. Kettering, the inventor of the electric starter. GM spent WWII turning out defense materials, including some 1,300 airplanes and one-fourth of all US aircraft engines. In the 1950s, GM introduced the V-8 engine, power steering and brakes, front seat safety belts, and the first car air-conditioning system. GM, like other carmakers, made most of the parts for its cars.

During the mid-1960s, GM diversified into home appliances, insurance, locomotives, electronics, ball bearings, and financing. Delco began to produce AM/FM car stereos. In 1961 J. T. Battenberg III (Delphi's current CEO) joined GM as a GM Institute student.

The oil crisis of the 1970s contributed to a drop in sales for GM. Additionally, new pollution-control standards forced the company to spend billions on compliance. In the early 1980s GM spent more than $60 billion on new model designs and plant updates. It bought Hughes Electronics and placed Delco under the Hughes umbrella. GM failed to keep up with competitors' technological developments in the 1980s. Lagging behind, it began venturing out of its own backyard to buy cheaper car components.

Devastating losses in the early 1990s forced GM to restructure. In 1991 it began organizing its parts operations into a separate business group. The next year Battenberg took control of the parts division and began streamlining and exiting noncore operations. During 1993 and 1994 the company shed some 40 parts operations. In 1994 GM formed Automotive Components Group (ACG) Worldwide; the next year GM changed ACG's name to Delphi. Under pressure to cut costs, Delphi sold four facilities that year.

GM began reporting Delphi's earnings separately in 1997, as a first step towards spinning it off. That year GM also transferred its Delco operations to Delphi, which was suffering from declining profits.

In 1998 United Auto Workers members at a Flint, Michigan, Delphi plant joined those from GM's metal-stamping plant across town in a devastating strike that lasted almost two months and reduced income by about $726 million. Also that year Delphi recorded a $430 million loss related to the sale of its coil spring, lighting, and seating businesses.

In early 1999 GM offered 18% of Delphi in an IPO; GM spun off the rest of Delphi's stock to GM shareholders later that year. Delphi also agreed the same year to buy the autoparts operations of Daewoo Group (South Korean) for $396 million.

Chairman, President, and CEO: J. T. Battenberg III,
age 55, $1,450,000 pay
VP and CFO: Alan S. Dawes, age 44, $608,000 pay
VP; President, Delphi South America: Volker J. Barth,
age 51
VP; President, Delphi Asia Pacific: William A. Ebbert,
age 56
VP; President, Delphi Chassis Systems: Guy C. Hachey,
age 43
VP; President, Delphi Packard Electric Systems:
David R. Heilman, age 54, $580,000 pay
VP; President, Delphi Interior Systems: Rodney O'Neal,
age 45
VP; President, Delphi Harrison Thermal Systems:
Ronald M. Pirtle, age 44
**VP; President, Delphi Energy & Engine Management
Systems:** Donald L. Runkle, age 53, $693,000 pay
VP; President, Delphi Saginaw Steering Systems:
Paul J. Tosch, age 58, $597,000 pay
VP; President, Delphi Automotive Systems Europe:
Jose M. Alapont
VP; President, Delphi Delco Electronics Systems:
David B. Wohleen, age 48
VP Mergers, Acquisitions, and Planning: John P. Arle,
age 51
VP Operations: James A. Bertrand, age 41
VP and Treasurer: John G. Blahnik, age 44
VP Purchasing: Ray C. Campbell, age 56
VP and Chief Information Officer: Peter H. Janak, age 59
VP Production Control and Logistics: Mark C. Lorenz,
age 48
VP Human Resources Management: Mark R. Weber,
age 50
Auditors: Deloitte & Touche LLP

LOCATIONS

HQ: Delphi Automotive Systems Corporation,
5725 Delphi Dr., Troy, MI 48098
Phone: 248-813-2000   **Fax:** 248-813-2523
Web site: http://www.delphiauto.com

Delphi Automotive Systems operates 168 manufacturing
facilities, 27 technical centers, and 51 sales offices
scattered throughout Africa, the Americas, Asia, Europe,
the Middle East, and the Pacific region.

PRODUCTS/OPERATIONS

1998 Sales

	% of total
GM-North America	62
GM-International	11
GM-SPO (Service Parts Organization)	6
Other customers	21
Total	**100**

1998 Sales

	$ mil.	% of total
Dynamics & propulsion	12,862	45
Safety, thermal, & electrical architecture	11,226	39
Electronics & mobile communication	4,823	16
Adjustments	(432)	—
Total	**28,479**	**100**

COMPETITORS

Autoliv
Collins & Aikman
Dana
Denso
Eaton
Federal-Mogul
ITT Industries
Johnson Controls
Lear
Magna International
Mannesmann AG
Meritor
Motorola
NSK
Robert Bosch
Siemens
TRW
Valeo
Visteon Automotive
  Systems
Yazaki

HISTORICAL FINANCIALS & EMPLOYEES

NYSE symbol: DPH FYE: December 31	Annual Growth	1989	1990	1991	1992	1993	1994	1995	1996	1997	1998
Sales ($ mil.)	(0.6%)	—	—	—	—	29,327	31,044	31,661	31,032	31,447	28,479
Net income ($ mil.)	—	—	—	—	—	948	975	1,307	853	215	(93)
Income as % of sales	—	—	—	—	—	3.2%	3.1%	4.1%	2.7%	0.7%	—
Employees	(1.4%)	—	—	—	—	—	—	—	—	200,463	197,568

STOCK PRICE HISTORY

HIGH/LOW/CLOSE

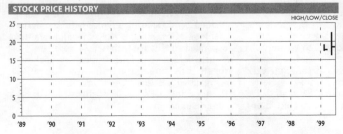

1998 FISCAL YEAR-END

Debt ratio: 99.7%
Return on equity: —
Cash ($ mil.): 995
Current ratio: 1.58
Long-term debt ($ mil.): 3,137

DELTA AIR LINES, INC.

OVERVIEW

After years of financial turbulence, Delta Air Lines may now, indeed, be ready when you are. The Atlanta-based airline (#3 in the US after UAL's United and AMR's American) has hubs in its hometown and Cincinnati, Dallas/Fort Worth, Los Angeles, New York City, and Salt Lake City. It serves about 150 US cities and more than 20 foreign countries. With its code-sharing partners, which include Austrian Airlines, China Southern Airlines, and Swissair, Delta reaches another 14 countries. Delta has a marketing alliance with United that links the carriers' frequent-flier programs.

Delta's low-fare carrier Delta Express is winging into Southwest Airlines' domain by offering service to Florida from Northeast and Midwest cities. Other subsidiaries include ASA Holdings, the parent of regional carrier Atlantic Southeast. Delta also has minority stakes in regional carriers Comair and Skywest, as well as 38% of computer reservation service WORLDSPAN. The airline has agreed to expand its Northeast regional jet service through a deal with Atlantic Coast.

After steady losses in the early 1990s, Delta regained profitability through extensive cost-cutting, but as a result employee morale and, not coincidentally, Delta's cherished reputation for customer service took a dive. While working to improve performance, Delta also plans to take on American in the Latin American market.

HISTORY

Delta Air Lines was founded in Macon, Georgia, in 1924 as the world's first crop-dusting service, Huff-Daland Dusters, to combat boll weevil infestation of cotton fields. It moved to Monroe, Louisiana, in 1925. In 1928 field manager C. E. Woolman and two partners bought the service and renamed it Delta Air Service after the Mississippi Delta region it served.

In 1929 Delta pioneered passenger service from Dallas to Jackson, Mississippi. Flying mail without a government subsidy, Delta finally got a US Postal Service contract in 1934 to fly from Fort Worth to Charleston via Atlanta. Delta moved to Atlanta in 1941. Woolman became president in 1945 and managed the airline until he died in 1966.

Delta continued to add flights, including a direct route from Chicago to New Orleans with its 1952 purchase of Chicago and Southern Airlines. Delta offered its first transcontinental flight in 1961. In 1972 the airline bought Northeast Airlines, thereby expanding service to New England and Canada; it added service to the UK in 1978, the year that the US airline industry was deregulated.

In 1982 Delta's employees pledged $30 million to buy a Boeing 767 jet, christened *The Spirit of Delta*, as a token of appreciation. In fiscal 1983 the company succumbed to the weak US economy and posted its first loss ever, but quickly became profitable again in 1985. It bought Los Angeles-based Western Air Lines in 1986.

Delta began service to Asia in 1987, the year that Ronald Allen, a longtime employee, became CEO. In 1990 Delta joined TWA and Northwest to form WORLDSPAN, a computer reservation service.

Despite a slump in 1990 earnings, in 1991 Delta bought gates, planes, and Canadian routes from Eastern, as well as Pan Am's New York-Boston shuttle, European routes, and Frankfurt hub. The move elevated Delta from domestic carrier to top international airline. In 1992 Pan Am and some of its creditors filed a $2.5 billion breach-of-contract lawsuit against Delta after it backed out of an agreement to fund Pan Am's reorganization, but a district court in 1994 ruled in Delta's favor. Delta's Eastern and Pan Am purchases contributed to a $2 billion loss between 1991 and 1994. Allen began a cost-reduction plan, lasting from 1994 to 1997, that cut many routes and 15,000 jobs. The airline also discontinued unprofitable international routes in 1995 and introduced no-frills Delta Express in 1996.

Allen was let go in 1997 and Leo Mullin, a former electric utility chief, replaced him. That year Delta's unprofitable eight-year-old code-sharing agreement with Singapore Airlines was dissolved, and the carrier began a Latin American expansion drive.

Delta held takeover talks with Continental in 1998, but Continental joined with Northwest instead. On the rebound, Delta signed a marketing accord with United under which the carriers joined their frequent-flier programs. Delta also formed a code-sharing alliance with Aeroperu and took a 35% stake (since diluted); Delta then expanded an alliance with AeroMexico.

In 1999 Delta and Air France — which together fly 20% of the trans-Atlantic traffic — reached a hallmark agreement: Air France chose Delta as its exclusive North American partner.

Chairman: Gerald Grinstein
President and CEO: Leo F. Mullin
CFO: Edward H. West
EVP and Chief Marketing Officer: Frederick W. Reid
EVP, Customer Service: Vicki B. Escarra
EVP, Human Resources: Robert L. Colman
EVP, Operations: Malcolm B. "Mac" Armstrong
SVP, Airport Customer Service: John N. Selvaggio
SVP, Cargo: Rick Nixon
SVP, Corporate Communications: Thomas J. Slocum
**SVP, Corporate Planning and Information
   Technologies:** Paul G. Matsen
SVP, Flight Operations: David S. Bushy
SVP, Governmental Affairs: D. Scott Yohe
SVP, Network Management: Mark A. P. Drusch
SVP, Sales and Distribution: Vincent F. Caminiti
SVP, Secretary, and General Counsel: Robert S. Harkey
SVP, Technical Operations: Ray Valeika
Treasurer: Michele Burns, age 41
Auditors: Arthur Andersen LLP

LOCATIONS

HQ: Hartsfield Atlanta International Airport,
   1030 Delta Blvd., Atlanta, GA 30320-6001
Phone: 404-715-2600   **Fax:** 404-715-5042
Web site: http://www.delta-air.com

Delta Air Lines serves the US and more than 30 other
countries (including code-sharing agreements).

Hub Locations

Atlanta	New York City
Cincinnati	Orlando, FL
Dallas-Fort Worth	Salt Lake City
Los Angeles	

PRODUCTS/OPERATIONS

1998 Sales

	$ mil.	% of total
Passenger	12,976	92
Cargo	582	4
Other	580	4
Total	**14,138**	**100**

1998 Aircraft

	No. Owned	No. Leased
Boeing 727	121	10
Boeing 737	1	72
Boeing 757	54	41
Boeing 767	48	32
L-1011	39	—
MD-11	8	7
MD-88	63	57
MD-90	16	—
Total	**350**	**219**

Selected Affiliates
The Delta Connection (carriers)
   Comair (21%)
   SkyWest (15%)

COMPETITORS

AirTran Holdings	Lufthansa
Alaska Air	Mesa Air
America West	Northwest Airlines
AMR	Qantas
British Airways	SAS
Continental Airlines	Southwest Airlines
Galileo International	TACA
Hawaiian Airlines	TWA
JAL	UAL
KLM	US Airways

HISTORICAL FINANCIALS & EMPLOYEES

NYSE symbol: DAL FYE: June 30	Annual Growth	1989	1990	1991	1992	1993	1994	1995	1996	1997	1998
Sales ($ mil.)	6.4%	8,090	8,582	9,171	10,837	11,997	12,077	12,194	12,455	13,590	14,138
Net income ($ mil.)	9.0%	461	303	(324)	(506)	(1,002)	(409)	408	156	854	1,001
Income as % of sales	—	5.7%	3.5%	—	—	—	—	3.3%	1.3%	6.3%	7.1%
Earnings per share ($)	3.4%	4.69	2.64	(3.87)	(5.30)	(11.16)	(5.16)	2.73	0.72	5.52	6.34
Stock price - FY high ($)	—	36.63	42.88	39.38	37.88	30.69	30.56	37.69	43.50	50.56	65.00
Stock price - FY low ($)	—	22.88	30.50	26.25	26.13	22.88	19.75	21.38	31.75	33.38	40.75
Stock price - FY close ($)	7.4%	33.94	36.56	34.31	27.13	24.19	22.63	36.88	41.50	41.31	64.63
P/E - high	—	8	16	—	—	—	—	14	60	9	10
P/E - low	—	5	12	—	—	—	—	8	44	6	6
Dividends per share ($)	(18.1%)	0.60	0.85	0.60	0.60	0.35	0.10	0.10	0.10	0.10	0.10
Book value per share ($)	0.1%	26.59	28.16	24.87	19.06	19.11	14.54	17.98	18.74	20.40	26.74
Employees	2.1%	58,784	61,675	66,512	70,907	73,533	71,412	59,717	60,289	63,441	70,846

STOCK PRICE HISTORY

HIGH/LOW/CLOSE

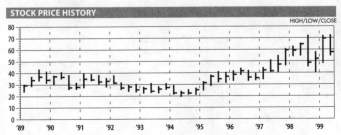

1998 FISCAL YEAR-END

Debt ratio: 29.8%
Return on equity: 24.9%
Cash ($ mil.): 1,077
Current ratio: 0.73
Long-term debt ($ mil.): 1,782
No. of shares (mil.): 150
Dividends
   Yield: 0.2%
   Payout: 1.6%
Market value ($ mil.): 9,724

DELUXE CORPORATION

OVERVIEW

Now that money can move at the speed of a mouse click, Deluxe Corporation wants to do more than keep its revenues in check. The Shoreview, Minnesota-based company remains the #1 check printer in the US (which, along with printing business forms, accounts for most of its sales). Deluxe also provides electronic funds transfer software and processing services for the financial and retail sectors (it's the largest third-party transaction processor for regional ATMs in the US). Deluxe's Payment Protection Systems unit provides account and check verification services and collections support (its Tandem Online service enables collection agents to track cases over the Internet). In addition, the company provides electronic benefits transfer services to state governments.

With the growing popularity of ATMs and debit cards, Deluxe plans to streamline its check printing operations to nine plants (from more than 60 less than a decade ago) and focus on financial services. It sold its greeting card, mail-order stationery, and direct marketing operations. Through acquisitions and alliances, Deluxe plans to leverage the information it collects about consumers to offer new services (such as one that combats fraud), as well as expand overseas.

HISTORY

Deluxe Corporation began in 1915 with the determination of William Hotchkiss, a newspaper publisher turned chicken farmer, to produce one product "better, faster, and more economically than anyone else." From his office in St. Paul, Minnesota, Hotchkiss set out to provide banks with business checks within 48 hours of receiving the order. Deluxe Check Printers made just $23 that year. However, when a new Federal Reserve Bank was established in Minneapolis, the region soon became a major national banking center.

During the 1920s Hotchkiss introduced the most successful product in Deluxe's history: the Handy, a pocket-sized check. As a private company, Deluxe avoided some effects of the 1929 stock market crash. During the Depression the company cut employee hours and pay, but no jobs.

George McSweeney, a sales manager, created the Personalized Check Program in 1939 and was named president two years later. During WWII he stabilized the company by printing ration forms for banks after persuading Washington to release Deluxe's paper supply. In the 1950s Deluxe was one of the first firms to implement the government's magnetic-ink character-recognition program.

By 1960 the company was selling its printing services to 99% of US commercial banks. Deluxe went public in 1965 and introduced its Distinctive line of checks, featuring American scenic designs, in 1969. The company integrated computers and advanced printing technology into production during the 1970s.

In the following decade Deluxe positioned itself to profit from the increasing automation of transactions. It bought Chex-Systems (account verification) in 1984, Colwell Systems (medical business forms) in 1985, A. O. Smith Data Systems (banking software) in 1986, and Current (mail-order greeting cards and checks) in 1987. It established a UK base in 1992 with Stockforms Ltd. (computer forms). Deluxe closed about a fourth of its check printing plants in 1993, the first layoffs in the firm's history.

When Gus Blanchard became president and CEO of Deluxe (the first outsider to do so) the following year, he began a reorganization. In 1996 he announced the company would close 26 check printing plants and eliminate 1,200 jobs. He pursued international business, entering into a joint venture with HCL Corporation, India's largest information technology company, to provide electronic financial services to that nation's banking system.

Deluxe sold Nelco (electronic filing services) and bought Fusion Marketing Group (customized database marketing services) in 1997. The next year, through a joint venture with Fair, Isaac & Co. and Acxiom Corp., Deluxe developed FraudFinder, a computerized system to rate a merchant's risk in accepting an individual's check or debit card. Increasing its focus on financial services, the company sold off its greeting card, specialty paper, and marketing database businesses for $114 million. Also in 1998 it began offering check ordering over the Internet and via voice recognition technology.

In 1999 the company bought eFunds, whose technology converts checks into an electronic transaction at the point of sale. Deluxe also bought the remaining stake of its venture with HCL in 1999, renaming it iDLX.

Chairman, President, and CEO: John A. Blanchard III, age 56, $1,800,000 pay
EVP: Lawrence J. Mosner, age 56, $1,320,000 pay
SVP Sales and Marketing: Gregory J. Bjorndahl
SVP and General Manager, Deluxe Paper Payment Systems: Ronald E. Eilers, age 51, $570,631 pay
SVP, Secretary, and General Counsel: John H. LeFevre, age 55, $540,500 pay
SVP and CFO: Thomas W. VanHimbergen, age 50, $705,000 pay
VP and Chief Information Officer: Warner F. Schlais, age 46
VP Human Resources: Sonia St. Charles, age 38
Auditors: Deloitte & Touche LLP

LOCATIONS

HQ: 3680 Victoria St. North, Shoreview, MN 55126-2966
Phone: 651-483-7111   **Fax:** 651-481-4163
Web site: http://www.deluxe.com

Deluxe Corporation has operations in Canada, India, the UK, and the US.

1998 Sales

	$ mil.	% of total
US	1,905	99
Other countries	27	1
Total	**1,932**	**100**

PRODUCTS/OPERATIONS

1998 Sales

	$ mil.	% of total
Deluxe Paper Payment Systems	1,278	66
Deluxe Direct	224	12
Deluxe Payment Protection Systems	214	11
Deluxe Electronic Payment Systems	129	7
Deluxe Government Systems	44	2
Deluxe Direct Response	43	2
Total	**1,932**	**100**

Selected Divisions and Subsidiaries
Chex Systems, Inc. (account verification services)
Deluxe Business Forms and Supplies (forms and checks)
Deluxe Payment Protection Systems, Inc. (check verification services)
eFunds Corporation (electronic transaction technology)
iDLX (India; customized software and financial service packages)
NRC Holding Corporation (collection services)

COMPETITORS

Adobe	MDC
American Banknote	Moore Corporation
Bowne	National Processing
De La Rue	New England Business
DST	Service
EDS	Standard Register
Equifax	Transaction Systems
First Data	VeriFone
Intuit	Wallace Computer
John Harland	

HISTORICAL FINANCIALS & EMPLOYEES

NYSE symbol: DLX FYE: December 31	Annual Growth	1989	1990	1991	1992	1993	1994	1995	1996	1997	1998
Sales ($ mil.)	4.4%	1,316	1,414	1,475	1,534	1,582	1,748	1,858	1,896	1,919	1,932
Net income ($ mil.)	(0.5%)	153	172	183	203	142	141	87	66	45	145
Income as % of sales	—	11.6%	12.2%	12.4%	13.2%	9.0%	8.1%	4.7%	3.5%	2.3%	7.5%
Earnings per share ($)	0.1%	1.79	2.03	2.18	2.41	1.71	1.71	1.06	0.79	0.55	1.80
Stock price - FY high ($)	—	35.75	35.88	48.50	49.00	47.88	38.00	34.00	39.75	37.00	38.19
Stock price - FY low ($)	—	24.00	26.63	32.63	38.13	31.75	25.63	25.75	27.00	29.75	26.06
Stock price - FY close ($)	0.7%	34.38	35.00	39.63	46.75	36.25	26.38	29.00	32.75	34.50	36.56
P/E - high	—	20	18	22	20	28	22	32	50	67	21
P/E - low	—	13	13	15	16	19	15	24	34	54	14
Dividends per share ($)	4.7%	0.98	1.10	1.22	1.34	1.42	1.46	1.48	1.48	1.48	1.48
Book value per share ($)	0.2%	7.40	8.04	8.91	9.90	9.71	9.89	9.48	8.69	7.50	7.57
Employees	(1.3%)	16,948	17,174	17,563	17,400	17,748	18,000	19,300	19,600	18,900	15,100

STOCK PRICE HISTORY

HIGH/LOW/CLOSE

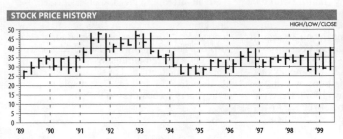

1998 FISCAL YEAR-END

Debt ratio: 14.9%
Return on equity: 23.9%
Cash ($ mil.): 269
Current ratio: 1.37
Long-term debt ($ mil.): 106
No. of shares (mil.): 80
Dividends
  Yield: 4.0%
  Payout: 82.2%
Market value ($ mil.): 2,942

DEXTER CORPORATION

OVERVIEW

Whether you're trying to create a primordial soup or just want a cup of tea, Dexter Corporation — the oldest company listed on the NYSE — can help. Founded before the United States existed, the Windsor Locks, Connecticut-based firm has grown into a billion dollar company focused on specialty materials for the aerospace, electronics, food packaging, and medical industries. The company lays claim to being the world's largest producer of both culture media and paper for tea bags.

Dexter's specialty polymers segment produces adhesives, coatings, and encapsulants used by the aerospace and electronics markets. It also produces materials used to make semiconductors and the segment's magnetic coating technologies are used in chip manufacture.

Dexter's 71%-owned Life Technologies subsidiary produces culture media, animal serum, and reagent supplements for growing and studying cells. The company's nonwoven materials products include tea and coffee packaging, fabrics for surgical drapes and gowns, and premoistened and dry wiping materials.

Dexter focuses on specialty product niches where it can use its proprietary technology. The company also has found new applications for its expertise. Magnetic coating techniques developed for the semiconductor industry have found applications in the production of architectural glass and in medical research. Heirs of founder Seth Dexter own about 6% of the company.

HISTORY

Seth Dexter founded Dexter Corporation in Connecticut in 1767. Dexter's great-great-great grandfather Thomas Dexter had arrived in America in 1630 and built a major farming estate. In 1784 Seth added a gristmill to his sawmill and timberland interests. Seth's son Charles Dexter began experimenting with papermaking, and in 1847 he reorganized the business as C. H. Dexter; it was renamed C. H. Dexter and Sons in 1867. Charles' son-in-law, Herbert Coffin, made paper production a major part of the company's business. He took over the company in 1886. His two sons, Arthur and Herbert, reincorporated Dexter as a partnership in 1914 following Herbert's death.

Continuing its tradition of innovation using paper materials, the company introduced the porous tea bag in the 1930s, as well as the first packaged sheets of toilet paper (soon discontinued). By 1936 when Arthur's son Dexter took over the business, the company was making airmail writing papers, catalog cover paper, and condenser tissues for the electrical industry.

To modernize the company's operations, David Coffin (a salesman by training who took over as Dexter president in 1958) placed an emphasis on marketing, sales, and cost controls. He also took the company on an acquisition drive, picking up Chemical Coatings (1961), Lacquer Products (1962), and Midland Industrial Finishes (1963). The company obtained more cash for acquisitions by going public on its 200th birthday (1967). Dexter subsequently bought chemical-related firms, including Hysol (1967), Puritan Chemical (1973), Howe and Bainbridge (1976), and

Mogul (1977). In 1983 the company acquired Bethesda Research Labs and formed Life Technologies. In 1986 Dexter entered the high-performance thermoplastics market with the purchase of Research Polymers International and Rutland Plastics.

The end of 220 years of family management came in 1988, when company veteran Grahame Walker took over the company from David Coffin, who was unable to persuade any of his three children to take the job. Walker took the company through a major restructuring and cut its divisions by half. In 1992 and 1993 the firm sold its water management, composites, and plastics lines and acquired Akzo Coatings International's US aerospace coatings business. The company scaled back its automotive businesses in 1995 (selling Acoustic Material and D&S Plastics International) to focus on its other businesses.

In 1997 Dexter's acquisitions included Kolack AG (specialty coatings, Switzerland), Herberts (can coatings, Austria), and Quantum Materials (die attach material for semiconductor packaging).

In an attempt to give the diversified company a cohesive image with both customers and employees, Dexter in 1998 adopted a new logo and tag line, "special material for special effects." The company also launched a hostile bid to buy the remaining 48% of Life Technologies stock, but had to settle for increasing its stake to 71%. In 1999 Dexter sold its packaging coatings business to Valspar.

Chairman and CEO: K. Grahame Walker, age 61, $824,835 pay
President and COO: David G. Gordon, age 47, $263,524 pay (prior to promotion)
SVP, Strategic and Business Development: John D. Thompson, age 49
Corporate VP; President, Electronic Materials: Ronald C. Benham, age 56
Corporate VP; President, Adhesive & Coating Systems: Jeffrey W. McClelland, age 56, $309,100 pay
Corporate VP; President, Magnetic Technologies: David Woodhead, age 58
VP and CFO: Kathleen Burdett, age 43, $318,670 pay
VP, General Counsel, and Secretary: Bruce H. Beatt, age 46
VP, Environmental and Process Management: John B. Blatz, age 47
VP, Overseas Business Development: Horst Geldmacher, age 50
VP Human Resources: Lawrence McClure, age 50
VP and Controller: Dale J. Ribaudo, age 41
President and CEO, Life Technologies: J. Stark Thompson, age 57
President, Dexter Nonwoven Materials Business: A. Duncan Middleton, age 53
Auditors: PricewaterhouseCoopers LLP

HQ: 1 Elm St., Windsor Locks, CT 06096
Phone: 860-292-7675 **Fax:** 860-292-7673
Web site: http://www.dexelec.com

Dexter operates about 25 plants in North America, Europe, and Asia.

1998 Sales

	$ mil.	% of total
Specialty Polymers	526	45
Life Sciences	362	31
Nonwovens	280	24
Total	**1,168**	**100**

Selected Products

Aerospace Market
Adhesives and structural materials
Coatings

Electronics Market
Assembly and advanced products
Electronics packaging products
Magnetic materials
Printed wiring board products
Quantum materials (conductive adhesives)

Life Technologies

Medical Market
Gibco BRL products

Nonwovens

Food-Packaging Market
Long-fiber products

Medical Market
Wet-formed and hydroentangled nonwovens

Celox Laboratories
Crown Cork & Seal
H.B. Fuller
Henkel
3M
Organogenesis
Polymer Group
PPG
Rohm and Haas
Uniroyal Technology
Valspar

NYSE symbol: DEX FYE: December 31	Annual Growth	1989	1990	1991	1992	1993	1994	1995	1996	1997	1998
Sales ($ mil.)	3.6%	849	908	938	951	887	975	1,089	1,100	1,147	1,168
Net income ($ mil.)	(3.3%)	43	42	(7)	38	24	38	41	49	56	32
Income as % of sales	—	5.1%	4.6%	—	4.0%	2.7%	3.9%	3.7%	4.4%	4.9%	2.7%
Earnings per share ($)	(2.5%)	1.70	1.71	(0.30)	1.57	0.99	1.55	1.66	2.03	2.41	1.35
Stock price - FY high ($)	—	34.75	24.50	26.13	28.13	28.88	26.00	26.88	33.63	43.94	43.38
Stock price - FY low ($)	—	20.13	18.00	18.50	20.88	20.38	19.88	20.38	23.13	28.75	23.50
Stock price - FY close ($)	4.1%	21.88	21.00	21.63	25.88	23.50	21.75	23.63	31.88	43.19	31.44
P/E - high	—	20	14	—	18	29	17	16	17	18	32
P/E - low	—	12	11	—	13	21	13	12	11	12	17
Dividends per share ($)	2.5%	0.80	0.88	0.88	0.88	0.88	0.88	0.88	0.88	0.94	1.00
Book value per share ($)	2.7%	13.14	14.24	12.99	12.98	12.87	14.11	15.26	15.94	16.09	16.69
Employees	(0.9%)	5,400	5,500	5,600	4,800	4,700	4,700	4,800	4,600	4,800	5,000

HIGH/LOW/CLOSE

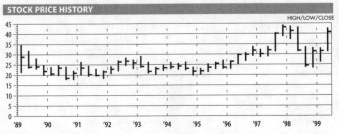

Debt ratio: 49.6%
Return on equity: 8.2%
Cash ($ mil.): 111
Current ratio: 2.07
Long-term debt ($ mil.): 382
No. of shares (mil.): 23
Dividends
  Yield: 3.2%
  Payout: 74.1%
Market value ($ mil.): 732

DHL WORLDWIDE EXPRESS

OVERVIEW

By bus, boat, or bicycle, from Albania to Kyrgyzstan, Qatar to Zimbabwe, DHL Worldwide Express delivers. The Redwood City, California-based logistics and express shipping company owns the world's largest air express company, holding the dominant market share for international traffic. Linking more than 225 countries, DHL has more than 17,500 delivery vehicles and its own fleet of more than 200 aircraft (but also uses other air carriers). The company is expanding its logistics management services which include Internet tracking and order fulfillment.

DHL operates as two separate companies. DHL Airways serves the US market but lags behind FedEx and UPS. Outside the US, the tables are turned. Brussels-based DHL International is the market leader in both Europe and Asia. It partners with its owners (Deutsche Post, Japan Airlines, and Lufthansa each own 25%) in strategic operating alliances to share facilities and routes.

Company co-founder Larry Lee Hillblom, now deceased, had a penchant for very young women that has delivered the air express courier into uncertainty. Part of his $550 million estate, which includes a 60% stake in DHL Airways, is going to four DNA-linked children born to barmaids in the Pacific Islands where Hillblom retired. The rest is slated for the University of California in the form of a medical research trust. The estate which paid out massive legal fees, is now suing its former lawyers.

HISTORY

In 1969 co-workers Adrian Dalsey (the "D" in DHL Worldwide Express), Larry Lee Hillblom (the "H"), and Robert Lynn (the "L") were looking for a way to improve the turnaround time for ships in ports. Their brainstorm was to fly shipping documents to ports for examination and processing before the ship arrived. This idea rapidly developed into an express delivery service between California and Hawaii, and Bank of America became a major customer.

Service was expanded to the Philippines in 1971. The next year the three original investors asked Hong Kong entrepreneur Po Chung to help them form DHL International, a global delivery network. Chung had no previous experience in the express delivery business, but he pioneered a simplified rate structure and the single network concept, which required that the company take full responsibility for picking up and delivering the package. By the end of 1972, service was extended to Australia, Hong Kong, Japan,and Singapore.

From its Pacific Basin origins, DHL expanded worldwide in the 1970s, moving into Europe in 1974, Latin America in 1977, and the Middle East and Africa in 1978.

An agreement with hotel franchisor Hilton in 1980 to provide daily pickup and international delivery garnered new outlets for DHL. The next year Hillblom, just retired from active management of the company, moved to the Pacific island of Saipan.

Having focused on its international network during its early years, DHL invested heavily in developing a delivery network within the US in 1983. It also extended its service to Eastern Europe. In 1985 — the year UPS and FedEx also began providing international express delivery — DHL and Western Union entered a venture to transmit documents by e-mail. The next year DHL established the first air express venture in China. Dalsey ran the company until his retirement in the mid-1980s (he died in 1994).

In 1990 DHL International sold 12.5% (later increased to more than 55%) of the company to Japan Airlines, Lufthansa (Germany), and Japanese securities firm Nissho Iwai (which sold its 5% stake back in 1999). Through its new owners, DHL boosted its customer base and improved its expertise in dealing with Japanese and German clients.

Hillblom presumably died in a 1995 plane crash in the Pacific Ocean, after having survived a crash two years earlier. As claimants came forward and lawyers stalled, the distribution of his sizable estate, including his holding of DHL, remained in dispute until late 1997.

The next year DHL opened a gateway in Moscow, and in 1997 the company became one of the first international air carriers to serve North Korea. Deutsche Post bought Hillblom's holding, a 25% stake in DHL International, in 1998. Lynn, DHL's last living co-founder, died that year.

In 1999 the company opened a bigger service center in Silicon Valley (its largest US center); began work on its larger, fully automated North American hub in Cincinnati; and formed an alliance with the US Post Office guaranteeing a priority mail service across the Atlantic. DHL also opened discussions with Macau on building an Asia/Pacific hub at Macau International Airport.

Executive Chairman: Patrick Lupo
CEO: Rob Kuijpers
SVP Sales and Marketing: Jeff Corbett
SVP Field Services and Customer Service:
 Larry Hughes
SVP Network Transportation: Steve Waller
Chairman, DHL Airways: Patrick Foley
CEO DHL Airways: Victor Guinasso, age 44
CEO Asia Region, DHL International: Charles Longley
CFO: Simon Clayton, age 42
SVP Secretary, and General Counsel, DHL Airways:
 Jed Orme
SVP Human Resources, DHL Airways: Garry Sellers
SVP Finance and CFO, DHL Airways: William Smartt
Director, Group Central Support: Bob Parker
Country Manager, Singapore: Charles Chan

HQ: 333 Twin Dolphin Dr., Redwood City, CA 94065
Phone: 650-593-7474   **Fax:** 650-593-1689
Web site: http://www.dhl.com

DHL Worldwide Express operates 33 hubs and about
3,000 stations in more than 225 countries.

Stations

	No.	% of total
Europe & Africa	1,470	50
Asia/Pacific	793	27
The Americas	595	20
Middle East	96	3
Total	**2,954**	**100**

Selected Services
Customs clearance
Desktop Shipping Services
DHLNET (electronic tracking and tracing system)
DHL Worldwide Priority Express (worldwide transport
 of non-document goods)
International Document Service (overnight service to
 major destinations)
Same Day Service (next-flight-out delivery for critical
 shipments)
USA Overnight
WorldMail (sorting and delivery of international mail)
Worldwide Express Logistics

Major Operating Companies
DHL Airways, Inc.
DHL International, Ltd. (Belgium, serving non-US
 markets)

Air Express	Fritz
Airborne Freight	Pittston BAX
American Freightways	Ratos
Bilspedition	SAirGroup
Circle International	Stinnes
CNF Transportation	TNT Post Group
Consolidated Delivery	UPS
Expeditors International	U.S. Postal Service
FDX	USFreightways

Private company FYE: December 31	Annual Growth	1989	1990	1991	1992	1993	1994	1995	1996	1997	1998
Estimated sales ($ mil.)	11.4%	1,900	2,000	2,200	2,800	3,000	3,100	3,800	4,200	4,800	5,000
Employees	13.1%	20,000	23,000	25,000	28,000	34,000	35,000	40,000	50,000	59,200	60,486

SALES HISTORY

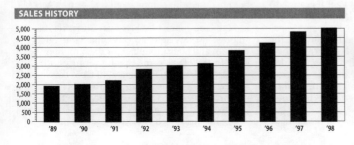

THE DIAL CORPORATION

OVERVIEW

Sink back in a gardenia bubble bath, light an air freshening candle, pop open a can of Vienna sausages, and you'll be relaxing in Dial style. The Scottsdale, Arizona-based consumer products company makes Dial, one of the US's best-selling soaps, and has leading brands in its five core product segments — personal care (Dial, Tone, Breck), laundry (Purex, Borateem, 20 Mule Team), specialty body care (Sarah Michaels, Freeman), air fresheners (Renuzit), and canned meats (Armour — the top selling brand of Vienna sausages).

Already a force in Canada, Dial has been expanding into Latin America, including Argentina (where it is #2 in laundry detergents), the Caribbean, Mexico, and Puerto Rico. Altogether, the company sells its products in more than 40 countries.

Domestically, Dial's emphasis is on building its core Dial, Purex, Renuzit, and Armour lines, as well as specialty body care items, which have higher profit margins than soaps and detergents and faster sales growth.

HISTORY

In the mid-1940s meatpacker Armour & Company developed a deodorant soap by adding the germicidal agent AT-7 to soap; this limited body odor by reducing bacteria on the skin. The new soap was named Dial because of its 24-hour protection against the odor-causing bacteria. Armour introduced the soap in 1948 in a full-page advertisement in the *Chicago Tribune*. The ad was printed on paper with scented ink and encouraged its readers to sample its refreshing fragrance by smelling the newspaper.

By the 1950s Dial was the best-selling deodorant soap in the US. The company adopted the slogan "Aren't you glad you use Dial? Don't you wish everybody did?" in 1953. In the 1960s Armour expanded the Dial line with deodorants and shaving creams.

Canadian bus company Greyhound bought Armour and its Dial brand in 1970. Greyhound kept the company's meatpacking (Armour Foods) and consumer products operations (Armour-Dial) and sold the rest of its assets. Armour-Dial moved its headquarters to Phoenix in 1971.

Greyhound's rapid diversification and frequent unit restructurings led to erratic profitability. In 1981 John Teets was appointed chairman of Greyhound and began selling unprofitable subsidiaries. After meatpackers struck at Armour plants in the mid-1980s, Teets shut 29 plants and sold its meatpacking operation to ConAgra (but kept its canned meat business). A similar labor feud at Greyhound led to the sale of the bus operations in 1987. Meanwhile, Teets was focusing on the company's more successful operations. Armour-Dial acquired laundry soap maker Purex Industries in 1985. Two years later it introduced Liquid Dial soap. In 1990 the company acquired the Breck hair products line from American Cyanamid.

To reflect its changing focus, the company changed its name to Dial in 1991. When it sold Motor Coach Industries to the public in 1993, it exited the US bus industry altogether. Also that year Dial bought Renuzit air fresheners from S.C. Johnson. The company introduced the Nature's Accents line of skin care products in 1995. Restructuring and writeoffs for inventory reductions caused a loss that year.

In a familiar scenario for US companies trying to increase stock value, Dial chose in 1996 to divide into two companies. Its services units became Viad, while its consumer products businesses continued to operate as Dial. Outsider Malcolm Jozoff — a veteran of Lenox and Procter & Gamble (P&G) — was brought in to head Dial. (Teets was named to head Viad but subsequently announced his retirement.)

The new Dial eliminated about 20% of its management and administrative jobs, centralized purchasing, reorganized its advertising and marketing units, and trimmed more than half of its 2,300 products to focus on its better-selling brands. Housecleaning continued when it sold its line of Brillo cleaning products to Church & Dwight (1997).

To expand its international sales, in 1997 Dial purchased Argentina's Nuevo Federal (soap, detergent) and then five more Argentine soap brands from P&G.

Dial retired its "Aren't you glad you use Dial?" slogan in 1998, hoping to lure younger consumers. To complement its Nature's Accents line, that year the company bought specialty bath care companies Freeman Cosmetic (natural skin care and hair care) and Sarah Michaels (bath and body products) for $185 million.

In 1999 Dial formed a joint venture with Germany's Henkel (Dial/Henkel LLC) to develop a new line of Purex detergent products for the North American market. The joint venture later purchased the Custom Cleaner home dry cleaning business from Creative Products Resource.

Chairman, President, and CEO: Malcolm Jozoff, age 59, $1,269,222 pay
SVP, Marketing and New Business: Jeffery B. Dias, age 47
SVP, Sales: Arthur E. Hanke, age 51
SVP, Product Supply: Daniel J. King, age 45
SVP, General Counsel, and Secretary: Jane E. Owens, age 45, $366,570 pay
SVP and CFO: Susan J. Riley, age 40, $490,762 pay
SVP, International/CMD: Mark R. Shook, age 44, $396,869 pay
SVP, Human Resources: Bernhard J. Welle, age 50, $339,545 pay
VP, Information Systems: Robert D. Forte
VP, Corporate Affairs: Nancy C. Stern
Auditors: Deloitte & Touche LLP

LOCATIONS

HQ: 15501 N. Dial Blvd., Scottsdale, AZ 85260-1619
Phone: 623-754-3425   **Fax:** 623-754-1098
Web site: http://www.dialcorp.com

Dial has major manufacturing operations in Argentina, Guatemala, Mexico, and the US.

1998 Sales

	$ mil.	% of total
US	1,360	89
Other countries	165	11
Total	**1,525**	**100**

PRODUCTS/OPERATIONS

Selected Brands

Air Fresheners	Cleaning and	Trend
Renuzit	Laundry	Vano
(adjustables,	Products	Zorro
aerosols,	20 Mule Team	
candles)	Borateem	**Food Products**
	Campos Verdes	Armour Star
Body, Hair, and	Cristal	(Vienna
Skin Care	Custom Cleaner	sausages, meat
Products	Dutch	spreads, hash,
Boraxo	Enzimax	chili, Appian
(handsoap)	Fels Naptha	Way Pizza Mix)
Breck	Gelatti	Cream (corn
Dial	Gran Federal	starch)
Freeman	Gran Llauro	
Liquid Dial	La France	
Nature's Accents	Limzul	
Pure & Natural	Purex	
Sarah Michaels	Sta-Flo	
Tone		

COMPETITORS

Alberto-Culver	Huish Detergents
Amway	International Home Foods
Benckiser	Intimate Brands
Body Shop	Johnson & Johnson
Church & Dwight	Mary Kay
Clorox	Nestle
Colgate-Palmolive	Procter & Gamble
ConAgra	Reckitt & Colman
Cosmair	S.C. Johnson
Del Labs	Scott's Liquid Gold
Garden Botanika	Unilever
GOJO	USA Detergents
Hormel	

HISTORICAL FINANCIALS & EMPLOYEES

NYSE symbol: DL FYE: December 31	Annual Growth	1989	1990	1991	1992	1993	1994	1995	1996	1997	1998
Sales ($ mil.)	3.5%	—	—	1,196	1,275	1,420	1,511	1,365	1,406	1,363	1,525
Net income ($ mil.)	5.3%	—	—	71	31	84	91	(27)	30	84	103
Income as % of sales	—	—	—	6.0%	2.4%	5.9%	6.0%	—	2.1%	6.1%	6.7%
Earnings per share ($)	75.8%	—	—	—	—	—	—	—	0.33	0.89	1.02
Stock price - FY high ($)	—	—	—	—	—	—	—	—	15.00	21.81	30.25
Stock price - FY low ($)	—	—	—	—	—	—	—	—	11.13	13.38	19.38
Stock price - FY close ($)	40.5%	—	—	—	—	—	—	—	14.63	20.81	28.88
P/E - high	—	—	—	—	—	—	—	—	45	25	30
P/E - low	—	—	—	—	—	—	—	—	34	15	19
Dividends per share ($)	100.0%	—	—	—	—	—	—	—	0.08	0.32	0.32
Book value per share ($)	60.3%	—	—	—	—	—	—	—	1.47	3.12	3.78
Employees	(1.8%)	—	—	4,279	4,197	4,000	3,995	3,985	2,800	2,533	3,759

STOCK PRICE HISTORY

HIGH/LOW/CLOSE

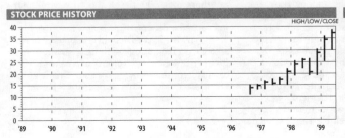

1998 FISCAL YEAR-END

Debt ratio: 41.8%
Return on equity: 26.3%
Cash ($ mil.): 12
Current ratio: 0.95
Long-term debt ($ mil.): 280
No. of shares (mil.): 103
Dividends
  Yield: 1.1%
  Payout: 31.4%
Market value ($ mil.): 2,980

DIEBOLD, INCORPORATED

OVERVIEW

No, Diebold does not star Bruce Willis. Its star performers are automated teller machines (ATMs), which account for about 60% of the company's sales. North Canton, Ohio-based Diebold is #2 in the US market for ATMs, having been displaced by world leader NCR. It also offers automated or staffed bank transaction facilities, such as the MicroBranch portable bank office, which can be installed in grocery stores and malls.

Diebold is taking its ATM technology into the health care market with MedSelect-RX, which stores, dispenses, and tracks patient medications and can link with other hospital systems such as billing and admissions. The company also develops smart cards and is still active in its original business: making safes.

The company is using acquisitions and alliances to duke it out with NCR for dominance of developing markets in Europe and Latin America. It is also broadening its services selection (nearly 40% of sales) by turning to home Internet transaction processing and other Web functions.

HISTORY

German immigrant Charles Diebold formed safe and vault maker Diebold Bahmann in Cincinnati in 1859. The Chicago Fire of 1871 gave the company an unexpected boost: All 878 of its safes in the area (and their contents) survived the inferno. The company relocated in 1872 to North Canton, Ohio, where it was incorporated in 1876. During the next two decades, it also made jails, gallows trapdoors, and padded cells for asylums. In the 1930s Diebold helped develop a bank lobby tear gas system, made in part to deter the notorious John Dillinger and his gang.

With safe sales dependent on the health of banks, the Great Depression led the company to diversify. Diebold made seven major acquisitions between 1936 and 1947 of bank and office equipment firms as well as other safe makers. In 1938 the company entered the office equipment business with the introduction of the Cardineer Rotary File System.

WWII government arms contracts helped boost Diebold from around $3 million in sales per year to $40 million in 1942. In 1944 former Prohibition G-man (and hero of the film *The Untouchables*) Eliot Ness joined Diebold's board, later becoming chairman and overseeing the 1946 takeover of York Safe, which had been the largest US safe maker before the war.

The 1947 acquisition of O. B. McClintock Co.'s bank equipment division moved Diebold into the drive-through teller window business. Sales of these windows and other bank equipment were stimulated by suburban growth in the 1950s. By 1957 business equipment represented about half of Diebold's business.

Diebold acquired Herring-Hall-Marvin Safe Co. of Hamilton, Ohio (safes and teller equipment) in 1959. An antitrust challenge to the merger resulted in a 1963 settlement agreement with the Justice Department under which Diebold agreed to sell Herring's safe and vault business and not to acquire any other such companies for five years.

Increased check use in the early 1960s led Diebold to enter check imprinting with the 1963 purchase of Consolidated Business Systems (business forms, magnetic imprinting ink for checks). Diebold went public the next year.

With security equipment sales slowing in the early 1970s, CEO Raymond Koontz gambled on ATMs, investing heavily in R&D. In 1973 Diebold introduced its first ATM. Sales were helped by long-standing relationships with banks, and within five years Diebold had 45% of the US ATM market. Robert Mahoney, who joined Diebold in 1982, replaced Koontz as CEO in 1985.

In 1990 Diebold formed InterBold, a joint venture with former rival IBM, to sell ATMs. Diebold benefited from, among other things, IBM's presence in Europe, Asia, and Latin America. In 1995 the company acquired Griffin Technology, moving into the market for campus systems.

Diebold acquired Safetell International Security in 1997, thereby expanding its presence in the Asia/Pacific region. In 1998, after InterBold canceled its agreement with IBM, Diebold brashly bought IBM's 30% interest in the venture, taking direct control over its global distribution. To cut costs, the company consolidated product lines and facilities and cut more than 500 jobs. But the InterBold purchase and heavy competition in the ATM market caused a decline in sales and earnings for 1998. The next year Diebold enhanced its smart card technology with its acquisition of Pioneer Systems, a developer of a campus ID card system that provides links to financial institutions as well as off-campus merchants.

OFFICERS

Chairman, President, and CEO: Robert W. Mahoney, age 62, $550,000 pay
EVP and CFO: Gerald F. Morris, age 55, $295,000 pay
SVP, Electronic Systems Development and Manufacturing: Alben W. Warf, age 60, $265,000 pay
SVP, International Sales and Service: Michael J. Hillock, age 47
SVP, North American Sales and Service: David Bucci, age 47, $190,000 pay (prior to promotion)
Group VP, Global Support Services: Charles J. Bechtel, age 53
VP and Corporate Controller: Robert L. Stockamp, age 55
VP, General Counsel, and Assistant Secretary: Warren W. Dettinger, age 45
VP; General Manager, Diebold Credit Corporation: Jeffrey J. Van Cleve
VP; General Manager, Security Products: Bartholomew J. Frazzitta, age 56, $184,000 pay
VP and Secretary: Charee Francis-Vogelsang, age 52
VP and Treasurer: Robert J. Warren, age 52
VP, Human Resources: Charles B. Scheurer, age 57
Auditors: KPMG LLP

LOCATIONS

HQ: 5995 Mayfair Rd., North Canton, OH 44720-8077
Phone: 330-490-4000   **Fax:** 330-490-4549
Web site: http://www.diebold.com

1998 Sales

	$ mil.	% of total
US	889	75
Other countries	297	25
Total	**1,186**	**100**

PRODUCTS/OPERATIONS

1998 Sales

	$ mil.	% of total
Products	750	63
Services	436	37
Total	**1,186**	**100**

Products
Access control and electronic monitoring systems
Alarm systems
Automated medication dispensing systems
Automated teller machines
Drive-up banking equipment
Safes and vaults
Security software systems
Smart card terminals
Transaction facilities

Services
Consulting and maintenance
Installation
Internet transaction processing
Project management
Remote monitoring and troubleshooting

COMPETITORS

Affiliated Computer
Bull
Cardinal Health
Dassault
De La Rue
Detection Systems
Fujitsu
Harris Corporation
Honeywell
Itautec Philco
Mosler
NCR
Olivetti
Sensormatic
Siemens
Tidel
Triton
Tyco International

HISTORICAL FINANCIALS & EMPLOYEES

NYSE symbol: DBD FYE: December 31	Annual Growth	1989	1990	1991	1992	1993	1994	1995	1996	1997	1998
Sales ($ mil.)	10.9%	469	476	506	544	623	760	863	1,030	1,227	1,186
Net income ($ mil.)	8.6%	36	27	36	23	48	64	76	97	123	76
Income as % of sales	—	7.7%	5.7%	7.1%	4.3%	7.8%	8.4%	8.8%	9.5%	10.0%	6.4%
Earnings per share ($)	8.2%	0.54	0.41	0.53	0.35	0.71	0.93	1.10	1.40	1.76	1.10
Stock price - FY high ($)	—	9.45	9.30	10.49	12.27	18.29	20.80	27.64	42.35	50.94	55.31
Stock price - FY low ($)	—	7.20	5.94	6.56	9.25	11.60	15.10	14.68	22.47	28.00	19.13
Stock price - FY close ($)	18.7%	7.62	6.93	9.55	11.97	17.88	18.30	24.64	41.94	50.63	35.69
P/E - high	—	18	23	20	35	26	22	25	30	29	50
P/E - low	—	13	14	12	26	16	16	13	16	16	17
Dividends per share ($)	8.4%	0.27	0.30	0.31	0.33	0.35	0.39	0.43	0.45	0.50	0.56
Book value per share ($)	6.6%	5.69	5.66	5.90	5.91	6.28	6.71	7.37	8.36	9.69	10.15
Employees	5.0%	4,183	3,184	3,858	3,975	4,202	4,731	5,178	5,980	6,714	6,489

STOCK PRICE HISTORY

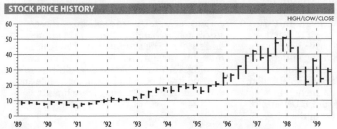

1998 FISCAL YEAR-END

Debt ratio: 2.9%
Return on equity: 10.9%
Cash ($ mil.): 43
Current ratio: 2.31
Long-term debt ($ mil.): 21
No. of shares (mil.): 69
Dividends
  Yield: 1.6%
  Payout: 50.9%
Market value ($ mil.): 2,458

DILLARD'S INC.

OVERVIEW

"Divide and conquer" could be Dillard's marching orders. The Little Rock, Arkansas-based company, the US's #3 operator of up-scale department stores (behind Federated and May), has about 340 stores, mostly in the Sunbelt and Midwest. Dillard's caters to middle- and upper-middle-income consumers, offering name-brand and private-label merchandise, with an emphasis on clothing and home furnishings.

Dillard's has pursued growth aggressively, opening new stores and acquiring other operations, including Mercantile Stores. The retailer often uses a successful double anchor concept: two stores in the same mall. Rather than

closing stores when it buys a store in a mall in which it already has a presence, Dillard's uses the additional space, placing women's and children's departments and home furnishings in one location and men's and juniors' departments in the other.

A history of complaints alleging racial bias has Dillard's trying to overcome the percep-tion that its stores discriminate against minority customers.

Members of the founding Dillard family run the company; they also own 99% of its Class B voting stock and thus elect two-thirds of the company's directors.

HISTORY

At age 12 William Dillard began working in his father's general store in Mineral Springs, Arkansas. After he graduated from Columbia University in 1937, the third-generation retailer spent seven months in the Sears, Roebuck manager training program in Tulsa, Oklahoma.

With $8,000 borrowed from his father, William opened his first department store in Nashville, Arkansas, in 1938. Service was one of the most important things he had to offer, he said, and he insisted on quality — he personally inspected every item and would settle for nothing but the best. William sold the store in 1948 to finance a partnership in Wooten's Department Store in Texarkana, Arkansas; he bought out Wooten and established Dillard's the next year.

Throughout the 1950s and 1960s, the company became a strong regional retailer, developing its strategy of buying well-established downtown stores in small cities; acquisitions in those years included Mayer & Schmidt (Tyler, Texas; 1956) and Joseph Pfeifer (Little Rock, Arkansas; 1963). Dillard's moved its headquarters to Little Rock after buying Pfeifer. When it went public in 1969 (the name was changed to Dillard Department Stores in 1964), it had 15 stores in three states.

During the early 1960s the company began computerizing operations to streamline inventory and information management. In 1970 Dillard added computerized cash registers, which gave management hourly sales figures.

The chain continued acquiring outlets (more than 130 over the next three decades, including stores owned by Stix, Baer & Fuller, Macy's, Joske's, and Maison Blanche). In a 1988 joint venture with Edward J. DeBartolo, Dillard bought a 50% interest in the 12

Higbee's stores in Ohio (buying the other 50% in 1992, shortly after Higbee's bought five former Horne's stores in Ohio).

In 1991 Vendamerica, a subsidiary of Vendex International and the only major nonfamily holder of the company's stock, sold its 8.9 million shares of Class A stock (25% of the class) in an underwritten public offering.

Its purchase of 12 Diamond stores from Dayton Hudson in 1994 gave it a small-event ticket-sales chain in the Southwest, which it renamed Dillard's Box Office. A lawsuit filed by the FTC against Dillard that year, claiming the company made it unreasonably difficult for company credit card holders to remove unauthorized charges from their bills, was dismissed the following year.

Dillard continued to grow; it opened 11 new stores in 1995 and 16 new stores in 1996 (entering Georgia and Colorado). The next year it opened 12 new stores and acquired 20, making its way into Virginia, California, and Wyoming. Also in 1997 the company changed its name back to Dillard's.

William retired in 1998 and William Dillard II took over the CEO position, while brother Alex became president. The company then paid $3.1 billion for Mercantile Stores, which operated 106 apparel and home design stores in the South and Midwest. To avoid redundancy in certain regions, Dillard's sold 26 of those stores and exchanged seven others for new Dillard's stores. The assimilation of Mercantile brought distribution problems that cut into earnings for fiscal 1999. As a result, Dillard's has said it will curb its buying for awhile and boost sales by emphasizing store brands.

Chairman: William Dillard, age 84
CEO: William Dillard II, age 54, $1,300,000 pay
President: Alex Dillard, age 49, $1,210,000 pay
EVP: Drue Corbusier, age 52, $695,000 pay
EVP; President Merchandising, Little Rock Division: Mike Dillard, age 47, $840,000 pay
SVP and CFO: James I. Freeman, age 49, $695,000 pay
VP: H. Gene Baker, age 60
VP; President Merchandising, St. Louis Division: Joseph P. Brennan
VP; President Merchandising, Phoenix Division: G. Kent Burnett, age 54
VP; President Merchandising, Tampa Division: David M. Doub, age 52
VP: T. R. Gastman, age 69
VP: Randal L. Hankins, age 48
VP; President Merchandising, Louisville Division: Robin Sanderford, age 52
VP: Paul J. Schroeder Jr., age 50
VP: Burt Squires, age 49
VP: Charles O. Unfried, age 52
VP: Richard B. Willey
VP: Gary Wirth
VP: Linda Zwern
Director Personnel: Joyce Wisner
Auditors: Deloitte & Touche LLP

LOCATIONS

HQ: 1600 Cantrell Rd., Little Rock, AR 72201
Phone: 501-376-5200   **Fax:** 501-376-5917
Web site: http://www.dillards.com

Dillard's has stores in 29 southern and midwestern states.

PRODUCTS/OPERATIONS

1999 Sales

	% of total
Women's & juniors' clothing	31
Men's clothing & accessories	20
Shoes, accessories & lingerie	20
Cosmetics	13
Home	9
Children's clothing	6
Leased departments	1
Total	**100**

COMPETITORS

AnnTaylor
Belk
Best Buy
Dayton Hudson
Federated
The Gap
Harcourt General
Heilig-Meyers
J. Crew
J. C. Penney
Kohl's
Lands' End
Levitz
The Limited
Marks & Spencer
May
Men's Wearhouse
Montgomery Ward
Nordstrom
Saks Inc.
Sears
Venator Group

HISTORICAL FINANCIALS & EMPLOYEES

NYSE symbol: DDS FYE: January 31	Annual Growth	1990	1991	1992	1993	1994	1995	1996	1997	1998	1999
Sales ($ mil.)	11.0%	3,049	3,606	4,036	4,714	5,131	5,546	5,918	6,228	6,632	7,797
Net income ($ mil.)	(1.0%)	148	183	206	236	241	252	167	239	258	135
Income as % of sales	—	4.9%	5.1%	5.1%	5.0%	4.7%	4.5%	2.8%	3.8%	3.9%	1.7%
Earnings per share ($)	(1.5%)	1.45	1.67	1.84	2.11	2.14	2.23	1.48	2.09	2.31	1.26
Stock price - FY high ($)	—	24.89	32.30	45.54	51.50	52.75	36.63	33.88	41.75	44.75	44.50
Stock price - FY low ($)	—	14.11	20.56	29.64	30.00	33.13	24.63	24.00	28.50	28.00	24.75
Stock price - FY close ($)	1.5%	21.65	29.97	41.13	49.00	35.88	26.25	28.75	29.88	35.13	24.81
P/E - high	—	17	19	25	24	25	16	23	20	19	35
P/E - low	—	10	12	16	14	15	11	16	14	12	20
Dividends per share ($)	11.5%	0.06	0.07	0.07	0.08	0.08	0.09	0.12	0.13	0.16	0.16
Book value per share ($)	11.2%	10.22	12.30	14.18	16.28	18.43	20.55	18.62	23.91	25.70	26.57
Employees	8.5%	26,304	31,786	32,132	33,883	35,536	37,832	40,312	43,470	44,616	54,921

STOCK PRICE HISTORY

HIGH/LOW/CLOSE

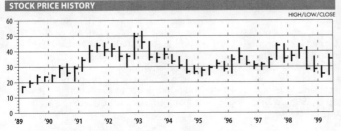

1999 FISCAL YEAR-END

Debt ratio: 55.6%
Return on equity: 4.8%
Cash ($ mil.): 72
Current ratio: 3.14
Long-term debt ($ mil.): 3,561
No. of shares (mil.): 107
Dividends
  Yield: 0.6%
  Payout: 12.7%
Market value ($ mil.): 2,653

DIME BANCORP, INC.

OVERVIEW

If you had a dime for every dime's worth of assets held by Dime Bancorp, you'd be the fifth-largest US thrift (Washington Mutual is #1).

The New York City-based holding company's Dime Savings Bank of New York is working to be a "super-community bank," striving to give its customers more attention than New York's money center banks and more products than traditional thrifts. The bank concentrates its activities in the New York metropolitan area, but its 1997 acquisition of North American Mortgage Company made Dime one of the top 10 US mortgage originators.

Dime's lending programs target low- and moderate-income borrowers, with a focus on home mortgage loans. The company also of-

fers consumer loans, brokerage services, and insurance products. It sells or securitizes most of its fixed-rate and consumer loans, retaining servicing.

Dime's business banking services include both a small-business lending program (for companies located in Dime branch neighborhoods with revenues of less than $5 million) and a commercial lending program (serving businesses with up to $25 million in sales).

The thrift now offers more bank-like consumer services including 24-hour telephone banking and automated teller machines. The bank uses database marketing to improve cross-selling of products.

HISTORY

Dime was founded in 1859 by William Edwards as a bank "for the common people," an institution where people could save money dime by dime (the bank's minimum deposit). During the Civil War, Dime pioneered banking by mail, allowing Union soldiers to deposit their pay.

It remained a community bank serving the middle and working classes through wars and depressions. Dime vastly increased its size in 1949 by acquiring 42,000 loans from the New York State Home Owners Association. In 1951, as the suburbs developed, it opened a branch in Nassau County.

The number of branches increased to 11 by 1978 after several small mergers and acquisitions. But Dime's real growth came in the 1980s, when thrifts were deregulated in response to soaring interest rates. Deregulation let thrifts make both larger consumer and commercial loans. Dime went overboard, making low-documentation loans; among the newly optional information was proof that the borrower could actually afford the monthly payments. As the economy soured, loan defaults rose, approaching 11% of total assets shortly after the arrival in 1988 of Richard Parsons as president — the first African-American to hold such a high-profile banking position. Parsons had no banking experience but had worked with Dime's chairman, Harry Albright, on Nelson Rockefeller's staff. Parsons turned Dime around by raising underwriting standards, managing or selling bad loans, cutting branches and staff, and outsourcing operations. In 1992 the bank was profitable for the first time since 1989. It merged with Anchor Bancorp in 1995. At the time of the merger (which was crucial to

Dime's emergence in New York), Parsons left Dime to become president of Time Warner.

Anchor Bancorp was founded in Brooklyn in 1869 as the Bay Ridge Savings Bank. It became the institution of choice for sailors serving New York's growing shipping industry. The thrift opened its first branch in 1926. In 1968, seeking a less-localized image, Bay Ridge changed its name to Anchor and in 1969 made its first acquisition. More followed in the 1970s and 1980s. Anchor acquired several banks in Georgia and Florida, buying 13 savings and loans between 1981 and 1986 and moving into mortgages. Then came the real estate crash and new capital regulations, which raised defaults and forced the company to adopt tough new capital-reserve standards.

Suddenly in the red, Anchor sold assets, first its out-of-state branches and then mortgage operations. Profitable once more by 1992, Anchor aimed to gain market share. Merging into Dime in 1995 made the new company one of the largest in the New York area.

The Anchor acquisition spurred further expansion in the New York area: Dime bought BFS Bankorp in 1997 and two years later acquired Lakeview Financial.

Eager to diversify its financial arsenal, Dime bought National Mortgage Investments of Griffin, Georgia, in 1996 and in 1997 acquired North American Mortgage Company. Together, these purchases catapulted Dime into the mortgage-banking major leagues. In addition to mortgage lending, Dime formed an insurance unit in 1999, offering property/casualty, title, and other insurance products. That year the company also bought Citigroup's auto finance business.

Chairman Emeritus: James M. Large Jr., age 66
Chairman, President, CEO, and COO: Lawrence J. Toal,
age 61, $1,954,810 pay
Chief Human Resources and Administrative Services
Executive: Arthur C. Bennett
Director Office of the Secretary and Senior Legal
Advisor: Gene C. Brooks, age 49
CFO: Anthony R. Burriesci, age 51, $776,720 pay
SVP and General Manager, Dime Insurance Group:
Melvin L. Cebrik, age 51
Treasurer and Asset and Liability Executive:
D. James Daras, age 45, $526,270 pay
Chief Information Officer: Thomas J. Ducca
General Counsel: James E. Kelley, age 47
CEO, Mortgage Banking: Fred B. Koons, age 54,
$877,310 pay
Corporate Auditor: John S. Lohmuller
General Manager, Commercial Real Estate Lending:
Murray F. Mascis
COO, Mortgage Banking: Richard A. Mirro
Chief Credit and Risk Management Officer:
Carlos R. Munoz, age 63, $556,520 pay
General Manager, Consumer Financial Services:
Peyton R. Patterson, age 42
Chief Marketing Officer: Amy J. Radin
Executive Center, External Affairs, and Investor
Relations Executive: Franklin L. Wright
SVP, Segmentation and Customer Information
Management: Kristine S. Reed
Auditors: KPMG LLP

HQ: 589 5th Ave., New York, NY 10017-1977
Phone: 212-326-6170   Fax: 212-326-6169
Web site: http://www.dime.com

1998 Assets

	$ mil.	% of total
Cash & equivalents	358	2
Mortgage-backed securities	2,964	13
Loans held for sale	3,885	17
Net loans	12,643	57
Other investments	689	3
Other assets	1,782	8
Total	**22,321**	**100**

1998 Sales

	$ mil.	% of total
Interest		
Real estate loans	1,074	55
Consumer loans	71	4
Business loans	14	1
Securities & other	262	13
Charges & fees	274	14
Other	251	13
Total	**1,946**	**100**

Astoria Financial	Merchants New York
Bank of New York	North Fork Bancorporation
Chase Manhattan	Queens County Bancorp
Citigroup	Reliance Bancorp
First of Long Island	Republic New York
Haven Bancorp	Sterling Bancorp
JSB Financial	Suffolk Bancorp

NYSE symbol: DME FYE: December 31	Annual Growth	1989	1990	1991	1992	1993	1994	1995	1996	1997	1998
Assets ($ mil.)	7.5%	11,652	10,842	9,898	8,773	9,276	9,996	20,327	18,870	21,848	22,321
Net income ($ mil.)	—	(92)	(136)	(237)	8	36	84	62	104	122	237
Income as % of assets	—	—	—	—	0.1%	0.4%	0.8%	0.3%	0.6%	0.6%	1.1%
Earnings per share ($)	—	(4.05)	(5.94)	(10.27)	0.32	0.90	0.26	0.57	0.96	1.12	2.06
Stock price - FY high ($)	—	17.75	10.75	6.75	7.38	10.50	10.75	13.38	16.88	30.38	33.06
Stock price - FY low ($)	—	8.75	2.13	1.19	3.13	5.75	7.38	7.38	10.63	14.50	17.13
Stock price - FY close ($)	11.0%	10.25	2.38	3.38	5.88	8.13	7.75	11.63	14.75	30.25	26.25
P/E - high	—	—	—	—	23	12	41	23	18	27	16
P/E - low	—	—	—	—	10	6	28	13	11	13	8
Dividends per share ($)	(12.0%)	0.60	0.45	0.00	0.00	0.00	0.00	0.00	0.00	0.12	0.19
Book value per share ($)	(8.5%)	27.66	21.12	11.11	11.41	10.37	9.98	9.79	9.76	11.30	12.42
Employees	12.2%	2,640	2,338	2,345	2,214	2,345	1,700	2,697	3,159	6,451	7,437

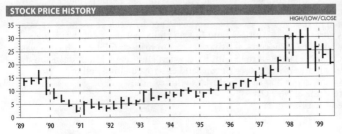
HIGH/LOW/CLOSE

Equity as % of assets: 6.2%
Return on assets: 1.1%
Return on equity: 17.1%
Long-term debt ($ mil.): 771
No. of shares (mil.): 112
Dividends
 Yield: 0.7%
 Payout: 9.2%
Market value ($ mil.): 2,929
Sales (mil.): $1,946

DOLE FOOD COMPANY, INC.

OVERVIEW

Bananas might be Dole Food's favorite fruit because they have "a-peel," but the firm — the world's largest producer of fresh fruit and vegetables — also grows and markets about 40 other fruits as well as more than 20 types of veggies. The Westlake Village, California-based company also produces canned juices and fruits, dried fruits, and nuts, almost entirely under the Dole name. Dole has operations in more than 90 countries worldwide. Chairman and CEO David Murdock owns about 24% of the company.

The company is taking advantage of its refrigerated distribution network to distribute new products, such as fresh flowers (of which it's the world's largest producer). In addition, Dole is introducing value-added products in fast growing grocery segments (such as precut vegetables and packaged salads) to become less vulnerable to erratic commodity markets.

HISTORY

James Dole embarked on an unlikely career in a faraway land when he graduated from Harvard College in 1899 and sailed to Hawaii. He bought 61 acres of farmland for $4,000 in 1900 and the next year organized the Hawaiian Pineapple Company, announcing that the island's pineapples would eventually be in every US grocery store.

Others had tried and failed to sell fresh fruit to the mainland. Dole decided he would succeed by canning pineapples. He built his first cannery in 1903 and in 1908 introduced a national magazine advertising campaign designed to make consumers associate Hawaii with pineapples (then considered an exotic fruit).

In 1922 Dole expanded his production by buying the island of Lanai, where he set up a pineapple plantation. He financed the purchase by selling a third interest in Hawaiian Pineapple to Waialua Agricultural Company, which was part of Castle & Cooke (C&C). Samuel Castle and Amos Cooke, missionaries to Hawaii, formed C&C in 1851 to manage their church's failing depository, which supplied outlying mission posts with staple goods. In 1858 they entered the sugar business and within 10 years served as agents for several Hawaiian sugar plantations and the ships that carried their cargoes.

C&C gained control of Hawaiian Pineapple in 1932 when it acquired an additional 21% interest in the business. The company began using the Dole name on packaging the next year. Dole became chairman of the board of the reorganized company in 1935 but pursued other business interests until he retired in 1948.

Hawaiian Pineapple was run separately until C&C bought the remainder in 1961. The company started pineapple and banana farms in the Philippines in 1963 to supply markets in East Asia. C&C began importing bananas when it purchased 55% of Standard Fruit of New Orleans in 1964. (It purchased the remainder four years later.)

Heavily in debt and limping from two hostile takeover attempts, C&C agreed in 1985 to merge with Flexi-Van, a container leasing company owned by David Murdock, who became C&C's CEO. Murdock, who brought capital and Flexi-Van's fleet of ships to transport produce, began trimming back, leaving C&C with its fruit and real estate operations. He also decided to end the company's pineapple operations on Lanai to concentrate on tourist properties there such as the Lodge at Koele and the Manele Bay Hotel, which opened in the early 1990s. The company took a $168 million writeoff on them in 1995, when it spun off its real estate and resort operations as Castle & Cooke.

C&C became Dole Food in 1991. The company expanded at home and internationally, adding SAMICA (Europe, dried fruits and nuts, 1992), an interest in Jamaica Fruit Distributors (UK, 1994), Dromedary (US, dates, 1994), and Chiquita's New Zealand produce operations (1995).

In 1995 Dole sold its juice business to Seagram's Tropicana Products division, keeping its pineapple juices and licensing the Dole name to Seagram. (PepsiCo bought Tropicana in 1998.) The next year Dole pioneered the packaged, single-serve salad concept.

Continuing to increase its presence in Europe, in 1998 Dole made several acquisitions, including 60% of SABA Trading, a Swedish importer and distributor of fruits and vegetables. That year it entered the fresh flower trade by acquiring four major growers and marketers.

Already vexed by weak economies in Asia and Russia and a worldwide glut of bananas that depressed prices, in late 1998 Dole was hit hard when Hurricane Mitch devastated crops and destroyed almost all of its Honduran facilities.

Chairman and CEO: David H. Murdock, age 75, $800,000 pay
President and COO: David A. DeLorenzo, age 52, $557,692 pay
VP Human Resources: George R. Horne, age 61
VP International Legal and Regulatory Affairs: Patrick A. Nielson, age 48
VP Taxes: David W. Perrigo
VP Finance and CFO: John W. Tate, age 48
VP, Corporate Secretary, and Corporate General Counsel: J. Brett Tibbitts, age 43, $252,308 pay
VP: Roberta Wieman, age 54
President of Dole Fresh Vegetables: Lawrence A. Kern, age 51, $501,923 pay
President of Dole Packaged Foods: Peter M. Nolan, age 56, $425,962 pay
Auditors: Arthur Andersen LLP

LOCATIONS

HQ: 31365 Oak Crest Dr., Westlake Village, CA 91361
Phone: 818-879-6600   **Fax:** 818-879-6615
Web site: http://www.dole.com

Dole Food has operations in more than 90 countries and sells its products worldwide.

PRODUCTS/OPERATIONS

1998 Sales

	$ mil.	% of total
Fresh fruit	2,692	61
Processed foods	835	19
Fresh vegetables	790	18
Other (flowers)	107	2
Total	**4,424**	**100**

Divisions and Selected Products

Dried fruit and	Oranges	Fresh-cut
nuts	Papayas	vegetables
Almonds	Peaches	Coleslaw
Dates	Pineapples	Peeled mini-
Prunes	Plantains	carrots
Raisins	Plums	Salad mixes
Fresh flowers	Pomegranates	Shredded
Alstroemeria	Raspberries	lettuce
Calla lillies	Strawberries	Packaged foods
Roses	Tangelos	Canned
Sunflowers	Tangerines	mandarin
Fresh fruit	Yucca	orange
Apples	Fresh vegetables	segments
Bananas	Artichokes	Canned mixed
Cantaloupe	Asparagus	fruits
Cherries	Broccoli	Canned
Coconuts	Carrots	mushrooms
Cranberries	Celery	Canned
Grapefruit	Lettuce	pineapple
Grapes	Onions	Juices
Kiwi	Potatoes	
Mangoes	Radishes	
Melons	Sugar peas	
Nectarines		

COMPETITORS

Cadbury Schweppes	Pro-Fac
Chiquita Brands	Seneca Foods
Coca-Cola	Sun-Diamond Growers
Del Monte	Sunkist
Fresh Del Monte Produce	Tri Valley Growers
Fyffes	United Foods
Ocean Spray	U.S.A. Floral Products

HISTORICAL FINANCIALS & EMPLOYEES

NYSE symbol: DOL FYE: December 31	Annual Growth	1989	1990	1991	1992	1993	1994	1995	1996	1997	1998
Sales ($ mil.)	5.6%	2,718	3,003	3,216	3,376	3,431	3,842	3,804	3,840	4,336	4,424
Net income ($ mil.)	(20.5%)	95	121	134	16	78	68	23	89	160	12
Income as % of sales	—	3.5%	4.0%	4.2%	0.5%	2.3%	1.8%	0.6%	2.3%	3.7%	0.3%
Earnings per share ($)	(20.6%)	1.60	2.03	2.24	0.26	1.30	1.14	0.40	1.47	2.65	0.20
Stock price - FY high ($)	—	45.25	38.63	48.00	40.00	37.88	35.50	38.63	43.75	50.06	57.31
Stock price - FY low ($)	—	25.38	26.25	28.00	26.00	25.88	22.50	23.00	30.88	33.75	28.06
Stock price - FY close ($)	(1.6%)	34.75	29.38	36.00	32.13	26.75	23.00	35.00	33.88	45.75	30.00
P/E - high	—	28	19	21	154	29	31	97	30	19	287
P/E - low	—	16	13	13	100	20	20	58	21	13	140
Dividends per share ($)	—	0.00	0.00	0.00	0.40	0.40	0.40	0.40	0.40	0.40	0.40
Book value per share ($)	(3.2%)	14.11	15.67	17.53	16.85	17.70	18.17	8.49	9.10	11.10	10.49
Employees	1.9%	45,000	51,000	50,000	50,000	45,300	46,000	43,000	46,000	44,000	53,500

STOCK PRICE HISTORY

HIGH/LOW/CLOSE

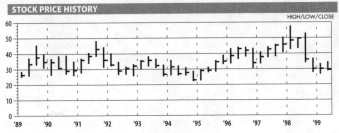

1998 FISCAL YEAR-END

Debt ratio: 64.2%
Return on equity: 1.9%
Cash ($ mil.): 35
Current ratio: 1.45
Long-term debt ($ mil.): 1,116
No. of shares (mil.): 59
Dividends
  Yield: 1.3%
  Payout: 200.0%
Market value ($ mil.): 1,779

DOLLAR GENERAL CORPORATION

OVERVIEW

Small town by small town, Dollar General is capturing customers by offering convenience without the high prices associated with convenience stores. The Nashville, Tennessee-based discount retailer operates about 4,000 stores in 24 southeastern and midwestern states. The fast-growing company's stores sell a limited selection of best-selling household basics, including cleaning supplies, housewares, stationery, nonperishable foods, and health and beauty aids, as well as basic apparel such as T-shirts. About half of its items sell for $1 or less; the highest-priced products go for about $35.

Because Dollar General's customers typically live in small towns (less than 25,000 people), the company doesn't advertise, only sending out direct mailings to announce new stores. It caters to lower- and middle-income customers who find shopping at the small, bare-bones stores (about 6,700 sq. ft.) easier and quicker than at supersized competitors such as Wal-Mart (which are often much farther away). Stores in larger cities (about 25% of its total) are located primarily in low-income neighborhoods.

Chairman, president, and CEO Cal Turner Jr., grandson of the retailer's founder, owns about 17% of Dollar General (and about 28% of its voting shares).

HISTORY

J.L. Turner was 11 when his father was killed during the 1890s in a Saturday night wrestling match. This forced J.L. to drop out of school and work on the family farm, which was weighted by a mortgage. By his 20s J.L., who never learned to read well, was running an area general store. Experiencing some success, he branched out and purchased two stores of his own. They failed. J.L. rebounded, going to work for a wholesaler. With the onset of the Depression, J.L. found he could buy out the inventories of failing merchants for next to nothing, using short-term bank loans that were quickly repaid.

In 1939 J.L. was joined by his son Cal. The two each put up $5,000 to start a new Scottsville, Kentucky-based dry goods wholesaling operation called, not surprisingly, J.L. Turner & Son. It was not until 1945, when the company experienced a glut of women's underwear, that it expanded into retail. J.L. Turner & Son sold off the dainties in their first store, located in Albany, Kentucky. Within a decade the company was operating 35 stores. In 1956 J.L. Turner & Son introduced its first experimental Dollar General Store — all items priced less than a dollar — in Springfield, Kentucky. Like the company's first stores, the dollar store concept would grow: Dollar General Stores numbered 255 a decade later.

Cal Jr., J.L.'s 25-year-old grandson, joined the family business in 1965 and became a director in 1966. The company changed its name to Dollar General and went public two years later. In 1977 Cal Jr. was named president and CEO. That year Dollar General acquired Arkansas-based United Dollar Stores.

The early 1980s saw Dollar General continue its acquisition-powered growth. The company bought Interco's 280-store P.N. Hirsch chain and the 203-store Eagle Family Discount chain in 1983 and 1985, respectively. To cope with expanded distribution demands, Dollar General opened an additional distribution center in Homerville, Georgia, the following year to help out the original Scottsville facility.

The acquisitions, led by Cal Jr.'s brother Steve, ended up costing the company dearly; Dollar General's 1987 stock price dropped nearly 85%. They also cost Steve his job in 1988: He was forced out by the company's new chairman, Cal Jr. In addition to ousting Steve, Cal Jr. replaced more than half of Dollar General's executives that year. The retailer began moving toward everyday low pricing (à la Wal-Mart) in the late 1980s.

Growth from then on was powered by internal expansion. In 1990 the company operated nearly 1,400 stores; by 1995 it had more than 2,000. To accommodate the growth, Dollar General built a third distribution center in Ardmore, Oklahoma, in 1995 and another in South Boston, Virginia, in 1997. Cal Jr.'s CEO-heir apparent, former Circle K COO Bruce Krysiak, joined the company as president that January, only to resign in December, a casualty of differing corporate visions.

Dollar General opted to stop advertising in 1998 and started opening new distribution centers to handle its increasing number of stores. In 1999 Dollar General announced it would move its Georgia distribution center to Florida sometime in 2000.

OFFICERS

Chairman, President, and CEO: Cal Turner Jr., age 59, $1,232,167 pay
EVP and CFO: Brian M. Burr, age 42
EVP, Chief Administrative Officer: Bob Carpenter, age 51, $368,833 pay
EVP, Operations: Leigh Stelmach, age 59, $525,750 pay
EVP, Operations: Earl Weissert, age 53
SVP, Company Growth and Development: Mike Ennis, age 45
SVP, Merchandising: Stonie O'Briant, age 44, $303,967 pay
VP, Distribution: Troy Fellers, age 57
VP, Merchandising Operations: Tom Hartshorn, age 48
VP, Information Services: Holger Jensen, age 52
VP, Human Resources and Employee Support Services: Susan Milana, age 49
VP, Controller: Randy Sanderson, age 44
VP, Distribution and Logistics: Jeff Sims, age 48
VP, General Merchandising Manager: Robert Warner, age 49
Treasurer: Wade Smith
Director, Investor Relations: Kiley Fleming
Auditors: Deloitte & Touche LLP

LOCATIONS

HQ: 104 Woodmont Blvd., Ste. 500, Nashville, TN 37205
Phone: 615-783-2000   **Fax:** 615-386-9937
Web site: http://www.dollargeneral.com

PRODUCTS/OPERATIONS

1999 Sales

	% of total
Hardlines	82
Softlines	18
Total	**100**

Selected Merchandise
Basic apparel
Cleaning supplies
Health and beauty aids
Housewares
Packaged foods
Seasonal goods
Stationery

COMPETITORS

Bill's Dollar Stores
Consolidated Stores
Costco Companies
Dollar Tree
Family Dollar Stores
Kmart
Mazel Stores
Montgomery Ward
One Price Clothing Stores
Target Stores
TJX
Value City
Wal-Mart

HISTORICAL FINANCIALS & EMPLOYEES

NYSE symbol: DG FYE: January 31	Annual Growth	1990	1991	1992	1993	1994	1995	1996	1997	1998	1999
Sales ($ mil.)	20.2%	615	653	754	921	1,133	1,449	1,764	2,134	2,627	3,221
Net income ($ mil.)	34.8%	12	15	22	36	49	74	88	115	145	182
Income as % of sales	—	2.0%	2.2%	2.8%	3.9%	4.3%	5.1%	5.0%	5.4%	5.5%	5.7%
Earnings per share ($)	31.0%	0.06	0.06	0.09	0.14	0.19	0.28	0.33	0.43	0.54	0.68
Stock price - FY high ($)	—	1.00	0.90	2.23	3.33	5.83	6.82	8.91	11.43	20.48	30.24
Stock price - FY low ($)	—	0.65	0.56	0.64	1.85	2.87	4.15	5.05	6.13	9.91	16.00
Stock price - FY close ($)	45.8%	0.67	0.71	2.00	3.01	4.57	6.76	6.52	10.16	18.62	19.95
P/E - high	—	17	15	25	24	31	24	27	27	38	44
P/E - low	—	11	9	7	13	15	15	15	14	18	24
Dividends per share ($)	19.6%	0.02	0.02	0.02	0.02	0.03	0.04	0.05	0.06	0.08	0.10
Book value per share ($)	22.8%	0.51	0.56	0.63	0.62	0.77	1.50	1.91	2.22	2.65	3.27
Employees	17.5%	7,000	8,000	8,000	10,300	10,400	18,000	22,000	25,400	27,400	29,820

STOCK PRICE HISTORY   HIGH/LOW/CLOSE

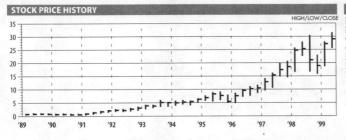

1999 FISCAL YEAR-END
Debt ratio: 0.1%
Return on equity: 25.1%
Cash ($ mil.): 22
Current ratio: 1.93
Long-term debt ($ mil.): 1
No. of shares (mil.): 222
Dividends
 Yield: 0.5%
 Payout: 14.7%
Market value ($ mil.): 4,427

DOMINION RESOURCES, INC.

OVERVIEW

Dominion Resources wants to dominate energy markets in the mid-Atlantic region of the US. The Richmond, Virginia-based energy holding company is already well on its way, having agreed to buy gas company Consolidated Natural Gas (CNG). Dominion's main subsidiary, Virginia Electric and Power, distributes and transmits electricity to more than 2 million customers in eastern Virginia (doing business as Virginia Power) and northeastern North Carolina (as North Carolina Power). The company is gaining about 2 million gas customers through the CNG deal and is adding

Ohio, Pennsylvania, and West Virginia to its service areas.

In anticipation of the energy market's deregulation — to be completed in Virginia in 2004 — Dominion is reorganizing. A new subsidiary, Dominion Generation, manages the firm's generation facilities in the US, the UK, and Latin America and handles its wholesale energy trading operations. Subsidiary Dominion Energy has 1.2 trillion cu. ft. of natural gas reserves in the US and Canada. Dominion Capital is the company's lending, investment, and financial services arm.

HISTORY

George Washington and James Madison were two of the founders of Dominion Resources' predecessor. In 1781 the Virginia General Assembly established the Appomattox Trustees to promote navigation on the Appomattox River. The trustees (including Washington and Madison) formed the Upper Appomattox Company canal operation in 1795 to secure water rights to the river. In 1888 the company took over several hydroelectric plants on the river and added a steam power facility.

Frank Jay Gould bought a successor company in 1909 through his Virginia Railway and Power Company (VR&P). The next year the firm acquired several electric streetcar lines and electric and gas utilities.

New York engineering firm Stone & Webster acquired VR&P in 1925 and placed it under Engineers Public Service (EPS), a new holding company. VR&P's name was changed to Virginia Electric and Power Company, and the firm bought several utilities in North Carolina. During the 1930s the automobile and the Depression killed the company's trolley lines.

In 1940 the government sued EPS under the Public Utility Holding Company Act of 1935 (which ushered in an era of regulated utility monopolies). EPS was forced to divest itself of everything but Virginia Power. Virginia Power, however, soon doubled its service territory by merging with the Virginia Public Service Company.

From 1950 to 1957 the number of electric customers increased by about half, and the company added new plants to keep up with demand. Always an innovator, it built the world's first extra-high-voltage transmission system.

Virginia Power's first nuclear plants went into service in the 1970s. By 1980, however, the firm was near bankruptcy. That year William Berry, who had completed a 23-year rise

through the ranks to become president, canceled two other nuclear units. He also became an early proponent of electric competition. In 1983 he formed Dominion Resources with Virginia Power as a subsidiary, then halted nearly all plant construction to emphasize transmission. Two years later Dominion Capital was formed; Dominion Energy followed in 1987.

In 1990, the year Thomas Capps took over as CEO, Dominion sold its natural gas distribution operations, and Dominion Energy formed joint ventures to develop natural gas reserves. The firm bought three natural gas companies in 1995, and the next year Dominion joined with Chesapeake Paper Products to build a cogeneration plant.

Dominion acquired UK power firm East Midlands Electricity in 1997. However, after it was hit by a hefty windfall tax by the newly elected Labour Party, and its hopes for mergers with other UK utilities were dashed, it sold East Midlands to PowerGen, just 18 months after acquiring it. Also in 1998, Dominion bought an Illinois power station from Unicom's Commonwealth Edison.

The following year Dominion agreed to buy Consolidated Natural Gas (CNG) in a $6.3 billion deal that will create one of the US's largest electric and gas utilities, with more than 4 million customers. Dominion reorganized in preparation for the merger and energy deregulation by separating its generation activities from its transmission, distribution, and retail operations, and the company agreed to sell its generation facilities in Latin America to Duke Energy.

Also in 1999, Virginia Power formed a consortium with Duke Power and French nuclear-fuel manufacturer COGEMA to convert weapons-grade plutonium into fuel for civilian nuclear reactors.

OFFICERS

Chairman, President, and CEO: Thomas E. Capps,
age 63, $1,389,344 pay
EVP and CFO: Edgar M. Roach Jr., age 50
EVP; President and CEO, Virginia Electric and Power:
Norman B. Askew, age 56, $875,089 pay
EVP; President, Dominion Capital:
David L. Heavenridge, age 52, $545,332 pay
EVP; President, Dominion Energy:
Thomas N. Chewning, age 53, $543,060 pay
SVP and Controller: James L. Trueheart, age 47
**SVP, Corporate Affairs; EVP, Virginia Electric and
Power:** Thomas F. Farrell II, age 44,
$553,760 pay (prior to promotion)
VP and General Counsel: James F. Stutts, age 54
**VP; VP, Information Technology, Virginia Electric and
Power:** William S. Mistr, age 51
VP and Treasurer: G. Scott Hetzer, age 42
EVP, Virginia Electric and Power: Robert E. Rigsby,
age 49
**SVP, Commercial Operations, Virginia Electric and
Power:** Larry M. Girvin, age 55
SVP, Dominion Capital: Charles E. Coudriet, age 52
SVP, Fossil and Hydro, Virginia Electric and Power:
William R. Cartwright, age 56
SVP, Human Resources, Virginia Power:
James A. White, age 55
SVP, Nuclear, Virginia Electric and Power:
James P. O'Hanlon, age 55
Corporate Secretary: Patricia A. Wilkerson, age 43
Director, Human Resources: Barbara S. Fasig
Auditors: Deloitte & Touche LLP

LOCATIONS

HQ: 120 Tredegar St., Richmond, VA 23219
Phone: 804-819-2000 **Fax:** 804-819-2233
Web site: http://www.domres.com

PRODUCTS/OPERATIONS

1998 Sales

	$ mil.	% of total
Virginia Power	4,285	70
Dominion UK		
(East Midlands)	1,009	17
Dominion Capital	409	7
Dominion Energy	383	6
Total	**6,086**	**100**

Selected Subsidiaries
Dominion Capital, Inc.
Dominion Energy, Inc.
Dominion Generation
Virginia Electric and Power Company

COMPETITORS

AEP	Imperial Oil
Alberta Energy	Koch
Allegheny Energy	LG&E Energy
Avista	Murphy Oil
BP Amoco	Peabody Group
Cabot Oil & Gas	PG&E
Carolina Power & Light	Range Resources
Cinergy	Reliant Energy
Chevron	Sempra Energy
Coastal	Shell Canada
Columbia Energy	Southern Company
Consolidated Natural Gas	Statoil Energy
Constellation Energy	Suncor
Group	Tom Brown
Devon Energy	Tractebel
Duke Energy	Unicom
Dynegy	United Utilities
El Paso Energy	UtiliCorp
Enron	Williams Companies

HISTORICAL FINANCIALS & EMPLOYEES

NYSE symbol: D FYE: December 31	Annual Growth	1989	1990	1991	1992	1993	1994	1995	1996	1997	1998
Sales ($ mil.)	5.8%	3,662	3,533	3,786	3,791	4,434	4,491	4,652	4,842	7,678	6,086
Net income ($ mil.)	3.0%	411	446	460	445	517	478	425	472	399	536
Income as % of sales	—	11.2%	12.6%	12.1%	11.7%	11.7%	10.6%	9.1%	9.7%	5.2%	8.8%
Earnings per share ($)	(0.0%)	2.76	2.92	2.94	2.76	3.12	2.81	2.45	2.65	2.15	2.75
Stock price - FY high ($)	—	31.93	32.60	38.19	41.00	49.50	45.38	41.63	44.38	42.88	48.94
Stock price - FY low ($)	—	26.93	27.60	29.85	34.13	38.25	34.88	34.88	36.88	33.25	37.81
Stock price - FY close ($)	4.4%	31.68	31.27	38.02	39.50	45.38	36.00	41.25	38.50	42.56	46.75
P/E - high	—	12	11	13	15	16	16	17	17	20	18
P/E - low	—	10	9	10	12	12	12	14	14	15	14
Dividends per share ($)	2.0%	2.15	2.23	2.31	2.40	2.48	2.55	2.58	2.58	2.58	2.58
Book value per share ($)	2.1%	22.68	23.42	24.41	25.21	26.38	26.60	26.88	27.17	26.84	27.33
Employees	(2.1%)	13,343	12,871	12,728	12,217	12,057	10,789	10,592	11,174	15,458	11,033

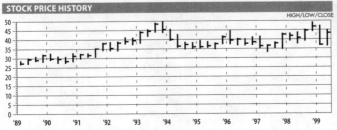

STOCK PRICE HISTORY HIGH/LOW/CLOSE

1998 FISCAL YEAR-END
Debt ratio: 45.8%
Return on equity: 10.1%
Cash ($ mil.): 426
Current ratio: 0.65
Long-term debt ($ mil.): 5,071
No. of shares (mil.): 195
Dividends
  Yield: 5.5%
  Payout: 93.8%
Market value ($ mil.): 9,093

DOMINO'S PIZZA, INC.

OVERVIEW

Creating its own definition of the domino effect, Domino's Pizza has spread a craving for pizza across the globe. Ann Arbor, Michigan-based Domino's is the world's #1 pizza delivery company and the #2 pizza chain overall (behind TRICON's Pizza Hut). The company boasts in excess of 6,200 stores (almost 90% are franchised) in more than 60 countries. Toppings vary from place to place — refried beans are popular in Mexico, while pie-lovers elsewhere favor pickled ginger (India), green peas (Brazil), canned tuna and corn (UK), and squid (Japan).

Domino's has built its reputation on speedy delivery (it focuses solely on delivery and has no "eat-in" restaurants), but the company also has begun to emphasize the quality of its fare. Domino's founder Thomas Monaghan, a devout Catholic, retired from the company in 1998 to concentrate on his religious activities. He sold 93% of his company to Boston-based investment firm Bain Capital.

HISTORY

Thomas Monaghan's early life was one of hardship. After growing up in an orphanage and numerous foster homes, Monaghan spent his young adult life experimenting, trying everything from a Catholic seminary to a stint in the Marine Corps.

In 1960 Monaghan borrowed $500 and bought DomiNick's, a failed pizza parlor in Ypsilanti, Michigan, which he operated with the help of his brother James. In 1961 James traded his share in the restaurant to his brother for a Volkswagen Beetle, but Thomas pressed on, learning the pizza business largely by trial and error. After a brief partnership with an experienced restaurateur, with whom he later had a falling out, Monaghan developed a strategy to sell only pizza and to locate stores near colleges and military bases. In 1965 the company changed its name to Domino's.

In the 1960s and 1970s, Monaghan endured setbacks that brought the company to the brink of bankruptcy. Among these were a 1968 fire that destroyed the Domino's headquarters and a 1975 lawsuit from Domino Sugar maker Amstar Corporation for trademark infringement. But the company won the ensuing legal battles and by 1978 it was operating 200 stores.

In the 1980s Domino's grew phenomenally. Between 1981 and 1983 the company doubled its number of US stores to 1,000; it went international in 1983, opening a store in Canada. The company's growth brought Monaghan a personal fortune. In 1983 he bought the Detroit Tigers baseball team and amassed one of the world's largest collections of Frank Lloyd Wright objects.

Domino's expansion continued in the mid-1980s. With sales figures mounting, the company introduced pan pizza (its first new product) in 1989. That year Monaghan put Domino's up for sale, but his practice of linking his personal and professional finances had gotten both the founder and company into such dire fiscal straits that no one wanted to buy the chain. Monaghan removed himself from direct management in 1989 and installed a new management group.

When company performance began to slide, Monaghan returned in 1991, having experienced a religious rebirth. He sold off many of his private holdings (including his resort island and his baseball team, which went to cross-town pizza rival Michael Ilitch of Little Caesar) to reinvigorate the company and reorganize company management.

In 1989, a Domino's driver, trying to fulfill the company's 30-minute delivery guarantee, ran a red light and collided with another car. The resulting $79 million judgment against the company in 1993 prompted Domino's to drop its famous 30-minute policy and replace it with a satisfaction guarantee.

Domino's introduced Buffalo Wings (chicken wings doused with hot sauce) in 1994, began a national advertising push for its Ultimate Deep Dish pizza the next year, and launched its Roma Herb flavored-crust pizza in 1996. The company revamped its logo and store interiors with a new look in 1997.

In 1998 Domino's introduced a delivery bag with a patented heating system designed to keep pies hot and crispy. Later that year, prompted by his decision to devote more time to religious pursuits, Monaghan retired from the business he had guided for nearly 40 years. He sold 93% of his company to investment firm Bain Capital. David Brandon, former CEO of sales promotion company Valassis Communications, replaced Monaghan as chairman and CEO in 1999.

OFFICERS

Chairman, President, and CEO: David A. Brandon
EVP Finance and Administration and CFO:
Harry J. Silverman, age 40, $3,345,116 pay
EVP Marketing and Product Development:
Cheryl A. Bachelder, age 42, $2,092,957 pay
EVP Domino's Pizza International: J. Patrick Doyle
EVP Corporate Operations: Patrick Kelly, age 46
EVP Franchise Operations: Stuart Mathis, age 43,
$2,143,185 pay
EVP Distribution: Michael D. Soignet, age 39,
$2,078,993 pay
SVP and Treasurer: Steve Benrubi
SVP Franchise Administration: Jim Stansik
VP Human Resources: Robert Clayton
VP Corporate Communications: Tim McIntyre
VP Training and Quality Compliance:
Patricia Moore Thomas
Auditors: Arthur Andersen LLP

LOCATIONS

HQ: 30 Frank Lloyd Wright Dr.,
Ann Arbor, MI 48106-0997
Phone: 734-930-3030   **Fax:** 734-668-1946
Web site: http://www.dominos.com

Domino's Pizza has operations in more than 60 countries.

PRODUCTS/OPERATIONS

1998 Sales

	$ mil.	% of total
Domestic distribution	599	51
Corporate stores	410	35
Domestic franchise royalties	112	9
International	56	5
Total	**1,177**	**100**

COMPETITORS

Bertucci's
Burger King
CEC Entertainment
CKE Restaurants
Godfather's Pizza
KFC
LDB Corp
Little Caesar
McDonald's
Papa John's
Pizza Hut
Pizza Inn
Round Table Pizza
Sbarro
Subway
Uno Restaurant
Wendy's
Whataburger

HISTORICAL FINANCIALS & EMPLOYEES

Private company FYE: December 31	Annual Growth	1989	1990	1991	1992	1993	1994	1995	1996	1997	1998
Sales ($ mil.)	7.7%	—	—	—	—	—	875	905	970	1,045	1,177
Net income ($ mil.)	382.4%	—	—	—	—	—	0	25	20	61	77
Income as % of sales	—	—	—	—	—	—	0.0%	2.8%	2.0%	5.8%	6.5%
Employees	—	—	—	—	—	—	—	—	—	—	14,200

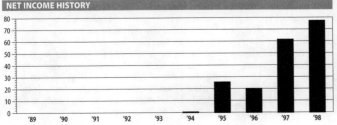

NET INCOME HISTORY

1998 FISCAL YEAR-END
Debit ratio: 100.0%
Return on equity: —
Cash ($ mil.): 0
Current ratio: 0.84
Long-term debt ($ mil.): 720

DONALDSON, LUFKIN & JENRETTE

OVERVIEW

Donaldson, Lufkin & Jenrette (DLJ) has made a name for itself in high-yield bond underwriting in the US, and has been trying its hand in Europe, where the market is still young. But this is just one area of expertise for the New York City-based firm.

DLJ's Banking Group offers investment banking, merchant banking, and management and underwriting for new security issues. Its Capital Markets Group provides research, securities trading, and sales services to institutional clients. This division also sponsors the Sprout Group of venture capital funds. Unlike the rest of the online trading

pack, the company's DLJdirect eschews the hoi polloi to go after wealthy investors.

Subsidiary Autranet distributes research and investment material to large institutional clients. The company's Pershing Division provides trade execution, clearing, and information management services to securities firms and investment advisers.

DLJ is more than 70%-owned by AXA Financial (formerly The Equitable Companies), a subsidiary of French insurer AXA. The French connection has spurred the company to boost overseas sales, largely by establishing new outposts.

HISTORY

In 1959, shortly after graduating from Harvard Business School, Dick Jenrette and partners Bill Donaldson and Dan Lufkin founded Donaldson, Lufkin & Jenrette (DLJ). Their first product, in-depth institutional equities research, was new to Wall Street. After establishing a strong reputation in equities research and trading, DLJ in 1970 became the first NYSE member firm to go public.

In the 1970s the deregulation of commissions and lower profits from research prompted DLJ to diversify. The company absorbed losses in proprietary trading and exited that business. DLJ found itself undercapitalized and in search of a suitor. In 1985 when The Equitable Companies (now AXA Financial) acquired DLJ, Jenrette was promoted to a top position in Equitable. John Chalsty became CEO of DLJ in 1986.

Under Equitable's wing, DLJ expanded into niche markets such as high-yield (or junk) bonds, merchant banking, and mortgage-backed securities. DLJ's cautious business approach left it largely unscathed by the 1987 stock market crash; as more swashbuckling firms laid off staff members, DLJ scooped them up. In 1989 the company launched PC Financial Network, later renamed DLJdirect. When Michael Milken's Drexel Burnham Lambert crumbled in 1991, DLJ again snapped up employees, as well as cheap junk bonds that later recovered their value. By 1993 DLJ was the #1 junk-bond underwriter in the country. DLJ capitalized on other firms' woes again in 1995 when it hired Latin American markets experts who had been cast out after the Mexican peso crash.

In the early 1990s Equitable was deeply in debt and looking for a way to raise capital. AXA came to the rescue with a cash infusion that

gave it control of Equitable after the latter's 1992 initial public offering (IPO), which raised $450 million. DLJ's IPO followed in 1995, when Equitable sold 20% of the company to the public. Jenrette retired as chairman of both Equitable and DLJ in 1996, and Chalsty took over as chairman of DLJ.

In 1996 the firm worked on major mergers and acquisitions transactions for such companies as El Paso Energy, GM Hughes, and Tenet Healthcare; it was lead manager on stock offerings by Host Marriott, Trump Hotels & Casino Resorts, and Price/Costco (now Costco Companies), among others. That year DLJ was also lead manager on the first NYSE-listed IPOs by Russian and German companies (the chickens came home to roost in 1998 when the Russian economy imploded).

DLJ opened offices in Mexico, Brazil, and Argentina and doubled its London staff in 1996 in an effort to expand into emerging European and Latin American markets. In 1997 it bought UK-based Phoenix Group (advisory and asset management services) and London Global Securities (securities lending). The following year the Banking Group made investments totaling more than $1 billion in an eclectic collection of companies (from industrial equipment to publishing). It also began looking at overseas opportunities for DLJdirect. DLJ president Joe Roby took over as CEO from Chalsty, who remained chairman.

DLJ allied with Sumitomo Bank in 1998 to operate an Internet brokerage in Japan and opened an international equities business in London. In 1999 DLJ issued a separate tracking stock for DLJdirect. Also that year, DLJ formed a joint venture with Charles Schwab, Fidelity Investments, and Spear, Leeds & Kellogg to sell Nasdaq stocks online.

OFFICERS

Chairman Emeritus, Co-Founder and Senior Advisor: Richard H. Jenrette
Co-Founder and Senior Advisor: William H. Donaldson
President and CEO: Joe L. Roby, age 59, $8,675,000 pay
Chairman: John S. Chalsty, age 65, $8,500,000 pay
EVP and CFO: Anthony F. Daddino, age 58, $3,500,000 pay
SVP and General Counsel: Michael A. Boyd, $920,000 pay
Chairman, DLJ Banking Group: Hamilton E. James, age 48
VC, DLJ Banking Group: Garrett M. Moran
Managing Director, Mergers and Aqcuisitions, DLJ Banking Group: Joel J. Cohen
Managing Partner, Sprout: Richard E. Kroon
Chairman, DLJ Financial Services Group: Richard S. Pechter, age 55
Managing Director, Institutional Equities Division: Stuart M. Robbins, age 55
Managing Director and COO, Fixed Income Division: David F. Delucia, age 46
President and CEO, DLJ International Group: James L. Alexandre
Chairman, DLJ International Group: Charles M. Hale
Secretary: Majorie S. White
SVP and Chief Accounting Officer: Michael M. Bendik, $990,000 pay
SVP and Director Human Resources : Gerald B. Rigg
Auditors: KPMG LLP

LOCATIONS

HQ: Donaldson, Lufkin & Jenrette, Inc., 277 Park Ave., New York, NY 10172
Phone: 212-892-3000   **Fax:** 212-892-7272
Web site: http://www.dlj.com

PRODUCTS/OPERATIONS

1998 Sales

	$ mil.	% of total
Interest	2,189	40
Fees	1,192	21
Underwriting	1,078	20
Commissions	855	16
Investment	126	2
Trading	(93)	—
Other	60	1
Total	**5,407**	**100**

Selected Subsidiaries
AMB Holdings Ltd. (formerly DLJ Pleiade, South Africa)
Autranet, Inc.
Bond Investment Partners, LLC
Calmco, Inc.
DLJdirect Inc.
Equine Technology and Analysis Inc.
London Global Securities (UK)
Pershing & Co., Inc.
Phoenix Securities (International) Ltd. (UK)
Scratch & Sniff Funding, Inc.
Snoga, Inc.
Wood, Struthers & Winthrop Management Corp.

COMPETITORS

A.G. Edwards
Ameritrade
Bear Stearns
Brown Brothers Harriman
Charles Schwab
Deutsche Banc Alex. Brown
E*TRADE
Goldman Sachs
J.P. Morgan
Lehman Brothers
Merrill Lynch
Morgan Stanley Dean Witter
Salomon Smith Barney Holdings

HISTORICAL FINANCIALS & EMPLOYEES

NYSE symbol: DLJ FYE: December 31	Annual Growth	1989	1990	1991	1992	1993	1994	1995	1996	1997	1998
Sales ($ mil.)	23.8%	—	—	1,215	1,664	2,285	2,009	2,759	3,491	4,640	5,407
Net income ($ mil.)	30.3%	—	—	58	147	186	123	179	291	408	371
Income as % of sales	—	—	—	4.8%	8.8%	8.1%	6.1%	6.5%	8.3%	8.8%	6.9%
Earnings per share ($)	19.6%	—	—	—	—	—	—	1.55	2.30	3.16	2.65
Stock price - FY high ($)	—	—	—	—	—	—	—	16.75	18.50	44.00	63.75
Stock price - FY low ($)	—	—	—	—	—	—	—	14.19	13.69	17.88	20.38
Stock price - FY close ($)	37.9%	—	—	—	—	—	—	15.63	18.00	39.75	41.00
P/E - high	—	—	—	—	—	—	—	11	8	14	24
P/E - low	—	—	—	—	—	—	—	9	6	6	8
Dividends per share ($)	—	—	—	—	—	—	—	0.00	0.25	1.40	0.25
Book value per share ($)	26.6%	—	—	—	—	—	—	10.25	11.99	16.64	20.79
Employees	16.1%	—	—	—	—	—	4,676	5,000	5,900	7,000	8,500

STOCK PRICE HISTORY

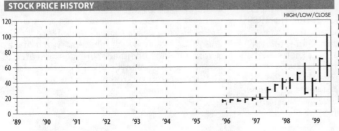

HIGH/LOW/CLOSE

1998 FISCAL YEAR-END

Debt ratio: 54.3%
Return on equity: 14.5%
Cash ($ mil.): —
Current ratio: —
Long-term debt ($ mil.): 3,482
No. of shares (mil.): 123
Dividends
  Yield: 0.6%
  Payout: 9.4%
Market value ($ mil.): 5,035

DOVER CORPORATION

OVERVIEW

Dover sees diversification as a way to keep its earnings from going off a cliff (white or otherwise). The New York City-based industrial conglomerate operates nearly 50 companies producing everything from garbage trucks (H.E.I.L.) to ink-jet printing equipment (Imaje).

Dover has four major divisions. Its largest, Dover Technologies, produces printed circuit board assembly equipment, communications and military components, and ink-jet printing equipment. Dover Industries, its second-largest segment, makes products for the automotive service, bulk transport, food service, machine tool, and waste-handling industries. About the same size as Dover Industries, Dover Diversified produces can-making machinery, compressors, food refrigeration and display cases, and heat-transfer equipment. Last, and least (but not by much), is Dover Resources. Its products include equipment for the automotive, fluid-handling, chemical, and petroleum industries.

Dover maintains a highly decentralized management culture, with a president for each business. Although Dover has maintained a long-term acquisitions strategy (60 companies since 1994), it has sold Dover Elevator, its best-known brand, to German manufacturer Thyssen Krupp to focus on specialized-machinery operations.

HISTORY

George Ohrstrom, a New York stockbroker, formed Dover in 1955 and took it public that year. Originally headquartered in Washington, DC, Dover consisted of four companies: C. Lee Cook (compressor seals and piston rings), Peerless (space-venting heaters), Rotary Lift (automotive lifts), and W.C. Norris (components for oil wells). In 1958 Dover made the first of many acquisitions and entered the elevator industry by buying Shepard Warner Elevator.

Dover continued to diversify throughout the 1960s. Acquisitions included OPW (gas pump nozzles) in 1961 and De-Sta-Co (industrial clamps and valves) in 1962. In 1964 OPW head Thomas Sutton became Dover's president and the company moved its headquarters to New York City. Dover acquired Groen Manufacturing (food industry products) in 1967 and Ronningen-Petter (filter-strainer units) in 1968.

During the 1970s Dover expanded beyond its core industries (building materials, industrial components and equipment). In 1975 it acquired Dieterich Standard, a maker of liquid-measurement instruments. Dieterich Standard's president, Gary Roubos, became Dover's president and COO in 1977 and its CEO in 1981. The company sold Peerless in 1977 and acquired electronics assembly equipment manufacturer Universal Instruments in 1979.

Electronics became an increasingly important part of Dover's business during the 1980s. The company acquired K&L Microwave, a maker of microwave filters used in satellites and cable TV equipment (1983), Dielectric Laboratories (microwave filter parts, 1985), and NURAD (microwave antennae, 1986). Between 1985 and 1990 Dover bought some 25 companies, including Weldcraft Products (welding equipment, 1985), Wolfe Frostop (salad bars, 1987), Weaver Corp. (automotive lifts, 1987), General Elevator (1988), Texas Hydraulics (1988), Security Elevator (1990), and Marathon Equipment (waste-handling equipment, 1990). In 1989 Roubos became the company's chairman.

The corporation spun off its DOVatron circuit board assembly subsidiary to shareholders in 1993 after finding that DOVatron was competing with important Dover customers. That same year Dover acquired H.E.I.L. (garbage trucks).

Dover purchased 10 companies in 1994, including Hill Refrigeration (commercial refrigeration cases) and Koolrad Design & Manufacturing (radiators for transformers, Canada). In 1995 it negotiated four joint ventures for elevator installations in China and bought France-based Imaje, S.A. (ink-jet printers and specialty inks) for $200 million. It was the largest purchase in the company's history.

The next year Dover purchased Everett Charles Technologies, a maker of electronic testing equipment. In 1997 the corporation and its subsidiaries purchased 17 companies, including Vitronics (soldering equipment for circuit board assembly). The company sold its Dover elevator unit — a popular brand but a management headache — to German steel giant Thyssen (now Thyssen Krupp) for $1.1 billion the next year.

Dover continued its acquisitive ways in 1999, picking up six more companies by midyear. Notable were Alphasem, which makes semiconductor-manufacturing equipment, and Graphic Microsystems, which took Dover into the market for pressroom equipment.

OFFICERS

Chairman, President and CEO: Thomas L. Reece,
age 56, $1,675,000 pay
VP Finance and Treasurer: John F. McNiff, age 56
VP, General Counsel, and Secretary:
Robert G. Kuhbach, age 51
VP Corporate Development: Robert A. Tyre, age 54
VP and Controller: George F. Messerole, age 53
VP Taxation: Charles R. Goulding, age 49
VP; President, Dover Industries: Lewis E. Burns,
age 60, $870,000 pay
VP; President, Dover Resources: Rudolf J. Herrmann,
age 48, $790,000 pay
Auditors: PricewaterhouseCoopers LLP

LOCATIONS

HQ: 280 Park Ave., New York, NY 10017-1292
Phone: 212-922-1640   **Fax:** 212-922-1656
Web site: http://www.dovercorporation.com

Dover's primary operations are in the US, but the
company has subsidiaries and affiliates in Brazil, Canada,
France, Germany, Japan, Mexico, the Netherlands,
Singapore, Sweden, Switzerland, and the UK.

1998 Sales

	$ mil.	% of total
The Americas		
US	2,498	63
Canada & other Americas	358	9
Europe	750	19
Asia	296	7
Other regions	76	2
Total	**3,978**	**100**

PRODUCTS/OPERATIONS

1998 Sales

	$ mil.	% of total
Dover Technologies		
Circuit board assembly/		
test equipment	745	19
Electronic components	282	7
Marking equipment	184	5
Dover Industries	1,012	25
Dover Diversified	958	24
Dover Resources	801	20
Adjustments	(4)	—
Total	**3,978**	**100**

COMPETITORS

Baker Hughes	Ingersoll-Rand
Crane	ITT Industries
Eaton	Mannesmann AG
Electro Scientific	Matsushita
Industries	Mitsui
Electrolux	Quad Systems
Emerson	Samsung
Esterline	Siemens
Flowserve	Tatung
Fujitsu	TDK
GE	Tecumseh Products
Hewlett-Packard	Tektronix
Hitachi	Tyco International
Hubbell	

HISTORICAL FINANCIALS & EMPLOYEES

NYSE symbol: DOV FYE: December 31	Annual Growth	1989	1990	1991	1992	1993	1994	1995	1996	1997	1998
Sales ($ mil.)	7.2%	2,120	2,210	2,196	2,272	2,484	3,085	3,746	4,076	4,548	3,978
Net income ($ mil.)	11.3%	144	156	128	130	158	202	278	390	405	379
Income as % of sales	—	6.8%	7.0%	5.8%	5.7%	6.4%	6.6%	7.4%	9.6%	8.9%	9.5%
Earnings per share ($)	12.8%	0.57	0.64	0.54	0.56	0.69	0.88	1.22	1.69	1.79	1.69
Stock price - FY high ($)	—	9.88	10.31	10.94	11.91	15.47	16.72	20.84	27.56	36.69	39.94
Stock price - FY low ($)	—	6.81	6.88	8.63	9.56	11.25	12.44	12.91	18.31	24.13	25.50
Stock price - FY close ($)	16.9%	9.00	9.94	10.44	11.47	15.19	12.91	18.44	25.25	36.13	36.63
P/E - high	—	17	16	20	21	22	19	17	16	20	24
P/E - low	—	12	11	16	17	16	14	11	11	13	15
Dividends per share ($)	9.3%	0.18	0.19	0.21	0.22	0.23	0.25	0.28	0.32	0.36	0.40
Book value per share ($)	12.5%	3.00	3.28	3.51	3.53	3.80	4.39	5.40	6.62	7.65	8.67
Employees	(8.1%)	50,049	20,461	18,898	18,827	20,445	22,992	25,332	26,234	28,758	23,350

STOCK PRICE HISTORY

HIGH/LOW/CLOSE

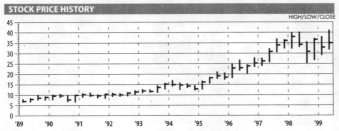

1998 FISCAL YEAR-END

Debt ratio: 24.2%
Return on equity: 19.8%
Cash ($ mil.): 97
Current ratio: 1.32
Long-term debt ($ mil.): 610
No. of shares (mil.): 220
Dividends
  Yield: 1.1%
  Payout: 23.7%
Market value ($ mil.): 8,074

THE DOW CHEMICAL COMPANY

OVERVIEW

Maker of Styrofoam brand insulation, Dursban insecticides, and a host of other plastics and chemicals, Dow Chemical probably will never win the corporate "good guy" award at a Sierra Club convention. Still, the Midland, Michigan-based company can boast about its ranking as the #2 US chemical company, after DuPont. The company produces a wide range of performance plastic products that go into making everything from footwear to automotive interiors. Dow also produces herbicides and chemicals used in dry cleaning, paint, and antifreeze. It is the world's #1 maker of caustic soda, chlorine, ethylene, polyethylene, and polystyrene.

To focus on chemicals, Dow has sold its pharmaceutical and consumer product lines, its engineering business, and a majority share in power-plant operator Destec Energy. Dow's agricultural biotech business is taking root, however, and it has acquired seed maker Mycogen and the remaining 40% of its pesticide joint venture with Eli Lilly. Dow has also gained a foothold in the growing market for polypropylene and polyethylene terephthalate, used by the automotive and packaging industries. Dow is buying rival Union Carbide to become the world's second largest chemical company.

HISTORY

Herbert Dow founded Dow Chemical in 1897 after developing a process to extract bromides and chlorides from underground brine deposits around Midland, Michigan. Its first product was chlorine bleach. Dow eventually overcame British and German monopolies on bleach, bromides, and other chemicals.

In the mid-1920s Dow rejected a takeover by DuPont. By 1930, the year of Herbert Dow's death, sales had reached $15 million. Dow started building new plants around the country in the late 1930s. Its Freeport, Texas, plant began the Texas Gulf Coast petrochemical complex.

Dow research yielded new plastics in the 1940s such as Saran Wrap, the company's first major consumer product. In 1952 the company built its first plant outside North America, in partnership with Japan (Asahi-Dow). By 1957 plastics represented 32% of sales, compared with 2% in 1940. Strong sales of plastics and silicone products propelled the company into the top ranks of US firms.

Dow entered the pharmaceutical field with the 1960 purchase of Allied Labs. To limit the cyclic effect of chemicals on profits, Dow expanded its interests in pharmaceuticals and consumer goods. In 1989 it merged its pharmaceutical division with Marion Labs to create Marion Merrell Dow (it sold its 71% stake to Hoechst in 1995). Also in 1989 it formed Dow-Elanco, a joint venture with Eli Lilly to produce agricultural chemicals.

Following allegations that it had put a breast implant on the market without proper testing, Dow Corning, a joint venture with glassmaker Corning and the #1 producer of silicone breast implants, stopped making the devices in 1992. Dow sold its Freeport refinery to Phibro Energy, a subsidiary of Salomon, in 1993. In 1995 a federal judge ordered Dow to pay a Nevada woman $14 million in damages — the first breast-implant verdict against the company as a sole defendant. Facing thousands of pending cases, Dow Corning filed for bankruptcy protection. (In 1998 Dow Corning agreed to pay $3.2 billion to settle most breast-implant claims.)

Dow entered the polypropylene and polyethylene terephthalate markets with the 1996 purchase of INCA International. Dow also bought a stake in seed developer Mycogen.

In 1997 Dow sold its 80% of Destec Energy and bought Eli Lilly's 40% stake in plant-science venture DowElanco (renamed Dow AgroSciences in 1998). Also in 1997 Dow joined Sinopec (China's biggest petrochemical company) to build an ethylene plant in China. Dow also bought South Africa's Sentrachem (crop protection products), but regulators made Dow sell part of it to Akzo Nobel.

In 1998 Dow sold its DowBrands unit — maker of bathroom cleaner (Dow), plastic bags (Ziploc), and plastic wrap (Saran Wrap) — to S.C. Johnson & Son and its Radian engineering unit to Dames & Moore (now a subsidiary of URS). Dow bought the rest of Mycogen (it became part of Dow AgroSciences) and then made a 10% investment in Illinois Foundation Seeds. It also formed an alliance with Biosource Technologies to develop improved crop traits and created licensing clearinghouse Advanced AgriTraits. In 1999 Dow bought out Hoechst South Africa's share in the two companies' polyolefins joint ventures. Later that year, Dow agreed to buy CanStates Holdings, Inc., and its subsidiary, ANGUS Chemical Company. Dow also agreed to buy Union Carbide for $9.3 billion.

OFFICERS

Chairman: Frank P. Popoff, age 63
President and CEO: William S. Stavropoulos, age 59, $1,583,338 pay
EVP; VP, Plastics, Hydrocarbons, and Energy: Anthony J. Carbone, age 58, $939,784 pay
EVP; President, Dow North America; VP, Chemicals: Michael D. Parker, age 52, $907,334 pay
EVP and CFO: J. Pedro Reinhard, age 53, $907,334 pay
VP Operations: Arnold A. Allemang, age 56, $661,684 pay
Business VP, Polystyrene: K. M. Bader
Business VP, Emulsion Polymers: T. J. Block
VP and Business Director, EDC/VCM and Electrochemical Management: P. H. Cook
VP, Automotive Materials: L. A. Denton
Business VP, Adhesives, Sealants, and Coatings: W. R. Donberg
Business VP, Insight Technology: E. F. Gambrell
VP and Director Research and Development: Richard M. Gross, age 51
VP and Controller: G. Michael Lynch, age 55
VP and Treasurer: Geoffrey E. Merszei, age 47
VP, Secretary, and General Counsel: John G. Scriven, age 56
VP Environment, Health and Safety, Human Resources, and Public Affairs: Lawrence J. Washington Jr., age 53
Auditors: Deloitte & Touche LLP

LOCATIONS

HQ: 2030 Dow Center, Midland, MI 48674
Phone: 517-636-1000   **Fax:** 517-636-1830
Web site: http://www.dow.com

Dow Chemical sells its products and services in 168 countries.

PRODUCTS/OPERATIONS

1998 Sales

	$ mil.	% of total
Performance plastics	5,076	28
Plastics	3,779	20
Performance chemicals	2,639	14
Chemicals	2,385	13
Agricultural products	2,352	13
Hydrocarbons & energy	1,479	8
Other	731	4
Total	**18,441**	**100**

COMPETITORS

Akzo Nobel	Huntsman
AlliedSignal	ICI
BASF AG	ITOCHU
Bayer AG	Lyondell Chemical
BP Amoco	Millennium Chemicals
Cargill	Mobil
Chevron	Monsanto
ConAgra	Novartis
DuPont	Occidental
Eastman Chemical	Olin
Elf Aquitaine	Phillips Petroleum
Exxon	PPG
FINA	Rohm and Haas
FMC	Royal Dutch/Shell
Henkel	Union Carbide
Hoechst AG	

HISTORICAL FINANCIALS & EMPLOYEES

NYSE symbol: DOW FYE: December 31	Annual Growth	1989	1990	1991	1992	1993	1994	1995	1996	1997	1998
Sales ($ mil.)	0.5%	17,600	19,773	18,807	18,971	18,060	20,015	20,200	20,053	20,018	18,441
Net income ($ mil.)	(6.9%)	2,487	1,384	942	(489)	644	938	2,071	1,907	1,808	1,310
Income as % of sales	—	14.1%	7.0%	5.0%	—	3.6%	4.7%	10.3%	9.5%	9.0%	7.1%
Earnings per share ($)	(5.1%)	9.20	5.10	3.46	(1.83)	2.31	3.35	7.62	7.60	7.70	5.76
Stock price - FY high ($)	—	72.25	75.75	58.00	68.00	62.00	79.25	78.00	92.50	102.63	101.44
Stock price - FY low ($)	—	55.53	37.00	44.13	51.00	49.00	56.50	61.38	68.25	75.75	74.69
Stock price - FY close ($)	2.7%	71.38	47.50	53.75	57.25	56.75	67.25	70.25	78.38	101.50	90.94
P/E - high	—	8	15	17	—	27	24	10	12	13	18
P/E - low	—	6	7	13	—	21	17	8	9	10	13
Dividends per share ($)	5.3%	2.18	2.60	2.60	2.60	2.60	2.60	2.60	2.80	3.00	3.24	3.48
Book value per share ($)	1.5%	29.55	32.33	34.88	29.58	29.27	29.63	29.33	32.99	33.82	33.71
Employees	(5.0%)	62,100	62,100	62,200	61,353	55,436	53,730	39,500	40,289	42,861	39,000

STOCK PRICE HISTORY

HIGH/LOW/CLOSE

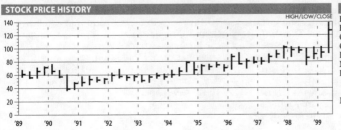

1998 FISCAL YEAR-END

Debt ratio: 35.2%
Return on equity: 17.6%
Cash ($ mil.): 123
Current ratio: 1.18
Long-term debt ($ mil.): 4,051
No. of shares (mil.): 220
Dividends
  Yield: 3.8%
  Payout: 60.4%
Market value ($ mil.): 20,041

DOW JONES & COMPANY, INC.

OVERVIEW

Dow Jones & Company has its finger on the pulse of the global economy. The New York City-based company publishes *The Wall Street Journal,* the financial daily whose circulation of nearly 1.8 million qualifies it as the most widely read newspaper in the US. Dow Jones rounds out its print publications with Asian and European versions of *The Wall Street Journal;* financial magazines *Barron's, Far Eastern Economic Review,* and *SmartMoney* (jointly owned with Hearst); and more than 30 community newspapers issued by its Ottaway Newspapers group.

While its print publications and community newspapers generate more than two-thirds of the company's revenues, Dow Jones also distributes information electronically to more than 1.1 million subscribers via Dow Jones Newswires, Dow Jones Interactive (an online service offering news from more than 6,000 publications), and The Wall Street Journal Interactive. Dow

Jones is an equal partner with NBC in CNBC Europe and CNBC Asia, and it provides content to CNBC in the US. The Dow Jones Indexes group develops and licenses index products such as the Dow Jones Industrial Average.

Dow Jones & Company is struggling to regroup following a botched attempt at branching into financial data. Sluggish ad revenues from its print products have also left the company hoping that growth in its online activities will shore up its bottom line. The company will get help in the Internet arena from rival Reuters, which has combined its Reuters Business Briefing online financial information business with Dow Jones Interactive in a new joint venture called Dow Jones Reuters Business Interactive. Members of the Bancroft family (heirs of early owner Clarence Barron) own 42% of Dow Jones and control 68% of the voting power. The Ottaway family owns nearly 5% of the company.

HISTORY

Charles Dow, Edward Jones, and Charles Bergstresser founded Dow Jones & Company in 1882. The company delivered handwritten bulletins of stock and bond trading news to subscribers in New York City. In 1883 Dow Jones started summarizing the trading day in the *Customers' Afternoon Letter,* which evolved into *The Wall Street Journal* (1889).

Jones sold out to his partners in 1899; three years later Dow and Bergstresser sold the company to Clarence Barron. In 1921 the company introduced *Barron's National Business and Financial Weekly*. Dow Jones suffered along with the financial industry during the Depression as circulation dropped from 50,000 in 1928 to 28,000 a decade later.

Bernard Kilgore, who was appointed managing editor in 1941, shaped the format of *The Wall Street Journal* that has endured until this day. During the 1960s, the company saw circulation figures for *The Wall Street Journal* exceed 1 million. With its acquisition of the Ottaway group and investments in the *Far Eastern Economic Review* and *The Asian Wall Street Journal* during the 1970s, Dow Jones expanded into community and international publications. It launched *The Wall Street Journal Europe* in 1983 and between 1985 and 1990 gradually acquired Telerate, a real-time financial data network that it renamed Dow Jones Markets.

In 1992 Dow Jones teamed with Hearst Corp. to launch *SmartMoney* magazine. A 1992 alliance with BellSouth to provide

telephone access to Dow Jones reports and a 1994 venture with American City Business Journals to publish a monthly magazine did not fare well, and both were discontinued in 1995.

In 1997 the company shut down its unprofitable Dow Jones Investor Network (a video news service started in 1993) and tried to revive the ailing Dow Jones Markets service by announcing a $650 million investment program to revamp the financial data unit. Also that year Dow Jones agreed to provide content to CNBC and teamed with NBC to launch CNBC in Europe and Asia.

Charges associated with Dow Jones Markets led to a sizable loss for 1997, and the company sold the unit to Bridge Information Systems for $510 million the following year. In 1998 the company inked deals to distribute its newswires through Reuters, Bloomberg, and Bridge.

In 1999 the company sold its EDGAR Direct SEC filings service to Primark. Dow Jones announced an expansion of *The Wall Street Journal Europe* and formed a joint venture with Reuters Group that combined their online news databases. It also launched the business-oriented Web portal dowjones.com. In addition, the company plans to offer *The Wall Street Journal Sunday,* a package of articles that will appear in 10 US newspapers.

OFFICERS

Chairman and CEO; Publisher, The Wall Street Journal: Peter R. Kann, age 56, $1,152,885 pay
EVP and CFO: Jerome H. Bailey, age 46, $534,605 pay
EVP, General Counsel, and Secretary: Peter G. Skinner, age 54, $705,296 pay
SVP Electronic Publishing: L. Gordon Crovitz
SVP; Chairman and CEO, Ottaway Newspapers: James H. Ottaway Jr., age 61, $561,138 pay
President, International: Karen Elliott House
President, Dow Jones Newswires: Paul J. Ingrassia
President, Dow Jones Indexes: David E. Moran
President, Dow Jones Interactive Publishing: Dorothea Coccoli Palsho
General Manager, The Wall Street Journal: Danforth W. Austin
Editor, the Wall Street Journal: Robert L. Bartley
Managing Editor, The Wall Street Journal: Paul Steiger
President and COO, Ottaway Newspapers: Joseph Richter
President and Editor, Barron's: Edwin A. Finn Jr.
VP and Chief Technology Officer: William A. Godfrey III
VP Finance: Thomas G. Hetzel, age 43
Treasurer: Thomas W. McGuirl
Comptroller: Lawrence K. Kinsella, age 42
VP Employee Relations: James A. Scaduto
VP Corporate Communications: Richard J. Tofel
Auditors: PricewaterhouseCoopers LLP

LOCATIONS

HQ: 200 Liberty St., New York, NY 10281
Phone: 212-416-2000   **Fax:** 212-416-4348
Web site: http://www.dj.com

Dow Jones & Company has operations in Asia, Europe, and the US.

PRODUCTS/OPERATIONS

1998 Sales

	$ mil.	% of total
Advertising	1,031	48
Information services	671	31
Circulation & other	456	21
Total	**2,158**	**100**

1998 Sales

	$ mil.	% of total
Print publishing	1,162	54
Electronic publishing	393	18
Community Newspapers	317	15
Dow Jones Markets (sold in 1998)	286	13
Total	**2,158**	**100**

COMPETITORS

Advance Publications
Associated Press
Bloomberg
Bridge Information
Data Broadcasting
Dialog Corporation
Dun & Bradstreet
EDGAR Online, Inc.
FactSet
Forbes
Gannett
Hoover's
Knight Ridder
LEXIS-NEXIS
MarketWatch.com
McGraw-Hill
Morgan Stanley Dean Witter
The Motley Fool
New York Times
News Corp.
Pearson
Reed Elsevier
Reuters
Telescan
TheStreet.com
Thomson Corporation
Time Warner
Times Mirror
Track Data
Tribune
UPI
Washington Post

HISTORICAL FINANCIALS & EMPLOYEES

NYSE symbol: DJ FYE: December 31	Annual Growth	1989	1990	1991	1992	1993	1994	1995	1996	1997	1998
Sales ($ mil.)	2.8%	1,688	1,720	1,725	1,818	1,932	2,091	2,284	2,482	2,573	2,158
Net income ($ mil.)	(33.2%)	317	107	72	108	148	178	190	190	(802)	8
Income as % of sales	—	18.8%	6.2%	4.2%	5.9%	7.6%	8.5%	8.3%	7.7%	—	0.4%
Earnings per share ($)	(32.6%)	3.15	1.06	0.71	1.06	1.47	1.79	1.94	1.95	(8.36)	0.09
Stock price - FY high ($)	—	42.50	33.75	30.63	35.38	39.00	41.88	40.13	41.88	55.88	59.00
Stock price - FY low ($)	—	29.25	18.13	21.63	24.50	26.75	28.13	30.63	31.88	33.38	41.56
Stock price - FY close ($)	4.2%	33.25	24.00	25.88	27.00	35.75	31.00	39.88	33.88	53.69	48.13
P/E - high	—	13	32	43	33	27	23	21	21	—	656
P/E - low	—	9	17	30	23	18	16	16	16	—	462
Dividends per share ($)	3.2%	0.72	0.76	0.76	0.76	0.80	0.84	0.92	0.96	0.96	0.96
Book value per share ($)	(9.7%)	13.94	14.23	14.20	14.41	14.96	15.33	16.47	17.22	8.08	5.54
Employees	(1.8%)	9,818	9,677	9,459	9,860	10,006	10,300	11,200	11,800	12,300	8,300

STOCK PRICE HISTORY

HIGH/LOW/CLOSE

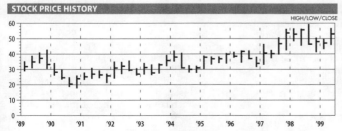

1998 FISCAL YEAR-END

Debt ratio: 22.7%
Return on equity: 1.6%
Cash ($ mil.): 143
Current ratio: 0.74
Long-term debt ($ mil.): 150
No. of shares (mil.): 92
Dividends
 Yield: 2.0%
 Payout: 1,066.7%
Market value ($ mil.): 4,426

DTE ENERGY COMPANY

OVERVIEW

Detroit-based DTE Energy keeps the assembly lines rolling in Motor City and the electricity flowing through Michigan power lines. The utility holding company's main subsidiary, Detroit Edison, generates, transmits, and distributes electricity to more than 2 million customers in southeastern Michigan. It has a generating capacity of more than 10,200 MW, mainly fossil-fueled. The utility also operates a nuclear plant, Fermi 2, and its huge investment in the nuke has left Detroit Edison stranded with high production costs. To drive down its prices as Michigan motors toward deregulation, DTE Energy has been approved to speed up the amortization of the nuke to recover its costs. Full electric competition in Michigan is slated for 2002.

Still focused on the heavily industrialized Great Lakes region, DTE Energy is moving into nonutility businesses such as wholesale power marketing and transporting coal for Detroit Edison and other industrial customers. DTE Energy is also cozying up to large commercial and industrial customers with services such as energy management and cooling system installation.

Environmental pursuits by DTE Energy include utility pole recycling and landfill gas recovery, and its Plug Power joint venture with GE is marketing fuel cell technology.

HISTORY

DTE Energy's predecessor threw its first switch in 1886 when the Edison Illuminating Company of Detroit was incorporated by George Peck and a group of local investors. Neighboring utility Peninsular Electric Light was formed in 1891, and both companies bought smaller utilities until they merged in 1903 to form Detroit Edison. A subsidiary of holding company North American Co., Detroit Edison was incorporated in New York to secure financing for power plants.

Detroit's growth in the 1920s and 1930s led the utility to build new plants and buy others in outlying areas. Detroit Edison acquired Michigan Electric Power, which had been divested from its holding company under the auspices of the Public Utility Holding Company Act of 1935, and was itself divested from North American in 1940.

The post-WWII boom prompted Detroit Edison to build more plants, most of them coal-fired. In 1953 it joined a consortium of 34 companies to build Fermi 1, an experimental nuclear plant, and brought it on line in 1963. Still strapped for power, Detroit Edison began building the huge, coal-fired Monroe plant, which went into service in 1970. In 1972 Fermi 1 had a partial core meltdown and was taken off line.

Detroit Edison began shipping low-sulfur Montana coal through its Wisconsin terminal in 1974, reducing the cost of obtaining the fuel. The next year it began building another nuke, Fermi 2. The nuke had cost more than $4.8 billion by the time it went on line in 1988. That year the utility began its landfill gas recovery operation (now DTE Biomass Energy), and John Lobbia became CEO.

A recession pounded automakers in the early 1990s, leading to cutbacks in electricity purchases. In 1992 Congress passed the Energy Policy Act, allowing wholesale power competition in the industry. In late 1993 a fire shut down Fermi 2 for almost two years. Michigan's public service commission (PSC) approved retail customer-choice pilot programs for its utilities in 1994. Detroit Edison and rival Consumers Energy (now CMS Energy) took the PSC to court.

DTE Energy became Detroit Edison's holding company in 1996. The next year it formed DTE Energy Trading to broker power and DTE-CoEnergy to provide energy-management services and sell power to large customers. It also formed Plug Power, a venture with Mechanical Technology, to develop fuel cells that convert natural gas to power without combustion.

In 1997 and 1998 the PSC, bolstered by state court decisions, issued orders to restructure Michigan's utilities. The transition to retail competition began in 1998. That year DTE and regional natural gas provider MichCon began collaborating on some operations, including billing and meter reading. DTE and GE formed a venture to sell and install Plug Power fuel cell systems. Also in 1998, Detroit Edison reached a settlement with 3,500 former employees claiming discrimination during 1993-94 layoffs, and Lobbia was succeeded by president Anthony Earley.

A higher court shot down the PSC's restructuring orders in 1999, but DTE and CMS (facing less-favorable proposed legislation) decided to voluntarily implement customer choice, using PSC guidelines. That year DOE selected DTE to install the world's first super power-cable, which could carry three times as much electricity as conventional copper.

Chairman, President, CEO, and COO, DTE Energy and Detroit Edison: Anthony F. Earley Jr., age 49, $868,503 pay

President and COO, DTE Energy Resources, DTE Energy and Detroit Edison: Gerard M. Anderson, age 40, $421,306 pay

President and COO, DTE Energy Distribution, DTE Energy and Detroit Edison: Robert J. Buckler, age 49, $425,606 pay

EVP and CFO, DTE Energy and Detroit Edison: Larry G. Garberding, age 60, $489,448 pay

SVP, DTE Energy and Detroit Edison: Michael E. Champley, age 50

SVP Nuclear Generation, Detroit Edison: Douglas R. Gipson, age 51, $335,210 pay

VP and Chief Information Officer: Lynne E. Halpin, age 47

VP and Controller, DTE Energy and Detroit Edison: David E. Meador, age 41

VP and Corporate Secretary, DTE Energy and Detroit Edison: Susan M. Beale, age 50

VP Corporate and Public Affairs, Detroit Edison: S. Martin Taylor, age 58

VP Corporate Communications, Detroit Edison: Michael C. Porter, age 45

VP Energy Delivery and Services, Detroit Edison: Ron A. May, age 47

VP and General Counsel, DTE Energy and Detroit Edison: Christopher C. Nern, age 54

VP Human Resources, Detroit Edison: Sandra J. Miller, age 55

VP Power Generation, Detroit Edison: William R. Roller, age 53

VP and Treasurer, DTE Energy and Detroit Edison: Leslie L. Loomans, age 55

Auditors: Deloitte & Touche LLP

HQ: 2000 2nd Ave., Detroit, MI 48226-1279
Phone: 313-235-4000   **Fax:** 313-235-0223
Web site: http://www.dteenergy.com

1998 Sales

	$ mil.	% of total
Electricity		
Commercial	1,553	37
Residential	1,253	30
Industrial	753	18
Other	343	8
Steam heating	319	7
Total	**4,221**	**100**

1998 Fuel Sources

	MW	% of total
Fossil	7,696	75
Nuclear	1,129	11
Pumped storage	924	9
Peak units	513	5
Total	**10,262**	**100**

AEP	Peabody Group
CMS Energy	PG&E
Duke Energy	SEMCO Energy
Dynegy	Southern Company
Enron	UtiliCorp
MCN	Wisconsin Energy
Northern States Power	WPS Resources

NYSE symbol: DTE FYE: December 31	Annual Growth	1989	1990	1991	1992	1993	1994	1995	1996	1997	1998
Sales ($ mil.)	3.1%	3,203	3,307	3,592	3,558	3,555	3,519	3,636	3,645	3,764	4,221
Net income ($ mil.)	0.4%	426	515	535	558	491	390	406	309	417	443
Income as % of sales	—	13.3%	15.6%	14.9%	15.7%	13.8%	11.1%	11.2%	8.5%	11.1%	10.5%
Earnings per share ($)	1.6%	2.65	3.26	3.64	3.79	3.34	2.67	2.80	2.13	2.88	3.05
Stock price – FY high ($)	—	25.88	30.25	35.38	35.25	37.13	30.25	34.88	37.25	34.75	49.25
Stock price – FY low ($)	—	17.13	23.50	27.75	30.25	29.88	24.25	25.75	27.63	26.13	33.44
Stock price – FY close ($)	6.0%	25.38	28.25	34.75	32.75	30.00	26.13	34.50	32.38	34.69	43.06
P/E – high	—	10	9	10	9	11	11	12	17	12	16
P/E – low	—	6	7	8	8	9	9	9	13	9	11
Dividends per share ($)	2.3%	1.68	1.76	1.86	1.96	2.04	2.06	2.06	2.06	2.06	2.06
Book value per share ($)	5.2%	16.14	17.63	19.37	21.18	22.42	22.96	23.68	23.73	24.55	25.49
Employees	(2.1%)	10,254	9,669	9,357	9,183	8,919	8,494	8,340	8,526	8,732	8,482

HIGH/LOW/CLOSE

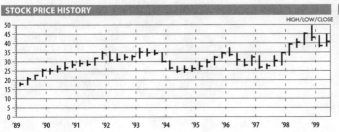

Debt ratio: 53.9%
Return on equity: 12.0%
Cash ($ mil.): 130
Current ratio: 0.89
Long-term debt ($ mil.): 4,323
No. of shares (mil.): 145
Dividends
  Yield: 4.8%
  Payout: 67.5%
Market value ($ mil.): 6,247

DUKE ENERGY CORPORATION

OVERVIEW

Duke Energy is duking it out with rivals for the title of king of the fast-consolidating energy industry. Based in Charlotte, North Carolina, Duke is the second-largest investor-owned utility, behind California's PG&E. The company's regulated utilities, Duke Power and Nantahala Power and Light, generate electricity (17,300-MW capacity, fueled almost entirely by nuclear power and coal) that is transmitted to 2 million customers in North and South Carolina.

Duke also owns and operates some 11,500 miles of natural gas pipeline, which connect the Gulf Coast region to the northeastern US, and the company gathers, processes, and markets natural gas and natural gas liquids.

Although the Carolinas haven't undergone deregulation in the electric industry, Duke is slugging it out in newly competitive markets worldwide. Its trading and marketing joint venture with Mobil markets natural gas and electricity to local utilities, industrial users, and power generators in the US and Canada. Duke Energy North America buys and builds power generators in Canada, Mexico, and the US; it has a generating capacity of 2,645 MW in California alone.

Internationally, the company is developing energy projects, focusing its efforts in the Asia/Pacific region and Latin America. Duke also provides engineering and construction services for power projects and has expanded beyond energy into real estate and telecommunications.

HISTORY

Surgeon W. Gill Wylie founded Catawba Power Company in 1899. The company's first hydroelectric plant in South Carolina was on line by 1904. The next year Wylie met with James "Buck" Duke (founder of the American Tobacco Company and Duke University's namesake) to discuss the future of electricity in the Carolinas, and the two formed Southern Power Company with Wylie as president.

In 1910 Buck Duke became president of Southern Power and organized Mill-Power Supply to sell electric equipment and appliances. He also began investing in textile mills that promised to buy Southern's electricity. The mills prospered as a result of the electric power, and Buck continued to bring in customers. He formed the Southern Public Utility Company in 1913 to buy other Piedmont-region utilities. Wylie died in 1924, the same year the company was renamed Duke Power; Buck Duke died the next year.

Growing after WWII, the company went public in 1950 and moved to the NYSE in 1961. It also formed its real estate arm, Crescent Resources, in the 1960s. Insulating itself from the effects of the 1970s energy crisis, Duke invested in coal mining and nuclear energy (it has three nuclear plants, the first completed in 1974).

In 1988 Duke began to develop power projects outside its home region, and it also bought neighboring utility Nantahala Power and Light. The next year it formed a joint venture with Fluor Daniel to provide engineering and construction services to power generators. Mill-Power Supply was sold in 1990.

By the 1990s Duke had moved into overseas markets, acquiring an Argentine power station in 1992. It also tried its hand at telecommunications, creating DukeNet Communications in 1994 to build fiber-optic systems, and in 1996 it teamed up with oil major Mobil to create a power trading and marketing business. As the US power industry traveled toward deregulation, Duke also sought natural gas operations to add to its holdings. It targeted PanEnergy Corp., which was formed in 1929 and owned a major pipeline system in the eastern half of the US. Duke Power bought PanEnergy in 1997 to form Duke Energy Corporation.

Seeing an opportunity in 1998, Duke formed Duke Communication to provide antenna sites to the fast-growing wireless communications industry. It also acquired a 52% stake in Electroquil, an electric power generating company in Guayaquil, Ecuador. That year it purchased a pipeline company in Australia from PG&E; it also bought three PG&E power plants to compete in California's deregulated electric utility marketplace.

Duke merged its pipeline business, Duke Energy Trading and Transport, with TEPPCO Partners and acquired gas processing operations from Union Pacific Resources. It sold Panhandle Eastern Pipe Line and gas-related assets in the Midwest to CMS Energy for $2.2 billion in 1999, and it made plans to build a pipeline extending from Alabama to Florida.

Outside the US, Duke Energy International planned to spend $1.2 billion for generation facilities in Argentina, Belize, Bolivia, Brazil, El Salvador, and Peru. The deals will more than double the company's international power generation holdings.

Chairman and CEO: Richard B. Priory, age 52,
$1,701,000 pay
President and COO: P. M. Anderson, $1,637,780 pay
EVP and CFO: Richard J. Osborne, age 48, $537,840 pay
EVP and Chief Administrative Officer: Ruth G. Shaw,
age 51
EVP, General Counsel, and Secretary:
Richard W. Blackburn, age 56, $597,600 pay
SVP and Treasurer: David L. Hauser
SVP, Corporate Planning: Donald H. Denton Jr.
SVP, Diversified Operations: Robert S. Lilien
SVP, Information Management: Cecil O. Smith Jr.
SVP, Retail Services, Duke Power: Jimmy R. Hicks
SVP, Strategic Planning and Development:
Leonard B. Gatewood
VP, Corporate Human Resources: Christopher C. Rolfe
Group President, Duke Power: William A. Coley, age 55,
$540,560 pay
Group President, Energy Services: Harvey J. Padewer,
age 51
Group President, Energy Transmission: Fred J. Fowler,
age 53, $597,600 pay
Auditors: Deloitte & Touche LLP

LOCATIONS

HQ: 526 S. Church St., Charlotte, NC 28202-1904
Phone: 704-594-6200   **Fax:** 704-382-3814
Web site: http://www.duke-energy.com

Duke Energy distributes electricity in North and South
Carolina and transports and stores natural gas in the Mid-
Atlantic and New England states. It also has power
generation facilities in California, Connecticut, Louisiana,
Missouri, and New York, as well as in Argentina, Australia,
Chile, Ecuador, Indonesia, and Peru.

PRODUCTS/OPERATIONS

1998 Sales

	$ mil.	% of total
Natural gas & petroleum	7,854	45
Electricity		
Utilities	4,586	26
Marketing & trading	2,788	16
Natural gas transport & storage	1,450	8
Other	932	5
Total	**17,610**	**100**

Selected Subsidiaries
Duke Energy Field Services
Duke Energy International (power generation projects)
Duke Energy North America (power generation projects)
Duke Energy Trading and Marketing (60%, energy
marketing in North America)
Duke Power (electric utility)

COMPETITORS

AEP	KeySpan Energy
Avista	Koch
BP Amoco	Peabody Group
Carolina Power & Light	PG&E
Chevron	Phillips Petroleum
Coastal	Reliant Energy
Columbia Energy	Southern Company
Consolidated Natural Gas	Texaco
Dynegy	Texas Utilities
El Paso Energy	Tractebel
Enron	TVA
Entergy	UtiliCorp
Exxon	Williams Companies

HISTORICAL FINANCIALS & EMPLOYEES

NYSE symbol: DUK FYE: December 31	Annual Growth	1989	1990	1991	1992	1993	1994	1995	1996	1997	1998
Sales ($ mil.)	19.1%	3,639	3,682	3,817	3,962	4,282	4,489	4,677	4,758	16,309	17,610
Net income ($ mil.)	9.1%	572	538	584	508	626	639	715	730	974	1,252
Income as % of sales	—	15.7%	14.6%	15.3%	12.8%	14.6%	14.2%	15.3%	15.3%	6.0%	7.1%
Earnings per share ($)	3.2%	2.57	2.40	2.60	2.21	2.11	2.26	2.68	2.85	2.50	3.40
Stock price - FY high ($)	—	28.25	32.38	35.00	37.50	44.88	43.00	47.88	53.00	56.56	71.00
Stock price - FY low ($)	—	21.38	25.50	26.75	31.38	35.38	32.88	37.38	43.38	41.88	48.94
Stock price - FY close ($)	9.6%	28.06	30.63	35.00	36.13	42.38	38.13	47.38	46.25	55.38	64.06
P/E - high	—	11	13	13	17	21	19	18	19	23	21
P/E - low	—	8	11	10	14	17	15	14	15	17	14
Dividends per share ($)	4.2%	1.52	1.60	1.68	1.76	1.84	1.92	2.00	2.08	2.16	2.20
Book value per share ($)	2.5%	18.05	18.84	19.86	20.26	21.17	22.13	23.36	24.25	20.96	22.45
Employees	1.4%	19,449	18,187	17,968	18,727	18,274	17,052	17,121	17,726	23,000	22,000

1996 and prior information is for Duke Power Company only.

STOCK PRICE HISTORY

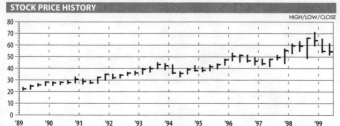

1998 FISCAL YEAR-END

Debt ratio: 42.6%
Return on equity: 15.4%
Cash ($ mil.): 80
Current ratio: 0.98
Long-term debt ($ mil.): 6,272
No. of shares (mil.): 363
Dividends
  Yield: 3.4%
  Payout: 64.7%
Market value ($ mil.): 23,254

DUN & BRADSTREET

OVERVIEW

Dun & Bradstreet hopes two is company since three was a crowd. After recently dividing into three publicly traded companies, the Murray Hill, New Jersey-based holding company has scaled back to just two operations. Its D&B subsidiary is one of the world's largest corporate credit, marketing, and accounts-receivable management agencies, reporting on more than 50 million businesses worldwide. Its Moody's Investors Service publishes credit ratings and other financial information on commercial and government entities in 100 countries.

After decades of acquisitions left D&B unfocused and debt-ridden, the company split into three separate public entities, selling market research firm ACNielsen and high-tech research specialist Cognizant. The reorganization also involved divestitures, including D&B Software and Donnelley's Southern California operations.

The company also spun off its Moody's and D&B units as a new Dun & Bradstreet Corporation, and turned one-time subsidiary R. H. Donnelley, which produces about 300 Yellow Pages phone directories in 13 states, into a separate, publicly traded company. It also sold Moody's financial publishing business to publishing venture Financial Communications. Since restructuring, D&B has played to its strengths: the ability to pull together and organize financial data to support decision making.

HISTORY

Dun & Bradstreet (D&B) originated as Lewis Tappan's Mercantile Agency, established in 1841 in New York City. One of the first commercial credit-reporting agencies, the Mercantile supplied wholesalers and importers with reports on their customers' credit histories. The company's credit reporters included four future US presidents (Lincoln, Grant, Cleveland, and McKinley). In the 1840s it opened offices in Boston, Philadelphia, and Baltimore, and in 1857 established operations in Montreal and London.

In 1859 Robert Dun took over the agency and changed its name to R.G. Dun & Co. The first edition of the *Dun's Book* (1859) contained information on 20,268 businesses; by 1886 the number had risen to over 1 million. Bradstreet Company, a rival firm founded in Cincinnati in 1849, merged with Dun in 1933; the Dun & Bradstreet name was adopted in 1939.

In 1961 D&B bought Reuben H. Donnelley Corp., a direct-mail advertiser and publisher of the Yellow Pages (first published 1886) and 10 trade magazines. In 1962 Moody's Investors Service (founded 1900) and *Official Airline Guides* (first published 1929; sold 1988) became part of D&B. The company computerized its records in the 1960s and eventually developed the largest private business database in the world. By 1975 it had a national network with a centralized database. Sales boomed when D&B created new products by repackaging information from its vast database (such as Dun's Financial Profiles, first published in 1979).

In the 1970s D&B began buying up other information, data, and publishing companies, including Technical Publishing (trade and professional publications, 1978) and National

CSS (computer services, 1979). This trend continued in the 1980s with the purchase of McCormack & Dodge (software, 1983), ACNielsen (1984), and IMS International (pharmaceutical sales data, 1988). In 1989 reports surfaced that D&B was overcharging customers for credit reports; it settled the resulting class-action suit in 1994.

The tide turned in the 1990s as D&B, finding that not all information was equally profitable, sold its specialty industry and consumer database companies and IMS's communications unit. But it still hoped to cash in on both the medical-information industry (by forming D&B HealthCare Information) and information technology (by buying a majority interest in high-tech consulting firm Gartner Group). In 1993 the company attempted to improve efficiency in its information-services businesses by consolidating 27 data centers worldwide into four automated centers.

But in 1996, after its second earnings decline in three years, management revamped the company, selling off ACNielsen and Cognizant. The next year it sold coupon processing and management firm NCH Promotional Services. In 1998, concluding that Yellow Pages are fundamentally different from credit information and bond-rating businesses, D&B spun off R. H. Donnelley (formerly Reuben H. Donnelley). D&B won a moral victory in 1999 when the Justice Department ended its three-year antitrust inquiry into Moody's bond-rating practices without filing any charges.

OFFICERS

Chairman and CEO; Chairman, Dun & Bradstreet:
Volney "Terry" Taylor, age 59, $1,698,903 pay
SVP and CFO: Frank S. Sowinski, age 42, $725,625 pay
SVP and Chief Communications Officer:
William F. Doescher
SVP and Chief Human Resources Officer: Peter J. Ross,
age 53
SVP and Chief Legal Counsel: Nancy L. Henry, age 53,
$492,872 pay
SVP and Chief Technology Officer: Elahe Hessamfar,
age 45, $742,030 pay
VP Benefits: Mary M. Orlando
VP Business Practices: Lucy A. Collett
VP and Controller; SVP Finance, Dun & Bradstreet:
Chester J. Geveda Jr., age 52, $443,648 pay
VP Organizational Performance and Inclusion:
Doretta Gasorek
VP Tax and Financial Planning: Daniel S. Miller
VP and Treasurer: Roxanne E. Parker
Secretary: Mitchell C. Sussis
President, Dun & Bradstreet US: Andre Dahan
**President, Dun & Bradstreet Europe, Africa, and
Middle East:** John Fry
**President, Dun & Bradstreet Asia Pacific, Canada, Latin
America, and RMS North America:** Michael R. Flock
President, Moody's Investors Service:
John Rutherfurd Jr.
Auditors: PricewaterhouseCoopers LLP

LOCATIONS

HQ: The Dun & Bradstreet Corporation,
1 Diamond Hill Rd., Murray Hill, NJ 07974-1218
Phone: 908-665-5000   **Fax:** 908-665-5803
Web site: http://www.dnbcorp.com

Dun & Bradstreet has operations in about 200 countries.

PRODUCTS/OPERATIONS

1998 Sales

	$ mil.	% of total
Dun & Bradstreet		
US	902	46
Europe	428	22
Asia Pacific/Canada/Latin America	89	5
Moody's Investor Service	496	26
Other	20	1
Total	**1,935**	**100**

Selected Subsidiaries
Dun & Bradstreet Computer Leasing, Inc.
Dunsnet Inc.
Moody's Investors Service, Inc.
Palmetto Assurance Ltd.

COMPETITORS

Acxiom
Dialog Corporation
Equifax
Experian
Fimalac
FinancialWeb.com
Harte-Hanks
infoUSA
M/A/R/C Group
Marmon Group
McGraw-Hill
Morningstar
Primark
Reuters
Value Line

HISTORICAL FINANCIALS & EMPLOYEES

NYSE symbol: DNB FYE: December 31	Annual Growth	1989	1990	1991	1992	1993	1994	1995	1996	1997	1998
Sales ($ mil.)	(8.5%)	4,322	4,818	4,643	4,751	4,710	4,896	5,415	2,159	2,154	1,935
Net income ($ mil.)	(7.9%)	586	508	509	554	38	630	321	(44)	160	280
Income as % of sales	—	13.6%	10.5%	11.0%	11.7%	0.8%	12.9%	5.9%	—	7.4%	14.5%
Earnings per share ($)	—	—	—	—	—	—	—	—	—	—	1.63
Stock price - FY high ($)	—	—	—	—	—	—	—	—	—	—	34.44
Stock price - FY low ($)	—	—	—	—	—	—	—	—	—	—	21.75
Stock price - FY close ($)	—	—	—	—	—	—	—	—	—	—	31.56
P/E - high	—	—	—	—	—	—	—	—	—	—	21
P/E - low	—	—	—	—	—	—	—	—	—	—	13
Dividends per share ($)	—	—	—	—	—	—	—	—	—	—	0.37
Book value per share ($)	—	—	—	—	—	—	—	—	—	—	(2.16)
Employees	(17.6%)	71,500	62,900	58,500	52,400	50,400	47,000	49,500	15,400	15,100	12,500

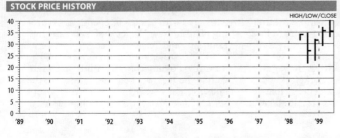

STOCK PRICE HISTORY
HIGH/LOW/CLOSE

1998 FISCAL YEAR-END
Debt ratio: 0.0%
Return on equity: —
Cash ($ mil.): 91
Current ratio: 0.56
Long-term debt ($ mil.): 0
No. of shares (mil.): 171
Dividends
 Yield: 1.2%
 Payout: 22.7%
Market value ($ mil.): 5,411

DYNEGY INC.

OVERVIEW

Formerly NGC, Dynegy (short for "dynamic energy" and pronounced DIE-negy) is living up to its new name by evolving from a natural gas marketer into a national, multidimensional energy and services provider. The Houston-based company is a giant natural gas wholesaler and power trader in the US. It also gathers and processes natural gas, produces natural gas liquids, and generates electricity. In addition, Dynegy markets coal, crude oil, electricity, natural gas liquids, and liquid petroleum gas. The company is also revving up to buy electric and natural gas utility Illinova.

Dynegy owns almost 50 gas processing plants; about 15 storage terminals; 17,000 miles of crude oil, natural gas, and LPG pipelines; and interests in three fractionation facilities. The company markets natural gas in Canada, the US, and the UK. Anticipating deregulation in the electricity marketplace, Dynegy is assembling a power portfolio with 31 gas-fired plants (6,800 MW), while forming alliances with regional utilities to get a jump on full retail competition.

Chevron holds 28% of Dynegy. BG plc (one of the companies that emerged from the British Gas split) and NOVA Chemicals each hold 25%; after the Illinova deal NOVA and BG are planning to reduce their stakes. Chairman Chuck Watson owns 6% of the company.

HISTORY

Dynegy, originally Natural Gas Clearinghouse, emerged from the deregulation of the natural gas industry. In 1978 the Natural Gas Policy Act reduced interstate pipeline companies' control over the marketplace. Federal Energy Regulatory Commission (FERC) Order 380 (1984) made gas prices on the open market competitive with those of pipeline companies. Natural Gas Clearinghouse was founded in late 1984 to match gas buyers and sellers without taking title. Chuck Watson became president and CEO in 1985. The company grew dramatically as deregulation secured larger volumes of gas for independent marketers.

The company developed financial instruments (such as natural gas futures) to provide customers with a hedge against wide fluctuations in natural gas prices. By 1990 Natural Gas Clearinghouse was trading natural gas futures on NYMEX. The company was the first independent gas marketer to act as the exclusive supply agent for a large local distributor. It also branched out by buying gas gathering and processing facilities, and it formed NGC Oil Trading and Transportation, a crude-oil marketer.

FERC Order 636 (1992) required most interstate pipeline companies to offer merchant sales, transportation, and storage as separate services, on the same terms that their own affiliates received. With the low-price advantage taken away from pipeline companies, Natural Gas Clearinghouse began selling more to local gas utilities.

In 1984 Natural Gas Clearinghouse set up partnerships with Canada's NOVA (Novagas Clearinghouse, a natural gas marketer) and British Gas (Accord Energy, an energy marketer), which gave those firms sizable stakes in the company. It also set up an electric power marketing unit, Electric Clearinghouse.

The company changed its name to NGC and went public in 1995 after it bought Trident NGL, an integrated natural gas liquids company. The next year NGC bought Chevron's natural gas business, giving Chevron a stake in NGC. It also acquired propane dealer LPG Services Group.

In 1997 NGC acquired Destec Energy, a leading independent power producer, and kept most of its US power plants but sold its international operations, lignite reserves, and Tiger Bay cogeneration plant. The company also formed alliances with regional players — IPL Energy's Consumersfirst in Canada, NICOR in the US Midwest, and All Energy in the northeastern US — to market its products through locally known entities. To do the same in the Southeast, NGC teamed up with AGL Resources and Piedmont Natural Gas in 1998 to form SouthStar Energy.

Taking the name Dynegy in 1998, the company allied with Florida Power to market wholesale electricity and gas. Meanwhile, it began developing new power plants in Georgia, Illinois, Kentucky, and North Carolina and bought a gas-powered facility in California (acquiring yet another in 1999) through a venture with NRG Energy. The company also partnered with Texaco to operate a gas processing plant in New Mexico and a pipeline in Louisiana and Texas.

In 1999 Dynegy agreed to pay about $4 billion for utility holding company Illinova, thereby gaining huge power generation assets in the Midwest. The new Dynegy will own or control some 15,000 MW of US generating capacity.

Chairman and CEO: Charles L. Watson, age 49,
$1,603,000 pay
President and COO: Stephen W. Bergstrom
SVP and CFO: John U. Clarke, age 46, $555,000 pay
SVP; President and COO, Dynegy Marketing and Trade:
Stephen W. Bergstrom, age 41, $1,200,000 pay
SVP; President and COO, Dynegy Midstream Services,
Limited Partnership: Stephen A. Furbacher, age 51
SVP, Secretary, and General Counsel:
Kenneth E. Randolph, age 42, $438,758 pay
Auditors: Arthur Andersen LLP

LOCATIONS

HQ: 1000 Louisiana, Ste. 5800, Houston, TX 77002
Phone: 713-507-6400   **Fax:** 713-507-3871
Web site: http://www.dynegy.com

Dynegy operates facilities in western Canada, the UK,
and the US.

1998 Sales

	$ mil.	$ of total
US	12,456	87
Canada	1,180	8
UK	622	5
Total	**14,258**	**100**

PRODUCTS/OPERATIONS

1998 Sales

	$ mil.	% of total
Wholesale gas and power	10,741	75
Liquids	3,517	25
Total	**14,258**	**100**

Selected Subsidiaries
DMT Holdings, Inc.
Dynegy Administrative Services Company
Dynegy Canada, Inc. (natural gas, natural gas liquids,
crude oil, and electricity marketing)
Dynegy Global Energy, Inc.
Dynegy GP Inc.
Dynegy Marketing and Trade (electric power and natural
gas marketing)
Dynegy Midstream, Inc. (natural gas liquids)
Dynegy Power Corp. (electricity and steam generation)
Dynegy Regulated Holdings, Inc.
Dynegy United Kingdom (natural gas, crude oil, and
LPG marketing)
Dynegy Upper Holdings, LLC

COMPETITORS

Avista	PG&E
BP Amoco	Phillips Petroleum
Coastal	Reliant Energy
Columbia Energy	Sempra Energy
Constellation Energy	Sonat
Group	Southern Company
Duke Energy	Statoil Energy
Edison International	Tejas Energy
El Paso Energy	Texas Utilities
Enron	Tractebel
Entergy	TVA
Koch	UtiliCorp
Mitchell Energy &	Western Gas
Development	Williams Companies
Peabody Group	

HISTORICAL FINANCIALS & EMPLOYEES

NYSE symbol: DYN FYE: December 31	Annual Growth	1989	1990	1991	1992	1993	1994	1995	1996	1997	1998
Sales ($ mil.)	30.1%	—	1,732	2,099	2,493	2,791	3,238	3,666	7,260	13,378	14,258
Net income ($ mil.)	18.4%	—	28	39	44	46	42	45	113	(103)	108
Income as % of sales	—	—	1.6%	1.9%	1.8%	1.6%	1.3%	1.2%	1.6%	—	0.8%
Earnings per share ($)	33.1%	—	—	—	—	—	0.21	0.82	0.83	0.00	0.66
Stock price - FY high ($)	—	—	—	—	—	—	12.25	11.75	24.75	24.13	17.50
Stock price - FY low ($)	—	—	—	—	—	—	8.00	8.38	8.63	14.75	9.38
Stock price - FY close ($)	1.0%	—	—	—	—	—	10.50	8.88	23.25	17.50	10.94
P/E - high	—	—	—	—	—	—	58	14	30	—	27
P/E - low	—	—	—	—	—	—	38	10	10	—	14
Dividends per share ($)	0.0%	—	—	—	—	—	0.05	0.04	0.06	0.05	0.05
Book value per share ($)	52.1%	—	—	—	—	—	1.29	5.00	6.95	6.24	6.92
Employees	22.8%	—	—	—	—	—	1,070	1,055	1,893	2,572	2,434

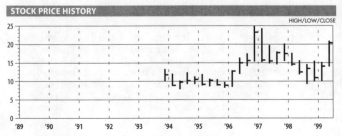

STOCK PRICE HISTORY	1998 FISCAL YEAR-END

HIGH/LOW/CLOSE	Debt ratio: 48.1%
	Return on equity: 10.3%
	Cash ($ mil.): 28
	Current ratio: 1.04
	Long-term debt ($ mil.): 1,047
	No. of shares (mil.): 152
	Dividends
	  Yield: 0.5%
	  Payout: 7.6%
	Market value ($ mil.): 1,664

E. & J. GALLO WINERY

OVERVIEW

"We don't want most of the business," E. & J. Gallo Winery chairman Ernest Gallo has said. "We want it all." A longtime producer of cheap jug wine such as Carlo Rossi and Gallo and fortified favorites such as Thunderbird, the world's largest wine maker has begun to siphon market share from upscale rivals by branching into more profitable middle- and premium-priced wines, including Indigo Hills and Gallo Estate. The Modesto, California-based company even sells premium wines without mentioning the Gallo name to distance them from their lowly cousins.

Already the leader in domestic table wines, with a 30% market share, Gallo sells wine in more than 80 countries and accounts for over half of US wine exports. It cultivates 4,000-plus acres of vineyards in prestigious Sonoma County, California, alone and buys grapes from other area growers. Gallo sells more than 30 brands of wine-based products in a wide price range, from alcohol-added wines and wine coolers to a growing number of upscale varietals that fetch up to $60 a bottle.

The founding Gallo family owns the company.

HISTORY

At first there were Ernest, Julio, and Joe, the three sons of Joe Gallo Sr., who left Italy for San Francisco around 1906. Joe Sr. started selling wine and then, after marrying the daughter of a commercial wine maker, began growing grapes. During Prohibition, Joe Sr. sent his grapes to Chicago, where Ernest and Julio sold them for use in legal home wine making.

Near the end of Prohibition, Joe Sr. and his wife were found dead in an apparent murder-suicide. In 1933 Ernest and Julio started their own business, E. & J. Gallo Winery, selling through the Chicago contacts they had made while selling grapes. Gallo soon became a popular local brand.

Ernest ran the business end, assembling a large distribution network and building a national brand, while Julio made the wine and Joe worked for them. In the early 1940s Gallo opened bottling plants in Los Angeles and New Orleans, using screw-cap bottles, which then seemed more hygienic and modern than corks. Gallo lagged during the war when alcohol was diverted for the military. Under Julio's supervision, it began upgrading its planting stock and refining its wine-making technology.

In the 1950s US wine tastes were generally unsophisticated, and sweet wines such as Italian Swiss Colony were the leaders. In an attempt to take this market, Gallo introduced Thunderbird, a fortified wine (its alcohol content is boosted to 20%), in 1957. In the 1960s Gallo spurred its growth by advertising heavily and keeping prices low. It introduced Hearty Burgundy, a jug wine, in 1964, along with Ripple. Gallo introduced the carbonated, fruit-flavored Boone's Farm Apple Wine in 1969, creating an interest in "pop" wines that lasted for a few years.

In 1974 the company introduced its first varietal wines, bearing the name of the grape from which they were made. In the 1970s Gallo field workers switched unions, from the United Farm Workers to the Teamsters. Repercussions included protests and boycotts, but sales were largely unaffected. From 1976 to 1982 Gallo operated under an FTC order limiting its control over wholesalers. The order was lifted after the industry's competitive balance changed.

Through the 1970s and 1980s, Gallo expanded its production of varietals; in 1988 it began adding vintage dates to the wines' labels. But it also kept a hand in the lower levels of the market, introducing Bartles & Jaymes wine coolers.

Beginning in 1986, the company fought a legal battle with Joe over the use of the Gallo name. After working for his brothers for years, Joe had been eased out and had started a dairy farm to make cheese. In 1992 he lost the use of his name for commercial purposes. Julio died the next year when his jeep overturned on a family ranch.

Heublein, which sells Jose Cuervo tequila, sued Gallo in 1995 for selling a "margarita" cooler, saying that only a drink containing tequila could be called a margarita. The case was settled in 1996 when Gallo agreed to downplay the margarita theme.

Further litigation followed that year when rival Kendall-Jackson sued Gallo for trademark infringement over Gallo's new wine brand, Turning Leaf (Kendall-Jackson claimed the Gallo wine tried to copy its Vintner's Reserve bottle and label). In 1997 a jury ruled in Gallo's favor. (A federal appeals court supported that decision in 1998.) Co-president David Gallo, son of Ernest, died of a heart attack at age 57 in 1997.

Chairman: Ernest Gallo
Co-President: James E. Coleman
Co-President: Joseph E. Gallo
Co-President: Robert J. Gallo
EVP, Marketing: Albion Fenderson
EVP and General Counsel: Jack B. Owens
VP, Controller and Assistant Treasurer: Tony Youga
VP, Human Resources: Mike Chase
VP, Information Systems: Kent Kushar
VP, Media: Sue McClelland
VP, National Sales: Gary Ippolito
VP and Secretary: Charles M. Crawford

LOCATIONS

HQ: 600 Yosemite Blvd., Modesto, CA 95354
Phone: 209-341-3111   **Fax:** 209-341-3569
Web site: http://www.gallo.com

E. & J. Gallo Winery has four wineries in the California counties of Fresno, Livingston, Modesto, and Sonoma and vineyards throughout the region.

PRODUCTS/OPERATIONS

Labels

Anapamu	Gallo Estate
Andre	Gallo Sonoma
Ballatore	Gossamer Bay
Bartles & Jaymes	Indigo Hills
Boone's Farm	Livingston Cellars
Burlwood	Marcelina
Carlo Rossi	Night Train Express
Copperidge	Peter Vella
E & J Brandy	The Reserve Cellars of
Ecco Domani	Ernest & Julio Gallo
Eden Roc	Sheffield
Ernest & Julio Gallo	Thunderbird
Ernest & Julio Gallo	Tott's
Sonoma Estate	Turning Leaf
Fairbanks	Zabaco
Gallo	

COMPETITORS

Allied Domecq	Kendall-Jackson
Anheuser-Busch	LVMH
Asahi Breweries	Pernod Ricard
Bacardi-Martini	R.H. Phillips
Beringer	Ravenswood Winery
Brown-Forman	Robert Mondavi
Canandaigua Brands	Seagram
Chalone Wine	Sebastiani Vineyards
Concha y Toro	Sutter Home
Diageo	Wine Group
Foster's Brewing	

HISTORICAL FINANCIALS & EMPLOYEES

Private company FYE: December 31	Annual Growth	1989	1990	1991	1992	1993	1994	1995	1996	1997	1998
Estimated sales ($ mil.)	4.6%	1,000	1,050	1,100	1,000	1,100	980	1,100	1,200	1,300	1,500
Employees	6.0%	2,950	3,000	3,000	3,000	4,000	4,000	4,000	5,000	5,000	5,000

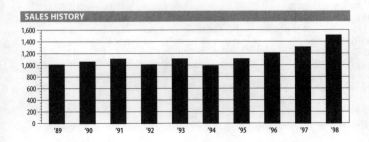

SALES HISTORY

THE EARTHGRAINS COMPANY

OVERVIEW

Man shall not live by bread alone, but if he had to, The Earthgrains Company would be happy. St. Louis-based Earthgrains is the US's second-largest wholesale baking company, after Interstate Bakeries. The company distributes its fresh baked goods and refrigerated dough products to retail grocers and food outlets in nearly 30 states, mostly in the southern US.

In addition to retail brands such as Rainbo (white breads, buns, and rolls), Grant's Farm (wheat breads), IronKids (high-fiber white bread), and Break Cake (snack cakes and sweets), Earthgrains offers more than 100 store brands of refrigerated dough, and it supplies buns, rolls, and other specialty breads to fast-food chains such as Burger King and Pizza Hut. Earthgrains also operates about 275 thrift stores.

The company's Bimbo subsidiary is one of the largest producers of fresh baked goods in Spain and Portugal. Earthgrains' EuroDough subsidiary is France's top refrigerated dough supplier; it also distributes its CroustiPate, HappyRoll, and store-brand products elsewhere in Western Europe, and it makes frozen dough products for Pillsbury.

Like good dough, the firm's presence has been rising as it expands through acquisitions in the US and Europe. Earthgrains' product lines have also grown as it adds higher-margin items such as potato bread, sesame seed bagels, and caramelized onion French bread.

HISTORY

The company today known as The Earthgrains Company was founded in 1925 by former Continental Baking president Winfield Campbell. When A. L. Taggart invested in the six-bakery company three years later, it was renamed Campbell Taggart Associated Bakeries. By 1929 it had 19 bakeries, and its brands included Betsy Ross, Colonial, Holsum, Kilpatrick, and Rainbo.

Campbell Taggart continued to grow by acquiring small, local bakeries. It added 25 bakeries during the 1930s alone. During the 1950s, as supermarkets began developing their own bakeries, many small operators went out of business or entered the folds of large bakers such as Campbell Taggart.

Through a 1971 joint venture with Mexican baker Grupo Industrial Bimbo, Campbell Taggart operated and eventually bought Bimbo, Spain's largest baking company. The company entered the premium-bread market in 1975 with its Earth Grains brand.

When the FTC hampered further company acquisitions of US bakeries, Campbell Taggart acquired the El Chico restaurant chain in 1977. El Chico began a rapid downward spiral due to overexpansion and Campbell Taggart's inexperience in the restaurant industry.

The situation was resolved when St. Louis-based brewer Anheuser-Busch bought the baking company for $560 million in 1982, arranging a hasty sale of El Chico to finalize the deal. By then the #2 baker in the US, Campbell Taggart helped the big beer company become more established in the food industry; the two enterprises shared yeast-making facilities and settled into what would be a 14-year marriage. Anheuser-Busch, deciding to focus on its core business, installed executive Barry Beracha as CEO of Campbell Taggart in 1993 and began preparing the bakery subsidiary to stand on its own. Between 1993 and 1995 Campbell Taggart spent $140 million on restructuring to address overcapacity. It shut down or sold 13 plants, laid off employees, and pruned marginal businesses. In 1996 Anheuser-Busch spun off its baking subsidiary as The Earthgrains Company.

Earthgrains opened a research and development facility and began eyeing potential acquisitions. During 1996 it picked up Heiner's Bakery and swapped a Virginia plant for Interstate Bakeries' Texas routes; in 1997 it bought New Mexico-based H & L Baking.

In 1998 Earthgrains bought bread wholesaler CooperSmith for $193 million, strengthening its southeastern presence. It also bought San Luis Sourdough, a baker selling specialty breads in California and Arizona, and it picked up South Carolina and Alabama plants from Southern Bakeries that year.

European expansion included the purchase of French dough maker Chevalier Servant in 1998, which became part of new subsidiary EuroDough. In 1999 EuroDough became the king biscuit of France's refrigerated dough suppliers when it bought Patrick Raulet. Earthgrains also purchased Spanish sweets baker Reposteira Martinez Group.

Also in 1999 Earthgrains offered bonuses of up to a year's salary to about 220 managers if the company can hit certain targets (including 5% sales growth and 13% earnings growth) over the next three years.

OFFICERS

Chairman and CEO: Barry H. Beracha, age 57,
$1,015,000 pay
President Worldwide Bakery Products:
John W. Iselin Jr., age 46,
$396,998 pay (prior to promotion)
**President Worldwide Refrigerated Dough Products,
Technology and Purchasing:** William H. Opdyke,
age 55, $332,674 pay
VP and CFO: Mark H. Krieger, age 45, $282,480 pay
EVP European Bakery Products: Xavier Argente, age 39
VP Corporate Planning and Development:
Bryan A. Torcivia, age 39
VP Diversified Products (US Bakery Products):
Larry Pearson, age 53
VP, General Counsel, and Coporate Secretary:
Joseph M. Noelker, age 50
VP Human Resources: Edward J. Wizeman, age 57
**VP Operations & Administration (US Refrigerated
Dough Products):** Todd A. Brown, age 51,
$272,283 pay
Auditors: PricewaterhouseCoopers LLP

LOCATIONS

HQ: 8400 Maryland Ave., St. Louis, MO 63105
Phone: 314-259-7000   **Fax:** 314-259-7036
Web site: http://www.earthgrains.com

The Earthgrains Company operates more than 40
bakeries in the US and about a dozen in Europe.

1999 Sales & Operating Income

	Sales		Operating Income	
	$ mil.	% of total	$ mil.	% of total
US	1,611	84	79	100
Europe	314	16	(6)	—
Total	**1,925**	**100**	**73**	**100**

PRODUCTS/OPERATIONS

US Brands
Bost's
Break Cake (snack cakes)
Colonial
Cooper's Mill
Country Recipe
Earth Grains
Grant's Farm
Heiner's
IronKids
Kern's
Merico (toaster pastries,
refrigerated dough)
Rainbo
San Luis Sourdough
Signature Line (gourmet
bread)
Smith's

Sunbeam (licensed brand)
Waldensian

European Brands
Bimbo
BimboCao (kids' chocolate
bun)
Bony (snack cakes)
CroustiPate (refrigerated
dough)
HappyRoll (refrigerated
dough)
Madame Brioche
Martinez
Semilla de Or
Silueta
Tigreton (snack cakes)

COMPETITORS

Bestfoods
Campbell Soup
Danone
Flowers Industries
Industrial Bimbo
Interstate Bakeries
Keebler
Kellogg
McKee Foods
Nabisco Holdings
Nestlé
Pillsbury
Sara Lee
Specialty Foods
Tasty Baking

HISTORICAL FINANCIALS & EMPLOYEES

NYSE symbol: EGR FYE: March 31	Annual Growth	1990	1991	1992	1993	1994	1995	1996	1997	1998	1999
Sales ($ mil.)	1.4%	—	—	—	1,766	1,741	1,721	1,665	1,663	1,719	1,925
Net income ($ mil.)	(0.3%)	—	—	—	39	(27)	11	(7)	16	36	38
Income as % of sales	—	—	—	—	2.2%	—	0.7%	—	1.0%	2.1%	2.0%
Earnings per share ($)	49.2%	—	—	—	—	—	—	—	0.40	0.85	0.89
Stock price - FY high ($)	—	—	—	—	—	—	—	—	14.34	23.75	37.25
Stock price - FY low ($)	—	—	—	—	—	—	—	—	7.28	12.31	20.13
Stock price - FY close ($)	33.2%	—	—	—	—	—	—	—	12.50	22.09	22.19
P/E - high	—	—	—	—	—	—	—	—	36	28	42
P/E - low	—	—	—	—	—	—	—	—	18	14	23
Dividends per share ($)	93.6%	—	—	—	—	—	—	—	0.04	0.09	0.15
Book value per share ($)	5.1%	—	—	—	—	—	—	—	13.51	14.11	14.92
Employees	4.9%	—	—	—	—	—	16,000	16,200	14,000	18,000	19,400

STOCK PRICE HISTORY

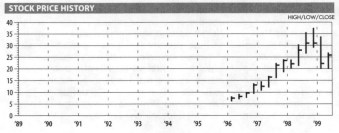

HIGH/LOW/CLOSE

1999 FISCAL YEAR-END

Debt ratio: 36.6%
Return on equity: 5.9%
Cash ($ mil.): 53
Current ratio: 1.36
Long-term debt ($ mil.): 369
No. of shares (mil.): 43
Dividends
  Yield: 0.7%
  Payout: 16.9%
Market value ($ mil.): 951

EASTMAN CHEMICAL COMPANY

OVERVIEW

Eastman Chemical can recall its past through photos — it was once part of film giant Eastman Kodak. The Kingsport, Tennessee-based company has developed into a major producer of chemicals, fibers, and plastics. It supplies industrial customers with materials used in the manufacture of items such as food and beverage containers, toothbrushes, garden hoses, chewing gum, swim and ski goggles, shower curtains, and suntan oils. The packaging and tobacco industries are Eastman's largest customers — Eastman Chemical is one of the world's largest makers of polyethylene terephthalate (PET), used to

make plastic packaging; it also churns out tons of the acetate tow used in cigarette filters.

Eastman Chemical veteran and CEO Earnest Deavenport has remolded the company from a Kodak division into a major independent player with a growing international presence. However, the company's earnings have been hurt by lower prices caused by competition and overcapacity and by the effects of financial problems in Asia, Russia, and Latin America. Eastman Chemical is retrenching by reducing capital investment while continuing its efforts to cut costs by $500 million by 2000.

HISTORY

Eastman Chemical went public on January 1, 1994, but it traces its roots back to the 19th century. George Eastman, after developing a method for dry-plate photography, established the Eastman Dry Plate and Film Company in 1884 in Rochester, New York (the name was changed to Eastman Kodak in 1892).

In 1886 Eastman hired Henry Reichenbach as his first scientist to help with the creation and manufacture of new photographic chemicals. As time passed, Reichenbach and the company's other scientists came up with chemicals that were either not directly related to photography or had uses in addition to photography. For instance, cellulose acetate, developed as a base for safety film, was used to coat airplane wings during WWII.

Eastman bought a wood distillation plant in Kingsport, Tennessee, in 1920 and formed the Tennessee Eastman Corporation to make methanol and acetone for the manufacture of photographic chemicals. The company, by this time called Kodak, introduced acetate yarn and Tenite, a cellulose ester plastic, in the early 1930s. In 1938 Kodak formed a joint venture with General Mills, called Distillation Products, to develop a process for molecular distillation, and the firm soon began supplying vitamin E products.

During WWII the company formed Holston Defense to make explosives for the US's armed forces. Kodak began to vertically integrate Tennessee Eastman's operations during the 1950s, acquiring A. M. Tenney Associates, Tennessee Eastman's selling agent for its acetate yarn products, in 1950. It also established Texas Eastman, opening a plant in Longview to produce ethyl alcohol and aldehydes, raw materials used in fiber and film production.

At the end of 1952, Kodak created Eastman

Chemical Products to sell alcohols, plastics, and fibers made by Tennessee Eastman and Texas Eastman.

That year Tennessee Eastman developed cellulose acetate filter tow, used in cigarette filters. In the late 1950s the company introduced Kodel polyester fiber. Kodak created Carolina Eastman Company in 1968, opening a plant in Columbia, South Carolina, to produce Kodel and other polyester products. It also created Eastman Chemicals Division to handle its chemical operations.

Eastman Chemicals introduced polyethylene terephthalate (PET) resin, used to make containers, in the late 1970s. It acquired biological and molecular instrumentation manufacturer International Biotechnologies in 1987.

Eastman Chemicals Division became Eastman Chemical Company in 1990. In 1993 it exited the polyester fiber business. When Kodak spun off Eastman Chemical in early 1994, the new company was saddled with $1.8 billion in debt.

In 1996 Eastman Chemical started production at a new PET plant in Mexico. Lower prices due to industry oversupply reduced the company's earnings for PET that year. The company won a $12 million patent-infringement suit against Goodyear in 1997 for Goodyear's use of Eastman's PET-making process. In 1998 company continued its international push, opening plants in Argentina, Malaysia, and the Netherlands. It also signed a joint venture with a Chinese company to produce resins for adhesive manufacturers. In 1999 Eastman Chemical added to its international locations, opening a manufacturing plant in Singapore and an office in Bangkok. It also paid $400 million for Lawter International, a maker of specialty chemicals for ink and coatings.

Chairman and CEO: Earnest W. Deavenport Jr., age 60, $1,266,331 pay
VC and EVP, Business Organizations: R. Wiley Bourne Jr., age 61, $652,487 pay
SVP: James L. Chitwood, age 55, $524,440 pay
SVP and General Counsel: Harold L. Henderson, age 63, $472,533 pay
SVP and CFO: James P. Rogers
VP Communications and Public Affairs: Betty W. DeVinney, age 54
VP and Comptroller: Patrick R. Kinsey, age 53
VP Human Resources and Health, Safety, Environment, and Security: B. Fielding Rolston, age 57
VP, Worldwide Manufacturing: Garland S. Williamson, age 54
Auditors: PricewaterhouseCoopers LLP

LOCATIONS

HQ: 100 N. Eastman Rd., Kingsport, TN 37660
Phone: 423-229-2000   **Fax:** 423-229-1351
Web site: http://www.eastman.com

Eastman Chemical's principal plants are located in Batesville, Arkansas; Columbia and Roebuck, South Carolina; Kingsport, Tennessee; Longview, Texas; and Rochester, New York; as well as in Cosoleacaque, Mexico; Hartlepool, Llangefni, and Workington, UK; Hong Kong; Kuantan, Malaysia; Pulau Sakra, Singapore; San Roque, Spain; Rotterdam, the Netherlands; and Toronto.

1998 Sales

	$ mil.	% of total
US	2,764	62
Other countries	1,717	38
Total	**4,481**	**100**

PRODUCTS/OPERATIONS

1998 Sales & Operating Income

	Sales		Operating Income	
	$ mil.	% of total	$ mil.	% of total
Specialty & performance	2,736	61	357	75
Core plastics	1,071	24	(40)	—
Chemical intermediates	674	15	117	25
Total	**4,481**	**100**	**434**	**100**

Selected Products

Specialty and Performance
Acetate tow
Acetate yarn
Cellulose esters
Chlorinated polyolefins
Ester-alcohol
Glycols
Hydrocarbon resins

Core Plastics
Cellulose acetate
PEN polymer

PET polyester and copolyester

Chemical Intermediates
Acids
Alcohols
Aldehydes
Hydroquinone
Plasticizers
Specialty ketones/nitriles

COMPETITORS

Akzo Nobel	GE	Mobil
AlliedSignal	Geon	Phillips
BASF AG	Hercules	Petroleum
Bayer AG	Hoechst AG	Rhône-Poulenc
BP Amoco	Huntsman	Royal
Chevron	ICI	Dutch/Shell
Dow Chemical	Laporte	S.C. Johnson
DSM	Lyondell	Union Carbide
DuPont	Chemical	Wellman
Exxon	Mitsubishi	

HISTORICAL FINANCIALS & EMPLOYEES

NYSE symbol: EMN FYE: December 31	Annual Growth	1989	1990	1991	1992	1993	1994	1995	1996	1997	1998
Sales ($ mil.)	3.6%	3,246	3,433	3,614	3,811	3,903	4,329	5,040	4,782	4,678	4,481
Net income ($ mil.)	(6.0%)	433	359	336	292	(209)	336	559	380	286	249
Income as % of sales	—	13.3%	10.5%	9.3%	7.7%	—	7.8%	11.1%	7.9%	6.1%	5.6%
Earnings per share ($)	4.9%	—	—	—	—	2.46	4.04	6.78	4.79	3.63	3.13
Stock price - FY high ($)	—	—	—	—	—	45.50	56.00	69.50	76.25	65.38	72.94
Stock price - FY low ($)	—	—	—	—	—	42.88	39.50	48.50	50.75	50.75	43.50
Stock price - FY close ($)	(0.2%)	—	—	—	—	45.25	50.50	62.38	55.25	59.56	44.75
P/E - high	—	—	—	—	—	18	14	10	16	18	23
P/E - low	—	—	—	—	—	17	10	7	11	14	14
Dividends per share ($)	—	—	—	—	—	0.00	1.20	1.62	1.70	1.76	2.20
Book value per share ($)	13.7%	—	—	—	—	12.85	15.59	19.11	21.12	22.40	24.45
Employees	(1.0%)	17,532	17,561	17,796	18,457	18,043	17,495	17,709	17,500	16,100	16,000

STOCK PRICE HISTORY
HIGH/LOW/CLOSE

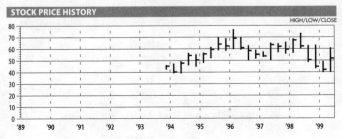

1998 FISCAL YEAR-END

Debt ratio: 46.0%
Return on equity: 12.9%
Cash ($ mil.): 29
Current ratio: 1.44
Long-term debt ($ mil.): 1,649
No. of shares (mil.): 79
Dividends
  Yield: 4.9%
  Payout: 70.3%
Market value ($ mil.): 3,540

EASTMAN KODAK COMPANY

OVERVIEW

Eastman Kodak has got the picture — cut costs or die. The venerable Rochester, New York-based photo products firm is trimming its noncore operations (notably copiers) and refocusing on film and digital imaging products. It's also cropping out about one-fifth of its employees.

Kodak, the #1 maker of film in the US, is shooting for a big share of the digital imaging market, which allows photos to be altered via computer and stored on the Internet. The company is striving to make photography an everyday occurrence in consumers' lives.

The company is also attempting to take the high ground in the world's fastest-growing film market by spending $1 billion in China for plant modernization and infrastructure. Meanwhile, Kodak is engaged in an increasingly fierce price-cutting competition in the US film market with global rival Fuji Photo.

HISTORY

After developing a method for dry-plate photography, George Eastman established The Eastman Dry Plate and Film Company in 1884. In 1888 it introduced its first camera, a small, easy-to-use device that was loaded with enough film for 100 pictures. To develop the film, owners mailed the camera to the company, which returned it with the pictures and more film. The firm settled on the name Eastman Kodak in 1892, after Eastman tried many combinations of letters starting and ending with "k," which he thought was a "strong, incisive sort of letter." The user-friendly Brownie camera followed in 1900. Three years later Kodak introduced a home-movie camera, projector, and film.

Ailing and convinced that his work was done, Eastman committed suicide in 1932. Kodak continued to dominate the photography industry with the introduction of color film (Kodachrome, 1935) and a handheld movie camera (1951). The company established US plants to produce the chemicals, plastics, and fibers used in its film production.

The Instamatic, introduced in 1963, became Kodak's biggest success. The camera's foolproof film cartridge eliminated the need for loading in the dark. By 1976 Kodak had sold an estimated 60 million Instamatics—50 million more cameras than all its competitors combined. Subsequent introductions included the Kodak instant camera (1976) and the unsuccessful disc camera (1982).

In the 1980s Kodak diversified into electronic publishing, batteries, floppy disks (Verbatim, 1985; sold 1990), pharmaceuticals (Sterling Drug, sold 1994), and do-it-yourself and household products (L&F Products, sold 1994).

Kodak entered a joint research and development project with four Japanese photo giants (Canon, Nikon, Minolta, and Fuji Photo) in 1992 to develop the Advanced Photography System. Also that year the company introduced the Photo CD, a CD capable of storing photographs. George Fisher, former chairman of Motorola,

became Kodak's chairman in 1993. Fisher began cutting debt by selling noncore assets. Kodak spun off Eastman Chemical in early 1994. In 1996 the company sold its money-losing copier sales and services business and its document management outsourcing operations to Danka Business Systems.

The following year Kodak created a new subsidiary when it bought the document management operations from Wang Laboratories (now part of Getronics) for $260 million. A severe drop in earnings that year contributed to Fisher's decision to cut nearly 20,000 workers from the payroll by 2000. Also in 1997 the World Trade Organization rejected Kodak's two-year-old complaint that Japan had denied the company fair access to its film market in favor of Fuji.

In 1998 the company formed deals that expanded its digital offerings, such as one that delivers pictures to America Online subscribers and a collaboration with Intel and Adobe Systems on Picture CD, which allows consumers to manipulate, print, and send personal photos from their computers. Kodak teamed up with online auction house eBay in 1999 to allow eBay users to display photos with their listings via Kodak's PhotoNet service.

Kodak acquired the medical imaging business of Imation for $530 million in 1998. That year the company unloaded more of its noncore operations, including its 450-store Fox Photo chain and drug delivery company NanoSystems; in 1999 it sold its copier production unit to Germany's Heidelberger Druckmaschinen for about $200 million and planned to sell Eastman Software.

In May 1999 Kodak agreed to pay $13 million in retroactive and current pay raises to 12% of its female and 33% of its black employees in response to internal complaints.

The company announced chairman and CEO George Fisher would give his CEO title to president and COO Daniel Carp in January 2000.

OFFICERS

Chairman and CEO: George M. C. Fisher, age 58, $3,710,000 pay
President and COO: Daniel A. Carp, age 50, $1,286,313 pay
EVP and Assistant COO: Carl F. Kohrt, age 55, $863,500 pay
EVP and Assistant COO: Eric L. Steenburgh, age 57
SVP: Richard T. Bourns, age 64, $618,510 pay
SVP of Business Strategy and Information Technology and Acting CFO: Jesse J. Greene Jr., age 54
SVP and Chief Marketing Officer: Carl E. Gustin Jr., age 47
SVP; President, Consumer Imaging: Robert J. Keegan, age 51
SVP and Director Human Resources: Michael P. Morley
SVP and General Counsel: Gary P. Van Graafeiland
Auditors: PricewaterhouseCoopers LLP

LOCATIONS

HQ: 343 State St., Rochester, NY 14650
Phone: 716-724-4000 **Fax:** 716-724-1089
Web site: http://www.kodak.com

Eastman Kodak has manufacturing plants in Australia, Brazil, Canada, China, France, Germany, India, Indonesia, Japan, Mexico, Russia, the UK, and the US.

1998 Sales

	$ mil.	% of total
US	6,417	48
Europe, Middle East & Africa	3,701	28
Asia/Pacific	2,009	15
Canada & Latin America	1,279	9
Total	**13,406**	**100**

PRODUCTS/OPERATIONS

1998 Sales

	$ mil.	% of total
Consumer Imaging	7,164	53
Kodak Professional	1,840	14
Health Imaging	1,526	11
Other Imaging	2,876	22
Total	**13,406**	**100**

Selected Products and Services

Consumer Imaging
Cameras
Film
Image enhancing software
Kiosks and scanning systems
Photographic chemicals and papers
Processing services
Projectors

Kodak Professional
Digital cameras
Films
Photographic chemicals and papers

Photographic services
Printers
Scanners

Health Imaging
Medical films
Photographic chemicals
Photographic services for health care professionals
Processing equipment

Other Imaging
Applications software
Audiovisual equipment
Microfilm products
Motion picture films

COMPETITORS

Agfa
Canon
Casio Computer
Fuji Photo
Hewlett-Packard
Leica Camera
Matsushita
3M
Minolta
Nikon
Corporation
Olympus Optical Co.
Philips Electronics
Polaroid
Ricoh
Seattle FilmWorks
Sharp
Sony
Xerox

HISTORICAL FINANCIALS & EMPLOYEES

NYSE symbol: EK FYE: December 31	Annual Growth	1989	1990	1991	1992	1993	1994	1995	1996	1997	1998
Sales ($ mil.)	(3.5%)	18,398	18,908	19,419	20,183	16,364	13,557	14,980	15,968	14,538	13,406
Net income ($ mil.)	11.3%	529	703	17	1,146	(1,515)	557	1,252	1,288	5	1,390
Income as % of sales	—	2.9%	3.7%	0.1%	5.7%	—	4.1%	8.4%	8.1%	0.0%	10.4%
Earnings per share ($)	11.2%	1.63	2.17	0.05	3.41	(4.64)	1.63	3.67	3.82	0.01	4.24
Stock price - FY high ($)	—	52.38	43.88	49.75	50.75	65.00	56.38	70.38	85.00	94.75	88.94
Stock price - FY low ($)	—	40.00	33.75	37.63	37.75	40.25	40.69	47.13	65.13	53.31	57.94
Stock price - FY close ($)	6.4%	41.13	41.63	48.25	40.50	56.25	47.75	67.00	80.25	60.56	72.00
P/E - high	—	32	20	995	15	—	35	19	22	9,475	21
P/E - low	—	25	16	753	11	—	25	13	17	5,331	14
Dividends per share ($)	(1.4%)	2.00	2.00	2.00	2.00	2.00	1.70	1.60	1.60	1.72	1.76
Book value per share ($)	(5.5%)	20.46	20.75	18.79	20.12	10.15	11.82	14.81	14.27	9.78	12.35
Employees	(5.1%)	137,750	134,450	133,200	132,600	110,400	96,300	96,600	94,800	97,500	86,200

STOCK PRICE HISTORY

HIGH/LOW/CLOSE

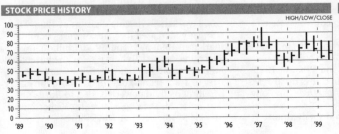

1998 FISCAL YEAR-END

Debt ratio: 11.2%
Return on equity: 34.9%
Cash ($ mil.): 457
Current ratio: 0.91
Long-term debt ($ mil.): 504
No. of shares (mil.): 323
Dividends
  Yield: 2.4%
  Payout: 41.5%
Market value ($ mil.): 23,241

EATON CORPORATION

OVERVIEW

Eaton plays for keeps — if it can't win, it doesn't play. The diversified Cleveland-based manufacturing company is nurturing businesses in which it holds a strong market share. Eaton's product line includes electric power distribution and control equipment, engine components, hydraulic products, and switches for aerospace, automotive, and marine use, among others. The company also makes ion-implanter equipment used by semiconductor manufacturers.

Eaton has been tweaking its operations to find the optimum product mix. It has acquired Aeroquip-Vickers, a maker of aerospace and auto components, and has entered an alliance to make automotive cylinder heads with Fiat subsidiary Teskid Group.

Eaton has more than 150 manufacturing facilities in 25 countries. A fourth of its sales are to customers outside the US. Eaton is expanding into the emerging markets of Asia, Eastern Europe, and Latin America.

HISTORY

In 1911 Joseph Eaton and Viggo Torbensen started the Torbensen Gear and Axle Company to make an internal-gear rear truck axle patented by Torbensen in 1902. The company moved from Newark, New Jersey, to Cleveland in 1914.

After Republic Motor Truck bought Torbensen (1917), Eaton formed the Eaton Axle Company (1919), repurchased Torbensen (1922), and by 1931 had bought 11 more auto parts businesses (adding bumpers, springs, heaters, and engine parts to its line). In 1932 the company became Eaton Manufacturing.

The Depression flattened automobile sales, and profits plummeted. Heavy wartime demand helped Eaton recover, and in 1946 the company bought Dynamatic (eddy-current drives). Eaton died in 1949.

To diversify, the company bought Fuller Manufacturing (truck transmissions, 1958), Dole Valve (1963), and Yale & Towne Manufacturing (locks and forklift trucks, 1963). The acquisitions augmented Eaton's international business, and foreign sales increased from virtually zero in 1961 to 20% of sales by 1966. That year the company changed its name to Eaton Yale & Towne (it adopted its present name in 1971).

Eaton sold the lock business in 1978 to Scovill Manufacturing and bought Cutler-Hammer (electronics), Kenway (automated storage and retrieval systems), and Samuel Moore (plastics and fluid power). By 1980 the company was supplying space shuttle landing systems and making traffic-control systems for airways and waterways.

Downturns in the truck and auto industries forced Eaton to close 30 plants and trim 23,000 jobs between 1979 and 1983. In 1982 the company reported its first loss in 50 years and decided to diversify as a high-technology firm and expand overseas.

From 1984 to 1993, Eaton spent almost $4 billion in capital improvements and R&D that enabled it to debut several new products. In 1986 it bought Consolidated Controls (precision instruments), Pacific-Sierra Research (computer and defense systems), and Singer Controls (valves and switches). Eaton also put its defense electronics business (AIL Systems) up for sale, but there was no buyer.

Eaton's acquisitions in the early 1990s included Nordhauser Ventil (automotive engine valves, Germany), Control Displays (flight-deck equipment), Heinemann Electric (hydraulic-magnetic circuit breakers), and the automotive switch business of diversified industrial heavyweight Illinois Tool Works. In 1994 Eaton's $1.1 billion purchase of Westinghouse's electrical distribution and control business tripled the size of Eaton's electrical power and controls operation.

In 1995 Eaton bought Emwest Products (electrical switch gear and controls, Australia); the IKU Group, a Dutch auto controls firm; and a golf grip maker in Thailand. The next year it purchased CAPCO Automotive Products, a Brazilian maker of truck transmissions. Eaton bought semiconductor equipment maker Fusion Systems in 1997. That year the company in turn sold its appliance-control business to Siebe PLC and sold a majority of its high-tech defense electronics subsidiary, AIL Systems, to management. In 1998 Eaton sold its heavy-axle and brake business to Dana and its suspension business to Oxford Automotive. Eaton closed and consolidated plants and laid off more than 1,000 workers in its chip division in 1998. The company increased its share of the hydraulics market in 1999 by spending $1.7 billion for Aeroquip-Vickers. To help pay for the purchase, Eaton has sold its engineered-fasteners business to TransTechnology for $173 million and is selling its fluid power division to Borg-Warner and is seeking a buyer for Vickers' former electronics-systems division.

OFFICERS

Chairman and CEO: Stephen R. Hardis, age 63, $1,920,211 pay
President and COO: Alexander M. Cutler, age 47, $1,355,519 pay
EVP and General Counsel: Gerald L. Gherlein, age 60, $661,819 pay
EVP, Chief Financial and Planning Officer: Adrian T. Dillon, age 45
SVP and Group Executive, Hydraulics, Semiconductor Equipment, and Specialty Controls: Brian R. Bachman, age 53
SVP and Group Executive, Automotive: Bruce E. Taylor
SVP and Group Executive, Truck Components: Thomas W. O'Boyle, age 56, $763,072 pay
SVP and Group Executive, Aeroquip: Howard M. Selland
SVP and Group Executive, Cutler-Hammer: David M. Wathen, age 46
VP Growth Initiatives: Randy Carson, age 48
VP, Human Resources: Susan J. Cook, age 51
VP and Treasurer: Robert E. Parmenter, age 46
VP, Semiconductor Equipment Operations: Mary G. Puma
VP and Controller: Billie K. Rawot, age 47
Auditors: Ernst & Young LLP

LOCATIONS

HQ: Eaton Center, Cleveland, OH 44114-2584
Phone: 216-523-5000   **Fax:** 216-523-4787
Web site: http://www.eaton.com

Eaton has more than 150 manufacturing facilities in 25 countries.

PRODUCTS/OPERATIONS

1998 Sales

	$ mil.	% of total
Industrial & commercial controls	2,320	35
Automotive components	1,943	30
Truck components	1,465	22
Hydraulics & other components	599	9
Semiconductor equipment	267	4
Divested operations	31	—
Total	**6,625**	**100**

COMPETITORS

A. O. Smith	Meritor
AlliedSignal	Metso
American Standard	Navistar
Applied Materials	PACCAR
Arvin Industries	Parker Hannifin
Borg-Warner Automotive	Powell Industries
Cooper Industries	Precision Castparts
Cummins Engine	Raytheon
Dana	Robert Bosch
Detroit Diesel	Rockwell International
Emerson	Sauer
Genus	Siemens
Honeywell	SPX
Hubbell	Thomas & Betts
Intermet	TRW
ITT Industries	United Technologies
Johnson Controls	Woodhead Industries
MascoTech	

HISTORICAL FINANCIALS & EMPLOYEES

NYSE symbol: ETN FYE: December 31	Annual Growth	1989	1990	1991	1992	1993	1994	1995	1996	1997	1998
Sales ($ mil.)	6.8%	3,671	3,639	3,381	3,869	4,401	6,052	6,822	6,961	7,563	6,625
Net income ($ mil.)	5.0%	225	179	74	(128)	187	333	399	349	410	349
Income as % of sales	—	6.1%	4.9%	2.2%	—	4.2%	5.5%	5.8%	5.0%	5.4%	5.3%
Earnings per share ($)	5.3%	3.01	2.53	1.10	(1.86)	2.45	4.35	5.08	4.46	5.24	4.80
Stock price - FY high ($)	—	33.75	32.19	33.13	41.63	55.38	62.13	62.50	70.88	103.38	99.63
Stock price - FY low ($)	—	26.50	20.38	23.31	30.88	38.25	43.88	45.25	50.38	67.25	57.50
Stock price - FY close ($)	10.6%	28.50	24.94	32.31	40.81	50.50	49.50	53.63	69.75	89.25	70.69
P/E - high	—	11	13	30	—	23	14	12	16	20	21
P/E - low	—	9	8	21	—	16	10	9	11	13	12
Dividends per share ($)	6.5%	1.00	1.05	1.10	1.10	1.22	1.20	1.50	1.60	1.72	1.76
Book value per share ($)	7.1%	15.51	16.81	16.92	13.67	15.50	21.54	25.45	28.02	27.72	28.69
Employees	2.8%	38,734	36,603	35,656	38,000	38,000	51,000	52,000	54,000	49,000	49,500

STOCK PRICE HISTORY

HIGH/LOW/CLOSE

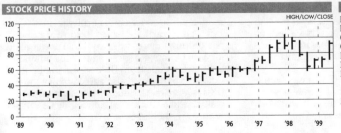

1998 FISCAL YEAR-END

Debt ratio: 36.7%
Return on equity: 17.0%
Cash ($ mil.): 80
Current ratio: 1.31
Long-term debt ($ mil.): 1,191
No. of shares (mil.): 72
Dividends
  Yield: 2.5%
  Payout: 36.7%
Market value ($ mil.): 5,068

EDISON INTERNATIONAL

OVERVIEW

Lights, camera, action! Deregulation — take one. Based in Southern California's Rosemead, Edison International lights up the set and keeps the cameras rolling. It also has its share of action as its home state welcomes competition to the electric utility industry. The holding company's largest subsidiary, Southern California Edison (SCE), distributes electricity to some 11 million people in central, coastal, and Southern California. Edison International also has energy interests and infrastructure investments overseas.

In response to deregulation, Edison International is divesting its California power plants, and independent power producer Edison Mission Energy (EME) is buying power plants in the Midwest and Northeast. EME has also extended the company's reach into Australia, Indonesia, Italy, New Zealand, the Philippines, Spain, Thailand, Turkey, and the UK.

Edison International is also pursuing nonutility opportunities. Its Edison Capital unit invests in public infrastructure, affordable housing, and energy operations worldwide — ranging from Latin American water systems to power facilities in South Africa. Its Edison Enterprises offers consumer services such as home security, appliance repair, electrical maintenance, and energy management.

HISTORY

In 1896 Elmer Peck, Walter Wright, William Staats, and George Baker organized the West Side Lighting Company to provide electricity to Los Angeles. The next year the firm merged with Los Angeles Edison Electric, which owned the rights to Thomas Edison's name and patents in its region. Baker was the first president. The new Edison Electric installed the first DC-power underground conduits in the Southwest.

In 1901 John Barnes Miller, the "Great Amalgamator," took charge. During Miller's 31-year reign the firm bought numerous Southern California utilities and built several power plants, including three hydroelectric plants. In 1909 it took the name Southern California Edison (SCE).

In 1917 SCE doubled its assets by buying Southern California electric interests from rival Pacific Light & Power. However, in 1912 the City of Los Angeles had decided to develop its own power distribution system, and by 1922 SCE's authority inside the city had ended.

A 1925 earthquake and the 1928 collapse of the St. Francis Dam severely damaged SCE's facilities, but SCE survived to finish consolidating its service territory with the 1964 purchase of California Electric Power.

Although SCE built 11 fossil-fueled power stations (1948-73), it also diversified its energy sources. In 1963 it broke ground on the San Onofre nuke with San Diego Gas & Electric (operations began in 1968), and in the late 1970s it began to build solar, geothermal, and wind power facilities.

Edison Mission Energy (EME) was founded in 1986 to develop, buy, and operate power plants around the world. The next year investment arm Edison Capital was formed, and SCEcorp became the holding company for SCE and the nonutility subsidiaries. EME began to build its portfolio in 1992 when it snagged a 51% stake in an Australian plant (now 100%-owned) and bought hydroelectric facilities in Spain, and again in 1995 when it bought UK hydroelectric company First Hydro. In 1995 it also kicked off a building regimen overseas, joining a consortium constructing a plant in Indonesia (increasing its stake to 40% in 1996) and beginning plants in Italy and Turkey.

The 1994 Northridge earthquake that cut power to 1 million SCE customers was nothing compared to the industry's seismic shifts. In 1996 SCEcorp became the more worldly sounding Edison International. California electricity markets opened to competition in 1998, and the utility decided to exit the low-margin power generation business in California: It sold 12 gas-fired plants for $1.2 billion. Overseas EME picked up 25% of a power plant being built in Thailand and a 50% stake in a cogeneration facility in Puerto Rico. In 1999 it bought 40% of Contact Energy, a New Zealand electric company.

Meanwhile, subsidiary Edison Select bought two California security firms in 1998, while Edison Capital invested in South African power projects and Latin American water projects. SCE got regulatory approval to offer telecommunications services in its utility territory in 1999. That year EME began looking at US opportunities, buying a Pennsylvania power plant for $1.8 billion and agreeing to buy Midwestern power plants from Unicom for $5 billion. Edison International also agreed to pay the UK's PowerGen $2 billion for two coal-fired plants, which will more than double its European power holdings.

Chairman and CEO, Edison International and Southern California Edison: John E. Bryson, age 55, $1,860,000 pay
EVP and General Counsel, Edison International and Southern California Edison: Bryant C. Danner, age 61, $848,500 pay
EVP and CFO, Edison International and Southern California Edison: Alan J. Fohrer, age 48, $760,000 pay
SVP and Treasurer, Edison International and Southern California Edison: Theodore F. Craver Jr., age 47
SVP Public Affairs, Edison International and Southern California Edison: Robert G. Foster, age 51
SVP Human Resources, Edison International and Southern California Edison: Lillian R. Gorman, age 45
SVP Customer Service: Pamela A. Bass, age 51
SVP Strategic Planning and New Business Development: William J. Heller, age 42
SVP Worldwide Operations: Ronald L. Litzinger
President and CEO, Edison Capital and Mission Land Company: Thomas R. McDaniel, age 49
President and CEO, Edison Mission Energy: Edward R. Muller, age 46, $822,000 pay
President and CEO, Edison Enterprises; Chairman and CEO, Edison Source and Edison Select; Chairman, President, and CEO, Edison Utility Services: Stephen E. Pazian, age 49
President and COO, Southern California Edison: Stephen E. Frank, age 57, $1,124,400 pay
EVP Generation Business Unit, Southern California Edison: Harold B. Ray, age 58, $727,000 pay
SVP Regulatory Policy and Affairs, Southern California Edison: John R. Fielder, age 53
SVP Trade and Distribution Business Unit, Southern California Edison: Richard M. Rosenblum, age 48
Auditors: Arthur Andersen LLP

HQ: 2244 Walnut Grove Ave., Rosemead, CA 91770
Phone: 626-302-1212   **Fax:** 626-302-2517
Web site: http://www.edison.com

1998 Sales

	$ mil.	% of total
Electric utility		
Ultimate consumers	7,105	70
Power exchange	1,348	13
Other	394	4
Diversified operations	1,361	13
Total	**10,208**	**100**

Selected Subsidiaries
Edison Capital (project financing, cash management, and venture capital for energy and infrastructure projects)
Edison Enterprises (retail products and services)
Edison Mission Energy (develops, owns, and operates cogeneration and independent power production projects)
Southern California Edison (electric utility)

AES	Portland General Electric
Dynegy	Protection One
El Paso Electric	Public Service (NM)
Enron	Sempra Energy
Entergy	Sierra Pacific Resources
MidAmerican Energy	Southern Company
PacifiCorp	TVA
PG&E	Tyco International

NYSE symbol: EIX FYE: December 31	Annual Growth	1989	1990	1991	1992	1993	1994	1995	1996	1997	1998
Sales ($ mil.)	5.1%	6,524	7,199	7,503	7,984	7,821	8,345	8,405	8,545	9,235	10,208
Net income ($ mil.)	(1.7%)	778	786	703	739	639	681	739	717	700	668
Income as % of sales	—	11.9%	10.9%	9.4%	9.3%	8.2%	8.2%	8.8%	8.4%	7.6%	6.5%
Earnings per share ($)	0.4%	1.78	1.80	1.61	1.66	1.42	1.52	1.65	1.63	1.73	1.84
Stock price - FY high ($)	—	20.50	20.13	23.69	23.81	25.75	20.50	18.00	20.38	27.81	31.00
Stock price - FY low ($)	—	15.50	16.75	18.00	20.13	19.88	12.38	14.38	15.00	19.38	25.13
Stock price - FY close ($)	3.9%	19.69	18.94	23.38	22.00	20.00	14.63	17.63	19.88	27.19	27.88
P/E - high	—	12	11	15	14	18	13	11	13	16	17
P/E - low	—	9	9	11	12	14	8	9	9	11	14
Dividends per share ($)	(2.2%)	1.26	1.30	1.34	1.38	1.41	1.21	1.00	1.00	1.00	1.03
Book value per share ($)	2.1%	12.10	12.59	12.91	13.30	13.31	13.73	14.34	14.90	14.71	14.55
Employees	(2.8%)	17,010	16,925	17,511	17,259	17,193	17,074	16,434	13,160	12,642	13,177

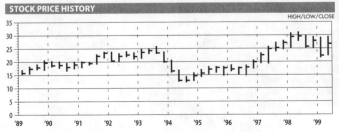

HIGH/LOW/CLOSE

1998 FISCAL YEAR-END
Debt ratio: 61.1%
Return on equity: 13.1%
Cash ($ mil.): 584
Current ratio: 0.73
Long-term debt ($ mil.): 8,008
No. of shares (mil.): 351
Dividends
  Yield: 3.7%
  Payout: 56.0%
Market value ($ mil.): 9,773

EG&G, INC.

OVERVIEW

EG&G didn't drop the A-bomb, but it helped make sure it would go off. Ironically, today the company makes equipment to detect bombs and explosives on airline passengers and in their luggage. The Wellesley, Massachusetts-based technology company, which worked on the trigger for the first atomic bomb, makes test and measurement instruments, engineered products, optoelectronics, and life sciences systems.

EG&G's instrument division's products include X-ray security systems used at airports around the world, food inspection devices, and radiation measurement instruments. The company's engineered products segment specializes in seals and valves for aerospace and semiconductor manufacturing. EG&G's optoelectronics products include light-emitting diodes and silicon panels. The Life Sciences unit makes diagnostic, drug discovery, and bio-analytical systems for use in the medical and pharmaceutical industries.

While acquisitions are positioning EG&G away from reliance on government service contracts (at one time representing three-fourths of the company's revenue), consolidation and divestitures are simplifying its operational structure. It sold, for example, its unit that provides technical services to the government and industrial customers.

The University of California owns about 7% of EG&G.

HISTORY

MIT professor Harold Edgerton invented the strobe light in 1931 while doing research on electric motors. After failing to sell the device to General Electric, he and former student Kenneth Germeshausen formed a consulting business using strobe lights and high-speed photography to solve manufacturing problems. As business picked up, they brought in another former student, Herbert Grier, and in 1947 formed Edgerton, Germeshausen and Grier. Their first contract was photographing nuclear weapons tests for the US government. The company went public in 1959 and changed its name to EG&G in 1966.

Over the next 30 years, EG&G bought scores of companies involved in electronic instruments and components, biomedical services, energy and nuclear weapons R&D, seal and gasket manufacturing, automotive testing, and various aspects of the aerospace industry. Key acquisitions included Reynolds Electrical & Engineering (1967), which provided support services for the Department of Energy (DOE) and the Department of Defense (including the nuclear weapon testing program); Sealol (1968), a maker of seals for industrial applications; and Automotive Research Associates (1973). Grier retired in 1976.

EG&G started providing support at the Kennedy Space Center in 1983. Company veteran John Kucharski became CEO in 1987 and chairman in 1988. That year EG&G secured a contract to operate the DOE's Mound facility in Miamisburg, Ohio, which was involved in R&D and production of components for nuclear weapons and generators used in spacecraft. In 1990 EG&G took over operation of the DOE's Rocky Flats nuclear weapon components production facility in Colorado. That year Edgerton died, at age 86.

The company bought the optoelectronics businesses of General Electric Canada in 1990, and the next year it purchased Heimann, a German maker of optoelectronic devices, from Siemens. EG&G acquired Finland's Wallac Group (analytical and diagnostic systems) from Procordia AB in 1993. The following year it bought IC Sensors and NoVOCs (environmental remediation).

The close of the Cold War put an end to DOE-sponsored nuclear weapon programs, and activists' questions about worker safety and environmental protection measures led to lawsuits against the company. In 1994 EG&G announced that it would discontinue the business (which accounted for about 50% of sales) as its contracts ran out. To accommodate this shift, the company began a costly reorganization that contributed to a loss that year.

In 1996 EG&G began testing its new airport security system for detecting plastic explosives (now marketed worldwide). The company in 1998 sold its mechanical components businesses (Sealol, Rotron) and created a separate Life Sciences unit. Kucharski retired that year and president Gregory Summe, a former AlliedSignal and General Electric executive, was named CEO (and later, chairman). EG&G in 1999 bought Lumen Technologies, a maker of specialty light sources, and the analytical instruments division of PE Corporation (formerly Perkin-Elmer) for $425 million — its largest purchase to date. (EG&G plans to take the PerkinElmer name.) The company also sold its technical services business to The Carlyle Group in a $250 million deal.

Chairman, President, and CEO: Gregory L. Summe,
age 42, $781,187 pay
SVP: Angelo D. Castellana, age 57, $583,578 pay
SVP and CFO: Robert F. Friel
SVP and General Counsel: Terrence L. Carlson
SVP, Human Resources: Richard F. Walsh, age 46
**VP; President, Engineered Products Strategic Business
Unit:** Robert A. Barrett, age 55
VP; President, Instruments Strategic Business Unit:
Robert J. Rosenthal, age 32
**VP; President, Optoelectronics Strategic Business
Unit:** John J. Engel, age 37
VP, Control and Treasury: Gregory D. Perry, age 38
VP, Investor Relations and Corporate Communications:
Deborah S. Lorenz, age 49
VP, Strategic Planning and Business Development:
Stephen P. De Falco, age 38
President, Life Sciences Strategic Business:
Patrik Dahlen, age 37
Treasurer: Daniel T. Heaney, age 45
Auditors: Arthur Andersen LLP

LOCATIONS

HQ: 45 William St., Wellesley, MA 02481
Phone: 781-237-5100　　**Fax:** 781-431-4255
Web site: http://www.egginc.com

EG&G has operations worldwide.

1998 Sales

	$ mil.	% of total
US	999	71
Germany	68	5
UK	48	3
Other countries	293	21
Total	**1,408**	**100**

PRODUCTS/OPERATIONS

1998 Sales

	$ mil.	% of total
Products	785	56
Services	623	44
Total	**1,408**	**100**

Products and Services

Optoelectronics
Airbag accelerometers
Beacons
Flashlamps
Flow control systems
Laser systems for light
sourcing applications
Photodetectors and sensors
Silicon detector panels for
X-ray imaging
Specialty lighting
Weapons trigger systems

Instruments
Automobile performance
and emissions testing
X-ray food inspection
systems (PakScan)

X-ray security screening
devices (Z-Scan)

Engineered Products
Seals and valves

Life Sciences
Bioanalytic assay
instruments (VICTOR)
Biotechnology and clinical
research instrumentation
Clinical diagnostic
screening instrument
systems
Diagnostic systems
(AutoDELFIA)

COMPETITORS

II-VI	Continental AG	Invensys
Aavid	Cookson Group	OSI Systems
AlliedSignal	DynCorp	PE Corporation
American	Hewlett-Packard	SGS
Science and	Honeywell	SPX
Engineering	International	Thermo Electron
AMP	Total Services	TRW

HISTORICAL FINANCIALS & EMPLOYEES

NYSE symbol: EGG FYE: December 31	Annual Growth	1989	1990	1991	1992	1993	1994	1995	1996	1997	1998
Sales ($ mil.)	(1.7%)	1,650	2,474	2,689	2,789	2,698	1,333	1,420	1,427	1,461	1,408
Net income ($ mil.)	4.3%	70	74	81	88	59	(6)	68	60	34	102
Income as % of sales	—	4.2%	3.0%	3.0%	3.1%	2.2%	—	4.8%	4.2%	2.3%	7.2%
Earnings per share ($)	7.1%	1.20	1.30	1.46	1.56	1.05	(0.10)	1.32	1.27	0.74	2.22
Stock price - FY high ($)	—	18.25	20.50	25.00	26.75	24.50	19.00	24.50	25.13	24.63	33.75
Stock price - FY low ($)	—	14.19	14.00	15.44	17.88	15.75	13.75	13.00	16.25	18.00	18.88
Stock price - FY close ($)	5.6%	17.00	15.50	24.88	19.63	18.38	14.13	24.25	20.13	20.81	27.81
P/E - high	—	15	16	17	17	23	—	19	20	33	15
P/E - low	—	12	11	11	11	15	—	10	13	24	9
Dividends per share ($)	2.4%	0.34	0.38	0.42	0.49	0.52	0.56	0.57	0.56	0.56	0.42
Book value per share ($)	4.5%	6.02	6.58	7.45	8.34	8.00	8.08	7.71	7.88	7.24	8.93
Employees	(8.9%)	30,000	35,000	37,000	34,000	32,000	25,000	15,000	15,000	14,000	13,000

STOCK PRICE HISTORY

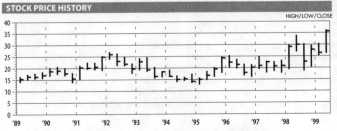

HIGH/LOW/CLOSE

1998 FISCAL YEAR-END

Debt ratio: 24.5%
Return on equity: 25.5%
Cash ($ mil.): 96
Current ratio: 1.08
Long-term debt ($ mil.): 130
No. of shares (mil.): 45
Dividends
　Yield: 1.5%
　Payout: 18.9%
Market value ($ mil.): 1,244

E. I. DU PONT DE NEMOURS

OVERVIEW

E. I. du Pont de Nemours (DuPont) lost its energy, but is far from feeling run down. The US's largest chemical company, DuPont has exited the energy business and is now completely focused on its high-performance materials, specialty chemicals, pharmaceuticals, and biotechnology products. The Wilmington, Delaware-based company developed and still produces familiar brand name materials such as Lycra, Teflon, Corian, Kevlar, and Dacron.

DuPont's chemical and material science products include specialty fibers (Lycra, nonwovens, advanced fibers), nylons (yarns, polymers, and intermediates, Stainmaster and Antron carpet fibers), and polyesters (Dacron, films, resins). This segment of DuPont's business also produces specialty polymers (photopolymer/electronic materials, packaging and industrial polymers, Corian), pigments and chemicals (white pigment, mineral products, specialty chemicals, fluorochemicals),

and performance coatings (engineering polymers, elastomers).

DuPont's life science businesses include crop protection products (herbicides, fungicides, insect control), biotechnology products (animal feed, food ingredients, seed products), and pharmaceuticals. The company's newly enlarged pharmaceuticals arm is focused on developing drugs to treat HIV, cardiovascular disease, central nervous system disorders, cancer, and arthritis. Its products include Sustiva, the first once-daily anti-HIV drug.

Seeking refuge from economic cycles, DuPont has largely left the energy business by spinning off Conoco. Meanwhile the company has been investing heavily in its life sciences businesses ($6 billion over two years). DuPont has also decided to move its polyester business into joint ventures with companies outside the US. The extended du Pont family owns about 15% of the company.

HISTORY

Eleuthére Irénée du Pont de Nemours, a Frenchman who had studied gunpowder manufacture under chemist Antoine Lavoisier, fled to America in 1800 after the French Revolution. In 1802 he founded a gunpowder plant on Delaware's Brandywine Creek.

Within a decade the DuPont plant was the largest of its kind in the US. After E. I.'s death in 1834, his sons Alfred and Henry took over. DuPont added dynamite and nitroglycerine in 1880, guncotton in 1892, and smokeless powder in 1894.

In 1902 three du Pont cousins bought DuPont and instituted a centralized structure with functionally organized departments — now widely adopted by big business. By 1906 DuPont controlled most of the US explosives market, but a 1912 antitrust decision forced it to sell part of the powder business. WWI profits were used to diversify into paints, plastics, and dyes.

DuPont acquired an interest in General Motors (GM) in 1917; the stake increased to 37% by 1922 (the company had to surrender its stake in 1962 due to antitrust regulations). In the 1920s the firm bought and improved French cellophane technology and began producing rayon. The company's inventions include neoprene synthetic rubber (1931), Lucite (1937), nylon (1938), Teflon (1938), and Dacron. The last du Pont to head the company resigned as chairman in 1972. DuPont got into

the energy business in the early 1980s, acquiring Conoco for $7.6 billion in 1981.

In 1991 DuPont and Merck created DuPont Merck Pharmaceutical to focus on non-US markets. After record earnings in 1994, DuPont spent $8.8 billion in 1995 to buy back shares of the company from Seagram. Also that year company veteran Jack Krol became CEO.

In 1997 DuPont purchased Protein Technologies International (soy proteins) from Ralston Purina and Imperial Chemical's polyester resins and intermediates operations (1997) and polyester film business (1998).

DuPont president Chad Holliday succeeded Krol as CEO in early 1998. That year DuPont purchased a 20% stake in Pioneer Hi-Bred International (corn seed) for $1.7 billion and Merck's 50% stake in DuPont Merck Pharmaceutical (now DuPont Pharmaceuticals) for $2.6 billion. DuPont's public offering of Conoco in 1998 raised $4.4 billion, the largest US IPO at the time.

In 1999 DuPont bought the Herberts paints and coatings unit from Hoechst. DuPont then announced it would issue a tracking stock for its life sciences operations, which got a boost when DuPont agreed to buy the remaining 80% of Pioneer Hi-Bred International for $7.7 billion. Making a clean break with its oil business, DuPont sold its remaining 70% stake in Conoco. Also in 1999, DuPont picked up 51% of Wirex, a Taiwan-based plastics company.

Chairman and CEO: Charles O. Holliday Jr., age 50,
$2,672,663 pay
**EVP; COO, Specialty Fibers and Performance Coatings
and Polymers:** Richard R. Goodmanson, age 51
**EVP; COO, Pharmaceuticals and Agriculture, and
Nutrition:** Kurt M. Landgraf, age 52, $1,135,400 pay
**EVP; COO, Pigments and Chemicals, Specialty
Polymers, Nylon, and Poylester:** Dennis H. Reilley,
age 46, $704,900 pay
SVP: Cinda A. Hallman
SVP: William F. Kirk
SVP and Chief Technology Officer: Joseph A. Miller Jr.,
age 57
SVP: Stacey J. Mobley, age 53, $699,200 pay
SVP Finance and CFO: Gary M. Pfeiffer, age 49
SVP Legal and General Counsel: Howard J. Rudge,
age 63
SVP: Eduard J. Van Wely, age 56, $1,107,300 pay
VP Global Operations, DuPont Fluoroproducts:
Richard J. Angiullo
VP Corporate Initiatives: Bruce A. Bachman
VP Pension Fund: Edward J. Bassett
VP Global Technology, DuPont Agricultural Enterprise:
Elmo M. Beyer
**VP and General Manager, DuPont Polyester Resins &
Intermediates:** Craig F. Binetti
**VP and General Manager, DuPont Crop Protection
Products:** James C. Borel
VP Corporate Human Resources: John D. Broyles
Auditors: PricewaterhouseCoopers LLP

HQ: E. I. du Pont de Nemours and Company,
1007 Market St., Wilmington, DE 19898
Phone: 302-774-1000   **Fax:** 302-774-7321
Web site: http://www.dupont.com

1998 Sales

	$ mil.	% of total
Performance coatings & polymers	4,607	17
Nylon enterprise	4,594	16
Specialty polymers	4,093	15
Pigment & chemicals	3,659	13
Specialty fibers	3,296	12
Agriculture & nutrition	3,156	11
Polyester enterprise	2,797	10
Pharmaceuticals	1,109	4
Other	445	2
Adjustments	(2,989)	
Total	**24,767**	**100**

Akzo Nobel	ICI
AlliedSignal	Koch
BASF AG	Lyondell Chemical
Bayer AG	Monsanto
Cargill	Novartis
Clorox	Novo Nordisk A/S
ConAgra	PPG
Dow Chemical	Rhône-Poulenc
Eastman Chemical	Rohm and Haas
FMC	Sherwin-Williams
Formosa Plastics	Siemens
Hercules	Union Carbide
Hoechst AG	W. R. Grace
Huntsman	

NYSE symbol: DD FYE: December 31	Annual Growth	1989	1990	1991	1992	1993	1994	1995	1996	1997	1998
Sales ($ mil.)	(3.0%)	32,617	36,591	34,692	33,145	32,621	34,042	36,508	38,349	39,730	24,767
Net income ($ mil.)	6.8%	2,480	2,310	1,403	(3,927)	565	2,727	3,293	3,636	2,405	4,480
Income as % of sales	—	7.6%	6.3%	4.0%	—	1.7%	8.0%	9.0%	9.5%	6.1%	18.1%
Earnings per share ($)	9.2%	1.77	1.70	1.04	(2.92)	0.40	1.98	2.77	3.18	2.08	3.90
Stock price - FY high ($)	—	21.06	21.19	25.00	27.44	26.94	31.19	36.50	49.69	69.75	84.44
Stock price - FY low ($)	—	14.34	15.69	16.38	21.75	22.25	24.13	26.31	34.81	46.38	51.69
Stock price - FY close ($)	11.2%	20.48	18.38	23.31	23.56	24.13	28.06	34.94	47.06	60.06	53.06
P/E - high	—	12	12	24	—	67	16	13	16	34	22
P/E - low	—	8	9	16	—	56	12	9	11	22	13
Dividends per share ($)	7.2%	0.73	0.81	0.84	0.87	0.88	0.91	1.02	1.12	1.23	1.37
Book value per share ($)	0.8%	11.35	12.08	12.29	8.54	8.11	9.24	7.08	9.29	9.57	12.18
Employees	(4.0%)	145,787	143,961	132,578	124,916	114,000	107,000	105,000	97,000	98,000	101,000

HIGH/LOW/CLOSE

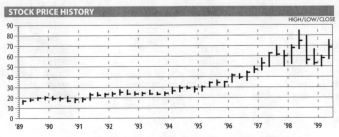

Debt ratio: 24.4%
Return on equity: 32.7%
Cash ($ mil.): 1,434
Current ratio: 0.80
Long-term debt ($ mil.): 4,495
No. of shares (mil.): 1,126
Dividends
  Yield: 2.6%
  Payout: 35.1%
Market value ($ mil.): 59,755

EL PASO ENERGY CORPORATION

OVERVIEW

El Paso Energy provides safe passage for oil and gas across del Norte. The Houston-based holding company gathers, transports, processes, and markets oil and natural gas. The 1998 purchase of DeepTech International, which had an interest in Leviathan Gas Pipeline, and El Paso's planned acquisition of Sonat will vault it ahead of Williams Companies as the leading gas transportation company (by volume) in the US. The purchase of Sonat also gives El Paso an exploration and production company, allowing it greater access to gas supplies.

The company owns two major intrastate pipelines that transport the gas to the US Midwest, Northeast, and West and to northern Mexico along a 28,000-mile system. Tennessee Gas Pipeline transports gas to the Midwest and East Coast, and El Paso Natural Gas oversees the western region (including interests in 14,000 miles of pipeline) in the Southeast.

El Paso's international unit has plowed millions of dollars into buying and building pipelines and power plants. El Paso Energy International has interests in South America, Europe, and the Asia/Pacific. El Paso Energy Marketing is also a major player in the energy marketing business, selling and trading natural gas, electricity, and oil in Canada, the US, and Mexico.

HISTORY

In 1928 Paul Kayser, a Houston attorney, started the El Paso Natural Gas Company and got the rights to sell natural gas to that West Texas town a year later. Despite the 1929 stock market crash, the company built a 200-mile pipeline, first connecting El Paso, Texas, with natural gas wells in Jal, New Mexico. In 1931 it laid pipe again to reach the copper mines of Arizona and Mexico, and three years later expanded to Phoenix and Tucson.

After WWII the company began a 700-mile pipeline to bring natural gas from Texas' Permian Basin to California. As the Golden State's population exploded, sales soared. El Paso also ventured into new business areas, first chemicals and later textiles, mining, land development, and insurance.

In 1974 the Supreme Court ruled that El Paso had to divest its pipeline holdings north of New Mexico and Arizona. Federal regulators had granted the company the right to buy the holdings two decades earlier but later rescinded. Other operations, such as fiber manufacturing, were posting losses, so the company jettisoned some non-gas businesses. El Paso received a boost in 1978 when the Natural Gas Policy Act allowed it more freedom to purchase its own reserves, but later weak demand, coupled with oversupply brought on by the spike in 1970s energy prices, cut its business by 1982.

Conglomerate Burlington Northern acquired El Paso Natural Gas in 1983. Many of its operations were spun off when Federal Energy Regulatory Commission Order 436 obliged gas pipelines to unbundle their sales and transportation business and open up interstate pipelines to third parties. It became mainly a gas transportation company.

El Paso became independent once more when Burlington spun it off in 1992. It entered the big leagues in 1996 by buying Tenneco Energy for $4 billion. With more than 16,000 miles of pipeline, Tenneco more than doubled El Paso's transportation capacity and gave it the only coast-to-coast natural gas pipeline in the US. El Paso Natural Gas began using the name El Paso Energy (in 1998 it restructured to place El Paso Natural Gas and four other business units under El Paso Energy, a new holding company) and moved from its namesake town to Houston, Tenneco's headquarters. In 1997 it sold Tenneco's oil and gas exploration unit to help pay off debt and bought a 29% stake in Capsa, an Argentine energy concern.

Refocusing on Gulf Coast assets, El Paso sold its Anadarko pipeline gas gathering system in Oklahoma and Texas in 1998, then bought DeepTech International and its stake in the Leviathan Gas Pipeline, the largest independent gas-gathering system in the Gulf of Mexico. The company also moved into the UK power market via a joint venture power plant project in Scotland.

In 1999 El Paso agreed to buy Sonat, a natural gas transportation and marketing firm that also has an exploration and production unit, in a $6 billion deal. It also announced plans to spend $150 million on building a 1,500-mile fiber-optic line, using about 750 miles of El Paso's rights-of-way between California and Texas, and to spend $1.5 billion on building a network of gas-fueled power generators that will be available in peak season. Boosting its power plant portfolio, the company also acquired 14 independent power plants from CalEnergy (now MidAmerican Energy).

Chairman, President, and CEO: William A. Wise, age 53, $1,600,000 pay
President, El Paso Natural Gas: Richard O. Baish, age 52, $698,500 pay
EVP and CFO: H. Brent Austin, age 44, $743,417 pay
EVP: Ralph Eads
EVP Human Resources and Administration: Joel Richards III, age 51, $577,500 pay
EVP and General Counsel: Britton White Jr., age 55, $675,584 pay
SVP: Mark A. Searles, age 42
President, El Paso Energy International: John D. Hushon, age 53
President, El Paso Energy Marketing: Greg G. Jenkins, age 41
President, El Paso Field Services: Robert G. Phillips, age 44
President, Tennessee Gas Pipeline: John W. Somerhalder II, age 43, $698,500 pay
Auditors: PricewaterhouseCoopers LLP

LOCATIONS

HQ: 1001 Louisiana, Houston, TX 77002
Phone: 713-420-2131   **Fax:** 713-420-6030
Web site: http://www.epenergy.com

El Paso Energy Corporation gathers natural gas in major producing areas of the US, including South and East Texas, North Louisiana, the Permian Basin in Texas and New Mexico, the San Juan Basin in New Mexico, and both onshore and offshore along the Gulf Coast. The company transports gas to the US Midwest, Northeast, and West and to northern Mexico. El Paso also has power plants interests in the Asia/Pacific region, Europe, and South America.

PRODUCTS/OPERATIONS

1998 Sales

	$ mil.	% of total
Energy marketing	4,323	75
Gas pipeline	728	13
Natural gas	473	8
Field services	194	3
Energy international	58	1
Other	6	—
Total	**5,782**	**100**

Subsidiaries
El Paso Energy International Co.
El Paso Energy Marketing Co.
El Paso Field Services Co.
El Paso Natural Gas Co.
Tennessee Gas Pipeline Co.

COMPETITORS

Avista
Coastal
Columbia Energy
Consolidated Natural Gas
Constellation Energy Group
Duke Energy
Dynegy
Enbridge
Enron
Entergy
Enterprise
Equitable Resources
Imperial Oil
K N Energy
MidAmerican Energy

Mitchell Energy & Development
Peabody Group
Petro-Canada
PG&E
Preussag
Reliant Energy
Sempra Energy
Southern Company
Statoil Energy
Tejas Energy
Tractebel
TransCanada PipeLines
UtiliCorp
Western Gas
Williams Companies

HISTORICAL FINANCIALS & EMPLOYEES

| NYSE symbol: EPG
FYE: December 31	Annual Growth	1989	1990	1991	1992	1993	1994	1995	1996	1997	1998
Sales ($ mil.)	34.3%	—	—	735	803	909	870	1,038	3,010	5,638	5,782
Net income ($ mil.)	6.7%	—	—	143	76	92	90	85	38	186	225
Income as % of sales	—	—	—	19.4%	9.5%	10.1%	10.3%	8.2%	1.3%	3.3%	3.9%
Earnings per share ($)	9.7%	—	—	—	1.06	1.23	1.23	1.24	0.52	1.59	1.85
Stock price - FY high ($)	—	—	—	—	15.75	20.19	20.94	16.25	26.63	33.75	38.94
Stock price - FY low ($)	—	—	—	—	10.13	15.13	14.81	12.38	14.31	24.44	24.69
Stock price - FY close ($)	14.4%	—	—	—	15.50	18.00	15.25	14.38	25.25	33.25	34.81
P/E - high	—	—	—	—	15	16	17	13	51	21	21
P/E - low	—	—	—	—	10	12	12	10	28	15	13
Dividends per share ($)	20.4%	—	—	—	0.25	0.54	0.59	0.65	0.69	0.72	0.76
Book value per share ($)	11.7%	—	—	—	9.01	9.60	9.98	10.40	13.93	16.37	17.53
Employees	4.1%	—	—	2,710	2,499	2,460	2,403	2,393	4,300	3,500	3,600

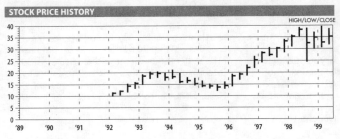

STOCK PRICE HISTORY
HIGH/LOW/CLOSE

1998 FISCAL YEAR-END
Debt ratio: 54.8%
Return on equity: 10.7%
Cash ($ mil.): 90
Current ratio: 0.56
Long-term debt ($ mil.): 2,552
No. of shares (mil.): 120
Dividends
  Yield: 2.2%
  Payout: 41.1%
Market value ($ mil.): 4,187

ELECTRONIC DATA SYSTEMS

OVERVIEW

Electronic Data Systems (EDS) has found a few potholes on the road to independence. Plano, Texas-based EDS is the largest independent computer management and services company in the US. (IBM is #1 overall.) The information technology (IT) services provider develops, assembles, and manages complex computer and telecom systems for major government and corporate clients. EDS's A.T. Kearney unit is itself a billion-dollar management consulting business.

EDS is expanding globally, with about 40% of sales generated outside the US. The company, which draws about half of sales through contracts with manufacturers, is seeking greater diversification through deals with governments and financial services, communications, health, and travel industry clients.

For more than a decade, EDS was a General Motors subsidiary (GM still accounts for about 25% of sales). The company struggled after its 1996 spinoff from GM, as its profits and stock slumped. Multibillion-dollar contracts, combined with a restructuring plan to trim thousands of jobs, have brightened prospects. Its purchase of MCI Systemhouse, the Canada-based IT services arm of MCI WorldCom, is just one part of a far-reaching alliance that has EDS swapping assets, employees, and services with the telecom giant.

HISTORY

After 10 years with computer powerhouse IBM, disgruntled salesman Ross Perot founded Electronic Data Systems (EDS) in 1962. IBM executives pooh-poohed Perot's idea of providing companies with electronic data processing management that would take data management worries off clients' hands.

Perot took five months to find his first customer, Collins Radio of Cedar Rapids, Iowa. In 1963 EDS pioneered the long-term, fixed-price contract with snack food maker Frito-Lay, writing a five-year contract instead of the 60- to 90-day contracts usually offered by service companies. EDS then got into Medicare and Medicaid claims processing (mid-1960s), data processing for insurance providers (1963), and data management for banks (1968) — moves that led it to become the #1 provider of data management services in all three of these markets.

EDS went public in 1968. It bought Wall Street Leasing (computer services) and established regional data centers and central data processing stations in the early 1970s to pioneer the notion of distributed processing. In 1976 EDS signed its first offshore contract, in Saudi Arabia, and a contract with the government of Iran. But by 1978 Iran was six months behind in its payments, and EDS halted operations there. When two EDS employees were later arrested amid the disorder of the Islamic revolution, Perot assembled a rescue team that spirited them out of the country.

On EDS's 22nd anniversary in 1984, General Motors (GM) bought the company for $2.5 billion. GM promised EDS its independence as well as contract work managing its lumbering data processing system. While EDS prospered, Perot and GM chairman Roger Smith's managerial styles differed, resulting in an uneasy alliance and, ultimately, divorce. GM bought Perot's EDS shares in 1986 for more than $700 million. (One result was that Perot's famously strict EDS dress code — no beards — loosened some.) Perot formed competitor Perot Systems in 1988.

EDS bought UK computer services company SD-Scicon two years later. In 1993 the company launched its management consulting service to leverage its systems business contacts. EDS scored big in 1994 with Xerox when it contracted to manage most of that company's information technology (IT) needs in a $3 billion deal. (EDS filed suit against Xerox five years later, citing nonpayment.) The next year EDS acquired management consulting firm A.T. Kearney and securities industry consultant FCI.

The company won independence from GM in mid-1996 in a spinoff that included paying $500 million to GM and an agreement to extend the automaker more favorable computer services contracts. In 1998 CEO Lester Alberthal resigned and was replaced by Cable & Wireless executive Richard Brown, who became chairman and CEO in 1999.

That year EDS agreed to exchange assets and services from its networking business for communications management services and employees from MCI WorldCom in an alliance worth an estimated $17 billion. As one part of that deal, EDS paid $1.65 billion to purchase MCI Systemhouse, a move that thrust EDS into e-commerce. Also in 1999 the company signed a 10-year, $2 billion deal to manage Nasdaq's stockbroker activity tracking systems.

Chairman and CEO: Richard H. Brown, age 51
President and COO: Jeffrey M. Heller, age 59
EVP: John A. Bateman, age 50
EVP: Hartmut W. Burger, age 55
EVP: John R. Castle Jr., age 56
EVP: Paul J. Chiapparone, age 59
EVP and CFO: James E. Daley, age 58
EVP of Leadership and Change Management:
 Troy W. Todd, age 70
EVP of US Operations: Douglas Frederick, age 49
SVP: J. Coley Clark, age 53
SVP: H. Paulett Eberhart, age 45
SVP, Secretary, and General Counsel:
 D. Gilbert Friedlander
SVP: Edward V. Yang, age 53
SVP of Strategic Planning and Business Development:
 Richard L. deNey, age 49
VP and Treasurer: Scott Krenz
VP and Interim Human Resources: John W. Wroten Jr.
Auditors: KPMG LLP

LOCATIONS

HQ: Electronic Data Systems Corporation,
 5400 Legacy Dr., Plano, TX 75024-3199
Phone: 972-604-6000 **Fax:** 972-605-2643
Web site: http://www.eds.com

Electronic Data Systems has operations in the US and 46 other countries.

1998 Sales

	$ mil.	% of total
US	10,303	61
UK	1,911	11
Other countries	4,677	28
Total	**16,891**	**100**

PRODUCTS/OPERATIONS

1998 Sales

	$ mil.	% of total
System & technology services	12,249	73
Business process management	3,282	19
Management consulting services	1,000	6
Other	360	2
Total	**16,891**	**100**

Services
Communications management
Customer equity management
Distributed systems
E-commerce and electronic data interchange
Enterprise applications
Enterprise customer management (Centrobe)
Information technology planning
Interactive marketing
Intranet (and Web site) development
Operations consulting
Process management
Procurement logistics
Remittance processing
Supply chain management
Systems planning
Systems development and implementation
Year 2000 consulting (CIO Services)

COMPETITORS

Andersen Worldwide	Computer Sciences	InaCom McKinsey &
Arthur D. Little	Deloitte Touche	Company
BT	Tohmatsu	Origin
Cambridge Technology	Ernst & Young	Perot Systems
Cap Gemini	Fiserv Getronics	Pricewaterhouse Coopers
Compaq	IBM	Unisys

HISTORICAL FINANCIALS & EMPLOYEES

NYSE symbol: EDS FYE: December 31	Annual Growth	1989	1990	1991	1992	1993	1994	1995	1996	1997	1998
Sales ($ mil.)	13.6%	5,374	6,022	7,029	8,155	8,507	10,052	12,422	14,441	15,236	16,891
Net income ($ mil.)	6.1%	435	497	548	636	724	822	939	432	731	743
Income as % of sales	—	8.1%	8.3%	7.8%	7.8%	8.5%	8.2%	7.6%	3.0%	4.8%	4.4%
Earnings per share ($)	5.7%	0.91	1.04	1.14	1.33	1.50	1.69	1.94	0.88	1.48	1.50
Stock price - FY high ($)	—	14.41	20.06	33.06	34.00	35.88	39.50	52.63	63.38	49.63	51.31
Stock price - FY low ($)	—	10.63	12.19	17.50	25.25	26.00	27.50	36.88	40.75	29.56	30.44
Stock price - FY close ($)	15.6%	13.66	19.31	31.50	32.88	29.25	38.38	52.00	43.25	43.94	50.19
P/E - high	—	16	19	29	26	24	23	27	72	34	34
P/E - low	—	12	12	15	19	17	16	19	46	20	20
Dividends per share ($)	10.7%	0.24	0.28	0.32	0.36	0.40	0.48	0.52	0.60	0.60	0.60
Book value per share ($)	14.0%	3.69	4.56	5.46	6.39	7.52	8.79	10.29	9.82	10.80	12.00
Employees	9.1%	55,000	59,900	65,800	70,500	70,000	70,000	96,000	100,000	110,000	120,000

STOCK PRICE HISTORY

HIGH/LOW/CLOSE

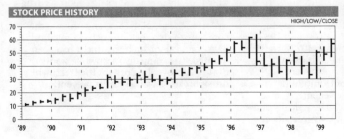

1998 FISCAL YEAR-END

Debt ratio: 16.7%
Return on equity: 12.6%
Cash ($ mil.): 1,039
Current ratio: 1.54
Long-term debt ($ mil.): 1,184
No. of shares (mil.): 493
Dividends
 Yield: 1.2%
 Payout: 40.0%
Market value ($ mil.): 24,750

ELI LILLY AND COMPANY

What's so bad about feeling good? For Eli Lilly and Company, not a thing.

The Indianapolis-based company is perhaps best-known these days for making Prozac, the world's best-selling antidepressant (it makes up 30% of Lilly's sales), but it also makes a wide variety of other pharmaceuticals, hormones, and nutritional products for humans and animals. Other products include Gemzar (for pancreatic cancer), Humalog (insulin), and Zyprexa (a schizophrenia treatment with possible applications for bipolar disorders and Alzheimer's). Eli Lilly's Evista debuted in early 1998 as an osteoporosis preventative (and gained headlines for a time as a possible breast cancer preventative). Its Kinetra joint venture with EDS is an electronic health care information network. The company has R&D alliances with other drug companies to pump products through its pipeline.

Lilly is anxious to extend the protected life span of Prozac (set to expire in 2003); in 1998 it bought rights to an improved formulation. The move, which could stave off competition for another decade, got the attention of the FTC as part of an inquiry into anticompetitive behavior. The Lilly Endowment, a charitable foundation, owns 16% of the company.

Colonel Eli Lilly, pharmacist and Union officer in the Civil War, started Eli Lilly & Company in 1876 with $1,300. His process of coating pills with gelatin led to sales of nearly $82,000 in 1881. Later, the company made gelatin capsules, which it still sells. Lilly died in 1898, and his son and two grandsons ran the business until 1953.

Eli Lilly began extracting insulin from the pancreases of hogs and cattle in 1923 (6,000 cattle or 24,000 hog glands made one ounce of the substance). Other company products created in the 1920s and 1930s included Merthiolate (an antiseptic), Seconal (a sedative), and treatments for pernicious anemia and heart disease. In 1947 the company began selling a drug to prevent miscarriages — diethylstilbestrol (DES). Eli Lilly researchers isolated the antibiotic erythromycin from a species of mold found in the Philippines in 1952; that decade the company was the major supplier of the Salk polio vaccine.

The company enjoyed a 70% share of the DES market by 1971, when researchers noticed that a rare form of cervical cancer afflicted many of the daughters of women who had taken the drug. The FDA restricted the drug's use and Eli Lilly found itself on the receiving (and frequently losing) end of a number of trailblazing product-liability suits that dragged on into the 1990s.

The firm diversified in the 1970s, buying Elizabeth Arden (cosmetics, 1971; sold 1987) and IVAC (medical instruments, 1977). New product introductions included Darvon (a prescription analgesic) and Ceclor (an antibiotic).

Eli Lilly's 1982 launch of Humulin (a synthetic insulin developed by Genentech) made it the first company to market a genetically engineered product. In 1986 Eli Lilly introduced Prozac and acquired Hybritech, a biotechnology firm (sold 1995 for a huge loss). In 1988 Lilly introduced Axid (antiulcerative). With Dow Chemical it founded DowElanco (pesticides and herbicides) in 1989.

Trying to find a new product outlet, the firm in 1994 bought PCS Health Systems (pharmacy benefit management) from what is now McKesson HBOC. But an FTC mandate to offer rival drugs and a lack of mail-order sales contributed to poor results, which ultimately led Eli Lilly to sell PCS to Rite Aid and back out of this arena completely in 1998.

Eli Lilly's 1995 purchase of medical communications network developer Integrated Medical Systems (now part of Kinetra), allowed the company to add another layer of service. Also in 1995 the company introduced ReoPro, a blood-clot inhibitor developed by Centocor that is used in angioplasties.

In 1997 Eli Lilly sold its DowElanco stake to Dow, leading to a loss that year. In 1998 the Lilly Endowment passed the Ford Foundation as the US's largest charity (largely due to Prozac sales). That year the company began trying to stop Chinese drugmakers from infringing on its patents for fluoxetine, Prozac's active ingredient.

In 1999 a US federal judge found that Eli Lilly illegally promoted its osteoporosis drug Evista as a breast cancer preventative similar to AstraZeneca's Nolvadex, and ordered the company to stop making such claims until FDA approval for such treatment had been granted. The company meanwhile wants the FDA to approve the drug for the treatment of osteoporosis as well as for its prevention.

Chairman, President, and CEO: Sidney Taurel, age 50, $2,674,741 pay
EVP and CFO: Charles E. Golden, age 52, $1,507,801 pay
EVP Science and Technology: August M. Watanabe, age 57, $1,525,058 pay
SVP Corporate Strategy and Policy: Mitchell E. Daniels Jr., age 49
SVP and General Counsel: Rebecca O. Goss, age 51, $936,285 pay
SVP Human Resources and Manufacturing: Pedro P. Granadillo, age 51, $1,048,777 pay
SVP Pharmaceutical Products: John C. Lechleiter, age 45
President, SERM and Skeletal Products: Bryce D. Carmine, age 47
President, Elanco Animal Health: Brendan P. Fox, age 55
President, Diabetes and Growth Disorders Products: James A. Harper, age 51
President, Internal Medicine Products: William R. Ringo Jr., age 53
President, Neuroscience Products: Gary Tollefson, age 48
VP and Chief Information Officer: Roy Dunbar
Auditors: Ernst & Young LLP

LOCATIONS

HQ: Lilly Corporate Center, Indianapolis, IN 46285
Phone: 317-276-2000 **Fax:** 317-277-6579
Web site: http://www.lilly.com

1998 Sales

	$ mil.	% of total
US	5,837	63
Western Europe	1,692	18
Other regions	1,708	19
Total	**9,237**	**100**

PRODUCTS/OPERATIONS

1998 Sales

	$ mil.	% of total
Prozac	2,811	30
Zyprexa	1,443	16
Anti-infectives	1,161	13
Insulins	1,155	13
Animal health	614	7
Axid	418	4
ReoPro	365	4
Gemzar	307	3
Humatrope	268	3
Evista	144	1
Other products	551	6
Total	**9,237**	**100**

COMPETITORS

Abbott Labs	Hoechst AG
American Home Products	Johnson & Johnson
Amgen	Merck
AstraZeneca	Novartis
BASF AG	Novo Nordisk A/S
Baxter	Pfizer
Bayer AG	Pharmacia & Upjohn
Boehringer Ingelheim	Rhône-Poulenc
Bristol-Myers Squibb	Roche Holding
Elf Aquitaine	Schering-Plough
Genentech	SmithKline Beecham
Glaxo Wellcome	Warner-Lambert

HISTORICAL FINANCIALS & EMPLOYEES

NYSE symbol: LLY FYE: December 31	Annual Growth	1989	1990	1991	1992	1993	1994	1995	1996	1997	1998
Sales ($ mil.)	9.2%	4,176	5,192	5,726	6,167	6,452	5,712	6,764	7,347	8,518	9,237
Net income ($ mil.)	9.3%	940	1,127	1,315	709	480	1,286	2,291	1,524	(385)	2,098
Income as % of sales	—	22.5%	21.7%	23.0%	11.5%	7.4%	22.5%	33.9%	20.7%	—	22.7%
Earnings per share ($)	9.9%	0.80	0.98	1.13	0.61	0.40	1.10	1.99	1.36	(0.35)	1.87
Stock price - FY high ($)	—	17.13	22.59	21.28	21.94	15.50	16.56	28.50	40.19	70.44	91.31
Stock price - FY low ($)	—	10.59	14.69	16.88	14.44	10.91	11.78	15.63	24.69	35.56	57.69
Stock price - FY close ($)	20.1%	17.13	18.31	20.88	15.19	14.84	16.41	28.13	36.50	69.63	88.88
P/E - high	—	21	23	19	36	39	15	14	30	—	49
P/E - low	—	13	15	15	24	27	11	8	18	—	31
Dividends per share ($)	10.0%	0.34	0.41	0.50	0.55	0.61	0.63	0.66	0.69	0.94	0.80
Book value per share ($)	2.0%	3.37	3.25	4.24	4.18	3.90	4.59	4.93	5.52	4.18	4.04
Employees	0.8%	27,800	29,500	30,800	32,200	32,700	24,900	26,800	29,200	31,100	29,800

STOCK PRICE HISTORY

HIGH/LOW/CLOSE

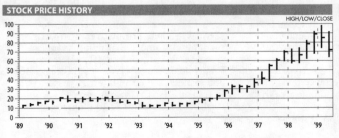

1998 FISCAL YEAR-END

Debt ratio: 33.0%
Return on equity: 47.4%
Cash ($ mil.): 1,496
Current ratio: 1.17
Long-term debt ($ mil.): 2,186
No. of shares (mil.): 1,096
Dividends
 Yield: 0.9%
 Payout: 42.8%
Market value ($ mil.): 97,448

EMC CORPORATION

OVERVIEW

EMC is squarely focused on data storage. Based in Hopkinton, Massachusetts, it is the #1 producer (ahead of IBM) of hardware and software for the storage and retrieval system market. Its refrigerator-sized Symmetrix RAID (redundant array of independent disks) storage systems combine small, independent disk drives to ensure data integrity. The company's products — which work both with larger mainframes and with UNIX and Windows NT systems — also let users manage remote data and share information from different types of networked computers. Known for its aggressive sales force, EMC markets its products to data-intensive customers, among them 90% of the major airlines and the 25 largest US banks. Other customers include Lucent Technologies and Gillette.

EMC continues to expand its capabilities and support. Jumping on opportunities to oversee corporate Internet data (especially e-commerce-related business), EMC now offers Web site setup and management services. To move into the market for mid-range storage, EMC is buying rival Data General. Such tactics have helped EMC increase earnings an average of 30% annually for the last five years.

A family business (co-founder Dick Egan, his wife Maureen, and his son John are board members; John's cousin Paul Noble Jr. is an EVP), EMC keeps costs down by not making any of the components in its machines, although engineers guarantee quality by testing the parts before assembly.

HISTORY

EMC was founded in 1979 by former Intel executive Dick Egan and his college roommate, Roger Marino (their initials gave the company its name). Feisty entrepreneur Egan, whose first job was shining shoes, served as a marine in Korea and later worked at MIT on the computer system for NASA's Apollo program. Egan also helped found Cambridge Memory Systems (later Cambex).

EMC was started with no business plan, only the idea that Egan and Marino would be better off working for themselves. At first they sold office furniture, which in short order led to contacts at technology companies and recognition that there was a niche market for add-on memory boards for minicomputers.

The firm grew steadily throughout the early 1980s and went public in 1986. Two years later Michael Ruettgers, a former COO of Technical Financial Services, joined the company as EVP of operations. Ruettgers spent his first year and a half at EMC dealing with a crisis that almost ruined the company: Defective disk drives in some of its products were losing customers' files. Ruettgers stepped up quality control and guided EMC through the crisis; in 1989 he became president and COO.

In the late 1980s the company expanded into data storage systems, developing one that employed small hard disks rather than the larger and more expensive disks and tapes used for IBM mainframes. EMC then separated itself from competitors by providing systems with a large cache — a temporary storage area that allows for quicker data retrieval.

EMC in 1990 pioneered RAID storage and eliminated nearly a dozen major product lines, focusing on storage for larger IBM computers in a bid to beat Big Blue by undercutting prices. The company introduced its original Symmetrix system, based on the new integrated cached disk array technology that held data from a variety of different computers. Marino left the company in 1990.

Ruettgers became EMC's CEO in 1992. The next year the company acquired Epoch Systems, a provider of data management software for the UNIX market, and in 1994 it bought storage products firm Array Technology and Magna Computer, a leader in tape storage technology for IBM's midrange computers. EMC also introduced its first storage product for open systems, the Centriplex series, and its sales passed the $1 billion mark.

With the 1995 acquisition of McDATA Corporation, a maker of high-performance information switching and computer connection products, EMC increased its presence in this fast-growing market. The next year it launched a digital video storage and retrieval system for the TV and film industry and introduced software that lets its systems work on a network instead of requiring a file server.

In 1997 the company formed an Internet services group to provide Web site management for customers. Expanding its international service presence, EMC in 1998 bought French technology services firm Groupe MCI and in 1999 opened an Internet services office in Ireland. Also that year it agreed to acquire rival Data General for $1.1 billion in stock.

Chairman: Richard J. Egan, age 63, $544,550 pay
President and CEO: Michael C. Ruettgers, age 56, $1,762,562 pay
EVP, Markets and Channels: Robert M. Dutkowsky, age 44, $1,229,402 pay
EVP, Products and Offerings: Paul E. Noble Jr., age 43, $484,064 pay
SVP: Richard P. Lehane
SVP, Chief Administrative Officer, and Treasurer: Colin G. Patteson, age 50, $494,476 pay
SVP: James B. Rothnie
SVP: Allan L. Scherr
SVP, Global Customer Service: Frank M. Hauck
SVP, Global Marketing: Cosmo Santullo
SVP, Global Sales and Services: Harold R. Dixon
SVP, Markets and Channel Operations: Charles J. Cavallaro
VP and General Counsel: Paul T. Dacier, age 41
VP and CFO: William J. Teuber Jr., age 47
VP, Recruitment and Training: Donald W. Amaya
Auditors: PricewaterhouseCoopers LLP

LOCATIONS

HQ: 35 Parkwood Dr., Hopkinton, MA 01748-9103
Phone: 508-435-1000   **Fax:** 508-497-6961
Web site: http://www.emc.com

EMC has more than 80 sales offices in the US, plus offices in 32 other countries.

1998 Sales

	% of total
North America	61
Europe, Middle East & Africa	31
Asia/Pacific & Latin America	8
Total	**100**

PRODUCTS/OPERATIONS

Products

Mainframe Systems
Symmetrix series 5000 family

Open Storage Systems
Symmetrix series 3000 family

Other
DataReach (database extraction and movement)
EMC Celerra File Server (for data storage)
EMC Celerra Media Server (for video content)
EMC CopyPoint (disaster recovery software)
EMC Data Manager (data backup and recovery)
EMC InfoMover (file transfer)
EMC PowerPath (performance management)
EMC TimeFinder (software that lets backups occur without disrupting running applications)
ESCON Director (network connectivity)
FDR (backup/restore)
Symmetrix Enterprise Storage Platform (stores data from mainframes and UNIX systems on a Symmetrix system)
Symmetrix Remote Data Facility (data mirroring between two Symmetrix systems)

COMPETITORS

Cambex	IBM
Compaq	MTI Technology
Data General	NCR
Dell Computer	Network Appliance
Exabyte	Procom Technology
Fujitsu	Seagate
Hewlett-Packard	Storage Technology
Hitachi	Sun Microsystems
Hyundai	Tricord Systems

HISTORICAL FINANCIALS & EMPLOYEES

NYSE symbol: EMC FYE: December 31	Annual Growth	1989	1990	1991	1992	1993	1994	1995	1996	1997	1998
Sales ($ mil.)	45.9%	132	171	232	349	783	1,378	1,921	2,274	2,938	3,974
Net income ($ mil.)	—	(19)	9	13	29	127	251	327	386	539	793
Income as % of sales	—	—	5.2%	5.6%	8.2%	16.2%	18.2%	17.0%	17.0%	18.3%	20.0%
Earnings per share ($)	—	(0.04)	0.02	0.03	0.05	0.15	0.28	0.34	0.40	0.52	0.75
Stock price - FY high ($)	—	0.26	0.41	0.55	1.52	4.88	6.00	6.84	9.09	16.28	43.31
Stock price - FY low ($)	—	0.11	0.14	0.20	0.45	1.28	3.13	3.25	3.72	7.94	12.00
Stock price - FY close ($)	88.7%	0.14	0.33	0.52	1.48	4.13	5.49	3.84	8.28	13.72	42.50
P/E - high	—	—	21	18	30	33	21	20	23	31	58
P/E - low	—	—	7	7	9	9	11	10	9	15	16
Dividends per share ($)	—	0.00	0.00	0.00	0.00	0.00	0.00	0.00	0.04	0.00	0.00
Book value per share ($)	38.8%	0.17	0.19	0.21	0.26	0.56	0.92	1.24	1.72	2.39	3.30
Employees	29.7%	936	1,142	1,155	1,500	2,452	3,375	4,100	4,800	6,400	9,700

STOCK PRICE HISTORY

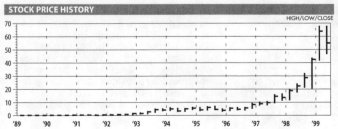

HIGH/LOW/CLOSE

1998 FISCAL YEAR-END

Debt ratio: 14.0%
Return on equity: 23.9%
Cash ($ mil.): 705
Current ratio: 4.75
Long-term debt ($ mil.): 539
No. of shares (mil.): 1,007
Dividends
  Yield: —
  Payout: —
Market value ($ mil.): 42,809

EMCOR GROUP, INC.

OVERVIEW

At EMCOR's core is construction. Norwalk, Connecticut-based EMCOR Group (whose name is short for Electrical Mechanical Corp.) is one of the world's largest specialty construction firms. Its metier is the design, installation, and operation of complex mechanical and electrical systems. Operating through 45 units in 19 US states, Canada, and the UK, as well as a few international joint ventures, EMCOR builds and maintains electric, lighting, security, and plumbing systems for commercial, industrial, and institutional customers. It also offers

on-site services, such as equipment and system installation and maintenance, for facilities.

Having righted the boat after a stint in bankruptcy court in 1994, EMCOR is again acquiring mechanical contracting companies. The firm has also allied with Duke Energy and PECO Energy to install more energy-efficient equipment for customers. Its UK subsidiary has enjoyed rapid growth in its facilities service business, and EMCOR would like to replicate that success in the US.

HISTORY

EMCOR's forerunner, Jamaica Water Supply Co., was incorporated in 1887 to supply water to some residents of Queens and Nassau Counties in New York. In 1902 it bought Jamaica Township Water Co., and by 1906 it was generating revenue — reaching $1.6 million by 1932. Over the next 35 years, the company kept pace with the population of its service area.

In 1966 the enterprise was acquired by Jamaica Water and Utilities, which then bought Sea Cliff Water Co. In 1969 and 1970 it acquired Welsbach (electrical contractors) and A to Z Equipment (construction trailer suppliers), and briefly changed its name in 1974 to Welsbach Corp. before becoming Jamaica Water Properties in 1976.

Diversification proved unprofitable, however, and in 1977 a major investor in the company, Martin Dwyer, and his son Andrew took over the management of the struggling firm. Although the company had posted million-dollar losses in 1979, it was profitable by 1980.

The Dwyers acquired companies in the electrical and mechanical contracting, security, telecommunications, computer, energy and environmental businesses. In 1985 Andrew Dwyer became president, and the company changed its name the next year to JWP.

Between 1986 and 1990 JWP acquired more than a dozen companies, including Extel (1986, telecommunications), Gibson Electric (1987, electrical contracting), Dynalectric (1988, specialty contracting), Drake & Scull (1989, British electrical contractor), NEECO, Compumat (1990, computer resellers), and Comstock Canada (1990, Canada's largest electrical and mechanical contractor).

In 1991 JWP capped its strategy of buying up US computer systems resellers by acquiring Businessland for $32 million plus assumption of $43 million of debt. It then bought French

microelectronics distributor SIVEA. Later that year JWP bought a 34% stake in Resource Recycling Technologies (a solid-waste recycler) and offered to buy the rest of the company through an exchange of stock in 1992.

JWP's shopping spree extended the firm's reach, but the company began to struggle when several sectors turned sour. A price war in the information services business and a weak construction market led to a loss of more than $600 million in 1992. That year president David Sokol resigned after questioning JWP's accounting practices. He turned over to the SEC a report that claimed inflated profits.

Cutting itself to about half its former size, the firm sold JWP Information Services (now Entex Information Services) in 1993. However, JWP continued to struggle, and in early 1994 it filed for bankruptcy. Emerging from Chapter 11 protection in December 1994, the reorganized company took the name EMCOR. That year Frank MacInnis, former CEO of electrical contractor Comstock Group, stepped in to lead EMCOR.

In 1995 the SEC, using Sokol's information, charged several former JWP executives with accounting fraud, claiming they had overstated profits to boost the value of their company stock and their bonuses. EMCOR later reached a nonmonetary settlement with the SEC. The company sold Jamaica Water Supply and Sea Cliff in 1996; it also achieved profitability that year.

As part of its growth-through-acquisition strategy, EMCOR acquired a number of firms in 1998 and 1999, including Romanoff Electric/Columbus (Ohio), Marelich Mechanical Co. and Mesa Energy Systems (California), John Miller Electric (Michigan), Energy Systems Industries (Massachusetts), and it agreed to buy Poole & Kent (Massachusetts) in 1999.

Chairman and CEO: Frank T. MacInnis, age 52,
$1,500,000 pay
President and COO: Jeffrey M. Levy, age 46,
$850,000 pay
EVP and CFO: Leicle E. Chesser, age 52, $725,000 pay
EVP, Secretary, and General Counsel:
Sheldon I. Cammaker, age 59, $621,160 pay
EVP: Thomas D. Cunningham, age 49, $425,000 pay
VP, Taxation: Sidney R. Bernstein
VP and Treasurer: R. Kevin Matz, age 40
VP and Controller: Mark A. Pompa, age 34
VP, Risk Management: Rex C. Thrasher
Staff VP, Human Resources: Jim Murphy
Auditors: Arthur Andersen LLP

LOCATIONS

HQ: 101 Merritt 7 Corporate Park, 7th Fl.,
Norwalk, CT 06851
Phone: 203-849-7800 **Fax:** 203-849-7820
Web site: http://www.emcorgroup.com

EMCOR Group operates through 45 units in Canada, the UK, and 19 US states, and through joint ventures in Hong Kong, Macau, Saudi Arabia, South Africa, and the United Arab Emirates.

1998 Sales & Operating Income

	Sales		Operating Income	
	$ mil.	% of total	$ mil.	% of total
US	1,503	68	52	91
UK	493	22	(1)	—
Canada	202	9	5	9
Other countries	12	1	(1)	—
Adjustments	—	—	(18)	—
Total	**2,210**	**100**	**37**	**100**

PRODUCTS/OPERATIONS

1998 Sales

	% of total
Construction services	80
Facilities services	20
Total	**100**

Selected Mechanical and Electrical Services
Bridge and tunnel lighting
Electrical power distribution systems
Facilities services
Heating, ventilation, and air-conditioning systems
Lighting systems
Low-voltage fire alarm, security, communications, and
process control systems
Piping and plumbing systems
Sheet metal fabrication
Street lighting and traffic signal systems

COMPETITORS

ABB Asea Brown Boveri   Johnson Controls
ABM Industries   MYR Group
BFC Construction   Nationwide Electric
Bechtel   Schneider
Building One Services   Stratesec
Dycom   United Technologies
Fluor   Quanta Services
Honeywell   Hoffman Corporation
Integrated Electrical
Services

HISTORICAL FINANCIALS & EMPLOYEES

Nasdaq symbol: EMCG FYE: December 31	Annual Growth	1989	1990	1991	1992	1993	1994	1995	1996	1997	1998
Sales ($ mil.)	2.7%	1,741	2,827	3,594	2,404	2,195	1,764	1,589	1,669	1,951	2,210
Net income ($ mil.)	(12.0%)	39	59	60	(617)	(114)	303	(11)	9	8	12
Income as % of sales	—	2.2%	2.1%	1.7%	—	—	17.2%	—	0.6%	0.4%	0.6%
Earnings per share ($)	—	—	—	—	—	—	—	(1.13)	0.96	0.74	1.11
Stock price - FY high ($)	—	—	—	—	—	—	—	9.63	17.38	22.25	23.13
Stock price - FY low ($)	—	—	—	—	—	—	—	9.38	9.38	12.75	12.50
Stock price - FY close ($)	18.8%	—	—	—	—	—	—	9.63	13.00	20.50	16.13
P/E - high	—	—	—	—	—	—	—	—	18	30	21
P/E - low	—	—	—	—	—	—	—	—	10	17	11
Dividends per share ($)	—	—	—	—	—	—	—	0.00	0.00	0.00	0.00
Book value per share ($)	17.6%	—	—	—	—	—	—	7.49	8.82	9.94	12.19
Employees	(0.6%)	15,800	19,700	22,400	14,000	14,000	14,000	12,000	12,000	14,000	15,000

STOCK PRICE HISTORY

HIGH/LOW/CLOSE

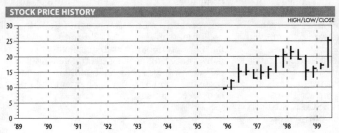

1998 FISCAL YEAR-END

Debt ratio: 49.5%
Return on equity: 10.3%
Cash ($ mil.): 83
Current ratio: 1.43
Long-term debt ($ mil.): 117
No. of shares (mil.): 10
Dividends
  Yield: —
  Payout: —
Market value ($ mil.): 159

EMERSON ELECTRIC CO.

OVERVIEW

Emerson is self-reliant, but not averse to joint ventures and acquisitions. St. Louis-based Emerson Electric makes a range of electrical, electromechanical, and electronic products. Products geared for commercial and industrial use include process control and monitoring systems, industrial motors and drives, industrial components and equipment, and electronics. Products sold in the construction-related and appliance market consist of fractional horsepower motors; heating, ventilating, and air-conditioning components; other appliance components; and tools. International sales account for about a third of total sales.

A major acquisition push has seen Emerson gobble up businesses (focusing on smaller firms) to broaden product lines. Joint ventures and acquisitions over the past five years account for annual sales of about $1.5 billion. Emerson is also focused on new products; almost a third of the company's sales come from products it has unveiled in the past five years, and the company is aiming for 35% by 2000.

HISTORY

Emerson Electric was founded in 1890 in St. Louis by brothers Alexander and Charles Meston, inventors who developed uses for the new alternating-current electric motor. The company was named after former Missouri judge and US marshal John Emerson, who financed the enterprise and became its first president. The company's best-known product was an adaptation of the electric motor — an electric fan — introduced in 1892. The firm also put its motors to use in player pianos, hair dryers, sewing machines, and water pumps. Between 1910 and 1920 the company helped develop the first forced-air circulating systems.

The Depression and labor problems in the 1930s brought the business close to bankruptcy, but new products, including a hermetic motor for refrigerators, revived it. Emerson's electric motors were adapted to new uses during WWII, including powering the gun turrets in B-24 bombers.

Emerson suffered in postwar years. Former football coach Wallace Persons took over as president in 1954 and reorganized Emerson's commercial product line to bring in customers from outside the consumer appliance market.

Beginning in the early 1960s, Persons bought a number of smaller companies in new areas, including thermostats and gas controls, power transmission products, and welding and cutting tools. He retired in 1974.

Persons handed off to former college football player Chuck Knight, who became CEO in 1974. Knight took Emerson into high-tech fields and expanded its hardware segment with six acquisitions between 1976 and 1986.

In 1989 Emerson expanded its electrical offerings through acquisitions, including a 45% stake in Hong Kong-based Astec (power supplies). The company spun off Hazeltine and other businesses in 1990 as ESCO Electronics. Emerson bought Fisher Controls International for $1.25 billion in 1992 and formed S-B Power Tool with Bosch. The company also acquired Buehler International (destructive testing equipment). The next year it sold the aerospace business of subsidiary Rosemount to BF Goodrich.

From 1993–95 Emerson set up operations in China and Eastern Europe. In 1995 Emerson sold its 50% stake in S-B Power Tool to Bosch. In 1996 Emerson and Caterpillar invested in plants in Northern Ireland through their power-generating equipment joint venture, F.G. Wilson. Production began at its Thailand compressor plant in 1997, and Emerson's Appleton Electric division agreed to form a joint venture with General Signal (acquired by SPX in 1998) to serve the electrical distribution industry. Also that year Emerson paid $165 million for Computational Systems, which makes equipment that detects potential problems in machinery at manufacturing or utility facilities.

In 1998 Emerson was accused of using strong arm tactics to acquire the 49% of UK-based Astec, a maker of electronic equipment, that it didn't already own. (Emerson backed down, changed its tactics, and completed the purchase early in 1999.) The company also paid about $265 million for CBS's Westinghouse Process Control division, the top supplier of systems to control power-generation companies in China and Eastern Europe. To enhance its monitoring, diagnostic, and testing capabilities, Emerson bought PC&E. In 1999 Emerson sold its F.G. Wilson stake to partner Caterpillar in exchange for that company's Kato Engineering electric generator subsidiary. It also paid $460 million for Daniel Industries, a maker of measurement and flow control equipment.

Chairman and CEO: C. F. Knight, age 63,
$3,400,000 pay
Senior VC and Chief Administrative Officer: A. E. Suter,
age 63, $1,040,000 pay
VC and Co-CEO: G. W. Tamke, age 51,
$1,150,000 pay (prior to promotion)
VC and President: J. G. Berges, age 51, $850,000 pay
VC: R. W. Staley, age 63, $725,000 pay
SEVP and COO: David N. Farr, age 44
EVP: J.-P. L. Montupet
EVP: L. W. Solley
SVP Finance and CFO: W. J. Galvin, age 52,
$770,000 pay
SVP Acquisitions and Development: R. M. Cox Jr.
SVP: J. A. Harmon
SVP Human Resources: P. A. Hutchison
SVP and Chief Technology Officer: R. D. Ledford
SVP: E. J. Lovelady
SVP: G. T. McKane
SVP: C. A. Peters
SVP Development: J. D. Switzer
SVP, Secretary, and General Counsel: W. W. Withers,
age 58
**VP Employee Relations and Chief Employment
Counsel:** J. R. Carius
Auditors: KPMG LLP

LOCATIONS

HQ: 8000 W. Florissant Ave., St. Louis, MO 63136
Phone: 314-553-2000   **Fax:** 314-553-3527
Web site: http://www.emersonelectric.com

Emerson Electric operates more than 350
manufacturing locations, primarily in the US and
Europe, and to a lesser extent in the Asia/Pacific region,
Canada, and Latin America.

PRODUCTS/OPERATIONS

1998 Sales & Pretax Income

	Sales		Pretax Income	
	$ mil.	% of total	$ mil.	% of total
Commercial & industrial	8,102	60	1,123	54
Appliance & construction	5,345	40	940	45
Corporate & other items	—	—	13	1
Adjustments	—	—	(152)	—
Total	**13,447**	**100**	**1,924**	**100**

COMPETITORS

ABB Asea Brown Boveri	MagneTek
Allegheny Teledyne	Mark IV
American Power	McDermott
Conversion	NEC
Black & Decker	Raytheon
Cooper Industries	Rockwell International
Daewoo	Rolls-Royce
Dana	Siemens
Eaton	Snap-on
GE	SPX
Hitachi	Stanley Works
Honeywell	Tecumseh Products
Illinois Tool Works	Toshiba
Ingersoll-Rand	United Technologies
Johnson Controls	

HISTORICAL FINANCIALS & EMPLOYEES

NYSE symbol: EMR FYE: September 30	Annual Growth	1989	1990	1991	1992	1993	1994	1995	1996	1997	1998
Sales ($ mil.)	7.4%	7,071	7,573	7,427	7,706	8,174	8,607	10,013	11,150	12,299	13,447
Net income ($ mil.)	8.5%	588	613	632	663	708	789	908	1,019	1,122	1,229
Income as % of sales	—	8.3%	8.1%	8.5%	8.6%	8.7%	9.2%	9.1%	9.1%	9.1%	9.1%
Earnings per share ($)	8.6%	1.32	1.38	1.42	1.48	1.58	1.76	2.03	2.25	2.50	2.77
Stock price - FY high ($)	—	19.13	22.19	25.19	29.00	31.19	32.94	37.69	45.81	60.38	67.44
Stock price - FY low ($)	—	14.13	15.38	16.06	22.69	25.13	26.94	28.63	34.31	43.75	49.75
Stock price - FY close ($)	14.9%	17.88	16.13	24.31	27.25	29.44	29.81	35.75	45.06	57.63	62.25
P/E - high	—	14	16	18	20	20	19	19	20	24	24
P/E - low	—	11	11	11	15	16	15	14	15	18	18
Dividends per share ($)	8.6%	0.56	0.63	0.66	0.69	0.72	0.78	0.89	0.98	1.08	1.18
Book value per share ($)	7.5%	6.90	6.69	7.27	8.31	8.71	9.71	10.88	11.96	12.30	13.24
Employees	4.9%	72,600	73,700	69,500	69,400	71,600	73,900	78,900	86,400	100,700	111,800

STOCK PRICE HISTORY

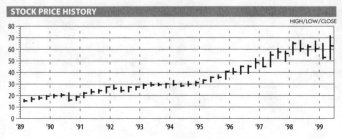

HIGH/LOW/CLOSE

1998 FISCAL YEAR-END

Debt ratio: 15.4%
Return on equity: 21.2%
Cash ($ mil.): 210
Current ratio: 1.24
Long-term debt ($ mil.): 1,057
No. of shares (mil.): 438
Dividends
  Yield: 1.9%
  Payout: 42.6%
Market value ($ mil.): 27,279

ENGELHARD CORPORATION

OVERVIEW

Like a medieval alchemist, Engelhard Corporation converts base materials into wealth. The Iselin, New Jersey-based company is a major producer of catalysts for the petroleum, chemical, and food industries. Engelhard has five business lines: environmental technologies (automotive catalysts), industrial commodities management (base- and precious-metal sales), paper and pigment additives (kaolin-based products for paper products), process technologies (chemical and petroleum catalysts), and specialty pigments and additives (chemicals used for automobile finishes, ceramics, cosmetics, inks, and other applications). Engelhard's biggest customer, the Ford Motor Company, accounts for 18% of sales. Engelhard owns five kaolin mines and the mineral rights to several other kaolin-rich properties.

In 1998 Engelhard began a productivity and supply-chain initiative that it hopes will save the company $100 million by 2001. While fixing or eliminating peripheral businesses, the company is focusing on its bread-and-butter operations in surface chemistry and materials science, especially its growth-leading environmental technologies division.

HISTORY

Charles Engelhard, a German immigrant, came to the US in 1891 to work as a representative for a platinum marketer. In a short time he managed to acquire stakes in Baker & Co. (platinum), Irving Smelting (gold and silver), Hanovia, and a number of other precious-metals firms. In 1902 he set up Engelhard Industries as a precious-metals fabricator.

During the early 1900s, Engelhard pioneered industrial uses of platinum (such as for lightbulb filaments) while also meeting more traditional demands in dentistry and ornamentation. But it wasn't until the 1920s that Engelhard secured a regular supply of the previously scarce element. Teaming up with Inco, he became the Canadian mining firm's sole US platinum dealer. In the 1930s Engelhard, working with DuPont, invented a process to mass-produce nitric acid using a platinum and rhodium catalyst. That decade the company also benefited from the development of the platinum spinnerette (used in machines that produced synthetic fibers). Engelhard acquired D.E. Makepeace (gold and silver sheet), Amersil (fused quartz), and National Electric Instruments (medical instruments) in the 1940s.

Charles Engelhard Jr. set up his own company, Precious Metals Development, in South Africa in 1949, shortly before his father's death in 1950. He built his business exporting gold in the 1950s. With shipments of bullion banned, gold could be shipped internationally only in the form of art objects. Consequently, Engelhard's company made solid-gold plates, bracelets, and the like for export to markets where the gold was then melted down again. The flamboyant Engelhard, an acquaintance of Ian Fleming, is said to have been the model for the writer's Auric Goldfinger character.

Engelhard expanded its chemicals business in 1963 with the purchase of a 20% stake in Minerals & Chemicals Philipp (MCP), a producer of kaolin and fuller's earth owned by Philipp Brothers. In 1967 Engelhard and MCP merged to become Engelhard Minerals and Chemicals Corp. (EMCC).

The fast-growing Philipp Brothers spun off EMCC as Engelhard Corporation in 1981. During the 1980s much of Engelhard's revenues came from selling fluid catalytic cracking materials to the petroleum industry. Engelhard acquired Harshaw/Filtrol Partnership (pigments and additives) in 1988. The company won a contract in 1992 to produce Russia's first automotive catalytic converters. It opened factories in Germany (1994) and South Africa (1995) and introduced automotive catalysts in Europe and the US.

Engelhard acquired Mearl Corp. (which makes pearlescent pigments and iridescent film) in 1996 for $272 million. That year automaker Ford pulled its support of Engelhard's smog-eating car project, claiming that the capacity of the Engelhard radiators to convert ozone into fresh air on contact was much overestimated.

A joint venture with UCAL Fuel Systems Ltd., called Engelhard Environmental Systems (India) Ltd., was formed in 1997 to make automotive-emission catalysts in India.

The next year Engelhard bought Mallinckrodt's catalyst businesses for $210 million. In 1999 Luxembourg-based Minorco sold its 32% stake in Engelhard. The same year Engelhard found itself the target of a Peruvian investigation into tax-fraud charges stemming from its gold operations in that country.

Chairman and CEO: Orin R. Smith, age 63,
$2,614,996 pay
President and COO: Barry W. Perry, age 52,
$1,002,744 pay
SVP and CFO: Thomas P. Fitzpatrick, age 60,
$837,500 pay
SVP Strategy and Corporate Development:
Joseph E. Gonnella, age 52, $641,500 pay
Group VP and General Manager, Chemical Catalysts:
James A. Martin
**Group VP and General Manager, Environmental
Technologies:** Edmund A. Stanczak Jr.
**Group VP and General Manager, Industrial
Commodities Management:** Ian P. McLean
Group VP and General Manager, Petroleum Catalysts:
Daniel W. Parker
VP and Chief Technical Officer: Robert J. Schaffhauser,
age 60, $672,796 pay
VP, General Counsel, and Secretary:
Arthur A. Dornbusch II, age 55
VP Human Resources: John C. Hess, age 46
VP, Investor Relations: Peter B. Martin, age 59
VP of Corporate Communications: Mark Dresner, age 47
VP; President, Engelhard Asia Pacific: George C. Hsu
Treasurer: Peter R. Rapin, age 44
Controller: David C. Wajsgras, age 38
Auditors: PricewaterhouseCoopers LLP

LOCATIONS

HQ: 101 Wood Ave., Iselin, NJ 08830
Phone: 732-205-5000   **Fax:** 732-321-1161
Web site: http://www.engelhard.com

Engelhard operates manufacturing facilities in Canada,
Finland, France, Germany, Italy, Japan, the Netherlands,
South Africa, the UK, and the US.

PRODUCTS/OPERATIONS

1998 Sales & Operating Income

	Sales		Operating Income	
	$ mil.	% of total	$ mil.	% of total
Industrial commodities management	2,347	56	48	16
Environmental technologies	559	13	83	27
Process technologies	533	13	79	25
Specialty pigments & additives	349	8	42	14
Paper pigments & additives	239	6	36	11
Other	148	4	21	7
Total	**4,175**	**100**	**309**	**100**

COMPETITORS

Akzo Nobel
BASF AG
Cambrex
Clariant
Corning
English China Clays
Hitox
ICI
MacDermid
Minerals Technologies
Nalco Chemical
NL Industries
OM Group
Penford

HISTORICAL FINANCIALS & EMPLOYEES

NYSE symbol: EC FYE: December 31	Annual Growth	1989	1990	1991	1992	1993	1994	1995	1996	1997	1998
Sales ($ mil.)	6.3%	2,403	2,942	2,436	2,400	2,151	2,386	2,840	3,184	3,631	4,175
Net income ($ mil.)	—	(78)	70	88	11	1	118	138	150	48	187
Income as % of sales	—	—	2.4%	3.6%	0.4%	0.0%	4.9%	4.8%	4.7%	1.3%	4.5%
Earnings per share ($)	—	(0.51)	0.47	0.58	0.08	0.00	0.82	0.94	1.03	0.33	1.29
Stock price - FY high ($)	—	7.68	7.01	10.16	16.24	19.96	21.01	32.50	26.13	23.75	22.81
Stock price - FY low ($)	—	5.12	5.01	5.04	9.27	12.90	13.92	14.92	17.88	17.06	15.75
Stock price - FY close ($)	14.6%	5.71	5.60	9.64	15.29	16.26	14.76	21.75	19.13	17.38	19.50
P/E - high	—	—	15	18	203	—	26	35	25	72	18
P/E - low	—	—	11	9	116	—	17	16	17	52	12
Dividends per share ($)	10.0%	0.17	0.20	0.22	0.25	0.28	0.31	0.35	0.36	0.38	0.40
Book value per share ($)	4.6%	4.21	4.73	5.01	4.38	3.69	4.31	5.13	5.79	5.43	6.29
Employees	(2.5%)	8,100	7,000	6,400	6,030	5,750	5,830	5,100	6,300	6,400	6,425

STOCK PRICE HISTORY

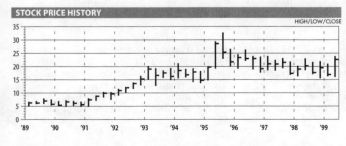

HIGH/LOW/CLOSE

1998 FISCAL YEAR-END

Debt ratio: 35.6%
Return on equity: 20.8%
Cash ($ mil.): 22
Current ratio: 1.07
Long-term debt ($ mil.): 497
No. of shares (mil.): 143
Dividends
  Yield: 2.1%
  Payout: 31.0%
Market value ($ mil.): 2,794

ENRON CORP.

OVERVIEW

Enron has done an end run around its energy rivals. The Houston-based company's playbook has expanded during the 1990s, transforming Enron from a gas pipeline company into a global energy powerhouse. The largest buyer and seller of natural gas in the US, Enron's pipeline network spans some 32,000 miles throughout North America. It also owns utility Portland General Electric (PGE), which has a generating capacity of more than 2,000 MW and serves some 700,000 customers in Oregon.

Enron's gas history and PGE have helped Enron refine its game plan as it tackles deregulating energy markets. The top wholesale power marketer in the US, Enron sells more than 18,000 megawatt-hours each day. The company markets and trades not only electricity but also natural gas, coal, and other energy commodities in the Americas, Australia, and Europe. It also provides risk management services, energy project financing, energy consulting, and engineering and construction services for energy infrastructure around the world. Playing the field, Enron owns interests in merchant power plants near New York City (New Jersey) and in Mississippi and Tennessee. Internationally, the company has stakes in power plants and pipelines in China, Europe, India, Latin America, and Southeast Asia.

The company continues to score points. Enron's communications arm is building a national fiber-optic, Internet protocol-based network. It also has plans to create a market for the trading of communications bandwidth. Enron's purchase of the UK's Wessex Water (now part of Azurix) led the company into the international water market. Enron also owns 13% of its oil and gas exploration and production spin-off, EOG Resources.

HISTORY

Enron traces its history through two well-established natural gas companies — Inter-North and Houston Natural Gas (HNG).

InterNorth began in 1930 as Northern Natural Gas, a Nebraska-based gas pipeline company. By 1950 it had doubled capacity, and in 1960 it started processing and transporting natural gas liquids. The company was renamed InterNorth in 1980 and bought Belco Petroleum three years later. InterNorth (with four partners) also built the Northern Border Pipeline to link Canadian fields with US markets.

HNG, formed in 1925 as a South Texas gas distributor, started developing oil and gas properties in 1953. It bought Houston Pipe Line Company in 1956 and Valley Gas Production in 1963. HNG sold its original distribution properties to Entex in 1976. In 1984 HNG, faced with a hostile takeover attempt by Coastal, brought in former Exxon executive Kenneth Lay as CEO. He refocused HNG on natural gas and added Transwestern Pipeline (California) and Florida Gas Transmission. By 1985 HNG operated the only transcontinental gas pipeline.

In 1985 InterNorth bought HNG for $2.4 billion, creating the US's largest natural gas pipeline system. Lay became CEO of the new company, called Enron (the first name choice, Enteron, was dropped after its meaning, "alimentary canal," was discovered), and the company moved its headquarters from Omaha to Houston. Laden with debt, Enron sold 50% of Citrus Corp. (owner of Florida Gas Transmission, 1986), 50% of Enron Cogeneration (electricity and steam power, 1988), and 16% of Enron Oil & Gas (exploration and production, 1989).

The company bought Tenneco's natural gas liquids and petrochemical operations in 1991. The next year Enron and three partners acquired control of a 4,100-mile pipeline in Argentina. Enron bought several gas businesses from gas giant Williams in 1993 and, as electricity markets worldwide began deregulating, began its power marketing business.

In 1997 Enron, which had been competing against electric utilities, bought its own, Portland General Electric. The next year Enron began power trading in Australia and became the first electric power marketer in Argentina. It also gained control of a Brazilian utility. The company continued to build its US portfolio in 1998, buying interests in power plants near New York City from Cogen Technologies.

Seeping into the international water market, in 1998 the company acquired UK firm Wessex Water and formed Azurix, a global water business, to own and operate its water and wastewater assets. Enron took Azurix public in 1999, retaining a 69% stake. It traded most of its stake in Enron Oil & Gas (now EOG Resources) for cash and the natural gas company's properties in China and India. In another international move, Enron formed a venture with SK Group in 1999 to distribute and market natural gas in South Korea.

Chairman and CEO: Kenneth L. Lay, age 56,
$4,416,667 pay
VC: Joseph W. Sutton, age 51,
$1,724,334 pay (prior to promotion)
President and COO: Jeffrey K. Skilling, age 45,
$3,066,667 pay
SVP, Board Communications: Rebecca C. Carter
SVP and CFO: Andrew S. Fastow, age 37
**SVP and Chief Accounting, Information, and
Administrative Officer:** Richard A. Causey, age 39
**SVP, Corporate Development; VC and Managing
Director, Enron Capital and Trade Resources:**
J. Clifford Baxter, age 40
SVP and General Counsel: James V. Derrick Jr., age 54
SVP, Human Resources: Doy G. "Rocky" Jones II
SVP, Investor Relations: Mark E. Koenig
**SVP, Marketing, Communications, and Human
Resources, Enron Energy Services:**
Elizabeth A. Tilney
SVP, Public Affairs: Steven J. Kean
SVP, Risk Assessment and Control: Richard B. Buy
**Chairman and CEO, Enron Capital and Trade
Resources - North America:** Kenneth D. Rice, age 40,
$1,462,500 pay
Chairman and CEO, Enron Energy Services:
Lou L. Pai, age 51
Chairman and CEO, Enron Gas Pipeline Group:
Stanley C. Horton, age 49
Auditors: Arthur Andersen LLP

HQ: 1400 Smith St., Houston, TX 77002-7369
Phone: 713-853-6161   **Fax:** 713-853-3129
Web site: http://www.enron.com

1998 Sales

	$ mil.	% of total
Wholesale energy	27,725	87
Transportation & distribution	1,849	6
Retail energy	1,072	3
Exploration & production	884	3
Corporate and other	516	1
Adjustments	(786)	—
Total	**31,260**	**100**

Selected Subsidiaries and Affiliates

Transportation and Distribution
Enron Transportation & Storage
Portland General Electric

Wholesale Energy Operations and Services
Enron Capital & Trade Resources
Enron International

New Businesses
Azurix (69%, international water business)
Enron Communications (fiber-optic network)

Avista	Sempra Energy
Black and Veatch	Sonat
Columbia Energy	Southern Company
Constellation Energy	Suez Lyonnaise des Eaux
Group	Tejas Energy
Duke Energy	Texas Utilities
Dynegy	Tractebel
El Paso Energy	TransTexas Gas
Entergy	UtiliCorp
Peabody Group	Vivendi
PG&E	Western Gas
Reliant Energy	Williams Companies

NYSE symbol: ENE FYE: December 31	Annual Growth	1989	1990	1991	1992	1993	1994	1995	1996	1997	1998
Sales ($ mil.)	13.7%	9,836	13,165	13,520	6,325	7,973	8,984	9,189	13,289	20,273	31,260
Net income ($ mil.)	13.4%	226	202	242	306	333	453	520	584	105	703
Income as % of sales	—	2.3%	1.5%	1.8%	4.8%	4.2%	5.0%	5.7%	4.4%	0.5%	2.2%
Earnings per share ($)	8.6%	0.48	0.43	0.51	0.60	0.63	0.85	0.97	1.08	0.16	1.01
Stock price - FY high ($)	—	7.63	7.84	9.61	12.53	18.50	17.31	19.69	23.75	22.56	29.38
Stock price - FY low ($)	—	4.44	6.28	6.20	7.66	11.09	13.38	14.00	17.31	17.50	19.06
Stock price - FY close ($)	16.5%	7.20	6.84	8.75	11.59	14.50	15.25	19.06	21.56	20.78	28.53
P/E - high	—	16	18	19	21	29	20	20	22	141	29
P/E - low	—	9	15	12	13	18	16	14	16	109	19
Dividends per share ($)	5.0%	0.31	0.31	0.32	0.34	0.36	0.38	0.41	0.43	0.46	0.48
Book value per share ($)	11.8%	3.84	4.00	4.21	4.98	4.97	5.44	6.03	7.03	8.81	10.45
Employees	11.1%	6,900	6,962	7,400	7,780	7,100	6,955	6,700	11,700	15,500	17,800

HIGH/LOW/CLOSE

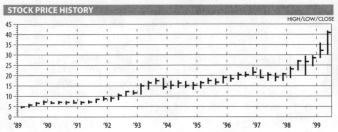

Debt ratio: 51.1%
Return on equity: 10.2%
Cash ($ mil.): 111
Current ratio: 0.97
Long-term debt ($ mil.): 7,357
No. of shares (mil.): 662
Dividends
  Yield: 1.7%
  Payout: 47.5%
Market value ($ mil.): 18,880

ENTERGY CORPORATION

OVERVIEW

Entergy is putting the energy back into its business. The New Orleans-based holding company, which owns five operating utilities, has a generating capacity of nearly 30,000 MW and and more than 15,000 miles of transmission lines. Entergy distributes electricity to about 2.5 million customers in Arkansas, Louisiana, Mississippi, and Texas.

Subsidiaries include Entergy Services, which manages the firm's domestic utilities, and Entergy Power, an energy marketing and trading operation. The company also sells natural gas to about 240,000 customers in New Orleans and Baton Rouge, Louisiana, and is building two power plants in the UK.

In the face of approaching full-scale retail competition for utilities, Entergy is abandoning its plan to try its hand at such nonregulated services as home security and telecommunications. Instead, the company is divesting its noncore operations in an effort to refocus on US power distribution. Entergy has sold its home security and energy consulting businesses and is selling its share in a telecom joint venture (a competitive local-exchange carrier) to partner Hyperion Telecommunications. In addition, the company has dumped its Australian distributor and most of its UK operations, not including the two plants under construction.

HISTORY

Arkansas Power & Light (AP&L, founded in 1913) consolidated operations with three other Arkansas utilities in 1926. Also that year, New Orleans Public Service Inc. (NOPSI, founded in 1922) merged with two other Big Easy electric companies. Louisiana Power & Light (LP&L) and Mississippi Power & Light (MP&L) were both formed in 1927, also through consolidation of regional utilities.

AP&L, LP&L, MP&L, NOPSI, and other utilities were combined into a Maine holding company, Electric Power and Light, which was dissolved in 1949. A new holding company, Middle South Utilities, emerged that year to take over the four utilities' assets.

In 1971 the company bought Arkansas-Missouri Power. In 1974 it brought its first nuclear plant on line and formed Middle South Energy (now System Energy Resources) to develop two more nuclear facilities, Grand Gulf 1 and 2. Unfortunately, Grand Gulf 1 was completed behind schedule (1985) and about 400% over budget. When Middle South tried to pass on the costs to its customers, controversy ensued. Construction of Grand Gulf 2 was halted, and the CFO, Edwin Lupberger, took charge in 1985. Two years later, nuke-related losses took the company to the brink of bankruptcy.

The company moved to settle the disputes by absorbing a $900 million loss on Grand Gulf 2 in 1989. To distance itself from the controversy, Middle South changed its name to Entergy. In 1991 NOPSI settled with the City of New Orleans over Grand Gulf 1 costs and was allowed to defer $90 million in construction expenses.

That year, as US regulators began to discuss breaking the utility industry monopoly, Entergy branched out into nonregulated industries and looked abroad for growth opportunities. In 1993 a consortium including Entergy acquired a 51% interest in Edesur, an electric utility in Buenos Aires. The next year Entergy signed a deal to build four power plants in China. In 1995 Entergy agreed to buy a 20% stake in a power plant under construction in India, but the state government soon halted the project, accusing the participating US companies of exploiting India.

Entergy completed its $1.2 billion acquisition of CitiPower, an Australian electric distributor, in 1996, and the next year it bought the UK's London Electricity for about $2.1 billion.

But diversification had drained funds. Lupberger resigned under shareholder pressure in 1998, and a new management team began selling noncore businesses. Entergy sold CitiPower and agreed to sell London Electricity. However, it contracted out construction on two UK power plants, to be owned by Entergy, and moved into Eastern Europe through a joint venture with Bulgaria's National Electricity Company to modernize a power plant.

NYMEX began trading electricity futures in 1998, using Entergy and Cinergy as contract-delivery points. Entergy also bought the Pilgrim nuclear reactor in Massachusetts, its first power plant outside of its utility territory, from BEC Energy (now NSTAR).

In 1999 Wayne Leonard, the former CFO of Cinergy, stepped in as CEO. Entergy sold the security monitoring business and agreed to sell its interest in a telecom joint venture to partner Hyperion Telecommunications. It also began looking for a buyer for its share of Edesur. Meanwhile, Arkansas enacted a bill for full retail competition by 2002.

Chairman: Robert v.d. Luft, age 63,
$1,234,771 pay (prior to title change)
VC: Jerry L. Maulden, age 62, $864,309 pay
CEO: J. Wayne Leonard, age 48, $1,558,259 pay
President: Donald C. Hintz, age 56, $693,225 pay
Group President and Chief Utility Operating Officer:
Frank F. Gallaher, age 53, $733,763 pay
EVP and CFO: C. John Wilder, age 40
**EVP; President and CEO Entergy Gulf States -
Louisiana and Entergy Louisiana:** Jerry D. Jackson,
age 54, $756,612 pay
SVP Human Resources: Gary Clary
SVP Retail Operations: Hugh McDonald
SVP, Secretary, and General Counsel:
Michael G. Thompson, age 58
SVP, Public Relations and Public Affairs:
Horace S. Webb
VP and Chief Accounting Officer: Nathan E. Langston,
age 50, $269,688 pay
VP and Treasurer: Steven C. McNeal, age 42,
$249,121 pay
VP Corporate Contributions: Deanna Rodriguez
VP, Entergy Nuclear: Danny R. Dan Keuter
Auditors: PricewaterhouseCoopers LLP

LOCATIONS

HQ: 639 Loyola Ave., New Orleans, LA 70113
Phone: 504-529-5262 **Fax:** 504-576-4428
Web site: http://www.entergy.com

PRODUCTS/OPERATIONS

1998 Sales

	$ mil.	% of total
Domestic electric	6,136	54
Competitive growth businesses	5,200	45
Natural gas	116	1
Steam products	43	—
Total	**11,495**	**100**

Selected Subsidiaries

Entergy Nuclear, Inc. (operates nuclear facilities)
Entergy Operations (provides management, technical,
and operating services to Entergy's five US utilities)
Entergy Power (power generation and wholesale
marketing)
Entergy Services, Inc. (provides administrative,
accounting, legal, and other services to Entergy's five
US utility companies)
EPMC (marketing and trading energy commodities)
System Energy Resources (owns 90% of Grand Gulf
Nuclear Station)

COMPETITORS

AES	Reliant Energy
Avista	Sempra Energy
Central and South West	Sithe Energies
Constellation Energy	Southern Company
Group	Statoil Energy
Duke Energy	Texas Utilities
El Paso Energy	Tractebel
Enron	TVA
Koch	UtiliCorp
Peabody Group	Williams Companies
PG&E	

HISTORICAL FINANCIALS & EMPLOYEES

NYSE symbol: ETR FYE: December 31	Annual Growth	1989	1990	1991	1992	1993	1994	1995	1996	1997	1998
Sales ($ mil.)	13.3%	3,724	3,982	4,051	4,117	4,485	5,963	6,274	7,164	9,562	11,495
Net income ($ mil.)	—	(473)	478	482	438	552	342	520	420	301	786
Income as % of sales	—	—	12.0%	11.9%	10.6%	12.3%	5.7%	8.3%	5.9%	3.1%	6.8%
Earnings per share ($)	—	(2.31)	2.44	2.64	2.48	3.16	1.49	2.13	1.83	1.03	3.00
Stock price – FY high ($)	—	23.25	23.63	29.88	33.63	39.88	37.38	29.25	30.50	30.25	32.44
Stock price – FY low ($)	—	15.50	18.00	21.88	26.13	32.50	21.25	20.00	24.88	22.38	23.25
Stock price – FY close ($)	3.3%	23.25	22.38	29.63	33.00	36.00	21.88	29.25	27.63	29.94	31.13
P/E – high	—	—	10	11	14	13	25	14	17	29	11
P/E – low	—	—	7	8	11	10	14	9	14	22	8
Dividends per share ($)	5.8%	0.90	1.05	1.25	1.45	1.65	1.80	1.80	1.80	1.80	1.50
Book value per share ($)	3.8%	20.68	22.34	23.53	24.43	28.27	27.93	28.41	28.51	27.23	28.82
Employees	(0.3%)	13,190	13,379	12,763	12,457	16,679	16,037	13,521	13,363	17,288	12,816

STOCK PRICE HISTORY

HIGH/LOW/CLOSE

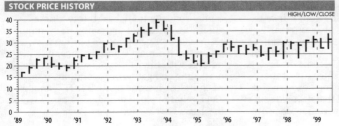

1998 FISCAL YEAR-END

Debt ratio: 46.1%
Return on equity: 11.1%
Cash ($ mil.): 1,185
Current ratio: 1.87
Long-term debt ($ mil.): 6,817
No. of shares (mil.): 247
Dividends
Yield: 4.8%
Payout: 50.0%
Market value ($ mil.): 7,677

EOTT ENERGY PARTNERS, L.P.

OVERVIEW

Crude oil is dirty stuff, but EOTT Energy Partners is willing to get it together and spread it around. The Houston-based public limited partnership is one of the largest independent gatherers and marketers of crude oil in North America. EOTT purchases about 450,000 barrels per day of crude oil, produced from about 40,000 leases in 18 US states. It buys mainly from independent producers (87%).

EOTT operates principally in the US's Gulf Coast, Southwest, Rocky Mountains, and Mid-Continent regions, but also has businesses on the West Coast and in Canada. Acting as an intermediary between supplier and buyer, it transports oil to refineries and other customers via 8,200 miles of pipelines and a fleet of 440 trucks. It markets refined oil products (fuels and unleaded gasoline) on the West Coast.

The firm, which has to operate on razor-thin profit margins, has been hammered by low oil prices, resulting in losses in 1997 and 1998. In order to get bigger to survive, EOTT has been making acquisitions; it has purchased pipelines and other gas gathering assets from Amerada Hess, CITGO, and Koch Industries, among others. These acquisitions allow EOTT to reach the major oil producing regions of the US and Canada.

The company's former parent, power giant Enron, has retained a 14% stake in EOTT; Enron's wholly owned subsidiary EOTT Energy Corp., EOTT's general partner, has a separate 29% stake.

HISTORY

EOTT Energy Partners was originally a part of Enron. Enron itself emerged from the combination of Houston Natural Gas (HNG), formed in 1925, and InterNorth, formed in 1930.

HNG, once a South Texas natural gas distributor, started developing oil and gas fields in 1953. In 1984 Coastal Corp. tried to take over HNG. HNG brought in former Exxon executive Kenneth Lay as CEO to help fend off the bid. Lay shifted HNG's direction toward concentrating almost solely on natural gas production and exploration.

Over in Omaha, Nebraska, Northern Natural Gas was a gas pipeline company that started processing and transporting natural gas liquids in 1960. It changed its name to InterNorth in 1980; three years later it bought Belco Petroleum, giving it considerable natural gas and oil reserves.

When InterNorth bought HNG for $2.4 billion in 1985, the US's largest natural gas system (38,000 miles) was created. The next year Lay became CEO of the newly named Enron and moved its headquarters from Omaha to Houston.

Under Lay's direction, Enron bought crude oil terminals and gathering and transportation systems. In 1987 it purchased a crude oil terminal and transportation facility from Fairway Crude and a year later bought Tesoro Petroleum's gathering and transportation businesses.

But Enron had bigger fish to fry. It planned to focus on natural gas and become the first natural gas major, and it wanted to exit the volatile commodity and trading side of the business. In 1992 it announced that it would spin off Enron Oil Trading & Transportation Company, which brought in high revenues but few profits. In the meantime, Enron acquired Shell's eastern New Mexico oil pipeline system in 1993.

Finally in 1994, Enron combined Enron Oil Trading & Transportation (which had been renamed EOTT Energy) with Enron Products Marketing Company and created EOTT Energy Partners as a separate public partnership. The IPO raised about $200 million. Philip Hawk took charge of the firm, which was one of the largest independent gatherers and marketers of crude oil in North America.

EOTT had troubles from the start; into the first half of 1995, it suffered through the worst industry refining margins in a decade. To stem the losses from its West Coast operation, EOTT renegotiated its contract with its key processor, Paramount Petroleum, agreeing to sell crude to Paramount and then market the fuel in exchange for a share of the revenues.

Nonetheless, EOTT made several acquisitions, including the $54 million purchase in 1996 of 600 miles of pipeline in Mississippi and Alabama from oil giant Amerada Hess and the 1997 purchase of 400 miles of pipeline in Louisiana and Texas from CITGO.

Following a financial loss in 1997, Hawk resigned in 1998 and was replaced by venture capital consultant Michael Burke. Burke guided EOTT toward upgrading its communications and streamlining its business processes. It almost tripled its pipeline mileage with the 1998 acquisition of crude oil marketing and gathering operations from Koch Industries, and in 1999 EOTT bought 2,000 miles of pipeline and other assets from the Texas-New Mexico Pipe Line.

Chairman: Edward O. Gaylord, age 67
President and CEO: Michael D. Burke, age 54,
$242,504 pay
VP, Human Resources and Administration:
Mary Ellen Coombe, age 48, $175,100 pay
VP and General Counsel: Stephen W. Duffy, age 45,
$185,100 pay
VP, Operations: Douglas P. Huth, age 52, $180,100 pay
VP and Secretary: Peggy B. Menchaca
Controller and Chief Accounting Officer:
Lori L. Maddox, age 34, $156,766 pay
Treasurer: Susan C. Ralph
Auditors: Arthur Andersen LLP

LOCATIONS

HQ: 1330 Post Oak Blvd., Ste. 2700, Houston, TX 77056
Phone: 713-993-5200   **Fax:** 713-993-5821
Web site: http://www.eott.com

EOTT Energy Partners operates in Canada and the US
states of Alabama, Arkansas, California, Colorado,
Florida, Kansas, Louisiana, Mississippi, Missouri,
Montana, Nebraska, New Mexico, North Dakota,
Oklahoma, South Dakota, Texas, Utah, and Wyoming.

PRODUCTS/OPERATIONS

1998 Sales

	$ mil.	% of total
North American crude oil	4,591	87
West Coast operations	586	11
Pipeline operations	7	—
Corporate & other	111	2
Total	**5,295**	**100**

Services
Gathering
Purchasing
Resale
Storage
Trading
Transporting

Selected Affiliates
EOTT Energy Canada LP
EOTT Energy Operating LP
EOTT Energy Pipeline LP

COMPETITORS

Amerada Hess	PDVSA
BP Amoco	PEMEX
Chevron	Phillips Petroleum
Coastal	Plains All American
Conoco	Pipeline
Devon Energy	Royal Dutch/Shell
Elf Aquitaine	Sunoco
Exxon	TEPPCO Partners
Imperial Oil	Texaco
Kerr-McGee	Ultramar Diamond
Koch	Shamrock
Mobil	Unocal
Occidental	USX-Marathon

HISTORICAL FINANCIALS & EMPLOYEES

NYSE symbol: EOT FYE: December 31	Annual Growth	1989	1990	1991	1992	1993	1994	1995	1996	1997	1998
Sales ($ mil.)	(4.9%)	—	7,886	8,236	7,697	6,359	4,557	5,088	7,470	7,646	5,295
Net income ($ mil.)	—	—	(14)	28	(19)	20	12	(61)	29	(14)	(4)
Income as % of sales	—	—	—	0.3%	—	0.3%	0.3%	—	0.4%	—	—
Earnings per share ($)	—	—	—	—	—	—	0.71	(3.54)	1.50	(0.75)	(0.21)
Stock price - FY high ($)	—	—	—	—	—	—	20.13	18.50	22.00	22.38	20.00
Stock price - FY low ($)	—	—	—	—	—	—	14.75	12.75	16.13	14.75	11.25
Stock price - FY close ($)	0.8%	—	—	—	—	—	15.25	18.25	21.88	17.13	15.75
P/E - high	—	—	—	—	—	—	28	—	15	—	—
P/E - low	—	—	—	—	—	—	21	—	11	—	—
Dividends per share ($)	21.2%	—	—	—	—	—	0.88	1.80	1.90	1.90	1.90
Book value per share ($)	(23.8%)	—	—	—	—	—	9.33	4.46	5.64	3.30	3.15
Employees	12.0%	—	—	—	850	900	800	828	966	1,500

STOCK PRICE HISTORY

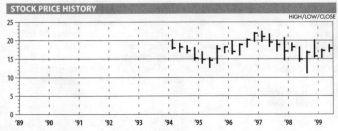

HIGH/LOW/CLOSE

1998 FISCAL YEAR-END

Debt ratio: 0.0%
Return on equity: —
Cash ($ mil.): 3
Current ratio: 0.66
Long-term debt ($ mil.): 0
No. of shares (mil.): 24
Dividends
  Yield: 12.1%
  Payout: —
Market value ($ mil.): 378

EQUIFAX INC.

OVERVIEW

Chances are good that Equifax is to blame if your application for that platinum card is denied.

As the US's largest consumer credit reporter, the Atlanta-based company has the goods on some 300 million credit holders worldwide. Equifax also approves checks, processes credit card transactions, provides database marketing consulting, and develops credit scoring software. Its customers include banks and other financial institutions, hotels, and retailers.

Equifax has used new technologies to build a database of consumers and their behavior in the US and the developed world. It owns Transax, a large check warranty company based in the UK. Because these markets (particularly the US) are mature, Equifax is targeting emerging markets

such as Latin America (where it is leading the US credit reporter charge). There is little consumer credit information infrastructure in these areas, but fast-growing economies have created a need for Equifax's services.

Through its Equifax Secure subsidiary, the company is working with such partners as Sun, Netscape, and IBM to develop products and services for the booming e-commerce industry.

Equifax and the credit reporting industry in general suffer perennial public relations problems relating to accuracy and distribution of personal information. In 1999 a new twist was added when it became known that some banks routinely withhold credit data on individuals in order to prevent competitors from targeting desirable customers.

HISTORY

Brothers Cator and Guy Woolford started Retail Credit Co. in Atlanta in 1899. They compiled credit records of local residents into their Merchants Guide, which they sold to retailers for $25 a year. The brothers extended their services to the insurance industry in 1901, investigating applicants' backgrounds. The company grew steadily and by 1920 had offices across the US and Canada. After several decades, Retail Credit branched into other information sectors, partly through acquisitions of regional credit reporters.

The company came under scrutiny in 1973 when the FTC filed an antimonopoly suit (dropped in 1982) against its consumer credit division and a complaint against its investigative practices (Retail Credit used field investigators to probe people's backgrounds). In 1976 the company became Equifax (short for "equitability in the gathering and presentation of facts").

In the 1980s and 1990s, Equifax continued to buy small businesses in the US and Europe. As the Information Age matured, businesses clamored for its services. By the end of the 1980s, Equifax had surpassed TRW (now part of Experian) as the largest provider of consumer information.

Receptive to consumer concerns in the late 1980s, the company ended list sales to US direct marketers and scrapped Marketplace, a 1991 joint venture with Lotus Development to compile a database of the shopping habits of 100 million Americans.

During the 1990s Equifax acquired regional credit and collection firms in Florida, Georgia, and Texas. The company restructured in 1992,

merging its US and Canadian operations, closing field offices, and expanding its international operations.

In 1992 and 1993 it settled cases with several states over intrusive and inaccurate credit and job reference reports. The California State Lottery ended its scratch ticket terminal contract with an Equifax unit, claiming the subsidiary ran substandard operations. The contract was reinstated in 1995 after Equifax threatened to sue, but the lottery business left a bad impression on Equifax. In 1996 it subcontracted most of its contract obligations to GTECH.

Also in 1996 Equifax exited the health care information business; the next year it spun off its insurance services business as Choicepoint. As part of this effort it reassigned CDB Infotek (acquired 1996) to ChoicePoint. After CDB was revealed to have illegally sold voter registration and social security number lists, shareholders questioned if Equifax's management was not aware of the scandal, or if it had bought CDB knowing that it would assume potential legal responsibility for the infractions (spokespeople were also caught giving contradictory explanations).

Equifax has been building its Latin American business, buying the remaining 50% of South American credit company DICOM (1997) and 80% of Brazil's largest credit information firm, Seguranca ao Credito e Informacoes (1998). In 1999 the company entered the UK credit card market with a card processing contract with IKANO Financial Services.

Chairman, President, and CEO: Thomas F. Chapman, age 55, $579,198 pay
EVP and Group Executive - North American Information Services: James J. Allhusen, age 50, $693,370 pay
EVP and Group Executive - Payment Services: Lee A. Kennedy, age 48, $604,411 pay
EVP and Group Executive - Latin America: William R. Phinney, age 60
EVP and Group Executive - Europe, and Chief Technology Officer: C. Richard Crutchfield, age 51, $299,924 pay
VP and Chief Administrative Officer: John T. Chandler
VP, Human Resources and Community Affairs: Karen H. Gaston
VP, Treasurer, and Controller: Philip J. Mazzilli, age 58
VP and CFO: David A. Post, age 46
VP and General Counsel: Bruce S. Richards, age 44
VP, Communications and Investor Relations and Secretary: Marietta Edmunds Zakas, age 40
Auditors: Arthur Andersen LLP

LOCATIONS

HQ: 1600 Peachtree St. NW, Atlanta, GA 30309
Phone: 404-885-8000   **Fax:** 404-885-8055
Web site: http://www.equifax.com

1998 Sales

	$ mil.	% of total
US	1,175	72
UK	184	12
Canada	97	6
Brazil	62	4
Other countries	103	6
Total	**1,621**	**100**

PRODUCTS/OPERATIONS

1998 Sales & Operating Income

	Sales		Operating Income	
	$ mil.	% of total	$ mil.	% of total
Information services	774	48	272	67
Payment services	518	32	105	26
Equifax Europe	215	13	1	—
Equifax Latin America	104	6	21	5
Other	10	1	9	2
Adjustments	—	—	(42)	—
Total	**1,621**	**100**	**366**	**100**

Selected Subsidiaries
Credence, Inc.
The Decisioneering Group, Inc.
Equifax Asia Pacific Holdings, Inc.
Equifax Credit Information Services, Inc.
Equifax Decision Systems, B.V.
Equifax Europe Inc.
Equifax Healthcare Information Services, Inc.
Equifax Holdings (Mexico) Inc.
Equifax Payment Services, Inc.
Equifax Properties, Inc.
Equifax Secure, Inc.
Equifax South America, Inc.
Equifax Ventures, Inc.
Financial Institution Benefit Assocation, Inc.
info, Inc.

COMPETITORS

The Associates	Marmon Group
Dun & Bradstreet	National Data
Experian	NOVA Corporation
Fair, Isaac	Total System Services
First Data	

HISTORICAL FINANCIALS & EMPLOYEES

NYSE symbol: EFX FYE: December 31	Annual Growth	1989	1990	1991	1992	1993	1994	1995	1996	1997	1998
Sales ($ mil.)	7.6%	840	1,079	1,094	1,134	1,217	1,422	1,623	1,811	1,366	1,621
Net income ($ mil.)	20.7%	36	64	5	85	64	120	148	178	184	193
Income as % of sales	—	4.2%	5.9%	0.5%	7.5%	5.2%	8.5%	9.1%	9.8%	13.4%	11.9%
Earnings per share ($)	15.4%	0.37	0.40	0.03	0.52	0.42	0.79	0.96	1.19	1.25	1.34
Stock price - FY high ($)	—	8.95	10.01	9.45	9.23	12.25	13.65	19.47	30.88	36.44	45.00
Stock price - FY low ($)	—	5.82	6.04	5.99	6.43	7.78	9.79	11.30	15.89	23.72	29.75
Stock price - FY close ($)	19.0%	7.16	7.27	7.10	9.23	12.25	11.80	19.13	27.41	35.44	34.19
P/E - high	—	24	25	315	18	29	17	20	26	29	34
P/E - low	—	16	15	200	12	19	12	12	13	19	22
Dividends per share ($)	2.9%	0.27	0.24	0.26	0.26	0.28	0.31	0.32	0.33	0.35	0.35
Book value per share ($)	0.4%	2.51	2.30	2.13	1.70	1.70	2.38	2.40	2.93	2.45	2.62
Employees	0.1%	13,900	14,200	12,400	12,400	12,800	14,200	13,400	14,100	10,000	14,000

STOCK PRICE HISTORY

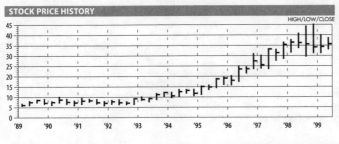

HIGH/LOW/CLOSE

1998 FISCAL YEAR-END
Debt ratio: 70.3%
Return on equity: 52.8%
Cash ($ mil.): 91
Current ratio: 1.24
Long-term debt ($ mil.): 870
No. of shares (mil.): 140
Dividends
  Yield: 1.0%
  Payout: 26.1%
Market value ($ mil.): 4,788

ERNST & YOUNG INTERNATIONAL

OVERVIEW

Even if accounting isn't the oldest profession, Ernst & Young is definitely one of its oldest practitioners.

The New York City-based concern has over 660 offices in more than 130 countries. The fourth-largest of the Big Five accounting firms (after PricewaterhouseCoopers, Andersen Worldwide, and KPMG International), Ernst & Young has abandoned its planned merger with KPMG, which would have made it #1.

The company's audit and accounting operations provide internal audit and accounting advice and oversight. The firm has one of the world's largest tax practices, particularly serving the needs of multinational clients that have to comply with multiple local tax laws. Ernst & Young's consulting services concentrate on corporate operations and information technology.

Most of the leading accounting firms have moved strongly into consulting in response to growing competition and legal entanglements evolving from audit standards. Ernst & Young has followed this trend by increasing its marketing efforts and stepping up its concentration on emerging markets, particularly in Asia.

HISTORY

The 1494 publication in Venice of Luca Pacioli's *Summa di Arithmetica* — the first published work dealing with double-entry bookkeeping — boosted the accounting profession, but it wasn't until the 19th century, as stock companies proliferated, that the industry took off.

Frederick Whinney joined the UK firm of Harding & Pullein in 1849. He became a name partner in 1859 and was followed into the business by his sons. The firm became Whinney, Smith & Whinney in 1894. The name lasted until 1965.

After WWII Whinney, Smith & Whinney formed an alliance with the American firm of Ernst & Ernst, which had been founded in Cleveland in 1903 by brothers Alwin and Theodore Ernst. The alliance, which recognized that the accountants' business clients were getting larger and becoming more international, provided that each firm would operate on the other's behalf within their respective markets.

The Whinney firm merged with Brown, Fleming & Murray in 1965 to become Whinney Murray. The merger also included the fledgling computer department set up by the latter firm to serve British Petroleum. Whinney Murray also formed joint ventures with other accounting firms to provide consulting services.

In 1979 Whinney Murray and Turquands Barton Mayhew — itself the product of a merger that began with a cricket match — united with Ernst & Ernst to form Ernst & Whinney, a firm with an international scope.

But Ernst & Whinney, a merger melting pot, wasn't finished. Ten years later, when it was the fourth-largest accounting firm, it merged with #5 Arthur Young.

Founded by Scotsman Arthur Young in 1895 in Kansas City, the firm was long known as "old reliable." Arthur Young fell on hard times in the 1980s because its audit relationships with failed savings and loans (S&Ls) led to expensive litigation.

The new firm of Ernst & Young faced a rocky start. At the end of 1990, it fended off rumors of collapse. The next year it pared back the payroll, thinning its ranks of partners and others. Ernst & Young agreed the next year to pay $400 million for allegedly mishandling the audits of four failed S&Ls.

Exhausted by the legal battles, in 1994 the firm replaced its pugnacious general counsel, Carl Riggio, with the more cost-conscious Kathryn Oberly.

In the mid-1990s Ernst & Young concentrated on building its consulting services, adding several new information software products. It also grew through acquisitions. In 1996 the firm bought Houston-based Wright Killen & Co., a petroleum and petrochemicals consulting firm, to form Ernst & Young Wright Killen. It also entered several new alliances that year, with Washington, DC-based ISD-Shaw, which provides banking industry consulting, and India's Tata Consulting, among others.

In 1997 Ernst & Young was sued for a record $4 billion for its alleged failure to effectively handle the restructuring of the now-closed Merry-Go-Round Enterprises retail chain in 1993; it settled the suit for $185 million in 1999. On the heels of a merger deal between Coopers & Lybrand and Price Waterhouse, Ernst & Young agreed that year to merge with KPMG International. At Ernst & Young's suggestion, however, the firms called off their pairing early in 1998, blaming the decision on the costly, time-consuming, and uncertain regulatory process they faced.

In 1999 Ernst & Young launched a worldwide media blitz aimed at raising awareness of the firm's full range of services.

Chairman: Philip A. Laskawy
CEO: William L. Kimsey
VC Finance, Technology, and Administration:
Hilton Dean
VC Assurance and Advisory Services: John F. Ferraro
VC Regional Integration and Planning:
Richard N. Findlater
VC Tax and Legal Services: Andrew B. Jones
VC Intrastructure: John G. Peetz Jr.
**VC Regional Integration and Entrepreneurial Growth
Companies:** Jean-Charles Raufast
VC Global Accounts: David A. Reed
VC Consulting Services: Antonio Schneider
VC Human Resources: Lewis A. Ting
Executive Partner: Paul J. Ostling
National Director SALT Practice and Procedure:
Prentiss Willson Jr.
General Counsel: Kathryn A. Oberly

LOCATIONS

HQ: 787 7th Ave., New York, NY 10019
Phone: 212-773-3000   **Fax:** 212-773-6350
Web site: http://www.eyi.com

Ernst & Young has more than 660 offices in over
130 countries.

1998 Sales

	$ mil.	% of total
Americas	6,200	57
Europe, Middle East & Africa	3,900	36
Asia/Pacific	800	7
Total	**10,900**	**100**

PRODUCTS/OPERATIONS

1998 Sales

	$ mil.	% of total
Audit	4,400	40
Consulting	4,000	37
Tax	2,500	23
Total	**10,900**	**100**

Representative Clients
American Express
BankAmerica
Coca-Cola
Eli Lilly
Hanson
Hoover's, Inc.
Knight Ridder
Lockheed Martin
Marubeni
McDonald's
Mobil
Time Warner
US Postal Service
USF&G
Wal-Mart

COMPETITORS

American Management
Andersen Worldwide
Arthur D. Little
Bain & Company
BDO International
Booz, Allen
Boston Consulting
Computer Sciences
Deloitte Touche Tohmatsu
EDS
Grant Thornton International
IBM
KPMG
Marsh & McLennan
McKinsey & Company
Perot Systems
Policy Management Systems
PricewaterhouseCoopers
Towers Perrin

HISTORICAL FINANCIALS & EMPLOYEES

Partnership FYE: September 30	Annual Growth	1989	1990	1991	1992	1993	1994	1995	1996	1997	1998
Sales ($ mil.)	11.2%	4,200	5,006	5,406	5,701	5,839	6,020	6,867	7,800	9,100	10,900
Employees	4.1%	—	61,591	61,173	58,900	58,377	61,287	68,452	72,000	79,750	85,000

SALES HISTORY

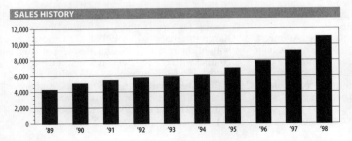

ERNST & YOUNG

THE ESTÉE LAUDER COMPANIES INC

OVERVIEW

Estée Lauder's products must work: Its customers are getting younger. The New York City-based company, a world leader in upscale skin care, makeup, and fragrances, captures nearly half of all US prestige cosmetics sales with its Estée Lauder, Clinique, and other brands. Estée Lauder has expanded its customer base to include younger, trendier shoppers with the acquisition of Sassaby's *jane* cosmetics brand (sold at mass merchants for a teen-friendly $2.99) and the hip Make-Up Art Cosmetics (M·A·C) line.

The company has also launched fragrances licensed from designer Tommy Hilfiger: Its tommy and tommy girl are among the top prestige fragrances sold in US department stores, as is Clinique's new happy fragrance. Estée Lauder's Origins and Aveda lines of botanical beauty products are aimed at environmentally conscious consumers. Other sales strategies include replacing department stores' traditional glass cosmetics counters with open displays (so that women can explore products more easily), launching Clinique counters in college bookstores, and creating an Origins catalog.

With a strong international presence (overseas sales in more than 100 countries bring in about 40% of business), Estée Lauder continues to expand. The Lauder family owns nearly 65% of the company, with the third generation now involved in running the firm.

HISTORY

Estée Lauder (then Josephine Esther Mentzer) started her beauty career by selling skin care products formulated by her Hungarian uncle, John Schotz, during the 1930s. Eventually she packaged and peddled her variations of his formulas, which included face cream and a cleansing oil.

With the help of her husband, Joseph Lauder, she set up her first office in Queens, New York, in 1944 and added lipstick, eye shadow, and face powder to the line. Joseph oversaw production, and Estée sold her wares to beauty salons and department stores, using samples and gifts to win customers. Throughout the 1950s Estée traveled cross-country, at first to sell her line to high-profile department stores like Neiman-Marcus, I. Magnin, and Saks, and later to train saleswomen in these stores.

She created her first fragrance, Youth Dew bath oil, in 1953. In the late 1950s many of the large US cosmetics houses introduced European skin care lines that had scientific-sounding names and supposedly advanced skin repair properties. Estée Lauder's contribution was Re-Nutriv cream. It sold for $115 a pound in 1960, the same year the firm hit the million-dollar profit mark. The cream's advertising campaign established the "Lauder look": sophisticated and tastefully wealthy, an image that Estée herself cultivated.

In 1964 Estée Lauder introduced Aramis, a fragrance for men, and in 1968, with the help of a *Vogue* editor, it launched Clinique, a hypoallergenic skin care line with a scientific image (sales staff wore white lab coats). In 1972 Estée's son Leonard became president; Estée remained CEO.

The company introduced two fragrances for women, White Linen and Cinnabar, in 1978. The next year Estée Lauder created Prescriptives skin care and makeup for young professional women. From 1978 to 1983 the company focused R&D on skin care products, resulting in top-selling Night Repair. Leonard was named CEO in 1983. By 1988 the company had captured a third of the US market in prestige cosmetics. Leonard's brother, Ronald, who had left Estée Lauder in 1983, returned after losing a bid to become mayor of New York in 1989.

Estée Lauder unveiled its Origins botanical cosmetics line in 1990. Also that year it recruited former Calvin Klein executive Robin Burns to head its domestic branch. The company launched the All Skins cosmetics line in 1991 and in 1994 bought a controlling stake in hip Make-Up Art Cosmetics (M·A·C).

Leonard became chairman in 1995. The company's IPO that year was structured to allow Estée and Ronald to avoid a potential $95 million tax bill (inspiring a 1997 revision of the federal tax law). In 1997 it bought botanical beauty products concern Aveda for $300 million, broadening distribution into 30,000 hair salons, and entered the mass market with its purchase of Sassaby (*jane* cosmetics).

In 1997 and 1998 the company reached deals to make and market cosmetics and fragrances for top designers, including Donna Karan International. In 1998 Estée Lauder bought the rest of M·A·C and, despite potential conflict with the retailers on which it depends, launched a Clinique products Web site.

The Lauder family in 1999 sold 3.4 million common shares, totaling a little over 4% of the company. In August 1999 Estée Lauder agreed to purchase rapidly growing Stila Cosmetics.

OFFICERS

Chairman and CEO: Leonard A. Lauder, age 65,
$5,617,000 pay
VC: Jeanette S. Wagner, $1,812,700 pay
President and COO: Fred H. Langhammer, age 54,
$3,300,000 pay
SVP and CFO: Robert J. Bigler, age 50
SVP, Secretary, and General Counsel: Saul H. Magram,
$1,791,400 pay
SVP Global Packaging: Roger Caracappa
SVP Corporate Human Resources:
Andrew J. Cavanaugh, age 51
SVP Global Operations: John B. Chilton
SVP Global Information Systems: John M. Corrigan
SVP Research and Development: Joseph Gubernick
**Chairman, Clinique Laboratories and Estée Lauder
International:** Ronald S. Lauder, age 54
President, Estée Lauder USA and Canada:
Daniel J. Brestle, age 53, $1,566,500 pay
President, Clinique USA and Canada: William P. Lauder
Auditors: Arthur Andersen LLP

LOCATIONS

HQ: 767 5th Ave., New York, NY 10153
Phone: 212-572-4200 **Fax:** 212-572-6633
Web site: http://www.elcompanies.com

1998 Sales & Operating Income

	Sales		Operating Income	
	$ mil.	% of total	$ mil.	% of total
Americas				
US	2,076	57	219	54
Other countries	129	4	29	7
Europe, Middle East				
& Africa	961	27	131	32
Asia/Pacific	452	12	30	7
Total	**3,618**	**100**	**409**	**100**

PRODUCTS/OPERATIONS

1998 Sales

	$ mil.	% of total
Makeup	1,320	36
Skin care	1,253	35
Fragrance	988	27
Hair care	57	2
Total	**3,618**	**100**

Selected Brands

Aramis	*jane*
Aveda	Kiton (licensed)
Bobbi Brown *essentials*	Lab Series for Men
Clinique	M·A·C
Creme de la Mer	Origins
Donna Karan (licensed)	Prescriptives
Estée Lauder	Tommy Hilfiger (licensed)

COMPETITORS

Adrien Arpel	Jean Philippe Fragrances
Alberto-Culver	Joh. A. Benckiser
Allou	L'Oréal
Amway	LVMH
Avon	Mary Kay
BeautiControl Cosmetics	Perfumania
Body Shop	Procter & Gamble
Bristol-Myers Squibb	Renaissance Cosmetics
Chanel	Revlon
Clarins	Shiseido
Coty	Tristar
Garden Botanika	Unilever
Helen of Troy	Wella
Intimate Brands	

HISTORICAL FINANCIALS & EMPLOYEES

NYSE symbol: EL FYE: June 30	Annual Growth	1989	1990	1991	1992	1993	1994	1995	1996	1997	1998
Sales ($ mil.)	7.6%	1,865	2,010	2,100	2,252	2,448	2,576	2,899	3,195	3,382	3,618
Net income ($ mil.)	29.4%	—	—	39	51	58	70	121	160	198	237
Income as % of sales	—	—	—	.1.9%	2.3%	2.4%	2.7%	4.2%	5.0%	5.8%	6.5%
Earnings per share ($)	22.8%	—	—	—	—	—	—	—	0.59	0.74	0.89
Stock price - FY high ($)	—	—	—	—	—	—	—	—	22.00	26.75	36.97
Stock price - FY low ($)	—	—	—	—	—	—	—	—	15.88	17.38	19.50
Stock price - FY close ($)	28.4%	—	—	—	—	—	—	—	21.13	25.13	34.84
P/E - high	—	—	—	—	—	—	—	—	37	36	42
P/E - low	—	—	—	—	—	—	—	—	27	23	22
Dividends per share ($)	—	—	—	—	—	—	—	—	0.09	0.17	0.13
Book value per share ($)	32.3%	—	—	—	—	—	—	—	1.68	2.32	2.94
Employees	4.8%	10,000	10,000	12,000	12,000	12,000	10,000	9,900	13,500	14,700	15,300

STOCK PRICE HISTORY

HIGH/LOW/CLOSE

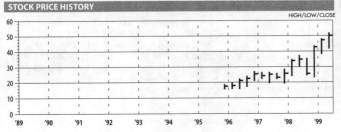

1998 FISCAL YEAR-END

Debt ratio: 28.7%
Return on equity: 34.0%
Cash ($ mil.): 278
Current ratio: 1.74
Long-term debt ($ mil.): 425
No. of shares (mil.): 237
Dividends
  Yield: 0.4%
  Payout: 14.6%
Market value ($ mil.): 8,244

THE E. W. SCRIPPS COMPANY

OVERVIEW

One of the oldest newspaper chains in the US, The E. W. Scripps Company has helped shape journalism for over a century. The Cincinnati-based company's portfolio includes 19 daily newspapers (*Denver Rocky Mountain News, The Commercial Appeal* of Memphis) with a combined circulation of about 1.3 million. Scripps also owns a handful of community newspapers (publishing weekly or semiweekly) and operates the Scripps Howard News Service, a wire service covering US and international news.

While newspapers generate nearly 60% of the company's revenue, Scripps' nine TV stations bring in more than 20%. Scripps is also active in cable TV through its ownership of Home & Garden Television (HGTV), its 59% ownership of the Food Network, and its 12% ownership of FOX Sports South. Through United Media, Scripps' licensing and syndication arm, the company syndicates more than 150 comic strips including *Dilbert* and the legendary *Peanuts*. Scripps Productions creates nonfiction cable programs. Scripps also has a 60% interest in Yellow Pages directories in four Southern states.

With its foothold in traditional media firmly established, Scripps is looking to broaden its profile in cable TV programming. In addition to stepping up its efforts to boost distribution of HGTV and the Food Network, Scripps is also planning to unveil its Do-it-Yourself cable network.

Trusts benefiting members of the Scripps family own about 60% of the company and control more than 90% of the voting shares.

HISTORY

Edward Willis "E. W." Scripps launched a newspaper empire in 1878 with his creation of *The Penny Press* in Cleveland. While adding to his string of inexpensive newspapers, Scripps demonstrated his fondness for economy by shunning "extras" such as toilet paper and pencils for his employees.

In 1907 Scripps gave the Associated Press a new rival, combining three wire services to form United Press. E. W. Scripps' health began deteriorating in the 1920s, and Roy Howard was tapped to become chairman. Howard's contribution to the burgeoning media enterprise was soon acknowledged when the company's name was changed to the Scripps Howard League. E. W. Scripps died in 1926, leaving a newspaper chain second in size only to the Hearst chain.

In the 1930s Scripps made a foray into radio, buying WCPO (Cincinnati) and KNOX (Knoxville, Tennessee). Roy Howard placed his son Jack in charge of Scripps' radio holdings; under Jack's leadership, Scripps branched into TV. Its first TV station, Cleveland's WEWS, began broadcasting in 1947. Scripps also made Charlie Brown a household name when it launched the *Peanuts* comic strip in 1950. By the time Charles Scripps (E. W. Scripps' grandson) became chairman and Jack Howard was appointed president in 1953, the company had amassed 19 newspapers and a handful of radio and TV stations.

United Press merged with Hearst's International News Service in 1958 to become United Press International (UPI). In 1963 Scripps took its broadcasting holdings public as Scripps Howard Broadcasting Company (Scripps retained controlling interest). Scripps Howard Broadcasting expanded its TV station portfolio in the 1970s and 1980s, buying KJRH (Tulsa, Oklahoma; 1971), KSHB (Kansas City, Missouri; 1977), KNXV (Phoenix; 1985), WFTS (Tampa; 1986), and WXYZ (Detroit; 1986).

With UPI facing mounting losses, Scripps sold the news service in 1982. Under the leadership of chief executive Lawrence Leser, Scripps began streamlining, jettisoning extraneous investments and refocusing on its core business lines. In 1988 after decades of family ownership, the company went public as The E. W. Scripps Company (the Scripps family retained a controlling interest).

In 1994 Scripps Howard Broadcasting merged back into E. W. Scripps Company. That year Scripps branched into cable TV when its Home & Garden Television network went on the air. Former newspaper editor William Burleigh became CEO in 1996. Scripps' 1997 purchase of the newspaper and broadcast operations of Harte-Hanks Communications marked the largest acquisition in its history. Scripps promptly traded Harte-Hanks' broadcasting operations for a controlling interest in the Food Network.

Scripps sold television production unit Scripps Howard Productions in 1998. The company sold its Dallas Community Newspaper Group in 1999 and prepared its Do-it-Yourself cable network for a debut later that year.

OFFICERS

Chairman, President and CEO: William R. Burleigh, age 63, $942,550 pay (prior to promotion)
EVP: Richard A. Boehne, age 42
SVP Corporate Development: Craig C. Standen, age 56, $416,305 pay
SVP Finance and Administration: Daniel J. Castellini, age 59, $443,260 pay
SVP Newspapers: Alan M. Horton, age 55, $559,000 pay
SVP Television: Paul F. "Frank" Gardner, age 56, $514,125 pay
President, Food Network: Eric Ober
President and CEO, Home and Garden Television: Kenneth W. Lowe
President and CEO, United Media: Douglas R. Stern
VP and Controller: J. Robert Routt, age 44
VP Human Resources: Gregory L. Ebel, age 43
VP Investor Relations and Communications: Timothy E. Strautberg, age 36
VP New Media: Neal F. Fondren, age 40
VP Newspapers: Stephen W. Sullivan, age 52
VP Newspaper Operations: Jeffrey J. Hively, age 45
VP Television: James M. Hart, age 57
Corporate Secretary: M. Denise Kuprionis, age 42
Treasurer: E. John Wolfzorn, age 53
Auditors: Deloitte & Touche LLP

LOCATIONS

HQ: 312 Walnut St., Cincinnati, OH 45201
Phone: 513-977-3000   **Fax:** 513-977-3721
Web site: http://www.scripps.com

The E. W. Scripps Company has operations in 17 states and Washington, DC.

PRODUCTS/OPERATIONS

1998 Sales

	$ mil.	% of total
Newspapers	865	59
Broadcast television	331	23
Cable television	149	10
Licensing & other media	96	7
Divested operating units	14	1
Total	**1,455**	**100**

1998 Sales

	$ mil.	% of total
Advertising	1,094	75
Circulation	154	11
Licensing	62	4
Joint operating agency distributions	48	3
Affiliate fees	38	3
Program production	11	1
Other	48	3
Total	**1,455**	**100**

COMPETITORS

Belo	Media General
Associated Press	MediaNews
CBS	New York Times
Copley Press	News Corp.
Dow Jones	Reuters
Freedom Communications	Times Mirror
Gannett	Tribune
Hearst	Washington Post
Knight Ridder	

HISTORICAL FINANCIALS & EMPLOYEES

NYSE symbol: SSP FYE: December 31	Annual Growth	1989	1990	1991	1992	1993	1994	1995	1996	1997	1998
Sales ($ mil.)	1.6%	1,266	1,297	1,300	1,263	1,206	1,220	1,030	1,122	1,242	1,455
Net income ($ mil.)	4.4%	89	48	65	106	129	123	94	157	158	131
Income as % of sales	—	7.1%	3.7%	5.0%	8.4%	10.7%	10.1%	9.1%	14.0%	12.7%	9.0%
Earnings per share ($)	(9.1%)	—	—	—	—	—	—	—	1.96	1.93	1.62
Stock price - FY high ($)	—	—	—	—	—	—	—	—	35.25	48.94	58.50
Stock price - FY low ($)	—	—	—	—	—	—	—	—	32.75	32.25	38.50
Stock price - FY close ($)	19.2%	—	—	—	—	—	—	—	35.00	48.44	49.75
P/E - high	—	—	—	—	—	—	—	—	18	25	36
P/E - low	—	—	—	—	—	—	—	—	17	17	24
Dividends per share ($)	—	—	—	—	—	—	—	—	0.00	0.39	0.54
Book value per share ($)	7.9%	—	—	—	—	—	—	—	11.70	13.01	13.61
Employees	(2.5%)	9,900	10,000	9,700	8,200	7,600	7,700	6,700	6,800	8,100	7,900

STOCK PRICE HISTORY

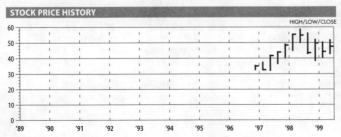

HIGH/LOW/CLOSE

1998 FISCAL YEAR-END

Debt ratio: 32.0%
Return on equity: 12.3%
Cash ($ mil.): 14
Current ratio: 0.76
Long-term debt ($ mil.): 502
No. of shares (mil.): 79
Dividends
  Yield: 1.1%
  Payout: 33.3%
Market value ($ mil.): 3,908

EXIDE CORPORATION

OVERVIEW

Exide combines positives and negatives in more ways than one. Based in Bloomfield Hills, Michigan, Exide is the world's #1 maker of lead-acid automotive and industrial batteries. The company sells primarily to the automotive aftermarket through NAPA, Kmart, Pep Boys, and other retailers, and to car manufacturers DaimlerChrysler, Fiat, and Volkswagen. Automotive batteries (65% of sales) include brands Exide, Prestolite, and Tudor.

Exide sells its industrial batteries to customers that include the navies of Germany, Israel, and Turkey. It sells nearly 100,000 tank batteries a year to the US Army. Exide also makes batteries for trucks, tractors, boats, and forklifts, as well as battery chargers, alternators, and lithium batteries.

Due to heavy debt and ongoing legal woes, Exide has slowed acquisitions to concentrate on battery markets that emphasize high margins over volume. Exide has been the subject of sale rumors, a recapitalization that didn't materialize, and an SEC probe. Former chairman and CEO Arthur Hawkins owns about 10% of Exide.

HISTORY

Exide got its start in 1888 when Thomas Edison founded the Electric Storage Battery Company (ESB) in Gloucester, New Jersey, to develop a battery as a backup for steam engines and dynamos. By 1890 ESB had installed the first practical battery backup in a Philadelphia utility, and that year it also provided batteries for the US's first streetcars. Sales picked up as the versatility of the battery was recognized, and in 1898 ESB batteries powered the US Navy's first submarine. The company was soon the world's top battery maker.

The Exide brand name debuted in 1901, and the firsts kept coming: the first automobile ignition battery (1903), the batteries used in the first transcontinental telephone services (1915), and the batteries used for the first air-conditioned train (1931). Exide batteries also powered Jean and Jeanette Piccard's first balloon ride into the stratosphere and Commander Richard Byrd's "Little America" Antarctic base, both in 1934.

WWII saw the beginning of ESB's vertical integration, with the purchases of a maker of battery chargers and testers (1938) and a maker of battery containers (1946). ESB also developed battery-powered torpedoes used in WWII.

In 1951 Exide batteries assured the continuous operation of many Bell Systems relay stations for the first coast-to-coast wireless telephone network. In 1957 it entered the dry-cell battery business by acquiring the Ray-O-Vac Company. NASA used Exide batteries throughout the Apollo missions of the 1960s and 1970s, including the 1969 moon landing.

Inco Limited of Toronto purchased ESB in 1974. Management reorganized ESB in 1978 as a holding company, ESB Ray-O-Vac. The Exide brand stagnated, losing market share. In 1980 ESB Ray-O-Vac became INCO Electro Energy, with Exide as a subsidiary.

Investors led by the Spectrum Group and First Chicago Investment rescued Exide's North American operations in 1983. In 1985 the company hired ITT executive Arthur Hawkins as CEO and began a turnaround. Exide bought General Battery in 1987 to become #1 in the US auto battery market. The company acquired Speedclip Manufacturing (battery cables, terminals, and accessories; 1989) and Shadwood Industries (automotive battery chargers, fully acquired 1991) and went public in 1993.

Exide expanded into Europe in the mid-1990s, spending more than $600 million to buy firms in France, Spain, and the UK, including two of Europe's largest battery makers, Tudor and CEAc. In 1997 Exide completed its European expansion by buying three battery-making units from Germany's CEAG AG.

Despite market dominance, Exide lost about 75% of its share value from 1996 to 1998. Some shareholders sued management, alleging misrepresentation, and the Florida Attorney General and the SEC launched probes into whether the company sold used batteries as new. (Exide settled with Florida without admitting wrongdoing for $3.3 million in 1999.) In 1998 management clumsily announced a recapitalization attempt and then changed its mind, and the FBI continued looking for more than 100,000 batteries unaccounted for since 1996.

Amidst these problems, Hawkins resigned as chairman and CEO and former Chrysler exec Robert Lutz replaced him. Exide also formed a joint venture with Schumacher, a top maker of battery chargers. In 1999 Exide canceled a contract with Sears (for which it made 4 million DieHard batteries a year) to focus on profits rather than volume.

Chairman, President, and CEO: Robert A. Lutz, age 67, $300,000 pay
Chairman, President, and CEO, Exide Holding Europe: Santiago Ramirez
President and COO: Alan C. Johnson, age 51
EVP and CFO: James M. Diasio, age 42, $135,758 pay
EVP and CFO, Exide Holding Europe: Ronald J. Gardhouse, age 52
EVP Human Resources: Jack J. Sosiak, age 60, $220,000 pay
VP and General Counsel: John R. Van Zile, age 47
VP and Controller: Kenneth S. Pawloski
VP and Treasurer: David Kelly
VP Manufacturing: Malcolm Gavant, age 55
Auditors: Arthur Andersen LLP

LOCATIONS

HQ: 645 Penn St., Reading, PA 19601
Phone: 610-378-0500   **Fax:** 610-378-0824
Web site: http://www.exideworld.com

Exide has operations in Belgium, Canada, France, Germany, Italy, Poland, Portugal, Spain, Sweden, Turkey, the UK, and the US.

1999 Sales

	$ mil.	% of total
US	837	35
Germany	453	19
France	262	11
UK	259	11
Spain	194	8
Italy	173	8
Other countries	196	8
Total	**2,374**	**100**

PRODUCTS/OPERATIONS

1999 Sales

	% of total
Aftermarket	83
OEMS	17
Total	**100**

1999 Sales

	% of total
Automotive batteries	65
Industrial batteries	31
Other products	4
Total	**100**

Selected Products
Automotive batteries (for agricultural equipment, buses, commercial trucks, construction equipment, and emergency and passenger vehicles)
Industrial batteries
  Traction batteries (for forklifts and mining locomotives)
Specialty batteries (for boats, garden equipment, golf carts, motorcycles, and wheelchairs)
  Standby/backup batteries
Other Products
  Battery accessories
  Battery chargers
  Booster cables

COMPETITORS

Delco Remy
Delphi Automotive Systems
General Motors
Interstate Batteries
Invensys
Johnson Controls
Matsushita
Pacific Dunlop
Varta
Yuasa

HISTORICAL FINANCIALS & EMPLOYEES

NYSE symbol: EX FYE: March 31	Annual Growth	1990	1991	1992	1993	1994	1995	1996	1997	1998	1999
Sales ($ mil.)	14.6%	694	743	570	579	680	1,199	2,343	2,333	2,273	2,374
Net income ($ mil.)	—	(25)	(19)	(9)	(10)	4	1	(9)	16	(10)	(130)
Income as % of sales	—	—	—	—	—	0.6%	0.1%	—	0.7%	—	—
Earnings per share ($)	—	—	—	—	—	0.41	0.06	(0.37)	0.77	(0.45)	(6.12)
Stock price - FY high ($)	—	—	—	—	—	42.25	57.50	53.88	30.25	31.25	21.75
Stock price - FY low ($)	—	—	—	—	—	20.00	32.75	23.25	16.00	14.63	5.38
Stock price - FY close ($)	(21.4%)	—	—	—	—	37.00	36.75	23.38	16.38	16.94	11.13
P/E - high	—	—	—	—	—	103	958	—	39	—	—
P/E - low	—	—	—	—	—	49	546	—	21	—	—
Dividends per share ($)	32.0%	—	—	—	—	0.02	0.08	0.08	0.08	0.08	0.08
Book value per share ($)	(8.6%)	—	—	—	—	11.11	20.67	21.03	17.41	13.83	7.08
Employees	11.0%	6,372	4,466	4,480	5,428	11,100	11,712	16,597	15,814	17,183	16,300

STOCK PRICE HISTORY

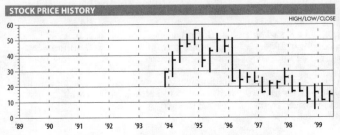

HIGH/LOW/CLOSE

1999 FISCAL YEAR-END

Debt ratio: 88.4%
Return on equity: —
Cash ($ mil.): 21
Current ratio: 1.83
Long-term debt ($ mil.): 1,155
No. of shares (mil.): 21
Dividends
  Yield: 0.7%
  Payout: —
Market value ($ mil.): 238

EXXON CORPORATION

OVERVIEW

This tiger has a large bite. Exxon is the world's largest oil and gas company, leaping over Royal Dutch/Shell, and the Irving, Texas-based company is readying itself to sink its teeth into Mobil. It is indeed a jungle out there. Low oil prices have squeezed the majors' profits, leading to industrywide mergers and cost-cutting, especially at the gas pump. Exxon hopes to save some $3 billion through its merger with Mobil.

Exxon — which has major oil and gas holdings in Germany, the Netherlands, Norway, the US, and the UK — boasts proved reserves of 1.1 billion barrels of oil equivalent. It is looking for new reserves in Azerbaijan, Brazil, Kazakhstan, Russia, and West Africa.

The company has more than 32,000 gas stations worldwide, mostly in Europe and the US. Every day Exxon sells about 70 million gallons of motor fuel to 8 million drivers. The company is introducing larger formats for its US gas stations, including bigger convenience stores.

Exxon also produces petrochemicals, including olefins and aromatics; mines coal, copper, and other minerals; and has electric power interests in China and Hong Kong. The company is expanding its operations in China, where it supplies asphalt, fuels, and lubricants, and is increasing marketing efforts in India and Vietnam for lube oil and lubricants.

HISTORY

John D. Rockefeller, a commodity trader, started his first oil refinery in 1863 in Cleveland. Realizing that the price of oil at the well would shrink with each new strike, Rockefeller chose to monopolize oil refining and transportation. He raised $1 million and in 1870 formed the Standard Oil Company. In 1882 Rockefeller and his associates created the Standard Oil Trust, which allowed the existing Standard Oil affiliates to be dissolved and new, ostensibly independent companies set up in different states, including the Standard Oil Company of New Jersey (Jersey Standard).

Initially capitalized at $70 million, the Standard Oil Trust controlled 90% of the petroleum industry. In 1911, after two decades of political and legal wrangling, the Supreme Court disbanded the trust into 34 companies, the largest of which was Jersey Standard.

Walter Teagle became president in 1917, secretly bought half of Humble Oil of Texas (1919), and expanded into South America. In 1928 Jersey Standard joined in the Red Line Agreement, which reserved most Middle East oil for a few companies. Teagle resigned in 1942 after Congress looked into a prewar research pact giving Farben of Germany patents for an essential lead in aviation fuel in exchange for a synthetic rubber formula (never received).

The 1948 purchase of a 30% stake in Arabian American Oil Company, combined with a 7% share of Iranian production bought in 1954, made Jersey Standard the world's #1 oil company at that time.

Other US companies still using the Standard Oil name objected to Jersey Standard's marketing in their territories as Esso (derived from the initials for Standard Oil). To end the confusion, in 1972 Jersey Standard became Exxon, a name change that cost $100 million.

Nationalization of oil assets by producing countries reduced Exxon's access to oil during the 1970s. Though it increased exploration that decade and the next, its reserves shrank.

Oil tanker *Exxon Valdez* spilled some 11 million gallons of oil into Alaska's Prince William Sound in 1989. Exxon spent billions on the cleanup, and in 1994 a federal jury in Alaska slapped Exxon with a $5 billion fine (which Exxon appealed in 1997).

In 1994 Exxon and Pertamina, the Indonesian state oil company, made a $40 billion pact to develop the giant Natuna gas field (50% owned by Exxon), and the next year Exxon signed a $15 billion agreement to develop three fields off Russia's Sakhalin Island.

Exxon made a major oil discovery in the Gulf of Mexico in 1996. That year it merged its worldwide oil and fuel additives business with that of Royal Dutch/Shell.

In 1997, under FTC pressure, Exxon agreed to run ads refuting past claims that its premium gas enables car engines to run more efficiently. The next year CEO Lee Raymond upset environmentalists when he publicly questioned the global warming theory. After its string of PR disasters, Exxon tried to save its image by raising money to save the world's tigers.

But image isn't everything. In 1998 Exxon agreed to buy Mobil in an $80 billion deal, one of the largest mergers in US history. Regulators worldwide were kept busy in 1999 deciding what assets would have to be sold by the new Exxon Mobil, which would be headed by Raymond.

Chairman and CEO: Lee R. Raymond, age 60,
$3,300,000 pay
SVP: Rene Dahan, age 57, $1,300,000 pay
SVP: Harry J. Longwell, age 57, $1,300,000 pay
SVP: Robert E. Wilhelm, age 58, $1,300,000 pay
President, Exxon Ventures (CIS): K. T. Koonce
VP Public Affairs: A. W. Atkiss
VP; President, Exxon Company, USA: A. L. Condray,
age 56
VP Human Resources: T. J. Hearn
VP and Controller: D. D. Humphreys, age 51
VP and General Counsel: Charles W. Matthews Jr.,
age 54
VP; President, Exxon Company International:
S. R. McGill, age 56
VP; President, Exxon Coal and Minerals Company:
J. T. McMillan, age 62
VP and Treasurer: Frank A. Risch, age 56
VP Washington Office: J. J. Rouse
VP; President, Exxon Chemical Company:
Daniel S. Sanders, age 59
VP Environment and Safety: F. B. Sprow
VP and General Tax Counsel: P. E. Sullivan, age 55
VP; President, Exxon Exploration Company:
J. L. Thompson, age 59
VP Investor Relations and Secretary: T. P. Townsend,
age 62
General Manager Corporate Planning: R. A. Brenneman
Auditors: PricewaterhouseCoopers LLP

LOCATIONS

HQ: 5959 Las Colinas Blvd., Irving, TX 75039-2298
Phone: 972-444-1000   **Fax:** 972-444-1882
Web site: http://www.exxon.com

PRODUCTS/OPERATIONS

1998 Sales & Net Income

	Sales		Net Income	
	$ mil.	% of total	$ mil.	% of total
Petroleum & natural gas	104,051	90	5,166	76
Chemicals	10,504	9	1,213	18
Other operations	862	1	384	6
Adjustments	(14,720)	—	(330)	—
Total	**100,697**	**100**	**6,433**	**100**

COMPETITORS

7-Eleven	Mobil
Amerada Hess	Norsk Hydro
Ashland	Occidental
BHP	PDVSA
BP Amoco	PEMEX
Caltex	Petrobras
Celanese	Phillips Petroleum
Chevron	Racetrac Petroleum
Costco Companies	Royal Dutch/Shell
Dow Chemical	Saudi Aramco
DuPont	Sunoco
Eastman Chemical	Texaco
Elf Aquitaine	Tosco
ENI	TOTAL FINA
Huntsman	Ultramar Diamond
ICI	Shamrock
Imperial Oil	Union Carbide
Kerr-McGee	Unocal
Koch	USX-Marathon
Lyondell Chemical	YPF Sociedad Anonima

HISTORICAL FINANCIALS & EMPLOYEES

NYSE symbol: XON FYE: December 31	Annual Growth	1989	1990	1991	1992	1993	1994	1995	1996	1997	1998
Sales ($ mil.)	1.7%	86,656	105,519	102,847	103,160	97,825	99,683	107,893	116,728	120,279	100,697
Net income ($ mil.)	7.0%	3,510	5,010	5,600	4,770	5,280	5,100	6,470	7,510	8,460	6,433
Income as % of sales	—	4.1%	4.7%	5.4%	4.6%	5.4%	5.1%	6.0%	6.4%	7.0%	6.4%
Earnings per share ($)	7.3%	1.37	1.98	2.23	1.89	2.09	2.03	2.58	2.99	3.37	2.58
Stock price - FY high ($)	—	25.81	27.56	30.94	32.75	34.50	33.69	43.00	50.63	67.25	77.31
Stock price - FY low ($)	—	20.75	22.44	24.81	26.88	28.88	28.06	30.06	38.81	48.25	56.63
Stock price - FY close ($)	12.7%	25.00	25.88	30.44	30.56	31.56	30.38	40.56	49.00	61.19	73.13
P/E - high	—	19	14	14	17	17	17	17	17	20	30
P/E - low	—	15	11	11	14	14	14	12	13	14	22
Dividends per share ($)	4.0%	1.15	1.24	1.34	1.42	1.44	1.46	1.50	1.96	1.63	1.64
Book value per share ($)	4.9%	11.68	12.89	13.71	13.29	13.74	14.84	16.10	17.41	17.69	17.98
Employees	(3.0%)	104,000	104,000	101,000	95,000	91,000	86,000	82,000	79,000	80,000	79,000

STOCK PRICE HISTORY

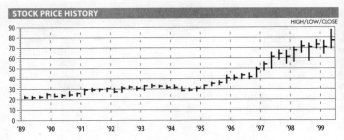

HIGH/LOW/CLOSE

1998 FISCAL YEAR-END

Debt ratio: 9.4%
Return on equity: 14.7%
Cash ($ mil.): 1,441
Current ratio: 0.91
Long-term debt ($ mil.): 4,530
No. of shares (mil.): 2,428
Dividends
  Yield: 2.2%
  Payout: 63.6%
Market value ($ mil.): 177,560

FAMILY DOLLAR STORES, INC.

OVERVIEW

For families on a budget, the buck stops at Family Dollar Stores. The Charlotte, North Carolina-based retail chain operates about 3,300 no-frills, low-overhead, small stores (6,000 to 8,000 sq. ft.) in 39 states from Maine to Florida and as far west as New Mexico. Family Dollar offers discounts on basic merchandise for family and home needs, including apparel, health and beauty aids, housewares, and school supplies. It keeps prices low by buying manufacturers' overruns, buying merchandise from vendors who overbought, buying via yearlong contracts, and arranging for manufacturing during factory downtimes. Since price is the most important factor for the company's target customer — a woman shopping for a family that makes less than $25,000 a year — most merchandise sells for less than $18.

In the face of increased competition from mass marketers such as Wal-Mart, the company has shifted to an everyday-low-pricing strategy (as opposed to making short-lived promotional offers). Family Dollar is expanding rapidly without accumulating long-term debt.

Founder and chairman Leon Levine and his family own about 22% of the firm.

HISTORY

Leon Levine came from a retailing family. His father, who founded The Hub, a general store-style department store in Rockingham, North Carolina, in 1908, died when Levine was 13, and the boy and his older brother Al helped his mother run the store. (Al went on to found the Pic 'n Pay self-service shoe stores in 1957.) In 1959, when he was 25, Levine (with his cousin Bernie) opened his own store in Charlotte, with nothing priced over a dollar, targeting lower- and middle-income families seeking good value for their money. The concept of low prices and small neighborhood stores was immediately popular, and Levine began adding stores. By 1970, when he took Family Dollar Stores public, it had 100 stores in five states. That year Levine brought his cousin Lewis into the business.

Family Dollar's profits plummeted in the mid-1970s as the chain's lower-income customers, hit by recession, cut back on spending — even though all merchandise was priced at $3 or less. Such pricing made for tight margins, so the company dropped the policy. Family Dollar also improved inventory controls to make operations more efficient and began moving into other states. Sales picked up, topping $100 million in 1977, and the next year the firm bought the 40-store Top Dollar chain from Sav-A-Stop.

As the 1980s began, Family Dollar had nearly 400 stores in eight southern states; rapidly expanding, it was adding more than 100 stores a year. But in an effort to boost margins, the company had lost its pricing edge, and it was almost oblivious to a new threat — Wal-Mart's truckload prices and quick domination of the southern discount retailing market.

After Family Dollar sales were flat in 1986 and dropped 10% in 1987, Levine finally took action. He found his prices were sometimes as much as 10% higher than Wal-Mart's and his stores often didn't have sufficient stocks of advertised products. He lowered prices, declaring that Family Dollar would not be undersold, and again instituted new inventory controls. But the action had not come quickly enough, argued president and COO Lewis, who left the company in 1987. (He was also upset over a huge salary disparity: Leon — noted for being a hard bargainer with suppliers — was making $1.8 million compared to Lewis' $260,000.) Also leaving was Leon's son Howard, who had joined the firm in 1981; he returned to the fold in 1996 and became CEO in 1998.

Family Dollar picked up momentum in the 1990s. It implemented a major renovation of stores and phased out a number of low-margin items such as motor oil and tools in favor of such high-margin items as toys and boom boxes. The company also accelerated its growth plans, opening stores in a number of new markets and setting up a second distribution center, in Arkansas, in 1994 to support its westward expansion. Also in 1994 Family Dollar began offering everyday low prices and scaled back its sales promotions.

The pace of expansion was steady during the late 1990s, as the company opened hundreds of new stores and closed underperforming locations. Family Dollar added 200 stores in fiscal 1995, 165 in fiscal 1996, and 186 in fiscal 1997. In fiscal 1998 it added 250 stores and opened a Virginia distribution center (its third). In fiscal 1999 Family Dollar began work on an Oklahoma distribution center and said it would add up to 350 stores, with at least 400 more on tap for fiscal 2000.

Chairman: Leon Levine, age 61, $1,492,450 pay
VC, CFO, and Chief Administrative Officer:
R. James Kelly, age 51, $706,950 pay
President, CEO, and COO: Howard R. Levine, age 39,
$513,278 pay
EVP, Secretary, and General Counsel:
George R. Mahoney Jr., age 56, $345,609 pay
SVP Distribution and Logistics: R. David Alexander Jr.,
age 41, $290,481 pay
SVP Information Technology: Albert S. Rorie, age 48
SVP Merchandising and Advertising: John J. Scanlon,
age 49
SVP Finance: C. Martin Sowers, age 40
SVP Store Operations: Phillip W. Thompson, age 49
VP Store Operations: Charles W. Broome, age 50
VP Store Development: Charles A. Brunjes, age 39
VP Asset Protection: Charles D. Curry, age 43
VP Logistics: Charles S. Gibson Jr., age 37
VP Distribution and Transportation:
Owen R. Humphrey, age 57
VP Real Estate: Gilbert A. LaFare, age 52
VP Human Resources: Dennis C. Merriam
VP Advertising and Sales Promotion: Edgar L. Paxton,
age 56
VP and General Merchandise Manager, Softlines:
Lou Scognamiglio, age 49
VP and General Merchandise Manager:
Richard P. Siliakus, age 39
VP Business Development: Kenneth T. Smith, age 36
Auditors: PricewaterhouseCoopers LLP

PRODUCTS/OPERATIONS

1998 Sales

	% of total
Hardlines (housewares, health aids, food)	67
Soft goods (apparel, shoes, linens)	33
Total	**100**

Selected Products

Apparel (men's, women's, children's, and infants')	Household products
	Housewares
Automotive supplies	Linens
Bedspreads	Paint
Blankets	School supplies
Candy	Shoes
Curtains	Snacks
Electronics	Toys
Health and beauty aids	

COMPETITORS

Ames	J. C. Penney
Bill's Dollar Stores	Kmart
BJs Wholesale Club	Mazel Stores
Bradlees	Rite Aid
Caldor	Sears
Consolidated Stores	ShopKo Stores
Costco Companies	Target Stores
CVS	Toys "R" Us
Dollar General	Value City
Dollar Tree	Walgreen
Drug Emporium	Wal-Mart

LOCATIONS

HQ: PO Box 1017, Charlotte, NC 28201-1017
Phone: 704-847-6961   **Fax:** 704-847-0189
Web site: http://www.familydollar.com

HISTORICAL FINANCIALS & EMPLOYEES

NYSE symbol: FDO FYE: August 31	Annual Growth	1989	1990	1991	1992	1993	1994	1995	1996	1997	1998
Sales ($ mil.)	13.5%	757	874	989	1,159	1,297	1,428	1,547	1,715	1,995	2,362
Net income ($ mil.)	19.1%	22	29	40	56	64	63	58	61	75	103
Income as % of sales	—	2.8%	3.3%	4.1%	4.8%	5.0%	4.4%	3.8%	3.5%	3.7%	4.4%
Earnings per share ($)	18.5%	0.13	0.18	0.25	0.34	0.39	0.38	0.35	0.35	0.44	0.60
Stock price - FY high ($)	—	2.67	2.54	4.56	7.25	8.21	6.59	6.59	6.42	11.75	21.88
Stock price - FY low ($)	—	1.71	1.61	1.48	3.84	5.42	3.67	3.29	3.67	5.34	10.31
Stock price - FY close ($)	21.2%	2.25	1.90	4.19	5.75	6.46	4.21	6.09	5.75	10.63	12.69
P/E - high	—	21	14	18	21	21	17	19	18	27	36
P/E - low	—	13	9	6	11	14	10	9	10	12	17
Dividends per share ($)	12.3%	0.06	0.07	0.07	0.08	0.10	0.11	0.13	0.14	0.16	0.17
Book value per share ($)	13.5%	1.08	1.18	1.36	1.62	1.91	2.18	2.40	2.61	2.75	3.36
Employees	10.1%	11,000	11,800	13,400	14,700	15,900	16,500	18,500	20,700	22,500	26,100

STOCK PRICE HISTORY

HIGH/LOW/CLOSE

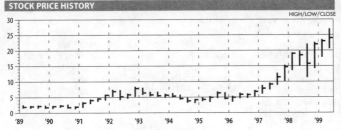

1998 FISCAL YEAR-END

Debt ratio: 0.0%
Return on equity: 17.9%
Cash ($ mil.): 134
Current ratio: 1.88
Long-term debt ($ mil.): 0
No. of shares (mil.): 172
Dividends
  Yield: 1.3%
  Payout: 28.3%
Market value ($ mil.): 2,186

FANNIE MAE

OVERVIEW

Fannie Mae may be holding your mortgage. Based in Washington, DC, Fannie Mae (formerly known as the Federal National Mortgage Association) is the leading buyer of single-family home mortgages. Fannie Mae buys mortgages from the originating lenders and repackages them as securities for sale, thereby creating liquidity in the mortgage market by cushioning lenders from fluctuations in interest rates and allowing them to offer mortgages to people who might not otherwise qualify.

Fannie Mae is a for-profit, publicly traded, government corporation with a federal mandate to make housing affordable for low- to middle-income families. As such, Fannie Mae enjoys the ability to borrow from the government at advantageous rates and is exempt from certain taxes (it also benefits from an implicit guarantee of federal support that makes its securities desirable).

Bureaucrats and mortgage market competitors have called for an end to Fannie Mae's federal hybrid status because it gives Fannie Mae an advantage over its fully private competitors in attracting investors and building market share. Exclusive arrangements between competitor Freddie Mac and leading mortgage originator Wells Fargo and other major lenders could jeopardize Fannie Mae's #1 status.

HISTORY

In 1938 President Franklin Roosevelt created Fannie Mae as part of the government-owned Reconstruction Finance Corporation to buy FHA (Federal Housing Administration) loans. Fannie Mae began buying VA (Veterans Administration) mortgages in 1948. It was rechartered as a partly private, partly governmental mixed-ownership corporation in 1954.

The Housing Act of 1968 divided the corporation into two entities: the Government National Mortgage Association (Ginnie Mae, which, as part of Housing and Urban Development, retained explicit US backing) and Fannie Mae, which went public (with only an implicit US guarantee). Fannie Mae retained its treasury backstop authority, whereby the secretary of the treasury can purchase up to $2.24 billion of the company's obligations.

The corporation introduced uniform conventional loan mortgage documents in 1970, began to buy conventional mortgages in 1972, and started buying condo and planned unit development mortgages in 1974. By 1976 it was buying more conventional loans than FHA and VA loans.

As interest rates rose in the 1970s, Fannie Mae's profits declined and by 1981 it was losing more than $1 million a day. Then it began offering mortgage-backed securities (MBSs) — popular as an investment product because of their implicit guarantee from the government. By 1982 the corporation funded 14% of US home mortgages.

Fannie Mae began borrowing money overseas and buying conventional multifamily and co-op housing loans in 1984. The next year it tightened credit rules and began issuing securities, such as yen-denominated securities, aimed at international investors. Fannie Mae issued its first real estate mortgage investment conduit (REMIC) securities (shares in mortgage pools of specific maturities and risk classes) and introduced a program to allow small lenders to pool loans with other lenders to create MBSs in 1987.

After CEO David Maxwell's 1991 retirement with a reported $29 million pension package, Fannie Mae's powerful Washington DC, lobby squelched calls to limit executive salaries. Other attempts to make it more competitive with private concerns were more successful. In 1992 Fannie Mae's capital requirements were raised; a new mandate also required the organization to lend greater support to inner-city buyers.

In the 1980s Fannie Mae struggled to improve its information systems, pouring more than $100 million into a mainframe data system that was obsolete before it went online. In the 1990s a more flexible client/server system replaced it, helping to handle the deluge of new loans and refinancings that came in 1993.

In 1997 Fannie Mae officially adopted its longtime nickname. The next year Fannie Mae named White House budget chief Franklin Raines to succeed CEO James Johnson at the end of the year. In 1999 it teamed up with the NAACP and Bank of America to boost home ownership among African-Americans. After scaling back its mortgage insurance requirement and requiring underwriters to use its software to sell loans, Fannie Mae faced increased criticism from mortgage lenders over what they perceived as the corporation's encroachment on their territory of loan origination.

Chairman and CEO: Franklin D. Raines, age 50,
$1,635,743 pay
President and COO: Lawrence M. Small, age 57,
$1,847,098 pay
VC: Jamie S. Gorelick, age 48, $1,346,625 pay
EVP and CFO: J. Timothy Howard, age 50, $888,750 pay
EVP and Chief Information Officer: William E. Kelvie,
age 51
EVP Housing and Community Development:
Robert J. Levin, age 43, $888,750 pay
EVP Single Family Mortgage Business: Ann D. Logan
EVP and Chief Credit Officer: Adolfo Marzol, age 38
SVP, Southeastern Region: Glenn T. Austin Jr., age 50
SVP Operations and Corporate Services:
William G. Ehrhorn, age 50
SVP, Midwestern Region: Elizabeth S. Harshfield
SVP Capital Markets: Lynda C. Horvath, age 46
SVP and Treasurer: Linda K. Knight, age 49
SVP, Southwestern Region: Thomas Lund, age 40
SVP Government and Industry Relations:
William R. Maloni, age 54
SVP Human Resources: Thomas R. Nides, age 38
SVP, Northeastern Region: Zach Oppenheimer, age 39
SVP Investor Relations: Jayne J. Shontell, age 44
SVP and Controller: Leanne Spencer, age 43
SVP and Deputy General Counsel: Ann M. Kappler
Auditors: KPMG LLP

LOCATIONS

HQ: 3900 Wisconsin Ave. NW,
Washington, DC 20016-2892
Phone: 202-752-7000   **Fax:** 202-752-3868
Web site: http://www.fanniemae.com

Fannie Mae operates throughout the US, with regional
offices in Atlanta; Chicago; Dallas; Pasadena, California;
and Philadelphia.

PRODUCTS/OPERATIONS

1998 Assets

	$ mil.	% of total
Cash & equivalents	743	—
Mortgage portfolio	415,223	86
Investments	58,515	12
Receivables	3,453	1
Other assets	7,080	1
Total	**485,014**	**100**

1998 Sales

	$ mil.	% of total
Mortgage interest	25,676	81
Other interest	4,319	14
Guaranty fees	1,229	4
Other income	275	1
Total	**31,499**	**100**

COMPETITORS

Bank of America
BANK ONE
Chase Manhattan
Citigroup
Countrywide Credit
First American Financial
First Union
Fleet
Freddie Mac
Mellon Bank
PNC Bank
Washington Mutual
Wells Fargo

HISTORICAL FINANCIALS & EMPLOYEES

NYSE symbol: FNM FYE: December 31	Annual Growth	1989	1990	1991	1992	1993	1994	1995	1996	1997	1998
Assets ($ mil.)	16.3%	124,315	133,113	147,072	180,978	216,979	272,508	316,550	351,041	391,673	485,014
Net income ($ mil.)	17.4%	807	1,173	1,547	1,623	1,873	2,132	2,144	2,725	3,056	3,418
Income as % of assets	—	0.6%	0.9%	1.1%	0.9%	0.9%	0.8%	0.7%	0.8%	0.8%	0.7%
Earnings per share ($)	17.1%	0.78	1.12	1.41	1.48	1.70	1.93	1.96	2.48	2.83	3.23
Stock price - FY high ($)	—	11.51	11.16	17.41	19.31	21.53	22.59	31.50	41.63	57.31	76.19
Stock price - FY low ($)	—	4.17	6.22	8.09	13.78	18.22	17.03	17.19	27.50	36.13	49.56
Stock price - FY close ($)	27.2%	8.47	8.91	17.25	19.09	19.63	18.22	30.97	37.63	57.06	74.00
P/E - high	—	15	10	12	13	13	12	16	17	20	24
P/E - low	—	5	6	6	9	11	9	9	11	13	15
Dividends per share ($)	27.2%	0.11	0.18	0.26	0.35	0.46	0.60	0.68	0.76	0.84	0.96
Book value per share ($)	18.1%	3.13	4.13	5.08	6.20	7.39	8.74	10.04	11.09	12.34	13.95
Employees	4.8%	2,500	1,900	2,763	3,000	3,200	3,500	3,280	3,400	3,400	3,800

STOCK PRICE HISTORY

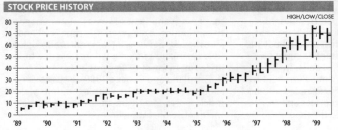

HIGH/LOW/CLOSE

1998 FISCAL YEAR-END

Equity as % of assets: 2.9%
Return on assets: 0.8%
Return on equity: 23.9%
Long-term debt ($ mil.): 254,878
No. of shares (mil.): 1,025
Dividends
  Yield: 1.3%
  Payout: 29.7%
Market value ($ mil.): 75,850
Sales (mil.): $31,499

FARMLAND INDUSTRIES, INC.

OVERVIEW

Farmland Industries helps its members farm land industriously. The Kansas City, Missouri-based enterprise is the #1 agricultural cooperative in the US and a major player in agribusiness worldwide, exporting agricultural products (primarily grain) to more than 90 countries. It will grow even larger when it merges with Cenex Harvest States, the nation's #2 agricultural co-op.

Farmland is owned by 1,500 local co-ops, comprising about 600,000 farmers in the US, Canada, and Mexico. In addition to processing members' crops, the co-op's operations include fertilizer plants, a petroleum refinery, grain elevators, feed mills, barges, 4,400 railcars, 1,000-plus trucks, and nearly 2,000 trailers. The co-op processes and markets beef and pork through its Farmland National Beef Packing and Farmland Foods subsidiaries. Farmland also has more than 60 joint ventures and alliances, including Country Energy (petroleum distribution) and Farmland Hydro (phosphate production).

HISTORY

US agriculture has always been sensitive to boom-and-bust cycles and to the ups and downs of raw commodity prices. After a golden age of supplying food for a world torn by WWI, the industry had a hard time during the 1920s. In 1929 President Herbert Hoover called a special session of Congress to deal with farm issues, resulting in passage of the far-reaching Agricultural Marketing Act (AMA). The act encouraged the formation of cooperatives as one means of bringing order to the marketplace, but a record grain harvest in 1928 and 1929 foiled its intent. The glut ground down prices, and later the Depression (and drought) dried up markets.

By the time of the AMA, Union Oil Company, Farmland Industries' predecessor, was already in the works. Union Oil was formed in 1929 to provide petroleum supplies to farmers in a period of rapid agricultural mechanization. In the early 1930s, as the government sought to regulate supply by introducing payments for taking land out of production, Union Oil increased the range of its co-op activities. It changed its name to Consumers Cooperative Association in 1935.

Farming did not revive until WWII, though price controls and supports remained an important feature of agricultural policy. Throughout this period the performance of Consumers Cooperative's growing membership of primary producers and local co-ops remained tied to raw commodity prices. In 1959, however, to decrease its reliance on commodity prices, Consumers Cooperative bought a pork processing plant in Denison, Iowa, and began making Farmbest meat products. It was a success, and four years later the co-op opened another plant in Iowa Falls. In 1966 Consumers Cooperative became Farmland Industries, and in the 1970s it expanded into beef production. However, when prices and consumption declined, it exited the field.

Overzealous expansion by American farmers in the 1970s was followed in the 1980s by an industrywide crisis. When the farm economy went down, it hurt the co-op's sales of inputs such as fertilizers. Cheap fertilizer imports, low crude oil prices, and high natural gas prices also took their toll, and the co-op lost more than $210 million in 1985 and 1986. James Rainey took over as CEO in 1986 and turned the operation around. Farmland began placing a greater emphasis on food processing and marketing, otherwise known as outputs.

Harry Cleberg succeeded Rainey in 1991. The co-op had stopped handling grains in 1985, after a period of volatile prices, but it profitably re-entered the market in 1992. The next year it bought the Tradigrain unit of British Petroleum (now BP Amoco). The purchase led Farmland into markets outside the US. Also in 1993 the co-op resumed beef processing and expanded its pork processing facilities. Farmland formed a joint venture in 1995 with fertilizer producer Mississippi Chemical (Farmland Trinidad Limited) and acquired the OhSe and Roegelein lunch meat brands from Hudson Foods.

In 1996 the co-op formed a joint venture with Strauss Veal Feeds to make specialty feeds. The next year Farmland formed OneSystem, a joint venture with Ernst & Young, to manage its data systems. The co-op also combined its meat and livestock businesses in 1997. The company formed partnerships in 1998 with ConAgra (Concourse Grain, grain marketing) and Cenex Harvest States Cooperatives (Country Energy, energy products) and absorbed SF Services, an agricultural cooperative. Farmland's income fell in 1998 due to low prices on many of its key products.

Farmland and Cenex's 1999 discussions about combining their grain operations yielded much more: an agreement in May to merge their entire operations.

Chairman: Albert J. Shivley
VC and VP: Jody Benzer
President and CEO: H. D. "Harry" Cleberg
EVP and CFO: Terry M. Campbell
SVP and Corporate Secretary: Bernard L. Sanders
EVP and COO, Grain and Grain Processing Businesses: John F. Berardi
EVP and COO, Meats Group: Gary E. Evans
EVP and COO, Ag Input Businesses: Robert W. Honse
VP Government Relations: William R. "Bill" Allen Jr.
VP and Controller: Merl Daniel
VP System Strategic Planning: Gerald "Jerry" Leeper
VP Human Resources: Holly D. McCoy
VP; Co-President, Country Energy: Ken D. Otwell
VP; President, Pork Division: George H. Richter
VP Crop Production: Stan Riemann
VP and Treasurer: Jeff Roberts
VP Administration: Drue M. Sander
VP Transportation: Fred E. Schrodt
VP; President, Feed and Grain Processing: Michael T. Sweat
VP and General Counsel: Robert B. Terry
Auditors: KPMG LLP

LOCATIONS

HQ: 3315 N. Oak Trafficway,
Kansas City, MO 64116-0005
Phone: 816-459-6000   **Fax:** 816-459-6979
Web site: http://www.farmland.com

Farmland Industries conducts business throughout the US and in more than 90 other countries.

PRODUCTS/OPERATIONS

1998 Sales & Operating Income

	Sales		Operating Income	
	$ mil.	% of total	$ mil.	% of total
Food marketing	3,656	42	55	32
Grain marketing	2,132	24	30	18
Crop production	1,158	13	48	28
Petroleum	1,137	13	28	16
Feed	550	6	11	6
Other	142	2	(4)	—
Total	**8,775**	**100**	**168**	**100**

Selected Subsidiaries and Joint Ventures

Concourse Grain, LLC (grain alliance with ConAgra)
Country Energy, LLC (energy products alliance with Cenex Harvest States Cooperatives)
Farmers Chemical Co. (fertilizer production)
Farmland-Atwood, LLC (50%, with ConAgra; risk management services)
Farmland Foods (99%, 11 food processing plants)
Farmland Hydro, LP (50%, with Norsk Hydro; phosphate fertilizer manufacturing)
Farmland Industrias SA de CV (marketing support services, Mexico)
Farmland Insurance Agency, Inc.
Farmland National Beef Packing Co., LP (76%)
Farmland Securities Co. (broker-dealer)
Farmland Transportation, Inc. (brokerage)
Heartland Wheat Growers LP (79%, wheat gluten and starch processing)
National Carriers, Inc. (79%, transportation brokerage)
OneSystem Group, LLC (50%, with Ernst & Young; information technology)
SF Phosphates Limited Co. (50%, fertilizer manufacturing)
SF Services Inc. (farm supply cooperative)
Tradigrain SA (international grain trading)
WILFARM, LLC (50%, with Wilbur-Ellis Co.; pesticides)

COMPETITORS

ADM	Hormel
Ag Processing	IBP
Agway	IMC Global
American Foods	JR Simplot
Cargill	Keystone Foods
Cenex Harvest States	Monsanto
CF Industries	Rose Packing
ConAgra	Royal Dutch/Shell
Continental Grain	Smithfield Foods
Exxon	Southern States
Gold Kist	Transammonia

HISTORICAL FINANCIALS & EMPLOYEES

Cooperative FYE: August 31	Annual Growth	1989	1990	1991	1992	1993	1994	1995	1996	1997	1998
Sales ($ mil.)	12.8%	2,975	3,378	3,638	3,429	4,723	6,678	7,257	9,789	9,148	8,775
Net income ($ mil.)	(5.6%)	99	49	43	62	(30)	74	96	126	135	59
Income as % of sales	—	3.3%	1.4%	1.2%	1.8%	—	1.1%	2.2%	1.3%	1.5%	0.7%
Employees	10.8%	6,372	6,691	7,126	7,616	8,155	12,000	12,700	14,700	14,600	16,100

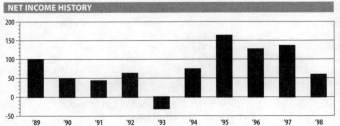

NET INCOME HISTORY

1998 FISCAL YEAR-END
Debt ratio: 44.4%
Return on equity: 6.4%
Cash ($ mil.): 7
Current ratio: 1.34
Long-term debt ($ mil.): 728

FDX CORPORATION

OVERVIEW

Just think of "FDX" as a fast way to express "FedEx." The Memphis-based package-delivery powerhouse is under the umbrella of FDX Corporation, the holding company formed in 1998 when Federal Express — probably the fastest-moving operation with "federal" in its name — bought trucking company Caliber System.

FDX's five main subsidiaries are led by FedEx, the world's #1 express transportation company, with 44,700 drop-off locations, more than 600 aircraft, and 40,900 vehicles. FedEx delivers more than 3 million express packages to about 200 countries each working day. Most items sent through FedEx reach the recipient within 48 hours; the company offers same-day delivery service in the US and limited delivery on Sunday. FedEx is a leader in the burgeoning Chinese air cargo market.

FedEx's services complement those of the Caliber companies: RPS, the US's #2 ground carrier of packages under 150 pounds; Viking Freight, a less-than-truckload (LTL) carrier (combining freight from several sources to form a load) serving the western US; and Roberts Express, the leading surface-expedited carrier in North America, which delivers time-critical shipments. FDX Global Logistics offers business services such as just-in-time delivery programs, order processing, and transportation management.

Founder and CEO Fred Smith owns about 7% of FDX.

HISTORY

FedEx was the brainchild of Vietnam veteran Fred Smith, who recognized in the late 1960s that the US was becoming a service-oriented economy with a need for reliable, overnight delivery services. When he presented FedEx's business concept in a Yale term paper, he got a C. But between 1969 and 1971 Smith found investors willing to contribute $40 million, used $8 million of family money, and received bank financing to total $90 million, making FedEx the largest startup funded by venture capital. Services to 22 US cities started in 1973 with overnight and second-day delivery and a $5-per-package Courier Pak envelope for expediting documents.

Several factors contributed to FedEx's success. Air passenger traffic grew rapidly, so parcel service became less important to commercial airlines; United Parcel Service union workers struck in 1974, disrupting service; and, finally, competitor REA Express went bankrupt. FedEx went public in 1978.

FedEx has had one fiasco. Believing hardcopy delivery services could be severely eroded by the burgeoning electronic mail market, the company invested heavily in ZapMail, a satellite-based network that provided two-hour document delivery. Failing to anticipate the impact of low-cost fax machines, FedEx lost over $300 million in 1986 on the now-disbanded ZapMail.

FedEx bought Island Courier Companies and Cansica (1987), SAMIMA (Italy, 1988), and three Japanese freight carriers (1988). In 1989 it spent $880 million for Tiger International (Flying Tigers line) and doubled overseas revenues to become the #1 air cargo company.

In 1991 FedEx introduced EXPRESSfreighter, an international air-express cargo service, but scrapped its loss-making European domestic pickup and delivery service in 1992. FedEx pilots rocked the boat in 1993 when they announced their decision to unionize: The announcement touched off protracted labor negotiations.

FedEx in 1995 became the first US express carrier with direct flights to China. The company also created Latin American and Caribbean divisions that year.

The next year FedEx introduced interNet-Ship, a service allowing users to print their own shipping labels and communicate with recipients via e-mail, and a software package called BusinessLink, which allows businesses to sell goods over the Internet that would then be delivered by FedEx.

In 1997 the company announced plans to create a hub at Charles de Gaulle Airport in Paris (its first hub in Europe) and another in Miami (to drive its expansion into Latin America). That year a strike at UPS gave the company an advantage: FedEx handled 850,000 extra packages a day. Increasing its pressure on UPS, the company bought Caliber System in early 1998, creating holding company FDX in the process. After being threatened with a pilots' strike during the 1998 holiday season, FedEx announced it would permanently outsource large portions of its flight operations. The pilots' union decided to call off the strike vote, but FedEx said it would stick to its backup plan.

The next year FDX took a first step into freight forwarding, acquiring GeoLogistics Air Services (renamed Caribbean Transport Services), which specializes in transportation of pharmaceutical equipment.

Chairman, President, and CEO: Frederick W. Smith,
age 54, $2,122,000 pay
EVP and CFO: Alan B. Graf Jr., age 44, $1,135,243 pay
**EVP Market Development and Corporate
Communications:** T. Michael Glenn, $973,791 pay
EVP and Chief Information Officer: Dennis H. Jones,
$1,100,810 pay
EVP, General Counsel, and Secretary:
Kenneth R. Masterson, $1,199,023 pay
SVP and Chief Personnel Officer: James A. Perkins
Corporate VP and Chief Accounting Officer:
James S. Hudson
President and CEO, Federal Express:
Theodore L. Weise
President and CEO, RPS: Daniel J. Sullivan
Auditors: Arthur Andersen LLP

LOCATIONS

HQ: 6075 Poplar Ave., Ste. 300, Memphis, TN 38119
Phone: 901-369-3600   **Fax:** 901-395-2000
Web site: http://www.fdxcorp.com

FDX Corporation's subsidiaries offer package delivery in
the US and about 200 other countries.

1999 Sales

	$ mil.	% of total
US	12,910	77
Other countries	3,863	23
Total	**16,773**	**100**

PRODUCTS/OPERATIONS

1999 Sales

	$ mil.	% of total
FedEx	13,979	84
RPS	1,878	11
Other	916	5
Total	**16,773**	**100**

FDX Subsidiaries:
Caliber Logistics, Inc. (logistics, warehouse
management, and order-fulfillment services)
Caliber Technology, Inc. (logistics, warehouse
management, and order-fulfillment services)
Caribbean Transport Services, Inc. (regional freight
forwarding of pharmaceutical equipment)
Federal Express Corp. (express package delivery)
Roberts Express, Inc. (surface-expedited carrier)
RPS, Inc. (small-package delivery)
Viking Freight, Inc. (regional freight carrier)

COMPETITORS

Air Express	Pittston BAX
Airborne Freight	Ryder
Burlington Northern	TNT Post Group
Santa Fe	UAL
Canadian Pacific	Union Pacific
CHR	UPS
CNF Transportation	U.S. Postal Service
CSX	USFreightways
DHL	Yellow Corporation
Norfolk Southern	

HISTORICAL FINANCIALS & EMPLOYEES

NYSE symbol: FDX FYE: May 31	Annual Growth	1990	1991	1992	1993	1994	1995	1996	1997	1998	1999
Sales ($ mil.)	10.2%	7,015	7,688	7,550	7,808	8,480	9,392	10,274	11,520	15,873	16,773
Net income ($ mil.)	20.7%	116	6	(114)	54	204	298	308	361	503	631
Income as % of sales	—	1.7%	0.1%	—	0.7%	2.4%	3.2%	3.0%	3.1%	3.2%	3.8%
Earnings per share ($)	16.1%	0.55	0.03	(0.53)	0.25	0.92	1.32	1.35	1.56	1.72	2.10
Stock price - FY high ($)	—	14.50	12.47	14.03	15.19	19.47	20.19	21.50	28.94	42.25	61.88
Stock price - FY low ($)	—	10.53	7.38	8.00	8.63	11.09	13.38	14.63	18.13	26.25	21.81
Stock price - FY close ($)	18.9%	11.56	10.03	10.19	12.25	19.13	14.97	19.16	26.19	32.06	54.81
P/E - high	—	26	416	—	61	21	15	16	19	25	29
P/E - low	—	19	246	—	35	12	10	11	12	15	10
Dividends per share ($)	—	0.00	0.00	0.00	0.00	0.00	0.00	0.00	0.00	0.00	0.00
Book value per share ($)	8.1%	7.76	7.78	7.38	7.63	8.61	10.09	11.32	12.89	13.44	15.68
Employees	5.8%	85,000	86,800	91,550	95,000	101,000	107,000	114,208	126,000	138,000	141,000

STOCK PRICE HISTORY

HIGH/LOW/CLOSE

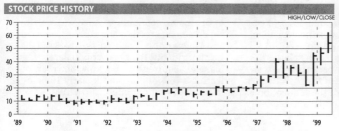

1999 FISCAL YEAR-END

Debt ratio: 22.6%
Return on equity: 13.5%
Cash ($ mil.): 325
Current ratio: 1.13
Long-term debt ($ mil.): 1,360
No. of shares (mil.): 297
Dividends
  Yield: —
  Payout: —
Market value ($ mil.): 16,303

FEDERAL-MOGUL CORPORATION

OVERVIEW

After sending its retail operation to the scrap heap, Federal-Mogul is embracing its core business of making and distributing auto parts. The Southfield, Michigan-based company's product line includes engine components and bearings, sealing products, fuel systems, lighting products, and ignition, brake, friction, and chassis products for cars, trucks, and construction equipment. Principle customers include automobile and equipment makers such as General Motors, Ford, DaimlerChrysler, BMW, Volkswagen, Caterpillar, and Cummins.

Federal-Mogul provides about 150,000 products to customers in the global automotive aftermarket — primarily independent warehouse distributors, but also local parts suppliers and retailers.

CEO Richard Snell wants to grow Federal-Mogul into the world's largest supplier of auto parts to reach his lofty target (the company calls it the "Big Hairy Audacious Goal") of $10 billion in sales by 2002. Snell has steered the company away from its misdirected venture into international auto parts retailing, which turned some of its retail aftermarket customers into competitors. Now the company is focusing on expanding its product line to include parts for the entire engine, including gaskets and other sealing compounds. As the major carmakers expand internationally, they expect suppliers to follow, so the company is boosting its international distribution capacity, mainly through acquisitions.

HISTORY

In 1899 J. Howard Muzzy and Edward Lyon formed the Muzzy-Lyon Company, and later, subsidiary Mogul Metal Company. The two modified a printer's old typecasting machine and developed a process for making replaceable die-cast engine bearings. Their first big order came in 1910, when Buick ordered 10,000 connecting rod bearings for the Buick 10. In 1924 Mogul Metal merged with Federal Bearing and Bushing to become Federal-Mogul Corporation. Following the merger, the company acquired Kansas City-based parts distributor Douglas-Dahlin Company.

In 1941 Federal-Mogul had about 50 manufacturing plants dedicated to the war effort, and by 1945 sales had doubled prewar levels. In 1955 the company acquired Bower Roller Bearing Company and changed its name to Federal-Mogul-Bower Bearings, Inc. By the late 1950s it had nearly 100 distribution centers, and sales had grown fourfold in 10 years.

The company began investing in international manufacturing facilities in the 1960s to safeguard against lower US car exports as more foreign cars entered the global marketplace. It changed its name back to Federal-Mogul in 1965 and moved its headquarters from Detroit to Southfield, Michigan, the following year. Following a recession in the mid-1970s, Federal-Mogul realized that it was too dependent on the big automotive manufacturers and began diversifying. It acquired the Mather Company, a maker of high-performance sealing products, in 1985. The next year it further broadened its offerings with the acquisition of Carter Automotive (fuel pumps) and Signal-Stat (lighting and safety components).

In 1989 Dennis Gormley became CEO. He continued the diversification-through-acquisition strategy and led the company into the automotive aftermarket. In 1992 Gormley proposed a push into retail, and that year Federal-Mogul bought the aftermarket business of TRW Inc. In its effort to become the AutoZone of the Third World, the company sold parts of its manufacturing business to finance its retail ventures. By 1996 it owned about 130 retail stores, primarily in Latin America. The company began to lose money, and that year Gormley resigned. His successor, Dick Snell, put an immediate end to the retail fiasco.

By 1998 Federal-Mogul had sold all of its retail holdings and was concentrating on providing parts for entire engine systems. That year it made two major acquisitions: Fel-Pro, a domestic maker of gaskets and other sealing products, for $720 million; and T&N plc, a British maker of engine bearings, pistons, and brake pads, for about $3 billion (it later sold T&N's engine-bearings business to rival Dana for $430 million).

Driving further into the aftermarket, Federal-Mogul paid $1.9 billion for the automotive business of Cooper Industries, maker of Champion spark plugs, Anco windshield wipers, Moog steering and suspension parts, and Wagner/Abex brake parts. UK-based LucasVarity put the brakes on Federal-Mogul's plans to acquire that company, however, rejecting a $6.4 billion offer in early 1999 in favor of a $7 billion offer from TRW.

Chairman and CEO: Richard A. Snell, age 57,
$3,414,096 pay
President and COO: Gordon A. Ulsh, age 53
EVP and CFO: Thomas W. Ryan, age 52, $987,589 pay
EVP, Sealing Systems: Wilhelm A. Schmelzer, age 58,
$953,589 pay
SVP, General Counsel, and Secretary:
James J. Zamoyski, age 52
SVP, Human Resources: Richard P. Randazzo, age 55,
$800,223 pay
VP and Controller: Kenneth P. Slaby, age 47
VP and Treasurer: David A. Bozynski, age 44
VP, Aftermarket Sales and Distribution, Asia Pacific:
David M. Wilson
VP, Aftermarket Sales and Distribution, Europe:
John McCormack
VP, Aftermarket Sales and Distribution, the Americas:
Edward J. O'Leary
VP, Corporate Communications: Kimberly A. Welch
VP, Corporate Development: Charles B. Grant, age 54
VP, Investor Relations: Bonnie J. Price
VP, Manufacturing Operations: Frank Tomes, age 56
VP, Strategic Planning and Marketing:
James C. "Jay" Burkhart, age 41
Auditors: Ernst & Young LLP

PRODUCTS/OPERATIONS

1998 Sales

	$ mil.	% of total
Powertrain systems	1,883	42
General products	1,636	37
Sealing systems	925	21
Divested activities	25	—
Total	**4,469**	**100**

COMPETITORS

Applied Industrial Technologies
Borg-Warner Automotive
Dana
Donnelly
Hahn Automotive Warehouse
Meritor
Motorcar Parts
Owosso
Robert Bosch
Tenneco
Twin Disc

LOCATIONS

HQ: 26555 Northwestern Hwy., Southfield, MI 48034
Phone: 248-354-7700   **Fax:** 248-354-8950
Web site: http://www.federal-mogul.com

Federal-Mogul's Powertrain Systems division operates
71 manufacturing facilities in 21 countries; its Sealing
Systems division operates 30 manufacturing facilities in
12 countries; and its General Products division operates
80 manufacturing facilities in 17 countries.

HISTORICAL FINANCIALS & EMPLOYEES

NYSE symbol: FMO FYE: December 31	Annual Growth	1989	1990	1991	1992	1993	1994	1995	1996	1997	1998
Sales ($ mil.)	17.0%	1,084	1,134	1,099	1,264	1,576	1,896	1,996	2,030	1,807	4,469
Net income ($ mil.)	5.4%	33	9	(5)	(84)	40	63	(10)	(211)	69	54
Income as % of sales	—	3.1%	0.8%	—	—	2.5%	3.3%	—	—	3.8%	1.2%
Earnings per share ($)	(2.6%)	1.22	0.20	(0.36)	(3.94)	1.02	1.38	(0.42)	(6.20)	1.61	0.96
Stock price - FY high ($)	—	28.81	22.50	19.13	20.13	30.00	37.63	23.75	24.50	47.63	72.00
Stock price - FY low ($)	—	18.63	10.25	12.25	14.50	16.00	18.63	16.75	16.13	21.63	33.00
Stock price - FY close ($)	12.3%	21.00	13.50	14.63	16.25	29.00	20.13	19.63	22.00	40.50	59.50
P/E - high	—	24	113	—	—	29	27	—	—	30	75
P/E - low	—	15	51	—	—	16	14	—	—	13	34
Dividends per share ($)	(19.4%)	0.91	0.92	0.92	0.48	0.48	0.48	0.48	0.48	0.48	0.13
Book value per share ($)	11.0%	10.54	10.21	8.67	6.48	6.60	12.99	12.02	5.39	7.92	26.91
Employees	17.7%	12,500	15,500	13,100	14,300	14,400	16,200	17,200	15,700	13,300	54,350

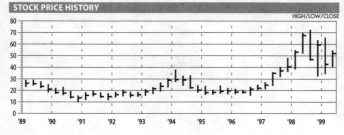

STOCK PRICE HISTORY HIGH/LOW/CLOSE

1998 FISCAL YEAR-END
Debt ratio: 61.2%
Return on equity: 3.0%
Cash ($ mil.): 77
Current ratio: 1.28
Long-term debt ($ mil.): 3,131
No. of shares (mil.): 67
Dividends
  Yield: 0.2%
  Payout: 13.5%
Market value ($ mil.): 4,000

FEDERATED DEPARTMENT STORES

OVERVIEW

The nation's #1 upscale department store operator wants to make more house calls. Including its venerable Bloomingdale's and Macy's chains, Federated Department Stores operates over 400 stores under such prestigious names as The Bon Marche, Burdines, Rich's, and Stern's. Upscale apparel, household goods, and gifts account for most of its sales. The fashion conscious also flock to its stores for cosmetics, fragrances, and other accessories.

Federated is breaking down its brick-and-mortar heritage by selling through such alternative retail channels as catalogs (Macy's by Mail, Bloomingdale's by Mail) and the Internet (Macys.com). To that end, it has acquired a stake in online e-registry service WeddingChannel.com and purchased Fingerhut Companies, which has a number of online interests and is the nation's #2 catalog retailer (after J. C. Penney).

Federated spends more than $150 million per year to advertise its private labels (including Alfani, I.N.C, and Tools of the Trade), which together account for about 10% of sales.

HISTORY

In 1929 Fred Lazarus, who controlled Columbus, Ohio's, giant F&R Lazarus department store and the John Shillito Company (the oldest department store west of the Alleghenies; 1830), met with three other great retailers on a yacht in Long Island Sound: Walter Rothschild of Brooklyn-based Abraham & Straus; Louis Kirstein of Boston-based Filene's; and Samuel Bloomingdale, head of Manhattan's Bloomingdale's. Lazarus, Rothschild, and Kirstein agreed to merge their stores into a loose federation. Bloomingdale joined the next year.

Though Federated set up headquarters in Cincinnati in 1945, it continued to be run by powerful merchants in each city where it operated. Under Lazarus' leadership, it was among the first to see the coming growth of the Sunbelt, acquiring Foley's (Houston, 1945), Burdines (Miami, 1956), Sanger's (Dallas, 1958), Bullock's and I. Magnin (California, 1964), and Rich's (Atlanta, 1976).

Federated's growth stalled after Lazarus' son Ralph stepped down in 1981. The company faced stiffer competition from rival department store operators and chains, including May Department Stores, Nordstrom, and Dillard's. By 1989 Federated was no longer a leader, although it was still financially strong.

Years before, when Federated was leader of the department store industry, Allied Stores was #2. Allied was made up mostly of stores that were in small towns or were #2 in their market, with a few leaders (Maas Brothers, The Bon Marche, Jordan Marsh). It had a mediocre track record until Thomas Macioce took the helm in 1971. He closed unprofitable stores, downsized others, and went on an acquisition spree (Brooks Brothers, AnnTaylor).

Campeau Corporation bought Allied and Federated in 1988. Saddled with more than $8 billion in debt from the purchase, both companies declared bankruptcy in 1990. Allen Questrom became Federated's CEO, and in 1992 the companies emerged from bankruptcy as Federated Department Stores.

The next year, after being rebuffed in a bid to merge with Macy's, Federated purchased 50% of Macy's unsecured debt, setting the stage for Federated's 1994 acquisition of the respected department store.

Rowland Macy opened a store under his name in Manhattan in 1858. After Macy's death, the Strauses, a New York china merchant family, bought the department store in 1896 and expanded it across the US. In 1986 chairman Edward Finkelstein led a $3.5 billion buyout of Macy's and took it private. Its debt load increased into the early 1990s, and Macy's entered bankruptcy proceedings in 1992.

In 1995 Federated bought the 82-store Broadway Stores and renamed 52 of them Macy's in 1996 (it also renamed 21 Bullock's and 18 Jordan Marsh stores).

Questrom quit (under longstanding tensions with Federated) in 1997, succeeded by president James Zimmerman. In 1998 the firm paid $10.6 million to settle complaints that it illegally collected debts from bankrupt credit card holders. Federated sold its Aeropostale and Charter Club (now Chelsea Campbell) specialty clothing stores in 1998 to a group led by division president Julian Geiger.

After relaunching the Macys.com Web site, Federated added a number of other hot Web retailing prospects in 1999 by purchasing Fingerhut Companies, which will provide it with back-end support for its budding e-commerce and catalog business. It also acquired a 20% stake in WeddingChannel.com, which offers bridal services online.

Chairman and CEO: James M. Zimmerman, age 55,
$2,172,000 pay
VC, Finance and Real Estate: Ronald W. Tysoe, age 46,
$1,015,900 pay
President and Chief Merchandising Officer:
Terry J. Lundgren, age 46, $1,567,200 pay
EVP Law and Human Resources: Thomas G. Cody,
age 57, $934,600 pay
EVP, Federated Marketing Services: Joseph Feczo, age 47
SVP, General Counsel, and Secretary:
Dennis J. Broderick, age 50
SVP Logistics and Operations: Jim Frede, age 55
SVP Planning and CFO: Karen M. Hoguet, age 42,
$541,800 pay
SVP Design and Construction: Rudolph V. Javosky
Chairman, Bloomingdale's: Michael Bould
President, Fingerhut Companies, Inc.:
William J. Lansing
Auditors: KPMG LLP

HQ: Federated Department Stores, Inc.,
7 W. 7th St., Cincinnati, OH 45202
Phone: 513-579-7000   **Fax:** 513-579-7555
Web site: http://www.federated-fds.com

Federated Department Stores has stores in Alabama,
Arizona, California, Connecticut, Delaware, Florida,
Georgia, Idaho, Illinois, Indiana, Kentucky, Louisiana,
Maine, Maryland, Massachusetts, Minnesota, Montana,
Nevada, New Hampshire, New Jersey, New Mexico, New
York, Ohio, Oregon, Pennsylvania, Rhode Island, South
Carolina, Tennessee, Texas, Virginia, Washington, West
Virginia, and Wyoming.

Store Chains
Bloomingdale's
The Bon Marche
Burdines
Goldsmith's
Lazarus
Macy's
Rich's
Stern's

Other Operations
Bloomingdale's by Mail (catalog business)
Fingerhut Companies Inc.
Macy's by Mail (catalog business)
Macys.com (electronic retail site)
WeddingChannel.com (20%)

Private Labels
Alfani
Charter Club
I.N.C
Tools of the Trade

American Retail	J. C. Penney	Polo
AnnTaylor	Jos. A. Bank	Saks Inc.
Bed Bath &	Lands' End	Sears
Beyond ·	The Limited	Spiegel
Belk	Marks & Spencer	Talbots
Brown Shoe	May	TJX
Dayton Hudson	Men's Wearhouse	Venator Group
Dillard's	Neiman Marcus	Zale
The Gap	Nine West	
J. Crew	Nordstrom	

NYSE symbol: FD FYE: January 31	Annual Growth	1990	1991	1992	1993	1994	1995	1996	1997	1998	1999
Sales ($ mil.)	8.5%	7,578	7,142	6,932	7,080	7,229	8,316	15,049	15,229	15,668	15,833
Net income ($ mil.)	—	(1,774)	(271)	(1,236)	113	193	188	75	266	536	662
Income as % of sales	—	—	—	—	1.6%	2.7%	2.3%	0.5%	1.7%	3.4%	4.2%
Earnings per share ($)	19.6%	—	—	—	1.01	1.50	1.40	0.39	1.24	2.41	2.96
Stock price - FY high ($)	—	—	—	—	21.50	25.00	25.25	30.13	37.00	48.88	56.19
Stock price - FY low ($)	—	—	—	—	11.25	17.38	17.88	18.75	26.13	31.63	32.81
Stock price - FY close ($)	12.7%	—	—	—	20.38	21.88	18.88	27.00	32.88	42.31	41.81
P/E - high	—	—	—	—	21	17	18	77	30	20	19
P/E - low	—	—	—	—	11	12	13	48	21	13	11
Dividends per share ($)	—	—	—	—	0.00	0.00	0.00	0.00	0.00	0.00	0.00
Book value per share ($)	8.8%	—	—	—	16.46	18.03	19.93	21.09	22.45	25.04	27.38
Employees	7.8%	60,300	54,200	78,900	73,000	67,300	111,700	119,100	117,100	114,700	118,800

HIGH/LOW/CLOSE

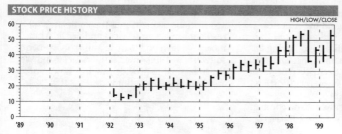

Debt ratio: 34.9%
Return on equity: 11.6%
Cash ($ mil.): 307
Current ratio: 1.95
Long-term debt ($ mil.): 3,057
No. of shares (mil.): 209
Dividends
  Yield: —
  Payout: —
Market value ($ mil.): 8,717

FIRST AMERICAN FINANCIAL

OVERVIEW

Act locally, think globally. First American Financial, whose First American Title Insurance subsidiary is the #1 title company in the US, turns the old saw around in its quest for a national database to centralize title records. To help it get there, the company has acquired such companies as Data Tree, owner of an extensive database of imaged property records. Smart Title Solutions, a joint venture with Experian Information Solutions, will also help First American Financial reach its goal: a central source for property titles, eliminating costly local searches.

Santa Ana, California-based First American also offers real estate tax monitoring, mortgage credit reporting, home warranty, and other services. The company is making use of its extensive databases to offer other services, such as employee screening and credit reporting for landlords. What First American doesn't already have, it buys — the firm is on an unabashed acquisition drive, fueled by a strong housing and real estate market.

Donald and Parker Kennedy (officers of First American and descendants of its founder) own about 5% of the firm.

HISTORY

In 1889, when Los Angeles was on its way to becoming a real city, the more countrified residents to the south (including the Irvine Company's founding family) formed Orange County, a peaceful realm of citrus groves where land transactions were assisted by title companies Orange County Abstract and Santa Ana Abstract. In 1894 the firms merged under the leadership of local businessman C. E. Parker. For three decades, the resulting Orange County Title limited its business to title searches.

In 1924, as real estate transactions became more complex (in part because of mineral-rights issues related to Southern California's oil boom), Orange County Title began offering title insurance and escrow services. The company remained under Parker family management until 1930, when H. A. Gardner took over and guided it through the Depression. In 1943 the company returned to Parker family control.

In 1957 the company began a major expansion beyond Orange County. The new First American Title Insurance and Trust name minimized the firm's local image and acknowledged its expansion into trust and custody operations. Donald Kennedy (C. E. Parker's grandson) took over in 1963 and took the company public the next year.

In 1968 First American Financial was formed as a holding company for subsidiaries First American Title Insurance and First American Trust. This structure facilitated growth as the firm began opening new offices and buying all or parts of other title companies, including Title Guaranty Co. of Wyoming, Security Title & Trust (San Antonio), and Ticore, Inc. (Portland, Oregon), all purchased in 1968.

The 1970s were a quiet time for the company, but it began growing again in the 1980s as savings and loan deregulation jump-started the commercial real estate market in Southern California. In addition to acquiring more title operations, First American diversified into home warranty and real estate tax services. In 1988, on the brink of the California meltdown, the company bought an industrial loan corporation to make commercial real estate loans.

Reduced property sales during California's early 1990s real estate crash and recession rocked company results. Fluctuating interest rates didn't help the tremulous bottom lines. In 1994 Donald Kennedy became chairman; his son Parker became president.

As part of its expansion effort, First American bought CREDCO (mortgage credit reporting) and Flood Data Services (flood zone certification) in 1995. A year later it acquired Ward Associates, a field inspection and property preservation service provider. In 1997 the company merged its real estate information subsidiaries with those of the Experian Information Solutions (a leading supplier of real estate data, and now a unit of Great Universal Stores); it also bought Strategic Mortgage Services (mortgage information and document preparation), whose software for escrow closing and for title plants (geographically sorted title indexes) formed the core of software operations for First American's title division.

Earnings jumped in 1998's hot real estate market. That year and the next, First American's acquisitions brought into the company's fold resident screening services and providers of mortgage loan and loan default management software. In 1999 American Financial and Wells Fargo teamed to provide title insurance and appraisal services nationwide.

OFFICERS

Chairman; VC, First American Title Insurance:
D. P. Kennedy, age 80, $472,300 pay
President; Chairman, First American Title Insurance:
Parker S. Kennedy, age 51, $858,320 pay
EVP and CFO: Thomas A. Klemens, age 48,
$674,026 pay
EVP and General Counsel: Craig I. DeRoy, age 46,
$667,226 pay
EVP; President, First American Title Insurance:
Gary L. Kermott
**EVP; President and CEO, First American Real Estate
Information Services:** John W. Long
VP, Secretary, and Corporate Counsel: Mark R. Arnesen,
age 46, $254,920 pay
Director Investor Relations: Denise M. Warren
Human Resources: Carolyn Knandle
Chairman, First American Home Buyers Protection:
Philip B. Branson
**President and CEO, First American Capital
Management:** William C. Conrad
President and CEO, First American Trust:
Jerald P. Lewis
President and CEO, First Security Thrift:
James Bresnan
President, First American Equity Loan Services:
Michael B. Hopkins
President, First American Home Buyers Protection:
Martin R. Wool
Auditors: PricewaterhouseCoopers LLP

LOCATIONS

HQ: The First American Financial Corporation,
114 E. 5th St., Santa Ana, CA 92701-4642
Phone: 714-558-3211   **Fax:** 714-541-6372
Web site: http://www.firstam.com

PRODUCTS/OPERATIONS

1998 Sales

	$ mil.	% of total
Title insurance	2,087	73
Real estate information	601	21
Home warranty	63	2
Consumer risk	57	2
Corporate	44	1
Trust & banking	25	1
Total	**2,877**	**100**

Selected Subsidiaries
CIC, Inc. (employee screening for employers)
Contour Software, Inc. (mortgage loan software)
Credit Net Communication, Inc. (75%, credit reporting
services)
First American Real Estate Information Services, Inc.
(flood zone determinations, mortgage credit reporting,
tax monitoring)
Excelis, Inc. (online loan servicing)
Realty Tax & Service Co.
Market Data Center, LLC (automated appraisal systems)
Smart Title Solutions (real estate services joint venture,
with Experian)
Strategic Mortgage Services, Inc. (mortgage credit
information, appraisal data, document preparation,
escrow closing, and title software)

COMPETITORS

Chicago Title
Fidelity National
Investors Title
LandAmerica Financial Group
Old Republic
PMI Group
Stewart Information

HISTORICAL FINANCIALS & EMPLOYEES

NYSE symbol: FAF FYE: December 31	Annual Growth	1989	1990	1991	1992	1993	1994	1995	1996	1997	1998
Sales ($ mil.)	17.0%	699	708	757	1,116	1,398	1,376	1,250	1,598	1,888	2,877
Net income ($ mil.)	34.8%	14	3	3	43	66	19	8	54	65	199
Income as % of sales	—	1.9%	0.5%	0.4%	3.9%	4.7%	1.4%	0.6%	3.4%	3.4%	6.9%
Earnings per share ($)	31.1%	0.29	0.07	0.07	1.01	1.29	0.37	0.15	1.03	1.21	3.32
Stock price - FY high ($)	—	3.74	3.15	2.83	5.94	8.72	8.33	6.11	9.13	16.60	43.00
Stock price - FY low ($)	—	2.46	1.44	1.39	2.62	5.00	3.55	3.66	5.50	6.97	15.92
Stock price - FY close ($)	31.8%	2.67	1.55	2.62	5.83	7.77	3.83	5.94	9.13	16.41	32.13
P/E - high	—	13	45	40	6	7	23	41	9	14	13
P/E - low	—	8	21	20	3	4	10	24	5	6	5
Dividends per share ($)	6.9%	0.11	0.08	0.08	0.08	0.11	0.13	0.13	0.15	0.16	0.20
Book value per share ($)	25.5%	1.58	3.20	3.34	2.40	5.54	5.44	5.89	6.78	7.89	12.13
Employees	12.1%	7,042	6,588	7,583	8,694	10,679	9,033	10,149	11,611	12,930	19,669

STOCK PRICE HISTORY

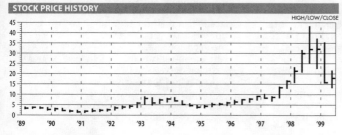

HIGH/LOW/CLOSE

1998 FISCAL YEAR-END

Debt ratio: 15.1%
Return on equity: 27.1%
Cash ($ mil.): —
Current ratio: —
Long-term debt ($ mil.): 130
No. of shares (mil.): 60
Dividends
  Yield: 0.6%
  Payout: 6.0%
Market value ($ mil.): 1,938

FIRST DATA CORPORATION

OVERVIEW

Atlanta-based First Data is first in bank card transaction processing in the US.

The company's business areas include processing applications, embossing cards, and providing billing services for banks that issue MasterCard and VISA credit cards. Other services include check processing (through TeleCheck, the nation's leading check authorization organization), money transfers (through its Western Union unit), merchant transaction processing (through its Paymentech joint venture with BANK ONE),

and investment processing services for mutual funds.

Having shed its noncore businesses, the company is now focused on building its payment instruments, card issuer services, and merchant processing services. The company continues to expand through partnerships with customers who outsource transaction and information processing services. Besides Paymentech, alliances include a joint venture with Microsoft intended to enhance First Data's standing in the evolving e-commerce market.

HISTORY

Both predecessors to today's First Data (First Financial Management and First Data Resources) developed from in-house data processing operations that became independent profit centers for their parent companies and were then spun off.

The older of the two companies, First Financial Management, arose out of the data processing department of the Georgia Railroad Bank & Trust Co. By the time it went public in 1983, First Financial was the largest banking data processor in the Southeast. It grew rapidly in a consolidating industry and in 1987 entered the credit card transaction processing business with the purchase of NaBANCO.

That year American Express created First Data Resources, a separate unit for its transaction processing functions, under the leadership of Henry Duques. Duques had built up the unit during the 1980s to process a variety of transactions for American Express' charge card processing business and its burgeoning financial services operations, which included the Boston Company (now part of Mellon Bank), Lehman Brothers (spun off in 1994), E. F. Hutton, and IDS.

While First Data was growing, First Financial remained active, buying Georgia Federal Bank in 1989 to facilitate the growth of its bank card business.

As the 1990s dawned, American Express' dreams of a financial services empire were crumbling. The businesses did not fit well with American Express, diverting attention from its core lines. However, First Data had become the largest bank card processing company in the US and a significant power in mutual fund transactions. In 1992 it was spun off.

First Financial began sharpening its focus on merchant (rather than bank) services. It bought TeleCheck (check authorization) in

1992 and began divesting its banking and bank services holdings.

In 1994 First Data and First Financial Management went head-to-head, vying to buy Western Union (founded 1855) from bankrupt parent New Valley Corporation. First Financial, with a $1.9 billion offer for the top consumer funds transfer company, was the victor in the bidding war (which also included Forstmann Little).

Although First Data's $6.5 billion merger with First Financial in 1995 raised antitrust concerns, the deal went through with only the stipulation of selling the MoneyGram (money transfer) services business. The new union gave First Data a 30% share of the fragmented credit card processing market and moved it into new service areas.

The company has continued to grow through strategic partnerships. First Data won a 10-year contract in 1996 to process credit and debit transactions for retail giant Wal-Mart — more than 5 billion each year. A 1997 pact added about 6 million accounts to First Data's mix; the company provides processing for credit cards issued by BANK ONE and its First USA subsidiary. First Data also expanded its geographical presence that year, agreeing to provide credit card processing for HSBC Holdings' banks in the UK, the US, and Hong Kong (First Data pulled out of Hong Kong in 1998). In 1998 the company added to its retirement-plan asset base with the acquisition of United States Pension Services.

In 1999 First Data and BANK ONE moved to strengthen their relationship: First Data bought up the shares of BANK ONE subsidiary Paymentech and folded that 48% stake into its existing joint venture with BANK ONE: Banc One Payment Services LLC.

In an effort to refocus on its electronic payment and commerce services, First Data agreed to sell its Investor Services Group to PNC Bank in 1999.

Chairman and CEO: Henry C. "Ric" Duques, age 55, $800,000 pay
President and COO: Charles T. Fote, age 50, $811,138 pay
EVP and CFO: Lee Adrean, age 47, $572,115 pay
EVP: Eula Adams, age 49
EVP: David P. Bailis, age 43, $598,367 pay
EVP: Robert J. Levenson, age 57, $518,558 pay
EVP and Chief Administrative Officer: Michael Whealy, age 46
SVP Client Services, First Data Investor Services: Debralee Goldberg
SVP Human Resources: Janet Harris
SVP and General Manager, Fund Accounting and Administration: John M. Stratton
VP and Controller: J. Allen Berryman
VP Financial Reporting: Kevin M. Connerty
VP and Division Manager, First Data Investor Services: Michael C. Kardok
Auditors: Ernst & Young LLP

LOCATIONS

HQ: 5660 New Northside Dr., Ste. 1400, Atlanta, GA 30328
Phone: 770-857-7001   **Fax:** 770-857-0404
Web site: http://www.firstdatacorp.com

First Data Corporation operates primarily in Australia, the UK, and the US.

PRODUCTS/OPERATIONS

1998 Sales

	$ mil.	% of total
Payment instruments	1,697	33
Card issuance	1,434	28
Merchant card processing	1,394	27
Other	585	12
Adjustments	8	—
Total	**5,118**	**100**

Business Segments and Selected Services

Card Issuer Services
Application processing
Bank card customer servicing
Chargeback services
Credit and consumer support
Credit-risk decision modeling services
Customized card promotion services
Target-marketing decision modeling services

Merchant Processing Services
Credit transaction processing services
Debit card transaction processing services
Delinquent account processing services

Payment Instruments
Bill payment services
Nonbank money transfer and payment services

COMPETITORS

The Associates	EDS	PMT Services
BA Merchant	Fiserv	Synovus
Services	MBNA	Total System
CheckFree	MoneyGram	Services
Concord EFS	National Data	Vestcom
Deluxe	NOVA	International
ECHO	Corporation	

HISTORICAL FINANCIALS & EMPLOYEES

NYSE symbol: FDC FYE: December 31	Annual Growth	1989	1990	1991	1992	1993	1994	1995	1996	1997	1998
Sales ($ mil.)	25.3%	672	845	1,026	1,205	1,490	1,652	4,081	4,934	4,979	5,118
Net income ($ mil.)	18.9%	98	103	118	141	173	208	(84)	637	357	466
Income as % of sales	—	14.6%	12.2%	11.5%	11.7%	11.6%	12.6%	—	12.9%	7.2%	9.1%
Earnings per share ($)	8.1%	—	—	—	0.65	0.71	0.85	(0.19)	1.37	0.79	1.04
Stock price - FY high ($)	—	—	—	—	17.19	21.13	25.31	35.63	44.00	46.13	36.06
Stock price - FY low ($)	—	—	—	—	10.63	15.63	20.25	23.00	30.38	25.00	19.69
Stock price - FY close ($)	10.8%	—	—	—	17.19	20.38	23.69	33.44	36.50	29.25	31.88
P/E - high	—	—	—	—	26	30	30	—	32	58	35
P/E - low	—	—	—	—	16	22	24	—	22	32	19
Dividends per share ($)	26.0%	—	—	—	0.02	0.06	0.06	0.06	0.06	0.06	0.08
Book value per share ($)	15.6%	—	—	—	3.61	4.33	4.60	7.04	8.28	8.18	8.62
Employees	8.7%	—	—	—	19,400	19,300	22,000	36,000	40,000	36,000	32,000

STOCK PRICE HISTORY   HIGH/LOW/CLOSE

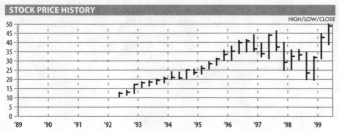

1998 FISCAL YEAR-END
Debt ratio: 29.5%
Return on equity: 12.4%
Cash ($ mil.): 460
Current ratio: 0.99
Long-term debt ($ mil.): 1,572
No. of shares (mil.): 436
Dividends
  Yield: 0.3%
  Payout: 7.7%
Market value ($ mil.): 13,884

FIRST UNION CORPORATION

OVERVIEW

In order to form a more perfect First Union, this company has acquired a slew of banks (more than 70 since 1985), spruced up its electronic offerings, and diversified its financial services. The Charlotte, North Carolina-based bank claims 16 million customers and some 2,400 locations. Following its 1998 acquisition of CoreStates Financial Corp, it is the sixth-largest in the US and is fulfilling its strategy of becoming a 50/50 mix of traditional (though technologically advanced) banking on one hand and investment, brokerage, financial, and insurance services on the other.

First Union's bank offerings include checking and savings accounts, mortgages and other consumer loans (among its other acquisitions was home equity loan giant The Money Store, acquired in 1998), and banking for small to midsized businesses. To compete with financial services mammoths such as Merrill Lynch and major insurance companies that have been invading the banking industry's turf since the early 1980s, First Union has moved into investment services for institutions and individuals with investment advice, mutual funds, retail brokerage, and corporate finance (including debt underwriting and asset financing). It has also moved into insurance sales, offering a variety of life policies.

CEO Edward Crutchfield's eat-or-be-eaten expansion program has left investors unimpressed with its ego; the bank has stumbled in integrating CoreStates and The Money Store and has failed to deliver promised big profits, bruising its bottom line and shareholder returns. First Union is looking to overcome the downturn by expanding its asset management operations and focusing on new technology to sell and deliver its services.

HISTORY

First Union traces it roots to the Union National Bank of Charlotte, North Carolina, formed in 1908. After acquiring First National Bank & Trust of Asheville, it changed its name to First Union National Bank of North Carolina in 1958. In 1967 the bank formed a holding company, First Union National Bancorp, which was renamed First Union in 1975.

Led by Edward Crutchfield, who became president in 1988 (and is now chairman and CEO), the bank's acquisition strategy (partly spurred by its rivalry with crosstown competitor NationsBank, now Bank of America) made it a powerhouse.

In 1991 First Union bought the failed Southeast Banks from the FDIC. Two years later it acquired First American Metro Corp. of Washington, DC. First Union assimilated more than 10 banks between 1994 and 1996 and was one of the first expansionist banks to install uniform data processing systems in all its regions. One of its largest trophies was First Fidelity.

Despite an acquisitions binge in the 1990s, First Fidelity could not ensure its safety against hostile takeovers, and in 1996 it merged with First Union.

Thereafter, First Union continued making acquisitions, including Connecticut-based Center Financial and Florida-based Home Financial. Its purchase of Virginia's Signet Banking Corporation in 1997 made it the largest bank in the state.

Also that year First Union moved into securities when the Federal Reserve gave it permission to underwrite equity warrants and preferred stock; in 1998 the company bought Wheat First Butcher Singer (brokerage) and Bowles Hollowell Conner & Co. (mergers and acquisitions advisory services). In addition, the bank moved more strongly into consumer finance with the purchase of the Money Store. But the year's big news was its purchase of CoreStates Financial, in a deal that added more than 500 branches on the East Coast. At the time, the merger was the largest in history. Yet the assimilation of CoreStates did not go as smoothly as previous mergers. More than 7,000 workers were informed that their services were no longer needed, and customers were hit by a slew of new fees.

In 1999 the cutbacks continued as First Union said it would cut its workforce by about 7%. More bad news followed when the bank twice warned its earnings would not meet projections — thanks, in part, to costs related to the CoreStates and Money Store acquisitions. First Union's stock dove, and investors filed two lawsuits alleging the bank covered up financial gaffes to inflate its value. Despite the backlash against its merger mania, the bank announced plans to buy securities brokerage EVEREN Capital, and is starting an electronic billing and payment company with Wells Fargo and Chase Manhattan.

Chairman and CEO: Edward E. Crutchfield, age 57,
$3,420,000 pay
VC: B. J. Walker, age 68
VC, President, and COO: G. Kennedy Thompson, age 47
EVP and CFO: Robert T. Atwood, age 58, $1,310,000 pay
EVP and Chief E-Commerce Officer: David Carroll
EVP, Consumer Banking Group: Jack Antonini
General Counsel: Mark C. Treanor, age 52
EVP, Human Resources: Don R. Johnson
**CEO, Congress Financial and Congress Talcott;
President, First Union Business Credit:**
William R. Davis
President, First Union - Mid-Atlantic Region:
Malcolm C. Everett III
VC: Benjamin P. Jenkins III
Chief Investment Officer, Capital Management Group:
Dennis Ferro
Auditors: KPMG LLP

HQ: 1 First Union Center, Charlotte, NC 28288-0570
Phone: 704-374-6565   **Fax:** 704-374-3425
Web site: http://www.firstunion.com

First Union has about 2,400 banking branches in the US,
primarily on the East Coast; the company also has
offices in Africa, the Asia/Pacific Region, Europe, North
America, and South America.

1998 Assets

	$ mil.	% of total
Cash & equivalents	28,637	12
Trading account	9,759	4
Securities available for sale	37,434	16
Other securities	2,025	1
Net loans	133,557	56
Other assets	25,951	11
Total	**237,363**	**100**

1998 Sales

	$ mil.	% of total
Interest & fees on loans	11,196	52
Other interest	3,792	18
Deposit account service charges	1,146	5
Capital management	1,720	8
Other	3,689	17
Total	**21,543**	**100**

Advanta	KeyCorp
The Associates	Keystone Financial
Bank of America	M&T Bank
Bank of New York	MBNA
Charles Schwab	Mellon Bank
Chase Manhattan	Merrill Lynch
Citigroup	National City
Commonwealth Bancorp	National Penn Bancshares
Countrywide Credit	Northwest Bancorp
First Virginia	PNC Bank
Fleet	Summit Bancorp
FMR	SunTrust
Fulton Financial	Susquehanna Bancshares
Household International	Wachovia

NYSE symbol: FTU FYE: December 31	Annual Growth	1989	1990	1991	1992	1993	1994	1995	1996	1997	1998
Assets ($ mil.)	24.9%	32,131	40,781	46,085	51,327	70,787	77,314	96,741	140,127	157,274	237,363
Net income ($ mil.)	30.9%	256	304	319	515	818	944	1,013	1,499	1,896	2,891
Income as % of assets	—	0.8%	0.7%	0.7%	1.0%	1.2%	1.2%	1.0%	1.1%	1.2%	1.2%
Earnings per share ($)	10.5%	1.20	1.26	1.28	1.86	2.09	2.25	2.38	2.58	2.99	2.95
Stock price - FY high ($)	—	13.50	11.00	15.50	22.44	26.56	24.00	29.75	38.88	53.00	65.94
Stock price - FY low ($)	—	9.81	6.88	6.75	14.56	18.63	19.50	20.69	25.56	36.31	40.94
Stock price - FY close ($)	21.8%	10.31	7.69	15.00	21.81	20.63	20.69	27.81	37.00	51.25	60.81
P/E - high	—	11	9	12	12	13	11	13	15	18	22
P/E - low	—	8	5	5	8	9	9	9	10	12	14
Dividends per share ($)	13.6%	0.50	0.54	0.56	0.64	0.75	0.86	0.98	1.10	0.90	1.58
Book value per share ($)	6.8%	9.69	11.60	12.31	13.97	15.19	15.24	17.93	17.41	18.91	17.49
Employees	16.8%	17,733	20,521	24,203	23,459	32,861	31,858	44,536	44,333	47,096	71,486

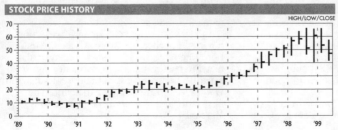

HIGH/LOW/CLOSE

Equity as % of assets: 7.2%
Return on assets: 1.5%
Return on equity: 16.8%
Long-term debt ($ mil.): 22,949
No. of shares (mil.): 982
Dividends
  Yield: 2.6%
  Payout: 53.6%
Market value ($ mil.): 59,715
Sales (mil.): $21,543

FIRSTAR CORP.

OVERVIEW

Star light, star bright, Firstar Corp. is burning bright.

The product of a merger between Milwaukee-based Firstar and Cincinnati-based Star Banc, Firstar spreads its stardust from more than 700 locations in several midwestern states, with outposts in Arizona and Florida.

Firstar offers consumer and business banking services, as well as brokerage and investment management, trust services, mortgage banking, consumer finance, lease financing, and insurance sales. The bank's fairly successful post-merger performance has been a bright star amid otherwise lackluster merger results within the industry, and investors are generally looking with favor upon its plan to buy Missouri-based Mercantile Bancorporation, which would add another 500 branches. CEO Jerry Grundhofer is also making complementary deals for long-term growth.

HISTORY

When Farmers and Millers Bank was founded in 1853, it operated out of a strongbox in a rented storefront. After surviving a panic in the 1850s, the bank became part of the national banking system in 1863 as First National Bank of Milwaukee. The bank grew along with Milwaukee, and in 1894 it merged with Merchants Exchange Bank (founded 1870).

In 1919 the bank merged again, with Wisconsin National Bank (founded in 1892), to form First Wisconsin National Bank of Milwaukee. The new bank was a leading financial institution in the area from the 1920s on.

First Wisconsin grew through acquisitions over the next decade, though the number of banks fell after the 1929 stock market crash; by the end of WWII it had 11 banks. Postwar growth was constrained by state and federal legislation, particularly by the 1956 Bank Holding Company Act (which proscribed acquisitions and branching). In the 1970s Wisconsin eased restrictions on intrastate branching and the bank began to grow again.

Growth accelerated in the late 1980s after Wisconsin and surrounding states legalized interstate banking in adjoining states in 1987. That year First Wisconsin acquired seven Minnesota banks and then moved into Illinois. The company focused on strong, well-run institutions. Also that year, it sold its headquarters and used the proceeds to fund more acquisitions. In 1988, in its first foray outside the Midwest, the company bought Metro Bancorp in Phoenix, targeting midwestern retirees moving to Arizona.

In 1989 First Wisconsin changed its name to Firstar. The company moved into Iowa in 1990 with its purchase of Des Moines-based Banks of Iowa, the second-largest banking institution in that state. In 1992 it bought rival Federated Bank Geneva (Wisconsin) Capital Corporation. The next year it swept up DSB Corporation in Deerfield, Illinois. In 1994 Firstar bought First Southeast Banking Corp., another Wisconsin bank, and merged it, along with Firstar Bank Racine and Firstar Bank Milwaukee, into one bank.

That year the company was hit with a $13 million charge to cover an operating loss stemming from a check-kiting fraud. The company tightened its controls after the episode, which it termed a "major disappointment."

Trying to strengthen its position against larger competitors, Firstar continued to make acquisitions in 1995 (Chicago bank First Colonial Bankshares and Investors Bank Corp. of Minneapolis/St. Paul) and in 1996 (Jacob Schmidt Company). But acquisitions left the company bloated with redundant operations. In 1996 Firstar began a restructuring designed to cut costs and increase margins. The restructuring project ended in 1997, but by then the company's performance lagged behind other midwestern banks considerably. In an effort to diversify, it announced an alliance with EVEREN Securities to enable it to offer debt underwriting and sales, fixed income products, and public finance advisory services. But it was too little, too late, and under pressure from major stockholders to seek a partner, Firstar began looking for a buyer.

It found Star Banc. Star Banc was established in 1863 as The First National Bank of Cincinnati under a bank charter signed by Abraham Lincoln. Over the years it added branches and acquired other banks. The company renamed all of its subsidiary banks Star Bank in 1988 and in 1989 took the name Star Banc.

In 1998 Star Banc chairman Jerry Grundhofer approached Firstar about a combination. Negotiations proceeded quickly, and a new Firstar was born. The move depressed earnings that year, but not enough to dampen Wall Street enthusiasm for the bank. The next year Firstar announced plans to buy Mercantile Bank.

Chairman: Roger L. Fitzsimonds, age 60, $1,062,100 pay
VC and COO: John A. Becker, age 56, $757,700 pay
VC and CFO: David M. Moffett, age 46, $656,500 pay
VC and Director of Information Services and Operations: William L. Chenevich
VC and Manager Wholesale Banking: Mark C. Wheeler Jr.
VC, Consumer Banking: Richard K. Davis, age 40, $656,500 pay
President and CEO: Jerry A. Grundhofer, age 54, $1,800,000 pay
EVP, Community Banking: Joseph A. Campanella, age 56
EVP, Credit Administration: John R. Heistad, age 52
EVP, Human Resources: Stephen E. Smith, age 51
EVP, Information Services: Ronald E. Roder, age 50
EVP, Metro Banking and In-Store Banking: Kathy P. Beechem, age 47
EVP, Mortgage Banking: Daniel A. Arrigoni, age 48
EVP, Operations: Timothy J. Fogarty, age 41
EVP, Retail Lending and Finance Company: Kenneth R. Griffith, age 51
EVP, Sales and Marketing: Jay B. Williams, age 47
EVP, Trusts and Investments: Daniel B. Benhase, age 39
SVP, General Counsel, and Secretary: Jennie P. Carlson
President and CEO, Firstar Investment Research and Management: Mary Ellen Stanek, age 42
Auditors: Arthur Andersen LLP

LOCATIONS

HQ: 777 E. Wisconsin Ave., Milwaukee, WI 53202
Phone: 414-765-4321   **Fax:** 414-287-3290
Web site: http://www.firstar.com

Firstar operates more than 700 branches in Arizona, Florida, Illinois, Indiana, Iowa, Kentucky, Minnesota, Ohio, Tennessee and Wisconsin.

PRODUCTS/OPERATIONS

1998 Assets

	$ mil.	% of total
Cash & equivalents	2,350	6
Treasury & agency securities	1,317	3
Mortgage-backed securities	3,168	8
State & municipal bonds	1,580	5
Net loans	25,742	66
Other investments	369	1
Other assets	4,220	11
Total	**38,746**	**100**

1998 Sales

	$ mil.	% of total
Interest income	2,642	75
Trust income	262	8
Mortgage banking	151	4
Fees	93	3
Other income	354	10
Total	**3,502**	**100**

COMPETITORS

Area Bancshares
BANK ONE
Camco Financial
Fifth Third Bancorp
First American
FirstMerit
Huntington Bancshares
Marshall & Ilsley
Mercantile Bancorporation
MidAmerica Bancorp
National City
National City Bancshares
Old Kent Financial
Old National Bancorp
Peoples Bancorp (OH)
Provident Financial Group
S.Y. Bancorp
TCF Financial
Union Planters
U. S. Bancorp
Wells Fargo

HISTORICAL FINANCIALS & EMPLOYEES

NYSE symbol: FSR FYE: December 31	Annual Growth	1989	1990	1991	1992	1993	1994	1995	1996	1997	1998
Assets ($ mil.)	23.1%	5,949	6,295	6,646	7,715	7,637	9,391	9,573	10,094	10,959	38,476
Net income ($ mil.)	24.9%	58	65	66	76	100	117	137	158	195	430
Income as % of assets	—	9.1%	9.8%	10.0%	11.9%	15.9%	17.0%	16.1%	17.5%	19.3%	12.3%
Earnings per share ($)	12.8%	0.22	0.25	0.25	0.28	0.37	0.43	0.50	0.58	0.73	0.65
Stock price - FY high ($)	—	2.99	2.59	3.05	4.38	4.37	4.96	6.90	10.44	19.54	31.28
Stock price - FY low ($)	—	2.05	1.61	1.66	2.69	3.66	3.71	4.02	6.22	9.88	17.61
Stock price - FY close ($)	32.6%	2.44	1.86	2.77	3.99	3.88	4.03	6.60	10.19	19.11	30.97
P/E - high	—	14	10	12	16	12	12	14	18	27	48
P/E - low	—	9	6	7	10	10	9	8	11	14	27
Dividends per share ($)	13.0%	0.10	0.10	0.11	0.11	0.13	0.15	0.17	0.20	0.25	0.30
Book value per share ($)	13.0%	1.79	1.92	2.06	2.23	2.48	2.66	3.05	3.28	3.54	5.37
Employees	7.3%	6,733	6,733	7,709	8,671	9,133	9,876	8,680	8,367	8,755	12,700

1997 and prior financial information is for "old" Firstar.

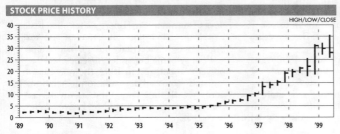

STOCK PRICE HISTORY
HIGH/LOW/CLOSE

1998 FISCAL YEAR-END
Debt ratio: 32.6%
Equity as % of assets: 9.2%
Return on assets: 1.7%
Return on equity: 12.2%
Long-term debt ($ mil.): 1,709
No. of shares (mil.): 657
Dividends
  Yield: 1.0%
  Payout: 46.2%
Market value ($ mil.): 20,344
Sales ($ mil.): 3,502

FIRSTENERGY CORP.

OVERVIEW

Competition has FirstEnergy acting like an electrified Tasmanian devil. The Akron, Ohio-based energy holding company is whirling through the northeastern US, picking up companies, putting down others, creating new subsidiaries, and even trading power plants. Formed when Ohio Edison bought Centerior Energy, FirstEnergy has a stable force in its regulated utility subsidiaries — Ohio Edison, Pennsylvania Power, Cleveland Electric Illuminating, and Toledo Edison. The four generate and distribute electricity to more than 2.2 million customers in central and northern Ohio and western Pennsylvania. FirstEnergy has a generating capacity of almost 12,000 MW,

of which nearly 70% is coal-powered and more than 30% nuclear-powered.

The company is preparing for the day when its customers can choose another electricity supplier. It has created new subsidiaries to handle its transmission assets and hopes to form a for-profit transmission company with fellow utility holding companies AEP, CMS Energy, and Dominion Resources.

Subsidiary FirstEnergy Trading & Power Marketing is also going after deregulated energy markets throughout the US. In an effort to provide a wider range of energy services, FirstEnergy is acquiring nonregulated companies, including electrical and mechanical contractors and natural gas company MARBEL Energy.

HISTORY

Ohio Edison came to light in 1893 as the Akron Electric Light and Power Company. After several mergers, the business went bankrupt and was sold in 1899 to Akron Traction and Electric Company, which became Northern Ohio Power and Light (NOP&L).

In 1930 Commonwealth and Southern (C&S) bought NOP&L and merged it with four other Ohio utility holding companies to form Ohio Edison. The new firm increased sales during the Depression by selling electric appliances (and continued to do so until the 1970s).

During WWII, heavy industrial growth within the company's service area increased demand for power. By 1949 the Public Utility Holding Company Act of 1935 (passed to rein in the uncontrolled utilities) had caught up with C&S and forced it to divest Ohio Edison. Rival Ohio Public Service was also divested from its holding company, and in 1950 Ohio Edison bought it.

The company continued expanding in the 1950s and early 1960s. In 1967 Ohio Edison and three other Ohio and Pennsylvania utilities formed the Central Area Power Coordination Group (CAPCO) to share new power plant costs, including the construction of the Beaver Valley nuclear plant (1970-76). Although the CAPCO partners agreed in 1980 to cancel four planned nukes, in 1985 Ohio Edison took part in building the Perry Unit 1 and Beaver Valley Unit 2 nuclear plants.

The federal Energy Policy Act of 1992 transformed the industry by allowing wholesale power competition. To satisfy new federal requirements, Ohio Edison formed a six-state transmission alliance in 1996 with fellow utilities Centerior Energy, Allegheny Power System,

and Dominion Resources' Virginia Power to coordinate their power grids.

Ohio Edison paid about $1.5 billion in 1997 for the slightly larger Centerior Energy, formed in 1986 as a holding company for Toledo Edison and Cleveland Electric, two utilities that served heavily industrialized and largely urban markets. Ohio Edison and Centerior, both burdened by high-cost generating plants, merged to cut costs, and the expanded energy concern was renamed FirstEnergy Corp.

The transmission issue arose again in 1997. FirstEnergy defected from fledgling transmission-coordination alliance Midwest ISO (Independent System Operator) to start a rival, Alliance, with 11 utility members.

Looking toward deregulation, FirstEnergy began buying mechanical construction, contracting, and energy management companies in 1997, including Roth Bros. and RPC Mechanical. It added nine more the next year. In 1998 FirstEnergy ventured into natural gas operations with its purchase of MARBEL Energy. The company also created separate subsidiaries for its nuclear and transmission assets.

The perils of the free market struck FirstEnergy in 1998. Power marketers Federal Energy Sales and the Power Co. of America couldn't deliver the juice to FirstEnergy during the hottest days of summer. FirstEnergy later sued Federal Energy for $25 million in damages. The next year it bought electricity outage insurance.

Pennsylvania began large-scale electric power competition in 1999, the year the Ohio legislature passed deregulation legislation. To comply with state laws, FirstEnergy agreed to trade power plants, including Beaver Valley, with DQE.

Chairman, FirstEnergy and Pennsylvania Power:
Willard R. Holland, age 62, $893,275 pay
President and CEO: H. Peter Burg, age 52,
$589,105 pay (prior to title change)
EVP and General Counsel: Anthony J. Alexander,
$459,018 pay
SVP: John A. Gill, $327,715 pay
VP and CFO: Richard H. Marsh
VP: Arthur R. Garfield
VP: Douglas S. Elliot
VP: Earl T. Carey, $306,012 pay
VP: Kathryn W. Dindo
VP: Mary Beth Carroll
VP: Stanley F. Szwed
**President and Chief Nuclear Officer, FirstEnergy
Nuclear Operating Company:** John P. Stetz
President, Pennsylvania Power: R. Joseph Hrach
Regional President, Central: Stephen E. Morgan
Regional President, Eastern: Lynn M. Cavalier
Regional President, Northern: Charles E. Jones
Regional President, Southern: Thomas A. Clark
Regional President, Western: James M. Murray
Corporate Secretary: Nancy C. Ashcom
Human Resources Coordinator: Renee Spino
Auditors: Arthur Andersen LLP

HQ: 76 S. Main St., Akron, OH 44308-1890
Phone: 330-384-5100   **Fax:** 330-384-3866
Web site: http://www.firstenergycorp.com

FirstEnergy serves electricity customers in central and
northern Ohio and western Pennsylvania.

1998 Sales

	$ mil.	% of total
Electric sales	4,980	85
Trading & power marketing	411	7
Facilities services	198	3
Other	272	5
Total	**5,861**	**100**

Electric Utility Subsidiaries
The Cleveland Electric Illuminating Company
(northeastern Ohio)
Ohio Edison Company (north central and northeastern
Ohio)
Pennsylvania Power Company (northwestern
Pennsylvania)
The Toledo Edison Company (northwestern Ohio)

Selected Unregulated Subsidiaries
American Transmission Systems, Inc. (transmission
assets)
FirstEnergy Facilities Services Group, Inc. (heating,
ventilating, air conditioning, and energy management)
FirstEnergy Trading & Power Marketing, Inc.
MARBEL Energy Corporation (natural gas exploration,
production, and marketing)

AEP	Dynegy
Allegheny Energy	Enron
Cinergy	Peabody Group
Conectiv	PG&E
DPL	PP&L Resources
DQE	Southern Company
Duke Energy	UtiliCorp

NYSE symbol: FE FYE: December 31	Annual Growth	1989	1990	1991	1992	1993	1994	1995	1996	1997	1998
Sales ($ mil.)	11.8%	2,155	2,226	2,359	2,332	2,370	2,368	2,466	2,470	2,821	5,861
Net income ($ mil.)	1.4%	361	282	265	277	25	304	317	315	306	411
Income as % of sales	—	16.8%	12.7%	11.2%	11.9%	1.0%	12.8%	12.9%	12.8%	10.8%	7.0%
Earnings per share ($)	(6.2%)	—	—	—	—	—	—	—	—	1.94	1.82
Stock price - FY high ($)	—	—	—	—	—	—	—	—	—	29.00	34.06
Stock price - FY low ($)	—	—	—	—	—	—	—	—	—	25.13	27.06
Stock price - FY close ($)	12.3%	—	—	—	—	—	—	—	—	29.00	32.56
P/E - high	—	—	—	—	—	—	—	—	—	15	19
P/E - low	—	—	—	—	—	—	—	—	—	13	15
Dividends per share ($)	—	—	—	—	—	—	—	—	—	0.00	1.50
Book value per share ($)	1.8%	—	—	—	—	—	—	—	—	22.39	22.80
Employees	(13.1%)	6,905	6,792	6,481	6,263	5,978	5,166	4,812	4,273	4,215	1,944

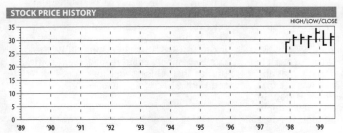

HIGH/LOW/CLOSE

Debt ratio: 54.0%
Return on equity: 7.6%
Cash ($ mil.): 78
Current ratio: 0.49
Long-term debt ($ mil.): 6,352
No. of shares (mil.): 237
Dividends
  Yield: 4.6%
  Payout: 82.4%
Market value ($ mil.): 7,719

FISHER SCIENTIFIC INTERNATIONAL

OVERVIEW

If the sight of a Bunsen burner gets you hot, Fisher Scientific International is your company. Hampton, New Hampshire-based Fisher is the world's leading provider of scientific equipment and instruments — everything from Erlenmeyer flasks to video/microscope systems. Fisher sells more than 260,000 products online and through catalogs. The company offers instruments and supplies from independent vendors, as well as its own products (40% of sales) including chemicals, clinical equipment, diagnostic tools, and laboratory workstations.

After decades of gobbling up complementary companies (and 44 consecutive years of increased sales), Fisher continues to use acquisitions (nearly 30 in the past seven years) to expand globally. Following a series of restructurings, Fisher is dropping its technology operations to focus on its original market niche — research and clinical labs.

An investor group led by LBO specialist Thomas H. Lee Company owns 52% of the company, and an investor group affiliated with Donaldson, Lufkin & Jenrette owns 16%.

HISTORY

In 1902, 20-year-old Chester Fisher bought the stockroom of Pittsburgh Testing Laboratories (established 1884) and formed Scientific Materials Co. The company's earliest products, supplied from Europe via New York, included simple tools such as microscopes, balances, and colorimeters. The company published its first catalog in 1904.

With the outbreak of WWI disrupting its European supply lines, Scientific Materials established its own R&D and manufacturing facilities in 1915. The company acquired Montreal-based Scientific Supplies in 1925 and the following year changed its name to Fisher Scientific Company. By 1935 Fisher had doubled its size, adding glass blowing operations and an instrument shop.

In 1940 the company acquired pioneering chemicals supplier Eimer & Amend (founded 1851), whose customers had included Thomas Edison and Henry Ford. Two years later Fisher supplied chemicals used in the Manhattan Project. In 1949 Chester's son Aiken became president.

Jonas Salk relied on Fisher reagents to develop the polio vaccine, introduced in 1955. In 1957 the company bought the laboratory apparatus division of E. Machlett & Son.

Chester died in 1965, the year the company went public, leaving Fisher to sons Aiken, Benjamin, and James. Fisher acquired pipette maker Pfeiffer Glass (1966), scientific teaching equipment maker Stansi Scientific (1967), optical instruments maker Jerrell-Ash Company (1968), and Hi-Pure Chemicals (1974).

Aiken retired as chairman in 1975 and was replaced by Benjamin. That year former Pfeiffer Glass president Edward Perkins was appointed president and CEO; he was the first nonfamily member to hold this position. In 1976 Fisher landed its largest order, supplying $8.75 million in teaching tools to Nigeria.

The next year Fisher bought the diagnostics division of American Cyanamid's Lederle Laboratories.

In 1980 Fisher acquired laboratory furniture company Conco Industries. But with earnings flat and the Fisher brothers aging, the company became vulnerable, and was purchased in 1981 by Allied Corporation (now AlliedSignal). Allied wanted Fisher to form the core of its new Health & Science Products unit, but by 1986 Allied was selling off nonstrategic businesses. Allied spinoff the Henley Group bought Fisher, then sold 57% of the renamed Fisher Scientific International (moving its headquarters from Pennsylvania to New Hampshire) to the public in 1991.

In 1992 Fisher bought Hamilton Scientific, the top US maker of laboratory workstations, and a majority interest in Kuhn + Bayer, a German supplier of scientific equipment.

In 1995 Fisher made its largest acquisition to date: Curtin Matheson Scientific, a leading US provider of diagnostic instruments. That year the company boosted its global presence by acquiring Fisons plc, a UK-based laboratory products supplier.

In 1997 the company consolidated several of its international operations and took a charge of nearly $52 million. The next year stockholders approved a recapitalization deal giving Thomas H. Lee Company a majority stake in the company. Fisher also bought Bioblock Scientific, a French distributor of scientific and laboratory instruments. A restructuring caused a second straight year of losses in 1998. In 1999 it spun off its ProcureNet (supply chain management software) unit to shareholders and announced plans to sell UniKix Technology (software).

Chairman and CEO: Paul M. Montrone, age 57,
$1,180,000 pay
VC, EVP, and CFO: Paul M. Meister, age 46,
$820,000 pay
President and COO: David Della Penta, age 51,
$632,442 pay
VP and Controller: Kevin P. Clark, age 36
VP, Secretary, and General Counsel: Todd M. DuChene,
age 35, $362,500 pay
VP, Communications: Amy L. Binder
VP, External Affairs: Charles R. Hogen Jr.
VP, Finance and Treasurer: Robert J. Gagalis, age 44
VP, Human Resources: David Renker
President, Fisher Health Care: Daniel A. Eckert
President, Fisher Research: Paul F. Patek
President, Fisher Safety: Charles V. Wozniak
President, Fisher Scientific Worldwide:
Denis N. Maiorani, age 50, $550,000 pay
President, Global Laboratory Products:
Thomas W. Baugh
Auditors: Deloitte & Touche LLP

LOCATIONS

HQ: 1 Liberty Ln., Hampton, NH 03842
Phone: 603-926-5911   **Fax:** 603-926-0222
Web site: http://www.fishersci.com

Fisher Scientific International has principal
manufacturing facilities in Arkansas, New Jersey, New
York, North Carolina, Pennsylvania, and Wisconsin, and
in Belgium and the UK. The company has principal
distribution centers in California, Georgia, Illinois, and
New Jersey, and in Australia, Belgium, Canada, France,
Germany, Malaysia, Mexico, Singapore, South Korea,
and the UK.

PRODUCTS/OPERATIONS

1998 Sales

	% of total
Proprietary products	40
Other vendors	60
Total	**100**

Selected Products
Ampules
Animal supplies
Applicators
Balances
Barometers
Beakers
Biotechnology equipment
Burners
Centrifuges
Clinical equipment
Conductivity equipment
Corks
Counters
Cryogenics equipment
Cylinders
Dialysis equipment
Erlenmeyer and other
flasks
Evaporators
Extraction equipment
Fermentation products
Filtration products
Flowmeters
Fluorometers
Gauges
Immunology equipment
Incubators
Microbiology equipment
Microscope supplies
Refrigeration equipment
Safety equipment
Syringes
Tachometers
Ultraviolet lamps
Waste disposal equipment
Water purification
equipment

COMPETITORS

Allegiance
AlliedSignal
Beckman Coulter
Carl-Zeiss-
Stiftung
DuPont
Dynatech
EG&G
Hach
ICI
J. Bibby & Sons
Mettler-Toledo
International
PE Corporation
Philip Harris
Rhône-Poulenc
Sybron
International
Thermo
Instrument
VWR
Waters
Corporation

HISTORICAL FINANCIALS & EMPLOYEES

NYSE symbol: FSH FYE: December 31	Annual Growth	1989	1990	1991	1992	1993	1994	1995	1996	1997	1998
Sales ($ mil.)	15.6%	—	705	758	814	978	1,127	1,436	2,144	2,175	2,252
Net income ($ mil.)	—	—	11	8	27	33	36	3	37	(31)	(50)
Income as % of sales	—	—	1.6%	1.0%	3.3%	3.3%	3.2%	0.2%	1.7%	—	—
Earnings per share ($)	—	—	—	0.10	0.33	0.40	0.44	0.04	0.38	(0.30)	(1.24)
Stock price - FY high ($)	—	—	—	3.10	6.25	7.23	7.75	6.95	9.55	10.25	22.50
Stock price - FY low ($)	—	—	—	2.75	3.10	5.35	4.58	4.93	6.65	7.03	9.53
Stock price - FY close ($)	30.5%	—	—	3.10	6.13	7.08	4.95	6.68	9.40	9.55	19.94
P/E - high	—	—	—	31	19	18	18	174	25	—	—
P/E - low	—	—	—	28	9	13	10	123	18	—	—
Dividends per share ($)	—	—	—	0.00	0.01	0.02	0.02	0.02	0.02	0.02	0.00
Book value per share ($)	—	—	—	1.40	1.89	2.26	2.73	2.78	3.84	8.67	(8.12)
Employees	10.9%	—	3,200	3,200	3,200	4,200	4,800	7,500	6,600	6,800	7,300

STOCK PRICE HISTORY

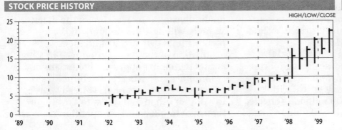
HIGH/LOW/CLOSE

1998 FISCAL YEAR-END

Debt ratio: 100.0%
Return on equity: —
Cash ($ mil.): 66
Current ratio: 1.24
Long-term debt ($ mil.): 1,022
No. of shares (mil.): 40
Dividends
  Yield: —
  Payout: —
Market value ($ mil.): 797

FLEET FINANCIAL GROUP, INC.

OVERVIEW

From dinghy to fleet to armada, Boston-based Fleet Financial Group has climbed the mast to its perch as New England's #1 bank. The voyage began in the early 1980s as the once-tiny Rhode Island bank boarded competitor Shawmut and sailed into Boston. Fleet is now poised to swallow #2 BankBoston; the resulting company, Fleet Boston, will be #8 in the US when the deal is complete. Lest Fleet leave competitors foundering in its wake, regulators have mandated the dry-docking or sale of about 300 branches of the merging banks.

Through some 1,200 New England, New Jersey, and New York branches, Fleet offers retail and commercial banking, investment services, and other traditional banking products. The bank is one of the US's largest loan servicers, especially of student loans and mortgages. Other lines of business include retail brokerage, commercial and asset-based lending, and government banking.

Fleet also absorbs businesses other than banks. With its acquisition of discount brokerage firm Quick & Reilly Group, Fleet has set a course for nonbanking services. Other purchases include leasing, specialist, credit card, and asset management businesses.

HISTORY

Fleet National Bank was founded in 1791 in Rhode Island as the Providence Bank. In 1968 Fleet became a subsidiary of Industrial Bancorp, which specialized in loans to jewelers in the Northeast. In the 1970s the bank diversified, acquiring consumer finance company Southern Discount of Atlanta in 1973 and mortgage banker Mortgage Associates of Milwaukee in 1974.

Terrence Murray was named CEO and the company became Fleet Financial Group in 1982; rapid expansion was to follow. Murray acquired Credico of New Jersey (consumer lending, 1983) and folded it into Atlanta-based Fleet Finance. Fleet began expanding its banking operations outside Rhode Island in 1984, buying 46 companies in the 1980s. Even its non-acquisitions were successes: The firm was outbid for bad-loan-heavy Conifer Group in 1986; the Pyrrhic victor was soon-to-be-defunct rival Bank of New England.

In 1988 Fleet bought Norstar for $1.3 billion, taking the name Fleet/Norstar. But its expansion and credit policies left it with risky loans that became bad assets when the economy went into recession. Fleet went into the red for 1990, but would soon capitalize on other banks' problems. With the help of Kohlberg Kravis Roberts (which owns about 9% of the bank), Fleet bought the failed Bank of New England (minus its bad loan portfolio) and two other banks from the FDIC in 1991. The company's name reverted to Fleet Financial Group, and it made six acquisitions in New England in 1992.

That year a *60 Minutes* report alleged that Fleet charged exorbitant home equity interest rates and fees to low-income, minority customers. In 1993 the company settled with Georgia, agreeing to pay $30 million to affected customers and to contribute $70 million to low-income housing programs. In 1996 Fleet Mortgage discontinued its practice of rewarding employees for making loans exceeding the company's base rates.

In 1995 Fleet merged with Shawmut National Bank. The merger doubled Fleet's customer base and strengthened its presence in New Jersey and New York, but organizational problems left many customers upset. In 1997 Fleet divested its subprime lending operation and bought mutual fund company Columbia Management.

In 1998 Fleet bought Florida-based Quick & Reilly, the #3 discount brokerage in the US, and with it Internet trading subsidiary Suretrade.com (which Fleet has contemplated spinning off). To compete with Citigroup's consumer credit cards, Fleet also bought credit card portfolios from Household International, Crestar Financial (now part of SunTrust), and Advanta. (Fleet has sued Advanta for allegedly puffing up the value of its portfolio.) Also that year, Fleet bought Merrill Lynch Specialists and merged it into its newly named Fleet Specialists, the largest specialist company on the New York Stock Exchange.

In 1999 the company paid a $1.9 million fine for illegal practices committed by Shawmut Investment Advisers before Fleet bought Shawmut. Also that year, Fleet Financial bought Sanwa Bank's US business credit division. The treasure of the Fleet, though, will be 400-branch BankBoston, replete with its own array of financial services; acquisition of the rival, announced in 1999, awaits regulatory approval. Politicians and community activists are watching Fleet's moves closely; the bank has already agreed to sell more than 300 (most to Sovereign Bancorp) to quell anti-competition concerns.

Chairman and CEO; Chairman, Fleet National Bank:
Terrence Murray, age 59, $4,479,361 pay
President and COO; President and CEO, Fleet National Bank: Robert J. Higgins, age 53, $2,160,346 pay
VC and Chief Administrative Officer; Chairman and CEO, Fleet Bank, N.A.: H. Jay Sarles, age 53, $1,833,481 pay
VC and Chief Credit Policy Officer: David L. Eyles, age 59
VC and CFO: Eugene M. McQuade, age 50
VC; Chairman, Fleet Trust and Investment Services: Gunnar S. Overstrom Jr., age 56, $1,627,673 pay
VC and Chief Technology Officer: Michael R. Zucchini, age 52, $1,532,255 pay
EVP, Secretary, and General Counsel: William C. Mutterperl, age 52
EVP Human Resources: M. Anne Szostak, age 48
SVP and Treasurer: Douglas L. Jacobs, age 51
SVP, Corporate Strategy and Development: Brian T. Moynihan, age 39
Chief Accounting Officer and Controller: Robert C. Lamb Jr., age 43
VP and Chief Information Officer: Roy Lowrance
President and CEO, Fleet Bank New Jersey: Douglas L. Kennedy
President, Fleet Capital Leasing: Ronald H. Chamides
Managing Director and Chief Investment Officer, Fleet Investment Advisors: Thomas M. O'Neill
Director, Investor Relations: Thomas R. Rice
Director, Corporate Auditing: Edwin J. Santos
Auditors: KPMG Peat Marwick LLP

HQ: 1 Federal St., Boston, MA 02110-2010
Phone: 617-346-4000   **Fax:** 617-346-0464
Web site: http://www.fleet.com

1998 Assets

	$ mil.	% of total
Cash & equivalents	5,738	6
Other securities	10,792	10
Net loans	67,844	65
Other assets	20,008	19
Total	**104,382**	**100**

1998 Sales

	$ mil.	% of total
Loan interest & fees	5,878	59
Other interest	887	9
Investment services	851	8
Fees & commissions	748	7
Capital markets	530	5
Processing	457	5
Credit cards	391	4
Other noninterest	260	2
Total	**10,002**	**100**

Bank of New York
BANK ONE
Bank of America
BankBoston
Charles Schwab
Chase Manhattan
Citigroup
Countrywide Credit
Deutsche Bank
First Union
FMR

J.P. Morgan
Mellon Bank
Merrill Lynch
National Discount Brokers Group
Olde Discount Brokers
Republic New York
SLM Holding
State Street
UST

NYSE symbol: FLT FYE: December 31	Annual Growth	1989	1990	1991	1992	1993	1994	1995	1996	1997	1998
Assets ($ mil.)	13.5%	33,441	32,507	45,445	46,939	47,923	48,757	84,432	85,518	85,535	104,382
Net income ($ mil.)	17.1%	371	(49)	98	280	488	613	610	1,139	1,303	1,532
Income as % of assets	—	1.1%	—	0.2%	0.6%	1.0%	1.3%	0.7%	1.3%	1.5%	1.5%
Earnings per share ($)	4.8%	1.65	(0.26)	0.34	0.89	1.51	1.88	0.79	1.99	2.37	2.52
Stock price - FY high ($)	—	15.44	13.81	13.13	16.94	18.94	20.69	21.63	28.13	37.59	45.38
Stock price - FY low ($)	—	11.88	4.44	4.81	12.13	14.13	14.94	14.94	18.81	24.38	30.00
Stock price - FY close ($)	14.6%	13.06	5.50	12.44	16.38	16.69	16.19	20.38	24.94	37.56	44.69
P/E - high	—	9	—	39	19	13	11	27	14	16	18
P/E - low	—	7	—	14	14	9	8	19	9	10	12
Dividends per share ($)	4.8%	0.64	0.53	0.58	0.40	0.48	0.65	0.80	0.86	0.90	0.98
Book value per share ($)	4.9%	9.93	8.82	9.08	9.75	11.42	11.11	11.35	12.33	14.05	15.31
Employees	7.7%	18,500	18,000	25,000	27,500	26,000	21,500	30,800	36,000	34,000	36,000

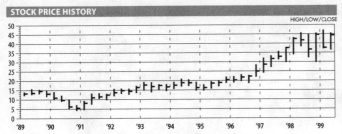

HIGH/LOW/CLOSE

Equity as % of assets: 8.4%
Return on assets: 1.6%
Return on equity: 17.6%
Long-term debt ($ mil.): 8,820
No. of shares (mil.): 570
Dividends
  Yield: 2.2%
  Payout: 38.9%
Market value ($ mil.): 25,454
Sales (mil.): $10,002

FLEETWOOD ENTERPRISES, INC.

OVERVIEW

Fleetwood Enterprises makes its customers feel at home, even when they're on the road. The Riverside, California-based company is the #1 US maker of recreational vehicles (RVs), travel trailers, and folding trailers and the #2 maker of manufactured housing after Champion Enterprises. Fleetwood Enterprises makes its vehicles (motor homes and folding and travel trailers) and homes (features may include vaulted ceilings, walk-in closets, and porches) in about 20 states in the US and also in Canada. The company also retails manufactured homes through more than 160 sites.

Fleetwood Enterprises remains a market leader, but the company has been slow to respond to market shifts brought on by increased price competition. However, the company is forecasting a bright future based on the growing number of people nearing retirement age (the typical RV customer).

The company has sold less-productive retail outlets and made a major push to boost its retailing strength by acquiring retailers, including HomeUSA, the top US manufactured-home retailer.

HISTORY

In 1950 John Crean started Coach Specialties Company, a California business that made Venetian blinds for use by motor home manufacturers. Headquartered in Riverside, this company was the forerunner of Fleetwood Enterprises, Crean's 1957 entry into the manufactured-housing industry. The company entered the RV market in 1964 by buying a small plant that produced the Terry travel trailer. The firm went public in 1965.

Between 1968 and 1973 sales grew nearly 55% annually. In 1969 the company bought motor home maker Pace Arrow to expand its offerings in the fast-growing RV market. An industrywide recession caused by the 1973 oil shock and subsequent credit crunch dropped Fleetwood Enterprises' stock from a 1972 high of $49.50 to $3.50 in 1974. Intensive cost-cutting helped position the company for the eventual upturn, and in 1976 it bought Avion Coach, a maker of luxury-class travel trailers and motor homes.

In 1980 Fleetwood Enterprises closed nine factories in response to a recession, high interest rates, and high gas prices. COO Glenn Kummer became president in 1982. Strong RV sales helped pull the company out of a mild recession in the mid-1980s.

Fleetwood Enterprises opened a credit office in Southern California in 1987 to finance customers' RV purchases, which enabled it to avoid riskier loans made to mobile-home buyers. The company added to its existing supply operations (fiberglass and lumber) by buying a maker of cabinet doors (1988) and a maker of aluminum windows (1989).

In 1989 the company became the first to surpass the $1 billion sales mark in RVs by increasing market share during an industry slump while continuing to avoid long-term debt. The company also added two new models to its RV line: the lower-priced Flair and the curved-wall Cambria. Also in 1989 Fleetwood Enterprises bought Coleman's folding-trailer business — the largest in the industry, with a 30% market share.

In 1990 the company received an order from Saudi Arabia for 2,000 manufactured homes. Unfortunately, recession and the Persian Gulf War inhibited demand for RVs and manufactured housing, but sales began to recover by mid-1991. Fleetwood Enterprises and Ford Motor Credit formed a joint venture that year to offer financing to manufactured-housing dealers.

The company bought 80% of Niesmann & Bischoff, a German maker of luxury motor homes, in 1992. The next year it finished a plant in Tennessee. It built a new plant near Waco, Texas, in 1994, and its travel trailer unit introduced a lightweight line for customers with limited towing capacity. Fleetwood Enterprises began producing manufactured homes in Wichita Falls, Texas, in 1995 and broke ground for a housing manufacturing center in Winchester, Kentucky.

The company streamlined its operations in 1996, selling its finance subsidiary, Fleetwood Credit, and its money-losing German RV subsidiary. In 1997 it became the first US homebuilder to construct a million houses.

Kummer succeeded Crean as chairman and CEO in 1998; Crean became chairman emeritus (he left to start another business in 1999). Also that year the company bought more than half a dozen retailers, including HomeUSA (65 outlets), Better Homes (Kansas), Central Homes (Oregon), and Jasper Homes, Classic City Homes, and America's Best Homes (all in Georgia). Acquisitions continued in 1999 with Viking Homes (New Mexico), JR's Mobile Homes (Illinois), and D&D Homes (California).

OFFICERS

Chairman and CEO: Glenn F. Kummer, age 65,
$1,386,091 pay
President and COO: Nelson W. Potter, age 56,
$1,624,793 pay
SVP, Finance and CFO: Paul M. Bingham, age 57,
$556,806 pay
SVP, Housing Group: Mallory S. Smith, age 57,
$890,811 pay
SVP, Recreational Vehicle Group: Richard E. Parks,
age 52, $744,499 pay
SVP, General Counsel, and Secretary: William H. Lear,
age 59
SVP, Retail Housing Division: John G. Pollis, age 59
VP, Finance, Retail Housing Division: Boyd R. Plowman
VP, Motor Homes: John R. Weiss, age 47
VP, Travel Trailers: Carl D. Betcher, age 52
VP, Folding Trailers: Patrick O. Scanlon
VP, Administration and Supply Subsidiaries:
Larry L. Mace, age 56
VP, Treasurer, and Assistant Secretary: Lyle N. Larkin,
age 54
VP, Housing Eastern Region: Charles E. Lott
VP, Housing Central Region: J. Wesley Chaney
VP, Housing Western Region: Charles A. Wilkinson
VP, Materials & Product Development, Housing Group:
Gary L. Johnson
VP, Marketing, Housing Group: Robert L. Jordan
Director of Human Resources: Dundee Kelbel
Auditors: Arthur Andersen LLP

LOCATIONS

HQ: 3125 Myers St., Riverside, CA 92503-5527
Phone: 909-351-3500   **Fax:** 909-351-3312
Web site: http://www.fleetwood.com

Fleetwood Enterprises operates about 60 RV and
manufactured-housing plants in 18 states and Canada.

PRODUCTS/OPERATIONS

1999 Sales

	$ mil.	% of total
Manufactured housing	1,718	49
Recreational vehicles		
Motor homes	1,064	31
Travel trailers	549	16
Folding trailers	116	3
Supply operations	43	1
Total	**3,490**	**100**

Selected Products
Manufactured housing (up to 3,175 sq. ft.)
Recreational vehicles
Motor homes (American Dream, American Eagle,
American Tradition, Bounder, Discovery, Flair,
Jamboree, Pace Arrow, Southwind, Tioga)
Travel trailers (Avion, Mallard, Prowler, Terry,
Westport, Wilderness)
Folding trailers

COMPETITORS

Cavco
Champion Enterprises
Clayton Homes
Coachmen Industries
Harley-Davidson
KIT Manufacturing
Oakwood Homes
Palm Harbor Homes
Skyline
Thor Industries
Winnebago

HISTORICAL FINANCIALS & EMPLOYEES

NYSE symbol: FLE FYE: April 30	Annual Growth	1990	1991	1992	1993	1994	1995	1996	1997	1998	1999
Sales ($ mil.)	9.4%	1,549	1,401	1,589	1,942	2,369	2,856	2,809	2,874	3,051	3,490
Net income ($ mil.)	7.7%	55	30	40	57	66	85	80	125	109	107
Income as % of sales	—	3.5%	2.2%	2.5%	2.9%	2.8%	3.0%	2.8%	4.3%	3.6%	3.1%
Earnings per share ($)	10.4%	1.21	0.69	0.88	1.23	1.40	1.82	1.71	3.19	3.01	2.94
Stock price - FY high ($)	—	14.75	16.81	24.00	26.88	26.00	27.25	29.00	37.25	48.00	46.44
Stock price - FY low ($)	—	11.00	7.88	14.06	12.69	16.50	17.75	18.13	24.13	25.88	23.25
Stock price - FY close ($)	6.8%	13.63	14.31	18.69	19.38	20.88	23.00	26.25	26.38	46.19	24.69
P/E - high	—	12	24	27	22	19	15	17	12	16	16
P/E - low	—	9	11	16	10	12	10	11	8	9	8
Dividends per share ($)	7.5%	0.37	0.41	0.44	0.46	0.50	0.55	0.59	0.63	0.67	0.71
Book value per share ($)	6.4%	9.51	9.78	10.26	11.01	11.88	13.20	14.22	12.40	11.96	16.67
Employees	6.4%	12,000	11,000	12,000	14,000	16,000	18,000	18,000	18,000	19,000	21,000

STOCK PRICE HISTORY   HIGH/LOW/CLOSE

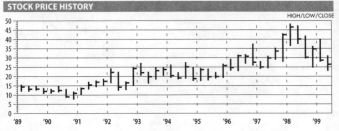

1999 FISCAL YEAR-END
Debt ratio: 8.6%
Return on equity: 18.3%
Cash ($ mil.): 26
Current ratio: 1.59
Long-term debt ($ mil.): 55
No. of shares (mil.): 35
Dividends
  Yield: 2.9%
  Payout: 24.1%
Market value ($ mil.): 869

FLEMING COMPANIES, INC.

OVERVIEW

Oklahoma City-based Fleming Companies weighs in as the nation's #2 wholesale food distributor (behind SUPERVALU), but it's trying to trim some fat. Fleming supplies brand-name and private-label food and general merchandise to more than 7,500 retailers (including some 3,000 supermarkets) across the US. Having lost several of its largest customers (Randall's Food Markets, Furr's Supermarkets), the company is undergoing a five-year effort to make itself more efficient, shedding unprofitable company-owned retail chains and consolidating distribution facilities.

Fleming serves independent retailers, franchised stores (under its IGA and Piggly Wiggly banners), Big Kmart and SuperKmart stores, warehouse stores, and convenience stores. It also owns about 260 stores that operate under a dozen or so banners, including ABCO Foods in Arizona and Rainbow Foods in Minnesota and Wisconsin. While the company sells the IGA and Piggly Wiggly private-label brands only to those chains, it sells its BestYet and Living Well labels to a number of its customers. Fleming also offers an array of marketing, consulting, and insurance services to food retailers.

HISTORY

Lux Mercantile, a Topeka, Kansas, wholesale grocery founded by O. A. Fleming, Gene Wilson, and Sam Lux, was incorporated in 1915. Three years later the company became Fleming-Wilson Mercantile.

Facing competition from chains, independent wholesalers and grocers banded together to provide competitive mass merchandising, advertising, and efficient store operations. Fleming's son Ned helped establish Fleming-Wilson as the first voluntary wholesaler west of the Mississippi (1927). The enterprise was renamed the Fleming Company (1941), and Ned became president (1945-64) and then chairman and CEO (1964-81). The company went public in 1959 and adopted the name Fleming Companies in 1972.

Fleming has grown by acquisitions since the 1930s, primarily of midwestern wholesale food distributors and supermarkets such as Grainger Brothers (1962, renamed the Fleming Co. of Nebraska); Associated Grocers of Arizona (1985); and Godfrey, with 32 Sentry supermarkets and four Sun warehouse markets (1987). The company also acquired a coffee company, a bakery, a wholesale drug firm, and several distribution centers.

The $600 million purchase in 1988 of Tennessee-based Malone & Hyde, the sixth-largest wholesale food distributor in the US (and owner of the Piggly Wiggly franchise), made Fleming the largest in that field for several years. Later that year the company sold Malone & Hyde's 99-store retail pharmacy subsidiary, M&A Drugs, for $55 million.

Fleming lost important customers when Albertson's began self-distributing in 1990 and when Alpha Beta stores merged with Lucky. However, in 1991 Fleming gained Texas-based Furr's Supermarkets as a customer when it purchased its warehouse and transportation assets. As the company saw its supermarkets losing market share to superstores and warehouses in 1993, it began a major restructuring that year (which encountered so much resistance it was delayed until 1998).

In 1994 Fleming added nearly 3,000 stores, including 175 company-owned outlets, with its $1.1 billion purchase of Scrivner, the US's #3 food wholesaler at the time, from German company Franz Haniel & Cie. It acquired ABCO Markets, a nearly bankrupt customer with 71 supermarkets in Arizona, in 1996. That year Fleming sold off underperforming units such as the 28-unit Brooks convenience store chain, cut its workforce again, and began consolidating its store brands.

Randall's Food Markets sued Fleming in 1998, alleging that the company overcharged them. Randall's was denied its claim but the contract between the two was terminated. (Comparable lawsuits filed by David's Supermarkets and Furr's Supermarkets were settled in 1997.)

With its performance flagging in 1998, Fleming ousted chairman and CEO Robert Stauth and eventually replaced him with Mark Hansen, former CEO of Wal-Mart's Sam's Club. Hansen promptly announced a five-year, $781 million program to improve profit margins by selling or closing seven supply centers, doing the same with Fleming's weaker stores, and boosting capital spending.

To that end, in 1999 the company put its Boogaarts Food Stores, Hyde Park Market, and Consumers Food & Drug chains up for sale. Fleming also began converting SuPeRSaVeR stores to its Sentry Foods banner in Wisconsin to streamline marketing efforts in that area.

OFFICERS

Chairman and CEO: Mark S. Hansen, age 44, $57,692 pay (partial-year salary)
EVP Food Distribution: E. Stephen Davis, age 58, $324,643 pay
EVP and CFO: John T. Standley
SVP, General Counsel, and Secretary: David R. Almond, age 58
SVP; Operating Group President: Ronald C. Anderson
SVP Sales and Business Development, Food Distribution: Mark K. Batenic, age 50
SVP; President, Rainbow Foods: Thomas A. Farello
SVP Real Estate and Store Development: Chuck Hall
SVP, Supply: Dick Judd
SVP Grocery, Frozen Food & Dairy: Richard H. Keeney
SVP Information Technology: Arlyn L. Larson
SVP Labor Relations: Richard C. Lynn
SVP Human Resources: Scott M. Northcutt, age 37
SVP; Group President, Price Impact Stores: John S. Runyan
SVP Retail Services: Dixon E. Simpson, age 56
SVP Retail Development Services: Robert W. Smith
Auditors: Deloitte & Touche LLP

LOCATIONS

HQ: 6301 Waterford Blvd., Oklahoma City, OK 73126
Phone: 405-840-7200 **Fax:** 405-841-8158
Web site: http://www.fleming.com

Fleming Companies serves more than 7,500 retailers (supermarkets among them) in 42 states, including about 260 company-owned stores, predominantly in the Midwest and on the East Coast. It has about 30 distribution centers in 23 states.

PRODUCTS/OPERATIONS

1998 Sales

	$ mil.	% of total
Food distribution	11,480	76
Retail	3,589	24
Total	**15,069**	**100**

Fleming Retail Group
ABCO Foods (Arizona)
Baker's (Nebraska and Oklahoma)
Boogaarts Food Stores (Kansas and Nebraska)
Consumers Food & Drug (Arkansas, Kansas, and Missouri)
Hyde Park Market (Florida)
New York Retail (Jubilee Foods and Market Basket stores in New York and Pennsylvania)
Penn Retail (Festival Foods and Jubilee Foods in Pennsylvania and Maryland)
Rainbow Foods (Minnesota and Wisconsin)
RichMar (90%, California)
Sentry Foods/SuPeRSaVeR (Wisconsin)
Thompson Food Basket (Illinois and Iowa)
University Foods (five Food 4 Less stores in Utah)

COMPETITORS

A&P	Meijer
Albertson's	Nash Finch
Associated Food	Publix
Associated Wholesale Grocers	Roundy's
C&S Wholesale	Royal Ahold
H-E-B	Safeway
Homeland Holding	Spartan Stores
Hy-Vee Food Stores	SUPERVALU
Kroger	Wakefern Food
McLane	Wal-Mart
	Winn-Dixie

HISTORICAL FINANCIALS & EMPLOYEES

NYSE symbol: FLM FYE: December 31	Annual Growth	1989	1990	1991	1992	1993	1994	1995	1996	1997	1998
Sales ($ mil.)	2.5%	12,045	11,933	12,902	12,938	13,092	15,754	17,502	16,487	15,373	15,069
Net income ($ mil.)	—	80	97	63	113	35	56	42	27	25	(511)
Income as % of sales	—	0.7%	0.8%	0.5%	0.9%	0.3%	0.4%	0.2%	0.2%	0.2%	—
Earnings per share ($)	—	2.54	2.93	1.50	3.06	0.96	1.51	1.12	0.71	0.67	(13.48)
Stock price - FY high ($)	—	40.00	37.63	40.63	35.13	34.38	30.00	29.88	20.88	20.38	20.75
Stock price - FY low ($)	—	27.50	28.00	29.88	27.25	23.75	22.63	19.13	11.50	13.44	8.63
Stock price - FY close ($)	(11.2%)	30.13	35.25	34.38	31.50	24.75	23.25	20.63	17.25	13.44	10.38
P/E - high		16	13	27	11	36	20	27	29	30	—
P/E - low		11	10	20	9	25	15	17	16	20	—
Dividends per share ($)	(24.5%)	1.00	1.03	1.14	1.20	1.20	1.20	1.20	0.36	0.08	0.08
Book value per share ($)	(4.8%)	22.95	25.03	27.01	28.90	28.90	28.78	28.72	28.47	28.48	14.79
Employees	6.1%	22,800	22,900	22,800	22,800	23,300	42,400	44,000	41,200	39,700	38,900

STOCK PRICE HISTORY
HIGH/LOW/CLOSE

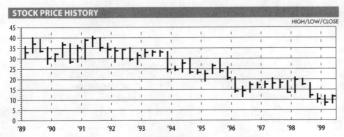

1998 FISCAL YEAR-END

Debt ratio: 72.5%
Return on equity: —
Cash ($ mil.): 6
Current ratio: 1.24
Long-term debt ($ mil.): 1,503
No. of shares (mil.): 39
Dividends
  Yield: 0.8%
  Payout: —
Market value ($ mil.): 400

FLORIDA PROGRESS CORPORATION

OVERVIEW

Florida Progress' nuclear plant is up and running again — and that's progress. Based in St. Petersburg, Florida, the utility holding company has been bedeviled by a troubled reactor and a lawsuit against its Mid-Continent Life Insurance subsidiary. CEO Dick Korpan has repeatedly said that the company is open to alliances and mergers, and a suitor has emerged: Carolina Power & Light has agreed to buy the company in an $8 billion deal.

Florida Power, a regulated utility, has a generating capacity of 7,700 MW and provides electricity to 1.3 million customers in west and central Florida; it also has an alliance with Dynegy to market power in the southeastern

US. Progress Capital holds the company's nonutility businesses, which include Electric Fuels' coal mining, river barge, and rail materials operations. Florida Progress also works with fellow utilities Cinergy and New Century Energies to operate Cadence Network, which provides energy management services to multistate companies.

The company's troubles have slowed competitive strategizing, but it is building up Electric Fuels through acquisitions. It has also dipped into telecommunications, forming a subsidiary to sell fiber-optic capacity to long-distance carriers, ISPs, and other large customers in Florida.

HISTORY

Florida Progress began providing its juice as the St. Petersburg Electric Light & Power Company in 1899. It changed its name to St. Petersburg Lighting in 1915, Pinellas County Power in 1923, and finally Florida Power in 1927. Florida Power's parent was General Gas & Electric, part of the Associated Gas & Electric System (AG&E) — Howard Hopson's utility empire that stretched from Florida and Georgia to New York and Pennsylvania.

In the 1920s and 1930s, Florida Power acquired several rival utilities. But the Public Utility Holding Company Act of 1935 (passed largely because of Hopson's pyramid scheme excesses) spelled doom for AG&E by limiting utility holding companies to one contiguous service area. AG&E's Florida and Georgia companies were merged, and after WWII Florida Power became independent, with Georgia Power & Light as a subsidiary.

In 1957 Florida Power sold Georgia Power & Light to Georgia Power. Florida Power fared well in the 1960s and in 1968 began building a nuclear unit (Crystal River).

Rising construction costs at Crystal River ended plans for a second reactor in 1970. Two years later engineer Andrew Hines became president, just before the OPEC oil embargo sent fuel prices soaring. At the time, 81% of Florida Power's fuel was imported oil. In 1975 the company began converting two oil-fired plants to coal and in 1976 formed Electric Fuels to supply fuel at bulk rates. By 1977 the Crystal River plant was on line, saving the company $46 million in fuel costs.

During the 1980s the company made an ill-fated decision to diversify and spent the 1990s paying for it. In 1981 it formed real estate and building materials companies and the next

year created Florida Progress as a holding company. It created an equipment leasing firm in 1983 (spun off as Echelon International in 1996) and bought Mid-Continent Life Insurance in 1986. In 1988 Florida Progress formed Progress Capital Holdings as the parent of its nonutility subsidiaries.

Jack Critchfield succeeded Hines in 1990 and began shedding subsidiaries unrelated to financial services, fuels, or power. Electric Fuels expanded in 1994, acquiring railcar equipment, leasing, and recycling businesses, and a barge facility.

In 1996 the reactor was shut down for safety reasons (it did not reopen until 1998, costing more than $100 million in repairs). In 1997 Florida Progress wrote off its $84 million investment in Mid-Continent after Oklahoma regulators forced the firm into receivership over alleged shortfalls in money reserves for future claims. Also that year Florida Progress and fellow utilities Cinergy and New Century Energies formed Cadence Network, which markets power and energy management services to national chains. The company bought a 5% stake in baseball's Tampa Bay Devil Rays, which played its first season in 1998.

Scottish Power flirted with the idea of buying Florida Progress in 1998 but decided against the purchase — too many problems for the price tag. That year no-nonsense Dick Korpan, a lawyer, became CEO, and Florida Power allied with Dynegy to market power in the southeastern US. Florida Progress also launched Progress Telecommunications.

In 1999 Florida Progress agreed to be bought by Carolina Power & Light for $5.3 billion in cash and stock and $2.7 billion in assumed debt.

Chairman, President, and CEO; Chairman, Florida Power: Richard Korpan, age 57, $1,244,766 pay
SVP, Energy Supply, Florida Power: Roy A. Anderson, age 50
SVP and CFO: Edward W. Moneypenny, age 57
Group VP, Energy and Transportation; President and CEO, Electric Fuels: Richard D. Keller, age 45, $641,926 pay
Group VP, Utility Group; President and CEO, Florida Power: Joseph H. Richardson, age 49, $803,658 pay
SVP, Energy SolutionsSM, Florida Power: Janice B. Case, age 46
SVP, Energy Delivery, Florida Power: Michael B. Foley Jr., age 55
SVP and CFO, Florida Power: Jeffrey R. Heinicka, age 44, $468,530 pay (prior to title change)
VP and General Counsel, Florida Progress and Florida Power: Kenneth E. Armstrong, age 51, $359,433 pay
VP, Human Resources: William G. Kelley
VP and Controller: John Scardino Jr.
VP, Acquisitions: James V. Smallwood
Secretary and Compliance Officer: Kathleen M. Haley
Auditors: KPMG LLP

LOCATIONS

HQ: 1 Progress Plaza, St. Petersburg, FL 33701
Phone: 727-824-6400   **Fax:** 727-820-5940
Web site: http://www.fpc.com

Florida Progress provides electricity in west and central Florida and parts of the Gulf Coast, including Orlando, St. Petersburg, and Clearwater. It also has power marketing operations in the southeastern US. Subsidiary Electric Fuels has operations in 22 US states, Canada, and Mexico.

PRODUCTS/OPERATIONS

1998 Sales

	$ mil.	% of total
Utility	2,648	73
Rail services	658	18
Energy and related services	174	5
Inland marine transportation	125	3
Other	19	1
Adjustments	(4)	—
Total	**3,620**	**100**

Selected Subsidiaries
Cadence Network (joint venture with New Century Energies and Cinergy offering energy management services to multistate companies)
Florida Power Corporation (electric utility)
Progress Capital Holdings (diversified businesses)
Electric Fuels Corporation
Progress Telecommunications Corporation (sells fiber-optic capacity in Florida)

COMPETITORS

ACF	Greenbrier
American Commercial	Ingram Industries
Lines	Peabody Group
Arch Coal	Southern Company
CONSOL Energy	Southern Union
Duke Energy	TECO Energy
Enron	Trinity Industries
Florida Public Utilities	Westinghouse Air Brake
FPL	Zeigler Coal

HISTORICAL FINANCIALS & EMPLOYEES

NYSE symbol: FPC FYE: December 31	Annual Growth	1989	1990	1991	1992	1993	1994	1995	1996	1997	1998
Sales ($ mil.)	6.1%	2,129	2,011	2,075	2,095	2,449	2,772	3,056	3,158	3,316	3,620
Net income ($ mil.)	4.7%	187	165	172	176	197	212	239	224	54	282
Income as % of sales	—	8.8%	8.2%	8.3%	8.4%	8.0%	7.6%	7.8%	7.1%	1.6%	7.8%
Earnings per share ($)	1.9%	2.45	2.14	2.13	2.06	2.24	2.28	2.50	2.32	0.56	2.90
Stock price - FY high ($)	—	26.85	27.01	31.52	33.25	36.38	33.63	35.75	36.50	39.25	47.13
Stock price - FY low ($)	—	22.18	22.34	24.43	27.93	31.25	24.75	29.38	31.50	27.75	37.69
Stock price - FY close ($)	5.9%	26.68	25.51	31.35	32.63	33.63	30.00	35.38	32.25	39.25	44.81
P/E - high	—	11	13	15	16	16	15	14	16	70	16
P/E - low	—	9	10	11	14	14	11	12	14	50	13
Dividends per share ($)	2.5%	1.72	1.78	1.85	1.91	1.95	1.99	2.02	2.06	2.10	2.14
Book value per share ($)	0.7%	17.93	18.37	19.14	19.85	20.40	20.85	21.55	19.84	18.30	19.13
Employees	(5.0%)	7,490	7,879	6,377	6,254	6,295	5,529	7,174	7,253	4,799	4,740

STOCK PRICE HISTORY

HIGH/LOW/CLOSE

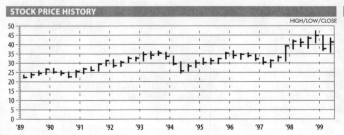

1998 FISCAL YEAR-END

Debt ratio: 54.3%
Return on equity: 15.1%
Cash ($ mil.): 3
Current ratio: 0.88
Long-term debt ($ mil.): 2,250
No. of shares (mil.): 97
Dividends
  Yield: 4.8%
  Payout: 73.8%
Market value ($ mil.): 4,362

FLOWERS INDUSTRIES, INC.

OVERVIEW

Driven by a knead to succeed, Flowers Industries is using flour power to make — what else? — bread. Thomasville, Georgia-based Flowers — the #3 wholesale baker in the US (behind Interstate Bakeries and Earthgrains) — owns Flowers Bakeries and Mrs. Smith's Bakeries, as well as about 55% of Keebler, the #2 cookie and cracker company in the US (behind Nabisco).

Flowers Bakeries makes fresh breads, rolls, and snack cakes and sells them to retailers in 16 states primarily located in the South and Southeast. Its Nature's Own brand is the best-selling bread in the US; other brands include Cobblestone Mill and BlueBird. Flowers Bakeries also rolls out hamburger buns for Burger King and private-label breads for retailers such as Winn-Dixie.

Mrs. Smith's Bakeries produces the #1 frozen-pie brand in the country, along with other fresh and frozen breads, cakes, and desserts for retail and food service customers. Among its national brands are Mrs. Smith's, Pet-Ritz, and Oregon Farms. The division also includes frozen fruits and batter-dipped vegetables under the Stilwell name.

Having long been a regional fresh bread baker, in the late 1990s Flowers bulked up on brand names by adding Mrs. Smith's and Keebler. Publicly traded Keebler is best known for its Fudge Shoppe cookies and Sunshine cracker lines (Cheeze-It, Hi-Ho) and accounts for nearly 60% of the company's sales. Flowers now competes in all areas of baked goods in both the retail and food service industries nationwide. Flowers is investing heavily in production line upgrades while closing less efficient plants and shifting production to more automated facilities.

HISTORY

Georgia native William Flowers and his brother Joseph opened the Flowers Ice Cream Co. in the winter resort town of Thomasville, Georgia, in 1914 to serve wealthy visitors from the North. Seeing that there was no bakery in the town (the nearest bakery was located more than 200 miles away), the brothers opened Flowers Baking Co. in 1919. During the 1920s William took charge of the bakery, while Joseph continued to run the ice-cream operation. In 1928 Flowers moved into the production of sweet rolls and cakes. As its reputation for high-quality baked goods spread, the firm established a regional network of customers. William died in 1934, and his 20-year-old son, Bill, took over.

Despite the difficult Depression years, Bill led the company in its first acquisition, a bakery in Florida. Flowers operated its bakeries around the clock during WWII to supply military bases in the Southeast. Bill's brother Langdon joined the firm after the war and helped take the company on a major expansion drive in the 1950s and 1960s.

Flowers acquired additional southeastern bakers in the mid-1960s and bought the Atlanta Baking Co. in 1967. The next year the company changed its name to Flowers Industries and went public.

In 1976 the company diversified, entering the frozen-food business by acquiring Stilwell Foods (frozen fruits, battered vegetables) in Oklahoma and its subsidiary, Rio Grande Foods, in Texas. The firm also expanded its fresh bread line. The following year Flowers introduced the Nature's Own brand of variety breads, which rapidly became a best-seller.

During the 1970s and 1980s, the company expanded beyond its southeastern regional base by acquiring bakeries in the Southwest and Midwest. Company veteran Amos McMullian became CEO in 1981 and chairman in 1985, when both Bill and Langdon retired. In 1989 Flowers bought out Winn-Dixie's bakery operations. The company launched a $377 million, six-year capital investment program in 1991 to upgrade and automate its bakeries.

Flowers began a major expansion strategy with the 1996 acquisition of Mrs. Smith's, the US's top frozen-pie brand, from J.M. Smucker (which had outbid Flowers when Kellogg originally sold it less than two years earlier). Later that year Flowers and joint venture partners Artal Luxembourg and Benmore acquired cookie maker Keebler (which, in turn, purchased Sunshine Biscuit Company, to become the #2 US cookie and cracker baker).

In 1997 the company acquired Allied Bakery Products, a baker of frozen breads and rolls for food service customers in the northeastern US.

When Flowers went public in 1998, it retained its controlling stake in Keebler. In May 1999 Flowers agreed to buy Home Baking Company, which serves food service clients in the southeastern states and the Caribbean.

Chairman and CEO: Amos R. McMullian, age 61,
$1,288,000 pay
VC; Chairman, Keebler Foods: Robert P. Crozer, age 52,
$985,347 pay
SVP and CFO: C. Martin Wood III, age 55, $347,954 pay
VP and General Counsel: Stephen R. Avera
VP of Public Affairs: Marta Jones Turner, age 45
President and COO, Flowers Bakeries: George E. Deese,
age 52, $502,600 pay
President and COO, Mrs. Smith's Bakeries:
Gary L. Harrison, age 61, $345,700 pay
President and CEO, Keebler Foods: Sam K. Reed
EVP, Flowers Bakeries: Allen L. Shiver
EVP, Mrs. Smith's Bakeries: George von Borstel
**Director of Human Resources; Director of Human
Resources, Flowers Bakeries:** Donald A. Thriffiley Jr.
Auditors: PricewaterhouseCoopers LLP

LOCATIONS

HQ: 1919 Flowers Circle, Thomasville, GA 31757
Phone: 912-226-9110 **Fax:** 912-225-3823
Web site: http://www.flowersindustries.com

Flowers Industries operates more than 40 production,
distribution, and sales companies in 20 states.

PRODUCTS/OPERATIONS

1998 Sales

	$ mil.	% of total
Keebler	2,226	58
Flowers Bakeries	950	25
Mrs. Smith's Bakeries	673	17
Other	(73)	—
Total	**3,776**	**100**

Selected Brands

Fresh Baked Goods Brands
BlueBird
Bunny
Butter Krust
Cobblestone Mill
Country Hearth
Evangeline Maid
Mrs. Freshley's (vending machine sales)
Nature's Own
Sunbeam

Frozen Products Brands
European Bakers Ltd.
Mrs. Smith's
Oregon Farms

Oronoque Orchard
Our Special Touch
Pet-Ritz
Pour-A-Quiche
Stilwell

Keebler Brands
Carr's (imported and distributed in the US)
Famous Amos
Girl Scout cookies
Keebler
Murray Sugar Free cookies
Olde New England (vending brownies)
Sunshine

COMPETITORS

Bestfoods
Campbell Soup
Earthgrains
George Weston
Interstate Bakeries
Lance

Marie Callender
McKee Foods
Mrs. Baird's Bakeries
Nabisco Holdings
Pillsbury

Procter & Gamble
Ralcorp
Rich Products
Sara Lee
Specialty Foods
Tasty Baking

HISTORICAL FINANCIALS & EMPLOYEES

NYSE symbol: FLO FYE: December 31	Annual Growth	1989	1990	1991	1992	1993	1994	1995	1996	1997	1998
Sales ($ mil.)	18.3%	835	825	879	962	990	1,129	1,239	1,438	713	3,776
Net income ($ mil.)	4.1%	29	24	32	39	30	42	31	62	28	42
Income as % of sales	—	3.5%	2.9%	3.6%	4.1%	3.0%	3.7%	2.5%	4.3%	3.9%	1.1%
Earnings per share ($)	1.7%	0.37	0.31	0.41	0.47	0.35	0.50	0.36	0.72	0.32	0.43
Stock price - FY high ($)	—	9.40	9.29	8.12	9.45	9.01	8.79	12.01	18.09	21.50	26.31
Stock price - FY low ($)	—	7.23	5.28	5.95	7.29	7.23	7.12	8.06	10.67	13.34	16.50
Stock price - FY close ($)	12.5%	8.29	7.45	7.84	7.34	8.12	8.68	10.76	16.88	20.56	23.94
P/E - high	—	25	30	20	20	26	18	33	25	67	61
P/E - low	—	20	17	15	16	21	14	22	15	42	38
Dividends per share ($)	7.0%	0.26	0.29	0.31	0.33	0.35	0.37	0.39	0.41	0.22	0.48
Book value per share ($)	8.3%	2.79	2.73	2.83	3.31	3.27	3.52	3.48	3.86	3.95	5.73
Employees	(4.6%)	—	9,200	10,915	8,900	8,400	8,200	7,500	7,600	7,300	6,300

1997 is a 6-month fiscal year.

STOCK PRICE HISTORY

HIGH/LOW/CLOSE

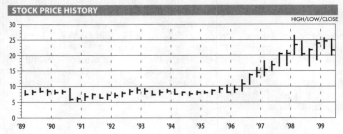

1998 FISCAL YEAR-END

Debt ratio: 64.5%
Return on equity: 7.3%
Cash ($ mil.): 57
Current ratio: 1.03
Long-term debt ($ mil.): 1,039
No. of shares (mil.): 100
Dividends
  Yield: 2.0%
  Payout: 111.6%
Market value ($ mil.): 2,393

FLUOR CORPORATION

OVERVIEW

Under the shadow of a worldwide economic slowdown, towering Fluor is looking for ways to flourish again. The Irvine, California-based company is one of the world's largest engineering and construction concerns. Subsidiary Fluor Daniel has grown a global garden: It provides design, construction, engineering, consulting, project and construction management, procurement, plant operations, maintenance, and other services to large clients worldwide. Subsidiary A. T. Massey Coal, which operates in Appalachia, controls about three-fourths of US metallurgical coal reserves.

Fluor is restructuring its business after a long expansion and decentralization drive in the early 1990s. The result was sky-high costs and eroding profit margins, from which Fluor is still recovering. Meanwhile, slowing construction demand brought on by the Asian economic crisis has caused the company to prune back further under CEO Philip Carroll.

Fluor has a hard row to hoe. It is shuttering 15 of its 75 offices, selling noncore assets, and thinning employee ranks. By hand-picking high-margin megaprojects, Fluor will cultivate its relationships with its top 200 customers — mainly government, mining, petrochemical, utility, and industrial clients — while allowing less profitable business to wither.

HISTORY

Fluor's history began in 1890 when the three Fluor brothers, immigrants from Switzerland, opened a Wisconsin lumber mill under the name Rudolph Fluor & Brothers; they soon branched into construction. In 1912 Simon Fluor struck out on his own, forming a construction firm in California. The new outfit soon began a relationship with Southern California Gas, leading it to specialize in oil and gas construction work. The company, incorporated as Fluor Construction in 1924, later began making engine mufflers. In 1930 it expanded outside California with a contract to build Texas pipelines.

After WWII, Middle East oil reserves came under aggressive development by Western companies. Fluor cashed in on the stampede, winning major contracts in Saudi Arabia. During the early 1960s it continued to emphasize oil and gas work, establishing a contract drilling unit, and in the 1970s it began work on giant energy projects.

In 1977 Fluor made its biggest purchase: Daniel International, a South Carolina engineering and construction firm with more than $1 billion in annual revenues. Charles Daniel had originally founded the contracting firm in 1934, and it subsequently began doing construction work, first for the textile industry, then for chemical, pharmaceutical, metals, and power industries.

Flush with cash, Fluor bought St. Joe Minerals in 1981. Analysts were predicting a great future for Fluor, but a drop in oil prices in the 1980s killed demand for the big projects that were its bread and butter. As metal prices fell, St. Joe didn't help the bottom line either. Bob Fluor, the last of the founding family to head the firm, died in 1984.

When David Tappan stepped in as CEO, he faced a $573 million loss the first year. The white-haired son of missionaries to China, Tappan — known as the Ice Man — dumped subsidiaries and halved the payroll. In 1986 he merged Daniel into Fluor's engineering unit, forming Fluor Daniel.

Leslie McCraw succeeded Tappan as CEO in 1991. McCraw saw Fluor as overly conservative, and three years later he began setting up offices around the world while decentralizing Fluor's structure (at one point it had 30 operating companies) and adding new business such as temporary staffing and equipment leasing. Fluor also shed some of its commodity companies, including its lead business in 1994. In 1996 Fluor's environmental services unit merged with Groundwater Technology and was spun off as a public company, Fluor Daniel GTI.

Fluor saw mixed results from its expansion. Amid fierce competition and pricing pressure, in early 1997 Fluor Daniel began cutting its overhead by reorganizing and selling noncore businesses. But the growing financial crisis in Asia was killing the bottom line.

Ill with cancer, McCraw stepped down in 1998, and Philip Carroll, who had overhauled Shell Oil, took over as CEO. Carroll began reorganizing Fluor into four business units and tagged $90 million to rebuild its internal information management systems. Fluor also unloaded its 52% stake in Fluor Daniel GTI to The IT Group for $36 million.

In 1999 the company announced it would cut 5,000 jobs and streamline 17 engineering, procurement, and construction operating companies into just five.

OFFICERS

Chairman and CEO: Philip J. Carroll Jr., age 61, $612,692 pay
EVP and CFO: Ralph F. Hake
SVP Law and Secretary: Lawrence N. Fisher, age 54, $467,005 pay
SVP Human Resources and Administration: Frederick J. Grisby Jr., age 51
Chairman and CEO, A. T. Massey Coal: Don L. Blankenship, age 48, $1,075,732 pay
Chairman, Fluor Constructors International: Richard A. Flinton
President and CEO, Fluor Signature Services: James O. Rollans, age 56, $736,985 pay
President, Chemicals and Life Sciences, Fluor Daniel: Eddie Lewis
President and CEO, Fluor Global Services: James C. Stein, age 55, $880,425 pay
President, Operations and Maintenance, Fluor Global Services: Ronald G. Peterson
Group President Diversified Services, Fluor Daniel: T. Jeff Putman
EVP and COO, A. T. Massey Coal: Bennett K. Hatfield
SVP Group Operations, A. T. Massey Coal: H. Drexel Short
VP and Chief Information Officer: Dennis W. Benner, age 57
VP Investor Relations: Lila J. Churney, age 46
VP and Treasurer: Stephen F. Hull
VP Corporate Relations: George K. Palmer, age 55
VP and Controller: Victor L. Prechtl
Auditors: Ernst & Young LLP

LOCATIONS

HQ: 1 Enterprise Dr., Aliso Viejo, CA 92656
Phone: 949-349-2000   **Fax:** 949-349-5271
Web site: http://www.fluor.com

PRODUCTS/OPERATIONS

1998 Sales

	$ mil.	% of total
Engineering & construction	12,378	92
Coal	1,127	8
Total	**13,505**	**100**

Selected Subsidiaries and Operating Groups
American Equipment Co. (construction equipment leasing worldwide)
A. T. Massey Coal Co., Inc. (bituminous, low-sulfur coal production)
Fluor Constructors International, Inc. (construction, management, and maintenance services)
Fluor Daniel Group
  Diversified Services
  Industrial Group
  Power and Government Group
  Process Group

COMPETITORS

ABB Asea Brown Boveri	Hyundai
AGRA	Kajima
J.S. Alberici	KTI
Ansaldo	Kvaerner
ARCADIS	McDermott
Arch Coal	Ogden
Bechtel	Peter Kiewit Sons'
Black and Veatch	Philip Services
Bouygues	Philipp Holzmann
CH2M Hill	Raytheon
Day & Zimmermann	Samsung
Foster Wheeler	Stone & Webster
Groupe GTM	Technip
Halliburton	

HISTORICAL FINANCIALS & EMPLOYEES

NYSE symbol: FLR FYE: October 31	Annual Growth	1989	1990	1991	1992	1993	1994	1995	1996	1997	1998
Sales ($ mil.)	8.9%	6,278	7,446	6,742	6,601	7,850	8,485	9,301	11,015	14,299	13,505
Net income ($ mil.)	9.0%	109	147	161	6	167	192	232	268	146	235
Income as % of sales	—	1.7%	2.0%	2.4%	0.1%	2.1%	2.3%	2.5%	2.4%	1.0%	1.7%
Earnings per share ($)	9.2%	1.35	1.81	1.97	0.07	2.04	2.34	2.81	3.21	1.75	2.97
Stock price - FY high ($)	—	36.75	49.25	54.75	48.13	46.88	56.25	59.50	71.88	75.88	52.50
Stock price - FY low ($)	—	18.63	28.50	31.38	35.25	38.00	38.63	41.25	54.75	40.25	33.50
Stock price - FY close ($)	3.4%	28.75	32.38	45.63	44.63	40.75	49.50	56.50	65.50	41.13	38.81
P/E - high	—	27	27	28	688	23	24	21	22	43	18
P/E - low	—	14	16	16	504	19	17	15	17	23	11
Dividends per share ($)	21.4%	0.14	0.24	0.32	0.40	0.48	0.52	0.60	0.68	0.76	0.80
Book value per share ($)	9.4%	9.03	10.75	12.58	10.81	12.72	14.79	17.20	19.93	20.79	20.19
Employees	12.3%	20,059	22,188	39,637	43,605	38,532	39,807	41,678	52,461	60,679	56,886

STOCK PRICE HISTORY

HIGH/LOW/CLOSE

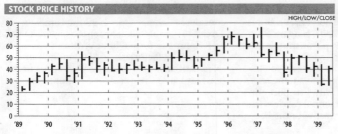

1998 FISCAL YEAR-END

Debt ratio: 16.5%
Return on equity: 15.4%
Cash ($ mil.): 341
Current ratio: 0.91
Long-term debt ($ mil.): 300
No. of shares (mil.): 76
Dividends
  Yield: 2.1%
  Payout: 26.9%
Market value ($ mil.): 2,933

FMC CORPORATION

OVERVIEW

Chairman and CEO Robert Burt continues to plant and prune in FMC's corporate garden in an effort to create a favorable financial landscape. Chicago-based FMC operates in five segments: energy systems (subsea products, drilling, engineering, metering and related services for the oil and natural gas industries), agricultural products (insecticides and herbicides), specialty chemicals (food and pharmaceutical additives), food and transportation systems (freezers, fryers, airline cargo loaders, deicers, and jetway passenger boarding bridges), and industrial chemicals (soda ash — #1 worldwide).

FMC's ongoing restructuring is aimed at emphasizing its operations in oil field subsea products, food-processing equipment, and agricultural products. The company operates more than 100 plants in 25 countries. FMC employees own about 16% of the company.

HISTORY

After retiring to California, inventor John Bean developed a pump to deliver a continuous spray of insecticide in 1884. This invention led to the Bean Spray Pump Company in 1904. In 1928 Bean Spray Pump went public and bought Anderson-Barngrover (food-growing and -processing equipment). The new company became Food Machinery Corporation in 1929. It bought Peerless Pump (agricultural and industrial pumps) in 1933.

During WWII the company started making military equipment. It entered the agricultural chemical field when it bought Niagara Sprayer & Chemical (1943). After the war it added Westvaco Chemical (1948) and changed its name to Food Machinery & Chemical.

The Bean family ran the company until 1956, when John Bean's grandson, John Crummey, retired as chairman. The enterprise extended its product line, buying such companies as Oil Center Tool (wellhead equipment, 1957), Sunland Industries (fertilizer and insecticides, 1959), and Barrett Equipment (automotive brake equipment, 1961).

In light of its growing diversification, the company changed its name to FMC in 1961. Major purchases in the 1960s included American Viscose (rayon and cellophane, 1963) and Link-Belt (equipment for power transmission and for bulk-material handling, 1967).

To be centrally located, FMC moved its headquarters from San Jose to Chicago in 1972. Through the 1970s and early 1980s the company sold several slow-growing businesses, including its pump and fiber divisions (1976), semiconductor division (1979), industrial packaging division (1980), Niagara Seed Operation (1980), and Power Transmission Group (1981).

It moved into other markets just as quickly, including mining (1979, through a joint venture in a Nevada gold mine with Freeport Minerals), Bradley armored personnel carriers (the early 1980s, through a contract with the US Army), and lithium (1985, by purchasing Lithium Corp. of America). In a 1986 antitakeover move, FMC gave employees a larger stake in the company.

In 1992 FMC bought Ciba-Geigy's flame-retardants and water-treatment businesses and combined its defense operations with Harsco as United Defense. The next year the company announced 1,200 job cuts, which brought down earnings. FMC's 1994 acquisitions included Abex's Jetway Systems Division (aircraft support systems) and Caterpillar's Automated Vehicle Systems group. The next year FMC formed a joint venture with Nippon Sheet Glass and Sumitomo Corp. to mine for soda ash.

In 1996 FMC made a deal with DuPont to commercialize new herbicides. To settle federal charges that FMC had inflated the price of its Bradley vehicle, the company agreed that year to pay the government $13 million.

The company in 1997 debuted its composite (nonmetallic) prototype armored vehicle. In the long shadow of reduced defense budgets, FMC and Harsco sold their stagnant defense operation for $850 million to the Carlyle Group investment firm. The delayed startup of an herbicide plant and a tough chemical market cut earnings that year.

The sale of its defense division didn't protect FMC from a $310 million damage award in a whistleblower suit against the company in 1998. A federal jury found that FMC had misled the Army about the safety of the Bradley armored infantry vehicle. The court later lowered the verdict to about $90 million and FMC considered an appeal. In 1999 the company agreed to combine its phosphorus operations with Solutia to form a joint venture (Astaris LLC) with 12 factories and $600 million in sales. FMC also sold its process additives unit to Great Lakes Chemical for $162 million.

OFFICERS

Chairman and CEO: Robert N. Burt, age 61,
$1,241,911 pay
President: Joseph H. Netherland, age 52,
$606,967 pay (prior to promotion)
EVP and CFO: Michael J. Callahan, age 60,
$556,564 pay
SVP: William J. Kirby, age 61
SVP, General Counsel, and Corporate Secretary:
J. Paul McGrath, age 58
VP; President, FMC Europe, Middle East, and Africa:
Alfredo Bernad
VP Communications: Patricia D. Brozowski
**VP; General Manager, FMC Food Tech and Jetway
Systems:** Charles H. Cannon Jr., age 46
VP; General Manager, Agricultural Products Group:
W. Kim Foster, age 50
VP; President, FMC Asia-Pacific: W. Reginald Hall,
age 62
VP; General Manager, Chemical Products Group:
Robert I. Harries, age 55
VP and Treasurer: Stephanie K. Kushner, age 43
VP and Controller: Ronald D. Mambu, age 49
VP Worldwide Marketing: James A. McClung, age 61
VP Human Resources: Michael W. Murray
VP Corporate Development: William H. Schumann,
age 48
VP and Chief Information Officer: Craig M. Watson
Auditors: KPMG LLP

LOCATIONS

HQ: 200 E. Randolph Dr., Chicago, IL 60601
Phone: 312-861-6000　　**Fax:** 312-861-5913
Web site: http://www.fmc.com

FMC operates 107 manufacturing facilities and mines
in 25 countries.

PRODUCTS/OPERATIONS

1998 Sales

	$ mil.	% of total
Energy systems	1,321	30
Industrial chemicals	974	21
Food & transportation	868	20
Agricultural products	648	15
Specialty chemicals	598	14
Adjustments	(31)	—
Total	**4,378**	**100**

COMPETITORS

Agrium	Hoechst AG
American Home Products	Ingersoll-Rand
Asahi Glass	Monsanto
Baker Hughes	Nestlé
BASF AG	Novartis
Cargill	Olin
Cyprus Amax	Rhône-Poulenc
Dow Chemical	Rohm and Haas
DuPont	Solvay
Electrolux	Sumitomo
General Chemical	Terra Industries
Halliburton	Union Pacific Resources
Hercules	USX-U.S. Steel

HISTORICAL FINANCIALS & EMPLOYEES

NYSE symbol: FMC FYE: December 31	Annual Growth	1989	1990	1991	1992	1993	1994	1995	1996	1997	1998
Sales ($ mil.)	2.8%	3,415	3,722	3,899	3,974	3,754	4,011	4,510	5,081	4,313	4,378
Net income ($ mil.)	(2.0%)	128	155	164	(76)	36	173	216	211	162	107
Income as % of sales	—	3.8%	4.2%	4.2%	—	1.0%	4.3%	4.8%	4.1%	3.8%	2.4%
Earnings per share ($)	(2.4%)	3.79	4.30	4.52	(2.06)	1.01	4.66	5.72	5.54	4.41	3.05
Stock price - FY high ($)	—	49.00	38.75	51.63	53.25	54.00	65.13	80.00	78.00	91.44	82.19
Stock price - FY low ($)	—	31.63	25.38	29.50	42.50	41.50	45.50	57.13	60.88	59.38	48.25
Stock price - FY close ($)	5.3%	35.25	31.88	47.88	49.50	47.13	57.75	67.63	70.13	67.31	56.00
P/E - high	—	13	9	11	—	53	14	14	14	21	27
P/E - low	—	8	6	7	—	41	10	10	11	13	16
Dividends per share ($)	—	0.00	0.00	0.00	0.00	0.00	0.00	0.00	0.00	0.00	0.00
Book value per share ($)	—	(2.05)	4.30	8.78	6.10	5.99	11.41	17.79	23.02	21.78	22.30
Employees	(4.3%)	24,110	23,882	23,150	22,097	20,696	21,344	22,164	22,048	16,805	16,216

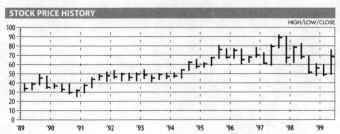

STOCK PRICE HISTORY — HIGH/LOW/CLOSE

1998 FISCAL YEAR-END

Debt ratio: 64.5%
Return on equity: 14.6%
Cash ($ mil.): 62
Current ratio: 1.19
Long-term debt ($ mil.): 1,326
No. of shares (mil.): 33
Dividends
　Yield: —
　Payout: —
Market value ($ mil.): 1,831

FMR CORP.

OVERVIEW

FMR Corp. is *semper fidelis* (ever faithful) to its core business. The Boston-based financial service conglomerate, better known as Fidelity Investments, is the world's #1 mutual fund company. With more than 15 million investors, FMR manages some 280 funds, including Magellan (the US's largest). Magellan's growing bulk raises the question of whether the leviathan fund can retain the nimbleness that historically gave it such impressive growth. FMR's nonfund products include on-line brokerage, life insurance, real estate management, and retirement services.

Chairman Ned Johnson has shuffled management and slimmed down nonfund assets amid sagging performance in a bull market. The Johnson family controls 49% of FMR; company executives control the rest. Abigail Johnson, Ned's daughter and heir apparent, is the largest single shareholder with about 25%.

HISTORY

In 1930 Fidelity Fund was formed by Anderson & Cromwell, a Boston money management firm. Edward Johnson became president of Fidelity Fund in 1943, when it had $3 million invested in Treasury bills. Johnson diversified into stocks, and by 1945 the fund had grown to $10 million. In 1946 he established Fidelity Management and Research to act as investment adviser to Fidelity Fund.

In the early 1950s Johnson hired Gerry Tsai, a young immigrant from Shanghai, to analyze stocks. He put Tsai in charge of Fidelity Capital Fund in 1957. Tsai's brash, go-go investment strategy in such speculative stocks as Xerox and Polaroid paid off; by the time he left to form his own fund in 1965, he was managing more than $1 billion.

The Magellan Fund started in 1962. The company entered the markets for corporate pension plans (FMR Investment Management) in 1964, retirement plans for self-employed individuals (Fidelity Keogh Plan) in 1967, and investors outside the US (Fidelity International) in 1968.

Holding company FMR was formed in 1972, and that year Johnson gave control of Fidelity to his son Ned, who vertically integrated FMR by selling directly to customers rather than through brokers and assuming back-office accounting from banks. The next year he formed Fidelity Daily Income Trust, the first money market fund to offer check writing.

Peter Lynch was hired as manager of the Magellan Fund in 1977. During his 13-year tenure, Magellan grew from $20 million to $12 billion in assets and outperformed all other mutual funds. Fidelity Brokerage Services was established in 1978, making Fidelity the first mutual fund company to offer discount brokerage services.

In 1980 the company launched a nationwide branch network and in 1986 entered the credit card business. The Wall Street crash of 1987 forced its Magellan Fund to liquidate almost $1 billion in stock in a single day. That year FMR moved into insurance by offering variable life, single premium, and deferred annuity policies. In 1989 the company introduced the low-expense Spartan Fund, targeted toward large, less-active investors.

Magellan's performance faded in the early 1990s, and the fund dropped from #1 performer in the industry to #3. Most of Fidelity's best performers were from its 36 select funds, which focus on narrow industry segments. FMR founded London-based COLT Telecom in 1993. In 1994 Ned Johnson gave his daughter and heir apparent, Abigail, a 25% stake in FMR.

Jeffrey Vinik resigned his position as manager of Magellan in 1996, one of more than a dozen fund managers to leave the firm that year and the next. Robert Stansky then took the helm of the $56 billion fund. Magellan had been criticized as being too large to be managed well, and FMR decided the next year to close it to new individual and institutional shareholders. That year, for the first time in its history, Fidelity hired an outside group, Bankers Trust (now part of Deutsche Bank), to manage its index mutual funds.

The company continued to do the management shuffle in 1998. Robert Pozen took over as head of mutual funds from Gary Burkhead, who moved to the CEO slot at the institutional group. Meanwhile, James Curvey moved from venture capital to oversee corporate daily operations. FMR sold Capital Publishing, which produced *Worth* magazine, in 1998 (after selling Wentworth art galleries in 1997). FMR also made its first steps into Japan and expanded its presence in Canada in 1998.

In 1999 the firm formed a joint venture with Charles Schwab; Donaldson, Lufkin & Jenrette; and Spear, Leeds & Kellogg to trade Nasdaq stocks online. Also that year, Fidelity agreed to sponsor a CBS news segment, "American Dream."

OFFICERS

Chairman and CEO: Edward C. Johnson III
President and COO: James C. Curvey
VC; President, Fidelity Personal Investments and Brokerage Group: J. Gary Burkhead
SVP and Chief of Administration and Government Affairs: David C. Weinstein
EVP and CFO: Stephen P. Jonas
VP and General Counsel: Lena G. Goldberg
President, Fidelity Corporate Systems and Services: Mark A. Peterson
President, Fidelity Investments Systems: Donald A. Haile
President, Fidelity-Wide Processing: Chuck Griffith
President, Fidelity Corporate Real Estate: Ronald C. Duff
President, Fidelity Security Services: George K. Campbell
EVP, Fidelty Investments Human Resources: Ilene B. Jacobs
President, Fidelity Management and Research Company: Robert C. Pozen
President and Chief Investment Officer, Strategic Advisors: William V. Harlow
President, Fidelity Investments Institutional Retirement Group: Robert L. Reynolds
President, Fidelity Investments Institutional Services: Kevin J. Kelly
President, Fidelity Ventures: Timothy T. Hilton
President, Fidelity Capital: Steven P. Akin
President, Fidelity International Limited: Barry R.J. Bateman
SVP, Fidelity Management & Research Company: Abigail P. Johnson, age 37
Auditors: PricewaterhouseCoopers LLP

LOCATIONS

HQ: 82 Devonshire St., Boston, MA 02109
Phone: 617-563-7000 **Fax:** 617-476-6150
Web site: http://www.fidelity.com

FMR Corp. maintains investor centers in 29 US states. It also has offices in Australia, Bermuda, Canada, France, Germany, Hong Kong, Japan, Luxembourg, the Netherlands, Taiwan, and the UK.

PRODUCTS/OPERATIONS

Selected Subsidiaries
Fidelity Brokerage Group
  Fidelity Brokerage Technology Group
  Fidelity Capital Markets
  National Financial Correspondent Services
Fidelity Capital
  BostonCoach
  Devonshire Custom Publishing
  Fidelity Capital Telecommunications & Technology
    COLT Telecom Group (nearly 60%)
  J. Robert Scott
  NetSuite Development
  Pembroke Real Estate
  Seaport Hotel at the World Trade Center
  World Trade Center Boston
Fidelity Financial Intermediary Services
Fidelity International Limited
  Fidelity Brokerage Services Japan LLC
  Fidelity Investments Canada Limited
  Fidelity Investments Management (H.K.) Limited (Hong Kong)
Fidelity Investments Institutional Retirement Group
  Fidelity Benefits Center
  Fidelity Group Pensions International
  Fidelity Management Trust Company
Fidelity Investments Life Insurance Company
Fidelity Investments Retail Group
  Fidelity Investments Premium Assets Group
Fidelity Technology & Processing Group
Strategic Advisers, Inc.

COMPETITORS

Aetna
Alliance Capital
AXA Financial
Barclays
Charles Schwab
Citigroup
First Union
Goldman Sachs
John Hancock
Lehman Brothers
MassMutual
Merrill Lynch
MetLife
Morgan Stanley Dean Witter
Northwestern Mutual
Paine Webber
Prudential
Raymond James Financial
T. Rowe Price
TIAA-CREF
TD Waterhouse Securities
USAA
Vanguard Group

HISTORICAL FINANCIALS & EMPLOYEES

Private company FYE: December 31	Annual Growth	1989	1990	1991	1992	1993	1994	1995	1996	1997	1998
Sales ($ mil.)	22.6%	1,083	1,272	1,474	1,824	2,570	3,530	4,277	5,080	5,878	6,770
Net income ($ mil.)	26.7%	53	32	89	125	225	315	431	423	536	446
Income as % of sales	—	4.9%	2.5%	6.0%	6.9%	8.8%	8.9%	10.1%	8.3%	9.1%	6.6%
Employees	17.6%	6,500	7,000	7,700	9,000	12,900	14,600	18,000	23,300	25,000	28,000

NET INCOME HISTORY

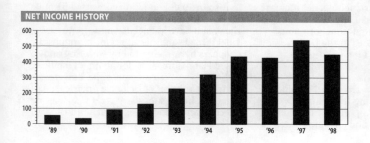

FOOD LION, INC.

OVERVIEW

Food Lion is no pussycat. The Salisbury, North Carolina-based company is aggressively expanding, upgrading existing stores, and building new stores in key markets. Having announced it would buy Hannaford Bros., a northeastern grocer with about 150 stores, the company restructured and is now a subsidiary of Delhaize America, which was formed as a holding company for its US supermarkets. Delhaize "Le Lion," one of Belgium's largest public companies, owns nearly 55% of Delhaize America's voting shares.

Food Lion operates more than 1,100 stores in 11 states. Located primarily in the Carolinas, Florida, and Virginia, the stores target low- and middle-income price-conscious shoppers. Food Lion's extensive private-label offerings (about 2,000 items) account for about 16% of its business. Food Lion once ran the more upscale Kash n' Karry chain (about 130 stores in Florida), which offers an expanded variety of grocery items and also runs nearly 20 Save 'n Pack warehouse-type stores in Florida. However, as part of the restructuring, Kash n' Karry has become a separate subsidiary of Delhaize America.

HISTORY

Food Lion was formed in Salisbury, North Carolina, in 1957 by three former Winn-Dixie employees — Wilson Smith, Ralph Ketner, and Ralph's brother Brown Ketner. They named the market Food Town and peddled stock in the new company at $10 per share to anyone in town who would buy.

The company struggled through its first 10 years of operation; by the end of 1967 it was foundering. That year Ralph pored over six months of store receipts and determined that if Food Town lowered the prices on all 3,000 items and sales increased 50%, the company would survive. The strategy paid off, and Food Town was reborn as a resolute cost cutter.

A Belgian grocery company, Delhaize "Le Lion," which used a lion as its symbol, began investing in Food Town in 1974. (By 1989 it owned 50.3% of the voting stock.) Food Town changed its name in 1983 to avoid confusion with another Food Town store in its market area. Ralph adopted the name Food Lion, not only because of the lion symbol of Delhaize, but also because he could save money by replacing only two letters in the company's signage. (Ralph resigned in 1993.)

In the 1980s Food Lion increased its number of stores from 106 to 663 — always following the company's low-price, cost-cutting formula. The grocery chain maintained its high growth rate, experiencing a net increase of 115 new stores in 1990 and 103 in 1991, the year it entered its first noncontiguous state by opening 41 stores in the Dallas/Fort Worth area. Food Lion opened 131 new stores in 1992, including outlets in Oklahoma and Louisiana.

That year *PrimeTime Live* aired a hidden-camera segment accusing the chain of unsanitary food handling, including soaking spoiled meat in bleach and changing dates on out-of-date foods. The company's income fell 98% the following year — and store openings slowed to only 84. It closed 87 unprofitable stores in 1994 (about 50 were in the Southwest, mostly in Texas and Oklahoma).

Food Lion filed a $2.5 billion lawsuit the next year against ABC News, claiming the network broke the law during its 1992 investigation. (A federal jury agreed in 1997, and it awarded $5.5 million in punitive damages to Food Lion. The award was later reduced to $315,000.)

In 1996 the chain surpassed its prescandal net income level, and it made two acquisitions: nine Food Fair supermarkets in North Carolina and the chronically troubled Kash n' Karry Food Stores, which added about 100 more upscale supermarkets (and more than 30 liquor stores) and bolstered its position in Florida. Food Lion then launched an aggressive remodeling program for the Kash n' Karry chain. The following year the company closed its last 61 stores in Texas, Oklahoma, and Louisiana.

Chairman, president, and CEO Tom Smith, a bagger for the original store in 1957 who became CEO in 1986, retired abruptly in April 1999. SVP Bill McCanless replaced him as president and CEO. Pierre-Olivier Beckers (CEO of Delhaize) was then named chairman.

Also in 1999 Food Lion converted 51 of its 95 Food Lion stores in Florida to the Kash n' Karry and Save 'n Pack formats. In August 1999 it made another move for more upscale shoppers by agreeing to buy New England-based Hannaford Bros. for about $3.6 billion. In September the company's shares were converted into shares of Delhaize America, a Delhaize "Le Lion" subsidiary created to acquire US companies, including Hannaford Bros.

OFFICERS

Chairman: Pierre-Olivier Beckers
CEO: R. William McCanless, age 41,
 $591,977 pay (prior to promotion)
President: Joseph C. Hall Jr., age 49,
 $621,576 pay (prior to promotion)
SVP of Merchandising: Pamela K. Kohn, age 34,
 $345,321 pay
VP of Information Technology and Chief Information Officer: A. Edward Benner Jr., age 57, $310,301 pay
VP of Procurement/Category Management:
 Robert J. Brunory, age 44
VP of Distribution: Bob Crosslin, age 44
VP of Real Estate and Store Development:
 Keith M. Gehl, age 40
VP of Human Resources: L. Darrell Johnson, age 46
VP of Finance and CFO: Laura C. Kendall, age 47
VP of Marketing: Elwyn G. Murray III, age 32
VP of Legal Affairs and Assistant Secretary:
 Lester C. Nail, age 39
VP of Diversity: Natalie M. Taylor, age 39
VP of Operations, Kash n' Karry Food Stores:
 Michael D. Byars, age 40
VP of Operations, Northern Division: W. Bruce Dawson,
 age 46
VP of Operations, Southern Division: David Morgan,
 age 48
VP of Operations, Central Division:
 Thomas J. Robinson, age 38
Director of Accounting and Corporate Controller:
 Carol M. Herndon, age 36
Director of Finance and Treasurer: Richard A. James,
 age 39
Director of Risk Management and Loss Prevention:
 Dewey R. Preslar Jr.
Auditors: PricewaterhouseCoopers LLP

LOCATIONS

HQ: 2110 Executive Dr., Salisbury, NC 28145-1330
Phone: 704-633-8250   **Fax:** 704-636-5024
Web site: http://www.foodlion.com

Food Lion operates more than 1,100 supermarkets in 11 states, primarily in the Carolinas, Virginia, and Florida.

1998 Stores

	No.
North Carolina	409
Virginia	266
Florida	186
South Carolina	112
Tennessee	81
Georgia	56
Maryland	49
West Virginia	17
Delaware	12
Kentucky	12
Pennsylvania	7
Total	**1,207**

WHAT

1998 Sales

	% of total
Retail grocery	84
Private label products	16
Total	**100**

COMPETITORS

A&P
Albertson's
Alex Lee
Bruno's
Houchens
IGA
Ingles Markets
Kroger
K-Va-T Food Stores
Publix
Rite Aid
Royal Ahold
Ruddick
SUPERVALU
Wal-Mart
Whole Foods
Winn-Dixie

HISTORICAL FINANCIALS & EMPLOYEES

Subsidiary FYE: December 31	Annual Growth	1989	1990	1991	1992	1993	1994	1995	1996	1997	1998
Sales ($ mil.)	9.0%	4,717	5,584	6,439	7,196	7,610	7,933	8,211	9,006	10,194	10,220
Net income ($ mil.)	7.7%	140	173	205	178	4	153	172	206	172	273
Income as % of sales	—	3.0%	3.1%	3.2%	2.5%	0.1%	1.9%	2.1%	2.3%	1.7%	2.7%
Employees	9.5%	40,736	47,276	53,583	59,721	65,494	64,840	69,345	73,170	83,871	92,125

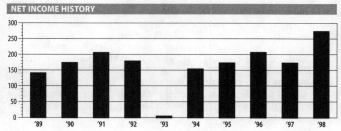

NET INCOME HISTORY

1998 FISCAL YEAR-END
Debt ratio: 36.6%
Return on equity: 17.0%
Cash ($ mil.): 124
Current ratio: 1.45
Long-term debt ($ mil.): 922

FOOD LION

FOODMAKER, INC.

OVERVIEW

With its perpetually smiling Ping-Pong ball-headed mascot, Foodmaker wants to bring its burgers back coast to coast. Based in San Diego, Foodmaker runs Jack in the Box, the #4 fast-food hamburger chain in the US. With more than 1,400 restaurants, 360 of which are franchised, the company sells burgers, fries, shakes, and other standard fare. It has developed a niche by including more adult-oriented items, such as the Teriyaki Bowl and the low-fat Chicken Fajita Pita, on its menu.

Foodmaker operates the chain in 12 western states (with most of its units in California and Texas), but has its eye on regaining the nationwide status it once held. To that end it opened more than 100 units in 1998 and is scouting new locations in the eastern US. It

also planned to change its corporate name to Jack in the Box.

Foodmaker brought back its Jack icon as the centerpiece of a new advertising campaign in 1995 to help rebuild Foodmaker's brand image, which was severely tarnished after hamburgers tainted with *E.coli* caused four customers to die and hundreds to fall ill; Foodmaker's insurance paid out around $85 million in personal injury settlements. The company responded by developing a stringent food safety program and by opening up its management style. The company is now working on reducing its debt load and focusing on controlled growth and expansion. It plans on adding some 100 new units in 1999 and is testing higher menu prices.

HISTORY

Robert Peterson founded his first restaurant, Topsy's Drive-In, in 1941 in San Diego. He soon renamed it Oscar's (his middle name) and began to expand the restaurant. By 1950 he had four Oscar's drive-in restaurants. That year he changed the name again to Jack in the Box and opened one of the country's first drive-through restaurants, which featured a speaker mounted in the chain's signature clown's head.

The drive-through concept took off, and by the late 1960s the company, renamed Foodmaker, operated about 300 Jack in the Box restaurants. In 1968 Peterson sold Foodmaker to Ralston Purina. To differentiate itself from competitors, Foodmaker added new food items, including the first breakfast sandwich (1969). The company continued to expand during the 1970s, and by 1979 it had more than 1,000 restaurants. That year it decided to concentrate on the western and southwestern US, selling 232 restaurants in the East and Midwest.

To attract more adult customers, in 1980 Foodmaker began remodeling its stores and adding menu items geared toward adult tastes. The company ran a series of TV ads showing its trademark clown logo being blown up. The ads were meant to show that Jack in the Box was not just for children anymore, but they drew protests from parents worried about the violence in the advertisements.

In 1985 Foodmaker's management acquired the company in a $450 million LBO. The company went public in 1987, but management took it private again the next year. Led by CEO Jack Goodall, Foodmaker expanded its number of franchises. (Unlike most of its competitors,

the company had previously owned almost all of its restaurants.) By 1987 about 30% of the company's 900 stores were owned by franchisees, compared to an average of about 75% for Burger King, McDonald's, and Wendy's.

The next year Foodmaker paid about $230 million for the Chi-Chi's chain of 200 Mexican restaurants. It made its first move outside the US in 1991, opening restaurants in Mexico and Hong Kong. The company went public again the following year.

In 1993 four people died and more than 700 became ill after eating *E. coli*-tainted hamburgers from Jack in the Box restaurants in several states, the largest such contamination in US history. Customers, shareholders, and franchisees sued Foodmaker, which in turn sued meat supplier and supermarket chain Vons and Vons' suppliers. Foodmaker's stock and profits plummeted, and the company subsequently enacted a stringent food safety program that became a model for the fast-food industry and won kudos from the FDA.

Foodmaker sold its Chi-Chi's chain to Family Restaurants (now Prandium) in 1994 for about $200 million and briefly held a stake in that company. In 1996 Goodall retired as CEO and Robert Nugent succeeded him. The next year Foodmaker announced a major expansion to add 200 Jack in the Box restaurants, primarily in the western US. Foodmaker put the *E. coli* episode farther behind it in 1998 when it accepted a $58.5 million settlement from Vons and others. Setting its sights back east, in 1999 the company announced that it would start building units in selected Southeastern markets.

Chairman: Jack W. Goodall, age 60
President and CEO: Robert J. Nugent, age 57, $1,075,000 pay
EVP, CFO, and Chief Administrative Officer: Charles W. Duddles, age 58, $587,900 pay
EVP Marketing and Operations: Kenneth R. Williams, age 56, $666,400 pay
EVP and Secretary: Lawrence E. Schauf, age 53, $469,500 pay
VP Operations and Domestic Franchising: Paul L. Schultz, age 44, $452,000 pay
VP Corporate Communications: Karen Bachmann
VP and Chief Information Officer: Donald C. Blough, age 50
VP Logistics: Bruce N. Bowers, age 52
VP Human Resources and Strategic Planning: Carlo E. Cetti, age 54
VP Marketing Communications: Bradford R. Haley, age 40
VP Restaurant Development: William F. Motts, age 55
VP Quality Assurance, Research and Development, and Product Safety: David M. Theno, age 48
VP New Products, Promotions, and Consumer Research: Linda A. Vaughan, age 40
VP Real Estate and Construction: Charles E. Watson, age 43
VP, Chief Accounting Officer, and Controller: Darwin J. Weeks, age 52
Treasurer: Harold L. Sachs
Corporate Counsel and Assistant Secretary: Victoria S. Brush
Corporate Counsel and Assistant Secretary: Michael J. Snider
Assistant Secretary: Shirley K. Heller
Auditors: KPMG LLP

HQ: 9330 Balboa Ave., San Diego, CA 92123-1516
Phone: 858-571-2121   **Fax:** 858-571-2101
Web site: http://www.jackinthebox.com

1998 Sales

	$ mil.	% of total
Restaurants	1,112	91
Distribution	26	2
Franchise rents & royalties	36	3
Other	50	4
Total	**1,224**	**100**

1998 Restaurants

	No.
Company-operated	1,069
Franchised	345
Total	**1,414**

Burger King	Sonic
Checkers Drive-In	Subway
CKE Restaurants	Taco Cabana
Dairy Queen	Triarc
Domino's Pizza	TRICON
IHOP	Wendy's
Long John Silver's	Whataburger
McDonald's	

NYSE symbol: FM FYE: September 30	Annual Growth	1989	1990	1991	1992	1993	1994	1995	1996	1997	1998
Sales ($ mil.)	3.8%	875	1,119	1,157	1,219	1,232	1,049	1,019	1,063	1,072	1,224
Net income ($ mil.)	33.4%	5	7	0	(42)	(98)	(40)	(69)	20	34	67
Income as % of sales	—	0.6%	0.6%	0.0%	—	—	—	—	1.9%	3.2%	5.4%
Earnings per share ($)	(7.3%)	—	—	—	2.62	(2.55)	(1.03)	(1.77)	0.51	0.86	1.66
Stock price - FY high ($)	—	—	—	—	18.50	14.00	10.75	7.25	10.25	21.00	21.06
Stock price - FY low ($)	—	—	—	—	9.13	7.50	5.00	3.25	4.75	7.75	12.56
Stock price - FY close ($)	7.1%	—	—	—	10.38	10.00	5.75	5.75	10.00	18.81	15.69
P/E - high	—	—	—	—	7	—	—	—	20	24	13
P/E - low	—	—	—	—	3	—	—	—	9	9	.8
Dividends per share ($)	—	—	—	—	0.00	0.00	0.00	0.00	0.00	0.00	0.00
Book value per share ($)	(9.3%)	—	—	—	6.47	3.64	2.59	0.81	1.32	2.25	3.61
Employees	5.0%	—	—	—	24,350	22,185	26,170	25,785	24,800	29,000	32,600

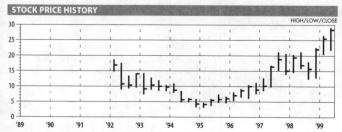

HIGH/LOW/CLOSE

Debt ratio: 70.0%
Return on equity: 48.7%
Cash ($ mil.): 10
Current ratio: 0.37
Long-term debt ($ mil.): 320
No. of shares (mil.): 38
Dividends
  Yield: —
  Payout: —
Market value ($ mil.): 595

FORD MOTOR COMPANY

OVERVIEW

In almost a century of car making, Ford Motor has produced enough vehicles — some 270 million — to put every man, woman, and child in the US today behind the wheel of a Ford. Parked in Dearborn, Michigan, Ford Motor is the world's largest truck maker — its F-Series pickup trucks lead the pack — and the #2 manufacturer of cars and trucks combined, behind General Motors. Its Aston Martin, Ford, Jaguar, Lincoln, and Mercury vehicles are made at 150 plants worldwide. Ford also owns a controlling (33%) interest in Mazda.

The company's Ford Motor Credit business is a world leader in auto financing and Ford's 81%-owned Hertz is the top car rental firm in the world. Ford plans to spin off Visteon, its car component business, in the year 2000.

After amassing about $24 billion in ready money, Ford went out and bought Volvo's passenger vehicle business. Volvo, with a reputation for producing cars that are particularly safe to drive, attracts more women and younger buyers than do Ford's other upscale brands, Jaguar and Lincoln. The Swedish brand also gives the company a larger European presence and fills the niche between its Ford and Lincoln nameplates. Ford has also expanded into the car repair market by acquiring Kwik-Fit Holdings, Europe's #1 car repair shop operator with 1,600 outlets.

The Ford family owns about 34% of the corporation's voting stock.

HISTORY

Henry Ford started the Ford Motor Company in 1903 in Dearborn, Michigan. In 1908 Ford introduced the Model T, produced on a moving assembly line that revolutionized both carmaking and manufacturing, period. By 1920 some 60% of all vehicles on the road were Fords.

In 1916 Ford omitted its customary dividend. Stockholders sued for payment, and in 1919 the company bought back all of its outstanding shares. It was 1956 before the Ford family again allowed outside ownership.

Ford bought Lincoln in 1922 and discontinued the Model T in 1927. Its replacement, the Model A (1932), was the first low-priced car with a V-8 engine. With Henry Ford's health failing, his son Edsel became president in 1932. Despite the introduction of the Mercury (1938), market share slipped behind GM and Chrysler. After Edsel's sudden death in 1943, his son, Henry II, took over and decentralized Ford, following the GM model. In 1950 the carmaker recaptured second place. Ford rolled out the infamous Edsel in 1958 and launched the Mustang in 1964.

Stung by the oil shocks of the 1970s, Ford cut its workforce by 33% and closed 15 plants during the 1980s. It also diversified into agricultural equipment with the purchase of New Holland (1986) and Versatile (1987). Ford added luxury sports cars to its lineup in 1987 by acquiring 75% of Aston Martin (it bought the rest in 1994). The 1988 introduction of the Taurus and Sable spurred Ford to its largest share of the US car market (21.7%) in 10 years. In 1989 it bought the Associates (financial services) and Jaguar (luxury cars).

In 1990 the company sold Ford Aerospace to Loral and merged New Holland with a Fiat subsidiary in 1991. The next year the company took a $7.4 billion charge relating to the future cost of retiree health care benefits.

Ford acquired Hertz in 1994 and in 1996 bought #3 rental agency Budget Rent a Car (sold 1997). Also that year it sold a 19% stake in finance unit Associates First Capital in an IPO and increased its stake in Mazda to one-third.

To focus on its medium- and light-truck production, Ford sold its heavy-duty truck unit to Daimler-Benz's Freightliner in 1997 for about $200 million. It also spun off 19% of Hertz in an IPO.

Ford began building a minibus line in China in 1997, beating GM in the race to produce vehicles for the Chinese market.

In 1998 Ford spun off the rest of Associates First Capital and acquired Cosworth's racing engines unit from Audi. Ford also sold off its direct stake in Kia Motors. Chairman, president, and CEO Alex Trotman retired in 1998. Henry Ford's great-grandson, William Ford Jr., succeeded him as chairman and Jacques Nasser became president and CEO.

Ford bought Volvo's carmaking operations for $6.45 billion in 1999, adding the brand to its new Premier Automotive Group (Aston Martin, Jaguar, and Lincoln). Ford bought the UK's Kwik-Fit Holdings for $1.6 billion to boost aftermarket services for new car buyers. Ford then began buying up junkyards in the US, and agreed to buy Mazda's credit division for $69 million. The company set up an $8 million fund that year for 700 to 900 female employees who suffered sexual harassment at two Ford plants in the Chicago area.

Chairman: William C. Ford Jr., age 41
President and CEO: Jacques A. Nasser, age 51,
  $6,050,000 pay (prior to promotion)
VC: W. Wayne Booker, age 64, $3,814,166 pay
VC and Chief of Staff: Peter J. Pestillo, age 60
EVP and CFO: John M. Devine, age 55
EVP; Chairman and CEO, Ford Motor Credit;
  President, Ford Financial Services: Phillipe Paillart,
  age 47
Group VP Manufacturing: James J. Padilla, age 52
Group VP; President, Visteon: Craig H. Muhlhauser
Group VP Product Development and Quality:
  Richard Parry-Jones, age 47
Group VP Marketing, Sales, and Service:
  Robert L. Rewey, age 60
Group VP Global Business: James D. Donaldson
Group VP Premier Automotive Group: Wolfgang Reitzle
VP; Chairman, Ford Motor Land Development:
  Wayne S. Doran
VP and Treasurer: Malcolm S. Macdonald
VP Human Resources: David L. Murphy
VP, General Counsel, and Secretary:
  John M. Rintamaki Jr.
VP; Chairman, Ford Werke: Rolf Zimmerman
Auditors: PricewaterhouseCoopers LLP

LOCATIONS

HQ: The American Rd., Dearborn, MI 48121-1899
Phone: 313-322-3000   **Fax:** 313-323-2959
Web site: http://www.ford.com

Ford has car and truck operations in 38 countries,
Ford Credit operates in 36 countries, Visteon operates
in 21 countries, and Hertz has operations in more than
140 countries.

PRODUCTS/OPERATIONS

1998 Sales

	$ mil.	% of total
Automotive sector		
Automotive	121,856	73
Visteon	17,762	11
Financial Services		
Ford Credit	19,303	12
Hertz	4,250	3
Other	2,269	1
Adjustments	(21,024)	—
Total	**144,416**	**100**

Selected Auto Brands

Aston Martin	Mazda (33%)
Ford	Mercury
Jaguar	Volvo
Lincoln	

COMPETITORS

AutoNation	Honda
BANK ONE	Hyundai
Bank of America	Isuzu
BMW	Johnson Controls
Boots Company	Mack Trucks
Budget Group	Mitsubishi
Cendant	Navistar
Chase Manhattan	Nissan
Citigroup	Peugeot
DaimlerChrysler	Saab Automobile
Denso	Suzuki
Dollar Thrifty Automotive	Toyota
Group	TRW
Fiat	Valeo
General Motors	Volkswagen

HISTORICAL FINANCIALS & EMPLOYEES

NYSE symbol: F FYE: December 31	Annual Growth	1989	1990	1991	1992	1993	1994	1995	1996	1997	1998
Sales ($ mil.)	4.6%	96,146	97,650	88,286	100,132	108,521	128,439	137,137	146,991	153,627	144,416
Net income ($ mil.)	21.5%	3,835	860	(2,258)	(7,385)	2,529	5,308	4,139	4,446	6,920	22,071
Income as % of sales	—	4.0%	0.9%	—	—	2.3%	4.1%	3.0%	3.0%	4.5%	15.3%
Earnings per share ($)	17.8%	4.06	0.92	(2.40)	(7.81)	2.10	4.44	3.33	3.64	5.62	17.75
Stock price - FY high ($)	—	18.80	16.31	14.28	16.23	21.95	23.28	21.83	24.73	33.37	61.44
Stock price - FY low ($)	—	13.74	8.30	7.76	9.21	14.28	17.02	16.10	18.09	19.92	28.30
Stock price - FY close ($)	16.8%	14.48	8.84	9.34	14.23	21.41	18.51	19.17	21.41	32.25	58.69
P/E - high	—	5	18	—	—	10	5	7	7	6	3
P/E - low	—	3	9	—	—	7	4	5	5	4	2
Dividends per share ($)	1.5%	1.50	1.50	0.98	0.80	0.80	0.91	1.23	1.47	1.65	1.72
Book value per share ($)	(2.5%)	24.04	24.56	23.47	15.07	15.61	21.14	21.16	22.55	25.55	19.16
Employees	(0.7%)	366,641	368,547	331,977	325,333	322,213	337,778	346,990	371,702	363,892	345,175

STOCK PRICE HISTORY

HIGH/LOW/CLOSE

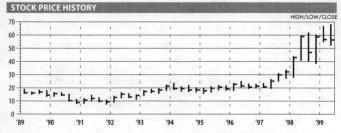

1998 FISCAL YEAR-END

Debt ratio: 76.1%
Return on equity: 94.3%
Cash ($ mil.): 4,836
Current ratio: 0.42
Long-term debt ($ mil.): 74,564
No. of shares (mil.): 1,222
Dividends
  Yield: 2.9%
  Payout: 9.7%
Market value ($ mil.): 71,719

FORT JAMES CORPORATION

OVERVIEW

Fort James wants to wipe up the competition, among other things. The Deerfield, Illinois-based maker of consumer paper products is the top tissue maker in North America (Kimberly-Clark is #1 worldwide). The company's leading brands include Brawny (#2 in paper towels, after Procter & Gamble's (P&G) Bounty), Mardi Gras and Northern (#1 and #3 in napkins), Green Forest (#1 in recycled tissue products), Quilted Northern (#2 in toilet paper, behind P&G's Charmin), and Dixie (disposable cups and plates). In addition to its brand-name goods, Fort James makes private-label tissue products for retailers.

The firm also makes printing paper (for brochures, catalogs, and manuals) and other paper products. To focus on its consumer offerings, Fort James sold its packaging unit that produces folding cartons and other packaging products.

Formerly known as James River, the company was reshaped by its 1997 purchase of recycled-paper maker Fort Howard in an effort to expand its product offerings and boost its international presence, especially in Europe. The deal combined James River's brand-management skill with Fort Howard's low-cost production and its strengths in the industrial and commercial markets.

HISTORY

When Richmond, Virginia-based Ethyl Corporation wanted to sell Albemarle Paper's Hollywood Mill in 1969, Ethyl executives Brenton Halsey and Robert Williams, some Albemarle employees, and a few investors joined forces to buy the mill, located on the James River in Richmond. Halsey was named chairman and CEO and Williams president and COO of the resulting company, James River Paper. In 1973 the company went public and became James River Corporation of Virginia.

Rather than build new pulp and paper enterprises, James River bought existing ones from other companies. These included 80% of Pepperell Paper (1971), Peninsular Paper (1974), and Weyerhaeuser Massachusetts (1975). In 1977 James River bought Curtis Paper, Rochester Paper, and Riegel Products. The company entered the industrial film products market in 1978 (buying Scott Graphics from Scott Paper) and the wood pulp business in 1980 (buying Brown Paper from Gulf + Western).

James River became the maker of Dixie cups, Northern towels and tissues, and Marathon folding cartons in 1982, when it bought Dixie/Northern paper and forest properties from American Can. The company bought the pulp and papermaking facilities of Diamond International (Vanity Fair products) in 1983. In 1986 it bought the pulp, papermaking, flexible packaging, and distribution businesses of Crown Zellerbach (one of the world's largest integrated paper companies) for $1.6 billion. The next year James River bought 50% of Kaysersberg, France's leading manufacturer of paper towel and tissue products. It sold its Nonwovens Group in 1990 and formed a joint venture (Jamont) with Italy's Gruppo Feruzzi and Finland's Nokia to gain a foothold in the European tissue market. (James River doubled its stake in Jamont to 86% in 1994.)

As part of a restructuring program, James River sold its specialty paper business to AEA Investors (1991). Halsey retired in 1992 and was succeeded as chairman and CEO by co-founder Williams. In 1993 James River bought Occidental Forest's 77% stake in Diamond Occidental Forest for $198 million, gaining 500,000 acres of forest.

In 1994 the firm sold its 50% interest in Coastal Paper Company, a lightweight-paper producer, and sold 47,000 acres of timberland. The next year Miles Marsh, formerly an executive with food maker Pet, Inc., replaced Williams as CEO. Also in 1995 James River acquired the plastic cutlery division of Benchmark Holdings, sold off its noncore businesses, and completed the spinoff of Crown Vantage, which consisted of a large part of the company's Communications Papers Business along with the specialty paper-based portion of the packaging business segment.

James River bought Fort Howard, a Green Bay, Wisconsin-based maker of paper towels and other sanitary papers, in 1997. Renamed Fort James, it began a major restructuring in 1998 that included several plant closures and layoffs of about 5% of its workforce. (Restructuring charges topped $500 million.) The company moved its corporate headquarters from Richmond to Deerfield, Illinois, that year and bought microwave packaging company Beckett Technologies.

In 1999 Fort James sold its packaging business to ACX Technologies for $830 million. Adding to its skin care products, Fort James then agreed to buy Demak'Up, the European cotton pads business of Procter & Gamble.

OFFICERS

Chairman and CEO: Miles L. Marsh, age 51, $2,344,221 pay
EVP and CFO: Ernst A. Haberli, age 50, $948,938 pay
SVP, General Counsel, and Corporate Secretary: Clifford A. Cutchins IV, age 50, $809,547 pay
SVP, Human Resources and Administration: Daniel J. Girvan, age 50
SVP and Treasurer: R. Michael Lempke, age 46
SVP, Planning and Strategy: Joseph W. McGarr, age 47
SVP and Controller: Joseph A. McGarr
VP and Chief Information Officer: Alan R. Guibord, age 52
VP, Marketing: Gary Kurlancheek, age 45
President, North American Consumer Products: Francis J. Florido, age 50
President, European Consumer Products: John F. Lundgren, age 47, $866,853 pay
President, North American Commercial Business: Daniel J. McCarty, age 47
President, Communications Papers: Joe R. Neil, age 60
President, North American Towel and Tissue Operations & Logistics and Packaging: B. Gregory Stroh, age 51
EVP, Dixie: William Schultz, age 37
Auditors: PricewaterhouseCoopers LLP

LOCATIONS

HQ: 1650 Lake Cook Rd., Deerfield, IL 60015-4753
Phone: 847-317-5000   **Fax:** 847-236-3755
Web site: http://www.fortjames.com

Fort James operates more than 60 manufacturing facilities in North America and Europe.

PRODUCTS/OPERATIONS

1998 Sales & Operating Income

	Sales $ mil.	Sales % of total	Operating Income $ mil.	Operating Income % of total
Tissue - North America	3,441	47	864	69
Tissue - Europe	1,869	25	236	19
Communications papers	797	10	2	—
Dixie	775	9	89	7
Packaging	718	9	56	5
Adjustments	(299)	—	(187)	—
Total	**7,301**	**100**	**1,060**	**100**

Selected Products

Tissue - North America
Bathroom tissue (Northern, Preference, Soft'n Gentle)
Facial tissue (Preference, Soft'n Gentle)
Napkins (Mardi Gras, Northern, Preference, Vanity Fair)
Paper towels (Brawny, Mardi Gras, Preference, So-Dri)
Recycled products (Envision, Green Forest)

Tissue - Europe
Bathroom tissue (Colhogar, Delica, Embo, Inversoft, Kittensoft, Lotus, Moltonel, Selpak, Tenderly)
Feminine hygiene (Vania)
Handkerchiefs
Kitchen towels (Okay, Selpak)
Lotus (facial tissues, baby wipes, and cotton swabs)

Communications Papers
Printing, copying, and publishing papers (Eureka!)

Dixie
Disposable cups, plates, cutlery

COMPETITORS

Dart Container	Procter & Gamble
Georgia-Pacific	Sweetheart Cup
Kimberly-Clark	Van Leer

HISTORICAL FINANCIALS & EMPLOYEES

NYSE symbol: FJ FYE: December 31	Annual Growth	1989	1990	1991	1992	1993	1994	1995	1996	1997	1998
Sales ($ mil.)	2.3%	5,950	3,392	4,562	4,728	4,650	5,417	6,800	5,691	7,259	7,301
Net income ($ mil.)	9.4%	222	10	78	(427)	(0)	(13)	126	157	(27)	498
Income as % of sales	—	3.7%	0.3%	1.7%	—	—	—	1.9%	2.8%	—	6.8%
Earnings per share ($)	(0.9%)	2.45	(0.08)	0.66	(5.55)	(15.56)	(0.96)	0.50	1.43	(0.28)	2.26
Stock price - FY high ($)	—	34.38	29.25	29.25	23.38	23.38	24.75	37.38	35.00	47.13	53.00
Stock price - FY low ($)	—	22.63	18.50	17.00	17.00	16.25	15.63	20.25	22.38	27.25	26.50
Stock price - FY close ($)	6.4%	22.88	26.25	20.00	18.50	19.25	20.25	24.13	33.13	38.25	40.00
P/E - high	—	14	—	44	—	—	—	75	24	—	23
P/E - low	—	9	—	26	—	—	—	41	16	—	12
Dividends per share ($)	0.0%	0.60	0.30	0.70	0.60	0.60	0.60	0.60	0.60	0.60	0.60
Book value per share ($)	(17.6%)	27.14	27.21	27.25	20.34	18.55	17.40	17.83	18.19	1.11	4.77
Employees	(5.6%)	46,000	46,000	38,000	38,000	35,000	33,800	27,000	23,000	29,000	27,500

STOCK PRICE HISTORY

HIGH/LOW/CLOSE

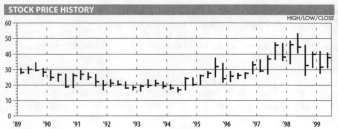

1998 FISCAL YEAR-END

Debt ratio: 77.6%
Return on equity: 47.3%
Cash ($ mil.): 5
Current ratio: 1.21
Long-term debt ($ mil.): 3,647
No. of shares (mil.): 221
Dividends
 Yield: 1.5%
 Payout: 26.5%
Market value ($ mil.): 8,820

FORTUNE BRANDS, INC.

OVERVIEW

Now smoke free, Fortune Brands can concentrate on keeping its brands as strong as a straight shot of bourbon. The Old Greenwich, Connecticut-based company, which made its early fortune in tobacco, in 1997 spun off UK subsidiary Gallaher, the #1 British tobacco firm (Benson & Hedges), to become completely free of tobacco.

Today, Fortune is indeed fortunate: 80% of sales come from a stable of 15 household name brands that are #1 or #2 in their categories. The company boasts many leading brands for both the home (Moen faucets, Master Lock padlocks, Aristokraft and Schrock cabinets) and office (Day-Timers personal planners, Swingline staplers). Fortune is also a leading US golf equipment maker (Titleist balls, Cobra clubs, and FootJoy golf shoes) and a leading US producer of distilled spirits, including Jim Beam bourbon and DeKuyper cordials.

Fortune has added more products to its lines both through new product introductions and acquisitions. Recent purchases have added office products, cabinets, and wine.

HISTORY

Fortune Brands began in 1864 as W. Duke and Sons, a small tobacco company started by Washington Duke, a North Carolina farmer. James Buchanan Duke joined his father's business at age 14 in 1870 and by age 25 was its president. James advertised to expanding markets, bought rival tobacco firms, and by 1904 controlled the industry. That year he merged all the competitive groups as American Tobacco Company. In a 1911 antitrust suit, the US Supreme Court dissolved American Tobacco into its original constituents, ordering them to operate independently.

James left American Tobacco the next year but remained president of British-American Tobacco Company (which he had founded in 1902). He established a $100 million trust fund composed mainly of holdings in his power company, Duke Power and Light (now Duke Energy Corporation), for Trinity College. The school became Duke University in 1924.

American Tobacco found a dynamic new leader in George Washington Hill, who became president in 1925. For the next 19 years until his death, George proved himself a consummate adman, pushing Lucky Strike, Pall Mall, and Tareyton cigarettes to top sales.

Smokers began switching to filter-tipped cigarettes in the 1950s because of health concerns. American Tobacco, however, ignored the trend and continued to rely on its popular filterless brands until the mid-1960s. In 1962 the firm sold J. Wix and Sons (Kensitas cigarettes) to UK tobacco firm Gallaher Group for a stake in Gallaher.

American Tobacco remained solely in the tobacco business until 1966, when it purchased Sunshine Biscuits (sold 1988) and Jim Beam Distillery. Reflecting its increasing diversity, the firm became American Brands in 1969. The next year it added Swingline (office supplies) and Master Lock. Meanwhile, American Brands increased its stake in Gallaher, controlling 100% by 1975. In 1976 the company acquired Acushnet (Titleist and Bulls Eye); it added FootJoy in 1986.

Threatened with a takeover by E-II Holdings (a conglomerate of brands split from Beatrice), American Brands bought E-II in 1988. It kept five of E-II's companies — Day-Timers (time management products), Aristokraft (cabinets), Waterloo (tool storage), Twentieth Century (plumbing supplies), and Vogel Peterson (office partitions; sold 1995) — and sold the rest (Culligan, Samsonite) to Riklis Family Corporation. Acquisitions in 1990 included Moen (faucets) and Whyte & Mackay (distillers). The company bought seven liquor brands in 1991 from Seagram, including Kessler (whiskey) and Ronrico (rum).

To distance itself from the tobacco business, American Brands' sold its American Tobacco subsidiary, including the Pall Mall and Lucky Strike brands, to onetime subsidiary B.A.T Industries (now British American Tobacco) in 1994. President and COO Thomas Hays became American Brands' CEO the next year. The firm acquired publicly held Cobra Golf in 1996.

The following year American Brands changed its name to Fortune Brands and completed the spinoff of its Gallaher tobacco subsidiary. In 1998 Fortune bought kitchen and bathroom cabinet maker Schrock from Electrolux, doubling its sales in that category. Also that year it bought Geyser Peak Winery and Apollo Presentation Products, a maker of overhead projectors.

Seeking to trim costs, in 1999 Fortune announced it would reduce its workforce by a third and relocate its headquarters to Lincolnshire, Illinois (the changes resulted in a $1.2 billion charge). In August 1999 Fortune formed MaxxiuM, a non-US wine/spirits sales and distribution joint venture, with Remy Cointreau and Highland Distillers.

Chairman and CEO: Thomas C. Hays
VC: John T. Ludes, $1,175,300 pay (prior to promotion)
President and COO: Norman H. Wesley, age 49
EVP Corporate: Gilbert L. Klemann II, age 48,
$775,700 pay
SVP and CFO: Craig P. Omtvedt
SVP Corporate Development: Charles H. McGill
SVP and Chief Administrative Officer:
Steven C. Mendenhall, $576,400 pay
SVP and General Counsel: Mark A. Roche
SVP Corporate Affairs: Robert J. Rukeyser, $621,100 pay
VP and Secretary: Louis F. Fernous Jr.
VP Human Resources: Anne C. Linsdau
VP and Associate General Counsel: Kenton R. Rose
VP and Chief Internal Auditor: Gary L. Tobison
Auditors: PricewaterhouseCoopers LLP

LOCATIONS

HQ: 1700 E. Putnam Ave.,
Old Greenwich, CT 06870-0811
Phone: 203-698-5000   **Fax:** 203-637-2580
Web site: http://www.fortunebrands.com

Fortune Brands has facilities in Australia, Canada,
Europe, Mexico, South Africa, Taiwan, Thailand, and the
US; it has a joint venture in China.

1998 Sales

	$ mil.	% of total
US	3,815	73
UK	552	10
Canada	236	5
Australia	158	3
Other countries	480	9
Total	**5,241**	**100**

PRODUCTS/OPERATIONS

Selected Brands

Home Products
Aristokraft (cabinets)
Master Lock (padlocks)
Moen (faucets)
Schrock (cabinets)
Waterloo (toolboxes)

Office Products
ACCO (office supplies)
Apollo (overhead
projectors)
Day-Timers (organizers)
Kensington (computer
accessories)
Perma Products (storage)
Swingline (staplers)
Wilson Jones (binders and
labels)

Spirits and Wine
After Shock (liqueur)
Calvert (gin)
Canadian Supreme
(whiskey)
Canyon Road (wine)
Chateaux (cordials)
Chinaco (tequila)
DeKuyper (cordials)

El Tosoro (tequila)
Geyser Peak (wine)
Gilbey's (gin and vodka)
Jim Beam (bourbon)
Kamchatka (vodka)
Kessler (whiskey)
Leroux (cordials)
Lord Calvert Canadian
Whisky
Old Crow (whiskey)
Old Grand-Dad (bourbon)
Old Taylor (whiskey)
Ronrico (rum)
Venezia (wine)
Whyte & Mackay (Scotch)
Windsor Canadian
(whiskey)
Wolfschmidt (vodka)

Golf Products
Bulls Eye (clubs)
Cobra (clubs)
DryJoy (shoes)
FootJoy (shoes and gloves)
Pinnacle (balls)
Titleist (balls, clubs, bags)
Weather-Sof (gloves)

COMPETITORS

Allied Domecq	Callaway Golf	Newell
American	Diageo	Rubbermaid
Standard	Franklin Covey	Seagram
Barcardi-Martini	Kohler	Stanley Works
Black & Decker	Masco	Taylor Made Golf
Brown-Forman		

HISTORICAL FINANCIALS & EMPLOYEES

NYSE symbol: FO FYE: December 31	Annual Growth	1989	1990	1991	1992	1993	1994	1995	1996	1997	1998
Sales ($ mil.)	(3.6%)	7,265	8,270	8,379	8,840	8,288	7,490	5,905	5,776	4,845	5,241
Net income ($ mil.)	(9.3%)	631	596	806	884	470	734	540	487	99	263
Income as % of sales	—	8.7%	7.2%	9.6%	10.0%	5.7%	9.8%	9.2%	8.4%	2.0%	5.0%
Earnings per share ($)	(7.6%)	3.04	2.84	3.74	4.13	2.29	3.77	2.86	2.76	0.56	1.49
Stock price - FY high ($)	—	25.87	26.31	30.10	31.52	25.68	24.25	29.86	31.68	38.00	42.25
Stock price - FY low ($)	—	19.36	19.51	22.52	24.65	18.01	18.57	23.15	25.20	30.18	25.25
Stock price - FY close ($)	3.9%	22.44	26.23	28.44	25.60	21.01	23.70	28.12	31.36	37.06	31.63
P/E - high	—	9	9	8	8	11	6	10	11	68	28
P/E - low	—	6	7	6	6	8	5	8	9	54	17
Dividends per share ($)	(4.3%)	1.26	1.41	1.59	1.81	1.97	1.99	2.00	2.50	1.41	0.85
Book value per share ($)	5.3%	15.34	18.13	20.42	21.14	21.09	22.93	21.43	21.52	23.31	24.34
Employees	(6.4%)	47,300	49,000	47,600	46,220	46,660	34,820	27,050	28,000	24,920	26,040

STOCK PRICE HISTORY

HIGH/LOW/CLOSE

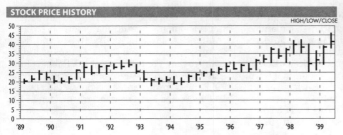

1998 FISCAL YEAR-END

Debt ratio: 19.3%
Return on equity: 6.4%
Cash ($ mil.): 40
Current ratio: 1.23
Long-term debt ($ mil.): 982
No. of shares (mil.): 168
Dividends
Yield: 2.7%
Payout: 57.0%
Market value ($ mil.): 5,311

FOSTER WHEELER CORPORATION

OVERVIEW

Foster Wheeler is fostering relations internationally. The Clinton, New Jersey-based company has a host of subsidiaries organized into three business groups: Engineering and Construction (designs and builds chemical, petroleum, and resource recovery plants), Energy Equipment (designs and manufactures steam generating equipment), and Power Systems (designs, builds, and operates cogeneration and independent power plants). Subsidiary

Foster Wheeler Environmental Corp. provides environmental remediation services.

Recognizing the prospective explosion in demand for power, especially overseas, CEO Richard Swift has led the company to make acquisitions that extend its technology and its foreign market presence, particularly in developing countries. (Overseas sales account for about three-fifths of Foster Wheeler's revenues.)

LOCATIONS

Foster Wheeler was created by the merger of two 19th-century family enterprises. In 1891 (concurrent with the commercialization of the steam turbine) brothers Frederick and Clifton Wheeler founded Wheeler Condenser & Engineering Co. in New York to build condensers, heat exchangers, and pumps for the marine and power industries. Three years later cousins Pell and Ernest Foster started the Water Works Supply Co. in New York. Ernest Foster had become intrigued by the use of superheated steam for power in Europe and hoped to exploit that technology in the US. In 1900 Water Works Supply became the Power Specialty Company.

Power Specialty acquired Wheeler Condenser & Engineering in 1927, and the merged business became the Foster Wheeler Corporation. That year the company's UK subsidiary was launched; in 1928 a Canadian branch became the company's second subsidiary. Foster Wheeler listed on the NYSE in 1929 and two years later bought the D. Connelly Boiler Co.

Foster Wheeler weathered the Depression with the help of US military contracts, and its experience working with the military helped it win record business during WWII. Following the war the pace of international expansion quickened with subsidiaries opening in Paris (1949); Milan, Italy (1957); and Madrid (1965). During the 1960s, shortages in many of Foster Wheeler's core industries (energy, fertilizer, and petrochemicals) boosted the company's sales and prompted a diversification program. In 1967 the company acquired Dallas-based Glitsch International, a manufacturer of specialty products for the auto, chemical, electronics, and oil industries.

The company formed Foster Wheeler Energy Corp. and Foster Wheeler International Corp. in 1973. That year it acquired Ullrich Copper, a fabricator of industrial copper products, and formed a subsidiary in Turkey. The company opened an office in Singapore in 1974

and in 1979 ducked a takeover attempt by McDonnell Douglas.

Foster Wheeler continued to grow internationally in the 1980s, with new subsidiaries in the UK and Thailand and an office in China. It moved its headquarters to New Jersey in 1987 and formed Foster Wheeler Constructors to handle projects in the Western Hemisphere. In the late 1980s, the company avoided a takeover attempt by New York investor Asher Edelman.

Foster Wheeler opened a subsidiary in Chile in 1991 and two years later organized its operation into three business groups. It also formed Foster Wheeler Power Machinery, a manufacturing joint venture in China.

The company acquired Enserch Environmental Corp. in 1994 and merged it with its own Environmental Services Division to form Foster Wheeler Environmental Corp. It also acquired Optimized Process Designs, which provides engineering and construction for the hydrocarbon processing industries. That year longtime company executive Richard Swift became CEO.

Foster Wheeler acquired Pyropower (a boilermaker) in 1995 from Finnish conglomerate Ahlstrom. The following year the company won a contract to build a polyethylene plant in the Philippines but lost a $316 million contract to build an incinerator (the largest in Canada) near Montreal.

In 1997 Foster Wheeler sold its Glitsch International subsidiary to Koch Engineering. A $10.5 million loss posted in 1997 was attributed to unexpected writeoffs on specific contracts and nonrecurring charges. Global sales continued to build in 1998, with new contracts in Turkey, Mexico, and China, but so did losses, mainly related to problems at the Robbins Resource Recovery waste-to-energy facility. In 1999 the company announced it would cut 1,600 jobs and slash its quarterly dividend 71%.

Chairman, President, and CEO: Richard J. Swift,
age 54, $725,000 pay
VC and CFO: David J. Roberts, age 54, $389,000 pay
SVP - Energy Equipment Group: Henry E. Bartoli,
age 52, $330,000 pay
SVP - Engineering and Construction Group:
John C. Blythe, age 51, $479,500 pay
(prior to promotion)
SVP - Power Systems Group: Claudio Ferrari, age 62
SVP and General Counsel: Thomas R. O'Brien, age 60
VP, Secretary, and Chief Compliance Officer:
Lisa F. Gardner, age 42
VP and Treasurer: Robert D. Iseman, age 50
VP Government Affairs: Sherry E. Peske
VP Human Resources and Administration:
James E. Schessler, age 53
VP Development, Pharmaceuticals, and Fine
Chemicals, Foster Wheeler USA: George Schnitzer
VP and Deputy General Counsel: Steven I. Weinstein
VP and Controller: George S. White, age 62
Director - Investor Relations: Scott W. Dudley Jr.
Director - Validation and General Manager - Puerto
Rico Operations, Pharmaceuticals and Fine
Chemicals Unit: Eduardo Guzman
Auditors: PricewaterhouseCoopers LLP

LOCATIONS

HQ: Perryville Corporate Park, Clinton, NJ 08809-4000
Phone: 908-730-4000   **Fax:** 908-730-4100
Web site: http://www.fwc.com

Foster Wheeler has operations in the US and 30
foreign countries.

1998 Sales

	$ mil.	% of total
Europe	2,806	59
US	1,878	39
Canada	71	1
Adjustments	(218)	—
Total	**4,537**	**100**

PRODUCTS/OPERATIONS

1998 Sales

	$ mil.	% of total
Engineering & Construction	3,459	73
Energy Equipment	1,111	23
Power Systems	184	4
Adjustments	(218)	—
Total	**4,537**	**100**

COMPETITORS

ABB Asea Brown Boveri	Morrison Knudsen
Bechtel	Ogden
Dresser-Rand	Parsons
Fluor	Perini
GE	Peter Kiewit Sons'
Halliburton	Raytheon
ITOCHU	Siemens
Jacobs Engineering	Stone & Webster
Mannesmann AG	Sumitomo
McDermott	Waste Management

HISTORICAL FINANCIALS & EMPLOYEES

NYSE symbol: FWC FYE: December 31	Annual Growth	1989	1990	1991	1992	1993	1994	1995	1996	1997	1998
Sales ($ mil.)	15.5%	1,243	1,661	1,992	2,495	2,583	2,234	3,042	4,006	4,060	4,537
Net income ($ mil.)	—	34	38	43	(46)	58	65	29	82	(11)	(32)
Income as % of sales	—	2.7%	2.3%	2.2%	—	2.2%	2.9%	0.9%	2.1%	—	—
Earnings per share ($)	—	0.95	1.08	1.22	(1.29)	1.61	1.82	0.78	2.02	(0.26)	(0.77)
Stock price - FY high ($)	—	22.00	28.75	34.00	32.88	35.88	45.13	43.50	47.25	48.13	32.25
Stock price - FY low ($)	—	14.25	17.75	20.25	23.00	25.88	26.63	29.38	33.50	26.13	11.75
Stock price - FY close ($)	(4.9%)	20.75	22.38	26.50	28.88	33.50	29.75	42.50	37.13	27.06	13.19
P/E - high	—	23	27	28	—	22	25	56	23	—	—
P/E - low	—	15	16	17	—	16	15	38	17	—	—
Dividends per share ($)	7.4%	0.44	0.49	0.53	0.59	0.65	0.72	0.77	0.81	0.84	0.84
Book value per share ($)	0.7%	13.21	14.50	15.13	10.87	11.21	12.75	15.46	16.95	15.21	14.05
Employees	3.8%	7,925	8,778	9,335	9,980	9,980	11,685	12,650	12,085	11,090	11,120

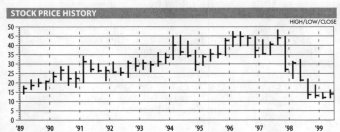

STOCK PRICE HISTORY
HIGH/LOW/CLOSE

1998 FISCAL YEAR-END
Debt ratio: 63.4%
Return on equity: —
Cash ($ mil.): 180
Current ratio: 1.12
Long-term debt ($ mil.): 991
No. of shares (mil.): 41
Dividends
  Yield: 6.4%
  Payout: —
Market value ($ mil.): 537

FOUNDATION HEALTH SYSTEMS

OVERVIEW

With the HMO business on shaky ground, Foundation Health Systems is scrambling to get its footing. Formed by the 1997 merger of Foundation Health Corporation and Health Systems International, Foundation Health Systems (FHS) serves some 6 million people in Arizona, California, Florida, and the Northeast. The Woodland Hills, California-based company's Health Plan Services unit offers HMO, PPO, Medicare, and Medicaid plans. The Government Contracts/Specialty Services unit administers government health care contracts and offers plans covering such specialty services as behavioral health, vision, and dental care.

The tremors that have caused FHS to wobble include rising medical costs, Medicare losses, and the failure of care providers. The company is shoring itself up with cost controls and other measures. As part of the cutbacks, FHS has sold its pharmaceutical services unit, two hospitals, and health plans in Colorado, Louisiana, New Mexico, Oklahoma, and Texas.

LOCATIONS

Foundation Health started as the not-for-profit Foundation Community Health Plan in the 1960s. In 1984 it was bought by AmeriCare Health, which had HMOs in six states. The acquisition was a coup: Foundation Health soon accounted for the bulk of AmeriCare's sales.

AmeriCare went public in 1985. The next year it lost to another firm the rights to that name. Redubbed Foundation Health, the company expanded into new states and unrelated businesses: commercial real estate, silk flowers, and furniture.

In late 1986 senior management led a $140 million LBO that left Foundation Health hobbled with debt when the industry was starting to slide. A 1988 Department of Defense (DOD) CHAMPUS contract brightened prospects, but the five-year, $3 billion contract to provide health care to 860,000 military retirees and dependents in California and Hawaii provided little short-term relief against the effects of high debt and rapid growth: the company lost money again.

The CEO slot had been vacant a year when Dan Crowley, a trained accountant with a good turnaround record, came aboard in 1989. He cut staff, slashed budgets, sold unrelated and nonperforming units, and kicked off a huge sales effort. To satisfy bankers and the DOD, which was threatening to rescind its contract, Crowley refinanced Foundation's debt. In a little over a year, Foundation Health recorded its best results ever. In 1990 the company went public.

Back on solid ground, the company began to expand its services and markets through acquisitions, including Western Universal Life Insurance (renamed Foundation Health Benefit Life Insurance, 1991), Occupational Health Services (employee assistance and substance abuse programs, 1992), and California Compensation Insurance (workers' compensation insurance, 1993).

Foundation Health found ways to compensate for the loss of almost half its revenues when the DOD contract was lost in 1993, but it also protested the decision, which was reversed two years later. The company regained the California/Hawaii contract, by then worth $2.5 billion. Also that year Foundation Health won a five-year, $1.8 billion DOD managed care contract for Oklahoma and parts of Arkansas, Louisiana, and Texas.

Meanwhile, the company had formed Integrated Pharmaceutical Services and acquired Miami-based CareFlorida Health Systems, Intergroup Healthcare, and Thomas-Davis Medical Centers during 1994.

In 1995 the company dropped an offer to buy Health Systems International. The next year it added behavioral health and employee assistance programs with the acquisition of Managed Health Network.

Renewed discussions with Health Systems International resulted in the companies merging to become Foundation Health Systems in 1997. Crowley — whose aggressive style garnered profits but was denounced as brutal by some critics — resigned after the merger. In 1998 the company pushed into the Northeast, acquiring Connecticut-based HMO Physicians Health Services. It then sold its workers' compensation insurance operations to Superior National Insurance. Chairman Malik Hasan (founder of Health Systems' nucleus, QualMed) resigned that year, partly because president Jay Gellert planned to focus on Arizona and California health plans, CHAMPUS, and behavioral health and pharmacy benefit management. The financial aftershocks of the companies' merger continued into 1999, when FHS began in earnest to prune non-core businesses, including pharmacy services and QualMed's Colorado operations. The company also agreed to sell its two hospitals to Healthplus Corp. in 1999.

Chairman: Richard W. Hanselman, age 71
President and CEO: Jay M. Gellert, age 45, $500,000 pay
EVP Medical Affairs and Chief Medical Officer:
Dale T. Berkbigler, age 50, $412,776 pay
President, FHS Central Division: J. Robert Bruce,
**President, FHS Workers' Compensation Services
Division:** Maurice Costa, age 51, $470,000 pay
President and CEO, FHS Northeast Division:
Karen A. Coughlin, age 51
EVP and CFO: Steven P. Erwin, age 55
President, FHS Arizona Division: Edward J. Munno Jr.
SVP Investor Relations: David Olson
President and CEO, FHS California Division:
Cora Tellez, age 49
SVP and Chief Technology Officer: Dale Terrell, age 58
**President and CEO, Government and Specialty Services
Divisions:** Gary S. Velasquez, age 39, $350,000 pay
SVP, Secretary, and General Counsel: B Curtis Westen,
SVP Human Resources: Karin D. Mayhew, age 48
President, Western Division: Michael D. Pugh
President and CEO, Health Net/Foundation Health:
Arthur M. Southam
SVP and Chief Medical Officer: Ross D. Henderson,
age 52
SVP Strategic Planning and Business Development:
Douglas C. Werner
President and CEO, Florida Health: Bruce Young
Auditors: Deloitte & Touche LLP

LOCATIONS

HQ: Foundation Health Systems, Inc.,
21600 Oxnard St., Woodland Hills, CA 91367
Phone: 818-676-6000   **Fax:** 818-676-8591
Web site: http://www.fhs.com

PRODUCTS/OPERATIONS

1998 Sales

	$ mil.	% of total
Health plan premiums	7,441	85
Government contracts	989	11
Specialty services	367	4
Total	**8,797**	**100**

Selected Services
Behavioral health services plans
Dental services plans
Government-sponsored managed care plans
Individual HMO plans
Medicaid HMO plans
Medicare HMO plans
Vision services plans
Workers' compensation

Selected Subsidiaries
AVP Vision Plans
DentiCare of California, Inc.
First Option Health Plan
Foundation Health PsychCare Services, Inc.
(behavioral health care)
Managed Health Networks, Inc. (behavioral health care)
Physician Health Services, Inc. (managed care services)

COMPETITORS

Aetna	CIGNA
Catholic Health East	Humana
Catholic Health Initiatives	Kaiser Foundation
Catholic Healthcare	Maxicare Health Plans
Network	PacifiCare
Catholic Healthcare	UnitedHealth Group
Partners	WellPoint Health
Catholic Healthcare West	Networks

HISTORICAL FINANCIALS & EMPLOYEES

NYSE symbol: FHS FYE: December 31	Annual Growth	1989	1990	1991	1992	1993	1994	1995	1996	1997	1998
Sales ($ mil.)	67.5%	—	142	283	436	1,957	2,306	2,732	3,204	7,121	8,797
Net income ($ mil.)	—	—	5	18	19	24	88	90	74	(187)	(165)
Income as % of sales	—	—	3.2%	6.4%	4.4%	1.2%	3.8%	3.3%	2.3%	—	—
Earnings per share ($)	—	—	—	1.21	1.12	1.00	0.88	1.55	0.67	(1.52)	(1.35)
Stock price - FY high ($)	—	—	—	14.25	22.00	20.50	36.75	34.25	37.13	33.94	32.63
Stock price - FY low ($)	—	—	—	10.25	10.00	10.00	15.88	24.88	19.38	22.06	5.88
Stock price - FY close ($)	(1.1%)	—	—	12.88	19.25	16.88	30.38	32.13	24.75	22.25	11.88
P/E - high	—	—	—	12	20	21	42	22	55	—	—
P/E - low	—	—	—	8	9	10	18	16	29	—	—
Dividends per share ($)	—	—	—	0.00	0.00	0.00	0.00	0.00	0.00	0.00	0.00
Book value per share ($)	1.5%	—	—	5.48	6.49	3.17	4.61	5.91	7.54	7.18	6.09
Employees	51.3%	—	509	511	2,367	2,455	2,700	2,500	3,825	15,200	14,000

1990–96 information is for Health Systems International.

STOCK PRICE HISTORY

HIGH/LOW/CLOSE

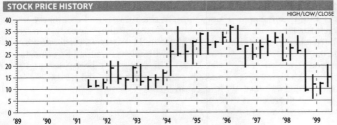

1998 FISCAL YEAR-END

Debt ratio: 62.8%
Return on equity: —
Cash ($ mil.): 764
Current ratio: 1.23
Long-term debt ($ mil.): 1,254
No. of shares (mil.): 122
Dividends
  Yield: —
  Payout: —
Market value ($ mil.): 1,452

FOX ENTERTAINMENT GROUP, INC.

OVERVIEW

Contrary to what Mulder and Scully might think, this is no conspiracy — it's just business. New York City-based Fox Entertainment is one of the world's largest entertainment conglomerates. A vertically integrated company, Fox Entertainment develops and produces programming that can be distributed through its own movie and TV studios, its TV network, or both (as with *The X-Files*). It also develops programming for third parties such as CBS and NBC. The company's Fox Television Network is one of the US's largest; it has 198 affiliates, 22 of which are company-owned. In addition, the company owns cable channels (Fox Sports Networks, Fox Family Worldwide), professional sports teams (Los Angeles Dodgers, New York Knicks), and sporting arenas (40% of New York

City's Madison Square Garden and 40% of Los Angeles' Staples Center).

The company and its Filmed Entertainment division (which includes Twentieth Century Fox production studios) are riding quite a wave of success, thanks in large part to *Titanic*, which it co-produced with Viacom's Paramount Pictures. Also, Fox Television Network — home to hits *Ally McBeal, The Simpsons,* and *King of the Hill* — is now the US's #2 channel in the coveted advertising demographic of adults between the ages of 18 and 49.

Fox Entertainment Group's 1998 IPO raised $2.8 billion; one of the largest offerings in American history. Rupert Murdoch's News Corporation owns 82% of the company.

LOCATIONS

Hungarian-born immigrant William Fox (originally Wilhelm Fried) purchased a New York City nickelodeon for $1,600 in 1904. He transformed the failing operation into a success and soon owned (with two partners) 25 theaters across the city. The partners also opened a film exchange, The Greater New York Rental Company, and then in 1913 began making their own movies through the Box Office Attraction Company.

Fox became the first to combine film production, leasing, and exhibition when he founded the Fox Film Corporation in 1915. Soon after, he moved the studio to California. One of the first to recognize the value of individual actors, Fox is credited with developing the "star system."

Throughout the 1920s, Fox Film continued to grow. The company began experiencing trouble in 1927, and by 1930 William Fox was forced out.

In 1935 the company merged with Twentieth Century Pictures, a studio started two years earlier by Darryl Zanuck, former head of production at Warner Brothers. Under Zanuck's leadership, the studio flourished in the 1930s and 1940s, producing such films as *The Grapes of Wrath* and *All About Eve.* By the early 1950s, however, TV was dulling some of Hollywood's shine. Zanuck left the studio in 1956 only to return in 1962 to help it recover from the disastrous *Cleopatra.*

The 1960s brought both good (*The Sound of Music*) and bad (*Tora! Tora! Tora!*). During this time Twentieth Century Fox emerged as a leading TV producer. By 1971 infighting between Darryl Zanuck and his son Richard, who had

been president of the studio, resulted in the resignation of both men. The studio prospered during the 1970s, culminating in 1977 with the production and release of box office hit *Star Wars.*

Oilman Marvin Davis bought Twentieth Century Fox for $722 million in 1981. In 1985 the studio was purchased by Murdoch. The next year Murdoch bought six TV stations from Metromedia and launched the Fox Broadcasting network.

Murdoch focused almost exclusively on TV and feature films throughout the 1990s. During the early 1990s Fox was riding high with *The Simpsons* and *Beverly Hills 90210* on TV and *Home Alone* in movie theaters. In 1996 and 1997, respectively, Murdoch created the Fox News Channel and purchased Pat Robertson's International Family Entertainment. The company also joined Liberty Media in 1996 to create a rival to Disney's ESPN sports network.

In 1998 Murdoch bought the Los Angeles Dodgers and acquired 40% of the Staples Center, thereby acquiring options to buy minority interests in the Los Angeles Kings and the Los Angeles Lakers. Also that year the company's investment in *Titanic* paid off: The movie won 11 Academy Awards. The following year News Corp. bought the 50% of the Fox/Liberty Networks business that it didn't already own from Liberty Media and transferred ownership to Fox (the operation was renamed Fox Sports Networks). The deal gave Liberty Media an 8% stake in News Corp. and raised News Corp.'s interest in Fox to 82%.

Chairman and CEO: K. Rupert Murdoch, age 67
President and COO: Peter Chernin, age 47
Co-COO: Chase Carey, age 44
SEVP and CFO: David F. DeVoe, age 51
SEVP and General Counsel: Arthur M. Siskind, age 59
**Chairman and CEO, Fox Broadcasting Company;
President, Fox Sports; Chairman, Fox/Liberty
Networks:** David Hill, age 52
Chairman, Fox Filmed Entertainment:
William Mechanic, age 48
Chairman and CEO, Fox Television Stations, Inc.:
Mitchell Stern, age 44
President, Fox Consumer Products: Patricia Wyatt
**President, Twentieth Century Fox Licensing &
Merchandising:** Steven M. Ross
Auditors: Arthur Andersen LLP

LOCATIONS

HQ: 1211 Avenue of the Americas, New York, NY 10036
Phone: 212-556-2400   **Fax:** 212-852-7145
Web site: http://www.fox.com

PRODUCTS/OPERATIONS

1998 Sales

	$ mil.	% of total
Filmed entertainment	3,876	55
TV broadcasting	3,075	44
Cable network programming	72	1
Total	**7,023**	**100**

Selected Operations

Canal Fox (entertainment cable channel, Latin America)
Cinecanal (20%; pay-television movie service,
    Latin America)
Fox Broadcasting Company
    Fox Television Network
Fox Family Worldwide (49.5%)
    Fox Family Channel
    Fox Kids Network
Fox Filmed Entertainment
    Fox 2000
    Fox Animation Studios
    Fox Searchlight Pictures
    Fox Studios Australia (50%)
    Fox Television Studios
    Regency Television (50%)
    Twentieth Century Fox Studios
    Twentieth Century Fox Television
    Twentieth Television
Fox Sports Networks
    Fox Sports International
    Fox Sports Net
    FX (general interest cable channel)
    Health Network (cable and Internet health
        information service)
    Regional Programming Partners (includes interests
        in regional cable sports channels, Madison Square
        Garden, Radio City Music Hall, the New York Knicks
        and New York Rangers)
Fox/Liberty Ventures
    Outdoor Life (34%, nature programming)
    Speedvision (34%, live racing events and related news)
    Staples Center (40%, sports complex in Los Angeles)
Fox News Channel
FXM: Movies From Fox
The Golf Channel (33%)
Los Angeles Dodgers (professional baseball organization)
Telecine (13%, pay-television service, Brazil)

COMPETITORS

Carsey-Werner	MGM	Universal
CBS	NBC	Studios
DreamWorks	Sony Pictures	USA Networks
SKG	Entertainment	Viacom
King World	Time Warner	Walt Disney
Liberty Media		

HISTORICAL FINANCIALS & EMPLOYEES

NYSE symbol: FOX FYE: June 30	Annual Growth	1989	1990	1991	1992	1993	1994	1995	1996	1997	1998
Sales ($ mil.)	24.3%	—	—	—	—	—	—	—	4,548	5,847	7,023
Net income ($ mil.)	(34.6%)	—	—	—	—	—	—	—	411	30	176
Income as % of sales	—	—	—	—	—	—	—	—	9.0%	0.5%	2.5%
Employees	—	—	—	—	—	—	—	—	—	—	10,000

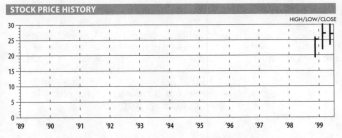

STOCK PRICE HISTORY
HIGH/LOW/CLOSE

1998 FISCAL YEAR-END
Debt ratio: 8.7%
Return on equity: 4.5%
Cash ($ mil.): 101
Current ratio: 1.27
Long-term debt ($ mil.): 375

FPL GROUP, INC.

OVERVIEW

For a Florida firm without any oranges, FPL Group produces a lot of juice. Based in Juno Beach, Florida, the energy holding company, through its main subsidiary, Florida Power & Light (FPL), generates, transmits, and distributes electricity to about 3.7 million customers. Its service territory includes Florida's east coast and the southern area of the state. FPL's power plants, mainly fossil-fueled and nuclear-powered, have a generating capacity of more than 18,000 MW. Its Energy Marketing and Trading unit brokers excess power for FPL and other US producers, primarily in the Southeast. FPL accounts for almost all of the group's revenues, and its outlook remains sunny because Florida doesn't have set plans for deregulation.

While FPL Group may not be looking for competition in its home state, it loves deregulating markets elsewhere. Subsidiary FPL Group Capital owns the firm's nonutility businesses, including FPL Energy and FPL Energy Services.

FPL Energy, an independent power producer (IPP), prefers green power: Much of its 4,185-MW generating capacity is produced by wind, gas, solar, and geothermal energy. The IPP owns plants in nine US states. It focuses its efforts in California, Virginia, and the northeastern states and is adding another 1,300 MW to its capacity in Iowa, Texas, and Washington. FPL Energy also owns plants in Colombia and Ireland.

FPL Energy Services provides energy management services (from energy supply to power audits to staff training) for large commercial and government clients in the eastern US.

LOCATIONS

During Florida's land boom of the early 1920s, new homes and businesses were going up fast. But electric utilities were few and far between, and no transmission lines linked one system to another.

In 1925 American Power & Light Company (AP&L), which operated utilities throughout the Americas, set up Florida Power & Light (FPL) to consolidate the state's electric assets. AP&L built transmission lines linking 58 communities from Miami to Stuart on the Atlantic Coast and from Arcadia to Punta Gorda on the Gulf.

FPL accumulated many holdings, including a limestone quarry, streetcars, phone companies, and water utilities, and purchases in 1926 and 1927 nearly doubled its electric properties. In 1927 the company used an electric pump to demonstrate how swamplands could be drained and cultivated.

During the 1940s and 1950s FPL sold its nonelectric properties. The Public Utility Holding Company Act of 1935 forced AP&L to spin off FPL in 1950. The company was listed on the NYSE that year.

FPL grew with Florida's booming population. In 1972 its first nuclear plant (Turkey Point, south of Miami) went on line. In the 1980s it began to diversify with the purchase of real estate firm W. Flagler Investment in 1981, and FPL Group was created in 1984 as a holding company. It subsequently acquired Telesat Cablevision (1985), Colonial Penn Group (1985, insurance), and Turner Foods (1988, citrus groves). FPL Group formed ESI Energy in 1985 to develop nonutility energy projects.

Diversification efforts didn't pan out, and in 1990 the firm wrote off about $750 million. That year, sticking to electricity, the utility snagged its first out-of-state power plant, in Georgia, acquiring a 76% stake (over five years). FPL Group sold its ailing Colonial Penn unit in 1991; two years later it sold its real estate holdings and some of its cable TV businesses.

The utility gave environmentalists cause to complain in 1995. First, the St. Lucie nuclear plant was fined by the NRC for a series of problems. FPL also wanted to burn orimulsion, a cheap, tarlike fuel. Barred by the governor and state cabinet from using the fuel, the utility finally gave up the fuel-ish plan in 1998.

In 1997 FPL Group created FPL Energy, an independent power producer (IPP), out of its ESI Energy and international operations; FPL Energy teamed up with Belgium-based Tractebel the next year to buy two gas-fired plants in Boston and Newark, New Jersey. In 1998 FPL Group planned a wind power facility to be built in Iowa and in 1999 announced the construction of two more wind plants in Wisconsin and Texas.

FPL Energy bought 35 generating plants from Central Maine Power for $846 million in 1999. The IPP later tried to back out of the deal, believing deregulation in New England had lowered the plants' value, but a judge forced it to complete the purchase. The acquisition, coupled with a rate cut, took a serious bite out of FPL's profits. FPL Group sold its Turner Foods citrus unit and the rest of its cable TV holdings that year.

Chairman and CEO, FPL Group and Florida Power & Light: James L. Broadhead, age 63, $2,000,000 pay
President: Roger Young, age 55
President, Florida Power & Light: Paul J. Evanson, age 57, $1,139,400 pay
President, FPL Energy: Michael W. Yackira, age 47, $706,000 pay
President, Nuclear Division, Florida Power & Light: Thomas F. Plunkett, age 59
President, Power Generation, FPL Group and Florida Power & Light: C. O. Woody, age 60, $547,700 pay
VP, Corporate Communications: Mary Lou Kromer
VP, Human Resources; SVP, Human Resources, Florida Power & Light: Lawrence J. Kelleher, age 51
VP, Tax: James P. Higgins
VP, Business Management, FPL Energy: Kenneth P. Hoffman
VP and CFO, FPL Energy: Peter D. Boylan
VP, Development, FPL Energy: Glenn E. Smith
VP, Engineering Construction and Project Management, FPL Energy: William A. Fries
VP, International Development, FPL Energy: Michael L. Leighton
VP, Operations East, FPL Energy: John W. Stanton
VP, Operations West, FPL Energy: James A. Keener
General Counsel and Secretary, FPL Group and Florida Power & Light: Dennis P. Coyle, age 60, $688,000 pay
Treasurer, FPL Group and Florida Power & Light: Dilek L. Samil, age 43
Auditors: Deloitte & Touche LLP

HQ: 700 Universe Blvd., Juno Beach, FL 33408
Phone: 561-694-4000 **Fax:** 561-694-4620
Web site: http://www.fplgroup.com

FPL Group provides electric utility services in Florida. It also has operating power plants in California, Maine, Massachusetts, New Jersey, Nevada, Oregon, Pennsylvania, South Carolina, and Virginia, as well as Colombia and Ireland. It has power plants under construction in Iowa, Texas, and Washington.

1998 Sales

	$ mil.	% of total
Electric operations		
Residential	3,580	54
Commercial	2,239	34
Industrial	197	3
Group sales	295	4
Other operations	350	5
Total	**6,661**	**100**

AES	Entergy	PECO Energy
Central and	Florida Progress	PG&E
South West	Florida Public	PowerGen
CMS Energy	Utilities	Reliant Energy
Conectiv	GreenMountain.	Sempra Energy
Duke Energy	com	Sithe Energies
Dynegy	MidAmerican	Southern
Edison	Energy	Company
International	National Power	TECO Energy
Enersis	Northern States	Thermo Ecotek
Enron	Power	Texas Utilities

NYSE symbol: FPL FYE: December 31	Annual Growth	1989	1990	1991	1992	1993	1994	1995	1996	1997	1998
Sales ($ mil.)	0.8%	6,180	6,289	5,249	5,193	5,316	5,423	5,593	6,037	6,369	6,661
Net income ($ mil.)	5.5%	410	(391)	241	467	429	519	553	580	618	664
Income as % of sales	—	6.6%	—	4.6%	9.0%	8.1%	9.6%	9.9%	9.6%	9.7%	10.0%
Earnings per share ($)	2.4%	3.12	(2.86)	1.48	2.65	2.30	2.91	3.16	3.33	3.57	3.85
Stock price - FY high ($)	—	36.75	36.50	37.25	38.38	41.00	39.13	46.50	48.13	60.00	72.56
Stock price - FY low ($)	—	29.00	26.13	28.13	32.00	35.50	26.88	34.00	41.50	42.63	56.06
Stock price - FY close ($)	6.0%	36.38	29.00	37.00	36.25	39.13	35.13	46.38	46.00	59.19	61.63
P/E - high	—	12	—	25	14	18	13	15	14	17	19
P/E - low	—	9	—	19	12	15	9	11	12	12	15
Dividends per share ($)	(1.3%)	2.26	2.34	2.39	2.43	2.47	1.88	1.76	1.84	1.92	2.00
Book value per share ($)	0.9%	26.11	19.63	19.64	20.99	21.57	22.51	23.81	25.17	26.66	28.37
Employees	(6.4%)	18,800	19,138	14,500	14,530	12,400	12,135	11,353	10,011	10,039	10,375

HIGH/LOW/CLOSE

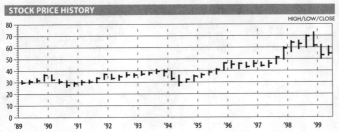

Debt ratio: 30.5%
Return on equity: 13.0%
Cash ($ mil.): 187
Current ratio: 0.77
Long-term debt ($ mil.): 2,347
No. of shares (mil.): 181
Dividends
 Yield: 3.2%
 Payout: 51.9%
Market value ($ mil.): 11,137

FRED MEYER, INC.

OVERVIEW

The dinner table has turned on Fred Meyer. Under the auspices of investor Ron Burkle, the Portland, Oregon-based company grew fat acquiring grocery chains. Now it finds itself swallowed by Kroger, the #1 US grocer, in a $13 billion acquisition that comes close to creating the first national supermarket chain. An operator of just multidepartment and jewelry stores a few years ago, Fred Meyer has gorged on food retailers, acquiring Smith's Food & Drug Centers, Quality Food Centers (QFC), and Ralphs Grocery. The company is one of the biggest food and drug retailers in the US, with more than 1,050 supermarkets, jewelry outlets, and multidepartment stores spanning from Alaska to Texas.

Fred Meyer's stores include about 135 Fred Meyer Marketplace superstores (averaging about 145,000 sq. ft.), mostly in the Northwest, which sell apparel, jewelry, home electronics, home improvement items, and groceries. It also operates about 300 Ralphs supermarkets and about 90 Food 4 Less warehouse stores in Southern California, about 150 Smith's Food & Drug Centers in eight western states, and about 90 QFC stores in the Seattle area. Its smaller chains include PriceRite in Las Vegas and Cala, Bell, and FoodsCo. in Northern California. Fred Meyer also has about 380 jewelry stores across the US under five names, including Fred Meyer Jewelers, Merksamer Jewelers, and Littman Jewelers (more than 100 are located in Fred Meyer Marketplace stores).

Supermarket investment powerhouse The Yucaipa Companies — headed by Burkle — exchanged its controlling 9% stake in Fred Meyer for a 2% stake in Kroger.

LOCATIONS

Fred Meyer worked in his dad's grocery store in New York before heading west at the age of 19. He began peddling coffee, tea, and spices door-to-door in Portland, Oregon, in 1909, and in 1915 he opened the Java Coffee Co., renting a stall at a public market that featured separate shopping areas for dairy products, meat, produce, and other items. He moved to a larger location in 1917 and added groceries on a cash-and-carry basis. Five years later he and his brother, Harry, opened their first grocery and variety store (Mybros Public Market) in downtown Portland. (They eventually parted over unresolved differences.)

Meyer opened the nation's first self-service drugstore in 1930 and the next year his first One-Stop Shopping in Hollywood, a Portland suburb, where customers could buy groceries, drugs, and general merchandise under one roof and get their cars serviced at the adjacent gas station. Meyer had six stores by the end of the decade and opened stores throughout Oregon and southern Washington over the next 30 years. Since it cost less to operate his stores, Meyer's prices were much lower than those of other markets.

In 1960 the 18-store chain went public with sales of $56 million. During the 1960s it added departments such as home improvement and garden centers. In 1973 its fine jewelry department became an independent jewelry salon inside the store and, in 1989, a separate 18-store chain. Several northwestern retailing acquisitions expanded Fred Meyer into Idaho, Alaska, and western Montana.

Kohlberg Kravis Roberts (KKR) took the company private in a $420 million management-led LBO in 1981. The investment firm then took it public in 1986, making the participants about $240 million. Albertson's veteran Robert Miller became CEO in 1991.

The company added almost 70 jewelry stores with two major acquisitions in 1996. The next year Fred Meyer bought 44 Fox Jewelry stores in the Midwest, and it also bought Smith's Food & Drug Centers, in which Ron Burkle and his investment company, The Yucaipa Companies, owned a 14% stake. Burkle became chairman of Fred Meyer and immediately went to work on new deals.

In March 1998 Fred Meyer acquired Yucaipa-controlled Ralphs Grocery, the dominant California grocery chain, and Seattle-area Quality Food Centers (QFC), which owned Hughes Family Markets in Southern California. (The company merged its Hughes stores into Ralphs, converting them to the Ralphs banner.) In October 1998 Smith's bought 13 stores in Wyoming and Montana from Albertson's and acquired 123 Littman and Barclay jewelry stores in 10 eastern states from Elangy. In December 1998 Ralphs sold five Falley's and 33 Food 4 Less stores in Kansas and Missouri to Associated Wholesale Grocers.

Fred Meyer sold the whole basket in May 1999 to Kroger for $13 billion in stock and debt, creating a chain with strongholds in the Midwest, South, and West.

Chairman: Ronald W. Burkle, age 46
VC and CEO: Robert G. Miller, age 54, $1,660,000 pay
President and COO: George Golleher, age 50, $1,553,939 pay
EVP Regulatory and Legal Affairs and Secretary: Roger A. Cooke, age 50
EVP Finance and Investor Relations: David R. Jessick, age 44
EVP Purchasing and Procurement: Kenneth A. Martindale, age 38, $619,995 pay
EVP Distribution and Manufacturing: George A. Schnug, age 53
EVP and Chief Administrative Officer: Kenneth Thrasher, age 47
SVP and CFO: John T. Standley, age 36
President, Ralphs: Sammy K. Duncan, age 47
President, QFC: Michael E. Huse, age 43
President, Food 4 Less: Harold McIntire, age 53
President and CEO, Smith's: Russell J. Dispense, age 51
President and CEO, Fred Meyer Stores: Mary F. Sammons, age 50, $630,800 pay
Auditors: Deloitte & Touche LLP

LOCATIONS

HQ: 3800 SE 22nd Ave., Portland, OR 97202
Phone: 503-232-8844   **Fax:** 503-797-5609
Web site: http://www.fredmeyerstores.com

Fred Meyer Marketplace stores are located in Alaska, Arizona, Idaho, Oregon, Utah, and Washington. Food 4 Less and Ralphs are located in Southern California. Bell, Cala, and FoodsCo. operate in Northern California. Quality Food Centers (QFC) are located in Oregon and Washington. Smith's Food & Drug Centers has locations in Arizona, Idaho, Montana, Nevada, New Mexico, Texas, Utah, and Wyoming. PriceRite operates in Las Vegas. Fred Meyer also operates specialty stores in 26 states.

PRODUCTS/OPERATIONS

Subsidiaries
Fred Meyer Stores Inc.
  Jewelry stores (Fox's Jewelers, Fred Meyer Jewelers, Merksamer Jewelers, Littman Jewelers, and Barclay Jewelers)
  Multidepartment stores (Fred Meyer, Fred Meyer Marketplace)
Quality Food Centers, Inc.
  Supermarkets (QFC)
Ralphs Grocery Company
  Conventional and warehouse stores (Bell, Cala)
  Supermarkets (Ralphs)
  Warehouse stores (Food 4 Less, FoodsCo.)
Smith's Food & Drug Centers Inc.
  Food and drug centers (Smith's)
  Warehouse stores (PriceRite)

COMPETITORS

Albertson's	May
Bashas'	Safeway
Circuit City	ShopKo Stores
Costco Companies	Signet
Dayton Hudson	Stater Bros.
Federated	TJX
Fleming Companies	Toys "R" Us
Furr's Supermarkets	Walgreen
Home Depot	Wal-Mart
J. C. Penney	Waremart
Kmart	Zale
Lowe's	

HISTORICAL FINANCIALS & EMPLOYEES

Subsidiary FYE: January 31	Annual Growth	1990	1991	1992	1993	1994	1995	1996	1997	1998	1999
Sales ($ mil.)	23.1%	2,285	2,476	2,703	2,854	2,979	3,128	3,429	3,725	5,481	14,879
Net income ($ mil.)	—	(7)	34	45	61	68	7	30	59	12	(163)
Income as % of sales	—		1.4%	1.7%	2.1%	2.3%	0.2%	0.9%	1.6%	0.2%	—
Employees	17.1%	22,200	21,700	24,200	24,000	25,000	27,000	27,000	28,000	85,000	92,000

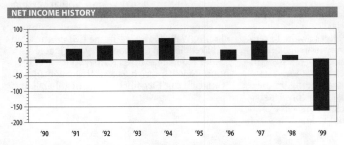

NET INCOME HISTORY

1999 FISCAL YEAR-END
Debt ratio: 68.3%
Return on equity: —
Cash ($ mil.): 178
Current ratio: 1.09
Long-term debt ($ mil.): 4,981

Fred Meyer, Inc.

FREDDIE MAC

McLean, Virginia-based Freddie Mac (once known as the Federal Home Loan Mortgage Corporation) is a shareholder-owned, government-sponsored enterprise established by the US Congress. Along with sister company Fannie Mae (formerly the Federal National Mortgage Association), Freddie Mac provides a continuous flow of funds for residential mortgages, helping Americans achieve the dream of home ownership. Although Freddie Mac is significantly smaller than Fannie Mae (with about half its asset value), it indirectly finances one out of every six homes in the US.

Freddie Mac provides liquidity in the housing market by buying mortgage lenders' loans (thus allowing them to make more loans) and repackaging them into securities. The company is prevented from originating loans, but its work in the secondary market allows home buyers to save up to 0.5% on their mortgage rate. Freddie Mac's automated systems for underwriting, networking, and tracking mortgage payments help reduce origination costs.

Although not part of the US government, Freddie Mac enjoys an implicit guarantee of government support should the company fall on hard times. Because of the perceived backing, investors are willing to lend to Freddie Mac at below-market rates. Consequently, private-sector competitors are growing more vocal with their complaints, claiming Freddie and Fannie unfairly use their special status to fund expansion into loan origination, insurance, and other areas outside the scope of their congressional charter.

LOCATIONS

Ah, the 1960s — free love, great tunes, and a war nobody wanted to pay for with taxes. By decade's end, inflation was rising dramatically and real income was starting to fall. Fearing a recession in the construction industry, Congress acted to increase the flow of money into the housing market by providing a new entity to buy home mortgages.

Fannie Mae had been buying mortgages since 1938, but it focused on Federal Housing Administration (FHA) and Veterans Administration loans. The Emergency Home Finance Act of 1970 created Freddie Mac and enlarged Fannie Mae's field of action to include conventional mortgages. Still, rising interest rates in the 1970s were brutal on the US real estate market and also damaged Freddie Mac.

In the early 1980s dealers devised a way to securitize the company's loans — which were seen as somewhat frumpy investments — by packaging them into more alluring, bond-like investments. (The implicit government guarantee made them even sexier.) When three major government securities dealers collapsed in 1985, ownership of some Freddie Mac securities was in doubt, and the Federal Reserve Bank of New York quickly automated registration of government securities.

Other organizational changes awaited Freddie Mac. In 1984 the company issued shares to members of the Federal Home Loan Bank (the overseer of US savings and loans); four years later the shares began limited trading on the NYSE. Finally, in 1989 legislation converted the shares to common stock. Because its shares were publicly traded, Freddie Mac's board of directors was expanded from three political appointees to 18 members.

In 1991 the rate of real estate defaults nationwide (which had increased in the wake of the late 1980s real estate crash) kindled concern about Freddie Mac's loss-reserve levels and fostered the fear that the company might need to tap its line of credit at the US Treasury. In response, Congress created the Office of Federal Housing Enterprise Oversight in 1992 to regulate Freddie Mac and Fannie Mae. Initial examinations, completed in 1995, sounded no alarms. In 1996 a Congressional Budget Office report questioned whether the government should continue implicitly guaranteeing the debt securities issued by Freddie Mac and Fannie Mae.

In 1997 Freddie Mac (which officially adopted its longtime nickname) joined GE Capital Mortgage Corporation (a unit of General Electric Capital) and First Union in a program to cut administration costs on federal housing subsidies.

In 1998 Freddie Mac launched a system that cut loan approval time from 30 days to two minutes (it agreed to develop a similar version for the FHA). The streamlining was crucial to agreements in which mortgage lenders (including Wells Fargo, #1 in the US) promised to sell Freddie Mac the loans they originated. In 1999 Freddie Mac hired former speaker of the house Newt Gingrich as a strategic consultant (Gingrich can't legally lobby until July 2000).

OFFICERS

Chairman and CEO: Leland C. Brendsel, age 56, $2,925,000 pay
President and COO: David W. Glenn, age 55, $1,610,000 pay
EVP Single Family Securitization Group: John D. Fisk, age 42, $655,677 pay
EVP and CFO: John P. Gibbons, age 47, $660,127 pay
EVP, Secretary, and General Counsel: Maud Mater, age 51
SVP and Chief Credit Officer: David A. Andrukonis, age 41
SVP Risk Assessment and Model Development: Donald J. Bisenius, age 40
SVP Portfolio Management: Henry J. Cassidy, age 55
SVP Finance: Vaughn A. Clarke, age 45
SVP Government Relations: R. Mitchell Delk, age 46
SVP Investor and Dealer Services: Kevin J. Finnerty, age 44
SVP and General Auditor: Melvin M. Kann, age 58
SVP Information Systems and Services: William I. Ledman, age 50
SVP Business Development: Peter F. Maselli, age 41
SVP Human Resources: Candice D. Mendenhall, age 49
SVP Corporate Finance and Chief Investment Officer: Gregory J. Parseghian, age 38
SVP Servicer Division: Paul T. Peterson, age 49
SVP and Corporate Controller: Gregory E. Reynolds
SVP Corporate Relations: Ann B. Schnare, age 51
SVP Multifamily Housing: Thomas J. Watt, age 59
Auditors: Arthur Andersen LLP

LOCATIONS

HQ: 8200 Jones Branch Dr., McLean, VA 22102-3110
Phone: 703-903-2000   **Fax:** 703-918-8403
Web site: http://www.freddiemac.com

PRODUCTS/OPERATIONS

1998 Assets

	$ mil.	% of total
Cash & equivalents	4,321	1
Asset-backed securities	7,124	2
Other investments	38,203	12
Mortgages, net	255,348	80
Other assets	16,425	5
Total	**321,421**	**100**

1998 Sales

	$ mil.	% of total
Mortgage interest	14,269	79
Other interest	2,369	13
Management & guarantee income	1,307	7
Other income	103	1
Total	**18,048**	**100**

COMPETITORS

Advanta	First Union
AIG	Fleet
Bank of New York	GE Capital
Chase Manhattan	KeyCorp
Citigroup	PNC Bank
Countrywide Credit	TELACU
Dime Bancorp	Washington Mutual
Fannie Mae	

HISTORICAL FINANCIALS & EMPLOYEES

NYSE symbol: FRE FYE: December 31	Annual Growth	1989	1990	1991	1992	1993	1994	1995	1996	1997	1998
Assets ($ mil.)	27.8%	35,462	40,579	46,860	59,502	83,880	106,199	137,181	173,866	194,597	321,421
Net income ($ mil.)	16.3%	437	414	555	622	786	983	1,091	1,243	1,395	1,700
Income as % of assets	—	1.2%	1.0%	1.2%	1.0%	0.9%	0.9%	0.8%	0.7%	0.7%	0.5%
Earnings per share ($)	18.9%	—	0.58	0.77	0.82	1.02	1.26	1.41	1.63	1.88	2.31
Stock price - FY high ($)	—	—	6.84	11.57	12.31	14.19	15.72	20.91	29.00	44.56	66.38
Stock price - FY low ($)	—	—	2.52	3.68	8.44	11.31	11.75	12.47	19.06	26.69	38.69
Stock price - FY close ($)	41.3%	—	4.06	11.45	12.09	12.47	12.63	20.88	27.59	41.94	64.44
P/E - high	—	—	12	15	15	14	12	15	18	24	29
P/E - low	—	—	4	5	10	11	9	9	12	14	17
Dividends per share ($)	17.7%	—	0.13	0.17	0.19	0.22	0.26	0.30	0.35	0.40	0.48
Book value per share ($)	18.5%	—	2.96	3.56	4.92	6.10	7.09	8.10	9.63	8.74	11.55
Employees	3.6%	—	—	—	—	2,929	3,380	3,320	3,194	3,258	3,503

STOCK PRICE HISTORY

HIGH/LOW/CLOSE

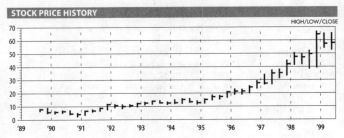

1998 FISCAL YEAR-END

Equity as % of assets: 2.5%
Return on assets: 0.7%
Return on equity: 21.2%
Long-term debt ($ mil.): 93,525
No. of shares (mil.): 695
Dividends
  Yield: 0.7%
  Payout: 20.8%
Market value ($ mil.): 44,797
Sales (mil.): $18,048

FREEPORT-MCMORAN

OVERVIEW

Fending off challenges by Indonesian environmentalists and human rights groups, Freeport-McMoRan Copper & Gold (FCX) keeps digging out profits from one of the world's largest gold and copper mines. The New Orleans-based firm's lifeblood flows from Indonesian contracts to explore and develop millions of acres in the country's Sudirman Range.

The company's P.T. Freeport Indonesia (PT-FI) subsidiary operates the vast open-pit Grasberg gold and copper mine, the world's largest gold mine. PT-FI also is developing other copper, gold, and silver ore deposits in the area. The Indonesian government owns a 9% stake in the mining operation. Former president Raden Suharto also owns a stake through P.T.

Indocopper Investama Corporation. British mining giant Rio Tinto (formerly RTZ) owns 14% of FCX. Other FCX subsidiaries include P.T. IRJA Eastern Minerals, which explores for minerals in Indonesia, and Atlantic Copper, which operates a copper smelter in Spain.

Political and environmental controversy continues to plague FCX, which is now without its major benefactor, President Suharto, who was forced to resign after more than 30 years in power. Not helping are low copper and gold prices. However, FCX is counting on low-cost operations and strong production to help it weather the rough times. The Grasberg mine is known as the lowest-cost copper producer in the world.

LOCATIONS

The Freeport Sulfur Company was formed in Texas in 1912 by Francis Pemberton, banker Eric Swenson, and several investors to develop a sulfur field. The next year Freeport Texas was formed as a holding company for Freeport Sulfur and other firms.

During the 1930s the company diversified. In 1936 Freeport pioneered a process to remove hydrocarbons from sulfur. The company joined Consolidated Coal in 1955 to establish the National Potash Company. In 1956 Freeport formed an oil and gas subsidiary, Freeport Oil.

Internationally, Freeport formed an Australian minerals subsidiary in 1964 and a copper-mining subsidiary in Indonesia in 1967. The company changed its name to Freeport Minerals in 1971 and merged with McMoRan Oil & Gas in 1982.

Utah-based oil and gas company McMoRan Explorations (later McMoRan Oil & Gas) was formed in 1969 by William McWilliams, Jim Bob Moffett, and Byron Rankin. In 1973 McMoRan formed an exploration and drilling alliance with Dow Chemical and signed a deal with Indonesia to mine in the remote Irian Jaya region. McMoRan went public in 1978.

Moffett became chairman and CEO of Freeport-McMoRan in 1984. The company formed Freeport-McMoRan Copper in 1987 to manage its Indonesian operations. The unit assumed its current name in 1991. Two years later it acquired Rio Tinto Minera, a copper-smelting business with operations in Spain.

To support expansion in Indonesia, FCX spun off its copper and gold division in 1994. In 1995 it formed an alliance with the UK's RTZ Corporation to develop its Indonesian

mineral reserves. Local riots that year closed the Grasberg Mine, and Freeport's political risk insurance was canceled. Despite these setbacks, higher metal prices and growing sales in 1995 helped the company double its operating income.

An Indonesian tribal leader filed a $6 billion lawsuit in 1996 charging FCX with environmental, human rights, and social and cultural violations. The company called the suit baseless but offered to set aside 1% of its annual revenues, worth about $15 million, to help local tribes. Tribal leaders rejected the offer, and in 1997 a judge dismissed the lawsuit. The ruling has been appealed.

In 1997 FCX pulled out of Bre-X Minerals' Busang gold mine project, which independent tests proved a fraud of historic proportions. Also in 1997 the company prepared plans to more than double production at the Grasberg Mine. Following a report by an independent consultant on ways to ease tension in Irian Jaya, FCX said it would increase workers' wages by 26% over the next two years.

Amid widespread rioting, Indonesia's embattled president Raden Suharto was forced out of office in 1998. The new government investigated charges of cronyism involving FCX.

In 1999 the company received permission from the Indonesian government to expand the Grasberg Mine and increase ore output to up to 300,000 metric tons per day. The quid pro quo arrangement could double the copper royalties and triple the gold royalties FCX must pay the Indonesian government.

**Chairman and CEO; President Commisioner, P.T.
  Freeport Indonesia:** James R. Moffett, age 60,
  $3,750,000 pay
VC: Rene L. Latiolais
President and COO; EVP, P.T. Freeport Indonesia:
  Richard C. Adkerson, age 52, $2,025,000 pay
SVP and CFO; EVP, P.T. Freeport Indonesia:
  Stephen M. Jones, age 49, $820,000 pay
**SVP and Chief Administrative Officer; EVP, P.T.
  Freeport Indonesia:** Michael J. Arnold, age 46
**SVP International Relations and Federal Government
  Affairs:** W. Russell King, age 49
SVP Stategic Planning; EVP, P.T. Freeport Indonesia:
  John A. Macken, age 47, $770,000 pay
SVP External Affairs: Paul S. Murphy, age 55
SVP Exploration; EVP, P.T. Freeport Indonesia:
  Steven D. Van Nort, age 58, $770,000 pay
SVP and Treasurer; Treasurer, P.T. Freeport Indonesia:
  Craig E. Saporito, age 47
Human Resources: Allison Lauricella
Auditors: Arthur Andersen LLP

HQ: Freeport-McMoRan Copper & Gold Inc.,
  1615 Poydras St., New Orleans, LA 70112
Phone: 504-582-4000   **Fax:** 504-582-1847
Web site: http://www.fcx.com

Freeport-McMoRan Copper & Gold conducts exploration
and development, mining, and processing of copper,
gold, and silver in Indonesia and operates a copper
smelting and refining plant in Spain.

Selected Products
Copper
Gold
Silver

Joint Venture
P.T. Smelting Co. (25%, smelting, Indonesia)

Selected Subsidiaries
Atlantic Copper Holding, SA (smelting and
  refining, Spain)
P.T. Freeport Indonesia Co. (82%, mining)
P.T. Indocopper Investama Corp.
  (49%, mining, Indonesia)
P.T. IRJA Eastern Minerals Corp.
  (95%, mining, Indonesia)

Anglo American
ASARCO
Barrick Gold
BHP
Carso
Centromin
Codelco
CVRD
Cyprus Amax
Gencor
Grupo Mexico
Homestake Mining
Inco Limited
Lonmin
Mueller Industries
Newmont Mining
Norddeutsche Affinerie
Phelps Dodge
Placer Dome
Rio Algom
Rio Tinto plc
Southern Peru Copper
Trelleborg
Virginia Indonesia
WMC Limited
Zambia Copper

NYSE symbol: FCX FYE: December 31	Annual Growth	1989	1990	1991	1992	1993	1994	1995	1996	1997	1998
Sales ($ mil.)	19.0%	368	434	468	714	926	1,212	1,834	1,905	2,001	1,757
Net income ($ mil.)	5.1%	99	93	96	130	51	130	254	226	245	154
Income as % of sales	—	26.8%	21.3%	20.6%	18.2%	5.5%	10.7%	13.8%	11.9%	12.2%	8.8%
Earnings per share ($)	(11.9%)	—	—	—	—	—	—	0.98	0.89	1.06	0.67
Stock price - FY high ($)	—	—	—	—	—	—	—	30.75	36.13	34.88	21.44
Stock price - FY low ($)	—	—	—	—	—	—	—	22.63	27.38	14.94	9.81
Stock price - FY close ($)	(28.1%)	—	—	—	—	—	—	28.13	29.88	15.75	10.44
P/E - high	·	—	—	—	—	—	—	31	41	33	32
P/E - low		—	—	—	—	—	—	23	31	14	15
Dividends per share ($)	(13.3%)	—	—	—	—	—	—	0.23	0.90	0.90	0.15
Book value per share ($)	—	—	—	—	—	—	—	1.35	1.49	(0.33)	(1.13)
Employees	4.8%	4,170	3,772	4,486	4,983	6,054	6,074	4,983	8,300	6,300	6,349

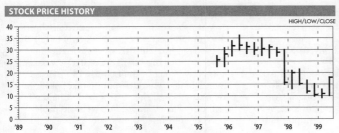

HIGH/LOW/CLOSE

Debt ratio: 79.4%
Return on equity: —
Cash ($ mil.): 6
Current ratio: 1.05
Long-term debt ($ mil.): 2,329
No. of shares (mil.): 219
Dividends
  Yield: 1.4%
  Payout: 22.4%
Market value ($ mil.): 2,281

FRUIT OF THE LOOM, LTD.

OVERVIEW

The underwear may not be as sexy as Victoria's, but it is the fruit of this company's loom. Chicago-based Fruit of the Loom is one of the largest makers of basic apparel in the US, producing about 32% of all men's and boys' and 15% of all women's and girls' underwear sold in the US. The company is also the #1 supplier to the screen print T-shirt market.

Fruit of the Loom makes briefs, boxers, panties, T-shirts, jackets, activewear, casual wear, and children's wear. Brand names include BVD, Fruit of the Loom, Gitano, Pro Player, and Wilson. The company also has

licenses for children's characters from *Batman*, *Star Wars*, and *Teletubbies*, as well as the names, trademarks, and logos of professional sports teams, colleges, and universities. Fruit of the Loom's products are sold primarily in North America (more than 80% of sales) to department stores, discount and mass merchandisers, wholesale clubs, and screen printers.

The company is a fully integrated manufacturer, spinning, knitting, sewing, and packaging its products. CEO William Farley has stepped down after years of depressed company earnings and a more recent product supply problem.

LOCATIONS

Fruit of the Loom began as a brand name used by Robert Knight's textile company, which he established in 1851. Knight's company adopted the Fruit of the Loom name in 1856. The brand, whose logo (an apple, grapes, gooseberries, and a cluster of leaves) was adopted in 1893, was first licensed to finished-garment makers in 1928.

Polish immigrant Jacob Goldfarb founded Union Underwear in 1926 and began making one-piece "unionsuits." In 1938 Goldfarb acquired a 25-year license to the Fruit of the Loom trademark. Newly outfitted with the license, Union introduced boxer shorts and knit underwear in the 1940s.

By the mid-1950s Union was the biggest US maker of men's briefs. In 1955 Goldfarb, then 60 and worried Union might be liquidated after he died, accepted a cash offer for his company from Philadelphia & Reading Corporation.

Philadelphia & Reading, which went on to buy Fruit of the Loom in 1961, had been a coal company until the mid-1950s, when investors led by Howard Newman transformed it into a holding company. In 1968 Philadelphia & Reading was bought by Northwest Industries, a conglomerate that included the North Western railroad.

The acquisition by Northwest funded Union's growth. Commercials featuring the "Fruit of the Loom Guys" (men dressed as fruit and leaves) debuted in 1975, and the next year the company acquired the BVD trademark for a separate line of underwear. The Underoos line (decorated underwear for children) was launched in 1978.

Deal maker William Farley bought Northwest in 1985 for $1.4 billion (most of it from junk bond specialist Drexel Burnham Lambert). Farley changed the company's name to Fruit of the Loom in 1987. It went public that

year, but Farley's own holding company, Farley, Inc., kept control. Under his ownership, the firm began to diversify, manufacturing socks (1986), sweatshirts, and increasing production of women's underwear (which it had begun selling in 1984).

Following a failed attempt to take over sheet maker West Point-Pepperell in 1989, Farley, Inc., shed businesses, trying to keep ahead of debt and interest payments.

In the early 1990s Fruit of the Loom became a leader in children's underwear, and in 1994 it acquired the Gitano fashion brand. The company lost nearly $230 million in 1995, partly because of charges incurred from closing six US plants and laying off more than 3,000 workers. That year, in an effort to reduce costs and streamline operations, it began moving production to the Caribbean and Central America.

Fruit of the Loom sold its hosiery division in 1996 to sock maker Renfro for $90 million and paid $22 million to rename Miami's Joe Robbie Stadium after its Pro Player line. The next year it took a $102 million charge to pay for a lawsuit judgment against a former unit, announced 7,700 more layoffs, and closed nine plants at a cost of $250 million. In June 1997 Farley sold more than 800,000 shares of his own stock in Fruit of the Loom just weeks before the company announced a disastrous second quarter.

With slackening demand, it curtailed production of fleece wear in 1998 only to fall short of demand in 1999. To cut costs further, in 1999 Fruit of the Loom created a new parent company (Fruit of the Loom, Ltd.) in the Cayman Islands, where corporate taxes are lower. By mid-1999 all the cutting hadn't paid off, and CEO Farley stepped down amid projections of continued poor earnings.

Chairman: William Farley
Acting CEO: Dennis Bookshester
EVP Sports Licensing: Douglas Kelly
EVP Operations: Edgar F. Turner, age 55
SVP Human Resources: Marett Cobb
SVP Sales: Dennis Murphy
SVP Marketing: John D. Wendler
VP, Treasurer, and Assistant Secretary:
Brian J. Hanigan, age 40
VP Finance, Acting CFO, and Assistant Secretary:
G. William Newton, age 46, $300,000 pay
VP, General Counsel, and Secretary: John J. Ray III,
age 40
VP Tax and Assistant Secretary: Walter J. Sluzas
President Retail: John W. Salisbury Jr., age 50,
$400,000 pay
President European Operations: Felix Sulzberger,
age 47, $415,000 pay
President Activewear: Vincent J. Tyra, age 33,
$300,000 pay
VP Merchandising and Design, Gitano: Sachin Batra
Auditors: Ernst & Young LLP

LOCATIONS

HQ: 5000 Sears Tower, 233 S. Wacker Dr.,
Chicago, IL 60606
Phone: 312-876-1724   **Fax:** 312-993-1749
Web site: http://www.fruit.com

Fruit of the Loom has manufacturing facilities in
Canada, El Salvador, Honduras, Ireland, Jamaica,
Morocco, the UK, and the US.

PRODUCTS/OPERATIONS

1998 Sales & Operating Income

	Sales		Operating Income	
	$ mil.	% of total	$ mil.	% of total
Retail products	1,095	50	103	39
Activewear	589	27	68	26
Sports & licensing	186	9	8	3
Other	300	14	83	32
Adjustments	—	—	(27)	—
Total	**2,170**	**100**	**235**	**100**

Selected Brand Names
Best
BVD
Cumberland Bay
Fans Gear
Fruit of the Loom
Gitano
Lofteez
Munsingwear
Official Fan
Pro Player
Screen Stars
Underoos
Wilson

Selected Products
Activewear
Casual wear
Children's wear
Jackets
Jeans
Sports-licensed
apparel
Sportswear
Underwear

COMPETITORS

Benetton
Bugle Boy
Calvin Klein
Delta Woodside
Donnkenny
The Gap
GIANT GROUP
Guess?
Intimate Brands
Jockey International
Levi Strauss
Mossimo
NIKE
Ocean Pacific
Oneita Industries
OshKosh B'Gosh
Reebok
Russell Corporation
Sara Lee
Starter
Tommy Hilfiger
Tultex
VF
Warnaco Group

HISTORICAL FINANCIALS & EMPLOYEES

NYSE symbol: FTL FYE: December 31	Annual Growth	1989	1990	1991	1992	1993	1994	1995	1996	1997	1998
Sales ($ mil.)	5.7%	1,321	1,427	1,628	1,855	1,884	2,298	2,403	2,447	2,140	2,170
Net income ($ mil.)	7.3%	72	77	111	179	208	60	(233)	151	(488)	136
Income as % of sales	—	5.5%	5.4%	6.8%	9.6%	11.0%	2.6%	—	6.2%	—	6.3%
Earnings per share ($)	6.0%	1.11	1.18	1.55	2.35	2.81	1.11	(3.07)	1.98	(6.55)	1.88
Stock price - FY high ($)	—	16.00	15.38	28.00	49.63	49.25	33.00	27.75	39.00	44.88	38.19
Stock price - FY low ($)	—	6.13	6.13	7.63	26.50	22.88	23.00	16.50	22.50	23.13	11.50
Stock price - FY close ($)	(0.8%)	14.88	8.88	27.63	48.63	24.13	27.00	24.25	37.88	25.63	13.81
P/E - high	—	14	13	18	21	18	30	—	20	—	20
P/E - low	—	6	5	5	11	8	21	—	11	—	6
Dividends per share ($)	0.0%	0.00	0.00	0.00	0.00	0.00	0.00	0.00	0.00	0.00	0.00
Book value per share ($)	4.1%	5.30	6.77	9.21	11.32	13.83	14.84	11.78	13.90	5.87	7.61
Employees	2.0%	26,000	27,700	26,700	31,100	35,000	37,400	33,300	32,900	28,500	31,000

STOCK PRICE HISTORY

HIGH/LOW/CLOSE

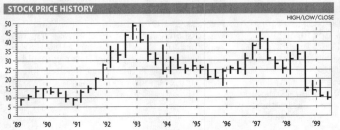

1998 FISCAL YEAR-END

Debt ratio: 60.9%
Return on equity: 24.8%
Cash ($ mil.): 1
Current ratio: 1.45
Long-term debt ($ mil.): 857
No. of shares (mil.): 72
Dividends
   Yield: —
   Payout: —
Market value ($ mil.): 996

FURNITURE BRANDS

OVERVIEW

Furniture Brands International is a centerpiece in the furniture industry's showroom. The St. Louis-based company, which is the US's #1 maker of residential furniture, has three major subsidiaries: Broyhill Furniture Industries, Lane Furniture Industries, and Thomasville Furniture Industries. Furniture Brands makes bedroom, dining room, and living room furniture, including chairs, home entertainment centers, love seats, recliners, sofas, tables, and accessories. Brands include Broyhill Premier; Pearson and Hickory (sold by Lane); and Founders, Highland House, and Creative Interiors (sold by Thomasville). In addition, Lane makes indoor/outdoor wicker and rattan furniture.

The company makes different brands for different segments of the market: Thomasville makes Ernest Hemingway furnishings for high-end shoppers, Thomasville's Creative Interiors unit makes ready-to-assemble furniture for mass marketers such as Wal-Mart and Target, and Broyhill is targeted for mid-range buyers.

Furniture Brands has remained profitable since emerging from bankruptcy in 1992 and shedding its non-furniture operations. Although the company takes a back seat to no one in the industry, its domestic market share is only about 10%. To avoid competing with retailers of its products, Furniture Brands has eschewed selling furniture over the Internet.

LOCATIONS

Although already a diversified firm, INTERCO's purchase of Ethan Allen in 1980 took the company in a direction that would eventually become its only business. INTERCO traces its roots back to the pairing of two shoe manufacturers and made a name for itself by running men's shoemaker and retailer IFlorsheim, which it acquired in 1953. It added other operations, including department stores and apparel, beginning in the 1960s. The Ethan Allen purchase gave INTERCO 24 furniture factories and 300 retail outlets.

The company grew its furniture business later in 1980 by purchasing Broyhill Furniture Industries, which was founded by J. E. Broyhill as Lenoir Chair Company in 1926. The Broyhill line first became popular during the 1930s. The Broyhill family built the company into the largest privately owned maker of furniture, with 20 manufacturing facilities when INTERCO bought it.

In 1986, after acquiring furniture maker Highland House (Hickory), INTERCO made its largest acquisition in the home furnishings and furniture market the next year when it gained control of the Lane Company for approximately $500 million. Founded in 1912 by Ed Lane to make cedar chests, Virginia-based Lane had grown into a full-line maker of furniture with 16 plants in operation. The acquisition of Lane lifted furniture and furnishings to 33% of INTERCO's total sales in 1987.

Meanwhile, INTERCO hadn't neglected its shoe business, adding Converse in 1986. Richard Loynd, the Converse CEO, served as INTERCO's CEO from 1989 to 1996. In 1988, under a takeover threat by the Rales brothers of Washington, DC, the company retained the investment banking firm of Wasserstein Perella, which advised payment of a $76 special dividend, for which INTERCO borrowed $1.8 billion via junk bonds. To repay the debt, the firm began selling off assets, including its apparel businesses and Ethan Allen. However, the sales yielded low prices and some businesses failed to attract buyers.

After fighting off the hostile takeover, INTERCO filed for bankruptcy in 1991 — one of the largest bankruptcy cases in US history. It also filed a malpractice suit against Wasserstein Perella when it emerged from Chapter 11; the suit was settled the following year, and Apollo Investment Fund acquired a large stake in the firm.

INTERCO sold the last of its 80-year-old shoemaking sole with the spinoff of its Florsheim and Converse units in 1994. The company acquired Thomasville Furniture from Armstrong World Industries for $331 million in 1993, a purchase that made it the leading shaker in residential furniture. The Finch brothers ran Thomasville, founded in 1904, until Armstrong acquired it in 1968.

W. G. "Mickey" Holliman became CEO in 1996, and INTERCO's board decided to change the company's name to Furniture Brands International to better reflect its remaining business. In 1997 Apollo Investment Fund, its largest shareholder, sold its 38% stake. The next year Furniture Brands and retailer Haverty Furniture signed a deal whereby Havertys would allocate up to half its retail space for the display of Furniture Brands' products.

OFFICERS

Chairman, President, and CEO:
Wilbert G. "Mickey" Holliman, age 61, $1,453,147 pay
VP, General Counsel, and Secretary: Lynn Chipperfield, age 47
VP, Treasurer, and CFO: David P. Howard, age 47
President and CEO, Action Industries: John T. Foy, age 51, $557,410 pay
President and CEO, Thomasville Furniture Industries: Christian J. Pfaff, age 50, $536,413 pay
Controller and Chief Accounting Officer: Steven W. Alstadt, age 44
Auditors: KPMG LLP

LOCATIONS

HQ: Furniture Brands International, Inc.,
101 S. Hanley Rd., St. Louis, MO 63105
Phone: 314-863-1100 **Fax:** 314-863-5306
Web site: http://www.furniturebrands.com

Furniture Brands International's products are sold worldwide, and the company has plants in Mississippi, North Carolina, Tennessee, and Virginia.

1998 Offices, Warehouses & Plants

	No.
North Carolina	40
Virginia	6
Mississippi	4
Missouri	1
Tennessee	1
Total	**52**

PRODUCTS/OPERATIONS

Selected Products
Case Goods Furniture
  Bedroom
  Dining room
  Living room
Occasional Furniture
  Accent items
  Freestanding home
    entertainment centers
  Home office items
  Wood tables

Stationary Upholstery
  Products
  Chairs
  Love seats
  Sectionals
  Sofas
Other
  Motion furniture
  Recliners
  Sleep sofas

COMPETITORS

Bassett Furniture
Bombay Company
Chromcraft Revington
DMI Furniture
Ethan Allen
Flexsteel
Kimball International
Klaussner Furniture Group
LADD Furniture
La-Z-Boy
LifeStyle Furnishings International
Masco
Pulaski Furniture
River Oaks Furniture
Room Plus
Rowe Companies
Sauder Woodworking
Stanley Furniture
Wellington Hall
WinsLoew Furniture

HISTORICAL FINANCIALS & EMPLOYEES

NYSE symbol: FBN FYE: December 31	Annual Growth	1989	1990	1991	1992	1993	1994	1995	1996	1997	1998
Sales ($ mil.)	1.9%	1,656	1,439	1,472	662	1,657	1,073	1,074	1,697	1,808	1,960
Net income ($ mil.)	—	(52)	(272)	(49)	21	45	38	28	47	67	98
Income as % of sales	—	—	—	—	3.2%	2.7%	3.6%	2.6%	2.8%	3.7%	5.0%
Earnings per share ($)	25.2%	—	—	—	—	—	0.74	0.56	0.76	1.15	1.82
Stock price - FY high ($)	—	—	—	—	—	—	8.38	9.25	15.00	21.50	34.13
Stock price - FY low ($)	—	—	—	—	—	—	6.13	5.50	8.25	13.63	12.94
Stock price - FY close ($)	41.7%	—	—	—	—	—	6.75	9.00	14.00	20.50	27.25
P/E - high	—	—	—	—	—	—	11	17	20	19	19
P/E - low	—	—	—	—	—	—	8	10	11	12	7
Dividends per share ($)	—	—	—	—	—	—	0.00	0.00	0.00	0.00	0.00
Book value per share ($)	9.8%	—	—	—	—	—	5.50	6.01	6.83	6.22	7.99
Employees	(10.1%)	54,000	22,100	19,800	19,750	20,045	20,400	20,700	20,800	20,700	20,700

STOCK PRICE HISTORY

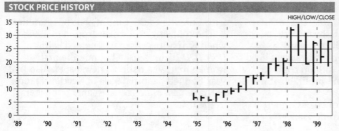

HIGH/LOW/CLOSE

1998 FISCAL YEAR-END

Debt ratio: 58.8%
Return on equity: 23.7%
Cash ($ mil.): 13
Current ratio: 4.05
Long-term debt ($ mil.): 589
No. of shares (mil.): 52
Dividends
  Yield: —
  Payout: —
Market value ($ mil.): 1,410

GANNETT CO., INC.

OVERVIEW

Gannett satisfies news junkies with a stash of nearly 90 papers. The Arlington, Virginia-based company is the nation's largest newspaper publisher; *USA TODAY*, Gannett's flagship paper, ranks second only to *The Wall Street Journal* in daily circulation (it is #1 if bulk sales to hotels and airports are included). Gannett's newspaper holdings include 75 dailies and boast a combined circulation of almost 7 million.

While newspapers generate about three-quarters of Gannett's revenue, the company also owns 21 TV stations. Multimedia Cable vision, Gannett's cable TV venture, provides cable services to 515,000 subscribers in Kansas,

Oklahoma, and North Carolina. (Gannett is selling Multimedia Cablevision to Cox Communications.) Gannett companies are also engaged in telemarketing, direct marketing, commercial printing, and advertising.

In the face of heightened competition brought about by the Internet, Gannett is branching into cyberspace. About 60 of its newspapers offer Web sites, and USATODAY.com has become a leader in online news delivery. It has also ventured outside the US through its purchase of 95% of UK newspaper publisher Newsquest (180 regional newspapers).

LOCATIONS

In 1906 Frank Gannett started building a newspaper empire when he and his associates purchased an interest in the *Elmira Gazette* (New York). In 1923 Gannett bought out his associates' interests and formed the Gannett Company. The company's history of technical innovation dates to the 1920s, when Frank Gannett invested in the development of the Teletypesetter; some of his newspapers were printing in color by 1938. His company continued to buy small and medium-sized dailies in the Northeast, and by the time Gannett died in 1957, the company had accumulated 30 newspapers.

In the 1960s Gannett expanded into a national newspaper chain as it kept acquiring local newspapers. It was not until 1966, however, that Gannett started its own newspaper, *TODAY* (now *FLORIDA TODAY*), in Cocoa Beach, Florida. Gannett went public in 1967.

The company went through its greatest expansion during the 1970s and 1980s under the direction of Allen Neuharth, who became CEO in 1973 and chairman in 1979. Gannett captured national attention in 1979 when it merged with Phoenix-based Combined Communications Corporation (CCC), another media conglomerate whose holdings included TV and radio stations, an outdoor advertising business, and the Louis Harris & Associates polling service.

In 1982 Gannett started *USA TODAY*, a national newspaper whose splashy format and mini-stories made it an industry novelty. Critics branded it "McPaper," but readers liked it, and circulation passed a million copies a day by the end of 1983. (It wasn't profitable until 1993, however.)

Neuharth retired as chairman of Gannett in 1989. In 1990 declines in newspaper

advertising, primarily among US retailers, broke the company's sequence of 89 consecutive quarters of earnings gains. USA TODAY-On-Demand, a fax news service, began in 1992. Gannett bought Multimedia Inc., a newspaper, TV, cable, and program syndication company, for about $2.3 billion in 1995. The purchase gave Gannett additional print and broadcast properties as well as an entry into cable TV.

USA TODAY Online, an electronic complement to *USA TODAY*, debuted in 1995. The next year Gannett teamed up with newspaper publisher Knight Ridder and privately held media firm Landmark Communications to form Internet service provider InfiNet. In 1996 Gannett sold pollster Louis Harris & Associates and its outdoor advertising operations and traded six radio stations to Jacor Communications for one Tampa TV station.

Gannett exited the radio industry in 1998 by selling its last five radio stations. That year it expanded its TV holdings through purchases of three stations in Maine and South Carolina. The company narrowed its focus by selling its Multimedia Security Service unit for $233 million. Gannett's integrity took a blow in 1998 when a reporter for one of its newspapers (*The Cincinnati Enquirer*) illegally obtained information for a report accusing Chiquita Brands International of unscrupulous business practices. Gannett retracted the story and settled with Chiquita to the tune of about $10 million.

The company broke new ground in 1999 when Karen Jurgensen was named editor of *USA TODAY*. Jurgensen became the first woman to head a national newspaper. Also that year Gannett acquired 95% of Newsquest, one of the largest regional newspaper publishers in the UK.

Chairman and CEO: John J. Curley, age 60,
$2,400,000 pay
VC and President: Douglas H. McCorkindale, age 59,
$2,225,000 pay
EVP and CFO: Larry F. Miller, age 60
**SVP Administration; President and Publisher, USA
TODAY:** Thomas Curley, age 50, $820,000 pay
SVP, Secretary, and General Counsel:
Thomas L. Chapple, age 51
SVP Human Resources: Richard L. Clapp, age 58
SVP Public Affairs and Government Relations:
Millicent A. Feller, age 51
SVP Labor Relations and Assistant General Counsel:
John B. Jaske, age 54
**Senior Group President, Gannett Pacific Newspaper
Group; President and Publisher, Reno (NV) Gazette-
Journal:** Susan Clark-Johnson, age 52
**Senior Group President, Gannett South Newspaper
Group; President and Publisher, FLORIDA TODAY:**
Michael J. Coleman, age 55
**Senior Group President, Gannett East Newspaper
Group; President and Publisher, The News Journal,
Wilmington, DE:** W. Curtis Riddle, age 47
VP Investor Relations and Treasurer: Gracia C. Martore,
age 46
Auditors: PricewaterhouseCoopers LLP

LOCATIONS

HQ: 1100 Wilson Blvd., Arlington, VA 22234
Phone: 703-284-6000   **Fax:** 703-558-4638
Web site: http://www.gannett.com

Gannett has operations in 45 US states, the District of
Columbia, Guam, and the UK.

PRODUCTS/OPERATIONS

1998 Sales

	$ mil.	% of total
Newspaper advertising	2,943	57
Newspaper circulation	1,010	20
Broadcasting	721	14
Cable & security	241	5
Other	206	4
Total	**5,121**	**100**

COMPETITORS

Advance Publications
Belo
Associated Press
AT&T Broadband &
  Internet Services
Bloomberg
CBS
Central Newspapers
Chronicle Publishing
Clear Channel
Comcast
Cox Enterprises
Dow Jones
E. W. Scripps
Freedom Communications
Hearst
Hollinger
Journal Communications

Knight Ridder
Landmark
  Communications
McClatchy Company
Media General
MediaNews
MediaOne Group
New York Times
News Corp.
Pulitzer
Reuters
Time Warner
  Entertainment
Times Mirror
Tribune
Viacom
Walt Disney
Washington Post

HISTORICAL FINANCIALS & EMPLOYEES

NYSE symbol: GCI FYE: December 31	Annual Growth	1989	1990	1991	1992	1993	1994	1995	1996	1997	1998
Sales ($ mil.)	4.3%	3,518	3,442	3,382	3,469	3,642	3,825	4,007	4,421	4,730	5,121
Net income ($ mil.)	10.8%	398	377	302	200	398	465	477	943	713	1,000
Income as % of sales	—	11.3%	11.0%	8.9%	5.8%	10.9%	12.2%	11.9%	21.3%	15.1%	19.5%
Earnings per share ($)	12.3%	1.23	1.17	0.99	0.69	1.35	1.60	1.69	3.33	2.50	3.50
Stock price - FY high ($)	—	24.94	22.25	23.50	27.00	29.13	29.50	32.44	39.38	61.81	75.13
Stock price - FY low ($)	—	17.25	14.75	17.56	20.63	23.38	23.06	24.75	29.50	35.69	47.63
Stock price - FY close ($)	12.8%	21.75	18.06	22.75	25.38	28.63	26.63	30.69	37.44	61.81	64.50
P/E - high	—	20	19	24	39	22	18	19	12	25	21
P/E - low	—	14	13	18	30	17	14	15	9	14	14
Dividends per share ($)	4.0%	0.54	0.60	0.62	0.63	0.65	0.67	0.69	0.71	0.73	0.77
Book value per share ($)	9.7%	6.20	6.49	5.35	5.47	6.49	6.52	7.63	10.37	12.26	14.26
Employees	0.8%	36,650	36,600	36,700	36,700	36,500	36,000	39,100	37,200	39,000	39,400

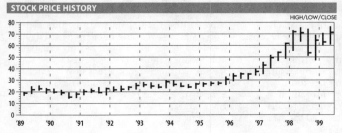

STOCK PRICE HISTORY — HIGH/LOW/CLOSE

1998 FISCAL YEAR-END
Debt ratio: 24.7%
Return on equity: 25.1%
Cash ($ mil.): 66
Current ratio: 1.25
Long-term debt ($ mil.): 1,307
No. of shares (mil.): 279
Dividends
  Yield: 1.2%
  Payout: 22.0%
Market value ($ mil.): 17,996

THE GAP, INC.

OVERVIEW

From infancy to affluence, The Gap has got you (or your body) covered. Based in San Francisco, the clothing company operates nearly 2,600 retail outlets under the names Gap, Gap-Kids, babyGap, GapBody, Banana Republic, and Old Navy Clothing Co. All of The Gap's merchandise is private label.

Lately the company has been the toast of the fashion retailing world, and Old Navy is a major reason. Started in 1994, Old Navy has quickly expanded to more than 400 locations. The outlets resemble upscale warehouses and offer casual family apparel at low prices and, at some locations, WWII-themed restaurants.

Also contributing to Gap's success is Banana Republic, which offers upscale clothing and accessories for the over-30 crowd. Both the Old Navy and Banana Republic divisions have been outperforming the three main Gap-branded chains. The company is also testing a format called GapBody, which offers casual intimate apparel and loungewear for men and women.

The Gap reaches international customers mainly through its Gap stores but plans to open more Banana Republic stores and introduce Old Navy overseas in coming years. Founders Donald and Doris Fisher own 21% of the company.

HISTORY

Donald Fisher and his wife, Doris, opened a small store in 1969 near what is now San Francisco State University. The couple named their store The Gap (after "the generation gap") and concentrated on selling Levi's jeans. The couple opened a second store in San Jose, California, eight months later, and by the end of 1970, there were six Gap stores. The Gap went public six years later.

In the beginning, the Fishers catered almost exclusively to teenagers, but in the 1970s they expanded into activewear that would appeal to a larger spectrum of customers. Nevertheless, by the early 1980s The Gap — which had grown to about 500 stores — was still dependent upon its largely teenage customer base. However, it was less dependent on Levi's (about 35% of sales), thanks to its growing stable of private labels.

In a 1983 effort to revamp the company's image, Donald hired Mickey Drexler, a former president of AnnTaylor with a spotless apparel industry track record, as The Gap's new president. Drexler immediately overhauled the motley clothing lines to concentrate on sturdy, brightly colored cotton clothing. He also consolidated the stores' many private clothing labels into the Gap brand. As a final touch, Drexler replaced circular clothing racks with white shelving so clothes could be neatly stacked and displayed.

Also in 1983 The Gap bought Banana Republic, a unique chain of jungle-themed stores that sold safari clothing. The company expanded the chain, which enjoyed tremendous success in the mid-1980s but slumped after the novelty of the stores wore off late in the decade. In response, Drexler introduced a broader range of clothes (including higher-priced leather items) and dumped the safari

lines in 1988. By 1990 Banana Republic was again profitable.

The first GapKids opened in 1985 after Drexler couldn't find clothing that he liked for his son. During the late 1980s and early 1990s, the company grew rapidly, opening its first stores in Canada and the UK. In 1990 it introduced babyGap in 25 GapKids stores, featuring miniature versions of its GapKids line. The Gap announced in 1991 it would no longer sell Levi's (which had fallen to less than 2% of total sales) and would go completely private label.

Earnings fell in fiscal 1993 because of Gap division losses brought on by low margins and high rents. The company shuffled management positions and titles as part of a streamlining effort. It rebounded in 1994, by concentrating on improving profit margins rather than sales and by launching Old Navy Clothing Co., named after a bar Drexler saw in Paris.

Banana Republic launched a line of bath and body products and opened its first two stores outside the US, both in Canada, in 1995.

Robert Fisher (the founders' son) became the new president of the Gap division (including babyGap and GapKids) in 1997 and was charged with reversing the segment's sales decline. The company refocused its Gap chain on basics (jeans, T-shirts, and khakis) and helped boost its performance with a high-profile advertising campaign focusing on those wares. Later in 1997 the Gap opened an online Gap store. The next year the retailer opened its first GapBody stores, introduced its only catalog (for Banana Republic), and opened a Torpedo Joe's restaurant—reminiscent of WWII mess halls—in an Old Navy flagship. The Gap plans to open 450 stores in 1999, including about 100 overseas.

OFFICERS

Chairman: Donald G. Fisher, age 70, $1,072,155 pay
President and CEO: Millard S. "Mickey" Drexler, age 54, $7,311,870 pay
COO: John B. Wilson, age 39, $2,259,000 pay
EVP and CFO: Heidi Kunz
EVP Supply Chain and Technology: Charles K. Crovitz, age 45, $1,009,245 pay
EVP; President, Gap Division: Robert J. Fisher, age 44, $3,005,271 pay
EVP Human Resources, Legal, and Corporate Administration: Anne B. Gust, age 41
SVP - Finance and Strategy: Warren R. Hashagen Jr., age 48
CEO, Banana Republic: Jeanne Jackson
President, International: Ken S. Pilot, age 38
Auditors: Deloitte & Touche LLP

LOCATIONS

HQ: 1 Harrison St., San Francisco, CA 94105
Phone: 415-427-2000   **Fax:** 650-874-7815
Web site: http://www.gapinc.com

The Gap sells casual apparel, shoes, and personal care items through nearly 2,600 stores in Canada, France, Germany, Japan, the UK, and the US.

PRODUCTS/OPERATIONS

1999 Stores

	No.
Gap	1,109
GapKids/babyGap	640
Old Navy Clothing Co.	407
Banana Republic	292
Total	**2,448**

Stores
babyGap (clothing for infants and toddlers)
Banana Republic (upscale clothing)
Gap (casual and active clothing)
GapBody (intimate apparel)
GapKids (clothing for children)
Old Navy Clothing Co. (lower-priced family clothing)

COMPETITORS

Abercrombie & Fitch	L.L. Bean
American Eagle Outfitters	May
Benetton	Nautica Enterprises
Bugle Boy	NIKE
Calvin Klein	Nordstrom
Dayton Hudson	OshKosh B'Gosh
Dillard's	Phillips-Van Heusen
Esprit de Corp.	Polo
Federated	Reebok
Fruit of the Loom	Saks Inc.
Guess?	Sears
Gymboree	Spiegel
J. C. Penney	TJX
J. Crew	Toys "R" Us
Lands' End	Venator Group
Levi Strauss	VF
The Limited	Wal-Mart

HISTORICAL FINANCIALS & EMPLOYEES

NYSE symbol: GPS FYE: January 31	Annual Growth	1990	1991	1992	1993	1994	1995	1996	1997	1998	1999
Sales ($ mil.)	21.4%	1,587	1,934	2,519	2,960	3,296	3,723	4,395	5,284	6,508	9,055
Net income ($ mil.)	26.8%	98	145	230	211	258	320	354	453	534	825
Income as % of sales	—	6.2%	7.5%	9.1%	7.1%	7.8%	8.6%	8.1%	8.6%	8.2%	9.1%
Earnings per share ($)	27.8%	0.10	0.15	0.24	0.22	0.27	0.33	0.37	0.47	0.58	0.91
Stock price - FY high ($)	—	2.28	3.17	8.81	8.35	6.36	7.33	7.57	10.83	18.35	43.36
Stock price - FY low ($)	—	1.31	1.45	2.97	4.17	3.78	4.28	4.41	6.88	8.49	17.57
Stock price - FY close ($)	42.8%	1.73	3.15	7.90	5.12	6.27	4.82	6.99	8.53	17.38	42.81
P/E - high	—	23	21	37	38	24	22	20	23	32	48
P/E - low	—	13	10	12	19	14	13	12	15	15	19
Dividends per share ($)	13.0%	0.03	0.03	0.05	0.05	0.06	0.07	0.07	0.09	0.09	0.09
Book value per share ($)	20.0%	0.36	0.49	0.71	0.91	1.15	1.41	1.69	1.79	1.79	1.84
Employees	19.1%	23,000	26,000	32,000	39,000	44,000	55,000	60,000	66,000	81,000	111,000

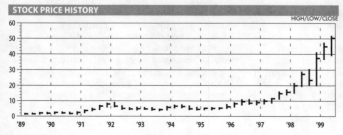

STOCK PRICE HISTORY
HIGH/LOW/CLOSE

1999 FISCAL YEAR-END

Debt ratio: 24.0%
Return on equity: 52.4%
Cash ($ mil.): 565
Current ratio: 1.21
Long-term debt ($ mil.): 497
No. of shares (mil.): 858
Dividends
  Yield: 0.2%
  Payout: 9.9%
Market value ($ mil.): 36,711

GATEWAY, INC.

OVERVIEW

Gateway is taking the straw out from behind its ears. The San Diego-based maker of PCs is #2 in the US, behind Dell, in direct computer marketing (a process that offers products directly to computer users ordering by phone or Web site, cutting markup costs and releasing new technology faster). The company also makes big-screen PCTVs, software, and peripherals for consumers (who account for more than half of sales) and businesses worldwide. Subsidiary Amiga is developing information appliances using the resilient, graphics-fueled Amiga PC technology. Gateway continues to move beyond its colorful bumpkin roots to establish a stronger industry presence.

When a push into the corporate market

fizzled under weak global sales, Gateway refocused efforts on its traditional small business and techno-savvy consumer customers, pushing training and other Internet services through its nearly 200 US Gateway Country technology test-drive showrooms.

To be taken more seriously, the company relocated its headquarters from South Dakota to high-tech California, changed its name (from Gateway 2000), played down its recognizable PC boxes (spotted like Holstein cows), and created an Internet access service (gateway.net), among other investments.

Laid-back chairman, CEO, and founder Ted Waitt owns 41% of Gateway.

HISTORY

Apparently college and billion-dollar PC retailers don't mix. Like his main competitor, Michael Dell, Ted Waitt dropped out of college to get into the computer business. Waitt had gone to Des Moines, Iowa, to see his roommates' band one weekend. He met a friend who was working for a computer retailer, liked the sound of the job, and left school to go to work. After nine months of on-the-job training, he quit to start his own company.

Using his grandmother's certificate of deposit as collateral, Waitt borrowed $10,000 and in 1985 set up shop in the South Dakota barn of his father, a fourth-generation cattleman. There, with his brother Norm and friend Mike Hammond, he founded the TIPC Network, which sold add-on parts by phone for Texas Instruments' PCs. However, Ted's goal was to sell PCs himself, and in 1987 the three men jumped into the fray. Ted and Hammond put together a fully configured computer system at a price that was near what other companies were charging for a bare-bones system; sales took off. The next year they changed the enterprise's name to Gateway 2000 to express the belief that their computers were the gateway to the 21st century.

The company's customer base was made up of sophisticated buyers willing to dig through catalogs to find the best price for the exact system they wanted, and much of the firm's success was rooted in Ted's ability to predict which standard features customers would want.

Gateway distinguished itself from competitors with eye-catching ads. Some featured cows, while others featured Gateway employees. His idea was to convince potential customers that if they bought a Gateway

computer, the firm would be around in the future to service it.

In 1990 Gateway moved to North Sioux City, South Dakota. Two years later Gateway introduced a line of notebook computers and created a new division to handle component add-ons. Gateway went public in 1993, and opened a manufacturing and service facility in Ireland. In 1994 it added retail showrooms in Europe.

In 1995 Gateway expanded into Australia when it purchased 80% of the country's largest computer maker. Gateway introduced a cross between a PC and a big-screen TV (called a PCTV) in 1996 and opened two US retail stores, modeled after those in Europe.

The next year Ted, balking at the thought of his staff becoming subordinate to Compaq's management, rejected a $7 billion takeover bid. Also in 1997 Gateway acquired corporate server manufacturer Advanced Logic Research (ALR) and the technology rights to the venerated Amiga, one of the industry's earliest PCs. Inventory excesses and a charge for the ALR buy caused earnings to decline in 1997.

Gateway dropped the "2000" from its name in 1998 to avoid appearing behind the times as the millennium approached. In a bolder move that year, Gateway established an agreement with Microsoft whereby Gateway customizes Windows 98 to promote its own Internet service (gateway.net) over the services of Microsoft-connected providers. Gateway in 1999 expanded its Web presence by investing in Internet sales specialist NECX to create an online peripherals store. It also formed an alliance with Internet investment powerhouse CMGI and made a $200 million investment in that company.

OFFICERS

Chairman and CEO: Theodore W. Waitt, age 36
President and COO: Jeffrey Weitzen, age 42
EVP and Chief Administrative Officer: David J. Robino, age 39
SVP and Chief Marketing Officer: Anil Arora, age 38
SVP; Regional Managing Director, Europe, Middle East, and Africa: R. Todd Bradley, age 40
SVP, Corporate Secretary, and General Counsel: William M. Elliott, age 64
SVP; Regional Managing Director, Asia Pacific: Frank Smilovic, age 49
SVP and CFO: John J. Todd, age 38
SVP and Chief Information Officer: James Pollard
SVP, Gateway Business: Van M. Andrews, age 47
SVP, Gateway Financial Services: Robert M. Spears
SVP, Gateway Products: Peter B. Ashkin, age 47
SVP, Global Business Development: Joseph J. Burke, age 41
SVP, Manufacturing: Michael D. Hammond, age 37
SVP, Strategy and New Ventures: Daniel E. Pittard
VP, Administration: Sandra Lawrence
VP, Global Human Resources: Gary Glandon
VP, Global Operations: Michael Dunne
VP, Manufacturing Operations: Bernard F. Ebert
VP, Marketing, Gateway Home: Bart Brown
Auditors: PricewaterhouseCoopers LLP

LOCATIONS

HQ: 610 Gateway Dr., North Sioux City, SD 57049
Phone: 605-232-2000   **Fax:** 605-232-2023
Web site: http://www.gateway.com

Gateway has manufacturing plants in Malaysia and the US, and other facilities in Australia, Austria, France, Germany, Hong Kong, Ireland, Japan, the Netherlands, New Zealand, Singapore, Sweden, and the UK.

1998 Sales

	$ mil.	% of total
US	6,413	86
Europe	570	8
Asia/Pacific	485	6
Total	**7,468**	**100**

PRODUCTS/OPERATIONS

Products

Add-On Products
Peripherals
CD-ROM drives
Fax modems
Monitors
Printers
Software (AmigaOS operating system)

Internet Access
gateway.net

Personal Computers
Desktops (Gateway Performance, Select, Essential, E-Series, and GP-Series lines)
PCTVs
Portables
Servers

COMPETITORS

Acer	Hewlett-Packard
America Online	IBM
Apple Computer	Micron Technology
Auspex Systems	Packard Bell
CNET	Sequent
Compaq	Texas Instruments
Dell Computer	Toshiba
Excite@Home	WebTV
Fujitsu	Yahoo!

HISTORICAL FINANCIALS & EMPLOYEES

NYSE symbol: GTW FYE: December 31	Annual Growth	1989	1990	1991	1992	1993	1994	1995	1996	1997	1998
Sales ($ mil.)	67.7%	71	276	627	1,107	1,732	2,701	3,676	5,035	6,294	7,468
Net income ($ mil.)	64.2%	4	17	39	106	151	96	173	251	110	346
Income as % of sales	—	5.6%	6.2%	6.2%	9.6%	8.7%	3.6%	4.7%	5.0%	1.7%	4.6%
Earnings per share ($)	25.2%	—	—	—	—	0.71	0.61	1.09	1.60	0.70	2.18
Stock price - FY high ($)	—	—	—	—	—	10.75	12.38	18.75	33.13	46.25	68.75
Stock price - FY low ($)	—	—	—	—	—	8.38	4.63	8.00	9.00	23.56	31.00
Stock price - FY close ($)	39.2%	—	—	—	—	9.81	10.81	12.25	26.78	32.75	51.19
P/E - high	—	—	—	—	—	15	20	17	21	66	32
P/E - low	—	—	—	—	—	12	8	7	6	34	14
Dividends per share ($)	—	—	—	—	—	0.00	0.00	0.00	0.00	0.00	0.00
Book value per share ($)	34.7%	—	—	—	—	1.94	2.60	3.73	5.31	6.03	8.59
Employees	71.5%	150	303	657	1,369	2,832	5,442	9,300	9,700	13,300	19,300

STOCK PRICE HISTORY

High/Low/Close

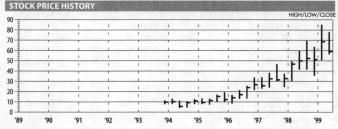

1998 FISCAL YEAR-END

Debt ratio: 0.3%
Return on equity: 25.8%
Cash ($ mil.): 1,170
Current ratio: 1.56
Long-term debt ($ mil.): 3
No. of shares (mil.): 157
Dividends
  Yield: —
  Payout: —
Market value ($ mil.): 8,015

HOOVER'S HANDBOOK OF AMERICAN BUSINESS 2000   **649**

GATX CORPORATION

OVERVIEW

GATX gets around. The Chicago-based holding company operates in five business segments: financial services, railcar leasing and management, bulk-liquid terminals and pipelines, logistics and warehousing, and Great Lakes shipping.

GATX Capital (34% of sales) leases railcars, locomotives, commercial and corporate jets, and information technology equipment. The company also provides asset-based financing and manages lease portfolios for third parties. Also in the leasing business is GATX's General American Transportation (29% of sales), one of the leading US lessors of railway tank cars. Its fleet includes nearly 100,000 cars.

Other units include GATX Terminals, which stores, handles, and transfers products for oil,

chemical, and other companies. It has 15 terminals in eight US states, four pipeline systems, and interests in 13 joint ventures in Asia, Europe, and Mexico. GATX Logistics, a major third-party provider of distribution and logistics support services for manufacturers and retailers in the US, has about 100 warehousing facilities. The 11 self-unloading vessels of GATX's American Steamship Company serve the steel, electric utility, and construction industries on the Great Lakes.

GATX has sold underperforming terminals in the UK and the US to streamline operations. To build its aircraft leasing business, the company has formed partnerships with Swissair, Gulfstream Aerospace, and Rolls Royce & Partners Finance.

HISTORY

Max Epstein, a worker in the Chicago Stockyards, founded the Atlantic Seaboard Dispatch in 1898. He used the $1,000 commission he received for arranging the sale of 20 old railway freight cars as a down payment to purchase 28 cars for himself. In 1902 he incorporated the firm as the German-American Car Co., which became the first to lease specialty railcars on a long-term basis.

By 1907 Epstein had 433 railway cars and had begun to specialize in building customized freight cars. In 1916 the firm offered stock under the name General American Tank Car (GATC); its railcars carried the initials GATX (the "X" meant that a car belonged to a private line). In 1925 GATC began a bulk-liquid storage business, which became GATX Terminals.

Epstein purchased 13 firms between 1926 and 1931. The Depression was good to GATC: Epstein declared that conditions allowed him to make better deals, and the petroleum and food hauled in GATC cars were always in demand, despite economic pressures. By the 1940s the company was the US's largest freight-car lessor. It also owned the US's largest public liquid-storage terminal facility and had begun operating cargo ships on the Great Lakes.

The company was the US's fourth-largest maker of freight cars by 1952. In 1954 GATC acquired Fuller Co., a builder of cement plants, which produced steady profits until its sale in 1986.

In 1968 GATC formed GATX Leasing, an airplane lessor (later GATX Capital, a principal subsidiary of GATX Financial Services). That year, as the demand for railcars plummeted,

the firm reduced manufacturing and began refocusing. In 1973 GATC acquired American Steamship, which helped expand its role in Great Lakes shipping. The company changed its name to GATX Corporation in 1975.

GATX exited manufacturing and became more service-oriented in the 1980s by expanding its railcar and aircraft fleets and bulk-liquid storage operations. It narrowly escaped several takeover attempts. GATX Terminals expanded rapidly toward the end of the 1980s.

The firm purchased Associated Unit Companies in 1989 (later the Unit Companies and then GATX Logistics) and Sealand Oil Services Ltd. (Scotland) in 1993. It continued to expand overseas by forming a joint venture with EnviroLease in 1994 to provide equipment for moving wastes and recyclables.

In 1995 the company leased the 1,200-tank-car fleet of Mexico's state-owned railroad, and the following year it bought a 65% stake in a bulk-liquid storage facility in Altamira, Mexico.

CEO James Glasser, head of GATX since 1978, turned over the reins to Ronald Zech in 1996. The next year mailing-machine maker Pitney Bowes sold part of its lease portfolio to GATX and put other equipment in a joint venture with the company.

A restructuring charge stemming mainly from the revaluation of GATX Terminals assets led to an overall loss for 1997. The company began moving that year to sell poorly performing terminals, and by 1999 it had sold six of its terminals in the UK.

OFFICERS

Chairman, President, and CEO: Ronald H. Zech, age 55, $1,073,057 pay
SVP and CFO: David M. Edwards, age 47, $493,333 pay
SVP Customer Solutions: Todd Carter
VP Corporate Development, General Counsel, and Secretary: David B. Anderson, age 57, $503,460 pay
VP Implementation Services: Todd Benton
VP Human Resources: William L. Chambers, age 61, $370,346 pay
VP Compensation, Benefits, and Corporate Human Resources: Gail L. Duddy, age 46
VP Finance: Brian A. Kenney, age 39, $291,155 pay
Controller and Chief Accounting Officer: Ralph L. O'Hara, age 54
VP of Corporate Strategy: Clifford Porzenheim, age 35
VP Locomotive Marketing: Al Smith
Treasurer: William Hasek
President, General American Transportation: D. Ward Fuller
President, GATX Capital: Jesse V. Crews
President, GATX Terminals: Anthony J. Andrukaitis
President, GATX Logistics: Joseph A. Nicosia
President, American Steamship: Ned A. Smith
Managing Director, GATX Liquid Logistics: Stephen H. Fraser
Auditors: Ernst & Young LLP

LOCATIONS

HQ: 500 W. Monroe St., Chicago, IL 60661-3676
Phone: 312-621-6200   **Fax:** 312-621-6698
Web site: http://www.gatx.com

PRODUCTS/OPERATIONS

1998 Sales & Operating Income

	Sales		Operating Income	
	$ mil.	% of total	$ mil.	% of total
Financial services	597	34	64	33
Railcar leasing & management	514	29	106	54
Terminals & pipelines	290	17	12	6
Logistics & warehousing	273	15	3	1
Great Lakes shipping	87	5	11	6
Other	5	—	(31)	—
Adjustments	(3)	—	(2)	—
Total	**1,763**	**100**	**163**	**—**

Primary Operations and Subsidiaries
Financial Services (GATX Capital Corporation)
Railcar Leasing and Management (General American Transportation Corporation)
Terminals and Pipelines (GATX Terminals Corporation)
Logistics and Warehousing (GATX Logistics, Inc.)
Great Lakes Shipping (American Steamship Company)

COMPETITORS

CHR	Newcourt Credit
CNF Transportation	NFC
CSX	Oglebay Norton
GE	Pakhoed
General Motors	Ryder
Greenbrier	Transtar
Johnstown America	Trinity Industries
Marmon Group	TTX
MidAmerican Energy	Van Ommeren

HISTORICAL FINANCIALS & EMPLOYEES

NYSE symbol: GMT FYE: December 31	Annual Growth	1989	1990	1991	1992	1993	1994	1995	1996	1997	1998
Sales ($ mil.)	10.8%	702	870	989	1,019	1,087	1,155	1,233	1,414	1,702	1,763
Net income ($ mil.)	8.1%	66	83	83	(17)	73	92	101	103	(51)	132
Income as % of sales	—	9.4%	9.5%	8.4%	—	6.7%	7.9%	8.2%	7.3%	—	7.5%
Earnings per share ($)	5.7%	1.59	1.77	1.76	(0.77)	1.52	1.90	2.07	2.10	(1.28)	2.62
Stock price - FY high ($)	—	18.94	17.88	20.13	16.88	21.13	22.31	27.13	25.63	36.69	47.56
Stock price - FY low ($)	—	13.38	8.81	10.75	12.13	15.69	19.13	20.19	21.50	23.75	26.25
Stock price - FY close ($)	9.3%	17.00	12.94	14.38	16.56	20.38	22.00	24.31	24.25	36.28	37.88
P/E - high	—	12	10	11	—	14	12	13	12	—	18
P/E - low	—	8	5	6	—	10	10	10	10	—	10
Dividends per share ($)	3.2%	0.75	0.55	0.60	0.65	0.70	0.77	0.80	0.86	0.92	1.00
Book value per share ($)	1.4%	13.18	14.48	15.71	14.21	14.66	16.56	17.77	19.03	13.39	14.89
Employees	6.2%	3,500	4,200	5,100	5,100	5,500	5,800	5,900	6,000	6,000	6,000

STOCK PRICE HISTORY

HIGH/LOW/CLOSE

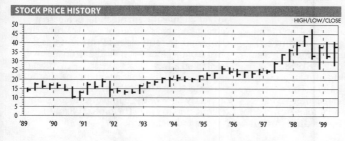

1998 FISCAL YEAR-END

Debt ratio: 79.4%
Return on equity: 18.0%
Cash ($ mil.): 95
Current ratio: 1.46
Long-term debt ($ mil.): 2,822
No. of shares (mil.): 49
Dividends
  Yield: 2.6%
  Payout: 38.2%
Market value ($ mil.): 1,864

GENENTECH, INC.

OVERVIEW

At Genentech the double helix has become a double-edged sword. Although the San Francisco-based company has several drug-development victories based on its recombinant DNA technology, it has also suffered defeats in the lab and the courtroom. Eight Genentech drugs are sold in the US; international sales are made by drug giant Hoffmann-La Roche, a subsidiary of Swiss druggernaut Roche Holding. After buying all outstanding shares and then spinning off 16% of Genentech, Roche Holding now owns 84%.

Its top seller is Activase, a blood-clot treatment for heart-attack victims. Other products include Herceptin (breast cancer), Protropin and Nutropin (growth hormone-related conditions), Pulmozyme (cystic fibrosis), and

Rituxan (non-Hodgkin's lymphoma). Genentech is developing antibodies to treat asthma and is testing new uses for its existing drugs. Genentech spends about one-third of its annual revenues on R&D.

While Activase has lost market share to competitors and to angioplasty (surgery that clears blood vessels), Rituxan's sales have rocketed since its 1997 FDA approval. Genentech's pipeline contains about a dozen drugs, some being developed with companies such as Pharmacia & Upjohn. The development of a drug for diabetics was halted when Genentech discovered it was not effective. The drugmaker's legal woes include a $50 million fine for overzealous marketing and a University of California lawsuit alleging patent infringement.

HISTORY

Venture capitalist Robert Swanson and molecular biologist Herbert Boyer founded Genentech in 1976 to commercialize Boyer's patented gene-splicing techniques that could mass-produce genetically-engineered substances. The company went public in 1980.

Genentech's market debut (the first FDA-approved biotech product) was a bioengineered form of human insulin, OK'd in 1982. Eli Lilly bought the license and sold it as Humulin. Genentech sold marketing rights for royalties and focused on research; the company next developed the human immune-system protein alpha interferon and licensed it to Hoffmann-La Roche, which sold the cancer treatment as Roferon-A. The first product to bear the Genentech name was its human growth hormone, Protropin, approved by the FDA in 1985.

After five years and $200 million, Genentech released Activase in 1988. Its $180 million in sales was the largest first-year take of any new drug at the time. The company won a patent infringement suit over US rights to Activase in 1990.

Roche Holding bought 60% of Genentech for $2.1 billion that year, including nearly $500 million to maintain the long-term research pipeline. In 1993 Genentech and Merck developed a compound to prevent activation of the RAS oncogene, which triggers cancerous cells in the pancreas, colon, and lung. Merck began human tests of anti-RAS drugs in 1998.

Genentech began shipping human growth hormone Nutropin in early 1994. The next year CEO Kirk Rabb was ousted after trying to secure a $2 million personal loan from Roche. Rabb was replaced by scientists Arthur

Levinson (seen as a sign of Roche's R&D commitment). That year the two companies signed an agreement that gave Roche Genentech's Canadian and European operations, with a provision allowing Roche to buy the rest of the company by mid-1999.

After spending $100 million in 10 years on AIDS-related research, in 1996 Genentech formed a separate company to develop its sidetracked HIV vaccine gp120. That year the FDA approved Activase for use as the first effective treatment for acute stroke, and in 1998 approved Rituxan (developed with IDEC Pharmaceuticals) to treat lymphoma. Rituxan is a monoclonal antibody, the first of its kind to be approved as a cancer treatment. That year the FDA also approved breast cancer drug Herceptin.

The next year saw the demise of Neuleze, a once-promising formulation designed to treat diabetes-related nerve damage (it didn't work); the company could take comfort in the accolades pouring in for Herceptin and the skyrocketing sales of Rituxan. Meanwhile, charges that Genentech marketed human growth hormone for non-approved uses led to a federal court fine of $50 million. That amount may be pocket change if Genentech loses a patent-infringement case brought by the University of California; the suit claims Protropin was developed from a cloned gene lifted from a university lab on a New Year's Eve some two decades ago. Also in 1999, Roche bought the shares of Genentech that it didn't own and then spun off nearly 20% of the company. Roche plans to continue to allow the biotech firm to operate independently.

OFFICERS

President, CEO, and Chairman: Arthur D. Levinson,
age 49, $1,600,000 pay
COO: William D. Young, age 54, $830,000 pay
EVP and CFO: Louis J. Lavigne Jr., age 51, $660,000 pay
SVP Development and Chief Medical Officer:
Susan D. Desmond-Hellmann, age 41, $620,000 pay
SVP Research: Dennis J. Henner, age 48, $471,979 pay
SVP Human Resources: Judith A. Heyboer, age 49
SVP General Counsel and Secretary:
Stephen G. Juelsgaard, age 50
VP Process Sciences: W. Robert Arathoon, age 47
VP Research Discovery: Joffre B. Baker, age 51
VP Quality: J. Joseph Barta, age 51
VP Medical Affairs: Stephen G. Dilly, age 40
VP Product Development: David Ebersman, age 29
VP Regulatory Affairs: Robert L. Garnick, age 49
VP Finance: Bradford S. Goodwin, age 44
VP Pharmacological Sciences: Paula M. Jardieu, age 48
VP Corporate Development: Edmon R. Jennings, age 52
VP Intellectual Property: Sean A. Johnston, age 40
VP Government Affairs: Walter K. Moore, age 47
VP Sales: Kimberly J. Popovits, age 40
Controller and Chief Accounting Officer:
John M. Whiting, age 44
Auditors: Ernst & Young LLP

LOCATIONS

HQ: 1 DNA Way, South San Francisco, CA 94080-4990
Phone: 650-225-1000   **Fax:** 650-225-6000
Web site: http://www.gene.com

PRODUCTS/OPERATIONS

1998 Sales

	$ mil.	% of total
Product sales		
Growth hormones	214	20
Activase	213	20
Rituxan	162	15
Pulmozyme	94	9
Herceptin	31	3
Actimmune	4	1
Royalties	229	21
Contract & other	115	11
Total	**1,062**	**100**

Selected Products
Actimmune (chronic granulomatous disease)
Activase (heart attacks, ischemic stroke)
Herceptin (breast cancer)
Nutropin (human growth hormone)
Protropin (human growth hormone)
Pulmozyme (cystic fibrosis)
Rituxan (non-Hodgkin's lymphoma)

Selected Licensed Products
Engerix-B (hepatitis B vaccine)
Humatrope (human growth hormone)
Humulin (human insulin)
Kogenate (factor VIII)
Posilac (bovine growth hormone)
Recombivax (hepatitis B vaccine)
Roferon-A (recombinant interferon alpha)

COMPETITORS

Abbott Labs
American Home Products
Amgen
Bayer AG
Biogen
Bristol-Myers Squibb
Chiron
DuPont
Eli Lilly
Genzyme
Glaxo Wellcome
Hoechst AG
Immunex
Johnson & Johnson
Merck
Novartis
Novo Nordisk A/S
Pfizer
Pharmacia & Upjohn
Rhône-Poulenc
Schering-Plough
SmithKline Beecham

HISTORICAL FINANCIALS & EMPLOYEES

NYSE symbol: DNA FYE: December 31	Annual Growth	1989	1990	1991	1992	1993	1994	1995	1996	1997	1998
Sales ($ mil.)	12.0%	383	447	467	544	650	753	857	905	948	1,062
Net income ($ mil.)	17.1%	44	(98)	44	21	59	124	146	118	129	182
Income as % of sales	—	11.5%	—	9.5%	3.8%	9.1%	16.5%	17.1%	13.1%	13.6%	17.1%
Employees	7.4%	1,790	1,923	2,202	2,331	2,510	2,738	2,842	3,071	3,242	3,389

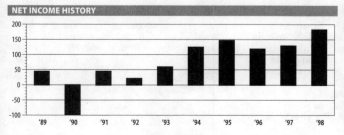

NET INCOME HISTORY

1998 FISCAL YEAR-END
Debt ratio: 6.0%
Return on equity: 7.8%
Cash ($ mil.): 281
Current ratio: 4.26
Long-term debt ($ mil.): 150

Genentech, Inc.
Genentech, Inc.
Genentech, Inc.
Genentech, Inc.

GENERAL DYNAMICS CORPORATION

OVERVIEW

After losing weight during some lean years, General Dynamics is gaining again — but insists it's all muscle. Through acquisitions, the Falls Church, Virginia-based defense supplier is venturing into systems integration and moving back into aviation. The company now operates in four primary areas: aviation (business jets), combat systems (tanks and amphibious assault vehicles), marine (warships and nuclear submarines), and information systems and technology (command and control systems). A group led by investor Warren Buffett owns about 6% of the company, and director Charles Goodman controls about 13%.

General Dynamics, which derives more than 80% of its revenue from the US government, is the US's top military shipbuilder. The company's Bath Iron Works subsidiary builds the Navy's class DDG 51 destroyers. Another subsidiary, Electric Boat, builds Seawolf class attack subs. The company's Land Systems subsidiary builds the M1 series tank.

The company has expanded into defense-related electronics after shedding its aircraft, missile, electronics, and space systems in the early 1990s due to post-Cold War defense cutbacks. The company's purchase of business-jet maker Gulfstream Aerospace moved it back into the aviation business.

HISTORY

In 1899 John Holland founded Electric Boat Company, a New Jersey ship and submarine builder. The company built ships, PT boats, and submarines during WWII, but faced with waning postwar orders, CEO John Jay Hopkins diversified with the 1947 purchase of aircraft builder Canadair. Hopkins formed General Dynamics in 1952, merging Electric Boat and Canadair and buying Consolidated Vultee Aircraft (Convair), a major producer of military and civilian aircraft, in 1954.

Electric Boat launched the first nuclear submarine, the *Nautilus,* in the mid-1950s. In 1955, at the urging of Howard Hughes, Convair began designing its first commercial jetliners. Weakened by the jetliners' production costs, General Dynamics merged with building-materials supplier Material Service Corporation (1959). Nuclear subs became a mainstay for the company, and it abandoned jetliners in 1961 after losses on the planes reached the staggering sum of $425 million.

During the 1960s General Dynamics developed the controversial F-111 fighter. Despite numerous problems, the aircraft proved financially and militarily successful (F-111s participated in the 1986 US bombing raid on Libya).

David Lewis became CEO in 1970. Under Lewis, the company won contracts for the US Navy's 688-class attack submarine (1971), liquefied natural gas tankers for Burmah Oil Company (1972), the Trident ballistic-missile submarine (1974), and the F-16 lightweight fighter aircraft (1975). The company sold Canadair in 1976 and bought Chrysler Defense, which had a contract to build the US Army's new M1 tank, in 1982. Lewis retired in 1985 amid federal investigations of overcharges to the government. The charges were dropped in 1996, and the US was ordered to pay the company $25 million in legal fees.

Under CEO Stanley Pace, the company bought Cessna Aircraft in 1986. The next year it won a contract to design and build the upper stage of the Titan IV space-launch rocket. In 1991 former astronaut William Anders became CEO. Facing defense cuts, Anders sold pieces of the company, including Cessna Aircraft (1992, to Textron), its missile operations (1992, to Hughes Aircraft), and its electronics business (1993, to the Carlyle Group).

Anders retired as CEO in 1993 and president James Mellor succeeded him. Mellor sold the company's space-systems business to Martin Marietta in 1994 before beginning a buying spree. General Dynamics bought shipbuilder Bath Iron Works (1995), Teledyne's combat vehicle unit (1996), Lockheed Martin's Defense Systems and Armament Systems units (1997), and defense electronics units from Ceridian and Lucent.

In 1998 it acquired National Steel and Shipbuilding to gain a major naval shipyard on the West Coast. In early 1999 the company made a $2 billion bid to buy rival submarine and warship maker Newport News Shipbuilding. The Pentagon rejected the deal, however, citing concerns that it would create a near monopoly in Navy shipbuilding. To strengthen its information systems business, General Dynamics bought GTE's military communications, electronic systems, and worldwide telecommunications services divisions in 1999. Also that year, General Dynamics bought business jet maker Gulfstream Aerospace.

Chairman and CEO: Nicholas D. Chabraja, age 56,
$2,100,000 pay
President and COO: James E. Turner Jr., age 64,
$1,125,000 pay
EVP: Gordon R. England, age 61, $800,000 pay
SVP and CFO: Michael J. Mancuso, age 56,
$675,000 pay
SVP, Law and Secretary: David A. Savner, age 54,
$550,000 pay
**SVP International, Planning, and Business
Development:** Michael W. Wynne, age 54
VP Government Relations: G. Kent Bankus, age 56
VP; President of Bath Iron Works: Allan C. Cameron,
age 52
**VP; President of General Dynamics Information
Systems:** James I. Finley, age 52
VP and Treasurer: David H. Fogg, age 43
VP Information Technology: Kenneth A. Hill, age 49
VP; President, Armament Systems: Linda P. Hudson,
age 48
VP; President of Armament Systems:
Kenneth J. Leenstra, age 61
VP; President of Advanced Technology Systems:
Charles E. McQueary, age 59
VP Human Resources and Administration:
W. Peter Wylie, age 59
Auditors: Arthur Andersen LLP

HQ: 3190 Fairview Park Dr.,
Falls Church, VA 22042-4523
Phone: 703-876-3000   **Fax:** 703-876-3125
Web site: http://www.gendyn.com

1998 Sales

	$ mil.	% of total
Marine		
Nuclear submarines	1,381	28
Surface combatants	936	19
Other marine	349	7
Combat systems		
Armored vehicles	915	18
Ordnance	257	5
Other combat	100	2
Information technology		
Communications systems	214	4
Avionics	204	4
Commercial	132	3
Maritime	110	2
Other information technology	136	3
Other	236	3
Total	**4,970**	**100**

Airbus	Newport News
Boeing	Shipbuilding
Bombardier	Peugeot
Dassault Aviation	Racal Electronics
Harris Corporation	Raytheon
Harsco	Renco
ITT Industries	Textron
Litton Industries	Titan
L-3 Communications	United Defense Industries
Lockheed Martin	Vickers
Marine Management	Westwood
Systems	

NYSE symbol: GD FYE: December 31	Annual Growth	1989	1990	1991	1992	1993	1994	1995	1996	1997	1998
Sales ($ mil.)	(7.5%)	10,043	10,173	8,751	3,472	3,187	3,058	3,067	3,581	4,062	4,970
Net income ($ mil.)	2.4%	293	(578)	505	815	885	238	321	270	316	364
Income as % of sales	—	2.9%	—	5.8%	23.5%	27.8%	7.8%	10.5%	7.5%	7.8%	7.3%
Earnings per share ($)	5.5%	1.76	(3.47)	3.03	8.93	2.13	1.76	1.95	2.13	2.50	2.86
Stock price - FY high ($)	—	10.77	8.21	9.68	19.21	25.19	23.81	31.50	37.75	45.75	62.00
Stock price - FY low ($)	—	7.57	3.38	3.61	9.50	18.41	19.00	21.19	28.50	31.56	40.25
Stock price - FY close ($)	24.9%	7.99	4.50	9.57	18.45	23.06	21.75	29.56	35.38	43.38	59.00
P/E - high	—	6	—	3	2	12	14	16	18	18	22
P/E - low	—	4	—	1	1	9	11	11	13	13	14
Dividends per share ($)	11.2%	0.25	0.25	0.25	0.37	12.95	0.68	0.74	0.81	0.82	0.65
Book value per share ($)	3.6%	12.78	9.06	11.81	15.15	9.41	10.45	12.39	13.58	15.22	17.51
Employees	(12.4%)	102,200	98,100	80,600	56,800	30,500	24,200	27,700	23,100	29,000	31,000

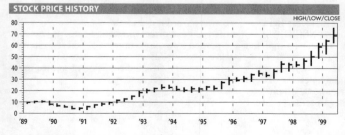

HIGH/LOW/CLOSE

Debt ratio: 10.1%
Return on equity: 16.4%
Cash ($ mil.): 127
Current ratio: 1.28
Long-term debt ($ mil.): 249
No. of shares (mil.): 127
Dividends
  Yield: 1.1%
  Payout: 22.7%
Market value ($ mil.): 7,475

GENERAL ELECTRIC COMPANY

OVERVIEW

From TV broadcasting to jet engines, financing, and power plants, General Electric (GE) has plugged in to several of the businesses that have shaped the 20th century. The Fairfield, Connecticut-based conglomerate is the fifth-largest US company (that other "general," General Motors, is #1).

GE's operating segments include aircraft engines (it vies with Rolls Royce and Pratt & Whitney for industry leadership), appliances, industrial products and systems (lighting, electrical distribution and control equipment, diesel-electric locomotives), plastics, power systems (gas turbines, steam turbine-generators, nuclear reactors), and technical products and services (medical imaging systems, data management). Its National

Broadcasting Company (NBC) is the #2 US TV network (behind CBS in TV ratings). GE Capital Services, which provides consumer and business financing, contributes nearly half of total revenues.

CEO Jack Welch, widely viewed as one of the best corporate leaders in the US, drives GE with the mandate to make the company #1 or #2 in every industry in which it operates. Under Welch, GE has become a seemingly unstoppable global growth engine: In 1998 sales rose, as usual, and the company invested $21 billion in 108 acquisitions. As the 21st century nears, Welch is pushing GE to continue expanding outside the US (particularly in Asia), to build the service businesses tied to many of its products, and to do more business on the Web.

HISTORY

General Electric (GE) was established in 1892 in New York, the result of a merger between Thomson-Houston and Edison General Electric. Charles Coffin was GE's first president, and Thomas Edison, who left the company in 1894, was one of the directors.

GE's financial strength (backed by the Morgan banking house) and its research focus contributed to its initial success. Early products included such Edison legacies as lightbulbs, elevators, trolleys, motors, toasters, and other appliances under the GE and Hotpoint labels. In the 1920s GE joined AT&T and Westinghouse in a radio broadcasting venture, Radio Corporation of America (RCA), but GE sold off its RCA holdings in 1930 because of an antitrust ruling (one of 65 antitrust actions against GE between 1911 and 1967).

By 1980 GE had reached $25 billion in revenues from plastics, consumer electronics, nuclear reactors, and jet engines. But it had become rigid and bureaucratic. Jack Welch became president in 1981 and shook up the company. He decentralized operations and adopted a strategy of pursuing only high-achieving ventures and dumping those that didn't perform. GE shed air-conditioning (1982), housewares (1984), and semiconductors (1988), and with the proceeds acquired Employers Reinsurance (1984), RCA, including NBC (1986), investment banker Kidder, Peabody (completed in 1990), and CGR medical equipment (1987).

In the early 1990s GE grew its lighting business. It bought mutual fund wholesaler GNA in 1993; GE Investment Management, which runs GE's pension assets, began selling mutual funds to the public.

GE sold scandal-plagued Kidder, Peabody to Paine Webber in 1994. General Electric Capital Services (GECS) expanded its lines, buying Amex Life Insurance (Aon's Union Fidelity unit) and Life Insurance Co. of Virginia in 1995 and life insurer First Colony the next year.

The company sold its struggling GEnie online service in 1996, forming an NBC and Microsoft venture, the MSNBC cable news channel, with better prospects. In 1997 GE Engine Services bought aircraft engine maintenance firms Greenwich Air Services and UNC.

GE acquired Lockheed Martin's medical imaging unit in 1997 and added to the medical systems business with the 1998 purchase of Marquette Medical Systems and Elbit Medical Imaging's Diasonics Vingmed Ultrasound unit.

In 1998 GECS became the first foreign company to enter Japan's life insurance market when it bought assets from Toho Mutual Life Insurance and set up GE Edison Life. Not every unit expanded in 1998, however. GE Power Systems began cutting 1,200 jobs as part of a restructuring, while 300 jobs were axed at NBC because of higher production costs for top shows, coupled with the loss of NFL broadcasting rights and the end of *Seinfeld*.

In 1999 GECS bought the 53% of Montgomery Ward it didn't already own, along with the retailer's direct marketing arm, as Wards emerged from bankruptcy. GE Power Systems agreed to buy Alstom's heavy-duty gas turbine business, and GE Medical Systems agreed to buy OEC Medical Systems.

Chairman and CEO: John F. Welch Jr., age 63,
$10,000,000 pay
VC and Executive Officer; Chairman and CEO, GE
Capital Services: Dennis D. Dammerman, age 53,
$3,100,000 pay
VC and Executive Officer: Eugene F. Murphy, age 63,
$2,300,000 pay
VC and Executive Officer: John D. Opie, age 61,
$3,133,333 pay
SVP, Human Resources: William J. Conaty, age 53
SVP, Research and Development: Lewis S. Edelheit,
age 56
SVP, General Counsel, and Secretary:
Benjamin W. Heineman Jr., age 55, $2,283,333 pay
SVP, Asia/Pacific: Goran S. Malm, age 52
SVP and Chief Information Officer: Gary M. Reiner,
age 44
SVP, Finance and CFO: Keith S. Sherin, age 40
SVP, GE Lighting: David L. Calhoun, age 41
SVP, GE Appliances: David M. Cote, age 46
SVP, GE Medical Systems: Jeffrey R. Immelt, age 43
SVP, GE Aircraft Engines: W. James McNerney Jr.,
age 49
SVP, GE Power Systems: Robert L. Nardelli, age 50
VP, Financial Planning and Analysis: Robert W. Nelson,
age 58
SVP, GE Plastics: Gary L. Rogers, age 54
SVP, GE Industrial Systems: Lloyd G. Trotter, age 53
VP and Controller: Philip D. Ameen, age 50
VP and Treasurer: James R. Bunt, age 57
Auditors: KPMG LLP

HQ: 3135 Easton Tpke., Fairfield, CT 06431-0001
Phone: 203-373-2211   Fax: 203-373-3131
Web site: http://www.ge.com

1998 Sales & Operating Income

	Sales		Operating Income	
	$ mil.	% of total	$ mil.	% of total
GE Capital Services				
Financing	48,694	46	—	—
Other	3,796	4	3,796	27
Industrial products	11,222	11	1,880	14
Aircraft engines	10,294	10	1,769	13
Power systems	8,466	8	1,306	9
Plastics	6,633	6	1,584	12
Major appliances	5,619	5	755	5
Technical	5,323	5	1,109	8
Broadcasting	5,269	5	1,349	10
Other	262	—	271	2
Adjustments	(5,975)	—	1,364	—
Total	**99,820**	**100**	**15,183**	**100**

ABB Asea Brown Boveri	News Corp.
AIG	Philips Electronics
Alstom	Polaroid
Bank of America	Raytheon
Caterpillar	Rockwell International
CIGNA	Rohm and Haas
Cooper Industries	Rolls-Royce
Electrolux	Siemens
General Motors	Textron
General Re	Thyssen Krupp
Hitachi	Time Warner
ITT Industries	Toshiba
Johnson Controls	United Technologies
Matsushita	U.S. Industries
Maytag	Viacom
Mitsubishi	Walt Disney
Mitsui	Whirlpool

NYSE symbol: GE FYE: December 31	Annual Growth	1989	1990	1991	1992	1993	1994	1995	1996	1997	1998
Sales ($ mil.)	7.1%	53,884	57,662	59,379	56,274	59,827	59,316	69,276	78,541	88,540	99,820
Net income ($ mil.)	10.0%	3,939	4,303	2,636	4,725	4,315	4,726	6,573	7,280	8,203	9,296
Income as % of sales	—	7.3%	7.5%	4.4%	8.4%	7.2%	8.0%	9.5%	9.3%	9.3%	9.3%
Earnings per share ($)	11.1%	1.09	1.22	0.76	1.39	1.26	1.38	1.93	2.16	2.46	2.80
Stock price - FY high ($)	—	16.19	18.88	19.53	21.88	26.75	27.44	36.56	53.06	76.56	103.94
Stock price - FY low ($)	—	10.88	12.50	13.25	18.19	20.22	22.50	24.94	34.75	47.94	69.00
Stock price - FY close ($)	22.7%	16.13	14.34	19.13	21.38	26.22	25.50	36.00	49.44	73.38	102.00
P/E - high	—	15	15	26	16	21	20	19	25	31	37
P/E - low	—	10	10	17	13	16	16	13	16	19	25
Dividends per share ($)	12.7%	0.41	0.47	0.51	0.56	0.63	0.75	0.82	0.92	1.04	1.20
Book value per share ($)	8.4%	5.77	6.21	6.27	6.86	7.55	7.73	8.88	9.46	10.55	11.89
Employees	0.0%	292,000	298,000	284,000	231,000	222,000	221,000	222,000	239,000	276,000	293,000

HIGH/LOW/CLOSE

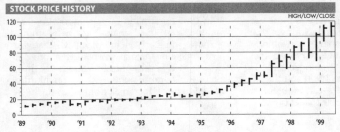

Debt ratio: 60.5%
Return on equity: 23.9%
Cash ($ mil.): 4,317
Current ratio: 1.72
Long-term debt ($ mil.): 59,663
No. of shares (mil.): 3,271
Dividends
  Yield: 1.2%
  Payout: 42.9%
Market value ($ mil.): 333,672

GENERAL INSTRUMENT

OVERVIEW

General Instrument is working to bring you 500 TV channels, even if there's nothing good on. The Horsham, Pennsylvania-based company (GI) is the top designer of the digital set-top boxes that give TVs interactive, telephony, and Internet access capabilities. The company also offers network transmission equipment to cable providers for upgrading their lines to handle interactive video and other bandwidth-intensive data. GI's satellite systems are geared for programmers, direct-to-home satellite networks, and business networks. The company has filed to take public Next Level

Communications, its majority-owned high-speed communications technology arm.

GI gained its leading market status through a long, close product partnership with cable giant TCI (now part of AT&T), which accounts for 31% of its sales. The company continues to thrive from alliances, including a pact with Sony (a GI shareholder) to develop systems incorporating Sony's home entertainment network technology.

AT&T's Liberty Media Group owns 21% of GI, which Motorola is buying.

HISTORY

General Instrument (GI) was founded in New York in 1923 by Abraham Blumenkrantz, an Austrian orphan who, at age 15, came to New York where his brother was a machine shop foreman. Blumenkrantz landed a job sweeping floors for $4 a week. He became a US citizen that year, at age 25, and started his own machine shop to manufacture the variable condensers that let radios tune into stations. The company, which became GI, was soon also making earphone jacks and tube sockets. It went public in 1939.

During WWII GI (sometimes called "Genius Incorporated" for its amazing innovations) supplied parts for bombs. In the 1940s it added phonograph record changers and television components to its growing product line. Over the next decade it would add more than a thousand items, including its first end product, a converter box for the recently introduced UHF (ultrahigh-frequency) TV channels. Blumenkrantz retired in 1955 but remained chairman of GI's finance committee. He died in 1961.

In 1967 GI entered the cable TV industry with its purchase of Jerrold Communications, a supplier of cable TV equipment. That year the company also bought American Totalisator, the world's top maker of pari-mutuel betting machines.

During the early 1970s GI acquired a collection of electronics firms, then began selling noncore assets to encourage its two most successful segments, cable TV and gaming. By the late 1970s GI was making a large portion of North America's betting and lottery machines.

Acquisitions in the 1980s included cable TV converter specialist Tocom (1983) and the TV equipment operations of M/A-COM (1986), including its industry-standard VideoCipher encryption system.

GI was bought in 1990 in an LBO by Forstmann Little & Co., which took the company public again in 1992. The following year Jerrold Communications and the VideoCipher operations were joined to create the company's GI Communications division. Cable and telecommunications equipment contracts boosted international sales, and in 1995 GI acquired Next Level Communications, a maker of digital telephone equipment; a related charge lowered earnings for the year. That year president and COO Richard Friedland was named CEO.

As a benefit to shareholders, Friedland in 1997 split GI into three separately traded companies: CommScope (TV cable), General Semiconductor (power semiconductors), and NextLevel Systems (network systems). Purchases that year boosted NextLevel's skills in network management, TV Internet access, and individualized TV programming. But a restructuring to streamline operations hurt 1997 earnings and led to Friedland's resignation; he was replaced by longtime executive Edward Breen.

A dozen cable companies placed a $4.5 billion order for NextLevel to make 15 million set-top boxes that year. As part of that deal, in 1998 the company made a separate pact with seasoned partner TCI and Sony to make and distribute the boxes. That year NextLevel Systems reclaimed the well-known GI name.

In 1999 Forstmann Little sold most of its remaining stake in GI, including a hefty amount of shares to Liberty Media Group. GI that year filed to take its majority-owned telephony subsidiary, Next Level Communications (by then a major R&D drain), public. Soon after, Motorola agreed to buy GI in an $11 billion deal.

OFFICERS

Chairman and CEO: Edward D. Breen, age 43,
$1,074,621 pay
EVP: Geoffrey S. Roman, age 46, $543,966 pay
EVP and Treasurer: Richard C. Smith, age 54,
$484,269 pay
**SVP; General Manager, Satellite and Broadcast Network
Systems:** Thomas J. Lynch, age 44
**SVP; General Manager, Advanced Network and Telecom
Systems:** Daniel M. Maloney, age 39
**SVP; General Manager, Transmission Network
Systems:** G. Bickley Remmey III, age 39
SVP; General Manager, Digital Network Systems:
David E. Robinson, age 39
SVP, Secretary, and General Counsel: Robert A. Scott,
age 48
SVP, Administration and Employee Resources:
Scott A. Crum, age 42
SVP, Finance and CFO: Eric M. Pillmore, age 45,
$433,645 pay
SVP, Manufacturing and Procurement:
Robert D. Cromack, age 55, $454,489 pay
Auditors: Deloitte & Touche LLP

LOCATIONS

HQ: General Instrument Corporation,
101 Tournament Dr., Horsham, PA 19044
Phone: 215-323-1000   **Fax:** 215-443-9454
Web site: http://www.gi.com

General Instrument's primary manufacturing facilities
are located in Mexico, Taiwan, and the US. The company
also has operations in Argentina, Australia, Brazil,
Canada, Chile, China, France, Germany, Hong Kong,
India, Japan, Saudi Arabia, Singapore, and the UK.

PRODUCTS/OPERATIONS

Selected Products

Broadband Network Systems
  Analog set-top boxes
  Cable modems (Surfboard)
  Computer and processing equipment
  Digital video, audio, and data processing equipment
  Distribution amplifiers
  Fiber-optic transmission equipment
  Network management software
  Programming content security tools
  Set-top boxes
  Signal processing equipment
  Subscriber authorization tools

Satellite and Broadcast Network Systems
  Analog and digital satellite uplink and
    downlink products
  Digital compression and transmission systems
  Digital satellite television systems
  HDTV encoding and decoding equipment
  Network management and access control tools

COMPETITORS

Adaptive Broadband	Hughes Electronics
ADC Telecommunications	Lucent
ADTRAN	Motorola
Alcatel	Nokia
ANTEC	Nortel Networks
Aware	PairGain
California Amplifier	Scientific-Atlanta
C-COR.net	Stanford Telecom
Cisco Systems	Tellabs
Ericsson	Vertex Communications
General DataComm	Zenith

HISTORICAL FINANCIALS & EMPLOYEES

NYSE symbol: GIC FYE: December 31	Annual Growth	1989	1990	1991	1992	1993	1994	1995	1996	1997	1998
Sales ($ mil.)	23.6%	—	—	—	557	783	1,275	1,533	1,756	1,764	1,988
Net income ($ mil.)	—	—	—	—	(39)	50	121	4	(96)	(16)	56
Income as % of sales	—	—	—	—	—	6.4%	9.5%	0.3%	—	—	2.8%
Earnings per share ($)	(400.0%)	—	—	—	—	—	—	—	—	(0.11)	0.33
Stock price - FY high ($)	—	—	—	—	—	—	—	—	—	21.50	36.94
Stock price - FY low ($)	—	—	—	—	—	—	—	—	—	12.63	16.44
Stock price - FY close ($)	89.8%	—	—	—	—	—	—	—	—	17.88	33.94
P/E - high	—	—	—	—	—	—	—	—	—	—	112
P/E - low	—	—	—	—	—	—	—	—	—	—	50
Dividends per share ($)	—	—	—	—	—	—	—	—	—	0.00	0.00
Book value per share ($)	19.4%	—	—	—	—	—	—	—	—	8.19	9.78
Employees	(4.8%)	—	—	—	—	—	—	—	8,600	7,350	7,800

STOCK PRICE HISTORY

HIGH/LOW/CLOSE

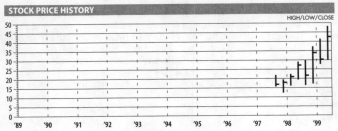

1998 FISCAL YEAR-END

Debt ratio: 0.0%
Return on equity: 3.4%
Cash ($ mil.): 149
Current ratio: 1.96
Long-term debt ($ mil.): 0
No. of shares (mil.): 169
Dividends
  Yield: —
  Payout: —
Market value ($ mil.): 5,728

GENERAL MILLS, INC.

OVERVIEW

Although its menu for success includes Wheaties, the Breakfast of Champions, Minneapolis-based General Mills is only #2 in US cereal sales, behind king Kellogg. Its Big G unit boasts Cheerios, Wheaties, and Trix cereals, while Betty Crocker's pantry is stocked with Gold Medal flour, Betty Crocker baking mixes, side dish mixes, and Hamburger Helper. Its snack lineup includes Pop Secret microwave popcorn, Chex Mix, an assortment of chewy fruit snacks, and Yoplait and Colombo yogurts. (The company is #2 in yogurt, behind Dannon.) General Mills also markets Betty Crocker cookbooks, licenses Betty Crocker housewares, and operates a food service division.

Weary from the cereal wars, the General is using new products (Chicken Helper, Go-Gurt) and acquisitions to bolster its ranks. The company has had mixed success in marketing its dessert and snack food brands overseas through joint ventures.

HISTORY

Cadwallader Washburn built his first flour mill in 1866 in Minneapolis, which eventually became the Washburn Crosby Company. After winning a gold medal for flour at an 1880 exposition, the company changed the name of its best flour to Gold Medal Flour.

In 1921 advertising manager Sam Gale created fictional spokeswoman Betty Crocker so that correspondence to housewives could go out with her signature. The firm introduced Wheaties cereal in 1924. James Bell, named president in 1925, consolidated the company with other US mills in 1928 to form General Mills, the world's largest miller. The companies operated independently of one another, with corporate headquarters coordinating advertising and merchandising.

General Mills began introducing convenience foods such as Bisquick (1931) and Cheerios (1941). During WWII it produced war goods such as ordnance equipment and developed chemical and electronics divisions.

When Edwin Rawlings became CEO in 1961, he closed half the flour mills and divested such unprofitable lines as electronics. This cost $200 million in annual sales but freed resources for such acquisitions as Kenner Products (toys, 1967) and Parker Brothers (board games, 1968), which made General Mills the world's largest toy company.

Through the next 20 years the company made many acquisitions, including Gorton's (frozen seafood, 1968), Monet (jewelry, 1968), Eddie Bauer (outerwear, 1971), and The Talbot's (women's clothing, 1973). It bought Red Lobster in 1970 and acquired the US rights to Yoplait yogurt in 1977. General Mills started its Olive Garden restaurant chain in 1983. When the toy and fashion divisions' profits fell in 1984, they were spun off as Kenner Parker Toys and Crystal Brands (1985). Reemphasizing food in 1989, the firm sold many businesses, including Eddie Bauer and Talbot's.

That year General Mills and Nestle entered the European cereal market as the Cereal Partners Worldwide joint venture (CPW, a major cereal maker outside North America). General Mills formed Snack Ventures Europe (one of the largest snack companies in Continental Europe) with PepsiCo in 1992.

As part of a cereal price war, in 1994 the company cut coupon promotion costs by $175 million and lowered prices on many cereals. But some retailers did not pass on the price cuts to consumers due to shortages that developed after the FDA found an unauthorized pesticide in some cereals. General Mills destroyed 55 million boxes of cereal at a cost of $140 million. Stephen Sanger became CEO in 1995. That year the company sold Gorton's to Unilever and spun off its restaurant business.

In 1996, for her 75th birthday, General Mills introduced a new Betty Crocker image: a computer composite of 75 women's faces. Earnings were down for 1997, partly because further price-war cuts reduced sales and partly due to the $570 million acquisition (the largest in its history) of Ralcorp Holdings' Chex snack and cereal lines. The next year General Mills sifted its Gold Medal flour line into its Betty Crocker division and created a convenience foods unit to house its yogurt and snack brands.

Early in 1999 the company bought Lloyd's Barbeque (ready-to-heat barbecued meats) and Farmhouse Foods (rice and pasta side dishes). It then locked up the North American rights to Olibra, an appetite suppressant made by Scotia Holdings that can be added to yogurt and other foods to make them seem more filling. Later in 1999 General Mills purchased Gardetto's Bakery (snack mixes) and announced it was pulling the plug on two overseas ventures to sell desserts and snacks.

Chairman and CEO: Stephen W. Sanger, age 53,
$1,740,263 pay
VC: Raymond G. Viault, age 55, $1,103,000 pay
President: Charles W. Gaillard, age 58, $1,0263,990 pay
EVP: Stephen R. Demeritt, age 55, $724,652 pay
EVP and CFO: James A. Lawrence, age 46
SVP; President, Big G: Y. Marc Belton, age 40
**SVP, Consumer Food Sales, Foodservice and Channel
Development:** Jeffrey J. Rotsch, age 49
SVP, Corporate Affairs and General Counsel:
Siri S. Marshall, age 51, $555, 309 pay
SVP, Corporate Relations: Austin P. Sullivan Jr., age 59
SVP, Financial Operations: Kenneth L. Thome, age 51
SVP, Global Convenience Foods: Jon L. Finley, age 45
SVP, Human Resources: Michael A. Peel, age 49
SVP, Innovation, Technology and Quality:
Danny L. Strickland, age 49
SVP, Investor Relations: Eric J. Larson, age 43
SVP, Operations: Randy G. Darcy, age 48
SVP; CEO, Cereal Partners Worldwide: Kendall J. Powell
SVP; President, New Ventures: Christina L. Shea,
age 46
VP; President, Foodservice: Robert L. Stretmater, age 55
VP; President, Snacks Unlimited: Peter J. Capell, age 42
VP; President, Yoplait-Colombo: Ian R. Friendly, age 38
Auditors: KPMG LLP

HQ: 1 General Mills Blvd., Minneapolis, MN 55426
Phone: 612-540-2311   **Fax:** 612-540-2445
Web site: http://www.generalmills.com

General Mills has operations throughout the US and
Canada. Its products can be found in more than 100
markets worldwide.

Selected Brand Names

Cereals
Cheerios
Chex
Cocoa Puffs
Golden Grahams
Kix

Lucky Charms
Oatmeal Crisp
Total
Trix
Wheaties

Desserts, Flour, and Baking Mixes
Betty Crocker
Bisquick
Gold Medal
La Pina, Red Band & Robin Hood (regional flour)

Dinner and Side-Dish Products
Bac*O's
Betty Crocker (Hamburger Helper, Suddenly Salad)

Snack Products and Beverages
Bugles snacks
Dunkaroos snacks
Fruit Roll-Ups
Nature Valley granola bars
Pop Secret microwave popcorn
Squeezit juice drinks
Sweet Rewards fat-free snack bars

Yogurt Products
Colombo
Yoplait

Bestfoods	Keebler	Procter &
Borden	Kellogg	Gamble
Campbell Soup	Kraft	Quaker Oats
ConAgra	Nabisco Holdings	Ralcorp
Danone	Nestle	Sara Lee
Heinz	Pillsbury	Unilever

NYSE symbol: GIS FYE: May 31	Annual Growth	1990	1991	1992	1993	1994	1995	1996	1997	1998	1999
Sales ($ mil.)	(0.4%)	6,448	7,153	7,778	8,135	8,517	5,027	5,416	5,609	6,033	6,246
Net income ($ mil.)	3.8%	381	473	496	506	470	367	476	445	422	535
Income as % of sales	—	5.9%	6.6%	6.4%	6.2%	5.5%	7.3%	8.8%	7.9%	7.0%	8.6%
Earnings per share ($)	4.3%	2.33	2.87	2.99	3.10	2.95	2.33	2.94	2.76	2.60	3.40
Stock price - FY high ($)	—	40.31	60.88	75.88	74.13	68.75	64.63	60.50	68.75	78.25	84.69
Stock price - FY low ($)	—	30.31	37.94	54.25	62.00	49.88	49.38	50.38	52.00	60.00	59.19
Stock price - FY close ($)	8.0%	40.31	58.75	63.50	65.25	54.75	51.88	57.38	63.25	68.25	80.38
P/E - high	—	17	21	25	24	23	28	21	25	30	25
P/E - low	—	13	13	18	20	17	21	17	19	23	17
Dividends per share ($)	7.8%	1.10	1.28	1.48	1.68	1.88	1.88	1.44	2.03	2.12	2.16
Book value per share ($)	(15.6%)	4.96	6.74	8.28	7.59	7.26	0.89	1.94	3.09	1.23	1.08
Employees	(21.8%)	97,238	108,077	111,501	121,290	125,700	9,882	9,800	10,200	10,200	10,660

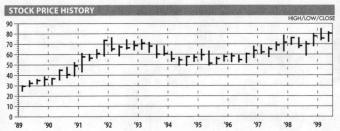

STOCK PRICE HISTORY — HIGH/LOW/CLOSE

1999 FISCAL YEAR-END
Debt ratio: 91.2%
Return on equity: 325.5%
Cash ($ mil.): 4
Current ratio: 0.65
Long-term debt ($ mil.): 1,702
No. of shares (mil.): 152
Dividends
  Yield: 2.7%
  Payout: 63.5%
Market value ($ mil.): 12,218

GENERAL MOTORS CORPORATION

OVERVIEW

Lead, follow, or get the hell out of the way — bumper sticker or business strategy? General Motors (GM), the world's #1 maker of cars and trucks, is doing a bit of all three. Detroit-based GM, whose North American brands include Buick, Cadillac, Chevrolet, GMC, Oldsmobile, Pontiac, and Saturn, has followed the industry trend toward consolidation and is trying to get out of the way of its own mega-bureaucracy by spinning off noncore units.

Even without vehicle sales, GM would boast a formidable array of businesses. Subsidiary Hughes Electronics makes communications equipment such as the digital satellite system for DIRECTV television; GMAC offers financing and insurance; Allison Transmission makes medium- and heavy-duty transmissions; and the GM Locomotive Group makes train locomotives and light armored vehicles. GM has spun off Delphi Automotive Systems, the world's #1 manufacturer of auto parts.

Outside of North America, GM's cars and trucks go under the Cadillac, Chevrolet, GMC, Holden, Isuzu (49%), Opel, Saab (a 50-50 joint venture with Investor AB), and Vauxhall nameplates. GM's NUMMI joint venture with Toyota makes cars for both companies.

After watching its US market share drop five points to 30% in the past decade, GM has consolidated its automotive operations under GM Automotive. GM is pushing truck production in the US, while scaling back on small cars. To boost non-US sales, GM has invested in plants overseas and has increased its stakes in Isuzu and Suzuki.

HISTORY

In the early years of the auto industry, hundreds of carmakers produced a few models. William Durant, who bought and reorganized failing Buick Motors in 1904, reasoned that manufacturers could benefit from banding together, and formed the General Motors Company in Flint, Michigan, in 1908.

Durant bought 17 companies (including Oldsmobile, Cadillac, and Pontiac) by 1910, the year a bankers syndicate forced him to step down. In 1915 he regained control through Chevrolet, a company he formed with race car driver Louis Chevrolet. GM created the GM Acceptance Corporation (auto financing) and bought businesses including Frigidaire (sold 1979) and Hyatt Roller Bearing.

With Hyatt came Alfred Sloan (president from 1923 to 1937), who built GM into a corporate colossus. By 1927 it was the industry leader. Overseas, it bought Vauxhall Motors (UK, 1925) and merged with Adam Opel (Germany, 1931). After the Depression, GM added defense products for WWII and diversified into areas such as home appliances and locomotives.

GM spent much of the 1970s making its cars meet federal pollution-control mandates. Under Roger Smith (CEO from 1981 to 1990) GM laid off thousands of workers in a massive restructuring.

In 1984 GM formed NUMMI with Toyota to see if Toyota's manufacturing techniques would work in the US. GM also bought Ross Perot's Electronic Data Systems (1984), Hughes Aircraft (1986), and 50% of Saab Automobile (1989). GM launched the Saturn car in 1990; that year Robert Stempel became CEO. In 1992

GM made what was the largest stock offering in US history and raised $2.2 billion. Culminating an early 1990s period of boardroom coups, John Smith replaced Stempel as CEO.

In 1995 GM sold its National Car Rental business to investors and spun off Electronic Data Systems in 1996. In 1997 GM sold the defense electronics business of Hughes Electronics to Raytheon and merged Hughes' electronic auto parts business with Delphi Automotive Systems.

In 1998 UAW walkouts at two Michigan GM parts plants forced the shutdown of virtually all North American GM production lines, costing the company about $2.8 billion. The same year, GM combined its North American and international operations and moved to unite the sales, marketing, and service operations for its five major brands. The company also agreed to build cars with Suzuki, increasing its 3% stake in the Japanese minicar maker to 10%.

In early 1999 GM spun off about 18% of Delphi Automotive Systems in an IPO that raised about $1.7 billion; the rest was spun off later that year. GM also boosted its stake in small truck partner Isuzu to 49%. Meanwhile, subsidiary Hughes Electronics agreed to buy Primestar's direct-to-home business for about $1.3 billion and subsidiary GMAC agreed to buy a commercial finance unit of the Bank of New York for $1.8 billion. Also that year a jury awarded $4.9 billion to six people burned when the fuel tank of their Chevrolet Malibu exploded in a rear-end collision. Although the judge reduced the amount to $1.1 billion, GM said it would appeal.

Chairman and CEO: John F. Smith Jr., age 61, $3.030.000 pay
VC: Harry J. Pearce, age 56, $1,562,000 pay
President and COO: G. Richard Wagoner Jr., age 46, $1,562,000 pay
EVP New Business Strategies: Louis R. Hughes, age 50, $1,450,000 pay
EVP and CFO: J. Michael Losh, age 52
EVP and Group Executive; President, General Motors Acceptance Corporation: John D. Finnegan, age 50
EVP; President, GM North America: Ronald L. Zarrella, age 49
SVP and General Counsel: Thomas A. Gottschalk
SVP North America Car Group and North American Manufacturing: Donald E. Hackworth
VP and Group Executive; President, GM Europe: Michael Burns
VP and Group Executive, Labor Relations: Gary L. Cowger
VP and Group Executive, General Motors Truck Group: Thomas J. Davis
VP and Group Executive, Design, Product, and Manufacturing Engineering, GM Europe: Peter H. Hanenberger
VP and Group Executive; President and CEO, Saab; President and CEO, Adam Opel: Robert W. Hendry
VP and Group Executive, GM Powertrain Group: Arvin F. Mueller
VP Global Human Resources and General Motors University: Kathleen S. Barclay
Auditors: Deloitte & Touche LLP

HQ: 100 Renaissance Center, Detroit, MI 48243
Phone: 313-556-5000 **Fax:** 313-556-5108
Web site: http://www.gm.com

1998 Sales

	$ mil.	% of total
Automotive products	143,031	89
Financial services	18,284	11
Total	**161,315**	**100**

Selected GM Brands

Buick	Oldsmobile
Cadillac	Opel and Vauxhall
Chevrolet	Pontiac
GMC	Saab
Holden	Saturn
Isuzu (49%)	

BMW
DaimlerChrysler
Fiat
Ford
Fuji Heavy Industries
Honda
Hyundai
Kia Motors
Mack Trucks
Mazda
Mitsubishi
Nissan
Peugeot
Renault
Suzuki
Toyota
Volkswagen
Volvo

NYSE symbol: GM FYE: December 31	Annual Growth	1989	1990	1991	1992	1993	1994	1995	1996	1997	1998
Sales ($ mil.)	3.0%	123,212	122,021	119,753	128,533	133,622	150,592	163,861	158,015	166,445	161,315
Net income ($ mil.)	(3.9%)	4,224	(1,986)	(4,453)	(23,498)	2,466	4,901	6,881	4,963	6,698	2,956
Income as % of sales	—	3.4%	—	—	—	1.8%	3.3%	4.2%	3.1%	4.0%	1.8%
Earnings per share ($)	(4.5%)	6.33	(4.09)	(7.97)	(38.28)	2.13	4.10	7.14	6.02	8.62	4.18
Stock price - FY high ($)	—	50.50	50.50	44.38	44.38	57.13	65.38	53.13	59.38	72.44	76.69
Stock price - FY low ($)	—	39.13	33.13	26.75	28.63	32.00	36.13	37.25	45.75	52.25	47.06
Stock price - FY close ($)	6.0%	42.25	34.38	28.88	32.25	54.88	42.13	52.88	55.75	60.75	71.56
P/E - high	—	8	—	—	—	27	16	7	10	8	18
P/E - low	—	6	—	—	—	15	9	5	8	6	11
Dividends per share ($)	(7.4%)	3.00	3.00	1.60	1.40	0.80	0.80	1.10	1.60	2.00	1.50
Book value per share ($)	(9.9%)	50.38	43.23	35.53	5.87	5.28	11.64	18.05	27.33	21.95	19.68
Employees	(2.9%)	775,100	761,000	756,300	750,000	710,800	728,000	745,000	647,000	608,000	594,000

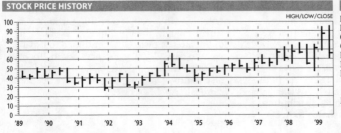

HIGH/LOW/CLOSE

Debt ratio: 77.8%
Return on equity: 19.7%
Cash ($ mil.): 10,869
Current ratio: 1.30
Long-term debt ($ mil.): 52,574
No. of shares (mil.): 761
Dividends
 Yield: 2.1%
 Payout: 35.9%
Market value ($ mil.): 54,469

GENUINE PARTS COMPANY

OVERVIEW

What do spark plugs, hydraulic hoses, note pads, and magnet wire have in common? They're all Genuine Parts. Atlanta-based Genuine Parts Company (GPC) is the largest member of the National Automotive Parts Association (NAPA), a voluntary trade association that distributes auto parts nationwide. Through more than 60 distribution centers, GPC distributes some 200,000 parts to about 5,600 NAPA Auto Parts stores in the US, including about 750 company-owned outlets. The company also serves about 650 corporate and associate resellers in Canada and distributes parts in Mexico through a joint venture with Grupo Auto Todo. GPC's Rayloc division rebuilds automotive parts.

In addition to the automotive market, GPC distributes parts for industrial equipment (including parts for transmissions, hydraulics, and irrigation equipment). With eight distribution centers, the division serves nearly 440 branches in the US and Canada.

GPC also distributes office products through the S. P. Richards Company, one of the oldest office supply wholesalers in the country. The division has three proprietary brands: Sparco, Nature Saver, and CompuCessory. GPC's newest subsidiary, EIS, manufactures and distributes electronic and electrical products such as copper foil, magnet wire, and thermal management materials.

HISTORY

Genuine Parts Company (GPC) got its start in Atlanta in 1928 when Carlyle Fraser bought a small auto parts store. That year GPC had the only loss in its history. Three years earlier a group that included Fraser had founded the National Automotive Parts Association (NAPA), an organization of automotive manufacturers, remanufacturers, distributors, and retailers.

The Depression was a boon for GPC because fewer new-car sales meant more sales of replacement parts. During the 1930s GPC's sales rose from less than $350,000 to more than $3 million. One tool the company developed to spur sales during the Depression was its monthly magazine, *Parts Pups*, which featured pretty girls and corny jokes (discontinued in the 1990s). The company acquired auto parts rebuilder Rayloc in 1931 and established parts distributor Balkamp in 1936.

WWII boosted sales at GPC because carmakers were producing for the war effort, but scarce resources limited auto parts companies to producing functional parts. GPC went public in 1948.

The postwar boom in car sales boosted GPC's sales in the 1950s and 1960s. It expanded during this period with new distribution centers across the country. The company bought Colyear Motor Sales (NAPA's West Coast distributor) in 1965 and introduced a line of filters and batteries in 1966 that were the first parts to carry the NAPA name.

GPC moved into Canada in 1972 when it bought Corbetts, a Calgary-based parts distributor. That acquisition included Oliver Industrial Supply. During the mid-1970s the company began to broaden its distribution businesses, adding S. P. Richards (office

products, 1975) and Motion Industries (industrial replacement parts, 1976). In the late 1970s GPC acquired Bearing Specialty and Michigan Bearing as part of Motion Industries.

In 1982 the company introduced its now familiar blue-and-yellow NAPA logo. Canadian parts distributor UAP (formerly United Auto Parts) and GPC formed a joint venture, UAP/NAPA, in 1988, with GPC acquiring a 20% stake in UAP.

During the 1990s GPC diversified its product lines and its geographic reach. Its 1993 acquisition of Berry Bearing made the company a leading distributor of industrial parts. The next year GPC formed a joint venture with Grupo Auto Todo of Mexico.

NAPA formed an agreement in 1995 with Penske Corporation to be the exclusive supplier of auto parts to nearly 900 Penske Auto Centers. GPC purchased Horizon USA Data Supplies that year as well, adding computer supplies to S. P. Richards' product mix.

A string of acquisitions in the late 1990s have increased GPC's industrial distribution business (including Midcap Bearing, Power Drives & Bearings, and Amarillo Bearing).

GPC paid $200 million in 1998 for EIS, a leading wholesale distributor of materials and supplies to the electrical and electronic industries. Late that year, after a 10-year joint venture, it bought the remaining 80% of UAP it didn't already own. GPC continued to expand its auto parts distribution network in 1999, acquiring Johnson Industries, an independent distributor of auto supplies for large fleets and car dealers.

OFFICERS

Chairman and CEO: Larry L. Prince, age 60, $1,378,535 pay
President and COO: Thomas C. Gallagher, age 51, $967,300 pay
EVP: Robert J. Breci, age 63, $531,360 pay
EVP Finance and Administration and Principal Financial and Accounting Officer: George W. Kalafut, age 64, $533,040 pay
SVP Finance: Jerry W. Nix
SVP Market Development: Robert J. Susor
SVP Sales: William E. Turnbull
SVP Human Resources: Edward Van Stedum, age 49
Group VP: Keith M. Bealmear, age 52, $458,800 pay
Group VP: Glenn M. Chambers, age 42
Group VP: Albert T. Donnon Jr., age 51
Auditors: Ernst & Young LLP

LOCATIONS

HQ: 2999 Circle 75 Pkwy., Atlanta, GA 30339
Phone: 770-953-1700   **Fax:** 770-956-2211
Web site: http://www.genpt.com

Genuine Parts Company has operations throughout much of the US and in Canada, Chile, and Mexico.

PRODUCTS/OPERATIONS

1998 Sales & Operating Profit

	Sales		Operating Profit	
	$ mil.	% of total	$ mil.	% of total
Automotive	3,262	49	344	53
Industrial	2,009	31	176	27
Office products	1,123	17	114	18
Electronics	220	3	12	2
Total	**6,614**	**100**	**646**	**100**

Selected Operations

Automotive Parts Group
Balkamp, Inc. (majority-owned subsidiary; distributes replacement parts and accessories for cars, heavy-duty vehicles, motorcycles, and farm equipment)
Grupo Auto Todo SA de CV (49% distribution and stores, Mexico)
Rayloc (remanufacturing)
UAP Inc. (auto parts distribution, Canada)

Industrial Parts Group
Berry Bearing Co.
Motion Industries, Inc.
Motion Industries, Inc. (Canada)

Office Products Group
S. P. Richards Co.

Electrical/Electronic Materials Group
EIS, Inc. (46 branch locations in the US and Mexico; products for electrical and electronic equipment, including adhesives, copper foil, and thermal management materials)

COMPETITORS

Applied Industrial Technologies
APS Holding
AutoZone
Boise Cascade Office Products
Ford
General Motors
General Parts
Hahn Automotive Warehouse
Ingersoll-Rand
PACCAR
Trak Auto
United Stationers
U.S. Office Products

HISTORICAL FINANCIALS & EMPLOYEES

NYSE symbol: GPC FYE: December 31	Annual Growth	1989	1990	1991	1992	1993	1994	1995	1996	1997	1998
Sales ($ mil.)	8.5%	3,161	3,319	3,435	3,669	4,384	4,858	5,262	5,721	6,005	6,614
Net income ($ mil.)	6.6%	200	207	208	220	258	289	309	330	342	356
Income as % of sales	—	6.3%	6.2%	6.0%	6.0%	5.9%	5.9%	5.9%	5.8%	5.7%	5.4%
Earnings per share ($)	6.2%	1.15	1.19	1.21	1.28	1.38	1.55	1.68	1.81	1.90	1.98
Stock price - FY high ($)	—	19.35	19.02	21.97	23.18	26.01	26.26	28.01	31.68	35.88	38.25
Stock price - FY low ($)	—	15.52	14.74	15.52	19.34	21.93	22.43	23.68	26.68	28.68	28.25
Stock price - FY close ($)	6.7%	18.69	16.91	21.69	22.68	25.10	24.01	27.35	29.68	33.94	33.44
P/E - high	—	17	16	18	18	19	17	17	18	19	19
P/E - low	—	13	12	13	15	16	14	14	15	15	14
Dividends per share ($)	7.6%	0.51	0.59	0.64	0.66	0.70	0.75	0.82	0.88	0.94	0.99
Book value per share ($)	8.9%	5.30	6.02	6.57	7.19	7.76	8.30	9.03	9.62	10.39	11.44
Employees	7.9%	16,195	16,383	17,107	18,400	18,400	21,285	22,500	24,200	24,500	32,000

STOCK PRICE HISTORY

HIGH/LOW/CLOSE

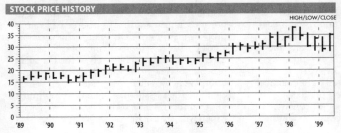

1998 FISCAL YEAR-END

Debt ratio: 22.3%
Return on equity: 17.3%
Cash ($ mil.): 85
Current ratio: 3.28
Long-term debt ($ mil.): 589
No. of shares (mil.): 180
Dividends
  Yield: 3.0%
  Payout: 50.0%
Market value ($ mil.): 6,003

GEORGIA-PACIFIC CORPORATION

OVERVIEW

As its name implies, Georgia-Pacific Corporation operates from sea to shining sea. The Atlanta-based company is the holding company for Georgia-Pacific Group, the US's #2 forest products company (behind International Paper) and The Timber Company, which conducts its timber and wood fiber operations. Georgia-Pacific Group is also one of the world's top building products companies, leading the country in wood panels, specialty chemicals, and wholesale building products distribution. It sells its gypsum wallboard, containerboard, office stationery products, and tissue under the Angel Soft, Coronet, Delta, and other brand names. Its Unisource Worldwide subsidiary distributes printing and imaging paper.

The Timber Company owns and leases approximately 5.4 million acres of forests, mainly in the southern US.

Faced with fiscal woes due to weak paper prices and continued troubles with its building products distribution, Georgia-Pacific split its operations into two tracking stocks of Georgia-Pacific Group and The Timber Company to shield its timber business from the cyclic paper market.

Georgia-Pacific concentrates on value-added products, such as tissue paper, that generate greater profits and make the company less vulnerable to foreign competition.

HISTORY

Owen Cheatham founded the Georgia Hardwood Lumber Company in Augusta, Georgia, in 1927 as a hardwood lumber wholesaler. By 1938 the company was operating five southern sawmills, and during WWII it became the largest lumber supplier to the US armed forces.

Georgia Hardwood bought a plywood mill in Bellingham, Washington, in 1947. Recognizing the potential of plywood, Cheatham acquired several more plywood mills in the late 1940s.

Cheatham began a land-buying spree in 1951 that would give Georgia Hardwood its first timberlands. The company moved its headquarters to Oregon three years later, adopting the Georgia-Pacific name in 1957. That year it embarked on a period of explosive growth. By 1960 Georgia-Pacific had a million acres of timberland.

In the 1960s the company acquired several competitors and diversified into containers, paperboard, tissue, and other products. The Federal Trade Commission forced Georgia-Pacific to sell 20% of its assets to reduce its size in 1972. The following year the company bought Boise Cascade's wood products operations, and in 1975 it acquired Exchange Oil and Gas.

Georgia-Pacific continued its diversification into chemicals in 1976 and introduced cheaper substitutes for plywood, such as waferboard. It acquired timberland in the South and modernized existing paper mills. In 1979 Georgia-Pacific bought Hudson Pulp and Paper and reached $5 billion in sales. The company returned to Georgia in 1982. Two years later Georgia-Pacific decided to sell most chemical operations unrelated to forest products.

In 1988 the company bought Brunswick Pulp and Paper in Georgia, increasing its southern timber holdings. The 1990 acquisition of Great Northern Nekoosa increased Georgia-Pacific's reliance on pulp and paper. To pay down debt, the company sold $1 billion of assets that year.

Georgia-Pacific sold 80% of Great Northern to Bowater in 1991 and gained the right to require Bowater to buy the remaining 20% of Great Northern (which Bowater subsequently did).

The firm sold its envelope business to the Sterling Group in 1994 and also sold its roofing line that year. In 1995 the pulp and paper industry rebounded from several sluggish years, which raised the price for the company's products and yielded higher profits. The trend was short-lived, however.

Georgia-Pacific more than doubled its gypsum production capacity in 1996 with the purchase of nine wallboard plants from Domtar. The following year Georgia-Pacific Corp. created separate stocks for its timber and building products businesses.

In 1998 Georgia-Pacific bought CeCorr, a US producer of corrugated sheets. The company plans to close a deal in 1999 for the purchase of Connelly Containers' packaging facility in Bala Cynwyd, Pennsylvania. In 1999 Georgia-Pacific paid $1.2 billion for North America's #1 paper distributor, Unisource Worldwide, trumping a previous agreement that Unisource had with propane distributor UGI. To raise money for a stock buyback, Georgia-Pacific sold 390,000 acres of Canadian timberlands to the Canadian province of New Brunswick for $41 million. Georgia-Pacific and Chesapeake also agreed to combine their tissue-making businesses into a joint venture — 90% owned by Georgia-Pacific, which will pay Chesapeake $730 million.

OFFICERS

Chairman, President, and CEO:
Alston D. "Pete" Correll, age 57, $1,449,600 pay
EVP Timber; President and CEO, The Timber Company: Donald L. Glass, age 50, $840,000 pay
EVP Pulp and Paperboard: Clint M. Kennedy, age 49
EVP Finance and CFO: John F. McGovern, age 52, $730,000 pay
EVP Wood Products and Distribution: Ronald L. Paul, age 55, $700,000 pay
EVP Wood Procurement, Gypsum, and Industrial Wood Products: John F. Rasor, age 55
EVP Paper and Chemicals: Lee M. Thomas, age 54, $650,000 pay
SVP Human Resources: Patricia A. Barnard
SVP Environmental, Government Affairs, and Communications: James E. Bostic Jr., age 51
SVP Law and General Counsel: James F. Kelley, age 57, $535,300 pay
VP and Treasurer: Danny W. Huff
VP and Controller: James E. Terrell, age 49
Auditors: Arthur Andersen LLP

LOCATIONS

HQ: Georgia-Pacific Center, 133 Peachtree St. NE, Atlanta, GA 30303
Phone: 404-652-4000   **Fax:** 404-584-1470
Web site: http://www.gp.com

Georgia-Pacific Corporation's Georgia-Pacific Group operates approximately 400 facilities in the US and Canada and its The Timber Company owns or manages more than 5 million acres of forests, mainly in the southern US.

PRODUCTS/OPERATIONS

1998 Sales & Operating Income

	Sales		Operating Income	
	$ mil.	% of total	$ mil.	% of total
Building products	5,792	35	603	50
Distribution	4,333	27	1	—
Pulp & paper	3,548	22	133	11
Containerboard	2,104	13	106	9
Timber	534	3	364	30
Adjustments	(2,975)	—	(273)	—
Total	**13,336**	**100**	**934**	**100**

Georgia-Pacific Group Products

Building Products	Pulp and Paper
Chemicals	Communications papers
Adhesives	Business forms
Specialty chemicals	Checks
Wood resins	Envelopes
Distribution	Stationery
Domestic building	Containerboard and
products wholesaler	packaging materials
Gypsum products	Bleached board
Industrial plaster	Corrugated packaging
Joint compound	Kraft paper
Wallboard	Linerboard
Lumber	Distribution
Wood panels	Printing and imaging
Hardboard	paper
Medium-density	Market pulp
fiberboard	Tissue papers
Oriented strand board	Bathroom tissues
Particleboard	Napkins
Plywood	Paper towels

COMPETITORS

Boise Cascade	Kimberly-Clark
Bowater	Mead
Champion International	Potlatch
Consolidated Papers	Rayonier
Fletcher Challenge Forests	Smurfit-Stone Container
Fort James	USG
Gaylord Container	Weyerhaeuser
International Paper	Willamette

HISTORICAL FINANCIALS & EMPLOYEES

Holding company FYE: December 31	Annual Growth	1989	1990	1991	1992	1993	1994	1995	1996	1997	1998
Sales ($ mil.)	3.1%	10,171	12,665	11,524	11,847	12,287	12,738	14,313	13,024	13,094	13,336
Net income ($ mil.)	(9.3%)	661	365	(79)	(124)	(77)	249	921	156	69	274
Income as % of sales	—	6.5%	2.9%	—	—	—	2.0%	6.4%	1.2%	0.5%	2.1%
Employees	(0.6%)	—	—	—	—	—	—	—	45,500	46,500	45,000

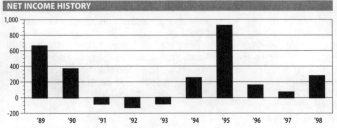

NET INCOME HISTORY

1998 FISCAL YEAR-END
Return on equity: 8.8%
Cash ($ mil.): 5
Current ratio: 1.00
Long-term debt ($ mil.): 4,125

THE GILLETTE COMPANY

OVERVIEW

Is Warren Buffett a blade man, or does he use a shaver? Either way, The Gillette Company (of which Buffett's Berkshire Hathaway owns around 9%) has what he needs. Boston-based Gillette is the world's #1 maker of shaving supplies for men and women. Buffett can also use Gillette's Paper Mate, Waterman, or Parker pens to jot down a shopping list of products which might include an Oral-B toothbrush and dental floss, Right Guard deodorant, Duracell batteries, and Braun shavers and appliances. If he makes a mistake, he can fix it with Liquid Paper correction fluid.

And big as it is stateside, Gillette is even bigger abroad: Almost two-thirds of sales are made overseas. The company meets its goal of maintaining the leadership spot in each of its markets with bold advertising campaigns and vigorous research and development operations (nearly half of sales come from products launched in the last five years). Gillette's newest star, perhaps the holy grail of smooth shaving, is the #1 selling Mach3 triple-bladed razor.

HISTORY

King Gillette, a salesman for the Baltimore Seal Company, originated the idea of a disposable razor blade in 1895 while shaving with a dull straight razor at his home in Brookline, Massachusetts. For the next six years, Gillette developed his idea yet could find no backers. Finally, in 1901 MIT machinist William Nickerson joined Gillette and perfected the safety razor. With the financial support of some wealthy friends, the two men formed The Gillette Safety Razor Company in Boston.

Gillette put his razor on the market in 1903 but sold only 51 sets. The good news spread fast, however, and the next year Gillette Safety Razor sold 90,844 sets. Gillette established his first overseas operation in London in 1905. Five years later Gillette sold most of his interest in the business (he remained president of the company until 1931) to pursue his utopian corporate theories, first described in his 1894 book *The Human Drift*.

The company introduced self-shaving to a generation of young men by selling shaving kits to the US military during WWI. In the 1920s Gillette Safety Razor distributed free razors through such outlets as banks (via the "Shave and Save" plan) and boxes of Wrigley's gum. The tactics brought millions of new customers. Foreign expansion continued, and by 1923 business overseas accounted for 30% of the firm's sales.

In 1939 Gillette Safety Razor paid $100,000 to obtain the radio broadcast rights for the World Series, initiating its long-standing commitment to advertising during sporting events. The company began diversifying in 1948 by purchasing Toni (home permanent kits), which became the Personal Care Division in 1971. In the 1950s it adopted its present name, The Gillette Company, introduced Foamy (shaving cream, 1953), and bought Paper Mate (pens, 1955).

During the 1960s and 1970s, product expansion continued (Right Guard deodorant, Cricket disposable lighters, Eraser Mate pens). It also acquired Braun, maker of electric shavers and appliances, in 1967 and Liquid Paper in 1979. In 1984 Gillette branched into dental care products with the purchase of Oral-B.

Attracted by Gillette's consumer brands, Revlon chairman Ron Perelman made a failed attempt to buy the company in 1986. Two years later the company overcame a proxy battle with investment firm Coniston Partners, eventually buying back Coniston's 6% stake. In 1989 Warren Buffett's Berkshire Hathaway acquired 11% of the company's stock (later reduced to approximately 9%).

Alfred Zeien took over as CEO in 1991 and gave each Gillette business the goal of seizing or maintaining the #1 spot in its market. It continued to expand its product base through the 1990s and found success in foreign markets. Gillette also continued to make acquisitions, but only in sectors where it could operate as the #1 or #2 player. It bought the Parker pen business in 1993 (making it the leading seller of premium-priced pens) and in 1996 added Duracell, the #1 battery maker.

Facing high costs and unstable international markets, in 1998 Gillette announced it would slash its worldwide workforce by 11%, closing 14 plants, 12 warehouses, and 30 offices. That year — after six years of preparation and an investment of roughly $750 million — the firm unveiled the triple-bladed Mach3 razor. By 1999 Gillette's razor-sharp investment began to pay off: The Mach3 had become the #1 US blade and razor. Also in 1999 CEO Zeien retired; COO Michael Hawley replaced him.

Chairman and CEO: Michael C. Hawley
EVP, Global Business Management, Gillette Grooming Products and Duracell: Edward F. DeGraan, age 55, $633,000 pay
EVP, Commercial Operations, Western Hemisphere: Robert G. King, age 53, $677,083 pay
EVP, Global Business Management, Diversified Group: Archibald Livis, age 60, $700,000 pay
EVP, Commercial Operations, Eastern Hemisphere: Jorgen Wedel, age 50
SVP, Finance and CFO: Charles W. Cramb, age 52
SVP, Global Business Management, Gillette Grooming Products and Duracell: Allan G. Boath
SVP, Personnel and Administration: Robert E. DiCenso
VP, Human Resources: Edward E. Guillet
Auditors: KPMG LLP

LOCATIONS

HQ: Prudential Tower Bldg., Boston, MA 02199
Phone: 617-421-7000   **Fax:** 617-421-7123
Web site: http://www.gillette.com

PRODUCTS/OPERATIONS

1998 Sales & Operating Income

	Sales		Operating Income	
	$ mil.	% of total	$ mil.	% of total
Blades & razors	3,028	30	1,153	50
Duracell products	2,576	26	597	26
Braun products	1,740	17	291	13
Toiletries	1,214	12	54	2
Stationery products	856	9	108	5
Oral-B	642	6	101	4
Adjustments	—	—	(515)	—
Total	**10,056**	**100**	**1,789**	**100**

Selected Brand Names

Blades and Razors
Atra
Custom Plus
Good News
Mach3
Sensor
SensorExcel
Trac II

Batteries
Duracell

Braun Division
Braun (small appliances)
Thermoscan (instant thermometers)
VitalScan (blood pressure monitors)

Toiletries
Dry Idea (antiperspirant)
Gillette Series (men's toiletries)
Right Guard (deodorant)

Satin Care (women's shaving gel)
Soft & Dri (antiperspirant)
White Rain (hair care products)

Stationery Products
Liquid Paper
Paper Mate
Parker
Waterman

Oral-B Division
Advantage (toothbrush)
Contura (toothbrush, overseas)
Gripper (children's toothbrush)
Oral-B (toothbrush and dental products)
Prudent (toothbrush, overseas)
Ultra Floss (dental floss)

COMPETITORS

American Safety Razor
A. T. Cross
BIC
Bristol-Myers Squibb
Carter-Wallace
Colgate-Palmolive
Dial
Johnson & Johnson
Pfizer
Philips Electronics
Procter & Gamble
Ralston Purina
Rayovac
Remington Products
SANYO
S.C. Johnson
SEB
SmithKline Beecham
Sunbeam
Unilever
Warner-Lambert
Waterford Wedgwood

HISTORICAL FINANCIALS & EMPLOYEES

NYSE symbol: G FYE: December 31	Annual Growth	1989	1990	1991	1992	1993	1994	1995	1996	1997	1998
Sales ($ mil.)	11.4%	3,819	4,345	4,684	5,163	5,411	6,070	6,795	9,698	10,062	10,056
Net income ($ mil.)	16.0%	285	368	427	513	288	698	824	949	1,427	1,081
Income as % of sales	—	7.5%	8.5%	9.1%	9.9%	5.3%	11.5%	12.1%	9.8%	14.2%	10.7%
Earnings per share ($)	12.1%	0.34	0.40	0.49	0.58	0.25	0.82	0.95	0.83	1.25	0.95
Stock price - FY high ($)	—	6.22	8.16	14.03	15.31	15.94	19.13	27.69	38.88	53.19	62.66
Stock price - FY low ($)	—	4.13	5.44	7.05	10.97	11.84	14.44	17.69	24.13	36.00	32.25
Stock price - FY close ($)	25.6%	6.14	7.84	14.03	14.22	14.91	18.72	26.06	38.88	50.22	47.81
P/E - high	—	18	20	29	26	64	23	29	47	43	66
P/E - low	—	12	14	14	19	47	18	19	29	29	34
Dividends per share ($)	13.0%	0.12	0.14	0.15	0.18	0.21	0.25	0.29	0.35	0.42	0.36
Book value per share ($)	52.5%	0.09	0.33	1.29	1.66	1.62	2.22	2.76	3.98	4.25	4.04
Employees	4.0%	30,400	30,400	31,200	30,900	33,400	32,800	33,500	44,100	44,000	43,100

STOCK PRICE HISTORY HIGH/LOW/CLOSE

1998 FISCAL YEAR-END
Debt ratio: 33.2%
Return on equity: 24.2%
Cash ($ mil.): 102
Current ratio: 1.56
Long-term debt ($ mil.): 2,256
No. of shares (mil.): 1,105
Dividends
  Yield: 0.8%
  Payout: 37.9%
Market value ($ mil.): 52,850

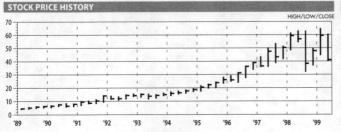

GOLDEN WEST FINANCIAL

OVERVIEW

Across the bay from such glittering financial names as Wells Fargo and Transamerica, sits dowdy, thrifty, Oakland, California-based Golden West Financial. The company's World Savings and Loan (the #2 US thrift behind Washington Mutual) has 250 banking branches in eight states, as well as some 250 loan offices in 26 states; half of the company's loan offices share premises with banking operations. Golden West prides itself on fiscal strength drawn from conservative management and cost controls (branches are small and spartan; ATMs didn't appear until 1998). Golden West Financial also owns Atlas Assets, which offers a line of no-load mutual funds.

Herbert and Marion Sandler, the husband-and-wife team that runs Golden West, have kept it financially healthy by sticking to the unglamorous business of providing deposit accounts and making home loans. The company retains most of its adjustable-rate mortgages, but sells its fixed-rate loans. The Sandlers own about 10% of Golden West; Marion's brother, Bernard Osher, has another 6%.

The disappearance of several significant rivals boosted Golden West's rank in the industry (#1 Washington Mutual keeps gobbling up such erstwhile competitors as Great Western Financial and H.F. Ahmanson). Nonetheless, #2 now will have to try harder, facing fiercer home-turf battles against more aggressive foes with deeper pockets.

HISTORY

World Savings and Loan Association was founded in 1912 as a stock savings and loan (S&L) association. In 1959 Trans-World Financial Co. was incorporated as its parent. The company chugged along until 1963, when Herbert and Marion Sandler bought it. Herbert was a lawyer who had worked with financial institutions, and Marion was a securities analyst.

Trans-World went public in 1968. Seven years later it merged with Golden West Financial, parent of Golden West Savings & Loan. The resulting holding company took the Golden West name, but the S&Ls became World Savings and Loan. In 1982 Golden West acquired First S&L Shares and its subsidiary, Majestic Savings & Loan.

During the 1970s and into the 1980s, when many S&Ls were whipsawed by soaring interest rates and a legacy of low fixed-rate mortgages, Golden West concentrated on the pedestrian business of collecting savings deposits and making primarily single-family mortgage loans.

When S&Ls were deregulated in the early 1980s, many institutions ill-advisedly rushed into commercial real estate. Golden West was there to pick up the pieces when regulators closed the erstwhile high-fliers. In 1985 the company moved into Texas with the acquisition of the failed Bell Savings Banc.

Golden West continued to buy pieces of defunct S&Ls, gaining good loans and deposits while the government retained the bad loans. Such acquisitions included all or part of Blue Valley Federal Savings (Missouri, 1990), American Savings (Colorado, 1990), Security Savings (Arizona, 1991), and Beach Federal Savings (Florida, 1991). These deals helped the company expand nationally at low cost. The Beach Federal Savings deal, for example, involved the acquisition of $1.5 billion in assets for $40 million.

When the recession came to California in the early 1990s, many of Golden West's competitors were devastated by real estate defaults. The company's earnings slipped as well, but because it had little exposure to commercial real estate, it remained strong enough to expand in Arizona (where the thrift and banking industry was wracked by failures). Golden West bought the Arizona operations of PriMerit Bank (seven branches) in 1993 and acquired selected deposits the next year from Polifly Savings & Loan, which extended its operations to New Jersey.

Golden West took advantage of new regulations that favored banks over S&Ls, buying Watchung Hills Bank for Savings (New Jersey), renaming it World Savings Bank, and opening bank branches on some of its S&L premises in California, Colorado, and New Jersey.

Meanwhile, back in California, the economy was looking up. Residential real estate roared back and Golden West rose with its market, more than doubling earnings in 1997 because of improved business, lower reserves for loan losses, and lower deposit insurance premiums. The trend continued through 1998 when the local housing market jump-started the demand for mortgages.

Suffering from stock downturns caused by fear of a Federal Reserve interest rate hike, Golden West repurchased 5% of its stock in 1999.

Co-Chairman and Co-CEO, Golden West Financial, World Savings and Loan, and World Savings Bank: Herbert M. Sandler, age 67, $1,074,868 pay
Co-Chairman and Co-CEO, Golden West Financial, World Savings and Loan, and World Savings Bank: Marion O. Sandler, age 68, $1,074,868 pay
President and Treasurer; SEVP, World Savings and Loan and World Savings Bank: Russell W. Kettell, age 55, $577,908 pay
SEVP; President and COO, World Savings and Loan and World Savings Bank: James T. Judd, age 60, $636,484 pay
EVP, Golden West Financial, World Savings and Loan, and World Savings Bank: Dirk S. Adams, age 47, $367,500 pay
EVP, Golden West Financial, World Savings and Loan, and World Savings Bank: J. L. Helvey, age 67
SVP and Secretary, Golden West Financial, World Savings and Loan, and World Savings Bank: Robert C. Rowe, age 43
Director Human Resources: Susan Lennox
Auditors: Deloitte & Touche LLP

LOCATIONS

HQ: Golden West Financial Corporation, 1901 Harrison St., Oakland, CA 94612
Phone: 510-446-3420   **Fax:** 510-446-4259

Golden West Financial has savings and lending operations in Arizona, California, Colorado, Florida, Illinois, Kansas, New Jersey, and Texas and lending offices in Connecticut, Delaware, Idaho, Maryland, Massachusetts, Michigan, Minnesota, Missouri, Nevada, New Mexico, North Carolina, Oregon, Pennsylvania, South Dakota, Utah, Virginia, Washington, and Wisconsin.

PRODUCTS/OPERATIONS

1998 Assets

	$ mil.	% of total
Cash & equivalents	251	1
Mortgage-backed securities	10,032	26
Other securities	377	1
Net loans	25,721	67
Other investments	1,248	3
Other	840	2
Total	**38,469**	**100**

1998 Sales

	$ mil.	% of total
Loan interest	2,254	73
Other interest	708	23
Service charges & fees	63	2
Other income	75	2
Total	**3,100**	**100**

Selected Subsidiaries
Atlas Advisers, Inc.
Atlas Assets, Inc. (mutual funds)
Atlas Securities, Inc.
World Mortgage Investors, Inc.
World Real Estate Investors, Inc.
World Savings and Loan Association

COMPETITORS

Bank of America
Bank of the West
BANK ONE
Chase Manhattan
Citigroup
Countrywide Credit
First Union
Fleet
FMR
Golden State Bancorp
Silicon Valley Bancshares
U. S. Bancorp
UnionBanCal
Washington Mutual
Wells Fargo

HISTORICAL FINANCIALS & EMPLOYEES

NYSE symbol: GDW FYE: December 31	Annual Growth	1989	1990	1991	1992	1993	1994	1995	1996	1997	1998
Assets ($ mil.)	7.8%	19,521	22,562	24,298	25,891	28,829	31,684	35,118	37,731	39,590	38,469
Net income ($ mil.)	11.9%	158	182	239	284	274	230	235	165	354	435
Income as % of assets	—	0.8%	0.8%	1.0%	1.1%	1.0%	0.7%	0.7%	0.4%	0.9%	1.1%
Earnings per share ($)	13.0%	2.51	2.87	3.76	4.46	4.28	3.71	3.94	2.80	6.13	7.52
Stock price - FY high ($)	—	33.75	35.25	44.25	46.25	50.38	46.00	57.50	68.75	97.94	114.50
Stock price - FY low ($)	—	15.38	17.63	22.25	35.50	37.13	34.25	34.75	49.00	58.88	69.81
Stock price - FY close ($)	14.6%	26.88	24.63	43.63	43.38	39.00	35.25	55.25	63.13	97.81	91.69
P/E - high	—	13	12	12	10	12	12	15	25	16	15
P/E - low	—	6	6	6	8	9	9	9	18	10	9
Dividends per share ($)	14.8%	0.15	0.17	0.19	0.23	0.27	0.31	0.35	0.40	0.46	0.52
Book value per share ($)	14.2%	16.61	19.27	22.82	27.02	32.31	34.14	38.70	40.99	47.28	54.95
Employees	7.2%	2,818	3,161	3,798	4,019	4,376	4,559	4,461	4,028	4,879	5,289

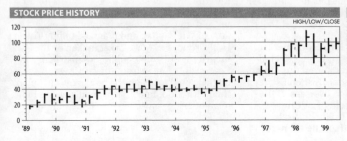

STOCK PRICE HISTORY HIGH/LOW/CLOSE

1998 FISCAL YEAR-END
Equity as % of assets: 8.1%
Return on assets: 1.1%
Return on equity: 13.9%
Long-term debt ($ mil.): 912
No. of shares (mil.): 57
Dividends
  Yield: 0.6%
  Payout: 6.9%
Market value ($ mil.): 5,214
Sales (mil.): $3,100

THE GOLDMAN SACHS GROUP, INC.

OVERVIEW

The Goldman Sachs Group has done enough initial public offerings (IPOs) to know when the getting is good, so in 1999 the company — the last major partnership on Wall Street — sold about 11% of itself to the public in the largest financial services IPO in history.

One of the top underwriters of US IPOs, Goldman Sachs' business lines include mergers and acquisitions, research, securities and commodities trading, foreign exchange, and real estate. In addition, proprietary trading remains one of its most lucrative activities.

Many of the firm's superlatives derive from the financial health and strength of the US economy rather than market share overseas. Currently, about one-quarter of the firm's sales come from overseas. The firm hopes to increase this number and is working in particular on taking advantage of the realignments occurring in the European Union.

The Kamehameha Schools/Bishop Estate of Hawaii trust owns about 5% of Goldman Sachs.

HISTORY

German immigrant and Philadelphia retailer Marcus Goldman moved to New York in 1869 and began buying customers' promissory notes from jewelers to resell to banks. Samuel Sachs, Goldman's son-in-law, came aboard in 1882, and the firm became Goldman, Sachs & Co. in 1885.

Two years later Goldman Sachs, through British merchant bankers Kleinwort Sons, offered its clients US-UK foreign exchange and currency services. To serve clients like Sears, Roebuck, it expanded to Chicago and St. Louis. In 1896 it joined the NYSE.

Before WWI the firm increased its contacts in Europe. Goldman's son Henry made the firm a major source of financing for US industry, and in 1906 it co-managed its first public offering, United Cigar Manufacturers (later General Cigar). By 1920 it had underwritten IPOs for Sears, B.F. Goodrich, and Merck.

Sidney Weinberg made partner in 1927 and remained active in the firm until his death in 1969. In the 1930s Goldman Sachs opened securities dealing and sales departments. After WWII it became a leader in investment banking, co-managing Ford's IPO in 1956.

Under Weinberg's son, John (first co-senior partner with John Whitehead, 1976), Goldman Sachs became a leader in mergers and acquisitions. In 1981 the acquisition of J. Aron Co. gave the firm significant presence in commodities, including precious metals. Contacts made through Aron helped it grow in South America. The next year it acquired First Dallas, Ltd. (landed merchant banking).

In the aftermath of the 1987 stock market crash, Goldman Sachs sought capital, including nonparticipatory interests from Sumitomo and the Kamehameha Schools/Bishop Estate.

Goldman Sachs expanded overseas in the 1990s, but there were problems: A Chinese project fell through after Goldman Sachs asked for a greater share than the Chinese were willing to grant, and in Russia it hitched its wagon to a government official who was booted out of office.

The 1994 bond crash and a decline in new debt issues led Goldman Sachs to lay off staff for the first time since the 1980s. Even partners began leaving (including senior partner Stephen Friedman, whom some blamed for the problems), taking their equity with them. Cost cuts, a stronger bond market, and the long bull market helped the firm rebound. Firm members also sought to protect themselves with limited liability partnership status, and they extended the period during which partners could cash out (thereby slowing the cash drain).

In 1996 Goldman Sachs bought UK pension manager CIN Management and Liberty Investment Management. The next year the firm acquired Commodities Corp. and began a new push into Asia.

After rejecting such a move at least six times in the previous 30 years, the partners in 1998 voted to sell the public a minority stake in the firm. Market volatility, however, led to a postponement. Goldman Sachs also suffered from involvement with Long-Term Capital Management; the New York Federal Reserve Bank persuaded the firm to contribute to the notorious hedge fund's bailout.

In 1999 Goldman Sachs moved aggressively into the Internet space: It began plans for an online brokerage; it set up Internet underwriting system GS-Online; it bought more than 20% of Wit Capital; and it agreed to buy The Hull Group, a major market maker. As it inched toward going public, co-chairman Jon Corzine was forced from the co-CEO spot, saying he would focus on the public offering plan, then retire. Goldman Sachs finally went public in an offering valued at close to $4 billion.

Co-Chairman and CEO: Henry M. Paulson Jr., age 53, $600,000 pay
Co-Chairman: Jon S. Corzine, age 52
VC: Robert J. Hurst Jr., age 53, $600,000 pay
President and Co-COO: John A. Thain, age 43, $600,000 pay
President and Co-COO: John L. Thornton, age 45, $600,000 pay
CFO: David A. Viniar, age 43, $600,000 pay
General Counsel: Robert J. Katz, age 51
General Counsel: Gregory K. Palm, age 50
Chief of Staff: Robin Neustein, age 45
Chief Information Officer: Leslie M. Tortora, age 42
Chief Administrative Officer: Barry L. Zubrow, age 46
Co-Head, Equities: Robert K. Steel
Co-Head, Equities; Deputy Chairman - Europe: Patrick J. Ward
Co-COO, Investment Banking: Steven M. "Mac" Heller
Co-COO, Investment Banking: Robert S. Kaplan
Co-COO, Investment Banking; Deputy Chairman - Europe: Peter A. Weinberg
Head, Leveraged Finance: Jon Winkelried
Co-Head, Merchant Banking: Richard A. Friedman
Co-Head, Merchant Banking: Daniel M. Neidich
VP Personnel: Bruce Larson
Auditors: PricewaterhouseCoopers LLP

HQ: 85 Broad St., New York, NY 10004
Phone: 212-902-1000   **Fax:** 212-902-3000
Web site: http://www.gs.com

The Goldman Sachs Group has offices from coast to coast in the US and in Canada, Mexico, and South America. Overseas, it has regional headquarters in Hong Kong, London, and Tokyo and offices throughout Asia and Europe.

1998 Sales

	$ mil.	% of total
The Americas	15,972	71
Europe	5,156	23
Asia	1,350	6
Total	**22,478**	**100**

1998 Sales

	$ mil.	% of total
Interest	15,010	67
Investment banking	3,368	15
Asset management & securities services	2,085	9
Trading & principal investments	2,015	9
Total	**22,478**	**100**

Significant Subsidiaries
Goldman, Sachs & Co.
Goldman Sachs (Asia) Finance Holdings L.L.C.
Goldman Sachs Capital Markets, L.P.
Goldman Sachs (Cayman) Holding Company (Cayman Islands)
Goldman, Sachs & Co. Bank (Switzerland)
Goldman, Sachs & Co. oHG (Germany)
Goldman Sachs Credit Partners, L.P. (Bermuda)
Goldman Sachs Holdings L.L.C. (49%, with Caterpillar Inc.)
Goldman Sachs International Bank (UK)
Goldman Sachs Holdings (Netherlands) B.V.
Goldman Sachs Mitsui Marine Derivative Products, L.P. (49%, with Mitsui Marine & Fire Insurance Co.)
Goldman Sachs (Japan) Ltd. (British Virgin Islands)
Goldman Sachs Mortgage Company
J. Aron Holdings, L.P.
J. Aron & Company

Bear Stearns	Lehman Brothers
Brown Brothers Harriman	Merrill Lynch
Canadian Imperial	Morgan Stanley Dean
Charles Schwab	Witter
Citigroup	Nomura Securities
Credit Suisse	Paine Webber
Deutsche Bank	Prudential
DLJ	Royal Bank of Canada
FMR	Salomon Smith Barney
ING	Holdings
J.P. Morgan	

NYSE symbol: GS FYE: November 30	Annual Growth	1989	1990	1991	1992	1993	1994	1995	1996	1997	1998
Sales ($ mil.)	8.6%	—	—	—	—	14,848	12,452	14,324	17,289	20,433	22,478
Net income ($ mil.)	36.7%	—	—	—	—	508	1,370	1,348	2,399	2,746	2,428
Income as % of sales	—	—	—	—	—	3.4%	11.0%	9.4%	13.9%	13.4%	10.8%
Employees	11.8%	—	—	—	—	8,103	8,998	8,159	8,977	10,622	14,170

Debt ratio: 75.9%
Return on equity: 38.5%
Cash ($ mil.): —
Current ratio: —
Long-term debt ($ mil.): 19,906

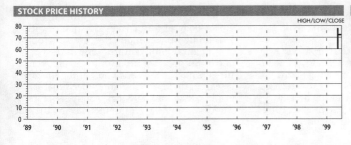

HIGH/LOW/CLOSE

80
70
60
50
40
30
20
10
0
'89 '90 '91 '92 '93 '94 '95 '96 '97 '98 '99

GOODYEAR TIRE & RUBBER

OVERVIEW

Goodyear is hoping for a good year. Akron, Ohio-based Goodyear Tire & Rubber is the world's #1 tire maker. Goodyear also makes industrial and consumer products from rubber, including belts, hoses, and tank tracks, and it produces a wide range of synthetic rubber, resins, and organic chemicals. The company's retail tire outlets provide auto repair services at more than 900 outlets.

Goodyear supplies tires to European and North American automakers; construction and agricultural equipment makers; and the replacement tire market. The company has leapfrogged rivals Bridgestone and Michelin to become #1 through its alliance with Japan's Sumitomo Rubber Industries — Goodyear took over Sumitomo's Dunlop brand tire operations in North America and Europe and took a 10% stake in the company in exchange for Goodyear's operations in Japan and $936 million in cash.

HISTORY

In 1898 Frank and Charles Seiberling founded a tire and rubber company in Akron, Ohio, and named it after Charles Goodyear (inventor of the vulcanization process, 1839). Goodyear targeted the automotive industry. The debut of the Quick Detachable tire and the Universal Rim (1903) made Goodyear the world's largest tire maker by 1916, the same year it introduced the pneumatic truck tire.

Goodyear began manufacturing in Canada in 1910 and over the next two decades expanded into Argentina, Australia, and the Dutch East Indies. It established its own rubber plantations in Sumatra (now part of Indonesia) in 1916.

Financial woes led to reorganization in 1921, and investment bankers forced the Seiberlings out. Succeeding caretaker management, Paul Litchfield began three decades as CEO in 1926. By that year Goodyear had become the world's largest rubber company.

By the 1930s Goodyear blimps served as floating billboards nationwide. During that decade Goodyear opened company stores, acquired tire maker Kelly-Springfield (1935), and began producing tires made from synthetic rubber (1937). After WWII, Goodyear was a leader in new technologies such as polyester tire cord (1962) and the bias-belted tire (1967). The company provided the tires used on the Apollo 14 Lunar Rover in 1970.

By 1980 Goodyear had introduced the all-weather Tiempo, the Eagle, and the Arriva and led the US market. These brands were all radial tires, an innovation introduced in the US by Michelin in 1966.

Thwarting British financier Sir James Goldsmith's takeover attempt in 1986, CEO Robert Mercer raised $1.7 billion by selling non-tire businesses (Motor Wheel, Goodyear Aerospace, and Celeron Oil) and by borrowing heavily.

Recession, overcapacity, and price-cutting in 1990 led to hard times for tire makers.

Goodyear's problems were worsened by heavy interest payments on debt incurred in its 1986 takeover defense. After suffering through 1990, its first money-losing year since the Depression, Goodyear lured Stanley Gault out of retirement. He ceased marketing tires exclusively through Goodyear's dealer network by selling tires through Wal-Mart, Kmart, and Sears. Gault also cut costs through layoffs, plant closures, and spending reductions and returned Goodyear to profitability in 1991.

The company increased its presence in the US retail market in 1995 when it began selling tires to 860 Penske Auto Centers and 300 Montgomery Ward auto centers. President Samir Gibara succeeded chairman Gault as CEO in 1996. That year the company bought the leading tire maker in Poland, T C Debica, and a 60% stake in South African tire maker Contred (it acquired the rest in 1998).

In 1997 Goodyear formed an alliance with Tokyo-based Sumitomo Rubber Industries under which the companies make and market tires for one another in Asia and North America. The company paid $120 million that year for a controlling stake in Sava Group, a Slovenian tire maker.

In 1998 Goodyear sold the Celeron subsidiary, which operated the All American Pipeline, to Plains Resources for about $420 million and acquired its remaining 26% stake in tire distributor Brad Ragan (53 commercial outlets in 19 states and 116 retail outlets in the South) for $20.7 million. In 1999 Goodyear formed a broad alliance with Sumitomo Rubber Industries, creating four geographical joint ventures (one in the US, one in Europe, two in Japan), one joint venture for purchasing, and another for sharing research. Goodyear also announced that it would cut about 2,800 jobs, about 3% of its workforce, in Asia, Latin America, and the US.

Chairman, President, and CEO: Samir F. Gibara, age 59, $1,571,299 pay
President of North American Tire: William J. Sharp, age 57, $696,168 pay (prior to title change)
President of Eastern Europe, Africa and Middle East Region: Michael J. Roney
President of European Union Region: Sylvain G. Valensi, age 56
EVP and CFO: Robert W. Tieken, age 59, $579,851 pay
VP and Secretary: James Boyazis, age 62
VP Public Affairs: John P. Perduyn, age 59
VP Materials Management: Richard P. Adante, age 52
VP Purchasing: Gary A. Miller, age 52
VP Human Resources and Total Quality Systems: Mike L. Burns, age 57
VP Finance, North America Tires: George E. Strickler, age 51
VP Corporate Research: Richard J. Steichen, age 55
VP and General Counsel: C. Thomas Harvie, age 56, $480,252 pay
VP, Goodyear Tire Latin America: John C. Polhemus, age 54
VP and Treasurer: Stephanie W. Bergeron, age 45
Auditors: PricewaterhouseCoopers LLP

WHERE

HQ: The Goodyear Tire & Rubber Company, 1144 E. Market St., Akron, OH 44316-0001
Phone: 330-796-2121   **Fax:** 330-796-2222
Web site: http://www.goodyear.com

Goodyear Tire & Rubber has about 90 plants in the US and in about 29 other countries. The company operates about 900 retail outlets in the US.

1998 Sales & Operating Income

	Sales		Operating Income	
	$ mil.	% of total	$ mil.	% of total
North America	6,234	48	379	34
Europe	2,911	22	302	27
Latin America	1,246	9	186	16
Asia	502	4	8	1
Other regions	2,257	17	251	22
Adjustments	(524)	—	(123)	—
Total	**12,626**	**100**	**1,003**	**100**

WHAT

Selected Products
Automotive equipment
Bias-ply tires
Chemical products
Conveyor belts
Industrial rubber products
Radial tires
Rubber
Synthetic rubber

KEY COMPETITORS

Bandag
Bridgestone
Continental AG
Cooper Tire & Rubber
Michelin
Midas
Pep Boys
Pirelli Tire

HISTORICAL FINANCIALS & EMPLOYEES

NYSE symbol: GT FYE: December 31	Annual Growth	1989	1990	1991	1992	1993	1994	1995	1996	1997	1998
Sales ($ mil.)	1.7%	10,869	11,273	10,907	11,785	11,643	12,288	13,166	13,113	13,155	12,626
Net income ($ mil.)	15.3%	189	(38)	97	(659)	388	567	611	102	559	682
Income as % of sales	—	1.7%	—	0.9%	—	3.3%	4.6%	4.6%	0.8%	4.2%	5.4%
Earnings per share ($)	11.3%	1.64	(0.33)	0.81	(4.62)	2.64	3.75	3.97	0.65	3.53	4.31
Stock price - FY high ($)	—	29.88	23.19	27.06	38.06	47.25	49.25	45.38	53.00	71.25	76.75
Stock price - FY low ($)	—	21.06	6.44	8.38	26.00	32.56	31.63	33.00	41.50	49.25	45.88
Stock price - FY close ($)	9.8%	21.75	9.44	26.75	34.19	45.75	33.63	45.38	51.38	63.63	50.44
P/E - high	—	18	—	33	—	18	13	11	82	20	18
P/E - low	—	13	—	10	—	12	8	8	64	14	11
Dividends per share ($)	3.2%	0.90	0.90	0.20	0.28	0.58	0.75	0.95	1.03	1.14	1.20
Book value per share ($)	2.9%	18.54	17.94	19.32	13.36	15.29	18.51	21.38	21.01	21.68	24.02
Employees	(1.5%)	111,489	107,671	99,952	95,712	91,754	90,712	87,930	88,903	95,472	96,950

STOCK PRICE HISTORY

HIGH/LOW/CLOSE

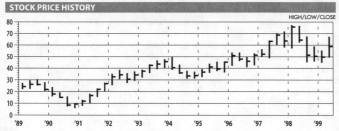

1998 FISCAL YEAR-END

Debt ratio: 24.1%
Return on equity: 18.2%
Cash ($ mil.): 239
Current ratio: 1.38
Long-term debt ($ mil.): 1,187
No. of shares (mil.): 156
Dividends
  Yield: 2.4%
  Payout: 27.8%
Market value ($ mil.): 7,866

GPU, INC.

OVERVIEW

As its customers prepare to pick new power providers, GPU is saying goodbye to its old generation. The Morristown, New Jersey-based holding company is leaving the electricity generation business to focus on power transmission. GPU is selling fossil-fueled facilities, its interest in the Three Mile Island (TMI) Unit 1 nuclear plant, and its Oyster Creek nuclear facility. GPU still owns the license for the defunct TMI Unit 2, which was responsible for the infamous 1979 accident.

GPU Energy delivers power through three utilities — Jersey Central Power & Light, Metropolitan Edison, and Pennsylvania Electric — to nearly 2 million customers in New Jersey and Pennsylvania. Electric competition has begun in both states, where unregulated subsidiary GPU Advanced Resources, a power marketer, pursues new retail customers. GPU is also moving into other distribution businesses, including natural gas, water, and telecommunications (it develops and manages telecom infrastructure).

GPU owns merchant power plants in Latin America and the US (925 MW), an Australian gas transmission system, electric distributors in Argentina, and Midland Electricity, a UK regional electric company.

HISTORY

GPU began as the Associated Gas & Electric Company (Ageco) in 1906. In 1922 Howard Hopson, a former New York utility regulator, and John Mange, Ageco's general manager, secretly bought up Ageco's stock. Mange became president and Hopson treasurer. Hopson came up with a pyramid scheme by which Ageco became one of the biggest US utility holding companies by 1929. His tactics (typical for the day) included overpaying for a firm, recording its inflated value, and issuing excessive securities on the strength of the write-up.

Throughout the Depression, Ageco stayed ahead of its banks and stockholders. But in 1935, largely because of Hopson's excesses, Congress passed the Public Utility Holding Company Act, ushering in six decades of regionalized and highly regulated utilities.

Ageco declared bankruptcy in 1940, but the SEC didn't approve its reorganization until after WWII. Under new management, Ageco became General Public Utilities (GPU) in 1946. In the 1950s GPU divested some of its properties and improved its power plants' efficiency.

In 1963 GPU became the first US utility to invest in a commercial nuclear plant, Oyster Creek (completed in 1969). Shortly afterward it began building Three Mile Island (TMI); Unit 1 went on line in 1974 and Unit 2 in 1978. A 1979 accident at TMI Unit 2 overheated the reactor core, damaged the plant, and released radioactive particles. It was shut down, and GPU faced bankruptcy. The Nuclear Regulatory Commission investigated and wrote sweeping new safety rules that raised the costs of nukes, causing many to be abandoned or converted to fossil fuel. GPU struggled financially until it was allowed to restart Unit 1 in 1985. Meanwhile, the cost of cleaning up Unit 2 (placed in long-term storage in 1993) rose to $1 billion.

GPU reorganized in 1994 and cut 1,350 jobs. At first the Pennsylvania Commonwealth Court wouldn't allow GPU to use its rates to recover the $184 million in future costs for TMI Unit 2, but the next year the Pennsylvania Supreme Court gave the okay.

The company acquired 50% of Solaris, an Australian power company, in 1995 and the next year, with Cinergy, bought Midlands Electricity, a regional electricity company (REC) in the UK. In 1996, the year Pennsylvania passed a deregulation bill, the firm changed its name to GPU, Inc. GPU formed telecommunications and power marketing businesses, and in 1997 it formed a solar electricity joint venture with AstroPower.

In early 1998 GPU bought Australian transmission company PowerNet but had to sell its stake in Solaris to avoid cross-ownership. GPU began to divest power plants that year, first agreeing to sell the TMI Unit 1 to AmerGen Energy for about $100 million, then 23 power plants to Sithe Energies for $1.72 billion. In 1999 GPU agreed to sell its Oyster Creek nuclear facility to AmerGen.

GPU and Cinergy sold off Midlands' power generation arm for $300 million in 1999, and GPU bought out Cinergy's interest in the REC's distribution activities. Midlands was also hit with a major rate cut, which sent GPU into the courts to request relief. GPU bought natural gas company Transmission Pipelines Australia for $690 million and renamed the unit GPU GasNet. It also bought Argentine electricity distributor Emdersa for $435 million. That year New Jersey opened its power markets to competition.

OFFICERS

Chairman, President, and CEO, GPU and GPU Service; Chairman and CEO, Genco, Jersey Central Power & Light, Metropolitan Edison, and Pennsylvania Electric; Chairman, GPU Nuclear, GPU International, GPU Power, GPU Capital, and GPU Electric: Fred D. Hafer, age 58, $988,077 pay

SVP and CFO, GPU, Jersey Central Power & Light, Metropolitan Edison, and Pennsylvania Electric; President, GPU Capital and GPU Electric: Bruce L. Levy, age 43, $512,075 pay

SVP and General Counsel, GPU, Jersey Central Power & Light, Metropolitan Edison, and Pennsylvania Electric: Ira H. Jolles, age 60, $479,085 pay

VP, Comptroller, and Chief Accounting Officer: Peter E. Maricondo, age 52

VP and Treasurer, GPU, Jersey Central Power & Light, Metropolitan Edison, and Pennsylvania Electric: Terrance G. Howson, age 50

Secretary, GPU, GPU Service, and Genco; Assistant Secretary, GPU Nuclear, Jersey Central Power & Light, Metropolitan Edison, and Pennsylvania Electric: M. A. Nalewako, age 64

Secretary, GPU, Jersey Central Power & Light, Metropolitan Edison, and Pennsylvania Electric: S. L. Guibord, age 50

President, Genco, GPU International, and GPU Power: Robert L. Wise, age 55, $408,000 pay

President and COO, Jersey Central Power & Light, Metropolitan Edison, and Pennsylvania Electric: Dennis Baldassari, age 49, $430,000 pay

Auditors: PricewaterhouseCoopers LLP

LOCATIONS

HQ: 300 Madison Ave., Morristown, NJ 07962-1911
Phone: 973-455-8200   **Fax:** 973-455-8377
Web site: http://www.gpu.com

1998 Sales

	$ mil.	% of total
US		
Utilities and subsidiaries	3,953	71
Power investments	179	3
Nonregulated retail	11	—
International		
UK	1,203	22
Australia	181	3
Other	66	1
Adjustments	(1,344)	—
Total	**4,249**	**100**

PRODUCTS/OPERATIONS

Selected Subsidiaries
GPU Energy
  Jersey Central Power & Light Company
  Metropolitan Edison Company
  Pennsylvania Electric Company
GPU Solar
GPU Telecom Services, Inc.
GPUI Group
  GPU International, Inc.
  GPU Electric, Inc.

COMPETITORS

AES	FPL	PECO Energy
Allegheny Energy	Iberdrola	PP&L Resources
Amerada Hess	New England	PSEG
Conectiv	Electric	Reliant Energy
Consolidated	Niagara Mohawk	South Jersey
Natural Gas	Northeast	Industries
DQE	Utilities	UGI
Dynegy	Orange &	
Endesa (Spain)	Rockland	
Enron	Utilities	

HISTORICAL FINANCIALS & EMPLOYEES

NYSE symbol: GPU FYE: December 31	Annual Growth	1989	1990	1991	1992	1993	1994	1995	1996	1997	1998
Sales ($ mil.)	4.3%	2,911	2,996	3,372	3,434	3,596	3,650	3,805	3,918	4,143	4,249
Net income ($ mil.)	2.7%	283	278	276	252	296	184	440	298	335	360
Income as % of sales	—	9.7%	9.3%	8.2%	7.3%	8.2%	5.1%	11.6%	7.6%	8.1%	8.5%
Earnings per share ($)	1.3%	2.51	2.51	2.49	2.27	2.65	1.42	3.79	2.47	2.77	2.83
Stock price - FY high ($)	—	23.63	23.63	27.25	27.88	34.75	31.63	34.00	35.25	42.75	47.19
Stock price - FY low ($)	—	18.13	19.25	21.75	24.25	25.75	23.75	26.25	30.13	30.75	35.19
Stock price - FY close ($)	7.2%	23.63	22.75	27.25	27.63	30.88	26.25	34.00	33.63	42.13	44.19
P/E - high	—	9	9	11	12	13	22	9	14	15	17
P/E - low	—	7	8	9	11	10	17	7	12	11	12
Dividends per share ($)	8.3%	1.00	1.25	1.45	1.58	1.65	1.78	1.86	1.93	1.99	2.05
Book value per share ($)	4.8%	17.78	19.83	20.81	21.47	22.83	22.32	25.36	25.27	25.65	27.07
Employees	(4.1%)	13,013	12,516	12,018	11,969	11,939	10,534	10,310	9,061	9,387	8,931

STOCK PRICE HISTORY

HIGH/LOW/CLOSE

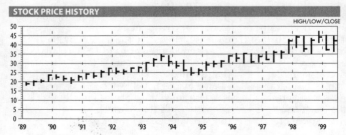

1998 FISCAL YEAR-END

Debt ratio: 49.2%
Return on equity: 10.4%
Cash ($ mil.): 73
Current ratio: 0.53
Long-term debt ($ mil.): 3,826
No. of shares (mil.): 128
Dividends
  Yield: 4.6%
  Payout: 72.4%
Market value ($ mil.): 5,656

GREAT A & P TEA COMPANY

OVERVIEW

Once "America's grocery store," blanketing cities from coast to coast, The Great Atlantic & Pacific Tea Company (A&P) now oversees a patchwork of about 750 stores in the northeastern and southern US and Canada. Although A&P remains its best-known chain, the Montvale, New Jersey-based company also runs Food Emporium and Waldbaum's in the New York City area, Farmer Jack in Michigan, and Super Fresh from New Jersey to Virginia. Other chains include Food Basics (franchised stores in Ontario, Canada), Kohl's in Wisconsin, and Sav-A-Center in several southern states.

Competitors' superstores have eaten into the sales of A&P's small and aging outlets. As a result, the company is remodeling old stores and aggressively expanding its own superstore prototype. A&P is focusing its growth on existing markets where it can achieve the #1 or #2 position, specifically New York, Detroit, New Orleans, and Ontario. To that end, A&P has exited weaker markets, including Richmond, Virginia, and Atlanta.

The company's Compass Foods division makes the Eight O'Clock, Bokar, and Royale brands of coffee (sold not only by A&P but by other food retailers). A&P is also expanding other profitable private-label offerings, primarily under its America's Choice and Master Choice brands.

President and CEO Christian Haub and his family own German retailer Tengelmann Group, which owns 55% of A&P.

HISTORY

George Gilman and George Hartford of Augusta, Maine, set up shop in 1859 on New York City's docks to sell tea at a 50% discount by eliminating middlemen. The Great American Tea Company advertised by drawing a red wagon through the city's streets. By 1869 the company, renamed The Great Atlantic & Pacific Tea Company (A&P), had 11 stores offering discounted items.

Gilman retired in 1878, and Hartford brought in his sons George and John. In 1912, when the company had 400 stores, John opened a store on a low-price, cash-and-carry format, without customer credit or premiums, which proved popular. When the company passed to the sons four years later, A&P had over 1,000 cash-and-carry stores.

The company expanded at a phenomenal pace during the 1920s and 1930s, growing to 15,900 stores by the mid-1930s; however, a movement by small retailers to restrict chain stores tarnished the country's view of A&P in particular. To improve the company's image, John initiated innovative marketing and customer service policies.

A&P grew in the 1940s by converting its stores to supermarkets, but an antitrust suit in 1949 and the company's reluctance to carry more nonfood items pushed it into decline. Management shut stores in California and Washington to shore up the northeastern stores.

In 1975, after a long period of poor sales and failed discount format attempts, the board chose a new CEO: former Albertson's president Jonathan Scott (who eventually left A&P to become president and CEO of American Stores).

Scott cut costs by closing stores and reducing the workforce, but the company's sales increases failed to keep ahead of inflation, and A&P lost $52 million in 1978.

A year later the Hartford Foundation sold its A&P holdings to the German Tengelmann Group, which in 1980 appointed English-born James Wood as CEO. A&P made several acquisitions, including Super Fresh (1982), Kohl's (1983), Pantry Pride (1984), Borman's (1989), Ontario's Miracle Food Mart (1990), and Atlanta's Big Star (1992).

Rivals' larger, newer, and cleaner supermarkets stripped away market share in New York City, Long Island, and Detroit in the early 1990s. In response, A&P closed hundreds of old stores, remodeled several hundred more, and planned openings of larger stores.

A 14-week strike in 1994 resulted in a complete shutdown of all 63 Miracle stores in Canada. In addition to lost sales, the company paid $17 million in labor settlement costs. In 1995 A&P began converting its Canadian Food Basics stores to franchises.

Christian Haub replaced Wood as CEO in 1998 (Wood remained as chairman), and A&P stepped up its modernization efforts by announcing plans to close or sell nearly 130 older stores, renovate 75 stores per year, and open as many as 200 superstores by 2001.

A&P announced plans in 1999 to roll out about 200 in-store Eight O'Clock Coffee Cafes. It also exited the Richmond, Virginia, and Atlanta markets. A&P will boost its presence in New Orleans with its planned purchase of six Schwegmann's stores, which will be converted to the Sav-A-Center banner.

OFFICERS

Chairman: James Wood, age 69, $527,098 pay
VC and CFO: Fred Corrado, $506,800 pay
VC Development & Strategic Planning: Aaron Malinsky, age 50, $476,923 pay
President and CEO: Christian W. E. Haub, $562,397 pay
SEVP and COO: Michael J. Larkin, age 57, $425,000 pay
EVP and Chief Merchandising Officer: George Graham, age 49
EVP International Store and Product Development: Peter J. O'Gorman, age 60
SVP People Resources and Services: Laurane Magliari
SVP Strategic Marketing: Cheryl M. Palmer, age 41
SVP, General Counsel, and Secretary: Robert G. Ulrich, age 64
VP Marketing and Corporate Affairs: Andrew Carrano
Chairman and Co-CEO, The Great Atlantic & Pacific Tea Company of Canada: John Dunne, age 60
Auditors: Deloitte & Touche LLP

LOCATIONS

HQ: The Great Atlantic & Pacific Tea Company, Inc., 2 Paragon Dr., Montvale, NJ 07645
Phone: 201-573-9700   **Fax:** 201-930-8144
Web site: http://www.aptea.com

The Great Atlantic & Pacific Tea Company operates supermarkets in the northeastern and southern US, the District of Columbia, and Ontario, Canada. It also has franchised stores in Canada.

1999 Sales

	$ mil.	% of total
US	8,276	81
Canada	1,516	15
Wholesale	387	4
Total	**10,179**	**100**

PRODUCTS/OPERATIONS

Store Names
A&P
Dominion
Farmer Jack
Food Basics
Food Emporium
Kohl's
Sav-A-Center
Super Foodmart
Super Fresh
Ultra Mart
Waldbaum's

Selected Subsidiaries
Borman's, Inc. d/b/a Farmer Jack
Compass Foods, Inc.
Family Center, Inc. d/b/a Family Mart
Futurestore Food Markets, Inc.
Kwik Save Inc.
Limited d/b/a A&P and New Dominion
LO-LO Discount Stores, Inc.
St. Pancras Company Limited
The Great Atlantic & Pacific Company of Canada

COMPETITORS

Albertson's
Food Lion
Giant Food
Grand Union
King Kullen Grocery
Kroger
Meijer
Pathmark
Penn Traffic
Rite Aid
Safeway
Schwegmann
Shaw's
ShopRite
Stop & Shop
Wakefern Food
Walgreen
Wal-Mart
Winn-Dixie

HISTORICAL FINANCIALS & EMPLOYEES

NYSE symbol: GAP FYE: February 28	Annual Growth	1990	1991	1992	1993	1994	1995	1996	1997	1998	1999
Sales ($ mil.)	(1.0%)	11,148	11,391	11,591	10,500	10,384	10,332	10,101	10,089	10,262	10,179
Net income ($ mil.)	—	147	151	71	(190)	4	(172)	57	73	63	(67)
Income as % of sales	—	1.3%	1.3%	0.6%	—	0.0%	—	0.6%	0.7%	0.6%	—
Earnings per share ($)	—	3.84	3.95	1.85	(4.96)	0.10	(4.49)	1.50	1.91	1.65	(1.75)
Stock price - FY high ($)	—	65.38	59.63	57.75	35.25	35.00	27.38	29.00	36.75	36.00	35.00
Stock price - FY low ($)	—	47.00	37.75	25.00	21.38	22.75	17.38	19.13	22.13	23.13	21.88
Stock price - FY close ($)	(4.8%)	49.13	52.75	31.38	23.38	26.38	19.25	22.50	29.75	30.44	31.56
P/E - high	—	17	15	31	—	350	—	19	19	22	—
P/E - low	—	12	10	14	—	228	—	13	12	14	—
Dividends per share ($)	(5.7%)	0.68	0.78	0.80	0.80	0.80	0.65	0.20	0.20	0.40	0.40
Book value per share ($)	(2.9%)	28.58	31.96	32.79	27.06	26.02	20.27	21.53	23.27	24.22	21.87
Employees	(1.0%)	91,000	99,300	94,600	90,000	94,000	92,000	89,000	84,000	80,000	83,400

STOCK PRICE HISTORY

HIGH/LOW/CLOSE

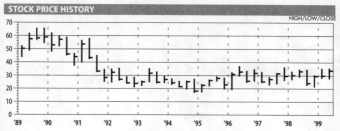

1999 FISCAL YEAR-END

Debt ratio: 50.2%
Return on equity: —
Cash ($ mil.): 137
Current ratio: 1.08
Long-term debt ($ mil.): 844
No. of shares (mil.): 38
Dividends
  Yield: 1.3%
  Payout: —
Market value ($ mil.): 1,208

THE GREEN BAY PACKERS, INC.

OVERVIEW

Say cheese! Given the playoff success of the Green Bay Packers over the last six seasons (including two Super Bowl appearances and one championship), the team's fans (or "Cheeseheads," as they're affectionately known) have plenty to smile about. Since 1960, every game played on the frozen tundra of Lambeau Field in Green Bay, Wisconsin, has been sold out, thanks to the team's adoring, cheddar-cheese-chapeau-wearing fans, some of whom are also shareholders. The legendary team is organized as a not-for-profit corporation that is publicly owned by more than 100,000 shareholders and governed by 45 directors and a seven-person executive committee. Its shares do not appreciate or pay dividends, and if the team is ever liquidated, proceeds go to the Green Bay Packers Foundation.

In the modern world of big-money sports, the Packers, who play in the NFL's smallest market, are able to hold their own because of the league's TV contracts and revenue sharing. But the franchise is falling behind in stadium revenues with a 40-year-old facility with limited luxury boxes and club seating (from which other NFL teams derive millions in revenue). The Packers and the city of Green Bay now must decide whether to renovate Lambeau Field or replace it.

HISTORY

In 1919 Curly Lambeau and George Calhoun met in the newsroom of the *Green Bay Press-Gazette* to organize a football team. After talking Lambeau's employer, Indian Packing Company, into buying equipment for the team, its name naturally became the Packers. The team's revenues came from fans passing the hat at games. The team became so successful and popular that coach Lambeau and two packing plant officials obtained a franchise from the new National Football League in 1921. Receipts didn't cover expenses, and the franchise folded at the end of the season.

When Lambeau and other backers repurchased the franchise again in 1922 for $250, bad weather was almost the team's downfall. Following a rainout, its insurance company wouldn't pay off; a storm later that year threatened to cancel another game and ruin the team. A. B. Turnbull, a *Press-Gazette* executive who was the first Packers president, convinced merchants in Green Bay to underwrite the team; the Packers became a corporation, and the game was played.

The Packers first stock offering followed in 1923, raising $5,000. The Packers went on to win three straight championships from 1929 to 1931, but its winning ways couldn't stem the tide of bad fortune. In 1934 the Packers lost a $5,000 lawsuit to a fan who fell from the bleachers. The club's insurance company went out of business, and the Packers were forced into receivership. Green Bay merchants raised $15,000 through the second stock sale in 1935 to revive the corporation.

Championships in 1936, 1939, and 1944 kept the team popular, but didn't seem to help financially. A 1949 intra-squad game raised $50,000 to keep the team afloat, and a 1950 stock drive (the team's third) raised another $118,000. Lambeau resigned from the Packers in 1950, and the team's football fortunes were temporarily sacked. Then came Vince Lombardi in 1959.

The legendary coach, known for his "winning isn't everything — it's the only thing" mantra, commanded a team that dominated the NFL in the 1960s, winning five championships and the first two Super Bowls in 1967 and 1968 (Super Bowl winning teams now receive the Vince Lombardi Trophy). City Stadium (built in 1957) was renamed Lambeau Field following Lambeau's death in 1965. Lombardi left coaching for the front office in 1968, and the team struggled to regain its luster during dismal seasons in the 1970s and 1980s.

In 1989 Bob Harlan, a former sports publicist who joined the Packers as assistant general manager in 1971, became president and CEO. Harlan named Ron Wolf general manager in midseason 1991, and Wolf hired Mike Holmgren as head coach in 1992. With the help of three-time NFL MVP quarterback Brett Favre, Holmgren led the team to the playoffs for six straight seasons from 1993 to 1998, including the Packers' third Super Bowl victory in 1997. The Packers returned to the Super Bowl the following year, but lost to the Denver Broncos.

The team raised more than $20 million for stadium improvements through its fourth stock offering in 1998. Holmgren then left the Packers after the 1998 season for a head coach/general manager job with the Seattle Seahawks. He was replaced by former Philadelphia Eagles head coach Ray Rhodes.

682

OFFICERS

President and CEO: Robert E. Harlan, age 63
EVP and General Manager: Ron Wolf, age 61
Head Coach: Ray Rhodes, age 49
SVP Adminstration: John Jones, age 47
VP and General Counsel: Lance Lopes, age 36
VP Player Personnel: Ken Herock
Executive Director Public Relations: Lee Remmel, age 75
Director Administrative Affairs: Mark Schiefelbein
Director Tickets: Mark Wagner
Marketing Director: Jeff Cieply
Auditors: Wipfli Ullrich Bertelson LLP

LOCATIONS

HQ: 1265 Lombardi Ave., Green Bay, WI 54304
Phone: 920-496-5700   **Fax:** 920-496-5738
Web site: http://www.packers.com

The Green Bay Packers play at Lambeau Field in Green Bay, Wisconsin.

PRODUCTS/OPERATIONS

Titles
Super Bowl Champions (1967-68, 97)
NFL Champions (1929-31, 36, 39, 44, 61-62, 65-67)
NFC Champions (1997-98)
NFC Central Division Champions (1972, 95-97)
NFC Wild Card (1993-94, 98)

COMPETITORS

Chicago Bears Football Club
Detroit Lions
Minnesota Vikings
Tampa Bay Buccaneers

HISTORICAL FINANCIALS & EMPLOYEES

Not-for-profit FYE: March 31	Annual Growth	1989	1990	1991	1992	1993	1994	1995	1996	1997	1998
Sales ($ mil.)	12.8%	28	30	42	45	54	66	62	70	75	83
Employees	8.3%	45	51	54	62	72	74	80	82	90	92

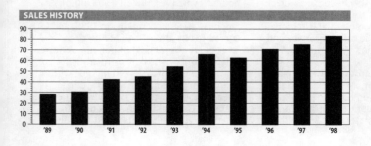

SALES HISTORY

GTE CORPORATION

OVERVIEW

Once crying merger most foul, GTE, the largest non-Baby Bell local phone company, has agreed to be bought by Bell Atlantic, the largest Bell, to form a scattered empire covering 39 US states. The Irving, Texas-based firm now serves more than 23 million local phone customers in 28 states. GTE and its affiliates also provide telecommunications services in Argentina, Canada, China, the Dominican Republic, Puerto Rico, and Venezuela.

GTE has cracked other markets. GTE Wireless offers cellular and PCS phone service to almost 5 million US subscribers; GTE is also buying almost half of Ameritech's wireless businesses in a venture with private investment firm Georgetown Partners. GTE.net offers Internet dial-up access to about 500,000 US consumers, and the Data Products and Services division offers Internet and data business services.

The Telecommunications Act of 1996 gave GTE carte blanche to compete. Armed with competitive local-exchange carrier (CLEC) certification in 24 US states, GTE is breaking into the Bells' territories in eight states, including California, Florida, and Texas, where it has its biggest operations. GTE also offers long-distance service to about 2.7 million customers nationwide; it owns about 25% of Qwest's coast-to-coast fiber-optic network and is building its own 17,000-mile fiber-optic network. It has cable franchises in Pinellas County, Florida, and Ventura County, California, and it is rolling out wireless cable service in Oahu, Hawaii.

To focus on high-growth opportunities, GTE plans to sell about 1.6 million US access lines and its Airfone (phone service for airline passengers) unit.

HISTORY

Sigurd Odegard and John O'Connell, former Wisconsin Railroad Commission staffers, formed Richland Center Telephone in Wisconsin in 1918. They created Associated Telephone Utilities in 1926 and bought a Long Beach, California, phone company which Odegard, on vacation, had noticed was for sale. Associated Telephone grew rapidly but was encumbered with debt during the Depression. Lenders took control in 1932 and moved headquarters from Chicago to New York. Beset with problems, the company went bankrupt, emerging as General Telephone (GT) in 1935.

Attorney David Power, named CEO in 1951, led GT to buy a 55% stake in Canadian phone firm BC Tel and later, in 1959, to buy Sylvania. Sylvania, founded in 1901 to repair burned-out lightbulbs, became a lighting and electronics manufacturer under GT, which was renamed General Telephone and Electronics (GTE).

GTE, long the largest non-Bell phone company, expanded from 1957 to 1967 by buying phone companies in Florida, the Southwest, and Hawaii. It sold the US consumer electronics business in 1981. Becoming GTE Corp. in 1982, it formed GTE Mobilnet (later renamed GTE Wireless) to provide cellular service and bought Southern Pacific's US Sprint long-distance business in 1983.

But GTE soon sold most of Sprint to partner United Telecommunications in 1989 and the rest in 1991 to refocus on lucrative local phone service. In 1991 it bought Contel: 30 phone companies serving 30 states. The $6.6 billion merger was then the biggest telecom deal ever, making GTE the #1 US local phone company. GTE also bought about 20% of Venezuelan phone company CANTV.

Charles Lee took over as CEO in 1992. GTE sold the lighting business in 1993 and its Spacenet satellite unit in 1994. That year a GTE-led consortium won a bid for Argentinian cellular licenses.

With the 1996 passage of the Telecommunications Act, GTE returned to the long-distance market. It also led Baby Bells to court to challenge the FCC's authority to limit the fees local carriers charged for access to their phone lines. (The FCC's powers were stalled in court until 1999.) GTE also established a venture to build paging networks in China.

In 1997 GTE formed a competitive local-exchange carrier to steal Bell business and bought BBN, which became the Data Products & Services division. GTE also made a $28 billion bid for long-distance player MCI, which spurned GTE in 1998 for WorldCom's $37 billion offer. Undaunted, GTE agreed to be bought by Bell Atlantic in a $53 billion deal. The prospective partners agreed to shed overlapping wireless operations in 1999, and GTE agreed to buy almost half of Ameritech's wireless operations for $3.3 billion in a venture with minority-owned investment firm Georgetown Partners. BC Telecom merged with TELUS and became BCT.TELUS, Canada's #2 telecom company; GTE kept a 27% stake. Also that year General Dynamics bought three GTE defense-electronics units for $1.05 billion.

Chairman and CEO: Charles R. Lee, age 59,
$2,523,146 pay
President: Kent B. Foster, age 55, $1,861,742 pay
VC and President - International: Michael T. Masin,
age 54, $1,702,035 pay
SEVP Market Operations, GTE Service Corporation:
Thomas W. White, age 52, $1,017,931 pay
EVP Strategic Development and Planning:
James A. Attwood, age 40
EVP Government and Regulatory Advocacy, and General
Counsel: William P. Barr, age 48, $899,262 pay
EVP Technology and Systems: Armen Der Marderosian,
age 61
EVP Human Resources and Administration:
J. Randall MacDonald, age 50
EVP Finance and CFO: Daniel P. O'Brien, age 44
SVP Public Affairs and Communications:
Mary Beth Bardin, age 44
Acting Treasurer: Jan L. Deur, age 54
VP Government and Regulatory Affairs:
Geoffrey C. Gould
VP Taxes: John P. Z. Kent
VP Marketing and Quality: Thomas F. Lysaught
VP and Controller: Paul R. Shuell, age 51
President, GTE Network Services: John C. Appel
President, GTE Communications Corporation:
Clarence F. Bercher
President, Technology and President, Labs:
David N. Campbell
President, GTE Wireless: Mark S. Feighner
Auditors: Arthur Andersen LLP

HQ: 1255 Corporate Dr., Irving, TX 75038
Phone: 972-507-5000   Fax: 972-507-5002
Web site: http://www.gte.com

1998 Sales

	$ mil.	% of total
Local services	5,814	19
Network access	5,316	18
Tolls	859	3
Directory services	3,259	11
External services	14,943	49
Adjustments	(4,718)	—
Total	25,473	100

Selected Subsidiaries

GTE Communications	GTE Internetworking
Corporation	GTE Network Services
GTE Data Products and	GTE Supply
Services	GTE Technology and
GTE Directories	Systems
Corporation	GTE Wireless

ALLTEL	IBM
America Online	MCI WorldCom
Ameritech	Microsoft
AmTec	Motorola
Asia Satellite	Nextel
Telecommunications	PrimeCo
AT&T	Rogers Communications
BCE	SBC Communications
BellSouth	Sprint
China Telecom	Telcel Celular CA
Cox Communications	Telecom Argentina
EDS	Telefonica
EarthLink	Telefonica de Argentina
Ericsson	Teleglobe
Frontier Corporation	U S WEST
Harris Corporation	Vodafone AirTouch

NYSE symbol: GTE FYE: December 31	Annual Growth	1989	1990	1991	1992	1993	1994	1995	1996	1997	1998
Sales ($ mil.)	4.3%	17,424	18,374	19,621	19,984	19,748	19,944	19,957	21,339	23,260	25,473
Net income ($ mil.)	4.9%	1,417	1,541	1,580	(754)	900	2,451	(2,144)	2,798	2,794	2,172
Income as % of sales	—	8.1%	8.4%	8.1%	—	4.6%	12.3%	—	13.1%	12.0%	8.5%
Earnings per share ($)	0.8%	2.08	2.26	1.75	(0.86)	0.93	2.55	(2.20)	2.88	2.90	2.24
Stock price - FY high ($)	—	35.56	36.00	35.00	35.75	39.88	35.25	45.13	49.25	52.25	71.81
Stock price - FY low ($)	—	21.44	23.50	27.50	28.88	34.13	29.50	30.00	37.75	40.50	46.56
Stock price - FY close ($)	7.1%	35.00	29.25	34.63	34.63	35.00	30.38	43.88	45.38	52.25	65.00
P/E - high	—	17	16	20	—	43	14	—	17	18	32
P/E - low	—	10	10	16	—	37	12	—	13	14	21
Dividends per share ($)	3.6%	1.37	1.49	1.61	1.73	1.84	1.88	1.88	1.88	1.88	1.88
Book value per share ($)	(3.1%)	12.01	12.90	12.21	10.61	10.14	10.86	7.05	7.62	8.39	9.06
Employees	(3.0%)	158,000	177,477	162,000	131,000	117,446	111,000	106,000	102,000	114,000	120,000

HIGH/LOW/CLOSE

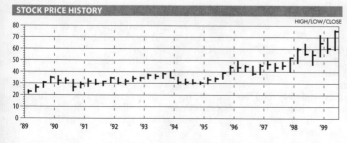

Debt ratio: 63.8%
Return on equity: 24.8%
Cash ($ mil.): 467
Current ratio: 0.65
Long-term debt ($ mil.): 15,418
No. of shares (mil.): 968
Dividends
  Yield: 2.9%
  Payout: 83.9%
Market value ($ mil.): 62,920

HALLIBURTON COMPANY

OVERVIEW

No matter where you are in the oil field of dreams, if you need it built, Halliburton will come. The Dallas-based company is the world's #1 provider of oil field services (with Schlumberger close behind). Halliburton makes oil field equipment and offers construction, engineering, and maintenance services, particularly for the petroleum industry, in more than 120 countries. It has three business groups: Energy Services, Engineering and Construction, and Dresser Equipment (the former Dresser Industries, acquired in 1998).

The Energy Services Group includes Brown & Root Energy Services, which provides engineering and construction for offshore and marine projects; Halliburton Energy Services, which offers well evaluation, drilling, and maintenance services for oil companies; and Landmark Graphics, which develops exploration-related software and provides information technology services.

In the Engineering and Construction Group, Kellogg Brown & Root primarily serves energy, petrochemical, and refinery clients, while Brown & Root Services provides engineering, construction, management, and technology services for non-energy businesses and government institutions. The Dresser Equipment Group makes meters, pumps, engines, automated controls, and other products for manufacturing, energy, and petrochemical companies.

Halliburton's field marshal is former US Defense Secretary Dick Cheney, who oversaw the laying off of more than 9,000 employees in 1998 and 1999 as the company absorbed Dresser Industries and endured reduced demand for its services because of the prolonged oil price slump.

HISTORY

Erle Halliburton began his oil career in 1916 at Perkins Oil Well Cementing. He moved to oil boomtown Burkburnett, Texas, to start his Better Method Oil Well Cementing Company in 1919. Halliburton used cement to hold a steel pipe in a well, which kept oil out of the water table, strengthened a well's walls, and reduced the risk of explosions. A widely recognized contribution today, his technique was considered useless at the time.

In 1920 Halliburton moved to Oklahoma. Incorporating Halliburton Oil Well Cementing Company in 1924, he patented his products and services, forcing oil companies to employ his firm if they wanted to cement wells. Among the company's acquisitions was Perkins, Erle's former employer.

Erle died in 1957. Between the 1950s and the 1970s Halliburton acquired oil services companies, and in 1962 it bought Houston construction giant Brown & Root, an expert in offshore platforms. After the 1973 Arab oil embargo Halliburton benefited from the surge in global oil exploration, and later, as drilling costs surged, it became a leader in well stimulation.

The oil industry slumped in 1982, and the firm halved its workforce. In 1985 Brown & Root, already suffering, coughed up $750 million to settle charges of mismanagement at the South Texas Nuclear Project.

In the 1990s Halliburton expanded abroad, opening a Moscow office in 1991. Two years later it acquired a directional drilling and services business and entered a joint venture with China National Petroleum Corporation. Brown & Root was named contractor in 1994 for the Gulf-South Asia Gas Project pipeline stretching from Qatar to Pakistan.

Richard Cheney, a former US defense secretary, became CEO in 1995. Continuing overseas expansion, Halliburton drilled the world's deepest horizontal well (18,860 ft.) in Germany in 1995; Brown & Root began providing engineering and logistics services to US Army peacekeeping troops in the Balkans in 1995 and won a major contract to develop an offshore Canadian oil field the next year; and Halliburton took a 26% stake in Scotland-based Petroleum Engineering Services in 1997. Halliburton also began trading services to Cairn Energy for a percentage of the oil recovered.

Halliburton had begun a major reorganization in 1993; by 1997 the independent divisions and companies were consolidated under the Halliburton umbrella. Halliburton nearly doubled its size in 1998 with its $7.7 billion acquisition of oil field equipment manufacturer Dresser Industries. Because of the Dresser acquisition and the oil price downturn in 1998 and 1999, Halliburton axed more than 9,000 workers.

In 1999 Brown & Root Energy Services won a contract to provide logistics support for the US Army in Albania. The Energy Services Group invested in oil field emergency-response firm Boots & Coots, and Kellogg Brown & Root took a stake in Japanese engineering firm Chiyoda.

Chairman: William E. Bradford, age 63, $2,673,708 pay
VC: Donald C. Vaughn, age 62, $1,699,417 pay
CEO: Richard B. Cheney, age 57, $2,337,961 pay
President and COO: David J. Lesar, age 45,
$1,228,210 pay
Shared Services VP-Finance: Louis A. Raspino, age 46
EVP and General Counsel: Lester L. Coleman, age 56,
$637,506 pay
EVP and CFO: Gary V. Morris, age 45
**SVP Strategic Account Management and Chief Health,
Safety, and Environment Officer:**
Lewis W. "Jody" Powers, age 52
President, Halliburton Energy Development:
Norman C. Chambers
President, Brown & Root Energy Services:
Larry E. Farmer
President, Halliburton Energy Services: Edgar Ortiz
President, Landmark Graphics Corporation:
Robert P. Peebler
President and CEO, Kellogg Brown & Root:
A. Jack Stanley
VP and Treasurer: Jerry H. Blurton, age 54
VP Human Resources: Paul M. Bryant
VP Administration: Celeste Colgan
VP Government Relations: David J. Gribbin III
VP, Secretary, and Corporate Counsel: Susan S. Keith
VP Investor Relations: Guy T. Marcus
VP and Controller: R. Charles Muchmore Jr., age 45
Auditors: Arthur Andersen LLP

LOCATIONS

HQ: 3600 Lincoln Plaza, 500 N. Akard St.,
Dallas, TX 75201-3391
Phone: 214-978-2600   **Fax:** 214-978-2611
Web site: http://www.halliburton.com

1998 Sales

	$ mil.	% of total
US	6,132	35
UK	2,247	13
Other countries	8,974	52
Total	**17,353**	**100**

PRODUCTS/OPERATIONS

1998 Sales

	$ mil.	% of total
Energy Services Group	9,009	52
Engineering & Construction Group	5,495	32
Dresser Equipment Group	2,849	16
Total	**17,353**	**100**

COMPETITORS

ABB Asea Brown Boveri	Nabors Industries
Baker Hughes	National-Oilwell
Bechtel	Nuovo Pignone Industrie
BJ Services	Meccaniche
Black and Veatch	Parsons
Caterpillar	Perini
Coflexip	Peter Kiewit Sons'
Cooper Cameron	R&B Falcon
Deere	Raytheon
Diamond Offshore	Schlumberger
Ensco	Smith International
Fluor	Stolt Comex Seaway
FMC	Stone & Webster
Foster Wheeler	Thyssen Krupp
Global Marine	Tuboscope
McDermott	Tyco International
Mitsubishi	Weatherford International

HISTORICAL FINANCIALS & EMPLOYEES

NYSE symbol: HAL FYE: December 31	Annual Growth	1989	1990	1991	1992	1993	1994	1995	1996	1997	1998
Sales ($ mil.)	13.3%	5,661	6,926	7,019	6,525	6,351	5,741	5,699	7,385	8,819	17,353
Net income ($ mil.)	—	135	197	27	(137)	(161)	178	168	300	454	(15)
Income as % of sales	—	2.4%	2.9%	0.4%	—	—	3.1%	3.0%	4.1%	5.2%	—
Earnings per share ($)	—	0.64	0.89	0.17	(0.63)	(0.61)	0.73	0.74	1.19	1.75	(0.03)
Stock price - FY high ($)	—	22.25	29.38	27.63	18.44	22.00	18.63	25.44	31.81	63.25	57.25
Stock price - FY low ($)	—	13.75	19.38	12.75	10.88	12.88	13.94	16.44	22.38	29.69	25.00
Stock price - FY close ($)	3.7%	21.38	22.81	14.25	14.38	15.94	16.56	25.31	30.13	51.88	29.63
P/E - high	—	35	33	163	—	—	26	34	27	36	—
P/E - low	—	21	22	75	—	—	19	22	19	17	—
Dividends per share ($)	0.0%	0.50	0.50	0.50	0.50	0.50	0.50	0.50	0.50	0.50	0.50
Book value per share ($)	(0.8%)	9.95	10.52	10.11	8.90	8.27	8.51	7.64	8.62	9.85	9.23
Employees	5.7%	65,500	77,000	73,400	69,200	64,700	57,200	57,300	60,000	70,750	107,800

STOCK PRICE HISTORY

HIGH/LOW/CLOSE

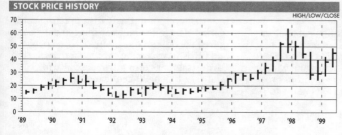

1998 FISCAL YEAR-END

Debt ratio: 25.2%
Return on equity: —
Cash ($ mil.): 203
Current ratio: 1.52
Long-term debt ($ mil.): 1,370
No. of shares (mil.): 440
Dividends
  Yield: 1.7%
  Payout: —
Market value ($ mil.): 13,037

HALLMARK CARDS, INC.

OVERVIEW

Hallmark Cards is the #1 producer of warm fuzzies. The Kansas City, Missouri-based company's greeting cards (sold under brand names such as Hallmark, Shoebox, and Ambassador) are sold in more than 47,000 US retail stores. About 7,500 of these stores bear the Hallmark or Hallmark Gold Crown name, but the company owns less than 5% of these stores, and the rest are franchised. Hallmark cards are distributed internationally in more than 100 countries.

While personal expression products bring in about three-quarters of Hallmark's revenue, the company has diversified into a host of other areas. Hallmark owns Binney & Smith, makers of Crayola brand crayons and markers, and mall-based portrait studio chain Picture

People (with more than 180 studios across 19 states). The company also produces television movies through is Hallmark Entertainment unit and offers Keepsake brand ornaments. Through its Web site, Hallmark.com, Hallmark offers electronic greeting cards.

Not resting on well-engraved laurels, Hallmark has announced its intention to triple its revenue by 2010. While it plans to continue expanding its greeting card empire, the company is also intent on stretching its reach into markets such as gifts and family entertainment. Members of the Hall family (including chairman Donald Hall, son of founder Joyce Hall) own two-thirds of Hallmark; company employees own the remainder.

HISTORY

Eighteen-year-old Joyce Hall started selling picture postcards from two shoe boxes in his room at the Kansas City, Missouri, YMCA in 1910. His brother Rollie joined him the next year, and the two added greeting cards (made by another company) to their line in 1912. The brothers opened Hall Brothers, a store that sold postcards, gifts, books, and stationery, but it was destroyed in a 1915 fire. The Halls got a loan, bought an engraving company, and produced their first original cards in time for Christmas.

In 1921 a third brother, William, joined the firm, which started stamping the backs of its cards with the phrase "A Hallmark Card." By 1922 Hall Brothers had salespeople in all 48 states and had begun offering gift wrap. The firm began selling internationally in 1931.

Hall Brothers patented the "Eye-Vision" display case for greeting cards in 1936 and sold it to retailers across the country. The company aired its first radio ad in 1938. The next year it introduced a friendship card, displaying a cart filled with purple pansies. The card became the company's best-seller. During WWII Joyce Hall convinced the government not to curtail paper supplies, arguing that his greeting cards were essential to the nation's morale.

The company opened its first retail store in 1950. The following year marked the first production of *Hallmark Hall of Fame,* TV's longest-running dramatic series and winner of more Emmy awards than any other program. Hall Brothers changed its name to Hallmark Cards in 1954.

Hallmark introduced paper party products

and started putting *Peanuts* characters on cards in 1960. Donald Hall, Joyce Hall's son, was appointed CEO in 1966. The following year the company began construction of Crown Center, which surrounded company headquarters in Kansas City. Disaster struck in 1981 when two walkways collapsed at the Crown Center's Hyatt Regency hotel, killing 114 and injuring 225.

Joyce Hall died in 1982, and Donald Hall became both chairman and CEO. Hallmark acquired Binney & Smith (Crayola Crayons, Magic Marker) in 1984. It introduced Shoebox Greetings, a line of nontraditional cards, in 1986. Irvine Hockaday replaced Donald Hall as CEO in 1986 (Donald Hall continued as chairman).

The company joined with Information Storage Devices in 1993 to market recordable greeting cards. It unveiled its Web site, Hallmark.com, in 1996 and began offering electronic greeting cards. That same year, Hallmark and Microsoft signed a five-year agreement to create personal expression products.

In 1997 Binney & Smith created a children's television series, *Crayola Kids Adventures,* featuring many product tie-ins. Hallmark's 1998 acquisition of UK-based Creative Publications boosted the company into the top spot in the British greeting card market. The following year the company acquired portrait studio chain Picture People and Christian greeting card maker DaySpring Cards. Hallmark also introduced Warm Wishes, a line of 99-cent cards.

Chairman: Donald J. Hall
President and CEO: Irvine O. Hockaday Jr.
President and CEO, Binney & Smith: Mark Schwab
President and CEO, Hallmark Entertainment:
  Robert Halmi Jr.
VP Administration and CFO: Robert J. Druten
VP Public Affairs and Communications: Steve Doyal
VP Human Resources: Ralph N. Christensen
Manager Corporate Media Relations: Julie O'Dell
Auditors: Arthur Andersen LLP

LOCATIONS

HQ: 2501 McGee St., Kansas City, MO 64108
Phone: 816-274-5111   **Fax:** 816-274-5061
Web site: http://www.hallmark.com

Hallmark Cards has operations in the US and the UK. Its products are distributed in more than 100 countries.

PRODUCTS/OPERATIONS

Selected Products
Albums
Calendars
Christmas ornaments
Collectibles
Electronic greetings
Gift wrap
Gifts
Greeting cards
Party goods
Personal expression software
Puzzles
Stickers
Writing paper

Selected Brands
Ambassador (greeting cards)
Hallmark Business Expressions (business greeting cards)
Keepsake Ornaments (holiday and other collectibles)
Mahogany (products celebrating African-American
  heritage)
Party Express (party products)
Shoebox (greeting cards)
Tree of Life (products celebrating Jewish heritage)

Selected Subsidiaries
Binney & Smith (Crayola brand crayons and markers)
DaySpring Cards (Christian greeting cards)
Hallmark Entertainment (television, movies, and
  home video
production)
The Picture People (portrait studio chain)
Tapper Candles

COMPETITORS

American Greetings
Andrews McMeel Universal
Blue Mountain Arts
Blyth Industries
CPI Corp.
CSS Industries
Dixon Ticonderoga
Gibson Greetings
Olan Mills
PCA International
Syratech
Time Warner
Viacom
Walt Disney

HISTORICAL FINANCIALS & EMPLOYEES

Private company FYE: December 31	Annual Growth	1989	1990	1991	1992	1993	1994	1995	1996	1997	1998
Estimated sales ($ mil.)	5.1%	2,487	2,742	2,850	3,100	3,400	3,800	3,400	3,600	3,700	3,900
Employees	5.3%	13,213	13,877	13,202	12,487	12,600	12,800	12,100	12,600	12,554	20,945

Employee numbers do not include all subsidiaries.

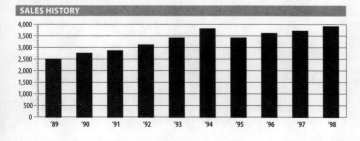

SALES HISTORY

H&R BLOCK, INC.

OVERVIEW

Only two things are certain in this life, and H&R Block has a stranglehold on one of them. The Kansas City, Missouri-based company is North America's leading tax preparer, serving about 14% of US taxpayers. The firm also prepares taxes in Canada, Australia, and the UK, and it provides refund anticipation loans.

H&R Block is rolling out other financial services to decrease its dependency on the April 15 deadline (tax operations account for about 85% of sales). It bought top-10 US accounting firm McGladrey & Pullen and combined it with its HRB Business Services subsidiary to create RSM McGladrey as part of a strategy to build a national accounting practice serving midsized companies. It is also increasing the number of its H&R Block Financial Centers, which offer tax preparation, financial planning, investment advice, and home mortgages. The company also has a division devoted to mortgages, and is moving into brokerage services, as well.

About 45% of H&R Block's 10,400 offices are franchised. H&R Block has two types of franchisees: major franchisees, which cover large cities and counties, and satellite franchisees, which are located in less populated areas and pay higher royalties.

HISTORY

Brothers Henry and Richard Bloch opened the United Business Company in Kansas City, Missouri, in 1946 to provide accounting services. As tax preparation began to monopolize their time, a client suggested they specialize in taxes. The Blochs bought two ads, which brought a stampede of customers.

In 1955 the company became H&R Block (the Blochs didn't want customers to read the name as "blotch"). Basing charges on the number and complexity of tax forms resulted in a low-fee, high-volume business. The first tax season was a success, and the next year the brothers successfully tested their formula in New York City. But neither brother wanted to move to New York, so they worked out a franchise-like agreement with local CPAs. It was the first step toward becoming a nationwide chain.

As the chain grew, H&R Block began training preparers at H&R Block Income Tax Schools. By 1969, when Richard retired, the company had over 3,000 offices in the US and Canada.

Henry began appearing in company ads in the 1970s; his reassuring manner inspired confidence and aided expansion. Fearing saturation of the tax preparer market, he pushed the company into new areas. H&R Block bought Personnel Pool of America in 1978 (taken public in 1994 as part of Interim Services) and two years later bought 80% of law office chain Hyatt Legal Services. Synergies between the tax operations and the legal clinics never developed, and in 1987 H&R Block sold its stake.

In 1980 the firm bought CompuServe, which evolved from a computer time-share firm to a major online service by the 1990s. H&R Block sought to integrate its two operating areas, hoping electronic filing and banking would increase its tax business.

In 1992 Henry was succeeded as president by his son, Thomas, who built on the nontax side of the business to try for more even revenue distribution. The next year the company bought MECA Software (personal finance software), mistakenly believing MECA's relationships with banks, based on its refund anticipation loan program, would help develop online banking services. It sold MECA to BankAmerica and NationsBank in 1994, and Thomas stepped down.

Also that year H&R Block bought Fleet Financial Group's Option One Mortgage, boosting its financial services. In an effort to build a national accounting practice in 1996, it formed HRB Business Services with the acquisition of Kansas City accounting firm Donnelly Meiners Jordan Kline; acquisitions of six more regional accounting firms followed. Frank Salizzoni became CEO in 1996.

After selling 20% of CompuServe to the public in 1996, H&R Block in 1998 sold its remaining interest to long-distance provider WorldCom (now MCI WorldCom) for $1.3 billion. In 1999 the firm sold its credit card operations and formed RSM McGladrey by purchasing the non-consulting assets of the #7 US accounting firm, McGladrey & Pullen, for $290 million.

The McGladrey & Pullen deal didn't please everyone. In May 1999 — even before the McGladrey deal had been reached — a group of franchisees sued H&R Block to ensure that they receive their fair share of royalties from any sales generated in their territories by both the accounting group and H&R Block's tax software. Later in 1999 H&R Block announced it would pay $850 million to buy Olde Financial Discount, a discount brokerage with some 180 offices in 35 states.

OFFICERS

Chairman: Henry W. Bloch, age 76
President and CEO: Frank L. Salizzoni, age 61,
$1,141,667 pay
EVP and COO: Mark A. Ernst, age 41, $618,507 pay
SVP and Chief Marketing Officer: David F. Byers, age 37
SVP and Chief Information Officer: James D. Rose,
age 48
SVP and CFO: Ozzie Wenich, age 56, $433,804 pay
VP and Corporate Controller: Cheryl L. Givens, age 33
VP Legal and Secretary: James H. Ingraham, age 45
VP Communications: Linda M. McDougall, age 46
VP and Treasurer; Director of Investor Relations:
Brian N. Schell, age 33
VP Human Resources: Doug D. Waltman, age 38
VP Government Relations: Robert A. Weinberger, age 55
VP and General Manager, Financial Services Group:
Bernard M. Wilson, age 37
VP Coporate Development; VP Mortgage Operations,
Block Financial Corporation: Bret G. Wilson, age 40
VP Business Development: Robert D. Wilson, age 40
President and CEO, Option One Mortgage Corporation:
Robert E. Dubrish, age 47, $556,045 pay
President, HRB Business Services: Terrance E. Putney
President, H&R Block Tax Services:
Thomas L. Zimmerman, age 49, $469,881 pay
Auditors: Deloitte & Touche LLP

PRODUCTS/OPERATIONS

Selected Business Units and Services

Business Services
Birchtree Financial Services (full-service investment firm)
Franchise Partner (low-interest credit for franchisees)
H&R Block Financial Advisors (financial planning and
investment advice)
RSM McGladrey (accounting firm serving midsized
businesses)

Financial Services
H&R Block Financial Centers (tax preparation, financial
planning, investment advice, and home mortgages)

Mortgage Operations
Assurance Mortgage Corporation of America
(conventional retail loans)
Companion Mortgage Corporation
Option One Mortgage Corporation

Tax Operations
Electronic filing
H&R Block Premium (tax preparation for customers
with more complicated returns)
H&R Block Tax Services (income tax preparation and
related services)
Income tax return preparation courses
Software products

LOCATIONS

HQ: 4400 Main St., Kansas City, MO 64111
Phone: 816-753-6900   **Fax:** 816-753-5346
Web site: http://www.handrblock.com

H&R Block operates throughout the US, and in
Australia, Canada, and the UK.

COMPETITORS

American Express	Grant Thornton
Andersen Worldwide	International
BDO International	Intuit
Century Business Services	Jackson Hewitt
Deloitte Touche Tohmatsu	KPMG
Ernst & Young	PricewaterhouseCoopers

HISTORICAL FINANCIALS & EMPLOYEES

NYSE symbol: HRB FYE: April 30	Annual Growth	1990	1991	1992	1993	1994	1995	1996	1997	1998	1999
Sales ($ mil.)	5.5%	938	1,061	1,226	1,382	1,119	1,234	765	1,806	1,196	1,522
Net income ($ mil.)	6.4%	124	140	162	181	201	107	177	48	392	215
Income as % of sales	—	13.2%	13.2%	13.2%	13.1%	17.9%	8.7%	23.2%	2.6%	32.8%	14.2%
Earnings per share ($)	7.0%	1.16	1.31	1.49	1.68	1.88	1.00	1.67	0.45	3.65	2.14
Stock price - FY high ($)	—	19.00	27.88	41.13	42.75	48.75	47.63	48.88	36.38	49.06	51.75
Stock price - FY low ($)	—	13.19	17.31	25.63	30.38	31.88	33.00	31.50	23.63	30.63	35.31
Stock price - FY close ($)	12.0%	17.31	25.81	32.38	34.63	42.50	42.13	35.25	32.25	45.00	48.13
P/E - high	—	16	21	28	25	26	48	29	81	13	24
P/E - low	—	11	13	17	18	17	33	19	53	8	17
Dividends per share ($)	5.0%	0.61	0.75	0.86	0.97	1.09	1.22	1.27	1.04	0.80	0.95
Book value per share ($)	9.6%	4.76	5.39	5.76	6.12	6.67	6.54	10.05	9.60	12.54	10.88
Employees	2.5%	69,000	81,000	89,400	82,000	82,800	85,000	79,000	78,900	83,500	86,500

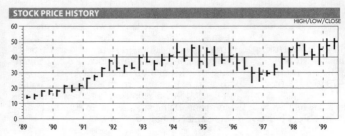

STOCK PRICE HISTORY — HIGH/LOW/CLOSE

1999 FISCAL YEAR-END
Debt ratio: 19.0%
Return on equity: 20.3%
Cash ($ mil.): 193
Current ratio: 1.96
Long-term debt ($ mil.): 250
No. of shares (mil.): 98
Dividends
  Yield: 2.0%
  Payout: 44.4%
Market value ($ mil.): 4,699

HANNAFORD BROS. CO.

OVERVIEW

Chilled by poor growth prospects in New England, Hannaford Bros. took a lesson from the birds and began heading south for what it hoped were warmer financial surroundings. The Scarborough, Maine-based company, which is being acquired by southeastern grocery chain Food Lion, runs about 150 supermarkets, most of which operate in New England and New York as Hannaford and Shop 'n Save. Since 1994 Hannaford has built or acquired stores in Virginia and the Carolinas that operate under the Hannaford name.

As it turns out, the retail climate has been just as chilly for Hannaford in Dixie. Finding it difficult to lure customers from well-established favorites like Ukrop's and Food Lion, Hannaford rethought its expansion plans and closed five stores in Virginia and two in North Carolina and wrote off $40 million of its $120 million investment in the Southeast. Since then the company has focused on building stores in the more urban areas of North Carolina and Virginia.

HomeRuns, Hannaford's experimental home delivery service in Boston, is still searching for ways to become profitable in the online grocery business.

HISTORY

Produce grower Arthur Hannaford moved from the farm to the waterfront in 1883 when he opened a fruit and vegetable wholesaling shop in Portland, Maine. Before long, his brother Howard joined him, and in 1902 they incorporated as Hannaford Bros. The brothers toughed out a score of nearby competitors, and over the years the company acquired a reputation as one of the region's foremost produce wholesalers.

At its employees' urging, Hannaford entered the grocery business in the late 1920s, and by 1934 the company was cooperating with several stores in the Clover Farm Group, an organization of independent retail grocers. (This affiliation helped support Hannaford during the Depression.) Hannaford likewise teamed up with Maine's Red & White grocery stores in 1939. The next year the Clover Farm stores took the Red & White name. (The alliance lasted until 1967.)

Although Hannaford merged with Maine wholesaler T.R. Savage Co. in 1955, the company was getting more involved with retailing. In 1959 it founded a subsidiary to lease fixtures that small retailers could use to spruce up stores for battles with corporate chains. Hannaford bought part of Sampson Supermarkets (31 Maine stores) in 1966. It introduced nonfood merchandise to the mix with a stake in Progressive Food Distributors (renamed Progressive Distributors) the following year.

The company went public in 1971. During the 1970s Hannaford established stores under the Shop 'n Save name, and it moved beyond food retailing in 1973 with its first Wellby drugstore.

Hugh Farrington, who as a boy had worked in his grandfather's Red & White store in New Hampshire, became president in 1984. (He added CEO to his duties in 1992.) The business passed $1 billion in sales in 1987, the year it placed its first stores in New York State.

Expanding its presence again in 1990, Hannaford bought 11 supermarkets in New Hampshire and Massachusetts. The chain reached $2 billion in sales in 1991. The next year it sold 34 of its 41 drugstores (by then known as Wellby Super Drug) to Rite Aid.

Hannaford entered the Carolinas in 1994 when it bought the 20-store, North Carolina-based Boney Wilson & Sons chain (Wilson's Supermarkets). A year later the company bought a dozen stores in Virginia from Farm Fresh and The Grocery Stores. Also in 1995 the chain consolidated its private-label lines from its various acquisitions with a rollout of its Hannaford brand.

In 1998 Hannaford closed seven stores in the Southeast to refocus on urban markets in North Carolina and Virginia and spent $50 million to build new stores and remodel others in the area. In April 1998 Hannaford's HomeRuns home shopping service suffered a setback when an adjacent building toppled and damaged its distribution facility.

Rumors spread about Hannaford's possible sale when Canada's Sobey family announced in May 1999 that they would not renew an agreement restricting the sale of their 26% stake in the company. (The family, which controls Canada's #2 food retailer, Empire Company, first began investing in Hannaford in 1975.) In August 1999 Food Lion, controlled by Belgian supermarket giant Delhaize "Le Lion," agreed to acquire the company in a roughly $3.6 billion deal. Delhaize is creating a new holding company, Delhaize America, to run the Food Lion and Hannaford chains.

Chairman: Walter J. Salmon, age 68
President and CEO: Hugh G. Farrington, age 54,
$670,402 pay
EVP Southeast Operations: Richard A. Anicetti, age 41,
$340,162 pay
EVP Sales & Northeast Operations: Ronald C. Hodge,
age 51, $371,158 pay
EVP Human Resources: Michael J. Strout
SVP, Secretary, and General Counsel:
Andrew P. Geoghegan, age 48
VP Real Estate: Arthur A. Aleshire
VP, Treasurer, and Controller: Garrett D. Bowne IV
VP Research: Steven H. Brinn
VP Perishables Merchandising: Shelley G. Broader
VP: Thomas B. Furber
VP Internal Audit and Loss Prevention:
Michael A. Harris
VP Engineering: Steven G. Hitchcock
VP and Chief Information Officer: William L. Homa
VP Non-Foods: Kenneth C. Johnson
VP Retail Services: Amos E. Merrow
VP Merchandising, Southeast Division:
Margaret M. Ham
VP Retail Operations, Western Division:
Beth M. Newlands Campbell
Auditors: PricewaterhouseCoopers LLP

LOCATIONS

HQ: 145 Pleasant Hill Rd., Scarborough, ME 04074
Phone: 207-883-2911   **Fax:** 207-885-3165
Web site: http://www.hannaford.com

Hannaford Bros. operates supermarkets in Maine,
Massachusetts, New Hampshire, New York, North
Carolina, South Carolina, Vermont, and Virginia.

PRODUCTS/OPERATIONS

Selected Store Departments
Bakery
Banking
Coffee bar
Deli
General merchandise
International cheeses
Meal center
Meat
Natural foods
Pharmacy
Poultry
Produce
Seafood
Video rental center

COMPETITORS

A&P	Penn Traffic
Ahold USA	Ruddick
BJs Wholesale Club	Safeway
Costco Companies	Shaw's
DeMoulas Super Markets	SUPERVALU
Food Lion	Ukrop's Super Markets
Golub	Wakefern Food
Grand Union	Wal-Mart
IGA	Wegmans Food Markets
Kmart	Winn-Dixie

HISTORICAL FINANCIALS & EMPLOYEES

NYSE symbol: HRD FYE: December 31	Annual Growth	1989	1990	1991	1992	1993	1994	1995	1996	1997	1998
Sales ($ mil.)	9.1%	1,521	1,688	2,008	2,066	2,055	2,292	2,568	2,958	3,226	3,324
Net income ($ mil.)	10.3%	39	42	43	49	57	62	70	75	60	95
Income as % of sales	—	2.6%	2.5%	2.2%	2.4%	2.8%	2.7%	2.7%	2.5%	1.8%	2.8%
Earnings per share ($)	9.1%	1.01	1.07	1.08	1.21	1.42	1.49	1.66	1.76	1.40	2.21
Stock price - FY high ($)	—	20.38	20.31	22.75	28.63	25.00	26.63	29.00	34.25	44.13	53.00
Stock price - FY low ($)	—	10.63	14.88	16.38	16.00	20.00	19.75	23.88	23.00	30.50	38.75
Stock price - FY close ($)	13.8%	16.50	18.00	22.75	22.25	21.50	25.38	24.63	34.00	43.44	53.00
P/E - high	—	20	19	21	24	18	18	17	19	32	24
P/E - low	—	11	14	15	13	14	13	14	13	22	18
Dividends per share ($)	14.3%	0.18	0.22	0.26	0.30	0.34	0.38	0.42	0.48	0.54	0.60
Book value per share ($)	12.4%	5.48	6.46	7.42	8.48	9.63	10.88	12.26	13.46	14.22	15.70
Employees	6.3%	13,652	16,681	15,960	14,472	14,713	16,551	20,400	22,000	22,400	23,600

STOCK PRICE HISTORY

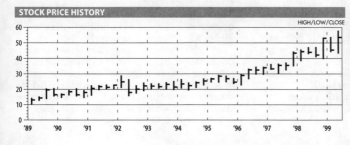

HIGH/LOW/CLOSE

1998 FISCAL YEAR-END

Debt ratio: 30.7%
Return on equity: 14.3%
Cash ($ mil.): 60
Current ratio: 1.14
Long-term debt ($ mil.): 294
No. of shares (mil.): 42
Dividends
 Yield: 1.1%
 Payout: 27.1%
Market value ($ mil.): 2,239

HARCOURT GENERAL, INC.

OVERVIEW

Harcourt General believes in the basics: reading, writing, and retail. Based in Boston burb Chestnut Hill, the company has two core businesses: publishing (Harcourt, Inc.) and upscale department stores (The Neiman Marcus Group). The company also owns Drake Beam Morin (outplacement services).

Harcourt, Inc. is among the world's largest publishing houses. It publishes school and college textbooks and instructional materials (Holt, Rinehart and Winston); books and journals for the life, physical, social, and computer sciences (Academic Press); medical books and periodicals (W. B. Saunders); and assessment materials (The Psychological Corporation). It also owns Steck-Vaughn Publishing and the Harcourt Trade Publishers imprint.

Harcourt General owns nearly 55% of The Neiman Marcus Group, which caters to the well-heeled through 31 Neiman Marcus stores, two Bergdorf Goodman stores, and its NM Direct catalog business. The company is spinning off most of its interest in Neiman Marcus to its shareholders. Harcourt General will retain a 10% stake and management control of the retailer.

The company is hoping to accomplish the twin goals of solidifying its existing publishing business and edging into new markets. Harcourt is also plugging into the digital age by creating an Internet university.

The family of chairman Richard Smith owns about 28% of Harcourt General.

HISTORY

Alfred Harcourt and Donald Brace, former classmates at Columbia University, quit their jobs at Henry Holt & Co. in 1919 and joined Will Howe to begin their own publishing firm in New York called Harcourt, Brace and Howe. Howe left in less than a year and the name became Harcourt, Brace and Co. In the following years the company published such notable works as *The Economic Consequences of Peace* by John Maynard Keynes and *Main Street* and *Arrowsmith* by Sinclair Lewis. Harcourt, Brace diversified into other areas of publishing in the 1920s, including religious works and high school and college textbooks.

Harcourt turned over the company to Brace in 1942. William Jovanovich joined the company in 1947, making $50 a week as a salesman. He became president of the firm eight years later, after the deaths of Harcourt (1954) and Brace (1955).

Jovanovich began diversifying Harcourt, Brace into other publishing and unrelated areas during the 1960s. It merged with World Book Company in 1960 to become the largest publisher of elementary, secondary, and college materials in the US and changed its name to Harcourt, Brace & World, Inc. Jovanovich took the company public that year. It entered the insurance business with the 1967 purchase of Harvest Publishing Co., which sold farm journals and life insurance (the insurance companies were sold in 1994). Jovanovich became chairman in 1970, and the company became Harcourt Brace Jovanovich (HBJ).

HBJ continued the acquisition spree throughout the 1970s and 1980s, including the purchase of theme parks (Sea World, 1976;

sold, 1989), publishers, and other services (The Psychological Corporation, 1970). Jovanovich retired as chairman in 1990.

In 1991 HBJ was acquired by General Cinema, a movie-theater pioneer founded in 1922 as Philip Smith Theatrical Enterprises and renamed in 1964. In 1984 General Cinema bought 37% of Carter Hawley Hale, which controlled Neiman Marcus (founded 1907).

General Cinema was renamed Harcourt General in 1993, and it spun off its General Cinema theaters as GC Companies. In 1995 Neiman Marcus sold its ailing Contempo Casuals subsidiary, and Harcourt General acquired Assessment Systems, a provider of computerized testing and licensing services.

Academic Press began making its journals available on the Internet in 1996. The following year Harcourt General bought National Education Corporation for about $854 million, topping Sylvan Learning Systems' bid for the education products and services provider. Also in 1997 it became a majority owner of Steck-Vaughn, but the acquisition caused Harcourt General to operate at a loss that year. In early 1998 the company bought the remaining 18% stake in Steck-Vaughn it didn't already own for $42.8 million. It also bolstered its publishing operations by paying $415 million for Times Mirror's health sciences unit, Mosby.

In 1999 Harcourt General said it would spin off most of its stake in Neiman Marcus. Its 1999 purchase of Knowledge Communication (professional development training tools offered via the Internet, intranets, and CD-ROM) expanded Harcourt's professional educational titles.

OFFICERS

Chairman, Harcourt General and The Neiman Marcus Group: Richard A. Smith, age 74, $1,628,000 pay (prior to title change)
President and Co-COO; CEO, Harcourt, Inc.: Brian J. Knez, age 41, $1,138,200 pay (prior to promotion)
President and Co-COO; CEO, The Neiman Marcus Group: Robert A. Smith, age 39, $1,138,200 pay (prior to promotion)
SVP and CFO, Harcourt General and The Neiman Marcus Group: John R. Cook, age 57, $682,000 pay
SVP, General Counsel, and Secretary, Harcourt General and The Neiman Marcus Group: Eric P. Geller, age 51, $564,825 pay
VP; VP and General Counsel, Harcourt, Inc.: Kathleen A. Bursley, age 44
VP, Corporate Relations, Harcourt General and The Neiman Marcus Group: Peter Farwell, age 55
VP and Treasurer, Harcourt General and The Neiman Marcus Group: Paul F. Gibbons, age 47
VP, Human Resources, Harcourt General and The Neiman Marcus Group: Gerald T. Hughes, age 42
VP and Controller, Harcourt General and The Neiman Marcus Group: Catherine N. Janowski, age 38
VP; President and COO, Harcourt, Inc.: James P. Levy, age 58
VP, General Auditor, Harcourt General and The Neiman Marcus Group: Michael F. Panutich, age 50
President and COO, The Neiman Marcus Group; Chairman and CEO, Neiman Marcus Stores: Burton Tansky
President and CEO, NM Direct: Bernie Feiwus
Chairman and CEO, Bergdorf Goodman: Stephen C. Elkin
Auditors: Deloitte & Touche LLP

LOCATIONS

HQ: 27 Boylston St., Chestnut Hill, MA 02467
Phone: 617-232-8200   **Fax:** 617-739-1395
Web site: http://www.harcourt-general.com

Harcourt General maintains corporate headquarters in Massachusetts, New York, and Texas, and has 31 Neiman Marcus stores in 28 US cities.

PRODUCTS/OPERATIONS

1998 Sales & Operating Income

	Sales		Operating Income	
	$ mil.	% of total	$ mil.	% of total
Speciality retail	2,373	56	213	48
Publishing	1,862	44	233	52
Adjustments	—	—	(35)	—
Total	**4,235**	**100**	**411**	**100**

COMPETITORS

Adecco	Nordstrom
Advance Publications	Pearson
Bertelsmann	Reed Elsevier
CBT Group	Right Management
Dayton Hudson	Saks Inc.
Dillard's	Scholastic
Federated	SkillSoft
Hearst	Spiegel
Houghton Mifflin	Thomson Corporation
John Wiley	Tiffany
Knowledge Universe	Time Warner
May	Tribune
McGraw-Hill	Viacom
News Corp.	

HISTORICAL FINANCIALS & EMPLOYEES

NYSE symbol: H FYE: October 31	Annual Growth	1989	1990	1991	1992	1993	1994	1995	1996	1997	1998
Sales ($ mil.)	9.2%	1,914	2,150	3,588	3,717	3,656	3,154	3,035	3,290	3,692	4,235
Net income ($ mil.)	(19.3%)	972	111	(293)	495	171	178	166	191	(115)	142
Income as % of sales	—	50.8%	5.2%	—	13.3%	4.7%	5.6%	5.5%	5.8%	—	3.3%
Earnings per share ($)	(19.1%)	13.16	1.51	(3.88)	6.25	2.15	2.22	2.16	2.62	(1.64)	1.96
Stock price - FY high ($)	—	28.50	28.50	24.75	30.00	46.13	44.00	45.75	57.00	56.25	61.94
Stock price - FY low ($)	—	19.25	16.50	18.00	16.50	28.13	30.25	32.13	38.00	42.63	41.88
Stock price - FY close ($)	6.9%	26.75	18.75	20.25	29.50	44.00	37.00	39.63	50.00	50.06	48.69
P/E - high	—	2	19	—	5	21	20	21	22	—	32
P/E - low	—	1	11	—	3	13	14	15	15	—	21
Dividends per share ($)	7.3%	0.41	0.45	0.49	0.53	0.57	0.61	0.65	0.69	0.73	0.77
Book value per share ($)	(5.8%)	22.28	23.35	6.24	12.08	13.58	13.43	12.93	14.52	11.93	13.02
Employees	(7.5%)	24,200	25,500	32,641	33,090	30,166	15,430	15,219	20,890	18,500	12,000

STOCK PRICE HISTORY

HIGH/LOW/CLOSE

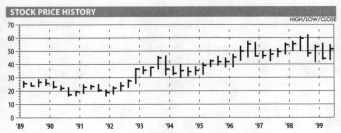

1998 FISCAL YEAR-END

Debt ratio: 65.1%
Return on equity: 15.3%
Cash ($ mil.): 115
Current ratio: 1.47
Long-term debt ($ mil.): 1,730
No. of shares (mil.): 71
Dividends
  Yield: 1.6%
  Payout: 39.3%
Market value ($ mil.): 3,458

HARLEY-DAVIDSON, INC.

OVERVIEW

"Put your ass on some class," reads one (not necessarily official) Harley-Davidson T-shirt. Offering loads of chrome and the telltale roar of a V-twin engine, the Harley is, to its cult of devotees, the ultimate American machine.

Milwaukee-based Harley-Davidson controls about half of the heavyweight motorbike market in the US; its 24 models are among the best known in the industry, including the Sportster, Electra Glide, Low Rider, Fat Boy, and Road King. The bikes are sold through a worldwide network of more than 900 dealers. Harley-Davidson also sells an attitude through its line of toys, jewelry, clothing (MotorClothes), and other goods licensed under the company names.

If Harley-Davidson has a problem, it's with supply, not demand. Devoted customers sometimes wait more than a year for a new bike. To address the lag time, the company plans to increase annual production from 155,000 to 200,000 bikes by 2003, which will mark the company's 100th anniversary. The company also has built a new plant in Kansas City, Missouri. However, the increased demand for Harley cruisers has spawned a spate of competing models from BMW, Polaris (known for its snowmobiles and watercraft), and Excelsior-Henderson (a resurrection of the Excelsior motorcycle company, defunct since 1931).

HISTORY

In 1903 William Harley and the Davidson brothers (Walter, William, and Arthur) of Milwaukee sold their first Harley-Davidson motorcycles, which essentially were motor-assisted bicycles that required pedaling uphill. Demand was high, and most sold before leaving the factory. Six years later the company debuted its trademark two-cylinder, V-twin engine. By 1913 the company had 150 competitors.

WWI created a demand for US motorcycles overseas that made international sales important. During the 1920s Harley-Davidson was a leader in innovative engineering, introducing models with a front brake and the "teardrop" gas tank that became part of the Harley look.

The Great Depression decimated the motorcycle industry. As one of only two remaining companies, Harley-Davidson survived by its exports and by sales to the police and military. To improve sales, the company added styling features like art deco decals and three-tone paint. The 1936 EL model, with its "knucklehead" engine (named for the shape of its valve covers), was a forerunner of today's models.

During WWII Harley-Davidson prospered from military orders. It introduced new models after the war that catered to a growing recreational market of consumers with money to spend: the K-model (1952), Sportster "superbike" (1957), and Duo-Glide (1958). Ever since competitor Indian gave up the ghost in the 1950s, Harley-Davidson has been the US's only major motorcycle manufacturer.

The company began making golf carts (since discontinued) in the early 1960s. It went public in 1965 and was bought by American Machine and Foundry (AMF) in 1969. But by the late 1970s, sales and quality were slipping. Certain that Harley-Davidson would lose to Japanese

bikes flooding the market, AMF put the company up for sale. There was no buyer until 1981, when Vaughn Beals and other AMF executives purchased it. Minutes away from bankruptcy in 1985, then-CFO Richard Teerlink convinced lenders to accept a restructuring plan.

Facing falling demand and increasing imports, Harley-Davidson made one of the greatest comebacks in US automotive history (helped in part by a punitive tariff targeting Japanese imports).

Using Japanese management principles, Harley-Davidson updated manufacturing methods, improved quality, and expanded the model line. Harley-Davidson again went public in 1986, and by the next year it had won back 25% of the US heavyweight motorcycle market, up from 16% in 1985.

In 1993 the company acquired a 49% stake in Eagle Credit (financing, insurance, and credit cards for dealers and customers; it bought the rest in 1995) and a 49% share of Wisconsin-based Buell Motorcycle (gaining a niche in the performance motorcycle market). The recreational vehicle business, Holiday Rambler, was sold to Monaco Coach Corp. in 1996.

Budget Rent a Car joined with Harley-Davidson in 1997 to launch a pilot motorbike rental program in Florida. It bought most of Buell's remaining stock in 1998. In 1999 the company announced plans to open an assembly plant in Brazil to increase sales in Latin America. It also announced plans to open the Harley-Davidson Experience Center, a $30 million, 110,000-sq.-ft. museum in Milwaukee.

Chairman, President and CEO; CEO, Harley-Davidson Motor: Jeffrey L. Bleustein, age 58, $1,140,260 pay
VP, Treasurer, and Controller; VP and Controller, Harley-Davidson Motor: James M. Brostowitz, age 47
VP, General Counsel, and Secretary; VP and General Counsel, Harley-Davidson Motor: Gail A. Lione, age 49
VP and CFO: James L. Ziemer, age 49, $502,134 pay
VP Purchasing, Harley-Davidson Motor: Garry S. Berryman
VP Marketing, Harley-Davidson Motor: Joanne M. Bischmann
VP Styling, Harley-Davidson Motor: William G. Davidson
VP Communications, Harley-Davidson Motor: Kathleen A. Demitros
VP Quality and Reliability, Harley-Davidson Motor: John D. Goll
VP International Trade and Regulatory Affairs, Harley-Davidson Motor: Timothy K. Hoelter
VP Parts, Accessories, and Customer Service, Harley-Davidson Motor: Ronald M. Hutchinson, age 52
VP Continuous Improvement, Harley-Davidson Motor: James A. McCaslin, age 50, $451,540 pay
Chairman and Chief Technical Officer, Buell: Erik F. Buell
Auditors: Ernst & Young LLP

HQ: 3700 W. Juneau Ave., Milwaukee, WI 53208
Phone: 414-342-4680   Fax: 414-343-8230
Web site: http://www.harley-davidson.com

Harley-Davidson operates manufacturing facilities in Wisconsin, Pennsylvania, and Missouri.

1998 Sales

	$ mil.	% of total
Harley-Davidson Motorcycles	1595	77
Parts & accessories	297	14
General merchandise	115	6
Buell Motorcycles	54	3
Other	3	—
Total	**2,064**	**100**

Selected Motorcycle Models
Dyna Glide
Electra Glide
Fat Boy
Heritage Springer
Low Rider
Road Glide
Road King
Softail
Sportster
Super Glide
Wide Glide

BMW
Excelsior-Henderson Motorcycle Manufacturing
Honda
Kawasaki Heavy Industries
Polaris Industries
Suzuki
Triumph Motorcycles
Yamaha Motor

NYSE symbol: HDI FYE: December 31	Annual Growth	1989	1990	1991	1992	1993	1994	1995	1996	1997	1998
Sales ($ mil.)	11.2%	791	865	940	1,105	1,217	1,542	1,351	1,531	1,763	2,064
Net income ($ mil.)	23.1%	33	38	37	54	(12)	104	113	166	174	214
Income as % of sales	—	4.2%	4.4%	3.9%	4.9%	—	6.8%	8.3%	10.8%	9.9%	10.3%
Earnings per share ($)	21.5%	0.24	0.26	0.26	0.36	0.50	0.63	0.74	0.94	1.13	1.38
Stock price - FY high ($)	—	2.69	4.30	7.59	9.69	11.88	14.94	15.06	24.75	31.25	47.50
Stock price - FY low ($)	—	1.52	1.67	2.22	5.44	7.88	10.81	11.00	13.19	16.69	23.88
Stock price - FY close ($)	39.0%	2.45	2.41	5.59	9.41	11.03	14.00	14.38	23.50	27.25	47.38
P/E - high	—	11	17	29	27	24	24	20	26	28	34
P/E - low	—	6	6	9	15	16	17	15	14	15	17
Dividends per share ($)	—	0.00	0.01	0.00	0.00	0.03	0.07	0.09	0.11	0.14	0.16
Book value per share ($)	22.0%	1.12	1.40	1.67	2.21	2.14	2.84	3.30	4.38	5.43	6.73
Employees	2.4%	5,000	5,000	5,300	5,800	6,000	6,700	4,800	5,200	6,060	6,200

HIGH/LOW/CLOSE

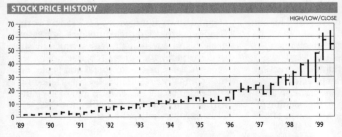

Debt ratio: 21.4%
Return on equity: 20.7%
Cash ($ mil.): 165
Current ratio: 1.80
Long-term debt ($ mil.): 280
No. of shares (mil.): 153
Dividends
 Yield: 0.3%
 Payout: 11.6%
Market value ($ mil.): 7,246

HARNISCHFEGER INDUSTRIES, INC.

OVERVIEW

Harnischfeger Industries can provide coal miners with everything but the canary. The St. Francis, Wisconsin-based holding company's subsidiaries make heavy machinery for underground coal mining (Joy Mining Machinery), surface mining (P&H Mining Equipment), and pulp and papermaking (Beloit). Although the company has manufacturing facilities in almost a dozen countries, the US generates more than half of sales.

Joy is a leading maker of mining machinery. P&H Mining manufactures equipment that includes electric mining shovels, draglines, and blasthole drills used to dig and load ores and minerals in mines and quarries. Harnischfeger's

mining equipment accounts for 59% of revenues. The company's pulp and papermaking machinery division consists of its 80% interest in Beloit Corporation. (The other 20% is owned by Mitsubishi Heavy Industries.) Beloit machinery accounts for the production of a significant share of the world's newsprint, printing paper, and paper towels. Harnischfeger also owns 20% of P&H Material Handling, a leading maker of overhead cranes.

Harnischfeger has struggled to cope with falling sales and earnings as its Asian customers retrench. Although it cut costs, Harnischfeger has had to seek Chapter 11 bankruptcy protection from its creditors.

HISTORY

In the mid-1880s German immigrant Henry Harnischfeger and partner Alonzo Pawling started a small machine and pattern shop in Milwaukee called Pawling and Harnischfeger (P&H). The company shipped its first overhead electric crane in 1888.

After a fire destroyed its main shop in 1903, P&H built a new plant in West Milwaukee in 1904 that became the world's leading manufacturer of overhead cranes. Pawling died in 1914, after which the company became Harnischfeger Corporation. In remembrance of Pawling, Harnischfeger kept its P&H trademark.

The highly cyclical heavy-equipment industry enjoyed a big upswing with WWI. To help weather industry downturns, Harnischfeger began selling excavating and mining equipment after the war.

Harnischfeger died in 1930, and his son Walter became president. The Depression meant hard times for the company, as it lost money every year from 1931 to 1939. Harnischfeger diversified into welding equipment, diesel engines, and prefabricated houses in the 1930s and 1940s.

WWII and the postwar period gave the company a boost. During that time it built new plants and began licensing foreign companies to build Harnischfeger cranes and excavators. Harnischfeger was listed on the AMEX in 1956. Walter became chairman in 1959, and his son, Henry, became president.

In the 1960s Harnischfeger streamlined operations, and by the end of the decade the company had only two divisions: construction and mining, and industrial and electrical. Harnischfeger was listed on the NYSE in 1971.

After the 1973 oil embargo, the opening of new coal reserves and the construction of oil

pipelines and mass transit systems boosted sales of Harnischfeger machinery. By the end of the 1970s, however, recession and high interest rates had taken their toll. On the verge of bankruptcy in the early 1980s, Harnischfeger was able to revive itself by trimming down, diversifying, and making key acquisitions.

In 1986 the firm purchased papermaking equipment firm Beloit, later selling a 20% interest to Mitsubishi and forming Harnischfeger Industries as a holding company. The manufacturer began moving away from systems handling in the early 1990s, selling its Harnischfeger Engineering unit.

Harnischfeger bought underground-mining equipment makers Joy Technologies in 1994 and Longwall International (through the acquisition of Dobson Park Industries) in 1995. The next year it bought Ingersoll-Rand's pulp machinery division.

In 1998 Harnischfeger sold an 80% stake in P&H Material Handling to Chartwell Investments and announced it was laying off about 20% of its workforce — about 3,100 jobs. Late in the year Asia Pulp and Paper Co. defaulted on a $300 million machinery purchase. In 1999 Harnischfeger rearranged the terms of $500 million in loans and obtained a $250 million term loan. In 1999 chairman and CEO Jeffery Grade, chairman since 1993, stepped down along with CFO Francis Corby. Grade spearheaded the company's aggressive growth strategy — a strategy stymied by slips in demand for the company's machinery because of weak prices for metal and paper. Former company president John Nils Hanson succeeded Grade as CEO. Unable to keep up with its bills, the company filed for Chapter 11 bankruptcy protection that year.

Chairman: Robert B. Hoffman
CEO: John N. Hanson, age 57
EVP for Law and Government Affairs and Secretary:
James A. Chokey, age 55, $254,400 pay
SVP; President of P&H Mining Equipment:
Robert W. Hale, age 52
SVP; President and COO of Joy: Wayne F. Hunnell,
age 52
SVP; President of Beloit: Mark E. Readinger, age 45,
$329,010 pay
VP and Controller: James C. Benjamin
VP Taxes: Gary E. Lakritz
VP Human Resources: Joseph A. Podawiltz
VP and Treasurer: Somerset R. Waters
Director Corporate Communications: David A. Brukardt
Auditors: PricewaterhouseCoopers LLP

LOCATIONS

HQ: 3600 S. Lake Dr., St. Francis, WI 53235-3716
Phone: 414-486-6400   **Fax:** 414-486-6747
Web site: http://www.harnischfeger.com

Harnischfeger Industries has manufacturing facilities in
Australia, Brazil, Canada, Chile, France, Italy, Poland,
South Africa, the UK, and the US.

1998 Sales

	$ mil.	% of total
US	1,556	58
Europe	439	17
Other regions	676	25
Adjustments	(629)	—
Total	**2,042**	**100**

PRODUCTS/OPERATIONS

1998 Sales

	$ mil.	% of total
Mining equipment	1,212	59
Pulp & paper machinery	830	41
Total	**2,042**	**100**

Selected Operations

Beloit (80%; pulp and papermaking machinery and
systems)
Horsburgh & Scott (custom-engineered gears, drives,
and replacement parts for industrial and mining
equipment)
Joy Mining Machinery (underground-mining equipment
such as roof supports, armored-face conveyors, and
continuous haulage systems)
P&H Material Handling (20%, overhead and portal
cranes, hoists, and container cranes)
P&H Mining Equipment (surface-mining equipment
such as electric shovels, walking draglines, blasthole
drills, dredge and dragline buckets, and hydraulic
excavators)

COMPETITORS

Bucyrus International
Caterpillar
Hitachi
Ingersoll-Rand
J.M. Voith
Komatsu
Marmon Group
Metso
Mitsui
Rowan
Tampella Corporation
Terex

HISTORICAL FINANCIALS & EMPLOYEES

NYSE symbol: HPH FYE: October 31	Annual Growth	1989	1990	1991	1992	1993	1994	1995	1996	1997	1998
Sales ($ mil.)	3.7%	1,467	1,762	1,584	1,376	1,235	1,117	2,152	2,864	3,089	2,042
Net income ($ mil.)	—	71	73	65	57	(18)	(48)	57	114	140	(19)
Income as % of sales	—	4.8%	4.1%	4.1%	4.1%	—	—	2.7%	4.0%	4.5%	—
Earnings per share ($)	—	2.17	2.27	2.08	1.95	(0.67)	(1.23)	1.23	2.37	2.60	(0.40)
Stock price - FY high ($)	—	22.38	25.00	22.00	22.88	22.75	26.50	39.38	42.13	50.00	40.00
Stock price - FY low ($)	—	14.38	12.38	12.88	16.13	17.13	18.50	24.75	28.63	37.94	6.13
Stock price - FY close ($)	(7.2%)	18.50	13.13	18.13	17.25	22.13	25.00	31.50	40.00	39.38	9.44
P/E - high	—	10	11	11	12	—	—	32	18	19	—
P/E - low	—	7	5	6	8	—	—	20	12	15	—
Dividends per share ($)	8.0%	0.20	0.20	0.40	0.40	0.40	0.40	0.40	0.40	0.40	0.40
Book value per share ($)	(1.3%)	15.90	18.38	19.82	21.15	18.01	16.24	11.51	13.71	15.76	14.13
Employees	1.4%	12,100	12,200	12,400	11,600	10,800	11,200	14,000	17,200	17,700	13,700

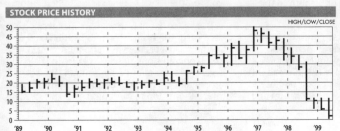

STOCK PRICE HISTORY
HIGH/LOW/CLOSE

1998 FISCAL YEAR-END
Debt ratio: 59.1%
Return on equity: —
Cash ($ mil.): 30
Current ratio: 1.43
Long-term debt ($ mil.): 963
No. of shares (mil.): 47
Dividends
 Yield: 4.2%
 Payout: —
Market value ($ mil.): 446

HARRAH'S ENTERTAINMENT, INC.

OVERVIEW

Harrah's Entertainment likes to spread its bets. The Memphis, Tennessee-based company is the second-largest gaming company in the world (behind Park Place Entertainment) and one of the most geographically diverse US casino operators, owning and/or managing land-based, dockside, riverboat, and Indian gaming casinos in 10 states and Australia.

Harrah's derives about 75% of its revenues from gambling at its casinos; its stateside locations are in Arizona, Illinois, Indiana, Kansas, Louisiana, Mississippi, Missouri, Nevada, New Jersey, and North Carolina. Its facilities boast more than 30,000 slot machines, 11,600 hotel rooms and suites, and about 90 restaurants.

The company is regrouping after a disastrous campaign to build a casino in New Orleans. However, Harrah's resumed construction on the casino after it lay dormant for three years; it is scheduled to open in late 1999. The company also plans to buy Players International and its riverboat casino operations in Illinois, Louisiana, and Missouri.

HISTORY

William Harrah and his father founded their first bingo parlor in Reno, Nevada, in 1937. Using the income from that business, Harrah opened his first casino, Harrah's Club, in downtown Reno in 1946. In 1955 and 1956 he bought several clubs in Stateline, Nevada (near Lake Tahoe). Harrah built the company by using promotions to draw middle-class Californians to his clubs.

During the 1960s the entrepreneur expanded his operations in Lake Tahoe, and in 1968 he built a 400-room hotel tower in Reno. Harrah's went public in 1971. After Harrah's death in 1978, the company expanded outside Nevada by building a hotel and casino in Atlantic City, New Jersey. It opened two years later.

Holiday Inns acquired Harrah's in 1980 for about $300 million. The hotelier already owned a 40% interest in River Boat Casino, which operated a casino next to a Holiday Inn in Las Vegas. When Holiday Inns acquired the other 60% of the casino/hotel in 1983, Harrah's took over management of it. Holiday Inns changed its name to Holiday Corporation in 1985. The following year UK brewer Bass plc put up $100 million for 10% of Holiday Corporation.

In 1988 Bass agreed to buy the Holiday Inn chain, completing the $2.2 billion acquisition in 1990. The rest of Holiday Corporation, including Harrah's, was renamed Promus under chairman Michael Rose. Promus moved its headquarters from Reno to Memphis the following year.

In the early 1990s Harrah's built a casino on Ak-Chin Indian land near Phoenix and opened riverboat casinos in Joliet, Illinois; Shreveport, Louisiana; and North Kansas City, Missouri. In 1995 Promus spun off its hotel operations as Promus Hotel Corporation and changed the name of its casino business to Harrah's Entertainment.

That year Harrah's gambled and lost. Big. Its Rivergate Casino, which would have been the world's biggest gambling facility, was shelved even before it was finished — a victim of Louisiana's Byzantine politics. Eager for the right to build what would be a $395 million, 200,000-sq.-ft. casino in the heart of New Orleans, Harrah's had made a number of ill-advised concessions to state and municipal officials. The company agreed not to offer hotel rooms or food at the casino (forgoing about 20% of anticipated revenues) to placate New Orleans' hospitality industry, and it promised to make an annual $100 million minimum payment to the state, in addition to 19% of the casino's revenues. In the end, the fiasco's price tag reached $900 million (only half of which went to casino construction costs), and Harrah's put the project into bankruptcy to stop the bleeding.

In 1997 Rose retired as chairman and was replaced by CEO Philip Satre. In 1998 Harrah's rolled out its version of frequent flier miles: the Total Gold program, which allows slot machine players to earn points redeemable for lodging, merchandise, and other perks. Also in 1998 Harrah's bought competitor Showboat Inc., with properties in Las Vegas and Atlantic City and management of a New South Wales, Australia, casino. A 1998 Louisiana Supreme Court ruling allowed the company to resume work on the New Orleans casino (albeit with a stake of less than 45%). Harrah's also invested in Las Vegas-based National Airlines that year.

In early 1999 Harrah's bought Rio Hotel & Casino (also a partner in National Airlines), which operates one upscale casino on the Las Vegas Strip, for about $525 million. It also agreed to buy riverboat casino operator Players International for $425 million.

Chairman and CEO: Philip G. Satre, age 49, $1,136,723 pay
EVP and COO: Gary W. Loveman, age 38, $476,923 pay
EVP and CFO: Colin V. Reed, age 51, $649,535 pay
SVP and General Counsel: E. O. Robinson Jr., age 59, $347,730 pay
SVP Corporate Human Resources: Marilyn Winn
SVP Information Technology and Brand Operations: John M. Boushy, age 44
President, Central Division: Anthony M. Sanfilippo
President, Eastern Division: Timothy J. Wilmott, age 40
President, New Orleans Division: Jay D. Sevigny
President, Rio Hotel and Casino: John M. Lipkowitz
President, Showboat Division: Herbert R. Wolfe
President, Western Division: J. Carlos Tolosa, age 49
SVP and General Manager, Harrah's Las Vegas: Tom Jenkin, age 44
VP Brand Management: Craig R. Hudson, age 40
Auditors: Arthur Andersen LLP

LOCATIONS

HQ: 1023 Cherry Rd., Memphis, TN 38117
Phone: 901-762-8600   **Fax:** 901-762-8637
Web site: http://www.harrahs.com

PRODUCTS/OPERATIONS

1998 Sales

	$ mil.	% of total
Casino	1,660	76
Food & beverages	232	10
Rooms	153	7
Management fees	65	3
Other	78	4
Adjustments	(184)	—
Total	**2,004**	**100**

COMPETITORS

Ameristar Casinos
Argosy Gaming
Aztar
Boyd Gaming
Greate Bay
Hollywood Casino
Hollywood Park
Hyatt
Isle of Capri Casinos
Mandalay Resort Group
Mashantucket Pequot Gaming
MGM Grand
Mirage Resorts
Park Place Entertainment
President Casinos
Starwood Hotels & Resorts Worldwide
Station Casinos
Sun International Hotels
Trump Hotels & Casinos

HISTORICAL FINANCIALS & EMPLOYEES

NYSE symbol: HET FYE: December 31	Annual Growth	1989	1990	1991	1992	1993	1994	1995	1996	1997	1998
Sales ($ mil.)	8.7%	945	1,004	1,031	1,113	1,252	1,339	1,550	1,588	1,619	2,004
Net income ($ mil.)	(4.5%)	155	23	30	53	86	78	79	99	99	102
Income as % of sales	—	16.4%	2.3%	2.9%	4.7%	6.9%	5.9%	5.1%	6.2%	6.1%	5.1%
Earnings per share ($)	16.2%	—	0.30	0.33	0.52	0.84	0.76	0.76	0.95	0.98	1.00
Stock price - FY high ($)	—	—	7.68	6.57	13.51	39.62	39.78	33.13	38.88	23.06	26.38
Stock price - FY low ($)	—	—	2.13	2.79	5.31	12.58	18.63	21.60	16.38	15.50	11.06
Stock price - FY close ($)	20.2%	—	3.60	5.28	13.21	32.94	22.23	24.25	19.88	18.88	15.69
P/E - high	—	—	26	20	26	47	52	44	41	24	26
P/E - low	—	—	7	8	10	15	25	28	17	16	11
Dividends per share ($)	—	—	0.00	0.00	0.00	0.00	0.00	0.00	0.00	0.00	0.00
Book value per share ($)	15.3%	—	2.67	3.70	4.20	5.24	6.09	5.70	6.99	7.28	8.33
Employees	5.9%	22,400	23,100	23,000	23,000	23,100	28,500	22,000	22,000	23,400	37,400

STOCK PRICE HISTORY

HIGH/LOW/CLOSE

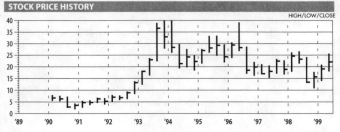

1998 FISCAL YEAR-END

Debt ratio: 70.1%
Return on equity: 12.0%
Cash ($ mil.): 159
Current ratio: 1.20
Long-term debt ($ mil.): 1,999
No. of shares (mil.): 102
Dividends
 Yield: —
 Payout: —
Market value ($ mil.): 1,603

HARRIS CORPORATION

OVERVIEW

Harris is hardly harassed by the demands of a changing world market. Originally a maker of printing presses, the Melbourne, Florida-based company's current products are high-tech. Its main operation, Lanier Worldwide, markets copying and fax systems, electronic imaging equipment, and health care information management systems, as well as other products and services. The company's electronic-systems sector develops communications and information systems used for air traffic control, space exploration, national defense, and utility energy management.

Harris also manufactures communications products such as microwave radios, which are used in cellular and PCS infrastructures, and digital telephone and TV (aka HDTV) equipment. Its communications products are used in a variety of markets, including aerospace, multimedia, automotive, and telecommunications.

The US government accounts for more than 20% of the company's sales.

Lanier Worldwide, which Harris is spinning off to shareholders, has stayed ahead of its competition by introducing new high-end office products, such as a digital color copier, and entering emerging markets such as digital TV. Harris' electronic systems sector has a joint venture with General Electric to manufacture railway control systems using Harris satellite-based global positioning systems, and to develop computer management systems for utilities.

The company's communications unit — soon to be Harris' main focus — is expanding into new markets, providing telecommunications equipment to countries such as Brazil, Indonesia, and Romania. As part of its new focus, Harris has also sold off its semiconductor operations.

HISTORY

Harris was founded in Niles, Ohio, in 1895 by brothers Alfred and Charles Harris, both jewelers and inventors. Among their inventions was a printing press that became Harris Automatic Press Company's flagship product.

Harris remained a small, family-run company until 1944, when engineer George Dively was hired as general manager. Under Dively the company began manufacturing bindery, typesetting, and paper-converting equipment while remaining a leading supplier of printing presses. In 1957 Harris merged with Intertype, a typesetter maker, and became known as Harris-Intertype Corporation.

During the 1960s and 1970s Harris-Intertype grew through acquisitions. In 1967 it bought electronics and data-processing equipment maker Radiation, a $50 million company heavily dependent upon government contracts, and relocated to Radiation's headquarters in Melbourne, Florida. The company also bought RF Communications (two-way radios, 1969), General Eletric's (GE) broadcast equipment line (1972), and UCC-Communications Systems (data-processing equipment, 1972). The company changed its name to Harris Corporation in 1974. In 1980 Harris bought Farinon, a manufacturer of microwave radio systems, and Lanier Business Products, the leading maker of dictating equipment. In 1983 it sold its printing equipment business.

Harris formed a joint venture with 3M called Harris/3M Document Products in 1986 to market copiers and fax machines, and in 1989 it acquired the entire operation, which became Lanier Worldwide. Other 1980s acquisitions included Scientific Calculations, a CAD software developer (1986), and GE's Solid State group (1988).

Harris won a $1.7 billion deal with the FAA in 1992 to modernize voice communications between airports and airplanes. Later that year Harris acquired Westronic, a supplier of automated control systems for electric utilities. In 1993 Harris formed a joint venture with China-based Shenzen Telecom Equipment to produce digital microwave radios.

In 1994 Harris began installing the world's largest private digital telephone network, along Russia's gas pipeline. That year it spun off its computer systems division.

In 1996 Harris became the first company to demonstrate a digital TV transmitter. That year it acquired NovAtel Communication, maker of cellular and wireless local-loop systems for rural areas, and bought a stake in the Chile-based Compania de Telefonos. In 1997 Lanier purchased litigation services company Quorum Group and bought a European maker of digital broadcasting products.

Lanier in 1998 bought Bayer's photocopier business, which duplicated Lanier's share of the European office equipment market. Hurt by a tough semiconductor market, Harris also began a worldwide layoff of 2,300 employees, about 8% of its workforce. The following year Harris sold its photomask manufacturing unit and its semiconductor business.

OFFICERS

Chairman Emeritus: Joseph A. Boyd
Chairman Emeritus: Richard B. Tullis
Chairman, President, and CEO: Phillip W. Farmer, age 60, $1,462,400 pay
SVP and CFO: Bryan R. Roub, age 57, $562,131 pay
President, Lanier Worldwide: Wesley E. Cantrell, age 63, $664,616 pay
President, Communications Sector: E. Van Cullens, age 52, $510,757 pay
President, Government Communications Systems Division: Robert K. Henry
President, Electronic Systems Sector: Jon E. Wohler
Deputy President, Electronic Systems Sector: Charles J. Herbert, age 62
VP, Secretary, and General Counsel: Richard L. Ballantyne, age 58
VP Internal Audit: James L. Christie, age 46
VP and Controller: Robert W. Fay, age 51
VP Human Resources and Corporate Relations: Nick E. Heldreth, age 56
VP Quality and New Processes: John G. Johnson, age 62
VP Investor Relations: Pamela Padgett, age 42
VP and General Manager of Aerospace Systems Division: Daniel R. Pearson
VP Corporate Development: Ronald R. Spoehel, age 40
VP and Treasurer: David S. Wasserman, age 55
VP Operations, Washington: Raymon M. White, age 60
Auditors: Ernst & Young LLP

LOCATIONS

HQ: 1025 W. NASA Blvd., Melbourne, FL 32919
Phone: 407-727-9100   **Fax:** 407-727-9344
Web site: http://www.harris.com

Harris has more than 35 manufacturing plants and about 430 offices worldwide.

PRODUCTS/OPERATIONS

1998 Sales

	$ mil.	% of total
Lanier Worldwide	1,257	32
Communications	970	25
Electronic Systems	953	25
Semiconductors	710	18
Total	**3,890**	**100**

Selected Products

Lanier Worldwide
Dictation systems
Facsimile units
Information management systems
Office copiers
Voice-recording products

Communications
Digital telephone switches
Microwave systems

Radio and television transmission systems
Two-way pagers

Electronic Systems
Air traffic control
Communications
Electronics systems testing
Energy management
Mobile radio networks
Space exploration

COMPETITORS

A.B.Dick	ITT Industries	Rockwell
Alcatel	Litton Industries	International
Canon	Lucent	Sharp
Casio Computer	Minolta	Siemens
Eastman Kodak	Motorola	Sony
Ericsson	Multigraphics	SPX
GEC	NEC	Sun
General Dynamics	Nortel Networks	Microsystems
GenRad	Northrop	Tektronix
Hitachi	Grumman	Thomson SA
Honeywell	Oce NV	Toshiba
Hyundai	Pitney Bowes	Viking Office
IKON	Raytheon	Products
		Xerox

HISTORICAL FINANCIALS & EMPLOYEES

NYSE symbol: HRS FYE: June 30	Annual Growth	1989	1990	1991	1992	1993	1994	1995	1996	1997	1998
Sales ($ mil.)	6.5%	2,214	3,053	3,040	3,004	3,099	3,336	3,444	3,621	3,797	3,890
Net income ($ mil.)	22.5%	21	131	20	75	111	112	155	178	208	133
Income as % of sales	—	1.0%	4.3%	0.6%	2.5%	3.6%	3.4%	4.5%	4.9%	5.5%	3.4%
Earnings per share ($)	22.4%	0.27	1.65	0.25	0.96	1.41	1.41	1.98	2.29	2.63	1.66
Stock price - FY high ($)	—	17.25	19.75	17.13	17.00	19.63	26.13	26.81	34.44	46.06	55.31
Stock price - FY low ($)	—	12.50	13.75	6.88	10.63	13.44	18.19	18.88	24.44	25.13	40.19
Stock price - FY close ($)	12.0%	16.06	17.19	12.94	13.75	19.38	22.06	25.81	30.50	42.00	44.69
P/E - high	—	64	12	69	18	14	19	14	15	18	33
P/E - low	—	46	8	28	11	10	13	10	11	10	24
Dividends per share ($)	8.0%	0.44	0.48	0.52	0.52	0.52	0.56	0.62	0.68	0.76	0.88
Book value per share ($)	5.7%	12.23	13.51	13.22	13.65	14.41	15.12	16.06	17.66	19.82	20.11
Employees	(2.3%)	35,100	33,400	30,700	28,300	28,300	28,200	26,600	27,600	29,000	28,500

STOCK PRICE HISTORY

HIGH/LOW/CLOSE

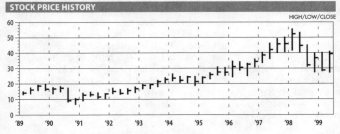

1998 FISCAL YEAR-END

Debt ratio: 32.3%
Return on equity: 8.3%
Cash ($ mil.): 184
Current ratio: 1.66
Long-term debt ($ mil.): 769
No. of shares (mil.): 80
Dividends
  Yield: 2.0%
  Payout: 53.0%
Market value ($ mil.): 3,576

HARTFORD FINANCIAL SERVICES

OVERVIEW

Like the stag in its logo, The Hartford Financial Services Group takes a heads-up stance.

The Hartford, Connecticut-based company provides personal and commercial property/casualty insurance (including homeowners and standard and nonstandard auto coverage) and sells reinsurance.

The company owns 81% of Hartford Life, the #1 writer of individual annuities in the US and a provider of disability insurance, investment management services, and both personal and group life insurance. Hartford Life also offers mutual funds managed by Wellington Management Group and Hartford itself.

With property/casualty sales stagnant, Hartford Life (about one-third of sales) is targeting the growing retirement savings market and seeks marketing alliances such as its agreement to provide auto and homeowners polices to members of the American Association of Retired Persons (AARP). The company is also focusing on building its small-business coverage.

HISTORY

In 1810 a group of Hartford, Connecticut, businessmen led by Walter Mitchell and Henry Terry founded the Hartford Fire Insurance Co. Thanks to frequent fires in America's wooden cities and executive ignorance of risk assessment and premium-setting, the firm was often on the edge of insolvency. (In 1835 stockholders staged a coup and threw out the management.) Still, each urban conflagration — including the Great Chicago Fire of 1871 — afforded the Hartford the opportunity to seek out and pay all its policyholders, thus allowing the company to learn underwriting under fire, as it were, and use such disasters to refine its rates.

As for the company's stag logo, it was initially a little deer, as shown on a policy sold to Abraham Lincoln in 1861. A few years later, however, Hartford began using the more majestic creature (from a Landseer painting) now familiar to customers. By the 1880s Hartford operated nationwide, as well as in Canada and Hawaii.

In 1882 an agent from Kansas named Mrs. Dodds asked the firm to consider "windstorm" policies. Her suggestion was met with disdain, but within a few years Hartford was writing tornado insurance. Other new types of coverage were also added (including auto, travel, and inland marine), particularly after the San Francisco earthquake of 1906.

The company survived both World Wars and the Depression but emerged in the 1950s in need of organization. It set up new regional offices and added life insurance, acquiring Columbian National Life (founded 1902), which became Hartford Life Insurance Co.

In 1969 Hartford was acquired by ITT (formerly International Telephone and Telegraph), whose CEO, Harold Geneen, was an avid conglomerateur. Consumer advocate Ralph Nader strongly opposed the acquisition — he led a court fight against the merger for years and

felt vindicated when ITT spun off Hartford in 1995. Others opposed it, too, because ITT had engineered the merger based on an IRS ruling (later revoked) that Hartford stockholders would not have to pay capital gains taxes on the purchase price of their stock.

Insurance operations were consolidated under the Hartford Life Insurance banner in 1978. Throughout the 1980s, Hartford Life remained one of ITT's strongest operations. A conservative investment policy kept Hartford safe from the junk bond and real estate manias of the 1980s.

Hartford reorganized its property/casualty operations along three lines in 1986, and in 1992 it organized its reinsurance business into one unit. The company faced some liability in relation to Dow Corning's breast-implant litigation, but underwriting standards after 1985 reduced its long-term risk. In 1994 the company began selling insurance products to AARP members under an exclusive agreement that runs through 2002. In 1996 the company finished its spinoff from ITT, which was acquired by Starwood Hotels & Resorts two years later.

To grow its reinsurance operation, Hartford acquired Orion Capital's reinsurance business in 1996. It posted a loss of $99 million, due in large part to asbestos and pollution liabilities. Late that year the firm changed its name to The Hartford Financial Services Group.

To shore up reserves and fund growth, in 1997 the company spun off 17% of Hartford Life in an IPO. The next year the Hartford expanded into nonstandard auto insurance, acquiring Omni Insurance Group. The company sold its London & Edinburgh Insurance Group to Norwich Union PLC. In 1999 Hartford acquired the reinsurance business of Vesta Fire Insurance, a subsidiary of Vesta Insurance Group.

OFFICERS

Chairman, President, and CEO: Ramani Ayer, age 51, $1,781,000 pay
VC; President and CEO, Hartford Life; President, International Operations: Lowndes A. "Lon" Smith, age 59, $1,638,417 pay
EVP and CFO: David K. Zwiener, age 44, $937,750 pay
EVP and Chief Investment Officer: Joseph H. Gareau, $659,200 pay
Group SVP and Chief Actuary, Property and Casualty Operations: Linda L. Bell
Group SVP, Information Technology: John T. Crawford
Group SVP, Human Resources: Helen G. Goodman
Group SVP, Claims, Property and Casualty: Paul R. Schwartzott
Group SVP and General Counsel: Michael S. Wilder
SVP Investor Relations: Stephen P. Minihan
VP and Corporate Secretary: Amy B. Gallent
President, Commerical Lines: Richard J. Quagliaroli
President, Business Insurance: Judith A. Blades
President, Hartford Specialty: David R. Bradley
CEO, Hartford Reinsurance Management: Dennis Zettervall
Auditors: Arthur Andersen LLP

LOCATIONS

HQ: The Hartford Financial Services Group, 690 Asylum Ave., Hartford, CT 06115-1900
Phone: 860-547-5000   **Fax:** 860-547-2680
Web site: http://www.thehartford.com

1998 Sales

	$ mil.	% of total
North America	13,201	88
UK	1,212	8
Other regions	609	4
Total	**15,022**	**100**

PRODUCTS/OPERATIONS

1998 Assets

	$ mil.	% of total
Cash & equivalents	123	—
Treasury & agency securities	2,165	1
Foreign governments' securities	1,692	1
State & municipal bonds	10,007	7
Corporate bonds	17,526	12
Stocks	1,066	1
Policy loans	6,687	4
Other investments	4,553	3
Assets in separate account	91,579	61
Other assets	15,234	10
Total	**150,632**	**100**

1998 Sales

	$ mil.	% of total
Life	5,788	39
Commercial	3,385	23
Personal	2,268	15
International	1,647	11
Reinsurance	716	5
Investment income & other	1,218	7
Total	**15,022**	**100**

COMPETITORS

AIG	MetLife
Allmerica Financial	Mutual of Omaha
Allstate	New York Life
American General	Northwestern Mutual
Berkshire Hathaway	Prudential
Chubb	SAFECO
Citigroup	St. Paul Companies
CNA Financial	State Farm
Lincoln National	USAA

HISTORICAL FINANCIALS & EMPLOYEES

NYSE symbol: HIG FYE: December 31	Annual Growth	1989	1990	1991	1992	1993	1994	1995	1996	1997	1998
Assets ($ mil.)	22.4%	24,493	32,014	37,771	54,180	66,179	76,765	93,855	108,840	131,743	150,632
Net income ($ mil.)	11.8%	372	328	431	(274)	537	632	562	(99)	1,332	1,015
Income as % of assets	—	1.5%	1.0%	1.1%	—	0.8%	0.8%	0.6%	—	1.0%	0.7%
Earnings per share ($)	21.8%	—	—	—	—	—	—	2.38	(0.42)	5.58	4.30
Stock price - FY high ($)	—	—	—	—	—	—	—	25.06	34.94	47.25	60.00
Stock price - FY low ($)	—	—	—	—	—	—	—	23.69	22.25	32.44	37.63
Stock price - FY close ($)	31.4%	—	—	—	—	—	—	24.19	33.75	46.78	54.88
P/E - high	—	—	—	—	—	—	—	11	—	8	14
P/E - low	—	—	—	—	—	—	—	10	—	6	9
Dividends per share ($)	—	—	—	—	—	—	—	0.00	0.60	0.80	0.83
Book value per share ($)	12.1%	—	—	—	—	—	—	20.07	19.22	25.79	28.25
Employees	2.2%	—	21,000	21,000	21,000	21,000	20,000	21,000	22,000	25,000	25,000

STOCK PRICE HISTORY
HIGH/LOW/CLOSE

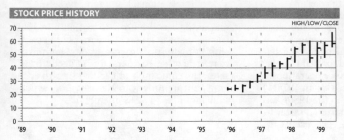

1998 FISCAL YEAR-END

Equity as % of assets: 4.3%
Return on assets: 0.7%
Return on equity: 15.8%
Long-term debt ($ mil.): 1,548
No. of shares (mil.): 227
Dividends
  Yield: 1.5%
  Payout: 19.3%
Market value ($ mil.): 12,479
Sales (mil.): $15,022

HARTFORD LIFE, INC.

OVERVIEW

Don't expect strippers at this stag party. Known for its stag logo, Simsbury, Connecticut-based Hartford Life hooks customers up with insurance and financial services to provide support following disability or retirement, or after a family member's death. Hartford Life is one of the key business groups of Hartford Financial Services Group, which owns 81% of the company.

Hartford Life's business segments are individual and group annuities (it's the US's largest individual annuities writer), individual life insurance (variable, universal, whole, and term),

and employee benefits (group life, disability, and accident insurance, as well as reinsurance). Employee benefits and investment products account for more than 60% of sales. The company distributes its products through some 1,300 broker-dealers and 450 banks. In addition to selling self-managed financial products, Hartford Life offers funds overseen by the Wellington Management Company.

To counter stagnant sales of annuities and life insurance, Hartford Life has turned to cross-selling. It is also building brand awareness and increasing distribution channels.

HISTORY

Connecticut businessmen founded The Hartford Fire Insurance Co. in 1810. Underwriting mistakes and frequent conflagrations in America's wooden cities left the young insurer at the brink of failure several times; an 1835 stockholder coup installed new management. Still, the company learned underwriting under fire, as it were. After each catastrophe (including the Great Chicago Fire of 1871) Hartford worked to find and pay policyholders; it also used such disasters to refine rates.

The company's original symbol (seen on a policy sold to Abraham Lincoln in 1861) was a little deer. Within a few years, however, the firm had lifted its now-familiar splendid stag from a painting by Edwin Landseer. By the 1880s Hartford operated throughout the US (as well as Hawaii) and Canada. In 1882, an Osage City, Kansas agent (Mrs. Dodd, an example of the insurance profession's early openness to women) suggested the company begin offering windstorm coverage. Her idea was coolly received, but Hartford nonetheless soon began writing tornado insurance. It added other types of coverage, including auto, travel, and inland marine, at a pace that quickened after the San Francisco earthquake of 1906.

The company survived both World Wars and the Depression; by the 1950s it restructured, setting up regional offices to coordinate local ones. It entered life insurance, buying Columbian National Life (Boston, founded in 1902) to form Hartford Life Insurance Co.

In 1969 International Telephone and Telegraph bought Hartford and formed ITT Hartford; it consolidated insurance operations as the Hartford Life Insurance Cos. in 1978. ITT Hartford was a bright spot in the 1980s, as bloated parent ITT lurched from disaster to disaster. One misstep — largely because it

was ahead of its time — was the company's purchase of interests in three stock brokerages, including one that is now part of First Union. Conservative investment policies insulated Hartford from the decade's junk-bond and real estate manias. Stung by slowing sales of death-benefit life insurance, the company moved into variable-rate annuities.

The Hartford continued building its life insurance operations. In 1995 ITT spun off Hartford Life as part of its voluntary dismemberment. Other resulting entities were manufacturer ITT Industries and a hospitality unit that is now part of Starwood Hotels & Resorts Worldwide.

In 1996 ITT Hartford became The Hartford Financial Services Group (The Hartford) and pumped up its life insurance operations in South America. It joined forces with Banco de Galicia y Buenos Aires (Argentina's largest private bank) to form insurer Galicia Vida Compania de Seguros; it also forged a marketing agreement with Swiss Life Insurance and Pension to offer employee benefits coverage in Brazil.

In 1997 The Hartford sold 17% of Hartford Life to the public to fund continued growth for the life insurer. The next year, Hartford Life bought out Mutual Benefit Life Insurance's 40% of International Corporate Marketing Group, an employer-owned life insurance marketing venture (formed in 1992). In 1999 Hartford ended an exclusive marketing pact with Putnam Investments, freeing both firms to pursue other partners. Citing declining sales, the company and Pacific Life also ended joint venture American Maturity Life, which sold annuities to AARP members.

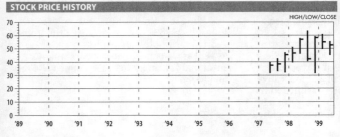

HARTMARX CORPORATION

OVERVIEW

Hartmarx is the nation's top maker of men's suits, but as Fridays go casual, the Chicago-based company has loosened its collar. Hartmarx built a name around its century-old Hart Schaffner & Marx and Hickey-Freeman brands of men's tailored clothing. Though suits and sports coats still account for about 65% of sales, Hartmarx has ventured into sportswear, including golf wear (Bobby Jones, Jack Nicklaus), slacks (Sansabelt), and accessories, which appeal to younger customers and those not tied to wearing a suit every day.

The company sells its apparel through department and specialty stores, golf shops, resorts, and catalogs in the US and in more than a dozen other countries. In addition to its own brands, it makes clothing under licenses from Tommy Hilfiger, Kenneth Cole, Perry Ellis, and others. Hartmarx also makes women's suits and separates (about one-tenth of sales) under labels such as Barrie Pace and the licensed Austin Reed name. Saudi Arabian investor Abdullah Taha Bakhsh owns about 15% of the company.

HISTORY

Harry Hart, 21, and his brother Max, 18, of Chicago, opened a men's clothing store, Harry Hart and Brother, in 1872. In 1887, after Marcus Marx and Joseph Schaffner had joined the company, the enterprise was renamed Hart Schaffner & Marx.

The young clothiers contracted with independent tailors to produce suits for their new store. Recognizing the potential of the wholesale garment industry, they began selling to other merchants and in 1897 launched a national ad campaign in leading publications.

A walkout by female workers in 1910 protesting low wages and poor working conditions in one of the company's 48 tailoring shops sparked a citywide garment workers' strike. Schaffner and Harry Hart successfully negotiated a settlement (not honored by other major Chicago companies) in January 1911.

Hart Schaffner & Marx in 1935 began a pattern of purchases over the next three decades that included Wallach Brothers (New York clothing chain), Hastings (a California clothier, 1952), Hanny's (Arizona, 1962), Hickey-Freeman (stores in Chicago, New York, and Detroit; 1964), and Field Brothers (New York, 1968). A 1970 antitrust decree forced it to sell 30 of its 238 men's clothing stores and refrain for 10 years from further purchases without court approval. The company made several approved purchases during the period. In 1981 Hart Schaffner & Marx bought the Country Miss chain and expanded into women's clothing. A year later it bought Kuppenheimer, a leading maker of lower-priced suits.

The company changed its name to Hartmarx in 1983, creating a holding company to oversee the variety of businesses it had acquired. A costly 1986 reorganization of administrative functions and the retail stores resulted in the loss of 800 jobs; earnings fell 42%. After a brief recovery in 1987 and 1988, earnings declined

by more than half to $17 million in 1989, largely because of a dramatic increase in wool prices. Further restructuring, in 1990 Hartmarx reorganized its women's lines into a new unit under the name Barrie Pace and began experimenting with placing Kuppenheimer outlets in Sears stores. It entered the golf wear industry the next year with the introduction of its Bobby Jones line; golf wear grew to $50 million in sales in just five years.

In spite of the financial birdie hit by golf wear, CEO Harvey Weinberg was ousted in 1992 due to continued losses (blamed largely on retail operations). COO Elbert Hand took the post and immediately upped the restructuring pace, expanding Hartmarx's core men's apparel business and further divesting retail operations. The company completely exited retailing in 1995, even as some of its retail customers (Barneys, Today's Man) filed for bankruptcy protection. It also closed 10 domestic factories and began moving production to countries such as Costa Rica and Mexico.

In 1996 Hartmarx bought Plaid Clothing Group, a bankrupt supplier of men's tailored clothing, which handled five name brands, including Burberrys, Evan-Picone, and Liz Claiborne's men's line. The following year the company defeated designer Nino Cerruti in a lawsuit to stop Hartmarx from manufacturing Cerruti clothing overseas; he claimed it cheapened the value of his label.

Adding to both its casual and tailored portfolios, in 1998 Hartmarx acquired the tropical sportswear wholesale business of Pusser's, as well as Canadian men's apparel manufacturer and Hartmarx licensee Coppley, Noyes and Randall.

OFFICERS

Chairman and CEO: Elbert O. Hand, age 59,
$1,135,699 pay
President and COO: Homi B. Patel, age 49,
$870,464 pay
EVP and CFO: Glenn R. Morgan, age 51, $348,338 pay
SVP, General Counsel, and Secretary:
Frederick G. Wohlschlaeger, age 48, $285,357 pay
VP and Treasurer: James E. Condon, age 48,
$178,573 pay
VP Compensation and Benefits: Linda J. Valentine,
age 48
President, Intercontinental Branded Apparel: Joe Conti
President, Plaid Clothing: Jim Murray
President, Hickey-Freeman Company: Howard Zenner
Group President: Steven J. Weiner
Manager Employee Relations: Lorraine Dickson
Auditors: PricewaterhouseCoopers LLP

LOCATIONS

HQ: 101 N. Wacker Dr., Chicago, IL 60606
Phone: 312-372-6300   **Fax:** 312-444-2710

Hartmarx operates nearly 20 plants in Canada, Costa
Rica, Mexico, and the US.

PRODUCTS/OPERATIONS

1998 Sales

	$ mil.	% of total
Tailored clothing	471.2	65
Sportswear	193.8	27
Women's apparel	60.0	8
Total	**725.0**	**100**

Owned Brands
Barrie Pace
Brannoch
Cambridge
Coppley
Desert Classic
Hart Schaffner
& Marx
Hawksley & Wight
Hickey-Freeman
Keithmoor
Palm Beach
Pusser's of the
West Indies
Racquet Club
Sansabelt
Society Brand Ltd.

Licensed Brands
Allyn Saint George
Austin Reed
Bobby Jones
Burberrys
Claiborne
Daniel Hechter
Evan-Picone
Gieves & Hawkes
Henry Grethel
Jack Nicklaus
J.G. Hook
Karl Lagerfeld
Kenneth Cole
KM by Krizia
Nino Cerruti
Perry Ellis
Pierre Cardin
Pringle
Robert Comstock
Tommy Hilfiger

COMPETITORS

Ashworth
Brooks Brothers
The Gap
Haggar
Lands' End
Levi Strauss
Nautica Enterprises
Oxford Industries
Perry Ellis International
Phillips-Van Heusen
Pietrafesa
Polo
Tropical Sportswear

HISTORICAL FINANCIALS & EMPLOYEES

NYSE symbol: HMX FYE: November 30	Annual Growth	1989	1990	1991	1992	1993	1994	1995	1996	1997	1998
Sales ($ mil.)	(6.3%)	1,297	1,296	1,215	1,054	732	718	595	610	718	725
Net income ($ mil.)	(1.9%)	17	(62)	(38)	(220)	6	16	3	25	25	15
Income as % of sales	—	1.3%	—	—	—	0.8%	2.2%	0.5%	4.0%	3.5%	2.0%
Earnings per share ($)	(8.0%)	0.89	(3.11)	(1.74)	(8.59)	0.20	0.50	0.10	0.74	0.74	0.42
Stock price - FY high ($)	—	28.13	20.75	13.25	8.63	8.25	7.50	6.88	6.50	10.13	9.00
Stock price - FY low ($)	—	20.13	5.50	6.63	3.00	5.13	5.00	4.25	3.75	4.88	4.38
Stock price - FY close ($)	(12.8%)	20.13	6.88	7.25	5.63	7.00	5.38	4.50	5.25	8.13	5.88
P/E - high	—	32	—	—	—	41	15	69	9	14	21
P/E - low	—	23	—	—	—	26	10	43	5	7	10
Dividends per share ($)	(100.0%)	1.18	0.90	0.60	0.00	0.00	0.00	0.00	0.00	0.00	0.00
Book value per share ($)	(11.6%)	18.37	14.60	11.32	2.73	3.41	3.95	4.11	4.86	5.62	6.06
Employees	(9.9%)	23,500	22,000	20,000	13,000	11,200	11,000	8,200	8,600	8,100	9,200

STOCK PRICE HISTORY

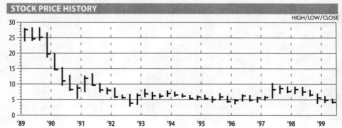

HIGH/LOW/CLOSE

1998 FISCAL YEAR-END

Debt ratio: 44.6%
Return on equity: 6.9%
Cash ($ mil.): 5
Current ratio: 3.50
Long-term debt ($ mil.): 170
No. of shares (mil.): 35
Dividends
  Yield: —
  Payout: —
Market value ($ mil.): 205

HASBRO, INC.

OVERVIEW

As any Jedi knows, the Force is a powerful thing, and Hasbro is hoping it can stand up to Barbie. Pawtucket, Rhode Island-based Hasbro, the #2 toy company behind Barbie-maker Mattel, makes toys, games, software, and puzzles. It has some of the best-known brand names in the industry, including *Star Wars* action figures, G.I. Joe, Playskool, Nerf, and Tonka. The company's Milton Bradley and Parker Brothers games include *Monopoly* and *Yahtzee*. Its Hasbro Interactive unit is doing well by converting vintage arcade games (*Frogger*, *Q*Bert*) and board games (*Monopoly*) into computer and video games.

Hasbro has tapped into the cross-marketing force of movies, paying at least $600 million (plus stock) for the right to make most of the toys for the *Star Wars* prequels. The company is also expanding into new areas — children's digital cameras (with chipmaker Intel) and television (the preschool show *It's Itsy Bitsy Time* with the Fox Family Channel). Wal-Mart and Toys "R" Us account for about 35% of Hasbro's sales.

Chairman and CEO Alan Hassenfeld, the third generation of Hassenfelds to control the company, owns about 9% of Hasbro; *Star Wars* creator George Lucas owns about 7%.

HISTORY

Henry and Hillel Hassenfeld formed Hassenfeld Brothers in Pawtucket, Rhode Island, in 1923 to distribute fabric remnants. By 1926 the company was manufacturing fabric-covered pencil boxes and shortly thereafter, pencils. Hassenfeld Brothers branched into the toy industry during the 1940s by introducing toy nurse and doctor kits. The company's toy division was the first to use TV to promote a toy product (Mr. Potato Head in 1952).

Expansion continued in the mid-1960s with the introduction of the G.I. Joe doll, which quickly became its primary toy line. Hassenfeld Brothers went public in 1968 and changed its name to Hasbro Industries. It bought Romper Room (TV productions) the next year.

In the 1970s the toy and pencil divisions, led by different family members, disagreed over the company's finances, future direction, and leadership. The dispute caused the company to split in 1980. The toy division continued to operate under the Hasbro name; the pencil division (Empire Pencil Corporation in Shelbyville, Tennessee), led by Harold Hassenfeld, became a separate corporation.

Hasbro expanded rapidly in the 1980s under new CEO Stephen Hassenfeld. He reduced the number of products by one-third to concentrate on developing a line of toys aimed at specific markets. During that decade the firm released a number of successful toys, including a smaller version of G.I. Joe (1982) and Transformers (small vehicles that transform into robots, 1984). Hasbro acquired Milton Bradley, a major producer of board games (*Chutes and Ladders*, *Candy Land*), puzzles, and preschool toys (Playskool) in 1984.

The company acquired Cabbage Patch Kids, *Scrabble*, *Parcheesi*, and other product lines from Coleco in 1989. Stephen died from AIDS that year. His brother Alan, who had spearheaded Hasbro's international sales growth in the late 1980s, became CEO.

Hasbro bought Tonka (whose brands included Kenner and Parker Brothers) for $486 million in 1991 and established operations in Greece, Mexico, and Hungary. The next year it set a marketing precedent by purchasing all commercial time during a 14-hour Thanksgiving weekend cartoon marathon on three Turner Broadcasting System networks.

In 1995 the company introduced the CD-ROM version of *Monopoly*. In 1996 Hasbro blocked a $5.2 billion hostile takeover attempt by Mattel, and the next year it beat them to an exclusive four-year deal to produce nearly all NFL-related toys and games. Hasbro also bought OddzOn Products (sports toys, Koosh balls).

Some of Hasbro's workers lost a round of corporate *Chutes and Ladders* in 1997 when the toy maker announced that it would cut about 2,500 jobs (20% of Hasbro's employees) over four years.

Expanding in the high-tech toys niche, in 1998 Hasbro bought Tiger Electronics (Giga Pets), the rights to some 75 Atari game titles (including *Missile Command* and *Centipede*), and MicroProse (3-D video games for PCs). The company also bought Galoob Toys, a fellow *Star Wars* prequel licensee and maker of Micro Machines and Pound Puppies. Tiger Electronics had the hit of the 1998 holiday season: a chattering interactive doll called Furby. Hasbro has plans for Furbies to speak Japanese, Spanish, and other languages.

In 1999 Hasbro agreed to pay $325 million for game maker and retailer Wizards of the Coast, which offers the card game Magic: The Gathering, and Pokémon trading cards.

Chairman and CEO: Alan G. Hassenfeld, age 50,
$1,437,216 pay (prior to title change)
VC: Harold P. Gordon, age 61, $786,672 pay
President and COO: Herbert M. Baum, age 62
EVP and CFO: John T. O'Neill, age 54, $736,672 pay
EVP Global Operations and Development:
Alfred J. Verrecchia, age 56,
$1,181,089 pay (prior to title change)
Deputy CFO: David Hargreaves
SVP and Controller: Richard B. Holt, age 57
SVP and Sector Head, Toys: Virginia H. Kent, age 44
SVP and General Counsel: Cynthia S. Reed, age 43
SVP and Chief Information Officer:
Douglas J. Schwinn, age 48
SVP and Treasurer: Martin R. Trueb, age 47
SVP and Sector Head, International Businesses:
George B. Volanakis, age 51
SVP Corporate Legal Affairs and Secretary:
Phillip H. Waldoks, age 46
SVP and Sector Head, Games: E. David Wilson
President, Hasbro Interactive: Tom Dusenberry
HR Head: Bob Carniaux
Auditors: KPMG LLP

LOCATIONS

HQ: 1027 Newport Ave., Pawtucket, RI 02861
Phone: 401-431-8697   **Fax:** 401-431-8535
Web site: http://www.hasbro.com

1998 Sales

	$ mil.	% of total
US	2,113	64
Other countries	1,191	36
Total	**3,304**	**100**

PRODUCTS/OPERATIONS

Selected Brands and Products

Action Man	Parker Brothers
Barney preschool toys	Play-Doh
Batman action figures	Playskool
Easy-Bake Oven	Pokémon (toys and
G.I. Joe action figures	collectibles)
Hasbro Interactive (CD-	Pound Puppies
ROM games)	Raggedy Ann and Raggedy
Larami Super Soaker	Andy dolls
Lincoln Logs	Spirograph
Lite-Brite	*Star Wars* action figures
Micro Machines	*Teletubbies*
Milton Bradley	Tiger Electronics
My Little Pony dolls	Tinkertoys
Nerf (soft play toys)	Tonka (toy trucks)
OddzOn	Transformers (small
Cap Candy	vehicles that transform
Koosh (soft play toys)	into robots)
Rubik's (puzzles)	Winner's Circle (die-cast
Vortex (sports products)	toy vehicles)

COMPETITORS

Acclaim Entertainment	Mattel
Applause Enterprises	Nintendo
Electronic Arts	Ohio Art
Equity Marketing	Play By Play
GT Interactive	SEGA
Havas	Sony
LEGO	Toymax International
LucasArts	Ty
Marvel Enterprises	

HISTORICAL FINANCIALS & EMPLOYEES

NYSE symbol: HAS FYE: December 31	Annual Growth	1989	1990	1991	1992	1993	1994	1995	1996	1997	1998
Sales ($ mil.)	9.9%	1,410	1,520	2,141	2,541	2,747	2,670	2,858	3,002	3,189	3,304
Net income ($ mil.)	9.4%	92	89	82	179	200	175	156	200	135	206
Income as % of sales	—	6.5%	5.9%	3.8%	7.1%	7.3%	6.6%	5.4%	6.7%	4.2%	6.2%
Earnings per share ($)	9.1%	0.46	0.46	0.42	0.89	0.96	0.85	0.77	0.98	0.68	1.01
Stock price - FY high ($)	—	7.23	6.38	12.13	15.96	18.02	16.29	15.68	20.91	24.34	27.30
Stock price - FY low ($)	—	4.52	3.34	4.49	10.29	12.51	12.40	12.62	12.84	15.26	18.67
Stock price - FY close ($)	17.7%	5.56	4.64	12.02	14.51	16.12	12.96	13.79	17.29	21.01	24.09
P/E - high	—	16	14	29	18	19	19	20	21	36	27
P/E - low	—	10	7	11	12	13	15	16	13	22	18
Dividends per share ($)	17.3%	0.05	0.06	0.07	0.09	0.10	0.12	0.14	0.17	0.21	0.21
Book value per share ($)	10.4%	4.05	4.56	4.93	5.64	6.47	7.09	7.77	8.55	9.19	9.91
Employees	2.2%	8,200	7,700	10,500	11,000	12,500	12,500	13,000	13,000	12,000	10,000

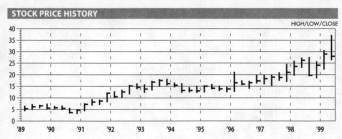

STOCK PRICE HISTORY — HIGH/LOW/CLOSE

1998 FISCAL YEAR-END
Debt ratio: 17.3%
Return on equity: 10.6%
Cash ($ mil.): 178
Current ratio: 1.31
Long-term debt ($ mil.): 407
No. of shares (mil.): 196
Dividends
  Yield: 0.9%
  Payout: 20.8%
Market value ($ mil.): 4,726

HEALTHSOUTH CORPORATION

OVERVIEW

HEALTHSOUTH is the Holiday Inn of standardized health care.

As the #1 US provider of outpatient surgery and rehabilitative health care services, the Birmingham, Alabama-based HEALTHSOUTH owns about 1,900 inpatient and outpatient rehabilitation facilities, outpatient surgery centers, diagnostic centers, and occupational medicine centers in the US, the UK, and Australia. The rehabilitation hospitals minister to patients requiring physical and other therapy to help them function following orthopedic injuries, sports and work-related injuries, and neurological/neuromuscular conditions. Patients receive nonemergency surgical procedures at the freestanding surgery centers. The diagnostic centers provide imaging services such as magnetic resonance imaging, X-rays, and mammograms. The occupational medicine centers cater exclusively to patients requiring treatment for work-related injuries or illnesses.

HEALTHSOUTH contracts with top insurers, managed care plans, and such major employers as Wal-Mart, Goodyear, and Winn-Dixie. It also has ongoing relationships with professional sports associations, universities, and high schools to provide sports medicine coverage of events and rehabilitative services for injured athletes. These partnerships the company hopes will build its brand recognition.

Hit hard by cuts in federal reimbursement rates and facing pressure from managed care companies, HEALTHSOUTH thought briefly about spinning off its inpatient services into HealthSouth Hospital Corp. so that it could concentrate on expanding its more profitable outpatient services.

HISTORY

A onetime service-station worker (when he was a 17-year-old married man with a baby on the way), Richard Scrushy got into the health care industry by working in respiratory therapy; he earned a degree in the subject in 1974. Recruited for a job with Lifemark, a Texas health care management firm, Scrushy saw the convergence of several trends: lowered reimbursements for medical care, a new emphasis on rehabilitation as a way to reduce the need for surgery and get employees back to work faster, and brand names practically everywhere but in health care. Scrushy decided to establish a national health care brand of rehabilitation hospitals, and in 1984 he and four of his co-workers founded Amcare and built its first outpatient center in Birmingham, Alabama.

From the beginning Scrushy wanted to make his rehabilitation centers less like hospitals and more like upscale health clubs. He also sought workers' compensation and rehabilitation contracts from self-insured companies and managed care operations. The strategies worked. The company had revenues of $5 million in 1985, the year it became HEALTHSOUTH. Other strategies included specializing in specific ailments, such as back problems and sports injuries, and using the same floor plan and furnishings for all HEALTHSOUTH locations to save money. The company went public in 1986.

By 1988 HEALTHSOUTH had nearly 40 facilities in 15 states and kept shopping for more. A merger with its biggest rival, Continental Medical Systems, fell through in 1992, but HEALTHSOUTH became the #1 provider of rehabilitative services the next year with its acquisition of most of the rehabilitation services of National Medical Enterprises. (Scrushy and other officers formed MedPartners, a physician management company, in 1993.) Additional acquisitions included ReLife (1994) and NovaCare's inpatient rehabilitation hospitals and Caremark's rehabilitation services (1995). HEALTHSOUTH became the #1 operator of outpatient surgery centers with its acquisition of Surgical Care Affiliates in 1995. The $1.1 billion stock swap was the company's largest acquisition ever.

In 1997 HEALTHSOUTH acquired Horizon/CMS Healthcare, the US's largest provider of specialty health care. After completing the Horizon/CMS deal, HEALTHSOUTH sold Horizon's 139 long-term-care facilities, 12 specialty hospitals, and 35 institutional pharmacies to Integrated Health Services Inc.; it kept about 30 inpatient and 275 outpatient rehabilitation facilities.

In the late 1990s, HEALTHSOUTH built its outpatient operations through acquisitions, buying nearly three dozen outpatient centers from ailing Columbia/HCA as well as National Surgery Centers, adding another 40 locations in 1998. In 1999 the company announced plans to acquire rival Mariner Post-Acute Network's American Rehability Services outpatient unit.

Chairman and CEO: Richard M. Scrushy, age 46,
$2,777,829 pay
President and COO: James P. Bennett, age 41,
$670,000 pay
EVP Administration and Secretary: Anthony J. Tanner,
age 50, $388,422 pay
EVP Finance and CFO: Michael D. Martin, age 38,
$415,826 pay
EVP Corporate Development: Thomas W. Carman,
age 47
President HEALTHSOUTH Outpatient Centers:
P. Daryl Brown, age 44, $386,212 pay
President HEALTHSOUTH Inpatient Operations:
Robert E. Thomson, age 51
President HEALTHSOUTH Surgery Centers:
Patrick A. Foster, age 52
Group SVP Finance and Corporate Controller:
William T. Owens, age 40
SVP, Corporate Counsel, and Assistant Secretary:
William W. Horton, age 39
SVP Operations Controller: Sharon B. Faulkner
SVP Operations and Controller, Outpatient Division:
H. Sonny Crumpler
SVP Operations, Diagnostic Division: David A. Jayne
SVP Operations, Surgery Division: Eugene E. Smith
Group VP Human Resources: Brandon O. "Brad" Hale
Auditors: Ernst & Young LLP

LOCATIONS

HQ: 1 HealthSouth Pkwy., Birmingham, AL 35243
Phone: 205-967-7116   **Fax:** 205-969-4719
Web site: http://www.healthsouth.com

HEALTHSOUTH operates more than 1,900 facilities in all
50 states, the District of Columbia, Australia, and the UK.

PRODUCTS/OPERATIONS

1998 Patient Care Facilities

	No.	% of total
Outpatient rehabilitation centers	1,181	67
Surgery centers	221	12
Inpatient rehabilitation facilities	125	7
Diagnostic centers	118	7
Medical centers	4	—
Other services	125	7
Total	**1,774**	**100**

1998 Sales

	$ mil.	% of total
Outpatient services	2,043	51
Inpatient & other clinical services	1,909	48
Other	54	1
Total	**4,006**	**100**

COMPETITORS

Beverly Enterprises
BJC Health
Columbia/HCA
Genesis Health Ventures
HCR Manor Care
Integrated Health Services
Mariner Post-Acute Network
NovaCare
Occupational Health & Rehab
Paracelsus Healthcare
Sun Healthcare
Tenet Healthcare
Vencor

HISTORICAL FINANCIALS & EMPLOYEES

NYSE symbol: HRC FYE: December 31	Annual Growth	1989	1990	1991	1992	1993	1994	1995	1996	1997	1998
Sales ($ mil.)	48.5%	114	181	226	407	482	1,127	1,557	2,437	3,017	4,006
Net income ($ mil.)	21.4%	8	13	22	30	7	53	79	221	331	47
Income as % of sales	—	7.1%	7.1%	9.9%	7.3%	1.4%	4.7%	5.1%	9.1%	11.0%	1.2%
Earnings per share ($)	(1.8%)	0.13	0.16	0.21	0.25	0.23	0.30	0.32	0.55	0.91	0.11
Stock price - FY high ($)	—	3.19	4.29	8.80	9.31	6.59	9.84	16.19	19.88	28.94	30.81
Stock price - FY low ($)	—	1.54	2.27	3.67	3.81	3.03	5.84	8.19	13.50	17.75	7.69
Stock price - FY close ($)	20.5%	2.88	4.17	8.80	6.59	6.31	9.11	14.56	19.31	27.75	15.44
P/E - high	—	25	27	42	37	29	33	51	36	32	280
P/E - low	—	12	14	17	15	13	19	26	25	20	70
Dividends per share ($)	—	0.00	0.00	0.00	0.00	0.00	0.00	0.00	0.00	0.00	0.00
Book value per share ($)	25.3%	1.07	1.68	2.49	2.52	2.54	3.12	4.77	4.75	7.99	8.13
Employees	35.8%	3,300	3,300	5,124	7,243	14,562	18,423	26,427	36,410	56,281	51,901

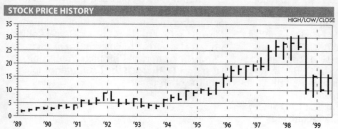

STOCK PRICE HISTORY   HIGH/LOW/CLOSE

1998 FISCAL YEAR-END
Debt ratio: 44.8%
Return on equity: 1.4%
Cash ($ mil.): 139
Current ratio: 3.36
Long-term debt ($ mil.): 2,781
No. of shares (mil.): 421
Dividends
  Yield: —
  Payout: —
Market value ($ mil.): 6,502

THE HEARST CORPORATION

Like legendary founder William Randolph Hearst's castle, The Hearst Corporation is sprawling. New York City-based Hearst owns 12 daily newspapers (*San Francisco Examiner, Houston Chronicle*) and 12 weeklies; about 20 US consumer magazines (*Cosmopolitan, Popular Mechanics, Esquire*); stakes in cable TV networks (A&E, ESPN); TV and radio stations (through Hearst-Argyle Television); a features and comic syndicate; and business publishers. Although it no longer owns Hearst Castle (deeded to the State of California in 1951), the

company has extensive real estate holdings. Hearst is also active on the Internet: Its online interests include Women.com Networks.

The company is owned by the Hearst family, but managed by a board of trustees (per William Randolph Hearst's will). Upon his death, Hearst left 99% of the company's common stock to two charitable trusts controlled by a 13-member board that includes five family and eight non-family members. The will includes an *in terrorem* clause that allows the trustees to disinherit any heir who contests the will.

William Randolph Hearst, son of a California mining magnate, started as a reporter, having been expelled from Harvard in 1884 for playing jokes on professors. In 1887 he became editor of the *San Francisco Examiner,* which his father had obtained as payment for a gambling debt. In 1895 he bought the *New York Morning Journal* and competed against the *New York World,* owned by Joseph Pulitzer, Hearst's first employer. The "yellow journalism" resulting from that rivalry characterized American-style reporting at the turn of the century.

Hearst branched into magazines (1903), film (1913), and radio (1928). Also during this time, it created the Hearst International News Service newswire (it was sold to E.W. Scripps' United Press in 1958 to form United Press International). The Hearst organization pioneered film journalism throughout the 1920s with the Hearst-Selig News Pictorial. In 1935 the company was at its peak, with newspapers in 19 cities (nearly 14% of total US daily and 24% of Sunday circulation), the largest syndicate (King Features), international news and photo services, 13 magazines, eight radio stations, and two motion picture companies. Two years later Hearst relinquished control of the company to avoid bankruptcy, selling movie companies, radio stations, magazines, and, later, most of his San Simeon estate to reduce debt. (Hearst's rise and fall inspired Orson Welles' 1941 film *Citizen Kane.*)

In 1948 Hearst became the owner of one of the US's first TV stations, WBAL-TV in Baltimore. When Hearst died in 1951, company veteran Richard Berlin became CEO. Berlin sold off failing newspapers but also moved into television and acquired more magazines.

Frank Bennack, president and CEO since 1979, expanded the company, acquiring

newspapers, publishing firms (notably William Morrow, 1981), TV stations, magazines (*Redbook,* 1982; *Esquire,* 1986), and 20% of cable sports network ESPN (1991). Hearst branched into video via a joint venture with Capital Cities/ABC (1981) and helped launch the Lifetime and Arts & Entertainment cable channels (1984).

In 1990 Hearst teamed up with *Izvestia* to start a newspaper in Russia. The following year the company launched a New England news network with Continental Cablevision. In 1992 Hearst brought on board former Federal Communications chairman Alfred Sikes, who quickly moved the company onto the Internet with the opening of the Hearst New Media Center at its New York headquarters in 1994. In 1996 Randolph A. Hearst (the sole surviving son of the founder) passed the title of chairman to nephew George Hearst. Broadcaster Argyle Television merged with Hearst's TV holdings in 1997 to form publicly traded Hearst-Argyle Television.

In 1999 Hearst combined its HomeArts Web site with Women.com to create one of the largest online networks for women (Women.com Networks then filed an IPO). It also announced projects with Walt Disney's Miramax Films (to publish new entertainment magazine *Talk*) and Oprah Winfrey's Harpo Entertainment (to published a new women's magazine). In 1999 the company sold its book publishing operations (Avon Books, William Morrow & Co.) to News Corp.'s HarperCollins unit. It also agreed to buy the *San Francisco Chronicle* from rival Chronicle Publishing. Hearst will either sell the *Examiner* or fold it into the other paper.

Chairman: George R. Hearst Jr.
President and CEO: Frank A. Bennack Jr.
EVP and COO: Victor F. Ganzi
Chairman and Co-CEO, Hearst-Argyle Television:
Bob Marbut, age 64
President, Hearst Magazines: Cathleen P. Black
President, King Features Syndicate:
T. R. "Rocky" Shepard III
VP; President, Hearst Newspapers: George B. Irish,
age 53
**VP; Group Head, Hearst Entertainment and
Syndication:** Raymond E. Joslin
VP; President, Hearst New Media and Technology:
Alfred C. Sikes
VP; President and Co-CEO, Hearst-Argyle Television:
John G. Conomikes, age 66
VP and CFO: Ronald J. Doerfler
VP and Chief Legal and Development Officer:
James M. Asher
VP and General Counsel: Jonathan E. Thackeray
VP Human Resources: Ruth Diem
SVP and Group Publishing Director, Hearst Magazines:
Anne S. Fuchs
SVP and Chief Marketing Officer, Hearst Magazines:
Michael A. Clinton

LOCATIONS

HQ: 959 8th Ave., New York, NY 10019
Phone: 212-649-2000   **Fax:** 212-765-3528
Web site: http://www.hearstcorp.com

PRODUCTS/OPERATIONS

Selected Operations

Broadcasting
Hearst-Argyle Television (56%)

Entertainment and Syndication
A&E Television Networks (37.5%, with ABC & NBC)
The History Channel
ESPN (20%)
King Features Syndicate
Lifetime Entertainment Services (50%, with ABC)
Locomotion (with Cisneros Group; all animation TV)
New England Cable News (with Media One)
TVA (minority investment; Brazilian pay-TV)

Magazines
Colonial Homes
CosmoGIRL!
Cosmopolitan
Country Living
Country Living Gardener
Esquire
Good Housekeeping
Harper's Bazaar
House Beautiful
Marie Claire (with Marie
Claire Album)
Motor Boating & Sailing
Popular Mechanics
Redbook
SmartMoney (with Dow
Jones)
Sports Afield
Talk (joint venture with
Disney's Miramax unit)
Town & Country
Victoria

New Media and Technology
Hearst New Media Center (orientation of employees in
new technologies)
Talk City (5%, online communities)
Women.com Networks (53%, Internet site geared
toward women)

Major Newspapers
Albany Times Union (New
York)
Beaumont Enterprise
(Texas)
Edwardsville Intelligencer
(Illinois)
Houston Chronicle
Huron Daily Tribune
(Michigan)
Laredo Morning Times
(Texas)
Midland Daily News
(Michigan)
*Midland Reporter-
Telegram* (Texas)
Plainview Daily Herald
(Texas)
San Antonio Express-News
San Francisco Examiner
Seattle Post-Intelligencer

COMPETITORS

Advance Publications
Belo
Bertelsmann
Bloomberg
CBS
Chronicle Publishing
Cox Enterprises
E. W. Scripps
Freedom Communications
Gannett
Hachette Filipacchi
Knight Ridder
McGraw-Hill

MediaNews
New York Times
News Corp.
PRIMEDIA
Reader's Digest
Reed Elsevier
Time Warner
Times Mirror
Tribune
Viacom
Walt Disney
Washington Post

HISTORICAL FINANCIALS & EMPLOYEES

Private company FYE: December 31	Annual Growth	1989	1990	1991	1992	1993	1994	1995	1996	1997	1998
Sales ($ mil.)	1.4%	2,094	2,138	1,888	1,973	2,174	2,299	2,513	2,568	2,833	2,375
Employees	(0.4%)	14,000	13,950	14,000	13,000	13,500	14,000	14,000	14,000	15,000	13,555

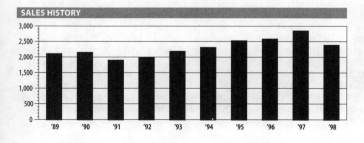

SALES HISTORY

The Hearst Corporation

HEILIG-MEYERS COMPANY

OVERVIEW

Heilig-Meyers doesn't care if your house is in the country or the city; it just wants to fill it with furniture. The Richmond, Virginia-based company is the #1 home furnishings retailer in the US, with more than 900 stores across the US and in Puerto Rico under the Heilig-Meyers, The RoomStore, and Berrios names. Heilig-Meyers offers furniture and accessories, consumer electronics, appliances, bedding, and services such as home delivery and repairs.

The company's core business consists of about 800 namesake stores, primarily located in towns that are more than 25 miles from major cities and have fewer than 50,000 people. Since its competitors generally are individual

mom-and-pop stores, the chain leverages its buying power to offer a wider selection and lower prices. About 80% of Heilig-Meyers' customers use its installment-credit plan. The company's 75 RoomStore locations display and sell furniture in complete room packages.

Heilig-Meyers has been compared to Wal-Mart for its similarly successful small-town strategy. It also sought new formats and a quick fit in metropolitan markets by purchasing several chains located in big cities. However, not every purchase has gone well with its existing corporate decor. Heilig-Meyers has sold its Rhodes chain and all but 7% of its stake in Mattress Discounters, the nation's largest bedding chain.

HISTORY

Brothers-in-law J. M. Meyers and W. A. Heilig, both Lithuanian immigrants, opened the first Heilig-Meyers in 1913 in Goldsboro, North Carolina. The pair opened their second store in Kinston, North Carolina, 15 years later. During the Depression the company stayed in business in part because it was flexible with its customers' financial constraints. Heilig-Meyers suffered its only Depression-era loss, $5,000, in 1931.

The partnership ended in 1946 with the men dividing up the stores and Meyers keeping the Heilig-Meyers name. Meyers' son Hyman became general manager and son Sidney became director of merchandising. The company moved its headquarters to Richmond, Virginia, in 1951. Soon after, Heilig-Meyers added stores, first in North Carolina and then throughout the Southeast. In 1970 the company merged with Virginia-based Thornton Stores, boosting its total number of stores to 28. Thornton's founder, George Thornton Jr., became chairman of the board of the combined company and held that position until his death in 1980.

Heilig-Meyers went public in 1972 to raise money for aggressive expansion plans. By 1980 the chain had 81 stores in four states. Three years later Heilig-Meyers prepared for the 1984 retirement of Hyman and Sidney by installing a new management team, including William DeRusha as chairman and CEO. DeRusha had been with the company for 30 years, working his way up from the mailroom under Hyman's wing. The company continued to expand rapidly under DeRusha. In the early 1990s Heilig-Meyers began to move into the Midwest. Expansion took the company to new areas in

1994, when it acquired 92 McMahan's Furniture stores in the Southwest and West. The following year Heilig-Meyers ventured outside the continental US for the first time, buying 17 Berrios Enterprises furniture stores in Puerto Rico.

Deciding to penetrate the big-city market, the company purchased successful chains with successful metropolitan formats. In 1996 it acquired low-price home furnishings retailer Rhodes, with stores in metropolitan areas in 15 southern, midwestern, and western states. (It later tried to reposition Rhodes as a more upscale chain.) The next year the retailer added The RoomStore, a 10-store Dallas-area chain, latching on to the relatively new concept of selling furniture in room-ready packages. It also bought 169-store Mattress Discounters for about $43 million in 1997.

But Heilig-Meyers suffered as it added the new businesses. The company decided to cut costs, closing about 40 stores in 1998, relocating others, and laying off several hundred employees. Also in 1998 Heilig-Meyers bought 24 stores from Reliable (converted to RoomStore outlets) and five Homemakers stores in Illinois from John M. Smyth.

To combat its second annual loss in fiscal year 1999, the company took several steps, including hiring former Sears executive Donald Shaffer as president and COO in 1999. It also sold its struggling Rhodes stores to managers and other investors for $110 million in 1999. Heilig-Meyers then sold all but a 7% stake in Mattress Discounters to that unit's managers and Bain Capital for $230 million. The company closed nearly 20 stores in the Chicago and Milwaukee markets in 1999.

Chairman and CEO: William C. DeRusha, age 49,
$700,000 pay
President and COO: Donald S. Shaffer, age 52
EVP and CFO: Roy B. Goodman, age 41, $220,770 pay
EVP, Heilig-Meyers: James F. Cerza Jr., age 51,
$410,000 pay
EVP, The RoomStore/Berrios: James R. Riddle, age 57,
$265,000 pay
EVP, The RoomStore/Berrios: Patrick D. Stern, age 42,
$330,000 pay
VP, Human Resources: Brent Langford
Auditors: Deloitte & Touche LLP

LOCATIONS

HQ: 12560 W. Creek Pkwy., Richmond, VA 23238
Phone: 804-784-7300 **Fax:** 804-784-7913
Web site: http://www.hmyco.com

1999 Stores

	No.
California	155
North Carolina	120
Illinois	98
Virginia	76
Georgia	75
Florida	61
Tennessee	60
Texas	58
South Carolina	50
Alabama	43
Maryland	42
Ohio	42
Other States	341
Puerto Rico	32
Total	**1,253**

PRODUCTS/OPERATIONS

1999 Sales

	$ mil.	% of total
Heilig-Meyers	1,296	53
Rhodes	457	19
The RoomStore	440	18
Mattress Discounters	238	10
Total	**2,431**	**100**

Store Names
Berrios (furniture chain in Puerto Rico)
Heilig-Meyers (furniture chain targeting small towns)
Homemaker (furniture stores in Chicago)
Mattress Discounters (7%; bedding retailer)
The RoomStore (furniture chain targeting midsized and
large markets)

COMPETITORS

Bombay Company	Levitz
Cost Plus	living.com
Dayton Hudson	May
Dillard's	Montgomery Ward
Ethan Allen	Pier 1 Imports
Euromarket Designs	Rooms To Go
Federated	Schottenstein Stores
Furniture.com	Seaman Furniture
Haverty Furniture	Sears
HomeLife	Service Merchandise
IKEA	Wal-Mart
J. C. Penney	Williams-Sonoma
Jennifer Convertibles	

HISTORICAL FINANCIALS & EMPLOYEES

NYSE symbol: HMY FYE: February 28	Annual Growth	1990	1991	1992	1993	1994	1995	1996	1997	1998	1999
Sales ($ mil.)	24.8%	331	377	437	550	864	956	1,139	1,342	2,160	2,431
Net income ($ mil.)	—	19	21	27	38	55	67	42	40	(55)	(2)
Income as % of sales	—	5.6%	5.5%	6.2%	6.9%	6.4%	7.0%	3.6%	3.0%	—	—
Earnings per share ($)	—	0.52	0.59	0.65	0.83	1.12	1.34	0.84	0.80	(0.98)	(0.03)
Stock price - FY high ($)	—	7.72	8.83	14.68	22.43	39.00	36.00	27.38	24.13	20.00	15.94
Stock price - FY low ($)	—	4.75	4.71	7.72	10.68	19.43	23.25	13.25	12.50	11.56	5.63
Stock price - FY close ($)	(0.1%)	6.53	7.79	14.07	19.93	33.00	23.63	14.00	14.13	15.50	6.50
P/E - high	—	15	15	23	27	35	27	33	30	—	—
P/E - low	—	9	8	12	13	17	17	16	16	—	—
Dividends per share ($)	9.9%	0.12	0.13	0.14	0.16	0.20	0.24	0.28	0.28	0.28	0.28
Book value per share ($)	8.6%	4.81	5.20	6.07	6.88	8.95	10.10	10.69	11.81	10.36	10.11
Employees	17.9%	5,320	5,910	6,700	7,850	10,536	13,063	14,383	18,200	23,100	23,500

HIGH/LOW/CLOSE

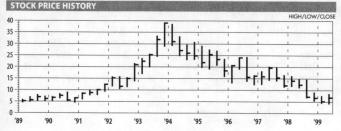

1999 FISCAL YEAR-END
Debt ratio: 47.5%
Return on equity: —
Cash ($ mil.): 67
Current ratio: 1.51
Long-term debt ($ mil.): 547
No. of shares (mil.): 60
Dividends
 Yield: 4.3%
 Payout: —
Market value ($ mil.): 389

HERCULES INCORPORATED

OVERVIEW

Zeus said to Hercules, "Shed your underperforming operations, my son, and get your strength from specialty chemicals and food products!" Hercules sold several divisions, including aerospace, and is now a global supplier of chemicals and related products that help make diapers dryer and duct tape stickier. Its Aqualon additives thicken toothpastes and paint, aid in oil-field drilling, and fill joints and cracks. Hercules supplies the pectin for half the world's jams and jellies, and it makes resins that keep paper towels strong when wet.

The aerospace operation may be gone, but it's not forgotten. In mid-1998 Hercules paid $55 million to avoid a trial in a 10-year-old whistle-blower lawsuit over allegations of lapses in quality-control inspections at its Utah nuclear rocket-motor plant.

Hercules is bulking up again. The acquisition of specialty chemical company BetzDearborn created the world's largest supplier of specialty chemicals for mill-wide performance, process, and water-treatment programs.

HISTORY

A 1912 federal court decision forced DuPont, which controlled two-thirds of US explosives production, to spin off half the business into two companies, Hercules Powder and Atlas Powder.

Hercules began operating explosives plants across the US in 1913. During WWI the company became the largest US producer of TNT. After the war Hercules diversified into nonexplosive products, such as nitrocellulose for the manufacture of plastics, lacquers, and films.

By the late 1920s Hercules' core business had changed from powders to chemicals. Hercules marketed its rosin products to dozens of industries, including the paper industry, the largest user.

In the early 1950s Hercules developed a new process for making phenol, used in plastics, paints, and pharmaceuticals. Its explosives department made important contributions in rocketry by developing propellants for Nike rockets and making motors for Minuteman and Polaris missiles. By the late 1950s Hercules was making chemical propellants, petrochemical plastics, synthetic fibers, agricultural and paper chemicals, and food additives.

During the 1960s and early 1970s, the company, renamed Hercules Incorporated (1966), increased plastic resin and fabricated plastic production and opened five new plants. Hercules also developed international markets and doubled export sales between 1962 and 1972. Following the 1970s energy crisis, Hercules reduced its dependence on commodity petrochemicals and expanded its specialty chemical and defense-related rocket propulsion businesses. In 1987 it sold its interest in the polypropylene resins business (HIMONT) and two years later took full ownership of the Aqualon Group, which had been a 50-50 joint venture with Germany's Henkel.

Hercules had a $96 million loss in 1989

from a $323 million charge to cover cost overruns on Titan IV, Delta II, and SRAM missile contracts. The 1991 explosion of the Titan IV during a test firing led to a suit against development partner Martin Marietta. The suit was dropped in 1993 when the US Air Force and Martin Marietta agreed to reimburse Hercules for its program investments and development costs.

Hercules sold its aerospace business (which accounted for 26% of 1994 sales) in 1995 to Alliant Techsystems for $440 million. The deal left Hercules with 30%-ownership of Alliant. The following year Hercules made an unsolicited bid for fellow chemical producer W. R. Grace, but Grace rejected the bid.

In 1997 Hercules and Mallinckrodt sold their Tastemaker joint venture. That year Hercules agreed to form a joint venture with Denmark-based Jacob Holm & Sons by combining its fibers operations with Jacob Holm's Danaklon Group. The company's 1997 offer to buy UK-based Allied Colloids (polymers, paper technology) was topped in early 1998 by Ciba Specialty Chemicals. Also in 1997 Hercules began selling its stake in Alliant.

Three separate whistleblower lawsuits alleging flawed inspections and billing irregularities at Hercules' former aerospace division cost the company $55 million, $4.5 million, and $4.4 million in settlements in 1998 and 1999. Also in 1998 the company bought the Houghton International paper chemical company and the Citrus Colloids pectin business. Hercules also acquired BetzDearborn, a maker of chemicals for paper production and wastewater treatment, for $2.4 billion and the assumption of $700 million in debt. Hercules said about 5% of the combined company's workforce would be cut by the end of 1999.

Chairman: R. Keith Elliott, age 57,
$1,280,880 pay (prior to title change)
President and CEO: Vincent J. Corbo, age 55,
$814,273 pay (prior to title change)
SVP and General Manager, Paper and Pulp:
Dominick W. DiDonna, age 50, $380,402 pay
SVP and CFO: George MacKenzie Jr., age 49,
$471,670 pay
SVP and General Manager, BetzDearborn Division:
Larry V. Rankin, age 55
SVP Corporate Development: Harry J. Tucci, age 58,
$430,850 pay
VP Human Resources: June B. Barry, age 47
VP External Affairs and International:
Thomas A. Ciconte, age 51
VP Law and General Counsel: Richard G. Dahlen, age 59
VP and General Manager, Resins Division:
Thomas W. Fredericks
VP, Marketing: Robert E. Gallant
VP and Controller: Vikram Jog, age 42
VP and Treasurer: Jan M. King, age 49
**President, Hercules Asia/Pacific and Hercules
Incorporated, Hong Kong:** John E. Montgomery
President, Hercules Europe: Klaus Petersen
VP and General Manager, Aqualon: Monika Riese-Martin
VP, Business Analysis and Assistant Controller:
Michael J. Scott, age 47
Corporate Secretary and Assistant General Counsel:
Israel J. Floyd, age 52
Auditors: PricewaterhouseCoopers LLP

LOCATIONS

HQ: Hercules Plaza, 1313 N. Market St.,
Wilmington, DE 19894-0001
Phone: 302-594-5000   **Fax:** 302-594-5400
Web site: http://www.herc.com

PRODUCTS/OPERATIONS

1998 Sales & Operating Income

	Sales		Operating Income	
	$ mil.	% of total	$ mil.	% of total
Functional products	863	41	215	51
Chemical & services	717	33	131	31
Chemical specialties	566	26	75	18
Adjustments	(1)	—	(229)	—
Total	**2,145**	**100**	**192**	**100**

Business Units

Functional Products
Aqualon (carboxymethylcellulose, hydroxypropylcellulose)
Food gums (agar, carrageenan, pectin)

Process Chemicals and Services
BetzDearborn (water treatment and process treatment)
Pulp and paper (performance additives)

Chemical Specialties
FiberVisions (biocomponent fibers, polyethylene and
polypropylene monocomponent fibers, textile fibers)
Resins (hydrocarbon resins, peroxides, rosin resins,
terpene resins, terpene specialties)

COMPETITORS

Akzo Nobel	Georgia-Pacific
Arizona Chemical	Great Lakes Chemical
BASF AG	Hoechst AG
Bayer AG	Hoffmann-La Roche
BP Amoco	Nalco Chemical
Dow Chemical	Procter & Gamble
DuPont	Rhône-Poulenc
Eastman Chemical	Union Carbide
Elf Aquitaine	US Filter
Exxon	W. R. Grace
FMC	

HISTORICAL FINANCIALS & EMPLOYEES

NYSE symbol: HPC FYE: December 31	Annual Growth	1989	1990	1991	1992	1993	1994	1995	1996	1997	1998
Sales ($ mil.)	(4.0%)	3,092	3,200	2,929	2,865	2,773	2,821	2,427	2,060	1,866	2,145
Net income ($ mil.)	—	(96)	96	95	168	(33)	274	333	325	319	9
Income as % of sales	—	—	3.0%	3.2%	5.9%	—	9.7%	13.7%	15.8%	17.1%	0.4%
Earnings per share ($)	—	(0.53)	0.68	0.67	1.21	(0.28)	2.23	2.87	2.98	3.13	0.10
Stock price - FY high ($)	—	17.40	13.82	16.77	21.23	38.25	40.46	62.25	66.25	54.50	51.38
Stock price - FY low ($)	—	12.78	8.53	10.57	14.86	21.06	32.09	38.21	42.75	37.75	24.63
Stock price - FY close ($)	8.6%	12.99	11.20	16.73	21.15	37.80	38.42	56.38	43.25	50.06	27.25
P/E - high	—	—	20	25	18	—	18	22	22	17	514
P/E - low	—	—	13	16	12	—	14	13	14	12	246
Dividends per share ($)	4.1%	0.75	0.75	0.75	0.75	0.75	0.75	0.84	0.92	1.00	1.08
Book value per share ($)	(9.5%)	13.57	13.80	13.68	13.36	11.16	11.10	9.97	8.75	7.18	5.54
Employees	(6.8%)	23,290	19,867	17,324	15,419	14,083	11,989	7,892	7,114	6,221	12,357

STOCK PRICE HISTORY

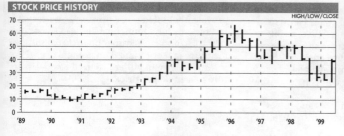

HIGH/LOW/CLOSE

1998 FISCAL YEAR-END

Debt ratio: 84.7%
Return on equity: 1.6%
Cash ($ mil.): 68
Current ratio: 0.94
Long-term debt ($ mil.): 3,096
No. of shares (mil.): 101
Dividends
  Yield: 4.0%
  Payout: 1,080.0%
Market value ($ mil.): 2,748

HERMAN MILLER, INC.

OVERVIEW

Though no relation to Glenn, Herman Miller still fronts a big band of office furniture, equipment, and services. The #2 maker of office furnishings (behind Steelcase and just ahead of Haworth), Herman Miller produces freestanding modular office partitions and furniture with a sleek, contemporary design — and an upscale price. The Zeeland, Michigan-based company manufactures furniture for the office, home, and health care industry, including seating, freestanding furniture, accents, clinical furniture, and filing and storage items.

It makes its products in the US, Mexico, and the UK and sells them worldwide through independent dealers and a direct sales staff. Herman Miller also sells its furniture online.

Herman Miller has long been revered for its innovative furniture designs and notable designers. Collectors particularly value pieces made by the company during the 1940s and 1950s. Herman Miller also prides itself on its employee participation and has received several awards for being one of America's best places to work.

HISTORY

In 1923 Herman Miller lent his son-in-law, D. J. De Pree, enough money to buy Star Furniture Company, started in 1905 in Zeeland, Michigan. (De Pree renamed the furniture maker after Miller.) Hard-pressed during the Depression, the company tried making contemporary furniture. Designer Gilbert Rohde led Herman Miller's transformation from traditional to more modern styles in the 1930s.

Rohde designed the company's first office component line, the Executive Office Group, which was introduced in 1942. Rohde died two years later, and in 1946 George Nelson was named Herman Miller's design director. Nelson not only continued the company's move to contemporary design but also brought in a number of notable designers, including Charles Eames and Isamu Noguchi.

Throughout its history, the company has maintained a reputation for being open to suggestions and comments from its workers. This policy dates back to De Pree's learning that one of his millwrights who had died had also been a poet; De Pree began to value his employees for their innate talents rather than just for the work they did for him.

Herman Miller grew, largely unimpeded by national competitors, except for neighboring Steelcase. In 1950 the company adopted the Scanlon plan, an employee participation plan that included bonuses based on helpful participation, such as cost-cutting suggestions.

De Pree retired in 1962 and was succeeded by his son, Hugh. Two years later Herman Miller introduced the Action Office, a collection of panels, work surfaces, and storage units that could be moved about to create custom-designed work spaces within an open-plan office; this line has been the company mainstay ever since.

The firm went public in 1970 and introduced its Ergon ergonomic chair in 1976.

Hugh retired in 1980 and was succeeded by his brother Max, who capped executive salaries at 20 times the average wage of factory-line workers. Max, the author of several books on management, including *Leadership Is an Art* and *Leadership Jazz*, believed that dominance by the De Pree family would hamper employee initiative and banned family members from the firm. In 1988 he became chairman and resigned from day-to-day management duties to pursue teaching opportunities.

Max's successor, 33-year company veteran Richard Ruch, began restructuring to sharpen Herman Miller's focus. Then the commercial real estate market collapsed and, with it, the need for new office furnishings. Earnings tumbled in 1991 and 1992. Ruch retired in 1992 to become VC and was succeeded by first-ever company outsider Kermit Campbell.

In 1994 Herman Miller acquired German furniture company Geneal. Earnings plummeted in 1995 and chairman Campbell was forced out after two months as head of the company. Despite his commitment to its traditionally employee-friendly corporate culture, CEO Michael Volkema led Herman Miller in a shake-up, cutting 180 jobs and closing underperforming plants. The company introduced its cubicle systems office furniture unit Miller SQA ("simple, quick, and affordable") in 1995.

Herman Miller and leading carpet tile maker Interface formed a joint venture in 1997 to provide integrated office furniture and carpeting systems for commercial clients. The next year the company became the first major office furniture maker to target customers over the Internet. Herman Miller acquired wood furniture maker Geiger Brickel in 1999.

OFFICERS

Chairman: David L. Nelson, age 69
President and CEO: Michael A. Volkema, age 43,
$1,009,280 pay
EVP, Casegoods and Seating: Dan Rosema, age 40
**EVP, Financial Services and Business Develpment, and
CFO:** Brian C. Walker, age 37, $448,684 pay
EVP; President, Herman Miller International:
Robert Frey, age 56, $383,979 pay
**EVP, Human Resources and Corporate
Communications:** Gene Miyamoto, age 44
EVP; President, Business Services Group:
Andrew C. McGregor, age 49, $577,715 pay
EVP and Chief Information Officer:
Christopher A. "Bix" Norman, age 51, $380,980 pay
EVP, Offer Development and Marketing:
Gary Van Spronsen, age 43
EVP, Product Research and Development:
Gary S. Miller, age 49
EVP, Sales and Distribution: David M. Knibbe, age 44
EVP, Strategic Planning: Vicki TenHaken, age 48
EVP, Systems and SQA: Mike Valz, age 47
VP, Legal Services, and Secretary:
James E. Christenson, age 52
Auditors: Arthur Andersen LLP

LOCATIONS

HQ: 855 E. Main Ave., Zeeland, MI 49464-0302
Phone: 616-654-3000   **Fax:** 616-654-5385
Web site: http://www.hermanmiller.com

Herman Miller designs, manufactures, and distributes
office furniture through subsidiaries in Australia,
Canada, France, Germany, Italy, Japan, Mexico, the
Netherlands, the UK, and the US. Through independent
dealers, the company's products are also offered in Asia,
the Middle East, and South America.

1999 Sales

	$ mil.	% of total
US	1,507	85
Other countries	259	15
Total	**1,766**	**100**

PRODUCTS/OPERATIONS

Selected Products
Accents
Clinical and administrative furniture
Freestanding furniture products
Modular systems (Action Office, Ethospace, Q System)
Seating (Aeron, Ambi, Equa, Ergon)
Storage (Meridian filing products)

COMPETITORS

Anderson Hickey
Bush Industries
Global Furniture
Haworth International
HighPoint Furniture
HON INDUSTRIES
Kimball International
Knoll
O'Sullivan Industries
Sauder Woodworking
Shelby Williams
Steelcase
Virco Mfg.

HISTORICAL FINANCIALS & EMPLOYEES

Nasdaq symbol: MLHR FYE: May 31	Annual Growth	1990	1991	1992	1993	1994	1995	1996	1997	1998	1999
Sales ($ mil.)	8.3%	865	879	805	856	953	1,083	1,284	1,496	1,719	1,766
Net income ($ mil.)	13.2%	47	14	(14)	22	40	4	46	74	128	142
Income as % of sales	—	5.4%	1.6%	—	2.6%	4.2%	0.4%	3.6%	5.0%	7.5%	8.0%
Earnings per share ($)	15.7%	0.45	0.14	(0.15)	0.22	0.40	0.04	0.46	0.77	1.39	1.67
Stock price - FY high ($)	—	5.91	6.09	5.63	6.59	8.75	7.34	8.59	18.81	36.25	30.75
Stock price - FY low ($)	—	4.44	3.75	3.75	3.69	5.94	4.81	5.34	7.31	17.06	15.63
Stock price - FY close ($)	16.4%	5.13	5.03	4.75	6.41	6.13	5.41	7.72	17.88	27.69	20.19
P/E - high	—	13	44	—	30	22	184	19	24	26	18
P/E - low	—	10	27	—	17	15	120	12	9	12	9
Dividends per share ($)	1.6%	0.13	0.13	0.13	0.13	0.13	0.13	0.13	0.13	0.15	0.15
Book value per share ($)	(1.7%)	3.07	3.08	2.78	2.84	3.01	2.89	3.12	3.12	2.58	2.63
Employees	4.5%	5,770	5,556	5,488	5,446	5,940	7,264	6,964	7,425	7,924	8,555

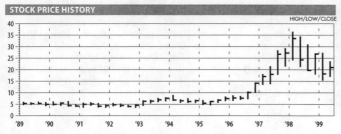

STOCK PRICE HISTORY
HIGH/LOW/CLOSE

1999 FISCAL YEAR-END
Debt ratio: 30.3%
Return on equity: 67.8%
Cash ($ mil.): 80
Current ratio: 1.00
Long-term debt ($ mil.): 91
No. of shares (mil.): 80
Dividends
  Yield: 0.7%
  Payout: 9.0%
Market value ($ mil.): 1,606

HERSHEY FOODS CORPORATION

OVERVIEW

A hard candy coating now surrounds Hershey Foods' rich chocolate center. The Hershey, Pennsylvania-based company is the #1 US producer of chocolates and chocolate-related grocery products. In addition to its sinfully popular Hershey's bars and Kisses, Reese's candies, Kit Kat, 5th Avenue, Almond Joy, and Milk Duds, the company is a growing presence in the hard- and non-chocolate candy market, with such brands as Good & Plenty and Jolly Rancher. Other offerings include Hershey's chocolate milk mix and Reese's peanut butter.

The company is expanding its products with new versions of old favorites, such as Jolly Rancher lollipops and a wafer-based version of

Reese's Peanut Butter Cups called ReeseSticks. Hershey is also wooing health-conscious chocoholics with reduced-fat versions of its established products, including Sweet Escapes lower-calorie candy bars and light sundae syrups. It has sold its pasta operations (eight brands, including American Beauty, Ronzoni, and Skinner) to focus on its candies.

Hershey's sweets are sold in more than 2 million retail outlets in North America alone (Wal-Mart accounts for 14% of sales). Hershey exports its products to more than 90 countries.

The Hershey Trust — which benefits the Milton Hershey School for disadvantaged children — controls 76% of the company's voting power.

HISTORY

Hershey Foods is the legacy of Milton Hershey, of Pennsylvania Dutch origin. Apprenticed in 1872 at age 15 to a candy maker, Hershey started Lancaster Caramel Company at age 30. In 1893, at the Chicago Exposition, he saw a new chocolate-making machine, and in 1900 he sold the caramel operations for $1 million to start a chocolate factory.

The factory was completed in 1905 in Derry Church, Pennsylvania, and it was renamed Hershey Foods the next year. Chocolate Kisses, individually hand wrapped in silver foil, were introduced in 1907. Two years later the candy man founded the Milton Hershey School, an orphanage; the company was donated to a trust in 1918 and for years existed solely to fund the school. Although Hershey is now publicly traded, the school still controls the majority of shareholder votes. William Dearden (chairman from 1976-84) was a Hershey School graduate, as are many Hershey employees.

Concerned more with benevolence than profits, Hershey had people building a hotel, golf courses, a library, theaters, a museum, a stadium, and other facilities during the Depression.

The candy company pioneered mass-production techniques for chocolates and developed much of the machinery for making and packaging its own products. At one time Hershey supplied its own sugar cane from Cuba and enlarged the world's almond supply sixfold through nut farm ownership. The Hershey bar became so universally familiar that it was used overseas during WWII as currency.

Milton refused to advertise, believing that quality would speak for itself. Even after his death in 1945, the company continued his

policy. Then, in 1970, facing a sluggish candy market and a diet-conscious public, the company lost share to Mars, and management relented.

During the 1960s and 1970s, Hershey diversified in order to stabilize the effects of changing commodity prices. The company got into the pasta business with its 1966 purchase of San Giorgio Macaroni, and it bought the Friendly Ice Cream chain in 1979 (sold 1988). The company expanded candy operations by bringing out large-sized bars (1980) and buying Cadbury's US candy business (Peter Paul, Cadbury, Caramello; 1988).

In 1990 Hershey formed a joint venture with Fujiya to distribute Hershey products in Japan and bought Ronzoni's pasta, cheese, and sauce operations. Kenneth Wolfe was named chairman and CEO in 1994.

The company acquired Henry Heide, a manufacturer of non-chocolate confectionery products, in 1995. Hershey boosted its presence in the non-chocolate candy market with the 1996 acquisition of the North American operations of Leaf (Good & Plenty, Jolly Rancher) from Finnish candy maker Huhtamaki Oy. In return, it sold Huhtamaki its struggling European confectionery interests.

In 1998 Hershey sued candy rival Mars, charging that Mars used packaging and colors for its M&Ms that are similar to those of Reese's Pieces. In early 1999 the company sold its pasta business to New World Pasta for $450 million. Also in 1999 Hershey Trust, wanting to diversify its holdings, sold $100 million of its stock to Hershey.

Chairman and CEO: Kenneth L. Wolfe, age 60,
$1,094,944 pay
VC, President, and COO: Joseph P. Viviano, age 60,
$820,642 pay
SVP, CFO, and Treasurer: William F. Christ, age 58,
$421,135 pay
SVP Confectionery and Grocery: Michael F. Pasquale,
age 51, $512,280 pay
SVP Operations: Raymond Brace, age 55
SVP Public Affairs, General Counsel, and Secretary:
Robert M. Reese, age 49
VP Information Technology Integration:
Richard E. Bentz
VP, Research Services and Special Operations:
Jay F. Carr, $377,124 pay
VP Human Resources: John R. Canavan, age 51
VP Procurement: Frank Cerminara
VP Research and Development: Charles L. Duncan
VP and General Manager Grocery: Dennis N. Eshleman
VP Financial Services: R. Montgomery Garrabrant
VP and General Manager, Chocolate: Michael H. Holmes
VP Manufacturing: Kenneth B. Kwiat
VP Sales: Milton T. Matthews
VP and General Manager Special Markets:
Anthony J. Pingitore
President, Hershey International: Patrice N. Le Maire
Auditors: Arthur Andersen LLP

HQ: 100 Crystal A Dr., Hershey, PA 17033
Phone: 717-534-6799   **Fax:** 717-534-6760
Web site: http://www.hersheys.com

Hershey Foods' main manufacturing facilities are located
in Hershey and Lancaster, Pennsylvania; Oakdale,
California; Robinson, Illinois; Stuarts Draft, Virginia; and
Smiths Falls, Ontario.

Candy
5th Avenue
Cadbury's Creme Eggs
Caramello
Chuckles
Glosette candy
Good & Fruity
Good & Plenty
Heath
Heide
Hershey's
Jolly Rancher
Jujyfruits
Kit Kat
Krackel
Milk Duds
Mr. Goodbar
Oh Henry!
PayDay
Peter Paul
RainBlo
Reese's
Rolo
Skor

Special Crisp
Super Bubble
Sweet Escapes
Symphony
Twizzlers
Whatchamacallit
Whoppers
York peppermint patties

Groceries
Brown Cow chocolate
  syrup
Chipits baking chocolate
Hershey's baking
  chocolate
Hershey's cocoa
Hershey's syrup
Luden's throat drops
Reese's peanut butter
Strawberry Cow
  strawberry syrup
Top Scotch butterscotch
  syrup

ADM
Brach's
Cadbury Schweppes
Campbell Soup
ConAgra
Favorite Brands
General Mills

Mars
Nabisco Holdings
Nestle
Philip Morris
Russell Stover
Tootsie Roll

NYSE symbol: HSY FYE: December 31	Annual Growth	1989	1990	1991	1992	1993	1994	1995	1996	1997	1998
Sales ($ mil.)	7.0%	2,421	2,716	2,899	3,220	3,488	3,606	3,691	3,989	4,302	4,436
Net income ($ mil.)	8.0%	171	216	220	243	193	184	282	273	336	341
Income as % of sales	—	7.1%	8.0%	7.6%	7.5%	5.5%	5.1%	7.6%	6.8%	7.8%	7.7%
Earnings per share ($)	10.5%	0.95	1.19	1.21	1.34	1.07	1.05	1.69	1.75	2.23	2.34
Stock price - FY high ($)	—	18.44	19.81	22.25	24.19	27.94	26.75	33.94	51.75	63.88	76.38
Stock price - FY low ($)	—	12.38	14.13	17.56	19.13	21.75	20.56	24.00	31.94	42.13	59.69
Stock price - FY close ($)	14.8%	17.94	18.75	22.19	23.50	24.50	24.19	32.50	43.75	61.94	62.19
P/E - high	—	19	17	18	18	26	25	20	30	29	33
P/E - low	—	13	12	15	14	20	20	14	18	19	26
Dividends per share ($)	10.7%	0.37	0.50	0.47	0.52	0.57	0.63	0.69	0.76	0.84	0.92
Book value per share ($)	1.8%	6.19	6.89	7.40	8.12	8.06	8.31	7.25	7.59	5.97	7.28
Employees	3.6%	11,800	12,700	14,000	13,700	14,300	15,600	14,800	15,300	16,200	16,200

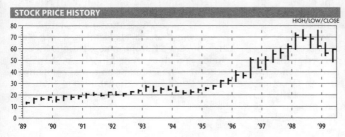

HIGH/LOW/CLOSE

Debt ratio: 45.8%
Return on equity: 32.7%
Cash ($ mil.): 39
Current ratio: 1.39
Long-term debt ($ mil.): 879
No. of shares (mil.): 143
Dividends
  Yield: 1.5%
  Payout: 39.3%
Market value ($ mil.): 8,902

THE HERTZ CORPORATION

OVERVIEW

If you've ever said, "Don't worry about it, it's a rental," guess who hurts: Park Ridge, New Jersey-based Hertz, one of the world's largest car rental companies. The Hertz Corporation operates a rental fleet of over 500,000 vehicles, with more than 6,000 locations in 140 countries. Its car rental revenues are split almost evenly between business and leisure travelers. Almost 90% of its US car rental revenue is generated from airport pickups, where it holds a 30% share of the market. Hertz also has car leasing and used-car sales operations. Ford Motor, which partially spun off Hertz in a 1997 IPO, owns about 81% of the company.

Subsidiary Hertz Equipment Rental is a major North American renter of construction

and industrial equipment, with more than 230 locations in 37 US states and Canada as well as about 50 locations in Europe. The company also administers insurance-related claims for other companies and purchases and resells telecommunications services primarily to small and medium-sized businesses.

The shift in ownership of car rental companies to the public equity markets has put a new emphasis on profitability, and rental prices have increased. To generate more sales, the company is stressing amenities, such as car phones and onboard satellite navigation systems. Hertz also plans to boost sales through acquisitions and through increased equipment rentals.

HISTORY

In 1918, 22-year-old John Jacobs opened a Chicago car rental business with 12 Model T Fords that he had repaired. By 1923, when John Hertz (president of Yellow Cab and Yellow Truck and Coach Manufacturing Company) bought Jacobs' business, it had revenues of about $1 million. Jacobs continued as top executive of the company, renamed Hertz Drive-Ur-Self System. Three years later General Motors (GM) acquired the company when it bought Yellow Truck from John Hertz. Hertz introduced the first car rental charge card in 1926, opened its first airport location at Chicago's Midway Airport in 1932, and initiated the first one-way (rent-it-here/leave-it-there) plan in 1933. The company expanded into Canada in 1938 and Europe in 1950.

Omnibus bought Hertz from GM in 1953, sold its bus interests, and focused on vehicle leasing and renting. The next year Omnibus changed its name to The Hertz Corporation and was listed on the NYSE. Also in 1954 the company purchased Metropolitan Distributors, a New York-based truck leasing firm. In 1961 Hertz began operations in South America. The company formed its Hertz Equipment Rental subsidiary in 1965. RCA bought Hertz two years later but allowed the company to maintain its board of directors and management. In 1972 it introduced the first frequent traveler's club, the #1 Club, which allowed the rental location to prepare a rental agreement before the customer arrived at the counter. Three years later Hertz began defining the company's image through TV commercials featuring football star/celebrity O. J. Simpson running through airports. (In 1994, following Simpson's arrest for the murder of

his ex-wife and her friend, Hertz canceled Simpson's contract — the TV ads had stopped in 1992.) Frank Olson became CEO in 1977 after serving in the same position at United Airlines.

United Airlines bought Hertz from RCA in 1985, then sold it in 1987 for $1.3 billion to Park Ridge, which had been formed by Hertz management and Ford Motor specifically for the purchase (Hertz was Ford's largest customer). In 1988 Ford, which held 80% of Park Ridge, sold 20% to Volvo North America for $100 million (Ford later reduced its stake to 49% when it sold shares to Volvo). Also that year Hertz sold its stock in the Hertz Penske truck leasing joint venture for $85.5 million and issued Penske a license to use its name.

Ford bought all the shares of Hertz it didn't already own in 1994. The next year it formed a unit to provide replacement cars for insurance companies. Taking advantage of heightened investor interest in rental car companies (stemming in part from the purchases of some competitors by HFS and AutoNation), Ford sold 17% of Hertz to the public in 1997.

Hertz acquired several equipment rental companies in 1998, including the Boireau Group (France, 26 locations) and Matthews Equipment (Canada, six locations). In 1999 the company's European acquisitions included French car rental franchise SST (14 locations) and German van rental company Yellow Truck (11 locations). Also in 1999 Hertz created a referral network with Toyota, Japan's #1 car dealer.

Chairman and CEO: Frank A. Olson, age 66,
$1,919,000 pay
President and COO: Craig R. Koch, age 52,
$1,059,000 pay
EVP, Marketing and Sales: Brian J. Kennedy, age 57,
$486,000 pay
**EVP; General Manager Vehicle Rental and Leasing, The
Americas and Asia/Pacific:** Joseph R. Nothwang,
age 52, $538,000 pay (prior to promotion)
EVP; President, Hertz Equipment Rental Corporation:
Gerald A. Plescia, age 43
EVP and CFO: Paul J. Siracusa, age 53, $454,000 pay
SVP, Quality Assurance and Administration:
Robert J. Bailey, age 64
SVP and General Counsel: Harold E. Rolfe, age 41
SVP, Employee Relations: Donald F. Steele, age 59
VP; President, Hertz Europe: Charles L. Shafer, age 55
Staff VP, Marketing: Frank E. Camacho
Staff VP, Facilities: Richard O. Cardinale
Staff VP and Deputy General Counsel:
Richard P. McEvily
Treasurer: Robert H. Rillings, age 58
Controller: Richard J. Foti, age 52
Auditors: PricewaterhouseCoopers LLP

LOCATIONS

HQ: 225 Brae Blvd., Park Ridge, NJ 07656-0713
Phone: 201-307-2000   **Fax:** 201-307-2644
Web site: http://www.hertz.com

1998 Sales

	$ mil.	% of total
US	3,283	77
Other countries	955	23
Adjustment	(84)	—
Total	**4,154**	**100**

PRODUCTS/OPERATIONS

1998 Sales

	$ mil.	% of total
Car rental	3,485	84
Industrial & construction equipment rental	631	15
Car leasing	38	1
Total	**4,154**	**100**

Selected Services
Car rentals
Claim management services (Hertz Claim Management)
Corporate telecommunications (Hertz Technologies)
Heavy equipment rental and leasing (Hertz Equipment
Rental)
Truck and van rental
Used-car sales

COMPETITORS

Accor
Atlas Copco
AutoNation
Budget Group
Cendant
Dollar Thrifty Automotive Group
Enterprise Rent-A-Car
National Equipment Services
Neff
Prime Service
Rental Service
Sixt
United Rentals
Volkswagen
Western Power

HISTORICAL FINANCIALS & EMPLOYEES

NYSE symbol: HRZ FYE: December 31	Annual Growth	1989	1990	1991	1992	1993	1994	1995	1996	1997	1998
Sales ($ mil.)	7.0%	2,253	2,667	2,626	2,816	2,855	3,294	3,401	3,589	3,815	4,154
Net income ($ mil.)	17.5%	65	90	52	55	53	91	105	159	202	277
Income as % of sales	—	2.9%	3.4%	2.0%	2.0%	1.9%	2.8%	3.1%	4.4%	5.3%	6.7%
Earnings per share ($)	37.1%	—	—	—	—	—	—	—	—	1.86	2.55
Stock price - FY high ($)	—	—	—	—	—	—	—	—	—	41.75	51.88
Stock price - FY low ($)	—	—	—	—	—	—	—	—	—	27.13	27.56
Stock price - FY close ($)	13.4%	—	—	—	—	—	—	—	—	40.25	45.63
P/E - high	—	—	—	—	—	—	—	—	—	22	20
P/E - low	—	—	—	—	—	—	—	—	—	15	11
Dividends per share ($)	100.0%	—	—	—	—	—	—	—	—	0.10	0.20
Book value per share ($)	23.1%	—	—	—	—	—	—	—	—	10.49	12.92
Employees	3.6%	18,000	18,700	18,100	18,000	17,950	19,200	19,500	21,000	21,700	24,800

STOCK PRICE HISTORY

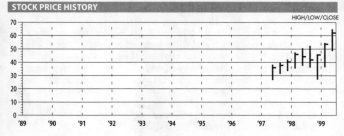

HIGH/LOW/CLOSE

1998 FISCAL YEAR-END

Debt ratio: 80.5%
Return on equity: 19.9%
Cash ($ mil.): 189
Current ratio: 1.34
Long-term debt ($ mil.): 5,760
No. of shares (mil.): 108
Dividends
  Yield: 0.4%
  Payout: 7.8%
Market value ($ mil.): 4,924

HEWLETT-PACKARD COMPANY

OVERVIEW

What's the sound when one of Silicon Valley's largest computer companies morphs itself to become more nimble? Platt! Palo Alto, California-based Hewlett-Packard (HP), the world's second-largest computer company (behind IBM), boasts more than 29,000 products. Computer operations, which account for nearly 85% of sales, include PCs, the servers that link them in corporate networks, printers and other peripherals, and maintenance and customer support services. Breaking HP away from its heritage, chairman Lewis Platt is spearheading the spinoff of its non-computer operations (test and measurement and medical equipment, among others) and selling part of the new unit (dubbed Agilent Technologies) to the public.

HP has used acquisitions and alliances to become more diverse, but at the price of slowed momentum. Platt, who will step down in the year 2000 when the company's restructuring is complete, is recreating HP as a speedy (albeit Johnny-come-lately) Internet specialist. HP's Internet Business Unit, encompassing subsidiary VeriFone, is designed to provide Web servers, software, and services to corporate customers.

The benign spirit of the founders has fostered a seductive corporate culture. In an industry where job changing is a way of life, the average tenure for HP employees is 11 years. The family of co-founder David Packard owns 12% of HP, much of it in a charitable trust similar in size to the Ford and Kellogg foundations. Co-founder Bill Hewlett and his family own about 6% of HP.

HISTORY

Encouraged by professor Frederick Terman (considered the founder of Silicon Valley), in 1938 Stanford engineers Bill Hewlett and David Packard started Hewlett-Packard (HP) out of a garage in Palo Alto, California, with $538. Hewlett was the idea man, while Packard served as manager; the two were so low-key that the company's first official meeting ended with no decision on exactly what to manufacture. Finding good people took priority over finding something to sell. The first product ended up being an audio oscillator. Walt Disney Studios, one of the first customers, bought eight to use in the making of *Fantasia*.

Demand for HP's electronic testing equipment during WWII spurred revenue growth from $34,000 in 1940 to nearly $1 million just three years later. The company expanded beyond the US during 1959, establishing a marketing organization in Switzerland and a manufacturing plant in West Germany. HP entered the medical field in 1961 by acquiring Sanborn Co., and the analytical instrumentation business in 1965 with the purchase of F&M Scientific. In 1969 Packard began serving two years as deputy secretary of defense.

In 1972 the company pioneered personal computing with the world's first handheld scientific calculator. Under the leadership of John Young, the founders' chosen successor (named CEO in 1978), HP introduced its first PCs, the first desktop mainframe, and the LaserJet printer. Its initial PCs were known for their rugged build, tailored for shop floors and factory operations. They were also nearly one-third more expensive than rival versions and, consequently, didn't enjoy strong sales.

By 1986 a five-year, $250 million effort — the most expensive research and development project in company history — had produced a family of HP computers based on the innovative and efficient RISC (reduced instruction set computing) architecture. The company licensed its RISC chip to Hitachi and Samsung to increase the availability of applications for its products. Hewlett retired in 1987. HP became a leader in workstations with the 1989 purchase of market pioneer Apollo Computers, despite technology delays with the merger that resulted in the loss of nearly $750 million in new business and a tumble in market share.

In 1992 HP acquired Texas Instruments' line of UNIX-based computers and made a new commitment to product cost-cutting. Lewis Platt, an EVP since 1987, was named president and CEO that year. The next year Packard retired. HP combined its PC, printer, UNIX workstation, and service operations in 1995.

To push expansion, HP bought most of software security firm SecureWare in 1996 and electronic commerce firm VeriFone the next year. Lower demand caused a drop below 20% growth for the first time in five years, and HP responded by reorganizing operations. Competition fueled a decrease in profits for fiscal 1998. In 1999 HP made plans to spin off its test and measurement and other non-computer operations under the name Agilent Technologies, and sell 15% of the new unit to the public. Platt announced his retirement that year and HP — becoming one of the first major US corporations headed by a woman — appointed Lucent executive Carleton Fiorina president and CEO.

OFFICERS

Chairman: Lewis E. Platt, age 58,
$1,910,700 pay (prior to title change)
CEO and President: Carleton S. "Carly" Fiorina, age 44
EVP, Finance and Administration and CFO:
Robert P. Wayman, age 53, $1,145,429 pay
EVP; General Manager, Measurement Organization:
Edward W. Barnholt, age 55, $875,242 pay
SVP, Corporate Affairs and General Counsel:
S. T. Jack Brigham III, age 59
Chief Scientist: Joel S. Birnbaum, age 61,
$698,091 pay (prior to title change)
VP; President and CEO, Computer Products:
Duane E. Zitzner, age 51
**VP; President and CEO, Enterprise Computing
Solutions:** Ann M. Livermore
VP; President and CEO, Inkjet Imaging Solutions:
Antonio M. Perez, age 53
VP; President and CEO, Laserjet Imaging Systems:
Carolyn M. Ticknor, $663,862 pay (prior to promotion)
VP and Controller: Raymond W. Cookingham, age 55
VP; General Manager, Automated Test Group:
William P. Sullivan
VP, Human Resources: Susan D. Bowick, age 50
Auditors: PricewaterhouseCoopers LLP

LOCATIONS

HQ: 3000 Hanover St., Palo Alto, CA 94304
Phone: 650-857-1501 **Fax:** 650-857-7299
Web site: http://www.hp.com

Hewlett-Packard operates major development
and production facilities in the US and 20 other
countries. It has sales and support offices in more
than 130 countries.

PRODUCTS/OPERATIONS

Products

Computers and Software
Business process management tools (HP Changengine)
Handheld PCs (Jornada series)
Internet communication software (Chai)
Internet photo management tools
Multimedia PCs (Pavilion series)
Network management (OpenView)
Notebooks
Operating systems (HP-UX)
PC servers (NetServer series)
PCs (Vectra, Brio series)
Personal workstations (Kayak series)
Servers (HP 9000 series)
Software development tools

Peripheral Products
Copy/print/scan/fax devices (OfficeJet)
Desktop sending device (Digital Sender)
PC photography tools (PhotoSmart)
Printer and computer drivers
Printers (DeskJet, LaserJet)
Scanners

COMPETITORS

Apple Computer	IBM	Sharp
Canon	Lexmark	Siemens
Compaq	International	Sony
Dell Computer	Motorola	Sun
Eastman Kodak	NCR	Microsystems
EMC	Oki Electric	Toshiba
Fisher Scientific	Packard Bell	Unisys
Fujitsu	Samsung	Xerox
Intel	Seiko Epson	

HISTORICAL FINANCIALS & EMPLOYEES

NYSE symbol: HWP FYE: October 31	Annual Growth	1989	1990	1991	1992	1993	1994	1995	1996	1997	1998
Sales ($ mil.)	16.5%	11,899	13,233	14,494	16,410	20,317	24,991	31,519	38,420	42,895	47,061
Net income ($ mil.)	15.1%	829	739	755	549	1,177	1,599	2,433	2,586	3,119	2,945
Income as % of sales	—	7.0%	5.6%	5.2%	3.3%	5.8%	6.4%	7.7%	6.7%	7.3%	6.3%
Earnings per share ($)	13.6%	0.88	0.77	0.76	0.55	1.17	1.54	2.31	2.46	2.95	2.77
Stock price - FY high ($)	—	15.38	12.59	14.16	21.25	22.31	24.72	48.31	57.69	72.94	82.38
Stock price - FY low ($)	—	11.41	6.44	6.22	11.16	13.50	17.53	22.97	36.81	42.75	47.06
Stock price - FY close ($)	19.7%	11.94	6.50	12.59	14.22	18.41	24.47	46.31	44.13	61.63	60.25
P/E - high	—	17	16	19	39	19	16	21	23	25	30
P/E - low	—	13	8	8	20	12	11	10	15	14	17
Dividends per share ($)	23.5%	0.09	0.11	0.12	0.19	0.23	0.28	0.35	0.44	0.52	0.60
Book value per share ($)	12.6%	5.73	6.52	7.22	7.47	8.42	9.54	11.61	13.25	15.52	16.66
Employees	3.1%	95,000	92,000	89,000	92,600	96,200	98,400	102,300	112,000	121,900	124,600

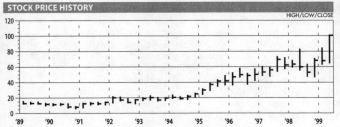

STOCK PRICE HISTORY HIGH/LOW/CLOSE

1998 FISCAL YEAR-END
Debt ratio: 10.9%
Return on equity: 17.4%
Cash ($ mil.): 4,046
Current ratio: 1.60
Long-term debt ($ mil.): 2,063
No. of shares (mil.): 1,015
Dividends
  Yield: 1.0%
  Payout: 21.7%
Market value ($ mil.): 61,178

HILLENBRAND INDUSTRIES, INC.

OVERVIEW

Life. Death. Corpse disposal. Batesville, Indiana-based Hillenbrand Industries serves the verities of existence from cradle to grave. The holding company operates three major subsidiaries. Hillenbrand's Health Care Group is spearheaded by its Hill-Rom subsidiary, a leading US supplier of hospital beds, infant incubators, and related equipment. The company's Forethought Financial Services provides burial insurance and trust services; through its Forethought Federal Savings Bank it also enables living customers to save up for their own funerals. And when it's time for the inevitable,

another Hillenbrand subsidiary will be there for you; Batesville Casket Company is the world's #1 casket maker and a leading provider of cremation products.

The company is focused on product innovation in its medical group, and it intends to grow by acquiring companies with complementary products and services. Hillenbrand also expects the aging of the baby boom generation to have a positive effect on both its health care and funeral businesses. The Hillenbrand family owns about 25% of the company.

HISTORY

In 1906 John A. Hillenbrand, a banker, newspaperman, and general-store owner in Batesville, Indiana, bought the ailing Batesville Casket Company (founded 1884) to save it from bankruptcy. Under Hillenbrand, and later his four sons (John W., who succeeded his father as president of the company; William; George; and Daniel), the casket company flourished.

In 1929 William Hillenbrand established the Hill-Rom Company in Batesville to make hospital furniture. Hill-Rom made its furniture out of wood — instead of tubular steel — and quickly became a leader in innovative hospital furnishings.

During the following decades George Hillenbrand created several patented products for both Batesville Casket and Hill-Rom. By the 1940s, for example, the company had developed corrosion-, air-, and water-resistant metal caskets. George constantly sought ways to improve manufacturing techniques and product quality, giving the company a sales and productivity edge over its competitors.

Daniel, the youngest son, became president of Batesville Casket in 1964 and consolidated Batesville Casket and Hill-Rom into Hillenbrand Industries five years later. Hoping to make it a more nationally (and eventually globally) competitive company, Daniel took Hillenbrand public in 1971.

The company acquired Dominion Metalware Industries (1972) and luggage maker American Tourister (1978; sold to Astrum International, maker of Samsonite luggage, in 1993). In 1984 it bought Medeco Security Locks and a year later purchased Support Systems International (SSI), provider of specialty rental mattresses for critically ill and immobile patients. (In 1994 SSI was integrated into what is now Hill-Rom.) Hillenbrand founded the Forethought Group in 1985 to provide special life insurance

to cover pre-arranged funerals and in 1991 entered the European market by acquiring Le Couviour, a French maker of hospital beds. The company also bought Block Medical, a maker of home infusion therapy products, that year. August Hillenbrand, nephew of Daniel, became CEO in 1989.

The company has been trying to gather all the caskets in one basket. In 1992 Batesville Casket bought casket producer Cormier & Gaudet (Canada). It then bought Bridge Casket Company (New Jersey); Lincoln Casket (Hamtramck, Michigan); and Industrias Arga, S.A. de C.V. (Mexico City), all in 1993. That year Hillenbrand also purchased L. & C. Arnold A.G., one of the biggest and oldest hospital furniture makers in Germany.

In 1996 the company sold its Block Medical subsidiary to I-Flow Corp., a marketer of infusion systems.

With the casket market flat in the mid-1990s, Hillenbrand grew its business by going after market share in cremation products and diversifying into retail. One venture, which specialized in funeral mementos, expired quietly. A bed store chain, Sleep Options (begun 1995), lived on, opening its seventh store in 1997. Also in 1997 Hillenbrand acquired AirShields (UK, infant incubators/warmers) and sought a federal thrift charter to enter the funeral and cemetery trust market. In 1998 Hill-Rom entered the medical gas delivery market and further expanded its international position when it acquired the UK-based MEDAES (medical gas distribution). Feeling secure in the prospects of its other businesses, Hillenbrand sold its Medeco lock unit to Sweden's Assa Abloy in 1998.

OFFICERS

Chairman: Daniel A. Hillenbrand, age 75
President and CEO: W. August Hillenbrand, age 58, $1,508,038 pay
SVP Finance: Tom E. Brewer, age 60, $547,965 pay
VP and CFO: Donald G. Barger Jr., age 56, $338,901 pay
President and CEO, Batesville Casket: David J. Hirt, age 52
President and CEO, The Hillenbrand Funeral Services Group: Frederick W. Rockwood, age 51
President and CEO, Hill-Rom: Walter M. Rosebrough, age 44
EVP and COO, Forethought Financial Services: Richard N. Coffin, age 52
VP Corporate Services: George E. Brinkmoeller, age 63
VP Corporate Development: Michael L. Buettner, age 41
VP and Treasurer: Mark R. Lanning, age 44
VP, Secretary, and General Counsel: Mark R. Lindenmeyer, age 52, $343,390 pay
VP Corporate Planning: J. Cameron Moss, age 42
VP Human Resources: David L. Robertson, age 53
VP Continuous Improvement: Robert J. Tennison, age 52, $367,227 pay
VP and Controller: James D. Van De Velde, age 52
Auditors: PricewaterhouseCoopers LLP

LOCATIONS

HQ: 700 State Rte. 46 East, Batesville, IN 47006-8835
Phone: 812-934-7000   **Fax:** 812-934-1963
Web site: http://www.hillenbrand.com

Hillenbrand Industries has facilities in Batesville, Indiana; Batesville and Vicksburg, Mississippi; Campbellsville, Kentucky; Charleston, South Carolina; Hatboro, Pennsylvania; Manchester, Tennessee; Nashua, New Hampshire; Norcross, Georgia; as well as in Canada, France, Germany, and Mexico.

PRODUCTS/OPERATIONS

1998 Sales

	$ mil.	% of total
Health care sales	748.0	38
Funeral services	541.0	27
Health care services	403.0	20
Insurance	309.0	15
Total	**2,001.0**	**100**

Selected Subsidiaries

Health Care
Hill-Rom, Inc.
  Air-Shields Holding, Inc.
  MEDAES Holdings, Inc.
Funeral Services
Batesville Casket Co., Inc.
  Batesville International Corporation
  Batesville Logistics, Inc.
  Batesville Manufacturing, Inc.
Forethought Financial Services, Inc.
  ForeLife Agency, Inc.
  Foresight Association, Inc.
  Forethought Federal Savings Bank
  Forethought Investment Management, Inc.
  Forethought Life Assurance Company
  Forethought Life Insurance Company
  Forethought National TrustBank

COMPETITORS

Graham-Field Health Products
Kinetic Concepts
Medline Industries
Sunrise Medical
York Group

HISTORICAL FINANCIALS & EMPLOYEES

NYSE symbol: HB FYE: November 30	Annual Growth	1989	1990	1991	1992	1993	1994	1995	1996	1997	1998
Sales ($ mil.)	6.5%	1,138	1,107	1,199	1,430	1,448	1,577	1,625	1,684	1,776	2,001
Net income ($ mil.)	10.5%	75	76	89	116	146	90	90	140	157	184
Income as % of sales	—	6.6%	6.8%	7.4%	8.1%	10.1%	5.7%	5.5%	8.3%	8.8%	9.2%
Earnings per share ($)	11.7%	1.01	1.03	1.23	1.62	2.04	1.26	1.27	2.02	2.28	2.73
Stock price - FY high ($)	—	21.38	24.00	30.31	43.63	48.63	43.63	33.13	40.25	48.63	64.69
Stock price - FY low ($)	—	13.19	15.06	17.88	29.31	36.50	26.63	27.00	31.88	33.88	44.38
Stock price - FY close ($)	11.7%	21.00	18.38	29.75	41.63	41.63	29.88	32.75	36.88	44.56	56.81
P/E - high	—	21	23	25	27	24	35	26	20	21	24
P/E - low	—	13	15	15	18	18	21	21	16	15	16
Dividends per share ($)	12.5%	0.25	0.28	0.29	0.35	0.45	0.57	0.60	0.62	0.66	0.72
Book value per share ($)	11.3%	5.46	5.96	6.75	7.65	8.98	9.72	10.63	11.44	12.93	14.26
Employees	1.6%	9,000	9,500	10,500	10,700	9,800	10,000	9,800	9,800	10,100	10,400

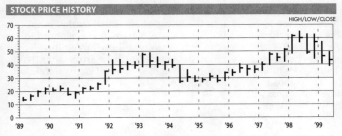

STOCK PRICE HISTORY   HIGH/LOW/CLOSE

1998 FISCAL YEAR-END
Debt ratio: 24.1%
Return on equity: 19.3%
Cash ($ mil.): 297
Current ratio: 2.29
Long-term debt ($ mil.): 303
No. of shares (mil.): 67
Dividends
  Yield: 1.3%
  Payout: 26.4%
Market value ($ mil.): 3,793

HILTON HOTELS CORPORATION

OVERVIEW

Explore the lineage of Hilton Hotels and you'll unearth a sizable chunk of the history of hotels in the US. When Conrad Hilton bought his first hotel in Cisco, Texas, in 1919, he sowed the seeds for what has become one of the leading hotel enterprises in the country. Headquartered in Beverly Hills, California, Hilton Hotels' lodging empire spans about 275 owned, partially owned, managed, or franchised hotels. Its franchised hotels operate under the Hilton, Hilton Garden Inn, and Hilton Suites names. Among Hilton's flagship hotels are New York's Waldorf-Astoria and Chicago's Palmer House (both are company-owned). More than 95% of Hilton's hotels are in the US (British leisure concern Hilton Group owns the rights to the Hilton name outside the US). Through its

Hilton Grand Vacations Company, Hilton also operates more than 20 vacation ownership resorts in Florida and Nevada. The firm's $4 billion purchase of Promus Hotels (operator of the Doubletree and Hampton Inn chains) will boost Hilton's holdings to about 1,700 properties.

In 1998 Hilton Hotels ended 28 years in the US casino business by spinning off its gaming interests in the form of Park Place Entertainment (the world's largest gaming concern). Renewing its focus on lodging, Hilton is pursuing hotel acquisitions. The company also plans to expand its North American franchising efforts. Chairman Barron Hilton, Conrad Hilton's son, owns about 9% of the company and controls an additional 6% through the charitable Conrad N. Hilton Fund.

HISTORY

Conrad Hilton got his start in hotel management by renting out rooms in his family's New Mexico home. He served as a state legislator and started a bank before leaving for Texas in 1919, hoping to make his fortune in banking. Hilton was unable to shoulder the cost of purchasing a bank, but, recognizing a high demand for hotel rooms, he made a quick change in strategy and bought his first hotel in Cisco, Texas. Over the next decade he bought seven more Texas hotels.

Hilton lost several hotels during the Depression, but he began rebuilding his hotel empire soon thereafter through purchases of hotels in California (1938), New Mexico (1939), and Mexico (1942). In 1942 he married starlet Zsa Zsa Gabor (they later divorced). Hilton Hotels Corporation was created and went public in 1946. Hilton achieved his goal of purchasing New York's Waldorf-Astoria (a hotel he labeled "the greatest of them all") in 1949. Hilton's first European hotel opened in Madrid in 1953. He paid $111 million for the 10-hotel Statler chain the following year.

Hilton took his company out of the overseas hotel business in 1964 by spinning off Hilton International. The company began franchising in 1965 to capitalize on its well-known name. Barron Hilton, Conrad Hilton's son, was appointed president in 1966 (he became chairman upon Conrad Hilton's death in 1979). In 1970 Hilton bought two Las Vegas hotels (the Las Vegas Hilton and the Flamingo Hilton), launching a gaming division. The company returned to the international hotel business with Conrad International Hotels in 1982. It opened its first suite-only Hilton Suites hotel in 1989.

In 1992 Hilton bought Bally's Casino Resort in Reno for $83 million. Hilton launched the *Hilton Queen of New Orleans,* its first riverboat casino, in 1994. Two years later Stephen Bollenbach, the former Walt Disney CFO who negotiated the $19 billion acquisition of Capital Cities/ABC, was named CEO, becoming the first nonfamily member to run the company. That year Hilton acquired Bally Entertainment and made plans to expand its Hilton Garden Inns hotel line.

In January 1997 Hilton formed an alliance with Ladbroke Group PLC (which owns the rights to the Hilton name internationally and now operates as Hilton Group) to unify the Hilton brand worldwide. Hilton's 1997 bid to acquire ITT, owner of Sheraton hotels and Caesars World, was thwarted when ITT accepted a higher offer by Starwood Hotels & Resorts. Hilton was disappointed again in 1998 when a deal with casino operator Circus Circus, which would have separated Hilton's hotel and casino operations, fell through. With a downturn in the gambling industry translating into sluggish results in Hilton's gaming segment, the company spun off its gaming interests as Park Place Entertainment in late 1998.

In 1999 Hilton revealed plans to branch into the extended-stay hotel market in the US, Canada, and Mexico. It also planned to open more than 65 Hilton Garden Inn properties across North America. Later that year Hilton agreed to buy Promus Hotel Corp. for $4 billion.

Chairman: Barron Hilton, age 71
President and CEO: Stephen F. Bollenbach, age 56, $997,967 pay
EVP; President, Hotel Operations: Dieter H. Huckestein, age 55, $675,131 pay
EVP, CFO, and Treasurer: Matthew J. Hart, age 46, $908,896 pay (prior to promotion)
EVP, General Counsel, and Secretary: Thomas E. Gallagher, age 54, $909,850 pay (prior to promotion)
SVP Architecture and Construction: Patrick B. Terwilliger
SVP and Controller: Robert M. La Forgia
SVP Corporate Affairs: Marc A. Grossman
SVP Development and Finance: Ted Middleton Jr.
SVP Diversity: Dorothy J. Porter
SVP Labor Relations and Personnel Administration: James M. Anderson
VP & Counsel: Mark A. Robertson
Chief Administrative Officer: Thomas E. Gallagher
Director of Corporate Employee Relations and Recruitment (HR): Bethany Ellis
Auditors: Arthur Andersen LLP

LOCATIONS

HQ: 9336 Civic Center Dr., Beverly Hills, CA 90210
Phone: 310-278-4321   **Fax:** 310-205-7678
Web site: http://www.hilton.com

Hilton Hotels has operations in Belgium, China, Egypt, Ireland, Singapore, Spain, Turkey, the UK, and the US.

PRODUCTS/OPERATIONS

1998 Sales

	$ mil.	% of total
Rooms	952	54
Food & beverages	414	23
Management & franchise fees	104	6
Other	299	17
Total	**1,769**	**100**

COMPETITORS

Accor
Bass
Canadian Pacific
Carlson
Cendant
Fairfield Communities
Four Seasons Hotels
Host Marriott
Hyatt
ILX Resorts
Marriott International
Promus Hotel
Rank
ResortQuest International
Ritz Carlton
Starwood Hotels & Resorts Worldwide
Sunterra
Trendwest Resorts
Vistana
Wyndham International

HISTORICAL FINANCIALS & EMPLOYEES

NYSE symbol: HLT FYE: December 31	Annual Growth	1989	1990	1991	1992	1993	1994	1995	1996	1997	1998
Sales ($ mil.)	6.6%	998	1,125	1,113	1,230	1,394	1,506	1,649	3,940	5,316	1,769
Net income ($ mil.)	11.7%	110	113	84	104	106	122	173	82	250	297
Income as % of sales	—	11.0%	10.0%	7.6%	8.4%	7.6%	8.1%	10.5%	2.1%	4.7%	16.8%
Earnings per share ($)	7.8%	0.57	0.59	0.44	0.54	0.56	0.63	0.89	0.41	0.94	1.12
Stock price - FY high ($)	—	28.88	21.09	12.47	13.31	15.25	18.50	19.94	31.75	35.81	35.50
Stock price - FY low ($)	—	12.09	6.59	8.56	9.94	10.38	12.44	15.09	15.28	24.00	12.50
Stock price - FY close ($)	(0.8%)	20.63	9.31	10.13	10.84	15.19	17.00	15.38	26.25	29.75	19.13
P/E - high	—	51	36	28	25	27	29	22	77	38	32
P/E - low	—	21	11	19	18	19	20	17	37	26	11
Dividends per share ($)	2.8%	0.25	0.35	0.30	0.30	0.30	0.30	0.30	0.31	0.32	0.32
Book value per share ($)	(18.5%)	4.60	4.86	5.01	5.25	5.53	5.86	6.49	12.82	13.66	0.73
Employees	(0.3%)	39,000	38,000	40,000	41,000	43,000	44,000	48,000	65,000	61,000	38,000

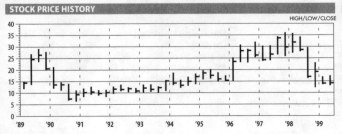

STOCK PRICE HISTORY
HIGH/LOW/CLOSE

1998 FISCAL YEAR-END
Debt ratio: 94.2%
Return on equity: 158.8%
Cash ($ mil.): 47
Current ratio: 0.93
Long-term debt ($ mil.): 3,037
No. of shares (mil.): 257
Dividends
  Yield: 1.7%
  Payout: 28.6%
Market value ($ mil.): 4,916

H.J. HEINZ COMPANY

OVERVIEW

Metaphorically speaking, H.J. Heinz is banging on the bottom of the bottle, trying to get more sales out of ketchup and its other traditional food products. Pittsburgh-based Heinz is a leading global food company with more than 5,700 products in six core categories: ketchup, condiments, and sauces; frozen foods; tuna; soups, beans, and pasta meals; infant foods; and pet food. Its stable of US retail market leaders includes Heinz ketchup (more than 50% US market share), Ore-Ida potatoes (45%), Star-Kist tuna (48%),

9-Lives cat food (26%), and Weight Watchers food products. It is also the #1 maker of private-label soup. Ketchup, condiments, and sauces account for nearly 25% of its sales.

With brands in mature markets back home, Heinz is expanding overseas through acquisitions and joint ventures. The company now derives nearly half of its sales from outside the US. Its top international markets are the UK, Canada, Australia, New Zealand, and Northern Europe.

HISTORY

In 1852 eight-year-old Henry J. Heinz started selling produce from the family garden to neighbors in Sharpsburg, Pennsylvania. The young entrepreneur formed a partnership with his friend L. C. Noble in 1869 bottling horseradish sauce in clear glass, but the business went bankrupt in 1875. The following year, with the help of his brother John and his cousin Frederick, Heinz created F. & J. Heinz; the enterprise developed ketchup (1876) and sweet pickles (1880). He gained financial control of the firm in 1888 and changed the name to the H.J. Heinz Company.

Heinz developed a reputation as an advertising and marketing genius. He introduced pickle pins, a popular promotion, at the 1893 Chicago World's Fair; coined the catchy "57 Varieties" slogan in 1897 (despite already having 60 products); and in 1900 raised New York City's first large electric advertising sign (a 40-ft. pickle). By 1905 Heinz was manufacturing food products in the UK.

After Heinz's death in 1919, the business, under the direction of his son and later his grandson, continued to rely on its traditional product lines for the next four decades, although some new ones were introduced, such as baby food in 1931. The company went public in 1946. Heinz changed its strategy in 1958 when it made its first acquisition, a Dutch food processor. Major purchases that followed included Star-Kist (tuna and pet food, 1963) and Ore-Ida (potatoes, 1965). In 1966 Burt Gookin became CEO, the first nonfamily member to hold that position.

The company bought Weight Watchers in 1978. The next year former rugby star Anthony O'Reilly became the company's fifth CEO. He intensified the focus on international expansion and presided over a string of acquisitions throughout the 1980s. O'Reilly became chairman in 1987.

Acquisitions in the 1990s included Wattie's Limited, New Zealand's largest food processing company (1992); Borden's food service business (1994); pet food divisions from Quaker Oats (1995); and Earth's Best organic baby food (1996).

Faced with weak sales growth in its stable markets and with opportunity beckoning from emerging markets, in 1997 Heinz launched a reorganization by announcing it would close or sell 25 plants. Globally, the company continued to grow through acquisitions while consolidating and upgrading remaining plants. It sold its Ore-Ida food service operations to McCain Foods but purchased Unilever's John West Foods (the UK's leading brand of tuna) and Polish ketchup maker Pudliszki.

William Johnson, who had turned around stagnant brands such as 9-Lives, succeeded O'Reilly as CEO in 1998. He began increasing brand marketing: Heinz resumed running TV ads for its ketchup after a five-year hiatus. Also that year the company sold its bakery products division (frozen, unbaked bagels and bread dough) to Pillsbury and bought the convenience meals business of Germany's Sonnen Basserman from Danone Group.

In 1999 Heinz announced a restructuring that, over several years, will involve the elimination of up to 4,000 jobs and the closure or sales of about 20 factories. It also involves the sale of the diet class business of Weight Watchers to European investment firm Artal Luxembourg for $735 million (it will keep the Weight Watchers frozen foods line). Also in 1999 the firm bought a majority stake in Indonesia's ABC Central Food, the world's #2 maker of soy sauce. Heinz then acquired Thermo Pac of Stone Mountain, Georgia, and Serv-A-Portion of Belgium to expand its global single-serve business.

Chairman: Anthony J. F. O'Reilly, age 63
President and CEO: William R. Johnson, age 50
EVP and CFO: Paul F. Renne, age 56
EVP; President, Europe: A. G. Malcolm Ritchie, age 45
EVP Global Manufacturing/Supply Chain and Frozen Foods: Richard H. Wamhoff, age 53
EVP: David R. Williams, age 56
SVP Strategy, Process, and Business Development: Michael J. Bertasso, age 49
SVP, General Counsel, and Secretary: Lawrence J. McCabe, age 64
SVP Corporate and Government Affairs: D. Edward I. Smyth, age 49
VP and Chief Administrative Officer: William C. Goode, age 58
Manager Human Resources: Gary Matson
Auditors: PricewaterhouseCoopers LLP

LOCATIONS

HQ: 600 Grant St., Pittsburgh, PA 15219
Phone: 412-456-5700 **Fax:** 412-456-6128
Web site: http://www.heinz.com

H.J. Heinz operates more than 30 domestic processing plants and more than 60 foreign plants.

1999 Sales

	$ mil.	% of total
North America	5,077	55
Europe	2,461	26
Asia/Pacific	1,012	11
Other regions	750	8
Total	**9,300**	**100**

PRODUCTS/OPERATIONS

Selected Brand Names

Food
Bagel Bites (frozen pizza snacks)
Chef Francisco (frozen soups)
College Inn (broths)
Eta (salad dressings and spreads, New Zealand)
Farley's (baby food, Europe)
Guloso (tomato products, Europe)
Heinz (ketchup, pickles, relishes, sauces, baby food)
John West (fish, Europe)
Ore-Ida (frozen potatoes)
Pablum (baby food, Canada)
Petit Navire (tuna and mackerel, Europe)
Plasmon (baby food, Europe)
Star-Kist (tuna)
The Budget Gourmet (frozen entrees and dinners)
Weight Watchers (diet foods, weight-loss programs)

Pet Food

9-Lives	Ken-L-Ration	Pupperoni
Amore	Kibbles 'n Bits	Reward
Cycle	Meaty Bone	Snausages
Gravy Train	Nature's Recipe	Wagwells
Jerky Treats	Pounce	

COMPETITORS

Bestfoods	Kraft Foods
Borden	Mars
Campbell Soup	McIlhenny
Colgate-Palmolive	Nabisco Holdings
ConAgra	Nestle
Del Monte	New World Pasta
Doane Pet Care Enterprises	Pillsbury
Hormel	Ralston Purina
International Home Foods	Slim-Fast
Jenny Craig	Vlasic Foods

HISTORICAL FINANCIALS & EMPLOYEES

NYSE symbol: HNZ FYE: April 30	Annual Growth	1990	1991	1992	1993	1994	1995	1996	1997	1998	1999
Sales ($ mil.)	4.8%	6,086	6,647	6,582	7,103	7,047	8,087	9,112	9,357	9,209	9,300
Net income ($ mil.)	(0.7%)	505	568	638	396	603	591	659	302	802	474
Income as % of sales	—	8.3%	8.5%	9.7%	5.6%	8.6%	7.3%	7.2%	3.2%	8.7%	5.1%
Earnings per share ($)	0.3%	1.26	1.42	1.59	1.00	1.56	1.58	1.75	0.81	2.15	1.29
Stock price - FY high ($)	—	23.93	27.43	32.43	30.35	26.60	28.68	36.63	44.88	59.94	61.75
Stock price - FY low ($)	—	16.42	19.59	23.43	23.51	20.51	21.09	27.43	29.75	41.13	44.56
Stock price - FY close ($)	9.4%	20.76	25.01	24.26	24.51	21.84	28.01	33.88	41.50	54.50	46.69
P/E - high	—	19	19	20	30	17	18	21	55	28	48
P/E - low	—	13	14	15	24	13	13	16	37	19	35
Dividends per share ($)	10.6%	0.54	0.62	0.70	0.78	0.86	0.94	1.04	1.14	1.24	1.34
Book value per share ($)	0.1%	4.96	5.85	6.21	6.09	6.26	6.77	7.34	6.65	6.10	5.02
Employees	0.4%	37,300	34,100	35,500	37,700	35,700	42,200	43,300	44,700	40,500	38,600

STOCK PRICE HISTORY

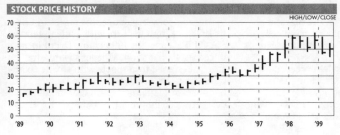

HIGH/LOW/CLOSE

1999 FISCAL YEAR-END

Debt ratio: 57.8%
Return on equity: 26.3%
Cash ($ mil.): 116
Current ratio: 1.04
Long-term debt ($ mil.): 2,472
No. of shares (mil.): 359
Dividends
  Yield: 2.9%
  Payout: 103.9%
Market value ($ mil.): 16,768

THE HOME DEPOT, INC.

OVERVIEW

The Home Depot has drawn a simple blueprint for success: Take the service and convenience of a mom-and-pop hardware shop and combine them in a store the size of an airplane hangar. The Atlanta-based home improvement chain (the largest in the US) operates about 800 stores and a handful of EXPO Design Center stores, large design showrooms that feature bath and kitchen products, appliances, and flooring and lighting items.

Home Depot stores average about 130,000 sq. ft. (including outside garden centers) and primarily cater to do-it-yourself (DIY) customers, but also to those who buy supplies and then hire third parties to complete projects, and — increasingly — professionals. (The company courts professional builders and contractors by giving them more individualized attention and special services such as same-day delivery.) Each store stocks more than 40,000 kinds of building materials, home improvement supplies, and lawn and garden equipment.

Like its dedicated DIY customers, Home Depot keeps adding on to and polishing its business plan. The rapidly expanding company intends to sell products through the Internet and is opening a handful of "hardware convenience stores" called Villager's Hardware. Blueprints also call for opening up to 200 EXPO stores over the next five to seven years. Home Depot is expanding its operations outside the US with stores in Canada and South America.

HISTORY

Bernard Marcus and Arthur Blank founded The Home Depot in 1978 after they were fired (under disputed circumstances) from Handy Dan Home Improvement Centers. They joined Handy Dan co-worker Ronald Brill to launch a "new and improved" home center for the do-it-yourselfer (DIY). (A potential major investment from Ross Perot fell through that year because the wealthy Texan wouldn't allow Home Depot to pick up the payments on Marcus' used Cadillac.) In 1979 they opened three stores in the fast-growing Atlanta area and expanded to four stores in 1980.

In 1981 Home Depot went public, opened four stores in South Florida, and posted sales of $50 million. After sales of $100 million in 1982, the company was named Retailer of the Year in the home building supply industry.

The chain entered Louisiana and Arizona next. By 1983 sales were more than $250 million. Home Depot also began installing computerized checkout systems, and by 1984 inventory reordering was computerized.

That year Home Depot's stock was listed on the NYSE, and the company acquired nine Bowater Home Centers in the South. Through subsequent stock and debenture offerings, Home Depot continued to grow, entering California, Handy Dan's home turf, with six new stores in 1985. However, the Bowater acquisition and rapid internal expansion caused Home Depot to record the only dip in earnings in its history that year.

Back on track in 1986, sales exceeded $1 billion in the firm's 60 stores. Home Depot began the current policy of "low day-in, day-out pricing" the following year, achieving Marcus' dream of eliminating sales events.

The company entered the competitive northeastern market with stores on Long Island in 1988 and opened its first EXPO Design Center in San Diego. The next year Home Depot added 22 stores, primarily in California, Florida, and New England.

Home Depot's sales continued to rise during the 1990-92 recession. The retailer opened more than 50 stores in 1990 and 1991. It acquired a 75% interest in Aikenhead's, a Canadian DIY chain, in 1994 and converted the outlets to the Home Depot name. (The company bought the remaining 25% in 1998.)

A series of gender-bias lawsuits plagued the company in 1994, as female workers claimed they were not trained, promoted, or paid on an equal basis with male employees. Home Depot reached a $65 million out-of-court settlement in that class-action suit in 1997, but not before the company was ordered to pay another female employee $1.7 million in a case in California.

Troubles aside, Home Depot roared past the 500-store mark in 1997. In mid-1997 Blank succeeded Marcus as the company's CEO; Marcus remained chairman. Home Depot bought National Blind & Wallpaper Factory (a mail-order firm) and Maintenance Warehouse (a direct-mail marketer) that year.

The company began opening stores in Chile in 1998 in a joint venture with Chilean retailer S.A.C.I. Falabella. In 1999 Home Depot introduced its 40,000-sq.-ft. Villager's Hardware stores, designed to compete with smaller hardware shops, in New Jersey. Home Depot bought Georgia Lighting, an Atlanta lighting designer, distributor, and retailer, in 1999.

OFFICERS

Chairman: Bernard Marcus, age 69, $2,900,000 pay
President, CEO, and COO: Arthur M. Blank, age 56, $2,900,000 pay
EVP and Chief Administrative Officer: Ronald M. Brill, age 55, $864,800 pay
EVP and CFO: Dennis J. Carey, age 52
EVP Merchandising: Pat Farrah, age 55
SVP Store Operations: Alan Barnaby
SVP Finance and Administration: Marshall L. Day, age 55
SVP Real Estate: Bryan J. Fields
SVP Information Services: Ronald B. Griffin
SVP Marketing and Communications: Richard A. Hammill
SVP Human Resources: Stephen R. Messana, age 54
SVP Strategic Business Development: W. Andrew McKenna, age 53, $776,397 pay
SVP Merchandising: Dennis J. Ryan
SVP Legal and Secretary: Lawrence A. Smith, age 51
SVP Advertising: Richard L. Sullivan
SVP Merchandising: Kenneth W. Ubertino
SVP Business Development: Robert J. Wittman
Group President and EVP - Operations: Larry M. Mercer, age 52
Group President - Diversified Business: David Suliteanu, age 46
Auditors: KPMG LLP

LOCATIONS

HQ: 2455 Paces Ferry Rd., Atlanta, GA 30339-4024
Phone: 770-433-8211   **Fax:** 770-384-2337
Web site: http://www.homedepot.com

1999 Stores

	No.
US	
California	106
Florida	72
Texas	63
Georgia	39
New York	38
Other States	428
Canada	43
Chile	2
Puerto Rico	1
Total	**753**

PRODUCTS/OPERATIONS

1999 Sales

	% of total
Building materials, lumber & floor & wall coverings	34
Plumbing, heating, lighting & electrical supplies	27
Seasonal & specialty items	15
Hardware & tools	14
Paint & other	10
Total	**100**

COMPETITORS

84 Lumber
Ace Hardware
Building Materials Holding
Carolina Holdings
Hechinger
HomeBase
Lanoga
Lowe's
Menard
Payless Cashways
Sears
Sherwin-Williams
Sutherland Lumber
TruServ
Wal-Mart
Wickes

HISTORICAL FINANCIALS & EMPLOYEES

NYSE symbol: HD FYE: January 31	Annual Growth	1990	1991	1992	1993	1994	1995	1996	1997	1998	1999
Sales ($ mil.)	30.5%	2,759	3,815	5,137	7,148	9,239	12,477	15,470	19,536	24,156	30,219
Net income ($ mil.)	34.5%	112	163	249	363	457	605	732	938	1,160	1,614
Income as % of sales	—	4.1%	4.3%	4.9%	5.1%	5.0%	4.8%	4.7%	4.8%	4.8%	5.3%
Earnings per share ($)	28.6%	0.11	0.15	0.20	0.28	0.34	0.44	0.51	0.65	0.78	1.06
Stock price - FY high ($)	—	2.88	4.94	11.99	17.16	16.85	16.17	16.68	19.84	30.81	62.00
Stock price - FY low ($)	—	1.54	2.59	4.69	9.93	11.67	12.38	12.21	14.17	16.51	30.63
Stock price - FY close ($)	41.8%	2.61	4.81	10.28	16.29	13.01	15.59	15.34	16.51	30.25	60.50
P/E - high	—	26	33	60	61	50	37	33	31	40	58
P/E - low	—	14	17	23	35	34	28	24	22	21	29
Dividends per share ($)	31.8%	0.01	0.02	0.02	0.03	0.04	0.05	0.07	0.08	0.10	0.12
Book value per share ($)	31.8%	0.50	0.64	1.34	1.73	2.09	2.53	3.49	4.13	4.85	5.92
Employees	27.6%	17,500	21,500	28,000	38,900	50,600	67,300	80,000	100,000	125,000	157,000

STOCK PRICE HISTORY

HIGH/LOW/CLOSE

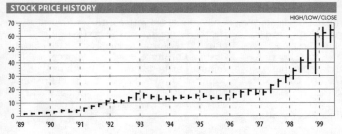

1999 FISCAL YEAR-END

Debt ratio: 15.2%
Return on equity: 18.5%
Cash ($ mil.): 62
Current ratio: 1.73
Long-term debt ($ mil.): 1,566
No. of shares (mil.): 1,475
Dividends
  Yield: 0.2%
  Payout: 11.3%
Market value ($ mil.): 89,265

HON INDUSTRIES INC.

OVERVIEW

Caught in the office during a blizzard? Mad at your office manager? Not to add fuel to the fire, but HON INDUSTRIES makes office furniture and the fireplace to burn it in. Based in Muscatine, Iowa, HON INDUSTRIES is the US's #1 maker of value-priced office furniture. Through subsidiaries BPI, Gunlocke, and Holga, the company makes desks and chairs, filing cabinets, office systems, shelving, and related products. Office products make up about 86% of revenues; one customer, United Stationers, accounts for 12% of HON INDUSTRIES' total sales.

The company's Hearth Technologies subsidiary makes products for the domestic pyrophile. It is the largest maker of wood- and gas-burning fireplaces, sold under the Heatilator and Heat-N-Glo names, and it also makes Aladdin stoves. Subsidiary HON Export markets the company's products outside the US and Canada.

HON INDUSTRIES distributes its wares through a national system of dealers, wholesalers, and retailers, as well as directly to governments. It is fueling growth through new value-priced products and acquisitions.

HISTORY

Friends Maxwell Stanley, Clement Hanson, and Wood Miller founded The Home-O-Nize Co. (a name that suggested "modernize" and "economize") in 1944 with the intention of making home freezers and steel kitchen cabinets. These two products were never made, however, because of a steel shortage.

The first Home-O-Nize product was an aluminum hood used in the installation of natural gas systems. More important than the aluminum hood was the aluminum scrap left behind, which the company made into beverage coasters. These coasters, which could be imprinted with a company's name, were sold to businesses to be given out as gifts. Home-O-Nize also transformed the aluminum scraps into boxes for file cards and, due to favorable response, decided to plunge into the office products business.

This move began in earnest in 1951, in an effort dramatically labeled "Operation Independence Home-O-Nize." Quasi-militaristic nomenclature aside, the effort was successful, and in 1952 the company started an unbroken string of profitable years. Helping this streak were such products as Unifile, a file cabinet that featured a single key that would lock all drawers simultaneously (1953). Home-O-Nize added cabinets, coat racks, and desks to its product line during this time and began marking all its products with the "H-O-N" label. Miller retired in 1958.

Home-O-Nize grew during the 1960s under the control of Stanley Howe, a Home-O-Nize employee since 1948. Howe had been appointed president in 1964 and made the company a national manufacturer by purchasing a plant in Georgia in 1967. The firm changed its name to HON INDUSTRIES the next year. Hanson left the company in 1969. HON INDUSTRIES continued its expansion

by purchasing California-based Holga Metal Products in 1971. Another California purchase followed, along with a 1972 acquisition in Pennsylvania and the opening of a plant in Virginia, which gave HON INDUSTRIES a considerable presence on both US coasts. Howe replaced Stanley as CEO in 1979.

In 1981 HON INDUSTRIES moved into the fireplace market by acquiring Heatilator, a leading brand of prefabricated fireplaces. By 1987, four decades after shipping its first product, HON INDUSTRIES had become a *FORTUNE* 500 company that many regarded as the most efficient maker of office furniture. (It could produce a desk a minute and a chair every 20 seconds.) HON INDUSTRIES acquired Gunlocke, a maker of wooden office furniture, two years later.

The rise of the office products superstore at the start of the 1990s did not go unnoticed by the company, which quickly positioned itself as a supplier to these businesses. Yet no action could spare HON INDUSTRIES from the office supply bust that occurred soon afterward, as oversupply and a lagging national economy dragged the industry downward.

Jack Michaels became the new CEO in 1991 as the company's sales dropped for the first time in decades. It adapted by investing in new products, and by 1992 sales were climbing again. In 1996 HON INDUSTRIES acquired rival fireplace maker Heat-N-Glo, which it merged with Heatilator to form Hearth Technologies. The next year it acquired three furniture makers: Allsteel, Bevis Custom Furniture, and Panel Concepts. The company further bolstered Hearth in 1998 by acquiring stove maker Aladdin Steel Products. Three of HON INDUSTRIES' smaller plants were closed in 1999 to cut costs.

Chairman Emeritus: Stanley M. Howe, age 75
Chairman, President, and CEO: Jack D. Michaels,
  age 61, $983,442 pay
VC: Richard H. Stanley, age 66
VP and CFO: David C. Stuebe, age 58, $414,307 pay
VP, New Business Development: W. Stephen Coder
VP, Member and Community Relations (HR):
  Jeffrey D. Fick, age 37
VP, General Counsel, and Secretary: James I. Johnson,
  age 50, $234,872 pay
VP and Controller: Melvin L. McMains, age 57
**VP, Marketing and International; President, HON
  Export Limited:** Thomas K. Miller, age 60,
  $227,379 pay
VP, Technical Development: David W. Strohl, age 55
President, The HON Company:
  George J. Koenigsaecker III, age 53, $545,365 pay
President, Holga Inc.: Brian R. Oken
President, BPI Inc.: Jean M. Reynolds
President, Hearth Technologies Inc.: Daniel C. Shimek
President, The Gunlocke Company: John M. Stevens
**President, Heatilator Division-Hearth Technologies
  Inc.:** David B. Cribb
**President, Aladdin Hearth Products Division-Hearth
  Technologies Inc.:** Alan J. Trusler
Treasurer: William F. Snydacker
Auditors: Arthur Andersen LLP

LOCATIONS

HQ: 414 E. 3rd St., Muscatine, IA 52761-7109
Phone: 319-264-7400   **Fax:** 319-264-7217
Web site: http://www.honi.com

HON INDUSTRIES sells its products primarily in the US
and Canada. Products are also sold in select countries,
mainly in Latin America and the Caribbean.

PRODUCTS/OPERATIONS

1998 Sales

	$ mil.	% of total
Office furniture	1,451	86
Hearth products	245	14
Total	**1,696**	**100**

Selected Products

Office Furniture
bookcases, credenzas, desks, filing cabinets, panel
  systems, seating, storage units, tables

Hearth Products
chimney venting systems, direct venting, fireplaces
  and stoves, fireplace inserts

Subsidiaries
BPI Inc. (panel systems products)
The Gunlocke Company (high quality wood
  office furniture)
Hearth Technologies Inc. (fireplaces)
Holga Inc. (shelving and storage systems)
HON Company (value-priced office furniture)
HON Export Limited (international sales)

COMPETITORS

Anderson Hickey	Kimball International
Bush Industries	Knoll
CFM Majestic	La-Z-Boy
Federal Prison Industries	Lennox
Fireplace Manufacturers	Martin Industries
Global Furniture	O'Sullivan Industries
Haworth International	Sauder Woodworking
Herman Miller	Steelcase
HighPoint Furniture	Tab Products
KI	

HISTORICAL FINANCIALS & EMPLOYEES

NYSE symbol: HNI FYE: December 31	Annual Growth	1989	1990	1991	1992	1993	1994	1995	1996	1997	1998
Sales ($ mil.)	12.2%	602	664	608	707	780	846	893	998	1,363	1,696
Net income ($ mil.)	16.2%	28	43	33	39	45	54	41	68	87	106
Income as % of sales	—	4.6%	6.5%	5.4%	5.5%	5.8%	6.4%	4.6%	6.8%	6.4%	6.3%
Earnings per share ($)	17.9%	0.39	0.65	0.51	0.59	0.70	0.87	0.67	1.13	1.45	1.72
Stock price - FY high ($)	—	9.94	11.50	10.25	11.75	14.63	17.00	15.63	21.38	32.13	37.19
Stock price - FY low ($)	—	4.38	6.75	6.63	8.25	10.75	12.00	11.50	9.25	16.00	20.00
Stock price - FY close ($)	10.9%	9.44	7.25	9.63	11.75	14.00	13.38	11.63	16.50	29.50	23.94
P/E - high	—	25	18	20	20	21	20	23	19	22	22
P/E - low	—	11	10	13	14	15	14	17	8	11	12
Dividends per share ($)	11.5%	0.12	0.15	0.18	0.19	0.20	0.22	0.24	0.25	0.28	0.32
Book value per share ($)	16.6%	1.87	2.03	2.32	2.52	2.81	3.17	3.56	4.25	6.19	7.48
Employees	4.8%	6,400	6,073	5,599	5,926	6,257	6,131	5,933	6,502	9,400	9,800

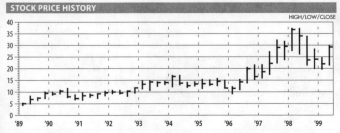

STOCK PRICE HISTORY HIGH/LOW/CLOSE

1998 FISCAL YEAR-END
Debt ratio: 22.7%
Return on equity: 23.0%
Cash ($ mil.): 18
Current ratio: 1.34
Long-term debt ($ mil.): 136
No. of shares (mil.): 62
Dividends
  Yield: 1.3%
  Payout: 18.6%
Market value ($ mil.): 1,478

HONEYWELL INC.

OVERVIEW

Honeywell has gone back to the sweet waters of automation and industrial controls, ending its ventures into mainframe computers and telecommunications. The Minneapolis-based company, which diversified electronics maker AlliedSignal is buying, has refocused on making thermostats, security systems, and other automation equipment. Honeywell provides high-tech control systems for private and commercial buildings, industry, and aircraft. A global leader in control technology, Honeywell's products are used extensively in homes, office buildings, and industrial facilities and in military and commercial aircraft.

The company also provides services that retrofit older buildings for energy efficiency. Honeywell also is making acquisitions, expanding its product lines to include airfield lighting-control and monitoring systems.

Honeywell's space and aviation segment, which had stumbled because of commercial aviation and government cutbacks, has seen new contracts from commercial airlines and the US military. It makes the cockpit display for Boeing's 777 aircraft and is selling that advanced technology to other aerospace electronics firms as a next-generation, industry-standard system. Honeywell's acquisition by AlliedSignal is expected to create a leading aerospace parts-and-electronics manufacturer.

HISTORY

An invention patented by Al Butz in 1885, the Damper Flapper, led to the building-regulation equipment that Honeywell still provides today. The Damper Flapper, forerunner of the thermostat, opened furnace vents automatically. Butz formed the Butz Thermo-Electric Regulator Co. to market the product but sold patent rights to investor William Sweatt in 1893. Sweatt led the company for the next four decades. The company eventually began producing a burner-control system for fire protection on oil and gas furnaces. Sweatt persuaded manufacturers to redesign furnaces to accommodate controls, thus establishing a new market.

In 1927 the company merged with Indiana-based chief competitor Mark Honeywell Heating Specialties as Minneapolis-Honeywell Regulator. (The company adopted its present name in 1964.)

Honeywell developed precision optics during WWII, when the US military sought its assistance in designing instrumentation and control systems for bombers. During the following decade, Honeywell used computers in control and guidance systems. It formed Datamatic Corporation (1955) with Raytheon to develop data processors. The company purchased GE's computer division in 1970 and also received 66% of a French company, Machines Bull. Honeywell bought Xerox's computer business in 1976. That year it merged Machines Bull with a computer company owned by the French government, which purchased Honeywell's interest (after threatening to nationalize it) in 1982. Honeywell bought Sperry Aerospace Group in 1986. The next year it renewed its ties with Bull to create Honeywell Bull. (Honeywell sold its interest in the Bull enterprise in 1991.)

The company won a $2 billion contract in 1990 to develop cockpit displays and flight management systems for Boeing's 777 jetliner. A recession in the company's key markets hurt sales in the early 1990s. In 1992 company acquired the Enviracaire Division of Environmental Air Control (air cleaners) and two regional security companies.

Honeywell spent $105 million on acquisitions in 1994 to expand its European services and its TotalPlant range of products. In 1995 Honeywell built its first plant in China.

The next year Honeywell and Trimble Navigation extended a pact to provide navigation equipment to airlines. In 1997 Honeywell bought Measurex, the #1 maker of papermaking measurement and control systems, and renamed it Honeywell-Measurex.

In 1998 Honeywell purchased Hughey & Phillips, a leader in airfield lighting-control and monitoring systems, and commercial security systems maker VVE Security. Honeywell also acquired Westinghouse Security Electronics from CBS and Data Instruments.

Following a decades long legal battle with Litton Industries, a jury in 1998 returned a $750 million verdict against Honeywell for monopolizing the commercial airplane guidance and navigation market; Honeywell won a reduction to $660 million on appeal in 1999 and vowed to seek a reversal of the verdict. Also in 1999 AlliedSignal agreed to buy Honeywell, and take its name, in a deal valued at about $14 billion. Honeywell immediately set out to boost its security business by agreeing to acquire C&K Systems, a maker of sensors for commercial buildings.

Chairman and CEO: Michael R. Bonsignore, age 57,
$2,028,366 pay
President and COO: Giannantonio Ferrari, age 59,
$1,146,344 pay
VP Communications: Frances B. Emerson
VP and Secretary: Kathleen M. Gibson
VP and General Counsel: Edward D. Grayson, age 60
VP and Controller: Philip M. Palazzari, age 51
VP of Government Affairs: Paula Prahl
VP Technology: Ronald E. Peterson
VP Human Resources and Chief Administrative Officer:
James T. Porter, age 47
VP Information Systems: William L. Sanders
VP and CFO: Larry W. Stranghoener, age 44
President, Honeywell Asia/Pacific:
Eduardo Castro-Wright
**President, Solutions and Services Business, Home and
Building Control:** J. Kevin Gilligan, age 44,
$647,127 pay
President, Honeywell Europe: William M. Hjerpe,
age 47, $735,982 pay
President, Honeywell Limited (Canada): P. F. Rankine
President, Space and Aviation Control:
Don K. Schwanz, age 54, $787,004 pay
President, Industrial Control: Markos I. Tambakeras,
age 47
President, Honeywell Consumer Products:
J. E. "Jack" Teela
**President, Products Business and Home and Building
Control:** Albrecht Weiss, age 47
VP and General Manager, Latin America Region:
Jaime J. Conesa
Auditors: Deloitte & Touche LLP

LOCATIONS

HQ: Honeywell Plaza, Minneapolis, MN 55408
Phone: 612-951-1000   **Fax:** 612-951-8537
Web site: http://www.honeywell.com

Honeywell has manufacturing plants in 19 countries
worldwide.

PRODUCTS/OPERATIONS

1998 Sales & Operating Income

	Sales		Operating Income	
	$ mil.	% of total	$ mil.	% of total
Home & building control	3,441	41	349	34
Industrial control	2,516	30	314	31
Space & aviation control	2,339	28	334	32
Other sales	131	1	31	3
Total	**8,427**	**100**	**1,028**	**100**

COMPETITORS

ABB Asea Brown Boveri
AlliedSignal
Emerson
GE
Invensys
Johnson Controls
Litton Industries
Rockwell International
Sextant Avionique
Siemens
Tyco International

HISTORICAL FINANCIALS & EMPLOYEES

NYSE symbol: HON FYE: December 31	Annual Growth	1989	1990	1991	1992	1993	1994	1995	1996	1997	1998
Sales ($ mil.)	3.7%	6,059	6,309	6,193	6,223	5,963	6,057	6,731	7,312	8,028	8,427
Net income ($ mil.)	(0.6%)	604	382	331	391	322	279	334	403	471	572
Income as % of sales	—	10.0%	6.1%	5.3%	6.3%	5.4%	4.6%	5.0%	5.5%	5.9%	6.8%
Earnings per share ($)	2.6%	3.55	2.52	2.35	1.80	2.38	2.15	2.58	3.11	3.65	4.48
Stock price - FY high ($)	—	22.94	28.09	32.75	37.94	39.38	36.88	49.50	69.88	80.75	96.38
Stock price - FY low ($)	—	14.88	17.66	20.50	30.19	31.00	28.25	30.75	44.38	63.88	58.63
Stock price - FY close ($)	14.8%	21.69	22.25	32.56	33.25	34.25	31.50	48.63	65.75	68.50	75.31
P/E - high	—	6	11	14	21	17	17	19	22	22	22
P/E - low	—	4	7	9	17	13	13	12	14	18	13
Dividends per share ($)	7.9%	0.57	0.70	0.77	0.84	0.91	0.97	1.01	1.06	1.09	1.13
Book value per share ($)	7.0%	11.99	11.99	13.25	13.10	13.48	14.57	16.09	17.86	18.93	22.05
Employees	(1.5%)	65,500	60,300	58,200	55,400	52,300	50,800	50,100	53,000	57,500	57,000

STOCK PRICE HISTORY

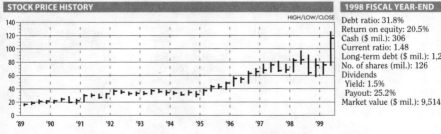

HIGH/LOW/CLOSE

1998 FISCAL YEAR-END

Debt ratio: 31.8%
Return on equity: 20.5%
Cash ($ mil.): 306
Current ratio: 1.48
Long-term debt ($ mil.): 1,299
No. of shares (mil.): 126
Dividends
  Yield: 1.5%
  Payout: 25.2%
Market value ($ mil.): 9,514

HORMEL FOODS CORPORATION

OVERVIEW

When Hormel Foods introduced SPAM in 1937, the company couldn't have known its canned ham would one day be considered an American icon worthy of museum display. Austin, Minnesota-based Hormel produces SPAM — two cans of which are now part of the Smithsonian Institution's permanent collection — as well as Cure 81 hams, Jennie-O turkey, and Always Tender fresh pork.

The US's #1 turkey processor and #3 pork processor (after Smithfield Foods and IBP), Hormel still counts on meat products for half of sales. However, it has branched into

higher-margin convenience, ethnic, and low-fat foods. Its consumer brands include Chi-Chi's Mexican foods, Dinty Moore beef stew, Stagg chili, Peloponnese Mediterranean foods, and House of Tsang sauces.

Hormel is expanding globally, forming joint ventures in Australia, China (the world's biggest market for pork), Mexico, and the Philippines. Keen to find room for growth in the mature US food market, Hormel is even eyeing nutraceuticals. The Hormel Foundation, a charitable trust formed during WWII, owns 43% of the company's stock.

HISTORY

George Hormel opened his Austin, Minnesota, slaughterhouse in an abandoned creamery in 1891. By 1900 Hormel had modernized his facilities to compete with larger meat processors. In 1903 the enterprise introduced its first brand name (Dairy Brand) and a year later began opening distribution centers nationwide. The scandal that ensued after the discovery in 1921 that an assistant controller had embezzled over $1 million almost broke the company, causing Hormel to initiate tighter controls. By 1924 it was processing more than a million hogs annually. Hormel introduced canned ham two years later.

Jay Hormel, George's son, became president in 1929; under his guidance Hormel introduced Dinty Moore beef stew (1936) and SPAM (1937). A Hormel executive won a contest, and $100, by submitting the name, a contraction of "spiced ham." During WWII, the US government bought over half of Hormel's output; it supplied SPAM to GIs and Allied forces. Soviet premier Nikita Khrushchev once remarked that the USSR could not have fed its army without lend-lease SPAM.

After WWII, Hormel sponsored a traveling entertainment group, the Hormel Girls, to promote products. In 1959 it introduced its Little Sizzlers pork sausage and sold its billionth can of SPAM. New products rolled out in the 1960s included Hormel's Cure 81 ham (1963). By the mid-1970s the firm had more than 750 products.

The company survived a violent, nationally publicized strike triggered by a pay cut in 1985. In the end, only 500 of the original 1,500 strikers returned to accept lower pay scales. Sensing the consumer shift towards poultry, Hormel purchased Jennie-O Foods in 1986. Later acquisitions included the House of Tsang and Oriental Deli (1992), Dubuque (processed

pork, 1993), and Herb-Ox (bouillon and dry soup mix, 1993). After more than a century as Geo. A. Hormel & Co., the company began calling itself Hormel Foods in 1993 to reflect its expansion into non-pork foods. Former General Foods executive Joel Johnson was named president and CEO that year (and chairman two years later).

Hormel proved it could take a joke with the 1994 debut of its tongue-in-cheek SPAM catalog, featuring dozens of SPAM-related products. But when a 1996 Muppets movie featured a real swine of a character named Spa'am, Hormel sued Jim Henson Productions; a federal court gave Spa'am the go-ahead.

Also in 1996 Hormel teamed up with Mexican food processor Grupo Herdez to sell Herdez sauces and other Mexican food products in the US. It then formed a joint venture with Indian food producer Patak Spices (UK) to market its products in the US. Late that year Hormel paid $64 million for a 21% interest in Spanish food maker Campofrio Alimentacion.

Earnings fell 34% in 1996, due in part to soaring hog prices. The next year Hormel sold its catfish business. Striving for consistency for its branded fresh pork, the company signed production contracts with hog growers, and ultimately paid premium rates during 1998 when hog prices fell due to a glutted market. Also that year Hormel recalled more than 2.2 million frozen hamburgers from warehouses because of possible bacterial contamination.

In 1998 the Smithsonian accepted two cans of SPAM (one from 1937, the other an updated 1997 version) for its History of Technology collection. SPAM sales soared in 1999 as nervous consumers stockpiled provisions for the millennium.

Chairman, President, and CEO: Joel W. Johnson,
age 55, $1,325,246 pay
EVP and CFO: Don J. Hodapp, age 60, $736,900 pay
EVP: Gary J. Ray, age 52, $628,400 pay
Group VP Meat Products: Stanley E. Kerber, age 60,
$532,750 pay
Group VP, Prepared Foods: Eric A. Brown, age 52
Group VP International and Corporate Development:
David N. Dickson, age 55
VP Foodservice: Steven G. Binder, age 41
VP Grocery Products: Richard A. Bross, age 47
VP Research and Development: Forrest D. Dryden,
age 55
VP; President, Hormel Foods International:
Ronald W. Fielding, age 46
VP Human Resources: James A. Jorgenson, age 53
VP, Treasurer, and Controller: Michael J. McCoy, age 51
VP Manufacturing: Gary C. Paxton, age 53
VP; President and CEO, Jennie-O Foods:
James N. Rieth, age 58
VP and General Counsel: Mahlon C. Schneider, age 59
VP Meat Products Sales: Robert A. Slavik, age 53
Auditors: Ernst & Young LLP

HQ: 1 Hormel Place, Austin, MN 55912-3680
Phone: 507-437-5611   **Fax:** 507-437-5489
Web site: http://www.hormel.com

Hormel Foods has processing and packaging facilities in
11 states and licensee agreements or joint ventures in
more than a dozen countries. It sells its products in
more than 50 countries.

1998 Sales

	% of total
Meat products	51
Prepared foods	28
Poultry & other	21
Total	**100**

Selected Brands

Chi-Chi's (Mexican foods)	Little Sizzlers (pork
Cure 81 (ham)	sausage)
Curemaster (ham)	Mrs. Paterson's Aussie Pies
Dinty Moore (beef stew)	(frozen meat pies)
Fast 'N Easy (precooked	Old Smokehouse (steak
hamburgers)	sauce)
Herb-Ox (bouillon and	Peloponnese
stock)	(Mediterranean foods)
Herdez (Mexican foods)	Quick Meal (frozen
Homeland (hard salami)	microwaveable
Hormel (bacon, bacon bits,	sandwiches)
chili, ham, hot dogs,	Range Brand (bacon)
pepperoni)	Sandwich Maker (lunch
House of Tsang (Oriental	meats)
foods)	SPAM (canned meat)
Jennie-O (turkey products)	Stagg (chili)
Light & Lean (reduced-fat	Wranglers (smoked franks)
products)	

Bestfoods	Foster Poultry	Smithfield Foods
Bob Evans	Goya	Thorn Apple
Bridgford Foods	IBP	Valley
Campbell Soup	Keystone Foods	Tyson Foods
Cargill	Perdue	WLR Foods
ConAgra	Pilgrim's Pride	
Farmland	Sara Lee	
Industries	Seaboard	

NYSE symbol: HRL FYE: October 31	Annual Growth	1989	1990	1991	1992	1993	1994	1995	1996	1997	1998
Sales ($ mil.)	3.8%	2,341	2,681	2,836	2,814	2,854	3,065	3,046	3,099	3,257	3,261
Net income ($ mil.)	7.9%	70	77	86	95	(27)	118	120	79	110	139
Income as % of sales	—	3.0%	2.9%	3.0%	3.4%	—	3.9%	4.0%	2.6%	3.4%	4.3%
Earnings per share ($)	8.2%	0.91	1.00	1.12	1.24	(0.35)	1.54	1.57	1.04	1.43	1.85
Stock price - FY high ($)	—	15.56	18.88	23.13	22.25	25.50	25.00	28.00	28.00	32.75	39.38
Stock price - FY low ($)	—	9.25	14.00	14.75	16.75	20.25	18.75	23.00	19.38	23.50	25.69
Stock price - FY close ($)	9.4%	14.56	14.88	19.50	21.25	22.63	24.50	23.00	23.63	30.06	32.56
P/E - high	—	17	19	21	18	—	16	18	27	23	21
P/E - low	—	10	14	13	14	—	12	15	19	16	14
Dividends per share ($)	13.2%	0.21	0.25	0.29	0.35	0.42	0.49	0.56	0.60	0.61	0.64
Book value per share ($)	6.8%	6.13	6.70	7.61	8.41	7.43	8.62	9.52	10.13	10.59	11.07
Employees	3.8%	8,000	8,300	8,300	8,300	10,800	9,500	10,600	11,000	11,000	11,200

HIGH/LOW/CLOSE

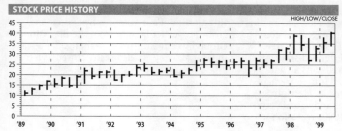

Debt ratio: 20.1%
Return on equity: 17.1%
Cash ($ mil.): 204
Current ratio: 2.68
Long-term debt ($ mil.): 205
No. of shares (mil.): 73
Dividends
  Yield: 2.0%
  Payout: 34.6%
Market value ($ mil.): 2,393

HOST MARRIOTT CORPORATION

OVERVIEW

Host Marriott is checking into luxury hotels. The Bethesda, Maryland-based company is returning to what it knows best — it has spun off more than 30 retirement communities and has reorganized as a real estate investment trust (REIT). The change put Host Marriott, which owns some 125 hotels, in a better tax position and gave it more leverage for future acquisitions.

The move comes in the wake of the most dramatic growth period since the company's founding: It has added more than 100 hotels since 1994. Host Marriott looks for properties in desirable urban, airport, and resort locations and then converts them to the recognizable Marriott and Ritz-Carlton brands to improve performance. Many of the company's acquisi-

tions are effected through its alliance with Marriott International, which manages the company's hotel and retirement communities and owns the Ritz-Carlton name. The company is also looking to acquire other brands.

Host Marriott and Marriott International both were once part of Marriott Corp.; the companies were spun off so each could enhance its value in the stock market. The split left Host Marriott with several chains of limited-service hotels. As part of a strategy to concentrate on luxury hotels, the company sold its limited-service chains to another REIT, which leases them to Marriott International.

The founding Marriott family owns more than 11% of the company; the Blackstone Group owns about 16%.

HISTORY

Newlyweds John and Alice Marriott left Marriott, Utah (founded by John's grandparents) in 1927 to open a root beer stand in Washington, DC. As a way to attract customers during the winter, they began selling tamales and tacos (recipes came from a cook at the Mexican Embassy). Dubbed the Hot Shoppe, the Marriotts built the business into a regional chain.

In 1937 the Marriotts began providing boxed lunches for airlines. Hot Shoppes entered the hospital food service business in 1955 and two years later opened its first hotel in Arlington, Virginia. John and Alice's son Bill became president in 1964. The company, which operated four hotels, 45 Hot Shoppes, and the airline catering business, became Marriott-Hot Shoppes.

In the 1960s the company acquired Bob's Big Boy restaurant chain (sold 1987), started Roy Rogers fast-food restaurants, and changed its name to Marriott Corp. Later, Marriott bought an Athenian cruise line (Oceanic; sold 1987). Bill Marriott became CEO in 1972.

Marriott diversified its hotel operations in the 1980s, moving into limited-service, middle-priced hotels with the launch of Courtyard by Marriott in 1983. To accelerate growth, the company began building hotels for sale, retaining their control through management contracts. In 1987 it acquired Residence Inn Company, which targeted extended-stay travelers. The company also expanded its airline catering business and moved into retirement facilities. To fund the expansion, Marriott formed limited partnerships and issued corporate bonds; when the late 1980s recession hit,

the company was deeply in debt. (About 1,800 of the investors in the limited partnerships have since sued, saying Marriott did not disclose all the risks involved in the investments.)

In 1993 Marriott Corp. divided into Marriott International (hotel management services) and Host Marriott (real estate and food service), leaving Host Marriott with most of the corporation's debt. Host Marriott began focusing on full-service hotels. It raised money to buy more hotels (many of which belonged to its old limited partnerships) by taking loans from Marriott International and selling assets (including 14 retirement properties and 30 Fairfield Inns). In late 1995 the company further refined its focus by spinning off its food service and concessions business as Host Marriott Services (now Italy-based restaurant operator Autogrill).

Host Marriott acquired three Ritz-Carlton hotels in 1995 (through Marriott International, which owns the Ritz-Carlton name) and in 1997 acquired the Forum Group, owner of 29 retirement communities. The next year it spun off Crestline Capital to own its retirement properties and to lease its hotels.

In 1999 the company expanded its hotel brands, adding controlling stakes in 13 luxury Ritz-Carlton, Four Seasons, Swissotel, and Hyatt properties bought from the Blackstone Group investment firm in exchange for a stake in Host Marriott. It also restructured as a real estate investment trust, or REIT.

Chairman: Richard E. Marriott, age 60, $406,630 pay
President and CEO: Terence C. Golden, age 54, $1,272,590 pay
EVP and COO: Christopher J. Nassetta, age 36, $669,485 pay
EVP and CFO: Robert E. Parsons Jr., age 43, $646,770 pay
SVP, Corporate Secretary, and General Counsel: Christopher G. Townsend, age 51, $334,651 pay
SVP and Treasurer: W. Edward Walter
SVP and Corporate Controller: Donald D. Olinger, age 40
SVP Taxes: Richard A. Burton
VP Human Resources: Arezu Ingle
Auditors: Arthur Andersen LLP

LOCATIONS

HQ: 10400 Fernwood Rd., Bethesda, MD 20817
Phone: 301-380-9000   **Fax:** 301-380-8413
Web site: http://www.hostmarriott.com

Host Marriott owns hotels in Canada and the US.

1998 Sales

	% of total
US	97
Other countries	3
Total	**100**

PRODUCTS/OPERATIONS

1998 Sales

	$ mil.	% of total
Hotels		
Rooms	2,220	64
Food & beverage	984	29
Other	238	7
Total	**3,442**	**100**

COMPETITORS

Accor North America
Bass
Boykin Lodging
Canadian Pacific
Carlson
Four Seasons Hotels
Hilton
Hyatt
Lodgian
Prime Hospitality
Promus Hotel
Starwood Hotels & Resorts Worldwide
Wyndham International

HISTORICAL FINANCIALS & EMPLOYEES

NYSE symbol: HMT FYE: December 31	Annual Growth	1989	1990	1991	1992	1993	1994	1995	1996	1997	1998
Sales ($ mil.)	11.4%	—	—	1,614	1,198	1,354	1,501	484	732	1,147	3,442
Net income ($ mil.)	—	—	—	(65)	(37)	(60)	(25)	(143)	(13)	50	47
Income as % of sales	—	—	—	—	—	—	—	—	—	4.4%	1.4%
Earnings per share ($)	(5.1%)	—	—	—	—	0.35	(0.26)	(0.90)	(0.07)	0.24	0.27
Stock price - FY high ($)	—	—	—	—	—	10.00	13.75	13.88	16.25	23.75	22.13
Stock price - FY low ($)	—	—	—	—	—	6.25	8.25	9.13	11.25	15.25	9.88
Stock price - FY close ($)	8.6%	—	—	—	—	9.13	9.63	13.13	16.00	19.63	13.81
P/E - high	—	—	—	—	—	29	—	—	—	99	82
P/E - low	—	—	—	—	—	18	—	—	—	64	37
Dividends per share ($)	—	—	—	—	—	0.00	0.00	0.00	0.00	0.00	0.00
Book value per share ($)	8.2%	—	—	—	—	3.91	4.62	4.23	5.58	5.89	5.81
Employees	(62.0%)	—	—	—	—	24,000	22,000	800	1,000	525	191

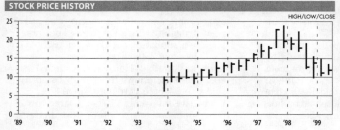

STOCK PRICE HISTORY HIGH/LOW/CLOSE

1998 FISCAL YEAR-END
Debt ratio: 79.6%
Return on equity: 3.6%
Cash ($ mil.): 436
Current ratio: 3.23
Long-term debt ($ mil.): 5,131
No. of shares (mil.): 226
Dividends
  Yield: —
  Payout: —
Market value ($ mil.): 3,116

HOUSEHOLD INTERNATIONAL, INC.

OVERVIEW

Household International has been cleaning the clutter out of its garage and is ready to concentrate on what it does best. The Prospect Heights, Illinois-based company is the US's #2 consumer finance firm (behind Associates First Capital) and one of the nation's largest home equity lenders. Household Finance and other subsidiaries serve working-class folks who may have trouble borrowing from banks. In addition to its highly profitable unsecured consumer loans and secured home equity loans, Household provides co-branded and private-label cards for retailers. The company, which has more than 1,600 US, Canadian, and UK offices, also offers credit life insurance and finances used cars, mainly through dealers.

Household solidified its spot in a rapidly consolidating industry by gobbling up rival Beneficial and the consumer finance unit of Transamerica (now owned by Dutch insurer AEGON NV).

To maintain its competitive edge, Household International has exited low-margin areas (branch banking, individual life and annuity products) to focus on such high-return (if risky) operations as unsecured loans. Shrinking profit margins are also behind the company's move to cut back its MasterCard and Visa operations in favor of private-label and affinity cards, which present greater cross-selling opportunities.

HISTORY

In 1878 Frank Mackey opened a finance company in Minneapolis to lend cash to workers between paychecks. In 1894, when the company had 14 midwestern offices, Mackey moved the headquarters to Chicago (it is now located in a suburb). The firm introduced installment payments on loans in 1905.

More than 30 such Mackey-controlled companies consolidated in 1925 as Household Finance Corporation (HFC), a public company. That year the firm paid its first quarterly dividend.

In 1930 HFC set up the Money Management Institute to teach people how to handle credit. (One pamphlet showed a family of five how to live on $150 a month.) HFC's banks froze the company's credit and stopped lending in 1931, but the freeze was lifted the next year and the company weathered the Depression. It made its first non-US purchase in 1933, buying Canada's Central Finance.

After WWII the unleashed demand for goods propelled HFC into the suburbs. By 1960 HFC had 1,000 offices and was advertising on TV.

HFC diversified into retailing in the 1960s: hardware stores (Coast to Coast, 1961), variety chains (Ben Franklin and TG&Y, 1965), vacuum jugs (King-Seeley Thermos, 1968), and car rentals (National, 1969). HFC also bought a savings and loan company, four banks, and Alexander Hamilton Life (1977). This strategy benefited the firm in the 1970s, when rising inflation rates made Household's traditional short-term, fixed-rate loans less profitable.

The company became Household International in 1981. During the mid-1980s chairman Donald Clark refocused Household on financial services, particularly consumer banking, and began divesting noncore operations. Between 1985 and 1988 it bought several finance companies and banks, including BGC Finance in Australia (exiting in 1994).

In the late 1980s Household began securitizing some of its receivables (as a bond-like security), freeing it of liability for delinquencies and defaults.

The firm began restructuring in 1994, eventually tossing out brokerage, first-mortgage, banking, and most insurance operations. It was fitting that Clark — who oversaw the expansion of the firm's financial services businesses — gave the reins of power to William Aldinger (who became chairman in 1996) just as Household was getting rid of the last of those businesses.

In 1996 Household increased its credit card reach through an affinity card program for AFL-CIO members and through an agreement to jointly manage Barnett Banks' card business in Florida and Georgia (a deal that came to a close when Barnett was purchased by what is now Bank of America). In 1997 Household bought the consumer finance operations of Transamerica and moved into the hot area of subprime auto loans through its purchase of ACC Consumer Finance. The following year the company paid around $8 billion for Beneficial Corporation, which in recent years had been struggling with an unfocused business plan. In assimilating Beneficial, Household cut 1,000 jobs and 250 offices.

In the late 1990s Household realigned its credit card operations. In 1998 the company sold a chunk of its card portfolio to Fleet Financial Group and in 1999 embarked on a program to build its subprime card offerings.

Chairman and CEO: William F. Aldinger, age 51,
$3,188,463 pay
**Group Executive Private Label, UK, Canada, Insurance,
US Consumer Banking, and Auto Finance:**
Lawrence N. Bangs, age 62, $1,240,385 pay
Group Executive US Consumer Finance: Gary Gilmer,
age 49, $1,254,809 pay
Group Executive, U.S. BankCard: Siddarth N. Mehta,
age 40, $959,615 pay
EVP and CFO: David A. Schoenholz, age 47,
$1,175,482 pay
SVP Human Resources: Colin P. Kelly, age 56
SVP, General Counsel, and Secretary:
Kenneth H. Robin, age 52
Managing Director and Treasurer: Edgar D. Ancona
Managing Director and CEO, HFC of Canada:
Thomas G. Arndt
**National Director, Pricing, Profit & Risk, Household
Retail Services USA:** Susan E. Artmann
VP Corporate Law and Assistant Secretary:
John W. Blenke, age 43
**Deputy Managing Director, COO, Household Retail
Services USA:** Charles A. Colip
Managing Director, HFC Sales: Thomas M. Detelich
Group Managing Director, Retail Finance:
Rocco J. Fabiano
Managing Director and Chief Information Officer:
Kenneth H. Harvey, age 38
VP Investor Relations: Craig A. Streem, age 49
Auditors: Arthur Andersen LLP

LOCATIONS

HQ: 2700 Sanders Rd., Prospect Heights, IL 60070
Phone: 847-564-5000   **Fax:** 847-205-7401
Web site: http://www.household.com

PRODUCTS/OPERATIONS

1998 Sales

	$ mil.	% of total
Finance income	5,604	64
Securitization income	1,549	18
Fee income	600	7
Insurance revenues	493	6
Investment income	161	2
Other interest	57	—
Other income	244	3
Total	**8,708**	**100**

Selected Subsidiaries
Hamilton Investments, Inc.
Household Bank, f.s.b.
Household Finance Corporation
  Beneficial Corporation
  HFC Card Funding Corporation
  HFC Revolving Corporation
  Household Automotive Finance Corporation
  Household Card Services, Inc.
  Household Consumer Loan Corporation
Household Finance Industrial Loan Company
Household Reinsurance Ltd. (Bermuda)

COMPETITORS

Advanta	FIRSTPLUS Financial
The Associates	Group
Bank of America	GE Capital
BANK ONE	MBNA
Capital One Financial	Mercury Finance
Chase Manhattan	Metris
Citigroup	Money Store
ContiFinancial	Providian Financial
Delta Financial	Wells Fargo
First Union	World Acceptance

HISTORICAL FINANCIALS & EMPLOYEES

NYSE symbol: HI FYE: December 31	Annual Growth	1989	1990	1991	1992	1993	1994	1995	1996	1997	1998
Sales ($ mil.)	10.7%	3,490	4,320	4,594	4,181	4,455	4,603	5,144	5,059	5,503	8,708
Net income ($ mil.)	9.1%	240	235	150	191	299	368	453	539	687	524
Income as % of sales	—	6.9%	5.4%	3.3%	4.6%	6.7%	8.0%	8.8%	10.6%	12.5%	6.0%
Earnings per share ($)	0.1%	1.02	0.96	0.52	0.64	0.95	1.17	1.43	1.77	2.16	1.03
Stock price - FY high ($)	—	10.91	8.87	10.49	10.07	13.47	13.24	22.77	32.68	43.29	53.69
Stock price - FY low ($)	—	7.72	3.23	4.58	6.91	8.97	9.49	11.95	17.32	26.18	23.00
Stock price - FY close ($)	18.4%	8.64	5.47	8.53	9.87	10.86	12.36	19.81	30.72	42.50	39.63
P/E - high	—	11	9	20	16	14	11	16	18	20	52
P/E - low	—	8	3	9	11	9	8	8	10	12	22
Dividends per share ($)	2.3%	0.36	0.36	0.37	0.38	0.39	0.41	0.43	0.47	0.53	0.44
Book value per share ($)	9.6%	5.63	6.34	6.38	6.46	7.30	7.58	9.22	10.09	14.03	12.88
Employees	5.5%	14,500	14,500	14,500	13,397	16,900	15,500	13,000	14,700	14,900	23,500

STOCK PRICE HISTORY

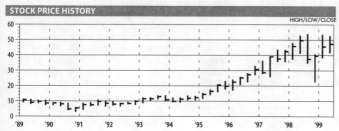

HIGH/LOW/CLOSE

1998 FISCAL YEAR-END

Debt ratio: 86.3%
Return on equity: 8.4%
Cash ($ mil.): —
Current ratio: —
Long-term debt ($ mil.): 40,357
No. of shares (mil.): 483
Dividends
  Yield: 1.1%
  Payout: 42.7%
Market value ($ mil.): 19,147

HUGHES ELECTRONICS

OVERVIEW

Hughes Electronics' operations are overflowing with space. The El Segundo, California-based, publicly traded unit of General Motors charts the heavens as a satellite and wireless communications company. Its Hughes Space and Communications operation (nearly 45% of sales) is the world's largest satellite maker, and is shifting focus from traditional defense markets toward entertainment and Internet transmissions. Telecommunications equipment arm Hughes Network Systems supplies wireless business networks and cellular mobile systems. The company also owns 81% of PanAmSat, a

19-satellite (with more expected by mid-2000) network.

Hughes has pared electronics interests while transforming itself into a subscriber-based communication services company. Its DIRECTV unit is the largest US satellite TV broadcaster, offering 210 channels of programming to more than 7 million customers. It is also developing the Spaceway global network, which will supply service providers' customers with two-way broadband video and data on demand.

Well-publicized satellite glitches and manufacturing delays have inspired Hughes to fine-tune its quality control efforts.

HISTORY

Hughes Electronics' roots go back to 1932, when Hughes Aircraft was founded to build experimental airplanes for Howard Hughes, who set a number of world airspeed records with the company's H-1 racer. During WWII the company began building a mammoth flying boat to serve as a troop carrier, but the *Spruce Goose* wasn't completed until 1947, when Hughes piloted it for its only flight (to silence critics who claimed it couldn't fly).

After WWII the company began moving into the growing defense electronics field. In 1953 it underwent a major shake-up when about 80 of its top engineers walked out, dissatisfied with Howard Hughes, who was becoming more distant and difficult.

The US Air Force threatened to cancel the company's contracts because of Hughes' erratic behavior, so he transferred the company's assets to the Howard Hughes Medical Institute (with himself as its sole trustee) and hired former Bendix Aviation executive Lawrence Hyland to run the company. Hyland rebuilt its research staff, and the institute produced the first beam of coherent laser light (1960) and placed the first communications satellite into geosynchronous orbit (1963). The Hughes-built Surveyor landed on the moon in 1966.

When Hughes died in 1976, a board of trustees was created to oversee the institute. In 1984 the Department of Defense canceled several missile contracts and the firm found it difficult to fund research and development.

The next year the institute sold Hughes Aircraft to General Motors (GM) for $5.2 billion. GM teamed its Delco Electronics auto parts unit with Hughes to form GM Hughes Electronics (GMHE). GMHE acquired General Dynamics' missile business in 1992 and installed former IBM executive Michael Armstrong as CEO. He

cut personnel by 25% and refocused the company on commercial electronics.

In 1995 GMHE became Hughes Electronics and launched its DIRECTV satellite service. That year the company strengthened its defense by acquiring CAE-Link (training and technical services) and Magnavox Electronic Systems (warfare and communications systems). The company in 1996 bought a majority stake in satellite communications provider PanAmSat.

In 1997 GM sold its defense electronics unit to Raytheon for $9.5 billion, and merged Hughes' Delco Electronics into GM subsidiary Delphi Automotive Systems, creating the world's largest automotive supplier. Armstrong left Hughes to head AT&T and was replaced by Michael Smith, brother of GM CEO John Smith.

In 1998 the company boosted its stake in PanAmSat to 81%. Hughes took a public relations hit that year when the control processors of several of its satellites failed. The most dramatic outage temporarily halted most US pager activity. Lower sales due to Asia's financial crisis and the additional PanAmSat investment contributed to a drop in profits for 1998.

To increase its customers and broadcast channels, Hughes in 1999 bought United States Satellite Broadcasting for $1.6 billion and the satellite business of rival PRIMESTAR (now PhoenixStar) for $1.3 billion. Also that year Hughes began building its Spaceway broadband satellite network (expected to launch in 2002). America Online invested $1.5 billion in the company, with plans to develop a satellite-based Internet service.

OFFICERS

Chairman and CEO: Michael T. Smith
VC: Steven D. Dorfman
President and COO: Charles H. Noski
EVP: Jack A. Shaw
SVP and CFO: Roxanne S. Austin
SVP: Eddy W. Hartenstein
SVP: Pradman P. Kaul
SVP: Tig H. Krekel
SVP Human Resources: Sandra Harrison
VP: Larry D. Hunter
VP and Treasurer: Mark McEachen
VP and Chief Information Officer, Hughes Electronics and Hughes Space and Communications: K. S. "Rhadha" Rhadhakrishnan, age 48
VP: Roderick M. Sherwood III
VP and General Counsel: Marcy J. K. Tiffany
VP Corporate Communications: George H. Jamison, age 42
VP Strategic Planning and Business Development: Mufit Cinali
Secretary: Jan L. Williamson
Controller: Michael J. Gaines
Auditors: Deloitte & Touche LLP

LOCATIONS

HQ: Hughes Electronics Corporation,
200 N. Sepulveda Blvd., El Segundo, CA 90245
Phone: 310-364-6000   **Fax:** 310-568-6390
Web site: http://www.hughes.com

Hughes Electronics has operations worldwide and a fleet of 19 communications satellites orbiting the earth.

PRODUCTS/OPERATIONS

1998 Sales

	$ mil.	% of total
Satellite manufacturing	2,493	42
Direct-to-home broadcast	1,814	30
Network systems	1,001	17
Satellite services	644	11
Other	12	—
Total	**5,964**	**100**

1998 Sales

	$ mil.	% of total
Products	3,360	56
Broadcasting, leasing & other services	2,604	44
Total	**5,964**	**100**

Operations
DIRECTV (direct broadcast satellite services)
Hughes Network Systems (telecommunications and satellite equipment)
Hughes Space and Communications (satellite manufacturing)
PanAmSat (81%-owned, satellite network operation)
Spaceway (broadband communications)

COMPETITORS

Alcatel	Lockheed Martin
ANTEC	Loral Space
AT&T Broadband &	Motorola
Internet Services	Orbital Sciences
COMSAT	Siemens
EchoStar	Teledesic
Communications	Teleglobe
GE	Time Warner
INTELSAT	Williams Companies
Iridium	

HISTORICAL FINANCIALS & EMPLOYEES

NYSE symbol: GMH FYE: December 31	Annual Growth	1989	1990	1991	1992	1993	1994	1995	1996	1997	1998
Sales ($ mil.)	(6.9%)	11,359	11,723	11,541	12,297	13,518	14,062	14,714	15,744	5,128	5,964
Net income ($ mil.)	(11.9%)	781	726	559	(922)	798	925	1,108	1,151	450	251
Income as % of sales	—	6.9%	6.2%	4.8%	—	5.9%	6.6%	7.5%	7.3%	8.8%	4.2%
Earnings per share ($)	(11.0%)	1.94	1.82	1.26	(0.11)	2.30	0.08	0.07	0.46	1.18	0.68
Stock price - FY high ($)	—	32.13	25.63	21.00	26.13	42.38	22.69	28.10	38.36	40.00	57.88
Stock price - FY low ($)	—	23.50	17.00	13.13	14.25	22.88	17.42	18.69	25.29	27.54	30.38
Stock price - FY close ($)	5.0%	25.50	17.63	14.75	25.75	39.00	19.60	27.61	31.61	36.94	39.69
P/E - high	—	17	14	17	—	18	284	401	83	34	85
P/E - low	—	12	9	10	—	10	218	267	55	23	45
Dividends per share ($)	(100.0%)	0.72	0.72	0.72	0.72	0.72	0.98	0.92	0.96	1.00	0.00
Book value per share ($)	(0.0%)	79.00	81.00	82.20	68.16	73.28	79.76	85.28	91.04	80.01	78.85
Employees	(16.1%)	73,200	93,600	92,900	89,300	78,000	77,100	84,000	86,000	15,000	15,000

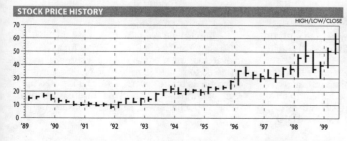

STOCK PRICE HISTORY
HIGH/LOW/CLOSE

1998 FISCAL YEAR-END
Debt ratio: 8.5%
Return on equity: 3.0%
Cash ($ mil.): 1,342
Current ratio: 1.91
Long-term debt ($ mil.): 779
No. of shares (mil.): 106
Dividends
  Yield: —
  Payout: —
Market value ($ mil.): 4,219

HUMANA INC.

OVERVIEW

Although it is one of the top health care providers in the US, Humana is finding that maintaining a balance between humane care and healthy earnings might be the trickiest operation of them all.

The Louisville, Kentucky-based firm provides services primarily through HMOs and PPOs, but it also serves Medicare and Medicaid patients and select military beneficiaries through a contract with the Department of Defense known as TRICARE. The company also offers workers' compensation, group life, and dental plans. Humana has more than 6 million members, with nearly one-quarter residing in Florida.

Struggling with rising medical costs (thanks, in part, to a mangled contract renewal with Columbia/HCA) and lowered reimbursement rates for Medicare (30% of its sales), Humana is raising premiums and exiting certain markets.

Chairman David Jones owns 5% of the company.

HISTORY

In 1961 David Jones and Wendell Cherry, two Louisville, Kentucky, lawyers, bought a nursing home as a real estate investment. Within six years their company, Extendicare, with only eight homes, had become the largest nursing home chain in the US.

Noticing that hospitals received more money per patient per day than nursing homes — and faced with a glutted nursing home market — the partners took their company public in 1968 to finance the buying of hospitals (one per month from 1968 to 1971). The company then sold its 40 nursing homes. Sales rose 13-fold in the next five years, and in 1973 the company changed its name to Humana.

By 1975 Humana had built 27 hospitals in the South and Southwest. It targeted young, privately insured patients, and kept its charity caseload and bad-debt expenses low. Three years later Humana, the #3 for-profit hospital operator in the country, moved up a notch when it bought #2 American Medicorp.

In 1983 the government began reimbursing Medicare payments (40% of the company's sales) based on fixed rates. Counting on its high hospital occupancy, in 1984 the company launched Humana Health Care Plans, rewarding doctors and patients who used Humana hospitals. However, hospital occupancy dropped, and the company closed several clinics. Humana's net income fell 75% in 1986.

The company responded by lowering premiums to attract employers. In 1990 Humana acquired Chicago's Michael Reese Hospital and an associated health plan, setting the stage for intense price competition with Blue Cross and Blue Shield in Chicago. Wendell Cherry died in 1991.

With hospital profits down, in 1993 Jones spun off Humana's 76 hospitals as Galen Healthcare, which Columbia bought to form the nucleus of Columbia/HCA Healthcare. Humana used the cash to expand its HMO membership, acquiring Group Health Association (an HMO in the Washington, DC, area) and CareNetwork (a Milwaukee HMO). The next year Humana added 1.3 million members with the acquisition of EMPHESYS, and the company's income, which had stagnated since the salad days of the late 1980s and early 1990s, seemed headed in the right direction.

In the mid-1990s cutthroat premiums failed to cover rising health care costs as the company's hospital use soared out of control, particularly in its newly acquired Washington, DC, market. Profits dropped 94%, and Humana's already tense relationship with doctors and members worsened. President and COO Wayne Smith and CFO Roger Drury resigned as part of a management shake-up, and newly appointed president Gregory Wolf offered to drop the company's gag clause after the Florida Physicians Association threatened to sue.

A reorganized Humana rebounded in 1997. The company pulled out of 13 unprofitable markets, including PrimeHealth of Alabama and its Washington, DC, health plan. Refocusing on core markets in the Midwest and Southeast, Humana acquired Physician Corporation of America (PCA) and ChoiceCare, a Cincinnati HMO. Wolf replaced Jones as CEO in 1997.

In a step intended to cut costs, Humana agreed in 1998 to be bought by United Health-Care (now UnitedHealth Group). The deal was abandoned, however, when United HealthCare took a $900 million charge in advance of the purchase. Humana found savings by pruning its Medicare HMO business instead.

Humana did everything *but* party in 1999. The company faced RICO charges for allegedly overcharging members for co-insurance; it agreed to repay $15 million in Medicare overpayments to the government; and it raised the ire of filmmaker Michael Moore after denying a member a life-saving pancreas transplant.

OFFICERS

Chairman: David A. Jones, age 67
SVP, Sales Marketing and Business Development: Kenneth J. Fasola, age 39, $490,456 pay
SVP and Chief Information Officer: Bruce J. Goodman
SVP, Human Resources: Bonnie C. Hathcock
SVP and General Counsel: Arthur P. Hipwell, $511,724 pay
SVP, Health System Management: Michael B. McAllister, age 46, $861,580 pay
SVP and CFO: James E. Murray, age 45
SVP, National Contracting: Bruce D. Perkins, age 44
SVP and Chief Medical Officer: Jerry D. Reeves, age 54, $540,978 pay
SVP, Specialty Products and Services and International Businesses: Kirk E. Rothrock, age 40
SVP, Market Segment Management: George W. Vieth Jr., age 43
Regional VP: Douglas R. Carlisle
VP, Investment Management and Treasurer: James W. Doucette
VP, Finance and Controller: David M. Krebs
VP, Women's Health: Mitzi R. Krockover
VP, Corporate Development: Thomas J. Liston
VP and Chief Actuary: David R. Nelson, age 44
VP, Corporate Communications: Thomas J. Noland Jr.
VP, Customer Service and Operations: Gregory K. Rotherham, age 42
Auditors: PricewaterhouseCoopers LLP

LOCATIONS

HQ: The Humana Bldg., 500 W. Main St., Louisville, KY 40202
Phone: 502-580-1000   **Fax:** 502-580-4188
Web site: http://www.humana.com

Humana operates in 15 states and Puerto Rico.

PRODUCTS/OPERATIONS

1998 Sales

	$ mil.	% of total
Commercial premiums	5,257	55
Medicare HMO	2,918	30
TRICARE	800	8
Medicaid & other	622	7
Total	**9,597**	**100**

COMPETITORS

Aetna
Cerulean
CIGNA
Foundation Health Systems
Kaiser Foundation
New York Life
Oxford Health Plans
PacifiCare
Prudential
UnitedHealth Group

HISTORICAL FINANCIALS & EMPLOYEES

NYSE symbol: HUM FYE: December 31	Annual Growth	1989	1990	1991	1992	1993	1994	1995	1996	1997	1998
Sales ($ mil.)	9.9%	4,088	4,852	5,865	4,043	3,137	3,654	4,605	6,677	7,880	9,597
Net income ($ mil.)	(7.3%)	256	310	355	123	89	176	190	12	173	129
Income as % of sales	—	6.3%	6.4%	6.1%	3.0%	2.8%	4.8%	4.1%	0.2%	2.2%	1.3%
Earnings per share ($)	(8.5%)	1.71	3.00	2.26	0.77	0.55	1.07	1.16	0.07	1.05	0.77
Stock price - FY high ($)	—	29.33	33.92	35.08	29.50	19.13	25.38	28.00	28.88	25.31	32.13
Stock price - FY low ($)	—	16.25	23.50	22.75	17.00	6.13	15.88	17.00	15.00	17.38	12.25
Stock price - FY close ($)	(5.4%)	29.33	28.08	26.88	20.50	17.75	22.63	27.38	19.00	20.75	17.81
P/E - high	—	17	11	16	38	35	24	24	413	24	42
P/E - low	—	10	8	10	22	11	15	15	214	17	16
Dividends per share ($)	(100.0%)	0.63	0.00	0.00	0.00	0.00	0.00	0.00	0.00	0.00	0.00
Book value per share ($)	1.3%	8.99	11.18	12.70	12.70	5.54	6.56	7.94	7.94	9.15	10.08
Employees	(12.7%)	55,100	62,000	70,500	65,800	10,100	12,000	16,800	18,300	19,500	16,300

STOCK PRICE HISTORY

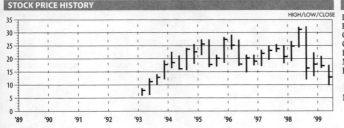

HIGH/LOW/CLOSE

1998 FISCAL YEAR-END

Debt ratio: 25.3%
Return on equity: 7.6%
Cash ($ mil.): 913
Current ratio: 1.18
Long-term debt ($ mil.): 573
No. of shares (mil.): 168
Dividends
　Yield: —
　Payout: —
Market value ($ mil.): 2,983

HYATT CORPORATION

OVERVIEW

Chicago-based Hyatt is high at the top of the list of major US hotel operators, with a few rivals, such as Marriott and Hilton. Hyatt manages or licenses more than 110 full-service luxury hotels and resorts in North America and the Caribbean through its Hyatt Hotels; Hyatt International, a separate company, operates 80 hotels and resorts in 35 countries. In addition, Hyatt manages casinos at several of its hotels and runs a retirement community subsidiary called Classic Residence by Hyatt.

Hyatt caters to business travelers,

convention-goers, and upscale destination-oriented vacationers. The company offers specially designed Business Plan rooms with fax machines and 24-hour access to copiers, printers, and other business necessities. Camp Hyatt targets family travelers with educational games, activities, and programs for children.

Led by chairman, president, and CEO Thomas Pritzker, the company is owned by the Pritzker family, one of the US's wealthiest families (its net worth is estimated by *Forbes* at nearly $14 billion).

HISTORY

In 1881 Nicholas Pritzker left Kiev for Chicago, where his family's ascent to the ranks of America's wealthiest families began.

Nicholas' son A. N. left the family law practice in the 1930s and began investing in a variety of businesses. He turned a 1942 investment (Cory Corporation) worth $25,000 into $23 million by 1967.

After WWII, A. N.'s son Jay followed in his father's wheeling-and-dealing footsteps. In 1953, with the help of his father's banking connections, Jay purchased Colson Company and recruited his brother Bob, an industrial engineer, to restructure a company that made tricycles and US Navy rockets. By 1990 Jay and Bob had added 60 industrial companies, with annual sales exceeding $3 billion, to the entity they called the Marmon Group.

In 1957 Jay bought a hotel called Hyatt House, located near the Los Angeles airport, from Hyatt von Dehn. Jay added five locations by 1961 and hired his gregarious youngest brother, Donald, to manage the hotel company.

Hyatt went public in 1967, but the move that opened new vistas for the hotel chain was the purchase that year of an 800-room hotel in Atlanta that both Hilton and Marriott had turned down. John Portman's design, incorporating a 21-story atrium, a large fountain, and a revolving rooftop restaurant, became a Hyatt trademark.

The Pritzkers formed Hyatt International in 1969 to operate hotels overseas, and the company grew rapidly in the US and abroad during the 1970s. Donald Pritzker died in 1972, and the family decided to take the company private in 1979.

Much of Hyatt's growth in the 1970s came from contracts to manage, under the Hyatt banner, hotels built by other investors. When Hyatt's cut on those contracts shrank in the 1980s, it launched its own hotel and resort

developments under Nick Pritzker, a cousin to Jay and Bob. In 1988, with US and Japanese partners, it built the Hyatt Regency Waikoloa on Hawaii's Big Island for $360 million — a record for a hotel.

Through Hyatt subsidiaries, the Pritzkers bought bedraggled Braniff Airlines in 1983 as it emerged from bankruptcy. After a failed 1987 attempt to merge the airline with PanAm, the Pritzkers sold Braniff in 1988. Hyatt opened Classic Residence by Hyatt, a group of upscale retirement communities, in 1989.

In 1993 Hyatt sold the majority of its 85% interest in Ticketmaster to Paul Allen, co-founder of Microsoft. Hyatt joined Circus Circus (now Mandalay Resort Group) in 1994 to launch the *Grand Victoria*, the nation's largest cruising gaming vessel, at Elgin, Illinois. The next year, as part of a new strategy to manage both freestanding golf courses and those near Hyatt hotels, the company opened its first freestanding course: an 18-hole par 71 championship course on Aruba.

Hyatt Regency hotels hosted both the Republican (San Diego) and the Democratic (Chicago) national conventions in 1996. That year Hyatt said it would build a 500-room resort and casino, with a Jack Nicklaus-designed championship golf course, at Lake Las Vegas — a development on a man-made lake 17 miles from town.

In 1997 the company acquired hotels in Atlanta, San Francisco, and Miami as part of a plan to buy up to 30 hotels by the year 2000. President Thomas Pritzker, Jay's son, took over as chairman and CEO of Hyatt following his father's death in early 1999. The company continues to expand through acquisitions and new resort construction.

Chairman, President and CEO; Chairman Hyatt International Corporation: Thomas J. Pritzker, age 48
VC; Chairman and President, Hyatt Development Corporation; President, Hyatt Equities: Nicholas J. Pritzker, age 53
SVP Finance and Adminstration: Frank Borg
Chairman and President, Classic Residence by Hyatt: Penny S. Pritzker, age 39
President, Hyatt Hotel Corporation: Doug Geoga
President, Hyatt International Corporation: Bernd Chorengel
EVP, Hyatt Development Corporation: Scott D. Miller
EVP, Hyatt Hotels Corporation: Ed Rabin
SVP, Human Resources, Hyatt Hotels Corporation: Linda Olson
SVP Sales, Hyatt Hotels Corporation: Chuck Floyd
SVP Marketing, Hyatt Hotels Corporation: Tom O'Toole
Divisional VP (Eastern), Hyatt Hotels Corporation: Alex Alexander
Divisional VP (Southern), Hyatt Hotels Corporation: Tim Lindgren
Divisional VP (Resorts), Hyatt Hotels Corporation: Victor Lopez
Divisional VP (Western), Hyatt Hotels Corporation: John Orr
Divisional VP (Central), Hyatt Hotels Corporation: Steve Sokal
Associate General Counsel: Mary Catherine Sexton

LOCATIONS

HQ: 200 W. Madison St., Chicago, IL 60606
Phone: 312-750-1234 **Fax:** 312-750-8550
Web site: http://www.hyatt.com

Hyatt Corporation and sister company Hyatt International own, manage, or license hotels in Africa, Asia, Australia, Europe, Latin America, the Middle East, and the US.

PRODUCTS/OPERATIONS

Selected Operations
Camp Hyatt (designed for the needs of traveling families)
Classic Residence by Hyatt (upscale retirement communities)
Hyatt Hotels and Resorts
Hyatt Vacation Ownership (time-share resorts)
Regency Casinos

COMPETITORS

Accor
Bass
Canadian Pacific
Carlson
Carnival
Cendant
Four Seasons Hotels
Granada Group
Helmsley
Hilton
Hilton Group
Host Marriott
Loews
Marriott International
Promus Hotel
Rank
Ritz Carlton
Starwood Hotels & Resorts Worldwide
Trump
Walt Disney

HISTORICAL FINANCIALS & EMPLOYEES

Private company FYE: January 31	Annual Growth	1990	1991	1992	1993	1994	1995	1996	1997	1998	1999
Sales ($ mil.)	1.0%	3,101	2,915	1,350	1,460	950	1,240	2,500	2,900	3,250	3,400
Employees	4.2%	55,195	49,820	51,275	52,275	47,000	54,000	65,000	80,000	80,000	80,000

1992–95 sales do not include revenue for franchised or managed hotels.

SALES HISTORY

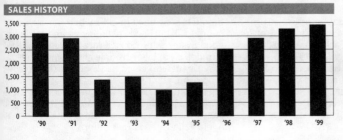

IBP, INC.

OVERVIEW

IBP produces the stuff of meat lovers' dreams and vegetarians' worst nightmares. Dakota Dunes, South Dakota-based IBP is the world's largest processor of fresh beef and a top US pork producer. More than 90% of the company's sales come from producing boxed meat and pork products at nearly 25 facilities, all located in western North America (one is in Canada; the rest are in the US). Nonedible remains are processed and sold to manufacturers of animal feed, leather, and pharmaceuticals. Subsidiary Thorn Apple Valley produces bacon, sliced hams, and hot dogs.

To guard against the vagaries of the meat market, IBP is expanding its value-added products business through acquisition. Through more than 20 facilities nationwide, the division makes value-added meat products (pizza toppings, taco fillings, deli products) and frozen, preprepared foods (hors d'oeuvres, soups, desserts, pizza crusts).

IBP customers include supermarkets, food service distributors, meat processors, and restaurants, among others. Although about 85% of its sales come from the US, the firm has operations in more than 50 countries worldwide.

Agribusiness giant Archer Daniels Midland owns about 14% of IBP.

HISTORY

A. D. Anderson and Currier Holman's experiences in the meatpacking business convinced them that the industry needed modernization. In 1960 they formed Iowa Beef Packers and, with their first plant in Denison, Iowa, broke with tradition. To cut costs and save time, the company built facilities in rural areas where cattle were raised and workers were less likely to unionize. Carefully monitored demand and more efficient slaughtering kept inventory from building up; almost as soon as a steer walked into a plant, it exited in a considerably less animated manner.

Iowa Beef Packers' highly automated plants were manned by local, unskilled workers with few benefits. Employees organized and in 1965 walked out over the right to strike. Two years later union relations were spoiled further when Iowa Beef Packers began cutting meat into smaller portions (minus fat and bone), thus reducing supermarkets' need for butchers. "Boxed beef," as it is called, soon became the standard among meat companies.

By 1969, when Iowa Beef Packers had eight plants in the Midwest, workers in Dakota City, Nebraska, struck over pay. When three Iowa plants shut down, the company sued the United Food and Commercial Workers for sabotage and other interference. Vandalism, death threats, shootings, and 56 bombings (one at a VP's home) ensued over several months in a struggle, sparked in part by demands for a raise of 20 cents an hour. Iowa Beef Packers eventually won $2.6 million in damages. In 1970 it changed its name to Iowa Beef Processors.

In the early 1970s Holman paid a mob-related meat broker almost $1 million to ensure that unions wouldn't interfere with New York City distribution. The company and Holman were convicted of bribery.

As Iowa Beef Processors expanded (Texas, 1975; Idaho and Washington, 1976; Kansas, 1980; and Illinois, 1983), it ran into more trouble. In the late 1970s it was investigated for anticompetitive practices, but the inquiry was eventually dropped. During the 1980s Iowa Beef Processors was fined $2.6 million and penalized by OSHA for not reporting workers' hand injuries caused by meat-cutting techniques.

Armand Hammer's Occidental Petroleum bought Iowa Beef Processors in 1981. The following year it changed its name to IBP and entered the pork business. In 1987, 49% of IBP was sold to the public. Hammer died in 1990, and the meat business was spun off to shareholders the next year.

IBP acquired Heinhold (hog marketing) in 1993 and beef-boning plants in Texas, Iowa, and Nebraska two years later. In 1996 Japanese consumers, scared by an E. coli outbreak and mad-cow disease, steered away from foreign meats, causing a dip in sales. An E. coli scare in 1998 forced IBP to recall 140 tons of ground beef.

Expanding further in 1997, IBP opened a pork processing plant in China and acquired Foodbrands America (pizza and deli meats), Bruss Company (premium meats), and Hudson Foods' hamburger plant.

The beefing up of the value-added meat products continued in 1999 when the company bought Russer Foods (deli meats) and H&M Food Systems (precooked meat products). IBP found itself in labor trouble again when the majority of workers at its Pasco, Washington, processing plant struck over wages and working conditions; the workers prevailed with an improved labor contract. In August the company acquired distressed meat producer Thorn Apple Valley for $117.5 million.

Chairman and CEO: Robert L. Peterson, age 66,
$5,568,006 pay
President and COO: Richard L. Bond, age 51,
$1,067,467 pay
President, Fresh Meats: Eugene D. Leman, age 56,
$672,300 pay
CFO; President, IBP Enterprises: Larry Shipley, age 43,
$549,150 pay
EVP, Manufacturing, Fresh Meats: James V. Lochner,
age 46
EVP, Fresh Meats Sales and Marketing:
Charles F. Mostek, age 51
EVP, Operations Services: Kenneth L. Rose, age 54
EVP, Manufacturing Support, Fresh Meats:
Jerry S. Scott, age 53
SVP, International: Roel G. M. Andriessen
SVP, Information Technology: Roger J. Jones
VP and Controller, IBP Enterprises: Craig J. Hart,
age 43, $162,083 pay
VP, Human Resources: Kenneth J. Kimbro
President and CEO, Foodbrands America, Inc.:
R. Randolph Devening, age 56, $1,917,650 pay
President, Value-Added Products: L. Jack Dunn Jr.
President, Value-Added Ground Meats: David C. Layhee,
age 54
President and COO, The Bruss Company:
Daniel L. Timm
EVP, Hides, Leather, and Skins:
Kenneth W. Browning Jr., age 49
SVP, Finance, Foodbrands America, Inc.:
Bryant P. Bynum
**SVP, Foodbrands America, Inc.; President, Continental
Deli Foods, Inc.:** Raymond J. Haefele
**SVP, Foodbrands America, Inc.; President, Doskocil
Food Service Company, LLC:** Thomas G. McCarley
Auditors: PricewaterhouseCoopers LLP

LOCATIONS

HQ: 800 Stevens Port Dr., Ste. 836,
Dakota Dunes, SD 57049
Phone: 605-235-2061   **Fax:** 605-235-2068
Web site: http://www.ibpinc.com

IBP has plants and sales offices in Canada, China, Japan,
Korea, Mexico, Russia, Taiwan, the UK, and the US.

1998 Sales

	$ mil.	% of total
US	10,953	86
Japan	785	6
Canada	422	3
Mexico	173	1
South Korea	134	1
Other countries	382	3
Total	**12,849**	**100**

PRODUCTS/OPERATIONS

1998 Sales

	$ mil.	% of total
Fresh meats	11,696	91
IBP Enterprises	1,153	9
Total	**12,849**	**100**

COMPETITORS

American Foods	Hormel
Bridgford Foods	Keystone Foods
Cargill	Seaboard
ConAgra	Smithfield Foods
Continental Grain	Thorn Apple Valley
Farmland Industries	Tyson Foods
Heinz	

HISTORICAL FINANCIALS & EMPLOYEES

NYSE symbol: IBP FYE: December 31	Annual Growth	1989	1990	1991	1992	1993	1994	1995	1996	1997	1998
Sales ($ mil.)	3.9%	9,129	10,185	10,388	11,128	11,671	12,075	12,668	12,539	13,259	12,849
Net income ($ mil.)	20.6%	35	48	1	64	90	182	258	199	117	190
Income as % of sales	—	0.4%	0.5%	0.0%	0.6%	0.8%	1.5%	2.0%	1.6%	0.9%	1.5%
Earnings per share ($)	20.8%	0.37	0.51	0.02	0.67	0.94	1.90	2.69	2.07	1.25	2.03
Stock price - FY high ($)	—	8.88	10.88	13.13	10.31	13.13	17.75	33.63	29.00	26.00	29.44
Stock price - FY low ($)	—	6.75	7.38	6.44	7.25	8.75	11.31	14.56	22.50	20.38	16.56
Stock price - FY close ($)	15.9%	7.69	10.44	7.31	10.06	12.94	15.13	25.25	24.25	20.94	29.13
P/E - high	—	24	21	657	15	14	9	13	14	21	15
P/E - low	—	18	14	322	11	9	6	5	11	16	8
Dividends per share ($)	(11.5%)	0.30	0.30	0.30	0.20	0.10	0.10	0.10	0.10	0.10	0.10
Book value per share ($)	12.5%	5.25	5.40	5.10	5.62	6.45	8.23	10.80	12.72	13.36	15.18
Employees	5.9%	23,793	25,290	26,500	27,500	29,200	30,700	34,000	34,000	38,000	40,000

STOCK PRICE HISTORY
HIGH/LOW/CLOSE

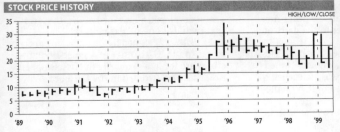

1998 FISCAL YEAR-END

Debt ratio: 29.1%
Return on equity: 13.6%
Cash ($ mil.): 27
Current ratio: 1.27
Long-term debt ($ mil.): 576
No. of shares (mil.): 92
Dividends
  Yield: 0.3%
  Payout: 4.9%
Market value ($ mil.): 2,689

IGA, INC.

Independent grocers have found they can boost their business by being a little less independent. More than 3,600 stores belong to Chicago-based IGA (which stands for "Independent Grocers Alliance" or "International Grocers Alliance"). The alliance is the world's largest voluntary supermarket network, with stores in 47 states and about 30 countries. Collectively, its members are one of the largest food operations in terms of sales in North America.

IGA is owned by 18 marketing and distribution companies worldwide, including Fleming Companies and SUPERVALU. In addition to flying the IGA Red Oval banner and having access to IGA Brand private-label products, members receive advertising and marketing services, educational programs, and volume discounts through the food distributors that control it. Roughly 200 rural stores in the alliance also sell gas.

The association continues its expansion overseas. The first US grocer to go into China and Singapore, IGA is now looking to move into Europe, focusing on signing up independent food retailers in Poland.

IGA was founded in Chicago in 1926 by a group led by accountant Frank Grimes. During the 1920s chains began to dominate the grocery store industry. Grimes, an accountant for many grocery wholesalers, saw an opportunity to develop a network of independent grocers that could compete with the burgeoning chains. Grimes and five associates — Gene Flack, Louis Groebe, W. K. Hunter, H. V. Swenson, and William Thompson — created IGA.

Their idea was to "level the playing field" for independent grocers and chain stores by taking advantage of volume buying and mass marketing. IGA originally acted as a purchasing agent for its wholesalers but eventually passed that duty to the wholesalers. The group's first members were Poughkeepsie, New York-based grocery distributor W. T. Reynolds Company and the 69 grocery stores it serviced.

IGA focused on adding distributors and retailers, and it soon added wholesaler Fleming-Wilson (now Fleming Companies) and Winston & Newell (now SUPERVALU). In 1930 it hired Babe Ruth as a spokesman; other celebrity endorsers during the period included Jackie Cooper, Jack Dempsey, and Popeye. IGA also sponsored a radio program called the *IGA Home Town Hour.*

In 1945 the company introduced the Foodliner format, a design for stores larger than 4,000 sq. ft. The next year IGA introduced the 30-ft.-by-100-ft. Precision Store — designed so customers had to pass all the other merchandise in the store to get to the dairy and bread sections.

Grimes retired as president in 1951. He was succeeded by his son, Don, who continued to expand the company. Don was succeeded in 1968 by Richard Jones, head of IGA member J. M. Jones Co.

Thomas Haggai was named chairman of the company in 1976. A Baptist minister, radio commentator, and former CIA employee, Haggai had come to the attention of Grimes in 1960 when he praised Christian Scientists in one of his radio broadcasts. Grimes, a Christian Scientist, asked Haggai to speak at an IGA convention and eventually asked him to join the IGA board. Haggai, who became CEO in 1986, tightened the restrictions for IGA members, weeding out many of the smaller, low-volume mom-and-pop stores making up much of the group's network.

Haggai also began a push for international expansion. In 1988 the organization signed a deal with Japanese food company C. Itoh (now ITOCHU) to open a distribution outlet in Tokyo. The company moved into Australia that year and into the Papua New Guinea market in 1990.

Three years later IGA began an international television advertising campaign, a first for the supermarket industry. The group licensed grocery stores in four Caribbean countries in 1994 and signed a deal to enter China. Additionally, IGA launched its first line of private-label products for an ethnic food market, introducing several Mexican food products.

The company signed a partnership in 1995 with Singapore's largest grocery store chain, NTUC Fairprice Co-operative, thereby gaining 47 stores in Singapore. In 1996 IGA opened stores in Hawaii and South Africa, and the next year it opened a store in Brazil. In 1998 the group developed a new format for its stores that included on-site gas pumps.

SUPERVALU signed 54 independent grocery stores to the IGA banner in August 1999; the stores are located primarily in Mississippi and Arkansas and Trinidad in the Caribbean.

OFFICERS

Chairman and CEO: Thomas S. Haggai
SVP: Duane Martin, age 32
VP, Benefit Trust: Ronald Bujko
VP, IGA International: Paul Goelzer
VP, IGA Brand and Equipment: Patrick Sylvester
VP, Communications & Events: Barbara G. Wiest
Director, Public Relations: Shannan Blagg
Human Resources: Juanita Brodkorb
Auditors: Arthur Andersen

LOCATIONS

HQ: 8725 W. Higgins Rd., Chicago, IL 60631-2773
Phone: 773-693-4520   **Fax:** 773-693-1271
Web site: http://www.igainc.com

IGA has operations in all 47 states and 32 other
countries, commonwealths, and territories.

PRODUCTS/OPERATIONS

Distributors/Owners
Bozzuto's, Inc.
C.I. Foods Systems Co., Ltd.
The Copps Corp.
Davids Ltd.
Fairway Foods of Michigan, Inc.
Fleming Companies, Inc.
Foodland Associated Ltd.
Great North Foods
IGA Brasil
IGA South Africa
Ira Higdon Grocery Co.
McLane Polska
Merchants Distributors, Inc.
Nash Finch Co.
Pearl River Distribution Ltd.
SUPERVALU INC.
Tripifoods, Inc.
W. Lee Flowers & Co., Inc.

Selected Joint Operations and Services
Advertising
Community service programs
Equipment purchase
IGA Brand (private-label products)
IGA Grocergram (in-house magazine)
Internet services
Marketing
Merchandising
Red Oval Family (manufacturer/IGA collaboration on
 sales and marketing efforts and other activities)
Volume buying

COMPETITORS

A&P
Albertson's
Associated Wholesale Grocers
BJs Wholesale Club
C&S Wholesale
Daiei
Delhaize
George Weston
Hannaford Bros.
H-E-B
Ito-Yokado
Kroger
Meijer
Penn Traffic
Publix
Roundy's
Royal Ahold
Safeway
Spartan Stores
Topco Associates
Wakefern Food
Wal-Mart
Winn-Dixie

HISTORICAL FINANCIALS & EMPLOYEES

Association FYE: December 31	Annual Growth	1989	1990	1991	1992	1993	1994	1995	1996	1997	1998
Sales ($ mil.)	6.3%	10,400	11,100	11,500	15,900	16,500	17,000	17,100	16,800	18,000	18,000
Employees	(10.9%)	—	—	—	—	—	—	130,000	128,000	135,000	92,000

1989-91 sales do not include Canada.

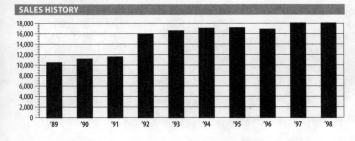

SALES HISTORY

IKON OFFICE SOLUTIONS, INC.

OVERVIEW

IKON is struggling to remain an object of uncritical devotion. Malvern, Pennsylvania-based business equipment specialist IKON Office Solutions is the #2 supplier and servicer of copiers, behind Xerox. Through acquisitions the firm has assembled a network of more than 1,000 independent copier and office technology dealers in North America and Europe. IKON's three divisions sell and lease Canon, Ricoh, and other name-brand copiers, fax machines, and office equipment; contract with legal firms and businesses to help manage huge quantities of documents; and offer information systems support.

A runaway acquisition strategy (more than 200 companies in three years) has left IKON's bottom line smudged in red and its stock price low on toner. After a management shake-up, a new team headed by president and CEO James Forese cut jobs, curtailed buying, and intensified a push of high-volume color and digital products.

IKON wants to duplicate the success it had before it changed its name from Alco Standard and spun off its Unisource paper distribution division in 1997. Its moves reflect a plan to become a one-stop office technology provider.

HISTORY

Tinkham Veale, a mechanical engineer from Cleveland, married the daughter of A. C. Ernst of the Ernst & Ernst accounting firm in 1941. Ernst helped Veale buy a stake in an engineered goods manufacturer, which prospered during WWII. Veale retired at age 37 to breed and race horses. He invested his earnings, became a millionaire by 1951, and joined the board of Alco Oil and Chemical (formerly Rainbow Production Company). In 1960 Veale and his associates formed a holding company, V & V Associates, and bought a large minority share in Alco.

Alco (renamed Alco Chemical in 1962) acquired four fertilizer companies and in 1965 (renamed Alco Standard) merged with V & V, which had bought stakes in several machinery producers. Veale then implemented the partnership strategy that would serve the company for 25 years: He bought small, privately owned businesses, usually with cash and Alco Standard stock, and let the owners continue to run them. By 1968 Alco Standard had bought 52 companies in this way and had branched into electrical, metallurgical, and distribution businesses.

Alco Standard expanded into coal mining in the 1970s by acquiring several coal properties. The company also bought several paper distributors and formed a national paper distributor called Unisource. The division's profitability prompted Alco Standard to enter other distribution businesses, including pharmaceuticals, steel products, auto parts, food service equipment, and liquor. By 1981 distribution provided 60% of earnings and 75% of sales.

Veale had also acquired several manufacturers (plastics, machinery, rubber, and chemicals), but they had not grown as rapidly as the distribution businesses. In 1984 he merged the

manufacturers into Alco Industries and sold the new company to its managers; he kept a minority stake. Ray Mundt (who succeeded Veale as chairman) switched Alco's focus in 1986 to office products and paper distribution, cutting seven divisions, including health services and ice cream.

John Stuart succeeded Mundt as CEO in 1993 (and as chairman in 1995) and oversaw a restructuring. Although a 1992 joint venture with European company IMM Office Systems (IMMOS) didn't work out, Alco did not walk away empty-handed: The dissolution agreement gave it two IMMOS subsidiaries, Denmark's Eskofot and France-based STR.

Alco Standard's largest purchase in 1995 was UK-based copier distribution and service firm Southern Business Group PLC — renamed A:Copy (UK) PLC — for $134 million. The company bought 97 businesses in fiscal 1996.

In 1997 Alco Standard spun off wholesale paper distribution unit Unisource Worldwide, which through years of acquisitions had by then amassed 100 local sales and service operations. After the spinoff, Alco Standard changed its name to IKON Office Solutions. It continued a searing rate of acquisitions, including 89 companies in fiscal 1997 and 34 more in fiscal 1998. Trouble integrating all of its purchases into a united company pushed IKON off its axis, and profits dropped for fiscal 1997. In 1998 EVP James Forese replaced Stuart as president and CEO. To reduce expenses, the company that year cut 1,500 positions. IKON suffered a loss in fiscal 1998 because of restructuring charges, and it made plans to cut 2,000 more jobs — 5% of its staff.

Chairman: Richard A. Jalkut
President and CEO: James J. Forese, age 63,
$450,000 pay
SVP and CFO: William S. Urkiel, age 53
SVP and Chief Information Officer: David M. Gadra,
age 50, $234,167 pay
SVP and General Counsel: Don H. Liu
SVP; President, Business Services:
Peter W. Shoemaker, age 56, $287,608 pay
SVP, President, Document Services: Lynn B. Graham,
age 51, $235,620 pay
SVP; President, IKON North America:
Dennis P. LeStrange
SVP Human Resources: Beth B. Sexton, age 43
SVP Marketing: Barbara A. Pellow, age 44
SVP Operations, Technology Services: Mitch Morgan,
age 39
VP and Controller: Michael J. Dillon, age 45
VP; President, IKON Europe: David D. Mills, age 40
VP; SVP, Technology Services: Paul Nellis, age 59
VP Finance: Michael H. Dudek, age 52
VP Strategic Partnerships: Dan Cohen, age 34
VP Supply Chain: Stephen R. LaHood, age 52
Secretary and Corporate Counsel: Karin M. Kinney,
age 38
Treasurer: J. F. Quinn, age 43
Auditors: Ernst & Young LLP

HQ: 70 Valley Stream Pkwy., Malvern, PA 19355
Phone: 610-296-8000 **Fax:** 610-408-7025
Web site: http://www.ikon.com

IKON Office Solutions has more than 1,000 offices in
Canada, Denmark, France, Germany, Mexico, the UK,
and the US.

1998 Sales

	$ mil.	% of total
Products	3,012	54
Service & rentals	2,310	41
Finance income	307	5
Total	**5,629**	**100**

Products and Services
Computer network management
Copy center and other contract outsourcing
Customized leasing and financial support
Digital business document support
Digital printers
Document storage
Electronic document management support
Electronic file conversion
Fax machines
Imaging equipment
Information technology consulting
Legal document support
Photocopiers
Print controllers
Project management
Technology training
Wireless software

Amplicon	Hewlett-Packard
BT Office Products	Kinko's
Corporate Express	Office Depot
Danka	Pitney Bowes
Global Imaging Systems	Sharp
Harris Corporation	Xerox

NYSE symbol: IKN FYE: September 30	Annual Growth	1989	1990	1991	1992	1993	1994	1995	1996	1997	1998
Sales ($ mil.)	3.5%	4,133	4,296	4,724	4,883	6,387	7,926	9,794	3,942	4,905	5,629
Net income ($ mil.)	—	171	106	118	96	0	71	203	211	130	(83)
Income as % of sales	—	4.1%	2.5%	2.5%	2.0%	0.0%	0.9%	2.1%	5.3%	2.7%	—
Earnings per share ($)	—	0.08	0.05	0.26	0.53	0.52	(0.09)	0.86	1.12	0.77	(0.76)
Stock price - FY high ($)	—	17.69	18.94	17.94	21.31	25.31	32.75	43.63	66.00	52.25	36.25
Stock price - FY low ($)	—	11.50	13.81	14.50	15.13	16.63	21.75	26.50	37.38	20.63	5.00
Stock price - FY close ($)	(9.4%)	17.44	15.13	16.94	17.94	22.00	31.06	42.38	49.88	25.56	7.19
P/E - high	—	221	379	69	40	49	—	51	59	68	—
P/E - low	—	144	276	56	29	32	—	31	33	27	—
Dividends per share ($)	(9.2%)	0.38	0.42	0.44	0.46	0.48	0.50	0.52	0.56	0.26	0.16
Book value per share ($)	1.3%	7.38	8.39	9.17	9.36	8.76	10.72	12.64	14.94	8.94	8.30
Employees	8.9%	19,800	20,900	18,800	23,500	28,500	30,600	36,500	31,300	41,000	42,600

HIGH/LOW/CLOSE

Debt ratio: 59.4%
Return on equity: —
Cash ($ mil.): 1
Current ratio: 1.29
Long-term debt ($ mil.): 2,087
No. of shares (mil.): 137
Dividends
 Yield: 2.2%
 Payout: —
Market value ($ mil.): 985

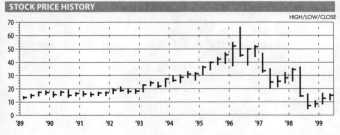

ILLINOIS TOOL WORKS INC.

OVERVIEW

Flexible plastic six-pack holders are such a fixture of daily life that it's hard to imagine a world without them. Before Chicago-based Illinois Tool Works (ITW) introduced the plastic holder in 1962, sodas presumably were rolling around loose or expensively confined in cardboard.

The international industrial products and equipment company operates in three business segments: engineered components (adhesives, polymers, welding equipment, and metal and plastic fasteners), specialty systems (spray guns, paint-curing systems, packaging systems, and strapping machinery), and leasing and investments. Brands include ZIP-PAK (resealable packaging), Paslode (fasteners), Miller (welding products), and DeVilbiss (spray-painting equipment).

ITW has expanded by acquiring companies, dumping their weaker products, and tweaking the efficiency of the new unit. ITW is making its biggest acquisition and entering a new field by agreeing to buy Premark International, which makes home appliances (West Bend), commercial kitchen equipment (Hobart), and fitness equipment (Precor). The company's more than 400 decentralized operating units are small and focused on specific markets. Although ITW has business interests in 35 countries, the US accounts for about two-thirds of its sales.

HISTORY

In the early years of the 20th century, Byron Smith, founder of Chicago's Northern Trust Company, recognized that rapid industrialization was outgrowing the capacity of small shops to supply machine tools. Smith encouraged two of his four sons to launch Illinois Tool Works (ITW) in 1912. Harold C. Smith became president of ITW in 1915 and expanded its product line into automotive parts.

ITW developed the Shakeproof fastener, the first twisted-tooth lock washer, in 1923. When Harold C. died in 1936, the torch passed to his son Harold B., who decentralized the company and exhorted salesmen to learn customers' businesses so they could develop solutions even before the customers recognized the problems. Smith plowed profits back into research as WWII spurred demand.

In the 1950s the company began exploring plastics and combination metal and plastic fasteners, as well as electrical controls and instruments, to become a leader in miniaturization. Its major breakthrough came in the early 1960s with the development of flexible plastic collars to hold six-packs of beverage cans. This item, under a new division called Hi-Cone, was ITW's most profitable offering.

Silas Cathcart became CEO in 1970. Smith's son, another Harold B., was president and COO until 1981 (he remains on the board of directors and is chairman of the board's executive committee). By the early 1980s ITW had become bureaucratic and susceptible to foreign competition. It was forced to lower prices to hold on to customers. Wary after the 1982 recession, ITW hired John Nichols as CEO. Nichols broadened the company's product line, introduced more-effective production methods, and doubled ITW's size by buying 27

companies, the largest being Signode Industries, bought for $524 million (1986). Nichols broke Signode into smaller units to speed development of 20 new products.

ITW acquired Ransburg Corporation (electrostatic finishing systems, 1989) and the DeVilbiss division of Eagle Industries (1990) and merged the two to form its Finishing Systems and Products division. In 1992 the company introduced the Ring Leader Recycling Program to recycle its plastic six-pack rings.

ITW acquired ownership of the Miller Group, a maker of arc welding equipment and related systems, through a stock swap in 1993. An 11% increase in car building in Europe in 1994 caused revenues of the company's engineered-components segment to grow dramatically, and that year 76% of its international sales derived from European operations.

In 1995 ITW named president James Farrell as CEO. He replaced Nichols as chairman in 1996. ITW acquired Hobart Brothers (welding products) and Medalists Industries (industrial fasteners) in 1996 and made 28 acquisitions and joint ventures in 1997. It entered the domestic spray-painting equipment business in 1998 by acquiring Binks Sames (now Sames Corporation). In 1999 ITW acquired industrial ink-jet maker Trident International. Also in 1999 ITW purchased a polyester film processing plant from South Korea's SKC and pneumatic nailing and stapling toolmaker Duo-Fast. ITW also sold its Irathane Systems urethane linings and moldings division to Industrial Rubber Products. ITW agreed to buy consumer products maker Premark International for $3.5 billion in 1999.

Chairman and CEO: W. James Farrell, age 56,
$1,477,500 pay
Chairman Executive Committee: Harold B. Smith, age 65
VC: Frank S. Ptak, age 55, $780,312 pay
EVP: Russell M. Flaum, age 48, $487,140 pay
EVP: Thomas J. Hansen, age 50
EVP: Dennis J. Martin, age 48
EVP: F. Ronald Seager, age 58, $604,650 pay
EVP: David B. Speer, age 47, $509,581 pay
EVP: Hugh J. Zentmyer, age 52
SVP, General Counsel, and Secretary:
Stewart S. Hudnut, age 59
SVP Human Resources: John Karpan, age 58
SVP and CFO: Jon C. Kinney, age 56
Auditors: Arthur Andersen LLP

LOCATIONS

HQ: 3600 W. Lake Ave., Glenview, IL 60025-5811
Phone: 847-724-7500   **Fax:** 847-657-4392
Web site: http://www.itwinc.com

Illinois Tool Works operates more than 200 plants and
offices in the US. Other principal international plants
are in Australia, Belgium, Canada, France, Germany,
Ireland, Italy, Japan, Malaysia, Spain, Sweden,
Switzerland, and the UK.

1998 Sales

	$ mil.	% of total
US	3,618	65
Europe	1,482	26
Asia	193	3
Other regions	355	6
Total	**5,648**	**100**

PRODUCTS/OPERATIONS

1998 Sales & Operating Income

	Sales		Operating Income	
	$ mil.	% of total	$ mil.	% of total
Specialty systems	3,049	51	504	47
Engineered products	2,728	46	504	47
Leasing & investments	150	3	71	6
Adjustments	(279)	—	—	—
Total	**5,648**	**100**	**1,079**	**100**

Selected Products

Engineered Components
Fasteners and assemblies
Fastening tools
Industrial fluids and adhesives
Plastic and metal components
Welding products

Industrial Systems and Consumables
Consumables for consumer and industrial packaging
Industrial spray-coating equipment and systems
Ink-jet and bar-coding systems
Marking, labeling, and identification systems
Quality-assurance equipment and systems

COMPETITORS

Armstrong World
BASF AG
Cooper Industries
Cordant Technologies
DuPont
ESAB
Hoechst AG
Ingersoll-Rand
3M
NCH
Nordson

Penn Engineering &
   Manufacturing
PPG
Sames
SPS Technologies
Stanley Works
Textron
TriMas
Tyco International
Union Carbide
W. R. Grace

HISTORICAL FINANCIALS & EMPLOYEES

NYSE symbol: ITW FYE: December 31	Annual Growth	1989	1990	1991	1992	1993	1994	1995	1996	1997	1998
Sales ($ mil.)	11.2%	2,173	2,544	2,640	2,812	3,159	3,461	4,152	4,997	5,220	5,648
Net income ($ mil.)	17.0%	164	182	181	192	207	278	388	486	587	673
Income as % of sales	—	7.5%	7.2%	6.8%	6.8%	6.5%	8.0%	9.3%	9.7%	11.2%	11.9%
Earnings per share ($)	15.0%	0.76	0.83	0.81	0.85	0.90	1.22	1.63	1.95	2.33	2.67
Stock price - FY high ($)	—	11.88	14.34	17.34	17.66	20.25	22.75	32.75	43.63	60.13	73.19
Stock price - FY low ($)	—	8.25	9.81	11.41	14.25	16.25	18.50	19.88	25.94	37.38	45.19
Stock price - FY close ($)	20.0%	11.22	12.06	15.94	16.31	19.50	21.88	29.50	39.94	60.13	58.00
P/E - high	—	16	17	21	21	23	19	20	22	26	27
P/E - low	—	11	12	14	17	18	15	12	13	16	17
Dividends per share ($)	15.4%	0.14	0.17	0.20	0.23	0.25	0.27	0.31	0.35	0.43	0.51
Book value per share ($)	14.1%	4.06	4.98	5.44	5.97	5.56	6.76	8.13	9.66	11.24	13.35
Employees	7.1%	15,700	18,400	18,700	17,800	19,000	19,500	21,200	24,400	25,700	29,200

STOCK PRICE HISTORY

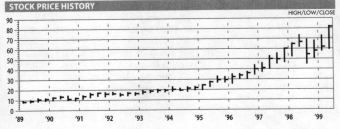

HIGH/LOW/CLOSE

1998 FISCAL YEAR-END

Debt ratio: 22.1%
Return on equity: 20.2%
Cash ($ mil.): 94
Current ratio: 1.50
Long-term debt ($ mil.): 947
No. of shares (mil.): 250
Dividends
  Yield: 0.9%
  Payout: 19.1%
Market value ($ mil.): 14,507

IMATION CORP.

OVERVIEW

Imation is sharpening its image. Headquartered in Oakdale, Minnesota, the company is a leading maker of data storage and computer diskettes, and other imaging products for the information technology industry. Its products also include information management tools, color proofing systems, printing and publishing software, imaging software for engineers, and photographic films (it is a top supplier of private-label brands but is planning to sell this business). Almost half of its sales come from outside the US.

Red ink and reorganization have been Imation's close companions since its 1996 spinoff from Post-it Notes and Scotch tape maker 3M. Chairman and CEO William Monahan took on an unfocused fledgling serving a number of stalled markets and stuck to its parents' conservative culture.

Monahan has overseen a series of workforce cuts (unheard of at 3M), revamped management, and divested Imation of its CD-ROM and medical imaging systems operations in an attempt to refresh earnings and refine focus.

HISTORY

Imation's ancestry stretches back to 1902, when five businessmen founded 3M in Two Harbors, Minnesota, to sell corundum to manufacturers for grinding wheels. Faced with stiff competition and the realization that its mining holdings contained the nearly worthless igneous rock anorthosite instead of corundum, the company shifted gears and began making sandpaper and abrasive wheels.

In a research-fueled corporate culture, 3M's engineers thrived, launching a long line of culturally implanted products including Scotch masking tape, the dry-printing photocopy process, Post-it adhesive notepads, and, in 1947, the first commercially viable magnetic recording tape. This ancestor of the cassette tape would mark 3M's leap into the business that later helped make Imation.

The genesis of Imation's other lines continued in the 1950s and 1960s when 3M ventured into photographic products. It jumped into color proofing systems and X-ray and other medical imaging technologies in the 1970s. When its diskette manufacturing business faced intense global competition in the 1980s, 3M expanded its efforts in the data storage products market.

Imation — a name taken from the words "imaging" and "information" — was born in 1996 when 3M spun off its low-performing data storage, imaging, and printing businesses. 3M's plan was to boost its sagging stock price and let the new company focus on customers, as opposed to the wider corporate goals of 3M (which retained its industrial and consumer and life science units and discontinued its audiotape and videotape business). About 75% of 3M's data storage and medical imaging employees made the move; the rest opted to take an early retirement. That year William Monahan, who began his career

in the early 1970s selling 3M data storage products on Wall Street and rose to serve as VP of the company's Electro and Communication Group, was named chairman and CEO.

In 1996 Imation also unveiled the LS-120 diskette for a drive that used both standard floppy disks (1.44 MB) and 120-MB, 3 1/2-in. disks. Hitachi, Matsushita, and Mitsubishi made products based on the technology. Also that year the company bought Seattle-based prepress software company Luminous Corporation, and was awarded its first non-3M patent for a minicartridge design.

While Imation struggled in an intensely competitive market with plummeting product prices, industry watchers questioned the company's commitment to new technology. Imation intensified restructuring efforts to pare operations and sharpen its focus. In 1997 it stepped up a new technology push by acquiring digital medical imaging specialist Cemax-Icon, as well as Internet service provider Imaginet, resulting in the creation of Imation Internet Studio (sold in 1999 to Gage Marketing Group when its strategies conflicted with Imation's).

With more losses in 1997 — despite a slew of new products and features — Imation in 1998 worked to turn around its financial results, slashing its workforce by 3,400. The company also sold its CD-ROM services unit to optical media company Metatec and its medical imaging systems to Eastman Kodak for about $520 million, partly to settle an intellectual-property lawsuit.

In 1999 Imation agreed to sell its photo color systems business (photographic film, single-use cameras) to Schroder plc affiliate Schroder Ventures, an equity adviser.

Chairman, President, and CEO: William T. Monahan, age 51, $530,040 pay
SVP, CFO, and Chief Administrative Officer: Robert L. Edwards, age 43, $357,291 pay
VP; President, Product Technologies: Barbara M. Cederberg, age 45, $224,910 pay
VP; President, Digital Solutions and Services: Michael A. Howard, age 49
VP and Treasurer: Galen K. Johnson
VP; President, Data Storage and Information Management: Steven D. Ladwig, age 41, $178,666 pay
VP, Secretary, and General Counsel: John L. Sullivan, age 44
VP, Corporate Communications and Investor Relations: Bradley D. Allen
VP, Human Resources: Jacqueline Chase
VP, International: David H. Wenck, age 55, $199,500 pay
Corporate Controller: Paul R. Zeller, age 38
Auditors: PricewaterhouseCoopers LLP

LOCATIONS

HQ: 1 Imation Place, Oakdale, MN 55128
Phone: 651-704-4000   **Fax:** 651-704-3444
Web site: http://www.imation.com

Imation markets its products in more than 60 countries, and has operations in Canada, France, Italy, the Netherlands, the UK, and the US.

1998 Sales

	$ mil.	% of total
US	1,123	55
Other countries	924	45
Total	**2,047**	**100**

PRODUCTS/OPERATIONS

1998 Sales

	$ mil.	% of total
Data storage & information management	714	35
Product technologies	575	28
Medical imaging systems	553	27
Digital solutions & services	144	7
Other	61	3
Total	**2,047**	**100**

Selected Products

Data Storage and Information Management
CD recordable
CD rewritable
Computer cartridge tapes
Computer diskettes (SuperDisk)
Data cartridges (Travan)
Drives

Photo Color
Disposable cameras
Film
Ink jet paper
Multipart business forms

Printing and Proofing
Asset management software
Conventional color proofing systems (Matchprint)
Digital color proofing systems (Rainbow)
Image setting and graphic arts products
Graphic arts films
Paper and other printing application accessories
Printing plates
Publishing software
Workflow automation software

COMPETITORS

Agfa	Hitachi Maxell	Polaroid
DuPont	IBM	Scitex
Eastman Kodak	Iomega	Sony
Fuji Photo	Konica	SyQuest

HISTORICAL FINANCIALS & EMPLOYEES

NYSE symbol: IMN FYE: December 31	Annual Growth	1989	1990	1991	1992	1993	1994	1995	1996	1997	1998
Sales ($ mil.)	(2.4%)	—	—	—	—	2,308	2,281	2,246	2,278	2,202	2,047
Net income ($ mil.)	(5.3%)	—	—	—	—	75	54	(97)	(21)	(180)	57
Income as % of sales	—	—	—	—	—	3.2%	2.4%	—	—	—	2.8%
Earnings per share ($)	—	—	—	—	—	—	—	—	(0.49)	(4.54)	1.45
Stock price - FY high ($)	—	—	—	—	—	—	—	—	33.38	31.88	19.94
Stock price - FY low ($)	—	—	—	—	—	—	—	—	19.25	15.13	13.56
Stock price - FY close ($)	(21.1%)	—	—	—	—	—	—	—	28.13	16.00	17.50
P/E - high	—	—	—	—	—	—	—	—	—	—	14
P/E - low	—	—	—	—	—	—	—	—	—	—	9
Dividends per share ($)	—	—	—	—	—	—	—	—	0.00	0.00	0.00
Book value per share ($)	(7.5%)	—	—	—	—	—	—	—	21.70	16.81	18.56
Employees	(18.9%)	—	—	—	—	—	—	12,000	9,400	9,800	6,400

STOCK PRICE HISTORY

HIGH/LOW/CLOSE

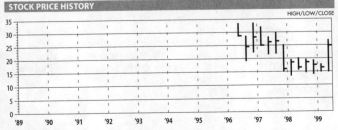

1998 FISCAL YEAR-END

Debt ratio: 4.1%
Return on equity: 7.5%
Cash ($ mil.): 64
Current ratio: 2.18
Long-term debt ($ mil.): 33
No. of shares (mil.): 41
Dividends
  Yield: —
  Payout: —
Market value ($ mil.): 718

IMC GLOBAL INC.

OVERVIEW

IMC Global digs phosphate. Based in Northbrook, Illinois, IMC turns phosphate rock into phosphate chemicals and potash, which is used in fertilizers. IMC also has mining and processing operations in Canada, the UK, and the US. IMC owns 52% of phosphate producer Phosphate Resource Partners (formerly Freeport-McMoRan Resource Partners). IMC's 1998 purchase of Harris Chemical makes it the world's #3 salt producer (behind Rohm and Haas' Morton Salt and Cargill).

IMC-Agrico Phosphates is part of the IMC-Agrico joint venture with Phosphate Resource Partners. The company is one of the world's leading producers of phosphate fertilizers and IMC's top revenues source. IMC-Agrico Feed Ingredients (also part of Phosphate Resource Partners) produces phosphate and potash feed supplements. IMC Kalium produces potash for agricultural and industrial use, for water softening, and for food-quality salt. IMC is building its international presence through acquisitions and joint ventures. It has also focused itself by selling noncore operations.

HISTORY

In 1897 engineer Thomas Meadows and his brother-in-law Oscar Dortch formed T.C. Meadows & Co. in Tennessee to exploit local phosphorus-rich rock. At the time major sources for potassium (potash) and nitrogen (nitrates) were in Germany and Chile. The company, renamed United States Agricultural Corporation in 1899, began mining in Florida, which was soon the center of the US phosphate industry.

Waldemar Schmidtmann, whose father controlled a major German potash mine, joined Meadows and Dortch in 1909 to form International Agricultural Corp. (IAC), which bought the elder Schmidtmann's mine. Despite an import ban during WWI, IAC's German potash supplies gave it a jump on US firms still searching for domestic potash sources. IAC pioneered a method of separating phosphate rocks from surrounding debris in 1929, doubling the life of rock reserves. By 1939 the company was the world's #1 miner of phosphate rock. US potash was commercially developed by Union Potash in the 1930s, and IAC bought Union Potash in 1939.

IAC changed its name to International Mineral & Chemical (IMC) in 1941. After WWII the use of western farming techniques (such as using commercial fertilizers) by markets in Asia helped sustain 20 years of growth. IMC entered the nitrate market through a 1963 joint venture with Northern Natural Gas of Omaha to build an ammonia plant.

In the 1970s and 1980s the dominance of Communist Bloc fertilizer firms in markets outside the US, the drop in fertilizer prices, and growing concern about the health risks of inorganic fertilizers caused IMC to suffer financially. In response, it bought Mallinckrodt (pharmaceuticals) and Pitman-Moore (animal health products) in 1986. IMC reorganized as a holding company with subsidiaries Mallinckrodt, IMC Fertilizer, and Pitman-Moore.

IMC Fertilizer went public in 1988 but struggled in the early 1990s due to plant explosions, lawsuits, and depressed prices. In 1992 it changed its name to IMC Global, and in 1993 it pooled its phosphate assets with those of Freeport-McMoRan Resource Partners (now Phosphate Resource Partners) to create IMC-Agrico.

To support Chinese expansion, IMC set up a World Food Production Conference in Beijing and opened a Hong Kong office in 1995. Late that year IMC became the world's #1 miner of phosphate rock and potash by buying Vigoro, a producer and distributor of potash, nitrogen-based fertilizers, and related goods.

In 1996 IMC-Agrico began to explore developing phosphate resources in China's Yunnan province. The next year it bought potash -producer Western AG-Minerals and mining company Freeport-McMoRan for $750 million.

IMC bought Harris Chemical for $1.4 billion in 1998. It exited the consumer and professional lawn and garden products market that year by selling IMC Vigoro to privately owned Pursell Industries.

IMC reorganized, and IMC-Agrico Crop Nutrients became IMC-Agrico Phosphates. IMC hired former Culligan Water CEO Doug Pertz as president. In 1999 it sold its IMC AgriBusiness distribution business to privately owned distributor Royster-Clark for about $300 million and announced plans to cut some 6% of its workforce. It also elected to close mines and plants in Florida and Louisiana.

OFFICERS

Chairman and CEO: Robert E. Fowler Jr., age 63, $1,450,754 pay
President and COO: Douglas A. Pertz, age 44
SVP, General Counsel, and Assistant Secretary: Phillip Gordon, age 55
SVP; President, IMC International: C. Steven Hoffman, age 50, $464,011 pay
SVP; President, IMC Crop Nutrients: John U. Huber, age 60, $673,124 pay
SVP and CFO: J. Bradford James, age 52, $526,969 pay
SVP Human Resources: B. Russell Lockridge, age 49
SVP, Environment, Health and Safety: Carolyn W. Merritt, age 52
SVP; President, IMC AgriBusiness: Robert M. Van Patten, age 53, $437,327 pay
SVP Corporate Development: Lynn F. White, age 46
VP of Tax and Assistant Treasurer: Louis J. Corna, age 51
VP and Treasurer: E. Paul Dunn Jr., age 45
VP and Controller: Anne M. Scavone, age 35
SVP, IMC-Agrico Feed Ingredients: Kermit E. McCormack, age 53
President, IMC Salt: Robert F. Clark, age 55
President, IMC Chemicals: John F. Tancredi, age 55
Auditors: Ernst & Young LLP

LOCATIONS

HQ: 2100 Sanders Rd., Northbrook, IL 60062
Phone: 847-272-9200 **Fax:** 847-205-4805
Web site: http://www.imcglobal.com

IMC Global has operations in Canada, the UK, and the US.

PRODUCTS/OPERATIONS

1998 Sales

	$ mil.	% of total
IMC-Agrico Phosphates	1,573	58
IMC Kalium	700	26
IMC Salt	175	6
IMC-Agrico Feed Ingredients	164	6
Other	84	4
Total	**2,696**	**100**

Selected Products

Boron chemicals	Potash
Concentrated phosphates	Salt
Feed supplements	Soda chemicals
Magnesium chloride	Sodium bicarbonate
Merchant-grade phosphoric acid	Sulphate of potash
Phosphate and potash feed supplements	

Selected Subsidiaries
IMC Kalium
IMC Salt
IMC-Agrico Feed Ingredients
IMC-Agrico Phosphates

COMPETITORS

Agrium	Norsk Hydro
Cargill	Potash Corporation
Dow Chemical	Rich Coast
K + S	Rohm and Haas
LESCO	Scotts
MDPA	Terra Industries
Mississippi Chemical	Tessenderlo Chemie

HISTORICAL FINANCIALS & EMPLOYEES

NYSE symbol: IGL FYE: December 31	Annual Growth	1989	1990	1991	1992	1993	1994	1995	1996	1997	1998
Sales ($ mil.)	10.4%	1,106	1,131	1,059	897	1,442	1,924	2,981	2,982	2,989	2,696
Net income ($ mil.)	—	83	96	(75)	(167)	(29)	115	144	193	63	(9)
Income as % of sales	—	7.5%	8.5%	—	—	—	6.0%	4.8%	6.5%	2.1%	—
Earnings per share ($)	—	1.57	1.93	(1.69)	(3.79)	(0.57)	1.94	1.56	2.03	0.67	(0.08)
Stock price - FY high ($)	—	19.88	23.44	34.00	22.94	24.63	27.31	43.25	44.50	42.50	39.50
Stock price - FY low ($)	—	15.56	15.19	21.19	12.19	13.00	17.06	27.00	33.13	29.63	17.81
Stock price - FY close ($)	2.2%	17.56	23.06	21.44	14.69	17.31	27.06	37.63	35.00	32.75	21.38
P/E - high	—	13	12	—	—	—	14	28	22	63	—
P/E - low	—	10	8	—	—	—	9	17	16	44	—
Dividends per share ($)	(5.6%)	0.54	0.54	0.54	0.41	0.00	0.15	0.29	0.32	0.16	0.32
Book value per share ($)	0.5%	15.56	16.12	13.96	9.76	11.12	12.92	19.42	14.32	16.98	16.27
Employees	7.2%	6,000	6,000	6,000	5,400	5,200	6,300	6,800	9,200	9,200	11,244

STOCK PRICE HISTORY
HIGH/LOW/CLOSE

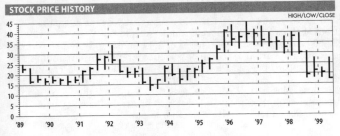

1998 FISCAL YEAR-END
Debt ratio: 58.6%
Return on equity: —
Cash ($ mil.): 111
Current ratio: 1.64
Long-term debt ($ mil.): 2,639
No. of shares (mil.): 114
Dividends
 Yield: 1.5%
 Payout: —
Market value ($ mil.): 2,444

INACOM CORP.

OVERVIEW

Omaha, Nebraska-based InaCom is taking the service road. A leading provider of technology management products and services, InaCom primarily sells customized computer systems, networks, and telecommunications equipment to midsized and large corporate clients. It also offers system support and systems integration services. The company operates through more than 1,000 company-owned and franchised business centers around the US.

Compaq, IBM, and Hewlett-Packard account for about two-thirds of InaCom's sales as it procures computer products, configures them for customers, and distributes them. It also offers phone systems and a variety of services as well as other voice, data, and video convergence equipment.

InaCom is moving away from the razor-thin margins of computer reselling and concentrating on its more lucrative technology management services. Its 1999 purchase of Vanstar, a rival reseller known for its broad range of services, is expected to push InaCom's annual sales near the $7 billion mark.

Warburg, Pincus Capital owns 23% of the company.

HISTORY

It was a case of computers before swine. In 1982 Valmont Industries, a manufacturer of irrigation systems and other products that was founded in 1946, created ValCom to sell computers and software to farmers, its primary customer base. The company sold PCs along with software such as Swine Management and Poultry Farm Management. But ValCom discovered that its customers were not interested in the hog software. In fact, most of the customers were not farmers at all but local bankers, lawyers, and store owners who bought PCs from the company because of the extensive training and service ValCom offered with the purchase. Bill Fairfield, head of ValCom, dropped the farming software to focus on selling hardware and services to small businesses.

ValCom expanded through both company-owned and franchised computer centers, and by 1984 it had 121 stores. A year later it introduced an online system to provide its stores with product information. In 1987 Valmont spun off ValCom to the public, with Bill Fairfield as CEO, and began the first of several acquisitions that added locations and new markets, including New Jersey's #1 computer chain, Clancy-Paul (1988). In 1990 it expanded its businesses to include value-added resellers and systems integrators, giving ValCom more than 300 locations.

ValCom nearly doubled in size in 1991 when it merged with computer reseller Inacomp Computer Centers, founded in 1976 by Rick Inatome. After graduating from Michigan State, Inatome borrowed $35,000 and opened a small computer store called Computer Mart in Clawson, Michigan. In 1979 the company became an authorized Apple dealer.

During the early 1980s Computer Mart began to focus on larger corporate accounts and changed its name to Inacomp Computer Centers. To expand its product offerings, it also became an authorized IBM dealer. Inacomp went public in 1983. The company expanded by buying computer store chains in California and Georgia, adding computer rentals, and opening computer superstores to serve its business customers.

Inacomp merged with ValCom in 1991 to become InaCom (Inatome insisted that his company's name come first). To provide more business services, InaCom added technical support for networking systems in 1992. It also signed a deal with systems integration consortium ICG to expand its services worldwide. The following year InaCom acquired Sears Business Centers and shifted its emphasis to direct-to-end-user shipments, streamlining its distribution system.

InaCom acquired the computer and service businesses of Chaparral Information Systems, a networking company, in 1994. InaCom posted a loss in 1994 due, in part, to the loss of a government contract. The next year the company agreed to sell and support Cisco Systems' internetworking products and Canon Computer Systems' printers and scanners.

The company acquired three technology management consulting companies in late 1996 and inked pacts in 1997 to distribute network security and management software for McAfee (now Network Associates) and multifunction fax and laser printer products for Brother. Also that year the company moved from Nasdaq to the NYSE. The 1998 purchases of AM Computer Systems and Inacomp of Torrance strengthened InaCom's services presence on both US coasts. The next year InaCom bought smaller rival Vanstar in a deal valued at $435 million; the acquisition gave Vanstar chairman William Tauscher a 4% stake in InaCom.

Chairman: Rick Inatome, age 45
President and CEO: Bill L. Fairfield, age 52, $724,272 pay
EVP and CFO: David C. Guenthner, age 49, $331,485 pay
SVP, Corporate Resources (HR): Larry Fazzini, age 51
SVP, Distribution and Operation: Leon Kerkman, age 39
SVP, Information Technology and Chief Information Officer: Jeff Hartigan, age 56
SVP, Life Cycle Services: Dennis Strittmatter, age 52
SVP, Sales: Richard Anderson
SVP, Technology Services: Chris Howard
VP and Treasurer: Richard Oshlo, age 51
Group Executive, Information Systems: Robert A. Schultz, age 56, $338,368 pay
Group Executive, Technology Service: George DeSola, age 52, $352,446 pay
Chief Technology Officer: Len Smith, age 47
President and General Manager, International Division: Cris Freiwald, age 44
President, Distribution and Operations and Secretary: Michael A. Steffan, age 47, $323,191 pay
SVP, Reseller Division: Pete Graziano
Auditors: KPMG Peat Marwick LLP

PRODUCTS/OPERATIONS

Products

Accessories	Modems
Video cards	Monitors
Cables	Network management
Carrying cases	Printer Servers
Mobile peripherals	Printers
Printer supplies	Scanners
CPUs	**Software**
Mobile	Applications
Desktop	Database
Server	E-mail
	Groupware
Networking	Network operating system
Bridges/routers	OS
Hubs	Software licensing
Network interface cards	Utilities
PCMCIA	
Switches	**Services**
	Consulting
Peripherals	Network Services
Digital cameras	Outsourcing
Faxes	System Customization
Mass storage	Training
Memory	

LOCATIONS

HQ: 10810 Farnam, Omaha, NE 68154
Phone: 402-392-3900   **Fax:** 402-758-4421
Web site: http://www.inacom.com

InaCom has distribution centers in California, Nebraska, and New Jersey, and affiliations in Africa, Asia, Canada, the Caribbean, Central America, Europe, Mexico, the Middle East, and South America.

COMPETITORS

Andersen	CompUSA	IBM
Worldwide	Dell Computer	Lucent
ASCII	EDS	Merisel
AT&T	ENTEX	Micro Warehouse
CDW Computer	Gateway	MicroAge
Centers	GE	PC Connection
Comark	IKON	Tech Data
CompuCom	Ingram Micro	Unisys

HISTORICAL FINANCIALS & EMPLOYEES

NYSE symbol: ICO FYE: December 31	Annual Growth	1989	1990	1991	1992	1993	1994	1995	1996	1997	1998
Sales ($ mil.)	31.6%	359	428	680	1,015	1,545	1,801	2,200	3,102	3,896	4,258
Net income ($ mil.)	23.7%	6	7	3	11	12	(2)	12	19	30	43
Income as % of sales	—	1.8%	1.6%	0.5%	1.1%	0.8%	—	0.5%	0.6%	0.8%	1.0%
Earnings per share ($)	5.5%	1.40	1.69	0.56	1.25	1.28	(0.22)	1.16	1.66	2.17	2.26
Stock price - FY high ($)	—	11.75	17.00	18.50	14.75	25.50	21.00	15.25	40.63	40.00	37.25
Stock price - FY low ($)	—	9.38	9.25	7.00	9.25	12.75	6.88	7.00	13.25	19.75	13.50
Stock price - FY close ($)	3.7%	10.75	12.50	10.00	14.50	13.50	7.00	14.13	40.00	28.06	14.88
P/E - high	—	8	10	33	12	20	—	13	24	18	16
P/E - low	—	7	5	13	7	10	—	6	8	9	6
Dividends per share ($)	—	0.00	0.00	0.00	0.00	0.00	0.00	0.00	0.00	0.00	0.00
Book value per share ($)	13.4%	8.19	9.81	11.07	12.24	13.92	13.75	14.85	16.29	21.94	25.35
Employees	44.5%	438	661	1,380	1,309	1,883	1,884	2,196	2,874	4,200	12,000

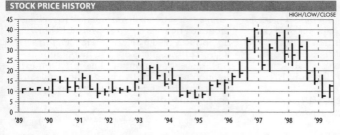

STOCK PRICE HISTORY HIGH/LOW/CLOSE

1998 FISCAL YEAR-END
Debt ratio: 32.2%
Return on equity: 10.0%
Cash ($ mil.): 54
Current ratio: 1.59
Long-term debt ($ mil.): 202
No. of shares (mil.): 17
Dividends
 Yield: —
 Payout: —
Market value ($ mil.): 250

INGERSOLL-RAND COMPANY

OVERVIEW

Ingersoll-Rand helped shape the face of America (or at least the ones on Mount Rushmore) with its rock drills and has kept a prominent profile ever since. The Woodcliff Lake, New Jersey-based company makes machinery and equipment in four business sectors: air and temperature control (refrigerant gas compressors), engineered products (pumps), hardware and tools (tools and locks), and specialty vehicles (golf carts and hydraulic excavators). Its more than two dozen brands include Blaw-Knox, Bobcat, Club Car, Fafnir, Steelcraft, Schlage, Torrington, and Worthington.

Ingersoll-Rand has obtained a diverse list of subsidiaries through acquisitions and divestitures. Nearly 40% of sales are outside of the US.

HISTORY

Simon Ingersoll invented the steam-driven rock drill in New York City in 1871. In 1874 he sold the patent to Jose Francisco de Navarro, who financed the organization of the Ingersoll Rock Drill Company. Three years later it merged with Sergeant Drill, a company created by Navarro's former foreman, Henry Clark Sergeant.

Meanwhile, the Rand brothers were forming an eponymous drill company. In 1905 the companies merged to become Ingersoll-Rand.

Ingersoll-Rand was initially engaged in producing air compressors and a basic line of rock drills. In 1912 the company added centrifugal compressors and turbo blowers. Further diversification and growth occurred with the purchase of A. S. Cameron Steam Pump Works and Imperial Pneumatic Tool Company (portable air tools).

After WWII Ingersoll-Rand, which had mostly served US mining operations, expanded internationally. From the 1960s on, the company diversified into specialized machinery and products. Acquisitions included Aldrich Pump (high-pressure plunger pumps, 1961), Torrington (antifriction bearings and textile machine needles, 1969), DAMCO (drilling rigs, 1973), Schlage Lock (door hardware, 1974), and Fafnir Bearings (1986). The purchases made Ingersoll-Rand the largest US bearing manufacturer.

The company also developed several new products, including small air compressors and water-jet systems capable of cutting steel and concrete. In 1986 Ingersoll-Rand joined with manufacturing titan Dresser Industries (Dresser-Rand, 49%) to produce gas turbines, compressors, and similar equipment. Ingersoll-Rand bought Aro (air-powered tools) and German ABG (paving-equipment) in 1990, and sold Schlage Electronics to Westinghouse the next year. Ingersoll-Rand and Dresser Industries combined pump operations (Ingersoll-Dresser Pump, 51%) in 1992.

After five years in charge, CEO Theodore Black retired in 1993; he was replaced by 16-year veteran James Perrella. That year the company purchased the German needle and cylindrical-bearing business of FAG Kugelfischer Georg Schafer, and it sold its underground coal-mining machinery business (to Long-Airdox) as well as its domestic jet-engine bearing operation. ECOAIR, a unit of MAN GHH, was among several 1994 acquisitions.

Ingersoll-Rand paid $1.5 billion in 1995 to acquire Clark Equipment, a deal that brought Melroe (skid-steer loaders), Clark-Hurth Components (axles and transmissions, sold in 1997), Club Car (golf cars), and Blaw-Knox Construction Equipment (asphalt paving equipment) on board. In 1996 Ingersoll-Rand bought Mascotech's Steelcraft Division, which makes steel doors used primarily in nonresidential construction. That year Ingersoll-Rand set up a holding company in China to handle investments and various operations there; it set up a similar company in Latin America the following year. Its 1997 purchases of the UK-based Newman Tonks Group and segments of the Master Lock unit of Fortune Brands boosted its architectural hardware line and extended its European and Asian distribution network. That year the company acquired Thermo King from Westinghouse (now CBS) for $2.6 billion.

In 1999 Ingersoll-Rand paid $160 million for Harrow Industries, a manufacturer of access controls technologies, architectural hardware, and decorative bath fixtures. Ingersoll's electronics division received a boost when the parent company entered into an agreement with Cadence Design Systems, the world's leading supplier of electronic design automation software. James Perrella announced he would step down as CEO in 1999, to be succeeded by Herbert Henkel, formerly of Textron. To focus on its core operations, Ingersoll-Rand announced its intention to sell its interests in two joint ventures — Dresser-Rand and Ingersoll-Dresser — with Halliburton.

OFFICERS

Chairman and CEO: James E. Perrella, age 63, $2,458,333 pay
President and COO: Herbert L. Henkel, age 50
EVP: Brian D. Jellison, age 53, $533,917 pay
EVP: Steven T. Martin, age 58, $588,653 pay
SVP and CFO: David W. Devonshire, age 53, $828,462 pay
VP and General Counsel: Patricia Nachtigal, age 52
VP, Strategic Technologies: Nicholas J. Pishotti, age 58
VP and Treasurer: William J. Armstrong
VP: Gerard V. Geraghty
VP: Charles R. Hoge
VP: Daniel E. Kletter
VP: Allen M. Nixon
VP Human Resources: Donald H. Rice
VP: Gerald E. Swimmer
VP: Marvin L. Walrath
Corporate Secretary: Ronald G. Heller
Controller: Stephen R. Shawley, age 46
Auditors: PricewaterhouseCoopers LLP

LOCATIONS

HQ: 200 Chestnut Ridge Rd., Woodcliff Lake, NJ 07675
Phone: 201-573-0123　　**Fax:** 201-573-3172
Web site: http://www.ingersoll-rand.com

Ingersoll-Rand operates 11 plants in Asia, five in Canada, 39 in Europe, seven in Latin America, and 60 in the US.

1998 Sales

	$ mil.	% of total
US	5,115	62
Other countries	3,177	38
Total	**8,292**	**100**

PRODUCTS/OPERATIONS

1998 Sales

	$ mil.	% of total
Air & temperature controls	2,236	27
Specialty vehicles	2,181	26
Engineered products	2,151	26
Hardware & tools	1,724	21
Total	**8,292**	**100**

COMPETITORS

AMSTED	Graco
Baker Hughes	Harnischfeger
Black & Decker	Hillenbrand
Case	Inductotherm Industries
Caterpillar	ITT Industries
Cooper Industries	Mannesmann AG
Crown Equipment	Nesco
Deere	Robert Bosch
Dover	SPX
Eaton	Stanley Works
Emerson	Thermo Electron
Fiat	Thyssen Krupp
FMC	Toshiba
Fortune Brands	Toyota
Gardner Denver	W.W. Grainger

HISTORICAL FINANCIALS & EMPLOYEES

NYSE symbol: IR FYE: December 31	Annual Growth	1989	1990	1991	1992	1993	1994	1995	1996	1997	1998
Sales ($ mil.)	10.2%	3,447	3,738	3,586	3,784	4,021	4,508	5,729	6,703	7,103	8,292
Net income ($ mil.)	10.8%	202	185	151	(234)	143	211	270	358	381	509
Income as % of sales	—	5.9%	5.0%	4.2%	—	3.5%	4.7%	4.7%	5.3%	5.4%	6.1%
Earnings per share ($)	10.4%	1.26	1.19	0.97	(1.50)	0.90	1.33	1.69	2.21	2.31	3.08
Stock price - FY high ($)	—	16.76	20.18	18.34	22.84	26.60	27.76	28.26	31.77	46.25	54.00
Stock price - FY low ($)	—	11.21	9.50	11.67	16.68	19.18	19.68	18.93	23.43	27.85	34.00
Stock price - FY close ($)	12.2%	16.76	12.42	18.34	19.43	25.51	21.01	23.43	29.68	40.50	47.25
P/E - high	—	13	17	19	—	30	21	17	14	20	18
P/E - low	—	9	8	12	—	21	15	11	11	12	11
Dividends per share ($)	4.9%	0.39	0.42	0.44	0.46	0.47	0.48	0.49	0.52	0.57	0.60
Book value per share ($)	7.1%	8.92	9.69	10.14	8.25	8.55	9.36	11.00	12.74	15.07	16.47
Employees	4.4%	31,623	33,722	31,117	35,308	35,143	35,932	41,133	40,100	46,600	46,500

STOCK PRICE HISTORY

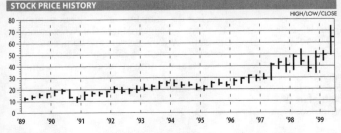

HIGH/LOW/CLOSE

1998 FISCAL YEAR-END

Debt ratio: 44.4%
Return on equity: 18.8%
Cash ($ mil.): 72
Current ratio: 1.31
Long-term debt ($ mil.): 2,166
No. of shares (mil.): 164
Dividends
　Yield: 1.3%
　Payout: 19.5%
Market value ($ mil.): 7,767

INGRAM INDUSTRIES INC.

OVERVIEW

Book 'em, Martha. Billionaire Martha Ingram heads Nashville-based Ingram Industries, whose Ingram Book Group is the US's largest wholesale distributor of trade books and audiobooks to retailers and a leading distributor to libraries. Ingram Book, through its some 11 fulfillment centers, can distribute 115 million titles a year. It serves some 32,000 retail outlets and represents over 12,000 publishers.

Although Ingram Book accounts for just over half of Ingram Industries' sales, the company also operates Ingram Marine Group, which ships grain, ore, and other products through its 2,600 barges, and

Ingram Insurance Group, which offers high-risk auto insurance in about 10 states through Permanent General Insurance.

Ingram Industries has undergone dramatic makeovers in the last few years. It spun off its largest segment, Ingram Micro (the world's largest distributor of microcomputer products) in 1996 and Ingram Entertainment (the US's top distributor of videotapes) in 1997.

Martha is America's wealthiest active businesswoman and she and her family own and run Ingram Industries. The Ingram family controls nearly 85% of Ingram Micro's voting stock.

HISTORY

Orrin Ingram and two partners founded the Dole, Ingram & Kennedy sawmill in 1857 in Eau Claire, Wisconsin, on the Chippewa River, about 50 miles upstream from the Mississippi River. By the 1870s the company, renamed Ingram & Kennedy, was selling lumber as far downstream as Hannibal, Missouri.

Ingram's success was noticed by Frederick Weyerhaeuser, a German immigrant in Rock Island, Illinois, who, like Ingram, had worked in a sawmill before buying one of his own. In 1881 Ingram and Weyerhaeuser negotiated the formation of Chippewa Logging (35%-owned by up-river partners, 65%-owned by down-river interests), which controlled the white pine harvest of the Chippewa Valley. In 1900 Ingram paid $216,000 for 2,160 shares in the newly formed Weyerhaeuser Timber Company. Ingram let his sons and grandsons handle the investment and formed O.H. Ingram Co. to manage the family's interests. He died in 1918.

In 1946 Ingram's descendants founded Ingram Barge, which hauled crude oil to the company's refinery near St. Louis. After buying and then selling other holdings, in 1962 the family formed Ingram Corp., consisting solely of Ingram Barge. Brothers Bronson and Fritz Ingram (the great grandsons of Orrin) bought the company from their father, Hank, before he died in 1963, and in 1964 they bought half of Tennessee Book, a textbook distributing company founded in 1935. In 1970 they formed Ingram Book Group to sell trade books to bookstores and libraries.

Ingram Barge won a $48 million Chicago sludge-hauling contract in 1971, but later the company was accused of bribing city politicians with $1.2 million in order to land the contract. The brothers stood trial in 1977 for authorizing the bribes; Bronson was acquitted,

but the court convicted Fritz on 29 counts. Before Fritz entered prison (he served 16 months of a four-year sentence), he and his brother split their company. Fritz took the energy operations and went bust in the 1980s. Bronson took the barge and book businesses and formed Ingram Industries.

This acquisitive, technologically savvy new company formed computer products distributor Ingram Computer in 1982 and between 1985 and 1989 bought all of the stock of Micro D, a computer wholesaler. Ingram Computer and Micro D merged to form Ingram Micro. In 1992 it acquired Commtron, the world's #1 wholesaler of prerecorded videocassettes, and merged it into Ingram Entertainment.

When Bronson died in mid-1995, his wife Martha became chairman (she had been the company's PR director) and began a dramatic restructuring. Ingram Industries closed its non-bookstore rack distributor (Ingram Merchandising) in 1995 and sold its oil-and-gas machinery subsidiary (Cactus Co.) in 1996. It spun off Ingram Micro in 1996, followed in 1997 by Ingram Entertainment. Ingram Industries purchased Christian books distributor Spring Arbor that year and also introduced an on-demand book publishing service (Lightning Print).

In late 1998 the company agreed to sell its book group to Barnes & Noble for $600 million, but the companies killed the deal in mid-1999 when it appeared that the FTC would do the same. With customers and competitors increasing distribution capacity in the western US, a resulting drop in business led Ingram Industries to cut more than 100 jobs at an Oregon warehouse in 1999.

Chairman: Martha Ingram, age 62
VC; Chairman, Ingram Book Group: John R. Ingram, age 36
President and CEO: Orrin H. Ingram II, age 37
VP, CFO, and Treasurer: Robert W. Mitchell
VP and Controller: Mary K. Cavarra
VP: Richard B. Patton
President, Ingram Periodicals: Julie Burns
President, Ingram Library Services and Ingram International: Martin Keeley
President and CEO, Ingram Book Group: Michael Lovett
President, Spring Arbor Distributors: Frances Salamon
Chief Administrative Officer, Spring Arbor Distributors: Steven Little
Human Resources: Dennis Delaney

HQ: 1 Belle Meade Place, 4400 Harding Rd., Nashville, TN 37205-2244
Phone: 615-298-8200   **Fax:** 615-298-8242
Web site: http://www.ingrambook.com

Selected Operations

Ingram Book Group
Ingram Book Company (wholesaler of trade books and audiobooks)
Ingram Customer Systems (computerized systems and services)
Ingram International (international distribution of books and audiobooks)
Ingram Library Services (distribution of books, audiobooks, and videos to libraries)
Ingram Periodicals (direct distributor of specialty magazines)
Ingram Publisher Services (distribution services for publishers)
Lighting Print (on-demand printing)
Retailer Services (book distributor to nontraditional book market)
Spring Arbor Distributors (product and services for Christian retailers)
White Bridge Communications (consumer marketing programs for publishers and retailers)

Ingram Insurance Group
Permanent General Insurance Co. (automobile insurance in California, Georgia, Indiana, Louisiana, Mississippi, Ohio, South Carolina, Tennessee, and Wisconsin)
Tennessee Insurance Company (insures Ingram affiliates)

Ingram Marine Group
Ingram Barge (ships grain, ore, and other products)
Ingram Materials Co. (produces construction materials such as sand and gravel)

Advanced Marketing
Allstate
American Commercial Lines
American Financial
Baker & Taylor
Chas. Levy
Hollywood Marine
Kirby
Koen Book Distributors
Progressive Corporation
SAFECO
State Farm
Thomas Nelson
Times Publishing

Private company FYE: December 31	Annual Growth	1989	1990	1991	1992	1993	1994	1995	1996	1997	1998
Sales ($ mil.)	(3.0%)	2,640	2,677	3,422	4,657	6,163	8,010	11,000	1,463	1,796	2,000
Employees	3.9%	4,600	5,400	6,526	8,407	9,658	10,000	13,000	5,300	6,362	6,500

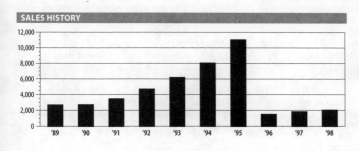

SALES HISTORY

INGRAM MICRO INC.

OVERVIEW

Like a plastic Pez container, Ingram Micro has a knack for dispensing. The Santa Ana, California-based company is the world's largest wholesale distributor of computer products. It offers more than 200,000 items (including PCs, mass storage and networking devices, CD-ROM drives, printers, and software) to 140,000 reseller customers worldwide. Its suppliers include Apple, Compaq, and IBM. Ingram Micro distributes its products through warehouses in North America, Europe, and Asia. More than one-third of its business comes from international sales.

With a history of summer-movie-plot-thin

profit margins, Ingram Micro has been challenged by the trend toward lower PC prices. Its response has been to streamline operations, boost Internet sales (eSolutions), and expand into build-to-order PC assembly. Unpretentious CEO Jerre Stead, who answers his own special 800 number for employees who want to complain or commend, and lists "Head Coach" on his business card, is pushing Ingram Micro's boundaries internationally through acquisitions.

The Ingram family owns about 48% of the company's stock but controls nearly 85% of the voting power.

HISTORY

There is no love lost between the former Micro D and Ingram Industries. Micro D was founded in Fountain Valley, California, in 1979 by husband-and-wife entrepreneurs Geza Csige and Lorraine Mecca. As the company grew, Mecca sought to merge the computer distributor with a partner that could take over daily operations. She relinquished control of Micro D to Linwood "Chip" Lacy in 1986 and sold her 51% share of the company to minority shareholder Ingram Distribution Group.

Sales bottomed out for Micro D that year. Lacy tightened Micro D's belt and took huge charges for outdated inventory it sold at a discount and overdue payments from customers that had gone bankrupt.

At the same time, Ingram Industries was busy merging recently acquired Ingram Software Distribution Services of Buffalo, New York, with Compton, California-based Softeam. The merger made the company one of the nation's largest wholesale distributors of computer software. Lacy saw Ingram's purchase of Micro D shares as a conflict of interest, but he was too busy returning Micro D to profitability: centralizing its marketing and distribution functions, cutting costs, and expanding its market to include more small retailers, which provided higher margins. Micro D went from the fourth-largest distributor of microcomputer products to #1 in just one year.

The surging PC market in the late 1980s fueled Micro D's growth. By 1988 the firm had expanded outside the US for the first time, acquiring Ottawa, Ontario-based Frantek Computer Products.

Ingram Industries offered to acquire the 41% of outstanding Micro D stock it did not own in 1988, but Lacy resisted, preferring to let Ingram wait. Though Ingram owned a majority of

Micro D stock, it only controlled three of seven seats on the board. Ingram was forced to play Lacy's game and finally acquired the company at a higher cost in 1989. The new company, which controlled 20% of the computer distribution market, was called Ingram Micro D. The merger was anything but smooth, and several Micro D executives jumped ship.

As the PC took hold in the US in the 1990s, Ingram Micro D became the dominant industry player, but relations between Lacy and the Ingram family never improved. The company shortened its name to Ingram Micro in 1991, and two years later, as it was hitting stride, Lacy announced plans to leave. To keep him, Ingram Industries' CEO Bronson Ingram (much to his distaste) promised to let Lacy take the company public.

Bronson Ingram died in 1995 and the next year his widow, Martha, forced Lacy's resignation. Lacy was replaced by Jerre Stead, formerly CEO of software maker Legent, who devised a compensation package for himself consisting solely of stock options (no salary). Ingram went public a few months after Stead took over.

In 1998 Ingram Micro forged a distribution alliance with Japanese computer giant SOFTBANK and bought a majority stake in German computer products distributor Macrotron. It also bought an assembly plant in the Netherlands to expand into build-to-order PC manufacturing. Amid softer PC sales industrywide, Ingram Micro in 1999 announced plans to lay off 1,400 employees (about 10% of its workforce), and signed a tentative deal (worth an estimated $10 billion) with CompUSA to be its primary PC manufacturer and distributor. Later that year the company — with its sales slipping and its stock slumping — announced it was in search of a new CEO.

Chairman and CEO: Jerre L. Stead, age 56
President and Worldwide COO: Jeffrey R. Rodek, age 45,
$778,868 pay
EVP and Worldwide CFO: Michael J. Grainger, age 46,
$468,750 pay
EVP; President, Frameworks: Douglas R. Antone
EVP; President, Ingram Micro Europe:
Gregory M. Spierkel, age 42
EVP; President, Ingram Micro North America:
Philip D. Ellett
EVP; President, Ingram Micro US: Robert D. Grambo,
age 34
**SVP, Chief Technology Officer and Chief Information
Officer; Co-Chair of eSolutions Group:** Richard J. Kish
SVP, Secretary, and General Counsel:
James E. Anderson Jr., age 51
SVP; President, Ingram Micro Asia/Pacific: Lai Fuan Foo
SVP; President, Ingram Micro Canada: Kevin M. Murai,
age 43
SVP; President, Ingram Micro Latin America:
Hans T. Koppen
SVP, Worldwide Human Resources: David M. Finley,
age 58
**SVP, Worldwide Marketing; Co-Chair of eSolutions
Group:** Guy P. Abramo, age 37
Auditors: PricewaterhouseCoopers LLP

LOCATIONS

HQ: 1600 E. St. Andrew Place, Santa Ana, CA 92799-5125
Phone: 714-566-1000   **Fax:** 714-566-7900
Web site: http://www.ingrammicro.com

1998 Sales

	$ mil.	% of total
US	14,393	65
Europe	5,624	26
Other regions	2,017	9
Total	**22,034**	**100**

PRODUCTS/OPERATIONS

Selected Products

Business application software	Printers
CD-ROM drives	Scanners
Computer supplies	Servers
Desktop and notebook PCs	Workstations
Entertainment software	
Mass storage devices	**Selected Services**
Modems	Electronic services
Monitors	Financing services
Network interface cards	Order fulfillment
Networking hubs, routers, and switches	System configuration
	Marketing services
	Technical education
	Technical support

COMPETITORS

Arrow Electronics	MicroAge
ASI Corp.	Microtech International
Avnet	Navarre
CHS Electronics	Pulsar Data Systems
InaCom	Scribona
Marshall Industries	Tech Data
Merisel	Wyle Electronics
Micro Warehouse	

HISTORICAL FINANCIALS & EMPLOYEES

NYSE symbol: IM FYE: December 31	Annual Growth	1989	1990	1991	1992	1993	1994	1995	1996	1997	1998
Sales ($ mil.)	40.7%	—	—	2,017	2,731	4,044	5,830	8,617	12,024	16,582	22,034
Net income ($ mil.)	35.0%	—	—	30	31	50	63	84	111	194	245
Income as % of sales	—	—	—	1.5%	1.1%	1.2%	1.1%	1.0%	0.9%	1.2%	1.1%
Earnings per share ($)	36.5%	—	—	—	—	—	—	—	0.88	1.32	1.64
Stock price - FY high ($)	—	—	—	—	—	—	—	—	28.13	34.75	54.63
Stock price - FY low ($)	—	—	—	—	—	—	—	—	20.00	19.00	26.63
Stock price - FY close ($)	24.0%	—	—	—	—	—	—	—	23.00	29.13	35.38
P/E - high	—	—	—	—	—	—	—	—	32	26	33
P/E - low	—	—	—	—	—	—	—	—	23	14	16
Dividends per share ($)	—	—	—	—	—	—	—	—	0.00	0.00	0.00
Book value per share ($)	26.5%	—	—	—	—	—	—	—	6.15	7.69	9.86
Employees	23.7%	—	—	—	—	—	—	7,604	9,008	12,000	14,400

STOCK PRICE HISTORY

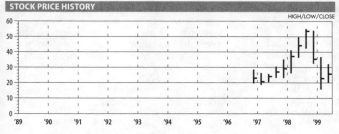

1998 FISCAL YEAR-END

Debt ratio: 54.6%
Return on equity: 17.5%
Cash ($ mil.): 97
Current ratio: 1.68
Long-term debt ($ mil.): 1,682
No. of shares (mil.): 142
Dividends
  Yield: —
  Payout: —
Market value ($ mil.): 5,023

INTEL CORPORATION

OVERVIEW

Just how inside is Intel? Its microprocessors — the brains of a computer — are found in about 80% of all PCs. Santa Clara, California-based Intel is the world's top semiconductor maker and a bellwether among high-tech companies. Compaq and Dell account for 13% and 11% of sales, respectively. Best-known for its PC microprocessors, Intel also makes embedded products (including microcontrollers and flash memories) for the communications, industrial equipment, and military markets.

The networking revolution is playing an increasingly important part in Intel's corporate makeup; the company has formed units to oversee its communications and networking chip and device (servers, hubs, routers) operations. Intel is using investments and acquisitions to expand into related markets. For example, it plans to provide data service centers that support Internet service providers with centralized banks of powerful servers. (Intel is also the world's largest e-commerce company, with more than $1 billion a month in online sales.)

Part of Intel's power lies in its partnership with Microsoft, the so-called "Wintel" alliance that has seen Microsoft's increasingly powerful software matched by beefed-up chips from Intel. The company is developing the powerful Merced, a much-anticipated 64-bit microprocessor, with Hewlett-Packard. With its power focus, Intel lost some market share when it was slow to produce its Celeron low-end chip for the burgeoning sub-$1,000 PC market.

Another Intel strength is its management, led by hallowed chairman Andrew Grove and CEO Craig Barrett. Co-founder Gordon Moore (whose famous Moore's Law positing that chip capabilities double every eighteen months has proven remarkably prescient) still serves as chairman emeritus. He owns about 5% of Intel.

HISTORY

In 1968 three engineers from Fairchild Semiconductor created Intel in Mountain View, California, to develop technology for silicon-based chips. ("Intel" is a contraction of Integrated Electronics, a name that was already in use.) Robert Noyce (co-inventor of the integrated circuit, 1958) and Gordon Moore handled long-range planning, while Andy Grove oversaw manufacturing.

Intel's sales grew as it supplied semiconductor memory for large computers (DRAM chips, which replace magnetic core memory storage, 1970; EPROM chips, which allow read-only memory to be erased and reused, 1971). This success funded Intel microprocessor designs that revolutionized the electronics industry. In 1979 Moore became Intel's chairman and Grove its president. (Grove became CEO in 1987.) When Intel's 8088 chip was chosen for IBM's PC in 1981, Intel's place as the microcomputer standards supplier was secured.

In 1985 cutthroat pricing by Japanese competitors forced Intel out of the DRAM market. The company refocused on proprietary PC chips. In its drive to set the industry standard, Intel licensed Advanced Micro Devices (AMD) and others to produce clones of the 286, only to see AMD capture more than half of that market by 1990. In response, Intel fiercely protected the technology of its highly successful 386 (1985) and 486 chips (1989), leading AMD to sue for breach of contract. Intel unveiled its Pentium chip in 1993. A mathematical flaw in the Pentium temporarily tarnished the company's image.

Intel and AMD settled several microcode court cases in 1995: AMD got the microcode license and Intel was awarded $58 million in damages. That year Intel's sixth-generation chip, the Pentium Pro, debuted.

Machines containing Intel's MMX Pentium and Pentium II microprocessors hit the shelves in 1997. That year Digital Equipment (now part of Compaq) accused Intel of using patented technology to develop the Pentium. To settle the suit Intel bought Digital's semiconductor operations and agreed to make Digital's Alpha chip technology available to rivals.

Grove handed the CEO reins to president Craig Barrett in 1998. That year Intel bought Chips and Technologies (graphics controllers) and unveiled its Celeron chip for sub-$1,000 PCs. The FTC also slapped Intel with an antitrust suit, accusing it of denying key technical data to customers that had challenged it on patent issues.

In 1999 Intel and the FTC reached a settlement, forcing Intel to soften some competitive tactics; the FTC continued its inquiry on a broader scale. That year Intel made a $100 million investment in top memory chip maker Samsung. It boosted its networking products segment by acquiring Shiva Corporation (now Intel Network Systems), Level One (for $2.2 billion; communications integrated circuits), and Dialogic ($770 million; computer telephony). The company said it would exit the market for PC graphics chips.

Chairman Emeritus: Gordon E. Moore, age 69
Chairman: Andrew S. Grove, age 62, $2,416,800 pay
President and CEO: Craig R. Barrett, age 59,
$2,244,000 pay
**EVP; General Manager, Intel Architecture Business
Group:** Paul S. Otellini, age 48, $1,056,000 pay
EVP; General Manager, New Business Group:
Gerhard H. Parker, age 55, $1,279,700 pay
SVP and CFO: Andy D. Bryant, age 48
SVP; Director, Corporate Business Development:
Leslie L. Vadasz, age 62, $1,134,800 pay
SVP; Director, Sales and Marketing Group:
Sean M. Maloney, age 42
SVP; General Manager, Content Group:
Ronald J. Whittier
**SVP; General Manager, Microprocessor Products
Group:** Albert Y. C. Yu, age 57
**SVP; General Manager, Technology and Manufacturing
Group:** Michael R. Splinter, age 48
VP; Director, Corporate Licensing: Robert T. Jenkins
VP; Director, Human Resources: Patricia Murray
VP; Director, New Business Development:
Kirby A. Dyess
VP; Director, Strategic Marketing: Dennis L. Carter
VP, Secretary, and General Counsel:
F. Thomas Dunlap Jr., age 47
Auditors: Ernst & Young LLP

LOCATIONS

HQ: 2200 Mission College Blvd.,
Santa Clara, CA 95052-8119
Phone: 408-765-8080   **Fax:** 408-765-6284
Web site: http://www.intel.com

1998 Sales

	$ mil.	% of total
North America	11,663	45
Europe	7,452	28
Asia/Pacific		
Japan	1,849	7
Other countries	5,309	20
Total	**26,273**	**100**

PRODUCTS/OPERATIONS

Selected Products

Chipsets
Communications servers
Computer telephony
   products
Digital imaging products
Embedded processors
Flash memories
Home networking
   products
Microcontrollers
Microprocessors
Network appliances

Network infrastructure
   products
Network interface cards
Network management
   products
Network processors
Systems management
   software
Video- and data-
   conferencing products
Virtual private network
   products

COMPETITORS

3Com
Acer
AMD
Atmel
Cisco Systems
Fujitsu
Hitachi
IBM
IDT
Lucent
Macronix International

Mitsubishi Electric
Motorola
National Semiconductor
NEC
Nortel Networks
Philips Electronics
Samsung Electronics
STMicroelectronics
Sun Microsystems
Texas Instruments
Toshiba

HISTORICAL FINANCIALS & EMPLOYEES

Nasdaq symbol: INTC FYE: December 31	Annual Growth	1989	1990	1991	1992	1993	1994	1995	1996	1997	1998
Sales ($ mil.)	26.7%	3,127	3,921	4,779	5,844	8,782	11,521	16,202	20,847	25,070	26,273
Net income ($ mil.)	35.6%	391	650	819	1,067	2,295	2,288	3,566	5,157	6,945	6,068
Income as % of sales	—	12.5%	16.6%	17.1%	18.2%	26.1%	19.9%	22.0%	24.7%	27.7%	23.1%
Earnings per share ($)	33.3%	0.13	0.20	0.25	0.31	0.65	0.66	1.01	1.45	1.94	1.73
Stock price – FY high ($)	—	2.25	3.25	3.70	5.72	9.28	9.19	19.59	35.38	51.00	63.09
Stock price – FY low ($)	—	1.43	1.75	2.36	2.91	5.34	6.34	7.88	12.45	31.44	32.83
Stock price – FY close ($)	44.5%	2.16	2.41	3.06	5.44	7.75	7.98	14.19	32.73	35.13	59.28
P/E – high	—	17	16	15	18	14	14	19	24	26	36
P/E – low	—	11	9	9	9	8	10	8	9	16	19
Dividends per share ($)	—	0.00	0.00	0.00	0.01	0.03	0.03	0.04	0.05	0.06	0.07
Book value per share ($)	26.3%	0.86	1.12	1.35	1.63	2.24	2.80	3.70	5.14	5.93	7.05
Employees	12.9%	21,700	23,900	24,600	25,800	29,500	32,600	41,600	48,500	63,700	64,500

STOCK PRICE HISTORY

HIGH/LOW/CLOSE

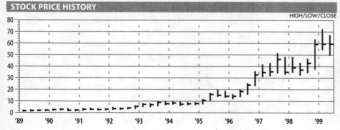

1998 FISCAL YEAR-END

Debt ratio: 2.9%
Return on equity: 26.0%
Cash ($ mil.): 2,038
Current ratio: 2.32
Long-term debt ($ mil.): 702
No. of shares (mil.): 3,315
Dividends
   Yield: 0.1%
   Payout: 4.0%
Market value ($ mil.): 196,513

INTERGRAPH CORPORATION

OVERVIEW

Intergraph is plotting its escape from the bottom of the financial charts. The Huntsville, Alabama-based company makes graphics-intensive hardware and software systems, primarily for customers in mapping and geographic information, architecture, engineering, and construction. The company has three subsidiaries: Intergraph Computer Systems (graphics accelerators, workstations), Intergraph Public Safety (computer-assisted dispatching systems), and VeriBest (electronic design automation software). Related services account for 30% of sales.

A wrenching and costly restructuring from UNIX-based to Windows NT-based design systems, in addition to legal disputes with key supplier Intel that left Intergraph canceling several projects, has taken a heavy toll on Intergraph. The company hasn't seen a profitable year since 1992.

Intergraph is plotting a new diagram as a leaner company. To cut costs the company has sold its engineering and document products lines and has begun to outsource its product manufacturing operations. Intergraph is also leaving the PC and server market behind and reorganizing around software, services, and graphics accelerators.

HISTORY

James and Nancy Meadlock and several other former IBM workers (all software developers for Saturn rockets) founded consulting firm M&S Computing in 1969. The first contract, a guidance system for the US Army Missile Command in Huntsville, Alabama, used the applications that later grew into Intergraph's computer graphics business.

The company's first commercial graphics system was for mapping applications (1973). Penetration of the architecture, engineering, and construction markets followed with the introduction of the Interactive Graphics Design System. M&S packaged the software with industry-accepted hardware while competitors stuck to more restricted proprietary versions.

In the late 1970s M&S began making its own computers to boost profit margins and compatibility across product lines. The company changed its name to Intergraph in 1980 and went public the following year. During the graphics boom of the early 1980s, Intergraph grew 40%-60% yearly. In 1984 it introduced the first dual-screen workstation.

Intergraph supported open systems by adopting the UNIX operating system and networking its workstations with standard technologies. The company powered the workstations with its RISC (reduced instruction set computer) microprocessor and anticipated demand for generic workstations unbundled from graphics software.

The company also absorbed key technologies by buying makers of CLIPPER chips (1987), scanning and plotting hardware (Optotronics, 1986; AnaTech, 1987), engineering software (Tangent Systems, 1988), and software development tools (Quintus, 1989). It also bought a 50% stake in Bentley Systems (creator of Intergraph's MicroStation software, 1987)

and acquired struggling Daisy Cadnetix (1990), making it a leading supplier to the electronic design automation industry.

Intergraph began a major transition in 1993 from UNIX-based systems to those based on Intel microprocessors and Microsoft operating systems. As part of its reorganization, Intergraph exited the microprocessor design business.

In 1994 the General Services Administration's appeals board upheld a $398 million US Navy contract awarded to Intergraph. The technology transition caused more losses for 1994.

Intergraph in 1995 unveiled technology that let graphics modules from multiple vendors work together. The company brought several new products to market in 1996, but losses associated with the technology turnaround continued.

In 1997 Intergraph launched a line of PCs designed for the low-end 3-D graphics market. Intergraph sued Intel in late 1997 over contract and patent issues and anticompetitive practices. Intel countersued, but Intergraph's position appeared to strengthen in 1998 when a preliminary injunction forced Intel to continue supplying technical information to Intergraph. (Intergraph continues to pursue its action against Intel even though the FTC and Intel reached a tentative settlement in a separate action involving alleged antitrust activities.)

Also in 1998 it sold its solid edge and engineering modeling system product lines to Electronic Data Systems, and turned over its manufacturing operations to contract manufacturer SCI Systems. The drawn out tussle with Intel worsened losses for that year. In 1999 Intergraph announced it would exit the PC and server business.

Chairman and CEO: James W. Meadlock, age 65,
$300,000 pay
President and COO: Manfred Wittler, age 58,
$443,280 pay (prior to promotion)
EVP: Lawrence F. Ayers Jr., age 66
EVP: Klass Borgers, age 54, $243,022 pay
EVP: Penman R. Gilliam, age 61
EVP and CFO: Larry J. Laster
EVP: Richard H. Lussier, age 53
EVP: Nancy B. Meadlock, age 60
**EVP; President and CEO, Intergraph Computer
Systems:** Wade C. Patterson, age 37, $320,368 pay
EVP: Stephen J. Phillips, age 57, $249,170 pay
EVP: William E. Salter, age 57
EVP: K. David Stinson Jr., age 45
EVP; CEO, Intergraph Public Safety: James F. Taylor Jr.
EVP: Robert E. Thurber, age 58
EVP: Edward A. Wilkinson, age 65
EVP: Allan B. Wilson, age 50
VP Corporate Human Resources: Milford B. French
Auditors: Ernst & Young LLP

LOCATIONS

HQ: Huntsville, AL 35894-0001
Phone: 256-730-2000 **Fax:** 256-730-2040
Web site: http://www.intergraph.com

1998 Sales

	$ mil.	% of total
US	505	49
Europe	318	31
Asia/Pacific	108	10
Other regions	102	10
Total	**1,033**	**100**

PRODUCTS/OPERATIONS

1998 Sales

	$ mil.	% of total
Systems	726	70
Maintenance & services	307	30
Total	**1,033**	**100**

Selected Products

Civil engineering-based software (SelectCAD)
Electronic design automation tools (VeriBest)
Graphics accelerators (Intense 3D, RealiZm)
Graphics workstations (TDZ, StudioZ, ExtremeZ)
Plant design software (SmartPlant)
Printers
Process and building-based hardware and software
  systems
Public safety-based hardware and software dispatch
  systems
State and local government-based applications
Transportation analysis software (MGE)
Utility-based geographical information systems

COMPETITORS

Autodesk	Mentor Graphics
Cadence	Parametric Technology
Compaq	Printrak
Dell Computer	Scitex
ECRM	SGI
Environmental Systems	Structural Dynamics
Research	Research
Evans & Sutherland	Sun Microsystems
Hewlett-Packard	Synopsys
IBM	TriTech Software Systems
Litton Industries	Unisys

HISTORICAL FINANCIALS & EMPLOYEES

Nasdaq symbol: INGR FYE: December 31	Annual Growth	1989	1990	1991	1992	1993	1994	1995	1996	1997	1998
Sales ($ mil.)	2.1%	860	1,045	1,195	1,177	1,050	1,041	1,098	1,095	1,124	1,033
Net income ($ mil.)	—	80	63	71	8	(116)	(70)	(45)	(69)	(70)	(20)
Income as % of sales	—	9.2%	6.0%	5.9%	0.7%	—	—	—	—	—	—
Earnings per share ($)	—	1.48	1.28	1.47	0.18	(2.51)	(1.56)	(0.98)	(1.46)	(1.46)	(0.41)
Stock price - FY high ($)		22.75	23.50	31.50	22.38	13.50	11.25	18.50	20.13	14.19	10.56
Stock price - FY low ($)		13.75	10.50	13.00	11.00	8.50	7.38	8.13	8.63	6.25	4.69
Stock price - FY close ($)	(11.5%)	17.25	13.75	17.75	13.25	10.63	8.13	15.75	10.25	10.00	5.75
P/E - high		15	18	21	124	—	—	—	—	—	—
P/E - low	—	9	8	9	61	—	—	—	—	—	—
Dividends per share ($)	—	0.00	0.00	0.00	0.00	0.00	0.00	0.00	0.00	0.00	0.00
Book value per share ($)	(5.9%)	12.58	14.36	15.80	15.49	12.98	11.66	10.76	9.38	6.34	7.30
Employees	(2.2%)	8,200	9,600	10,300	10,300	9,500	9,200	8,400	8,200	7,700	6,700

STOCK PRICE HISTORY

HIGH/LOW/CLOSE

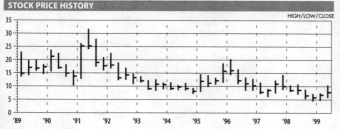

1998 FISCAL YEAR-END

Debt ratio: 14.3%
Return on equity: —
Cash ($ mil.): 95
Current ratio: 1.78
Long-term debt ($ mil.): 60
No. of shares (mil.): 49
Dividends
  Yield: —
  Payout: —
Market value ($ mil.): 280

IBM

Big Lou saved Big Blue. Armonk, New York-based International Business Machines (IBM) still logs on as the world's biggest computer firm. The company makes software (#2 behind Microsoft), PCs, mainframe and server systems, notebooks, microprocessors, networking equipment (a business it's getting out of), and peripherals, among its 40,000 products. IBM, whose increasingly valued services business accounts for 35% of sales, is the planet's largest provider of technical support. Subsidiary Lotus Development wrote the book on spreadsheet and business software, while Tivoli Systems specializes in developing tools that manage corporate computer networks.

IBM has grown synonymous with PCs — and the phrase, "insular establishment of button-down drones." CEO Louis Gerstner has spent his tenure erasing both stereotypes. Gerstner, who became head of the ailing, artifact-status firm in 1993, slashed costs and nonstrategic divisions, cut the workforce, shook up entrenched management, reinvented the mainframe as a business network workhorse, and pushed services.

In the face of dwindling PC sales IBM is emphasizing the Internetworked world through acquisitions (most notably the purchase of a controlling stake in Web site development software firm NetObjects). IBM also has intensified sales of its stand-alone computer parts, a strategy that has resulted in lucrative deals with fellow computer manufacturers and would-be rivals such as Hewlett-Packard and Dell Computer.

In 1914 National Cash Register's star salesman, Thomas Watson, left to rescue the flagging Computing-Tabulating-Recording Company, the pioneer in US punch card processing. Watson aggressively marketed C-T-R's tabulators, supplying them to the US government during WWI and tripling company revenues to almost $15 million by 1920. The company became International Business Machines (IBM) in 1924 and soon dominated the global market for tabulators, time clocks, and electric typewriters. It was the US's largest office machine firm by 1940.

IBM perfected electromechanical calculation (the Harvard Mark I, 1944) but initially dismissed the potential of computers. When Remington Rand's UNIVAC computer (1951) began replacing IBM machines, IBM quickly responded.

The company unveiled its first computer in 1952. With its superior research and development (R&D) and marketing, IBM built a market share near 80% in the 1960s and 1970s. The firm's innovations included the STRETCH systems, which eliminated vacuum tubes (1960) and the first compatible family of computers, the System/360 (1964). IBM also developed floppy disk storage (1971) and the first laser printer for computers (1975). The introduction of the IBM PC in 1981 ignited the PC industry; a barrage of PC clones followed. Through it all IBM was the subject of a 12-year, massive government antitrust investigation that ended in 1982.

The shift to smaller, open systems, along with greater competition in all of IBM's segments, caused wrenching change. Instead of responding to the market need for cheap PCs and practical business applications, IBM stubbornly stuck with mainframes, and rivals began capitalizing on Big Blue's technology. After posting profits of $6.6 billion in 1984, the company began a slow slide. It sold many noncomputer businesses, including its copier division to Kodak in 1988 and its Lexmark typewriter and supplies business to Clayton, Dubilier & Rice in 1991. Closing the book on its heritage, IBM even shuttered the last of its punch card plants that year.

In 1993 CEO John Akers was replaced with Louis Gerstner, the first outsider to run the company. Among his myriad restructuring changes, Gerstner demanded that $1 billion be cut from the R&D budget, causing an exodus of scientists from IBM and creating an operation geared more toward quick turnaround than lengthy research (though the company still leads the business world in patents each year). In 1994 Big Blue reported its first profit in four years. IBM that year began making computer chips designed by Cyrix.

Beefing up its software offerings, IBM bought spreadsheet software pioneer Lotus for $3.5 billion in 1995 and network management specialist Tivoli Systems in 1996. In 1998 AT&T bought IBM's Global Network unit, which provides multinational corporations with international data links, for $5 billion. In 1999 IBM agreed to buy Sequent Computer Systems, whose servers help businesses handle heavy on-line transaction processing and Internet communications. That year IBM bowed out of the networking hardware business, making plans to sell its intellectual property to Cisco Systems.

OFFICERS

Chairman and CEO: Louis V. Gerstner Jr., age 57, $9,375,000 pay
SVP and CFO: Douglas L. Maine, age 50
SVP and General Counsel: Lawrence R. Ricciardi, age 58, $1,342,500 pay
SVP and Group Executive, IBM Global Services: Samuel J. Palmisano, age 47, $1,381,250 pay
SVP and Group Executive, Personal Systems Group: David M. Thomas, age 49
SVP and Group Executive, Sales and Distribution Group: William A. Ethrington, age 57
SVP and Group Executive, Server Group: Robert M. Stephenson, age 60, $1,456,250 pay
SVP and Group Executive, Technology Group: James T. Vanderslice, age 58
SVP Human Resources: J. Thomas Bouchard, age 58
SVP Marketing: Abby F. Kohnstamm, age 45
SVP Research: Paul M. Horn, age 52
SVP Strategy: J. Bruce Harreld, age 48
SVP Technology and Manufacturing: Nicholas M. Donofrio, age 53
Auditors: PricewaterhouseCoopers LLP

LOCATIONS

HQ: International Business Machines Corporation, New Orchard Rd., Armonk, NY 10504
Phone: 914-499-1900   **Fax:** 914-765-7382
Web site: http://www.ibm.com

1998 Sales

	$ mil.	% of total
US	35,303	43
Japan	8,567	10
Other countries	37,797	47
Total	**81,667**	**100**

PRODUCTS/OPERATIONS

1998 Sales

	$ mil.	% of total
Hardware	35,419	43
Services	28,916	35
Software	11,863	15
Financing	2,877	4
Enterprise investments & other	2,592	3
Total	**81,667**	**100**

Products
Hard disk drives
LAN adapters
Microelectronics
Monitors and other service parts
Network computers
Notebook computers
PCs
Printers and supplies
Servers
Software
Storage systems
Workstations

Services
Business recovery
Connectivity support
Consulting
Custom integration
Internet support
Outsourcing
Product training
Support
Systems management

COMPETITORS

Acer
Apple Computer
Bull
Canon
Compaq
Computer Associates
Data General
Dell Computer
EDS
eMachines
Fujitsu
Gateway
Hewlett-Packard
Hitachi
Intel
Lexmark
International
Micron
Electronics
Microsoft
Motorola
Novell
Oki Electric
Oracle
Packard Bell
SAP
SGI
Sun Microsystems
Texas Instruments
Toshiba
Unisys

HISTORICAL FINANCIALS & EMPLOYEES

NYSE symbol: IBM FYE: December 31	Annual Growth	1989	1990	1991	1992	1993	1994	1995	1996	1997	1998
Sales ($ mil.)	3.0%	62,710	69,018	64,792	64,523	62,716	64,052	71,940	75,947	78,508	81,667
Net income ($ mil.)	6.0%	3,758	6,020	(2,827)	(4,965)	(8,101)	3,021	4,178	5,429	6,093	6,328
Income as % of sales	—	6.0%	8.7%	—	—	—	4.7%	5.8%	7.1%	7.8%	7.7%
Earnings per share ($)	8.2%	1.62	2.63	(1.24)	(2.17)	(3.56)	1.24	1.77	2.51	3.01	3.29
Stock price - FY high ($)	—	32.72	30.78	34.94	25.09	14.97	19.09	28.66	41.50	56.75	94.97
Stock price - FY low ($)	—	23.34	23.63	20.88	12.19	10.16	12.84	17.56	20.78	31.78	47.81
Stock price - FY close ($)	16.4%	23.53	28.25	22.25	12.59	14.13	18.38	22.84	37.88	52.31	92.19
P/E - high	—	20	12	—	—	—	15	16	17	19	29
P/E - low	—	14	9	—	—	—	10	10	8	11	15
Dividends per share ($)	(10.7%)	1.19	1.21	1.21	1.21	0.40	0.25	0.25	0.33	0.39	0.43
Book value per share ($)	(5.2%)	16.75	18.74	16.20	12.09	8.02	9.50	10.12	10.52	10.10	10.36
Employees	(3.0%)	383,220	373,816	344,396	301,542	256,207	219,839	225,347	240,615	269,465	291,067

STOCK PRICE HISTORY

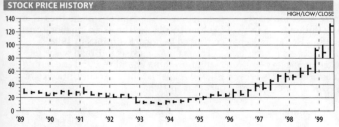

HIGH/LOW/CLOSE

1998 FISCAL YEAR-END

Debt ratio: 44.4%
Return on equity: 33.0%
Cash ($ mil.): 5,375
Current ratio: 1.15
Long-term debt ($ mil.): 15,508
No. of shares (mil.): 1,852
Dividends
  Yield: 0.5%
  Payout: 13.1%
Market value ($ mil.): 170,719

INTERNATIONAL FLAVORS

OVERVIEW

A rose by any name would smell sweeter if New York City-based International Flavors & Fragrances (IFF) had anything to do with it. A leading producer of flavorings and fragrances, IFF markets primarily to cosmetics manufacturers, personal care product makers, and food companies. IFF has manufacturing, sales, and distribution facilities in more than 35 countries.

IFF's flavors are sold to makers of prepared foods, dairy products, beverages, confectionery products, and pharmaceuticals. Its fragrance customers include producers of perfumes, cosmetics, deodorants, detergents, hair care products, and soaps. IFF's fragrances account for

about 60% of sales. The compounds used in the company's products are made both synthetically and from natural ingredients such as flowers and fruits. IFF also sells its excess synthetic ingredients to other companies.

The economic slowdown in Asia has depressed sales. Other factors affecting IFF's stagnating sales include the Russian financial collapse and the strength of the US dollar. Still, IFF's sales outside the US account for 70% of revenues, as emerging markets such as Eastern Europe have shown great demand for flavorings and fragrances.

HISTORY

International Flavors & Fragrances (IFF) began in 1909 when Dutch immigrant and perfumer A. L. van Ameringen and William Haebler formed a fragrance company, van Ameringen-Haebler, in New York City.

The company produced the fragrance for Youth Dew, Estée Lauder's first big cosmetics hit, in 1953. One biographer of Estée Lauder linked her romantically with van Ameringen after her 1939 divorce (she later remarried Joseph Lauder). The business association with van Ameringen's company endured, and by the late 1980s it had produced an estimated 90% of Estée Lauder's fragrances.

In 1958 van Ameringen-Haebler bought Polak & Schwartz, a Dutch firm, and changed the name of the combined companies to International Flavors & Fragrances. The US market for fragrances grew as consumers bought items such as air fresheners and manufacturers began adding fragrances to household items such as laundry detergent.

Henry Walter, who became CEO when van Ameringen retired in 1963, expanded IFF's presence overseas, with its highest foreign sales occurring in Europe and Latin America. Walter boasted, "Most of the great soap fragrances have been ours." So have many famous French perfumes. But most perfume companies wanted to cultivate product mystique, preventing IFF from taking credit for its scents.

Most of IFF's products were made for manufacturers of consumer goods. But under Walter's direction in the 1970s, IFF's R&D personnel experimented to find scents for museum exhibits and participated in Masters & Johnson's research on the connection between sex and smell. Said Walter, "Our business is sex and hunger."

During the early 1980s IFF conducted

fragrance research for relieving stress, lowering blood pressure, and alleviating depression. In 1982 IFF researchers developed a way to bind odors to plastic, a process used by makers of garbage bags and toys.

In 1985 Walter retired, and Eugene Grisanti (now president and chairman of the board) became CEO. Grisanti reorganized IFF, giving the VPs more decision-making power. After a three-year creative slump, IFF created fragrances for several prestigious perfumes, such as Eternity and Halston, in 1988. In 1991 IFF started operations in Turkey and Argentina and opened its third office in China.

IFF enhanced its position in dairy flavors in 1991 with the purchase of Wisconsin-based Auro Tech. It opened an office in Moscow in 1992. The following year IFF successfully synthesized the fragrance of growing flowers for perfumes through its Living Flower process.

In 1994 IFF inaugurated its flavor and fragrance facility in China (Guangzhou) and began building an aroma chemical plant there (Hangzhou). The company reasserted its leadership in the US fragrance market in 1996 with the launch of two IFF-originated fragrances: Elizabeth Taylor's Black Pearls and Escada's Jardin de Soleil. In 1997 (after net profitability fell from 17.3% in 1995 to 13.2%), IFF announced the closing of its Union Beach, New Jersey, plant and the transfer of that plant's production to plants in Spain and the UK and to other US plants. The Asian currency crisis continued to impact earnings in 1998.

The economic crisis in Brazil, weak demand for aroma chemicals, and the strong US dollar against the euro continued to hurt earnings in 1999.

Chairman, President, and CEO: Eugene P. Grisanti,
age 69, $1,365,000 pay
VP; President, Flavor Division: Robert G. Corbett, age 44
VP; President, Fragrance Division:
Stuart R. Maconochie, age 59, $602,893 pay
VP: Ronald S. Fenn, age 61
VP: Philip P. Gaetano, age 39
VP and Director of Research: Judith C. Giordan, age 45
VP: Sophia Grojsman
**VP and Area Manager, Fragrances Europe, Africa and
Middle East:** Carlos A. Lobbosco, age 59, $529,026 pay
VP: Lewis G. Lynch Jr., age 63
VP: Jose Antonio Rodriguez, age 55
VP and Area Manager, Fragrances North America:
Timothy Schaffner, age 49, $427,000 pay
VP and CFO: Douglas J. Wetmore, age 41
VP Law and Regulatory Affairs and Secretary:
Stephen A. Block, age 54
Treasurer: James P. Huether
VP and Area Manager, Flavors North America:
Kenneth G. Hunter
**VP and Area Manager, Flavors Europe, Africa, and
Middle East:** Ian A. Neil
VP and Area Manager, Fragrances Latin America:
Robert J. Gordon
VP and Area Manager, Flavors Latin America:
Jose R. D'Aprile
VP and Area Manager, Fragrances Far East:
Frans A. M. Nijnens
VP and Area Manager, Flavors Far East: Neil Humphreys
Auditors: PricewaterhouseCoopers LLP

LOCATIONS

HQ: International Flavors & Fragrances Inc.,
521 W. 57th St., New York, NY 10019
Phone: 212-765-5500   **Fax:** 212-708-7132

PRODUCTS/OPERATIONS

Fragrance Uses	Flavor Uses
Air fresheners	Alcoholic beverages
Aftershave lotions	Animal foods
Colognes	Baked goods
Cosmetic creams	Candies
Deodorants	Convenience foods
Detergents	Dairy products
Hair care products	Desserts
Laundry soap	Diet foods
Lipsticks	Drink powders
Lotions	Ethnic foods
Perfumes	Marinades
Powders	Pharmaceuticals
Soaps	Prepared foods
Toilet waters	Soft drinks

COMPETITORS

BASF AG
Bayer AG
Bush Boake
Elf Aquitaine
Hauser
Henkel
Hercules
Joh. A. Benckiser
MacAndrews & Forbes
McCormick
Roche Holding
Unilever
Wrigley

HISTORICAL FINANCIALS & EMPLOYEES

NYSE symbol: IFF FYE: December 31	Annual Growth	1989	1990	1991	1992	1993	1994	1995	1996	1997	1998
Sales ($ mil.)	5.5%	870	963	1,017	1,126	1,189	1,315	1,440	1,436	1,427	1,407
Net income ($ mil.)	4.4%	139	157	169	171	203	226	249	190	218	204
Income as % of sales	—	15.9%	16.3%	16.6%	15.1%	17.0%	17.2%	17.3%	13.2%	15.3%	14.5%
Earnings per share ($)	5.0%	1.22	1.37	1.47	1.48	1.77	2.02	2.22	1.70	1.99	1.90
Stock price - FY high ($)	—	25.81	25.02	34.92	38.71	39.79	47.88	55.88	51.88	53.44	51.88
Stock price - FY low ($)	—	16.07	18.19	22.89	31.47	32.97	35.63	45.13	40.75	39.88	32.06
Stock price - FY close ($)	7.8%	22.56	24.81	34.17	36.21	37.88	46.25	48.00	45.00	51.50	44.19
P/E - high	—	21	18	24	26	22	24	25	31	27	27
P/E - low	—	13	13	16	21	19	18	20	24	20	17
Dividends per share ($)	9.8%	0.64	0.72	0.80	0.91	1.00	1.08	1.24	1.36	1.44	1.48
Book value per share ($)	3.2%	6.69	7.84	8.38	8.47	7.96	9.04	10.06	9.79	9.17	8.91
Employees	1.1%	4,217	4,184	4,218	4,242	4,371	4,570	4,650	4,630	4,640	4,670

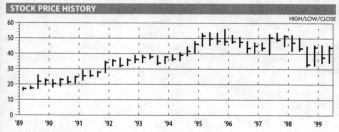

STOCK PRICE HISTORY   HIGH/LOW/CLOSE

1998 FISCAL YEAR-END
Debt ratio: 0.5%
Return on equity: 21.6%
Cash ($ mil.): 115
Current ratio: 3.11
Long-term debt ($ mil.): 4
No. of shares (mil.): 106
Dividends
  Yield: 3.3%
  Payout: 77.9%
Market value ($ mil.): 4,686

INTERNATIONAL MULTIFOODS

OVERVIEW

International Multifoods is counting on that spare change in your pocket. The US's #1 distributor to the vending industry, the Wayzata, Minnesota-based food processor distributes more than 8,000 products — including candy, snacks, pastries, and beverages — to about 20,000 vending machine operators, coffee service operators, and others. It also distributes food and supplies to independent restaurants, sandwich shops, movie theaters, and other concessionaires.

The company's U.S. Foods unit produces commercial baking mixes, frozen batters, and doughs for in-store and food service baking

operations. In Canada its Robin Hood Multifoods unit produces the #1 brand of consumer flours and baking mixes (Robin Hood) and the leading brand of pickles and condiments (Bick's). It also sells hot cereals (Old Mill, Purity).

Once one of the Big Three in the flour business (with General Mills and Pillsbury), International Multifoods shifted focus a few times before landing on its current mix of businesses that predominately serve the food service industry.

Agricultural processor Archer Daniels Midland owns nearly 9% of International Multifoods.

HISTORY

When Francis Bean's first flour mill went bankrupt, he rented a small mill and started the New Prague Flouring Mill Co. in 1892 in New Prague, Minnesota. Four years later the owner wanted the rented mill back, so Bean had to start over once again. The people of the town put up more than $30,000 to help him build a new mill, which retained the old name. Bean added more mills (including two in Canada in the early 1900s) and changed the company's name to International Milling (IM) in 1910.

Christmas in 1911 was a memorable time for Bean — and key to IM's corporate culture, as the story has been passed down. More than 20 years after his original mill had gone bankrupt, Bean sought out all of its unpaid creditors. He paid them both the principal and the interest that had accrued over the years, although he had no legal obligation to pay the debts that had long since been wiped off the books; the total came to more than $200,000.

IM added new mills in the 1920s, including ones in Iowa and New York. During WWII it helped the country meet the increased need for flour and also developed Alcomeal, a wheat product used to make grain alcohol for the production of synthetic rubber.

The company continued to expand, adding more mills (15 during and just after the war), enhancing its product line (acquiring an animal feed maker in 1951), and developing new services (it was the first miller to deliver bulk flour directly to commercial bakeries).

Exporting around the world by the late 1950s, IM decided to concentrate its efforts in Venezuela, where it held more than a third of the market. It went public in 1964 and began diversifying through more than 40 acquisitions ranging from a meat processing plant to Mr. Donut stores, with a particular emphasis on

consumer companies. The International Multifoods name was adopted in 1970 to reflect the shift from commodities to consumer items.

In 1984 the company bought Vendors Supply of America, the largest US vending distributor. It then began purchasing food service operations (Fred's Frozen Foods in 1986 and Pueringer Distributing in 1987, among others) while selling off most of its consumer products, flour mills, seafood restaurants, and animal feed businesses. In 1993, two years after deciding to focus on value-added food products in the US, International Multifoods switched its strategy and began selling its prepared foods operations.

International Multifoods bought Leprino Foods' specialty food distribution business — with an emphasis on supplying pizza restaurants — in 1994 (its largest acquisition ever, at about $100 million). The next year it added Alum Rock Foodservice.

The company was plagued with high turnover in 1995 and 1996, losing about a dozen top executives. Former Kellogg executive Gary Costley was named CEO in late 1996 in an attempt to stem the hemorrhage. International Multifoods also suffered from lowered vending margins as volume fell, pricing pressures increased, and the customer mix changed.

In 1997 the company shut down its unprofitable poultry exporting business. To better focus on its North American operations, in 1999 International Multifoods sold its Venezuelan operations, including MONACA (consumer foods) and Alimentos Super-S (animal feeds); the sales contributed to most of the company's loss in 1999.

Chairman, President, and CEO: Gary E. Costley, age 55, $663,893 pay
SVP Finance and CFO; President, Latin America Operations: William L. Trubeck, age 52, $419,900 pay (prior to promotion)
VP Communications: Jill W. Schmidt, age 40
VP; President, Multifoods Distribution Group: Jeffrey E. Boies, age 54, $464,367 pay
VP; President, North America Foods: Robert S. Wright, age 52, $303,066 pay
VP, Secretary, and General Counsel: Frank W. Bonvino, age 57, $326,900 pay
VP and Treasurer: Anthony T. Brausen, age 39
VP and Controller: Dennis R. Johnson, age 47
President, Robin Hood Multifoods: Donald H. Twiner, age 58
VP Human Resources, Robin Hood Multifoods: Roderick C. Morrison
Director Human Resources: Joyce Traver
Assistant Treasurer: Gregory J. Keup, age 41
Auditors: KPMG Peat Marwick LLP

LOCATIONS

HQ: International Mulitfoods Corporation, 200 E. Lake St., Wayzata, MN 55391
Phone: 612-594-3300   **Fax:** 612-594-3343
Web site: http://www.multifoods.com

International Multifoods has processing and distribution centers throughout the US and Canada.

PRODUCTS/OPERATIONS

1999 Sales

	$ mil.	% of total
Distribution	1,846	80
Food manufacturing	451	20
Total	**2,297**	**100**

Selected Operations and Brand Names

Multifoods Distribution Group
Food Service Distribution (cheeses, cleaning supplies, meats, paper goods, pizza ingredients, snacks)
Vending Distribution (candy, coffee service supplies, frozen and refrigerated products, hot beverages, juices, pastries, snacks)

North America Foods
Robin Hood Multifoods (Canada)
  Baking mixes (Robin Hood)
  Condiments (Bick's, Habitant, Gattuso, Woodman's)
  Flour (Robin Hood, Brodie, Cream of the West, Monarch)
  Hot cereals (Robin Hood, Old Mill, Red River, Purity)
  Pickles and Relishes
U.S. Foods
  Bakery mix products (Jamco, Multifoods)
  Frozen batters and doughs (Fantasia, Gourmet Baker)

COMPETITORS

ADM	Heinz
Alliant Foodservice	Nabisco Group Holdings
AmeriServe	Pillsbury
Bunge International	Quaker Oats
CSM	Sara Lee
Flowers Industries	SYSCO
General Mills	U.S. Foodservice
Gordon Food Service	

HISTORICAL FINANCIALS & EMPLOYEES

NYSE symbol: IMC FYE: February 28	Annual Growth	1990	1991	1992	1993	1994	1995	1996	1997	1998	1999
Sales ($ mil.)	1.1%	2,075	2,192	2,281	2,224	2,225	2,295	2,523	2,596	2,612	2,297
Net income ($ mil.)	—	25	35	22	41	(13)	57	24	3	20	(132)
Income as % of sales	—	1.2%	1.6%	1.0%	1.9%	—	2.5%	1.0%	0.1%	0.8%	—
Earnings per share ($)	—	1.31	1.81	1.12	2.10	(0.72)	3.16	1.32	0.15	1.08	(6.98)
Stock price - FY high ($)	—	22.26	26.60	31.52	28.88	26.38	19.63	23.88	22.00	32.44	31.44
Stock price - FY low ($)	—	16.09	16.34	23.88	23.25	16.75	15.13	17.25	15.13	20.00	15.13
Stock price - FY close ($)	3.1%	16.51	25.68	26.38	25.75	17.38	18.63	18.63	21.13	27.94	21.69
P/E - high	—	17	15	28	14	—	6	18	147	30	—
P/E - low	—	12	9	21	11	—	5	13	101	19	—
Dividends per share ($)	0.1%	0.79	0.82	0.79	0.80	0.80	0.80	0.80	0.80	0.80	0.80
Book value per share ($)	(1.4%)	15.69	16.41	16.18	16.65	12.92	16.16	16.66	16.08	16.51	13.86
Employees	(3.2%)	9,015	9,140	8,341	8,390	8,390	7,495	7,115	7,176	6,807	6,743

STOCK PRICE HISTORY

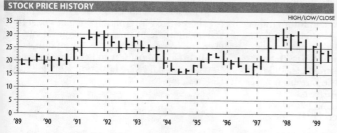

HIGH/LOW/CLOSE

1999 FISCAL YEAR-END

Debt ratio: 31.8%
Return on equity: —
Cash ($ mil.): 14
Current ratio: 1.29
Long-term debt ($ mil.): 121
No. of shares (mil.): 19
Dividends
  Yield: 3.7%
  Payout: —
Market value ($ mil.): 407

INTERNATIONAL PAPER COMPANY

OVERVIEW

More diverse and less international than its name suggests (75% of sales are in the US), International Paper is the world's largest forest products company. The Purchase, New York-based company's products include printing and writing papers, packaging, and paperboard. Non-paper products include wood products, chemicals (Arizona Chemical), and oil and gas. The company controls more than 7 million acres of forest in the US and, through a subsidiary, more than 800,000 acres in New Zealand.

International Paper distributes paper, office supplies, and printing and graphics arts supplies through subsidiary xpedx in North America. Subsidiaries Aussedat Rey (France), Scaldia (the Netherlands), and Impap (Poland) serve Europe.

International Paper is focusing on its core paper, packaging, distribution, and forest products businesses. As a zealous participant in the industry's global consolidation, it pursues acquisitions and alliances worldwide, such as its purchase of rival Union Camp.

HISTORY

Eighteen northeastern pulp and paper firms consolidated in 1898 to lower costs. The resulting International Paper began with 20 mills in Maine, Massachusetts, New Hampshire, New York, and Vermont. The mills relied on forests in New England and Canada for wood pulp. When Canadian provinces enacted legislation to stop the export of pulpwood in 1919, International Paper formed Canadian International Paper.

In the 1920s International Paper built a hydroelectric plant on the Hudson River. Between 1928 and 1941 the company called itself International Paper & Power. It entered the kraft paper market (paper sacks) in 1925 with the purchase of the Bastrop Pulp & Paper kraft paper mill (Louisiana). Mass production emerged with the Fourdrinier paper machine, which could make paper in a continuous sheet.

During the 1940s and 1950s, the company bought Agar Manufacturing (shipping containers, 1940), Single Service Containers (Pure-Pak milk containers, 1946), and Lord Baltimore Press (folding cartons, 1958). It diversified in the 1960s and 1970s, buying Davol (hospital products, 1968; sold to C. R. Bard in 1980), American Central (land development, 1968; sold to developers in 1974), and General Crude Oil (gas and oil, 1975; sold to Mobil Oil in 1979).

In the 1980s International Paper modernized its plants to focus on less-cyclical products and became the industry's low-cost producer. After selling Canadian International Paper in 1981, the company bought Hammermill Paper (office paper, 1986), Arvey (paper manufacturing and distribution, 1987), and Masonite (composite wood products, 1988). International Paper entered the European paper market in 1989 by buying Aussedat Rey (France), Ilford Group (UK), and Zanders (West Germany). Its 1990 purchases included

Dixon Paper (distributor of paper and graphic arts supplies), Nevamar (laminates), and the UK's Cookson Group (printing plates).

International Paper expanded globally and domestically in the early 1990s, with acquisitions such as Scaldia Papier (the Netherlands, 1991) and Western Paper (1992), and investments in Carter Holt Harvey (New Zealand) and Scitex (Israel), a leading maker of electronic prepress systems. In 1994 International Paper formed a joint venture in a Chinese packaging plant and bought two Mexican paper-distributing companies. The next year it bought Seaman-Patrick Paper and Carpenter Paper (paper distribution), Micarta (high-pressure laminates), and DSM (inks and adhesives, resins). In 1996 it bought Federal Paper Board, a forest- and paper-products firm.

To lower costs, International Paper began downsizing in 1997 and sold $1 billion in marginal assets and cut its workforce by 10%. Branching its US box-making operations into the South and Midwest, International Paper bought Weston Paper & Manufacturing in 1998; it also bought Mead's distribution business for $263 million, then the company announced it would close 25 plants in the combined enterprise. The company also sold xpedx's grocery supply business to Bunzl in 1998, and announced plans to close several plants in the US and Australia and cut about 2,000 jobs by early 1999.

To preserve competition, in 1999 federal regulators axed International Paper's deal to sell its laminate business to Formica. However, the company did sell its Fountainhead solid-surfacing business to Formica. International Paper paid $7.9 billion in 1999 for rival Union Camp.

Chairman and CEO: John T. Dillon, age 60, $1,742,500 pay

EVP, Operations Group: C. Wesley Smith, age 59, $762,083 pay

EVP, Legal and External Affairs: James P. Melican, age 58, $745,000 pay

EVP, Consumer Packaging: David W. Oskin, age 56, $687,917 pay

EVP, Specialty Businesses: Milan J. Turk, age 60, $580,000 pay

EVP Human Resources: Marianne M. Parrs, age 55

SVP and CFO: John Faraci, age 49

SVP and General Counsel: William B. Lytton, age 50

VP and Controller: Andrew R. Lessin, age 56

Auditors: Arthur Andersen LLP

LOCATIONS

HQ: 2 Manhattanville Rd., Purchase, NY 10577
Phone: 914-397-1500   **Fax:** 914-397-1596
Web site: http://www.ipaper.com

International Paper has production facilities in 50 countries and sells its products in 130 countries.

1998 Sales

	$ mil.	% of total
US	14,810	76
Europe	2,894	15
Pacific Rim	1,647	8
Other regions	190	1
Total	**19,541**	**100**

PRODUCTS/OPERATIONS

1998 Sales

	$ mil.	% of total
Distribution	5,510	28
Packaging	4,970	25
Printing papers	4,120	21
Forest products	3,020	16
Specialty products	1,665	9
Adjustments	256	1
Total	**19,541**	**100**

Selected Business Units and Products

Distribution Businesses
Aussedat Rey (France)
Impap (Poland)
Scaldia (The Netherlands)
Xpedx (North America)

Packaging
Bleached board
Containerboard
Folding cartons
Kraft packaging

Printing Papers
Coated papers
Newsprint

Forest Products
Lumber products
Panel products
Particleboard
Treated pilings
Treated poles

Specialty Products
Chemicals and petroleum
Door facings and sidings
  (Craftmaster)
High-pressure laminates
Specialty industrial papers
Tissue

COMPETITORS

Amcor	Fort James	Smurfit-Stone
Boise Cascade	Georgia-Pacific	Container
Buhrmann	Kimberly-Clark	Temple-Inland
Canadian Pacific	Mead	UPM-Kymmene
Champion	3M	Westvaco
International	Nippon Paper	Weyerhaeuser
Fletcher	Jefferson Smurfit	Willamette
Challenge		

HISTORICAL FINANCIALS & EMPLOYEES

NYSE symbol: IP FYE: December 31	Annual Growth	1989	1990	1991	1992	1993	1994	1995	1996	1997	1998
Sales ($ mil.)	6.2%	11,378	12,960	12,703	13,598	13,685	14,966	19,797	20,143	20,096	19,541
Net income ($ mil.)	(13.4%)	864	569	184	86	289	357	1,153	303	(151)	236
Income as % of sales	—	7.6%	4.4%	1.4%	0.6%	2.1%	2.4%	5.8%	1.5%	—	1.2%
Earnings per share ($)	(16.4%)	3.86	2.61	0.83	0.35	1.17	1.43	4.50	1.04	(0.50)	0.77
Stock price - FY high ($)	—	29.38	29.88	39.13	39.25	34.94	40.25	45.69	44.63	61.00	55.25
Stock price - FY low ($)	—	22.56	21.38	25.25	29.25	28.31	30.31	34.13	35.63	38.63	35.50
Stock price - FY close ($)	5.3%	28.25	26.75	35.38	33.31	33.88	37.69	37.88	40.50	43.13	44.81
P/E - high	—	8	11	47	112	30	28	10	43	—	72
P/E - low	—	6	8	30	84	24	21	8	34	—	46
Dividends per share ($)	2.9%	0.77	0.84	0.84	0.84	0.84	0.84	0.92	1.00	1.00	1.00
Book value per share ($)	2.3%	23.68	25.67	25.57	25.22	25.12	25.87	29.87	31.13	28.82	28.98
Employees	2.6%	63,500	69,000	70,500	73,000	72,500	70,000	81,500	87,000	82,000	80,000

STOCK PRICE HISTORY

HIGH/LOW/CLOSE

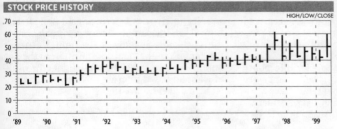

1998 FISCAL YEAR-END

Debt ratio: 37.4%
Return on equity: 2.7%
Cash ($ mil.): 477
Current ratio: 1.65
Long-term debt ($ mil.): 6,407
No. of shares (mil.): 307
Dividends
  Yield: 2.2%
  Payout: 129.9%
Market value ($ mil.): 13,763

THE INTERPUBLIC GROUP

OVERVIEW

Interpublic knows a brand image is priceless. The New York City-based Interpublic Group of Companies, the world's second-largest advertising group (behind #1 Omnicom), offers clients such as MasterCard International, Coca-Cola, and Burger King one-stop shopping for advertising and marketing services. Its creative ad work is done primarily through global agencies McCann-Erickson WorldGroup, Ammirati Puris Lintas, and The Lowe Group, as well as through a number of stand-alone agencies (Dailey & Associates; Hill, Holiday, Connors, Cosmopulos). The company also provides direct marketing through DraftWorldwide and is one of the top public relations firms in the world.

Operating as a cluster of competing agencies within a holding company, Interpublic has been able to offer a variety of creative approaches to its clients. But this strategy leads to problems when different units work for rival clients. Mercedes-Benz parent Daimler-Chrysler cited concerns over work other Interpublic units do for rival General Motors when it yanked the $100 million Mercedes-Benz account from Lowe & Partners in 1999.

Much of Interpublic's recent growth has come through the acquisition of media and marketing service companies such as Initiative Media Worldwide (merged with Western International to form Western Initiative Media Worldwide). It has also beefed up its new media services.

HISTORY

In 1911 Standard Oil ad exec Harrison McCann opened an agency and signed his first client, Standard Oil of New Jersey (later Exxon). As automobile and petroleum products became integral parts of American life, McCann's ad business boomed. In 1930 his firm merged with Alfred Erickson's agency, forming the McCann-Erickson Company. At the end of the decade, the firm hired Marion Harper, a top Yale graduate, as a mail room clerk. In 1948 Harper became president.

Harper began acquiring other ad agencies and by 1961 controlled more than 20 companies. That year he unveiled his concept of an advertising holding company for subsidiaries that would use the parent firm's financial and informational resources but operate separately, allowing them to work on accounts for competing products. He named the company The Interpublic Group after a German research company that was owned by the former H. K. McCann Co.

The advertising conglomerate continued expanding, buying Afamal (the largest ad firm in Africa) in 1962 and Erwin, Wasey, Ruthrauff & Ryan in 1963, making it the #1 agency. But Harper's management capabilities weren't up to the task, and with the company facing bankruptcy in 1967, the board of directors replaced him with Robert Healy. Healy was able to save Interpublic and return it to profitability. In 1971 the company went public.

The 1970s were fruitful years for Interpublic; its ad teams created memorable campaigns for Coke ("It's the Real Thing" and "Have a Coke and a Smile") and Miller Beer ("Miller Time" and Miller Lite ads). After Philip Geier became chairman in 1980, the company gained a stake in Lowe Howard-Spink (1983; it later became The Lowe Group) and bought Lintas International (1987). Interpublic bought the rest of The Lowe Group in 1990.

In 1993 the firm was dealt a blow when Coca-Cola (a client since 1942) hired Creative Artists Agency to develop a new image. The next year Interpublic bought Western International Media, the largest independent media buyer in the US (now Western Initiative Media Worldwide), and Ammirati & Puris (merged with Lintas to form Ammirati Puris Lintas).

As industry consolidation picked up in 1996, Interpublic kept pace with acquisitions of PR company Weber Group and DraftWorldwide, the world's #1 independently owned direct marketing agency. In 1997 it bought a majority stake in Addis-Wechsler & Associates (now Industry Entertainment), one of Hollywood's top artist management and film production companies. Interpublic also formed Octagon, a sports marketing and management group, following the purchases of agencies Advantage International (US) and API Group (UK).

In 1998 Interpublic acquired Carmichael Lynch (US) and Hill, Holliday, Connors, Cosmopulos (US). It also boosted its PR presence with its purchase of International Public Relations (UK), the parent company of public relations networks Shandwick and Golin/Harris. Interpublic strengthened its position in the online world in 1999 when it bought 20% of Stockholm-based Internet services company Icon Medialab International.

OFFICERS

Chairman, President, and CEO: Philip H. Geier Jr.,
age 64, $2,495,000 pay
VC Finance and Operations: Eugene P. Beard, age 63,
$2,150,000 pay
**Chairman, CEO, and Chief Creative Officer, Ammirati
Puris Lintas Worldwide:** Martin F. Puris, age 60,
$1,720,000 pay
Chairman and CEO, The Lowe Group: Frank B. Lowe,
age 57, $1,833,333 pay
Chairman and CEO, McCann-Erickson WorldGroup:
John J. Dooner Jr., age 50, $2,060,000 pay
SVP Human Resources: C. Kent Kroeber, age 60
SVP Planning and Business Development:
Barry R. Linsky, age 57
VP and Controller: Frederick Molz, age 42
VP, General Counsel, and Secretary:
Nicholas J. Camera, age 52
Auditors: PricewaterhouseCoopers LLP

LOCATIONS

HQ: The Interpublic Group of Companies, Inc.,
1271 Avenue of the Americas, New York, NY 10020
Phone: 212-399-8000   **Fax:** 212-399-8130
Web site: http://www.interpublic.com

The Interpublic Group of Companies has offices in more
than 120 countries.

1998 Sales

	$ mil.	% of total
US	1,925	50
Europe	1,269	34
Asia/Pacific	326	8
Latin America	232	6
Other regions	92	2
Total	**3,844**	**100**

PRODUCTS/OPERATIONS

Advertising Networks
Ammirati Puris Lintas Inc. (New York City)
The Lowe Group (UK)
McCann-Erickson WorldGroup (New York City)

Marketing and Communications
Allied Communications Group (New York City)
DraftWorldwide, Inc. (Chicago)
Octagon (New York City)
Western Initiative Media Worldwide (Los Angeles)

Independent Agencies
Angotti Thomas Hedge (New York City)
Austin Kelly Advertising (Atlanta)
Campbell-Ewald (Warren, MI)
Campbell Mithun Esty (Minneapolis)
Carmichael Lynch (Minneapolis)
Dailey & Associates (Los Angeles)
Goldberg Moser O'Neill (San Francisco)
Gotham Inc. (New York City)
Hill, Holliday, Connors, Cosmopulos (Boston)
Long Haymes Carr (Winston-Salem, NC)
The Martin Agency (Richmond, VA)

COMPETITORS

Ackerley Group	MacManus Group
Creative Artists	Omnicom Group
Dentsu	Publicis
Grey Advertising	True North
Havas Advertising	WPP Group
IMG	Young & Rubicam
Leo Burnett	

HISTORICAL FINANCIALS & EMPLOYEES

NYSE symbol: IPG FYE: December 31	Annual Growth	1989	1990	1991	1992	1993	1994	1995	1996	1997	1998
Sales ($ mil.)	13.2%	1,257	1,368	1,678	1,804	1,794	1,984	2,180	2,538	3,126	3,844
Net income ($ mil.)	17.9%	71	80	95	87	125	93	130	205	239	310
Income as % of sales	—	5.6%	5.9%	5.6%	4.8%	7.0%	4.7%	6.0%	8.1%	7.6%	8.1%
Earnings per share ($)	13.7%	0.35	0.40	0.44	0.39	0.56	0.41	0.56	0.85	0.95	1.11
Stock price - FY high ($)	—	6.32	6.34	9.55	11.92	11.88	11.96	14.47	16.76	26.50	40.31
Stock price - FY low ($)	—	4.06	4.88	5.63	8.59	7.96	9.17	10.59	13.22	15.67	22.56
Stock price - FY close ($)	24.8%	5.44	5.84	9.55	11.63	10.67	10.71	14.47	15.84	24.91	39.88
P/E - high	—	18	16	22	31	21	29	26	20	28	36
P/E - low	—	12	12	13	22	14	22	19	16	16	20
Dividends per share ($)	11.4%	0.11	0.13	0.14	0.15	0.17	0.19	0.21	0.23	0.25	0.29
Book value per share ($)	11.0%	1.77	2.31	2.59	2.27	2.51	2.79	3.14	3.58	4.23	4.53
Employees	9.8%	14,700	16,800	16,800	16,800	17,600	18,200	19,700	21,700	27,100	34,000

STOCK PRICE HISTORY

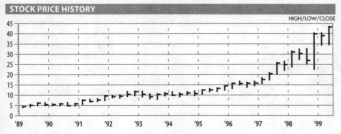

HIGH/LOW/CLOSE

1998 FISCAL YEAR-END

Debt ratio: 28.6%
Return on equity: 24.5%
Cash ($ mil.): 809
Current ratio: 1.03
Long-term debt ($ mil.): 507
No. of shares (mil.): 279
Dividends
  Yield: 0.7%
  Payout: 26.1%
Market value ($ mil.): 11,129

INTERSTATE BAKERIES

OVERVIEW

It's no Wonder that a Hostess would show her Home Pride by serving breads and sweet treats made by Interstate Bakeries, the largest US wholesale bread and snack cake producer. The Kansas City, Missouri-based company operates about 70 bakeries, making a variety of sliced breads, rolls, bagels, buns, English muffins, cereal bars, snack cakes, doughnuts, and a growing croutons/dry stuffing mix line. Its national and regional brands include Dolly Madison, Hostess (Twinkies and Ho-Hos), Merita, and Mrs. Cubbison's. The company's Wonder white bread and Home Pride wheat bread are the top two US bread brands. Its

baked goods are delivered to more than 200,000 supermarkets and other food outlets; unsold products are delivered to its 1,500 bakery thrift stores. The company is also a licensed baker and distributor of Roman Meal and Sun-Maid bread products.

Interstate Bakeries jumped to the #1 US position in 1995 when it bought rival Continental Baking (including the popular Wonder and Hostess brands). As part of the deal, Continental's previous owner, Ralston Purina, now owns 42% of Interstate Bakeries (but must reduce its stake to 15% by mid-2000).

HISTORY

Interstate Bakeries was founded in Kansas City, Missouri, in 1930 by Ralph Leroy Nafziger. In 1937 it merged with its local rival, Schulze Baking, beginning a strategy of growth through acquisitions and mergers. Interstate Bakeries acquired Supreme Baking of Los Angeles in 1943, and in 1950 the company added O'Rourke Baking, of Buffalo, New York, to its operations.

The company entered the cake business in 1954 with the purchases of the Ambrosia Cake, Remar Baking, and Butter Cream Baking companies. It added more layers when it acquired Campbell-Sell Baking (1958) and the Kingston Cake Bakery (1959).

In 1968 Interstate Bakeries purchased the Millbrook bread division of Nabisco. That year it expanded into the processed food business, buying Baker Canning, a vegetable canner (sold 1974).

Interstate Bakeries itself became the object of an acquisition in 1975. DPF, of Hartsdale, New York, an IBM computer-leasing venture that had recorded a $43 million loss over four years, was seeking a low-risk, low-tech acquisition. As the nation's third-largest wholesale baker, Interstate Bakeries fit the bill. The company attempted to block the sale, but DPF prevailed. It spun off its computer business in 1981 and took the Interstate Bakeries name.

New CEO Dale Putman focused on improving plant efficiency, but the company recorded declining profits and was saddled with debt. In 1984, in hopes of turning the company around, Interstate Bakeries tapped General Mills executive Robert Hatch as president. Faced with $36 million in outstanding loan payments, Hatch paid banks from an overfunded $37 million pension fund.

Interstate Bakeries was taken private in 1987 through an LBO by IBC Holdings, a

group formed by Interstate Bakeries' management. The company acquired American Bakeries' Merita/Cotton's Bakeries division that year, and Merita president Charles Sullivan was named CEO. The company again went public in 1991. Sullivan decentralized operations, and in 1995 Interstate Bakeries acquired its biggest rival, Ralston Purina's Continental Baking.

Continental was founded as the Ward Baking Co. in New York City in 1849. In 1921 William Ward, grandson of the company's founder, formed United Bakeries, which was renamed Continental Baking in 1924. By 1925, the year Continental bought Taggart Baking (maker of Wonder Bread), it had become the US's largest bakery. Continental was sold to hotel and defense conglomerate ITT in 1968. The health-conscious 1970s were hard on Continental, maker of Hostess cupcakes and Twinkies, and in 1984 ITT sold Continental to Ralston Purina, which created a new class of stock in 1993 for separate trading of the company.

To comply with a US Justice Department order related to the Continental acquisition, in 1997 Interstate Bakeries sold its Chicago Butternut Bakery and a Southern California white bread brand, Weber. That year it bought San Francisco French Bread.

In 1998 Interstate Bakeries bought New England-based John J. Nissen Baking. It made an especially sweet deal when it bought talk-show hostess Rosie O'Donnell's favorite cake maker, Drake's (Ring Dings, Yodels), from Canada's Culinar. Not satiated with the Drake's purchase, in July 1999 the company tried to buy the rest of Culinar, which owns the Canadian trademark for Hostess. However, Montreal-based cheese company Saputo eventually outbid Interstate Bakeries, keeping Culinar Canadian.

Chairman and CEO: Charles A. Sullivan, age 64, $1,124,211 pay
President and COO: Michael D. Kafoure, age 50, $560,329 pay
VP, Secretary, and General Counsel: Ray S. Sutton, age 61, $281,447 pay
SVP and CFO: Frank W. Coffey, age 56
SVP, Corporate Marketing: Mark D. Dirkes, age 52, $193,798 pay
SVP, Engineering: Brian A. Poulter
SVP, Purchasing: Brian E. Stevenson, age 44, $198,066 pay
VP and Corporate Controller: John F. McKenny, age 49
VP, National Account Sales: Terry A. Stephens
VP, Research and Development: Theresa S. Cogswell
VP and Treasurer: Paul E. Yarick, age 60
EVP, Central Division: Robert P. Morgan
EVP, Eastern Division: James R. Widler
EVP, Western Division: Richard D. Willson
SVP, Central Division-North: Thomas S. Bartoszewski
SVP, Central Division-South: Timothy W. Cranor
SVP, Eastern Division-North: Michael E. Colgan
SVP, Eastern Division-South: Bobby J. McClellan
SVP, Western Division-South: Thomas E. Wilson
Director, Human Resources: Russell Baker
Auditors: Deloitte & Touche LLP

PRODUCTS/OPERATIONS

Selected Brands
Beefsteak
Braun's
Bread du Jour
Buttermaid
Butternut
Colombo
Cotton's Holsum
DiCarlo
Dolly Madison
Eddy's
Emperor Norton
Holsum
Home Pride
Hostess
J.J. Nissen
Marie Callender's
Merita
Millbrook Farms
Mrs. Cubbison's
Parisian
Roman Meal
Sun-Maid
Sweetheart
Toscana
Wonder

Selected Products
Bagels
Bread (white, wheat, crusty, sourdough, raisin, reduced calorie)
Breakfast pastries
Buns
Cereal bars
Croutons
Cupcakes
Doughnuts (Donettes)
English muffins
Rolls
Shortcakes
Snack cakes (Devil Dogs, Ding-Dongs, Ho-Hos, Ring Dings, Sno-Balls, Twinkies, Yankee Doodles, Yodels, Zingers)
Snack pies
Stuffing
Sweet rolls
Variety cakes

LOCATIONS

HQ: Interstate Bakeries Corporation, 12 E. Armour Blvd., Kansas City, MO 64111
Phone: 816-502-4000   **Fax:** 816-502-4155

Interstate Bakeries operates about 70 bakeries in 31 states.

COMPETITORS

Bestfoods
Campbell Soup
Earthgrains
Flowers Industries
George Weston
Industrial Bimbo
International Home Foods
International Multifoods
Keebler
Kellogg
McKee Foods
Philip Morris
Quaker Oats
Sara Lee
Specialty Foods
Tasty Baking

HISTORICAL FINANCIALS & EMPLOYEES

NYSE symbol: IBC FYE: May 31	Annual Growth	1990	1991	1992	1993	1994	1995	1996	1997	1998	1999
Sales ($ mil.)	13.7%	1,093	1,107	1,146	1,166	1,143	1,223	2,878	3,212	3,266	3,459
Net income ($ mil.)	—	(17)	(8)	16	17	16	21	25	97	128	126
Income as % of sales	—	—	—	1.4%	1.4%	1.4%	1.7%	0.9%	3.0%	3.9%	3.6%
Earnings per share ($)	20.6%	—	—	0.47	0.39	0.39	0.53	0.35	1.28	1.71	1.74
Stock price - FY high ($)	—	—	—	9.69	10.56	8.75	8.13	13.88	27.94	38.00	35.00
Stock price - FY low ($)	—	—	—	7.50	7.19	5.81	5.94	7.19	12.63	26.88	20.13
Stock price - FY close ($)	16.5%	—	—	7.50	8.50	6.00	7.31	13.81	26.88	32.63	21.88
P/E - high	—	—	—	21	27	22	15	40	22	22	20
P/E - low	—	—	—	16	18	15	11	21	10	16	12
Dividends per share ($)	7.4%	—	—	0.17	0.24	0.25	0.25	0.25	0.27	0.28	0.28
Book value per share ($)	9.2%	—	—	4.65	4.81	4.77	5.04	6.17	7.17	7.77	8.60
Employees	11.8%	—	13,900	14,000	14,000	14,000	35,000	30,000	32,000	34,000	34,000

STOCK PRICE HISTORY

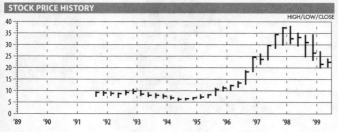

1999 FISCAL YEAR-END

Debt ratio: 37.9%
Return on equity: 20.9%
Cash ($ mil.): 0
Current ratio: 0.98
Long-term debt ($ mil.): 369
No. of shares (mil.): 70
Dividends
  Yield: 1.3%
  Payout: 16.1%
Market value ($ mil.): 1,535

INTIMATE BRANDS, INC.

OVERVIEW

Intimate Brands is proving that less really can be more, saleswise. The rapidly growing Columbus, Ohio-based company sells lingerie, underwear, and other clothing at its Victoria's Secret stores and through more than 400 million Victoria's Secret Catalogues a year. Subsidiary Bath & Body Works, its fastest-growing unit, offers bath and skin care products and other toiletries. Combined, the chains have nearly 2,000 stores. Another subsidiary, Gryphon, develops private-label personal care products for both the company and other retailers, and it helps Intimate Brands to bring new products to market quickly.

The bodacious sales at Victoria's Secret are entirely from private-label merchandise, including bra brands such as Perfect Silhouette,

Angels, and the Miracle Bra. In addition to bras, the company's cups runneth over thanks to new and expanded lines, including cosmetics and hosiery. About 60% of the customers at the Victoria's Secret Web site are male — *surely* not enticed by its attractive models.

Bath & Body Works is the US's top bath-shop chain, ahead of niche originator The Body Shop. Also stocking private-label products, stores have a rustic country farmhouse decor complete with gingham-clad employees. Its 60 or so White Barn Candle Co. stores (formerly Bath & Body Works Home) sell candles, room sprays, and other housewares.

Billionaire CEO Leslie Wexner owns 26% of mall retailer The Limited, which in turn owns 84% of Intimate Brands.

HISTORY

Slipping into the first piece of what would become Intimate Brands, The Limited acquired Victoria's Secret from Roy Raymond in 1982. Uncomfortable shopping in stores for lingerie for his wife, Raymond founded Victoria's Secret in San Francisco in 1977. The secret? Forget the cold metal department store racks and sell lingerie in a Victorian boudoir fantasy environment with lots of lace and classical music.

The first Victoria's Secret Catalogue was published in 1978. When Raymond sold the firm for $4 million, its mail-order operation and five stores had become synonymous with sexy — but not tacky — lingerie. (Raymond committed suicide in 1993 by jumping off the Golden Gate Bridge.)

To further play up the English fantasy image, new owner, Anglophile, and then-bachelor Leslie Wexner added a fictitious London address (No. 10 Margaret Street, London W1) to catalogs, store signs, and shopping bags. In addition, the catalog was revamped. Pictures of erotically posed couples gave way to demurely posed supermodels. In contrast to this British image, The Limited created the Cacique brand in 1988 to offer French-styled lingerie.

In 1990 The Limited acquired British cosmetics chain Penhaligon's from Laura Ashley. That year it launched Bath & Body Works as part of the Express chain. UK-based rival The Body Shop had opened its first US store just two years earlier and accused Bath & Body Works of flattering its store design too sincerely. When the companies settled out of court in 1991, Bath & Body Works already had 95 stores.

Victoria's Secret then tackled the market for traditionally unsexy cotton panties. Added to its offerings in 1993, Victoria's version of the underwear contributed $150 million to the firm's sales by 1996. In 1994 Victoria's Secret's sales were pushed up, in part, by the introduction of the Miracle Bra. (Sara Lee, however, outmarketed the company with its Wonderbra.)

Gryphon was formed in the late 1980s, which developed products solely for The Limited's company retailers until 1995, when it began looking for third-party development opportunities.

With the women's apparel industry sagging through the mid-1990s, The Limited unhooked Intimate Brands (one of its most successful divisions) in a late 1995 spinoff. By 1996 intimate apparel accounted for only 40% of the pages in the Victoria's Secret Catalogue, and half the pages pictured sportswear.

The company sold its UK-based Penhaligon's stores in 1997 and continued its aggressive expansion of Bath & Body Works by adding 170 stores. A year later Intimate Brands closed the 118-store Cacique chain, but it began testing a new chain, Lingerie for Legs, featuring that hosiery line, as well as swimwear and bodywear. It also launched VictoriasSecret.com in 1998 and converted about 50 Bath & Body Works stores into its new home furnishings concept, White Barn Candle Co.

Intimate Brands formed Intimate Beauty Corp. in 1999 to develop cosmetics to be sold through existing retail channels.

Chairman and CEO: Leslie H. Wexner, age 61, $2,565,546 pay
VC; VC and Chief Administrative Officer, The Limited: Kenneth B. Gilman, age 52, $1,872,073 pay
EVP & Chief Human Resources Officer: Arnie Kanarick
VP Finance and CFO: Philip E. Mallott, age 41
VP Investor Relations and Communications: Debbie J. Mitchell
President and CEO, Intimate Beauty Corporation: Robin R. Burns
President and CEO, Victoria's Secret Catalogue: Cynthia A. Fields, age 49, $987,070 pay
President and CEO, Victoria's Secret Stores: Grace A. Nichols, age 52, $1,380,750 pay
President and CEO, Bath & Body Works: Beth M. Pritchard, age 52, $1,660,048 pay
President and Chief Marketing Officer, Brand and Creative Services: Edward G. Razek
President and CEO, Gryphon: Robert J. Ruttenberg
EVP Operations & Administration, Victoria's Secret Stores: Wendy E. Burden
EVP Operations & Administration, Victoria's Secret Catalogue: Hank Fisher
VP Marketing, Victoria's Secret Stores: Jill Beraud
VP Public Relations, Victoria's Secret: Monica Mitro
Auditors: PricewaterhouseCoopers LLP

LOCATIONS

HQ: 3 Limited Pkwy., Columbus, OH 43216
Phone: 614-415-8000   **Fax:** 614-479-7094
Web site: http://www.intimatebrands.com

Intimate Brands has international sales through its Victoria's Secret Catalogue, has Victoria's Secret stores across the US, and has Bath & Body Works stores in the US and the UK.

PRODUCTS/OPERATIONS

1999 Sales

	$ mil.	% of total
Victoria's Secret		
Stores	1,829	47
Catalogue	759	19
Bath & Body Works	1,272	33
Other	26	1
Total	**3,886**	**100**

Operations

Retail
Bath & Body Works (personal care products and gifts)
Intimate Beauty (fragrances, cosmetics, and bath and personal care products)
Victoria's Secret (lingerie, swimwear, shirts, blouses, sweaters, pants, skirts, coats, dresses, and shoes)
White Barn Candle Company (candles, fragrances, and home furnishings)

Other
Gryphon (development of bath and personal care products for Intimate Brands' stores)
Victoria's Secret Catalogue (international mail order sales of lingerie, apparel, and personal care products)

COMPETITORS

Alberto-Culver	Frederick's of	Procter &
Amway	Hollywood	Gamble
Avon	Garden Botanika	Ross Stores
Benetton	Johnson &	Sara Lee
Body Shop	Johnson	Spiegel
Colgate-	L'Oréal	TJX
Palmolive	Maidenform	VF
Dayton Hudson	Mary Kay	Warnaco Group
Dillard's	May	Wolford
Estee Lauder	Nordstrom	Yankee Candle
Federated		

HISTORICAL FINANCIALS & EMPLOYEES

NYSE symbol: IBI FYE: January 31	Annual Growth	1990	1991	1992	1993	1994	1995	1996	1997	1998	1999
Sales ($ mil.)	18.3%	—	—	1,200	1,325	1,631	2,517	2,517	2,997	3,618	3,886
Net income ($ mil.)	20.8%	—	—	106	102	133	204	204	258	289	400
Income as % of sales	—	—	—	8.9%	7.7%	8.1%	8.1%	8.1%	8.6%	8.0%	10.3%
Earnings per share ($)	20.0%	—	—	—	—	—	—	0.92	1.02	1.14	1.59
Stock price - FY high ($)	—	—	—	—	—	—	—	18.50	24.63	25.63	41.38
Stock price - FY low ($)	—	—	—	—	—	—	—	13.38	14.00	17.00	18.00
Stock price - FY close ($)	39.3%	—	—	—	—	—	—	14.75	17.75	25.31	39.88
P/E - high	—	—	—	—	—	—	—	20	24	22	26
P/E - low	—	—	—	—	—	—	—	15	14	15	11
Dividends per share ($)	67.1%	—	—	—	—	—	—	0.12	0.48	0.52	0.56
Book value per share ($)	35.1%	—	—	—	—	—	—	1.06	1.59	2.22	2.62
Employees	25.7%	—	—	—	—	—	22,000	39,300	43,900	50,000	55,000

STOCK PRICE HISTORY

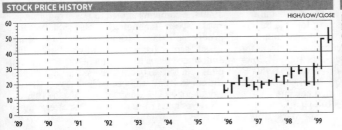

HIGH/LOW/CLOSE

1999 FISCAL YEAR-END

Debt ratio: 27.9%
Return on equity: 62.1%
Cash ($ mil.): 388
Current ratio: 1.82
Long-term debt ($ mil.): 250
No. of shares (mil.): 246
Dividends
  Yield: 1.4%
  Payout: 35.2%
Market value ($ mil.): 9,806

IOMEGA CORPORATION

OVERVIEW

Iomega has a Zip on its shoulders. The Roy, Utah-based company's removable data storage devices — most notably the Zip drive, which has sold more than 21 million units worldwide — offer generous storage capacity and portability. The company also makes the Jaz drive, which stores up to 2 GB, and Clik!, a disk-based storage product for use with handheld computers, cellular phones, and digital cameras.

Computer makers like Apple, Dell, Hewlett-Packard, and IBM make Iomega's Zip drives standard features in their PCs and account for half of Iomega's sales. The company also sells its products through distributors (Ingram Micro accounts for 16% of sales) and retailers.

One of the fastest-growing US companies of the late 1990s, Iomega has taken investors on a bumpy ride: Its stock has risen and dropped in the last few years due to competition and management turmoil. Iomega has fought a hail of product problems and lawsuits, including allegations questioning its technology and services.

Longtime chairman David Dunn owns 9% of Iomega through Idanta Partners, of which he is a managing partner.

HISTORY

David Bailey and David Norton started Iomega (an offshoot of an IBM research facility in Tucson, Arizona) in 1980 with the backing of Idanta Partners, a venture fund controlled by the Bass family of Texas. Its first product, the Bernoulli Box (developed and abandoned by IBM), was a disk drive system used by the government and based on an aerodynamic principle named after 18th-century Swiss mathematician Daniel Bernoulli. In 1983 Iomega launched the storage drive for PC users. Its success was attributed to the fact that it could be removed from the disk casing and featured technology impervious to dirt (unlike rival systems). The company went public that year.

Earnings rose to $2.5 million in 1984, but by 1987 poor management and lagging sales led to a $37 million loss. The company closed its plants for four months, cut nearly half its employees, and shifted focus to tape backup systems. CEO Michael Kucha, an early Iomega investor, cut costs across the board except in development. By 1988 the company looked healthy again.

Hewlett-Packard veteran Fred Wenninger replaced Kucha in 1989 and tweaked Iomega's manufacturing and design processes to save time. Earnings reached $14 million in 1990, but within three years the Bernoulli system's niche market caused another financial downturn and round of layoffs.

General Electric marketing heavyweight Kim Edwards took over as CEO in 1994 and immediately began redirecting Iomega beyond its technology-driven roots. In 1995 Iomega transformed the consumer market for external storage devices with its 100 MB, low-cost Zip drive and its Jaz drive, which holds 10 times the data of the Zip. Shirts and other items bearing the Iomega logo became company moneymakers. "After Bill Gates, Edwards has done the best job of marketing in the computer industry," one analyst wrote. Sales surged more than tenfold between 1994 ($141.4 million) and 1997 ($1.74 billion), and the company became the subject of intense speculation and commentary by participants on the Motley Fool bulletin boards on America Online and the Web.

Expanding overseas, Iomega partnered with electronics giant Seiko Epson in 1995 to market Zip drives in Japan. The company kept producing smaller and more powerful storage devices, and convincing computer manufacturers to include Zip drives in their products. In late 1996 Iomega eliminated hundreds of jobs in Utah and moved manufacturing operations to Malaysia.

The following year the company recalled 75,000 Jaz storage disks to replace a malfunctioning component that could damage data. It also had trouble keeping up with customer demand: In 1997 Iomega faced a breach-of-warranty suit (settled in 1998) by users who complained of delays in telephone service and the resulting hefty call charges.

In 1998 Edwards resigned as CEO amid slipping sales, poor quality control, and rising marketing expenses. To settle a patent-infringement suit with French rival Nomai, Iomega that year paid $45 million for a majority stake in that company and for related technologies. Later that year Rockwell International executive Jodie Glore took over as CEO. The entire year's turmoil left Iomega in the red for fiscal 1998. In 1999 the company agreed to buy struggling rival SyQuest Technology. It also sold its Ditto product line (tape backup systems) to Canada-based Tecmar Technologies International, and announced plans to close its San Diego and Milpitas, California, operations. As part of this plan, the company announced later that year that it would cut its workforce by 9%. Also in 1999 Glore resigned from the CEO post after only 10 months on the job.

Chairman, Acting President, and Acting CEO:
David J. Dunn, age 68
CFO: Philip G. Husby
EVP and Chief Marketing Officer: James A. Taylor,
age 52, $498,041 pay
EVP, Global Operations: John L. Conely Sr.
SVP, Strategic Business Development:
Anton J. Radman Jr., age 46
SVP, Secretary, and General Counsel: Laurie B. Keating,
age 45
**SVP, Product Development and Chief Technology
Officer:** James C. Kelly, age 41
VP; General Manager, Zip/Jaz Product Management:
David Henry
VP and Associate General Counsel: Charlotte L. Miller
VP and Treasurer: Robert J. Simmons, age 36
VP, Customer Satisfaction: Roxie Craycraft, age 44
VP, Human Resources: Kevin O'Connor, age 40
VP, Software Solutions: Germaine Ward
Senior Director, Treasurer: Tracy M. Welch
Director, Investor Relations: Tyler Thatcher
Auditors: Arthur Andersen LLP

LOCATIONS

HQ: 1821 W. Iomega Way, Roy, UT 84067
Phone: 801-778-1000   **Fax:** 801-332-3804
Web site: http://www.iomega.com

Iomega has manufacturing plants in Malaysia and the US.

1998 Sales

	$ mil.	% of total
US	1,112	66
Germany	95	5
Other countries	487	29
Total	**1,694**	**100**

PRODUCTS/OPERATIONS

1998 Sales

	$ mil.	% of total
Zip	1,183	70
Jaz	417	24
Ditto	81	5
Clik!	2	—
Other	11	1
Total	**1,694**	**100**

Products
Clik! drives and disks (40MB)
Jaz drives and disks (1GB to 2GB)
Zip drives and disks (100MB to 250MB)
ZipCD (650MB; CD-rewritable drive and disks)

Selected OEM Customers

Apple	Hewlett-Packard	Packard Bell
Compaq	IBM	Sharp
Dell	Micron	Siemens
Fujitsu	Electronics	Sony
Gateway	NEC Corporation	

COMPETITORS

Advanced Digital	Maxtor
Information	NEC
Castlewood Systems	OR Technology
Compaq	Overland Data
EMC	Quantum
Exabyte	Samsung
Fuji Photo	Seagate
Fujitsu	Sony
Hewlett-Packard	Storage Technology
Hitachi	SyQuest
IBM	Toshiba
Imation	Western Digital

HISTORICAL FINANCIALS & EMPLOYEES

NYSE symbol: IOM FYE: December 31	Annual Growth	1989	1990	1991	1992	1993	1994	1995	1996	1997	1998
Sales ($ mil.)	35.6%	109	120	137	139	147	141	326	1,213	1,740	1,694
Net income ($ mil.)	—	11	14	12	5	(15)	(2)	9	57	115	(54)
Income as % of sales	—	10.3%	11.6%	9.0%	3.4%	—	—	2.6%	4.7%	6.6%	—
Earnings per share ($)	—	0.05	0.06	0.05	0.02	(0.07)	(0.01)	0.03	0.21	0.42	(0.20)
Stock price – FY high ($)	—	0.26	0.42	0.60	0.75	0.55	0.30	4.47	27.56	16.75	13.75
Stock price – FY low ($)	—	0.12	0.20	0.27	0.32	0.16	0.13	0.27	2.85	7.06	2.94
Stock price – FY close ($)	49.2%	0.20	0.36	0.57	0.49	0.17	0.27	4.05	8.69	12.44	7.31
P/E – high	—	5	7	12	38	—	—	149	131	40	—
P/E – low	—	2	3	5	16	—	—	9	14	17	—
Dividends per share ($)	—	0.00	0.00	0.00	0.00	0.00	0.00	0.00	0.00	0.00	0.00
Book value per share ($)	27.5%	0.17	0.24	0.29	0.30	0.23	0.22	0.27	1.31	1.75	1.56
Employees	21.8%	—	1,006	1,153	1,270	1,077	886	1,667	2,926	4,816	4,865

STOCK PRICE HISTORY   HIGH/LOW/CLOSE

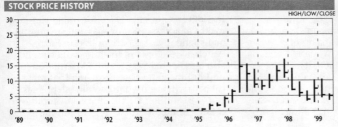

1998 FISCAL YEAR-END
Debt ratio: 10.8%
Return on equity: —
Cash ($ mil.): 90
Current ratio: 1.63
Long-term debt ($ mil.): 50
No. of shares (mil.): 267
Dividends
 Yield: —
 Payout: —
Market value ($ mil.): 1,955

ITT INDUSTRIES, INC.

OVERVIEW

ITT Industries is pumped up to defend its core markets. Based in White Plains, New York, the diversified manufacturer's Pumps & Complementary Products unit is the world's largest maker of water and sewage pumps; it also makes exchangers and related devices. The Defense Products & Services unit makes air traffic control systems, jamming devices, combat radios, night-vision devices, and satellite instruments. Its Connectors & Switches division produces connectors, switches, and cabling for telecommunications and computer use. The Specialty Products unit supplies valves, switches, specialty shock absorbers, fluid-handling materials, and tubing used in industrial, aerospace, and transportation applications.

The company has sold most of ITT Automotive (once two-thirds of sales) to limit exposure to the highly cyclical market for auto parts. ITT Industries is using the proceeds to expand its other divisions.

HISTORY

Colonel Sosthenes Behn founded International Telephone and Telegraph (ITT) in 1920 to build a global telephone company. After three small acquisitions, Behn bought International Western Electric (renamed International Standard Electric, or ISE) from AT&T in 1925, making ITT an international maker of phone equipment. In the late 1920s ITT bought Mackay, a US company that made telegraph, cable, radio, and other equipment.

In the 1930s sales outside the US made up two-thirds of revenues. To increase US opportunities during WWII, Behn arranged for a Mackay subsidiary, Federal Telegraph (later Federal Electric), to become part of ITT. Behn took charge of Federal and created Federal Telephone & Radio Laboratories. Meanwhile, ISE scientists who fled war-torn Europe gravitated to ITT's research and development operations and laid the foundation for its high-tech electronics business.

By the 1950s ITT was a diverse and unwieldy collection of companies. In the mid-1950s ISE, ITT's biggest unit, developed advanced telephone switching equipment. ITT researchers pioneered transistor technology, but management failed to turn the advances into market successes.

During the 1960s and 1970s ITT added several companies that would become part of ITT Industries. Auto-parts makers included Teves (brakes, West Germany), Ulma (trim, Italy), and Altissimo (lights and accessories, Italy). Electronics acquisitions included Cannon Electric (electrical connectors) and National Computer Products (satellite communications). Fluid-technology companies included Bell & Gossett (the US's #1 maker of commercial and industrial pumps). When ITT bought Sheraton's hotel chain in 1968, it also got auto-parts supplier Thompson Industries. By 1977 ITT's Engineered Products division consisted of nearly 80 automotive and electrical companies. In 1979 ITT began selling all or part of 250 companies, including the last of its telecommunications operations.

In the 1980s ITT became a major supplier of antilock brakes and, with the 1988 purchase of the Allis-Chalmers pump business, an international force in fluid technology. ITT's Defense & Electronics segment earned contracts to make equipment used in the Persian Gulf War. In 1994 ITT Automotive purchases solidified its position as the world's top maker of electric motors and wiper systems.

In 1995 ITT split into three independent companies: ITT Corporation (hospitality, entertainment, and information services; now part of Starwood Hotels & Resorts), ITT Hartford (insurance; now Hartford Financial Services), and ITT Industries (auto parts, defense and electric systems, and fluid-control products).

When ITT Automotive's 1996 sales were less than predicted, the company began to focus on smaller divisions. In 1997 ITT sold its seat subsystem operations to rival Lear and acquired Goulds Pumps, making ITT the world's largest pump maker. After the $815 million takeover, ITT announced in 1998 that it would cut 1,000 jobs and close five plants in its pump division. Also that year it reorganized into four segments: Connectors & Switches, Defense Products & Services, Pumps & Complementary Products, and Specialty Products. The company sold its automotive electrical systems unit to Valeo for $1.7 billion and its brake and chassis unit to Germany's Continental for about $1.9 billion. In 1999 ITT bought Hydro Air Industries (a maker of accessories for spas and swimming pools) and invested $25 million in Earth-Watch, a developer of imaging satellites. ITT also agreed that year to pay $119 million for a unit of Singapore-based San Teh that makes rubber switches used in mobile telephones and $191 million for the space and communications unit of Stanford Telecommunications.

Chairman, President, and CEO: Travis Engen, age 54, $2,293,871 pay
President and COO: Louis J. Giuliano, age 52, $1,043,074 pay
EVP; President and CEO, ITT Fluid Technology: Richard J. Labrecque, age 60, $622,194 pay
SVP and Director of Corporate Development: Martin Kamber, age 50
SVP and General Counsel: Vincent A. Maffeo, age 48
VP and Director of Corporate Relations: Thomas R. Martin, age 45
SVP and Director of Human Resources: James P. Smith Jr., age 56
VP and Director of Investor Relations: Ralph D. Allen, age 57
VP; President, Industrial Pump Group: Robert L. Ayers
VP, Associate General Counsel, and Assistant Secretary: Robert W. Beicke
VP; President, ITT Flygt: Leif E. Carlsson
VP, Secretary, and Associate General Counsel: Gwenn L. Carr
VP and General Auditor: Robert J. Eason
VP and Treasurer: Donald E. Foley, age 47
VP; President, ITT Cannon Worldwide: Gerard Gendron, age 46
VP; President Industrial Products, ITT Fluid Technology: Richard J. M. Hamilton
VP and Director, Operations Analysis: Wilberto S. Montes de Oca
Auditors: Arthur Andersen LLP

LOCATIONS

HQ: 4 W. Red Oak Ln., White Plains, NY 10604
Phone: 914-641-2000   **Fax:** 914-696-2950
Web site: http://www.ittind.com

1998 Sales

	$ mil.	% of total
US	2,570	58
Western Europe	1,228	27
Asia/Pacific	281	6
Other regions	414	9
Total	**4,493**	**100**

PRODUCTS/OPERATIONS

1998 Sales

	$ mil.	% of total
Pumps & complementary products	1,767	39
Defense products	765	17
Connectors & switches	578	13
Defense services	528	12
Fluid-handling products	362	8
Brakes	151	3
Engineered valves	117	3
Shock absorbers	92	2
Marine products	88	2
Measuring devices	17	—
Other	28	1
Total	**4,493**	**100**

COMPETITORS

Alliant	GenCorp	Siemens
Techsystems	Harris	SPX
AlliedSignal	Corporation	Swagelok
British	KSB	Texas
Aerospace	Litton Industries	Instruments
Daniel Industries	Mannesmann AG	Thomson SA
Ebara	Raytheon	TRW
FMC	Robert Bosch	United Dominion
GEC	SCI Systems	Industries

HISTORICAL FINANCIALS & EMPLOYEES

NYSE symbol: IIN FYE: December 31	Annual Growth	1989	1990	1991	1992	1993	1994	1995	1996	1997	1998
Sales ($ mil.)	(6.8%)	—	—	—	6,845	6,621	7,758	8,884	8,718	8,777	4,493
Net income ($ mil.)	—	—	—	—	(260)	913	1,033	658	223	108	1,533
Income as % of sales	—	—	—	—	—	13.8%	13.3%	7.4%	2.6%	1.2%	34.1%
Earnings per share ($)	29.9%	—	—	—	—	—	—	6.18	1.85	0.89	13.55
Stock price - FY high ($)	—	—	—	—	—	—	—	24.25	28.63	33.69	40.88
Stock price - FY low ($)	—	—	—	—	—	—	—	21.25	21.50	22.13	28.13
Stock price - FY close ($)	18.3%	—	—	—	—	—	—	24.00	24.50	31.38	39.75
P/E - high	—	—	—	—	—	—	—	4	15	38	3
P/E - low	—	—	—	—	—	—	—	3	12	25	2
Dividends per share ($)	—	—	—	—	—	—	—	0.00	0.45	0.60	0.60
Book value per share ($)	36.2%	—	—	—	—	—	—	5.36	6.75	6.94	13.55
Employees	(7.6%)	—	—	—	53,000	50,000	58,400	59,000	59,000	58,500	33,000

STOCK PRICE HISTORY

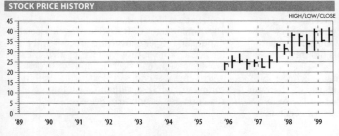

HIGH/LOW/CLOSE

1998 FISCAL YEAR-END

Debt ratio: 28.4%
Return on equity: 117.9%
Cash ($ mil.): 881
Current ratio: 1.11
Long-term debt ($ mil.): 516
No. of shares (mil.): 96
Dividends
 Yield: 1.5%
 Payout: 4.4%
Market value ($ mil.): 3,815

JACOBS ENGINEERING GROUP INC.

OVERVIEW

Jacobs Engineering Group continues to climb the ladder. The Pasadena, California-based engineering and design firm builds facilities, such as manufacturing plants, for companies in the chemical, oil refining, semiconductor, pulp and paper, pharmaceutical, and biotechnology industries. Chemical and petroleum industry projects account for about half of revenues.

The company also manages construction activities for commercial, industrial, federal, and other large customers and provides process plant maintenance services. It manages the Department of Energy's Oak Ridge, Tennessee, facilities with Bechtel Group through the

Bechtel Jacobs joint venture. Government projects, primarily environmental engineering, account for 8% of its revenues.

Jacobs Engineering is using acquisitions as rungs in its upward path. It has strengthened its overseas operations by acquiring French firm Serete Group and a controlling interest in its Indian affiliate Jacobs H&G (formerly Humphreys & Glasgow). Jacobs Engineering also has acquired Sverdrup, a US construction, architecture, and engineering firm best known for its transportation projects.

Founder and chairman Joseph Jacobs owns 14% of the company.

HISTORY

Joseph Jacobs graduated from the Polytechnic Institute of Brooklyn in 1942 with a doctorate degree in engineering. He went to work for Merck, designing processes for pharmaceutical production. Later he moved to Chemurgic Corp. near San Francisco, where he worked until 1947, when he founded Jacobs Engineering as a consulting firm. Jacobs supplemented his consulting work by selling industrial equipment, avoiding any apparent conflict of interest by simply telling his clients what he was doing.

When equipment sales outstripped consulting work, Jacobs hired four salesmen by 1954 and Stan Krugman, an engineer, who soon became his right-hand man. Two years later, the company got its first big chemical design job; it was for Kaiser Aluminum. The following year Jacobs incorporated his sole proprietorship.

Until 1960, the company had avoided actual construction work; then it won a contract to design and build a potash flotation plant and Jacobs Engineering became a fully integrated design and construction firm. In 1967 the company opened its first regional office but kept management decentralized to replicate the small size and hard-hitting qualities that had made its home office successful. Three years later Jacobs Engineering went public.

The firm continued its expansion by merging with Houston-based Pace Companies, which specialized in petrochemical engineering design, in 1974. That year Jacobs Engineering became Jacobs Engineering Group and began construction in Ireland of its first major overseas chemical plant.

By 1977 the firm's sales had reached $250 million. A decade of lobbying paid off that year when the firm won a contract for the Arab Potash complex in Jordan. Jacobs began to

withdraw from his firm's operations in the early 1980s, but the 1982-1983 recession and poor management decisions pounded the company's earnings. Jacobs returned from retirement in 1985, fired 14 VPs, cut the staff in half, and returned the firm to the pursuit of smaller process plant jobs and specialty construction.

Jacobs abandoned an attempt in 1986 to take the company private, then began to make acquisitions to improve the firm's construction expertise.

In 1992 Jacobs relinquished his role as CEO to president Noel Watson. The next year the company expanded its international holdings by acquiring H&G Process Contracting and H&G Contractors in England.

The firm's $38 million purchase of CRS Sirrine Engineers (engineering design) and CRSS Constructors (construction management) in 1994 was the largest at that point in its history and opened up new markets in the paper and semiconductor industries. By 1995 Jacobs Engineering was consolidating its acquisitions and working on a record backlog.

Jacobs Engineering spent the rest of the decade making acquisitions. In 1996 it purchased a 49% interest in European engineering specialist Serete Group (it bought the rest the next year). In 1997 it gained control of Indian engineering affiliate Humphreys & Glasgow (now Jacobs H&G), increasing its 40% stake to 70%, and bought CPR Engineering, a specialist in pulp and paper converting processes. It also formed a joint venture with Krupp UHDE to provide design, engineering, and construction management services in Mexico. In 1999 the company paid $198 million for St. Louis construction and design firm Sverdrup.

OFFICERS

Chairman: Joseph J. Jacobs, age 82, $882,200 pay
VC: Richard E. Beumer
President and CEO: Noel G. Watson, age 62, $1,133,510 pay
EVP Operations: William R. Kerler, age 69, $711,010 pay
EVP Operations: Richard J. Slater, age 52, $516,780 pay
EVP Operations: Thomas R. Hammond, age 47, $513,080 pay
EVP, Sverdrup Operations: James C. Uselton
SVP Quality and Safety: Andrew E. Carlson, age 65
SVP Federal Programs: Michael J. Higgins, age 54
SVP General Sales and Marketing: Craig L. Martin, age 49
SVP Finance and Administration and Treasurer: John W. Prosser Jr., age 53
SVP and Controller: Nazim G. Thawerbhoy, age 51
Group VP, Field Services: Donald J. Boutwell, age 61
Group VP Central Region: Robert M. Clement, age 50
Group VP, Buildings and Infrastructure: Warren M. Dean, age 54
Group VP, Northern Region: George A. Kunberger Jr., age 46
Group VP International Operations: Gregory J. Landry, age 50
Group VP International Operations: John McLachlan, age 52
Group VP, Federal Operations: Roger L. Williams, age 60
Director Corporate Human Resources: William Gebhardt
Auditors: Ernst & Young LLP

LOCATIONS

HQ: 1111 S. Arroyo Pkwy., Pasadena, CA 91105
Phone: 626-578-3500 **Fax:** 626-578-6916

1998 Sales

	$ mil.	% of total
US	1,677	80
Europe	411	20
Other regions	13	—
Total	**2,101**	**100**

PRODUCTS/OPERATIONS

1998 Sales

	$ mil.	% of total
Construction	1,012	48
Engineering	822	39
Maintenance	267	13
Total	**2,101**	**100**

COMPETITORS

BE&K	Kvaerner
Bechtel	Morrison Knudsen
CH2M Hill	Parsons
Fluor	Peter Kiewit Sons'
Foster Wheeler	Raytheon
Halliburton	Roy F. Weston
ICF Kaiser	Stone & Webster
IT Group	Turner Corporation

HISTORICAL FINANCIALS & EMPLOYEES

NYSE symbol: JEC FYE: September 30	Annual Growth	1989	1990	1991	1992	1993	1994	1995	1996	1997	1998
Sales ($ mil.)	11.4%	794	882	1,036	1,106	1,143	1,166	1,723	1,799	1,781	2,101
Net income ($ mil.)	20.4%	10	14	20	27	29	19	32	40	47	54
Income as % of sales	—	1.3%	1.6%	2.0%	2.4%	2.5%	1.6%	1.9%	2.2%	2.6%	2.6%
Earnings per share ($)	17.7%	0.48	0.64	0.86	1.11	1.15	0.75	1.27	1.56	1.80	2.08
Stock price - FY high ($)	—	6.88	13.63	28.88	36.50	31.00	26.88	25.75	29.38	32.56	34.25
Stock price - FY low ($)	—	4.81	5.56	8.63	21.63	20.00	18.00	16.88	19.63	21.25	24.69
Stock price - FY close ($)	20.0%	6.03	9.13	27.63	29.13	23.25	24.38	24.88	22.50	30.63	31.00
P/E - high	—	14	21	34	33	27	36	20	19	18	16
P/E - low	—	10	9	10	19	17	24	13	13	12	12
Dividends per share ($)	—	0.00	0.00	0.00	0.00	0.00	0.00	0.00	0.00	0.00	0.00
Book value per share ($)	20.4%	2.73	3.69	4.59	5.92	7.02	7.99	9.37	11.01	12.53	14.50
Employees	5.9%	10,280	11,220	10,750	12,300	13,100	13,140	14,500	14,150	15,870	17,240

STOCK PRICE HISTORY

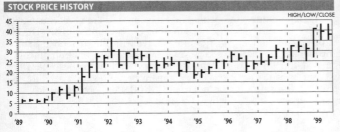

HIGH/LOW/CLOSE

1998 FISCAL YEAR-END

Debt ratio: 6.6%
Return on equity: 14.6%
Cash ($ mil.): 101
Current ratio: 1.54
Long-term debt ($ mil.): 26
No. of shares (mil.): 26
Dividends
 Yield: —
 Payout: —
Market value ($ mil.): 794

J.B. HUNT TRANSPORT SERVICES

OVERVIEW

Other companies can keep on trucking if they wish — J.B. Hunt Transport Services, however, is hunting for a bigger share of the market for freight transportation services: intermodal (train/truck) shipping, logistics, and contract services. The Lowell, Arkansas-based company is the US's largest publicly traded truckload carrier (privately held Schneider National is #1 overall). With 10,500 drivers, 8,900 tractors, and more than 22,000 containers, J.B. Hunt trucks across the US, Canada, and Mexico. Founder Johnnie Bryan Hunt owns 40% of the firm.

The carrier has dumped its hazardous-waste transport and small-package divisions to concentrate on trucking and logistics. As other truck companies have struggled to keep qualified drivers, J.B. Hunt has raised drivers' wages, a strategy that has paid off through lower recruiting, training, and accident expenses.

But trucking's just part of the picture. J.B. Hunt Logistics offers services to manage a company's entire supply chain, including its products, packages, and truck routes. It also has an Internet tracking system that allows trucks to identify the freight waiting to be moved and to post their available equipment and capacity. Another business unit, Dedicated Contract Services, puts together customized delivery systems for large clients using the trucking company's equipment and drivers.

HISTORY

Founder Johnnie Bryan Hunt's history is a classic tale of rolling from rags to riches, with a little help from a Rockefeller. Hunt's family members were sharecroppers; he left school at age 12 during the Depression to work for his uncle's Arkansas sawmill. In the late 1950s, after driving trucks for more than nine years, Hunt noticed that the rice mills along his eastern Arkansas route were burning rice hulls. Believing that the hulls could be used as poultry litter, Hunt got a contract to haul away the hulls and began selling them to chicken farmers. In 1961 he began the J.B. Hunt Company with help from future Arkansas governor Winthrop Rockefeller's Winrock grass company, where Hunt bought sod for one of his side businesses. He developed a machine to compress the rice hulls, which made their transportation profitable, and within a few years the company was the world's largest producer of rice hulls for poultry litter.

Still looking for new opportunities, Hunt bought some used trucks and refrigerated trailers in 1969, though the company continued to focus on its original business. In the 1970s it found that the ground rice hulls made a good base for livestock vitamins and medications. Buyers of the ground hulls included Pfizer and Eli Lilly. J.B. Hunt, with Pfizer's backing, soon began selling a vitamin premix to feed companies.

In the 1980s, J.B. Hunt's trucking division grew dramatically and became lucrative as the trucking industry was deregulated. In 1981 and 1982 the Hunt trucking business had higher margins than most trucking firms. In 1983, when J.B. Hunt Transport Services, Inc. went public, Hunt sold the rice hull business to concentrate on trucking.

By 1986 J.B. Hunt was the nation's third-largest irregular-route trucking company. The time was ripe to expand, and the company began trucking in Canada (1988) and Mexico (1989). It also formed an alliance in 1989 with Santa Fe Pacific Railroad (now Burlington Northern Santa Fe) to provide intermodal services between the West Coast and the Midwest.

The company began adding computers to its trucks in 1992 to improve data exchange and communication on the road. J.B. Hunt also formed a joint venture with Latin America's largest transportation company, Transportacion Maritima Mexicana. Founder Hunt retired in 1995 and became Senior Chairman.

J.B. Hunt tried hauling automobiles in 1996 but abandoned the idea when it found that cars were easily dented on intermodal trailers. More in line with the trucking company's long-term goals was an effort to stabilize its roster of drivers. The company raised wages by one-third in 1997 to counteract driver shortages and high turnover. That year J.B. Hunt sold its underperforming flatbed-trucking unit (renamed Charger Inc.).

In 1998 J.B. Hunt reaped the benefits from its efforts to retain drivers with greater profits; it also formed expansion plans that included opening new terminals, thereby decreasing the need for long cross-country drives. The logistics unit worked with IBM to launch a suite of Java-based applications to track shipments for third-party carriers, and the next year the trucking company began testing a satellite system from ORBCOMM Global to track empty trailers.

Senior Chairman: J. B. Hunt, age 72, $375,000 pay
Chairman: Wayne Garrison, age 46, $375,000 pay
VC: J. Bryan Hunt Jr.
President and CEO: Kirk Thompson, age 45, $469,615 pay
EVP, Marketing: Paul R. Bergant, age 52
EVP, Operations: A. Craig Harper, age 41
EVP, Equipment and Properties: Bob D. Ralston, age 52
EVP, Finance and CFO: Jerry W. Walton, age 52, $292,308 pay
SVP of Supply Chain Integration: Joel Sutherland
VP Personnel: Mark Greenway
President, J.B. Hunt Logistics; EVP, Integrated Solutions: Jun-Sheng Li, age 40
President, Dedicated Contract Services: John N. Roberts III, age 34
VP, J.B. Hunt Logistics: David Roth
Chief Information Officer: Robert E. Logan, age 60, $299,485 pay
Secretary: Johnelle Hunt, age 67
Auditors: KPMG LLP

LOCATIONS

HQ: J.B. Hunt Transport Services, Inc.,
615 J.B. Hunt Corporate Dr., Lowell, AR 72745
Phone: 501-820-0000   **Fax:** 501-820-8397
Web site: http://www.jbhunt.com

J.B. Hunt Transport Services provides truckload service to the 48 contiguous US states, Mexico, and the Canadian provinces of British Columbia, Ontario, and Quebec.

PRODUCTS/OPERATIONS

1998 Sales & Operating Income

	Sales		Operating Income	
	$ mil.	% of total	$ mil.	% of total
Van/Intermodal	1,379	72	81	77
JBHL	317	17	8	7
DCS	212	11	17	16
Other	8	—	(3)	—
Adjustments	(74)	—	—	—
Total	**1,842**	**100**	**103**	**100**

Operating Groups
Van/Intermodal
J.B. Hunt Logistics (JBHL)
Dedicated Contract Services (DCS)

COMPETITORS

Air Express	Fritz
APL	Hub Group
Burlington Northern	Landstar System
Santa Fe	Norfolk Southern
Cannon Express	Ocean Group
CHR	Pittston BAX
Circle International	Ryder
CNF Transportation	Schneider National
CSX	Union Pacific
Eagle USA	UPS
Expeditors International	U.S. Xpress
FDX	Werner

HISTORICAL FINANCIALS & EMPLOYEES

Nasdaq symbol: JBHT FYE: December 31	Annual Growth	1989	1990	1991	1992	1993	1994	1995	1996	1997	1998
Sales ($ mil.)	15.4%	509	580	733	912	1,021	1,208	1,352	1,487	1,554	1,842
Net income ($ mil.)	4.8%	31	30	28	39	38	40	(2)	22	11	47
Income as % of sales	—	6.0%	5.2%	3.8%	4.3%	3.7%	3.3%	—	1.5%	0.7%	2.5%
Earnings per share ($)	4.4%	0.87	0.85	0.80	1.08	1.00	1.05	(0.06)	0.58	0.31	1.28
Stock price - FY high ($)	—	17.34	15.51	20.51	26.00	26.75	25.75	20.13	22.13	19.25	38.88
Stock price - FY low ($)	—	11.34	9.67	11.34	16.25	17.25	15.00	12.75	13.75	13.38	12.31
Stock price - FY close ($)	6.4%	13.17	11.67	20.01	23.25	23.25	15.25	16.75	14.00	18.75	23.00
P/E - high	—	20	18	26	24	27	25	—	38	62	30
P/E - low	—	13	11	14	15	17	14	—	24	43	10
Dividends per share ($)	2.5%	0.16	0.16	0.19	0.20	0.20	0.20	0.20	0.20	0.20	0.20
Book value per share ($)	8.8%	4.95	5.52	6.19	8.10	8.95	9.81	9.35	9.61	9.48	10.55
Employees	7.6%	7,380	8,479	9,445	11,201	10,476	11,837	12,020	11,575	11,780	14,250

STOCK PRICE HISTORY

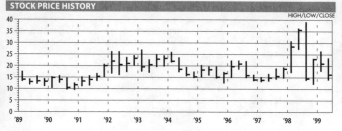

HIGH/LOW/CLOSE

1998 FISCAL YEAR-END

Debt ratio: 52.6%
Return on equity: 12.5%
Cash ($ mil.): 9
Current ratio: 1.09
Long-term debt ($ mil.): 417
No. of shares (mil.): 36
Dividends
  Yield: 0.9%
  Payout: 15.6%
Market value ($ mil.): 819

J. C. PENNEY COMPANY, INC.

OVERVIEW

Under pressure to make a quick change, J. C. Penney Company is exiting the dressing room in some new duds with a slightly different look. To boost sales at its 1,150 or so troubled JCPenney department stores, the Plano, Texas-based company is expanding upon and re-emphasizing what made it popular in the early 1990s: private-label clothing.

To do this, J. C. Penney is creating stores-within-stores — a favorite concept among upscale retailers — to feature its eight key private-label brands, including the popular Arizona Jean Co. line, which is expanding into new categories. The company hopes to lure back customers from discount stores such as Target and hot specialty retailers such as The Gap.

Although the department stores have struggled, the company still boasts the largest catalog operation in the US (The JCPenney BIG BOOK) and the Eckerd drugstore chain, with 2,900 stores (Eckerd accounts for about one-third of sales). J. C. Penney plans to add another 575 new and relocated stores to Eckerd by 2001. To better realize Eckerd's value on the stock market, it plans to sell about 20% of the chain through a tracking stock.

Burdened by debt, J. C. Penney also hopes to raise money by selling its $4 billion credit card business.

HISTORY

In 1902 James Cash Penney and two former employers opened the Golden Rule, a dry goods store, in Kemmerer, Wyoming. Penney bought out his partners in 1907 and opened stores that sold soft goods in small towns. Basing his customer service policy on his Baptist heritage, he held employees (called "associates") to a high moral code.

The firm incorporated in Utah in 1913 as the J. C. Penney Company, with headquarters in Salt Lake City, but it moved to New York City the next year to improve buying and financial operations. It expanded to nearly 1,400 stores in the 1920s and went public in 1929. The company grew during the Depression with its reputation for high quality and low prices.

J. C. Penney rode the postwar boom, and by 1951 sales had surpassed $1 billion. It introduced credit plans in 1958 and entered catalog retailing in 1962 with its purchase of General Merchandise Co. The next year JCPenney added hard goods, which allowed it to compete with Sears and Montgomery Ward.

The company formed JCPenney Insurance in the mid-1960s and bought Thrift Drug in 1969. The chain continued to grow, and in 1973, two years after Penney's death, there were 2,053 stores. Also in the 1970s J. C. Penney began its ill-fated foray overseas by buying chains in Belgium and Italy in hopes of duplicating its US formula — giant department stores.

It bought Delaware-based First National Bank in 1983 (renamed JCPenney National Bank in 1984) to issue MasterCard and Visa cards. JCPenney stores refocused on soft goods during the 1980s and stopped selling automotive services, appliances, paint, hardware, and fabrics in 1983. It discontinued sporting goods, consumer electronics, and photographic equipment in 1987.

The next year JCPenney Telemarketing was formed to take catalog phone orders and provide telemarketing services for other companies. Also in 1988 the company moved its headquarters to Plano, Texas.

JCPenney tried to move upmarket in the 1980s, enlisting the services of fashion designer Halston. The line failed, however, so the company developed its own brands.

James Oesterreicher was named CEO in 1995. After facing many delays (including the devaluation of the peso), J. C. Penney opened its first Mexican department store in Monterrey that year. Facing a slow-growing department store business back home, it then bought 272 drugstores from Fay's Inc. and 200 more from Rite Aid. In 1997 it acquired Eckerd (nearly 1,750 stores) for $3.3 billion, converting its other drugstores to the Eckerd name. The company also sold its $740 million credit card portfolio of JCPenney National Bank to Associates First Capital and dealt its bank branches to First National Bank of Wyoming in 1997.

The retailer struggled in 1998, swallowing slumps in sales and a $70 million charge for consolidating its drugstore operations. J. C. Penney also closed 75 underperforming department stores that year. In late 1998 the company bought a controlling stake in the 21-location Brazilian department store chain Lojas Renner for $33 million, continuing its expansion in Latin America.

With its stock value falling, J. C. Penney announced in 1999 it would sell 20% of Eckerd in the form of a tracking stock; the company also announced it was selling its credit card business in 1999.

Chairman and CEO: James E. Oesterreicher, age 57, $1,062,121 pay
EVP and Chief Human Resources and Administration Officer: Gary L. Davis, age 56
EVP, Secretary, and General Counsel: Charles R. Lotter, age 61, $450,900 pay
EVP and CFO: Donald A. McKay, age 53
EVP and COO, JCPenney Stores, Merchandising and Catalog: Vanessa Castagna, age 49
SVP and Chief Information Officer: David V. Evans, age 53
SVP and Chief Marketing Officer: Stephen Farley
SVP; Director of JCPenney Stores: Michael W. Taxter
VP and Director of Systems Architecture and Technical Support: Rick Conley
VP and Director of Retail Marketing and Catalog Systems: Andy Cowan
VP; President and CEO of JCPenney Direct Marketing Services: Robert Romasco
VP and Director of Corporate and Financial Systems: Eldridge White
Chairman, President, and CEO of Eckerd: Francis A. Newman, age 50, $733,541 pay
Auditors: KPMG LLP

LOCATIONS

HQ: 6501 Legacy Dr., Plano, TX 75024-3698
Phone: 972-431-1000   **Fax:** 972-431-1977
Web site: http://www.jcpenney.net

J. C. Penney Company operates about 1,150 JCPenney retail stores in Chile, Mexico, Puerto Rico, and the US; 21 Brazilian department stores under the name Renner; and approximately 2,900 drugstores in the American northeastern, southeastern, and Sunbelt regions. It has six catalog distribution centers.

PRODUCTS/OPERATIONS

1999 Sales

	$ mil.	% of total
JCPenney stores	15,402	50
JCPenney catalog	3,929	13
Drugstores	10,325	34
Direct marketing	1,022	3
Total	**30,678**	**100**

1999 Stores

	No.
Eckerd	2,756
JCPenney	1,148
Renner	21
Total	**3,925**

Selected Private Labels

Arizona Jean Co.	JCPenney Home Collection
Crazy Horse by Liz	Jones Wear (exclusive
Claiborne (exclusive	third-party brand)
third-party brand)	St. John's Bay
Hunt Club	Stafford
Jacqueline Ferrar	

COMPETITORS

Ames	Federated	Nine West
Bed Bath &	The Gap	Rite Aid
Beyond	J. Crew	Ross Stores
Belk	J. Jill Group	Saks Inc.
Bradlees	Kmart	Sears
Brown Shoe	Kohl's	Spiegel
Costco	Lands' End	TJX
Companies	The Limited	Venator Group
CVS	Longs	Walgreen
Dayton Hudson	May	Wal-Mart
Dillard's	Montgomery	
Dress Barn	Ward	

HISTORICAL FINANCIALS & EMPLOYEES

NYSE symbol: JCP FYE: January 31	Annual Growth	1990	1991	1992	1993	1994	1995	1996	1997	1998	1999
Sales ($ mil.)	7.4%	16,103	16,365	16,201	18,009	18,983	20,380	21,419	23,649	29,618	30,678
Net income ($ mil.)	(3.3%)	802	577	448	777	940	1,057	838	565	566	594
Income as % of sales	—	5.0%	3.5%	2.8%	4.3%	5.0%	5.2%	3.9%	2.4%	1.9%	1.9%
Earnings per share ($)	(3.2%)	2.93	2.17	0.20	2.95	3.24	4.05	3.33	2.25	2.10	2.19
Stock price - FY high ($)	—	37.81	35.44	29.13	40.19	56.38	59.00	50.00	57.00*	68.25	78.75
Stock price - FY low ($)	—	25.38	18.69	23.56	27.06	36.00	39.88	41.13	46.25	44.88	38.13
Stock price - FY close ($)	1.7%	33.44	25.56	27.38	35.81	52.38	41.50	48.88	47.38	67.38	39.00
P/E - high	—	13	16	146	14	16	15	15	25	33	36
P/E - low	—	9	9	118	9	10	10	12	21	21	17
Dividends per share ($)	8.0%	1.09	1.32	1.32	1.32	1.41	1.62	1.86	2.04	2.13	2.17
Book value per share ($)	4.7%	17.78	18.29	17.20	19.11	21.59	23.31	24.59	24.67	27.09	26.78
Employees	3.2%	198,000	196,000	185,000	192,000	193,000	202,000	205,000	252,000	260,000	262,000

STOCK PRICE HISTORY

HIGH/LOW/CLOSE

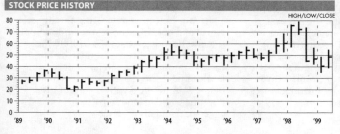

1999 FISCAL YEAR-END

Debt ratio: 49.9%
Return on equity: 8.9%
Cash ($ mil.): 96
Current ratio: 1.86
Long-term debt ($ mil.): 7,143
No. of shares (mil.): 250
Dividends
 Yield: 5.6%
 Payout: 99.1%
Market value ($ mil.): 9,750

JO-ANN STORES, INC.

OVERVIEW

Jo-Ann Stores has sewn up the leadership of the fabric store market. The Hudson, Ohio-based company is the #1 specialty fabric retailer in the US, well ahead of Hancock Fabrics. Formerly called Fabri-Centers of America, Jo-Ann sells fabrics, craft supplies, decorating and floral items, and seasonal goods at about 1,050 locations in 49 states. The company's stores operate mostly under the Jo-Ann Fabrics and Crafts name and are located mainly in strip shopping centers.

Recognizing that sewing these days is more often a hobby than a necessity, the company is luring creative customers with arts and crafts and home decorating items (thank you, Martha Stewart). Jo-Ann has picked up the thread of specialty retailing's "bigger is better" trend. It is pinning its hopes for future growth on its Jo-Ann etc (experience the creativity) stores, which average about 47,000 sq. ft. — more than three times the size of its traditional stores. Jo-Ann etc stores offer a range of non-sewing items as well as extras such as pottery classes. For now, though, the large stores bring in less than 10% of Jo-Ann's sales.

Chairman, president, and CEO Alan Rosskamm and his mother, Betty (an SVP), control 17% of Jo-Ann's voting power; SVP Alma Zimmerman and her family control 7%.

HISTORY

Jo-Ann Stores' predecessor began in 1943 when the German immigrant Rohrbach family started Cleveland Fabric with the help of fellow immigrants, the Reichs. Alma, daughter of the Rohrbachs, worked at the store and was joined by Betty Reich in 1947.

Betty's and Alma's respective husbands, Martin Rosskamm and Freddy Zimmerman, also joined the company. At the urging of Martin (who eventually became chairman), Cleveland Fabric opened more stores, mainly in malls. As it moved beyond Cleveland, it adopted a new store name — Jo-Ann — devised from the names of Alma and Freddy's daughter Joan and Betty and Martin's daughter Jackie Ann. It changed its name to Fabri-Centers of America in 1968 and went public the following year.

The very postwar boom that brought Alma and Betty into the workforce worked against the company in the 1970s, as women tucked away their sewing baskets in favor of jobs outside their homes. Specialty fabric stores found their niche as department stores, responding to the trend, stopped offering sewing supplies. But they soon faced competition from fabric superstores and heavily discounted ready-made clothing.

Martin and Betty's son Alan took over as president and CEO in 1985 and began to modernize the company and the stores. Trained in real estate law, he began focusing on opening larger stores in strip shopping centers, which offered cheaper leasing than malls. He also added a new computer system for inventory, laid off some administrative workers, and closed underperforming stores. The company had about 625 stores by mid-1989.

As its industry consolidated, Fabri-Centers held on, despite missteps such as its 1984 launch of the Cargo Express housewares chain (that money-losing venture, which had about 40 stores at its peak, ended in 1994). The firm became the nation's largest fabrics and crafts chain in 1994 when it bought 300-plus Cloth World stores from Brown Group. At the close of that deal, Fabri-Centers had nearly 1,000 stores in every state except Hawaii.

In 1995 Fabri-Centers opened a store on its home turf in Hudson, Ohio, that offered not only a range of fabric and craft items, but also home decorating merchandise, furniture, craft classes, and day care. At three times the size of its other stores, the Jo-Ann etc superstore helped the company pull in non-sewers looking for art supplies, picture frames, and decorating ideas. Jo-Ann etc became the focus of the company's growth.

Fabri-Centers paid $3.8 million in 1997 to settle SEC charges that it had overstated its profits during a 1992 debt offering. In 1998 it paid nearly $100 million for ailing Los Angeles-based fabric and craft company House of Fabrics, adding about 260 locations and strengthening its presence on the West Coast. Fabri-Centers then renamed itself Jo-Ann Stores and began placing all of its stores under the Jo-Ann name.

Jo-Ann continued relocating traditional stores and opening new stores while snipping underperforming locations. In 1999 the company signed a pact with Martha Stewart Living Omnimedia to sell fancy decorating fabrics under the Martha Stewart Home name. Jo-Ann's deal with the decorating doyenne could extend to patterns, wall coverings, and other items.

Chairman, President and CEO: Alan Rosskamm, age 49, $448,107 pay
EVP and CFO: Brian P. Carney, age 38, $295,052 pay
EVP, Merchandising, Marketing and Inventory Management: Jane Aggers, age 50, $344,946 pay
EVP, Stores and Business Development: David E. Bolen, age 46, $268,047 pay
SVP; General Merchandise Manager Fashion Apparel, Decorating: Lee Barnard
SVP and Chief Information Officer: Les Duncan, age 50, $224,839 pay
SVP, Human Resources: Rosalind Thompson
SVP, Inventory Management: Bruce Schwallie
SVP, Logistics: Anthony Dissinger
SVP; General Merchandise Manager, Crafting: M. J. Marlinski
SVP, Real Estate: John Stec
SVP and Secretary: Betty Rosskamm
SVP: Alma Zimmerman
SVP and Assistant Secretary: Justin Zimmerman
VP and Controller: Jim Kerr
VP; General Merchandise Manager, Sewing: Mark Krebbs
VP, Marketing: Barbara Semen
VP, Real Estate: James Phillips
VP, Store Effectiveness: Carolyn Tackett
VP, Store Planning and Construction: Daniel Maguire
Auditors: Arthur Andersen LLP

LOCATIONS

HQ: 5555 Darrow Rd., Hudson, OH 44236
Phone: 330-656-2600   **Fax:** 330-463-6675
Web site: http://www.joann.com

Jo-Ann Stores operates about 1,050 fabric and craft stores throughout the US.

1999 Stores

	No.
California	129
Ohio	83
Texas	73
Michigan	64
Florida	61
Pennsylvania	61
New York	51
Illinois	49
Washington	38
Indiana	34
Massachusetts	26
Oregon	26
Minnesota	25
Virginia	24
Maryland	23
Wisconsin	23
Connecticut	20
Arizona	19
Colorado	17
Georgia	16
New Jersey	16
Utah	15
Other states	165
Total	**1,058**

COMPETITORS

A.C. Moore
FNC Holdings
Garden Ridge
Hancock Fabrics
Hobby Lobby
Kmart
Michaels Stores
MJDesigns
Pier 1 Imports
Rag Shops
Target Stores
Wal-Mart

HISTORICAL FINANCIALS & EMPLOYEES

NYSE symbol: JAS.A FYE: January 31	Annual Growth	1990	1991	1992	1993	1994	1995	1996	1997	1998	1999
Sales ($ mil.)	15.7%	333	386	469	574	582	677	835	929	975	1,243
Net income ($ mil.)	5.0%	9	11	18	4	2	12	18	25	31	14
Income as % of sales	—	2.6%	2.9%	3.7%	0.7%	0.4%	1.7%	2.1%	2.6%	3.2%	1.1%
Earnings per share ($)	1.9%	0.58	0.72	0.98	0.22	0.11	0.63	0.90	1.26	1.54	0.69
Stock price - FY high ($)	—	5.29	9.75	23.63	22.50	9.63	9.13	16.13	17.00	27.81	31.88
Stock price - FY low ($)	—	3.67	4.96	9.44	5.00	6.25	5.81	8.19	9.88	15.75	13.00
Stock price - FY close ($)	13.3%	4.96	9.50	20.50	8.19	8.75	8.19	13.63	16.00	24.38	15.25
P/E - high	—	9	14	24	102	88	14	18	13	18	46
P/E - low	—	6	7	10	23	57	9	9	8	10	19
Dividends per share ($)	—	0.00	0.00	0.00	0.00	0.00	0.00	0.00	0.00	0.00	0.00
Book value per share ($)	14.7%	4.50	5.15	7.67	7.84	8.02	8.81	9.80	11.13	14.58	15.47
Employees	14.5%	6,500	6,510	10,300	11,400	11,400	17,600	17,200	17,100	16,400	22,000

STOCK PRICE HISTORY

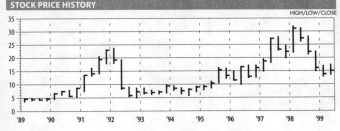

HIGH/LOW/CLOSE

1999 FISCAL YEAR-END

Debt ratio: 41.3%
Return on equity: 5.3%
Cash ($ mil.): 20
Current ratio: 2.34
Long-term debt ($ mil.): 183
No. of shares (mil.): 17
Dividends
 Yield: —
 Payout: —
Market value ($ mil.): 255

JOHN HANCOCK MUTUAL LIFE

OVERVIEW

John Hancock Mutual Life Insurance has products designed to offer comfort in your old age and security to your survivors.

The Boston-based company's largest business is life insurance, but as baby boomers move toward retirement age, the company has put more emphasis on retirement savings products. These include annuities, proprietary mutual funds, and long-term-care insurance. One of the largest investors in the US, John Hancock offers institutional asset management services, providing clients with specialty funds in such industries as timber and agriculture.

John Hancock is demutualizing (converting to a stock company) by early 2000, and is trying to clean up its image before its IPO. The company's name has been tainted by policyholder lawsuits and a lobbying scandal that just won't go away. Even its association with the Olympics has been tarred by the Salt Lake City bribery scandal. To distance the insurer from the problems surrounding the Games, company president David D'Alessandro has been loudly calling for members of the International Olympic Committee to resign.

HISTORY

In 1862 Albert Murdock and other Boston businessmen founded John Hancock Mutual Life Insurance Company, named after a signer of the Declaration of Independence. The firm added agents in Connecticut, Illinois, Missouri, and Pennsylvania in 1865.

The following year the policyholder-owned company began making annual distributions of surplus to paid-up members. It became the first US mutual life insurer to offer industrial insurance (small-face-value weekly premium life insurance) in 1879. Hancock was also a pioneer in granting dividends and cash surrender values (the amount returned to the policyholder when a policy is canceled) with industrial insurance. In 1902 its weekly premium agencies began selling annual premium insurance.

Hancock added annuities in 1922, group insurance in 1924, and individual health insurance in 1957. In 1968 it formed John Hancock Advisers (mutual funds) and John Hancock International Group Program (group health and life insurance overseas). It added property/casualty insurance operations (with Sentry Insurance) in the early 1970s.

Despite these forays into new areas, Hancock's mainstay remained whole-life insurance. In the late 1970s, as interest rates soared, members borrowed on their policies at low rates to invest at higher rates, draining company funds. This convinced the company that it had to diversify.

It did so through acquisitions, including brokerages and bond specialists. Other business additions included equipment leasing, universal life, and credit cards. The company also made risky direct investments in the booming real estate market.

Despite the new business lines, Hancock's position in the industry declined during the 1980s. In the 1990s the company was hit by a downturn in the real estate industry that forced it to establish hefty reserves against defaults, which contributed to declining earnings. As a result, it sold its banking and credit card operations, as well as its property/casualty business.

Hancock expanded overseas by acquiring interests in insurers in Singapore and Thailand. (In 1998 the company also began collaborating with Vietnam Insurance Company to operate in that country.) John Hancock was among many in the industry subjected to increased fraud scrutiny in the mid-1990s. In 1994 it agreed to pay more than $1 million in federal and state fines for treating Massachusetts state senators to sporting events and dinners over a period of six years (a policyholder suit about this is still outstanding).

But the problems went even deeper. In 1996 Hancock was fined $1 million by the State of New York because agents persuaded consumers that life insurance policies were retirement savings products. To help restore public trust, the company fined and laid off agents and altered their compensation plans. But problems continued in 1997 when Massachusetts began investigating the company in the wake of a $350 million settlement of a class-action policyholder civil suit.

John Hancock initiated new sales strategies to bypass agents entirely, including direct mail, telemarketing, and online (through a groundbreaking pact with Microsoft). It sold its health care operations to WellPoint Health Networks in 1997. The next year the company announced it would demutualize. In 1999 John Hancock was among the first insurers approved to sell life insurance in China.

OFFICERS

Chairman and CEO: Stephen L. Brown
VC and Chief Investment Officer: Foster L. Aborn
President and COO: David F. D'Alessandro
CFO: Thomas E. Moloney
EVP Corporate Sector: Diane M. Capstaff
SVP and Controller: Earl W. Baucom
SVP Business Insurance Group: Nancy F. Bern
SVP and Demutualization Project Director:
  John M. DeCiccio
SVP Real Estate Investment Group: Edward P. Dowd
SVP Mergers and Acquisitions: John T. Farady
SVP Alternative Channels and Product Management:
  Kathleen M. Graveline
**SVP Corporate Law, Corporate Compliance, and Deputy
General Counsel:** Bruce E. Skrine
VP Human Resources: A. Page Palmer
Chief Information Officer: Robert F. Walters
General Counsel: Richard S. Scipione
**Chairman and CEO, John Hancock International
Holdings:** Derek Chilvers
SVP John Hancock Signature Services: David A. King
SVP Signator Financial Network: Robert A. Marra
SVP JH Financial Institutions: Peter F. Mawn
SVP JH Management Co.: Paul L. Sweeney
Auditors: Ernst & Young LLP

LOCATIONS

HQ: John Hancock Mutual Life Insurance Company,
  200 Clarendon St., Boston, MA 02117
Phone: 617-572-6000   **Fax:** 617-572-6451
Web site: http://www.jhancock.com

John Hancock Mutual Life Insurance operates throughout the US and in Belgium, Indonesia, Ireland, Malaysia,
Singapore, Thailand, the UK, and other countries.

PRODUCTS/OPERATIONS

1998 Assets

	$ mil.	% of total
Cash & equivalents	1,395	2
Bonds	24,875	37
Stocks	2,347	3
Mortgage loans	8,716	13
Real estate	1,885	3
Policy loans	1,826	3
Assets in separate account	24,042	36
Other assets	1,993	3
Total	**67,079**	**100**

1998 Sales

	$ mil.	% of total
Premiums, annuity considerations & pension fund contributions	10,116	74
Net investment income	3,118	23
Other income	419	3
Total	**13,653**	**100**

COMPETITORS

AIG	MetLife
Allmerica Financial	Morgan Stanley Dean
American General	Witter
AXA Financial	MONY
Charles Schwab	Mutual of Omaha
Conseco	National Life Insurance
FMR	New York Life
GenAmerica	Northwestern Mutual
Guardian Life	Phoenix Home Life
Hartford	Principal Financial
Jefferson-Pilot	Prudential
Kemper Insurance	Prudential Corporation
Lincoln National	TIAA-CREF
MassMutual	Transamerica
Merrill Lynch	

HISTORICAL FINANCIALS & EMPLOYEES

Mutual company FYE: December 31	Annual Growth	1989	1990	1991	1992	1993	1994	1995	1996	1997	1998
Assets ($ mil.)	8.4%	32,344	35,332	38,105	41,242	46,468	49,805	54,505	58,361	62,125	67,079
Net income ($ mil.)	11.7%	232	224	233	141	199	183	341	314	414	627
Income as % of assets	—	0.7%	0.6%	0.6%	0.3%	0.4%	0.4%	0.6%	0.5%	0.7%	0.9%
Employees	(7.2%)	15,655	16,000	16,500	13,903	16,500	16,000	7,996	9,453	6,362	7,959

NET INCOME HISTORY

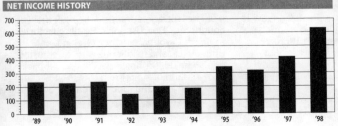

1998 FISCAL YEAR-END

Equity as % of assets: 7.0%
Return on assets: 1.0%
Return on equity: 13.3%
Long-term debt ($ mil.): 0
Sales (mil.): $13,653

JOHNS MANVILLE CORPORATION

OVERVIEW

Having insulated itself against asbestos litigation, Johns Manville is remodeling its business. The Denver-based company is the US's second-largest maker of building insulation (behind Owens Corning). It also manufactures commercial and industrial roofing systems, air-filtration equipment, and fibers and nonwoven mats used in roofing and flooring. Johns Manville is the world's #1 maker of fiberglass wall fabric.

To distance itself from its history as the world's top maker of asbestos, the firm adopted the name of its Schuller subsidiary in 1996. However, few people recognized the name and the company soon returned to the Johns Manville name.

Under a federal court settlement, a liability trust fund owns nearly 77% of the company. The trust has paid around $1.8 billion in recent years to settle asbestos injury claims filed by about 190,000 claimants. Another 135,000 claims remain unsettled.

Johns Manville has reorganized into three units: insulation, roofing, and engineered products (filtration products and mats and fibers). The company is using acquisitions and joint ventures to increase its presence in non-US markets. After years of downsizing, Johns Manville plans to buy companies that complement existing product lines.

HISTORY

H. W. Johns founded a roofing materials business in Brooklyn, New York in 1858. In 1868 he patented a line of asbestos products. The company merged in 1901 with Manville Covering, which had been founded in 1886 in Milwaukee to make pipe coverings and insulation.

Thomas Manville headed the new company, named Johns Manville, until he died in 1925. His brother Hiram bought most of the stock and in 1927 sold 53% of the company to J.P. Morgan & Co. for about $20 million. Under Morgan the company focused on building materials and moved away from earlier diversification ventures into markets for such items as automobile horns, fire extinguishers, and spark plugs.

Johns Manville moved to Colorado in 1973. The next year 448 WWII shipyard workers filed the first major asbestos health suits against the company. (Inhaled, asbestos causes asbestosis, a serious lung disease.) Johns Manville bought paper producer Olinkraft in 1979 and in 1981 shortened its name to Manville.

By 1982 it had settled more than 4,100 suits, but it still faced a backlog of nearly 17,000 more. Bankruptcy ensued. While in bankruptcy, Manville closed its plastic pipe and residential roofing operations and stopped all asbestos-related activities. In 1985 Manville acquired Eastex Packaging (forest products). A reorganization plan finalized in 1988 created a trust fund to cover asbestos-related claims filed before mid-1985 and to bar any future claims. Manville began paying the trust $75 million a year.

The firm purchased carton and paperboard companies in three countries in 1990.

Manville's US and European filtration and minerals groups were combined as Celite in 1991. That year Alleghany Corporation bought Celite, and Manville became a holding company. Its Manville Forest Products and Manville Sales divisions were renamed Riverwood International and Schuller International and became subsidiaries. In 1991 Riverwood bought packaging, equipment, and marketing companies in Brazil (M.E.A.D.), Spain (Jorba and Syspack), Minnesota (Minnesota Automation), and New Jersey (Jak-et-Pak).

In 1992 Manville sold 19.5% of Riverwood International in a $172 million public offering. In 1993 it bought Steinachglas, a glass-mat maker in eastern Germany, and swapped its residential roofing business for Corning's commercial roofing unit.

Manville sold its remaining 80% of Riverwood to investors Clayton, Dubilier & Rice for $1.1 billion in 1996 and renamed itself Schuller Corporation. That year the company acquired Dibiten USA and Dibiten Mexico, makers of bitumen roofing products. It also bought NRG Barriers and IMCOA, makers of foam insulation products. In 1997 the company changed its name back to Johns Manville and bought Mitex (the world's #1 maker of fiberglass wall fabric), HPG International's roofing business, and Ergon Nonwovens, a maker of filtration products. In 1999 the firm bought four Hoechst polyester fiber factories in South Carolina, Northern Ireland, and China to expand its fiberglass roofing business.

Also in 1999 Johns Manville bought back $167 million of stock from its asbestos-claim trust fund after the fund couldn't find a third-party buyer.

OFFICERS

Chairman, President, and CEO:
Charles L. "Jerry" Henry, age 57, $2,100,000 pay
SVP and CFO: John P. Murphy, age 52, $502,875 pay
SVP and Corporate General Counsel:
John J. Klocko III, age 59, $203,437 pay
SVP and General Manager, Engineered Products Group:
Harvey L. Perry Jr., age 44, $495,206 pay
SVP Corporate Development and Investor Relations:
Kenneth L. Jensen
SVP Human Resources and Purchasing:
Ron L. Hammons
SVP, Insulation Group: Thomas L. Caltrider, age 48,
$640,750 pay
VP and General Manager, Commercial and Industrial Insulations: Michael R. Harrison
VP and General Manager, Commercial and Industrial Roofing Systems Group: Bartley E. Roggensack Jr.
VP and General Manager, Engineered Products Division: Marvin Mitchell
VP and General Manager, Johns Manville Europe:
Paul F. Hahmann
VP and Treasurer: Mary Rhinehart
VP, Assistant General Counsel, and Secretary:
Dion Persson
VP Research and Development: John A. Coppola
VP Taxes: David S. Cope
Controller: John M. Rosebery
Auditors: PricewaterhouseCoopers LLP

LOCATIONS

HQ: 717 17th St., Denver, CO 80202
Phone: 303-978-2000   **Fax:** 303-978-2041
Web site: http://www.jm.com

Johns Manville operates more than 50 manufacturing facilities in North America, Europe, and Asia.

PRODUCTS/OPERATIONS

1998 Sales & Operating Income

	Sales		Operating Income	
	$ mil.	% of total	$ mil.	% of total
Insulation	731	41	118	42
Roofing systems	562	32	48	17
Engineered products	488	27	78	28
Adjustments	—	—	36	13
Total	**1,781**	**100**	**280**	**100**

Selected Products

Building Products
Building insulation (residential and commercial)
Commercial and industrial roofing systems
(roofing materials)
Mechanical insulations (pipe and duct insulation)

Engineered Products
Mats and fibers (fiberglass mats for roofing and
flooring substrates, plastics reinforcements,
and wall coverings)
Specialty insulation and filtration
Thermal and acoustic insulation for aircraft,
automobiles, marine vessels, and HVAC equipment

COMPETITORS

Armstrong World	Guardian Industries
Carlisle Companies	Irex
CLARCOR	Louisiana-Pacific
Donaldson	Lydall
Elcor	NCI Building Systems
Flanders Corporation	Owens Corning
GAF	PPG
Georgia-Pacific	Saint-Gobain
GreenStone Industries	USG

HISTORICAL FINANCIALS & EMPLOYEES

NYSE symbol: JM FYE: December 31	Annual Growth	1989	1990	1991	1992	1993	1994	1995	1996	1997	1998
Sales ($ mil.)	(2.3%)	2,192	2,245	2,025	2,224	2,276	2,560	1,392	1,552	1,648	1,781
Net income ($ mil.)	(0.9%)	197	111	35	36	48	37	116	90	150	181
Income as % of sales	—	9.0%	4.9%	1.7%	1.6%	2.1%	1.4%	8.3%	5.8%	9.1%	10.2%
Earnings per share ($)	(2.4%)	1.39	0.79	0.15	0.13	0.21	0.10	0.73	0.20	0.92	1.12
Stock price - FY high ($)	—	10.50	9.38	8.50	10.88	9.75	10.13	15.25	15.25	13.94	18.13
Stock price - FY low ($)	—	6.88	4.38	4.00	7.63	6.50	7.00	8.25	7.75	9.25	9.63
Stock price - FY close ($)	6.8%	9.13	4.63	7.88	8.63	8.50	9.00	13.00	10.63	10.06	16.44
P/E - high	—	8	12	57	84	46	101	21	76	15	16
P/E - low	—	5	6	27	59	31	70	11	39	10	9
Dividends per share ($)	—	0.00	0.00	0.00	1.04	1.04	0.00	0.00	6.03	0.13	0.18
Book value per share ($)	(7.3%)	9.87	12.57	5.39	5.98	6.05	7.20	8.15	3.59	4.29	4.97
Employees	(6.3%)	17,000	18,000	16,000	15,800	16,000	13,600	7,500	8,100	8,300	9,500

STOCK PRICE HISTORY

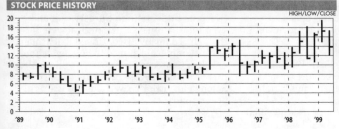

HIGH/LOW/CLOSE

1998 FISCAL YEAR-END

Debt ratio: 42.6%
Return on equity: 22.9%
Cash ($ mil.): 12
Current ratio: 1.45
Long-term debt ($ mil.): 587
No. of shares (mil.): 159
Dividends
  Yield: 1.1%
  Payout: 16.1%
Market value ($ mil.): 2,614

JOHNSON & JOHNSON

Johnson & Johnson keeps making & making more & more products.

The New Brunswick, New Jersey, company is one of the largest health care products manufacturers in the world. It is one of the US's top-three makers of prescription drugs (with Merck and Bristol-Myers Squibb); its pharmaceutical division produces contraceptives (Ortho-Novum) and dermatologicals (Retin-A), and is developing Evra, a female contraceptive patch worn on the skin. Its consumer unit

makes Band-Aids and Neutrogena skin care products, Reach toothbrushes, Tylenol and Motrin. The professional products segment makes ACUVUE contact lenses.

Through a broad range of acquisitions, as well as through alliances with small companies developing specialized products, Johnson & Johnson has established a presence in several medical sectors, in anticipation of new treatment patterns integrating drugs, medical devices, and diagnostics.

HISTORY

Brothers James and Edward Mead Johnson founded their medical products company in 1885 in New Brunswick, New Jersey. In 1886 Robert joined his brothers to make and sell the antiseptic surgical dressings he developed. The company bought gauze maker Chicopee Manufacturing in 1916. In 1921 it introduced two of its classic products, the Band-Aid and Johnson's Baby Cream.

Robert Jr. became chairman in 1932 and served until 1963. A US Army general in WWII, he believed in decentralization; managers were given substantial freedom, a principle still used today. Product lines in the 1940s included Ortho (birth control products) and Ethicon (sutures). In 1959 Johnson & Johnson bought McNeil Labs, which launched Tylenol (acetaminophen) as an over-the-counter drug the next year. Foreign acquisitions included Switzerland's Cilag-Chemie (1959) and Belgium's Janssen (1961). The company focused on consumer products in the 1970s, gaining half the feminine protection market and making Tylenol the top selling painkiller.

Johnson & Johnson bought Iolab, a developer of intraocular lenses used in cataract surgery in 1980. A few years later, trouble hit when someone laced Tylenol capsules with cyanide in 1982, killing eight people. The company's response is now a damage control classic: It immediately recalled 31 million bottles and totally redesigned its packaging to prevent future tampering. It cost $240 million, but it saved the Tylenol brand. The next year the drug Zomax was linked to five deaths and was pulled.

New products in the 1980s included ACUVUE (disposable contact lenses) and Retin-A. The company bought LifeScan (blood monitoring products for diabetics) in 1986. In 1989 Johnson & Johnson began a joint venture with Merck to sell Mylanta and other drugs bought from ICI Americas.

Johnson & Johnson continued its acquisition

and diversification strategy in the 1990s, entering new markets and building its presence in particular sectors. After introducing the first daily-wear, disposable contact lenses in 1993, it bought skin care products maker Neutrogena (1994) to enhance its consumer lines. To diversify its medical product line and better compete for hospital business, the company acquired Mitek Surgical Products in 1995. It bought heart disease product maker Cordis in 1996. That year the FDA cleared the company's Renova wrinkle and fade cream. The company also began selling Confide, an at-home HIV test, but faced with low demand and other troubles, took it off the market the next year.

In 1997 Johnson & Johnson acquired the over-the-counter rights to Motrin from Pharmacia & Upjohn in exchange for a variety of consumer products. In 1998 the company won FDA approval for the Indigo LaserOptic system (for treating prostate enlargement) and sucralose, an artificial sweetener. That year it bought DePuy and launched Benecol, a margarine said to cut "bad" cholesterol by up to 15%.

The year 1998 ended on a sour note: Benecol ran into regulatory problems (but was approved in 1999), rights to an anemia drug were lost, and the company's share of the coronary stent market fell. In response, it cut jobs and announced that it would consolidate plants worldwide.

In 1999 it purchased S.C. Johnson & Son's skin care business, including the Aveeno line. That year three patent infringement suits between its Ethicon Endo-Surgery unit and Tyco International's U.S. Surgical were settled. The company discontinued its Hismanal antihistamine and agreed to buy biotechnology firm Centocor for nearly $5 billion. Also that year, the FDA approved the company's Splenda low-calorie sweetener for use as a general-purpose sweetener.

Chairman and CEO: Ralph S. Larsen, age 60,
$2,626,796 pay
VC: Robert N. Wilson, age 58, $1,782,886 pay
VP Finance: Robert J. Darretta, age 52
VP Administration (HR): Russell C. Deyo, age 49
VP and General Counsel: Roger S. Fine, age 56
**Worldwide Chairman, Health Systems and Diagnostics
Group:** Ronald G. Gelbman, age 51, $1,051,363 pay
VP Science and Technology: Robert Z. Gussin
VP and Chief Information Officer: JoAnn H. Heisen,
age 49
Corporate Controller: Clarence E. Lockett
VP Public Affairs: Willard D. Nielsen
Treasurer: John A. Papa
Secretary and Assistant General Counsel:
Michael H. Ullmann
VP Business Development: James R. Utaski
Auditors: PricewaterhouseCoopers LLP

HQ: 1 Johnson & Johnson Plaza,
New Brunswick, NJ 08933
Phone: 732-524-0400 **Fax:** 732-524-3300
Web site: http://www.jnj.com

Johnson & Johnson has operating companies in more
than 36 countries and markets its products in more
than 175.

1998 Sales

	$ mil.	% of total
US	12,562	53
Europe	6,317	27
Africa & Asia/Pacific	2,688	11
Canada & Latin America	2,090	9
Total	**23,657**	**100**

1998 Sales & Operating Profit

	Sales		Operating Profit	
	$ mil.	% of total	$ mil.	% of total
Professional products	8,569	36	941	22
Pharmaceuticals	8,562	36	3,016	69
Consumer products	6,526	28	414	9
Other	—	—	(102)	—
Total	**23,657**	**100**	**4,269**	**100**

Selected Products

Pharmaceuticals	Consumer Products
Eprex (antianemia agent)	Imodium A-D
Leustatin (leukemia	Monistat
treatment)	Mylanta
Nizoral (antifungal)	Pepcid AC (with Merck)
Retin-A (acne cream)	Reach (toothbrush)
Risperdal (antipsychotic)	Tylenol

Abbott Labs	Hoechst AG
American Home Products	Kimberly-Clark
Bausch & Lomb	Medtronic
Baxter	Merck
Bayer AG	3M
Beckman Coulter	Monsanto
Bristol-Myers Squibb	Novartis
Carter-Wallace	Pfizer
Colgate-Palmolive	Pharmacia & Upjohn
Dade Behring	Procter & Gamble
Dial	Rhône-Poulenc
Eli Lilly	St. Jude Medical
Genentech	SmithKline Beecham
Gillette	Unilever
Glaxo Wellcome	United States Surgical

NYSE symbol: JNJ FYE: December 31	Annual Growth	1989	1990	1991	1992	1993	1994	1995	1996	1997	1998
Sales ($ mil.)	10.3%	9,757	11,232	12,447	13,753	14,138	15,734	18,842	21,620	22,629	23,657
Net income ($ mil.)	12.2%	1,082	1,143	1,461	1,030	1,787	2,006	2,403	2,887	3,303	3,059
Income as % of sales	—	11.1%	10.2%	11.7%	7.5%	12.6%	12.7%	12.8%	13.4%	14.6%	12.9%
Earnings per share ($)	12.1%	0.80	0.85	1.08	0.32	1.36	1.55	1.82	2.12	2.41	2.23
Stock price - FY high ($)	—	14.88	18.53	29.06	29.34	25.19	28.25	46.19	54.00	67.31	89.75
Stock price - FY low ($)	—	10.38	12.78	16.34	21.50	17.81	18.00	26.81	41.56	48.63	54.44
Stock price - FY close ($)	21.2%	14.84	17.94	28.63	25.25	22.44	27.38	42.75	49.75	65.88	83.88
P/E - high	—	19	22	27	92	19	18	25	25	28	40
P/E - low	—	13	15	15	67	13	12	15	20	20	24
Dividends per share ($)	14.8%	0.28	0.33	0.39	0.45	0.51	0.57	0.64	0.74	0.85	0.97
Book value per share ($)	14.0%	3.11	3.68	4.22	3.94	4.33	5.54	6.98	8.13	9.19	10.11
Employees	1.3%	83,100	82,200	82,700	84,900	81,600	81,500	82,300	89,300	90,500	93,100

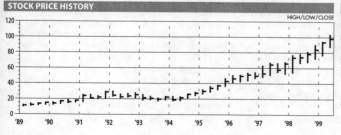

HIGH/LOW/CLOSE

Debt ratio: 8.5%
Return on equity: 22.5%
Cash ($ mil.): 1,927
Current ratio: 1.36
Long-term debt ($ mil.): 1,269
No. of shares (mil.): 1,344
Dividends
  Yield: 1.2%
  Payout: 43.5%
Market value ($ mil.): 112,739

JOHNSON CONTROLS, INC.

OVERVIEW

Don't panic, but Johnson Controls has you surrounded. The Milwaukee-based company makes seats, interiors, and batteries for automobiles and environmental control systems for commercial buildings. Seats and interior products such as door panels, instrument panels, and consoles account for about 90% of sales — 40% from GM, Ford, and Daimler-Chrysler. About 85% of Johnson Controls' batteries are sold through the replacement market (Sears, AutoZone). The company also makes specialty batteries and sells original equipment batteries to carmakers and is developing a battery that's a tenth the size of regular car batteries.

The controls business makes security systems, temperature controls, and integrated facility management for businesses. It also keeps both American generals and Russian bureaucrats comfy by equipping the Pentagon and the Kremlin.

Rapid growth in the car interior and seating business has come through acquisitions and carmakers' increasing outsourcing of component production. Johnson Controls boasts more than 250 subsidiaries.

HISTORY

Professor Warren Johnson developed the electric telethermoscope in 1880 so that janitors at Whitewater, Wisconsin's State Normal School could regulate room temperatures without disturbing classrooms. His device — the thermostat — used mercury to move a heat element that opened and shut a circuit. Milwaukee hotelier William Plankinton believed in Johnson's invention and invested $150,000 to begin production.

The two men formed Johnson Electric Service Company in 1885; sold the marketing, installation, and service rights; and concentrated on manufacturing. Johnson invented other devices, including tower clocks. He also experimented with the telegraph, forming American Wireless Telegraph in 1900. He abandoned the venture when he became intrigued with the automobile.

Johnson began producing steam-powered cars. He won the US Postal Service's first automotive contract but never gained support within his own company. He continued to look elsewhere for financing until his death in 1911.

The renamed Johnson Services regained full rights to its thermostats in 1912, and new president Harry Ellis sold all other businesses. During the Depression the company produced economy systems, which automatically regulated building temperatures. During WWII Johnson Services aided the war effort, building weather data gatherers and test radar sets.

In the 1960s Johnson Services began to develop centralized control systems — introduced in 1967 — for temperature, fire alarm, lighting, and security regulation. The firm was renamed Johnson Controls in 1974 and acquired automotive battery manufacturer Globe-Union in 1978.

Johnson Controls bought auto seat makers Hoover Universal and Ferro Manufacturing in 1985. It expanded its controls business through the purchases of ITT's European controls group (1982) and Pan Am World Services (1989), a provider of facilities management to the US government.

The company sold its car door components business in 1990 and bought battery maker Varta's Canadian plant. The next year Johnson Controls bought several European car seat component manufacturers, and in 1992 it bought a Welsh plastic manufacturer and a Czech seat-cover producer.

The battery unit faced a major setback in 1994 when Sears dropped the company as its battery maker. Two years later, however, the firm's battery business was recharged by an exclusive supply contract with mass merchandiser Target.

In 1996 Johnson Controls bought most of Roth Freres (auto components) and Prince Automotive (interior systems and components) for $1.35 billion, becoming a major interior systems integrator. In 1997 the company sold its plastic container operations to Germany's VIAG for about $650 million and regained its Sears business with a three-year deal to make DieHard batteries. That year it used nonunion workers during a United Auto Workers strike, but Ford refused to accept the seats, speeding the strike's resolution.

In 1998 the firm paid $600 million for Becker Group, a US automotive interior parts maker with 70% of its sales in Europe. It also bought Creative Control Designs, a designer of HVAC and lighting control systems, and Commerfin SpA, an Italian door systems maker. Also that year the company sold its plastics machinery division to Cincinnati Milacron (now named Milacron) and agreed to sell its industrial batteries unit to C&D Technologies.

Chairman and CEO: James H. Keyes, age 58, $1,782,250 pay
President and COO: John M. Barth, age 52, $995,498 pay
SVP and CFO: Stephen A. Roell, age 48, $643,752 pay
VP Corporate Technology: Steven J. Bomba, age 61
VP Human Resources: Susan F. Davis, age 45
VP, Secretary, and General Counsel: John P. Kennedy, age 55
VP Corporate Development and Strategy: William P. Killian, age 63
VP Corporate Communications: Denise M. Zutz, age 47
Corporate VP and President, Automotive Operations Europe, Asia, and Africa: Giovanni "John" Fiori, age 55, $643,458 pay
Corporate VP and President, North American Operations, Automotive Systems Group: Michael F. Johnston, age 51, $628,330 pay
Corporate VP and Treasurer: Ben C. M. Bastianen, age 54
Corporate VP and Corporate Controller: Patrick J. Dennis, age 47
Corporate VP, Product Engineering Worldwide: Lou Kincaid, age 51
Auditors: PricewaterhouseCoopers LLP

LOCATIONS

HQ: 5757 N. Green Bay Ave., Milwaukee, WI 53201
Phone: 414-228-1200 **Fax:** 414-228-2302
Web site: http://www.jci.com

Johnson Controls' automotive segment has production facilities throughout the US and in 34 other countries.

PRODUCTS/OPERATIONS

1998 Sales & Operating Income

	Sales		Operating Income	
	$ mil.	% of total	$ mil.	% of total
Automotive systems	9,264	74	530	80
Controls	3,323	26	134	20
Total	**12,587**	**100**	**664**	**100**

Selected Products

Automotive Segment
Batteries
Door systems
Electronics
Instrument panels
Overhead systems
Seating systems

Control Products
Actuators
Control panels, consoles, and instrumentation
Dampers

Digital electronic controllers
Electronic sensors and controls
Facility management systems
Heating products
Personal environment systems
Pneumatic controls
Refrigeration controls
Valves

COMPETITORS

Alcatel
Collins & Aikman
Eagle-Picher
Eaton
Exide
Faurecia
General Motors
Hitachi
Honeywell

Invensys
Landis & Gyr
Lear
Magna International
Pacific Dunlop
SPX
Textron
United Technologies
Varta

HISTORICAL FINANCIALS & EMPLOYEES

NYSE symbol: JCI FYE: September 30	Annual Growth	1989	1990	1991	1992	1993	1994	1995	1996	1997	1998
Sales ($ mil.)	14.6%	3,684	4,504	4,559	5,157	6,182	6,871	8,330	10,009	11,145	12,587
Net income ($ mil.)	14.8%	98	92	95	123	16	165	196	235	289	338
Income as % of sales	—	2.6%	2.1%	2.1%	2.4%	0.3%	2.4%	2.4%	2.3%	2.6%	2.7%
Earnings per share ($)	13.0%	1.21	1.03	1.06	1.37	0.08	1.80	2.13	2.55	3.12	3.63
Stock price - FY high ($)	—	23.38	17.94	17.56	21.88	29.56	30.88	33.00	38.25	49.81	61.88
Stock price - FY low ($)	—	15.88	9.50	8.56	15.19	19.31	22.44	22.88	28.88	35.38	42.19
Stock price - FY close ($)	11.6%	17.38	9.88	16.63	19.94	27.19	24.88	31.63	37.50	49.56	46.50
P/E - high	—	19	17	17	16	370	17	15	15	16	17
P/E - low	—	13	9	8	11	241	12	11	11	11	12
Dividends per share ($)	5.3%	0.58	0.60	0.62	0.64	0.68	0.72	0.78	0.82	0.86	0.92
Book value per share ($)	7.7%	10.92	10.93	11.24	12.66	11.29	12.79	16.30	16.30	18.60	21.24
Employees	8.5%	42,600	43,500	42,700	46,800	50,100	54,800	59,200	65,800	72,300	89,000

STOCK PRICE HISTORY

HIGH/LOW/CLOSE

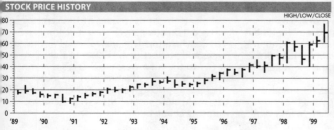

1998 FISCAL YEAR-END

Debt ratio: 33.9%
Return on equity: 18.7%
Cash ($ mil.): 134
Current ratio: 0.79
Long-term debt ($ mil.): 998
No. of shares (mil.): 85
Dividends
 Yield: 2.0%
 Payout: 25.3%
Market value ($ mil.): 3,944

JONES APPAREL GROUP, INC.

OVERVIEW

Jones Apparel Group isn't content with keeping up — it wants to set the pace. The Bristol, Pennsylvania-based firm has transformed itself from a supplier of designer-alternative career wear into a provider of a wide range of women's clothing and shoes. Jones also offers men's casual sportswear.

It offers about 20 brands of moderately priced sportswear, business wear, casuals, and shoes, including Jones New York, Nine West, Evan-Picone, Todd Oldham, Rena Rowan, Saville, Easy Spirit, and several brands licensed from Polo Ralph Lauren. Its products are manufactured — mainly by third parties — in Asia, Latin America, and the US. Jones also licenses its Jones New York and Evan-Picone brand

names to other makers of women's and men's apparel and accessories.

The company's 1999 acquisition of footwear designer Nine West Group more than doubled its size. The deal significantly increased Jones' retail presence, adding about 1,500 Nine West stores to the company's half dozen retail stores and more than 200 outlet locations. Jones plans to take advantage of the increased retail space by selling clothing in Nine West stores and cross-marketing its footwear and apparel brands.

Founder and CEO (and occasional movie producer) Sidney Kimmel owns about 12% of the company.

HISTORY

When diversifying chemical firm W. R. Grace & Co. began a brief foray into the fashion world in 1970, it hired Sidney Kimmel to run the show. Kimmel had worked in a knitting mill in the 1950s and served as president of women's sportswear maker Villager in the 1960s. He and his companion, designer Rena Rowan, created Grace's fashionable but moderately priced Jones New York line.

Kimmel and Grace accountant Gerard Rubin bought Grace's fashion division in 1975, incorporating it as Jones Apparel Group. Jones expanded quickly by bringing out new labels and licensing others, such as Christian Dior. Talks to sell the company to underwear maker Warnaco fell through in 1981.

Tapping into two trends of the early 1980s, Jones offered the sweatsuit fashions of Norma Kamali and in 1984 acquired the license for the Gloria Vanderbilt line from Murjani. Swan-adorned Gloria Vanderbilt jeans had been must-haves early in the decade, but the deal turned into an ugly duckling as costs beyond Jones' control pushed the company into the red. (Meanwhile, Kimmel produced the films *9 1/2 Weeks* and *Clan of the Cave Bear* and led a group that briefly controlled the Famous Amos Cookie Co.)

Creditors forced Jones to unload most of its brands — all but Jones New York, Saville, and Christian Dior — and cut jobs, and by 1988 it was profitable again. Kimmel bought Rubin's interest in the company in 1989 and took Jones public in 1991, retaining about half of the stock.

In the early 1990s, as recession-minded shoppers looked for bargains and the American workplace became more casual, Jones again took off. The company expanded with new

lines, such as Rena Rowan (inexpensive suits) and Jones & Co. (career casuals). Jones moved into women's accessories with the 1993 purchase of the Evan-Picone brand name.

Two years later the company struck its first licensing agreement with Polo Ralph Lauren, for the Lauren by Ralph Lauren line of women's sportswear. Propelled by the new line, Jones reached a billion dollars in sales in 1996. The company ended its long-held licensing agreement with Christian Dior the next year.

Jones licensed Ralph by Ralph Lauren, a lower-priced juniors' line, in 1998. Also in 1998 it purchased Sun Apparel, picking up the rights to Todd Oldham and Polo jeans, and in 1999 it bought the remaining clothing, footwear, cosmetics, and apparel rights to the youth-oriented Oldham name.

The firm then made its biggest acquisition by far when it paid $1.4 billion for shoe designer and retailer Nine West Group (Easy Spirit, Enzo Angiolini, Bandolino, Amalfi).

Nine West began in 1977 when footwear industry veterans Jerome Fisher and Vincent Camuto founded a wholesale operation. By the time of its 1993 IPO, Nine West offered shoes with designer looks but moderate prices at major department stores as well as about 250 company-owned stores. The purchase of U.S. Shoe's footwear operations in 1995 created a $1.4 billion company. Excess inventory and underwhelming demand led Nine West to cut jobs and production in 1998 and 1999.

With the Nine West purchase, Jones inherited an FTC investigation into the footwear designer's pricing policies. The company said it would close several Nine West facilities, cutting about 1,900 jobs.

Chairman and CEO: Sidney Kimmel, age 71
President: Jackwyn Nemerov, age 47, $1,500,000 pay
CFO: Wesley R. Card, age 51, $650,000 pay
EVP Marketing: Irwin Samelman, age 68,
$1,350,000 pay
VP Design: Rena Rowan
Chairman and CEO, Nine West: Mark Schwartz
President and CEO, Sun Apparel: Eric A. Rothfeld,
age 47, $643,894 pay
Director Human Resources: Aida Tejero-DeColli
Auditors: BDO Seidman, LLP

LOCATIONS

HQ: 250 Rittenhouse Circle, Bristol, PA 19007
Phone: 215-785-4000 **Fax:** 215-785-1795
Web site: http://www.jny.com

Jones Apparel Group's products are manufactured
primarily by contractors in Asia, Latin America, and the
US. They are sold in more than 55 countries in Asia,
Europe, and North and South America.

PRODUCTS/OPERATIONS

1998 Sales

	$ mil.	% of total
Career sportswear	646	39
Casual sportswear	454	27
Lifestyle collection	413	25
Suits, dresses & other	156	9
Total	**1,669**	**100**

1998 Nine West Stores

	No.
Nine West & Nine West outlet	445
Easy Spirit & Easy Spirit outlet	259
Banister	129
Stein Mart (leased)	86
Enzo Angiolini	81
9 & Co.	63
cK/Calvin Klein	6
International stores	430
Total	**1,499**

Selected Brands

9 & Co.	Luca B. for Pappagallo
Amalfi	Nine West
Bandolino	Pied a Terre
Calico	Polo (licensed)
cK/Calvin Klein (licensed)	Ralph by Ralph Lauren
Easy Spirit	(licensed)
Enzo Angiolini	Rena Rowan
Evan-Picone	Saville
JNY Sport	Selby
Jones & Co.	The Shoe Studio Group
Jones New York	Limited
Lauren by Ralph Lauren	Todd Oldham
(licensed)	Westies

COMPETITORS

AnnTaylor	Carole Little	Payless
Bally	Donna Karan	ShoeSource
Berkshire	Ellen Tracy	St. John Knits
Hathaway	Etienne Aigner	Sara Lee
Bernard Chaus	Gucci	Skechers U.S.A.
Brown Shoe	Kenneth Cole	Steven Madden
Calvin Klein	Liz Claiborne	
Candie's	Maxwell Shoe	

HISTORICAL FINANCIALS & EMPLOYEES

NYSE symbol: JNY FYE: December 31	Annual Growth	1989	1990	1991	1992	1993	1994	1995	1996	1997	1998
Sales ($ mil.)	25.8%	—	—	334	437	541	633	776	1,021	1,373	1,669
Net income ($ mil.)	24.1%	—	—	34	41	50	55	64	81	122	155
Income as % of sales	—	—	—	10.2%	9.5%	9.2%	8.7%	8.2%	7.9%	8.9%	9.3%
Earnings per share ($)	24.3%	—	—	0.32	0.40	0.49	0.52	0.60	0.76	1.13	1.47
Stock price - FY high ($)	—	—	—	7.47	10.50	10.25	8.94	9.91	18.69	28.72	37.75
Stock price - FY low ($)	—	—	—	3.41	5.75	4.66	5.50	5.66	8.91	16.06	15.88
Stock price - FY close ($)	16.9%	—	—	7.38	9.53	7.47	6.44	9.84	18.69	21.50	22.06
P/E - high	—	—	—	23	26	21	17	17	25	25	26
P/E - low	—	—	—	11	14	10	11	9	12	14	11
Dividends per share ($)	—	—	—	0.00	0.00	0.00	0.00	0.00	0.00	0.00	0.00
Book value per share ($)	31.0%	—	—	0.87	1.33	1.87	2.40	3.01	3.62	4.26	5.74
Employees	39.9%	—	—	—	1,160	1,475	2,325	2,560	2,945	3,135	8,685

STOCK PRICE HISTORY

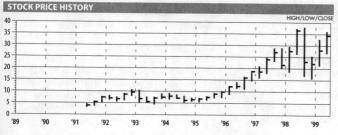

HIGH/LOW/CLOSE

1998 FISCAL YEAR-END

Debt ratio: 41.1%
Return on equity: 26.1%
Cash ($ mil.): 129
Current ratio: 3.63
Long-term debt ($ mil.): 415
No. of shares (mil.): 103
Dividends
  Yield: —
  Payout: —
Market value ($ mil.): 2,283

J.P. MORGAN & CO. INCORPORATED

New York City-based J.P. Morgan has traded in its commercial banking dowager's tiara for the foxy ops of equities and investment banking.

The silk stocking institution's other operations include debt- and foreign exchange-based trading (it's the world's largest dealer in derivatives), and asset management. J.P. Morgan makes more than half of its revenues in Europe and Latin America.

The company has dumped the frump by squeezing into the tight-fitting "bulge bracket" — the top echelon reserved for lead underwriters of public offerings. J.P. Morgan's services also include mergers and acquisitions advising

(it advised on the Exxon/Mobil merger announced in 1998). The bank has even extended its individual asset management operations down market (to people with $1 million or even less) and dipped a toe into the consumer market through its acquisition of 45% of mutual fund manager American Century Companies.

But there are questions as to whether this staid spinster can revamp her culture to cope with the competitive, sales-oriented realities of the fin-de-siecle financial world fast enough to remain single or whether she will be forced into a marriage of convenience.

HISTORY

Junius Spencer Morgan became a partner in George Peabody's London bank in 1854. Within a decade Morgan had gained control and renamed the firm J.S. Morgan and Co. Morgan's son started his own firm, J. Pierpont Morgan and Co., in New York in 1862. Connections on both sides of the pond brought profits and power as the firms funneled European capital into the US. When Congress bickered in 1877 over the Hayes-Tilden election and didn't get around to paying the Army, a Morgan affiliate came up with the funds.

After Junius died in 1890, his son united the London and New York businesses as J.P. Morgan & Co. Morgan himself had become the personification of Wall Street, and after financing and restructuring much of the American railroad network, the firm went on to help create U.S. Steel, General Electric, and International Harvester.

In 1907 J. Pierpont played the role of central banker, marshaling a group of bankers to stop a financial panic. (This action spurred legislation that led to the 1913 formation of the Federal Reserve system.) His influence was pervasive: A 1912 federal investigation found that Morgan partners held 72 directorships in 47 corporations, with total resources of $10 billion.

J. P. Morgan Jr. became senior partner of the firm upon his father's death in 1913. He yielded control to partner Thomas Lamont, who, emulating Morgan's 1907 feat, tried to stem the 1929 market crash. Unsuccessfully.

The 1933 Glass-Steagall Act forced the company to split up into a commercial bank, J.P. Morgan, and a securities company, Morgan Stanley.

The bank merged with Guaranty Trust Co. of New York in 1959 and became a holding company. In the 1960s J.P. Morgan was the

most active trader in government securities. As corporations abandoned bank loans in favor of debt issues, J.P. Morgan sought new sources of income in the 1970s. After restructuring in 1987, Morgan pushed into mergers and acquisitions. In 1991 regulators allowed a unit of the company to both trade and underwrite corporate equities (making it the first bank able to underwrite equity securities since 1933).

In the nineties, the bank's performance closely followed the market, taking especially hard hits in the 1994 bond crash and the 1998 Russian default, which followed hard on the heels of the Asian credit crisis. (It was an investor, and consequently a major participant, in the bailout of Long-Term Capital Management.) The company was also rocked in 1997 by the Bre-X Minerals fiasco, in which J.P. Morgan became financial adviser to a Canadian mining company that wrongly claimed to have found an enormous gold deposit in Borneo.

Despite its head start in equities, the bank's goal of challenging the top three securities firms (Merrill Lynch, Goldman Sachs, and Morgan Stanley Dean Witter) remained elusive: Competitors were merging, other banks followed it into equities, and its traditional focus on the elite meant that it missed out on the lucrative consumer market. Accordingly, in 1998 J.P. Morgan bought a 45% stake in American Century Investments.

Shrugging off trials in emerging markets, in 1999 the company opened an office in India and continued to boost its share in Latin American debt markets. That year J.P. Morgan also bought a stake in Archipelago Holdings, an electronic communications network designed to compete with the major US equity exchanges.

Chairman and CEO: Douglas A. "Sandy" Warner III, age 52, $1,875,000 pay
VC and Global Head of Investment Banking Group: Walter A. Gubert, age 51, $1,550,000 pay
Managing Director and Chief Administrative Officer; Managing Director, J.P. Morgan Securities: Thomas B. Ketchum, age 48, $1,362,500 pay
CFO: Peter D. Hancock
Managing Director, Secretary, and General Counsel: Rachel F. Robbins, age 48
Managing Director and Head of Bank Mergers and Acquisitions: Gail Rogers
Managing Director and Global Head of Equities: Clayton S. Rose
Managing Director and Head of Credit Markets and Credit Portfolio: Nicholas S. Rohatyn
Managing Director and Head of Europe, Middle East, and Africa: Joseph P. MacHale
Chief Information Officer: Peter A. Miller
Managing Director of Human Resources: Nancy Baird Harwood
Auditors: PricewaterhouseCoopers LLP

LOCATIONS

HQ: 60 Wall St., 46th Fl., New York, NY 10260-0060
Phone: 212-483-2323   **Fax:** 212-648-5213
Web site: http://www.jpmorgan.com

1998 Sales

	% of total
North America	47
Europe, Africa & the Middle East	34
Asia/Pacific	11
Latin America	8
Total	**100**

PRODUCTS/OPERATIONS

1998 Assets

	$ mil.	% of total
Cash & equivalents	35,214	13
Treasury & agency securities	35,264	14
Foreign investment	968	—
Trading account, net	113,896	44
Net loans	25,025	10
Other assets	50,700	19
Total	**261,067**	**100**

1998 Sales

	$ mil.	% of total
Interest	12,641	69
Trading	2,362	13
Investment banking	1,401	7
Fees & commissions	748	4
Other	1,273	7
Total	**18,425**	**100**

COMPETITORS

American Express	Deutsche Bank
Bank of America	Goldman Sachs
Barclays	HSBC Holdings
Bear Stearns	Merrill Lynch
Canadian Imperial	Paine Webber
Chase Manhattan	Royal Bank of Canada
Citigroup	Salomon Smith Barney
Credit Lyonnais	Holdings
Credit Suisse First Boston	UBS
Dai-Ichi Kangyo	

HISTORICAL FINANCIALS & EMPLOYEES

NYSE symbol: JPM FYE: December 31	Annual Growth	1989	1990	1991	1992	1993	1994	1995	1996	1997	1998
Assets ($ mil.)	12.7%	88,964	93,103	103,468	102,941	133,888	154,917	184,879	222,026	262,159	261,067
Net income ($ mil.)	—	(1,275)	1,005	1,146	1,382	1,586	1,215	1,296	1,574	1,465	963
Income as % of assets	—	—	1.1%	1.1%	1.3%	1.2%	0.8%	0.7%	0.7%	0.6%	0.4%
Earnings per share ($)	—	(7.04)	5.21	5.80	6.92	7.80	6.02	6.42	7.63	7.17	4.71
Stock price – FY high ($)	—	48.13	47.25	70.50	70.50	79.38	72.00	82.50	100.13	125.75	148.75
Stock price – FY low ($)	—	34.00	29.63	40.50	51.50	59.38	55.13	56.13	73.50	93.13	72.13
Stock price – FY close ($)	10.2%	44.00	44.38	68.63	65.75	69.38	56.13	80.25	97.63	112.88	105.06
P/E – high	—	—	9	12	10	10	12	13	13	18	32
P/E – low	—	—	6	7	7	8	9	9	10	13	15
Dividends per share ($)	9.6%	1.66	1.82	1.98	2.18	2.40	2.72	3.00	3.24	3.59	3.80
Book value per share ($)	12.0%	21.78	25.29	29.41	34.30	48.50	48.34	53.21	58.07	60.74	60.38
Employees	1.1%	14,207	12,968	13,323	14,368	15,193	17,055	15,613	15,527	16,943	15,674

STOCK PRICE HISTORY

HIGH/LOW/CLOSE

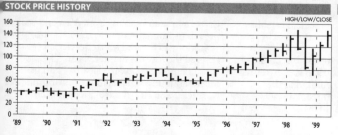

1998 FISCAL YEAR-END

Equity as % of assets: 4.0%
Return on assets: 0.4%
Return on equity: 9.1%
Long-term debt ($ mil.): 27,607
No. of shares (mil.): 175
Dividends
  Yield: 3.6%
  Payout: 80.7%
Market value ($ mil.): 18,386
Sales (mil.): $18,425

KAISER FOUNDATION

OVERVIEW

This Kaiser isn't German, but it still reigns—as the largest not-for-profit HMO in the US.

Oakland, California-based Kaiser Foundation Health Plan has an integrated care model, offering both hospital and physician care, through a network of hospitals and physician practices operating under the Kaiser Permanente name. Kaiser serves nearly 9 million members in 18 states and the District of Columbia.

Kaiser once had sole possession of the HMO market, but it now faces increased competition from such for-profit care providers as Aetna, CIGNA, and UnitedHealth Group, which do no face the dilemma of operating hospitals while trying to contain costs by limiting admissions. Back-to-back losses have prompted Kaiser to raise rates, divest underperforming units, and pursue enrollment growth through alliances.

HISTORY

Henry Kaiser — shipbuilder, war profiteer, builder of the Hoover and Grand Coulee dams, and founder of Kaiser Aluminum — was a bootstrap capitalist who did well by doing good. A high school dropout from upstate New York, Kaiser moved to Spokane, Washington, in 1906 and went into road construction. During the Depression, he headed the consortium that built the great WPA dams.

It was in building the Grand Coulee dam that, in 1938, Kaiser teamed with Dr. Sidney Garfield. Garfield had devised a prepayment health plan in 1933 for workers on California public works projects.

In WWII Kaiser moved into steelmaking and shipbuilding, turning out some 1,400 bare-bones Liberty ships (at the rate of 1 per day at peak production). On the theory that healthy workers produce more than sick ones, Kaiser called on Garfield to set up onsite clinics, funded by the US government as part of operating expenses. Garfield was released from military service by President Roosevelt for that purpose.

After the war, the clinics became war surplus. Kaiser and his wife bought them — at a 99% discount — through the new Kaiser Hospital Foundation. His vision was to provide the public with low-cost, prepaid medical care. He created the Health Plan — the self-supporting entity that would administer the system — and the Group Medical Organization, Permanente (named after Kaiser's first cement plant site).

He then endowed the Health Plan with $200,000. This health plan, the classic HMO model, was criticized by the medical establishment as socialized medicine performed by "employee" doctors.

But the plan flourished, becoming California's #1 medical system. In 1958 Kaiser retired to Hawaii and started his health plan there. But physician resistance limited national growth; HMOs were illegal in some states well into the 1970s.

As health care costs rose, Congress legalized HMOs in all states. Kaiser expanded in the 1980s; as it moved outside its traditional geographic areas the company contracted for space in hospitals rather than building them. Growth slowed as competition increased.

Some health care costs in California fell in the early 1990s as more medical procedures were performed on an outpatient basis. Specialists flooded the state, and as price competition among doctors and hospitals heated up, many HMOs landed advantageous contracts. Kaiser, with its own highly paid doctors, was unable to realize the same savings and was no longer the best deal in town. Its membership stalled.

To boost membership and control expenses, in 1996 Kaiser instituted a controversial program in which nurses earned bonuses for cost-cutting. Critics said the program could lead to a decrease in care quality; Kaiser later became the focus of investigations into wrongful death suits linked to cost-cutting in California (where it has since beefed up staffing and programs) and Texas (where it has agreed to pay $1 million in fines).

In 1997, to fend off for-profit competitors, Kaiser and Washington-based Group Health Cooperative of Puget Sound formed Kaiser/Group Health to handle the companies' administrative services in the Northwest. Kaiser also tried to boost membership by lowering premiums, but the strategy proved *too* effective: Costs linked to an unwieldy 20% enrollment surge brought a loss in 1997 — Kaiser's first annual loss ever. A second year in the red prompted Kaiser to sell its Texas operations to Sierra Health Services. It also entered the Florida market via an alliance with Miami-based AvMed Health Plan. In 1999 Kaiser announced plans to sell its unprofitable Northeast and North Carolina operations.

Chairman and CEO: David M. Lawrence
President and COO: Richard G. Barnaby
VP and CFO: L. Dale Crandall
VP and Chief Information Officer:
Timothy E. Sullivan
VP and General Counsel: Kirk E. Miller
VP Government Relations: Steven R. Zatkin
VP Labor/Management Partnerships: Gary Fernandez
VP New Business Development: James A. Lane
VP Strategic Development and Human Resources:
James B. Williams
VP Communications: James H. Hill
Chief Administrative Officer: Robert M. Crane
VP and President, Southwest Division:
William A. Gillespie
**SVP and Chief Marketing Officer, Medicare and
Commercial Operations:** Kathy Swenson

LOCATIONS

HQ: Kaiser Foundation Health Plan, Inc.,
1 Kaiser Plaza, Oakland, CA 94612
Phone: 510-271-5910   **Fax:** 510-271-6493
Web site: http://www.kaiserpermanente.org

Kaiser Foundation Health Plan operates in 18 states and
the District of Columbia.

1998 Membership

	No.
California	5,800,000
Central East	734,000
Northeast	617,000
Northwest	440,000
Rocky Mountain	433,000
Southeast	372,000
Hawaii	212,000
Total	**8,608,000**

PRODUCTS/OPERATIONS

1998 Membership

	% of total
Private-sector employees	59
State/local government employees	18
Individuals	10
Federal government employees	9
Education employees	4
Total	**100**

Selected Operations

Kaiser Foundation
Kaiser Foundation Health Plan (health coverage)
Kaiser Foundation Hospitals (community hospitals and
outpatient facilities)
Kaiser Foundation Research Institute
Permanente Medical Groups

Permanente Medical Groups
Kaiser Foundation Health Plan of Georgia, Inc.
Kaiser Foundation Health Plan of Hawaii, Inc.
Kaiser Foundation Health Plan of North Carolina, Inc.
Kaiser Foundation Health Plan of the Northeast, Inc.
Kaiser Permanente California
Kaiser Permanente Colorado Denver/Boulder
Kaiser Permanente Colorado Springs
Kaiser Permanente Kansas City
Kaiser Permanente Mid-Atlantic States
Kaiser Permanente Northwest
Kaiser Permanente Ohio

COMPETITORS

Aetna	Foundation Health
Catholic Health East	Systems
Catholic Health Initiatives	Humana
Catholic Healthcare	Oxford Health Plans
Network	PacifiCare
Catholic Healthcare	Sierra Health
Partners	UnitedHealth Group
Catholic Healthcare West	WellPoint Health
CIGNA	Networks
Columbia/HCA	

HISTORICAL FINANCIALS & EMPLOYEES

Not-for-profit FYE: December 31	Annual Growth	1989	1990	1991	1992	1993	1994	1995	1996	1997	1998
Sales ($ mil.)	9.5%	6,857	8,443	9,823	11,032	11,930	12,268	12,290	13,241	14,500	15,500
Net income ($ mil.)	—	159	381	486	796	848	816	550	265	(270)	(288)
Income as % of sales	—	2.3%	4.5%	4.9%	7.2%	7.1%	6.7%	4.5%	2.0%	—	—
Employees	3.2%	—	—	—	82,858	84,885	84,845	85,000	90,000	100,000	100,000

NET INCOME HISTORY

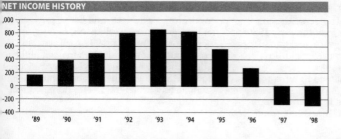

KAUFMAN AND BROAD

OVERVIEW

Kaufman and Broad rhymes with abode, and that's what the company builds. Poetry in motion, Kaufman and Broad Home vaulted into the upper echelon of US home builders with its 1999 purchase of Lewis Homes, the nation's largest privately held home builder. Now one of the top three (with Centex and D.R. Horton), the Los Angeles-based company operates in seven states from the West Coast to the Texas Gulf Coast. It builds about 10,000 homes each year, primarily single-family dwellings for first-time buyers and first-time move-up buyers, but it has begun developing and financing low-income apartment housing as well.

Outside the US, Kaufman and Broad has operations in Mexico City and Paris; it is a leading builder of homes and commercial buildings in and around Paris. It also offers financing for home buyers through its Kaufman and Broad Mortgage subsidiary.

Kaufman and Broad is led by dynamic CEO Bruce Karatz, who uses everything from gospel singers in the boardroom to a boxing match (his own) to inspire employees. Kaufman and Broad is known for its many innovations in design, financing, and promotion. Moving away from speculative building of look-alike homes, the company assembles New Home Showrooms that display standard features and options — and the prices of each of those items — allowing prospective home buyers to customize their homes. Showroom homes range in price from $80,000 to about $500,000.

It was the first in the industry to offer a "lease-to-own" option for new home buyers and the first to create a mortgage company for its customers. It has a reputation for attention-getting promotional stunts, notably when it built a replica of the home in the hit TV show *The Simpsons*, right down to a never-used door, for a national ad campaign.

HISTORY

Kaufman and Broad Building Co. was founded in Detroit in 1957 by Eli Broad and Donald Kaufman. Broad, an accountant, parlayed an initial $25,000 investment into sales of $250,000 on the first weekend of business. By the end of its first year, Kaufman and Broad was posting revenues of $1.7 million.

The company expanded rapidly and went public in 1961. A year later it was the first home builder to be listed on the stock exchange. It moved into California in 1963. Buying up smaller builders, it rapidly became a top US home builder, expanding into New York, San Francisco, and Chicago. In 1965 it formed a mortgage subsidiary to arrange loans for its customers.

In the early 1970s Kaufman and Broad went into Europe and Canada. Sales passed the $100 million mark in 1971, and the company diversified, buying Sun Life Insurance. Housing operations were renamed Kaufman and Broad Development Group (KBDG).

In 1980 the flamboyant Bruce Karatz, who had joined the firm in 1972, was appointed president of KBDG. Karatz steered the company through the recession of the early 1980s, focusing on California, France, and Canada. KBDG acquired Bati-Service, a major French developer of affordable homes, in 1985.

The company was renamed Kaufman and Broad Home Corporation in 1986. Three years later it reorganized into two separate billion-dollar companies: Broad Inc. (now SunAmerica), an insurance firm with Eli Broad as its chairman and CEO, and Kaufman and Broad Home, with Karatz as CEO (and later chairman), which was spun off to shareholders in 1989.

When the California real estate market crashed in 1990, earnings plummeted for the next two years. Karatz decided to diversify by buying up strong regional builders. Kaufman and Broad entered Arizona, Colorado, and Nevada in 1993 and Utah in 1994. Profits dropped in 1995 and 1996 because of weakness in the California and Paris markets and the company's winding down of Canadian operations. But expansion continued, including the acquisition of Rayco, a Texas builder, in 1996.

Borrowing from the methods of Rayco, Kaufman and Broad began surveying home buyers for suggestions to incorporate into new designs. In 1998 the company began to build its New Home Showrooms; there are now 14, and another one is under construction. The corporation continued its expansion drive in 1998 when it paid about $165 million for Dover/Ideal, PrideMark, and Estes, privately held builders based in Houston, Denver, and Tucson, respectively. In 1999 Kaufman and Broad bought Lewis Homes, a major California builder and the #1 builder in Las Vegas, for about $545 million. The purchase makes Kaufman and Broad the top US home builder by volume.

Chairman, President, and CEO: Bruce Karatz, age 53, $2,688,338 pay
EVP; President and CEO, Kaufman and Broad France; President, European Operations: Guy Nafilyan, age 54
SVP and Regional General Manager: Glen Barnard, age 54, $876,749 pay
SVP and Regional General Manager; President, Kaufman and Broad Coastal and Kaufman and Broad of San Diego: William R. Cardon, age 55
SVP Marketing: M. Jeffrey Charney
SVP and CFO: Michael F. Henn, $710,825 pay
SVP and Regional General Manager: Lisa G. Kalmbach, $736,488 pay
SVP: Randall W. Lewis, age 47
SVP and Regional General Manager; President, Kaufman and Broad of Arizona: Jeffrey T. Mezger, age 43
SVP and General Counsel: Barton P. Pachino, age 39
SVP Business Development: Albert Z. Praw, age 50, $947,313 pay
SVP Human Resources: Gary A. Ray, age 40
President, Kaufman and Broad Multi-Housing Group: Michael A. Costa
President, Kaufman and Broad Mortgage: Mark Crivelli
President, Kaufman y Broad de Mexico: Hipolito Gerard
President, Colorado Division: Dennis Welsch, age 41
VP and Controller: William R. Hollinger, age 40
VP Management Development and Planning: Kathleen L. Knoblauch
VP Investor Relations: Mary M. McAboy, age 46
Corporate Secretary and Associate Corporate Counsel: Kimberly N. King
Auditors: Ernst & Young LLP

HQ: Kaufman and Broad Home Corporation, 10990 Wilshire Blvd., Los Angeles, CA 90024
Phone: 310-231-4000   **Fax:** 310-231-4222
Web site: http://www.kaufmanandbroad.com

Kaufman and Broad Home Corporation builds single-family homes in Arizona, California, Colorado, Nevada, New Mexico, Texas, and Utah and in France and Mexico. It also engages in multifamily and commercial construction in France.

1998 Sales

	$ mil.	% of total
California	1.106	46
Other US	1,042	43
International	255	11
Total	**2,403**	**100**

Beazer Homes
Capital Pacific
Centex
David Weekley Homes
D.R. Horton
Fortress Group
Inco Homes
Lennar
Presley
Pulte
Ryland
Shapell Industries
Standard Pacific
U.S. Home

NYSE symbol: KBH FYE: November 30	Annual Growth	1989	1990	1991	1992	1993	1994	1995	1996	1997	1998
Sales ($ mil.)	7.4%	1,265	1,366	1,221	1,094	1,238	1,308	1,367	1,754	1,844	2,403
Net income ($ mil.)	1.8%	81	40	27	28	40	47	29	(61)	58	95
Income as % of sales	—	6.4%	2.9%	2.2%	2.6%	3.2%	3.6%	2.1%	—	3.2%	4.0%
Earnings per share ($)	(0.2%)	2.36	1.21	0.79	0.77	0.96	1.09	0.73	(1.54)	1.45	2.32
Stock price - FY high ($)	—	21.75	15.25	17.00	25.00	22.25	25.50	16.00	16.88	23.13	35.00
Stock price - FY low ($)	—	9.88	5.38	7.00	11.38	15.25	12.25	10.88	11.25	11.75	17.13
Stock price - FY close ($)	6.8%	13.88	7.00	13.38	15.50	20.13	12.75	13.00	12.88	21.69	25.19
P/E - high	—	9	13	22	32	23	23	22	—	16	15
P/E - low	—	4	4	9	15	16	11	15	—	8	7
Dividends per share ($)	(26.5%)	4.80	0.30	0.30	0.38	0.30	0.30	0.30	0.30	0.30	0.30
Book value per share ($)	6.5%	6.76	8.46	8.97	8.61	12.76	12.46	12.80	8.77	9.82	11.86
Employees	14.2%	1,060	1,060	792	820	942	1,330	1,220	1,730	2,040	3,500

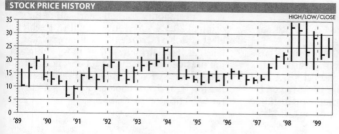

HIGH/LOW/CLOSE

Debt ratio: 61.8%
Return on equity: 20.1%
Cash ($ mil.): 63
Current ratio: 4.61
Long-term debt ($ mil.): 769
No. of shares (mil.): 40
Dividends
  Yield: 1.2%
  Payout: 12.9%
Market value ($ mil.): 1,007

KEEBLER FOODS COMPANY

OVERVIEW

Keebler's funny little elf shoes are stepping on Nabisco's heels. Plump from acquisitions and kid-friendly treats, Elmhurst, Illinois-based Keebler Foods is the US's #2 maker of cookies and crackers. And even though it only comes up to Nabisco's shins saleswise, a few of Nabisco's snack lines have been crumbling, allowing Keebler to nibble away at its rival's market share.

Its Keebler and Sunshine labels include leading products such as Fudge Shoppe fudge-covered cookies, Sandies shortbread cookies, Cheez-It snack crackers, Famous Amos cookies, and Ready Crust pie crusts. The company also makes Kellogg's Pop Tarts and NutriGrain bars and imports Carr's specialty crackers. Keebler is the leading maker of private-label cookies and crackers for the grocery and food service markets and the largest supplier of Girl Scout cookies.

The company is extending its already popular Cheez-It and Fudge Shoppe lines, while sprucing up less glamorous products such as Wheatables and Vienna Fingers. It also has given its Hydrox sandwich cookie line a complete makeover and new name: Droxies. While gunning for wider distribution into convenience stores, club stores, and vending machines, Keebler is also looking to boost its market share through acquisitions and new product development.

Bakery firm Flowers Industries owns 55% of Keebler.

HISTORY

Keebler Foods began in 1853, when baker Godfrey Keebler opened a shop in Philadelphia and became known for his cookies and crackers. As transportation and product packaging improved, so did the need for a regional bakery delivery system. So, in 1927, Keebler joined with several other bakeries — including Strietmann in Ohio, developer of the Zesta cracker brand; Hekmann in Michigan; Supreme in Illinois; and Bowman in Colorado — to form the United Biscuit Company of America.

By 1944 United Biscuit comprised 16 bakeries serving almost the entire country. The company began custom-baking Pop-Tarts for Kellogg in 1963 and changed its name to the quirkier, more memorable Keebler Foods in 1966. Two years later it began using the Keebler elves, led by spokes-elf Ernie Keebler, in its packaging and television advertising.

United Biscuits Holdings, one of the UK's largest food companies (and no relation to the US-based United Biscuit), acquired Keebler in 1974. It became a truly national firm in 1983 when it began distributing on the West Coast. The next year Keebler, along with Nabisco and Frito-Lay, introduced a line of soft cookies. Procter & Gamble (P&G) sued, alleging that its Duncan Hines soft cookie recipe had been stolen. In 1989 Keebler and Nabisco each agreed to pay $53 million to P&G (Frito-Lay agreed to pay $19 million).

The company entered the salty-snack business during the 1980s with brands such as Tato Skins and O'Boisies potato chips. A 1993 price war sparked by Keebler backfired on the company, leading to a restructuring in 1994. Tough competition from Frito-Lay forced Keebler to sell its salty-snack business two years later. Shortly thereafter, United Biscuits sold Keebler to INFLO, a holding company formed by Artal Luxembourg, Flowers Industries, and top Keebler execs. At the same time, Keebler's frozen foods unit was sold to Windsor Foods.

In 1996 the company acquired #3 cookie and cracker company Sunshine Biscuits, including the Ohio dairy that makes the cheese for Cheez-It crackers. Sunshine Biscuits — whose brands also included Hi-Ho and Hydrox (the original, pre-Oreo chocolate sandwich cookie launched in 1908) — began as the Loose-Wiles Biscuit Company, formed in Kansas City in 1902 by Jacob and Joseph Loose and industrialist John Wiles. Sunshine was acquired by the American Tobacco Company (later American Brands) in 1966, then sold to G.F. Industries in 1988.

After its 1996 acquisition of Sunshine, Keebler worked quickly to blend the two firms' operations, eliminating nearly 1,800 positions, closing two plants, and converting another one to cracker production.

Keebler went public in January 1998; as part of the move, Flowers Industries took a controlling stake in the company. Later that year Luxembourg sold off nearly all of his original 20.5% stake. After the IPO, Keebler elected Robert Crozer (VC of Flowers Industries) as its chairman, with Sam Reed remaining president and CEO. In its first acquisition since the IPO, Keebler bought President Baking (Girl Scout cookies, Famous Amos) for $450 million in 1998.

OFFICERS

Chairman: Robert P. Crozer, age 52
CEO and President: Sam K. Reed, age 52, $1,883,000 pay
CFO and SVP-Finance: E. Nichol McCully, age 44, $690,000 pay
SVP-Operations: James T. Willard, age 58, $610,000 pay
VP-Operations Finance and Planning: Jeff Ablin
VP-Logistics: John Balog
VP; President, Mother's Cookies: William G. Bayers
VP; President, Murray Biscuit: Jerry D. Cavitt
VP-Human Resources: Alan Gambrel
VP-New Business Development: Bruce B. Grieve
VP and Treasurer: Lori Marin
VP, Secretary, and General Counsel: Thomas E. O'Neill
VP and General Manager-Keebler Foodservice Division: Dave Pfanzelter
VP-Specialty Products: David Shanholtz
VP-Finance and Corporate Controller: James T. Spear
VP-Corporate Planning and Development: Steven B. Woolf
President-Specialty Products: Jack M. Lotker, age 55, $486,000 pay
President-Keebler Brands: David B. Vermylen, age 48, $816,500 pay
President and COO-Bake-Line Products, Inc.: Harry J. Walsh
Auditors: PricewaterhouseCoopers LLP

LOCATIONS

HQ: 677 Larch Ave., Elmhurst, IL 60126
Phone: 630-833-2900   **Fax:** 630-530-8773
Web site: http://www.keebler.com

Keebler Foods' operations include 19 manufacturing facilities and shipping centers and more than 60 distribution centers in the US.

Selected Manufacturing Facilities

Athens, GA	Columbus, GA	Louisville, KY
Augusta, GA	Denver	Macon, GA
Birmingham, AL	Des Plaines, IL	Marietta, GA
Charlotte, NC	Florence, KY	North Little
Chicago	Grand Rapids, MI	Rock, AR
Cincinnati	Kansas City, KS	Sayreville, NJ
Cleveland, TN	Lake Bluff, IL	

Other Operation
Fremont, OH (dairy)

PRODUCTS/OPERATIONS

Selected Products

Keebler-Brand Products
Chips Deluxe cookies
Club crackers
Droxies cookies
Fudge Shoppe cookies
Graham Selects crackers
Keebler ice-cream cones
Munch'ems crackers
Ready Crust pie crusts
Sandies cookies
Town House crackers
Vienna Fingers cookies
Wheatables crackers
Zesta crackers

Sunshine-Brand Products
Cheeze-It crackers
Heads and Tails animal cheese crackers
Hi-Ho crackers
Sunshine Krispy crackers

Other Products
Carr's (imported and distributed in the US)
Famous Amos
Girl Scout cookies
Murray Sugar Free cookies
Olde New England (vending brownies)

COMPETITORS

Austin Quality Foods	Delicious Brands	McKee Foods
Bestfoods	Frito-Lay	Nabisco Holdings
Campbell Soup	General Mills	Ralcorp
Danone	Interbake Foods	Specialty Foods
	Lance	Tasty Baking

HISTORICAL FINANCIALS & EMPLOYEES

NYSE symbol: KBL FYE: December 31	Annual Growth	1989	1990	1991	1992	1993	1994	1995	1996	1997	1998
Sales ($ mil.)	6.2%	—	—	—	—	1,650	1,600	1,579	1,747	2,065	2,227
Net income ($ mil.)	—	—	—	—	—	(147)	(23)	(158)	11	57	95
Income as % of sales	—	—	—	—	—	—	—	—	0.6%	2.8%	4.3%
Earnings per share ($)	—	—	—	—	—	—	—	—	—	—	1.08
Stock price - FY high ($)	—	—	—	—	—	—	—	—	—	—	37.81
Stock price - FY low ($)	—	—	—	—	—	—	—	—	—	—	23.88
Stock price - FY close ($)	—	—	—	—	—	—	—	—	—	—	37.63
P/E - high	—	—	—	—	—	—	—	—	—	—	35
P/E - low	—	—	—	—	—	—	—	—	—	—	22
Dividends per share ($)	—	—	—	—	—	—	—	—	—	—	0.00
Book value per share ($)	—	—	—	—	—	—	—	—	—	—	3.93
Employees	10.7%	—	—	—	—	—	—	9,000	9,300	9,500	12,200

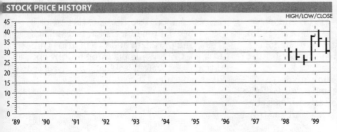

STOCK PRICE HISTORY   HIGH/LOW/CLOSE

1998 FISCAL YEAR-END
Debt ratio: 62.2%
Return on equity: 28.8%
Cash ($ mil.): 24
Current ratio: 0.81
Long-term debt ($ mil.): 542
No. of shares (mil.): 84
Dividends
  Yield: —
  Payout: —
Market value ($ mil.): 3,153

KELLOGG COMPANY

OVERVIEW

Packaging grrrREAT mornings in a box is Kellogg's business. The Battle Creek, Michigan-based breakfast giant makes seven of the world's top 10 cereal brands, including such morning classics as Frosted Flakes, Corn Flakes, Rice Krispies, Two Scoops Raisin Bran, Special K, and Froot Loops. As cereal sales slip and time-pressed consumers grow impatient with the traditional cereal-milk combo, Kellogg is relying increasingly on convenience foods such as Eggo waffles, Nutri-Grain cereal bars, and Pop-Tarts.

Kellogg has snapped under the pressure of periodic cereal price wars (since 1988, its US market share has slipped from 40% to 32%, just ahead of General Mills) and crackled under fierce store-brand competition (its top cereals are among the easiest to imitate). Kellogg is experimenting with new single-serve distribution channels for its products, such as gas stations and vending machines.

The W. K. Kellogg Foundation, one of the world's largest charities, owns 34% of the company. The Gund family, which sold its coffee business (later Sanka) to Kellogg in 1927, owns about 12%.

HISTORY

Will Keith (W. K.) Kellogg first made wheat flakes in 1894 while working for his brother, Dr. John Kellogg, at Battle Creek, Michigan's, famed homeopathic sanitarium. While doing an experiment with grains (for patients' diets), the two men were interrupted; by the time they returned to the dough, it had absorbed water. They rolled it anyway, toasted the result, and accidentally created the first flaked cereal. John sold the flakes via mail order (1899) in a partnership that W. K. managed. In 1906 W. K. started his own firm to produce corn flakes.

As head of the Battle Creek Toasted Corn Flake Company, W. K. competed against 42 cereal companies in Battle Creek (one run by former patient C. W. Post) and roared to the head of the pack with his innovative marketing ideas. A 1906 *Ladies' Home Journal* ad helped increase demand from 33 cases a day earlier that year to 2,900 a day by year-end. The next year W. K. formed campaigns around his cereal's main ingredient, corn grit, termed "The Sweetheart of the Corn." He was the first to use full-color magazine ads and widespread consumer sampling. One ad, then considered risque, offered a free box of cereal to every woman who winked at her grocer.

Another of W. K.'s innovations was the Waxtite inner lining to keep cereal fresh (1914). He continued to introduce classic cereals, such as Bran Flakes (1915), All-Bran (1916), and Rice Krispies (1928). International expansion began in Canada (1914) and followed in Australia (1924) and England (1938). In 1930 W. K. established the W. K. Kellogg Foundation, giving it the majority of his interest in Kellogg.

Diversifying a little, the company introduced the Pop-Tart in 1964 and acquired Eggo waffles in the 1970s. By the early 1980s Kellogg's US market share hit a low, due to strong competition from General Mills and other rivals. The company pitched new cereals to health-conscious adults and aggressively pursued the fast-growing European market.

Kellogg spent the mid-1990s reengineering itself, creating the USA Convenience Foods Division and selling such noncore assets as its carton container and Argentine snack-foods makers (1993). It teamed with ConAgra in 1994 to create a cereal line sold under the latter's popular Healthy Choice label.

But in 1996 Kellogg was crying in its milk after losing ground in its two largest markets. It was hurt in the US and UK by stiff store-brand competition and a price war. Kellogg was forced to slash prices an average of 19% on 16 brands after Kraft Foods lowered its Post-brand cereal prices.

Also in 1996 the company created a functional foods division to market foods that will prevent and treat diseases (exposing the products to close regulatory scrutiny). Kellogg also acquired Lender's (bagels) that year.

In 1997 and 1998 the company opened or bought operations in Australia (Day Dawn), the UK, Asia, and Latin America. Kellogg introduced the Ensemble line of cholesterol-reducing entrees, pasta, and baked goods, as well as its "Haagen-Dazs of cereals," Country Inn Specialties.

The company slashed about 25% of its salaried North American workforce and hiked prices on about two-thirds of its cereals in 1998. Several top officers left in 1998 and 1999, and president and COO Carlos Gutierrez became CEO. While planning to introduce additional non-cereal products, he discussed selling the Lender's division.

Chairman: Arnold G. Langbo, age 62,
$1,027,500 pay (prior to title change)
President and CEO: Carlos M. Gutierrez, age 45,
$557,390 pay (prior to promotion)
EVP; President, Kellogg North America: John D. Cook,
age 45
EVP; President, Kellogg Asia/Pacific:
Jacobus "Koos" Groot, age 48
EVP; President, Kellogg Europe: Alan F. Harris, age 44
EVP, New Business Development: William J. Mayer
EVP, Services and Technology: Donald W. Thomason
SVP, Research and Development: Donna J. Banks,
age 42
SVP: Jay W. Shreiner, age 49
SVP, Corporate Affairs: Joseph M. Stewart, age 56
SVP, Global Supply Chain: Michael J. Teale, age 54,
$420,810 pay
VP, Human Resources: James W. Larson
Auditors: PricewaterhouseCoopers LLP

HQ: 1 Kellogg Sq., Battle Creek, MI 49016-3599
Phone: 616-961-2000   **Fax:** 616-961-2871
Web site: http://www.kelloggs.com

1998 Sales & Operating Income

	Sales $ mil.	% of total	Operating Income $ mil.	% of total
North America	4,176	62	832	69
Europe	1,698	25	212	18
Latin America	511	8	107	9
Asia/Pacific	377	5	48	4
Other regions	—	—	(233)	—
Total	**6,762**	**100**	**966**	**100**

Selected Brands

Cereals	
All-Bran	Kellogg's Cinnamon
Apple Jacks	Mini-Buns
Apple Raisin Crisp	Kellogg's Corn Flakes
Bran Buds	Kellogg's Frosted Bran
Common Sense	Kellogg's Frosted Flakes
Complete Bran Flakes	Kellogg's Low Fat Granola
Corn Pops	Kellogg's Squares
Country Inn Specialties	Kellogg's Two Scoops
Cracklin' Oat Bran	Raisin Bran
Crispix	Muesli
Cruncheroos	Nut & Honey Crunch
Froot Loops	Product 19
Frosted Mini-Wheats	Rice Krispies
Fruitful Bran	Smacks
Just Right	Smart Start
	Special K

Other Products
Croutettes (stuffing mix)
Eggo (frozen waffles)
Ensemble (cholesterol-reducing entrees, baked goods)
Kellogg's Corn Flake Crumbs (breading)
Kellogg's Nutri-Grain (cereal bars, frozen waffles)
Lender's (bagels)
Pop-Tarts (toaster pastries)
Special K (frozen waffles)

Associated	Interstate	Nestle
British Foods	Bakeries	Pillsbury
Earthgrains	Kraft Foods	Quaker Oats
General Mills	Malt-O-Meal	Ralcorp
Gilster-Mary Lee	Nabisco	Sara Lee
Grist Mill	Holdings	Wessanen

NYSE symbol: K FYE: December 31	Annual Growth	1989	1990	1991	1992	1993	1994	1995	1996	1997	1998
Sales ($ mil.)	4.2%	4,652	5,181	5,787	6,191	6,295	6,562	7,004	6,677	6,830	6,762
Net income ($ mil.)	0.7%	470	503	606	431	681	705	490	531	546	503
Income as % of sales	—	10.1%	9.7%	10.5%	7.0%	10.8%	10.7%	7.0%	8.0%	8.0%	7.4%
Earnings per share ($)	0.6%	1.17	1.04	1.26	0.90	1.47	1.58	1.12	1.25	1.32	1.23
Stock price - FY high ($)	—	20.41	19.38	33.50	37.69	33.94	30.38	39.75	40.31	50.47	50.19
Stock price - FY low ($)	—	14.44	14.69	17.50	27.19	23.63	23.69	26.25	31.00	32.00	28.50
Stock price - FY close ($)	8.1%	16.91	18.97	32.69	33.50	28.38	29.06	38.63	32.81	49.63	34.13
P/E - high	—	17	19	27	42	23	19	35	32	38	41
P/E - low	—	12	14	14	30	16	15	23	25	24	23
Dividends per share ($)	8.8%	0.43	0.48	0.54	0.60	0.66	0.70	0.75	0.81	0.87	0.92
Book value per share ($)	(4.6%)	3.35	3.94	4.49	4.10	3.76	4.08	3.67	3.06	2.43	2.20
Employees	(1.9%)	17,268	17,239	17,017	16,551	16,151	15,657	14,487	14,511	14,339	14,498

HIGH/LOW/CLOSE

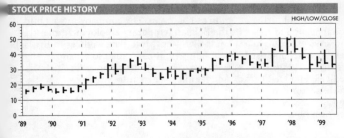

Debt ratio: 64.5%
Return on equity: 56.5%
Cash ($ mil.): 136
Current ratio: 0.87
Long-term debt ($ mil.): 1,615
No. of shares (mil.): 405
Dividends
  Yield: 2.7%
  Payout: 74.8%
Market value ($ mil.): 13,823

KELLY SERVICES, INC.

OVERVIEW

Kelly Services may be a permanent fixture in the personnel services market, but the people it places are free to move around. The Troy, Michigan-based company is the second-largest temporary staffing company in the US (behind Manpower). Kelly Services provides more than 750,000 temps to almost 200,000 clients in 19 countries. The company helps reduce its customers' cost of hiring new help during peak business periods by handling the hiring process for them and charging its customers an hourly rate for each assigned temp. What was once a business that only supplied female clerical help has expanded to include light-industrial, technical, and professional employees of both genders, including information technology specialists, engineers, and accountants. It even has an operation that places lawyers (The Law Registry) and scientists (Kelly Scientific Resources), and its Kelly Assisted Living Services unit provides personal care and daily living assistance to people who need care at home. The company also has consolidated its engineering staffing operations into Kelly Engineering Resources. Chairman and CEO Terence Adderley owns about 51% of Kelly Services.

HISTORY

William Russell Kelly, a college dropout and former car salesman, went to Detroit after WWII to seek his fortune. An owner of modern business equipment, he set up Russell Kelly Office Services in his Detroit office in 1946 to provide copying, typing, and inventory services for other businesses; first-year sales from 12 customers totaled $847.

Although companies began to acquire their own machines, Kelly knew that they still needed people to work at their offices. He reincorporated his rapidly expanding business as Personnel Service in 1952 and opened the company's first branch office, in Louisville, Kentucky, in 1955; by the end of that year he had 35 offices throughout the US. In 1957 the company was renamed Kelly Girl Service to reflect its all-female workforce.

In the 1960s Kelly ventured beyond office services and began placing, among others, convention hostesses, blue-collar workers, data processors, door-to-door marketers, and drafters. Kelly Girl went public in 1962, boasting 148 branches at the time, and in 1966 the company adopted its present name, Kelly Services. Its first non-US office opened in Toronto in 1968, and one in Paris followed in 1972.

A tough US economy in the 1970s saw a surge in corporate interest in temporary employees. Employers saw the benefits of hiring "Kelly Girls" to meet seasonal needs and special projects. In 1976 Kelly Services acquired a modest health care services company and used it to form Kelly Home Care. In the 1980s this division abandoned the Medicaid and Medicare markets and shifted to private-sector care. Renamed Kelly Assisted Living Services in 1984, the unit offered aides to perform household duties and nurses to conduct home visits for the elderly and disabled. Also in the 1980s Kelly Services began hiring retired people as part of its ENCORE Program.

The company developed specialty services in the US in the 1990s. In 1994 it acquired ComTrain (testing and training software products) and Your Staff (an employee-leasing company providing companies with entire human resources departments, including benefits and payroll services). In 1995 it bought the Wallace Law Registry (later renamed The Law Registry), which provides lawyers, paralegals, and clerks. Kelly also established Kelly Scientific Resources to place science professionals. In 1996 that subsidiary acquired Oak Ridge Research Institute, which provided scientists to the defense and energy industries.

International expansion has been a central focus for Kelly. Since 1988 more than a dozen acquisitions have expanded the company in Australia, Europe, New Zealand, and elsewhere. In response to new legislation allowing companies to hire temporary workers, the company opened five offices in Italy. It also acquired a personnel placement firm in Russia in 1997.

William Kelly died at the age of 92 in 1998, and the company named president and CEO Terence Adderley (his adopted son) to replace him as chairman. The company moved into the Belgian temporary employment market later that year through new offices in Brussels and Antwerp. It continued to expand in 1999 with new acquisitions planned for Australia and its initial entry into Sweden.

Chairman, President, and CEO: Terence E. Adderley,
age 65, $1,164,000 pay
VP Field Operations, Sales and Marketing:
Carl T. Camden, age 44, $682,500 pay
VP and Chief Administration and Technology Officer:
Tommi A. White, age 48, $682,500 pay
VP and CFO: William K. Gerber, age 45, $568,968 pay
VP, Secretary, and General Counsel:
George M. Reardon, age 51
VP Administration: James H. Bradley
VP and Managing Director, UK and Ireland:
Grahame C. H. Caswell
**VP and General Manager, Strategic Customer
Relationships:** Joan M. Brancheau
VP and Division General Manager: Clayton B. Bullock
VP and Division Group Manager: Arlene G. Grimsley
VP and Division General Manager: Alfredo Maselli
VP and Division General Manager: Andrew R. Watt
VP and Division General Manager: Michael S. Webster
VP Science and Healthcare Services Group:
Rolf E. Kleiner
VP Technical Services Group: Larry J. Seyfarth
VP Service Delivery: Theresa A. Dolbert
VP Human Resources: David Beckstrand
Auditors: PricewaterhouseCoopers LLP

HQ: 999 W. Big Beaver Rd., Troy, MI 48084
Phone: 248-362-4444   **Fax:** 248-813-3990
Web site: http://www.kellyservices.com

Kelly Services has more than 1,800 offices in Australia,
Belgium, Canada, Denmark, France, Germany, Ireland,
Italy, Luxembourg, Mexico, the Netherlands, New
Zealand, Norway, Puerto Rico, Russia, Spain,
Switzerland, the UK, and the US.

1998 Sales

	$ mil.	% of total
US commercial staffing	2,536	62
International	964	24
Professional, technical & staffing alternatives	592	14
Total	**4,092**	**100**

Selected Services
Kelly Engineering Resources (aeronautical, automotive,
  chemical, electrical, mechanical, and process
  engineers)
Kelly Management Services (mail and shipping, payroll,
  and accounts payable management)
Kelly Scientific Resources (science staffing in biology,
  chemistry, geology, biochemistry, and physics)
Kelly Services (temporary employees in areas of office
  services, marketing, technical, accounting, and other
  professional services)
Kelly Staff Leasing (human resources management)
KellySelect (temporary to full-time employee service)
Partnered Staffing (on-site management of temporary
  workforce)

Adecco
Administaff
Interim Services
Manpower
Olsten
On Assignment
Randstad Holding
Staff Builders
Staff Leasing
Volt Information

Nasdaq symbol: KELYA FYE: December 31	Annual Growth	1989	1990	1991	1992	1993	1994	1995	1996	1997	1998
Sales ($ mil.)	12.9%	1,378	1,471	1,438	1,723	1,955	2,363	2,690	3,302	3,853	4,092
Net income ($ mil.)	2.0%	71	71	39	39	45	61	70	73	81	85
Income as % of sales	—	5.1%	4.8%	2.7%	2.3%	2.3%	2.6%	2.6%	2.2%	2.1%	2.1%
Earnings per share ($)	1.9%	1.89	1.90	1.02	1.04	1.18	1.61	1.83	1.91	2.12	2.23
Stock price - FY high ($)	—	33.60	32.20	33.40	35.00	36.60	32.00	37.00	32.50	38.75	38.50
Stock price - FY low ($)	—	21.45	21.80	21.60	22.20	22.00	23.00	24.50	25.25	23.25	23.75
Stock price - FY close ($)	0.1%	31.40	26.20	25.20	35.00	27.75	27.50	27.75	27.00	30.00	31.75
P/E - high	—	18	17	33	34	31	20	20	17	18	17
P/E - low	—	11	11	21	21	19	14	13	13	11	11
Dividends per share ($)	7.9%	0.46	0.53	0.58	0.58	0.63	0.70	0.78	0.83	0.87	0.91
Book value per share ($)	7.7%	7.55	8.98	9.44	9.74	10.23	11.37	12.52	13.58	14.67	14.72
Employees	2.7%	583,900	578,800	553,900	584,000	634,300	665,000	660,600	692,100	750,000	740,000

STOCK PRICE HISTORY   HIGH/LOW/CLOSE

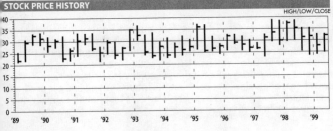

1998 FISCAL YEAR-END
Debt ratio: 0.0%
Return on equity: 15.7%
Cash ($ mil.): 60
Current ratio: 1.69
Long-term debt ($ mil.): 0
No. of shares (mil.): 37
Dividends
  Yield: 2.9%
  Payout: 40.8%
Market value ($ mil.): 1,160

KERR-MCGEE CORPORATION

OVERVIEW

Kerr-McGee hasn't run out of energy, but lately it gets a bigger kick from chemicals. The Oklahoma City-based company explores for and produces oil and natural gas (37% of sales) and produces inorganic chemicals (44% of sales).

Kerr-McGee's oil and gas activities take place in China, the Gulf of Mexico, Indonesia, Thailand, the UK sector of the North Sea, and Yemen; its Gulf of Mexico and North Sea operations account for nearly 90% of production. With its purchase of Oryx Energy, the company became one of the US's largest nonintegrated upstream oil and gas companies. The firm is also boosting its exploration activities. Kerr-McGee produces inorganic industrial and

specialty chemicals, heavy minerals, and timber products. It has grabbed a 10% world market share with its primary chemical product, titanium dioxide (a white pigment used in paint, plastics, and paper).

The company has pursued a decade-long strategy of selling off energy-related lines that no longer fit with its core business, including coal mining, oil refining and marketing, and nuclear fuels manufacturing, though it is still mired in the cleanup of old nuclear plant sites. Kerr-McGee is also selling off noncore chemical operations to concentrate on its growing titanium dioxide business.

HISTORY

In 1929 partners Robert Kerr (later an Oklahoma governor and U.S. senator) and James Anderson founded Anderson & Kerr Drilling Company in Ada, Oklahoma. They moved the business to Oklahoma City the following year.

Renamed A & K Petroleum in 1932, the company went public in 1935. Anderson sold his stake the following year. Renamed Kerlyn Oil in 1937, the company recruited Dean McGee, Phillips Petroleum's chief geologist, who in 1938 made a major oil find in Arkansas. Kerlyn made a big oil strike in Oklahoma in 1943. Two years later it bought its first refinery and began exploring for oil in the Gulf of Mexico. Kerlyn became Kerr-McGee Oil Industries in 1946.

Kerr-McGee diversified in the early 1950s by acquiring four natural gas-processing plants in Oklahoma and Texas. When atomic bomb production during the Cold War boosted uranium demand, Kerr-McGee began mining uranium in Arizona. In 1954 McGee became president and CEO. Kerr-McGee became a fully integrated oil company with the 1955 purchase of Deep Rock Oil, which operated service stations in the Midwest, as well as pipeline and refining facilities. In 1957 it bought Triangle Refineries and Cato Oil and Grease Company (sold in 1995).

By the 1960s Kerr-McGee (renamed Kerr-McGee Corporation in 1965) was doing contract drilling in the US and overseas. It entered the timber and industrial chemicals businesses by acquiring two railroad tie plants and several fertilizer companies. The 1967 acquisition of American Potash & Chemical gave Kerr-McGee two industrial chemical plants and a California lake from which it extracted brine to make soda ash, boron, sodium sulfate, and potash.

Kerr-McGee began mining coal in 1969. It

opened more uranium plants and bought Southwestern Refining Co. in 1974. Problems plagued the company's nuclear program in the 1970s and 1980s. Karen Silkwood, a plutonium plant employee who accused the company of safety breaches, was killed in a mysterious car accident in 1974. An explosion at Kerr-McGee's nuclear fuel plant in Gore, Oklahoma, killed a worker and injured dozens in 1986.

While Kerr-McGee diversified, its oil and gas reserves dwindled. It also sold its potash and phosphate mines, uranium interests, and contract drilling operations. The company unloaded its marketing and refining assets in 1995 by selling its four oil refineries, a pipeline gathering system and trucking operation, and 51 filling stations.

Company veteran Luke Corbett became chairman and CEO in 1997. That year Kerr-McGee sold its onshore oil and natural gas exploration and production businesses to Devon Energy. The $353 million deal gave Kerr-McGee a 31% stake in Devon, which was later reduced to 14%.

In 1998 the company acquired a majority stake in Bayer's European titanium dioxide pigment operations and bought the North Sea oil and gas reserves of Gulf Canada Resources for $418 million. Kerr-McGee also sold part of its coal-mining operations to American Coal Co. for about $200 million and sold the rest to Rio Tinto for $400 million. Positioning itself as one of the largest independent oil and gas exploration and production companies in the US, Kerr-McGee bought Oryx Energy for about $2.4 billion in 1999. Also that year Kerr-McGee bought out the interests in oil and gas producer Sun Energy Partners that it didn't already own.

OFFICERS

airman: Robert L. Keiser, age 56
: Tom J. McDaniel, age 60, $378,269 pay
O: Luke R. Corbett, age 52, $868,077 pay
P and CFO: John C. Linehan, age 59, $378,269 pay
P Worldwide Exploration and Production
Operations: Kenneth W. Crouch, age 55, $288,846 pay
P Strategic Planning: Michael G. Webb, age 51
P, Kerr-McGee Chemical: W. Peter Woodward, age 50
Safety and Environmental Affairs:
George D. Christiansen, age 54
Human Resources: Julius C. Hilburn, age 48
and Controller: Deborah A. Kitchens, age 42
, General Counsel, and Corporate Secretary:
Gregory F. Pilcher
General Administration: Jean B. Wallace, age 45
and Treasurer: J. Michael Rauh, age 49
sistant Secretary and Deputy General Counsel:
John F. Reichenberger
uditors: Arthur Andersen LLP

LOCATIONS

Q: Kerr-McGee Center, 123 Robert S. Kerr Ave.,
Oklahoma City, OK 73102
hone: 405-270-1313   **Fax:** 405-270-3029
eb site: http://www.kerr-mcgee.com

err-McGee explores for and produces oil and gas
nshore in Algeria, Ecuador, Indonesia, Thailand, the
K, the US, and Yemen, as well as offshore China,
abon, the Gulf of Mexico, Thailand, and the UK sector
f the North Sea. It owns chemical plants in the US and
olds stakes in titanium dioxide plants in Australia,
elgium, Germany, and Saudi Arabia. It produces timber
roducts in plants in Illinois, Indiana, Mississippi,
lissouri, Oregon, and Texas.

PRODUCTS/OPERATIONS

1998 Sales

	$ mil.	% of total
Chemicals	933	67
Exploration & production	463	33
Total	**1,396**	**100**

Selected Subsidiaries

Chemicals
Kerr-McGee Chemical GmbH
Kerr-McGee Chemical LLC
Kerr-McGee Pigments Limited
KMCC Western Australia Pty. Ltd.

Oil and Gas
Kerr-McGee China Petroleum Ltd.
Kerr-McGee Oil & Gas Corporation
Kerr-McGee Oil (U.K.) PLC
Kerr-McGee Resources (U.K.) Limited

COMPETITORS

Amerada Hess	Millennium Chemicals
ARCO	Mobil
Ashland	NL Industries
BHP	Nord Resources
BP Amoco	Occidental
Burlington Resources	Phillips Petroleum
Chevron	Royal Dutch/Shell
Coastal	Texaco
DuPont	TOTAL FINA
Exxon	Unocal
Kemira Oy	USX-Marathon

HISTORICAL FINANCIALS & EMPLOYEES

NYSE symbol: KMG FYE: December 31	Annual Growth	1989	1990	1991	1992	1993	1994	1995	1996	1997	1998
Sales ($ mil.)	(8.4%)	3,087	3,683	3,274	3,382	3,281	3,353	1,801	1,931	1,711	1,396
Net income ($ mil.)	(11.9%)	156	150	102	(101)	77	90	(31)	220	194	50
Income as % of sales	—	5.1%	4.1%	3.1%	—	2.3%	2.7%	—	11.4%	11.3%	3.6%
Earnings per share ($)	(11.6%)	3.20	3.01	2.10	(2.08)	1.57	1.74	(0.60)	4.43	4.04	1.06
Stock price - FY high ($)	—	52.00	53.63	46.88	46.38	56.00	51.00	64.00	74.13	75.00	73.19
Stock price - FY low ($)	—	37.38	42.38	35.13	35.63	41.75	40.00	44.00	55.75	55.50	36.19
Stock price - FY close ($)	(3.1%)	50.75	44.88	38.63	45.00	45.25	46.25	63.50	72.00	63.31	38.25
P/E - high	—	16	18	22	—	36	29	—	17	19	69
P/E - low	—	12	14	17	—	27	23	—	13	14	34
Dividends per share ($)	4.5%	1.21	1.38	1.48	1.52	1.52	1.52	1.52	1.64	1.76	1.80
Book value per share ($)	(0.5%)	29.44	30.77	31.43	27.96	29.27	28.95	27.73	28.31	30.20	28.26
Employees	(9.1%)	7,942	6,756	6,072	5,866	5,812	5,524	3,976	3,851	3,746	3,367

STOCK PRICE HISTORY

HIGH/LOW/CLOSE

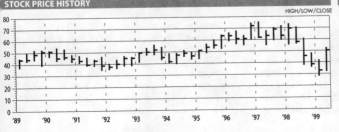

1998 FISCAL YEAR-END

Debt ratio: 40.3%
Return on equity: 3.8%
Cash ($ mil.): 114
Current ratio: 1.40
Long-term debt ($ mil.): 901
No. of shares (mil.): 47
Dividends
  Yield: 4.7%
  Payout: 169.8%
Market value ($ mil.): 1,804

KEYCORP

OVERVIEW

Cleveland-based KeyCorp is unlocking the door to a new identity as a nationwide financial services organization.

Regulatory changes and strategic acquisitions are moving the superregional bank into new markets — investment banking, financial advice, securities underwriting, and even stock brokerage (through a partnership with discount broker Charles Schwab.) Central to this strategy is the company's move, allowed by the Riegle-Neal Act, to unify 10 of its 12 separately chartered state banks as KeyBank, N.A. This helps cut costs by consolidating operations and standardizing products. KeyCorp, already a community banking powerhouse, has more than 1,000 offices across the northern US.

KeyCorp's National Consumer Finance division provides education, home equity, and auto loans, as well as credit cards to customers nationwide. Key Corporate Capital administers 401(k) plans, offers health insurance to small businesses (through alliances), finances commercial real estate, and leases high-tech equipment. Key Capital Partners offers investment management, insurance, brokerage services, and investment banking (through its 1998 purchase of Cleveland's McDonald & Company Investments).

HISTORY

KeyCorp predecessor Commercial Bank of Albany was chartered in 1825. In 1865 it joined the new national banking system and became National Commercial Bank of Albany. After WWI National Commercial consolidated with Union National Bank & Trust as National Commercial Bank and Trust, which then merged with First Trust and Deposit in 1971.

In 1973 Victor Riley became president and CEO. Under Riley, National Commercial grew during the 1970s and 1980s through acquisitions. Riley sought to make the company a regional powerhouse but was thwarted when several New England states passed legislation barring New York from buying banks in the region.

As a result, the company, renamed Key Bank in 1979, turned west, targeting small towns with less competition. Thus situated, it prospered, despite entering Alaska just in time for the 1986 oil price collapse. Its folksy image and small-town success earned it a reputation as the "Wal-Mart of banking."

Meanwhile, in Cleveland, Society for Savings followed a different path. Founded as a mutual savings bank in 1849, the institution succeeded from the start. It survived the Civil War and the postwar economic turmoil, and built Cleveland's first skyscraper in 1890. It continued to grow even during the Depression, and became the largest savings bank outside the Northeast in 1949.

In 1955 the bank formed a holding company, Society National. Society grew through the acquisitions of smaller banks in Ohio until 1979, when Ohio allowed branch banking in contiguous counties. Thereafter, Society National opened branches as well. In the mid-1980s and the early 1990s, the renamed Society Corporation began consolidating its operations and continued growing.

A 1994 merger with Society more than doubled assets for the surviving KeyCorp; compatibility of the two companies' systems and software simplified consolidation. The company sold its mortgage-servicing unit to Nations-Bank (now Bank of America) in 1995 and over the next year bought investment management, finance, and investment banking companies.

In 1997 KeyCorp began trimming its branch network, divesting 200 offices. At the same time, it expanded its consumer lending business by buying Champion Mortgage.

In cooperation with USF&G (now part of The St. Paul Companies) and three HMOs, KeyCorp began offering health insurance for employees of its small-business customers, a market underserved by large insurance companies. In 1998 joint ventures placed KeyCorp ATMs in gas stations in Arizona, California, and Nevada and provided KeyCorp's US customers with banking services in the former Soviet bloc (in concert with Germany's Commerzbank). That year the company acquired Leasetec, a firm that leases computer storage systems globally through its StorageTek subsidiary, and also McDonald & Company Investments, whose investment banking and brokerage operations may help KeyCorp reach its goal of earning half of all revenues from fee income. Also in 1998, KeyCorp began offering business lines of credit to customers of Costco Companies, the largest wholesale club retailer in the US. In 1999 KeyCorp began offering electronic business services by partnering with Econex, an e-commerce portal that provides software and services to the bank's business customers.

Chairman and CEO: Robert W. Gillespie, age 54,
$2,067,500 pay
President and COO: Henry L. Meyer III, age 49,
$1,187,501 pay
EVP and Chief Banking Officer: Gary R. Allen, age 50,
$750,000 pay
EVP, Strategic and Operational Services:
James E. Bennett III, age 56
Group EVP, Key Corporate Capital: James S. Bingay
Group EVP, Key Consumer Finance: James A. Fishell
Group EVP and Chief Technology Officer:
Allen J. Gula Jr., age 44
EVP; President, Key Capital Partners:
Robert B. Heisler Jr., age 50
Group EVP and Chief Human Resource Officer:
Thomas E. Helfrich, age 48
Group EVP, Key Client Services: Robert G. Jones, age 42
EVP and CFO: K. Brent Somers, age 50, $792,500 pay
EVP, Secretary, and General Counsel:
Thomas C. Stevens, age 49, $760,000 pay
Chairman, Key Capital Partners:
William B. Summers Jr., age 48
Chairman, Key Asset Management: William G. Spears
President and CEO, Key Asset Management:
Richard J. Buoncore
VP Strategic Management: David R. Campbell
VP Corporate Communications: W. John Fuller
VP and Chief Accounting Officer: Lee G. Irving, age 50
VP Corporate Relations: Michael J. Monroe
VP Investor Relations: Vernon L. Patterson
Auditors: Ernst & Young LLP

LOCATIONS

HQ: 127 Public Sq., Cleveland, OH 44114-1306
Phone: 216-689-6300   **Fax:** 216-689-7009
Web site: http://www.keybank.com

PRODUCTS/OPERATIONS

1998 Assets

	$ mil.	% of total
Cash & equivalents	3,296	4
Mortgage-backed securities	4,314	5
Other securities	1,940	2
Net loans	61,112	77
Other assets	9,358	12
Total	**80,020**	**100**

1998 Sales

	$ mil.	% of total
Loan interest	4,935	70
Other interest	590	8
Trust income	335	5
Charges & fees	374	5
Investment banking income	239	3
Insurance & brokerage income	111	2
Other	516	7
Total	**7,100**	**100**

COMPETITORS

American Express	Fleet
Bank of America	GE
Bank of New York	General Motors
BANK ONE	Merrill Lynch
BankBoston	National Bancorp of Alaska
Charles Schwab	Northern Trust
Chase Manhattan	SunTrust
Citigroup	Wells Fargo
First Union	Zions Bancorporation

HISTORICAL FINANCIALS & EMPLOYEES

NYSE symbol: KEY FYE: December 31	Annual Growth	1989	1990	1991	1992	1993	1994	1995	1996	1997	1998
Assets ($ mil.)	24.8%	10,903	15,110	15,405	24,978	27,007	66,798	66,339	67,621	73,699	80,020
Net income ($ mil.)	27.7%	110	158	163	301	347	854	825	783	919	996
Income as % of assets	—	1.0%	1.0%	1.1%	1.2%	1.3%	1.3%	1.2%	1.2%	1.2%	1.2%
Earnings per share ($)	7.5%	1.16	1.18	1.23	1.20	1.43	1.70	1.71	1.67	2.07	2.23
Stock price – FY high ($)	—	10.13	8.81	13.13	16.72	18.63	16.88	18.63	27.13	36.59	44.88
Stock price – FY low ($)	—	8.25	6.00	7.63	12.13	13.63	11.81	12.38	16.69	23.94	23.38
Stock price – FY close ($)	15.8%	8.53	8.06	12.38	16.06	14.88	12.50	18.13	25.25	35.41	32.00
P/E – high	—	9	7	11	14	13	10	11	16	18	20
P/E – low	—	7	5	6	10	10	7	7	10	12	10
Dividends per share ($)	10.0%	0.40	0.44	0.46	0.49	0.56	0.64	0.72	0.76	0.84	0.94
Book value per share ($)	5.7%	8.29	7.67	8.45	7.75	8.68	9.44	10.68	10.92	11.83	13.63
Employees	17.8%	5,935	8,752	7,919	12,451	29,983	29,211	29,563	26,963	24,595	25,862

STOCK PRICE HISTORY

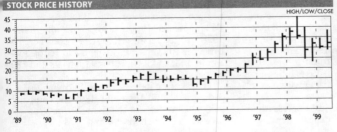

HIGH/LOW/CLOSE

1998 FISCAL YEAR-END

Equity as % of assets: 7.7%
Return on assets: 1.3%
Return on equity: 16.2%
Long-term debt ($ mil.): 12,967
No. of shares (mil.): 452
Dividends
 Yield: 2.9%
 Payout: 42.2%
Market value ($ mil.): 14,478
Sales (mil.): $7,100

KIMBERLY-CLARK CORPORATION

OVERVIEW

The world's #1 maker of tissue products, Kimberly-Clark gets up close and personal. With popular brands such as Kleenex, Huggies, and Kotex, the Irving, Texas-based company generates more than 90% of revenues from sales of its tissue and personal care products. However, it also is increasing its presence in the health care product business through acquisitions.

Kimberly-Clark manufactures paper-based personal care products (baby wipes, diapers, feminine pads, incontinence items, and training and youth pants), away-from-home products (wipes and washroom materials), consumer tissue products (facial tissue, bathroom tissue, and paper towels), and medical products (surgical face masks and wound dressings).

Other brand names by the company include Depend, GoodNites, Kotex, New Freedom, Pull-Ups, Poise, Kleenex Cottonelle, Kleenex Viva, Kimwipes, Scott, and Wypall. Kimberly-Clark's newsprint, printing papers, premium business and correspondence papers, and specialty and technical papers are marketed under the Neenah Paper, Classic Crest, and Classic brands.

Kimberly-Clark moved into the medical products business in 1997 with its purchase of Tecnol Medical Products. Its agreement to buy Ballard Medical Products will add disposable respiratory, gastroenterology, and cardiology care products, including the #1 brand of respiratory-suction catheters, Trach Care, to its product line.

HISTORY

In 1872 John Kimberly, Charles Clark, Havilah Babcock, and Frank Shattuck founded Kimberly, Clark & Company in Neenah, Wisconsin, to manufacture newsprint from rags. The company incorporated as Kimberly & Clark Company in 1880 and built a pulp and paper plant on the Fox River in 1889.

In 1914 the company developed cellu-cotton, a cotton substitute used by the US Army as surgical cotton during WWI. Army nurses began using cellu-cotton pads as disposable sanitary napkins, and six years later the company introduced Kotex, the first disposable feminine hygiene product. Kleenex, the first throwaway handkerchief, followed in 1924, and soon many Americans were referring to all sanitary napkins as Kotex and facial tissues as Kleenex. Kimberly & Clark joined with the New York Times Company in 1926 to build a newsprint mill (now Spruce Falls Power and Paper) in Ontario, Canada. Two years later the company went public as Kimberly-Clark.

The firm expanded internationally during the 1950s, opening plants in Mexico, Germany, and the UK. It began operations in 17 more foreign locations in the 1960s.

Before retiring in 1971, CEO Guy Minard sold the four mills that handled Kimberly-Clark's unprofitable coated-paper business and entered the paper towel and disposable diaper markets. Minard's successor, Darwin Smith, introduced Kimbies diapers in 1968, but they leaked and were withdrawn from the market. An improved version came out in 1976, followed by Huggies, a premium-priced diaper with elastic leg bands, two years later.

The company formed Midwest Express Airlines from its corporate flight department in

1984 (a business it exited in 1996). Smith moved Kimberly-Clark's headquarters from Neenah to Irving, Texas, the following year.

In 1991 Kimberly-Clark and the New York Times Company sold Spruce Falls Power and Paper. Smith retired as chairman in 1992 and was succeeded by Wayne Sanders, who was largely responsible for designing Huggies Pull-Ups (introduced in 1989). Kimberly-Clark entered a joint venture to make personal care products in Argentina in 1994 and also bought the feminine hygiene units of VP-Schickedanz (Germany) and Handan Comfort and Beauty Group (China).

Kimberly-Clark bought Scott Paper in 1995 for $9.4 billion, which boosted its market share in bathroom tissue from 5% to 31% and its share in paper towels from 6% to 18%, but led to some headaches as the company absorbed Scott's operations.

In 1997 Kimberly-Clark bought diaper operations in Spain and Portugal and disposable surgical face masks maker Tecnol Medical Products. A tissue price war in Europe and overcapacity problems led to Kimberly-Clark's 1997 announcement that year that it would reduce its workforce by 7%.

To expand its disposable medical goods business, the company agreed in 1998 to acquire Ballard Medical Products for $764 million. In 1998 and 1999 it agreed to sell 800,000 acres of timber in Alabama, Mississippi, and Tennessee, a pulp mill, and its fleet of 19 tugboats and 120 barges.

Augmenting its presence in Germany, Switzerland, and Austria, in 1999 the company paid $365 million for the tissue business of Swiss-based Attisholz Holding.

OFFICERS

Chairman and CEO: Wayne R. Sanders, age 51, $1,317,488 pay
VP and CFO: John W. Donehower, age 52, $516,800 pay
VP Law and Government Affairs and General Counsel: O. George Everbach, age 60, $526,800 pay
VP: Mark R. Hunsader
VP (HR): Bruce J. Olson
Chairman and Managing Director, Kimberly-Clark de Mexico: Claudio X. Gonzalez
Group President, Global Health Care/Nonwovens: Robert E. Abernathy, age 44
Group President, Tissue, Pulp, and Paper: Thomas J. Falk, age 40, $714,425 pay
Group President, Asia/Pacific: Paul S. Geisler, age 57
Group President, Personal Care Products: Kathi P. Seifert, age 49, $526,288 pay
Auditors: Deloitte & Touche LLP

LOCATIONS

HQ: 351 Phelps Dr., Irving, TX 75038
Phone: 972-281-1200   **Fax:** 972-281-1435
Web site: http://www.kimberly-clark.com

Kimberly-Clark has operations in the US and 39 other countries. Its products are sold in 150 countries.

1998 Sales

	$ mil.	% of total
US	8,018	62
Europe	2,471	19
Asia, Latin America & Africa	1,689	13
Canada	785	6
Adjustments	(665)	—
Total	**12,298**	**100**

PRODUCTS/OPERATIONS

1998 Sales

	$ mil.	% of total
Tissue-based products	6,706	54
Personal care products	4,578	37
Health care & other	1,047	9
Adjustments	(33)	—
Total	**12,298**	**100**

Selected Tissue-Based Products
Baby wipes (Huggies)
Bathroom and facial tissue (Kleenex, Cottonelle)
Commercial wipes (Kimwipes)
Paper napkins (Kleenex)
Paper towels (Kleenex Cottonelle, Scott)

Selected Personal Care Products
Disposable diapers (Huggies, Pull-Ups)
Feminine hygiene products (Kotex, New Freedom)

Incontinence products (Depend, Poise)

Selected Newsprint and Paper Products
Business and writing papers (Neenah)
Newsprint
Printing papers
Specialty and technical papers

Selected Medical Products
FluidShield (face masks)
Hand-Aid (wrist supports)
Jumbo-Plus (ice packs)
Paddle Strip (wound dressing)

COMPETITORS

Allegiance
Bristol-Myers Squibb
CONMED
Drypers
DSG International
Fort James
Johnson & Johnson

Medline Industries
3M
Paragon Trade Brands
Playtex
Potlatch
Procter & Gamble

HISTORICAL FINANCIALS & EMPLOYEES

NYSE symbol: KMB FYE: December 31	Annual Growth	1989	1990	1991	1992	1993	1994	1995	1996	1997	1998
Sales ($ mil.)	8.8%	5,734	6,407	6,777	7,091	6,973	7,364	13,789	13,149	12,547	12,298
Net income ($ mil.)	11.9%	424	432	508	135	511	535	33	1,404	902	1,166
Income as % of sales	—	7.4%	6.7%	7.5%	1.9%	7.3%	7.3%	0.2%	10.7%	7.2%	9.5%
Earnings per share ($)	5.3%	1.32	1.35	1.59	0.42	0.41	1.34	0.06	2.48	1.61	2.11
Stock price - FY high ($)	—	18.84	21.44	26.13	31.63	31.00	30.00	41.50	49.81	56.88	59.44
Stock price - FY low ($)	—	14.34	15.38	19.00	23.13	22.31	23.50	23.63	34.31	43.25	35.88
Stock price - FY close ($)	12.8%	18.38	21.00	25.34	29.50	25.94	25.19	41.38	47.63	49.31	54.50
P/E - high	—	14	16	16	75	76	22	692	20	35	28
P/E - low	—	11	11	12	55	54	18	394	14	27	17
Dividends per share ($)	5.9%	0.59	0.68	0.73	0.82	0.85	0.88	0.90	0.92	0.95	0.99
Book value per share ($)	1.2%	6.46	7.07	7.87	6.81	7.63	8.10	11.39	8.01	7.42	7.22
Employees	3.6%	39,664	39,954	41,286	42,902	42,131	42,707	55,341	54,800	57,000	54,700

STOCK PRICE HISTORY

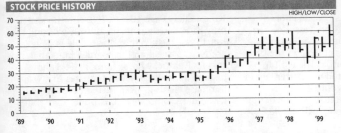

HIGH/LOW/CLOSE

1998 FISCAL YEAR-END

Debt ratio: 34.7%
Return on equity: 30.0%
Cash ($ mil.): 144
Current ratio: 0.89
Long-term debt ($ mil.): 2,068
No. of shares (mil.): 538
Dividends
  Yield: 1.8%
  Payout: 46.9%
Market value ($ mil.): 29,335

KING RANCH, INC.

OVERVIEW

King Ranch's property is Texas-sized (not really, but it is larger than all of Rhode Island). The company's 825,000-acre namesake ranch (managed from Houston corporate headquarters) still conducts the farming and ranching that made it famous, but it has beefed up its revenues with oil and gas exploration (royalties account for a majority of sales), a sod farm, retail leather goods, and tourism. Newfangled activities include "ecotours" through the ranch, home to more than 60,000 cattle and 200 animal species.

Considered the birthplace of the American ranching industry, King Ranch has also introduced the new highly fertile breed of beef cattle: the King Ranch Santa Cruz, which is one-fourth Gelbvieh, one-fourth Red Angus, and one-half Santa Gertrudis. But raising animals isn't the only thing King Ranch cottons to — this sprawl of four noncontiguous ranches is also one of the US's largest cotton producers.

Like a good western movie, some things ride into the sunset at King Ranch. The company sold its 670-acre Kentucky Thoroughbred breeding and racing farm, which has produced Triple Crown and Kentucky Derby winners. About 85 descendants of the company's founder, Richard King, own King Ranch.

HISTORY

King Ranch was founded in 1853 by former steamboat captain Richard King and his wife, Henrietta, the daughter of a Brownsville, Texas, missionary. On the advice of his friend Robert E. Lee, King used his steamboating profits and occasional strong-arm tactics to buy land — miles of flat, brush-filled, coastal plain and desert south of Corpus Christi, Texas, valued at pennies an acre.

The next year King relocated the residents of an entire drought-ravaged village to the ranch and employed them as ranch hands, known ever after as *kinenos* ("King's men"). The Kings built their homestead in 1858 at a site recommended by Lee.

King Ranch endured attacks from Union guerrillas during the Civil War and Mexican bandits after the war. Times were tough, but King was up to the challenge, always traveling armed and with outriders.

In 1867 the ranch used its famed Running W brand for the first time. After King's death in 1885, Robert Kleberg, who married King's daughter Alice, managed the 1.2 million-acre ranch for his mother-in-law. Henrietta died in 1925 and left three-fourths of the ranch to Alice. Before Robert's death in 1932, control of the ranch passed to sons Richard and Bob. In 1933 Bob negotiated an exclusive oil and gas lease with Houston-based Humble Oil, which later became part of Exxon. For protection, King Ranch incorporated two years later.

While Richard served in Congress, Bob ran the ranch. He developed the Santa Gertrudis, the first breed of cattle ever created in the US, by crossing British shorthorn cattle with Indian Brahmas. The new breed was better suited to the hot, dry South Texas climate.

Bob made King Ranch a leading breeder of quarter horses, which worked cattle, and Thoroughbreds, which he raced. He bought Kentucky Derby winner Bold Venture in 1936 and a Kentucky breeding farm in 1946. That year a King Ranch horse, Assault, won racing's Triple Crown.

When Bob died in 1974, the family asked James Clement, husband of one of the founders' great-granddaughters, to become CEO and bypassed Robert Shelton, a King relative and orphan whom Bob had raised as his own son. Shelton severed ties with the ranch in 1977 over a lawsuit he filed against Exxon, and partially won, alleging underpayment of royalties. (Clement and Shelton died within days of each other in 1994.)

Under Clement, King Ranch became a multinational corporation. In 1980 it formed King Ranch Oil and Gas to explore for and produce oil and gas in five states and the Gulf of Mexico. In 1988 Clement retired, and Kimberly-Clark executive Darwin Smith became the first CEO not related to the founders. Smith left after one year, and the reins passed to petroleum geologist Roger Jarvis and then to Jack Hunt in 1995. King Ranch opened a visitor center in 1990 and launched "ecotours" in 1994.

In 1997 the company faced a lawsuit alleging that in 1883 Robert Kleberg and Richard King conspired to cheat one of King's early partners out of property. Also that year Alice Kleberg East, the last remaining grandchild of the Kings, died at age 104. In 1998 Tio Kleberg, the only King descendant still actively working the ranch, was pushed from the saddle of daily operations to a seat on the board. King Ranch sold its Kentucky horse farm in 1998 and teamed up with Collier Enterprises that year to purchase citrus grower Turner Foods from utility holding company FPL Group.

OFFICERS

Chairman: Abraham Zaleznik
President and CEO: Jack Hunt
VP, CFO, and Treasurer: Bill Gardiner
VP Audit: Richard Nilles
VP, Secretary, and General Counsel: Steve Petti
VP Livestock: Paul Genho
Manager Personnel: Rickey Blackman

LOCATIONS

HQ: 1415 Louisiana St., Ste. 2300,
Houston, TX 77002-7352
Phone: 713-752-5700   **Fax:** 713-752-0088
Web site: http://www.king-ranch.com

King Ranch operates ranching and farming interests in South Texas as well as in Arizona, Florida, and Brazil. Its King Ranch Oil and Gas subsidiary has operations in the Gulf of Mexico, Louisiana, Mississippi, Oklahoma, and Texas.

Selected Agricultural Operations
Arizona
  6,000 acres (alfalfa, onions, and honeydew melons)
Florida
  3,300 acres (St. Augustine sod)
  12,000 acres (sugar cane)
  42,000 acres (orange and grapefruit groves)
Texas
  60,000 acres (cotton)

PRODUCTS/OPERATIONS

Selected Operations
Bluebonnet Warehousing Corporation (public warehouse facilities)
King Ranch Museum
King Ranch Nature Tour Program
King Ranch Oil and Gas, Inc.
King Ranch Saddle Shop (leather products)
Running W Citrus Limited Partnership (southern Florida citrus groves)

Thoroughbred Horses
Assault (1946 Triple Crown winner)
Bold Venture (1936 Kentucky Derby and Preakness Stakes winner)
Chicaro
Gallant Bloom
High Gun
Middleground (1950 Kentucky Derby and Belmont Stakes winner)

COMPETITORS

Alico
AZTX Cattle
Cactus Feeders
Calcot
Devon Energy
Koch
Southern States
Southwestern Irrigated Cotton
Tejon Ranch

HISTORICAL FINANCIALS & EMPLOYEES

Private company FYE: December 31	Annual Growth	1989	1990	1991	1992	1993	1994	1995	1996	1997	1998
Sales ($ mil.)	7.2%	160	160	165	330	250	250	250	250	300	300
Employees	8.0%	350	350	350	700	700	700	700	700	700	700

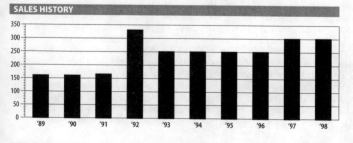

SALES HISTORY

KING WORLD PRODUCTIONS, INC.

OVERVIEW

If *Wheel of Fortune* distributor King World Productions were to buy a vowel, it would probably be an "O" for *The Oprah Winfrey Show*. Distributing Winfrey's perennially top-rated talk show provides more than 40% of the company's revenues; another 39% comes from distributing the nation's #1 and #2 game shows, *Wheel of Fortune* and *Jeopardy!*, respectively. These three are the US's highest-rated syndicated daily shows and are seen in virtually every US TV market. King World, based in Los Angeles, also produces and distributes *Inside Edition, The Roseanne Show, Hollywood Squares,* and *The Martin Short Show* (debuting in the fall of 1999). In addition, it owns a library of more than 60 movies and 200 TV shows.

The company markets its shows outside the US and develops new shows for foreign markets through its King World International subsidiary. It also sells advertising time (mainly in the shows King World distributes) through King World Media Sales and produces children's programming through King World Kids. Subsidiary King World Direct produces infomercials and develops direct-response marketing campaigns.

The King family, including chairman Roger and CEO Michael, owns about 23% of the company; Oprah Winfrey, nearly 6%. The company will soon be part of the Tiffany Network following its acquisition by CBS.

HISTORY

Charles and Lucille King established King World Productions in 1964 to syndicate films and TV programs to TV stations. They began by acquiring rights to distribute reruns, such as those of the *Little Rascals*. Charles' sons Roger and Michael took over the business after his death in 1973. In lean times they worked out of their kitchen, and Michael parked cars for extra cash.

In 1978 the Kings bought subdistribution rights to game shows *Joker's Wild* and *Tic Tac Dough*. After a failed attempt to distribute a talk show in 1982, the Kings returned to game shows, paying Merv Griffin a $50,000 advance for the rights to syndicate *Wheel of Fortune* in evening time slots. Through aggressive selling, heavy advertising support, and careful promotion of letter-turner Vanna White, *Wheel* began an astounding reign as the top game show.

In 1984 King World nearly tripled its fees for *Wheel*, by then broadcast over 181 stations, and launched *Jeopardy!*, a remake of the successful network game show also acquired from Griffin. It went public the same year and acquired rights to the Leo A. Gutman library of films and TV series, which included *Branded* and the *Charlie Chan* and *Mr. Moto* film series.

Heavy spending on market research paid off, helping the company customize sales pitches to TV stations, select shows for syndication, and build confidence among TV program producers. Consequently, the producer of *The Oprah Winfrey Show* chose King World to launch *Oprah* nationally in 1986. By the end of the year, *Wheel* and *Jeopardy!* were the top two syndicated TV shows, and *Oprah* entered the top 10. In 1988 King World bought the CBS-TV affiliate in Buffalo, New York.

Along with its successes were several minor failures, including *Headline Chasers, Rock 'n Roll Evening News,* and *Instant Recall*. King World wrote off its 1990 investment in Financial News Network in 1991, when FNN failed. King World launched its first in-house production in 1989 with *Inside Edition*. Other productions had limited runs: *Arts & Entertainment Revue* (1990-92) and a new *Candid Camera* series (1991-92). The company entered children's programming in 1992 with the cartoon *Wild West C.O.W.-Boys of Moo Mesa*. The next year it agreed to produce infomercials for Sears and launched *Inside Edition* spinoff *American Journal* and *The Les Brown Show* (which was soon replaced by *Rolonda*).

In 1995 the company sold its CBS-TV affiliate. That year media master Turner Broadcasting talked about, then decided against, acquiring King World. The potential suitor in 1996 was Ronald Perelman's New World Communications, but that deal also failed to materialize, and King World started an alliance with Chicago publisher and broadcaster Tribune by taking over distribution of *The Geraldo Rivera Show* (which the host gave up to join NBC in 1997).

King World successfully weathered the growing competition brought on by broadcast deregulation. In 1998 it announced that *Wheel of Fortune* and *Jeopardy!* were renewed until the year 2004. Also that year the company launched a pair of new shows: a talk show hosted by comedian Roseanne and a new version of *Hollywood Squares*. The company also signed an agreement with Oprah Winfrey to distribute her show through the 2001-02 season. In 1999 CBS agreed to buy the company for $2.5 billion.

OFFICERS

Chairman: Roger King, age 54, $5,311,663 pay
VC, CEO, and Interim President: Michael King, age 50, $5,311,663 pay
EVP Research: Moira Farrell
SVP and CFO: Steven A. LoCascio, age 40
SVP Business Affairs and General Counsel: Jonathan Birkhahn, age 45
SVP Corporate Communications: Randi Cone
SVP Network Programming: Merrill Karpf
SVP Strategic Planning and Acquisitions: Robert King
SVP Production: Andy Lassner
SVP Administration: Robert V. Madden, age 50
President, King World Media Sales: Steven R. Hirsch, age 49, $725,000 pay
President, First-Run Programming and Production: Andrew Friendly, age 47, $645,000 pay
President, Merchandising and Licensing: Kevin Allyn
President, King World International: Fred Cohen, age 54
President, Advertising and Promotion: Donald Prijatel,
Director Human Resources: Brenda Young
VP and Corporate Secretary: Diana King, age 48
Auditors: Arthur Andersen LLP

LOCATIONS

HQ: 12400 Wilshire Blvd., Ste. 1200, Los Angeles, CA 90025
Phone: 310-826-1108　　**Fax:** 310-207-2179
Web site: http://www.kingworld.com

1998 Sales

	% of total
US	94
Other countries	6
Total	**100**

PRODUCTS/OPERATIONS

1998 Sales

	% of total
The Oprah Winfrey Show	42
Wheel of Fortune	21
Jeopardy	18
Inside Edition	7
American Journal	4
King World Direct	1
Other	7
Total	**100**

First-Run Syndicated Programs
American Journal
(discontinued after 1997-98 season)
Hollywood Squares
Inside Edition
Jeopardy!
The Oprah Winfrey Show
The Roseanne Show
Wheel of Fortune

Program Library
Branded
Charlie Chan
The East Side Kids
The Guns of Will Sonnett
Little Rascals
Mr. Moto
Sherlock Holmes
Topper

COMPETITORS

ABC	News Corp.
A&E Networks	Pearson
Carsey-Werner	Sony
CBS	Time Warner
dick clark productions	Tribune
DreamWorks SKG	Universal Studios
Kushner-Locke	Viacom
NBC	Walt Disney

HOW MUCH

NYSE symbol: KWP FYE: August 31	Annual Growth	1989	1990	1991	1992	1993	1994	1995	1996	1997	1998
Sales ($ mil.)	6.2%	396	454	476	503	474	481	574	663	671	684
Net income ($ mil.)	6.7%	76	84	91	95	102	88	117	150	143	136
Income as % of sales	—	19.2%	18.5%	19.0%	18.9%	21.5%	18.4%	20.4%	22.6%	21.4%	19.9%
Earnings per share ($)	6.6%	1.01	1.08	1.15	1.22	1.33	1.17	1.57	1.99	1.91	1.79
Stock price - FY high ($)	—	11.21	15.01	17.25	15.63	19.25	22.06	22.25	22.56	20.47	30.81
Stock price - FY Low ($)	—	6.88	9.06	10.06	10.81	12.00	16.63	16.25	16.38	17.00	19.19
Stock price - FY close ($)	7.5%	10.92	10.00	14.00	12.31	18.56	18.88	19.00	17.63	19.88	21.00
P/E - high	—	11	14	15	13	14	19	14	11	11	17
P/E - low	—	7	8	9	9	9	14	10	8	9	11
Dividends per share ($)	—	0.00	0.00	0.00	0.00	0.00	0.00	0.00	0.00	0.10	0.00
Book value per share ($)	34.9%	0.82	1.94	3.17	4.50	5.28	6.24	7.83	9.89	10.70	12.18
Employees	3.0%	319	449	474	246	405	430	430	490	487	418

STOCK PRICE HISTORY

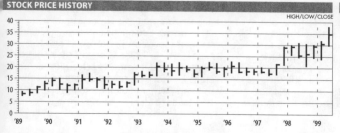

HIGH/LOW/CLOSE

1998 FISCAL YEAR-END

Debt ratio: 0.0%
Return on equity: 15.4%
Cash ($ mil.): 189
Current ratio: 3.18
Long-term debt ($ mil.): 0
No. of shares (mil.): 72
Dividends
　Yield: —
　Payout: —
Market value ($ mil.): 1,520

KMART CORPORATION

OVERVIEW

Like an overstuffed shopping cart in a narrow aisle, Kmart hasn't been easy to turn around, but the once shaky retail chain (#3 in the US, behind Wal-Mart and Sears) is beginning to get on a roll. Based in Troy, Michigan, Kmart sells to low- and middle-income families through about 2,160 discount stores in all 50 states, Puerto Rico, the US Virgin Islands, and Guam.

As part of its turnaround, the firm has been converting old Kmart stores into Big Kmart outlets, which feature an expanded selection of merchandise, including small grocery sections dubbed "Kmart Pantry." About 190 stores too small to be converted will be remodeled as

"best of" Kmart, featuring only the best-selling merchandise. Among the company's retail operations are its 100-plus Super Kmart stores, which are similar to Wal-Mart's Supercenter stores and offer a full line of groceries and general merchandise.

Another factor greasing Kmart's wheels is its successful stable of private-label brands, led by the Martha Stewart Everyday home fashion line. In addition to expanding the Martha Stewart brand into new areas such as patio furniture and gardening tools, Kmart is revamping other house brands, which include Sesame Street children's clothes and Route 66 apparel.

HISTORY

Sebastian Kresge and John McCrorey opened five-and-dime stores in Memphis and Detroit in 1897. When the partners split two years later, Kresge got Detroit and McCrorey took Memphis. By the time Kresge incorporated as S. S. Kresge Company in 1912, it had become the second-largest dime store chain in the US, with 85 stores. Kresge expanded rapidly in the next several decades, forming S. S. Kresge, Ltd., in 1929 to operate stores in Canada. In the late 1920s and 1930s, the company opened stores in suburban shopping centers. By the 1950s Kresge was one of the largest general merchandise retailers in the US.

A marketing study prompted management to enter discount retailing in 1958, and three unprofitable locations were transformed into Jupiter Discount stores in 1961. The company judged this a success and opened the first Kmart discount store in Detroit in 1962; by 1966 the company had more than 160 Kmart stores. Kresge formed a joint venture with G. J. Coles & Coy (later Coles Myer) to operate Kmart stores in Australia (1968). The company expanded the Kmart format swiftly in the 1970s, opening more than 270 stores in 1976 alone. With about 95% of its sales coming from Kmart stores, the company changed its name to Kmart in 1977.

Kmart diversified during the 1980s and early 1990s, adding various retailers, including Walden Book Company, then the #1 US bookstore chain, and Builders Square (formerly Home Centers of America) in 1984; PayLess Drug Stores Northwest in 1985; PACE Membership Warehouse in 1989; The Sports Authority in 1990; a 90% stake in OfficeMax by 1991; and the Borders bookstore chain in 1992.

Meanwhile, in 1987 the company sold most of its remaining Kresge and Jupiter locations in the US to McCrory's, the chain started by Kresge's former partner. In 1990 Kmart launched its one-stop Super Kmart Centers.

In 1994 and 1995, amid falling earnings, the company spun off OfficeMax and The Sports Authority; sold the PACE operations to Wal-Mart, its 21.5% interest in Coles Meyer to that company, and its US automotive service centers to Penske; and divested its Borders Group to the public. In 1995 CEO Joseph Antonini — architect of the diversification strategy — was replaced by Floyd Hall. More than 200 US stores were closed.

The company sold Kmart Mexico, a joint venture with El Puerto de Liverpool, and an 87.5% stake in Kmart Canada in 1997. Also in 1997 it unveiled the new Big Kmart format, increasing the emphasis on home fashions and children's goods and adding groceries. The company also sold woebegone 162-store Builders Square to Leonard Green & Partners (owners of the Hechinger chain) for a mere $10 million, but retained a $761 million liability for the stores' lease obligations (when Hechinger filed for bankruptcy in 1999, Kmart announced it would likely assume the obligations of 115 stores).

Hudson's Bay Co. bought all of Kmart Canada in 1998 for about $168 million. Also that year Kmart began offering merchandise online. Kmart also opened 45 outlets (acquired from bankrupt Venture Stores) as new Big Kmart stores in 1998. As part of the company's effort to expand its grocery selections, in 1999 it signed a deal with food distributors SUPER-VALU and Fleming to supply dry groceries and other goods to all of its stores.

OFFICERS

Chairman, President, and CEO: Floyd Hall, age 60, $2,679,000 pay
Vice Chairman: Michael Bozic, age 58
EVP and President, Super Kmart:
 Laurence L. Anderson, age 57, $735,000 pay
EVP Human Resources and Administration:
 Warren F. Cooper, age 54, $705,000 pay
EVP Store Operations: Donald W. Keeble, age 50, $775,000 pay
EVP and General Counsel: Anthony N. Palizzi, age 56
SVP and General Merchandise Manager Hardlines:
 William N. Anderson, age 51
SVP and CFO: Martin E. Welch III, age 50
SVP Merchandise Planning and Replenishment:
 Ernest L. Heether, age 53
SVP Store Operations: Paul J. Hueber, age 50
SVP General Merchandise Manager Home:
 Cecil B. Kearse, age 46
SVP and General Merchandise Manager, Health and Beauty Care, Pharmacy, Consumables: Jerry J. Kuske, age 47
SVP Logistics: James P. Mixon, age 54
SVP and General Merchandise Manager Apparel:
 E. Jackson Smailes, age 56
SVP Global Operations, Corporate Brands and Quality Assurance: William D. Underwood, age 58
Auditors: PricewaterhouseCoopers LLP

LOCATIONS

HQ: 3100 W. Big Beaver Rd., Troy, MI 48084
Phone: 248-643-1000   **Fax:** 248-643-5636
Web site: http://www.kmart.com

Kmart operates more than 2,160 retail stores in all 50 states and Guam, Puerto Rico, and the US Virgin Islands.

PRODUCTS/OPERATIONS

1999 Stores

	No.
Big Kmart	1,840
Traditional Kmart	219
Super Kmart	102
Total	**2,161**

Selected Private Labels
American Fare (health care products)
B.A.S.S. (fishing gear)
BenchTop (tools)
Jaclyn Smith (ladies apparel)
Kathy Ireland collection (ladies apparel)
Martha Stewart Everyday (home fashions)
Penske Auto Center (automotive)
Route 66 (casual wear and shoes)
Sesame Street (kid's clothing and merchandise)
Thom McAn (shoes)
White-Westinghouse (small appliances)

COMPETITORS

Ames	Montgomery Ward
AutoZone	Ross Stores
Bed Bath & Beyond	Sears
Best Buy	Service Merchandise
BJs Wholesale Club	Target Stores
Circuit City	TJX
Costco Companies	Toys "R" Us
Dollar General	Walgreen
J. C. Penney	Wal-Mart
Linens 'n Things	

HISTORICAL FINANCIALS & EMPLOYEES

NYSE symbol: KM FYE: January 31	Annual Growth	1990	1991	1992	1993	1994	1995	1996	1997	1998	1999
Sales ($ mil.)	1.5%	29,533	32,070	34,580	37,724	34,156	34,025	34,389	31,437	32,183	33,674
Net income ($ mil.)	5.4%	323	756	859	941	(974)	296	(571)	(220)	249	518
Income as % of sales	—	1.1%	2.4%	2.5%	2.5%	—	0.9%	—	—	0.8%	1.5%
Earnings per share ($)	2.5%	0.81	1.89	2.02	2.06	(2.40)	0.67	(1.25)	(0.46)	0.51	1.01
Stock price - FY high ($)	—	22.44	18.50	25.62	28.12	25.75	19.75	16.25	16.00	15.25	20.87
Stock price - FY low ($)	—	16.19	11.69	15.25	20.87	19.25	12.50	5.75	6.00	10.25	10.75
Stock price - FY close ($)	0.6%	16.62	15.50	24.50	23.25	19.62	13.62	5.87	11.12	11.00	17.56
P/E - high	—	28	10	13	14	—	29	—	—	30	21
P/E - low	—	20	6	8	10	—	19	—	—	20	11
Dividends per share ($)	(100.0%)	0.78	0.85	0.88	0.91	0.95	0.96	0.61	0.00	0.00	0.00
Book value per share ($)	(0.3%)	12.45	13.47	14.63	15.71	12.10	12.86	10.85	10.45	11.12	12.12
Employees	(3.0%)	365,000	373,000	349,000	358,000	344,000	348,000	307,000	265,000	261,000	278,525

STOCK PRICE HISTORY

HIGH/LOW/CLOSE

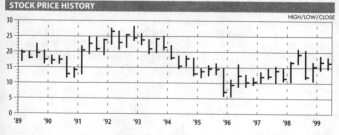

1999 FISCAL YEAR-END

Debt ratio: 30.5%
Return on equity: 8.7%
Cash ($ mil.): 710
Current ratio: 2.12
Long-term debt ($ mil.): 2,629
No. of shares (mil.): 493
Dividends
 Yield: —
 Payout: —
Market value ($ mil.): 8,663

KNIGHT RIDDER

OVERVIEW

The top story for Knight Ridder, the nation's #2 newspaper chain (behind Gannett), is the Internet. The fast-growing influence of the World Wide Web convinced the firm to move its headquarters from Miami to San Jose, California, to capitalize on progressive thinking in Silicon Valley. Knight Ridder publishes 31 daily newspapers, including *The Philadelphia Inquirer, The Miami Herald,*, the *San Jose Mercury News, The Kansas City Star,* and the *Fort Worth Star-Telegram*. It also owns 21 non-daily papers.

Diversification led the company into cable and specialized information services, but CEO Anthony Ridder (great-grandson of Ridder Publications founder Herman Ridder) has shed the company's non-newspaper operations, taking the firm back to its roots. Seen as a pioneer in online newspapering, Knight Ridder is expanding its electronic services as a way to catch advertisers who are expected to leave hard-copy classifieds in favor of the Internet. Hopes are that its online activities will turn a profit within a few years. The firm offers about 45 Web sites (29 of which are newspaper related) under its Real Cities umbrella.

HISTORY

Knight Ridder began in 1974 with the merger of Knight Newspapers and Ridder Publications, then the #2 and #3 newspaper groups by circulation.

Knight Newspapers began in 1903 when lawyer-turned-editor Charles Knight purchased the *Akron Beacon Journal*. He died in 1933, leaving the paper to his sons, Jack and Jim. With their guidance the company grew to include 16 metropolitan dailies, including *The Miami Herald* (1937), the *Detroit Free Press* (1940), and *The Philadelphia Inquirer* (1969).

Ridder Publications was founded in 1892 when Herman Ridder bought a German-language newspaper, the *Staats-Zeitung* in New York. He expanded in 1926 with the purchase of the *Journal of Commerce*, a New York shipping daily founded in 1827. Over the next 50 years the company grew to 19 dailies and eight weeklies, mostly in the West.

After the Knight-Ridder merger, Knight's Lee Hills became chairman and CEO, and Ridder's Bernard Ridder became VC.

During the 1970s and 1980s, the company expanded into TV, radio, and book publishing. The company bought HP Books in 1979 (sold in 1987) and formed TKR Cable with TCI in 1981. A year later Knight Ridder launched VU/TEXT (online news retrieval), followed in 1983 by Viewtron, America's first consumer videotext system. In 1988 the firm bought DIALOG, the world's largest online full-text service, from Lockheed. Broadcast properties were sold in 1989.

A newspaper battle between Knight Ridder's *Detroit Free Press* and Gannett's *The Detroit News* in the 1980s ended with the two papers signing a joint operating agreement in 1989 and merging some operations.

Knight Ridder joined the Tribune Company (with whom it operates a news service) in 1992 to deliver business news electronically to PC users. The next year the *San Jose Mercury News,* working with America Online, became the first newspaper to integrate online services with a daily paper. Purchases in 1993 included Data-Star (European online service), Equinet (Australian online service), and EFE-COM (Spain, financial news; renamed KRF/Iberia).

The company sold the *Journal of Commerce* in 1995. Chairman and CEO James Batten died of cancer that year and was succeeded by Anthony Ridder, the first Ridder family member to run the company. Ridder immediately began to sharpen the focus on newspapers. In 1996 Knight Ridder formed MediaStream, which develops archives for Web sites. That year the company sold its financial news unit, Knight Ridder Financial, to Global Financial Information (part of the investor group of Welsh, Carson, Anderson & Stowe).

In 1997 the firm bought four newspapers from Walt Disney (including *The Kansas City Star* and the *Fort Worth Star-Telegram*) and swapped its Boulder, Colorado newspaper for two California newspapers. It also sold several newspapers and sold the Knight Ridder Information unit to M.A.I.D plc. Knight Ridder moved its headquarters to San Jose, California, in 1998. That year it bought Hills Newspapers, a group of weeklies in California, and sold its interest in TKR Cable to partner AT&T Broadband & Internet Services. It joined other powerhouse media companies, including Gannett and Times-Mirror, in 1998 to form Classified Ventures, an online real estate and auto classifieds service.

OFFICERS

Chairman and CEO: P. Anthony Ridder, age 58, $1,225,242 pay
VP Finance and CFO: Ross Jones, age 56, $671,133 pay
VP Human Resources: Mary Jean Connors, age 46, $568,670 pay
VP Operations: Frank McComas, age 53, $672,271 pay
VP Operations: Steve Rossi, age 49, $458,551 pay (prior to promotion)
VP and Chief Information Officer: David Starr, age 48
VP and Controller: Gary R. Effren, age 42
VP Corporate Relations and Secretary: Polk Laffoon IV, age 53
VP Finance and Advanced Technology: Tally C. Liu, age 48
VP and General Counsel: Karen Stevenson, age 48
VP Marketing: Mike Rogers
VP News: Jerry Ceppos
VP News: Marty Claus, age 50
VP Production and Facilities: Larry D. Marbert, age 45
VP Research: Virginia Dodge Fielder, age 50
VP Senior Labor and Employment Counsel: Marshall Anstandig, age 50
VP and Treasurer: Alan G. Silverglat, age 52
Auditors: Ernst & Young LLP

LOCATIONS

HQ: 50 W. San Fernando St., San Jose, CA 95113
Phone: 408-938-7700   **Fax:** 408-938-7766
Web site: http://www.kri.com

Knight Ridder has newspapers in 28 markets in 17 states.

PRODUCTS/OPERATIONS

1998 Sales

	$ mil.	% of total
Advertising	2,363	76
Circulation	588	19
Other	141	5
Total	**3,092**	**100**

Selected Investments and Joint Ventures
Classified Ventures (online classifieds venture with the Tribune, Gannett, Times-Mirror, Washington Post, and three others)
Detroit Newspaper Agency (50%, joint venture with Gannett)
InfiNet (33%, Internet access provider)
Newspapers First (31%, advertising sales)
Ponderay Newsprint Co. (14%, newsprint mill in Washington)
Seattle Times Co. (49.5%, newspapers)
Southeast Paper Manufacturing Co. (33%, newsprint mill in Georgia)
Tesserae Information Systems, Inc. (33%, software producer)

COMPETITORS

ABC
Advance Publications
Belo
Associated Press
Cox Enterprises
Dow Jones
E. W. Scripps
Gannett
Hearst
Media General
New York Times
News Corp.
Reuters
Thomson Corporation
Times Mirror
Tribune
Washington Post

HISTORICAL FINANCIALS & EMPLOYEES

NYSE symbol: KRI FYE: December 31	Annual Growth	1989	1990	1991	1992	1993	1994	1995	1996	1997	1998
Sales ($ mil.)	3.5%	2,268	2,305	2,237	2,330	2,451	2,649	2,752	2,775	2,877	3,092
Net income ($ mil.)	8.2%	180	149	132	41	148	171	160	268	413	366
Income as % of sales	—	7.9%	6.5%	5.9%	1.8%	6.0%	6.5%	5.8%	9.7%	14.4%	11.8%
Earnings per share ($)	8.9%	1.73	1.47	1.28	0.37	1.34	1.58	1.60	2.75	4.08	3.73
Stock price - FY high ($)	—	29.19	29.00	28.75	32.06	32.50	30.50	33.31	42.00	57.13	59.63
Stock price - FY low ($)	—	21.44	18.50	21.88	25.75	25.31	23.25	25.25	29.88	35.75	40.50
Stock price - FY close ($)	6.4%	29.19	22.88	26.44	29.00	29.88	25.25	31.25	38.25	52.00	51.13
P/E - high	—	17	20	22	87	24	19	21	15	14	16
P/E - low	—	12	13	17	70	19	15	16	11	9	11
Dividends per share ($)	3.1%	0.61	0.66	0.70	0.70	0.70	0.72	0.74	0.77	0.80	0.80
Book value per share ($)	10.1%	8.91	9.05	10.72	10.75	11.33	11.58	11.43	12.12	18.99	21.21
Employees	0.5%	21,000	21,000	20,000	20,000	20,000	21,000	22,800	24,000	22,000	22,000

STOCK PRICE HISTORY HIGH/LOW/CLOSE

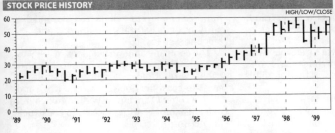

1998 FISCAL YEAR-END
Debt ratio: 44.4%
Return on equity: 22.0%
Cash ($ mil.): 27
Current ratio: 0.80
Long-term debt ($ mil.): 1,329
No. of shares (mil.): 78
Dividends
  Yield: 1.6%
  Payout: 21.4%
Market value ($ mil.): 4,005

KOCH INDUSTRIES, INC.

OVERVIEW

Among really big privately owned businesses, Koch (pronounced "coke") is the real thing. Wichita, Kansas-based Koch Industries, which has extensive operations in oil and gas, agriculture, and chemicals, is the second-largest private company in the US, after grain merchant Cargill.

Koch's petroleum operations include the purchasing, gathering, and trading of crude oil. The company's two refineries in Minnesota and Texas process about 540,000 barrels of crude a day, making it a leading producer of gasoline and petrochemicals. Koch also owns gas gathering systems and about 35,000 miles of pipeline between Texas and Canada, and it purchases, processes, and markets natural gas liquids.

Agricultural businesses include Purina Mills, the leading commercial animal feed producer in the US, and cattle ranches in Kansas, Montana, and Texas. Koch expanded its cattle-feeding operations in 1998, but pulled back as beef prices stayed low, selling four feedlots in 1998 and 1999.

Through its 50% ownership of the KoSa joint venture with Mexico's Saba family, Koch is one of the world's leading polyester producers. Koch also produces paraxylene and high-octane missile fuels. Other lines of businesses include asphalt production, dry bulk ocean transport of minerals, and the manufacture of equipment for the chemical industry.

Slumping crude oil, cattle, and hog prices have hammered Koch in 1998 and 1999, and the company has laid off several hundred employees. The family-run enterprise is owned by brothers Charles and David Koch.

HISTORY

Fred Koch grew up poor in Texas and worked his way through MIT. In 1928 Koch developed a process to refine more gasoline from crude oil, but when he tried to market his invention, the major oil companies sued him for patent infringement. Koch eventually won the lawsuits (after 15 years in court), but the controversy made it tough to attract many US customers. In 1929 Koch took his process to the USSR but, disenchanted with Stalinism, he returned home to become a founding member of the anticommunist John Birch Society.

Koch launched Wood River Oil & Refining in Illinois (1940) and bought the Rock Island refinery in Oklahoma (1947). Though he would later sell the refineries, he folded the remaining purchasing and gathering network into Rock Island Oil & Refining.

After Koch's death in 1967, his 32-year-old son Charles took the helm and renamed the company Koch Industries in honor of his father. With the help of his father's confidant, Sterling Varner, Charles began a series of acquisitions, adding petrochemical and oil trading service operations.

During the 1980s Koch was thrust into various arenas, legal and political. Charles' brother David, also a Koch Industries executive, ran for US vice president on the Libertarian ticket in 1980. That year the other two Koch brothers, Frederick and William (David's fraternal twin), launched a takeover attempt, but Charles retained control, and William was fired from his job as VP.

The brothers traded lawsuits, and in a 1983 settlement Charles and David bought out the dissident family members for just over $1 billion. William and Frederick continued to challenge their brothers in court, claiming they had been shortchanged in the deal (the two estranged brothers eventually lost their case in 1998). In 1987 they even sued their mother over her distribution of trust fund money.

Despite this legal wrangling, Koch Industries continued to expand, purchasing a Corpus Christi, Texas, refinery in 1981. It expanded its pipeline system, buying Bigheart Pipe Line in Oklahoma (1986) and two systems from Santa Fe Southern Pacific (1988).

In 1991 Koch purchased the Corpus Christi marine terminal, pipelines, and gathering systems of Scurlock Permian (a unit of Ashland Oil). In 1992 the company bought United Gas Pipe Line (renamed Koch Gateway Pipeline) and its pipeline system extending from Texas to Florida. Koch acquired USX-Delhi Group, a natural gas processor and transporter, in 1997.

In 1998 Koch bought Purina Mills, the largest US producer of animal feed, and formed the KoSa joint venture with Mexico's Saba family to buy Hoechst's Trevira polyester unit. Lethargic energy and livestock prices in 1998 and 1999, however, led Koch to lay off several hundred employees, sell its feedlots, and divest portions of its natural gas gathering and pipeline systems.

The company announced plans in 1999 to take advantage of its pipeline assets by contributing right-of-way for an 11,000-mile coast-to-coast fiber-optic network. Koch and PF Telecom of Vancouver, Washington, agreed to form a joint venture, PF.Net, to construct the network.

Chairman and CEO: Charles G. Koch
President and COO: William W. Hanna
EVP: Richard H. Fink
EVP Chemical Technology: David H. Koch
EVP Finance and Administration and Treasurer:
  F. Lynn Markel
EVP International: Joe W. Moeller
EVP Operations: Bill R. Caffey
EVP and Special Counsel: Donald L. Cordes
SVP Capital Services: Paul W. Brooks
SVP Chemicals: Cy S. Nobles
SVP Gas Liquids: S. E. Odell
SVP Crude Oil and Energy Services: Kyle D. Vann
VP Agriculture: D. E. Watson
VP Capital Services: J. C. Pittenger
VP Chemical Technology: John M. Van Gelder
VP Human Resources: Paul Wheeler
VP Information Technology: M. Brad Hall
VP, Koch Industries and Koch Petroleum Group:
  Seth Vance
Auditors: KPMG LLP

LOCATIONS

HQ: 4111 E. 37th St. North, Wichita, KS 67220-3203
Phone: 316-828-5500   **Fax:** 316-828-5739
Web site: http://www.kochind.com

Koch Industries operates worldwide.

PRODUCTS/OPERATIONS

Selected Operations
Koch Agriculture Group
  Koch Beef Company (livestock and ranches)
  Purina Mills (animal feed)
Koch Capital Services Group (financial and capital
  market management)
Koch Chemicals Group
  Koch Chemicals (paraxylene)
    KoSa (polyester, 50%)
  Koch Microelectronic Service Company
    (semiconductor chemicals)
  Koch Specialty Chemicals (high-octane missile fuel)
Koch Chemical Technology Group (specialty equipment
  and services for refining and chemical industry)
Koch Energy Group
  Koch Energy Trading
  Koch Gateway Pipeline Company
  Koch Midstream Enterprises (gas gathering systems
    and pipelines)
Koch Gas Liquids Group
Koch Mineral Services Group (bulk ocean transportation
  and fuel supply)
Koch Petroleum Group (crude oil and refined products)
  Koch Materials Company (asphalt)
Koch Ventures Group (investment in noncore
  businesses)

COMPETITORS

ADM	EOTT Energy	Royal
Ashland	Partners	Dutch/Shell
Avista	Exxon	Southern
BP Amoco	Imperial Oil	Company
Cargill	Kerr-McGee	Statoil Energy
Chevron	King Ranch	Sunoco
Coastal	Lyondell	Tosco
Columbia Energy	Chemical	Tractebel
Conoco	Mobil	Ultramar
Continental	Motiva	Diamond
Grain	Enterprises	Shamrock
Duke Energy	Occidental	USX-Marathon
Dynegy	Peabody Group	UtiliCorp
Elf Aquitaine	PEMEX	Williams
Equilon	PG&E	Companies
Enterprises	Phillips	
Enron	Petroleum	
Entergy	Reliant Energy	

HISTORICAL FINANCIALS & EMPLOYEES

Private company FYE: December 31	Annual Growth	1989	1990	1991	1992	1993	1994	1995	1996	1997	1998
Sales ($ mil.)	9.1%	16,000	17,190	19,250	19,914	20,000	23,725	25,200	30,000	36,200	35,000
Employees	8.0%	8,000	9,300	10,000	12,000	12,000	12,000	12,500	13,000	15,600	16,000

SALES HISTORY

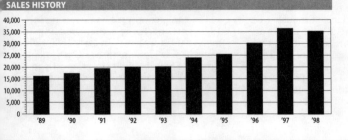

KOCH

KOHL'S CORPORATION

OVERVIEW

Department store operators don't look forward to treading on hot Kohl's. The Menomonee Falls, Wisconsin-based chain operates more than 230 family-oriented department stores (primarily in the Midwest and the Mid-Atlantic). Targeting middle-income customers, it sells moderately priced apparel and shoes for men, women, and children; accessories; and housewares.

Kohl's has become one of the fastest-growing and most successful US department store chains by offering convenience and brand-name merchandise at low prices. The company has merchandising relationships that allow it to carry top brands not typically available to discounters. It sells them at lower prices than department stores by controlling costs. Its one-floor stores (averaging about 85,000 sq. ft.) have fewer departments than

full-line department stores and cost-saving features such as central registers. By locating stores primarily in strip malls, Kohl's benefits by receiving cheaper rents; its customers benefit by having easier access to its stores. Kohl's carries brands such as NIKE, Haggar, Springmaid, and Levi's. Its private-label lines, including the Genuine Sonoma brand, account for about 20% of sales.

After several years of expanding on its native midwestern turf and in the mid-Atlantic area, Kohl's is aggressively moving west, opening its first stores in the St. Louis, Denver, and Dallas-Fort Worth areas. It is also renovating 33 former Caldor stores in the New York City area. The company plans to have 300 stores by the end of 2000.

Chairman William Kellogg owns about 7% of the company.

HISTORY

Max Kohl (father of Sen. Herbert Kohl of Wisconsin) opened his first grocery store in Milwaukee in the late 1920s, and over the years he and his three sons developed it into a chain; in 1938 Kohl's incorporated.

Kohl opened a department store (half apparel, half hard goods) in 1962 next door to a Kohl's grocery. In the mid-1960s he hired William Kellogg, a twentysomething buyer in the basement discount department at Milwaukee's Boston Store, for his expertise in budget retailing. Kellogg came from a retailing family (his father was VP of merchandising at the Boston Store; the younger Kellogg had joined that firm out of high school). Kohl and Kellogg began developing the pattern for the store, carving out a niche between upscale department stores and discounters (offering department store quality at discount store prices).

The Kohl family entered real estate development in 1970, building the largest shopping center in the Milwaukee area. By 1972 the family's 65 food stores and five department stores were generating about $90 million in yearly sales. That year the Kohls sold 80% of the two operations to British-American Tobacco's Brown & Williamson Industries division (later called BATUS), the first in a string of department store acquisitions that would eventually include Marshall Field's and Saks Fifth Avenue.

BATUS bought the rest of Kohl's in 1978. Herb and Allen Kohl left the business to concentrate on real estate and politics, and Kellogg was named president and CEO. The next

year BATUS separated the food and department store operations, and it eventually sold the food store chain (to A&P in 1983).

Kohl's discount image did not fit in with BATUS's other retail operations, so it decided to sell the department store chain. In 1986 Kellogg and two other executives, with the backing of mall developers Herbert and Melvin Simon, led an LBO to acquire the chain's 40 stores and a distribution center; annual sales were about $288 million.

Two years later Kohl's acquired 26 Main-Street department stores from Federated Department Stores, moving the company into new cities such as Chicago and Detroit. When Kohl's went public in 1992, it had 81 stores in six states, and sales topped $1 billion.

In 1995 Kohl's completed its phaseout of electronics. The next year it began its mid-Atlantic expansion by opening stores in North Carolina. Sales topped $2 billion in fiscal 1997, and same-store sales were up more than 11%. Early in 1997 the firm acquired a former Bradlees store to enter New Jersey and later opened stores in Delaware, New York State, Philadelphia, and Washington, DC.

The chain continued its expansion in 1998, entering Tennessee and building its mid-Atlantic presence. In early 1999 Kohl's named Larry Montgomery as CEO, and it agreed to buy about 30 stores, mostly in the New York City area, from bankrupt Caldor.

OFFICERS

Chairman: William S. Kellogg, age 55, $1,482,732 pay
VC and CEO: R. Lawrence Montgomery, age 50, $699,054 pay (prior to promotion)
President: Kevin B. Mansell, age 46, $547,800 pay (prior to promotion)
COO and Secretary: John F. Herma, age 51, $779,879 pay
EVP Merchandise Planning and Logistics: Caryn A. Blanc, age 41
EVP, Chief Information Officer: John J. Lesko, age 46
EVP, General Merchandise Manager and Product Development: Richard Leto, age 47
EVP, CFO: Arlene Meier, age 47
EVP, General Merchandise Manager: Jack E. Moore Jr., age 44
EVP, Regional Director of Stores and Store Administration: Jeffrey Rusinow, age 44
EVP Human Resources: Donald H. Sharpin, age 50
EVP Marketing: Gary Vasques, age 51
Auditors: Ernst & Young LLP

LOCATIONS

HQ: N56 W17000 Ridgewood Dr., Menomonee Falls, WI 53051
Phone: 414-703-7000   **Fax:** 414-703-6143
Web site: http://www.kohls.com

Kohl's has distribution centers in Menomonee Falls, Wisconsin; Findlay, Ohio; and Winchester, Virginia.

1999 Stores

	No.
Illinois	33
Ohio	31
Wisconsin	27
Pennsylvania	17
Michigan	16
Indiana	15
Minnesota	13
Virginia	9
Maryland	8
North Carolina	8
Kansas	7
Other states	36
Total	**213**

PRODUCTS/OPERATIONS

1999 Sales

	% of total
Apparel	62
Accessories & shoes	18
Soft home & housewares	12
Hardlines	8
Total	**100**

COMPETITORS

Ames	J. C. Penney	Service
Belk	Kmart	Merchandise
BJs Wholesale	May	ShopKo Stores
Club	Men's Wearhouse	Syms
Bradlees	Montgomery	TJX
Dayton Hudson	Ward	Value City
Designs	Ross Stores	Wal-Mart
Dillard's	Saks Inc.	
Federated	Sears	

HISTORICAL FINANCIALS & EMPLOYEES

NYSE symbol: KSS FYE: January 31	Annual Growth	1990	1991	1992	1993	1994	1995	1996	1997	1998	1999
Sales ($ mil.)	19.9%	—	863	1,006	1,097	1,306	1,554	1,926	2,388	3,060	3,682
Net income ($ mil.)	37.6%	—	15	17	27	54	69	73	103	141	192
Income as % of sales	—	—	1.7%	1.7%	2.4%	4.1%	4.4%	3.8%	4.3%	4.6%	5.2%
Earnings per share ($)	35.6%	—	—	0.14	0.22	0.33	0.46	0.49	0.68	0.91	1.18
Stock price - FY high ($)	—	—	—	5.63	8.72	13.03	13.81	14.19	21.00	37.69	67.75
Stock price - FY low ($)	—	—	—	3.31	3.31	7.75	9.50	9.97	13.38	19.44	34.06
Stock price - FY close ($)	43.4%	—	—	5.44	8.69	12.09	10.88	14.09	19.44	34.69	67.75
P/E - high	—	—	—	40	40	39	30	29	31	41	57
P/E - low	—	—	—	24	15	23	21	20	20	21	29
Dividends per share ($)	—	—	—	0.00	0.00	0.00	0.00	0.00	0.00	0.00	0.00
Book value per share ($)	33.8%	—	—	0.95	1.47	1.79	2.27	2.78	3.50	6.05	7.34
Employees	14.8%	—	—	12,900	13,940	14,900	17,600	21,200	25,500	32,200	33,800

STOCK PRICE HISTORY

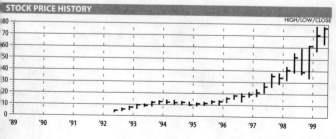

HIGH/LOW/CLOSE

1999 FISCAL YEAR-END

Debt ratio: 21.1%
Return on equity: 16.5%
Cash ($ mil.): 3
Current ratio: 2.47
Long-term debt ($ mil.): 311
No. of shares (mil.): 158
Dividends
  Yield: —
  Payout: —
Market value ($ mil.): 10,731

KPMG INTERNATIONAL

OVERVIEW

KPMG is taking off the gloves in its struggle for leadership in the bare-knuckled field of international accountancy.

The third-largest of the Big Five accounting firms (after PricewaterhouseCoopers and Andersen Worldwide), Montvale, New Jersey-based KPMG International is forging a 21st-century identity as the technological champion in its field.

Traditionally a confederation of accounting firms based in more than 150 nations, KPMG is strengthening ties among its more than 800 offices and organizing them into two groups, KPMG Americas (North and South America and Australasia) and KPMG Europe (Europe, Africa, Asia, and the Middle East). It is the only one of the Big Five whose practice is larger outside the US.

Even more radically, KPMG plans to take its US consulting business public. KPMG, the most Internet-savvy of the accounting/consulting firms, hopes that a major investment in online-related services will distinguish it from the pack. Cisco Systems is investing about $1 billion for a 20% stake in the new entity (should it receive regulatory clearance).

KPMG's plans, which include a move into legal services, have raised concerns about the conflict of interest involved when KPMG audits companies that the consulting or legal groups may view as potential clients.

HISTORY

Peat Marwick was founded in 1911 when William Peat, a London accountant, met James Marwick on a westbound Atlantic crossing. University of Glasgow alumni Marwick and Roger Mitchell had formed Marwick, Mitchell & Company in New York in 1897. Peat and Marwick agreed to ally their firms temporarily, and in 1925 they merged permanently as Peat, Marwick, Mitchell, & Copartners.

In 1947 William Black became senior partner, a position he held until 1965. He guided the firm's 1950 merger with Barrow, Wade, Guthrie, one of the US's oldest firms, and built its consulting practice. Peat Marwick restructured its international practice as PMM&Co. (International) in 1972 and reformed it as Peat Marwick International in 1978.

The following year several European accounting firms, led by Klynveld Kraayenhoff (The Netherlands) and Deutsche Treuhand (Germany), discussed forming an international accounting federation. Needing an American member, the European firms encouraged the merger of two American firms founded around the turn of the century, Main Lafrentz & Hurdman Cranstoun. Main Hurdman & Cranstoun soon joined the Europeans to form Klynveld Main Goerdeler (KMG), named after two of the member firms and the chairman of Deutsche Treuhand, Reinhard Goerdeler. Other members were C. Jespersen (Denmark), Thorne Riddel (Canada), Thomson McLintok (UK), and Fides Revision (Switzerland).

Peat Marwick merged with KMG in 1987 to form Klynveld Peat Marwick Goerdeler (KPMG). KPMG immediately lost 10% of its business owing to the departure of competing client companies.

In 1990 the firm began consolidating operations, a move which brought about a flood of departures that the firm attempted to stem by emphasizing increased profit per partner.

In the 1990s the Big Six fell victim to legal actions resulting from the growing belief that auditors should actively search for clients' accounting misdeeds instead of simply certifying the proper form of accounts. Among KPMG's largest problems were suits stemming from its audits of defunct S&Ls and litigation relating to the bankruptcy of Orange County, California. Despite these setbacks, the firm expanded its consulting division with the acquisition of Barefoot, Marrinan & Associates, a banking consultancy, in 1996.

In 1997, after Price Waterhouse and Coopers & Lybrand announced their merger, KPMG and Ernst & Young announced one of their own. But fears that regulators would find the merger anticompetitive and that the two cultures would not mesh smoothly led the firms to abandon the effort in 1998.

The creation of PricewaterhouseCoopers (PwC) and increasing competition on the consulting sides of the Big Five brought a realignment of loyalties in their separate national practices. KPMG Consulting lost its Belgian group to PwC and its French group to Computer Sciences Corporation. Its Canadian consulting group was nearly wooed away by Andersen Worldwide's audit group. (The plan was foiled by the ever-sullen Andersen Consulting group and by KPMG's promises of more money to build the business.)

Against this background, KPMG undertook a reorganization and entered its alliance with Cisco Systems.

airman: Colin Sharman
O: Paul C. Reilly
O: Joseph E. Heintz
gional Executive Partner, Europe, Middle East, and Africa: Colin Holland
gional Executive Partner, Americas: Lou Miramontes
gional Executive Partner, Asia/Pacific: John Sim
ernational Managing Partner, Assurance: Hans de Munnik
ernational Managing Partner, Consulting: im McGuire
ernational Managing Partner, Tax and Legal: Hartwick Lubmann
ernational Managing Partner, Financial Advisory Services: Gary Colter
ternational Managing Partner, Markets: Alistair Johnston
ternational Managing Partner, Infrastructure and Resources: Don Christiansen
airman and CEO, KPMG LLP: Stephen G. Butler
puty Chairman, KPMG LLP: Robert W. Alspaugh
, Consulting, KPMG LLP: Randolph C. Blazer
ief Administrative Officer, KPMG LLP: Michael J. Reagan
ief Marketing Officer, KPMG LLP: Timothy R. Pearson
eneral Counsel, KPMG LLP: Claudia L. Taft
rtner, Human Resources, KPMG LLP: Timothy P. Flynn

Q: 345 Park Ave., New York, NY 10154
one: 212-909-5000   **Fax:** 212-909-5299
eb site: http://www.kpmg.com

MPG has operations in more than 800 cities in more an 150 countries.

Selected Areas of Industry Expertise
Banking and finance
Building and construction
Energy and natural resources
Government
Health care and life sciences
Industrial products
Information, communications, and entertainment
Insurance
Retail and consumer products
Transportation

Representative Clients
Aetna U.S. Healthcare
Apple Computer
AT&T Broadband & Internet Services
Bankers Trust
City of New York
Motorola
NBC
Oxford Health Plans
PepsiCo
Pfizer
PhyCor
Smithsonian Institution
Tenet
Wells Fargo

Andersen Worldwide	Gemini Consulting
Aon	H&R Block
Arthur D. Little	Hewitt Associates
Bain & Company	IBM
BDO International	Marsh & McLennan
Booz, Allen	McKinsey & Company
Boston Consulting	Perot Systems
Deloitte Touche Tohmatsu	PricewaterhouseCoopers
EDS	Towers Perrin
Ernst & Young	Watson Wyatt

Partnership FYE: September 30	Annual Growth	1989	1990	1991	1992	1993	1994	1995	1996	1997	1998
ales ($ mil.)	10.5%	4,300	5,368	6,011	6,150	6,000	6,600	7,500	8,100	9,200	10,600
mployees	2.6%	68,000	77,300	75,000	73,488	76,200	76,200	72,000	77,000	83,500	85,300

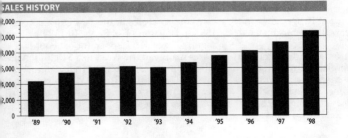

THE KROGER CO.

The Kroger Co. is at the top of the food chain. The Cincinnati-based company is the largest supermarket chain in the country, with more than 2,200 grocery stores from coast to coast — the closest the US has to a national supermarket chain. Kroger also operates about 800 convenience stores and some 380 jewelry stores (bringing its store total to about 3,400).

Its namesake chain — which has outlets in about 20 southern, mid-Atlantic, and midwestern states — has a dominating presence in a number of Ohio and Tennessee cities, as well as a sizable share of the market in large cities such as Dallas-Forth Worth and Atlanta. Kroger's Dillon Companies subsidiary runs more than 260 grocery stores, primarily in Arizona, Colorado, Kansas, and Missouri, under such names as Dillon Food Stores, City Markets, King Soopers, and Sav-Mor. The subsidiary also runs the company's convenience

stores, including Mini-Mart and Turkey Hill Minit Markets, among others.

Kroger's 1999 acquisition of Fred Meyer not only added three supermarket chains (Ralphs, Smith's Food & Drug Centers, and QFC), it gave the company several new retailing formats: multidepartment stores (Fred Meyer Marketplace), limited selection warehouse outlets (Food 4 Less, PriceRite), and jewelry stores (under the Fred Meyer, Merksamer, and Littman names). The purchase gave Kroger a significant presence in the western US.

As a result of the Fred Meyer acquisition, by 2003 Kroger expects to reap roughly $225 million in savings, mostly from its distribution and manufacturing operations. The grocer also owns about 43 food processing facilities that supply its supermarkets with private-label products, which account for about 25% of grocery sales. Employees own about 18% of Kroger.

Bernard Kroger was 22 when he started the Great Western Tea Company in 1883 in Cincinnati. Kroger lowered prices by cutting out middlemen, sometimes by making products such as bread. Growing to 40 stores in Cincinnati and northern Kentucky, the company became Kroger Grocery and Baking Company in 1902. It expanded into St. Louis in 1912 by acquiring 25 stores and grew rapidly during the 1910s and 1920s by purchasing smaller, cash-strapped companies. Kroger sold his holdings in the company for $28 million in 1928, the year before the stock market crash, and retired.

The company acquired Piggly Wiggly stores in Kentucky, Michigan, Missouri, Ohio, Oklahoma, and Tennessee in the late 1920s and bought most of Piggly Wiggly's corporate stock, which it held until the early 1940s. The chain reached its largest number of stores — a whopping 5,575 — in 1929 (the Depression later trimmed that total). A year later Kroger manager Michael Cullen suggested opening self-service, low-price supermarkets, but company executives demurred. Cullen left Kroger and began King Kullen, the first supermarket. If he was ahead of his time at Kroger, it wasn't by much; within five years, the company itself had 50 supermarkets.

During the 1950s Kroger acquired companies with stores in Texas; Georgia; and Washington, DC. It added New Jersey-based Sav-on drugstores in 1960, and it opened its first SupeRx drugstore in Ohio in 1961. The company began opening larger supermarkets in 1971; between

1970 and 1980 Kroger's store count increased only 5%, but its selling space nearly doubled.

In 1983 the grocer bought Kansas-based Dillon Food Stores (supermarkets and convenience stores) and Kwik Shop convenience stores. Kroger sold most of its interests in the Hook and SupeRx drug chains (which became Hook-SupeRx) in 1987 and focused on its food-and-drug stores (it sold its remaining stake to Revco in 1994). The next year it faced two separate takeover bids from the Herbert Haft family and from Kohlberg Kravis Roberts. The company warded off the raiders by borrowing $4.1 billion to pay a special dividend to shareholders and to buy shares for an employee stock plan.

To reduce debt, Kroger sold most of its equity in Price Saver Membership Wholesale Clubs, 95 food stores, 29 liquor stores, and its Fry's California stores. In 1990 the company made its first major acquisition since the 1988 restructuring by buying 29 Great Scott! supermarkets in Michigan. Joseph Pichler became CEO that year.

Kroger sold its Time Saver Stores unit (116 convenience stores in the New Orleans area) in 1995 to Houston's E-Z Serve. In 1999 Kroger acquired Fred Meyer, operator of about 800 stores mainly in the West, in a $13 billion deal. The company also is buying Indiana grocery retailer The John C. Groub Co., which operates nearly 30 stores under the Jay C, Foods Plus, and Ruler names.

Chairman and CEO: Joseph A. Pichler, age 59, $1,194,935 pay
VC and COO: Robert G. Miller
President and COO: David B. Dillon, age 47, $817,540 pay
EVP and Chief Information Officer: Michael S. Heschel, age 57, $548,940 pay
SVP, Secretary, and General Counsel: Paul W. Heldman, age 47
SVP: Don W. McGeorge, age 44
SVP and CFO: W. Rodney McMullen, age 38, $449,762 pay
SVP: James R. Thorne, age 52
Group VP of Corporate Affairs: Lynn Marmer, age 46
VP of Human Resources: Reuben Shaffer
VP and Treasurer: Lawrence M. Turner, age 51
SVP, West Coast Operations: Warren F. Bryant, age 53, $510,553 pay (prior to promotion)
President Manufacturing, SVP: Geoffrey J. Covert
Group VP Food Procurement: Darrell Webb, age 41
President, Turkey Hill Minit Markets: Jim Leonard
President, Mid-Atlantic Marketing: Pete Williams
SVP Food Group, Fred Meyer: Michael Ellis
Auditors: PricewaterhouseCoopers LLP

LOCATIONS

HQ: 1014 Vine St., Cincinnati, OH 45202
Phone: 513-762-4000 **Fax:** 513-762-1160
Web site: http://www.kroger.com

Kroger operates supermarkets in 31 states and convenience stores in 15 states.

PRODUCTS/OPERATIONS

1998 Sales

	$ mil.	% of total
Grocery stores	26,423	94
Convenience stores	1,003	3
Other	777	3
Total	**28,203**	**100**

Kroger Stores

Convenience Stores
Jr. Food Stores
Kwik Shop
Loaf 'N Jug
Mini-Mart
Quik Stop Markets
Tom Thumb Food Stores
Turkey Hill Minit Markets

Jewelry Stores
Barclay Jewelers
Fox's Jewelers
Fred Meyer Jewelers
Littman Jewelers
Merksamer Jewelers

Multidepartment Stores
Fred Meyer Marketplace

Supermarkets and Warehouse Stores
Bell Markets
Cala Foods
City Markets
Dillon Food Stores
Food 4 Less
FoodsCo.
Fry's Food Stores
Gerbes Supermarkets
King Soopers
Kroger
PriceRite
Quality Food Centers (QFC)
Ralphs
Sav-Mor
Smith's Food & Drug Centers

COMPETITORS

7-Eleven
A&P
Albertson's
Costco Companies
Food Lion
IGA
Kmart
Meijer
Raley's
Rite Aid
Royal Ahold
Safeway
Stater Bros.
Tosco
Walgreen
Wal-Mart
Winn-Dixie
Zale

HISTORICAL FINANCIALS & EMPLOYEES

NYSE symbol: KR FYE: December 31	Annual Growth	1989	1990	1991	1992	1993	1994	1995	1996	1997	1998
Sales ($ mil.)	4.4%	19,104	20,261	21,351	22,145	22,384	22,959	23,938	25,171	26,567	28,203
Net income ($ mil.)	—	(73)	83	80	(6)	(12)	242	303	350	412	411
Income as % of sales	—	—	0.4%	0.4%	—	—	1.1%	1.3%	1.4%	1.5%	1.5%
Earnings per share ($)	—	(0.24)	0.24	0.22	(0.02)	0.01	0.49	0.61	0.67	0.79	0.77
Stock price – FY high ($)	—	4.94	4.25	6.13	5.28	5.44	6.72	9.44	11.88	18.66	30.41
Stock price – FY low ($)	—	2.09	2.66	3.16	2.81	3.50	4.84	5.84	8.38	11.34	17.00
Stock price – FY close ($)	26.3%	3.69	3.56	4.94	3.66	5.03	6.03	9.34	11.63	18.38	30.25
P/E – high	—	—	18	28	—	544	14	15	18	24	39
P/E – low	—	—	11	14	—	350	10	10	13	14	22
Dividends per share ($)	—	0.00	0.00	0.00	0.00	0.00	0.00	0.00	0.00	0.00	0.00
Book value per share ($)	—	(9.09)	(8.36)	(7.84)	(7.38)	(5.71)	(4.85)	(3.23)	(2.33)	(1.54)	(0.75)
Employees	2.5%	170,000	170,000	170,000	190,000	190,000	200,000	205,000	212,000	212,000	213,000

STOCK PRICE HISTORY

HIGH/LOW/CLOSE

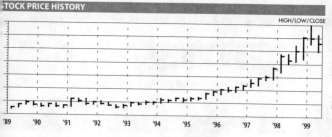

1998 FISCAL YEAR-END

Debt ratio: 113.7%
Return on equity: —
Cash ($ mil.): 121
Current ratio: 0.84
Long-term debt ($ mil.): 3,229
No. of shares (mil.): 514
Dividends
Yield: —
Payout: —
Market value ($ mil.): 15,546